This Is Who We Were:
In The 1910s

This Is Who We Were:
In The 1910s

Based on material from Grey House Publishing's
Working Americans Series by Scott Derks

Grey House
Publishing

PUBLISHER: Leslie Mackenzie
EDITORIAL DIRECTOR: Laura Mars
ASSOCIATE EDITORS: Diana Delgado; Sandy Towers
PRODUCTION MANAGER: Kristen Thatcher
MARKETING DIRECTOR: Jessica Moody
COMPOSITION: David Garoogian

Grey House Publishing, Inc.
4919 Route 22
Amenia, NY 12501
518.789.8700
FAX 845.373.6390
www.greyhouse.com
e-mail: books @greyhouse.com

While every effort has been made to ensure the reliability of the information presented in this publication, Grey House Publishing neither guarantees the accuracy of the data contained herein nor assumes any responsibility for errors, omissions or discrepancies. Grey House accepts no payment for listing; inclusion in the publication of any organization, agency, institution, publication, service or individual does not imply endorsement of the editors or publisher.

Errors brought to the attention of the publisher and verified to the satisfaction of the publisher will be corrected in future editions.

Publisher's Cataloging-In-Publication Data
(Prepared by The Donohue Group, Inc.)

This is who we were. In the 1910s / [edited by] Grey House Publishing. —
    [First edition].

    pages : illustrations ; cm

    "Based on material from Grey House Publishing's Working Americans Series by Scott Derks."
    Includes bibliographical references and index.
    ISBN: 978-1-61925-177-9

1. United States—Economic conditions—1865-1918. 2. United States-Economic conditions—1918-1945. 3. United States—Social conditions—1865-1918. 4. United States—Social conditions—1918-1932. 5. United States—Civilization—1865-1918. 6. United States—Civilization—1918-1945. 7. United States—History—1865-1921. 8. Nineteen tens. I. Based on (work) Derks, Scott. Working Americans. II. Grey House Publishing, Inc. III. Title: In the 1910s

HC106 .T45 2014
330.973

TABLE OF CONTENTS

Section One: Profiles

This section contains 28 profiles of individuals and families living and working in the 1910s. It examines their lives at home, at work, and in their neighborhoods. Based upon historic materials, personal interviews, and diaries, the profiles give a sense of what it was like to live in the years 1910 to 1919.

Section Two: Historical Snapshots

This section includes lists of important "firsts" for America, from technical advances and political events to new products and top selling books. Combining serious American history with fun facts, these snapshots present an easy-to-read overview of what happened in the 1910s.

Section Three: Economy of the Times

This section looks at a wide range of economic data, including food, clothing, transportation, housing and other selected prices, with reprints of actual advertisements for products and services of the time. It includes figures for the following categories, plus a valuable year-by-year listing of the value of a dollar.

Section Four: All Around Us—What We Saw, Wrote, Read & Listened To

This section includes reprints of newspaper and magazine articles, speeches, and other items designed to help readers focus on what was on the minds of Americans in the 1910s. These original pieces show how popular opinion was formed, and how American life was affected.

Section Five: Census Data

This section includes state-by-state comparative tables and reprints from the 1920 Census.

ESSAY ON THE 1910s

America was booming during the second decade of the century. Economically and politically, anything seemed possible. America's upper class enjoyed world-class train and automobile transportation and spent considerable time discovering new forms of entertainment. An emerging middle class took on more managerial duties, freeing factory owners and stockholders to travel and flex their entrepreneurial muscles. Millions of dollars were poured into libraries, parks, and literacy classes, designed to uplift the immigrant masses flooding to American shores in search of economic opportunity. Schools were called upon to manage social change by "Americanizing" the foreigners. Instead of creative play, kindergartens stressed order and discipline to instill a strong work ethic.

Between 1910 and 1913, some 11 million immigrants—an all-time record—entered the United States. The wages of unskilled workers fell, but the number of jobs increased dramatically. Earnings of skilled workers rose substantially and resulted in a backlash focused on protecting American workers' jobs. As a result, a series of anti-immigration laws was passed, culminating in 1917 with the end of unrestricted entry of immigrants into the United States. From the beginning of World War I until 1919, the number of new immigrants fell sharply while the war effort demanded more and more workers. Accordingly, wages for low-skilled work rose rapidly, forcing managers to find new and more streamlined ways to get the jobs done.

During the decade, motorized tractors changed the lives of farmers, while electricity extended the day of urban dwellers. Powered trolley cars, vacuum cleaners, hair dryers, and electric ranges moved onto the modern scene. Wireless communication connected San Francisco to New York and New York to Paris. In 1915, the Bell system alone operated six million telephones, which were considered essential in most middle class homes as the decade drew to a close.

In the midst of these dynamics, the Progressive Movement, largely a product of the rising middle class, began to shape the decade, raising questions about work safety, the rights of individuals, the need for clean air and fewer work hours. The results were significant and widespread. South Carolina prohibited the employment of children under 12 years old in mines, factories, and textile mills. Delaware began to frame employer's liability laws. Direct election of U.S. senators was approved. Communities argued over the right of women to vote and the lawfulness of alcohol consumption.

One of the biggest stories of the decade, however, was America's unabashed love affair with the automobile. By 1916, the Model T cost less than half of its 1908 price, and most everyone dreamed of owning a car.

The music scene continued to evolve. Opera grew in popularity and church music expanded its reach and sophistication. The sale of pianos hit a new high, ragtime neared its peak, and the patriotic spirit ignited by America's entry into World War I resulted in dozens of rousing or romantic songs. Movies were also maturing during the period. Some 25 percent of the population, including many newly arrived immigrants, went weekly to the nickelodeon to marvel at the exploits of Charlie Chaplin, Mary Pickford, and Douglas Fairbanks.

In the midst of blazing prosperity and positive social awareness, America felt the consequences of rapid change. Divorce was on the rise, with one in 12 marriages ending in divorce in 1911, compared with one in 85 in 1905. The discovery of a quick treatment for syphilis was hailed as both a miracle and an enticement to sin. As the technology and sophistication of silent movies improved, the Missouri Christian Endeavor Society tried to ban films that included kissing. The rapidly expanding economy began resulting in inequities of wealth—affluence for the few and hardship for the many. The average salary of $750 a year was rising, but not fast enough for the majority of Americans.

The second half of the decade was marked by the Great War, later known as the First World War. Worldwide, it cost more than nine million lives and swept away four empires—German, Austro-Hungarian, Russian, and Ottoman—and the traditional aristocratic style of leadership in Europe. It bled the treasuries of Europe dry and made the United States the richest country in the world.

When the war broke out in Europe, American exports were required to support the allied war effort, driving the well-oiled American industrial engine into high gear. When America's physical entry into the war in 1917 required the drafting of two million men, women were given their first taste of economic independence. Millions of women stepped forward to produce the materials needed by a nation. As a result, when the men came back from Europe, America was a changed place for both the well-traveled soldier and the newly trained female worker, yet women possessed full suffrage in only Wyoming, Colorado, Utah, and Idaho.

The war forced the United States to become a full participant in the world economy. Tariffs on imported goods were reduced, and exports reached all-time highs, so that at the end of the 1910s, the American economy was prospering.

INTRODUCTION

This Is Who We Were: In The 1910s is an offspring of our 13-volume *Working Americans* series, which was devoted, volume by volume, to Americans by class, occupation, or social cause. This new edition is devoted to one decade—the 1910s. It represents various economic classes, dozens of occupations, and all regions of the country, and is a comprehensive look at the decade that was shaped by the automobile, electricity, immigration, and World War I, through the eyes and ears of everyday Americans, not the words of historians or politicians.

This Is Who We Were: In The 1910s presents 28 profiles of individuals and families—their life at home, on the job, and in their neighborhood—with lots of photos and historical images of the time. These authentic stories portray both struggling, and successful Americans, and capture a wide range of thoughts and emotions.

The profiles, together with the other sections outlined below, present a complete picture of what it was like to live in America in the 1910s, from the Russian immigrant who worked in a Pittsburgh steel factory, to well-known entertainers and athletes, to World War I servicemen.

Section One: Profiles

Each of the 28 profiles in Section One begins with a brief introduction that anchors the text to the decade. Then, each profile is arranged in three categories: Life at Home; Life at Work; Life in the Community.

Section Two: Historical Snapshots

Section Two is made up of three long, bulleted lists of significant events and milestones. In chronological order—Early 1910s, Mid 1910s and Late 1910s—these offer an amazing range of firsts and turning points in American history, including a few "can you believe it?" facts, such as:
- $700 tuition at Harvard University
- adoption of the 19th Amendment, granting women suffrage
- Orville Wright's record breaking airplane flight
- discovery of the ozone layer
- linkage of high-cholesterol diets to heart problems
- introduction of a test measuring intelligence, and the term IQ
- first successful blood transfusion using stored blood
- adoption of daylight savings time

Section Three: Economy of the Times

One of the most interesting things about researching an earlier time is learning how much things cost and what people earned. This section offers this information in spades. Each of three categories—Consumer Expenditures, Annual Income of Standard Jobs, and Selected Prices—offers actual figures from three specific years during the 1910s for easy comparison and study.

At the end of Section Three is a Value of a Dollar Index that compares the buying power of $1.00 in 2013 to the buying power of $1.00 in every year prior, back to 1860, helping to put the economic data in *This Is Who We Were: In The 1910s* into context.

Section Four: All Around Us

There is no better way to put your finger on the pulse of a country than to read its magazines and newspapers. This section offers 60 original articles, book excerpts, speeches, and advertising copy that influenced American thought in the 1910s. With articles declaring "Why Girls Go Wrong," "Our Responsibility in the War," "The Darker Side of Driving," and "Meeting the Child Labor Problem," this section is the eyes and ears of America in the 1910s.

Section Five: Census Data

This section includes two elements, both invaluable in helping to define the decade of the 1910s. First, 10 State-by-State comparative tables that rank data from the 1910, 1920, and 2010 Census. Topics include Population, Foreign-Born, and Homeownership Rate. Second, actual reprints from the 1920 Census of Population, including a United States Summary and detailed statistics on various topics, such as Color or Race, Marital Condition, Mother Tongue of the Foreign-Born White Population, Inability to Speak English, and Dwellings and Families.

This Is Who We Were: In The 1910s ends with a comprehensive Bibliography, arranged by 13 topics from African Americans to World War I, and a detailed Index.

The editors thank all those who agreed to be interviewed and share their personal photos for this book. We also gratefully acknowledge the Prints & Photographs Collections of the Library of Congress.

Russian American Steelworker in 1910

Velimir Rzhevsky, a 28-year-old Russian worker, worked beyond his normal 72-hour week to earn enough money to bring his 20-year-old sweetheart to America so they could marry. He was employed by U.S. Steel in Pittsburgh, Pennsylvania, where his job was manning the blast furnace.

Life at Home

- When he came to the United States from Voronezh, Russia, Velimir planned to work, save his money, and return to the motherland, but he decided to stay in America.
- After three years of working in the steel mill, Velimir was able to save enough money to bring his fiancée, Vera, from Kiev, Russia, to Pittsburgh.
- Velimir and Vera were recently married in an Orthodox wedding.
- For two years Velimir had worked an average 80 hours per week, often asking for overtime beyond his normal 72 hours; now he wanted to work less.
- Overtime hours were paid at the regular rate, not an increased rate.
- Velimir and Vera lived in a three-room tenement house in the McKees Rocks section of Pittsburgh.
- They had no electricity or indoor toilet.
- Vera was shocked by the poor produce and meat available and by its high price.
- From Velimir's savings, they recently purchased a bed, made of iron and painted white, a table, and a rug.
- Then Velimir began saving money to bring his younger brother to Pittsburgh; in Russia his brother made the equivalent of $0.50 a day.
- Velimir and Vera were considering taking in single male Russian boarders in order to add to their income; most of the Russians working in the steel industry were single and lived in boardinghouses.
- Vera would do the cooking and washing for the boarders as well as for her own family.
- Boarders would pay $0.75 to $1.00 a week for a place to sleep and the little cooking and washing that they cared to have done.
- Typically boarding houses kept food accounts based on what everyone ate; every two weeks the sum was divided equally among the boarders. The bill for two weeks normally amounted to $3.00 a man, so the average boarder spent only $10 a month on room and maintenance.

Velimir Rzhevsky

- Vera had already earned some extra money as a seamstress.
- A Russian worker for the YWCA had helped her find customers and adjust to life in her new country.
- Like most immigrants (78 percent), Velimir and Vera each had burial insurance; theirs was through the Russian Brotherhood Society.
- Velimir had little time for anything beyond work and sleep, but he and his friends sometimes played cards for amusement.
- Vera and Velimir sometimes attended a dance or went to a movie, but these were rare occasions.
- Velimir occasionally purchased a "penny-paper" to look at the pictures and practice reading English.
- Socially and at work, Velimir and Vera associated almost exclusively with other Russians and had little contact with native-born Americans other than second-generation Russian Americans.
- They knew little of American culture, but they understood that things would be different for their children, who would be educated in free American public schools.
- Physically Velimir was very strong, as were most steel men.
- After their marriage Velimir and Vera attended the Orthodox Church, called in the United States the Russian Greek Orthodox Catholic Church, which was well funded and well attended, particularly by men, who far outnumbered Russian women in the community.

Life at Work

- Velimir worked for U.S. Steel as an unskilled laborer in the blast furnace section. In 1910 he worked 46 weeks during the year—7 days a week, 12 hours per day.
- The average work week in non-farm industries in 1910 was 51 hours.
- The blast furnace was known for its low hourly rates, but Velimir chose it because it offered relatively steady work throughout the year.
- Approximately 45 percent of the blast furnace workers earned between $0.16 and $0.18 per hour; 39 percent made between $0.19 and $0.25 per hour.
- Velimir earned $0.18 per hour.

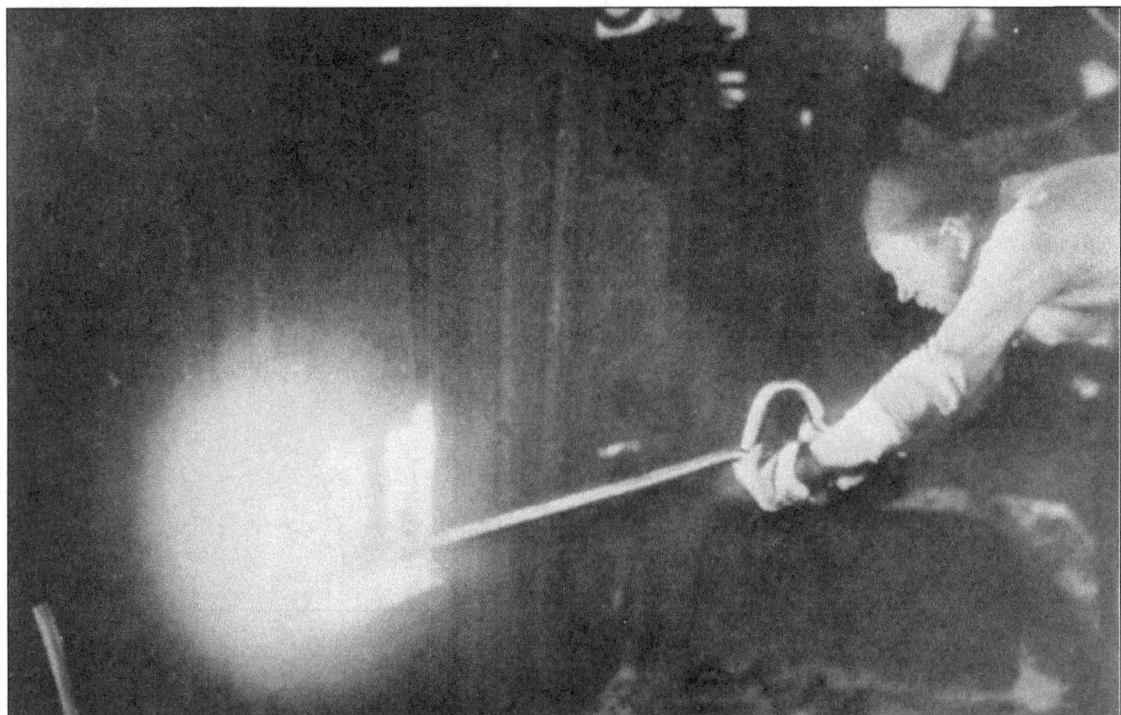

Velimir worked for U.S. Steel in the blast furnace.

- Over 1900-1910, the cost of retail prices for food had risen 33 percent, while wages in the steel industry went up just 17.5 percent.
- Velimir's job was to unload the oar cars by running the cars on high trestles and then, by opening the hoppers, allow the ore to run down into the piles below.
- When he first came to work, the old-style furnace was filled by hand; the temperatures from the furnace could run as high as 118 degrees Fahrenheit.
- Newer machinery gave workers less exposure to the heat.
- Velimir and the other workers still had to be wary of the toxic fumes produced by the furnace as well as "flame ups" from the furnace, which could severely burn a man.
- Many of the on-the-job injuries were eye injuries.
- The labor force consisted of relatively unskilled laborers, recruited from the ranks of recent immigrants, most of whom came from rural areas and were accustomed to farm work.
- The skilled positions within the mills generally were held by English, Scottish, German, Irish, and Welsh workers. Many had learned the trade abroad before immigrating to the United States.
- The skilled workmen were machinists, millwrights, electricians, bricklayers, and locomotive and stationary engineers.

Many unskilled laborers in the steel mills were immigrants from rural areas.

Fatigued steelworkers were subject to on-the-job injuries.

- Nationwide a handful of companies controlled all of the steel and iron work.
- The industry employed approximately 275,000 people; of these, approximately six thousand belonged to either the Sons of Vulcan union or the Amalgamated Association of Iron, Steel and Tin Workers. Velimir belonged to neither.
- The Amalgamated Association was very weak and nearly bankrupt in 1910 after major battles with both Carnegie Steel Company and United States Steel Corporation.
- The majority of steel workers were employed 12 hours per day, and Velimir was among the 30 percent who worked seven days a week.
- Some companies, notably U.S. Steel in Pittsburgh, moved to reduce the work week from seven to six days.
- Many workers objected to the reduction in the work week because it reduced their pay.
- Others objected because the day off was during the week, not on Sunday, and thus they had "nothing to do," with their friends at work at the mills, their

Most steelworkers often worked long hours in a single day so that the mill could run continuously.

children at school, and their wives busy with their regular household duties.

- The hardest part of the schedule, the workmen reported, was not working 7 days but working 12 hours at a stretch.
- After a 12-hour shift, workers often were asked to fill in for workers who failed to show up for work, adding overtime and creating an 18- to 24-hour day.
- There was some discussion of changing from two 12-hour shifts to three 8-hour shifts, recognizing that the steel mill must run continuously.
- Reformers urged the industry to adopt the shorter hours and keep worker's pay constant, citing a survey that found that in the production of steel, labor constituted only 17 percent of the total cost of production.
- The same survey showed that 30 percent of the employees worked some overtime each week, normally 6 hours per week on top of a regular 72-hour week.
- Steel mills often stopped production entirely; 60 percent of all steelworkers were laid off for up to four weeks each year.
- The increasing use of machinery within the industry led to the displacement of workers in some unskilled jobs; still, unskilled workers comprised about half of the work force.
- Although many ethnic groups were represented at Velimir's mill, the company liked to hire Poles and Slovaks because they were "strong, steady and capable of being trained rapidly."
- The duties of the unskilled laborers included handling the materials produced in the steel process and cleaning up the site, mostly by clearing slag and scrap.
- Semiskilled workers—the fastest-growing job category—normally were machine operators.
- No female or child labor was used within the industry; most companies insisted that employees be at least 16 years old, and at least one company would hire only individuals 18 and older.
- Steel work was considered too physically challenging for women.
- A bonus fund, based on production, was established at the steel mill for supervisory and professional employees; it was not available to the work force, causing discontent.

- U.S. Steel made efforts to "make partners, practically, of its workers" through a stock purchase plan.
- The great majority of steelworkers were 20 to 44 years old; only 13 percent of the work force was 45 years old or older.
- The foreman did all hiring of unskilled workers; Velimir's foreman was Russian but had been with the company for many years.
- For unskilled workers, few employment records were kept beyond a worker's name, the nature of his work, and the rate to be paid.
- For skilled workers, the steel mills had a centralized employment department where extensive records were kept.
- Steelworkers were paid semimonthly; most industries at the time pay weekly.
- According to the U.S. Bureau of Labor's report on conditions of employment in the iron and steel industry, mandated by Congress in June 1910, one U.S. Steel competitor "owns every dwelling in the community, and also owns every acre of land in the immediate vicinity upon which a dwelling could be constructed. It also owns the only railroad entering the community."
- The same steel mill also owned the only store in the community as well as a bakery, a dairy, a truck farm, and an abattoir.
- More generally, a voluntary retirement program started at age 60 after 20 years of service; a man who worked 25 years and averaged $60.00 a month for the last 10 years of his service would receive $15.00 a month in retirement.

Russian immigrants were comforted by familiar religious leaders.

Life in the Community: Pittsburgh, Pennsylvania

- Allegheny County, Pennsylvania, where Pittsburgh was located, produced 19 percent of the nation's pig iron and 27 percent of its steel.

Eastern European men made up a significant portion of the population of common laborers in the Carnegie plants of Pennsylvania.

- Other prominent steel-producing communities included Allentown, Pennsylvania; Ironton, Ohio; Birmingham, Alabama; St. Louis, Missouri; and Pueblo, Colorado.
- In 1910 the primary use of steel was for railroad rails, followed by structural shapes, steel plates, and rods for reinforced concrete work.
- Newly arrived immigrants dominated the bottom ranks of the steel industry; in 1907, 11,694 of the 14,359 common laborers working in the Carnegie plants of Allegheny County were Eastern Europeans.
- More Russian-born immigrants to the United States found work in the steel industry than in any other economic sector except mining.
- Approximately 32 percent of the laborers could not speak English.
- In 1880 Slavs, Lithuanians, Hungarians, and Italians formed less than 1 percent of the population of Pittsburgh; by 1910 they represented 13 percent.
- The U.S. Immigration Commission classified all workers who earned less than $1.50 a day as unskilled;

The family of an immigrant steelworker

by that measure 50 percent of Italians and Slavs, 70 percent of Croatians, and 85 percent of Serbs and Bulgarians were unskilled.

- "Hungry" immigrants often were accused of undermining American workers; "These guys have no pride," one craftsman said, "they are not ruled by custom. When the foreman demands it, they throw down the saw and the hammer and take up the wheelbarrow."
- Alcohol consumption, especially among immigrant men without wives, was very high; drunk and disorderly charges were common.
- When determining whether the worker would be paid by the piece or by the hour, the rule was, "If the machine depends upon the man for speed, we put on piece work; if the machine drives the man, we pay him by the day."
- Of 500 industrial fatalities in Allegheny County in one year, 293 of the victims were foreign-born.
- Both U.S. Steel and Pittsburgh Steel Company introduced accident prevention programs; no state or local regulations governed deaths on the job.
- The geographical contours of the region had an influence on keeping the foreign population within certain limited districts.
- The beds of two rivers, the Allegheny and the Monongahela, cut into the Allegheny range, leaving a narrow strip of "usable" land on either side of their banks; thus the topography offered limited sites for dwellings, mills, and factories.
- Clustering the worker's homes near the plant was considered an advantage to the employer, keeping the "crude labor force within easy call." It was asserted that "night work and the cost of carfare help keep the mass of men employed in common labor near the mills and on the congested low lands."
- A strike in 1909 at the Pressed Steel Car Company in McKee's Rock was continuing to attract media attention. The *Wall Street Journal* called the company's methods "sordid and inhuman."
- The *New York Evening Post* accused the Pressed Steel of "grinding out" profits "at the expense of the laborers."

- As a result a government investigation was launched.
- In September 1910 the *American Federationist*, the magazine of the American Federation of Labor, proclaimed, "Public opinion at the present moment is arrayed against the working conditions in the steel industry."
- Even in the mines the working conditions were better than they were in the steel industry.
- Reformers in Pittsburgh opened schools for immigrant children and clubs were formed to teach the workers English.
- Still, the punishing work hours endured by most immigrant steelworkers put "Americanization"— and other educational, civic, and social activities—virtually out of their reach.
- The National Slovak Society had 50,000 members; the Polish National Alliance boasted 75,000.
- The Italian organizations focused on citizenship; in 1910 four-fifths of all Italians in Pittsburgh who had been in the country five years were naturalized; many quickly become voters, giving the Italians a powerful voice in city business.
- Pittsburgh banks, discovering that immigrants were savers, created foreign exchange departments headed by men who could speak the languages of the immigrants.
- One banker doing business with the Serbs noted that each pay day, he sent between $20,000 and $25,000 to the old country.
- The fraternal organizations among the Slavs, Lithuanians, and Italians promoted thrift, provided insurance, and helped those who were sick or in need.

Many immigrant workers learned English as a way to assimilate into American society.

Immigrant families lived in unsanitary tenement districts.

Medical Education Reformer in 1910

Abraham Flexner authored the groundbreaking 1910 "Flexner Report," which revolutionized medical education and radically reduced the number of medical schools in the United States.

Life at Home

- Abraham Flexner was not a doctor; he was a secondary school teacher and principal in Louisville, Kentucky.
- Abraham's father, Moritz, was born in Neumark, Bohemia, in 1820; Moritz spent his teenage years in Strasbourg, where he lived with an uncle, a rabbi.
- Abraham's mother, Esther Abraham, was born in 1834, one of six children, in the village of Roden near Saarlouis in the Rhineland; getting an education meant she had to share her textbooks with her brothers and sister.
- After immigrating to America, Moritz first tried New Orleans and then settled in Louisville, Kentucky.
- Moritz was a hat merchant, and Esther was a seamstress.
- Abraham was born in 1866, the sixth of their nine children.
- Education for their children was at the heart of their ambitions; Abraham's parents repeatedly said, "Our children will justify us."
- Severe financial losses in the Panic of 1873 forced the Flexners to abandon their dreams of sending all their sons to college; simply to make ends meet, they were forced to move several times, into smaller and smaller homes.
- To help support the family, the teenage Abraham worked at the Louisville library six days a week, from 2:30 in the afternoon to 10 in the evening; he made $16 a month.
- He used the time to read hundreds of books and keep up with national affairs through *Nation*, the *Saturday Review* and several city newspapers.
- Abraham also wrote to the editors, including one letter that championed the secret ballot and its adoption by Kentucky.
- He prepared himself carefully for each project; he liked to quote Pasteur's remark, "chance favors the well-prepared mind."
- Following a pattern going back two generations, Abraham delighted in reading

Abraham Flexner

aloud his literary favorites: Shakespeare's *Hamlet*, Keats's "Ode on a Grecian Urn," and Wordsworth's "Ode: Intimations of Immortality."
- The older boys took menial jobs to help support the household, while Abraham and his three younger siblings were able to remain in school.
- Abraham was the first of the children to finish high school.
- With assistance and encouragement from his older brother, Abraham attended Johns Hopkins University in 1884, entering at age 17.
- Revered institutions such as the University of Virginia and Vanderbilt University were impoverished and still hobbled as a result of the Civil War.
- In Baltimore merchant Johns Hopkins had left $7 million, nearly his entire fortune, to endow a university and to fund the building of a hospital, which he wanted to be associated with the university.
- Abraham fully understood that his money would run out after two years, so he graduated in two years by taking a double load of courses.
- Johns Hopkins stressed postgraduate education—then very rare in the United States—and Abraham hoped to continue his studies, but the fellowship he sought eluded him.
- He returned to Louisville to teach Latin and Greek at Louisville High School before founding, in 1890, an experimental school, which had no formal exams or grades but excelled at preparing students for prestigious colleges.
- Abraham wanted a place to test his ideas about education.
- He believed that education should be marked by small classes, personal attention, and hands-on teaching.
- With the success of his school, Flexner was able to help his older brother Simon to attend Johns Hopkins and to support his sister Mary so that she could attend Bryn Mawr College.
- In addition, Abraham's wife, playwright Anne Crawford, a former pupil in his school and a graduate of Vassar College, had found financial success on Broadway with the production of her play "Mrs. Wiggs of the Cabbage Patch."
- This, too, enabled Abraham to pursue a master's degree in psychology from Harvard and to spend a year at the universities of Berlin and Heidelberg.
- Despite his initial enthusiasm, he left Harvard after a year, disappointed in his professors and assistantship.
- Never to earn an advanced degree, Flexner embarked instead upon an extended period of observation of all types of schools and universities, in both New York and Europe.
- In 1908, Abraham published his first book, *The American College: A Criticism*.
- Strongly critical of many aspects of American higher education, it was especially scathing in regard to the university lecture as a method of instruction.
- According to Abraham, lectures enabled colleges to "handle cheaply by wholesale a large body of students who would be otherwise unmanageable, and thus give the lecturer time for research."
- This book received little notice except from the president of the Carnegie Foundation for the Advancement of Teaching, Dr. Henry S. Pritchett.
- Pritchett soon offered Abraham the opportunity to conduct a survey of medical schools, even though Flexner not only had never attended a medical school but had never so much as been inside one.
- Thus he joined the research staff at the Carnegie Foundation in 1908.

Life at Work
- When Abraham Flexner stepped into the role of medical school evaluator, he knew he would be vulnerable to attack, especially if his reports were negative.
- As it turned out, most of them were.

Harvard Medical College

- In 1910 he published the Flexner Report, which was funded by the Carnegie Foundation.
- The report examined the state of American medical education and led to far-reaching reforms in the way doctors were trained.
- At an American Medical Association convention in Chicago, Abraham declared that two-thirds of America's medical schools were dangerous to the profession and to the public.
- His report caused an uproar.
- Ultimately the Flexner Report triggered reforms in the standards, organization and curriculum of North American medical schools.
- The Flexner Report caused more than 100 medical schools to close down, and most of the remaining schools were reorganized to conform to the educational model Flexner advocated.
- The number of medical schools fell from 155 to 31 as the American Medical Association took steps to eliminate uncertified for-profit medical schools.
- But that was why Henry Pritchett had wanted Abraham to take the lead, perceiving that as an analyst Abraham was incisive, incorruptible, and beholden to no one.
- To Pritchett, Abraham Flexner was a "layman educator" capable of completing a key assignment in the Carnegie Foundation's larger institutional classification scheme, such as differentiating colleges from secondary schools, and universities from colleges.
- Abraham was paid $5,000 a year.
- He began in Chicago, where he found that the reports of the American Medical Association were credible, painstaking documents that went to great lengths to be diplomatic.
- Prepared by a committee of physicians from medical schools, the reports were tactful and cautious—but Abraham was not a doctor, and he was under no obligation to be diplomatic.
- Abraham's next trip was to Tulane University in New Orleans; keenly conscious of his own ignorance and inexperience, he wanted make his start in a location well removed from New York.

Abraham Flexner reported on medical school requirements, faculty, financial support, laboratories, and relationships with hospitals.

- His assignment was to view an institution from an educational standpoint: its entrance requirements, the number and training of its faculty, its financial resources and stability, the quality of its laboratories, and its relationship with its training hospitals.
- Abraham found that entrance requirements were often ignored and that many of the faculty members were local doctors rather than college professors.
- Equipment, he discovered, was often both inadequate and poorly maintained.
- Many students were pronounced to be medical doctors even though they had had little practical experience, owing to minimal access to hospital patients.
- Abraham was fearless.
- After a trip to St. Louis to see the medical school of Washington University, where Dr. Pritchett had been a professor of astronomy, Abraham wrote, "Its medical department is entirely out of harmony with the spirit and equipment of the rest of the university. Unless this department is to be a drag and a reproach, one of two courses should be adopted: The department must be either abolished or reorganized."
- At Bowdoin College in Maine, he produced a similar scorched-earth report, even though the president of Bowdoin was a trustee of the Carnegie Foundation.
- Abraham found that many of the schools were "essentially private ventures, moneymaking in spirit and in object."
- One criticism regularly leveled at his approach was that his inspection tours, which rarely took more than a few hours, were inadequate and superficial.
- He was accused of trying to reduce the number of new doctors in order to limit competition for physicians already in practice.

- Abraham nevertheless became known as the "severest critic and the best friend American medicine ever had."
- The Flexner Report led to the closure of most rural medical schools and all but two of America's African American medical colleges.
- It also set the stage for modern American medical education.

Life in the Community: Louisville, Kentucky

- At the dawn of the twentieth century, Louisville was struggling to be a cosmopolitan city.
- One hundred years earlier, the recently invented steamboat had brought new life to Louisville via the Mississippi River.
- Until then, most of the cargo on the Mississippi was going downstream.
- In 1815 the *Enterprise*, captained by Henry Miller Shreve, became the first steamboat to travel northward from New Orleans to Louisville, showing the commercial potential of the steamboat in making upriver shipping practical.
- Industry and manufacturing flocked to Louisville; its population grew rapidly, tripling between 1810 and 1820.
- By 1830 its growth would surpass that of Lexington, making it the state's largest city.
- The completion of the Louisville and Portland Canal in 1830 allowed boats to circumvent the Falls of the Ohio and travel through from Pittsburgh to New Orleans.
- In 1831 Catherine Spalding moved from Bardstown to Louisville and established Presentation Academy, a Catholic school for girls; she also established the St. Vincent Orphanage, which was later renamed St. Joseph Orphanage.
- In 1839 a precursor of the modern Kentucky Derby was held at Old Louisville's Oakland Race Course.
- More than ten thousand spectators attended the two-horse race, in which Grey Eagle lost to Wagner—36 years before the first Kentucky Derby.
- The Kentucky School for the Blind in Louisville was founded in 1839.
- Following the 1850 Census, Louisville was reported to be the nation's tenth-largest city; Kentucky was the eighth most populous state.
- The Louisville and Nashville Railroad (L&N) Company was founded in 1850 by James Guthrie, who also was involved in the founding of the University of Louisville.
- When the railroad was completed in 1859, Louisville's strategic location at the Falls of the Ohio became central to the city's development and cemented its importance in the rail and water freight transportation business.
- Part of that business was the slave trade.
- Before the Civil War, Louisville conducted one of the largest slave markets in the United States; shifting agricultural patterns had left what was seen as an excess of slaves in parts of the Upper South and a shortage in the Deep South.
- Kentucky slave traders sold 2,500-4,000 slaves annually; the expression "sold down the river" originated as a lament of Eastern slaves who were sold in Louisville and shipped south on the Mississippi River.

Louisville, Kentucky

Louisville Colonials baseball team

- Kentucky officially declared its neutrality early in the Civil War but heavily supported the Union army.
- The first Kentucky Derby was held on May 17, 1875, at the Louisville Jockey Club track (later renamed Churchill Downs).
- One year later, professional baseball launched its National League; the Louisville Grays team was a charter member.
- In 1877 the Southern Baptist Theological Seminary relocated to Louisville from Greenville, South Carolina, where it had been founded in 1859.
- Its new campus, at Fourth and Broadway, downtown, was underwritten by a group of Louisville business leaders eager to add the promising graduate-professional school to the city's resources.
- It grew quickly, attracting students from all parts of the nation, and by the early twentieth century, it was the second largest accredited seminary in the United States.
- On August 1, 1883, President Chester A. Arthur opened the first annual Southern Exposition.
- Exhibitions included the largest to-date installation of incandescent light bulbs, which had recently been invented by Thomas Edison, a former Louisville resident.
- Downtown Louisville began a modernization period in the 1890s, with Louisville's second skyscraper, the Columbia Building, opening on January 1, 1890.
- One year later, landscape architect Frederick Law Olmsted was commissioned to design Louisville's system of parks.
- Two Louisville sisters, Patty and Mildred J. Hill, both schoolteachers, wrote the song "Good Morning to All" for their kindergarten class; the song did not become popular, and the lyrics were later changed to the more recognizable, "Happy Birthday to You."
- Early in the twentieth century, controversy over political corruption came to a head in the 1905 mayoral election, called the most corrupt in city history.
- The Waverly Hills Sanatorium was opened in 1910 to house tuberculosis patients.

"Medical Education in America, Rethinking the Training of American Doctors," Abraham Flexner, *Atlantic, June 1910*

The American medical school is now well along in the second century of its history. It began, and for many years continued to exist, as a supplement to the apprenticeship system still in vogue during the seventeenth and eighteenth centuries. The likely youth of that period, destined to a medical career, was at an early age indentured to some reputable practitioner, to whom his service was successively menial, pharmaceutical, and professional; he ran his master's errands, washed the bottles, mixed the drugs, spread the plasters, and finally, as the stipulated term drew toward its close, actually took part in the daily practice of his preceptor-bleeding his patients, pulling their teeth, and obeying a hurried summons in the night. The quality of the training varied within large limits with the capacity and conscientiousness of the master. Ambitious spirits sought, therefore, a more assured and inspiring discipline. Beginning early in the eighteenth century, having served their time at home, they resorted in rapidly increasing numbers to the hospitals and lecture-halls of Leyden, Paris, London, and Edinburgh. The difficulty of the undertaking proved admirably selective, for the students who crossed the Atlantic gave a good account of themselves. Returning to their native land, they sought opportunities to share with their less fortunate or less adventurous fellows the rich experience gained as they "walked the hospitals" of the old world. The voices of the great masters of that day thus reechoed in the recent western wilderness. High scientific and professional ideals impelled the youthful enthusiasts, who bore their lighted torches safely back across the waters.

Out of these early assays in medical teaching, the American medical school developed. As far back as 1750, informal classes and demonstrations, mainly in anatomy, are matters of record. Philadelphia was then the chief centre of medical interest. There, in 1762, William Shippen the younger, after a sojourn of five years abroad, began, in the very year of his return home, a course of lectures on midwifery. In the following autumn, he announced a series of anatomical lectures "for the advantage of the young gentlemen now engaged in the study of physic in this and the neighboring provinces, whose circumstances and connections will not admit of their going abroad for improvement to the anatomical schools in Europe; and also for the entertainment of any gentlemen who may have the curiosity to understand the anatomy of the Human Frame."

From these detached courses, the step to an organized medical school was taken at the instigation of Shippen's friend and fellow student abroad, John Morgan, who in 1765 proposed to the trustees of the College of Philadelphia the creation of a professorship in the theory and practice of medicine. At the ensuing Commencement, Morgan delivered a noble and prophetic discourse, still pertinent, upon the institution of medical schools in America. The trustees were favorable to the suggestion; the chair was established, and Morgan himself was its first occupant. Soon afterwards, Shippen became professor of anatomy and surgery. Thirteen years previously, the Pennsylvania Hospital, conceived by Thomas Bond, had been established through the joint efforts of Bond himself and Benjamin Franklin. Realizing that the student "must Join Examples with Study, before he can be sufficiently qualified to prescribe for the sick, for Language and Books alone can never give him Adequate Ideas of Diseases and the best methods of Treating them," Bond now argued successfully on behalf of bedside training for the medical students. "There the Clinical professor comes in to the Aid of Speculation and demonstrates the Truth of Theory by Facts," he declared in words that a century and a half later still warrant repetition; "he meets his pupils at stated times in the Hospital, and when a case presents adapted to his purpose, he asks all those Questions which lead to a certain knowledge of the Disease and parts Affected; and if the Disease baffles the power of Art and the Patient falls a Sacrifice to it, he then brings his Knowledge to the Test, and fixes Honour or discredit on his Reputation by exposing all the Morbid parts to View, and Demonstrates by what means it produced Death, and if perchance he finds something unexpected, which Betrays an Error in Judgement, he, like a great and good man, immediately acknowledges the mistake, and, for the benefit of survivors, points out other methods by which it might have been more happily treated."

The writer of these sensible words fitly became our first professor of clinical medicine, with unobstructed access to the one hundred and thirty patients then in the hospital wards. Subsequently, the faculty of the new school was increased and greatly strengthened when Adam Kuhn, trained by Linnaeus, was made professor of materia medica, and Benjamin Rush, already at twenty-four on the threshold of his brilliant career, became professor of chemistry.

Our first medical school was thus soundly conceived as organically part of an institution of learning and intimately connected with a large public hospital. The instruction aimed, as already pointed out, not to supplant, but to supplement apprenticeship. A year's additional training, carrying the bachelor's degree, was offered to students who, having demonstrated a competent knowledge of Latin, mathematics, natural and experimental philosophy, and having served a sufficient apprenticeship to some reputable practitioner in physic, now completed a prescribed lecture curriculum, with attendance upon the practice of the Pennsylvania Hospital for one year. This course was well calculated to round off the young doctor's preparation, reviewing and systematizing his theoretical acquisitions, while considerably extending his practical experience....

Since that day medical colleges have multiplied without restraint, now by fission, now by sheer spontaneous generation. Between 1810 and 1840, twenty-six new medical schools sprang up; between 1840 and 1876, forty-seven more; and the number actually surviving in 1876 has been since then much more than doubled. First and last, the United States and Canada have in little more than a century produced four hundred and forty-seven medical schools, many, of course, short-lived, and perhaps fifty still-born. One hundred and fifty-six survive today. Of these, Illinois, prolific mother of thirty-nine medical colleges, still harbors in the city of Chicago fourteen; forty-two sprang from the fertile soil of Missouri, ten of them still "going" concerns; the Empire State produced forty-three, with eleven survivors; Indiana, twenty-seven, with two survivors; Pennsylvania, twenty, with eight survivors; Tennessee, eighteen, with eleven survivors. The city of Cincinnati brought forth about twenty, the city of Louisville eleven.

These enterprises-for the most part, they can be called schools or institutions only by courtesy-were frequently set up regardless of opportunity or need, in small towns as readily as in large, and at times, almost in the heart of the wilderness. No field, however limited, was ever effectually pre-empted. Wherever and whenever the roster of untitled practitioners rose above half a dozen, a medical school was likely at any moment to be precipitated. Nothing was really essential but professors. The laboratory movement is comparatively recent, and Thomas Bond's wise words about clinical teaching were long since out of print. Little or no investment was therefore involved. A hall could be cheaply rented, and rude benches were inexpensive. Janitor service was unknown and is even now relatively rare. Occasional dissections in time supplied a skeleton-in whole or in part-and a box of odd bones. Other equipment there was practically none.

The teaching was, except for a little anatomy, wholly didactic. The schools were essentially private ventures, money-making in spirit and object. Income was simply divided among the lecturers, who reaped a rich harvest besides, through the consultations which the loyalty of their former students threw into their hands. "Chairs" were therefore valuable pieces of property, their prices varying with what was termed their "reflex" value; only recently a professor in a now defunct Louisville school, who had agreed to pay three thousand dollars for the combined chair of physiology and gynecology, objected strenuously to a division of the professorship assigning him physiology, on the ground of "failure of consideration," for the "reflex" which constituted the inducement to purchase went obviously with the other subject. No applicant for instruction who could pay his fees or sign his note was turned down. State boards were not as yet in existence. The school diploma was itself a license to practice. The examinations brief, oral, and secret-plucked almost none at all; even at Harvard, a student for whom a majority of nine professors "voted" was passed. The man who had settled his tuition bill was thus practically assured of his degree, whether he had regularly attended lectures or not. Accordingly, the business throve....

In the wave of commercial exploitation which swept the entire profession, so far as medical education is concerned, the original university departments were practically torn from their moorings. The medical schools of Harvard, Yale, Pennsylvania, became, as they expanded, virtually independent of the institutions with which they were legally united, and have had in our own day to be painfully won back to their former status. For years they managed their own affairs, disposing of professorships by common agreement, segregating and dividing fees along proprietary lines. In general, these indiscriminate and irresponsible conditions continued at their worst until well into the eighties. To this day, it is as easy to establish a medical school as a business college, though the inducement and tendency to do so have greatly weakened.

Meanwhile, the entire situation had fundamentally altered. The preceptorial system, soon moribund, had become nominal. The student registered in the office of a physician whom he never saw again. He no longer read his master's books, submitted to his quizzing, or rode with him in the countryside in the enjoyment of valuable bedside opportunities. All the training that a young doctor got before beginning his practice had now to be procured within the medical school. The school was no longer a supplement; it was everything. Meanwhile, the practice of medicine was itself becoming quite another thing. Progress in chemical, biological, and physical science was increasing the physician's resources, both diagnostic and remedial. Medicine, hitherto empirical, was beginning to develop a scientific basis and method. The medical schools had thus a different function to perform; it took them upwards of half a century to wake up to the fact. The stethoscope had been in use for over thirty years before its first mention in the catalogue of the Harvard Medical School in 1868-69; the microscope is first mentioned the following year.

The schools simply had not noticed at all when the vital features of the apprentice system dropped out. They continued along the old channel, their ancient methods aggravated by rapid growth in the number of students, and by the lowering in the general level of their education and intelligence. Didactic lectures were given in huge, badly-lighted amphitheatres, and in these discourses the instruction almost wholly consisted. Personal contact between teacher and student, between student and patient, was lost. No consistent effort was made to adapt medical training to changed circumstances. Many of the schools had no clinical facilities whatsoever, and the absence of adequate clinical facilities is, to this day, not prohibitive. The school session had indeed been lengthened to two sessions; but they were of only sixteen to twenty weeks each. Moreover, the course was not graded, and the two classes were not separated. A student had two chances to hear one set of lectures-and for the privilege paid two sets of fees. To this traffic, many of the ablest practitioners in the country were parties, and with little or no realization of its enormity at that! "It is safe to say," said Henry J. Bigelow, professor of surgery at Harvard, in 1871, "that no successful school has thought proper to risk large existing classes and large receipts in attempting a more thorough education."

I recall that on one occasion, when I was in high school, I came home and complained to [my father] of what I conceived to be the injustice of one of my teachers. He heard me out patiently and then walked away without a word. I was greatly puzzled.

After breakfast he said to me, "I'll walk to school with you today." We left our home together on Sixth Street near Broadway, walking a block to Chestnut Street and then down to the old high school building at Ninth Street. Nothing was said, but I continued to wonder what he intended to do. On reaching the school, he went to the office of the principal, Prof. Ashley B. Hurt, a very competent school executive and excellent Greek scholar. Prof. Hurt greeted us and asked us to be seated. My father said, "I need only a few moments, Prof. Hurt. My son has complained to me of what he regards as the injustice of one of his teachers. I should like you and all the teachers to know that if any question arises between my son and his teachers, I shall always regard his teachers as being in the right."

Not a word was said in explanation. My father arose, shook hands with Prof. Hurt, bade me good-by, and left. It was no wonder that I never complained again. On the contrary, I became more assiduous in my studies and made a very credible record as a high school student. I should not say that this mode of procedure is necessarily correct in all cases, but it shows a strain of common sense capable of very wide application.

—Abraham Flexner: An Autobiography

Ohio Inventor in 1911

James Murray Spangler's most important upright suction sweeper sale was to his first cousin, whose husband, William "Boss" Hoover, was intrigued by the new invention, patent number 889,823.

Life at Home

- One of ten children born to William Spangler and his wife, Elizabeth Lind Spangler, James Murray Spangler was born in 1848 and grew up in Ohio.
- He collected his first business experience selling gentlemen's furnishings in Akron.
- James married Elestra Amanda Holtz, called Lettie, in May 1874; they would have three children, two sons, Clarence and Francis, and a daughter, Jennie.
- James Murray Spangler loved to tinker.
- In 1887, when he was 34, he created a new and useful improvement for grain harvester by removing the standard tailboard and installing a sliding tailboard to better regulate the width of the platform and permit the harvester to be adjusted for wheat stalks of different lengths.
- In 1893, when he was 47, James invented a combined hay rake and tedder in one machine, thereby providing more hay-spreading efficiency at a reduced cost.
- He was sure that farmers would readily see the advantages of his invention.
- Raising capital was often difficult, however, and running a successful, growing and profitable business was even harder.
- The company he formed to sell this second invention was unsuccessful.
- Four years later, in 1897, James was granted a patent on a velocipede wagon.
- This time he sold his invention and had the joy of seeing his creation do well in the marketplace for a while.
- His fourth invention was an upright vacuum cleaner, created after he turned 60 years old.
- This last invention finally made him financially secure.
- At the time of this invention, James had moved from New Berlin, Ohio, to Canton, Ohio, to work temporarily as a janitor at the Zollinger Department Store, located in the Folwell Building in downtown Canton.
- While handling the messy cleanup with a broom and carpet sweeper, he developed the idea for an upright vacuum cleaner.
- The tedious, daily labor of sweeping the dust and dirt aggravated James's asthmatic condition.
- Inspired by the mechanics of a rotary street sweeper, James decided to mount a sewing machine motor onto

James Murray Spangler

the carpet sweeper; fan blades would blow dirt out of the rear of the cleaner and into a cloth bag to collect the dirt that was vacuumed up.

- Thus was born the electric carpet sweeper, which James called a "suction sweeper."
- It was not the first vacuum cleaner, but it was certainly the first one practical for home use.
- Housekeeping was hard work in 1907, the year the upright vacuum cleaner was invented.
- Cooking a meal on cast-iron or steel stove required constant attention; throughout the day a stove had to be continually fed with coal or wood consuming up to 50 pounds a day.
- Poultry and fish purchased live from the market had to be killed, plucked or scaled.
- Soot and smoke from wood-burning stoves blackened the walls and dirtied draperies and carpets.
- Gas and kerosene lamps left smelly deposits of soot on the furniture and curtains.
- Laundry, one of the most detestable of household chores, often consumed most of Mondays and Tuesdays.
- At the same time, processed foods were appearing, including canned pickles and sauerkraut from the H.J. Heinz Company and condensed soups from the Joseph Campbell Company.
- By the turn of the century, the carpet sweeper was commonly used, various forms of washing machines were being introduced, and by 1903 the electric iron was invented, followed by the first commercially successful electric toaster in 1909.

Life at Work

- James's upright suction sweeper basically consisted of an electric fan to generate suction, rotating brushes to loosen dirt, a pillowcase for a filter and a broomstick for a handle.
- James first tested his invention and applied for a patent in 1907; after a number of modifications, his device was patented on June 2, 1908.
- He had already formed a partnership with a friend, C. Ray Harned, and in October 1907, capitalized with $5,000 invested by F. G. Folwell and W. H. Folwell, the Electric Suction Sweeper Company was founded to manufacture James's design.
- Production began in fall 1907.
- James was aided by his son Clarence, who helped him assemble the machines, and his daughter, who made the dust bags.
- James assembled just two to three machines a week; he bought the motors himself, using his home as collateral.
- Despite the slow rate of manufacture, production soon exceeded sales, which supposedly were being handled by Ray Harned.
- James quickly ran out of money and found himself in danger of losing his home.
- At the same time, his cousin Susan's husband, William "Boss" Hoover, was looking to diversify out of the leather business.
- Automobiles, electric trolleys and other modern inventions were cutting into his profits; he saw that the market for horse collars and harnesses had peaked.
- He was ready to expand his product lines in a changing marketplace when he was introduced to the suction sweeper, which his wife had purchased.
- He quickly came to believe that the electric suction sweeper would "sell itself if we can get the ladies to try it."
- In August 1908 Boss Hoover formed a partnership with James to build the new device.
- He assumed the debts of the Electric Suction Sweeper Company and acquired the patent from James, who served as salaried superintendent but shared in the invention's royalties.
- The Electric Suction Sweeper Company became the Hoover Suction Sweeper Company.
- Hoover set aside a corner of his North Canton factory for the production of sweepers, supervised by Spangler.

- After many months of experiments and numerous improvements, James Spangler and Boss Hoover introduced American housewives to the vacuum sucking cleaner by offering a ten-day free home trial—assuming, of course, that the house had electricity.
- Less than 20 percent of American homes were wired for electricity, but the new energy source was spreading quickly.
- Current was supplied as AC current or DC current, depending on the local source of electricity; at first, until current was standardized as AC in 1910, Hoover and Spangler had to supply models for each.
- Small motors powered by electricity had entered the household market in 1891 when a rotary fan was introduced by the Westinghouse Electric & Manufacturing Company.
- Soon the power of the electric motor was being applied to washing machines, sewing machines, refrigerators, dishwashers, can openers, coffee grinders, eggbeaters, hair dryers and knife sharpeners.
- Advertisers stated, "Electric servants can be depended on to do the muscle part of washing, ironing, cleaning and sewing. Go to your leading electric shop to solve your servant problem."
- Using a network of local retailers to support its advertising campaign, Hoover developed a system of national retailers for the distribution of the vacuums.
- By the end of 1908, the company had sold 372 of its Model Os.
- In 1911 the company became international when Boss Hoover opened a branch in Canada.
- The vacuum cleaner offered an alternative from the annual ritual of spring cleaning, in which all the furniture was removed from the house so that the carpets and rugs could be taken outside to be beaten clean.
- Various metal and wood and rug beaters had been created for this unpleasant and exhausting task.
- Year-round indoor gas lighting and the smoke it emitted created a layer of dust that added an extra week's work to the average spring cleaning; open windows from spring to fall, most without screens, added their own complications.
- But as soon as mechanization took housewives one step toward less physical labor, Americans embarked on a newfound passion for greater hygiene and cleanliness.
- This obsession with microbes coincided with a trend toward houses possessing more light-admitting windows that highlighted any lingering dirt.
- Advertisements and medical pronouncements—including those of the Hoover Suction Sweeper Company—emphasized the dire dangers of household filth.
- Vacuum cleaner advertisements in particular portrayed the dangers that lurked in uncaptured dirt.

Life in the Community: Canton, Ohio

- Founded in 1805 on the West and Middle branches of the Nimishillen Creek, Canton, Ohio, was named for Canton, China (now Guangzhou) by Bezaleel Wells, the surveyor who platted the town.
- Canton did not become a city until 1838.
- It rapidly became a manufacturing center for farm implements at a time when agricultural activity in Ohio was expanding.
- Ohio's wealth of natural resources was attracting investors in transportation canals and railroads.
- Canton residents, however, rejected an offer by Ohio and Erie Canal planners to route the canal through Canton, believing that a canal's standing water would generate diseases.
- The city likewise refused the offer of the Cleveland and Pittsburgh Railroad to run its track through Canton provided the city committed $10,000 to the cost of construction.
- The railroad therefore built the track through Alliance, some 18 miles east of Canton; Alliance reaped the benefits of being on the transportation corridor.
- In the Civil War era, Canton became a center of iron production, and its industries thrived.
- Steel became a major product of the area, thanks to a plentiful supply of water.

Dedication ceremony of the McKinley Monument

- Canton's industrial base attracted immigrants eager for work, particularly Italians, Greeks, Spaniards, Romanians and Russians.
- After the war Canton also became known for watch production; the Hampden Watch Manufacturing Company and the Dueber Watch Case Manufacturing Company, both owned by John Dueber moved to Canton in 1889.
- In its first year Dueber-Hampden, as the sister companies were popularly known, employed nearly ten percent of Canton's population.

- The company's needs were important factors in the city's rapid economic expansion, and Canton's population doubled.
- In nearby New Berlin (later North Canton), William H. "Boss" Hoover moved his tannery business in 1873 from the family farm east of town to the center of the village.
- There he ran a successful leather business before he branched into the manufacturing of vacuum cleaners.
- Canton's weekly newspaper, the *Canton Repository*—founded by John Saxton in 1815 as the *Ohio Repository*—became a daily in 1892.
- The Saxtons were fervent abolitionists and strongly supported education for women; James Saxton, son of the newspaper's founder, was an early supporter of the Republican Party and probably part of the Underground Railroad network in northeastern Ohio.
- Politically the staunchly Republican newspaper was a longtime supporter of future president William McKinley.
- McKinley, who began to practice law in Canton around 1867, married Ida Saxton, John Saxton's granddaughter, in January 1871.
- McKinley was elected to the U.S. House of Representatives in 1876 and lived in Canton during his successful campaigns for Ohio governor (1891, 1893).
- In 1896 McKinley's "front porch campaign"—waged from Canton, very deliberately from the home Ida and William McKinley lived in when they were first married—brought national attention to Canton.
- Reporters descended on the city.
- The McKinley campaign released a biography of Ida Saxton McKinley, who as an adult suffered from epilepsy and other illnesses—some probably associated with her medical treatment—in order to counter rumors that she was mentally ill.
- McKinley was re-elected in 1900, again campaigning from Canton but this time less actively.
- On September 9, 1901, McKinley was shot by Leon Czolgosz, an anarchist, at the Pan-American Exposition in Buffalo, New York; he died six days later, on September 14.
- A three-day funeral train cortege proceeded from Buffalo to Washington, District of Columbia, to Canton.
- The McKinley Monument, where the president was eventually buried along with his wife, who died in May 1907, was dedicated on September 30, 1907.
- The dedication ceremony brought President Theodore Roosevelt, who was the main speaker, and a host of dignitaries to Canton.
- Canton's streetcar system began in December 1884 with the Canton Street Railway's horsedrawn cars; the system was electrified in January 1890.
- The Canton-Akron Consolidated Railway was assembled from predecessors built between 1892 and 1903.
- Canton's streetcar railways were operated by the Northern Ohio Traction and Light Company, which acquired the Canton-Akron Consolidated in 1906 and also was a major power producer for the region.
- Meanwhile the Stark Electric Railway in 1902 ran an interurban line from Canton to Alliance to Sebring, parallel to the Pennsylvania Railroad line. Stark Electric was also a power producer.
- Ohio led the states in interurban railway mileage, with 28,000 miles in service by 1908.
- A decade later the street was paved in brick, and soon the streetcar lines were replaced by automobile traffic.
- Canton was a lively center of early baseball, with an unnamed team belonging to the Ohio State League as early as 1887. Teams came and went, as did leagues.
- In 1890 the Canton team, defending champions of the minor league-level Tri-State League, sold Denton T. "Cy" ["Cyclone"] Young to the National League's Cleveland Spiders for, rumor had it,

$300; the Canton team folded almost immediately afterward, and the Tri-State League disbanded at the end of the season.

- Canton was also a football hotbed; schools and athletic clubs played numerous games. The Canton Bulldogs of the professional Ohio League played in 1904–1906 and then disbanded. In 1911 a new Canton team, the Professionals, took the field.

❧❧❧❧❧❧❧❧

Vacuum Cleaner Timeline

1869 In his Chicago basement, Ives W. McGaffey invented the "whirlwind," a handpumped, non-electric vacuum cleaner made of wood and canvas.

1901 British engineer Cecil Booth pioneered the concept of sucking dust using an electrical pump; the contraption weighed more than 100 pounds.

1905 Chapman Skinner in San Francisco created the first portable electric vacuum; it weighed 92 pounds and used a fan 18 inches in diameter to produce the sucking action.

1907 James Murray Spangler invented a portable electric upright vacuum cleaner that used a cloth bag to collect dust.

1910 The Hoover Vacuum Cleaner Company manufactured a vacuum cleaner that weighed only 10 pounds.

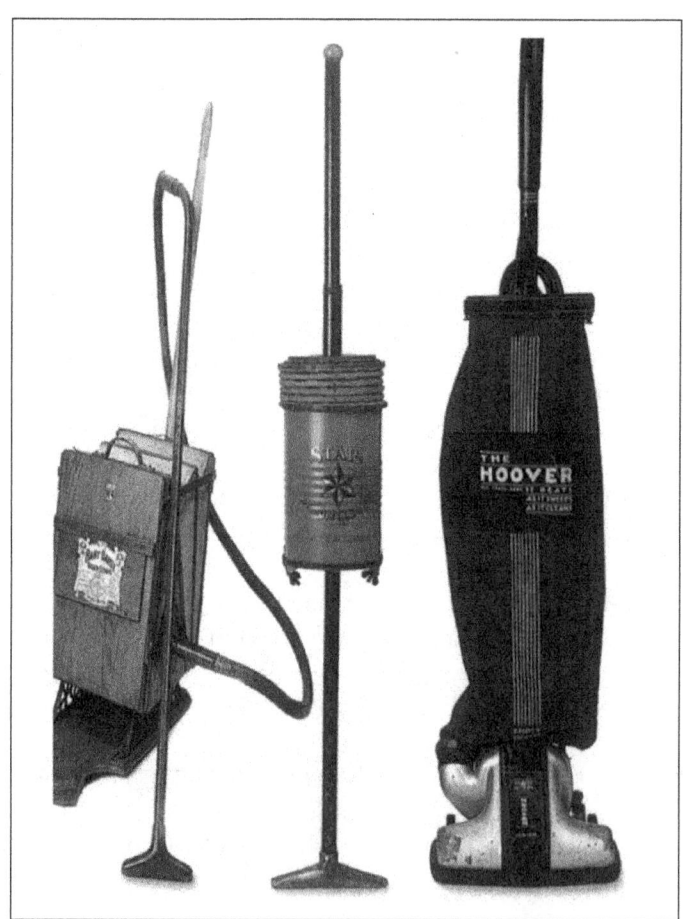

Filmmaker and Inventor in 1911

David Rosen and his wife, Ruth, were at the forefront of the emerging technology of making short feature films and distributing them to the thousands of nickelodeons springing up nationwide. It was their dream that Denver, Colorado, would become the center of the moviemaking industry.

Life at Home

- David and Ruth Rosen's home in downtown Denver accommodated a photography studio, darkroom, and space for David to work on his inventions.
- Originally from Pennsylvania, David had left home at age 16 to travel to the West.
- He met Ruth, who was from New York state, in Colorado Springs, and after marrying they settled in Denver.
- David worked in newspapers and photography before turning to moviemaking in 1902.
- The family owned a four-cylinder Buick, which cost $1,750, a symbol of their prosperity.
- Since Ruth had no desire to learn how to drive the automobile, David always drove, occasionally hiring a driver to take her on trips.
- The Rosens' two children, Richard and Esther, enjoyed the constantly changing nature of their parents' work as well as its social side; the Rosens frequently welcomed people in the film industry to their home.
- Richard was developing an interest in the technical demands of the filmmaking industry.
- Both children attended a Denver public school; Esther was in second grade, but she still found it difficult to conform to school discipline when she had so much freedom at home.
- Ruth was outspoken on women's rights and proud of her record of voting in every election since women in Colorado received the right to vote in 1894.
- Much of Ruth's free time was spent volunteering with fraternal associations such as the Eastern Star, which was affiliated with the Masons and was open to both men and women; to be eligible for membership, women were required to have a significant relationship—wife, mother, or sister, for example—with a Master Mason.

David Rosen

The Rosens collected wicker furniture.

- David was a Master Mason as well as a member of the Elks and an El Jebel Shriner; he had contributed to the building fund for the Shriners' Mosque at 18th Avenue and Sherman Street in Denver and attended its dedication in November 1907.
- The Rosens also collected wicker furniture; David first began using wicker as a photography prop, and the couple later purchased several pieces, including a library table and a Japanese sofa.
- In the summer of 1911, David and Ruth both took an interest in an ocean-to-ocean automobile trip organized by a Philadelphia automobile sales executive named John Guy Monihan, the advertising manager for the Premier Motor Manufacturing Company.
- The convoy of Premiers consisted of one pilot car driven by a professional driver employed by Premier; ten cars driven by private motor enthusiasts; and one Premier "commissary truck," also driven by a Premier driver, carrying parts, supplies, and baggage.
- The commissary truck was not with the convoy for the entire trip; it joined the other Premiers in Indianapolis and was shipped ahead by rail at least once.
- The travelers for the most part found comfortable accommodations along the way and had to set up a "tent village," for which they had made elaborate preparations, only once.
- As the Premiers progressed from Atlantic City, New Jersey, to Los Angeles, California, Monihan sent regular telegram dispatches to the press.
- Despite initial misgivings, the travelers found the roads in the West to be more than adequate; Monihan commented that the worst roads they experienced actually were in Pennsylvania.

The Rosens often had friends for dinner.

- In addition to C. Francis Jenkins, the inventor of the movie camera, who filmed some of the journey, and J. C. Bell, a professional photographer, the group of motorists included at least eight women and three boys, among them Jenkins's wife and Monihan's wife and son.
- The trip was completed in less than 60 days.
- David would have liked to film the Denver portion of the trip, but when the convoy reached Denver on July 15, David was away on a long-scheduled business trip.
- The Premier company published a 52-page booklet, *Ocean to Ocean Tour of the Premierites Told by Wire and Photo,* to publicize the journey.

Life at Work

- David began his training as a still photographer working for newspapers.
- For most of the 1800s, newspaper illustrations were made from engravings; in the later years of the century, photos often guided the engraver.
- In 1894 the *Rocky Mountain News* moved from engravings to halftone photographs, making an investment in equipment and photographers and popularizing the new technique.
- Having gained some experience in newspapers, in 1896 David formed a photographic company to take still pictures of trains and Colorado scenes.
- He loved promoting Colorado; his friends joked that he was the state's unofficial spokesman.

- David also began experimenting with innovations such as high-speed shutters, to capture objects in motion, and panoramic photography, to capture the majesty of the West.
- He also manufactured an X-ray tube, experimenting with X-ray photography for a time, and developed a "detectophone," which could be placed in a room to transmit sounds over a telephone line to a listener.
- To meet current demand, David distributed his photographs using the current rage, postcards, which provided a way for friends to exchange greetings without writing extended missives.
- By 1902 David had turned to the motion picture industry, developed by Thomas Edison and George Eastman.
- His early films featured Colorado's mountainous railroads, spectacular views of the state, and Native American dances, which he filmed on the Ute reservation at Ignacio.
- Like most films, David's movies had little plot; the public was so mesmerized by the action on the screen that no plot was needed.
- David's background and experimentation in high-speed still photography prepared him well for the new technology.

A TABLE SPOON.

David's photographs were also used on postcards.

- He was intrigued by the prospect of taking movies from the arcades to the big screen, or silver screen, as it had become known.

David's equipment enabled him to create short films from clips of daily life.

- David secured financial backing from a pioneering movie producer from Chicago who believed that the scenery and sunshine of Colorado could make it the movie capital of America.
- The Chicago-based company provided national distribution for the short films David produced.
- Typically David's short films were one- to three-and-one-half minutes long and might include clips from a train, a fire, and a mountain range, all cut together to create fast action.
- New York City boasted more than a thousand moviehouses where short features, called the "poor man's grand opera," were shown.
- To gain acceptance for his movie activities, David contracted with the City of Denver for summertime entertainment; his short movies, shown in the city park, featured girls skipping rope, trains passing deep cliffs, and cowboys riding horses.
- The public response was overwhelming' the newspapers carried daily stories concerning upcoming films and the latest films in the making.
- During the first summer they were shown, more than 30,000 people rode the trolley on a single day to see the new moving pictures.

- During the presidential election of 1908, between William Howard Taft and William Jennings Bryan, short features were shown to the crowds outside the newspaper office as people waited for election updates to be flashed on a screen.
- As the role of movies developed, David joined with nine other film producers to control film production and distribution.
- His company was subsequently sued for a violation of antitrust laws.
- One of David's latest movie projects almost ended disastrously; while shooting alongside a river, a cameraman and rider were nearly washed away by a flash flood.
- All filming was done outdoors; when stunts were needed, cowboys were hired, and action scenes often included gunfire using live bullets.
- Recently a small movie company had been established to produce films in Hollywood, California; David was worried that this company could lure some business away from Colorado.

Life in the Community: Denver, Colorado

- Denver came to life in 1858 when gold was discovered along the South Platte River, located at the foot of the Rocky Mountains, which served as a 14,000-foot barrier to travel further west.
- Denver soon became a territorial capital with a reputation as the richest, raciest community between St. Louis and San Francisco.
- In 1869 Dan Castello's Circus left the railroad at Cheyenne, Wyoming, and took four days to make the 85-mile trek to Denver; the trip cost the life of the troupe's baby elephant, but the circus performed in Denver.
- Thespian Edwin Booth toured the West presenting Shakespeare's tragedies; this touch of class appealed to the Western audiences so much that Booth earned $25,000 a month on tour.
- By 1880 the city's population had passed 36,000, and it then tripled, to 106,000, by 1890; Denver accounted for one-third of the state's population.
- Using the wealth provided by gold and later silver, businessmen quickly built banks and railroads to attract additional businesses and to lure the tokens of culture, such as opera, so prized in the East.
- By 1871, using locally available natural gas, streetlights illuminated the city.

The bustling streets of Denver, Colorado

- Eight years later, the first telephones, called "galvanic muttering machines," were available to the city's elite.
- By 1880 electric lights began to replace gas lighting, and five years later attempts were made to install an electric streetcar.
- In 1892 world-trotting journalist Richard Harding Davis called the city "a smaller New York in an encircling range of white-capped mountains."
- The discovery of coal and iron launched a steel industry, turning Denver into an industrial powerhouse and the world's manufacturing center for mining machinery.

The vast, arid stretches of the High Plains did not discourage auto enthusiasts.

- The city's business community displayed its newfound wealth with huge mansions—some costing more than a quarter of a million dollars—perched on the high ground in the southeastern part of the city; the four-story, white marble-columned mansion of David H. Moffat, a railroad magnate and banker, at Eighth Avenue and Grant Street had 42 rooms and included a $25,000 stained-glass window ordered from Tiffany & Company.
- Denver's recently completed civic center was part of a plan to make Denver "one of the most beautiful cities of the world."
- In 1911 enrollment in the city's public schools had increased by 287 students over the previous year, for a total of 30,059 public school students.
- In the summer of 1911, Denver was divided over Methodist bishop H. W. Warren's pronouncement that Dr. Frederick Vining Fisher, pastor of the Methodist church at Ogden, Utah, should resign because of an article concerning Mormonism that Fisher had published in *Outlook* magazine; Bishop Warren said that the article appeared to be a defense of Mormonism.
- Despite the controversy, Fisher enjoyed the strong support of his congregation, and he did not resign.
- Geologists were predicting that Colorado's coal supply would last 31,000 years at the current production rate of 12 million tons a year.
- During the 1911 session of the legislature, proposals before the elected officials included the Headless Ballot law, intended to kill straight ticket voting; a public utility law giving the state the power to regulate all public and quasi-public corporations; an anti-pass law forbidding railroads from giving, or others from receiving, free transportation; a law making it a felony to carry concealed weapons; and a law to protect miners in their work.

Trains were vital to the economic development of Denver.

High School Football Player in 1911

Jonas Bergman, the son of a major mill owner in Everett, Washington, was obsessed with all things connected with football, which he believed to be his destiny.

Life at Home

- Sixteen-year-old Jonas Bergman loved being the oldest son in a family of seven, which included eight-year-old twin sisters.
- He enjoyed being the leader and dreaming up plans for everyone, especially at Christmastime.
- Every year when he and his sisters and brothers decorated the giant Christmas tree, he got to decide who put which ornaments on the tree.
- It was the special job of the youngest and the oldest to put on the first string of popcorn and berries along the lower limbs of the fir tree, but Jonas alone got to place the angel on the top.
- His mother told everyone that her children were the finest tree trimmers in the Western states.
- At Easter Jonas also takes a lead role in reading *Ben-Hur, A Tale of the Christ* to the smaller children.
- Most of the year, a well-illustrated edition of *Ben-Hur* sits on the shelf, next to the Bible; but during the Christian season of Lent, a nightly reading was held.
- Both his mother and father were raised on a tradition of reading this historical romance novel, written in 1880 by Lew Wallace.
- The book, which told of the effect of the life and death of Jesus Christ on a Hebrew merchant, quickly became a national bestseller, and reading it evolved into an Easter tradition in many homes.
- The year Jonas turned 14, a touring company had actually staged the theatrical version of *Ben-Hur* in Everett; it was attended by the entire family.
- Jonas also loved to pass along his boyhood secrets, and he recently showed his five-year- old brother how to twiddle his thumbs; Jonas challenged the little boy to twiddle backward and forward with his eyes closed and not fall over.
- At home the evening meal was an important family time, and no excuses were accepted for not being in attendance.

Jonas Bergman

- Jonas, his sisters, and his brothers were to stand behind their chairs at opposite sides of the table until their parents took their seats, one at each end of the table; then they took their seats.
- All heads were bowed as Mr. Bergman said grace.
- Invariably, in front of Jonas's father were ten dinner plates—blue willow on weekdays and Haviland china on Sundays.
- If the main course was roast or fowl, Mr. Bergman did the carving at the table and served the food on everyone's plate.
- Always to his left there sat a bowl of potatoes or stuffing, while on his right was a bowl of fresh or home-canned vegetables, depending on the season.
- The children were forbidden to announce that they didn't like something being served; if a child indicated that a certain food is not his favorite, Father put less on his or her plate, but the child was expected to eat it all.
- In front of Jonas's mother was placed the salad or fruit of the day, and at her left was a pot of hot tea in a highly glazed black pottery teapot with enameled flowers—for the adults only.
- All of the family's milk cames from Hembree, the family cow, even though quality milk was now available all year around in Everett.
- Jonas's father was born in Sweden and raised in rural Wisconsin.
- He married a Swedish American girl and immersed himself in the timber industry, jumping at the opportunity to move West, where thousands of acres of virgin forest still existed.
- He now managed investments in Everett for John D. Rockefeller and was co-owner of the largest shingle-manufacturing mill in the United States.
- During the past decade, red cedar shingles, milled for distribution nationwide, had been one of the lumber industry's most profitable products.
- Nevertheless shingles were often subject to wide price swings based on competition and availability.
- In 1911 the shingle plant was doing well; business was comparable to what it had been in 1906, when the San Francisco earthquake and ensuing fires opened up considerable demand for shingles for the city's rebuilding.
- In one year, the price of logs, lumber, and shingles had doubled.
- Jonas's father employed 165 shingle weavers who produced more than a million shingles during each ten-hour shift.
- In Everett, the term "shingle weaver" applied to sawyers, filers, and packers, who worked together as a crew to produce cedar roofing shingles.
- While stacking the slices of cedar into overlapping bundles, a skilled packer could work so rapidly that he appeared to be weaving the shingles together—hence the name "shingle weaver."
- From the mid-1880s, investors from the East—including John D. Rockefeller—had speculated heavily in the possibilities offered by Everett, Washington; many succeeded in their ventures, but few succeeded for long in this rough market.
- Growing up in Everett, Jonas enjoyed the freedom afforded by the town, his father's position, and his own intrepid spirit.
- In Everett adventurous boys could hop onto logs that were floated down the Snohomish River, swim out to the sandbar in mid-channel, or catch snakes along the riverbank.
- Like many boys in the area, Jonas took great pride in his ability to identify the various mill whistles along the waterfront—the Ferry-Baker, Clough-Hartley, Hulbert, Eclipse, and others each had a distinctive sound.
- At the noontime whistle, when other young boys in the town ran pails filled with their fathers' lunch to the mill, Jonas ate at home with his father, who routinely took an hour-long nap after lunch before returning to work.

- Jonas's mother often spent her afternoons taking a walk; she was still wearing black in mourning for her baby, Garrison, who had died the previous year when a measles epidemic swept through the Northwest, claiming, in Everett, 17 children under age 2.
- The town's best photographer was hired to shoot a picture of Garrison as he lay in his casket; Jonas's mother kept the picture by her bed, which was also draped in black.
- Several days a week, the mothers of the victims walked to the cemetery together to put flowers on their children's graves.

Life at School

- Jonas enjoyed school but was obsessed with football, believing it represented his future.
- Ever since he first read *Walter Camp's Book of Foot-ball*, he had been convinced that he should play football in college, maybe at Yale.
- He longed to be the star quarterback, especially now that the rules had been changed to allow the quarterback to cross the line of scrimmage whenever he pleased.
- Over the previous 25 years, the rules of football had specified that: "The quarterback is obligated, when running the ball across the line of scrimmage, to be at least five yards away from the center."
- That had now been changed, and it was not the only significant rule shift, although not all of the changes were positive, in Jonas's view.
- As of 1910 flying tackles were prohibited, because of they caused so many injuries to both tackler and runner.
- The new rule stated, "A player in tackling must have at least one foot on the ground."
- Jonas agrees with Walter Camp's comment on this new rule: "If a man, therefore, is endeavoring to go around an end and a (defensive) halfback is running at full speed to reach him, it is going to be a very difficult question as to what will happen, for we all know that a man running at speed has both feet off the ground at once, and if it is a close thing, either the halfback must tackle when he is on the run, or lose his man if he stops."

Jonas's obsession with football began when he read Walter Camp's Book of Foot-ball.

- The second rule that was causing trouble was the new one on passing, stating: "No player of either side while in the act of catching a forward pass shall be tackled, thrown, pushed, pulled, shouldered or straight-armed until he shall have caught the ball and taken more than one step in any direction."
- Jonas believed this rule must be changed; after all, interference was the signature of American football and crucial to preventing the other player from catching the ball.
- At night Jonas and his father worked together to design "weight plays," such as Harvard's flying wedge, that concentrated the weight of the attack upon a point in the opponent's line that could not be quickly supported.
- To support Jonas's fascination with the sport, his father cleared a large field near his mill and helped create an industrial league.
- Most of the other players were the mill's sawyers and lumbermen, who were not especially averse to experiencing or causing pain; they took pain for granted.
- Now that a field was available, industrial teams were forming at many of the mills in the area, with games always scheduled for Sunday afternoons—the workers' only day for recreation.

EDWARD H. COY
Yale

THOMAS L. SHEVLIN
Yale

WALTER W. HEFFELFINGER
Yale

Jonas hoped to become a star quarterback at Yale.

- Spirited competition, fights, and rivalries already were commonplace, with more than one broken arm or leg resulting from these Sunday outings.
- Jonas, one of the few players who had actually read the rules, attempted to explain them before each game; everyone, including massive-bodied lumberjacks, listened to the boss's boy.
- They had also agreed that he should be the quarterback.
- His high-school had a team as well, but the industrial league was more competitive and more fun for a boy getting ready to go East to college.
- Even though his grades were relatively poor, he was sure that when he graduated from the eleventh grade in a year, Yale would be more than happy to accept him.
- After all, his uncle had graduated from Yale, and his father had plenty of money.
- Besides, playing for a school whose mascot was a bulldog seemed right; Jonas liked the Yale cheer: "Bulldog, bulldog, bow, wow, wow!"

A view of the waterfront in Everett, Washington

Life in the Community: Everett, Washington

- Six days a week, the mills' whistles blew at six in the morning, giving a working man an hour to build a fire, have his breakfast and smoke his pipe before embarking on a ten-hour day in the lumber industry.
- Everett boasted 95 manufacturing plants, including 11 lumber mills, 16 shingle mills, 17 combination lumber-shingle mills, a paper mill, an iron factory, several manufacturers of logging and milling machinery, shipyards, an arsenic plant, breweries, and dozens of companies related to the sawdust economy.
- More than 5,000 of the city's 35,000 men, women, and children earned their wages in mills and factories—a ratio more similar to that found in the industrial East than elsewhere in the rural West.
- A quarter of the people in the city were foreign-born, while another quarter had foreign parentage; on the streets of Everett, Norwegian, Swedish, German, Italian and Greek could all be heard.
- In 1909 the Norwegians had agreed to close their private school when the public schools introduced the Norwegian language as a regular part of the high-school curriculum.
- Most homes were built on the 25-foot lots offered by the Everett Improvement Company—two lots if the family was affluent—and were designed by the carpenters who built them, a tradition that inspired considerable creativity as carpenters competed with one another to build the most interesting houses.
- Everett had 40 churches, many based more on nationality than on theology.
- Of the six large Lutheran congregations, only one held services in English; the others conducted their services in German, Norwegian, or Swedish.
- Everett had four fraternal lodges—most of them with women's auxiliaries; 25 labor unions; and dozens of reform clubs, political clubs, women's clubs, book clubs, historical societies, and professional organizations, most of which held regular meetings, picnics, smokers, clambakes, dances, and parties.
- In addition, the YMCA sponsored classes in English, bookkeeping, and arithmetic.

Many jobs in Everett were associated with the lumber industry.

Sawyers were often exposed to dangerous working conditions while cutting and transporting logs.

- The city was already heavily unionized; currently the "Wobblies"—the Industrial Workers of the World—were actively recruiting members among the lumber workers.
- Shingle weavers had recently begun sending money to assist IWW members arrested in Spokane, Washington, for organizing workers.
- Union men in Everett addressed each other as "brother," and when one union member fell ill, aid for the family was typically provided by many others.
- Help was often needed; shingle-making was dangerous work.
- To cut a cedar log into bolts that could fit the carriage of the shingle saw, a man pushed the log forward at waist height with his knee and hands, risking the danger of falling into the blade.
- The sawyer on the upright machine faced similar danger from two whirling blades; the blade on his left sliced the blocks that came automatically from the bolter, ripping 60 slices a minute.
- To make the operation work, the sawyer cleared his saw with his left hand, then passed the slices of wood over to his right hand, with which he then shaped the shingle on the trimmer saw and passed it down a chute to the packer.
- During the operation, sawdust clouded his eyes, nose, and throat; still, a good sawyer took great pride in his ability to cut and trim 30,000 shingles in a ten-hour shift.
- Despite the dangers, shingle weaver jobs were prized; the average pay of $4.50 a day was significantly higher than the $2.25 that lumber mill workers typically made.
- Everett got its start in the 1880s after the Northern Pacific Railroad linked its rails from Lake Superior to the Columbia River and then to Puget Sound, attracting nearly a hundred thousand people to the region during a two-year period.

- Washington achieved statehood in 1889, as thousands roamed the new territory looking for fortunes in lumber, wheat, gold, and new development.
- Speculation was so rampant that a piece of land selling in 1891 for $4,000 was quickly resold for $128,000—and eventually $500,000—as 1892 drew to a close.
- But the early speculation turned to despair in the Panic of 1893, when wages fell 60 percent and the schools that survived had only enough funds to operate for three months; thousands were driven into bankruptcy and fled the city.
- A new city had since formed on the foundation of the railroads of James J. Hill, the lumbering might of Frederick Weyerhaeuser, and the investments of John D. Rockefeller.
- In 1900 Weyerhaeuser purchased 900,000 acres of timber from the Northern Pacific land grants at $6.00 an acre, or about $0.10 per thousand feet of wood.
- The resulting lumber mill was the largest in the world, by 1911 processing 70 million feet of timber a year.

Settlers in Washington hoped to find economic fortune.

Hand-Cigar Maker in 1912

The family of Agustín Rodenas, from Cuba, was supported by the booming cigar making industry in the Ybor City section of Tampa, Florida. Both Agustín and his wife, Luisa, worked in the cigar industry, although Luisa often worked shorter hours so that she could care for their two children, Inez and Raúl.

Life at Home

- The Rodenas family lived in a one-story house very close to the house of their neighbors on either side.
- Although the houses in the area were close together, common areas were set aside for gardens to grow vegetables, cutting the family's food bill by 30 percent.
- Italian vegetable vendors also toured the neighborhood with additional fruits and vegetables.
- Windows were left open. None of the homes was heated, owing to the climate of Florida.
- Conversations between neighbors often took place from window to window, rather than yard to yard; secrets were whispered to prevent anyone else from hearing.
- One woman revealed that a friend boiled and stirred hot water in the kitchen during hard times so that more affluent neighbors would think that stew was cooking.
- The ethnic make-up of the neighborhood was both Cuban and Spanish; no single ethnic group exclusively dominated any area of ever-changing Ybor City.
- Parades, picnics, and festivals were important to the energy and social action of the society, and they were held often.
- Seventh Avenue was a social magnet for the Rodenas family, who never missed the evening stroll down the street on a Saturday night, when the whole community promenaded there and socialized.
- Lining the street were the *chavateros*, who invited housewives to bring their knives for sharpening; *mondongo* men, who sold kidneys; the *heladeros*, who offered fruit-flavored sherbets; and the *maniseros*, who sold peanuts along the crowded thoroughfare.
- The *maniseros* were of particular interest to Raúl and his friends.
- At age 13, Inez was already well aware that the evening stroll often was a time for courtship.

Agustín Rodenas

- As one young woman later recalled, "Mother would take us walking up and down Seventh Avenue and all the boys would be standing on the curb and the mothers would look like little hens watching their chicks so that nobody would look at us or touch us—the boys would go wild trying to get a word with us."
- Another girl said, "If you even sat on the porch outside, somebody had to be there. Marriage was the only way to get out from under the skirts of the mothers—so the first male to come along and smile at us, we would marry him. And there is not divorce."
- Apart from the evening stroll, the social life of the family—especially the men—centered on El Centro Asturiano, the social club of the Cuban cigar workers.
- This club, like most Latin clubs, protected and promoted the idea of the supreme Latin male; women's auxiliaries existed to serve the male members.
- One Latin writer said that any male who stayed home should be considered "hen-pecked and only half a man."
- The men normally saw their children only during the evening meal, after which they headed to the club to enjoy the gaming tables and the company of the other men.
- El Centro Asturiano had approximately three thousand members.
- According to the newspapers, "On Sunday the Cantinas of Ybor City reverberated with the sound of Cubans playing dominoes and cards and club halls are commonly filled to capacity."
- The club's amenities included a library of more than five thousand books, a staircase made of Mexican onyx, and a dance hall with a marble floor and magnificent chandeliers.
- There was also a bowling alley and a gymnasium for club members.
- The family looked forward to the club's annual picnics. In 1911 more than six thousand people—members, their families, and their guests—attended the picnic at Sulphur Springs, causing the trolley company to press all of its cars into service. "Every nationality is represented," reported the *Tampa Morning Tribune*.
- But in June 1912, El Centro Asturiano burned down.
- All of its members were granted full membership privileges in a rival club, El Centro Español, operated by the Italian cigar makers.
- The Rodenas family, like many in the community, paid $1.50 per month for social benefits and total medical protection through La Benefica Española; through the efforts of Cuban cigar workers, a hospital described as the first "electric ambulance" is built.
- Yellow fever was a constant threat to the family, along with typhoid, dengue fever, malaria, and tuberculosis—as was typical of communities with large numbers of immigrants.
- When cigar workers contracted tuberculosis, requiring a long convalescence, the medical package offered through the club provided for $415 and transportation to a Havana sanatorium.
- Church attendance among Cuban cigar makers was poor, and donations to the Catholic Church were low, even as large social clubs were being constructed.
- Of the approximately "10,000 souls" identified by the Catholic church as potential communicants, only 160 came to Mass on Easter, traditionally the most important holy day of the church year.
- Nevertheless, women and some men often refused to work during high Christian holidays such as Holy Week—the week before Easter—or Ascension Thursday.
- The Rodenas family lived within walking distance of the cigar factory.

Life at Work

- Agustín worked as a hand cigar maker; his pay averaged out at about $0.45 per hour, and he worked about 46 hours weekly.
- Cigar makers were paid at a piece rate, not hourly; Agustín made more than a thousand cigars each week, mostly perfectos.
- The average worker's pay amounted to approximately $0.29 per hour.

- Luisa worked as a bander; she made about $11.50 per week, which was the average wage for that type of worker in the industry.
- Luisa frequently worked fewer hours than Agustín, about 40, so that she could tend the children. Cigar workers throughout the country set their own hours and protected that privilege vociferously.
- Unlike in the more ethnically diversified industrial cities of the North, Florida's late 19th-century cigar communities were founded by Spanish-speaking immigrants.
- They produced one item, handmade cigars made from Cuban tobacco.
- Among the total population of Tampa, 82 percent of Cuban males worked in the cigar industry, compared with 45 percent of the Italian men and 78 percent of the Spanish men.
- Ventilation was extremely controversial in cigar factories. Usually the windows remained closed despite the heat. Open windows caused a draft for the men, who sat in virtually the same position all day. More important, the fresh air dried out the tobacco and made it harder to work with, resulting in lower production.
- Cigar makers wanted to make cigars with tobacco that was dry but pliable.
- The smell of a cigar factory was intense and overpowering; recalling their first days on the job, workers often mentioned the nausea and intoxication caused by the thick, penetrating smell, which made it "difficult for them to walk in a straight line."
- The tobacco produced a fine brown dust that settled everywhere, contributing to the fact that cigar workers' mortality rate from tuberculosis was second only to that of stonecutters.
- Cigar makers changed their clothing in the morning and donned an apron to begin work. The tobacco stained everything that was not covered.
- The apprenticeship of an aspiring cigar maker often lasted three years, with pay of only $5.00 a week.

Women took on supporting roles in the cigar industry.

Decorative labels helped to identify and sell cigars.

Unloading barrels of tobacco leaves was a first step in cigar production.

- Even young cigar makers were expected to smoke their own cigars to test the quality of the product they produced.
- All wages were paid weekly, in cash, on Saturdays. The pay was based on how many cigars the worker produced, measured per thousand.
- For what was called "Spanish" hand work, using only Clear Havana tobacco, a cigar maker who made a thousand four-and-a-half-inch-long cigars would be paid $17.00 for straight work, $18.00 for shaped cigars, and $21.00 for perfectos, the hardest to make.
- The Ybor City factory clearly had a class system, with packers and selectors at the top.
- The packers and selectors looked down on cigar makers such as Agustín, who in turn considered themselves superior to strippers and banders.
- Other cigar industry jobs included bunch maker, roller, and steamer.
- The cigar making industry was considered a travelling fraternity. Like carpenters, hatters, and printers, many cigar makers traveled from factory to factory, knowing a good cigar maker could get a job almost anywhere in the country.
- The cigar makers of Ybor City, however, distrusted the German influences they perceived in the national unions.
- The unions themselves excluded some nationalities, including "Chinese coolies," and male union members often distrusted women workers, whom they believed could be disloyal and were capable of undermining worker solidarity.
- Cigars produced in Ybor City were considered "high end," or more expensive, and the workers there had a strong sense of themselves as craft workers.

- Beginning about 1907, however, they faced increasing competition from cigar makers pushing $0.05 and $0.10 cigars.
- Several "cheap cigar" manufacturers relocated from New York City to Tampa in 1910 and 1911.
- Increasingly, as the market for cheaper cigars grew, manufacturers reorganized production methods to produce the cheaper cigars using a mold and a more mechanized process; this was referred to as team work.
- For the more expensive cigars, "Spanish work," in which a single person was responsible for making a cigar, continued to be the production model, but the more expensive cigars were steadily losing market share in favor of the less expensive ones.
- Of the 11,541 total factory employees, 64.6 percent were females, although it was unusual for a married woman to work there; only 20 percent of the working Cuban women were married.
- Women usually were employed in support roles and were given little encouragement to become cigar makers.
- A study of women cigar workers showed that they worked more irregular hours; many married women arrived early and worked quickly so they could leave work and get home in time to meet their children arriving home after school.
- Nationally, female membership in the Cigar Makers International Union (CMIU), was 10 percent at best, although the percentage tended to rise during strikes.
- Employers often hired women, who were accustomed to receiving lower pay, for team work production.
- When the CMIU organized the Jacob A. Mayer Company in Pennsylvania in 1907, 30 women were fired because the union did not allow team work.

Paid lectors entertained and educated cigar workers.

Jobs within the cigar industry included bunch maker, roller, and steamer.

- It was customary within the industry for cigar makers to take home three cigars at the end of each weekday and six on Saturday; a cigar maker created "smokers" for his own personal use as part of his pay.
- Some female cigar makers took home free cigars to their husbands or boyfriends.
- The pressure to produce cigars was so high that many workers did not take the time to go to the restroom, fearing that, as one worker said, "you are going to lose 10 minutes and you are going to lose 10 to 15 cigars or 20." Therefore, the worker continued, "Many times you waited until you got home."
- Cigar workers became educated thanks to the industry tradition of lectors, one of the most prestigious professions in the cigar industry.
- Lectors, or readers, were hired to entertain the cigar roller. They were paid by the workers, and the more popular the lector, the higher the salary he could command.
- Lectors usually were seated in a chair elevated above the cigar-roller tables so their voices could easily be heard throughout the room.
- They began the day by reading excerpts from a local newspaper and a newspaper from Spain or Cuba, followed by a reading from a novel or the works of a political philosopher.
- Cigar workers, many of whom were unable to read and write, could quote Shakespeare, Voltaire, Zola, and Dumas.
- The lector custom was not widespread outside Tampa, except in the Jewish cigar making shops in New York.
- Future labor leader Samuel Gompers served as a lector before becoming the head of the American Federation of Labor.
- In 1912 the Rodenas family was still struggling to repay debts acquired during the Cigar Strike of 1910.

Women workers in the cigar factory

- The cigar factory was not unionized, but in 1909–1910, the CMIU began intensive organizing efforts in Tampa, and membership in the union tripled over this period.
- Owing to CMIU efforts, workers received an across-the-board pay increase in 1910.
- But at the beginning of August 1910, when the owners refused to institute union shops or to formally recognize the union, the workers called a general strike.
- At the start of the strike, nearly 1,000 unionized construction workers, printers, machinists, and longshoremen marched with more than 2,000 cigar workers to a rally in Ybor City that attracted 5,000.
- The ethnically diverse audience heard speakers in English, Spanish, and Italian encouraging the men and women to strike.
- Tampa's Cigar Manufacturers Association, the owners' group, officially locked the workers out on September 3.
- After a factory bookkeeper was shot when he arrived at the factory for work on September 13, two Italian immigrants were arrested in connection with the shooting.
- Hours later the two were lynched by well-organized vigilantes.
- An investigator later found that the lynchings were planned and executed in cold blood with the collusion of some police, in order to intimidate strikers.
- The bookkeeper died; no charges were ever filed against the vigilantes.
- As the strike wore on, union leaders were arrested and the union hall and union newspaper were closed by the authorities.
- Some factories were reopened in mid-October, but few workers reported for work.
- By the end of January 1911, their union funds exhausted, the workers returned to the factories.

Life in the Community: Tampa and Ybor City, Florida

- The arrival of the railroad in Tampa, located on Florida's west coast on Tampa Bay, in 1884 had transformed the small community's economic prospects.

- Cigars were first made in Tampa in 1886, in Ybor City, a neighborhood established by Vicente Martínez Ybor just to the northeast of the city center.
- Ybor, Eduardo Manrara, and Serafín Sánchez, all originally from Spain, had moved their cigar factories to Tampa from Key West, Florida, to avoid labor problems.
- Key West had had a cigar making industry since 1869, when cigar makers left Cuba because of the turmoil of the Second Cuban War for Independence.
- The great fire of 1886 in Key West contributed to Ybor's move to Tampa. Many in Key West feared a repeat of the devastation.
- The climate of Tampa, on the west coast of Florida, was characterized by high humidity and was therefore well suited to the making of cigars.
- The incentives offered by Ybor attracted thousands of immigrants to the cigar-making trade.

Cigar labels attracted cigar consumers.

- The industrial work force comprised almost exclusively Spanish, Cuban, and Italian immigrants, who did not have to compete with entrenched ethnic groups, such as the Irish and the Germans, from earlier migrations.
- Cigar manufacturing expanded even further in the 1890s when many more factories relocated to Tampa from New York and Key West.
- Eleven Key West factories moved to Tampa following the fire; 13 from New York also relocated to the city.
- By 1895 approximately 10,000 Cubans resided in Florida—approximately 2.3 percent of the state's population.
- The Cuban population included many Afro-Cubans; there was little racial discrimination in Ybor City in the early years, although the Afro-Cubans generally were unskilled workers and entered the industry at the lowest levels.
- The Italian workers, too, tended to get low-paying jobs in the cigar factories; unlike the Spanish and the Cubans, the Italians usually had no prior experience in the specialized cigar making industry.
- By 1900 Tampa had become the leading manufacturing city in Florida, thanks largely to its production of millions of pure Havana cigars.
- By 1909 Florida's cigar industry employed 12,280 wage earners; the industry manufactured products valued at $21.5 million, 29.6 percent of the total value of the state's manufactured products.
- The 1910 census listed 58,725 male cigar makers nationwide, of whom 18,032 were born of native parents.
- Among unionized cigar makers in New York City, separate union locals were created for the Bohemians, Jews, and Spanish-speaking cigar makers.

- In terms of workers employed, New York was the industry's foremost urban center, with a total of 22,416 workers, followed by Tampa, with 8,061; Philadelphia, 6,216; Detroit, 4,354; Chicago, 4,161; Pittsburgh, 3,061; Baltimore, 2,648; and Cincinnati, 2,437. Together other cities employed 86,224, for a total of 139,578 cigar workers nationwide.
- In 1910 approximately 38,000 people lived in Tampa, up from 15,800 residents in 1900.
- West Tampa, where the Rodenas family lived, boasted 10 cigar factories, a $20,000 opera house, and streetcar service.
- One observer commented, "West Tampa is just like the wild west, a frontier town. There are cockfights, boxing matches, horses tied to hitching posts in front of cantinas. West Tampa is called La Caimaneri'a, or 'place of gators.'"
- Latin cigar makers who strayed beyond the Ybor City district of Tampa often encountered social boundaries; "A Latin can't cross Twenty-second street," according to one writer.
- Signs reading "No Dogs or Latins Allowed" or "No Dagoes" were posted in Tampa by the Anglo population.

The front arcarde of the Cherokee Club, a social club in Ybor City.

Engineer for a Textile Manufacturing Company in 1913

Paul Chéreau worked as an engineer for the Amoskeag Manufacturing Company in Manchester, New Hampshire; he started as an office boy and worked his way up to plant construction and machinery improvement. He lived with his wife, Patrice, and their five children in a house provided by the company.

Life at Home

- The Chéreaus lived in a large home built and maintained by Amoskeag for officers of the company.
- The eldest son, also named Paul, was attending Yale College in New Haven, Connecticut.
- Marie, the elder of the two Chéreau daughters, had expressed a strong desire to go on to college, and the couple was discussing whether they would be willing to pay for college for the two girls.
- Paul and Patrice did not entirely agree on which school Marie should attend.
- Patrice wanted Marie to remain close to home, and Marie herself dreamed of the freedom as well as the education that a secular college such as Mount Holyoke or Smith would give her.
- But Paul preferred the idea of sending Marie to a Catholic college or academy, probably in Canada.
- The Congregation of Notre Dame of Quebec had won permission in 1908 to open a college for young women, opening the way for them to go on to university studies.

- Paul was not at all sure that he approved of women pursuing higher education.
- But if Marie was determined to go to college, he thought it would be better for her to do so under the firm and experienced direction of the sisters, who had supervised Catholic education in Quebec since the days of New France.
- The three younger children were as lively and intelligent as young Paul and Marie, and both Patrice and Paul were fiercely protective and proud of all five of their children.
- Yet because he viewed silence as a strength, Paul rarely showed emotion toward his children.
- He also prided himself on his memory and expected his wife and children to remember each of his requests; he did not like to repeat himself.
- He loved dressing well, and many of his clothes were purchased during trips to Boston or ordered from John M. Smyth Company in Chicago.
- In addition to maintaining a full work schedule, he was often away from home serving on boards, both governmental and church.

Paul Chéreau

Paul's wife, Patrice

- Paul's grandparents were originally from France; his family lived first in Quebec before moving to Manchester when he was a child.
- His high, consistent wages allowed him to invest in high-grade bonds; he managed his money very conservatively and was skeptical of the stock market.
- The only stock Paul owned was that of Amoskeag Manufacturing, some of which he purchased and some of which he was given.
- Paul made it a practice to check the company stock price every day.
- Amoskeag Manufacturing experimented with profit sharing and stock-option plans, attempting to include all workers; the workers, however, tended to suspect that the company stock program was actually a way to hold down wages.
- Total wages were an important factor in Amoskeag's financial operation, constituting 35 percent of the total cost of mill operations.
- The annual stockholder's meeting was always held in one of the mill buildings in Manchester; more than a thousand people had attended the 1912 annual meeting and received a free meal.
- The family recently purchased a car for trips into the country.
- Except when young Paul was home from Yale, only Paul drove, however; Patrice thought that women should not handle machinery.

Life at Work

- The Amoskeag Manufacturing Company facilities encompassed 30 major mills, each of which was as large as a standard, stand-alone mill elsewhere; the buildings covered eight million square feet.
- The company was totally self-sufficient in its operations, including power generation and construction capabilities.
- By 1912 Amoskeag had almost 15,000 employees producing close to five hundred miles of cloth a day.
- In 1913 Amoskeag employed 17,000 workers, making it the largest textile plant in the United States—and possibly in the world.
- Amoskeag's total operating profit in 1913 was $1.1 million, an increase over that of 1912; the combined annual production of cotton and worsted cloth was 231.6 million square yards.
- The company had earned a solid reputation for producing excellent yarns with a high fiber count, making them superior goods.

The Chéreaus' youngest daughter dreamed of going to college.

A large office staff managed the mills.

- Paul joined Amoskeag as an office boy; he was expected to arrive at daylight and start coal fires to provide heat; he then swept the office, picked up the mail, and delivered handwritten orders for cotton, wool, machinery, and other items needed in Boston.
- Next he worked in the payroll department while going to school at night.
- Paul's supervisors noticed his abilities and work ethic, and he was regularly promoted.
- Eventually he became an engineer for Amoskeag with responsibility for textile machinery and new construction.
- Like all of the company's managers, Paul was expected to negotiate the best price for whatever he purchased; Amoskeag was known for its success in making advantageous deals for cotton, supplies, and machinery.
- By 1913 Paul was in charge of installing new textile equipment; he loved the precision of quality machines, which produced fewer errors and less waste and also required less supervision.
- Most of the equipment at Amoskeag had been manufactured and installed between 1881 and 1900.
- By 1913 the company had 60 men working in its foundry to make replacement parts for its aging machinery.
- Weavers nevertheless wanted the newest machines; if a weaver's five or six looms were running well, he could walk around, chat with others, and even read.
- Machines in poor repair required more work and more downtime; because employees were paid according to the amount of cloth they produced, weavers assigned such machines were unable to earn top pay.
- The Amoskeag facility was so large that when Paul was pressed for time, he often used a company taxi to go from his office to the cloth room or to a mill that was experiencing problems.
- Mill management operated by means of a centralized, well-defined hierarchy of authority.

- The company was feeling pressure from cotton goods produced in the South; Paul thought that most of the Southern textile mills produced inferior cloth.
- In 1912 Amoskeag management was forced to increase wages because a strike in Lawrence, Massachusetts, was gaining support among workers in Manchester and walkouts were beginning.
- Amoskeag's 10 percent, across-the-board wage increase effectively ended labor unrest in its mills.
- Paul was convinced that if the United States had not overreacted to immigration, willing workers from Europe would have been available to take mill jobs at any wage.
- Then the Southern mills, which now spent less on payroll than Amoskeag, would not have been able to undersell the company.
- Moreover, fashion changes seemed to be coming more and more quickly, further harming profits; Paul frequently had to respond to demands from buyers to change patterns, weaves, and styles in order to chase every fad.
- He well knew the consequences: when styles changed frequently, it was usually the manufacturer that accumulated too much costly inventory.
- Further, manufacturing to custom order in a changing market often caused wide fluctuations in production and considerable downtime for both workers and machines; in short, it was not good business.
- Paul was puzzled that gingham, an Amoskeag mainstay, was losing popularity; designers told him that because of its rigidity of pattern and weave, gingham was being used less.
- Printed cloth, on the other hand, was enjoying wide use because of its flexibility in finishing and styling.
- After the passage of the New Hampshire child labor law of 1911, it was rare to find children younger than 12 working at the mill; the law allowed children 12 and above to work during school vacations, and at age 14, children could begin to work full-time.
- French Canadians were considered to be particularly well-suited to textile work because of their large families; family members followed one another into the mills.
- Recruitment of French Canadians to work in Manchester was made easier by the railroad route running between Montreal and Boston.
- The French Canadians filled skilled and semiskilled jobs, while the overseer jobs were given to native-born Americans, whose origins were English, Scottish, second-generation Irish, German, and Swedish.

Workers crossed the bridge from the factory into town.

The vast Amoskeag complex sat on the banks of the Merrimack River.

- Adapting to immigrant workers, supervisors by 1913 were accustomed to speaking French; the Polish and Greek workers often relied on translators hired by the company.
- A paymaster commented that, "most of the people who worked in the mill couldn't talk English, but they knew their coinage. They could tell the difference between a silver dollar and a quarter."
- The average weekly pay was $17.50.
- In 1905 Amoskeag opposed the state of New Hampshire's efforts to reduce the workweek from 60 hours to 58.
- To cope with the ever-changing and expanding work force, Amoskeag introduced an employment office in 1911; it was intended to centralize the hiring process for all workers and to keep systematic records of all hirings, firings, and reasons for leaving.
- Management also used the employment office to attempt to control the diversity of the departments by controlling turnover.
- Turnover was a constant in mill operations; by one estimate, some two percent of the Amoskeag work force left every week.
- A centralized system allowed management to screen out troublemakers and labor agitators.
- The mill provided a textile club, a textile school, a cooking school for girls, and free dental service.
- The curriculum of the textile school included mechanical drawing, shorthand, typewriting, mathematics, automobile construction, and practical weaving.
- The company also maintained a small hospital staffed by a doctor and nine nurses; the staff made home visits to employees and families without charge.
- Cloth from the mill was provided to families in need so that they could make clothing.
- The company also provided rental privileges pertaining to three- to five-story brick homes located along the streets leading to the center of town.
- Originally designed as boardinghouses for the "mill girls" of the 1840s, the buildings were remodeled for family use; rent was only $1 per room per month—substantially below the market rate for the rest of the city.
- To qualify for housing, workers had to have large families with more than one member employed by the mill.
- The houses were so popular that some families stayed on the housing waiting lists for months or even years.
- The closeness of the houses to the mill allowed working women to quickly cross the bridges dividing factory and town to check on their children during breaks.

The mill provided training sessions for both male and female workers.

- By 1913 about 20 percent of the Amoskeag work force lived in corporate housing.
- The company took a paternalistic view of its workers and expected loyalty in return; association with unions that would disturb this relationship was strongly discouraged.
- The children of workers played at Amoskeag playgrounds, which included a swimming pool, baseball diamond, and, in winter, a skating rink; gardening by children and adults was encouraged.
- Over just the past year, nearly $30,000 was spent to transform these recreational grounds into one of the city's premier attractions.

Life in the Community: Manchester, New Hampshire
- The Amoskeag Company founded the city of Manchester in 1837 and dominated the economy of the city.
- The city and company were planned and developed by a group of Boston-based entrepreneurs.
- *Amoskeag* meant "abundance of fish" in the Pennacook dialect of the Abenaki language.
- The same waterfall viewed by the native Pennacook people as a source of pure water became the engine that drove the operations of the textile machinery.
- The Boston entrepreneurs purchased the waterpower for the entire length of the Merrimack River, New England's second largest river, and 15,000 acres were set aside across from the Amoskeag Falls as the site for the planned city and mill.

The Amoskeag Mills

- The Amoskeag complex was a unique and highly successful attempt at total planning, both of the mill and the city.
- The solid, red-brick factory walls flanked the Merrimack River for more than a mile on one side of the river, and for a half-mile on the other.
- The solid wall of the mill facing the cluster of corporation-owned worker boardinghouses was constructed in a style that resembled that of a walled medieval city.
- Manchester's arrangement of streets, brick homes, and bridges gave it the honor of being the "handsomest manufacturing city in the world."
- It was founded on the nineteenth-century belief in providing for the complete life of the new industrial man.
- The community was named after Manchester, England, already famous as the world's largest textile city.
- The developers envisioned a community of young, unmarried women, mostly from rural New England, working together in the mills and living together in the boardinghouses.
- The company regulated the workers' behavior during work and after hours; the boardinghouses were closed and locked at 10 p.m., church attendance was compulsory, and alcoholic consumption was prohibited.
- To stimulate the development of the city, Amoskeag auctioned off land for stores and homes and gave land to churches and social clubs to encourage their development.
- Congregationalists, Universalists, and Baptists were the first to obtain lots for building churches or meeting houses, commencing in 1839.
- To avoid overcrowding, the corporation employed deed restrictions that limited the number and size of houses in residential areas; the corporation also dictated the types of materials it considered suitable for construction in the commercial areas of the city.
- After the Civil War, Irish immigrant families willing to work for less than the "mill girls" began to predominate in the labor force.
- The company also began recruiting skilled gingham weavers in Scotland; the quality of work at Amoskeag was improved by the initial 80 "Scotch girls," who eventually were joined by many of their relatives emigrating from Scotland to work at Amoskeag.
- In 1880 the manufacture of cotton goods was concentrated in New England, the location of 80 percent of the nation's spindles; by 1913, however, this dominance had eroded to 54 percent.
- The new cellulose-based fiber called Viscose, regarded as an artificial silk, accounted for only 0.1 percent of the mill's consumption of all fibers in 1913.
- Beginning in the 1880s, the Amoskeag Company annexed and purchased all of the surrounding mills, and by 1905 the company had become the only large textile corporation in the city.
- Workers in Manchester often said, "Amoskeag is Manchester."

- In 1913 the assessed value of Amoskeag represented slightly less than one-quarter of the total assessed value of all of Manchester, New Hampshire.
- Unlike other textile towns, Amoskeag did not have a company store; in 1913 Manchester was a lively city full of private shops, movie houses, and dance halls.
- Known for its clean air and tree-lined avenues, Manchester was the fifth largest city in New England, boasting a population of more than 70,000.
- In addition to the mill and shops, Manchester had two shoe factories and a cigar industry; most of the cigar workers were Belgian.
- The shoe factory provided the city with some economic diversity; many families made an effort to ensure that they had at least one member working at the shoe factory so as not to be entirely dependent on textile employment.
- The population of Manchester began to change in the early 1900s as large numbers of French-speaking Canadian immigrants, escaping the poverty of the farms, came to work at the textile company.
- As had their predecessors, new immigrant groups quickly organized in parishes.
- The Roman Catholic diocese of Manchester had been formed in 1884 from a portion of the diocese of Portland, Maine; at that time, all of the 37 priests of the Manchester diocese were required to speak both English and French.
- Years before that, in 1871, Québécois priests had established a French-speaking Roman Catholic parish, St. Augustin, in Manchester; Manchester's Irish Catholics already had a parish, St. Joseph's, founded in 1869.
- In 1902 some 850 Polish immigrants founded their first parish, St. Hedwig's.
- The 1910 census recorded that 42 percent of Manchester's residents were foreign-born, with French Canadians representing 19.6 percent, followed by the Irish, at 5 percent; Greeks, at 1.9 percent; and Poles, at 1.5 percent.
- The immigrant work force was concentrated at the mills; the percentages of immigrant workers at the mills was considerably higher than the percentages of immigrants residing in Manchester at large.
- In December 1912—a month in which, owing to relatively low turnover, it took on many fewer new employees than usual—the mill hired 360 workers, of whom 51 percent were French [Canadian]; 13 percent, Irish; 11 percent, Greek; 8 percent, native-born Americans; 8 percent, Polish; and the remainder English, German, Scottish, Swedish, Lithuanian, and Russian.
- Future president William Howard Taft toured Amoskeag in February 1908; on a return trip to Manchester in March 1912, he was greeted by vast crowds, among them 12,000 schoolchildren.
- Previous presidents had visited Manchester, including Abraham Lincoln, just prior to his election in 1860; Ulysses S. Grant, in 1869; Rutherford B. Hayes, in 1877; and Theodore Roosevelt, in 1902.

The streets of Manchester, New Hampshire

Retired Automobile Company Executive in 1913

Henry Jorgensen accumulated his wealth through Michigan copper and lumber investments, then in the manufacture of Oldsmobile automobiles and engines. Thereafter he traveled with his wife, Phoebe; enjoyed life on the eastern shore of Maine; and pursued his new passion, rediscovering his heritage in Scandinavia.

Life at Home

- The Jorgensens lived in Detroit in a 5,000-square-foot, three-story home with buff-colored brick trimmed with red sandstone.
- The hip roof was covered with green slate, and at the corners were impressive Victorian towers.
- The interior of the house had paneled walls, decorated ceilings, and marquetry floors with four-tone borders throughout; on the first floor, the house also featured a music hall, separate library, and complete study.
- A mural of a partially draped woman swinging on a garland of flowers was painted in the arched stairwells leading to the second floor, where it blended with the 18-foot stained-glass window.
- The second story, which had ten bedrooms, featured a walnut-paneled music room dominated by a large pipe organ, which Phoebe took great pride in playing for her children, grandchildren, and guests.
- The floor of the massive room was covered with an oriental rug from Turkey.
- Henry had recently added an "automobile room" to the house, at the right rear of the first floor; the trade journal *Automobile* pointed out that with the rapidly growing popularity of the automobile, the best houses of the future might contain this kind of room.
- Born in 1840 in Lansing, Michigan, Henry took an early interest in politics, winning office in the Michigan House of Representatives before running unsuccessfully for statewide office in his late twenties.
- Leaving southern Michigan in 1869, he went to Copper County, in the state's upper peninsula, where he made a fortune.
- Beginning modestly enough as a merchant in Houghton, he participated in the organization of several copper mining companies.
- To keep the copper moving, he put his energy into expanding the transportation resources of the area, and he was successful in bringing to

Henry Jorgensen

completion the Portage Lake and Lake Superior ship canal.

- He also helped organize two railroads: the Marguette, Houghton and Ontonagon and the Copper Range.
- When he was approached by a friend at the turn of the century about investing in horseless carriages, he was 59 years old, already rich, and in semiretirement.
- Initially Henry regarded horseless carriages as an interesting idea requiring relatively little capital—about $10,000—even if the risk was high.
- The creation of the Olds Motor Company to manufacture the Oldsmobile automobile and the Olds engine allowed Henry to work with David, one of his two sons.
- His son Carl joined the company in 1899, becoming president after founder Ransom Olds left in 1904 in a dispute over control.
- Because Henry was always focused on work and promoting the economy of Michigan, he and Phoebe rarely traveled during his working years.

Henry's wife, Phoebe, and his young family

- One of the family's first trips abroad, in June 1911, was an excursion to England to attend the coronation of King George V a year after the death of his father, King Edward VII.
- The long, luxurious cruise across the ocean provided Henry with a lot of "thinking time"; he found this so congenial that they subsequently took two cruises a year, frequently visiting Denmark and Sweden and occasionally Russia.
- Henry believed his great-grandfather had come from Copenhagen, so he hired a university professor to research the records.
- Henry and Phoebe also enjoyed spending summers at their home on the eastern shore of Maine, which was good for his health; they could relax, walk the harbor area, and visit the beaches.
- They often took their grandchildren and great-grandchildren to the shore with them, along with a handful of servants and nannies.
- One of their newest obsessions was the sound produced by the new and vastly improved phonographs now on the market; they had one at each of their homes.

Four of a Kind raising a pair.

The Jorgensens spent careferee summers at the shore.

Life at Work

- Henry Jorgensen made a fortune in Michigan copper and lumber in the years following the Civil War; for the past few years, he had been investing in real estate in Detroit and in new inventions that caught his fancy.
- In 1897 he became acquainted with Ransom Olds of Lansing, Michigan, through a friend who had already put money into Olds's company.
- Olds desperately needed capital to keep alive his dream of making an affordable automobile, which he called the Oldsmobile.
- Originally from Lansing, Henry had a long history of partnering with friends for investment purposes; in the 1880s, he was part of a group of investors who started City National Bank.
- Initially, in 1897, he came into the Olds company with four other investors, each of whom put in $10,000; 18 months later he became the dominant player in the new company and active in its running.
- By 1899 the nominal capital in the company was $350,000, of which $200,000 was paid in; a total of $400 was invested by Olds himself, the rest by Jorgensen.
- To help Henry watch his investment, his son David was named secretary and treasurer of the new company.
- As a businessman, Jorgensen's initial interest was in the Olds gasoline engine, which was already selling well; he was also intrigued by the possibilities of the horseless carriage.
- At first, he did not like the other term gaining popularity, a French term that his partner Ransom Olds favored: *automobile.*
- The investment in the Oldsmobile was often vexing for investor and inventor alike.
- Inventor Ransom Olds found that inviting others to invest brought much-needed capital but unwanted advice as well; he was often frustrated that outside investors wanted to make money from a product about which they knew little or nothing.
- During an early board meeting, Olds was told, "We want you to make one perfect horseless carriage." Ultimately, the minutes of the meeting reflected a desire to make a "nearly perfect" horseless carriage.

Henry kept a picture of his two daughters with him at work.

- A master at publicity, Olds promoted his new car constantly; in 1897 Olds's brother Wallace gained nationwide headlines when he drove the company's one motor vehicle from Lansing to Grand Lede and back, making the 12-mile return trip in one hour and 15 minutes.
- By 1901 Oldsmobile was one of the biggest names in the fledgling industry; the car sold for $650 at a time when an imported, top-of-the-line French automobile cost up to $17,000.
- By 1902 the Olds company had selling agents throughout the East and Midwest, plus a few in the South and West.
- The Olds dealer in Denver, Colorado, reported that he sold 15 cars in the first four weeks of the year, 6 of them to doctors.
- That year the company sold 3,700 vehicles; by 1903 Oldsmobile ads referred to "5,000 satisfied" customers.
- The nation's total automobile output in 1903 by all companies was 9,000 cars.
- Sales for the Oldsmobile totaled $2.3 million in 1903, up five times over the sales results of $410,000 in 1901.
- The curved-dash Olds was the talk of the industry.
- To conserve cash while growing so rapidly, Olds Motor Works insisted that the burden of funding salaries at the factory be passed along to the dealer.
- Dealers' deposits often paid half the sum necessary to bring out a full year's production; in turn, to get their cash back as rapidly as possible, dealers required that their customers pay cash also.
- Olds believed that selling on credit only encouraged customers to be careless with a car they did not own and were paying for in installments.
- Working together, Olds, Jorgensen and his son streamlined the business, especially the manufacturing process; in January 1904, *Scientific American* singled out the Olds Motor Works as an operation that exemplified the new trend in automobile manufacturing.
- Unfortunately, by the time the article appeared, Ransom Olds had left the company after a battle of wills.
- Believing that the Oldsmobile runabout was beginning to be regarded as an inferior product, Henry wanted to replace the inexpensive model with a bigger, heavier, more expensive vehicle that was more reliable.
- Olds blamed the problems on inexperienced repairmen who did not understand the complexity of an automobile.
- Upon leaving, Olds created a new company and a new car, the REO; the name was derived Ransom E. Olds' initials.
- Henry and his sons, however, continued to manufacture Oldsmobiles.
- By 1907 the REO and the Oldsmobile were each being manufactured in a factory in Lansing, Michigan, creating fierce competition.
- According to *Motor Age*, "Everyone works either for one or the other of the two motorcar factories, has a friend who does or knows a friend's friend who expects soon to be employed. So strong is the rivalry between the two factories, however, that the man who leaves skimmed milk at the door of the Olds employee knows better than to solicit trade from the family whose breadwinner dallies with an envelope from the REO paymaster."
- By 1908 the REO's sales soared well ahead of Oldsmobile's; Oldsmobile produced only a thousand cars that year.
- Henry pumped more than a million dollars into the firm to keep it going, but in November 1908, he, David, and the stockholders accepted an offer from William Durant to merge Olds Motor Works with a new company known as General Motors—a merger that handsomely rewarded the Jorgensen family.
- Henry enjoyed dabbling in "inventions of progress"; he also had investments in a local automobile brake company called Lockheed Brakes.

- His interest in inventions even extended to bathroom fixtures; to the enormous frustration of his wife, he keeps changing the faucets in the bathroom, experimenting with the latest ideas in compression valves versus fuller ball valves.
- Henry was interested in the Sanitary Movement, which was pushing for greater bathroom cleanliness and focusing on the use of porcelain-enameled iron bathtubs and sinks, along with the elimination of extensive use of microbe-harboring wood in the bathroom.

Life in the Community: Detroit, Michigan

- Detroit was founded on the Detroit River in 1701 by Antoine de la Mothe Cadillac.
- He called the settlement Fort Pontchartrain, and for more than a hundred years it was the most important military and trading station on the Great Lakes.
- Real development of Detroit began after the War of 1812.
- By 1830 Detroit was the nation's fifty-third largest city; by 1910 it was the nation's ninth-largest, and it was growing.
- From 1900 until 1910, while the population of the state of Michigan grew 16 percent, the population of the city of Detroit increased 63 percent, to 492,695 inhabitants.
- The city's key economic drivers included the pharmaceuticals industry, most notably by Parke, Davis and Company; the paint and varnish industry, which began in Detroit in the 1890s; and automobile manufacturing.

A 4 p.m. change of work shift at the Ford Motor Company assembly plant in Detroit, 1910s.

- Thirty different makes of passenger cars, trucks, and tractors were manufactured by 29 separate companies; another 129 companies were devoted exclusively to the manufacture of parts and accessories.
- In addition, Detroit supplied 95 percent of the state's meat products and 86 percent of its structural steel.
- In all, Detroit's factories were valued at more than $254 million and were supplied by 15 railroads with a combined capacity of 2,989 cars.
- Railroad service in and out of Detroit was seriously hampered in 1913 by a bottleneck of line connections through Toledo, where terminals were so congested during much of the year that losses were sustained by Detroit shippers.
- Outbound freight by steamship was currently 250 million pounds annually, with the potential for more.
- The growth of the immigrant population forced many merchants to prepare signs and instructions in various languages.
- Across the city and the state, as elsewhere in the country, sheet music by writer Irving Berlin was everywhere; his songs ranged from a song entitled "Snookey Ookums" to tales of the "Devil's Ball."
- The campaign for good roads continued to rage; every new car owner became "a voter for good roads," the *Ford Times* said.
- Motorists had the American Automobile Association, which became a powerful lobbying force, although many groups seeking quality roads did not want federal assistance.
- The *Engineering News* remarked, "It needs but the slightest knowledge of Congressional methods and precedents to perceive that the first grant of federal aid to highway work will be the opening of a drain out of the Treasury which may easily menace national solvency."
- The fiscal 1913 Post Office Appropriation Bill included a grant of $500,000 in federal aid for the improvement of rural post roads, provided each federal dollar was matched two for one by the states.
- At the Jorgensens' other home, along the eastern shore of Maine, the very wealthy residents of Long Island and Bar Harbor were actively talking about "giving back" to the poor.
- Part of their motivation, however, was to make sure America's working class did not rise up in revolt against conspicuous wealth.
- Andrew Carnegie, who popularized the concept of giving through the "gospel of wealth," said that money must be used to ease the social ills of the world.
- Banker Jacob H. Schiff was said to demonstrate this "gospel" through the giving of least 10 percent of everything he made to both Jewish and non-Jewish causes; wealthy lawyer Louis Marshall believed in giving through the Talmudic doctrine, "Twice blessed is he who gives in secret," so all his gifts were given anonymously.
- But some of the very rich were also finding creative—and expensive—ways to celebrate and to get into the society pages of prestigious newspapers; Mrs. W. Watt Sherman gave her daughter Mildred a party at which a huge swan floated on an artificial lake surrounded by 1,300 guests, and when the débutante took her bow, the giant swan exploded, scattering 10,000 pink roses into the air.
- At Newport, Norman R. de Whitehouse recently hired the U.S. Navy to assist with the coming-out party of his daughter Alice; warships moored offshore used their search lamps to light up the dance floor so everyone could enjoy an extended evening of dancing under the stars.

"Making Your Money Do Double Work, How a Shrewd Speculative Investor Made One Security Carry Another," by C.H. Provost, *The Magazine of Wall Street, June 1913*

"During the early part of May I decided that the market had seen its worst, and as I had been saving up a long while in anticipation of bargains some time this year, I decided to put my money into securities. My available funds amounted to $6,000, and you can imagine how carefully I scanned the list and delved into earnings and other statistics in an effort to secure the greatest obtainable safety and probable profit. Following the teachings of this magazine and bearing in mind Mr. Carnegie's admonition, 'put all your eggs into one basket, then watch the basket,' I made up my mind that I would pick out the one stock which would be nearest to my personal requirements, and this is how I came to my decision-as near as I can remember my mental processes at the time. First, I wanted a dividend payer, and second, something that would move. Starting at the top of the list I passed Amalgamated Copper because there were other stocks which would net more on the investment, and with equal chances for improvement in price. American Beet Sugar and American Can were non-dividend payers, so they didn't interest me. Car Foundry with its two-percent dividend didn't yield enough and was too slow a mover. I didn't like any of the industrial preferred stocks, as their varying investment qualities keep them all within a narrow range, and I wanted my principal to grow rapidly as soon as the turn in the market came. American Smelting, I admitted, contained possibilities, but somehow I found it an unsatisfactory stock to deal in. Every time I touch it I promise that it shall be the last. American Sugar Refining is more or less of a bet on the tariff. American Telephone and Telegraph looked very good to me indeed with its eight-percent dividends and occasional 'rights.' I reasoned that if it should advance to its former high price, that it would be about 20 points above this level. Twenty points on a stock selling at 120 odd is about a 16 percent increase on the investment, while on a stock selling at 50 it is a 40 percent increase. All other things being equal therefore, I favored a low-priced stock.

This resolution naturally eliminated high-priced issues like American Tobacco, Canadian Pacific, Sears Roebuck, etc., which further narrowed the list.... Chesapeake & Ohio were at a stage where doubts as to continuance of dividends appeared frequently in the public press. Other people said the road's credit was poor ...I threw out Pennsylvania [Railroad], notwithstanding the recent decline, owing to its price being above par, and I decided that I would await a possible chance in Southern Pacific, having in mind the aforesaid idea. This simmered the whole proposition down to two stocks-Chesapeake & Ohio [Railroad] and U.S. Steel common.

UNCLE SAM, TO CONGRESS: "Toss it aboard—haven't time to stop."—Philadelphia *Record*.

Turning over in mind the merits and demerits of Chesapeake & Ohio, I remembered that while its five-percent dividend made it look cheap around 64, there was a possibility that the trouble in placing its bond might make a dividend cut necessary. Hence, I decided that this was a point in favor of

Steel, and while it is unknown what effect the tariff will have on the earnings of the steel corporation, orders now on hand are sufficient to carry it well along into the fall with earnings in excess of dividend requirements.... To put it another way, it occurred to me that with good crops, which are promised, and the removal of the European war menace, business conditions during the next six months might not be as bad as some of the tariff howlers have predicted, and that Steel was one of the stocks which should respond quickly to any recognition of improved conditions.... To sum the whole

MAY THE NEW DEAL BE A SQUARE DEAL.
—Chicago *Tribune.*

thing up, I made up my mind to buy 100 Steel common and pay for it.... While the stock was being transferred, the thought occurred to me that I wasn't making my money work hard enough. If my judgment on Steel was correct, then it was time to buy other things-some of these high-grade stocks for instance, which wouldn't decline very much unless everything went to pieces. Accordingly I went back over the list and finally cut out everything but American Telephone and Pennsylvania.... I turned the whole matter over in my mind and decided to buy Telephone because it was the soundest and yielded the largest return. I then put my 100 shares of Steel up as margin for the purchase of the Telephone, figuring out that if, during the next year, my anticipation of higher prices was realized I would come out, on dividends alone, about as follows:

Dividend on 100 U.S. Steel. $500
Dividend on 100 American Telephone $800
. . . . $1,300

Carrying charges on $12,800 at five percent. $640

Net income from the combined operation $660

From this I concluded that my net return on the $6,000 investment in U.S. Steel would be 11 percent, even if these two stocks did not move from their present prices during the entire year.... So long as there was no reason for me to change my opinion, I would hold this same position, and if everything came out all right there would be an advance from 10 to 15 points on these two stocks, depending on circumstances. Ten points would be $2,000, or a 33 1/3 percent increase on my original capital. Fifteen points in each would amount to 50 percent on my original capital, and that was what I had originally started out to find. Thus I am making my money do double work."

Young Swedish Immigrant in 1913

Swedish-born Karin Moberg found she had to adapt to life in America very quickly after arriving in the United States to meet her father for the first time.

Life at Home

- Seven-year-old Karin Moberg was born in 1906 in the town of Karlskrona, Sweden, named for King Karl XI.
- Originally the town's name was spelled Carlskrona; the name meant "Carl's crown."
- From the time of Karin's birth, she and her mother, Selma, lived in a one-room apartment, number 11, Ronnebygatan—Karlskrona's main street.
- The corner of the single room was taken up by a floor-to-ceiling white porcelain fireplace with glittery-bright brass doors.
- The apartment had white-painted furniture made of birch.
- There was a round table flanked by chairs; the chair backs had a blue-and-white design that Karin liked enormously.
- Selma and Karin often took a short walk from their home to the Baltic Sea, where there were green benches by the water.
- There her mother would take out some handiwork and Karin would play in the sand, roll her hoop, or bounce a ball.
- Karin especially enjoyed running over to an inlet where the white swans swam regally, always with an eye out for some bread that might be cast to them.
- Selma was well respected as the town seamstress, and her work was much favored.
- Karin was proud of her mother.
- Years before, Selma had been trained as an apprentice to the top seamstress in southern Sweden.
- From Selma's tiny home, she made dresses, men's suits, and underwear; she often went to the customers' homes for fittings.
- Selma was also trained to knit, crochet, and embroider, as well as to create beautiful cut work.

Seven-year old Karin Moberg

- Often when someone needed a dress quickly, before the specified time, Selma would sew, sew, sew throughout the night, sitting at her faithful Singer trundle sewing machine until the work was done.
- Karin had been taught never, ever, to touch the materials or clothing being prepared.
- Her father, Lennart Moberg, was in the merchant marines, stationed in Buenos Aires, Argentina.
- Karin was seven years old before Lennart first saw her—and the meeting came about only then because of an accident on board ship.
- A highly trained ship's mechanic, Lennart was burned when a steam boiler blew up at sea.
- He was taken to the Norwegian Hospital in Brooklyn, New York, where he required an operation and a long period of recovery.
- Naturally, his ship had to continue on its schedule; Lennart was left behind in New York City.
- That's when he made the decision to remain in the "land of opportunity."
- He began working several jobs, including one at an automobile plant, so that he could send for his wife and the daughter he had never seen.
- Karin and her mother left the harbor of Gothenburg on the west coast of Sweden and arrived in New York City ten days later.
- Karin was so excited about seeing her father for the first time that she developed a severe nosebleed and was unable to go to the rail to look for him below in the throng.
- Instead, at the moment she had awaited her entire life, she was sitting in a deck chair with a nurse in attendance—blood spatters marring her precious new outfit.

Life at Work

- Lennart Moberg was adamant that his daughter become as Americanized as possible—as soon as possible.
- He even considered moving somewhere other than Minnesota because Swedes were so concentrated there she might cling to the old ways.
- He told her that he would never make her work in factories like the Italian children; if she learned to be a seamstress like her mother, she might even marry an American boy.
- "It is my job to earn money; I don't want your pay from a factory," he told her.
- Karin was told always to study hard and value her education; book learning was the ticket to a good life in America.
- Since the Elementary School Act of 1842, promoted by the Lutheran Church, illiteracy had become rare in Sweden.
- For decades the ability of Swedes to read and write had made them attractive to states seeking new settlers.
- As soon as Karin learned English, her father would not allow her to speak in Swedish to anyone, even at home.
- She also learned what other things not to do in America.
- All her life she had been expected to curtsy to adults when she met them on the street—a habit she continued in America—but not for long.
- Her father told her it was no longer appropriate; curtsying wasn't done in America.
- But the transition was not always easy; homesickness would overcome Karin and her mother at the strangest moments.
- One day, out of the blue, Selma asked Lennart in what direction Sweden was located; when he showed her, she stood looking in that direction and began to weep.
- Then, without a word, she dried her tears, picked up her sewing and never spoke of the incident again.
- A short time later, the Moberg family left for Minnesota to join the automobile industry in that state.
- Karin thought the idea of the six-day train ride was exciting.

- But when the day came, she didn't like the way her white gloves turned black from the coal smoke or being told repeatedly not to talk to the other passengers wandering the aisles of the train.
- Mostly it was boring.
- For more than a decade, the practical farmers of Minnesota had been tinkering in their barns with horseless carriages, Moto buggies, cycle cars, or automobiles—whichever name was in vogue.
- While living in New York, Lennart had grown intrigued by gasoline-powered internal combustion engines, especially those of the Oldsmobile, which he admired.
- Nationwide, a dizzying assortment of handmade cars and innovative technologies were being created by hundreds of manufacturers dabbling in steam-, electricity- and gas-powered autos.
- Lennart believed that the gas-powered autos represented the future, and he wanted to be a part of it—a crucial reason why he picked Minneapolis as their home.

Immigrant children often worked in factories.

- Innovation was rampant, with no clear standards for basic vehicle architecture, body types, construction materials, or controls.
- Most cars operated at a single speed using a chain drive technology, similar to a bicycle's.
- Recent innovations had included an electric selfstarter, an independent suspension, and four-wheel brakes.
- In all, 15 different kinds of vehicles were being built in Minnesota, including the Michaelson, a fast-traveling cycle car designed for racing.
- More than a hundred U.S. firms were producing little autos to cash in on the fad.
- The Michaelson Minneapolis Motorcycle Company was already known for its motorcycles, introduced a few years earlier; building fast cars would be even more fun.
- Getting employment for skilled Swedish mechanics in Minnesota was relatively easy; making ends meet was not.
- The cost of housing, food, transportation, even the expectations of the church, stretched the budget for the Mobergs.
- Lennart reluctantly agreed that Selma could reestablish her seamstress business—much to her delight.
- After seven years of living independently, she found that being told what she could and could not do was burdensome.
- She often felt guilty about this resentment, knowing she had often told Karin that everything would be fine once she and Lennart were together again.

Automobile factories hired many immigrants.

Life in the Community: Minneapolis, Minnesota

- Historically, Minnesota had been an immigration state.
- Drawn by the lure of inexpensive farmland and a growing industrial base, settlers from New England as well as immigrants from Norway, Sweden, Ireland, and Germany settled in Minnesota prior to 1850.
- By 1896 official election instructions were being issued in nine languages: English, German, Norwegian, Swedish, Finnish, French, Czech, Italian, and Polish.
- The pace of immigration accelerated in Minnesota at the turn of the twentieth century.
- While the foreign-born population in the rest of the United States was approximately 15 percent in the 1890s, 40 percent of Minnesota's population was foreign-born.
- This wave of immigration to Minnesota peaked in about 1910, when more than 60 percent of the immigrants came from Sweden, Norway, and Germany.
- The city of Minneapolis grew up around Saint Anthony Falls, the only waterfall on the Mississippi River.
- Thanks to this water power, Minneapolis was described as the "greatest direct-drive waterpower center the world has ever seen."
- The city's importance also grew because Minneapolis was home to 34 flour mills that processed grains grown throughout the Great Plains and shipped to Minneapolis by rail.
- By 1905 Minneapolis delivered almost 10 percent of the country's flour and grist.
- At peak production, a single mill made enough flour for 12 million loaves of bread each day.
- In 1905 a retired telephone company executive from New England named Charles J. Glidden launched a long-distance tour event intended to demonstrate the reliability of the new automobiles.
- The tour was organized as an annual event by the nascent American Automobile Association; the Glidden tour was the largest of several such efforts.

Many immigrants from Norway, Sweden, Ireland, and Germany settled in Minnesota.

- The promoters knew that the tours would draw attention to the need for improved roads; as yet few locales boasted all-weather roads.
- At first the tours were the projects of automobile enthusiasts like Glidden; later the manufacturers saw their opportunity to publicize their models and sponsored the efforts.
- The route for the Glidden tour varied from one year to the next; in 1909 the tour route from Detroit to Kansas City traversed Chicago, Minneapolis, and Denver.
- In July 1913 the tour commenced from a garage on Hennepin Avenue in Minneapolis; its destination was Glacier Park.
- Other auto enthusiasts joined the tour for portions of the route, and journalists accompanying the tour group assembled a daily four-page commemorative "newspaper" called the *Glacier Park Blazer*.
- The Minneapolis Millers of the eight-team American Association baseball league played home games at Nicollet Park in Minneapolis; the Millers's decades-long double-A ball rivals were the St. Paul Saints.
- In 1912 a new steel-and-concrete stadium in Nicollet Park replaced the old wooden structure.
- That year, under manager Joseph D. "Pongo Joe" Cantillon, the Minneapolis Millers won the league championship for the third year running.

The Pillsbury plant at St. Anthony Falls in Minneapolis, Misnnesota.

Professional Golfer in 1913

Francis Ouimet was fascinated by golfers and their sporting equipment, and he grew to adulthood at the same time golf was maturing into a visible, competitive sport in the United States.

Life at Home

- Twenty-year-old Francis Ouimet had grown up reading Harry Vardon's book *The Complete Golfer* and collecting the "Vardon Flyer" golf balls that he discovered on the golf course near his home.
- Now he was scheduled to play against his hero—a man 23 years his senior—in the most important tournament of his life.
- The newspapers billed the 1913 U.S. Open as a battle between the rising American amateur and the golf star of Britain.
- The Country Club, in Brookline, Massachusetts, the Boston suburb where Francis was born, was home to one of the first golf courses in America.
- The Country Club was also his father's occasional employer, providing the French-Canadian immigrant with work as a coachman or gardener.
- The English Protestant oppression because of which his father had fled Canada was replaced in Boston by Yankee intolerance of immigrant "Frenchies."
- From his two-story clapboard house directly across the street from the Country Club, Francis could see the 17th fairway and green.
- Francis and his brother Wilfred designed their own golf course in an overgrown cow pasture near their house; the first hole required a 100-yard carry off the tee over a creek to a small, oval green.
- The second hole was a par three; the third hole crossed back over the creek to a circular green in their own backyard.
- Tin cans from the kitchen served as cups, and the two boys carved their own clubs; badly hit golf shots from the Country Club supplied them with a sufficient number of golf balls.
- The Country Club first opened its doors in 1882; six years later it added golf to complement archery, tennis, polo, ice-skating, curling, and an annual horse racing season.

Francis Ouimet

- The club started with a six-hole course; it generated so much interest that three more holes were added within a year.
- Twenty sheep were imported from Devonshire, England, to keep the fairways clipped.
- In Brookline the popularity of the sport was exploding; Francis spent hours watching golfers chip and putt their way past his window while he dreamed of perfecting his swing.
- For most of the nation, however, golf was a curiosity, a game for the British, the wealthy, and the powerful.
- For most Americans, the typical 56-hour work week left little leisure for the time-consuming—and expensive—game of golf.
- The cost of lessons, $0.75 an hour, was beyond Francis's reach, as were custom clubs, at $2.50 each, or a golf bag, at $4.00.
- Rubber tees sold for $0.25 each, and the price for Haskell golf balls was three for a dollar at the pro shop.
- When he was eight years old, at Wright & Ditson's Sporting Goods store, Francis succeeded in trading three dozen found golf balls for a fairway two wood, called the cut-down brassie.
- His second club was a five iron known as a mashie, followed by a chipping wedge, or niblick.

A young Francis Ouimet with his older brother, Wilfred

- At age nine Francis began to caddie during the summer, an occupation that not only gave him spending money but provided an opportunity to study golfers up close, in a variety of situations.
- He quickly soaked up an insider's knowledge of the course and its rules.
- His mother was not pleased.
- "No good will come from this, Francis," she would say. "Golf can never offer you any kind of life or living."
- When Francis turned 16, he was required to give up caddying at the Country Club in order to retain his amateur status.
- United States Golf Association rules forbade amateur players from receiving money for any service connected with the sport.
- Francis planned to make golf the center of his life, but his father had other ideas.
- After years of struggling economically, his father demanded that Francis quit school and start working to help support the family.
- Golf was never to be spoken of again.
- Francis—the captain of the high-school golf team, the finest prodigy to emerge from the Brookline Country Club—began work as a $0.10 an hour stock boy.
- At 17 he secretly borrowed $25 from his mother to enter the prestigious National Amateur match, which was to be played in Brookline, but after a summer away from golf, he failed to qualify.
- It was a pattern that would repeat itself over the next two years, despite a change in jobs and the discovery of Harry Vardon's first book, *The Complete Golfer*.
- Francis committed the book to memory.

- Vardon's advice improved Francis's hand action and timing, developments that increased the length of his drives off the tee—when he had time to pursue his passion.

Life at Work

- As 1913 approached, Francis Ouimet was working at the Boston sporting goods store Wright & Ditson, owned by a former professional athlete eager to see his $15 a week sales clerk do well at his passion.
- They both thought winning the National Amateur Golf Tournament—the sport's most coveted American title—was critical and also possible.
- At 20 years old, Francis believed the 1913 contest was his final opportunity.
- Together the store owner and Francis formulated a step-by-step tactical plan that emphasized not only the physical side of winning, but the psychological side as well.
- For the first time Francis could practice without fear and with absolute commitment, believing that his shots would fly straight and his putts would fall.
- He qualified for the National Amateur Tournament by winning the Massachusetts Amateur Championship in a walk.
- In the clutch Francis kept his cool; his opponents did not.
- From its inception in 1894, the National Amateur Tournament had been strictly a match-play event that matched hole-by-hole scoring, not total score.
- In 1913 the prestigious tournament doubled in size when 141 players showed up for the competition held at the Garden City Golf Club in Garden City, New York.
- Garden City's 6,800-yard course, built in 1898, was renowned for its length, punitive bunkers, and small greens.
- The first two days of play reduced the field to 32 golfers.
- Francis was so exhilarated that feeling frightened didn't occur to him, and he easily made the cut.
- Then he was paired in match play against a previous National Amateur champion and won in a close match.
- Francis was eliminated in the quarterfinals, but he was invited to play in the U.S. Open, a tournament largely populated by professionals that was scheduled to be played at a familiar place: Brookline Country Club.
- The United States Golf Association's Open Championship began tournament play in 1881.
- Only the Kentucky Derby could lay claim to a longer history of continuous sports contests.
- Francis's hero Harry Vardon was scheduled to play in this year's contest.
- Harry Vardon and fellow Briton Ted Ray arrived with great fanfare, and critics agreed they had an excellent chance to recapture the U.S. Open trophy for Britain.
- In all, 23 amateurs had been accepted at Brookline, where they were welcome to use the Country Club clubhouse.
- Ironically, as an amateur, Francis was allowed to use the clubhouse, while his hero Harry Vardon was not; tradition excluded professionals, who were regarded as working class, from the facilities.

Francis grew up around the Country Club, where his father worked.

- On the first day of the tournament, Francis learned that his regular caddie had deserted him for a more popular, more financially capable pro.
- So for the most important tournament of his life Francis picked Eddie Lowery, a 10-year-old schoolboy, who was playing hooky from school, to be his caddie.
- Covering the event were hundreds of reporters, supported by a crowd of nine thousand who followed Harry Vardon's every move—even though many were watching the first golf match of their lives.
- Course marshals shouted through megaphones to control the stampede on the course, to little avail.
- The crowd watching Francis's round swelled to a thousand, including former President William Howard Taft, and six hundred automobiles crowded the Country Club lot.
- After overcoming first-hole jitters, Francis posted a 77—six shots behind the leader on the first 18—followed by a 74 in the afternoon round to finish the first day in fifth place, four strokes back.
- The second day was played in a driving rainstorm, which the British golfers considered to be to their advantage.

Francis entered the National Amateur Tournament but was eliminated in the quarterfinals.

- Francis's mother furtively watched from her house across the street from the 17th hole, and Eddie Lowery, his elementary-school caddie, skipped school again.
- Francis's morning rounds on the second day produced a 74 and gave him the lead, ahead of both Ted Ray and Harry Vardon.
- Francis had shot the lowest round and picked up four strokes on the two best players in the world.
- The press still didn't give Francis any chance of winning the tournament, and with good reason.
- On the final scheduled round of the tournament, Francis allowed his doubts to overpower his confidence, and after the first ten holes, the young amateur had not only lost his lead but was down two strokes.
- The gallery of nearly ten thousand began to smell his defeat, and many wandered away, convinced that Francis had lost his golden opportunity.
- Then, on the par-four 13th hole, which measured 339 uphill yards, Francis chipped in a birdie from the green to regain one stroke, causing the crowd to cheer so loudly that his mother could hear it from her front porch.
- On the par-three 16th hole, Francis went for another birdie, but he had to struggle for par.
- The newspapers would later describe the crowd as being half-mad with tension; Francis needed to pick up one stroke on the next two holes in order to tie the British champions and be eligible for a playoff the next day.
- When Francis dropped in a 20-foot putt from above the hole, the roar of the crowd could be heard two miles away.
- Harry Vardon told the press, "Coming when it did, I count it as one of the master strokes of golf."
- Francis parred the 18th hole: the stage was set for an 18-hole playoff with Ray and Vardon.
- British journalist Bernard Darwin described his own emotions in the *London Times*: "After sober reflection I state my conviction that if I live the length of a dozen lives I should never again be the spectator of such an amazing, thrilling and magnificent finish to an Open championship."
- No amateur had ever won the U.S. Open, and Harry Vardon had never lost to an amateur.
- Even though the rain continued on Saturday, more than 12,000 spectators descended on the course.

- The three golfers, while polite, barely spoke to one another, and after nine holes all three men were at even-par 38.
- At the 10th hole, Francis went up by one stroke, and for the first time he began to imagine that he could defeat the two British stars.
- On the 12th hole, the young American went up two strokes.
- His opponents kept waiting for him to crack under the pressure.
- At the 370-yard, par-four 15th hole, Ted Ray took a double bogey; then the championship was down to Francis Ouimet and Harry Vardon.
- When Francis teed off on the 17th hole, he could see his mother watching from her front porch.
- Overcome by anxiety, she had left the course when the crowd became almost uncontrollable at the prospect that Francis might win the U.S. Open.
- On the green of the 17th hole, Francis had an 18-foot putt that went downhill and to the right.
- He barely touched it, and slowly the ball rolled down the slope and fell in for a birdie three.

Francis being carried by his fans after winning the U.S. Open. His young caddie, Eddie Lowery is front and center.

- As they approached the final hole, Francis led Vardon by three strokes and Ray by seven.
- Francis fired a perfect drive to the center of the fairway on the 18th hole, and his second shot cleared the bunker and landed on the green.
- The first putt rolled within nine inches of the cup and, as the second putt dropped in, the entire crowd exploded with excitement.
- Francis was hoisted onto the shoulders of his fans and carried to the clubhouse for the victory ceremony.
- There he saw his father proudly waving his approval.
- As an amateur, Francis received no compensation; Harry Vardon's second-place finish earned him $300.
- The USGA offered a total purse of $900 for the tournament, with $300 allotted for first place and $20 for 10th place.

Life in the Community: Brookline, Massachusetts

- Originally settled as farmland in the 1630s, Brookline, Massachusetts, was located between the Charles and the Muddy river.
- Founded as a hamlet within Boston and initially called Muddy River Hamlet, Brookline was incorporated separately in 1705 and resisted several subsequent attempts by Boston to annex it.
- The town contributed three companies of volunteers for the famous Revolutionary War battles in Lexington and Concord.
- During the 1800s Boston's wealthy merchant class began building summer homes in the area.

HAYMARKET SQ., THE BOSTON CITY HOSPITAL RELIEF STATION AND NORTH STATION, BOSTON, MASS.

Brookline, Massachusetts, was linked to Boston through a system of turnpikes and planked roads.

- Prominent architect H. H. Richardson, whose style was dubbed Richardson Romanesque, was based in Brookline.
- In 1883 Frederick Law Olmsted, the nation's foremost landscape architect, moved to Brookline to be close to Richardson, with whom he frequently collaborated.
- At his Brookline home, Fairsted, Olmsted established the first full-scale professional office for landscape design.
- Olmsted's famed "Emerald Necklace" linked system of parks and wetlands lay partly in Boston and partly in Brookline.
- After Olmsted's death in 1903, his sons John and Frederick continued his landscape design practice at Fairsted.
- Turnpikes and planked roads from Boston brought the town ever closer; two main arteries were the Boston Post Road and the Boston and Worcester Turnpike.
- By the early 1900s Brookline was linked to Boston by an electrified trolley car.
- *The London Times* described the Country Club course as a "very pretty spot (with) picturesque valleys and wooded hills and rocky promontories in one or two places. It's not a big course, yet a very sound one quite difficult enough for any reasonable being."
- From the beginning the Country Club, one of the five founding clubs of the United States Golf Association, was a strong supporter of amateur golf.

Golf Timeline

1894 The United States Golf Association (USGA) was founded to govern the game.

The size of the cup was standardized at 4.25 inches in diameter.

1895 The first official U.S. Amateur Championship was won by Charles MacDonald.

Spalding became the first American company to manufacture golf balls.

The first U.S. Women's Amateur Championship was won by Mrs. Charles S. Brown.

1896 Harry Vardon won the first of his six British Open titles.

1897 *Golf magazine began publication.*

Yale University won the first collegiate golf tournament played in the U.S.

The Royal & Ancient Golf Club's Rules of Golf Committee was formed.

William McKinley became the first sitting U.S. president to play the game of golf.

1898 The U.S. Open was expanded from 36 holes to 72 holes.

The term "birdie" was coined during a round at Atlantic City Country Club in New Jersey.

The British Open introduced a cut in the number of golfers eligible to continue after 36 holes of play.

Coburn Haskell invented the "Haskell," a wound, rubber-cored golf ball.

1899 Harvard Dental School faculty member George Grant patented the wooden tee.

The Western Open was played for the first time.

1900 Golf was made an Olympic sport.

Persimmon wood became a popular material for golf club heads.

John B. Coles Tappan, captain of Nassau Country Club in New York, invented the Nassau bet, also known as "best nines."

British champion Harry Vardon's U.S. exhibition tour spurred interest in golf in America.

Goodrich Rubber Company's patented process of winding rubber threads around the core of a Haskell ball, caused a decline in the use of balls made with gutta percha-sap from trees in the Maylay peninsula that is boiled and molded around the rubber core.

1901 Walter Travis won the U.S. Amateur playing a Haskell ball, the first player to win a major using the wound, rubber-core ball.

The first nine holes of what would become known as Pinehurst No. 2 were opened at North Carolina's Pinehurst Resort.

1902 Grooves were added to the clubfaces of irons.

Willie Anderson became the first player to break 300 in a U.S. tournament.

1903 Walter Travis won the last of his three U.S. Amateur titles.

Oakmont Country Club opened near Pittsburgh, Pennsylvania.

Spalding Company switched from gutta percha to balata to cover their Haskell rubber-core balls, a latex rubber from South American trees.

1904 The British Open format changed from two days of 36 holes each, to three days of 00 holes each.

Walter Travis was the first U.S. citizen to win the British Amateur.

1905 The "Dympl" ball was patented by William Taylor, who discovered that balls with depressions, rather than bumps, fly higher and farther.

The Vardon Grip was explained in Harry Vardon's book, *The Complete Golfer.*

1907 Frenchman Arnaud Massy became the first player from outside the British Isles to win the British Open.

1909 The Royal & Ancient (R&A) Rules of Golf Committee began issuing rulings on what equipment was legal to use in major tournaments.

Dorothy Campbell became the first golfer to win the U.S. Women's Amateur and British Women's Amateur in the same year.

1910 Steel-shafted clubs, developed by Arthur Knight, began replacing hickory in the manufacture of golf club The USGA broke from an R&A equipment ruling, by keeping center-shafted putters legal.

1911 The USGA determined par yardages: par three, up to 225 yards; par four, 225-425 yards; par five; 426-600 yards; par six, 601 yards and up.

The Royal & Ancient rejected steel-shafted clubs as illegal.

1913 American amateur Francis Ouimet defeated British stars Harry Vardon and Ted Ray in a playoff for the U.S. Open.

ớ๑<ớ๑<ớ๑<ớ๑<ớ๑<

"Francis Ouimet Hero of the U.S. Golf World,"
The Fresno Bee, September 27, 1913

Telegrams and letters of congratulations from golf enthusiasts all over the United States are pouring in on Francis Ouimet, the youthful winner of the 19th championship tournament for the United States Golf Association in Brookline, Massachusetts, last week. In keeping the championship in this country Ouimet defeated Vardon and Ray, the leading golf experts of England.

For more reasons than one the victory of Ouimet is noteworthy. This is the first time in the history of golf that an American has defeated the best of England in a championship tournament. And, besides, Ouimet is a mere youth, not yet 21.

Both Vardon and Ray have unstinted praise for the youthful champion. They declare that he beat them fairly and squarely and echo the sentiment of *The London Times* that *"all other feelings are extinguished in admiration for the wonderful feat of Ouimet, who proved himself to be one of the game's greatest of golfers."*

Ouimet is a native of Brookline. His parents are poor and the boy was forced at an early age to eke out the family income by working as a caddy in the very field where he won the great triumph Saturday. From his 13th year till he graduated from the Brookline High School a year ago, he was a familiar figure in the Brookline links. His play first attracted wide attention in the amateur championship open this year which Jerome D. Travers won.

Young Singer of Spirituals in 1913

Sarah Washington grew up surrounded by the sounds of her mother singing "the old songs"— spirituals employing new words for old tunes that bridged the past and present.

Life at Home

- Sarah Washington was born into a desperately impoverished area of Denmark, South Carolina, in 1897.
- Yet she only learned she was poor at age nine, when she visited her rich cousins in Sumter, South Carolina.
- Sarah was astonished that one cousin owned three dresses and two pairs of shoes and could draw water from a pump inside the kitchen.
- While on the same trip, she saw a building that actually had electricity and would light up at night.
- More important, she became aware of the good things in her own life.
- Sarah quickly decided that her own church in Denmark was much more fun than her cousins' in Sumter.
- The people in Sumter were too dignified to sing and clap and dance; in Denmark, Sarah loved nothing more than being swept away by the magical singing of a praise meeting.
- Sarah decided right then she liked best a God who permitted his worshipers to make a loud, joyful noise.
- Besides, there was no reason that the devil should have all the best tunes.
- She didn't care that her cousins looked down on spirituals, seeing them as associated with "slave ways"; spiritual singing was meant to be fun.
- At home Sarah's mother daily breathed fresh life into the old spirituals.
- If the water turned sour, that dilemma joined the song being sung; when the rain arrived in sheets, that, too, was added; and if the cotton crop was excellent, her mother's jubilation came alive in song.
- In this way a spiritual tune was always under construction in Sarah's house.
- As one of 11 children, Sarah didn't have to be told when the crops were poor and money tight.

Sarah Washington

- Between planting season, deer season, sicknesses of her younger brothers and sisters, and demands that she help at home, Sarah rarely attended school more than 60 days a year.
- Sarah learned all the standard spirituals from the neighborhood ladies: "Deep River," Nobody Knows the Trouble I've Seen," "Little David Play Yo' Harp," and "Shout All Over God's Heab'n."
- Then she created her own spiritual songs—most dwelling on the woes she encountered herself—using the familiar biblical allusions, carefully crafted during the days of slavery.
- "Then Moses said to Israel/When they stood upon the shore/'Your enemy you see today/You will never see no more'/Old Pharoah and his host/Got lost in the Red Sea."
- Now that she was turning 16 and was ready to leave school, Sarah knew that her future included marriage, babies, and more farm work.
- But she wanted to sing spirituals.

Sarah didn't realize how poor she was until she visited a city.

Life at Work

- Spirituals and spiritual singing arrived in North America with the first African slaves, who were snatched from their homelands and deposited—with all their customs, habits, and aspirations—on the isolated plantations of the South.
- Over time, African rhythms blended with English words, and songs evolved—drenched in pain, expressing a yearning for freedom, and filled with double meanings.
- Many spirituals were used to communicate escape plans or safe routes, or simply to convey resentment against the slave owner.
- Historically spirituals constituted a living folk art, with no authors, composers, or lyricists; nothing was written down, and spirituals had no fixed or authoritative text.
- Spirituals belonged to the community.
- Writer W. E. B. Du Bois called spirituals "sorrow songs," "the music of an unhappy people, of the children of disappointment; they tell of death and suffering and unvoiced longing toward a truer world."
- Spirituals were improvisational.

City life was astounding for Sarah.

- Usually a lead singer sang one line and the others would repeat it or reply with a familiar chorus in an antiphony.
- Anyone could add new verses, and the best of those survived through a kind of musical natural selection.
- When singing spirituals, there was no separation between artist and audience, no distinction between creator and performer.
- The religious music of African-Americans also included the ring shout, the song sermon, the Jubilee, and the Gospel song.
- The ring shout survived because it did not violate the Protestant prohibitions against dancing and drumming, yet a ring shout is "danced" with the whole body, including hands, feet, and hips.
- The most common spirituals employed the call-and-response pattern, which Sarah's mother had perfected.
- The songs most familiar to white audiences—"Nobody Knows the Trouble I've Seen," "Go Down Moses," and "Swing Low, Sweet Chariot"—represented a mixture of European and African music.

Sarah's schoolmates

- Many of the songs had strong biblical allusions, especially to popular Old Testament stories that included conquest and personal achievement.
- "He delivered David from de lion's den/Jonah from de belly of de whale/And de Hebrew children from de fiery furnace/Why not everything, man?"
- An early custom of the rural African American church was "lining out" the song, whereby the preacher read the words before the congregation sang them.
- Over time, in the churches where hymn books were few and literacy low, the congregation learned the words by heart.
- Musically, this folk style of singing allowed everyone to sing the tune in unison without concern for harmony.
- Spirituals came to the attention of the non-African American public in the 1860s after they were described in popular publications such as the *Atlantic Monthly,* and in 1867 they were collected into a book, *Slave Songs for the United States.*
- In 1871 the Fisk Jubilee Singers, of Fisk College in Nashville, Tennessee, began to spread the message of spirituals through their nationwide tours, establishing spirituals in the national consciousness.
- In addition to raising enough funds to keep the college open, the Fisk Jubilee Singers popularized the "Negro spiritual" as a genre and made it part of American popular culture.
- Thanks to the presence in Denmark of a school for African Americans called Voorhees, Sarah saw an opportunity to avoid the trap of a too-early marriage and a plan to realize her desire to sing spirituals.
- The financially struggling Voorhees, created in the image of Booker T. Washington's famed Tuskegee Institute, was founded on the principle of self-help.
- What if, Sarah asked herself, she could form a touring spiritual singing group similar to the Fisk Jubilee Singers that would support the college and herself?

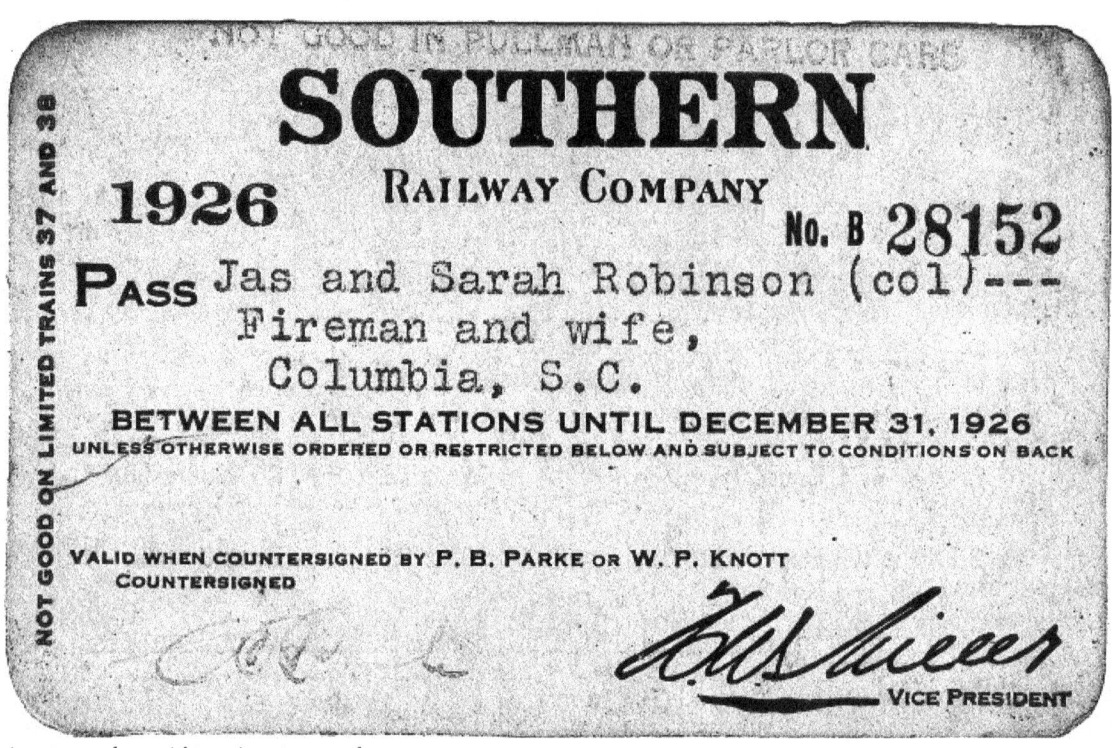

A train pass for an African American couple

- Already she had organized the youth choir of her church and an all-girl choir school, and she spent most of her days dreaming up new words for old songs.
- Why not, indeed?
- Voorhees was envisioned and created by Elizabeth Evelyn Wright, who was 23 when she came to Bamberg County.
- A native of Georgia, Wright had found her inspiration while studying at Tuskegee Institute.
- Tuskegee gave her a mission in life: being "the same type of woman as Mr. Washington was of a man."
- Knowing the importance of education, Wright moved to South Carolina with the intention of establishing schools for African Americans in the rural areas.
- She survived repeated threats, attacks, and arson.
- In April 1893 Wright's first attempt at creating a school for blacks—in McNeill, South Carolina, where she had gone at the invitation of Mrs. Almira Steele, a white trustee at Tuskegee—ended in a blazing fire.
- Wright's second attempt in McNeill ended when an arsonist, opposed to secondary education for African Americans, burned all the lumber purchased for a new building.
- Then, when she negotiated the purchase of a property in McNeill with existing buildings, all the buildings on the land were torched.
- Convinced that education was the path to black prosperity, Wright moved her vision to Denmark, eight miles from the new county seat of Bamberg.
- There, with the aid of Stanwix G. Mayfield, a leading white state senator, and a recommendation letter from Booker T. Washington, Wright founded the Denmark Industrial School in 1897—the year Sarah was born.
- Operating on the second floor of a general store building in the Sato district of Denmark, the school was modeled on Tuskegee.
- Only 14 students enrolled the first year, but in 1898 the school had 270 students.

- New Jersey philanthropist Ralph Voorhees and his wife donated $5,000 to buy the land and construct the first building of the school's permanent home; the school opened there in 1902.
- It was the only high school and industrial school for blacks in the area and soon was named Voorhees Industrial School to honor its primary benefactors.
- Wright, who had suffered from ill health during her time in Tuskegee, died at John Harvey Kellogg's Battle Creek, Michigan, sanitarium in December 1906, at age 34.
- About the same time Vorhees was founded, black urban intellectuals were beginning to bemoan the potential loss of spiritual singing, predicting that, as the literacy increased throughout the South, the old ways would be lost.
- Yet the crushing oppression of Jim Crow laws, designed to strip African Americans of most of their rights, was having an opposite impact: rural blacks, suffering more, were singing more, not less.
- By 1913 the notorious "black codes" of Jim Crow—state and local laws and regulations intended to oppress African Americans and keep them in a condition little better than slavery—had strengthened the African American church, especially the rural African American church.
- The African American church was the one institution white society couldn't touch.
- There black preachers, black deacons, and black women in huge hats held uncontested sway at least one day a week.
- Sarah understood that the singing of spirituals and gospel songs, rooted in the churches, was essential to African Americans' celebration of life.
- Sarah proposed to the leaders of Voorhees that a touring choir be formed from among its students and faculty.
- Her plan was for the first gathering of the Voorhees Jubilee Voices to take place in Columbia, South Carolina, the state capital, where a large paying audience was available.
- Her goal was to earn $100 for Vorhees, enough to prove her ability.
- Within days, the college was buzzing about the young girl who wanted to duplicate the success of the Fisk Jubilee Singers; many people, however, were discomfited that one so young had gained the initiative.
- Within a week Sarah had talked her uncle into driving her the 45 miles to Columbia in his horse and buggy.
- Three Baptist preachers in Columbia agreed to help launch the Voorhees Jubilee Voices—provided their choir could sing, also.
- Two more choirs were added later in the week, and suddenly Sarah was in charge of the biggest songfest—it would feature 120 singers—in years.
- Several attempts to push her aside were made by the more experienced men, but Sarah refused to budge.
- Instead she focused on building a still-bigger network and leading the newly created Voorhees Jubilee Voices.
- One of the more challenging aspects of her task was to get everyone to agree on a repertoire in which words would actually be sung.
- A former teacher got her a travel pass that allowed her to ride the train to Columbia; it carried the teacher's name, address, and racial designation: "col," for "colored."
- Three weeks before the event, Sarah actually persuaded the state newspaper to write a story about the coming "Negro spiritual gathering"—a feat the black Baptist ministers had declared to be impossible.
- Three days before the event, Sarah took her uncle's horse and buggy to Columbia, along with her supplies, convinced she would need the time to decorate the church.
- But two days were consumed simply in getting there; rain washed out roads and frightened her horse.

- Sarah slept in the buggy one night in the pouring rain, since no other accommodations were available, and she knew no one.
- Wet, cold, and insecure, Sarah arrived in Columbia on the morning of the big event to find the ministers energized, the choirs prepared, and more than 500 tickets sold at $0.25 each.
- First, she broke into tears—and then she broke into song.
- And the entire gathering joined in "Go Down, Moses."
- The event itself was a dream; the choirs and choir leaders meshed well, the audience was engaged, and the music was, Sarah thought, heavenly.
- Scheduled to last two hours, the concert lasted three.
- No one wanted the music to stop.

Life in the Community: Denmark, South Carolina

- In 1913 Denmark, South Carolina, was a farming community of approximately 750 people, evenly divided between whites and blacks.
- The town was originally known as Graham; it was named after the Z. G. Graham family, which sold 17 acres to the Charleston-Hamburg Railroad in 1837 for a rail siding named Graham's Turnout.
- By 1913 three railway companies crisscrossed the town, the name of which had been changed to Denmark, after a major railway promoter.
- Cotton dominated the fields of South Carolina in 1913; cotton's value was greater than that of all other South Carolina agricultural products combined.
- Cotton production in the Palmetto State rose from 224,000 bales in 1870 to nearly one million in 1913.

Denmark, South Carolina

Three railroads operated in the town.

- At the same time, rice production fell dramatically in the coastal regions of the state, as mechanized farming in the Southwestern states proved to give them a competitive advantage.
- "Bright leaf" tobacco—a gold-leafed variety, less vigorous than the commonly used darker variety, that thrived on poor soils and was flue-cured—was introduced into the state in the 1890s and transformed agriculture in the region, thanks to a boom in tobacco usage accompanying the introduction of machine-made cigarettes.
- But after the Civil War and into the 1900s, farmers' lives were most affected by the expansion of South Carolina railroad system.
- Nearly every town in the state was connected to others by rail.
- The time and energy required to get supplies in, and crops out, was dramatically decreased.
- Road improvements began in 1895, after the state legislature permitted counties to use convict labor to do the work.
- By 1913 the state had more than 20,000 automobiles.
- Overall the biggest economic change was the growth of textile manufacturing, which employed cheap white labor drawn from a pool of poor rural farmers eager to escape the vagaries and isolation of agricultural life.
- Public education, for blacks and whites, remained a low priority; in the rural areas, the typical school operated for only a few months a year.
- In 1907 the legislature allocated $8.00 per white enrollee annually and $1.57 per black pupil.
- In the same year, state-supported high schools for whites were created; no high schools were funded for African Americans.
- In 1911 the state's first rural elementary school superintendent reported, "The Negro schoolhouses are miserable beyond description…most of the teachers are absolutely untrained."

Imagery in Plantation-Based Spirituals

Satan = slave owner
King Jesus = slave benefactor
Babylon = winter
Hell = traveling farther south
Jordan (River) = first steps to freedom
Israelites = enslaved African-Americans
Egyptians = slaveholders
Canaan = land of freedom
Heaven = Canada or points north
Home = Africa

Spiritual: "Changed My Name"

I tol' Jesus it would be all right
If He changed mah name

Jesus tol' me I would have to live humble
If He changed mah name

Jesus tol' me that the world would be 'gainst me
If He changed mah name

But I tol' Jesus it would be all right
If He changed mah name

Spiritual: "Going to Set Down and Rest Awhile"

Going to set down and rest awhile
When my good Lord calls me.

Sister Mary went to heaven
And she went there to stay
And she didn't go to come back no more.

She sang a song that the angels couldn't sing
"Hosanna, carry on."

Little children, don't you moan,
When my good Lord calls me.

O, Zion!
When my good Lord calls me.

Aspiring Young Tennis Player in 1914

Sally Waayne was lucky to have an enlightened father who helped her perfect her tennis game; her father even devised a tennis court for her with a borrowed net and sticky tape.

Life at Home

- Sally Waayne grew up in Zeeland, Michigan, as the only child of a single father.
- Her father, Gordon, was a popular cigar maker in a community dominated by furniture manufacturing.
- Her mother died shortly after Sally's birth, a horrible event that left Gordon Waayne devastated and unable to work for weeks.
- His closest friends told him a man couldn't raise a girl and encouraged him to send Sally to his sister's house.
- Possessing a keen mind and a long-nurtured ability to do as he pleased, Gordon agreed he couldn't properly raise a girl, so he decided he would raise Sally as a boy.
- Sally grew up loving baseball—especially the Chicago Cubs—hunting in the deep woods, and playing lawn tennis.
- Zeeland, a small, close-knit Dutch community 20 miles from Grand Rapids, still clung to its Old World language, customs and traditions.
- Zeeland's community leaders were exceedingly proud of its work ethic, cultural roots, and proud isolation.
- They resisted a national move to reduce the typical work week from 54 to 48 hours.
- Zeeland was hardly the ideal environment for a girl who dressed like a boy and knew the vital statistics of baseball players such as Joe Tinker, Johnny Evans, and Frank Chance.
- It did not escape the attention of the neighbors that Sally could easily whip boys as well as girls at tennis.
- When Sally was eight years old, the community's religious leaders formally took Gordon aside and demanded conformity or banishment from services.
- From that day on, Gordon and Sally faithfully spent Sundays perfecting her backhand and practicing the skills she needed to score aces off first serves.

Sally Waayne

- Because his cigars were of the highest quality, Gordon continued to prosper instead of being boycotted for his actions; the preachers could only grumble.
- By the time she reached high school, where she was a competent but somewhat disengaged student, Sally had attracted the attention of the local newspaper.
- She was 16 when the opportunity of a lifetime landed in her lap.
- Three-time U.S. Open champion Mary K. Browne—Sally's idol—was planning an exhibition in Grand Rapids and needed some area competition—preferably from local women and girls.
- As a 5-foot, 2-inch right-hander, Sally was the same height as Mary, who was also a right-hander.
- In recent years Mary had dominated the U.S. Championships at Philadelphia, scoring triples, singles, doubles, and mixed titles in 1912, 1913, and 1914.
- Now 23 years old, Mary was known for her aggressive play and her tendency to play "more like a man" than a woman.
- Trained by male players on the fast, unyielding surfaces of California's asphalt courts, Browne was always prepared, even eager, to settle matters quickly by means of sharp, decisive volleying duels at the net.
- Most of her female opponents preferred a long-volley, backcourt game that emphasized flawless play, not powerful serves and overhead smashes.
- Mary had been tutored by her brother Nat and her father, and she was nurtured by a California culture that accepted women's athletics.
- In one of the most demanding days in tennis annals, Mary played 82 games in the course of winning the 1912 singles, doubles, and mixed finals titles all in the same afternoon—much of the time in a downpour.
- "The rain was coming down in torrents, and still we went on," Mary was quoted in the local paper as saying. "Our rackets were mushy and our clothes soaked."
- Sally had never been so excited in her life as when her father told her she was not only going to meet Mary K. Browne, she was going to play a match against the champion.

Life at Work

- Sally Waayne could barely concentrate on school work once she learned she would be opposing Mary K. Browne in a tennis match.
- Sally had never seen a champion play, but she imagined the game would be faster and sharper than the matches she was accustomed to, even against older players.
- Mary would be in the area to compete in the 1914 Western Lawn Tennis Championship at Lake Forest, Illinois, only a train ride away.
- According to the tennis magazine articles, Mary unhesitatingly hit smashes from anywhere on the court and was known to chase down a lob while running backwards, only to crash it back across the net for an easy point.
- Her opponents were amazed to see her so often crashing the net.
- Stroke for stroke, Mary was known for her sound fundamentals and for understanding court technique; her returns were hard and accurate.
- She didn't like to lose, and she didn't like to play all the time.
- To keep fresh, she intentionally skipped tournaments so that she would always be enthusiastic about the game she loved.
- Everything Sally read about Mary Browne increased her excitement.
- Thanks to her father, she, too, had developed an intimidating serve, a powerful forehand, an adequate backhand, and a strong sense of where the ball would be returned.
- The newspaper said that Sally's style was unmatched by any female player—except Mary Browne.
- For weeks Sally practiced relentlessly, until blisters threatened to swell her hands and feet.

Driving to play a match in Grand Rapids was Sally's first long car ride.

- When Sally was called to help fix supper, her plea was always the same: "Please, just one more serve."
- By the time the day of the match arrived, Sally felt that she was as well prepared as she could be and at the top of her game.
- The day of the match was filled with firsts—her first long car ride, her first trip to Grand Rapids, and her first official tennis shoes.
- When she fretted about being outclassed and embarrassed, her dad reminded her that the 1913 Kentucky Derby winner, Donerail, had been given a 92.5-to-1 chance of winning the $5,000 first prize.
- Compared with those odds, he said, he was eager to place a $2 wager on his girl.
- The first serve was the hardest for Sally.
- She rocketed a first shot to Mary Browne—and was amazed at how easily it was returned.
- For Mary Browne the exhibition match was a chance to promote women's tennis; for Sally the match was a dream come true.
- For the first two sets, Sally held her own, displaying a solid ground game and managing a passing shot that left the champion flatfooted.
- The crowded roared, cheering for the 16-year-old local girl.
- After that, every point was a fierce battle.
- Sally had never played someone who dominated the net so completely.
- After Mary won the match, the two met at the net to exchange congratulations.
- Mary looked Sally in the eye and graciously said, "You remind me of myself. Congratulations on a good effort."

Life in the Community: Zeeland, Michigan

- Zeeland, Michigan, was settled in 1847 by a group of Dutch immigrants who were in search of religious freedom.
- Jannes Van De Luyster, a wealthy landowner, sold all his holdings in the Netherlands in order to purchase the site of the original village—some 16,000 acres—from the U.S. government.
- He named the community after the settlers' home province in the Netherlands, a province known for its conservatism and strict orthodox Calvinism.
- Liberalizing trends in the Dutch Reformed Church and the interference of King William I in church governance—the Dutch Reformed Church was not formally a state church but had close ties to the government—had led a number of conservative Dutch Calvinists to secede.
- Van De Luyster, a pious evangelical, was among them; the Seceders, as they were known, were fined for holding their own services and were subject to harassment and expulsion.
- At first the Seceders' leadership, chiefly clerics, opposed emigration, but by 1844-1845 they had changed their views and were forming emigration societies—including, in February 1847, the Zeeland Association for Emigration to the United States of America.
- Van De Luyster paid the sea passage of settlers who could not afford the cost, as did another Zeeland Seceder, Jan Steketee.
- In 1847 three ships embarked for the United States, carrying about 460 immigrants in all; en route, some 30 of them died.
- After some hesitation about where their settlement should be located, they made their way to Holland, Michigan, and thereafter to the site of Zeeland.
- Food was scarce in the early months, and disease, especially malaria, afflicted the new settlement.
- From the outset the native Ottawa people helped the newcomers to adjust to the severe climate of the area.
- In addition to introducing the settlers to hunting techniques appropriate to the new community's forest setting, the Ottawa taught them how to fell trees, an essential skill for clearing land for crops and building shelters.
- By the fall of 1847 the settlers had erected about 120 log homes with split-log floors.
- The first sizeable building to be assembled was a church, dedicated in May 1848; it was used as a school on weekdays.
- Students were instructed in English and in Dutch.
- A brickyard was established in 1848; brickmaking became on important regional industry.
- During the next 25 years, Zeeland acquired a sawmill and a wagon factory in addition to blacksmith shops, grocery stores, and a post office.
- The steam railroad arrived in Zeeland in 1872, prompting most businesses to move from Cross Street to North Main Street in order to take advantage of railroad traffic.
- The first regular interurban rail service to Grand Rapids began in 1901.
- The sale of alcohol was banned in Zeeland at the turn of the century, although most citizens seemed more concerned about the temptations they associated with movies than about the evils of drink.
- Friday-night concerts at a band stand in a town park were always well attended.
- The village officially became a city in 1907; its population was then almost 3,000.
- By that time Zeeland boasted a two-story brick kindergarten building and a two-story brick grade school.
- The city's economy revolved around four furniture factories and one large manufacturing plant.
- The community was strictly religious; building a public dance hall was prohibited.
- During the second half of the nineteenth century, nearby Grand Rapids, which was also settled by the Dutch, became a major lumbering center and premier furniture manufacturing city.
- Grand Rapids earned the nickname "Furniture City."

Chief Surgeon and Scion of the Virginia Aristocracy in 1915

The son of a wealthy Virginia landowner, Stuart Ramsdell was president of the Association of Seaboard Air Line Railway Surgeons as well as chief surgeon for the railway. Ramsdell and his wife, Charlotte, both traced their roots to the founders of Virginia.

Life at Home

- Both Stuart and Charlotte claimed membership in the First Families of Virginia, which was restricted to socially prominent and wealthy individuals who were "lineal descendants of an ancestor who aided in the establishment of the first permanent English colony, Virginia, 1607–1624."
- Many of the First Families were descended from Pocohontas.
- Charlotte loved to point out—especially when in New England—that her forebears arrived on American shores 13 years before the Mayflower even landed.
- Just as important, of the 105 men in the original Jamestown, Virginia, expedition of 1607, 35 carried the all-important status of gentleman, whereas the settlers who came aboard the Mayflower, as Charlotte liked to say, were "just hard-working people—hatters, tailors, merchants, wool combers, weavers, and the like."
- The latter were not to be found among the ancestors of the First Families.
- A graduate of Princeton and a railroad executive, Stuart was less invested in his ancestry and less inclined than Charlotte to make fun of the Yankees he met.
- On weekends, they loved to go fox hunting; Charlotte especially relished the aristocratic pageantry of this equine fashion show, while Stuart liked setting aside the logistical problems of railroad disasters for a while to enjoy sitting astride a well-trained, powerful horse.
- Charlotte lived for the formal balls in Petersburg, Richmond and Washington, to which they frequently were invited.
- Recently the Ramsdells had attended a society ball in Washington at which Charlotte met Countess Cellere, wife of the Italian ambassador, and Mme. de Riano, wife of the Spanish ambassador.
- Mme. de Riano was wearing a silvery gray satin gown with drapery of gold-brocade chiffon; her hat was trimmed with pale blue-gray, white-tipped goura feathers.

Stuart Ramsdell

- Charlotte had to explain to Stuart the unique desirability of goura feathers; much-coveted, they were the plumes of the Victoria crowned pigeon and originated in New Guinea.
- Charlotte felt well-turned-out in her gown of dark blue chiffon with falling folds over soft blue silk, bordered by a deep edging of cream and dark-blue lace; she topped her ensemble with a smart hat of shiny black straw trimmed with a wreath of natural-toned dahlias.
- During the same trip, the Ramsdells attended the very private marriage of Mrs. Mabelle Swift Moore, widow of Mr. Clarence Moore, a victim of the *Titanic* disaster three years earlier; Mabelle married Axel Christian Preheu Wickfeld, a Danish resident of New York.
- Clarence Moore had been Master of Hounds of the Chevy Chase, Maryland, Hunt, and the Ramsdells had often entertained the Moores at their Petersburg mansion; Charlotte and Mabelle had been close friends since their school days at Mount Vernon Seminary.
- Like many of the more professional men whose work revolved around the railroad, Stuart loved precision, embodied in his goldcase Waltham pocket watch—a gift from his father upon Stuart's graduation from medical school.

James, the Ramsdells' oldest son attended Groton school.

- Not only was the watch very accurate but it had buttons on the edge of the case to activate two separate stopwatch hands, useful in recording events or counting a pulse.
- James, the Ramsdells' elder son, was in his second year at Groton, one of the most aristocratic of New England's private schools.
- Groton's founder, the Reverend Endicott Peabody, was connected to one of the oldest families of New England, while the school's chief financial banker was multimillionaire J. Pierpont Morgan.
- Assured by Stuart of the importance of these connections, Charlotte had reluctantly assented to sending James into the heart of Yankee territory.
- She planned to keep her younger sons, Charles and Robert, closer to home; she was uncertain about where to send her daughter, Martha, but thought that Mount Vernon Seminary might be the best choice.
- Groton was well-known for its educational quality and its determination to be a spiritual extension of a well-born boy's own family.
- Upholding the belief that a Spartan lifestyle built character, Groton directors required undergraduates to sleep in unheated cells without doors, wash up in long, communal black sinks with cold water, and eat meals featuring such unappetizing fare as cold poached cod and "sure-death hash."

Stuart Ramsdell loved the precision embodied in his Waltham pocket watch.

- Groton boys wore stiff white collars and black patent-leather pumps to dinner; no one was allowed to stand with his hands in his pockets, and close friendships were discouraged.
- A favorite form of punishment was known as pumping; an erring student was taken into the lavatory and literally pumped full of water.
- Former U.S. president Teddy Roosevelt, a bold leader, was often cited by the school as the type of leader the school produced.
- Groton's founder and rector, Rev. Endicott Peabody, was a cousin of Roosevelt's first wife, Alice; Roosevelt himself was home-schooled, but he was an early supporter of the school and sent his four sons to Groton.

Life at Work

- In 1914 there were 10,150 people killed and more than 190,000 injured on railroads in the United States.
- Stuart Ramsdell was pushing for every railroad to employ a surgical staff, strenuously insisting that a "surgical organization is of paramount importance today to the successful operation of trains."
- With increasing locomotion speed, accidents likewise were increasing, resulting in more injuries and deaths.
- It was now possible for a train such as the Twentieth-Century Limited to make the trip from Chicago and New York in just 20 hours.
- Stuart had come to believe that once a railway accident occurred, early and careful transportation of victims was necessary; shock resulted more often from railway injuries than from any other class of accidents.

- Although the idea was new, Stuart was convinced that administering first aid would decrease deaths by controlling bleeding and trauma.
- He also was insisting that every train and every station have a "First Aid Package," including instructions on how to use the medicine in the box and explaining the proper use of a stretcher.
- He supported a rule that all employees should be examined every five years and be required to pass the same physical exam used by the Army and Navy; union management was resisting the requirement, believing it would be used to eliminate workers.
- The Seaboard Air Line Railway Company, Stuart's employer, was chartered in 1900 as the successor to the Richmond, Petersburg and Carolina Railroad Company, which owned the 102-mile line from Richmond, Virginia, to Norlina, North Carolina.
- Charlotte's family held a sizeable percentage of the stock of the Richmond, Petersburg and Carolina, and the family profited handsomely from the transaction.

Lurid depictions of railroad accidents were used to pitch casualty insurance.

- The Ramsdells enjoyed a very comfortable income of approximately $60,000 a year, including Stuart's salary as chief surgeon, dividends from their own railroad stocks, and revenues from the 11,000 acres they had inherited between them.
- The Seaboard Air Line Railway Company's 18,949 railroad cars included 143 passenger- and 284 freight locomotives.
- Stockholders had recently gathered in Petersburg, Virginia, to approve the reorganization of the Seaboard Air Line with its Carolina, Atlantic & Western Railway subsidiary, creating the Seaboard Air Line Railway Company.
- The Bureau of Railway Economics reported that the net operating income of U.S. railroads had increased 21.3 percent in the East; operating revenues per mile of line averaged $1,191 nationwide.
- The railroads were opposing a plan by the postmaster general concerning payment for mail transportation.
- Twelve railroad executives in New Haven, Connecticut, including William Rockefeller, were now being tried in federal court for conspiracy to monopolize railroad, steamship, and trolley transportation traffic in New England.

Life in the Community: Petersburg, Virginia

- Within a mile of Petersburg's city limits was the site of the Battle of the Crater, which took place during "our late unpleasantness," as city fathers liked to call the Civil War.
- It was at the Battle of the Crater that Lieutenant Colonel Henry Pleasants, a Union officer under General Grant, conceived the idea of digging a tunnel under the Confederate works in order to break the Union siege of the city.

- The tunnel was excavated by a regiment of Pennsylvania coal miners; in the early morning of July 30, 1864, approximately 8,000 pounds of gunpowder were detonated in the largest manmade explosion that had ever been created.
- The works were destroyed, and 278 Confederate soldiers were killed.
- Despite the 300-foot-wide breach, the poorly led Union infantry troops were repulsed by Confederate soldiers led by Brigadier General William Mahone.
- Shortly before the attack, Union general George Meade had overruled the decision of General Ambrose Burnside to have United States Colored Troops (USCT) lead the attack; unlike the African American troops, the white regiment sent in its place had not been trained for the combat situation.
- As a general policy, the Confederate government had decreed that captured USCT officers would be treated as criminals fomenting slave rebellion; rank-and-file black soldiers were to be killed on the battlefield or, if captured, returned to slavery, sold, or sent to labor on Confederate works.
- At the Battle of the Crater, when the soldiers of the USCT eventually were sent into combat, they were treated with particular ferocity, even after the Union surrender.
- Nevertheless, one Confederate private later recounted, they "fought like bulldogs and died like soldiers."
- Congress was considering the purchase of Crater Farm and adjacent land for the creation of a national battlefield park.
- Within the city proper is Old Blandford Cemetery, where 30,000 Confederate dead were "sleeping their last sleep," as it was put by W. E. Poole, acting mayor of the city.
- Located on Market Street was the Wallace House, where General Grant and President Abraham Lincoln discussed the terms of surrender prior to General Grant's meeting with General Robert E. Lee at Appomattox.

Executives and representatives of the White Star Line, owner of the RMS Titanic. Chairman and managing director, J. Bruce Ismay is at right.

- Petersburg acquired the sobriquet of the "Cockade City" during the Battle of 1812 after President Madison thanked a company of Petersburg men for their gallantry, saying they had won for their city "the proud appellation of the Cockade City of the Union."
- Founded in the early 1700s, Pocohontas Island, located within the city limits on a peninsula jutting into the Appomattox River, was the home of the oldest free black settlement in Virginia; it was incorporated into Petersburg in 1782.
- After the Civil War, an influx of freed slaves into the settlement caused overcrowding and unemployment, with the attendant social and health problems.
- Conditions for Pocohontas Island residents gradually improved, as they did for Petersburg at large, yet the community was especially vulnerable to economic downturns.
- By 1914 an exodus of black residents was very evident, part of the Great Migration of Southern African Americans to the North in search of jobs and a better life.
- The comic strip *Bringing up Father* was a favorite across the Petersburg; nearly everyone claimed to know someone like the newly wealthy Jiggs, who couldn't seem to leave his immigrant worker roots behind, or his wife Mary, who couldn't wait to use their newfound wealth to unlock the doors of society.
- Also very popular were vaudeville shows combining live entertainment with moving picture shows, especially westerns and comedies.
- The city leaders were again discussing the installation of an electric streetcar or trolley; the first in the nation had been created as long ago as 1887, by engineer Julian Sprague of nearby Richmond, Virginia.
- War was under way in Europe; everyone was talking about when and if America should join the fight.
- Many in Petersburg believed the conflict to be strictly a European matter, best settled by Europeans.
- Some people thought the war would be good for American business; leaders in the banking community knew that world commercial and financial leadership might be "thrust within its grasp by war."
- Furthermore, as a columnist for *Life* magazine noted, it was "being whispered, for instance, that the war is going to kill feminism and cubism, and all the other strenuous and angular isms, and bring the good old simple life back into favor."
- In 1914 the Daughters of the American Revolution had moved a solid rock basin from the north bank of the Appomattox River to Petersburg's Central Park so it could be better displayed; tradition held that Pocahontas was "wont to take her morning bath" in the basin.
- The basin was described in Henry Howe's *Historical Collections of Virginia* of 1852.
- Thanks to predictions of very favorable crop production, most of which would be shipped by rail, many of the "better" people of Petersburg were aggressively buying railroad stocks; the earnings of the New Haven Railroad were expected to be strong, thanks to the shipping needs of industries doing war business in New England.
- Throughout Southern states, such as Virginia, optimism about the economy was high in the expectation that cotton prices would be good; Fairfax Harrison, president of the Southern Railway Company, declared, "At current prices the profit to the farmer on a bale of cotton is probably greater than in some years."
- Advertisements appearing in the local newspaper touted the use of radium on plants and grass lawns to make them grow better; the Radium Fertilizer Company claimed that radium would increase vegetable yields by 39 percent.

African American U.S. Army Major in 1916

Major Rudy West, who toured the world as a soldier, was called upon to lead his men into Mexico and capture bandit-political leader Pancho Villa; Villa's men had killed 19 Americans during a raid in New Mexico.

Life at Home

- Rudy West grew up on the Illinois side of the Mississippi River, near St. Louis, in the community of Belleville.
- He was the youngest son of a minister and blacksmith and his seamstress wife; they had been born slaves but learned to read, and they valued God, hard work, education, and a little savings under the mattress.
- They taught their youngest child to love learning, sports, and music.
- Rudy spent many happy hours playing the battered keyboard of an upright piano at his father's church.
- Although Rudy was an excellent student, few opportunities were available to him beyond his community school.
- Then he learned about West Point.
- While working as a clerk in an insurance company, he read that his congressman was holding competitive exams for an appointment to the United States Military Academy at West Point.
- Few blacks had ever attended the academy, and fewer still had graduated.
- Relatives warned him about racism—being ostracized and even hated and cursed.
- During the midst of a community prayer meeting, the call came from the Lord, Rudy believed, to take the exam.
- After a tense day of test-taking in a drafty hall with a dozen white candidates, Rudy learned his score was the highest—the appointment was his!
- Passing the academy's entrance exam was all that lay ahead.
- His family and members of the congregation pooled their money for the trip to West Point and to hire a tutor to prepare him for the test.
- Instead of offering hostility and harassment, the other prospective cadets simply ignored him.

Major Rudy West

Rudy was sent to the Southwest in 1916.

- After only a few weeks in New York, isolated and homesick, Rudy wanted to return home; only because so many had sacrificed so much to send him there did he stay.
- He passed the test with room to spare and entered West Point in 1885.
- Rudy endured four years of abusive hazing, convinced it would make him both a better man and a better soldier.
- He was only the third black student to achieve a diploma.
- His assignments were limited to the military's black units—the 9th and 10th Cavalry and the 24th and 25th Infantry.
- By 1903 the U.S. Army was responsible for a number of national parks created by President Theodore Roosevelt; Rudy was made superintendent of two of the parks, located in California.
- His following three-year assignment was in Port-au-Prince, Haiti, as military attaché to gather intelligence and construct maps of the island terrain.
- Then a placement came in the newly formed Intelligence Office at Army Headquarters in Washington, District of Columbia; it was a dream assignment.
- Within the growing black middle class of the nation's capital, Rudy found friendship, comfort, and a place to be himself.

The barracks in Fort Huachuca, Arizona, were spacious and comfortable.

Rudy and his men were responsible for two national parks in California.

- An accomplished linguist capable of speaking Greek, French, Spanish, and German, he attracted a wide circle of friends.
- It was at a Washington party that he met his wife.
- Unfortunately, soon after the formerly confirmed bachelor walked down the aisle with his new bride, he was shipped to the Philippines, forced to leave behind his home in the capital, his friends, and his now-pregnant wife.
- In the Philippines he watched the slow, agonizing process of forming a democracy; in 1907 under U.S. rule, the Philippines became the first Asian state to establish a national legislature.
- Rudy learned about exotic diseases and the songs they inspired: "I've the dobie itch and Moro stitch/The jim-jams and the fever/The burning fart and the Samar dart/And maybe a kris in my liver!"
- He discovered that Manila's San Miguel beer was excellent, but three drinks of Filipino wine were dangerous.
- On his next assignment, as attaché in Monrovia, Liberia, his wife was allowed to accompany him.
- They were finding great joy living in a nation of former slaves when new orders arrived.
- In 1916 Rudy was assigned to Fort Huachuca, Arizona; his wife, and their three sons could remain with him.
- He was put in command of a squadron of the 10th Cavalry.
- Just as he was anticipating the chance to hunt mule deer, word arrived that American civilians had come under attack from Mexico.

Life at Work

- Information was sketchy, but on March 9, the Mexican political leader and bandit Francisco "Pancho" Villa had led a force of men across the United States border and attacked the community of Columbus, New Mexico.
- Buildings were burned, stores and homes looted, women raped, and 19 soldiers and civilians killed.

Pancho Villa was ordered captured or killed by President Wilson.

- President Woodrow Wilson, long troubled by uneasy relations with Mexico, immediately ordered a punitive expedition into Mexico to capture or kill Villa.
- Six regiments, including four cavalry and two infantry, all under the command of Brigadier General John Pershing, were ordered out.
- Rudy West and the 10th, who were only 250 miles away from Columbus, immediately saddled up, taking care to order two wagons loaded with rations, ammunition, and a double supply of horseshoes.
- In accordance with a tradition dating to the Indian Wars of 30 years before, the band played while the troops filed off the post.
- Both the 7th and 10th Cavalry first gathered at Colbertson's Ranch before crossing the border into the Mexican state of Chihuahua on March 16.
- In all, 1,500 men were made available to General Pershing; few expected the expedition to last a year.
- Under Rudy's command—he was an excellent horseman with a love of the outdoors—the 10th Cavalry was able to move faster than its supply line and subsisted on what they brought or could buy from the locals.
- After travelling 252 miles—30 miles a day—from Huachuca, the 10th was ordered to board a Mexican train to speed their journey south.
- One lieutenant described the trip as less than pleasant: "Our troubles in patching and nailing up the cars, getting materials for camps, collecting wood for the wood-burning engine and getting started late in the afternoon with the animals inside the freight cars and officers and men on top in truly Mexican style, were exceeded, if possible, only by the troubles in keeping the engine going by having the men get off and chop mesquite to burn in it, only to find the wood must be used to send the engine someplace for water, and so on ad infinitum."
- On the morning of April 1, the 10th encountered a force of Villa's men.

- Rudy felt invigorated by the brief engagement; when the Mexicans broke and ran, his troop pursued the invaders for two hours before trapping them in a ravine.
- There the soldier in him wanted to attack, but as an officer, he knew he must wait for the remainder of the regiment to improve their position.
- When the assault occurred, the infantry controlled the rim of the canyon so they could fire down.
- A machine gun covered the ground, and the 10th was free to charge into the ravine.
- Excited by the prospect of being part of the first cavalry charge since the Spanish-American War, Rudy relished the chance to draw his .45 and yell at the top of his lungs.
- The Mexicans fled.
- None of his men was hit; their horses, though, did not enjoy the skirmish.
- One horse was wounded, one dropped from exhaustion, and a third died the next night.
- During the next few days, with rumors rampant that Villa was dead or wounded, the expedition continued.
- Chasing Villa's men required treks through mountains and high deserts at altitudes of up to ten thousand feet.
- There the 10th Cavalry was assaulted by stinging snow and sleet, laced with sand; with freezing nights and days filled with dust, they quickly discovered why the region was called the "windiest place in the world."
- A dust storm could last 24 hours, making cooking impossible and sleep unlikely.
- The men were equipped with .30-caliber Springfield rifles, which weighed slightly more than eight pounds and took ammunition in five-round clips. The men believed the Springfield was far easier to load than the old Krag-Jorgensen rifles, the first U.S. military weapon to use smokeless powder.

Rudy and the 10th Cavalry travelled in brutal conditions, searching for Villa and his men.

- Other equipment changes, many instituted since 1910, were designed to put as much of the soldier's load as possible onto his back and remove bags that might bang against the legs.
- Reconnaissance for General Pershing was provided by four aircraft flying between the cavalry units and enemy lines, with Pershing himself delivering information.
- Mostly, though, the planes were of little use.
- Rudy and his men found themselves faced with an unstable and dangerous foe—angry Mexican citizens inflamed by the American invasion.
- The problems began on April 12 in Parral, Villa's hometown.
- Major Frank Tompkins entered the small community; it was filled with Mexican government troops who were officially allied with the Americans in pursuit of Villa and his men.
- When Tompkins attempted to secure supplies, trouble broke out.
- The seething resentment against the American invasion erupted in gunfire.
- The American troops were trapped by engaged Mexican townspeople and Mexican military.
- Only a few miles away when trouble started, the 10th Cavalry immediately mounted their horses and rode into the fray, dispersing the violence without losing a man.
- When Rudy returned to camp, he was greeted with a letter from the quartermaster general, demanding to know why the hides of slaughtered animals were not sold as called for by Army regulations.

The 10th Cavalry were exhausted as they entered Villa's hometown.

Life in the Community: Mexico

- As foreign investment in Mexico grew and the foreigners became wealthy using Mexican resources, native Mexicans began complaining that "Mexico was the mother of foreigners, and only a stepmother to Mexicans."
- Over half the nation's population—Indians and mestizos—were sharecroppers, with little hope of climbing out of debt.
- The Mexican Revolution against foreign influence started shortly after Porfirio Díaz became president of Mexico for the eighth time on October 4, 1910.
- By 1912 the country had become a battlefield of warring factions; the foreign oil companies, among many outsiders, were outraged.
- By 1913, when strongman Victoriano Huerta swept into power, the German, British, and Spanish governments quickly recognized his rule, but the United States was more cautious.
- The Zapatistas, an army of peasants who occasionally took time away to look after their corn and chili patches, combined with revolutionary armies led by Pancho Villa and Venustiano Carranza under the slogan, "Death to Huerta, down with the foreigners, Mexico for the Mexicans."

- By April 1914 the revolutionary armies controlled all of Mexico except the capital and a small area on the oil-rich coast.
- When the rebels took Tampico, the United States ordered the U.S Navy fleet into Veracruz, Mexico, to seize the port and occupy the city.
- Hatred of foreigners erupted in riots everywhere; American flags were torn and stamped upon in gutters, and businesses were stoned.
- Despite this American soldiers stayed, often working in the community to improve conditions.
- In Veracruz, when Army General Frederick Funston cleaned up the water supply, improved sewage, and imported 2,500 garbage cans from the United States, the death rate among city residents plummeted.
- In July, after President Huerta had fled the country and Carranza was installed as the new president, Villa and Zapata refused to demobilized their troops or accept Carranza as their leader.
- By 1916 Mexico was again a battleground, Mexican money was worthless, and citizens were often on the move to avoid the warring factions.
- With most jobs paying in devalued currency, many men attached themselves to whatever troops were sweeping through the area.

Mexican Invasion Calendar,
The Outlook, July 5, 1916

- March 9, 1916: Nineteen Americans were killed and about 20 wounded in a raid on Columbus, New Mexico, by Mexican bandits, supposedly led by General Villa.
- March 15: An American column under General Pershing crossed the border in pursuit of raiders. It was generally understood by the American public that this incursion was made with the consent of the Carranza government, that the Mexican de facto government would cooperate with the United States in the bandit hunt, and that American troops would be withdrawn as soon as the marauders who had attacked Columbus were killed or captured.
- April 19: General Pershing's expedition reached its "farthest south" by the arrival of two troops of the 13th Cavalry at Parral, about 400 miles from the border, where they were ambushed by Carranzista soldiers and townsmen and forced to retreat, with the loss of two killed and seven wounded. This virtually ended the pursuit of Villa by the Americans, and led to the dispatch of heavy reinforcements to General Pershing and a general contraction of his lines.
- April 29: Conferences began at Juarez, Mexico, and El Paso, Texas, between Alvaro Obregon representing Carranza, and Generals Scott and Funston representing the United States.
- May 15: Mexicans raided the "Big Bend" district of Texas, killing seven Americans.
- May 11: The conferences at Juarez and El Paso were discontinued, with no substantial agreement reached. About the same time, American cavalrymen captured 14 Mexicans alleged to have taken part in the raid on Glen Springs in the "Big Bend," and a little later other cavalrymen killed a number of the companions of these captured bandits.
- May 31: The American government received a note from the Carranza government stating that the Pershing expedition had gone into Mexico without the consent of Carranza, and asking for "the immediate withdrawal of American troops which are now in Mexican territory."
- June 11: Mexicans raided an American ranch near Laredo, Texas, with the result that 1,600 American regulars were drawn from the Engineer Corps of the Coast Artillery to further reinforce the defenses of the U.S. border.
- June 14-21: Texas soil was twice again raided by Mexicans. President Wilson's summons to the militia of all states, except the three border states already called, resulted on June 18. Sixteen warships were sent to watch Mexican ports.
- June 20: The president's reply to Carranza's demand for the withdrawal of U.S. troops was issued. The American government refused and, while admitting that "American troops had crossed the international boundary in hot pursuit of the Columbus raiders, and without notice to or the consent of your government," served notice that any attempt by the de facto government to expel the American soldiers by force would be followed by "the gravest consequences."

**"Riding Mexican Trains through Chihuahua, Mexico,
in Search of Pancho Villa," by Captain Rodney**

It was a train by courtesy, nothing else. Six cattle cars were hitched to a wood-burning engine for which there was no fuel. Our first job was to rebuild the train, for great holes had been burned in the floors. Most of the cars had no doors, and every time the engine moved, the sides of the cars opened out just as the sticks in a fan separate. When we finally got the horses loaded, we placed bales of hay along the tops of the cars so the men would not fall off when asleep; then we set to work with camp hatchets to cut a supply of fuel for the engine. In this way, we finally got started, after demolishing a set of loading pens for fuel for which the government later had to pay $1,900. Then, we started, but it was only a start. From time to time a man would roll off the roof, or sparks from the engine would set fire to the hay bales; then the engine would stop for water and we had to cut down telegraph poles for fuel, and when we got the fuel, the water was gone. It took us 24 hours to run 25 miles, and we finally reached our destination about three hours after we would have reached it had we marched. At a little wood station called Rucio, we finally got the horses off the train. As there was no ramp for unloading, the train was stopped in a railway cut and we got the horses out by the simple process of pushing them out of the open car doors. Then, we started on our cross-country march to San Miguel rancho, where rumor said Villa had been hiding.

❧❧❧❧❧❧❧❧

"Villa's Invasion,"
The Literary Digest, March 18, 1916

Villa's descent of March 9 upon American soil was a surprise to readers of American newspapers, yet there has been presented evidence that it had been planned some time in advance. United States Army officers in command along the Mexican border were, of course, prepared for the worst, although in Columbus itself there had been no trouble during the past three years. An interesting story of Villa's preliminary movements, and of the ways of the man who ventured to go to war with the United States on his own account, was given in the story of an American woman who was his prisoner for several days preceding the Columbus battle. Mrs. Maud Hawk Wright, wife of an American ranch owner in Mexico, was visited on March 1 by a Villista officer Servantes. Their supplies and horses were taken, and Mr. Wright and the baby were sent away. The Villistas took Mrs. Wright prisoner, joined the main body, and compelled her to accompany them on a nine days' forced march. From the first, says Mrs. Wright:

"I knew that Villa intended to attack Columbus. It was freely discussed by the men and the officers. Some of the latter told me that Villa intended to kill every American he could find, but they pointed to me as an example of their decision not to harm women. Later, as we approached the border from Boca Grande, these same officers told me that Villa-his rage growing as he neared the boundary-would make torches of every woman and child, as well as of every man, in Columbus.

Villa and his men assemble for another attack.

"'He intended,' they said, 'to kill everybody in the United States, and would be helped by Japan and Germany.' At Boca Grande I saw evidence of their determination. I did not see the three American cowboys named McKinney, Corbett, and O'Neill slain, but I saw officers wearing their clothing. That was after Villa had sent out 20 men to break up the Palomas cattle roundup and supply the hungry column with meat....

"We left Boca Grande yesterday and crossed the border west of Columbus before four o'clock.

"As we entered the ditch leading past the American army camp below Columbus, the captain of my company told me that he and the 20 officers had crossed the border yesterday as spies, and found that only a few American soldiers were in the camp, that the others were farther west.

"I was in the line Villa threw along the railroad tracks after his troops swept eastward through the United States cavalry. A bullet hit the saddle of my horse as I stood dismounted behind it. Villa sent his men across the tracks into the town. Soon I saw buildings on fire. Then, the American troops apparently got into action, and in a little while the Mexicans came back.... I went back with the retreating forces until I reached a point near the house where Mr. Moore was killed and his wife wounded. Here Villa came upon me. Again I asked him to set me free.

"'You go; you are at liberty,' he said. I went to the Moores' house and found Mr. Moore lying facing down on the steps, dead; his wife was in a nearby field, wounded. She had seen her husband shot, but did not know he was dead."

Teacher and Americanization Advocate in 1916

Emily Strandhope thought that if Americans were not careful, the Greeks, Italians, and Russians would overrun the United States and reduce English to a minority language.

Life at Home

- Emily Strandhope heard the call at an early age; in retrospect, she decided that the vision arrived at age 15 while she was at the open-air market not far from her home in Brooklyn, New York.
- She had been sent to the market for some carrots, cabbage, and flour.
- None were in sight, and when she asked the vendor, he replied in German that he didn't understand her request; she turned to the next vendor and he, too, spoke no English.
- That's when Emily decided that she was being called to Americanize the immigrant hordes flocking to the United States.
- Fixing the immigrant problem would save America from the anarchists and Bolsheviks, and the best way to do that was to teach the foreigners English and compel them to use it.
- The quicker they learned to speak nothing but English, the better off everyone would be.
- From 1870 to 1916, about 27 million immigrants arrived at America's shores looking for work, education and opportunity.
- The lure of American-style education was so great that, on days after a steamship landed in New York Harbor, the city's schools would often experience an enrollment hike of 125 pupils.
- Emily was sure that education was necessary if the American way of life was to be preserved.
- She attended Teachers College at Columbia University with this conviction in mind.
- There, she learned of the emerging idea called "kindergarten."
- The idea of schools for "infants" had been circulating in Europe, mostly in Germany, since the turn of the last century, but the first American "kindergarten"—a name coined about 1840 by Friedrich Fröbel, in Thuringia, Germany—did not open until 1856, in Wisconsin.
- This first American kindergarten was conducted in German; not until Elizabeth Palmer Peabody

Emily Strandhope

opened a kindergarten in Boston in 1860 was there a formal English-language school for children ages 4 to 6.

- Ironically, Elizabeth Palmer Peabody herself had a reading knowledge of ten languages.
- Emily saw that kindergartens could not only educate the very young but provide the moral training so clearly lacking, she thought, in the slums of New York.
- In school children could be taught disciplines such as cleanliness, politeness, obedience and regularity.
- Some schools even installed showers to meet the needs of the dirty, neglected urban children.
- These steps were all necessary, Emily had read, because among the immigrants, critical influences like the family, church and community had collapsed.
- Emily knew that a child who lived for years in the misery of a crowded tenement home would, as an adult, become too comfortable with corruption and immorality.
- Emily was, in effect, saving America from itself, and she was often disappointed that her family and friends did not fully comprehend how important her work was or how much she was sacrificing for the country.
- She didn't hesitate to scrub children clean when they arrived dirty, and she washed their hair to reduce lice infestations.
- She also regularly swatted children on their backsides when she heard them speaking in their native language.
- Emily's own upbringing had not prepared her for these tasks, but she was determined to do whatever was necessary to put her students on the right path.
- Early in her career, she had read an article in the *Atlantic Monthly* that called for schools to organize themselves along business principles.
- The article's author identified the ideal teacher as one who would rigidly "hew to the line."
- His ideal school was a place strictly governed by a rigid routine, and he repeatedly stressed in his article a need for "unquestioned obedience."
- Emily had no wish to be well liked by her students—popularity was a dangerous game that helped no one.
- Her parents supported her mission, but her sisters were often exasperated by her single-mindedness.
- When she was 24, Emily turned down a marriage proposal from a solid working man; married women were expected to give up teaching—and Emily had no intention of doing that.
- Now, at 36, she was a spinster with no prospects on the horizon, and she was perfectly content.
- At least, she thought, the onset of World War I had drastically curtailed the number of new immigrants coming to America; now was the time to tamp down the Statue of Liberty's symbolic welcome flame and cope with the immigrants America had already.
- One of the answers was kindergarten and the chance to "straighten the crooked sticks" while they were young.
- Emily had even helped several young children by changing the spelling of their names to make them more American; when one parent objected, Emily told her "it was for her own good."
- The first free public-school kindergarten in the United States opened in St. Louis, Missouri, in 1873, with the specific purpose of dealing with urban poverty.
- Forty-three years later, the educational reform movement had evolved; in addition to preparing young children academically and socially for school, kindergartens focused on improving parenting skills—especially in the poverty-stricken urban neighborhoods where so many immigrants lived.

Life at Work

- Every day Emily Strandhope contended with the influence of the Gary Plan, which so many of her colleagues—especially the younger ones—wanted to implement in city schools.

- She was sure that the Gary Plan was destined to fail in New York City, where the student population was diverse, multiple languages were embedded in the culture, and the children were less manageable than in the Midwest, where the Gary Plan originated.
- First established in 1906 in Gary, Indiana, the Gary Plan model kept students in motion; children moved from class to class, learned technical subjects such as automobile repair, and took physical education classes.
- Superintendent William Wirt, the plan founder, wanted his students to be kept busy.
- He viewed the self-sufficient family farm as containing all of the characteristics necessary for a student's development—particularly vocational training, physical activity, and character growth.
- Work and productivity characterized rural life, Wirt believed, and he thought that the rapid urbanization occurring in the early twentieth century threatened the rural values necessary for children's total development.
- Wirt aimed to create in the public schools a kind of haven in which to instill the values of family, work, and productivity among urban students and to produce an efficient, orderly society of solid, productive citizens.
- For older students he pioneered classes in animal care and husbandry, auto mechanics shop and business.
- All of a school's space was used all the time; he called it "Work-Study-Play."
- On the Gary Plan, students helped to run the school from the print shop to the cafeteria.
- Wirt's goal was to "make every working man a scholar and every scholar a working man."
- Emily, however, considered Wirt's ideas an invitation to bedlam; in her experience children learned best when they were sitting still, facing forward, and paying attention.
- When a student's hands got too busy, she argued, his or her brain went dead.
- Emily had learned to read people's characters at an early age, and this applied to students as well as to adults.
- There was only enough time to help the promising ones, she declared proudly, and that is how she wanted to spend her time.
- She was not one to follow that latest educational fad, she proclaimed.
- Now that she had taught for more than 16 years, she was firm in her conviction that classes with 45 children were too big, and making teachers instruct in only one subject robbed them of the opportunity to engage the whole student.
- While the Gary Plan was still being tested on younger children, it was merchandised from the newsstand, pulpit, and lecture circuit, and it was quickly adopted as gospel by the proponents of the scientific management movement.
- More ominously, as Emily saw it, Wirt's ideas were lauded in administrative circles and soundly praised by John and Evelyn Dewey in their 1915 book *Schools of Tomorrow*.
- In 1912, in an article entitled "Elimination of Waste in Education," a contributor to *Elementary School Teacher* had gong even further.
- Teaching, the article forecast, would become a specialized scientific calling conducted by preapproved agents of the school's central business office.
- Classroom teachers, the author claimed, would teach their subject over and over to groups of children circulating through the school building on a precise time schedule.
- Early in 1914, the Federal Bureau of Education had endorsed the Gary Plan, and to Emily's extreme dismay, it was implemented in dozens of schools in Brooklyn.
- Rather to her surprise, many New York City parents, especially the parents of Jewish students, staged a spontaneous rebellion against extension of the Gary Plan.
- A program that looked like a complete and comprehensive education in Gary, Indiana, looked to many New Yorkers like a government-sponsored training program for factory workers.
- This was not the future they wanted for their children.

- The new-fangled ideas about education, they thought, were not going to give children the tools they needed to get ahead in America.
- They wanted the schools to produce moral, educated children.
- Many agreed with Emily that only strict discipline would accomplish that.
- Emily had found allies in the very last place she expected to find them.

Life in the Community: Brooklyn, New York

- The Dutch were the first Europeans to settle on the western end of Long Island, which they found inhabited by a Native American people, the Lenape.
- The Dutch lost the area, which they called Breuckelen, in the British conquest of New Netherland in 1664; over time, the name evolved from Breuckelen to Brockland to Brocklin to Brookline to Brookland, and, eventually, to Brooklyn.
- During the first half of the nineteenth century, Brooklyn experienced significant growth along the economically strategic East River waterfront across from New York City; Brooklyn's population expanded more than threefold between 1800 and 1820, doubled again in the 1820s, and doubled yet again during the 1830s.
- Then, in 1854, the City of Brooklyn annexed the City of Williamsburg, an event that allowed Brooklyn to grow from a substantial community of 36,236 to an influential city of 96,838.
- The building of rail links, such as the Brighton Beach Line in 1878, heralded explosive growth, and in the space of a decade, Brooklyn annexed the towns of New Lots, in 1886; Flatbush, Gravesend, and New Utrecht, in 1894; and Flatlands, in 1896.
- The Brooklyn Bridge, completed in 1883, linked Manhattan to Brooklyn, and in 1894, Brooklyn residents voted by a slight majority to join with Manhattan, the Bronx, Queens, and Richmond (later Staten Island) to become the five boroughs of the modern New York City.
- When the Williamsburg Bridge opened in 1903, it was the largest suspension bridge in the world.
- Five years later, in 1908, the city's first subway began running trains between Brooklyn and Manhattan; in 1909, the Manhattan Bridge was completed.
- Brooklyn nevertheless continued to maintain a distinct culture.
- Many Brooklyn neighborhoods were enclaves where particular ethnic groups and cultures predominated.
- The Brooklyn Academy of Music opened in Brooklyn Heights in 1861; the academy moved to Fort Greene in 1908; performances celebrating that occasion included Isadora Duncan dancing to three movements of Beethoven's Symphony No. 7, played by the New York Symphony Orchestra conducted by Walter Damrosch.
- In addition to music and dance performances, the academy offered lectures by luminaries such as Booker T. Washington, Jacob Riis, and former U.S. president William Howard Taft.
- The Brooklyn Museum, which quickly became known especially for its Egyptian antiquities, opened in 1897 in a Beaux Arts-style building designed by the famed architectural firm McKim, Mead, and White; sculptor Daniel Chester French, famous for his work at the Lincoln Memorial in Washington, District of Columbia, contributed pediment- and cornice sculptures.
- Baseball was firmly entrenched in Brooklyn by the 1850s; it was the home of half the 16 member teams attending the National Association of Base Ball Players's first convention, in 1857.
- Ebbets Field opened in 1913 on the site of a former Flatbush garbage dump colloquially known as Pigtown.
- In 1916 the Ebbets-based Brooklyn Robins—a team known be a variety of names over the years but finally as the Brooklyn Dodgers—won their first National League pennant, but in the World Series, they were demolished by Babe Ruth and his Boston Red Sox teammates.
- Center-fielder Casey Stengel was the Robins' standout offensive player in the series.

Star of the New York Metropolitan Opera in 1916

With her glorious voice and glamorous style, soprano opera singer Geraldine Farrar, the daughter of a onetime professional baseball player, became a reigning figure of the New York Metropolitan Opera.

Life at Home

- Opera singer Geraldine Farrar's clothes, food, and travels—and every word she spoke—were chronicled in the New York press.
- They invariably discussed her beauty and acting ability and the intimate timbre of her singing voice.
- She was paid a salary second only to that of tenor Enrico Caruso.
- She insisted she was not a singer but a singing actor.
- Among her fans was a large following of young women, who were nicknamed "Gerry-flappers."
- Born in Melrose, Massachusetts, in 1882, Geraldine began studying music with her mother, Henrietta Barnes Farrar, at the tender age of three; both her parents sang in the church choir.
- Her father, Sidney Farrar, had a hardware store; as a young man he had played professional baseball in Philadelphia.
- When Geraldine decided that she liked the black "devilish" piano keys best and refused to play the white "angel" keys, her mother bribed her with a tricycle to play "regular."
- A lover of animals as a child, she dressed the family cats, dogs, alligators, rabbits, bullfinch, and robin in elaborate costumes.
- Then, at 10 years old, her dramatic side emerged after a boy who had paid her special attention tragically drowned while ice skating; for six weeks, Geraldine acted the widow
- She dressed in black, eschewed all gaiety, and went to school with a black fringed handkerchief to wipe her weepy eyes.
- She made her public singing debut at 12, portraying the legendary soprano Jenny Lind at a springtime carnival.
- When her moment arrived, the prima donna in Geraldine insisted on first singing an aria from *Faust* before breaking into "Home, Sweet Home," the song she was scheduled to sing.

Geraldine Farrar

- As a teen her temper was sharp and her moods dark; she took to wearing black-and-white checked stockings when she wanted to be left alone.
- After studying in Boston, she moved to New York City to work with American soprano Emma Thursby.
- She auditioned successfully for the Metropolitan Opera, but her mother encouraged her to turn down the offer until she was more fully prepared.
- To gain sufficient funds for Geraldine to study in Germany, her father sold his hardware store and the family borrowed $30,000 from a Boston benefactor—all of which was repaid within two years of the family's return to the United States.
- The family sailed to Europe on a cattle boat.
- While in Paris, Geraldine went to Leo Reutlinger, a famous fashion photographer, and demanded professional rates.

Geraldine's family sailed to Europe on a cattle boat so that she could study in Germany.

- When Reutlinger objected that she was unknown, Geraldine replied, "But I am going to be famous."
- Her first professional opera performance abroad, in 1901, was in the role of Marguerite in Charles Gounod's *Faust*, at the Berlin Hofoper; she sang her role in Italian, while the rest of the cast performed in German.
- Nineteen-year-old Geraldine created such a sensation at her debut that she remained with the company for four years.
- Many German opera lovers were captivated by a soprano who was neither fat nor 40; others condemned the very idea of an American singing Italian in the great German Royal Hall.
- Geraldine became a pupil of Lilli Lehmann and appeared in the title roles of Ambroise Thomas's *Mignon* and Jules Massenet's *Manon*, as well as Juliette in Gounod's *Roméo et Juliette*.
- In 1903, when Kaiser Wilhelm II invited her to perform at his palace, she accepted the opportunity but refused to wear black or lavender as dictated by the court (which was in mourning).
- Nor would she agree to wear long gloves.
- Kaiser Wilhelm relented and she performed.
- Her admirers in Berlin included Crown Prince Wilhelm of Germany, igniting a storm of German press concerning a possible relationship.
- Before she ended her stay in Europe, Geraldine performed in Italy with Enrico Caruso; she was overwhelmed by the power and clarity of his voice.

Geraldine began studying music at three years old and made her public singing debut when she was twelve.

Life at Work

- After years away from the United States, Geraldine Farrar made her debut in *Roméo et Juliette* on November 26, 1906—at the New York Metropolitan Opera, the place she had always dreamed of performing.
- Personally recruited by Metropolitan Opera general manager Heinrich Conried, Geraldine returned to glorious reviews and quickly became a reigning figure in New York opera.
- The press described her clothing, her moods, her every word; she was truly a star.
- She appeared in the first Met performance of Giacomo Puccini's *Madama Butterfly* in 1907, a role she would dominate for the next decade.
- To prepare, she "slaved with ardor and enthusiasm" to master the style, gestures and mannerisms of a Japanese woman, with the help of a Japanese actress.
- To meet all her ambitions and offers, Geraldine performed in New York, Paris, and Berlin that year; she was continually afraid that her voice would disappear or her energy would give out.
- At one point in January 1908, Geraldine performed four times in six days, bouncing from *Faust* to *Butterfly* to *Pagliacci*.
- Fatigue took its toll, and during her third season at the Met, she fought with Italian conductor Arturo Toscanini over nearly everything; the estrangement was complete after the opening performance of *Madama Butterfly*, when they both, as she later wrote, "lost our manners and tempers in a high-handed fashion."
- The press helped fan the flames with dozens of stories about the artistic dispute—frequently quoting anonymous sources.
- Geraldine was prepared to flee New York, but then Toscanini made warm overtures and became an important musical impresario for the star.

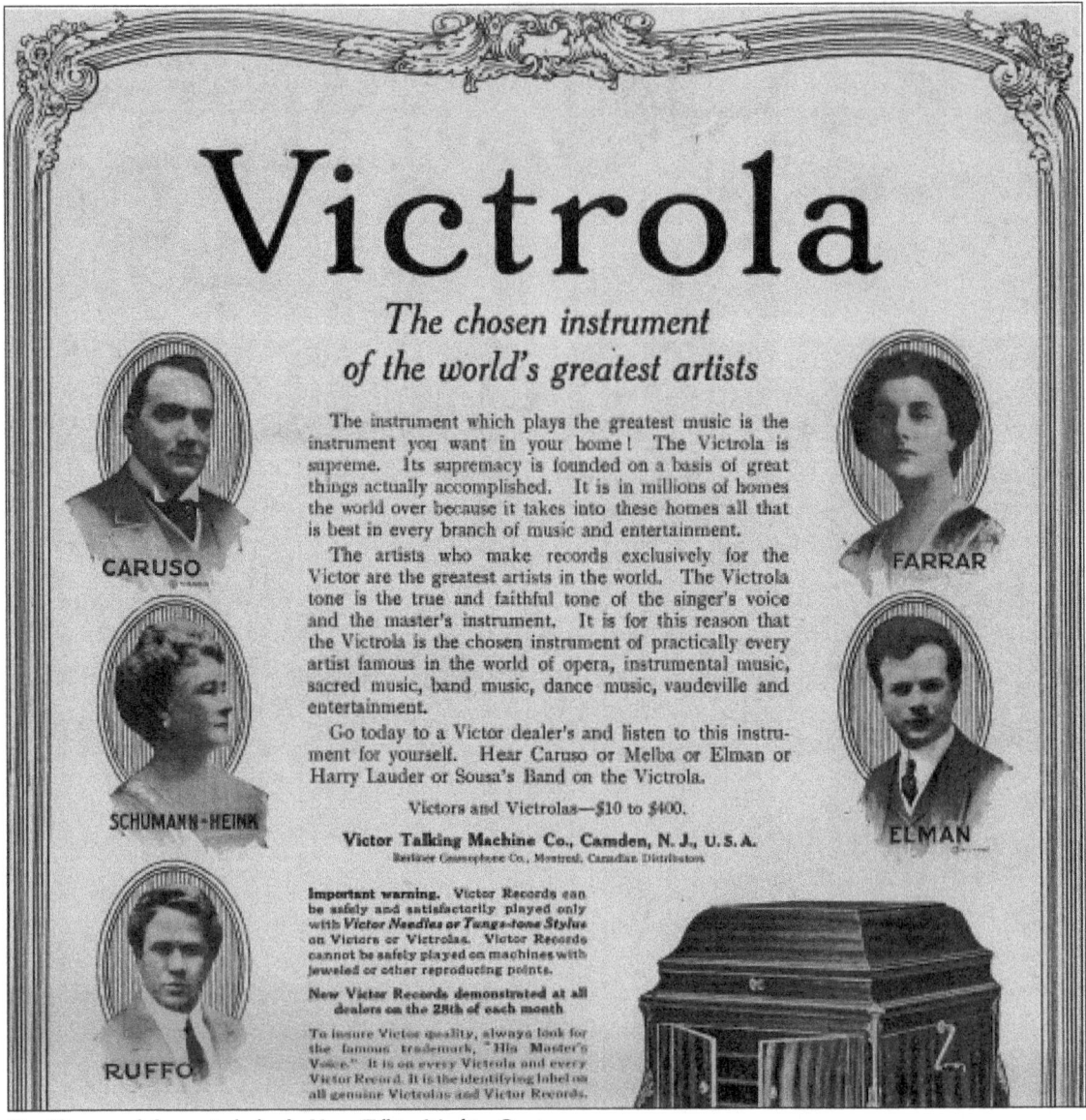

Geraldine recorded extensively for the Victor Talking Machine Company.

- Geraldine had a seven-year love affair with Toscanini; it ended after she demanded that he leave his family.
- Toscanini abruptly resigned his position as principal conductor of the Metropolitan Opera in 1915.
- Geraldine created the title roles in Pietro Mascagni's *Amica* (Monte Carlo, 1905); Umberto Giordano's *Madame Sans-Gêne* (New York, 1915); as well as the Goosegirl in Engelbert Humperdinck's *Die Königskinder* ("The Goosegirl," New York, 1910)
- In 1914 Caruso and Geraldine performed together in Georges Bizet's *Carmen,* which would become one of her career triumphs.
- One seasoned New York critic gushed, "She was indeed a vision of loveliness, never aristocratic, yet never vulgar, a seductive, languorous, passionate Carmen of the romantic gypsy blood. It was full of imagination and delicate touches of art. And above all, it was beautifully sung."
- During her career Farrar recorded extensively for the Victor Talking Machine Company, and she was often featured prominently in that firm's advertisements.

Geraldine considered herself a "singing actor" since her performances were laced with drama, passion, and emotion.

- She shocked many of her fans by agreeing to appear in silent movies, which were filmed between opera seasons.
- The silent movies included a 1915 adaptation of Bizet's *Carmen*.
- On the moving picture screen, it was her acting, not her voice, that counted.
- While most bel canto singers sacrificed dramatic action to tonal perfection, Farrar was more interested in the emotional than in the purely lyrical aspects of her roles.
- Her marriage to cinema actor Lou Tellegen on February 8, 1916, was celebrated in the press—and closely chronicled as it fell apart.

Life in the Community: New York City
- In 1916, with a population of 4.6 million, New York was emerging as one of the world's great seaports.
- The war in Europe had also transformed the city into the world's money center—a designation that previously had been bestowed on London.
- In 1880 a group of prominent and extremely wealthy businessmen formed a new organization expressly for promoting opera in the city.
- The completion of the Metropolitan Opera House three years later brought stability to the New York music scene.
- Located between Thirty-ninth and Fortieth streets on the West Side, and taking up the entire block to Seventh Avenue, the Metropolitan Opera House opened on October 22, 1883, with Henry E. Abbey as manager.
- Being too large in size for ordinary theatre, the house was devoted almost exclusively to grand opera.
- It was also the scene of many great gatherings on patriotic occasions, of many public balls, and of concerts, as well as several fairs.
- Its interior was destroyed by fire in September 1892 but was rebuilt the following year.

Metropolitan Opera House, Broadway, New York City.

- Metropolitan Opera orchestra seats sold for $5.00; a one-sided, 78 rpm recording of Enrico Caruso singing "Celeste Aida" cost $3.00.
- Opera lovers would attend live performances multiple times to become thoroughly familiar with a production's sounds and nuances.
- Operas performed in Italian tended to lose money, while German-language operas were moneymakers.
- The competition was Oscar Hammerstein's opera company, Hammerstein's booked talent and facilities were first class. cigar-producing
- Hammerstein, a German immigrant, was an inventor; the machines he devised to make cigars earned him a fortune, which supported his writing, plays, and theaters.
- In 1889 he opened his first theater, the Harlem Opera House, on 125th Street, featuring operas sung in German.
- New York's music infrastructure also included Carnegie Hall, completed in 1891; the famed Russian composer Pyotr Ilyich Tchaikovsky conducted his own Coronation March at the opening.
- In 1892 Antonín Dvoøák became Director of the National Conservatory of Music, where he promoted Native American and African American folk music.
- New York's position as a center for European classical music was established early, thanks to the New York Philharmonic, formed in 1842.
- In the opening decades of the twentieth century, New York City's music scene spawned and supported Tin Pan Alley, Broadway theaters, Yiddish theater, vaudeville, ragtime, operetta, jazz, the music of the Gullah people, and the Impressionist and Post-Romantic music of European composers.

Review by Richard Aldrich,
The New York Times, November 27, 1916

Miss Farrar comes back to her native land as one of the American singers who have made name and fame for themselves abroad. It is not always easy to establish the same success in this country, and it may be that all she does will not meet with quite so unqualified acceptance as it has abroad. But she went far upon that road in what she accomplished last evening. She made a most agreeable impression in her impersonation of Juliette, for she is full of excellent instincts, making for the best things as a lyric actress. She has a charming personality, a graceful and winning one, and her stage presence is alluring and with much of the girlishness of Juliette.

It has been said that by the time an actress has learned the art of denoting the passion and the ecstatic emotion of Juliette, she could rarely still be in possession of the juvenile charm that the part needs. But Miss Farrar has it, and has at the same time skill and resource in stagecraft. She is a singer of remarkable gifts. Her voice is a full and rich soprano, lyric in its nature and flexibility, yet rather darkly colored and with not a little of the dramatic quality and with a power of dramatic nuance that she uses in the main skillfully. Her singing is generally free and spontaneous in delivery, well phrased and well enunciated, yet she is not a wholly finished vocalist, and there were matters in her singing that could not meet with entire approbation, as in the duet in the fourth act, where she sang with a certain constraint.

There will be more interesting and more important music of the exhibition of her artistic powers before the season is much further advanced, but there was ample cause in her Juliette of last evening for the high expectations that have been raised for her in the musical public of New York.

From the review by Henry Krehbiel,
The New York Tribune, November 26, 1916

Miss Farrar was most graciously received, and was then permitted with kind encouragement to win her way to popular approval. She won that approval, and she won more: She achieved her place among those whom a Metropolitan audience recognizes as in the foremost of the world's operatic artists. She appeared as a beautiful vision; youthful, charming in face, figure, movement and attitude. She sang with a voice of exquisite quality in the middle register, and one that was vibrant with feeling almost always. She acted like one whose instincts for the stage were full and eager, but also like one who, not needing to learn what to do, had neglected to learn that it is possible to do too much. Had she been one-half less consciously demonstrative, whenever she stepped out of the dramatic picture, one-half less sweeping in her movements and gestures when she was in the picture, she would have been twice as admirable to her compatriots who were rejoicing in her success, and twice as convincing to those who were sitting in judgment upon an artist for whom the trumps of acclaim have been so loudly sounded that their din will make calm listening difficult for some time to come. But she has won a welcome that must have emphatic expression. The few crudities in her vocalization are pushed into notice by the very excellence of her merits. Red and warm blood flows in her voice and pulses in harmony with the emotions of the play. She is eloquently truthful in declamation, and correct taste dictates her choice of nuance and vocal color. It is only when she forces her upper tones that sensuous charm leaves her voice in a measure and one deplores the departure all the more because the voice is of a carrying power that makes strenuousness unnecessary.

"Carmen Again Today at Palace,"
The Racine Journal News (Wisconsin), May 22, 1916

Today is the second and last showing of that great photo dramatization of the greatest play, *Carmen*, which attracted such tremendous crowds Sunday at the Palace Theater. This is the only real picturization of *Carmen*, and the fact that so renowned an artiste as Geraldine Farrar appears in the leading role made so many anxious to see it that the limited seating capacity of the Palace was inadequate to accommodate half the crowds who came Sunday. The special music arranged for this great picture is charming, and the management of the Palace is to be highly commended for bringing to Racine such a magnificent attraction in both the picture and music.

Several scenes in this picture are so startling that it fairly brings the audience to their feet. The fight scene in the cigarette factory between Carmen and Anita King is the most realistic ever staged, and in fact is real in one instance when Miss Farrar is dangerously wounded in the terrific fight during which Miss King accidentally cut her with the dagger, and Miss Farrar was confined to a hospital for two months following the taking of this picture.

Geraldine Farrar is the highest-salaried female opera star, having received $5,000 for a single performance. Her favorite role is that of Carmen. The string of pearls which Miss Farrar wears in this picture was given to her by Kaiser Wilhelm of Germany. She is a favorite of the nobility, has appeared at the Royal Opera House in Berlin, and has also appeared before all the crowned heads of Europe. It was rumored that she was engaged to the Crown Prince, who is now leading the terrific assault on Verdun. It was only after he was exiled to the Royal Palace in Potsdam that he gave up the vivacious queen of the opera.

Farm Family's First High-School Student in 1916

After a childhood spent working on his father's tobacco farm in Kentucky, Wilfred Mathieson was given the opportunity to become the first person in his family to graduate high school—at the cost of leaving home to attend school in a neighboring town.

Life at Home

- Born at home in his parents' bed, Wilfred Mathieson, at age 16, began attending high school in Greenburg, a neighboring community, over his father's strong objections.
- His father had long assumed that his son would quit school when he finished the eighth grade and help on the tobacco farm.
- He expected the other children to do likewise and does not want to give any of them the wrong impression concerning their duty to the family.
- "The boy's become too valuable on the farm to be going off to school and looking at a book," Wilfred overheard his father tell his mother.
- Wilfred's father himself had left school in the fourth grade to help tend the family farm—and because of the fight he had with a new teacher over rock throwing.
- But Wilfred's mother was determined that her promising son would be the first person in the family to complete high school.
- She arranged for Wilfred to live with her second cousin, Buford Forbes, in Greenburg.
- Before Wilfred left for school, he gave away some of his possessions: little brother Buford got a slingshot, Sarah got his gardening trowel, and to Talbert, the youngest child, he gave a piglet to take care of.
- Like most of the families in the neighborhood, the Mathiesons were small-scale farmers—the one-horse kind who depended on light, air-cured Burley tobacco for cash and homegrown vegetables and farm-raised livestock for food.
- Wilfred began farming with his parents at age six; his first job was planting, which requires considerable stooping—a skill well-suited to children of about that age.

Wilfred Mathieson

Wilfred gave Talbert, his youngest brother, a piglet to take care of when he left for school.

- Plants were set out in rows about three feet apart, wide enough for a horse or mule to pass through.
- Wilfred would bend over and push a peg into the ground, pull a plant from a bucket, push it into the hole and drag dirt around it; then he would move two feet and stoop again.
- After planting came weeding, using a hoe.
- He found that worming, the removal of tobacco worms by hand, could be made somewhat less boring than weeding.
- Last tobacco season, to show off for a girl, he pulled a three-inch-long worm off a leaf, put it in his mouth, and bit the head off.
- She was impressed, he believed.
- Even though he had been around tobacco his entire life, Wilfred did not smoke; his mother warned him that if he drank coffee or smoked cigarettes, he would be headed straight for perdition.
- When he went off to school, Wilfred was given store-bought clothes for the first time, after a lifetime of wearing hand-me-down shirts and homemade pants—often constructed of denim material so stiff it would hardly bend.
- He even received a suit for Sundays; his mother wanted Wilfred to look respectable for church.
- Until recently, he had worn his homemade pants at a three-quarter length—six inches below the knee—to protect them from farm muck and keep them out of water.
- Even now Wilfred's stockings were entirely homemade, from the carding, spinning, and dyeing of the wool to the knitting.
- Wilfred's hats likewise were made from wool; they assumed the shape of a cone when wet, which was referred to on the farm as "going to seed."
- He wore stiff-bottomed, brogan-type shoes made of rough leather and held together in front with a buckle.
- Because his mother did not want him walking the mile to the nearest school alone, Wilfred started school when his younger brother turned six and the boys could go together.
- The elementary school had eight grades in two rooms for 48 children; it was considered a modern school because the children were divided by skill level and age.

Wilfred's father always assumed that his son would quit school and help out on the tobacco farm.

- The school term extended for three months, or about 61 days each year; the rest of the time, the building was used for storing farm supplies, including feed and fertilizer.
- From the beginning, Wilfred loved going to school, and at the end of the first grade, he received a New Testament Bible for perfect attendance.
- Since his earliest years, Wilfred had been particularly interested in growing herbs; mint was his first favorite, and he prided himself on his ability to tell the difference between spearmint and peppermint.
- Wilfred delighted in the herbs' distinctive tastes and pungent smells; he liked using them for flavoring food and even for making candy.
- He especially enjoyed helping his mother use the herbs in her jams and pickles; locally his mother's preserves were highly regarded.
- For several years before Wilfred left home, his grandmother had been teaching him all she knew about using herbs to make medicines, beginning with using mint and water to create a refreshing tea that was also useful for treating stomach troubles.
- Wilfred found the effects of these concoctions endlessly interesting, almost magical; his grandmother was pleased with his progress in learning the exacting art of using medicinal herbs, some of which the family grew and others of which had to be gathered in the wild.
- Wilfred had become adept at recognizing the wild herbs and distinguishing them from similar-looking plants that might be poisonous; he knew when to pick them, how to prepare them, and how to store them safely.
- Sage was used for seasoning meats and for making a soothing tea; catnip not only entertained the barn cats but was good for colic; boneset was used topically to ease muscle and joint pain and was especially good for arthritis.
- Wilfred was proud of his ability to create the perfect asthma medicine used by his little sister; instructed by his grandmother, he made it from jimsonweed, which, when dried, mixed with saltpeter, burned, and then inhaled, brought her relief.

- Wilfred's grandmother warned him against experimenting with herbs he did not know and especially against drinking teas or extracts he wasn't sure about; medicinal herbs might bring harm as well as good, and, she cautioned, ignorance could lead to disaster, even death.
- Some people thought that in the modern era, growing and using medicinal herbs was obsolete, since extracts and powders such as Goody Headache Powder could be purchased in any general store.
- Farmers such as the Mathiesons, however, were used to self-reliance; moreover, they tended to be skeptical about the nostrums available at the stores in town, although a persuasive traveling salesman could occasional overcome their doubts.

Wilfred's younger siblings

- Before leaving for school, to entertain the younger children, Wilfred showed them how to "fish" for chickens; with the little ones gathered all around him, he cut a notch in a grain of corn, tied it to a piece of cotton thread and tossed it to the family chickens.
- Every time one of the chickens swallowed the corn, Wilfred would give the string a jerk and out would pop the grain of corn again.
- The boys fell on the ground laughing.
- Some hungry but confused chickens swallowed the corn several times before abandoning the potential meal.
- The game was a roaring success until the family rooster, objecting to losing his supper, flew at the children with his wings ferociously beating, scaring little Talbert.
- Wilfred also liked to entertain the little ones by whittling popguns when the chinaberries were right for use as ammunition, and he showed Buford how to make wooden whistles when the hickory bark slipped.
- Before Wilfred left home, his granny pulled him aside and said, "Don't forget the Lord when you get to the city."
- She gave him a Bible with his name engraved on the cover.
- Now that he was away, his father had the younger brothers looking for snakes, because a fresh-killed snake laid across a tree limb was guaranteed to bring rain—something the farm desperately needed; a black snake hung

The Mathieson property

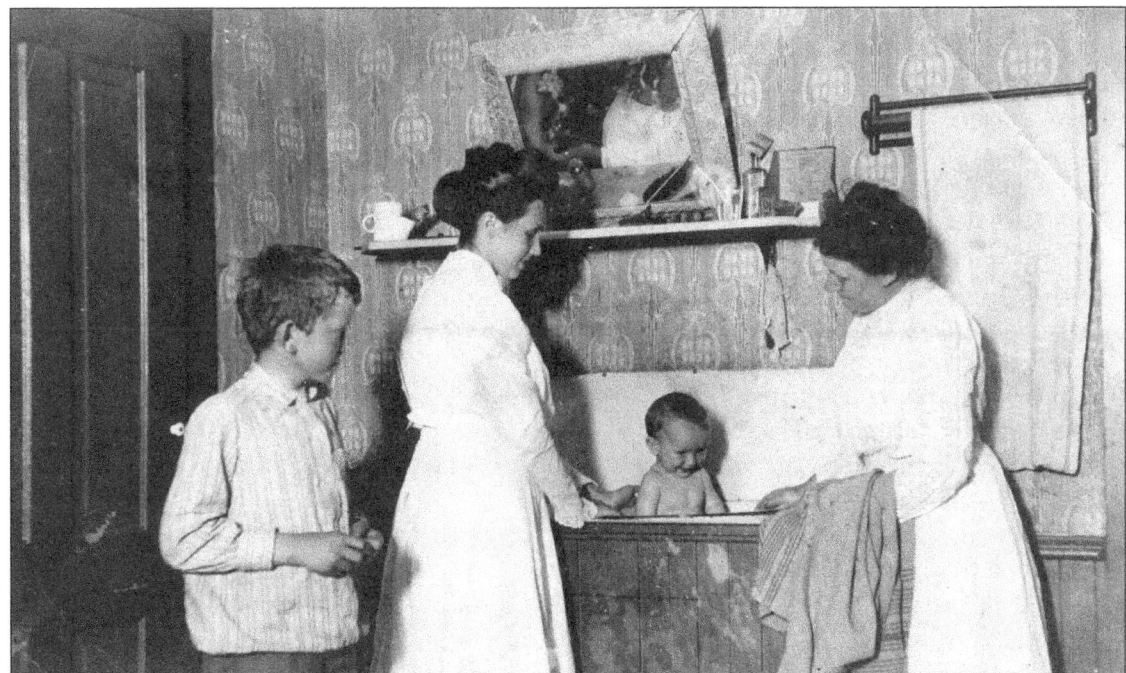

Wilfred's large family meant a lot of responsibilities both on the farm and in the house.

in a persimmon tree brought the best luck of all.
- At the Forbes's house, Wilfred swept floors, cleared the table after meals, washed dishes, and did odd jobs to earn his room and board; the Forbes family rented the upstairs rooms in their rambling house to three single women, whose rent covered meals and general maintenance.
- Wilfred dried the dishes with dishtowels made from feed sacks, which often had attractive printed designs; at home his mother had used the feed sack fabric for handkerchiefs and children's clothes, and she saved the scraps for quilting.
- Wilfred's bed was a cot in the living room, and he walked to school each day.
- Mr. Forbes was a successful cotton salesman; he believed that any young man who had "get up and go" could prosper.
- He was confident that he could teach Wilfred the important things in life and free him from the yoke of farming forever.
- At the Forbes's home, the boy was surrounded by books; the family even subscribed to publications such as *American Magazine,* filled with stories on how to be successful in business and life.
- A special benefit of the move to Greenburg was the Saturday movies; since his arrival Wilfred had seen a dozen two-reelers, thrilling to runaway trains, chase scenes, and cowboy showdowns.
- Recently, when Wilfred watched the movie *The Birth of a Nation,* the farmer next to him got so excited during certain scenes that he pulled out a loaded pistol and waved it around.
- Wilfred expected the man to shoot at the screen at any moment.

Life at School
- Wilfred's new school was a big brick building, boasting two stories; best of all, the school term was seven full months.
- In addition to offering courses in subjects such as world history, English literature, and algebra, the school had a small chemistry lab; the lab immediately drew Wilfred's interest.
- But he had found some of what was being taught startling and hard to accept.

- Growing up, Wilfred had spent many afternoons listening to old-timers tell about how the South whipped the Yankees during the "war of northern aggression."
- As a border state, Kentucky had divided its allegiance, giving more recruits to the Union than did Ohio, and more to the Confederacy than Florida.
- But in history class at Greenburg High School, Wilfred learned that despite all the stories, which had always ended with the South's victory, the South in fact had lost the war.
- Wilfred's other problem was girls—they all treated him like a farm hick and wouldn't have anything to do with him—all except Sara, a very sweet, churchgoing girl who let him walk her home some days.
- Twice he was allowed to sit with her on her front-porch swing—while her mother was present, of course—and once he caught a June bug for her.
- He tied a thread to its leg and they both laughed themselves silly while the June bug flew around and around making a determined buzzing sound.
- Still, Wilfred is convinced that if only he were smarter or owned more than two pairs of pants, the other girls—and the boys, too—would like him better.
- Starting when he was a little boy working in the fields, Wilfred had collected flint points and arrowheads from the freshly plowed furrows.
- His father bragged for years that his eldest son was the best rock hound in Kentucky; his boy, he would say, could spot quality arrowheads in a hailstorm.
- A shoebox full of arrowheads was one of the very few possessions Wilfred had brought with him to Greenburg.

Wilfred enjoyed collecting arrowheads in the fields near his home.

Educational reform in Kentucky was intended to increase the number of schools and school attendance.

- In Greenburg Wilfred discovered that he was not the only person interested in ancient Indian arrowheads.
- Two other boys in his class had impressive collections, including arrowheads from as far away as Ohio and Illinois; already Wilfred had swapped dozens of his childhood finds for big, carefully carved dovetail points that took his breath away.
- When Wilfred felt lonely, he found it comforting to sit for a while with the old men at the Greenburg general store, which also served as a post office; it was just three blocks away from the school.
- Even though he didn't know these men well, they were happy to share their tales with him; the tales were a familiar reminder of home, as were their gentle running arguments about whose mule had the most pulling power, which hog was the biggest, and who grew the finest sorghum cane.

Life in the Community: Greenburg, Kentucky

- Educational reform was evident throughout Kentucky; the number of high schools alone more than tripled between 1908, when there were 50, to more than 160 in 1916.
- Over that time the state passed truancy laws to increase the percentage of children attending school, standardized the educational requirements for teachers, created a state textbook commission, fixed the minimum salary of public-school teachers—$75 a month—and enhanced the powers of school boards.
- For many years lumbering was a critical industry in the Kentucky's Green River region; many of the area's hardwood trees supplied cross ties for the ever-expanding railroads.
- From the 1890s the number of steamboat travelers on the Green River gradually increasing from a few thousand annually to nearly 20,000 a year.
- Passengers included women going to Evansville to shop, businessmen on fishing trips, young people going to Massey Springs on the Barren River to dance, athletic teams traveling to meet their rivals, and traveling salesmen bound for various Kentucky towns to peddle their wares.

- Many people came to the western portion of the state to see Mammoth Cave, a major tourist attraction; some even spent $8.00 to take the four-day tour of the natural phenomenon, which included steamboat transportation, entertainment, and meals in addition to the actual cave tours.
- Many children in the area were suffering from pellagra, the hallmark of which was a butterfly rash that could spread across the victim's face.
- Most farmers in the area believed pellagra was caused by eating moldy corn; a few, however, blamed it on the flood of immigrants who had been coming to America from southern Europe, bringing unknown diseases with them.
- Across the South, 75,000 to 165,000 cases were suspected, out of a population of 32.5 million; about five percent of those who contracted pellagra would die from dementia or from the dehydration caused by diarrhea.
- Joseph Goldberger, a doctor known for his work with malaria, had come through the region a while back, doing research concerning what he called the "three-M Southern diet of meal, molasses and meat"—which was cheap, fast, and filling.
- Goldberger claimed that poor diet might cause the disease, but as an outsider he was not considered trustworthy.
- Based on the 1910 national census, 5,516,163 Americans could not read—a number that exceeded the entire population of Denmark.
- Beginning about 1911, dozens of counties in Kentucky opened their schoolhouses in the evenings for adult education; a program called "Moonlight Schools" was designed to eliminate illiteracy, which the state pledged to eradicate by the 1920 census.
- By 1916 some 1,600 men and women had enrolled in the program.
- Arithmetic, geography, history, civics, agriculture, horticulture, home economics, and road building were among the subjects taught; reading assignments dealt with topics such as seed-testing, crop rotation, plumbing, the value of a daily bath, extermination of the fly, and cooking and safe food-preservation techniques.
- Progress was also being made in the building of good roads; throughout the state the newspapers were calling on Kentucky to join the automobile age by constructing hard-surfaced roads fit for year-round car travel.

Creator of the Campbell Kids in 1917

Streetcar advertising was in its infancy when freelance illustrator Grace Wiederseim was first asked to design an ad for Joseph Campbell's Preserve Company.

Life at Home

- Born on October 14, 1877, Viola Grace Gebbie was the third daughter of George Gebbie and his wife, Mary Jane Fitzgerald Gebbie, who were the parents of seven children—six daughters and one son.
- George Gebbie, a lithographer, was Philadelphia's first art printer; he had immigrated to the United States from Scotland in 1862, listing his occupation as bookseller in his immigration papers.
- After landing in Quebec and working in upstate New York for a short time, he arrived in Philadelphia; he was naturalized in 1869.
- Gebbie was a Scots Presbyterian; his wife was a strict Roman Catholic, and all six of the Gebbie girls attended Catholic schools.
- Grace grew up in the sophisticated environment of art publishing; her father's library held numerous volumes of belles-lettres and Greek and Roman classics, many illustrated.
- Her sisters and a niece, Mary A. Hays Huber, who authored the comic strip "Kate and Karl," all had drawing talent.
- Growing up, the sisters learned from each other and from an older relative; drawing cartoon figures was simply another way to amuse one another.
- Grace's early education was in private and church schools, including the Convent of Notre Dame, in Philadelphia, and the Convent of Eden Hall, in Torresdale, Pennsylvania.
- Grace was 15 years old when her father died in 1892.
- Three years later, Grace began her formal art training from the Philadelphia School of Design for Women, where the artist Robert Henri was a faculty member.
- Grace Gebbie enrolled in Henri's Antiques class, described in the college catalog as "Drawing from the antique, artistic anatomy, composition, Crayon portraits."
- The school was founded to prepare women for a successful career in industrial design at a time when "No nice girl should go to art school."

Grace Wiederseim

An immigrant family—including a 9-year-old girl—making Campbell's Kid doll legs.

- Grace was married for the first time in 1900, to Theodore Wiederseim, an advertising executive for a Philadelphia streetcar company.

Life at Work

- Grace Gebbie Wiederseim's artistic career began at a young age; by the time she was 18 years old, she was freelancing as a commercial artist.
- Often her drawings depicted small-fry characters with round faces, pug noses, and full figures; they resembled Grace herself.
- In 1869 Joseph A. Campbell, a fruit merchant, and Abraham Anderson, an icebox manufacturer, founded Campbell's, which originally produced a line of canned tomatoes, vegetables, jellies, soups, condiments, and minced meats.
- Rapid industrialization of America's cities had transformed rural economies; food was now being grown a long distance from its consumers.
- This demanded that less perishable foods be created, capable of surviving the ever-widening distances separating the farm from the urban dinner table.
- Campbell and Anderson believed that canned foods were the answer.
- Their cannery was located between the fertile fields near Camden, New Jersey, and nearby Philadelphia, a regional transportation hub.
- Campbell's was especially known for its canned beefsteak tomatoes; the product exemplified a blending of Anderson's tinsmith skills with Campbell's farming background.
- The company's big break came in 1897.
- Dr. John T. Dorrance, a chemist with degrees from the Massachusetts Institute of Technology and the University of Göttingen, in Germany, developed a commercially viable method for condensing soup by halving the quantity of its heaviest ingredient: water.
- Dorrance had recently returned from Europe, where he had developed a taste for Continental soups.
- Franco-American and the Hutchins Company were both already making ready-to-eat soups with some success, while Borden had perfected the process for evaporating milk.

- Dorrance reasoned that if Campbell's created a condensed ready-to-eat soup, the product would be cheaper to ship, take less room in the store, and could be sold for less to the busy housewife.
- Within a year of the invention, Joseph Campbell's Preserve Company was selling five varieties of condensed soups, all easily identified by its can's bright red and white color scheme.
- Herberton Williams, a Campbell's executive, had convinced the company to adopt the look based on the crisp colors of the Cornell University football team's uniforms.
- At the Exposition Universelle de 1900 in Paris, the soups were awarded the Gold Medallion for Excellence.

One year after creating condensed ready-to-eat soup, Campbell's sold five varieties.

- Campbell's wanted to attract the attention of women, who had started to become streetcar regulars.
- The National Biscuit Company had its recognizable figure in Zu Zu, the ginger snap clown; Sunny Jim hawked Force what flakes cereal; and everyone knew Nipper, the alertly listening terrier looking into the horn of the Edison-Bell phonograph in the logo of the Victor Talking Machine Company.
- At her husband's urging, in 1904 Grace Wiederseim designed two plump and adorable little children that he could pitch to the company for a series of Campbell's streetcar ads; thus were born the "funny babies," as Grace called them, known to the world as the Campbell's Kids.

All American kids wanted to be Campbell Kids.

- Her rosy-cheeked, cherub-faced youngsters were an immediate hit both for the streetcar line and for Campbell's.
- Their first magazine appearance was in the *Ladies' Home Journal* in 1905.
- Before long, the beloved Kids were everywhere—in books and on pajamas, postcards, games, dishes, and piggybanks, and much more.
- And every American child wanted to be a Campbell's Kid.
- The sales of Campbell's products soared behind the marketing force of Grace's unsigned creative realizations of idyllic American childhood.
- In 1905—the year after the debut of the Campbell's Kids—the company was advertising "21 kinds of Campbell's Soup—16 million sold in 1904."

- Campbell's had invested heavily in advertising since its inception, a proclivity that only accelerated with the success of the ubiquitous Campbell's Kids.
- The "Kids" had no individual names, nor were they of any specific age.
- There was no set number of Campbell's Kids, nor were their relationships to each other ever explained.
- Yet they symbolized the ideals of health and wholesomeness; the public intuitively grasped that Grace's pudgy tots proclaimed the quality and wholesomeness of Campbell's soups.
- The company was inundated with requests for posters of the Campbell's Kids streetcar ads; it decided to fulfill every request, charging just $0.15 per poster—the cost of postage.
- The first Campbell's Kids doll was issued in 1909, quickly followed by a second doll, created by the E. I. Horsman Company, in 1910.
- Two years later, both the Sears, Roebuck and the Montgomery Ward catalogs featured the cute dolls.
- They were sold by the thousands for $1.00 each.
- That same year, Campbell's added the word *Soup* to its corporate name, an acknowledgment of the role soup products played in the company's profitability.
- Next came pictures of the pudgy toddlers on bridge tallies and even lapel pins that declared, "I am a Campbell's Kid."
- Under Grace's direction, the Kids began giving etiquette lessons to children and they advised housewives on domestic matters through company-published booklets such as *Help for the Hostess*.
- Meanwhile, the Campbell's Kids, as depicted in the company's paid advertising, were actively testing early versions of the automobile, the airplane, and the telephone.
- Campbell's girls demanded the right to vote; Campbell's boys put on Charlie Chaplin mustaches and pretended to be in the movies.
- Through it all, Grace continued creating.
- Early on, Grace created comics for the *Philadelphia Press* entitled *Dolly Drake and Bobby Blake*.
- As her work in cartooning expanded, Grace developed *The Terrible Tales of Captain Kiddo* in collaboration with her sister, Margaret G. Hays.
- In the midst of this, Grace divorced Theodore Wiederseim in 1911 and promptly married W. Heyward Drayton III.

The Campbell's Kids

- While the Joseph Campbell Company was busy using Grace's clever illustrations to sell soup to the nation, Grace Drayton continued to illustrate for various magazines.
- In 1913, she created a new character, Dolly Dingle, for the popular publication *Pictorial Review*.
- With her shoe-button eyes and baby curls, Dolly Dingle instantly won the hearts of the American public.
- Grace's paper dolls in the Dolly Dingle series were printed in full color in the *Pictorial Review*.
- Dolly Dingle's adventures included traveling around the world to visit children in distant lands; these foreign friends came complete with costumes and emblems of their native lands.
- Travel by steamer had never been easier, and even stay-at-home Americans turned into globetrotters visiting Egypt, Rome, and the Holy Land.
- As 1916 came to a close, with the shadow of American involvement in World War I looming, Grace began, after 12 years, to relinquish control of her "funny babies" so that she could concentrate on Dolly Dingle.
- By that time, the Campbell's Kids were so critical to the image of the company that Roy Williams of the Philadelphia *Public Ledger* was hired to take over the main drawing duties, leaving Grace more time to create.

Life in the Community: Philadelphia, Pennsylvania

- The history of Philadelphia, Pennsylvania, goes back to 1682, when the city was founded by William Penn.
- Philadelphia quickly grew into an important colonial city, and during the American Revolution it was the site of the First and the Second Continental Congress.
- At the beginning of the nineteenth century, Philadelphia was one of the nation's first diversified industrial centers.
- On the eve of the Civil War, Philadelphia's population was 565,529; by 1870 it was 674,022, and by 1876, the city was estimated to be the home of 817,000 people.
- A large portion of the growth came from immigrants, mostly German and Irish.
- In 1870 census figures showed that about 27 percent of Philadelphia's population had been born outside the United States.
- By the 1880s immigration from Russia, Eastern Europe, and Southern Europe had begun to rival immigration from Western Europe.
- Many of Philadelphia's major industries of that era were transportation-related, including the Baldwin Locomotive Works, William Cramp and Sons Ship & Engine Building Company, and the Pennsylvania Railroad.
- There were numerous iron- and steel manufacturers, including Philadelphia-owned iron and steel works outside the city—most notably the Bethlehem Iron Company.
- Nevertheless, the largest industry in Philadelphia was textiles.

Philadelphia was an important colonial city and one of the first U.S. industrial centers.

Major department stores dominated Philadelphia's Market Street.

- Philadelphia produced more textiles than any other U.S. city, and in 1904 textiles employed more than 35 percent of the city's workers.
- The cigar, sugar, and oil industries also were of great economic importance to the city.
- Department stores such as Gimbel's, Lit Brothers and the elegant Strawbridge and Clothier sprang up along Market Street.
- In the beginning of the twentieth century, Philadelphia's reputation suffered; it was known for political corruption.
- The Republican-controlled political machine, run by Israel Durham, permeated all parts of city government.
- In some quarters Philadelphia was also dismissed as stuffy and reactionary.
- *Harper's Magazine* commented: "The one thing unforgivable in Philadelphia is to be new, to be different from what has been."

Civilian Relief Worker in War-Torn France in 1918

As World War I wore on in Europe, Livia Sedgwick's lifelong passion for helping the children of her city's poor brought her to the front in war-torn France; there she found injured people and frightened children, including a young orphan named Marie.

Life at Home

- Livia Sedgwick had always loved children.
- Growing up in Springfield, Massachusetts, she often helped her mother with children at the town's largest mill, which was owned by Livia's father.
- Together, she and her mother would throw parties on special occasions, hold health and hygiene clinics, and arrange for tutorials for those who had fallen behind in their schoolwork.
- Livia especially relished teaching English to the immigrant children; they were always eager to learn.
- Livia's father did not understand this fascination with helping the less fortunate, but he recognized that his wife and daughter found it satisfying and that their efforts made for a happier and more loyal work force.
- Even after Livia graduated—with honors—from Smith College and spent a year touring Europe, her interest continued.
- In fact, her desire to help poor children only intensified after her marriage to Edward Sedgwick and their move to Hartford, Connecticut, where Edward was an insurance company executive.
- Both her family and the Sedgwicks held considerable interests in the company.
- Once she was settled in her large house in one of Hartford's newest and nicest neighborhoods, Livia began focusing on the needs of the city's poorest families.
- She organized, lectured and recruited friends for the effort.
- After more than eight years passed without Livia having a child of her own, she increasingly began to see the city's poor as "her" children.
- The arrival of the Great War in Europe brought with it a daily barrage of death, starvation, and dislocation in Europe.
- Livia followed every word, especially as Edward's focus on his work increased and the couple's relationship grew more distant.

Livia Sedgwick

- By 1916, before America's entry into the war, Livia was convinced that her energies were needed in Europe, but she was unsure of how to proceed, how it would appear to others, and how she could get across the ocean in wartime.
- Early in 1917 Edward joined the war effort as a "dollar-a-year man" in Washington, District of Columbia, where his executive management skills were invaluable.
- His assignment was procurement—locating and purchasing the thousands of items needed for combat, from ammunition and airplanes to military clothing.
- Proud as Livia was of his contribution, she was also keenly aware that the time between Edward's visits and his letters was growing longer.

A street in Hartford, Connecticut, where Livia lived after she married.

- Just before Memorial Day, while having lunch with a friend and fellow Smith alumna, Livia learned that Harriet Boyd Hawes, who had taught Greek archaeology at Smith just before Livia's time there, was leading a recruiting drive for a Smith College Relief Unit.
- Hawes had become well known in archeological circles for her work on Greek Bronze and Iron Age settlements in the Aegean, especially on the island of Crete; she discovered Gournia, a Minoan settlement, and when her team excavated the town, she became the first woman to lead a major field project in Greece. The American Exploration Society later published her findings.
- In 1915 and 1916, Hawes had already undertaken relief work in Europe.
- Designed to be independent of the much larger Red Cross, the Smith College Relief Unit's specific goal was to aid French civilians in overcoming the hardships of war.
- That very afternoon Livia wired Hawes that she was interested in participating.
- Only the next day did she think to call Edward; he was not pleased, but he said he would not stand in her way.
- Within days, Livia was interviewed by a panel; Hawes only wanted serious-minded women of proven ability.
- Livia's fluency in French, her knowledge of Europe, and her past experience in social work among the poor impressed the committee.
- She was soon notified that she would be accepted for service upon the payment of $300 for uniform, travel, and sundries; she was also required to provide $55 a month for her own support.
- After closing up the houses in Hartford and Old Sagbrook, on Long Island Sound, Livia sailed for France.
- Her parents proudly saw her off, and to her delight, Edward sent a supportive telegram from Washington.

Life at Work

- Livia and 17 other Smith graduates, ranging in age from 20 to 40, set sail for France from New York in late 1917, each determined to be of service to her country.
- Every member of the Smith College Relief Unit was fluent in French, and many possessed special expertise in health, transportation, agriculture, or social work.

- To support the effort, the unit brought two trucks, a car, six portable houses, carpenter's tools, parts for the cars and trucks, cots, blankets, clothing, and food for the French.
- Within weeks of arriving, the unit had established itself in the town of Grécourt, just a few miles from the French front lines.
- Called the "Ladies of Grécourt," the unit set itself the task of assisting 16 neighboring villages, their populations totaling 1,650.
- Farms were restocked, war wounds treated, and woodworking classes created to help villagers rebuild their war-damaged homes.
- A sewing and knitting shop was set up to provide employment for four women.
- Livia did what she had always done—work with the children.
- She established a library for them and found that they loved the escape of reading.
- Day after day she worked with government officials to reopen schools and ensure the fair distribution of food.
- Some days she was convinced that her greatest enemies were not the Germans but the French bureaucrats.
- Mostly she listened to young children, frequently girls, talk about their lives, their families, becoming a woman, and being afraid.
- Livia spent enormous energy planning Christmas parties for each of the villages.
- Using her own money, she purchased large quantities of food and drink.
- Most important, she made sure each and every child was able to open an individually wrapped Christmas present.
- Many of the children wept with joy—for a moment, the war had gone away.
- Livia's other project was more personal: a girl named Marie.
- Marie, whose parents were killed in an explosion, had lost her right leg to an artillery shell.
- Eager, intelligent, and resilient, Marie was devoted to Livia and wanted to learn English.
- Livia began exploring the arcane and convoluted regulations that might make it possible for her to take Marie back to Hartford with her.
- She did not discuss the possibility with the little girl; if she were unable to cut through the red tape of the French bureaucracy, the lost opportunity would only mean more disappointment for Marie.

Livia and other Smith College graduates arrived in France to serve their country.

Livia saw the refugee children as her own, and her desire to help them intensified.

- Occasionally soldiers would pass through the town and offer gifts.
- Recently a French officer had sent a wagon of pigs, while an English unit provided a load of duckboard platforming to line the muddy village streets.
- Another group of soldiers explained how the ladies could "read" their undergarments on a sunny day to rid them of lice.
- Livia was exhausted, filthy, and happier than she had ever been.
- As spring arrived, signs were everywhere that the war was drawing nearer.
- Some nights the artillery fire was so loud that she was unable to sleep.
- Then, almost without warning, word came that the village must be abandoned.
- The relief unit was ordered to leave as the Red Cross carried out the evacuation.
- Livia and her colleagues made dozens of trips transporting the sick, the disabled, and the children on muddy roads clogged with refugees, livestock, and retreating soldiers.
- As each group of children was delivered to safety, Livia returned to the village for more.
- Only the crash of German shells stopped the work.
- In the midst of the turmoil, Edward, who had always wanted children, wrote to Livia saying how much he wanted to bring Marie to the United States.
- He began assisting with the complex paperwork involved in adopting a French orphan.
- A doctor in New York, whom Livia and Edward knew because he, too, had a summer house on Long Island Sound, had agreed to fit Marie with a prosthetic leg.
- But first Livia needed to complete her work.
- After Marie was entrusted to a group of nuns caring for children, Livia moved to a field hospital to help the many, many wounded.
- A large number of the patients came from units in New England; there were even a few who had once worked in her father's mills.

New technological devices of destruction made World War I particularly gruesome.

- Some soldiers were missing limbs, several were suffering the aftereffects of a mustard gas attack, and others simply had the flu, which had already killed so many people worldwide, even in the United States.
- During the day, Livia treated and comforted the wounded; at night she listened to their stories.
- Matter-of-factly, they spoke of lost friends, cold trenches, and fear so strong it smelled; of tanks, airplane dogfights, barbed-wire battlefields, and their dreams of home.
- She helped them write letters home and awaited letters from Marie, still with the nuns and safely away from the front, and from Edward, in Washington.
- Marie wrote often in her looping cursive handwriting, always working hard to include some English words in her message.
- Edward wrote that Marie's passage to America could be secured once the war ended.
- To Marie Livia wrote encouraging messages; to Edward she wrote about brave men who cried themselves to sleep.

Life in the Community: Grécourt, Picardy, France

- Grécourt was a small agricultural community in the Somme department of Picardy in northeastern France.
- The principal crops of the region were sugar beets, wheat, oats, fodder beets, and potatoes.
- Just 10 miles to the south was the cathedral town of Noyon; its magnificent twelfth- and thirteenth-century cathedral was built on the site of a still-earlier cathedral that was destroyed by fire in 1131.
- The great sixteenth-century Reformed theologian Jean Calvin was born in Noyon.
- Soissons, less than 30 miles from Grécourt, to the southeast of Noyon and like it a cathedral town, suffered extremely heavy damage during World War I.
- The Cathedral of Saint-Gervais and Saint-Protais in Soissons contained a number of distinguished works of art, including a fifteenth-century tapestry; *Adoration of the Shepherds,* a painting by Peter Paul Rubens; and stained glass windows dating from the thirteenth century.

- The western end of the cathedral, with its tower, sustained considerable damage, but the choir end, with its tapestry and stained glass, and the north transept, the location of the Rubens painting, were spared.
- Affiliated with the American Fund for French Wounded, the Smith College Relief Unit was assigned by the French government to Grécourt and instructed to establish a base there in the ruins of the eleventh-century Château Robécourt, just 15 miles from the front-line trenches of the Somme.
- The baroness gladly entrusted to the unit the remains of the château, which had been occupied for some time by German officers.
- The baroness thanked the unit for their efforts to help France and its "unhappy inhabitants."
- Traveling from Paris, the unit first encountered evidence of war around Noyon: a trench, tangled wire, wooden crosses marking the graves of the fallen.
- Although it was nearly midnight when the unit arrived, all of the remaining villagers of Grécourt—fewer than 30 women and children—turned out to welcome them.
- The villagers actually lived in the château's stables; in the village itself, only the small church was still standing.
- The destruction caused by bombardment and combat lay all around, and the unit saw that pure vandalism had added to the general distress.
- The retreating German army had quite deliberately reduced Grécourt and all of the villages around it to ruins in order to make it as difficult as possible for the returning French to provide themselves with the necessities of food and shelter.
- Wells had been poisoned and buildings that had not already been dynamited were burned.
- The Army had erected a barracks for the unit on the château lawn; over the following months, the unit, with help from American, French, and British authorities, rehabilitated parts of the château.
- The damp but whitewashed cellar became a storeroom and the chief center of the unit's activities; a repaired orangerie, its shattered glass replaced with oiled paper, became dispensary, garage, carpentry shop, and meeting hall.
- Control of the area was still bitterly contested, over the course of the Great War, it changed hands several times.
- In 1917, after the disastrous offensive known as the Second Battle of the Aisne, or the Chemin des Dames ("Ladies' Path"), thoroughly demoralized soldiers in Soissons mutinied, refusing to return to the front.
- Soissons fell to the Germans again in the spring of 1918; it was not finally liberated until the summer.
- Artillery and machine guns, not rifles, were the biggest killers on the battlefield during World War I.
- The influenza outbreak of 1917-1918 killed 52,000 American soldiers, sailors, and Marines, almost equaling the toll on the battlefield.

General "John" B. Pershing

Polish War Refugee in 1918

When Josephine Glueck came to America from Poland, she found unemployment, parents who had immigrated 17 years earlier, siblings she was not aware of, and the determination to establish her own business.

Life at Home

- Josephine Glueck grew up in Tarnów, Poland, dreaming of what it would be like to have a mother—just to talk to.
- When Josephine was 20 months old, her mother, Josie, and father, Samuel, immigrated to the United States, leaving Josephine and her sister Eva in the care of their grandmother.
- Every month their parents sent money to support their two daughters—but never the necessary immigration papers for them to go to America and be a family again.
- Josephine's opportunity to emigrate did not take place until she was 17 years old, and even then the journey was necessitated by the ugliness of war.
- When Josephine was born at the turn of the century, Tarnów occupied a border position in the northern Austro-Hungarian Empire.
- After years of waiting to join her parents, she and Eva decided to leave Poland when the outbreak of World War I was followed in Poland by intolerable persecution of civilians.
- Poland's loss of independence in the late eighteenth century had already scattered its people throughout Europe and the United States.
- They were driven away by both the political uncertainty and the transition from an agricultural economy to an industrial society—a development unfamiliar and unwelcome to many.
- Of the millions of Poles who immigrated to North America prior to World War I, most viewed the United States as a temporary home.
- By the time World War I erupted in 1914, large Polish communities existed in Pittsburgh, Detroit, Buffalo, Milwaukee, and Chicago.
- Chicago proudly claimed to be the third-largest Polish-populated city in the world.
- Josephine's parents had come to America believing they would stay only a short time; they were known as *za chlebem*, or

Josephine Glueck

Josephine and her sister, Eva, anxiously awaited inspection on the docks.

for-bread immigrants, those who planned to earn a nest egg and return home.

- In Poland Samuel Glueck, Josephine and Eva's father, was educated at a trade school and then opened a business for himself.
- The need for capital sparked the idea of emigration to America; a few years of earning good money would make everything possible in Poland, he told his customers before he left.
- At first he was to be the only immigrant; his wife and children would be left behind.
- But when his mother-in-law volunteered to raise the girls temporarily, he decided that between them, he and Josie could make more money faster and then return to Poland sooner.
- On the day they left, Samuel and Josie chose not to wake their two daughters; they did not feel capable of surviving an emotional parting.
- Josephine awoke on the morning her parents left to find a weeping grandmother struggling to be brave.
- As a child Josephine worked hard in school so she would be worthy when the summons to America finally came.
- Her sister Eva's strategy was to be delightfully entertaining; at this Eva frequently succeeded.
- Eva was known as the fun one, while Josephine was the serious sister who always had her nose in a book.
- Then World War I erupted, their grandmother died, remittances from the United States stopped, and their village became a war zone.
- First Russian soldiers passed through the area, commandeering their home and barn.
- The Russians were followed by Polish soldiers who took everything they could see, including Josephine and Eva's last loaf of bread.
- The Polish people were caught in a crossfire of territorial hatred.
- The sisters had run out of options and patience; the time to discover America had arrived.
- They elected to leave Poland in January 1918, right after the Christmas celebration.
- Neither wanted to miss the traditional Christmas Eve dinner, or Wigila, with its 13-course Polish meal—each course representing Christ and the 12 apostles.

- Knowing this was their last holiday in Poland, the girls were careful to properly display the family paper cuttings, or *wycinanki,* used throughout the home to celebrate the birth of Jesus.
- Fashioned with ordinary sheep shears and traditional craftsmanship, the paper cutouts symbolized to the girls everything precious about Poland.
- At the last moment, Josephine decided to take one of the cutouts with her as a remembrance of the homeland she might never see again.
- A few weeks later, Josephine and Eva left in the middle of the night.
- They knew that the authorities would come looking for them; their talents as the town bread baker's assistants made them valuable.
- In preparation for their escape, they sold an old cow, a few chickens, and a wood lathe to raise money for the voyage; otherwise, they left most of their worldly possessions behind.
- They walked or rode carts for 39 days; Josephine reached the docks feeling dirty and exhausted.
- She was terrified of undergoing the physical exam required for emigrants.
- A three-year-old farm injury to her leg had left her with a limp that might be pronounced enough to make her ineligible for immigration.
- Even a humorous vendor selling pears that he referred to as "ladies legs" could not break the tension.

After her arrival in America, Josephine's father told her to work as a live-in maid.

Josephine's father—"Hungarian Handyman"—found success managing a mechanical repair business.

- At the docks the sisters suddenly realized that most of the other passengers had shaved their heads to demonstrate they didn't have lice; this reality made them both feel even more uncertain and terrified.
- But the medical examination itself was cursory, less personal than Josephine had been led to believe.
- Best of all, it was over quickly.
- Without ever looking up or acknowledging Josephine's broad smile, the ship's clerk issued an official paper that said she was headed to the United States of America—after 15 years of waiting.
- The woman directly ahead of Eva in line was unable to demonstrate her ability to read in any language—a new requirement for immigration to the United States—and the distraught woman was rejected despite her shaved head and tearful pleas.
- Boarding the ship with that official document in her hand was the happiest moment Josephine had experienced in years.

The Ocean Voyage

- The ocean voyage was an adventure to be remembered, even in third-class accommodations, despite the determination of the gang of Spanish children to steal everything they could lay their hands on.
- Josephine was horrified when the gang snatched the brand-new Christmas doll of a terrified seven-year-old Polish girl and sent it flying over the rail, just to be mean.
- The same group of boys took a paint box set from an 11-year-old boy, who plaintively cried, "My grandfather gave me that for Christmas!"
- The chaos continued after they landed at Ellis Island in New York Harbor.
- There the two teenaged girls waited for five days to be claimed; a sponsor in the United States was required before they could leave.
- On the first day they were at Ellis Island, a Frenchwoman walked up and slapped Eva across the face, supposedly for taking her seat; Eva wore the welt for three days.
- On the second day, their suitcases full of clothes were stolen, including all their underwear embroidered with the family name.
- Josephine realized that after waiting so long to see her parents again, she would have to greet them in a dirty dress.
- At night, however, the sisters attended a beautiful theater on Ellis Island, provided for the immigrants who were still being processed.
- Josephine was dazzled to be near the stage of an opera star and hear "La Donna è Mobile" sung by a wonderful professional tenor.
- After the evening concert, everyone would be lined up for Graham crackers and milk containing Ex-Lax.
- After the second day, the sisters took the crackers and threw away the milk.
- But in the tension of waiting, conflicts were inevitable.
- On the fourth day, the sisters got into a shouting match with a German translator who was scolding them in Russian, a language they detested.
- Quickly Josephine was learning that those without the native language didn't possess a voice.
- Never had she felt so lost, stupid, and unsure about her decision to come to the United States.
- During the day, food was provided to the waiting immigrants; Josephine enjoyed the pickled herring and onions, but she found hot dogs baffling.
- In the cafeteria, immigration officials had established for Jewish immigrants a separate line and special food tables that looked much more inviting.
- When her parents finally arrived, late and apologetic, she realized for the first time that she had two brothers and one sister whom she had never met, or even been told about.
- The reunion on Ellis Island was enthusiastic and awkward.
- Her mother spoke excitedly in Polish and English, the small children shouted at each other and yanked one another's coats;

Immigrants arriving at Ellis Island in New York Harbor

Josephine and Eva struggled to fit into a family they didn't know existed.

- Almost immediately their father told them that they would have to work if they planned to stay in America; he was not going to support loafers.
- They were informed that he had landed both of them jobs as live-in maids in Sandwich and had signed a one-year commitment on their behalf.
- Eva's only response was to cry, while Josephine remained silent.
- Josephine's first day on the job did not go well.
- Instead of simply doing the cleaning job she had been given, she was eager to demonstrate her skills as a baker, especially her ability to produce luscious breads.
- This skill threatened the position of the well-established Italian staff, which had no interest in learning anything from a Polish greenhorn fresh off the boat.
- The first time she attempted to enter the kitchen, the three cooks shooed her out as though she were an errant chicken; the second time, she was threatened with a broom handle.
- The third attempt was rewarded with a bucketful of soapy water.
- That night the mistress of the house gave her a stern lecture about the need to get along with others; because the scolding was entirely in English, Josephine understood not a word.
- She lasted a week before she was fired, to the outrage of her father.
- Within a month, Eva, too, had lost her job.
- They vowed to learn English quickly and open a bakery together in Boston.
- They thought it was all too evident that their parents were ashamed to acknowledge that they had Polish children who spoke the Polish language and knew only the traditional Polish ways.
- For years, to escape discrimination, her parents had denied they were Polish; the appearance of their two daughters straight from Poland had made liars of them.
- Samuel was proud of his accomplishments in America and did not wish to see them threatened.
- Shortly after arriving 15 years earlier, with no relatives or friends to rely on, he had found work in the woods of Virginia.
- Each morning he rose at 5 a.m. to cut phenomenally tall trees from the lush woods to be hauled by train to sawmills near the coast.
- Samuel often worked hauling logs until 9 or 10 p.m. in those early years, always dreaming of being his own boss again.
- One day some equipment at the sawmill broke down, halting work; even though he had never worked on this type of belt-driven machinery before, he understood its mechanics.
- Within an hour he had the equipment humming again and production back under way; the next day he was taken off the logging train and assigned to equipment maintenance.

The growing community of Sandwich, Massachusetts

- Within weeks Samuel was nicknamed the "Hungarian handyman," and the rumor spread that he was capable of fixing anything; he didn't bother to set the ethnic record straight.
- In three years he had created the reputation he needed to set up his own heavy equipment business in Sandwich.
- The future was to be found in America, not in Poland.
- His new children would be Americans, who understood American ways and didn't cling to the past.

Life in the Community: Sandwich, Massachusetts

- A decade earlier, Samuel Glueck had been busy repairing a broken driveshaft when he received an offer he never expected.
- Two Sandwich, Massachusetts, businessmen offered to finance and equip a mechanical repair facility for him if he would relocate to their community, which was located on Cape Cod.
- The Sandwich community was growing steadily and needed someone to service equipment for the commercial fishing and truck-farming industries that were the mainstays of the economy.
- They told him they would finance the entire business and allow him to buy them out after five years.
- Their goal was to support the community; they would charge no interest so long as he agreed to stay in Sandwich for at least five years.
- They even offered him a two-bedroom house to rent near the shop they proposed to build to his specifications.
- Only in America, he kept telling his wife—only in America.
- Within four years he had repaid the loan, hired three additional workers, and begun contributing regularly to the Catholic Church he attended.
- Sandwich was located in southeastern Massachusetts at the base of Cape Cod.
- Bordered by Cape Cod Bay, Sandwich was 57 miles southeast of Boston; 61miles east of Providence, Rhode Island; and 238 miles from New York City.
- Sandwich was incorporated in 1639; it was the first European settlement on Cape Cod to incorporate.
- The town was well known for its beaches along Cape Cod Bay; the beaches stretched for miles and provided wonderful views of the vessels that pass through on their way to or from the Boston area.
- Commercial fishermen and lobstermen appeared daily on the docks at the Sandwich Marina, the only harbor along the canal.
- In Sandwich Samuel had a captive audience, eager to employ his mechanical skills and approving of his earnest efforts to be successful.

Moderato

There's a   lit-tle spark of love still   burn-ing,   and   yearn-ing down in
There's a   lit-tle spark of love still   burn-ing,   and   yearn-ing down in
lit-tle spark   of love still   burn-ing,   and   yearn-ing down in

Young Popular Song Composer in 1918

In 1913 Alonzo "Zo" Elliott had made musical history from his dorm room at Yale College, where he composed what became one of the most successful songs of the World War I era, "There's a Long, Long Trail A-Winding."

Life at Home

- Alonzo "Zo" Elliott wrote "There's a Long, Long Trail A-Winding" as a lark and a last-minute entry for a fraternity skit.
- The song ended up earning $3 million in sheet music sales.
- By 1918 Zo's song was on the lips of millions of soldiers eager to leave the fighting in France behind and dream while singing: "I forget that you're not with me yet/When I think I see you smile."
- The future musician was born in Manchester, New Hampshire, of Puritan stock; Zo's father was a banker and his mother a graduate of the Boston Conservatory of Music.
- She provided Zo with his first music lessons, yet she never pushed him to be a musician.
- "Although my musical mother had what was virtually a professional training, she did not try to persuade my father that music was the only profession for a man," Zo said.
- Zo was educated at St. Paul's School in Concord, New Hampshire; Phillips Academy in Andover, Massachusetts; and Yale University.
- While at Yale, in the years before the start of World War I in Europe, Zo met Stoddard King, who was to become his collaborator on "There's a Long, Long Trail A-Winding."
- Born in Spokane, Washington, Stoddard had gained Zo's respect because he was obliged to work his way through college.
- Zo and Stoddard were both prospective members of the fraternity Zeta Psi, and both became interested in the dramatic productions of the fraternity.
- Their first collaboration was in 1911, when they both worked on a production of John Gay's *Beggar's Opera.*
- By the spring 1913 semester, Zo and King desperately wanted to be sent as delegates to a Zeta Psi "smoker" in Boston.
- This was an important step in achieving full-fledged participation in "Greek life": fraternity recruits were expected to wear a coat and tie for

Zo Elliot (right)

145

the occasion, at which were given a presentation about the fraternity and invited to smoke a cigar along with their peers.

- Delegates to the smoker were to have their expenses paid and were excused from classes.
- But to be elected for the honor, they had to prove themselves entertainers by preparing an act to entertain their fraternity brothers.
- One morning Zo was in Connecticut Hall at college, reading Baron de Ségur's report of Napoleon's retreat from Moscow, when he went to the piano and spontaneously improvised the chorus of "There's a Long, Long Trail A-Winding."
- When Stoddard King arrived a few minutes later, Zo confided, "I have a song with a 'sticky' harmony."
- *Sticky harmony* was college slang for a tune to which a tenor part, usually starting a third above, could be added.
- The melody appealed to King immediately, and almost as quickly as Zo had composed the tune, the two came up with the words.
- Traditionally, the words to songs were written first, followed by the melody—but not always.

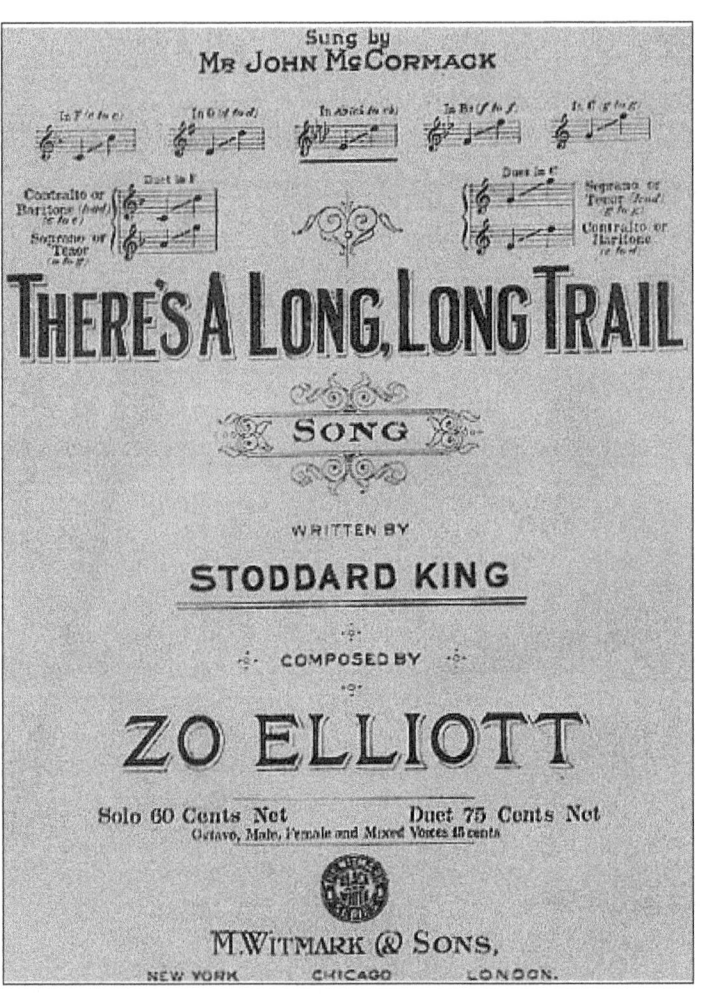

- In the case of Gilbert and Sullivan's operettas, Sullivan usually wrote the melodies first; Gilbert then mortised the words and song together.
- King had a gift similar to Gilbert's, and he took Zo's melody in a different direction.
- When composing his tune, Zo was picturing Napoleon at the end of his tragic trail to Moscow; King saw the trail as leading to home and romance.
- The following week, when it was time for the two aspiring frat brothers to perform their song at the Zeta Psi banquet in Boston, Zo took a painful fall while ascending the steps to the stage.
- The results, in the midst of the college festivities, were jeers, cheers, and calls to "do it again."
- Zo and Stoddard King were so flustered after the hubbub they had raised that all they could do was sing the chorus.
- Then, to their great surprise, the tune captured everyone's imagination, and one of the fraternity boys demanded the words so they could heartily sing along.
- It was a huge hit that night.
- But New York's music publishers failed to share Zeta Psi's enthusiasm for the song; Zo and Stoddard submitted the song to practically every sheet music publisher in New York, with no success.

Life at Work

- After graduation from Yale, Alonzo "Zo" Elliott entered Trinity College in Cambridge, England, where he went shopping at a music store for a piano.
- "In trying the instruments, I played the song," Zo recalled. "The proprietor was a tune scout for a London publisher, and he sent for his chief to come to Cambridge to hear it."
- Claude Yearsley, representing West and Company, liked what he heard, and the song was published in December 1913.
- Sales were slow until the outbreak of World War I in Europe, when British soldier boys were pouring into France to fight Germans in the "war to end all wars."
- Several Canadian soldiers saw the gorgeous song sheet cover of a trail leading down a mountain valley, read the words, and were homesick; this song had perfectly captured their loneliness and emotional response to being far away from home with no assurance of ever returning.
- After the song became the rage in every London music hall, a New York house took a gamble on it.
- And sales exploded.
- In all, more than five million song sheets featuring "There's a Long, Long Trail A-Winding" were sold, earning $3 million.
- Sheet music, which cost from $0.25 to $0.60 per song, was a big business despite the emerging competition of phonograph machines.
- Millions of families entertained themselves by gathering around the piano after dinner to sing.
- Following the Civil War, more than 25,000 new pianos were sold annually in the United States, and by 1887, it was estimated that more than 500,000 youths were studying piano.
- As a result, the demand for sheet music grew rapidly, and more and more publishers entered the market.
- As the twentieth century began, New York was emerging as the center of popular music publishing as well as an important center for the musical and performing arts.
- Popular song composers were hired under contracts that gave the publisher exclusive rights to the composer's works.
- Publishers surveyed the market to determine what style of song was selling best, and then they directed the composers under contract to compose in that style.
- Songs were tested with both performers and listeners to determine which would be published and which would go into the trash bin; composers complained that music was becoming an industry more than an art.
- Once a song was published, song pluggers—performers who worked in music shops playing the latest

Irving Berlin was a popular song composer in 1918.

releases—were hired, and popular performers were persuaded to play the new songs in their acts to give the music public exposure.

- And Zo's music passed the popularity test—first with the English Tommies, who had entered the Great War three years before the United States.
- In Oklahoma's Fort Sill, thousands of raw recruits began to swelter to it.
- At Camp Devens in Massachusetts, thousands more shivered to it.
- The song was a favorite of President Woodrow Wilson and was sung after dinner at the White House.
- At Camp Gordon in Georgia, men shaved to it, groomed horses to it, and built roads to it.
- They sang it whether they wanted to or not.
- The government's official morale-boosters made it compulsory for soldiers to sing.
- By the time America entered the war in 1917, the American song first published in England united the Tommies who had ploughed through Flanders's mud with the doughboys who marched through the black night into the Argonne.

Elsie Janis, the "sweetheart" of the AEF.

- Soldiers herded aboard transports and troop trains and recruits who dug straddle ditches and loaded ammunition had one song that helped more than any other to see them through the war.
- By then, the words had changed to "There's a long, long trail that's winding/Into no man's land in France/Where shrapnel shells are bursting/And where we must advance./There'll be lots of drills and hiking/Before our dreams come true/But someday we'll show the Kaiser/ What machine-gun boys can do. WOW."
- Singing undeniably helped the soldiers cope with their wartime experiences, from the mundane to the exalted to the devastating.
- Irving Berlin expressed soldiers' grumpiness with "Oh, How I Hate to Get Up in the Morning"; Geoffrey O'Hara created "K_K_K_Katy" to capture spontaneity; George M. Cohen fashioned the rallying cry of the soldier with "Over There"—a song written by Cohen as he traveled from Long Island to Manhattan the morning after Wilson's war address.
- And in leaky barracks and smoky cafés as well as on endless marches, "There's a Long, Long Trail A-Winding" was sung rowdily and nostalgically.
- Tenor Enrico Caruso sang it in Liberty Loan drives; in France, Elsie Janis, the "sweetheart of the AEF" (American Expeditionary Force), sang it from the back of a truck.
- It was played when the first U.S. troops to land in England marched in review before Ambassador Page and Admiral Sims.
- As recounted in the *New York Times* on March 29, 1917, British soldiers sang it in February 1917 when their transport ship, the *Tyndareus*, struck a mine off Cape Agulhas, the southernmost tip of

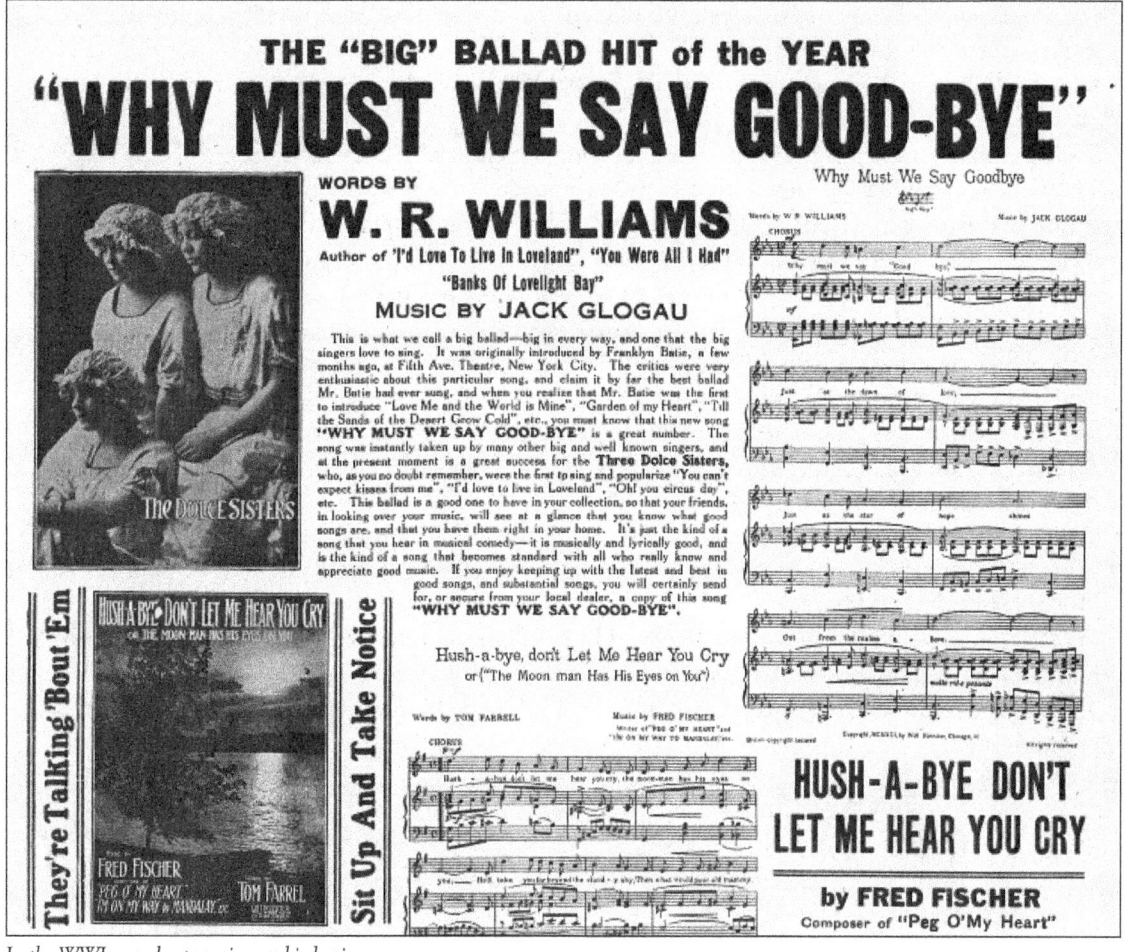

In the WWI era, sheet music was big business.

Africa; as the ship began to sink, "some one started 'The Long Trail,' and in a few seconds the whole gathering from end to end of the ship had taken up the haunting refrain of the latest marching song." All were rescued, including Paddy, the regimental dog.

- Troops even sang it after the Armistice when they marched across the bridge into Cologne.

Life in the Community: New York, New York

- Already a major manufacturing hub, New York City became the world's financial center once the war in Europe was under way, replacing both London and Paris.
- After America officially joined the war in Europe, the city of New York quickly focused on "women power," which one government brochure called "One of the Increasingly Valuable and Undeveloped Assets of our Country."
- By December 1917 women filled the office chairs of thousands of newly minted American soldiers.
- New Yorkers, flouting the injunction "time is money," fell in love with the pageantry displayed in the dozens of war parades staged at the city's very center.
- New Yorkers even accepted a mayoral curfew decree that shortened the night by closing restaurants, bars, and theaters by 1 a.m.
- After the start of the Great War, German-Americans were frequently suspected of being too sympathetic to the German Empire.

- Former president Theodore Roosevelt denounced "hyphenated Americanism," insisting that dual loyalties were impossible in wartime.
- Nationwide, about 1 percent of the country's 480,000 "enemy aliens" of German birth were imprisoned in 1917-1918.
- Charges included spying for Germany or endorsing the German war effort.
- Thousands of Germans in New York City were compelled to buy War Bonds to show their loyalty.
- In fear of sabotage, the Red Cross barred individuals with German last names from joining.
- In Collinsville, Illinois, German-born Robert Prager, a suspected spy, was dragged from jail and lynched; in Minnesota, a minister was tarred and feathered when he was overheard praying in German with a dying woman.
- Across the country orchestras replaced music by the German composer Richard Wagner with works by the French composer Hector Berlioz.
- Streets with German-sounding names were rechristened: Germania Avenue became Pershing Avenue; Berlin, Michigan, changed its name to Marne, Michigan, in honor of those who fought in the Battle of Marne.
- Nebraska banned instruction in any language except English.
- In response, German-Americans often "Americanized" their names: Schmidt became Smith, while Müller evolved into Miller.
- On November 11, 1918, the Armistice signed by Germany and the Allies at Compiègne in northern France ended fighting on the Western Front, effectively ending the war.
- Total war casualties were estimated at 10 million dead, 21 million wounded, and 7.7 million missing or imprisoned.

Fighters who broke the Hindenburg Line paraded down Fifth Avenue in NYC.

There's a Long, Long Trail A-Winding

Nights are growing very lonely,
Days are very long;
I'm a-growing weary only
List'ning for your song.
Old remembrances are thronging
Through my memory
Till it seems the world is full of dreams
Just to call you back to me.

Chorus:
There's a long, long trail a-winding
Into the land of my dreams,
Where the nightingales are singing
And a white moon beams.
There's a long, long night of waiting
Until my dreams all come true;
Till the day when I'll be going down
That long, long trail with you.

All night long I hear you calling,
Calling sweet and low;
Seem to hear your footsteps falling,
Ev'rywhere I go.
Tho' the road between us stretches
Many a weary mile,
I forget that you're not with me yet
When I think I see you smile.

Chorus:
There's a long, long trail a-winding
Into the land of my dreams,
Where the nightingales are singing
And a white moon beams.
There's a long, long night of waiting
Until my dreams all come true;
Till the day when I'll be going down
That long, long trail with you.

The (Tin Pan) Alley's strident songs and nervous dance tunes, its blurbs and ballads and banalities, are as evanescent as the encircling smoke in which they are ground out in accordance with constantly changing recipes. In one essential, however, there is no change, for this frankly commercial pursuit involves a ceaseless and eager following of the taste of the crowd-the indiscriminate and undiscriminating crowd-an inseparable part of the American scene.

—William Fisher, *One Hundred and Fifty Years of Music Publishing in the United States*

Recorded Popular Songs from WWI Era: 1914-1918

- By the Beautiful Sea
- Keep the Home-Fires Burning (Till the Boys Come Home)
- Missouri Waltz (Hush-a-Bye, Ma Baby)
- The Aba Daba Honeymoon
- When You Wore a Tulip and I Wore a Big Red Rose
- Are You From Dixie? (Cause I's From Dixie, Too!)
- Battle in the Sky
- I Didn't Raise My Boy to Be a Soldier
- Nola (A Silhouette for the Piano)
- Pack Up Your Troubles in Your Old Kit-Bag and Smile, Smile, Smile
- Thank God for a Garden
- When the Lusitania Went Down
- If You Were the Only Girl in the World
- Mother's Good Night Song
- The Hero of the European War
- Me and My Gal
- Good-bye Broadway, Hello France!
- Hail! Hail! The Gang's All Here (What the Deuce Do We Care?)
- Time for Ev'ry Boy to Be a Soldier
- Over There
- The Battle Song of Liberty
- I'm Always Chasing Rainbows
- In Flanders Fields the Poppies Grow
- Keep the Trench Fires Going for the Boys Out There
- Oh! How I Hate to Get Up in the Morning
- Over The Sea, Boys
- Rock-a-Bye Your Baby With a Dixie Melody
- Somebody Stole My Gal
- Yanks With the Tanks (Will Go Through the German Ranks)
- Till We Meet Again
- We Don't Want the Bacon (What We Want Is a Piece of the Rhine)
- When Pershing's Men Go Marching Into Picardy

First-Generation Russian American Millworker in 1919

Ivan Perova lived with his wife, Lyudmila, and his three children in Lawrence, Massachusetts, where he worked in a textile mill. The Lawrence mills fed the clothing industry of New York City, which made the United States a leading nation in the ready-made clothing industry.

Life at Home

- Ivan Perova was his family's sole wage earner, so Lyudmila was able to care for the children and do all the housework, including sewing and laundry.
- Lyudmila was a second-generation Lithuanian America, and several members of her family worked at the mills.
- The Perovas' children were still very young. Piotr, the eldest, would soon start school.
- Although Ivan and Lyudmila sometimes spoke Russian between themselves, for the most part they spoke English at home, and they always used English when the children were present.
- Ivan's English was improving, and Lyudmila's was fairly good.
- The family rented a tenement apartment consisting of four rooms. The rooms were unheated.
- The tenement had gas and an indoor toilet, but no bathtub was available.
- Families living at a minimum standard, like the Perovas, usually burned about three tons of coal a year. The average cost of chestnut (medium-sized anthracite) and stove coal was $14.00 a ton.
- Some of the Perovas' neighbors did not buy coal in ton or half-ton lots but rather in the more expensive smaller quantities available in bags from the neighborhood stores.
- Coal was stored in the tenement cellars, where rubbish frequently accumulated and the lack of light meant that kerosene lamps were needed to see. Many people simply used lit matches for light.
- Fire risk was often on Ivan's mind, and his children were forbidden to go to the cellar.
- Lyudmila tended the kitchen fire herself and did not allow the children near it.
- She knew that in families in which both parents worked, even very young children, returning from school to an empty tenement in which the fire had been allowed to die out, often relit the fire themselves, whether or not they had been shown how to do it safely.

Ivan Perova

Families often lived in crowded tenement buildings with limited outdoor space.

- Gas, which was generally used for lighting and cooking, cost $1.25 per thousand cubic feet. The Perovas spent an average of $2.00 a month for gas.
- In the spring and autumn, the Perovas preferred to burn cordwood instead of coal.
- The rooms in the Perovas' tenement were dimly lit, with the little natural light in their apartment coming from a narrow alley.
- About 15 percent of the Lawrence mills employees took transportation to and from work. Streetcar fares were $0.10 a trip, and jitneys cost $0.07. Ivan tried to avoid spending money on transportation.
- Fashion and custom required that women's hair be worn long; short-haired women, like long-haired men, were associated with radicalism and possibly free love. Lyudmila usually braided her long hair and pinned it up.
- Cigarette smoking was rapidly increasing in popularity. Fatima cigarettes cost $0.23 for a pack of 20. Ivan occasionally bought a pack.

Life at Work

- Of the 35,750 mill workers in Lawrence, 23,034—Ivan among them—were foreign born, and of these only 5,100 were naturalized. About 1,800 had taken out their first papers, but more than 16,000, or nearly 70 percent, were aliens.
- Because of his Russian origin, Ivan was sometimes accused of being a Bolshevik, and he had begun the naturalization process partly in order to distance himself from such taunts.
- Ivan began as an unskilled worker but soon began to acquire proficiency with the mill machinery he was required to operate.
- The ideas of socialists and labor organizers circulated among the workers, although they were divided by language and myriad cultural barriers.

Most of the mill workers were foreign born and divided by language and ethnicity.

- English was a second language for more than 70 percent of the work force; about half of the workers spoke English "fairly well."
- The general appearance of the mill workers indicated that "American customs" were "exercising a considerable influence on their standard of living," one survey said.
- The New England mill system utilized the "family system," according to which immigrant men, women, and children all worked alongside one another.
- The mills of Lawrence were beginning to use the "scientific management" concepts developed in the 1880s, including the introduction of cost accounting systems, a time clock for workers, more managerial control and regimentation, production and inventory controls, and incentive wage plans to stimulate production.
- In 1912 the radical labor group Industrial Workers of the World (IWW) had led a large and violent strike in Lawrence. The strike—dubbed the Bread and Roses Strike—attempted to publicize the fact that the woolen industry, which enjoyed the highest protection under the Payne-Aldrich tariff, was paying starvation wages. Male operatives earned a maximum of $10 for a 54-hour week.
- This was the first major American strike in which foreign workers were organized and in which women and children played a vital role.
- Mill management wrongly believed that the workers, divided by language and ethnicity, would not be able to organize in opposition to the pay cuts imposed when legislation required the mill owners to reduce the work week from 56 hours to 54.
- The strike lasted two months and drew a Congressional investigation that revealed the squalid conditions in the mills.
- Damaging publicity induced the mill owners to settle; workers not only had the pay cuts reversed but received a raise in pay.
- A second major strike began in February 1919.
- In 1919 the United Textile Workers and Central Labor Union succeeded in getting the length of the workweek further reduced, from 54 hours to 48 hours—but at the price of an overall wage cut
- Most adult male mill workers already earned less than $1,000 per year, whereas the War Labor Board had defined a living wage as $1,500 per year
- Despite his misgivings about being labeled a Bolshevik, Ivan was among the approximately 17,000 immigrant workers who walked out of the mills throughout Lawrence on February 3, although the United Textile Workers had not formally called a strike.

- The strikers were organized in 20 separate ethnic groups. Few were unionized workers.
- Ethnic business owners supported the strike, accepting coupons as payment for their goods; strikers boycotted stores that did not cooperate.
- Ivan and Lyudmila received some relief from the strike fund, but they struggled as the strike wore on.
- Police violence, arrests, fines, and even kidnappings met the strikers' efforts to hold meetings and picket the mills.
- In April Governor Calvin Coolidge imposed arbitration, but no settlement was reached.
- Unbeknownst to the strikers, the United Textile Workers began negotiations with the mill owners.
- By this time the owners wanted to settle the strike but would not negotiate directly with the strikers.
- Meanwhile, the strike's funding was dwindling.
- In mid-May, just as the strikers were about to capitulate, the United Textile Workers announced that they had struck a deal with the owners that would reduce the work week to 48 hours while obtaining for workers a 15 percent pay increase—more than the strikers had been demanding.
- The strike ended on May 23.
- Ivan was elated. He knew that such an outcome would have been impossible in Russia.

Life in the Community: Lawrence, Massachusetts

- In 1915 the population of Lawrence was 90,259, of whom only 12,034 were native-born of native parents.
- The city's 41,347 foreign-born residents included 8,587 Italians, 5,443 French Canadians, 5,154 English, 5,084 Irish, 3,022 Poles, and 3,603 Russians (a category then including Lithuanians, Finns, and Jews).
- Not only was the leading industry in Lawrence the manufacturing of textiles—chiefly woolens, although cotton goods were made at several plants—but the city had been planned and come into existence specifically for this purpose.
- Nearly all the people of Lawrence lived within a mile and a half of the city hall.
- The city was arranged on the hills rising from the Merrimack River Valley; the hill topography worked against the development of ethnic neighborhood groupings.
- On the flat land in the center of the city was a crowded and undesirable tenement district.
- According to the 1911 survey of Lawrence commissioned by the White Fund, "Though all defective houses are not at the center, and all center houses are not defective, the city's pressing housing needs are at the center. ... Lawrence is by more than one half a city of tenements."
- "The density of the apartments in the central district," noted the White Fund's analyst, "is about four and one-half times the density in the rest of North Lawrence and more than twelve times the density in South Lawrence," a trend that was increasing as new buildings were crammed into the central district.
- The city's houses were made of wood, thus, again according to the White Fund analyst, "piling risk upon risk" of fire losses, which the analyst regarded as inevitable.
- Lawrence thus far had been remarkably fortunate with regard to fire disasters, although as of 1911 some 97 percent of its houses were made of wood—more than in any other city in the state.
- Many were four-story buildings, which were both structurally weaker and so dangerous in a fire that insurers placed them in a different category than houses of one- to three floors.
- In the 1911 survey, the city engineer identified sewage disposal as among the city's most acute problems; at that time, "The sewage from all the sewers," according to the engineer, was "discharged in a crude state into the river."
- The more prosperous people of all races live on the higher land.
- The downtown stores and markets shared the meat and grocery business of Lawrence, with a large number of stores situated in the separate neighborhoods.
- Clothing stores were confined to the downtown district.

During the 1912 "Bread and Roses" strike, strikers sent their children to live with sympathizers in New York City.

- Motion picture houses in Lawrence charged $0.10 in the afternoon and normally $0.20 in the evening; the local daily newspaper cost $0.02, and the Boston Sunday paper was $0.07.
- Doctors charged $2.00 for an office call and $3.00 for a house visit.
- A considerable portion of the city's social life was conducted through the city's approximately three hundred clubs and fraternal societies; Lawrence had more such organizations than any other city of comparable size.
- Some of the lodges also offered their members sick or death benefit privileges.
- Approximately 70 percent of the wage earners and their families had burial insurance.
- Lawrence was predominantly Roman Catholic, and the churches were well supported.
- About one-third of the children attended Catholic parochial schools. The church charged $0.60 a month per child.
- In addition to Roman Catholic churches, there were several Protestant churches, for Germans and Swedes, among others, and five churches of the Greek or other Eastern rite.
- Automobiles were still a luxury of the affluent; most were open, since the sedan, or closed car, had not gained popularity.
- In 1919 there were seven million cars on the road in the United States, a number that clearly was growing rapidly.
- The average speed limit in most states was 15 miles an hour in residential areas and six miles an hour on curves.
- There were no automatic traffic lights to regulate traffic.

Tenement buildings were often dangerous, giving rise to a host of social ills as depicted here.

Dress Manufacturing Company Owner in 1919

As the owner of a dress manufacturing company that sold its goods exclusively to Sears, Roebuck, Allan Kincaid was able to buy a home for his family in a fashionable part of Chicago. He acquired a car and vacationed at family resorts in the country. He and his wife, Gladys, had two boys.

Life at Home

- The war years brought prosperity to the nation, and since the retail giant Sears, Roebuck & Co., for which Allan manufactured dresses, was doing especially well, Allan's business was thriving.
- The family was considering taking an extended vacation in London and Paris, but Allan was concerned about inflation eating into their savings, and he was also unsure of how long he could leave his business.
- He dressed very conservatively, preferring a hat and coat every day, and the more prosperous he became, the more conservative the clothing he chose.
- At age 6 his youngest son, Michael, loved to dress up like his father.
- Their two-story brick home was furnished with antiques Allan inherited from his mother; most came from her native Germany, and although Gladys loved having good furniture, she wished it were not so big and heavy.
- Allan avidly read the business pages of the *Chicago Daily Tribune,* and he was astonished at how high prices rose following the end of the Great War; he hoped this trend was temporary.
- The cost of living was a frequent topic of conversation at the Kincaids' dinner table and at Allan's men's club in downtown Chicago.
- Gladys was unhappy about rising prices but was very pleased that sugar, unavailable during the war, was obtainable again.
- The progress of the Peace Conference was making Allan uncomfortable; he thought that President Woodrow Wilson was naïve, but he was convinced that the Germans could not be excluded from future affairs.
- As a second-generation German American, Allan was careful in his comments during the First World War; he did not lose any business, he thought, but he rarely spoke of the old country anymore.

Allan Kincaid

The Sears, Roebuck & Co. building (background) in Chicago, Illinois

- After 1916, orchestras avoided presenting music composed by Germans—even works by Richard Wagner and Ludwig von Beethoven.
- Financial institutions with German names Americanized them, and the teaching of the German language was discontinued in many schools.
- Sauerkraut was referred to as "liberty cabbage," and hamburgers became "liberty steak."
- In 1919 fashion decreed that women's skirts, which were tight at the ankles, must stop at six inches above the ground; Kincaid's spring 1919 line, featured in the Sears, Roebuck catalogs, dared to go slightly higher.
- *Vogue* magazine predicted that skirts would soon become even shorter, declaring, "Not since the days of the Bourbons has the woman of fashion been visible so far above the ankle."
- Gladys always wore stockings—nearly always black, but occasionally tan to match her shoes—and stockings were never flesh-colored.
- Her makeup included powder, but like most well-brought-up women, she frowned on rouge.
- To go shopping, a hat was required, preferably with a veil pinned neatly in the back.
- Gladys's bathing suit consisted of an outer tunic of silk or cretonne over a tight knitted undergarment, worn, of course, with long stockings.
- At their monthly dinner and dance at a local hotel, sponsored by Allan's men's club, Gladys noticed several women smoking openly, not caring if anyone saw them; she commented to Allan on how brazen they were.
- Gladys believed that the First World War, known widely as the Great War, had ushered in too much change.

- The realities of the new Constitutional amendment mandating Prohibition were becoming clear; what liquor was still available was expensive, but shortly it would not be available at all.
- Allan still liked a good drink in the evening and did not look forward to being denied his evening shot, but Gladys, who regarded drinking as sinful, was quite pleased that Prohibition had been approved.
- Allan was concerned that Bolshevism was taking over, and he heartily concurred with an advertisement recently run by Swift and Company that read, "Everything that falsely encourages unrest also encourages Bolshevism. Misunderstanding of American industrial organization, and its benefits to mankind, leads to unrest, dissatisfaction, and radicalism."
- Allan was pleased that the government had relinquished control of the railroads; he never liked purchasing tickets at the United States Railroad Administration Consolidated ticket office.

Life at Work

- World War I was very good for Allan's business and for Sears, Roebuck in general.
- Rising prosperity fueled a desire for the "extras"; for many women that meant owning dresses beyond just the "necessary."
- Women who went to work to support the war were particularly interested in dressing well; many spent at least some of the money they earned on themselves—for the first time.
- In 1919 Allan discerned the first signs of what could become a recession as inflation threatened to drive the price of many goods out of the reach of the average consumer; sales of dresses, always a luxury, were declining slightly.

Women working in the Sears Roebuck shipping department

- Allan found the economic picture confusing; his future felt less secure than it had two years ago.
- On the one hand, after the end of the war, farm prices plummeted, including the price of the cotton he used to make many of the dresses he manufactured; during 1919 cotton slumped from a wartime high of $0.35 per pound to $0.16—a problem for farmers, but a boon for dressmakers dependent on this raw product.
- At the same time, inflation was driving most of Allan's costs higher.
- Moreover, the threat of strikes was constant; workers nationwide were desperate to keep up with the rapidly rising cost of living, yet thousands of men and women were being thrown out of wartime industries as government contracts for war materials—of all kinds—were canceled.
- With the threat of unions hovering everywhere, all of the 79 women who worked for Allan knew that he would fire anyone who spoke about unions in his presence.
- Several chain department stores had asked for his spring dresses; Allan was wondering whether he should diversify his client base.
- Selling directly and exclusively to Sears had served him well for more than a decade, so he was unsure of the best direction; loyalty counted for something, he believed.
- In spring 1919 Sears, anticipating an increase in pregnancies, requested that his dress line include several new maternity dresses; the number of catalog pages devoted to the sale of baby goods was also been increased as more men returned from the war in Europe.
- At the same time, Allan had come to think that some of Sears's top managers had gone soft, taking more of an interest in their golf game and in having drinks at the club than in selling his dresses.
- From experience he knew that when mercantile companies slumped or failed, the suppliers were the first to be hurt financially.
- Allan did not want to see his carefully accumulated reserves swallowed up in a long downturn.
- His business arrangement with Sears was efficient and successful; he made quality dresses and Sears, with its national reach, took care of marketing and sales, distributing his dresses across the nation.
- Gladys thought Allan should modernize his office; advertisements for the "Dictaphone" appearing regularly in the *Chicago Daily Tribune* claimed that "The businessman who says: 'Yes, I should like a Dictaphone demonstration—but some other time' is the very man who needs the demonstration now. He is putting it off because he's busy. And a demonstration shows that The Dictaphone saves hours every day in dictating and transcribing letters."
- Allan agreed with many of the men at his club that now that the United States had won the war, all socialists and communists should be expelled from the country.
- Labor was so out of control that Boston had actually experienced a police strike, challenging the widely held idea that public servants had no right to endanger the public safety by going on strike; Allan expected Chicago to experience similar problems if radical ideas were not stopped.
- He especially disliked the International Workers of the World, or IWW; the "Wobblies," as they were known, surely intended to kill capitalism—and not, as they claimed, just to raise workers' wages and improve conditions.
- Despite the evident prosperity around him, Allan distrusted the stock market and considered stock speculation to be dangerous.
- Disregarding the early signs of trouble ahead, everyone at the club was talking about getting rich in the stock market; whereas earlier in the year, 1.5 million shares a day were exchanged on the market, by late 1919 volume surpassed 2 million shares per day.
- Stock speculation had driven the cost of a seat on the New York Stock Exchange to between $60,000 and $110,000.
- Several of Allan's friends at the club had taken up golf—a sport he considered foolish; he had been known to ask aloud why any grown man would spend time knocking a little white ball around the ground.

Life in the Community: Chicago, Illinois

- Almost a third of Chicago's 2.7 million residents were foreign-born; more than a million were Catholics, and another 125,000 were Jews.
- In late 1919 the city was still in turmoil over the riots following the drowning in July of an African-American boy whose raft was stoned by whites after straying into a white swimming area of a city beach on Lake Michigan.
- Over seven days the rioting cost the lives of 23 blacks and 15 whites; 537 people were injured, while thousands—mostly African Americans—were left homeless by the fires that raged throughout the city.
- As was the case elsewhere, immigrant groups in Chicago had consistently banded together both to preserve their Old World ties and to become Americans; Chicago's Irish, Polish, Lithuanian, Greek, German, and Russian neighborhoods, among others, were clearly defined.
- The various groups fiercely competed for housing and employment, and these pressures were acute even before the Great Migration of African Americans to the North from the rural South brought a huge influx of blacks into the city.
- In 1919 most of the rioting took place on the city's South Side.
- A reporter for the *Chicago Daily News* named Carl Sandburg asserted that, "one section of the city ... supplied more white hoodlums than any other section. It was the district around the stockyards and packing houses."
- As Sandburg observed, infant mortality was seven times higher in that district than it was in the Lake Shore area just a mile away, and he pointed to the "gaunt involuntary poverty from which issues the hoodlum."
- At the same time, the population of Chicago's Black Belt residential district, already overcrowded and slum-ridden, more than doubled during the war years, and increasingly blacks were forced to seek housing in "white" areas in which one or more ethnic group predominated.
- During the riots, members of Ragen's Colts, an Irish gang, disguised themselves in blackface and torched Polish and Lithuanian neighborhoods in the Back of the Yards district; they intended both

White rioters in Chicago in the "red" summer of 1919

to strike at their Eastern European immigrant rivals and to incite them to attack African Americans, which the Poles and Lithuanians had hitherto avoided doing.

- The animosity between Poles and Lithuanians was a more immediate issue for them than the conflict between "whites" and "blacks"; they did not especially identify with the "whites" involved.
- Gangs formed among all of the major ethnic groups in the city as well as among African Americans; intra-ethnic gang conflict was commonplace.
- The gangs were also entwined in the city's political patronage networks.
- About 78,000 people were employed in the downtown area known as "The Loop."
- Colleges, pressed for cash because of inflation, were beginning to use the money-raising methods learned during the Liberty Loan campaigns.
- The war, which ended on November 11, 1918, had lasted 1,563 days, claimed the lives of some 10 million worldwide, and wounded 20 million others.
- When the armistice was declared, people poured into the streets to celebrate, as shopkeepers tacked up signs reading, "Closed for the Kaiser's funeral."
- At that time, more than 3.5 million men were in uniform; 2 million were in Europe.
- Even the call of patriotism could not stifle labor disputes; during the conflict there were 6,000 strikes, and the pace of labor unrest appeared to be quickening.
- Inflation drove prices faster than wages, resulting in extensive labor strikes as the high cost of living affected every household; food, rent, clothing, and taxes were all rising.
- Milk jumped from $0.09 to $0.15 a quart over the five wartime years.

Even before inheriting a lumber fortune, Agnes Forcelle, the wife of a prominent Presbyterian minister, had the means to travel abroad. The family went to Hawaii as missionaries and to Paris as first-class tourists.

Life at Home

- The Forcelle family lived in Chevy Chase, Maryland, where Agnes's husband, Albert, served as a Presbyterian minister.
- Three years earlier, Agnes's mother had passed away; she left an estate of more than $300,000, considerably increasing the family's economic freedom.
- Agnes's maternal grandfather made a fortune in the timber industry, and he later more than doubled his wealth through real estate; the vast land holdings he had acquired for timber became valuable to developers near rapidly growing cities and towns.
- Agnes's father, a promising young manager, married her mother, an only child, and the couple inherited both the timber business and the real estate interests.
- Trained well by his father in law, Agnes's father proved to be a shrewd and forward-thinking businessman.
- The family lived in upstate New York, where the timber interests and paper mills were located, but they also had a house in New York City, since Agnes's father transacted much business there.
- By the middle of the nineteenth century, New York led the states in timber production; by the 1870s, a million logs per year were transported down the Hudson River to sawmills and paper mills.
- Especially after his only son died of tuberculosis as a child, Agnes's father saw to it that she received a first-rate education.
- He even tutored her himself; she was an eager student and showed an aptitude for business while still in her teens.
- Agnes frequently traveled with her father for both business and pleasure; she visited England a half dozen times before her marriage and even accompanied her father to India.

Agnes Forcelle

The Forcelles loved to travel, especially to Europe.

- She fell in love with New York theater as a child and often returned to New York City to enjoy plays and opera.
- Because her parents had always shared their wealth generously, Agnes and her husband and daughter frequently traveled to Europe for vacations, even when Martha was quite young.
- Martha went to Miss Hall's, a private boarding school, and hated the experience.
- At age 25, Martha had begun working toward her master's degree after completing her undergraduate education at George Washington University.
- Now that the war was over, Martha and her mother planned to repeat their 1913 grand tour of Europe, taking one last trip together before Martha's marriage.
- As one of 12 children from a middle-class family in Springfield, Massachusetts, Albert in his younger years did not have the wealth to travel on his own.
- After graduation from Yale in 1878, Albert spent two years as principal of Connecticut's Rockville High School; he then entered Yale Divinity School, graduating in 1885.
- He spent the next two years touring the world as a guide, tutor, and companion to a wealthy young man, the son of a Yale alumnus.
- Tracing her lineage to William Bradford, the second signer of the Mayflower Compact, Agnes was proud to be a member of both the Colonial Daughters and the Society of Mayflower descendants.
- During the war, when foreign travel was restricted, the Forcelles took up the hobby of collecting American art pottery—a passion that appealed to many well-to-do Americans they knew.
- The popularity of these ceramic vessels, created for beauty rather than utility, was largely driven by a rebellion against the machine-made blandness of mass-produced objects.
- In their quest for pottery, the Forcelles had taken the train to New Orleans, where they bought several pieces of Newcomb pottery; Agnes's favorite piece depicted a misty moon shining through moss-draped trees.
- Agnes was particularly interested in works produced in the Arts and Crafts style, and she liked the idea of supporting Newcomb Pottery, which was associated with the art and design department of Newcomb College, the women's branch of Tulane University.

- On another trip, they went to Chicago to buy Roseville pottery, made in Roseville and Zanesville, Ohio; Agnes was drawn to the new Sylvan line, with its incised depictions of animals and vegetation and its muted colors.
- During the Chicago trip, they visited the theater and opera, and they bought several very subtle Tiffany bowls with leaves and flowers etched onto a monochromatic background.
- In New York they found a wonderful three-handled vase, glazed one color inside and unglazed outside, made by the studio of Louis C. Tiffany.

Agnes with her daughter, Martha

Life at Work

- During his many years as a Presbyterian pastor, Albert had moved around quite a bit: he served for 5 years in churches in upstate New York and in Allston, Massachusetts, near Boston; 4 years in Hawaii; and then 13 years in Rye, New York before taking his current pulpit in Chevy Chase, Maryland.
- Before the turn of the century, the Forcelles lived in the newly acquired U.S. territory of Hawaii, where Albert served as a Presbyterian missionary.
- There they learned some of the language and collected furniture made by local craftsmen; they also welcomed American troops passing through during the Spanish American War.
- While in Rye, a New York City suburb, Albert secured contributions from property owners to build sidewalks and improve the public library.
- During World War I, the Forcelles' home had been a center for visiting pastors and soldiers.
- It was even a temporary refuge for the Korean government in exile, a dangerous political position; the Japanese government had a price of $300,000 on the head of Korean dissident Syngman Rhee.
- Albert enjoyed studying at Yale and often returned there; from the pulpit, he enjoys telling how in 1638 the Rev. John Davenport and the merchant Theophilus Eaton founded the New Haven Colony to establish a Puritan "Bible State," in which "the word of God shall be the onely rule to be attended into in ordering the affayres of government."
- Albert felt particularly at home at Connecticut Hall, the building that marked Yale's first foray into the Gothic Revival architectural style.
- Currently, a building program was under way at his church in Chevy Chase; the builder was a local man and a friend of Albert known for constructing meaningful worship spaces using only the finest stone.
- During the flu epidemic of 1918, several children of the parish had died within days of each other; their parents and grandparents all contributed funds for an expanded Sunday School building in their memory.
- With the women of the church, Albert was also working on outreach programs to help the starving people of Armenia, formerly a part of the extensive Turkish Empire.
- In 1915 American ambassador Henry Morgenthau had appealed for assistance to help save the Armenia people from extermination at the hands of the Turks, and in August 1919 Congress issued a charter for the American Committee for Relief in the Near East, which had been formed from several different aid organizations active in the region.

- Albert delegated management of his church's initiative to Agnes, who was very accomplished in the art of keeping committees moving steadily toward a goal without ruffling feathers.
- Prior to the war, Albert's church had been actively engaged in the Christian Helpers League, designed to help down-and-out men, who were often alcoholics.
- Working with several Presbyterian churches, the League in 1915 had provided meals to 11,352 people, baths to 4,834, clothing to 64, medical care to 102, and jobs to 100; records showed that 5,442 of those served also attended religious services.
- With the war over, Washington society was attempting to regain its footing.
- President Woodrow Wilson remained out of the public eye after suffering a massive stroke on October 2, 1919; Mrs. Wilson devoted all of her time to his care.
- Prior to the president's illness, Albert and Agnes, had been honored by a personal invitation from Mrs. Wilson to lunch at the White House, in recognition of what they had done during the war.
- They were aware that the president's health continued to be weak; the cabinet and the press had been told that he was suffering from "nervous exhaustion."
- Nonetheless, visits by Belgian and British nobility had dressed up the Washington social season.
- A reception for H.R.H. Edward Albert, Prince of Wales, held at the Congressional Library "brought out the gowns and jewels," according to the *Washington Post*.
- Agnes was not especially interested in keeping up with fashion, but even she enjoyed reading about how Cora, Countess of Stafford, the former Mrs. Colgate of New York, had arrived in white satin with diamond tiara and corsage ornaments, while Lady Newborough, who had been passing the past few months with American friends, wore "black velvet on modish lines, with diamonds and pearls."
- After the anxiety of the war years and the ongoing controversies of the war's aftermath, it was a relief to indulge in frivolous pursuits.

The Forcelles took a trip to Notre Dame in France.

Life in the Community: Chevy Chase, Maryland

- Germany accepted the principles of the President Wilson's Fourteen Points—his plan for peace enunciated in January 1918—at the Armistice in November 1918, but the eventual peace treaty, the Treaty of Versailles—the formal diplomatic document ending the war—substantially departed from the Fourteen Points.
- Germany was not party to the negotiations and called the result a *diktat*.
- Many thought that the Treaty of Versailles went too far in its strictures on Germany and its demands that Germany pay enormous reparations and accept sole responsibility for the war.
- Nevertheless, Wilson supported it.
- Over the summer and fall of 1919, Senator Henry Cabot Lodge, the chairman of the Senate Foreign Relations Committee, led Republican efforts in Congress to add amendments to the treaty that would have hobbled the proposed League of Nations.
- Wilson strongly opposed these efforts to alter the document; it had been worked out with the Allies at the Paris Peace Conference in difficult negotiations that sought to accommodate the victors' very different aims.
- The Paris Peace Conference was to establish the League of Nations independently of the treaty.
- The president's strenuous efforts to enlist public opinion in the treaty's favor and secure ratification without any changes had seriously impaired his health and contributed to his present condition.
- Women's clubs, created for the purpose of mind improvement, continued to study key issues such as English and French women's war work, prohibition, and national efficiency
- General John J. Pershing was still basking in the glow of victory, even though Ohio Representative Sherwood had attracted a firestorm of criticism for suggesting that Pershing was "not on the firing line during the great battles of the western front."
- General Pershing was popular with America's mothers; the normally unsentimental general gave the celebration of Mother's Day a boost in 1918 by ordering all his commanding officers to have "every officer and soldier in the American Expeditionary Forces to write home on Mother's Day."

Washington struggled to return to normalcy in the aftermath of World War I.

- The soldiers were instructed to write "Mother's Letter" on the envelopes so the Army Postal Service could spot them more easily and speed them home.
- According to the Stars and Stripes, one transport alone carried approximately 1.4 million letters from France to the United States that year.
- Pershing also took time to thank the women who worked to aid the war effort.
- During the war, women took a critical role in book drives to create libraries overseas, and even gathered peach stones to combat the effects of poisonous gases; seven pounds of pits were needed to filter a single gas mask, and a million men required masks.
- Many women's groups were now turning their attention to widespread starvation in Europe and the threat of socialism taking hold in America.
- Chevy Chase was developed beginning the 1880s as one of the earliest planned "streetcar suburbs."
- Until the advent of the streetcar, most people lived close to their place of work, but railroads and electric streetcars had made it possible to separate homes from crowded industrial districts.
- Major George Armes originated the plan to buy up farmland and extend Connecticut Avenue, but Armes needed partners to provide the money to execute the plan as well as to ensure that the needed approvals from local governments were forthcoming.
- With two ambitious Nevadans, Francis G. Newlands and William Stewart, Armes formed the Chevy Chase Land Company.
- Newlands, an heir to the Comstock Lode fortune, went on to represent Nevada in both houses of the U.S. Congress, and Stewart, too, was a U.S. senator from Nevada.
- Newlands was the sponsor of the Newlands Reclamation Act of 1902, which launched irrigation projects throughout the Western states.
- Newlands and Stewart bought up thousands of acres along the planned route of Connecticut Avenue.
- They built a streetcar line out to Chevy Chase Lake, an amusement park with an artificial lake created to drawn residents to their planned "home suburb of Washington." By 1892, the trolley line was in service.
- They hired the firm of Frederick Law Olmsted as consultants; Olmsted advocated the separation of "business premises from domestic premises."
- The partners advertised large homes in a park-like setting, promising wide streets, sidewalks, and parks along with city amenities such as running water, sewers, electricity and telephone service.
- By the end of 1901, 49 expansive and expensive homes intended to appeal to the upper class were ready for sale, and the first Chevy Chase residents were among the social elite.
- In 1916 the Chevy Chase Land Company opened up their model suburb to the middle class, having constructed smaller, lower-cost homes that nevertheless preserved the character of the suburb.
- Newlands ran for president in 1912; his platform called for the disenfranchisement of black men and a whites-only immigration policy.
- The 1916 advertisements for Chevy Chase appealed to the "discriminating" buyer, which was understood to mean that African Americans and Jews would be excluded.

Non-Commissioned Officer Serving in Russia in 1919

Bull Rawicz reluctantly left his new wife to fight for his country, but nothing prepared him for a journey into Russia to battle the Bolsheviks—after World War I had ended.

Life at Home

- Bull Rawicz was enormously pleased with his life on the day the U.S. Army draft notice arrived.
- Newly married, Bull was dreaming of children and a chance to attend business school—courtesy of his new father-in-law.
- Imagine, a Rawicz in a three-piece businessman's suit!
- Born into the Polish community of Hamtramck, Michigan, a Detroit suburb, Bull was raised in a large apartment with his siblings, parents, paternal grandparents, and widowed uncle.
- Most of his extended family lived within a few blocks of his apartment building.
- Principally, their lives revolved around the family, work, their ethnically Polish Roman Catholic Church, and the traditional Polish food cooked by his mother, sisters, and grandmother.
- Bull's father was a shift supervisor at an iron foundry; his uncle the foreman of a mechanical crew at a rail yard.
- His mother had been a seamstress but primarily managed the home, occasionally doing special sewing jobs.
- Bull's ancestors were skilled laborers and foremen in the Polish city of Biaystok; the family immigrated to the United States in the 1890s.
- Although no Polish state had existed for 120 years, his family considered themselves Polish and spoke Polish at home.
- Bull got his name when he started school and was found to be markedly taller and stockier than the other students.
- His friends all agreed that Bull, although hardworking and intelligent, was not an exceptional student; what he lacked, they said, was curiosity.
- After high school graduation, Bull joined a rivet gang; his job was to drive the rivets manually into the steel beams used to construct the tall buildings of Detroit.
- Soon after securing the job, Bull married Jadwiga, a girl he had known since childhood.

Bull Rawicz

Bull was eager to defend America, the country that has given his family so much.

- Also from Biaystok, her people were small business owners, and they boasted a priest in the family.
- Some neighbors whispered that marriage to Bull was beneath Jadwiga, but her father knew the Rawicz men were hard-working, frugal, and respectable.
- Nevertheless, Jadwiga considered Bull's current job unsuitable for a family man.
- Therefore her father offered to send Bull to management courses at a business college.
- That's when the draft notice arrived.
- Bull had been playing his accordion at a Knights of Columbus dance, a favorite social occasion for his family, when he was told to report for duty.
- He was eager to defend America—the country he felt had given him and his family so much.
- Still, he was afraid.
- He had a young wife, whom he did not want to leave; furthermore, he had never been outside of Wayne County, Michigan.
- Bull was sworn in with the other Wayne County draftees in June 1918 and soon was on his way to Camp Custer in Battle Creek, Michigan.
- A large group of friends and family—many saying they thought the war would be over quickly—saw him off at the station, wishing him a safe return.

Life at Work
- After only three weeks of training, Bull was sent to Camp Mills on Long Island in New York state, where he was met with a telegram informing him that his wife was expecting a child.
- He was thrilled.
- His excitement was immediately tinged with anxiety, however.
- He could not be there to help, although he was supremely confident that the family would take good care of his bride.

- As the other regiments embarked for France, Bull's 339th Infantry waited.
- Eighty-five percent of the men in the regiment were from Michigan, and of those, 70 percent were from metropolitan Detroit.
- Many American soldiers were introduced to the concept of regular tooth-brushing by military training during the Great War.
- The 339th was sent to England, where they were ordered to exchange their rifles for long, light, less accurate bolt-action rifles.
- This type of rifle was used by the Imperial Russian Infantry, or so Bull had been told.
- They were also issued heavy woolen clothing and heavy-soled canvas Shackleton boots reserved for use in arctic climates.
- Shackleton boots were clumsy and extremely unpopular with the troops; one veteran wrote that the "Charlie Chaplin walk has nothing on the Shakleton gliding-wabble. ... Aw, Shakletons."
- Quickly a rumor spread that the 339th was being sent to Russia.
- To Bull this made no sense; Russia had withdrawn from the war months ago, after the overthrow of the czar.
- Nonetheless, on August 25, the 339th boarded transports in Newcastle Harbor and set off for northern Russia.
- The men were told they were not to be an offensive force but were being sent to protect from the Bolsheviks the supplies and equipment sent by the Allies to the Imperial Army.
- The equipment was now stored in the northern port cities of Murmansk and Arkhangelsk.

Bull's 339th Infantry prepared while they waited to be sent to France.

President Woodrow Wilson addressed Congress on the war.

- The 339th was placed under the command of the British.
- Their stated goal was to defeat the Bolos, as the Bolsheviks were called.
- Bull had little use for Russians; Russia had been party to splitting up Poland more than a century before he was born.
- As a child, however, he had learned a fair amount of Russian from older members of his family who had grown up in Russian-dominated Poland; at least he would be in a country where he could speak the language.
- Bull wrote two letters a day—one to his parents and one to his wife—even though he could not mail them until they made landfall.
- For his parents he composed a chronicle of each day's events, coupled with assurances of his good health.
- To Jadwiga he wrote longer letters about their future together and about names for the baby; Bull wanted the child's name to be both American and recognizably Catholic.
- On September 4, 1918, his convoy arrived in Arkhangelsk Harbor.
- The First Battalion, which included Bull's company, stayed aboard ship for a couple of days while the other troops disembarked.
- When their time finally came, the First Battalion did not go on guard duty in Arkhangelsk, as expected, but were loaded onto filthy, stinking barges.

- For five days they cruised up the river, which some of the soldiers said reminded them of the lower reaches of the Mississippi River—though few had actually ever seen the lower reaches of the Mississippi.
- From what Bull and his company could see, the country seemed to be one giant swamp filled with vermin.
- He had never imagined that there could be so many cockroaches; the barge swarmed with them.
- When the barges finally landed, his company was first put on guard duty but was soon told to back up a British unit in action a little farther south of the town.
- The fight was fierce, but the arrival of the American reinforcements caused the Bolos to retreat.
- Although there were no casualties in Bull's company, they felt initiated into battle.
- A few days later, half the company, including Bull, and a few allied Russian troops took a steamer up the Dvina river onto the Vaga, a large tributary.
- They sought to occupy the town of Shenkursk, a summer resort now filled with upper-class refugees from St. Petersburg.
- They stayed only a short while; orders came from the British Command to proceed farther up-river to "stir up the enemy."
- The small force set out again and were soon under heavy fire from the banks.
- As bullets thumped around it, the steamer pulled close to the shore.
- The troops jumped out, waded to shore and dispersed the Bolos.
- Struggling over the marshy ground with the ever-present insects, they then embarked on a march to the interior.
- Soon Bolsheviks from throughout the region marshaled for a battle and began pursuing the Americans.
- Finally, as their rations neared an end, Bull's battalion engaged a sizable force of the enemy, inflicting twice as many casualties as they had men.

Bull and his regiment were sent to Russia to protect supplies from the Bolsheviks.

The 339th Infantry was based for a time in the resort town of Shenkursk.

- Again, Bull escaped injury.
- Through the fight, he registered his first confirmed kill; drawing a careful bead on the enemy troops, he was able to drop several of them in their tracks.
- The small force backtracked until they reached the village of Ust Padenga, about 15 miles south of Shenkursk, where they were ordered to stop.
- They guarded the village—the southern outpost of the Allied forces—until November, when they were finally relieved for a brief period to return to the relative security of Shenkursk.
- Here Bull took the opportunity to practice his Russian language skills.
- He was also able to play at a couple of dances on a borrowed accordion.
- He received—finally—mail from home, including a letter from Jadwiga agreeing to the names Matthew James for a boy and Mary Elizabeth for a girl; she thought the names were beautiful.
- News also arrived that the armistice had been signed on the Western Front; the Great War was over!
- The men rejoiced and hoped that they would soon get their orders to go home.
- But the port at Archangelsk remained frozen, and they heard they would not be able to get home until spring.
- Bull grew anxious and frustrated, and finally broke down and cried.
- If their return was delayed until spring, he would not be able to get home in time to see his first child born.
- Soon those concerns were washed away; instead of going home, they were sent back into battle at Ust Padenga.
- When they arrived, they were ordered to attack the city on January 19, the dead of the Russian winter.
- First Bull and his regiment began with a heavy artillery bombardment, followed by a charge against thousands of white-clad Bolos—almost invisible against the snow.
- Casualties rose quickly.
- After the Bolos were repulsed for the third time and the British-American force had lost half its company, orders came to abandon the town.

- On the fourth night of the engagement, Bull and the remaining troops crept from Ust Padenga, ablaze from a Bolo shell, down the frozen Vaga until they reached Shenkursk.
- The journey took two days.
- Soon they were nearly surrounded again by the enemy, who anticipated the Allied retreat.
- One night, however, undetected by the enemy, the entire force plus a large number of civilians left Shenkursk by a secret road and slowly retreated from town to town along the Vaga.
- They were in the town of Kitsa when spring finally broke and the Bolsheviks withdrew, afraid they would become bogged down in the melting snow.

World War I left countless towns and cities in shattered ruins.

- Spring also meant that Bolshevik boats would be able to patrol the river and attack the British-American army.
- Kitsa was abandoned.
- In mid-May, Bull's squadron was on patrol when it was swept by sniper fire, but they were able to suppress it and the sniper surrendered.
- He was immediately shot, according to British orders that no accommodations for prisoners be made.
- A few days later, all the Americans boarded a river steamer that took them to Archangelsk—the first leg toward home.
- There, they received a month's worth of back mail; Bull found a letter announcing the birth of his first child, Mary Elizabeth, on March 26, 1919.

Life in the Community: Arkhangelsk, Russia

- To support the war effort, the American government amassed an army eventually totaling 4 million; the Navy numbered 600,000 more, and the Marine Corps, nearly 80,000.
- The United States was involved with the Great War against Germany and Austria for 30 months but played a significant battlefield role in France, Belgium, and Italy for only 8 months.
- Commander John "Blackjack" Pershing complained that, because most of the American troops were raised in towns and cities, many had little familiarity with firearms and were poor marksmen.
- During World War I, while the Russians fought Germany alongside the Allies, their counterparts in Russia began to run out of supplies; the cost of staples such as bread rose dramatically, quickly spiraling out of control.
- Bread riots began, leading to the March Revolution.
- As a result a provisional government was set up in 1917, but it soon fell apart.
- The Bolsheviks, under the leadership of Lenin and Trotsky, seized power.
- As a result, the Soviet government signed the Treaty of Brest-Litovsk with Germany and pulled out of the war.

- The European Allies then began secretly planning to join with the anti-Soviet forces within Russia to overthrow the Bolshevik government and reopen the Eastern Front.
- If successful, this ploy would necessarily draw German military resources away from the Western Front, where they were now concentrated.
- Trotsky, however, successfully engineered the Red Army to include experienced former officers of the Czarist government.
- As a result the Russian army was too large and well-trained to be defeated by the paltry forces the Allies had allocated.
- President Wilson had had to be pressed by Marshal Ferdinand Foch to involve Americans in the Arkhangelsk mission at all, and he ordered that their role be confined to protecting the Allied supplies supposedly stockpiled in Arkhangelsk.
- The delay in executing the plan gave the Bolsheviks more time to strengthen their forces in the area.
- The Northern Russian Expedition—also known as the American North Russia Expeditionary Force (ANREF) and the American Expeditionary Force North Russia (AEFNR)—consisted of the 339th Infantry ("Detroit's Own"), one battalion of the 310th Engineers, the 337th Ambulance Company, and the 337th Field Hospital Company.
- On arrival in Arkhangelsk, the Northern Russian Expedition found that the Bolsheviks had already captured the munitions and supplies and moved them south.
- The mission was then reconfigured by the British commander as "active defense" of Arkhangelsk, involving offensive military operations.
- These entailed sending relatively small units hundreds of miles into the Russian hinterlands in the depths of winter, with deep snow making most roads impassable and temperatures of 20 degrees below zero Fahrenheit often rendering artillery useless.
- Keeping what was essentially an American and Canadian force under British command proved to be constant source of friction.
- With communications tenuous at best, orders sent by commanders hundreds of miles away often were negated by the situation on the ground; troops were sent to hold positions at great cost, only to be ordered subsequently to abandon them.
- It was a "grim fight against terrible odds," according to one account.
- The original commander was eventually replaced by a British general who attempted to restore the mission's declared defensive character.
- By that time the Bolsheviks had learned that the Northern Russian Expedition was a much smaller force than they had thought, and since ordinary citizens in the United States, Britain, and Canada were protesting against its continued presence in Russia, reinforcements would not be forthcoming.
- It had also become clear that no effective anti-Bolshevik force could be gathered in northern Russia.
- The "Spanish flu" had claimed 70 lives even before the expedition reached Arkhangelsk; over the winter the flu epidemic spread in the northern Russian towns and villages, bringing further misery and death to soldiers and villagers alike.
- In February 1919 President Wilson ordered that American forces be withdrawn from northern Russia as soon as Arkhangelsk Harbor became navigable.
- In late May the first half of a British relief force arrived in Arkhangelsk, and in June the Americans sailed for France and then for the United States.
- During the withdrawal, the ANREF dubbed itself the Polar Bear Expedition.
- The ANREF was disbanded in August 1919.
- The last British forces withdrew from northern Russia in October.
- In all the U.S. government declared American World War I casualties to be 116,516; battle deaths totaled 53,402; other deaths, including disease, totaled 55,114; total wounded tallied at 204,002; and fatalities worldwide for all nations were placed at 10 million.

Wartime Secretary for the YMCA in France in 1919

As a secretary for the YMCA, Robert Meek had witnessed his share of horror in the Great War, even though he himself never fired a shot.

Life at Home

- Robert Meek had been back from the Great War almost eight months before he decided to talk about his war experiences.
- All around him soldiers, young and old, were telling war stories about death and destruction, mustard gas and airplane duels.
- The grit and glory of their tales were different from the turmoil, triumph, and sadness he had experienced.
- The fighting he witnessed in France was brutish, and it left its participants psychologically wounded and mentally exhausted.
- Robert never fired a shot in the Great War; he spent his time in France as a secretary for the YMCA, trying to boost the morale of the troops by playing exhibition baseball games, organizing recreational events, and showing films to U.S. troops.
- This essential role was much praised in Poitiers, France, where he was stationed for 16 months, but it sounded trivial to those in the States who wanted to know how many Germans he had killed and how many French girls he had kissed.
- As a result, he rarely discussed the war.
- That changed at a dinner party at his uncle's house in Sheboygan, Wisconsin, at which three soldiers who had never left the United States talked about what they would have done had they been in the trenches.
- On hearing that Robert had served in France as a YMCA secretary, their tone grew condescending.
- Feeling both nauseated and angered, Robert was moved to respond.
- As though on a lecture circuit, he began reciting vital statistics.
- "The YMCA performed 90 percent of all service work with the American Expeditionary Forces in Europe," he began. "YMCA workers suffered 286

Robert Meek

Before the war, Robert played baseball whenever he could.

casualties; six men and two women were killed in action.

- "The 319 citations and decorations earned by YMCA workers include the French Legion d'Honneur, the Order of the British Empire, the Distinguished Service Cross and the Distinguished Service Medal."
- The soldiers shifted uncomfortably as Robert continued.
- "During the war 26,000 men and women were paid to serve with the YMCA. They guided 35,000 volunteers attending to the spiritual, social, and physical needs of the troops.
- "The YMCA operated 26 R&R leave centers in France, providing respite for 1,944,300 American officers and men.
- "The YMCA's 4,000 'huts' and tents were used for recreation and religious services."
- Robert paused, took a deep breath, and went on.
- "The YMCA staffed 8,000 troop trains. It mobilized 1,470 entertainers overseas to perform for the troops.
- "It is now in the process of distributing 80,000 educational scholarships to veterans of the Great War."
- "We didn't shoot Germans," he said louder than he had intended, "but we did live in trenches, we watched men die, and we feared for our lives.
- "We helped the men remember what they were fighting for, and that's good enough for me and I hope it is good enough for you."
- With that said, Robert got up, apologized to his uncle for leaving the dinner table early, and walked outside.

Life at Work

- Before the war, Robert Meek lived a dual life—tailor by day and baseball player by night.
- He was passionate about catching ground balls and executing perfect bunts to advance the runner.

Robert quit his job as a tailor to become a YMCA secretary in France.

One of the duties of the YMCA was to distribute medication to sick and wounded soldiers.

- It was his dream to be discovered one day and play in the majors as a lead-off batter and right-handed shortstop.
- He also enjoyed his work fitting and sewing fine men's clothing.
- This combination of occupations landed him the assignment of YMCA secretary in France.
- One of his customers was the chairman of the YMCA Board and would, he told Robert, soon be in the thick of the fighting.
- The Young Men's Christian Association's relief work dated to the Civil War era, when 15 YMCA associations formally gathered to coordinate efforts to alleviate the suffering of the sick and wounded.
- When advised of these plans, President Abraham Lincoln wrote to YMCA leaders of his support, stating, "I sincerely hope your plan may be as successful as it is just and generous in conception."
- During its four years of operations during the Civil War, the commission recruited an estimated 5,000 volunteer "delegates" who served without pay in every theater of the war.
- It was the nation's first large-scale civilian volunteer service corps.
- Some volunteers served as surgeons, nurses, chaplains, and chaplains' assistants, while others distributed emergency medical supplies, food, and clothing.
- They built and operated special-diet kitchens in hospitals, brought books and prefabricated chapels to soldiers, taught enlisted men to read and write, maintained a hotel for soldiers on furlough, and provided free meals.
- The YMCA tradition of serving troops beyond U.S. borders began during the Spanish-American War in 1898, when YMCA staff and volunteers were dispatched to Cuba, Puerto Rico, and the Philippines.
- The YMCA supplies, including medicine and office materials, reached Cuba before those of the U.S. Army, and early dispatches from Teddy Roosevelt's Rough Riders were written on YMCA stationery.
- Prior to the war, the YMCA had developed mobile canteens and recreational facilities, expanding their expertise in service to the armed forces.
- This expertise then blossomed into a massive program of morale and "welfare" services for the military—on the home front, but particularly overseas.

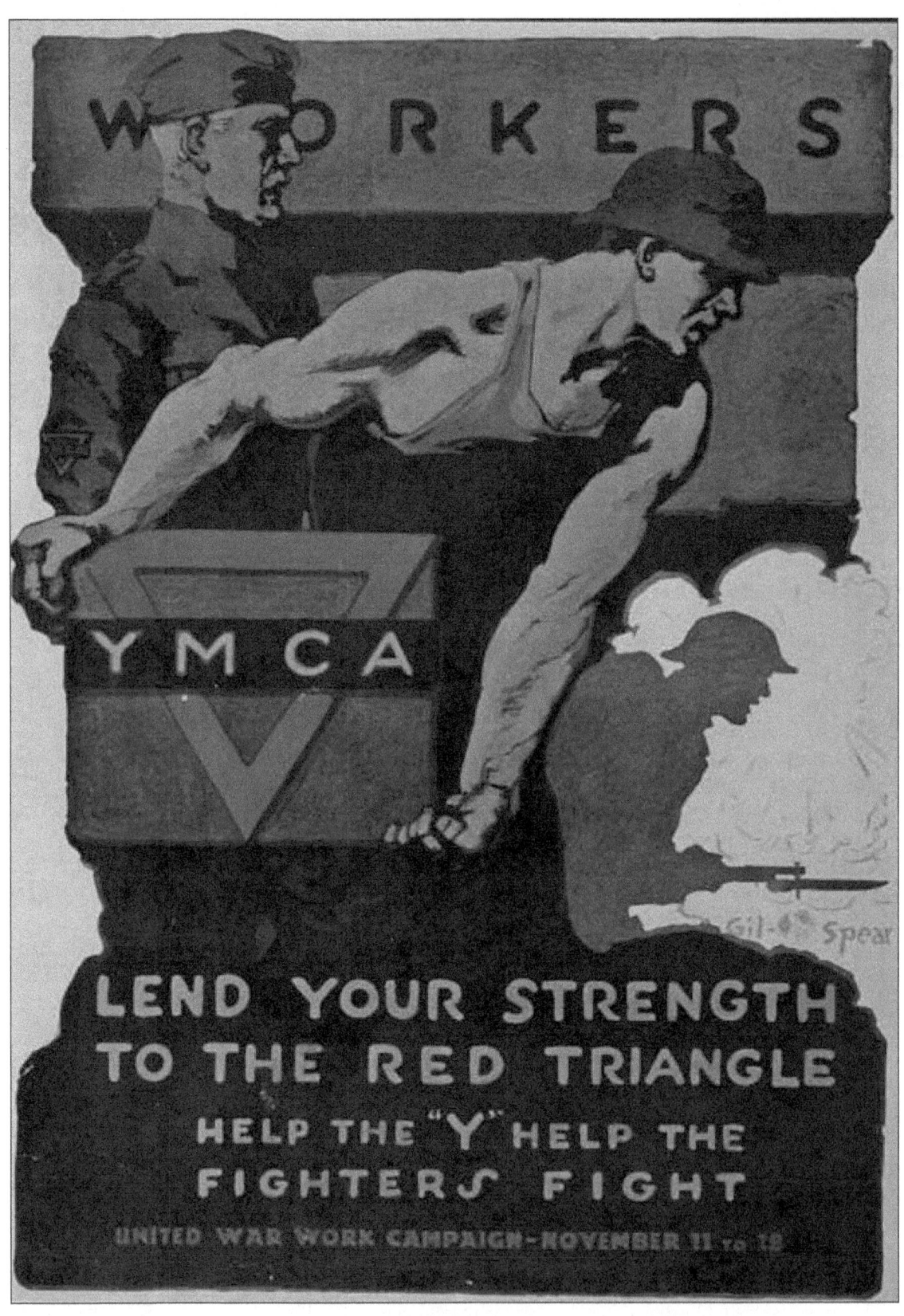

- When war was declared in 1917, the YMCA immediately volunteered its support, and President Woodrow Wilson immediately accepted it.
- The YMCA assumed responsibilities on a scale that had never in the history of the United States been attempted by a nonprofit, community-based organization.
- Robert's particular skills were prized: as he listened to homesick soldiers, he was unusually successful in both conveying empathy and giving them concrete suggestions for coping with their feelings.
- He not only organized baseball games but motivated his teams to achieve a high level of play, thereby drawing ever-increasing interest in the games among the soldier-spectators.
- Under the conditions prevailing at the Western Front, this was a remarkable accomplishment.
- Having been relieved for a while of the constant pressure of combat and the anticipation of combat, the soldiers returned to their posts in a better frame of mind, making them more effective soldiers.
- Robert arrived in France during some of the most intense fighting.
- On two occasions he had breakfast with a young man in the morning, only to find that he had to write a heartfelt "I'm-sorry-about-the-death-of-your-son" letter that night.
- On some days the pace of killing was brutal, while on other days the soldiers were consumed by boredom, which opened the door to tension and fear.
- Robert quickly discovered that a game of catch with the YMCA's baseballs would inject new life into the saddest doughboy.
- Twice a year a traveling U.S. Army-sponsored baseball team would arrive and play.
- Composed of former professional baseball players and the best amateurs in the Army, they typically won easily.
- These games created a much-needed diversion from the fighting.
- A ballgame was particularly successful if a rivalry was involved, such as on one occasion when a group of flyboys and their mechanics came into camp.
- Within hours the entire camp knew that the pilots—the hotshots of the air—had challenged Robert's nine to a baseball game.
- Bats and gloves were in short supply, so the teams shared their equipment.
- Robert led off with a single to left field, stole second, and advanced to third on a ground ball to first as hundreds of soldiers watched.
- Robert's first sergeant then blasted a shot into deep center, and when the inning ended, Robert's team—the American Expeditionary Army—was up, 4-0.
- In the fifth inning, the game was tied, 5–5, and the flyboys had two on and no outs.
- Robert snared a vicious line drive up the middle, stepped on second for out number two and threw out the retreating runner at first for a triple play.
- The celebration had barely begun when a major arrived to assemble the troops.
- The Germans were on the move again.
- The next day Robert's team lost its catcher to enemy fire.
- The YMCA showed movies that night to help the soldiers temporarily forget what they had seen, but most of the team wanted to talk about the game that got cut short.

Pilots loved the diversion of the baseball games that Robert organized for the troops.

- If only the game went nine innings; if only Robert was not in position to complete the triple play; if only the catcher had not been in the trench that was shelled.
- Robert tried to concentrate on the movie—*Shoulder Arms,* starring Charlie Chaplin and Edna Purviance—but ended up writing letters home to Sheboygan, Wisconsin.
- The catcher, too, was from Sheboygan, where the German language was still widely spoken, so Robert wrote the "regrets" letter to his family in German.

America and the Great War

- The World War began in August 1914, lasted until November 11, 1918.
- It encompassed 28 warring nations with a total population of 1,575,135,000—90 percent of the Earth's population.
- The Great War lasted four years, three months, and 15 days, for a total of 1,567 days, and the combined armies in this "gigantic test of civilization" reached a total of 59,176,800 soldiers.
- Battle deaths were 7,781,800, the wounded reached 18,681,200, prisoners and missing comprised 7,081,500.
- Total casualties topped 33,543,500.
- Direct financial cost to all nations was $249 billion, with indirect costs to commerce and trade adding $151 billion.
- America's participation in the war began on April 6, 1917, almost three years after the fighting began, and lasted 19 months, when 4,800,000 men were placed under arms.
- Of these, 2,000,000 men were transported over 3,000 miles across the sea and landed in France in the darkest days of the world crisis.
- On the war effort, America spent $22 billion, loaned its allies more than $10 billion and placed its powerful industrial system at the disposal of the Allied cause.

The YMCA supported troops by organizing a variety of activities to boost their morale.

African American Entrepreneur in 1919

Madam C. J. Walker learned at a young age how to survive tough situations—a necessary skill for a female pioneer African American entrepreneur.

Life at Home

- Sarah Breedlove McWilliams Walker was 37 years old before she launched the hair care business that made her one of the richest African American women in America.
- She was born on the Burney plantation in Delta, Louisiana, on December 23, 1867, to Owen and Minerva Breedlove, former slaves who worked as sharecroppers on the cotton plantation.
- Sarah was the first in her family to be born outside of slavery.
- The shack in which the family lived had no windows, no water, no toilet, one door, and a dirt floor.
- Built from cottonwood logs gathered on the plantation, the cabin had a fireplace used for cooking and warmth that dominated one wall of the one-room structure.
- The shanty's other prominent feature was the bedstead, topped with a homespun mattress sack stuffed with Spanish moss, gathered from trees in the area.
- Though now sharecroppers and no longer slaves, the Breedlove family still lived in a dangerous and hostile environment.
- Venomous snakes and mosquitoes, the latter of which caused diseases such as malaria and yellow fever, were always lurking in the sweltering, swampy climate of the Delta.
- From the day she was born, Sarah Breedlove spent nearly every moment with her parents.
- As a baby, she was strapped to her mother's back while Minerva worked in the fields.
- At the age of four, Sarah had learned to work alongside her parents, drilling holes in the field where she carefully dropped cotton seeds.
- Each year she received material from the plantation owner for her one sackcloth dress.
- Sarah had no time to attend school even if one had existed; instead, she learned to pick cotton and pick it well.
- An orphan at age seven, she had few options, and she was moved across the Mississippi River to Vicksburg, Mississippi, with her sister Louvenia and her sister's abusive husband, Jesse Powell, in 1876.

Sarah Walker, a.k.a. "Madam C.J. Walker"

Being a laundress was physically demanding, and Sarah couldn't compete with washing machines.

- Life in Vicksburg was hard for the Breedlove sisters; work was scarce and the shanty in which they lived was crowded.
- After the birth of Louvenia's son Willie, her husband became increasingly hostile; there was never enough money or food to sustain the growing family.
- To escape the volatile situation in her sister's home, Sarah became a live-in domestic worker for a white family who provided her with meals, lodging, and a small salary.
- Too young to cook, she laid fires, dusted, mopped, washed dishes, scoured pots and pans, changed bed linens, polished boots, and took in washing and ironing.
- In 1882, at age 14, she married Moses McWilliams and left her domestic position to work as a laundress.
- "I married at the age of 14 in order to get a home of my own," Sarah explained years later.
- In the 1880s machines were taking over the laundry business even in Vicksburg, where a new Chinese laundry advertised the newest vacuum-type washing machines.
- Sarah realized she could not compete with the steam laundries on the grounds of speed and productivity; instead she kept her customers by offering reliability and professionalism.
- Sarah Breedlove McWilliams gave birth to a daughter she named Lelia on June 6, 1885; just two years later she found herself a widow and a single parent.
- After the sudden death of her husband, who was rumored to be one of 95 black men lynched nationwide in 1888, she left Vicksburg for St. Louis, Missouri, where her brother Alexander was a barber.
- The steamboat trip up the Mississippi River consumed a week and cost $4.00 for a mother and child.

- St. Louis was a city filled with black entrepreneurs, including nearly 300 black barbers who shaved their white customers daily.
- Within a decade the barbering business would dramatically change when King Gillette introduced the easy-to-use safety razor, designed for home use.
- Alexander lived in the mostly black Mill Creek Valley section of the city.
- The two-story tenement apartment in which Sarah lived with her brother and her young daughter was a one-room affair which served as a kitchen and sleeping room.
- Sarah soon took a job in a steam laundry.
- A survey by the St. Louis public schools showed that of 5,076 black parents, 22.6 percent worked as laundresses and 42.6 percent were laborers.
- White steam-laundry owners considered blacks particularly suited to the task, given their legendary tolerance for heat and sweltering conditions.
- The work required Sarah to stand over hot tubs of boiling water all day, stirring the laundry with a long stick, a task demanding great strength and stamina.
- She was married again, briefly, in 1894.
- At age 35, when she began her new career in hair care products, Sarah was making $1.50 a day.

Sarah was married at the age of 14.

- She was living on $468 a year; after deducting $8.00 a month for rent and $3.00 a week for food, she was left with $216 a year for fuel, medicine, transportation, clothing, church donations, and all other expenses.

Life at Work

- Sarah Breedlove McWilliams was on the edge of becoming entirely bald when she was introduced to Annie Turnbo hair care products for black women.
- Annie Turnbo's agents sold her brand of hair straightener door-to-door.
- For years, like many African-American women, Sarah had shampooed her hair only monthly—less often in the wintertime—and she suffered from acute dandruff, lice, eczema, and psoriasis.
- In addition, she had used harsh lye soaps, goose fat, and meat drippings to straighten her hair; the lye and sulfur had burned her skin and destroyed her hair follicles, resulting in hair loss.
- To hide her condition, Sarah often wore a scarf in the fashion she had learned on the farm.
- Even within the black community, long, straight hair denoted prosperity and beauty, while poor hair care marked a woman as coming from the country; rural women were presumed to be unsophisticated and uneducated.
- Eager to cure her baldness, Sarah had tried a variety of concoctions, including several that promised to simultaneously grow and straighten her hair.
- Most failed miserably.
- But after using the Pope-Turnbo Wonderful Hair Grower made by Annie Turnbo and experiencing miraculous results, Sarah joined the army of women selling Pope-Turnbo products door-to-door.
- As part of her front-porch sales pitch, Sarah told the story of how the Wonderful Hair Grower had changed her life.
- She quickly became their leading saleswoman.

- The Pope-Turnbo promotional literature made the connection between beautiful hair and prosperity very clear.
- "Clean scalps mean clean bodies. Better appearance means greater business opportunities, higher social standing, cleaner living and beautiful homes," the brochure said.
- Turnbo's competitors hawked hair straighteners and shampoos with names such as Kinkilla, Kink-No-More, and Straightine.
- The Boston-based Ozono promised in its advertisements to take the "Kinks out of Knotty, Kinky, Harsh, Curly, Refractory, Troublesome Hair."
- Some products were so patently dangerous—or useless—that black-owned newspapers refused to carry their advertising.
- Most black intellectuals, including Booker T. Washington, disdained the hair-straightening products sold to Negro women.
- But that had little impact on Sarah's success in St. Louis or Denver, when she took her sales operation farther west.
- In July 1905, with $1.50 in savings, 37-year-old Sarah moved to Denver, where she worked as a cook for druggist E. L. Scholtz and moonlighted selling Turnbo's products.
- Even though the State of Colorado's entire population of 540,000 was smaller than that of the city of St. Louis, Sarah sensed opportunity in the mining town.
- She used $0.25 of her $1.50 savings to buy business cards advertising Pope-Turnbo Wonderful Hair Grower, now available in Denver; as orders arrived, Sarah reinvested the profits in more advertising.
- She found the city welcoming: women could vote, and there was less racial animosity toward African Americans than she had encountered elsewhere (although Denver's Chinese population was increasing dramatically, and the Chinese were despised).
- Then Scholtz suggested that she provide him with a sample of the Wonderful Hair Grower so that he could analyze it and help her devise a formula of her own.

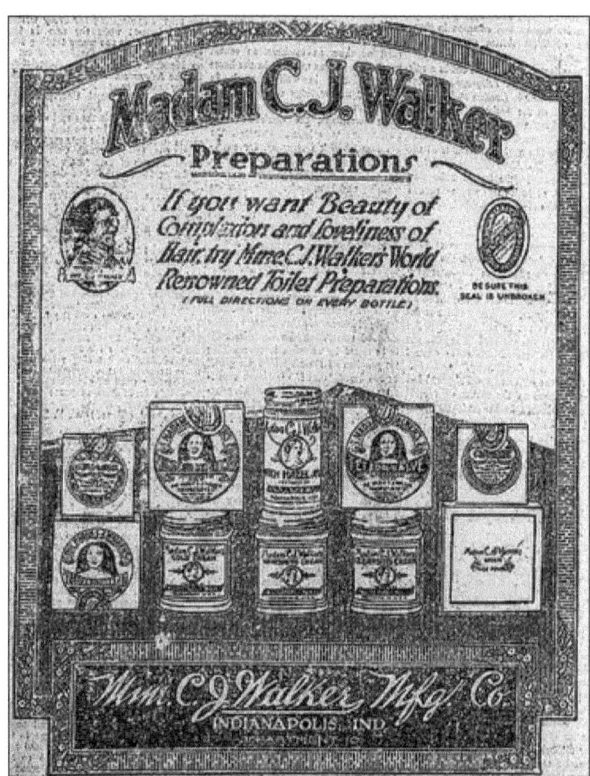

Druggist E.L. Scholtz helped Sarah devise her hair care product.

- Consequently a new company was launched, featuring a wide variety of hair care products.
- Later Sarah would say that the magical concoction came to her in a series of dreams brought by a man with very specific instructions; competitor Annie Turnbo thought otherwise.
- Turnbo, however, had not trademarked her product; she did so in 1906, under the name Poro—a West African word denoting a discipline promoting physical and spiritual enhancement.
- In 1906 Sarah married Charles Joseph Walker, a salesman, and developed her own line of hair care products under the name Madam C. J. Walker; that year she tripled her income, to $3,652.
- For the next 18 months, Sarah and her husband demonstrated and sold their products throughout the South, systematically canvassing the region where 90 percent of the nation's African Americans still lived.

- In each city they would contact the Baptist or African Methodist Episcopal (AME) Church, rent the best house they could afford, introduce themselves to the local black fraternal organizations, arrange a demonstration at the church or lodge, hold classes to train agents, and take orders for Madam C. J. Walker's Wonderful Hair Grower.
- Then they would travel on to their next stop.
- "All the people who know me are just wild about my hair," Sarah was told by one customer; "I have to take it down and let them see and feel it for themselves. I tell you, I am quite an advertisement here for your goods."
- In the summer of 1907, the volume of orders had become so great Sarah decided to relocate the business to Pittsburgh, where 16 rail lines offered convenient shipping nationwide—a critical component of her mail-order business.

Sarah pledged $1,000 to help build a YMCA for the black youth in Indianapolis.

- In 1908 Madam Walker earned $6,672, nearly twice the previous year's earnings; one year later she took home $8,782.
- She attracted the attention of the Pennsylvanian Negro Business Directory, which called her "one of the most successful businesswomen of the race in this community."
- When women saw her photo and heard her life story, they clamored to take her course and sit for treatments; for thousands of maids and laundresses, Sarah symbolized the progress possible even for black women without a formal education.
- After two and a half years in Pittsburgh, the peripatetic Madam Walker was ready to relocate again, this time to Indianapolis, where a small article in the *Indianapolis Recorder* described her as "the noted Hair Culturist."
- "Hair culturist" was Sarah's preferred description for her work.
- Advertisements placed by Sarah advised women "calling for treatments will kindly bring comb, brush and two towels"; consultations were free, while scalp treatments cost $1.00 and tins of her Wonderful Hair Grower sold for $0.50 each.
- There she built a manufacturing facility, employed three dozen women and constructed a beautiful six-bedroom house for herself; her income exceeded $10,000.
- Indianapolis was the nation's largest inland manufacturing center, with banks willing to finance startup companies.
- The city's central location gave Sarah access to Chicago and Cincinnati as well as to her markets in the South and East.
- Press notices preceded her arrival in Indianapolis as she toured the city in her chauffeur-driven $1,500 Pope-Waverly electric runabout.
- Following the opening of her factory, her sales soared to $250,000 annually, and Sarah could legitimately claim to have the largest black-owned company in the United States.

- And still she hustled for more business, attending dozens of black-sponsored conventions and gatherings to lecture on hair care.
- Constantly searching for new customers, the restless Madam Walker was always adding to her commissioned workforce of 950 saleswomen.
- She personally trained agents throughout the South and designed their own advertising.
- Meanwhile her marriage to C. J. Walker was disintegrating; it ended in 1912.
- Sarah discovered the power and pleasure of philanthropy.
- In 1911, when the concept of building YMCAs for black youth was in its infancy, Sarah stepped forward to accept the challenge laid down by Sears, Roebuck executive Julius Rosenwald to build a YMCA in Indianapolis.
- Sarah made a pledge of $1,000—setting the standard for others, especially in the white community, to match.
- The *Indianapolis Freeman* declared her to be the "First Colored Woman in the United States to Give $1,000 to Colored YMCA Building" and featured her in an article that was read throughout the nation.
- Next, Sarah became involved with the National Association of Colored Women, through which she met and helped support Mary McLeod Bethune, a proponent of education of black girls.
- Sarah's $5,000 donation to the NAACP Anti-Lynching Campaign was the largest in the campaign's history.
- She also joined a delegation that traveled to Washington to protest the blight of lynching and President Woodrow Wilson's silence on the matter.
- Moved by men and women willing to better themselves, Sarah promoted a Valentine's Day charity benefit for Indianapolis's only black harpist—a 15-year-old girl who had lost her mother at the age of nine.
- She also supported family members, including her daughter, who worked in the business; a sister-in-law; four nieces; and her elder sister.
- Nevertheless, despite her continuing business success and philanthropic donations, African American leader Booker T. Washington continued to ignore her and her company—largely because of his disdain for hair straightening products.
- As a diversion from business, Sarah often attended movies to watch silent romances, Westerns, and comedies featuring entrepreneurs who had found success.
- The movie theaters also propelled her to leave Indianapolis for New York; after the owner of the Isis Theatre arbitrarily increased ticket prices from $0.10 to a quarter "for colored people," Sarah vowed to move.
- During 1914 and 1915, she traveled extensively, especially in the West, giving lectures on hair care and making donations, particularly scholarships for worthy students.
- Often, especially in California, Sarah had more invitations for speaking engagements than she could fulfill; everywhere she went, she trained new agents, sold Wonderful Hair Grower, and laid the groundwork for new business.
- By the time Sarah moved her operation to Harlem, in New York City, she employed ten thousand commissioned agents, making her the largest employer of black women in America.
- The agents were organized into Walker Clubs that rewarded their members based on contributions raised for charities well as on total sales.
- By 1916 Sarah had real estate investments in Indiana, Michigan and Oklahoma and in the city of Los Angeles; according to her federal tax returns, her business and real estate interests gave her a net worth of $600,000.
- Sarah moved into a beautifully renovated brownstone on West 136th Street and Lenox Avenue, but she saw a flood of poor, undereducated women in need of her services throughout Harlem.

Harlem, New York

- For women seeking something other than domestic or factory work, Madam C. J. Walker offered an alternative: selling Walker's Scientific Scalp Treatment for the chance to earn between $15 and $40 per week.
- And for working women, making the most money they had made in their lives, Sarah offered an urban, modern look for $1.75 per tin.
- Her goal, she said repeatedly, was to grow hair and confidence.
- Potential agents were tempted by written testimonials: "It is a Godsend to unfortunate women who are walking in the rank-and-file that I had walked. It's helped me financially since 1910. We have to been able to purchase a home and overmeet our obligations."
- Despite the luxury she had created for herself in New York City, Sarah spent the last three years of her life traveling for the war effort, seeking to encourage the patriotic service of Negro men.
- She also took the opportunity to train additional agents.
- On several occasions her travels were halted by nervous exhaustion and her failing health.
- For her final crusade, Sarah returned to the issue of lynching, armed with a report that said 3,200 people had been lynched in the United States between 1889 and 1918; the vast majority were black men, and almost all the lynchings took place in the South.
- In 1918 alone, 63 African-Americans, including five women, as well as four white men, had been lynched.
- To that cause alone Sarah pledged $5,000, one of many charitable gifts she made "to help my race."

Life in the Community: Harlem, New York

- Until the early 1870s, Harlem had been a distant rural village of mostly poor farmers in the northern end of Manhattan Island.
- But at the end of that decade, with the launching of the city's first elevated train, Harlem became the city's first suburb.
- Soon thereafter, contractors built opulent brownstones, and Harlem became known for its many mansions.
- An expansion of the Interborough Rapid Transit Line brought a second wave of growth, principally fueled by Irish and Jewish families.
- But when the overheated real estate market collapsed in 1905, West Harlem was saturated with vacant apartments, which became the home of middle-class blacks eager to escape the tenements of the Tenderloin and the San Juan Hill districts.
- In 1911 the prosperous St. Philip's Episcopal Church, an all-black congregation, engineered a million-dollar real estate transaction in Harlem that became the symbolic beachhead for the black presence.

Many African Americans worked in factories.

- Three years later, when Sarah gave her first serious thoughts to a New York move, Harlem was home to 50,000 African Americans.
- A National Urban League report said, "Negroes as a whole are...better housed in Harlem than any other part of the country."
- At the same time, large numbers of African Americans were being pushed from the South by the floods of 1915 and the boll weevil infestations of 1916.
- Many were pulled to Northern cities, including New York City, where they found employment at factory jobs left vacant when the two-decade-long flood of European immigrants was halted by the beginning of World War I.
- Many African Americans found they could make as much as $8.00 a day in a Northern city after a lifetime of making only $0.40 a day farming in the South.
- Black churches, newspapers, YMCAs, and advocacy groups such as the National League on Urban Conditions sprang up.
- Manhattan's population topped two million.
- Manhattan could claim the world's tallest buildings, from the 60-story terra-cotta Woolworth Building on Broadway and Park to the 50-story Metropolitan Life Insurance Building farther uptown on Madison Avenue near 23rd Street.

Home Builder for Out-of-Town Teachers in 1919

Before Joshua Blevins got a contract to construct small homes for out-of-town teachers, he had never heard of a teacherage, much less realized they were needed.

Life at Home

- In the closing days of World War I, Joshua Blevins grew to love the sights, sounds, and smells of France, but it was great to get back to central Texas, where the air was sweet and the sunsets uniformly spectacular.
- During most of his 18 months in France, Joshua had led a 7- to 12-man construction crew in a small village outside Paris, building or rebuilding housing for the American troops and the flood of refugees pouring through the area.
- As a result of wartime conditions, he had learned how to adapt quickly to changing situations, build with the existing materials, and be flexible when emergencies arose.
- It was the perfect combination of skills and training for the third-grade school dropout whose new job was the construction of 32 teacherages across central Texas.
- By 1919 more than 3,000 teacherages had been constructed nationwide.
- The movement was ignited in 1905 after a young female teacher who could not afford proper housing commandeered a cookhouse wagon in Walla Walla County, Washington, for her living quarters.
- The 20-foot wagon, covered only in canvas, let in the rain and snow—and attracted newspaper stories concerning her unusual housing arrangement, much to the embarrassment of the community.
- With the backing of the school board, a two-room cottage was built for the teacher on school property, sparking a national movement to assist rural communities by building teacherages.
- Women routinely were paid 50 percent less than men.
- Teachers frequently found they could not live on their poor wages—one of the reasons that teacherages became necessary.

Joshua Blevins

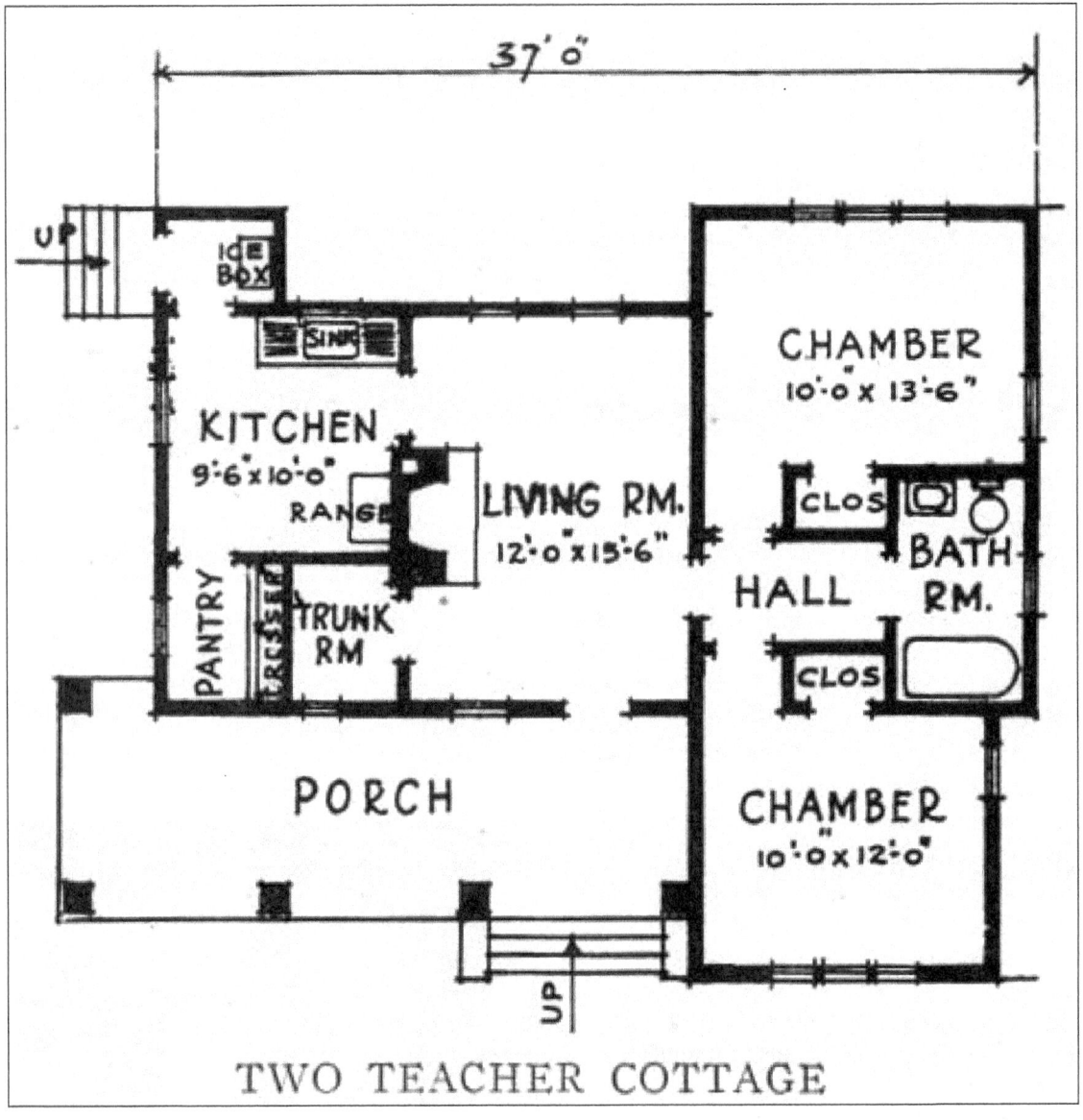

TWO TEACHER COTTAGE

- By 1919 Texas was one of the nation's leaders in providing housing for its predominately female teachers in rural communities.
- At the center of this movement was the General Federation of Women's Clubs; its 100,000 members embraced school reform as a natural extension of their role as mothers.
- The women's clubs lobbied for improved teacher training, an end to political patronage in the selection of school superintendents, school consolidations, better facilities, and quality instructional materials for students.
- Much of their focus was on rural schools, where facilities lagged and the instruction was often poor; typically, illiteracy was twice as great in rural areas as it was in urban ones.
- A primary concern was that poor rural schools would continue to drive a flood of ill-prepared youth into the city streets in search of jobs; this would weaken both the urban and the farm economies.
- Good schools were seen as the best way to shore up the American tradition of family farms in the agricultural economy.
- Achieving good schools demanded changes in teacher recruitment and school-lesson hours.

Rural areas had little to offer teachers and students.

- The average school term nationally lasted 150 days; in rural Texas, the average number of school days totaled 106, while some schools offered instruction only 63 days a year.
- Joshua himself had intermittently attended a school like that until he dropped out to work on the family farm.
- The school gave him the rudiments of mathematics, but his early training in repairing farm buildings and finding ways to make broken-down machinery work were what got him into construction work in the Army.
- Rigorous Army training had made him an exacting craftsman; he found his work very satisfying and had no intention of returning to the farm.

Life at Work

- When Joshua Blevins began construction of his first teacherage in a town 20 miles from his home in Marlin, Texas, he had a clear vision of how to construct two- and three-room cottages for under $100, a sum that would ensure him a profit.
- But that was before he fully understood how much help he was to receive.
- When he arrived for the first morning of work—hauling all his tools and supplies in a 12- foot cart pulled by a horse—he was met by a committee of women representing the school superintendent's office.
- They were so excited about the prospect of a livable home for their teacher that they had brought a gaggle of sullen teenage boys and several elderly servants to assist.
- Against all objections from Joshua, the "helpers" pulled everything from the wagon.

Joshua's teachers' homes became visible symbols of improved education.

- Joshua was beside himself; he was careful and methodical by nature, and his years of experience had taught him that setting up properly was as critical to the exacting work of building a house as was using quality lumber.
- It didn't matter; the welcoming committee was immensely proud of their contribution, even when the boys picked up several very precise tools and used them in mock sword fights.
- Joshua had a contract to build 32 units in cities stretching across central Texas; he had to complete all of the buildings over the summer, before school began again after Labor Day.
- Joshua took a deep breath and mumbled to himself, "Yes. I survived bombs and buffoons in France. I will survive even this."
- Joshua discovered that many of the club ladies disapproved of him smoking, too, but fortunately they lacked the courage to ask him to stop.
- As far as Joshua was concerned, the automated cigarette rolling machine was one of the greatest inventions in the history of man.
- On his second day on the job, Joshua was greeted by schoolchildren and their mothers; the mothers seemed to think that they possessed a world of knowledge—albeit little experience—about how he should proceed.
- Worse, they made little effort to keep their children out of his wood pile and away from his tools.
- Day two, like day one, went more slowly than planned; day three brought the prospective teacher occupant herself with a list of preferences, including her ideas about window dressings, the height of steps, and the location of the outhouse.
- All Joshua could say was, "One down and 31 to go."
- It was a process that was repeated over and over.
- By the time he built the ninth teacher's home, he fully realized that Texas communities truly wanted to offer good education, and that his building was a visible symbol of that desire.

Townspeople added their own improvements to make the teacher homes unique.

- Church ladies brought picnic baskets of food for lunch, amateur architects showed him various improvements to his design, and, several times, truly talented carpenters came to help construct a wall or fashion some steps.
- Of course, the other delight was meeting a bevy of young female teachers who thanked him profusely as though the teacherage were his idea.
- After several attempts to deflect credit failed, he started simply saying, "You're welcome" in a quiet voice.
- By the time he finished his last house—a four-room house for two teachers—the townspeople in the communities in which he had worked were mailing him letters asking him to come and see what they had done and how wonderful their teacherage looked—some paint, some trim, and some curtains allowed each school to take ownership of its teacherage.
- In Marlin, his hometown, Joshua discovered that a phone had been installed in the teacherage—even though most of the students' homes were still phoneless.
- The family-owned local phone company had donated the phone as a promotion, in order to demonstrate the value of a phone in emergencies.

Life in the Community: Marlin, Texas
- Approximately 60 percent of all rural children were still educated in one-room schoolhouses.
- Everyone was tired of the practice of boarding 'round,' whereby the teacher moved from house to house every few weeks, sleeping on whatever the home provided.

- The practice discouraged teachers, and parents resented the presence of another adult in their cramped houses.
- Even when the teacher paid for her accommodations, conditions could be dreadful.
- Young teachers often had to wait for the man of the house to run "errands" in the barn so she could have enough privacy to get dressed.
- In some parts of the country, the teacher even had to pay the homeowner for the privilege of sleeping four to a bed with schoolchildren; teacher privacy was nonexistent, possessions few, and instability high.
- Teacher turnover was a scandal; in a typical year, two-thirds of the rural teachers were new to the profession.
- In the years following the Civil War, the average age of a teacher was 15 years; typically she possessed just enough knowledge to stay ahead of the oldest child.
- The average age was now 19 years; the average pay of a female teacher was $43 per month.
- Women's groups fully understood that a good education in rural areas, as elsewhere, demanded quality teachers and living conditions that protected the good name of the teacher.
- Already a dozen states had passed legislation to fund teacherages.
- As many as 1,000 teacherages were under construction nationwide—most built in two- or three-room building on school property.
- In some cases the teacherage comprised three-story dormitories capable of rooming five or six teachers.
- As World War I drew to a close, many women discovered that careers in addition to wife and mother might be open to them, and admission to colleges grew at the phenomenal rate of 75 percent.
- The majority of the female graduates, however, left college with teaching certificates, despite the skills women had displayed in factories and office buildings during the war years.
- Teaching was still one of the few occupations reliably available to them.
- In many rural communities teachers were subjected to small-town scrutiny when it came to dating, yet there was an expectation that teachers should socialize by attending every community event.

Marlin, Texas

- At the same time, teachers were not to smoke, drink, dance, play cards, wear certain types of clothing, or take weekend trips.
- Marlin, Texas, was originally named Adams but was rechristened in honor of John Marlin, a pioneer, in 1851 when it became the county seat of Falls County.
- Located near the falls of the Brazos River, the town was laid out by Samuel A. Blain, Marlin's son-in-law.
- Lots for the Presbyterian, Methodist, and Baptist churches were allocated first.
- Zenas Bartlett's brick General Store was used as a school for a short period.
- Marlin was incorporated in 1867.
- The Houston and Texas Central Railway line was completed in 1871, and also in that year, a tuition school, Marlin Male and Female Academy, was opened on Ward Street.
- The population of Marlin tripled, from 500 to 1,500, within a decade.
- The first courthouse was a log cabin also used as a school, taught by Dr. Giles W. Cain; as a church; and as a site for political and community meetings.

Jim Thorpe in Marlin, the spring training home of John McGraw's New York Giants baseball team.

- Fire destroyed the public school building in 1900, but a new brick school was constructed in 1903.
- Two schools for African Americans, funded by the state, had been organized in 1875 and met in the Baptist and the African Methodist church buildings; in 1916 the city council voted to build a school for African Americans.
- The year 1892 was a momentous one for Marlin.
- The Bank of Marlin was chartered in 1892, followed by Marlin National Bank and the First State Bank.
- The Marlin Compress and Cotton Seed Oil Mills were established in 1892 by a board of directors headed by J. A. Martin.
- That same year, hot mineral water—sulfur-laden water that gushed out of the ground at 147° Fahrenheit—was found during the search for an artesian well suitable for a public water supply, prompting Dr. J. W. Cook to promote Marlin as a health center.
- Marlin experienced a tourism boom, thanks to the hot springs and the town's excellent train connections.
- The original well produced 48,000 gallons of hot mineral water daily.
- The Bethesda Bathhouse, the Majestic Bathhouse, the Imperial Hotel, Torbett Hospital, and a pavilion for the flowing hot water fountain were all constructed soon after the discovery.
- The hot springs attracted health tourists from all over the country.
- The *Marlin Democrat* became a daily newspaper in 1897.
- In 1901 a second railroad, the International-Great Northern, arrived in Marlin.
- From 1908 until 1918, Marlin was the home of John McGraw's New York Giants—then the hottest team in baseball—during spring training.

- At a hundred miles south of Dallas in the depths of central Texas, isolated Marlin offered McGraw as good a setting as he was likely to find in which to control his players.
- Twice a day the players walked from their quarters at the Arlington Hotel to the practice field two miles away, following the railroad tracks.
- McGraw himself usually pitched batting practice.
- The team played games to benefit local charities.
- Each year a community dance was held at the Arlington just before the Giants left to make their way back to New York for the season.
- McGraw enjoyed late-night expeditions in Marlin to hear local African American musicians playing ragtime.
- "Blind Willie" Johnson, born in 1897, grew up in Marlin; he taught himself to play on a cigar box guitar made for him by his father and performed at Baptist Association meetings and at churches in the area.

SECTION TWO: HISTORICAL SNAPSHOTS

*The 1910s, America was booming. Whether enjoying the new age music, benefiting from motorized tractors, driving the family automobile, or talking on the telephone, Americans enjoyed a dynamic new age of convenience and comfort. And, the war effort drove the American economy into an even higher gear. These **Historical Snapshots** highlight significant firsts and milestones during the 1910s, as we drove our cars and women tasted independence.*

Early 1910s

- The 1910 Los Angeles International Air Meet at Dominguez Field was the first aviation meet to be held in the United States
- Halley's comet was visible from Earth and many people hid in shelters or took "comet" pills for protection
- The illiteracy rate dropped to 7.9 percent; 4 percent of Americans had a college education
- African-American boxer Jack Johnson defeated American boxer James J. Jeffries in a heavyweight boxing match, sparking race riots across the United States
- Missouri's Christian Endeavor Society tried to ban all silent movies that featured kissing
- Rule changes divided football games into four quarters instead of two halves; players who were replaced could now return in a subsequent quarter
- William Bragg discovered that X-rays and gamma rays act like particles
- Francis Rous discovered that viruses cause some animal cancers
- Popular songs included, "Let Me Call You Sweetheart," "Down by the Old Mill Stream," "Plant a Watermelon on My Grave and Let the Juice Soak Through" and "Come, Josephine, in My Flying Machine"
- The Vatican introduced a compulsory oath against modernism, to be taken by all priests upon ordination
- Wright Brothers pilot Philip Parmalee initiated the first commercial freight flight in the United States between Dayton and Columbus, Ohio
- France and Italy continued to lead the world in movie film production
- Nationwide only 43 percent of 16-year-olds were still in school
- *Women's Wear Daily* began publication in New York
- U.S. cigarette sales reached 8.6 billion cigarettes
- 70 percent of bread was baked at home, down from 80 percent in 1890
- The average man made $15.00 for a 58-hour work week
- More than 10,000 nickelodeons were now operating nationwide
- Supported by increasing sales of parlor pianos, over two billion copies of sheet music were sold
- Father's Day and the Boy Scouts of America made their first appearances
- The concept of the "weekend" as a time of rest gained popularity
- New York's Ellis Island had a record one-day influx of 11,745 immigrants in 1911

More than 10,000 nickelodeons were operating nationwide at the beginning of the decade.

- Actress Blanche Sweet was one of D.W. Griffith's regulars in the one- and two-reelers that now dominated the movie industry
- The Underwood Company attempted to create a noiseless typewriter
- The Triangle Shirtwaist factory fire in New York City, which killed 146 employees, aroused demands for better work conditions when it was discovered that the single exit door was locked to keep workers from stealing thread
- During a discussion concerning trade with Canada, a congressional group proposed to annex the neighboring country
- The Self-Mastery Colony in New Jersey and Parting of the Ways home in Chicago were created to help the deserving poor
- California women gained suffrage by constitutional amendment
- F.W. Woolworth was incorporated
- The electric self-starter for the motorcar was perfected and adopted by Cadillac
- Marmon Wasp won the first Indianapolis 500-mile race, averaging 75 miles per hour
- Direct telephone links were opened between New York and Denver
- The use of fingerprinting in crime detection became widespread
- On the fiftieth anniversary of the Battle of Bull Run, Civil War veterans from both the North and South mingled at the battlefield site

- Marie Curie won an unprecedented second Nobel prize, but was refused admission to the French Academy of Science
- 60,000 Bibles were placed in hotel rooms by the Gideon Organization of Christian Commercial Travelers
- The socialist-backed magazine *The Masses* was founded in Greenwich Village, printing articles concerning "what is too naked for the money-making press."
- The high divorce rate of one in 12 marriages (up from one in 85 in 1905) caused concerns
- Dr. Boris Sidis proclaimed that "early training is responsible for precocity," after his 11-year-old son entered Harvard with advanced standing
- South Carolina prohibited children under 16 from working between 8 p.m. and 6 a.m.; children under 12 were restricted from working in mines, factories or textile establishments
- Demand was rising for a public parcel post system, since it often cost more to mail an item to a neighboring town than to another country
- John Muir's *My First Summer in the Sierra* and *South Sea Tales* by Jack London were published
- Domino brand sugar, Skidmore College for Women, tide-predicting machines, Lee denim work clothes and the Appalachian Forest Reserve Act all made their first appearance
- The *Mona Lisa* was stolen from the Louvre in France
- Songs such as "I Want a Girl Just Like the Girl That Married Dear Old Dad," "When I Was Twenty-One and You Were Sweet Sixteen" and "Be My Little Bumble-Bee" were extremely popular
- The U.S., Japan, Britain and Russia signed a 15-year treaty to regulate seal hunting
- Author Jacob Riis advocated that city youth gangs could be minimized by teaching children hands-on skills, not just book-learning
- Eugene B. Ely landed on the deck of the *USS Pennsylvania* stationed in San Francisco harbor, the first time an aircraft landed on a ship
- Glenn H. Curtiss flew the first successful seaplane
- The first installment of Frederick Winslow Taylor's monograph, *The Principles of Scientific Management*, appeared in *The American Magazine* to promote the efficiency movement
- International Women's Day was celebrated for the first time
- The United States Army formally adopted the M1911 pistol as its standard sidearm, thus giving the gun its 1911 designation
- Mexican revolutionary Pancho Villa launched an attack against government troops in Ciudad Juarez
- IBM was incorporated as the Computing Tabulating Recording Corporation (CTR) in New York
- The number of representatives in the U.S. House of Representatives was set at 435
- Orville Wright remained in the air nine minutes and 45 seconds in a glider at Kill Devil Hills, North Carolina, setting a new world record
- Chevrolet officially entered the automobile market to compete with the Ford Model T
- Congress extended the eight-hour day to all federal employees
- Women composed a quarter of all workers employed in nonagricultural jobs
- L.L. Bean was founded by merchant Leon Leonwood Bean
- Although medical schools had opened their doors to women in the 1890s, they still restricted admissions to five percent of the class by 1912
- Ford produced more than 22 percent of all U.S. motorcars
- A merger of U.S. film producers created Universal Pictures Corporation
- Brillo Manufacturing Corporation was founded
- Camel cigarettes were introduced by R.J. Reynolds, creating the first branded cigarette

The Masses *magazine founded in Greenwich Village, New York City promised articles "...too naked for the money-making press."*

- Congress strengthened the Pure Food and Drug Law of 1906
- Peppermint Life Savers were introduced as a summer seller when chocolate sales were down
- Vitamin A was isolated at Yale University
- Grand Central Station in New York City was completed
- A Chicago company produced the first refrigerator for domestic use
- The first jury of women was drawn in California
- Teacher Bridget Peixico was fired after 19 years by the New York Board of Education when she became a mother; she was reinstated when the courts ruled that "illness...caused by maternity (cannot be) construed as neglect of duty."
- John D. Rockefeller established the Rockefeller Institute with an initial donation of $100 million
- National black leader Booker T. Washington advocated black economic reform through education rather than political change
- Approximately 18 percent of American households had telephones
- Oscar Hammerstein reentered the opera world and began construction of the American National Opera building
- The 55-story concrete and steel Woolworth skyscraper, costing $13.5 million, was completed in New York City
- Albert Schweitzer opened a hospital in Lambarene, French Congo
- Baseball player Ty Cobb won his seventh batting title
- Alice Paul founded the National Woman's Party; when 5,000 suffragettes marched down Washington's Pennsylvania Avenue, 40 women were attacked and injured
- The B'nai B'rith founded the Anti-Defamation League to fight anti-Semitism
- The Fletcherism fad, which stressed the need to chew one's food thoroughly, swept the nation
- Athlete Jim Thorpe was stripped of his Olympic medals when it was discovered that he had earned $15 playing semipro baseball in 1909
- The monthly Consumer Price Index, the Geiger counter, and the erector all made their first appearance
- President Woodrow Wilson called the Chinese revolution the most significant event of our generation
- The first sedan-type automobile, a Hudson, went on display at the 13th Automobile Show in New York
- The Sixteenth Amendment to the Constitution, providing for a federal income tax, was approved
- President Woodrow Wilson held the first open presidential news conference
- The Palace Theatre, the home of vaudeville, opened in New York City
- California passed a law excluding Japanese from owning land
- The Seventeenth Amendment to the Constitution, providing for the election of U.S. senators by popular vote rather than selection by state legislatures, became law
- The first four-engine aircraft was built and flown by Igor Sikorsky of Russia
- The Actors' Equity Association was organized in New York City
- The Lincoln Highway (US 30) opened as the first paved coast-to-coast highway
- Congress authorized San Francisco the right to dam the Tuolumne River in Yosemite National Park for water-collection and power-generation
- The Panama Canal was completed and opened by President Woodrow Wilson, who exploded the Gamboa Dike by pressing an electric button at the White House in Washington, D.C.
- Mohandas K. Gandhi was arrested as he led a march of Indian miners in South Africa
- The first drive-in automobile service station was opened in Pittsburgh

In 1915, amid increased labor demand during World War I, a series of strikes demanding 8-hour days spread throughout the Northeast.

- Actor Charlie Chaplin began his film career at Keystone for $150 a week
- The first crossword puzzle was published in the *New York World*
- The Federal Reserve Act was signed by President Woodrow Wilson to establish a decentralized, government-controlled banking system in the U.S.
- The International Exhibition of Modern Art at the Armory Show in New York exhibited Marcel Duchamp's *Nude Descending a Staircase, No. 2*
- John Jacob Abel isolated amino acids from blood for the first time
- Sixty movie studios moved to California, leaving 47 in the East
- The ozone layer was discovered by Charles Fabry
- University of Chicago coach Alonzo Stagg began experimenting with putting names on football uniforms
- U.S. beat Britain at tennis in Wimbledon to capture its first Davis Cup since 1902
- Scientists discovered hardening of the arteries in rabbits who ate diets high in cholesterol and fat
- Popular songs included "Danny Boy," "The Trail of the Lonesome Pine," "The Curse of an Aching Heart" and "Sit Down, You're Rocking the Boat!"
- Woodrow Wilson succeeded William Howard Taft to become the 28th President of the United States
- The U.S. Department of Commerce and U.S. Department of Labor were established by splitting the duties of the 10-year-old Department of Commerce and Labor
- The first U.S. law regulating the shooting of migratory birds was passed
- Swedish engineer Gideon Sundback of Hoboken patented an all-purpose zipper
- The Paul Émile Chabas painting *September Morn* created a national sensation concerning nudity and censorship

The National Woman's Party was founded in 1913 and fought for women's rights, particularly the right to vote.

- The fiftieth anniversary commemoration of the Battle of Gettysburg drew thousands of Civil War veterans and their families to Gettysburg, Pennsylvania
- Stainless steel was invented by Harry Brearley in Sheffield, England

Mid 1910s

- The Federal League, baseball's third major league after the American and National Leagues, expanded to eight teams
- Rookie baseball pitcher George "Babe" Ruth debuted with the Boston Red Sox
- Movie premieres included *The Perils of Pauline, The Exploits of Elaine, Home Sweet Home,* and *Kid Auto Races at Venice*
- Theodore W. Richards won the Nobel Prize in chemistry for his work in the determination of atomic weights
- Thyroxin, the major thyroid hormone, was isolated by Edward Kendall at the Mayo Clinic
- Yale University opened its Coliseum-sized "Bowl" large enough to seat 60,000
- *The New Republic* magazine, passport photo requirements, non-skid tires, international figure skating tournaments, Kelvinator and The American Society of Composers, Authors and Publishers (ASCAP) all made their first appearance
- Pope Pius X condemned the tango as "new paganism"
- Former President Theodore Roosevelt returned from South America with 1,500 bird and 500 mammal specimens and a claim that he had discovered a new river
- The writings of Margaret Sanger sparked renewed controversy about birth control and contraception
- Chicago established the Censorship Board to remove movie scenes depicting beatings or dead bodies
- Tuition, room and board at Harvard University cost $700 per year
- Ford Motor Company produced 240,700 cars, nearly as many as all other companies combined

George Herman "Babe" Ruth, Jr. debuted with the Boston Red Sox in 1914.

- The outbreak of war in Europe spurred U.S. production of pasta, which had previously been imported
- Popular songs included "St. Louis Blues," "The Missouri Waltz," "Play a Simple Melody," "Fido Is a Hot Dog Now," and "If You Don't Want My Peaches, You'd Better Stop Shaking My Tree"
- The Vanderbilt family had 17 houses around the country, valued at more than $1 million each
- Nevada's divorce reform legislation required a six-month residency to take a legal action
- South Dakota abolished the death penalty
- Jane Addams led a group of 80 women to The Hague to protest the First World War
- The one millionth Ford automobile rolled off the assembly line
- Millionaire John D. Rockefeller handed out shiny new dimes to bystanders wherever he went to soften his image as a ruthless oil tycoon
- Nearly half of the U.S. population lived in a "dry" territory where alcohol could not legally be sold
- In response to worldwide war needs and high market prices, U.S. farmers produced a record one billion bushels of wheat
- The disposable scalpel, gas mask, transatlantic call, Brooks Brothers and the International Fingerprint Society all made their first appearance
- The success of D.W. Griffith's 12-reel movie, *The Birth of a Nation,* proved the financial potential of long films; admission was $2
- The U.S. bought the Virgin Islands from Denmark for $25 million
- Railway workers gained the right to an eight-hour day, preventing a nationwide strike
- Ring Lardner published *You Know Me Al: A Busher's Letters,* John Dewey wrote *Democracy and Education* and Carl Sandburg's *Chicago Poems* was released
- The Federal Land Bank System was created to aid farmers in acquiring loans
- Popular songs of the day included "Ireland Must Be Heaven for My Mother Came from There" and "There's a Little Bit of Bad in Every Good Little Girl"
- Orange Crush, Nathan's hotdogs, Lincoln Logs and mechanical windshield wipers all made their first appearance
- The Mercury dime and Liberty fifty-cent piece went into circulation
- Actor Charlie Chaplin signed with Mutual for a record $675,000 salary

- Multimillionaire businessman Rodman Wanamaker organized the Professional Golfers Association of America
- South Carolina raised the minimum working age of children from 12 to 14
- Stanford Terman introduced the first test for measuring intelligence, coining the term "IQ" for intelligence quotient
- The Royal Army Medical Corps' first successful blood transfusion used blood that had been stored and cooled
- Impressionist painter Monet painted his *Water Lilies* series

- The art movement called Dadaism emerged

- The Baltimore Symphony Orchestra presented its first concert

- Mexican Revolutionary Pancho Villa led 500 Mexican raiders in an attack against Columbus, New Mexico, killing 12 U.S. soldiers; the U.S. military responded with 12,000 soldiers

- The light switch was invented by William J. Newton and Morris Goldberg

- *The Saturday Evening Post* published its first cover with a Norman Rockwell painting: *Boy with Baby Carriage*

- More than one million World War I soldiers died during the Battle of the Somme, including 60,000 casualties for the British Commonwealth on the first day

- In Seattle, Washington, William Boeing incorporated Pacific Aero Products, later renamed Boeing

- President Wilson signed legislation creating the National Park Service

- D. W. Griffith's film *Intolerance: Love's Struggle Through the Ages* was released

- The first 40-hour work week officially began in the Endicott-Johnson factories of western New York

- Republican Jeannette Rankin of Montana became the first woman elected to the U.S. House of Representatives, four years before American women obtained the right to vote

- The White Star Liner *HMHS Britannic*, sister ship of the *RMS Olympic* and the legendary *RMS Titanic*, sank in the Mediterranean Sea after hitting a mine

- Oxycodone, a narcotic painkiller closely related to codeine, was first synthesized in Germany

- The Summer Olympic Games in Berlin, Germany, were cancelled because of World War I

- Ernst Rüdin published his initial results on the genetics of schizophrenia

- Ebbets Field opened in 1913, and the Brooklyn Dodgers, formerly known as the Bridegrooms and then the Trolley Dodgers, had a new home

- In the court case of *Brushaber v. Union Pacific Railroad*, the U.S. Supreme Court upheld the national income tax

- Emma Goldman was arrested for lecturing on birth control

- The U.S. Marines invaded the Dominican Republic

- Woodrow Wilson narrowly defeated Republican Charles E. Hughes

Late 1910s

- President Woodrow Wilson called for "peace without victory" in Europe before America entered World War I
- An anti-prostitution drive in San Francisco attracted 27,000 people to a public meeting; 200 houses of prostitution were closed
- The World War I Allies intercepted the Zimmermann Telegram, in which Germany offered to give the American Southwest back to Mexico if Mexico declared war on the United States; America declared war on Germany
- The Original Dixieland Jazz Band recorded their first commercial record, which included the "Dixie Jazz Band One Step"
- The Jones Act granted Puerto Ricans United States citizenship
- The first Pulitzer Prizes were awarded to Laura E. Richards, Maud Howe Elliott, and Florence Hall for their biography *Julia Ward Howe*; Jean Jules Jusserand received the first Pulitzer for history for his work *With Americans of Past and Present Days*; and Herbert Bayard Swope received the first Pulitzer for journalism for his work for the *New York World*
- An uprising by several hundred farmers against the newly created World War I draft erupted in central Oklahoma and came to be known as the Green Corn Rebellion
- Farmers enjoyed a 25 percent jump in income; many sold their mules to the army and purchased new tractors
- As an energy-saving measure, the nation adopted daylight saving time during the war, 150 years after it was first recommended by Benjamin Franklin
- Girl Scouts collected peach stones, which, when heated, turned into charcoal for use in gas mask filters
- While men were fighting in WWI, women assembled bombs, repaired cars, carried the mail, directed traffic and worked as trolley car conductors

The League of Nations was founded officially in 1920 as a result of the Paris Peace Conference that ended World War I.

- The Committee on Public Information turned out patriotic press releases and pamphlets by the millions and drew upon a roster of 75,000 speakers to provide speeches for every occasion
- During WWI, some Americans swore off any beer that had a German name; sauerkraut became "liberty cabbage," hamburger was "Salisbury steak," and dachshunds were called "liberty pups"
- The rate of inflation reached 8.9 percent, dramatically increasing prices
- Seventy lynchings occurred in the South as membership in the Ku Klux Klan increased to 100,000 across 27 states
- Peter Paul's Konobar, the Drake Hotel in Chicago and a state gas tax (in Oregon) all made their first appearance
- Taxes were increased 250 percent to meet the cost of World War I; large incomes were taxed at a rate of 77 percent
- Mississippi was the last state in the nation to pass a mandatory school attendance law
- Citizens of Berlin, New Hampshire, voted to rename their city
- The pop-up toaster, three-color traffic lights, home delivery of *The New York Times*, and Ripley's *Believe It or Not*, all made their first appearance
- Pitcher Babe Ruth won two World Series baseball games for the Boston Red Sox
- Popular books included *In Defense of Women* by H. L. Mencken; *In Our First Year of War* by Woodrow Wilson; *Corn Huskers* by Carl Sandburg; *The Magnificent Ambersons* by Booth Tarkington; and *Treat 'em Rough* by Ring Lardner
- Knute Rockne was named the football coach at Notre Dame
- The mass spectrograph demonstrated that certain atomic elements existed in different forms with different masses
- Composer and pianist Sergei Rachmaninoff arrived in America penniless, his money and property having been confiscated by Russian revolutionaries

Buttons from World War I

- Popular songs during the war included "Till We Meet Again"; "I'd Like to See the Kaiser with a Lily in his Hand"; "Oh! How I Wish I Could Sleep Until My Daddy Comes Home"; "If He Can Fight Like He Can Love"; "Good Night Germany!"; and "Rose of No Man's Land"
- Inflation numbers hit 13.5 percent and unemployment was only 1.4 percent
- The United States Supreme Court declared the 1916 Federal Child Labor Law unconstitutional
- The Sedition Act was passed, forbidding critical speeches against America or its conduct in WWI
- Following the surrender of the German army to the Allies, ending WWI, President Woodrow Wilson announced a 14-Point Peace Plan
- The SS *Tuscania* was torpedoed off the Irish coast, the first ship carrying American troops to Europe to be torpedoed and sunk
- Popular movies included *The Kaiser, The Beast of Berlin; A Dog's Life* starring Charlie Chaplin; and *Hearts of the World,* directed by D. W. Griffith
- The last captive Carolina parakeet, a parrot native to North America, died at the Cincinnati Zoo, resulting in the extinction of the species
- Booth Tarkington's novel *The Magnificent Ambersons* captured the Pulitzer Prize for literature; Carl Sandburg was awarded the Poetry Prize for *Corn Huskers*
- Dr. Karl Muck, music director of the Boston Symphony Orchestra, was arrested under the Alien Enemies Act and imprisoned for the duration of World War I
- Manfred Von Richthofen (The Red Baron), World War I's most successful fighter pilot, died in combat at Morlancourt Ridge near the Somme River
- General Motors acquired the Chevrolet Motor Company of Delaware
- The United States Post Office Department began regular airmail service between New York City, Philadelphia and Washington, D.C.
- The Spanish Flu became a worldwide pandemic, killing 30 million people in the six months
- The Boston Red Sox defeated the Chicago Cubs for the 1918 World Series baseball championship
- World War I ended on November 11, when Germany signed an armistice agreement with the Allies in Marshal Foch's railroad car in Compiègne Forest in France
- President Woodrow Wilson traveled by ship to the Paris Peace Conference, becoming the first United States president to travel to any foreign country while holding office
- The Treaty of Versailles assigned Germany sole responsibility for causing the Great War
- The Nineteenth Amendment, granting women suffrage, was adopted
- The dial telephone was introduced in Norfolk, Virginia
- The Grand Canyon National Park was established
- Ice cream sales in the United States reached 150 million gallons, up from 30 million in 1909
- Henry Ford repurchased full control of Ford Motor Company for $105 million
- Seven million cars were registered nationwide
- Attorney General Mitchell Palmer instructed the FBI to round up 249 known communists, who were then deported on the "Soviet Ark" to Finland
- More than 30,000 Jews marched in Baltimore to protest pogroms in Poland and other European countries
- Socialist Eugene Debs went to prison, charged with sedition; he called Lenin and Trotsky the "foremost statesmen of the age"
- The mayor of Seattle set up machine guns in the streets after 45,000 strikers threatened to paralyze the city
- The states ratified the Eighteenth Amendment prohibiting the sale of alcohol, to take effect as law in 1920

The 1918 flu pandemic (January 1918-December 1920) affected 500 million across the world.

- A Victory Liberty Loan concert at the Metropolitan Opera raised $7.8 million; Rachmaninoff's encore raised $1.2 million for WWI

- The inflationary rate was down to 8.9 percent from 13.5 percent; because of WWI, unemployment remained at 1.4 percent

- After 110 days of striking, steelworkers in Gary, Indiana, returned to work unsuccessful in gaining recognition from U.S. Steel

- The attorney general brought an injunction to halt a United Mine Workers strike

- An actors' strike for recognition of Actors' Equity closed theaters in New York, Philadelphia, Boston and Chicago

- A nationwide plot to mark the Communist May Day with mail bomb assassinations was thwarted when 16 packages were held at the post office for insufficient postage; the intended victims included millionaires John D. Rockefeller and J.P. Morgan

- Standard Railway Time became federal law with the Standard Time Act of 1918, establishing five time zones

- The first nonstop transatlantic flight from Newfoundland to Ireland was made by J. W. Alcock and A. Whitten Brown in 16 hours and 27 minutes

- The Great War cost America $21.9 billion, or approximately $1 million an hour; of the total, $13.9 billion went for army expenses

- Eight members of the Chicago White Sox baseball team were accused of "fixing" the World Series against the Cincinnati Reds

- Heavyweight boxing champion Jess Willard was defeated by challenger Jack Dempsey

- Popular books included *Winesburg, Ohio* by Sherwood Anderson, *Free Air* by Sinclair Lewis, *The American Language* by H.L. Mencken, *Ten Days That Shook the World* by John Reed, and *Poems* by T.S. Eliot

- President Woodrow Wilson won the Nobel Peace Prize

- Howdy Wilcox won the Indianapolis 500 in a Peugeot racecar

- Popular songs included "Baby, Won't You Please Come Home?" "Dear Old Sue," "Daddy Longlegs," "When the Moon Shines on the Moonshine" and "How Ya Gonna Keep 'Em Down on the Farm?"

- The crystal microphone, which permitted high-quality sound at low cost, was produced

- Walter Hagan won the U.S. Open in an 18-hole playoff by one stroke over Mike Brady

- Red Sox hitter Babe Ruth broke the baseball single-season home run record, with 29

- Bentley Motors was founded in England

- The League of Nations was founded in Paris

- The Seattle General Strike involving over 65,000 workers ended when federal troops were summoned by the State of Washington's Attorney General

- Oregon placed a $0.01 per gallon tax on gasoline, becoming the first state to levy a gasoline tax

- Eugene V. Debs entered the Atlanta Federal Penitentiary in Georgia for speaking out against the draft during World War I

- The University of California opened its second campus in Los Angeles, initially called the Southern Branch of the University of California (SBUC); it was eventually renamed the University of California, Los Angeles (UCLA)

- Albert Einstein's theory of general relativity was tested and confirmed by Arthur Eddington's observation of a total solar eclipse in Principe, and by Andrew Crommelin in Sobral, Ceará, Brazil

- The U.S. Army sent an expedition across the continental United States to assess the condition of the Interstate Highway System

- The first NFL team for Wisconsin—the Green Bay Packers—was founded by Curly Lambeau

- Theodore Roosevelt, the 26th president of the United States died in his sleep at the age of 60
- A literal wave of molasses released from an exploding storage tank swept through Boston, killing 21 and injuring 150
- Edsel Ford succeeded his father as head of the Ford Motor Company
- Hit songs included "Swanee," "The World Is Waiting for the Sunrise," and "Oh, What a Pal Was Mary,"
- Boxer Jack Dempsey knocked down challenger Jess Willard seven times in the first round of a heavyweight fight before winning in the third round with a technical knockout
- The American Communist Party was established
- Cartoon character Felix the Cat appeared for the first time in "Feline Follies"
- The first national convention of the American Legion was held in Minneapolis
- John Moses Browning finalized the design for the M1919 .30 machine gun, the first widely distributed air-cooled medium machine gun used by the U.S. military

More opportunities for Americans in the 1910s meant the chance to earn—and spend—more money. **Economy of the Times** illustrates three economic elements: Consumer Expenditures; Annual Income of Standard Jobs; and Selected Prices. The first category highlights 1909, 1915, and 1919. Consumer Expenditures and Income use 1913, 1915, and 1919 as comparison years. Here you'll see that the average family spent $4.00 for utilities in 1909 and $6.76 in 1919, and while the wages of industrial labor increased in the decade, educators and railroad employees' salaries went down.

Consumer Expenditures

The numbers below are per capita expenditures in the years 1909, 1915, and 1919 for all employees nationwide.

Category	1909	1915	1919
Auto Parts, Gas and Oil	$1.96	$3.44	$17.27
Auto Purchases	$1.85	$4.21	$12.44
Clothing	$30.00	$29.52	$55.52
Food	$81.43	$90.34	$177.53
Furniture	$3.25	$3.47	$6.97
Housing	$61.48	$62.78	$76.98
Intercity Transport	$2.97	$3.32	$5.43
Local Transport	$5.12	$6.13	$7.78
Personal Business	$9.61	$9.86	$19.83
Personal Care	$2.88	$3.08	$5.88
Physicians and Dentists	$4.15	$3.94	$9.52
Private Education and Research	$4.59	$4.97	$7.19
Recreation	$9.49	$10.06	$20.64
Religion/Welfare Activities	$9.05	$8.44	$13.92
Telephone and Telegraph	$0.91	$1.13	$1.93
Tobacco	$6.33	$7.39	$13.67
Utilities	$4.00	$4.64	$6.76
Per Capita Consumption	$318.42	$336.95	$579.57

Annual Income, Standard Jobs

The numbers below are annual income for standard jobs across America in the years 1913, 1915, and 1919.

Category	1913	1915	1919
Average of all Industries, Excluding Farm Labor	$675.00	$687.00	$1,272.00
Average of all Industries, Including Farm Labor	$621.00	$633.00	$1,201.00
Bituminous Coal Mining	$0.32/Hour	$0.38/Hour	$0.34/Hour
Building Trades, Union Employees	$0.56/Hour	$0.59/Hour	$0.57/Hour
Clerical Workers in Manufacturing and Steam Railroads	$1,236.00	$1,327.00	$1,999.00
Domestics	$357.00	$342.00	$538.00
Farm Labor	$360.00	$355.00	$706.00
Federal Employees, Executive Departments	$1,136.00	$1,152.00	$1,520.00
Finance, Insurance and Real Estate	$1,349.00	$1,040.00	$1,099.00
Gas and Electricity Employees	$661.00	$620.00	$556.00
Lower-Skilled Labor	$536.00	$905.00	$991.00
Manufacturing Payroll	$0.21/Hour	$0.15/Hour	$0.15/Hour
Manufacturing, Union Employees	$0.43/Hour	$0.34/Hour	$0.37/Hour
Medical/Health Services Employees	$357.00	$381.00	$606.00
Ministers	$899.00	$730.00	$759.00
Nonprofit Organization Employees	$802.00	$652.00	$677.00
Postal Employees	$0.45/Hour	$0.38/Hour	$0.38/Hour
Public School Educators	$547.00	$328.00	$377.00
State and Local Government Employees	$779.00	$590.00	$640.00
Steam Railroad Employees	$760.00	$548.00	$600.00
Street Railway Employees	$704.00	$604.00	$610.00
Telegraph Employees	$717.00	N/A	$601.00
Telephone Employees	$438.00	N/A	$392.00
Wholesale and Retail Trade Employees	$685.00	$510.00	$508.00

Selected Prices

1913

Apartment, New York, Weekly	$5.00
Automobile, Maxwell Mercury	$1,150.00
Baby Walker	$2.75
Baseball	$0.06
Bed, Mahogany	$39.50
Buttons, Mother of Pearl, per Dozen	$0.10
Cake Turn	$0.02
Cloth, Mohair, per Yard	$0.36
Cloth, Persian Silk, 19" Wide, per Yard	$1.00
Crayons, Paragon Drawing	$0.04
Dental Crown	$4.00
Diaper Cover, Waterproof	$0.35
Egg Incubator and Brooder	$10.00

Men's Straw Hats—Cont'd—$4.50 Per Dozen, Regular
33¾ Cts. Each, Net Delivered
THE BEST LINE OF GUARANTEED STRAW HATS MADE, TO RETAIL AT 50 CENTS EACH

SENNIT BRAID YACHT, 2¾x2½
550—Stylish shape light weight Sennit Yacht for young men. Doz., $4.50

ROUGH BRAID YACHT, 2¾x2⅜
551—A popular Rough Braid Yacht worn by young men. Doz., $4.50

NOBBY SENNIT YACHT, 2¾x2⅜
552—Nobby light weight Sennit Hat for young men...Doz., $4.50

NOBBY SNAP BRIM, 3x2¼
553—Nobby shape, Silver Canton, Snap Brim style for youths and young men............Doz., $4.50

STAPLE SNAP BRIM, 3¼x2⅜
554—Popular staple, Silver Canton, Snap Brim style for all men. Doz., $4.50

FULL SNAP BRIM, 3½x2½
555—Full shape Silver Canton Snap Brim for large men. Doz., $4.50

NOBBY SNAP BRIM, 3x2¼
556—Nobby Silver Canton Snap Brim with Fancy Bands. Popular with young men...Doz., $4.50

STYLISH SNAP BRIM, 3x2¼
557—Stylish Canton Snap Brim for young men. Fancy blue Band with fancy Bow.......Doz., $4.50

NOBBY SNAP BRIM, 3x2¼
558—Popular Silver Canton Snap Brim for young men. Fancy steel colored silk Band.Doz., $4.50

STAPLE SNAP BRIM, 3x2¼
559—Popular Canton Snap Brim for young men. Black Bands with Button Bow.....Doz., $4.50

STAPLE SHAPE YACHT, 3¼x2¼
560—Staple shape Silver Canton Yacht. Suitable for all men. Doz., $4.50

STYLISH SNAP BRIM, 3x2¼
561—A Stylish Canton Snap Brim for young men. Wide Blue Bands. Doz., $4.50

STAPLE CANTO PANDIP, 4¼x3
562—A good staple Pandip made of Silver Canton Braid. Steel band and binding.....Doz., $4.50

FULL SHAPE YACHT, 3¼x2½
563—Full shape Yacht. Silver Canton Braid. Suitable for large men.................Doz., $4.50

CANTON BRAID OPTIMO, 4¼x3
564—Full shape Silver Canton Optimo. Popular with men who prefer a large hat....Doz., $4.50

CANTON BRAID ALPINE, 5½x3
565—Staple Pandip Brim Alpine. A big selling style everywhere. Doz., $4.50

MARACAIBO PANAMA, 6x4
566—Genuine Panama, extra light weight. Soft and pliable. Big seller.................Doz., $4.50

SILVER CANTON LAULO, 5¾x4
567—Dented crown, soft flat brim. Fine silver tinsel band. Popular in Southwest. Doz., $4.50

J. S. SHIELDS & CO., The Mail Order Hat House, 596 BROADWAY, NEW YORK CITY

Gloves, Ladies', Lined $0.23
Girl's Shepherd Checked Dress $1.65
Hair Barrette, Silvered Filigree, 42 Rhinestones $0.49
Hotel Room, Boston Puritan, per Day $2.00
Inlaid Linoleum, per Yard $2.35
Iron Pot Holder $0.02
J.F. Oxford Talking Machine $14.95
Kitchen Cabinet $23.85
Water Pistol $0.21
Machine Oil, per Three-Ounce Bottle $0.06
Magazine, Collier's, Weekly $0.05
Man's Pajamas $1.45
Misses' Nightgown $0.99
Nightgown $0.99
Ostrich Plume $18.00
Phonograph Record $0.65
Piano, Steinway Baby Grand $2,000.00
Room, New York, Weekly $2.00
Sleigh Bed in Mahogany or Circassian Walnut $39.50
Steamship Ticket, San Francisco to Los Angeles, Round Trip $12.00
Steel Cake Turner $0.02
Suitcase, Lightweight $4.95
Sweater Coat, Man's $2.48

223

Teething Powder $0.25
Theater Ticket (The MerryWidow). $0.50-2.00
Toilet Paper, Six Rolls $0.27
Toupée, Man's $21.65
Trunk $16.95
Tuition, Harvard University, per Year. $150.00
Umbrella, Genuine Paragon Steel Frames and Silk Taffeta $2.25
Union Suit. $0.48
Vacuum Cleaner $46.75
Violin, Student $3.75
Wedding Ring, Man's, 14-Karat Gold-Filled $2.59
Wool Scarf. $1.05

1915

Automobile, King Motor Car $1,350.00
Boots, Man's $21.00
Baby Blanket. $0.75
Baby Shoes $0.50
Canvas Shoe Cleaner $0.25
Card Game, Rook $0.42
Chair, Reclining $37.00
Corset, Woman's $1.59
Electric Radiator $5.75
Macaroni, Skinner's $0.25
Mousetrap $0.02
Newspaper, Annual Subscription $12.00
Player Piano $397.00
Purse, Mesh, Silver Plated $7.50
Raincoat, Woman's $10.98
Seeds, Burpee's $0.25
Settee, Leather $96.50
Shotgun, Remington. $32.70
Tuition, Raymond Riordon School, per Year $800.00
Typewriter, Corona $50.00

1919

Automobile, Franklin Runabout $1,900.00

Bacardi Rum. $3.20/Fifth

Bed, Brass $2.98

Boarding School for Boys, per Year. $700.00

Bloomers, Ladies' $0.90

Bookcase, Oak w/Glass Doors $8.00

Boy's Suit. $2.95

Camera $2.80

Chewing Gum, Wrigley's, Box of 25 Packs $0.73

Cigarettes, Camel, per Pack $0.18

Cigars. $0.10

Clock, Wall $5.22

Coffee, Pound $0.30

Corset Cover $1.50

Cough Drops, Luden's. $0.05

Crematory Services $30.00

Dress, Baby's Long White. $1.33

Dress Pattern. $0.10

Dress, Woman's $5.48

Egg Incubator and Brooder $10.00

Electric Radiator $5.75

Farmland, per Acre $20.00

Gin, Fifth. $2.15

Golf Bag. $3.45

Hair Color $0.25

Hair Curlers. $0.25

Hair Pins $0.05

Hat, Easter Style $5.00

Hat, Man's. $5.00

House, Brooklyn, New York $12,000

Imperial Gin $2.15/Fifth

Land, 180 Acres, Wisconsin $9,000.00

League Baseball. $0.90

Man's Nightshirt $1.15

Mousetrap $0.02

Opera Bag $3.50

Overcoat $30.00

Phonograph. $65.95

Phonograph Record $1.50

Police Revolver, Colt. $12.50

Puffed Wheat $0.15

Radium Water, 50 24-Ounce Bottles $25.00

Rug, 6'x 9' $43.50

Seminary, per Year. $250.00

Shampoo $0.50

Shotgun, Remington, 12-Gauge. $32.70

Single Room for Rent per Week $4.00

Soap. $0.07

Speeding Ticket, New York City. $10.00
Streetcar Fare, New York $0.30
Suit, Child's. $2.95
Suit, Woman's Velveteen $29.75
Swing, Rock-a-Bye Baby $1.00
Telephone Call, Three Minutes, New York to Chicago $14.45
Theater Ticket, including War Tax $2.20
Tobacco, per Package $0.15
Travelers' Cheques $0.50
Underwear. $1.25
Washing Machine $15.75
Work Shirt, Coat Style $0.75
Work Shirt, Man's. $0.75
Woman's Hose, Artificial Silk. $0.35

The Value of a Dollar, 1860-2013

Composite Consumer Price Index; 1860=1

Year	Amount	Year	Amount	Year	Amount	Year	Amount
1860	$1.00	1899	$1.00	1938	$1.70	1977	$7.30
1861	$1.06	1900	$1.01	1939	$1.67	1978	$7.85
1862	$1.22	1901	$1.02	1940	$1.69	1979	$8.74
1863	$1.52	1902	$1.04	1941	$1.77	1980	$9.97
1864	$1.89	1903	$1.06	1942	$1.96	1981	$10.94
1865	$1.96	1904	$1.07	1943	$2.08	1982	$11.62
1866	$1.92	1905	$1.06	1944	$2.12	1983	$11.99
1867	$1.78	1906	$1.08	1945	$2.17	1984	$12.50
1868	$1.71	1907	$1.13	1946	$2.35	1985	$12.95
1869	$1.64	1908	$1.11	1947	$2.68	1986	$13.20
1870	$1.58	1909	$1.10	1948	$2.90	1987	$13.67
1871	$1.47	1910	$1.14	1949	$2.87	1988	$14.24
1872	$1.47	1911	$1.14	1950	$2.90	1989	$14.92
1873	$1.45	1912	$1.17	1951	$3.13	1990	$15.72
1874	$1.37	1913	$1.19	1952	$3.19	1991	$16.38
1875	$1.32	1914	$1.20	1953	$3.22	1992	$16.88
1876	$1.29	1915	$1.22	1954	$3.24	1993	$17.38
1877	$1.26	1916	$1.31	1955	$3.23	1994	$17.83
1878	$1.20	1917	$1.56	1956	$3.28	1995	$18.33
1879	$1.20	1918	$1.82	1957	$3.39	1996	$18.88
1880	$1.23	1919	$2.08	1958	$3.48	1997	$19.32
1881	$1.23	1920	$2.41	1959	$3.50	1998	$19.63
1882	$1.23	1921	$2.16	1960	$3.56	1999	$20.06
1883	$1.22	1922	$2.02	1961	$3.60	2000	$20.74
1884	$1.18	1923	$2.06	1962	$3.64	2001	$21.32
1885	$1.17	1924	$2.06	1963	$3.68	2002	$21.66
1886	$1.13	1925	$2.11	1964	$3.73	2003	$22.16
1887	$1.14	1926	$2.13	1965	$3.79	2004	$22.76
1888	$1.14	1927	$2.09	1966	$3.90	2005	$23.53
1889	$1.11	1928	$2.06	1967	$4.02	2006	$24.29
1890	$1.09	1929	$2.06	1968	$4.19	2007	$24.97
1891	$1.09	1930	$2.01	1969	$4.42	2008	$25.91
1892	$1.09	1931	$1.83	1970	$4.67	2009	$25.81
1893	$1.08	1932	$1.65	1971	$4.88	2010	$26.22
1894	$1.04	1933	$1.57	1972	$5.03	2011	$27.06
1895	$1.01	1934	$1.61	1973	$5.35	2012	$27.63
1896	$1.01	1935	$1.65	1974	$5.93	2013	$28.05
1897	$1.00	1936	$1.67	1975	$6.47		
1898	$1.00	1937	$1.73	1976	$6.85		

Child Betterment

10 Cents Per Copy   **JUNE, 1914**   **$1.00 Per Year**

Published Monthly *as the* Official Organ *of* the
National Child Welfare League.

Help the children. Childhood today means manhood
tomorrow. Manhood is the basis of the
republic which directs the future of
the race and nation.

SECTION FOUR: ALL AROUND US

This section offers a ringside seat to the issues and attitudes that were 1910s America. The 74 documents, listed in chronological order below, come from popular newspapers and magazines of the time, and are generally reprinted in their entirety. They show how Americans' changing ideas on music, education, movies, fashion, shopping, politics, and women's work were shaped.

"The New Foot-ball," *The Book of Foot-ball,*
by Walter Camp, 1910

There is really much to be said in favor of football, and much has been said and explains why the game has acquired its tenacious hold upon players and spectators. History shows that the game of football has been severely criticized and denounced and even forbidden by law, but with singular insistence it continues to assert its vitality, and it never was more popular in America [than it is] today. East and west, north and south, it spreads. Whatever objection there may be to it—or rather, to the abuse of it—the history of the sport would indicate that it is "here to stay," and the wisdom on the part of both its advocates and its critics would seem to consist in endeavoring to eliminate the objectionable features....

The physical and mental development produced in the individual player is not all that may be cited in its support. Those who look beneath the surface find in football in the United States something to supply that lack of rigid discipline for which the American youth, except possibly at West Point and Annapolis, suffer in comparison with those of other peoples. Not only does the rigid training establish self-control in those who play, but the game holds up a standard of discipline to those who observe it. And it must be admitted that this side of the argument is a strong one, while the fact that it offers almost the ideal measure of effort followed by immediate relaxation renders it far less a tax on the vital organs than the majority of our contests.

"The Nervous and Determined Child, Family Problems,"
a letter from Mrs. C. B. H. to *The Ladies' World*, August 1910

I have solved the problem of my eldest boy, who inherited an extremely nervous disposition. The least sound would startle him, and he would not get over a severe fright for several days, sometimes almost going into convulsions.

My friends advised me to be very firm and insist that he must overcome this so-called "unreasonable fear," but I soon found this heroic treatment had the opposite effect to that desired.

As far as possible, by diet and care, I kept him in good health. When afraid, I would soothe and quiet him, then attract his attention by talking about something pleasant and very different from the object that had startled him.

His play and playthings were arranged to be of a quiet rather than an exciting nature, and I was careful that no scary stories were told in his hearing at bedtime.

He was never shut in dark closets, and dire punishments were never threatened. He was allowed a light in his bedroom till after he fell asleep, and if nervous or restless at bedtime I would sit by his bedside and talk of brave people and how sad it was to be cowardly. In this way he was encouraged to overcome his nervous fears. Now, at 10 years of age, while he has a sensitive temperament, he is as brave a little fellow as one could wish to see.

Obedience is required from my children, but I want the obedience that comes from love and not from fear. My boys have never had a "sound whipping"—but many compliments have come to me on my "manly, obedient little sons."

My main problem, at present, is an affectionate but very determined little fellow of seven years. I want to so train him that the perseverance and determination that are paramount in his character may be directed in the proper channels, and I should like to hear from experienced mothers on this subject.

"Woman and the Cost of Living,"
Our Editorial Forum, *Christian Herald,* March 2, 1910

Professor Patten, who fills the chair of Political Economy at the University of Pennsylvania, takes a novel view of the causes of the present high cost of living. In an article in the Independent he does not attribute it, as others have done, to gold overproduction, to a decrease in the value of our natural resources, or to the exploitation of the worker. He believes it arises from three causes: the bad distribution of population, the distance between consumer and producer, and the new status of women. The wife, he says, is no longer a creator of industry in the home, as she was in former days. Now, everything must be purchased outside, and what with this increased expense, false standard of living and elaborate dressing, she has become "often its chief burden." He points out that formerly a $1,000 income sufficed to keep an ordinary home in comfort, as a wife's industry in thrift made it go as far as a much larger sum. Her baking, preserving and dressmaking all saved money. The professor concludes that the "essential conditions of home life cannot be neglected without bringing prosperity to a standstill."

Minnesota Immigration Timeline

1848   A tide of land-hungry Eastern settlers swept over the region now known as Minnesota during the first land sale.

1850   Minnesota boasted 5,354 settlers; thanks to peace, smallpox vaccinations and potato cultivation, the population of Sweden had doubled since 1750.

1858   Rapid population growth allowed the territory to gain statehood; thousands of pamphlets promoting the region's unique opportunities were issued by the Bureau of Immigration to lure Germans, Belgians, Scandinavians, French and Swiss.

1868   The growing network of railroads lured European immigrants, particularly Scandinavians and Irish, to Minnesota.

1880   The U.S. Census showed a population in Minnesota of 780,773, of which 71 percent were Europeans of the first or second generation. Literacy among Swedes, Norwegians and Danish immigrants exceeded 70 percent.

1890   Immigration to Minnesota reached its height.

Norwegians rarely settled in areas of Swedish concentration.

Census figures showed Germany leading all nations in the numbers it was sending to Minnesota.

1900   To fill the labor needs of the packing plants, manufacturers sent agents to recruit workers in the Balkan countries as far north as Poland and Lithuania.

1910   Swedish immigrants became the largest non-native nationality in Minnesota.

Although the British Isles and Norway surpassed Sweden in the number of immigrants coming to America, in proportion to Sweden, 1.4 million Swedish first- and second-generation immigrants were listed as living in the U.S. compared to Sweden's population of 5.5 million.

**"Curious Paths Taken by the Immigrants, Interesting
Peculiarities of Incoming Foreigners as Shown by
Reports Just Released by the Government,"
The New York Times, February 13, 1910**

When a man gets so much money that he can lose $5 million and not know it's gone, he's got a lot of money. But this same man, if he feels wronged, can so concentrate his mind on the loss of $0.50 that he will yowl like a cat with a pinched tale. He sort of loses, for the moment, all sense of proportion, and can remember nothing except that someone has frisked him for half a dollar.

Big countries in some respects are like big men. Most of the days of the year this country does not worry much about the immigration question. We simply swallow up immigrants as fast as they come and forget they are here. But periodically we get into the frame of mind of the millionaire gentleman who was unlawfully, outrageously, and scandalously made to part with the price of a couple pounds of meat. We look about us and see nothing but Scandinavians, Mongolians, Italians, and Hungarians. We go through streets where we can understand no more what is spoken than as if we were attending a convention of parrots, blackbirds, and blue jays. And we say to ourselves—just like this—"this immigrant business has got to stop."

Such another period is upon us. The announcement that 957,000 foreigners took up their abode here last year has brought back all of the old uneasiness. Which makes it well to reassure ourselves with a few facts.

The fact is that this country is in about as much danger of being overrun by foreigners as the Atlantic Ocean is of being drowned out by the Mississippi River. The foreigners come here by the thousand, the tens of thousands, and the millions. They bring their wives, their babies, their stepfathers, and their mothers-in-law. They clutter up the benches in Battery Park until the native-born American citizens can hardly see over their heads to the Statue of Liberty. They fill the second-class coaches that run to the West. They settle in Chicago, Detroit, St. Paul, Sacramento, and Wahoo, Nevada. And by the time they are all at the anchor, no one can tell what has become of them. They don't seem to be here.

Contrary to public opinion, it is a statistical fact that the percentage of foreign-born citizens in American cities is becoming less and less. It isn't, of course, that immigration is falling off. On the contrary, immigration is falling on. During the last 10 years precisely 7,959,135 foreigners came to this country. Either the other countries are becoming so bad or this country is becoming so good that we can count upon an average of about a million a year.

But in the face of this fact the percentage of foreign-born inhabitants is constantly decreasing for the reason that America, as a producer of population, is such a wonderful country. There are so many millions here already that their offspring simply swamp a relatively small incoming tide from across the ocean.

Some people, for instance, hardly consider New York an American city. A recent visitor from London returned to his hometown and told the folks that there didn't seem to be many Americans in New York. The Kaiser greeted some Manhattan Germans with the remark that he was glad to welcome fellow countrymen from the city that, next to Berlin, possessed the largest German population in the world.

All of which, in its essence, is more or less true. This is a cosmopolitan town. Its size and the fact that it is the first spot that the immigrant hits ... make it so. But the truth requires the statement of the fact that there are not only quite a number of native-born persons here but that they are constantly increasing their relative number.

In 1870, when the total population of New York was a little less than a million, 44 percent of the population was foreign. A man going down the street, for instance, could shake dice with himself as to whether the next person he met would be an American or foreigner. But, in order to not lose money he would have had to make the betting about even, because there were 419,000 foreigners in town to only 523,000 Americans.

When the last census was taken there were 1,270,000 foreigners here. But there were also 2,167,000 native-born American persons whose names went on the list. In other words, the percentage of foreign-born residents had fallen from 44 percent in 1870 to 37 percent in 1900, notwithstanding the fact that the number of foreigners had tripled.

During the same time, the percentage of foreigners in Chicago fell from 48 to 34, Philadelphia dropped from 27 to 22, St. Louis from 36 to 19, and Baltimore from 21 to 13. Boston held its own to a decimal the percentage of foreigners in 1900, as in 1870, being 35.1…. Atlanta showed the smallest percentage of foreigners, only 2.8. Southern cities generally ranked exceedingly low. North Dakota has the highest percentage of foreigners and Georgia the lowest, North Dakota 35, as against 42 in 1900, and Georgia .6 as against .7.

It is an interesting, though perhaps not surprising, fact to discover that it is the American city that plays hob with the foreigner. Put him out in the country and he will do better in the matter of population than the native-born American. But in the city he is compelled to live in a manner in which no American, or at least few Americans, will consent to live. He is huddled into tenements where his children die and he himself contracts tuberculosis.

What these handicaps do to his population figures may be understood when it is explained that, in the 21 cities for which statistics have been given, there was, between 1870 and 1900, an average decrease of 14 percent in the foreign-born population. The average fell from 38 to 24. But the foreigner did much better in the country than he did in the city that the average for the United States fell only from 14.4 in 1870 to 13.7 in 1900.

All of which suggests what the foreigner might be able to do if he were enabled to compete on equal terms, if he were not forced to live where he and his children are ever menaced by death. Yet as matters stand, inexorable America is assimilating the foreigner and decreasing his relative importance as a population element.

It is interesting to note the manner in which the various states attract the different nationalities. Take the Turks, for instance. It is almost necessary to get out extradition papers to induce a Turk to go to Arkansas.

When the 1900 census was taken there were in the United States 9,910 countrymen of the Sudan, but the whole state of Arkansas could show but one Turk. The Turk who comes to this country is more likely to head straight for Massachusetts. Nobody knows the reason. It may be because Massachusetts is so much like Turkey, or because it is so different from Turkey; it all depends on why the Turk left home. At any rate, the old Bay State heads the list of preferred American places for Turks with an Ottoman population of 2,896. New York is the second choice with 1,915.

Arkansas is also shunned by the Portuguese. The records do not show that there are any Portuguese in the state. These little kingdomers, like the Turks, prefer Massachusetts, which leads the list with more than 13,000. There are only 30,000 Portuguese in the whole country, of whom California and Massachusetts have almost the entire number, California with 12,000 figuring as a close second.

A Roumanian, on the other hand, cannot be taken into Massachusetts unless he is sealed in a boxcar and shipped over the border before he can beat his way through the roof. There are only 128 Roumanians in the state, though there are 10,000 in New York, 1,200 in Pennsylvania, and enough in other places to bring the total for the country up to 15,000. Next to Massachusetts the Roumanian gives the whole wide berth to Maine, Nevada, and Vermont. In these three states there is not a single one of his nationality.

Scotchmen prefer New York, will take Pennsylvania if they can get their first choice, and, if denied both, will turn to Massachusetts. The only states the Scotchmen really fight shy of are Southern states. There are 233,000 Scotchmen In the country, but the Southern states, as a rule, have only 300 or 400 apiece, while New York has 33,000. Even Kansas has more than 4,000.

When a Dutchman comes here the only thing he can see in the country is Michigan. There are 104,000 Hollanders in the United States, of whom Michigan has 80,000. Years ago the Dutch formed a settlement west of Grand Rapids on the shore of Lake Michigan. They prospered and sent home favorable reports, and other Dutchmen joined them. To this day they have retained their compact social organization, and almost all of their old habits of mind. Being a deeply religious people, for instance, many of them regard life insurance as an indication of a lack of faith in the Lord's promise to provide, and, therefore, as a commodity, it is very wicked to buy. Insurance agents have come out of the Dutch belt in Michigan looking more emaciated and generally rundown than Dr. Cook did when he boarded the *Hans Egede* to return from the "boreal centre." Yet the Dutch are among the best citizens in Michigan. Their eyes are always on the main chance....

In the same way that the Dutch have formed the habit of going to Michigan, the Swedes have formed the habit of going to Minnesota. Give a Swede car fare to West Virginia and he would jump off the train to walk to the late Gov. Johnson's old state. There are only 132 Swedes in all of West Virginia, while Minnesota has more than 115,000. Illinois, with 100,000, comes in second in Swedish affections....

"Auto Industry Center Is Here. Motor Car Manufacturers See New York's Approval of Their Products," *The New York Times*, January 17, 1910

Although in actual output of motor cars, New York does not rank very high compared with some manufacturing communities, the Garden and Palace shows during the past two weeks have clearly shown that Manhattan is the automobile center of the country. This is not only because there are probably more machines in actual use here than in any other one place, but automobile manufacturers all over the country, like those in other branches of industry, first seek metropolitan approval of their products.

The Garden show brought visitors to New York from all over the United States, and there were one or two instances of enthusiastic motorists coming here from London and Paris primarily to witness this American exhibit. These foreigners are not only impressed with the Garden show, but were surprised at the high-class exhibits in all the show rooms on both sides of the automobile row on upper Broadway, where New Yorkers may see an automobile show any time of the year.

The record of the 1909 show, which was attended during the week by 116,000, was left hopelessly in the rear. It is estimated yesterday that every day last week as many as 25,000 persons visited the show, 10,000 are in the morning and afternoon sessions and 15,000 at night. One of the show officials said yesterday that an estimate of 150,000 would be very conservative.

New York Evening Mail, July 10, 1910

These are the saddest of possible words:

"Tinker to Evers to Chance."
Trio of bear cubs, and fleeter than birds,
Tinker and Evers and Chance.
Ruthlessly pricking our gonfalon bubble,
Making a Giant hit into a double
Words that are heavy with nothing but trouble:
"Tinker to Evers to Chance."

༺·ഀ·ഀ·ഀ·ഀ·ഀ·ഀ·ഀ·ഀ༻

"Milledgeville Citizens Take Part in Funeral of Aged Negress," The Atlanta Constitution, January 12, 1910

Milledgeville, Ga., January 11 (Special). For the second time in the recent history of Milledgeville has a negro been buried with some of our most prominent white citizens acting as pallbearers. In both instances, it was the funeral of an old colored mammy; this time it was Aunt Amy Latimer. The pallbearers were Judge G. T. Whilden, recorder; Dr. J. E. Kidd, W. W. Stembridge, George H. Brantley, L. H. Andrews, C I. Morris. Last Sunday, Dr. B. J. Simmons, one of the most successful negroes of this state, was buried in this city. He had accumulated some $20,000 in the last 15 years from the practice of medicine. He represented all the most that a progressive man of his race had accomplished in this community. The white people of this city did not ignore his success. He received considerable consideration in many ways as an evidence that his ability was recognized. Quite a number of our citizens attended his funeral, but it safe to say that there is no comparison to be made of the feelings of the white people over the passing away of these two members of another race. Aunt Amy had accumulated little or nothing. It was not what she had, but what she was and what she had been that opened the hearts of her white friends and made them mindful of her even after death. Aunt Amy had been in the valley and shadow with many a good mother in this community. Her tender, humble sympathy and gentle services were not to be forgotten. Her voice had first announced the arrival of many a bouncing boy or girl. The white women sent wreaths and roses.

༺·ഀ·ഀ·ഀ·ഀ·ഀ·ഀ·ഀ·ഀ༻

"Get Songs That Really Help People" Says Mr. Alexander, Fort Wayne Weekly Sentinel, December 14, 1910

Go to Princess rink any evening during the services of the Chapman-Alexander evangelistic campaign in Ft. Wayne, and you will come away with a better comprehension why Charles M. Alexander has come to be known as one of the very foremost directors of gospel the world has ever known.

Mr. Alexander doesn't merely sing—he preaches while he sings and while he is directing the choir or the audience in the rendition of the swinging hymns that carry a personal message. True, his preaching is by methods quite apart from those one usually sees in the pulpit, but it's preaching, nevertheless. No other man does this sort of thing quite as Dr. Chapman does it. From the outset, he takes his audiences completely into his confidence.

Perhaps Mr. Alexander's most striking characteristic is his ability to make people readily see and carry home the gospel message, which he says is in every song that is really worthwhile.

The whole force of this tremendous enthusiasm is thrown into his work, and a listless or indifferent spirit in the audience is completely incomprehensible when Mr. Alexander is interpolating between the verses of the hymns and his running fire original interpretation....

"I began to look around to see how it could help the most men in the best way, and I decided that my work lay in helping them by song. I found out that a hymn set to music is like a sermon on wheels, and soon became more and more firmly convinced of the power of a gospel hymn to reach and save people," he said.

"Where you get your hymns?"

"From the wide world. Here, there and everywhere. From all sorts of people in all kinds of places. The man who sets out to make a collection of gospel songs never knows when he might find a treasure. I can tell you stories enough to fill columns about the origins of some of the songs that have been sung in this mission. I received through the mail the music of "What Will You Do With Jesus?" And it has become a great invitational song that Mrs. Asher uses with such power. Then I shall never forget how "Don't Stop Praying" had its birth. I also received it through the post; the sender told me it had been refused by two music publishers. I was so struck with it that I asked the writer to call and see me. She came, and told me that she had a very great trouble. She prayed for help, but help did not seem to be coming. Still she kept praying, and one morning at breakfast she opened a letter that lifted the whole trouble from her. She was so convinced her faith been justified, and so inspired by that belief, that before she got up from the table she wrote the words and music to "Don't Stop Praying" almost exactly as they stand today."

"Girls' Affairs," an attempt to unravel some of the perplexities that come to girls in their relation to the other sex, *The Ladies' Home Journal,* April 1911

"I have a friend whom I have known a long time. We are very sympathetic, and like the same books and people. He comes often to see me and seems to enjoy himself. He takes me out, too, and we always have good times together. The other young folks in our set seem to think we are engaged. The girls talk to him as if he belonged to me, and the rest of the fellows have stopped coming to see me. But really there isn't anything to it yet. He has never said a word and I don't know what to make of it. My sister says perhaps he is waiting for me to say something. What would you do?

"Answer: This is a difficult situation. The first question for you to ask yourself is whether you really have a right to think your friend means to come to more serious purposes. It may be that he enjoys your society in a frank way and has no idea that anything more can be expected. If so I do not think much of his cleverness. It is certainly quite natural that your other friends should consider the matter settled, and this is why it is either ungenerous or stupid of him to let such a situation continue. Sometimes a man does this out of pure thoughtlessness. He forgets that while he is monopolizing a girl she may lose other friends and other chances. The girl is rather helpless under it too. She cannot say to him: Are you in earnest? What do you mean to do? All the best sentiment and tradition are against such a course. If she were to take things into her own hands in this way she would never feel happy or at rest about it. No, there is nothing direct that can be done. But you might try a little judicious discipline. Do not be at home one of the usual times he calls. Try absent treatment for a while. Don't sit in the parlor waiting for him every night, like a ripe plum ready to drop into his mouth when he says the word. He will value your society more when he finds it is not easy to get and that you have other friends who want to see you."

Abstract of Reports of the Immigration Commission, 1911

"While social conditions affect the situation in some countries, the present immigration from Europe to the United States is in the largest measure due to economic causes. It should be stated, however, that emigration from Europe is not now an absolute economic necessity, and as a rule those who emigrate to the United States are impelled by a desire for betterment rather than by the necessity for escaping intolerable conditions."

ঌ৯ঌ৯ঌ৯ঌ৯ঌ৯

**"Public Shows Are Endorsed by Public Speaker, Professor Libby
Approves of People Spending Time and Money for
Entertainment," *The Denver Post,* March 11, 1911**

"Man cannot live by bread alone; he needs the moving picture. This is not a literal quotation from the lecture of Prof. M.F. Libby, Chair of Philosophy at the state university, given at the public library last night, but it is an authentic extract from the gist of the professor's remarks.

'It is not a bad sign,' declared Professor Libby, 'when people spend more for amusement than for the necessities of life. Man cannot live by bread alone. We are too much inclined toward Philistinism, (sic) or I may even say we are inclined to be pharisaical about this proposition. Go into the moving picture shows and see for yourself. These people are squandering money on the artistic impulses that are not educating, but what's the difference? Art is the play of grown-ups....' Denver is classed as an intellectual center by Professor Libby, whose investigation shows that one-sixth of the books taken from the Denver public library are the old standards."

"Motion Pictures of Colorado Scenes Now on Screens, First Showing in Denver Brings Cheers from Business Men," *The Denver Post,* September 7, 1911

"Denver and Colorado in moving pictures, full of action, life, picturesqueness, and beauty will now be shown upon the canvas of the world by the William H. Swanson Film Company. The firm was run off at the Princess Theater yesterday for the first time, bearing the authority of the Denver Chamber of Commerce and viewed by members of that body, together with the Denver press.

It was a success. Hundreds of reproductions will be sent throughout the world for the delectation of the patrons of moving picture theaters. Thursday the film will be on the regular program of the Princess. It will also be released throughout the country.... The pictures open with the great industrial pageant that moved through the streets on July 18. One of the features of the big parade was *The Denver Post* Boys and Girls' Band with 70 pieces. As these young musicians moved through the thoroughfares, which were banked on either side by thousands of spectators, all of whom are shown in the film, they were greeted with enthusiastic applause."

❧❧❧❧❧❧❧❧

Excerpts from *"Helpful Hints in English,"* by James C. Fernald, Funk and Wagnalls Company, 1911

I don't think so. Never say, "I don't think," exclaims the purist. "Any rational person is always thinking." Doubtless, my dear purist, but, not always thinking the same way that you do. Consult your dictionary and you will find that "think" has more than one meaning; it may mean "to carry on the process of thought" in which sense we are "always thinking"; or it may mean "to entertain a particular opinion," in which sense I may never think your way. You think that tree is a maple; I do not think (entertain the opinion) that it is; in other words, "I don't think so." In that case, would it not be better to say, "I think not"? That depends on what you mean. The two expressions are not identical; "I don't think so" means I am doubtful of the affirmative; "I think not" means I am almost sure of the negative.

Woman, women: With reference to organizations and movements, the singular (woman) is commonly preferred, as "The Woman's (not Women's) Christian Temperance Union"; "woman suffrage," not "women suffrage." Woman, so used, is generic, denoting all "womankind," just as man is generic in the sentence "Man is mortal." But we say, "Votes for women"; there are to be as many women as there are votes for them; "Votes for woman" might suggest plural voting; but "The ballot for woman" is correct. We may say either "A woman's college" or "A college for women," but not a "Women's college." "Woman's nature"; is the nature inseparable from womanhood? "Women's opinions" are the opinions of a large part of the sex, thought of as individuals.

❧❧❧❧❧❧❧❧

"Boy Scouting—What It Really Is," by F. A. Crosby, *The World Today,* February 1911

"Be Prepared," the motto of the "Boy Scout," signifies fully the purpose of the scout movement as it is being grafted from the parent English stock, where it first took shape, to that more live and adaptable, but perhaps less sturdy shoot, the American boy. Whether it is to be ready in will and training to help an old lady safely cross a busy crossing; to give "first aid" to an

injured companion; or to repel an invasion by a hostile nation, the American youth may well take as his slogan, "Be Prepared." This does not mean merely gaining a fund of information from the leader, book and nature, but unconsciously developing a resourcefulness which will always stand him in stead and which our average city bred boy lacks to a great degree.

The American boy used to live in the country, or in close proximity to it, and a healthy environment and nature's schooling gave him a practical knowledge and a resourcefulness which have brought forth empire-builders. This boy could ride, swim, hunt and skate; he was handy with tools; knew nature's secrets in field and wood; had chores to do. He was self-reliant and well developed in body and brain. Because of a careful rearing in a real home he was respectful and obedient, the right material from which to build a nation, and from which come nation-builders.

There is the danger of our losing this type of boy through the change due to modern social and industrial conditions. Modern standards of living may conduce to a higher type of civilization, but the adolescent boy, with his many semibarbarous instincts, is being forced onward too rapidly, like a hothouse plant, toward and into this stage of refinement, to the exclusion of his natural impulses. His wide interest in nature—persons, beasts, plants at work—is being dwarfed by narrow nature study from books; his personal interest in athletics is being superseded by a mania for "beating" in spectacular contests; his desire to make things and see them work is in danger of being smothered by too much theoretical instruction. Likewise, the normal boy's natural religious instincts, his altruistic impulses are too crude and deep-seated to be found and nurtured by many of our modern religious forms and prejudices.

Any scheme of ideas that will help to bring back to our city boy's life his inherent rights and desires of achievement, adventure, observation and knowledge of nature, is well worth careful study. The Boy Scout movement is such a scheme. Although its ideals can better be attained in the country, yet its adaptation to the city has been proved, and is only in its beginnings. Scouting is an educational movement, to be promoted by and in conjunction with other institutions, not an independent organization.

ENGLISH BOY SCOUTS GETTING DINNER READY

Domestic Labor-Saving Invention Timeline

1844 Linus Yale of Springfield, Massachusetts, received a patent for a "Door Lock."

1846 Elias Howe, Jr. of Cambridge, Massachusetts, received the first American patent for a "Sewing Machine" that used a lock stitch.

1848 William C. Young of Baltimore, Maryland, received a patent for an "Ice Cream Freezer."

1850 Joel Houghton of Ogden, New York, received the first U.S. patent for a "Table Furniture Cleaning Machine" for washing dishes; it featured hand-turned beaters to move water against tableware set in a basket in a tub of hot water.

1851 Dr. John Gorrie of New Orleans, Louisiana, received a patent for an "Ice Machine" which he described as a "new and useful Machine for the Artificial Production of Ice and for general Refrigeratory Purposes."

Isaac M. Singer of New York, New York, received a patent for a "Sewing Machine" that featured a rocking double treadle; used a flying shuttle instead of a rotary shuttle with the needle mounted vertically and a presser foot to hold the cloth in place; Singer later introduced business innovations such as installment buying, after-sale servicing, and trade-in allowances.

1857 James T. Henry and William P. Campbell of Philadelphia, Pennsylvania, received a patent for a "Closet Cistern" described as "…combining the basin of a water closet with a valved chamber, cistern, and communicating pipes…that the soil may be readily and effectually disposed of, and all offensive smells obviated."

1858 Hamilton E. Smith of Philadelphia, Pennsylvania, received a U.S. patent for a "Washing Machine" that cycled reheated water and contained a reciprocating plunger and two horizontal diaphragms in the tub which moved vertically with the action of the plunger.

1859 George B. Simpson of Washington, DC, received a patent for an "Electrical Heating Apparatus" which generated heat by passing electricity through wire coils.

1866 Orrin L. Hopson and Eli J. Manville of Waterbury, Connecticut, and Herman P. Brooks of Wolcottville, Connecticut, received a patent for an "Improved Machine for Reducing Pointing Wires" and organized the Excelsior Needle Company.

1867 Sheldon B. Everitt of Ansonia, Connecticut, received a patent for a "Tea Kettle."

1868 Amariah M. Hills of Hockanum, Connecticut, received a patent for an "Improvement in Lawn-Mowers" described as a "device for mowing grass by hand, and is more especially designed for mowing lawns."

1869 Ives W. McGaffey of Chicago, Illinois, received a patent for a "Sweeping Machine" called the "whirlwind" vacuum cleaner; the first suction-type vacuum cleaner was a light, hand-powered device for surface cleaning consisting of a handle to turn a pulley which used a belt to drive a fan in a casing, thus producing a strong current of air, "controlled to take up dust and dirt, and carry the fine particles into a porous air-chamber, so constructed as to allow the air to escape while the dust is retained"; McGaffey started the American Carpet Cleaning Company.

Cornelius Swartwout of Troy, New York, patented a "Waffle Iron."

1871   Mary Florence Potts of Ottumwa, Iowa, received a patent for a "Sad Iron" with a detachable handle for pressing irons; it was widely manufactured and licensed in the U.S. and Europe with advertising featuring her picture.

1873   Josiah George Jennings, sanitary engineer from Palace Wharf, Stangate, England, received a patent for "Water Closets" in which the "pan discharges itself by a side opening into the upright limb of a siphon-trap."

Ludwig M. N. Wolf of Avon, Connecticut, received a patent for "Lamp-Brackets for Sewing Machines," which the Singer Sewing Machine Company introduced to meet the needs of those who wished to sew at night.

Anthony Iske of Lancaster, Pennsylvania, received the first U.S. patent for "Machines for Slicing Dried Beef."

1875   Francis Torrance, James W. Arrott, and John Fleming in Pittsburgh, Pennsylvania, formed the Standard Manufacturing Company, making cast-iron bathtubs, washstands and water closets.

1876   Melville R. Bissell of Grand Rapids, Michigan, received a U.S. patent for a "Carpet-Sweeper"; he was attempting to eradicate the effect on his wife's health of dust from packing materials at his crockery shop; hog bristles bound with string were dipped in hot pitch, inserted in brush rollers, and trimmed with scissors.

1879   Black American inventor Thomas Elkins of Albany, New York, received a patent for a "Refrigerating Apparatus" for "food or corpses," which provided a convenient container and method of chilling using the evaporation of water.

1881   John Reece of Boston, Massachusetts, received patent for a "Button Hole Sewing Machine."

1882   Henry W. Seely of New York received a patent for an "Electric Flat-Iron" that weighed almost 15 pounds.

1883   Thomas J. Clark and John K. Stewart developed hair and wool clipping machines for shearing sheep and grooming horses in Dundee, Illinois.

Jonas Cooper of Washington, DC, received a patent for a "Shutter and Fastening" for inside shutters.

1885   Rufus M. Eastman of Boston, Massachusetts, received a patent for a "Mixer for Cream, Eggs, and Liquors," or electric mixer.

1886   Josephine G. Cochran of Shelbyville, Illinois, received a patent for a "Dish Washing Machine."

1888   Edward Katzinger founded a commercial baking pan company in Chicago, Illinois, later registered as "ECKO."

1890   George K. Cooke of Jamaica, New York, received a patent for a "Gas-Burner" known as a "self-lighter," having a main and auxiliary jet.

Daniel Johnson received a patent for a "Grass-Receiver for Lawn-Mowers."

Daniel McCree of Chicago, Illinois, received a patent for a "Portable Fire-Escape."

1891   Cyrenus Wheeler, Jr. of Auburn, New York, received a patent for a "Clothes-Wringer."

1892   Sarah Boone of New Haven, Connecticut, received a patent for an "Ironing Board" for sleeves.

George T. Sampson of Dayton, Ohio, received a patent for a "Clothes Dryer."

1893   Lyde W. Benjamin of Boston, Massachusetts, received a patent for a "Broom Moistener and Bridle" that kept the broom moist while sweeping without being so wet as to drip but to prevent the dust from rising.

Black American inventor Fredrick J. Loudin of Revanna, Ohio, received a patent for a "Fastener for the Meeting-Rails of Sashes."

1894   Frederick J. Loudin of Ravenna, Ohio, received a patent for a "Key-Fastener" which prevented a burglar from disengaging the key from outside the door by inserting something through the keyhole.

Simeon Newsome of Detroit, Michigan, received a patent for an "Oil Heater or Cooker."

1895   Robert H. Gray of Lexington, Kentucky, received a patent for a "Cistern-Cleaner."

1899   Benjamin F. Jackson of Cambridge, Massachusetts, received a patent for a "Gas-Burner" in which air was supplied "under pressure and in which all parts of the burner-tube…got the same amount of air and consequently maintained an even combustion, thereby producing a more efficient burner and one having a longer life."

John Albert Burr of Agawam, Massachusetts, received a patent for a "Lawn-Mower."

Albert T. Marshall of Brockton, Massachusetts, received a patent for an "Automatic Refrigerating Apparatus" ("relates to the class of refrigerating-machines which ordinarily employ anhydrous ammonia as a refrigerating medium"): a household refrigerator.

John S. Thurman of St. Louis, Missouri, received a patent for a "Pneumatic Carpet-Renovator," a gasoline-powered, motor-driven vacuum cleaner drawn by horses door to door.

1901   Hubert Cecil Booth, a bridge engineer, developed first power-driven vacuum cleaner named "Puffing Billy."

1902   Willis Haviland Carrier, chief engineer of Buffalo Forge Company from 1902 to 1915, completed drawings recognized as the world's first scientific air conditioning system.

1906   Alfred C. Fuller, entrepreneur from Nova Scotia, founded the Fuller Brush Company.

1907   Maytag introduced the first wringer washing machine, "Pastime Washer."

1910   Louis H. Hamilton, Chester Beach, and Fred Osius formed Hamilton Beach Manufacturing Company to develop "universal" motor-driven appliances and introduced its first product: the electric hand-held massager.

William M. Frost of Eureka, Montana, received the first U.S. patent for an "Electric Insect Destroyer."

1911   Louis, Frederick, and Emory Upton founded Upton Machine Company in St. Joseph, Michigan, to produce an electric, motor-driven wringer washer; the company later became the Whirlpool Corporation.

**"A Place Where a Way Has Been Found to Cut Down Drudgery
and Make Life Easy—Social Science Worked Out Practically by a
Connecticut Couple,"** *The New York Times,* **May 7, 1911**

The kitchenette is the last word, Mr. Charles Barnard thinks, in cooking convenience. Things must be carefully arranged so when the mistress of the stove can stand in one place and find ready to her hand all she needs, at a cost of only one or two steps there seems to have been gained a distinct advantage over the "nice roomy kitchen."

Every kitchen, Mr. and Mrs. Barnard declare, should be small, and if there is plenty of space to start, it would be partitioned off and made into a sitting room for the servant. No servant should have to eat in the kitchen. It lessens the appetite and gives her no sense of rest.

It is precisely a sense of rest that the servant needs, says Mr. Barnard, just like the woman who does her own cooking. Fatigue is a poison. Nobody can be "always tired" and keep well. But the body will throw off the poison in a short time if it is given a chance. It must not ever be allowed to accumulate.

For this reason the steps of the housekeeper have to be carefully considered. No exercise is more beneficial than housework if it does not develop into drudgery and bring about a fatigue that cannot be thoroughly recovered from before the next "stint" is undertaken. Hence, the value of the kitchenette, and Mr. Barnard goes even further, and would have much of the simpler meals, like breakfast, cooked over alcohol gas burners, on the table.

Watching the coffee and the toast and the eggs is not a very difficult operation on the face of it, but it has to be done right to the minute or disaster follows. The average maid, getting up with the lark, is pretty tired before she has prepared the meal for the family, even though she sustains herself with the inevitable cup of tea. And when a woman is tired she is liable to let things burn or to take out the eggs before or after they have reached the proper point.

"A woman should get a meal," said Mr. Barnard, "according to the up-to-date methods used in such a trade as bricklaying, for instance. Not long ago the mason picked up his own bricks. Now they find the bricks piled for them at such a height that they do not have to stoop. When a man stoops for a brick he has to pick up not only the brick itself, but about one hundred pounds in addition, the weight of his inclined body.

"So careful managers have done away with that sort of thing. What is more, the bricklayers stop work every hour or two for five or 10 minutes. It is not a long time, but it suffices for rest. Then they go back to their work fresh, and freshness means efficiency. A tired person cannot work well....

"The conservation of energy is the theory of the day, the application of economy of motion to the work that has hitherto been done in a haphazard fashion. There is every reason in the world why this same theory should be applied to the kitchen. Not only should the kitchen be planned so as to save steps, and such things as can comfortably be done on the table transferred there, but the cook should have to sit down and rest at intervals. There shouldn't be minutes here and there stolen perhaps when a careful eye is turned the other way, but regular rest times. "Another idea we carry out is to cook some meats and vegetables in the dish in which they are to be served. It is possible to buy dishes of good shape and color that will stand great heat. The casserole solves many a difficulty. When the meat or vegetables are cooked, there is nothing to do but set them on the table, and thus the extra washing of pots and pans is saved."

Working along this line, Mr. and Mrs. Barnard got hold of steam cookers, and tried them, with great success. The way in which the steam cooker works is simple enough. The cooker is arranged like a double boiler, with holes in the sides of the inside pot. The steam enters these holes, condenses as it strikes the colder stuff inside, and gives up its heat. This device is admirable for vegetables and stews, and if it is desired, the dish in which the food is to be served may be put in the top and the utensil left perfectly clean. It does not take long, either.

What with the small, scientifically arranged kitchen, with the fireless cooker doing the work for soups and roasts that the gas stove has started, with the steam cooker preparing the other things without danger of their burning, and saving the washing of pots, and the alcohol gas stove doing all that is required of it, the Barnard kitchen is a little wonder. And yet they had not a single "city advantage" to start with, and they are not rich people.

There are a dozen other details that might be described before the kitchenette is left, but there are other parts of the house that must not be forgotten. There is the sweeping and dusting department of housekeeping, always a nuisance, and in these days of automobiles to stir up the dust of country roads, more of a problem than ever.

Of course, the Barnards do not use a broom. That implement does, indeed, belong to the Middle Ages. They have a vacuum cleaner, and twice a month they go over the whole house. Every day it is brushed up lightly with a dustless brusher, but twice a month cleaning with the vacuum apparatus keeps it immaculate. The cleaner is of fair size. There is a sort of pump arrangement that is carried from one room to the other, with a pipe attachment. The pump could be worked by a child of three and anybody who can lift an eighth of two or three pounds can run the suction end of the thing over the carpet.

One person can do the cleaning alone, but two, one to work the pump and the other to guide the suction pipe, do the work much more quickly. Any woman with a child to help or two hours of somebody's time twice a month can do a spring cleaning that would outdo all rug beating and never feel a moment's fatigue over it. That is not all the vacuum cleaner will do, for it draws the dust out of furniture with a special arrangement and out of clothes with another. One has to be careful, however, about selecting a cleaner, though now there are a number of makes that are really good, in addition to some that are distinctly bad.

The scrubbing of the floor is another obsolete item in the Barnard household. There are several mops that do the work just as well as any woman could. One long mop has a rubber end that acts like the grip of a hand. They put a thick piece of burlap on the floor and rub it back and forth with the long rubber-tipped mop and, behold, the floor is as clean as if some woman had broken her back over it. Similarly, the mop-handle is used for dusting the floors and walls. Only in this case not burlap but a dustless duster is attached. The dustless duster absorbs the dust. It can't be shaken out, for some occult reason there was not time to inquire into. Every now and then the duster is washed and then the dust leaves it, but it dries out perfectly good and still ready for more work.

☙❧☙❧☙❧☙❧

"Instructor in the Kindergarten Department of the Normal College, New York," *Munsey's Magazine,* **February 1911**

Marian's mother stands in the doorway of the kindergarten room, facing Miss Blank, a frown of perplexity creasing her brow.

"I'd like to ask your advice, Miss Blank," she says. "It's about Marian. I want to know how you manage her in school. She's a good enough child at home, only we can't make her mind!"

And Marian, clinging to mother's hand, hears that she cannot be made to mind, and swells visibly with pride at the smartness of her small self.

Another time it is Henrietta's mother who comes with her tale of disobedience, to drink of the well of Miss Blank's wisdom.

"I just don't know what to do with Henrietta," she says. "She is so impudent to everyone, and answers back so, that I have to send her away from the table almost every meal. I told her," continued the mother blandly, "that you are coming to visit us some time, and you won't like her if she is naughty at the table. I wish you would tell her so, too, and ask her not to be so saucy at table. She would do it for you!"

As there was no invitation to a meal following this request, Miss Blank wonders how long her influence over the somewhat troublesome child would last if she, too, should seek to discipline Henrietta by means of lies....

When all teachers of little children can duplicate such cases many times over, there is a significant fact concealed somewhere in the evidence. For, without doubt, the first, most important lesson a child has to learn is to obey—and to obey immediately and unquestionably.

Now, the modern child does not obey immediately and unquestionably. That is beyond dispute. This failure to do so would seem to be due to the modern parent's inability to command wisely, for the reason of a child's misbehavior may nearly always be found in the attitude of the people who have authority over him. There is too little examination into the motives of his acts, too little relation to the punishment to the offense. Too often, discipline means physical coercion, or futile threats which the mother or nurse has no power or intention of carrying out.

How wearily often have we heard, in streetcar, ferry, or train, an anxious mother in a rasping voice commanding Willie to "come away from the window," or she will "throw him out"? How many times have we seen small arms almost dragged from their sockets, small hands slapped, even spanking administered publicly, not because of the real disobedience, but because Willie or Johnny or Mary wished to gratify some perfectly legitimate interest which did not appeal to the adult!

As corporal punishment has the sanction of history and the weight of custom behind it, it is not to be passed over lightly and unadvisedly. "Spare the rod and spoil the child" is a doctrine that has been adhered to militarily through many generations—though, be it said, often times with such untoward results that it usually seems that the parent or guardian is aiming not at the betterment of the child, but the easiest way to rid herself a troublesome duty.

The net result of whipping in all its forms is not to create a better, more amenable spirit in the child, for which he will learn to right for the love of the right, but on the contrary, when the child does respond to this physical discipline, it is from fear—the lowest of the motives and the farthest removed the ideal one.

If we recall our own whipped selves, I fancy that most of us will admit that our first feeling on those sad occasions of reproof was one of flying rage—rage that someone who was bigger and stronger than ourselves was taking advantage of our weakness and getting the best of us in the only way it was possible to get the best of us. Our will was as strong as her or his hands. If it wasn't, the issue would never have been raised, so on the face of it, spanking is a confession of failure.

It is as if the one in authority said to the child, "I am master this way, at any rate," and any normal child is just as well aware of this as you are. You were quite well aware of it in your early days, and though you may have minded if the punishment hurt enough, your resulting emotion was not sorrow for the fault and a determination "not to do so anymore." It was, in all probability, a fierce sullenness and rage at your own powerlessness to hit back. These feelings, I imagine, must form a large part of the mental context of every whipped child, and it is hardly necessary to point out that they are neither healthy nor constructive feelings.

There is also the sense of loss of dignity—how painful a feeling to a sensitive child!—which he takes long to forgive. I remember one little boy who refused to speak to his mother for a week after she given him his first-and only-spanking, because he felt his pride and self-respect had been hurt beyond repair. These are delicate matters to tamper with in the growing child, and he who does so is laying up for himself lack of esteem and loss of authority, if not actual feelings of dislike. We none of us love him who makes us lose our self-respect.

Is corporal punishment never to be practiced, then? Must we always "spare the rod and spoil the proverb"?

Never, we should say, upon a child more than three or four years old. Previous to the age, the child is somewhat like a small animal, and immediate physical reaction is often the best way to correct the baby's faults, as immediate present is all that interested it. But this does not necessarily mean a whipping. If your child is in a tantrum, you'll bring him around far sooner if you take his two arms in yours and holding so firmly be used for power. The very fact that he is in the grasp of someone stronger than he, will have a soothing effect.

But, of course, this presupposes control within you, and how pitifully seldom this scene in one administering punishment! How often the red face and flashing eyes, a loud voice and intemperate speech, tell of a judgment in abeyance and a spirit in the worst possible case for the dealing out of justice!…

The fact that so many parents fail where so many teachers succeed in representing these things to a child is, I think, for a very simple reason, and that is that the child has absolute faith in the justice of the teacher. He means what he says, but she says what she means, but a given order must be obeyed, and that she carries out which she promises. Certainly this in the mind of the child is fruitful in two ways. It establishes the right attitude toward obedience and develops a child respect for rightful authority.

Conditions of Employment in the Iron and Steel Industry, 1913

"The general lack of effort for the improvement of the communities in which the employees of the steel industry live may in part be attributed to the fact that practically all the employees are adult males. No women are employed in the mills, and very few children. Since the workmen are so largely grown men, the steel manufacturers have felt no responsibility beyond that of paying the established scale of wages. Further-more, since the manufacturer or managers are brought into contact with the women and children of the community only indirectly, if at all, it is not surprising that very little notice has been taken of the conditions under which they live.

Another reason which may have a bearing on the general indifference of the managers of steel plants toward the communities in which they are situated is that the labor force is not generally recruited from among the native population but from the more recently arrived immigrants.

Finally, the apparent cause of the failure of most of the plans for education, recreation, or general improvement of the adult employees is the schedule of the working hours. Libraries and night schools are at best unattractive at the end of a 12-hour day, and all forms of amusement, except those stimulating, are likely to be passed by. Good libraries exist in many of the towns, but in all cases, the steel workers' patronage is extremely limited. In many cases cards are issued in the name of the steel workers, but the books are drawn by their wives and children."

"Soccer Meeting Next Thursday,"
The Atlanta Constitution, September 28, 1913

The soccer players of Atlanta will hold a meeting at Spalding's store Thursday night at 8 o'clock for the purpose of perfecting organization for the coming season. All those interested in soccer are invited to be present.

Soccer plans in Atlanta this winter will be on a larger scale than ever before. It is the plan of the soccerites to organize a four-team league and Spalding will give a handsome silver loving cup for the winning team.

The Scottish Society in Atlanta is taking an interest in the game, and the chances are that they will have a team in the league this season.

༄ஐ༄ஐ༄ஐ༄ஐ༄ஐ

"Sunny Weather,"
The Titusville Herald (Pennsylvania), December 31, 1913

PASS CHRISTIAN, MISSISSIPPI—President Wilson's vacation is greatly improving his health. As he climbed over the bunkers at the golf links today there was a resiliency in his step and a vigor in his walk that revealed to those who have been constantly observing him how much he has been benefited by a week of rest and recreation in the mild gulf climate.

The President played 18 holes of golf again today and seemed to enjoy the exercise. He is growing accustomed to the stubby grass upon the links, with its retarding effect on the roll of drives, and made a much better score today than usual.

༄ஐ༄ஐ༄ஐ༄ஐ༄ஐ

"Chum Bob's Talk for the Fans,"
Evening Independent (Massillon, Ohio), December 31, 1913

Perhaps one of the most novel golf clubs in the country is being organized out in Tacoma, Washington. The caddies of the Tacoma Golf and Country Club have formed themselves into a mutual organization and are playing the royal and ancient game on a field in the neighborhood of Manitou Park. The new club will be known as the Manitou Park Golf Club. Almost any day after school is out the youngsters may be seen playing over the field.

༄ஐ༄ஐ༄ஐ༄ஐ༄ஐ

"The Patent Cycle," by John Boyle, Jr.,
The Magazine of Wall Street, June 1913

When an inventor has completed his invention and desires to protect the same by a patent, he usually secures the services of a patent solicitor, who prepares a specification and drawings of the invention. These papers, together with the first fee of $15, are filed in the Patent Office and are designated as applications for patents. On receipt of an application by the Patent Office, it is assigned to the examiner having in charge the art to which the invention relates, who examines the same to determine the scope of the invention which the inventor is entitled to claim. As a result of his examination, he hands down a decision on the application, setting forth any objections and citing prior anticipating patents.

The applicant for a patent is allowed by law one year in which to reply to any official action. This latitude can be taken advantage of to keep the application in the office until such time as is most opportune to take out the patent. The famous Selden automobile patent was filed in 1879, and was issued in 1895. Another Selden patent, an off-shoot of this same application of 1879, was issued in 1912, 33 years after the invention was first filed in the Patent Office. But in the case of the *U.S. v. American Bell Telephone Co.,* which was a suit by the government to annul one of the telephone patents which had been pending in the Patent Office 14 years before issuing, the U.S. Supreme Court held that, inasmuch as the law expressly gave this latitude, it was perfectly legal for an applicant to avail himself of the same.

After varied correspondence between the office and the applicant on the question principally of the scope of the invention, it is finally decided to allow the application to go to patent. During all this correspondence, the applicant has been permitted one year in which to respond to official actions, although in the majority of cases the applicants do not avail themselves of this right. In fact, it might be said that it is only a small number of applicants that take the full legal limit of time in which to respond to official actions.

After the applicant has received notice of the allowance of his application for a patent, he has six months in which to pay the final fee of $20. Should he fail to pay the same within the prescribed time, the application becomes forfeited. But it is not dead yet, only sleeping, for he may renew this forfeited application at any time within two years from the date of the original allowance of the same. Upon payment of the final fee, the application goes to patent and bears a date of about a month later than the payment. These various and liberal time limits permitted applicants in the prosecution of their cases are brought out here to show the great elasticity of the system, and how it can be readily adapted to either hasten the issue of a patent during a period of prosperity, or delay the issue of the same during a period of depression.

❧❧❧❧❧❧❧❧

Booker T. Washington Quotations

The plantation songs known as "spirituals" are the spontaneous outburst of intense religious fervor…. They breathe a childlike faith in a personal Father, and glow with the hope that the children of bondage will ultimately pass out of the wilderness of slavery into the land of freedom. In singing of a deliverance which they believed would surely come, with bodies swaying, with the enthusiasm born of a common experience and of a common hope, they lost sight for the moment of the auction block, of the separation of mother and child, of sister and brother. There is in the plantation songs the pathos and the beauty that appeals to a wide range of tastes, and their harmony makes abiding impressions upon persons of the highest culture. The music of these songs goes to the heart because it comes from the heart.

No race can prosper till it learns that there is as much dignity in tilling a field as in writing a poem.

Nothing ever comes to one that is worth having except as a result of hard work.

One man cannot hold another man down in the ditch without remaining down in the ditch with him.

Success in life is founded upon attention to the small things rather than to the large things, to the everyday things nearest to us rather than to the things that are remote and uncommon.

Success is to be measured not so much by the position that one has reached in life as by the obstacles which he has overcome.

The individual who can do something that the world wants done will, in the end, make his way regardless of his race.

There are two ways of exerting one's strength: one is pushing down, the other is pulling up.

"Working Women and Wages,"
The Outlook, March 29, 1913

The employment of girls and women in factories, department stores, and all such out-of-the home industries is comparatively new, says *Life.* "It has nearly all come with the immense development of machinery during the last two generations and with the demand for cheap labor which has followed. Commercial organizations such as has given us the department stores is a form of machinery and has come along with all the other machines," *Life* adds.

At present, girls are the cheapest article in the labor market, and are used enormously in industrial exploitation. If it gets around that girls have a potential value to society which makes it uneconomic to use them up in service and scrap them like worn-out machines, it may raise hob with a lot of industries that are run by cheap girl-power at present.

When Jane Addams enlisted in the Progressive Movement sometime prior to the formal opening of the last presidential campaign, says the Los Angeles *Express,* her critics demanded that she confine her activities to the field of accredited philanthropy. "Her answer to these critics was an appeal for relief for the victims of an industrial system that refused to take account of the right of working girls and children to food, shelter, and safety." The Progressive National platform calls for "minimum wage standards for workingwomen to provide a living wage in all industrial occupations." But the New York *Sun* warns us that "a generous concern for the underpaid or the unfortunate should not blind the great mass of us to the fact that any artificial system of wages must result in cruel displacements of labor."

Letter to the Editor: "Why Girls Go Wrong, One of the Unskilled Class Tells Her Story," *The New York Times*, March 13, 1913

I have for some time been reading in the papers and listening to men from the pulpits and platforms argue and express their opinions as to "Why girls go wrong," and while some of these opinions and arguments are the result of guessing, others, such as low wages, dismal home surroundings, etc., are true, but I have been waiting to read or hear of the greatest and most tragic of all causes why girls go wrong, and find that even the costly investigation at Chicago has failed to bring it out....

For an unskilled working girl it is difficult enough to find employment except at a job paying $4 or $5 a week, but when she is also unfortunate enough to not have a home and applies to a storekeeper or any businessman for a least responsible position that pays near a living wage, she makes an unfortunate impression and is turned away. The longer she is out of work, the more she appears a doubtful character to those to whom she applies for work, and she is often asked, "How have you been living, being out of work and having no home?" These continual insults when seeking work are alone enough to suggest to a girl to do what she is suspected of having done. Is it any wonder if, after tramping the streets searching for work in a dispirited mood, girls yield to the temptations held out to them by flirts, mashers, white slavers, and others who seek their prey among this class of girls? And it is this class that is inevitably doomed to the underworld.

Though I have stood on the brink of the precipice for the last five years, the reason I have not yet fallen is the fact that I have a power of endurance which thousands who do fall have not, to prove that those who may be skeptical I am compelled to relate some of my own experiences. When I was 17 I lost my only friend, and it was necessary for me to get employment at once. Not having been taught any kind of work, the best job I could get was in the office of a department store at five dollars per week. I cooked my own coffee in the morning, which cost about two cents a cup, and purchased three rolls for two cents, one of which I had for breakfast and two for lunch, and another cup of coffee for which I paid three cents at the store lunch counters....

Having no one to depend on in case of emergency, I managed to save a least one dollar weekly. In the month of November another department store offered me seven dollars per week. Then I looked as big as all New York to me, and, of course, I accepted the job, but I did not know that help taken in that time in the year was laid off on Christmas Eve. While working there I learned of that fact, so I lived even more economically than before and walked about 40 blocks to and from work in order to save.

After a few days I had taken a place in a restaurant on West Street as cashier, but had to leave it at the end of a few weeks on account of the talk and insults I heard from sailors, drunkards, and ruffians who patronized the place.

Though I was awake most of the night and up at 5 a.m. daily scanning the advertisements, everywhere I went I found a large army of girls, young and old, applying to answer an advertisement that called for one person, and one who lived at home and was neat and cheerful was the one always taken on. It was about four months before I was successful in getting another job, which was in another department store at six dollars per week. While I was out of work, though I cut out the $0.12 suppers and lived on $0.10 or less a day, all I had saved was spent.

Because of these experiences, I decided to take up a course in bookkeeping at night. In order to do this, I tried more than ever before to save, and after attending school for two months I was compelled to leave, as I became sick, according to the doctors from lack of nourishment, and had to pay doctors what I saved on food to pay a tuition fee, and Christmas Eve I was again laid off in the next store to which I went. It was then again after three months before I got another job in a department store, for these stores did not take on help after Christmas and Easter season. Then, because of my worried state of mind, I made errors in my work and was dismissed. It now became almost impossible for me to work, even in department stores, or when a superintendent looked over my application he would remark, "How is it you have worked in so many places for so short a time and each only to be laid off, dismissed? And you are not living at home. We want people with better records." So the only time I can get work now is during the busy seasons, Christmas and Easter, and I have to exist on what I save then for the rest of the year and do odd jobs occasionally, such as addressing envelopes and making $0.75 per thousand.

Domestic work has at times been suggested to me, but until recently I regarded it as very humble work, and since I have changed my opinion I have not any more the strength for such work. Thus have I been existing for the last six years, during which time I had more than one offer from gentlemen with money to be a friend to me. As I have said above, while I possess the power to endure misery, as well as my higher ideals which have kept me from falls, hundreds situated as I am and to whom society is cold and cruel have fallen.

A victim of existing social conditions
New York

ॐ◌ॐ◌ॐ◌ॐ◌ॐ

I board where there are eight children and parents, and only two rooms in the house. I must do as the families do about washing, as there is but one basin, and no place to go to wash but out the door. I have not had the luxury of either lamp or candle, their only light being a cup of grease with a rag for a wick…. I occupy a room with three of the children, and a niece who boards there. The other room serves as a kitchen, parlor, and bedroom for the rest of the family.

—Letter to activist Catharine Beecher

ॐ◌ॐ◌ॐ◌ॐ◌ॐ

"Entertainment Ideas for New Year's,"
by Laura A. Smith, *Today's*, January 1914, An Immigration Party

IMMIGRATION PARTY
Will Land at Ellis Island, U.S.A. (date)
Wear the costume of some foreign land.
Prepare to show your money to the Inspectors,
Uncle Sam and Columbia,
Host and Hostess

Lay a gangplank from the street to the porch where the immigrants are to be 'inspected.' As they enter this hall they pass some blue-capped inspectors who ask them why they have come to the United States and other questions that will call forth witty answers, ask them to show their 'money,' and pass them on to white-clad 'doctors.' They turn little flashlights into the eyes of the immigrants and bid them stick out their tongues, then the immigrants pass into the United States. Here Uncle Sam, Columbia, a colored Mammy and other characters greet them. Uncle Sam's hand is a glove filled with cotton which collapses when one shakes hands with him. Columbia's hand is greased and Mammy's kiss leaves a smudge of burnt cork on the face. Baseball players, Indians, confidence men, suffragettes (militant) and other friends can help greet the immigrants when the crowd is a large one. Each newcomer receives a little flag to pin on her costume when she has become a citizen of the United States."

"Immigrant Wage-Earners," by Peter Roberts, 1914

"Religious ceremonies and observations have the strongest hold upon Poles, Lithuanians, Croatians, and Servians. We have seen that the number of men, all in the prime of life, so intent upon the religious exercises that the least movement of the priest at the altar found immediate response in every member of the audience. The ritual of the church has a deep hold upon Slav and Lithuanian; often the men go to confession at six in the morning in order that they may go to communion the day following. When men are so employed that they cannot attend mass on Sundays, they will attend one on Saturdays. The home must be consecrated once a year; and hundreds take their baskets laden with provisions to church on Easter morning that the priest may bless the feast they hope to enjoy that day."

"The day laborer of a generation ago is gone—a change which has been swifter and more complete in Pittsburgh than in many other of our industrial centers. 'Where are your Irish, your Welsh? Your Germans? Your Americans?' I asked an old mill hand. 'Go to the city hall and the police station,' he said. 'Some of them are still in the better paid jobs in the mills but mostly you'll have to look for them among the doctors and lawyers, office holders, clerks, accounts, salesmen. You'll find them there.'"

The day laborer in the mills today is a Slav. The foreign-born of the steel district include, it is true, representatives of every European nation, but I shall deal here only with the races from Southeastern Europe, which for twenty-five years have been steadily displacing the Teutonic and Keltic peoples in the rough work of the industries. The tendency of the Italians is to go into construction, railroad work, and the mines, rather than into the plant and yards; my group narrows itself down to the dominate Magyar, Slav and Lithuanian…

Roughly speaking, one-quarter of the population of Pittsburgh is foreign-born. The foreign is nowhere more at home than here, and nowhere has he been more actively welcomed by employers. The conflict of customers and habits, varying standards of living, prejudices, antipathies, all due to the confluence of representatives of different races of men, may be witnessed here. The whole territory is thrown into a stern struggle for subsistence and wage standards by the displacements due to these resistless accretions to the ranks of the workers. The moral and religious life of the city is equally affected by this inflow of peoples. The most backward of them are superstitious and ignorant, victims of cunning knaves and unscrupulous parasites. Their religious training differs widely from that of peoples of Protestant antecedents, and institutions that were dear to the founders of the city are fast being undermined by the customs of immigrants from south-eastern Europe."

ॐॐॐॐॐॐॐ

"Meeting the Child Labor Problem," by Mabel Potter Daggett, In the Spotlight, Women and Events in the World Drama, *Today's Woman*, January 1914

When we put on the statute books the law against child labor, we found ourselves confronted with a new difficulty. What about the child who must work or starve? There have been various expedients to meet this situation. Sometimes a woman's club has provided a "scholarship" that paid the child a factory wage when he was taken from work to school. In some states now this assistance is regularly arranged by the Department of Education that buys a child's time in which he may go to school, just as for a long while it has been customary to buy his schoolbooks at public expense. United States Commissioner of Education, Hon. P. O. Claxton, has recently proposed another plan. He would offset the need for the child's wage by an increase in the family purse through home gardening. He suggests that the school term be increased to 12 months and that half of each day be devoted to teaching the child to raise vegetables, chickens, cows and pigs, the instruction to be given in the home backyard. These home agricultural products, by the savings effected in the daily marketing, would more than compensate for the loss of the child's factory wage.

The plan, it appears, would work until it reaches the cities where there aren't any backyards. High up in the tenements there wouldn't be room for the pig and the cow and the chickens and for but very few vegetables in the limited area of a window garden where the slum geranium grows. We have recently been finding out that all of the child labor isn't confined to cotton mills. Children as young as three years of age in the New York tenements are engaged with the rest of the family in making artificial forget-me-nots at a rate of 540 for $0.05. In over 30,000 licensed tenement houses in New York, little girls and boys are making flowers and feathers and dolls' clothes for the trade.

శోశోశోశోశోశోశో

"Baby's Upbuilding," by Edith V. Hart, *Child Betterment,*
The Official Organ of the National Child Welfare League, June 1914

"Baby comes into the world a helpless, dependent creature, with no habits, and no impressions. That into which his mind is to develop is plastic—like a wax record, ready to retain such impressions as are made upon it. But on the future of your infant boy or girl you place great store. You try to lift aside the veil of the years unborn and see the wonderful success of your own flesh and blood.

As a mother, your very tenderness and love may handicap the child. The fostering care you bestow upon your little one may induce weakness, bad habits, and disease and retard physical and moral growth through all after-years."

It was just like a dream, how my sister and I were running away from the town where we were. And I remember the bullets shooting. They were taking the straw for the cows and we were behind that, and the bullets be just like over there in the ground, we were running away and we were praying. They took us away some way out and my grandmother was sick in bed. When we got back she was dead. Dead in bed, and nobody to attend to her. It was 1914. I must've been between four and a half and five years old.

—Valeria Kozacka Demusz, 1975 interview concerning Polish conditions in 1914

"Nationwide Mortality Probe," *Child Betterment*, June 1914

About 300,000 babies under one year of age die yearly in the United States. Fully 150,000 of these could be saved by applying methods of care already known and widely practiced. But while the death rate for the entire population is slowly but surely declining, the death rate for children under one year is, if anything, rising. One babe in every eight born in this country dies before it is a year old. In certain localities the ratio is far worse than that. In one American city, for which statistics have been gathered, babies die in the poor neighborhoods at the rate of 373 per 1,000 born, or more than one in every three; while in the good residence districts in the same city, the rate is 154 per 1,000. Even that is high compared to the death rate in New Zealand, where for babies under one year it is only 68 for each 1,000. We have, therefore, in infant mortality a nationwide problem, and it is to have a nationwide probe. The new Children's Bureau of the Department of Commerce and Labor will make one of its chief activities for some time to come the study of infant mortality. With the new year, it will begin a house-to-house canvass of the entire nation, to verify numbers, scan conditions, seek causes, and obtain a basis on which to formulate remedies. Among the special matters to be studied is the housing of families, the feeding of infants, the sanitary conditions of neighborhoods, and the physical and mental health of parents as well as children. No doubt great results will follow this careful and scientific study of the main problems relating to the causes of illness and death among juveniles.

Women in Sports Timeline

1882 The National Croquet Association was formed to revise and standardize the rules.

1883 Matilda Howell won her first national archery title, a feat she would repeat 17 times between 1883 and 1907.

1883 The first baseball "Ladies Day" was held by the New York Giants, where both escorted and unescorted women were allowed into the park for free.

1884 Women's singles tennis was added to Wimbledon.

1885 The Association of Collegiate Alumnae published a study which refuted the widely held belief that college study impaired a woman's physical health and ability to bear children.

Roller skating rinks were built in almost every city and small town around the country at a total cost of $20 million.

1886 The first women's lacrosse game was played.

1887 Ellen Hansell was crowned the first Women's Singles Tennis Champion at the U.S. Open.

1888 The modern "safety" bicycle was invented with a light frame, two equal-sized wheels and a chain drive, encouraging women to join cycling clubs.

The Amateur Athletic Union was formed to establish standards and uniformity in amateur sports.

1889 The first women's six-day bicycle race ended at Madison Square Garden in New York City.

1891 The Shinnecock Hills Golf Club on Long Island opened its doors to women.

1892 The journal *Physical Education,* a publication of the YMCA, said that women needed physical strength and endurance, and dismissed the popular idea that women were too weak to exercise.

Gymnastics instructor Senda Berenson Abbott adapted James Naismith's basketball rules for women and introduced the game to her students at Smith College; the rules confined each player to one-third of the court.

The Sierra Club of California welcomed women members as it organized.

1893 Katharine Lee Bates climbed to the top of Pike's Peak and was inspired to compose the poem "America, the Beautiful."

1895 The first Women's Amateur Golf Championship was held, with 13 golfers competing at the Meadow Brook Club, Hempstead, New York.

1895 Frances Willard, president of the Woman's Christian Temperance Union (WCTU), published *A Wheel Within a Wheel,* a best-selling account of learning to ride a bicycle.

The first women's softball team was formed at Chicago's West Division High School.

Volleyball was invented in Holyoke, Massachusetts.

The American Bowling Congress was organized, and established equipment standards and rules.

1896 Women bought 30 percent of all new bicycles.

The first women's intercollegiate basketball championship was played between Stanford and the University of California at Berkeley.

At the first modern Olympics in Athens, a woman, Melpomene, barred from the official race, ran the same course as the men, finishing in four hours, 30 minutes. Baron Pierre de Coubertin, founder of the modern Olympics, said, "It is indecent that the spectators should be exposed to the risk of seeing the body of a women being smashed before their very eyes. Besides, no matter how toughened a sportswoman may be, her organism is not cut out to sustain certain shocks."

1898 Lizzie Arlington became the first woman to sign a professional baseball contract, appearing in her first professional game pitching for the Philadelphia Reserves.

1899 Ping pong, or table tennis, was invented.

1900 Physical education instructors strongly opposed competition among women, fearing it would make them less feminine.

   Nineteen women competed in the modern Olympic Games in Paris, France, in just three sports: tennis, golf and croquet.

1901 Field hockey was introduced to women in the United States by Constance M. K. Applebee, a British physical education teacher.

1902 Mrs. Adolph Landenburg introduced the split skirt for horseback riding in Saratoga Springs, New York.

1903 Eleanor Roosevelt enrolled in the Junior League of New York, where she taught calisthenics and dancing to immigrants.

1904 Matilda Howell won three gold medals in archery at the St. Louis Olympic Games.

1906 Lula Olive Gill became the first woman jockey to win a horse race in California.

   Skater Madge Syers became the first woman world figure skating champion.

1907 The first organized bowling league for women began in St. Louis, Missouri.

1908 The anthem of baseball, "Take Me Out to the Ball Game," was written about a young girl's love of the game.

1910 Dr. Clelia Duel Mosher debunked several popular myths of female health, including one claiming women breathe differently from men, which makes them unfit for strenuous exercise.

   For the second consecutive year, Hazel Hotchkiss won the singles, doubles and mixed doubles titles at the U.S. Lawn Tennis Association's championships.

   Australia's Annette Kellerman was arrested for swimming in Boston Harbor in an "indecent" one-piece swimsuit exposing her legs.

1911 Helene Britton became the first woman owner of a major league team, the St. Louis Cardinals.

1912 Swimming and diving debuted at the Stockholm Olympic Games, with 57 women from 11 nations competing.

   American college women eagerly took up the latest sports craze: wall scaling.

   Eleanora Sears completed her first marathon walk of 108 miles in 19 hours and 50 minutes.

1914 The American Olympic Committee formally opposed women's athletic competition in the Olympics.

   Women's basketball rules changed to allow half-court play, expanded from the original one-third court rules.

   The first national swimming championships were held with women allowed to register by the Amateur Athletic Union (AAU).

Lyrics to "If You Don't Want My Peaches, You'd Better Stop Shaking My Tree," by Irving Berlin, 1914

Mary Snow had a beau
Who was bashful and shy
She simply couldn't make the boy propose
No matter how she'd try
Mary grew tired of waiting
So she called her beau to one side
While he stood there biting his fingernails
Mary cried:

If you don't want my peaches
You'd better stop shaking my tree

Let me say that you're mighty slow
You're as cold as an Eskimo

There's a thousand others waiting
Waiting to propose to me

So, if you don't want my peaches
You'd better stop shaking my tree

Mary's Pa and her Ma
Soon came into the room

They took a look at Mary's beau and cried
"You ought to be a groom
Of course, it's none of our bus'ness
But she'd make a lovely bride"
He just answered "I'll think it over" but
Mary cried:

So, if you don't want my peaches
You'd better stop shaking my tree

&·&·&·&·&·&·&·&

Speech: "Traumatic Neurasthenia," by Joseph M. Burke, M.D., Chief Surgeon of Association of Seaboard Air Line Railway Surgeons

"The reasons impelling me to present you with this paper on 'traumatic neurasthenia,' or 'railway spine,' is that long experience in my official capacity compels me, in justice of the railways I service, to give you some facts by which you may be guided, and which will prove helpful to you in the differentiation of the true condition from mythical fake cases.

The appalling frequency with which juries render large verdicts against railroads is abhorrent and abominable; in fact, their prejudices cannot be removed by any testimony the company presents, and the conclusion must necessarily be, therefore, that they do not believe one iota of the evidence sworn to by any of the medical witnesses produced by a railroad. There are no doubt some exceptions to this general rule, and it may be that the verdicts against railroads could be condoned because of the impression made on juries by the glib tongue of a 'shyster lawyer' or an 'ambulance chaser,' who will have the assistance of some unscrupulous fool or knave, or maybe, one who could, if he would, be an ornament to our ranks, but is shrewd and cunning and swears on the stand without compromise, that physical neurasthenia is a mental condition, there is something material existing which is unexplainable, and at the same time will openly admit the verdict of the jury as rendered will determine the amount of his fee. We can readily, therefore, put the blame of the prejudices existing among jurors on the educated and better class of people, as without their assistance and coaching, action in law would rarely be had.

It is true the antipathy toward railroads was originally infused within the minds of the general public by the demagogic, petty politicians, who would proclaim that the wealth of the railroads

was in the hands of the few, and that this wealth would someday grind every man, woman and child into smithereens. Such statements were and are now believed by some persons, without their reasoning for one minute that but for the railroads we would be as barren as when Columbus discovered this great land of ours. Each and every one should gratefully recognize that our progress and civilization are indebted to that wealth which serves as so helpful an adjunct to our well-being in everyday life.

The railroads are daily paying out large sums of money to persons who get something for nothing, and this is due to the circumstances enumerated above. This condition, in my opinion, will continue unless the U.S. Government intervenes through the Interstate Commerce Commission and appoints an unbiased, non-political commission of competent physicians to decide whether a person is injured or not."

❦❧❦❧❦❧❦❧

"Ripley Says the World as a Whole Is Getting Poorer," *The Wall Street Journal*, May 22, 1915

"E.P. Ripley, president of the *Atchison,* says to the *Wall Street Journal:* 'The European war situation is no worse than I thought it would be by this time when I went to California last fall for the winter. The world as a whole is getting poorer. The balance of trade at the moment is much in our favor, and some of us are getting much richer on account of others' misfortune, but does that mean our permanent good? I cannot conceive it so.

'Many things are in our favor now, however, among them being the saving of many millions by keeping our rich people at home. Europe is consuming an enormous amount of foodstuffs at high prices, and may do so for another year. The immediate result is prosperity for a small portion of our people and disaster to another and quite considerable portion. If we should be drawn into the war, the sort of prosperity which the war has given to us would shrink rapidly. But I cannot see any excuse for our being drawn into it.'"

"Do You Know That—"
Royster's Almanac, 1915

"There are 7,397,533,000,000 tons of coal in the world, according to a careful estimate by the editor of *Coal Age*.

Apples, pears, lemons, oranges and limes are of great value in improving a muddy complexion. Raw tomatoes have a fine effect on the liver.

The amount of iron ore mined in the United States last year is officially estimated at 58 million to 60 million long tons, a new high record.

If new gas mantles be dipped into vinegar and hung up to dry before being placed upon the gas fixtures, they will give a more brilliant light and last longer.

A famous German physician proves that infantile paralysis is often carried from one household to another by domestic animals, such as chickens, ducks and steers.

The railroads of Great Britain kill in accidents, for which the passenger is in no way responsible, one passenger for every 72 million carried, while those of the United States kill one for every 4.9 million passengers carried."

"Mail Order vs. Country Store,"
The Wall Street Journal, May 1915

"Is the country store doomed to go, because of the pressure which is being brought to bear upon it through the mail order houses? The advocates of the fixed-price method of retailing regard the rural village shop as one of the vital links in the merchandising economy of a farm community. Yet here comes along a rural witness against it, charging the village or country store with being the cause of much of the decay in farm life. 'I charge the country store with being a nuisance on three charges,' writes a Pennsylvania farmer to the Department of Agriculture. 'One of these is the abominable loafing system it tolerates; another is the debasing language used among the loafing clientele; and the third is the neglect of the home duties by the men, leaving the burden to fall on the womenfolk to the impairment of the health and the stability of the home.'"

"Women Students Spend More than Men at University of Wisconsin Despite Their Free Amusements," *The Washington Post,* May 15, 1915

"Women students spend more than men at the University of Wisconsin, and the same is probably true of other coeducational state universities. Less than $500 a year is spent by the average Wisconsin University student, and that suffices to carry him through in comfort, according to a comprehensive survey that has recently been made at the Madison institution....

The fact that women spend considerably more than men students may occasion some surprise when it is recalled that women at state universities are exceptionally well-treated by men students as far as amusements and entertainment go, so that the average 'coed' is not often obligated to purchase her own tickets to football or the theater, and she seldom pays for a dance."

⊱⊰⊱⊰⊱⊰⊱⊰

The Outlook Magazine, on the Woman's Suffrage Parade down Fifth Avenue, New York, in 1915, witnessed by 250,000 people

"I didn't walk in New York's first suffrage parade because my mother wouldn't let me. Next year, in 1913, I wanted to march, but my husband asked me not to. This fall I decided that it was 'up to me' to suffer for democracy.

Three o'clock on the afternoon of October 23, and a glorious day. Every band in greater New York and some beyond blows like the breeze today. First it's 'Tipperary,' and then 'Tipperary' again, and once more, 'Tipperary.'

After 50 false alarms, suddenly down the line comes the signal, 'Make ready.' Quickly we slip into place. The marshals look us over, straighten out bends and kinks, and then as the band strikes up, begin to count time, 'Left, left, left!' My heart is thumping louder than the band. Dear heaven, we're there!

By the time we had gone two blocks I had forgotten everything I had expected to feel. All my girlhood, Mother had repeated that a lady should never allow herself to be conspicuous. To march up Fifth Avenue had promised to flout directly one's early training. I was mistaken. There's no notoriety about it. When it's done along with twenty-five thousand other women, nothing could seem more natural. Embarrassment is left at the street corner, and one is just a spar, a singing, swinging part of a great stream, all flowing in the same direction toward the same goal....

As we marched along I did not see the crowd. I never heeded the many policemen battling with the encroaching throng. Once when we were marking time, an indignant woman burst through the sidelines and demanded of an overworked officer, 'How can I get to the Grand Central Station in time to take my train?' 'Well, ma'am,' he drawled, 'I don't see any better way than for you to fall into line and march there.' 'What, I in a suffrage parade!' she shrieked. 'I won't so demean myself,' and flounced away. Another time I'd have thought that funny, but as we took up our procession I wondered what she meant. Thousands and thousands of women walking in protest before the bar of public opinion—could that be an unworthy thing? Could this, my new elation, multiplied twenty thousandfold, carry no impression on those who watched? Would even a czar of autocratic Russia dare to disregard so great a demonstration of his people?"

"Paderewski Estate Ruined, Letter to Pianist Also Tells of Starvation of Polish People," *The New York Times*, October 17, 1915

All that remains of the estate of Ignance Paderewski in the Tarnow district of Poland are the stumps of the trees that once formed the park and forest, many of them planted by the pianist…. Everything else has been swept away by the war, according to a letter from a friend in Poland to Paderewski.

Mme. Paderewski said yesterday that the people of this country had little conception of what war had done to Poland.

"There are millions starving today in Poland," she said. "Whole towns have been destroyed and people without food and shelter. My husband has received a letter in which his friend says there are 2,000,000 persons living as best they can upon the site that was until a few months ago the city of Wroclawek, in Russian Poland. This multitude is without food and almost unprotected from the severity of the weather. In all of Galicia it is now hard to find a human habitation…. Caught between contending armies, those who had not fled were wiped out by the fighting between November and August.

"From all parts of Poland the cry is now going up for food. In the effort to stay the pangs of hunger, mothers are feeding their children a mixture of chalk and water in place of milk.

"Miss Henrietta Ely of Philadelphia, who is one of the few women allowed to enter Poland recently, has just returned to this country. She came in to see me the other day, and I cried as I listened to her. Miss Ely said that she very often could not eat because of the sight of the starving children, who gathered about to watch the visitors eat and beg food from them. Poland is desolate, and, to quote Miss Ely, beside her, Belgium is a country filled with prosperity."

Paderewski is head and organizer of the National American Committee for Polish Victims Relief Fund, and on Saturday afternoon, October 23, before his show upon recital in Carnegie Hall, he will speak on "Poland, past and present." The entire receipts will go to the relief fund.

❧❦❧❦❧❦❧❦

How do you explain the fact that so many people had their names changed at Ellis Island? They had to. They spoke very badly, were very nervous. Inspectors would say, where do you come from? And they would say Berlin. The inspector would put the name down Berliner. The name was not Berliner. That's not a name.

All the "witz's" and "ski's" got their names from their fathers. For example, Meyerson is the son of Meyer. We knew that, and changed the names here because they were spelled so badly. For instance, a Polish name would be Skyzertski, and they didn't even know how to spell it, so it would be changed to Sanda, to names like that. It was much easier that way.

Then there are names like "Vladimir." That would be Walter in American, or Willie, something like that. Vladimir was strictly a Russian name, you know; they often were very anxious to Americanize quickly.

And sometimes the children and parents would use first names; they would call the father Adam and it became Mr. Adam and that was the way they went through.

—Ellis Island Inspector Helen Barr, *Island of Hope, Island of Tears*

"The Darker Side of Driving,"
Morrison County (Minnesota) Historical Society

In June 1913, there were 140 automobiles in Morrison County. The newspaper published lists of car owners and the makes of the cars they owned because the automobile was such a novelty at this time.

By August 1915, there were 562 automobiles in the county and around 86,000 cars in the state.

Some driving disasters were caused by the design of vehicles and poor roads. Early cars were top heavy and had no seat belts or air bags. Roads were unpaved, bumpy and dusty, and had no shoulders or dividing lines. Just as many car catastrophes were caused by human error.

Holding political office is no guarantee of safety from automobile accidents. In May 1910, Little Falls alderman, J. F. Bastien, was struck in downtown Little Falls while crossing the street. "Due only to the fact that the car was moving at a slow rate of speed and that Mr. Bastien had presence of mind enough to cause him to clutch at the hood of the machine saved him from being severely injured."

The first auto fatality occurred in the county on April 22, 1913. Warren Farrow and Frank Kerich were on their way to Little Falls from Pierz on the Pierz Road (now Highway 27) when the accelerator stuck. In trying to free the pedal, Farrow took his eyes off the road and the car "turned turtle" over an eight-foot embankment. Kerich, the passenger, was thrown from the car and was crushed as it rolled. Farrow was thrown free of the car and became unconscious. When he awoke hours later, he crawled to a home a half-mile away to get help. It was one o'clock in the morning by the time he reached the Mike Thommes house. News of the accident reached Coroner N. W. Chance, who brought Charles Farrow and F. P. Farrow (Warren Farrow's father) to the scene to retrieve Kerich's body and the automobile.

∽∾∽∾∽∾∽∾∽

"Shoulder Socket Is All That Keeps Girl Players
from Beating Men Tennis Champions,"
Reno Evening Gazette (Nevada), July 5, 1915

The "lady of the racket and ball" is the belle of the summer season.

You'll meet her everywhere, not only at the country clubs, but in the public parks, and the playgrounds, in vacant back lots, in side streets as well as in private courts on the boulevards.

"High Society" no longer has a mortgage on the good game of tennis. It's every woman's game and almost every woman, and just about every girl you know is playing it this summer.

To be sure, there are men who say that women will never make great tennis players, not that they haven't the brain and the muscle to make McLaughlin, Daugherty and the rest of the men

champs notice them. But woman's real handicap on the tennis court is her shoulder socket.

Yep. That's it. Woman's shoulder socket is deeper than man's. That's nature's fault, not woman's. The shoulder ball sets in too far to permit the quick "punchy" cannonball service characteristic of the best men players. No woman, say the main critics, can ever play as well as McLaughlin; her shoulder socket won't let her.

But aside from a little thing like that, the tennis girl is a regular trump in the game of outdoor sports, and judging by the way she's devoting herself to the racket and ball this summer, she'll add to the great glory achieved by Mary Browne of Los Angeles, who is national woman champion, and she'll do it in spite of her funny shoulder socket.

ॐ♋ॐ♋ॐ♋ॐ♋

"The New Seasons,"
Croonborg's Gazette of Fashions, August 1915

We are passing through social, political and commercial conditions the like of which the world has never seen.

The situation in Europe and our present relations with pestiferous Mexico, which are rapidly approaching a focus in spite of the peace at any price policy of the Wilson administration, make even the stoutest hearts serious.

It now appears that the great European war may be dragged on indefinitely, or at least to the limit of the borrowing power of the nations engaged in the godless struggle.

There are three ways in which the European holocaust affects every tailor and everyone who wears clothes. Most important of all is the condition that has been brought about in the woolen and fabric markets.

Abroad the first care of the warring nations is to provide for the man at the front. Statistics go to show that the life of a uniform is only about six weeks' duration.

English industrial figures show that 80 percent of the woolen mills in Great Britain are monopolized solely for the purpose of clothing the English army and navy. A similar condition exists in other countries.

As far as fashion tendencies are concerned, they lean undeniably toward solid colors and quiet tones. Gone are all the freakish or "flashy" touches in design. The clothes of the fall and winter seasons will reflect the somber minds of American businessmen who view conditions abroad with trepidation and business possibilities at home with some misgivings....

Merchant tailors may build high hopes upon one feature of prevailing conditions, for, while the importation of raw and manufactured woolens has increased to a great extent according to government statistics, there's been a tremendous falling off in the importation of ready-made clothing. This was inevitable, of course, the foreign factories being neither tied up with orders from their own government nor being put out of commission altogether. The foreign-made clothes have enjoyed considerable vogue in this country. There is little doubt that the patrons of the "made in England," "made in Paris" or the "made in Berlin" articles of apparel will turn to the American merchant tailor and custom cutter for more solid comfort and for better style....

It is not generally appreciated that the tailoring trade is the third largest industry in the United States. When it has been thoroughly organized from top to bottom, there is no doubt that it will take its stand amongst the most important organizations in the country.

"Our Responsibility in the War,"
The Christian Herald, April 7, 1915

To a very large portion of the American people, the fact is becoming increasingly apparent that, while we are acclaimed by the whole world as neutrals, we are in reality one of the principal participants in the European strife. By our shipments of weapons and ammunition we are assisting materially in keeping up the slaughter. How we can logistically claim to be a peace-loving and humane nation, and still supply the means of destroying thousands of human lives, is a problem which the American people must ultimately square with their own conscience....

Almost from the beginning of hostilities, our war materiel-producing plants have been coining money, at the cost in human lives, at a tremendous rate. From September 1 to December 31, 1914, exports of war materiel totaled $49,466,092, being an increase over the same months in the proceeding year of $37,751,255. The September increase was slightly over a million, the increase of October was $6,973,964, the November increase was $12,554,957, the December increase was $17,209,495. The figures for January and February of the current year are not available, but it is known they maintain the rising ratio.

In its issue of March 4, *The New York World* gives an amazing description of the martial activities of the plants in the industrial communities of Western Pennsylvania, eastern Ohio and West Virginia, known collectively as the "Pittsburg district." No sooner had the war begun than these plants sprang into sudden activity, working double and triple shifts and continually increasing their workforce until it is estimated that not less than 150,000 men are now employed in turning out war orders....

There was a bill before the late Congress, providing for an arms embargo, but it came to nothing for the reason given by U.S. Sen. Moses E. Clapp (Minnesota) in a letter to one of his correspondents, which he said: "The spectacle of the United States sending shiploads of food and clothing to the orphaned and widowed people of Europe, and at the same time sending shiploads of guns and ammunition to make more widows and orphans, is one of those grotesque contrasts we sometimes find." And he added: "There is so much money invested in the making and the sale of arms and war munitions that we have simply been powerless to get anywhere with the bill."

**Letter to the Editor: "The Gary Plan: A Backward S,"
by Isidore Springer, Principal, Public School 25, Brooklyn,
The New York Times, January 6, 1915**

Very few educational movements have aroused so much interesting discussion among the public and education circles as the Gary Plan. We find editorials and newspapers advocating very strenuously its adoption. Directors of educational associations seem to find it a cure-all for all educational ills. In view of this constant agitation, I believe it is time to consider the Gary Plan, not in the light of partnership, but in view of educational history and practice, and seek to find whether this movement or plan is in harmony with the trend of educational thought during the past two decades.

I do not wish to be considered as an opponent of the Gary Plan, nor an exponent of the Ettinger or any other plan. It is simply my purpose to consider this plan in light of the various educational movements that had been discussed and proved worthy to be incorporated as a part of the educational program. I beg, therefore, to make a brief summary of the various movements that have been occupying the public attention and discussion for the past 20 years: to note, if possible, the common tendency or meaning; to examine, in such a light, the Gary Plan, and so determine whether this plan is a step forward and therefore in harmony with the main currents of educational history, or whether, on the contrary, this plan is not an about-face to what has gone before and practically nullifies educational progress for the past 20 years.

The graded class, which was called into being by the organization of large city schools, presented many problems which soon demanded solution. An attempt to solve the problem of mass instruction, with its attendant evils of disregard of the individual, was by formation of special classes, such as the "C" classes, or, English to foreign classes; "E" classes, classes which should help the backward pupils; and the ungraded classes, which would take care of the mentally unfit. A further attempt at this solution took the form of the organization in every class of groups, and the provision of the educational busy work for the members of the group not reciting.

In 1912, the Committee of Inquiry of the Board of Estimate and Apportionment began an investigation of the city schools with a view of determining wherein these schools were inefficient and uneconomical. This inquiry had been called forth by the then public discussion as to the prevalence of overage and retarded children in schools of the city of New York. It will be remembered by even the general reader that this question of overage became so heated as to, at times, assume an acrimonious stage. Conferences were called by the city superintendent, various committees were appointed, and important progress was made to solve the problem of retardation. It was seen that retarded and overage children were an economic loss to the city, and the prevention of retardation would result in a gain to the city, both economically and socially. The committee appointed by the Board of Estimate and Apportionment presented a report that showed that part-time and overcrowded classes were causes of retardation.

If we examine carefully, then, these various movements which have been deemed worthy of being incorporated as part of the educational practice of the day, I think it will be found that all these agitations seemed to have a basis, whether consciously or not, in a desire that the interests of society are best served when the needs and capacity of the individual are considered and developed....

In other words, the past two decades will be known in educational history as the period of the individualization of instruction.

Now let us consider the relation of the Gary Plan to this movement. The Gary Plan calls for the economical and wider use of the school plan by providing for schools of large size and large numbers of children in each class. Fundamentally considered, the Gary Plan is a plan for part-time schools, with many of the objectionable features of part-time schools culminating by incorporating ancillary activities, such as swimming pools, libraries, shops, etc. The Gary Plan does not present a single innovation in school methods or show a new approach toward individual instruction, but is simply a departmental schedule so drawn up as to accommodate two groups of classes in one building, a scheme which was attempted for many years in New York under the part-time school.

The Gary idea, and planning for large schools, from 64 to 128 classes, creates such a tremendous educational machine that the individual is lost. The direct relation between the supervisor in the class is reduced to a minimum. The close personal touch that should exist between principal and children must disappear. The supervisor becomes administrative officer, a business manager. The school becomes an educational factory.

The greatest danger, however, is the overcrowding of classrooms. The question of the number of children in the class that makes for efficient instruction has been the subject of a number of experiments recently. It has been proved almost conclusively that the ideal class should have 30 to 35. The Gary Plan, fundamentally a plan of economy, calls for classes of 45 and more.

The possibility of a close study of the individual with the view of determining his needs and issues, teaching, instead of becoming an art based on scientific pedagogy, degenerates into the peddling of information....

Finally, the Gary Plan, however attractive it may be made, is a double session plan, or part-time plan, and therefore brings with it the attendant evils of retardation and overage. Our evaluation of the Gary Plan leads us to the conclusion that it is a distinct backward step in educational history. The problems for retardation and overage which promised to be solved again become in imminent danger. The process of individualized education, the process of the study of the individual, to know his capacities, and to adopt himself to the service of society according to its needs, is halted, and American education becomes reactionary because of a policy of financial entrenchment.

ॐ◌ॐ◌ॐ◌ॐ◌ॐ◌ॐ

A Dutch Fork Farm Boy, a memoir by J. M. Eleazer

The finest milk cow we ever had got her neck broken while being driven to water. The water hole was down below the barn in a clump of cedars. She had been hitched out that day and a colored boy on horseback was driving her to water before taking her in that afternoon. When he hit the cedars he started chasing her full speed with her chain dragging. The galloping horse stepped on the chain, tripped her and broke her neck.

To the old folks, that was a tragedy of the first rank. But not to us kids. Hidden in the dense cedars, we watched the buzzards there for days, until nothing but a clean skeleton remained.

We saw none of the gruesomeness of it. Our observations were of a sort of scientific nature. To us that was a marvel of nature. It would have taken at least two mules that we did not have to pull her away. And much work to dig a hole big enough to bury her in the stone hills. So the buzzards came along and saved us all of that.

When we tired of watching the busy gang of them on the carcass, we would lie on our backs on the grass behind the cedars and look into the languid May skies. At first we would see only a dot. Then it grew larger into a buzzard. It would glide around and around, seldom flapping a wing, gradually descending. And when it landed there was always a slight flurry among the scores that were already there, as it dived into the feast.

Kentucky Tales

Down our way we can never forgive Mrs. Harriet Beecher Stowe for writing Uncle Tom's Cabin, not because she painted Southern slavery in such black colors but because she has Eliza crossing the Ohio River to get out of Kentucky. To this day, we hold that Eliza made the mistake of her life.

—Irvin S. Cobb, *American Magazine*, 1916

ॐॐॐॐॐॐ

The people of Kentucky are determined that when the next census is taken, there shall not be found one man or woman in the state who cannot read and write. They are fighting illiteracy as they might some terrible plague. In fact, they have come to realize that illiteracy is a plague, and that to allow it to exist is dangerous to the commonwealth.

—William F. De Moss, *Illustrated World*, 1916

ॐॐॐॐॐॐ

"A Wonderful Discovery,"
The Youth's Companion, November 1, 1916

When Roentgen announced his discovery of what has since become known as X-rays, no one could anticipate the value of the instrument that he placed in the hands of physicians and surgeons. But great as the value of that instrument is, it is strictly limited. Although it gives correct and most useful views of the bones of our frame, it delineates unsatisfactorily the soft parts of the body; and in a great number of cases a complete knowledge of those is of supreme importance.

Now news comes from England of an invention and discovery much more remarkable than any of Roentgen's. By an ingenious use of the electric current generated within the body in combination with two other electric currents in x-ray tubes, the living tissues are made to make their own pictures. They actuate a needle, which makes a diagram of any desired organ on a revolving cylinder covered with waxed paper…. The story seems well-nigh incredible, but is well-authenticated. It is accepted as true by the *British Medical Journal*, one of the best medical authorities in England.

ॐॐॐॐॐॐ

"The Submarine Issue,"
The Youth's Companion, November 16, 1916

How shall the submarine be treated? Is it entitled to the same privileges and subject to the same restrictions as a vessel that sails on the surface, or, in the absence of any international agreement on the subject, shall it be regarded as an outlaw of the sea? That is the question that complicates, and threatens to embitter, the relations between the belligerent nations and more than one of the neutral nations. Norway has answered it by excluding all military submarines from its waters, unless they come, helpless, in search of asylum, and by ruling that submarine merchantman must only enter those waters on the surface and flying the flag of its nation.

Although that decision is less sweeping than the Allies would like, it has angered Germany. Germans insist the submarine shall have every consideration that other vessels have, besides the right to use their special advantage of invisibility whenever they choose to do so. Unable to persuade Norway to take that view, they are trying the efficacy of violence. In no other way can we account for the busy campaign the German submarines are waging against Norwegian shipping. The excuse is that the destroyed vessels were carrying contraband of war, but that does not explain why English ships, the ships of an actual enemy, shall be almost neglected while this determined destruction of neutral vessels goes on. It will be interesting to see whether the German policy induces Norway to abandon its position or goads it into open hostility to Germany.

 споспоспоспоспо

"The Woman's Game, Tennis for Women," Miss Molla Bjurstedt, 1916

"Take the net as soon as you can and don't let her pass you." I heard this instruction given to a young girl by a man ranking in the first ten. The girl took the advice eagerly as though it were new and unusual. A few weeks later I saw her play; she was faithfully following the principle in so far as reaching the net was concerned, but she was being passed at will. Her opponent, who had not nearly so much tennis ability, was winning rather easily.

The admonition to play the volley game is perfectly sound; the style is most effective if you can play it.

I have never known a girl or woman who could play a net game in singles to three hard sets who could reach the net, volley consistently, and keep the pace. And yet I do not know how many thousands are trying to progress in the style of the game under the impression that first-class tennis is not to be achieved without imitating Mr. Maurice McLaughlin. Mr. McLaughlin, at his best, is a marvelous player; he can do things which an ordinary human being is foolish to attempt. And he must be in the most splendid physical and mental condition to play this particular game. No other man has ever yet been able to put over a railroad serve, follow up to the net, and play the ball almost continuously in the air; it demands more energy and endurance than even the trained man possesses....

If the men in the first flight cannot play the hard serving, smashing game, how foolish it is for the average girl to experiment with it!

споспоспоспоспо

"Liner *Cymric* Is Torpedoed Off Irish Coast, Great White Star Vessel Was Bound to Liverpool from New York," *The New York Times*, May 9, 1916

LONDON, May 8—The 13,000-ton White Star Line steamship *Cymric*, which for some time has been engaged in freight service, has been torpedoed by a German submarine, according to advices received here.

The *Cymric* left New York April 29 with an enormous cargo of war munitions. As she usually makes the voyage from New York to Liverpool in ten days, she was therefore within a day or two of her destination. It is considered probable, in the absence of definite details, that the disaster to the *Cymric* occurred off the west coast of Ireland, but whether on the northerly or southerly route cannot be stated.

The fate of the steamship is not yet known, although an early message received in London reported that the *Cymric* was sinking. The crew aboard numbered about 100 men, but the steamer carried no passengers.

The dispatch filed at Queenstown would seem to indicate that the *Cymric* had been attacked off the southwest or south coast of Ireland, possibly not far from where the Lusitania went down.

When the *Cymric* sailed from this port on April 29 she carried a crew of 110 officers and men and one of the largest cargoes of munitions of war yet shipped. None of these men is definitely known to be an American, although it was said unofficially yesterday that there were probably twenty Americans among them. J. J. MacPherson, the British Vice Consul in charge of shipping, said that eight new men were shipped on the *Cymric* for her last voyage, and that none of these was American. During the vessel's stay here twelve of her crew deserted and these eight were shipped to replace them.

In addition to the regular crew, three officers and two seamen of other British vessels, who had been stranded in this port, were being sent home.

According to the line's officials, the *Cymric* was in their service, denial being made that she had been taken over by the British Government. There was a very small amount of commercial goods shipped on the vessel, practically the entire cargo consisting of more than 18,000 tons of munitions and other war materiel. While no intimate details of the munitions could be obtained yesterday, the manifest showed that the *Cymric* carried:

8 cases of firearms.
13 cases of guns.
80 cases of rifles.
820 cases of Gaines (gun covers).
590 cases of primers.
2,163 pieces of forgings.
11,049 cases of empty shells.
300 cases of cartridge cases.
40 cases of aeroplanes and parts.
81 cases of tractors and parts.
62 cases of lathes.
7,554 barrels of lubricating oil.
60 cases of steel tubes.
107 cases of copper tubes.
1,768 plates of spelter.
20 cases of gun parts.
6 cases of bayonets.
624 cases of rubber boots and shoes.
220 cases of fuse heads.
7 cases of empty projectiles.
122 cases of forgings.
8,600 cases of cartridges.
6,720 cases of fuses.
18 cases of automobiles.
1,247 cases of agricultural machinery.
1,231 bundles of shovels.
831 bales of leather.
400 reels of barbed wire.
21,908 bars of copper.
1,056 cases of brass rods.

Captain F. E. Beadnell, who has been in the service of the White Star Line for more than twenty years and who was formerly commander of the *Baltic,* was in command of the *Cymric*.

The vessel was built by Harland & Wolff, Ltd., in Belfast, and was launched in 1898. She has a gross tonnage of 13,370 and is 585 feet long, with a beam of 64 feet and a depth of about 38 feet.

Never a fast vessel, the *Cymric* is rated as a ten- or eleven-day ship, and was one day from port at the time it was reported that she was sinking. For the last six weeks she has not carried passengers, and when in that service, only had accommodations for one class. The *Cymric* has had several narrow escapes from submarines during her previous voyages. On March 28, 1915, she was less than twenty miles away from the *Falaba* when the latter was torpedoed, having sailed a short time before that vessel. Captain Beadnell received the *Falaba's* call for help, but was forced to obey the Admiralty instructions and refrain from going to her assistance.

On Sept 26, 1915, when the *Cymric* reached here, members of her crew said that she was escorted into Liverpool by a cruiser and two torpedo boats, and announced that they believed that the Hesperian was torpedoed in mistake for their vessel, as both looked alike.

When the *Cymric* arrived here on Jan. 23, 1916, carrying $100,000 in gold and $26,250,000 in American securities, Captain Beadnell said that he had received a wireless warning shortly after clearing from Liverpool, that there were German submarines about and warning him to be on the lookout. This warning came from the Admiral at Queenstown, and the *Cymric* was met by three heavily armed patrol boats, which escorted her for more than fifty miles, or to the end of the danger zone. On that trip she carried a number of passengers.

৵৽৵৽৵৽৵৽

"Wilson the Political Weather Vane," *The Melting Pot,* May 1916

President Wilson was in favor of a single presidential term. Now he is against it.

President Wilson was in favor of the Garrison Continental Army plan. Now he is against it.

President Wilson was opposed to increasing the Navy. Now he demands that the Navy be made the largest in the world.

Preston Wilson was opposed to young men spending time in military training. Now he demands that 400,000 be trained.

President Wilson was opposed to a Tariff Commission. Now he demands a Tariff Commission.

President Wilson was in favor of free Panama Canal tolls. After his election, he compelled the Democratic majority to repeal the free tolls law....

President Wilson was for women's suffrage in New Jersey and against women's suffrage in Washington.

President Wilson was opposed to preparedness as late as last year. Now he is preaching preparedness fervently....

To us, it seems that President Wilson has no fixed principles or convictions upon any subject under the sun, and that he is consistent only in advocating anything that promises to promote his re-election in his personal ambitions.

—From the Los Angeles Examiner

"The Holy Inquisition in Power in Boston,"
The Melting Pot, October 1916

The Holy Inquisition is now in power in the Roman Catholic city of Boston.

The haters of free speech, with help of a judge of their stripe on the bench, have defied the supposedly constitutional rights of an American citizen and sentenced to prison the young student and a newspaperman for giving a papal sneak a leaflet on birth control.

The following account, taken from *The Masses,* tells the story:

Van Kleck Allison, 22 years, a former Columbia student and newspaperman, was sentenced to three years in the penitentiary in Boston on July 20, for having given a lying plainclothes man a leaflet on birth control.

The officer told Allison that he was a married man in poor circumstances, and that his wife was giving birth to another child. He could not afford more children and asked for methods.

Allison was sentenced on four counts. Three were on the leaflet given to the officer, and one was for publishing an article on birth control by Dr. W. J. Robinson and Allison's newsmagazine, *The Flame.*

The trial was horrible. The district attorney said that women present in the courtroom ought to blush for their womanhood. Judge Murray had the verdict ready right after district attorney concluded. Judge Murray said birth control was a blow to the foundations of Divine Law.

Appeal has been taken. The fight is on.

"Celebrating Yale,"
The Youth's Companion, November 16, 1916

The great Bowl at Yale was the scene last month of one of the most elaborate and impressive pageants ever staged—although as a spectacle some persons prefer the Harvard-Yale game to be played in the same place next week. The pageant was in celebration of the 200th anniversary of Yale's moving from Saybrook to New Haven. About 7,000 persons took part in the episodes that pictured important events in the history of Yale and Connecticut, and nearly 70,000 spectators looked on. The 200th anniversary that Yale is celebrating covers a long period, for the New Haven colony began to think of having a college as early as 1644, when it began contributing to the support of Harvard. It had no name until 1718, when the first building erected for use in New Haven was named for its benefactor, Elihu Yale, a native of Boston, who gained his fortune in India.

"New York's Fourth,"
The Outlook, July 12, 1916

Six years ago, Mayor Gaynor decided to give the people of New York a "safe and sane fourth." To replace the accustomed joys of burned fingers, blazing homes, and ruined eyes, he devised a series of popular and interesting entertainments.

This year, the mayor's "Independence Day Committee" has grown to permanent strength, and it arranged an elaborate programme for the day which would make accessible to every citizen a steady performance as varied as a three-ring circus from morning till night. It districted the city so as to provide "block celebrations" for 20 geographical units, each of which included band concerts, dancing, patriotic addresses, and the "movies." In 200 public schools, Independence Day exercises were held from 10:30 to noon, while song rallies took place out of doors in places ranging from the Bronx to Staten Island.

The day started with a flag-raising at the Old Block House in Central Park at 5:30 in the morning, followed by a band concert in the Park at eight o'clock, with speeches and songs. At 10 in Union Square, there were songs again from workingmen, most of them cloak and suit makers, now on strike. The Declaration of Independence was being read when two of the strikers came late into the range of the speakers' voices. As they listened, they were evidently puzzled at the words they heard; one turned to the other and asked if it was a manifesto from the Mexican workers to their American brethren. "No," said his companion. "I think it is an Irish revolutionary document of some kind...."

The small boy, although forbidden explosives, was happy all day with athletic competitions arranged throughout the city by the mayor's Independence Day Committee. In 36 public parks youngsters ran races, jumped both broad and high, put the shot, dashed gaily for 40, 50, for 60 yards. Swimming contests were won and lost, and grown folks strove with children in potato races and obstacle runs. In Chinatown, Wing Lee won the one-lap race for boys up to 110 pounds, while his brother, Non Lee, took second place in the 60-yard dash. In Washington Square, little Italian girls drilled and danced the morning away.

In the evening, 15,000 people went up to the stadium at City College for an elaborate programme of music, oratory, and tableaux. Madame Gadski sang the "The Star-Spangled Banner," while the audience applauded equally "Paul Revere's Ride" and the "Child Labor" pageant. That night, all of Thirty-ninth St. between Fifth and Sixth Ave. was turned into a dancing floor for the girls and their friends of the Vacation Association. A huge screen was hung on one side of the street, and those who would not dance could watch the pictures thrown there until midnight.

"Rapid Dish Washer,"
Today's Housewife, June 1917

"If all housewives were asked what part of housework is the most trying I am quite sure they would answer 'dishwashing.' A machine, therefore, that relieves women of the drudgery of this work should be of great interest to every homemaker.

At first view, the Rapid Electric Dish Washer appears to be only a beautiful kitchen table with silvery top and spacious lower compartment. Upon lifting the lid, which extends across a portion of the top, one sees a most interesting interior, consisting of removable racks for dishes, so made that there are spaces for all kinds of china and utensils. All one has to do in order to operate this machine is to scrape the dishes, place them in their proper compartments, pour in eight quarts of boiling water, in which a good washing powder has been mixed, close the lid tight, turn on the current—and go about one's other duties.

In 15 minutes the dishes are clean, and you can press the lever that allows the water to escape through a drainpipe. Then pour in eight quarts of clear, boiling hot water for rinsing the dishes, and switch on the current again for two or three minutes. The rinse water is drained off, and the result, if the water has been hot enough, will be shining, clean dishes that require no wiping with a towel. One of the great advantages of this machine is that it is adaptable to a small family as well as a large one, and is a special boon for company dinners and when canning multiplies dishwashing. It is self-cleaning, as the process of washing the dishes throws the water at high speed in every direction, cleaning all of the inner spaces and racks at the same time that it washes the dishes. The cost of running it is also inconsiderable, averaging about one cent per hour for the electricity. The electrical cord may be attached to any lighting fixture.

If one desires, she may easily connect the drainpipe of the dishwasher with the sewage system, thus disposing of the water without the use of a pail. There may be a hot water connection as well, but this is not advisable unless extremely hot water is available. The price is $40."

慡慡慡慡

"Thousands of Aeroplanes to Break the Deadlock in Europe," *Current Opinion*, August 1917

Why not make it the fixed aim of the United States, says Admiral Peary, to be "the first air-power in the world"? If we will only concentrate upon aircraft, he adds, as von Tirpitz concentrated on submarines, "we will not only have an answer to the submarine menace, but we will have an unequivocal decision of the war, and that within a short time." The suggestion has evidently kindled the American imagination as well as appealed to its common sense. Congress has responded by the passage, in the Lower House, without a dissenting vote, after only four hours of discussion, of a bill appropriating $640 million to build a great air fleet and train an army of aviators. Five universities started courses of instruction several months ago and began graduating students last month, 200 a week being expected to receive their certificates of graduation from now on.... In one month's time, 2,000 workmen have erected half a million dollars' worth of buildings at Rantoul, Illinois, for a training field; 3,000 men were at work at the same time near Dayton, Ohio; and 2,000 at work near Mt. Clemens, Michigan. The appropriation bill in Congress does not mention the number of aeroplanes or aviators to be provided. That is to remain a military secret. But the president of the Aereo Club is talking of 100,000 planes and 25,000 men to operate them.

慡慡慡慡

"Flower of Nation's Younghood to Be Selected to Battle for Democracy, Ten Million Men Enrolled for Service," *Toledo Weekly Blade*, June 14, 1917

The government at Washington now has 10 million names of citizens from which to select an army to fight for the cause which this nation represents in the world war. Registration day, the first of its kind in the history of the United States, was a success in every way. Eligibles went quietly to the booths and had their names and ages entered on the rolls of the government. Except for a few isolated cases, there was no trouble.

Many states fell behind the Census Bureau's estimates of eligibles. In others, the registration far exceeded the estimates. In many places registration privileges were extended for two days to any who did not understand what was required of them or could not give reasonable excuses for not registering on Tuesday. The next steps in the government's plan will be the selection of those who actually are to bear arms from others who will remain at home because of dependents or to do the work on the farm or in the factory that must be carried on to maintain the nation at war....

There will be no weaklings in the armies sent to France. The flower of the nation's youth from a physical viewpoint will be selected to fight the battle for democracy. It will be an army of athletes. In determining physical fitness, the examining physicians will observe the strict standards that have prevailed in the American army for many years. As a result of the enforcement of these physical requirements, an average of only one in four applicants for enlistment in the regular army is accepted. It is estimated, however, that the young men who have registered for the selective draft will be of a higher physical grade than those who have sought enlistment in the army hitherto, and that less than five percent will measure up to the required standard.

$\approx \approx \approx \approx \approx \approx \approx$

"What Our Red Cross Is Doing in France,"
by Marion G. Scheitlin, *American Review of Reviews*, December 1917

To a recent news cablegram sent by the American Red Cross Commission in France to the War Council in Washington, there was appended this sentence:

"If the American people could only get a picture of the misery among those daily driven out of their homes and dumped in poverty among other parts of the country—oftentimes terribly sick or mutilated—they would gladly do all in their power to help...."

This is not an appeal for aid; it was an involuntary expression—aye, prayer—of unselfish men, drawn from them by the picture on which they had gazed since the War Council sent them to France. A ghastlier picture was never limned by the brush of Verestchagin. This picture—a panorama of France, of Belgium, created by the insensate and insatiate savagery of the Hun—is in great measure dimmed by distance to most of us in America....

It has taken Prussianism nearly three and one half years to create this picture. If peace were to come today, it would take 10 times three and one half years to erase it; and there would still remain some ineffaceable blotches. But while the paint is still fresh and the blood-red coloring still vivid, let us try to visualize it as best we may. Perhaps the best way is to take some pages from the archives of the Red Cross in the form of communications from its workers afield....

All in a day's work, a Red Cross official sends this report:

"There arrived last week at Evian, where the repatriates from France and Belgium are received back into France, a train loaded with Belgian children. There were 680 of them—thin, sickly, from four to 12 years of age—children of men who refused to work for the Germans and of mothers who let their children go rather than to let them starve. They poured off the train, little ones clinging to the older ones, girls all crying, boys trying to cheer. They had come all the long way alone. On the platform were the Red Cross workers to greet them. Those children who could walk at all marched along crying, 'Meat, meat, we are going to have meat.' Their little claw-like hands were significant, but a doctor said, 'We have them in time; a few weeks of proper feeding and they will pull up.' Thirty percent of the older repatriates die the first month from exhaustion. The children can and must be saved."

Two such trains pull into Evian every day. They are laden with the too-young and the too old—untilled grist for the Prussian industrial mill. Kultur weighs its victims only in the scale of possible usefulness to the Veterland. The humans in its power are reduced to terms of thaler, mark and pfennig. The grandchildren too young to work and the grandparents too old to work for Germany are cast into the discard and loaded for France. Germany needs its food. It cannot afford to reduce rations of its fighting men by feeding, however meagerly, useless children and equally useless old people. If they have to starve, it were better they starved in France. And starve many of them unquestionably would were it not for Evian, Troche, and the Red Cross.

At Evian the Red Cross took over a public building, and at Troche, 20 miles from Limoges, it turned the famous monastery at La Grande Chartreuse into a haven of rest and recuperation for the very young and the very old repatriates. At these two stations, about 1,500 to 2,000 haggard, hopeless little children and aged persons arrive daily. And 30 percent of the older ones die during the first month in spite of all the tender mercies of the Red Cross can do!

☙❧☙❧☙❧☙❧

"The Greatest Woman in the Courts," by Fred Hawthorne, *Outing*, October 1917

There is a marked divergence in the style of game played by these two feminine wonders in the courts. Miss Browne is distinctly the net player, armed with a brilliant, severe overhead game, the ability to force her openings, to make cunning change of pace. In no single department is she weak, but her greatest effectiveness comes when she operates from just inside the service-court line, there to bring off her sharp overhead shots or to execute low volleys at acute angles across the fore-court, in the style made famous by Frederick B. Alexander.

As a matter of fact, Miss Browne's game is typically a man's. She is always prepared, even eager, to settle matters quickly by sharp, decisive volleying duels at the net, and she can smash wonderfully well from any position in the court. I've seen her more than once take a deep lob while running backwards, as McLaughlin used to do, and then crash it back for a "kill."

Her game is the result of long and careful instruction by such masters of the racket as Tom Bundy, her brother, Nat, and other stars from the Coast, and today the little Californian is a far greater player than when she held the national title.

☙❧☙❧☙❧☙❧

"Million Letters in the Mails Today Bearing Magic Words 'With the Colors,'" *The Cambridge City Tribune* (Indiana), November 22, 1917

It was evening on the broad Hempstead Plains, Long Island, where the Rainbow division was spending its last night before embarking for France. It had been raining hard in the afternoon—a cold, steady autumn downpour—and there was nothing to suggest the rainbow in the outward aspect of the camp. Lines and lines of sodden canvas housed 27,000 men, gathered from 27 different states. The ground was dotted with tools and quagmires. Under the wet canvas it was damp and cold, with penetrating chill. Lit by flickering candles, tents were far from cheerful shelter from man's last night in his native land.

But there were seven big tents where electric lights and friendliness made the night pleasant. In each of these a soldier was drumming on a piano; others were reading books and magazines; hundreds were writing letters home. Behind the raised counter at one end, three or four young men were busy passing out notepaper and envelopes, selling stamps and weighing parcels, which the men were sending home. One of the soldiers said to me as I stood in the tent used chiefly by men from Iowa: "We came all the way here from the morning, and we're mighty lonely. Then we found this YMCA on the job, and it's been more than a home for us. It gave us what we wanted when we needed it most. We'll never forget it. The boy's best friend is the YMCA.

How close these benches were packed with men, bending over the long tables absorbed in their writing! What an appeal to the sympathies these great groups of soldiers make! Fine, clean-cut, upstanding fellows, some of them mere boys, one thinks immediately of the sacrifice they have made for the rest of us, how precious they are to someone back home. Somewhere, in a far-off farm or village or city street, their parents or brothers or wives who would give all they possess for one glimpse of the sunburned faces as you and I see them on their last night before going across. And it was with the throb of the heart that I watched them, bent over their letter paper, in one after another of those seven big tents.

These were the tents of the YMCA. On that last night in America, the association was serving the soldiers in the best of all ways—giving them an opportunity to write home. On previous nights they had enjoyed boxing bouts, movies, concerts, dramatics and a score of healthy entertainment as well as religious meetings. But on the last night, home ties were strongest. And perhaps that is the keynote of the splendid work the YMCA is keeping among our men in uniform—keeping them in touch with home.

In these times there are some letters that mean more to us than any we have ever read before. They are written on sheets of paper stamped with the stars and stripes and the red triangle of the YMCA, and they bear the magic words, "With the Colors." There are many more than a million such letters in the mail now while you read this. Perhaps one is on its way to you. Each one of our 16 cantonments, where the new national army is being trained, is using more than a million sheets of this paper every month. In the draft army alone that means 16,000,000 filaments of love each month reaching out from the great encampment where the men are being trained into the greatest army this nation has ever dreamed of and binding them to the hearts at home. Multiply that by thinking of all the other places where Uncle Sam has men with the flag—and Navy yards, on the high seas, and arsenals and officers training camps and "over there" in France. In all these places men are writing home. Those unassuming little sheets of notepaper gladden millions of hearts a day.

Commercial Canning Timeline

1795 Napoleon offered 12,000 francs to anyone who could devise a way of preserving food for his army and navy.

1809 Nicolas Appert of France devised an idea of packing food into special "bottles," like wine.

1810 Nicolas Appert was awarded the 12,000-franc prize from the French Government after he invented the method of preserving food through sterilization; Appert published the *Book for all Households,* which was translated into English and published in New York.

Peter Durand of England received a patent from King George III that included pottery, glass and tinplated iron for use as food containers.

1812 Thomas Kensett of England established a small packing plant in New York to can oysters, meats, fruits and vegetables in hermetically sealed containers.

1818 Peter Durand introduced his tinplated iron can to America.

1819 Thomas Kensett and Ezra Gagett started selling their products in tinplate cans.

1825 Kensett received an American patent for tinplated cans.

1830 Huntley and Palmer of England began selling biscuits and cakes in decorated cans.

1846 Henry Evans introduced dies to increase production speeds tenfold.

1847 Allan Taylor patented a machine for stamping cylindrical can ends.

1849 Henry Evans was granted a patent for the pendulum press, capable of making a can end in a single operation; production speeds improved from five or six cans per hour to 50-60 per hour.

1856 Gail Borden was granted a patent on canned condensed milk.

1858 Ezra J. Warner of Waterbury, Connecticut, patented the first can opener

1866 E.M. Lang of Maine was granted a patent for sealing tin cans by dropping bar solder in measured drops on can ends.

       J. Osterhoudt patented the tin can with a key opener.

1870 William Lyman patented a can opener with a rotating wheel, which cut along the top rim of the can.

       Hinged-lid tin cans were introduced.

1875 Arthur A. Libby and William J. Wilson of Chicago developed the tapered can for canning corned beef.

       Sardines were first packed in cans.

1877 The simplified "side seamer" for cans came into use.

1880-1890 Automatic can-making machinery debuted.

1892 Tobacco cans were introduced.

1894 AMS Machine Company began manufacturing locked double-seam cans.

1898 George W. Cobb Preserving Company perfected the sanitary can.

1901 The American Can Company was formed.

1909 Tuna canning began in California.

1914 Continuous ovens, used to dry inked tinplate, were introduced.

1917 The Bayer Company introduced pocket-sized cans for aspirin.

       Key-opening collar-cans for coffee were introduced.

Food Brand and Product Introductions

1872 Blackjack chewing gum

1876 Premium soda crackers (later Saltines)

1881 Pillsbury Flour

1885 Dr Pepper

1886 Coca-Cola

1887 Ball-Mason jars

1888 Log Cabin Syrup

1889   Aunt Jemima pancake mix
       Calumet Baking Powder
       McCormick spices
       Pabst Brewing Company

1890   Knox Gelatine
       Libby introduces keys on its cans of meat
       Lipton tea

1891   Del Monte
       Fig Newtons
       Quaker Oats Company

1893   Cream of Wheat
       Good & Plenty
       Juicy Fruit gum

1894   Chili powder

1895   Shredded coconut
       Triscuit

1896   Cracker Jack
       Michelob beer
       S&W canned foods
       Tootsie Roll

1897   Campbell's Condensed Soup
       Campbell's Tomato Soup
       Grape-Nuts
       Jell-O

1898   Nabisco
       Nabisco graham crackers
       Shredded Wheat

1899   Wesson oil

1900   Chiclets
       Cotton candy
       Hershey's chocolate bar

1901   Instant coffee

1902   Barnum's Animal Crackers
       Karo corn syrup

1903   Pepsi
       Best Foods
       Canned tuna
       Sanka
       Sunshine Biscuits

1904   Banana split
       Campbell's Kids
       Campbell's pork and beans
       Canada Dry ginger ale
       Peanut butter
       Popcorn

1905   Epsicle (later Popsicle)
         Holly Sugar
         Royal Crown Cola

1906   A1 Sauce
         Bouillon cube
         Kellogg's Corn Flakes

1907   Hershey's Kisses

1908   Dixie cup
         Hydrox
         Monosodium glutamate

1909   Quaker puffed
         wheat and rice
         Tillamook Cheese

1910   Tea bag

1911   Crisco
         Mazola Corn Oil

1912   Cracker Jack prize
         Hamburger buns
         Hellmann's Mayonnaise
         Life Savers
         Lorna Doone Shortbread Cookies
         Morton Salt
         Ocean Spray Cranberry Sauce
         Vitamin pills

Whitman's Sampler
Oreos

1913 Campbell's Cream of Celery Soup
Peppermint Life Savers

1914 Doublemint gum
Fruit cocktail
Morton Salt girl

1915 Processed cheese
Pyrex bakeware

1916 Fortune cookie
Kellogg's All-Bran Cereal
Mr. Peanut
Orange Crush

1917 Clark Bar
Moon Pie

1918 Campbell's Vegetable Beef Soup
Contadina Tomato Sauce
French dip sandwich
Welch's first jam, Grapelade

"Asks $5,000 for Red Hair. Miss Gottdank Sues When Peroxide Fails to Make Tresses Golden," *The New York Times,* January 4, 1917

The efficacy of peroxide as a hair bleach was brought into question before Supreme Court Justice Erlanger and a jury yesterday when Miss Katie Gottdank, 16 years old, of 230 Second Street, asked $5,000 damages from Julius Kalish Inc., Grand Street druggists. Miss Gottdank complained that, in trying to transform herself from a maiden with hair of chestnut hue into a blonde, she lost part of her hair, and what she had left became brick red.

The plaintiff testified that, when she used one bottle of peroxide without seeing evidence of blondness, the manager of the drug concern advised her to try more, and she kept on doing it until she had poured the contents of five bottles over her locks. She exhibited a shoebox full of hair which, she said, had fallen out during the treatment.

The defendant contended that the plaintiff had failed to prove that the injury to her hair was due to the peroxide and offered to prove that peroxide alone could not cause the hair to become brittle and break off. Miss Gottdank's grandfather, Carl Weisshar, a barber and wig-maker, was called as an expert witness for the young woman, but he was unable to qualify because he admitted that he knew nothing about the effect of peroxide on hair. Justice Erlanger took under consideration a motion to dismiss the complaint because of lack of proof that the young woman's loss of hair was due to the peroxide.

"New York City in War Time,"
by Arthur Hepburn, *Vanity Fair,* December 1917

New York in war time has revealed herself in her true light. She has shown an adaptability to strange and trying conditions which has surprised even those who knew her best.

Already the greatest manufacturing center in the world, our coming into the war made New York the money center, the distributing center, the very hub of the universe as far as resources were concerned. London and Paris sank to the level of mere distributing points…. If the Kaiser is a bad sleeper, and he ought to be, he must be haunted in the mid-hours of the night by visions of the skyscrapers of lower Manhattan Island, for they symbolize the staying power which he should dread most of all.

ॐॐॐॐॐॐॐॐ

"The Fight against Venereal Disease,"
The New Republic, November 30, 1918

When the history of America's participation in the Great War comes to be written, no finer achievement will be recorded to her credit than the unending battle against sex indulgence and venereal disease in the army. The success of the efforts to repress prostitution on this side of the Atlantic is already fairly well known. Now that peace is at hand, some account can be given of the measures taken by General Pershing to protect the American Expeditionary Forces from this menace.

"The federal government has pledged its word that as far as care and vigilance can accomplish the result, the men committed to its charge will be returned to the homes and communities that so generously gave them with no scars except those won in honorable conflict." These were the words of President Wilson in April 1918. Through the Surgeon General of the Army and War Department Commission on Training Camp Activities, the government has carried out a programme for combating prostitution and venereal disease without parallel in any other country. It was founded on the proved principle that sexual continence was not only possible for soldiers, but was highly desirable from the standpoint of physical efficiency, morals and morale. Its chief features were education of men; repression of disorderly resorts; provision of healthful, interesting and constructive recreation; prophylaxis, or early treatment for men who

had exposed themselves; punishment for those exposed who failed to take prophylaxis; and, finally, expert treatment for those who either came into the army already infected or broke through all the barriers set up by the military authorities.

On the other side of the water a similar programme was instituted, but an exception had to be made of the feature of law enforcement—repression of prostitution. The foreign governments with which it was necessary for us to deal held views about prostitution very different than ours. The French believed in "toleration" and "regulation." For generations they had been used to licensed brothels and registered prostitutes, inspected with greater or less care by medical officers. They felt that an army could not get along without sexual indulgence, and that to attempt to carry out such a policy was to court discontent, a lowering of morale and health standards, and perhaps even mutiny. So sincerely did they hold this belief that prostitution facilities for our soldiers were officially offered to the American High Command.

"The Business of Clothing the Army,"
by Edward Hungerford, *Harper's Monthly Magazine*, April 1918

The biggest business in the land—as well as the most versatile—has its headquarters in the rather unbusiness-like city of Washington. We Americans are accused by some of our neighbors of the habit of exaggeration, and perhaps they are right. Yet today, it is hard to find sufficient superlatives to characterize our Uncle Sam as a businessman, at least if one considers the spry old gentleman in dimensions of size. In recent years he has become rather adept in big business, despite a supposed and traditional antipathy to it. But since he plunged into the Great War, his big business has become bigger business, in all probably the biggest single business that the world has ever known. His unofficial budget for the first year of his part in the international conflict provided for an expenditure of $20 billion, or about as much as the British Empire has expended during the first three years of the war. And England had not stinted herself, in men or in money. For the second year, Uncle Sam may not spend as much—perhaps not two thirds of his initial annual expenditure, which has bought many things that should have been purchased years before had we only been properly prepared, such as training camps, fighting ships, merchant vessels, dry docks and navy yards and coast defenses....

Today, Washington is the busiest city in the land. Its Southern inertia is disappearing. Offices are open and busy until late into the evening, whole departments alight long after dark. Even through the hottest months of last summer, there was bustle in the town. The old-time official Washington has ceased explaining that things could not be done and has watched the "dollar-a year men" go ahead and do them....

In the past decade or two our manufacturing efficiency, speaking broadly, has been greatly multiplied. The practical sermons of the efficiency experts have been heeded. And some of the homelier industries, yet industries tremendously important to the fitting out of an army, have been enabled to meet their supreme test in these trying days. Today, when one hears that the spindles and the looms of the United States will be called upon to weave five million blankets for the soldiers for a coming winter, he knows that modern efficiency will render them not only able to meet the test, but will insure they absolutely do meet it. As a matter of fact, up to February 9 of the present year, more than 7.9 million blankets and 800,000 comforters had been delivered to the army as a result of its war-time contracts. Uncle Sam, in his purchases, has been a huge merchant.

"Withdraw from Russia!"
The Dial, December 14, 1918

It is safe to say that the average American citizen would be thoroughly shocked at knowing the kind of imperialistic and anti-democratic game which is being played by our own and our allies' armies in Russia. These are facts and we think it high time that they be told. We do not believe that our own government wants the restoration of the monarchy in Russia or that it would support a demonstrable unpopular government forever. The American government would like to see in Russia a liberal and commercial republic like ourselves—a quiet, respectable government with which we could do business. Undoubtedly. But what we should like and what we are, as a matter of cold fact, getting are two widely different things. It is no secret that powerful parties in Japan are advocating the unostentatious annexation of large sections of Siberia, and that they have no interest in seeing any stable popular government arise east of the Urals. It is no secret that England trembles for Persia, Afghanistan, and India, and that the Tory party would gladly crush the Russian Revolution if it exhibited any tendency towards proselytism in foreign countries (as it has). It is no secret that a certain section of French governmental opinion cares not a fig what sort of a reactionary government there is in Russia, provided only that it is a government that will immediately repay the foreign loan. In a word, our intervention in Russia may have been undertaken with the best of intentions, *but the practical situation with which we are faced today is either to support reaction and imperialism or—to withdraw our troops.* Russian intervention has become for America a tragic anachronism since the defeat of Germany. We have neither a national nor an international interest which today legitimately sanctions the presence of our troops on Russian soil. It is false to our traditions to be fighting a workingman's republic, even if we do not approve of its form or its manners. It is not in accordance with any doctrine of American national policy for us to be engaged in crushing a revolution or in crucifying the hopes and aspirations of a great and mighty people. It is really difficult to believe that this is the same country which in Washington's time almost had a civil war because this government refused to intervene in the French Revolution, *on behalf of the revolutionists.* And not even the most severe critics of the present leaders of the Soviet government have said one-tenth as many bitter things as were said of Robespierre and Marat in their day. No; to help crush a revolution is not in accordance with the real American tradition.

For that reason, we demand of our government that our troops now in Russia be immediately withdrawn. We are asking no more than British Labor and French Labor and Italian Labor have already officially demanded of their governments. We are asking no more than President Wilson has again and again promised to the Russian peoples…. We are asking no more than most would ask, if they knew the facts, and do ask, those who are aware of them—the soldiers who entered this war inspired by an honest ideal to defeat the menace of German autocracy and to bring freedom to the oppressed peoples of this world. Those who have given their lives on the battlefields of France will rise to reproach us if we are now false to our trust.

స్త్రోస్త్రోస్త్రోస్త్రోస్త్రో

"Whisky Sold as Hair Tonic. Detectives in Sailors' Uniforms Arrest Bronx Barber,"
The New York Times, March 14, 1918

Detectives Ferguson and Albrecht of the newly created Division of National Defense of the New York Police Department put on naval uniforms yesterday and visited the barbershop of Nicholas Serra at 1019 East 170th street, the Bronx, where they found several blue-jackets having bottles filled with "hair tonic" from a large-sized demijohn.

In their turn, Ferguson and Albrecht both presented bottles and asked for "hair tonic." After making sure by sampling it that the "hair tonic" was cheap whiskey, the two detectives drew automatic revolvers and told Serra that he was under arrest. Five barbers in the shop had razors in their hands, but made no effort to interfere with the detectives. Serra was later arraigned before United States Commissioner Hitchcock and released on bail of $500.

"Why Should You Be Punished for Not Living in New York?," *Pictorial Review*, January 1918

A blow has been struck at every magazine reader in America. After July 1, 1918, you will pay more for every magazine and newspaper you wish to read. And this because you do not happen to live within 150 miles of the place of publication. You who live in Texas or California will have to pay one price. You who live in Idaho or Colorado will have to pay another, while, all of you who live in Illinois or Tennessee will have to pay still another price. Why? Because the War Revenue Bill recently passed by Congress contains a clause compelling magazines and newspapers being mailed on the zone system after July 1, 1918. Think how you in California, Washington, and Texas will feel when you have to pay something like $2.20 for this magazine that has cost you only $1.50. And while you are paying $2.20, subscribers within 150 miles from New York to still be paying only $1.50.

The zone system had already been defeated in the United States Senate. It was tacked onto the War Revenue Bill against the wishes of the majority of the conferees. It had no place there. It was not needed there. It was reported by the newspapers that the only reason it was there was due to political manipulation. Strong pressure was brought to bear. Delay in passing the War Revenue Bill would have hampered the government in its war program.

The members of the conference were powerless. They did not wish to prevent the War Revenue Bill from passing, so they had to yield. This is how this unjustified imposition on magazine readers came to be included in the War Revenue Bill where did not belong.

"After the Christmas Dinner, Bright Things of All Times That People Have Laughed Over," *The Ladies' Home Journal*, December 1918

Couldn't Faze Ethel
Ethel had her quick wit working that minute! She was sitting, after the Christmas dinner, with a gallant captain in a charmingly decorated recess. On her knee was a diminutive niece, placed there pour les convenances. In the adjoining room, with the door open, were the rest of the company. Finally the little niece was heard to say in a jealous and very audible voice: "Auntie, kiss me, too."

"Certainly, dear," returned Ethel. "But you should say twice, dear; two was not grammar."

A Prodigy
A gentleman living outside of Chicago went into the city of his office each day. When he was leaving home in the morning before Christmas, his wife said she would like him to bring a banner for her Sunday school class to use at an entertainment that evening, but that she did not know the wording and size needed. They agreed that she should send him a telegram during the day, giving him these two items. Consequently, before starting for home in the

afternoon, he went to the nearby telegraph office and found quite an excitement over the message which had just been received and which read: "Unto us a child is born. Three feet wide and six feet long."

Much Better
"Is your father's stomachache better?" asked the teacher, the day after Christmas.

"Yessum," replied the boy, "It isn't aching half as loud as it did."

She Knew, Sweet Dear
The young bride went to the grocery store to do her Christmas marketing. She was determined that the grocer should not take advantage of her youth and inexperience.

"These eggs are dreadfully small," she criticized.

"I know it," he answered. "But that's the kind the farmer brings me. They are just fresh from the country this morning."

"Yes," said the bride, "and that's the trouble with those farmers; they are so anxious to get their eggs sold that they take them off the nest too soon!"

Faith and Works
One Monday morning two little girls, aged seven and nine, were on their way to school. Fearing they would be tardy, the seven-year-old said to the nine-year-old: "Let's kneel down and pray that we won't be late."

The nine-year-old said to the seven-year-old: "Let's keep hiking and pray as we hike."

Better the First Time
A man asked a friend, who was hard of hearing, if he would lend him five dollars, to tide him over Christmas.

"What?" asked the friend.

"Will you lend me 10 dollars?"

"Oh, yes," replied the friend, "but I wish now I had heard you the first time."

Revenge
The druggist danced and chortled until the bottles danced on the shelves.

"What's up?" asked the soda clerk. "Have you been taking something?"

"No. But do you remember when our water pipes were frozen last Christmas?"

"Yes, but what?"

"Well, the plumber who fixed them has just come to have a prescription filled."

One on the Teacher
Boy: "Can a person be punished for something he hasn't done?"

Teacher: "Of course not."

Boy: "Well, I haven't done my geometry."

SECTION FIVE: CENSUS DATA

This section begins with 10 state-by-state comparative tables that rank data from the 1910, 1920, and 2010 census, designed to help define the times during which the families profiled in Section One lived. Table topics are listed below. Following the state-by-state tables are reprints directly from the 1920 Census of Population, including a United States Summary and statistics on various topics listed below. This data is portrayed by maps, tables, graphs, charts and narrative, helping to visualize the environment of the 1910s. Note that the original reprints show two page numbers: the number at the top of the page is from the original Census document.

Total Population

Area	Population			1910		1920		2010	
	1910	1920	2010	Area	Rank	Area	Rank	Area	Rank
Alabama	2,138,093	2,348,174	4,779,736	New York	1	New York	1	California	1
Alaska	64,356	55,036	710,231	Pennsylvania	2	Pennsylvania	2	Texas	2
Arizona	204,354	334,162	6,392,017	Illinois	3	Illinois	3	New York	3
Arkansas	1,574,449	1,752,204	2,915,918	Ohio	4	Ohio	4	Florida	4
California	2,377,549	3,426,861	37,253,956	Texas	5	Texas	5	Illinois	5
Colorado	799,024	939,629	5,029,196	Massachusetts	6	Massachusetts	6	Pennsylvania	6
Connecticut	1,114,756	1,380,631	3,574,097	Missouri	7	Michigan	7	Ohio	7
D.C.	331,069	437,571	601,723	Michigan	8	California	8	Michigan	8
Delaware	202,322	223,003	897,934	Indiana	9	Missouri	9	Georgia	9
Florida	752,619	968,470	18,801,310	Georgia	10	New Jersey	10	North Carolina	10
Georgia	2,609,121	2,895,832	9,687,653	New Jersey	11	Indiana	11	New Jersey	11
Hawaii	191,874	255,881	1,360,301	California	12	Georgia	12	Virginia	12
Idaho	325,594	431,866	1,567,582	Wisconsin	13	Wisconsin	13	Washington	13
Illinois	5,638,591	6,485,280	12,830,632	Kentucky	14	North Carolina	14	Massachusetts	14
Indiana	2,700,876	2,930,390	6,483,802	Iowa	15	Kentucky	15	Indiana	15
Iowa	2,224,771	2,404,021	3,046,355	North Carolina	16	Iowa	16	Arizona	16
Kansas	1,690,949	1,769,257	2,853,118	Tennessee	17	Minnesota	17	Tennessee	17
Kentucky	2,289,905	2,416,630	4,339,367	Alabama	18	Alabama	18	Missouri	18
Louisiana	1,656,388	1,798,509	4,533,372	Minnesota	19	Tennessee	19	Maryland	19
Maine	742,371	768,014	1,328,361	Virginia	20	Virginia	20	Wisconsin	20
Maryland	1,295,346	1,449,661	5,773,552	Mississippi	21	Oklahoma	21	Minnesota	21
Massachusetts	3,366,416	3,852,356	6,547,629	Kansas	22	Louisiana	22	Colorado	22
Michigan	2,810,173	3,668,412	9,883,640	Oklahoma	23	Mississippi	23	Alabama	23
Minnesota	2,075,708	2,387,125	5,303,925	Louisiana	24	Kansas	24	South Carolina	24
Mississippi	1,797,114	1,790,618	2,967,297	Arkansas	25	Arkansas	25	Louisiana	25
Missouri	3,293,335	3,404,055	5,988,927	South Carolina	26	South Carolina	26	Kentucky	26
Montana	376,053	548,889	989,415	Maryland	27	West Virginia	27	Oregon	27
Nebraska	1,192,214	1,296,372	1,826,341	West Virginia	28	Maryland	28	Oklahoma	28
Nevada	81,875	77,407	2,700,551	Nebraska	29	Connecticut	29	Connecticut	29
New Hampshire	430,572	443,083	1,316,470	Washington	30	Washington	30	Iowa	30
New Jersey	2,537,167	3,155,900	8,791,894	Connecticut	31	Nebraska	31	Mississippi	31
New Mexico	327,301	360,350	2,059,179	Colorado	32	Florida	32	Arkansas	32
New York	9,113,614	10,385,227	19,378,102	Florida	33	Colorado	33	Kansas	33
North Carolina	2,206,287	2,559,123	9,535,483	Maine	34	Oregon	34	Utah	34
North Dakota	577,056	646,872	672,591	Oregon	35	Maine	35	Nevada	35
Ohio	4,767,121	5,759,394	11,536,504	South Dakota	36	North Dakota	36	New Mexico	36
Oklahoma	1,657,155	2,028,283	3,751,351	North Dakota	37	South Dakota	37	West Virginia	37
Oregon	672,765	783,389	3,831,074	Rhode Island	38	Rhode Island	38	Nebraska	38
Pennsylvania	7,665,111	8,720,017	12,702,379	New Hampshire	39	Montana	39	Idaho	39
Rhode Island	542,610	604,397	1,052,567	Montana	40	Utah	40	Hawaii	40
South Carolina	1,515,400	1,683,724	4,625,364	Utah	41	New Hampshire	41	Maine	41
South Dakota	583,888	636,547	814,180	Vermont	42	D.C.	42	New Hampshire	42
Tennessee	2,184,789	2,337,885	6,346,105	D.C.	43	Idaho	43	Rhode Island	43
Texas	3,896,542	4,663,228	25,145,561	New Mexico	44	New Mexico	44	Montana	44
Utah	373,351	449,396	2,763,885	Idaho	45	Vermont	45	Delaware	45
Vermont	355,956	352,428	625,741	Arizona	46	Arizona	46	South Dakota	46
Virginia	2,061,612	2,309,187	8,001,024	Delaware	47	Hawaii	47	Alaska	47
Washington	1,141,990	1,356,621	6,724,540	Hawaii	48	Delaware	48	North Dakota	48
West Virginia	1,221,119	1,463,701	1,852,994	Wyoming	49	Wyoming	49	Vermont	49
Wisconsin	2,333,860	2,632,067	5,686,986	Nevada	50	Nevada	50	D.C.	50
Wyoming	145,965	194,402	563,626	Alaska	51	Alaska	51	Wyoming	51
United States	92,228,496	106,021,537	308,745,538	United States	–	United States	–	United States	–

Source: U.S. Census Bureau, 1910 Census of Population; U.S. Census Bureau, 1920 Census of Population; U.S. Census Bureau, Census 2010

White Population

Area	Percent of Population			1910		1920		2010	
	1910	1920	2010	Area	Rank	Area	Rank	Area	Rank
Alabama	57.47	61.62	68.53	New Hampshire	1	New Hampshire	1	Vermont	1
Alaska	n/a	n/a	66.68	Maine	2	Vermont	1	Maine	2
Arizona	83.91	87.22	73.01	Vermont	3	Maine	3	West Virginia	3
Arkansas	71.84	73.04	77.00	Wisconsin	4	Wisconsin	4	New Hampshire	4
California	95.04	95.27	57.59	Iowa	5	Minnesota	5	Iowa	5
Colorado	98.05	98.35	81.31	Minnesota	6	Iowa	6	Wyoming	6
Connecticut	98.58	98.41	77.57	Michigan	7	North Dakota	7	North Dakota	7
D.C.	71.32	74.70	38.47	Nebraska	8	Massachusetts	8	Montana	8
Delaware	84.57	86.37	68.89	Massachusetts	9	Nebraska	9	Idaho	9
Florida	58.95	65.89	75.04	North Dakota	10	Idaho	10	Kentucky	10
Georgia	54.88	58.33	59.74	Connecticut	11	Connecticut	11	Wisconsin	11
Hawaii	n/a	n/a	24.74	New York	12	Colorado	12	Nebraska	12
Idaho	98.04	98.56	89.09	Utah	13	Utah	13	Utah	13
Illinois	98.02	97.13	71.53	Rhode Island	14	Rhode Island	14	South Dakota	14
Indiana	97.74	97.22	84.33	Colorado	15	Michigan	15	Minnesota	15
Iowa	99.30	99.17	91.31	Idaho	16	Oregon	15	Indiana	16
Kansas	96.65	96.59	83.80	Illinois	17	New York	17	Kansas	17
Kentucky	88.56	90.23	87.79	Indiana	18	Wyoming	18	Oregon	18
Louisiana	56.82	60.97	62.56	Ohio	19	Montana	19	Missouri	19
Maine	99.68	99.70	95.23	Pennsylvania	20	Washington	20	Ohio	20
Maryland	82.04	83.10	58.18	Oregon	21	South Dakota	21	Pennsylvania	21
Massachusetts	98.77	98.73	80.41	Washington	22	Indiana	22	Rhode Island	22
Michigan	99.11	98.18	78.95	Kansas	23	Illinois	23	Colorado	23
Minnesota	99.21	99.24	85.30	South Dakota	24	Ohio	24	Massachusetts	24
Mississippi	43.74	47.69	59.13	New Jersey	25	Pennsylvania	25	Michigan	25
Missouri	95.19	94.74	82.80	Wyoming	26	Kansas	26	Connecticut	26
Montana	95.89	97.33	89.44	Montana	27	New Jersey	27	Tennessee	27
Nebraska	99.00	98.68	86.12	Missouri	28	California	28	Washington	28
Nevada	90.72	91.33	66.16	California	29	Missouri	29	Arkansas	29
New Hampshire	99.85	99.83	93.89	West Virginia	30	West Virginia	30	Florida	30
New Jersey	96.40	96.24	68.58	New Mexico	31	New Mexico	31	Arizona	31
New Mexico	93.06	92.87	68.37	Nevada	32	Nevada	32	Oklahoma	32
New York	98.39	97.95	65.75	Kentucky	33	Kentucky	33	Illinois	33
North Carolina	68.01	69.70	68.47	Oklahoma	34	Oklahoma	34	Texas	34
North Dakota	98.75	98.93	90.02	Delaware	35	Arizona	35	Delaware	35
Ohio	97.65	96.74	82.69	Arizona	36	Delaware	36	New Jersey	36
Oklahoma	87.17	89.79	72.16	Texas	37	Texas	37	Virginia	36
Oregon	97.37	98.18	83.65	Maryland	38	Maryland	38	Alabama	38
Pennsylvania	97.42	96.71	81.92	Tennessee	39	Tennessee	39	North Carolina	39
Rhode Island	98.14	98.28	81.41	Arkansas	40	D.C.	40	New Mexico	40
South Carolina	44.82	48.61	66.16	D.C.	41	Arkansas	41	Alaska	41
South Dakota	96.55	97.27	85.90	North Carolina	42	Virginia	42	Nevada	42
Tennessee	78.33	80.67	77.56	Virginia	43	North Carolina	43	South Carolina	42
Texas	82.25	84.02	70.40	Florida	44	Florida	44	New York	44
Utah	98.19	98.33	86.09	Alabama	45	Alabama	45	Louisiana	45
Vermont	99.53	99.83	95.29	Louisiana	46	Louisiana	46	Georgia	46
Virginia	67.41	70.06	68.58	Georgia	47	Georgia	47	Mississippi	47
Washington	97.12	97.28	77.27	South Carolina	48	South Carolina	48	Maryland	48
West Virginia	94.73	94.09	93.90	Mississippi	49	Mississippi	49	California	49
Wisconsin	99.43	99.43	86.20	Alaska	n/a	Hawaii	n/a	D.C.	50
Wyoming	96.13	97.81	90.71	Hawaii	n/a	Alaska	n/a	Hawaii	51
United States	88.62	89.44	72.41	United States	–	United States	–	United States	–

Source: U.S. Census Bureau, 1910 Census of Population; U.S. Census Bureau, 1920 Census of Population; U.S. Census Bureau, Census 2010

Black Population

Area	Percent of Population			1910		1920		2010	
	1910	1920	2010	Area	Rank	Area	Rank	Area	Rank
Alabama	42.48	38.36	26.18	Mississippi	1	Mississippi	1	D.C.	1
Alaska	n/a	n/a	3.28	South Carolina	2	South Carolina	2	Mississippi	2
Arizona	0.98	2.40	4.05	Georgia	3	Georgia	3	Louisiana	3
Arkansas	28.13	26.95	15.43	Louisiana	4	Louisiana	4	Georgia	4
California	0.91	1.13	6.17	Alabama	5	Alabama	5	Maryland	5
Colorado	1.43	1.20	4.01	Florida	6	Florida	6	South Carolina	6
Connecticut	1.36	1.52	10.14	Virginia	7	Virginia	7	Alabama	7
D.C.	28.53	25.13	50.71	North Carolina	8	North Carolina	8	North Carolina	8
Delaware	15.41	13.60	21.36	D.C.	9	Arkansas	9	Delaware	9
Florida	41.01	34.02	15.96	Arkansas	10	D.C.	10	Virginia	10
Georgia	45.11	41.66	30.46	Tennessee	11	Tennessee	11	Tennessee	11
Hawaii	n/a	n/a	1.57	Maryland	12	Maryland	12	Florida	12
Idaho	0.20	0.21	0.63	Texas	13	Texas	13	New York	13
Illinois	1.93	2.81	14.55	Delaware	14	Delaware	14	Arkansas	14
Indiana	2.23	2.76	9.12	Kentucky	15	Kentucky	15	Illinois	15
Iowa	0.67	0.79	2.93	Oklahoma	16	Oklahoma	16	Michigan	16
Kansas	3.20	3.27	5.88	West Virginia	17	West Virginia	17	New Jersey	17
Kentucky	11.43	9.76	7.78	Missouri	18	Missouri	18	Ohio	18
Louisiana	43.10	38.94	32.04	New Jersey	19	New Jersey	19	Texas	19
Maine	0.18	0.17	1.18	Kansas	20	Kansas	20	Missouri	20
Maryland	17.93	16.86	29.45	Pennsylvania	21	Pennsylvania	21	Pennsylvania	21
Massachusetts	1.13	1.18	6.63	Ohio	22	Ohio	22	Connecticut	22
Michigan	0.61	1.64	14.17	Indiana	23	Illinois	23	Indiana	23
Minnesota	0.34	0.37	5.17	Illinois	24	Indiana	24	Nevada	24
Mississippi	56.17	52.23	37.02	Rhode Island	25	Arizona	25	Kentucky	25
Missouri	4.78	5.24	11.58	Wyoming	26	New York	26	Oklahoma	26
Montana	0.49	0.30	0.41	New York	27	Rhode Island	27	Massachusetts	27
Nebraska	0.64	1.02	4.54	Colorado	28	Michigan	28	Wisconsin	28
Nevada	0.63	0.45	8.10	Connecticut	29	New Mexico	29	California	29
New Hampshire	0.13	0.14	1.14	Massachusetts	30	Connecticut	30	Kansas	30
New Jersey	3.54	3.71	13.70	Arizona	31	Colorado	31	Rhode Island	31
New Mexico	0.50	1.59	2.07	California	32	Massachusetts	32	Minnesota	32
New York	1.47	1.91	15.86	Iowa	33	California	33	Nebraska	33
North Carolina	31.63	29.83	21.48	Nebraska	34	Nebraska	34	Arizona	34
North Dakota	0.11	0.07	1.18	Nevada	35	Iowa	35	Colorado	35
Ohio	2.34	3.23	12.20	Michigan	36	Wyoming	36	Washington	36
Oklahoma	8.30	7.37	7.40	Washington	37	Washington	37	West Virginia	37
Oregon	0.22	0.27	1.81	New Mexico	38	Nevada	38	Alaska	38
Pennsylvania	2.53	3.26	10.85	Montana	39	Minnesota	39	Iowa	39
Rhode Island	1.76	1.66	5.72	Vermont	40	Utah	40	New Mexico	40
South Carolina	55.16	51.36	27.90	Minnesota	41	Montana	41	Oregon	41
South Dakota	0.14	0.13	1.25	Utah	42	Oregon	42	Hawaii	42
Tennessee	21.65	19.32	16.66	Oregon	43	Idaho	43	South Dakota	43
Texas	17.71	15.91	11.85	Idaho	44	Wisconsin	44	Maine	44
Utah	0.31	0.32	1.06	Maine	45	Maine	45	North Dakota	44
Vermont	0.46	0.16	1.00	South Dakota	46	Vermont	46	New Hampshire	46
Virginia	32.55	29.88	19.39	New Hampshire	47	New Hampshire	47	Utah	47
Washington	0.53	0.51	3.57	Wisconsin	48	South Dakota	48	Vermont	48
West Virginia	5.26	5.90	3.41	North Dakota	49	North Dakota	49	Wyoming	49
Wisconsin	0.12	0.20	6.32	Alaska	n/a	Hawaii	n/a	Idaho	50
Wyoming	1.53	0.71	0.84	Hawaii	n/a	Alaska	n/a	Montana	51
United States	10.66	9.87	12.61	United States	–	United States	–	United States	–

Source: U.S. Census Bureau, 1910 Census of Population; U.S. Census Bureau, 1920 Census of Population; U.S. Census Bureau, Census 2010

American Indian/Alaska Native Population

Area	Percent of Population 1910	1920	2010	1910 Area	Rank	1920 Area	Rank	2010 Area	Rank
Alabama	0.04	0.02	0.59	Arizona	1	Arizona	1	Alaska	1
Alaska	n/a	n/a	14.77	Nevada	2	Nevada	2	New Mexico	2
Arizona	14.29	9.87	4.64	New Mexico	3	New Mexico	3	South Dakota	3
Arkansas	0.03	0.01	0.76	Oklahoma	4	Oklahoma	4	Oklahoma	4
California	0.69	0.51	0.97	South Dakota	5	South Dakota	5	Montana	5
Colorado	0.19	0.15	1.11	Montana	6	Montana	6	North Dakota	6
Connecticut	0.01	0.01	0.31	North Dakota	7	North Dakota	7	Arizona	7
D.C.	0.02	0.01	0.35	Idaho	8	Idaho	8	Wyoming	8
Delaware	0.00	0.00	0.47	Wyoming	9	Wyoming	9	Washington	9
Florida	0.01	0.05	0.38	Washington	10	Washington	10	Oregon	10
Georgia	0.00	0.00	0.33	Utah	11	Utah	11	Idaho	11
Hawaii	n/a	n/a	0.31	Oregon	12	Oregon	12	North Carolina	12
Idaho	1.07	0.72	1.37	California	13	California	13	Nevada	13
Illinois	0.00	0.00	0.34	Minnesota	14	North Carolina	14	Utah	13
Indiana	0.01	0.00	0.28	Wisconsin	15	Minnesota	15	Minnesota	15
Iowa	0.02	0.02	0.36	North Carolina	16	Wisconsin	15	Colorado	16
Kansas	0.14	0.13	0.99	Nebraska	17	Nebraska	17	Nebraska	17
Kentucky	0.01	0.00	0.23	Michigan	18	Michigan	18	Kansas	18
Louisiana	0.05	0.06	0.67	Colorado	19	Colorado	18	California	19
Maine	0.12	0.11	0.65	Kansas	20	Kansas	20	Wisconsin	20
Maryland	0.00	0.00	0.35	Maine	21	Maine	21	Arkansas	21
Massachusetts	0.02	0.01	0.29	New York	22	Louisiana	22	Texas	22
Michigan	0.27	0.15	0.63	Mississippi	22	Mississippi	22	Louisiana	23
Minnesota	0.44	0.37	1.15	Rhode Island	24	New York	24	Maine	24
Mississippi	0.07	0.06	0.51	Louisiana	24	Texas	24	Michigan	25
Missouri	0.01	0.01	0.46	Alabama	26	Florida	24	Alabama	26
Montana	2.86	2.00	6.32	Virginia	27	Virginia	27	Rhode Island	27
Nebraska	0.29	0.22	1.01	Arkansas	27	Rhode Island	28	New York	28
Nevada	6.40	6.34	1.19	Massachusetts	29	Iowa	28	Mississippi	29
New Hampshire	0.01	0.01	0.24	Pennsylvania	29	Alabama	28	Delaware	30
New Jersey	0.01	0.00	0.33	Iowa	29	South Carolina	28	Missouri	31
New Mexico	6.29	5.41	9.38	D.C.	29	Massachusetts	32	South Carolina	32
New York	0.07	0.05	0.55	Texas	29	Connecticut	32	Florida	33
North Carolina	0.36	0.46	1.28	South Carolina	29	New Hampshire	32	Virginia	34
North Dakota	1.12	0.97	5.44	Connecticut	35	Vermont	32	Iowa	35
Ohio	0.00	0.00	0.22	New Jersey	35	D.C.	32	Maryland	36
Oklahoma	4.52	2.83	8.58	New Hampshire	35	Missouri	32	D.C.	36
Oregon	0.76	0.59	1.39	Vermont	35	Arkansas	32	Vermont	36
Pennsylvania	0.02	0.00	0.21	Missouri	35	New Jersey	39	Illinois	39
Rhode Island	0.05	0.02	0.58	Indiana	35	Illinois	39	New Jersey	40
South Carolina	0.02	0.02	0.42	Florida	35	Pennsylvania	39	Georgia	40
South Dakota	3.28	2.57	8.82	Kentucky	35	Ohio	39	Tennessee	42
Tennessee	0.01	0.00	0.32	Tennessee	35	Delaware	39	Hawaii	43
Texas	0.02	0.05	0.68	Illinois	44	Maryland	39	Connecticut	43
Utah	0.84	0.60	1.19	Ohio	44	Indiana	39	Massachusetts	45
Vermont	0.01	0.01	0.35	Delaware	44	West Virginia	39	Indiana	46
Virginia	0.03	0.04	0.37	Maryland	44	Kentucky	39	New Hampshire	47
Washington	0.96	0.67	1.54	West Virginia	44	Tennessee	39	Kentucky	48
West Virginia	0.00	0.00	0.20	Georgia	44	Georgia	39	Ohio	49
Wisconsin	0.43	0.37	0.96	Alaska	n/a	Hawaii	n/a	Pennsylvania	50
Wyoming	1.02	0.69	2.37	Hawaii	n/a	Alaska	n/a	West Virginia	51
United States	0.29	0.23	0.95	United States	–	United States	–	United States	–

Source: U.S. Census Bureau, 1910 Census of Population; U.S. Census Bureau, 1920 Census of Population; U.S. Census Bureau, Census 2010

Asian Population

Area	Percent of Population			1910		1920		2010	
	1910	1920	2010	Area	Rank	Area	Rank	Area	Rank
Alabama	0.00	0.00	1.12	California	1	California	1	Hawaii	1
Alaska	n/a	n/a	5.37	Nevada	2	Nevada	2	California	2
Arizona	0.82	0.51	2.76	Oregon	3	Washington	3	New Jersey	3
Arkansas	0.00	0.01	1.24	Washington	4	Oregon	4	New York	4
California	3.36	3.09	13.05	Wyoming	5	Wyoming	5	Nevada	5
Colorado	0.33	0.30	2.76	Arizona	6	Utah	6	Washington	6
Connecticut	0.05	0.05	3.79	Montana	7	Arizona	7	Maryland	7
D.C.	0.13	0.16	3.50	Idaho	8	Idaho	8	Virginia	8
Delaware	0.02	0.02	3.18	Utah	9	Montana	9	Alaska	9
Florida	0.03	0.03	2.42	Colorado	10	Colorado	10	Massachusetts	10
Georgia	0.01	0.01	3.25	New Mexico	11	D.C.	11	Illinois	11
Hawaii	n/a	n/a	38.60	D.C.	12	New Mexico	12	Minnesota	12
Idaho	0.69	0.50	1.22	Massachusetts	13	New York	13	Texas	13
Illinois	0.04	0.05	4.57	New York	14	Nebraska	14	Connecticut	14
Indiana	0.01	0.01	1.58	Rhode Island	15	Massachusetts	15	Oregon	15
Iowa	0.01	0.01	1.74	Nebraska	15	Connecticut	16	D.C.	16
Kansas	0.01	0.01	2.38	Connecticut	17	New Jersey	16	Georgia	17
Kentucky	0.00	0.00	1.13	New Jersey	17	Illinois	16	Delaware	18
Louisiana	0.04	0.03	1.55	Illinois	19	Rhode Island	19	Rhode Island	19
Maine	0.02	0.02	1.02	Louisiana	19	Minnesota	20	Arizona	20
Maryland	0.03	0.03	5.52	Pennsylvania	21	North Dakota	20	Colorado	20
Massachusetts	0.08	0.07	5.34	South Dakota	21	Michigan	20	Pennsylvania	22
Michigan	0.01	0.03	2.41	Maryland	21	Pennsylvania	20	Florida	23
Minnesota	0.02	0.03	4.04	Florida	21	South Dakota	20	Michigan	24
Mississippi	0.01	0.02	0.87	North Dakota	25	Texas	20	Kansas	25
Missouri	0.02	0.02	1.64	Minnesota	25	Maryland	20	Wisconsin	26
Montana	0.77	0.37	0.63	New Hampshire	25	Florida	20	North Carolina	27
Nebraska	0.06	0.08	1.77	Maine	25	Louisiana	20	New Hampshire	28
Nevada	2.25	1.88	7.24	Delaware	25	New Hampshire	29	Utah	29
New Hampshire	0.02	0.02	2.16	Missouri	25	Maine	29	Nebraska	30
New Jersey	0.05	0.05	8.25	Texas	25	Ohio	29	Iowa	31
New Mexico	0.15	0.12	1.37	Wisconsin	32	Delaware	29	Oklahoma	32
New York	0.07	0.09	7.33	Michigan	32	Missouri	29	Ohio	33
North Carolina	0.00	0.00	2.19	Ohio	32	Oklahoma	29	Missouri	34
North Dakota	0.02	0.03	1.03	Iowa	32	Virginia	29	Indiana	35
Ohio	0.01	0.02	1.67	Kansas	32	Mississippi	29	Louisiana	36
Oklahoma	0.01	0.02	1.73	Indiana	32	Wisconsin	37	Tennessee	37
Oregon	1.65	0.96	3.69	West Virginia	32	Iowa	37	New Mexico	38
Pennsylvania	0.03	0.03	2.75	Oklahoma	32	Kansas	37	South Carolina	39
Rhode Island	0.06	0.04	2.89	Virginia	32	Indiana	37	Vermont	40
South Carolina	0.00	0.01	1.28	Georgia	32	West Virginia	37	Arkansas	41
South Dakota	0.03	0.03	0.93	Mississippi	32	Arkansas	37	Idaho	42
Tennessee	0.00	0.00	1.44	Vermont	43	Georgia	37	Kentucky	43
Texas	0.02	0.03	3.84	Kentucky	43	South Carolina	37	Alabama	44
Utah	0.67	0.74	2.00	Arkansas	43	Vermont	45	North Dakota	45
Vermont	0.00	0.00	1.27	Alabama	43	Kentucky	45	Maine	46
Virginia	0.01	0.02	5.50	Tennessee	43	Alabama	45	South Dakota	47
Washington	1.39	1.54	7.15	South Carolina	43	Tennessee	45	Mississippi	48
West Virginia	0.01	0.01	0.67	North Carolina	43	North Carolina	45	Wyoming	49
Wisconsin	0.01	0.01	2.27	Alaska	n/a	Hawaii	n/a	West Virginia	50
Wyoming	1.32	0.79	0.79	Hawaii	n/a	Alaska	n/a	Montana	51
United States	0.16	0.17	4.75	United States	–	United States	–	United States	–

Source: U.S. Census Bureau, 1910 Census of Population; U.S. Census Bureau, 1920 Census of Population; U.S. Census Bureau, Census 2010

Foreign-Born Population

Area	Percent of Population 1910	1920	2010	1910 Area	Rank	1920 Area	Rank	2010 Area	Rank
Alabama	0.9	0.8	3.4	Rhode Island	1	Rhode Island	1	California	1
Alaska	n/a	n/a	7.2	Massachusetts	2	Massachusetts	2	New York	2
Arizona	23.9	24.1	14.2	New York	3	Connecticut	3	New Jersey	3
Arkansas	1.1	0.8	4.3	Connecticut	4	New York	4	Nevada	4
California	24.7	22.1	27.2	North Dakota	5	Arizona	5	Florida	5
Colorado	16.2	12.7	9.8	Minnesota	6	New Jersey	6	Hawaii	6
Connecticut	29.6	27.4	13.2	New Jersey	7	California	7	Texas	7
D.C.	7.5	6.7	13.0	Montana	8	Nevada	8	Massachusetts	8
Delaware	8.6	8.9	8.2	California	9	New Hampshire	9	Arizona	9
Florida	5.4	5.6	19.2	Nevada	10	Minnesota	10	Illinois	10
Georgia	0.6	0.6	9.6	Arizona	11	North Dakota	10	Maryland	11
Hawaii	n/a	n/a	17.7	New Hampshire	12	Michigan	12	Connecticut	11
Idaho	13.1	9.4	5.9	Washington	13	Washington	13	D.C.	13
Illinois	21.4	18.7	13.6	Wisconsin	14	Illinois	14	Washington	14
Indiana	5.9	5.2	4.4	Illinois	15	Wisconsin	15	Rhode Island	15
Iowa	12.3	9.4	4.1	Michigan	16	Montana	16	Virginia	16
Kansas	8.0	6.3	6.3	Wyoming	17	Pennsylvania	17	Colorado	17
Kentucky	1.8	1.3	3.1	Pennsylvania	18	Maine	18	New Mexico	18
Louisiana	3.2	2.6	3.6	Utah	19	Oregon	19	Oregon	18
Maine	14.9	14.0	3.3	South Dakota	20	Wyoming	19	Georgia	20
Maryland	8.1	7.1	13.2	Oregon	21	Utah	21	Utah	21
Massachusetts	31.5	28.3	14.5	Colorado	22	South Dakota	22	Delaware	21
Michigan	21.3	19.9	5.9	Maine	23	Colorado	23	North Carolina	23
Minnesota	26.2	20.4	7.0	Nebraska	24	Vermont	24	Alaska	24
Mississippi	0.5	0.5	2.2	Vermont	25	Ohio	25	Minnesota	25
Missouri	7.0	5.5	3.7	Idaho	26	Nebraska	26	Kansas	26
Montana	25.2	17.4	2.0	Ohio	27	Idaho	27	Michigan	27
Nebraska	14.8	11.6	5.9	Iowa	28	Iowa	27	Idaho	27
Nevada	24.1	20.7	19.3	Delaware	29	Delaware	29	Nebraska	27
New Hampshire	22.5	20.6	5.3	Maryland	30	New Mexico	30	Pennsylvania	30
New Jersey	26.0	23.5	20.3	Kansas	31	Texas	31	New Hampshire	31
New Mexico	7.1	8.3	9.7	D.C.	32	Maryland	32	Oklahoma	32
New York	30.2	27.2	21.7	New Mexico	33	D.C.	33	South Carolina	33
North Carolina	0.3	0.3	7.4	Missouri	34	Kansas	34	Wisconsin	34
North Dakota	27.1	20.4	2.4	Texas	35	Florida	35	Tennessee	35
Ohio	12.6	11.8	3.8	Indiana	36	Missouri	36	Indiana	35
Oklahoma	2.4	2.0	5.2	Florida	37	Indiana	37	Arkansas	37
Oregon	16.8	13.7	9.7	West Virginia	38	West Virginia	38	Iowa	38
Pennsylvania	18.8	16.0	5.6	Louisiana	39	Louisiana	39	Vermont	39
Rhode Island	33.0	29.0	12.6	Oklahoma	40	Oklahoma	40	Ohio	40
South Carolina	0.4	0.4	4.7	Kentucky	41	Virginia	41	Missouri	41
South Dakota	17.3	13.0	2.3	Virginia	42	Kentucky	42	Louisiana	42
Tennessee	0.9	0.7	4.4	Arkansas	43	Arkansas	43	Alabama	43
Texas	6.2	7.8	16.1	Alabama	44	Alabama	43	Maine	44
Utah	17.6	13.2	8.2	Tennessee	44	Tennessee	45	Wyoming	45
Vermont	14.0	12.6	4.0	Georgia	46	Georgia	46	Kentucky	45
Virginia	1.3	1.4	10.8	Mississippi	47	Mississippi	47	North Dakota	47
Washington	22.4	19.6	12.7	South Carolina	48	South Carolina	48	South Dakota	48
West Virginia	4.7	4.2	1.3	North Carolina	49	North Carolina	49	Mississippi	49
Wisconsin	22.0	17.5	4.6	Alaska	n/a	Hawaii	n/a	Montana	50
Wyoming	19.9	13.7	3.1	Hawaii	n/a	Alaska	n/a	West Virginia	51
United States	14.7	13.2	12.7	United States	–	United States	–	United States	–

Source: U.S. Census Bureau, 1910 Census of Population; U.S. Census Bureau, 1920 Census of Population; U.S. Census Bureau, Census 2010

Urban Population

Area	Percent of Population			1910		1920		2010	
	1910	1920	2010	Area	Rank	Area	Rank	Area	Rank
Alabama	17.3	21.7	55.0	D.C.	1	D.C.	1	D.C.	1
Alaska	9.5	5.6	60.5	Rhode Island	2	Rhode Island	2	New Jersey	2
Arizona	31.0	36.1	86.7	Massachusetts	3	Massachusetts	3	California	3
Arkansas	12.9	16.6	52.0	New York	4	New York	4	Massachusetts	4
California	61.8	67.9	93.2	New Jersey	5	New Jersey	5	Rhode Island	5
Colorado	50.3	48.2	82.0	Connecticut	6	California	6	Nevada	6
Connecticut	65.6	67.8	87.9	California	7	Illinois	6	Hawaii	7
D.C.	100.0	100.0	100.0	Illinois	8	Connecticut	8	Florida	8
Delaware	48.0	54.2	80.1	Pennsylvania	9	Pennsylvania	9	Connecticut	9
Florida	29.1	36.5	89.3	Ohio	10	Ohio	10	Illinois	10
Georgia	20.6	25.1	70.7	Washington	11	Michigan	11	Arizona	11
Hawaii	30.7	36.1	90.0	New Hampshire	12	Maryland	12	Maryland	12
Idaho	21.5	27.6	63.8	Maryland	13	New Hampshire	13	New York	13
Illinois	61.7	67.9	87.3	Colorado	14	Washington	14	Utah	14
Indiana	42.4	50.6	72.1	Delaware	15	Delaware	15	Colorado	15
Iowa	30.6	36.4	61.4	Michigan	16	Indiana	16	Washington	16
Kansas	29.1	34.8	71.1	Utah	17	Oregon	17	Texas	17
Kentucky	24.3	26.2	55.9	Oregon	18	Colorado	18	Delaware	18
Louisiana	30.0	34.9	72.1	Wisconsin	19	Utah	19	Ohio	19
Maine	35.3	39.0	36.6	Indiana	20	Wisconsin	20	Oregon	20
Maryland	50.8	60.0	86.4	Missouri	21	Missouri	21	Pennsylvania	21
Massachusetts	89.0	90.0	91.1	Minnesota	22	Minnesota	22	New Mexico	22
Michigan	47.2	61.1	72.2	Montana	23	Maine	23	Michigan	23
Minnesota	41.0	44.1	68.3	Maine	24	Florida	24	Indiana	24
Mississippi	11.5	13.4	48.7	Arizona	25	Iowa	25	Louisiana	24
Missouri	42.3	46.6	68.3	Hawaii	26	Arizona	26	Virginia	26
Montana	35.5	31.3	52.0	Iowa	27	Hawaii	26	Kansas	27
Nebraska	26.1	31.3	68.4	Louisiana	28	Louisiana	28	Georgia	28
Nevada	16.3	19.7	90.6	Wyoming	29	Kansas	29	Nebraska	29
New Hampshire	51.8	56.5	55.6	Kansas	30	Texas	30	Minnesota	30
New Jersey	76.4	79.9	94.7	Florida	30	Montana	31	Missouri	30
New Mexico	14.2	18.0	73.7	Vermont	32	Nebraska	31	Wisconsin	32
New York	78.9	82.7	85.6	Nebraska	33	Vermont	33	Oklahoma	33
North Carolina	14.4	19.2	59.1	Kentucky	34	Wyoming	34	Idaho	34
North Dakota	11.0	13.6	54.0	Texas	35	Virginia	35	Tennessee	35
Ohio	55.9	63.8	78.9	Virginia	36	Idaho	36	Wyoming	36
Oklahoma	19.2	26.5	65.1	Idaho	37	Oklahoma	37	Iowa	37
Oregon	45.6	49.8	77.9	Georgia	38	Kentucky	38	South Carolina	38
Pennsylvania	60.4	65.1	76.4	Tennessee	39	Tennessee	39	Alaska	39
Rhode Island	91.0	91.9	90.9	Oklahoma	40	West Virginia	40	North Carolina	40
South Carolina	14.8	17.5	61.2	West Virginia	41	Georgia	41	Kentucky	41
South Dakota	13.1	16.0	51.6	Alabama	42	Alabama	42	New Hampshire	42
Tennessee	20.2	26.1	63.6	Nevada	43	Nevada	43	Alabama	43
Texas	24.1	32.4	80.7	South Carolina	44	North Carolina	44	North Dakota	44
Utah	46.3	48.0	85.4	North Carolina	45	New Mexico	45	Arkansas	45
Vermont	27.8	31.2	33.6	New Mexico	46	South Carolina	46	Montana	45
Virginia	23.1	29.2	71.4	South Dakota	47	Arkansas	47	South Dakota	47
Washington	53.0	54.8	81.3	Arkansas	48	South Dakota	48	Mississippi	48
West Virginia	18.7	25.2	46.4	Mississippi	49	North Dakota	49	West Virginia	49
Wisconsin	43.0	47.3	65.8	North Dakota	50	Mississippi	50	Maine	50
Wyoming	29.6	29.4	62.4	Alaska	51	Alaska	51	Vermont	51
United States	45.6	51.2	77.6	United States	–	United States	–	United States	–

Source: U.S. Census Bureau, 1910 Census of Housing; U.S. Census Bureau, 1920 Census of Housing; U.S. Census Bureau, Census 2010

Rural Population

Area	Percent of Population 1910	1920	2010	1910 Area	Rank	1920 Area	Rank	2010 Area	Rank
Alabama	82.7	78.3	45.0	Alaska	1	Alaska	1	Vermont	1
Alaska	90.5	94.4	39.5	North Dakota	2	Mississippi	2	Maine	2
Arizona	69.0	63.9	13.3	Mississippi	3	North Dakota	3	West Virginia	3
Arkansas	87.1	83.4	48.0	Arkansas	4	South Dakota	4	Mississippi	4
California	38.2	32.1	6.8	South Dakota	5	Arkansas	5	South Dakota	5
Colorado	49.7	51.8	18.0	New Mexico	6	South Carolina	6	Arkansas	6
Connecticut	34.4	32.2	12.1	North Carolina	7	New Mexico	7	Montana	6
D.C.	0.0	0.0	0.0	South Carolina	8	North Carolina	8	North Dakota	8
Delaware	52.0	45.8	19.9	Nevada	9	Nevada	9	Alabama	9
Florida	70.9	63.5	10.7	Alabama	10	Alabama	10	New Hampshire	10
Georgia	79.4	74.9	29.3	West Virginia	11	Georgia	11	Kentucky	11
Hawaii	69.3	63.9	10.0	Oklahoma	12	West Virginia	12	North Carolina	12
Idaho	78.5	72.4	36.2	Tennessee	13	Tennessee	13	Alaska	13
Illinois	38.3	32.1	12.7	Georgia	14	Kentucky	14	South Carolina	14
Indiana	57.6	49.4	27.9	Idaho	15	Oklahoma	15	Iowa	15
Iowa	69.4	63.6	38.6	Virginia	16	Idaho	16	Wyoming	16
Kansas	70.9	65.2	28.9	Texas	17	Virginia	17	Tennessee	17
Kentucky	75.7	73.8	44.1	Kentucky	18	Wyoming	18	Idaho	18
Louisiana	70.0	65.1	27.9	Nebraska	19	Vermont	19	Oklahoma	19
Maine	64.7	61.0	63.4	Vermont	20	Montana	20	Wisconsin	20
Maryland	49.2	40.0	13.6	Kansas	21	Nebraska	20	Minnesota	21
Massachusetts	11.0	10.0	8.9	Florida	21	Texas	22	Missouri	21
Michigan	52.8	38.9	27.8	Wyoming	23	Kansas	23	Nebraska	23
Minnesota	59.0	55.9	31.7	Louisiana	24	Louisiana	24	Georgia	24
Mississippi	88.5	86.6	51.3	Iowa	25	Arizona	25	Kansas	25
Missouri	57.7	53.4	31.7	Hawaii	26	Hawaii	25	Virginia	26
Montana	64.5	68.7	48.0	Arizona	27	Iowa	27	Indiana	27
Nebraska	73.9	68.7	31.6	Maine	28	Florida	28	Louisiana	27
Nevada	83.7	80.3	9.4	Montana	29	Maine	29	Michigan	29
New Hampshire	48.2	43.5	44.4	Minnesota	30	Minnesota	30	New Mexico	30
New Jersey	23.6	20.1	5.3	Missouri	31	Missouri	31	Pennsylvania	31
New Mexico	85.8	82.0	26.3	Indiana	32	Wisconsin	32	Oregon	32
New York	21.1	17.3	14.4	Wisconsin	33	Utah	33	Ohio	33
North Carolina	85.6	80.8	40.9	Oregon	34	Colorado	34	Delaware	34
North Dakota	89.0	86.4	46.0	Utah	35	Oregon	35	Texas	35
Ohio	44.1	36.2	21.1	Michigan	36	Indiana	36	Washington	36
Oklahoma	80.8	73.5	34.9	Delaware	37	Delaware	37	Colorado	37
Oregon	54.4	50.2	22.1	Colorado	38	Washington	38	Utah	38
Pennsylvania	39.6	34.9	23.6	Maryland	39	New Hampshire	39	New York	39
Rhode Island	9.0	8.1	9.1	New Hampshire	40	Maryland	40	Maryland	40
South Carolina	85.2	82.5	38.8	Washington	41	Michigan	41	Arizona	41
South Dakota	86.9	84.0	48.4	Ohio	42	Ohio	42	Illinois	42
Tennessee	79.8	73.9	36.4	Pennsylvania	43	Pennsylvania	43	Connecticut	43
Texas	75.9	67.6	19.3	Illinois	44	Connecticut	44	Florida	44
Utah	53.7	52.0	14.6	California	45	California	45	Hawaii	45
Vermont	72.2	68.8	66.4	Connecticut	46	Illinois	45	Nevada	46
Virginia	76.9	70.8	28.6	New Jersey	47	New Jersey	47	Rhode Island	47
Washington	47.0	45.2	18.7	New York	48	New York	48	Massachusetts	48
West Virginia	81.3	74.8	53.6	Massachusetts	49	Massachusetts	49	California	49
Wisconsin	57.0	52.7	34.2	Rhode Island	50	Rhode Island	50	New Jersey	50
Wyoming	70.4	70.6	37.6	D.C.	51	D.C.	51	D.C.	51
United States	54.4	48.8	22.4	United States	–	United States	–	United States	–

Source: U.S. Census Bureau, 1910 Census of Housing; U.S. Census Bureau, 1920 Census of Housing; U.S. Census Bureau, Census 2010

Males per 100 Females

Area	Males per 100 Females			1910 Area	Rank	1920 Area	Rank	2010 Area	Rank
	1910	1920	2010						
Alabama	101.0	99.8	94.3	Nevada	1	Nevada	1	Alaska	1
Alaska	n/a	n/a	108.5	Wyoming	2	Wyoming	2	Wyoming	2
Arizona	138.2	121.9	98.7	Montana	3	Arizona	3	North Dakota	3
Arkansas	106.0	104.5	96.5	Arizona	4	Montana	4	Nevada	4
California	125.5	112.4	98.8	Washington	5	Idaho	5	Utah	5
Colorado	116.9	110.3	100.5	Oregon	6	Washington	6	Montana	6
Connecticut	102.3	101.5	94.8	Idaho	7	Oregon	7	Colorado	7
D.C.	91.3	87.0	89.5	California	8	South Dakota	8	Idaho	8
Delaware	104.6	104.1	93.9	North Dakota	9	California	9	Hawaii	9
Florida	110.0	104.7	95.6	South Dakota	10	New Mexico	10	South Dakota	10
Georgia	100.1	99.6	95.4	Colorado	11	North Dakota	11	Washington	11
Hawaii	n/a	n/a	100.3	New Mexico	12	Michigan	12	California	12
Idaho	132.5	118.2	100.4	Minnesota	13	Colorado	13	Arizona	13
Illinois	106.8	103.9	96.2	Oklahoma	14	Minnesota	14	Minnesota	14
Indiana	105.0	103.3	96.8	West Virginia	15	Oklahoma	15	Nebraska	14
Iowa	106.6	104.7	98.1	Utah	16	West Virginia	16	Wisconsin	14
Kansas	110.0	105.7	98.4	Nebraska	17	Nebraska	17	Texas	17
Kentucky	103.0	103.2	96.8	Kansas	18	Texas	18	Kansas	17
Louisiana	101.7	100.9	95.9	Florida	18	Utah	19	Iowa	19
Maine	103.2	102.5	95.8	Wisconsin	20	Wisconsin	20	Oregon	20
Maryland	98.9	101.3	93.6	Texas	20	Kansas	21	Oklahoma	20
Massachusetts	96.7	96.3	93.7	Michigan	22	Ohio	22	New Mexico	22
Michigan	107.3	110.8	96.3	Illinois	23	Iowa	23	New Hampshire	23
Minnesota	114.6	109.1	98.5	Iowa	24	Florida	23	West Virginia	23
Mississippi	101.6	100.4	94.4	Arkansas	25	Arkansas	25	Vermont	25
Missouri	105.1	102.5	96.0	Pennsylvania	26	Delaware	26	Indiana	26
Montana	152.1	120.5	100.8	Vermont	27	Illinois	27	Kentucky	26
Nebraska	111.2	107.9	98.5	Missouri	28	Indiana	28	Arkansas	28
Nevada	179.2	148.4	102.0	Indiana	29	Pennsylvania	29	Virginia	29
New Hampshire	100.9	100.5	97.3	Delaware	30	Kentucky	29	Michigan	29
New Jersey	102.9	101.5	94.8	Ohio	31	Vermont	31	Illinois	31
New Mexico	115.3	112.1	97.7	Maine	32	Maine	32	Missouri	32
New York	101.2	99.8	93.8	Kentucky	33	Missouri	32	Louisiana	33
North Carolina	99.2	99.9	95.0	New Jersey	34	Virginia	34	Maine	34
North Dakota	122.4	112.0	102.1	Connecticut	35	Connecticut	35	Florida	35
Ohio	104.4	105.4	95.4	Tennessee	36	New Jersey	35	Georgia	36
Oklahoma	113.7	109.0	98.0	Louisiana	37	Maryland	37	Ohio	36
Oregon	133.2	113.4	98.0	Mississippi	38	Louisiana	38	Pennsylvania	38
Pennsylvania	105.9	103.2	95.1	New York	39	Tennessee	38	Tennessee	38
Rhode Island	99.3	97.0	93.4	Alabama	40	New Hampshire	40	North Carolina	40
South Carolina	98.5	99.2	94.7	New Hampshire	41	Mississippi	41	New Jersey	41
South Dakota	118.9	112.6	100.1	Virginia	41	North Carolina	42	Connecticut	41
Tennessee	102.1	100.9	95.1	Georgia	43	New York	43	South Carolina	43
Texas	107.4	106.9	98.4	Rhode Island	44	Alabama	43	Mississippi	44
Utah	111.5	106.8	100.9	North Carolina	45	Georgia	45	Alabama	45
Vermont	105.3	103.0	97.1	Maryland	46	South Carolina	46	Delaware	46
Virginia	100.9	102.4	96.3	South Carolina	47	Rhode Island	47	New York	47
Washington	136.3	118.1	99.3	Massachusetts	48	Massachusetts	48	Massachusetts	48
West Virginia	111.6	108.9	97.3	D.C.	49	D.C.	49	Maryland	49
Wisconsin	107.4	106.4	98.5	Alaska	n/a	Hawaii	n/a	Rhode Island	50
Wyoming	168.8	131.3	104.1	Hawaii	n/a	Alaska	n/a	D.C.	51
United States	106.0	104.0	96.7	United States	–	United States	–	United States	–

Source: U.S. Census Bureau, 1910 Census of Population; U.S. Census Bureau, 1920 Census of Population; U.S. Census Bureau, Census 2010

Homeownership

Area	Percent of Population			1910		1920		2010	
	1910	1920	2010	Area	Rank	Area	Rank	Area	Rank
Alabama	35.1	35.0	69.7	North Dakota	1	North Dakota	1	West Virginia	1
Alaska	n/a	n/a	63.1	New Mexico	2	Wisconsin	2	Minnesota	2
Arizona	49.2	42.8	66.0	South Dakota	3	South Dakota	3	Michigan	3
Arkansas	46.6	45.1	66.9	Idaho	4	Idaho	4	Iowa	3
California	49.5	43.7	56.0	Utah	5	Minnesota	5	Delaware	5
Colorado	51.5	51.6	65.5	Wisconsin	6	Montana	6	Maine	6
Connecticut	37.3	37.6	67.5	Maine	7	Utah	7	New Hampshire	7
D.C.	25.2	30.3	42.0	Minnesota	8	Maine	8	Vermont	8
Delaware	40.7	44.7	72.0	Michigan	9	New Mexico	9	Utah	9
Florida	44.2	42.5	67.3	Oregon	10	Michigan	10	Idaho	10
Georgia	30.5	30.9	65.7	Montana	11	Iowa	11	Indiana	11
Hawaii	n/a	n/a	57.7	Nebraska	12	Vermont	12	Alabama	12
Idaho	68.1	60.9	69.9	Kansas	12	Nebraska	13	Pennsylvania	13
Illinois	44.1	43.8	67.4	Vermont	14	Kansas	14	Mississippi	13
Indiana	54.8	54.8	69.8	Iowa	15	Oregon	15	South Carolina	15
Iowa	58.4	58.1	72.1	Washington	16	Indiana	15	Wyoming	15
Kansas	59.1	56.9	67.7	Indiana	17	Washington	17	Missouri	17
Kentucky	51.6	51.6	68.7	Wyoming	18	Wyoming	18	Kentucky	18
Louisiana	32.2	33.7	67.3	Nevada	19	Colorado	19	New Mexico	19
Maine	62.5	59.6	71.3	Kentucky	20	Ohio	19	Tennessee	20
Maryland	44.0	49.9	67.5	Colorado	21	Kentucky	19	Wisconsin	21
Massachusetts	33.1	34.8	62.3	Virginia	21	Virginia	22	South Dakota	21
Michigan	61.7	58.9	72.1	Ohio	23	Maryland	23	Montana	23
Minnesota	61.9	60.7	73.1	New Hampshire	24	New Hampshire	24	Kansas	24
Mississippi	34.0	34.0	69.6	Missouri	25	Missouri	25	Ohio	25
Missouri	51.1	49.5	68.8	California	26	Tennessee	26	Maryland	26
Montana	60.0	60.5	68.0	West Virginia	26	Nevada	27	Connecticut	26
Nebraska	59.1	57.4	67.2	Arizona	28	North Carolina	28	Illinois	28
Nevada	53.4	47.6	58.8	North Carolina	29	West Virginia	29	Florida	29
New Hampshire	51.2	49.8	70.9	Tennessee	30	Oklahoma	30	Oklahoma	29
New Jersey	35.0	38.3	65.4	Arkansas	31	Pennsylvania	31	Louisiana	29
New Mexico	70.6	59.4	68.5	Oklahoma	32	Arkansas	32	Virginia	32
New York	31.0	30.7	53.3	Texas	33	Delaware	33	Nebraska	32
North Carolina	47.3	47.4	66.7	Florida	34	Illinois	34	Arkansas	34
North Dakota	75.7	65.3	65.4	Illinois	35	California	35	North Carolina	35
Ohio	51.3	51.6	67.6	Maryland	36	Arizona	36	Arizona	36
Oklahoma	45.4	45.5	67.3	Pennsylvania	37	Texas	36	Georgia	37
Oregon	60.1	54.8	62.1	Delaware	38	Florida	38	Colorado	38
Pennsylvania	41.6	45.2	69.6	Connecticut	39	New Jersey	39	New Jersey	39
Rhode Island	28.3	31.1	60.7	Alabama	40	Connecticut	40	North Dakota	39
South Carolina	30.8	32.2	69.3	New Jersey	41	Alabama	41	Washington	41
South Dakota	68.2	61.5	68.1	Mississippi	42	Massachusetts	42	Texas	42
Tennessee	47.0	47.7	68.2	Massachusetts	43	Mississippi	43	Alaska	43
Texas	45.1	42.8	63.7	Louisiana	44	Louisiana	44	Massachusetts	44
Utah	64.8	60.0	70.5	New York	45	South Carolina	45	Oregon	45
Vermont	58.5	57.5	70.7	South Carolina	46	Rhode Island	46	Rhode Island	46
Virginia	51.5	51.1	67.2	Georgia	47	Georgia	47	Nevada	47
Washington	57.3	54.7	63.9	Rhode Island	48	New York	48	Hawaii	48
West Virginia	49.5	46.8	73.4	D.C.	49	D.C.	49	California	49
Wisconsin	64.6	63.6	68.1	Alaska	n/a	Hawaii	n/a	New York	50
Wyoming	54.5	51.9	69.3	Hawaii	n/a	Alaska	n/a	D.C.	51
United States	45.9	45.6	65.1	United States	–	United States	–	United States	–

Source: U.S. Census Bureau, 1910 Census of Population; U.S. Census Bureau, 1920 Census of Population; U.S. Census Bureau, Census 2010

DEPARTMENT OF COMMERCE
BUREAU OF THE CENSUS

SAM. L. ROGERS, Director
RESIGNED APRIL 18, 1921

W. M. STEUART, Director
APPOINTED APRIL 14, 1921

FOURTEENTH CENSUS OF THE UNITED STATES TAKEN IN THE YEAR 1920

POPULATION

1920

NUMBER AND DISTRIBUTION OF INHABITANTS

PREPARED UNDER THE SUPERVISION OF WILLIAM C. HUNT
CHIEF STATISTICIAN FOR POPULATION

Bureau of the Census
Library

WASHINGTON
GOVERNMENT PRINTING OFFICE
1921

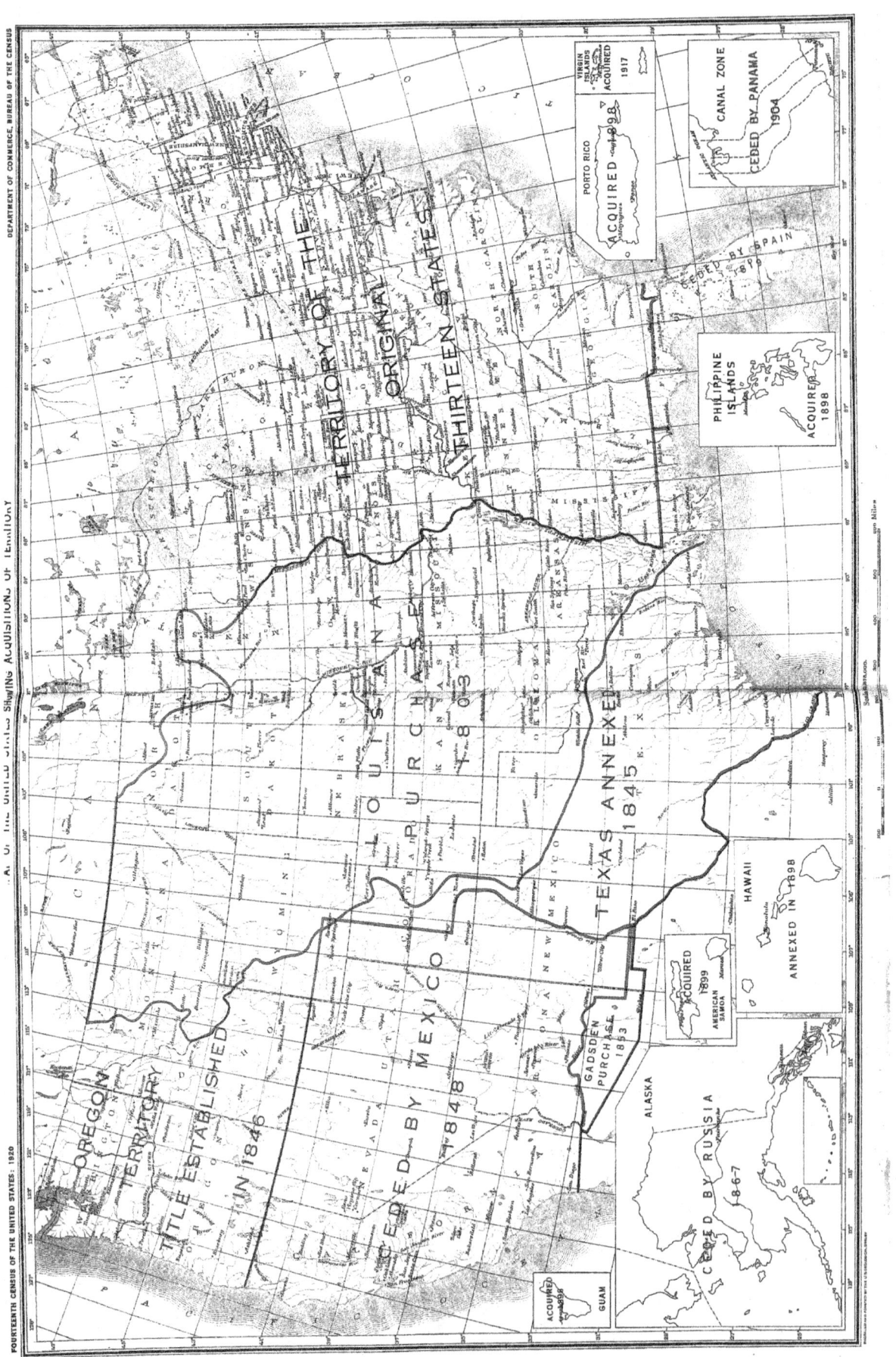

SUMMARY OF RESULTS.

POPULATION OF THE UNITED STATES AND OF ITS OUTLYING POSSESSIONS.

In 1920 the aggregate population of the United States with its outlying possessions was nearly 118,000,000. The distribution of this population is shown by Table 1.

The United States with its outlying possessions occupies approximately 6.7 per cent of the world's land area and embraces approximately 6.9 per cent of its population.*

TABLE 1.—POPULATION OF THE UNITED STATES AND OUTLYING POSSESSIONS: 1920 AND 1910.

AREA.	Gross area (land and water) in square miles.	POPULATION.	
		1920	1910
United States, with outlying possessions	3,743,529	117,859,495	101,146,530
Continental United States	3,026,789	105,710,620	91,972,266
Outlying possessions	716,740	12,148,875	9,174,264
Alaska	590,884	55,036	64,356
American Samoa	77	8,056	[1] 7,251
Guam	210	13,275	11,806
Hawaii	6,449	255,912	191,909
Panama Canal Zone	527	22,858	[1] 62,810
Porto Rico	3,435	1,299,809	1,118,012
Military and naval, etc., services abroad [2]		117,238	55,608
Philippine Islands	115,026	[3] 10,350,640	[4] 7,635,426
Virgin Islands of the United States	132	[5] 26,051	[6] 27,086

[1] Population in 1912.
[2] Comprises military, Red Cross, and consular services abroad, and naval service abroad or in American waters but not on fixed station. See explanation in text below.
[3] Population December 31, 1918.   [4] Population in 1903.   [5] Population November 1, 1917.   [6] Population in 1911.

* The area and population of the United States are compared with the area and population of other countries and of the continental divisions of the earth in the following table, which gives separate figures for the 11 countries or empires each having a population, according to the latest census or estimate available, in excess of 25,000,000. The areas, except for the United States, are taken from the Statesman's Year-Book for 1920. The population figures for the British Empire, Russia, France, Japan, Netherlands, Italy, and Poland were secured from the embassies or legations of those countries. The population shown for China is the usual estimate of 400,000,000, but other estimates range from 340,000,000 to 440,000,000. The figures for the remaining foreign countries were obtained from the Statesman's Year-Book for 1920. The figures for population do not in all cases relate to the year 1920, and in general those for both population and area must be regarded merely as estimates or approximations.

REGION OR COUNTRY.	Area in square miles.	Population.	PER CENT DISTRIBUTION.	
			Area.	Population.
Aggregate	55,885,000	1,720,000,000	100.0	100.0
Continental divisions:				
Asia	17,052,000	890,000,000	30.5	51.7
Europe	3,821,000	475,000,000	6.8	27.6
North America	8,040,000	145,000,000	14.4	8.4
South America	7,018,000	61,000,000	12.6	3.5
Africa	11,605,000	140,000,000	20.8	8.1
Australia and Oceania	3,457,000	9,000,000	6.2	0.5
Polar Regions	4,892,000		8.8	
Countries (including dependencies):				
British Empire	12,780,000	445,388,000	22.9	25.9
China	4,171,000	400,000,000	7.5	23.3
Russia	8,248,000	166,107,000	14.8	9.7
United States	3,743,000	117,859,000	6.7	6.9
France	4,751,000	96,109,000	8.5	5.6
Japan	316,000	78,000,000	0.6	4.5
Germany	172,000	55,086,000	0.3	3.2
Netherlands	796,000	54,027,000	1.4	3.1
Italy	562,000	38,000,000	1.0	2.2
Brazil	3,276,000	30,492,000	5.9	1.8
Poland	141,000	30,072,000	0.3	1.7
Other countries	16,920,000	208,770,000	30.3	12.1

The item "Military and naval, etc., services abroad" represents the following classes of persons: Officers and enlisted men in the military service abroad; persons in the service of the American Red Cross abroad, or in the consular service of the United States abroad, together with members of their families, including servants, who were actually residing with them at their posts of duty; officers and enlisted men in the naval service abroad or in American waters but not on fixed station. Persons in the military service in the United States were enumerated as residents of the states, counties, and minor civil divisions in which their posts of duty were located, and the members of their families were enumerated where they actually resided.

The growth of population since 1790 is shown in Table 2, which gives the population at each census and the increase during each decade for the country as a whole, exclusive of outlying territory.

Since the Twelfth Census was taken as of June 1, 1900, the Thirteenth as of April 15, 1910, and the Fourteenth as of January 1, 1920, the period between the Twelfth and Thirteenth Census dates was nine years and ten and one-half months, and that between the Thirteenth and Fourteenth Census dates was nine years and eight and one-half months. It may be estimated that the population increase from April 15 to June 1, 1910, the end of a full decennial period from

14   POPULATION.

the Twelfth Census date, was not less than 200,000, a number sufficient to raise the decennial rate of increase from 21 to 21.3 per cent. Similarly, it may be estimated that the population increase from January 1 to April 15, 1920, the end of a full decennial period from the Thirteenth Census date, was more than 400,000, which, added to the increase between the census dates, would represent a decennial rate of 15.4 per cent.

TABLE 2.—POPULATION OF THE UNITED STATES, EXCLUSIVE OF OUTLYING POSSESSIONS: 1790–1920.

| CENSUS YEAR. | Population. | INCREASE OVER PRECEDING CENSUS. | | Per cent of increase with correction [1] for 1870 and 1880. |
		Number.	Per cent.	
1920	105,710,620	13,738,354	14.9	14.9
1910	91,972,266	15,977,691	21.0	21.0
1900	75,994,575	13,046,861	20.7	20.7
1890	62,947,714	12,791,931	25.5	25.5
1880	50,155,783	11,597,412	30.1	26.0
1870	38,558,371	7,115,050	22.6	26.6
1860	31,443,321	8,251,445	35.6	35.6
1850	23,191,876	6,122,423	35.9	35.9
1840	17,069,453	4,203,433	32.7	32.7
1830	12,866,020	3,227,567	33.5	33.5
1820	9,638,453	2,398,572	33.1	33.1
1810	7,239,881	1,931,398	36.4	36.4
1800	5,308,483	1,379,269	35.1	35.1
1790	3,929,214			

[1] See explanation in text below.

Some explanation is necessary in regard to the revised percentages given in the last column of Table 2 for the decades 1860–1870 and 1870–1880. The percentages of increase shown for these decades for the country as a whole were materially affected by the small increase recorded for the Southern states at the census of 1870. The evidence is conclusive, however, that the enumeration of 1870 was incomplete in those states, and that their population was, in consequence, understated. The census returns, therefore, give for the decade 1860–1870 a rate of increase which is undoubtedly below, and for the decade 1870–1880 one which is undoubtedly above, the true rate. An estimate of the true population of the country in 1870 was made in the census report for 1890 (Population, Part I, pp. xi, xii, and xvi). In that report the number of omissions in the census of 1870 was estimated to have exceeded 1,200,000, and the true population of the country in 1870 was accordingly estimated to have been 39,818,449 instead of 38,558,371, the number derived from the 1870 returns. On the basis of this revised population total, the increase for the decade 1860–1870 became 8,375,128, or 26.6 per cent (instead of 7,115,050, or 22.6 per cent), and that for the succeeding decade, 10,337,334, or 26 per cent (instead of 11,597,412, or 30.1 per cent).

As stated in the introduction, Indians and other persons in Indian Territory and on Indian reservations were enumerated for the first time in 1890. Consequently the entire population of these areas in 1890—that is, 325,464, and not simply the excess of the 1890 over the 1880 population (which can not be determined)—enters into the aggregate population increase given in Table 2 for the decade 1880–1890. Since this increase is therefore partly attributable to extension of the area of enumeration in 1890, it does not accurately indicate the growth of population within the area enumerated in either 1880 or 1890. The increase within the area enumerated in 1880 may be determined by eliminating from the 1890 population these 325,464 Indians and other persons. The population in 1890 of the area enumerated in 1880 within the limits of continental United States was 62,622,250, which gives an increase for the decade 1880–1890, within this area, of 12,466,467, or 24.9 per cent. This is probably a more nearly correct statement of the increase than that based on the face of the returns (12,791,931, or 25.5 per cent) without taking into account the extension of the area of enumeration.

For each of the earlier decades in which the area enumerated has been extended, the increase may also be similarly determined by excluding the population of the areas newly added. The results of such a calculation are shown in Table 3. While the rates so computed do not differ very materially from those given in Table 2, the modifications result in making the percentage increases for the first seven decades more nearly uniform. The exceptionally high rates shown in Table 2 for the decades ending, respectively, in 1800, 1810, 1850, and 1860 are accounted for in some measure by extensions of the area of enumeration. Since, however, the population within these added areas in each given decade has undoubtedly grown to a greater or less extent by net migration from other sections of the country—which obviously lessened the population growth to an equal extent in those sec-

UNITED STATES AND OUTLYING POSSESSIONS.   15

tions—the rate obtained by excluding the population of these areas is somewhat below, as the unadjusted rate in Table 2 is somewhat above, the true rate for the country as a whole. The error arises, in the one case, from including in the increase the population of the added areas at the beginning of the decade, and, in the other case, from excluding the migrants from the population at the end of the decade. In Table 3 the estimated population for 1870 has been used in reckoning the increases for the decades ending in 1870 and 1880. To complete the table, increases have been included from Table 2 for decades in which there was no change in the area of enumeration.

TABLE 3.—INCREASE WITHIN AREA ENUMERATED AT PRECEDING CENSUS: 1800–1920.

CENSUS YEAR.	Total decennial increase.	Population of area enumerated first in year specified.	INCREASE WITHIN AREA ENUMERATED AT PRECEDING CENSUS.	
			Number.	Per cent.
1920	13,738,354	....	13,738,354	14.9
1910	15,977,691	....	15,977,691	21.0
1900	13,046,861	....	13,046,861	20.7
1890	12,791,931	325,464	12,466,467	24.9
1880	¹ 10,237,334	....	10,337,334	26.0
1870	¹ 8,375,128	....	8,375,128	28.6
1860	8,251,445	182,528	8,068,917	34.8
1850	6,122,423	391,410	5,731,013	33.0
1840	4,203,433	49,563	4,153,870	32.3
1830	3,227,567	40,048	3,187,519	33.1
1820	2,398,572	....	2,398,572	33.1
1810	1,931,308	97,401	1,833,907	34.5
1800	1,379,269	61,128	1,318,141	33.5

¹ Estimated increase (see p. 14).

Since it includes a net gain by immigration, the growth of the aggregate population from census to census exceeds the natural increase, or excess of births over deaths.

Summarizing, it may be noted that during each of the seven decades from 1790 to 1860 the population increased with remarkable uniformity by approximately one-third; that during each of the next three decades, from 1860 to 1890, the increase was approximately one-fourth; that during the two decades following the decennial rate of growth was slightly more than one-fifth; and that during the last decade, 1910–1920, the rate was only a little more than one-seventh. The decline in the decennial rate of increase, therefore, has not been gradual from decade to decade but has taken place in three abrupt breaks downward—between 1860 and 1870, between 1890 and 1900, and between 1910 and 1920, each of the four specified rates of growth, except the last, having been maintained with little change for two or more decades.

It may be noted also that, with the exception of that for the last decade, the numerical increase during each ten-year period has been greater than that for any preceding one (using, for the purpose of comparison, the estimated increase between 1860 and 1870, as given in Table 3). Moreover, the numerical increase during the decade 1910–1920 was greater than that for any other decade except the one immediately preceding.

POPULATION BY DIVISIONS AND STATES.

Distribution of the population and rank of states and divisions.—Table 8 (pp. 20 and 21) shows the population and rank according to population of each geographic division and each state from the earliest census to 1920. It will be noted from that table that there has been no change between 1910 and 1920 in rank among the leading six states—New York, Pennsylvania, Illinois, Ohio, Texas, and Massachusetts—but Michigan, which ranked eighth at the census of 1910, now ranks seventh, and California, which ranked twelfth in 1910, now ranks eighth, both these states having passed Missouri, which ranked seventh in 1910 and now ranks ninth. There has been no change in the rank of the leading four states since 1890. It is also to be noted that no state has maintained the same rank without interruption from 1790 to 1920. New York has had first place at each census beginning with that of 1820; Pennsylvania has ranked second in all census years from 1790 to 1920, except 1810 and 1820, when it ranked third; Illinois did not attain third place until 1890; Ohio, which now ranks fourth, has held that position continuously since 1890, but ranked third from 1840 to 1880; Texas did not reach fifth position until 1910; and Massachusetts has ranked sixth only in 1850, 1890, 1910, and 1920.

Nearly one-fifth of the total population of the country in 1790 was returned from Virginia, which ranked first among the states in that year as well as in 1800 and 1810.

In 1790 Maine was a district of Massachusetts; Vermont had not been admitted to the Union; the areas now constituting West Virginia and Kentucky formed parts of Virginia; the area now constituting Tennessee formed the greater part of the Territory South of the River Ohio; the area under the jurisdiction of Georgia extended westward to the Mississippi River; and the area now constituting Ohio, Indiana, Illinois, Michigan, Wisconsin, northeastern and northwestern Minnesota, northeastern North Dakota, and a small section of northeastern South Dakota was known as the Territory Northwest of the Ohio River. Florida and a strip along the southern border of Georgia as then constituted, together with the region west of the Mississippi River, were held by Spain. Although Maine, Vermont, Kentucky, and Tennessee were not in existence as states of the Union in 1790, the census returns for that year showed separately the population of the areas now constituting those states. No enumeration was made of the Territory Northwest of the Ohio River. Practically the total population returned in 1790, numbering 3,929,214, with the excep-

POPULATION.

16

tion of 109,368 inhabitants of the region which now constitutes Kentucky and Tennessee, lived in the area embraced within the limits of the three Atlantic Seaboard divisions—New England, Middle Atlantic, and South Atlantic.

Not more than 5 per cent of the population of the country in 1790 lived west of the Appalachian Mountains, the geographic distribution of the population giving an average depth of settlement, or distance of habitation from the coast, of 255 miles.

The geographic distribution of the population by divisions and sections at the censuses of 1850, 1890, 1900, 1910, and 1920 is shown by percentages in Table 4, which gives also the population in 1920 of each section and division.

TABLE 4.—PER CENT DISTRIBUTION OF POPULATION, BY SECTIONS AND DIVISIONS: 1890-1920, AND 1850.

SECTION AND DIVISION.	Population: 1920	PER CENT OF TOTAL POPULATION.				
		1920	1910	1900	1890	1850
United States	105,710,620	100.0	100.0	100.0	100.0	100.0
The North	63,631,845	60.2	60.6	62.3	63.3	60.5
New England	7,400,909	7.0	7.1	7.4	7.5	11.8
Middle Atlantic	22,261,144	21.1	21.0	20.3	20.2	25.4
East North Central	21,475,543	20.3	19.8	21.0	21.4	19.5
West North Central	12,544,249	11.9	12.7	13.6	14.2	3.8
The South	33,125,803	31.3	32.0	32.3	31.8	38.7
South Atlantic	13,990,272	13.2	13.3	13.7	14.1	20.2
East South Central	8,893,307	8.4	9.1	9.9	10.2	14.5
West South Central	10,242,224	9.7	9.6	8.6	7.5	4.1
The West	8,902,972	8.4	7.4	5.4	4.9	0.8
Mountain	3,336,101	3.2	2.9	2.2	1.9	0.3
Pacific	5,566,871	5.3	4.6	3.2	3.0	0.5
East of the Mississippi River	74,021,175	70.0	70.4	72.4	73.4	91.4
West of the Mississippi River	31,689,445	30.0	29.6	27.6	26.6	8.6

In this table, as in other tables where figures are presented for geographic sections, the term "the North" denotes the 21 states lying north of the southern boundary of Pennsylvania, the Ohio River, and the southern boundaries of Missouri and Kansas, and east of the western boundaries of Kansas, Nebraska, and the Dakotas; "the South" signifies the 16 states and the District of Columbia lying south of the North and east of New Mexico; and "the West" refers to the 11 states lying west of the North and the South. (See map, p. 8.)

Data for 1850 are included in Table 4 as representing conditions immediately after the last considerable accession to the area of the United States. As already pointed out, a very large area lying west of the Mississippi River was not enumerated at the census of 1850; in fact, the extent of this unenumerated area was approximately as great as that of the area canvassed by the enumerators. Since this unenumerated area was, however, practically all unsettled territory, its scanty population if taken into account could not materially affect the percentages shown in Table 4.

It will be noted from the table that the North had substantially the same proportion of the population

of the United States in 1920 as in 1850, whereas the South's percentage has decreased materially and the West's has increased greatly.

Table 5 shows the rank of the states according to population at each of the last three censuses.

TABLE 5.—RANK OF STATES ACCORDING TO POPULATION: 1920, 1910, AND 1900.

STATE.	Population: 1920	RANK IN POPULATION.		
		1920	1910	1900
New York	10,385,227	1	1	1
Pennsylvania	8,720,017	2	2	2
Illinois	6,485,280	3	3	3
Ohio	5,759,394	4	4	4
Texas	4,663,228	5	5	6
Massachusetts	3,852,356	6	6	7
Michigan	3,668,412	7	8	9
California	3,426,861	8	12	21
Missouri	3,404,055	9	7	5
New Jersey	3,155,900	10	11	16
Indiana	2,930,390	11	9	8
Georgia	2,895,832	12	10	11
Wisconsin	2,632,067	13	13	13
North Carolina	2,559,123	14	16	15
Kentucky	2,416,630	15	14	12
Iowa	2,404,021	16	15	10
Minnesota	2,387,125	17	19	19
Alabama	2,348,174	18	18	18
Tennessee	2,337,885	19	17	14
Virginia	2,309,187	20	20	17
Oklahoma	2,028,283	21	23	[1]30
Louisiana	1,798,509	22	24	23
Mississippi	1,790,618	23	21	20
Kansas	1,769,257	24	22	22
Arkansas	1,752,204	25	25	25
South Carolina	1,683,724	26	26	24
West Virginia	1,463,701	27	28	28
Maryland	1,449,661	28	27	26
Connecticut	1,380,631	29	31	29
Washington	1,356,621	30	30	34
Nebraska	1,296,372	31	29	27
Florida	968,470	32	33	33
Colorado	939,629	33	32	32
Oregon	783,389	34	35	36
Maine	768,014	35	34	31
North Dakota	646,872	36	37	40
South Dakota	636,547	37	36	38
Rhode Island	604,397	38	38	35
Montana	548,889	39	40	43
Utah	449,396	40	41	42
New Hampshire	443,083	41	39	37
District of Columbia	437,571	42	43	41
Idaho	431,866	43	45	46
New Mexico	360,350	44	44	44
Vermont	352,428	45	42	39
Arizona	334,162	46	46	47
Delaware	223,003	47	47	45
Wyoming	194,402	48	48	48
Nevada	77,407	49	49	49

[1] The territory of Oklahoma in 1900 ranked 38 and Indian Territory 30. The rank given in Table 5 for 1900 is based upon the population of Indian Territory and Oklahoma combined.

In the section east of the Mississippi River, 6 states and the District of Columbia gained in rank between 1910 and 1920, 11 states made no change, and 9 lost in rank; and in the section west of the Mississippi, 9 states gained in rank, 7 made no change, and 6 lost in rank.

Growth of population.—The decennial increases, by number and per cent, for the several divisions and states during each decade from 1790 to 1920 are given in Table 9 (pp. 22 and 23). For convenience the figures for the last two decades are repeated in Table 6, the divisions and states being arranged in the order of their rates of increase during the decade 1910–1920. The maps on page 19 show graphically

DIVISIONS AND STATES.

the relative rates of growth in the several states for the decades 1910–1920 and 1900–1910.

It will be seen from Table 6 that in 20 states and the District of Columbia the rates of increase were greater than that for the United States, that in 25 states the rates of increase were smaller than that for the country as a whole, and that in 3 states the population decreased. Of the most populous 10 states, 6 (Illinois, Ohio, Texas, Michigan, California, and New Jersey) show greater rates of increase than the country as a whole and 4 (New York, Pennsylvania, Massachusetts, and Missouri) show smaller rates.

In 15 states the population increased less than 10 per cent, or decreased. Five of these—South Dakota, Maine, Vermont, New Hampshire, and Nevada—had fewer than 800,000 inhabitants each, their combined population being only 2,277,479, but each of the remaining 10 had more than 1,000,000 inhabitants and their combined population was 22,495,911.

The states with relatively high rates of increase are scattered over the entire country, from Idaho and California in the West to Connecticut and Florida in the East; and, similarly, the states whose population increased at low rates, or decreased, are scattered from Nevada in the Mountain division and South Dakota and Nebraska in the West North Central division to Maine in the New England and Mississippi in the East South Central division. Of the 20 states whose population increased more rapidly than that of the United States, 8 are east and 12 are west of the Mississippi River; and of the 28 states whose population increased less rapidly than that of the country as a whole, or decreased, 18 are east and 10 are west of the Mississippi. Of the last-mentioned 10 states, however, 4, which border on the Mississippi, lie in the eastern half of the country.

Of the 21 Northern states only 6 (Connecticut, New Jersey, Ohio, Illinois, Michigan, and Minnesota) and of the 16 Southern states only 5 (West Virginia, North Carolina, Florida, Oklahoma, and Texas) increased in population more rapidly than the United States as a whole; but of the 11 Western states, all but 2 (New Mexico and Nevada) show increases at greater rates than that for the entire country. The westward migration which has been so distinguishing a characteristic of the country's growth showed a pronounced decline during the last decade. Between 1900 and 1910 all the Western states increased at rates far in excess of the average for the United States, the rate for Utah being the only one which was less than twice as great as that for the country as a whole; but between 1910 and 1920 only 5 of the Western states—Arizona, California, Idaho, Montana, and Wyoming—increased at rates more than double that for the United States.

40454°—21——2

TABLE 6.—INCREASE IN POPULATION, FOR TWO DECADES, BY DIVISIONS AND STATES, RANKED ACCORDING TO RATE OF GROWTH FROM 1910 TO 1920.

[A minus sign (−) denotes decrease.]

DIVISION AND STATE.	INCREASE IN POPULATION.			
	Number.		Per cent.	
	1910–1920	1900–1910	1910–1920	1900–1910
DIVISION.				
Pacific	1,374,567	1,775,612	32.8	73.5
Mountain	702,584	958,860	26.7	57.3
East North Central	3,224,922	2,265,040	17.7	14.2
West South Central	1,457,690	2,252,244	16.6	34.5
Middle Atlantic	2,945,252	3,801,214	15.2	25.0
United States	13,738,354	15,977,691	14.9	21.0
South Atlantic	1,795,377	1,751,415	14.7	16.8
New England	848,228	960,664	12.9	17.2
West North Central	906,328	1,290,498	7.8	12.5
East South Central	483,406	862,144	5.7	11.4
STATE.				
Arizona	129,808	81,423	63.5	66.2
Montana	172,836	132,724	46.0	54.5
California	1,049,312	892,496	44.1	60.1
Wyoming	48,437	53,434	33.2	57.7
Idaho	106,272	163,822	32.6	101.3
District of Columbia	106,502	52,351	32.2	18.8
Michigan	858,239	389,191	30.5	16.1
Florida	215,851	224,077	28.7	42.4
New Jersey	618,733	653,498	24.4	34.7
Connecticut	265,875	206,336	23.9	22.7
Oklahoma [1]	371,128	866,764	22.4	109.7
Ohio	992,273	609,576	20.8	14.7
Utah	76,045	96,602	20.4	34.9
West Virginia	242,582	262,319	19.9	27.4
Texas	766,686	847,832	19.7	27.8
Washington	214,631	623,887	18.8	120.4
Colorado	140,605	259,324	17.6	48.0
Oregon	110,624	259,229	16.4	62.7
North Carolina	352,836	312,477	16.0	16.5
Illinois	846,689	817,041	15.0	16.9
Minnesota	311,417	324,314	15.0	18.5
Massachusetts	485,940	561,070	14.4	20.0
New York	1,271,613	1,844,720	14.0	25.4
Pennsylvania	1,054,906	1,362,996	13.8	21.6
Wisconsin	298,207	264,818	12.8	12.8
North Dakota	69,816	257,910	12.1	80.8
Virginia	247,575	207,428	12.0	11.2
Maryland	154,315	107,302	11.9	9.0
Rhode Island	61,787	114,054	11.4	26.6
Arkansas	177,755	262,885	11.3	20.0
South Carolina	168,324	175,084	11.1	13.1
Georgia	286,711	392,790	11.0	17.7
Delaware	20,681	17,587	10.2	9.5
New Mexico	33,049	131,901	10.1	67.6
Alabama	210,081	309,396	9.8	16.9
South Dakota	52,659	182,318	9.0	45.4
Nebraska	104,158	125,914	8.7	11.8
Louisiana	142,121	274,763	8.6	19.9
Indiana	229,514	184,414	8.5	7.3
Iowa	179,250	−7,082	8.1	−0.3
Tennessee	153,096	164,173	7.0	8.1
Kentucky	126,725	142,731	5.5	6.6
Kansas	78,308	220,454	4.6	15.0
Maine	25,643	47,905	3.5	6.9
Missouri	110,720	186,670	3.4	6.0
New Hampshire	12,511	18,984	2.9	4.6
Mississippi	−6,496	245,844	−0.4	15.8
Vermont	−3,523	12,315	−1.0	3.6
Nevada	−4,468	39,540	−5.5	93.4

[1] Includes population of Indian Territory for 1900.

Table 7 presents a comparison, in percentages, of the distribution of the total population in 1920, 1910, and 1850, among the several sections and geographic divisions, with the distribution of the increase in population during the last two decades and during the 70-year period 1850–1920.

18   POPULATION.

The North's proportion of the total population varied only to a slight degree between 1850 and 1920, and its proportion of the total increase during the 70-year period was exactly the same as its proportion of the total population at the end of the period. Thus the loss through migration to the West was counterbalanced by immigration. For the South, however, the disparity between the proportion of the increase and the proportion of the total population was very much greater. That section had 38.7 per cent of the total for the country in 1850, and 31.3 per cent in 1920, but its proportion of the increase during the 70-year period was only 29.3 per cent. During recent decades, however, the disparity has not been so great. In fact, between 1900 and 1910 the difference between the proportion of the increase and the proportion of the total population was less for the South than for the North.

TABLE 7.—PER CENT DISTRIBUTION OF TOTAL POPULATION AND OF INCREASE, BY SECTIONS AND DIVISIONS: 1910–1920, 1900–1910, AND 1850–1920.

SECTION AND DIVISION.	Increase in population: 1910–1920	PER CENT DISTRIBUTION—					
		Of total population: 1920	Of increase: 1910–1920	Of total population: 1910	Of increase: 1900–1910	Of total population: 1850	Of increase: 1850–1920
United States.....	13,738,354	100.0	100.0	100.0	100.0	100.0	100.0
The North..........	7,924,730	60.2	57.7	60.6	52.4	60.5	60.2
New England.......	848,228	7.0	6.2	7.1	6.0	11.8	5.7
Middle Atlantic.....	2,945,252	21.1	21.4	21.0	24.2	25.4	19.8
East North Central..	3,224,922	20.3	23.5	19.8	14.2	19.5	20.5
West North Central...	906,328	11.9	6.6	12.7	8.1	3.8	14.1
The South..........	3,736,473	31.3	27.2	32.0	30.5	38.7	29.3
South Atlantic......	1,795,377	13.2	13.1	13.3	11.0	20.2	11.3
East South Central...	483,406	8.4	3.5	9.1	5.4	14.5	6.7
West South Central..	1,457,690	9.7	10.6	9.6	14.1	4.1	11.3
The West..........	2,077,151	8.4	15.1	7.4	17.1	0.8	10.6
Mountain..........	702,584	3.2	5.1	2.9	6.0	0.3	4.0
Pacific............	1,374,567	5.3	10.0	4.6	11.1	0.5	6.6
East of the Mississippi River.............	9,297,185	70.0	67.7	70.4	60.7	91.4	64.0
West of the Mississippi River.............	4,441,169	30.0	32.3	29.6	39.3	8.6	36.0

Ten states—Florida, Iowa, Kansas, Massachusetts, New Jersey, New York, North Dakota, Rhode Island, South Dakota, and Wyoming—took state censuses in 1915. In the case of Iowa the enumeration related to December 31, 1914, and in the cases of the other states the census dates ranged from March 1 to July 1. The provisions of law under which these state censuses were taken and the practices followed in making the enumerations varied greatly. The returns in certain cases were made up by local assessors, incidentally to the performance of other duties, and were admittedly more or less inaccurate or incomplete. In other states, however, the work was done by enumerators especially appointed for the purpose, and the reports are detailed and accurate.*

* The following table shows, for each of the 10 states which took a census in 1915, the population in 1920 and 1910 as ascertained at the Federal censuses, and in 1915 as ascertained at the state census, together with the numbers and rates of increase for the 5-year periods 1910–1915 and 1915–1920:

STATE.	POPULATION.			INCREASE.[1]			
				1915–1920		1910–1915	
	1920 (Federal census).	1915 (State census).	1910 (Federal census).	Number.	Per cent.	Number.	Per cent.
Total....	24,617,449	23,135,075	21,535,055	1,482,374	6.4	1,600,020	7.4
Florida.........	968,470	921,618	752,619	46,852	5.1	168,999	22.5
Iowa...........	2,404,021	2,358,066	2,224,771	45,955	1.9	133,295	6.0
Kansas.........	1,769,257	1,672,545	1,690,949	96,712	5.8	−18,404	−1.1
Massachusetts..	3,852,356	3,693,310	3,366,416	159,046	4.3	326,894	9.7
New Jersey....	3,155,900	2,844,342	2,537,167	311,558	11.0	307,175	12.1
New York......	10,385,227	9,687,744	9,113,614	697,483	7.2	574,130	6.3
North Dakota..	646,872	636,994	577,056	9,878	1.6	59,938	10.4
Rhode Island..	604,397	595,986	542,610	8,411	1.4	53,376	9.8
South Dakota..	636,547	582,765	583,888	53,782	9.2	−1,123	−0.2
Wyoming......	194,402	141,705	145,965	52,697	37.2	−4,260	−2.9

[1] A minus sign (−) denotes decrease.

It will be seen that, for the 10 states taken as a group, the increase between 1915 and 1920 was somewhat less than that between 1910 and 1915; that in the cases of New Jersey and New York there was no great difference between the increases during the two 5-year periods; that for Florida, Iowa, Massachusetts, North Dakota, and Rhode Island the increases were much smaller between 1915 and 1920 than during the preceding 5 years; and that Kansas, South Dakota, and Wyoming show decreases between 1910 and 1915, followed by increases. The decline in the rates of increase in Massachusetts and Rhode Island is readily attributable to the falling off in immigration, which had been an important factor in their growth prior to 1915.

DIVISIONS AND STATES.

PERCENTAGE OF INCREASE OR DECREASE IN TOTAL POPULATION, BY STATES: 1910–1920.

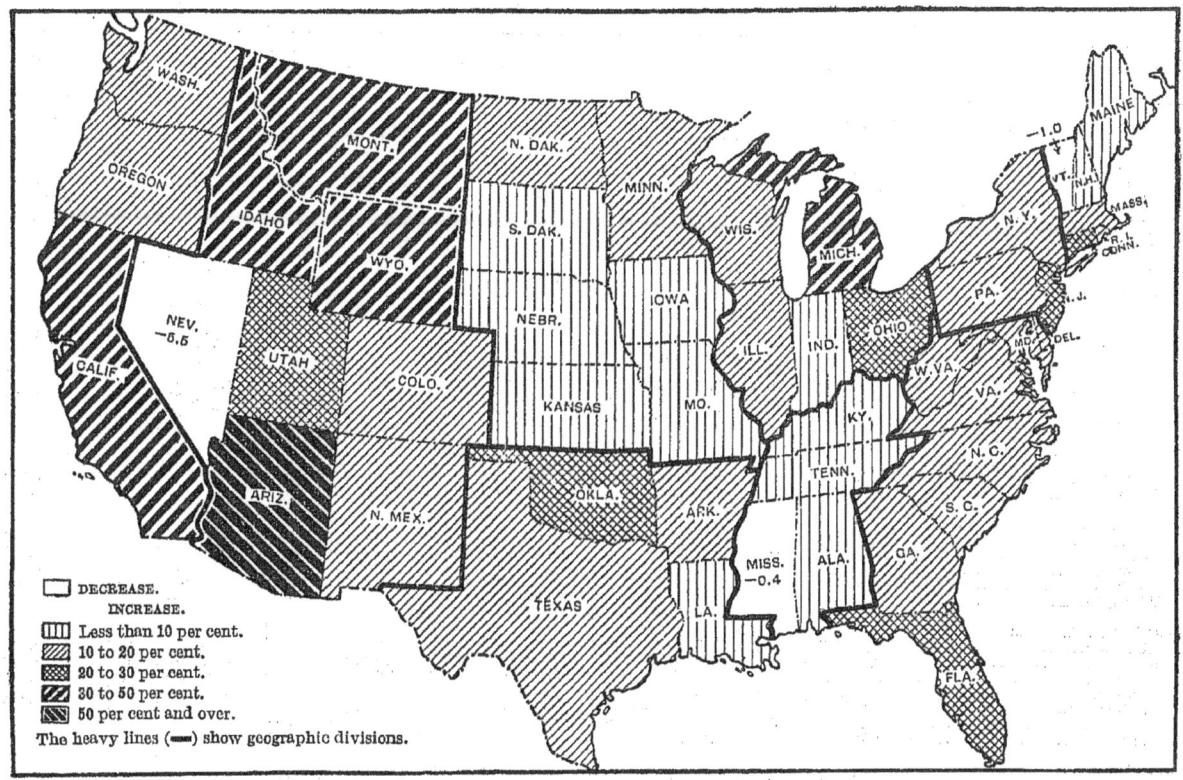

PERCENTAGE OF INCREASE OR DECREASE IN TOTAL POPULATION, BY STATES: 1900–1910.

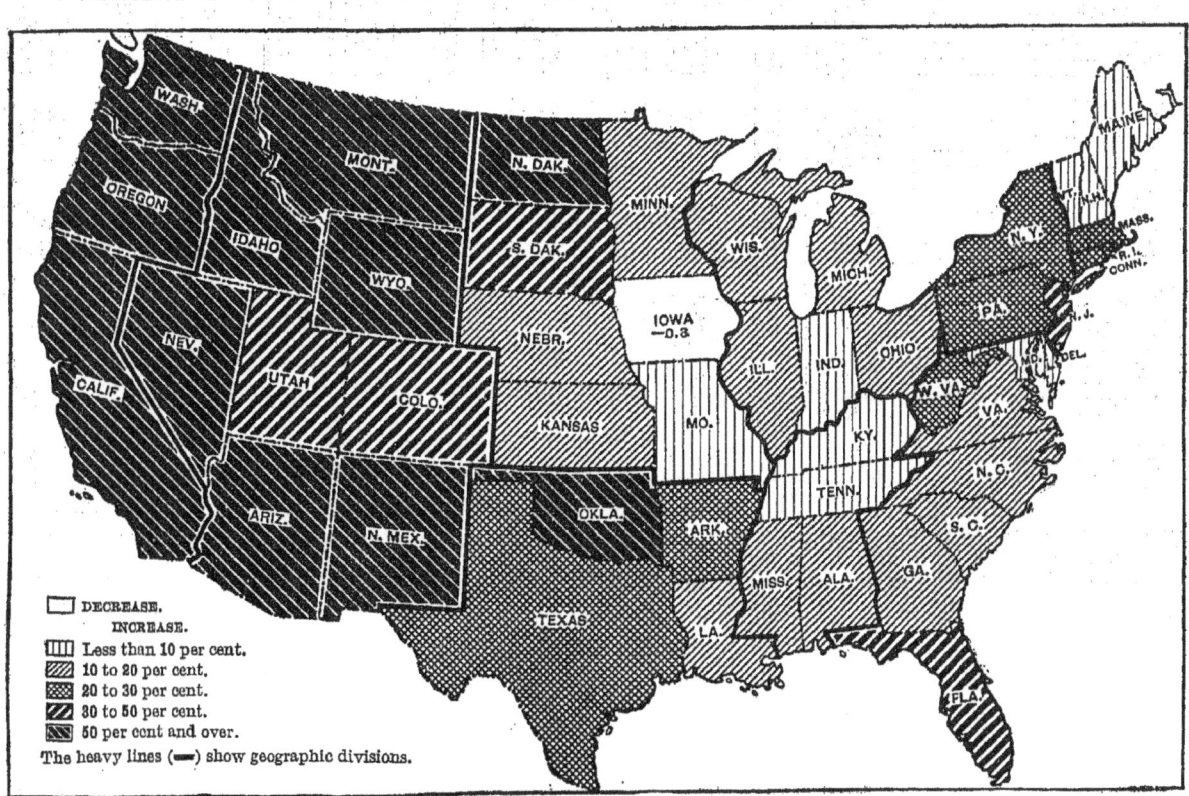

POPULATION.

20

TABLE 8.—POPULATION OF THE UNITED STATES, BY DIVISIONS

	DIVISION AND STATE.	1920 Population.	Rank.	1910 Population.	Rank.	1900 Population.	Rank.	1890 [1] Population.	Rank.	1880 Population.	Rank.	1870 Population.	Rank.
1	United States	105,710,620	......	91,972,266	......	75,994,575	......	62,947,714	......	50,155,783	......	38,558,371	......
	GEOGRAPHIC DIVISIONS:												
2	New England	7,400,909	VII	6,552,681	VII	5,592,017	VII	4,700,749	VII	4,010,529	VI	3,487,924	VI
3	Middle Atlantic	22,261,144	I	19,315,892	I	15,454,678	II	12,700,220	II	10,496,878	II	8,810,806	II
4	East North Central	21,475,543	II	18,250,621	II	15,985,581	I	13,478,305	I	11,206,668	I	9,124,517	I
5	West North Central	12,544,249	IV	11,037,021	IV	10,347,423	IV	8,932,112	III	6,157,443	IV	3,856,594	V
6	South Atlantic	13,990,272	III	12,194,895	III	10,443,480	III	8,857,922	IV	7,597,197	III	5,853,610	III
7	East South Central	8,893,307	VI	8,409,901	VI	7,547,757	V	6,429,154	V	5,585,151	V	4,404,445	IV
8	West South Central	10,242,224	V	8,784,534	V	6,532,290	VI	4,740,983	VI	3,334,220	VII	2,029,965	VII
9	Mountain	3,336,101	IX	2,633,517	IX	1,674,657	IX	1,213,935	IX	653,119	IX	315,385	IX
10	Pacific	5,566,871	VIII	4,192,304	VIII	2,416,692	VIII	1,888,334	VIII	1,114,578	VIII	675,125	VIII
	NEW ENGLAND:												
11	Maine	768,014	35	742,371	34	694,466	31	661,086	30	648,936	27	626,915	23
12	New Hampshire	443,083	41	430,572	39	411,588	37	376,530	38	346,991	31	318,300	31
13	Vermont	352,428	45	355,956	42	343,641	39	332,422	37	332,286	32	330,551	30
14	Massachusetts	3,852,356	6	3,366,416	6	2,805,346	7	2,238,947	6	1,783,085	7	1,457,351	7
15	Rhode Island	604,397	38	542,610	38	428,556	35	345,506	36	276,531	33	217,353	32
16	Connecticut	1,380,631	29	1,114,756	31	908,420	29	746,258	29	622,700	28	537,454	25
	MIDDLE ATLANTIC:												
17	New York	10,385,227	1	9,113,614	1	7,268,894	1	6,003,174	1	5,082,871	1	4,382,759	1
18	New Jersey	3,155,900	10	2,537,167	11	1,883,669	16	1,444,933	18	1,131,116	19	906,096	17
19	Pennsylvania	8,720,017	2	7,665,111	2	6,302,115	2	5,258,113	2	4,282,891	2	3,521,951	2
	EAST NORTH CENTRAL:												
20	Ohio	5,759,394	4	4,767,121	4	4,157,545	4	3,672,329	4	3,198,062	3	2,665,260	3
21	Indiana	2,930,390	11	2,700,876	9	2,516,462	8	2,192,404	8	1,978,301	6	1,680,637	6
22	Illinois	6,485,280	3	5,638,591	3	4,821,550	3	3,826,352	3	3,077,871	4	2,539,891	4
23	Michigan	3,668,412	7	2,810,173	8	2,420,982	9	2,093,890	9	1,636,937	9	1,184,059	13
24	Wisconsin	2,632,067	13	2,333,860	13	2,069,042	13	1,693,330	14	1,315,497	16	1,054,670	15
	WEST NORTH CENTRAL:												
25	Minnesota	2,387,125	17	2,075,708	19	1,751,394	19	1,310,283	20	780,773	26	439,706	28
26	Iowa	2,404,021	16	2,224,771	15	2,231,853	10	1,912,297	10	1,624,615	10	1,194,020	11
27	Missouri	3,404,055	9	3,293,335	7	3,106,665	5	2,679,185	5	2,168,380	5	1,721,295	5
28	North Dakota	646,872	36	577,056	37	319,146	40	190,983	42	} 135,177	40	4 14,181	45
29	South Dakota	636,547	37	583,888	36	401,570	38	348,600	6 35				
30	Nebraska	1,296,372	31	1,192,214	29	1,066,300	27	1,062,656	26	452,402	30	122,993	36
31	Kansas	1,769,257	24	1,690,949	22	1,470,495	22	1,428,108	19	996,096	20	364,399	29
	SOUTH ATLANTIC:												
32	Delaware	223,003	47	202,322	47	184,735	45	168,493	43	146,608	38	125,015	35
33	Maryland	1,449,661	28	1,295,346	28	1,188,044	26	1,042,390	27	934,943	23	780,894	20
34	District of Columbia	437,571	42	331,069	43	278,718	41	230,392	40	177,624	36	131,700	34
35	Virginia	2,309,187	20	2,061,612	20	1,854,184	17	1,655,980	15	1,512,565	14	1,225,163	10
36	West Virginia	1,463,701	27	1,221,119	28	958,800	28	762,794	28	618,457	29	442,014	27
37	North Carolina	2,559,123	14	2,206,287	16	1,893,810	15	1,617,949	16	1,399,750	15	1,071,361	14
38	South Carolina	1,683,724	26	1,515,400	26	1,340,316	24	1,151,149	23	995,577	21	705,606	22
39	Georgia	2,895,832	12	2,609,121	10	2,216,331	11	1,837,353	12	1,542,180	13	1,184,109	12
40	Florida	968,470	32	752,619	33	528,542	33	391,422	32	269,493	34	187,748	33
	EAST SOUTH CENTRAL:												
41	Kentucky	2,416,630	15	2,289,905	14	2,147,174	12	1,858,635	11	1,648,690	8	1,321,011	8
42	Tennessee	2,337,885	19	2,184,789	17	2,020,616	14	1,767,518	13	1,542,359	12	1,258,520	9
43	Alabama	2,348,174	18	2,138,093	18	1,828,697	18	1,513,401	17	1,262,505	17	996,992	16
44	Mississippi	1,790,618	23	1,797,114	21	1,551,270	20	1,289,000	21	1,131,597	18	827,922	18
	WEST SOUTH CENTRAL:												
45	Arkansas	1,752,204	25	1,574,449	25	1,311,564	25	1,128,211	24	802,525	25	484,471	26
46	Louisiana	1,798,509	22	1,656,388	24	1,381,625	23	1,118,588	25	939,946	22	726,915	21
47	Oklahoma	2,028,283	21	1,657,155	23	8 790,391	9 30	8 258,657	6 39				
48	Texas	4,663,228	5	3,896,542	5	3,048,710	6	2,235,527	7	1,591,749	11	818,579	19
	MOUNTAIN:												
49	Montana	548,889	39	376,053	40	243,329	43	142,924	45	39,159	45	20,595	43
50	Idaho	431,866	43	325,594	45	161,772	46	88,548	46	32,610	46	14,999	44
51	Wyoming	194,402	48	145,965	48	92,531	48	62,555	48	20,789	47	9,118	47
52	Colorado	939,629	33	799,024	32	539,700	32	413,249	31	194,327	35	39,864	41
53	New Mexico	360,350	44	327,301	44	195,310	44	160,282	44	119,565	41	91,874	37
54	Arizona	334,162	46	204,354	46	122,931	47	88,243	6 47	40,440	44	9,658	46
55	Utah	449,396	40	373,351	41	276,749	42	210,779	41	143,963	39	86,786	39
56	Nevada	77,407	49	81,875	49	42,335	49	47,355	49	62,266	43	42,491	40
	PACIFIC:												
57	Washington	1,356,621	30	1,141,990	30	518,103	34	357,232	34	75,116	42	23,955	42
58	Oregon	783,389	34	672,765	35	413,536	36	317,704	33	174,768	37	90,923	38
59	California	3,426,861	8	2,377,549	12	1,485,053	21	1,213,398	22	864,694	24	560,247	24

[1] Includes population (325,464) of Indian Territory and Indian reservations, specially enumerated in 1890, but not included in the general report on population for 1890.
[2] Includes persons (6,100 in 1840 and 5,318 in 1830) on public ships in the service of the United States, not credited to any division or state.
[3] Population of area taken to form state of Missouri in 1821; part of Louisiana territory in 1810.
[4] Population of that part of Dakota territory taken to form North Dakota: 1880, 36,909; 1870, 2,405. Population of part taken to form South Dakota: 1880, 98,268; 1870, 11,776.
[5] Dakota territory.

DIVISIONS AND STATES.   21

AND STATES, WITH RANK ACCORDING TO POPULATION: 1790–1920.

1860 Population.	Rank.	1850 Population.	Rank.	1840 Population.	Rank.	1830 Population.	Rank.	1820 Population.	Rank.	1810 Population.	Rank.	1800 Population.	Rank.	1790 Population.	Rank.	
31,443,321	.....	23,191,876	.....	[2]17,069,453	.....	[2]12,866,020	.....	9,638,453	.....	7,239,881	.....	5,308,483	.....	3,929,214	.....	1
3,135,283	V	2,728,116	V	2,234,822	V	1,954,717	III	1,660,071	III	1,471,973	III	1,233,011	III	1,009,408	II	2
7,458,985	I	5,808,735	I	4,526,260	I	3,587,664	II	2,699,845	II	2,014,702	II	1,402,565	II	958,632	III	3
6,926,884	II	4,523,260	III	2,924,728	III	1,470,018	V	792,719	V	272,324	V	51,006	V			4
2,169,832	VI	880,335	VII	428,814	VII	140,455	VII	66,586	VII	19,783	VII					5
5,364,703	III	4,679,090	II	3,925,209	II	3,615,752	I	3,061,063	I	2,674,891	I	2,286,494	I	1,851,806	I	6
4,020,991	IV	3,363,271	IV	2,575,445	IV	1,815,969	IV	1,190,489	IV	708,590	IV	335,407	IV	109,368	IV	7
1,747,667	VII	940,251	VI	449,985	VI	246,127	VI	167,680	VI	77,618	VI					8
174,923	IX	72,927	IX													9
444,053	VIII	105,891	VIII													10
628,279	22	583,169	16	501,793	13	309,456	12	298,335	12	228,705	11	151,719	14	96,540	11	11
326,073	27	317,976	22	284,574	22	269,328	18	244,161	15	214,460	10	183,858	11	141,885	10	12
315,098	28	314,120	23	291,948	21	280,652	17	235,981	16	217,895	15	154,465	13	85,425	12	13
1,231,066	7	994,514	6	737,699	8	610,408	8	523,287	7	472,040	5	422,815	5	378,787	4	14
174,620	29	147,545	28	108,830	24	97,199	23	83,059	20	76,931	17	69,122	16	68,825	15	15
460,147	24	370,792	21	309,978	20	297,675	16	275,248	14	261,942	9	251,002	8	237,946	8	16
3,880,735	1	3,097,394	1	2,428,921	1	1,918,608	1	1,372,812	1	959,049	2	589,051	3	340,120	5	17
672,035	21	480,555	19	373,306	18	320,823	14	277,575	13	245,562	12	211,149	10	184,139	9	18
2,906,215	2	2,311,786	2	1,724,033	2	1,318,233	2	1,049,458	3	810,091	3	602,365	2	434,373	2	19
2,339,511	3	1,980,329	3	1,519,407	3	937,903	4	581,434	5	230,760	13	45,365	18			20
1,350,428	6	988,416	7	685,866	10	343,031	13	147,178	18	24,520	21	5,641	21			21
1,711,951	4	851,470	11	476,183	14	157,445	20	55,211	24	12,282	24					22
749,113	16	307,654	20	212,267	23	31,639	27	8,896	27	4,762	25					23
775,881	15	305,391	24	30,945	30											24
172,023	30	6,077	36													25
674,913	20	192,214	27	43,112	29											26
1,182,012	8	682,044	13	383,702	16	140,455	21	66,586	23	[3]19,783	23					27
[5]4,837	42															28, 29
28,841	30															30
107,206	33															31
112,216	32	91,532	30	78,085	26	76,748	21	72,749	22	72,674	19	64,273	17	59,096	16	32
687,049	19	583,034	17	470,019	15	447,040	11	407,350	10	380,546	8	341,548	7	319,728	6	33
75,080	35	51,687	33	43,712	28	39,834	25	33,039	25	24,023	22	14,093	19			34
1,596,318	5	1,421,661	4	1,239,707	4	1,211,405	3	1,065,366	2	974,600	1	880,200	1	747,610	1	35
																36
992,622	12	869,039	10	753,419	7	737,987	5	638,829	4	555,500	4	478,103	4	393,751	3	37
703,708	18	668,507	14	594,398	11	581,185	9	502,741	8	415,115	6	345,591	6	249,073	7	38
1,057,286	11	906,185	9	691,392	9	516,823	10	340,989	11	252,433	11	162,686	12	82,548	13	39
140,424	31	87,445	31	54,477	27	34,730	26									40
1,155,684	9	982,405	8	770,828	6	687,917	6	564,317	6	406,511	7	220,955	9	73,677	14	41
1,109,801	10	1,002,717	5	829,210	5	681,904	7	422,823	9	261,727	10	105,602	15	35,691	17	42
964,201	13	771,623	12	590,756	12	309,527	15	127,901	19							43
791,305	14	606,526	15	375,651	17	136,621	22	75,448	21	40,352	20	8,850	20			44
435,450	25	209,897	26	97,574	25	30,388	28	14,273	26	[7]1,062	26					45
708,002	17	517,762	18	352,411	19	215,739	19	153,407	17	76,556	18					46
																47
601,215	23	212,592	25													48
																49
																50
																51
34,277	38	61,547	32													52
93,516	34															53
																54
40,273	37	11,380	35													55
6,857	41															56
11,594	40															57
52,465	36	13,294	34													58
379,994	26	92,597	29													59

[6] For 1890 the rank of South Dakota advances from 37 to 35 and that of Arizona from 48 to 47 when the population specially enumerated is included; and that of Oklahoma advances from 46 to 39 when the population of Indian Territory and Indian reservations specially enumerated is included.

[7] Population of area taken to form Arkansas territory in 1819; part of Louisiana territory in 1810.

[8] Includes population of Indian Territory, as follows: 1900, 392,060; 1890, 180,182.

[9] The territory of Oklahoma in 1900 ranked 38 and Indian Territory 39. In computing the rank for 1900 the population of Indian Territory was included with that of Oklahoma.

22

POPULATION.

TABLE 9.—INCREASE IN POPULATION OF THE

[A minus sign (−) denotes decrease.]

	DIVISION AND STATE.	1910–1920		1900–1910		1890–1900		1880–1890		1870–1880		1860–1870	
		Number.	Per cent.	Number.	Per cent.	Number.	Per cent.	Number.	Per cent.	Number.	Per cent.	Number.	Per cent.
1	United States	13,738,354	14.9	15,977,691	21.0	13,046,861	20.7	12,791,931	25.5	11,597,412	30.1	7,115,050	22.6
	GEOGRAPHIC DIVISIONS:												
2	New England	848,228	12.9	960,664	17.2	891,208	19.0	690,220	17.2	522,605	15.0	352,641	11.2
3	Middle Atlantic	2,945,252	15.2	3,861,214	25.0	2,748,458	21.6	2,209,342	21.0	1,686,072	19.1	1,361,821	18.1
4	East North Central	3,224,922	17.7	2,255,040	14.2	2,507,276	18.6	2,271,637	20.3	2,082,151	22.8	2,107,633	31.7
5	West North Central	906,328	7.8	1,290,408	12.5	1,415,311	15.8	2,774,609	45.1	2,300,849	59.7	1,686,762	77.7
6	South Atlantic	1,795,377	14.7	1,751,415	16.8	1,585,558	17.9	1,260,725	16.6	1,743,587	29.8	488,907	9.1
7	East South Central	483,406	5.7	862,144	11.4	1,118,603	17.4	844,003	15.1	1,180,706	26.8	383,454	9.5
8	West South Central	1,457,690	16.6	2,252,244	34.5	1,791,307	37.8	1,406,763	42.2	1,304,255	64.3	282,208	16.2
9	Mountain	702,584	26.7	958,860	57.3	460,722	38.0	590,816	85.9	337,734	107.1	140,462	80.3
10	Pacific	1,374,567	32.8	1,775,612	73.5	528,358	28.0	773,756	69.4	439,453	65.1	231,072	52.0
	NEW ENGLAND:												
11	Maine	25,643	3.5	47,905	6.9	33,380	5.0	12,150	1.9	22,021	3.5	−1,364	−0.2
12	New Hampshire	12,511	2.9	18,984	4.6	35,058	9.3	29,539	8.5	28,091	9.0	−7,773	−2.4
13	Vermont	−3,528	−1.0	12,315	3.6	11,219	3.4	136	(²)	1,735	0.5	15,453	4.0
14	Massachusetts	485,940	14.4	561,070	20.0	566,309	25.3	455,862	25.6	325,734	22.4	220,285	18.4
15	Rhode Island	61,787	11.4	114,054	26.6	83,050	24.0	68,975	24.9	59,178	27.2	42,733	24.5
16	Connecticut	265,875	23.9	200,336	22.7	162,162	21.7	123,558	19.8	85,246	15.9	77,307	16.8
	MIDDLE ATLANTIC:												
17	New York	1,271,613	14.0	1,844,720	25.4	1,265,720	21.1	920,363	18.1	700,112	16.0	502,024	12.9
18	New Jersey	618,733	24.4	653,498	34.7	438,736	30.4	313,817	27.7	225,020	24.8	234,061	34.8
19	Pennsylvania	1,054,906	13.8	1,362,996	21.6	1,044,002	19.9	975,222	22.8	760,940	21.6	615,736	21.2
	EAST NORTH CENTRAL:												
20	Ohio	992,273	20.8	609,576	14.7	485,216	13.2	474,267	14.8	532,802	20.0	325,749	13.9
21	Indiana	229,514	8.5	184,414	7.3	324,058	14.8	214,103	10.8	297,664	17.7	330,209	24.5
22	Illinois	846,689	15.0	817,041	16.9	995,198	26.0	718,481	24.3	537,980	21.2	827,940	48.4
23	Michigan	858,239	30.5	389,191	16.1	327,092	15.6	456,053	27.9	452,878	38.2	434,946	58.1
24	Wisconsin	298,207	12.8	264,818	12.8	375,712	22.2	377,833	28.7	200,827	24.7	278,789	35.9
	WEST NORTH CENTRAL:												
25	Minnesota	311,417	15.0	324,314	18.5	441,111	33.7	529,510	67.8	341,067	77.6	207,083	155.6
26	Iowa	179,250	8.1	−7,082	−0.3	319,556	16.7	287,082	17.7	430,595	36.1	510,107	76.9
27	Missouri	110,720	3.4	186,670	6.0	427,480	16.0	510,805	23.6	447,085	26.0	539,283	45.6
28	North Dakota	69,816	12.1	257,910	80.8	128,163	67.1	404,406	200.2	120,096	853.2	9,341	193.2
29	South Dakota	52,659	9.0	182,318	45.4	52,970	15.2	610,254	134.9	329,409	267.8	94,152	326.5
30	Nebraska	104,158	8.7	125,591	11.8	3,644	0.3	432,012	43.4	631,697	173.4	257,193	349.9
31	Kansas	78,308	4.6	220,451	15.0	42,387	3.0						
	SOUTH ATLANTIC:												
32	Delaware	20,681	10.2	17,587	9.5	16,242	9.6	21,885	14.9	21,503	17.3	12,709	11.4
33	Maryland	154,315	11.9	107,302	9.0	145,654	14.0	107,447	11.5	154,049	19.7	93,845	13.7
34	District of Columbia	106,502	32.2	52,351	18.8	48,326	21.0	52,708	29.7	45,024	34.9	56,620	75.4
35	Virginia	247,575	12.0	207,428	11.2	198,204	12.0	143,415	9.5	170,443	30.0	−371,155	−23.3
36	West Virginia	242,582	19.9	262,310	27.4	190,006	25.7	144,337	23.3	328,389	30.7	442,014	
37	North Carolina	352,836	16.0	312,477	16.5	275,861	17.1	218,199	15.6	280,971	41.1	78,739	7.9
38	South Carolina	168,324	11.1	175,084	13.1	189,167	16.4	155,572	15.6	358,071	30.2	1,808	0.3
39	Georgia	286,711	11.0	392,790	17.7	378,978	20.6	295,173	19.1	81,745	43.5	126,823	12.0
40	Florida	215,851	28.7	224,077	42.4	137,120	35.0	121,029	45.2			47,324	33.7
	EAST SOUTH CENTRAL:												
41	Kentucky	126,725	5.5	142,731	6.6	288,539	15.5	209,045	12.7	327,670	24.8	165,327	14.3
42	Tennessee	153,096	7.0	164,173	8.1	253,008	14.3	225,159	14.6	283,839	22.6	148,710	13.4
43	Alabama	210,081	9.8	309,396	16.9	315,206	20.8	250,896	19.9	265,513	26.6	32,791	3.4
44	Mississippi	−6,496	−0.4	245,844	15.8	261,670	20.3	158,003	14.0	303,075	36.7	36,617	4.6
	WEST SOUTH CENTRAL:												
45	Arkansas	177,755	11.3	262,885	20.0	183,353	16.3	325,686	40.6	318,054	65.6	49,021	11.3
46	Louisiana	142,121	8.6	274,763	19.9	233,037	23.5	178,642	19.0	213,031	29.3	18,913	2.7
47	Oklahoma	371,128	22.4	860,704	109.7	531,734	205.6	258,657					
48	Texas	766,686	19.7	847,832	27.8	813,183	36.4	643,778	40.4	773,170	94.5	214,364	35.5
	MOUNTAIN:												
49	Montana	172,836	46.0	132,724	54.5	100,405	70.3	103,765	265.0	18,564	90.1	20,595	
50	Idaho	106,272	32.6	163,822	101.3	73,224	82.7	55,938	171.5	17,611	117.4	14,999	
51	Wyoming	48,437	33.2	53,434	57.7	29,976	47.9	41,766	200.9	11,671	128.0	9,118	
52	Colorado	140,605	17.6	259,324	48.0	126,451	30.6	218,022	112.7	154,463	387.5	5,587	16.3
53	New Mexico	33,049	10.1	131,001	67.6	35,028	21.9	40,717	34.1	27,091	30.1	−1,642	−1.8
54	Arizona	129,808	63.5	81,423	66.2	34,688	39.3	47,803	118.2	30,782	318.7	9,658	
55	Utah	76,045	20.4	96,602	34.9	65,970	31.3	60,816	46.4	57,177	65.0	46,513	115.5
56	Nevada	−4,468	−5.5	39,540	93.4	−5,020	−10.6	−14,011	−23.9	10,775	46.5	35,634	510.7
	PACIFIC:												
57	Washington	214,631	18.8	623,887	120.4	160,871	45.0	282,116	375.6	51,161	213.6	12,301	106.6
58	Oregon	110,624	16.4	259,220	62.7	95,832	30.2	142,936	81.8	83,845	92.2	38,458	73.3
59	California	1,049,312	44.1	892,406	60.1	271,655	22.4	348,704	40.3	304,447	54.3	180,263	47.4

[1] In computing the decennial increases from 1820 to 1850, persons on public ships in 1830 and 1840 (see Table 8) were included.   [2] Less than one-tenth of 1 per cent.

DIVISIONS AND STATES.

UNITED STATES, BY DIVISIONS AND STATES: 1790–1920.

[A minus sign (−) denotes decrease.]

1850–1860		1840–1850		1830–1840		1820–1830		1810–1820		1800–1810		1790–1800		
Number.	Per cent.	Number.	Per cent.	Number.	Per cent.	Number.	Per cent.	Number.	Per cent.	Number.	Per cent.	Number.	Per cent.	
8,251,445	35.6	¹6,122,423	35.9	¹4,203,433	32.7	¹3,227,567	33.5	2,398,572	33.1	1,931,398	36.4	1,379,269	35.1	1
407,167	14.9	493,294	22.1	280,105	14.3	294,646	17.7	188,098	12.8	238,962	19.4	223,603	22.2	2
1,500,250	26.5	1,372,475	30.3	938,596	26.2	887,810	32.9	685,143	34.0	612,137	43.6	443,933	40.3	3
2,403,624	53.1	1,598,532	54.7	1,454,710	99.0	677,299	85.4	520,395	191.1	221,318	433.9	51,006		4
1,289,497	140.5	453,521	106.3	286,359	203.9	73,809	110.9	46,803	236.6	19,783				5
685,613	14.7	753,701	19.2	279,547	7.7	584,689	19.1	386,172	14.4	338,397	17.0	434,688	23.5	6
657,720	19.6	787,826	30.6	759,476	41.8	625,480	52.5	481,889	68.0	373,183	111.3	226,039	206.7	7
807,416	85.9	490,266	109.0	203,858	82.8	78,447	46.8	90,062	116.0	77,618				8
101,996	130.9	72,927												9
338,162	310.3	105,801												10
45,110	7.7	81,376	16.2	102,338	25.6	101,120	33.9	69,630	30.4	76,980	50.7	55,179	57.2	11
8,097	2.5	33,402	11.7	15,246	5.7	25,167	10.3	29,701	13.8	30,602	16.6	41,973	29.6	12
978	0.3	22,172	7.6	11,296	4.0	44,671	18.9	18,086	8.3	63,430	41.1	69,040	80.8	13
236,552	23.8	256,815	34.8	127,201	20.9	87,121	16.6	51,247	10.9	49,195	11.6	44,058	11.6	14
27,075	18.4	38,715	35.6	11,031	12.0	14,140	17.0	6,128	8.0	7,809	11.3	297	0.4	15
89,355	24.1	60,814	19.6	12,303	4.1	22,427	8.1	13,306	5.1	10,940	4.4	13,056	5.5	16
783,341	25.3	668,473	27.5	510,313	26.6	545,796	39.8	413,763	43.1	369,998	62.8	248,931	73.2	17
182,480	37.3	116,249	31.1	52,483	16.4	43,248	15.6	32,013	13.0	34,413	16.3	27,010	14.7	18
594,429	25.7	587,753	34.1	375,800	27.9	298,775	28.5	239,367	29.5	207,726	34.5	167,992	38.7	19
350,182	18.1	460,862	30.3	581,564	62.0	356,469	61.3	350,674	152.0	185,395	408.7	45,365		20
362,012	36.6	302,550	44.1	342,845	99.9	195,853	133.1	122,658	500.2	18,879	331.7	5,641		21
800,481	101.1	375,287	78.8	318,738	202.4	102,234	185.2	42,029	349.5	12,282				22
351,459	88.4	185,387	87.3	180,628	570.0	22,743	255.7	4,134	86.8	4,762				23
470,490	154.1	274,446	886.9	30,945										24
														25
165,946	2,730.7	6,077												26
482,699	251.1	149,102	345.8	43,112										27
499,968	73.3	208,342	77.8	243,247	173.2	73,869	110.9	46,803	236.6	19,783				28
														29
4,837														30
28,841														31
107,206														
20,684	22.6	13,447	17.2	1,337	1.7	3,099	5.5	75	0.1	8,401	13.1	5,177	8.8	32
104,015	17.8	113,015	24.0	22,979	5.1	39,050	9.7	26,804	7.0	38,998	11.4	21,820	6.8	33
23,303	45.3	7,975	18.2	3,878	0.7	6,795	20.6	9,016	37.5	9,930	70.5	14,093		34
174,657	12.3	181,864	14.7	28,392	2.8	146,039	13.7	90,766	9.3	94,400	10.7	132,590	17.7	35
														36
123,583	14.2	115,620	15.3	15,432	2.1	90,158	15.5	83,329	15.0	77,307	16.2	84,352	21.4	37
35,201	5.3	74,109	12.5	13,213	2.3	78,444	15.6	87,020	21.1	69,524	20.1	96,518	38.8	38
151,101	16.7	214,793	31.1	174,500	33.8	175,834	51.6	88,556	35.1	89,747	55.2	80,138	97.1	39
52,079	60.0	32,968	60.5	19,747	56.9	34,730									40
173,279	17.6	202,577	26.0	91,911	13.4	123,600	21.9	157,806	38.8	185,556	84.0	147,278	199.9	41
107,084	10.7	173,507	20.9	147,306	21.6	259,081	61.3	161,096	61.6	156,125	147.8	69,911	195.0	42
192,578	25.0	180,867	30.6	281,220	90.9	181,626	142.0	127,901						43
184,770	30.5	230,875	61.5	239,030	175.0	61,173	81.1	35,096	87.0	31,502	356.0	8,850		44
														45
225,553	107.5	112,323	115.1	67,180	221.1	16,115	112.9	13,211	1,244.0	1,062				46
190,240	36.7	165,351	40.9	136,072	63.4	62,332	40.6	70,851	100.4	76,556				47
														48
391,623	184.2	212,592												49
														50
														51
														52
31,277														53
31,969	51.9	61,547												54
														55
28,893	253.9	11,380												56
6,857														
														57
11,594		13,294												58
39,171	294.7	92,597												59
287,397	310.4													

¹ Decrease due to loss of territory, West Virginia having been detached from Virginia and admitted as a separate state in 1863.

24

POPULATION.

AREA AND DENSITY OF POPULATION.

AREA.

United States as a whole.—The gross area, land and water, of the territory under the jurisdiction of the United States at the Fourteenth Census was 3,743,529 square miles. The outlying territories had an area of 716,740 square miles, and constituted 19.1 per cent, or approximately one-fifth, of the aggregate area. The area in 1790 was 892,135 square miles, or somewhat less than one-fourth of the present area, and embraced substantially all the territory between Canada and Florida and between the Atlantic Ocean and the Mississippi River, together with the drainage basin of the Red River of the North. This original area and the areas of successive accessions of territory from 1790 to 1920 are shown in Table 10. In 1803 the area of the country was nearly doubled by the Louisiana Purchase; and between 1840 and 1850 three large accessions of territory resulted in further increases aggregating 1,204,896 square miles, equivalent to two-thirds of the former area. (See map following p. 6. On this map the northeastern boundary shown for Texas is that established at the time of the Louisiana Purchase in 1803. A different boundary between the United States and the Spanish possessions was established by the Florida Purchase treaty of 1819; and when Texas was admitted to the Union in 1845 it included, in addition to its present area, parts of New Mexico, Oklahoma, Kansas, and Colorado, and a small part of southern Wyoming. Its boundaries were fixed as at present in 1850.)

TABLE 10.—ACCESSIONS OF TERRITORY: 1790 TO 1920.

ACCESSION.	Gross area (land and water) in square miles.	PER CENT DISTRIBUTION. Aggregate area.	PER CENT DISTRIBUTION. Area of the United States.
Aggregate, 1920	3,743,529	100.0	
United States	3,026,789	80.9	100.0
Territory in 1790 [1]	892,135	23.8	29.5
Louisiana Purchase (1803)	827,987	22.1	27.4
Florida (1819)	58,666	1.6	1.9
By treaty with Spain (1819)	13,435	0.4	0.4
Texas (1845)	389,166	10.4	12.9
Oregon (1846)	286,541	7.7	9.5
Mexican Cession (1848)	529,189	14.1	17.5
Gadsden Purchase (1853)	29,670	0.8	1.0
Outlying possessions	716,740	19.1	
Alaska (1867)	590,884	15.8	
Hawaii (1898)	6,449	0.2	
Philippine Islands (1899)	115,026	3.1	
Porto Rico (1899)	3,435	0.1	
Guam (1899)	210	[2]	
Samoa (1900)	77	[2]	
Panama Canal Zone (1904)	527	[2]	
Virgin Islands of the United States (1917)	132	[2]	

[1] Includes drainage basin of Red River of the North, not a part of any accession, but in the past sometimes considered a part of the Louisiana Purchase.
[2] Less than one-tenth of 1 per cent.

Table 11 shows the aggregate area of the United States at each census from 1790 to 1920 and gives separate figures for outlying possessions.

TABLE 11.—AREA OF THE UNITED STATES AND OUTLYING POSSESSIONS: 1790–1920.

CENSUS YEAR.	Gross area (land and water) in square miles.	Per cent of area in 1920.	AREA OF UNITED STATES EXCLUSIVE OF OUTLYING POSSESSIONS. Gross area (land and water) in square miles.	AREA OF UNITED STATES EXCLUSIVE OF OUTLYING POSSESSIONS. Per cent of area in 1920.	AREA OF UNITED STATES EXCLUSIVE OF OUTLYING POSSESSIONS. Land (square miles).	AREA OF UNITED STATES EXCLUSIVE OF OUTLYING POSSESSIONS. Water [1] (square miles).	Gross area of outlying possessions (square miles).
1920	3,743,529	100.0	3,026,789	100.0	2,073,774	53,015	716,740
1910	3,743,397	100.0	3,026,789	100.0	2,073,890	52,899	716,608
1900	3,742,870	100.0	3,026,789	100.0	2,074,159	52,630	716,081
1890	3,617,673	96.6	3,026,789	100.0	2,073,965	52,824	590,884
1880	3,617,673	96.6	3,026,789	100.0	2,073,965	52,824	590,884
1870	3,617,673	96.6	3,026,789	100.0	2,073,965	52,824	590,884
1860	3,026,789	80.9	3,026,789	100.0	2,073,965	52,824	
1850	2,997,119	80.1	2,997,119	99.0	2,044,337	52,782	
1840	1,792,223	47.9	1,792,223	59.2	1,753,588	38,635	
1830	1,792,223	47.9	1,792,223	59.2	1,753,588	38,635	
1820	1,792,223	47.9	1,792,223	59.2	1,753,588	38,635	
1810	1,720,122	46.0	1,720,122	56.8	1,685,865	34,257	
1800	892,135	23.8	892,135	29.5	867,980	24,155	
1790	892,135	23.8	892,135	29.5	867,980	24,155	

[1] Does not include water surface of oceans, Gulf of Mexico, or Great Lakes, lying within jurisdiction of United States.

Divisions and states.—Table 12 shows, for 1920, the gross area and the land and water area, respectively, of the states, ranked according to gross area.

Seven states, each of which embraces within its limits over 100,000 square miles of territory and all lying west of the Mississippi River, have an aggregate gross area of 1,022,418 square miles, or approximately one-third of the total area of the United States. Texas, the largest of these, with 265,896 square miles of land and water, has an area more than four times that of the entire New England group and more than two hundred and thirteen times that of Rhode Island, the smallest state. California, the next largest state, with an extent of territory about three-fifths as great as that of Texas, nearly equals in area the New England and Middle Atlantic states combined. The aggregate area of these two states exceeds that of the Atlantic Seaboard states from Maine to Florida. The five remaining states with areas exceeding 100,000 square miles are in the Mountain division, and one other state in this division—Wyoming—falls just below that limit. Twenty-one states, 14 of which are located west of the Mississippi River, have areas ranging from 50,000 to 100,000 square miles, and 20 states have areas less than 50,000 square miles. The 22 states west of the Mississippi have an average area of 97,514 square miles, as against an average of only 33,900—a little more than one-third as great—for the 26 states east of that river.

AREA AND DENSITY.   25

TABLE 12.—LAND AND WATER AREA OF STATES, ACCORDING TO RANK IN GROSS AREA: 1920.

STATE.	Rank in gross area.	AREA IN SQUARE MILES.		
		Gross.	Land.	Water.[1]
United States................	....	3,026,789	2,973,774	53,015
Texas.............................	1	265,896	262,398	3,498
California........................	2	158,297	155,652	2,645
Montana..........................	3	146,997	146,131	866
New Mexico......................	4	122,634	122,503	131
Arizona...........................	5	113,956	113,810	146
Nevada............................	6	110,690	109,821	869
Colorado..........................	7	103,948	103,658	290
Wyoming..........................	8	97,914	97,548	366
Oregon............................	9	96,699	95,607	1,092
Utah..............................	10	84,990	82,184	2,806
Minnesota........................	11	84,682	80,858	3,824
Idaho.............................	12	83,888	83,354	534
Kansas............................	13	82,158	81,774	384
South Dakota.....................	14	77,615	76,868	747
Nebraska..........................	15	77,520	76,808	712
North Dakota.....................	16	70,837	70,183	654
Oklahoma.........................	17	70,057	69,414	643
Missouri..........................	18	69,420	68,727	693
Washington.......................	19	69,127	66,836	2,291
Georgia...........................	20	59,265	58,725	540
Florida...........................	21	58,666	54,861	3,805
Michigan..........................	22	57,980	57,480	500
Illinois..........................	23	56,665	56,043	622
Iowa..............................	24	56,147	55,586	561
Wisconsin.........................	25	56,066	55,256	810
Arkansas..........................	26	53,335	52,525	810
North Carolina...................	27	52,426	48,740	3,686
Alabama..........................	28	51,998	51,279	719
New York..........................	29	49,204	47,654	1,550
Louisiana.........................	30	48,506	45,409	3,097
Mississippi.......................	31	46,865	46,362	503
Pennsylvania......................	32	45,126	44,832	294
Virginia..........................	33	42,627	40,262	2,365
Tennessee.........................	34	42,022	41,687	335
Ohio..............................	35	41,040	40,740	300
Kentucky..........................	36	40,598	40,181	417
Indiana...........................	37	36,354	36,045	309
Maine.............................	38	33,040	29,895	3,145
South Carolina...................	39	30,989	30,495	494
West Virginia.....................	40	24,170	24,022	148
Maryland..........................	41	12,327	9,941	2,386
Vermont...........................	42	9,564	9,124	440
New Hampshire.....................	43	9,341	9,031	310
Massachusetts.....................	44	8,266	8,039	227
New Jersey........................	45	8,224	7,514	710
Connecticut.......................	46	4,965	4,820	145
Delaware..........................	47	2,370	1,965	405
Rhode Island......................	48	1,248	1,067	181
District of Columbia..............	49	70	60	10

[1] Does not include water surface of oceans, Gulf of Mexico, or Great Lakes, lying within jurisdiction of United States.

Table 13 shows, by sections and divisions, the gross area, rank in area, and percentage of total area, together with the average area of the states within each section and division.

TABLE 13.—GROSS AREA, BY SECTIONS AND DIVISIONS: 1920.

SECTION AND DIVISION.	Rank in gross area.	Gross area (square miles).	Per cent of total gross area.	Number of states.	Average gross area of states.
United States.................	....	3,026,789	100.0	[1] 48	[1] 63,057
The North......................	....	935,462	30.9	21	44,546
New England................	9	66,424	2.2	6	11,071
Middle Atlantic.............	8	102,554	3.4	3	34,185
East North Central..........	6	248,105	8.2	5	49,621
West North Central.........	2	518,379	17.1	7	74,054
The South......................	....	902,187	29.8	[1] 16	[1] 56,382
South Atlantic..............	5	282,910	9.3	[1] 8	[1] 35,355
East South Central..........	7	181,483	6.0	4	45,371
West South Central.........	3	437,794	14.5	4	109,449
The West.......................	....	1,189,140	39.3	11	108,104
Mountain....................	1	865,017	28.6	8	108,127
Pacific.....................	4	324,123	10.7	3	108,041
East of the Mississippi River......	....	881,476	29.1	[1] 26	[1] 33,900
West of the Mississippi River......	....	2,145,313	70.9	22	97,514

[1] Exclusive of District of Columbia.

The North, with 60.2 per cent of the total population of the United States in 1920, comprises only 30.9 per cent of the total area. The corresponding proportions for the South are far less divergent, being 31.3 per cent for population and 29.8 per cent for area. For the West, in which only 8.4 per cent of the total population of the United States was enumerated in 1920, the proportion of the total area is 39.3 per cent. The region east of the Mississippi River, with 70 per cent of the population in 1920, occupies only 29.1 per cent of the area of the country, whereas the region west of the Mississippi, with 30 per cent of the population, comprises 70.9 per cent of the area.

Table 14 shows, for each state and territory in continental United States, the total land area at each census from 1790 to 1920, inclusive.

26

POPULATION.

TABLE 14.—LAND AREA OF THE UNITED STATES IN SQUARE MILES, BY STATES AND TERRITORIES: 1790-1920.

STATE OR TERRITORY.	1920	1910	1900	1890	1880	1870	1860	1850	1840	1830	1820	1810	1800	1790
United States......	[1] 2,973,774	[2] 2,973,890	[3] 2,974,159	2,973,965	2,973,965	2,973,965	[4] 2,973,965	[5] 2,944,337	1,753,588	1,753,588	[6] 1,753,588	[7] 1,685,865	867,980	[8] 867,980
Alabama [9]........	51,279	51,279	51,279	51,279	51,279	51,279	51,279	51,279	51,279	51,279	51,279	....	....	....
Arizona [10]........	113,810	[11] 113,810	113,840	113,840	113,840	113,840	....	52,525	....	....	[12] 105,275	(12)	....	....
Arkansas [12]......	52,525	52,525	52,525	52,525	52,525	52,525	52,525	52,525	52,525	52,525	[12] 105,275	(12)	....	....
California [13].....	155,652	[14] 155,652	[15] 156,092	155,900	155,900	155,900	155,900	155,900	....	....	....	....	....	....
Colorado [16]......	103,658	103,658	103,658	103,658	103,658	103,658	[16] 103,658	....	....	....	....	....	....	....
Connecticut........	4,820	4,820	4,820	4,820	4,820	4,820	4,820	4,820	4,820	4,820	4,820	4,820	4,820	4,820
Delaware...........	1,965	1,965	1,965	1,965	1,965	1,965	1,965	1,965	1,965	1,965	1,965	1,965	1,965	1,965
District of Columbia [17]	60	60	[18] 60	58	58	58	58	58	[17] 90	90	90	90	90	....
Florida [19]........	54,861	54,861	54,861	54,861	54,861	54,861	54,861	54,861	54,861	54,861	[19] 54,861	....	[20] 111,877	[20] 145,196
Georgia [20]........	58,725	58,725	58,725	58,725	58,725	58,725	58,725	58,725	58,725	58,725	58,725	58,725	[20] 111,877	[20] 145,196
Idaho [21]..........	83,354	83,354	83,354	83,354	83,354	83,354	[21] 83,360	....	....	....	....	....	....	....
Illinois [22]........	56,043	[22] 56,043	56,002	56,002	56,002	56,002	56,002	56,002	56,002	56,002	56,002	[22] 192,381	....	....
Indiana [24]........	36,045	[25] 36,045	35,885	35,885	35,885	35,885	35,885	35,885	35,885	35,885	35,885	[24] 42,033	[24] 252,084	....
Iowa [26]..........	55,586	55,586	55,586	55,586	55,586	55,586	55,586	55,586	[26] 191,056	....	....	....	....	....
Kansas [27]........	81,774	81,774	81,774	81,774	81,774	81,774	[27] 81,774	....	....	....	....	....	....	....
Kentucky [23]......	40,181	40,181	40,181	40,181	40,181	40,181	40,181	40,181	40,181	40,181	40,181	40,181	40,181	[28] 40,181
Louisiana [29].....	45,409	45,409	45,409	45,409	45,409	45,409	45,409	45,409	45,409	45,409	45,409	[29] 34,065	....	....
Maine [30]..........	29,895	29,895	29,895	29,895	29,895	29,895	29,895	29,895	29,895	29,895	29,895	[30] 29,895	[30] 29,895	[30] 29,895
Maryland...........	9,941	9,941	9,941	9,941	9,941	9,941	9,941	9,941	9,941	9,941	9,941	9,941	[31] 9,941	9,000
Massachusetts.....	8,039	8,039	8,039	8,039	8,039	8,039	8,039	8,041	8,041	8,041	8,041	8,041	8,041	8,041
Michigan [32].......	57,480	57,480	57,480	57,480	57,480	57,480	57,480	57,480	57,480	[32] 186,052	[32] 186,052	[32] 42,025	....	....
Minnesota [33]......	80,858	80,858	80,858	80,858	80,858	80,858	80,858	80,858	[33] 163,457	....	....	....	....	....
Mississippi [34]....	46,362	46,362	46,362	46,362	46,362	46,362	46,362	46,362	46,362	46,362	46,362	[34] 97,041	[34] 33,319	....
Missouri [35].......	68,727	68,727	68,727	68,727	68,727	68,727	68,727	68,727	68,727	[35] 65,618	[35] 65,618	(35)	....	....
Montana [36].......	[37] 146,131	146,201	146,201	146,201	146,201	[36] 146,195	....	....	....	....	....	....	....	....
Nebraska [38]......	76,808	76,808	[38] 76,808	76,808	76,808	76,172	[38] 118,915	....	....	....	....	....	....	....
Nevada [39]........	109,821	109,821	109,821	109,821	109,821	109,821	[39] 61,200	....	....	....	....	....	....	....
New Hampshire....	9,031	9,031	9,031	9,031	9,031	9,031	9,031	9,031	9,031	9,031	9,031	9,031	9,031	9,031
New Jersey........	7,514	7,514	7,514	7,514	7,514	7,514	7,514	7,514	7,514	7,514	7,514	7,514	7,514	7,514
New Mexico [40]....	122,503	122,503	122,503	122,503	122,503	122,503	[40] 247,782	[40] 230,548	....	....	....	....	....	....
New York..........	47,654	47,654	47,654	47,654	47,654	47,654	47,654	47,652	47,652	47,652	47,652	47,652	47,652	47,652
North Carolina.....	48,740	48,740	48,740	48,740	48,740	48,740	48,740	48,740	48,740	48,740	48,740	48,740	48,740	48,740
North Dakota [41]..	70,183	70,183	70,183	70,183	(41)	(41)	(41)	....	....	....	....	....	....	....
Ohio [42]...........	40,740	40,740	40,740	40,740	40,740	40,740	40,740	40,740	40,740	[42] 40,228	40,228	40,228	[42] 40,228	....
Oklahoma [43].....	69,414	69,414	[43] 38,624	38,624	....	....	....	....	....	....	....	....	....	....
Oregon [44]........	95,607	95,607	95,607	95,607	95,607	95,607	95,607	[44] 282,257	....	....	....	....	....	....
Pennsylvania [45]..	44,832	44,832	44,832	44,832	44,832	44,832	44,832	44,832	44,832	44,832	44,832	44,832	44,832	[45] 44,832
Rhode Island......	1,067	1,067	1,067	1,067	1,067	1,067	1,067	1,067	1,067	1,067	1,067	1,067	1,067	1,067
South Carolina.....	30,495	30,495	30,495	30,495	30,495	30,495	30,495	30,495	30,495	30,495	30,495	30,495	30,495	30,495
South Dakota [46]..	76,808	76,808	76,808	76,808	(46)	(46)	(46)	....	....	....	....	....	....	....
Tennessee [47].....	41,687	41,687	41,687	41,687	41,687	41,687	41,687	41,687	41,687	41,687	41,687	41,687	41,687	[47] 40,977
Texas [48]..........	262,398	262,398	262,398	262,398	262,398	262,398	262,398	[49] 262,398	[49] 262,398	....	....	....	....	....
Utah [49]..........	82,184	82,184	82,184	82,184	82,184	82,184	82,184	[49] 230,610	....	....	....	....	....	....
Vermont [50].......	9,124	9,124	9,124	9,124	9,124	9,124	9,124	9,124	9,124	9,124	9,124	9,124	9,124	9,124
Virginia [51].......	40,262	40,262	40,262	40,262	40,262	40,262	[51] 64,284	[51] 64,284	64,252	64,252	64,252	64,252	[51] 64,252	[51] 64,284
Washington [52]....	66,836	66,836	66,836	66,836	66,836	66,836	[52] 183,254	....	....	....	....	....	....	....
West Virginia [53]..	24,022	24,022	24,022	24,022	24,022	24,022	....	....	....	....	....	....	....	....
Wisconsin [54].....	55,256	55,256	55,256	55,256	55,256	55,256	55,256	55,256	[54] 82,643	....	....	....	....	....
Wyoming [55]......	[56] 97,548	97,594	97,594	97,594	97,594	97,594	....	....	....	....	....	....	....	....
Territory Northwest of Ohio River [57]...	....	....	....	....	....	....	....	....	....	....	....	25,855	[57] 318,167	
Territory South of Tennessee [58]....	....	....	....	....	....	....	....	....	....	....	....	....	5,200	....
Missouri territory [59]	....	....	....	....	....	....	....	....	608,565	[59] 608,565	[59] 777,940	....	....	
Indian Territory and unorganized territory [60]	....	....	30,790	30,790	69,414	69,414	69,414	535,003	511,907	52,750	....	....	....	
Dakota territory [61]	....	....	....	....	147,687	147,687	312,094	....	....	....	....	....	....	

EXPLANATORY NOTES REGARDING ORGANIZATION OF STATES AND CHANGES IN AREA.

[1] Reduction of 116 square miles due to building of Pathfinder and Shoshone Reservoirs (46 square miles of water surface) in Wyoming and several reservoirs in connection with irrigation projects (70 square miles of water surface) in Montana.

[2] Net reduction of 269 square miles due to drainage of lakes and swamps in Illinois and Indiana (201 square miles of land), building of Roosevelt and Laguna Reservoirs in Arizona (30 square miles of water surface), and overflow of Colorado River into Salton Sea in California (440 square miles of water surface).

[3] Increase of 194 square miles due to reclamation of 2 square miles of Potomac River Flats in District of Columbia and 192 square miles of Lake Tulare in California.

[4] Includes Gadsden Purchase (29,628 square miles) in 1853.

[5] Includes Texas annexation (385,590 square miles) in 1845; Oregon territory (282,257 square miles) in 1846; and Mexican Cession (522,902 square miles) in 1848.

[6] Includes Florida Purchase (54,861 square miles) and other territory gained by treaty with Spain (12,802 square miles) in 1819.

[7] Includes Louisiana Purchase of 1803 (817,885 square miles), comprising territory of Orleans, 34,065 square miles, territory of Louisiana, 777,940 square miles, and 5,880 square miles of territory in dispute between United States and Spain, attached to Mississippi territory in 1812. (See map following p. 6.)

[8] Includes drainage basin of Red River of the North and Souris River (45,417 square miles).

[9] ALABAMA.—Organized as a territory in 1817 from part of Mississippi territory; admitted as a state in 1819.

[10] ARIZONA.—Organized as a territory in 1863 from part of New Mexico territory; admitted as a state in 1912.

[11] Decrease of 25 square miles due to building of Roosevelt Reservoir and 5 square miles due to building of Laguna Reservoir.

320

EXPLANATORY NOTES REGARDING ORGANIZATION OF STATES AND CHANGES IN AREA—Continued.

[12] ARKANSAS.—Organized as a territory in 1819 from part of Missouri territory; then included greater part of present area of Oklahoma; admitted as a state in 1836. (See note 59.)

[13] CALIFORNIA.—Ceded by Mexico in 1848; admitted as a state in 1850.

[14] Decrease of 440 square miles due to overflow of Colorado River into Salton Sea.

[15] Increase of 192 square miles due to reclamation of part of Lake Tulare, Calif.

[16] COLORADO.—Organized as a territory in 1861 from parts of territories of Utah, New Mexico, Kansas, and Nebraska; admitted as a state in 1876. Area shown for 1860 refers to 1861.

[17] DISTRICT OF COLUMBIA.—Formed in 1791 from parts of Maryland and Virginia; part south of Potomac retroceded to Virginia in 1846.

[18] Increase of 2 square miles due to reclamation of Potomac River Flats in District of Columbia.

[19] FLORIDA.—Purchased from Spain in 1819; territorial government established in 1822; admitted as a state in 1845. Area shown for 1820 refers to 1822.

[20] GEORGIA.—Included, in 1800, area now constituting northern parts of Alabama and Mississippi; in 1790, greater part of present area of those states.

[21] IDAHO.—Organized in 1863 from parts of territories of Washington, Dakota, and Nebraska; area reduced in 1864 by organization of Montana territory and in 1868 by organization of Wyoming territory; 6 square miles transferred to Montana in 1873; admitted as a state in 1890.

[22] ILLINOIS.—Formed as a territory in 1809 from part of Indiana territory; then included area now constituting Wisconsin, western part of Upper Peninsula of Michigan, northeastern and northwestern Minnesota, eastern and northern North Dakota, and small section of northeastern South Dakota; admitted as a state in 1818.

[23] Increase of 41 square miles due to drainage of lakes and swamps.

[24] INDIANA.—Formed as a territory in 1800 from part of Territory Northwest of the Ohio River; then included area now constituting Illinois, Wisconsin, western and northwestern Michigan, northeastern and northwestern Minnesota, eastern and northern North Dakota, and small section of northeastern South Dakota; area shown for 1810 includes part of present area of Illinois; admitted as a state in 1816.

[25] Increase of 160 square miles due to drainage of lakes and swamps.

[26] IOWA.—Organized in 1838 from part of Wisconsin territory; then included area now constituting that part of Minnesota lying west of the Mississippi River, and those parts of North and South Dakota lying east of the Missouri and White Earth Rivers; admitted as a state in 1846.

[27] KANSAS.—Organized as a territory in 1854 from unorganized territory originally part of Louisiana Purchase; then included part of present area of Colorado; admitted as a state in 1861. Area shown for 1860 refers to 1861.

[28] KENTUCKY.—Organized as a state from part of Virginia and admitted to Union in 1792. Area given for 1790 refers to 1792.

[29] LOUISIANA.—Organized as Orleans territory in 1804 from part of Louisiana Purchase; admitted to Union as state of Louisiana in 1812. Area given for 1810 includes 4,611 square miles of territory in dispute between United States and Spain, attached to Louisiana in 1812, and excludes 11,344 square miles gained by treaty with Spain in 1819.

[30] MAINE.—Under jurisdiction of Massachusetts until 1820, when admitted to Union as a separate state.

[31] MARYLAND.—Area reduced in 1791 by formation of District of Columbia.

[32] MICHIGAN.—Organized as a territory in 1805 from part of Indiana territory; then comprised Lower Peninsula and eastern end of Upper Peninsula; part of remainder of Upper Peninsula added in 1816; limits extended in 1818 to include area formerly part of Illinois territory and now constituting Wisconsin, northeastern and northwestern Minnesota, eastern and northern North Dakota, and small section of northeastern South Dakota; limits further extended in 1834 westward to Missouri and White Earth Rivers and southward to northern boundary of Missouri. Admitted as a state in 1837.

[33] MINNESOTA.—Organized as a territory in 1849 from unorganized area formerly within limits of Iowa and Wisconsin territories; then included area now constituting North and South Dakota east of Missouri and White Earth Rivers. Admitted as a state in 1858.

[34] MISSISSIPPI.—Organized as a territory from part of Georgia in 1798; then comprised area now constituting southern parts of Alabama and Mississippi; area now constituting northern Alabama and Mississippi (formerly a part of Georgia) added in 1804. Alabama organized as a separate territory and Mississippi admitted as a state in 1817. Area shown for 1810 includes 5,880 square miles of territory treated as part of Louisiana Purchase, but in dispute between United States and Spain, attached to Mississippi territory in 1812.

[35] MISSOURI.—Organized as a state from part of Missouri territory and admitted to Union in 1821; area increased in 1837 by Platte Purchase, now forming northwestern part of state. Area shown for 1820 refers to 1821. (See note 59.)

[36] MONTANA.—Organized as a territory from part of Idaho territory in 1864; 6 square miles transferred from Idaho in 1873; admitted as a state in 1889.

[37] Decrease of 70 square miles due to building of several reservoirs in connection with irrigation projects.

[38] NEBRASKA.—Organized in 1854 from unorganized territory, originally part of Louisiana Purchase; then included area now constituting parts of North and South Dakota, Montana, Wyoming, and Colorado; area greatly reduced in 1861 by organization of Dakota and Colorado territories and in 1863 by organization of Idaho territory. Admitted as a state in 1867. Small area, formerly part of Dakota territory, annexed in 1882. Area shown for 1860 is that of territory as constituted in 1861, then including nearly half of present state of Wyoming.

[39] NEVADA.—Organized as a territory from part of Utah territory in 1861; then comprised that part of present area of state lying west of 39th meridian from Washington and north of 37th parallel. Admitted as a state in 1864, with eastern boundary fixed at 38th meridian from Washington; present boundaries established in 1866. Area shown for 1860 refers to 1861.

[40] NEW MEXICO.—Organized as a territory in 1850 from region ceded by Mexico in 1848; at time of organization included areas now constituting southeastern Colorado, Arizona north of Gila River, and Nevada south of 37th parallel; area increased in 1854 by Gadsden Purchase, reduced in 1861 by organization of Colorado territory, and reduced to present limits in 1863 by organization of Arizona territory. Admitted as a state in 1912. Area shown for 1860 is that of territory as constituted in 1861, after organization of Colorado territory.

[41] NORTH DAKOTA.—Organized as a state from part of Dakota territory and admitted to Union in 1889. (See note 61.)

[42] OHIO.—Organized as a state from part of Territory Northwest of the Ohio River and admitted to Union in 1803. Present boundary between Ohio and Michigan established in 1836. Area shown for 1800 refers to 1803.

[43] OKLAHOMA.—Organized in 1890 as a territory from part of Indian Territory; organized as a state from Oklahoma territory and Indian Territory and admitted to Union in 1907.

[44] OREGON.—Oregon region occupied jointly by United States and Great Britain from 1818 to 1846; title established in 1846. Organized as a territory in 1848; then included area now constituting Washington, Idaho, and parts of Montana and Wyoming lying west of crest of Rocky Mountains; area reduced in 1853 by organization of Washington territory. Admitted as a state in 1859 with area reduced to present limits.

[45] PENNSYLVANIA.—Includes 314 square miles ceded to the United States by New York in 1781 and sold to Pennsylvania in 1792.

[46] SOUTH DAKOTA.—Organized as a state from part of Dakota territory and admitted to Union in 1889. (See note 61.)

[47] TENNESSEE.—Organized as Territory South of the River Ohio in 1790 from area ceded in that year to United States by North Carolina, together with 5,290 square miles of territory ceded in 1787 by South Carolina (now in northern Mississippi, Alabama, and Georgia); admitted as a state, with boundaries as at present, in 1796.

[48] TEXAS.—Independent republic of Texas annexed and admitted to Union as a state in 1845. Then included area now constituting portions of New Mexico, Oklahoma, Kansas, Colorado, and small part of southern Wyoming. Present boundaries established in 1850.

[49] UTAH.—Organized as a territory in 1850 from region ceded by Mexico in 1848; then included area now constituting western Colorado, southwestern Wyoming, and greater part of Nevada; area reduced by organization of Colorado and Nevada territories in 1861 and Idaho territory in 1863, by transfers of territory to Nevada in 1864 and 1866, and by organization of Wyoming territory in 1868, leaving Utah with present boundaries. Area shown for 1860 refers to 1861. Admitted as a state in 1896.

[50] VERMONT.—Independent republic of Vermont admitted to Union as a state in 1791.

[51] VIRGINIA.—Area shown for 1790 excludes area of Kentucky, organized from Virginia in 1792; area reduced in 1791 by formation of District of Columbia; in 1846 part of District of Columbia south of Potomac River retroceded to Virginia; area shown for 1860 and prior years includes present area of West Virginia, admitted as a separate state in 1863.

[52] WASHINGTON.—Organized as a territory in 1853 from part of Oregon territory; then included area now constituting northern Idaho and Montana west of crest of Rocky Mountains; area extended in 1859 by addition of region now constituting southern Idaho and Wyoming west of crest of Rocky Mountains, formerly part of Oregon territory; area reduced to present limits in 1863 by organization of Idaho territory. Admitted as a state in 1889.

[53] WEST VIRGINIA.—Formed from part of Virginia and admitted as a state in 1863.

[54] WISCONSIN.—Organized as a territory in 1836 from part of Michigan territory; then included area now constituting Minnesota, Iowa, and North and South Dakota east of Missouri and White Earth Rivers; area reduced in 1838 by organization of Iowa territory; area shown for 1840 includes that now constituting part of Minnesota northeast of Mississippi River; admitted as a state in 1848.

[55] WYOMING.—Organized as a territory in 1868 from Dakota and Idaho territories; admitted as a state in 1890.

[56] Decrease of 46 square miles due to building of Pathfinder and Shoshone Reservoirs.

[57] Region between Ohio and Mississippi Rivers and Great Lakes, together with drainage basin of Red River of the North, named, in 1787, Territory Northwest of the Ohio River; then comprised area now constituting Ohio, Indiana, Illinois, Michigan, Wisconsin, northeastern and northwestern Minnesota, northern and eastern North Dakota, and small section of northeastern South Dakota. Area greatly reduced by organization of Indiana territory in 1800. Area shown for 1800 excludes that of Ohio, admitted as a state in 1803.

[58] Ceded to United States in 1787 by South Carolina; included in Territory South of the River Ohio from 1790 to 1796; now in northern Georgia, Mississippi, and Alabama. (See note 47.)

[59] Formed from Louisiana Purchase; known as Louisiana territory from 1805 to 1812 and as Missouri territory from 1812 to 1834. Area shown for 1810 comprised all of original Louisiana Purchase except territory of Orleans (later state of Louisiana) and 5,880 square miles in dispute between United States and Spain, attached to Mississippi territory in 1812. (See map following p. 6.) Part taken to form Arkansas territory (including greater part of present area of Cklahoma) in 1819; 1,518 square miles of territory gained by treaty with Spain added in 1819; part taken to form state of Missouri in 1821; part north of Missouri and east of Missouri and White Earth Rivers annexed to Michigan territory in 1834; remainder known as Indian Country from 1834 to 1854. Area shown for 1820 excludes that of state of Missouri, admitted to Union in 1821. (See note 60.)

[60] Comprised, in 1830, areas detached from Arkansas territory in 1824 and 1828; from 1834 to 1850, that part of Louisiana Purchase lying west of western boundaries of Arkansas and Missouri and west of Missouri and White Earth Rivers; from 1850 to 1854 included also part of original area of Texas and part of territory ceded by Mexico in 1848. Upon organization of territories of Kansas and Nebraska in 1854 area of Indian Country was reduced to that of Indian Territory, now Oklahoma. (See map following p. 6.)

[61] Organized in 1861 from part of Nebraska territory and from unorganized territory included in Minnesota territory from 1849 to 1858; at time of organization included those parts of Montana and Wyoming lying east of crest of Rocky Mountains. Area west of present western boundaries of North and South Dakota transferred to territory of Idaho in 1863; greater part of present area of Wyoming transferred to Dakota in 1864; western boundary established at present western limits of North and South Dakota in 1868, upon organization of Wyoming territory; small area annexed to Nebraska in 1882. (See notes 41 and 46.)

28

POPULATION.

POPULATION PER SQUARE MILE.

United States as a whole.—Table 15 shows, for the United States exclusive of outlying possessions, the total population, land area in square miles, and density of population, or population per square mile of land area, at each census from 1790 to 1920; and the diagram below also shows the density of population at each census.

The decrease in density between 1800 and 1810 and between 1840 and 1850 was due in each case to large accessions of sparsely populated territory. With these exceptions, the number of inhabitants per square mile has increased during each decade from 4.5 in 1790 to 35.5 in 1920.

TABLE 15.—POPULATION PER SQUARE MILE, FOR THE UNITED STATES, EXCLUSIVE OF OUTLYING POSSESSIONS: 1790–1920.

CENSUS YEAR.	Population.	Land area in square miles.	Population per square mile.
1920	105,710,620	2,973,774	35.5
1910	91,972,266	2,973,890	30.9
1900	75,994,575	2,974,159	25.6
1890	62,947,714	2,973,965	21.2
1880	50,155,783	2,973,965	16.9
1870	38,558,371	2,973,965	13.0
1860	31,443,321	2,973,965	10.6
1850	23,191,870	2,944,337	7.9
1840	17,069,453	1,753,588	9.7
1830	12,866,020	1,753,588	7.3
1820	9,638,453	1,753,588	5.5
1810	7,239,881	1,685,865	4.3
1800	5,308,483	867,980	6.1
1790	3,929,214	867,980	4.5

POPULATION PER SQUARE MILE: 1790–1920.

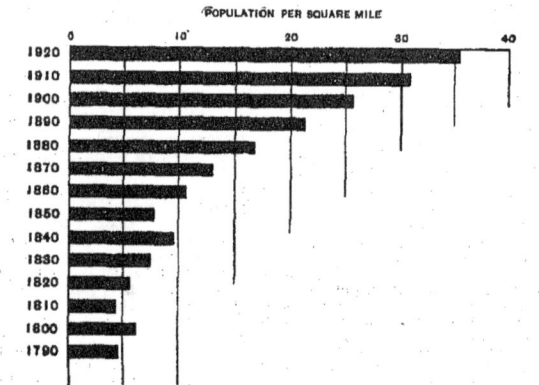

Divisions and states.—The population per square mile in the United States and in each state and territory at each census from 1790 to 1920, inclusive, is shown in Table 18 (p. 31). In preparing this table the population of each state or territory as returned at a given census has been divided by the land area in square miles of the state or territory as constituted at the time that census was taken. This in certain cases differed greatly from the present area of the state, and in some instances the enumerators did not canvass the entire area of a territory. For example, in 1850 the greater part of the region now constituting Arizona was a part of the territory of New Mexico, but was not canvassed by the enumerators. In computing the density of population of New Mexico in 1850, however, the total land area of the territory as then constituted has been used as the divisor.

POPULATION PER SQUARE MILE, BY STATES: 1920 AND 1910.

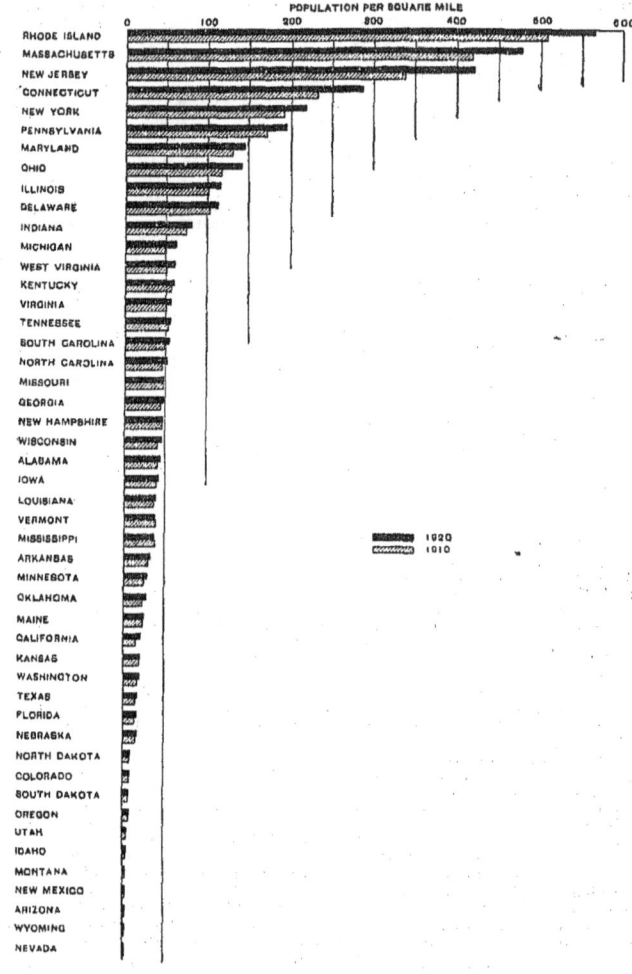

Table 16 shows, for each geographic division and each state, the population and land area in 1920 and the density of population, or population per square mile, for each of the last three censuses. The density of population for the last two censuses is shown also by the diagram above and by the maps on page 30. The density of population for counties in 1920 is indicated by the map headed "Population per square mile, by counties: 1920," on page 88.

AREA AND DENSITY.   29

TABLE 16.—POPULATION PER SQUARE MILE, BY DIVISIONS AND STATES: 1920, 1910, and 1900.

[Based on Table 8, p. 20, and Table 14, p. 26.]

DIVISION AND STATE.	Population: 1920	Land area (square miles): 1920	POPULATION PER SQUARE MILE.		
			1920	1910	1900
United States	105,710,620	2,973,774	35.5	30.9	25.6
GEOGRAPHIC DIVISIONS:					
New England	7,400,909	61,976	119.4	105.7	90.2
Middle Atlantic	22,261,144	100,000	222.6	193.2	154.5
East North Central	21,475,543	245,564	87.5	74.3	65.2
West North Central	12,544,249	510,804	24.6	22.8	20.3
South Atlantic	13,990,272	269,071	52.0	45.3	38.8
East South Central	8,893,307	179,509	49.5	46.8	42.0
West South Central	10,242,224	429,746	23.8	20.4	15.2
Mountain	3,336,101	859,009	3.9	3.1	1.9
Pacific	5,566,871	318,095	17.5	13.2	7.6
NEW ENGLAND:					
Maine	768,014	29,895	25.7	24.8	23.2
New Hampshire	443,083	9,031	49.1	47.7	45.6
Vermont	352,428	9,124	38.6	39.0	37.7
Massachusetts	3,852,356	8,039	479.2	418.8	349.0
Rhode Island	604,397	1,067	566.4	508.5	401.6
Connecticut	1,380,631	4,820	286.4	231.3	188.5
MIDDLE ATLANTIC:					
New York	10,385,227	47,654	217.9	191.2	152.5
New Jersey	3,155,900	7,514	420.0	337.7	250.7
Pennsylvania	8,720,017	44,832	194.5	171.0	140.6
EAST NORTH CENTRAL:					
Ohio	5,759,394	40,740	141.4	117.0	102.1
Indiana	2,930,390	36,045	81.3	74.9	70.1
Illinois	6,485,280	56,043	115.7	100.6	86.1
Michigan	3,668,412	57,480	63.8	48.9	42.1
Wisconsin	2,632,067	55,256	47.6	42.2	37.4
WEST NORTH CENTRAL:					
Minnesota	2,387,125	80,858	29.5	25.7	21.7
Iowa	2,404,021	55,586	43.2	40.0	40.2
Missouri	3,404,055	68,727	40.5	47.9	45.2
North Dakota	646,872	70,183	9.2	8.2	4.5
South Dakota	636,547	76,868	8.3	7.6	5.2
Nebraska	1,296,372	76,808	16.9	15.5	13.9
Kansas	1,769,257	81,774	21.6	20.7	18.0
SOUTH ATLANTIC:					
Delaware	223,003	1,965	113.5	103.0	94.0
Maryland	1,449,661	9,941	145.8	130.3	119.5
District of Columbia	437,571	60	7,292.9	5,517.8	4,645.3
Virginia	2,309,187	40,262	57.4	51.2	46.1
West Virginia	1,463,701	24,022	60.9	50.8	39.9
North Carolina	2,559,123	48,740	52.5	45.3	38.9
South Carolina	1,683,724	30,495	55.2	49.7	44.0
Georgia	2,895,832	58,725	49.3	44.4	37.7
Florida	968,470	54,861	17.7	13.7	9.6
EAST SOUTH CENTRAL:					
Kentucky	2,416,630	40,181	60.1	57.0	53.4
Tennessee	2,337,885	41,687	56.1	52.4	48.5
Alabama	2,348,174	51,279	45.8	41.7	35.7
Mississippi	1,790,618	46,362	38.6	38.8	33.5
WEST SOUTH CENTRAL:					
Arkansas	1,752,204	52,525	33.4	30.0	25.0
Louisiana	1,798,509	45,409	39.6	36.5	30.4
Oklahoma[1]	2,028,283	69,414	29.2	23.9	11.4
Texas	4,663,228	262,398	17.8	14.8	11.6
MOUNTAIN:					
Montana	548,889	146,131	3.8	2.6	1.7
Idaho	431,866	83,354	5.2	3.9	1.9
Wyoming	194,402	97,548	2.0	1.5	0.9
Colorado	939,629	103,658	9.1	7.7	5.2
New Mexico	360,350	122,503	2.9	2.7	1.6
Arizona	334,162	113,810	2.9	1.8	1.1
Utah	449,396	82,184	5.5	4.5	3.4
Nevada	77,407	109,821	0.7	0.7	0.4
PACIFIC:					
Washington	1,356,621	66,836	20.3	17.1	7.8
Oregon	783,389	95,607	8.2	7.0	4.3
California	3,426,861	155,652	22.0	15.3	9.5

[1] Includes population of Indian Territory for 1900.

Table 17 lists the states (disregarding the District of Columbia) in the order of their density of population in 1920.

In five states the density of population in 1920 was more than 200 per square mile; in five other states, between 100 and 200; in one state, slightly more than 80; in 26 states, between 15 and 65; and in 11 states, less than 10.

The combined population (42,453,437) of the 10 states having more than 100 inhabitants per square mile and of the District of Columbia in 1920 constituted slightly more than two-fifths (40.2 per cent) of the total population of the United States, while their combined land area (222,675 square miles) represented hardly more than one-fourteenth (7.5 per cent) of the entire land area of the country.

TABLE 17.—POPULATION PER SQUARE MILE, FOR STATES IN ORDER OF RANK: 1920.

STATE.	Population per square mile.	STATE.	Population per square mile.
Rhode Island	566.4	Louisiana	39.6
Massachusetts	479.2	Mississippi	38.6
New Jersey	420.0	Vermont	38.6
Connecticut	286.4	Arkansas	33.4
New York	217.9	Minnesota	29.5
Pennsylvania	194.5	Oklahoma	29.2
Maryland	145.8	Maine	25.7
Ohio	141.4	California	22.0
Illinois	115.7	Kansas	21.6
Delaware	113.5	Washington	20.3
Indiana	81.3	Texas	17.8
Michigan	63.8	Florida	17.7
West Virginia	60.9	Nebraska	16.9
Kentucky	60.1	North Dakota	9.2
Virginia	57.4	Colorado	9.1
Tennessee	56.1	South Dakota	8.3
South Carolina	55.2	Oregon	8.2
North Carolina	52.5	Utah	5.5
Missouri	49.5	Idaho	5.2
Georgia	49.3	Montana	3.8
New Hampshire	49.1	Arizona	2.9
Wisconsin	47.6	New Mexico	2.9
Alabama	45.8	Wyoming	2.0
Iowa	43.2	Nevada	0.7

The 11 states having fewer than 10 inhabitants per square mile are all west of the Mississippi River, 8 being in the Mountain division (constituting its entire area), 2 in the West North Central division, and 1 in the Pacific division. The combined land area of these 11 states (1,101,667 square miles) forms almost three-eighths (37 per cent) of the entire land area of the United States, while their combined population (5,402,909) represented only about one-twentieth (5.1 per cent) of the total population of the country in 1920.

The density of population of the several outlying possessions in 1920 was as follows: Alaska, one-tenth of 1 per square mile; American Samoa, 104.6; Guam, 63.2; Hawaii, 39.7; Panama Canal Zone,[1] 64; Porto Rico, 378.4; Philippine Islands,[2] 90; Virgin Islands,[1] 197.4. The density of population of Alaska is only about one-seventh as great as that for Nevada, the most sparsely populated state. American Samoa is nearly as densely populated as Delaware; Guam and the Panama Canal Zone may be compared with Michigan; Hawaii, with Louisiana; Porto Rico, with New Jersey; the Philippine Islands, with Indiana; and the Virgin Islands, with Pennsylvania.

[1] In calculating the density of population for the Panama Canal Zone and for the Virgin Islands the land area has been used, but for the other outlying possessions the land area has not been computed, and the density figures are therefore based on the gross area. The density stated for the Virgin Islands refers to Nov. 1, 1917.
[2] Refers to Dec. 31, 1918.

POPULATION.

POPULATION PER SQUARE MILE, BY STATES: 1920.

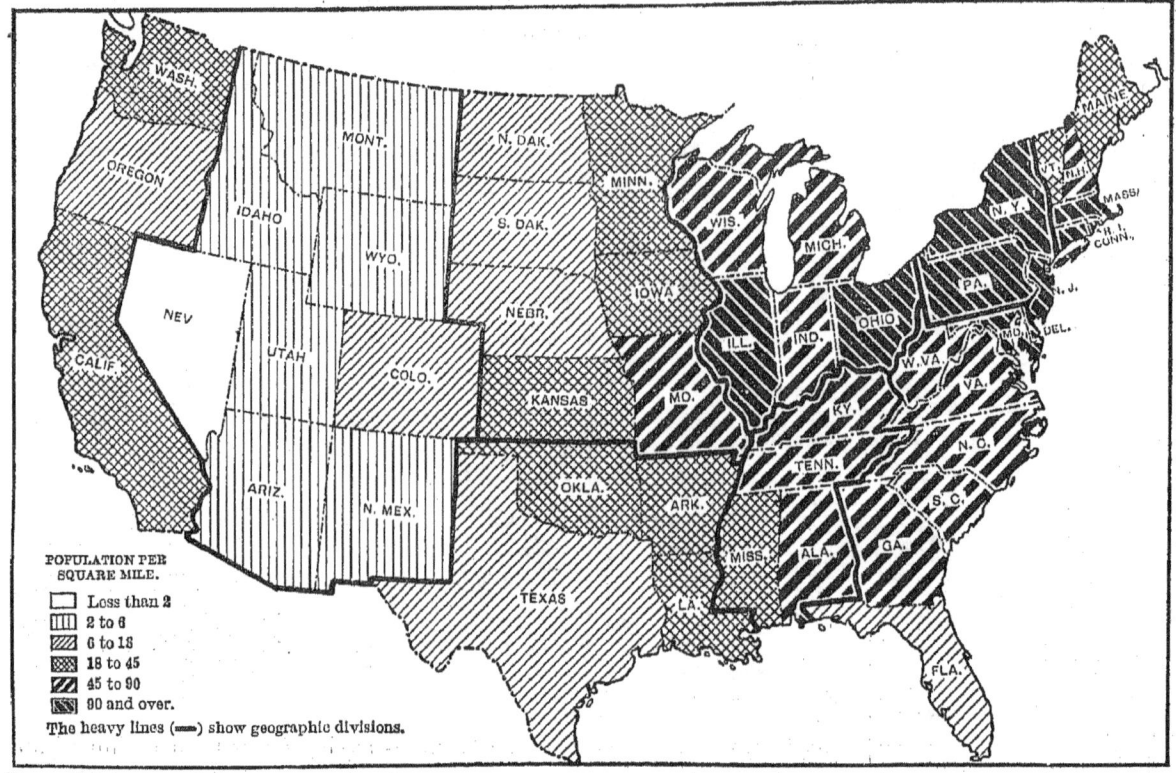

POPULATION PER SQUARE MILE, BY STATES: 1910.

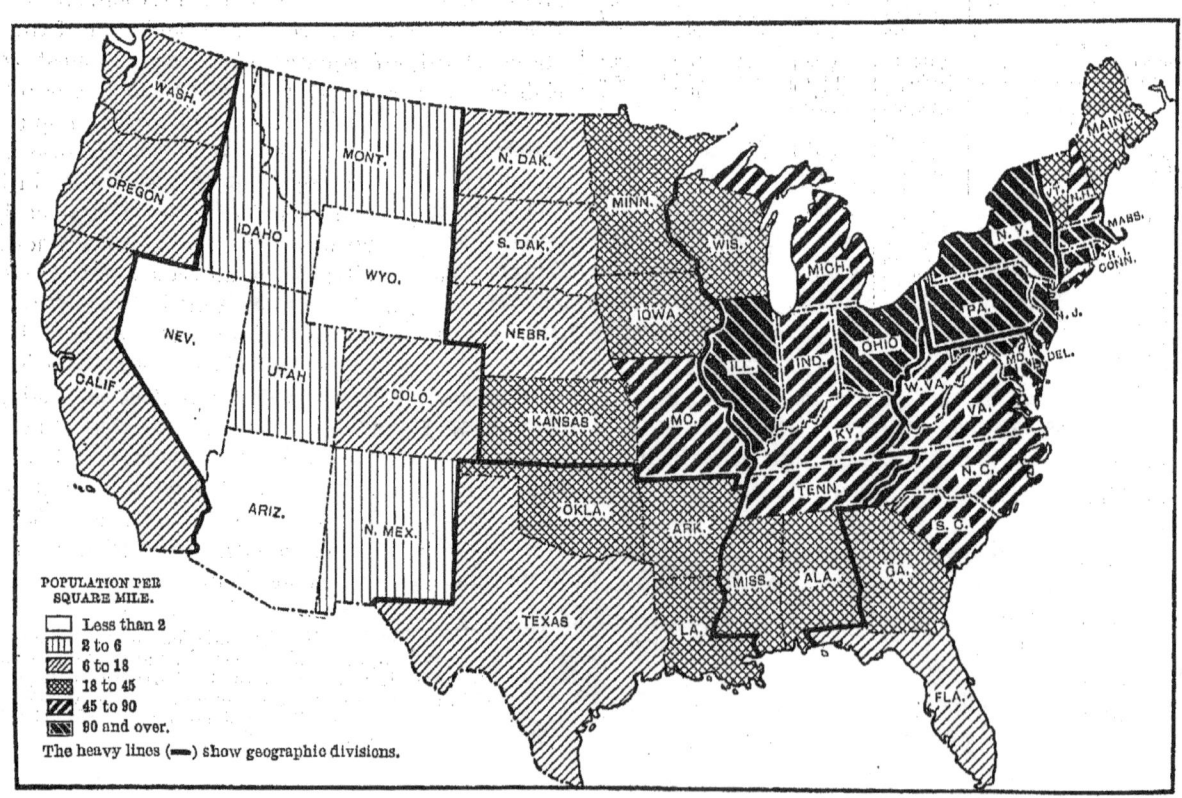

AREA AND DENSITY.

31

TABLE 18.—POPULATION PER SQUARE MILE, BY STATES: 1790–1920.

[Based on Tables 8 and 14.]

STATE.	1920	1910	1900	1890	1880	1870	1860	1850	1840	1830	1820	1810	1800	1790
United States	35.5	30.9	25.6	21.2	16.9	13.0	10.6	7.9	9.7	7.3	5.5	4.3	6.1	4.5
Alabama	45.8	41.7	35.7	29.5	24.6	19.4	18.8	15.0	11.5	6.0	2.5			
Arizona	2.0	1.8	1.1	0.8	0.4	0.1								
Arkansas	33.4	30.0	25.0	21.5	15.3	9.2	8.3	4.0	1.9	0.6	0.1	(¹)		
California	22.0	15.3	9.5	7.8	5.5	3.6	2.4	0.6						
Colorado	9.1	7.7	5.2	4.0	1.9	0.4	0.3							
Connecticut	286.4	231.3	188.5	154.8	129.2	111.5	95.5	76.9	64.3	61.8	57.1	54.3	52.1	49.4
Delaware	113.5	103.0	94.0	85.7	74.6	63.6	57.1	46.0	39.7	39.1	37.0	37.0	32.7	30.1
District of Columbia	7,292.9	5,517.8	4,645.3	3,972.3	3,062.5	2,270.7	1,294.5	891.2	485.7	442.6	367.1	266.9	156.6	
Florida	17.7	13.7	9.6	7.1	4.9	3.4	2.6	1.0	1.0	0.6				
Georgia	49.3	44.4	37.7	31.3	26.3	20.2	18.0	15.4	11.8	8.8	5.8	4.3	1.5	0.6
Idaho	5.2	3.9	1.9	1.1	0.4	0.2								
Illinois	115.7	100.6	86.1	68.3	55.0	45.4	30.6	15.2	8.5	2.8	1.0	0.1		
Indiana	81.3	74.9	70.1	61.1	55.1	46.8	37.6	27.5	19.1	9.6	4.1	0.6	(²)	
Iowa	43.2	40.0	40.2	34.4	29.2	21.5	12.1	3.5	0.2					
Kansas	21.6	20.7	18.0	17.5	12.2	4.5	1.3							
Kentucky	60.1	57.0	53.4	46.3	41.0	32.9	28.8	24.4	19.4	17.1	14.0	10.1	5.5	1.8
Louisiana	30.6	36.5	30.4	24.6	20.7	16.0	15.6	11.4	7.8	4.8	3.4	2.2		
Maine	25.7	24.8	23.2	22.1	21.7	21.0	21.0	19.5	16.8	13.4	10.0	7.7	5.1	3.2
Maryland	145.8	130.3	119.5	104.9	94.0	78.6	69.1	58.6	47.3	45.0	41.0	38.3	34.4	32.0
Massachusetts	479.2	418.8	349.0	278.5	221.8	181.3	153.1	123.7	91.7	75.9	65.1	58.7	52.6	47.1
Michigan	63.8	48.9	42.1	36.4	28.5	20.6	13.0	6.9	3.7	0.2	(²)			
Minnesota	29.5	25.7	21.7	16.2	9.7	5.4	2.1	(²)						
Mississippi	38.6	38.8	33.5	27.8	24.4	17.9	17.1	13.1	8.1	2.9	1.6	0.4	0.3	
Missouri	49.5	47.9	45.2	39.0	31.6	25.0	17.2	9.9	5.6	2.1	1.0	(¹)		
Montana	3.8	2.6	1.7	1.0	0.3	0.1								
Nebraska	16.9	15.5	13.9	13.8	5.9	1.6	0.2							
Nevada	0.7	0.7	0.4	0.4	0.6	0.4	0.1							
New Hampshire	49.1	47.7	45.6	41.7	38.4	35.2	36.1	35.2	31.5	29.8	27.0	23.7	20.4	15.7
New Jersey	420.0	337.7	250.7	192.3	150.5	120.6	89.4	65.2	49.7	42.7	36.9	32.7	28.1	24.5
New Mexico	2.9	2.7	1.6	1.3	1.0	0.7	0.4	0.3						
New York	217.9	191.2	152.5	126.0	106.7	92.0	81.4	65.0	51.0	40.3	28.8	20.1	12.4	7.1
North Carolina	52.5	45.3	38.9	33.2	28.7	22.0	20.4	17.8	15.5	15.1	13.1	11.4	9.8	8.1
North Dakota	9.2	8.2	4.5	2.7	(³)	(³)	(³)							
Ohio	141.4	117.0	102.1	90.1	78.5	65.4	57.4	48.6	37.3	23.3	14.5	5.7	1.1	
Oklahoma	20.2	⁴ 23.9	⁴ 11.4	⁴ 3.7										
Oregon	8.2	7.0	4.3	3.3	1.8	1.0	0.5	(²)						
Pennsylvania	194.5	171.0	140.6	117.3	95.5	78.6	64.8	51.6	38.5	30.1	23.4	18.1	13.4	9.7
Rhode Island	566.4	508.5	401.6	323.8	259.2	203.7	163.7	138.3	102.0	91.1	77.8	72.1	64.8	64.5
South Carolina	55.2	49.7	44.0	37.7	32.6	23.1	23.1	21.9	19.5	19.1	16.5	13.6	11.3	8.2
South Dakota	8.3	7.6	5.2	4.5	(⁵)	(³)	(³)							
Tennessee	56.1	52.4	48.5	42.4	37.0	30.2	26.6	24.1	19.9	16.4	10.1	6.3	2.5	0.8
Texas	17.8	14.8	11.6	8.5	6.1	3.1	2.3	0.8						
Utah	5.5	4.5	3.4	2.6	1.8	1.1	0.3	(²)						
Vermont	38.6	39.0	37.7	36.4	36.4	36.2	34.5	34.4	32.0	30.8	25.9	23.9	16.9	9.4
Virginia	57.4	51.2	46.1	41.1	37.6	30.4	24.8	22.1	19.3	18.9	16.6	15.2	13.7	11.6
Washington	20.3	17.1	7.8	5.3	1.1	0.4	0.1							
West Virginia	60.9	50.8	39.9	31.8	25.7	18.4								
Wisconsin	47.6	42.2	37.4	30.6	23.8	19.1	14.0	5.5	0.4					
Wyoming	2.0	1.5	0.9	0.6	0.2	0.1								

¹ Land area included in Louisiana territory.
² Less than one-tenth of 1.
³ Dakota territory: 1880, 0.9; 1870, 0.1; 1860, less than one-tenth of 1.
⁴ Oklahoma and Indian Territory combined.

ACRES PER INHABITANT.

United States as a whole.—The density of population may be indicated also by average area per inhabitant, expressed in acres. This average for the United States has been reduced from 30.2 acres in 1890 to 25 in 1900, to 20.7 in 1910, and to 18 in 1920, the total reduction for 30 years being about 40 per cent.

Divisions and states.—Table 19 shows, by divisions and states, the total population and the land area in acres in 1920 and the number of acres per inhabitant in 1920, 1910, and 1900. The changes in the number of acres per inhabitant are, of course, simply the converse of those in the number of inhabitants per square mile.

32

POPULATION.

TABLE 19.—NUMBER OF ACRES PER INHABITANT, BY DIVISIONS AND STATES: 1920, 1910, AND 1900.

DIVISION AND STATE.	Population: 1920	Land area in acres: 1920	ACRES PER INHABITANT.			DIVISION AND STATE.	Population: 1920	Land area in acres: 1920	ACRES PER INHABITANT.		
			1920	1910	1900				1920	1910	1900
United States	105,710,620	1,903,215,360	18.0	20.7	25.0	SOUTH ATLANTIC:					
GEOGRAPHIC DIVISIONS:						Delaware	223,003	1,257,600	5.6	6.2	6.8
New England	7,400,909	39,664,640	5.4	6.1	7.1	Maryland	1,449,661	6,362,240	4.4	4.9	5.4
Middle Atlantic	22,261,144	64,000,000	2.9	3.3	4.1	District of Columbia	437,571	38,400	0.1	0.1	0.1
East North Central	21,475,543	157,160,960	7.3	8.6	9.8	Virginia	2,309,187	25,767,680	11.2	12.5	13.9
West North Central	12,544,249	326,914,560	26.1	28.1	31.6	West Virginia	1,463,701	15,374,080	10.5	12.6	16.0
South Atlantic	13,990,272	172,205,440	12.3	14.1	16.5	North Carolina	2,559,123	31,193,600	12.2	14.1	16.5
East South Central	8,893,307	114,885,760	12.9	13.7	15.2	South Carolina	1,683,724	19,516,800	11.6	12.9	14.6
West South Central	10,242,224	275,037,440	26.9	31.3	42.1	Georgia	2,895,832	37,584,000	13.0	14.4	17.0
Mountain	3,336,101	549,705,760	164.8	208.8	328.3	Florida	968,470	35,111,040	36.3	46.7	66.4
Pacific	5,566,871	203,580,800	36.6	48.6	84.4	EAST SOUTH CENTRAL:					
NEW ENGLAND:						Kentucky	2,416,630	25,715,840	10.6	11.2	12.0
Maine	768,014	19,132,800	24.9	25.8	27.6	Tennessee	2,337,885	26,679,680	11.4	12.2	13.2
New Hampshire	443,083	5,779,840	13.0	13.4	14.0	Alabama	2,348,174	32,818,560	14.0	15.3	17.9
Vermont	352,428	5,839,360	16.6	16.4	17.0	Mississippi	1,790,618	29,071,680	16.6	16.5	19.1
Massachusetts	3,852,356	5,144,960	1.3	1.5	1.8	WEST SOUTH CENTRAL:					
Rhode Island	604,397	682,880	1.1	1.3	1.6	Arkansas	1,752,204	33,616,000	19.2	21.4	25.6
Connecticut	1,380,631	3,084,800	2.2	2.8	3.4	Louisiana	1,798,509	29,061,760	16.2	17.5	21.0
MIDDLE ATLANTIC:						Oklahoma	2,028,283	44,424,960	21.9	26.8	56.2
New York	10,385,227	30,498,560	2.9	3.3	4.2	Texas	4,663,228	167,934,720	36.0	43.1	55.1
New Jersey	3,155,900	4,808,960	1.5	1.9	2.6	MOUNTAIN:					
Pennsylvania	8,720,017	28,692,480	3.3	3.7	4.6	Montana	548,889	93,523,840	170.4	248.8	384.5
EAST NORTH CENTRAL:						Idaho	431,866	53,346,560	123.5	163.8	320.8
Ohio	5,759,394	26,073,600	4.5	5.5	6.3	Wyoming	194,402	62,430,720	321.1	427.9	675.0
Indiana	2,930,390	23,068,800	7.9	8.5	9.1	Colorado	939,629	66,341,120	70.6	83.0	122.9
Illinois	6,485,280	35,867,520	5.5	6.4	7.4	New Mexico	360,350	78,401,920	217.6	230.5	401.4
Michigan	3,668,412	36,787,200	10.0	13.1	15.2	Arizona	334,162	72,838,400	218.0	356.4	592.7
Wisconsin	2,632,067	35,363,840	13.4	15.2	17.1	Utah	449,396	52,597,760	117.0	140.0	190.1
WEST NORTH CENTRAL:						Nevada	77,407	70,285,440	908.0	858.4	1,600.2
Minnesota	2,387,125	51,749,120	21.7	24.9	29.5	PACIFIC:					
Iowa	2,404,021	35,575,040	14.8	16.0	15.9	Washington	1,356,621	42,775,040	31.5	37.5	82.6
Missouri	3,404,055	43,985,280	12.9	13.4	14.2	Oregon	783,389	61,188,480	78.1	91.0	148.0
North Dakota	646,872	44,917,120	69.4	77.8	140.7	California	3,426,861	99,617,280	29.1	41.9	67.3
South Dakota	636,547	49,195,520	77.3	84.3	122.5						
Nebraska	1,296,372	49,157,120	37.9	41.2	46.1						
Kansas	1,769,257	52,335,360	29.6	31.0	35.6						

CENTER OF POPULATION AND MEDIAN LINES.[1]

On the basis of the Fourteenth Census returns the center of population and the median point for the United States have been determined for January 1, 1920. In these calculations no account is taken of the area and population of Alaska and of other outlying territory. The location of the center at the dates of the several censuses from 1790 to 1920 and the movement of the point from census to census are indicated by the tables and maps of this section, which includes also a map on which are drawn the median parallel of latitude and the median meridian of longitude for 1920.

[1] **Definition of terms.**—The term "center of population" as used in census publications has a somewhat technical significance, different from that frequently attached to it. The center is often understood to be the point of intersection of a north and south line which divides the population equally, with an east and west line which likewise divides it equally. This point of intersection is, in a certain sense, a center of population; it is here, however, designated the median point to distinguish it from the point technically defined as the center.

The center of population may be said to represent the center of gravity of the population. If the surface of the United States be considered as a rigid level plane without weight, capable of sustaining the population distributed thereon, individuals being assumed to be of equal weight and the plane to be supported, as on a pivotal point, at its center of gravity, the influence of each individual in maintaining the equilibrium of the plane would be directly proportional to his distance from the pivotal point or center of gravity. This is the point referred to by the term "center of population" as used in this chapter. The median point, on the other hand, is in no sense a center of gravity but may be described as the numerical center of population. In determining the median point, distance is not taken into account, and the location of the units of population is considered only in relation to the intersecting median lines—as being north or south of the median parallel and east or west of the median meridian. Extensive changes in the geographic distribution of the population may take place without affecting the median point, whereas the center of population responds to the slightest population change in any section of the country. To illustrate, since the median point lies east of Minnesota, a million persons could move from Minnesota to Oregon without affecting the median point, while the removal of 500 persons from one town in Indiana to another, across the north and south line passing through the median point, would change the location of the point. On the other hand, the removal of a million persons from Minnesota to Oregon would have a very considerable effect on the center of population, since, in terms of the above analogy, the influence of each individual in maintaining the equilibrium of the plane would increase in proportion to his distance from the cen-

ter of gravity. If all the people in the United States were to be assembled at one place, the center of population would be the point which they could reach with the minimum aggregate travel, assuming that they all traveled in direct lines from their residences to the meeting place. This would not be true of the median point.

Method of determining the center of population.—In locating the center of population it is first assumed to be approximately at a certain point. Through this point a parallel and a meridian are drawn, crossing the entire country. In determining the center of population in 1920 the same point was selected as in 1910, namely, the intersection of the parallel of 39 degrees north latitude with the meridian of 86 degrees west longitude, which lines were taken as the axes of moments.

The product of the population of a given area by its distance from the assumed parallel is called a north or south moment, and the product of the population of the area by its distance from the assumed meridian is called an east or west moment. In calculating north and south moments the distances are measured in minutes of latitude; in calculating east and west moments it is necessary to use miles, on account of the unequal length of the degrees and minutes of longitude in different latitudes. The population of the country is grouped by "square degrees"—that is, by areas included between consecutive parallels and meridians—as they are convenient units with which to work. The population of the principal cities is then deducted from that of the respective square degrees in which they lie, and treated separately. The center of population of each square degree is assumed to be at its geographical center, except where such an assumption is manifestly incorrect; in these cases the position of the center of population of the square degree is estimated as nearly as possible. The population of each square degree north or south of the assumed parallel is multiplied by the distance of its center from that parallel; a similar calculation is made for the principal cities; and the sum of the north moments and the sum of the south moments are ascertained. The difference between these two sums, divided by the total population of the country, gives a correction to the latitude. In a similar manner the sums of the east and of the west moments are ascertained and from them the correction in longitude is made.

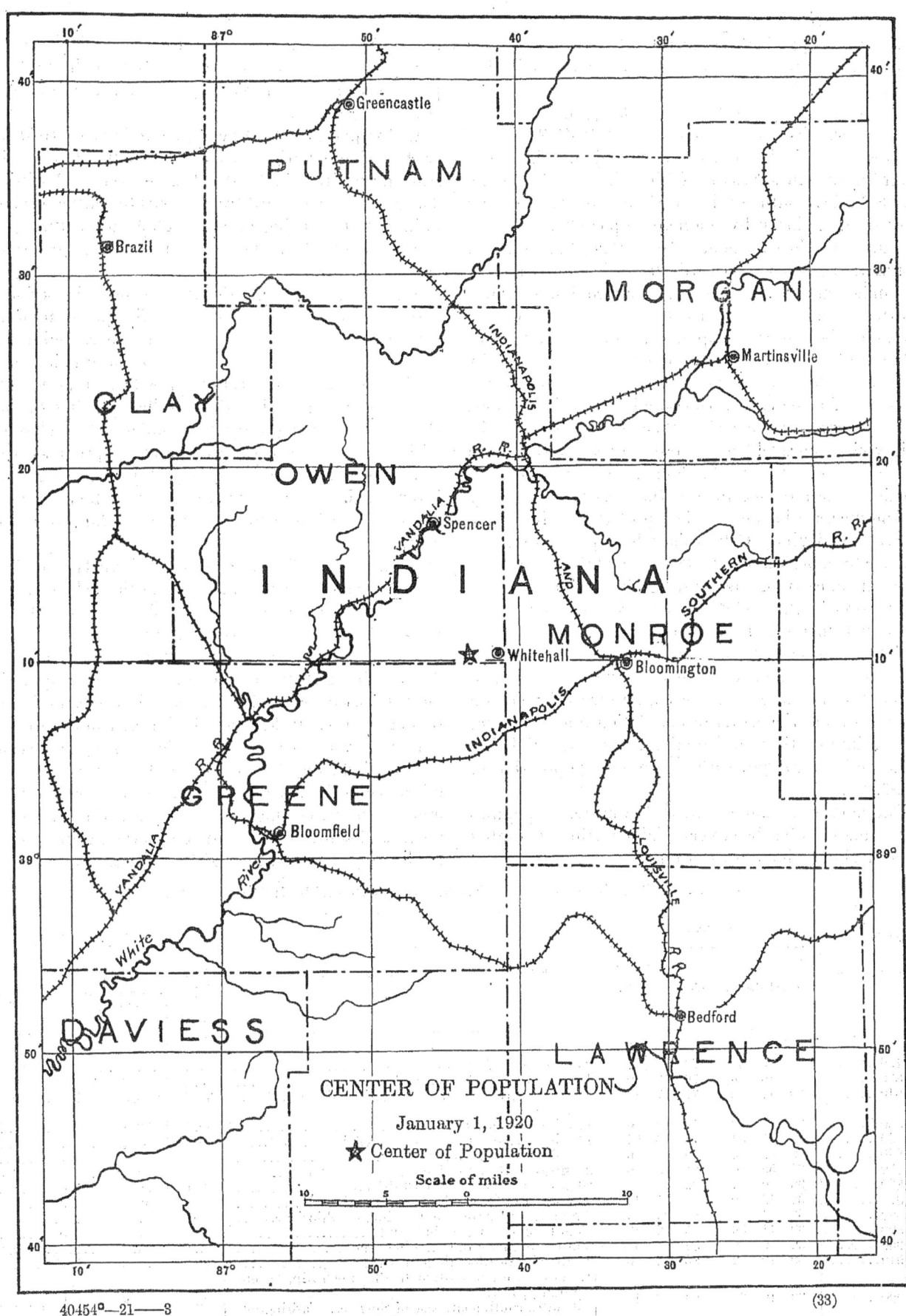

CENTER OF POPULATION

January 1, 1920

★ Center of Population

Scale of miles

34

POPULATION.

Center of population: 1920.—At the Fourteenth Census the center of population was in the following position:

Latitude.........................39° 10′ 21″ N.
Longitude.......................86° 43′ 15″ W.

This point is in southwestern Indiana, in Owen County, 1.9 miles west of Whitehall, Clay township, and 8.3 miles south-southeast of Spencer, Washington township, as shown by the map on page 33.

During the last decade, 1910 to 1920, the center of population moved westward 10′ 55″, approximately 9.8 miles, and northward 9″, or approximately two-tenths of a mile. This was the least movement ever made by the center of population in any decade since 1790, and was only about one-fourth as great as its movement between 1900 and 1910. (See Table 20, below.) The increase in the population of New York, Pennsylvania, and certain other states north of the thirty-ninth parallel has substantially counterbalanced the increase in Texas, Oklahoma, and southern California. The advance toward the west is due largely to the increase in the population of the Pacific Coast states—particularly California, whose population was greater by more than 1,000,000 in 1920 than in 1910—their distance from the center giving any increase of population in those states much greater weight than an equal increase in the populous eastern states, which are nearer the center. The cities of Seattle, San Francisco, and Los Angeles, with a combined population of 1,398,661, exert a greater influence on the location of the center of population than the cities of Baltimore, Boston, Buffalo, Cleveland, Philadelphia, and Pittsburgh, with a combined population of 5,197,624.

The northward movement of the center of population since 1900 has been very slight, having amounted to only about nine-tenths of a mile.

Location of center at prior censuses.—Table 20 and the map on page 35 show the location of the center of population and its proximity to important places at each Federal census.

In the period of 130 years, from 1790 to 1920, the center of population advanced westward 567 miles from its position in 1790, 23 miles east of Baltimore. The progress westward from census to census has been uninterrupted, being greatest, 80.6 miles, during the decade 1850–1860, and least, 9.8 miles, during the decade 1910–1920.

The net advance southward during this period of 130 years was only 7.5 miles. The position of the center in 1790 was the extreme northern point, and the position in 1830 the extreme southern point, occupied at any of the several censuses from 1790 to 1920, the distance separating the parallels passing through these points being only 21.5 miles. The closeness with which the center throughout its progress westward has clung to the thirty-ninth parallel of latitude is remarkable. In 1790 it was less than 20 miles north of this parallel, and in 1830 less than 2.5 miles south of it.

In each of the first four decades, from 1790 to 1830, the center moved westward and southward, the aggregate advance westward during this period of 40 years being 166.6 miles, and the aggregate advance southward, as noted above, 21.5 miles. During the nine decades from 1830 to 1920 the center of population moved northward and southward, but considering the period as a whole the net deviation from the course due west was very slight. The aggregate advance westward during this period of 90 years was 400.4 miles, while the net advance northward was only 14.1 miles. In traversing this distance the deviations north and south from a course due west were confined to the very narrow range of 16.1 miles.

TABLE **20.**—POSITION OF THE CENTER OF POPULATION: 1790 TO 1920.

CENSUS YEAR.	LOCATION.		APPROXIMATE LOCATION BY IMPORTANT TOWNS.	MOVEMENT IN MILES DURING PRECEDING DECADE.			
	North latitude.	West longitude.		From point to point in direct line.	West-ward.	North-ward.	South-ward.
	° ′ ″	° ′ ″					
1790......	39 16 30	76 11 12	23 miles east of Baltimore, Md............				
1800......	39 16 6	76 56 30	18 miles west of Baltimore, Md............	40.6	40.6	....	0.5
1810......	39 11 30	77 37 12	40 miles northwest by west of Washington, D. C. (in Va.).	36.9	36.5	....	5.3
1820......	39 5 42	78 33 0	16 miles east of Moorefield, W. Va.[1].........	50.5	50.1	....	6.7
1830......	38 57 54	79 16 54	19 miles west-southwest of Moorefield, W. Va.[1].....	40.4	39.4	....	9.0
1840......	39 2 0	80 18 0	16 miles south of Clarksburg, W. Va.[1].........	55.0	54.8	4.7	....
1850......	38 59 0	81 19 0	23 miles southeast of Parkersburg, W. Va.[1]......	54.8	54.7	....	3.5
1860......	39 0 24	82 48 48	20 miles south by east of Chillicothe, Ohio.........	80.6	80.6	1.6	....
1870......	39 12 0	83 35 42	48 miles east by north of Cincinnati, Ohio	44.1	42.1	13.3	....
1880......	39 4 8	84 39 40	8 miles west by south of Cincinnati, Ohio (in Ky.)..	58.1	57.4	....	9.1
1890......	39 11 56	85 32 53	20 miles east of Columbus, Ind....................	48.6	47.7	9.0	....
1900......	39 9 36	85 48 54	6 miles southeast of Columbus, Ind..............	14.6	14.4	....	2.8
1910......	39 10 12	86 32 20	In the city of Bloomington, Ind...................	39.0	38.9	0.7	....
1920......	39 10 21	86 43 15	{ 1.9 miles west of Whitehall, Clay township, Owen County, Ind. 8.3 miles south-southeast of Spencer, Washington township, Owen County, Ind.	9.8	9.8	0.2	....

[1] West Virginia formed part of Virginia until 1861.

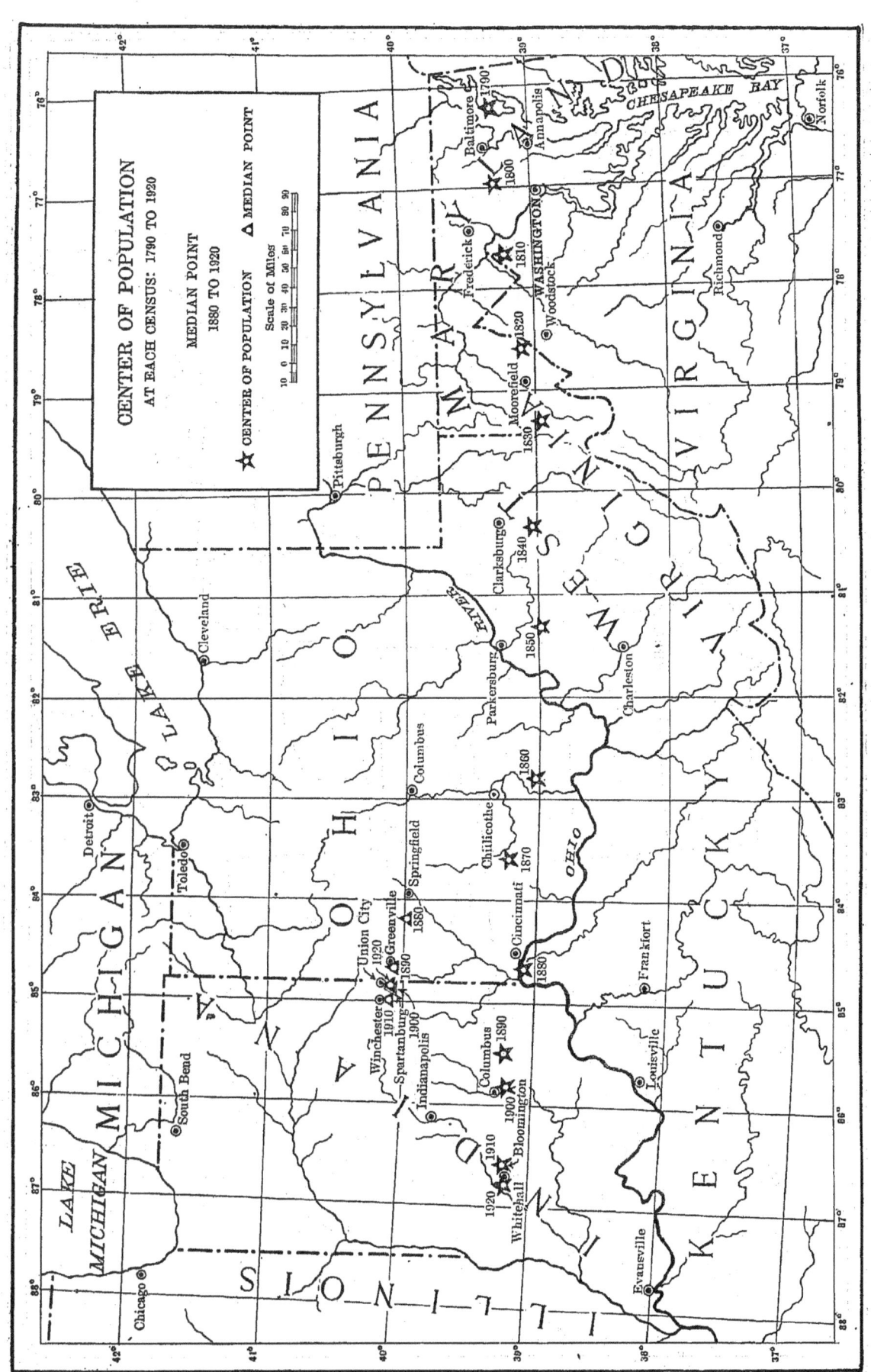

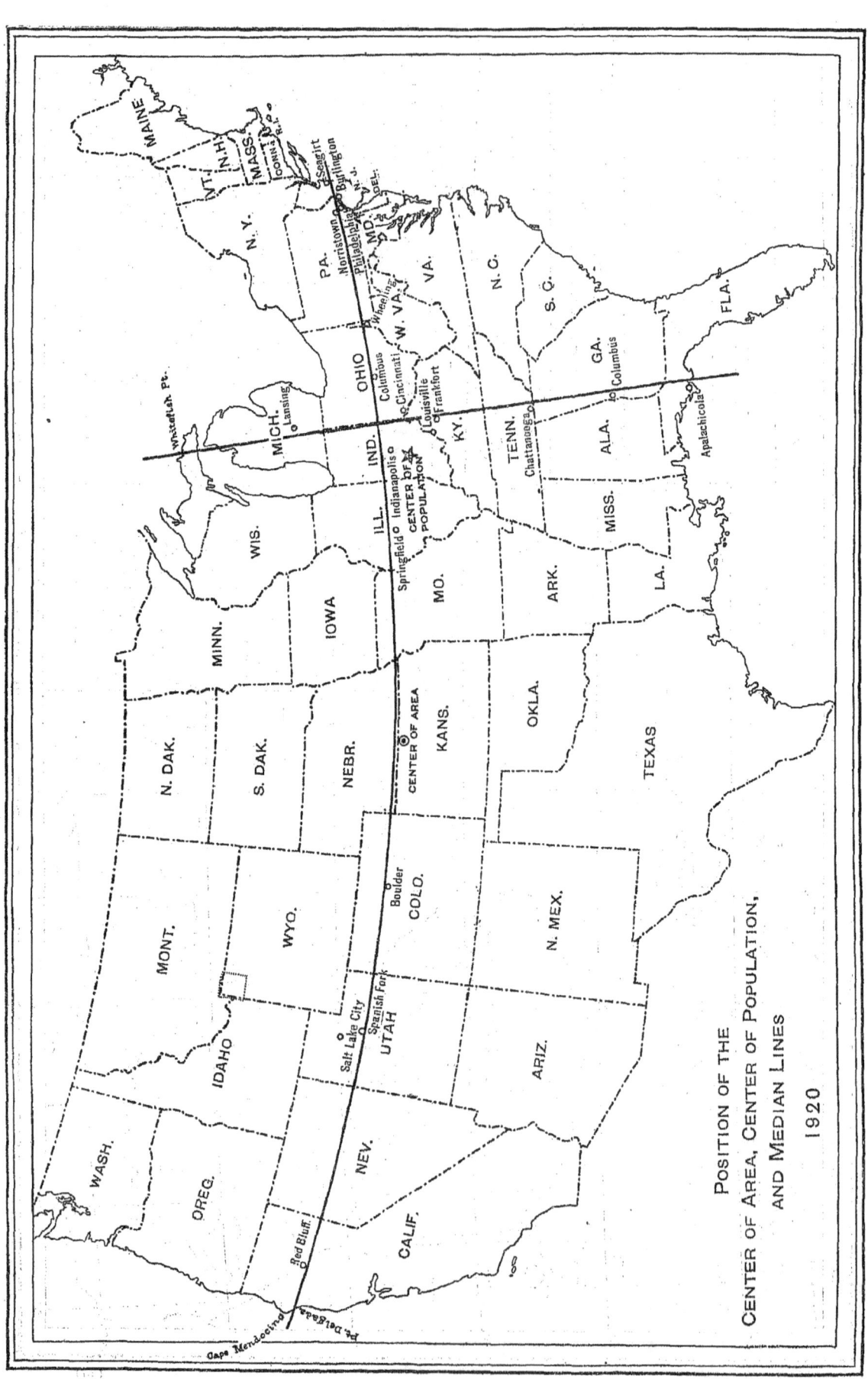

POSITION OF THE
CENTER OF AREA, CENTER OF POPULATION,
AND MEDIAN LINES

1920

CENTER OF POPULATION AND MEDIAN LINES.   37

Center of area.—In connection with the location of the center of population it is of interest to note also the position of what may be termed the center of area—that is, the point on which the surface of the United States would balance if it were a plane of uniform weight per unit of area. This point is located in northern Kansas, 10 miles north of Smith Center, the county seat of Smith County (approximate latitude 39° 55′, longitude 98° 50′), and is therefore about three-fourths of a degree (51 miles) north and about 12⅛ degrees (647 miles) west of the center of population. Its location is shown by the map on page 36. This would be the center of population if the inhabitants of the United States were distributed uniformly throughout its territory. In locating the center of area, no account is taken of Alaska and other outlying possessions.

Median lines.—The geographic distribution of the population is also indicated by the location of median lines. A parallel of latitude is determined which divides the country in such a manner that half the population is north of that parallel and half is south of it; and, similarly, a meridian of longitude is determined which evenly divides the population east and west.[2]

During the four decades from 1880 to 1920 there was little change in the location of the median parallel, its movement being so slight that it could not be accurately indicated on a small map. The movement of the median meridian, however, was much greater. During the 30 years from 1880 to 1910 this movement amounted to 45 miles, the westward progress of the meridian being uninterrupted, although diminishing from decade to decade; but between 1910 and 1920 a reverse movement took place, with the result that the position of the meridian in the later year was 8.8 miles east of its position in 1910. This eastward movement was due entirely to the relatively considerable increase in the population of the Atlantic Coast states.

TABLE **21.**—MEDIAN LINES: 1880–1920.

CENSUS YEAR.	Median parallel, north latitude.			Median meridian, west longitude.			MOVEMENT IN MILES DURING PRECEDING DECADE.		
							Median parallel, northward.	Median meridian, westward.	Median meridian, eastward.
	°	′	″	°	′	″			
1880	39	57	00	84	7	12			
1890	40	2	51	84	40	1	6.6	27.0	
1900	40	4	22	84	51	29	2.4	10.8	
1910	40	6	24	84	59	59	2.3	7.5	
1920	40	6	25	84	49	59	0.019		8.8

The latitude and longitude of the median lines at the several censuses from 1880 to 1920 are shown by Table 21, and their location in 1920 is indicated on the map on page 35.

It may be observed that while each median line exactly bisects the population as a whole it does not necessarily bisect the population at any given point or through any given section of its course. The median parallel does not bisect even approximately the population living either east or west of the Mississippi River. Similarly, the median meridian does not bisect the population of either the northern or the southern section of the country. As the result, no one of the four sections into which the intersecting median lines divide the country contains exactly or approximately one-quarter of the total population. The diagonally opposite sections, however, are necessarily exactly equal in population.[1] The population of the north-

eastern section equals that of the southwestern, and, similarly, the population of the southeastern equals that of the northwestern. The northeastern and southwestern sections each contain, in fact, a population of approximately 31,450,000, while the southeastern and northwestern sections each have about 21,400,000 inhabitants.

Median point.—The point at which the median lines described in the preceding paragraph intersect is designated as the "median point" of the population. It is, in other words, the junction of the line dividing the population equally north and south with the line dividing it equally east and west, and is, therefore, a point quite distinct from the center of population and having no definite or fixed relation to it. As already indicated, the changes in the median point reflect only the difference between the growth of population east of it and the growth west of it and the difference between the growth north and south of it. Other differences in relative growth do not affect its location.

---

[1] The mathematical demonstration of this is simple. If A, B, C, and D represent, respectively, the population of the northwestern, northeastern, southeastern, and southwestern sections, then:

A+B=½ population of U. S.
B+C=½ population of U. S.
A+B=B+C.
Therefore A=C.
Similarly it may be proven that B=D.

[2] In locating these median lines it is necessary, in case of the "square degrees" of latitude and longitude which are traversed by the lines themselves, to assume that the population is evenly distributed throughout these square degrees or to make an estimated adjustment where this is obviously not the case.

38   POPULATION.

In 1920 the median point was located at latitude 40° 6′ 25″ north and longitude 84° 49′ 59″ west, 6 miles slightly west of south of Union City, Randolph County, Ind. Its eastward movement during the decade was 8.8 miles and its northward movement nineteen-thousandths of a mile. Comparing its movement since 1910 with that of the center of population, it will be noted that while each moved slightly to the northward, the center of population moved westward 9.8 miles, as against an eastward movement of 8.8 miles on the part of the median point. These opposite movements bring out strikingly the difference between the significance of the center of population and that of the median point. The calculations to determine the location of the two points are made on entirely different bases, and the results are not comparable. The effect of the increase of 1,000,000 in the population of California was much less on the location of the median point than on that of the center of population, for the reason that in determining the location of the center of population the size of each of the various population groups and both its distance and direction from the center are taken into account, whereas in the case of the median point only the size of the group and its direction from the point are considered. The median point in 1920 was situated 121 miles to the northeast of the center of population.

The exact position of the median point in 1920 is shown by the median lines on the map on page 36, and its location at each of the last five censuses is indicated by the map on page 35. Its approximate location with reference to certain places was as follows:

In 1880, 16 miles due west of Springfield, Ohio.
In 1890, 5 miles southwest of Greenville, Ohio.
In 1900, in Spartanburg, Randolph County, Ind.
In 1910, 3 miles south of Winchester, Ind.
In 1920, 6 miles slightly west of south of Union City, Ind.

POPULATION OF COUNTIES.

The primary divisions of the several states constituting continental United States are, in general, termed counties, but in Louisiana these divisions are known as parishes. There are also a few cities which are independent of the county organizations and thus constitute primary divisions of the states, namely, Baltimore in Maryland, St. Louis in Missouri, and 20 cities in Virginia. There are no counties in the District of Columbia, the county organization having been abolished in 1874. The total number of counties or equivalent divisions in continental United States in 1920 was 3,065.

Tables 22–25 present statistics as to increases and decreases in population within identical county areas between 1910 and 1920. In these tables the number of areas considered is only 2,874, made up as follows: 2,789 individual counties; 63 combinations of two or more counties, comprising a total of 234 counties; 2 independent cities (Baltimore and St. Louis); and 20 combinations of independent cities in Virginia with the counties in which located. The 63 combinations of two or more counties have been made for the purpose of showing the true rates of increase or decrease within identical areas in cases where new counties were formed from parts of others between 1910 and 1920. (Mere transfers of territory from one county to another have been disregarded, since the areas thus transferred are, as a rule, small in proportion to the areas of the entire counties, the transfers having been made in many cases solely for the purpose of rectifying boundary lines.) The 20 combinations of independent cities in Virginia with the counties in which located have been made in order to secure statistics comparable with those for the counties in other states.

In 1,082 counties and combinations, representing 37.6 per cent of the total number considered, the population decreased during the decade 1910–1920.

These 1,082 counties and combinations had an aggregate area of 908,803 square miles, representing 30.6 per cent of the total land area of the United States. The extent of this area of decreasing population and the geographic distribution of the counties composing it are of significance when considered in conjunction with the relatively high rates of population growth during the decade in most urban communities and in a few of the rural districts.

Table 22 shows, by geographic sections and divisions, the distribution of the area of decreasing population.

Table 23 shows, by divisions and states, the aggregate area of the counties in which the population decreased.

TABLE 22.—LAND AREA OF COUNTIES AND COMBINATIONS OF COUNTIES SHOWING DECREASES IN POPULATION SINCE 1910, BY SECTIONS AND DIVISIONS: 1920.

SECTION AND DIVISION.	TOTAL LAND AREA.		COUNTY AREAS SHOWING DECREASES IN POPULATION SINCE 1910.		
	Square miles.	Per cent distribution.	Total land area (square miles).	Per cent distribution.	Per cent of total land area for section or division.
United States...........	2,973,774	100.0	908,803	100.0	30.6
The North..................	918,344	30.9	351,335	38.7	38.3
New England..............	61,976	2.1	16,415	1.8	26.5
Middle Atlantic...........	100,000	3.4	43,922	4.8	43.9
East North Central........	245,564	8.3	112,266	12.4	45.7
West North Central.......	510,804	17.2	178,732	19.7	35.0
The South..................	878,326	29.5	288,372	31.7	32.8
South Atlantic............	269,071	9.0	62,344	6.9	23.2
East South Central........	179,509	6.0	76,514	8.4	42.6
West South Central.......	429,746	14.5	149,514	16.5	34.8
The West..................	1,177,104	39.6	269,096	29.6	22.9
Mountain.................	859,009	28.9	183,449	20.2	21.4
Pacific...................	318,095	10.7	85,647	9.4	26.9
East of the Mississippi River...	856,120	28.8	311,461	34.3	36.4
West of the Mississippi River...	2,117,654	71.2	597,342	65.7	28.2

POPULATION OF COUNTIES.   39

TABLE 23.—LAND AREA OF COUNTIES AND COMBINATIONS OF COUNTIES SHOWING DECREASES IN POPULATION SINCE 1910, BY DIVISIONS AND STATES: 1920.

DIVISION AND STATE.	Total land area in square miles.	COUNTY AREAS SHOWING DECREASES IN POPULATION SINCE 1910.		DIVISION AND STATE.	Total land area in square miles.	COUNTY AREAS SHOWING DECREASES IN POPULATION SINCE 1910.	
		Total land area (square miles).	Per cent of total land area for division or state.			Total land area (square miles).	Per cent of total land area for division or state.
United States	2,973,774	908,803	30.6	SOUTH ATLANTIC:			
GEOGRAPHIC DIVISIONS:				Delaware	1,965	1,530	77.9
New England	61,976	16,415	26.5	Maryland	9,941	5,312	53.4
Middle Atlantic	100,000	43,922	43.9	District of Columbia	60		
East North Central	245,564	112,206	45.7	Virginia	40,262	13,572	33.7
West North Central	510,804	178,732	35.0	West Virginia	24,022	5,182	21.6
South Atlantic	269,071	62,344	23.2	North Carolina	48,740	4,017	8.2
East South Central	179,509	76,514	42.6	South Carolina	30,495	3,898	12.8
West South Central	429,746	149,514	34.8	Georgia	58,725	16,808	28.6
Mountain	859,009	183,449	21.4	Florida	54,861	12,025	21.9
Pacific	318,095	85,647	26.9	EAST SOUTH CENTRAL:			
NEW ENGLAND:				Kentucky	40,181	19,804	49.5
Maine	20,895	5,582	18.7	Tennessee	41,687	15,746	37.8
New Hampshire	9,031	4,392	48.6	Alabama	51,279	15,915	31.0
Vermont	9,124	5,549	60.8	Mississippi	46,362	24,959	53.8
Massachusetts	8,039	567	7.1	WEST SOUTH CENTRAL:			
Rhode Island	1,067	325	30.5	Arkansas	52,525	18,152	34.6
Connecticut	4,820			Louisiana	45,409	17,454	38.4
MIDDLE ATLANTIC:				Oklahoma	69,414	27,216	39.2
New York	47,654	29,145	61.2	Texas	262,398	86,692	33.0
New Jersey	7,514	1,231	16.4	MOUNTAIN:			
Pennsylvania	44,832	13,546	30.2	Montana	146,131	8,676	5.9
EAST NORTH CENTRAL:				Idaho	83,354	1,071	1.3
Ohio	40,740	17,674	43.4	Wyoming	97,548	15,354	15.7
Indiana	36,045	24,662	68.4	Colorado	103,658	17,203	16.6
Illinois	56,043	28,523	50.9	New Mexico	122,503	55,703	45.5
Michigan	57,480	31,019	54.0	Arizona	113,810		
Wisconsin	55,256	10,388	18.8	Utah	82,184	5,271	6.4
WEST NORTH CENTRAL:				Nevada	109,821	80,171	73.0
Minnesota	80,858	4,919	6.1	PACIFIC:			
Iowa	55,586	14,399	25.9	Washington	66,836	21,586	32.3
Missouri	68,727	53,775	78.2	Oregon	95,607	33,069	34.6
North Dakota	70,183	11,914	17.0	California	155,652	30,992	19.9
South Dakota	76,808	30,009	39.0				
Nebraska	76,808	20,245	26.4				
Kansas	81,774	43,471	53.2				

Table 24 shows the rates of increase or decrease for the county combinations which have been made because of the formation of certain counties from parts of others between 1910 and 1920.

TABLE 24.—PERCENTAGE OF INCREASE FOR COMBINED COUNTIES: 1910–1920.

[A minus sign (—) denotes decrease.]

COUNTY COMBINATIONS.	POPULATION.		PER CENT OF INCREASE: 1910–1920		COUNTY COMBINATIONS.	POPULATION.		PER CENT OF INCREASE: 1910–1920	
	1920	1910	For the combined counties.	For each county, disregarding changes in area.		1920	1910	For the combined counties.	For each county, disregarding changes in area.
ARIZONA:					FLORIDA—Continued.				
Greenlee	15,302				Broward	5,135			
Graham	10,148	23,999		—57.7	Okeechobee	2,132			
Total for combined counties	25,510	23,999	0.3		Dade	42,753	11,933		258.3
COLORADO:					Osceola	7,195	5,507		30.7
Alamosa	5,148				Palm Beach	18,654	5,577		234.5
Conejos	8,416	11,285		—25.4	St. Lucie	7,886	4,075		93.5
Costilla	5,032	5,498		—8.5	Total for combined counties	83,755	27,092	209.2	
Total for combined counties	18,596	16,783	10.8		Flagler	2,442			
Crowley	6,383				St. Johns	13,061	13,208		—1.1
Otero	22,623	20,201		12.0	Volusia	23,374	16,510		41.6
Total for combined counties	29,006	20,201	43.6		Total for combined counties	38,877	29,718	30.8	
Moffat	5,129				Okaloosa	9,360			
Routt	8,948	7,561		18.3	Santa Rosa	13,670	14,897		—8.2
Total for combined counties	14,077	7,561	86.2		Walton	12,119	16,460		—26.4
FLORIDA:					Total for combined counties	35,149	31,357	12.1	
Bay	11,407				Pinellas	28,265			
Washington	11,828	16,403		—27.9	Hillsborough	88,257	78,374		12.6
Total for combined counties	23,235	16,403	41.7		Total for combined counties	116,522	78,374	48.7	
					Seminole	10,986			
					Orange	19,890	19,107		4.1
					Total for combined counties	30,876	19,107	61.6	

POPULATION.

TABLE 24.—PERCENTAGE OF INCREASE FOR COMBINED COUNTIES: 1910–1920—Continued.

[A minus sign (−) denotes decrease.]

COUNTY COMBINATIONS.	POPULATION. 1920	POPULATION. 1910	PER CENT OF INCREASE: 1910–1920 For the combined counties.	For each county, disregarding changes in area.
GEORGIA:				
Atkinson	7,656			
Clinch	7,984	8,424		−5.2
Coffee	18,653	21,953		−15.0
Total for combined counties	34,293	30,377	12.9	
Bacon	6,460			
Appling	10,594	12,318		−14.0
Pierce	11,934	10,749		11.0
Ware	28,361	22,957		23.5
Total for combined counties	57,349	46,024	24.6	
Barrow	13,188			
Gwinnett	30,327	28,824		5.2
Jackson	24,654	30,169		−18.3
Walton	24,216	25,393		−4.6
Total for combined counties	92,385	84,386	9.5	
Bleckley	10,532			
Pulaski	11,587	22,835		−49.3
Total for combined counties	22,119	22,835	−3.1	
Candler	9,228			
Evans	6,594			
Treutlen	7,064			
Wheeler	9,817			
Bulloch	26,133	26,464		−1.3
Emanuel	25,862	25,140		2.9
Montgomery	9,167	19,638		−53.3
Tattnall	14,502	18,509		−21.9
Total for combined counties	108,967	89,811	21.3	
Cook	11,180			
Berrien	15,573	22,772		−31.6
Lowndes	26,521	24,436		8.5
Total for combined counties	53,274	47,208	12.8	
IDAHO:				
Adams	2,906			
Washington	9,424	11,101		−15.1
Total for combined counties	12,300	11,101	11.6	
Benewah	6,997			
Kootenai	17,878	22,747		−21.4
Total for combined counties	24,875	22,747	9.4	
Bonneville	17,501			
Butte	2,940			
Camas	1,730			
Clark	1,886			
Franklin	8,650			
Jefferson	9,441			
Madison	9,167			
Power	5,105			
Teton	3,921			
Bingham	18,810	23,306		−21.4
Blaine	4,473	8,387		−46.7
Cassia	15,659	7,197		117.6
Fremont	10,380	24,606		−57.8
Oneida	6,723	15,170		−55.7
Total for combined counties	115,886	78,666	47.3	
Boundary	4,474			
Bonner	12,957	13,588		−4.6
Total for combined counties	17,431	13,588	28.3	
Caribou	2,191			
Bannock	27,532	19,242		43.1
Total for combined counties	29,723	19,242	54.5	
Clearwater	4,993			
Lewis	5,851			
Nez Perce	15,253	24,860		−38.6
Total for combined counties	26,097	24,860	5.0	
Gem	6,427			
Payette	7,021			
Valley	2,524			
Boise	1,822	5,250		−65.3
Canyon	26,932	25,323		6.4
Idaho	11,749	12,384		−5.1
Total for combined counties	56,475	42,957	31.5	

COUNTY COMBINATIONS.	POPULATION. 1920	POPULATION. 1910	PER CENT OF INCREASE: 1910–1920 For the combined counties.	For each county, disregarding changes in area.
IDAHO—Continued.				
Gooding	7,548			
Jerome	5,729			
Minidoka	9,035			
Lincoln	3,446	12,676		−72.8
Total for combined counties	25,758	12,676	103.2	
KENTUCKY:				
McCreary	11,676			
Pulaski	34,010	35,986		−5.5
Wayne	16,208	17,518		−7.5
Whitley	27,749	31,982		−13.2
Total for combined counties	89,643	85,486	4.9	
LOUISIANA:				
Allen	18,382			
Beauregard	20,767			
Jefferson Davis	18,999			
Calcasieu	32,807	62,767		−47.7
Total for combined parishes	90,955	62,767	44.9	
Evangeline	23,485			
St. Landry	51,697	66,661		−22.4
Total for combined parishes	75,182	66,661	12.8	
MISSISSIPPI:				
Humphreys	19,192			
Holmes	34,513	39,088		−11.7
Sharkey	14,190	15,694		−9.6
Sunflower	46,374	28,787		61.1
Washington	51,092	48,933		4.4
Yazoo	37,149	46,672		−20.4
Total for combined counties	202,510	179,174	13.0	
Stone	6,528			
Harrison	32,855	34,658		−5.2
Total for combined counties	39,383	34,658	13.6	
Walthall	13,455			
Pike	28,725	37,272		−22.9
Marion	17,144	15,599		9.9
Total for combined counties	59,324	52,871	12.2	
MONTANA:				
Big Horn	7,015			
Musselshell	12,030			
Stillwater	7,630			
Treasure	1,990			
Wheatland	5,619			
Carbon	15,279	13,962		9.4
Fergus	28,344	17,385		63.0
Meagher	2,622	4,190		−37.4
Rosebud	8,002	7,985		0.2
Sweet Grass	4,926	4,029		22.3
Yellowstone	20,600	22,944		20.0
Total for combined counties	123,057	70,495	74.6	
Blaine	9,057			
Glacier	4,178			
Hill	13,958			
Liberty	2,416			
Phillips	9,311			
Pondera	5,741			
Roosevelt	10,347			
Sheridan	13,847			
Toole	3,724			
Chouteau	11,051	17,191		−35.7
Teton	5,870	9,546		−38.5
Valley	11,542	13,630		−15.3
Total for combined counties	101,042	40,367	150.3	
Carter	3,972			
Fallon	4,548			
Garfield	5,368			
McCone	4,747			
Powder River	3,357			
Prairie	3,084			
Richland	8,080			
Wibaux	3,113			
Custer	12,194	14,123		−13.7
Dawson	9,239	12,725		−27.4
Total for combined counties	59,211	26,848	120.5	
Mineral	2,327			
Missoula	24,041	23,596		1.9
Total for combined counties	26,368	23,596	11.7	

POPULATION OF COUNTIES.

41

TABLE 24.—PERCENTAGE OF INCREASE FOR COMBINED COUNTIES: 1910-1920—Continued.

[A minus sign (−) denotes decrease.]

COUNTY COMBINATIONS.	POPULATION. 1920	POPULATION. 1910	PER CENT OF INCREASE: 1910-1920 For the combined counties.	PER CENT OF INCREASE: 1910-1920 For each county, disregarding changes in area.	COUNTY COMBINATIONS.	POPULATION. 1920	POPULATION. 1910	PER CENT OF INCREASE: 1910-1920 For the combined counties.	PER CENT OF INCREASE: 1910-1920 For each county, disregarding changes in area.
NEBRASKA:					**SOUTH DAKOTA:**				
Arthur	1,412				Bennett	1,924	96		(¹)
McPherson	1,692	2,470		−31.5	Shannon	2,003			
Total for combined counties	3,104	2,470	25.7		Washabaugh	1,166			
NEVADA:					Washington	1,521			
Mineral	1,848				Pine Ridge Indian Reservation		6,607		
Esmeralda	2,410	9,369		−74.3	Total for combined counties	6,614	6,703	−1.3	
Total for combined counties	4,258	9,369	−54.6		Haakon	4,596			
Pershing	2,803				Jackson	2,472			
Humboldt	3,743	6,825		−45.2	Stanley	2,908	14,975		−80.6
Total for combined counties	6,546	6,825	−4.1		Total for combined counties	9,976	14,975	−33.4	
NEW MEXICO:					Jones	3,004			
De Baca	3,196				Lyman	6,591	10,848		−39.2
Lea	3,545				Total for combined counties	9,595	10,848	−11.6	
Chaves	12,075	16,850		−28.3	**TEXAS:**				
Eddy	9,116	12,400		−26.5	Brooks	4,560			
Guadalupe	8,015	10,927		−26.6	Jim Hogg	1,914			
Roosevelt	9,548	12,064		−45.7	Willacy	1,033			
Total for combined counties	42,495	52,241	−18.7		Cameron	36,662	27,158		35.0
Hidalgo	4,338				Duval	8,251	8,964		−8.0
Grant	21,939	14,813		48.1	Hidalgo	38,110	13,728		177.6
Total for combined counties	26,277	14,813	77.4		Starr	11,089	13,151		−15.7
NEW YORK:					Zapata	2,929	3,809		−23.1
Bronx	732,016				Total for combined counties	104,548	66,810	56.5	
New York	2,284,103	2,762,522		−17.3	Culberson	912			
Total for combined counties	3,016,119	2,762,522	9.2		Hudspeth	962			
NORTH CAROLINA:					El Paso	101,877	52,599		93.7
Avery	10,335				Total for combined counties	103,751	52,599	97.2	
Caldwell	19,984	20,579		−2.9	Jim Wells	6,587			
Mitchell	11,278	17,245		−34.6	Kleberg	7,837			
Watauga	13,477	13,556		−0.6	Nueces	22,807	21,955		3.9
Total for combined counties	55,074	51,380	7.2		Total for combined counties	37,231	21,955	69.6	
Hoke	11,722				Real	1,461			
Cumberland	35,064	35,284		−0.6	Bandera	4,001	4,921		−18.7
Robeson	54,674	51,945		5.3	Edwards	2,283	3,768		−39.4
Total for combined counties	101,460	87,229	16.3		Kerr	5,842	5,505		6.1
NORTH DAKOTA:					Total for combined counties	13,587	14,194	−4.3	
Golden Valley	4,832				**UTAH:**				
Slope	4,940				Daggett	400			
Billings	3,126	10,186		−69.3	Uintah	8,470	7,050		20.1
Total for combined counties	12,898	10,186	26.6		Total for combined counties	8,870	7,050	25.8	
Grant	9,553				Duchesne	9,093			
Sioux	3,308				Wasatch	4,625	8,920		−48.2
Morton	18,714	25,289		−26.0	Total for combined counties	13,718	8,920	53.8	
Total for combined counties	31,575	25,289	24.9		**WASHINGTON:**				
OKLAHOMA:					Pend Oreille	6,363			
Cotton	16,679				Stevens	21,005	25,297		−14.6
Comanche	26,629	41,489		−35.8	Total for combined counties	27,968	25,297	10.6	
Total for combined counties	43,308	41,489	4.4		**WYOMING:**				
OREGON:					Campbell	5,233			
Deschutes	9,622				Crook	5,524	6,492		−14.9
Jefferson	3,211				Weston	4,631	4,960		−6.6
Crook	3,424	9,315		−63.2	Total for combined counties	15,388	11,452	34.4	
Total for combined counties	16,257	9,315	74.5		Goshen	8,064			
SOUTH CAROLINA:					Platte	7,421			
Allendale	10,098				Laramie	20,699	26,127		−20.8
Jasper	9,868				Total for combined counties	36,184	26,127	38.5	
Barnwell	23,081	34,209		−32.5	Hot Springs	5,164			
Beaufort	22,269	30,355		−26.6	Washakie	3,106			
Hampton	19,550	25,126		−22.2	Big Horn	12,105	8,886		36.2
Total for combined counties	90,866	89,690	1.3		Fremont	11,820	11,822		(²)
McCormick	10,444				Park	7,298	4,909		48.7
Abbeville	27,139	34,804		−22.0	Total for combined counties	39,493	25,617	54.2	
Edgefield	23,928	28,281		−15.4	Lincoln	12,487			
Greenwood	35,791	34,225		4.6	Uinta	6,611	16,982		−61.1
Total for combined counties	103,302	97,310	6.2		Total for combined counties	19,098	16,982	12.5	
					Niobrara	6,321			
					Converse	7,871	6,294		25.1
					Total for combined counties	14,192	6,294	125.5	

¹ Per cent not shown where base is less than 100.   ² Decrease of less than one-tenth of 1 per cent.

42   POPULATION.

Table 25 shows the number of counties or county combinations in each state which increased and the number which decreased in population between 1910 and 1920, with rates of increase for the former.

TABLE 25.—NUMBER OF COUNTIES CLASSIFIED ACCORDING TO RATE OF INCREASE OF POPULATION FROM 1910 TO 1920, BY DIVISIONS AND STATES.

DIVISION AND STATE.	Total number of counties: 1920.	Number of counties (or combinations) considered.	NUMBER OF COUNTIES (OR COMBINATIONS) IN WHICH, SINCE 1910, THE POPULATION HAS—		NUMBER OF COUNTIES (OR COMBINATIONS) IN WHICH, SINCE 1910, THE POPULATION HAS INCREASED—				
			Decreased.	Increased.	Less than 5 per cent.	From 5 to 15 per cent.	From 15 to 25 per cent.	From 25 to 50 per cent.	50 per cent or more.
United States	3,065	2,874	1,082	1,792	408	625	312	290	157
GEOGRAPHIC DIVISIONS:									
New England	67	67	22	45	16	20	5	4	
Middle Atlantic	150	149	56	93	22	27	27	14	3
East North Central	436	436	224	212	60	73	34	33	12
West North Central	619	607	240	367	98	133	63	52	21
South Atlantic	558	496	140	356	80	142	67	50	17
East South Central	364	353	163	190	58	81	30	15	6
West South Central	469	450	160	290	46	80	51	58	46
Mountain	269	189	42	144	16	35	22	37	34
Pacific	133	130	35	95	12	25	13	27	18
NEW ENGLAND:									
Maine	16	16	5	11	7	3	1		
New Hampshire	10	10	5	5	2	2	1		
Vermont	14	14	8	6	5	1			
Massachusetts	14	14	3	11		8	2	1	
Rhode Island	5	5	1	4		3		1	
Connecticut	8	8		8	2	3	1	2	
MIDDLE ATLANTIC:									
New York	62	61	32	29	10	5	9	3	2
New Jersey	21	21	3	18	2	3	5	7	1
Pennsylvania	67	67	21	46	10	19	13	4	
EAST NORTH CENTRAL:									
Ohio	88	88	39	49	15	15	9	7	3
Indiana	92	92	64	28	8	9	7	3	1
Illinois	102	102	56	46	18	17	3	7	1
Michigan	83	83	48	35	6	10	6	7	6
Wisconsin	71	71	17	54	13	22	9	9	1
WEST NORTH CENTRAL:									
Minnesota	86	86	9	77	10	32	20	13	2
Iowa	99	99	27	72	31	28	7	6	
Missouri	[1]115	[1]115	89	[1]26	9	[1]11	2	4	
North Dakota	53	49	10	39	10	8	10	7	4
South Dakota	68	61	15	46	7	22	9	5	3
Nebraska	93	92	33	59	19	17	7	10	6
Kansas	105	105	57	48	12	16	8	7	5
SOUTH ATLANTIC:									
Delaware	3	3	2	1			1		
Maryland	[2]24	[2]24	13	[2]11	3	5	2	1	
District of Columbia	1	1		1				1	
Virginia	[3]120	[4]100	37	63	26	24	4	7	2
West Virginia	55	55	15	40	9	13	4	10	4
North Carolina	100	95	10	85	15	30	24	15	1
South Carolina	46	39	4	35	5	22	5	3	
Georgia	155	137	45	92	20	40	23	8	1
Florida	54	42	14	28	2	8	4	5	9
EAST SOUTH CENTRAL:									
Kentucky	120	117	61	56	20	25	4	3	4
Tennessee	95	95	37	58	23	22	7	6	
Alabama	67	67	21	46	9	20	12	5	
Mississippi	82	74	44	30	6	14	7	1	2
WEST SOUTH CENTRAL:									
Arkansas	75	75	25	50	3	25	11	9	2
Louisiana	64	60	27	33	8	12	3	9	1
Oklahoma	77	76	27	49	6	10	12	11	10
Texas	253	239	81	158	29	42	25	29	33
MOUNTAIN:									
Montana	51	20	4	16	1	5	3	3	4
Idaho	44	17	1	16	1	6	3	3	3
Wyoming	[5]22	12	3	9		2	1	3	3
Colorado	63	59	15	44	6	10	6	12	10
New Mexico	29	23	7	16	4	4	1	5	2
Arizona	14	13		13		1	1	4	7
Utah	29	27	2	25	4	5	6	6	4
Nevada	17	15	10	5		2	1	1	1
PACIFIC:									
Washington	39	38	13	25	4	8	3	7	3
Oregon	36	34	8	26	2	8	5	10	1
California	58	58	14	44	6	9	5	10	14

[1] Includes independent city of St. Louis.   [2] Includes independent city of Baltimore.   [3] Includes 20 independent cities.   [4] Includes 20 combinations of counties with independent cities located therein.   [5] Includes Yellowstone National Park.

Table 49, page 93, shows the population of the 48 states, by counties or equivalent divisions, for 1920 as shown by the returns of the Fourteenth Census, and for prior census years as far back as 1850 or the earliest year covered by any decennial census for a given county. The varying rates of increase in the population of counties from 1910 to 1920 are shown graphically by the map headed "Per cent of increase or decrease in total population, by counties: 1910–1920," on page 90.

URBAN AND RURAL.   43

URBAN AND RURAL POPULATION.

DEFINITION OF TERMS.

The Census Bureau classifies as urban population that residing in cities and other incorporated places having 2,500 inhabitants or more, and in towns of that size in Massachusetts, New Hampshire, and Rhode Island. In most sections of the country all or practically all densely populated areas having 2,500 inhabitants or more are incorporated separately as municipalities, variously known as cities, towns, villages, boroughs, etc. In the three New England states just named, however, this is not the case.

In Massachusetts and Rhode Island it is not the practice—as it is in practically all the other states—to incorporate, as separate municipalities, the relatively densely populated portions of "towns" (which are the primary divisions of the counties), and no town as a whole is incorporated as a municipality until it attains a population greatly in excess of 2,500. In New Hampshire a similar condition exists, although there are in the state two incorporated villages, each of which has fewer than 2,500 inhabitants. For this reason those towns having 2,500 or more inhabitants in the three states named are treated as urban, although portions of their areas are rural in character. The urban areas in the three states in question, as classified by the census, thus contain a certain number of inhabitants who in other sections of the country would be segregated as rural. Nevertheless, in most of the Massachusetts, New Hampshire, and Rhode Island towns having 2,500 inhabitants or more by far the greater part of the population resides within the more densely settled areas, so that the proportion classed as urban, considering each state as a whole, is not greatly exaggerated by the practice adopted. Statistics for individual counties in these states were omitted in Table 50, however, on account of the undoubted exaggeration in certain counties.

Urban population being thus defined, the remainder of the country is classed as rural, consisting of all unincorporated territory and all incorporated places having fewer than 2,500 inhabitants, except in Massachusetts, New Hampshire, and Rhode Island, where it consists of all towns under 2,500.

The statistics as to urban and rural population in this section relate only to the United States, exclusive of outlying possessions.

PROPORTIONS URBAN AND RURAL.

United States as a whole.—The proportions of the total population of the United States living in urban and in rural territory, as reported at each of the last five censuses, are shown in Table 26.

The rapid increase from census to census in the proportion which the urban population forms of the total, as shown by Table 26, is the continuation of a tendency which has been manifested conspicuously in the United States ever since 1820. It would be extremely difficult, if at all possible, even to approximate closely from the earlier census reports the population residing in urban territory as now defined, and therefore no such compilation has been attempted for censuses prior to that of 1880. The census report for 1880, however, contained a comparative statement showing the population living in places of 8,000 inhabitants or more at each census back to 1790; and, as affording an indication of the growth of urban population from the earliest to the latest census, so much of this statement as applies to the censuses prior to 1880 is reproduced in Table 27 in conjunction with comparable figures for the last five censuses, 1880 to 1920, covering the population of incorporated places (and of towns in Massachusetts, New Hampshire, and Rhode Island) having the same size limit, 8,000 inhabitants.

TABLE 26.—URBAN AND RURAL POPULATION OF THE UNITED STATES: 1880–1920.

CLASS.	1920	1910	1900	1890	1880
Total, number...	105,710,620	91,972,266	75,994,575	62,947,714	50,155,783
Urban..............	54,304,603	42,166,120	30,380,433	22,298,359	14,358,167
Rural..............	51,406,017	49,806,146	45,614,142	40,649,355	35,797,616
Total, per cent...	100.0	100.0	100.0	100.0	100.0
Urban..............	51.4	45.8	40.0	35.4	28.6
Rural..............	48.6	54.2	60.0	64.6	71.4

TABLE 27.—POPULATION IN PLACES OF 8,000 INHABITANTS OR MORE: 1790–1920.

CENSUS YEAR.	Total population.	PLACES OF 8,000 INHABITANTS OR MORE.		
		Population.	Number of places.	Per cent of total population.
1920..............	105,710,620	46,307,640	924	43.8
1910..............	91,972,266	35,570,334	768	38.7
1900..............	75,994,575	25,018,335	547	32.9
1890..............	62,947,714	18,244,239	445	29.0
1880..............	50,155,783	11,365,698	285	22.7
1870..............	38,558,371	8,071,875	226	20.9
1860..............	31,443,321	5,072,256	141	16.1
1850..............	23,191,876	2,897,586	85	12.5
1840..............	17,069,453	1,453,994	44	8.5
1830..............	12,866,020	864,509	26	6.7
1820..............	9,638,453	475,135	13	4.9
1810..............	7,239,881	356,920	11	4.9
1800..............	5,308,483	210,873	6	4.0
1790..............	3,929,214	131,472	6	3.3

POPULATION IN PLACES OF 8,000 INHABITANTS OR MORE AT EACH CENSUS: 1790–1920.

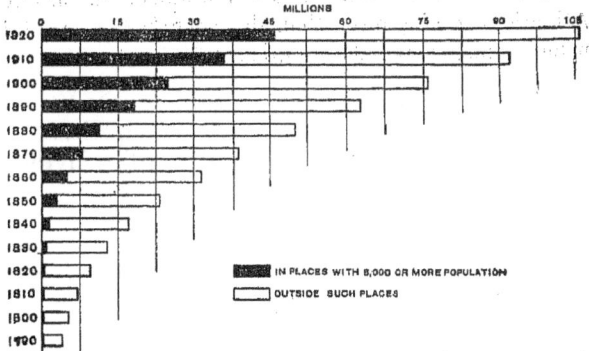

IN PLACES WITH 8,000 OR MORE POPULATION

OUTSIDE SUCH PLACES

POPULATION.

44

It will be seen from Table 27 and from the accompanying diagram that in 1790 only about one-thirtieth of the population of the country resided in places having 8,000 inhabitants or more, but that the proportion which this class of the population formed of the total increased to nearly one-twentieth in 1810, one-eighth in 1850, almost one-third in 1900, and nearly four-ninths in 1920.

The following diagram shows the proportions urban—that is, residing in places having 2,500 inhabitants or more—and rural in the total population at each census from 1880 to 1920.

URBAN AND RURAL POPULATION: 1880–1920.

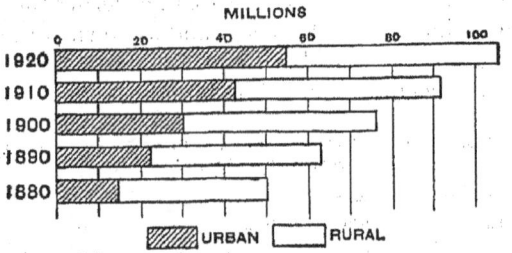

Divisions and states.—Table 28 shows, for 1920, by geographic sections and divisions, the urban and rural population, the per cent urban, and the per cent distribution of each class.

TABLE 28.—URBAN AND RURAL POPULATION, BY SECTIONS AND DIVISIONS: 1920.

SECTION AND DIVISION.	Urban.	Rural.	Per cent urban.	PER CENT DISTRIBUTION.	
				Urban.	Rural.
United States.........	54,304,603	51,406,017	51.4	100.0	100.0
The North...................	40,314,312	23,367,533	63.3	74.2	45.5
New England............	5,805,073	1,535,836	79.2	10.8	3.0
Middle Atlantic.........	16,672,595	5,588,549	74.9	30.7	10.9
East North Central.......	13,049,272	8,426,271	60.8	24.0	16.4
West North Central.....	4,727,372	7,816,877	37.7	8.7	15.2
The South..................	9,303,828	23,821,975	28.1	17.1	46.3
South Atlantic..........	4,338,792	9,651,480	31.0	8.0	18.8
East South Central.......	1,994,207	6,899,100	22.4	3.7	13.4
West South Central......	2,970,829	7,271,395	29.0	5.5	14.1
The West.................	4,686,463	4,216,509	52.6	8.6	8.2
Mountain................	1,214,980	2,121,121	36.4	2.2	4.1
Pacific..................	3,471,483	2,095,388	62.4	6.4	4.1
East of the Mississippi River.	41,919,939	32,101,236	56.6	77.2	62.4
West of the Mississippi River.	12,384,664	19,304,781	39.1	22.8	37.6

It will be noted that one division alone, the Middle Atlantic, contains more than three-tenths of the total urban population of the country, and that this division and the East North Central together contain considerably more than half the total urban population.

Table 29 shows, by geographic divisions, the density of the rural population in 1920. The density figures in this table have been based on the total land area, no deduction being made for areas classified as urban. Outside of New England the urban area in the divisional aggregates is too inconsiderable to have any material effect on the results; and since in New England the urban area is exaggerated only in the states of Massachusetts, New Hampshire, and Rhode Island, the resultant error in the figures for the division as a whole is not great.

TABLE 29.—DENSITY OF RURAL POPULATION, BY DIVISIONS: 1920.

DIVISION.	Land area in square miles.	RURAL POPULATION.	
		Total.	Per square mile.
United States..................	2,973,774	51,406,017	17.3
New England..................	61,976	1,535,836	24.8
Middle Atlantic..............	100,000	5,588,549	55.9
East North Central..........	245,564	8,426,271	34.3
West North Central.........	510,804	7,816,877	15.3
South Atlantic..............	269,071	9,651,480	35.9
East South Central..........	179,509	6,899,100	38.4
West South Central.........	429,746	7,271,395	16.9
Mountain...................	859,009	2,121,121	2.5
Pacific....................	318,095	2,095,388	6.6

The distribution, by states, of the rural population in 1920 is indicated by the map headed "Rural population per square mile, by counties: 1920," on page 89. In the preparation of this map the county has been taken as the unit; that is, the rural population of each county has been assumed to be uniformly distributed throughout the county.

Table 30 (p. 46) shows, by divisions and states, the urban and rural population as returned at the last four censuses. In the New England and Middle Atlantic divisions the proportions urban in the total population are much greater than in any other division, being, in 1920, approximately four-fifths and three-fourths, respectively. Among the individual states Rhode Island and Massachusetts rank first and second in this respect. It must be borne in mind, however, that the census method of classifying the urban and rural population in Massachusetts, Rhode Island, and New Hampshire results in some exaggeration of the figures for the former class, as already pointed out. Among the divisions, the smallest proportions of urban population are found in the South, but the eight states having less than one-

URBAN AND RURAL.

fifth of their population urban—North Carolina, South Carolina, Mississippi, Arkansas, North Dakota, South Dakota, New Mexico, and Nevada—are scattered through the three southern divisions, the West North Central division, and the Mountain division.

It will be noted that, although the South is far more densely populated than the West (see Table 16), the urban element in its total population is proportionally much smaller than in the West. In fact, in each of the three southern divisions the urban proportion is smaller than in either of the two western divisions.

In every geographic division the proportion urban increased between 1910 and 1920, and the same is true of every state except Colorado, Montana, and Wyoming. Because of the decreases in these three states, the Mountain division as a whole shows a decidedly smaller increase in the proportion urban during the past decade than appears for any other division.

The maps on page 48 and the diagram in the next column show the per cent urban in the total population in 1920 and 1910, respectively, for each of the states, and the diagram on page 49 indicates the percentage of urban population in each census year from 1890 to 1920. As shown by the map and by Table 30, the proportion urban in the total population is now more than one-half in 15 states, namely, California, Connecticut, Delaware, Illinois, Indiana, Maryland, Massachusetts, Michigan, New Hampshire, New Jersey, New York, Ohio, Pennsylvania, Rhode Island, and Washington.

States and counties.—Table 50 (p. 150) shows, by states and counties, the urban and rural population for 1920, 1910, and 1900, together with the percentage which the urban population represented of the total in each year, the percentages of increase in each class, and the rural population per square mile in 1920.

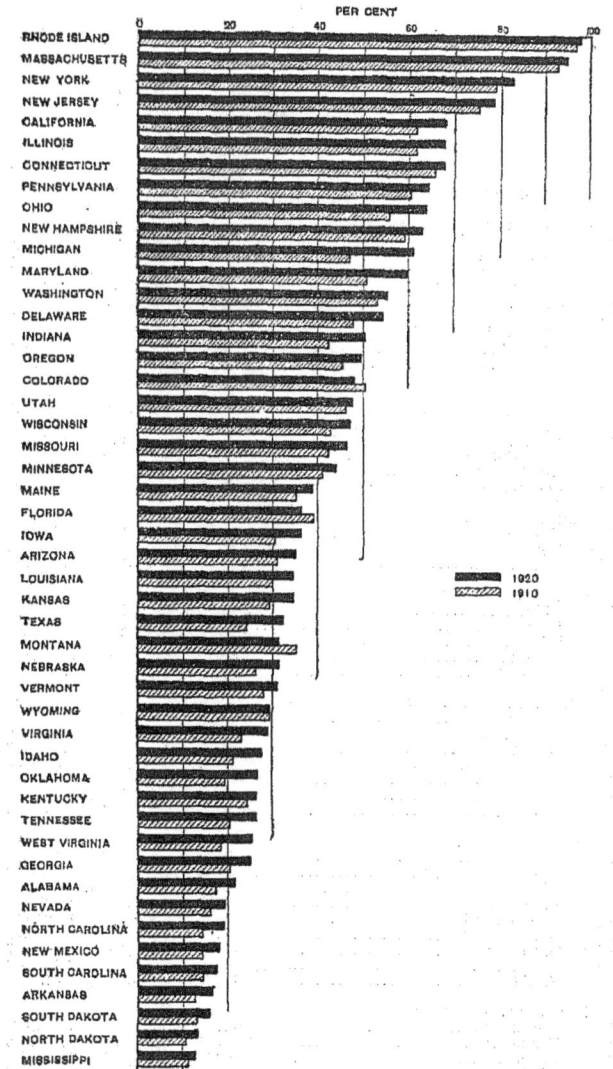

PER CENT URBAN IN TOTAL POPULATION, BY STATES: 1920 AND 1910.

POPULATION.

46

TABLE 30.—URBAN AND RURAL POPULATION,

DIVISION AND STATE.	1920 Total population.	1920 Urban population.	1920 Rural population. Total.	1920 Rural In incorporated places.	1920 Rural In unincorporated territory.	1910 Total population.	1910 Urban population.	1910 Rural population. Total.	1910 Rural In incorporated places.	1910 Rural In unincorporated territory.
1 United States	105,710,620	54,304,603	51,406,017	8,969,241	42,436,776	91,972,266	42,166,120	49,806,146	8,169,149	41,636,997
GEOGRAPHIC DIVISIONS:										
2 New England	7,400,909	5,865,073	1,535,836	83,355	1,452,481	6,552,681	4,908,082	1,554,590	77,636	1,476,963
3 Middle Atlantic	22,261,144	16,672,595	5,588,549	1,075,503	4,513,046	19,315,892	13,723,373	5,592,519	1,084,043	4,508,476
4 East North Central	21,475,543	13,049,272	8,426,271	2,007,078	6,419,193	18,250,621	9,017,271	8,633,350	1,952,985	6,680,365
5 West North Central	12,544,249	4,727,372	7,816,877	2,074,005	5,742,872	11,637,921	3,873,716	7,764,205	1,862,331	5,901,874
6 South Atlantic	13,990,272	4,338,792	9,651,480	1,175,440	8,476,031	12,194,895	3,092,153	9,102,742	1,084,383	8,038,359
7 East South Central	8,893,307	1,994,207	6,899,100	693,195	6,205,905	8,409,901	1,574,229	6,835,672	657,692	6,177,980
8 West South Central	10,242,224	2,970,829	7,271,395	980,585	6,290,810	8,784,534	1,957,456	6,827,078	771,238	6,055,840
9 Mountain	3,336,101	1,214,980	2,121,121	477,245	1,643,876	2,633,517	947,511	1,686,006	335,515	1,350,491
10 Pacific	5,566,871	3,471,483	2,095,388	402,826	1,092,562	4,192,304	2,382,329	1,809,975	363,326	1,446,649
NEW ENGLAND:										
11 Maine	768,014	299,569	468,445	19,049	449,396	742,371	262,248	480,123	18,020	461,194
12 New Hampshire	443,083	279,761	163,322	1,551	161,771	430,572	255,099	175,473	1,340	174,133
13 Vermont	352,428	109,976	242,452	52,187	190,265	355,956	98,917	257,039	45,555	211,484
14 Massachusetts	3,852,356	3,650,248	202,108	....	202,108	3,366,416	3,125,367	241,049	....	241,049
15 Rhode Island	604,397	589,180	15,217		15,217	542,610	524,654	17,956		17,956
16 Connecticut	1,380,631	936,339	444,292	10,568	433,724	1,114,756	731,797	382,959	11,812	371,147
MIDDLE ATLANTIC:										
17 New York	10,385,227	8,589,844	1,795,383	346,877	1,448,506	9,113,614	7,185,494	1,928,120	352,294	1,575,826
18 New Jersey	3,155,900	2,474,936	680,964	148,702	532,262	2,537,167	1,907,210	629,957	149,700	480,167
19 Pennsylvania	8,720,017	5,607,815	3,112,202	579,924	2,532,278	7,665,111	4,630,669	3,034,442	581,959	2,452,483
EAST NORTH CENTRAL:										
20 Ohio	5,759,394	3,677,136	2,082,258	472,754	1,609,504	4,767,121	2,665,143	2,101,978	452,030	1,649,948
21 Indiana	2,930,390	1,482,855	1,447,535	295,040	1,152,495	2,700,876	1,143,835	1,557,041	300,047	1,256,394
22 Illinois	6,485,280	4,403,153	2,082,127	680,740	1,401,387	5,638,591	3,476,929	2,161,662	675,502	1,486,160
23 Michigan	3,668,412	2,241,560	1,426,852	286,644	1,140,208	2,810,173	1,327,044	1,483,129	285,955	1,197,174
24 Wisconsin	2,632,067	1,244,568	1,387,499	271,900	1,115,599	2,333,860	1,004,320	1,329,540	238,851	1,090,689
WEST NORTH CENTRAL:										
25 Minnesota	2,387,125	1,051,593	1,335,532	368,269	967,263	2,075,708	850,294	1,225,414	326,166	899,248
26 Iowa	2,404,021	875,495	1,528,526	477,801	1,050,725	2,224,771	680,054	1,544,717	438,715	1,106,002
27 Missouri	3,404,055	1,586,903	1,817,152	389,711	1,427,441	3,293,335	1,398,817	1,894,518	359,452	1,535,066
28 North Dakota	646,872	88,239	558,633	126,708	431,925	577,056	63,236	513,820	98,261	415,559
29 South Dakota	636,547	101,872	534,675	145,745	388,930	583,888	76,673	507,215	117,871	389,344
30 Nebraska	1,296,372	405,306	891,066	275,568	615,498	1,192,214	310,852	881,362	243,292	638,070
31 Kansas	1,769,257	617,964	1,151,293	290,293	861,000	1,690,949	493,790	1,197,159	278,574	918,585
SOUTH ATLANTIC:										
32 Delaware	223,003	120,767	102,236	31,679	70,557	202,322	97,085	105,237	29,027	76,210
33 Maryland	1,449,661	869,422	580,239	70,145	510,094	1,295,346	658,192	637,154	68,788	568,366
34 District of Columbia	437,571	437,571	....	....	....	331,069	331,069	....	....	....
35 Virginia	2,309,187	673,984	1,635,203	120,783	1,514,420	2,061,612	476,529	1,585,083	113,016	1,472,067
36 West Virginia	1,463,701	369,007	1,094,694	134,128	960,566	1,221,119	228,242	992,877	132,398	860,479
37 North Carolina	2,559,123	490,370	2,068,753	240,753	1,828,000	2,206,287	318,474	1,887,813	218,482	1,669,331
38 South Carolina	1,683,724	293,987	1,389,737	148,303	1,241,434	1,515,400	224,832	1,290,568	129,360	1,161,208
39 Georgia	2,895,832	727,859	2,167,973	296,795	1,871,178	2,609,121	538,650	2,070,471	285,803	1,784,668
40 Florida	968,470	355,825	612,645	132,863	479,782	752,619	219,080	533,539	87,509	446,030
EAST SOUTH CENTRAL:										
41 Kentucky	2,416,630	633,543	1,783,087	197,551	1,585,536	2,289,905	555,442	1,734,463	188,872	1,545,591
42 Tennessee	2,337,885	611,226	1,726,659	131,174	1,595,485	2,184,789	441,045	1,743,744	133,940	1,609,804
43 Alabama	2,348,174	509,317	1,838,857	188,595	1,650,262	2,138,093	370,431	1,767,662	164,511	1,603,151
44 Mississippi	1,790,618	240,121	1,550,497	175,875	1,374,622	1,797,114	207,311	1,589,803	170,369	1,419,434
WEST SOUTH CENTRAL:										
45 Arkansas	1,752,204	290,497	1,461,707	196,550	1,265,157	1,574,449	202,681	1,371,768	174,764	1,197,004
46 Louisiana	1,798,509	628,163	1,170,346	129,055	1,041,291	1,656,388	496,516	1,159,872	100,802	1,059,070
47 Oklahoma[1]	2,028,283	539,480	1,488,803	291,972	1,196,831	1,657,155	320,155	1,337,000	230,367	1,106,633
48 Texas	4,663,228	1,512,689	3,150,539	363,008	2,787,531	3,896,542	938,104	2,958,438	256,305	2,702,133
MOUNTAIN:										
49 Montana	548,889	172,011	376,878	69,699	307,179	376,053	133,420	242,633	35,186	207,447
50 Idaho	431,866	119,037	312,829	77,442	235,387	325,594	69,898	255,696	50,375	190,321
51 Wyoming	194,402	57,348	137,054	46,267	90,787	145,965	43,221	102,744	22,866	79,878
52 Colorado	939,629	453,259	486,370	115,103	371,267	799,024	401,840	394,184	90,757	207,427
53 New Mexico	360,350	64,960	295,390	30,119	265,271	327,301	46,571	280,730	17,613	263,117
54 Arizona	334,162	117,527	216,635	15,122	201,513	204,354	63,260	141,094	16,406	124,688
55 Utah	449,396	215,584	233,812	108,437	125,375	373,351	172,934	200,417	80,644	119,773
56 Nevada	77,407	15,254	62,153	15,056	47,097	81,875	13,367	68,508	6,668	61,840
PACIFIC:										
57 Washington	1,356,621	748,735	607,886	130,211	477,675	1,141,990	605,530	536,460	120,532	415,928
58 Oregon	783,389	391,019	392,370	98,938	293,432	672,765	307,000	365,705	89,742	275,963
59 California	3,426,861	2,331,729	1,095,132	173,677	921,455	2,377,540	1,469,730	907,810	153,052	754,758

[1] Includes population of Indian Territory for 1900 and 1890.

URBAN AND RURAL.   47

BY DIVISIONS AND STATES: 1890–1920.

1900			1890			1920		1910		1900		1890		
Total population.	Urban population.	Rural population.	Total population.	Urban population.	Rural population.	Per cent urban.	Per cent rural.	Per cent urban.	Per cent rural.	Per cent urban.	Per cent rural.	Per cent urban.	Per cent rural.	
75,994,575	30,380,433	45,614,142	62,947,714	22,298,359	40,649,355	51.4	48.6	45.8	54.2	40.0	60.0	35.4	64.6	1
5,592,017	4,053,427	1,538,590	4,700,749	3,130,899	1,569,850	79.2	20.8	76.3	23.7	72.5	27.5	66.8	33.2	2
15,454,678	10,075,883	5,378,795	12,706,220	7,333,772	5,372,448	74.9	25.1	71.0	29.0	65.2	34.8	57.7	42.3	3
15,985,581	7,219,975	8,765,606	13,478,305	5,097,181	8,381,124	60.8	39.2	52.7	47.3	45.2	54.8	37.8	62.2	4
10,347,423	2,946,544	7,400,879	8,932,112	2,308,819	6,623,293	37.7	62.3	33.3	66.7	28.5	71.5	25.8	74.2	5
10,443,480	2,282,632	8,210,848	8,857,922	1,728,019	7,129,903	31.0	69.0	25.4	74.6	21.4	78.6	19.5	80.5	6
7,547,757	1,131,056	6,416,701	6,429,154	817,308	5,611,846	22.4	77.6	18.7	81.3	15.0	85.0	12.7	87.3	7
6,532,290	1,057,197	5,475,093	4,740,983	715,999	4,024,984	29.0	71.0	22.3	77.7	16.2	83.8	15.1	84.9	8
1,674,657	541,363	1,133,294	1,213,935	355,627	858,308	36.4	63.6	36.0	64.0	32.3	67.7	29.3	70.7	9
2,416,692	1,122,356	1,294,336	1,888,334	801,735	1,086,599	62.4	37.6	56.8	43.2	46.4	53.6	42.5	57.5	10
694,466	232,827	461,639	661,086	173,781	487,305	39.0	61.0	35.3	64.7	33.5	66.5	26.3	73.7	11
411,588	226,269	185,319	376,530	192,479	184,051	63.1	36.9	59.2	40.8	55.0	45.0	51.1	48.9	12
343,641	75,831	267,810	332,422	50,638	281,784	31.2	68.8	27.8	72.2	22.1	77.9	15.2	84.8	13
2,805,346	2,567,098	238,248	2,238,947	2,003,854	235,093	94.8	5.2	92.8	7.2	91.5	8.5	89.5	10.5	14
428,556	407,647	20,909	345,506	326,602	18,904	97.5	2.5	96.7	3.3	95.1	4.9	94.5	5.5	15
908,420	543,755	364,665	716,258	392,545	353,713	67.8	32.2	65.6	34.4	59.9	40.1	52.6	47.4	16
7,268,894	5,298,111	1,970,783	6,003,174	3,899,737	2,103,437	82.7	17.3	78.8	21.2	72.9	27.1	65.0	35.0	17
1,883,669	1,329,162	554,507	1,444,933	876,638	568,295	78.4	21.6	75.2	24.8	70.6	29.4	60.7	39.3	18
6,302,115	3,448,610	2,853,505	5,258,113	2,557,397	2,700,716	64.3	35.7	60.4	39.6	54.7	45.3	48.6	51.4	19
4,157,545	1,998,382	2,159,163	3,672,329	1,504,390	2,167,939	63.8	36.2	55.9	44.1	48.1	51.9	41.0	59.0	20
2,516,462	862,680	1,653,773	2,192,404	590,039	1,602,365	50.6	49.4	42.4	57.6	34.3	65.7	26.9	73.1	21
4,821,550	2,616,368	2,205,182	3,826,352	1,710,172	2,116,180	67.9	32.1	61.7	38.3	54.3	45.7	44.7	55.3	22
2,420,982	952,323	1,468,659	2,093,890	730,204	1,363,596	61.1	38.9	47.2	52.8	39.3	60.7	34.9	65.1	23
2,069,042	790,213	1,278,829	1,693,330	562,286	1,131,044	47.3	52.7	43.0	57.0	38.2	61.8	33.2	66.8	24
1,751,394	598,100	1,153,294	1,310,283	443,049	867,234	44.1	55.9	41.0	59.0	34.1	65.9	33.8	66.2	25
2,231,853	572,386	1,659,467	1,912,297	405,764	1,506,533	36.4	63.6	30.6	69.4	25.6	74.4	21.2	78.8	26
3,106,665	1,128,104	1,978,561	2,679,185	856,966	1,822,219	46.6	53.4	42.5	57.5	36.3	63.7	32.0	68.0	27
319,146	23,413	295,733	190,983	10,643	180,340	13.6	86.4	11.0	89.0	7.3	92.7	5.6	94.4	28
401,570	40,936	360,634	348,600	28,555	320,045	16.0	84.0	13.1	86.9	10.2	89.8	8.2	91.8	29
1,066,300	252,702	813,598	1,062,656	291,641	771,015	31.3	68.7	26.1	73.9	23.7	76.3	27.4	72.6	30
1,470,495	330,903	1,139,592	1,428,108	272,201	1,155,907	34.9	65.1	29.2	70.8	22.5	77.5	19.1	80.9	31
184,735	85,717	99,018	168,493	71,067	97,426	54.2	45.8	48.0	52.0	46.4	53.6	42.2	57.8	32
1,188,044	591,206	596,838	1,042,390	495,702	546,688	60.0	40.0	50.8	49.2	49.8	50.2	47.6	52.4	33
278,718	278,718	......	230,392	230,392	......	100.0	....	100.0	....	100.0	....	100.0	....	34
1,854,184	340,007	1,514,117	1,655,980	282,721	1,373,259	29.2	70.8	23.1	76.9	18.3	81.7	17.1	82.9	35
958,800	125,465	833,335	762,794	81,365	681,429	25.2	74.8	18.7	81.3	13.1	86.9	10.7	89.3	36
1,893,810	186,790	1,707,020	1,617,949	115,759	1,502,190	19.2	80.8	14.4	85.6	9.9	90.1	7.2	92.8	37
1,340,316	171,256	1,169,060	1,151,149	116,183	1,034,966	17.5	82.5	14.8	85.2	12.8	87.2	10.1	89.9	38
2,216,331	346,382	1,869,949	1,837,353	257,472	1,579,881	25.1	74.9	20.6	79.4	15.6	84.4	14.0	86.0	39
528,542	107,031	421,511	391,422	77,358	314,064	36.7	63.3	29.1	70.9	20.3	79.7	19.8	80.2	40
2,147,174	467,668	1,679,506	1,858,635	356,713	1,501,922	26.2	73.8	24.3	75.7	21.8	78.2	19.2	80.8	41
2,020,616	326,639	1,693,977	1,767,518	238,394	1,529,124	26.1	73.9	20.2	79.8	16.2	83.8	13.5	86.5	42
1,828,697	216,714	1,611,983	1,513,401	152,235	1,361,166	21.7	78.3	17.3	82.7	11.9	88.1	10.1	89.9	43
1,551,270	120,035	1,431,235	1,289,600	69,966	1,219,634	13.4	86.6	11.5	88.5	7.7	92.3	5.4	94.6	44
1,311,564	111,733	1,199,831	1,128,211	73,159	1,055,052	16.6	83.4	12.9	87.1	8.5	91.5	6.5	93.5	45
1,381,625	366,288	1,015,337	1,118,588	283,845	834,743	34.9	65.1	30.0	70.0	26.5	73.5	25.4	74.6	46
790,391	58,417	731,974	258,657	9,484	249,173	26.6	73.4	19.3	80.7	7.4	92.6	3.7	96.3	47
3,048,710	520,759	2,527,951	2,235,527	349,511	1,886,016	32.4	67.6	24.1	75.9	17.1	82.9	15.6	84.4	48
243,329	84,554	158,775	142,924	38,787	104,137	31.3	68.7	35.5	64.5	34.7	65.3	27.1	72.9	49
161,772	10,003	151,769	88,548	......	88,548	27.6	72.4	21.5	78.5	6.2	93.8	......	100.0	50
92,531	26,657	65,874	62,555	21,484	41,071	29.5	70.5	29.0	70.4	28.8	71.2	34.3	65.7	51
539,700	260,651	279,049	413,249	185,905	227,344	48.2	51.8	50.7	49.3	48.3	51.7	45.0	55.0	52
195,310	27,381	167,929	160,282	9,970	150,312	18.0	82.0	14.2	85.8	14.0	86.0	6.2	93.8	53
122,931	19,495	103,436	88,243	8,302	79,941	35.2	64.8	31.0	69.0	15.9	84.1	9.4	90.6	54
276,749	105,427	171,322	210,779	75,155	135,624	48.0	52.0	46.3	53.7	38.1	61.9	35.7	64.3	55
42,335	7,195	35,140	47,355	16,024	31,331	19.7	80.3	16.3	83.7	17.0	83.0	33.8	66.2	56
518,103	211,477	306,626	357,232	127,178	230,054	55.2	44.8	53.0	47.0	40.8	59.2	35.6	64.4	57
413,536	133,180	280,356	317,704	85,093	232,611	49.9	50.1	45.6	54.4	32.2	67.8	26.8	73.2	58
1,485,053	777,699	707,354	1,213,398	589,464	623,934	68.0	32.0	61.8	38.2	52.4	47.6	48.6	51.4	59

POPULATION.

8

PER CENT URBAN IN TOTAL POPULATION, BY STATES: 1920.

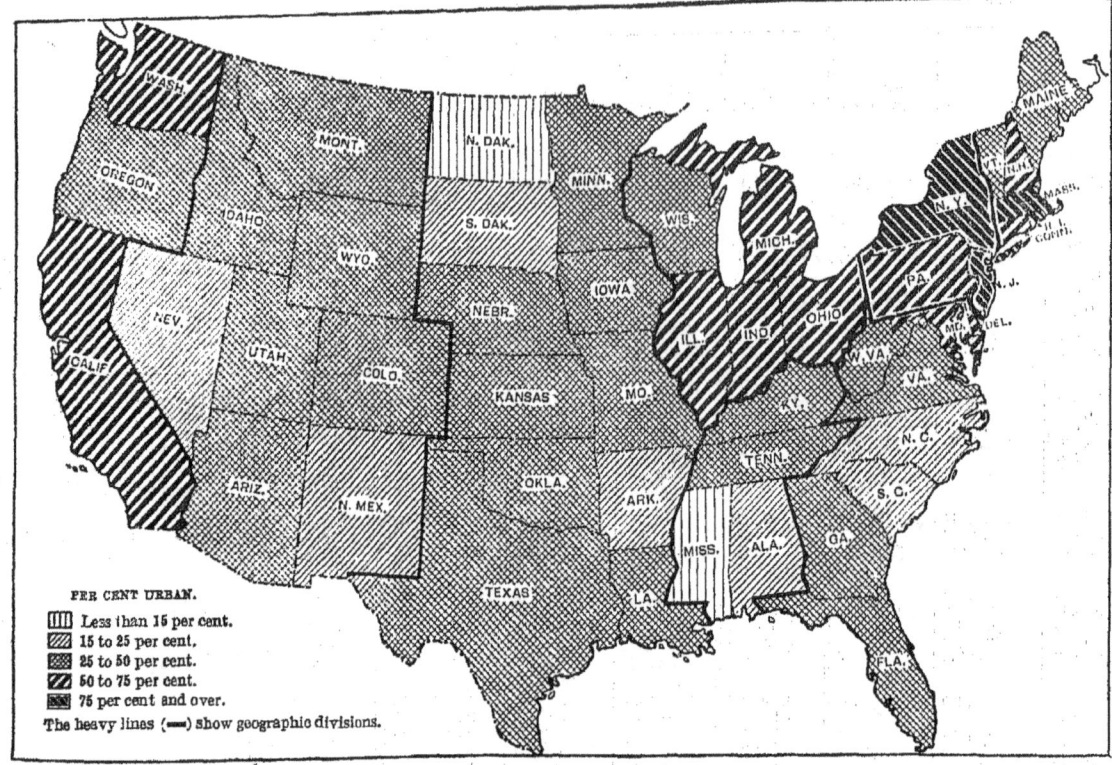

PER CENT URBAN IN TOTAL POPULATION, BY STATES: 1910.

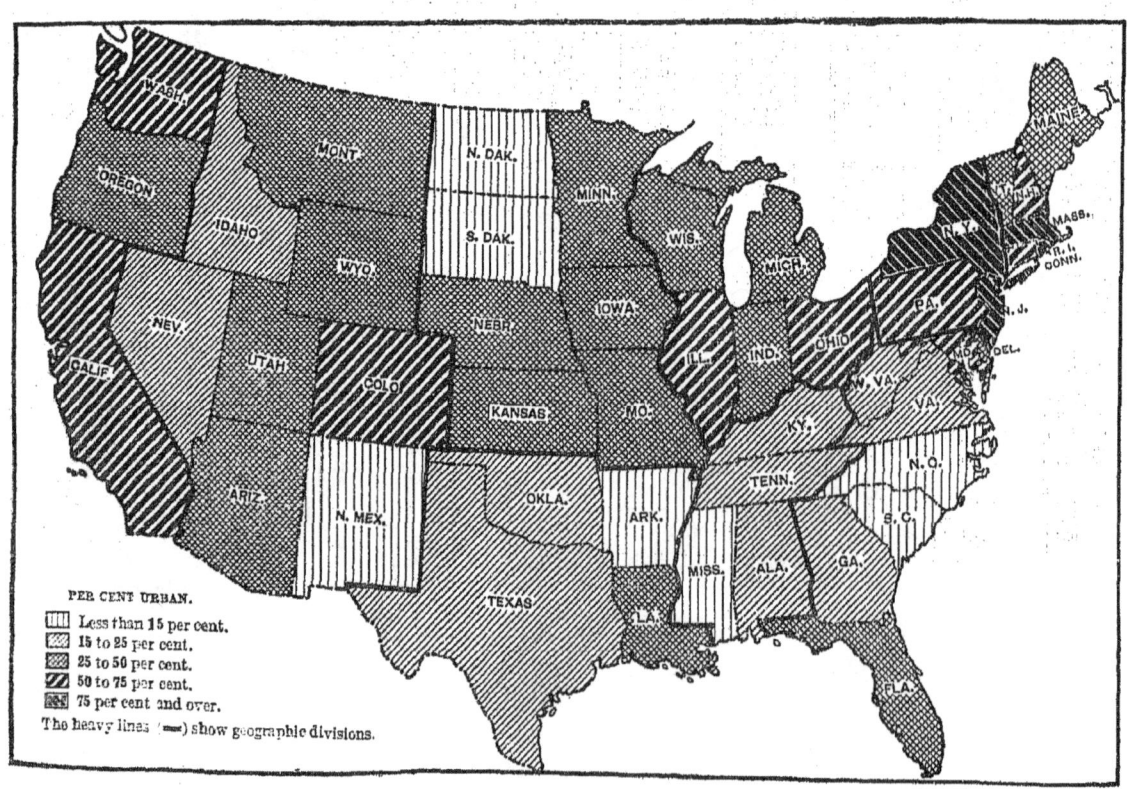

URBAN AND RURAL.

PER CENT URBAN IN TOTAL POPULATION, BY STATES: 1890–1920.

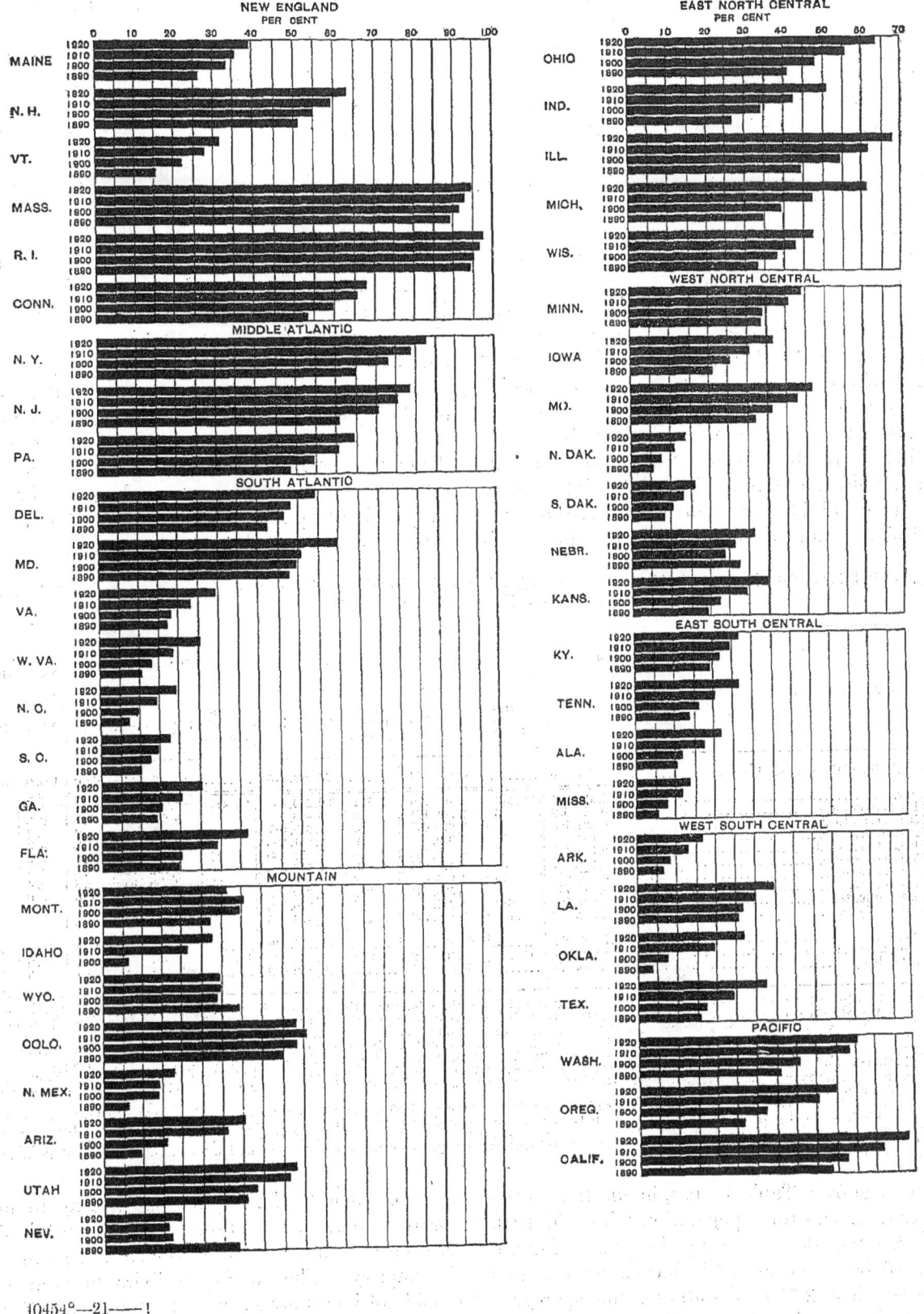

50   POPULATION.

COMMUNITIES CLASSIFIED ACCORDING TO SIZE.

United States as a whole.—In addition to classifying the population according to the broad groupings urban and rural, a further and more detailed analysis may be made by comparing the proportions of the total population residing in communities of specified size groups at each of the last four censuses. In making any study of this comparison, it must be kept in mind that the figures for a given group of cities at one census do not relate to exactly the same cities as those for the corresponding group at another census, since many places, as their population increases (or, in a few cases, decreases), pass from one group to another at successive censuses.

Table 31 shows, for the United States as a whole, the number of places constituting each of the specified classes at each of the last four censuses, the combined population of each group, and the percentage which the population of each group represented of the total for the country. Under the heading "Urban territory," which in the previous discussion has been considered as a unit, the communities of 2,500 inhabitants or more are subdivided, according to size, into nine classes of places, and the population of the rural territory is also subdivided by distinguishing the population of incorporated places having fewer than 2,500 inhabitants from that of unincorporated territory. The urban classes for 1920, 1910, and 1900 consist of incorporated municipalities in all parts of the country and of towns in Massachusetts, New Hampshire, and Rhode Island. At the census of 1890 separate returns for urban communities were not confined to incorporated places, and, as the incorporated places were not distinguished from the unincorporated, the number of the former class can not be exactly determined for that year. The number of places having 2,500 or more inhabitants which are not incorporated as municipalities is, however, very small except in Massachusetts, New Hampshire, and Rhode Island. For the urban class, therefore, the figures for 1890 are fairly comparable with those for the other census years covered by the table. In order to make the figures for incorporated places having fewer than 2,500 inhabitants in 1890 comparable with the corresponding figures for the more recent censuses, the number of such places in 1890 has been estimated according to the method adopted in compiling the census reports for 1900. (See note 3, Table 31.)

TABLE 31.—DISTRIBUTION OF POPULATION IN GROUPS OF CITIES CLASSIFIED ACCORDING TO SIZE, AND IN RURAL TERRITORY: 1890–1920.

CLASS OF PLACES.	1920		1910		1900		1890		PER CENT OF TOTAL POPULATION.			
	Number of places.	Population.	Number of places.	Population.	Number of places.	Population.	Number of places.	Population.	1920	1910	1900	1890
Total population of the United States		105,710,620		91,972,266		75,994,575		62,947,714	100.0	100.0	100.0	100.0
Urban territory	[1] 2,787	54,304,603	[1] 2,313	42,166,120	[1] 1,801	30,380,433	[1] 1,417	22,298,359	51.4	45.8	40.0	35.4
Places of 1,000,000 or more	3	10,145,532	3	8,501,174	3	6,429,474	3	3,662,115	9.6	9.2	8.5	5.8
Places of 500,000 to 1,000,000	9	6,223,769	5	3,010,607	3	1,645,087	1	800,343	5.9	3.3	2.2	1.3
Places of 250,000 to 500,000	13	4,540,838	11	3,949,839	9	2,861,296	7	2,447,608	4.3	4.3	3.8	3.9
Places of 100,000 to 250,000	43	6,519,187	31	4,840,458	23	3,272,490	17	2,781,894	6.2	5.3	4.3	4.4
Places of 50,000 to 100,000	76	5,265,747	59	4,178,915	40	2,709,338	30	2,022,822	5.0	4.5	3.6	3.2
Places of 25,000 to 50,000	143	5,075,041	119	4,026,045	82	2,800,627	66	2,208,780	4.8	4.4	3.7	3.6
Places of 10,000 to 25,000	459	6,942,742	367	5,524,434	280	4,338,250	228	3,420,247	6.6	6.0	5.7	5.4
Places of 5,000 to 10,000	721	4,997,794	612	4,254,856	468	3,220,766	339	2,372,717	4.7	4.6	4.2	3.8
Places of 2,500 to 5,000	1,820	4,593,953	1,106	3,879,732	893	3,103,105	726	2,505,827	4.3	4.2	4.1	4.0
Rural territory		51,406,017		49,806,146		45,614,142		40,649,355	48.6	54.2	60.0	64.6
Incorporated places of less than 2,500	[2] 12,905	8,969,241	11,832	8,169,149	8,030	6,301,533	[3] 6,400	4,757,974	8.5	8.9	8.3	7.6
Other rural territory		42,436,776		41,636,997		39,312,609		35,891,381	40.1	45.3	51.7	57.0

[1] The total number of places of certain classes for the United States as a whole is less than the sum of the numbers shown for the individual states of the country, for the reason that each of three cities lies in two adjoining states, namely, Bristol (Virginia and Tennessee), Texarkana (Arkansas and Texas), and Union City (Indiana and Ohio), and is counted in each state. Moreover, one of these cities lies in two geographic divisions (South Atlantic and East South Central), and is counted in both. Each of these cities consists of two incorporated municipalities, but each is, from the statistical standpoint, one city and should be classed according to its total population. In each case that part of the population living in each state, whatever its number, is credited to the group of cities to which, according to its total population, the city belongs. Classed in this manner, Bristol fell in 1920 and 1910 in the class of cities having 10,000 to 25,000 inhabitants, and in 1900 and 1890 in the 5,000–10,000 class; Texarkana fell, in 1920, 1910, and 1900, in the 10,000–25,000 class, and in 1890 in the 5,000–10,000 class; and Union City fell at each census from 1890 to 1920 in the 2,500–5,000 class.

[2] Includes 48 places not returned separately.

[3] The number of incorporated places can not be exactly determined from the returns of the 1890 census, at which incorporated places were not distinguished from unincorporated ones, and very small places, whether incorporated or not, were not enumerated separately. It has been assumed that those places were incorporated in 1890 which were returned separately in that year and were returned in 1900 as incorporated. (See Reports of the Twelfth Census: 1900, Population, Vol. 1, p. lviii.) The figures given for 1890 in this table for incorporated places having fewer than 2,500 inhabitants may, therefore, include the population of some unincorporated places and exclude that of some incorporated places.

It will be seen from Table 31 that, in addition to the 51.4 per cent of the total population which in 1920 resided in communities classed by the Census Bureau as urban, 8.5 per cent resided in incorporated places having fewer than 2,500 inhabitants, the aggregate for the two classes being 63,273,844, or 59.9 per cent of the total population. Although this aggregate does not include the population residing in unincorporated villages, it approximates the total of what may be described as the agglomerated population of the country. The population living in rural territory outside of incorporated places—numbering 42,436,776 and constituting 40.1 per cent of the total—although it includes a small proportion living in villages, is in

URBAN AND RURAL.   51

the main a scattered population and is more essentially rural in character than the total rural given in Table 31, which includes the inhabitants of small incorporated places. It may be noted that the conditions of environment and of occupation for the population of small as well as of large municipalities are essentially different from those which prevail in distinctly rural districts.

The group of cities having 1,000,000 or more inhabitants has comprised the same three cities—New York, Chicago, and Philadelphia—at each of the four censuses covered by the table; but each of the other groups has been made up of an increasing number of cities from census to census. The proportion which the population of each group forms of the total for the country has also increased from census to census, with very few exceptions. The only exception for the decade 1910–1920 appears in the case of the group comprising cities of 250,000 to 500,000, which contained 4.3 per cent of the total population in each of the two census years. The explanation is to be found in the passage of four important cities—Buffalo, Detroit, Los Angeles, and San Francisco—from this group to that next above, the aggregate population of these four cities being considerably greater than that of the six cities which entered the group from that next below during the same period.

In Table 32 the cities are grouped so as to throw into one aggregate the total population living in all cities having more than the specified minimum.

TABLE 32.—NUMBER AND POPULATION OF PLACES OF EACH SPECIFIED SIZE: 1890–1920.

CLASS OF PLACES.	1920	1910	1900	1890
Number of places of specified size:				
25,000 or more..............	287	228	160	124
100,000 or more.............	68	50	38	28
250,000 or more.............	25	19	15	11
500,000 or more.............	12	8	6	4
1,000,000 or more...........	3	3	3	3
Population living in places of specified size:				
25,000 or more..............	37,770,114	28,507,098	19,718,312	13,980,568
100,000 or more.............	27,429,326	20,302,138	14,208,347	9,697,960
250,000 or more.............	20,910,130	15,461,680	10,935,857	6,916,066
500,000 or more.............	16,369,301	11,511,841	8,074,561	4,468,458
1,000,000 or more...........	10,145,532	8,501,174	6,429,474	3,662,115
Percentage of total population living in places of specified size:				
25,000 or more..............	35.7	31.0	25.9	22.2
100,000 or more.............	25.9	22.1	18.7	15.4
250,000 or more.............	19.8	16.8	14.4	11.0
500,000 or more.............	15.5	12.5	10.6	7.1
1,000,000 or more...........	9.6	9.2	8.5	5.8

It will be noted that the proportion of the population living in cities having 500,000 inhabitants or more has more than doubled since 1890. This great increase is due in part, however, to the fact that the number of cities having more than 500,000 inhabitants was three times as great in 1920 as in 1890. The increase, from 5.8 per cent in 1890 to 9.6 per cent in

1920, in the proportion which the population living in cities having 1,000,000 inhabitants or more forms of the total, becomes more striking when it is remembered that this results entirely from the growth of the three cities—New York, Chicago, and Philadelphia—which have composed this group since 1890.

Divisions and states.—The population, in 1920, of urban places, classified in five size groups, and of rural districts, is shown by geographic sections and divisions in Table 34, from which the percentages in Table 33 are derived. The number of urban groups shown in these tables has been reduced to five because of the very great differences which appear among the several divisions with respect to the distribution of the urban population among communities of various sizes. Only two of the nine divisions contained cities having more than 1,000,000 inhabitants in 1920, and one division contained no city having 250,000 or more inhabitants. The grouping adopted is such as to show for each division at least two cities belonging to each group.

TABLE 33.—PER CENT OF POPULATION IN URBAN PLACES OF SPECIFIED SIZES AND IN RURAL DISTRICTS, BY SECTIONS AND DIVISIONS: 1920.

SECTION AND DIVISION.	URBAN PLACES OF—					Rural districts.
	100,000 or more.	25,000 to 100,000.	10,000 to 25,000.	5,000 to 10,000.	2,500 to 5,000.	
United States..........	25.9	9.8	6.6	4.7	4.3	48.6
The North.............	34.0	11.7	7.9	5.4	4.3	36.7
New England...........	29.8	23.0	14.3	8.1	4.2	20.8
Middle Atlantic.........	47.4	10.6	7.6	5.0	4.3	25.1
East North Central.......	31.6	12.5	7.2	5.5	4.1	39.2
West North Central.......	17.0	5.8	5.6	4.3	4.9	62.3
The South..............	10.3	6.3	4.2	3.3	4.0	71.9
South Atlantic..........	12.6	8.0	3.8	3.1	3.4	69.0
East South Central.......	7.8	4.1	3.9	2.8	3.8	77.6
West South Central.......	9.3	5.9	5.0	3.9	4.8	71.0
The West...............	26.4	8.7	6.2	5.5	5.8	47.4
Mountain..............	11.2	5.3	6.8	6.6	6.5	63.6
Pacific................	35.5	10.8	5.8	4.8	5.4	37.6
East of the Mississippi River..	29.7	11.1	7.0	4.8	4.0	43.4
West of the Mississippi River.	17.2	6.7	5.6	4.5	5.1	60.9

It will be seen from Table 33 that the concentration of the population in cities of 100,000 and over is greatest in the Middle Atlantic and the Pacific divisions, bordering on the Atlantic and the Pacific seaboards, respectively. Disregarding the Pacific division, by far the greatest concentration in large cities is found in the Northern states east of the Mississippi River. In the North as a whole the proportion in cities of 100,000 or more was over three times as great as in the South and was more than one-fourth greater than in the West. In the section east of the Mississippi River the corresponding proportion was nearly three-fourths greater than in that west of the Mississippi.

POPULATION.

TABLE 34.—NUMBER AND POPULATION OF URBAN PLACES OF SPECIFIED SIZES, AND POPULATION OF RURAL DISTRICTS, BY SECTIONS AND DIVISIONS: 1920.

SECTION AND DIVISION.	URBAN PLACES OF—										Rural districts—population.
	100,000 or more.		25,000 to 100,000.		10,000 to 25,000.		5,000 to 10,000.		2,500 to 5,000.		
	Number of places.	Population.	Number of places.	Population.	Number of places.	Population.	Number of places.	Population.	Number of places.	Population.	
United States	68	27,420,326	219	10,340,788	¹459	6,942,742	721	4,997,794	¹1,320	4,593,053	51,408,017
The North	45	21,660,731	158	7,467,964	328	5,000,569	487	3,425,197	786	2,759,851	23,367,533
New England	11	2,203,306	35	1,699,018	68	1,054,768	85	598,045	93	309,936	1,535,836
Middle Atlantic	15	10,549,599	48	2,353,654	111	1,697,000	158	1,113,921	272	958,412	5,588,549
East North Central	12	6,775,993	61	2,681,461	101	1,543,115	166	1,172,577	246	876,126	8,426,271
West North Central	7	2,131,833	14	733,831	48	705,677	78	540,654	175	615,377	7,816,877
The South	15	3,416,347	44	2,034,608	95	1,393,804	161	1,083,858	387	1,315,216	23,821,975
South Atlantic	6	1,769,625	25	1,119,452	36	534,462	64	436,404	142	478,849	9,651,480
East South Central	4	694,390	7	367,926	23	343,900	37	247,470	98	340,521	6,899,100
West South Central	5	952,332	12	607,225	36	515,442	60	399,984	147	495,846	7,271,395
The West	8	2,352,248	17	778,221	37	548,369	73	488,739	147	518,886	4,216,509
Mountain	2	374,601	5	176,623	16	227,902	32	218,948	62	216,906	2,121,121
Pacific	6	1,977,647	12	601,598	21	320,467	41	269,791	85	301,980	2,095,388
East of the Mississippi River	48	21,992,913	176	8,221,511	338	5,173,254	510	3,568,417	851	2,993,844	32,101,236
West of the Mississippi River	20	5,436,413	43	2,119,277	121	1,769,488	211	1,429,377	469	1,030,109	19,304,781

¹ See note 1 to Table 31, p. 50.

In the North as a whole, in the section east of the Mississippi River considered as a whole, and in each of the three northern divisions lying east of the Mississippi, the proportion of the population in each group of cities is greater than in the group next below; but in the South as a whole, in each southern division separately, and in each division west of the Mississippi River except the Mountain division, the proportion was greater for cities of 2,500 to 5,000 than for those of 5,000 to 10,000.

The population of the several divisions and states at the last four Federal censuses is distributed among urban places grouped according to specified limits of population, and rural districts, in Table 35. Including the District of Columbia, which is wholly urban and is independent of any state, the 287 urban places having 25,000 inhabitants or more in 1920 are distributed among 41 states, the 7 states in which there were no cities above this size being Idaho, Mississippi, Nevada, New Mexico, North Dakota, Vermont, and Wyoming.

URBAN AND RURAL.

53

TABLE 35.—NUMBER AND AGGREGATE POPULATION OF URBAN PLACES OF SPECIFIED SIZES, AND POPULATION OF RURAL DISTRICTS, BY DIVISIONS AND STATES: 1890–1920.

[The total number of cities of certain classes for the United States as a whole, and for certain geographic divisions, is less than the sum of the numbers shown for the individual states of the country or of the divisions, as explained in note 1 to Table 31, p. 50.]

DIVISION, STATE, AND CENSUS YEAR.	100,000 or more Number of places	Population.	25,000 to 100,000 Number of places	Population.	10,000 to 25,000 Number of places	Population.	5,000 to 10,000 Number of places	Population.	2,500 to 5,000 Number of places	Population.	Rural districts—population.	100,000 or more	25,000 to 100,000	10,000 to 25,000	5,000 to 10,000	2,500 to 5,000	Rural districts.
UNITED STATES:																	
1920	68	27,429,326	219	10,340,788	1 459	6,942,742	721	4,997,794	1 1,320	4,593,953	51,406,017	25.9	9.8	6.6	4.7	4.3	48.6
1910	50	20,302,138	178	8,204,960	1 367	5,524,434	612	4,254,856	1 1,106	3,879,732	49,806,146	22.1	8.9	6.0	4.6	4.2	54.2
1900	38	14,208,347	122	5,509,965	1 280	4,338,250	1 468	3,220,766	1 893	3,103,105	45,614,142	18.7	7.3	5.7	4.2	4.1	60.0
1890	28	9,697,960	96	4,291,608	228	3,429,247	1 339	2,372,717	1 726	2,506,827	40,649,355	15.4	6.8	5.4	3.8	4.0	64.6
GEOGRAPHIC DIVISIONS.																	
NEW ENGLAND:																	
1920	11	2,203,306	35	1,609,018	68	1,054,768	85	598,045	93	309,936	1,535,836	29.8	23.0	14.3	8.1	4.2	20.8
1910	8	1,606,984	33	1,601,269	56	851,779	89	628,603	87	309,447	1,554,599	24.5	24.4	13.0	9.6	4.7	23.7
1900	5	1,067,800	25	1,250,258	51	810,334	88	604,527	90	320,508	1,538,590	19.1	22.4	14.5	10.8	5.7	27.5
1890	2	580,623	22	1,026,947	41	647,318	63	448,489	122	430,522	1,560,850	12.4	21.8	13.8	9.5	9.3	33.2
MIDDLE ATLANTIC:																	
1920	15	10,549,599	48	2,353,654	111	1,697,009	158	1,113,921	272	958,412	5,588,540	47.4	10.6	7.6	5.0	4.3	25.1
1910	11	8,599,877	44	2,110,782	91	1,310,807	130	875,771	223	787,136	5,592,519	44.5	10.9	7.0	4.5	4.1	29.0
1900	11	6,465,480	29	1,315,158	67	1,027,611	93	636,600	179	631,034	5,378,795	41.8	8.5	6.6	4.1	4.1	34.8
1890	9	4,440,905	23	1,084,175	52	770,956	75	547,893	139	483,843	5,372,448	35.0	8.5	6.1	4.3	3.8	42.3
EAST N. CENTRAL:																	
1920	12	6,775,993	61	2,681,461	101	1,543,115	166	1,172,577	1 246	876,126	8,426,271	31.6	12.5	7.2	5.5	4.1	39.2
1910	10	4,761,966	38	1,553,809	88	1,390,143	154	1,086,197	1 232	819,156	8,633,350	26.1	8.5	7.6	6.0	4.5	47.3
1900	8	3,403,810	23	935,320	70	1,252,955	130	899,043	1 211	728,847	8,765,606	21.3	5.9	7.8	5.6	4.6	54.8
1890	6	2,173,891	16	698,122	64	947,440	95	652,288	1 178	625,440	8,381,124	16.1	5.2	7.0	4.8	4.6	62.2
WEST N. CENTRAL:																	
1920	7	2,131,833	14	733,831	48	705,677	78	540,654	175	615,377	7,816,877	17.0	5.8	5.6	4.3	4.9	62.3
1910	5	1,575,658	17	801,931	33	455,439	71	498,769	156	541,919	7,764,205	13.5	6.9	3.9	4.3	4.7	66.7
1900	6	1,310,307	12	448,447	22	335,850	59	402,293	132	449,617	7,400,879	12.7	4.3	3.2	3.9	4.3	71.5
1890	5	1,022,832	9	354,998	20	312,545	41	286,188	98	332,256	6,623,293	11.5	4.0	3.5	3.2	3.7	74.2
SOUTH ATLANTIC:																	
1920	6	1,769,025	25	1,119,452	1 36	534,462	64	436,404	142	478,849	9,651,480	12.6	8.0	3.8	3.1	3.4	69.0
1910	4	1,172,021	16	712,387	1 27	444,714	58	397,081	105	365,950	9,102,742	9.6	5.8	3.6	3.3	3.0	74.6
1900	2	787,679	9	514,853	27	429,391	1 31	203,328	84	297,385	8,210,818	7.5	4.9	4.1	1.9	2.8	78.6
1890	2	664,831	8	409,189	19	286,374	1 21	145,079	68	222,546	7,129,903	7.5	4.6	3.2	1.0	2.5	80.5
EAST S. CENTRAL:																	
1920	4	694,390	7	367,926	1 23	343,900	37	247,470	98	340,521	6,899,100	7.8	4.1	3.9	2.8	3.8	77.6
1910	4	598,082	7	289,285	15	220,364	33	229,933	67	236,565	6,835,672	7.1	3.4	2.6	2.7	2.8	81.3
1900	2	307,051	9	348,494	7	98,512	22	154,241	65	222,758	6,416,701	4.1	4.6	1.3	2.0	3.0	85.0
1890	1	161,129	6	264,388	9	147,837	16	111,454	39	132,500	5,611,846	2.5	4.1	2.3	1.7	2.1	87.3
WEST S. CENTRAL:																	
1920	5	952,332	12	607,225	1 36	515,442	60	399,984	147	495,846	7,271,395	9.3	5.9	5.0	3.9	4.8	71.0
1910	1	339,075	12	636,814	127	354,582	33	220,386	117	397,599	6,827,078	3.9	7.2	4.0	2.6	4.5	77.7
1900	1	287,104	6	243,376	1 13	174,907	22	156,377	56	195,433	5,475,093	4.4	3.7	2.7	2.4	3.0	83.8
1890	1	242,039	5	158,255	9	118,470	1 14	94,704	32	102,522	4,024,984	5.1	3.3	2.5	2.0	2.2	84.9
MOUNTAIN:																	
1920	2	374,001	5	176,623	16	227,902	32	218,948	62	210,906	2,121,121	11.2	5.3	6.8	6.6	6.5	63.6
1910	1	213,381	5	230,995	12	144,593	25	174,020	54	184,522	1,686,006	8.1	8.8	5.5	6.6	7.0	64.0
1900	1	133,859	3	112,158	7	99,787	11	71,664	38	123,895	1,133,294	8.0	6.7	6.0	4.3	7.4	67.7
1890	1	106,713	1	44,843	7	97,218	8	47,185	18	59,668	858,308	8.8	3.7	8.0	3.9	4.9	70.7
PACIFIC:																	
1920	6	1,977,647	12	601,598	21	320,467	41	269,791	85	301,980	2,095,388	35.5	10.8	5.8	4.8	5.4	37.6
1910	6	1,435,094	6	267,688	19	307,013	19	135,096	65	237,438	1,809,975	34.2	6.4	7.3	3.2	5.7	43.2
1900	2	445,261	6	341,901	7	108,903	13	92,693	38	133,508	1,294,336	18.4	14.1	4.5	3.8	5.5	53.6
1890	1	298,997	6	250,691	7	101,080	7	39,437	32	111,530	1,086,599	15.8	13.3	5.4	2.1	5.9	57.5
NEW ENGLAND.																	
Maine:																	
1920			3	127,041	5	77,189	11	76,095	6	19,244	468,445	....	16.5	10.1	9.9	2.5	61.0
1910			2	84,818	5	81,615	11	74,084	6	21,731	480,123	....	11.4	11.0	10.0	2.9	64.7
1900			1	50,145	6	96,867	10	66,759	5	19,056	461,639	....	7.2	13.9	9.6	2.7	66.5
1890			1	36,425	5	77,024	7	48,154	3	12,178	487,305	....	5.5	11.7	7.3	1.8	73.7
New Hampshire:																	
1920			2	106,703	6	86,976	6	43,747	13	42,275	163,322	....	24.1	19.6	9.9	9.5	36.9
1910			2	96,068	6	78,044	6	40,074	12	40,913	175,473	....	22.3	18.1	9.3	9.5	40.8
1900			1	56,987	4	67,374	7	53,926	14	47,982	185,319	....	13.8	16.4	13.1	11.7	45.0
1890			1	44,126	3	49,105	6	42,584	18	56,664	184,051	....	11.7	13.0	11.3	15.0	48.9
Vermont:																	
1920					3	47,741	6	41,714	5	20,521	242,452	....	....	13.5	11.8	5.8	68.8
1910					3	44,748	5	33,658	6	20,511	257,039	....	....	12.6	9.5	5.8	72.2
1900					2	30,139	6	37,572	2	8,120	267,810	....	....	8.8	10.9	2.4	77.9
1890					1	14,590	2	13,706	6	22,342	281,784	....	....	4.4	4.1	6.7	84.8
Massachusetts:																	
1920	7	1,521,583	20	1,028,383	39	594,111	47	321,312	56	184,859	202,108	39.5	26.7	15.4	8.3	4.8	5.2
1910	5	1,146,990	20	1,008,488	30	450,898	49	342,831	48	170,156	241,049	34.1	30.0	13.4	10.2	5.2	7.2
1900	3	784,176	17	852,988	27	413,698	46	310,720	57	205,516	238,248	28.0	30.4	14.7	11.1	7.3	8.5
1890	1	448,477	15	706,723	21	319,886	35	250,050	77	278,718	235,093	20.0	31.6	14.3	11.2	12.4	10.5
Rhode Island:																	
1920	1	237,595	4	167,406	6	96,361	8	61,345	8	26,473	15,217	39.3	27.7	15.9	10.1	4.4	2.5
1910	1	224,326	4	143,525	4	69,776	9	63,951	7	23,112	17,956	41.3	26.5	12.9	11.8	4.3	3.3
1900	1	175,597	2	67,435	5	87,405	7	49,008	8	28,202	20,909	41.0	15.7	20.4	11.4	6.6	4.9
1890	1	132,146	1	27,633	4	78,403	8	57,240	9	31,180	18,904	38.2	8.0	22.7	16.6	9.0	5.5
Connecticut:																	
1920	3	444,128	6	269,425	9	152,390	7	53,832	5	16,564	444,292	32.2	19.5	11.0	3.9	1.2	32.2
1910	2	235,659	5	268,375	8	126,698	9	74,041	8	27,024	382,959	21.1	24.1	11.4	6.6	2.4	34.4
1900	1	108,027	4	222,703	7	114,851	12	86,542	4	11,632	364,665	11.9	24.5	12.6	9.5	1.3	40.1
1890			4	212,040	7	108,310	5	36,755	9	35,440	353,713	....	28.4	14.5	4.9	4.7	47.4

1 See note 1 to Table 31, p. 50.

POPULATION.

54

TABLE 35.—NUMBER AND AGGREGATE POPULATION OF URBAN PLACES OF SPECIFIED SIZES, AND POPULATION OF RURAL DISTRICTS, BY DIVISIONS AND STATES: 1890-1920—Continued.

[See note at head of this table, p. 53.]

DIVISION, STATE, AND CENSUS YEAR.	100,000 or more — Number of places	100,000 or more — Population	25,000 to 100,000 — Number of places	25,000 to 100,000 — Population	10,000 to 25,000 — Number of places	10,000 to 25,000 — Population	5,000 to 10,000 — Number of places	5,000 to 10,000 — Population	2,500 to 5,000 — Number of places	2,500 to 5,000 — Population	Rural districts—population.	Per cent 100,000 or more	Per cent 25,000 to 100,000	Per cent 10,000 to 25,000	Per cent 5,000 to 10,000	Per cent 2,500 to 5,000	Per cent Rural districts
MIDDLE ATLANTIC.																	
New York:																	
1920	6	6,807,810	16	755,097	36	540,139	30	200,606	81	286,192	1,795,383	65.6	7.3	5.2	1.0	2.8	17.3
1910	5	5,646,249	16	685,322	30	439,571	25	162,373	72	251,979	1,928,120	62.0	7.5	4.8	1.8	2.8	21.2
1900	4	4,060,571	8	396,462	28	458,937	26	184,029	56	198,112	1,970,783	55.9	5.5	6.3	2.5	2.7	27.1
1890	4	2,711,204	9	442,324	22	346,523	30	221,375	49	178,311	2,103,437	45.2	7.4	5.8	3.7	3.0	35.0
New Jersey:																	
1920	5	1,084,100	16	718,899	18	267,130	35	242,399	47	162,408	680,964	34.4	22.8	8.5	7.7	5.1	21.6
1910	3	740,848	11	623,079	18	271,936	21	142,066	35	129,281	629,957	20.2	24.6	10.7	5.6	5.1	24.8
1900	3	557,074	7	349,073	14	218,271	16	107,651	27	96,493	554,507	20.6	18.5	11.6	5.7	5.1	29.4
1890	2	344,833	5	275,530	9	125,899	10	74,334	16	56,042	568,295	23.9	10.1	8.7	5.1	3.9	39.3
Pennsylvania:																	
1920	4	2,657,689	16	870,658	57	889,740	93	670,916	144	509,812	3,112,202	30.5	10.1	10.2	7.7	5.8	35.7
1910	3	2,212,780	17	802,381	43	638,300	84	571,332	116	405,876	3,034,442	28.9	10.5	8.3	7.5	5.3	39.6
1900	4	1,847,235	14	569,623	25	350,403	51	344,920	96	336,429	2,853,505	20.3	9.0	5.6	5.5	5.3	45.3
1890	3	1,390,868	9	366,321	21	298,534	35	252,184	74	249,490	2,700,718	26.5	7.0	5.7	4.8	4.7	51.4
EAST NORTH CENTRAL.																	
Ohio:																	
1920	7	2,171,635	14	535,822	29	456,388	44	317,584	[1]54	195,707	2,082,258	37.7	9.3	7.9	5.5	3.4	36.2
1910	5	1,390,839	9	393,371	23	360,984	45	321,860	[1]57	198,089	2,101,978	29.2	8.3	7.6	6.8	4.2	44.1
1900	4	965,052	5	241,866	19	305,089	43	299,714	[1]55	186,661	2,159,103	23.2	5.8	7.3	7.2	4.5	51.9
1890	2	558,261	7	349,709	14	199,186	29	199,899	[1]56	197,365	2,167,039	15.2	9.5	5.4	5.4	5.4	59.0
Indiana:																	
1920	1	314,194	11	559,351	19	298,280	23	166,968	[1]30	144,062	1,447,535	10.7	19.1	10.2	5.7	4.0	49.4
1910	1	233,650	4	245,421	26	339,996	26	188,790	[1]37	135,978	1,557,041	8.7	9.1	12.6	7.0	5.0	57.6
1900	1	169,164	4	176,794	14	218,623	23	161,751	[1]38	136,357	1,653,773	6.7	7.0	8.7	6.4	5.4	65.7
1890	1	105,436	3	116,366	10	143,945	18	119,441	[1]31	104,851	1,002,365	4.8	5.3	6.6	5.4	4.8	73.1
Illinois:																	
1920	1	2,701,705	16	700,310	27	406,143	47	324,046	80	270,949	2,082,127	41.7	10.8	6.3	5.0	4.2	32.1
1910	1	2,185,283	11	434,395	20	331,285	41	286,079	71	239,887	2,161,662	38.8	7.7	5.9	5.1	4.3	38.3
1900	1	1,698,575	6	216,570	19	319,195	27	182,236	61	199,792	2,205,182	35.2	4.5	6.6	3.8	4.1	45.7
1890	1	1,099,850	2	72,518	19	294,926	15	99,207	41	143,671	2,116,180	28.7	1.9	7.7	2.6	3.8	55.3
Michigan:																	
1920	2	1,131,312	12	583,309	14	179,991	32	225,476	33	121,472	1,426,852	30.8	15.9	4.9	6.1	3.3	38.9
1910	2	578,337	7	261,592	15	203,817	24	166,749	31	116,549	1,483,129	20.6	9.3	7.3	5.9	4.1	52.8
1900	1	285,704	4	182,718	14	212,890	22	158,649	30	112,392	1,468,650	11.8	7.5	8.8	6.6	4.6	60.7
1890	1	205,876	3	134,439	11	160,098	18	125,549	30	104,332	1,363,596	9.8	6.4	7.6	6.0	5.0	64.8
Wisconsin:																	
1920	1	457,147	8	302,669	12	202,313	20	138,503	41	143,936	1,387,490	17.4	11.5	7.7	5.3	5.5	52.7
1910	1	373,857	7	219,030	10	160,061	18	122,719	37	128,663	1,329,540	16.0	9.4	6.9	5.3	5.5	57.0
1900	1	285,315	4	117,372	13	197,158	15	96,693	28	93,675	1,278,829	13.8	5.7	9.5	4.7	4.5	61.8
1890	1	204,468	1	25,090	10	149,285	15	108,222	21	75,221	1,131,044	12.1	1.5	8.8	6.4	4.4	66.8
WEST NORTH CENTRAL.																	
Minnesota:																	
1920	2	615,280	1	98,917	8	111,525	16	114,851	32	111,020	1,335,532	25.8	4.1	4.7	4.8	4.7	55.9
1910	2	516,152	1	78,466	5	60,219	16	115,083	24	80,374	1,225,414	24.9	3.8	2.9	5.5	3.9	59.0
1900	2	365,783	1	52,969	3	42,631	11	72,066	20	64,651	1,153,204	20.9	3.0	2.4	4.1	3.7	65.9
1890	2	297,894	1	33,115	2	29,488	6	40,362	12	42,210	867,234	22.7	2.5	2.2	3.1	3.2	66.2
Iowa:																	
1920	1	126,468	6	285,053	11	192,629	18	114,802	45	156,543	1,528,526	5.3	11.9	8.0	4.8	6.5	63.6
1910			8	330,091	9	137,107	9	59,402	43	153,454	1,544,717		14.8	6.2	2.7	6.9	69.4
1900			6	218,259	8	129,096	10	70,618	46	154,413	1,659,407		9.8	5.8	3.2	6.9	74.4
1890			4	145,082	7	115,234	8	56,582	27	88,866	1,506,533		7.6	6.0	3.0	4.6	78.8
Missouri:																	
1920	2	1,097,307	3	147,472	8	110,146	16	109,337	34	122,041	1,817,152	32.2	4.3	3.2	3.2	3.6	53.4
1910	2	935,410	3	144,677	5	70,753	17	120,938	35	127,039	1,894,518	28.4	4.4	2.1	3.7	3.9	57.5
1900	3	841,999	1	26,023	12	51,278	18	120,291	25	88,543	1,978,501	27.1	0.8	1.7	3.9	2.9	63.7
1890	2	584,486	1	52,324	3	48,775	11	73,573	27	97,808	1,822,219	21.8	2.0	1.8	2.7	3.7	68.0
North Dakota:																	
1920					3	46,447	3	18,889	6	22,903	558,033			7.2	2.9	3.5	86.4
1910					2	26,809	3	16,788	5	19,689	513,820			4.6	2.9	3.4	89.0
1900							2	17,241	2	6,172	205,733				5.4	1.9	92.7
1890							1	5,664	1	4,979	180,340				3.0	2.6	94.4
South Dakota:																	
1920			1	25,202	1	14,537	6	41,994	8	20,139	534,675		4.0	2.3	6.6	3.2	84.0
1910					2	24,847	4	27,708	7	24,118	507,215			4.3	4.7	4.1	86.9
1900					1	10,266	1	6,210	7	24,460	360,034			2.6	1.5	6.1	89.8
1890					1	10,177			6	18,378	320,045			2.9		5.3	91.8
Nebraska:																	
1920	1	191,601	1	54,948	1	36,060	9	65,048	17	57,649	891,066	14.8	4.2	2.8	5.0	4.4	68.7
1910	1	124,096	2	70,232	1	10,326	9	61,670	14	44,528	881,362	10.4	5.9	0.9	5.2	3.7	73.9
1900	1	102,555	2	66,170			7	48,004	11	35,973	813,508	9.6	6.2		4.5	3.4	76.3
1890	1	140,452	1	55,154	3	39,361	5	38,811	6	17,863	771,015	13.2	5.2	3.7	3.7	1.7	72.6
Kansas:																	
1920	1	101,177	2	122,239	14	194,333	10	75,733	35	124,482	1,151,293	5.7	6.0	11.0	4.3	7.0	65.1
1910			3	178,465	9	125,378	13	97,180	28	92,707	1,197,159		10.6	7.4	5.7	5.5	70.8
1900			2	85,026	10	102,579	10	67,863	21	75,435	1,139,592		5.8	7.0	4.6	5.1	77.5
1890			2	69,323	4	69,530	10	71,196	19	62,152	1,155,907		4.9	4.9	5.0	4.4	80.9

[1] See note 1 to Table 31, p. 50.

URBAN AND RURAL.

55

TABLE 35.—NUMBER AND AGGREGATE POPULATION OF URBAN PLACES OF SPECIFIED SIZES, AND POPULATION OF RURAL DISTRICTS, BY DIVISIONS AND STATES: 1890–1920—Continued.

[See note at head of this table, p. 53.]

DIVISION, STATE, AND CENSUS YEAR.	100,000 or more No.	100,000 or more Pop.	25,000 to 100,000 No.	25,000 to 100,000 Pop.	10,000 to 25,000 No.	10,000 to 25,000 Pop.	5,000 to 10,000 No.	5,000 to 10,000 Pop.	2,500 to 5,000 No.	2,500 to 5,000 Pop.	Rural districts pop.	% 100,000+	% 25,000–100,000	% 10,000–25,000	% 5,000–10,000	% 2,500–5,000	% Rural
SOUTH ATLANTIC.																	
Delaware:																	
1920	1	110,168							3	10,599	102,236	49.4				4.8	45.8
1910			1	87,411					3	9,674	105,237		43.2			4.8	52.0
1900			1	76,508					3	9,209	99,018		41.4			5.0	53.6
1890			1	61,431					3	9,636	97,426		36.5			5.7	57.8
Maryland:																	
1920	1	733,826	2	57,901	2	22,280	3	21,037	10	34,378	580,239	50.6	4.0	1.5	1.5	2.4	40.0
1910	1	558,485			3	48,757	4	27,734	7	23,214	637,154	43.1		3.8	2.1	1.8	49.2
1900	1	508,957			2	30,719	4	28,842	7	22,688	596,838	42.8		2.6	2.4	1.9	50.2
1890	1	434,439			2	22,847	2	15,797	7	22,619	546,688	41.7		2.2	1.5	2.2	52.4
District of Columbia:																	
1920	1	437,571										100.0					
1910	1	331,069										100.0					
1900	1	278,718										100.0					
1890	1	230,392										100.0					
Virginia:																	
1920	2	287,444	5	201,907	[1] 5	67,639	9	58,694	18	53,300	1,635,203	12.4	8.7	2.9	2.5	2.5	70.8
1910	1	127,628	4	165,010	[1] 6	95,532	6	36,764	15	51,595	1,585,083	6.2	8.0	4.6	1.8	2.5	76.0
1900			2	131,674	7	130,300	[1] 6	38,261	12	39,826	1,514,117		7.1	7.0	2.1	2.1	81.7
1890			2	116,259	6	96,460	[1] 5	29,910	12	40,092	1,373,259		7.0	5.8	1.8	2.4	82.9
West Virginia:																	
1920			4	173,862	6	88,494	6	40,052	19	66,599	1,094,694		11.9	6.0	2.7	4.6	74.8
1910			2	72,802	4	62,724	6	49,803	13	42,913	992,877		6.0	5.1	4.1	3.5	81.3
1900			1	38,878	3	34,725	4	24,231	8	27,691	833,335		4.1	3.6	2.5	2.9	86.9
1890			1	34,522	1	10,108	4	22,376	5	14,359	681,429		4.5	1.3	2.9	1.9	89.3
North Carolina:																	
1920			4	156,609	10	153,903	13	89,970	28	89,888	2,068,753		6.1	6.0	3.5	3.5	80.8
1910			2	59,762	5	80,283	13	96,184	20	73,245	1,887,813		2.7	4.0	4.4	3.3	85.6
1900					6	87,447	6	42,181	16	57,162	1,707,020			4.6	2.2	3.0	90.1
1890					4	54,526	3	21,346	11	39,887	1,502,190			3.4	1.3	2.5	92.8
South Carolina:																	
1920			2	105,481	4	67,303	8	56,967	18	64,236	1,389,737		6.3	4.0	3.4	3.8	82.5
1910			2	85,152	2	33,258	9	60,737	12	45,085	1,290,568		5.6	2.2	4.0	3.0	85.2
1900			1	55,807	3	44,363	4	22,056	12	49,030	1,169,060		4.2	3.3	1.6	3.7	87.2
1890			1	54,955	1	15,353	2	14,151	10	31,724	1,034,966		4.8	1.3	1.2	2.8	90.9
Georgia:																	
1920	1	200,616	4	219,920	7	101,857	14	95,937	33	109,529	2,167,973	0.9	7.6	3.5	3.3	3.8	74.9
1910	1	154,839	3	146,769	5	72,233	14	90,403	22	74,406	2,070,471	5.9	5.6	2.8	3.5	2.9	79.4
1900			3	183,557	3	51,131	7	47,757	18	63,937	1,869,940		8.3	2.3	2.2	2.9	84.4
1890			3	142,022	2	40,049	5	35,907	12	39,434	1,579,881		7.7	2.2	2.0	2.1	86.0
Florida:																	
1920			4	203,772	2	32,986	11	73,747	13	45,320	612,645		21.0	3.4	7.6	4.7	63.3
1910			2	95,481	2	42,927	6	35,456	13	45,216	533,539		12.7	5.7	4.7	6.0	70.9
1900			1	28,429	3	50,700			8	27,902	421,511		5.4	9.6		5.3	79.7
1890					3	47,031	1	5,532	8	24,795	314,004			12.0	1.4	6.3	80.2
EAST SOUTH CENTRAL.																	
Kentucky:																	
1920	1	234,891	3	127,972	4	69,057	14	100,317	29	101,306	1,783,087	9.7	5.3	2.9	4.2	4.2	73.8
1910	1	223,928	3	118,678	4	60,688	12	84,079	20	68,009	1,734,463	9.8	5.2	2.7	3.7	3.0	75.7
1900	1	204,731	3	97,608	3	42,907	8	56,616	19	65,806	1,670,506	9.5	4.5	2.0	2.6	3.1	78.2
1890	1	161,129	1	37,371	3	59,282	7	50,631	14	48,300	1,501,922	8.7	2.0	3.2	2.7	2.6	80.8
Tennessee:																	
1920	2	280,693	2	135,713	[1] 3	39,349	7	43,536	33	111,935	1,726,659	12.0	5.8	1.7	1.9	2.8	73.9
1910	2	241,469	2	80,950	[1] 2	22,927	5	33,479	18	62,220	1,742,744	11.1	3.7	1.0	1.5	2.8	79.8
1900	1	102,320	3	143,650	[1] 2	14,511	[1] 3	20,754	14	45,398	1,693,077	5.1	7.1	0.7	1.0	2.2	83.6
1890			3	169,763	[1] 2	32,574	[1] 3	16,618	6	19,439	1,520,124		9.6	1.8	0.9	1.1	86.5
Alabama:																	
1920	1	178,806	2	104,241	7	99,298	8	50,461	21	76,516	1,838,857	7.6	4.4	4.2	2.1	3.3	78.3
1910	1	132,685	2	89,657	4	47,864	6	41,695	15	58,530	1,707,662	6.2	4.2	2.2	2.0	2.7	82.7
1900			3	107,230			7	49,462	17	60,022	1,611,983		5.9		2.7	3.3	88.1
1890			2	57,254	1	21,883	4	31,627	12	41,471	1,361,166		3.8	1.4	2.1	2.7	89.9
Mississippi:																	
1920					9	136,201			15	50,764	1,550,497			7.6	3.0	2.8	86.6
1910					5	88,885	10	70,680	14	47,746	1,589,803			4.9	3.9	2.7	88.5
1900					3	41,004	4	27,409	15	51,532	1,431,235			2.6	1.8	3.3	92.3
1890					3	34,098	2	12,578	7	23,200	1,219,634			2.6	1.0	1.8	94.6
WEST SOUTH CENTRAL.																	
Arkansas:																	
1920			2	94,012	[1] 4	53,280	8	53,135	27	90,070	1,461,707		5.4	3.0	3.0	5.1	83.4
1910			1	45,941	[1] 5	70,304	3	21,143	19	65,293	1,371,768		2.9	4.5	1.3	4.1	87.1
1900			1	38,307	[1] 3	27,997	2	15,523	9	29,906	1,199,831		2.9	2.1	1.2	2.3	91.5
1890			1	25,874	1	11,311	[1] 4	26,755	8	9,219	1,055,052		2.3	1.0	2.4	0.8	93.5
Louisiana:																	
1920	1	387,219	1	43,874	4	65,055	8	52,377	24	79,638	1,170,346	21.5	2.4	3.6	2.9	4.4	65.1
1910	1	339,075	1	28,015	4	47,768	5	29,491	15	52,167	1,159,872	20.5	1.7	2.9	1.8	3.1	70.0
1900	1	287,104			2	27,282	4	24,571	8	27,331	1,015,337	20.8		2.0	1.8	2.0	73.5
1890	1	242,039			2	22,457			6	19,349	834,743	21.6		2.0		1.7	74.6
Oklahoma: [2]																	
1920			3	193,647	9	123,617	15	104,193	36	118,023	1,488,803		9.5	6.1	5.1	5.8	73.4
1910			2	89,483	6	79,583	6	44,072	32	107,217	1,337,000		5.4	4.8	2.7	6.5	80.7
1900					2	20,043	1	5,681	10	32,693	731,974			2.5	0.7	4.1	92.6
1890							1	5,333	1	4,151	240,173				2.1	1.6	96.3
Texas:																	
1920	4	565,113	6	275,692	[1] 20	273,490	29	190,279	60	208,115	3,150,539	12.1	5.9	5.9	4.1	4.5	67.6
1910			8	473,375	[1] 13	157,127	19	134,680	51	172,922	2,958,438		12.1	4.0	3.5	4.4	75.9
1900			5	205,069	[1] 7	99,585	29	110,602	29	105,503	2,527,951		6.7	3.3	3.6	3.5	82.9
1890			4	132,381	6	84,711	[1] 10	62,616	22	69,803	1,886,016		5.9	3.8	2.8	3.1	84.4

[1] See note 1 to Table 31, p. 50.　　　[2] Includes population of Indian Territory for 1900 and 1890.

POPULATION.

TABLE 35.—NUMBER AND AGGREGATE POPULATION OF URBAN PLACES OF SPECIFIED SIZES, AND POPULATION OF RURAL DISTRICTS, BY DIVISIONS AND STATES: 1890–1920—Continued.

[See note at head of this table, p. 53.]

DIVISION, STATE, AND CENSUS YEAR.	PLACES HAVING A POPULATION OF—											Rural districts—population.	PER CENT OF TOTAL POPULATION LIVING IN—					
	100,000 or more		25,000 to 100,000		10,000 to 25,000		5,000 to 10,000		2,500 to 5,000				Places of—					Rural districts.
	Number of places.	Population.	Number of places.	Population.	Number of places.	Population.	Number of places.	Population.	Number of places.	Population.			100,000 or more	25,000 to 100,000	10,000 to 25,000	5,000 to 10,000	2,500 to 5,000	
MOUNTAIN.																		
Montana:																		
1920			1	41,611	5	75,594	6	37,127	5	17,679		376,878		7.6	13.8	6.8	3.2	68.7
1910			1	39,165	5	59,497	3	16,015	5	18,743		242,633		10.4	15.8	4.3	5.0	64.5
1900			1	30,470	2	25,700	1	9,453	6	18,931		158,775		12.5	10.6	3.9	7.8	65.3
1890					2	21,557			4	14,230		104,137			17.2		10.0	72.9
Idaho:																		
1920					2	36,394	7	47,544	11	35,099		312,829			8.4	11.0	8.1	72.4
1910					1	17,358	4	27,702	7	24,838		255,696			5.3	8.5	7.6	78.5
1900							1	5,957	1	4,046		151,769				3.7	2.5	93.8
1890												88,548						100.0
Wyoming:																		
1920					2	25,276	3	21,932	3	10,140		137,054			13.0	11.3	5.2	70.5
1910					1	11,320	3	22,423	3	9,478		102,744			7.8	15.4	6.5	70.4
1900					1	14,087	1	8,207	1	4,363		65,874			15.2	8.9	4.7	71.2
1890					1	11,690	1	6,388	1	3,406		41,071			18.7	10.2	5.4	65.7
Colorado:																		
1920	1	256,491	2	73,155	3	32,870	5	34,748	15	55,995		486,370	27.3	7.8	3.5	3.7	6.0	51.8
1910	1	213,381	2	73,473	1	10,204	7	52,558	16	55,224		394,184	26.7	9.2	1.3	6.6	6.9	49.3
1900	1	133,859	1	26,157	3	43,687	2	11,495	13	43,453		279,049	21.8	5.2	8.1	2.1	8.1	51.7
1890	1	106,713			3	46,082	3	15,792	6	17,318		227,344	25.8		11.2	3.8	4.2	55.0
New Mexico:																		
1920					1	15,157	3	19,813	8	29,990		205,390			4.2	5.5	8.3	82.0
1910					1	11,020	2	11,244	7	24,307		280,730			3.4	3.4	7.4	85.8
1900							2	11,841	5	15,540		167,929				6.1	8.0	86.0
1890							1	6,185	1	3,785		150,312				3.9	2.4	93.8
Arizona:																		
1920			1	29,053	1	20,292	6	43,063	7	25,119		216,635		8.7	6.1	12.9	7.5	64.8
1910			2	24,327	4	27,631	3	11,302				141,094			11.9	13.5	5.5	69.0
1900					2	13,075	2	6,420	4	3,152		103,436				10.6	5.2	84.1
1890					1	5,150	1					79,941				5.8	3.6	90.6
Utah:																		
1920	1	118,110	1	32,804	1	10,303	2	14,721	12	39,646		233,812	26.3	7.3	2.3	3.3	8.8	52.0
1910			2	118,357			2	16,447	12	38,130		200,417		31.7		4.4	10.2	53.7
1900			1	53,531	1	16,313	2	11,036	8	23,947		171,322		19.3	5.9	4.2	8.7	61.0
1890			1	44,843	1	14,889	1	5,159	3	10,264		135,624		21.3	7.1	2.4	4.9	64.3
Nevada:																		
1920					1	12,016			1	3,238		62,153			15.5		4.2	80.3
1910					1	10,867			1	2,500		68,508			13.3		3.1	83.7
1900									2	7,195		35,140					17.0	83.0
1890							1	8,511	2	7,513		31,331				18.0	15.9	66.2
PACIFIC.																		
Washington:																		
1920	2	419,749	3	150,194	5	72,074	7	47,544	18	50,174		607,886	30.9	11.1	5.3	3.5	4.4	44.8
1910	2	341,596	1	83,743	5	96,218	4	31,778	15	52,195		538,460	29.0	7.3	8.4	2.8	4.6	47.0
1900			3	155,233	1	10,049	2	14,672	9	31,523		306,626		30.0	1.9	2.8	6.1	59.2
1890			2	78,843	1	10,922			7	28,413		230,054		22.1	5.6		8.0	64.4
Oregon:																		
1920	1	258,288			3	42,299	8	50,445	11	39,987		392,370	33.0		5.4	6.4	5.1	50.1
1910	1	207,214			1	14,094	5	30,210	11	46,542		365,705	30.8		2.1	5.8	6.9	54.4
1900			1	90,426			2	15,044	8	27,710		280,356		21.9		3.6	6.7	67.8
1890			1	46,385	1	10,532	2	11,313	6	16,863		232,611		14.6	3.3	3.6	5.3	73.2
California:																		
1920	3	1,299,610	9	451,404	13	206,094	26	171,802	56	202,819		1,095,132	37.9	13.2	6.0	5.0	5.9	32.0
1910	3	886,284	5	183,945	13	196,701	10	64,108	39	138,701		907,810	37.3	7.7	8.3	2.7	5.8	38.2
1900	2	445,261	2	96,242	6	98,854	9	62,977	21	74,365		707,854	30.0	6.5	6.7	4.2	5.0	47.6
1890	1	298,997	3	125,463	5	70,626	5	28,124	19	66,254		623,934	24.6	10.3	5.8	2.3	5.5	51.4

Proportion of urban population living in each class of urban places.—Table 36 shows, for the United States as a whole, for the last four censuses, the proportion which the population of each urban class formed, not of the total population of the country, but of the urban population alone.

It will be noted that the proportion of the urban population in the smaller cities—those having from 2,500 to 25,000 inhabitants—has been decreasing from census to census, while the proportions in the other classes of cities have fluctuated somewhat.

TABLE 36.—DISTRIBUTION OF URBAN POPULATION IN GROUPS OF CITIES CLASSIFIED ACCORDING TO SIZE: 1890–1920.

CLASS OF PLACES.	URBAN POPULATION.				PER CENT OF TOTAL URBAN POPULATION.			
	1920	1910	1900	1890	1920	1910	1900	1890
Total	54,304,603	42,166,120	30,380,433	22,298,359	100.0	100.0	100.0	100.0
1,000,000 or more	10,145,532	8,501,174	6,429,474	3,662,115	18.7	20.2	21.2	16.4
100,000 to 1,000,000	17,283,794	11,800,964	7,778,873	6,035,845	31.8	28.0	25.6	27.1
25,000 to 100,000	10,340,788	8,204,960	5,509,965	4,291,608	19.0	19.5	18.1	19.2
2,500 to 25,000	16,534,489	13,659,022	10,662,121	8,308,791	30.4	32.4	35.1	37.3

URBAN AND RURAL.   57

INCREASE IN URBAN AND RURAL POPULATION.

In Table 50 (p. 150) the percentages of increase or decrease in the urban and rural population of the states and counties represent merely the difference between the population of the urban and the rural territory as constituted in a given census year and of the urban and the rural territory, respectively, as constituted in the preceding census year. As already pointed out, however, the territory treated as urban in one census year includes some small cities which were treated as rural at the time of the preceding census. In a few cases also, where small cities decreased in population, the reverse change took place. Similarly, a given group of urban places, classified according to size, may not contain exactly the same cities in one census year as in another. In order, therefore, to present fairly the contrast between specified size groups of urban communities and between urban and rural communities in regard to their *rates of growth*, it is necessary to consider the changes in population which have taken place from one decennial census to another in the *same territory*. For this purpose the population totals, in 1920, for the several groups of urban places as constituted in 1920, and for the rural territory as constituted in that year, are compared with the totals for the same territory in 1910 (so far as reported separately at that census). This method avoids the disturbing effect on the rate of growth which otherwise would arise from the passage of certain communities from the rural to the urban or from the urban to the rural class, or from one urban group to another.

It should be noted in this connection that even if there were no difference between urban and rural communities and between the various groups of urban communities in respect of rate of growth, there would nevertheless be a constantly decreasing proportion of rural population and a constantly increasing proportion of population in the largest cities so long as the population of the country as a whole was increasing. Were there no movement from country to city, from city to country, or from one class of urban communities to another, no disturbing effect from immigration, and no difference between different classes of communities in regard to natural increase resulting from excess of births over deaths, there would still be, in a growing population, a constant passage of certain communities from the rural to the urban class and from each urban class to the one next above. The rural municipalities, maintaining a rate of growth uniform with that of the country as a whole, would, one by one, pass the limit of 2,500 inhabitants fixed as the dividing line between urban and rural communities, and the urban communities would similarly pass the dividing line between one size group and another. Thus the proportion of rural population would decrease gradually from census to census and the proportion which the population of

the size group containing the largest cities formed of the total for the country would increase, while no great changes would take place in the proportions for the intermediate groups. As a matter of fact, however, in the United States the urban communities have far greater rates of growth than the rural communities, and the rapid increase in the proportion of urban population is due largely to this difference in rates of growth.

United States as a whole.—Table 37 shows, for the United States as a whole and for each geographic section, the increase between 1910 and 1920 in the population of the urban and of the rural territory as constituted in 1920.

It will be noted that, despite the decreases in population shown by so many counties between 1910 and 1920 (see Table 25, p. 42), nevertheless the population of the territory rural in 1920 showed an increase for each of the three geographic sections.

TABLE 37.—POPULATION OF URBAN AND RURAL TERRITORY AS CONSTITUTED IN 1920, WITH INCREASE, BY GEOGRAPHIC SECTIONS: 1920 AND 1910.

CLASS.	POPULATION.		INCREASE. 1910–1920	
	1920	1910	Number.	Per cent.
United States.............	105,710,620	91,972,266	13,738,354	14.9
Territory urban in 1920............	54,304,603	43,193,184	11,111,419	25.7
Territory rural in 1920.............	51,406,017	48,779,082	2,626,935	5.4
THE NORTH:[1]				
Territory urban in 1920........	40,314,312	32,726,851	7,587,461	23.2
Territory rural in 1920........	23,367,533	23,030,264	337,269	1.5
THE SOUTH:[1]				
Territory urban in 1920........	9,303,828	7,006,692	2,297,136	32.8
Territory rural in 1920........	23,821,975	22,382,638	1,439,337	6.4
THE WEST:[1]				
Territory urban in 1920........	4,686,463	3,459,641	1,226,822	35.5
Territory rural in 1920........	4,216,509	3,366,180	850,329	25.3

[1] For territory comprised in the North, South, and West, see map, p. 8.

The corresponding rates of increase, during the decade 1900–1910, in the population of the United States as a whole and in that of the total urban and the total rural territory as constituted in 1910 were as follows:

CLASS.	Population in 1910.	Per cent of increase: 1900–1910.
United States...........:	91,972,266	21.0
Territory urban in 1910.................	42,623,383	34.8
Territory rural in 1910.................	49,348,883	11.2

Table 38 shows, for the country as a whole, the increase between 1910 and 1920 in the urban territory and in the rural territory as constituted in 1920, the urban territory being subdivided into nine groups of cities classified according to size.

The rate of increase in the population of the territory urban in 1920 was nearly five times as great as that in the population of the territory rural in 1920. The

POPULATION.

cities having 500,000 to 1,000,000 inhabitants and those of 25,000 to 250,000 increased at materially greater rates than those in the remaining groups.

TABLE 38.—POPULATION OF URBAN CLASSES AND OF RURAL TERRITORY AS CONSTITUTED IN 1920, WITH INCREASE: 1920 AND 1910.

CLASS OF PLACES.	Number of places in 1920.	POPULATION.		INCREASE: 1910-1920	
		1920	1910	Number.	Per cent.
United States....	....	105,710,620	91,972,266	13,738,354	14.9
Territory urban in 1920..	[1] 2,787	54,304,603	43,193,184	11,111,419	25.7
Places having in 1920—					
1,000,000 or more.....	3	10,145,532	8,505,411	1,640,121	19.3
500,000 to 1,000,000...	9	6,223,769	4,664,460	1,559,309	33.4
250,000 to 500,000.....	13	4,540,838	3,712,128	828,710	22.3
100,000 to 250,000.....	43	6,519,187	5,087,486	1,431,701	28.1
50,000 to 100,000......	76	5,265,747	3,999,370	1,266,377	31.7
25,000 to 50,000........	143	5,075,041	3,777,417	1,297,624	34.4
10,000 to 25,000........	459	6,942,742	5,617,089	1,325,653	23.6
5,000 to 10,000.........	721	4,997,794	4,051,188	946,606	23.4
2,500 to 5,000..........	1,320	4,593,953	3,778,635	815,318	21.6
Territory rural in 1920...	....	51,406,017	48,779,082	2,626,935	5.4

[1] See note 1 to Table 31, p. 50.

Divisions and states.—Table 39 shows, by divisions and states, the increase between 1910 and 1920 in urban and rural territory as constituted in 1920, the urban territory being subdivided into three groups of cities classified according to size.

The only division which showed a decrease in population for the territory rural in 1920 was the East North Central, for which a decline of six-tenths of 1 per cent appears. In the Mountain division the rate of increase in the population of the territory rural in 1920 not only exceeded that for the territory urban in 1920 in the same division, but also exceeded the average rate of increase in the population of the territory urban in 1920 throughout the entire United States.

In 15 states the population of the territory rural in 1920 decreased during the decade. Of these states, 5 were in New England, 1 in the Middle Atlantic group, 3 in the East North Central, 2 in the West North Central, 2 in the South Atlantic, 1 in the East South Central, and 1 in the Mountain division. The states in which the groups of cities having 100,000 inhabitants or more in 1920 increased at rates more than twice as great as that for the entire population of the United States, both urban and rural (14.9 per cent), numbered 10, namely, Connecticut, Ohio, Indiana, Michigan, Iowa, Maryland, Virginia, Alabama, Texas, and California.

URBAN AND RURAL.

PERCENTAGE OF INCREASE IN POPULATION OF TERRITORY URBAN IN 1920, BY STATES: 1910–1920.

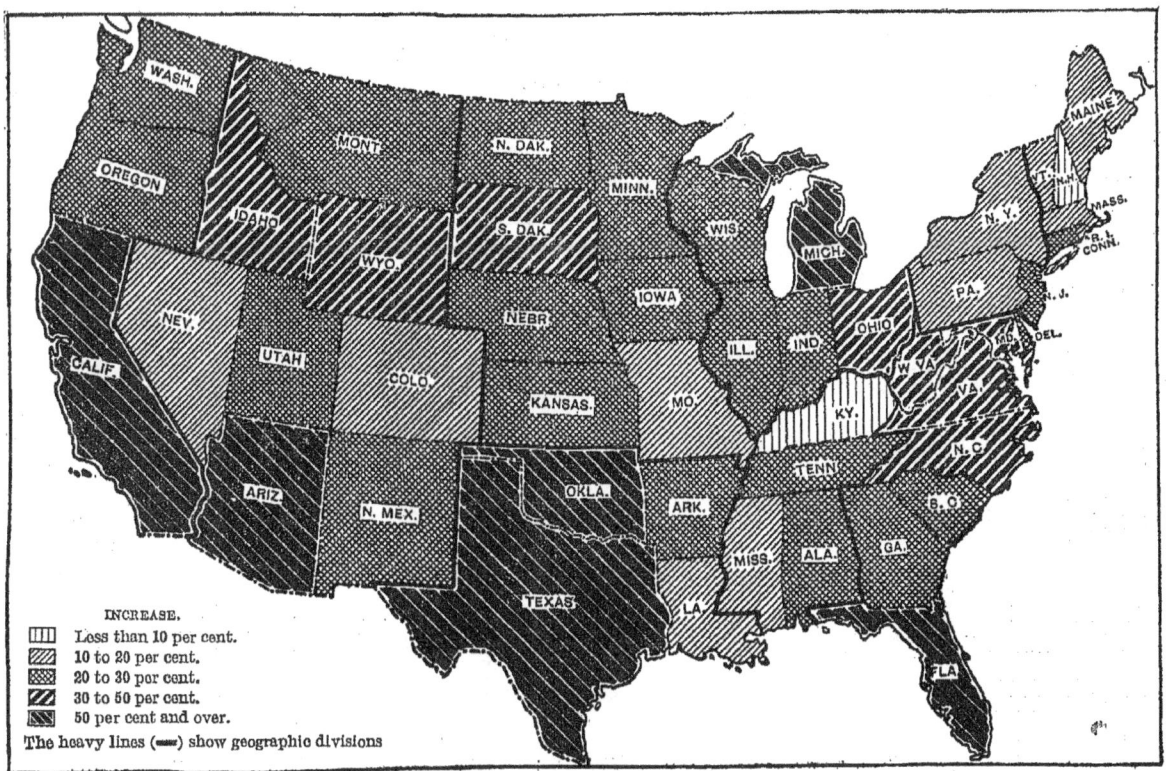

INCREASE.

- �III Less than 10 per cent.
- ▨ 10 to 20 per cent.
- ▩ 20 to 30 per cent.
- ▨ 30 to 50 per cent.
- ▨ 50 per cent and over.

The heavy lines (▬) show geographic divisions

PERCENTAGE OF INCREASE IN POPULATION OF TERRITORY RURAL IN 1920, BY STATES: 1910–1920.

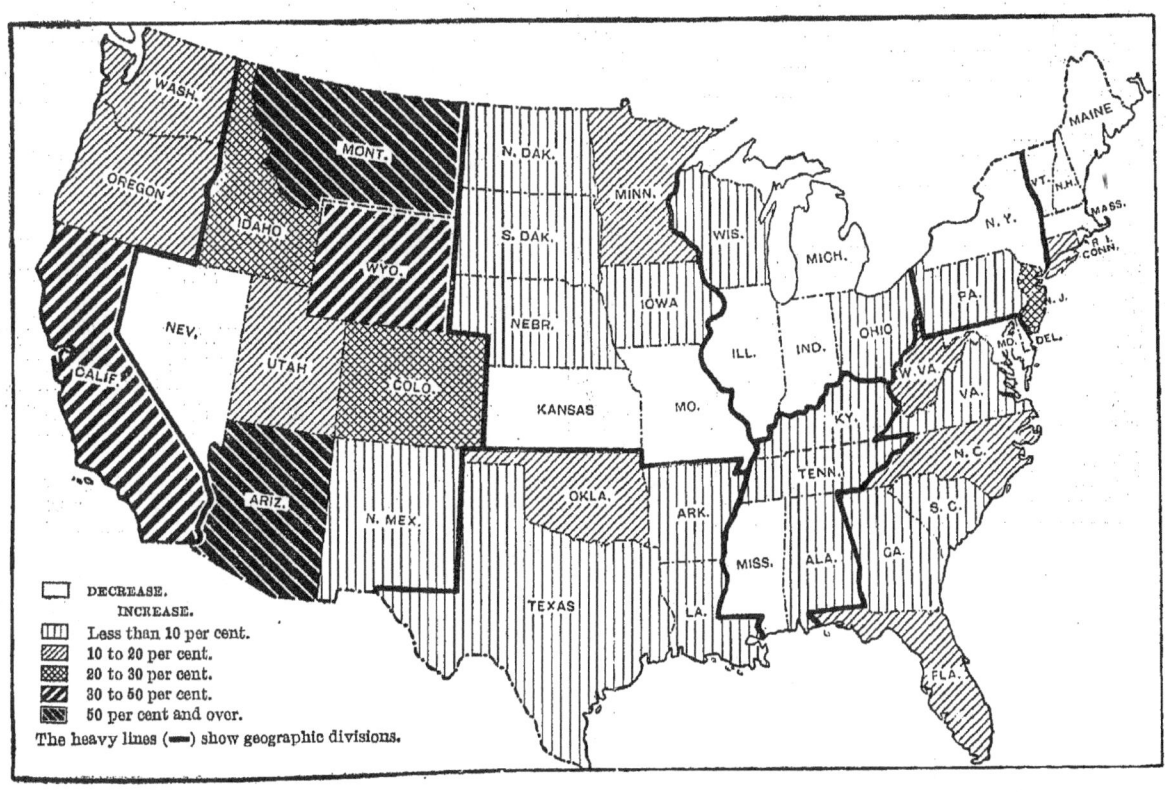

☐ DECREASE.

INCREASE.

- �III Less than 10 per cent.
- ▨ 10 to 20 per cent.
- ▩ 20 to 30 per cent.
- ▨ 30 to 50 per cent.
- ▨ 50 per cent and over.

The heavy lines (▬) show geographic divisions.

POPULATION.

60

TABLE 39.—POPULATION OF URBAN CLASSES AND OF RURAL TERRITORY AS CONSTITUTED

[A minus sign (−) denotes decrease.]

	DIVISION AND STATE	TOTAL TERRITORY URBAN IN 1920.				PLACES OF 100,000 OR MORE IN 1920.			
		Number of places.	Population.		Per cent of increase.	Number.	Population.		Per cent of increase.
			1920	1910			1920	1910	
1	United States	[1]2,787	54,304,603	43,193,184	25.7	68	27,429,326	21,969,485	24.9
	GEOGRAPHIC DIVISIONS:								
2	New England	292	5,865,073	5,030,761	16.6	11	2,203,306	1,906,984	15.5
3	Middle Atlantic	604	16,672,595	13,977,635	19.3	15	10,549,599	8,970,142	17.6
4	East North Central	[1]586	13,049,272	9,770,332	33.6	12	6,775,993	4,948,920	36.9
5	West North Central	322	4,727,372	3,948,123	19.7	7	2,131,833	1,776,492	20.0
6	South Atlantic	[1]273	4,338,792	3,240,199	33.9	6	1,769,625	1,330,089	33.0
7	East South Central	[1]169	1,991,207	1,672,974	19.2	4	691,390	599,755	15.8
8	West South Central	[1]260	2,970,829	2,093,519	41.9	5	952,332	680,889	38.6
9	Mountain	117	1,214,980	976,926	24.4	2	374,601	306,158	22.4
10	Pacific	165	3,471,483	2,482,715	39.8	6	1,977,647	1,444,056	37.0
	NEW ENGLAND:								
11	Maine	25	299,569	264,976	13.1				
12	New Hampshire	27	279,761	256,515	9.1				
13	Vermont	11	109,976	99,378	10.7				
14	Massachusetts	109	3,650,248	3,160,678	15.5	7	1,521,583	1,348,084	12.9
15	Rhode Island	27	589,180	527,106	11.8	1	237,595	221,326	5.9
16	Connecticut	30	936,339	722,108	29.7	3	444,128	334,574	32.7
	MIDDLE ATLANTIC:								
17	New York	169	8,589,844	7,235,908	18.7	6	6,807,810	5,727,090	18.9
18	New Jersey	121	2,474,936	1,992,978	24.2	5	1,084,100	932,201	16.3
19	Pennsylvania	314	5,607,815	4,748,749	18.1	4	2,657,689	2,309,951	15.1
	EAST NORTH CENTRAL:								
20	Ohio	148	3,677,136	2,704,844	35.9	7	2,171,635	1,572,304	38.1
21	Indiana	93	1,482,855	1,159,522	27.9	1	314,194	233,650	31.5
22	Illinois	171	4,403,153	3,584,261	21.6	2	2,701,705	2,189,520	23.4
23	Michigan	93	2,241,560	1,348,516	66.2	2	1,131,312	579,580	95.2
24	Wisconsin	82	1,244,568	1,023,159	21.6	1	457,147	373,857	22.3
	WEST NORTH CENTRAL:								
25	Minnesota	59	1,051,593	871,916	20.6	2	615,280	516,152	19.2
26	Iowa	81	875,495	706,223	24.0	1	126,468	86,368	46.4
27	Missouri	63	1,586,903	1,391,953	14.0	2	1,097,307	935,410	17.3
28	North Dakota	12	88,239	68,364	29.1				
29	South Dakota	14	101,872	76,203	33.7				
30	Nebraska	31	405,306	323,634	25.2	1	191,601	156,231	22.6
31	Kansas	62	617,964	509,830	21.2	1	101,177	82,331	22.9
	SOUTH ATLANTIC:								
32	Delaware	4	120,767	97,085	24.4	1	110,168	87,411	26.0
33	Maryland	18	869,422	663,838	31.0	1	733,826	558,485	31.4
34	District of Columbia	1	437,571	331,069	32.2	1	437,571	331,069	32.2
35	Virginia	39	673,984	496,268	35.8	2	287,444	198,285	45.0
36	West Virginia	35	369,007	259,064	42.4				
37	North Carolina	55	490,370	350,072	40.1				
38	South Carolina	32	293,987	210,486	22.2				
39	Georgia	59	727,859	569,621	27.8	1	200,616	151,839	29.6
40	Florida	30	355,825	232,693	52.9				
	EAST SOUTH CENTRAL:								
41	Kentucky	51	633,543	576,780	9.8	1	234,891	223,928	4.9
42	Tennessee	47	611,226	487,030	25.5	2	280,603	243,142	15.4
43	Alabama	89	509,317	396,437	28.5	1	178,806	132,685	34.8
44	Mississippi	32	240,121	212,747	12.9				
	WEST SOUTH CENTRAL:								
45	Arkansas	41	290,497	230,863	25.8				
46	Louisiana	38	628,163	528,873	18.8	1	387,219	339,075	14.2
47	Oklahoma	63	539,480	339,285	59.0				
48	Texas	119	1,512,689	994,498	52.1	4	565,113	347,814	62.5
	MOUNTAIN:								
49	Montana	17	172,011	139,162	23.6				
50	Idaho	20	119,037	83,865	41.9				
51	Wyoming	8	57,348	43,479	31.9				
52	Colorado	26	453,259	396,201	14.4	1	256,491	213,381	20.2
53	New Mexico	12	64,960	52,156	24.5				
54	Arizona	15	117,527	73,365	60.2				
55	Utah	17	215,584	175,331	23.0	1	118,110	92,777	27.3
56	Nevada	2	15,254	13,367	14.1				
	PACIFIC:								
57	Washington	35	748,735	619,752	20.8	2	419,740	312,378	22.6
58	Oregon	23	391,019	319,954	22.2	1	258,288	213,251	21.1
59	California	107	2,331,729	1,543,000	51.1	3	1,299,610	888,427	46.3

[1]See note 1 to Table 31, p. 50.

URBAN AND RURAL.

61

IN 1920, WITH PER CENT OF INCREASE, BY DIVISIONS AND STATES: 1920 AND 1910.

[A minus sign (−) denotes decrease.]

	PLACES OF 25,000 TO 100,000 IN 1920.				PLACES OF 2,500 TO 25,000 IN 1920.				TERRITORY RURAL IN 1920.			
Number.	Population 1920	Population 1910	Per cent of increase.	Number.	Population 1920	Population 1910	Per cent of increase.	Number.	Population 1920	Population 1910	Per cent of increase.	
219	10,340,788	7,776,787	33.0	¹2,500	16,534,489	13,446,912	23.0	51,406,017	48,779,082	5.4		1
35	1,699,018	1,413,007	20.2	246	1,962,749	1,710,770	14.7	1,535,836	1,521,920	0.9		2
48	2,353,654	1,892,960	24.3	541	3,769,342	3,114,533	21.0	5,588,549	5,338,257	4.7		3
61	2,681,461	1,868,594	43.5	¹513	3,591,818	2,952,818	21.6	8,426,271	8,480,289	−0.6		4
14	733,831	595,460	23.2	301	1,861,708	1,576,141	18.1	7,816,877	7,689,798	1.7		5
25	1,119,452	780,248	43.5	¹242	1,449,715	1,129,862	28.3	9,651,480	8,954,096	7.8		6
7	367,926	299,989	22.6	¹158	931,891	773,230	20.5	6,893,100	6,730,927	2.4		7
12	607,225	367,664	65.2	¹243	1,411,272	1,038,966	35.8	7,271,395	6,691,015	8.7		8
5	170,623	151,037	16.9	110	663,750	519,731	27.7	2,121,121	1,656,591	28.0		9
12	601,598	407,798	47.5	147	892,238	630,861	41.4	2,095,388	1,709,589	22.6		10
3	127,041	109,621	15.9	22	172,528	155,355	11.1	408,445	477,395	−1.9		11
2	106,763	96,068	11.1	25	172,998	160,447	7.8	163,322	174,057	−6.2		12
				14	109,976	99,378	10.7	242,452	256,578	−5.5		13
20	1,028,383	864,274	19.0	142	1,100,282	948,320	16.0	202,108	205,738	−1.8		14
4	167,406	138,003	21.3	22	184,179	164,777	11.8	15,217	15,504	−1.9		15
6	269,425	205,041	31.4	21	222,786	182,493	22.1	444,292	392,648	13.2		16
16	755,097	626,016	20.6	147	1,026,937	881,962	16.4	1,795,383	1,877,706	−4.4		17
16	718,809	553,179	30.0	100	671,937	507,598	32.4	680,964	544,189	25.1		18
16	879,658	713,765	23.2	294	2,070,468	1,725,033	20.0	3,112,202	2,916,362	6.7		19
14	535,822	365,551	46.6	¹127	969,679	766,989	26.4	2,082,258	2,062,277	1.0		20
11	559,351	302,180	42.6	¹81	609,310	533,683	14.2	1,447,535	1,541,354	−6.1		21
10	700,310	542,834	29.0	154	1,001,138	801,007	21.8	2,082,127	2,104,330	−1.1		22
12	583,309	326,728	78.5	79	526,939	442,229	19.2	1,426,852	1,461,627	−2.4		23
8	302,069	241,202	25.4	73	484,752	408,010	18.8	1,387,499	1,310,701	5.9		24
1	98,917	78,466	26.1	56	337,396	277,298	21.7	1,335,532	1,203,792	10.9		25
0	285,053	218,146	30.7	74	463,974	401,709	15.5	1,528,526	1,518,558	0.7		26
3	147,472	144,677	1.9	58	342,124	311,886	9.7	1,817,152	1,901,382	−4.4		27
				12	88,239	68,364	29.1	558,633	508,692	9.8		28
1	25,202	14,094	78.8	13	76,670	62,109	23.4	534,675	507,685	5.3		29
1	54,948	43,973	25.0	29	158,757	123,430	28.6	891,066	868,580	2.6		30
2	122,239	96,134	27.2	59	394,548	331,365	19.1	1,151,293	1,181,110	−2.5		31
				3	10,599	9,674	9.6	102,236	105,237	−2.9		32
2	57,001	38,346	51.0	15	77,695	67,007	16.0	580,239	631,508	−8.1		33
												34
5	201,007	141,890	42.3	¹32	184,633	156,003	18.3	1,535,203	1,565,344	4.5		35
4	173,362	114,838	51.4	31	195,145	144,220	35.3	1,094,604	962,055	13.8		36
4	156,600	101,224	54.7	51	333,761	248,848	34.1	2,068,753	1,856,215	11.5		37
2	105,481	85,947	22.7	30	188,506	154,539	22.0	1,389,787	1,274,914	9.0		38
4	219,920	174,060	26.3	54	307,323	240,716	27.7	2,167,973	2,039,497	6.3		39
4	203,772	123,934	64.4	26	152,053	108,759	39.8	612,645	519,926	17.8		40
3	127,972	120,420	6.3	47	270,680	232,403	16.5	1,783,087	1,713,145	4.1		41
2	135,713	89,903	51.0	¹43	194,820	153,985	26.5	1,726,659	1,697,759	1.7		42
2	104,241	89,657	16.3	38	226,270	174,095	30.0	1,838,857	1,741,658	5.6		43
				32	240,121	212,747	12.9	1,550,497	1,584,367	−2.1		44
2	94,012	70,590	33.2	¹39	196,485	160,264	22.6	1,461,707	1,343,586	8.8		45
1	43,874	28,015	56.6	36	197,070	161,783	21.8	1,170,346	1,127,515	3.8		46
3	193,047	107,665	79.9	60	345,833	231,620	49.3	1,488,803	1,317,870	13.0		47
6	275,692	161,385	70.8	¹109	671,884	485,299	38.4	3,150,539	2,902,044	8.6		48
1	41,611	39,165	6.2	16	130,400	99,997	30.4	376,878	236,891	59.1		49
				20	119,037	83,865	41.9	312,829	241,720	29.4		50
				8	57,348	43,470	31.9	137,054	102,486	33.7		51
2	73,155	75,158	−2.7	23	123,613	107,662	14.8	486,870	402,823	20.7		52
				12	64,960	52,156	24.5	295,390	275,145	7.4		53
1	29,053	11,134	160.9	14	88,474	62,231	42.2	216,635	130,989	65.4		54
1	32,804	25,580	28.2	15	64,670	56,974	13.5	233,812	198,020	18.1		55
				2	15,254	13,367	14.1	62,153	68,508	−9.3		56
3	150,194	132,855	13.1	30	178,792	144,510	23.7	607,886	522,238	16.4		57
				22	132,731	106,708	24.4	392,370	352,811	11.2		58
9	451,404	274,943	64.2	95	580,715	379,639	53.0	1,095,132	834,540	31.2		59

¹See note 1 to Table 31, p. 50.

POPULATION.

62

CITIES AND THEIR SUBURBS.

In presenting population statistics for cities the Bureau of the Census must necessarily deal with them as political units, showing for each city the population actually residing within its municipal boundaries. In many cases, however, the number of inhabitants enumerated within the municipal boundaries gives an inadequate idea of the population grouped about one urban center. In fact, in only a few of the large cities do the municipal boundaries closely define the urban area. Immediately beyond the political limits of many cities, and connected with them by rapid-transportation systems, are densely populated suburban districts which industrially and socially are parts of the cities themselves, differing only in the matter of governmental organization.

It is desirable to show the magnitude of each of the principal urban areas taken as a whole. Statistics have, therefore, been compiled showing, for each city in the United States having 100,000 inhabitants or more, the population within the city limits and the population in adjoining communities that may be considered as intimately associated with the urban centers. Two sets of computations have been made:

(1) For each city having 100,000 inhabitants or more within its municipal boundaries a computation has been made to determine the combined population of the city itself and of the suburban territory within 10 miles of the city boundaries. The areas thus mapped out may be briefly defined as "cities and adjacent territory."

(2) In the case of each city having within its own boundaries 200,000 inhabitants or more, there has been delimited what may be termed a "metropolitan district," which includes, in addition to the city itself, only those sections of the adjacent territory which may be considered as urban in character.

METHOD OF DEFINING DISTRICTS.

In outlining the two classes of districts the civil divisions within the 10-mile limit are first selected and their population and area ascertained. Such civil divisions as are divided by a line drawn within 10 miles of the city boundaries are included if one-half of their population or one-half of their area lies within the 10-mile limit. State boundaries are disregarded, so that in some cases the adjacent territory and the metropolitan district lie partly in one state and partly in another. The area within the 10-mile limit just defined is the "adjacent territory." It differs considerably, of course, from the territory included between the city boundaries and a line drawn parallel to them at an exact distance of 10 miles, because in delimiting the adjacent territory no civil divisions are subdivided. The outline of the area, therefore, must conform to the boundaries of the political divisions which lie along the outer limits of the included area. Because of this fact the boundaries of the adjacent territory thus defined may vary considerably from point to point in their actual distance from the city limits.

The "metropolitan district," which, as previously noted, has as its nucleus a city having at least 200,000 inhabitants, comprises the population and area of the central city itself and of those minor civil divisions lying within the adjacent territory which at the last census had 150 or more inhabitants per square mile. Where the density of population was less than this the division was considered as rural rather than urban in character and as not properly a part of the metropolitan district. This limit of density, however, was not always rigidly applied; in a few instances a minor civil division having a density of less than 150 per square mile has been included, because it was nearly or completely surrounded by other divisions the density of which would require their inclusion. The exceptions in such cases are considered to be justified in order to avoid undue irregularity in the outlines of the districts or gaps lying wholly within their area.

It is safe to say that these deviations from the rule have had very little effect upon the population totals for the districts and have yielded on the whole more consistent and satisfactory results than would have been obtained by the application of any rigid rule. In fact, absolute exactness in applying a density limit is out of the question, because in a few cases the areas of the minor civil divisions as measured from the maps and data available are not absolutely correct.

In general, the city with its adjacent territory, as here defined, includes, in addition to the central city, all cities, towns, villages, or other civil divisions located within 10 miles beyond the boundaries of the central city, while the metropolitan district includes, besides the central city, only those divisions within the 10-mile limit in which the population at the last census was at least 150 per square mile. The civil divisions comprised within these limits, so far as they were returned separately in 1920, are given in detail in the statements which follow Tables 40 and 41 (pp. 65–71 and 73–75).

METROPOLITAN DISTRICTS.

Table 40 shows, for 1920 and 1910, the population of the 29 metropolitan districts containing individual cities having 200,000 inhabitants or more, distinguishing the population living within the city proper from that outside the city. The total population of each city with all its "adjacent territory" is also shown. The 29 metropolitan districts comprise 32 central cities and their suburban territory, there being 3 districts each of which includes 2 cities so large that both together are treated as constituting the urban center of the district. These cities are Minneapolis and St. Paul; Kansas City, Kans., and Kansas City, Mo.; and San Francisco and Oakland. Two cities having more than 200,000 inhabitants each—Newark and Jersey

CITIES AND THEIR SUBURBS. 63

City—do not appear separately in the table, being included within the metropolitan district of New York.

The importance of the suburbs of great cities is brought out clearly by the combined statistics for the 29 metropolitan districts, which appear at the beginning of the table. It will be seen that the area of the suburban territory outside the central cities represents fully three-fourths of the entire area of the metropolitan districts, and that the population of these suburbs in 1920 constituted nearly one-fourth of the entire population of the districts. Moreover, during the 10-year period covered by the table the rate of increase in the population of the suburban areas was considerably greater than the corresponding rate for the central cities.

In addition to the population of the 29 metropolitan districts themselves the census returns for 1920 show an aggregate population of 949,961 residing in territory adjacent to the central cities but not included in the metropolitan districts—that is, in civil divisions which lie wholly or in greater part within 10 miles of the boundaries of the central cities, but in which the density of population was not sufficient to justify treating them as strictly urban. The total population residing in 1920 either in cities having 200,000 inhabitants or more or within approximately 10 miles of such cities constituted 28.6 per cent of the total population of the United States.

It will be noted from Table 40 that great differences appear among the several metropolitan districts in regard to the proportion which the population outside the central city represents of the total population of the district. These differences are due to the fact that some of the large cities have made no annexations of territory for many years, while others have made extensive annexations, with the result that most of the densely populated areas within the metropolitan districts have been added to the cities themselves. The column in the table giving the areas of the various districts brings out the wide variations in the density of population of the central cities, some of which have several times as many inhabitants per acre as others. This difference in policy among the cities in regard to the extension of municipal boundaries makes it the more obviously necessary to exclude thinly settled areas in the neighborhood of the cities in calculating the true metropolitan population, for, in the case of a city of relatively great area, there is necessarily also a large area lying within 10 miles beyond the municipal limits, many portions of which are likely to be rural rather than urban in character. The table emphasizes the well-known fact that many of the large cities have a materially different rank when their suburbs are taken into account from that which they hold when only the population living within their municipal boundaries is considered.

TABLE 40.—AREA AND POPULATION OF CENTRAL CITY, METROPOLITAN DISTRICT, AND ADJACENT TERRITORY, FOR CITIES OF 200,000 INHABITANTS OR MORE: 1920 AND 1910.

[Population shown for central cities for each census year does not include that of annexations made subsequently to census date, but total population given for each district for 1920 and 1910 relates to same area.]

DISTRICT.	Area in acres: 1920	POPULATION.		Per cent of increase:[1] 1910–1920	DISTRICT.	Area in acres: 1920	POPULATION.		Per cent of increase:[1] 1910–1920
		1920	1910				1920	1910	
Total for 29 metropolitan districts	6,816,110.3	29,238,582	23,045,544	26.9	BUFFALO.				
In central cities (32 cities)	1,518,715.9	22,111,380	17,673,818	25.1	Metropolitan district	140,015.0	602,847	493,290	22.2
Outside central cities	5,297,394.4	7,127,202	5,371,726	32.7	In city proper	24,894.3	506,775	423,715	19.6
					Outside	115,120.7	96,072	69,575	38.1
Cities and adjacent territory	13,369,925.9	30,188,543	23,870,351	26.5	City and adjacent territory	306,223.0	623,865	511,147	22.1
Adjacent territory	11,851,210.0	8,077,163	6,196,533	30.3	Adjacent territory	281,328.7	117,090	87,432	33.9
AKRON.					CHICAGO.				
Metropolitan district	113,912.0	285,113	104,320	173.3	Metropolitan district	469,569.6	3,178,924	2,455,942	29.4
In city proper	14,520.0	208,435	69,067	201.8	In city proper	123,382.9	2,701,705	2,185,283	23.6
Outside	99,392.0	76,678	35,253	117.5	Outside	346,186.7	477,219	270,659	76.3
City and adjacent territory	348,664.0	305,696	122,915	148.7	City and adjacent territory	594,410.4	3,201,301	2,472,712	29.5
Adjacent territory	334,144.0	97,261	53,848	80.6	Adjacent territory	471,027.5	499,596	287,429	73.8
ATLANTA.					CINCINNATI.				
Metropolitan district	85,266.2	249,226	185,235	34.5	Metropolitan district	211,938.4	606,850	567,876	6.9
In city proper	16,773.4	200,616	154,839	29.6	In city proper	45,529.6	401,247	363,591	10.4
Outside	68,492.8	48,610	30,396	59.9	Outside	166,408.8	205,603	204,285	0.6
City and adjacent territory	364,723.0	279,235	208,075	34.2	City and adjacent territory	527,812.2	681,287	637,156	6.9
Adjacent territory	347,949.6	78,619	53,236	47.7	Adjacent territory	482,282.6	280,040	273,565	2.4
BALTIMORE.					CLEVELAND.				
Metropolitan district	244,160.0	787,458	663,810	18.6	Metropolitan district	148,846.9	925,720	622,571	48.7
In city proper	50,560.0	733,826	558,485	31.4	In city proper	36,089.0	790,841	560,663	42.1
Outside	193,600.0	53,632	105,325	−49.1	Outside	112,757.9	128,879	61,908	108.2
City and adjacent territory	432,448.0	814,395	689,841	18.1	City and adjacent territory	351,584.0	951,579	643,854	47.8
Adjacent territory	381,888.0	80,569	131,356	−38.7	Adjacent territory	315,495.0	154,738	83,191	86.0
BOSTON.					COLUMBUS.				
Metropolitan district	365,073.3	1,772,254	1,531,138	15.7	Metropolitan district	80,689.0	260,338	199,146	30.7
In city proper	27,870.0	748,060	670,585	11.6	In city proper	14,449.0	237,031	181,511	30.6
Outside	337,203.3	1,024,194	860,553	19.0	Outside	66,240.0	23,307	17,635	32.2
City and adjacent territory	392,016.6	1,801,320	1,556,671	15.7	City and adjacent territory	347,318.0	284,841	222,521	28.0
Adjacent territory	364,146.6	1,053,260	886,086	18.9	Adjacent territory	332,864.0	47,810	41,010	16.6

[1] A minus sign (—) denotes decrease.

POPULATION.

64

TABLE 40.—AREA AND POPULATION OF CENTRAL CITY, METROPOLITAN DISTRICT, AND ADJACENT TERRITORY, FOR CITIES OF 200,000 INHABITANTS OR MORE: 1920 AND 1910—Continued.

[Population shown for central cities for each census year does not include that of annexations made subsequently to census date, but total population given for each district for 1920 and 1910 relates to same area.]

DISTRICT.	Area in acres: 1920	POPULATION. 1920	POPULATION. 1910	Per cent of increase:[1] 1910-1920
DENVER.				
Metropolitan district	46,205.0	264,232	219,314	20.5
In city proper	37,085.0	256,491	213,381	20.2
Outside	9,120.0	7,741	5,933	30.5
City and adjacent territory	510,438.4	259,465	240,657	20.3
Adjacent territory	473,353.4	32,974	27,276	20.9
DETROIT.				
Metropolitan district	175,253.8	1,165,153	514,086	126.6
In city proper	49,839.0	993,678	465,766	113.3
Outside	125,414.8	171,475	48,320	254.9
City and adjacent territory	295,906.6	1,181,057	522,740	125.9
Adjacent territory	246,067.6	187,379	56,974	228.9
INDIANAPOLIS.				
Metropolitan district	153,918.9	339,105	254,494	33.2
In city proper	27,893.9	314,194	233,650	34.5
Outside	126,025.0	24,911	20,844	19.5
City and adjacent territory	465,542.4	367,317	283,226	29.7
Adjacent territory	437,648.5	53,123	49,576	7.2
KANSAS CITY (MO. AND KANS.).				
Metropolitan district	264,006.7	477,354	369,276	29.3
In city proper (Kansas City, Mo.)	37,395.0	324,410	248,381	30.6
In city proper (Kansas City, Kans.)	10,138.1	101,177	82,331	22.9
Outside	216,473.6	51,767	38,564	34.2
Cities and adjacent territory	604,077.1	502,242	393,245	27.7
Adjacent territory	556,544.0	76,655	62,533	22.6
LOS ANGELES.				
Metropolitan district	831,605.0	879,008	464,841	89.1
In city proper	234,037.0	576,673	319,198	80.7
Outside	597,568.0	302,335	145,643	107.6
City and adjacent territory	941,870.6	880,853	406,462	88.8
Adjacent territory	707,833.6	303,980	147,264	106.4
LOUISVILLE.				
Metropolitan district	214,126.9	318,159	294,606	8.0
In city proper	14,348.8	234,891	223,928	4.9
Outside	199,778.1	83,268	70,678	17.8
City and adjacent territory	472,505.6	340,985	317,743	7.3
Adjacent territory	458,156.8	106,094	93,815	13.1
MILWAUKEE.				
Metropolitan district	128,287.3	537,797	431,417	24.6
In city proper	16,184.9	457,147	373,857	22.3
Outside	112,102.4	80,590	57,560	40.0
City and adjacent territory	219,519.3	546,822	440,206	24.2
Adjacent territory	203,334.4	89,675	66,349	35.2
MINNEAPOLIS-ST. PAUL.				
Metropolitan district	94,303.0	629,216	526,256	19.6
In city proper (Minneapolis)	31,834.0	380,582	301,408	26.3
In city proper (St. Paul)	33,389.0	234,698	214,744	9.3
Outside	29,080.0	13,936	10,104	37.9
Cities and adjacent territory	638,859.4	679,864	571,707	18.9
Adjacent territory	573,636.4	64,584	55,555	16.3
NEW ORLEANS.				
Metropolitan district	126,240.0	397,915	348,109	14.3
In city proper	113,920.0	387,219	339,075	14.2
Outside	12,320.0	10,696	9,034	18.4
City and adjacent territory	361,625.6	419,679	367,235	14.3
Adjacent territory	247,705.6	32,460	28,160	15.3
NEW YORK.				
Metropolitan district	751,887.3	7,910,415	6,566,859	20.5
In city proper	191,360.0	5,620,048	4,766,883	17.9
Outside	560,527.3	2,290,367	1,799,976	27.2
City and adjacent territory	875,515.2	8,034,349	6,657,946	20.7
Adjacent territory	684,155.2	2,414,301	1,891,063	27.7

DISTRICT.	Area in acres: 1920	POPULATION. 1920	POPULATION. 1910	Per cent of increase:[1] 1910-1920
PHILADELPHIA.				
Metropolitan district	483,439.4	2,407,234	1,983,300	21.4
In city proper	81,920.0	1,823,779	1,549,008	17.7
Outside	401,519.4	583,455	434,298	34.3
City and adjacent territory	645,329.8	2,428,728	2,004,185	21.2
Adjacent territory	563,409.8	604,949	455,177	32.9
PITTSBURGH.				
Metropolitan district	422,039.9	1,207,504	1,033,052	16.9
In city proper	25,517.2	588,343	533,905	10.2
Outside	396,522.7	619,161	499,147	24.0
City and adjacent territory	499,223.9	1,216,464	1,041,385	16.8
Adjacent territory	473,706.7	628,121	507,480	23.8
PORTLAND, OREG.				
Metropolitan district	160,762.0	299,882	240,005	24.9
In city proper	40,442.0	258,288	207,214	24.6
Outside	120,320.0	41,594	32,791	26.8
City and adjacent territory	440,742.8	329,246	264,303	24.6
Adjacent territory	400,300.8	70,958	57,089	24.3
PROVIDENCE.				
Metropolitan district	126,469.4	444,228	395,972	12.2
In city proper	11,388.0	237,595	224,326	5.9
Outside	115,081.4	206,633	171,646	20.4
City and adjacent territory	271,590.4	551,502	489,772	12.6
Adjacent territory	260,202.4	313,907	265,446	18.3
ROCHESTER.				
Metropolitan district	118,391.8	320,966	248,512	29.2
In city proper	18,891.0	295,750	218,149	35.6
Outside	99,500.8	25,216	30,363	-17.0
City and adjacent territory	338,084.6	342,999	272,741	25.8
Adjacent territory	319,193.6	47,249	54,592	-13.5
ST. LOUIS.				
Metropolitan district	197,757.1	952,012	828,733	14.9
In city proper	39,040.0	772,897	687,029	12.5
Outside	158,717.1	179,115	141,704	26.4
City and adjacent territory	456,357.4	1,014,457	881,025	15.0
Adjacent territory	417,317.4	241,560	194,896	23.9
SAN FRANCISCO-OAKLAND.				
Metropolitan district	286,500.8	801,477	686,873	29.8
In city proper (San Francisco)	26,880.0	506,676	416,912	21.5
In city proper (Oakland)	29,248.0	216,261	150,174	44.0
Outside	230,372.8	168,540	119,787	40.7
Cities and adjacent territory	381,880.0	900,921	692,654	30.1
Adjacent territory	325,752.0	177,084	125,568	41.7
SEATTLE.				
Metropolitan district	145,638.4	357,950	255,622	40.0
In city proper	37,478.4	315,312	237,194	32.9
Outside	108,160.0	42,638	18,428	131.4
City and adjacent territory	381,606.4	383,324	274,907	39.4
Adjacent territory	344,128.0	68,012	37,803	79.9
TOLEDO.				
Metropolitan district	59,661.2	263,717	180,375	46.2
In city proper	18,010.0	243,164	168,497	44.3
Outside	41,651.2	20,553	11,878	73.0
City and adjacent territory	336,890.0	294,248	208,872	40.9
Adjacent territory	318,880.0	51,084	40,375	26.5
WASHINGTON.				
Metropolitan district	170,146.0	506,588	380,508	33.1
In city proper	38,408.4	437,571	331,069	32.2
Outside	131,737.6	69,017	49,439	39.6
City and adjacent territory	567,166.2	540,702	413,458	30.8
Adjacent territory	528,757.8	103,131	82,389	25.2

[1] A minus sign (—) denotes decrease.

CITIES AND THEIR SUBURBS. 65

CIVIL DIVISIONS COMPRISED WITHIN METROPOLITAN DISTRICT AND ADJACENT TERRITORY OF EACH CENTRAL CITY.

AKRON DISTRICT.

METROPOLITAN DISTRICT.

Medina County.

Wadsworth twp., excl. Wadsworth village and part of Western Star village	1,225
Wadsworth village	4,742
Western Star village (part of)	86

Portage County.

Franklin twp., excl. Kent village	1,289
Kent village	7,070
Mogadore village (part of)	204

Summit County.

Akron city	208,435
Barberton city	18,811
Coventry twp., excl. Kenmore village	3,128
Cuyahoga Falls village	10,200
Kenmore village	12,683
Mogadore village (part of)	547
Norton twp., excl. Barberton city and part of Western Star village	2,848
Portage twp	1,589
Springfield twp., excl. part of Mogadore village	6,962
Tallmadge twp	5,207
Western Star village (part of)	87

ADJACENT TERRITORY OUTSIDE METROPOLITAN DISTRICT.

Medina County.

Granger twp	858
Sharon twp	1,087

Portage County.

Brimfield twp	893
Suffield twp., excl. part of Mogadore village	1,470

Stark County.

Lake twp	3,073

Summit County.

Bath twp	1,031
Boston twp., excl. Peninsula village	875
Clinton village	312
Copley twp	1,519
Franklin twp., excl. Clinton village	1,600
Green twp	1,702
Hudson twp., excl. Hudson village	803
Hudson village	1,134
Northampton twp	936
Peninsula village	520
Richfield twp	971
Silver Lake village	120
Stow twp., excl. Silver Lake village	1,619

ATLANTA DISTRICT.

METROPOLITAN DISTRICT.

Dekalb County.

Atlanta city (part of)	8,430
Decatur town	6,150
East Lake town	611
Kirkwood town	2,934
Mil. Dist. 531, Decatur, excl. Decatur town and part of East Lake town	3,882
Mil. Dist. 1379, Edgewood	(1)
Mil. Dist. 1586, Kirkwood, excl. Kirkwood town and part of East Lake town	10
Mil. Dist. 1666, East Atlanta	734

Fulton County.

Atlanta city (part of)	192,186
College Park town	3,622
East Point town	5,241
Hapeville town	1,631
Mil. Dist. 469, Cooks	3,397
Mil. Dist. 630, Black Hall	3,348
Mil. Dist. 1328, Collins	4,494
Mil. Dist. 1332, East Point, excl. East Point town	1,042
Mil. Dist. 1348, South Bend	6,377
Mil. Dist. 1362, Peachtree	1,123
Mil. Dist. 1422, Edgewood	1,063
Mil. Dist. 1511, Battle Hill	1,494
Mil. Dist. 1589, Hapeville, excl. Hapeville town	1,457

ADJACENT TERRITORY OUTSIDE METROPOLITAN DISTRICT.

Campbell County.

Mil. Dist. 499, Red Oak	1,406
Mil. Dist. 731, Sandtown	730
Mil. Dist. 1204, Union	617

40454°—21——5

ATLANTA DISTRICT—Con.

ADJACENT TERRITORY—con.

Clayton County.

Forest Park town	308
Mil. Dist. 548, Riverdale, excl. Riverdale town	1,095
Mil. Dist. 1189, Adamson	1,497
Mil. Dist. 1406, Ellenwood, excl. Rex town	881
Mil. Dist. 1446, Oak	1,059
Mil. Dist. 1644, Forest Park, excl. Forest Park town	1,024
Rex town	101
Riverdale town	159

Cobb County.

Mil. Dist. 1292, Smyrna, excl. Smyrna town	1,399
Mil. Dist. 1395, Howells	584
Mil. Dist. 1568, Vinings	373
Smyrna town	791

Dekalb County.

Chamblee town	253
Clarkston town	501
Doraville town	152
Mil. Dist. 524, Shallow Ford	611
Mil. Dist. 536, Panthersville	1,708
Mil. Dist. 572, Browning	1,250
Mil. Dist. 637, Evans	1,075
Mil. Dist. 686, Cross Keys, excl. Chamblee town	4,689
Mil. Dist. 1327, Clarkston, excl. Clarkston town	1,129
Mil. Dist. 1849, Mill	863
Mil. Dist. 1416, Doraville, excl. Doraville town	429

Fulton County.

Mil. Dist. 479, Bryants	1,040
Mil. Dist. 722, Buckhead	2,603
Mil. Dist. 1100, Oak Grove	784
Mil. Dist. 1289, Adamsville	898

BALTIMORE DISTRICT.

METROPOLITAN DISTRICT.

Anne Arundel County.

Dist. 3	4,881
Dist. 5	3,893

Baltimore city.

The city	733,826

Baltimore County.

Dist. 1	9,819
Dist. 3	3,987
Dist. 9	6,664
Dist. 12	4,162
Dist. 13	4,588
Dist. 14	3,500
Dist. 15	12,138

ADJACENT TERRITORY OUTSIDE METROPOLITAN DISTRICT.

Baltimore County.

Dist. 2	4,755
Dist. 4	5,499
Dist. 8	5,570
Dist. 11	5,196

Howard County.

Dist. 1, Elk Ridge	2,483
Dist. 2, Ellicott City, excl. Ellicott City	2,188
Ellicott City	1,246

BOSTON DISTRICT.

METROPOLITAN DISTRICT.

Essex County.

Lynn city	99,148
Marblehead town	7,324
Nahant town	1,318
Peabody city	19,552
Salem city	42,529
Saugus town	10,874
Swampscott town	8,101

Middlesex County.

Arlington town	18,665
Belmont town	10,749
Cambridge city	109,694
Everett city	40,120
Framingham town	17,033
Lexington town	6,350
Lincoln town	1,042
Malden city	49,103
Medford city	39,038
Melrose city	18,204
Natick town	10,907
Newton city	46,054
Sherborn town	1,558
Somerville city	93,091
Stoneham town	7,873
Wakefield town	13,025

BOSTON DISTRICT—Con.

METROPOLITAN DISTRICT—con.

Middlesex County—Con.

Waltham city	30,915
Watertown town	21,457
Wayland town	1,935
Weston town	2,282
Winchester town	10,485
Woburn city	16,574

Norfolk County.

Braintree town	10,580
Brookline town	37,748
Canton town	5,945
Dedham town	10,792
Dover town	867
Medfield town	3,595
Milton town	9,382
Needham town	7,012
Norwood town	12,627
Quincy city	47,876
Randolph town	4,756
Sharon town	2,467
Walpole town	5,446
Wellesley town	6,224
Westwood town	1,858
Weymouth town	15,057

Suffolk County.

Boston city	748,060
Chelsea city	43,184
Revere city	28,823
Winthrop town	15,455

ADJACENT TERRITORY OUTSIDE METROPOLITAN DISTRICT.

Essex County.

Lynnfield town	1,165

Middlesex County.

Burlington town	885
Reading town	7,439

Norfolk County.

Avon town	2,176
Holbrook town	3,161
Stoughton town	6,865

Plymouth County.

Hingham town	5,604
Hull town	1,771

BUFFALO DISTRICT.

METROPOLITAN DISTRICT.

Erie County.

Amherst town, excl. Williamsville village	4,533
Blasdell village	1,401
Buffalo city	506,775
Cheektowaga town, excl. Sloan village and part of Depew village	9,230
Depew village	5,850
Hamburg town, excl. Blasdell and Hamburg villages	4,070
Hamburg village	3,185
Kenmore village	3,160
Lackawanna city	17,918
Lancaster town, excl. Lancaster village and part of Depew village	2,165
Lancaster village	6,059
Sloan village	1,791
Tonawanda city	10,068
Tonawanda town, excl. Kenmore village	2,345
West Seneca town	7,002
Williamsville village	1,753

Niagara County.

North Tonawanda city	15,482

ADJACENT TERRITORY OUTSIDE METROPOLITAN DISTRICT.

Erie County.

Aurora town, excl. East Aurora village	1,609
Clarence town	2,660
East Aurora village	3,703
East Hamburg town	3,120
Elma town	1,986
Grand Island town	728

Niagara County.

La Salle village	3,813
Niagara town, excl. La Salle village	360
Pendleton town	1,175
Wheatfield town	1,834

CHICAGO DISTRICT.

METROPOLITAN DISTRICT (IN ILLINOIS).

Cook County.

Bellwood village	1,881
Berwyn city	14,150

CHICAGO DISTRICT—Con.

METROPOLITAN DISTRICT—con.

Cook County—Con.

Bloom twp., excl. Chicago Heights city, Glenwood, and South Chicago Heights villages, and parts of Homewood and Steger villages	1,816
Blue Island city	11,424
Bremen twp., excl. Robbins and Tinley Park villages and parts of Hazel Crest and Posen villages	4,711
Broadview village	430
Brookfield village	3,589
Burnham village	795
Burr Oak village	1,237
Calumet twp., excl. Burr Oak village and parts of Blue Island city and Riverdale village	1,151
Chicago city	2,701,705
Chicago Heights city	19,653
Chicago Ridge village	176
Cicero town	44,995
Des Plaines village	3,451
Dolton village	2,076
East Hazel Crest village	394
Elmwood Park village	1,380
Evanston city	37,234
Evergreen Park village	705
Forest Park village	10,768
Franklin Park village	914
Glencoe village	3,381
Glenwood village	738
Harvey city	9,216
Hazel Crest village	438
Hillside village	555
Hinsdale village (part of)	127
Hodgkins village	206
Homewood village	1,389
Justice village	183
Kenilworth village	1,188
La Grange village	6,525
La Grange Park village	1,684
Lansing village	1,409
Leyden twp., excl. Elmwood Park, Franklin Park, River Grove, and Schiller Park villages	1,761
Lyons twp., excl. Hodgkins, Justice, La Grange, and Summit villages and parts of Brookfield, Hinsdale, Lyons, Riverside, Spring Forest, and Western Springs villages	947
Lyons village	2,564
Maine twp., excl. Des Plaines and Riverview villages, and Park Ridge city	1,823
Maywood village	12,072
Melrose Park village	7,147
Morton Grove village	1,079
Mount Greenwood village	1,441
New Trier twp., excl. Glencoe, Kenilworth, Wilmette, and Winnetka villages	1,783
Niles twp., excl. Morton Grove, Niles, Niles Center, and Tessville villages	1,966
Niles village	1,258
Niles Center village	763
Norwood Park twp	6,897
Oak Lawn village	489
Oak Park village	39,858
Park Ridge city	8,383
Phoenix village	1,933
Posen village	947
Proviso twp., excl. Bellwood, Broadview, Forest Park, Hillside, La Grange Park, Maywood, and Melrose Park villages, and parts of Brookfield and Western Springs villages	980
River Forest village	4,358
River Grove village	484
Riverdale village	1,166
Riverside twp., excl. parts of Brookfield, Lyons, and Riverside villages	459
Riverside village	2,532
Riverview village	334
Robbins village	431
Schiller Park village	390
South Chicago Heights village	949
South Holland village	1,247
Spring Forest village	134
Stickney twp., excl. Stickney village	327
Stickney village	550
Summit village	4,019
Tessville village	355
Thornton twp., excl. Harvey and West Hammond cities, Burnham, Dolton, East Hazel Crest, Lansing, Phoenix, South Holland, and Thornton villages, and parts of Hazel Crest, Homewood, Posen, and Riverdale villages	3,372

[1] No population.

POPULATION.

CIVIL DIVISIONS COMPRISED WITHIN METROPOLITAN DISTRICT AND ADJACENT TERRITORY OF EACH CENTRAL CITY—Con.

CHICAGO DISTRICT—Con.

METROPOLITAN DISTRICT—con.
Cook County—Con.

Thornton village	767
Tinley Park village	493
West Hammond city	7,492
Western Springs village	1,258
Wilmette village	7,814
Winnetka village	6,694
Worth twp., excl. Chicago Ridge, Evergreen Park, Mount Greenwood, and Oak Lawn villages, and parts of Blue Island city and Worth village	1,443
Worth village	240

Du Page County.

Downers Grove twp., excl. Downers Grove village and part of Hinsdale village	1,811
Downers Grove village	3,543
Hinsdale village (part of)	3,915

METROPOLITAN DISTRICT (IN INDIANA).
Lake County.

Calumet twp., excl. Griffith town and part of Gary city	771
East Chicago city	35,967
Gary city	55,378
Griffith town	630
Hammond city	36,004
Hessville town	1,480
Highland town	542
Munster town	605
Whiting city	10,145

ADJACENT TERRITORY OUTSIDE METROPOLITAN DISTRICT (IN ILLINOIS).
Cook County.

Arlington Heights village	2,250
Elk Grove twp., excl. part of Mount Prospect village	1,102
Glenview village	760
Mount Prospect village	349
Northfield twp., excl. Glenview and Shermerville villages	2,124
Palos twp., excl. Palos Park village and parts of Spring Forest, and Worth villages	831
Palos Park village	240
Shermerville village	554
Wheeling twp., excl. Arlington Heights and Wheeling villages, and part of Mount Prospect village	2,537
Wheeling village	313

Du Page County.

Addison twp., excl. Addison, Bensenville, and Itasca villages, and part of Elmhurst city	1,202
Addison village	510
Bensenville village	650
Elmhurst city	4,594
Itasca village	339
Lombard village	1,331
Villa Park village	854
York twp., excl. Lombard and Villa Park villages, and part of Elmhurst city	1,837

CINCINNATI DISTRICT.
METROPOLITAN DISTRICT (IN OHIO).
Hamilton County.

Addyston village	1,448
Anderson twp., excl. Newtown village	2,450
Arlington Heights village	730
Cheviot village	4,108
Cincinnati city	401,247
Cleves village	1,454
Columbia twp., excl. Terrace Park village and parts of Madeira, Milford, and Silverton villages and Norwood city	2,899
Deer Park village	824
Delhi twp.	1,953
Elmwood Place village	3,991
Glendale village	1,759
Green twp., excl. Cheviot village	3,942
Lockland village	4,007
Madeira village	600
Miami twp., excl. Addyston, Cleves, and North Bend villages	798
Montgomery village	378
Mount Healthy village	2,255
Newtown village	534
North Bend village	597
North College Hill village	1,104
Norwood city	24,966
Reading village	4,540
St. Bernard city	6,312
Sharonville village	753
Silverton village	795

CINCINNATI DISTRICT—Con.
METROPOLITAN DISTRICT—con.
Hamilton County—Con.

Springfield twp., excl. Glendale, Mount Healthy, North College Hill, and Wyoming villages, and parts of Arlington Heights and Lockland villages	4,516
Sycamore twp., excl. Deer Park, Montgomery, Reading, and Sharonville villages, and parts of Arlington Heights, Lockland, Madeira, and Silverton villages	3,388
Terrace Park village	410
Wyoming village	2,323

METROPOLITAN DISTRICT (IN KENTUCKY).
Campbell County.

Bellevue city	7,379
Clifton town	2,065
Cote Brilliante town	489
Dayton city	7,646
Fort Thomas town	5,028
Mag. Dist. 1, excl. Clifton and Southgate towns and part of Newport city	244
Mag. Dist. 3, Outlying, excl. Bellevue and Dayton cities and Cote Brilliante town	915
Mag. Dist. 4, Cold Springs, excl. Fort Thomas town	1,793
Newport city	29,317
Southgate town	699

Kenton County.

Bromley town	736
Covington city	57,121
Fort Mitchell town	169
Ludlow town	4,582
Mag. Dist. 2, excl. part of Covington city	1,646
Mag. Dist. 3, excl. Bromley, Fort Mitchell, and Ludlow towns, and part of Covington city	1,940

ADJACENT TERRITORY OUTSIDE METROPOLITAN DISTRICT (IN OHIO).
Butler County.

Fairfield twp.	2,527
Hamilton city	39,675
Ross twp.	1,239
Union twp.	1,593

Clermont County.

Loveland village (part of)	1,017
Miami twp., excl. parts of Loveland and Milford villages	2,312
Milford village (part of)	1,454
Pierce twp., excl. part of Amelia town	1,182
Union twp.	1,659

Hamilton County.

Colerain twp.	2,801
Crosby twp.	758
Loveland village (part of)	521
Milford village (part of)	71
Symmes twp., excl. part of Loveland village	998
Whitewater twp.	1,467

Warren County.

Deerfield twp., excl. Mason village	2,059
Loveland village (part of)	19
Mason village	816

ADJACENT TERRITORY OUTSIDE METROPOLITAN DISTRICT (IN KENTUCKY).
Boone County.

Burlington town	198
Florence town	268
Mag. Dist. 1, Burlington, excl. Burlington town	1,703
Mag. Dist. 6, Florence, excl. Florence town	1,674

Campbell County.

Alexandria town	316
Mag. Dist. 5, Alexandria, excl. Alexandria and Melbourne towns	2,577
Melbourne town	337

Kenton County.

Elsmere town	919
Erlanger town	711
Independence town	153
Mag. Dist. 4, excl. Elsmere and Erlanger towns	1,381
Mag. Dist. 5, excl. Independence town	1,942

CLEVELAND DISTRICT.
METROPOLITAN DISTRICT.
Cuyahoga County.

Beachwood village	225
Bedford twp., excl. Bedford village	1,905

CLEVELAND DISTRICT—Con.
METROPOLITAN DISTRICT—con.
Cuyahoga County—Con.

Bedford village	2,677
Berea village	2,959
Bratenahl village	1,000
Brook Park village	861
Brooklyn twp., excl. Linndale village	422
Brooklyn Heights village	605
Cleveland city	796,841
Cleveland Heights village	15,236
Cuyahoga Heights village	739
East Cleveland city	27,292
East View village	606
Euclid village	3,363
Euclidville village	288
Fairview village	642
Garfield Heights village	2,550
Goldwood twp., excl. Fairview village	318
Idlewood village	131
Independence twp.	304
Independence village	1,074
Lakewood city	41,732
Linndale village	400
Maple Heights village	1,732
Middleburgh twp., excl. Berea village	2,004
Newburgh Heights village	2,957
North Randall village	652
Richmond Heights village	265
Rocky River village	1,861
Shaker Heights village	1,616
South Euclid village	1,005
Valley View village	403
Warrensville twp., excl. East View and North Randall villages	1,784
West Park village	8,581

ADJACENT TERRITORY OUTSIDE METROPOLITAN DISTRICT.
Cuyahoga County.

Bay village	751
Brecksville twp.	1,305
Chagrin Falls twp., excl. Chagrin Falls village	240
Chagrin Falls village	2,237
Dover village	1,754
Glenwillow village	200
Mayfield twp.	1,363
North Olmsted village	1,419
Olmsted twp., excl. Olmsted Falls village	1,098
Olmsted Falls village	374
Orange twp.	945
Parma twp.	2,345
Parma Heights village	310
Royalton twp.	1,262
Solon twp.	887
Strongsville twp.	1,285

Lake County.

Kirtland twp.	957
Wickliffe village	1,508
Willoughby twp., excl. Wickliffe and Willoughby villages	1,521
Willoughby village	2,656

Summit County.

Macedonia village	531
Northfield village	861

COLUMBUS DISTRICT.
METROPOLITAN DISTRICT.
Franklin County.

Bexley village	1,342
Blendon twp., excl. Westerville village	995
Clinton twp., excl. East Linden and Linden Heights villages	3,453
Columbus city	237,031
East Columbus village	1,328
East Linden village	724
Franklin twp., excl. Grandview Heights and Marble Cliff villages	4,362
Gahanna village	347
Grandview Heights village	1,185
Hanford village	160
Linden Heights village	1,731
Marble Cliff village	216
Marion twp., excl. Bexley and Hanford villages, and part of East Columbus village	2,798
Mifflin twp., excl. Gahanna village and part of East Columbus village	2,186
Westerville village	2,480

ADJACENT TERRITORY OUTSIDE METROPOLITAN DISTRICT.
Delaware County.

Orange twp.	890

COLUMBUS DISTRICT—Con.
ADJACENT TERRITORY—con.
Franklin County.

Brown twp.	659
Canal Winchester village	791
Dublin village	211
Grove City village	905
Groveport village	671
Hamilton twp., excl. Lockbourne village	1,602
Harrisburg village	258
Hilliard village	451
Jackson twp., excl. Grove City village	1,634
Jefferson twp.	1,211
Lockbourne village	279
Madison twp., excl. Canal Winchester and Groveport villages	2,033
New Albany village	200
Norwich twp., excl. Hilliard village	1,126
Perry twp., excl. Upper Arlington village	1,689
Plain twp., excl. New Albany village	808
Pleasant twp., excl. Harrisburg village	1,418
Prairie twp.	1,476
Reynoldsburg village	491
Sharon twp., excl. Worthington village	1,621
Truro twp., excl. Reynoldsburg village and part of East Columbus village	1,949
Upper Arlington village	620
Washington twp., excl. Dublin village	805
Worthington village	705

DENVER DISTRICT.
METROPOLITAN DISTRICT.
Arapahoe County.

Englewood city	4,356
Pct. 5, N. Englewood, excl. part of Englewood city	140
Pct. 6, S. W. Englewood, excl. part of Englewood city	143
Pct. 10, S. E. Englewood, excl. part of Englewood city	479
Pct. 19, N. Englewood, excl. part of Englewood city	63

Denver County.

Denver city	256,491

Jefferson County.

Edgewater town	664
Lakeside town	36
Mountain View town	372
Pct. 22, Manhattan, excl. part of Edgewater town	642
Pct. 27, Wheat Ridge	846

ADJACENT TERRITORY OUTSIDE METROPOLITAN DISTRICT.
Adams County.

Aurora town (part of)	507
Pct. 6, First Creek	146
Pct. 9, Henderson	631
Pct. 10, Lower Platte	408
Pct. 11, Irondale	1,201
Pct. 12, Colfax, excl. part of Aurora town	1,128
Pct. 13, Eastlake	916
Pct. 14, Lower Clear Creek	770
Pct. 15, Westminster, excl. Westminster town	493
Pct. 16, Retreat Park	689
Pct. 17, College	514
Westminster town	235

Arapahoe County.

Aurora town (part of)	386
Littleton town	1,636
Pct. 1, W. Sheridan, excl. part of Sheridan town	1,345
Pct. 2, E. Sheridan, excl. part of Sheridan town	144
Pct. 3, Glendale	580
Pct. 4, S. E. Littleton, excl. part of Littleton town	232
Pct. 7, Dry Creek	189
Pct. 8, N. Littleton, excl. part of Littleton town	220
Pct. 9, Broadway	382
Pct. 11, Melvin	154
Pct. 12, S. W. Littleton, excl. part of Littleton town	244
Pct. 16, Aurora, excl. part of Aurora town	191
Pct. 18, Sullivan	235
Sheridan town	455

Boulder County.

Pct. 26, Broomfield	167

CITIES AND THEIR SUBURBS.

67

CIVIL DIVISIONS COMPRISED WITHIN METROPOLITAN DISTRICT AND ADJACENT TERRITORY OF EACH CENTRAL CITY—Con.

DENVER DISTRICT—Con.

ADJACENT TERRITORY—Con.
Douglas County.

Pct. 2, Platte	315
Pct. 15, Kelley	523

Jefferson County.

Arvada town	915
Golden city	2,484
Morrison town	195
Pct. 1, Grant	594
Pct. 2, Vasquez	717
Pct. 3, Montana	632
Pct. 4, Morrison, excl. Morrison town	228
Pct. 9, Golden No. 1, excl. part of Golden city	43
Pct. 10, Golden No. 2, excl. part of Golden city	163
Pct. 11, Golden No. 3, excl. part of Golden city	61
Pct. 12, Golden No. 4, excl. part of Golden city	52
Pct. 13, Ralston	237
Pct. 16, Maple Grove	341
Pct. 19, Semper	363
Pct. 20, Lakewood	683
Pct. 21, E. Arvada, excl. part of Arvada town	718
Pct. 25, W. Arvada, excl. part of Arvada town	628
Pct. 26, Fairmont	431
Pct. 29	562

DETROIT DISTRICT.

METROPOLITAN DISTRICT.
Macomb County.

Erin twp., excl. part of Fraser village	2,599
Fraser village	247
Grosse Pointe Shores village (part of)	16

Oakland County.

Ferndale village	2,640
Royal Oak twp., excl. Ferndale and Royal Oak villages	6,785
Royal Oak village	6,007

Wayne County.

Dearborn twp., excl. Dearborn village	2,786
Dearborn village	2,470
Detroit city	993,678
Ecorse twp., excl. Ecorse, Ford, Oakwood, and River Rouge villages	2,411
Ecorse village	4,394
Ford village	4,294
Gratiot twp.	975
Greenfield twp.	2,643
Grosse Pointe twp., excl. Grosse Pointe, Grosse Pointe Farms, and Grosse Pointe Park villages, and part of Grosse Pointe Shores village	477
Grosse Pointe village	2,084
Grosse Pointe Farms village	1,649
Grosse Pointe Park village	1,355
Grosse Pointe Shores village (part of)	503
Hamtramck twp., excl. Hamtramck village	672
Hamtramck village	48,615
Highland Park city	46,499
Monguagon twp., excl. Trenton village	1,593
Oakwood village	1,900
River Rouge village	9,822
Springwells twp.	2,466
Trenton village	1,682
Wyandotte city	13,851

ADJACENT TERRITORY OUTSIDE METROPOLITAN DISTRICT.
Macomb County.

Lake twp., excl. part of Grosse Pointe Shores village	1,330
Warren twp., excl. Warren village	3,238
Warren village	326

Oakland County.

Southfield twp.	1,319
Troy twp.	2,520

Wayne County.

Grosse Isle twp.	802
Redford twp., excl. Redford village	3,812
Redford village	1,389
Taylor twp.	1,168

INDIANAPOLIS DISTRICT.

METROPOLITAN DISTRICT.
Marion County.

Beech Grove town	1,459
Broad Ripple town	1,552
Center twp., excl. Woodruff Place town and parts of Beech Grove town and Indianapolis city	2,436

INDIANAPOLIS DISTRICT—Con.

METROPOLITAN DISTRICT—Con.
Marion County—Con.

Clermont town	240
Indianapolis city	314,194
Perry twp., excl. Southport and University Heights towns, and parts of Beech Grove town and Indianapolis city	3,818
Ravenswood town	5
Southport town	458
University Heights town	477
Warren twp., excl. parts of Beech Grove town and Indianapolis city	3,151
Washington twp., excl. Broad Ripple and Ravenswood towns and part of Indianapolis city	3,142
Wayne twp., excl. Clermont town and part of Indianapolis city	7,015
Woodruff Place town	1,158

ADJACENT TERRITORY OUTSIDE METROPOLITAN DISTRICT.
Boone County.

Eagle twp., excl. Zionsville town	969
Zionsville town	957

Hamilton County.

Carmel town	598
Clay twp., excl. part of Carmel town	960
Delaware twp., excl. Fishers Station town and part of Carmel town	964
Fishers Station town	142

Hancock County.

Buck Creek twp.	1,153
New Palestine town	442
Sugar Creek twp., excl. New Palestine town	1,213

Hendricks County.

Brownsburg town	1,063
Guilford twp., excl. Plainfield town	1,789
Lincoln twp., excl. Brownsburg town	735
Plainfield town	1,373
Washington twp.	1,302

Johnson County.

Bargersville town	290
Greenwood town	1,907
Pleasant twp., excl. Greenwood and Whiteland towns	1,259
White River twp., excl. Bargersville town	1,752
Whiteland town	388

Marion County.

Castleton town	208
Decatur twp.	1,636
Franklin twp., excl. part of Beech Grove town	2,444
Lawrence twp., excl. Castleton town	2,919
Pike twp.	1,749

KANSAS CITY DISTRICT (MISSOURI AND KANSAS).

METROPOLITAN DISTRICT (IN MISSOURI).
Clay County.

Avondale village	314
Birmingham town	175
Gallatin twp., excl. Avondale village, and Birmingham and North Kansas City towns	2,497
North Kansas City town	870

Jackson County.

Blue twp., excl. Independence city and part of Kansas City	13,801
Brooking twp., excl. part of Kansas City	1,767
Grandview town	410
Independence city	11,686
Kansas City, Mo	324,410
Washington twp., excl. Grandview town	3,501

METROPOLITAN DISTRICT (IN KANSAS).
Wyandotte County.

Kansas City, Kans	101,177
Quindaro twp.	3,435
Rosedale city	7,674
Shawnee twp.	3,650
Wyandotte twp.	1,987

ADJACENT TERRITORY OUTSIDE METROPOLITAN DISTRICT (IN MISSOURI).
Clay County.

Liberty city	3,097
Liberty twp., excl. Liberty city	1,920

Jackson County.

Lees Summit city	1,467
Prairie twp., excl. Lees Summit city	2,859

KANSAS CITY DISTRICT—Con.

ADJACENT TERRITORY—Con.
Platte County.

May twp.	868
Parkville city	619
Pettis twp., excl. Parkville city	1,440
Waldron twp.	407

ADJACENT TERRITORY OUTSIDE METROPOLITAN DISTRICT (IN KANSAS).
Johnson County.

Lenexa city	472
Mission twp.	2,539
Monticello twp.	1,094
Oxford twp.	1,351
Shawnee twp., excl. Lenexa city	2,450

Wyandotte County.

Bonner Springs city	1,626
Delaware twp., excl. Edwardsville city	1,480
Edwardsville city	203
Prairie twp.	986

LOS ANGELES DISTRICT.

METROPOLITAN DISTRICT.
Los Angeles County.

Alhambra city	9,096
Arcadia city	2,239
Belvedere twp., excl. part of Monterey Park city	6,330
Beverly Hills city	674
Burbank city	2,913
Burbank twp., excl. Burbank, Eagle Rock, and Glendale cities and parts of Los Angeles and Pasadena cities	5,502
Cahuenga twp., excl. Beverly Hills city and part of Los Angeles city	4,588
Calabasas twp.	401
Compton city	1,478
Compton twp., excl. Compton city	4,879
Culver city	503
Downey twp.	5,562
Eagle Rock city	2,256
El Monte city	1,283
El Monte twp., excl. El Monte city and part of Monterey Park city	2,766
El Segundo city	1,563
Gardena twp.	6,331
Glendale city	13,536
Hermosa Beach city	2,327
Huntington Park city	4,513
Inglewood city	3,286
Inglewood twp., excl. Inglewood city and part of Los Angeles city	2,399
Lankershim twp., excl. part of Los Angeles city	1,725
Lomita twp., excl. part of Los Angeles city	3,531
Long Beach city	55,593
Long Beach twp., excl. Long Beach city	5,769
Los Angeles city	576,673
Los Angeles twp., excl. part of Los Angeles city	942
Malibu twp., excl. part of Los Angeles city	3,793
Manhattan Beach city	859
Monrovia city	5,480
Monterey Park city	4,108
Pasadena city	45,354
Pasadena twp., excl. Arcadia and Sierra Madre cities and part of Pasadena city	8,027
Redondo twp., excl. El Segundo, Hermosa Beach, Manhattan Beach, and Redondo Beach cities, and part of Los Angeles city	4,131
Redondo Beach city	4,913
San Antonio twp., excl. Huntington Park, Vernon, and Watts cities, and part of Monterey Park city	22,605
San Fernando city	3,204
San Gabriel city	2,640
San Gabriel twp., excl. Alhambra, San Gabriel, and San Marino cities, and part of Monterey Park city	2,218
San Marino city	594
Santa Monica city	15,252
Sierra Madre city	2,026
South Pasadena city	7,652
Venice city	10,385
Venice twp., excl. Culver and Venice cities and part of Los Angeles city	1,495
Vernon city	1,005
Watts city	4,529

ADJACENT TERRITORY OUTSIDE METROPOLITAN DISTRICT.
Los Angeles County.

Saugus and New Hall precincts (Soledad twp.)	1,645

LOUISVILLE DISTRICT.

METROPOLITAN DISTRICT (IN KENTUCKY).
Jefferson County.

Highland Park town	3,979
Jeffersontown town	350
Louisville city	234,891
Mag. Dist. 2, excl. Jeffersontown town	10,310
Mag. Dist. 3, excl. Highland Park and Oakdale towns	12,415
Mag. Dist. 4	11,474
Oakdale town	3,193

METROPOLITAN DISTRICT (IN INDIANA).
Clark County.

Clarksville town	2,322
Claysburg town	437
Jeffersonville city	10,098
Jeffersonville twp., excl. Jeffersonville city and Clarksville, Claysburg, and Port Fulton towns	1,799
Port Fulton town	971

Floyd County.

New Albany city	22,992
New Albany twp., excl. New Albany city	2,923

ADJACENT TERRITORY OUTSIDE METROPOLITAN DISTRICT (IN KENTUCKY).
Jefferson County.

Anchorage town	447
Mag. Dist. 1, excl. Anchorage town	9,305

Oldham County.

Mag. Dist. 1, Goshen	657
Mag. Dist. 5, Beard, excl. Pewee Valley town	1,207
Mag. Dist. 6, Brownsboro	539
Pewee Valley town	649

ADJACENT TERRITORY OUTSIDE METROPOLITAN DISTRICT (IN INDIANA).
Clark County.

Sellersburg town	915
Silver Creek twp., excl. Sellersburg town	1,222
Utica twp.	1,275

Floyd County.

Franklin twp.	653
Georgetown town	401
Georgetown twp., excl. Georgetown town	1,159
Lafayette twp.	1,368

Harrison County.

Elizabeth town	193
Franklin twp., excl. Lanesville town	1,189
Lanesville town	269
Posey twp., excl. Elizabeth town	1,378

MILWAUKEE DISTRICT.

METROPOLITAN DISTRICT.
Milwaukee County.

Cudahy city	6,725
Granville town	2,875
Greenfield town	6,293
Lake town	8,876
Milwaukee city	457,147
Milwaukee town	2,006
North Milwaukee city	3,047
Oak Creek town	2,292
Shorewood village	2,650
South Milwaukee city	7,598
Wauwatosa city	5,818
Wauwatosa town	15,082
West Allis city	13,745
West Milwaukee village	2,101
Whitefish Bay village	882

ADJACENT TERRITORY OUTSIDE METROPOLITAN DISTRICT.
Milwaukee County.

Franklin town	1,712

Waukesha County.

Brookfield town	1,973
Menomonee town	2,175
Menomonee Falls village	1,019
New Berlin town	1,042
New Butler village	564

MINNEAPOLIS—ST. PAUL DISTRICT.

METROPOLITAN DISTRICT.
Dakota County.

South St. Paul city	6,860
West St. Paul city	2,962

Hennepin County.

Edina village	1,833
Minneapolis city	380,582
St. Louis Park village	2,281

Ramsey County.

St. Paul city	234

POPULATION.

68

CIVIL DIVISIONS COMPRISED WITHIN METROPOLITAN DISTRICT AND ADJACENT TERRITORY OF EACH CENTRAL CITY—Con.

MINNEAPOLIS-ST. PAUL DISTRICT—Con.

ADJACENT TERRITORY OUTSIDE METROPOLITAN DISTRICT.

Anoka County.

Anoka city	4,287
Anoka twp	548
Blaine twp	550
Columbia Heights village	2,968
Fridley twp	533

Dakota County.

Burnsville twp	419
Egan twp	857
Invergrove twp	1,210
Invergrove village	363
Lebanon twp	361
Mendota twp	757
Mendota village	193
Rosemount twp	599
Rosemount village	310

Hennepin County.

Bloomington twp	1,330
Brooklyn twp	948
Brooklyn Center village	788
Champlin twp	583
Crystal village	814
Deephaven village	238
Eden Prairie twp	983
Golden Valley village	830
Maple Grove twp	1,083
Minnetonka twp	2,298
Osseo village	433
Plymouth twp	1,275
Richfield village	2,411
Robbinsdale village	1,369
Wayzata village	633
West Minneapolis village	3,055

Ramsey County.

Mounds View twp	1,058
New Brighton village	368
New Canada twp	1,729
North St. Paul village	1,979
Rose twp	1,562
White Bear twp	1,138
White Bear Lake village	2,022

Washington County.

Afton twp	807
Afton village	183
Baytown twp	584
Cottage Grove twp	667
Dellwood village	87
Denmark twp	645
Grant twp	600
Lakeland twp	590
Newport twp., excl. St. Paul Park village	131
Newport village	453
Oakdale twp	1,163
St. Paul Park village	900
Woodbury twp	956

NEW ORLEANS DISTRICT.

METROPOLITAN DISTRICT.

Jefferson Parish.

Gretna city	7,197
Ward 1, excl. part of Gretna city	245
Ward 3, excl. part of Gretna city	1,206
Ward 7	2,048

Orleans Parish.

New Orleans city	387,219

ADJACENT TERRITORY OUTSIDE METROPOLITAN DISTRICT.

Jefferson Parish.

Kenner town	1,882
Ward 4, incl. Westwego village	4,083
Ward 5	1,134
Ward 8	1,546
Ward 9, excl. Kenner town	758
Westwego village	(1)

Plaquemines Parish.

Ward 1	1,105
Ward 6	604

St. Bernard Parish.

Ward 1	1,464
Ward 2	1,499
Ward 3	1,050
Ward 4	291
Ward 5	270

St. Tammany Parish.

Pearl River village	364
Slidell town	2,958
Ward 8, excl. Pearl River village	1,115
Ward 9, excl. Slidell town	1,641

NEW YORK DISTRICT.

METROPOLITAN DISTRICT (IN NEW YORK).

Bronx County.

Bronx borough (part of New York city)	732,016

NEW YORK DISTRICT—Con.

METROPOLITAN DISTRICT—con.

Kings County.

Brooklyn borough (part of New York city)	2,018,356

Nassau County.

Cedarhurst village	2,838
East Rockaway village	2,005
Farmingdale village	2,091
Floral Park village	2,097
Freeport village	8,599
Garden City village	2,420
Glen Cove city	8,664
Great Neck Estates village	339
Hempstead town, excl. Cedarhurst, East Rockaway, Freeport, Garden City, Hempstead, Lawrence, Long Beach, Lynbrook, Rockville Center, and Woodsburgh villages, and part of Floral Park village	32,999
Hempstead village	6,382
Lawrence village	2,861
Long Beach village	282
Lynbrook village	4,371
Mineola village	3,016
North Hempstead town, excl. Great Neck Estates, Mineola, Plandome, Saddle Rock, and Sands Point villages and part of Floral Park village	21,795
Oyster Bay town, excl. Farmingdale and Sea Cliff villages	16,097
Plandome village	319
Rockville Center village	6,262
Saddle Rock village	71
Sands Point village	284
Sea Cliff village	2,108
Woodsburgh village	220

New York County.

Manhattan borough (part of New York city)	2,284,103

Queens County.

Queens borough (part of New York city)	469,042

Richmond County.

Richmond borough (part of New York city)	116,531

Westchester County.

Ardsley village	730
Bronxville village	3,055
Dobbs Ferry village	4,401
Eastchester town, excl. Bronxville and Tuckahoe villages	2,808
Elmsford village	1,635
Greenburg town, excl. Ardsley, Dobbs Ferry, Elmsford, Hastings-upon-Hudson, Irvington and Tarrytown villages	3,181
Hastings-upon-Hudson village	5,526
Irvington village	2,701
Larchmont village	2,468
Mamaroneck town, excl. Larchmont village and part of Mamaroneck village	1,797
Mamaroneck village	6,571
Mount Vernon city	42,726
New Rochelle city	36,213
North Pelham village	2,355
Pelham village	1,056
Pelham Manor village	1,754
Scarsdale village	3,506
Tarrytown village	5,807
Tuckahoe village	3,509
White Plains city	21,031
Yonkers city	100,176

METROPOLITAN DISTRICT (IN NEW JERSEY).

Bergen County.

Alpine borough	350
Bergenfield borough	3,667
Bogota borough	3,906
Carlstadt borough	4,472
Cliffside Park borough	5,709
Closter borough	1,840
Cresskill borough	942
Delford borough	1,286
Demarest borough	654
Dumont borough	2,537
East Rutherford borough	5,463
Edgewater borough	3,530
Englewood city	11,627
Englewood Cliffs borough	594
Fairview borough	4,882
Fort Lee borough	5,761
Hackensack town	17,667
Harrington Park borough	627
Hasbrouck Heights borough	2,895
Haworth borough	748
Leonia borough	2,979
Little Ferry borough	2,715
Lodi borough	8,175

NEW YORK DISTRICT—Con.

METROPOLITAN DISTRICT—con.

Bergen County—Con.

Lodi twp	987
Lyndhurst twp	9,515
Moonachie borough	1,194
North Arlington borough	1,767
Northvale borough	827
Norwood borough	820
Old Tappan borough	404
Palisades twp	3,833
Palisades Park borough	2,633
Ridgefield borough	1,560
Ridgefield Park village	8,575
Riverside borough	1,077
Rutherford borough	497
Teaneck twp	4,192
Tenafly borough	3,585
Teterboro borough	24
Wallington borough	5,715
Wood Ridge borough	1,923

Essex County.

Belleville town	15,660
Bloomfield town	22,019
East Orange city	50,710
Glen Ridge borough	4,620
Irvington town	25,480
Montclair town	28,810
Newark city	414,524
Nutley town	9,421
Orange city	33,268
South Orange twp	5,283
South Orange village	7,274

Hudson County.

Bayonne city	76,754
East Newark borough	3,057
Guttenberg town	6,726
Harrison town	15,721
Hoboken city	68,166
Jersey City	298,103
Kearny town	26,724
North Bergen twp	23,344
Secaucus town	5,423
Union town	20,651
Weehawken town	14,485
West Hoboken town	40,074
West New York town	29,926

Middlesex County.

East Brunswick twp	1,857
Helmetta borough	687
Highland Park borough	4,806
Metuchen borough	3,334
Milltown borough	2,573
Perth Amboy city	41,707
Raritan twp	5,419
Roosevelt borough	11,047
Sayreville twp	7,181
South Amboy city	7,807
South River borough	6,596
Spotswood borough	704
Woodbridge twp	18,423

Monmouth County.

Atlantic Highlands borough	1,620
Highlands borough	1,731
Keansburg borough	1,321
Keyport borough	4,415
Matawan borough	1,910
Matawan twp	1,856
Middletown twp	5,917
Raritan twp	1,659

Passaic County.

Clifton city	26,470
Little Falls twp	3,310
Passaic city	63,841
Paterson city	135,875
West Paterson borough	1,858

Union County.

Clark twp	791
Cranford twp	6,001
Elizabeth city	95,783
Garwood borough	2,084
Hillside twp	5,267
Kenilworth borough	1,312
Linden borough	1,756
Linden twp	6,612
Rahway city	11,042
Roselle borough	5,787
Roselle Park borough	5,438
Union twp	3,062
Westfield town	9,063

ADJACENT TERRITORY OUTSIDE METROPOLITAN DISTRICT (IN NEW YORK).

Rockland County.

Grand-View-on-Hudson village	175
Nyack village	4,444
Orangetown town, excl. Grand-View-on-Hudson, Nyack, Piermont, and South Nyack villages	6,266
Piermont village	1,600
South Nyack village	1,799

NEW YORK DISTRICT—Con.

ADJACENT TERRITORY—con.

Westchester County.

Harrison town	5,006
Port Chester village	16,573
Rye town, excl. Port Chester and Rye villages and part of Mamaroneck village	903
Rye village	5,308

ADJACENT TERRITORY OUTSIDE METROPOLITAN DISTRICT (IN NEW JERSEY).

Bergen County.

East Paterson borough	2,441
Emerson borough	973
Garfield city	19,381
Hillsdale twp	1,720
Maywood borough	1,618
Midland twp	2,203
Rivervale twp	583
Saddle River twp	2,815
Washington twp	194
Westwood borough	2,507

Essex County.

Milburn twp	4,633

Middlesex County.

Madison twp	1,808
New Brunswick city	32,779

Monmouth County.

Holmdel twp	1,100
Marlboro twp	1,710

Union County.

Fanwood borough	724
Mountainside borough	403
Scotch Plains twp	2,343
Springfield twp	1,715

PHILADELPHIA DISTRICT.

METROPOLITAN DISTRICT (IN PENNSYLVANIA).

Bucks County.

Bensalem twp	2,912
Bristol borough	10,273
Bristol twp	5,027
Hulmeville borough	491
Langhorne borough	1,067
Langhorne Manor borough	207
Middletown twp	1,805
Newtown borough	1,703
Newtown twp	725
South Langhorne borough	557

Chester County.

Easttown twp	2,307
Tredyffrin twp	4,470

Delaware County.

Aldan borough	1,136
Aston twp	2,107
Chester city	58,030
Chester twp	675
Clifton Heights borough	3,409
Collingdale borough	3,834
Colwyn borough	1,859
Darby borough	7,922
Darby twp	3,077
East Lansdowne borough	1,561
Eddystone borough	2,670
Glenolden borough	1,044
Haverford twp	6,691
Lansdowne borough	4,707
Lower Chichester twp	2,581
Marcus Hook borough	5,324
Marple twp	900
Media borough	4,109
Middletown twp	4,304
Millbourne borough	419
Morton borough	1,212
Nether Providence twp	2,344
Newtown twp	837
Norwood borough	2,353
Parkside borough	374
Prospect Park borough	2,536
Radnor twp	8,181
Ridley twp	6,342
Ridley Park borough	2,313
Rutledge borough	711
Sharon Hill borough	1,780
Springfield twp	1,208
Swarthmore borough	2,350
Tinicum twp	2,500
Trainer borough	1,367
Upland borough	2,486
Upper Chichester twp	1,577
Upper Darby twp	8,950
Upper Providence twp	1,246
Yeadon borough	1,308

Montgomery County.

Abington twp	8,684
Ambler borough	3,004
Bridgeport borough	4,680
Bryn Athyn borough	392

¹Not returned separately.

CITIES AND THEIR SUBURBS.

CIVIL DIVISIONS COMPRISED WITHIN METROPOLITAN DISTRICT AND ADJACENT TERRITORY OF EACH CENTRAL CITY—Con.

PHILADELPHIA DISTRICT—Con.

METROPOLITAN DISTRICT—con.

Montgomery County—Con.

Cheltenham twp	11,015
Conshohocken borough	8,481
East Norriton twp	643
Hatboro borough	1,102
Jenkintown borough	3,366
Lower Gwynedd twp	1,363
Lower Merion twp	23,866
Lower Moreland twp	1,126
Narberth borough	3,704
Norristown borough	32,319
North Wales borough	2,041
Plymouth twp	3,201
Rockledge borough	1,029
Springfield twp	3,374
Upper Dublin twp	3,045
Upper Gwynedd twp	1,534
Upper Merion twp	4,005
Upper Moreland twp	2,195
West Conshohocken borough	2,331
West Norriton twp	1,375
Whitemarsh twp	3,436
Whitpain twp	1,826

Philadelphia County.

Philadelphia city	1,823,779

METROPOLITAN DISTRICT (IN NEW JERSEY).

Burlington County.

Beverly city	2,562
Beverly twp	2,794
Burlington city	9,049
Burlington twp	1,520
Chester twp	7,273
Cinnaminson twp	1,587
Delran twp	1,475
Northampton twp	5,901
Palmyra twp	3,834
Riverside twp	6,018
Riverton borough	2,341
Westhampton twp	478
Willingboro twp	601

Camden County.

Audubon borough	4,740
Barrington borough	1,338
Camden city	116,309
Centre twp	4,004
Clementon twp	3,491
Collingswood borough	8,714
Gloucester city	12,162
Gloucester twp	3,097
Haddon twp	2,708
Haddon Heights borough	2,950
Haddonfield borough	5,646
Laurel Springs borough	911
Magnolia borough	1,245
Merchantville borough	2,749
Oaklyn borough	1,148
Pensauken twp	6,474
Woodlynne borough	1,515

Gloucester County.

Deptford twp	2,224
Greenwich twp	1,751
Mantua twp	2,002
National Park borough	1,000
Paulsboro borough	4,352
Pitman borough	3,385
Wenonah borough	918
West Deptford twp	1,781
Westville borough	2,380
Woodbury city	5,801
Woodbury Heights borough	481

ADJACENT TERRITORY OUTSIDE METROPOLITAN DISTRICT (IN PENNSYLVANIA).

Bucks County.

Ivyland borough	263
Northampton twp	1,325
Southampton twp	1,379
Warminster twp	700
Warwick twp	472
Wrightstown twp	741

Delaware County.

Edgemont twp	474

Montgomery County.

Horsham twp	1,180
Montgomery twp	787
Worcester twp	1,364

ADJACENT TERRITORY OUTSIDE METROPOLITAN DISTRICT (IN NEW JERSEY).

Burlington County.

Mount Laurel twp	1,667

Camden County.

Delaware twp	2,331
Voorhees twp	1,805

Gloucester County.

East Greenwich twp	1,483
Harrison twp	1,633
Logan twp	1,510
Swedesboro borough	1,838
Woolwich twp	973

PITTSBURGH DISTRICT.

METROPOLITAN DISTRICT.

Allegheny County.

Aleppo twp	397
Aspinwall borough	3,170
Avalon borough	5,277
Baldwin twp	4,928
Bellevue borough	8,198
Ben Avon borough	2,198
Ben Avon Heights borough	130
Bethel twp	2,406
Braddock borough	20,879
Braddock twp	1,215
Brentwood borough	1,695
Bridgeville borough	3,092
Carnegie borough	11,516
Carrick borough	10,504
Castle Shannon borough	2,353
Chalfant borough	1,044
Chartiers twp	5,934
Cheswick borough	471
Clairton borough	6,264
Collier twp	4,651
Coraopolis borough	6,162
Crafton borough	5,954
Crescent twp	980
Dormont borough	6,455
Dravosburg borough	2,204
Duquesne city	19,011
East Deer twp	3,506
East McKeesport borough	2,430
East Pittsburgh borough	6,527
Edgewood borough	3,181
Edgeworth borough	1,373
Elizabeth borough	2,703
Elizabeth twp	6,563
Emsworth borough	2,165
Etna borough	6,341
Forward twp	4,932
Frazer twp	1,035
Glassport borough	6,959
Glenfield borough	2,156
Greentree borough	1,043
Harmar twp	1,230
Hays borough	2,231
Haysville borough	173
Heidelberg borough	2,094
Homestead borough	20,452
Indiana twp	2,298
Ingram borough	2,900
Jefferson twp	5,009
Kennedy twp	760
Kilbuck twp	177
Knoxville borough	7,201
Leet twp	627
Leetsdale borough	2,311
Liberty borough	601
Lincoln twp	739
Lower St. Clair twp	51
McKees Rocks borough	16,713
McKeesport city	46,781
Mifflin twp	11,267
Millvale borough	8,031
Moon twp	1,700
Mount Lebanon twp	2,258
Mount Oliver borough	5,575
Munhall borough	6,418
Neville twp	1,272
North Braddock borough	14,928
North Clairton borough	1,270
North Fayette twp	5,000
North Versailles twp	4,844
Oakdale borough	1,611
Oakmont borough	4,512
O'Hara twp	4,672
Osborne borough	358
Overbrook borough	2,185
Patton twp	3,624
Penn twp	8,342
Pitcairn borough	5,738
Pittsburgh city	588,343
Plum twp	3,855
Port Vue borough	2,538
Rankin borough	7,301
Reserve twp	2,605
Robinson twp	3,453
Ross twp	4,949
Rosslyn Farms borough	315
St. Clair borough	6,585
Scott twp	4,927
Sewickley borough	4,955
Shaler twp	6,306
Sharpsburg borough	8,921
Snowden twp	2,889
South Fayette twp	9,221
South Versailles twp	303
Springdale borough	2,929
Springdale twp	910
Stowe twp	10,665
Swissvale borough	10,908
Tarentum borough	8,925
Thornburg borough	300
Trafford borough (pt. of)	132
Turtle Creek borough	8,138
Union twp	1,598
Upper St. Clair twp	1,458
Verona borough	3,938
Versailles borough	1,936
Versailles twp	2,241

PITTSBURGH DISTRICT—Con.

METROPOLITAN DISTRICT—con.

Allegheny County—Con.

Wall borough	2,426
West Deer twp	5,290
West Elizabeth borough	890
West Homestead borough	3,435
Westview borough	2,797
Westwood borough	478
Whitaker borough	1,881
Wilkins twp	3,455
Wilkinsburg borough	24,403
Wilmerding borough	6,441
Wilson borough	3,243

Washington County.

Cecil twp	5,843
Finleyville borough	609
Union twp	3,661

Westmoreland County.

Arnold borough	6,120
Irwin borough	3,235
New Kensington borough	11,987
North Huntington twp	8,360
North Irwin borough	908
Parnassus borough	3,816
Trafford borough (pt. of)	2,727

ADJACENT TERRITORY OUTSIDE METROPOLITAN DISTRICT.

Allegheny County.

Franklin twp	847
Hampton twp	1,720
McCandless twp	1,465
Ohio twp	404
Pine twp	685
Richland twp	1,361
Sewickley twp	164
Sewickley Heights twp	654

Washington County.

Peters twp	1,660

PORTLAND DISTRICT.

METROPOLITAN DISTRICT (IN OREGON).

Clackamas County.

Ardenwald pct	559
Canemah pct	366
Clackamas pct	609
Concord pct	504
Gladstone city	1,069
Gladstone pct. No. 1, excl. part of Gladstone city	82
Gladstone pct. No. 2, excl. part of Gladstone city	78
Harmony pct. No. 1	504
Harmony pct. No. 2	731
Jennings Lodge pct	558
Milwaukie town	1,172
Milwaukie Heights pct	885
Mount Pleasant pct	553
Oak Grove pct. No. 1	314
Oak Grove pct. No. 2	363
Oregon City	5,686
Oswego city	1,818
West Linn pct. No. 1, excl. part of West Linn town	49
West Linn pct. No. 2, excl. part of West Linn town	80
West Linn town	1,628
Willamette pct. No. 2	210

Multnomah County.

Portland city	258,288
Pct. 299, Swift	301
Pct. 300, Columbia	1,747
Pct. 301, Russellville	843
Pct. 302, North Kelly Butte	321
Pct. 303, South Kelly Butte	842
Pct. 304, Mount Scott	437
Pct. 316, Sauvies Island	149
Pct. 317, Holbrook	478
Pct. 318½, Germantown	228
Pct. 319, Sylvan	365
Pct. 320, Mount Zion	227
Pct. 321, Bertha	465
Pct. 322, Ryan	551
Pct. 322½	557
Pct. 323, Maplewood	471
Pct. 324, West Portland	379
Pct. 325, Riverdale	382
Pct. 325½, Kilpatrick Collins	566
Pct. 326, Brentwood	699
Pct. 326½, Kendall	659
Pct. 327, Errol Heights	412

METROPOLITAN DISTRICT (IN WASHINGTON).

Clarke County.

Vancouver city	12,637

ADJACENT TERRITORY OUTSIDE METROPOLITAN DISTRICT (IN OREGON).

Clackamas County.

Abernathy pct	361
Damascus pct	864
Evergreen pct	417

PORTLAND DISTRICT—Con.

ADJACENT TERRITORY—con.

Clackamas County—Con.

Maple Lane pct	548
Parkplace pct	658
Sunnyside pct	440
Tualatin pct	570

Multnomah County.

Fairview town	184
Gresham town	1,103
Pct. 305, Fairview, excl. Fairview town	428
Pct. 306, Rockwood	629
Pct. 307, Sycamore	362
Pct. 308, South Gresham, excl. part of Gresham town	333
Pct. 309, West Gresham, excl. part of Gresham town	39
Pct. 309½, East Gresham, excl. part of Gresham town	194
Pct. 310, Troutdale, excl. Troutdale town	662
Troutdale town	191

Washington County.

Aloha pct	957
Beaverton town	580
Cedar Mill pct	686
Connell pct	541
East Beaverton pct., excl. part of Beaverton town	514
East North Plains pct	561
Garden Home pct	615
Hillsboro city	2,468
Kinton pct	374
Metzger pct	524
Mulloy pct	198
North East Hillsboro pct., excl. part of Hillsboro city	288
North Tigard pct	543
North West Hillsboro pct., excl. part of Hillsboro city	284
Orenco pct., excl. Orenco town	338
Orenco town	335
Reedville pct	533
South East Hillsboro pct., excl. part of Hillsboro city	320
South Tigard pct	680
South West Hillsboro pct., excl. part of Hillsboro city	114
Tualatin pct., excl. Tualatin town	487
Tualatin town	234
West Beaverton pct., excl. part of Beaverton town	507

ADJACENT TERRITORY OUTSIDE METROPOLITAN DISTRICT (IN WASHINGTON).

Clarke County.

Barberton pct	485
Camas town	1,843
East Columbia pct	758
Fourth Plain pct	741
Fruit Valley pct	517
Harney pct	469
Jaggy pct	379
Lake Shore pct	513
Minnehaha pct	776
Preston pct	580
Proebstel pct	432
Salmon Creek pct	619
West Columbia pct	588

PROVIDENCE DISTRICT.

METROPOLITAN DISTRICT.

Bristol County.

Barrington town	3,897

Kent County.

Warwick town	13,481
West Warwick town	15,461

Providence County.

Central Falls city	24,174
Cranston city	29,407
Cumberland town	10,077
East Providence town	21,793
Johnston town	6,855
Lincoln town	9,543
North Providence town	7,697
Pawtucket city	64,248
Providence city	237,595

ADJACENT TERRITORY OUTSIDE METROPOLITAN DISTRICT (IN RHODE ISLAND).

Bristol County.

Bristol town	11,375
Warren town	7,841

Kent County.

East Greenwich town	3,290

Providence County.

North Smithfield town	3,200
Scituate town	3,006
Smithfield town	3,199
Woonsocket city	43,496

POPULATION.

CIVIL DIVISIONS COMPRISED WITHIN METROPOLITAN DISTRICT AND ADJACENT TERRITORY OF EACH CENTRAL CITY—Con.

PROVIDENCE DISTRICT—Con.

ADJACENT TERRITORY OUTSIDE METRO-POLITAN DISTRICT (IN MASSACHU-SETTS).

Bristol County.

Attleboro city	19,731
North Attleborough town	6,238
Seekonk town	2,898

ROCHESTER DISTRICT.

METROPOLITAN DISTRICT.

Monroe County.

Brighton town	2,911
East Rochester village	3,901
Fairport village	4,626
Gates town	1,419
Greece town	3,350
Irondequoit town	5,123
Perinton town, excl. Fairport village and part of East Rochester village	1,205
Pittsford town, excl. Pittsford village and part of East Rochester village	1,353
Pittsford village	1,328
Rochester city	295,750

ADJACENT TERRITORY OUTSIDE METROPOLITAN DISTRICT.

Monroe County.

Chili town	1,780
Henrietta town	1,910
Hilton village	827
Honeoye Falls village	1,107
Mendon town, excl. Honeoye Falls village	1,402
Ogden town, excl. Spencerport village	1,755
Parma town, excl. Hilton village	2,096
Penfield town	2,087
Rush town	2,091
Scottsville village	784
Spencerport village	926
Webster town, excl. Webster village	2,729
Webster village	1,247
Wheatland town, excl. Scottsville village	1,292

ST. LOUIS DISTRICT.

METROPOLITAN DISTRICT (IN MISSOURI).

St. Louis city.

The city	772,897

St. Louis County.

Carondelet twp., incl. part of North Glendale town, but excl. part of Glendale town, and parts of Kirkwood and Webster Groves cities	15,123
Central twp., incl. part of North Glendale town, but excl. Clayton, Maplewood, Richmond Heights, Uniondale, and University cities, Shrewsbury town, and parts of Glendale town and Kirkwood and Webster Groves cities	26,580
Clayton city	3,028
Glendale town	749
Kirkwood city	4,422
Maplewood city	7,431
North Glendale town	(1)
Richmond Heights city	2,136
Shrewsbury town	845
Uniondale city	1,315
University city	6,792
Webster Groves city	9,474

METROPOLITAN DISTRICT (IN ILLINOIS).

Madison County.

Granite City	14,757
Madison village	4,996
Nameoki town	1,181
Nameoki twp., excl. Nameoki town and parts of Granite City and Madison village	1,123
Venice city	3,895
Venice twp., excl. Venice city, and parts of Granite City and Madison village	107

St. Clair County.

Brooklyn village	1,685
Canteen twp., excl. Fairmont City and Washington Park villages	579
Centerville twp.	3,132
East St. Louis city	66,767
Fairmont City village	1,056
National City village	426
Washington Park village	1,516

ST. LOUIS DISTRICT—Con.

ADJACENT TERRITORY OUTSIDE METROPOLITAN DISTRICT (IN MISSOURI).

St. Charles County.

Portage Des Sioux twp., excl. Portage Des Sioux village	1,836
Portage Des Sioux village	283

St. Louis County.

Bonhomme twp., excl. Fenton village, Valley Park city, and part of Kirkwood city	5,749
Bridgeton town	121
Fenton village	146
Ferguson city	1,874
St. Ferdinand city	682
St. Ferdinand twp., excl. Bridgeton town and Ferguson and St. Ferdinand cities	9,624
Valley Park city	899

ADJACENT TERRITORY OUTSIDE METROPOLITAN DISTRICT (IN ILLINOIS).

Madison County.

Alton city	24,682
Bethalto village	471
Choteau twp.	818
East Alton village	1,669
Wood River twp., excl. East Alton and Wood River villages and part of Bethalto village	3,296
Wood River village	3,476

Monroe County.

Columbia pct., excl. Columbia village	894
Columbia village	1,592
New Hanover pct.	445

St. Clair County.

Dupo village	1,393
East Carondelet village	311
Stookey twp.	1,069
Sugar Loaf twp., excl. Dupo and East Carondelet villages	1,115

SAN FRANCISCO—OAKLAND DISTRICT.

METROPOLITAN DISTRICT.

Alameda County.

Alameda city	23,806
Albany city	2,462
Berkeley city	56,036
Eden twp., excl. Hayward town and San Leandro city	8,793
Emeryville town	2,390
Hayward town	3,487
Oakland city	216,261
Oakland twp., excl. Albany and Berkeley cities, Emeryville town, and parts of Oakland and Piedmont cities	1,259
Piedmont city	4,282
San Leandro city	5,703

Contra Costa County.

El Cerito town	1,505
Richmond city	16,843
Twp. 7, excl. El Cerito town	226

Marin County.

Belvedere town	616
Corte Madera town	607
Larkspur town	612
Mill Valley town	2,554
Ross town	727
San Anselmo town	2,475
San Rafael city	5,512
San Rafael twp., excl. Corte Madera, Larkspur, Ross, and San Anselmo towns, and San Rafael city	4,237
Sausalito town	2,790
Sausalito twp., excl. Belvedere, Mill Valley, and Sausalito towns	3,045

San Francisco County.

San Francisco city	506,676

San Mateo County.

Daly City	3,779
San Bruno city	1,562
South San Francisco city	4,411
Twp. 1, excl. Daly City, San Bruno, and South San Francisco cities	3,821

ADJACENT TERRITORY OUTSIDE METROPOLITAN DISTRICT.

Contra Costa County.

Martinez town	3,858
Twp. 1, excl. Martinez town	1,105
Twp. 3, excl. Walnut Creek town	1,884
Twp. 10	2,059
Walnut Creek town	538

SEATTLE DISTRICT.

METROPOLITAN DISTRICT.

King County.

Avondale pct.	279
Bellevue pct.	878
Black River pct.	505
Boddy pct.	397
Bossert pct.	185
Duwamish pct.	860
Earlington pct.	408
Enatie pct.	157
Endolyne pct.	733
Foster pct.	1,025
Greenwood pct.	723
Haller Lake pct.	592
Hill pct.	373
Hollywood pct.	286
Juanita pct.	694
Kirkland town	1,354
Lake City pct.	326
Lake Forest pct.	543
Lake View pct.	92
McGilvra pct.	289
McKinley pct.	519
Maple Leaf pct.	871
Meadow Point pct.	800
Medina pct.	440
Mercer pct.	580
Mountain View pct.	1,021
North Park pct.	2,255
Oak Lake pct.	1,459
Richmond pct.	687
Riverton pct.	1,035
Rose Hill pct.	1,194
Seahurst Park pct.	1,159
Seattle city	315,312
Stewart pct.	288
Sunnydale pct.	1,219
Tukwila town	453
Union pct.	1,155
Woodinville pct.	410

Kitsap County.

Annapolis pct.	783
Bremerton city	8,918
Bremerton pct., excl. Bremerton city	618
Eagle Harbor pct.	1,187
Island Center pct.	245
Port Blakely pct.	1,384
Port Madison pct.	604
Rolling Bay pct.	524
Veterans pct. No. 1	298
Veterans pct. No. 2	401

Snohomish County.

Currie pct.	241
Edmonds city	936
Richmond pct.	212

ADJACENT TERRITORY OUTSIDE METROPOLITAN DISTRICT.

King County.

Bothell pct. No. 1, excl. part of Bothell town	123
Bothell pct. No. 2, excl. part of Bothell town	260
Bothell town	613
Burton pct.	421
Cedar Mountain pct.	209
Cedar River pct.	647
Christopher pct.	822
Coal Field pct.	264
Cove pct.	387
Des Moines pct.	751
Dockton pct.	388
Dolphin pct.	176
Elliott pct.	139
Hazlewood pct.	123
Highland pct.	168
Houghton pct.	327
Inglewood pct.	204
Island pct.	68
Kennydale pct.	646
Kent city	2,282
Lisabuela pct.	201
Maury pct.	275
Meeker pct.	872
Monohon pct.	332
Newcastle pct.	804
Newport pct.	107
Orilla pct.	544
Quartermaster pct.	361
Redmond pct., excl. Redmond town	734
Redmond town	438
Renton town	3,301
Springbrook pct.	464
Squak pct.	160
Star Lake pct.	158
Suise Creek pct.	383
Swan Lake pct.	83
Vashon pct.	524
Wilburton pct.	286

SEATTLE DISTRICT—Con.

ADJACENT TERRITORY—Con.

Kitsap County.

Colby pct.	497
Fragaria pct.	220
Harper pct.	424
Kingston pct.	590
Long Lake pct.	200
Manette pct.	688
Olalla pct.	433
Suquamish pct.	617
Tracyton pct.	458
Waterman pct.	339

Snohomish County.

Allen pct.	368
Bear Creek pct.	141
Cedar Valley pct.	780
Fernwood pct.	475

TOLEDO DISTRICT.

METROPOLITAN DISTRICT.

Lucas County.

Adams twp.	4,735
Maumee village	3,195
Toledo city	243,164
Washington twp.	8,440

Wood County.

Ross twp.	4,183

ADJACENT TERRITORY OUTSIDE METROPOLITAN DISTRICT (IN OHIO).

Lucas County.

Jerusalem twp.	1,297
Monclova twp.	991
Oregon twp.	3,500
Springfield twp.	1,415
Sylvania twp., excl. Sylvania village	1,919
Sylvania village	1,222
Waterville village	779

Ottawa County.

Allen twp.	1,006
Clay twp., excl. Genoa village	1,067
Genoa village	971

Wood County.

Haskins village	427
Lake twp., excl. Millbury and Walbridge villages	1,122
Middleton twp., excl. Haskins village	1,290
Millbury village	232
Perrysburg twp., excl. Perrysburg village	2,275
Perrysburg village	2,429
Troy twp.	1,050
Walbridge village	584

ADJACENT TERRITORY OUTSIDE METROPOLITAN DISTRICT (IN MICHIGAN).

Monroe County.

Bedford twp.	2,689
Erie twp.	1,226
Whiteford twp.	1,741

WASHINGTON DISTRICT.

METROPOLITAN DISTRICT (DISTRICT OF COLUMBIA).

Washington city.

The city	437,571

METROPOLITAN DISTRICT (IN MARYLAND).

Montgomery County.

Dist. 7, Bethesda, excl. Glen Echo and Somerset towns, Northwest Park village and part of Garrett Park town	4,221
Dist. 13, Wheaton, excl. Kensington town and part of Takoma Park town	4,110
Glen Echo town	235
Kensington town	874
Northwest Park village	50
Somerset town	200
Takoma Park town (pt. of)	2,845

Prince Georges County.

Bladensburg town	597
Capitol Heights town	1,194
Dist. 2, Bladensburg, excl. Bladensburg town	1,476
Dist. 6, Spalding	2,557
Dist. 12, Oxon Hill	1,528
Dist. 13, Kent	1,686
Dist. 16, Hyattsville, excl. Hyattsville town	505
Dist. 17, Chillum, excl. Mount Rainier town and part of Takoma Park town	2,383
Dist. 18, Seat Pleasant, excl. Capitol Heights town	3,476

[1] Not returned separately.

CITIES AND THEIR SUBURBS.   71

WASHINGTON DISTRICT—Con.
METROPOLITAN DISTRICT—Con.
Prince Georges County—Con.

Dist. 19, Riverdale	1,809
Hyattsville town	2,675
Mount Rainier town	2,462
Takoma Park town (pt. of)	323

METROPOLITAN DISTRICT (IN VIRGINIA).
Alexandria city.

The city	18,060

Arlington County.

Arlington dist	8,547
Jefferson dist., excl. Potomac town	2,668
Potomac town	1,000

WASHINGTON DISTRICT—Con.
METROPOLITAN DISTRICT—Con
Arlington County—Con.

Washington dist., excl. part of Falls Church town	3,536

ADJACENT TERRITORY OUTSIDE METRO-POLITAN DISTRICT (IN MARYLAND).
Montgomery County.

Dist. 4, Rockville, excl. Rockville town and part of Garrett Park town	2,189
Dist. 5, Colesville	2,301
Dist. 10, Potomac	1,125
Garrett Park town	159
Rockville town	1,145

WASHINGTON DISTRICT—Con.
ADJACENT TERRITORY—con.
Prince Georges County.

Bowie town	677
Dist. 1, Vansville	3,203
Dist. 3, Marlboro, excl. Upper Marlboro town	1,109
Dist. 5, Piscataway, excl. Piscataway village	1,810
Dist. 7, Queen Anne	1,790
Dist. 9, Surratts	1,111
Dist. 14, Bowie, excl. Bowie town	1,760
Dist. 15, Mellwood	1,456
Piscataway village	38
Upper Marlboro town	385

WASHINGTON DISTRICT—Con.
ADJACENT TERRITORY OUTSIDE METRO-POLITAN DISTRICT (IN VIRGINIA).
Arlington County.

Falls Church town (pt. of)	289

Fairfax County.

Fairfax town	516
Falls Church dist., excl. part of Falls Church town	2,407
Falls Church town (pt. of)	1,370
Mount Vernon dist	3,826
Providence dist., excl. Fairfax and Vienna towns, and part of Falls Church town	4,675
Vienna town	773

CITIES OF 100,000 TO 200,000 INHABITANTS AND THEIR ADJACENT TERRITORY.

Table 41 shows, for 1920 and 1910, for each city having from 100,000 to 200,000 inhabitants, the population within the city proper, the population in other civil divisions all or more than half of which—either in area or in population—lie within 10 miles of the city boundaries, and the combined population of the city and such adjacent territory. In five cases cities of 100,000 to 200,000 do not appear in this table because they form parts of metropolitan districts. These cities are Paterson, N. J., and Yonkers, N. Y.; which form part of the New York district; Cambridge, Mass., which is included in the Boston district; Camden, N. J., which forms part of the Philadelphia district; and Kansas City, Kans., which is included in the Kansas City district. (See Table 40.) Moreover, in three cases there are one or more cities within the adjacent territory which approximate in population the central city itself. In such cases the names of the smaller cities are inserted in parentheses immediately below those of the central cities from whose boundaries the distances are determined.

For reasons already stated, it should not be considered that the total population shown by Table 41 is strictly urban in character, or that the figures afford an accurate comparison of the relative importance of the several cities as centers of urban population. They do, however, indicate the relative importance approximately. The area of the adjacent territory outside the central cities represents 95.3 per cent of the entire area of the districts, while its population in 1920 constituted 38.1 per cent of the entire population of the districts.

It is noteworthy that, whereas the population of the suburban districts of the metropolitan areas shown in Table 40 increased at a considerably greater rate during the decade than did the population of the central cities themselves, the reverse is true of the cities and adjacent areas shown in Table 41; in fact, the average rate of increase in the adjacent areas was less than two-thirds as great as in the central cities.

The fact that the population of the adjacent territory is larger relatively to that of the central cities covered by Table 41 than it is in the case of the larger cities shown in Table 40 should not be misunderstood. This does not imply that the smaller cities have relatively more important suburbs than the larger. It is due to two causes, namely, (1) that the smaller the size of the city the greater is the proportion which the adjacent area forms of the total; (2) that in Table 41 a number of cities are included, principally in New York state and in New England, in whose adjacent territory there are other cities of large size which can not in any true sense be considered suburbs. For example, Troy and Schenectady can not be considered as suburbs of Albany, but these three cities combined, together with other adjacent territory, constitute what may in a sense be regarded as a single urban community

POPULATION.

TABLE 41.—AREA AND POPULATION OF CENTRAL CITY AND OF ADJACENT TERRITORY, FOR CITIES OF 100,000 TO 200,000 INHABITANTS: 1920 AND 1910.

[Population shown for central cities for each census year does not include that of annexations made subsequently to census date, but total population given for each district for 1920 and 1910 relates to same area.]

DISTRICT.	Area in acres: 1920	POPULATION. 1920	POPULATION. 1910	Per cent of increase:[1] 1910-1920
Total for 29 districts	10,097,292.3	6,898,418	5,312,730	26.1
Total in central cities (30 cities)	469,903.0	4,143,265	3,165,314	30.9
Total outside central cities	9,627,389.3	2,555,153	2,147,416	19.0
ALBANY. (Including Troy and Schenectady.)				
Total in city and outside	418,195.2	382,959	357,467	7.1
In Albany	11,924.1	113,344	100,253	13.1
Outside Albany	406,271.1	269,615	257,214	4.8
BIRMINGHAM.				
Total in city and outside	399,443.2	290,884	208,066	39.8
In city proper	31,346.6	178,806	132,685	34.8
Outside city proper	368,096.6	112,078	75,381	48.7
BRIDGEPORT.				
Total in city and outside	191,130.0	190,043	132,554	43.4
In city proper	9,370.0	143,555	102,054	40.7
Outside city proper	181,760.0	46,488	30,500	52.4
DALLAS.				
Total in city and outside	123,725.0	184,515	112,008	64.7
In city proper	14,605.0	158,976	92,104	72.6
Outside city proper	109,120.0	25,539	19,904	28.3
DAYTON.				
Total in city and outside	347,547.0	210,177	163,646	28.4
In city proper	10,107.0	152,559	116,577	30.9
Outside city proper	337,440.0	57,618	47,069	22.4
DES MOINES.				
Total in city and outside	435,069.2	154,231	111,584	38.2
In city proper	33,597.2	126,468	86,368	46.4
Outside city proper	401,472.0	27,763	25,216	10.1
FALL RIVER-NEW BEDFORD.				
Total in cities and outside	416,404.0	333,130	296,935	12.2
In Fall River	21,723.0	120,485	119,295	1.0
In New Bedford	12,206.0	121,217	96,652	25.4
Outside Fall River and New Bedford	382,475.0	91,428	80,988	12.9
FORT WORTH.				
Total in city and outside	299,280.0	136,691	93,699	45.9
In city proper	10,553.4	106,482	73,312	45.2
Outside city proper	288,726.6	30,209	20,387	48.2
GRAND RAPIDS.				
Total in city and outside	315,360.0	171,204	145,632	17.6
In city proper	11,211.0	137,634	112,571	22.3
Outside city proper	304,149.0	33,570	33,061	1.5
HARTFORD.				
Total in city and outside	320,057.3	300,423	225,024	33.5
In city proper	10,162.9	138,036	98,915	39.6
Outside city proper	309,894.4	162,387	126,109	28.8
HOUSTON.				
Total in city and outside	497,504.0	168,351	103,584	62.5
In city proper	23,338.0	138,276	78,800	75.5
Outside city proper	474,166.0	30,075	24,784	21.3
LOWELL. (Including Lawrence.)				
Total in city and outside	365,108.0	313,206	283,741	10.4
In Lowell	8,308.0	112,759	106,294	6.1
Outside Lowell	356,800.0	200,447	177,447	13.0
MEMPHIS.				
Total in city and outside	454,098.0	214,169	181,143	18.2
In city proper	14,994.0	162,351	131,105	23.8
Outside city proper	439,104.0	51,818	50,038	3.6
NASHVILLE.				
Total in city and outside	347,724.8	169,194	150,902	12.1
In city proper	11,544.0	118,342	110,364	7.2
Outside city proper	336,180.8	50,852	40,538	25.4

DISTRICT.	Area in acres: 1920	POPULATION. 1920	POPULATION. 1910	Per cent of increase:[1] 1910-1920
NEW HAVEN.				
Total in city and outside	229,096.0	264,829	211,640	25.1
In city proper	11,400.0	162,537	133,005	21.7
Outside city proper	218,236.0	102,292	78,635	31.1
NORFOLK. (Including Portsmouth and Newport News.)				
Total in city and outside	269,689.6	303,278	205,445	47.6
In Norfolk	4,771.8	115,777	67,452	71.6
Outside Norfolk	264,917.8	187,501	137,993	35.9
OMAHA.				
Total in city and outside	373,330.0	249,999	207,820	20.3
In city proper	23,034.0	191,601	124,096	54.4
Outside city proper	349,696.0	58,398	83,733	-30.3
READING.				
Total in city and outside	314,103.5	169,655	153,960	10.2
In city proper	6,090.7	107,784	96,071	12.2
Outside city proper	308,012.8	61,871	57,889	6.9
RICHMOND.				
Total in city and outside	396,224.0	205,807	168,854	21.9
In city proper	15,360.0	171,667	127,628	34.5
Outside city proper	380,864.0	34,140	41,226	-17.2
SALT LAKE CITY.				
Total in city and outside	437,504.0	150,006	119,903	25.2
In city proper	32,704.0	118,110	92,777	27.3
Outside city proper	404,800.0	31,956	27,126	17.8
SAN ANTONIO.				
Total in city and outside	379,366.1	191,100	100,852	74.0
In city proper	22,860.5	161,379	96,614	67.0
Outside city proper	356,505.6	29,781	13,238	125.0
SCRANTON.				
Total in city and outside	331,446.5	347,793	314,998	10.4
In city proper	12,361.7	137,783	129,867	6.1
Outside city proper	319,084.8	210,010	185,131	13.4
SPOKANE.				
Total in city and outside	405,600.0	127,492	124,838	2.1
In city proper	24,819.0	104,437	104,402	(2)
Outside city proper	380,781.0	23,055	20,436	12.8
SPRINGFIELD, MASS.				
Total in city and outside	392,003.0	332,762	258,092	28.9
In city proper	20,451.0	129,614	88,926	45.8
Outside city proper	371,552.0	203,148	169,166	20.1
SYRACUSE.				
Total in city and outside	325,401.6	227,502	185,327	22.8
In city proper	11,782.0	171,717	137,249	25.1
Outside city proper	313,619.6	55,845	48,078	16.2
TRENTON.				
Total in city and outside	233,386.0	181,197	143,207	26.4
In city proper	4,490.0	119,289	96,815	23.2
Outside city proper	228,896.0	61,908	46,482	33.2
WILMINGTON.				
Total in city and outside	243,496.7	171,703	134,004	27.3
In city proper	4,495.1	110,168	87,411	26.0
Outside city proper	239,001.6	61,535	47,493	29.6
WORCESTER.				
Total in city and outside	398,953.6	208,551	228,271	17.6
In city proper	23,731.0	179,754	145,986	23.1
Outside city proper	375,222.6	88,797	82,285	7.9
YOUNGSTOWN.				
Total in city and outside	436,446.0	287,387	179,535	60.1
In city proper	15,902.0	132,358	79,066	67.4
Outside city proper	420,544.0	155,029	100,469	54.8

[1] A minus sign (—) denotes decrease.

[2] Less than one-tenth of 1 per cent.

CITIES AND THEIR SUBURBS.

78

CIVIL DIVISIONS COMPRISED WITHIN ADJACENT TERRITORY OF EACH CENTRAL CITY.

ALBANY DISTRICT.

CENTRAL CITY AND ADJACENT TERRITORY.

Albany County.

Albany city	113,344
Altamont village	797
Bethlehem town	4,430
Coeymans town, excl. Ravena village	2,054
Cohoes city	22,987
Colonie town	10,196
Green Island village	4,411
Guilderland town, excl. Altamont village	2,320
New Scotland town, excl. Voorheesville village	1,856
Ravena village	2,093
Voorheesville village	614
Watervliet city	16,073

Rensselaer County.

Brunswick town	2,812
Castleton village	1,595
East Greenbush town	1,558
North Greenbush town	1,408
Poestenkill town	1,002
Rensselaer city	10,823
Sandlake town	1,916
Schodack town, excl. Castleton village	2,397
Troy city	72,013

Saratoga County.

Clifton Park town	1,983
Waterford town, excl. Waterford village	1,915
Waterford village	2,637

Schenectady County.

Niskayuna town	3,149
Rotterdam town	7,853
Schenectady city	88,723

BIRMINGHAM DISTRICT.

CENTRAL CITY AND ADJACENT TERRITORY.

Jefferson County.

Bessemer city	18,674
Birmingham city	178,806
Boyles town	1,364
Brighton city	3,665
Brookside town	666
Cardiff town	463
Fairfield city	5,003
Graysville town	(1)
Inglenook town	1,590
Irondale town	809
Leeds town	1,600
Lipscomb town	1,605
Pinkney City town	(1)
Pct. 2, excl. part of Bessemer city	5,177
Pct. 7	5,104
Pct. 8	1,977
Pct. 9, excl. part of Birmingham city	7,688
Pct. 10, excl. part of Birmingham city	1,173
Pct. 11, excl. Boyles and Tarrant City towns	2,052
Pct. 12, excl. Leeds town	645
Pct. 13	1,561
Pct. 15	1,842
Pct. 18, excl. Brookside and Cardiff towns	1,583
Pct. 20, excl. Irondale town	2,372
Pct. 22	1,647
Pct. 24	560
Pct. 25	2,042
Pct. 29, incl. Sandusky town, but excl. part of Birmingham city	1,925
Pct. 30	8,198
Pct. 31	1,017
Pct. 33, excl. Lipscomb town and part of Bessemer city	2,962
Pct. 34, excl. part of Birmingham city	108
Pct. 36, excl. part of Birmingham city	249
Pct. 38, incl. Graysville and Pinkney City towns	1,661
Pct. 39	3,153
Pct. 40	1,070
Pct. 41	1,200
Pct. 42, excl. part of Birmingham city	2,502
Pct. 44	1,016
Pct. 45, excl. part of Birmingham city	3,194
Pct. 47	2,286
Pct. 49	
Pct. 52, excl. part of Birmingham city	1 6,893
Pct. 50	3,292
Pct. 51	1,229
Pct. 54, excl. Inglenook town and part of Birmingham city	259
Pct. 55, excl. Brighton city	1,910
Sandusky town	(1)

BIRMINGHAM DISTRICT—Con.

CENTRAL CITY, ETC.—con.

Jefferson County—Con.

Tarrant City town	734

Shelby County.

Pct. 12, Acton	1,076
Pct. 13, Bold Springs	282

BRIDGEPORT DISTRICT.

CENTRAL CITY AND ADJACENT TERRITORY.

Fairfield County.

Bridgeport city	143,555
Easton town	1,017
Fairfield town	11,475
Monroe town	1,161
Redding town	1,315
Shelton city	9,475
Stratford town	12,347
Trumbull town	2,597
Weston town	703
Westport town	5,114
Wilton town	1,284

DALLAS DISTRICT.

CENTRAL CITY AND ADJACENT TERRITORY.

Dallas County.

Cement city	878
Cockrell Hill town	459
Dallas city	158,976
Dalworth Park town	332
Grand Prairie town	1,263
Highland Park city	2,321
Just. Pct. 1, excl. Highland Park city and part of Dallas city	6,312
Just. Pct. 4, excl. Mesquite town	5,124
Just. Pct. 7, excl. Cement city, and Cockrell Hill, Dalworth Park, and Grand Prairie towns, and part of Dallas city	8,176
Mesquite town	674

DAYTON DISTRICT.

CENTRAL CITY AND ADJACENT TERRITORY.

Greene County.

Bath twp., excl. Fairfield and Osborn villages	1,738
Beaver Creek twp.	2,229
Bellbrook village	286
Fairfield village	329
Osborn village	1,059
Sugar Creek twp., excl. Bellbrook village	907

Miami County.

Bethel twp.	1,570

Montgomery County.

Butler twp., excl. Vandalia village	2,212
Centerville village	335
Dayton city	152,559
Englewood village	351
Farmersville village	479
Harrison twp.	7,880
Jackson twp., excl. Farmersville village and part of New Lebanon village	1,824
Jefferson twp.	6,401
Mad River twp.	3,283
Madison twp., excl. Trotwood village	3,003
Miami twp., excl. Miamisburg and West Carrollton villages	2,786
Miamisburg village	4,383
New Lebanon village	273
Oakwood village	1,473
Perry twp., excl. part of New Lebanon village	2,225
Randolph twp., excl. Englewood village	2,564
Trotwood village	422
Van Buren twp., excl. Oakwood village	5,740
Vandalia village	257
Washington twp., excl. Centerville village	1,230
Wayne twp.	949
West Carrollton village	1,430

DES MOINES DISTRICT.

CENTRAL CITY AND ADJACENT TERRITORY.

Dallas County.

Boone twp.	735
Granger town	324
Grant twp., excl. Granger town	650
Walnut twp., excl. Waukee town	634
Waukee town	375

Polk County.

Allen twp.	452
Altoona town	502
Ankeny town	648
Beaver twp., excl. Mitchellville town	800

DES MOINES DISTRICT—Con.

CENTRAL CITY, ETC.—con.

Polk County—Con.

Bloomfield twp., excl. Fort Des Moines town	2,284
Bondurant town	274
Camp twp., excl. Runnells town	995
Clay twp., excl. Altoona town	597
Clover Hill town	469
Crocker twp., excl. Ankeny town	1,388
Delaware twp.	990
Des Moines city	126,468
Douglas twp., excl. part of Bondurant town	988
Fort Des Moines town	1,020
Four Mile twp.	808
Franklin twp., excl. part of Bondurant town	658
Grimes town	524
Jefferson twp., exc. part of Grimes town	2,062
Mitchellville town	752
Runnells town	369
Saylor twp.	1,482
Urbandale town	298
Walnut twp., excl. Clover Hill town	837
Webster twp., excl. Urbandale town, and part of Grimes town	978

Warren County.

Allen twp., excl. Carlisle town	437
Carlisle town	640
Greenfield twp., excl. Spring Hill town	853
Hartford town	218
Linn twp., excl. Norwalk town	810
Norwalk town	331
Palmyra twp.	540
Richland twp., excl. Hartford town	543
Spring Hill town	489

FALL RIVER–NEW BEDFORD DISTRICT.

CENTRAL CITIES AND ADJACENT TERRITORY (IN MASSACHUSETTS).

Bristol County.

Acushnet town	3,075
Berkley town	935
Dartmouth town	6,493
Dighton town	2,574
Fairhaven town	7,291
Fall River city	120,485
Freetown town	1,532
New Bedford city	121,217
Rehoboth town	2,065
Somerset town	3,520
Swansea town	2,334
Taunton city	37,137
Westport town	3,115

Plymouth County.

Lakeville town	1,419
Marion town	1,288
Mattapoisett town	1,277
Middleborough town	8,453
Rochester town	1,047

CENTRAL CITIES AND ADJACENT TERRITORY (IN RHODE ISLAND).

Newport County.

Little Compton town	1,389
Portsmouth town	2,590
Tiverton town	3,894

FORT WORTH DISTRICT.

CENTRAL CITY AND ADJACENT TERRITORY.

Tarrant County.

Fort Worth city	106,482
Just. Pct. 1, excl. Fort Worth city and Niles City and Polytechnic towns	18,208
Just. Pct. 4	3,901
Just. Pct. 6	980
Just. Pct. 7	2,066
Niles City town	716
Polytechnic town	4,338

GRAND RAPIDS DISTRICT.

CENTRAL CITY AND ADJACENT TERRITORY.

Kent County.

Ada twp.	1,048
Algoma twp., excl. part of Rockford village	1,043
Alpine twp.	1,363
Byron twp.	2,202
Cannon twp.	837
Cascade twp.	1,035
East Grand Rapids village	1,310
Gaines twp.	1,343
Grand Rapids city	137,634

GRAND RAPIDS DISTRICT—Con.

CENTRAL CITY, ETC.—con.

Kent County—Con.

Grand Rapids twp., excl. East Grand Rapids village	3,950
Grandville village	799
Paris twp.	2,036
Plainfield twp., excl. part of Rockford village	1,841
Rockford village	1,143
Walker twp.	2,833
Wyoming twp., excl. Grandville village	5,702

Ottawa County.

Georgetown twp.	2,385
Tallmadge twp.	1,226
Wright twp.	1,474

HARTFORD DISTRICT.

CENTRAL CITY AND ADJACENT TERRITORY.

Hartford County.

Avon town	1,534
Berlin town	4,298
Bloomfield town	2,394
East Granby town	1,056
East Hartford town	11,648
East Windsor town	3,741
Farmington borough	1,021
Farmington town, excl. Farmington borough	2,823
Glastonbury town	5,592
Hartford city	138,036
Manchester town	18,370
New Britain city	59,316
Newington town	2,381
Plainville town	4,114
Rocky Hill town	1,633
Simsbury town	2,958
South Windsor town	2,142
West Hartford town	8,854
Wethersfield town	4,342
Windsor town	5,620
Windsor Locks town	3,554

Middlesex County.

Cromwell town	2,454
Portland town	3,644

Tolland County.

Rockville city	7,726
Vernon town, excl. Rockville city	1,172

HOUSTON DISTRICT.

CENTRAL CITY AND ADJACENT TERRITORY.

Harris County.

Harrisburg town	1,461
Houston city	138,276
Independence Heights town	715
Just. Pct. 1, excl. Houston city and Independence Heights town	13,661
Just. Pct. 2, excl. Harrisburg, La Porte, Magnolia Park, and Park Place towns	5,305
Just. Pct. 8	3,534
La Porte town	889
Magnolia Park town	4,080
Park Place town	430

LOWELL DISTRICT.

CENTRAL CITY AND ADJACENT TERRITORY (IN MASSACHUSETTS).

Essex County.

Andover town	8,268
Lawrence city	94,270
Methuen city	15,189
North Andover town	6,265

Middlesex County.

Acton town	2,162
Bedford town	1,362
Billerica town	3,646
Burlington town	885
Carlisle town	463
Chelmsford town	5,682
Concord town	6,461
Dracut town	5,280
Dunstable town	353
Groton town	2,185
Littleton town	1,277
Lowell city	112,759
North Reading town	1,286
Tewksbury town	4,450
Tyngsborough town	1,044
Westford town	3,170
Wilmington town	2,581

CENTRAL CITY AND ADJACENT TERRITORY (IN NEW HAMPSHIRE).

Hillsborough County.

Hudson town	1,954
Nashua city	28,379
Pelham town	974

Rockingham County.

Salem town	2,315
Windham town	542

POPULATION.

74

CIVIL DIVISIONS COMPRISED WITHIN ADJACENT TERRITORY OF EACH CENTRAL CITY—Continued.

MEMPHIS DISTRICT.

CENTRAL CITY AND ADJACENT TERRITORY
(IN TENNESSEE).

Shelby County.

Bartlett town	271
Civ. Dist. 4, excl. part of Memphis city	9,358
Civ. Dist. 6, excl. part of Memphis city	2,797
Civ. Dist. 7, excl. part of Memphis city	7,089
Civ. Dist. 8	5,905
Civ. Dist. 9, excl. Bartlett and Raleigh towns	7,385
Civ. Dist. 10	6,740
Memphis city	162,351
Raleigh town	287

CENTRAL CITY AND ADJACENT TERRITORY
(IN ARKANSAS).

Crittenden County.

Edmonson town	325
Jasper twp	2,587
Mississippi twp	136
Mound City twp	1,011
Proctor twp., excl. Edmonson town	3,236

CENTRAL CITY AND ADJACENT TERRITORY
(IN MISSISSIPPI).

De Soto County.

Beat 2, excl. Pleasant Hill village	4,441
Pleasant Hill village	190

NASHVILLE DISTRICT.

CENTRAL CITY AND ADJACENT TERRITORY.

Davidson County.

Civ. Dist. 2	3,187
Civ. Dist. 3	2,899
Civ. Dist. 4	3,554
Civ. Dist. 5	1,637
Civ. Dist. 6	7,269
Civ. Dist. 7	4,946
Civ. Dist. 8	7,524
Civ. Dist. 9	1,500
Civ. Dist. 10	3,072
Civ. Dist. 11	5,874
Civ. Dist. 12	3,545
Civ. Dist. 13	2,285
Civ. Dist. 14	2,181
Nashville city	118,342

Williamson County.

Civ. Dist. 7	500
Civ. Dist. 15	879

NEW HAVEN DISTRICT.

CENTRAL CITY AND ADJACENT TERRITORY.

New Haven County.

Ansonia city	17,643
Beacon Falls town	1,593
Bethany town	411
Branford borough	2,619
Branford town, excl. Branford borough	4,008
Derby city	11,238
East Haven town	3,520
Guilford borough	1,612
Guilford town, excl. Guilford borough	1,191
Hamden town	8,611
Milford town, excl. Woodmont borough	9,973
New Haven city	162,537
North Branford town	1,110
North Haven town	1,968
Orange town	16,614
Seymour town	6,781
Wallingford borough	9,648
Wallingford town, excl. Wallingford borough	2,362
Woodbridge town	1,170
Woodmont borough	220

NORFOLK DISTRICT.

CENTRAL CITY AND ADJACENT TERRITORY.

Elizabeth City County.

Chesapeake dist., excl. Phoebus town	6,997
Hampton city	6,138
Kecoughtan town	1,198
Phoebus town	3,043
Wythe dist., excl. Kecoughtan town	7,873

Nansemond County.

Sleepy Hole dist	3,491

Newport News city.

The city	35,596

Norfolk city.

The city	115,777

Norfolk County.

Deep Creek dist	6,938
South Norfolk town	7,724

NORFOLK DISTRICT—Con.

CENTRAL CITY, ETC.—con.

Norfolk County—Con.

Tanners Creek dist	24,331
Washington dist., excl. South Norfolk town	8,586
Western Branch dist	4,727

Portsmouth city.

The city	54,387

Princess Anne County.

Kempsville dist	5,053

Warwick County.

Denbigh dist	1,228
Newport dist	7,047

York County.

Poquoson dist	3,144

OMAHA DISTRICT.

CENTRAL CITY AND ADJACENT TERRITORY
(IN NEBRASKA).

Douglas County.

Bennington village	314
Benson pct	1,145
Douglas pct., excl. Ralston village	2,351
Dundee pct	439
East Omaha pct	380
Florence pct	645
Jefferson pct., excl. Bennington village	627
McArdle pct	771
Millard pct., excl. Millard village	513
Millard village	300
Omaha city	191,601
Ralston village	455
Union pct	986

Sarpy County.

Bellevue pct., excl. Bellevue village	769
Bellevue village	695
Fairview pct	450
Gilmore pct	1,095
Highland pct	1,262
Hobo Island	63
La Platte pct	387
Papillion pct., excl. Papillion village	524
Papillion village	666
Richland pct	494

Washington County.

Fort Calhoun twp., excl. Fort Calhoun village	1,022
Fort Calhoun village	309

CENTRAL CITY AND ADJACENT TERRITORY
(IN IOWA).

Mills County.

St. Mary twp	141

Pottawattamie County.

Council Bluffs city	36,162
Crescent twp	752
Garner twp	1,415
Hazel Dell twp	904
Kane twp., excl. Council Bluffs city	225
Lewis twp	1,265
Rockford twp	872

READING DISTRICT.

CENTRAL CITY AND ADJACENT TERRITORY.

Berks County.

Alsace twp	756
Amity twp	1,315
Bern twp	1,110
Bernville borough	302
Birdsboro borough	3,299
Brecknock twp	782
Centre twp	1,245
Centreport borough	134
Cumru twp	3,137
Earl twp	829
Exeter twp	2,847
Fleetwood borough	1,652
Heidelberg twp	800
Lower Alsace twp	1,158
Lower Heidelberg twp	919
Maidencreek twp	1,880
Mohnton borough	1,640
Mount Penn borough	1,370
Muhlenberg twp	5,220
North Heidelberg twp	533
Oley twp	1,876
Ontelaunee twp	1,070
Penn twp	876
Perry twp	1,690
Pike twp	648
Reading city	107,784
Richmond twp	1,608
Robeson twp	2,315
Robesonia borough	1,203
Rockland twp	978
Ruscombmanor twp	1,060
Shillington borough	2,175

READING DISTRICT—Con.

CENTRAL CITY, ETC.—con.

Berks County—Con.

Sinking Spring borough	1,270
South Heidelberg twp	2,236
Spring twp	2,103
Union twp	1,279
Wernersville borough	797
West Leesport borough	410
West Reading borough	2,921
Wyomissing borough	2,062

Lancaster County.

Adamstown borough	800
Brecknock twp	1,559

RICHMOND DISTRICT.

CENTRAL CITY AND ADJACENT TERRITORY.

Chesterfield County.

Dale dist	2,045
Manchester dist	4,251
Midlothian dist	2,499

Hanover County.

Henry dist	6,373

Henrico County.

Brookland dist	5,200
Fairfield dist	6,370
Tuckahoe dist	3,476
Varina dist	3,926

Richmond city.

The city	171,667

SALT LAKE CITY DISTRICT.

CENTRAL CITY AND ADJACENT TERRITORY.

Davis County.

Bountiful city	2,063
Bountiful pct., excl. Bountiful city	398
West Bountiful pct	573

Morgan County.

Canyon Creek pct	439

Salt Lake County.

Midvale city	2,209
Murray city	4,584
Pct. 1	2,833
Pct. 2	2,082
Pct. 3	5,547
Pct. 4	5,807
Pct. 5	3,070
Pct. 6, excl. Midvale city	1,751
Salt Lake City	118,110

SAN ANTONIO DISTRICT.

CENTRAL CITY AND ADJACENT TERRITORY.

Bexar County.

Just. Pct. 1, excl. San Antonio city	4,095
Just. Pct. 2	1,768
Just. Pct. 3	6,403
Just. Pct. 6	9,903
Just. Pct. 7	7,612
San Antonio city	161,379

SCRANTON DISTRICT.

CENTRAL CITY AND ADJACENT TERRITORY.

Lackawanna County.

Abington twp	438
Archbald borough	8,003
Benton twp	846
Blakely borough	6,564
Carbondale city	18,640
Carbondale twp	1,652
Clarks Green borough	350
Clarks Summit borough	1,404
Clifton twp	191
Covington twp	613
Dalton borough	786
Dickson City borough	11,049
Dunmore borough	20,250
Elmhurst borough	361
Glenburn borough	289
Jefferson twp	571
Jermyn borough	3,326
La Plume borough	259
Lackawanna twp	3,050
Madison twp	590
Mayfield borough	3,832
Moosic borough	4,364
Moscow borough	702
Newton twp	1,464
North Abington twp	333
Old Forge borough	12,237
Olyphant borough	10,236
Ransom twp	894
Roaring Brook twp	212
Scott twp	1,315
Scranton city	137,783
South Abington twp	990
Spring Brook twp	450
Taylor borough	9,876
Throop borough	6,072

SCRANTON DISTRICT—Con.

CENTRAL CITY, ETC.—con.

Lackawanna County—Con.

West Abington twp	194
Winton borough	7,583

Luzerne County.

Avoca borough	4,950
Dupont borough	4,876
Duryea borough	7,776
Exeter borough	4,176
Exeter twp	513
Franklin twp	427
Hughestown borough	2,244
Jenkins twp	5,722
Laflin borough	473
Pittston city	18,497
Pittston twp	3,581
West Pittston borough	6,008
West Wyoming borough	1,938
Wyoming borough	3,682
Yatesville borough	709

Wyoming County.

Clinton twp	397
Exeter twp	111
Factoryville borough	628
Falls twp	1,154
Overfield twp	396

SPOKANE DISTRICT.

CENTRAL CITY AND ADJACENT TERRITORY.

Spokane County.

Cheney town	1,252
Chester twp	362
Colbert twp	412
Duncan twp	366
East Cheney twp	255
East Spokane twp	1,200
Five Mile twp	474
Foot Hills twp	450
Four Lakes twp	580
Green Bluff twp	533
Hillyard city	3,942
Marshall twp	612
Mead twp	1,188
Medical Lake town	2,545
Mica twp	287
Moran twp	667
Nine Mile twp	161
Opportunity twp	3,278
Peone twp	248
Pleasant Prairie twp	651
South Moran twp	401
Spence twp	360
Spokane city	104,437
Stevens twp	410
Valleyford twp	602
Wayside twp	488
West Spokane twp	1,319

SPRINGFIELD DISTRICT.

CENTRAL CITY AND ADJACENT TERRITORY
(IN MASSACHUSETTS).

Hampden County.

Agawam town	5,023
Chicopee city	36,214
East Longmeadow town	2,362
Hampden town	624
Holyoke city	60,203
Longmeadow town	2,618
Ludlow town	7,470
Monson town	4,826
Palmer town	9,896
Southwick town	1,194
Springfield city	129,614
West Springfield town	13,443
Westfield town	18,604
Wilbraham town	2,780

Hampshire County.

Belchertown town	2,058
Easthampton town	11,261
Granby town	779
South Hadley town	5,527
Southampton town	814

CENTRAL CITY AND ADJACENT TERRITORY
(IN CONNECTICUT).

Hartford County.

Enfield town	11,719
Suffield town	4,070

Tolland County.

Somers town	1,673

SYRACUSE DISTRICT.

CENTRAL CITY AND ADJACENT TERRITORY.

Onondaga County.

Baldwinsville village	3,085
Camillus town, excl. Camillus village	2,097
Camillus village	808
Cicero town	2,536
Clay town	2,485
De Witt town, excl. East Syracuse and Eastwood villages	3,979

CITIES AND THEIR SUBURBS.

75

CIVIL DIVISIONS COMPRISED WITHIN ADJACENT TERRITORY OF EACH CENTRAL CITY—Continued.

SYRACUSE DISTRICT—Con.

CENTRAL CITY, ETC.—con.

Onondaga County—Con.

East Syracuse village	4,106
Eastwood village	2,194
Fayetteville village	1,584
Geddes town, excl. Solvay village	643
La Fayette town, excl. part of Onondaga Indian Reservation	1,293
Liverpool village	1,831
Manlius town, excl. Fayetteville, Manlius, and Minoa villages	2,852
Manlius village	1,296
Marcellus town, excl. Marcellus village	1,865
Marcellus village	989
Minoa village	867
Onondaga Indian Reservation	475
Onondaga town, excl. part of Onondaga Indian Reservation	6,620
Pompey town	1,882
Salina town, excl. Liverpool village	2,426
Solvay village	7,352
Syracuse city	171,717
Van Buren town, excl. part of Baldwinsville village	1,077

TRENTON DISTRICT.

CENTRAL CITY AND ADJACENT TERRITORY (IN NEW JERSEY).

Burlington County.

Bordentown city	4,371
Bordentown twp	500
Chesterfield twp	1,133
Fieldsboro borough	530
Florence twp	7,100
Mansfield twp	1,517

Mercer County.

Ewing twp	3,475
Hamilton twp	14,580
Hopewell borough	1,339
Hopewell twp	3,249
Lawrence twp	3,686
Pennington borough	965
Princeton borough	5,917
Princeton twp	1,424
Trenton city	119,289
Washington twp	1,161
West Windsor twp	1,389

CENTRAL CITY AND ADJACENT TERRITORY (IN PENNSYLVANIA).

Bucks County.

Falls twp	1,789
Lower Makefield twp	1,201

TRENTON DISTRICT—Con.

CENTRAL CITY, ETC.—con.

Bucks County—Con.

Morrisville borough	3,039
Tullytown borough	572
Upper Makefield twp	1,013
Yardley borough	1,262

WILMINGTON DISTRICT.

CENTRAL CITY AND ADJACENT TERRITORY (IN DELAWARE).

New Castle County.

Bellefonte town	291
Elsmere town	620
New Castle city	3,854
Newark town	2,183
Newport town	676
Rep. Dist. 6, excl. Bellefonte town	6,160
Rep. Dist. 7, excl. Elsmere and Newport towns	5,002
Rep. Dist. 8	4,052
Rep. Dist. 9, excl. Newark town	1,738
Rep. Dist. 10, excl. New Castle city	2,532
Wilmington city	110,168

CENTRAL CITY AND ADJACENT TERRITORY (IN NEW JERSEY).

Gloucester County.

Logan twp	1,510

Salem County.

Lower Penns Neck twp	2,149
Mannington twp	1,456
Oldmans twp	1,328
Pennsgrove borough	6,060
Salem city	7,435
Upper Penns Neck twp	6,259

CENTRAL CITY AND ADJACENT TERRITORY (IN PENNSYLVANIA).

Chester County.

Birmingham twp	334
Kennett twp	863
Kennett Square borough	2,398
New Garden twp	1,619
Pennsbury twp	545

Delaware County.

Bethel twp	558
Birmingham twp	676
Concord twp	1,237

WORCESTER DISTRICT.

CENTRAL CITY AND ADJACENT TERRITORY

Middlesex County.

Hopkinton town	2,289

Worcester County.

Auburn town	3,891
Berlin town	868
Boylston town	794
Charlton town	1,995
Clinton town	12,979
Grafton town	6,887
Holden town	2,970
Lancaster town	2,461
Leicester town	3,635
Millbury town	5,653
North Brookfield town	2,610
Northborough town	1,753
Northbridge town	10,174
Oakham town	477
Oxford town	3,820
Paxton town	489
Princeton town	682
Rutland town	1,743
Shrewsbury town	3,708
Spencer town	5,930
Sterling town	1,305
Sutton town	2,578
Upton town	1,693
West Boylston town	1,624
Westborough town	5,789
Worcester city	179,754

YOUNGSTOWN DISTRICT.

CENTRAL CITY AND ADJACENT TERRITORY (IN OHIO).

Mahoning County.

Austintown twp	1,989
Beaver twp	2,299
Boardman twp., excl. part of Poland village	2,709
Canfield twp., excl. Canfield village	1,002
Canfield village	806
Coitsville twp., excl. East Youngstown village and part of Struthers village	6,729
East Youngstown village	11,237
Ellsworth twp	670

YOUNGSTOWN DISTRICT—Con.

CENTRAL CITY, ETC.—con.

Mahoning County—Con.

Green twp., excl. part of Washingtonville village	1,417
Jackson twp	1,029
Lowellville village	2,214
New Middletown village	168
Poland twp., excl. Lowellville village and parts of Poland and Struthers villages	2,931
Poland village	561
Springfield twp., excl. New Middletown village	1,945
Struthers village	5,847
Youngstown city	132,358

Trumbull County.

Brookfield twp	4,553
Girard village	6,556
Howland twp., excl. part of Warren city	1,176
Hubbard twp., excl. Hubbard village	2,017
Hubbard village	3,320
Liberty twp., excl. Girard village	2,684
Lordstown twp	695
McDonald village	621
Niles city	13,080
Vienna twp	961
Warren city	27,050
Warren twp., excl. part of Warren city	1,469
Weathersfield twp., excl. McDonald village and Niles city	3,333

CENTRAL CITY AND ADJACENT TERRITORY (IN PENNSYLVANIA).

Lawrence County.

Bessemer borough	1,417
Mahoning twp	3,627
North Beaver twp	1,973
Pulaski twp	1,554

Mercer County.

Hickory twp	4,569
Sharon city	21,747
Sharpsville borough	4,674
Shenango twp	1,279
West Middlesex borough	1,349
Wheatland borough	1,742

Table 42 gives a condensed summary of the statistics in Tables 40 and 41. While an appreciable proportion of the population of the adjacent territory is more or less rural in character, nevertheless the table gives a comprehensive idea of the importance of the leading urban areas of the country.

The total population in 1920 of the 58 districts covered by this table was 36,886,961, or 34.9 per cent of the total population of the United States. It will be noted that the average rates of increase during the decade in the population of the central cities and of the adjacent territory were similar.

TABLE 42.—TOTAL AREA AND POPULATION OF CENTRAL CITIES AND OF ADJACENT TERRITORY: 1920 AND 1910.

	Area in acres: 1920	POPULATION.		Percent of increase: 1910-1920
		1920	1910	
Total in 58 districts (comprising cities and adjacent territory)	23,467,218.2	36,886,961	29,183,081	26.4
Total in 62 central cities	1,988,618.9	26,254,645	20,839,132	26.0
Total in adjacent territory [1]	21,478,599.3	10,632,316	8,343,949	27.4
Total in 68 cities of 100,000 or more	2,036,620.2	27,429,326	21,859,160	25.5
Total in adjacent territory outside 68 cities of 100,000 or more	21,428,598.0	9,457,635	7,323,021	29.1

[1] Adjacent territory includes 6 cities of 100,000 and over, as follows: Jersey City, Newark, Paterson, and Yonkers, in metropolitan district of New York; Camden, in metropolitan district of Philadelphia; and Cambridge, in metropolitan district of Boston.

POPULATION.

76

POPULATION OF INDIVIDUAL CITIES.

This section presents summary tables showing the population of individual cities having 100,000 inhabitants or more at each census from 1790 to 1920, and of cities having 25,000 inhabitants or more at each census from 1850 to 1920. The population of all cities, boroughs, villages, and other municipalities (and of towns in Massachusetts, New Hampshire, and Rhode Island which had 2,500 inhabitants or more in 1920) is shown for 1920, 1910, and 1900 in Table 51 (p. 178), in which the arrangement is alphabetical by states. This table shows also the population in 1920 of wards of cities having 5,000 inhabitants or more. In Table 52 those incorporated places (and those towns in the three states above named) which had 2,500 inhabitants or more in 1920 are classified according to size in four groups, the arrangement within each group being alphabetical by states.

Unless otherwise explained by footnote, the population shown for each city in any census year is that of the city as constituted at the time the census was taken. It should be kept in mind, therefore, that in many instances the growth shown by the figures may have been due in part to annexations of suburban territory. In cases where parts of townships or other county subdivisions have been annexed to incorporated places, the population of such annexed territory can not be determined separately; but where an incorporated place or an entire township has been annexed, the population, in 1910 and 1900, of such annexed territory is shown in footnotes to Table 53, to which cross references are made by footnotes to Table 51.

Cities of 250,000 inhabitants or more.—Table 43 shows, for each of the last four census years, the population, rank, and decennial increase in population for the 25 cities having, in 1920, more than 250,000 inhabitants, the cities being listed in the order of their rank in 1920.

TABLE 43.—POPULATION, RANK, AND DECENNIAL INCREASE FOR CITIES HAVING, IN 1920, 250,000 INHABITANTS OR MORE: 1890-1920.

[Except as explained in footnotes, population shown for each census year does not include that of territory subsequently annexed.]

CITY.	POPULATION.				RANK.				INCREASE.					
									1910–1920		1900–1910		1890–1900	
	1920	1910	1900	1890	1920	1910	1900	1890	Number.	Per cent.	Number.	Per cent.	Number.	Per cent.
New York	5,620,048	4,766,883	3,437,202	[1] 2,507,414	1	1	1	1	853,165	17.9	1,329,681	38.7	929,788	37.1
Chicago	2,701,705	2,185,283	1,698,575	1,099,850	2	2	2	2	516,422	23.6	486,708	28.7	598,725	54.4
Philadelphia	1,823,779	1,549,008	1,293,697	1,046,964	3	3	3	3	274,771	17.7	255,311	19.7	246,733	23.6
Detroit	993,678	465,766	285,704	205,876	4	9	13	15	527,912	113.3	180,062	63.0	79,828	38.8
Cleveland	796,841	560,663	381,768	261,353	5	6	7	10	236,178	42.1	178,895	46.9	120,415	46.1
St. Louis	772,897	687,029	575,238	451,770	6	4	4	5	85,868	12.5	111,791	19.4	123,468	27.3
Boston	748,060	670,585	560,892	448,477	7	5	5	6	77,475	11.6	109,693	19.6	112,415	25.1
Baltimore	733,826	558,485	508,957	434,439	8	7	6	7	175,341	31.4	49,528	9.7	74,518	17.2
Pittsburgh	588,343	533,905	[2] 451,512	[3] 343,904	9	8	11	13	54,438	10.2	82,393	18.2	107,608	31.3
Los Angeles	576,673	319,198	102,479	50,395	10	17	36	57	257,475	80.7	216,719	211.5	52,084	103.4
Buffalo	506,775	423,715	352,387	255,664	11	10	8	11	83,060	19.6	71,328	20.2	96,723	37.8
San Francisco	506,676	416,912	342,782	298,997	12	11	9	8	89,764	21.5	74,130	21.6	43,785	14.6
Milwaukee	457,147	373,857	285,315	204,468	13	12	14	16	83,290	22.3	88,542	31.0	80,847	39.5
Washington	437,571	331,069	278,718	230,392	14	16	15	14	106,502	32.2	52,351	18.8	48,326	21.0
Newark	414,524	347,469	246,070	181,830	15	14	16	17	67,055	19.3	101,399	41.2	64,240	35.3
Cincinnati	401,247	363,591	325,902	296,908	16	13	10	9	37,656	10.4	37,689	11.6	28,994	9.8
New Orleans	387,219	339,075	287,104	242,039	17	15	12	12	48,144	14.2	51,971	18.1	45,065	18.6
Minneapolis	380,582	301,408	202,718	164,738	18	18	19	18	79,174	26.3	98,690	48.7	37,980	23.1
Kansas City, Mo.	324,410	248,381	163,752	132,716	19	20	22	24	76,029	30.6	84,629	51.7	31,036	23.4
Seattle	315,312	237,194	80,671	42,837	20	21	48	70	78,118	32.9	156,523	194.0	37,834	88.3
Indianapolis	314,194	233,650	169,164	105,436	21	22	21	27	80,544	34.5	64,486	38.1	63,728	60.4
Jersey City	298,103	267,779	206,433	163,003	22	19	17	19	30,324	11.3	61,346	29.7	43,430	26.6
Rochester	295,750	218,149	162,608	133,896	23	25	24	22	77,601	35.6	55,541	34.2	28,712	21.4
Portland	258,288	207,214	90,426	46,385	24	28	42	61	51,074	24.6	116,788	129.2	44,041	94.9
Denver	256,491	213,381	133,859	106,713	25	27	25	26	43,110	20.2	79,522	59.4	27,146	25.4

[1] Includes population (992,113) of territory annexed between 1890 and 1900.

[2] Includes population of Allegheny: 129,896 in 1900; 105,287 in 1890.

Six cities—Kansas City, Mo., Seattle, Indianapolis, Rochester, Portland, and Denver—entered this group between 1910 and 1920. The rank of the largest 3 cities has remained unchanged since 1890, but Detroit, which ranked fifteenth in 1890, thirteenth in 1900, and ninth in 1910, advanced to fourth position in 1920. Cleveland also gained in rank from census to census during the 30-year period. Ten cities gained in rank between 1910 and 1920. The greatest advance shown for any of the cities in this group is that which appears for Los Angeles—from fifty-seventh position in 1890 to thirty-sixth in 1900, seventeenth in 1910, and tenth in 1920.

Cities of 100,000 inhabitants or more.—The cities having 100,000 inhabitants or more, as returned at the census of 1920, numbered 68. Eighteen of these cities passed the 100,000 limit between 1910 and 1920, namely, Akron, Ohio, Camden, N. J., Dallas, Tex., Des Moines, Ia., Fort Worth, Tex., Hartford, Conn., Houston, Tex., Kansas City, Kans., New Bedford, Mass., Norfolk, Va., Reading, Pa., Salt Lake City, Utah, San Antonio, Tex., Springfield, Mass., Trenton, N. J., Wilmington, Del., Yonkers, N. Y., and Youngstown, Ohio.

Table 46 shows the population of each of the 68 cities having 100,000 or more inhabitants in 1920, with

INDIVIDUAL CITIES.

comparative figures for all earlier censuses and rates of decennial increase from 1830 to 1920.

The diagram below presents, for 1920 and 1910, a comparison of the population of the 68 cities having more than 100,000 inhabitants in 1920.

POPULATION OF CITIES HAVING, IN 1920, 100,000 INHABITANTS OR MORE: 1920 AND 1910.

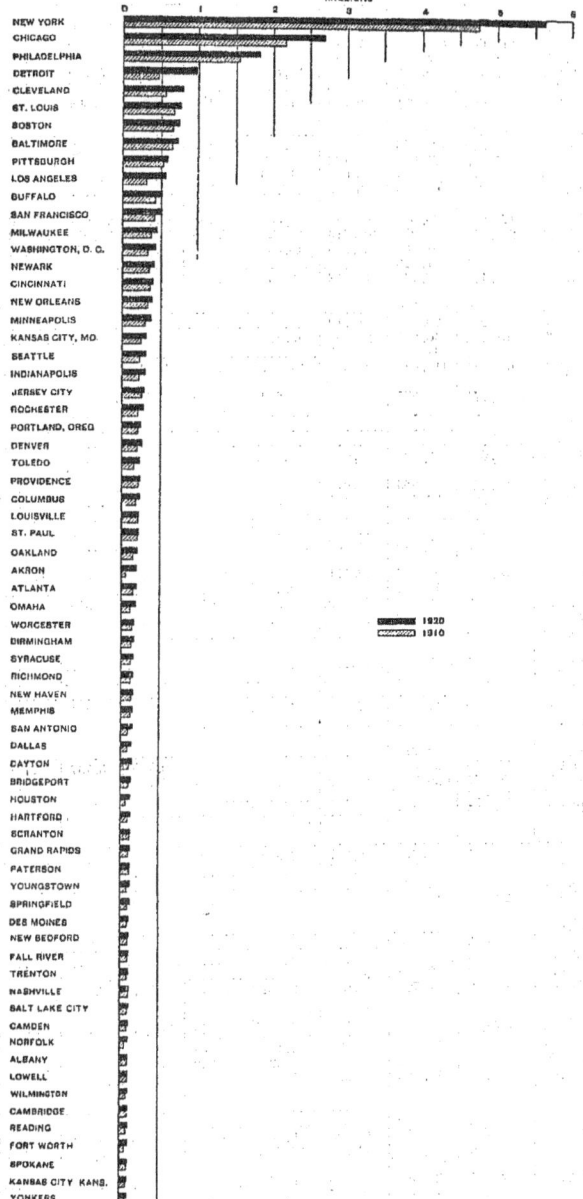

Table 47 shows, for each Federal census from 1850 to 1920, the population of the largest 50 cities, in the order of their rank at each of the several censuses. A considerable number of cities which ranked among the largest 50 at some of the earlier censuses have since been supplanted by others which have increased more rapidly in population, and a number of cities whose names appear in the lists for previous census years have since been consolidated with larger cities.

Cities of 25,000 inhabitants or more.—The cities having 25,000 inhabitants or more in 1920 numbered 287, 58 cities having entered this class since 1910. Table 44 shows, by geographic sections, the number of cities having 25,000 inhabitants or more in which the population increased and the number in which the population decreased during the decade 1910–1920, the former group being subdivided into 7 classes according to rates of increase.

TABLE 44.—NUMBER OF CITIES HAVING 25,000 INHABITANTS OR MORE IN 1920, GROUPED ACCORDING TO RATE OF INCREASE.

RATE OF INCREASE.	United States.	SECTION.		
		The North.[1]	The South.[1]	The West.[1]
Total...............................	287	203	59	25
Cities increasing during decade 1910–1920...	280	197	58	25
100 per cent and over.................	[2]25	[2]17	6	2
70–100 per cent.....................	19	7	8	4
50–70 per cent......................	19	12	7	......
30–50 per cent......................	70	48	16	6
20–30 per cent......................	56	41	9	6
10–20 per cent......................	53	43	8	2
Under 10 per cent...................	38	29	4	5
Cities decreasing during decade 1910–1920...	7	6	1	......

[1] For territory comprised in the North, South, and West, see map, p. 8.
[2] Includes Clifton, N. J., incorporated since 1910 from rural territory (Acquackanonk township, Passaic County).

Of the 25 cities which increased at rates greater than 100 per cent between 1910 and 1920, 17 are in the North, 6 in the South, and 2 in the West. These 25 cities, however, include Norwalk, Conn., whose nominal increase was due mainly to an annexation of territory, and Bethlehem, Pa., whose nominal increase resulted principally from a consolidation with South Bethlehem. The increase computed for each city as constituted in 1920 would be much less than 100 per cent.

Table 45 lists the 23 cities, excluding Norwalk and Bethlehem, which increased at rates greater than 100 per cent, in the descending order of their rates of increase, and presents for each the population in 1920 and the rate of increase between 1910 and 1920.

Table 48 shows the population, at each census from 1850 to 1920, of the cities having 25,000 inhabitants or more in 1920, together with the decennial increase during the two decades from 1900 to 1920.

TABLE 45.—CITIES HAVING 25,000 INHABITANTS OR MORE IN 1920 WHICH INCREASED IN POPULATION MORE THAN 100 PER CENT BETWEEN 1910 AND 1920.

Rank	CITY (unless otherwise specified).	Population: 1920	Per cent of increase: 1910–1920
1	Hamtramck village, Mich..................	48,615	1,266.0
2	Highland Park, Mich....................	46,499	1,028.6
3	Miami, Fla.....................	29,571	440.5
4	Wichita Falls, Tex............	40,079	388.8
5	Tulsa, Okla.....................	72,075	296.4
6	Gary, Ind.....................	55,378	229.6
7	Long Beach, Calif................	55,593	212.2
8	Cicero town, Ill................	44,995	209.1
9	Clarksburg, W. Va............	27,869	202.9
10	Akron, Ohio....................	208,435	201.8
11	East Cleveland, Ohio...........	27,292	197.3
12	Lakewood, Ohio................	41,732	174.9
13	Phoenix, Ariz.................	29,053	160.9
14	Warren, Ohio.................	27,050	144.1
15	Flint, Mich....................	91,599	137.6
16	Pontiac, Mich.................	34,273	135.8
17	Clifton, N. J..................	26,470	123.0
18	West New York town, N. J........	29,926	120.7
19	Irvington town, N. J...........	25,480	114.5
20	Knoxville, Tenn..............	77,818	114.1
21	Detroit, Mich.................	993,678	113.3
22	Winston-Salem, N. C...........	48,395	113.2
23	Oak Park village, Ill..........	39,858	105.0

POPULATION.

TABLE 46.—POPULATION OF CITIES HAVING, IN 1920, 100,000 INHABITANTS

[Except as explained in footnotes, population shown for each census year does not include that of territory subsequently annexed.]

CITY.	1920	1910	1900	1890	1880	1870	1860	1850	1840	1830	1820	1810	1800	1790
New York, N. Y.[1]	5,620,048	4,766,883	3,437,202	2,507,414	1,911,698	1,478,103	1,174,779	696,115	391,114	242,278	152,056	119,734	79,216	49,401
Manhattan borough	2,284,103	2,331,542	1,850,093	1,441,216	1,164,673	942,292	813,669	515,547	312,710	202,589	123,706	96,373	60,515	33,131
Bronx borough	732,016	430,980	200,507	88,908	51,980	37,393	23,593	8,032	5,346	3,023	2,782	2,267	1,755	1,781
Brooklyn borough	2,018,356	1,634,351	1,166,582	838,547	599,495	419,921	279,122	138,882	47,613	20,535	11,187	8,303	5,740	4,495
Queens borough	469,042	284,041	152,999	87,050	56,559	45,468	32,903	18,593	14,480	9,049	8,246	7,444	6,642	6,159
Richmond borough	116,531	85,969	67,021	51,693	38,991	33,029	25,492	15,061	10,965	7,082	6,135	5,347	4,564	3,835
Chicago, Ill.	2,701,705	2,185,283	1,698,575	1,099,850	503,185	298,977	109,260	29,963	4,470					
Philadelphia, Pa.	1,823,779	1,549,008	1,293,697	1,046,964	847,170	674,022	565,529	121,376	93,665	80,462	63,802	53,722	41,220	28,522
Detroit, Mich.	993,678	465,766	285,704	205,876	116,340	79,577	45,619	21,019	9,102	2,222	1,422			
Cleveland, Ohio	796,841	560,663	381,768	261,353	160,146	92,829	43,417	17,034	6,071	1,076	606			
St. Louis, Mo.	772,897	687,029	575,238	451,770	350,518	310,864	160,773	77,860	16,469					
Boston, Mass.[2]	748,060	670,585	560,892	448,477	362,839	250,526	177,840	136,881	93,383	61,392	43,298	33,787	24,937	18,320
Baltimore, Md.	733,826	558,485	508,957	434,439	332,313	267,354	212,418	169,054	102,313	80,620	62,738	46,555	26,514	13,503
Pittsburgh, Pa.[3]	588,343	533,905	451,512	343,904	235,071	139,256	77,923	67,863	31,204	15,369	7,248	4,768	1,565	
Los Angeles, Calif.	576,673	319,198	102,479	50,395	11,183	5,728	4,385	1,610						
Buffalo, N. Y.	506,775	423,715	352,387	255,664	155,134	117,714	81,129	42,261	18,213	8,668	2,095			
San Francisco, Calif.	506,676	416,912	342,782	298,997	233,959	149,473	56,802	[4]34,776						
Milwaukee, Wis.	457,147	373,857	285,315	204,468	115,587	71,440	45,246	20,061	1,712					
Washington, D. C.[5]	437,571	331,069	278,718	230,392	177,624	109,199	61,122	40,001	23,364	18,826	13,247	8,208		
Newark, N. J.	414,524	347,469	246,070	181,830	136,508	105,059	71,941	38,894	17,290					
Cincinnati, Ohio	401,247	363,591	325,902	296,908	255,139	216,239	161,044	115,435	46,338	24,831	9,642	2,540		
New Orleans, La.	387,219	339,075	287,104	242,039	216,090	191,418	168,675	116,375	102,193	46,082	27,176	17,242		
Minneapolis, Minn.	380,582	301,408	202,718	164,738	46,887	13,066	2,564							
Kansas City, Mo.	324,410	248,381	163,752	132,716	55,785	32,260	4,418							
Seattle, Wash.	315,312	237,194	80,671	42,837	3,533	1,107								
Indianapolis, Ind.	314,194	233,650	169,164	105,436	75,056	48,244	18,611	8,091	2,692					
Jersey City, N. J.	298,103	267,779	206,433	163,003	120,722	82,546	29,226	6,856	3,072					
Rochester, N. Y.	295,750	218,149	162,608	133,896	89,366	62,386	48,204	36,403	20,191	9,207				
Portland, Oreg.	258,288	207,214	90,426	46,385	17,577	8,293	2,874							
Denver, Colo.	256,491	213,381	133,859	106,713	35,629	4,759								
Toledo, Ohio	243,164	168,497	131,822	81,434	50,137	31,584	13,768	3,829	1,222					
Providence, R. I.	237,595	224,326	175,597	132,146	104,857	68,904	50,666	41,513	23,171	16,833	11,767	10,071	7,614	6,380
Columbus, Ohio	237,031	181,511	125,560	88,150	51,647	31,274	18,554	17,882	6,048	2,435				
Louisville, Ky.	234,891	223,928	204,731	161,129	123,758	100,753	68,033	43,194	21,210	10,341	4,012	1,357	359	200
St. Paul, Minn.	234,698	214,744	163,065	133,156	41,473	20,030	10,401	1,112						
Oakland, Calif.	216,261	150,174	66,960	48,682	34,555	10,500	1,543							
Akron, Ohio	208,435	69,067	42,728	27,601	16,512	10,006	3,477	3,266						
Atlanta, Ga.	200,616	154,839	89,872	65,533	37,409	21,789	9,554	2,572						
Omaha, Nebr.[6]	191,601	124,096	102,555	140,452	30,518	16,083	1,883							
Worcester, Mass.	179,754	145,986	118,421	84,655	58,291	41,105	24,960	17,049	7,497	4,173	2,962	2,577	2,411	2,095
Birmingham, Ala.	178,806	132,685	38,415	26,178	3,086									
Syracuse, N. Y.	171,717	137,249	108,374	88,143	51,792	43,051	28,119	22,271						
Richmond, Va.	171,667	127,628	85,050	81,388	63,600	51,038	37,910	27,570	20,153	16,060	12,067	9,735	5,737	3,761
New Haven, Conn.	162,537	133,605	108,027	81,298	[7]62,882	[7]50,840	[7]39,267	[7]20,345	12,960	10,180	7,147	5,772	4,049	
Memphis, Tenn.	162,351	131,105	102,320	64,495	33,592	40,226	22,623	8,841						
San Antonio, Tex.	161,379	96,614	53,321	37,673	20,550	12,256	8,235	3,488						
Dallas, Tex.	158,976	92,104	42,638	38,067	10,358									
Dayton, Ohio	152,559	116,577	85,333	61,220	38,678	30,473	20,081	10,977	6,067	2,950	1,000	383		
Bridgeport, Conn.	143,555	102,054	70,996	48,866	27,643	18,969	[7]13,299	[7]7,500	3,204					
Houston, Tex.	138,276	78,800	44,633	27,557	16,513	9,382	4,845	2,396						
Hartford, Conn.	138,036	98,915	79,850	53,230	42,015	37,180	[7]20,152	[7]17,966	9,468	7,074	4,726	3,955		
Scranton, Pa.	137,783	129,867	102,026	75,215	45,850	35,092	9,223							
Grand Rapids, Mich.	137,634	112,571	87,565	60,278	32,016	16,507	8,085	2,686						
Paterson, N. J.	135,875	125,600	105,171	78,347	51,031	33,579	19,586							
Youngstown, Ohio	132,358	79,066	44,885	33,220	15,435	8,075	2,759	2,802						
Springfield, Mass.	129,614	88,926	62,059	44,179	33,340	26,703	15,199	11,766	10,985	6,784	3,914	2,767	2,312	1,574
Des Moines, Iowa	126,468	86,368	62,139	50,093	22,408	12,035	3,965							
New Bedford, Mass.	121,217	96,652	62,442	40,733	26,845	21,320	22,300	16,443	12,087	7,592	3,947	5,651	4,361	3,313
Fall River, Mass.	120,485	119,295	104,863	74,398	48,961	26,766	14,026	11,524	6,738	4,158	1,594	1,206		
Trenton, N. J.	119,289	96,815	73,307	57,458	29,910	22,874	17,228	6,461	4,035	3,925	3,942	3,002		
Nashville, Tenn.	118,342	110,364	80,865	76,168	43,350	25,865	16,988	10,165	6,929	5,566				
Salt Lake City, Utah	118,110	92,777	53,531	44,843	20,768	12,854	8,236							
Camden, N. J.	116,309	94,538	75,935	58,313	41,659	20,045	14,358	9,479	3,371					
Norfolk, Va.	115,777	67,452	46,624	34,871	21,966	19,229	14,620	14,326	10,920	9,814	8,478	9,193	6,926	2,959
Albany, N. Y.	113,344	100,253	94,151	94,923	90,758	69,422	62,367	50,763	33,721	24,209	12,630	10,762	5,349	3,498
Lowell, Mass.	112,759	106,294	94,969	77,696	59,475	40,928	36,827	33,383	20,796	6,474				
Wilmington, Del.	110,168	87,411	76,508	61,431	42,478	30,841	21,258	13,979	8,367					
Cambridge, Mass.	109,694	104,839	91,886	70,028	52,669	39,634	26,060	15,215	8,409	6,072	3,295	2,323	2,453	2,115
Reading, Pa.	107,784	96,071	78,961	58,661	43,278	33,930	23,162	15,743	8,410	5,856	4,332	(8)	2,386	
Fort Worth, Tex.	106,482	73,312	26,688	23,076	6,663									
Spokane, Wash.	104,437	104,402	36,848	19,922										
Kansas City, Kans.	101,177	82,331	51,418	38,316	3,200									
Yonkers, N. Y.	100,176	79,803	47,931	32,033	18,892									

[1] Population shown is for New York and its boroughs as now constituted.
[2] Hyde Park town annexed to Boston city since 1910. Combined population: 1910, 686,092; 1900, 574,136; 1890, 458,670; 1880, 390,927; 1870, 254,002. Hyde Park not returned separately at earlier censuses.
[3] Includes population of Allegheny, as follows: 1900, 129,896; 1890, 105,287; 1880, 78,682; 1870, 53,180; 1860, 28,702; 1850, 21,262; 1840, 10,089; and 1830, 2,801. Allegheny not returned separately at earlier censuses.
[4] Population as reported by state census of 1852; returns for 1850 for San Francisco were destroyed by fire.

INDIVIDUAL CITIES.

OR MORE, 1790-1920, AND DECENNIAL INCREASE, 1830-1920.

79

[A minus sign (−) denotes decrease.]

INCREASE IN POPULATION.

1910-1920		1900-1910		1890-1900		1880-1890		1870-1880		1860-1870		1850-1860		1840-1850		1830-1840		
Number.	Per cent.	Number.	Per cent.	Number.	Per cent.	Number.	Per cent.	Number.	Per cent.	Number.	Per cent.	Number.	Per cent.	Number.	Per cent.	Number.	Per cent.	
853,165	17.9	1,329,681	38.7	929,788	37.1	595,716	31.2	483,595	29.3	303,324	25.8	478,664	68.8	305,001	78.0	148,836	61.4	1
−47,439	−2.0	481,449	26.0	408,877	28.4	276,543	23.7	222,381	23.6	128,623	15.8	208,122	57.8	202,837	64.9	110,121	54.4	
301,036	69.8	230,473	114.9	111,599	125.5	36,928	71.0	14,587	39.0	13,800	58.5	15,561	193.7	2,686	50.2	2,323	76.8	
384,005	23.5	467,769	40.1	328,035	39.1	239,052	39.9	179,574	42.8	140,799	50.4	140,240	101.0	91,269	191.7	27,078	131.9	
185,001	65.1	131,042	85.6	65,949	75.8	30,491	53.9	11,091	24.4	12,565	38.2	14,310	77.0	4,113	28.4	5,431	60.0	
30,562	35.6	18,948	28.3	15,328	29.7	12,702	32.6	5,962	18.1	7,537	29.6	10,431	69.3	4,096	37.4	3,883	54.8	
516,422	23.6	486,708	28.7	598,725	54.4	590,665	118.6	204,208	68.3	180,717	173.6	79,297	264.6	25,493	570.3			2
274,771	17.7	255,311	19.7	246,733	23.6	199,794	23.6	173,148	25.7	108,493	19.2	444,153	365.9	27,711	29.6	13,203	16.4	3
527,912	113.3	180,002	63.0	79,828	38.8	89,536	77.0	36,763	46.2	33,958	74.4	24,600	117.0	11,917	130.9	6,880	309.6	4
236,178	42.1	178,895	46.9	120,415	46.1	101,207	63.2	67,317	72.5	49,412	113.4	26,383	154.9	10,963	180.6	4,095	464.2	5
85,808	12.5	111,791	19.4	123,468	27.3	101,252	28.9	80,654	12.8	150,091	93.4	52,913	106.5	61,391	372.8			6
77,475	11.6	109,693	19.6	112,415	25.1	85,688	23.6	112,313	44.8	72,686	40.9	40,959	29.9	43,498	46.6	31,091	52.1	7
175,341	31.4	49,528	9.7	74,518	17.2	102,126	30.7	64,959	24.3	54,936	25.9	43,364	25.7	66,741	65.2	21,693	26.9	8
54,438	10.2	82,393	18.2	107,608	31.3	108,833	46.3	95,815	68.8	61,333	78.7	10,060	14.8	36,659	117.5	15,835	103.0	9
257,475	80.7	216,719	211.5	52,084	103.4	39,212	350.6	5,455	95.2	1,343	30.6	2,775	172.4					10
53,060	19.6	71,328	20.2	96,723	37.8	100,530	64.8	37,420	31.8	36,585	45.1	38,868	92.0	24,048	132.0	9,545	110.1	11
89,764	21.5	74,130	21.6	43,785	14.6	65,038	27.8	84,486	56.5	92,671	163.1	22,026	63.3					12
83,290	22.3	88,542	31.0	80,847	39.5	88,881	76.9	44,147	61.8	26,194	57.9	25,185	125.5	18,349	1,071.8			13
106,502	32.2	52,351	18.8	48,326	21.0	52,768	29.7	68,425	62.7	48,077	78.7	21,121	52.8	16,637	71.2	4,538	24.1	14
67,055	19.3	101,399	41.2	64,240	35.3	46,322	33.2	31,449	29.9	33,118	46.0	33,047	85.0	21,604	125.0			15
37,656	10.4	37,689	11.6	28,994	9.8	41,769	16.4	38,900	18.0	55,195	34.3	45,609	39.5	69,097	149.1	21,507	86.6	16
48,144	14.2	51,971	18.1	45,065	18.6	25,949	12.0	24,672	12.9	22,743	13.5	52,300	44.9	14,182	13.9	56,111	121.8	17
79,174	26.3	98,600	48.7	37,980	23.1	117,851	251.4	33,821	258.8	10,502	409.6							18
76,029	30.6	84,629	51.7	31,036	23.4	76,331	137.9	23,525	72.9	27,842	630.2							19
78,118	32.9	156,523	194.0	37,834	88.3	39,304	1,112.5	2,426	219.2									20
80,544	34.5	64,486	38.1	63,728	60.4	30,380	40.5	26,812	55.6	29,633	159.2	10,520	130.0	5,399	200.6			21
30,324	11.3	61,346	29.7	43,430	26.6	42,281	35.0	38,176	46.2	53,320	182.4	22,370	326.3	3,784	123.2			22
77,601	35.6	55,541	34.2	28,712	21.4	44,530	49.8	26,980	43.2	14,182	29.4	11,801	32.4	16,212	80.3	10,984	119.3	23
51,074	24.6	116,788	129.2	44,041	94.9	28,808	163.9	9,284	111.9	5,419	188.6							24
43,110	20.2	79,522	59.4	27,146	25.4	71,084	199.5	30,870	648.7									25
74,067	44.3	36,675	27.8	50,388	61.9	31,207	62.4	18,553	58.7	17,816	129.4	9,939	259.6	2,607	213.3			26
13,269	5.9	48,720	27.8	43,451	32.9	27,269	26.0	35,953	52.2	18,238	36.0	9,153	22.0	18,342	79.2	6,338	37.7	27
55,520	30.6	55,951	44.6	37,410	42.4	36,503	70.7	20,373	65.1	12,720	68.6	672	3.8	11,834	195.7	3,613	148.4	28
10,963	4.9	19,197	9.4	43,602	27.1	37,371	30.2	23,005	22.8	32,720	48.1	24,839	57.5	21,084	103.6	10,809	105.1	29
19,954	9.3	51,679	31.7	29,909	22.5	91,683	221.1	21,443	107.1	9,629	92.6	9,289	835.3					30
66,087	44.0	83,214	124.3	18,278	37.5	14,127	40.9	24,055	229.1	8,957	580.5							31
139,368	201.8	26,339	61.6	15,127	54.8	11,089	67.2	6,506	65.0	6,529	187.8	211	6.5					32
45,777	29.6	64,907	72.3	24,339	37.1	28,124	75.2	15,620	71.7	12,235	128.1	6,982	271.5					33
67,505	54.4	21,541	21.0	−37,897	−27.0	109,934	360.2	14,435	89.8	14,200	754.1							34
33,768	23.1	27,565	23.3	33,760	39.9	26,364	45.2	17,186	41.8	16,145	64.7	7,911	46.4	9,552	127.4	3,324	79.7	35
46,121	31.8	94,270	245.4	12,237	46.7	23,092	748.3											36
34,468	25.1	28,875	26.6	20,231	23.0	36,351	70.2	8,741	20.3	14,932	53.1	5,848	26.3					37
44,039	31.5	42,578	50.1	3,602	4.5	17,788	28.0	12,562	24.6	13,128	34.6	10,340	37.5	7,417	36.8	4,093	25.5	38
28,932	21.7	25,578	23.7	26,729	32.9	18,416	29.3	12,042	23.7	11,573	29.5	18,922	93.0	7,385	57.0	2,780	27.3	39
31,246	23.8	28,785	28.1	37,825	58.6	30,903	92.0	−6,634	−16.5	17,603	77.8	13,782	155.9					40
64,765	67.0	43,203	81.2	15,648	41.5	17,123	83.3	8,294	67.7	4,021	48.8	4,747	136.1					41
60,872	72.6	49,466	116.0	4,571	12.0	27,709	267.5											42
35,982	30.9	31,244	36.6	24,113	39.4	22,542	58.3	8,205	26.9	10,392	51.3	9,104	82.9	4,910	80.9	3,117	105.7	43
41,501	40.7	31,058	43.7	22,130	45.3	21,223	76.8	8,674	45.7	5,670	42.6	5,739	75.9	4,266	129.5			44
59,476	75.5	34,107	76.6	17,076	62.0	11,044	66.9	7,131	76.0	4,537	93.6	2,449	102.2					45
39,121	39.6	19,065	23.9	26,020	50.0	11,215	26.7	4,835	13.0	8,028	27.5	11,186	62.3	8,498	89.8	2,394	33.8	46
7,916	6.1	27,841	27.3	26,811	35.6	20,365	64.0	10,758	30.7	25,860	280.5							47
25,063	22.3	25,006	28.6	27,287	45.3	28,262	88.3	15,500	94.0	8,422	104.2	5,399	201.0					48
10,275	8.2	20,429	10.4	26,824	34.2	27,316	53.5	17,452	52.0	13,993	71.4	−43	−1.5					49
53,292	67.4	34,181	76.2	11,665	35.1	17,785	115.2	7,360	91.1	5,316	192.7	3,433	29.2	781	7.1	4,201	81.9	50
40,688	45.8	26,887	43.3	17,880	40.5	10,839	32.5	6,637	24.9	11,504	75.7							51
40,100	46.4	24,229	39.0	12,046	24.0	27,685	123.5	10,373	86.2	8,070	203.5							52
24,565	25.4	34,210	54.8	21,709	53.3	13,888	51.7	5,525	25.9	−980	−4.4	5,857	35.6	4,356	36.0	4,495	59.2	53
1,190	1.0	14,432	13.8	30,465	40.9	25,437	52.0	22,195	82.9	12,740	90.8	2,502	21.7	4,786	71.0	2,580	62.0	54
22,474	23.2	23,508	32.1	15,849	27.6	27,548	92.1	7,036	30.8	5,646	32.8	10,767	166.6	2,426	46.7	110	2.8	55
7,978	7.2	20,499	30.5	4,697	6.2	32,818	75.7	17,485	67.6	8,877	52.3	6,823	67.1	3,236	46.7	1,363	24.5	56
25,333	27.3	39,246	73.3	8,688	19.4	24,075	115.9	7,914	61.6	4,618	56.1			6,108	181.2			57
21,771	23.0	18,603	24.5	17,622	30.2	16,654	40.0	21,614	107.8	5,687	39.6	4,879	51.5	3,406	31.2	1,106	11.3	58
48,325	71.6	20,828	44.7	11,753	33.7	12,905	58.7	2,737	14.2	4,609	31.5	294	2.1					59
13,091	13.1	6,102	6.5	−772	−0.8	4,165	4.6	21,336	30.7	7,055	11.3	11,604	22.9	17,042	50.5	9,512	39.3	60
6,465	6.1	11,325	11.9	17,273	22.2	18,221	30.6	18,547	45.3	4,101	11.1	3,444	10.3	12,587	60.5	14,322	221.2	61
22,761	26.0	10,903	14.3	15,077	24.5	18,953	44.6	11,637	37.7	9,583	45.1	7,279	52.1	5,612	67.1			62
4,855	4.6	12,953	14.1	21,858	31.2	17,359	33.0	13,035	32.9	13,574	52.1	10,845	71.3	6,806	80.9	2,337	38.5	63
11,713	12.2	17,110	21.7	20,300	34.6	15,383	35.5	9,348	27.6	10,768	46.5	7,419	47.1	7,333	87.2	2,554	43.6	64
33,170	45.2	46,624	174.7	3,612	15.7	16,413	246.3											65
35	(9)	67,554	183.3	16,926	85.0													66
18,848	22.9	30,013	60.1	13,102	34.2	35,116	1,097.4											67
20,373	25.5	31,872	66.5	15,898	49.6	13,141	69.6											68

[5] Population as returned from 1880 to 1920 is for District of Columbia, with which city is now coextensive.
[6] Omaha and South Omaha cities consolidated since 1910. Combined population: 1910, 150,355; 1900, 128,556; 1890, 148,514. South Omaha not returned separately at earlier censuses.
[7] Population of town, including city; town and city not returned separately.
[8] Not returned separately.
[9] Less than one-tenth of 1 per cent.

80

POPULATION.

TABLE 47.—LARGEST FIFTY CITIES AT EACH CENSUS FROM 1850 TO 1920, ARRANGED IN ORDER OF RANK.

[For population of largest fifty cities in 1840, see Reports of the Thirteenth Census, 1910, Vol. I, Table 57, p. 82.]

Rank.	1920 CITY.	Population.	1910 CITY.	Population.	1900 CITY.	Population.	1890 CITY.	Population.	Rank.
1	New York, N. Y	5,620,048	New York, N. Y	4,766,883	New York, N. Y.[1]	3,437,202	New York, N. Y.[1]	1,515,301	1
2	Chicago, Ill	2,701,705	Chicago, Ill	2,185,283	Chicago, Ill	1,698,575	Chicago, Ill	1,099,850	2
3	Philadelphia, Pa	1,823,779	Philadelphia, Pa	1,549,008	Philadelphia, Pa	1,293,097	Philadelphia, Pa	1,046,964	3
4	Detroit, Mich	993,678	St. Louis, Mo	687,029	St. Louis, Mo	575,238	Brooklyn, N. Y.[1]	806,343	4
5	Cleveland, Ohio	796,841	Boston, Mass	670,585	Boston, Mass	560,892	St. Louis, Mo	451,770	5
6	St. Louis, Mo	772,897	Cleveland, Ohio	560,663	Baltimore, Md	508,957	Boston, Mass	448,477	6
7	Boston, Mass	748,060	Baltimore, Md	558,485	Cleveland, Ohio	381,768	Baltimore, Md	434,439	7
8	Baltimore, Md	733,826	Pittsburgh, Pa	533,905	Buffalo, N. Y	352,387	San Francisco, Calif	298,997	8
9	Pittsburgh, Pa	588,343	Detroit, Mich	465,766	San Francisco, Calif	342,782	Cincinnati, Ohio	296,908	9
10	Los Angeles, Calif	576,673	Buffalo, N. Y	423,715	Cincinnati, Ohio	325,902	Cleveland, Ohio	261,353	10
11	Buffalo, N. Y	506,775	San Francisco, Calif	416,912	Pittsburgh, Pa.[2]	321,616	Buffalo, N. Y	255,664	11
12	San Francisco, Calif	506,676	Milwaukee, Wis	373,857	New Orleans, La	287,104	New Orleans, La	242,039	12
13	Milwaukee, Wis	457,147	Cincinnati, Ohio	363,591	Detroit, Mich	285,704	Pittsburgh, Pa.[2]	238,617	13
14	Washington, D. C	437,571	Newark, N. J	347,469	Milwaukee, Wis	285,315	Washington, D. C	230,392	14
15	Newark, N. J	414,524	New Orleans, La	339,075	Washington, D. C	278,718	Detroit, Mich	205,876	15
16	Cincinnati, Ohio	401,247	Washington, D. C	331,069	Newark, N. J	246,070	Milwaukee, Wis	204,468	16
17	New Orleans, La	387,219	Los Angeles, Calif	319,198	Jersey City, N. J	206,433	Newark, N. J	181,830	17
18	Minneapolis, Minn	380,582	Minneapolis, Minn	301,408	Louisville, Ky	204,731	Minneapolis, Minn	164,738	18
19	Kansas City, Mo	324,410	Jersey City, N. J	267,779	Minneapolis, Minn	202,718	Jersey City, N. J	163,003	19
20	Seattle, Wash	315,312	Kansas City, Mo	248,381	Providence, R. I	175,597	Louisville, Ky	161,129	20
21	Indianapolis, Ind	314,194	Seattle, Wash	237,194	Indianapolis, Ind	169,164	Omaha, Nebr	140,452	21
22	Jersey City, N. J	298,103	Indianapolis, Ind	233,650	Kansas City, Mo	163,752	Rochester, N. Y	133,896	22
23	Rochester, N. Y	295,750	Providence, R. I	224,326	St. Paul, Minn	163,065	St. Paul, Minn	133,156	23
24	Portland, Oreg	258,288	Louisville, Ky	223,928	Rochester, N. Y	162,608	Kansas City, Mo	132,716	24
25	Denver, Colo	256,491	Rochester, N. Y	218,149	Denver, Colo	133,859	Providence, R. I	132,146	25
26	Toledo, Ohio	243,164	St. Paul, Minn	214,744	Toledo, Ohio	131,822	Denver, Colo	106,713	26
27	Providence, R. I	237,595	Denver, Colo	213,381	Allegheny, Pa.[2]	129,896	Indianapolis, Ind	105,436	27
28	Columbus, Ohio	237,031	Portland, Oreg	207,214	Columbus, Ohio	125,560	Allegheny, Pa.[2]	105,287	28
29	Louisville, Ky	234,891	Columbus, Ohio	181,511	Worcester, Mass	118,421	Albany, N. Y	94,923	29
30	St. Paul, Minn	234,698	Toledo, Ohio	168,497	Syracuse, N. Y	108,374	Columbus, Ohio	88,150	30
31	Oakland, Calif	216,261	Atlanta, Ga	154,839	New Haven, Conn	108,027	Syracuse, N. Y	88,143	31
32	Akron, Ohio	208,435	Oakland, Calif	150,174	Paterson, N. J	105,171	Worcester, Mass	84,655	32
33	Atlanta, Ga	200,616	Worcester, Mass	145,986	Fall River, Mass	104,863	Toledo, Ohio	81,434	33
34	Omaha, Nebr	191,601	Syracuse, N. Y	137,249	St. Joseph, Mo	102,979	Richmond, Va	81,388	34
35	Worcester, Mass	179,754	New Haven, Conn	133,605	Omaha, Nebr	102,555	New Haven, Conn	81,298	35
36	Birmingham, Ala	178,806	Birmingham, Ala	132,685	Los Angeles, Calif	102,479	Paterson, N. J	78,347	36
37	Syracuse, N. Y	171,717	Memphis, Tenn	131,105	Memphis, Tenn	102,320	Lowell, Mass	77,696	37
38	Richmond, Va	171,667	Scranton, Pa	129,867	Scranton, Pa	102,026	Nashville, Tenn	76,168	38
39	New Haven, Conn	162,537	Richmond, Va	127,628	Lowell, Mass	94,969	Scranton, Pa	75,215	39
40	Memphis, Tenn	162,351	Paterson, N. J	125,600	Albany, N. Y	94,151	Fall River, Mass	74,398	40
41	San Antonio, Tex	161,379	Omaha, Nebr	124,096	Cambridge, Mass	91,886	Cambridge, Mass	70,028	41
42	Dallas, Tex	158,976	Fall River, Mass	119,295	Portland, Oreg	90,426	Atlanta, Ga	65,533	42
43	Dayton, Ohio	152,559	Dayton, Ohio	116,577	Atlanta, Ga	89,872	Memphis, Tenn	64,495	43
44	Bridgeport, Conn	143,555	Grand Rapids, Mich	112,571	Grand Rapids, Mich	87,565	Wilmington, Del	61,431	44
45	Houston, Tex	138,276	Nashville, Tenn	110,364	Dayton, Ohio	85,333	Dayton, Ohio	61,220	45
46	Hartford, Conn	138,036	Lowell, Mass	106,294	Richmond, Va	85,050	Troy, N. Y	60,956	46
47	Scranton, Pa	137,783	Cambridge, Mass	104,839	Nashville, Tenn	80,865	Grand Rapids, Mich	60,278	47
48	Grand Rapids, Mich	137,634	Spokane, Wash	104,402	Seattle, Wash	80,671	Reading, Pa	58,661	48
49	Paterson, N. J	135,875	Bridgeport, Conn	102,054	Hartford, Conn	79,850	Camden, N. J	58,313	49
50	Youngstown, Ohio	132,358	Albany, N. Y	100,253	Reading, Pa	78,961	Trenton, N. J	57,458	50

[1] Greater New York formed between 1890 and 1900 by consolidation of New York, Brooklyn, and other territory. Figures for 1890 and previous census years show population of New York as then constituted (same as present borough of Manhattan in 1870 and prior years).
[2] Allegheny annexed to Pittsburgh in 1907. Separate figures for Pittsburgh and Allegheny given for 1900 and previous census years.

INDIVIDUAL CITIES.

TABLE 47.—LARGEST FIFTY CITIES AT EACH CENSUS FROM 1850 TO 1920, ARRANGED IN ORDER OF RANK—Con.

[For population of largest fifty cities in 1840, see Reports of the Thirteenth Census, 1910, Vol. I, Table 57, p. 82.]

Rank	1880 CITY.	Population.	1870 CITY.	Population.	1860 CITY.	Population.	1850 CITY.	Population.	Rank
1	New York, N. Y.[1]	1,206,299	New York, N. Y.[1]	942,292	New York, N. Y.[1]	813,669	New York, N. Y.[1]	515,547	1
2	Philadelphia, Pa.	847,170	Philadelphia, Pa.	674,022	Philadelphia, Pa.	565,529	Baltimore, Md.	169,054	2
3	Brooklyn, N. Y.[1]	566,663	Brooklyn, N. Y.[1]	396,099	Brooklyn, N. Y.[1]	266,661	Boston, Mass.	136,881	3
4	Chicago, Ill.	503,185	St. Louis, Mo.	310,864	Baltimore, Md.	212,418	Philadelphia, Pa.	121,376	4
5	Boston, Mass.	362,839	Chicago, Ill.	298,977	Boston, Mass.	177,840	New Orleans, La.	116,375	5
6	St. Louis, Mo.	350,518	Baltimore, Md.	267,354	New Orleans, La.	168,675	Cincinnati, Ohio	115,435	6
7	Baltimore, Md.	332,313	Boston, Mass.	250,526	Cincinnati, Ohio	161,044	Brooklyn, N. Y.[1]	96,838	7
8	Cincinnati, Ohio	255,139	Cincinnati, Ohio	216,239	St. Louis, Mo.	160,773	St. Louis, Mo.	77,860	8
9	San Francisco, Calif.	233,959	New Orleans, La.	191,418	Chicago, Ill.	109,260	Spring Garden, Pa.[6]	58,894	9
10	New Orleans, La.	216,090	San Francisco, Calif.	149,473	Buffalo, N. Y.	81,129	Albany, N. Y.	50,763	10
11	Washington, D. C.	177,624	Buffalo, N. Y.	117,714	Newark, N. J.	71,911	Northern Liberties, Pa.[6]	47,223	11
12	Cleveland, Ohio	160,146	Washington, D. C.	109,199	Louisville, Ky.	68,033	Kensington, Pa.[6]	46,774	12
13	Pittsburgh, Pa.[2]	156,389	Newark, N. J.	105,059	Albany, N. Y.	62,367	Pittsburgh, Pa.[2]	46,601	13
14	Buffalo, N. Y.	155,134	Louisville, Ky.	100,753	Washington, D. C.	61,122	Louisville, Ky.	43,194	14
15	Newark, N. J.	136,508	Cleveland, Ohio	92,829	San Francisco, Calif.	56,802	Charleston, S. C.	42,985	15
16	Louisville, Ky.	123,758	Pittsburgh, Pa.[2]	86,076	Providence, R. I.	50,666	Buffalo, N. Y.	42,261	16
17	Jersey City, N. J.	120,722	Jersey City, N. J.	82,546	Pittsburgh, Pa.[2]	49,221	Providence, R. I.	41,513	17
18	Detroit, Mich	116,340	Detroit, Mich	79,577	Rochester, N. Y.	48,204	Washington, D. C.	40,001	18
19	Milwaukee, Wis.	115,587	Milwaukee, Wis.	71,440	Detroit, Mich.	45,619	Newark, N. J.	38,894	19
20	Providence, R. I.	101,857	Albany, N. Y.	69,422	Milwaukee, Wis.	45,246	Southwark, Pa.[6]	38,799	20
21	Albany, N. Y.	90,758	Providence, R. I.	68,904	Cleveland, Ohio	43,417	Rochester, N. Y.	36,403	21
22	Rochester, N. Y.	89,366	Rochester, N. Y.	62,386	Charleston, S. C.	40,522	San Francisco, Calif.	[7] 34,776	22
23	Allegheny, Pa.[2]	78,682	Allegheny, Pa.[2]	53,180	New Haven, Conn.	[3] 39,267	Lowell, Mass.	33,383	23
24	Indianapolis, Ind.	75,056	Richmond, Va.	51,038	Troy, N. Y.	39,235	Williamsburgh, N. Y.[8]	30,780	24
25	Richmond, Va.	63,600	New Haven, Conn.	[3] 50,840	Richmond, Va.	37,910	Chicago, Ill.	29,963	25
26	New Haven, Conn.	[3] 62,882	Charleston, S. C.	48,956	Lowell, Mass.	36,827	Troy, N. Y.	28,785	26
27	Lowell, Mass.	59,475	Indianapolis, Ind.	48,244	Mobile, Ala.	29,258	Richmond, Va.	27,570	27
28	Worcester, Mass.	58,291	Troy, N. Y.	46,465	Jersey City, N. J.	29,226	Moyamensing, Pa.[6]	26,979	28
29	Troy, N. Y.	56,747	Syracuse, N. Y.	43,051	Hartford, Conn.	[3] 29,152	Syracuse, N. Y.	22,271	29
30	Kansas City, Mo.	55,785	Worcester, Mass.	41,105	Allegheny, Pa.[2]	28,702	Allegheny, Pa.[2]	21,262	30
31	Cambridge, Mass.	52,669	Lowell, Mass.	40,928	Syracuse, N. Y.	28,119	Detroit, Mich.	21,019	31
32	Syracuse, N. Y.	51,792	Memphis, Tenn.	40,226	Portland, Me.	26,341	Portland, Me.	20,815	32
33	Columbus, Ohio.	51,647	Cambridge, Mass.	39,634	Cambridge, Mass.	26,060	Mobile, Ala.	20,515	33
34	Paterson, N. J.	51,031	Hartford, Conn.	37,180	Roxbury, Mass.[5]	25,137	New Haven, Conn.	[3] 20,345	34
35	Toledo, Ohio	50,137	Scranton, Pa.	35,092	Charlestown, Mass.	25,065	Salem, Mass.	20,264	35
36	Charleston, S. C.	49,984	Reading, Pa.	33,930	Worcester, Mass.	24,960	Milwaukee, Wis.	20,061	36
37	Fall River, Mass.	48,961	Paterson, N. J.	33,579	Reading, Pa.	23,162	Roxbury, Mass.	18,364	37
38	Minneapolis, Minn.	46,887	Kansas City, Mo.	32,260	Memphis, Tenn.	22,623	Hartford, Conn.	[3] 17,966	38
39	Scranton, Pa.	45,850	Mobile, Ala.	32,034	Utica, N. Y.	22,529	Columbus, Ohio.	17,882	39
40	Nashville, Tenn.	43,350	Toledo, Ohio.	31,584	New Bedford, Mass.	22,300	Utica, N. Y.	17,565	40
41	Reading, Pa.	43,278	Portland, Me.	31,413	Savannah, Ga.	22,292	Charlestown, Mass.	17,216	41
42	Wilmington, Del.	42,478	Columbus, Ohio.	31,274	Salem, Mass.	22,252	Worcester, Mass.	17,049	42
43	Hartford, Conn.	42,015	Wilmington, Del.	30,841	Wilmington, Del.	21,258	Cleveland, Ohio.	17,034	43
44	Camden, N. J.	41,659	Dayton, Ohio	30,473	Manchester, N. H.	20,107	New Bedford, Mass.	16,443	44
45	St. Paul, Minn.	41,473	Lawrence, Mass.	28,921	Dayton, Ohio	20,081	Reading, Pa.	15,743	45
46	Lawrence, Mass.	39,151	Utica, N. Y.	28,804	Paterson, N. J.	19,586	Savannah, Ga.	15,312	46
47	Dayton, Ohio	38,678	Charlestown, Mass.[4]	28,323	Lynn, Mass.	19,083	Cambridge, Mass.	15,215	47
48	Lynn, Mass.	38,274	Savannah, Ga.	28,235	Indianapolis, Ind.	18,611	Bangor, Me.	14,432	48
49	Atlanta, Ga.	37,409	Lynn, Mass.	28,233	Columbus, Ohio.	18,554	Norfolk, Va.	14,326	49
50	Denver, Colo.	35,629	Fall River, Mass.	26,766	Petersburg, Va.	18,266	Lynn, Mass	14,257	50

[3] Population of town, including city; town and city not returned separately.
[4] Annexed to Boston in 1874.
[5] Annexed to Boston in 1867.
[6] Annexed to Philadelphia in 1854.
[7] According to state census of 1852; returns for 1850 destroyed by fire.
[8] Annexed to Brooklyn in 1854.

40454°—21——6

82

POPULATION.

TABLE 48.—POPULATION OF CITIES HAVING, IN 1920, 25,000 INHABITANTS OR MORE, 1850–1920; AND DECENNIAL INCREASE, 1900–1920.

[Except as explained in footnotes, population shown for each census year does not include that of territory subsequently annexed. For comparative figures for earlier years than those shown in this table, see Reports of the Twelfth Census, 1900, Vol. I, Table 6, p. 430, and Table 7, p. 434.]

[A minus sign (—) denotes decrease.]

CITY.	POPULATION.								INCREASE.			
									1910–1920		1900–1910	
	1920	1910	1900	1890	1880	1870	1860	1850	Number.	Per cent.	Number.	Per cent.
ALABAMA.												
Birmingham	178,806	132,685	38,415	26,178	3,086				46,121	34.8	94,270	245.4
Mobile	60,777	51,521	38,469	31,076	29,132	32,034	29,258	20,515	9,256	18.0	13,052	33.9
Montgomery	43,464	38,136	30,346	21,883	16,713	10,588	8,843	8,728	5,328	14.0	7,790	25.7
ARIZONA.												
Phoenix	29,053	11,134	5,544	3,152					17,919	160.9	5,590	100.8
ARKANSAS.												
Fort Smith	28,870	23,975	11,587	11,311	3,099	2,227	1,532	964	4,895	20.4	12,388	106.9
Little Rock	65,142	45,941	38,307	25,874	13,138	12,380	3,727	2,167	19,201	41.8	7,634	19.9
CALIFORNIA.												
Alameda	28,806	23,383	16,464	11,165	5,708	1,557	460		5,423	23.2	6,910	42.0
Berkeley	56,036	40,434	13,214	5,101					15,602	38.6	27,220	206.0
Fresno	45,086	24,892	12,470	10,818	1,112				20,194	81.1	12,422	99.6
Long Beach	55,593	17,809	2,252	564					37,784	212.2	15,557	690.8
Los Angeles	576,673	319,198	102,479	50,395	11,183	5,728	4,385	1,610	257,475	80.7	216,719	211.5
Oakland	216,261	150,174	66,960	48,682	34,555	10,500	1,543		66,087	44.0	83,214	124.3
Pasadena	45,354	30,291	9,117	4,882					15,063	49.7	21,174	232.2
Sacramento	65,908	44,696	29,282	26,396	21,420	16,283	13,785	6,820	21,212	47.5	15,414	52.6
San Diego	74,683	39,578	17,700	16,159	2,637	2,300	731		35,105	88.7	21,878	123.6
San Francisco	506,676	416,912	342,782	298,997	233,959	149,473	56,802	34,776	89,764	21.5	74,130	21.6
San Jose	39,642	28,946	21,500	18,060	12,567	9,089			10,696	37.0	7,446	34.6
Stockton	40,296	23,253	17,506	14,424	10,282	10,066	3,679		17,043	73.3	5,747	32.8
COLORADO.												
Colorado Springs [2]	30,105	29,078	21,085	11,140	4,226				1,027	3.5	7,993	37.9
Denver	256,491	213,381	133,859	106,713	35,629	4,759			43,110	20.2	79,522	59.4
Pueblo	43,050	[3] 41,747	28,157	24,558	3,217				1,303	3.1	13,590	48.3
CONNECTICUT.												
Bridgeport	143,555	102,054	70,996	48,866	27,643	18,969	[4] 13,299	[4] 7,560	41,501	40.7	31,058	43.7
Hartford	138,036	98,915	79,850	53,230	42,015	37,180	[4] 29,152	[4] 17,966	39,121	39.6	19,065	23.9
Meriden	29,867	27,265	24,296	21,652	15,540				2,602	9.5	2,969	12.2
New Britain	59,316	43,916	25,998	16,519	11,800				15,400	35.1	17,918	68.9
New Haven	162,537	133,605	108,027	81,298	[4] 62,882	[4] 50,840	[4] 39,267	[4] 20,345	28,932	21.7	25,578	23.7
New London	25,688	19,659	17,548	13,757	10,537	9,576	10,115	8,991	6,029	30.7	2,111	12.0
Norwalk [5]	27,743	6,954	6,125	(6)	5,308				20,789	299.0	829	13.5
Stamford	35,096	25,138	15,997						9,958	39.6	9,141	57.1
Waterbury	91,715	73,141	45,859	28,646	17,806	10,826			18,574	25.4	27,282	59.5
DELAWARE.												
Wilmington	110,168	87,411	76,508	61,431	42,478	30,841	21,258	13,979	22,757	26.0	10,903	14.3
DISTRICT OF COLUMBIA.												
Washington [7]	437,571	331,069	278,718	230,392	177,624	109,199	61,122	40,001	106,502	32.2	52,351	18.8
FLORIDA.												
Jacksonville	91,558	57,699	28,429	17,201	7,650	6,912	2,118	1,045	33,859	58.7	29,270	103.0
Miami	29,571	5,471	1,681						24,100	440.5	3,790	225.5
Pensacola	31,035	22,982	17,747	11,750	6,845	3,347	2,876	2,164	8,053	35.0	5,235	29.5
Tampa	51,608	37,782	15,839	5,532	720	796			13,826	36.6	21,943	138.5
GEORGIA.												
Atlanta	200,616	154,839	89,872	65,533	37,409	21,789	9,554	2,572	45,777	29.6	64,967	72.3
Augusta	52,548	41,040	39,441	33,300	21,891	15,389	12,493	(8)	11,508	28.0	1,599	4.1
Columbus	31,125	20,554	17,614	17,303	10,123	7,401	9,621	5,942	10,571	51.4	2,940	16.7
Macon	52,995	40,665	23,272	22,746	12,749	10,810	8,247	5,720	12,330	30.3	17,393	74.7
Savannah	83,252	65,064	54,244	43,189	30,709	28,235	22,292	15,312	18,188	28.0	10,820	19.9
ILLINOIS.												
Aurora	36,397	29,807	24,147	19,688	11,873	11,162	6,011		6,590	22.1	5,660	23.4
Bloomington	28,725	25,768	23,286	20,484	17,180	14,590	7,075	1,594	2,957	11.5	2,482	10.7
Chicago	2,701,705	2,185,283	1,698,575	1,099,850	503,185	298,977	109,260	29,963	516,422	23.6	486,708	28.7
Cicero town	44,995	14,557	16,310	10,204	5,182	1,545	1,272		30,438	209.1	−1,753	−10.7
Danville	33,776	27,871	16,354	11,491	7,733	4,751	1,632		5,905	21.2	11,517	70.4
Decatur	43,818	31,140	20,754	16,841	9,547	7,161	3,839	736	12,678	40.7	10,386	50.0
East St. Louis	66,767	58,547	29,655	15,169	9,185	5,644			8,220	14.0	28,892	97.4
Elgin	27,454	25,976	22,433	17,823	8,787	5,441	2,797		1,478	5.7	3,543	15.8
Evanston	37,234	24,978	19,259	(6)	4,400				12,256	49.1	5,719	29.7
Joliet	38,442	34,670	29,353	23,264	11,657	7,263	7,104	2,659	3,772	10.9	5,317	18.1
Moline	30,734	24,199	17,248	12,000	7,800	4,166	2,028		6,535	27.0	6,951	40.3
Oak Park village	39,858	19,444							20,414	105.0		
Peoria	76,121	66,950	56,100	41,024	29,259	22,849	14,045	5,095	9,171	13.7	10,850	19.3
Quincy	35,978	36,587	36,252	31,494	27,268	24,052	13,718	6,902	−609	−1.7	335	0.9
Rock Island	35,177	24,335	19,493	13,634	11,659	7,890	5,130	1,711	10,842	44.6	4,812	24.8
Rockford	65,651	45,401	31,051	23,584	13,129	11,049	6,979		20,250	44.6	14,350	46.2
Springfield	59,183	51,678	34,159	24,963	19,743	17,364	9,320	4,533	7,505	14.5	17,519	51.3

[1] Population as reported by state census of 1852; returns for San Francisco for 1850 were destroyed by fire.

[2] Colorado City and Colorado Springs city consolidated since 1910. Combined population: 1910, 33,411; 1900, 23,999; 1890, 12,928; 1880, 4,573. Colorado city not returned separately at earlier censuses.

[3] The population in 1910 shown for Pueblo in the Thirteenth Census reports includes the population of certain territory outside the city limits. The population of this area was 2,531 in 1920 and 2,648 in 1910. The combined population of the city of Pueblo and of this outside area was 45,581 in 1920 and 44,395 in 1910. The area in question was not returned separately in 1900 and earlier census years.

[4] Population of town, including city; town and city not returned separately.

[5] Norwalk and South Norwalk cities consolidated and made coextensive with Norwalk town since 1910; combined population, 15,922 in 1910 and 12,716 in 1900.

[6] Not returned separately.

[7] Population as returned from 1880 to 1920 is for the District of Columbia, with which the city of Washington is now coextensive.

[8] Not returned separately in 1850; population in 1852, according to a census taken by local authorities, 10,217.

INDIVIDUAL CITIES.

83

TABLE 48.—POPULATION OF CITIES HAVING, IN 1920, 25,000 INHABITANTS OR MORE, 1850-1920, AND DECENNIAL INCREASE, 1900-1920—Continued.

[Except as explained in footnotes, population shown for each census year does not include that of territory subsequently annexed. For comparative figures for earlier years than those shown in this table, see Reports of the Twelfth Census, 1900, Vol. I, Table 6, p. 430, and Table 7, p. 434.]

[A minus sign (−) denotes decrease.]

| CITY. | POPULATION. | | | | | | | | INCREASE. | | | |
	1920	1910	1900	1890	1880	1870	1860	1850	1910-1920 Number.	Per cent.	1900-1910 Number.	Per cent.
INDIANA.												
Anderson	20,707	22,476	20,178	10,741	4,126	3,126	1,196	383	7,291	32.4	2,298	11.4
East Chicago	35,067	19,098	3,411	1,255					16,869	88.3	15,687	459.9
Evansville	85,264	69,647	59,007	50,756	29,280	21,830	11,484	3,235	15,617	22.4	10,640	18.0
Fort Wayne	88,549	63,933	45,115	35,393	26,880	17,718	(¹)	4,282	22,616	35.4	18,818	41.7
Gary	55,378	16,802							38,576	229.6		
Hammond	36,004	20,925	12,376	5,428					15,079	72.1	8,549	69.1
Indianapolis	314,194	233,650	169,164	105,436	75,056	48,244	18,611	8,091	80,544	34.5	64,486	38.1
Kokomo	30,067	17,010	10,609	8,261	4,042	2,177	1,040		13,057	76.8	6,401	60.3
Muncie	36,524	24,005	20,942	11,345	5,219	2,992	1,782	666	12,519	52.2	3,063	14.6
Richmond	26,765	22,324	18,226	16,608	12,742	9,445	6,603	1,443	4,441	19.9	4,098	22.5
South Bend	70,983	53,684	35,999	21,819	13,280	7,206	3,832	1,652	17,299	32.2	17,685	49.1
Terre Haute	66,083	58,157	36,673	30,217	26,042	16,103	8,594	4,051	7,926	13.6	21,484	58.6
IOWA.												
Cedar Rapids	45,566	32,811	25,656	18,020	10,104	5,940	1,830		12,755	38.9	7,155	27.9
Council Bluffs	36,162	29,292	25,802	21,474	18,063	10,020	2,011		6,870	23.5	3,490	13.5
Davenport	56,727	43,028	35,254	26,872	21,831	20,038	11,267	1,848	13,699	31.8	7,774	22.1
Des Moines	126,468	86,368	62,139	50,093	22,408	12,035	3,965		40,100	46.4	24,229	39.0
Dubuque	39,141	38,494	36,297	30,311	22,254	18,434	13,000	3,108	647	1.7	2,197	6.1
Sioux City	71,227	47,828	33,111	37,806	7,366	3,401			23,399	48.9	14,717	44.4
Waterloo	36,230	26,693	12,580	6,674	5,630	4,337			9,537	35.7	14,113	112.2
KANSAS.												
Kansas City	101,177	82,331	51,418	38,316	3,200				18,846	22.9	30,913	60.1
Topeka	50,022	43,684	33,608	31,007	15,452	5,790	759		6,338	14.5	10,076	30.0
Wichita	72,217	52,450	24,671	23,853	4,911				19,707	37.7	27,779	112.6
KENTUCKY.												
Covington	57,121	53,270	42,988	37,371	29,720	24,505	16,471	9,408	3,851	7.2	10,332	24.1
Lexington	41,534	35,099	26,369	21,567	16,656	14,801	9,321	(¹)	6,435	18.3	8,730	33.1
Louisville	234,891	223,928	204,731	161,129	123,758	100,753	68,033	43,194	10,963	4.9	19,197	9.4
Newport	29,317	30,309	28,301	24,918	20,433	15,087	10,046	5,895	−992	−3.3	2,008	7.1
LOUISIANA.												
New Orleans	387,219	339,075	287,104	242,039	216,090	191,418	168,675	116,375	48,144	14.2	51,971	18.1
Shreveport	43,874	28,015	16,013	11,979	8,009	4,607	2,190	1,728	15,859	56.6	12,002	75.0
MAINE.												
Bangor	25,978	24,803	21,850	19,103	16,856	18,289	16,407	14,432	1,175	4.7	2,953	13.5
Lewiston	31,791	26,247	23,761	21,701	19,083	13,600	7,424	3,584	5,544	21.1	2,486	10.5
Portland	69,272	58,571	50,145	36,425	33,810	31,413	26,341	20,815	10,701	18.3	8,426	16.8
MARYLAND.												
Baltimore	733,826	558,485	508,957	434,439	332,313	267,354	212,418	169,054	175,341	31.4	49,528	9.7
Cumberland	29,837	21,839	17,128	12,729	10,693	8,056	4,078	6,073	7,998	36.6	4,711	27.5
Hagerstown	28,064	16,507	13,591	10,118	6,627	5,779	4,132	3,879	11,557	70.0	2,916	21.5
MASSACHUSETTS.												
Boston[2]	748,060	670,585	560,892	448,477	362,839	250,526	177,840	136,881	77,475	11.6	109,693	19.6
Brockton	66,254	56,878	40,063	27,294	13,608	8,007	6,584	3,939	9,376	16.5	16,815	42.0
Brookline town *	37,748	27,792	19,935	12,103	8,057	6,650	5,164	2,516	9,956	35.8	7,857	39.4
Cambridge	109,694	104,839	91,886	70,028	52,669	39,634	26,060	15,215	4,855	4.6	12,953	14.1
Chelsea	43,184	32,452	34,072	27,909	21,782	18,547	13,395	6,701	10,782	33.1	−1,620	−4.8
Chicopee	36,214	25,401	19,167	14,050	11,286	9,607	7,261	8,291	10,813	42.6	6,234	32.5
Everett	40,120	33,484	24,336	11,068	4,159	2,220			6,636	19.8	9,148	37.6
Fall River	120,485	119,295	104,863	74,398	48,961	26,766	14,026	11,524	1,190	1.0	14,432	13.8
Fitchburg	41,029	37,826	31,531	22,037	12,429	11,260	7,805	5,120	3,203	8.5	6,295	20.0
Haverhill	53,884	44,115	37,175	27,412	18,472	13,092	9,995	5,877	9,769	22.1	6,940	18.7
Holyoke	60,203	57,730	45,712	35,637	21,915	10,733	4,997	3,245	2,473	4.3	12,018	26.3
Lawrence	94,270	85,892	62,559	44,654	39,151	28,921	17,639	8,282	8,378	9.8	23,333	37.3
Lowell	112,759	106,294	94,969	77,696	59,475	40,928	36,827	33,383	6,465	6.1	11,325	11.9
Lynn	99,148	89,336	68,513	55,727	38,274	28,233	19,083	14,257	9,812	11.0	20,823	30.4
Malden	49,103	44,404	33,664	23,031	12,017	7,367	5,865	3,520	4,699	10.6	10,740	31.9
Medford	39,038	23,150	18,244	11,079	7,573	5,717	4,842	3,749	15,888	68.6	4,906	26.9
New Bedford	121,217	96,652	62,442	40,733	26,845	21,320	22,300	16,443	24,505	25.4	34,210	54.8
Newton	46,054	39,806	33,587	24,379	16,995	12,825	8,382	5,258	6,248	15.7	6,219	18.5
Pittsfield	41,763	32,121	21,766	17,281	13,364	11,112	8,045	5,872	9,642	30.0	10,355	47.6
Quincy	47,876	32,642	23,890	16,723	10,570	7,442	6,778	5,017	15,234	46.7	8,743	36.6
Revere	28,823	18,219	10,395	5,668	2,263	1,197	921	935	10,604	58.2	7,824	75.3
Salem	42,529	43,697	35,956	30,801	27,563	24,117	22,252	20,264	−1,168	−2.7	7,741	21.6
Somerville	93,091	77,236	61,643	40,152	24,933	14,685	8,025	3,540	15,855	20.5	15,593	25.3
Springfield	129,614	88,926	62,059	44,179	33,340	26,703	15,199	11,766	40,688	45.8	26,867	43.3
Taunton	37,137	34,259	31,036	25,448	21,213	18,629	15,376	10,441	2,878	8.4	3,223	10.4
Waltham	30,915	27,834	23,481	18,707	11,712	9,065	6,397	4,464	3,081	11.1	4,353	18.5
Worcester	179,754	145,986	118,421	84,655	58,291	41,105	24,960	17,049	33,768	23.1	27,565	23.3
MICHIGAN.												
Battle Creek	36,164	25,267	18,563	13,197	7,063	5,838	(¹)	1,064	10,897	43.1	6,704	36.1
Bay City	47,554	45,166	27,628	27,839	20,693	7,064	1,583		2,388	5.3	17,538	63.5
Detroit	993,678	465,766	285,704	205,876	116,340	79,577	45,619	21,019	527,912	113.3	180,062	63.0
Flint	91,599	38,550	13,103	9,803	8,409	5,386	2,950		53,049	137.6	25,447	194.2
Grand Rapids	137,634	112,571	87,565	60,278	32,016	16,507	8,085	2,686	25,063	22.3	25,006	28.6
Hamtramck village	48,615	3,559							45,056	1,266.0		
Highland Park	46,490	4,120	427						42,379	1,028.6	3,693	864.9
Jackson	48,374	31,433	25,180	20,798	16,105	11,447	4,799	2,363	16,941	53.9	6,253	24.8
Kalamazoo	48,487	39,437	24,404	17,853	11,937	9,181	6,070	2,507	9,050	22.9	15,033	61.6
Lansing	57,327	31,229	16,485	13,102	8,319	5,241	3,074		26,098	83.6	14,744	89.4
Muskegon	36,570	24,062	20,818	22,702	11,262	6,002			12,508	52.0	3,244	15.6
Pontiac	34,273	14,532	9,769	6,200	4,509	4,867			19,741	135.8	4,763	48.8
Port Huron	25,944	18,863	19,158	13,543	8,883	5,973	4,371		7,081	37.5	−295	−1.5
Saginaw	61,903	50,510	42,345	46,322	10,525	7,460	1,099		11,393	22.6	8,165	19.3

* Unincorporated.

¹ Not returned separately.

² Hyde Park town annexed to Boston city since 1910. Combined population: 1910, 686,092; 1900, 574,136; 1890, 458,670; 1880, 369,927; 1870, 254,662. Hyde Park not returned separately at earlier censuses.

POPULATION.

84

TABLE 48.—POPULATION OF CITIES HAVING, IN 1920, 25,000 INHABITANTS OR MORE, 1850–1920, AND DECENNIAL INCREASE, 1900–1920—Continued.

[Except as explained in footnotes, population shown for each census year does not include that of territory subsequently annexed. For comparative figures for earlier years than those shown in this table, see Reports of the Twelfth Census, 1900, Vol. I, Table 6, p. 430, and Table 7, p. 434.]

[A minus sign (−) denotes decrease.]

CITY.	POPULATION.								INCREASE.			
									1910–1920		1900–1910	
	1920	1910	1900	1890	1880	1870	1860	1850	Number.	Per cent.	Number.	Per cent.
MINNESOTA.												
Duluth	98,917	78,466	52,969	33,115	[1] 838	3,131	80		20,451	26.1	25,497	48.1
Minneapolis	380,582	301,408	202,718	164,738	46,887	13,066	2,564		79,174	26.3	98,690	48.7
St. Paul	234,698	214,744	163,065	133,156	41,473	20,030	10,401	1,112	19,954	9.3	51,679	31.7
MISSOURI.												
Joplin	29,902	32,073	26,023	9,943	7,038				−2,171	−6.8	6,050	23.2
Kansas City	324,410	248,381	163,752	132,716	55,785	32,260	4,418		76,029	30.6	84,629	51.7
St. Joseph	77,939	77,403	102,979	52,324	32,431	19,565	8,932		536	0.7	−25,576	−24.8
St. Louis	772,897	687,029	575,238	451,770	350,518	310,864	160,773	77,860	85,868	12.5	111,791	19.4
Springfield	39,631	35,201	23,267	21,850	6,522	5,555	(²)	415	4,430	12.6	11,934	51.3
MONTANA.												
Butte	41,611	39,165	30,470	10,723	3,363				2,446	6.2	8,695	28.5
NEBRASKA.												
Lincoln	54,948	43,973	40,169	55,154	13,003				10,975	25.0	3,804	9.5
Omaha [3]	191,601	124,096	102,555	140,452	30,518	16,083	1,883		67,505	54.4	21,541	21.0
NEW HAMPSHIRE.												
Manchester	78,384	70,063	56,987	44,126	32,630	23,536	20,107	13,932	8,321	11.9	13,076	22.9
Nashua	28,379	26,005	23,898	19,311	13,397	10,543	10,065	5,820	2,374	9.1	2,107	8.8
NEW JERSEY.												
Atlantic City	50,707	46,150	27,838	13,055	5,477	1,043	687		4,557	9.9	18,312	65.8
Bayonne	76,754	55,545	32,722	19,033	9,372				21,209	38.2	22,823	69.7
Camden	116,309	94,538	75,935	58,313	41,659	20,045	14,358	9,479	21,771	23.0	18,603	24.5
Clifton	26,470											
East Orange	50,710	34,371	21,506						16,339	47.5	12,865	59.8
Elizabeth	95,783	73,409	52,130	37,764	28,229	20,832	11,567		22,374	30.5	21,279	40.8
Hoboken	68,166	70,324	59,364	43,648	30,999	20,297	9,662		−2,158	−3.1	10,960	18.5
Irvington town	25,480	11,877	5,255	(²)	1,677				13,603	114.5	6,622	126.0
Jersey City	298,103	267,779	206,433	163,003	120,722	82,546	29,226	6,856	30,324	11.3	61,346	29.7
Kearny town	26,724	18,659	10,896						8,065	43.2	7,763	71.2
Montclair town	28,810	21,550	13,962						7,260	33.7	7,588	54.3
New Brunswick	32,779	23,388	20,006	18,603	17,166	15,058	11,256		9,391	40.2	3,382	16.9
Newark	414,524	347,469	246,070	181,830	136,508	105,059	71,941	38,894	67,055	19.3	101,399	41.2
Orange	33,268	29,630	24,141	18,844	13,207	9,348	8,877		3,638	12.3	5,489	22.7
Passaic	63,841	54,773	27,777	13,028	6,532				9,068	16.6	26,996	97.2
Paterson	135,875	125,600	105,171	78,347	51,031	33,579	19,586		10,275	8.2	20,429	19.4
Perth Amboy	41,707	32,121	17,699	9,512	4,808	2,861	2,302		9,586	29.8	14,422	81.5
Plainfield	27,700	20,550	15,369	11,267	8,125	5,005	3,224		7,150	34.8	5,181	33.7
Trenton	119,289	96,815	73,307	57,458	29,910	22,874	17,228	6,461	22,474	23.2	23,508	32.1
West Hoboken town	40,074	35,403	23,094						4,671	13.2	12,309	53.3
West New York town	29,926	13,560	5,267						16,366	120.7	8,293	157.5
NEW YORK.												
Albany	113,344	100,253	94,151	94,923	90,758	69,422	62,367	50,763	13,091	13.1	6,102	6.5
Amsterdam	33,524	31,267	20,929	17,336	9,466	5,426			2,257	7.2	10,338	49.4
Auburn	36,192	34,668	30,345	25,858	21,924	17,225	10,986	9,548	1,524	4.4	4,323	14.2
Binghamton	66,800	48,443	39,647	35,005	17,317	12,692	8,325		18,357	37.9	8,796	22.2
Buffalo	506,775	423,715	352,387	255,664	155,134	117,714	81,129	42,261	83,060	19.6	71,328	20.2
Elmira	45,393	37,176	35,672	30,893	20,541	15,863			8,217	22.1	1,504	4.2
Jamestown	38,917	31,297	22,892	16,038	9,357	5,336	3,155		7,620	24.3	8,405	36.7
Kingston	26,688	25,908	24,535	21,261	18,344	6,315			780	3.0	1,373	5.6
Mount Vernon	42,726	30,919	21,228	10,830	4,586	2,700			11,807	38.2	9,691	45.7
New Rochelle	36,213	28,867	14,720	9,057	5,276	3,915	3,519	2,458	7,346	25.4	14,147	96.1
New York [4]	5,620,048	4,766,883	3,437,202	2,507,414	1,911,698	1,478,103	1,174,779	696,115	853,165	17.9	1,329,681	38.7
Manhattan borough	2,284,103	2,331,542	1,850,093	1,441,216	1,164,673	942,292	813,669	515,547	−47,439	−2.0	481,449	26.0
Bronx borough	732,016	430,980	200,507	88,908	51,980	37,393	23,593	8,032	301,036	69.8	230,473	114.9
Brooklyn borough	2,018,356	1,634,351	1,166,582	838,547	599,495	419,921	279,122	138,882	384,005	23.5	467,769	40.1
Queens borough	469,042	284,041	152,999	87,050	56,559	45,468	32,903	18,593	185,001	65.1	131,042	85.6
Richmond borough	116,531	85,969	67,021	51,693	38,991	33,029	25,492	15,061	30,562	35.6	18,948	28.3
Newburgh	30,366	27,805	24,943	23,087	18,049	17,014			2,501	9.2	2,862	11.5
Niagara Falls	50,760	30,445	19,457						20,315	66.7	10,988	56.5
Poughkeepsie	35,000	27,936	24,029	22,206	20,207	20,080	14,726		7,064	25.3	3,907	16.3
Rochester	295,750	218,149	162,608	133,896	89,366	62,386	48,204	36,403	77,601	35.6	55,541	34.2
Rome	26,341	20,497	15,343	14,991	12,194	11,000			5,844	28.5	5,154	33.6
Schenectady	88,723	72,826	31,682	19,902	13,655	11,026	9,579	8,921	15,897	21.8	41,144	129.9
Syracuse	171,717	137,249	108,374	88,143	51,792	43,051	28,119	22,271	34,468	25.1	28,875	26.6
Troy	72,013	76,813	60,651	60,956	56,747	46,465	39,235	28,785	−4,800	−6.2	16,162	26.6
Utica	94,156	74,419	56,383	44,007	33,914	28,804	22,529	17,565	19,737	26.5	18,036	32.0
Watertown	31,285	26,730	21,696	14,725	10,697	9,336			4,555	17.0	5,034	28.2
Yonkers	100,176	79,803	47,931	32,033	18,892				20,373	25.5	31,872	66.5
NORTH CAROLINA.												
Asheville	28,504	18,762	14,694	10,235	2,616	1,400			9,742	51.9	4,068	27.7
Charlotte	46,338	34,014	18,091	11,557	7,094	4,473	2,265	1,065	12,324	36.2	15,923	88.0
Wilmington	33,372	25,748	20,976	20,056	17,350	13,446	9,552	7,264	7,624	29.6	4,772	22.7
Winston-Salem [5]	48,395	[5] 22,700	[5] 13,650	[5] 10,729	[5] 4,194	[5] 443			25,695	113.2	9,050	66.3

[1] Excludes Duluth village (population, 2,645), which was set apart by act of legislature Feb. 23, 1877, but which again became part of city by act of Mar. 2, 1887.
[2] Not returned separately.
[3] Omaha and South Omaha cities consolidated since 1910. Combined population: 1910, 150,355; 1900, 128,556; 1890, 148,514. South Omaha not returned separately at earlier censuses.
[4] Population shown is for New York and its boroughs as now constituted.
[5] Winston city and Salem town consolidated as Winston-Salem since 1910. Figures shown for 1910, 1900, 1890, and 1880 represent combined population of Winston and Salem; population given for 1870 is that of Winston alone.

INDIVIDUAL CITIES.

85

TABLE 48.—POPULATION OF CITIES HAVING, IN 1920, 25,000 INHABITANTS OR MORE, 1850-1920, AND DECENNIAL INCREASE, 1900-1920—Continued.

[Except as explained in footnotes, population shown for each census year does not include that of territory subsequently annexed. For comparative figures for earlier years than those shown in this table, see Reports of the Twelfth Census, 1900, Vol. I, Table 6, p. 430, and Table 7, p. 434.]

[A minus sign (−) denotes decrease.]

| CITY. | POPULATION. | | | | | | | | INCREASE. | | | |
	1920	1910	1900	1890	1880	1870	1860	1850	1910-1920 Number.	Per cent.	1900-1910 Number.	Per cent.
OHIO.												
Akron	208,435	69,067	42,728	27,601	16,512	10,006	3,477	3,266	139,368	201.8	26,339	61.6
Canton	87,091	50,217	30,667	26,189	12,258	8,660	4,041	2,603	36,874	73.4	19,550	63.7
Cincinnati	401,247	363,591	325,902	296,908	255,139	216,239	161,044	115,435	37,656	10.4	37,689	11.6
Cleveland	796,841	560,663	381,768	261,353	160,146	92,829	43,417	17,034	236,178	42.1	178,895	46.9
Columbus	237,031	181,511	125,560	88,150	51,647	31,274	18,554	17,882	55,520	30.6	55,951	44.6
Dayton	152,559	116,577	85,333	61,220	38,678	30,473	20,081	10,977	35,982	30.9	31,244	36.6
East Cleveland	27,292	9,179	2,757	(1)	2,876	(1)	3,011	....	18,113	197.3	6,422	232.9
Hamilton	39,675	35,279	23,914	17,565	12,122	11,081	7,223	3,210	4,396	12.5	11,365	47.5
Lakewood	41,732	15,181	3,355	....	....	....	....	....	26,551	174.9	11,826	352.5
Lima	41,326	30,508	21,723	15,981	7,567	4,500	1,989	757	10,818	35.5	8,785	40.4
Lorain	37,295	28,883	16,028	4,863	1,595	....	....	....	8,412	29.1	12,855	80.2
Mansfield	27,824	20,768	17,640	13,473	9,859	8,029	4,581	3,557	7,056	34.0	3,128	17.7
Marion	27,891	18,232	11,862	8,327	3,899	2,531	1,844	1,311	9,659	53.0	6,370	53.7
Newark	26,718	25,404	18,157	14,270	9,600	6,698	4,675	3,654	1,314	5.2	7,247	39.9
Portsmouth	33,011	23,481	17,870	12,394	11,321	10,592	6,268	4,011	9,530	40.6	5,611	31.4
Springfield	60,840	46,921	38,253	31,895	20,730	12,652	7,002	5,108	13,919	29.7	8,668	22.7
Steubenville	28,508	22,391	14,349	13,394	12,093	8,107	6,154	6,140	6,117	27.3	8,042	56.0
Toledo	243,164	168,497	131,822	81,434	50,137	31,584	13,768	3,829	74,667	44.3	36,675	27.8
Warren	27,050	11,081	8,529	5,973	4,428	3,457	2,402	(1)	15,969	144.1	2,552	29.9
Youngstown	132,358	79,066	44,885	33,220	15,435	8,075	2,759	2,802	53,292	67.4	34,181	76.2
Zanesville	29,569	28,026	23,538	21,009	18,113	10,011	9,229	7,929	1,543	5.5	4,488	19.1
OKLAHOMA.												
Muskogee [2]	30,277	25,278	4,254	....	....	....	....	....	4,999	19.8	21,024	494.2
Oklahoma City [2]	91,295	64,205	10,037	4,151	....	....	....	....	27,090	42.2	54,168	539.7
Tulsa [2]	72,075	18,182	1,390	....	....	....	....	....	53,893	296.4	16,792	1,208.1
OREGON.												
Portland	258,288	207,214	90,426	46,385	17,577	8,293	2,874	....	51,074	24.6	116,788	129.2
PENNSYLVANIA.												
Allentown	73,502	51,913	35,416	25,228	18,063	13,884	8,025	3,779	21,589	41.6	16,497	46.6
Altoona	60,331	52,127	38,973	30,337	19,710	10,610	3,591	....	8,204	15.7	13,154	33.8
Bethlehem [3]	50,358	12,837	7,293	6,762	5,193	4,512	2,866	1,516	37,521	292.3	5,544	76.0
Chester	58,030	38,537	33,988	20,226	14,997	9,485	4,631	1,667	19,493	50.6	4,549	13.4
Easton	33,813	28,523	25,238	14,481	11,924	10,987	8,944	7,250	5,290	18.5	3,285	13.0
Erie	93,372	66,525	52,733	40,634	27,737	19,646	9,419	5,858	26,847	40.4	13,792	26.2
Harrisburg	75,917	64,186	50,167	39,385	30,762	23,104	13,405	7,834	11,731	18.3	14,019	27.9
Hazleton	32,277	25,452	14,230	11,872	6,935	4,317	1,707	....	6,825	26.8	11,222	78.9
Johnstown	67,327	55,482	35,936	21,805	8,380	6,028	4,185	1,269	11,845	21.3	19,546	54.4
Lancaster	53,150	47,227	41,459	32,011	25,769	20,233	17,603	12,360	5,923	12.5	5,768	13.9
McKeesport	46,781	42,694	34,227	20,741	8,212	2,523	2,106	1,392	4,087	9.6	8,467	24.7
New Castle	44,938	36,280	28,339	11,600	8,418	6,164	1,882	....	8,658	23.9	7,941	28.0
Norristown borough	32,319	27,875	22,265	19,791	13,063	10,753	8,848	6,024	4,444	15.9	5,610	25.2
Philadelphia	1,823,779	1,549,008	1,293,697	1,046,964	847,170	674,022	565,529	121,376	274,771	17.7	255,311	19.7
Pittsburgh [4]	588,343	533,905	451,512	343,904	235,071	139,256	77,923	67,863	54,438	10.2	82,393	18.2
Reading	107,784	96,071	78,961	58,661	43,278	33,930	23,162	15,743	11,713	12.2	17,110	21.7
Scranton	137,783	129,867	102,026	75,215	45,850	35,092	9,223	....	7,916	6.1	27,841	27.3
Wilkes-Barre	73,833	67,105	51,721	37,718	23,339	10,174	4,253	2,723	6,728	10.0	15,384	29.7
Williamsport	36,198	31,860	28,757	27,132	18,934	16,030	5,664	1,615	4,338	13.6	3,103	10.8
York	47,512	44,750	33,708	20,793	13,940	11,003	8,605	6,803	2,762	6.2	11,042	32.8
RHODE ISLAND.												
Cranston	29,407	21,107	13,343	8,099	5,940	4,822	7,500	4,311	8,300	39.3	7,764	58.2
Newport	30,255	27,149	22,441	19,457	15,693	12,521	10,508	9,563	3,106	11.4	4,708	21.0
Pawtucket	64,248	51,622	39,231	27,633	19,030	6,619	4,200	3,753	12,626	24.5	12,391	31.6
Providence	237,595	224,326	175,597	132,146	104,857	68,904	50,666	41,513	13,269	5.9	48,729	27.8
Woonsocket	43,496	38,125	28,204	20,830	16,050	11,527	....	....	5,371	14.1	9,921	35.2
SOUTH CAROLINA.												
Charleston	67,957	58,833	55,807	54,955	49,984	48,956	40,522	42,985	9,124	15.5	3,026	5.4
Columbia	37,524	26,319	21,108	15,353	10,036	9,298	8,052	6,060	11,205	42.6	5,211	24.7
SOUTH DAKOTA.												
Sioux Falls	25,202	14,094	10,266	10,177	2,164	....	....	....	11,108	78.8	3,828	37.3
TENNESSEE.												
Chattanooga	57,895	44,604	30,154	29,100	12,892	6,093	....	2,076	13,291	29.8	14,450	47.9
Knoxville	77,818	36,346	32,637	22,535	9,693	8,682	(1)	2,076	41,472	114.1	3,709	11.4
Memphis	162,351	131,105	102,320	64,495	33,592	40,226	22,623	8,841	31,246	23.8	28,785	28.1
Nashville	118,342	110,364	80,865	76,168	43,350	25,865	16,988	10,165	7,978	7.2	29,499	36.5
TEXAS.												
Austin	34,876	29,860	22,258	14,575	11,013	4,428	3,494	629	5,016	16.8	7,602	34.2
Beaumont	40,422	20,640	9,427	3,296	....	....	....	....	19,782	95.8	11,213	118.9
Dallas	158,976	92,104	42,638	38,067	10,358	....	....	....	66,872	72.6	49,466	116.0
El Paso	77,560	39,279	15,906	10,338	736	....	....	....	38,281	97.5	23,373	146.9
Fort Worth	106,482	73,312	26,688	23,076	6,663	....	....	....	33,170	45.2	46,624	174.7
Galveston	44,255	36,981	37,789	29,084	22,248	13,818	7,307	4,177	7,274	19.7	−808	−2.1
Houston	138,276	78,800	44,633	27,557	16,513	9,382	4,845	2,396	59,476	75.5	34,167	76.6
San Antonio	161,379	96,614	53,321	37,673	20,550	12,256	8,235	3,488	64,765	67.0	43,293	81.2
Waco	38,500	26,425	20,686	14,445	7,295	....	....	....	12,075	45.7	5,739	27.7
Wichita Falls	40,079	8,200	2,480	1,987	....	....	....	....	31,879	388.8	5,720	230.6
UTAH.												
Ogden	32,804	25,580	16,313	14,889	6,069	3,127	1,464	....	7,224	28.2	9,267	56.8
Salt Lake City	118,110	92,777	53,531	44,843	20,768	12,854	8,236	....	25,333	27.3	39,246	73.3

[1] Not returned separately.

[2] For population as enumerated at special census of 1907, see Table 52, p. 320.

[3] South Bethlehem borough and Bethlehem borough consolidated and incorporated as Bethlehem city since 1910. Combined population: 1910, 32,810; 1900, 23,999; 1890, 19,823; 1880, 10,118; 1870, 8,068. South Bethlehem not returned separately in 1860 and 1850.

[4] Includes population of Allegheny, as follows: 1900, 129,896; 1890, 105,287; 1880, 78,682; 1870, 53,180; 1860, 28,702; 1850, 21,262.

86

POPULATION.

TABLE 48.—POPULATION OF CITIES HAVING, IN 1920, 25,000 INHABITANTS OR MORE, 1850–1920, AND DECENNIAL INCREASE, 1900–1920—Continued.

[Except as explained in footnotes, population shown for each census year does not include that of territory subsequently annexed. For comparative figures for earlier years than those shown in this table, see Reports of the Twelfth Census, 1900, Vol. I, Table 6, p. 430, and Table 7, p. 434.]

[A minus sign (−) denotes decrease.]

CITY.	POPULATION.								INCREASE.			
									1910–1920		1900–1910	
	1920	1910	1900	1890	1880	1870	1860	1850	Number.	Per cent.	Number.	Per cent.
VIRGINIA.												
Lynchburg	30,070	29,494	18,891	19,709	15,959	6,825	6,853	8,071	576	2.0	10,603	56.1
Newport News	35,596	20,205	19,635						15,391	76.2	570	2.9
Norfolk	115,777	67,452	46,624	34,871	21,966	19,229	14,620	14,326	48,325	71.6	20,828	44.7
Petersburg	31,012	24,127	21,810	22,680	21,656	18,950	18,266	14,010	6,885	28.5	2,317	10.6
Portsmouth	54,387	33,190	17,427	13,268	11,390	10,590	9,496	8,122	21,197	63.9	15,763	90.5
Richmond	171,667	127,628	85,050	81,388	63,600	51,038	37,910	27,570	44,039	34.5	42,578	50.1
Roanoke	50,842	34,874	21,495	16,159	[1] 669				15,968	45.8	13,379	62.2
WASHINGTON.												
Bellingham	25,585	24,298	[2] 11,062	[2] 8,135					1,287	5.3	13,236	119.7
Everett	27,644	24,814	7,838						2,830	11.4	16,976	216.6
Seattle	315,312	237,194	80,671	42,837	3,533	1,107			78,118	32.9	156,523	194.0
Spokane	104,437	104,402	36,848	19,922					35	[3]	67,554	183.3
Tacoma	96,965	83,743	37,714	36,006					13,222	15.8	46,029	122.0
WEST VIRGINIA.												
Charleston	39,608	22,996	11,099	6,742	4,192	3,162	1,520	1,050	16,612	72.2	11,897	107.2
Clarksburg	27,869	9,201	4,050	3,008	2,307	[4]	895		18,668	202.9	5,151	127.2
Huntington	50,177	31,161	11,923	10,108	3,174				19,016	61.0	19,238	161.4
Wheeling	56,208	41,641	38,878	34,522	30,737	19,280	14,083	11,435	14,567	35.0	2,763	7.1
WISCONSIN.												
Green Bay	31,017	25,236	18,684	9,069	7,464	4,666	2,275		5,781	22.9	6,552	35.1
Kenosha	40,472	21,371	11,606	6,532	5,039	4,309	3,990	3,455	19,101	89.4	9,765	84.1
La Crosse	30,421	30,417	28,895	25,090	14,505	7,785	3,860		4	[3]	1,522	5.3
Madison	38,378	25,531	19,164	13,426	10,324	9,176	6,611	1,525	12,847	50.3	6,307	33.2
Milwaukee	457,147	373,857	285,315	204,468	115,587	71,440	45,246	20,061	83,290	22.3	88,542	31.0
Oshkosh	33,162	33,062	28,284	22,836	15,748	12,663	6,086		100	0.3	4,778	16.9
Racine	58,593	38,002	29,102	21,014	16,031	9,880	7,822	5,107	20,591	54.2	8,900	30.6
Sheboygan	30,955	26,398	22,962	16,359	7,314	5,310	4,262		4,557	17.3	3,436	15.0
Superior	39,671	40,384	31,091	11,983					−713	−1.8	9,293	29.9

[1] Population of Big Lick town; name changed to Roanoke between 1880 and 1890.
[2] Population of Fairhaven and New Whatcom cities combined.
[3] Less than one-tenth of 1 per cent.
[4] Not returned separately.

POPULATION OF MINOR CIVIL DIVISIONS.

The political units into which the counties or equivalent divisions are subdivided are collectively termed "minor civil divisions." In most states these minor civil divisions comprise two classes, which are termed primary and secondary. The primary divisions are variously known as townships, towns (unincorporated), election precincts, beats, etc. In most states the smaller cities and other municipalities form parts of the primary minor civil divisions in which they are located, and are therefore termed secondary divisions; but in Pennsylvania all incorporated places, regardless of their size, are independent political units, not forming parts of any civil divisions smaller than a county; in New Jersey all incorporated places form primary divisions except 3 cities, 1 town, and 2 villages, each of which is coextensive with the township in which located; and in certain other states some of the small municipalities are primary divisions and others are secondary divisions. The large cities in a few cases are coextensive with the counties in which located; Baltimore and St. Louis are independent of the counties; and of the remainder, aside from the Virginia cities, part constitute primary and part secondary minor civil divisions. In Virginia all the cities except two, regardless of their size, are independent of the counties.

Table 53 shows, for states and counties, the population of all primary minor civil divisions, so far as reported separately at the census of 1920, with comparative figures so far as available for 1910 and 1900. The secondary divisions, all of which are incorporated places and therefore appear in Table 51, are not shown separately in Table 53.

Such general explanations and definitions as are needed in regard to the minor civil divisions in any state are made in a headnote at the beginning of the section for that state; and explanations in regard to individual minor civil divisions are made in footnotes.

POPULATION.   87

OUTLYING POSSESSIONS.

All available statistics as to number and distribution of the inhabitants of the several outlying possessions enumerated at the Fourteenth Census have been brought together in Table 54. (The Philippines and the Virgin Islands were not enumerated at the Fourteenth Census, but the totals shown by the latest enumerations made of these possessions are given in Table 1, p. 13.)

Alaska.—Alaska was purchased by the United States from Russia in March, 1867. The first enumeration of its population by the United States was made in 1880 and consisted of a canvass of all accessible settlements, supplemented by estimates—based mainly upon records or upon the personal knowledge of missionary priests—for those regions which could not be visited by the canvassers. A similar practice was followed in 1890, but the area actually canvassed in that year was larger than that visited in 1880, and at each subsequent census the enumeration has been more nearly complete and accurate. Alaska has no county organization, but the judicial districts into which the territory is divided are treated for census purposes as equivalent to county areas. The primary minor civil divisions are termed recorders' districts. In Table 54 comparative figures for 1910 only are given in the case of the judicial and recorders' districts, since the population of these districts can not generally be accurately determined from the census reports for earlier years.

Hawaii.—Hawaii, formerly an independent republic, was annexed to the United States in August, 1898. The first Federal census of the territory was taken in 1900, as a part of the decennial census of that year. The comparative figures for 1890 which appear in Table 54 were derived from a census taken as of December 28, 1890, under the direction of the Hawaiian Government. The territory is divided into 5 counties, whose primary civil divisions comprise 27 election districts and the island of Midway. Separate statistics for the population of the 9 inhabited islands of the archipelago are also given.

Porto Rico.—Porto Rico was ceded by Spain to the United States December 10, 1898, and was first enumerated at a Federal decennial census in 1910. A special census had been taken, however, under the direction of the War Department in 1899. Porto Rico is divided into 76 municipalities, each of which, except San Juan, which is wholly urban, comprises both urban and rural districts, known as barrios. As a rule a municipality consists of a single urban settlement and outlying rural districts, but in a few cases there is, besides the principal settlement which gives the name to the municipality, another detached settlement, termed for census purposes a village. In some cases a town consists of two or more barrios, but in most of the smaller municipalities a single barrio, usually designated as "pueblo," constitutes the town settlement. The distinction between the urban and rural barrios is a physical and not a political one, there being no difference in governmental status between the two classes of communities. Most of the barrios are either wholly urban or wholly rural in character, but a few comprise both urban and rural territory.

Guam.—The island of Guam was ceded by Spain to the United States December 10, 1898, but was not enumerated at a Federal decennial census until 1920, when the canvass was made under the direction of the naval governor in accordance with plans prescribed by the Director of the Census. Previous enumerations had been made, however, under the direction of the governor. For administrative purposes the island is divided into 6 districts, namely, Agana, Agat, Inarajan, Merizo, Sumay, and Yona. The enumerators did not make separate returns for these districts, however, and accordingly Table 54 presents the distribution of the population of the island by barrios, cities, and towns.

American Samoa.—American Samoa came into the possession of the United States by the Tripartite Treaty of November 14, 1899, entered into by the United States, Great Britain, and Germany, but was not enumerated at a Federal decennial census until 1920, when the canvass was made under the direction of the naval governor in accordance with plans prescribed by the Director of the Census. Previous enumerations had been made, however, under the direction of the governor. For administrative purposes American Samoa is divided into three districts— Eastern District of Tutuila, Western District of Tutuila, and Manua District—which in turn are divided into counties. Table 54 shows the distribution of the population by districts, counties, and villages.

Panama Canal Zone.—The Panama Canal Zone came into the possession of the United States by treaty between the United States and the Republic of Panama, signed November 18, 1903, but was not enumerated at a Federal decennial census until 1920, when the canvass was made under the direction of the governor in accordance with plans prescribed by the Director of the Census. A number of previous enumerations had been made, however, under the direction of the governor. The zone is divided for administrative purposes into the Balboa district and the Cristobal district. No minor civil divisions exist.

POPULATION PER SQUARE MILE, BY COUNTIES: 1920.

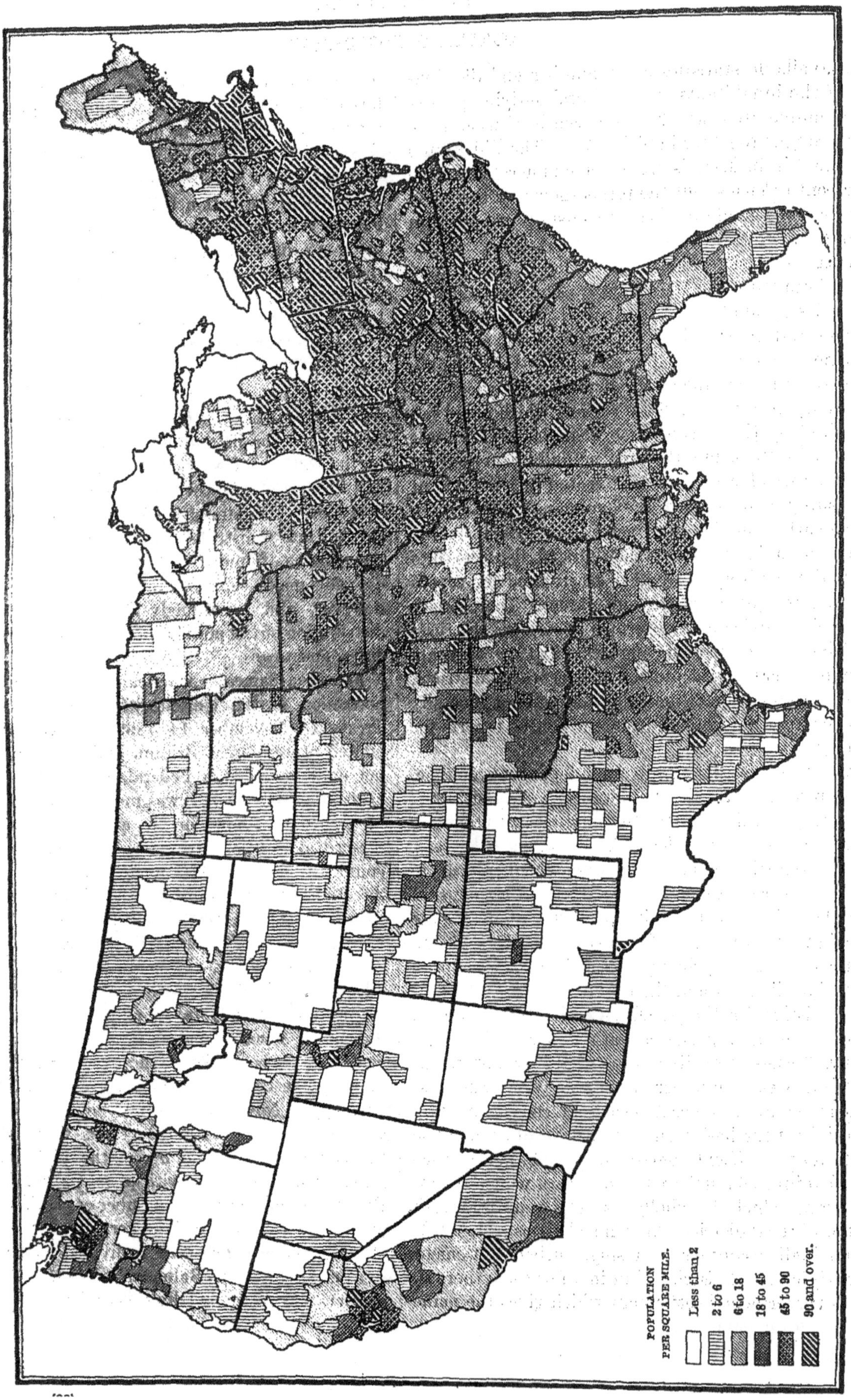

POPULATION
PER SQUARE MILE.

Less than 2

2 to 6

6 to 18

18 to 45

45 to 90

90 and over.

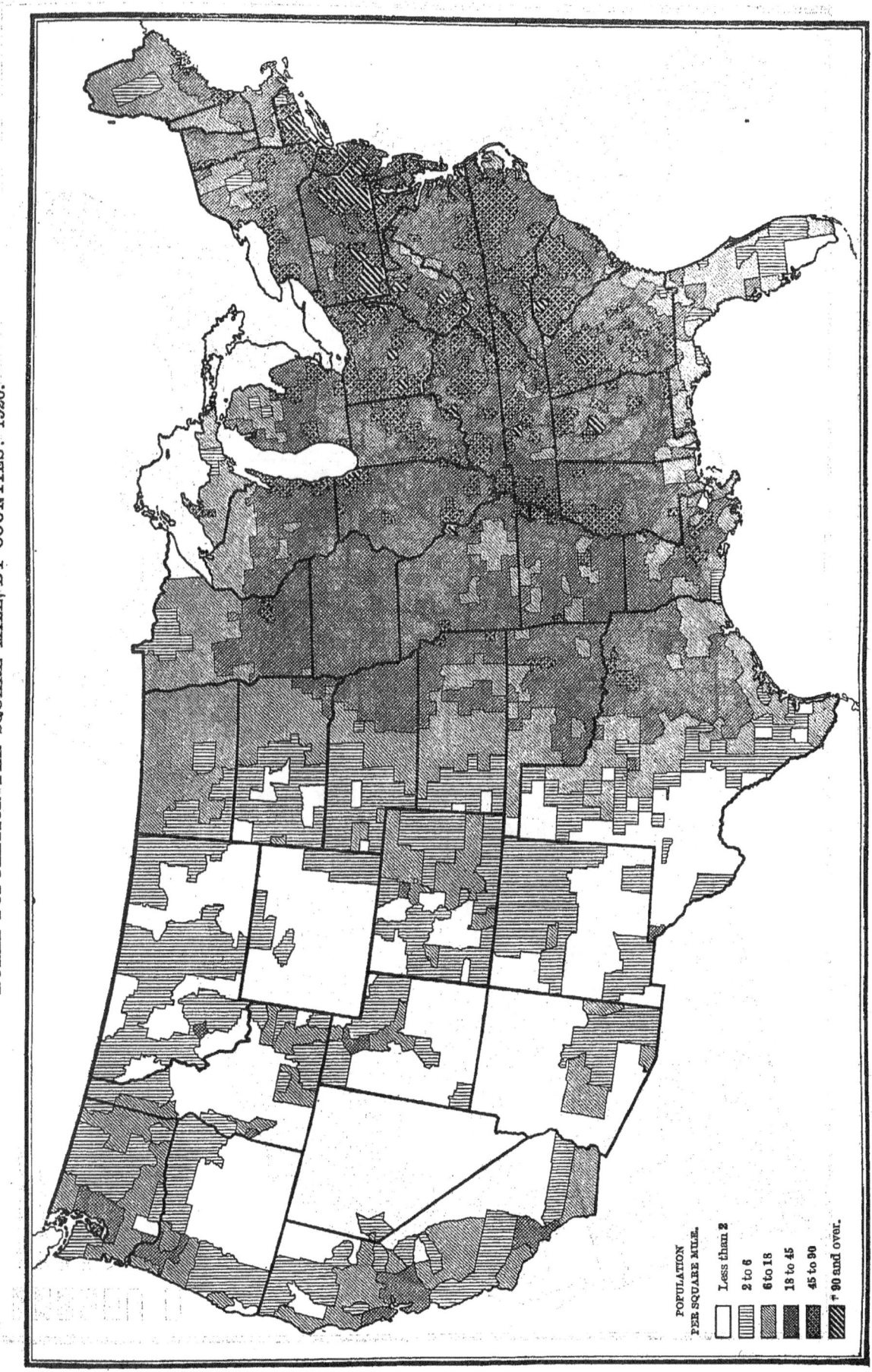

RURAL POPULATION PER SQUARE MILE, BY COUNTIES: 1920.

POPULATION
PER SQUARE MILE.

Less than 2
2 to 6
6 to 18
18 to 45
45 to 90
90 and over.

PER CENT OF INCREASE OR DECREASE IN TOTAL POPULATION, BY COUNTIES: 1910–1920.

DECREASE.
INCREASE.
Less than 5 per cent.
5 to 15 per cent.
15 to 25 per cent.
25 to 50 per cent.
50 to 75 per cent.
75 per cent and over.

CHAPTER I

COLOR OR RACE, NATIVITY, AND PARENTAGE

CHAPTER I.—COLOR OR RACE, NATIVITY, AND PARENTAGE.

INTRODUCTION.

This chapter presents statistics relative to color or race, nativity, and parentage of the population of the United States, exclusive of outlying possessions, as returned at the Fourteenth Decennial Census, with comparative figures for prior censuses. Detailed statistics regarding the population of all the outlying possessions except the Philippines and the Virgin Islands [1] are given in the reports for those possessions, which have been published in the form of separate bulletins and as sections of Volume III of the Fourteenth Census reports.

The classification by color or race generally distinguishes six groups, namely, white, Negro, Indian, Chinese, Japanese, and "all other." In classifying the population by nativity all persons born in the United States or in any of the outlying possessions are regarded as native and all other persons as foreign born. The classification by parentage includes three groups, as follows: (1) Native parentage—both parents born in the United States or in any of the outlying possessions; (2) foreign parentage—both parents born outside of the United States or outlying possessions; (3) mixed parentage—one parent native and the other foreign born.

The distinction as to parentage is generally confined to the native white population, so that in most of the tables there are six principal classes: (1) Native whites of native parentage; (2) native whites of foreign parentage; (3) native whites of mixed parentage; (4) foreign-born whites; (5) Negroes; and (6) all others. The last-named group is frequently omitted from the tables, as it comprises radically different subclasses and yet in the aggregate is unimportant in most parts of the United States. In tables where the numbers are important the Indians, Chinese, and Japanese are shown separately.

UNITED STATES AS A WHOLE.

Tables 1 to 4 (pp. 29 and 30) present statistics relating to the United States as a whole.

Correction for 1870.—The corrected figures for 1870 in Table 1 and for the decades 1860–1870 and 1870–1880 in Table 2 are based on estimates of the true population in 1870, the census taken in that year having been generally deficient in the Southern states. The number of omissions in these states in 1870 is estimated to have been 1,260,000, comprising 748,000 whites and 512,000 Negroes. (See Reports of the Eleventh Census, Population, Part I, pp. xi, xii, and xvi.)

White population.—The proportion of whites in the total population, which was approximately four-fifths in 1790, has increased at each succeeding census, except for an insignificant decrease in 1810 as compared with 1800. (See Table 1.) The increase during the first 40 years was much slower, however, than that during the remainder of the period covered by the table.

Accepting the estimate for 1870 as approximately correct, each decade since 1890, except the decade 1910–1920, has shown for the white population a numerical increase greater than that for the decade immediately preceding; and the percentage of increase for the white population has exceeded that for the Negro population in every decade since 1810.

In considering the growth of the white population it must be kept in mind that in the case of only one of the four nativity and parentage classes is the increase due in any measure to the excess of births over deaths within the class itself. The number of natives of native parentage is increased in part by the children born to natives of native parentage and in part by the children of the natives of foreign or of mixed parentage; the number of natives of mixed parentage is increased by the children of intermarriages between the native and the foreign born; the number of natives of foreign parentage, by the children born to immigrants after their arrival in this country; and the number of foreign born, by immigration. During any given period, therefore, the increase in the number of natives of native parentage is the sum of (1) the natural increase within that class, due to excess of births over deaths, and (2) the number of children born to natives of foreign or mixed parentage; the increase in the number of natives of mixed parentage is the excess of births from marriages between natives and immigrants over deaths among natives of mixed parentage, and is, in general, proportional to the number of mixed marriages; the increase in the number of natives of foreign parentage is the excess of the number of children born in the United States to foreign-born parents over the number of deaths among natives of foreign parentage;

[1] These two possessions were not enumerated in 1920, a census of the Philippines having been taken by the Philippine Government as of December 31, 1918, and a special census of the Virgin Islands having been taken by the Census Bureau as of November 1, 1917.

16   POPULATION.

and the increase in the number of foreign born is the excess of net immigration over the number of deaths among the foreign born. Of the four classes of whites, therefore, the natives of native parentage constitute the only one whose increase is affected in any degree by its own reproductivity, since the children born in this country to each of the other classes belong to a class different from that to which their parents belong (except that in some cases one parent of a native of mixed parentage is also a native of mixed parentage). While the increase in the number of native whites of native parentage must, so long as there is any element of foreign birth or parentage in the population, necessarily exceed the natural increase by excess of births over deaths within this class, the numerical increase of any of the other classes may or may not exceed the natural increase which would result if the children were included in the same class with the parents. The numerical increases within the several nativity and parentage classes, therefore, bear no specific relationship to the natural increase.

It is possible to estimate the natural increase of the white population between 1910 and 1920 by subtracting from the total increase in that element the excess of white immigration over white emigration plus the estimated excess of births over deaths in the families of white immigrants arriving in this country during the decade. The excess of white immigration over white emigration between April 15, 1910, and January 1, 1920, was approximately 3,350,000. The excess of births over deaths in the families of white immigrants who arrived in this country between 1910 and 1920 may be roughly estimated at 250,000. Thus the total estimated increase in the white population due to excess of immigration over emigration between 1910 and 1920 was 3,600,000. Subtracting this number from the total increase in the white population during the decade, 13,088,958, leaves approximately 9,490,000 as the natural increase which presumably would have taken place had there been no immigration nor emigration during the decade. This represents a rate of 11.6 per cent. The corresponding increase in the Negro population, which was affected to only a slight extent by immigration and emigration, was 635,368, or 6.5 per cent.

Negro population.—The distinction between white and colored is the only racial classification which has been carried through all the 14 censuses. There is some doubt whether the small number of taxed Indians were counted with the white or with the colored population prior to 1860.

Accepting as substantially correct the estimate for 1870 (see p. 15), the proportion of Negroes in the total population has decreased at each census since 1810. Attention should be called to the pronounced fluctuations in the indicated rates of increase for the Negroes between 1880 and 1910. (See Table 2.) Again ac-

cepting the estimated figures for 1870, the decennial rate of increase for this class of the population, as shown by the returns for succeeding censuses, dropped from 22 per cent during the decade 1870–1880 to 13.5 per cent between 1880 and 1890, rose to 18 per cent during the following decade, and declined to 11.2 per cent between 1900 and 1910. Such abrupt changes in the growth of a class of the population which is not materially affected by immigration seem highly improbable and practically force the conclusion that the enumeration of Negroes in 1890 was deficient.

The number of omissions at the census of 1890 can not be accurately determined, but on the assumption that the decline in the rate of increase from the decade 1870–1880 through the next two decades was constant, the rates for the last five decades would be as follows: [1]

1870–1880	22. 0 per cent.
1880–1890	17. 9 per cent.
1890–1900	13. 8 per cent.
1900–1910	11. 2 per cent.
1910–1920	6. 5 per cent.

Such data as are available indicate that the decline in the rate of increase for the Negro population is due to a considerable falling off in the birth rate, while the death rate has not changed to so great an extent. The greater part of the Negro population is in states which do not maintain adequate birth-registration systems, and a considerable proportion is also outside the death-registration area; but such birth and mortality statistics for the Negroes as are believed to be trustworthy have been carefully examined and compared with the corresponding statistics for the white population. There is no question that the birth rates for both races have been declining during recent decades, and in the case of the Negroes this decline has not been offset by a decline in the death rate to so great an extent as in the case of the white population.

Black and mulatto population.—Considerable uncertainty necessarily attaches to the classification of Negroes as black and mulatto, since the accuracy of the distinction made depends largely upon the judgment and care employed by the enumerators. Moreover, the fact that the definition of the term "mulatto" adopted at different censuses has not been entirely uniform doubtless affects the comparability of the figures in some degree. At the census of 1920 the instructions were to report as "black" all full-blooded Negroes and as "mulatto" all Negroes having some proportion of white blood. The instructions were substantially the same at the censuses of 1910 and 1870, but the term "black" as employed in 1890 denoted all persons "having three-

---

[1] The undercount of 1890 is discussed in more detail on pages 27 and 28 of the bureau's report, "Negro Population in the United States, 1790–1915."

COLOR OR RACE, NATIVITY, AND PARENTAGE.

17

fourths or more black blood," other persons with any proportion of Negro blood being classed as "mulattoes," "quadroons," or "octoroons." In 1900 and in 1880 no classification of Negroes as black or mulatto was attempted, and at the censuses of 1860 and 1850 the terms "black" and "mulatto" appear not to have been defined.

According to the census returns, the proportion of mulattoes in the Negro population increased from 12 per cent to 15.2 per cent during the 20-year period from 1870 to 1890 and continued to increase to 20.9 per cent during the following 20-year period, but decreased to 15.9 per cent during the 10-year period from 1910 to 1920. Thus on the face of the returns the proportion of mulattoes in 1920, although nearly one-fourth smaller than in 1910, was nevertheless slightly larger than that in 1890. (See Table 9.)

It is likely that the explanation of the relatively large proportion of mulattoes shown for 1910 may be found in part in the fact that a larger proportion of the Negro population was canvassed by Negro enumerators in that year than in any other census year. It is probable that the practice of returning as black those mulattoes who had but a small admixture of white blood was greater among the white than among the Negro enumerators. Moreover, the Negro enumerators may have taken somewhat greater care than did the white enumerators to ascertain whether Negroes whom they were not able to interview personally were blacks or mulattoes. The difference between the proportions mulatto in 1920 and in 1910, as shown by the returns, can not, however, be accounted for as resulting wholly or mainly from these causes.

In order to ascertain the probable effect of the employment of Negro enumerators in 1910 upon the proportion of the Negro population returned as mulattoes in that year as compared with 1920, a special tabulation was made for the 16 Southern states and the District of Columbia and for 10 Northern states—Massachusetts, New York, New Jersey, Pennsylvania, Ohio, Michigan, Indiana, Illinois, Missouri, and Kansas—in all of which a part of the Negro population was canvassed by Negro enumerators in 1910. The total Negro population of the area covered was 10,303,399 in 1920 and 9,714,770 in 1910, or between 98 and 99 per cent of the total Negro population of the United States in each year. The number of enumeration districts in this area in which Negro enumerators were employed in 1910 was 2,055. This special tabulation brought out the following facts:

Considering as one group those counties in each of which three or more Negro enumerators were employed in 1910, the percentage mulatto in the Negro population decreased from 21.8 in that year to 16.1 in 1920; considering as another group those counties in each of which one or two Negro enumerators were

employed, the percentage mulatto decreased from 21 to 14.2; and considering as a third group those counties in which white enumerators only were employed, the percentage decreased from 19.6 to 15.9. Thus the decrease in the counties in which white enumerators only were employed in 1910 was nearly two-thirds as great as the decrease in those counties in each of which three or more Negro enumerators were employed in that year.

Moreover, in every one of the 26 states covered by the comparison a decrease in the percentage mulatto between 1910 and 1920 is shown for the group of counties in which white enumerators only were employed in 1910, and in a number of cases this decrease was equal to or greater than that for the groups of counties in which Negro enumerators were employed in 1910.

It appears, therefore, that the employment of Negro enumerators in certain counties in 1910 and of white enumerators only in 1920 had some effect in reducing the proportion of mulattoes in the Negro population, as shown by the returns for 1920 in comparison with those for 1910, but that this was not the sole nor principal cause of the indicated decrease.

Indian population.—The census of 1860 was the first at which Indians were distinguished from the other classes, but no enumeration was made of the Indians in Indian Territory or on Indian reservations until 1890. Prior to that time the enumeration of Indians was confined to those found living among the general population of the various states and not in Indian Territory or on reservations. The returns for Indians are subject to some degree of uncertainty because of the practice of treating as Indians all persons having any trace of Indian blood. Such persons in some cases can not be distinguished by their appearance from pure-blooded white persons, and as a result some of them have doubtless been reported as white at one census and as Indian at another, since the enumerators are not always able to interview directly the persons whom they enumerate but are obliged to secure information regarding them from other persons. Moreover, at the census of 1910 a special effort was made to secure a complete enumeration of all persons having any perceptible amount of Indian blood, for the purpose of preparing a special report showing tribal relations, purity of Indian blood, etc.; and it is probable that this resulted in the enumeration as Indians of a considerable number of persons who would ordinarily have been reported as whites. For these reasons the changes indicated by the returns of the last four censuses may not altogether correspond to the facts.

Native and foreign-born population.—The distinction between native and foreign born is of no great significance except for the white population. The proportion foreign born among the Negroes and Indians is

18   POPULATION.

very slight. On the other hand, the proportion native among the other nonwhite races enumerated is small, although materially greater than the proportion foreign born among the Negroes and Indians. Moreover, in the cases of these races the distinction based on nativity has little significance.

The proportion foreign born in the total population increased during the two decades between 1850 and 1870, and alternately decreased and increased from decade to decade during the following 50 years. (See Table 4.) The decline in this proportion between 1910 and 1920 was greater than the change—either increase or decrease—which took place during any preceding decade since 1860.

The rates of increase in the total population and in the native population have declined from decade to decade since 1870. (See Tables 2 and 3.) The foreign-born population has gained in number from census to census, but the rate of increase has fluctuated greatly. The smallness of its increase during the decade 1910–1920 was due to the great reduction in the volume of immigration during the period of the World War, the net additions through immigration during the entire decade having been only a little more than 400,000 in excess of the number of deaths of foreign-born persons.

No corrections of the 1870 figures (see p. 15) have been inserted in Tables 3 and 4. It may be assumed that the omissions in the South at the census taken in that year were almost wholly of native population. Although there undoubtedly may have been a few omissions in the relatively small foreign-born population of the South, they could hardly have been numerous enough to affect the proportions for the country as a whole; but it is evident that the omission of native population would have an appreciable effect upon the proportions native and foreign born in the total population and in the white population and in the rate of increase of the natives. The true percentages native in the total population and in the white population in 1870 were, therefore, slightly larger, and the true percentages foreign were slightly smaller, than those shown (see Table 4); and the true rates of increase between 1860 and 1870 in the total natives and native whites were somewhat larger, while those for the decade 1870–1880 were somewhat smaller, than the rates given (see Table 3).

The statistics as to the nativity of the Chinese (see Table 4) are inaccurate to some extent, for the reason that a considerable number of Chinese report themselves as natives of this country when in fact they are of foreign birth.

In Table 4 both the natives and the foreign born in each color or race class are distributed according to parentage. Naturally, however, this classification has little significance for the foreign born because very nearly all such persons are of foreign parentage. A small number, however, are of mixed parentage, having one parent a native of the United States and the other foreign born.

In Table 4 the population of mixed parentage is further subdivided into two classes, namely, those who had native mothers and foreign-born fathers and those who had native fathers and foreign-born mothers. It may be noted that the former class greatly outnumbers the latter, which is merely a natural result of the fact that among immigrants males outnumber females, and of the further fact that among the male immigrants the proportion unmarried on arrival in this country is abnormally large.

DIVISIONS AND STATES.

Statistics for divisions and states are given in Tables 5 to 12, inclusive.

White and Negro population.—In making use of the statistics for both the white and the Negro population, the defective enumeration in the South in 1870 must be kept in mind (see p. 15); and in considering the growth during the decades 1880–1890 and 1890–1900 the probable incompleteness of the enumeration of Negroes in 1890 should not be overlooked (see p. 16). Significant comparisons between the growth of the white and of the Negro population are, however, afforded by the increases during the past two decades. (See Table 12.) During each of those decades the white population increased more rapidly than the Negro in the three southern divisions, where Negroes are most numerous; in fact, in the East South Central division an increase among the whites between 1910 and 1920 was accompanied by a decrease among the Negroes. Furthermore, between 1910 and 1920 every Southern state except West Virginia showed a greater rate of increase for the white than for the Negro population, or an increase among the whites together with a decrease among the Negroes.

As already stated (see p. 16), the distinction between blacks and mulattoes is not always obvious nor easily drawn, and the classification therefore involves a considerable amount of uncertainty, being necessarily dependent to a large degree upon personal judgment and care exercised by the enumerators. In general, the percentage of mulattoes among Negroes is somewhat larger in the Northern and Western states than in the South, although for some reason the Middle Atlantic division constitutes an exception among the Northern divisions. The proportion of mulattoes decreased between 1910 and 1920 in every geographic division, in every Southern state, and in every Northern or Western state except Vermont, Nebraska, Wyoming, Washington, and Oregon. (See Table 9.)

The following statement shows the Negro population of each of the three geographic sections in 1920,

COLOR OR RACE, NATIVITY, AND PARENTAGE.   19

1910, and 1900, together with the increase during each decade:

SECTION.	NEGRO POPULATION.			INCREASE.			
	1920	1910	1900	1910-1920		1900-1910	
				Number.	Per cent.	Number.	Per cent.
Total..........	10,463,131	9,827,763	8,833,994	635,368	6.5	993,769	11.2
The South [1]........	8,912,231	8,749,427	7,922,969	162,804	1.9	826,458	10.4
The North [2]........	1,472,309	1,027,674	880,771	444,635	43.3	146,903	16.7
The West [3]........	78,591	50,662	30,254	27,929	55.1	20,408	67.5

[1] South Atlantic, East South Central, and West South Central divisions.
[2] New England, Middle Atlantic, East North Central, and West North Central divisions. The boundary line between the North and the South is formed by the southern boundaries of New Jersey and Pennsylvania, the Ohio River, and the southern boundaries of Missouri and Kansas.
[3] Mountain and Pacific divisions. The West is that part of the country lying beyond the western boundaries of North and South Dakota, Nebraska, Kansas, Oklahoma, and Texas.

Native and foreign-born population.—The census of 1850 was the first at which the classification of the population by nativity was made. The native population includes practically all the Negroes and Indians, the latter having been first completely enumerated at the census of 1890, while the foreign-born population is mainly white but includes most of the Chinese, Japanese, and "all other."

It must be kept in mind in making use of the nativity statistics that unless the foreign-born population of a division or state is constantly recruited by immigration (or by the migration into that division or state of persons who have previously immigrated to the United States) it will decrease, for the reason that its numbers will be continually reduced by death, while the children born in this country to foreign-born parents are additions to the native population.

The only states in which the proportion foreign born in the total population increased between 1910 and 1920 are Delaware, Virginia, Florida, Texas, New Mexico, and Arizona. (See Table 10.) In Virginia the foreign-born element constitutes a very small proportion of the total population, and in Texas, New Mexico, and Arizona the increase was due largely to Mexican immigration. Thus Delaware is the only state in which the proportion foreign born is at all important and in which the increase was due directly or indirectly to European immigration.

Statistics relating to the nativity and parentage of the white population, by divisions and states, are given in Tables 5, 6, 7, and 12.

It may be noted that in every geographic division the native whites of foreign parentage and those of mixed parentage are together more numerous than the foreign-born whites, but the difference is less conspicuous in the New England, Middle Atlantic, and Pacific divisions than elsewhere. (See Table 5.) The relation between the number of foreign-born whites and the number of native whites of foreign or mixed parentage in any division or state depends largely upon the time at which it received its most important accessions from immigration. In the West North Central division, for example, to which immigration during the past three decades has been much less rapid than in earlier years, the native whites of foreign or mixed parentage have shown an increasing preponderance over the foreign-born whites from census to census since 1890, the former group in 1920 being nearly two and one-half times as numerous as the latter; but in the New England and Middle Atlantic divisions, which have been receiving large numbers of immigrants during the past four decades, except during the period of the World War, there is much less disparity between the two classes.

Very great differences appear among the individual states in regard to the composition of the white population; but only in Arizona were the foreign-born whites more numerous than the native whites of foreign or mixed parentage in 1920, due, as stated above, to Mexican immigration, and in no state did they equal in number the native whites of native parentage.

The size of the mixed-parentage and foreign-parentage classes in comparison with each other affords an indication of the extent to which the foreign born have intermarried with the natives. This varies greatly in different sections of the country, but in every division and in every state except North Carolina, Mississippi, and Arkansas the natives of foreign parentage outnumbered those of mixed parentage in 1920. (See Table 5.)

Increase.—In considering Table 6 it should be remembered that the increase in any given class within any one division or state by no means represents the natural growth by excess of births over deaths. Aside from the factors which have already been mentioned as contributing to the growth of the several elements, and particularly the white classes, in the country as a whole (see p. 15), the growth in individual divisions and states is largely affected by interstate migration.

PRINCIPAL CITIES.

Statistics for individual cities are presented in Tables 13 to 19, inclusive. Tables 13, 14, 15, and 16 relate to cities having 100,000 inhabitants or more and correspond to Tables 5, 6, 7, and 12, for divisions and states.

Table 17, for cities having from 25,000 to 100,000 inhabitants, is similar to Table 16 except for the omission of the decennial-increase figures.

Table 18, which gives statistics for the Indian, Chinese, and Japanese population of cities having 25,000 inhabitants or more, corresponds to Table 11, for divisions and states, except that it does not include figures for the "all other" group.

Table 19, which presents statistics for the Negro population of selected cities, corresponds in some measure to Table 8, for divisions and states, but is

20 POPULATION.

narrower in scope. The cities covered by this table are those in which the total population in 1920 was 10,000 or more and in which the Negro population in that year was at least 5,000 or at least 10 per cent of the total population.

Statistics for the black and mulatto population of the eleven cities having more than 50,000 Negro inhabitants in 1920 are presented in Table 9 in connection with the corresponding statistics for divisions and states.

URBAN AND RURAL POPULATION.

Since marked differences exist between urban and rural communities in regard to the color or race, nativity, and parentage of the population, separate statistics for the urban and rural population are given in Tables 20 to 24, inclusive. In Tables 20, 21, and 22 the urban class is not subdivided; in Table 23, for geographic divisions, the urban communities are grouped into five subclasses according to size; and in Table 24, for states, they are grouped into four subclasses according to size. In drawing the distinction between urban and rural population, all incorporated places (and all towns in Massachusetts, Rhode Island, and New Hampshire) having 2,500 inhabitants or more are treated as urban and the remainder of the country as rural.

In Massachusetts and Rhode Island it is not the practice, as in practically all the other states, to incorporate, as separate municipalities, the relatively densely populated portions of "towns" (which are the primary divisions of the counties), and no town as a whole is incorporated as a municipality until it attains a population greatly in excess of 2,500; and in New Hampshire a similar condition exists, although the state contains two incorporated villages, each of which has fewer than 2,500 inhabitants. For this reason those towns having 2,500 or more inhabitants in the three states named are treated as urban, although portions of their areas are rural in character. The urban areas in the three states in question, as classified by the census, thus contain relatively small numbers of inhabitants who in other sections of the country would be segregated as rural. Nevertheless, in most of the Massachusetts, New Hampshire, and Rhode Island towns having 2,500 inhabitants or more by far the greater part of the population resides within the more densely settled areas, so that tho proportion classed as urban is not greatly exaggerated by the practice adopted.

COLOR OR RACE, NATIVITY, AND PARENTAGE.

PER CENT OF NATIVE WHITE OF NATIVE PARENTAGE IN TOTAL POPULATION, BY STATES: 1920.

[District of Columbia, 54.7 per cent, not shown separately on the map.]

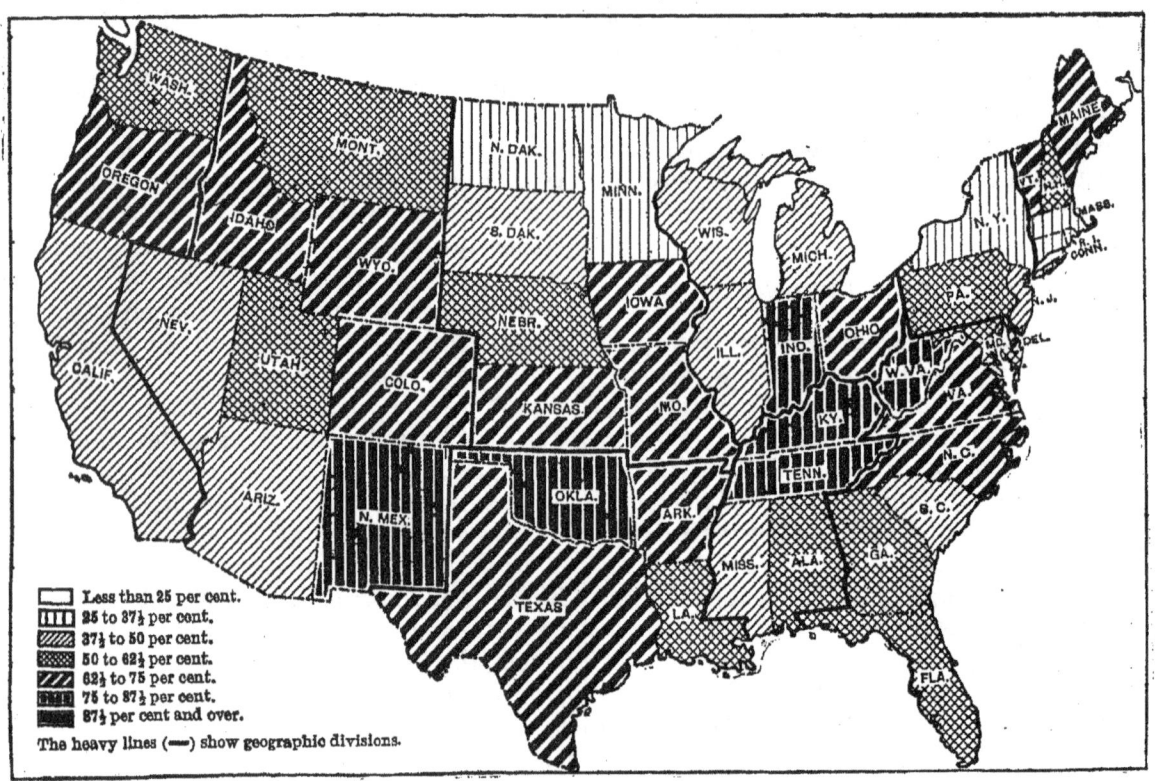

Less than 25 per cent.
25 to 37½ per cent.
37½ to 50 per cent.
50 to 62½ per cent.
62½ to 75 per cent.
75 to 87½ per cent.
87½ per cent and over.

The heavy lines (—) show geographic divisions.

PER CENT OF NATIVE WHITE OF NATIVE PARENTAGE IN WHITE POPULATION, BY STATES: 1920.

[District of Columbia, 73.3 per cent, not shown separately on the map.]

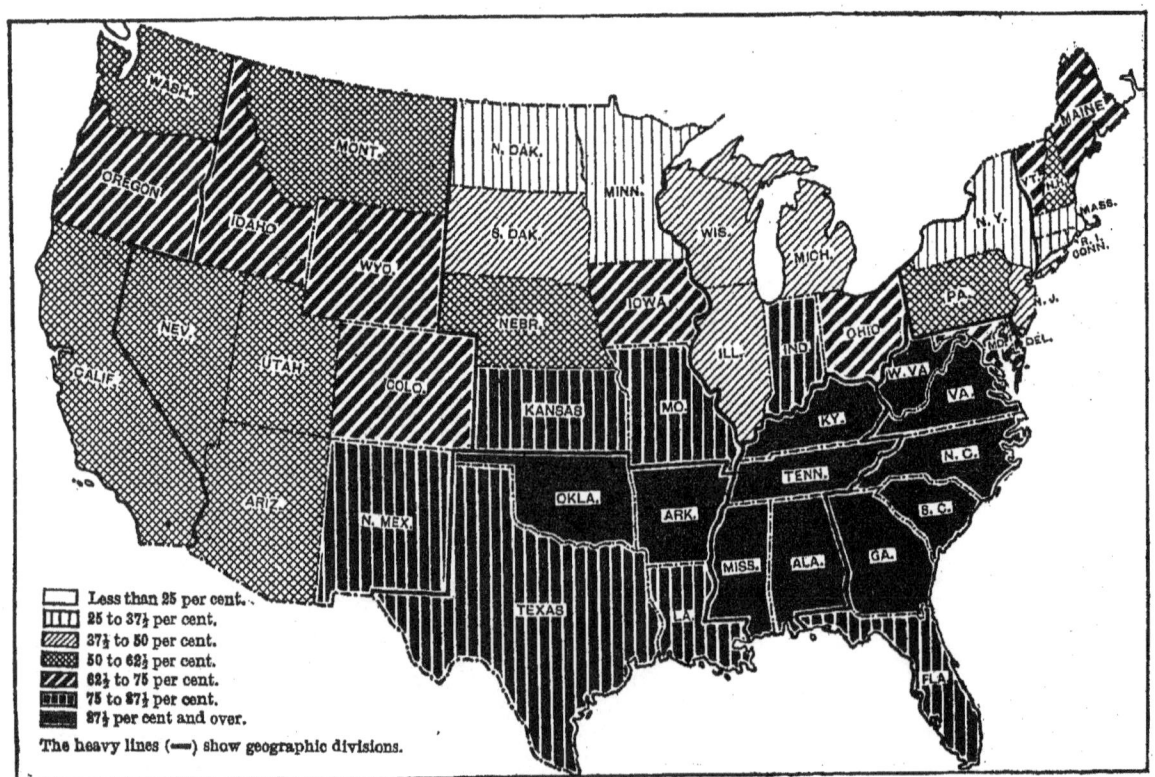

Less than 25 per cent.
25 to 37½ per cent.
37½ to 50 per cent.
50 to 62½ per cent.
62½ to 75 per cent.
75 to 87½ per cent.
87½ per cent and over.

The heavy lines (—) show geographic divisions.

POPULATION.

PER CENT OF FOREIGN-BORN WHITE IN TOTAL POPULATION, BY STATES: 1920.

[District of Columbia, 6.5 per cent, not shown separately on the map.]

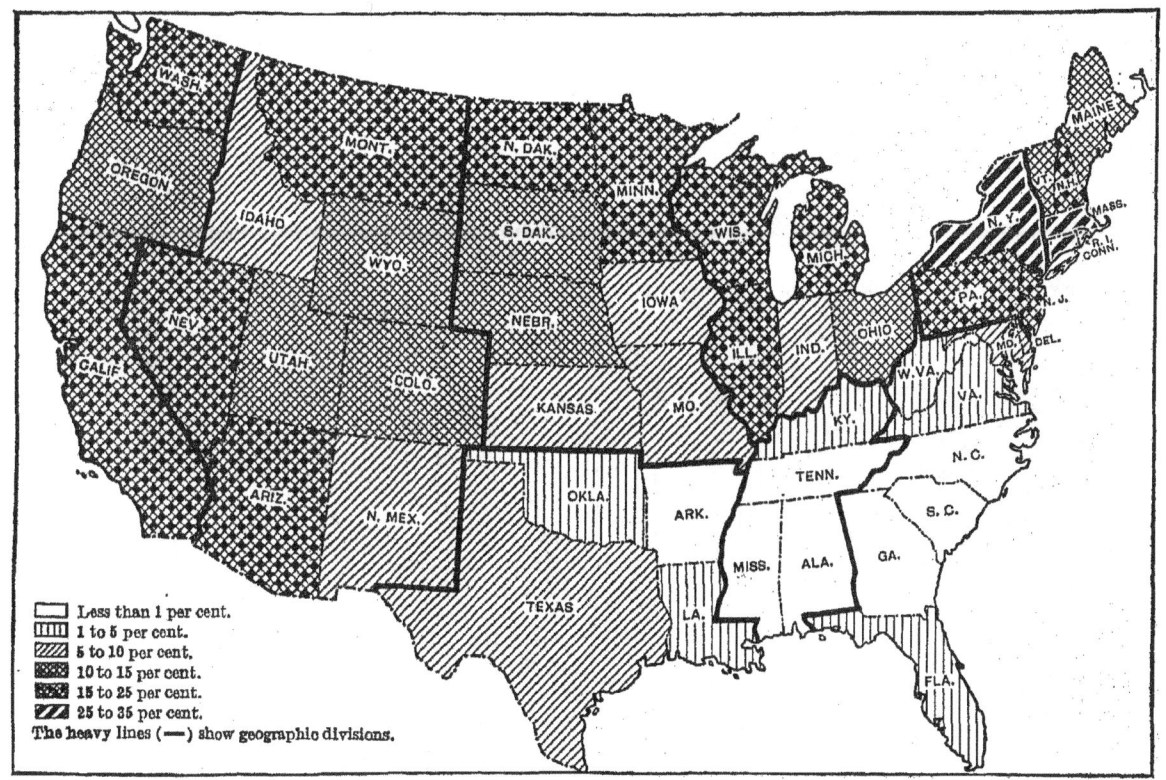

Less than 1 per cent.
1 to 5 per cent.
5 to 10 per cent.
10 to 15 per cent.
15 to 25 per cent.
25 to 35 per cent.
The heavy lines (—) show geographic divisions.

PER CENT OF NEGROES IN TOTAL POPULATION, BY STATES: 1920.

[District of Columbia, 25.1 per cent, not shown separately on the map.]

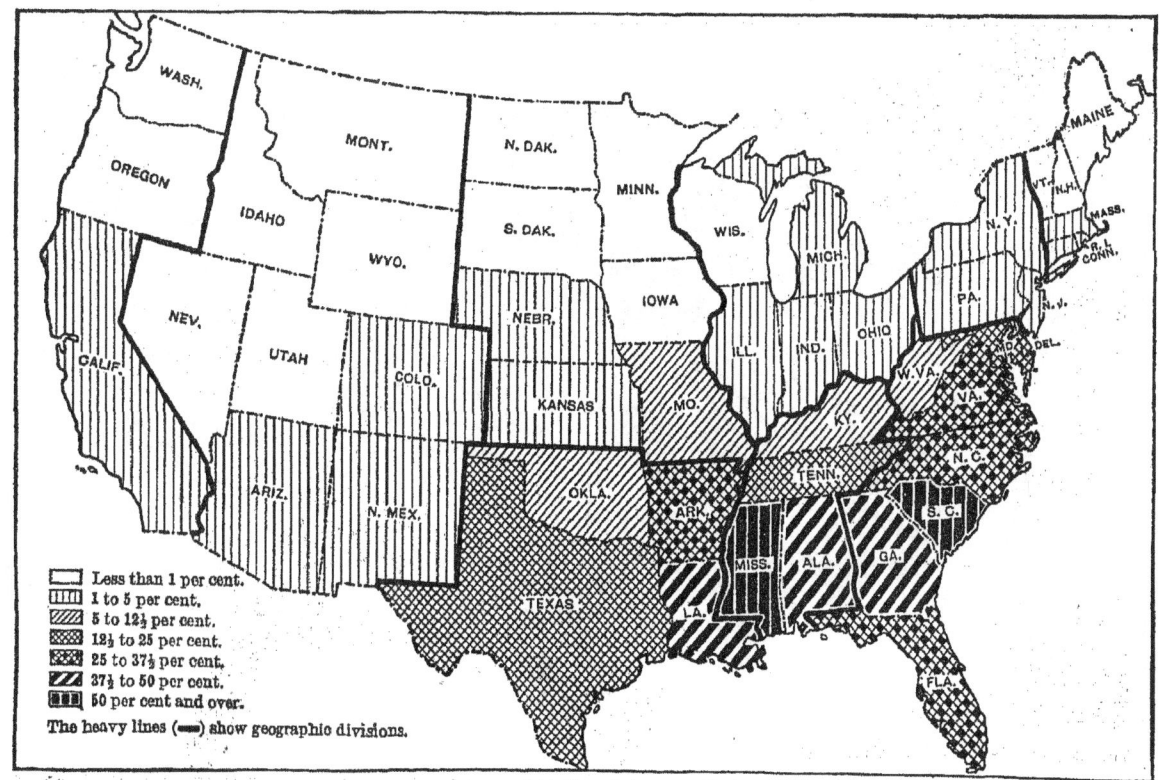

Less than 1 per cent.
1 to 5 per cent.
5 to 12½ per cent.
12½ to 25 per cent.
25 to 37½ per cent.
37½ to 50 per cent.
50 per cent and over.

The heavy lines (—) show geographic divisions.

COLOR OR RACE, NATIVITY, AND PARENTAGE.   23

PER CENT OF NATIVE WHITE OF FOREIGN OR MIXED PARENTAGE IN TOTAL POPULATION, BY STATES: 1920.

[District of Columbia, 13.4 per cent, not shown separately on the map.]

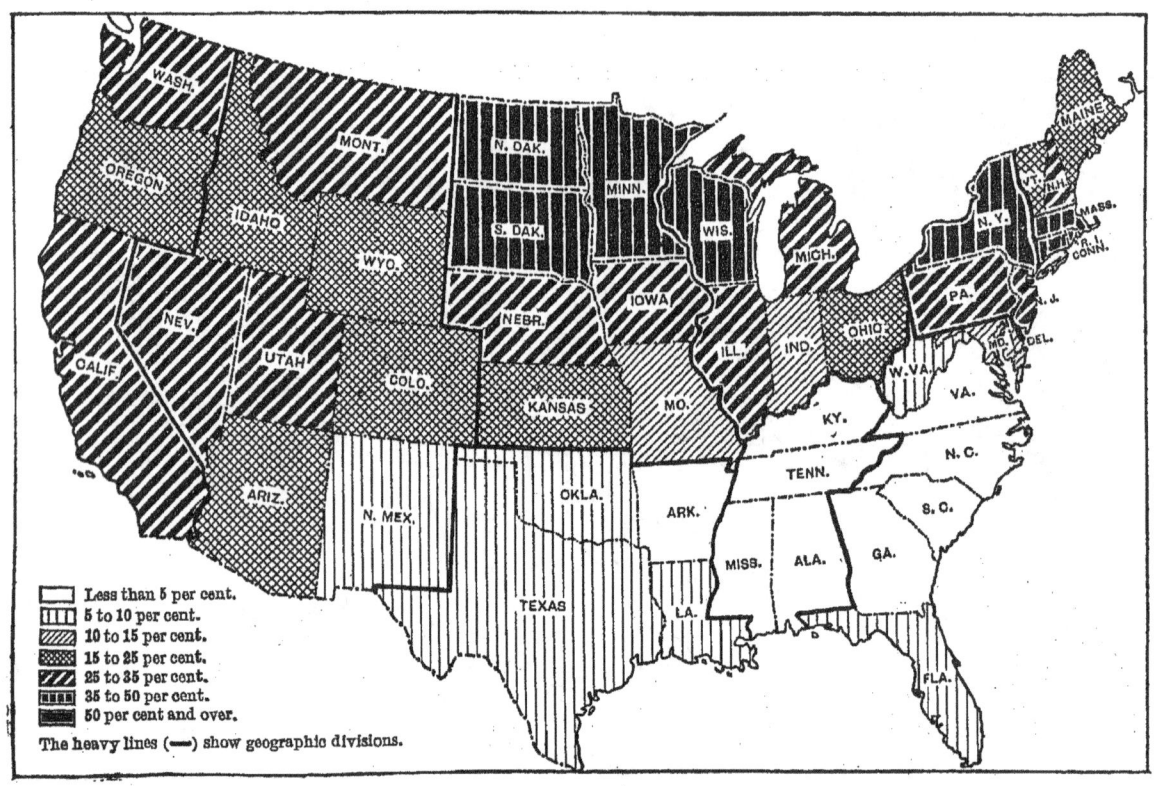

PER CENT OF FOREIGN-BORN WHITE AND NATIVE WHITE OF FOREIGN OR MIXED PARENTAGE COMBINED IN TOTAL POPULATION, BY STATES: 1920.

[District of Columbia, 19.9 per cent, not shown separately on the map.]

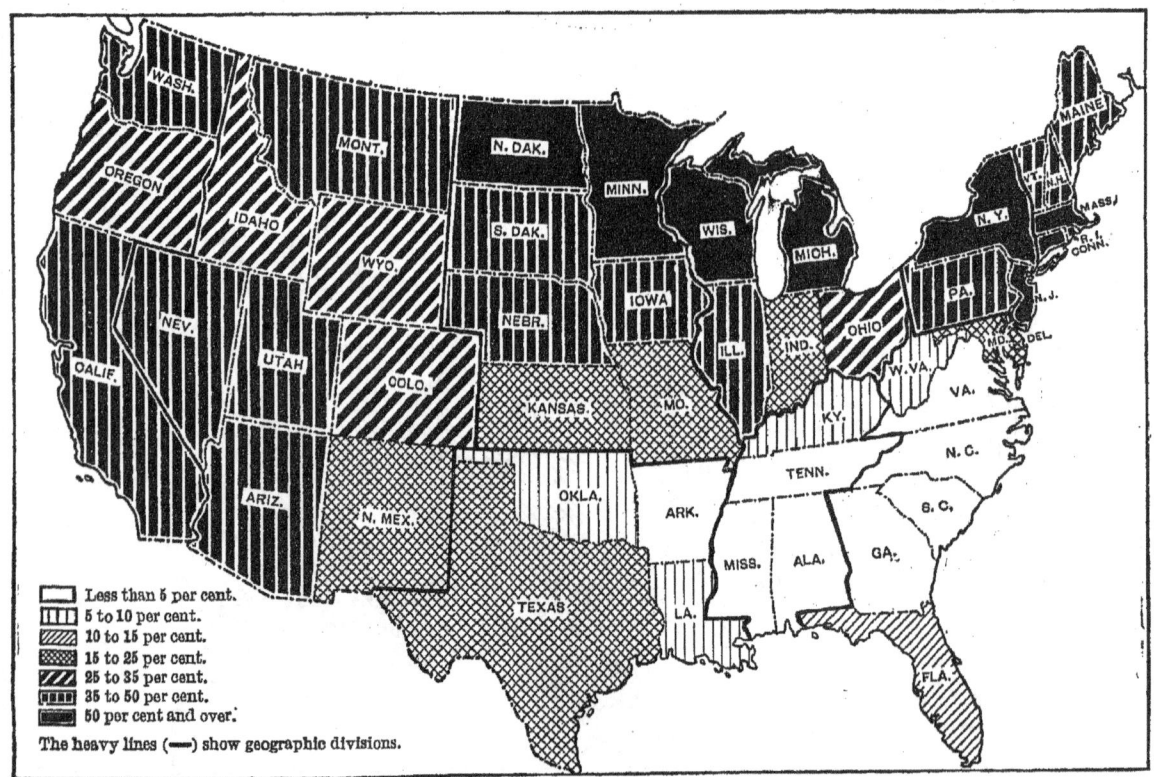

POPULATION.

TOTAL POPULATION AND DISTRIBUTION BY CLASSES: 1850–1920.

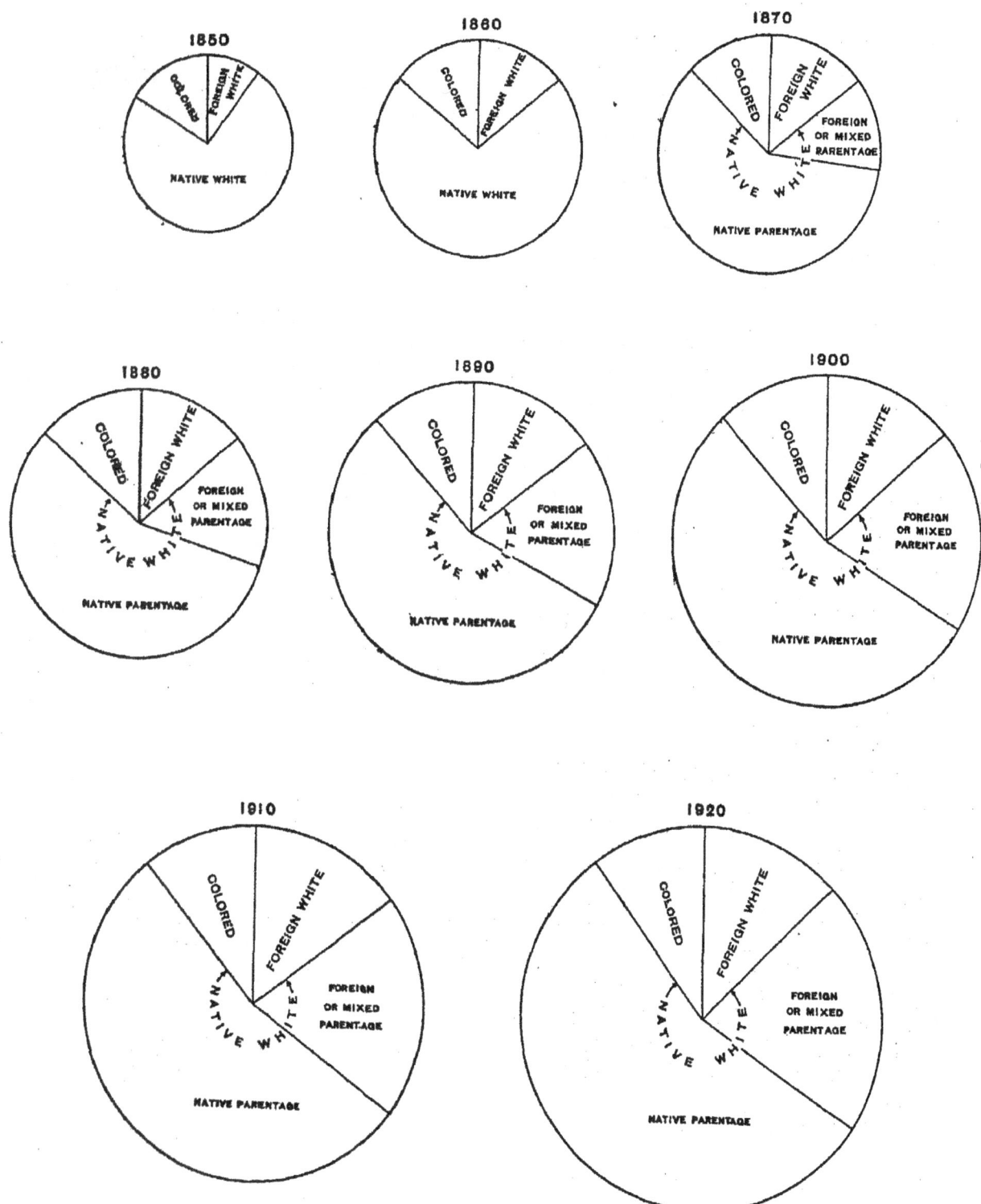

COLOR OR RACE, NATIVITY, AND PARENTAGE.

COLOR OR RACE, NATIVITY, AND PARENTAGE, BY STATES: 1920 AND 1910.

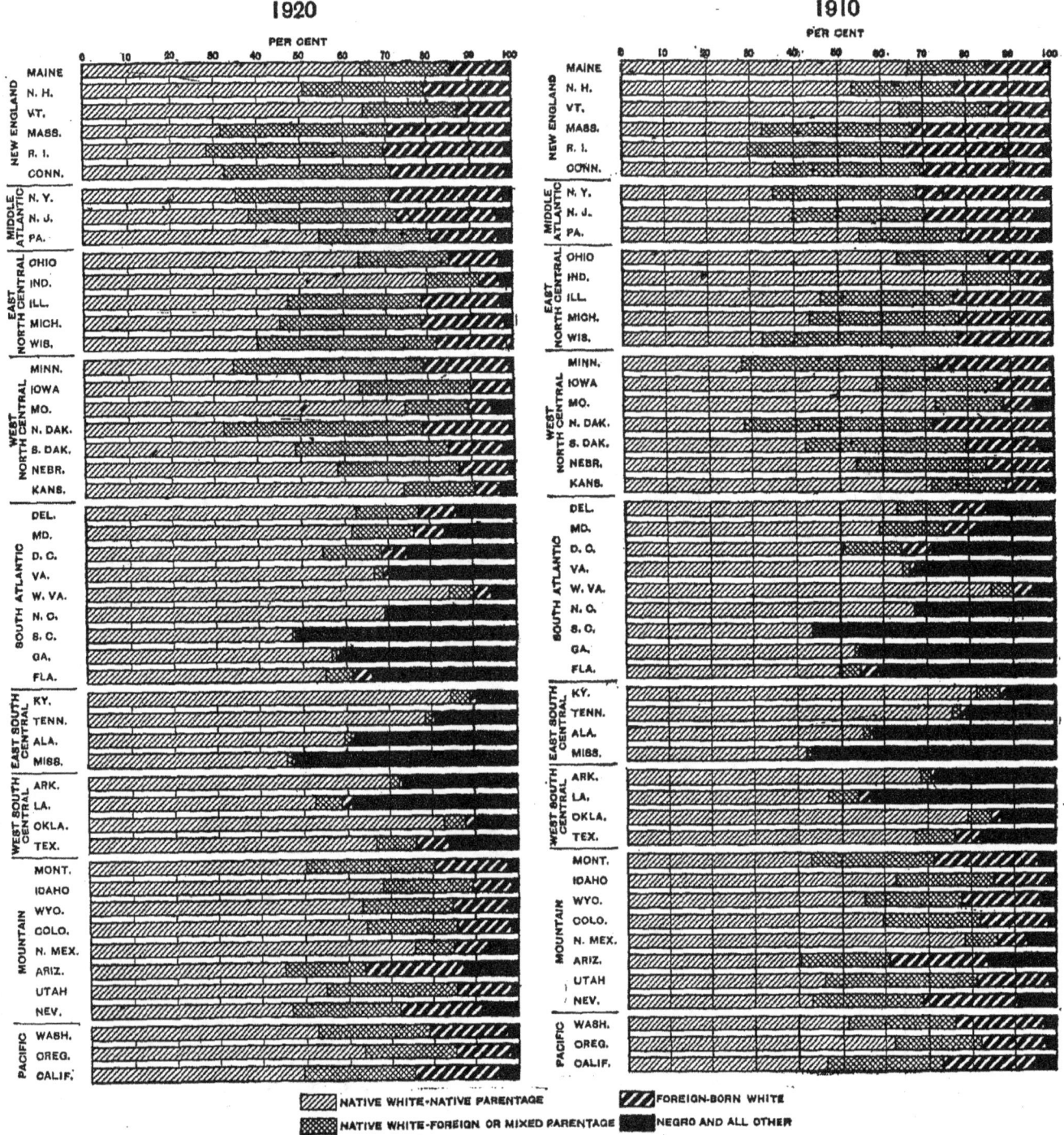

26

POPULATION.

FOREIGN-BORN POPULATION, BY STATES: 1920 AND 1910.

NEGRO POPULATION, BY STATES: 1920 AND 1910.

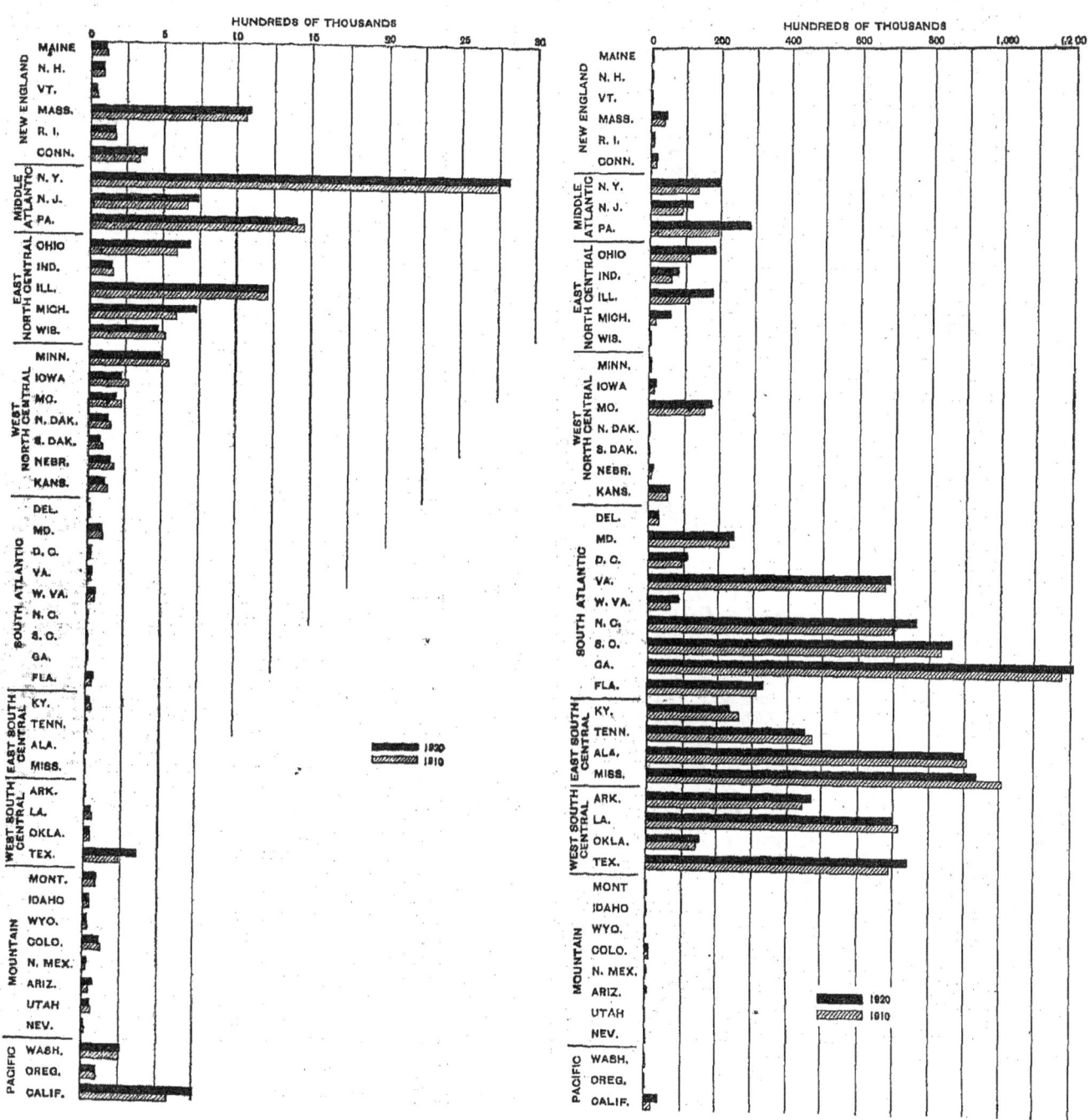

COLOR OR RACE, NATIVITY, AND PARENTAGE.

COLOR OR RACE, NATIVITY, AND PARENTAGE, FOR CITIES HAVING, IN 1920, 100,000 INHABITANTS OR MORE: 1920 AND 1910.

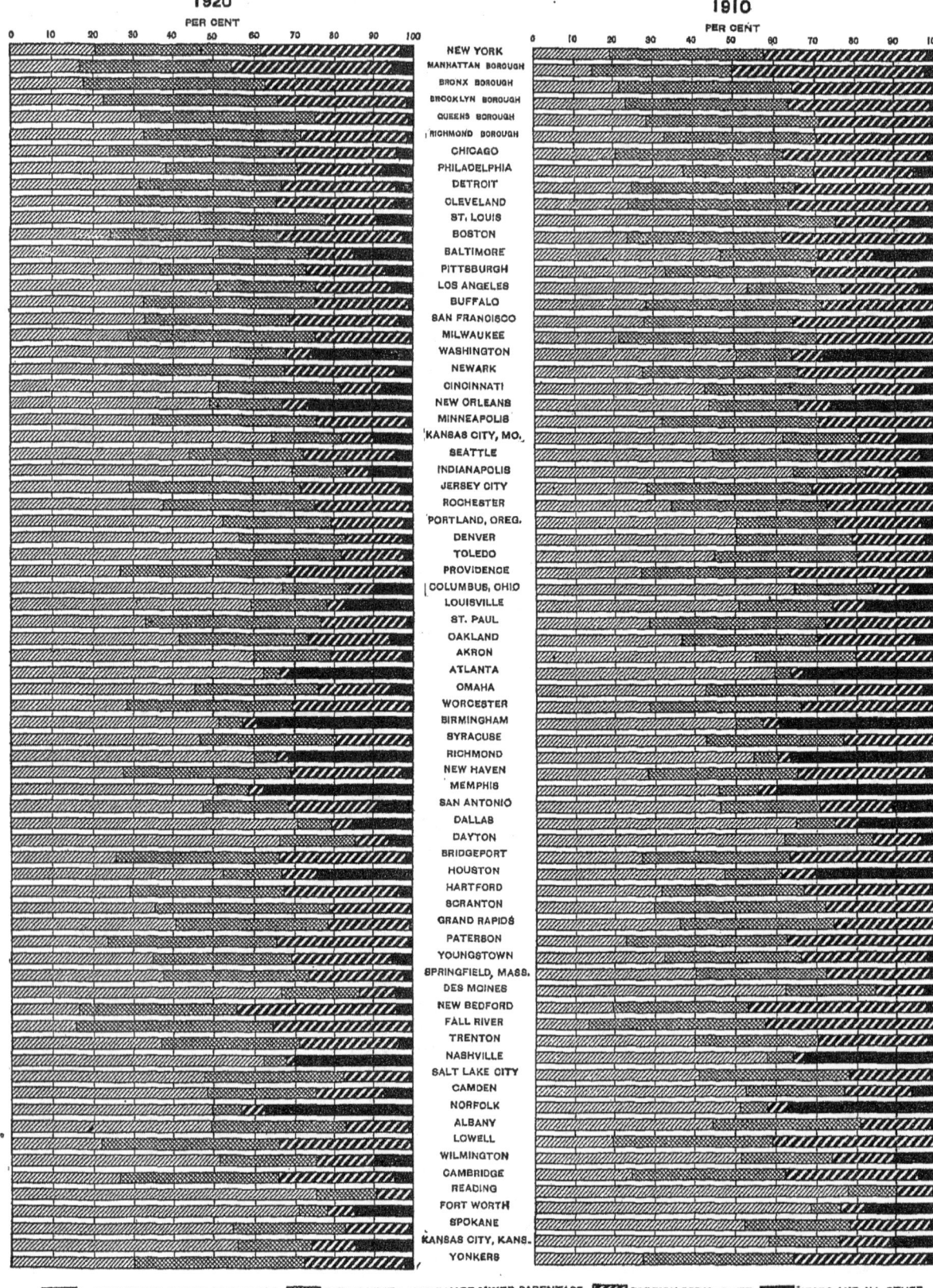

COLOR OR RACE, NATIVITY, AND PARENTAGE.   29

TABLE 1.—COLOR OR RACE, FOR THE UNITED STATES: 1790–1920.

[Figures are given under each class for all census years for which data are available.]

CENSUS YEAR.	Total population.	White.	Negro.			Indian.	Chinese.	Japanese.	All other.	PER CENT OF TOTAL POPULATION.						PER CENT OF TOTAL NEGRO.	
			Total.	Black.	Mulatto.					White.	Negro.	Indian.	Chinese.	Japanese.	All other.	Black.	Mulatto.
1920	105,710,620	94,820,915	10,463,131	8,802,577	1,660,554	244,437	61,639	111,010	¹9,488	89.7	9.9	0.2	0.1	0.1	(²)	84.1	15.9
1910	91,972,266	81,731,957	9,827,763	7,777,077	2,050,686	265,683	71,531	72,157	³3,175	88.9	10.7	0.3	0.1	0.1	(²)	79.1	20.9
1900	75,994,575	66,809,196	8,833,994			237,196	89,863	24,326		87.9	11.6	0.3	0.1	(²)			
1890	62,947,714	55,101,258	⁴7,488,676	6,337,980	1,132,060	248,253	107,488	2,039		87.5	11.9	0.4	0.2	(²)		84.8	15.2
1880	50,155,783	43,402,970	6,580,793			⁵66,407	105,465	148		86.5	13.1	0.1	0.2	(²)			
1870 ⁶	38,558,371	33,589,377	4,880,009	4,295,960	584,049	⁵25,731	63,199	55		87.1	12.7	0.1	0.2	(²)		88.0	12.0
1870 ⁷	39,818,449	34,337,292	5,392,172			⁵25,731	63,199	55		86.2	13.5	0.1	0.2	(²)			
1860	31,443,321	26,922,537	4,441,830	3,853,467	588,363	⁵44,021	34,933			85.6	14.1	0.1	0.1			86.8	13.2
1850	23,191,876	19,553,068	3,638,808	3,233,057	405,751					84.3	15.7					88.8	11.2
1840	17,069,453	14,195,805	2,873,648							83.2	16.8						
1830	12,866,020	10,537,378	2,328,642							81.9	18.1						
1820	9,638,453	7,866,797	1,771,656							81.6	18.4						
1810	7,239,881	5,862,073	1,377,808							81.0	19.0						
1800	5,308,483	4,306,446	1,002,037							81.1	18.9						
1790	3,929,214	3,172,006	757,208							80.7	19.3						

[1] Comprises 5,603 Filipinos, 2,507 Hindus, 1,224 Koreans, 110 Hawaiians, 19 Malays, 17 Siamese, 6 Samoans, and 2 Maoris.
[2] Less than one-tenth of 1 per cent.
[3] Comprises 160 Filipinos, 2,545 Hindus, 462 Koreans, and 8 Maoris.
[4] Includes 18,636 Negroes enumerated in Indian Territory, not distinguished as black or mulatto.
[5] Exclusive of Indians in Indian Territory and on Indian reservations, not enumerated at censuses prior to 1890.
[6] As enumerated.
[7] Estimated corrected figures. See explanation, p. 15.

TABLE 2.—INCREASE, BY COLOR OR RACE, FOR THE UNITED STATES: 1790–1920.

[A minus sign (—) denotes decrease.]

DECADE.	TOTAL POPULATION.		WHITE.		NEGRO.		INDIAN.		CHINESE.		JAPANESE.		ALL OTHER.	
	Number.	Per cent.	Number.	Per cent.	Number.	Per cent.	Number.	Per cent.	Number.	Per cent.	Number.	Per cent.	Number.	Per cent.
1910–1920	13,788,354	14.9	13,088,958	16.0	635,368	6.5	−21,246	−8.0	−9,892	−13.8	38,853	53.8	6,313	198.8
1900–1910	15,977,691	21.0	14,922,761	22.3	993,769	11.2	28,487	12.0	−18,352	−20.4	47,831	196.6	3,175	
1890–1900	13,046,861	20.7	11,707,938	21.2	1,345,318	18.0	−11,057	−4.5	−17,625	−16.4	22,287	1,093.0		
1880–1890	¹12,466,467	24.9	¹11,580,920	26.7	⁵889,247	13.5	³−7,601	−11.4	²2,010	1.9	1,891	1,277.7		
1870–1880	11,597,412	30.1	9,813,593	29.2	1,700,784	34.9	⁵40,676	158.1	42,266	66.9	93	(⁴)		
1870–1880 ⁵	10,337,334	26.0	9,065,678	26.4	1,188,621	22.0	⁵40,676	158.1	42,266	66.9	93	(⁴)		
1860–1870 ⁵	8,375,128	26.6	7,414,755	27.5	950,342	21.4	³−18,290	−41.5	28,266	80.9	55			
1860–1870	7,115,050	22.6	6,666,840	24.8	438,179	9.9	³−18,290	−41.5	28,266	80.9	55			
1850–1860	8,251,445	35.6	7,369,469	37.7	803,022	22.1	³44,021		34,933					
1840–1850	6,122,423	35.9	5,357,263	37.7	765,160	26.6								
1830–1840	4,203,433	32.7	3,658,427	34.7	545,006	23.4								
1820–1830	3,227,567	33.5	2,670,581	33.9	556,986	31.4								
1810–1820	2,398,572	33.1	2,004,724	34.2	393,848	28.6								
1800–1810	1,931,398	36.4	1,555,627	36.1	375,771	37.5								
1790–1800	1,379,269	35.1	1,134,440	35.8	244,829	32.3								

[1] Exclusive of 325,464 persons (117,368 whites, 18,636 Negroes, 189,447 Indians, and 13 Chinese) specially enumerated in 1890 in Indian Territory and on Indian reservations.
[2] See note 1.
[3] Exclusive of Indians in Indian Territory and on Indian reservations, not enumerated prior to 1890.
[4] Per cent not shown, base being less than 100.
[5] Estimated corrected increase. See explanation, p. 15.

TABLE 3.—INCREASE, BY NATIVITY OF TOTAL POPULATION AND BY NATIVITY AND PARENTAGE OF WHITE POPULATION, FOR THE UNITED STATES: 1850–1920.

[For numbers on which increase is based, see Table 4.]

DECADE.	TOTAL POPULATION.				WHITE POPULATION.									
	Native.		Foreign born.		Native.								Foreign born.	
					Total.		Native parentage.		Foreign parentage.		Mixed parentage.			
	Number.	Per cent.	Number.	Per cent.	Number.	Per cent.	Number.	Per cent.	Number.	Per cent.	Number.	Per cent.	Number.	Per cent.
1910–1920	13,333,548	17.0	404,806	3.0	12,721,749	18.6	8,933,382	18.1	2,778,228	21.5	1,010,139	16.9	367,209	2.3
1900–1910	12,803,081	19.5	3,174,610	30.7	11,791,033	20.8	8,539,213	20.9	2,284,031	21.5	967,789	19.3	3,131,728	30.7
1890–1900	11,955,145	22.3	1,091,716	11.8	10,615,988	23.1	6,473,646	18.8	2,547,251	31.5	1,595,081	46.7	1,091,950	12.0
1880–1890	¹9,896,863	22.8	²2,569,604	38.5	¹9,018,732	24.5	¹5,789,924	20.3	1,721,250	27.0	1,507,558	78.9	2,562,188	39.1
1870–1880 ²	10,484,698	31.8	1,112,714	20.0	8,747,626	31.1	5,797,027	25.5	2,196,671	52.7	753,928	65.2	1,065,967	19.4
1860–1870 ²	5,686,518	20.8	1,428,532	34.5	5,269,881	23.1							1,396,959	34.1
1850–1860	6,357,350	30.3	1,894,095	84.4	5,513,251	31.8							1,856,218	82.3

[1] Exclusive of population specially enumerated in 1890 in Indian Territory and on Indian reservations.
[2] Enumeration in 1870 incomplete. See pp. 15 and 18.

30 POPULATION.

TABLE 4.—NATIVITY AND PARENTAGE OF TOTAL POPULATION AND OF EACH COLOR OR RACE CLASS, FOR THE UNITED STATES: 1850–1920.

[Figures are given under each class for all census years for which data are available. The term "native parentage" includes those persons having both parents native; "foreign parentage," those having both parents foreign born; and "mixed parentage," those having one parent native and the other foreign born.]

CLASS OF POPULATION AND CENSUS YEAR.	POPULATION.		NATIVE POPULATION.					FOREIGN-BORN POPULATION.					One or both parents native.	One or both parents foreign born.
	Native.	Foreign born.	Native parentage.	Foreign parentage.	Mixed parentage.			Native parentage.	Foreign parentage.	Mixed parentage.				
					Total.	Father foreign.	Mother foreign.			Total.	Father foreign.	Mother foreign.		
Total:														
1920	91,789,928	13,920,692	68,994,682	15,764,366	7,030,880	4,564,295	2,466,585	(1)	13,832,797	87,895	57,609	30,286	76,113,457	36,715,938
1910	78,456,380	13,515,886	59,491,427	12,949,181	6,015,772	3,946,435	2,069,337	(1)	13,429,955	85,931	49,519	36,412	65,593,130	32,480,839
1900	65,653,299	10,341,276	49,956,178	10,650,802	5,040,319	3,362,228	1,678,091	9,458	10,269,085	62,733	46,198	16,535	55,074,688	26,028,039
1890	53,698,154	9,249,560												
1880	43,475,840	6,679,943												
1870 [2]	32,991,142	5,567,229												
1860	27,304,624	4,138,697												
1850	20,947,274	2,244,602												
White:														
1920	81,108,161	13,712,754	58,421,957	15,694,539	6,991,665	4,539,776	2,451,889	(1)	13,627,161	85,593	56,568	29,025	65,499,215	36,398,958
1910	68,386,412	13,345,545	49,488,575	12,916,311	5,981,526	3,923,845	2,057,681	(1)	13,261,666	83,879	48,594	35,285	55,553,980	32,243,382
1900	56,595,379	10,213,817	40,949,362	10,632,280	5,013,737	3,346,652	1,667,085	8,854	10,143,607	61,356	45,340	16,016	46,033,309	25,850,980
1890	45,979,391	9,121,867	34,475,716	8,085,019	3,418,656	2,378,729	1,039,927	105,809	8,926,762	89,206	45,964	43,242	38,089,477	20,519,643
1880	36,843,291	6,559,679	28,568,424	6,363,769	1,911,098									
1870 [2]	28,095,665	5,493,712	22,771,397	4,167,098	1,157,170									
1860	22,825,784	4,096,753												
1850	17,312,533	2,240,535												
Negro:														
1920	10,389,328	73,803	10,334,151	25,843	29,334	18,193	11,141	(1)	72,630	1,173	780	393	10,364,658	128,980
1910	9,787,424	40,339	9,748,424	14,560	24,425	15,332	9,093	(1)	38,887	1,452	703	749	9,774,316	79,324
1900	8,813,658	20,336	8,779,267	9,198	25,193	15,720	9,473	538	18,690	1,108	656	452	8,806,106	54,189
Indian:														
1920	238,138	6,299	230,410	2,719	5,009	3,542	1,467	(2)	6,137	162	128	34	235,531	14,027
1910	262,930	2,753	253,481	1,900	7,549	5,497	2,052	(1)	2,407	346	192	154	261,376	12,202
1900	234,983	2,213	227,272	1,358	6,353	4,882	1,471	47	1,937	229	172	57	233,901	9,877
Chinese:														
1920	18,532	43,107	2,391	11,952	4,189	2,249	1,940	(1)	42,210	897	73	824	7,477	50,248
1910	14,935	56,596	738	12,076	2,121	1,634	487	(1)	56,368	228	20	208	3,087	70,703
1900	9,010	80,853	245	7,762	1,003	946	57	12	80,817	24	19	5	1,284	89,606
Japanese:														
1920	29,672	81,338	212	28,948	512	446	66	(1)	81,276	62	54	8	786	110,798
1910	4,502	67,655	44	4,313	145	127	18	(1)	67,629	26	10	16	215	72,113
1900	269	24,057	32	204	33	28	5	7	24,034	16	11	5	88	24,287
All other:														
1920	6,097	3,391	5,501	365	171	89	82	(1)	3,383	8	6	2	5,740	3,927
1910	177	2,998	150	21	6		6	(1)	2,998				156	3,025

CLASS OF POPULATION AND CENSUS YEAR.	PER CENT OF TOTAL OF EACH CLASS.							PER CENT OF TOTAL NATIVE OF EACH CLASS.			PER CENT OF TOTAL FOREIGN BORN OF EACH CLASS.	
	Population.		Native population.			Foreign-born population.		Native.			Foreign born.	
	Native.	Foreign born.	Native parentage.	Foreign parentage.	Mixed parentage.	Foreign parentage.	Mixed parentage.	Native parentage.	Foreign parentage.	Mixed parentage.	Foreign parentage.	Mixed parentage.
Total:												
1920	86.8	13.2	65.3	14.9	6.7	13.1	0.1	75.2	17.2	7.7	99.4	0.6
1910	85.3	14.7	64.7	14.1	6.5	14.6	0.1	75.8	16.5	7.7	99.4	0.6
1900	86.4	13.6	65.7	14.0	6.6	13.5	0.1	76.1	16.2	7.7	99.3	0.6
1890	85.3	14.7										
1880	86.7	13.3										
1870 [2]	85.6	14.4										
1860	86.8	13.2										
1850	90.3	9.7										
White:												
1920	85.5	14.5	61.6	16.6	7.4	14.4	0.1	72.0	19.4	8.6	99.4	0.6
1910	83.7	16.3	60.5	15.8	7.3	16.2	0.1	72.4	18.0	8.7	99.4	0.6
1900	84.7	15.3	61.3	15.9	7.5	15.2	0.1	72.4	18.8	8.9	99.3	0.6
1890	83.4	16.6	62.6	14.7	6.2	16.2	0.2	75.0	17.6	7.4	97.9	1.0
1880	84.9	15.1	65.8	14.7	4.4			77.5	17.3	5.2		
1870 [2]	83.6	16.4	67.8	12.4	3.4			81.0	14.8	4.1		
1860	84.8	15.2										
1850	88.5	11.5										
Negro:												
1920	99.3	0.7	98.8	0.2	0.3	0.7	(3)	99.5	0.2	0.3	98.4	1.6
1910	99.6	0.4	99.2	0.1	0.2	0.4	(3)	99.6	0.1	0.2	96.4	3.6
1900	99.8	0.2	99.4	0.1	0.3	0.2	(3)	99.6	0.1	0.3	91.9	5.4
Indian:												
1920	97.4	2.6	94.3	1.1	2.0	2.5	0.1	96.8	1.1	2.1	97.4	2.6
1910	99.0	1.0	95.4	0.7	2.8	0.9	0.1	96.4	0.7	2.9	87.4	12.6
1900	99.1	0.9	95.8	0.6	2.7	0.8	0.1	96.7	0.6	2.7	87.5	10.3
Chinese:												
1920	30.1	69.9	3.9	19.4	6.8	68.5	1.5	12.9	64.5	22.6	97.9	2.1
1910	20.9	79.1	1.0	16.9	3.0	78.8	0.3	4.9	80.9	14.2	99.6	0.4
1900	10.0	90.0	0.3	8.6	1.1	89.9	(3)	2.7	86.1	11.1		
Japanese:												
1920	26.7	73.3	0.2	26.0	0.5	73.2	0.1	0.7	97.6	1.7	99.9	0.1
1910	6.2	93.8	0.1	6.0	0.2	93.7	(3)	1.0	95.8	3.2	100.0	(3)
1900	1.1	98.9	0.1	0.8	0.1	98.8	0.1	11.9	75.8	12.3		
All other:												
1920	64.3	35.7	58.6	3.8	1.8	35.7	0.1	91.2	6.0	2.8	99.9	0.1
1910	5.6	94.4	4.7	0.7	0.2	94.4		84.7	11.9	3.4	100.0	0.2

[1] In 1920 and 1910 all persons born in foreign territory, both parents being natives of the United States, were classified as American citizens born abroad and were included in the native class.
[2] Enumeration in 1870 incomplete. See pp. 15 and 18.
[3] Less than one-tenth of 1 per cent.

COLOR OR RACE, NATIVITY, AND PARENTAGE. 31

TABLE 5.—COLOR OR RACE, NATIVITY, AND PARENTAGE, BY DIVISIONS AND STATES: 1920.

DIVISION AND STATE.	Total population: 1920	COLOR OR RACE.						NATIVITY.		WHITE POPULATION BY NATIVITY AND PARENTAGE.				
		White.	Negro.	Indian.	Chinese.	Japanese.	All other.	Native.	Foreign born.	Native white. Total.	Native parentage.	Foreign parentage.	Mixed parentage.	Foreign-born white.
United States	105,710,620	94,820,915	10,463,131	244,437	61,639	111,010	9,488	91,789,928	13,920,692	81,108,161	58,421,957	15,694,539	6,991,665	13,712,754
GEOGRAPHIC DIVISIONS:														
New England	7,400,909	7,316,079	79,051	1,715	3,602	347	115	5,514,964	1,885,945	5,445,425	2,803,149	1,906,340	735,936	1,870,654
Middle Atlantic	22,261,144	21,641,840	600,183	5,940	8,812	3,266	1,103	17,300,726	4,960,418	16,729,265	9,631,012	5,397,951	1,700,302	4,912,575
East North Central	21,475,543	20,938,862	514,554	15,695	5,043	927	462	18,243,402	3,232,141	17,715,583	11,790,370	4,043,692	1,881,521	3,223,279
West North Central	12,544,249	12,225,387	278,521	37,263	1,678	1,215	185	11,168,596	1,375,653	10,853,426	7,475,548	2,126,126	1,251,752	1,371,961
South Atlantic	13,990,272	9,648,940	4,325,120	13,678	1,824	360	355	13,659,735	330,537	9,333,020	8,779,416	353,643	190,961	315,920
East South Central	8,893,307	6,367,547	2,523,532	1,623	542	35	28	8,820,318	72,989	6,295,608	6,092,782	115,484	87,342	71,939
West South Central	10,242,224	8,115,727	2,063,579	60,618	1,534	578	188	9,777,396	464,828	7,656,394	6,959,785	415,799	280,810	459,333
Mountain	3,336,101	3,212,899	30,801	76,899	4,339	10,792	371	2,808,481	467,620	2,759,674	2,002,508	451,132	306,034	453,225
Pacific	5,566,871	5,353,634	47,790	31,011	34,265	93,490	6,081	4,436,310	1,130,561	4,319,766	2,887,387	884,372	548,007	1,033,868
NEW ENGLAND:														
Maine	768,014	765,695	1,310	839	161	7	2	660,200	107,814	658,346	495,780	86,150	76,416	107,349
New Hampshire	443,083	442,331	621	28	95	8	......	351,686	91,397	351,098	225,512	81,039	44,547	91,233
Vermont	352,428	351,817	572	24	11	4	......	307,870	44,558	307,291	228,325	42,100	36,866	44,526
Massachusetts	3,852,356	3,803,524	45,466	555	2,544	191	76	2,763,808	1,088,548	2,725,990	1,230,773	1,093,258	401,959	1,077,534
Rhode Island	604,397	593,980	10,036	110	225	35	11	429,208	175,189	420,491	173,553	182,660	64,258	173,499
Connecticut	1,380,631	1,358,732	21,046	159	566	102	26	1,002,192	378,439	982,219	449,206	421,133	111,880	376,513
MIDDLE ATLANTIC:														
New York	10,385,227	10,172,027	198,483	5,503	5,793	2,686	735	7,559,852	2,825,375	7,385,915	3,668,266	2,844,083	873,566	2,786,112
New Jersey	3,155,900	3,037,087	117,132	100	1,190	325	66	2,413,414	742,488	2,298,474	1,212,675	829,058	256,741	738,613
Pennsylvania	8,720,017	8,432,726	284,568	337	1,829	255	302	7,327,460	1,392,557	7,044,876	4,750,071	1,724,810	569,995	1,387,850
EAST NORTH CENTRAL:														
Ohio	5,759,394	5,571,893	186,187	151	941	130	92	5,078,942	680,452	4,893,196	3,669,122	838,251	385,823	678,697
Indiana	2,930,390	2,849,071	80,810	125	283	81	20	2,779,062	151,328	2,698,203	2,329,544	227,066	141,593	150,868
Illinois	6,485,280	6,299,333	182,274	194	2,776	472	231	5,274,696	1,210,584	5,092,382	3,066,563	1,467,036	558,783	1,206,951
Michigan	3,668,412	3,601,627	60,082	5,614	792	184	113	2,939,120	729,292	2,874,992	1,670,447	775,288	429,257	726,635
Wisconsin	2,632,067	2,616,938	5,201	9,611	251	60	6	2,171,582	460,485	2,156,810	1,054,694	736,051	366,065	460,128
WEST NORTH CENTRAL:														
Minnesota	2,387,125	2,368,936	8,809	8,761	508	85	26	1,900,336	486,795	1,882,772	827,627	708,126	347,019	486,164
Iowa	2,404,021	2,384,181	19,005	529	235	29	42	2,178,027	225,994	2,158,534	1,528,553	376,710	253,271	225,647
Missouri	3,404,055	3,225,044	178,241	171	412	135	52	3,217,220	186,835	3,039,018	2,536,936	300,064	202,018	186,026
North Dakota	646,872	639,954	467	6,254	124	72	1	515,009	131,863	508,451	207,966	203,973	96,512	131,503
South Dakota	636,547	619,147	832	16,384	142	38	4	554,013	82,534	536,756	308,598	141,341	86,817	82,391
Nebraska	1,296,372	1,279,219	13,242	2,888	189	804	30	1,145,707	150,665	1,129,567	757,064	231,948	140,555	149,652
Kansas	1,769,257	1,708,906	57,925	2,276	68	52	30	1,658,290	110,967	1,598,328	1,308,804	163,964	125,560	110,578
SOUTH ATLANTIC:														
Delaware	223,003	192,615	30,335	2	43	8	......	203,102	19,901	172,805	139,876	23,288	9,641	19,810
Maryland	1,449,661	1,204,737	244,479	32	371	29	13	1,346,482	103,179	1,102,560	893,088	143,203	66,209	102,177
District of Columbia	437,571	326,860	109,966	37	461	103	144	408,206	29,365	298,312	239,488	35,129	23,695	28,548
Virginia	2,309,187	1,617,909	690,017	824	278	56	103	2,277,482	31,705	1,587,124	1,534,494	30,514	22,116	30,785
West Virginia	1,463,701	1,377,235	86,345	7	98	10	6	1,401,596	62,105	1,315,329	1,232,857	56,625	25,847	61,906
North Carolina	2,559,123	1,783,779	763,407	11,824	88	24	1	2,551,851	7,272	1,776,680	1,765,203	5,737	5,740	7,099
South Carolina	1,683,724	818,538	864,719	304	93	15	55	1,677,142	6,582	812,137	799,418	7,025	5,694	6,401
Georgia	2,895,832	1,689,114	1,206,365	125	211	9	8	2,879,268	16,564	1,672,928	1,642,697	16,371	13,860	16,186
Florida	968,470	638,153	329,487	518	181	106	25	914,606	53,864	595,145	532,295	35,751	27,099	43,008
EAST SOUTH CENTRAL:														
Kentucky	2,416,630	2,180,560	235,938	57	62	9	4	2,385,724	30,906	2,149,780	2,039,134	65,931	44,715	30,780
Tennessee	2,337,885	1,885,993	451,758	56	57	8	13	2,322,237	15,648	1,870,515	1,832,757	20,423	17,335	15,478
Alabama	2,348,174	1,447,032	900,652	405	59	18	8	2,330,147	18,027	1,429,370	1,394,129	19,591	15,650	17,662
Mississippi	1,790,618	853,962	935,184	1,105	364	....	3	1,782,210	8,408	845,943	826,762	9,539	9,642	8,019
WEST SOUTH CENTRAL:														
Arkansas	1,752,204	1,279,757	472,220	106	113	5	3	1,738,067	14,137	1,265,782	1,226,692	19,030	20,060	13,975
Louisiana	1,798,509	1,096,611	700,257	1,066	387	57	131	1,752,082	46,427	1,051,740	941,724	67,016	43,000	44,871
Oklahoma	2,028,283	1,821,194	149,408	57,337	261	67	16	1,987,851	40,432	1,781,226	1,679,107	53,083	49,036	39,968
Texas	4,663,228	3,918,165	741,694	2,109	773	449	38	4,299,396	363,832	3,557,646	3,112,262	276,670	168,714	360,519
MOUNTAIN:														
Montana	548,889	534,260	1,658	10,956	872	1,074	69	453,298	95,591	440,640	275,803	101,918	62,919	93,620
Idaho	431,866	425,668	920	3,098	585	1,569	26	391,119	40,747	386,705	294,252	47,920	44,533	38,963
Wyoming	194,402	190,146	1,375	1,343	252	1,194	92	167,835	26,567	164,891	122,884	25,234	16,773	25,255
Colorado	939,629	924,103	11,318	1,383	291	2,464	70	820,491	119,138	807,149	603,041	130,059	74,049	116,954
New Mexico	360,350	334,673	5,733	19,512	171	251	10	330,542	29,808	305,596	273,317	18,865	13,414	29,077
Arizona	334,162	291,449	8,005	32,989	1,137	550	32	253,596	80,566	213,350	151,145	39,534	22,671	78,099
Utah	449,396	441,901	1,446	2,711	342	2,936	60	390,196	59,200	385,446	245,781	75,901	63,764	56,455
Nevada	77,407	70,699	346	4,907	689	754	12	61,404	16,003	55,897	36,285	11,701	7,911	14,802
PACIFIC:														
Washington	1,356,621	1,319,777	6,883	9,061	2,363	17,387	1,150	1,091,329	285,292	1,069,722	711,706	214,618	143,398	250,055
Oregon	783,389	769,146	2,144	4,590	3,090	4,151	268	675,745	107,644	666,995	497,726	95,827	73,442	102,151
California	3,426,861	3,264,711	38,763	17,360	28,812	71,952	5,263	2,669,286	757,625	2,583,049	1,677,955	573,927	331,167	681,682

32

POPULATION.

TABLE 6.—INCREASE, BY COLOR OR RACE, NATIVITY, AND PARENTAGE, BY DIVISIONS AND STATES: 1910–1920.

[Per cent not shown where base is less than 100. A minus sign (—) denotes decrease.]

DIVISION AND STATE.	TOTAL POPULATION.		WHITE.		NEGRO.		INDIAN, CHINESE, JAPANESE, AND ALL OTHER.		NATIVE WHITE.						FOREIGN-BORN WHITE.	
									Native parentage.		Foreign parentage.		Mixed parentage.			
	Number.	Per cent.	Number.	Per cent.	Number.	Per cent.	Number.	Per cent.	Number.	Per cent.	Number.	Per cent.	Number.	Per cent.	Number.	Per cent.
United States....	13,738,354	14.9	13,086,958	16.0	635,368	6.5	14,028	3.4	8,933,382	18.1	2,778,228	21.5	1,010,139	16.9	367,209	2.8
GEOGRAPHIC DIVISIONS:																
New England	848,228	12.9	835,565	12.9	12,745	19.2	-82	-1.4	189,730	7.3	445,775	30.5	143,792	24.3	56,268	3.1
Middle Atlantic	2,945,252	15.2	2,761,388	14.6	182,313	43.6	1,551	8.8	1,168,051	13.8	1,284,875	31.2	222,066	15.0	86,396	3.1
East North Central	3,224,922	17.7	3,011,240	16.8	213,718	71.0	-36	-0.2	2,038,402	20.9	593,677	17.2	223,102	13.5	156,059	5.1
West North Central	906,328	7.8	878,766	7.7	35,859	14.8	-3,297	-7.6	951,861	14.6	23,423	1.1	139,752	12.6	-241,270	-15.0
South Atlantic	1,795,377	14.7	1,577,837	19.5	212,632	5.2	5,408	50.1	1,438,211	19.6	79,192	28.9	34,569	20.9	25,365	8.7
East South Central	483,406	5.7	613,221	10.7	-128,981	-4.9	-834	-27.2	640,290	11.7	-8,431	-6.8	-3,720	-4.1	-14,918	-17.2
West South Central	1,457,699	16.6	1,394,236	20.7	79,153	4.0	-15,699	-20.0	1,192,335	20.7	51,767	14.2	39,559	16.4	110,574	31.7
Mountain	702,584	26.7	692,444	27.5	9,334	43.5	806	0.9	535,884	36.5	81,123	21.9	59,122	23.9	16,315	3.7
Pacific	1,374,567	32.8	1,329,761	33.0	18,595	63.7	26,211	18.8	778,617	36.9	226,827	34.5	151,897	38.3	172,420	20.0
NEW ENGLAND:																
Maine	25,643	3.5	25,700	3.5	-53	-3.9	-4	-0.4	873	0.2	12,695	17.3	14,916	24.3	-2,784	-2.5
New Hampshire	12,511	2.9	12,425	2.9	57	10.1	29	28.4	-4,719	-2.0	13,438	19.9	9,031	25.4	-5,325	-5.5
Vermont	-3,528	-1.0	-2,481	-0.7	-1,049	-64.7	2	......	-1,057	-0.5	2,593	6.6	1,315	3.7	-5,335	-19.7
Massachusetts	485,940	14.4	478,598	14.4	7,411	19.5	-69	-2.0	127,344	11.5	246,438	29.1	78,332	24.2	26,484	2.5
Rhode Island	61,787	11.4	61,488	11.5	507	5.3	-208	-35.3	13,732	8.6	38,390	26.6	13,892	27.6	-4,526	-2.5
Connecticut	265,875	23.9	259,835	23.6	5,872	38.7	168	24.5	53,557	13.5	132,221	45.8	26,303	30.7	47,754	14.5
MIDDLE ATLANTIC:																
New York	1,271,613	14.0	1,205,182	15.4	64,292	47.9	2,139	17.0	437,941	13.6	602,246	26.9	108,155	14.1	56,840	2.1
New Jersey	618,733	24.4	591,193	24.2	27,372	30.5	168	11.1	292,766	20.1	253,047	43.9	54,955	27.2	80,425	12.2
Pennsylvania	1,054,906	13.8	965,013	12.9	90,649	46.7	-756	-21.7	527,344	12.5	429,582	33.2	58,956	11.5	-50,869	-3.5
EAST NORTH CENTRAL:																
Ohio	992,273	20.8	916,996	19.7	74,735	67.1	542	70.2	635,863	21.0	166,976	24.9	32,705	9.3	81,452	13.6
Indiana	229,514	8.5	209,110	7.9	20,490	34.0	-86	-14.5	199,456	9.4	16,058	7.6	2,050	1.5	-8,454	-5.3
Illinois	846,689	15.0	772,371	14.0	73,225	67.1	1,093	42.4	466,008	17.9	234,881	19.1	67,091	13.6	4,391	0.4
Michigan	858,239	30.5	816,380	29.3	42,967	251.0	-1,108	-14.2	445,606	36.4	163,969	26.8	75,694	21.4	131,111	22.0
Wisconsin	298,207	12.8	296,383	12.8	2,301	79.3	-477	-4.6	291,469	38.2	11,793	1.6	45,582	14.2	-52,441	-10.2
WEST NORTH CENTRAL:																
Minnesota	311,417	15.0	309,709	15.0	1,725	24.4	-17	-0.2	252,546	43.9	40,666	6.1	73,343	26.8	-56,846	-10.5
Iowa	179,250	8.1	174,990	7.9	4,032	26.9	228	37.6	225,027	17.3	-18,831	-4.8	16,631	7.0	-47,837	-17.5
Missouri	110,720	3.4	90,112	2.9	20,789	13.2	-181	-19.0	149,101	6.2	-11,963	-3.8	-4,156	-2.0	-42,870	-18.7
North Dakota	69,816	12.1	70,099	12.3	-150	-24.3	-133	-2.0	45,505	28.0	23,919	13.3	25,330	35.6	-24,655	-15.8
South Dakota	52,659	9.0	55,376	9.8	15	1.8	-2,732	-14.2	62,946	25.6	-1,704	-1.2	12,371	16.6	-18,237	-18.1
Nebraska	104,158	8.7	98,926	8.4	5,553	72.2	-321	-7.6	114,989	17.9	-2,722	-1.2	12,872	10.0	-26,213	-14.9
Kansas	78,308	4.6	74,554	4.6	3,895	7.2	-141	-5.5	101,747	8.4	-5,942	-3.5	3,361	2.8	-24,612	-18.2
SOUTH ATLANTIC:																
Delaware	20,681	10.2	21,513	12.6	-846	-2.7	14	......	12,067	9.4	5,722	32.6	1,334	16.1	2,390	13.7
Maryland	154,315	11.9	142,098	13.4	12,229	5.3	-12	-2.6	126,461	16.4	12,882	9.9	4,752	7.7	-1,997	-1.9
District of Columbia	106,502	32.2	90,732	38.4	15,520	16.4	250	50.5	72,777	43.7	8,607	32.5	5,151	27.8	4,197	17.2
Virginia	247,575	12.0	228,100	16.4	18,921	2.8	554	78.4	209,256	15.8	8,901	41.2	5,786	35.4	4,157	15.6
West Virginia	242,582	19.9	220,418	19.1	22,172	34.6	-8	-6.2	190,750	18.3	21,218	59.9	3,616	16.3	4,834	8.5
North Carolina	352,836	16.0	283,268	18.9	65,564	9.4	4,004	50.5	279,485	18.8	1,851	47.6	775	15.6	1,157	19.5
South Carolina	168,324	11.1	139,377	20.5	28,876	3.5	71	17.9	137,448	20.8	1,266	22.0	316	5.9	347	5.7
Georgia	286,711	11.0	257,312	18.0	29,378	2.5	21	6.3	251,639	18.1	3,139	23.7	1,420	11.4	1,114	7.4
Florida	215,851	28.7	194,519	43.8	20,818	6.7	514	162.7	158,328	42.3	15,606	77.5	11,419	72.8	9,166	27.1
EAST SOUTH CENTRAL:																
Kentucky	126,725	5.5	152,609	7.5	-25,718	-9.8	-166	-55.7	175,940	9.4	-10,592	-13.8	-3,466	-7.2	-9,273	-23.2
Tennessee	153,096	7.0	174,561	10.2	-21,330	-4.5	-135	-50.2	178,151	10.8	-149	-0.7	-460	-2.6	-2,981	-16.1
Alabama	210,081	9.8	218,200	17.8	-7,630	-0.8	-489	-49.9	216,670	18.4	1,924	10.9	900	6.1	-1,294	-6.8
Mississippi	-6,496	-0.4	67,851	8.6	-74,303	-7.4	-44	-2.9	69,529	9.2	386	4.2	-694	-6.7	-1,370	-14.6
WEST SOUTH CENTRAL:																
Arkansas	177,755	11.3	148,731	13.2	29,329	6.6	-305	-57.3	149,183	13.8	643	3.5	1,839	10.1	-2,934	-17.4
Louisiana	142,121	8.6	155,525	16.5	-13,617	-1.9	213	14.9	165,137	21.3	-1,373	-2.0	-1,328	-3.0	-6,911	-13.3
Oklahoma	371,128	22.4	376,663	26.1	11,796	8.6	-17,331	-23.1	368,704	28.1	3,206	6.4	4,869	11.0	-118	-0.3
Texas	766,686	19.7	713,317	22.3	51,645	7.5	1,724	104.8	509,312	19.6	49,291	21.7	34,179	25.4	120,535	50.2
MOUNTAIN:																
Montana	172,836	46.0	173,680	48.2	-176	-9.6	-668	-4.9	113,676	70.1	33,312	48.6	24,716	64.7	1,976	2.2
Idaho	106,272	32.6	106,447	33.3	269	41.3	-444	-7.8	90,653	44.5	7,845	19.6	9,413	26.8	-1,464	-3.6
Wyoming	48,437	33.2	49,828	35.5	-860	-38.5	-531	-15.6	42,188	52.3	5,483	27.8	4,020	31.5	-1,863	-6.9
Colorado	140,605	17.6	140,688	18.0	-135	-1.2	52	1.3	127,905	26.9	15,312	13.3	7,368	11.0	-9,897	-7.8
New Mexico	33,049	10.1	30,079	9.9	4,105	252.1	-1,135	-5.4	17,708	6.9	4,455	30.9	1,493	12.5	6,423	28.4
Arizona	129,808	63.5	119,981	70.0	5,996	298.5	3,831	12.4	68,677	83.3	13,417	51.4	6,612	41.2	31,275	66.8
Utah	76,045	20.4	75,318	20.5	302	26.4	425	7.6	74,118	24.1	1,918	2.6	6,220	10.8	-6,938	-10.9
Nevada	-4,468	-5.5	-3,577	-4.8	-167	-32.6	-724	-10.2	959	2.7	-619	-5.0	-720	-8.3	-3,197	-17.8
PACIFIC:																
Washington	214,631	18.8	210,666	19.0	825	13.6	3,140	11.7	126,320	21.6	39,773	22.7	35,715	33.2	8,858	3.7
Oregon	110,624	16.4	114,056	17.4	652	43.7	-4,084	-25.2	80,875	19.4	16,491	20.8	17,540	31.4	-850	-0.8
California	1,049,312	44.1	1,005,039	44.5	17,118	79.1	27,155	28.2	571,422	51.6	170,563	42.3	98,642	42.4	164,412	31.8

COLOR OR RACE, NATIVITY, AND PARENTAGE.

33

TABLE 7.—PER CENT DISTRIBUTION OF TOTAL POPULATION BY COLOR OR RACE, NATIVITY, AND PARENTAGE, AND OF WHITE POPULATION BY NATIVITY AND PARENTAGE, BY DIVISIONS AND STATES: 1920.

DIVISION AND STATE.	PER CENT OF TOTAL POPULATION.										PER CENT OF TOTAL WHITE POPULATION.				
			Indian, Chinese, Japanese, and all other.	Native.	Foreign born.	Native white.				Foreign-born white.	Native white.				Foreign-born white.
	White.	Negro.				Total.	Native parentage.	Foreign parentage.	Mixed parentage.		Total.	Native parentage.	Foreign parentage.	Mixed parentage.	
United States......	89.7	9.9	0.4	86.8	13.2	74.7	55.3	14.8	6.6	13.0	85.5	61.6	16.6	7.4	14.5
GEOGRAPHIC DIVISIONS:															
New England.........	98.9	1.1	0.1	74.5	25.5	73.6	37.9	25.8	9.9	25.3	74.4	38.3	26.1	10.1	25.6
Middle Atlantic.......	97.2	2.7	0.1	77.7	22.3	75.2	43.3	24.2	7.6	22.1	77.3	44.5	24.9	7.9	22.7
East North Central...	97.5	2.4	0.1	84.9	15.1	82.5	54.9	18.8	8.8	15.0	84.6	56.3	19.3	9.0	15.4
West North Central...	97.5	2.2	0.3	89.0	11.0	86.5	59.6	16.9	10.0	10.9	88.8	61.1	17.4	10.2	11.2
South Atlantic........	69.0	30.9	0.1	97.6	2.4	66.7	62.8	2.5	1.4	2.3	96.7	91.0	3.7	2.1	3.3
East South Central...	71.6	28.4	(1)	99.2	0.8	70.8	68.5	1.3	1.0	0.8	98.9	95.7	1.8	1.4	1.1
West South Central...	79.2	20.1	0.6	95.5	4.5	74.8	68.0	4.1	2.7	4.5	94.3	85.8	5.1	3.5	5.7
Mountain.............	96.3	0.9	2.8	86.0	14.0	82.7	60.0	13.5	9.2	13.6	85.9	62.3	14.0	9.5	14.1
Pacific..............	96.2	0.9	3.0	79.7	20.3	77.6	51.9	15.9	9.8	18.6	80.7	53.9	16.5	10.2	19.3
NEW ENGLAND:															
Maine...............	99.7	0.2	0.1	86.0	14.0	85.7	64.6	11.2	9.9	14.0	86.0	64.7	11.3	10.0	14.0
New Hampshire......	99.8	0.1	(1)	79.4	20.6	79.2	50.9	18.3	10.1	20.6	79.4	51.0	18.3	10.1	20.6
Vermont.............	99.8	0.2	(1)	87.4	12.6	87.2	64.8	11.9	10.5	12.6	87.3	64.9	12.0	10.5	12.7
Massachusetts........	98.7	1.2	0.1	71.7	28.3	70.8	31.9	28.4	10.4	28.0	71.7	32.4	28.7	10.6	28.3
Rhode Island.........	98.3	1.7	0.1	71.0	29.0	69.6	28.7	30.2	10.6	28.7	70.8	29.2	30.8	10.8	29.2
Connecticut..........	98.4	1.5	0.1	72.6	27.4	71.1	32.5	30.5	8.1	27.3	72.3	33.1	31.0	8.2	27.7
MIDDLE ATLANTIC:															
New York............	97.9	1.9	0.1	72.8	27.2	71.1	35.3	27.4	8.4	26.8	72.6	36.1	28.0	8.6	27.4
New Jersey...........	96.2	3.7	0.1	76.5	23.5	72.8	38.4	26.3	8.1	23.4	75.7	39.9	27.3	8.5	24.3
Pennsylvania.........	96.7	3.3	(1)	84.0	16.0	80.8	54.5	19.8	6.5	15.9	83.5	56.3	20.5	6.8	16.5
EAST NORTH CENTRAL:															
Ohio.................	96.7	3.2	(1)	88.2	11.8	85.0	63.7	14.6	6.7	11.8	87.8	65.9	15.0	6.9	12.2
Indiana..............	97.2	2.8	(1)	94.8	5.2	92.1	79.5	7.7	4.8	5.1	94.7	81.8	8.0	5.0	5.3
Illinois..............	97.1	2.8	0.1	81.3	18.7	78.5	47.3	22.6	8.6	18.6	80.8	48.7	23.3	8.9	19.2
Michigan............	98.2	1.6	0.2	80.1	19.9	78.4	45.5	21.1	11.7	19.8	79.8	46.4	21.5	11.9	20.2
Wisconsin...........	99.4	0.2	0.4	82.5	17.5	81.9	40.1	28.0	13.9	17.5	82.4	40.3	28.1	14.0	17.6
WEST NORTH CENTRAL:															
Minnesota...........	99.2	0.4	0.4	79.6	20.4	78.9	34.7	29.7	14.5	20.4	79.5	34.9	29.9	14.6	20.5
Iowa................	99.2	0.8	(1)	90.6	9.4	89.8	63.6	15.7	10.5	9.4	90.5	64.1	15.8	10.6	9.5
Missouri.............	94.7	5.2	(1)	94.5	5.5	89.3	74.5	8.8	5.9	5.5	94.2	78.7	9.3	6.3	5.8
North Dakota........	98.9	0.1	1.0	79.6	20.4	78.6	32.1	31.5	14.9	20.3	79.5	32.5	31.9	15.1	20.5
South Dakota........	97.3	0.1	2.6	87.0	13.0	84.3	48.5	22.2	13.6	12.9	86.7	49.8	22.8	14.0	13.3
Nebraska............	98.7	1.0	0.3	88.4	11.6	87.1	58.4	17.9	10.8	11.5	88.3	59.2	18.1	11.0	11.7
Kansas..............	96.6	3.3	0.1	93.7	6.3	90.3	74.0	9.3	7.1	6.2	93.5	76.6	9.6	7.3	6.5
SOUTH ATLANTIC:															
Delaware............	86.4	13.6	(1)	91.1	8.9	77.5	62.7	10.4	4.3	8.9	89.7	72.6	12.1	5.0	10.3
Maryland............	83.1	16.9	(1)	92.9	7.1	76.1	61.6	9.9	4.6	7.0	91.5	74.1	11.9	5.5	8.5
District of Columbia..	74.7	25.1	0.2	93.3	6.7	68.2	54.7	8.0	5.4	6.5	91.3	73.3	10.7	7.2	8.7
Virginia.............	70.1	29.9	0.1	98.6	1.4	68.7	66.5	1.3	1.0	1.3	98.1	94.8	1.9	1.4	1.9
West Virginia........	94.1	5.9	(1)	95.8	4.2	89.9	84.2	3.9	1.8	4.2	95.5	89.5	4.1	1.9	4.5
North Carolina.......	69.7	29.8	0.5	99.7	0.3	69.4	69.0	0.2	0.2	0.3	99.6	99.0	0.3	0.3	0.4
South Carolina.......	48.6	51.4	(1)	99.6	0.4	48.2	47.5	0.4	0.3	0.4	99.2	97.7	0.9	0.7	0.8
Georgia.............	58.3	41.7	(1)	99.4	0.6	57.8	56.7	0.6	0.5	0.6	99.0	97.3	1.0	0.8	1.0
Florida..............	65.9	34.0	0.1	94.4	5.6	61.5	55.0	3.7	2.8	4.4	93.3	83.4	5.6	4.2	6.7
EAST SOUTH CENTRAL:															
Kentucky............	90.2	9.8	(1)	98.7	1.3	89.0	84.4	2.7	1.9	1.3	98.6	93.5	3.0	2.1	1.4
Tennessee............	80.7	19.3	(1)	99.3	0.7	80.0	78.4	0.9	0.7	0.7	99.2	97.2	1.1	0.9	0.8
Alabama.............	61.6	38.4	(1)	99.2	0.8	60.9	59.4	0.8	0.7	0.8	98.8	96.3	1.4	1.1	1.2
Mississippi...........	47.7	52.2	0.1	99.5	0.5	47.2	46.2	0.5	0.5	0.4	99.1	96.8	1.1	1.1	0.9
WEST SOUTH CENTRAL:															
Arkansas.............	73.0	27.0	(1)	99.2	0.8	72.2	70.0	1.1	1.1	0.8	98.9	95.9	1.5	1.6	1.1
Louisiana............	61.0	38.9	0.1	97.4	2.6	58.5	52.4	3.7	2.4	2.5	95.9	85.9	6.1	3.9	4.1
Oklahoma...........	89.8	7.4	2.8	98.0	2.0	87.8	82.8	2.6	2.4	2.0	97.8	92.2	2.9	2.7	2.2
Texas...............	84.0	15.9	0.1	92.2	7.8	76.3	66.7	5.9	3.6	7.7	90.8	79.4	7.1	4.3	9.2
MOUNTAIN:															
Montana............	97.3	0.3	2.4	82.6	17.4	80.3	50.2	18.6	11.5	17.1	82.5	51.6	19.1	11.8	17.5
Idaho...............	98.6	0.2	1.2	90.6	9.4	89.5	68.1	11.1	10.3	9.0	90.8	69.1	11.3	10.5	9.2
Wyoming............	97.8	0.7	1.5	86.3	13.7	84.8	63.2	13.0	8.6	13.0	86.7	64.6	13.3	8.8	13.3
Colorado............	98.3	1.2	0.4	87.3	12.7	85.9	64.2	13.8	7.9	12.4	87.3	65.3	14.1	8.0	12.7
New Mexico.........	92.9	1.6	5.5	91.7	8.3	84.8	75.8	5.2	3.7	8.1	91.3	81.7	5.6	4.0	8.7
Arizona.............	87.2	2.4	10.4	75.9	24.1	63.8	45.2	11.8	6.8	23.4	73.2	51.9	13.6	7.8	26.8
Utah................	98.3	0.3	1.3	86.8	13.2	85.8	54.7	16.9	14.2	12.6	87.2	55.6	17.2	14.4	12.8
Nevada.............	91.3	0.4	8.2	79.3	20.7	72.2	46.9	15.1	10.2	19.1	79.1	51.3	16.6	11.2	20.9
PACIFIC:															
Washington..........	97.3	0.5	2.2	80.4	19.6	78.9	52.5	15.8	10.6	18.4	81.1	53.9	16.3	10.9	18.9
Oregon.............	98.2	0.3	1.5	86.3	13.7	85.1	63.5	12.2	9.4	13.0	86.7	64.7	12.5	9.5	13.3
California...........	95.3	1.1	3.6	77.9	22.1	75.4	49.0	16.7	9.7	19.9	79.1	51.4	17.6	10.1	20.9

1 Less than one-tenth of 1 per cent.

54

POPULATION.

TABLE 8.—WHITE AND NEGRO POPULATION, 1920, 1910, AND 1900, AND PER CENT NEGRO, 1850–1920, BY DIVISIONS AND STATES.

DIVISION AND STATE.	1920			1910			1900			PER CENT NEGRO IN TOTAL POPULATION.							
	Total population.[1]	White.	Negro.	Total population.[1]	White.	Negro.	Total population.[1]	White.	Negro.	1920	1910	1900	1890	1880	1870	1860	1850
United States....	105,710,620	94,820,915	10,463,131	91,972,266	81,731,957	9,827,763	75,994,575	66,809,196	8,833,994	9.9	10.7	11.6	11.9	13.1	12.7	14.1	15.7
GEOGRAPHIC DIVISIONS:																	
New England.......	7,400,909	7,316,079	79,051	6,552,681	6,480,514	66,306	5,592,017	5,527,026	59,099	1.1	1.0	1.1	0.9	1.0	0.9	0.8	0.8
Middle Atlantic.....	22,261,144	21,641,840	600,183	19,315,892	18,880,452	417,870	15,454,678	15,110,862	325,921	2.7	2.2	2.1	1.8	1.8	1.7	1.8	2.1
East North Central..	21,475,543	20,938,862	514,554	18,250,621	17,927,622	300,836	15,985,581	15,710,053	257,842	2.4	1.6	1.6	1.5	1.6	1.4	0.9	1.0
West North Central..	12,544,249	12,225,387	278,521	11,637,921	11,351,621	242,662	10,347,423	10,065,817	237,909	2.2	2.1	2.3	2.5	3.3	3.7	5.6	10.3
South Atlantic......	13,990,272	9,648,940	4,325,120	12,194,895	8,071,603	4,112,488	10,443,480	6,706,058	3,729,017	30.9	33.7	35.7	36.8	38.7	37.0	38.4	39.8
East South Central..	8,893,307	6,307,547	2,523,532	8,409,901	5,754,326	2,652,513	7,547,757	5,044,847	2,499,886	28.4	31.5	33.1	33.0	34.5	33.2	34.7	33.4
West South Central..	10,242,224	8,115,727	2,063,579	8,784,534	6,721,491	1,984,426	6,532,290	4,771,065	1,694,066	20.1	22.6	25.9	29.1	32.6	36.4	36.9	39.2
Mountain..........	3,336,101	3,212,899	30,801	2,633,517	2,520,455	21,467	1,674,657	1,579,855	15,590	0.9	0.8	0.9	1.1	0.8	0.5	0.1	0.1
Pacific............	5,566,871	5,353,634	47,790	4,192,304	4,023,873	29,195	2,416,692	2,293,613	14,064	0.9	0.7	0.6	0.7	0.6	0.7	1.0	1.1
NEW ENGLAND:																	
Maine...........	768,014	765,695	1,310	742,371	739,995	1,363	694,466	692,226	1,319	0.2	0.2	0.2	0.2	0.2	0.3	0.2	0.2
New Hampshire.....	443,083	442,331	621	430,572	429,906	564	411,588	410,791	662	0.1	0.1	0.2	0.2	0.2	0.2	0.2	0.2
Vermont..........	352,428	351,817	572	355,956	354,298	1,621	343,641	342,771	826	0.2	0.5	0.2	0.3	0.3	0.3	0.2	0.2
Massachusetts......	3,852,356	3,803,524	45,466	3,366,416	3,324,926	38,055	2,805,346	2,769,764	31,974	1.2	1.1	1.1	1.0	1.0	1.0	0.8	0.9
Rhode Island........	604,397	593,980	10,036	542,610	532,492	9,529	428,556	419,050	9,092	1.7	1.8	2.1	2.1	2.3	2.3	2.3	2.5
Connecticut........	1,380,631	1,358,732	21,046	1,114,756	1,098,897	15,174	908,420	892,424	15,226	1.5	1.4	1.7	1.6	1.9	1.8	1.9	2.1
MIDDLE ATLANTIC:																	
New York..........	10,385,227	10,172,027	198,483	9,113,614	8,966,845	134,191	7,268,894	7,156,881	99,232	1.9	1.5	1.4	1.2	1.3	1.2	1.3	1.6
New Jersey.........	3,155,900	3,037,087	117,132	2,537,167	2,445,894	89,760	1,883,669	1,812,317	69,844	3.7	3.5	3.7	3.3	3.4	3.4	3.8	4.9
Pennsylvania.......	8,720,017	8,432,726	284,568	7,665,111	7,467,713	193,919	6,302,115	6,141,664	156,845	3.3	2.5	2.5	2.0	2.0	1.9	2.0	2.3
EAST NORTH CENTRAL:																	
Ohio..............	5,759,394	5,571,893	186,187	4,767,121	4,654,897	111,452	4,157,545	4,060,204	96,901	3.2	2.3	2.3	2.4	2.5	2.4	1.6	1.3
Indiana...........	2,930,390	2,849,071	80,810	2,700,876	2,639,961	60,320	2,516,462	2,458,502	57,505	2.8	2.2	2.3	2.1	2.0	1.5	0.9	1.1
Illinois............	6,485,280	6,299,333	182,274	5,638,591	5,526,962	109,049	4,821,550	4,734,873	85,078	2.8	1.9	1.8	1.5	1.5	1.1	0.5	0.6
Michigan..........	3,668,412	3,601,627	60,082	2,810,173	2,785,247	17,115	2,420,982	2,398,563	15,816	1.6	0.6	0.7	0.7	0.9	1.0	0.9	0.7
Wisconsin..........	2,632,067	2,616,938	5,201	2,333,860	2,320,555	2,900	2,069,042	2,057,911	2,542	0.2	0.1	0.1	0.1	0.2	0.2	0.2	0.2
WEST NORTH CENTRAL:																	
Minnesota..........	2,387,125	2,368,936	8,809	2,075,708	2,059,227	7,084	1,751,394	1,737,036	4,959	0.4	0.3	0.3	0.3	0.2	0.2	0.2	0.6
Iowa..............	2,404,021	2,384,181	19,005	2,224,771	2,209,191	14,973	2,231,853	2,218,667	12,693	0.8	0.7	0.6	0.6	0.6	0.5	0.2	0.2
Missouri..........	3,404,055	3,225,044	178,241	3,293,335	3,134,932	157,452	3,106,665	2,944,843	161,234	5.2	4.8	5.2	5.6	6.7	6.9	10.0	13.2
North Dakota......	646,872	639,954	467	577,056	569,855	617	319,146	311,712	286	0.1	0.1	0.1	0.2	0.3			
South Dakota......	636,547	619,147	832	583,888	563,771	817	401,570	380,714	465	0.1	0.1	0.1	0.2	0.3	0.7		
Nebraska..........	1,296,372	1,279,219	13,242	1,192,214	1,180,293	7,689	1,066,300	1,056,526	6,269	1.0	0.6	0.6	0.8	0.5		0.3	
Kansas...........	1,769,257	1,708,906	57,925	1,690,949	1,634,352	54,030	1,470,495	1,416,319	52,003	3.3	3.2	3.5	3.5	4.3	4.7	0.6	
SOUTH ATLANTIC:																	
Delaware..........	223,003	192,615	30,335	202,322	171,102	31,181	184,735	153,977	30,697	13.6	15.4	16.6	16.8	18.0	18.2	19.3	22.3
Maryland..........	1,449,661	1,204,737	244,479	1,295,346	1,062,639	232,250	1,188,044	952,424	235,064	16.9	17.9	19.8	20.7	22.5	22.5	24.9	28.3
District of Columbia.	437,571	326,860	109,966	331,069	236,128	94,446	278,718	191,532	86,702	25.1	28.5	31.1	32.8	33.6	33.0	19.1	26.6
Virginia..........	2,309,187	1,617,909	690,017	2,061,612	1,389,809	671,096	1,854,184	1,192,855	660,722	29.9	32.6	35.6	38.4	41.8	41.9		
West Virginia......	1,463,701	1,377,235	86,345	1,221,119	1,156,817	64,173	958,800	915,233	43,499	5.9	5.3	4.5	4.3	4.2	4.1	34.4	37.1
North Carolina.....	2,559,123	1,783,779	763,407	2,206,287	1,500,511	697,843	1,893,810	1,263,603	624,469	29.8	31.6	33.0	34.7	38.0	36.6	36.4	36.4
South Carolina.....	1,683,724	818,538	864,719	1,515,400	679,161	835,843	1,340,316	557,807	782,321	51.4	55.2	58.4	59.8	60.7	58.9	58.6	58.9
Georgia...........	2,895,832	1,689,114	1,206,365	2,609,121	1,431,802	1,176,987	2,216,331	1,181,294	1,034,813	41.7	45.1	46.7	46.7	47.0	46.0	44.1	42.4
Florida...........	968,470	638,153	329,487	752,619	443,634	308,669	528,542	297,333	230,730	34.0	41.0	43.7	42.5	47.0	48.8	44.6	46.0
EAST SOUTH CENTRAL:																	
Kentucky..........	2,416,630	2,180,560	235,938	2,289,905	2,027,951	261,656	2,147,174	1,862,309	284,706	9.8	11.4	13.3	14.4	16.5	16.8	20.4	22.5
Tennessee..........	2,337,885	1,885,993	451,758	2,184,789	1,711,432	473,088	2,020,616	1,540,186	480,243	19.3	21.7	23.8	24.4	26.1	25.6	25.5	24.5
Alabama..........	2,348,174	1,447,032	900,652	2,138,093	1,228,832	908,282	1,828,697	1,001,152	827,307	38.4	42.5	45.2	44.8	47.5	47.7	45.4	44.7
Mississippi........	1,790,618	853,962	935,184	1,797,114	786,111	1,009,487	1,551,270	641,200	907,630	52.2	56.2	58.5	57.6	57.5	53.7	55.3	51.2
WEST SOUTH CENTRAL:																	
Arkansas..........	1,752,204	1,279,757	472,220	1,574,449	1,131,026	442,891	1,311,564	944,580	366,856	27.0	28.1	28.0	27.4	26.3	25.2	25.6	22.7
Louisiana..........	1,798,509	1,096,611	700,257	1,656,388	941,086	713,874	1,381,625	729,612	650,804	38.9	43.1	47.1	50.0	51.5	50.1	49.5	50.7
Oklahoma[2].......	2,028,283	1,821,194	149,408	1,657,155	1,444,531	137,612	790,391	670,204	55,684	7.4	8.3	7.0	8.4				
Texas.............	4,663,228	3,918,165	741,694	3,896,542	3,204,848	690,049	3,048,710	2,426,669	620,722	15.9	17.7	20.4	21.8	24.7	31.0	30.3	27.5
MOUNTAIN:																	
Montana..........	548,889	534,260	1,658	376,053	360,580	1,834	243,329	226,283	1,523	0.3	0.5	0.6	1.0	0.9	0.0		
Idaho............	431,866	425,668	920	325,594	319,221	651	161,772	154,495	293	0.2	0.2	0.2	0.2	0.2	0.4		
Wyoming..........	194,402	190,146	1,375	145,965	140,318	2,235	92,531	89,051	940	0.7	1.5	1.0	1.5	1.4	2.0		
Colorado..........	939,629	924,103	11,318	799,024	783,415	11,453	539,700	529,046	8,570	1.2	1.4	1.6	1.5	1.3	1.1	0.1	
New Mexico.......	360,350	334,673	5,733	327,301	304,594	1,628	195,310	180,207	1,610	1.6	0.5	0.8	1.2	0.8	0.2	0.1	(3)
Arizona...........	334,162	291,449	8,005	204,354	171,468	2,009	122,931	92,903	1,848	2.4	1.0	1.5	1.5	0.4	0.3		
Utah.............	449,396	441,901	1,446	373,351	366,583	1,144	276,749	272,465	672	0.3	0.3	0.2	0.3	0.2	0.1	0.2	0.4
Nevada...........	77,407	70,699	346	81,875	74,276	513	42,335	35,405	134	0.4	0.6	0.3	0.5	0.8	0.8	0.7	
PACIFIC:																	
Washington........	1,356,621	1,319,777	6,883	1,141,990	1,109,111	6,058	518,103	496,304	2,514	0.5	0.5	0.5	0.4	0.4	0.9	0.3	
Oregon............	783,389	769,146	2,144	672,765	655,090	1,492	413,536	394,582	1,105	0.3	0.2	0.3	0.4	0.3	0.4	0.2	1.6
California..........	3,426,861	3,264,711	38,763	2,377,549	2,259,672	21,645	1,485,053	1,402,727	11,045	1.1	0.9	0.7	0.9	0.7	0.8	1.1	1.0

[1] Includes Indians, Chinese, Japanese, and all other. [2] Includes population of Indian Territory for 1900 and 1890. [3] Less than one-tenth of 1 per cent.

COLOR OR RACE, NATIVITY, AND PARENTAGE.

35

TABLE 9.—NEGRO POPULATION, DISTINGUISHED AS BLACK OR MULATTO, 1920, 1910, AND 1890, WITH PER CENT MULATTO, 1920, 1910, 1890, 1870, 1860, AND 1850, BY DIVISIONS AND STATES, AND FOR CITIES HAVING, IN 1920, MORE THAN 50,000 NEGROES.

[Classification as black and mulatto not available for 1900 or 1880; not available for cities prior to 1910.]

DIVISION, STATE, OR CITY.	1920			1910			1890			PER CENT MULATTO IN TOTAL NEGRO.					
	Total Negro.	Black.	Mulatto.	Total Negro.	Black.	Mulatto.	Total Negro.	Black.	Mulatto.	1920	1910	1890	1870	1860	1850
United States.....	10,463,131	8,802,577	1,660,554	9,827,763	7,777,077	2,050,686	[1]7,488,676	6,337,980	1,132,060	15.9	20.9	15.2	12.0	13.2	11.2
GEOGRAPHIC DIVISIONS:															
New England........	79,051	63,734	15,317	66,306	44,156	22,150	44,580	30,001	14,579	19.4	33.4	32.7	23.6	28.5	24.8
Middle Atlantic......	600,183	530,350	69,833	417,870	335,901	81,969	225,326	177,174	48,152	11.6	19.6	21.4	14.9	23.1	21.4
East North Central....	514,554	408,197	106,357	300,836	201,027	99,809	207,023	130,024	76,999	20.7	33.2	37.2	29.2	40.9	52.0
West North Central....	278,521	226,567	51,954	242,062	173,031	69,631	224,089	167,307	56,782	18.7	28.7	25.3	16.0	20.4	15.9
South Atlantic........	4,325,120	3,627,737	697,383	4,112,488	3,256,669	855,819	3,262,690	2,823,905	438,785	16.1	20.8	13.4	10.4	11.9	10.0
East South Central....	2,523,532	2,143,871	379,661	2,652,513	2,145,458	507,055	2,119,797	1,830,762	289,035	15.0	19.1	13.6	11.1	11.7	8.9
West South Central....	2,063,579	1,743,116	320,463	1,984,426	1,586,440	397,986	[1]1,378,090	1,102,330	197,124	15.5	20.1	14.5	13.1	13.5	13.2
Mountain...........	30,801	25,235	5,566	21,467	15,332	6,135	12,971	8,334	4,637	18.1	28.6	35.7	30.4	37.0	(2)
Pacific.............	47,790	33,770	14,020	29,195	19,063	10,132	14,110	8,143	5,967	29.3	34.7	42.3	37.3	37.8	21.3
NEW ENGLAND:															
Maine.............	1,310	884	426	1,363	737	626	1,190	507	683	32.5	45.9	57.4	36.9	47.8	34.0
New Hampshire.....	621	439	182	564	356	208	614	248	366	29.3	36.9	59.6	24.8	51.2	35.4
Vermont...........	572	327	245	1,621	1,185	436	937	521	416	42.8	26.9	44.4	26.7	27.1	28.7
Massachusetts.......	45,466	35,562	9,904	38,055	24,100	13,955	22,144	14,108	8,036	21.8	36.7	36.3	30.6	32.0	25.8
Rhode Island.......	10,036	7,919	2,117	9,529	6,350	3,179	7,393	5,396	1,997	21.1	33.4	27.0	23.3	25.2	19.9
Connecticut........	21,046	18,603	2,443	15,174	11,428	3,746	12,302	9,221	3,081	11.6	24.7	25.0	27.7	22.0	23.4
MIDDLE ATLANTIC:															
New York..........	198,483	171,507	26,976	134,191	103,583	30,608	70,092	54,852	15,240	13.6	22.8	21.7	10.7	15.9	16.6
New Jersey.........	117,132	103,684	13,448	89,760	75,553	14,207	47,638	40,436	7,202	11.5	15.8	15.1	11.6	13.7	15.4
Pennsylvania.......	284,568	255,159	29,409	193,919	156,765	37,154	107,596	81,886	25,710	10.3	19.2	23.9	19.7	33.6	28.6
EAST NORTH CENTRAL:															
Ohio.............	186,187	148,234	37,953	111,452	72,203	39,249	87,113	50,078	37,035	20.4	35.2	42.5	28.2	45.5	56.4
Indiana...........	80,810	66,812	13,998	60,320	45,767	14,553	45,215	31,557	13,658	17.3	24.1	30.2	28.6	47.7	47.2
Illinois...........	182,274	138,634	43,640	109,049	72,221	36,828	57,028	40,346	16,082	23.9	33.8	29.3	25.5	47.1	46.1
Michigan..........	60,082	50,463	9,619	17,115	9,079	8,036	15,223	7,036	8,187	16.0	47.0	53.8	45.7	49.6	43.3
Wisconsin.........	5,201	4,054	1,147	2,900	1,757	1,143	2,444	1,007	1,437	22.1	39.4	58.8	24.4	62.9	46.8
WEST NORTH CENTRAL:															
Minnesota.........	8,809	6,563	2,246	7,084	4,468	2,616	3,683	1,981	1,702	25.5	36.9	46.2	32.3	65.3	(2)
Iowa.............	19,005	15,555	3,450	14,973	11,329	3,644	10,685	7,503	3,182	18.2	24.3	29.8	19.0	53.1	46.5
Missouri..........	178,241	148,339	29,902	157,452	112,762	44,690	150,184	114,730	35,445	16.8	28.4	23.6	15.0	19.9	15.7
North Dakota......	467	355	112	617	460	157	373	153	220	24.0	25.4	59.0	} (2)		
South Dakota......	832	547	285	817	521	296	541	310	231	34.3	36.2	42.7			......
Nebraska..........	13,242	9,620	3,022	7,689	5,602	2,087	8,913	6,091	2,822	27.4	27.1	31.7	6.5	(2)	......
Kansas...........	57,925	45,588	12,337	54,030	37,889	16,141	49,710	36,530	13,180	21.3	29.9	26.5	22.3	42.7	......
SOUTH ATLANTIC:															
Delaware..........	30,335	27,822	2,513	31,181	27,475	3,706	28,386	24,837	3,549	8.3	11.9	12.5	9.8	13.8	8.5
Maryland..........	244,479	213,186	31,293	232,250	189,098	43,152	215,657	181,296	34,361	12.8	18.6	15.9	13.6	14.6	13.0
District of Columbia..	109,966	81,502	28,464	94,446	61,494	32,952	75,572	55,736	19,836	25.9	34.9	26.2	18.5	38.0	29.7
Virginia..........	690,017	525,846	164,171	671,096	448,186	222,910	635,438	512,997	122,441	23.8	33.2	19.3	14.1	} 17.0	15.1
West Virginia......	86,345	69,073	17,272	64,173	43,294	20,879	32,690	23,336	9,354	20.0	32.5	28.6	24.1		
North Carolina.....	763,407	637,981	125,426	697,843	553,720	144,123	561,018	483,817	77,201	16.4	20.7	13.8	9.6	12.4	10.8
South Carolina.....	864,719	748,250	116,469	835,843	701,462	134,381	688,934	621,781	67,153	13.5	16.1	9.7	6.7	6.9	4.3
Georgia...........	1,206,365	1,037,153	169,212	1,176,987	972,782	204,205	858,815	773,682	85,133	14.0	17.3	9.9	7.9	8.4	6.3
Florida...........	320,487	280,924	42,563	308,669	259,158	49,511	166,180	146,423	19,757	12.9	16.0	11.9	12.4	9.4	9.3
EAST SOUTH CENTRAL:															
Kentucky..........	235,938	194,444	41,494	261,656	195,713	65,943	268,071	216,085	51,986	17.6	25.2	19.4	20.1	20.1	14.6
Tennessee.........	451,758	368,852	82,906	473,088	354,391	118,697	430,678	356,215	74,463	18.4	25.1	17.3	9.4	14.8	9.8
Alabama..........	900,652	767,533	133,119	908,282	756,872	151,410	678,489	601,009	77,420	14.8	16.7	11.4	8.8	8.3	6.8
Mississippi........	935,184	813,042	122,142	1,009,487	838,482	171,005	742,559	657,393	85,166	13.1	16.9	11.5	10.2	8.5	6.6
WEST SOUTH CENTRAL:															
Arkansas..........	472,220	410,624	61,596	442,891	361,520	81,371	309,117	269,487	39,630	13.0	18.4	12.8	10.1	12.7	14.2
Louisiana.........	700,257	583,550	116,707	713,874	561,297	152,577	559,193	468,240	90,953	16.7	21.4	16.3	15.5	13.6	12.9
Oklahoma.........	149,408	122,011	27,397	137,612	98,269	39,343	[1]21,609	2,156	817	18.3	28.6	27.5	......	......	......
Texas............	741,694	626,931	114,763	690,049	565,354	124,695	488,171	422,447	65,724	15.5	18.1	13.5	11.0	13.8	13.6
MOUNTAIN:															
Montana..........	1,658	1,275	383	1,834	1,223	611	1,490	1,086	404	23.1	33.8	27.1	25.1	......	......
Idaho............	920	738	182	651	425	226	201	100	101	19.8	34.7	50.2	......	......	......
Wyoming..........	1,375	1,016	359	2,235	1,942	293	922	671	251	26.1	13.1	27.2	47.5	......	......
Colorado..........	11,318	8,568	2,750	11,453	7,815	3,638	6,215	4,056	2,159	24.3	31.8	34.7	40.4	(2)	(2)
New Mexico........	5,733	4,949	784	1,628	1,189	439	1,956	970	986	13.7	27.0	50.4	32.6	(2)	(2)
Arizona...........	8,005	7,314	691	2,009	1,561	448	1,357	932	425	8.6	22.3	31.3	......	......	......
Utah.............	1,446	1,117	329	1,144	854	290	588	379	209	22.8	25.3	35.5	28.0	(2)	(2)
Nevada...........	346	258	88	513	323	190	242	140	102	25.4	37.0	42.1	18.8	(2)	......
PACIFIC:															
Washington........	6,883	3,936	2,947	6,058	4,218	1,840	1,602	1,044	558	42.8	30.4	34.8	72.0	(2)	......
Oregon...........	2,144	1,480	664	1,492	1,058	434	1,186	557	629	31.0	29.1	53.0	25.1	48.4	78.3
California.........	38,763	28,354	10,409	21,645	13,787	7,858	11,322	6,542	4,780	26.9	36.3	42.2	36.5	37.7	9.0
SELECTED CITIES.															
Atlanta, Ga........	62,796	46,515	16,281	51,902	35,071	16,831	28,098	......	......	25.9	32.4				
Baltimore, Md......	108,322	93,179	15,143	84,749	66,508	18,241	67,104	......	......	14.0	21.5				
Birmingham, Ala....	70,230	59,653	10,577	52,305	41,102	11,203	11,254	......	......	15.1	21.4				
Chicago, Ill........	109,458	79,432	30,026	44,103	25,760	18,343	14,271	......	......	27.4	41.6				
Memphis, Tenn......	61,181	49,927	11,254	52,441	38,592	13,849	28,706	......	......	18.4	26.4				
New Orleans, La.....	100,930	78,496	22,434	89,262	58,782	30,480	64,491	......	......	22.2	34.1				
New York, N.Y......	152,467	130,918	21,549	91,709	68,914	22,795	33,888	......	......	14.1	24.9				
Philadelphia, Pa....	134,229	124,883	9,346	84,459	70,479	13,980	39,371	......	......	7.0	16.6				
Richmond, Va.......	54,041	40,288	13,753	46,733	28,088	18,645	32,330	......	......	25.4	39.9				
St. Louis, Mo.......	69,854	59,728	10,126	43,960	29,004	14,956	26,865	......	......	14.5	34.0				
Washington, D.C....	109,966	81,502	28,464	94,446	61,494	32,952	75,572	......	......	25.9	34.9				

[1] Includes 18,636 Negroes enumerated in Indian Territory, not distinguished as black or mulatto.
[2] Per cent not shown, base being less than 100.

36

POPULATION.

TABLE 10.—NATIVE AND FOREIGN-BORN POPULATION, 1920, 1910, AND 1900, AND PER CENT FOREIGN BORN, 1850–1920, BY DIVISIONS AND STATES.

DIVISION AND STATE.	1920 Total population.	1920 Native.	1920 Foreign born.	1910 Total population.	1910 Native.	1910 Foreign born.	1900 Total population	1900 Native.	1900 Foreign born.	1920	1910	1900	1890	1880	1870	1860	1850
United States...	105,710,620	91,789,928	13,920,692	91,972,266	78,456,380	13,515,886	75,994,575	65,653,299	10,341,276	13.2	14.7	13.6	14.7	13.3	14.4	13.2	9.7
GEOGRAPHIC DIVISIONS:																	
New England......	7,400,909	5,514,964	1,885,945	6,552,681	4,727,571	1,825,110	5,592,017	4,146,780	1,445,237	25.5	27.9	25.8	24.3	19.8	18.6	15.0	11.2
Middle Atlantic...	22,261,144	17,300,726	4,960,418	19,315,892	14,464,719	4,851,173	15,454,678	12,137,119	3,317,559	22.3	25.1	21.5	21.6	19.3	21.3	20.8	17.3
East North Central..	21,475,543	18,243,402	3,232,141	18,250,621	15,176,855	3,073,766	15,985,581	13,360,355	2,625,226	15.1	16.8	16.4	18.6	17.1	18.2	17.3	12.2
West North Central..	12,544,249	11,168,596	1,375,653	11,637,921	10,021,226	1,616,695	10,347,423	8,814,175	1,533,248	11.0	13.9	14.8	17.3	16.2	17.4	16.0	11.3
South Atlantic...	13,990,272	13,659,735	330,537	12,194,895	11,894,901	299,994	10,443,480	10,227,450	216,030	2.4	2.5	2.1	2.4	2.3	2.9	3.0	2.2
East South Central..	8,893,307	8,820,318	72,989	8,409,901	8,322,076	87,825	7,547,757	7,457,189	90,568	0.8	1.0	1.2	1.6	1.7	2.4	2.5	1.5
West South Central..	10,242,224	9,777,396	464,828	8,784,534	8,432,342	352,192	6,532,290	6,265,203	267,087	4.5	4.0	4.1	4.6	5.4	6.4	7.3	9.3
Mountain...........	3,336,101	2,868,481	467,620	2,633,517	2,180,195	453,322	1,674,657	1,372,688	301,969	14.0	17.2	18.0	21.2	24.6	27.6	13.8	5.8
Pacific............	5,566,871	4,436,310	1,130,561	4,192,304	3,236,495	955,809	2,416,692	1,872,340	544,352	20.3	22.8	22.5	27.2	30.4	33.5	34.9	21.6
NEW ENGLAND:																	
Maine............	768,014	660,200	107,814	742,371	631,809	110,562	694,466	601,136	93,330	14.0	14.9	13.4	11.9	9.1	7.8	6.0	5.5
New Hampshire.....	443,083	351,686	91,397	430,572	333,905	96,667	411,588	323,481	88,107	20.6	22.5	21.4	19.2	13.3	9.3	6.4	4.5
Vermont..........	352,428	307,870	44,558	355,956	306,035	49,921	343,641	298,894	44,747	12.6	14.0	13.0	13.3	12.3	14.3	10.4	10.7
Massachusetts......	3,852,356	2,763,808	1,088,548	3,366,416	2,307,171	1,059,245	2,805,346	1,959,022	846,324	28.3	31.5	30.2	29.4	24.9	24.2	21.1	16.5
Rhode Island.......	604,397	429,208	175,189	542,610	363,469	179,141	428,556	294,037	134,519	29.0	33.0	31.4	30.8	26.8	25.5	21.4	16.2
Connecticut........	1,380,631	1,002,192	378,439	1,114,756	785,182	329,574	908,420	670,210	238,210	27.4	29.6	26.2	24.6	20.9	21.1	17.5	10.4
MIDDLE ATLANTIC:																	
New York..........	10,385,227	7,559,852	2,825,375	9,113,614	6,365,603	2,748,011	7,268,894	5,368,469	1,900,425	27.2	30.2	26.1	26.2	23.8	26.0	25.8	21.2
New Jersey.........	3,155,900	2,413,414	742,486	2,537,167	1,876,379	660,788	1,883,669	1,451,785	431,884	23.5	26.0	22.9	22.8	19.6	20.9	18.3	12.2
Pennsylvania.......	8,720,017	7,327,460	1,392,557	7,665,111	6,222,737	1,442,374	6,302,115	5,316,865	985,250	16.0	18.8	15.6	16.1	13.7	15.5	14.8	13.1
EAST NORTH CENTRAL:																	
Ohio..............	5,759,394	5,078,942	680,452	4,767,121	4,168,747	598,374	4,157,545	3,698,811	458,734	11.8	12.6	11.0	12.5	12.3	14.0	14.0	11.0
Indiana...........	2,930,390	2,779,002	151,328	2,700,876	2,541,213	159,663	2,516,462	2,374,341	142,121	5.2	5.9	5.6	6.7	7.3	8.4	8.8	5.0
Illinois...........	6,485,280	5,274,696	1,210,584	5,638,591	4,433,277	1,205,314	4,821,550	3,854,803	966,747	18.7	21.4	20.1	22.0	19.0	20.3	19.0	13.1
Michigan..........	3,668,412	2,939,120	729,292	2,810,173	2,212,623	597,550	2,420,982	1,879,329	541,653	19.9	21.3	22.4	26.0	23.7	22.6	19.0	13.8
Wisconsin.........	2,632,067	2,171,582	460,485	2,333,860	1,820,995	512,865	2,069,042	1,553,071	515,971	17.5	22.0	24.9	30.7	30.8	34.6	35.7	36.2
WEST NORTH CENTRAL:																	
Minnesota.........	2,387,125	1,900,330	486,795	2,075,708	1,532,113	543,595	1,751,394	1,246,076	505,318	20.4	26.2	28.9	35.7	34.3	36.5	34.1	32.5
Iowa.............	2,404,021	2,178,027	225,994	2,224,771	1,951,006	273,765	2,231,853	1,925,933	305,920	9.4	12.3	13.7	16.9	16.1	17.1	15.7	10.9
Missouri..........	3,404,055	3,217,220	186,835	3,293,335	3,063,556	229,779	3,106,665	2,890,286	216,379	5.5	7.0	7.0	8.8	9.8	12.9	13.6	11.2
North Dakota......	646,872	515,009	131,863	577,056	420,402	156,654	319,146	206,055	113,091	20.4	27.1	35.4	42.7	49.6		34.0	36.7
South Dakota......	636,547	554,013	82,534	583,888	483,098	100,790	401,570	313,062	88,508	13.0	17.3	22.0	26.4	34.2			
Nebraska..........	1,296,372	1,145,707	150,665	1,192,214	1,015,552	176,662	1,066,300	888,953	177,347	11.6	14.8	16.6	19.1	21.5	25.0	22.0	
Kansas...........	1,769,257	1,658,290	110,967	1,690,049	1,555,409	135,450	1,470,495	1,343,810	126,685	6.3	8.0	8.6	10.4	11.1	13.3	11.8	
SOUTH ATLANTIC:																	
Delaware..........	223,003	203,102	19,901	202,322	184,830	17,492	184,735	170,925	13,810	8.9	8.6	7.5	7.8	6.5	7.3	8.2	5.7
Maryland..........	1,449,661	1,346,482	103,179	1,295,346	1,190,402	104,944	1,188,044	1,094,110	93,934	7.1	8.1	7.9	9.0	8.9	10.7	11.3	8.7
District of Columbia.	437,571	408,206	29,365	331,069	306,167	24,902	278,718	258,599	20,119	6.7	7.5	7.2	8.1	9.6	12.3	16.6	9.5
Virginia...........	2,309,187	2,277,482	31,705	2,061,612	2,034,555	27,057	1,854,184	1,834,723	19,461	1.4	1.3	1.0	1.1	1.0	1.1	2.2	1.6
West Virginia......	1,463,701	1,401,596	62,105	1,221,119	1,163,901	57,218	958,800	936,349	22,451	4.2	4.7	2.3	2.5	3.0	3.9		
North Carolina.....	2,559,123	2,551,851	7,272	2,206,287	2,200,195	6,092	1,893,810	1,889,318	4,492	0.3	0.3	0.2	0.2	0.3	0.5	0.3	0.3
South Carolina.....	1,683,724	1,677,142	6,552	1,515,400	1,509,221	6,179	1,340,316	1,334,788	5,528	0.4	0.4	0.4	0.5	0.8	1.1	1.4	1.3
Georgia...........	2,895,832	2,879,268	16,564	2,609,121	2,593,644	15,477	2,216,331	2,203,928	12,403	0.6	0.6	0.6	0.7	0.7	0.9	1.1	0.7
Florida............	968,470	914,606	53,864	752,619	711,986	40,633	528,542	504,710	23,832	5.6	5.4	4.5	5.9	3.7	2.6	2.4	3.2
EAST SOUTH CENTRAL:																	
Kentucky..........	2,416,630	2,385,724	30,906	2,289,905	2,249,743	40,162	2,147,174	2,096,925	50,249	1.3	1.8	2.3	3.2	3.6	4.8	5.2	3.2
Tennessee.........	2,337,885	2,322,237	15,648	2,184,789	2,166,182	18,607	2,020,616	2,002,870	17,746	0.7	0.9	0.9	1.1	1.1	1.5	1.9	0.6
Alabama..........	2,348,174	2,330,147	18,027	2,138,093	2,118,807	19,286	1,828,697	1,814,105	14,592	0.8	0.9	0.8	1.0	0.8	1.0	1.3	1.0
Mississippi.........	1,790,618	1,782,210	8,408	1,797,114	1,787,344	9,770	1,551,270	1,543,289	7,981	0.5	0.5	0.5	0.6	0.8	1.4	1.1	0.8
WEST SOUTH CENTRAL:																	
Arkansas..........	1,752,204	1,738,067	14,137	1,574,449	1,557,403	17,046	1,311,564	1,297,275	14,289	0.8	1.1	1.1	1.3	1.3	1.0	0.8	0.7
Louisiana.........	1,798,509	1,752,082	46,427	1,656,388	1,603,622	52,766	1,381,625	1,328,722	52,903	2.6	3.2	3.8	4.4	5.8	8.5	11.4	13.2
Oklahoma [1]	2,028,283	1,987,851	40,432	1,657,155	1,616,713	40,442	790,391	769,853	20,538	2.0	2.4	2.6	1.1				
Texas............	4,663,228	4,299,396	363,832	3,896,542	3,654,604	241,938	3,048,710	2,869,353	179,357	7.8	6.2	5.9	6.8	7.2	7.6	7.2	8.3
MOUNTAIN:																	
Montana..........	548,889	453,298	95,591	376,053	281,340	94,713	243,329	176,262	67,067	17.4	25.2	27.6	32.2	29.4	38.7		
Idaho............	431,866	391,119	40,747	325,594	283,016	42,578	161,772	137,168	24,604	9.4	13.1	15.2	10.7	30.6	52.6		
Wyoming..........	194,402	167,835	26,567	145,965	116,945	29,020	92,531	75,116	17,415	13.7	19.9	18.8	23.8	28.1	38.5		
Colorado..........	939,629	820,491	119,138	799,024	669,437	129,587	539,700	448,545	91,155	12.7	16.2	16.9	20.3	20.5	16.6	7.8	
New Mexico.......	360,350	330,542	29,808	327,301	304,155	23,146	195,310	181,685	13,625	8.3	7.1	7.0	7.0	6.7	6.1	7.2	3.5
Arizona...........	334,162	253,596	80,566	204,354	155,589	48,765	122,931	98,698	24,233	24.1	23.9	19.7	21.3	39.7	60.1		
Utah.............	449,396	390,396	59,200	373,351	307,529	65,822	276,749	222,972	53,777	13.2	17.6	19.4	25.2	30.6	35.4	31.7	18.0
Nevada...........	77,407	61,404	16,003	81,875	62,184	19,691	42,335	32,242	10,093	20.7	24.1	23.8	31.1	41.2	44.2	30.1	
PACIFIC:																	
Washington........	1,356,621	1,091,329	265,292	1,141,990	885,749	256,241	518,103	406,739	111,364	19.6	22.4	21.5	25.2	21.0	21.0	27.1	
Oregon...........	783,389	675,745	107,644	672,765	559,629	113,136	413,536	347,788	65,748	13.7	16.8	15.9	18.0	17.5	12.8	9.8	7.7
California.........	3,426,861	2,669,236	757,625	2,377,549	1,791,117	586,432	1,485,053	1,117,813	367,240	22.1	24.7	24.7	30.2	33.9	37.5	38.6	23.5

[1] Includes population of Indian Territory for 1900 and 1890.

COLOR OR RACE, NATIVITY, AND PARENTAGE. 37

Table 11.—INDIANS, CHINESE, JAPANESE, AND "ALL OTHER," BY DIVISIONS AND STATES: 1920, 1910, AND 1900.

DIVISION AND STATE.	INDIAN.			CHINESE.			JAPANESE.			ALL OTHER.[1]	
	1920	1910	1900	1920	1910	1900	1920	1910	1900	1920	1910
United States........	244,437	265,683	237,196	61,639	71,531	89,863	111,010	72,157	24,326	9,488	3,175
GEOGRAPHIC DIVISIONS:											
New England............	1,715	2,076	1,600	3,602	3,499	4,203	347	272	89	115	14
Middle Atlantic..........	5,940	7,717	6,959	8,812	8,189	10,490	3,266	1,643	446	1,103	21
East North Central......	15,695	18,255	15,027	5,043	3,415	2,533	927	482	126	462	11
West North Central......	37,263	41,406	42,339	1,678	1,195	1,135	1,215	1,000	223	185	37
South Atlantic..........	13,673	9,054	6,585	1,824	1,582	1,791	360	156	29	355	12
East South Central......	1,623	2,612	2,590	542	414	427	35	26	7	28	10
West South Central......	60,618	76,767	65,574	1,534	1,303	1,555	578	428	30	188	119
Mountain................	76,899	75,338	66,155	4,339	5,614	7,950	10,792	10,447	5,107	371	196
Pacific.................	31,011	32,458	30,367	34,265	46,320	59,779	93,490	57,703	18,269	6,681	2,755
NEW ENGLAND:											
Maine...................	839	802	798	161	108	119	7	13	4	2	....
New Hampshire.........	28	34	22	95	67	112	8	1	1	....	....
Vermont................	24	26	5	11	8	39	4	3	....	....	....
Massachusetts...........	555	688	587	2,544	2,582	2,968	191	151	53	76	14
Rhode Island...........	110	284	35	225	272	366	35	33	13	11	....
Connecticut............	159	152	153	566	462	599	102	71	18	26	....
MIDDLE ATLANTIC:											
New York...............	5,503	6,046	5,257	5,793	5,266	7,170	2,686	1,247	354	735	19
New Jersey.............	100	168	63	1,190	1,139	1,393	325	206	52	66	....
Pennsylvania...........	337	1,503	1,639	1,829	1,784	1,927	255	190	40	302	2
EAST NORTH CENTRAL:											
Ohio...................	151	127	42	941	569	371	130	76	27	92	....
Indiana................	125	279	243	283	276	207	81	38	5	20	2
Illinois...............	194	188	16	2,776	2,103	1,503	472	285	80	231	4
Michigan...............	5,614	7,519	6,354	792	241	240	184	49	9	113	2
Wisconsin..............	9,611	10,142	8,372	251	226	212	60	34	5	6	3
WEST NORTH CENTRAL:											
Minnesota..............	8,761	9,053	9,182	508	275	166	85	67	51	26	2
Iowa...................	529	471	382	235	97	104	29	36	7	42	3
Missouri...............	171	313	130	412	535	449	135	99	9	52	4
North Dakota...........	6,254	6,486	6,968	124	39	32	72	59	148	1	....
South Dakota...........	16,384	19,137	20,225	142	121	165	38	42	1	4	....
Nebraska...............	2,888	3,502	3,322	189	112	180	804	590	3	30	28
Kansas.................	2,276	2,444	2,130	68	16	39	52	107	4	30	....
SOUTH ATLANTIC:											
Delaware...............	2	5	9	43	30	51	8	4	1	....	....
Maryland...............	32	55	3	371	378	544	29	24	9	13	....
District of Columbia.....	37	68	22	461	369	455	103	47	7	144	11
Virginia...............	824	539	354	278	154	243	56	14	10	103	....
West Virginia..........	7	36	12	98	90	56	10	3	....	6	....
North Carolina.........	11,824	7,851	5,687	88	80	51	24	2	....	1	....
South Carolina.........	304	331	121	93	57	67	15	8	....	55	....
Georgia................	125	95	19	211	233	204	9	4	1	8	....
Florida................	518	74	358	181	191	120	106	50	1	25	1
EAST SOUTH CENTRAL:											
Kentucky...............	57	234	102	62	52	57	9	12	....	4	....
Tennessee..............	56	216	108	57	43	75	8	8	4	13	2
Alabama................	405	909	177	59	62	58	18	4	3	8	4
Mississippi............	1,105	1,253	2,203	364	257	237	....	2	....	3	4
WEST SOUTH CENTRAL:											
Arkansas...............	106	460	66	113	62	62	5	9	....	3	1
Louisiana..............	1,066	780	593	387	507	599	57	31	17	131	110
Oklahoma[2]...........	57,337	74,825	64,445	261	139	58	67	48	....	16	....
Texas..................	2,109	702	470	773	595	836	449	340	13	38	8
MOUNTAIN:											
Montana................	10,956	10,745	11,343	872	1,285	1,739	1,074	1,585	2,441	69	24
Idaho..................	3,098	3,488	4,226	585	859	1,467	1,569	1,363	1,291	26	12
Wyoming................	1,343	1,486	1,686	252	246	461	1,194	1,596	393	92	84
Colorado...............	1,383	1,482	1,437	291	373	599	2,464	2,300	48	70	1
New Mexico.............	19,512	20,573	13,144	171	248	341	251	258	8	10	....
Arizona................	32,989	29,201	26,480	1,137	1,305	1,419	550	371	281	32	....
Utah...................	2,711	3,123	2,623	342	371	572	2,936	2,110	417	60	20
Nevada.................	4,907	5,240	5,216	689	927	1,352	754	864	228	12	55
PACIFIC:											
Washington.............	9,061	10,997	10,039	2,363	2,709	3,629	17,387	12,929	5,617	1,150	186
Oregon.................	4,590	5,090	4,951	3,090	7,363	10,397	4,151	3,418	2,501	268	312
California.............	17,360	16,371	15,377	28,812	36,248	45,753	71,952	41,356	10,151	5,263	2,257

[1] Comprises Filipinos, Hindus, Koreans, Hawaiians, Malays, Siamese, Samoans, and Maoris, in 1920; Filipinos, Hindus, Koreans, and Maoris, in 1910.
[2] Includes population of Indian Territory for 1900.

38

POPULATION.

TABLE 12.—COLOR OR RACE, NATIVITY, AND PARENTAGE, WITH DECENNIAL INCREASE, BY DIVISIONS AND STATES: 1920, 1910, AND 1900.

[A minus sign (−) denotes decrease.]

DIVISION OR STATE AND CLASS OF POPULATION.	POPULATION.			DECENNIAL INCREASE.				PER CENT DISTRIBUTION.					
				1910–1920		1900–1910		Total population.			White population.		
	1920	1910	1900	Number.	Per cent.	Number.	Per cent.	1920	1910	1900	1920	1910	1900
UNITED STATES.													
Total	105,710,620	91,972,266	75,994,575	13,738,354	14.9	15,977,691	21.0	100.0	100.0	100.0			
White	94,820,915	81,731,957	66,809,196	13,088,958	16.0	14,922,761	22.3	89.7	88.9	87.9	100.0	100.0	100.0
Negro	10,463,131	9,827,763	8,833,994	635,368	6.5	993,769	11.2	9.9	10.7	11.6			
Ind., Chi., Jap., and all other	426,574	412,546	351,385	14,028	3.4	61,161	17.4	0.4	0.4	0.5			
Native white	81,108,161	68,386,412	56,595,379	12,721,749	18.6	11,791,033	20.8	76.7	74.4	74.5	85.5	83.7	84.7
Native parentage	58,421,957	49,488,575	40,949,362	8,933,382	18.1	8,539,213	20.9	55.3	53.8	53.9	61.6	60.5	61.3
Foreign parentage	15,694,539	12,916,311	10,632,280	2,778,228	21.5	2,284,031	21.5	14.8	14.0	14.0	16.6	15.8	15.9
Mixed parentage	6,991,665	5,981,526	5,013,737	1,010,139	16.9	967,789	19.3	6.6	6.5	6.6	7.4	7.3	7.5
Foreign-born white	13,712,754	13,345,545	10,213,817	367,209	2.8	3,131,728	30.7	13.0	14.5	13.4	14.5	16.3	15.3
GEOGRAPHIC DIVISIONS.													
NEW ENGLAND.													
Total	7,400,909	6,552,681	5,592,017	848,228	12.9	960,664	17.2	100.0	100.0	100.0			
White	7,316,079	6,480,514	5,527,026	835,565	12.9	953,488	17.3	98.9	98.9	98.8	100.0	100.0	100.0
Negro	79,051	66,306	59,099	12,745	19.2	7,207	12.2	1.1	1.0	1.1			
Ind., Chi., Jap., and all other	5,779	5,861	5,892	−82	−1.4	−31	−0.5	0.1	0.1	0.1			
Native white	5,445,425	4,666,128	4,090,154	779,297	16.7	575,974	14.1	73.6	71.2	73.1	74.4	72.0	74.0
Native parentage	2,803,149	2,613,419	2,511,110	189,730	7.3	102,309	4.1	37.9	39.9	44.9	38.3	40.3	45.4
Foreign parentage	1,906,340	1,460,565	1,117,093	445,775	30.5	343,472	30.7	25.8	22.3	20.0	26.1	22.5	20.2
Mixed parentage	735,936	592,144	461,951	143,792	24.3	130,193	28.2	9.9	9.0	8.3	10.1	9.1	8.4
Foreign-born white	1,870,654	1,814,386	1,436,872	56,268	3.1	377,514	26.3	25.3	27.7	25.7	25.6	28.0	26.0
MIDDLE ATLANTIC.													
Total	22,261,144	19,315,892	15,454,678	2,945,252	15.2	3,861,214	25.0	100.0	100.0	100.0			
White	21,641,840	18,880,452	15,110,862	2,761,388	14.6	3,769,590	24.9	97.2	97.7	97.8	100.0	100.0	100.0
Negro	600,183	417,870	325,921	182,313	43.6	91,949	28.2	2.7	2.2	2.1			
Ind., Chi., Jap., and all other	19,121	17,570	17,895	1,551	8.8	−325	−1.8	0.1	0.1	0.1			
Native white	16,729,265	14,054,273	11,808,746	2,674,992	19.0	2,245,527	19.0	75.2	72.8	76.4	77.3	74.4	78.1
Native parentage	9,631,012	8,462,961	7,406,579	1,168,051	13.8	1,056,382	14.3	43.3	43.8	47.9	44.5	44.8	49.0
Foreign parentage	5,397,951	4,113,076	3,143,021	1,284,875	31.2	970,055	30.9	24.2	21.3	20.3	24.9	21.8	20.8
Mixed parentage	1,700,302	1,478,236	1,259,146	222,066	15.0	219,090	17.4	7.6	7.7	8.1	7.9	7.8	8.3
Foreign-born white	4,912,575	4,826,179	3,302,116	86,396	1.8	1,524,063	46.2	22.1	25.0	21.4	22.7	25.6	21.9
EAST NORTH CENTRAL.													
Total	21,475,543	18,250,621	15,985,581	3,224,922	17.7	2,265,040	14.2	100.0	100.0	100.0			
White	20,938,862	17,927,622	15,710,053	3,011,240	16.8	2,217,569	14.1	97.5	98.2	98.3	100.0	100.0	100.0
Negro	514,554	300,836	257,842	213,718	71.0	42,994	16.7	2.4	1.6	1.6			
Ind., Chi., Jap., and all other	22,127	22,163	17,686	−36	−0.2	4,477	25.3	0.1	0.1	0.1			
Native white	17,715,583	14,860,402	13,080,756	2,855,181	19.2	1,779,646	13.5	82.5	81.4	81.9	84.6	82.0	83.3
Native parentage	11,790,370	9,751,968	8,488,016	2,038,402	20.9	1,263,952	14.9	54.9	53.4	53.1	56.3	54.4	54.0
Foreign parentage	4,043,692	3,450,015	3,110,784	593,677	17.2	339,231	10.9	18.8	18.9	19.5	19.3	19.2	19.8
Mixed parentage	1,881,521	1,658,419	1,490,956	223,102	13.5	167,463	11.2	8.8	9.1	9.3	9.0	9.3	9.5
Foreign-born white	3,223,279	3,067,220	2,629,297	156,059	5.1	446,923	17.1	15.0	16.8	16.4	15.4	17.1	16.7
WEST NORTH CENTRAL.													
Total	12,544,249	11,637,921	10,347,423	906,328	7.8	1,290,498	12.5	100.0	100.0	100.0			
White	12,225,387	11,351,621	10,065,817	873,766	7.7	1,285,804	12.8	97.5	97.5	97.3	100.0	100.0	100.0
Negro	278,521	242,662	237,909	35,859	14.8	4,753	2.0	2.2	2.1	2.3			
Ind., Chi., Jap., and all other	40,341	43,638	43,697	−3,297	−7.6	−59	−0.1	0.3	0.4	0.4			
Native white	10,853,426	9,738,390	8,534,712	1,115,036	11.4	1,203,678	14.1	86.5	83.7	82.5	88.8	85.8	84.8
Native parentage	7,475,548	6,523,687	5,660,903	951,861	14.6	862,784	15.2	59.8	56.1	54.7	61.1	57.5	56.2
Foreign parentage	2,126,126	2,102,703	1,933,117	23,423	1.1	169,586	8.8	16.9	18.1	18.7	17.4	18.5	19.2
Mixed parentage	1,251,752	1,112,000	940,692	139,752	12.6	171,308	18.2	10.0	9.6	9.1	10.2	9.8	9.3
Foreign-born white	1,371,061	1,613,231	1,531,105	−241,270	−15.0	82,126	5.4	10.9	13.9	14.8	11.2	14.2	15.2
SOUTH ATLANTIC.													
Total	13,990,272	12,194,895	10,443,480	1,795,377	14.7	1,751,415	16.8	100.0	100.0	100.0			
White	9,648,940	8,071,603	6,706,058	1,577,337	19.5	1,365,545	20.4	69.0	66.2	64.2	100.0	100.0	100.0
Negro	4,325,120	4,112,488	3,729,017	212,632	5.2	383,471	10.3	30.9	33.7	35.7			
Ind., Chi., Jap., and all other	16,212	10,804	8,405	5,408	50.1	2,399	28.5	0.1	0.1	0.1			
Native white	9,333,020	7,781,048	6,497,175	1,551,972	19.9	1,283,873	19.8	66.7	63.8	62.2	96.7	96.4	96.9
Native parentage	8,779,416	7,341,205	6,107,314	1,438,211	19.6	1,233,891	20.2	62.8	60.2	58.5	91.0	91.0	91.1
Foreign parentage	353,643	274,451	233,871	79,192	28.9	40,580	17.4	2.5	2.3	2.2	3.7	3.4	3.5
Mixed parentage	199,961	165,392	155,990	34,569	20.9	9,402	6.0	1.4	1.4	1.5	2.1	2.0	2.3
Foreign-born white	315,920	290,555	208,883	25,365	8.7	81,672	39.1	2.3	2.4	2.0	3.3	3.6	3.1
EAST SOUTH CENTRAL.													
Total	8,893,307	8,409,901	7,547,757	483,406	5.7	862,144	11.4	100.0	100.0	100.0			
White	6,367,547	5,754,326	5,044,847	613,221	10.7	709,479	14.1	71.6	68.4	66.8	100.0	100.0	100.0
Negro	2,523,532	2,652,513	2,499,886	−128,981	−4.9	152,627	6.1	28.4	31.5	33.1			
Ind., Chi., Jap., and all other	2,228	3,062	3,024	−834	−27.2	38	1.3	(1)	(1)	(1)			
Native white	6,295,608	5,667,469	4,955,165	628,139	11.1	712,304	14.4	70.8	67.4	65.7	98.9	98.5	98.2
Native parentage	6,092,782	5,452,492	4,725,774	640,290	11.7	726,718	15.4	68.5	64.8	62.6	95.7	94.8	93.7
Foreign parentage	115,484	123,915	131,048	−8,431	−6.8	−7,133	−5.4	1.3	1.5	1.7	1.8	2.2	2.6
Mixed parentage	87,342	91,062	98,343	−3,720	−4.1	−7,281	−7.4	1.0	1.1	1.3	1.4	1.6	1.9
Foreign-born white	71,939	86,857	89,682	−14,918	−17.2	−2,825	−3.2	0.8	1.0	1.2	1.1	1.5	1.8

¹ Less than one-tenth of 1 per cent.

COLOR OR RACE, NATIVITY, AND PARENTAGE.   39

TABLE 12.—COLOR OR RACE, NATIVITY, AND PARENTAGE, WITH DECENNIAL INCREASE, BY DIVISIONS AND STATES: 1920, 1910, AND 1900—Continued.

[A minus sign (−) denotes decrease.]

DIVISION OR STATE AND CLASS OF POPULATION.	POPULATION.			DECENNIAL INCREASE.				PER CENT DISTRIBUTION.					
				1910-1920		1900-1910		Total population.			White population.		
	1920	1910	1900	Number.	Per cent.	Number.	Per cent.	1920	1910	1900	1920	1910	1900
GEOGRAPHIC DIVISIONS—Con.													
WEST SOUTH CENTRAL.													
Total	10,242,224	8,784,534	6,532,290	1,457,690	16.6	2,252,244	34.5	100.0	100.0	100.0			
White	8,115,727	6,721,491	4,771,065	1,394,236	20.7	1,950,426	40.9	79.2	76.5	73.0	100.0	100.0	100.0
Negro	2,063,579	1,984,426	1,694,066	79,153	4.0	290,360	17.1	20.1	22.6	25.9			
Ind., Chi., Jap., and all other	62,918	78,617	67,159	−15,699	−20.0	11,458	17.1	0.6	0.9	1.0			
Native white	7,656,394	6,372,732	4,507,055	1,283,662	20.1	1,865,677	41.4	74.8	72.5	69.0	94.3	94.8	94.5
Native parentage	6,959,785	5,767,449	4,028,944	1,192,336	20.7	1,738,505	43.2	68.0	65.7	61.7	85.8	85.8	84.4
Foreign parentage	415,799	364,032	285,781	51,767	14.2	78,251	27.4	4.1	4.1	4.4	5.1	5.4	6.0
Mixed parentage	280,810	241,251	192,330	39,559	16.4	48,921	25.4	2.7	2.7	2.9	3.5	3.6	4.0
Foreign-born white	459,333	348,759	264,010	110,574	31.7	84,749	32.1	4.5	4.0	4.0	5.7	5.2	5.5
MOUNTAIN.													
Total	3,336,101	2,633,517	1,674,657	702,584	26.7	958,860	57.3	100.0	100.0	100.0			
White	3,212,899	2,520,455	1,579,855	692,444	27.5	940,600	59.5	96.3	95.7	94.3	100.0	100.0	100.0
Negro	30,801	21,467	15,590	9,334	43.5	5,877	37.7	0.9	0.8	0.9			
Ind., Chi., Jap., and all other	92,401	91,595	79,212	806	0.9	12,383	15.6	2.8	3.5	4.7			
Native white	2,759,674	2,083,545	1,291,494	676,129	32.5	792,051	61.3	82.7	79.1	77.1	85.9	82.7	81.7
Native parentage	2,002,508	1,466,624	855,101	535,884	36.5	611,523	71.5	60.0	55.7	51.1	62.3	58.2	54.1
Foreign parentage	451,132	370,009	266,255	81,123	21.9	103,754	39.0	13.5	14.0	15.9	14.0	14.7	16.9
Mixed parentage	306,034	246,912	170,138	59,122	23.9	76,774	45.1	9.2	9.4	10.2	9.5	9.8	10.8
Foreign-born white	453,225	436,910	288,361	16,315	3.7	148,549	51.5	13.6	16.6	17.2	14.1	17.3	18.3
PACIFIC.													
Total	5,566,871	4,192,304	2,416,692	1,374,567	32.8	1,775,612	73.5	100.0	100.0	100.0			
White	5,353,634	4,023,873	2,293,613	1,329,761	33.0	1,730,260	75.4	96.2	96.0	94.9	100.0	100.0	100.0
Negro	47,790	29,195	14,664	18,595	63.7	14,531	99.1	0.9	0.7	0.6			
Ind., Chi., Jap., and all other	165,447	139,236	108,415	26,211	18.8	30,821	28.4	3.0	3.3	4.5			
Native white	4,319,766	3,162,425	1,821,122	1,157,341	36.6	1,341,303	73.7	77.6	75.4	75.4	80.7	78.6	79.4
Native parentage	2,887,387	2,108,770	1,165,621	778,617	36.9	943,149	80.9	51.9	50.3	48.2	53.9	52.4	50.8
Foreign parentage	884,372	657,545	411,310	226,827	34.5	246,235	59.9	15.9	15.7	17.0	16.5	16.3	17.9
Mixed parentage	548,007	396,110	244,191	151,897	38.3	151,919	62.2	9.8	9.4	10.1	10.2	9.8	10.6
Foreign-born white	1,033,868	861,448	472,491	172,420	20.0	388,957	82.3	18.6	20.5	19.6	19.3	21.4	20.6
NEW ENGLAND.													
Maine.													
Total	768,014	742,371	694,466	25,643	3.5	47,905	6.9	100.0	100.0	100.0			
White	765,695	739,995	692,226	25,700	3.5	47,769	6.9	99.7	99.7	99.7	100.0	100.0	100.0
Negro	1,310	1,363	1,319	−53	−3.9	44	3.3	0.2	0.2	0.2			
Ind., Chi., Jap., and all other	1,009	1,013	921	−4	−0.4	92	10.0	0.1	0.1	0.1			
Native white	658,346	629,862	599,291	28,484	4.5	30,571	5.1	85.7	84.8	86.3	86.0	85.1	86.6
Native parentage	495,780	494,907	493,082	873	0.2	1,825	0.4	64.6	66.7	71.0	64.7	66.9	71.2
Foreign parentage	86,150	73,455	58,306	12,695	17.3	15,149	26.0	11.2	9.9	8.4	11.3	9.9	8.4
Mixed parentage	76,416	61,500	47,903	14,916	24.3	13,597	28.4	9.9	8.3	6.9	10.0	8.3	6.9
Foreign-born white	107,349	110,133	92,935	−2,784	−2.5	17,198	18.5	14.0	14.8	13.4	14.0	14.9	13.4
New Hampshire.													
Total	443,083	430,572	411,588	12,511	2.9	18,984	4.6	100.0	100.0	100.0			
White	442,331	429,906	410,791	12,425	2.9	19,115	4.7	99.8	99.8	99.8	100.0	100.0	100.0
Negro	621	564	662	57	10.1	−98	−14.8	0.1	0.1	0.2			
Ind., Chi., and Jap.	131	102	135	29	28.4	−33	−24.4	(1)	(1)	(1)			
Native white	351,098	333,348	322,830	17,750	5.3	10,518	3.3	79.2	77.4	78.4	79.4	77.5	78.6
Native parentage	225,512	230,231	242,614	−4,719	−2.0	−12,383	−5.1	50.9	53.5	58.9	51.0	53.6	59.1
Foreign parentage	81,039	67,601	53,282	13,438	19.9	14,319	26.9	18.3	15.7	12.9	18.3	15.7	13.0
Mixed parentage	44,547	35,516	26,934	9,031	25.4	8,582	31.9	10.1	8.2	6.5	10.1	8.3	6.6
Foreign-born white	91,233	96,558	87,961	−5,325	−5.5	8,597	9.8	20.6	22.4	21.4	20.6	22.5	21.4
Vermont.													
Total	352,428	355,956	343,641	−3,528	−1.0	12,315	3.6	100.0	100.0	100.0			
White	351,817	354,298	342,771	−2,481	−0.7	11,527	3.4	99.8	99.5	99.7	100.0	100.0	100.0
Negro	572	1,621	826	−1,049	−64.7	795	96.2	0.2	0.5	0.2			
Ind., Chi., and Jap.	39	37	44	2	(2)	−7	(2)	(1)	(1)	(1)			
Native white	307,291	304,437	298,077	2,854	0.9	6,360	2.1	87.2	85.5	86.7	87.3	85.9	87.0
Native parentage	228,325	229,382	225,381	−1,057	−0.5	4,001	1.8	64.8	64.4	65.6	64.9	64.7	65.8
Foreign parentage	42,100	39,507	38,239	2,593	6.6	1,268	3.3	11.9	11.1	11.1	12.0	11.2	11.2
Mixed parentage	36,866	35,548	34,457	1,318	3.7	1,091	3.2	10.5	10.0	10.0	10.5	10.0	10.1
Foreign-born white	44,526	49,861	44,694	−5,335	−10.7	5,167	11.6	12.6	14.0	13.0	12.7	14.1	13.0
Massachusetts.													
Total	3,852,356	3,366,416	2,805,346	485,940	14.4	561,070	20.0	100.0	100.0	100.0			
White	3,803,524	3,324,926	2,769,764	478,598	14.4	555,162	20.0	98.7	98.8	98.7	100.0	100.0	100.0
Negro	45,466	38,055	31,974	7,411	19.5	6,081	19.0	1.2	1.1	1.1			
Ind., Chi., Jap., and all other	3,366	3,435	3,608	−69	−2.0	−173	−4.8	0.1	0.1	0.1			
Native white	2,725,990	2,273,876	1,929,650	452,114	19.9	344,226	17.8	70.8	67.5	68.8	71.7	68.4	69.7
Native parentage	1,230,773	1,103,429	1,032,264	127,344	11.5	71,165	6.9	31.9	32.8	36.8	32.4	33.2	37.3
Foreign parentage	1,093,258	846,820	650,694	246,438	29.1	196,126	30.1	28.4	25.2	23.2	28.7	25.5	23.5
Mixed parentage	401,959	323,627	246,692	78,332	24.2	76,935	31.2	10.4	9.6	8.8	10.6	9.7	8.9
Foreign-born white	1,077,534	1,051,050	840,114	26,484	2.5	210,936	25.1	28.0	31.2	29.9	28.3	31.6	30.3

[1] Less than one-tenth of 1 per cent.   [2] Per cent not shown, base being less than 100.

40

POPULATION.

TABLE 12.—COLOR OR RACE, NATIVITY, AND PARENTAGE, WITH DECENNIAL INCREASE, BY DIVISIONS AND STATES: 1920, 1910, AND 1900—Continued.

[A minus sign (—) denotes decrease.]

DIVISION OR STATE AND CLASS OF POPULATION.	POPULATION.			DECENNIAL INCREASE.				PER CENT DISTRIBUTION.					
				1910-1920		1900-1910		Total population.			White population.		
	1920	1910	1900	Number.	Per cent.	Number.	Per cent.	1920	1910	1900	1920	1910	1900
NEW ENGLAND—Continued.													
Rhode Island.													
Total	604,397	542,610	428,556	61,787	11.4	114,054	26.6	100.0	100.0	100.0			
White	593,980	532,492	419,050	61,488	11.5	113,442	27.1	98.3	98.1	97.8	100.0	100.0	100.0
Negro	10,036	9,529	9,092	507	5.3	437	4.8	1.7	1.8	2.1			
Ind., Chi., Jap., and all other	381	589	414	—208	—35.3	175	42.3	0.1	0.1	0.1			
Native white	420,481	354,467	285,278	66,014	18.6	69,189	24.3	69.6	65.3	66.6	70.8	66.6	68.1
Native parentage	173,553	159,821	144,986	13,732	8.6	14,835	10.2	28.7	29.5	33.8	29.2	30.0	34.6
Foreign parentage	182,660	144,270	104,057	38,390	26.6	40,183	38.6	30.2	26.6	24.3	30.8	27.1	24.8
Mixed parentage	64,268	50,376	36,205	13,892	27.6	14,171	39.1	10.6	9.3	8.4	10.8	9.5	8.6
Foreign-born white	173,499	178,025	133,772	—4,526	—2.5	44,253	33.1	28.7	32.8	31.2	29.2	33.4	31.9
Connecticut.													
Total	1,380,631	1,114,756	908,420	265,875	23.9	206,336	22.7	100.0	100.0	100.0			
White	1,358,732	1,098,897	892,424	259,835	23.6	206,473	23.1	98.4	98.6	98.2	100.0	100.0	100.0
Negro	21,046	15,174	15,226	5,872	38.7	—52	—0.3	1.5	1.4	1.7			
Ind., Chi., Jap., and all other	853	685	770	168	24.5	—85	—11.0	0.1	0.1	0.1			
Native white	982,219	770,138	655,028	212,081	27.5	115,110	17.6	71.1	69.1	72.1	72.3	70.1	73.4
Native parentage	449,206	395,649	372,783	53,557	13.5	22,866	6.1	32.5	35.5	41.0	33.1	36.0	41.8
Foreign parentage	421,133	288,912	212,485	132,221	45.8	76,427	36.0	30.5	25.9	23.4	31.0	26.3	23.8
Mixed parentage	111,880	85,577	69,760	26,303	30.7	15,817	22.7	8.1	7.7	7.7	8.2	7.8	7.8
Foreign-born white	376,513	328,759	237,396	47,754	14.5	91,363	38.5	27.3	29.5	26.1	27.7	29.9	26.6
MIDDLE ATLANTIC.													
New York.													
Total	10,385,227	9,113,614	7,268,894	1,271,613	14.0	1,844,720	25.4	100.0	100.0	100.0			
White	10,172,027	8,966,845	7,156,881	1,205,182	13.4	1,809,964	25.3	97.9	98.4	98.5	100.0	100.0	100.0
Negro	198,483	134,191	99,232	64,292	47.9	31,959	35.2	1.9	1.5	1.4			
Ind., Chi., Jap., and all other	14,717	12,578	12,781	2,139	17.0	—203	—1.6	0.1	0.1	0.2			
Native white	7,385,915	6,237,573	5,267,358	1,148,342	18.4	970,215	18.4	71.1	68.4	72.5	72.6	69.6	73.6
Native parentage	3,668,256	3,230,325	2,851,513	437,941	13.6	378,812	13.3	35.3	35.4	39.2	36.1	36.0	39.8
Foreign parentage	2,844,083	2,241,837	1,761,868	602,246	26.9	479,969	27.2	27.4	24.6	24.2	28.0	25.0	24.6
Mixed parentage	873,566	765,411	653,977	108,155	14.1	111,434	17.0	8.4	8.4	9.0	8.6	8.5	9.1
Foreign-born white	2,786,112	2,729,272	1,889,523	56,840	2.1	839,749	44.4	26.8	29.9	26.0	27.4	30.4	26.4
New Jersey.													
Total	3,155,900	2,537,167	1,883,669	618,733	24.4	653,498	34.7	100.0	100.0	100.0			
White	3,037,087	2,445,894	1,812,317	591,193	24.2	633,577	35.0	96.2	96.4	96.2	100.0	100.0	100.0
Negro	117,132	89,760	69,844	27,372	30.5	19,916	28.5	3.7	3.5	3.7			
Ind., Chi., Jap., and all other	1,681	1,513	1,508	168	11.1	5	0.3	0.1	0.1	0.1			
Native white	2,298,474	1,787,706	1,382,267	510,768	28.6	405,439	29.3	72.8	70.5	73.4	75.7	73.1	76.3
Native parentage	1,212,675	1,009,909	825,973	202,766	20.1	183,936	22.3	38.4	39.8	43.8	39.9	41.3	45.6
Foreign parentage	829,058	576,011	402,856	253,047	43.9	173,118	43.0	26.3	22.7	21.4	27.3	23.6	22.2
Mixed parentage	256,741	201,786	153,401	54,955	27.2	48,385	31.5	8.1	8.0	8.1	8.5	8.2	8.5
Foreign-born white	738,613	658,188	430,050	80,425	12.2	228,138	53.0	23.4	25.9	22.8	24.3	26.9	23.7
Pennsylvania.													
Total	8,720,017	7,665,111	6,302,115	1,054,906	13.8	1,362,996	21.6	100.0	100.0	100.0			
White	8,432,726	7,467,713	6,141,664	965,013	12.9	1,325,049	21.6	96.7	97.4	97.5	100.0	100.0	100.0
Negro	284,568	193,919	156,845	90,649	46.7	37,074	23.6	3.3	2.5	2.5			
Ind., Chi., Jap., and all other	2,723	3,479	3,606	—756	—21.7	—127	—3.5	(¹)	(¹)	0.1			
Native white	7,044,876	6,028,994	5,159,121	1,015,882	16.8	869,873	16.9	80.8	78.7	81.9	83.5	80.7	84.0
Native parentage	4,750,071	4,222,727	3,729,093	527,344	12.5	493,634	13.2	54.5	55.1	59.2	56.3	56.5	60.7
Foreign parentage	1,724,810	1,295,228	978,260	429,582	33.2	316,968	32.4	19.8	16.9	15.5	20.5	17.3	15.9
Mixed parentage	569,995	511,039	451,768	58,956	11.5	59,271	13.1	6.5	6.7	7.2	6.8	6.8	7.4
Foreign-born white	1,387,850	1,438,719	982,543	—50,869	—3.5	456,176	46.4	15.9	18.8	15.6	16.5	19.3	16.0
EAST NORTH CENTRAL.													
Ohio.													
Total	5,759,394	4,767,121	4,157,545	992,273	20.8	609,576	14.7	100.0	100.0	100.0			
White	5,571,893	4,654,897	4,060,204	916,996	19.7	594,693	14.6	96.7	97.6	97.7	100.0	100.0	100.0
Negro	186,187	111,452	96,901	74,735	67.1	14,551	15.0	3.2	2.3	2.3			
Ind., Chi., Jap., and all other	1,314	772	440	542	70.2	332	75.5	(¹)	(¹)	(¹)			
Native white	4,893,196	4,057,652	3,602,304	835,544	20.6	455,348	12.6	85.0	85.1	86.6	87.8	87.2	88.7
Native parentage	3,669,122	3,033,259	2,651,440	635,863	21.0	381,819	14.4	63.7	63.6	63.8	65.9	65.2	65.3
Foreign parentage	838,251	671,275	612,518	166,976	24.9	58,757	9.6	14.6	14.1	14.7	15.0	14.4	15.1
Mixed parentage	385,823	353,118	338,346	32,705	9.3	14,772	4.4	6.7	7.4	8.1	6.9	7.6	8.3
Foreign-born white	678,697	597,245	457,900	81,452	13.6	139,345	30.4	11.8	12.5	11.0	12.2	12.8	11.3
Indiana.													
Total	2,930,390	2,700,876	2,516,462	229,514	8.5	184,414	7.3	100.0	100.0	100.0			
White	2,849,071	2,639,961	2,458,502	209,110	7.9	181,459	7.4	97.2	97.7	97.7	100.0	100.0	100.0
Negro	80,810	60,320	57,505	20,490	34.0	2,815	4.9	2.8	2.2	2.3			
Ind., Chi., Jap., and all other	509	595	455	—86	—14.5	140	30.8	(¹)	(¹)	(¹)			
Native white	2,698,203	2,480,639	2,316,642	217,564	8.8	163,998	7.1	92.1	91.8	92.1	94.7	94.0	94.2
Native parentage	2,329,544	2,130,088	1,952,194	199,456	9.4	177,894	9.1	79.5	78.9	77.6	81.8	80.7	79.4
Foreign parentage	227,066	211,008	215,785	16,058	7.6	—4,777	—2.2	7.7	7.8	8.6	8.0	8.0	8.8
Mixed parentage	141,593	139,543	148,662	2,050	1.5	—9,119	—6.1	4.8	5.2	5.9	5.0	5.3	6.0
Foreign-born white	150,868	159,322	141,861	—8,454	—5.3	17,461	12.3	5.1	5.9	5.6	5.3	6.0	5.8

¹ Less than one-tenth of 1 per cent.

COLOR OR RACE, NATIVITY, AND PARENTAGE.

41

TABLE 12.—COLOR OR RACE, NATIVITY, AND PARENTAGE, WITH DECENNIAL INCREASE, BY DIVISIONS AND STATES: 1920, 1910, AND 1900—Continued.

[A minus sign (−) denotes decrease.]

DIVISION OR STATE AND CLASS OF POPULATION.	POPULATION.			DECENNIAL INCREASE.				PER CENT DISTRIBUTION.					
				1910-1920		1900-1910		Total population.			White population.		
	1920	1910	1900	Number.	Per cent.	Number.	Per cent.	1920	1910	1900	1920	1910	1900
EAST NORTH CENTRAL—Continued.													
Illinois.													
Total	6,485,280	5,638,591	4,821,550	846,689	15.0	817,041	16.9	100.0	100.0	100.0			
White	6,299,333	5,526,962	4,734,873	772,371	14.0	792,089	16.7	97.1	98.0	98.2	100.0	100.0	100.0
Negro	182,274	109,049	85,078	73,225	67.1	23,971	28.2	2.8	1.9	1.8			
Ind., Chi., Jap., and all other	3,673	2,580	1,599	1,093	42.4	981	61.4	0.1	(1)	(1)			
Native white	5,092,382	4,324,402	3,770,238	767,980	17.8	554,164	14.7	78.5	76.7	78.2	80.8	78.2	79.6
Native parentage	3,066,563	2,600,555	2,271,765	466,008	17.9	328,790	14.5	47.3	46.1	47.1	48.7	47.1	48.0
Foreign parentage	1,467,036	1,232,155	1,070,211	234,881	19.1	161,944	15.1	22.6	21.9	22.2	23.3	22.3	22.6
Mixed parentage	558,783	491,692	428,262	67,091	13.6	63,430	14.8	8.6	8.7	8.9	8.9	8.9	9.0
Foreign-born white	1,206,951	1,202,560	964,635	4,391	0.4	237,925	24.7	18.6	21.3	20.0	19.2	21.8	20.4
Michigan.													
Total	3,668,412	2,810,173	2,420,982	858,239	30.5	389,191	16.1	100.0	100.0	100.0			
White	3,601,627	2,785,247	2,398,563	816,380	29.3	386,684	16.1	98.2	99.1	99.1	100.0	100.0	100.0
Negro	60,082	17,115	15,816	42,967	251.0	1,299	8.2	1.6	0.6	0.7			
Ind., Chi., Jap., and all other	6,703	7,811	6,603	−1,108	−14.2	1,208	18.3	0.2	0.3	0.3			
Native white	2,874,992	2,189,723	1,858,367	685,269	31.3	331,356	17.8	78.4	77.9	76.8	79.8	78.6	77.5
Native parentage	1,670,447	1,224,841	1,026,714	445,606	36.4	198,127	19.3	45.5	43.6	42.4	46.4	44.0	42.8
Foreign parentage	775,288	611,319	533,547	163,969	26.8	77,772	14.6	21.1	21.8	22.0	21.5	21.9	22.2
Mixed parentage	429,257	353,563	298,106	75,694	21.4	55,457	18.6	11.7	12.6	12.3	11.9	12.7	12.4
Foreign-born white	726,635	595,524	540,196	131,111	22.0	55,328	10.2	19.8	21.2	22.3	20.2	21.4	22.5
Wisconsin.													
Total	2,632,067	2,333,860	2,069,042	298,207	12.8	264,818	12.8	100.0	100.0	100.0			
White	2,616,938	2,320,555	2,057,911	296,383	12.8	262,644	12.8	99.4	99.4	99.5	100.0	100.0	100.0
Negro	5,201	2,900	2,542	2,301	79.3	358	14.1	0.2	0.1	0.1			
Ind., Chi., Jap., and all other	9,928	10,405	8,589	−477	−4.6	1,816	21.1	0.4	0.4	0.4			
Native white	2,156,810	1,807,986	1,542,206	348,824	19.3	265,780	17.2	81.9	77.5	74.5	82.4	77.9	74.9
Native parentage	1,054,694	763,225	585,903	291,469	38.2	177,322	30.3	40.1	32.7	28.3	40.3	32.9	28.5
Foreign parentage	736,051	724,258	678,723	11,793	1.6	45,535	6.7	28.0	31.0	32.8	28.1	31.2	33.0
Mixed parentage	366,065	320,503	277,580	45,562	14.2	42,923	15.5	13.9	13.7	13.4	14.0	13.8	13.5
Foreign-born white	460,128	512,569	515,705	−52,441	−10.2	−3,136	−0.6	17.5	22.0	24.9	17.6	22.1	25.1
WEST NORTH CENTRAL.													
Minnesota													
Total	2,387,125	2,075,708	1,751,394	311,417	15.0	324,314	18.5	100.0	100.0	100.0			
White	2,368,936	2,059,227	1,737,036	309,709	15.0	322,191	18.5	99.2	99.2	99.2	100.0	100.0	100.0
Negro	8,809	7,084	4,959	1,725	24.4	2,125	42.9	0.4	0.3	0.3			
Ind., Chi., Jap., and all other	9,380	9,397	9,399	−17	−0.2	−2	(2)	0.4	0.5	0.5			
Native white	1,882,772	1,516,217	1,232,101	366,555	24.2	284,116	23.1	78.9	73.0	70.3	79.5	73.6	70.9
Native parentage	827,027	575,081	425,780	252,546	43.9	149,301	35.1	34.7	27.7	24.3	34.9	27.9	24.5
Foreign parentage	708,126	667,400	597,800	40,666	6.1	69,660	11.7	29.7	32.2	34.1	29.9	32.4	34.4
Mixed parentage	347,019	273,676	208,521	73,343	26.8	65,155	31.2	14.5	13.2	11.9	14.6	13.3	12.0
Foreign-born white	486,164	543,010	504,935	−56,846	−10.5	38,075	7.5	20.4	26.2	28.8	20.5	26.4	29.1
Iowa.													
Total	2,404,021	2,224,771	2,231,853	179,250	8.1	−7,082	−0.3	100.0	100.0	100.0			
White	2,384,181	2,209,191	2,218,667	174,990	7.9	−9,476	−0.4	99.2	99.3	99.4	100.0	100.0	100.0
Negro	19,005	14,973	12,693	4,032	26.9	2,280	18.0	0.8	0.7	0.6			
Ind., Chi., Jap., and all other	835	607	493	228	37.6	114	23.1	(1)	(1)	(1)			
Native white	2,158,534	1,935,707	1,912,885	222,827	11.5	22,822	1.2	89.8	87.0	85.7	90.5	87.8	86.2
Native parentage	1,528,553	1,303,526	1,261,068	225,027	17.3	42,458	3.4	63.6	58.6	56.5	64.1	59.0	56.8
Foreign parentage	376,710	395,541	419,123	−18,831	−4.8	−23,582	−5.6	15.7	17.8	18.8	15.8	17.9	18.9
Mixed parentage	253,271	236,640	232,694	16,631	7.0	3,946	1.7	10.5	10.6	10.4	10.6	10.7	10.5
Foreign-born white	225,647	273,484	305,782	−47,837	−17.5	−32,298	−10.6	9.4	12.3	13.7	9.5	12.4	13.8
Missouri.													
Total	3,404,055	3,293,335	3,106,665	110,720	3.4	186,670	6.0	100.0	100.0	100.0			
White	3,225,044	3,134,932	2,944,843	90,112	2.9	190,089	6.5	94.7	95.2	94.8	100.0	100.0	100.0
Negro	178,241	157,452	161,234	20,789	13.2	−3,782	−2.3	5.2	4.8	5.2			
Ind., Chi., Jap., and all other	770	951	588	−181	−19.0	363	61.7	(1)	(1)	(1)			
Native white	3,039,018	2,906,036	2,729,068	132,982	4.6	176,968	6.5	89.3	88.2	87.8	94.2	92.7	92.7
Native parentage	2,536,936	2,387,835	2,204,874	149,101	6.2	182,961	8.3	74.5	72.5	71.0	78.7	76.2	74.9
Foreign parentage	300,064	312,027	319,110	−11,963	−3.8	−7,083	−2.2	8.8	9.5	10.3	9.3	10.0	10.8
Mixed parentage	202,018	206,174	205,084	−4,156	−2.0	1,090	0.5	5.9	6.3	6.6	6.3	6.6	7.0
Foreign-born white	186,026	228,896	215,775	−42,870	−18.7	13,121	6.1	5.5	7.0	6.9	5.8	7.3	7.3
North Dakota.													
Total	646,872	577,056	319,146	69,816	12.1	257,910	80.8	100.0	100.0	100.0			
White	639,954	569,855	311,712	70,099	12.3	258,143	82.8	98.9	98.8	97.7	100.0	100.0	100.0
Negro	467	617	286	−150	−24.3	331	115.7	0.1	0.1	0.1			
Ind., Chi., Jap., and all other	6,451	6,584	7,148	−133	−2.0	−564	−7.9	1.0	1.1	2.2			
Native white	508,451	413,697	199,122	94,754	22.9	214,575	107.8	78.6	71.7	62.4	79.5	72.6	63.9
Native parentage	207,966	162,461	65,811	45,505	28.0	96,650	146.9	32.1	28.2	20.6	32.5	28.5	21.1
Foreign parentage	203,973	180,054	102,680	23,919	13.3	77,374	75.4	31.5	31.2	32.2	31.9	31.6	32.9
Mixed parentage	96,512	71,182	30,631	25,330	35.6	40,551	132.4	14.9	12.3	9.6	15.1	12.5	9.8
Foreign-born white	131,503	156,158	112,590	−24,655	−15.8	43,568	38.7	20.3	27.1	35.3	20.5	27.4	36.1

1 Less than one-tenth of 1 per cent.   2 Decrease of less than one-tenth of 1 per cent.

42

POPULATION.

TABLE 12.—COLOR OR RACE, NATIVITY, AND PARENTAGE, WITH DECENNIAL INCREASE, BY DIVISIONS AND STATES: 1920, 1910, AND 1900—Continued.

[A minus sign (—) denotes decrease.]

DIVISION OR STATE AND CLASS OF POPULATION.	POPULATION.			DECENNIAL INCREASE.				PER CENT DISTRIBUTION.					
				1910-1920		1900-1910		Total population.			White population.		
	1920	1910	1900	Number.	Per cent.	Number.	Per cent.	1920	1910	1900	1920	1910	1900
WEST NORTH CENTRAL—Continued.													
South Dakota.													
Total	636,547	583,888	401,570	52,659	9.0	182,318	45.4	100.0	100.0	100.0			
White	619,147	563,771	380,714	55,376	9.8	183,057	48.1	97.3	96.6	94.8	100.0	100.0	100.0
Negro	832	817	465	15	1.8	352	75.7	0.1	0.1	0.1			
Ind., Chi., Jap., and all other	16,568	19,300	20,391	-2,732	-14.2	-1,091	-5.4	2.6	3.3	5.1			
Native white	536,756	463,143	292,385	73,613	15.9	170,758	58.4	84.3	79.3	72.8	86.7	82.2	76.8
Native parentage	308,598	245,652	136,191	62,946	25.6	109,461	80.4	48.5	42.1	33.9	49.8	43.6	35.8
Foreign parentage	141,341	143,045	110,915	-1,704	-1.2	32,130	29.0	22.2	24.5	27.6	22.8	25.4	29.1
Mixed parentage	86,817	74,446	45,279	12,371	16.6	29,167	64.4	13.6	12.8	11.3	14.0	13.2	11.9
Foreign-born white	82,391	100,628	88,329	-18,237	-18.1	12,299	13.9	12.9	17.2	22.0	13.3	17.8	23.2
Nebraska.													
Total	1,296,372	1,192,214	1,066,300	104,158	8.7	125,914	11.8	100.0	100.0	100.0			
White	1,279,219	1,180,293	1,056,526	98,926	8.4	123,767	11.7	98.7	99.0	99.1	100.0	100.0	100.0
Negro	13,242	7,689	6,269	5,553	72.2	1,420	22.7	1.0	0.6	0.6			
Ind., Chi., Jap., and all other	3,911	4,232	3,505	-321	-7.6	727	20.7	0.3	0.4	0.3			
Native white	1,129,567	1,004,428	879,409	125,139	12.5	125,019	14.2	87.1	84.2	82.5	88.3	85.1	83.2
Native parentage	757,064	642,075	553,524	114,989	17.9	88,551	16.0	58.4	53.9	51.9	59.2	54.4	52.4
Foreign parentage	231,948	234,670	221,983	-2,722	-1.2	12,687	5.7	17.9	19.7	20.8	18.1	19.9	21.0
Mixed parentage	140,555	127,683	103,902	12,872	10.0	23,781	22.9	10.8	10.7	9.7	11.0	10.8	9.8
Foreign-born white	149,652	175,865	177,117	-26,213	-14.9	-1,252	-0.7	11.5	14.8	16.6	11.7	14.9	16.8
Kansas.													
Total	1,769,257	1,690,949	1,470,495	78,308	4.6	220,454	15.0	100.0	100.0	100.0			
White	1,708,906	1,634,352	1,416,319	74,554	4.6	218,033	15.4	96.6	96.7	96.3	100.0	100.0	100.0
Negro	57,925	54,030	52,003	3,895	7.2	2,027	3.9	3.3	3.2	3.5			
Ind., Chi., Jap., and all other	2,426	2,567	2,173	-141	-5.5	394	18.1	0.1	0.2	0.1			
Native white	1,598,328	1,499,162	1,289,742	99,166	6.6	209,420	16.2	90.3	88.7	87.7	93.5	91.7	91.1
Native parentage	1,308,804	1,207,057	1,013,655	101,747	8.4	193,402	19.1	74.0	71.4	68.9	76.6	73.9	71.6
Foreign parentage	163,964	169,906	161,506	-5,942	-3.5	8,400	5.2	9.3	10.0	11.0	9.6	10.4	11.4
Mixed parentage	125,560	122,199	114,581	3,361	2.8	7,618	6.6	7.1	7.2	7.8	7.3	7.5	8.1
Foreign-born white	110,578	135,190	126,577	-24,612	-18.2	8,613	6.8	6.2	8.0	8.6	6.5	8.3	8.9
SOUTH ATLANTIC.													
Delaware.													
Total	223,003	202,322	184,735	20,681	10.2	17,587	9.5	100.0	100.0	100.0			
White	192,615	171,102	153,977	21,513	12.6	17,125	11.1	86.4	84.6	83.4	100.0	100.0	100.0
Negro	30,335	31,181	30,697	-846	-2.7	484	1.6	13.6	15.4	16.6			
Ind., Chi., and Jap	53	39	61	14	(1)	-22	(1)	(2)	(2)	(2)			
Native white	172,805	153,682	140,248	19,123	12.4	13,434	9.6	77.5	76.0	75.9	89.7	89.8	91.1
Native parentage	139,876	127,809	118,029	12,067	9.4	9,780	8.3	62.7	63.2	63.9	72.6	74.7	76.7
Foreign parentage	23,288	17,566	14,767	5,722	32.6	2,799	19.0	10.4	8.7	8.0	12.1	10.3	9.6
Mixed parentage	9,641	8,307	7,452	1,334	16.1	855	11.5	4.3	4.1	4.0	5.0	4.9	4.8
Foreign-born white	19,810	17,420	13,729	2,390	13.7	3,691	26.9	8.9	8.6	7.4	10.3	10.2	8.9
Maryland.													
Total	1,449,661	1,295,346	1,188,044	154,315	11.9	107,302	9.0	100.0	100.0	100.0			
White	1,204,737	1,062,639	952,424	142,098	13.4	110,215	11.6	83.1	82.0	80.2	100.0	100.0	100.0
Negro	244,479	232,250	235,064	12,229	5.3	-2,814	-1.2	16.9	17.9	19.8			
Ind., Chi., Jap., and all other	445	457	556	-12	-2.6	-99	-17.8	(2)	(2)	(2)			
Native white	1,102,560	958,465	859,280	144,095	15.0	99,185	11.5	76.1	74.0	72.3	91.5	90.2	90.2
Native parentage	893,088	766,627	680,049	126,461	16.4	86,578	12.7	61.6	59.2	57.2	74.1	72.1	71.4
Foreign parentage	143,203	130,321	119,158	12,882	9.9	11,133	9.3	9.9	10.1	10.0	11.9	12.3	12.5
Mixed parentage	66,269	61,517	60,043	4,752	7.7	1,474	2.5	4.6	4.7	5.1	5.5	5.8	6.3
Foreign-born white	102,177	104,174	93,144	-1,997	-1.9	11,030	11.8	7.0	8.0	7.8	8.5	9.8	9.8
District of Columbia.													
Total	437,571	331,069	278,718	106,502	32.2	52,351	18.8	100.0	100.0	100.0			
White	326,860	236,128	191,532	90,732	38.4	44,596	23.3	74.7	71.3	68.7	100.0	100.0	100.0
Negro	109,966	94,446	86,702	15,520	16.4	7,744	8.9	25.1	28.5	31.1			
Ind., Chi., Jap., and all other	745	495	484	250	50.5	11	2.3	0.2	0.1	0.2			
Native white	298,312	211,777	172,012	86,535	40.9	39,765	23.1	68.2	64.0	61.7	91.3	89.7	89.8
Native parentage	239,488	166,711	134,073	72,777	43.7	32,638	24.3	54.7	50.4	48.1	73.3	70.6	70.0
Foreign parentage	35,129	26,522	22,449	8,607	32.5	4,073	18.1	8.0	8.0	8.1	10.7	11.2	11.7
Mixed parentage	23,695	18,544	15,490	5,151	27.8	3,054	19.7	5.4	5.6	5.6	7.2	7.9	8.1
Foreign-born white	28,548	24,351	19,520	4,197	17.2	4,831	24.7	6.5	7.4	7.0	8.7	10.3	10.2
Virginia.													
Total	2,309,187	2,061,612	1,854,184	247,575	12.0	207,428	11.2	100.0	100.0	100.0			
White	1,617,909	1,389,809	1,192,855	228,100	16.4	196,954	16.5	70.1	67.4	64.3	100.0	100.0	100.0
Negro	690,017	671,096	660,722	18,921	2.8	10,374	1.6	29.9	32.6	35.6			
Ind., Chi., Jap., and all other	1,261	707	607	554	78.4	100	16.5	0.1	(2)	(2)			
Native white	1,587,124	1,363,181	1,173,787	223,943	16.4	189,394	16.1	68.7	66.1	63.3	98.1	98.1	98.4
Native parentage	1,534,494	1,325,238	1,141,213	209,256	15.8	184,025	16.1	66.5	64.3	61.5	94.8	95.4	95.7
Foreign parentage	30,514	21,613	17,099	8,901	41.2	4,514	26.4	1.3	1.0	0.9	1.9	1.6	1.4
Mixed parentage	22,116	16,330	15,475	5,786	35.4	855	5.5	1.0	0.8	0.8	1.4	1.2	1.3
Foreign-born white	30,785	26,628	19,068	4,157	15.6	7,560	39.6	1.3	1.3	1.0	1.9	1.9	1.6

1 Per cent not shown, base being less than 100.　　2 Less than one-tenth of 1 per cent.

COLOR OR RACE, NATIVITY, AND PARENTAGE.   43

TABLE 12.—COLOR OR RACE, NATIVITY, AND PARENTAGE, WITH DECENNIAL INCREASE, BY DIVISIONS AND STATES: 1920, 1910, AND 1900—Continued.

[A minus sign (−) denotes decrease.]

DIVISION OR STATE AND CLASS OF POPULATION.	POPULATION.			DECENNIAL INCREASE.				PER CENT DISTRIBUTION.					
				1910–1920		1900–1910		Total population.			White population.		
	1920	1910	1900	Number.	Per cent.	Number.	Per cent.	1920	1910	1900	1920	1910	1900
SOUTH ATLANTIC—Continued.													
West Virginia.													
Total	1,463,701	1,221,119	958,800	242,582	19.9	262,319	27.4	100.0	100.0	100.0			
White	1,377,235	1,156,817	915,233	220,418	19.1	241,584	26.4	94.1	94.7	95.5	100.0	100.0	100.0
Negro	86,345	64,173	43,499	22,172	34.6	20,674	47.5	5.9	5.3	4.5			
Ind., Chi., Jap., and all other	121	129	68	−8	−6.2	61	(1)	(2)	(2)	(2)			
Native white	1,315,329	1,099,745	892,854	215,584	19.6	206,891	23.2	89.9	90.1	93.1	95.5	95.1	97.6
Native parentage	1,232,857	1,042,107	843,981	190,750	18.3	198,126	23.5	84.2	85.3	88.0	89.5	90.1	92.2
Foreign parentage	56,625	35,407	26,838	21,218	59.9	8,569	31.9	3.9	2.9	2.8	4.1	3.1	2.9
Mixed parentage	25,847	22,231	22,035	3,616	16.3	196	0.9	1.8	1.8	2.3	1.9	1.9	2.4
Foreign-born white	61,906	57,072	22,379	4,834	8.5	34,693	155.0	4.2	4.7	2.3	4.5	4.9	2.4
North Carolina.													
Total	2,559,123	2,206,287	1,893,810	352,836	16.0	312,477	16.5	100.0	100.0	100.0			
White	1,783,779	1,500,511	1,263,603	283,268	18.9	236,908	18.7	69.7	68.0	66.7	100.0	100.0	100.0
Negro	763,407	697,843	624,469	65,564	9.4	73,374	11.7	29.8	31.6	33.0			
Ind., Chi., Jap., and all other	11,937	7,933	5,738	4,004	50.5	2,195	38.3	0.5	0.4	0.3			
Native white	1,776,080	1,494,569	1,259,209	282,111	18.7	235,360	18.7	69.4	67.7	66.5	99.6	99.6	99.7
Native parentage	1,765,203	1,485,718	1,250,811	279,485	18.8	234,907	18.8	69.0	67.8	66.0	99.0	99.0	99.0
Foreign parentage	5,737	3,886	3,321	1,851	47.6	565	17.0	0.2	0.2	0.2	0.3	0.3	0.3
Mixed parentage	5,740	4,965	5,077	775	15.6	−112	−2.2	0.2	0.2	0.3	0.3	0.3	0.4
Foreign-born white	7,099	5,942	4,394	1,157	19.5	1,548	35.2	0.3	0.3	0.2	0.4	0.4	0.3
South Carolina.													
Total	1,683,724	1,515,400	1,340,316	168,324	11.1	175,084	13.1	100.0	100.0	100.0			
White	818,538	679,161	557,807	139,377	20.5	121,354	21.8	48.6	44.8	41.6	100.0	100.0	100.0
Negro	864,719	835,843	782,321	28,876	3.5	53,522	6.8	51.4	55.2	58.4			
Ind., Chi., Jap., and all other	467	396	188	71	17.9	208	110.6	(2)	(2)	(2)			
Native white	812,137	673,107	552,436	139,030	20.7	120,671	21.8	48.2	44.4	41.2	99.2	99.1	99.0
Native parentage	799,418	661,970	540,766	137,448	20.8	121,204	22.4	47.5	43.7	40.3	97.7	97.5	96.9
Foreign parentage	7,025	5,759	5,936	1,266	22.0	−177	−3.0	0.4	0.4	0.4	0.9	0.8	1.1
Mixed parentage	5,694	5,378	5,734	316	5.9	−356	−6.2	0.3	0.4	0.4	0.7	0.8	1.0
Foreign-born white	6,401	6,054	5,371	347	5.7	683	12.7	0.4	0.4	0.4	0.8	0.9	1.0
Georgia.													
Total	2,895,832	2,609,121	2,216,331	286,711	11.0	392,790	17.7	100.0	100.0	100.0			
White	1,689,114	1,431,802	1,181,294	257,312	18.0	250,508	21.2	58.3	54.9	53.3	100.0	100.0	100.0
Negro	1,206,365	1,176,987	1,034,813	29,378	2.5	142,174	13.7	41.7	45.1	46.7			
Ind., Chi., Jap., and all other	353	332	224	21	6.3	108	48.2	(2)	(2)	(2)			
Native white	1,672,928	1,416,730	1,169,273	256,198	18.1	247,457	21.2	57.8	54.3	52.8	99.0	98.9	99.0
Native parentage	1,642,697	1,391,058	1,144,360	251,639	18.1	246,698	21.6	56.7	53.3	51.6	97.3	97.2	96.9
Foreign parentage	16,371	13,232	12,006	3,139	23.7	1,226	10.2	0.6	0.5	0.5	1.0	0.9	1.0
Mixed parentage	13,860	12,440	12,907	1,420	11.4	−467	−3.6	0.5	0.5	0.6	0.8	0.9	1.1
Foreign-born white	16,186	15,072	12,021	1,114	7.4	3,051	25.4	0.6	0.6	0.5	1.0	1.1	1.0
Florida.													
Total	968,470	752,619	528,542	215,851	28.7	224,077	42.4	100.0	100.0	100.0			
White	638,153	443,634	297,333	194,519	43.8	146,301	49.2	65.9	58.9	56.3	100.0	100.0	100.0
Negro	329,487	308,669	230,730	20,818	6.7	77,939	33.8	34.0	41.0	43.7			
Ind., Chi., Jap., and all other	830	316	479	514	162.7	−163	−34.0	0.1	(2)	0.1			
Native white	595,145	409,792	278,076	185,353	45.2	131,716	47.4	61.5	54.4	52.6	93.3	92.4	93.5
Native parentage	532,295	373,967	254,032	158,328	42.3	119,935	47.2	55.0	49.7	48.1	83.4	84.3	85.4
Foreign parentage	35,751	20,145	12,267	15,606	77.5	7,878	64.2	3.7	2.7	2.3	5.6	4.5	4.1
Mixed parentage	27,099	15,680	11,777	11,419	72.8	3,903	33.1	2.8	2.1	2.2	4.2	3.5	4.0
Foreign-born white	43,008	33,842	19,257	9,166	27.1	14,585	75.7	4.4	4.5	3.6	6.7	7.6	6.5
EAST SOUTH CENTRAL.													
Kentucky.													
Total	2,416,630	2,289,905	2,147,174	126,725	5.5	142,731	6.6	100.0	100.0	100.0			
White	2,180,560	2,027,951	1,862,309	152,609	7.5	165,642	8.9	90.2	88.6	86.7	100.0	100.0	100.0
Negro	235,938	261,656	284,706	−25,718	−9.8	−23,050	−8.1	9.8	11.4	13.3			
Ind., Chi., Jap., and all other	132	298	159	−166	−55.7	139	87.4	(2)	(2)	(2)			
Native white	2,149,780	1,987,898	1,812,176	161,882	8.1	175,722	9.7	89.0	86.8	84.4	98.6	98.0	97.3
Native parentage	2,039,134	1,863,194	1,673,413	175,940	9.4	189,781	11.3	84.4	81.4	77.9	93.5	91.9	89.9
Foreign parentage	65,931	76,523	86,236	−10,592	−13.8	−9,713	−11.3	2.7	3.3	4.0	3.0	3.8	4.6
Mixed parentage	44,715	48,181	52,527	−3,466	−7.2	−4,346	−8.3	1.9	2.1	2.4	2.1	2.4	2.8
Foreign-born white	30,780	40,053	50,133	−9,273	−23.2	−10,080	−20.1	1.3	1.7	2.3	1.4	2.0	2.7
Tennessee.													
Total	2,337,885	2,184,789	2,020,616	153,096	7.0	164,173	8.1	100.0	100.0	100.0			
White	1,885,993	1,711,432	1,540,186	174,561	10.2	171,246	11.1	80.7	78.3	76.2	100.0	100.0	100.0
Negro	451,758	473,088	480,243	−21,330	−4.5	−7,155	−1.5	19.3	21.7	23.8			
Ind., Chi., Jap., and all other	134	269	187	−135	−50.2	82	43.9	(2)	(2)	(2)			
Native white	1,870,515	1,692,973	1,522,600	177,542	10.5	170,373	11.2	80.0	77.5	75.4	99.2	98.9	98.9
Native parentage	1,832,757	1,654,606	1,481,636	178,151	10.8	172,970	11.7	78.4	75.7	73.3	97.2	96.7	96.2
Foreign parentage	20,423	20,572	21,281	−149	−0.7	−700	−3.3	0.9	0.9	1.1	1.1	1.2	1.4
Mixed parentage	17,335	17,795	19,683	−460	−2.6	−1,888	−9.6	0.7	0.8	1.0	0.9	1.0	1.3
Foreign-born white	15,478	18,459	17,586	−2,981	−16.1	873	5.0	0.7	0.8	0.9	0.8	1.1	1.1

[1] Per cent not shown, base being less than 100.   [2] Less than one-tenth of 1 per cent.

POPULATION.

TABLE 12.—COLOR OR RACE, NATIVITY, AND PARENTAGE, WITH DECENNIAL INCREASE, BY DIVISIONS AND STATES: 1920, 1910, AND 1900—Continued.

[A minus sign (−) denotes decrease.]

DIVISION OR STATE AND CLASS OF POPULATION.	POPULATION.			DECENNIAL INCREASE.				PER CENT DISTRIBUTION.					
				1910-1920		1900-1910		Total population.			White population.		
	1920	1910	1900	Number.	Per cent.	Number.	Per cent.	1920	1910	1900	1920	1910	1900
EAST SOUTH CENTRAL—Con.													
Alabama.													
Total	2,348,174	2,138,093	1,828,697	210,081	9.8	309,396	16.9	100.0	100.0	100.0			
White	1,447,032	1,228,832	1,001,152	218,200	17.8	227,680	22.7	61.6	57.5	54.7	100.0	100.0	100.0
Negro	900,652	908,282	827,307	−7,630	−0.8	80,975	9.8	38.4	42.5	45.2			
Ind., Chi., Jap., and all other	490	979	238	−489	−49.9	741	311.3	(1)	(1)	(1)			
Native white	1,429,370	1,209,876	980,814	219,494	18.1	223,062	22.6	60.9	56.6	54.0	98.8	98.5	98.6
Native parentage	1,394,129	1,177,459	956,658	216,670	18.4	220,801	23.1	59.4	55.1	52.3	96.3	95.8	95.6
Foreign parentage	19,591	17,667	15,186	1,924	10.9	2,481	16.3	0.8	0.8	0.8	1.4	1.4	1.5
Mixed parentage	15,650	14,750	14,970	900	6.1	−220	−1.5	0.7	0.7	0.8	1.1	1.2	1.5
Foreign-born white	17,662	18,956	14,338	−1,294	−6.8	4,618	32.2	0.8	0.9	0.8	1.2	1.5	1.4
Mississippi.													
Total	1,790,618	1,797,114	1,551,270	−6,496	−0.4	245,844	15.8	100.0	100.0	100.0			
White	853,962	786,111	641,200	67,851	8.6	144,911	22.6	47.7	43.7	41.3	100.0	100.0	100.0
Negro	935,184	1,009,487	907,630	−74,303	−7.4	101,857	11.2	52.2	56.2	58.5			
Ind., Chi., Jap., and all other	1,472	1,516	2,440	−44	−2.9	−924	−37.9	0.1	0.1	0.2			
Native white	845,943	776,722	633,575	69,221	8.9	143,147	22.6	47.2	43.2	40.8	99.1	98.8	98.8
Native parentage	826,762	757,233	614,067	69,529	9.2	143,166	23.3	46.2	42.1	39.6	96.8	96.3	95.8
Foreign parentage	9,539	9,153	8,345	386	4.2	808	9.7	0.5	0.5	0.5	1.1	1.2	1.3
Mixed parentage	9,642	10,336	11,163	−694	−6.7	−827	−7.4	0.5	0.6	0.7	1.1	1.3	1.7
Foreign-born white	8,019	9,389	7,625	−1,370	−14.6	1,764	23.1	0.4	0.5	0.5	0.9	1.2	1.2
WEST SOUTH CENTRAL.													
Arkansas.													
Total	1,752,204	1,574,449	1,311,564	177,755	11.3	262,885	20.0	100.0	100.0	100.0			
White	1,279,757	1,131,026	944,580	148,731	13.2	186,446	19.7	73.0	71.8	72.0	100.0	100.0	100.0
Negro	472,220	442,891	366,856	29,329	6.6	76,035	20.7	27.0	28.1	28.0			
Ind., Chi., Jap., and all other	227	532	128	−305	−57.3	404	315.6	(1)	(1)	(1)			
Native white	1,265,782	1,114,117	930,394	151,665	13.6	183,723	19.7	72.2	70.8	70.9	98.9	98.5	98.5
Native parentage	1,226,692	1,077,509	897,608	149,183	13.8	179,841	20.0	70.0	68.4	68.4	95.9	95.3	95.0
Foreign parentage	19,030	18,387	15,199	643	3.5	3,188	21.0	1.1	1.2	1.2	1.5	1.6	1.6
Mixed parentage	20,060	18,221	17,527	1,839	10.1	694	4.0	1.1	1.2	1.3	1.6	1.6	1.9
Foreign-born white	13,975	16,909	14,186	−2,934	−17.4	2,723	19.2	0.8	1.1	1.1	1.1	1.5	1.5
Louisiana.													
Total	1,798,509	1,656,388	1,381,625	142,121	8.6	274,763	19.9	100.0	100.0	100.0			
White	1,096,611	941,086	729,612	155,525	16.5	211,474	29.0	61.0	56.8	52.8	100.0	100.0	100.0
Negro	700,257	713,874	650,804	−13,617	−1.9	63,070	9.7	38.9	43.1	47.1			
Ind., Chi., Jap., and all other	1,641	1,428	1,209	213	14.9	219	18.1	0.1	0.1	0.1			
Native white	1,051,740	889,304	677,759	162,436	18.3	211,545	31.2	58.5	53.7	49.1	95.9	94.5	92.9
Native parentage	941,724	776,587	569,962	165,137	21.3	206,625	36.3	52.4	46.9	41.3	85.9	82.5	78.1
Foreign parentage	67,016	68,389	63,317	−1,373	−2.0	5,072	8.0	3.7	4.1	4.6	6.1	7.3	8.7
Mixed parentage	43,000	44,328	44,480	−1,328	−3.0	−152	−0.3	2.4	2.7	3.2	3.9	4.7	6.1
Foreign-born white	44,871	51,782	51,853	−6,911	−13.3	−71	−0.1	2.5	3.1	3.8	4.1	5.5	7.1
Oklahoma.[2]													
Total	2,028,283	1,657,155	790,391	371,128	22.4	866,764	109.7	100.0	100.0	100.0			
White	1,821,194	1,444,531	670,204	376,663	26.1	774,327	115.5	89.8	87.2	84.8	100.0	100.0	100.0
Negro	149,408	137,612	55,684	11,796	8.6	81,928	147.1	7.4	8.3	7.0			
Ind., Chi., Jap., and all other	57,681	75,012	64,503	−17,331	−23.1	10,500	16.3	2.8	4.5	8.2			
Native white	1,781,226	1,404,447	649,814	376,779	26.8	754,633	116.1	87.8	84.8	82.2	97.8	97.2	97.0
Native parentage	1,679,107	1,310,403	601,552	368,704	28.1	708,851	117.8	82.8	79.1	76.1	92.2	90.7	89.8
Foreign parentage	53,063	49,877	24,683	3,206	6.4	25,194	102.1	2.6	3.0	3.1	2.9	3.5	3.7
Mixed parentage	49,036	44,167	23,579	4,869	11.0	20,588	87.3	2.4	2.7	3.0	2.7	3.1	3.5
Foreign-born white	39,968	40,084	20,390	−116	−0.3	19,694	96.6	2.0	2.4	2.6	2.2	2.8	3.0
Texas.													
Total	4,663,228	3,896,542	3,048,710	766,686	19.7	847,832	27.8	100.0	100.0	100.0			
White	3,918,165	3,204,848	2,426,669	713,317	22.3	778,179	32.1	84.0	82.2	79.6	100.0	100.0	100.0
Negro	741,694	690,049	620,722	51,645	7.5	69,327	11.2	15.9	17.7	20.4			
Ind., Chi., Jap., and all other	3,369	1,645	1,319	1,724	104.8	326	24.7	0.1	(1)	(1)			
Native white	3,557,646	2,964,864	2,249,088	592,782	20.0	715,776	31.8	76.3	76.1	73.8	90.8	92.5	92.7
Native parentage	3,112,262	2,602,950	1,959,762	509,312	19.6	643,188	32.8	66.7	66.8	64.3	79.4	81.2	80.8
Foreign parentage	276,670	227,379	182,582	49,291	21.7	44,797	24.5	5.9	5.8	6.0	7.1	7.1	7.5
Mixed parentage	168,714	134,535	106,744	34,179	25.4	27,791	26.0	3.6	3.5	3.5	4.3	4.2	4.4
Foreign-born white	360,519	239,984	177,581	120,535	50.2	62,403	35.1	7.7	6.2	5.8	9.2	7.5	7.3
MOUNTAIN.													
Montana.													
Total	548,889	376,053	243,329	172,836	46.0	132,724	54.5	100.0	100.0	100.0			
White	534,260	360,580	226,283	173,680	48.2	134,297	59.3	97.3	95.9	93.0	100.0	100.0	100.0
Negro	1,658	1,834	1,523	−176	−9.6	311	20.4	0.3	0.5	0.6			
Ind., Chi., Jap., and all other	12,971	13,639	15,523	−668	−4.9	−1,884	−12.1	2.4	3.6	6.4			
Native white	440,640	268,936	163,910	171,704	63.8	105,026	64.1	80.3	71.5	67.4	82.5	74.6	72.4
Native parentage	275,803	162,127	92,937	113,676	70.1	69,190	74.4	50.2	43.1	38.2	51.6	45.0	41.1
Foreign parentage	101,918	68,606	46,246	33,312	48.6	22,360	48.4	18.6	18.2	19.0	19.1	19.0	20.6
Mixed parentage	62,919	38,203	24,727	24,716	64.7	13,476	54.5	11.5	10.2	10.2	11.8	10.6	10.4
Foreign-born white	93,620	91,644	62,373	1,976	2.2	29,271	46.9	17.1	24.4	25.6	17.5	25.4	27.6

1 Less than one-tenth of 1 per cent.

2 Includes population of Indian Territory for 1900.

COLOR OR RACE, NATIVITY, AND PARENTAGE.   45

TABLE 12.—COLOR OR RACE, NATIVITY, AND PARENTAGE, WITH DECENNIAL INCREASE, BY DIVISIONS AND STATES: 1920, 1910, AND 1900—Continued.

[A minus sign (−) denotes decrease.]

DIVISION OR STATE AND CLASS OF POPULATION.	POPULATION.			DECENNIAL INCREASE.				PER CENT DISTRIBUTION.					
				1910–1920		1900–1910		Total population.			White population.		
	1920	1910	1900	Number.	Per cent.	Number.	Per cent.	1920	1910	1900	1920	1910	1900
MOUNTAIN—Continued.													
Idaho.													
Total	431,866	325,594	161,772	106,272	32.6	163,822	101.3	100.0	100.0	100.0			
White	425,668	319,221	154,495	106,447	33.3	164,726	106.6	98.6	98.0	95.5	100.0	100.0	100.0
Negro	920	651	293	269	41.3	358	122.2	0.2	0.2	0.2			
Ind., Chi., Jap., and all other	5,278	5,722	6,984	−444	−7.8	−1,262	−18.1	1.2	1.8	4.3			
Native white	380,705	278,794	132,605	107,911	38.7	146,189	110.2	89.5	85.6	82.0	90.8	87.3	85.8
Native parentage	294,252	203,599	89,851	90,653	44.5	113,748	126.6	68.1	62.5	55.5	69.1	63.8	58.2
Foreign parentage	47,920	40,075	23,373	7,845	19.6	16,702	71.5	11.1	12.3	14.4	11.3	12.6	15.1
Mixed parentage	44,533	35,120	19,381	9,413	26.8	15,739	81.2	10.3	10.8	12.0	10.5	11.0	12.5
Foreign-born white	38,063	40,427	21,890	−1,464	−3.6	18,537	84.7	9.0	12.4	13.5	9.2	12.7	14.2
Wyoming.													
Total	194,402	145,965	92,531	48,437	33.2	53,434	57.7	100.0	100.0	100.0			
White	190,146	140,318	89,051	49,828	35.5	51,207	57.6	97.8	96.1	96.2	100.0	100.0	100.0
Negro	1,375	2,235	940	−860	−38.5	1,295	137.8	0.7	1.5	1.0			
Ind., Chi., Jap., and all other	2,881	3,412	2,540	−531	−15.6	872	34.3	1.5	2.3	2.7			
Native white	164,891	113,200	72,469	51,691	45.7	40,731	56.2	84.8	77.6	78.3	86.7	80.7	81.4
Native parentage	122,884	80,696	47,982	42,188	52.3	32,714	68.2	63.2	55.3	51.9	64.6	57.5	53.9
Foreign parentage	25,234	19,751	15,450	5,483	27.8	4,301	27.8	13.0	13.5	16.7	13.3	14.1	17.4
Mixed parentage	16,773	12,753	9,037	4,020	31.5	3,716	41.1	8.6	8.7	9.8	8.8	9.1	10.1
Foreign-born white	25,255	27,118	16,582	−1,863	−6.9	10,536	63.5	13.0	18.6	17.9	13.3	19.3	18.6
Colorado.													
Total	939,629	799,024	539,700	140,605	17.6	259,324	48.0	100.0	100.0	100.0			
White	924,103	783,415	529,046	140,688	18.0	254,369	48.1	98.3	98.0	98.0	100.0	100.0	100.0
Negro	11,318	11,453	8,570	−135	−1.2	2,883	33.6	1.2	1.4	1.6			
Ind., Chi., Jap., and all other	4,208	4,156	2,084	52	1.3	2,072	99.4	0.4	0.5	0.4			
Native white	807,149	656,564	438,571	150,585	22.9	217,993	49.7	85.9	82.2	81.3	87.3	83.8	82.9
Native parentage	603,041	475,136	311,335	127,905	26.9	163,801	52.6	64.2	59.5	57.7	65.3	60.6	58.8
Foreign parentage	130,059	114,747	79,692	15,312	13.3	35,055	44.0	13.8	14.4	14.8	14.1	14.6	15.1
Mixed parentage	74,049	66,681	47,544	7,368	11.0	19,137	40.3	7.9	8.3	8.8	8.0	8.5	9.0
Foreign-born white	116,954	126,851	90,475	−9,897	−7.8	36,376	40.2	12.4	15.9	16.8	12.7	16.2	17.1
New Mexico.													
Total	360,350	327,301	195,310	33,049	10.1	131,991	67.6	100.0	100.0	100.0			
White	334,673	304,594	180,207	30,079	9.9	124,387	69.0	92.9	93.1	92.3	100.0	100.0	100.0
Negro	5,733	1,628	1,610	4,105	252.1	18	1.1	1.6	0.5	0.8			
Ind., Chi., Jap., and all other	19,944	21,079	13,493	−1,135	−5.4	7,586	56.2	5.5	6.4	6.9			
Native white	305,596	281,940	166,946	23,656	8.4	114,994	68.9	84.8	86.1	85.5	91.3	92.6	92.6
Native parentage	273,317	255,609	149,029	17,708	6.9	106,580	71.5	75.8	78.1	76.3	81.7	83.9	82.7
Foreign parentage	18,865	14,410	9,677	4,455	30.9	4,733	48.9	5.2	4.4	5.0	5.6	4.7	5.4
Mixed parentage	13,414	11,921	8,240	1,493	12.5	3,681	44.7	3.7	3.6	4.2	4.0	3.9	4.6
Foreign-born white	29,077	22,654	13,261	6,423	28.4	9,393	70.8	8.1	6.9	6.8	8.7	7.4	7.4
Arizona.													
Total	334,162	204,354	122,931	129,808	63.5	81,423	66.2	100.0	100.0	100.0			
White	291,449	171,468	92,903	119,981	70.0	78,565	84.6	87.2	83.9	75.6	100.0	100.0	100.0
Negro	8,005	2,009	1,848	5,996	298.5	161	8.7	2.4	1.0	1.5			
Ind., Chi., Jap., and all other	34,708	30,877	28,180	3,831	12.4	2,697	9.6	10.4	15.1	22.9			
Native white	213,350	124,644	70,508	88,706	71.2	54,136	76.8	63.8	61.0	57.4	73.2	72.7	75.9
Native parentage	151,145	82,468	44,830	68,677	83.3	37,638	84.0	45.2	40.4	36.5	51.9	48.1	48.3
Foreign parentage	39,534	26,117	15,466	13,417	51.4	10,651	68.9	11.8	12.8	12.6	13.6	15.2	16.6
Mixed parentage	22,671	16,059	10,212	6,612	41.2	5,847	57.3	6.8	7.9	8.3	7.8	9.4	11.0
Foreign-born white	78,099	46,824	22,395	31,275	66.8	24,429	109.1	23.4	22.9	18.2	26.8	27.3	24.1
Utah.													
Total	449,396	373,351	276,749	76,045	20.4	96,602	34.9	100.0	100.0	100.0			
White	441,901	366,583	272,465	75,318	20.5	94,118	34.5	98.3	98.2	98.5	100.0	100.0	100.0
Negro	1,446	1,144	672	302	26.4	472	70.2	0.3	0.3	0.2			
Ind., Chi., Jap., and all other	6,049	5,624	3,612	425	7.6	2,012	55.7	1.3	1.5	1.3			
Native white	385,446	303,190	219,661	82,256	27.1	83,529	38.0	85.8	81.2	79.4	87.2	82.7	80.6
Native parentage	245,781	171,663	104,026	74,118	43.2	67,637	65.0	54.7	46.0	37.6	55.6	46.8	38.2
Foreign parentage	75,901	73,983	69,204	1,918	2.6	4,779	6.9	16.9	19.8	25.0	17.2	20.2	25.4
Mixed parentage	63,764	57,544	46,431	6,220	10.8	11,113	23.9	14.2	15.4	16.8	14.4	15.7	17.0
Foreign-born white	56,455	63,393	52,804	−6,938	−10.9	10,589	20.1	12.6	17.0	19.1	12.8	17.3	19.4
Nevada.													
Total	77,407	81,875	42,335	−4,468	−5.5	39,540	93.4	100.0	100.0	100.0			
White	70,699	74,276	35,405	−3,577	−4.8	38,871	109.8	91.3	90.7	83.6	100.0	100.0	100.0
Negro	346	513	134	−167	−32.6	379	282.8	0.4	0.6	0.3			
Ind., Chi., Jap., and all other	6,362	7,086	6,796	−724	−10.2	290	4.3	8.2	8.7	16.1			
Native white	55,897	56,277	26,824	−380	−0.7	29,453	109.8	72.2	68.7	63.4	79.1	75.8	75.8
Native parentage	36,285	35,326	15,111	959	2.7	20,215	133.8	46.9	43.1	35.7	51.3	47.6	42.7
Foreign parentage	11,701	12,320	7,147	−619	−5.0	5,173	72.4	15.1	15.0	16.9	16.6	16.6	20.2
Mixed parentage	7,911	8,631	4,566	−720	−8.3	4,065	89.0	10.2	10.5	10.8	11.2	11.6	12.9
Foreign-born white	14,802	17,999	8,581	−3,197	−17.8	9,418	109.8	19.1	22.0	20.3	20.9	24.2	24.2

46

POPULATION.

TABLE 12.—COLOR OR RACE, NATIVITY, AND PARENTAGE, WITH DECENNIAL INCREASE, BY DIVISIONS AND STATES: 1920, 1910, AND 1900—Continued.

[A minus sign (—) denotes decrease.]

DIVISION OR STATE AND CLASS OF POPULATION.	POPULATION.			DECENNIAL INCREASE.				PER CENT DISTRIBUTION.					
				1910–1920		1900–1910		Total population.			White population.		
	1920	1910	1900	Number.	Per cent.	Number.	Per cent.	1920	1910	1900	1920	1910	1900
PACIFIC.													
Washington.													
Total.........	1,356,621	1,141,990	518,103	214,631	18.8	623,887	120.4	100.0	100.0	100.0	......	......	......
White.........	1,319,777	1,109,111	496,304	210,666	19.0	612,807	123.5	97.3	97.1	95.8	100.0	100.0	100.0
Negro.........	6,883	6,058	2,514	825	13.6	3,544	141.0	0.5	0.5	0.5	......	......	......
Ind., Chi., Jap., and all other.......	29,961	26,821	19,285	3,140	11.7	7,536	39.1	2.2	2.3	3.7	......	......	......
Native white.........	1,069,722	867,914	394,179	201,808	23.3	473,735	120.2	78.9	76.0	76.1	81.1	78.3	79.4
Native parentage.........	711,706	585,386	265,088	126,320	21.6	320,318	120.8	52.5	51.3	51.2	53.9	52.8	53.4
Foreign parentage.........	214,618	174,845	79,422	39,773	22.7	95,423	120.1	15.8	15.3	15.3	16.3	15.8	16.0
Mixed parentage.........	143,398	107,683	49,689	35,715	33.2	57,994	116.7	10.6	9.4	9.6	10.9	9.7	10.0
Foreign-born white.........	250,055	241,197	102,125	8,858	3.7	139,072	136.2	18.4	21.1	19.7	18.9	21.7	20.6
Oregon.													
Total.........	783,389	672,765	413,536	110,624	16.4	259,229	62.7	100.0	100.0	100.0	......	......	......
White.........	769,146	655,090	394,582	114,056	17.4	260,508	66.0	98.2	97.4	95.4	100.0	100.0	100.0
Negro.........	2,144	1,492	1,105	652	43.7	387	35.0	0.3	0.2	0.3	......	......	......
Ind., Chi., Jap., and all other.......	12,099	16,183	17,849	−4,084	−25.2	−1,666	−9.3	1.5	2.4	4.3	......	......	......
Native white.........	666,995	552,089	340,721	114,906	20.8	211,368	62.0	85.1	82.1	82.4	86.7	84.3	86.3
Native parentage.........	497,726	416,851	256,125	80,875	19.4	160,726	62.8	63.5	62.0	61.9	64.7	63.6	64.9
Foreign parentage.........	95,827	79,336	49,058	16,491	20.8	30,278	61.7	12.2	11.8	11.9	12.5	12.1	12.4
Mixed parentage.........	73,442	55,902	35,538	17,540	31.4	20,364	57.3	9.4	8.3	8.6	9.5	8.5	9.0
Foreign-born white.........	102,151	103,001	53,861	−850	−0.8	49,140	91.2	13.0	15.3	13.0	13.3	15.7	13.7
California.													
Total.........	3,426,861	2,377,549	1,485,053	1,049,312	44.1	892,496	60.1	100.0	100.0	100.0	......	......	......
White.........	3,264,711	2,259,672	1,402,727	1,005,039	44.5	856,945	61.1	95.3	95.0	94.5	100.0	100.0	100.0
Negro.........	38,763	21,645	11,045	17,118	79.1	10,600	96.0	1.1	0.9	0.7	......	......	......
Ind., Chi., Jap., and all other.......	123,387	96,232	71,281	27,155	28.2	24,951	35.0	3.6	4.0	4.8	......	......	......
Native white.........	2,583,049	1,742,422	1,086,222	840,627	48.2	656,200	60.4	75.4	73.3	73.1	79.1	77.1	77.4
Native parentage.........	1,677,955	1,106,533	644,428	571,422	51.6	462,105	71.7	49.0	46.5	43.4	51.4	49.0	45.9
Foreign parentage.........	573,927	403,364	282,830	170,563	42.3	120,534	42.6	16.7	17.0	19.0	17.6	17.9	20.2
Mixed parentage.........	331,167	232,525	158,964	98,642	42.4	73,561	46.3	9.7	9.8	10.7	10.1	10.3	11.3
Foreign-born white.........	681,662	517,250	316,505	164,412	31.8	200,745	63.4	19.9	21.8	21.3	20.9	22.9	22.6

CHAPTER II
SEX DISTRIBUTION

CHAPTER II.—SEX DISTRIBUTION.

INTRODUCTION.

The distribution by sex of the white population of the United States has been ascertained at every Federal census, but data on this subject for the total population were collected for the first time in 1820.

The distribution of population by sex is a fundamental classification essential to a proper interpretation of almost every other phase of population statistics. The sex distinction is accordingly presented in other chapters of this volume in correlation with other population statistics, and this chapter is devoted mainly to a consideration of the relative numerical importance of the two sexes in different sections of the country and in the principal color or race, nativity, and parentage classes of the population.

The returns as to sex are probably more nearly accurate than those for any other population census inquiry. There is no ambiguity of terms, and rarely any motive to misrepresent the facts; and very few errors are likely to be made regarding the sex of persons enumerated. It is possible, of course, that the sex distribution shown by the returns may be affected slightly by omissions or duplications which may be relatively more numerous for one sex than for the other, but it is not believed that such errors are of sufficient frequency to influence appreciably the sex ratio for the total population of all races or for the total white population.

For the several classes of the white population, however, there is likely to be a margin of error due to incorrect returns as to nativity and parentage. It is not improbable that some persons of foreign birth are erroneously reported as of native birth, or even as of native parentage, and that some persons of native birth but of foreign or mixed parentage are erroneously included with those of native parentage. Such errors are more likely to occur in the case of males than in the case of females, for the reason that the former predominate among the foreign born and among the floating population, for both of which classes accurate information is difficult to obtain.

Total population.—The statistics on sex distribution for the population of the United States, exclusive of outlying possessions, as returned at the Fourteenth Decennial Census, are summarized in Table 1, and comparative figures are presented for prior censuses. Statistics of sex distribution for the population of all

the outlying possessions except the Philippines and the Virgin Islands [1] are given in the reports for those possessions, which have been published in the form of separate bulletins and as sections of Volume III of the Fourteenth Census Reports.

The following statement shows the excess of males in the total population for each census year beginning with 1820, sex distribution having been ascertained for the white population only at the censuses of 1810, 1800, and 1790.

CENSUS YEAR.	Excess of males.	CENSUS YEAR.	Excess of males.	CENSUS YEAR.	Excess of males.
1920...........	2,090,242	1880...........	881,857	1840...........	307,611
1910...........	2,692,288	1870...........	428,759	1830...........	198,958
1900...........	1,038,321	1860...........	727,087	1820...........	154,757
1890...........	[1] 1,526,488	1850...........	483,444		

[1] Distribution by sex partly estimated for Indian Territory.

This preponderance of males is due in part to the fact that the total population includes a considerable proportion of foreign-born persons, among whom the males greatly outnumber the females; but in the most important class of the native population, namely, the native whites of native parentage, there is also a marked excess of males.

White population.—The preponderance of males over females in the white population is due in part to the abnormal sex distribution of the foreign-born white, but among the native whites also the males outnumbered the females in 1920 by 696,505. This excess, however, occurs only among the native whites of native parentage, the foreign-parentage and mixed-parentage groups both showing an excess of females in 1920. (See Table 1.)

This preponderance of males among the native whites of native parentage has appeared at each census beginning with that for 1890, at which the sex distinction between native and foreign parentage was first made. For all native whites combined an excess of males has also been shown at each census beginning with 1850, when the classification according to nativity was first made.

The reduction in the sex ratio for the total native white population between 1910 and 1920 was more

[1] These two possessions were not enumerated in 1920, a census of the Philippines having been taken by the Philippine Government as of December 31, 1918, and a special census of the Virgin Islands having been taken by the Census Bureau as of November 1, 1917.

104   POPULATION.

pronounced than any prior change, either increase or decrease, since 1880. This reduction is the result of various causes, including emigration, war losses, and increase in military and naval services stationed abroad at the time the census was taken and therefore not included in the population of continental United States.

The sex ratios for the native whites of native parentage, of foreign parentage, and of mixed parentage all declined to approximately the same extent; but the declines in the case of the native whites of foreign parentage and of mixed parentage were in line with those which had taken place during previous decades, whereas in the case of native whites of native parentage the decline between 1910 and 1920 followed increases during preceding decades.

The ratio for the foreign-born whites declined much more sharply than that for the native whites, but nevertheless was higher in 1920 than in any census year between 1850 and 1910. The decline was presumably due mainly to a large excess of males among the foreign-born whites who emigrated from the United States during the decade.

Negro population.—Differing from all other races, the Negroes have shown an excess of females over males at every census since and including that of 1840, although the returns for 1820 and 1830 showed a preponderance of males. The excess of females was most pronounced, according to the figures, in 1870, but it is generally recognized that the census taken in that year was very defective in the Southern states, and it is likely that among the Negroes the underenumeration was somewhat greater in the case of males than in the case of females.

The abnormal sex ratio appearing for the mulattoes is undoubtedly due to the inaccuracy of the returns for this subclass. In both 1910 and 1920 the black population showed an excess of males, while among the mulattoes the females, as reported, considerably outnumbered the males, the excess for 1920 being greater than that for any of the three earlier census years—1910, 1870, and 1860—for which data are available. (At the censuses of 1900 and 1880 the Negro population was not classified as black and mulatto; in 1890 the definition applied to the term "mulatto" was different from that applied in 1920 and 1910; in 1870 the word was used in substantially the same sense as at the last two censuses; and in 1860 it appears not to have been defined.)

It is possible that the explanation of the peculiar sex ratio shown for the mulattoes is to be found in the incorrect return of certain mulattoes as blacks, the error having been greater in the case of males than in that of females. Since the blacks are far more numerous than the mulattoes, the enumerators were likely to return as blacks those Negroes whom they did not see in person, and since the Negro women at home were more apt to be seen by the enumerators than were the men, the erroneous return of mulattoes as blacks probably occurred more frequently in regard to men than in regard to women.

Indian population.—At every census except that of 1870 the Indian population has shown an excess of males. No attempt was made, however, to secure a complete enumeration of this race prior to 1890, and it is doubtful whether the figures for earlier census years are of any material value as showing the true sex ratio of the total Indian population. The more recent returns also are subject to a somewhat greater margin of error than are those for the other races, due to the effort to treat as Indian all persons having any trace of Indian blood. It is likely that some persons in whom the admixture of Indian blood was so slight as not to be readily noticeable were erroneously reported as white, and there may have been differences between the two sexes in regard to the frequency of such errors.

Chinese, Japanese, and "all other" population.—Among the Chinese, Japanese, and other minor elements of the population the excess of males is very great, although there has been a pronounced decrease in the sex ratio from census to census since 1890 in the case of the Chinese and since 1900 in the case of the Japanese. The great majority of persons of the Chinese, Japanese, and "all other" races in the United States are immigrants, and among these immigrants the males are greatly in excess of the females.

Urban and rural population.—Since marked differences exist between urban and rural communities in regard to the sex distribution of their population, separate statistics are given for the two classes of communities in Table 9, for geographic divisions. Statistics for the several color or race, nativity, and parentage classes of the urban and rural population are not here presented for individual states, but the sex distribution of these classes in the urban and rural communities of each state (without classification of the urban communities according to size) is shown in Table 1 of the state bulletin and of the appropriate section of Volume III. In drawing the distinction between urban and rural population, all incorporated places (and all towns in Massachusetts, Rhode Island, and New Hampshire) having 2,500 inhabitants or more are treated as urban and the rest of the country as rural.

In Massachusetts and Rhode Island it is not the practice, as in practically all the other states, to incorporate, as separate municipalities, the relatively densely populated portions of "towns" (which are the primary divisions of the counties), and no town as a whole is incorporated as a municipality until it attains a population greatly in excess of 2,500; and in New Hampshire a similar condition exists, although there are in the state two incorporated villages, each of which has fewer than 2,500 inhabitants. For this reason those towns having 2,500 or more inhabitants

SEX DISTRIBUTION.

in the three states named are treated as urban, although portions of their areas are rural in character. The urban areas in the three states in question, as classified by the census, thus contain relatively small numbers of inhabitants who in other sections of the country would be segregated as rural. Nevertheless, in most of the Massachusetts, New Hampshire, and Rhode Island towns having 2,500 inhabitants or more by far the greater part of the population resides within the more densely settled areas, so that the proportion classed as urban is not greatly exaggerated by the practice adopted.

The ratio of males to females is decidedly higher in rural than in urban communities, not only for the total population but for each of its elements except the numerically unimportant group "Indian, Chinese, Japanese, and all other." (See Table 9.) In the case of this group the explanation of the higher ratio in urban than in rural communities is found in the fact that the Chinese, whose sex distribution is abnormal, the males being very greatly in excess of the females, are found mainly in urban communities, whereas the Indians, whose sex distribution is normal, live principally in rural communities. The Japanese, among whom the excess of males is abnormal, although not to so great an extent as among the Chinese, are nearly equally divided between urban and rural.

This difference between urban and rural communities in regard to the sex distribution of the principal classes of the population—which exists despite the fact that the foreign born, among whom the males considerably outnumber the females, are more numerous in urban than in rural communities—is doubtless due primarily to the fact that the cities afford many more opportunities for the gainful employment of women than do the rural districts.

POPULATION.

RATIO OF MALES TO FEMALES IN TOTAL POPULATION, BY STATES: 1920.

[District of Columbia, females in excess, not shown separately on the map.]

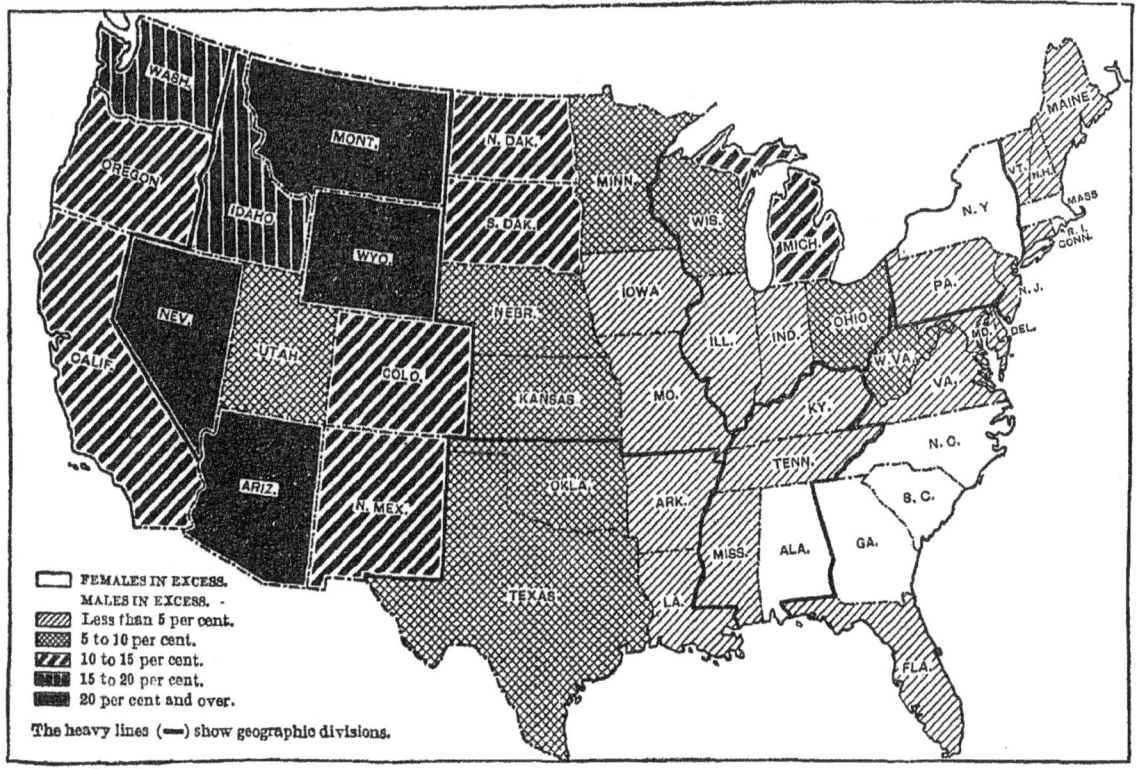

FEMALES IN EXCESS.
MALES IN EXCESS.
- Less than 5 per cent.
- 5 to 10 per cent.
- 10 to 15 per cent.
- 15 to 20 per cent.
- 20 per cent and over.

The heavy lines (—) show geographic divisions.

RATIO OF MALES TO FEMALES IN TOTAL POPULATION, BY STATES: 1910.

[District of Columbia, females in excess, not shown separately on the map.]

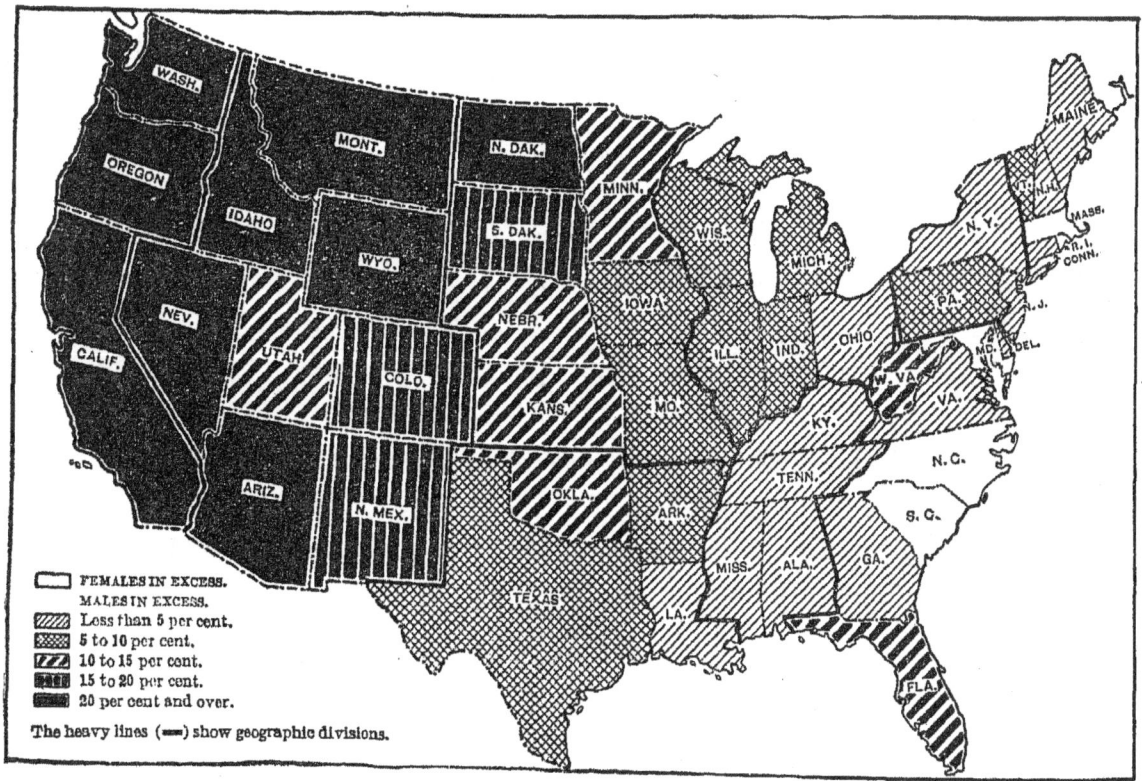

FEMALES IN EXCESS.
MALES IN EXCESS.
- Less than 5 per cent.
- 5 to 10 per cent.
- 10 to 15 per cent.
- 15 to 20 per cent.
- 20 per cent and over.

The heavy lines (—) show geographic divisions.

SEX DISTRIBUTION.

107

TABLE 1.—SEX DISTRIBUTION AND RATIO OF MALES TO FEMALES, BY POPULATION CLASSES, FOR THE UNITED STATES: 1790-1920.

[Figures are given under each class for all census years for which data are available.]

CLASS OF POPULATION AND CENSUS YEAR.	Both sexes.	Male.	Female.	PER CENT.[1] Male.	PER CENT.[1] Female.	Males to 100 females.[2]
Total population:						
1920	105,710,620	53,900,431	51,810,189	51.0	49.0	104.0
1910	91,972,266	47,332,277	44,639,989	51.5	48.5	106.0
1900	75,994,575	38,816,448	37,178,127	51.1	48.9	104.4
1890	62,947,714	32,237,101	30,710,613	51.2	48.8	105.0
1880	50,155,783	25,518,820	24,636,963	50.9	49.1	103.6
1870	38,558,371	19,493,565	19,064,806	50.6	49.4	102.2
1860	31,443,321	16,085,204	15,358,117	51.2	48.8	104.7
1850	23,191,876	11,837,660	11,354,216	51.0	49.0	104.3
1840	17,069,453	8,688,532	8,380,921	50.9	49.1	103.7
1830	12,866,020	6,532,489	6,333,531	50.8	49.2	103.1
1820	9,638,453	4,896,605	4,741,848	50.8	49.2	103.3
White:						
1920	94,820,915	48,430,655	46,390,260	51.1	48.9	104.4
1910	81,731,957	42,178,245	39,553,712	51.6	48.4	106.6
1900	66,809,196	34,201,735	32,607,461	51.2	48.8	104.9
1890	55,101,258	28,270,379	26,830,879	51.3	48.7	105.4
1880	43,402,970	22,130,900	21,272,070	51.0	49.0	104.0
1870	33,589,377	17,029,088	16,560,289	50.7	49.3	102.8
1860	26,922,537	13,811,387	13,111,150	51.3	48.7	105.3
1850	19,553,068	10,026,402	9,526,666	51.3	48.7	105.2
1840	14,195,805	7,255,544	6,940,261	51.1	48.9	104.5
1830	10,537,378	5,366,213	5,171,165	50.9	49.1	103.8
1820	7,866,797	3,995,809	3,870,988	50.8	49.2	103.2
1810	5,862,073	2,988,130	2,873,943	51.0	49.0	104.0
1800	4,306,446	2,195,305	2,111,141	51.0	49.0	104.0
1790	3,172,006	1,615,434	1,556,572	50.9	49.1	103.8
Native white—						
1920	81,108,161	40,902,333	40,205,828	50.4	49.6	101.7
1910	68,386,412	34,654,457	33,731,955	50.7	49.3	102.7
1900	56,595,379	28,686,450	27,908,929	50.7	49.3	102.8
1890	45,979,301	23,318,521	22,660,870	50.7	49.3	102.9
1880	36,843,291	18,609,265	18,234,026	50.5	49.5	102.1
1870	28,095,665	14,086,509	14,009,156	50.1	49.9	100.6
1860	22,825,784	11,619,157	11,206,627	50.9	49.1	103.7
1850	17,312,533	8,786,968	8,525,565	50.8	49.2	103.1
Native parentage—						
1920	58,421,957	29,636,781	28,785,176	50.7	49.3	103.0
1910	49,488,575	25,229,218	24,259,357	51.0	49.0	104.0
1900	40,949,362	20,849,847	20,099,515	50.9	49.1	103.7
1890	34,475,716	17,536,950	16,938,766	50.9	49.1	103.5
Foreign or mixed parentage—						
1920	22,686,204	11,265,552	11,420,652	49.7	50.3	98.6
1910	18,897,837	9,425,239	9,472,598	49.9	50.1	99.5
1900	15,646,017	7,886,603	7,809,414	50.1	49.9	101.0
1890	11,503,675	5,781,571	5,722,104	50.3	49.7	101.0
Foreign parentage—						
1920	15,694,539	7,810,531	7,884,008	49.8	50.2	99.1
1910	12,916,311	6,456,793	6,459,518	50.0	50.0	100.0
1900	10,632,280	5,341,350	5,290,930	50.2	49.8	101.0
Mixed parentage—						
1920	6,991,665	3,455,021	3,536,644	49.4	50.6	97.7
1910	5,981,526	2,968,446	3,013,080	49.6	50.4	98.5
1900	5,013,737	2,495,253	2,518,484	49.8	50.2	99.1
Foreign-born white—						
1920	13,712,754	7,528,322	6,184,432	54.9	45.1	121.7
1910	13,345,545	7,523,788	5,821,757	56.4	43.6	129.2
1900	10,213,817	5,515,285	4,698,532	54.0	46.0	117.4
1890	9,121,867	4,951,858	4,170,009	54.3	45.7	118.7
1880	6,559,679	3,521,635	3,038,044	53.7	46.3	115.9
1870	5,493,712	2,942,570	2,551,133	53.6	46.4	115.3
1860	4,096,753	2,192,230	1,904,523	53.5	46.5	115.1
1850	2,240,535	1,239,434	1,001,101	55.3	44.7	123.8

CLASS OF POPULATION AND CENSUS YEAR.	Both sexes.	Male.	Female.	PER CENT.[1] Male.	PER CENT.[1] Female.	Males to 100 females.[2]
Negro:						
1920	10,463,131	5,209,436	5,253,695	49.8	50.2	99.2
1910	9,827,763	4,885,881	4,941,882	49.7	50.3	98.9
1900	8,833,994	4,386,547	4,447,447	49.7	50.3	98.6
1890	7,488,676	3,735,603	3,753,073	49.9	50.1	99.5
1880	6,580,793	3,253,115	3,327,678	49.4	50.6	97.8
1870	4,880,009	2,393,263	2,486,746	49.0	51.0	96.2
1860	4,441,830	2,216,744	2,225,086	49.9	50.1	99.6
1850	3,638,808	1,811,258	1,827,550	49.8	50.2	99.1
1840	2,873,648	1,432,088	1,440,660	49.9	50.1	99.5
1830	2,328,642	1,166,276	1,162,366	50.1	49.9	100.3
1820	1,771,656	900,790	870,860	50.8	49.2	103.4
Black [3]—						
1920	8,802,577	4,444,514	4,358,063	50.5	49.5	102.0
1910	7,777,077	3,922,332	3,854,745	50.4	49.6	101.8
1870	4,295,960	2,115,367	2,180,593	49.2	50.8	97.0
1860	3,853,467	1,936,536	1,916,931	50.3	49.7	101.0
Mulatto [3]—						
1920	1,660,554	764,922	895,632	46.1	53.9	85.4
1910	2,050,686	963,549	1,087,137	47.0	53.0	88.6
1870	584,049	277,806	306,153	47.6	52.4	90.8
1860	588,363	280,208	308,155	47.6	52.4	90.9
Indian:						
1920	244,437	125,068	119,369	51.2	48.8	104.8
1910	265,683	135,133	130,550	50.9	49.1	103.5
1900	237,196	119,484	117,712	50.4	49.6	101.5
1890	248,253	125,710	122,534	50.6	49.4	102.6
1880	66,407	33,985	32,422	51.2	48.8	104.8
1870	25,731	12,534	13,197	48.7	51.3	95.0
1860	44,021	23,924	20,007	54.3	45.7	119.0
Chinese:						
1920	61,639	53,891	7,748	87.4	12.6	695.5
1910	71,531	66,856	4,675	93.5	6.5	1,430.1
1900	89,863	85,341	4,522	95.0	5.0	1,887.2
1890	107,488	103,620	3,868	96.4	3.6	2,678.9
1880	105,465	100,686	4,779	95.5	4.5	2,106.8
1870	63,199	58,633	4,566	92.8	7.2	1,284.1
1860	34,933	33,149	1,784	94.9	5.1	1,858.1
Japanese:						
1920	111,010	72,707	38,303	65.5	34.5	189.8
1910	72,157	63,070	9,087	87.4	12.6	694.1
1900	24,326	23,341	985	96.0	4.0	2,369.6
1890	2,039	1,780	269	87.3	12.7	687.3
1880	148	134	14	90.5	9.5	.....
1870	55	47	8	.....	.....	.....
All other:						
1920	9,488	8,674	814	91.4	8.6	1,065.6
1910	3,175	3,092	83	97.4	2.6	.....
Filipinos—						
1920	5,603	5,232	371	93.4	6.6	1,410.2
1910	160	144	16	90.0	10.0	.....
Hindus—						
1920	2,507	2,409	98	96.1	3.9	.....
1910	2,545	2,526	19	99.3	0.7	.....
Koreans—						
1920	1,224	923	301	75.4	24.6	306.6
1910	462	419	43	90.7	9.3	.....
Maoris—						
1920	2	2	.....			
1910	8	3	5			
Hawaiians—						
1920	110	75	35	68.2	31.8	.....
1910						
Malays—						
1920	19	17	2			
Samoans—						
1920	6	4	2			
Siamese—						
1920	17	12	5			

[1] Per cent not shown where base is less than 100.
[2] Ratio not shown where number of females is less than 100.
[3] Distinction between blacks and mulattoes for Negro population not made in 1880 or 1900; distribution by sex for black population (6,337,980) and mulatto population (1,132,080) not made for 1890.

108

POPULATION.

TABLE 2.—SEX DISTRIBUTION AND RATIO OF MALES TO FEMALES, FOR WHITE AND NEGRO POPULATION, BY DIVISIONS AND STATES: 1920 AND 1910.

DIVISION AND STATE.	TOTAL POPULATION. 1920 Male.	1920 Female.	1910 Male.	1910 Female.	Males to 100 females. 1920	1910	WHITE. 1920 Male.	1920 Female.	Males to 100 females. 1920	1910	NEGRO. 1920 Male.	1920 Female.	Males to 100 females. 1920	1910
United States	53,900,431	51,810,189	47,332,277	44,639,989	104.0	106.0	48,430,655	46,390,200	104.4	106.6	5,209,436	5,253,695	99.2	98.9
GEOGRAPHIC DIVISIONS:														
New England	3,672,591	3,728,318	3,295,114	3,287,567	98.5	99.3	3,627,911	3,688,168	98.4	99.2	40,155	38,896	103.2	97.8
Middle Atlantic	11,206,445	11,054,699	9,813,266	9,502,626	101.4	103.3	10,890,488	10,751,352	101.3	103.4	301,147	299,036	100.7	94.9
East North Central	11,035,041	10,440,502	9,392,839	8,857,782	105.7	106.0	10,748,049	10,190,813	105.5	106.0	273,026	241,528	113.0	108.3
West North Central	6,459,067	6,085,182	6,092,855	5,545,666	106.1	109.9	6,293,744	5,931,643	106.1	109.9	143,762	134,759	106.7	107.8
South Atlantic	7,035,843	6,954,429	6,134,605	6,060,290	101.2	101.2	4,893,290	4,755,650	102.9	103.2	2,133,377	2,191,743	97.3	97.5
East South Central	4,471,690	4,421,617	4,245,169	4,164,732	101.1	101.9	3,226,512	3,141,035	102.7	103.6	1,243,795	1,270,737	97.2	98.4
West South Central	5,265,829	4,976,395	4,544,595	4,240,029	105.8	107.2	4,203,877	3,911,850	107.5	109.3	1,029,457	1,034,122	99.5	100.4
Mountain	1,789,299	1,546,802	1,478,018	1,155,499	115.7	127.9	1,717,709	1,495,190	114.9	127.4	19,726	11,075	178.1	121.3
Pacific	2,964,626	2,602,245	2,365,906	1,826,398	113.9	129.5	2,829,075	2,524,550	112.1	125.4	24,991	22,799	109.6	120.4
NEW ENGLAND:														
Maine	388,752	379,262	377,052	365,319	102.5	103.2	387,455	378,240	102.4	103.2	716	594	120.5	105.6
New Hampshire	222,112	220,071	216,290	214,282	100.5	100.9	221,667	220,664	100.5	100.9	333	288	115.6	104.3
Vermont	178,854	173,574	182,568	173,388	103.0	105.3	178,504	173,313	103.0	104.9	320	252	127.0	261.8
Massachusetts	1,890,014	1,962,342	1,655,248	1,711,168	96.3	96.7	1,864,317	1,939,207	96.1	96.6	22,912	22,554	101.6	97.1
Rhode Island	297,524	306,873	270,314	272,296	97.0	99.3	292,131	301,849	96.8	99.2	5,096	4,940	103.2	95.1
Connecticut	695,335	685,296	563,642	551,114	101.5	102.3	683,837	674,895	101.3	102.3	10,778	10,268	105.0	91.0
MIDDLE ATLANTIC:														
New York	5,187,350	5,197,877	4,584,597	4,529,017	99.8	101.2	5,031,010	5,091,017	99.8	101.3	95,418	103,065	92.6	91.3
New Jersey	1,590,075	1,565,825	1,286,463	1,250,704	101.5	102.9	1,531,146	1,505,941	101.7	103.1	57,432	59,700	96.2	94.5
Pennsylvania	4,429,020	4,290,997	3,942,206	3,722,905	103.2	105.9	4,278,332	4,154,394	103.0	106.1	148,297	136,271	108.8	97.7
EAST NORTH CENTRAL:														
Ohio	2,955,960	2,803,414	2,434,758	2,332,363	105.4	104.4	2,854,064	2,717,220	105.1	104.3	100,160	86,027	116.4	108.5
Indiana	1,489,074	1,441,316	1,383,295	1,317,581	103.3	105.0	1,446,825	1,402,246	103.2	104.9	41,817	38,903	107.2	106.0
Illinois	3,304,833	3,180,447	2,911,674	2,726,917	103.9	106.8	3,207,773	3,091,560	103.8	106.6	93,835	88,439	106.1	109.1
Michigan	1,928,436	1,739,976	1,454,534	1,356,639	110.8	107.3	1,890,265	1,711,362	110.5	107.2	34,249	25,833	132.6	111.1
Wisconsin	1,356,718	1,275,349	1,208,578	1,125,282	106.4	107.4	1,348,522	1,268,416	106.3	107.4	2,905	2,236	132.6	103.7
WEST NORTH CENTRAL:														
Minnesota	1,245,537	1,141,588	1,108,511	967,197	109.1	114.6	1,235,728	1,133,208	109.0	114.5	4,851	3,958	122.6	144.2
Iowa	1,229,392	1,174,629	1,148,171	1,076,600	104.7	106.6	1,218,711	1,165,470	104.6	106.5	10,121	8,884	113.9	118.5
Missouri	1,723,319	1,680,736	1,687,813	1,605,522	102.5	105.1	1,631,697	1,593,347	102.4	105.1	90,991	87,250	104.3	104.6
North Dakota	341,673	305,199	317,554	259,592	112.0	122.4	338,031	301,923	112.0	122.6	276	191	144.5	161.4
South Dakota	337,120	299,427	317,112	266,776	112.6	118.9	328,197	290,950	112.8	119.5	475	357	133.1	134.1
Nebraska	672,805	623,567	627,782	564,432	107.9	111.2	663,230	615,980	107.7	111.0	7,309	5,933	123.2	124.2
Kansas	909,221	860,036	885,912	805,037	105.7	110.0	878,150	830,756	105.7	110.1	29,739	28,186	105.5	107.3
SOUTH ATLANTIC:														
Delaware	113,755	109,248	103,435	98,887	104.1	104.6	98,049	94,566	103.7	104.4	15,655	14,680	106.6	105.5
Maryland	729,455	720,266	644,225	651,121	101.3	98.9	605,601	599,136	101.1	99.2	123,453	121,026	102.0	97.7
District of Columbia	203,543	234,028	158,050	173,019	87.0	91.3	152,031	174,829	87.0	94.9	50,855	59,111	86.0	82.2
Virginia	1,168,492	1,140,695	1,035,348	1,026,264	102.4	100.9	825,133	792,776	104.1	102.8	342,536	347,481	98.6	97.1
West Virginia	763,100	700,601	644,044	577,075	108.9	111.6	715,869	661,366	108.2	110.5	47,120	39,216	120.2	132.8
North Carolina	1,279,062	1,280,061	1,098,476	1,107,811	99.9	99.2	899,031	884,748	101.6	101.2	373,965	389,442	96.0	94.8
South Carolina	838,293	845,431	751,842	763,558	99.2	98.5	415,823	402,715	103.3	102.4	422,185	442,534	95.4	95.4
Georgia	1,444,823	1,451,009	1,305,019	1,304,102	99.6	100.1	854,109	835,005	102.3	102.4	590,443	615,922	95.9	97.2
Florida	495,320	473,150	394,166	358,453	104.7	110.0	327,644	310,509	105.5	110.2	167,156	162,331	103.0	109.5
EAST SOUTH CENTRAL:														
Kentucky	1,227,494	1,189,136	1,161,709	1,128,196	103.2	103.0	1,108,853	1,071,707	103.5	103.2	118,548	117,390	101.0	101.0
Tennessee	1,173,967	1,163,918	1,103,491	1,081,208	100.9	102.1	951,224	934,789	101.8	103.3	222,639	229,119	97.2	97.6
Alabama	1,173,105	1,175,069	1,074,209	1,063,884	99.8	101.0	733,039	713,903	102.7	103.8	439,779	460,873	95.4	97.2
Mississippi	897,124	893,494	905,760	891,354	100.4	101.6	433,396	420,566	103.1	104.7	462,829	472,355	98.0	99.2
WEST SOUTH CENTRAL:														
Arkansas	895,228	856,976	810,026	764,423	104.5	106.0	658,169	621,588	105.9	107.7	236,895	235,325	100.7	101.7
Louisiana	903,335	895,174	835,275	821,113	100.9	101.7	557,498	539,113	103.4	104.3	344,794	355,463	97.0	98.3
Oklahoma	1,058,044	970,239	881,578	775,577	109.0	113.7	952,691	868,503	109.7	114.7	76,294	73,114	104.3	109.5
Texas	2,409,222	2,254,006	2,017,626	1,878,916	106.9	107.4	2,035,519	1,882,046	108.1	109.0	371,474	370,220	100.3	100.0
MOUNTAIN:														
Montana	299,941	248,948	226,872	149,181	120.5	152.1	291,592	242,668	120.2	152.2	962	696	138.2	136.3
Idaho	233,919	197,947	185,546	140,048	118.2	132.5	230,136	195,532	117.7	131.3	585	335	174.6	157.3
Wyoming	110,359	84,043	91,670	54,295	131.3	168.8	107,501	82,645	130.1	165.6	863	512	168.6	223.4
Colorado	492,731	446,898	430,097	368,327	110.3	116.9	484,245	439,858	110.1	116.4	5,834	5,484	106.4	105.0
New Mexico	190,456	169,594	175,245	152,056	112.1	115.3	175,350	159,323	110.1	115.8	4,593	1,140	402.9	120.9
Arizona	183,602	150,560	118,574	85,780	121.9	138.2	159,345	132,104	120.6	142.9	5,859	2,146	273.0	110.4
Utah	232,051	217,345	196,463	176,488	106.8	111.5	227,232	214,689	105.9	110.1	834	612	136.3	152.5
Nevada	46,240	31,167	52,551	29,324	148.4	179.2	42,308	28,391	149.0	181.5	196	150	130.7	105.2
PACIFIC:														
Washington	734,701	621,920	658,663	483,327	118.1	136.3	711,693	608,084	117.0	134.2	3,957	2,926	135.2	160.9
Oregon	416,334	367,055	384,265	288,500	113.4	133.2	407,159	361,987	112.5	130.1	1,197	947	126.4	155.0
California	1,813,591	1,613,270	1,322,978	1,054,571	112.4	125.5	1,710,223	1,554,488	110.0	120.1	19,837	18,926	104.8	109.3

SEX DISTRIBUTION.

109

TABLE 3.—SEX DISTRIBUTION, 1920, AND RATIO OF MALES TO FEMALES, 1920 AND 1910, FOR THE WHITE POPULATION BY NATIVITY AND PARENTAGE, BY DIVISIONS AND STATES.

DIVISION AND STATE.	Native White — Native parentage 1920 Male	Female	Males to 100 females 1920	1910	Foreign parentage 1920 Male	Female	Males to 100 females 1920	1910	Mixed parentage 1920 Male	Female	Males to 100 females 1920	1910	Foreign-born White 1920 Male	Female	Males to 100 females 1920	1910
United States	29,636,781	28,785,176	103.0	104.0	7,810,531	7,884,003	99.1	100.0	3,455,021	3,538,044	97.7	98.5	7,528,322	6,184,432	121.7	129.2
GEOGRAPHIC DIVISIONS:																
New England	1,388,963	1,414,186	98.2	98.1	935,127	971,213	96.3	96.3	359,085	377,851	94.8	95.2	945,786	924,918	102.3	104.8
Middle Atlantic	4,788,608	4,842,404	98.9	98.9	2,658,961	2,738,990	97.1	97.1	825,353	874,919	94.3	94.9	2,617,566	2,295,009	114.1	120.9
East North Central	5,991,476	5,798,894	103.3	102.9	2,016,078	2,027,614	99.4	99.1	931,161	950,360	98.0	97.7	1,809,334	1,413,945	128.0	131.3
West North Central	3,810,076	3,665,472	103.9	106.6	1,076,084	1,050,042	102.5	104.3	628,562	623,190	100.9	101.6	779,022	592,930	131.4	141.3
South Atlantic	4,433,700	4,345,716	102.0	102.1	176,458	177,185	99.6	98.1	97,989	101,972	96.1	96.9	185,143	130,777	141.6	146.9
East South Central	3,086,676	3,006,106	102.7	103.5	55,361	60,123	92.1	93.8	42,382	44,980	94.3	95.6	42,093	29,846	141.0	139.2
West South Central	3,587,989	3,371,796	106.4	108.2	212,320	203,479	104.3	105.8	142,791	138,019	103.5	104.2	260,777	198,556	131.3	138.8
Mountain	1,055,895	946,613	111.5	119.8	234,201	216,931	108.0	115.2	156,240	149,794	104.3	109.0	271,373	181,852	149.2	189.6
Pacific	1,493,398	1,393,989	107.1	117.4	445,941	438,431	101.7	108.4	272,458	275,549	98.9	104.2	617,278	416,590	148.2	181.9
NEW ENGLAND:																
Maine	250,299	245,481	102.0	101.9	43,382	42,708	101.4	101.8	37,967	38,449	98.7	101.6	55,807	51,542	108.3	111.1
New Hampshire	112,848	112,664	100.2	99.2	40,039	41,000	97.7	96.3	21,936	22,611	97.0	96.6	46,844	44,389	105.5	110.4
Vermont	115,392	112,933	102.2	102.7	21,184	20,916	101.3	100.2	18,217	18,649	97.7	96.5	23,711	20,815	113.9	127.3
Massachusetts	601,525	629,248	95.6	95.2	534,066	558,292	95.8	95.9	194,597	207,452	93.8	94.0	533,319	544,215	98.0	99.5
Rhode Island	86,368	87,185	99.1	99.6	88,057	94,003	94.3	95.6	30,942	33,326	92.8	94.1	86,164	87,335	98.7	103.6
Connecticut	222,531	226,675	98.2	97.6	206,899	214,234	96.6	96.1	54,516	57,364	95.0	95.1	199,891	176,622	113.2	116.7
MIDDLE ATLANTIC:																
New York	1,821,141	1,847,125	98.6	98.9	1,395,548	1,448,535	96.3	96.4	421,746	451,820	93.3	94.5	1,442,575	1,343,537	107.4	110.5
New Jersey	605,157	607,518	99.6	98.9	409,035	420,023	97.4	97.4	125,299	131,442	95.3	95.4	391,655	346,958	112.9	118.2
Pennsylvania	2,362,310	2,387,761	98.9	98.9	854,378	870,432	98.2	98.3	278,308	291,687	95.4	95.4	783,336	604,514	129.6	145.5
EAST NORTH CENTRAL:																
Ohio	1,800,779	1,808,343	102.9	101.5	413,305	424,946	97.3	96.2	189,236	196,587	96.3	95.8	391,344	287,353	136.2	137.8
Indiana	1,175,902	1,153,642	101.9	102.8	112,924	114,142	98.9	100.4	69,819	71,774	97.3	97.7	88,180	62,688	140.7	156.4
Illinois	1,552,087	1,514,476	102.5	103.9	724,616	742,420	97.6	98.5	273,806	281,977	96.1	97.4	657,264	549,687	119.6	127.3
Michigan	866,769	803,678	107.9	104.2	394,176	381,112	103.4	100.6	215,514	213,743	100.8	99.1	413,806	312,829	132.3	127.4
Wisconsin	535,939	518,755	103.3	103.2	371,057	364,994	101.7	101.3	182,786	183,279	99.7	98.6	258,740	201,388	128.5	130.8
WEST NORTH CENTRAL:																
Minnesota	424,834	402,793	105.5	110.2	358,334	349,792	102.4	103.8	173,972	173,047	100.5	100.0	278,588	207,576	134.2	144.0
Iowa	775,407	753,146	103.0	103.8	189,603	187,017	101.4	102.7	126,546	126,725	99.9	99.2	127,065	98,582	128.9	135.7
Missouri	1,283,069	1,253,867	102.3	104.2	146,528	153,536	95.4	97.9	98,682	103,336	95.5	97.5	103,418	82,608	125.2	135.9
North Dakota	108,334	99,632	108.7	121.6	104,728	99,245	105.5	111.5	49,583	46,920	105.7	109.1	75,386	56,117	134.3	145.8
South Dakota	161,080	146,618	110.5	118.2	74,127	67,214	110.3	111.6	44,480	42,337	105.1	108.5	47,610	34,781	136.0	145.8
Nebraska	389,049	368,015	105.7	108.5	118,286	113,662	104.1	105.2	71,618	68,937	103.9	103.8	84,277	65,375	128.9	136.7
Kansas	667,403	641,401	104.1	107.4	84,388	79,576	106.0	107.5	63,081	61,879	102.9	104.2	62,678	47,900	130.9	149.9
SOUTH ATLANTIC:																
Delaware	70,517	69,359	101.7	102.5	11,479	11,800	97.2	98.0	4,684	4,957	94.5	96.9	11,369	8,441	134.7	132.4
Maryland	448,287	444,801	100.8	99.0	70,267	72,936	96.3	94.9	32,419	33,850	95.8	94.7	54,628	47,549	114.9	108.9
District of Columbia	109,872	129,616	84.8	93.4	16,549	18,580	89.1	79.1	10,468	13,227	79.1	89.7	15,142	13,406	112.9	113.0
Virginia	778,053	756,441	102.9	101.6	16,545	13,969	118.4	110.6	11,484	10,632	108.0	104.4	19,051	11,734	162.4	169.0
West Virginia	632,425	600,432	105.3	106.3	28,591	28,034	102.0	102.2	12,943	12,904	100.3	100.5	41,910	19,996	209.6	261.8
North Carolina	888,953	876,250	101.4	101.0	2,932	2,805	104.5	100.4	2,805	2,935	95.6	97.0	4,341	2,758	157.4	170.5
South Carolina	405,120	394,298	102.7	102.0	3,678	3,347	109.9	95.2	2,930	2,764	106.0	99.2	4,095	2,306	177.6	159.3
Georgia	828,637	814,060	101.8	101.9	8,522	7,849	108.6	103.6	6,946	6,914	100.5	98.9	10,004	6,182	161.8	171.4
Florida	271,836	260,459	104.4	107.6	17,805	17,856	100.2	102.7	13,310	13,789	96.5	99.7	24,603	18,405	133.7	157.0
EAST SOUTH CENTRAL:																
Kentucky	1,039,134	1,000,000	103.9	103.8	30,816	35,115	87.8	90.3	21,424	23,291	92.0	93.2	17,479	13,301	131.4	117.2
Tennessee	923,544	909,213	101.6	103.0	10,158	10,265	99.0	98.5	8,501	8,834	96.2	97.2	9,021	6,457	139.7	152.4
Alabama	704,980	689,149	102.3	103.2	9,695	9,896	98.0	100.4	7,739	7,911	97.8	98.5	10,625	7,037	151.0	165.9
Mississippi	419,018	407,744	102.8	101.2	4,692	4,847	96.8	100.8	4,718	4,924	95.8	99.9	4,968	3,051	162.8	173.7
WEST SOUTH CENTRAL:																
Arkansas	628,856	597,830	105.2	106.8	10,360	8,661	119.7	118.8	10,353	9,707	106.7	107.0	8,591	5,384	159.6	168.3
Louisiana	478,415	463,309	103.3	104.2	31,923	35,093	91.0	94.2	20,352	22,648	89.9	92.3	26,808	18,063	148.4	133.9
Oklahoma	873,888	805,219	108.5	113.1	28,271	24,812	113.9	118.7	25,601	23,435	100.2	113.4	24,931	15,037	165.8	178.1
Texas	1,606,830	1,505,432	106.7	107.5	141,757	134,913	105.1	105.8	86,485	82,220	105.2	105.0	200,447	160,072	125.2	132.6
MOUNTAIN:																
Montana	147,662	128,141	115.2	139.6	53,379	42,539	110.0	124.4	32,322	30,597	105.6	116.5	58,229	35,391	164.5	233.4
Idaho	155,973	138,279	112.8	123.0	25,781	23,139	110.5	123.4	23,505	21,028	111.8	114.0	24,877	14,086	176.6	227.5
Wyoming	68,042	54,842	124.1	151.8	13,535	11,699	115.7	139.3	8,990	7,783	115.5	130.9	16,934	8,321	203.5	287.2
Colorado	313,759	289,282	108.5	112.0	65,574	64,485	101.7	105.4	36,693	37,356	98.2	101.1	68,219	48,735	140.0	160.1
New Mexico	141,937	131,380	108.0	111.1	9,715	9,150	106.2	116.1	6,853	6,561	104.4	113.6	16,845	12,232	137.7	189.6
Arizona	82,435	68,710	120.0	135.0	20,497	19,037	107.7	122.3	11,756	10,915	107.7	113.7	44,657	33,442	133.5	188.4
Utah	125,360	120,421	104.1	108.2	39,185	36,716	106.7	105.8	31,812	31,952	99.6	101.1	30,875	25,580	120.7	131.0
Nevada	20,727	15,558	133.2	161.3	6,535	5,166	126.5	147.2	4,309	3,602	119.6	132.6	10,737	4,065	264.1	331.4
PACIFIC:																
Washington	374,555	337,151	111.1	124.2	111,145	103,473	107.4	116.4	72,875	70,523	103.3	110.0	153,118	96,937	158.0	199.7
Oregon	258,647	239,079	108.2	121.6	49,146	46,681	105.3	116.5	37,056	36,388	101.8	108.7	62,310	39,841	156.4	209.9
California	860,196	817,759	105.2	112.4	285,650	288,277	99.1	103.6	162,527	168,640	96.4	100.7	401,850	279,812	143.6	169.6

110   POPULATION.

TABLE 4.—SEX DISTRIBUTION, 1920, AND RATIO OF MALES TO FEMALES, 1920 AND 1910, FOR INDIAN, CHINESE, JAPANESE, AND "ALL OTHER" POPULATION, BY DIVISIONS AND STATES.

DIVISION AND STATE.	INDIAN.				CHINESE.				JAPANESE.				ALL OTHER.[1]			
	1920		Males to 100 females.[2]		1920		Males to 100 females.[2]		1920		Males to 100 females.[2]		1920		Males to 100 females.[2]	
	Male.	Female.	1920	1910	Male.	Female.	1920	1910	Male.	Female.	1920	1910	Male.	Female.	1920	1910
United States......	125,068	119,369	104.8	103.5	53,891	7,748	695.5	1,430.1	72,707	38,303	189.8	694.1	8,674	814	1,065.6	
GEOGRAPHIC DIVISIONS:																
New England........	848	867	97.8	103.5	3,301	301	1,096.7		284	63			92	23		
Middle Atlantic.....	3,068	2,872	106.8	113.5	8,067	745	1,082.8	2,763.3	2,647	619	427.6	664.2	1,028	75		
East North Central...	8,166	7,529	108.5	108.8	4,623	420	1,100.7	3,121.7	750	177	423.7		427	35		
West North Central..	18,026	18,337	103.2	102.6	1,525	153	996.7		946	269	351.7		164	21		
South Atlantic........	6,923	6,759	102.6	102.5	1,638	186	880.6		285	75			330	25		
East South Central....	854	769	111.1	107.8	475	67			27	8			27	1		
West South Central...	30,542	30,076	101.5	101.5	1,402	132	1,062.1		405	173	234.1		146	42		
Mountain............	39,863	37,096	107.3	104.5	3,913	426	918.5	2,154.6	7,825	2,967	263.7	2,505.2	323	48		
Pacific..............	15,938	15,073	105.7	101.8	28,947	5,318	544.3	1,133.6	59,538	33,952	175.4	601.8	6,137	544	1,128.1	
NEW ENGLAND:																
Maine................	420	419	100.2	108.9	153	8			7				1	1		
New Hampshire.......	13	15			93	2			6	2						
Vermont.............	15	9			11				4							
Massachusetts........	262	293	89.4	104.8	2,307	237	973.4		149	42			67	9		
Rhode Island........	59	51		89.3	201	24			31	4			6	5		
Connecticut..........	79	80			536	30			87	15			18	8		
MIDDLE ATLANTIC:																
New York............	2,816	2,687	104.8	103.5	5,240	553	947.6	2,519.9	2,190	496	441.5	646.7	676	59		
New Jersey..........	56	44			1,132	58			247	78			62	4		
Pennsylvania........	196	141	139.0	154.7	1,695	134	1,264.9		210	45			290	12		
EAST NORTH CENTRAL:																
Ohio................	94	57			876	65			104	26			82	10		
Indiana.............	73	52		121.4	276	7			66	15			17	3		
Illinois.............	108	86			2,523	253	997.2		374	98			220	11		
Michigan............	2,941	2,673	110.0	111.7	717	75			162	22			102	11		
Wisconsin...........	4,950	4,661	106.2	106.5	231	20			44	16			6			
WEST NORTH CENTRAL:																
Minnesota...........	4,424	4,337	102.0	102.3	448	60			66	19			20	6		
Iowa................	289	249	112.4	182.0	218	17			23	6			39	3		
Missouri............	87	84		99.4	383	29			115	23			46	6		
North Dakota........	3,183	3,071	103.6	98.8	119	5			63	9			1			
South Dakota........	8,295	8,089	102.5	99.4	124	18			26	12			3	1		
Nebraska............	1,459	1,429	102.1	103.0	169	20			611	193	316.6		27	3		
Kansas..............	1,198	1,078	111.1	132.8	64	4			42	10			28	2		
SOUTH ATLANTIC:																
Delaware............	2				41	2			8							
Maryland............	18	14			350	21			22	7			11	2		
District of Columbia...	20	17			417	44			90	13			130	14		
Virginia............	423	461	105.5	112.2	254	24			45	11			101	2		
West Virginia.......	4	3			85	13			9	1			4	2		
North Carolina.......	5,972	5,852	102.1	102.0	75	13			18	6			1			
South Carolina.......	145	159	91.2	99.4	76	17			11	4			53	2		
Georgia.............	68	57			187	24			9				7	1		
Florida.............	271	247	109.7		153	28			73	33			23	2		
EAST SOUTH CENTRAL:																
Kentucky............	27	30		112.7	56	6			7	2			3	1		
Tennessee...........	33	23		98.2	51	6			7	1			13			
Alabama............	211	194	108.8	99.8	55	4			13	5			8			
Mississippi..........	583	522	111.7	114.9	313	51							3			
WEST SOUTH CENTRAL:																
Arkansas............	61	45		88.5	97	16			3	2			3			
Louisiana...........	550	516	106.6	97.5	346	41			48	9			99	32		
Oklahoma...........	28,750	28,587	100.6	101.5	243	18			54	13			12	4		
Texas..............	1,181	928	127.3	117.3	716	57			300	149	201.3		32	6		
MOUNTAIN:																
Montana............	5,679	5,277	107.6	109.4	805	67			842	232	362.9		61	8		
Idaho...............	1,577	1,521	103.7	102.7	542	43			1,058	511	207.0		21	5		
Wyoming............	715	628	113.9	104.7	246	6			952	242	393.4		82	10		
Colorado............	734	649	113.1	120.5	252	39			1,601	863	185.5	2,029.6	65	5		
New Mexico..........	10,149	9,363	108.4	102.6	161	10			200	51			3	7		
Arizona.............	17,628	15,961	106.7	106.4	963	174	553.4		383	167	229.3		24	8		
Utah...............	1,442	1,269	113.6	115.4	314	28			2,174	762	285.3		55	5		
Nevada.............	2,479	2,428	102.1	101.0	630	59			615	139	442.4		12			
PACIFIC:																
Washington.........	4,552	4,509	101.0	99.6	2,088	275	759.3	1,325.8	11,322	6,065	186.7	665.9	1,089	61		
Oregon.............	2,301	2,289	100.5	99.1	2,629	461	570.3	2,200.9	2,802	1,349	207.7	1,062.6	246	22		
California..........	9,085	8,275	109.8	104.3	24,230	4,582	528.8	1,017.0	45,414	26,538	171.1	562.8	4,802	461	1,041.6	

[1] Comprises Filipinos, Hindus, Koreans, Maoris, Hawaiians, Malays, Samoans, and Siamese.   [2] Ratio not shown where number of females is less than 100.

SEX DISTRIBUTION.

TABLE 5.—SEX DISTRIBUTION, 1920, AND RATIO OF MALES TO FEMALES, 1920, 1910, AND 1900, FOR POPULATION CLASSES, BY DIVISIONS AND STATES.

DIVISION OR STATE AND CLASS OF POPULATION.	Male: 1920	Female: 1920	MALES TO 100 FEMALES.[1]		
			1920	1910	1900
UNITED STATES.					
Total	53,900,431	51,810,189	104.0	106.0	104.4
White	48,430,655	46,390,260	104.4	106.6	104.9
Negro	5,209,436	5,253,695	99.2	98.9	98.6
Ind., Chi., Jap., and all other	260,340	166,234	156.6	185.7	185.2
Native white	40,902,333	40,205,828	101.7	102.7	102.8
Native parentage	29,636,781	28,785,176	103.0	104.0	103.7
Foreign parentage	7,810,531	7,884,008	99.1	100.0	101.0
Mixed parentage	3,455,021	3,536,644	97.7	98.5	99.1
Foreign-born white	7,528,322	6,184,432	121.7	129.2	117.4
GEOGRAPHIC DIVISIONS.					
NEW ENGLAND.					
Total	3,672,591	3,723,318	98.5	99.3	97.7
White	3,627,911	3,688,168	98.4	99.2	97.6
Negro	40,155	38,896	103.2	97.8	93.6
Ind., Chi., Jap., and all other	4,525	1,254	360.8	415.0	640.2
Native white	2,682,175	2,763,250	97.1	97.1	97.7
Native parentage	1,388,963	1,414,186	98.2	98.1	98.1
Foreign parentage	935,127	971,213	96.3	96.3	96.9
Mixed parentage	358,085	377,851	94.8	95.2	96.9
Foreign-born white	945,736	924,918	102.3	104.8	97.5
MIDDLE ATLANTIC.					
Total	11,206,445	11,054,699	101.4	103.3	100.9
White	10,890,488	10,751,352	101.3	103.4	100.8
Negro	301,147	299,036	100.7	94.9	96.1
Ind., Chi., Jap., and all other	14,810	4,311	343.5	326.7	413.0
Native white	8,272,022	8,456,343	97.8	98.0	98.5
Native parentage	4,788,608	4,842,404	98.9	98.0	99.1
Foreign parentage	2,658,901	2,738,990	97.1	97.1	97.8
Mixed parentage	825,353	874,949	94.3	94.9	96.1
Foreign-born white	2,617,566	2,295,009	114.1	120.9	109.8
EAST NORTH CENTRAL.					
Total	11,035,041	10,440,502	105.7	106.0	104.7
White	10,748,049	10,190,813	105.5	106.0	104.6
Negro	273,026	241,528	113.0	108.3	109.0
Ind., Chi., Jap., and all other	13,966	8,161	171.1	148.6	143.3
Native white	8,938,715	8,776,808	101.8	101.4	102.1
Native parentage	5,991,476	5,798,894	103.3	102.9	103.3
Foreign parentage	2,016,078	2,027,614	99.4	99.1	101.1
Mixed parentage	931,161	950,360	98.0	97.7	97.5
Foreign-born white	1,809,334	1,413,945	128.0	131.3	118.4
WEST NORTH CENTRAL.					
Total	6,459,067	6,085,182	106.1	109.9	109.7
White	6,293,744	5,931,643	106.1	109.9	109.8
Negro	143,762	134,759	100.7	107.8	104.0
Ind., Chi., Jap., and all other	21,561	18,780	114.8	112.5	104.9
Native white	5,514,722	5,338,704	103.3	105.5	106.5
Native parentage	3,810,076	3,665,472	103.9	106.6	107.6
Foreign parentage	1,076,084	1,050,042	102.5	104.3	105.0
Mixed parentage	628,562	623,190	100.9	101.6	103.1
Foreign-born white	770,022	592,039	131.4	141.3	130.5
SOUTH ATLANTIC.					
Total	7,035,843	6,954,429	101.2	101.2	100.6
White	4,893,290	4,755,650	102.9	103.2	101.7
Negro	2,133,377	2,191,743	97.3	97.5	96.9
Ind., Chi., Jap., and all other	9,176	7,036	130.4	135.6	154.4
Native white	4,708,147	4,624,873	101.8	101.8	101.1
Native parentage	4,433,700	4,345,716	102.0	102.1	101.3
Foreign parentage	176,458	177,185	99.6	98.1	98.0
Mixed parentage	97,989	101,972	96.1	96.9	97.2
Foreign-born white	185,143	130,777	141.6	146.9	123.3
EAST SOUTH CENTRAL.					
Total	4,471,690	4,421,617	101.1	101.9	101.0
White	3,226,512	3,141,035	102.7	103.6	103.4
Negro	1,243,795	1,279,737	97.2	98.4	98.9
Ind., Chi., Jap., and all other	1,383	845	163.7	137.9	136.6
Native white	3,184,419	3,111,189	102.4	103.1	103.0
Native parentage	3,086,076	3,006,106	102.7	103.5	103.3
Foreign parentage	55,361	60,123	92.1	93.8	97.6
Mixed parentage	42,382	44,960	94.3	95.6	98.0
Foreign-born white	42,093	29,846	141.0	139.2	130.1
WEST SOUTH CENTRAL.					
Total	5,265,829	4,976,395	105.8	107.2	106.7
White	4,203,877	3,911,850	107.5	109.3	109.3
Negro	1,029,457	1,034,122	99.5	100.4	99.9
Ind., Chi., Jap., and all other	32,495	30,423	106.8	105.7	103.5
Native white	3,943,100	3,713,294	106.2	107.9	108.0
Native parentage	3,587,989	3,371,796	106.4	108.2	108.4
Foreign parentage	212,320	203,479	104.3	105.8	104.5
Mixed parentage	142,791	138,019	103.5	104.2	103.8
Foreign-born white	260,777	198,556	131.3	138.8	134.3

DIVISION OR STATE AND CLASS OF POPULATION.	Male: 1920	Female: 1920	MALES TO 100 FEMALES.[1]		
			1920	1910	1900
GEOGRAPHIC DIVISIONS—Continued.					
MOUNTAIN.					
Total	1,789,299	1,546,802	115.7	127.9	128.0
White	1,717,709	1,495,190	114.9	127.4	127.2
Negro	19,726	11,075	178.1	121.3	140.4
Ind., Chi., Jap., and all other	51,864	40,537	127.9	144.3	142.1
Native white	1,446,336	1,313,338	110.1	117.6	120.0
Native parentage	1,055,895	946,613	111.5	119.8	122.8
Foreign parentage	234,201	216,931	108.0	115.2	118.2
Mixed parentage	156,240	149,794	104.3	109.0	109.6
Foreign-born white	271,373	181,852	149.2	189.6	166.1
PACIFIC.					
Total	2,964,626	2,602,245	113.9	129.5	128.2
White	2,829,075	2,524,559	112.1	125.4	122.2
Negro	24,991	22,799	109.6	120.4	121.1
Ind., Chi., Jap., and all other	110,560	54,887	201.4	395.4	441.3
Native white	2,211,797	2,107,969	104.9	113.8	113.6
Native parentage	1,493,398	1,393,989	107.1	117.4	118.1
Foreign parentage	445,941	438,431	101.7	108.4	107.0
Mixed parentage	272,458	275,549	98.9	104.2	104.4
Foreign-born white	617,278	416,590	148.2	181.9	162.9
NEW ENGLAND.					
Maine.					
Total	388,752	379,262	102.5	103.2	102.2
White	387,455	378,240	102.4	103.2	102.1
Negro	716	594	120.5	105.6	103.2
Ind., Chi., Jap., and all other	581	428	135.7	137.2	141.1
Native white	331,648	326,698	101.5	101.8	101.5
Native parentage	250,299	245,481	102.0	101.9	101.2
Foreign parentage	43,382	42,768	101.4	101.8	102.4
Mixed parentage	37,967	38,449	98.7	101.6	102.6
Foreign-born white	55,807	51,542	108.3	111.1	106.7
New Hampshire.					
Total	222,112	220,971	100.5	100.9	99.6
White	221,667	220,664	100.5	100.9	99.5
Negro	333	288	115.6	104.3	97.6
Ind., Chi., and Jap	112	19	......	......	......
Native white	174,823	176,275	99.2	98.3	98.9
Native parentage	112,848	112,664	100.2	99.2	99.3
Foreign parentage	40,039	41,000	97.7	96.3	98.4
Mixed parentage	21,936	22,611	97.0	96.6	96.6
Foreign-born white	46,844	44,389	105.5	110.4	101.9
Vermont.					
Total	178,854	173,574	103.0	105.3	103.9
White	178,504	173,313	103.0	104.9	103.9
Negro	320	252	127.0	261.8	122.0
Ind., Chi., and Jap	30	9	......	......	......
Native white	154,793	152,498	101.5	101.6	101.5
Native parentage	115,392	112,033	102.2	102.7	101.9
Foreign parentage	21,184	20,916	101.3	100.2	101.1
Mixed parentage	18,217	18,649	97.7	96.5	99.2
Foreign-born white	23,711	20,815	113.9	127.3	121.4
Massachusetts.					
Total	1,890,014	1,962,342	96.3	96.7	95.1
White	1,864,317	1,939,207	96.1	96.6	94.9
Negro	22,912	22,554	101.6	97.1	95.2
Ind., Chi., Jap., and all other	2,785	581	479.3	714.0	1,090.8
Native white	1,330,998	1,394,992	95.4	95.3	95.9
Native parentage	601,525	629,248	95.6	95.2	95.7
Foreign parentage	534,966	558,292	95.8	95.9	96.2
Mixed parentage	194,507	207,452	93.8	94.0	95.8
Foreign-born white	533,319	544,215	98.0	99.5	92.6
Rhode Island.					
Total	297,524	306,873	97.0	99.3	96.5
White	292,131	301,849	96.8	99.2	96.5
Negro	5,096	4,940	103.2	95.1	89.3
Ind., Chi., Jap., and all other	297	84	......	263.6	......
Native white	205,967	214,514	96.0	97.1	96.7
Native parentage	86,368	87,185	99.1	99.6	98.0
Foreign parentage	88,657	94,003	94.3	95.6	95.3
Mixed parentage	30,942	33,326	92.8	94.1	95.6
Foreign-born white	86,164	87,335	98.7	103.6	96.1
Connecticut.					
Total	695,335	685,296	101.5	102.3	100.0
White	683,837	674,895	101.3	102.3	100.1
Negro	10,778	10,269	105.0	91.0	90.8
Ind., Chi., Jap., and all other	720	133	541.4	......	......
Native white	483,946	498,273	97.1	96.8	97.6
Native parentage	222,531	226,075	98.2	97.6	97.9
Foreign parentage	206,899	214,284	96.6	96.1	97.3
Mixed parentage	54,516	57,364	95.0	95.1	96.0
Foreign-born white	199,801	176,622	113.2	116.7	107.2

[1] Ratio not shown where number of females is less than 100.

112

POPULATION.

TABLE 5.—SEX DISTRIBUTION, 1920, AND RATIO OF MALES TO FEMALES, 1920, 1910, AND 1900, FOR POPULATION CLASSES, BY DIVISIONS AND STATES—Continued.

DIVISION OR STATE AND CLASS OF POPULATION.	Male: 1920	Female: 1920	MALES TO 100 FEMALES.[1] 1920	1910	1900
MIDDLE ATLANTIC.					
New York.					
Total	5,187,350	5,197,877	99.8	101.2	98.9
White	5,081,010	5,091,017	99.8	101.3	98.9
Negro	95,418	103,065	92.6	91.3	88.6
Ind., Chi., Jap., and all other	10,922	3,795	287.8	276.4	367.3
Native white	3,638,435	3,747,480	97.1	97.5	97.8
Native parentage	1,821,141	1,847,125	98.6	98.9	98.9
Foreign parentage	1,395,548	1,448,535	96.3	96.4	96.9
Mixed parentage	421,746	451,820	93.3	94.5	95.5
Foreign-born white	1,442,575	1,343,537	107.4	110.5	101.9
New Jersey.					
Total	1,590,075	1,565,825	101.5	102.9	100.0
White	1,531,146	1,505,941	101.7	103.1	100.1
Negro	57,432	59,700	96.2	94.5	93.5
Ind., Chi., Jap., and all other	1,497	184	813.6	1,029.1	......
Native white	1,139,491	1,158,983	98.3	98.0	97.8
Native parentage	605,157	607,518	99.6	98.9	98.3
Foreign parentage	409,035	420,023	97.4	97.4	97.7
Mixed parentage	125,299	131,442	95.3	95.4	95.4
Foreign-born white	391,655	346,958	112.9	118.2	107.8
Pennsylvania.					
Total	4,429,020	4,290,997	103.2	105.9	103.5
White	4,278,332	4,154,394	103.0	106.1	103.4
Negro	148,297	136,271	108.8	97.7	102.4
Ind., Chi., Jap., and all other	2,391	332	720.2	441.9	402.9
Native white	3,494,996	3,549,880	98.5	98.4	99.3
Native parentage	2,362,310	2,387,761	98.9	98.9	99.5
Foreign parentage	854,378	870,432	98.2	98.3	99.5
Mixed parentage	278,308	291,687	95.4	95.4	97.2
Foreign-born white	783,336	604,514	129.6	145.5	128.0
EAST NORTH CENTRAL.					
Ohio.					
Total	2,955,980	2,803,414	105.4	104.4	102.3
White	2,854,664	2,717,229	105.1	104.3	102.2
Negro	100,160	86,027	116.4	108.5	106.5
Ind., Chi., Jap., and all other	1,156	158	731.6	......	......
Native white	2,463,320	2,429,876	101.4	100.1	100.5
Native parentage	1,860,779	1,808,343	102.9	101.5	101.6
Foreign parentage	413,305	424,946	97.3	96.2	97.7
Mixed parentage	189,236	196,587	96.3	95.8	97.1
Foreign-born white	391,344	287,353	136.2	137.8	116.8
Indiana.					
Total	1,489,074	1,441,316	103.3	105.0	104.4
White	1,446,825	1,402,246	103.2	104.9	104.3
Negro	41,817	38,993	107.2	106.0	105.8
Ind., Chi., Jap., and all other	432	77	......	337.5	250.0
Native white	1,358,645	1,339,558	101.4	102.3	103.3
Native parentage	1,175,902	1,153,642	101.9	102.8	103.6
Foreign parentage	112,924	114,142	98.9	100.4	103.0
Mixed parentage	69,819	71,774	97.3	97.7	99.3
Foreign-born white	88,180	62,688	140.7	156.4	123.8
Illinois.					
Total	3,304,833	3,180,447	103.9	106.8	105.3
White	3,207,773	3,091,560	103.8	106.6	105.1
Negro	93,835	88,439	106.1	109.1	112.9
Ind., Chi., Jap., and all other	3,225	448	719.9	1,183.6	......
Native white	2,550,509	2,541,873	100.3	101.5	102.5
Native parentage	1,552,087	1,514,476	102.5	103.9	104.5
Foreign parentage	724,616	742,420	97.6	98.5	100.0
Mixed parentage	273,806	284,977	96.1	97.4	98.5
Foreign-born white	657,264	549,687	119.6	127.3	115.8
Michigan.					
Total	1,928,436	1,739,976	110.8	107.3	106.6
White	1,890,265	1,711,362	110.5	107.2	106.5
Negro	34,249	25,833	132.6	111.1	108.2
Ind., Chi., Jap., and all other	3,922	2,781	141.0	110.1	118.9
Native white	1,476,459	1,398,533	105.6	102.4	102.8
Native parentage	866,769	803,678	107.9	104.2	103.8
Foreign parentage	394,176	381,112	103.4	100.6	102.4
Mixed parentage	215,514	213,743	100.8	99.1	100.1
Foreign-born white	413,806	312,829	132.3	127.4	120.5
Wisconsin.					
Total	1,356,718	1,275,349	106.4	107.4	106.6
White	1,348,522	1,268,416	106.3	107.4	106.6
Negro	2,965	2,236	132.6	103.7	126.2
Ind., Chi., Jap., and all other	5,231	4,697	111.4	111.4	112.0
Native white	1,089,782	1,067,028	102.1	101.6	102.1
Native parentage	535,939	518,755	103.3	103.2	103.9
Foreign parentage	371,057	364,994	101.7	101.3	104.6
Mixed parentage	182,786	183,279	99.7	98.6	93.0
Foreign-born white	258,740	201,388	128.5	130.8	121.0
WEST NORTH CENTRAL.					
Minnesota.					
Total	1,245,537	1,141,583	109.1	114.6	113.9
White	1,235,728	1,133,208	109.0	114.5	113.9
Negro	4,851	3,958	122.6	144.2	133.6
Ind., Chi., Jap., and all other	4,958	4,422	112.1	109.1	104.5
Native white	957,140	925,632	103.4	105.7	107.2
Native parentage	424,834	402,793	105.5	110.2	112.2
Foreign parentage	358,334	349,792	102.4	103.8	105.1
Mixed parentage	173,972	173,047	100.5	100.9	108.2
Foreign-born white	278,588	207,576	134.2	144.0	132.2
Iowa.					
Total	1,229,392	1,174,629	104.7	106.6	107.6
White	1,218,711	1,165,470	104.6	106.5	107.5
Negro	10,121	8,884	113.9	118.5	118.2
Ind., Chi., Jap., and all other	560	275	203.6	242.9	165.1
Native white	1,091,646	1,066,888	102.3	103.0	104.8
Native parentage	775,407	753,140	103.0	103.8	105.6
Foreign parentage	189,699	187,017	101.4	102.7	103.8
Mixed parentage	126,540	126,725	99.9	99.2	102.2
Foreign-born white	127,065	98,582	128.9	135.7	126.7
Missouri.					
Total	1,723,319	1,680,736	102.5	105.1	105.6
White	1,631,697	1,593,347	102.4	105.1	105.8
Negro	90,901	87,250	104.2	102.4	101.5
Ind., Chi., Jap., and all other	631	139	454.0	419.7	......
Native white	1,528,279	1,510,739	101.2	103.0	104.5
Native parentage	1,283,069	1,253,867	102.3	104.2	105.5
Foreign parentage	146,528	153,536	95.4	97.9	100.5
Mixed parentage	98,682	103,336	95.5	97.5	100.0
Foreign-born white	103,418	82,608	125.2	135.9	124.3
North Dakota.					
Total	341,673	305,199	112.0	123.4	125.3
White	338,031	301,923	112.0	122.6	125.8
Negro	276	191	144.5	161.4	153.1
Ind., Chi., Jap., and all other	3,366	3,085	109.1	101.8	104.0
Native white	262,045	245,806	106.9	114.9	117.4
Native parentage	108,334	99,632	108.7	121.6	130.9
Foreign parentage	104,728	99,245	105.5	111.5	111.1
Mixed parentage	49,583	46,929	105.7	109.1	111.9
Foreign-born white	75,386	56,117	134.3	145.8	142.4
South Dakota.					
Total	337,120	299,427	112.6	118.9	116.6
White	328,197	290,950	112.8	119.5	117.8
Negro	475	357	133.1	134.1	140.9
Ind., Chi., Jap., and all other	8,448	8,120	104.0	100.9	95.4
Native white	280,587	250,169	109.5	114.5	112.8
Native parentage	161,980	146,618	110.5	118.2	117.0
Foreign parentage	74,127	67,214	110.3	111.6	110.1
Mixed parentage	44,480	42,337	105.1	108.5	107.8
Foreign-born white	47,610	34,781	136.9	145.8	136.4
Nebraska.					
Total	672,805	623,567	107.9	111.2	112.5
White	663,230	615,989	107.7	111.0	112.5
Negro	7,309	5,933	123.2	124.2	116.1
Ind., Chi., Jap., and all other	2,266	1,645	137.8	141.7	116.4
Native white	578,953	550,614	105.1	107.1	109.5
Native parentage	389,049	368,015	105.7	108.5	111.5
Foreign parentage	118,286	113,662	104.1	105.2	106.4
Mixed parentage	71,618	68,937	103.9	103.8	105.6
Foreign-born white	84,277	65,375	128.9	136.7	128.8
Kansas.					
Total	909,221	860,036	105.7	110.0	109.5
White	878,150	830,756	105.7	110.1	109.7
Negro	29,739	28,186	105.5	107.3	104.2
Ind., Chi., Jap., and all other	1,332	1,094	121.8	143.1	135.9
Native white	815,472	782,850	104.2	107.1	107.7
Native parentage	667,403	641,401	104.1	107.4	108.0
Foreign parentage	84,388	79,576	106.0	107.5	107.8
Mixed parentage	63,681	61,879	102.9	104.2	104.2
Foreign-born white	62,678	47,900	130.9	149.9	132.9
SOUTH ATLANTIC.					
Delaware.					
Total	113,755	109,248	104.1	104.6	104.0
White	98,049	94,566	103.7	104.4	104.0
Negro	15,655	14,680	106.6	105.5	103.5
Ind., Chi., and Jap.	51	2	......	......	......
Native white	86,680	86,125	100.6	101.6	102.4
Native parentage	70,517	69,359	101.7	102.5	102.9
Foreign parentage	11,479	11,809	97.2	98.0	100.0
Mixed parentage	4,684	4,957	94.5	96.9	100.0
Foreign-born white	11,369	8,441	134.7	132.4	121.5

[1] Ratio not shown where number of females is less than 100.

SEX DISTRIBUTION. 113

TABLE 5.—SEX DISTRIBUTION, 1920, AND RATIO OF MALES TO FEMALES, 1920, 1910, AND 1900, FOR POPULATION CLASSES, BY DIVISIONS AND STATES—Continued.

DIVISION OR STATE AND CLASS OF POPULATION.	Male: 1920	Female: 1920	Males to 100 Females.[1] 1920	1910	1900
SOUTH ATLANTIC—Continued.					
Maryland.					
Total.....	729,455	720,206	101.3	98.9	98.4
White.....	605,601	599,136	101.1	99.2	98.7
Negro.....	123,453	121,026	102.0	97.7	96.8
Ind., Chi., Jap., and all other....	401	44			
Native white.....	550,973	551,587	99.9	98.1	98.4
Native parentage.....	448,287	444,801	100.8	99.0	99.1
Foreign parentage.....	70,267	72,936	96.3	94.9	96.0
Mixed parentage.....	32,419	33,850	95.8	94.7	95.3
Foreign-born white.....	54,628	47,549	114.0	108.9	101.9
District of Columbia.					
Total.....	203,543	234,028	87.0	91.3	90.0
White.....	152,031	174,829	87.0	94.9	94.8
Negro.....	50,855	59,111	86.0	82.2	79.3
Ind., Chi., Jap., and all other.....	657	88			
Native white.....	136,889	161,423	84.8	93.1	93.2
Native parentage.....	109,872	129,616	84.8	93.4	94.0
Foreign parentage.....	16,549	18,580	89.1	91.9	91.9
Mixed parentage.....	10,468	13,227	79.1	89.7	88.8
Foreign-born white.....	15,142	13,406	112.9	113.0	109.7
Virginia.					
Total.....	1,168,492	1,140,695	102.4	100.9	99.7
White.....	825,133	792,776	104.1	102.8	101.9
Negro.....	342,536	347,481	98.6	97.1	95.9
Ind., Chi., Jap., and all other.....	823	438	187.9	167.8	267.9
Native white.....	806,082	781,042	103.2	101.8	101.1
Native parentage.....	778,053	756,441	102.9	101.6	100.9
Foreign parentage.....	16,545	13,969	118.4	110.6	110.1
Mixed parentage.....	11,484	10,632	108.0	104.4	103.1
Foreign-born white.....	19,051	11,734	162.4	169.0	171.1
West Virginia.					
Total.....	783,100	700,601	108.9	111.6	108.6
White.....	715,869	661,366	108.2	110.5	107.4
Negro.....	47,129	39,216	120.2	132.8	137.3
Ind., Chi., Jap., and all other.....	102	19			
Native white.....	673,959	641,370	105.1	106.1	106.2
Native parentage.....	632,425	600,432	105.3	106.3	106.4
Foreign parentage.....	28,591	28,034	102.0	102.2	103.0
Mixed parentage.....	12,943	12,904	100.3	100.5	101.0
Foreign-born white.....	41,910	19,996	209.6	201.8	172.4
North Carolina.					
Total.....	1,279,082	1,280,001	99.9	99.2	98.3
White.....	899,031	884,748	101.6	101.2	100.1
Negro.....	373,965	389,442	96.0	94.8	94.6
Ind., Chi., Jap., and all other.....	6,066	5,871	103.3	103.9	102.0
Native white.....	894,690	881,990	101.4	101.0	99.9
Native parentage.....	888,053	876,250	101.4	100.4	99.9
Foreign parentage.....	2,932	2,805	104.5	100.4	99.5
Mixed parentage.....	2,805	2,935	95.6	97.0	100.0
Foreign-born white.....	4,341	2,758	157.4	170.5	161.2
South Carolina.					
Total.....	838,293	845,431	99.2	98.5	98.4
White.....	415,823	402,715	103.3	102.4	101.6
Negro.....	422,185	442,534	95.4	95.4	96.2
Ind., Chi., Jap., and all other.....	285	182	156.6	125.0	
Native white.....	411,728	400,409	102.8	102.0	101.3
Native parentage.....	405,120	394,298	102.7	102.0	101.4
Foreign parentage.....	3,678	3,347	109.9	95.2	92.4
Mixed parentage.....	2,930	2,764	106.0	99.2	97.2
Foreign-born white.....	4,095	2,306	177.6	159.3	142.8
Georgia.					
Total.....	1,444,823	1,451,009	99.6	100.1	99.1
White.....	854,109	835,005	102.3	102.4	100.8
Negro.....	590,443	615,922	95.9	97.2	97.1
Ind., Chi., Jap., and all other.....	271	82			
Native white.....	844,105	828,823	101.8	101.9	100.4
Native parentage.....	828,637	814,060	101.8	101.9	100.5
Foreign parentage.....	8,522	7,849	108.6	103.6	98.9
Mixed parentage.....	6,946	6,914	100.5	98.9	96.5
Foreign-born white.....	10,004	6,182	161.8	171.4	153.7
SOUTH ATLANTIC—Continued.					
Florida.					
Total.....	495,320	473,150	104.7	110.0	108.7
White.....	327,644	310,509	105.5	110.2	108.5
Negro.....	167,156	162,331	103.0	109.5	108.7
Ind., Chi., Jap., and all other.....	520	310	167.7		199.4
Native white.....	303,041	292,104	103.7	107.0	106.6
Native parentage.....	271,836	260,459	104.4	107.6	107.1
Foreign parentage.....	17,895	17,856	100.2	102.7	101.7
Mixed parentage.....	13,310	13,789	96.5	90.7	100.5
Foreign-born white.....	24,603	18,405	133.7	157.6	140.8
EAST SOUTH CENTRAL.					
Kentucky.					
Total.....	1,227,494	1,189,136	103.2	103.0	103.1
White.....	1,108,853	1,071,707	103.5	103.2	103.7
Negro.....	118,548	117,390	101.0	101.0	99.6
Ind., Chi., Jap., and all other.....	93	39		161.4	
Native white.....	1,091,374	1,058,406	103.1	103.0	103.5
Native parentage.....	1,039,134	1,000,000	103.9	103.8	104.2
Foreign parentage.....	30,816	35,115	87.8	90.3	94.4
Mixed parentage.....	21,424	23,291	92.0	93.2	96.1
Foreign-born white.....	17,479	13,301	131.4	117.2	111.6
Tennessee.					
Total.....	1,173,967	1,163,918	100.9	102.1	102.2
White.....	951,224	934,769	101.8	103.3	103.3
Negro.....	222,639	229,119	97.2	97.6	98.6
Ind., Chi., Jap., and all other.....	104	30		144.5	
Native white.....	942,203	928,312	101.5	102.0	103.0
Native parentage.....	923,544	909,213	101.6	103.0	103.0
Foreign parentage.....	10,158	10,265	99.0	98.5	103.1
Mixed parentage.....	8,501	8,834	96.2	97.2	101.0
Foreign-born white.....	9,021	6,457	139.7	152.4	141.1
Alabama.					
Total.....	1,173,105	1,175,069	99.8	101.0	100.5
White.....	733,039	713,993	102.7	103.8	102.8
Negro.....	439,779	460,873	95.4	97.2	97.9
Ind., Chi., Jap., and all other.....	287	203	141.4	115.2	
Native white.....	722,414	706,956	102.2	103.1	102.1
Native parentage.....	704,980	689,149	102.3	103.2	102.0
Foreign parentage.....	9,695	9,896	98.0	100.4	105.5
Mixed parentage.....	7,739	7,911	97.8	98.5	90.5
Foreign-born white.....	10,625	7,037	151.0	165.9	100.1
Mississippi.					
Total.....	897,124	893,494	100.4	101.6	101.5
White.....	433,396	420,566	103.1	104.7	103.9
Negro.....	462,829	472,355	98.0	99.2	99.8
Ind., Chi., and all other.....	899	573	156.9	149.3	125.3
Native white.....	428,428	417,515	102.6	104.1	103.1
Native parentage.....	419,018	407,744	102.8	104.2	103.2
Foreign parentage.....	4,692	4,847	96.8	100.8	101.4
Mixed parentage.....	4,718	4,924	95.8	99.9	100.2
Foreign-born white.....	4,968	3,051	162.8	173.7	193.4
WEST SOUTH CENTRAL.					
Arkansas.					
Total.....	895,228	856,976	104.5	106.0	106.1
White.....	658,169	621,588	105.9	107.7	107.7
Negro.....	236,895	235,325	100.7	101.7	102.1
Ind., Chi., Jap., and all other.....	164	63		113.7	
Native white.....	649,578	616,204	105.4	107.0	107.0
Native parentage.....	628,850	597,830	105.2	106.8	106.7
Foreign parentage.....	10,360	8,661	119.7	118.8	122.1
Mixed parentage.....	10,353	9,707	106.7	107.0	112.3
Foreign-born white.....	8,591	5,384	159.6	168.3	108.9
Louisiana.					
Total.....	903,335	895,174	100.9	101.7	101.1
White.....	557,498	539,113	103.4	104.3	103.5
Negro.....	344,794	355,463	97.0	98.3	98.8
Ind., Chi., Jap., and all other.....	1,043	598	174.4	226.8	328.7
Native white.....	530,690	521,050	101.9	102.8	102.0
Native parentage.....	478,415	463,309	103.3	104.2	103.7
Foreign parentage.....	31,923	35,093	91.0	94.2	94.2
Mixed parentage.....	20,352	22,648	89.9	92.3	93.4
Foreign-born white.....	26,808	18,063	148.4	133.0	125.3

[1] Ratio not shown where number of females is less than 100.

75647°—22——8

POPULATION.

114

TABLE 5.—SEX DISTRIBUTION, 1920, AND RATIO OF MALES TO FEMALES, 1920, 1910, AND 1900, FOR POPULATION CLASSES, BY DIVISIONS AND STATES—Continued.

DIVISION OR STATE AND CLASS OF POPULATION.	Male: 1920	Female: 1920	MALES TO 100 FEMALES.[1]		
			1920	1910	1900
WEST SOUTH CENTRAL—Continued.					
Oklahoma.[2]					
Total	1,058,044	970,239	109.0	113.7	115.3
White	952,691	868,503	109.7	114.7	117.9
Negro	76,294	73,114	104.3	109.5	106.0
Ind., Chi., Jap., and all other	29,059	28,622	101.5	102.0	98.6
Native white	927,760	853,466	108.7	113.3	116.7
Native parentage	873,888	805,219	108.5	113.1	116.4
Foreign parentage	28,271	24,812	113.9	118.7	121.8
Mixed parentage	25,601	23,435	109.2	113.4	118.0
Foreign-born white	24,931	15,037	165.8	178.1	194.4
Texas.					
Total	2,409,222	2,254,006	106.9	107.4	107.4
White	2,035,519	1,882,646	108.1	109.0	103.4
Negro	371,474	370,220	100.3	100.0	99.9
Ind., Chi., Jap., and all other	2,229	1,140	195.5	314.4	488.8
Native white	1,835,072	1,722,574	106.5	107.3	107.8
Native parentage	1,606,830	1,505,432	106.7	107.5	108.3
Foreign parentage	141,757	134,913	105.1	105.8	104.7
Mixed parentage	86,485	82,229	105.2	105.0	104.1
Foreign-born white	200,447	160,072	125.2	132.6	131.6
MOUNTAIN.					
Montana.					
Total	299,941	248,948	120.5	152.1	160.3
White	291,592	242,668	120.2	152.2	159.7
Negro	962	696	138.2	136.3	149.3
Ind., Chi., Jap., and all other	7,387	5,584	132.3	150.5	170.8
Native white	233,363	207,277	112.6	132.1	141.1
Native parentage	147,662	128,141	115.2	139.6	149.7
Foreign parentage	53,379	48,539	110.0	124.4	137.0
Mixed parentage	32,322	30,597	105.6	116.5	120.0
Foreign-born white	58,229	35,391	164.5	238.4	225.5
Idaho.					
Total	233,919	197,947	118.2	132.5	136.5
White	230,136	195,532	117.7	131.3	134.0
Negro	585	335	174.6	157.3	130.7
Ind., Chi., Jap., and all other	3,198	2,080	153.8	216.0	211.0
Native white	205,259	181,446	113.1	121.9	126.0
Native parentage	155,973	138,270	112.8	123.0	127.9
Foreign parentage	25,781	22,139	116.5	123.4	128.7
Mixed parentage	23,505	21,028	111.8	114.0	114.9
Foreign-born white	24,877	14,086	176.6	227.5	197.2
Wyoming.					
Total	110,359	84,043	131.3	168.8	169.4
White	107,501	82,645	130.1	165.6	168.2
Negro	863	512	168.6	223.4	204.2
Ind., Chi., Jap., and all other	1,995	886	225.2	335.8	206.0
Native white	90,567	74,324	121.9	147.1	156.9
Native parentage	68,042	54,842	124.1	151.8	163.0
Foreign parentage	13,535	11,699	115.7	139.3	148.5
Mixed parentage	8,990	7,783	115.5	130.0	141.1
Foreign-born white	16,934	8,321	203.5	287.2	231.9
Colorado.					
Total	492,731	446,898	110.3	116.9	120.9
White	484,245	439,858	110.1	116.4	120.8
Negro	5,834	5,484	106.4	105.0	109.2
Ind., Chi., Jap., and all other	2,652	1,556	170.4	421.5	191.5
Native white	416,026	391,123	106.4	109.7	114.5
Native parentage	313,759	289,282	108.5	112.0	117.4
Foreign parentage	65,574	64,485	101.7	105.4	110.2
Mixed parentage	36,693	37,356	98.2	101.1	103.0
Foreign-born white	68,219	48,735	140.0	160.1	158.1
New Mexico.					
Total	190,456	169,894	112.1	115.3	114.4
White	175,350	159,323	110.1	115.8	114.1
Negro	4,593	1,140	402.9	120.9	174.3
Ind., Chi., Jap., and all other	10,513	9,431	111.5	107.3	113.4
Native white	158,505	147,091	107.8	111.5	110.8
Native parentage	141,937	131,380	108.0	111.1	110.5
Foreign parentage	9,715	9,150	106.2	116.1	118.6
Mixed parentage	6,853	6,561	104.5	113.6	107.6
Foreign-born white	16,845	12,232	137.7	189.6	165.7

DIVISION OR STATE AND CLASS OF POPULATION.	Male: 1920	Female: 1920	MALES TO 100 FEMALES.[1]		
			1920	1910	1900
MOUNTAIN—Continued.					
Arizona.					
Total	183,602	150,560	121.9	138.2	140.4
White	159,345	132,104	120.6	142.9	146.6
Negro	5,859	2,146	273.0	110.4	281.0
Ind., Chi., Jap., and all other	18,398	16,310	112.8	117.0	117.1
Native white	114,688	98,662	116.2	129.3	139.3
Native parentage	82,435	68,710	120.0	135.0	146.3
Foreign parentage	20,497	19,037	107.7	122.3	131.4
Mixed parentage	11,756	10,915	107.7	113.7	122.7
Foreign-born white	44,657	33,442	133.5	188.4	172.9
Utah.					
Total	232,051	217,345	106.8	111.5	104.9
White	227,232	214,669	105.9	110.1	104.0
Negro	834	612	136.3	152.5	208.3
Ind., Chi., Jap., and all other	3,985	2,064	193.1	258.2	177.4
Native white	196,357	180,080	103.8	106.2	104.4
Native parentage	125,360	120,421	104.1	108.2	105.6
Foreign parentage	39,185	36,716	100.7	105.8	104.6
Mixed parentage	31,812	31,952	99.6	101.1	101.4
Foreign-born white	30,875	25,580	120.7	131.0	102.5
Nevada.					
Total	46,240	31,167	148.4	179.2	153.0
White	42,308	28,391	149.0	181.5	151.3
Negro	196	150	130.7	105.2	
Ind., Chi., Jap., and all other	3,736	2,626	142.3	163.4	162.1
Native white	31,571	24,326	129.8	153.4	131.9
Native parentage	20,727	15,558	133.2	161.3	142.5
Foreign parentage	6,535	5,166	126.5	147.2	122.0
Mixed parentage	4,309	3,602	119.6	132.6	114.5
Foreign-born white	10,737	4,065	264.1	331.4	240.5
PACIFIC.					
Washington.					
Total	734,701	621,920	118.1	136.3	142.2
White	711,693	608,084	117.0	134.2	139.0
Negro	3,957	2,926	135.2	160.9	171.8
Ind., Chi., Jap., and all other	19,051	10,910	174.6	262.9	260.9
Native white	558,575	511,147	109.3	120.8	128.4
Native parentage	374,555	337,151	111.1	124.2	133.9
Foreign parentage	111,145	103,473	107.4	110.4	120.9
Mixed parentage	72,875	70,523	103.3	110.0	113.0
Foreign-born white	153,118	96,937	158.0	199.7	191.4
Oregon.					
Total	416,334	367,055	113.4	133.2	129.0
White	407,150	361,987	112.5	130.1	122.8
Negro	1,197	947	126.4	155.0	158.2
Ind., Chi., Jap., and all other	7,978	4,121	193.6	410.5	490.2
Native white	344,849	322,146	107.0	119.5	116.8
Native parentage	258,647	239,079	108.2	121.6	118.3
Foreign parentage	49,146	46,681	105.3	116.5	115.8
Mixed parentage	37,056	36,386	101.8	108.7	108.4
Foreign-born white	62,310	39,841	156.4	209.0	169.6
California.					
Total	1,813,591	1,613,270	112.4	125.5	123.5
White	1,710,223	1,554,488	110.0	120.1	116.6
Negro	19,837	18,926	104.8	104.8	109.2
Ind., Chi., Jap., and all other	83,531	39,856	209.6	448.4	511.2
Native white	1,308,373	1,274,676	102.6	108.7	107.7
Native parentage	860,196	817,759	105.2	112.4	112.1
Foreign parentage	285,650	288,277	99.1	103.6	102.0
Mixed parentage	162,527	168,640	96.4	100.7	101.0
Foreign-born white	401,850	270,812	143.6	169.6	153.8

[1] Ratio not shown where number of females is less than 100.
[2] Ratios for 1900 based upon combined population of Oklahoma and Indian Territory.

SEX DISTRIBUTION.

115

Table 6.—SEX DISTRIBUTION AND RATIO OF MALES TO FEMALES, FOR WHITE AND NEGRO POPULATION, FOR CITIES HAVING, IN 1920, 100,000 INHABITANTS OR MORE: 1920 AND 1910.

CITY.	TOTAL POPULATION.						WHITE.				NEGRO.			
	1920		1910		Males to 100 females.		1920		Males to 100 females.		1920		Males to 100 females.	
	Male.	Female.	Male.	Female.	1920	1910	Male.	Female.	1920	1910	Male.	Female.	1920	1910
Akron, Ohio	121,160	87,266	36,604	32,463	138.9	112.8	117,481	85,237	137.8	112.7	3,554	2,026	175.4	119.0
Albany, N. Y.	54,674	58,670	48,270	51,983	93.2	92.9	53,975	58,061	93.0	92.8	635	604	105.1	92.0
Atlanta, Ga.	96,457	104,159	74,501	80,338	92.6	92.7	67,435	70,350	95.9	99.2	28,993	33,803	85.8	81.0
Baltimore, Md.	361,560	372,266	268,195	290,290	97.1	92.4	308,321	316,806	97.3	93.6	52,889	55,433	95.4	85.5
Birmingham, Ala.	89,015	89,791	67,268	65,417	99.1	102.8	54,832	53,718	102.1	107.3	34,160	36,070	94.7	96.3
Boston, Mass.	368,756	379,304	320,703	310,882	97.2	96.7	359,403	371,082	96.9	96.4	8,295	8,055	103.0	96.6
Bridgeport, Conn.	73,709	69,846	52,549	49,505	105.5	106.1	72,386	68,834	105.2	106.2	1,220	1,008	121.0	97.3
Buffalo, N. Y.	253,654	253,121	212,502	211,213	100.2	100.6	250,973	251,069	100.0	100.5	2,522	1,989	126.8	111.1
Cambridge, Mass.	52,428	57,266	50,161	54,678	91.6	91.7	49,800	54,456	91.5	91.6	2,535	2,790	90.6	89.8
Camden, N. J.	59,212	57,007	47,396	47,142	103.7	100.5	54,856	52,897	103.7	100.8	4,304	4,196	102.6	94.3
Chicago, Ill.	1,369,017	1,331,788	1,125,764	1,059,519	102.9	106.3	1,311,243	1,277,926	102.6	106.1	55,913	53,515	104.5	105.9
Cincinnati, Ohio	194,342	206,905	177,511	186,080	93.9	95.4	179,144	191,953	93.3	95.0	15,145	14,934	101.4	101.8
Cleveland, Ohio	413,398	383,443	289,262	271,301	107.8	106.6	394,337	367,689	107.2	106.5	18,733	15,718	119.2	105.7
Columbus, Ohio	118,810	118,221	91,452	90,059	100.5	101.5	106,905	107,876	99.2	100.6	11,798	10,393	113.4	113.9
Dallas, Tex.	79,506	79,470	46,499	45,605	100.0	102.0	67,629	67,259	100.6	101.2	11,828	12,195	97.0	92.9
Dayton, Ohio	77,114	75,445	58,848	57,729	102.2	101.9	72,308	71,187	101.6	101.8	4,776	4,249	112.4	104.6
Denver, Colo.	131,905	124,585	107,395	105,986	105.9	101.3	128,221	121,423	105.6	100.8	3,009	3,000	102.1	95.6
Des Moines, Iowa	62,178	64,290	43,135	43,233	96.7	99.8	59,342	61,515	96.4	99.6	2,771	2,741	101.1	103.5
Detroit, Mich.	540,248	453,439	240,354	225,412	119.1	106.6	515,989	436,076	118.3	106.6	23,605	17,233	137.0	108.3
Fall River, Mass.	57,918	62,567	57,627	61,668	92.6	93.4	57,716	62,398	92.5	93.3	152	163	93.3	96.1
Fort Worth, Tex.	56,366	50,116	39,007	34,305	112.5	113.7	48,247	42,219	114.3	115.7	8,010	7,886	101.6	104.3
Grand Rapids, Mich.	67,516	70,118	55,539	57,042	96.3	97.4	66,908	69,564	96.2	97.3	555	535	103.7	100.1
Hartford, Conn.	69,106	68,930	49,211	49,704	100.3	99.0	66,832	66,819	100.0	99.1	2,137	2,002	103.6	84.1
Houston, Tex.	69,048	69,228	40,126	38,674	99.7	103.8	52,621	51,647	101.9	111.2	16,391	17,566	93.3	88.3
Indianapolis, Ind.	155,839	158,355	116,069	117,581	98.4	98.7	138,362	141,049	98.1	98.7	17,378	17,300	100.5	98.1
Jersey City, N. J.	150,416	147,687	137,457	130,322	101.8	105.5	146,229	143,780	101.7	105.4	4,099	3,901	105.1	102.7
Kansas City, Kans.	51,798	49,379	42,772	39,558	104.9	108.1	44,615	42,088	106.0	109.3	7,130	7,275	98.0	99.1
Kansas City, Mo.	162,362	162,048	126,414	121,967	100.2	103.6	146,741	146,776	100.0	103.8	15,472	15,217	101.5	101.7
Los Angeles, Calif.	285,175	291,408	162,669	156,529	97.8	103.9	268,231	278,236	96.3	101.3	7,389	8,190	90.2	94.0
Louisville, Ky.	112,159	122,732	108,548	115,380	91.4	94.1	93,037	101,732	91.5	94.2	19,094	20,993	91.0	93.7
Lowell, Mass.	54,271	58,488	51,525	54,769	92.8	94.1	54,098	58,411	92.6	94.0	100	70	80.7[1]	92.9[1]
Memphis, Tenn.	79,116	83,235	66,270	64,835	95.1	102.2	50,132	50,981	98.3	108.9	28,935	32,246	89.5	95.2
Milwaukee, Wis.	228,614	228,533	189,488	184,369	100.0	102.8	227,310	227,514	99.9	102.8	1,233	1,000	123.8	137.1
Minneapolis, Minn.	189,215	191,367	157,345	144,063	98.9	109.2	186,852	189,513	98.6	108.9	2,133	1,794	118.9	131.1
Nashville, Tenn.	56,004	62,338	52,155	58,209	89.8	89.6	39,827	42,876	92.9	94.7	16,173	19,460	83.1	80.0
New Bedford, Mass.	59,388	61,829	47,731	48,921	96.1	97.6	56,565	59,577	94.9	97.2	2,756	2,242	122.9	100.1
New Haven, Conn.	80,221	82,316	66,695	66,910	97.5	99.7	77,822	79,904	97.3	99.7	2,269	2,304	98.5	92.5
New Orleans, La.	189,026	198,193	163,230	175,836	95.4	92.8	141,790	144,126	98.4	95.6	46,919	54,011	85.9	84.7
New York, N. Y.	2,802,638	2,817,410	2,382,482	2,384,401	99.5	99.9	2,723,217	2,736,246	99.5	100.0	72,351	80,116	90.3	85.0
Bronx borough	364,208	367,808	217,120	213,800	99.0	101.5	361,748	365,242	99.0	100.1	2,269	2,534	89.5	86.6
Brooklyn borough	1,007,879	1,010,497	809,791	824,500	99.7	98.2	991,274	993,670	99.8	98.3	15,197	16,715	90.9	82.2
Manhattan borough	1,135,708	1,148,995	1,166,659	1,164,883	98.9	100.2	1,078,536	1,090,320	98.9	100.2	51,912	57,221	90.7	86.2
Queens borough	233,410	235,002	144,205	139,846	99.1	103.1	230,998	232,663	99.3	103.3	2,238	2,882	77.7	81.9
Richmond borough	61,423	55,108	44,707	41,262	111.5	108.3	60,611	54,342	111.5	108.6	735	764	96.2	83.1
Newark, N. J.	209,200	205,324	173,380	174,080	101.9	99.6	200,348	196,875	101.8	99.8	8,552	8,425	101.5	89.6
Norfolk, Va.	60,018	55,750	32,867	34,585	107.6	95.0	38,077	34,149	111.5	99.7	21,794	21,598	100.9	90.4
Oakland, Calif.	111,954	104,307	78,222	71,952	107.3	108.7	103,922	100,082	103.8	103.9	3,029	2,460	123.1	112.0
Omaha, Nebr.[2]	98,954	92,047	79,303	70,992	106.8	111.8	93,151	87,895	106.0	111.1	5,598	4,717	118.7	120.5
Paterson, N. J.	67,218	68,027	62,430	63,161	98.8	98.9	66,452	67,802	98.0	98.9	731	820	89.1	85.6
Philadelphia, Pa.	907,633	916,146	760,463	788,545	99.1	96.4	839,296	848,884	98.9	96.8	67,132	67,097	100.1	87.6
Pittsburgh, Pa.	295,260	292,083	273,580	260,316	101.4	105.1	276,025	274,236	100.7	104.8	19,013	17,812	111.8	108.8
Portland, Oreg.	132,115	126,173	118,808	88,346	104.7	134.5	128,430	124,531	103.1	127.4	833	723	115.2	139.1
Providence, R. I.	115,154	122,441	110,288	114,038	94.0	96.7	112,150	119,606	93.8	96.6	2,850	2,805	101.6	94.1
Reading, Pa.	53,198	54,586	47,576	48,495	97.5	98.1	52,698	54,153	97.3	98.0	491	433	113.4	108.2
Richmond, Va.	80,631	91,036	60,905	66,723	88.6	91.3	55,896	61,678	90.6	95.1	24,696	29,345	84.2	85.0
Rochester, N. Y.	145,494	150,256	108,352	109,797	96.8	98.7	144,689	149,400	96.8	98.7	744	835	89.1	93.2
St. Louis, Mo.	383,402	389,495	340,068	340,961	98.4	101.5	347,605	354,950	97.9	101.3	35,359	34,495	102.5	101.7
St. Paul, Minn.	117,368	117,330	111,800	102,935	100.0	108.6	115,427	115,744	99.7	108.6	1,829	1,547	118.2	133.5
Salt Lake City, Utah	58,697	59,413	47,583	45,194	98.8	105.3	57,832	58,949	98.1	104.0	392	326	120.2	143.2
San Antonio, Tex.	80,782	80,597	47,865	48,749	100.2	98.2	73,741	73,058	100.9	99.9	6,842	7,499	91.2	84.5
San Francisco, Calif.	272,703	233,973	236,901	180,011	116.6	131.6	260,885	229,137	113.9	125.8	1,362	1,052	129.5	166.1
Scranton, Pa.	67,519	70,234	65,591	64,276	96.2	102.0	67,243	69,971	96.1	102.0	300	263	114.1	116.4
Seattle, Wash.	167,601	147,711	136,773	100,421	113.5	136.2	159,279	143,301	111.1	131.2	1,671	1,223	136.6	154.5
Spokane, Wash.	52,329	52,108	57,513	46,889	100.4	122.7	51,706	51,674	100.1	121.6	382	345	110.7	117.8
Springfield, Mass.	63,722	65,892	43,221	45,705	96.7	94.6	62,232	64,567	96.4	94.6	1,339	1,311	102.1	83.2
Syracuse, N. Y.	85,935	85,782	68,806	68,443	100.2	100.5	85,207	85,165	100.0	100.5	677	583	116.1	106.2
Toledo, Ohio	125,518	117,646	84,691	83,806	106.7	101.1	122,255	115,130	106.2	101.0	3,184	2,507	127.0	99.7
Trenton, N. J.	60,639	58,650	50,231	46,584	103.4	107.8	58,330	56,572	103.1	107.4	2,241	2,074	108.1	123.1
Washington, D. C.	203,543	234,028	158,050	173,019	87.0	91.3	152,031	174,829	87.0	94.9	50,855	59,111	86.0	82.2
Wilmington, Del.	56,180	53,988	43,938	43,473	104.1	101.1	50,574	48,808	103.6	101.9	5,598	5,178	107.5	93.6
Worcester, Mass.	89,586	90,168	73,424	72,562	99.4	101.2	88,898	89,493	99.3	101.2	608	650	93.5	84.9
Yonkers, N. Y.	49,010	51,166	40,103	39,700	95.8	101.0	48,061	50,117	95.9	101.1	898	1,042	86.2	89.6
Youngstown, Ohio	70,770	61,588	43,640	35,417	114.9	123.2	66,774	58,821	113.5	123.2	3,900	2,762	141.2	124.1

[1] Ratio not shown, number of females being less than 100.
[2] Includes, for 1910, population of South Omaha, consolidated with Omaha since 1910.

116

POPULATION.

TABLE 7.—SEX DISTRIBUTION, 1920, AND RATIO OF MALES TO FEMALES, 1920 AND 1910, FOR THE WHITE POPULATION BY NATIVITY AND PARENTAGE, FOR CITIES HAVING, IN 1920, 100,000 INHABITANTS OR MORE.

CITY.	Native parentage 1920 Male	Female	Males to 100 females 1920	1910	Foreign parentage 1920 Male	Female	Males to 100 females 1920	1910	Mixed parentage 1920 Male	Female	Males to 100 females 1920	1910	Foreign-born white 1920 Male	Female	Males to 100 females 1920	1910
Akron, Ohio	72,485	52,594	137.8	110.4	14,565	13,780	105.7	94.0	5,824	5,581	104.4	97.4	24,607	13,282	185.3	149.9
Albany, N.Y.	27,226	29,039	93.8	93.3	12,682	11,352	88.4	89.6	5,091	6,010	84.7	88.8	8,976	8,600	103.6	98.9
Atlanta, Ga.	60,913	64,035	95.1	97.8	2,327	2,488	93.5	94.5	1,495	1,789	83.6	86.5	2,700	2,038	132.5	150.4
Baltimore, Md.	185,737	192,643	96.4	92.6	56,318	60,421	93.2	91.6	22,235	23,855	93.2	91.5	44,034	39,877	110.4	100.6
Birmingham, Ala.	46,261	45,950	100.7	105.3	3,307	3,370	98.1	102.8	1,765	1,813	97.4	99.1	3,499	2,585	135.4	145.8
Boston, Mass.	89,608	91,913	97.8	96.1	116,910	121,331	96.4	97.4	34,825	36,089	94.9	96.0	117,770	121,149	97.2	95.8
Bridgeport, Conn.	18,668	18,148	102.9	102.2	23,121	23,973	96.4	94.3	5,318	5,578	95.3	98.6	25,279	21,135	119.6	122.3
Buffalo, N.Y.	82,313	82,822	99.4	100.2	74,705	79,654	93.8	94.1	29,207	31,811	91.8	91.9	64,748	56,782	114.0	112.8
Cambridge, Mass.	13,508	15,542	86.9	88.8	15,879	16,404	96.8	95.6	5,199	5,619	92.5	92.7	15,219	16,885	90.1	90.2
Camden, N.J.	28,376	27,873	101.8	98.6	11,294	11,523	98.0	98.7	4,100	4,325	94.8	90.7	11,086	9,176	120.8	110.1
Chicago, Ill.	322,022	319,940	100.9	103.8	434,112	454,054	95.7	95.9	122,145	130,175	93.8	95.6	431,764	373,718	115.5	121.1
Cincinnati, Ohio	101,319	105,286	96.2	97.9	36,620	43,691	83.8	85.6	19,413	21,941	88.5	91.6	21,792	21,035	103.6	105.9
Cleveland, Ohio	107,693	104,554	103.0	101.6	121,995	124,534	98.0	95.6	31,574	32,138	98.2	95.4	133,075	106,463	125.0	124.6
Columbus, Ohio	78,836	80,233	98.3	99.7	11,644	12,558	92.7	92.2	7,312	8,083	90.5	87.8	9,113	6,942	131.3	135.6
Dallas, Tex.	55,785	56,724	98.3	103.1	4,065	3,954	102.8	98.5	2,682	2,948	91.0	88.1	5,097	3,633	140.3	142.2
Dayton, Ohio	50,926	50,070	101.7	99.9	8,950	9,937	90.1	88.8	5,038	5,463	92.2	89.7	7,394	5,717	129.3	144.0
Denver, Colo.	75,229	69,449	108.3	100.2	20,675	22,387	92.4	94.9	11,421	12,863	88.8	90.4	20,896	16,724	124.9	115.8
Des Moines, Iowa	41,163	43,198	95.3	99.1	7,241	8,025	90.2	88.9	4,727	5,309	89.0	91.6	6,211	5,013	123.9	123.8
Detroit, Mich.	170,624	143,373	119.0	105.4	125,202	121,833	102.8	94.0	51,068	50,608	100.8	96.5	169,005	120,202	140.7	122.9
Fall River, Mass.	9,176	9,992	91.8	92.9	21,887	23,348	93.7	95.0	6,319	7,061	89.5	93.4	20,334	21,997	92.4	92.1
Fort Worth, Tex.	39,539	35,976	109.9	110.9	2,415	2,111	114.4	116.8	1,555	1,511	102.9	106.3	4,738	2,621	180.8	205.4
Grand Rapids, Mich.	27,445	28,634	95.8	95.9	16,512	18,267	90.4	88.8	7,952	9,307	85.4	84.9	14,009	13,356	112.3	110.4
Hartford, Conn.	19,843	20,484	96.9	96.9	20,386	21,368	95.4	95.5	5,133	5,800	88.5	93.1	21,470	19,197	111.8	106.4
Houston, Tex.	36,157	36,276	99.7	109.8	5,512	5,689	97.0	99.1	3,843	4,170	92.0	97.5	6,809	5,203	130.9	149.8
Indianapolis, Ind.	108,588	110,709	98.1	97.2	12,600	13,979	90.1	92.1	7,815	8,762	89.2	87.8	9,359	7,599	123.2	134.4
Jersey City, N.J.	44,007	43,076	102.2	102.7	48,116	50,504	95.3	98.0	13,894	14,431	96.3	96.5	40,212	35,760	112.4	120.5
Kansas City, Kans.	28,689	27,886	102.9	104.2	6,040	6,109	98.9	97.0	3,036	3,287	92.4	97.4	6,850	4,806	142.5	102.9
Kansas City, Mo.	103,801	105,333	98.5	102.6	17,202	17,981	95.7	95.6	10,361	11,519	89.9	92.0	15,377	11,943	128.8	132.3
Los Angeles, Calif.	142,121	152,337	93.3	99.8	41,282	45,526	90.7	92.7	24,040	28,901	85.3	86.3	60,188	51,869	116.0	131.8
Louisville, Ky.	67,500	71,903	93.9	96.2	12,002	15,074	79.6	85.7	7,653	9,016	84.9	80.4	5,882	5,739	102.5	103.5
Lowell, Mass.	11,810	12,866	91.8	89.3	17,781	19,260	92.3	93.4	6,041	6,711	90.0	91.7	18,466	19,574	94.8	97.3
Memphis, Tenn.	40,818	41,977	97.2	108.5	3,746	3,925	95.4	95.9	2,302	2,570	89.6	92.9	3,266	2,509	130.2	147.4
Milwaukee, Wis.	65,054	65,791	98.9	98.0	72,222	80,497	89.7	91.1	29,331	31,861	92.1	93.7	60,703	49,365	123.0	128.0
Minneapolis, Minn.	66,416	66,762	99.5	111.4	50,273	58,551	85.9	92.3	21,761	24,570	88.6	93.3	48,402	39,680	122.1	132.8
Nashville, Tenn.	35,652	38,370	92.9	95.2	1,637	2,016	81.2	81.0	1,251	1,390	90.0	91.1	1,287	1,100	117.0	111.4
New Bedford, Mass.	9,687	10,411	93.0	92.7	17,706	18,673	94.8	97.7	5,308	5,608	93.6	92.1	23,804	24,825	96.1	99.9
New Haven, Conn.	21,445	22,856	94.3	94.8	26,492	28,210	93.9	94.6	6,253	6,774	92.3	92.9	23,532	22,154	106.2	111.4
New Orleans, La.	91,570	96,071	95.4	97.6	19,148	22,658	84.5	87.5	12,575	14,902	84.4	84.7	15,497	10,495	147.7	112.1
New York, N.Y.	575,847	588,987	97.8	98.0	919,740	953,273	96.5	96.3	207,540	222,529	93.3	93.9	1,020,090	971,457	105.0	105.1
Bronx borough	66,172	66,508	99.4	100.6	131,452	136,928	96.0	95.7	28,668	30,201	94.9	96.4	135,456	131,515	103.0	109.8
Brooklyn borough	226,063	230,177	98.2	95.4	314,079	359,338	95.8	95.3	79,605	86,404	92.1	92.2	341,527	317,780	107.5	105.0
Manhattan borough	188,954	199,325	94.8	99.1	355,145	365,309	97.2	96.9	65,981	72,112	91.5	93.5	408,505	453,574	103.3	103.6
Queens borough	74,416	74,026	99.3	100.6	72,145	75,255	95.9	97.8	27,305	27,938	97.7	98.3	57,132	54,544	104.7	115.1
Richmond borough	20,242	17,961	112.7	105.3	16,919	16,443	102.9	101.9	5,981	5,874	101.8	101.7	17,469	14,064	124.2	122.6
Newark, N.J.	56,465	56,948	99.2	96.1	65,567	67,808	96.7	94.1	16,402	17,030	96.3	93.7	61,914	55,089	112.4	110.6
Norfolk, Va.	29,524	28,235	104.6	94.5	2,774	2,433	114.0	98.4	1,340	1,333	100.5	86.2	4,439	2,148	206.7	141.5
Oakland, Calif.	45,443	44,836	101.4	99.9	21,154	22,907	92.3	92.2	11,833	12,609	93.4	91.2	25,492	19,670	129.6	130.6
Omaha, Nebr.[1]	44,332	42,193	105.1	109.3	20,241	21,213	95.4	98.2	8,668	9,018	96.1	101.1	19,919	15,471	128.7	134.5
Paterson, N.J.	15,378	16,446	93.5	94.2	21,539	22,543	95.5	95.1	6,330	6,873	92.1	93.5	23,205	21,940	105.8	107.0
Philadelphia, Pa.	344,382	354,400	97.2	95.1	219,690	227,381	96.6	95.4	69,706	74,694	93.3	91.7	205,518	192,409	106.8	102.9
Pittsburgh, Pa.	107,253	109,277	98.1	99.0	76,444	81,137	94.2	95.2	26,961	28,923	93.2	95.0	65,367	54,890	119.1	128.7
Portland, Oreg.	67,180	69,036	97.3	123.7	20,492	21,443	95.6	107.9	13,414	14,282	93.9	100.0	27,344	19,770	138.3	172.7
Providence, R.I.	30,646	33,082	92.6	93.2	36,516	39,532	92.4	93.3	10,909	12,120	90.0	92.8	34,079	31,872	97.7	103.3
Reading, Pa.	39,371	41,629	94.6	94.1	5,828	6,088	95.7	96.2	2,042	2,310	87.3	91.8	5,457	4,096	133.2	145.8
Richmond, Va.	48,611	54,315	89.6	93.6	2,817	3,030	93.0	94.3	1,905	2,229	85.5	92.3	2,533	2,104	120.4	127.2
Rochester, N.Y.	54,847	57,129	96.0	97.4	37,474	40,971	91.5	90.8	15,376	16,791	91.6	91.4	36,992	34,329	107.8	112.6
St. Louis, Mo.	178,475	181,007	98.6	99.9	74,412	83,567	89.0	91.2	38,512	43,403	88.7	93.2	56,266	46,973	119.8	126.9
St. Paul, Minn.	39,171	38,207	102.5	111.9	33,024	37,166	88.9	97.2	15,229	16,779	90.8	93.2	28,003	23,592	118.7	126.2
Salt Lake City, Utah	28,191	28,043	100.5	110.9	11,598	11,917	97.3	97.8	8,306	9,292	89.4	95.4	9,737	9,697	100.4	104.0
San Antonio, Tex.	37,928	38,371	98.8	100.0	10,137	10,024	92.8	94.0	6,182	6,611	93.5	94.5	19,494	17,152	113.7	107.7
San Francisco, Calif.	88,737	78,442	113.1	126.9	61,388	61,260	95.5	100.8	27,842	29,153	95.5	101.7	82,918	57,282	144.8	162.4
Scranton, Pa.	23,589	25,126	93.9	96.7	21,543	23,674	91.0	92.6	6,972	7,742	90.1	92.6	15,139	13,429	112.7	127.2
Seattle, Wash.	71,333	68,368	104.3	126.1	27,286	27,392	99.6	105.7	16,881	17,445	96.8	101.2	43,779	30,096	145.5	170.6
Spokane, Wash.	28,322	29,002	97.7	115.3	7,920	8,646	91.6	105.7	6,001	6,663	90.1	102.8	9,463	7,363	128.5	171.5
Springfield, Mass.	23,856	25,089	95.1	92.7	16,054	16,537	94.8	92.4	6,449	7,164	90.0	92.3	15,873	15,377	103.2	100.7
Syracuse, N.Y.	39,807	40,265	98.9	98.3	19,816	21,066	94.1	90.3	8,151	8,946	91.1	90.2	17,433	14,888	117.1	123.2
Toledo, Ohio	63,758	60,267	105.7	99.0	25,039	26,062	96.1	95.1	11,707	12,377	94.6	92.7	21,751	16,394	132.7	120.2
Trenton, N.J.	21,862	22,333	97.9	98.9	15,991	16,190	98.8	98.0	4,000	4,453	89.8	98.9	16,477	13,596	121.2	132.2
Washington, D.C.	109,872	129,616	84.8	93.4	16,549	18,580	89.1	93.4	10,468	13,227	79.1	89.7	15,142	13,406	112.0	113.0
Wilmington, Del.	28,419	28,449	99.9	98.2	9,353	9,779	95.6	95.8	3,455	3,648	94.7	93.2	9,347	6,932	134.8	127.5
Worcester, Mass.	24,816	25,900	95.8	95.2	27,803	29,038	95.7	94.4	8,405	9,011	93.3	95.6	27,874	25,544	109.1	115.1
Yonkers, N.Y.	14,565	15,494	94.0	95.7	15,577	16,703	93.3	94.6	4,929	5,210	94.6	95.7	12,990	12,710	102.2	113.6
Youngstown, Ohio	23,755	22,704	104.6	100.6	16,991	17,468	97.3	98.3	5,331	5,512	96.7	96.4	20,697	13,137	157.5	180.6

[1] Includes, for 1910, population of South Omaha, consolidated with Omaha since 1910.

CHAPTER III
AGE DISTRIBUTION

CHAPTER III.—AGE DISTRIBUTION.

INTRODUCTION.

At every census some attempt has been made to distribute the population by age, but at the early censuses the age grouping was not elaborate. In 1790 the only age distribution was that for white males, those 16 years of age and over being distinguished from those under 16. In 1800 and 1810 the white males and females were distributed into five age groups. In 1820 the white males were distributed into six age groups, the white females into five, and the slaves and free colored into four. In 1830 and 1840 the whites were distributed into age groups of 5 or 10 years, and the slaves and free colored into six broader age groups. In 1850 and 1860 the whites, slaves, and free colored were distributed according to sex into 5-year groups up to and including 19 years and into 10-year groups from 20 to 100 years, and those under 1 year of age were separately classified. In 1860 the Chinese and civilized Indians were distributed in the same way. In 1870 the native, foreign born, native white, colored, foreign-born white, Chinese, and civilized Indians were distributed by single years to and including 4 years of age, and thereafter by 5-year age periods; 18 and 19 (one period), 20, and 21–24 years were also classified separately. In 1880 and at each subsequent census the total population classified by nativity and color has been tabulated according to single years of age; and, beginning with 1890, the native whites classified according to parentage have been similarly tabulated by single years.

For various uses to which census material is put, statistics in regard to age are of great importance. Mortality rates attain their full value only when the population can be distributed according to sex and age. Satisfactory birth rates and marriage rates can be computed only when statistics with regard to sex, age, and marital condition are available. The voting strength depends upon the age distribution, and the military strength on the distribution according to sex and age. The differences in the age distribution of the native and foreign-born population are important in their bearing on the economic, social, and political effects of immigration. Statistics of school attendance and illiteracy would have much less value if age were not taken into account. In fact, there are very few questions in vital statistics or sociology which can be studied with intelligence until the age distribution of the population has been determined.

The statistics of age distribution for continental United States are here given in detail. Those for the outlying possessions enumerated at the Fourteenth Census are presented in the sections pertaining to those possessions in Volume III of the Fourteenth Census Reports.

UNITED STATES AS A WHOLE.

Distribution by single years of age.—If a country were entirely removed from communication with the rest of the world the age distribution of the population would be determined wholly by births and deaths, and, since death is continually depleting the population, the number of survivors at any given age would normally be less than the number at any younger age, although irregularities might result from any decided diminution in the number of births in any year or group of years or by an excessive rate of mortality among those born in some particular year or group of years. (See Table 9, p. 162, and diagram, p. 151.) Where a country is receiving or losing a large number of migrants every year, however, the age distribution undergoes a change. Since a large proportion of migrants are in the more active years of life, a country which had been losing considerable numbers by emigration would show abnormally small proportions in the adult ages, while a country, like the United States, which had been receiving large numbers of immigrants would show abnormally large proportions of adults. Migration, however, while affecting the age distribution in general, would not lead to any decided irregularities for single years, such as are shown by Table 9 and by the diagram on page 151.

Irregularities of this character are due in large part to errors in the census returns. These errors result from three causes: (1) Some persons do not know their exact age. (2) The enumerators are obliged in many cases to obtain information relating to the person enumerated from a third person, either some member of the family found at home or a person in charge of a hotel or boarding house, who can give the age only approximately. (3) In certain instances, apparently more frequent among women than among men, the age is intentionally misstated. Where the age is not accurately known there is a tendency to report it as a multiple of 2 or of 5, and especially, in the case of ages above 20, as a multiple of 10. There is also a tendency to concentrate on age 21 for men. In gen-

146   POPULATION.

eral, the degree of inaccuracy is greater for adults than for children and youth, and is greatest for those classes of the population in which the proportion of illiterates is greatest. The returns also undoubtedly exaggerate the number of centenarians, particularly among the Negroes and Indians.

Distribution by 5-year periods and broad groups.—In order to neutralize the effect of concentration upon multiples of 2 and 5, the age statistics presented in most of the tables are given by 5-year periods or for broader age groups. Tables 9, 10, and 11, which relate to the United States as a whole, are the only ones in which the distribution by single years is given for all ages; but in Tables 13 and 15 the single-year distribution for persons under 25 is given for states and for cities of 500,000 or more, respectively. In general, the distribution by single years is unquestionably more nearly accurate for the younger than for the older ages; and it is only for the younger ages that variations from year to year are of great importance. In the older periods of life the changes that come with advancing years are more gradual, so that the differences between individual years are slight, and it is sufficient for most purposes if the figures can be presented with approximate accuracy by 5-year or broader age groups.

Effect of immigration on age distribution.—The abnormal constitution of the foreign-born white class affects materially the age distribution of the population as a whole. Were it not for immigration, the total population of the United States would show a somewhat smaller proportion of adults and a somewhat larger proportion of children and youth. (See Tables 3 and 4, pp. 156 and 157, and diagram, p. 151.)

Of the eight diagrams presented on pages 152 and 153, no two are identical in form, and the only one whose shape has not been perceptibly influenced by immigration, either directly or indirectly, is that representing the Negro population, although the diagram for the native whites of native parentage has not been greatly affected by this factor. The extraordinary character of the age distribution of the foreign-born whites, which is also brought out in the age-period tables, is clearly apparent in the diagram for that class.

Since the native white group includes the American-born children of foreign-born parents, the age distribution of this group is itself affected indirectly by immigration. The extent to which it has been so affected is not, however, easy to determine, depending largely upon variations in the volume of immigration. A great wave of immigration would normally be followed by a very material increase in the proportion of children in the native population; but if the immigration continued in undiminished volume the effect would become less marked as time went by. On the other hand, a sudden cessation or decline in immigra-

tion would be followed by an immediate falling off in the proportion of children in the native population, but here again the effect would tend to disappear with the passage of time if immigration were not resumed on its earlier scale.

The influence of immigration upon the age composition of the native population is, of course, most direct and obvious for those classes which are composed of persons one or both of whose parents were immigrants; that is, the native whites of foreign parentage and the native whites of mixed parentage. Even the age distribution of the native white population of native parentage is, however, indirectly affected by immigration, since the children of the native whites of foreign or mixed parentage are included in the class of native whites of native parentage. The Negroes, of course, are not affected by immigration to any appreciable extent.

A very considerable change has taken place since 1900 in the age distribution of the native whites of foreign or mixed parentage. Probably the chief cause of this change is to be found in the increase in the volume of immigration, which was much greater in proportion to the total population during the later than during the earlier half of the nineteenth century. It is but natural, therefore, that in 1900 there should be relatively few natives 50 years of age and over whose parents were born abroad, and that the proportion of such persons should increase from census to census. (See Table 7.)

Changes in the age distribution of the foreign-born whites from one census to another are materially affected both by the volume of immigration and by differences in the age distribution of the immigrants arriving at different periods.

Among the Chinese and Japanese the age distribution is abnormal to a still greater extent than among the foreign-born whites. The great bulk of both these races are immigrants, most of whom are unmarried men or men who have left their families in their native countries.

Age distribution of Negroes and Indians.—The age distribution of the Negroes and Indians, which is practically unaffected by immigration, is roughly similar to that of the native whites. Among the Negroes, however, the proportion of children under 5 is considerably smaller than in any of the native white classes, while the proportions in the age periods from 10 to 29 years are larger than the corresponding ones for either the native whites of native parentage or those of foreign parentage. The proportion of Negro children under 5 decreased to a marked extent between 1910 and 1920. (See Tables 4 and 7.)

Among the Indians the proportion of children is larger, and that of persons in the age groups from 15 to 44 is smaller, than in the case of either the native

AGE DISTRIBUTION.

whites or the Negroes. The chief, and perhaps the sole, explanation of this fact is to be found in the effect of intermixture of white and Indian blood. The children born of marriages between whites and Indians are all classified as Indians, while only one of the parents in each such marriage is thus classified. Since these intermarriages are becoming increasingly frequent, the number of persons of Indian-white mixed blood is increasing and is relatively greater among children than among older persons. The inclusion of these children with the Indian population, together with the exclusion of one parent in each case, increases the proportion of children and diminishes the proportion of adults in the Indian population. (See Table 5.)

Age distribution by sex.—Separate figures are given for each sex in most of the tables in this chapter. In addition, the age distribution for each sex in the total population and in each class of the population is shown by 5-year periods, in the diagrams on pages 152 and 153. In order to permit ready comparison of the proportions of males and females in each age period, the percentages shown for the sexes in connection with each diagram are based on the total population in the group or class to which the diagram relates, and not on the totals for the sexes separately. For example, the diagram relating to the native white population of native parentage shows that men in the age period 25–29 formed 4.1 per cent of the total native white population of native parentage, of both sexes, whereas Table 7 shows that men in this age period formed 8 per cent of the total native white males of native parentage.

Differences in age distribution as between males and females in the total population of the country are to be expected, by reason of the fact that the foreign born, whose age distribution is abnormal, include many more males than females. This condition explains in part the fact that in the total population a larger proportion of the males than the females are in the ages 30 to 69, inclusive, while the proportion under 30 years of age is greater among females than among males. (See Table 4.)

This difference in age distribution as between the sexes in the total population, however, is not wholly attributable to the presence of the foreign born, there being also considerable differences among the native classes. Starting with a moderate excess of males over females in the three age periods under 15 years, the returns for the native whites of native parentage show a practical equality of the sexes in the 15–19 period, an excess of females in the 20–29 periods, an excess of males in the 30–74 periods, and an excess of females in the periods above 74. Among the native whites of foreign parentage and of mixed parentage, however, the females outnumber the males

in most of the age groups, especially in the foreign-parentage class. (See Table 8.)

The marked excess of females shown by the returns for the 20–24 age period in the class of native whites of native parentage is due in large part to understatement of ages. The native white women of native parentage enumerated as in this age period in 1920 (2,629,889) outnumbered the native white females of native parentage in the age period 10–14, as enumerated in 1910 (2,623,627). (See Table 6.) This is a manifest impossibility, since the 20–24 group in 1920, if correctly enumerated, would be made up solely of the survivors of the 10–14 group in 1910, assuming that group also to have been correctly enumerated. No similar inconsistency appears for native white males of native parentage, nor for either males or females in the class of native whites of foreign or mixed parentage. Moreover, in the age period 20–24 the women outnumbered the men in 1920, not only among the native whites of foreign or mixed parentage but even among the foreign-born whites, although in general the males predominate among the foreign born. Thus it can not be assumed that any considerable number of foreign-born white women or native white women of foreign or mixed parentage in the 20–24 age period were incorrectly returned as native white of native parentage. It is obvious, therefore, either that the number of native white females of native parentage enumerated in 1910 as in the age period 10–14 was too small, or that the native white women of native parentage enumerated in 1920 as in the 20–24 period included a considerable number who were actually 25 years of age or more. The latter supposition is by far the more probable. A similar inconsistency is disclosed by a comparison between the 1910 returns for native white women of native parentage in the 20–24 age period and the 1900 returns for the corresponding class of females in the 10–14 period.

It may be that in the age periods from 45 to 69, in which a pronounced excess of men over women is shown for the native white population of native parentage, this excess is exaggerated in some measure by the erroneous classification of foreign-born white men or native white men of foreign or mixed parentage as native white of native parentage. This seems probable, in view of the small excess of men or the excess of women in the corresponding age groups for the native whites of foreign parentage and of mixed parentage.

For the foreign-born whites the age distribution of the males is decidedly different from that of the females, the former being greatly in excess in the age periods from 25 to 69. (See Table 8.)

The age distribution of males and females among the Negroes, as reported, presents a peculiar condition. According to the returns there was in 1920 a slight

148   POPULATION.

excess of females below the age of 15, a much larger excess in the age periods from 15 to 34, and a small excess in the 35–44 periods. From the ages of 45 to 69, however, there was a very great excess of men, followed by a moderate excess in the 70–79 periods and an excess of women in the ages above 79. The ratio of males to females for the Negroes in the 45–49 period (138.7 to 100) was higher than the foreign-born white ratio for any age period. The number of Negro men enumerated as in this age period in 1920 (320,506) was almost exactly the same as the number reported for the age period 35–39 in 1910 (320,450). This, of course, is an impossibility, for the reason that, disregarding the slight effect of immigration, the group of Negro men 45 to 49 years of age in 1920 would be made up solely of the survivors of those in the 35–39 age period in 1910. Inconsistencies of this character are due, wholly or in large part, to errors in estimating ages which can not be ascertained exactly by the enumerators. (See Tables 6 and 8.)

The age distribution by sex shown for the Negroes by the statistics for 1910 was somewhat similar to that indicated by the 1920 figures, but the excess of men from 45 to 69 years of age was less pronounced in the earlier than in the later year.

The remarkable excess of males over females shown in the 45–59 age periods for the Indians is doubtless due in considerable measure to inaccurate returns. (See Table 8.)

There is naturally an extraordinary difference between the two sexes in regard to age distribution in the case of the Chinese, Japanese, and "all other" population, due to the very great excess of males over females among the immigrants of these classes.

The probable errors in the statistics as to the age distribution of the two sexes are by no means confined to the census of 1920, prior censuses also having shown conspicuous inconsistencies in this respect, some of which at least can apparently be attributable only to erroneous returns.

Median age.—The median age is that age which divides the population into two equal groups, one-half being older and one-half younger than the median. The first tabular statement shows, for 1920, the median age for each important class of the population, disregarding persons of unknown ages.

The difference between the median ages of the two sexes for all classes combined is due in part to the fact that among the foreign born, whose median age is much higher than that of the natives, the males are considerably in excess of the females.

The comparatively low median ages of the native whites of foreign and of mixed parentage is due to the increase in the volume of immigration up to 1914. This resulted in a relatively rapid increase from year to year in the number of families in which one or both parents were foreign born, and therefore in the number of children born in such families. In consequence, the younger element of the native whites of foreign and of mixed parentage is disproportionately large and the older element disproportionately small.

	Total.	Male.	Female.
All classes............................	25.2	25.8	24.7
White..................................	25.6	26.1	25.1
Native white.......................	22.4	22.4	22.3
Native parentage...............	22.7	22.8	22.5
Foreign parentage..............	21.6	21.4	21.7
Mixed parentage...............	21.8	21.3	22.2
Foreign-born white.................	40.0	40.1	39.9
Negro.................................	22.3	22.8	22.0
Indian................................	19.7	20.4	19.0
Chinese...............................	40.2	42.7	19.4
Japanese..............................	30.2	34.1	24.0

The median ages of the total population and of the white population show uninterrupted increases since 1820. These increases have been due to two causes: First, an increase in average length of life; second, a reduction in the birth rate, which has resulted in a decrease in the proportion of young persons in the total population.

The statement below shows, for all classes combined and for the white and colored population separately, disregarding persons of unknown ages, the median ages in 1920 and earlier census years.

CENSUS YEAR.[1]	ALL CLASSES.			WHITE.			COLORED (NEGRO, INDIAN, CHINESE, JAPANESE, AND "ALL OTHER").		
	Both sexes.	Male.	Female.	Both sexes.	Male.	Female.	Both sexes.	Male.	Female.
1920..........	25.2	25.8	24.7	25.6	26.1	25.1	22.5	23.0	21.9
1910..........	24.0	24.6	23.5	24.4	24.9	23.9	21.0	21.5	20.6
1900..........	22.9	23.3	22.4	23.4	23.8	22.9	19.7	20.0	19.5
1890..........	21.4	21.8	21.0	21.9	21.3	21.6	17.8	17.9	17.8
1880..........	20.9	21.1	20.6	21.3	21.6	21.0	18.0	18.0	18.0
1870..........	20.1	20.2	20.1	20.4	20.5	20.3	18.5	18.2	18.8
1860..........	19.4	19.7	19.0	19.7	20.1	19.3	17.7	17.8	17.5
1850..........	18.8	19.1	18.6	19.1	19.5	18.8	17.3	17.3	17.4
1840..........	17.8	17.8	17.7	17.9	17.9	17.8	17.3	17.0	17.5
1830..........	17.2	17.1	17.3	17.2	17.2	17.3	16.9	16.7	17.1
1820..........	16.7	16.6	16.7	16.5	16.5	16.6	17.2	16.9	17.4
1810..........	....	....	....	16.0	15.9	16.1	....	....	....
1800..........	....	....	....	16.0	15.7	16.3	....	....	....
1790..........	....	....	....	....	15.9	....	....	....	....

[1] Before 1880 ages were not tabulated by single years. In 1790 the ages of only the white males were ascertained, and in only two groups, under 16 and over 16. At successive censuses new details were added to the age classification, and since 1830 the ages of that part of the population in which the median age falls have been tabulated in 5-year groups. For the censuses before 1880 it has been assumed for the purpose of computing the median age that the proportions at the single years of age within the groups were the same as in 1900. For the colored population, which included only the Negroes at censuses prior to 1870, the age distribution of the Negroes in 1900 has been used as the standard.

AGE DISTRIBUTION.

DIVISIONS AND STATES.

Statistics for divisions and states are given in Tables 12 to 14. In Table 12 the states are shown by the geographic divisions adopted by the Census Bureau, but in Table 13, for convenience of reference, the order is alphabetical.

Very considerable differences exist among the nine geographic divisions of the country and among the individual states in regard to the age distribution of the total population and of specific classes of the population. The differences in regard to the total population are in part attributable to variations in the composition according to color or race, nativity, and parentage. Thus. a large proportion foreign born tends to produce a relatively large proportion of adults in the total population.

The differences among the divisions and states with regard to specific classes of the population are due to various factors. Interstate migration has a great influence upon age distribution. Adults, particularly the younger adults, are relatively much more numerous among migrants than in the total population, and therefore a division or state which has lost extensively through interstate migration is likely to have a smaller proportion of persons in the younger and middle ages of adult life in its native population than one which has gained by such migration. The distribution of ages in the urban population is usually decidedly different from that in the rural population, partly by reason of migration from country to city, and consequently the age constitution of the total population of a given class in a state or division is much affected by the proportions urban and rural. Again, the age composition of the several native classes is affected by differences in birth rates and in death rates and by differences in the extent to which changes have taken place in these rates from one time to another. Finally, the age distribution of the foreign born and of the natives of foreign or mixed parentage in any given state or section of the country depends in considerable measure upon the period of time during which immigration to that state or section was most rapid.

PRINCIPAL CITIES.

Statistics for individual cities are presented in Tables 15 to 17. Table 15, for cities having 500,000 inhabitants or more, corresponds to Table 13, for divisions and states, except for the omission of comparative figures for 1910; Table 16 shows quinquennial age periods and single years under 5 for cities having 100,000 inhabitants or more and gives a somewhat condensed age grouping for cities having from 25,000 to 100,000 inhabitants; and Table 17 presents a broad age grouping for all cities having 25,000 inhabitants or more.

URBAN AND RURAL COMMUNITIES.

Since marked differences exist between urban and rural communities in regard to the age distribution of their population, separate statistics are given for the two classes of communities in Table 18. In drawing the distinction between urban and rural population, all incorporated places (and all towns in Massachusetts, Rhode Island, and New Hampshire) having 2,500 inhabitants or more are treated as urban and the remainder of the country as rural.

In Massachusetts and Rhode Island it is not the practice, as in practically all the other states, to incorporate, as separate municipalities, the relatively densely populated portions of "towns" (which are the primary divisions of the counties), and no town as a whole is incorporated as a municipality until it attains a population greatly in excess of 2,500; and in New Hampshire a similar condition exists, although the state contains two incorporated villages, each of which has fewer than 2,500 inhabitants. For this reason those towns having 2,500 or more inhabitants in the three states named are treated as urban, although portions of their areas are rural in character. The urban areas in the three states in question, as classified by the census, thus contain relatively small numbers of inhabitants who in other sections of the country would be segregated as rural. Nevertheless, in most of the towns having 2,500 inhabitants or more in Massachusetts, Rhode Island, and New Hampshire by far the greater part of the population resides within the more densely settled areas, so that the proportion classed as urban, considering the New England division as a whole, is not greatly exaggerated by the practice adopted.

The pronounced differences between urban and rural communities in regard to the age distribution of their population are in part attributable to differences in the color or race, nativity, and parentage composition of their population, but there are also pronounced differences between them in regard to the age composition of individual population classes. The opportunities to be found in urban communities have attracted large numbers of persons in the more active ages, and, because of the effect of this cityward migration on age distribution, it is impossible to draw directly from the statistics any trustworthy conclusions as to the relative fecundity or the relative longevity of the native whites of native parentage in the two classes of communities.

The age distribution of the foreign-born whites and of the native whites of foreign or mixed parentage in urban and in rural areas, respectively, has been influenced to a very considerable extent by the period—whether recent or remote—during which immigration into these areas has been most rapid.

150

POPULATION.

A large proportion of the earlier immigration went to the rural districts, but most of the recent immigration has gone to the cities.

The age distribution of the Negroes in urban and in rural areas is affected by the very considerable country-to-city migration of persons of this race in the active-age periods, and probably also by differences in birth and death rates between the two classes of communities.

The following statement brings out the marked differences between the urban and rural communities in regard to the sex distribution of the population in the age groups given in Table 18.

It will be seen that females, particularly in the adult ages, form a materially larger proportion of the population in urban than in rural communities, notwithstanding the fact that the foreign-born whites—a class in which males are greatly in the majority—are concentrated mainly in cities.

AGE GROUP.	MALES TO 100 FEMALES: 1920	
	Urban population.	Rural population.
All ages	100.4	108.0
Under 5 years	101.9	103.0
5 to 9 years	100.5	103.0
10 to 14 years	98.4	104.6
15 to 19 years	92.0	104.2
20 to 44 years	101.0	105.3
45 years and over	102.2	123.8

AGE DISTRIBUTION.

DISTRIBUTION BY SINGLE YEARS OF AGE FOR THE TOTAL POPULATION, BY SEX: 1920.

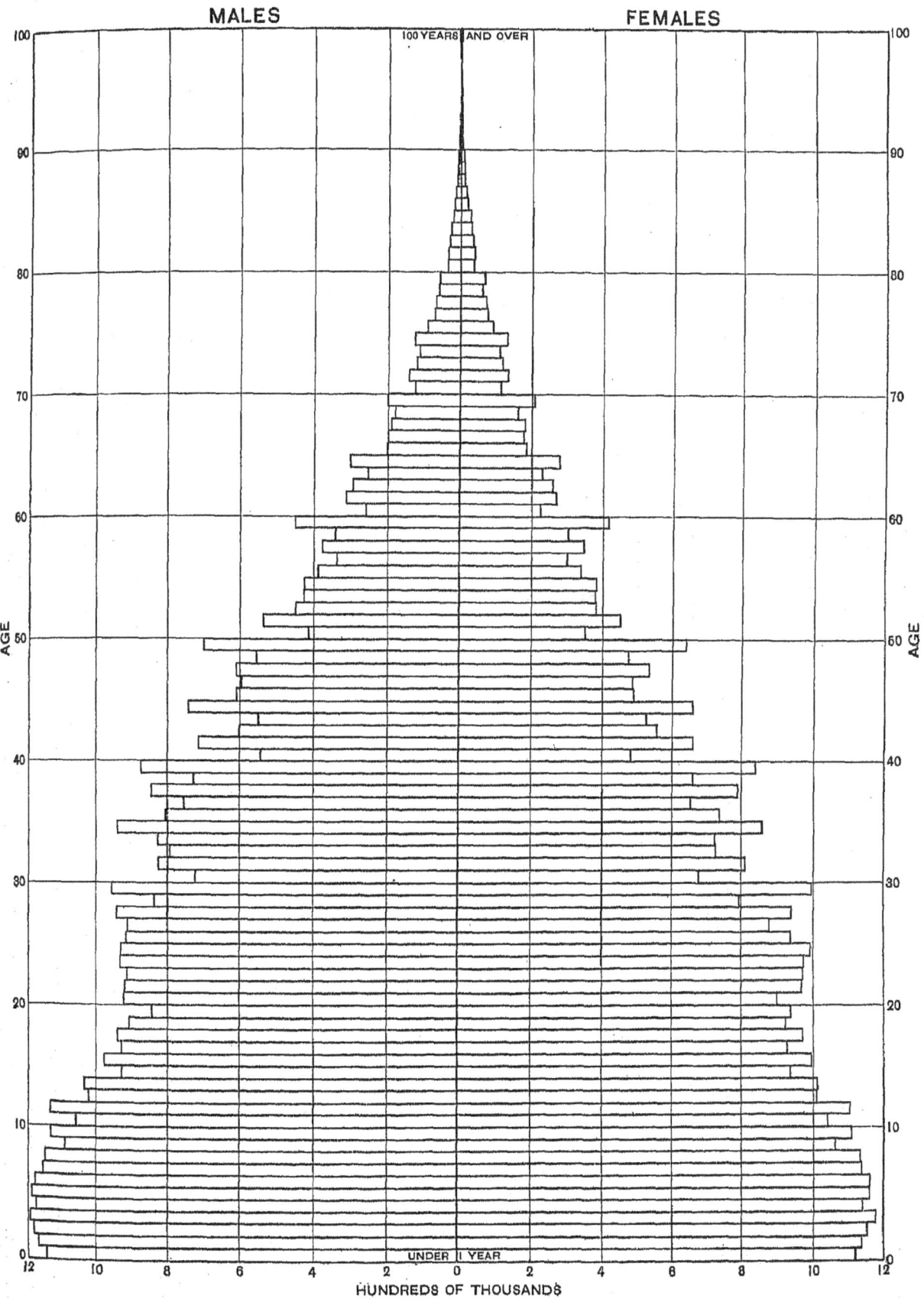

MALES   FEMALES

100 YEARS AND OVER

AGE

AGE

UNDER 1 YEAR

HUNDREDS OF THOUSANDS

152

POPULATION.

DISTRIBUTION BY AGE PERIODS FOR TOTAL POPULATION

TOTAL POPULATION.

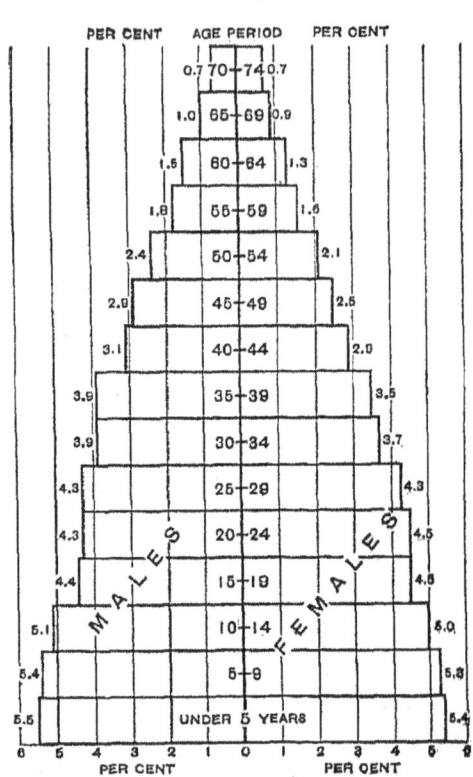

TOTAL WHITE.

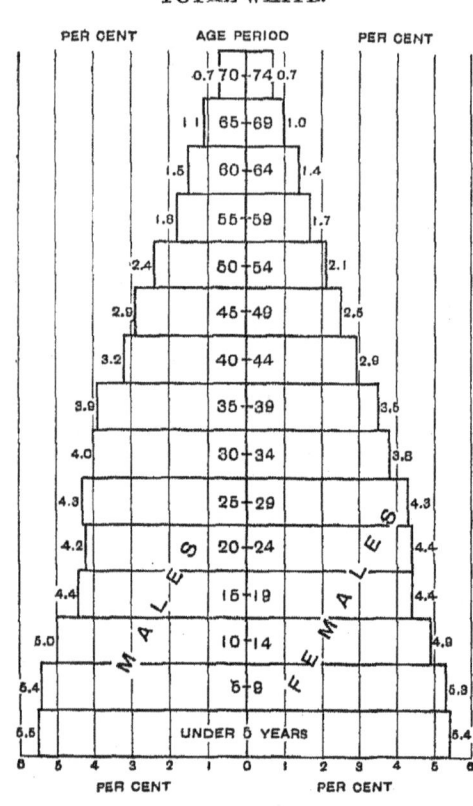

NEGRO.

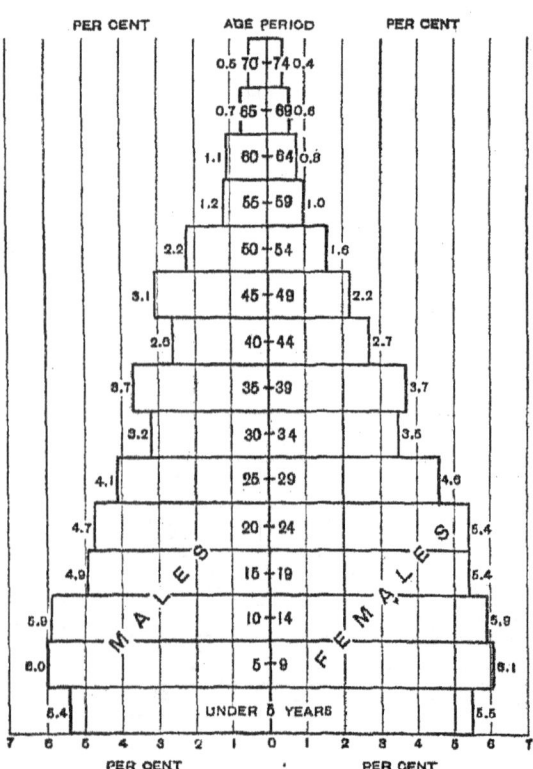

FOREIGN-BORN WHITE.

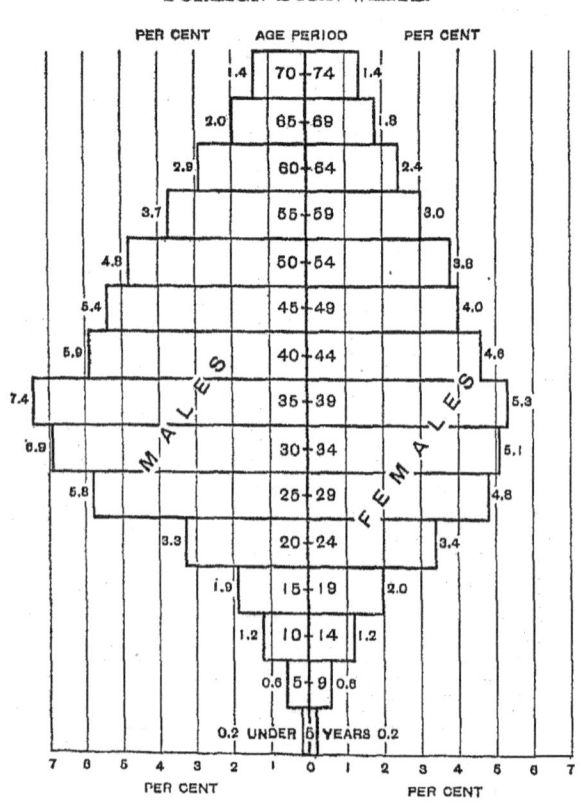

AGE DISTRIBUTION.

153

AND FOR PRINCIPAL POPULATION CLASSES, BY SEX: 1920.

NATIVE WHITE.

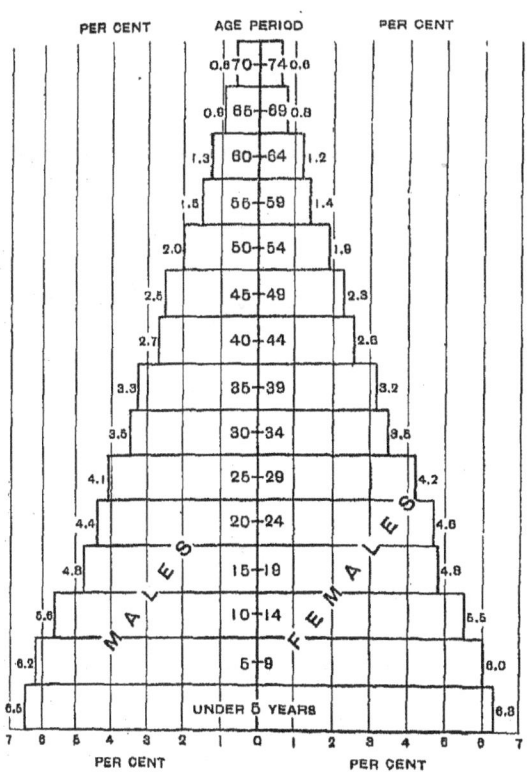

NATIVE WHITE OF NATIVE PARENTAGE.

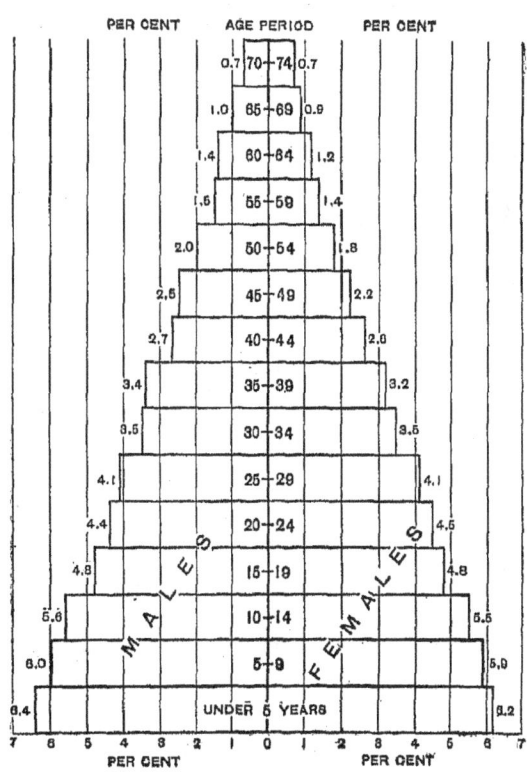

NATIVE WHITE OF FOREIGN PARENTAGE.

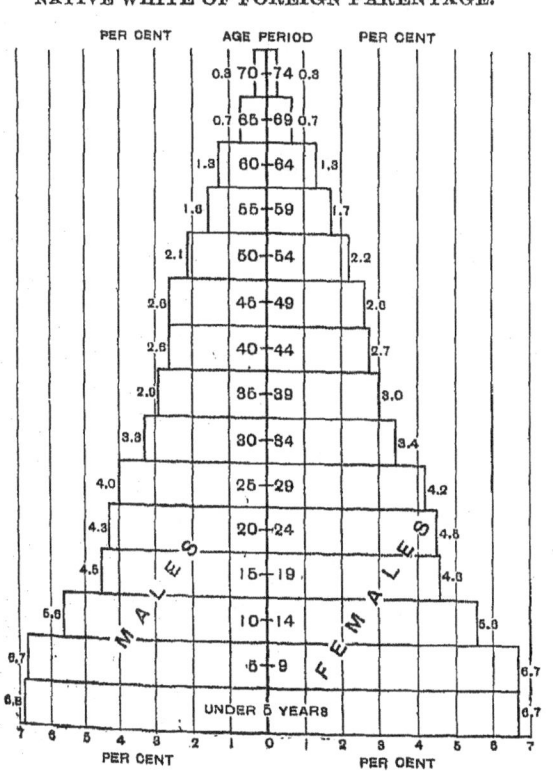

NATIVE WHITE OF MIXED PARENTAGE.

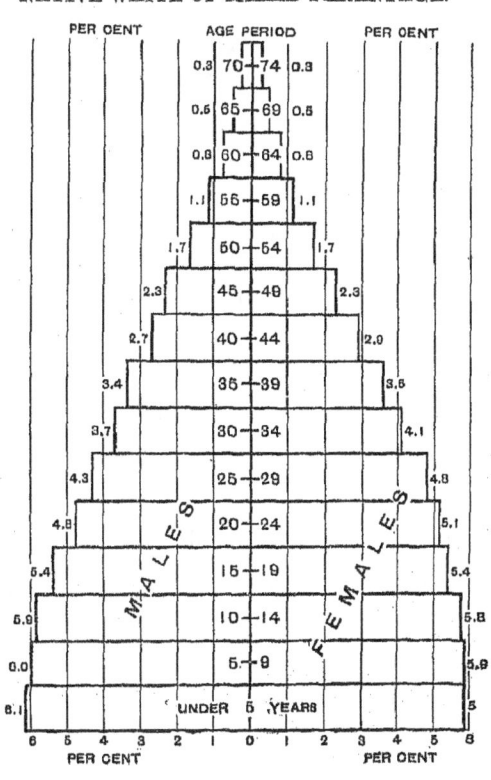

154

POPULATION.

TABLE 1.—DISTRIBUTION BY AGE PERIODS FOR THE TOTAL POPULATION, BY SEX, FOR THE UNITED STATES: 1850-1920.

SEX AND AGE PERIOD.	POPULATION.								PER CENT DISTRIBUTION.							
	1920	1910	1900	1890	1880	1870	1860	1850	1920	1910	1900	1890	1880	1870	1860	1850
BOTH SEXES.																
All ages	105,710,620	91,972,266	75,994,575	¹62,622,250	50,155,783	38,558,371	31,443,321	23,191,876	100.0	100.0	100.0	100.0	100.0	100.0	100.0	100.0
Under 5 years	11,573,230	10,631,364	9,170,628	7,634,693	6,914,516	5,514,713	4,842,496	3,497,773	10.9	11.6	12.1	12.2	13.8	14.3	15.4	15.1
Under 1 year	2,257,255	2,217,312	1,916,892	1,566,734	1,447,983	1,100,475	934,583	629,446	2.1	2.4	2.5	2.5	2.9	2.9	3.0	2.7
5 to 9 years	11,398,075	9,760,632	8,574,123	7,573,998	6,479,660	4,814,713	4,171,200	3,241,268	10.8	10.6	11.7	12.1	12.9	12.5	13.3	14.0
10 to 14 years	10,641,137	9,107,140	8,080,234	7,033,509	5,715,186	4,766,189	3,720,780	2,890,629	10.1	9.9	10.6	11.2	11.4	12.4	11.8	12.5
15 to 19 years	9,430,556	9,003,603	7,556,089	6,557,583	5,011,415	4,040,588	3,361,495	2,529,792	8.9	9.9	9.9	10.5	10.0	10.5	10.7	10.9
20 to 24 years	9,277,021	9,056,984	7,335,016	6,196,676	5,087,772	3,748,299			8.8	9.8	9.7	9.9	10.1	9.7		
25 to 29 years	9,086,491	8,180,003	6,529,441	5,227,777	4,080,621	3,075,118	5,726,400	4,277,318	8.6	8.9	8.6	8.3	8.1	8.0	18.2	18.4
30 to 34 years	8,071,193	6,972,185	5,556,039	4,578,639	3,368,943	2,502,829			7.6	7.6	7.3	7.3	6.7	6.6		
35 to 39 years	7,775,281	6,396,100	4,964,781	3,896,161	3,000,419	2,314,976	4,021,248	2,825,819	7.4	7.0	6.5	6.2	6.0	6.0	12.8	12.2
40 to 44 years	6,345,557	5,261,587	4,247,166	3,185,518	2,468,811	1,939,712			6.0	5.7	5.6	5.1	4.9	5.0		
45 to 49 years	5,763,620	4,469,197	3,454,612	2,731,640	2,089,445	1,578,932	2,614,330	1,846,660	5.5	4.9	4.5	4.4	4.2	4.1	8.3	8.0
50 to 54 years	4,734,873	3,900,791	2,942,829	2,326,262	1,839,883	1,367,969			4.5	4.2	3.9	3.7	3.7	3.5		
55 to 59 years	3,549,124	2,786,951	2,211,172	1,672,336	1,271,434	876,552	1,585,879	1,109,540	3.4	3.0	2.9	2.7	2.5	2.3	5.0	4.8
60 to 64 years	2,982,548	2,267,150	1,791,363	1,458,034	1,104,219	778,971			2.8	2.5	2.4	2.3	2.2	2.1		
65 to 69 years	2,068,475	1,679,593	1,302,926	1,010,110	725,876	484,353	888,809	609,926	2.0	1.8	1.7	1.6	1.4	1.3	2.8	2.6
70 to 74 years	1,395,636	1,113,728	883,841	701,751	495,442	344,358			1.3	1.2	1.2	1.1	1.0	0.9		
75 to 79 years	856,560	667,302	519,857	393,062	281,065	175,686	348,890	257,234	0.8	0.7	0.7	0.6	0.6	0.5	1.1	1.1
80 to 84 years	402,779	321,754	251,512	203,851	146,362				0.4	0.3	0.3	0.3	0.3			
85 to 89 years	156,539	122,816	88,600	75,240	49,835	129,077	93,552	77,382	0.1	0.1	0.1	0.1	0.1	0.3	0.3	0.3
90 to 94 years	39,980	33,473	23,092	23,645	16,100				(²)	(²)	(²)	(²)	(²)			0.1
95 to 99 years	9,579	7,391	6,266	5,648	4,763	16,653	13,778	11,695	(²)	(²)	(²)	(²)	(²)	(²)	(²)	
100 years and over	4,267	3,555	3,504	3,981	4,016	3,522	2,953	2,555	(²)	(²)	(²)	(²)	(²)	(²)	(²)	(²)
Age unknown	148,699	169,055	200,584	162,165		5,161	51,511	14,285	0.1	0.2	0.3	0.3		(²)	0.2	0.1
MALES.																
All ages	53,900,431	47,332,277	38,816,448	¹32,067,880	25,518,820	19,493,565	16,085,204	11,837,660	100.0	100.0	100.0	100.0	100.0	100.0	100.0	100.0
Under 5 years	5,857,461	5,380,595	4,633,612	3,884,869	3,507,709	2,797,257	2,449,547	1,769,460	10.9	11.4	11.9	12.1	13.7	14.3	15.2	14.9
Under 1 year	1,141,939	1,123,409	969,257	799,373	734,024	557,617	471,804	318,226	2.1	2.4	2.5	2.5	2.9	2.9	2.9	2.7
5 to 9 years	5,753,001	4,924,123	4,479,396	3,830,352	3,275,131	2,437,442	2,109,545	1,640,407	10.7	10.4	11.5	11.9	12.8	12.5	13.1	13.9
10 to 14 years	5,369,306	4,601,753	4,083,041	3,574,787	2,907,481	2,435,585	1,900,868	1,473,116	10.0	9.7	10.5	11.1	11.4	12.5	11.8	12.4
15 to 19 years	4,673,792	4,527,282	3,750,451	3,248,711	2,476,088	1,989,695	1,650,012	1,237,680	8.7	9.6	9.7	10.1	9.7	10.2	10.3	10.5
20 to 24 years	4,527,045	4,580,290	3,624,580	3,104,893	2,554,684	1,835,946			8.4	9.7	9.3	9.7	10.0	9.4		
25 to 29 years	4,538,233	4,214,348	3,323,543	2,698,311	2,109,741	1,515,671	2,911,558	2,194,469	8.4	9.0	8.6	8.4	8.3	7.8	18.1	18.5
30 to 34 years	4,130,783	3,656,768	2,901,321	2,425,964	1,744,308	1,273,633			7.7	7.7	7.5	7.6	6.8	6.5		
35 to 39 years	4,074,361	3,367,016	2,616,865	2,051,044	1,527,159	1,179,366	2,129,017	1,490,135	7.6	7.1	6.7	6.4	6.0	6.1	13.2	12.6
40 to 44 years	3,285,543	2,786,350	2,255,916	1,654,604	1,243,773	990,021			6.1	5.9	5.8	5.2	4.9	5.1		
45 to 49 years	3,117,550	2,378,916	1,837,836	1,418,102	1,078,695	839,578	1,392,223	967,573	5.8	5.0	4.7	4.4	4.2	4.3	8.7	8.2
50 to 54 years	2,535,545	2,110,013	1,564,622	1,208,922	966,702	740,360			4.7	4.5	4.0	3.8	3.8	3.8		
55 to 59 years	1,880,065	1,488,437	1,145,257	871,663	674,927	469,495	835,350	575,685	3.5	3.1	3.0	2.7	2.6	2.4	5.2	4.9
60 to 64 years	1,581,800	1,185,966	917,167	758,710	584,858	407,491			2.9	2.5	2.4	2.4	2.3	2.1		
65 to 69 years	1,079,817	863,994	667,669	525,627	379,498	250,662	455,754	309,515	2.0	1.8	1.7	1.6	1.5	1.3	2.8	2.6
70 to 74 years	796,301	561,644	449,609	363,642	250,001	173,036			1.3	1.2	1.2	1.1	1.0	0.9		
75 to 79 years	419,965	331,280	261,579	199,093	138,601	86,282	172,563	127,460	0.8	0.7	0.7	0.6	0.5	0.4	1.1	1.1
80 to 84 years	185,903	153,745	122,273	97,862	67,941				0.3	0.3	0.3	0.3	0.3			
85 to 89 years	69,272	56,335	40,742	34,063	21,908	60,042	43,790	36,727	0.1	0.1	0.1	0.1	0.1	0.3	0.3	0.3
90 to 94 years	16,383	14,553	9,858	9,848	6,351				(²)	(²)	(²)	(²)	(²)			
95 to 99 years	3,869	3,045	2,417	2,186	1,855	6,922	5,854	5,183	(²)	(²)	(²)	(²)	(²)	(²)	(²)	(²)
100 years and over	1,561	1,380	1,271	1,398	1,409	1,286	1,233	1,077	(²)	(²)	(²)	(²)	(²)	(²)	(²)	(²)
Age unknown	92,875	114,443	127,423	103,529	....	3,795	27,890	9,173	0.2	0.2	0.3	0.3	......	(²)	0.2	0.1
FEMALES.																
All ages	51,810,189	44,639,989	37,178,127	¹30,554,370	24,636,963	19,064,806	15,358,117	11,354,216	100.0	100.0	100.0	100.0	100.0	100.0	100.0	100.0
Under 5 years	5,715,769	5,250,768	4,537,016	3,749,824	3,406,807	2,717,456	2,392,949	1,728,313	11.0	11.8	12.2	12.3	13.8	14.3	15.6	15.2
Under 1 year	1,115,316	1,093,933	947,635	767,361	713,959	542,858	462,779	311,220	2.2	2.5	2.5	2.5	2.9	2.8	3.0	2.7
5 to 9 years	5,645,074	4,836,509	4,394,727	3,743,646	3,204,529	2,377,271	2,061,655	1,600,861	10.9	10.8	11.8	12.3	13.0	12.5	13.4	14.1
10 to 14 years	5,271,831	4,505,387	3,997,193	3,458,722	2,807,705	2,350,604	1,819,912	1,417,513	10.2	10.1	10.8	11.3	11.4	12.3	11.8	12.5
15 to 19 years	4,756,764	4,536,321	3,805,638	3,308,852	2,535,327	2,050,893	1,711,483	1,292,112	9.2	10.2	10.2	10.8	10.3	10.8	11.1	11.4
20 to 24 years	4,749,976	4,476,694	3,710,436	3,091,783	2,533,088	1,912,353			9.2	10.0	10.0	10.1	10.3	10.0		
25 to 29 years	4,548,258	3,965,655	3,205,898	2,529,466	1,970,880	1,559,447	2,814,842	2,082,849	8.8	8.8	8.6	8.3	8.0	8.2	18.3	18.3
30 to 34 years	3,940,410	3,315,417	2,654,718	2,152,966	1,624,635	1,289,196			7.6	7.4	7.1	7.0	6.6	6.8		
35 to 39 years	3,700,920	3,029,084	2,347,916	1,845,117	1,473,260	1,135,610	1,892,231	1,335,684	7.1	6.8	6.3	5.9	6.0	6.0	12.3	11.8
40 to 44 years	3,060,014	2,475,237	1,991,250	1,530,914	1,225,038	949,691			5.9	5.5	5.4	5.0	5.0	5.0		
45 to 49 years	2,646,070	2,090,281	1,616,776	1,313,538	1,010,750	739,354	1,222,107	879,087	5.1	4.7	4.3	4.3	4.1	3.9	8.0	7.7
50 to 54 years	2,199,328	1,790,778	1,378,207	1,117,340	873,181	627,609			4.2	4.0	3.7	3.7	3.5	3.3		
55 to 59 years	1,669,059	1,298,514	1,065,915	800,673	596,507	407,057	750,529	533,855	3.2	2.9	2.9	2.6	2.4	2.1	4.9	4.7
60 to 64 years	1,400,748	1,081,184	874,196	699,324	519,361	371,480			2.7	2.4	2.4	2.3	2.1	1.9		
65 to 69 years	988,658	815,599	635,257	484,483	346,378	233,691	433,055	300,411	1.9	1.8	1.7	1.6	1.4	1.2	2.8	2.6
70 to 74 years	688,735	552,084	434,232	338,109	245,441	171,322			1.3	1.2	1.2	1.1	1.0	0.9		
75 to 79 years	436,595	336,022	258,278	193,969	142,464	89,404	176,327	129,774	0.8	0.8	0.7	0.6	0.6	0.5	1.1	1.1
80 to 84 years	216,876	168,009	129,239	105,989	78,421				0.4	0.4	0.3	0.3	0.3			
85 to 89 years	87,267	66,483	47,858	41,177	27,927	69,035	49,762	40,655	0.2	0.1	0.1	0.1	0.1	0.4	0.3	0.4
90 to 94 years	23,597	18,920	14,134	13,797	9,749				(²)	(²)	(²)	(²)	(²)			
95 to 99 years	5,710	4,346	3,849	3,462	2,908	9,731	7,924	6,512	(²)	(²)	(²)	(²)	(²)	0.1	0.1	0.1
100 years and over	2,706	2,175	2,233	2,583	2,607	2,236	1,720	1,478	(²)	(²)	(²)	(²)	(²)	(²)	(²)	(²)
Age unknown	55,824	54,612	73,161	58,636	....	1,366	23,621	5,112	0.1	0.1	0.2	0.2	......	(²)	0.2	(²)

¹ Exclusive of 325,464 persons (169,221 males and 156,243 females) specially enumerated in 1890 in Indian Territory and on Indian reservations, for whom statistics of age are not available.
² Less than one-tenth of 1 per cent.

TABLE 2.—DISTRIBUTION BY BROAD AGE GROUPS FOR POPULATION CLASSES, BY SEX, FOR THE UNITED STATES: 1920 AND 1910.

CLASS OF POPULATION AND AGE GROUP.	POPULATION.						PER CENT DISTRIBUTION.						MALES TO 100 FEMALES.	
	1920			1910			1920			1910				
	Both sexes.	Male.	Female.	Both sexes.	Male.	Female.	Both sexes.	Male.	Female.	Both sexes.	Male.	Female.	1920	1910
All classes[1]	**105,710,620**	**53,900,431**	**51,810,189**	**91,972,266**	**47,332,277**	**44,639,989**	**100.0**	**100.0**	**100.0**	**100.0**	**100.0**	**100.0**	**104.0**	**106.0**
Under 5 years	11,573,230	5,857,461	5,715,769	10,631,364	5,380,596	5,250,768	10.9	10.9	11.0	11.6	11.4	11.8	102.5	102.5
5 to 14 years	22,039,212	11,122,307	10,916,905	18,867,772	9,525,876	9,341,896	20.8	20.6	21.1	20.5	20.1	20.9	101.9	102.0
15 to 24 years	18,707,577	9,200,837	9,506,740	18,120,587	9,107,572	9,013,015	17.7	17.1	18.3	19.7	19.2	20.2	96.8	101.0
25 to 44 years	31,278,522	16,028,920	15,249,602	26,809,875	14,054,482	12,755,393	29.6	29.7	29.4	29.1	29.7	28.6	105.1	110.2
25 to 34 years	17,157,684	8,669,016	8,488,668	15,152,188	7,901,116	7,251,072	16.2	16.1	16.4	16.5	16.7	16.2	102.1	109.0
35 to 44 years	14,120,838	7,359,904	6,760,934	11,657,687	6,153,366	5,504,321	13.4	13.7	13.0	12.7	13.0	12.3	108.9	111.8
45 to 64 years	17,030,165	9,114,960	7,915,205	13,424,089	7,163,332	6,260,757	16.1	16.9	15.3	14.6	15.1	14.0	115.2	114.4
45 to 54 years	10,498,493	5,653,095	4,845,398	8,369,988	4,488,929	3,881,059	9.9	10.5	9.4	9.1	9.5	8.7	116.7	115.7
55 to 64 years	6,531,672	3,461,865	3,069,807	5,054,101	2,674,403	2,379,698	6.2	6.4	5.9	5.5	5.7	5.3	112.8	112.4
65 years and over	4,933,215	2,483,071	2,450,144	3,949,524	1,985,976	1,963,548	4.7	4.6	4.7	4.3	4.2	4.4	101.3	101.1
Native white—Native parentage[1]	**58,421,957**	**29,636,781**	**28,785,176**	**49,488,575**	**25,229,218**	**24,259,357**	**100.0**	**100.0**	**100.0**	**100.0**	**100.0**	**100.0**	**103.0**	**104.0**
Under 5 years	7,366,530	3,741,194	3,625,336	6,546,282	3,326,237	3,220,045	12.6	12.6	12.6	13.2	13.2	13.3	103.2	103.3
5 to 14 years	13,433,572	6,803,480	6,630,092	11,185,298	5,669,886	5,515,412	23.0	23.0	23.0	22.6	22.5	22.7	102.6	102.8
15 to 24 years	10,775,753	5,344,295	5,431,458	9,771,977	4,885,442	4,886,535	18.4	18.0	18.9	19.7	19.4	20.1	98.4	100.0
25 to 44 years	15,776,025	7,968,863	7,807,162	12,946,441	6,642,210	6,304,231	27.0	26.9	27.1	26.2	26.3	26.0	102.1	105.4
25 to 34 years	8,860,843	4,421,983	4,438,860	7,450,675	3,788,166	3,662,509	15.2	14.9	15.4	15.1	15.0	15.1	99.6	103.4
35 to 44 years	6,915,182	3,546,880	3,368,302	5,495,766	2,854,044	2,641,722	11.8	12.0	11.7	11.1	11.3	10.9	105.3	108.0
45 to 64 years	8,239,032	4,354,663	3,884,369	6,740,000	3,547,325	3,192,675	14.1	14.7	13.5	13.6	14.1	13.2	112.1	111.1
45 to 54 years	4,989,713	2,649,866	2,339,847	4,022,103	2,122,657	1,899,446	8.5	8.9	8.1	8.1	8.4	7.8	113.2	111.8
55 to 64 years	3,249,319	1,704,797	1,544,522	2,717,897	1,424,668	1,293,229	5.6	5.8	5.4	5.5	5.6	5.3	110.4	110.2
65 years and over	2,738,876	1,365,527	1,373,349	2,201,068	1,089,349	1,111,719	4.7	4.6	4.8	4.4	4.3	4.6	99.4	98.0
Native white—Foreign parentage[1]	**15,694,539**	**7,810,531**	**7,884,008**	**12,916,311**	**6,456,793**	**6,459,518**	**100.0**	**100.0**	**100.0**	**100.0**	**100.0**	**100.0**	**99.1**	**100.0**
Under 5 years	2,124,350	1,072,885	1,051,465	1,819,847	917,613	902,234	13.5	13.7	13.3	14.1	14.2	14.0	102.0	101.7
5 to 14 years	3,870,731	1,944,735	1,925,996	2,944,114	1,479,402	1,464,712	24.7	24.9	24.4	22.8	22.9	22.7	101.0	101.0
15 to 24 years	2,814,123	1,383,857	1,430,266	2,691,109	1,326,580	1,364,529	17.9	17.7	18.1	20.8	20.5	21.1	96.8	97.2
25 to 44 years	4,094,449	2,017,298	2,077,151	3,663,022	1,818,392	1,844,630	26.1	25.8	26.3	28.4	28.2	28.6	97.1	98.6
25 to 34 years	2,338,688	1,150,323	1,188,365	1,963,218	971,470	991,748	14.9	14.7	15.1	15.2	15.0	15.4	96.8	98.0
35 to 44 years	1,755,761	866,975	888,786	1,699,804	846,922	852,882	11.2	11.1	11.3	13.2	13.1	13.2	97.5	99.3
45 to 64 years	2,418,332	1,208,166	1,210,166	1,631,035	829,486	801,549	15.4	15.5	15.3	12.6	12.8	12.4	99.8	103.5
45 to 54 years	1,489,610	745,976	743,634	1,192,088	604,926	587,162	9.5	9.6	9.4	9.2	9.4	9.1	100.3	103.0
55 to 64 years	928,722	462,190	466,532	438,947	224,560	214,387	5.9	5.9	5.9	3.4	3.5	3.3	99.1	104.7
65 years and over	364,554	179,375	185,179	159,599	81,224	78,375	2.3	2.3	2.3	1.2	1.3	1.2	96.9	103.6
Native white—Mixed parentage[1]	**6,991,665**	**3,455,621**	**3,536,044**	**5,981,526**	**2,968,446**	**3,013,080**	**100.0**	**100.0**	**100.0**	**100.0**	**100.0**	**100.0**	**97.7**	**98.5**
Under 5 years	838,057	423,778	414,279	854,278	432,860	421,418	12.0	12.3	11.7	14.3	14.6	14.0	102.3	102.7
5 to 14 years	1,651,018	833,214	817,804	1,607,330	810,227	797,103	23.6	24.1	23.1	26.9	27.3	26.5	101.9	101.6
15 to 24 years	1,454,834	715,997	738,837	1,387,574	682,402	705,172	20.8	20.7	20.9	23.2	23.0	23.4	96.9	96.8
25 to 44 years	2,059,616	986,381	1,073,235	1,547,087	747,242	799,845	29.5	28.5	30.3	25.9	25.2	26.5	91.9	93.4
25 to 34 years	1,175,111	559,355	615,756	942,108	450,513	491,595	16.8	16.2	17.4	15.8	15.2	16.3	90.8	91.6
35 to 44 years	884,505	427,026	457,479	604,979	296,729	308,250	12.7	12.4	12.9	10.1	10.0	10.2	93.3	96.3
45 to 64 years	833,541	419,843	413,698	486,351	246,736	239,615	11.9	12.2	11.7	8.1	8.3	8.0	101.5	103.0
45 to 54 years	558,931	280,968	277,963	330,769	167,414	163,355	8.0	8.1	7.9	5.5	5.6	5.4	101.1	102.5
55 to 64 years	274,610	138,875	135,735	155,582	79,322	76,260	3.9	4.0	3.8	2.6	2.7	2.5	102.3	104.0
65 years and over	151,369	74,189	77,180	95,987	47,438	48,549	2.2	2.1	2.2	1.6	1.6	1.6	96.1	97.7
Foreign-born white[1]	**13,712,754**	**7,528,322**	**6,184,432**	**13,345,545**	**7,523,788**	**5,821,757**	**100.0**	**100.0**	**100.0**	**100.0**	**100.0**	**100.0**	**121.7**	**129.2**
Under 5 years	44,984	22,857	22,127	102,507	51,940	50,567	0.3	0.3	0.4	0.8	0.7	0.9	103.3	102.7
5 to 14 years	501,246	252,926	248,320	656,839	331,955	324,884	3.7	3.4	4.0	4.9	4.4	5.6	101.9	102.2
15 to 24 years	1,454,786	716,258	738,528	2,104,142	1,175,674	928,468	10.6	9.5	11.9	15.8	15.6	15.9	97.0	126.6
25 to 44 years	6,271,742	3,550,778	2,720,964	5,879,979	3,442,770	2,437,209	45.7	47.2	44.0	44.1	45.8	41.9	130.5	141.3
25 to 34 years	3,105,838	1,738,906	1,366,932	3,168,411	1,879,244	1,289,167	22.6	23.1	22.1	23.7	25.0	22.1	127.2	145.8
35 to 44 years	3,165,904	1,811,872	1,354,032	2,711,568	1,563,526	1,148,042	23.1	24.1	21.9	20.3	20.8	19.7	133.8	136.2
45 to 64 years	4,001,505	2,202,387	1,799,118	3,392,518	1,894,735	1,497,783	29.8	30.5	29.1	25.4	25.2	25.7	127.4	126.5
45 to 54 years	2,467,052	1,395,969	1,071,083	2,071,415	1,182,711	888,704	18.0	18.5	17.3	15.5	15.7	15.3	130.3	133.1
55 to 64 years	1,624,453	806,418	728,035	1,321,103	712,024	609,079	11.8	11.9	11.8	9.9	9.5	10.5	123.1	116.9
65 years and over	1,328,227	679,384	648,843	1,183,349	607,008	576,341	9.7	9.0	10.5	8.9	8.1	9.9	104.7	105.3
Negro[1]	**10,463,131**	**5,209,436**	**5,253,695**	**9,827,763**	**4,885,881**	**4,941,882**	**100.0**	**100.0**	**100.0**	**100.0**	**100.0**	**100.0**	**99.2**	**98.9**
Under 5 years	1,143,699	568,633	575,066	1,263,288	629,320	633,968	10.9	10.9	10.9	12.9	12.9	12.8	98.9	99.3
5 to 14 years	2,503,121	1,247,592	1,255,529	2,401,819	1,197,249	1,204,570	23.9	23.9	23.9	24.4	24.5	24.4	99.4	99.4
15 to 24 years	2,138,062	1,000,585	1,137,477	2,091,211	990,102	1,101,109	20.4	19.2	21.7	21.3	20.3	22.3	88.0	89.9
25 to 44 years	2,941,236	1,415,444	1,525,792	2,638,178	1,304,098	1,334,080	28.1	27.2	29.0	26.8	26.7	27.0	92.8	97.8
25 to 34 years	1,607,604	755,931	851,673	1,549,316	753,968	795,348	15.4	14.5	16.2	15.8	15.4	16.1	88.8	94.8
35 to 44 years	1,333,632	659,513	674,119	1,088,862	550,130	538,732	12.7	12.7	12.8	11.1	11.3	10.9	97.8	102.1
45 to 64 years	1,380,797	789,791	591,006	1,108,103	595,554	512,549	13.2	15.2	11.2	11.3	12.2	10.4	133.6	116.2
45 to 54 years	950,699	548,501	402,198	711,070	379,315	332,664	9.1	10.5	7.7	7.2	7.8	6.7	136.4	114.0
55 to 64 years	430,098	241,290	188,808	396,124	216,239	179,885	4.1	4.6	3.6	4.0	4.4	3.6	127.8	120.2
65 years and over	332,713	173,881	158,832	294,124	152,482	141,642	3.2	3.3	3.0	3.0	3.1	2.9	109.5	107.7
Indian[1]	**244,437**	**125,068**	**119,369**	**265,683**	**135,133**	**130,550**	**100.0**	**100.0**	**100.0**	**100.0**	**100.0**	**100.0**	**104.8**	**103.5**
Under 5 years	33,346	16,591	16,755	40,384	20,202	20,182	13.6	13.3	14.0	15.2	14.9	15.5	99.0	100.1
5 to 14 years	64,339	32,156	32,183	67,934	34,548	33,386	26.3	25.7	27.0	25.6	25.6	25.6	99.9	103.5
15 to 24 years	45,426	23,123	22,303	50,330	25,877	24,453	18.6	18.5	18.7	18.9	19.1	18.7	103.7	105.8
25 to 44 years	55,336	28,805	26,531	60,175	30,840	29,335	22.6	23.0	22.2	22.6	22.8	22.5	108.6	105.1
25 to 34 years	30,011	15,521	14,490	33,380	16,993	16,387	12.3	12.4	12.1	12.6	12.6	12.6	107.1	103.7
35 to 44 years	25,325	13,284	12,041	26,795	13,847	12,948	10.4	10.6	10.1	10.1	10.2	9.9	110.3	106.9
45 to 64 years	32,060	17,481	14,579	32,925	17,055	15,870	13.1	14.0	12.2	12.4	12.6	12.2	119.9	107.5
45 to 54 years	19,534	10,751	8,783	19,230	10,017	9,213	8.0	8.6	7.4	7.2	7.4	7.1	122.4	108.7
55 to 64 years	12,526	6,730	5,796	13,695	7,038	6,657	5.1	5.4	4.9	5.2	5.2	5.1	116.1	105.7
65 years and over	13,139	6,512	6,627	12,986	6,130	6,856	5.4	5.2	5.6	4.9	4.5	5.3	98.3	89.4
Chinese, Japanese, and all other[1]	**182,137**	**135,272**	**46,865**	**146,863**	**133,018**	**13,845**	**100.0**	**100.0**	**100.0**	**100.0**	**100.0**	**100.0**	**288.6**	**960.8**
Under 5 years	22,264	11,523	10,741	4,778	2,424	2,354	12.2	8.5	22.9	3.3	1.8	17.0	107.3	103.0
5 to 14 years	15,185	8,204	6,981	4,438	2,609	1,829	8.3	6.1	14.9	3.0	2.0	13.2	117.5	142.6
15 to 24 years	24,593	16,722	7,871	24,244	21,495	2,749	13.5	12.4	16.8	16.5	16.2	19.9	212.5	781.9
25 to 44 years	80,118	61,351	18,767	74,993	68,930	6,063	44.0	45.4	40.0	51.1	51.8	43.8	326.9	1,136.9
25 to 34 years	39,589	26,997	12,592	45,080	40,762	4,318	21.7	20.0	26.9	30.7	30.6	31.2	214.4	944.0
35 to 44 years	40,529	34,354	6,175	29,913	28,168	1,745	22.3	25.4	13.2	20.4	21.2	12.6	556.3	1,614.2
45 to 64 years	34,898	32,629	2,269	33,157	32,441	716	19.2	24.1	4.8	22.6	24.4	5.2	1,438.0	4,530.9
45 to 54 years	22,954	21,064	1,890	22,404	21,889	515	12.6	15.6	4.0	15.3	16.5	3.7	1,114.5	4,250.3
55 to 64 years	11,944	11,565	379	10,753	10,552	201	6.6	8.5	0.8	7.3	7.9	1.5	3,051.5	5,249.8
65 years and over	4,337	4,203	134	2,411	2,345	66	2.4	3.1	0.3	1.6	1.8	0.5	3,136.6	(2)

[1] Totals include persons of unknown age.

[2] Ratio not shown, number of females being less than 100.

156 — POPULATION.

TABLE 3.—DISTRIBUTION BY AGE PERIODS FOR POPULATION CLASSES, BY SEX, FOR THE UNITED STATES: 1920.

AGE PERIOD.	ALL CLASSES.			WHITE.			NEGRO.			INDIAN, CHINESE, JAPANESE, AND ALL OTHER.		
	Both sexes.	Male.	Female.	Both sexes.	Male.	Female.	Both sexes.	Male.	Female.	Both sexes.	Male.	Female.
All ages	105,710,620	53,900,431	51,810,189	94,820,915	48,430,655	46,390,260	10,463,131	5,209,436	5,253,695	426,574	260,340	166,234
Under 5 years	11,573,230	5,857,461	5,715,769	10,373,921	5,260,714	5,113,207	1,143,699	568,633	575,066	55,610	28,114	27,496
Under 1 year	2,257,235	1,141,939	1,115,316	2,017,767	1,023,270	994,497	227,660	112,660	115,000	11,828	6,009	5,819
5 to 9 years	11,398,075	5,753,001	5,645,074	10,087,245	5,099,205	4,988,040	1,266,207	631,341	634,866	44,623	22,455	22,168
10 to 14 years	10,641,137	5,369,306	5,271,831	9,369,322	4,735,150	4,634,172	1,236,914	616,251	620,663	34,901	17,905	16,996
15 to 19 years	9,430,556	4,673,792	4,756,764	8,314,155	4,141,831	4,172,324	1,083,215	513,416	569,799	33,186	18,545	14,641
20 to 24 years	9,277,021	4,527,045	4,749,976	8,185,341	4,018,576	4,166,765	1,054,847	487,109	567,678	36,833	21,300	15,533
25 to 29 years	9,096,491	4,548,233	4,548,258	8,141,690	4,094,301	4,047,389	909,739	424,352	485,387	35,062	19,580	15,482
30 to 34 years	8,071,193	4,130,783	3,940,410	7,338,790	3,776,266	3,562,524	697,865	331,579	366,286	34,538	22,938	11,600
35 to 39 years	7,775,281	4,074,361	3,700,920	6,965,805	3,665,341	3,300,464	773,931	383,587	390,344	35,545	25,433	10,112
40 to 44 years	6,345,557	3,285,543	3,060,014	5,755,547	2,987,412	2,768,135	559,701	275,926	283,775	30,309	22,205	8,104
45 to 49 years	5,763,620	3,117,550	2,646,070	5,188,640	2,779,175	2,408,865	551,589	320,506	231,083	23,991	17,869	6,122
50 to 54 years	4,734,873	2,535,545	2,199,328	4,317,266	2,293,604	2,023,662	399,110	227,995	171,115	18,497	13,946	4,551
55 to 59 years	3,549,124	1,880,065	1,669,059	3,305,671	1,740,661	1,565,010	229,980	129,153	100,827	13,473	10,251	3,222
60 to 64 years	2,982,548	1,581,800	1,400,748	2,771,433	1,461,619	1,309,814	200,118	112,137	87,981	10,997	8,044	2,953
65 to 69 years	2,068,475	1,079,817	988,658	1,924,296	998,779	925,517	137,035	76,184	60,851	7,144	4,854	2,290
70 to 74 years	1,395,036	706,301	688,735	1,298,738	655,916	642,822	91,579	47,411	44,168	4,719	2,974	1,745
75 to 79 years	856,560	419,965	436,595	801,678	391,383	410,295	52,352	27,172	25,180	2,530	1,410	1,120
80 to 84 years	402,779	185,903	216,876	373,066	172,064	201,002	28,122	13,049	15,073	1,591	790	801
85 to 89 years	156,539	69,272	87,267	143,536	63,308	80,228	12,281	5,620	6,661	722	344	378
90 to 94 years	39,980	16,383	23,597	33,713	13,852	19,861	5,847	2,340	3,507	420	191	229
95 to 99 years	9,579	3,869	5,710	6,831	2,706	4,125	2,562	1,087	1,475	186	76	110
100 years and over	4,267	1,561	2,706	1,168	467	701	2,935	1,018	1,917	164	76	88
Age unknown	148,699	92,875	55,824	123,663	78,325	45,338	23,503	13,510	9,993	1,533	1,040	493

AGE PERIOD.	NATIVE WHITE.									FOREIGN-BORN WHITE.		
	Native parentage.			Foreign parentage.			Mixed parentage.			Both sexes.	Male.	Female.
	Both sexes.	Male.	Female.	Both sexes.	Male.	Female.	Both sexes.	Male.	Female.			
All ages	58,421,957	29,636,781	28,785,176	15,694,539	7,810,531	7,884,008	6,991,665	3,455,021	3,536,644	13,712,754	7,528,322	6,184,432
Under 5 years	7,366,530	3,741,194	3,625,336	2,124,350	1,072,885	1,051,465	838,057	423,778	414,279	44,084	22,857	22,127
Under 1 year	1,453,404	737,923	715,481	396,780	200,361	196,419	163,014	82,649	80,365	4,569	2,337	2,232
5 to 9 years	6,977,863	3,534,092	3,443,771	2,107,263	1,058,518	1,048,745	832,235	420,821	411,414	169,884	85,774	84,110
10 to 14 years	6,455,709	3,269,388	3,186,321	1,763,468	886,217	877,251	818,783	412,393	406,390	331,302	167,152	164,210
15 to 19 years	5,599,046	2,797,477	2,801,569	1,429,368	707,722	721,646	757,799	377,362	380,437	527,942	259,270	268,672
20 to 24 years	5,176,707	2,546,818	2,629,889	1,384,755	676,135	708,020	697,035	338,635	358,400	926,844	456,988	469,856
25 to 29 years	4,764,802	2,367,312	2,397,490	1,286,562	631,349	655,213	635,963	303,552	332,411	1,454,363	792,088	662,275
30 to 34 years	4,096,041	2,054,671	2,041,370	1,052,126	518,974	533,152	539,148	255,803	283,345	1,651,475	946,818	704,657
35 to 39 years	3,815,852	1,962,634	1,853,218	924,617	459,056	465,561	487,531	234,974	252,557	1,737,805	1,008,677	729,128
40 to 44 years	3,099,330	1,584,246	1,515,084	831,144	407,919	423,225	396,974	192,052	204,922	1,428,099	803,195	624,904
45 to 49 years	2,753,013	1,463,247	1,289,766	813,043	409,412	403,631	322,309	162,093	160,216	1,299,675	744,423	555,252
50 to 54 years	2,236,700	1,186,619	1,050,081	676,567	336,564	340,003	236,622	118,875	117,747	1,167,377	651,546	515,831
55 to 59 years	1,719,190	899,029	820,161	519,246	257,752	261,494	158,513	80,091	78,422	908,722	503,789	404,933
60 to 64 years	1,530,129	805,768	724,361	409,476	204,438	205,038	116,097	58,784	57,313	715,731	392,629	323,102
65 to 69 years	1,126,722	584,783	541,939	208,359	103,405	104,954	69,989	35,191	34,798	519,226	275,400	243,826
70 to 74 years	784,183	395,582	388,601	90,854	44,781	46,073	42,376	20,821	21,555	381,325	194,732	186,593
75 to 79 years	487,797	234,584	253,213	43,198	21,058	22,140	24,196	11,571	12,625	246,487	124,170	122,317
80 to 84 years	228,018	103,493	124,525	16,029	7,333	8,696	10,084	4,537	5,547	118,935	56,701	62,234
85 to 89 years	87,530	37,459	50,071	4,862	2,230	2,632	3,671	1,615	2,056	47,473	22,004	25,469
90 to 94 years	20,159	7,922	12,237	975	440	535	862	367	495	11,717	5,123	6,594
95 to 99 years	3,853	1,475	2,378	240	110	130	159	72	87	2,579	1,040	1,530
100 years and over	614	229	385	37	18	19	32	15	17	485	205	280
Age unknown	92,169	58,759	33,410	8,000	4,215	3,785	3,230	1,619	1,611	20,264	13,732	6,532

AGE DISTRIBUTION.　　157

TABLE 4.—PER CENT DISTRIBUTION BY AGE PERIODS FOR PRINCIPAL POPULATION CLASSES, BY SEX, FOR THE UNITED STATES: 1920.

AGE PERIOD.	ALL CLASSES. Both sexes	Male	Female	WHITE. Both sexes	Male	Female	NEGRO. Both sexes	Male	Female	NATIVE WHITE. Native parentage. Both sexes	Male	Female	Foreign parentage. Both sexes	Male	Female	Mixed parentage. Both sexes	Male	Female	FOREIGN-BORN WHITE. Both sexes	Male	Female
All ages	100.0	100.0	100.0	100.0	100.0	100.0	100.0	100.0	100.0	100.0	100.0	100.0	100.0	100.0	100.0	100.0	100.0	100.0	100.0	100.0	100.0
Under 5 years	10.9	10.9	11.0	10.9	10.9	11.0	10.9	10.9	10.9	12.6	12.6	12.6	13.5	13.7	13.3	12.0	12.3	11.7	0.3	0.3	0.4
Under 1 year	2.1	2.1	2.2	2.1	2.1	2.1	2.2	2.2	2.2	2.5	2.5	2.5	2.5	2.6	2.5	2.3	2.4	2.3	(1)	(1)	(1)
5 to 9 years	10.8	10.7	10.9	10.6	10.5	10.8	12.1	12.1	12.1	11.9	11.9	12.0	13.4	13.6	13.3	11.9	12.2	11.6	1.2	1.1	1.4
10 to 14 years	10.1	10.0	10.2	9.9	9.8	10.0	11.8	11.8	11.8	11.1	11.0	11.1	11.2	11.3	11.1	11.7	11.9	11.5	2.4	2.2	2.7
15 to 19 years	8.9	8.7	9.2	8.8	8.6	9.0	10.4	9.9	10.8	9.6	9.4	9.7	9.1	9.1	9.2	10.8	10.9	10.8	3.9	3.4	4.3
20 to 24 years	8.8	8.4	9.2	8.6	8.3	9.0	10.1	9.4	10.8	8.9	8.6	9.1	8.8	8.7	9.0	10.0	9.8	10.1	6.8	6.1	7.6
25 to 29 years	8.6	8.4	8.8	8.6	8.5	8.7	8.7	8.1	9.2	8.2	8.0	8.3	8.2	8.1	8.3	9.1	8.8	9.4	10.6	10.5	10.7
30 to 34 years	7.6	7.6	7.6	7.7	7.8	7.7	6.7	6.4	7.0	7.0	6.9	7.1	6.7	6.6	6.8	7.7	7.4	8.0	12.0	12.6	11.4
35 to 39 years	7.4	7.6	7.1	7.3	7.6	7.1	7.4	7.4	7.4	6.5	6.6	6.4	5.9	5.9	5.9	7.0	6.8	7.1	12.7	13.4	11.8
40 to 44 years	6.0	6.1	5.9	6.1	6.2	6.0	5.3	5.3	5.4	5.3	5.3	5.3	5.2	5.2	5.4	5.6	5.7	5.8	10.4	10.7	10.1
45 to 49 years	5.5	5.8	5.1	5.5	5.7	5.2	5.3	6.2	4.4	4.7	4.9	4.5	5.2	5.2	5.1	4.6	4.7	4.5	9.5	9.9	9.0
50 to 54 years	4.5	4.7	4.2	4.6	4.7	4.4	3.8	4.4	3.3	3.8	4.0	3.6	4.3	4.3	4.3	3.4	3.4	3.3	8.5	8.7	8.3
55 to 59 years	3.4	3.5	3.2	3.5	3.6	3.4	2.2	2.5	1.9	2.9	3.0	2.8	3.3	3.3	3.3	2.3	2.3	2.2	6.6	6.7	6.5
60 to 64 years	2.8	2.9	2.7	2.9	3.0	2.8	1.9	2.2	1.7	2.6	2.7	2.5	2.6	2.6	2.6	1.7	1.7	1.6	5.2	5.2	5.2
65 to 69 years	2.0	2.0	1.9	2.0	2.1	2.0	1.3	1.5	1.2	1.9	2.0	1.9	1.3	1.3	1.3	1.0	1.0	1.0	3.8	3.7	3.9
70 to 74 years	1.3	1.3	1.3	1.4	1.4	1.4	0.9	0.9	0.8	1.3	1.3	1.4	0.6	0.6	0.6	0.6	0.6	0.6	2.8	2.6	3.0
75 to 79 years	0.8	0.8	0.8	0.8	0.8	0.9	0.5	0.5	0.5	0.8	0.8	0.9	0.3	0.3	0.3	0.3	0.3	0.4	1.8	1.6	2.0
80 to 84 years	0.4	0.3	0.4	0.4	0.4	0.4	0.3	0.3	0.3	0.4	0.3	0.4	0.1	0.1	0.1	0.1	0.1	0.2	0.9	0.8	1.0
85 to 89 years	0.1	0.1	0.2	0.2	0.1	0.2	0.1	0.1	0.1	0.1	0.1	0.2	(1)	(1)	(1)	0.1	(1)	0.1	0.3	0.3	0.4
90 to 94 years	(1)	(1)	(1)	(1)	(1)	(1)	0.1	(1)	0.1	(1)	(1)	(1)	(1)	(1)	(1)	(1)	(1)	(1)	0.1	0.1	0.1
95 to 99 years	(1)	(1)	(1)	(1)	(1)	(1)	(1)	(1)	(1)	(1)	(1)	(1)	(1)	(1)	(1)	(1)	(1)	(1)	(1)	(1)	(1)
100 years and over	(1)	(1)	(1)	(1)	(1)	(1)	(1)	(1)	(1)	(1)	(1)	(1)	(1)	(1)	(1)	(1)	(1)	(1)	(1)	(1)	(1)
Age unknown	0.1	0.2	0.1	0.1	0.1	0.2	0.2	0.3	0.2	0.2	0.2	0.1	0.1	0.1	(1)	0.1	0.1	0.2	0.1	0.2	0.1

[1] Less than one-tenth of 1 per cent.

TABLE 5.—DISTRIBUTION BY AGE PERIODS FOR INDIAN, CHINESE, JAPANESE, AND "ALL OTHER" POPULATION, BY SEX, FOR THE UNITED STATES: 1920.

AGE PERIOD.	NUMBER. Indian. Both sexes	Male	Female	Chinese. Both sexes	Male	Female	Japanese. Both sexes	Male	Female	All other.[1] Both sexes	Male	Female	PER CENT DISTRIBUTION. Indian. Both sexes	Male	Female	Chinese. Both sexes	Male	Female	Japanese. Both sexes	Male	Female
All ages	244,437	125,068	119,369	61,639	53,891	7,748	111,010	72,707	38,303	9,488	8,674	814	100.0	100.0	100.0	100.0	100.0	100.0	100.0	100.0	100.0
Under 5 years	33,346	16,591	16,755	2,898	1,480	1,418	19,029	9,853	9,176	337	190	147	13.6	13.3	14.0	4.7	2.7	18.3	17.1	13.6	24.0
Under 1 year	6,416	3,236	3,180	622	299	323	4,704	2,428	2,276	86	46	40	2.6	2.6	2.7	1.0	0.6	4.2	4.2	3.3	5.9
5 to 9 years	34,166	16,931	17,235	2,511	1,370	1,141	7,743	4,048	3,695	203	106	97	14.0	13.5	14.4	4.1	2.5	14.7	7.0	5.6	9.6
10 to 14 years	30,173	15,225	14,948	2,005	1,223	782	2,569	1,379	1,190	154	78	76	12.3	12.2	12.5	3.3	2.3	10.1	2.3	1.9	3.1
15 to 19 years	25,417	12,710	12,707	2,760	2,161	599	3,081	1,820	1,261	667	593	74	10.4	10.2	10.6	4.5	4.0	7.7	3.9	4.2	3.3
20 to 24 years	20,009	10,413	9,596	4,845	4,122	723	9,636	4,535	5,101	2,343	2,230	113	8.2	8.3	8.0	7.9	7.6	9.3	8.7	6.2	13.3
25 to 29 years	16,537	8,558	7,979	5,279	4,543	736	11,270	4,600	6,670	1,976	1,879	97	6.8	6.8	6.7	8.6	8.4	9.5	10.2	6.3	17.4
30 to 34 years	13,474	6,963	6,511	4,682	4,093	589	15,253	10,819	4,434	1,129	1,063	66	5.5	5.6	5.5	7.6	7.6	7.6	13.7	14.9	11.6
35 to 39 years	13,707	7,213	6,494	5,319	4,789	530	15,304	12,309	3,025	1,125	1,062	63	5.6	5.8	5.4	8.6	8.9	6.8	13.9	17.0	7.9
40 to 44 years	11,618	6,071	5,547	5,345	4,913	432	12,762	10,670	2,092	584	551	33	4.8	4.9	4.6	8.7	9.1	5.6	11.5	14.7	5.5
45 to 49 years	10,806	5,987	4,819	5,527	5,242	285	7,181	6,184	997	477	456	21	4.4	4.8	4.0	9.0	9.7	3.7	6.5	8.5	2.6
50 to 54 years	8,728	4,764	3,964	6,045	5,850	195	3,515	3,129	386	209	203	6	3.6	3.8	3.3	9.8	10.9	2.5	3.2	4.3	1.0
55 to 59 years	6,573	3,594	2,979	5,594	5,476	118	1,214	1,094	120	92	87	5	2.7	2.9	2.5	9.1	10.2	1.5	1.1	1.5	0.3
60 to 64 years	5,953	3,136	2,817	4,504	4,416	88	489	443	46	51	49	2	2.4	2.5	2.4	7.3	8.2	1.1	0.4	0.6	0.1
65 to 69 years	4,655	2,429	2,226	2,303	2,261	42	151	134	17	35	30	5	1.9	1.9	1.9	3.7	4.2	0.5	0.1	0.2	(2)
70 to 74 years	3,455	1,748	1,707	1,217	1,188	29	31	26	5	16	12	4	1.4	1.4	1.4	2.0	2.2	0.4	(2)	(2)	(2)
75 to 79 years	2,150	1,049	1,101	355	344	11	12	6	6	13	11	2	0.9	0.8	0.9	0.6	0.6	0.1	(2)	(2)	(2)
80 to 84 years	1,457	666	791	129	120	9	2	2	.....	3	2	1	0.6	0.5	0.7	0.2	0.2	0.1	(2)	(2)	.....
85 to 89 years	674	298	376	42	40	2	5	5	.....	1	1	.....	0.3	0.2	0.3	0.1	0.1	(2)	(2)	(2)	.....
90 to 94 years	409	180	229	8	8	.....	.....	.....	.....	3	3	.....	0.2	0.1	0.2	(2)	(2)	.....	.....	.....	.....
95 to 99 years	179	69	110	7	7	.....	.....	.....	.....	.....	.....	.....	0.1	0.1	0.1	(2)	(2)	.....	.....	.....	.....
100 years and over	160	73	87	4	3	1	.....	.....	.....	.....	.....	.....	0.1	0.1	0.1	(2)	(2)	(2)	.....	.....	.....
Age unknown	791	400	391	260	242	18	412	330	82	70	68	2	0.3	0.3	0.3	0.4	0.4	0.2	0.4	0.5	0.2

[1] Comprises Filipinos, Hawaiians, Hindus, Koreans, Malays, Maoris, Samoans, and Siamese.　　[2] Less than one-tenth of 1 per cent.

158

POPULATION.

TABLE 6.—DISTRIBUTION BY AGE PERIODS FOR POPULATION

AGE PERIOD AND CENSUS YEAR.	ALL CLASSES.			WHITE.			NEGRO.			INDIAN, CHINESE, JAPANESE, AND ALL OTHER.		
	Both sexes.	Male.	Female.	Both sexes.	Male.	Female.	Both sexes.	Male.	Female.	Both sexes.	Male.	Female.
All ages:												
1920	105,710,620	53,900,431	51,810,189	94,820,915	48,430,655	46,390,260	10,463,131	5,209,436	5,253,695	426,574	260,340	166,234
1910	91,972,266	47,332,277	44,639,989	81,731,957	42,178,245	39,553,712	9,827,763	4,885,881	4,941,882	412,546	268,151	144,395
1900	75,994,575	38,816,448	37,178,127	66,809,196	34,201,735	32,607,461	8,833,994	4,386,547	4,447,447	351,385	228,166	123,219
Under 5 years:												
1920	11,573,230	5,857,461	5,715,769	10,373,921	5,260,714	5,113,207	1,143,699	568,633	575,066	55,610	28,114	27,496
1910	10,631,364	5,380,596	5,250,768	9,322,914	4,728,650	4,594,264	1,263,288	629,320	633,968	45,162	22,626	22,536
1900	9,170,628	4,633,612	4,537,016	7,919,952	4,011,455	3,908,497	1,215,655	604,487	611,168	35,021	17,670	17,351
5 to 9 years:												
1920	11,398,075	5,753,001	5,645,074	10,087,245	5,099,205	4,988,040	1,266,207	631,341	634,866	44,623	22,455	22,168
1910	9,760,632	4,924,123	4,836,509	8,475,173	4,285,366	4,189,807	1,246,553	619,175	627,378	38,906	19,582	19,324
1900	8,874,123	4,479,396	4,394,727	7,638,326	3,862,349	3,775,977	1,202,758	600,410	602,348	33,039	16,637	16,402
10 to 14 years:												
1920	10,641,137	5,369,306	5,271,831	9,369,322	4,735,150	4,634,172	1,236,914	616,251	620,663	34,901	17,905	16,996
1910	9,107,140	4,601,753	4,505,387	7,918,408	4,006,104	3,912,304	1,155,266	578,074	577,192	33,406	17,575	15,891
1900	8,080,234	4,083,041	3,997,193	6,959,238	3,519,303	3,439,935	1,091,990	548,642	543,348	29,006	15,096	13,910
15 to 19 years:												
1920	9,430,556	4,673,792	4,756,764	8,314,155	4,141,831	4,172,324	1,083,215	513,416	569,799	33,186	18,545	14,641
1910	9,063,603	4,527,282	4,536,321	7,968,391	3,999,143	3,969,248	1,060,416	507,945	552,471	34,796	20,194	14,602
1900	7,556,089	3,750,451	3,805,638	6,543,189	3,258,090	3,285,099	982,022	473,750	508,272	30,878	18,611	12,267
20 to 24 years:												
1920	9,277,021	4,527,045	4,749,976	8,155,341	4,018,576	4,166,765	1,054,847	487,169	567,678	36,833	21,300	15,533
1910	9,056,984	4,580,290	4,476,694	7,986,411	4,070,955	3,915,456	1,030,795	482,157	548,638	39,778	27,178	12,600
1900	7,335,016	3,624,580	3,710,436	6,335,044	3,145,481	3,189,563	969,172	458,921	510,251	30,800	20,178	10,622
25 to 29 years:												
1920	9,086,491	4,538,233	4,548,258	8,141,690	4,094,301	4,047,389	909,739	424,352	485,387	35,062	19,580	15,482
1910	8,180,003	4,244,348	3,935,655	7,257,136	3,792,224	3,464,912	881,227	421,805	459,422	41,640	30,319	11,321
1900	6,529,441	3,323,543	3,205,898	5,762,980	2,942,882	2,820,098	737,479	360,597	376,882	28,982	20,064	8,918
30 to 34 years:												
1920	8,071,193	4,130,783	3,940,410	7,338,790	3,776,266	3,562,524	697,865	331,579	366,286	34,538	22,938	11,600
1910	6,972,185	3,656,768	3,315,417	6,267,276	3,297,169	2,970,107	668,089	332,163	335,926	36,820	27,436	9,384
1900	5,556,039	2,901,321	2,654,718	5,004,444	2,619,446	2,384,998	524,607	262,130	262,477	26,988	19,745	7,243
35 to 39 years:												
1920	7,775,281	4,074,361	3,700,920	6,965,805	3,665,341	3,300,464	773,931	383,587	390,344	35,545	25,433	10,112
1910	6,396,100	3,367,016	3,029,084	5,731,845	3,024,002	2,707,843	633,449	320,450	312,999	30,806	22,564	8,242
1900	4,964,781	2,616,865	2,347,916	4,460,575	2,360,348	2,100,227	474,687	233,371	241,316	29,519	23,146	6,373
40 to 44 years:												
1920	6,345,557	3,285,543	3,060,014	5,755,547	2,987,412	2,768,135	559,701	275,926	283,775	30,309	22,205	8,104
1910	5,261,587	2,786,350	2,475,237	4,780,272	2,537,219	2,243,053	455,413	229,680	225,733	25,902	19,451	6,451
1900	4,247,166	2,255,916	1,991,250	3,852,143	2,055,176	1,796,967	367,216	179,090	188,126	27,807	21,650	6,157
45 to 49 years:												
1920	5,763,620	3,117,550	2,646,070	5,188,040	2,779,175	2,408,865	551,589	320,506	231,083	23,991	17,869	6,122
1910	4,469,197	2,378,916	2,090,281	4,061,062	2,161,848	1,899,214	385,909	199,928	185,981	22,226	17,140	5,086
1900	3,454,612	1,837,836	1,616,776	3,105,678	1,651,972	1,453,706	326,384	168,495	157,889	22,550	17,369	5,181
50 to 54 years:												
1920	4,734,873	2,535,545	2,199,328	4,317,266	2,293,604	2,023,662	399,110	227,995	171,115	18,497	13,946	4,551
1910	3,900,791	2,110,013	1,790,778	3,555,313	1,915,860	1,639,453	326,070	179,387	146,683	19,408	14,766	4,642
1900	2,042,820	1,564,622	1,616,776	2,633,981	1,396,035	1,237,946	290,987	155,188	135,799	17,861	13,399	4,462
55 to 59 years:												
1920	3,549,124	1,880,065	1,669,059	3,305,671	1,740,661	1,565,010	229,980	129,153	100,827	13,473	10,251	3,222
1910	2,786,951	1,488,437	1,298,514	2,564,206	1,363,821	1,200,385	209,622	115,090	94,532	13,123	9,526	3,507
1900	2,211,172	1,145,257	1,065,915	2,021,217	1,040,235	980,982	179,176	97,323	81,853	10,779	7,699	3,080
60 to 64 years:												
1920	2,982,548	1,581,800	1,400,748	2,771,433	1,461,619	1,309,814	200,118	112,137	87,981	10,997	8,044	2,953
1910	2,267,150	1,185,966	1,081,184	2,069,323	1,076,753	992,570	186,502	101,149	85,353	11,325	8,064	3,261
1900	1,791,363	917,167	874,196	1,620,658	825,213	795,445	161,687	85,961	75,726	9,018	5,993	3,025
65 to 69 years:												
1920	2,068,475	1,079,817	988,658	1,924,296	998,779	925,517	137,035	76,184	60,851	7,144	4,854	2,290
1910	1,679,503	863,994	815,509	1,549,954	792,310	757,644	123,550	67,956	55,594	5,999	3,728	2,271
1900	1,302,926	667,669	635,257	1,195,295	608,715	586,580	102,671	56,018	46,653	4,960	2,936	2,024
70 to 74 years:												
1920	1,395,036	706,301	688,735	1,298,738	655,916	642,822	91,579	47,411	44,168	4,719	2,974	1,745
1910	1,113,728	561,644	552,084	1,030,884	518,888	511,996	78,839	40,584	38,255	4,005	2,172	1,833
1900	883,841	449,609	434,232	808,097	411,658	396,439	72,382	36,235	36,147	3,362	1,716	1,646
75 to 79 years:												
1920	856,560	419,965	436,595	801,678	391,383	410,295	52,352	27,172	25,180	2,530	1,410	1,120
1910	667,302	331,280	336,022	620,992	307,446	313,546	44,018	22,667	21,351	2,292	1,167	1,125
1900	519,857	261,579	258,278	477,720	240,284	237,436	40,420	20,475	19,945	1,717	820	897
80 to 84 years:												
1920	402,779	185,903	216,876	373,066	172,064	201,002	28,122	13,049	15,073	1,591	790	801
1910	321,754	153,745	168,009	294,555	141,301	153,254	25,579	11,696	13,883	1,620	748	872
1900	251,512	122,273	129,239	224,717	110,087	114,630	25,527	11,655	13,872	1,268	531	737
85 to 89 years:												
1920	156,539	69,272	87,267	143,536	63,308	80,228	12,281	5,620	6,661	722	344	378
1910	122,818	56,335	66,483	110,936	50,843	60,093	11,166	5,164	6,002	716	328	388
1900	88,600	40,742	47,858	78,027	35,838	42,189	10,083	4,713	5,370	490	191	299
90 to 94 years:												
1920	39,980	16,383	23,597	33,713	13,852	19,861	5,847	2,340	3,507	420	191	229
1910	33,473	14,553	18,920	27,161	11,970	15,191	5,850	2,394	3,456	462	189	273
1900	23,992	9,858	14,134	18,319	7,607	10,712	5,293	2,085	3,208	380	166	214
95 to 99 years:												
1920	9,579	3,869	5,710	6,831	2,706	4,125	2,562	1,087	1,475	186	76	110
1910	7,391	3,045	4,346	4,757	1,935	2,822	2,447	1,017	1,430	187	93	94
1900	6,266	2,417	3,849	3,707	1,405	2,302	2,434	958	1,476	125	54	71
100 years and over:												
1920	4,267	1,561	2,706	1,168	467	701	2,935	1,018	1,917	164	76	88
1910	3,555	1,380	2,175	764	326	438	2,675	1,004	1,671	116	50	66
1900	3,504	1,271	2,233	837	330	507	2,553	886	1,667	114	55	59
Age unknown:												
1920	148,699	92,875	55,824	123,663	78,325	45,338	23,503	13,510	9,993	1,533	1,040	493
1910	169,055	114,443	54,612	134,224	94,112	40,112	31,040	17,076	13,964	3,791	3,255	536
1900	200,584	127,423	73,161	145,052	97,826	47,220	48,811	25,157	23,654	6,721	4,440	2,281

AGE DISTRIBUTION.

159

CLASSES, BY SEX, FOR THE UNITED STATES: 1920, 1910, AND 1900.

AGE PERIOD AND CENSUS YEAR.	NATIVE WHITE.									FOREIGN-BORN WHITE.		
	Total.			Native parentage.			Foreign or mixed parentage.					
	Both sexes.	Male.	Female.	Both sexes.	Male.	Female.	Both sexes.	Male.	Female.	Both sexes.	Male.	Female.
All ages:												
1920	81,108,161	40,902,333	40,205,828	58,421,957	29,636,781	28,785,176	22,686,204	11,265,552	11,420,652	13,712,754	7,528,322	6,184,432
1910	68,386,412	34,654,457	33,731,955	49,488,575	25,229,218	24,259,357	18,897,837	9,425,239	9,472,598	13,345,545	7,523,788	5,821,757
1900	56,595,379	28,086,450	27,908,929	40,949,362	20,849,847	20,099,515	15,646,017	7,836,603	7,809,414	10,213,817	5,515,285	4,698,532
Under 5 years:												
1920	10,328,937	5,237,857	5,001,080	7,366,530	3,741,194	3,625,336	2,962,407	1,496,663	1,465,744	44,984	22,857	22,127
1910	9,220,407	4,670,710	4,543,607	6,546,282	3,320,237	3,226,045	2,674,125	1,350,473	1,323,652	102,507	51,940	50,567
1900	7,867,583	3,984,888	3,882,695	5,464,881	2,773,201	2,691,680	2,402,702	1,211,087	1,191,615	52,360	26,507	25,802
5 to 9 years:												
1920	9,917,361	5,013,431	4,903,930	6,977,863	3,534,092	3,443,771	2,939,498	1,479,339	1,460,159	169,884	85,774	84,110
1910	8,176,664	4,134,714	4,041,950	5,801,015	2,909,230	2,891,785	2,315,649	1,165,484	1,150,165	298,509	150,652	147,857
1900	7,491,134	3,788,622	3,702,512	5,174,220	2,623,791	2,550,429	2,316,914	1,164,831	1,152,083	147,192	73,727	73,465
10 to 14 years:												
1920	9,037,900	4,567,998	4,469,902	6,455,709	3,269,388	3,186,321	2,582,251	1,298,610	1,283,641	331,362	167,152	164,210
1910	7,560,078	3,824,801	3,735,277	5,324,283	2,700,656	2,623,627	2,235,795	1,124,145	1,111,650	358,330	181,303	177,027
1900	6,647,673	3,361,671	3,286,002	4,660,390	2,364,797	2,295,593	1,987,283	996,874	990,409	311,565	157,032	153,033
15 to 19 years:												
1920	7,786,213	3,882,501	3,903,652	5,599,046	2,797,477	2,801,509	2,187,167	1,085,084	1,102,083	527,942	259,270	268,672
1910	7,294,630	3,647,389	3,647,241	5,080,055	2,552,528	2,536,527	2,205,575	1,094,801	1,110,714	673,761	351,754	322,007
1900	5,981,443	2,986,709	2,994,734	4,234,953	2,122,635	2,112,318	1,746,490	864,074	882,416	561,746	271,381	290,365
20 to 24 years:												
1920	7,258,407	3,561,588	3,696,909	5,176,707	2,546,818	2,629,889	2,081,700	1,014,770	1,067,020	926,844	456,088	400,856
1910	6,556,030	3,247,035	3,308,995	4,682,922	2,332,014	2,350,008	1,873,108	914,121	958,987	1,430,381	823,920	606,461
1900	5,415,502	2,689,295	2,726,207	3,805,609	1,903,864	1,901,745	1,609,953	785,431	824,522	910,482	456,185	463,296
25 to 29 years:												
1920	6,687,327	3,302,213	3,385,114	4,764,802	2,367,312	2,397,490	1,922,525	934,901	987,624	1,454,303	792,088	662,275
1910	5,594,440	2,801,648	2,792,792	4,049,074	2,046,597	2,002,477	1,545,366	755,051	790,315	1,662,696	990,576	672,120
1900	4,605,751	2,353,361	2,312,390	3,208,642	1,634,867	1,573,775	1,457,109	718,404	738,615	1,097,220	589,521	507,708
30 to 34 years:												
1920	5,687,315	2,829,448	2,857,867	4,096,041	2,054,671	2,041,370	1,591,274	774,777	816,497	1,651,475	946,818	704,657
1910	4,761,561	2,408,501	2,353,060	3,401,601	1,741,569	1,660,032	1,359,960	666,932	693,028	1,505,715	888,668	617,047
1900	3,830,761	1,958,744	1,872,017	2,659,360	1,372,529	1,286,831	1,171,401	586,215	585,186	1,173,683	660,702	512,981
35 to 39 years:												
1920	5,228,000	2,656,664	2,571,336	3,815,852	1,962,634	1,853,218	1,412,148	694,030	718,118	1,737,805	1,008,677	729,128
1910	4,323,752	2,211,995	2,111,757	3,045,381	1,580,130	1,465,242	1,278,371	631,850	646,515	1,408,003	812,007	596,086
1900	3,283,009	1,687,544	1,595,465	2,299,571	1,192,071	1,107,500	983,438	495,473	487,965	1,177,506	672,804	504,762
40 to 44 years:												
1920	4,327,448	2,184,217	2,143,231	3,099,330	1,584,246	1,515,084	1,228,118	599,971	628,147	1,428,099	803,195	624,904
1910	3,470,797	1,785,700	1,691,097	2,450,385	1,273,905	1,176,480	1,020,412	511,795	514,617	1,303,475	751,519	551,956
1900	2,880,031	1,497,876	1,388,155	2,104,551	1,096,825	1,007,726	781,480	401,051	380,429	966,112	557,300	408,812
45 to 49 years:												
1920	3,888,365	2,034,752	1,853,613	2,753,013	1,463,247	1,289,766	1,135,352	571,505	563,847	1,299,675	744,423	555,252
1910	2,914,702	1,505,393	1,409,309	2,071,976	1,081,912	990,064	842,726	423,481	419,245	1,146,360	656,455	489,905
1900	2,265,458	1,183,506	1,081,952	1,787,607	937,254	850,353	477,851	246,252	231,599	840,220	468,466	371,754
50 to 54 years:												
1920	3,149,880	1,642,058	1,507,831	2,236,700	1,186,619	1,050,081	913,189	455,430	457,759	1,107,377	651,546	515,831
1910	2,630,258	1,389,604	1,240,654	1,950,127	1,040,745	909,382	680,131	348,859	331,272	925,055	526,250	398,709
1900	1,830,589	955,956	874,633	1,551,811	811,724	740,087	278,778	144,232	134,546	803,392	440,079	363,313
55 to 59 years:												
1920	2,396,949	1,236,872	1,160,077	1,719,190	899,029	820,161	677,759	337,843	339,916	908,722	503,789	404,933
1910	1,870,686	983,711	886,975	1,400,463	780,243	701,220	380,223	194,468	185,755	603,520	380,110	313,410
1900	1,378,214	694,994	683,220	1,204,610	605,625	598,985	173,004	89,369	84,235	643,003	345,241	297,762
60 to 64 years:												
1920	2,055,702	1,068,990	986,712	1,530,129	805,768	724,361	525,573	263,222	262,351	715,731	392,629	323,102
1910	1,441,740	744,839	696,901	1,227,434	635,425	592,009	214,306	109,414	104,892	627,583	331,914	295,669
1900	1,075,627	539,430	536,197	965,900	483,454	482,446	109,727	55,970	53,751	545,031	285,783	259,248
65 to 69 years:												
1920	1,405,070	723,379	681,691	1,126,722	584,783	541,939	278,348	138,596	139,752	519,226	275,400	243,826
1910	1,061,557	536,894	524,663	931,607	470,750	460,857	129,950	66,144	63,806	488,397	255,416	232,981
1900	784,555	395,274	389,281	720,110	361,980	358,130	64,445	33,294	31,151	410,740	213,441	197,299
70 to 74 years:												
1920	917,413	461,184	456,229	784,183	395,582	388,601	133,230	65,602	67,628	381,325	194,732	186,593
1910	693,917	346,137	347,780	623,594	310,780	312,814	70,323	35,357	34,966	336,967	172,751	164,216
1900	525,772	263,590	262,182	488,649	244,574	244,075	37,123	19,016	18,107	282,325	148,068	134,257
75 to 79 years:												
1920	555,191	267,213	287,978	487,797	234,584	253,213	67,394	32,629	34,765	246,487	124,170	122,317
1910	412,780	202,034	210,746	378,823	185,109	193,714	33,957	16,925	17,032	208,212	105,412	102,800
1900	318,804	157,351	161,453	296,201	146,108	150,093	22,603	11,243	11,360	158,910	82,933	75,983
80 to 84 years:												
1920	254,131	115,363	138,768	228,018	103,493	124,525	26,113	11,870	14,243	118,935	56,701	62,234
1910	193,265	91,039	102,226	179,251	84,278	94,973	14,014	6,761	7,253	101,290	50,262	51,028
1900	155,642	74,697	80,945	144,314	69,087	75,227	11,328	5,610	5,718	69,075	35,390	33,085
85 to 89 years:												
1920	96,063	41,304	54,759	87,530	37,459	50,071	8,533	3,845	4,688	47,473	22,004	25,469
1910	73,503	32,762	40,741	67,966	30,166	37,800	5,537	2,596	2,941	37,433	18,081	19,352
1900	55,860	25,036	30,824	51,542	22,992	28,550	4,318	2,044	2,274	22,167	10,802	11,365
90 to 94 years:												
1920	21,996	8,729	13,267	20,159	7,922	12,237	1,837	807	1,030	11,717	5,123	6,594
1910	18,127	7,777	10,350	16,632	7,041	9,591	1,495	736	759	9,034	4,193	4,841
1900	12,998	5,268	7,730	11,940	4,815	7,125	1,058	453	605	5,321	2,339	2,982
95 to 99 years:												
1920	4,252	1,657	2,595	3,853	1,475	2,378	399	182	217	2,579	1,049	1,530
1910	3,034	1,168	1,866	2,756	1,045	1,711	278	123	155	1,723	767	956
1900	2,295	796	1,499	2,077	695	1,382	218	101	117	1,412	609	803
100 years and over:												
1920	683	262	421	614	229	385	69	33	36	485	205	280
1910	471	200	271	439	180	259	32	20	12	293	126	167
1900	446	152	294	393	129	264	53	23	30	391	178	213
Age unknown:												
1920	103,399	64,593	38,806	92,169	58,759	33,410	11,230	5,834	5,396	20,264	13,732	6,532
1910	108,013	74,406	33,607	97,509	68,769	28,740	10,504	5,637	4,867	26,211	19,706	6,505
1900	120,172	81,690	38,482	112,031	76,830	35,201	8,141	4,860	3,281	24,880	16,136	8,744

160

POPULATION.

TABLE 7.—PER CENT DISTRIBUTION BY AGE PERIODS FOR PRINCIPAL POPULATION CLASSES, BY SEX, FOR THE UNITED STATES: 1920, 1910, AND 1900.

AGE PERIOD AND CENSUS YEAR.	ALL CLASSES. Both sexes.	Male.	Female.	WHITE. Both sexes.	Male.	Female.	NEGRO. Both sexes.	Male.	Female.	NATIVE WHITE. Total. Both sexes.	Male.	Female.	Native parentage. Both sexes.	Male.	Female.	Foreign or mixed parentage. Both sexes.	Male.	Female.	FOREIGN-BORN WHITE. Both sexes.	Male.	Female.
All ages:																					
1920	100.0	100.0	100.0	100.0	100.0	100.0	100.0	100.0	100.0	100.0	100.0	100.0	100.0	100.0	100.0	100.0	100.0	100.0	100.0	100.0	100.0
1910	100.0	100.0	100.0	100.0	100.0	100.0	100.0	100.0	100.0	100.0	100.0	100.0	100.0	100.0	100.0	100.0	100.0	100.0	100.0	100.0	100.0
1900	100.0	100.0	100.0	100.0	100.0	100.0	100.0	100.0	100.0	100.0	100.0	100.0	100.0	100.0	100.0	100.0	100.0	100.0	100.0	100.0	100.0
Under 5 years:																					
1920	10.9	10.9	11.0	10.9	10.9	11.0	10.9	10.9	10.9	12.7	12.8	12.7	12.6	12.6	12.6	13.1	13.3	12.8	0.3	0.3	0.4
1910	11.6	11.4	11.8	11.4	11.2	11.6	12.9	12.9	12.8	13.5	13.5	13.5	13.2	13.2	13.3	14.2	14.3	14.0	0.8	0.7	0.9
1900	12.1	11.9	12.2	11.9	11.7	12.0	13.8	13.8	13.7	13.9	13.9	13.9	13.3	13.3	13.4	15.4	15.5	15.3	0.5	0.5	0.5
5 to 9 years:																					
1920	10.8	10.7	10.9	10.6	10.5	10.8	12.1	12.1	12.1	12.2	12.3	12.2	11.9	11.9	12.0	13.0	13.1	12.8	1.2	1.1	1.4
1910	10.6	10.4	10.8	10.4	10.2	10.6	12.7	12.7	12.7	12.0	11.9	12.0	11.8	11.8	11.9	12.3	12.4	12.1	2.2	2.0	2.5
1900	11.7	11.5	11.8	11.4	11.3	11.6	13.6	13.7	13.5	13.2	13.2	13.3	12.6	12.6	12.7	14.8	14.9	14.8	1.4	1.3	1.0
10 to 14 years:																					
1920	10.1	10.0	10.2	9.9	9.8	10.0	11.8	11.8	11.8	11.1	11.0	11.1	11.1	11.0	11.1	11.4	11.5	11.4	2.4	2.2	2.7
1910	9.9	9.7	10.1	9.7	9.5	9.9	11.8	11.8	11.7	11.1	11.0	11.1	10.8	10.7	10.8	11.8	11.9	11.7	2.7	2.4	3.0
1900	10.6	10.5	10.8	10.4	10.3	10.5	12.4	12.5	12.2	11.7	11.7	11.8	11.4	11.3	11.4	12.7	12.7	12.7	3.1	2.9	3.3
15 to 19 years:																					
1920	8.9	8.7	9.2	8.8	8.6	9.0	10.4	9.9	10.8	9.6	9.5	9.7	9.6	9.4	9.7	9.6	9.6	9.6	3.9	3.4	4.3
1910	9.9	9.6	10.2	9.7	9.5	10.0	10.8	10.4	11.2	10.7	10.5	10.8	10.3	10.1	10.5	11.7	11.6	11.7	5.0	4.7	5.5
1900	9.9	9.7	10.2	9.8	9.5	10.1	11.1	10.8	11.4	10.6	10.4	10.7	10.3	10.2	10.5	11.2	11.0	11.3	5.5	4.9	6.2
20 to 24 years:																					
1920	8.8	8.4	9.2	8.6	8.3	9.0	10.1	9.4	10.8	8.9	8.7	9.2	8.9	8.6	9.1	9.2	9.0	9.3	6.8	6.1	7.6
1910	9.8	9.7	10.0	9.8	9.7	9.9	10.5	9.9	11.1	9.6	9.4	9.8	9.5	9.2	9.7	9.9	9.7	10.1	10.7	11.0	10.4
1900	9.7	9.3	10.0	9.5	9.2	9.8	11.0	10.5	11.5	9.6	9.4	9.8	9.3	9.1	9.5	10.3	10.0	10.6	9.0	8.3	9.9
25 to 29 years:																					
1920	8.6	8.4	8.8	8.6	8.5	8.7	8.7	8.1	9.2	8.2	8.1	8.4	8.2	8.0	8.3	8.5	8.3	8.6	10.6	10.5	10.7
1910	8.9	9.0	8.8	8.9	9.0	8.8	9.0	8.6	9.3	8.2	8.1	8.3	8.2	8.1	8.3	8.2	8.0	8.3	12.5	13.2	11.5
1900	8.6	8.6	8.6	8.6	8.6	8.6	8.2	8.2	8.5	8.2	8.2	8.3	7.8	7.8	7.8	9.3	9.2	9.5	10.7	10.7	10.8
30 to 34 years:																					
1920	7.6	7.7	7.6	7.7	7.8	7.7	6.7	6.4	7.0	7.0	6.9	7.1	7.0	6.9	7.1	7.0	6.9	7.1	12.0	12.6	11.4
1910	7.6	7.7	7.4	7.7	7.8	7.5	6.8	6.8	6.8	7.0	7.0	7.0	6.9	6.9	6.8	7.2	7.1	7.3	11.3	11.8	10.6
1900	7.3	7.5	7.1	7.5	7.7	7.3	5.9	6.0	5.9	6.8	6.8	6.7	6.5	6.6	6.4	7.5	7.5	7.5	11.5	12.0	10.9
35 to 39 years:																					
1920	7.4	7.6	7.1	7.3	7.6	7.1	7.4	7.4	7.4	6.4	6.5	6.4	6.5	6.6	6.4	6.2	6.2	6.3	12.7	13.4	11.8
1910	7.0	7.1	6.8	7.0	7.2	6.8	6.4	6.6	6.3	6.3	6.4	6.3	6.3	6.3	6.0	6.8	6.7	6.8	10.6	10.8	10.2
1900	6.5	6.7	6.3	6.7	6.9	6.4	5.4	5.3	5.4	5.8	5.9	5.7	5.6	5.7	5.5	6.3	6.3	6.2	11.5	12.2	10.7
40 to 44 years:																					
1920	6.0	6.1	5.9	6.1	6.2	6.0	5.3	5.3	5.4	5.3	5.3	5.3	5.3	5.3	5.3	5.4	5.3	5.5	10.4	10.7	10.1
1910	5.7	5.9	5.5	5.8	6.0	5.7	4.6	4.7	4.6	5.1	5.2	5.0	5.0	5.0	4.8	5.4	5.4	5.4	9.8	10.0	9.5
1900	5.6	5.8	5.4	5.8	6.0	5.5	4.2	4.1	4.2	5.1	5.2	5.0	5.1	5.3	5.0	5.0	5.1	4.9	9.5	10.1	8.7
45 to 49 years:																					
1920	5.5	5.8	5.1	5.5	5.7	5.2	5.3	6.2	4.4	4.8	5.0	4.6	4.7	4.9	4.5	5.0	5.1	4.9	9.5	9.9	9.0
1910	4.9	5.0	4.7	5.0	5.1	4.8	3.9	4.1	3.8	4.3	4.3	4.2	4.2	4.3	4.1	4.5	4.5	4.4	8.6	8.7	8.4
1900	4.5	4.7	4.3	4.6	4.8	4.5	3.7	3.8	3.6	4.0	4.1	3.9	4.4	4.5	4.2	3.1	3.1	3.0	8.2	8.5	7.9
50 to 54 years:																					
1920	4.5	4.7	4.2	4.6	4.7	4.4	3.8	4.4	3.3	3.9	4.0	3.8	3.8	4.0	3.6	4.0	4.0	4.0	8.5	8.7	8.3
1910	4.2	4.5	4.0	4.3	4.5	4.1	3.3	3.7	3.0	3.8	4.0	3.7	3.9	4.1	3.7	3.6	3.7	3.5	6.9	7.0	6.9
1900	3.9	4.0	3.7	3.9	4.1	3.8	3.3	3.5	3.1	3.2	3.3	3.1	3.8	3.9	3.7	1.8	1.8	1.7	7.9	8.0	7.7
55 to 59 years:																					
1920	3.4	3.5	3.2	3.5	3.6	3.4	2.2	2.5	1.9	3.0	3.0	2.9	3.0	3.0	2.8	3.0	3.0	3.0	6.6	6.7	6.5
1910	3.0	3.1	2.9	3.1	3.2	3.0	2.1	2.4	1.9	2.7	2.8	2.6	3.0	3.1	2.9	2.0	2.1	2.0	5.2	5.1	5.4
1900	2.9	3.0	2.9	3.0	3.0	3.0	2.0	2.2	1.8	2.4	2.4	2.4	2.9	2.9	3.0	1.1	1.1	1.1	6.3	6.3	6.3
60 to 64 years:																					
1920	2.8	2.9	2.7	2.9	3.0	2.9	1.9	2.2	1.7	2.5	2.6	2.5	2.6	2.7	2.5	2.3	2.3	2.3	5.2	5.2	5.2
1910	2.5	2.5	2.4	2.5	2.6	2.5	1.9	2.1	1.7	2.1	2.1	2.1	2.5	2.5	2.4	1.1	1.2	1.1	4.7	4.4	5.1
1900	2.4	2.4	2.4	2.4	2.4	2.4	1.8	2.0	1.7	1.9	1.9	1.9	2.4	2.3	2.4	0.7	0.7	0.7	5.8	5.2	5.5
65 to 69 years:																					
1920	2.0	2.0	1.9	2.0	2.1	2.0	1.3	1.5	1.2	1.7	1.8	1.7	1.9	2.0	1.9	1.2	1.2	1.2	3.8	3.7	3.9
1910	1.8	1.8	1.8	1.9	1.9	1.9	1.3	1.4	1.1	1.6	1.5	1.6	1.9	1.9	1.9	0.7	0.7	0.7	3.7	3.4	4.0
1900	1.7	1.7	1.7	1.8	1.8	1.8	1.2	1.3	1.0	1.4	1.4	1.4	1.8	1.7	1.8	0.4	0.4	0.4	4.0	3.9	4.2
70 to 74 years:																					
1920	1.3	1.3	1.3	1.4	1.4	1.4	0.9	0.9	0.8	1.1	1.1	1.1	1.3	1.3	1.4	0.6	0.6	0.6	2.8	2.6	3.0
1910	1.2	1.2	1.2	1.3	1.2	1.3	0.8	0.8	0.8	1.0	1.0	1.0	1.3	1.3	1.3	0.4	0.4	0.4	2.5	2.3	2.8
1900	1.2	1.2	1.2	1.2	1.2	1.2	0.8	0.8	0.8	0.9	0.9	0.9	1.2	1.2	1.2	0.2	0.2	0.2	2.8	2.7	2.9
75 to 79 years:																					
1920	0.8	0.8	0.8	0.8	0.8	0.9	0.5	0.5	0.5	0.7	0.7	0.7	0.8	0.8	0.9	0.3	0.3	0.3	1.8	1.6	2.0
1910	0.7	0.7	0.8	0.8	0.7	0.8	0.4	0.5	0.4	0.6	0.6	0.6	0.7	0.7	0.8	0.2	0.2	0.2	1.6	1.4	1.8
1900	0.7	0.7	0.7	0.7	0.7	0.7	0.5	0.5	0.4	0.6	0.5	0.6	0.7	0.7	0.7	0.1	0.1	0.1	1.6	1.5	1.8
80 to 84 years:																					
1920	0.4	0.3	0.4	0.4	0.4	0.4	0.3	0.3	0.3	0.3	0.3	0.3	0.4	0.3	0.4	0.1	0.1	0.1	0.9	0.8	1.0
1910	0.3	0.3	0.4	0.4	0.3	0.4	0.3	0.2	0.3	0.3	0.3	0.3	0.3	0.3	0.4	0.1	0.1	0.1	0.8	0.7	0.9
1900	0.3	0.3	0.3	0.3	0.3	0.4	0.3	0.3	0.3	0.3	0.3	0.3	0.4	0.3	0.4	0.1	0.1	0.1	0.7	0.7	0.7
85 to 89 years:																					
1920	0.1	0.1	0.2	0.2	0.1	0.2	0.1	0.1	0.1	0.1	0.1	0.1	0.1	0.1	0.2	(1)	(1)	(1)	0.3	0.3	0.4
1910	0.1	0.1	0.1	0.1	0.1	0.1	0.1	0.1	0.1	0.1	0.1	0.1	0.1	0.1	0.1	(1)	(1)	(1)	0.3	0.3	0.3
1900	0.1	0.1	0.1	0.1	0.1	0.1	0.1	0.1	0.1	0.1	0.1	0.1	0.1	0.1	0.2	(1)	(1)	(1)	0.2	0.2	0.2
90 to 94 years:																					
1920	(1)	(1)	(1)	(1)	(1)	(1)	0.1	(1)	0.1	(1)	(1)	(1)	(1)	(1)	(1)	(1)	(1)	(1)			
1910	(1)	(1)	(1)	(1)	(1)	(1)	0.1	0.1	0.1	(1)	(1)	(1)	(1)	(1)	(1)	(1)	(1)	(1)	0.1	0.1	0.1
1900	(1)	(1)	(1)	(1)	(1)	(1)	0.1	0.1	0.1	(1)	(1)	(1)	(1)	(1)	(1)	(1)	(1)	(1)	0.1	(1)	0.1
95 to 99 years:																					
1920	(1)	(1)	(1)	(1)	(1)	(1)	(1)	(1)	(1)	(1)	(1)	(1)	(1)	(1)	(1)	(1)	(1)	(1)	(1)	(1)	(1)
1910	(1)	(1)	(1)	(1)	(1)	(1)	(1)	(1)	(1)	(1)	(1)	(1)	(1)	(1)	(1)	(1)	(1)	(1)	(1)	(1)	(1)
1900	(1)	(1)	(1)	(1)	(1)	(1)	(1)	(1)	(1)	(1)	(1)	(1)	(1)	(1)	(1)	(1)	(1)	(1)	(1)	(1)	(1)
100 years and over:																					
1920	(1)	(1)	(1)	(1)	(1)	(1)	(1)	(1)	(1)	(1)	(1)	(1)	(1)	(1)	(1)	(1)	(1)	(1)	(1)	(1)	(1)
1910	(1)	(1)	(1)	(1)	(1)	(1)	(1)	(1)	(1)	(1)	(1)	(1)	(1)	(1)	(1)	(1)	(1)	(1)	(1)	(1)	(1)
1900	(1)	(1)	(1)	(1)	(1)	(1)	(1)	(1)	(1)	(1)	(1)	(1)	(1)	(1)	(1)	(1)	(1)	(1)	(1)	(1)	(1)
Age unknown:																					
1920	0.1	0.2	0.1	0.1	0.2	0.1	0.2	0.3	0.2	0.1	0.2	0.1	0.2	0.2	0.1	(1)	0.1	(1)	0.1	0.2	0.1
1910	0.2	0.2	0.1	0.2	0.2	0.1	0.3	0.3	0.3	0.2	0.2	0.1	0.2	0.2	0.1	(1)	0.1	(1)	0.1	0.2	0.1
1900	0.3	0.3	0.2	0.2	0.3	0.1	0.6	0.6	0.5	0.2	0.3	0.1	0.3	0.4	0.1	0.1	0.1	(1)	0.2	0.3	0.2

¹ Less than one-tenth of 1 per cent.

AGE DISTRIBUTION. 161

TABLE 8.—MALES TO 100 FEMALES, BY AGE PERIODS, FOR POPULATION CLASSES, FOR THE UNITED STATES: 1920 AND 1910.

[Ratio not shown where number of females is less than 100.]

| AGE PERIOD. | ALL CLASSES. | | TOTAL WHITE. | | NATIVE WHITE. | | | | | | FOREIGN-BORN WHITE. | | NEGRO. | | INDIAN. | |
| | | | | | Native parentage. | | Foreign parentage. | | Mixed parentage. | | | | | | | |
	1920	1910	1920	1910	1920	1910	1920	1910	1920	1910	1920	1910	1920	1910	1920	1910
All ages	104.0	106.0	104.4	106.6	103.0	104.0	99.1	100.0	97.7	98.5	121.7	129.2	99.2	98.9	104.8	103.5
Under 5 years	102.5	102.5	102.9	102.9	103.2	103.3	102.0	101.7	102.3	102.7	103.3	102.7	98.9	99.3	99.0	100.1
5 to 9 years	101.9	101.8	102.2	102.3	102.0	102.7	100.9	101.0	102.3	102.0	102.0	101.9	99.4	98.7	98.2	100.9
10 to 14 years	101.8	102.1	102.2	102.4	102.0	102.9	101.0	101.0	101.5	101.3	101.8	102.4	99.3	100.2	101.0	100.6
15 to 19 years	98.3	99.8	99.3	100.8	99.0	100.6	98.1	98.3	99.2	99.1	96.5	105.2	90.1	91.9	100.0	105.3
20 to 24 years	95.3	102.3	96.4	104.0	96.8	99.3	95.4	96.0	94.5	94.1	97.3	135.9	85.8	87.9	108.5	100.5
25 to 29 years	99.8	107.8	101.2	109.4	98.7	102.2	96.4	97.7	91.3	91.3	119.6	147.4	87.4	91.8	107.3	103.8
30 to 34 years	104.8	110.3	106.0	111.0	100.7	104.9	97.3	98.2	90.3	92.0	134.4	141.0	90.5	98.9	106.9	103.6
35 to 39 years	110.1	111.2	111.1	111.7	105.0	107.8	98.6	98.9	93.0	94.8	138.3	136.2	98.3	102.4	111.1	108.5
40 to 44 years	107.4	112.6	107.9	113.1	101.6	108.3	96.4	99.8	93.7	98.3	128.5	136.2	97.2	101.7	109.4	105.0
45 to 49 years	117.8	113.8	115.4	113.8	113.5	109.3	101.4	101.2	101.2	100.3	134.1	134.0	138.7	107.5	124.2	106.7
50 to 54 years	115.3	117.8	113.3	116.9	113.0	114.4	99.0	105.3	101.0	105.3	126.3	132.0	133.2	122.3	120.2	111.0
55 to 59 years	112.6	114.0	111.2	113.6	109.6	112.6	98.6	104.4	102.1	105.6	121.4	121.3	128.1	121.7	120.0	107.0
60 to 64 years	112.9	109.7	111.6	108.5	111.2	107.3	99.7	105.4	102.6	101.8	121.5	112.3	127.5	118.5	111.3	104.4
65 to 69 years	109.2	105.9	107.9	104.6	107.9	102.1	98.5	105.4	101.1	100.4	112.9	109.6	125.2	122.2	100.1	101.6
70 to 74 years	102.6	101.7	102.0	101.3	101.8	99.3	97.2	102.4	96.6	99.0	101.4	105.2	107.3	106.1	102.4	85.7
75 to 79 years	96.2	98.6	95.4	98.1	92.0	95.6	95.1	102.6	91.7	95.4	101.5	102.5	107.9	106.2	95.3	87.6
80 to 84 years	85.7	91.5	85.6	92.2	83.1	88.7	84.3	97.3	81.8	89.2	91.1	98.5	86.6	84.2	84.2	70.9
85 to 89 years	79.4	84.7	78.9	84.6	74.8	79.8	84.7	93.3	78.6	83.3	86.4	93.4	84.4	80.0	79.3	78.6
90 to 94 years	69.4	76.9	69.7	78.8	64.7	73.4	82.2	108.8	74.1	85.3	77.7	86.6	66.7	69.3	78.6	67.8
95 to 99 years	67.8	70.1	65.6	68.6	62.0	61.1	84.6	......	......	......	68.6	80.2	73.7	71.1	62.7	....
100 years and over	57.7	63.4	66.6	74.4	59.5	69.5	......	......	......	......	73.2	75.4	53.1	60.1	....	....

75647°—22——11

CHAPTER IV

MARITAL CONDITION

CHAPTER IV.—MARITAL CONDITION.

INTRODUCTION.

Inquiry regarding marital condition was made for the first time at the Federal census of 1880, but the results were not tabulated. The earliest Federal statistics on the subject, therefore, are those for 1890.

The terms "married," "widowed," and "divorced" refer only to the marital status of the population at the time when the census was taken. A person who has been widowed or divorced but has remarried is reported as married, so that the returns for widowed and divorced persons do not represent the total number of living persons who have been widowed or divorced. Moreover, it is probable that some divorced persons are erroneously reported as single, some as married, and some as widowed, so that the census returns understate somewhat the actual number of divorced persons who have not remarried.

The number of persons under 15 years of age who are married, widowed, or divorced is naturally insignificant. The statistics on marital condition, therefore, usually relate only to persons 15 years of age and over, but in some of the tables figures are given also for persons under 15 years of age.

For a small number of persons the marital condition was not ascertained by the enumerators. In some of the tables no figures are given for these persons, but they are in all cases included in the totals on which are based the percentages single, married, widowed, and divorced. These percentages would not be appreciably different, however, if based exclusively upon the number of persons whose marital condition was reported, as the number for whom information on this subject was not secured amounted to only a little more than one-fifth of 1 per cent of the total population 15 years of age and over.

Other things being equal, the proportion married in the total population will be greater in a community where the sexes are numerically equal than in one where either sex outnumbers the other. In the latter case it is obvious that a larger number of persons of the sex which is in excess will remain single. Considering one sex alone, however, it is evident that the probability of marriage will increase as that sex falls below and will decrease as it rises above a numerical equality with the other sex.

The statistics on marital condition presented here are limited to continental United States. Those for the outlying possessions enumerated at the Fourteenth Census are presented in the sections pertaining to those possessions in Volume III of the Fourteenth Census Reports.

UNITED STATES AS A WHOLE.

Total population.—The excess of men over women in the adult population of the United States has a most important bearing upon the statistics of marital condition and accounts in part for the fact that the number of single men exceeded by 3,350,663 the number of single women. A further explanation of this disparity, however, is found in the tendency of men to marry at later ages than women, so that there would be more single men than single women in a population in which the sexes were numerically equal.

In the total population the number of married men exceeded the number of married women by 530,333. This condition is due in the main to the presence in the United States of many foreign-born married men who had left their wives in their home countries.

The excess of widows over widowers is probably due in some measure to more frequent remarriages among men than among women, and to the greater longevity of women than of men; but without doubt the principal cause of this excess is the fact that men usually marry at later ages than women, so that in the majority of cases the marriage relation is broken by the death of the husband rather than by the death of the wife. In other words, the excess of single men over single women has as a natural correlative an excess of widows over widowers. (See Table 2.)

Color or race, nativity, and parentage classes, by age.—No satisfactory analysis of statistics on marital condition can be made without considering age composition. In a population in which the sex distribution is normal, the proportion which the number of persons who are or have been married forms of the total number of adults depends on three factors: (1) The age at which marriage takes place, (2) the age distribution of the population, and (3) the number who permanently remain single. As a rule, the first and second factors have greater weight than the third in causing the differences which appear in the statistics for different classes or communities. In all cases the proportion of married, widowed, or divorced persons combined is smaller among young than among older persons; consequently differences between classes or communities in regard to the proportion married, widowed, or divorced in the total number of adults may result merely from differences in age distribution and may not appear when comparisons are confined to specific age groups.

The distribution according to marital condition varies considerably among the several classes of the native

384   POPULATION.

population, and the distribution of the foreign-born population differs materially from that of the native classes, both because of its abnormal age composition and because of its marked excess of males over females. (See Table 3.)

Naturally the excess of single men over single women is most pronounced in those classes in which the ratio of males to females is highest, namely, the foreign-born whites and the native whites of native parentage. In the case of the foreign-born white population 15 years of age and over in 1920 the number of single males was more than twice as large as the number of single females. (See Table 2.)

The statistics give no direct information with regard to intermarriage among the several classes of the white population. In view of the fact that these classes intermarry more or less, there is not necessarily an approximate equality between the number of married men and the number of married women within any one class.

In each class of the white population, and also among the Negroes, the number of widows was more than twice as large as the number of widowers, from causes already noted with respect to the total population; and for each native white class and for Negroes an excess of divorced women over divorced men is shown. This excess of divorced women is due, of course, to the greater frequency of remarriage among divorced men.

It will be noted that the proportion married was considerably smaller for each sex among the native whites of foreign or mixed parentage than among the native whites of native parentage. This difference, which appears for each age group and for each individual year of age for which figures are presented, is due in some measure, but not wholly, to the facts that a much larger proportion of native whites of foreign or mixed parentage than of native whites of native parentage live in urban communities and that in general the proportion married is smaller in the urban than in the rural population.

Although the total foreign-born white male population 15 years of age and over shows a larger percentage of married men than the corresponding total in the native white population of native parentage, the percentages of married men in the latter class are found to exceed those in the former when the comparison is made for specific age groups or individual years of age.

Among the Chinese and Japanese the proportions of married men are smaller and of married women are larger than among the native whites of native parentage, the Negroes, or the Indians. The proportion married is especially small among the Chinese men and especially large among the Japanese women. The abnormal distribution of the Chinese and Japanese population according to marital condition is due to the facts that most of the Chinese and Japanese in the United States are immigrants, and that among these immigrants the males greatly outnumber the females. (See Tables 2 and 3.)

DIVISIONS AND STATES.

Considerable differences in marital condition are found when one section of the country is compared with another, not only when the comparison is made with regard to the population as a whole but also when particular classes are taken into consideration. The marital condition of each sex in the total population of a given division or state may be materially affected by the sex, age, color or race, nativity, and parentage composition of the total; and in the case of any particular class the marital condition of each sex may be materially affected by the sex and age composition of the class or, when intermarriage between classes is common, of the total population within the division or state.

The marital condition of the total population or of any class may be affected by interstate migration, both directly by differences between persons of different marital classes in regard to the disposition to migrate, and indirectly through the influence of migration upon sex and age distribution. There are no statistics bearing specifically on this point, but it may be presumed that unattached persons—single men and women or widowed or divorced persons without children—are more likely to migrate than those with families. This being the case, and other things being equal, relatively fewer unmarried persons will be found in states and divisions which lose more than they gain through interstate migration than in those which gain more than they lose.

Another factor affecting marital condition in divisions and states as compared with one another is the relative importance of urban population. The sex and age distribution of the urban population differs from that of the rural population, and the proportion of unmarried persons is larger, as a rule, especially among women, in cities than in rural communities. A state in which the proportion of urban population is large is, therefore, likely to have a somewhat larger proportion of single persons in its adult population than a state which is predominantly rural.

The marital condition of the foreign-born population of the several states depends to some extent upon the period of time during which immigration has been most rapid and is influenced by differences among the countries which have contributed chiefly to the foreign-born population. The period of time at which immigration has been most rapid also indirectly affects the marital condition of the natives of foreign or mixed parentage, since it affects the age distribution of that class.

MARITAL CONDITION.

Thus the causes of differences among the divisions or states in regard to marital condition are exceedingly complex, and in some cases conflict with one another. For example, the effect of a relatively large number of young persons in the adult population of a certain division or state, which would tend to reduce the proportion married in the total adult population, may be offset by the presence of a relatively large rural population, in which the proportion of married persons is generally larger than in the urban population.

PRINCIPAL CITIES.

Statistics for the 68 cities having 100,000 inhabitants or more in 1920 are presented, in Tables 12 to 16, inclusive, in substantially the same detail as those given in Tables 6 to 11 for geographic divisions and states; while for the 219 cities having 25,000 to 100,000 inhabitants a less detailed presentation is made in Table 17.

Differences in marital condition among the cities result from the same causes which operate to produce differences among the states. The marital condition of each sex in any city is influenced in large measure by the sex and age distribution and the racial composition of the population.

URBAN AND RURAL COMMUNITIES.

Since marked differences exist between urban and rural communities in regard to the composition and marital condition of their population, separate statistics are given for the two classes of communities in Tables 18 to 23. In drawing the distinction between urban and rural population, all incorporated places (and all towns in Massachusetts, Rhode Island, and New Hampshire) having 2,500 inhabitants or more are treated as urban and the remainder of the country as rural.

In Massachusetts and Rhode Island it is not the practice, as in practically all the other states, to incorporate, as separate municipalities, the relatively densely populated portions of "towns" (which are the primary divisions of the counties), and no town as a whole is incorporated as a municipality until it attains a population greatly in excess of 2,500; and in New Hampshire a similar condition exists, although the state contains two incorporated villages, each of which has fewer than 2,500 inhabitants. For this reason those towns having 2,500 or more inhabitants in the three states named are treated as urban, although portions of their areas are rural in character. The urban areas in the three states in question, as classified by the census, thus contain relatively small numbers of inhabitants who in other sections of the country would be segregated as rural. Nevertheless, in most of the towns having 2,500 inhabitants or more in Massachusetts, Rhode Island, and New Hampshire by

far the greater part of the population resides within the more densely settled areas, so that the proportion classed as urban, considering each state as a whole, is not greatly exaggerated by the practice adopted.

In the case of every population class covered by the statistics, marriage, on the part of women, is less common or is deferred longer in cities than in rural communities. For all classes of the male population combined, and for each class considered separately, except the foreign-born white men, the tendency is in the same direction but is much less pronounced. Basing the comparison on all classes of the population combined, the proportion of married males 15 years of age and over was only slightly larger in 1920 in rural territory than in urban territory, whereas for women the corresponding difference was considerable. This condition is due, wholly or in part, to the fact that the ratio of males to females is considerably higher in rural than in urban communities, there being an actual excess of females in many cities. (See Table 21.)

It will be noted by reference to Tables 21 and 22 that the percentage of married males in the combined age group 15 to 24 in the native white population of native parentage was slightly larger in urban than in rural communities, although the age periods 15–19 and 20–24, considered separately, show larger percentages for rural than for urban communities. The explanation of this apparent contradiction lies in the fact that persons in the age period 15–19, among whom the proportion married is small, are relatively more numerous in rural than in urban communities. As a result, the proportion married in the combined group 15–24 is reduced by the inclusion of the 15–19 group to a greater extent in rural than in urban communities.

It will also be noted that for all classes of the male population combined the percentage married in the combined 15–24 group was larger in rural than in urban communities, whereas for each population class shown in the table, considered separately, the corresponding percentage was larger in urban than in rural communities. The paradoxical condition is due to the facts that the proportion of married persons 15 to 24 years of age is much smaller for the native white population of foreign or mixed parentage than for any other class covered by the table, and that persons of this class are much more numerous in urban than in rural communities, whereas the number of males 15 to 24 years of age in all classes of the population combined differ but slightly as between urban and rural communities. The inclusion of a relatively large number of native white males of foreign or mixed parentage in the urban population 15 to 24 years of age, together with the inclusion of a much smaller number of such males in the rural population, therefore, reduces the proportion of married persons in the total male population 15 to 24 years of age to a greater extent in urban than in rural communities.

386

POPULATION.

MARITAL CONDITION OF THE POPULATION 15 YEARS OF AGE AND OVER, BY SEX AND AGE PERIODS, FOR PRINCIPAL POPULATION CLASSES: 1920.

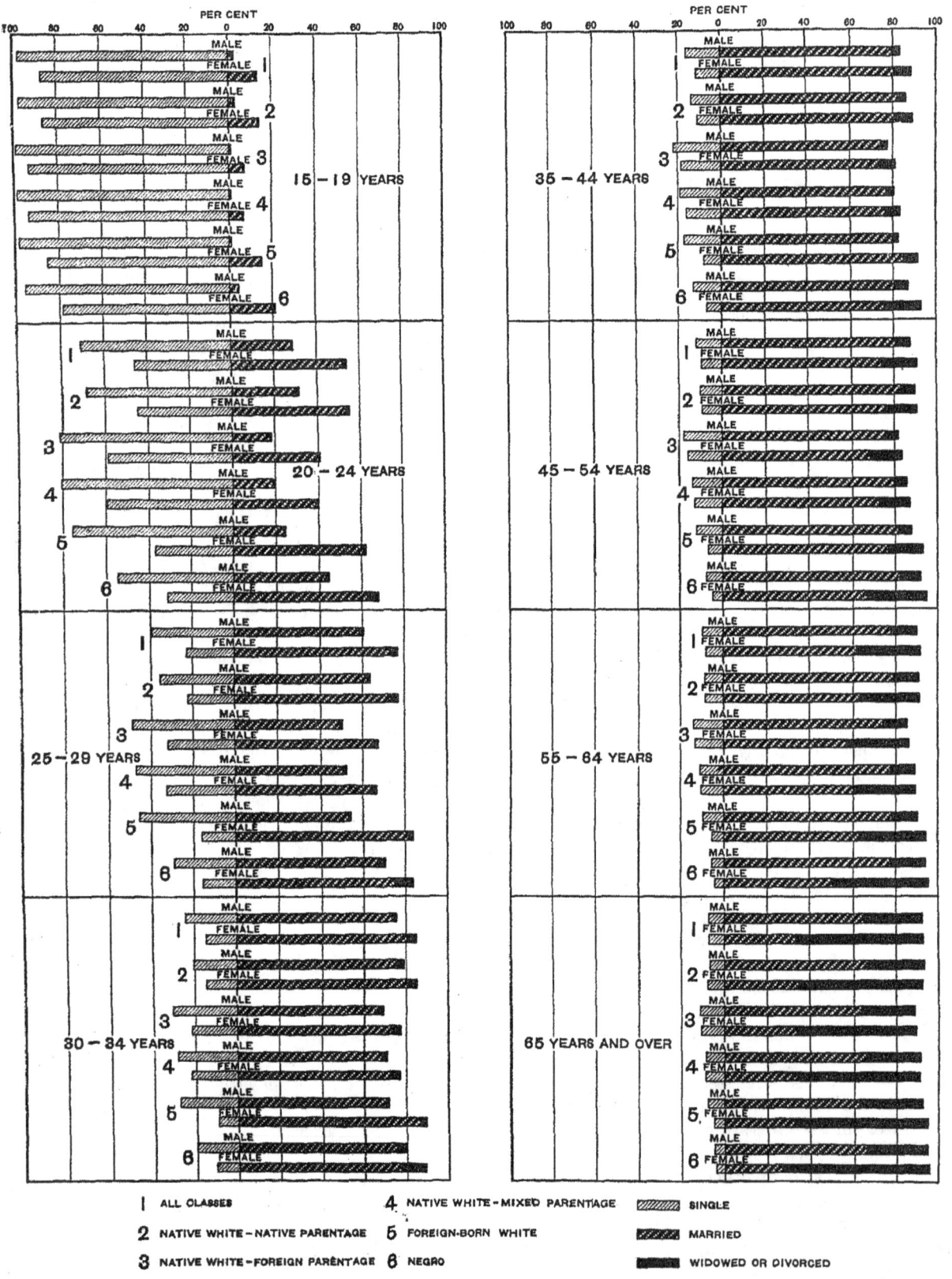

1	ALL CLASSES	4	NATIVE WHITE-MIXED PARENTAGE
2	NATIVE WHITE-NATIVE PARENTAGE	5	FOREIGN-BORN WHITE
3	NATIVE WHITE-FOREIGN PARENTAGE	6	NEGRO

SINGLE
MARRIED
WIDOWED OR DIVORCED

MARITAL CONDITION.

387

TABLE 1.—MARITAL CONDITION OF THE POPULATION 15 YEARS OF AGE AND OVER, BY SEX, FOR POPULATION CLASSES, FOR THE UNITED STATES: 1890–1920.

[Per cent not shown where base is less than 100.]

CLASS OF POPULATION AND CENSUS YEAR.	MALES 15 YEARS OF AGE AND OVER.								FEMALES 15 YEARS OF AGE AND OVER.							
	Total.[1]	Single.		Married.		Widowed.		Di-vorced.	Total.[1]	Single.		Married.		Widowed.		Di-vorced.
		Number.	Per cent.	Number.	Per cent.	Number.	Per cent.			Number.	Per cent.	Number.	Per cent.	Number.	Per cent.	
All classes:																
1920	36,020,603	12,967,565	35.1	21,849,266	59.2	1,758,308	4.8	235,284	35,177,515	9,610,002	27.3	21,318,933	60.6	3,917,625	11.1	273,304
1910	32,425,805	12,550,129	38.7	18,092,000	55.8	1,471,390	4.5	150,162	30,047,325	8,933,170	29.7	17,684,687	58.9	3,176,228	10.6	185,068
1900	25,620,399	10,297,940	40.2	13,955,650	54.5	1,177,976	4.6	84,290	24,219,191	7,566,530	31.2	13,810,057	57.0	2,717,715	11.2	114,047
1890[2]	20,777,872	8,655,711	41.7	11,205,205	53.9	815,437	3.9	49,100	19,002,178	6,233,316	31.8	11,124,785	56.8	2,154,593	11.0	71,883
White:																
1920	33,335,586	11,782,065	35.3	19,608,113	59.1	1,549,104	4.6	207,663	31,654,841	8,772,732	27.7	19,210,238	60.7	3,399,662	10.7	228,565
1910	29,158,125	11,360,282	39.0	16,253,040	55.7	1,274,388	4.4	135,203	26,857,337	8,091,240	30.1	15,852,011	59.0	2,705,990	10.1	150,801
1900	22,808,628	9,173,430	40.2	12,455,858	54.6	1,026,387	4.5	72,761	21,483,052	6,747,306	31.4	12,310,767	57.3	2,291,872	10.7	91,737
1890	18,534,187	7,732,832	41.7	9,902,010	53.9	721,971	3.9	43,829	17,401,915	5,575,143	32.0	9,924,785	57.0	1,831,772	10.5	61,125
Negro:																
1920	3,393,211	1,104,877	32.6	2,050,407	60.4	200,734	5.9	26,680	3,423,100	825,258	24.1	2,039,181	59.6	507,961	14.8	43,871
1910	3,059,312	1,083,472	35.4	1,749,228	57.2	180,970	6.2	20,146	3,103,344	823,090	26.6	1,775,049	57.2	459,831	14.8	33,286
1900	2,633,008	1,033,285	39.2	1,422,886	54.0	151,233	5.7	11,026	2,690,583	803,083	29.9	1,443,817	53.7	414,107	15.4	22,033
1890	2,110,721	842,764	39.8	1,175,513	55.5	91,083	4.3	5,212	2,175,550	652,314	30.0	1,187,434	54.6	320,194	14.7	10,888
Indian:																
1920	76,321	26,450	34.7	43,095	56.5	5,711	7.5	680	70,431	16,238	23.1	43,923	62.4	9,217	13.1	826
1910	80,383	27,391	34.1	46,154	57.4	5,319	6.6	679	76,982	16,324	21.2	49,095	63.8	10,071	13.1	959
1900	72,076	24,323	33.7	41,067	57.0	4,074	6.9	418	71,497	14,350	20.1	43,906	61.4	11,458	16.0	870
1890	19,911	7,990	40.1	9,803	49.5	1,241	6.2	45	18,412	4,717	25.6	10,543	57.3	2,541	13.8	67
Chinese:																
1920	49,818	23,096	46.4	24,782	49.7	1,355	2.7	66	4,407	962	21.8	3,040	69.1	371	8.4	15
1910	64,394	34,330	53.3	26,440	41.1	1,130	1.8	45	2,955	680	23.0	2,016	68.2	229	7.7	5
1900	83,633	48,007	58.6	31,794	38.0	1,310	1.6	19	3,204	778	24.3	2,157	67.3	259	8.1	3
1890	102,322	70,625	69.0	20,720	20.1	530	0.5	13	3,074	993	32.3	1,951	63.5	85	2.8	3
Japanese:																
1920	57,427	24,423	42.5	31,250	54.4	1,118	1.9	154	24,242	1,604	6.6	22,193	91.5	388	1.6	23
1910	60,536	42,688	70.5	15,018	26.3	495	0.8	80	6,648	908	13.7	5,581	84.0	96	1.4	17
1900	23,054	17,905	77.7	4,045	17.5	72	0.3	6	855	413	48.3	410	48.0	19	2.2	4
1890	1,731	1,500	86.7	199	11.5	12	0.7	1	227	149	65.6	72	31.7	6	2.6	
All other:																
1920	8,300	6,054	72.9	1,619	19.5	226	2.7	32	494	108	21.9	352	71.3	26	5.3	4
1910	3,055	1,966	64.4	911	29.8	79	2.6	3	59	13		35		11		
1900																
1890																
Native white:																
1920	26,083,047	9,927,618	38.1	14,705,171	56.7	1,111,115	4.3	175,713	25,740,856	7,936,933	30.8	15,086,735	58.6	2,480,407	9.6	200,909
1910	22,018,232	9,091,366	41.3	11,821,805	53.7	889,662	4.0	112,144	21,411,031	7,007,139	33.1	12,228,008	57.1	1,905,878	8.9	130,250
1900	17,551,269	7,627,637	43.5	9,100,302	51.8	693,940	4.0	50,415	17,037,720	5,878,706	34.5	9,464,321	55.5	1,589,287	9.3	79,219
1890	13,953,598	6,262,921	44.9	7,142,105	51.2	483,646	3.5	34,722	13,594,996	4,787,000	35.2	7,489,730	55.1	1,256,018	9.2	52,146
Native white—Native parentage:																
1920	19,092,107	6,776,518	35.5	11,244,289	58.9	874,821	4.6	134,789	18,529,748	5,258,490	28.4	11,195,865	60.4	1,885,000	10.2	152,743
1910	16,233,095	6,185,324	38.1	9,144,000	56.3	728,883	4.5	87,456	15,523,900	4,644,122	29.9	9,219,385	59.4	1,523,560	9.8	100,053
1900	13,088,058	5,105,203	39.7	7,103,922	55.0	587,804	4.5	47,093	12,501,813	3,893,417	31.0	7,251,375	57.7	1,332,334	10.6	62,585
1890	10,880,185	4,350,200	40.1	6,030,205	55.4	432,260	4.0	30,182	10,530,675	3,226,180	30.6	6,132,027	58.2	1,120,959	10.6	44,284
Native white—Foreign or mixed parentage:																
1920	6,990,940	3,151,100	45.1	3,550,882	50.8	236,294	3.4	40,924	7,211,108	2,668,443	37.0	3,890,870	54.0	595,407	8.3	48,166
1910	5,785,137	2,900,042	50.2	2,677,706	46.3	160,779	2.8	24,688	5,887,131	2,453,017	41.7	3,008,623	51.1	382,318	6.5	30,206
1900	4,463,211	2,432,374	54.5	1,996,380	42.7	100,055	2.4	11,422	4,475,907	1,985,289	44.4	2,212,946	49.4	256,953	5.7	16,634
1890	3,073,413	1,903,721	61.9	1,111,810	36.2	51,386	1.7	4,540	3,064,321	1,561,726	51.0	1,357,712	44.3	135,959	4.4	7,862
Native white—Foreign parentage:[3]																
1920	4,792,911	2,141,310	44.7	2,445,291	51.0	171,612	3.6	26,197	4,906,547	1,791,271	36.5	2,648,054	54.0	431,821	8.8	29,535
1910	4,059,778	1,989,127	49.0	1,926,075	47.4	117,046	2.9	16,471	4,092,572	1,660,120	40.6	2,123,165	52.0	276,348	6.8	18,987
Native white—Mixed parentage:[3]																
1920	2,198,029	1,009,790	45.9	1,105,591	50.3	64,682	2.9	14,727	2,304,561	877,172	38.1	1,242,816	53.9	163,586	7.1	18,631
1910	1,725,359	916,915	53.1	751,631	43.6	43,733	2.5	8,217	1,794,559	792,897	44.2	880,458	49.1	105,970	5.9	11,219
Foreign-born white:																
1920	7,252,539	1,855,047	25.6	4,902,942	67.6	438,049	6.0	31,950	5,913,985	835,799	14.1	4,123,503	69.7	919,255	15.5	27,656
1910	7,139,893	2,268,916	31.8	4,432,135	62.1	384,726	5.4	23,059	5,446,306	994,110	18.3	3,624,003	66.5	800,112	14.7	20,542
1900	5,257,359	1,545,793	29.4	3,355,556	63.8	320,438	6.2	13,346	4,445,332	868,600	19.5	2,855,446	64.2	702,585	15.8	12,518
1890	4,580,589	1,469,911	32.1	2,850,805	62.2	238,325	5.2	9,107	3,806,919	787,237	20.7	2,435,046	63.0	574,854	15.1	8,979

[1] Total includes persons whose marital condition was not reported.
[2] Figures for 1890 are exclusive of 325,464 persons (169,221 males and 156,243 females) specially enumerated in Indian Territory and on Indian reservations, for whom statistics of marital condition are not available.
[3] Not reported separately in 1900 or 1890.

388

POPULATION.

TABLE 2.—MARITAL CONDITION OF THE TOTAL POPULATION, BY SEX AND AGE PERIODS, FOR POPULATION CLASSES, FOR THE UNITED STATES: 1920.

CLASS OF POPULATION AND AGE PERIOD.	MALES.						FEMALES.					
	Total.	Single.	Married.	Widowed.	Divorced.	Marital condition not reported.	Total.	Single.	Married.	Widowed.	Divorced.	Marital condition not reported.
All classes	53,900,431	20,944,067	21,852,439	1,758,426	235,319	110,240	51,810,189	26,243,696	21,324,487	3,917,894	273,361	50,751
Under 15 years of age	16,979,768	16,976,442	3,173	118	35		16,632,674	16,626,794	5,554	269	57	
15 years and over	36,920,663	12,967,565	21,849,266	1,758,308	235,284	110,240	35,177,515	9,616,902	21,318,933	3,917,625	273,304	50,751
15 to 19 years	4,673,792	4,567,770	96,374	1,830	759	7,059	4,756,764	4,137,650	596,542	12,239	6,017	4,316
20 to 24 years	4,527,045	3,200,623	1,280,318	20,511	10,280	15,313	4,749,976	2,164,051	2,483,697	65,414	28,582	8,232
25 to 29 years	4,538,233	1,789,721	2,662,124	51,470	22,850	12,062	4,548,258	1,048,285	3,336,501	117,387	41,243	4,842
30 to 34 years	4,130,783	995,869	3,023,357	74,454	28,080	9,023	3,940,410	588,119	3,155,854	152,803	40,188	3,356
35 to 44 years	7,359,904	1,188,586	5,873,308	220,700	63,592	13,718	6,760,934	767,882	5,426,434	485,493	75,027	6,098
45 to 54 years	5,673,095	677,420	4,580,656	329,976	56,162	9,481	4,845,398	404,838	3,587,794	739,058	48,502	5,146
55 to 64 years	3,461,865	337,592	2,697,429	386,587	34,249	6,008	3,069,807	257,029	1,878,478	906,362	23,451	4,487
65 years and over	2,483,071	182,211	1,607,187	668,656	18,506	6,511	2,450,144	173,442	830,160	1,430,621	9,609	6,312
Age unknown	92,875	27,773	29,113	4,124	800	31,065	55,824	15,606	23,473	8,158	625	7,962
White	48,430,655	26,874,811	19,700,899	1,549,269	207,695	97,981	46,330,260	23,503,448	19,214,680	3,399,884	228,604	43,644
Under 15 years of age	15,095,069	15,092,146	2,786	105	32		14,735,419	14,730,718	4,442	222	30	
15 years and over	33,335,586	11,782,665	19,698,113	1,549,164	207,663	97,981	31,654,841	8,772,732	19,210,238	3,399,662	228,565	43,644
15 to 19 years	4,141,831	4,058,144	75,854	1,275	548	6,010	4,172,324	3,677,820	470,552	7,180	4,165	3,007
20 to 24 years	4,018,576	2,916,983	1,066,140	14,402	7,808	13,243	4,166,765	1,980,872	2,115,727	41,979	21,258	6,929
25 to 29 years	4,094,361	1,655,994	2,368,084	40,782	18,965	10,476	4,047,389	970,746	2,956,906	83,030	32,620	4,087
30 to 34 years	3,776,269	920,897	2,760,747	62,336	24,405	7,881	3,562,524	549,172	2,861,120	116,013	33,396	2,823
35 to 44 years	6,652,753	1,088,263	5,312,851	183,604	56,103	11,992	6,068,599	720,176	4,901,943	378,031	63,326	5,123
45 to 54 years	5,072,779	627,420	4,107,564	279,270	50,191	8,334	4,432,527	444,810	3,313,121	627,200	42,949	4,447
55 to 64 years	3,202,280	319,371	2,497,936	347,739	31,826	5,408	2,874,824	248,842	1,778,768	821,658	21,581	3,975
65 years and over	2,298,475	171,704	1,487,186	616,530	17,168	5,887	2,284,551	166,673	784,359	1,319,140	8,810	5,569
Age unknown	78,325	23,949	21,751	3,226	649	28,750	45,338	13,621	18,742	5,431	460	7,084
Negro	5,269,436	2,920,711	2,050,782	200,747	26,692	10,504	5,253,695	2,654,719	2,040,252	508,006	43,889	6,829
Under 15 years of age	1,816,225	1,815,834	375	13	3		1,830,595	1,829,461	1,071	45	18	
15 years and over	3,392,211	1,104,877	2,050,407	200,734	26,689	10,504	3,423,100	825,258	2,039,181	507,961	43,871	6,829
15 to 19 years	513,416	491,643	20,043	545	210	975	569,799	448,160	114,109	4,980	1,802	679
20 to 24 years	487,160	267,595	209,353	5,977	2,404	1,840	567,678	179,411	356,740	23,086	7,190	1,251
25 to 29 years	424,352	123,413	285,395	10,386	3,778	1,380	485,387	76,280	366,012	33,886	8,476	733
30 to 34 years	331,570	66,188	249,241	11,646	3,554	950	366,286	38,354	284,336	36,405	6,678	513
35 to 44 years	659,513	87,260	527,996	35,637	7,227	1,393	674,110	46,906	508,417	106,270	11,497	939
45 to 54 years	548,501	42,948	449,997	48,845	5,774	937	402,198	19,683	206,087	110,246	5,501	681
55 to 64 years	241,290	13,967	187,471	37,066	2,310	476	188,808	7,973	95,665	82,872	1,810	488
65 years and over	173,881	8,444	113,864	49,770	1,284	519	158,832	6,516	43,271	107,586	757	702
Age unknown	13,510	3,419	7,047	862	148	2,034	9,993	1,876	4,484	2,630	160	843
Indian	125,068	75,190	43,102	5,711	680	385	119,369	65,136	43,961	9,219	826	227
Under 15 years of age	48,747	48,740	7				48,938	48,898	38	2		
15 years and over	76,321	26,450	43,095	5,711	680	385	70,431	16,238	43,923	9,217	826	227
15 to 19 years	12,719	12,281	371	10	1	47	12,707	10,271	2,279	78	50	29
20 to 24 years	10,413	6,686	3,472	112	63	80	9,596	3,109	6,005	311	129	42
25 to 29 years	8,558	2,782	5,372	267	93	44	7,979	1,046	6,379	404	138	12
30 to 34 years	6,963	1,325	5,176	350	84	28	6,511	469	5,544	374	107	17
35 to 44 years	13,284	1,589	10,615	871	168	41	12,041	541	10,280	991	194	29
45 to 54 years	10,751	871	8,661	1,069	129	21	8,783	292	6,968	1,400	104	13
55 to 64 years	6,730	484	5,018	1,123	91	14	5,796	188	3,803	1,725	58	22
65 years and over	6,512	332	4,207	1,878	50	45	6,627	243	2,470	3,833	41	40
Age unknown	400	100	203	31	1	65	391	79	189	95	5	23
Chinese	53,891	27,167	24,784	1,355	66	519	7,748	4,302	3,047	371	15	13
Under 15 years of age	4,073	4,071	2				3,341	3,340	1			
15 years and over	49,818	23,096	24,782	1,355	66	519	4,407	962	3,046	371	15	13
15 to 19 years	2,161	2,098	60			3	599	517	82			
20 to 24 years	4,122	3,395	700	7	2	18	723	237	470	12	2	2
25 to 29 years	4,543	2,894	1,606	7	2	34	736	72	642	18	4	
30 to 34 years	4,093	2,011	2,020	18	2	42	589	28	518	40	3	
35 to 44 years	9,702	3,861	5,605	129	14	93	962	50	817	89	4	2
45 to 54 years	11,092	3,702	6,986	283	27	94	480	24	342	109	2	3
55 to 64 years	9,892	3,340	5,949	491	14	98	206	17	126	62		1
65 years and over	3,971	1,678	1,810	419	4	60	94	10	44	39		1
Age unknown	242	117	46	1	1	77	18	7	5	2		4
Japanese	72,707	39,700	31,253	1,118	154	482	38,303	15,663	22,195	388	23	34
Under 15 years of age	15,280	15,277	3				14,061	14,059	2			
15 years and over	57,427	24,423	31,250	1,118	154	482	24,242	1,604	22,193	388	23	34
15 to 19 years	3,081	3,033	42			6	1,261	822	437	1		1
20 to 24 years	4,535	3,965	521	5	3	41	5,101	392	4,672	26	3	8
25 to 29 years	4,600	3,159	1,364	19	11	47	6,670	129	6,480	48	5	8
30 to 34 years	10,819	4,774	5,870	82	23	70	4,434	91	4,278	59	3	3
35 to 44 years	23,039	6,719	15,739	383	69	129	5,117	111	4,892	105	6	3
45 to 54 years	9,313	2,212	6,569	432	40	60	1,383	29	1,256	92	4	2
55 to 64 years	1,537	377	992	153	7	8	166	9	114	40	2	1
65 years and over	173	39	93	41			28		11	17		
Age unknown	330	145	60	3	1	121	82	21	53			8
All other	8,674	6,423	1,619	226	32	369	814	428	352	26	4	4
Under 15 years of age	374	374					320	320				
15 years and over	8,300	6,054	1,619	226	32	369	494	108	352	26	4	4

MARITAL CONDITION.

389

TABLE 2.—MARITAL CONDITION OF THE TOTAL POPULATION, BY SEX AND AGE PERIODS, FOR POPULATION CLASSES, FOR THE UNITED STATES: 1920—Continued.

CLASS OF POPULATION AND AGE PERIOD.	MALES.						FEMALES.					
	Total.	Single.	Married.	Widowed.	Divorced.	Marital condition not reported.	Total.	Single.	Married.	Widowed.	Divorced.	Marital condition not reported.
Native white	40,902,333	24,744,249	14,797,713	1,111,197	175,744	73,430	40,205,828	22,397,555	15,090,874	2,480,581	200,946	35,872
Under 15 years of age	14,819,286	14,816,631	2,542	82	31		14,464,072	14,460,022	4,139	174	37	
15 years and over	26,083,047	9,927,618	14,795,171	1,111,115	175,713	73,430	25,740,856	7,936,933	15,086,735	2,480,407	200,909	35,872
15 to 19 years	3,882,561	3,802,817	72,596	1,100	525	5,454	3,903,652	3,448,580	441,075	6,081	4,001	3,315
20 to 24 years	3,561,588	2,572,115	957,845	13,071	7,414	11,143	3,696,909	1,800,735	1,826,378	37,514	20,130	6,152
25 to 29 years	3,302,213	1,207,209	2,045,904	34,680	17,587	6,833	3,385,114	864,463	2,416,371	70,549	30,278	3,453
30 to 34 years	2,829,448	660,521	2,093,412	49,285	21,729	4,501	2,857,807	480,115	2,251,085	94,213	30,138	2,316
35 to 44 years	4,840,881	771,123	3,876,456	138,614	47,865	6,823	4,714,567	609,821	3,753,495	292,189	55,256	3,806
45 to 54 years	3,676,810	456,505	2,969,817	203,915	41,462	5,111	3,361,444	371,035	2,490,682	459,417	36,136	3,274
55 to 64 years	2,305,862	230,177	1,797,141	249,639	25,315	3,590	2,146,789	208,242	1,321,603	506,399	17,597	2,048
65 years and over	1,619,091	118,725	1,064,921	418,207	13,278	3,000	1,635,708	134,947	570,646	910,165	6,073	3,977
Age unknown	64,593	18,426	17,079	2,475	538	26,075	38,806	12,095	15,400	4,280	400	6,631
Native white—Native parentage	29,636,781	17,319,288	11,246,113	874,882	134,808	61,690	28,785,176	15,520,296	11,190,314	1,885,144	152,772	27,650
Under 15 years of age	10,544,674	10,542,770	1,824	61	19		10,255,428	10,251,866	3,449	144	29	
15 years and over	19,092,107	6,776,518	11,244,280	874,821	134,789	61,690	18,529,748	5,268,490	11,195,865	1,885,000	152,743	27,650
15 to 19 years	2,797,477	2,727,715	64,392	990	470	3,910	2,801,569	2,417,110	372,924	5,878	3,498	2,159
20 to 24 years	2,546,818	1,747,256	774,580	10,805	6,146	7,971	2,620,883	1,175,208	1,404,020	30,185	16,307	4,109
25 to 29 years	2,367,312	844,867	1,476,829	26,795	13,740	5,081	2,397,490	544,242	1,774,694	53,239	23,045	2,270
30 to 34 years	2,054,671	427,445	1,569,007	37,123	16,671	3,465	2,041,370	360,636	1,646,968	69,656	22,529	1,681
35 to 44 years	3,540,880	491,663	2,909,662	104,520	30,216	5,403	3,368,302	342,258	2,747,693	200,067	41,182	2,797
45 to 54 years	2,649,806	280,785	2,184,378	149,899	30,809	3,995	2,339,847	215,435	1,780,111	315,266	26,560	2,466
55 to 64 years	1,704,797	149,315	1,347,772	185,552	19,260	2,898	1,544,522	130,390	975,230	423,318	13,313	2,322
65 years and over	1,365,527	91,915	902,207	356,027	11,026	3,452	1,373,349	108,365	480,833	774,000	5,909	3,543
Age unknown	58,759	15,557	15,095	2,141	451	25,515	33,410	9,701	18,383	3,692	331	6,303
Native white—Foreign or mixed parentage	11,265,552	7,424,961	3,551,600	236,315	40,936	11,740	11,420,652	6,877,259	3,891,560	595,437	48,174	8,222
Under 15 years of age	4,274,612	4,273,861	718	21	12		4,200,544	4,208,816	690	30	8	
15 years and over	6,990,940	3,151,100	3,550,882	236,294	40,924	11,740	7,211,108	2,668,443	3,890,870	595,407	48,166	8,222
15 to 19 years	1,085,084	1,075,102	8,204	170	55	1,544	1,102,083	1,031,470	68,151	803	503	1,156
20 to 24 years	1,014,770	824,859	183,205	2,206	1,268	3,172	1,067,020	631,527	422,358	7,329	3,763	2,043
25 to 29 years	934,901	462,342	469,075	7,885	3,847	1,752	987,024	320,221	641,677	17,310	7,233	1,183
30 to 34 years	774,777	233,076	523,445	12,102	5,058	1,036	816,407	179,570	604,117	24,557	7,609	635
35 to 44 years	1,294,001	279,400	967,387	34,085	11,649	1,420	1,340,205	242,258	1,005,802	83,122	14,074	808
45 to 54 years	1,020,944	175,720	785,439	54,016	10,653	1,116	1,021,597	150,500	710,571	144,151	9,567	1,009
55 to 64 years	601,005	80,862	449,369	64,087	6,055	602	602,267	77,912	346,864	173,081	4,284	808
65 years and over	253,564	26,810	162,714	61,340	2,252	448	262,350	20,582	89,813	144,466	1,064	620
Age unknown	5,834	2,800	1,984	334	87	569	5,306	2,304	2,017	588	60	328
Native white—Foreign parentage	7,810,531	5,158,428	3,445,770	171,627	26,205	8,501	7,884,008	4,768,233	2,648,525	431,841	29,543	5,866
Under 15 years of age	3,017,620	3,017,118	470	15	8		2,977,461	2,976,902	471	20	8	
15 years and over	4,792,911	2,141,310	2,445,291	171,612	26,197	8,501	4,906,547	1,791,271	2,648,054	431,821	29,535	5,866
15 to 19 years	707,722	701,037	4,896	116	35	1,038	721,046	674,705	45,336	490	257	708
20 to 24 years	676,135	551,584	119,851	1,422	685	2,203	708,620	417,140	283,156	4,764	2,105	1,455
25 to 29 years	631,349	308,422	314,187	5,155	2,309	1,276	655,213	210,542	428,236	11,349	4,279	807
30 to 34 years	518,974	159,156	347,908	8,047	3,008	735	533,162	117,035	395,145	16,013	4,529	430
35 to 44 years	866,075	196,345	630,104	23,292	7,136	1,038	888,786	160,790	650,869	55,977	8,465	715
45 to 54 years	745,976	135,801	561,888	40,274	7,153	857	743,634	120,476	509,085	106,657	6,201	615
55 to 64 years	462,190	65,414	342,016	49,010	4,315	535	466,582	63,214	264,796	135,059	2,961	502
65 years and over	179,375	20,572	113,805	43,155	1,440	313	185,170	19,654	101,009	101,009	688	310
Age unknown	4,215	2,076	1,426	241	56	416	3,785	1,085	1,400	413	50	228
Native white—Mixed parentage	3,455,021	2,266,533	1,105,830	64,688	14,731	3,239	3,536,644	2,109,026	1,243,035	163,596	18,631	2,356
Under 15 years of age	1,256,992	1,256,743	239	6	4		1,232,083	1,231,854	219	10		
15 years and over	2,198,029	1,009,790	1,105,591	64,682	14,727	3,239	2,304,561	877,172	1,242,816	163,586	18,631	2,356
15 to 19 years	377,362	373,465	3,308	63	20	506	380,437	350,705	22,815	313	246	358
20 to 24 years	338,635	272,975	63,414	784	583	879	358,400	214,387	139,202	2,565	1,658	588
25 to 29 years	303,552	143,920	154,888	2,730	1,538	476	332,411	106,679	213,441	5,961	2,954	376
30 to 34 years	255,803	73,920	175,477	4,115	1,900	301	283,345	62,544	208,072	8,544	3,080	205
35 to 44 years	427,926	83,115	328,223	10,793	4,513	382	457,479	75,498	348,933	27,145	5,600	294
45 to 54 years	280,968	39,916	223,551	13,742	3,500	259	277,963	36,024	200,886	37,494	3,366	193
55 to 64 years	138,875	15,448	107,353	14,177	1,740	157	135,735	14,698	81,568	38,022	1,323	124
65 years and over	74,189	6,238	48,819	18,185	812	135	77,180	6,928	20,391	43,367	376	118
Age unknown	1,619	703	558	93	31	144	1,611	709	608	175	19	100
Foreign-born white	7,528,322	2,130,502	4,903,186	438,072	31,951	24,551	6,184,432	1,105,893	4,123,806	919,303	27,658	7,772
Under 15 years of age	275,783	275,515	244	23	1		270,447	270,094	303	48	2	
15 years and over	7,252,539	1,855,047	4,902,942	438,049	31,950	24,551	5,913,985	835,799	4,123,503	919,255	27,656	7,772
15 to 19 years	259,270	255,327	3,258	106	23	556	268,672	229,240	38,477	490	164	292
20 to 24 years	456,988	344,808	108,205	1,331	394	2,100	469,856	174,137	289,849	4,405	1,128	777
25 to 29 years	702,088	358,785	422,180	6,102	1,878	3,643	662,275	106,283	540,535	12,481	2,342	634
30 to 34 years	946,818	290,376	667,335	13,051	2,676	3,380	704,657	69,057	610,035	21,800	3,258	507
35 to 44 years	1,811,872	317,080	1,436,395	44,990	8,238	5,169	1,354,032	110,355	1,148,448	85,842	8,070	1,317
45 to 54 years	1,395,009	170,915	1,137,747	75,355	8,729	3,223	1,071,083	72,875	822,439	167,783	6,813	1,173
55 to 64 years	896,418	80,104	700,795	98,100	6,511	1,818	728,035	40,600	457,165	225,259	3,984	1,027
65 years and over	679,384	52,979	422,205	198,203	3,890	1,987	648,843	31,726	213,713	399,975	1,887	1,592
Age unknown	13,732	5,523	4,672	751	111	2,675	6,532	1,526	3,342	1,151	60	453

POPULATION.

TABLE 3.—PER CENT DISTRIBUTION BY MARITAL CONDITION OF THE TOTAL POPULATION, BY SEX AND AGE PERIODS, FOR POPULATION CLASSES, FOR THE UNITED STATES: 1920.

[Per cent not shown where base is less than 100.]

CLASS OF POPULATION AND AGE PERIOD.	MALES Single	Married	Widowed	Divorced	FEMALES Single	Married	Widowed	Divorced
All classes	55.6	40.5	3.3	0.4	50.7	41.2	7.6	0.5
Under 15 years of age	100.0	(1)	(1)	(1)	100.0	(1)	(1)	(1)
15 years and over	35.1	59.2	4.8	0.6	27.3	60.6	11.1	0.8
15 to 19 years	97.7	2.1	(1)	(1)	87.0	12.5	0.3	0.1
20 to 24 years	70.7	28.3	0.5	0.2	45.6	52.3	1.4	0.6
25 to 29 years	39.4	58.7	1.1	0.5	23.6	73.4	2.6	0.9
30 to 34 years	24.1	73.2	1.8	0.7	14.9	80.1	3.9	1.0
35 to 44 years	16.1	79.8	3.0	0.9	11.4	80.3	7.2	1.1
45 to 54 years	12.0	81.0	5.8	1.0	9.6	74.0	15.3	1.0
55 to 64 years	9.8	77.9	11.2	1.0	8.4	61.2	29.5	0.8
65 years and over	7.3	64.7	26.9	0.7	7.1	33.9	58.4	0.4
Age unknown	29.9	31.3	4.4	0.9	28.0	42.0	14.6	1.1
White	55.5	40.7	3.2	0.4	50.7	41.4	7.3	0.5
Under 15 years of age	100.0	(1)	(1)	(1)	100.0	(1)	(1)	(1)
15 years and over	35.3	59.1	4.6	0.6	27.7	60.7	10.7	0.7
15 to 19 years	98.0	1.8	(1)	(1)	88.1	11.5	0.2	0.1
20 to 24 years	72.6	26.5	0.4	0.2	47.5	50.8	1.0	0.5
25 to 29 years	40.4	57.8	1.0	0.5	24.0	73.1	2.1	0.8
30 to 34 years	24.4	73.1	1.7	0.6	15.4	80.3	3.3	0.9
35 to 44 years	16.4	79.9	2.8	0.8	11.9	80.8	6.2	1.0
45 to 54 years	12.4	81.0	5.5	1.0	10.0	74.7	14.1	1.0
55 to 64 years	10.0	78.0	10.9	1.0	8.7	61.9	28.6	0.8
65 years and over	7.5	64.7	26.8	0.7	7.3	34.3	57.7	0.4
Age unknown	30.6	27.8	4.1	0.6	30.0	41.3	12.0	1.0
Negro	56.1	39.4	3.9	0.5	50.5	38.8	9.7	0.8
Under 15 years of age	100.0	(1)	(1)	(1)	99.9	0.1	(1)	(1)
15 years and over	32.6	60.4	5.9	0.8	24.1	59.6	14.8	1.3
15 to 19 years	95.8	3.9	0.1	(1)	78.7	20.0	0.9	0.3
20 to 24 years	54.9	43.0	1.2	0.5	31.6	62.8	4.1	1.3
25 to 29 years	29.1	67.3	2.4	0.9	15.7	75.4	7.0	1.7
30 to 34 years	20.0	75.2	3.5	1.1	10.5	77.6	9.9	1.8
35 to 44 years	13.2	80.1	5.4	1.1	7.0	75.4	15.8	1.7
45 to 54 years	7.8	82.0	8.9	1.1	4.9	66.2	27.4	1.4
55 to 64 years	5.8	77.7	15.4	1.0	4.2	50.7	43.9	1.0
65 years and over	4.9	65.5	28.6	0.7	4.1	27.2	67.7	0.5
Age unknown	25.3	52.2	6.4	1.1	18.8	44.9	26.3	1.0
Indian	60.1	34.5	4.6	0.5	54.6	36.8	7.7	0.7
Under 15 years of age	100.0	(1)	(1)	(1)	99.9	(1)	(1)	(1)
15 years and over	34.7	56.5	7.5	0.9	23.1	62.4	13.1	1.2
15 to 19 years	96.6	2.9	0.1	(1)	80.8	17.9	0.6	0.4
20 to 24 years	64.2	33.3	1.1	0.6	32.4	62.6	3.2	1.3
25 to 29 years	32.5	62.8	3.1	1.1	13.1	79.9	5.1	1.7
30 to 34 years	19.0	74.3	5.0	1.2	7.2	85.1	5.7	1.6
35 to 44 years	12.0	79.9	6.6	1.3	4.5	85.4	8.2	1.6
45 to 54 years	8.1	80.6	9.9	1.2	3.3	79.3	16.0	1.2
55 to 64 years	7.2	74.6	16.7	1.4	3.2	65.6	29.8	1.0
65 years and over	5.1	64.6	28.8	0.8	3.7	37.3	57.8	0.6
Age unknown	25.0	50.8	7.8	0.8	20.2	48.3	24.3	1.3
Chinese	50.4	46.0	2.5	0.1	55.5	39.3	4.8	0.2
Under 15 years of age	100.0	(1)			100.0	(1)		
15 years and over	46.4	49.7	2.7	0.1	21.8	69.1	8.4	0.3
15 to 19 years	97.1	2.8			86.3	13.7		
20 to 24 years	82.4	17.0	0.2	(1)	32.8	65.0	1.7	0.3
25 to 29 years	63.7	35.4	0.2	(1)	9.8	87.2	2.4	0.5
30 to 34 years	49.1	49.4	0.4	0.1	4.8	87.9	6.8	0.5
35 to 44 years	39.8	57.8	1.3	0.1	5.2	84.9	9.3	0.4
45 to 54 years	33.4	63.0	2.6	0.2	5.0	71.3	22.7	0.4
55 to 64 years	33.8	60.1	5.0	0.1	8.3	61.2		
65 years and over	42.3	45.6	10.6	0.1				
Age unknown	48.3	19.0	0.4	0.4				
Japanese	54.6	43.0	1.5	0.2	40.9	57.9	1.0	0.1
Under 15 years of age	100.0	(1)			100.0	(1)		
15 years and over	42.5	54.4	1.9	0.3	6.6	91.5	1.6	0.1
15 to 19 years	98.4	1.4			65.2	34.7	0.1	
20 to 24 years	87.4	11.5	0.1	0.1	7.7	91.6	0.5	0.1
25 to 29 years	68.7	29.7	0.4	0.2	1.9	97.2	0.7	0.1
30 to 34 years	44.1	54.3	0.8	0.2	2.1	96.5	1.3	0.1
35 to 44 years	29.2	68.3	1.7	0.3	2.2	95.6	2.1	0.1
45 to 54 years	23.8	70.5	4.6	0.4	2.1	90.8	6.7	0.3
55 to 64 years	24.5	64.5	10.0	0.5	5.4	68.7	24.1	1.2
65 years and over	22.5	53.8	23.7					
Age unknown	43.9	18.2	0.9	0.3				
All other	74.1	18.7	2.6	0.4	52.6	43.2	3.2	0.5
Under 15 years of age	100.0	(1)			100.0			
15 years and over	72.9	19.5	2.7	0.4	21.9	71.3	5.3	0.8

CLASS OF POPULATION AND AGE PERIOD.	MALES Single	Married	Widowed	Divorced	FEMALES Single	Married	Widowed	Divorced
Native white	60.5	36.2	2.7	0.4	55.7	37.5	6.2	0.5
Under 15 years of age	100.0	(1)	(1)	(1)	100.0	(1)	(1)	(1)
15 years and over	38.1	56.7	4.3	0.7	30.8	58.6	9.6	0.8
15 to 19 years	97.9	1.9	(1)	(1)	88.3	11.3	0.2	0.1
20 to 24 years	72.2	26.9	0.4	0.2	48.9	49.4	1.0	0.5
25 to 29 years	39.3	58.9	1.1	0.5	25.5	71.4	2.1	0.9
30 to 34 years	23.3	74.0	1.7	0.8	16.8	78.8	3.3	1.1
35 to 44 years	15.0	80.1	2.9	1.0	12.9	79.6	6.2	1.2
45 to 54 years	12.4	80.8	5.5	1.1	11.1	74.1	13.7	1.1
55 to 64 years	10.0	77.9	10.8	1.1	9.7	61.6	27.8	0.8
65 years and over	7.3	65.8	25.8	0.8	8.3	34.9	56.2	0.4
Age unknown	28.5	26.4	3.8	0.8	31.2	39.7	11.0	1.0
Native white—Native parentage	58.4	37.9	3.0	0.5	53.9	38.9	6.5	0.5
Under 15 years of age	100.0	(1)	(1)	(1)	100.0	(1)	(1)	(1)
15 years and over	35.5	58.9	4.6	0.7	28.4	60.4	10.2	0.8
15 to 19 years	97.5	2.3	(1)	(1)	86.3	13.3	0.2	0.1
20 to 24 years	68.6	30.4	0.4	0.2	44.7	53.4	1.1	0.6
25 to 29 years	35.7	62.4	1.1	0.6	22.7	74.0	2.2	1.0
30 to 34 years	20.8	76.4	1.8	0.8	14.7	80.7	3.4	1.1
35 to 44 years	13.9	82.0	2.9	1.0	10.9	81.6	6.2	1.2
45 to 54 years	10.6	82.4	5.7	1.2	9.2	76.1	13.5	1.1
55 to 64 years	8.8	79.1	10.9	1.1	8.4	63.1	27.4	0.9
65 years and over	6.7	66.1	26.1	0.8	7.9	35.0	56.4	0.4
Age unknown	26.5	25.7	3.6	0.8	29.0	40.1	11.1	1.0
Native white—Foreign or mixed parentage	65.9	31.5	2.1	0.4	60.2	34.1	5.2	0.4
Under 15 years of age	100.0	(1)	(1)	(1)	100.0	(1)	(1)	(1)
15 years and over	45.1	50.8	3.4	0.6	37.0	54.0	8.3	0.7
15 to 19 years	99.1	0.8	(1)	(1)	93.6	6.2	0.1	(1)
20 to 24 years	81.3	18.1	0.2	0.1	59.2	39.6	0.7	0.4
25 to 29 years	48.4	50.2	0.8	0.4	32.4	65.0	1.8	0.7
30 to 34 years	30.1	67.6	1.6	0.7	22.0	74.0	3.0	0.9
35 to 44 years	21.6	74.8	2.6	0.9	18.0	74.7	6.2	1.0
45 to 54 years	17.1	76.5	5.3	0.9	15.3	69.6	14.1	0.9
55 to 64 years	13.5	74.8	10.7	1.0	12.9	57.5	28.7	0.7
65 years and over	10.6	64.2	24.2	0.9	10.1	34.2	55.1	0.4
Age unknown	49.2	34.0	5.7	1.5	44.4	37.4	10.9	1.3
Native white — Foreign parentage	66.0	31.3	2.2	0.4	60.5	33.6	5.5	0.4
Under 15 years of age	100.0	(1)	(1)	(1)	100.0	(1)	(1)	(1)
15 years and over	44.7	51.0	3.6	0.5	36.5	54.0	8.8	0.6
15 to 19 years	99.1	0.7	(1)	(1)	93.5	6.3	0.1	(1)
20 to 24 years	81.6	17.7	0.2	0.1	58.9	40.0	0.7	0.3
25 to 29 years	48.9	49.8	0.8	0.4	32.1	65.4	1.7	0.7
30 to 34 years	30.7	67.0	1.6	0.6	22.0	74.1	3.0	0.8
35 to 44 years	22.6	73.7	2.7	0.8	18.8	73.9	6.3	1.0
45 to 54 years	18.2	75.3	5.4	1.0	16.2	68.5	14.3	0.8
55 to 64 years	14.2	74.0	10.8	0.9	13.5	56.8	28.9	0.6
65 years and over	11.5	63.5	24.1	0.8	10.6	34.2	54.6	0.4
Age unknown	49.3	33.8	5.7	1.3	44.5	37.2	10.9	1.3
Native white—Mixed parentage	65.6	32.0	1.9	0.4	59.6	35.1	4.6	0.5
Under 15 years of age	100.0	(1)	(1)	(1)	100.0	(1)	(1)	....
15 years and over	45.9	50.3	2.9	0.7	38.1	53.9	7.1	0.8
15 to 19 years	99.0	0.9	(1)	(1)	93.8	6.0	0.1	0.1
20 to 24 years	80.6	18.7	0.2	0.5	59.8	38.8	0.7	0.5
25 to 29 years	47.4	51.0	0.9	0.5	33.0	64.2	1.8	0.9
30 to 34 years	28.9	68.6	1.6	0.8	22.1	73.8	3.0	1.1
35 to 44 years	19.5	76.9	2.5	1.1	16.5	76.3	5.9	1.2
45 to 54 years	14.2	79.6	4.9	1.2	13.0	72.3	13.5	1.2
55 to 64 years	11.1	77.3	10.2	1.1	10.8	60.1	28.0	0.5
65 years and over	8.4	65.8	24.5	1.1	9.0	34.2	56.2	0.5
Age unknown	49.0	34.5	5.7	1.9	44.0	37.7	10.9	1.2
Foreign-born white	28.3	65.1	5.8	0.4	17.9	66.7	14.9	0.4
Under 15 years of age	99.9	0.1	(1)	(1)	99.9	0.1	(1)	....
15 years and over	25.6	67.6	6.0	0.4	14.1	69.7	15.5	0.5
15 to 19 years	98.5	1.3	(1)	(1)	85.3	14.3	0.2	0.1
20 to 24 years	75.5	23.7	0.3	0.1	37.1	61.6	1.0	0.2
25 to 29 years	45.3	53.3	0.8	0.2	16.0	81.6	1.9	0.4
30 to 34 years	27.5	70.5	1.4	0.3	9.8	86.6	3.1	0.5
35 to 44 years	17.5	79.3	2.5	0.5	8.2	84.8	6.3	0.6
45 to 54 years	12.2	81.5	5.4	0.6	6.8	76.8	15.7	0.6
55 to 64 years	10.0	78.2	10.9	0.7	5.6	62.8	30.9	0.5
65 years and over	7.8	62.2	29.2	0.6	4.9	32.9	61.6	0.3
Age unknown	40.2	34.0	5.5	0.8	23.4	51.2	17.6	0.9

1 Less than one-tenth of 1 per cent.

MARITAL CONDITION.

391

TABLE 4.—MARITAL CONDITION OF THE POPULATION 15 TO 34 YEARS OF AGE, BY SEX AND SINGLE YEARS, FOR PRINCIPAL POPULATION CLASSES, FOR THE UNITED STATES: 1920 AND 1910.

CLASS OF POPULATION AND AGE.	Total.	SINGLE. Number.	Per cent.	MARRIED. Number.	Per cent.	Widowed or divorced.	Marital condition not reported.	Total.	SINGLE. Number.	Per cent.	MARRIED. Number.	Per cent.	Widowed or divorced.	Marital condition not reported.
		MALES: 1920							MALES: 1910					
All classes:[1]														
15 years	925,670	923,997	99.8	1,609	0.2	82	....	862,475	858,522	99.5	531	0.1	60	3,362
16 years	976,834	973,468	99.7	3,222	0.3	144	....	925,246	918,028	99.2	993	0.1	96	6,129
17 years	926,033	918,008	99.1	7,609	0.8	266	....	900,649	891,324	99.0	3,466	0.4	166	5,693
18 years	938,646	909,332	96.9	24,944	2.7	770	3,600	949,876	930,457	98.0	13,321	1.4	393	5,705
19 years	906,690	842,905	93.0	58,909	6.5	1,327	3,459	889,036	849,736	95.6	33,566	3.8	742	4,992
20 years	843,501	732,213	86.8	105,369	12.5	2,426	3,493	899,372	814,735	90.6	77,658	8.6	1,888	5,091
21 years	920,779	719,816	78.2	193,663	21.0	4,168	3,132	937,420	776,575	82.8	152,208	16.2	3,386	5,161
22 years	918,849	648,916	70.6	260,630	28.4	6,207	3,136	925,234	695,600	75.2	219,949	23.8	5,163	4,522
23 years	911,705	574,761	63.0	326,245	35.8	7,906	2,793	906,182	603,256	66.6	292,308	32.3	6,074	4,544
24 years	932,311	524,917	56.3	394,511	42.3	10,024	2,759	912,082	541,905	59.4	357,880	39.2	8,436	3,771
25 years	932,333	462,811	49.6	454,791	48.8	12,210	2,521	918,733	486,148	52.9	418,325	45.5	10,683	3,577
26 years	915,495	403,477	44.1	495,055	54.2	13,435	2,628	899,196	411,521	47.3	443,475	51.0	11,064	3,136
27 years	910,809	349,753	38.4	543,508	59.7	15,079	2,469	818,862	341,528	41.7	463,158	56.6	11,569	2,607
28 years	943,054	326,869	34.6	596,013	63.3	17,402	2,470	901,975	343,254	38.1	540,990	60.0	14,872	2,859
29 years	835,942	246,811	29.5	570,957	68.3	16,200	1,974	735,582	233,080	31.8	487,577	66.3	12,407	1,912
30 years	950,567	277,588	29.0	654,280	68.4	22,244	2,455	973,592	310,707	31.9	638,582	65.6	21,050	3,253
31 years	724,643	178,608	24.7	528,367	72.9	16,015	1,563	600,222	155,515	25.9	431,291	71.9	11,930	1,477
32 years	826,738	201,562	24.4	602,328	72.9	21,073	1,775	745,053	194,918	26.1	531,582	71.3	17,326	1,827
33 years	795,555	171,147	21.5	602,059	75.7	20,738	1,611	663,778	147,525	22.2	498,557	75.1	16,381	1,315
34 years	827,280	166,874	20.2	636,323	76.9	22,464	1,619	673,523	143,155	21.3	511,232	75.9	17,711	1,425
Native white—Native parentage:														
15 years	561,320	560,321	99.8	955	0.2	44	....	504,547	502,428	99.6	234	(²)	29	1,856
16 years	588,313	586,290	99.7	1,935	0.3	88	....	530,805	526,914	99.3	575	0.1	44	3,272
17 years	554,815	549,577	99.1	5,083	0.9	155	....	513,800	508,438	99.0	2,246	0.4	80	3,036
18 years	555,858	536,783	96.6	16,670	3.0	400	2,005	521,571	509,997	97.8	8,551	1.6	181	2,842
19 years	537,171	494,744	92.1	39,749	7.4	773	1,905	481,805	456,690	94.8	22,212	4.6	372	2,525
20 years	480,567	417,792	85.3	68,577	14.0	1,320	1,878	468,836	417,472	89.0	48,044	10.2	899	2,421
21 years	538,528	410,990	80.8	123,437	22.9	2,354	1,747	493,820	399,257	80.8	90,294	18.3	1,750	2,525
22 years	513,123	349,503	68.1	158,545	30.9	3,460	1,615	462,186	334,735	72.4	122,876	26.6	2,474	2,101
23 years	501,825	301,383	60.1	194,715	38.8	4,344	1,383	458,257	280,947	63.3	163,160	35.6	3,300	1,850
24 years	503,775	267,588	53.1	220,306	45.5	5,533	1,348	449,809	240,074	55.6	193,926	43.1	4,210	1,699
25 years	490,375	225,827	46.1	256,950	52.4	6,440	1,158	433,588	211,365	48.7	215,833	49.8	4,918	1,472
26 years	482,089	194,082	40.2	280,357	58.0	7,430	1,120	425,405	181,783	42.9	234,643	55.4	5,628	1,351
27 years	478,647	165,413	34.6	303,826	63.5	8,366	1,042	398,942	148,817	37.3	243,087	60.9	5,937	1,101
28 years	483,036	148,406	30.7	324,209	67.1	9,400	1,021	424,053	148,673	33.8	272,496	64.2	7,388	1,196
29 years	432,205	111,130	25.7	311,487	72.1	8,899	740	380,009	101,381	27.7	257,427	70.3	6,387	814
30 years	465,522	118,151	25.4	335,288	72.0	11,111	972	430,495	123,404	28.7	296,275	68.8	9,503	1,253
31 years	377,883	80,526	21.3	287,810	76.2	8,857	684	302,229	67,224	22.2	228,187	75.5	6,193	625
32 years	407,537	85,700	21.0	309,923	76.0	11,172	676	355,300	81,072	22.8	264,673	74.5	8,835	720
33 years	395,788	72,745	18.4	311,543	78.7	10,955	545	323,007	62,200	19.3	251,843	78.0	8,341	558
34 years	407,941	70,257	17.2	325,397	70.8	11,099	588	330,538	60,803	18.4	260,001	78.7	9,037	607
Native white—Foreign or mixed parentage:														
15 years	217,665	217,364	99.9	280	0.1	21	....	215,448	214,677	99.6	91	(²)	8	672
16 years	229,349	228,875	99.8	458	0.2	16	....	234,541	232,005	99.3	94	(²)	11	1,441
17 years	216,114	215,387	99.7	692	0.3	35	....	222,945	221,430	99.3	180	0.1	17	1,300
18 years	213,207	210,572	98.8	1,804	0.8	73	758	219,106	217,085	99.1	787	0.4	31	1,203
19 years	208,749	202,904	97.2	4,970	2.4	89	786	202,821	199,200	98.2	2,474	1.2	59	1,079
20 years	196,071	184,813	93.8	11,102	5.7	210	780	191,310	183,446	95.9	6,789	3.5	121	954
21 years	207,208	182,598	88.1	23,580	11.4	392	638	195,005	177,502	90.7	10,970	8.7	209	924
22 years	201,611	167,729	82.0	35,648	17.4	611	623	180,635	153,079	84.8	20,332	14.6	379	745
23 years	204,073	152,776	74.9	49,777	24.4	968	552	175,143	135,332	77.3	38,562	22.0	605	644
24 years	201,907	136,043	67.8	63,098	31.3	1,287	579	171,528	120,215	70.1	49,884	29.1	808	621
25 years	195,074	117,884	60.4	75,087	38.5	1,675	428	164,629	104,023	63.2	59,019	35.8	1,056	531
26 years	195,292	105,080	53.8	87,747	44.9	2,061	404	159,483	91,727	57.5	66,070	41.4	1,244	442
27 years	190,438	89,579	47.0	98,052	51.5	2,467	340	147,062	75,082	51.5	69,936	47.4	1,373	371
28 years	183,714	77,645	42.3	102,991	56.1	2,757	321	151,508	72,706	48.0	76,650	50.6	1,825	327
29 years	170,383	62,154	36.5	105,198	61.7	2,772	259	131,709	53,571	40.7	76,185	57.8	1,716	237
30 years	174,244	61,120	35.1	109,431	62.8	3,427	266	153,650	63,306	41.2	87,576	57.0	2,460	308
31 years	147,332	44,661	30.3	90,033	67.6	2,864	174	114,943	38,449	33.5	74,491	64.8	1,843	160
32 years	154,506	47,290	30.6	103,519	67.0	3,477	220	136,400	47,507	34.8	86,131	63.1	2,013	209
33 years	146,913	40,538	27.6	102,633	69.9	3,532	210	128,262	38,635	30.1	86,754	67.6	2,709	104
34 years	151,782	39,467	26.0	108,229	71.3	3,920	166	133,017	38,744	29.0	91,604	68.5	3,052	157
Foreign-born white:														
15 years	40,280	40,168	99.7	107	0.3	5	....	37,069	36,844	99.4	80	0.2	10	135
16 years	49,626	49,395	99.5	221	0.4	10	....	49,421	48,985	99.1	90	0.2	12	334
17 years	51,501	51,230	99.4	266	0.5	26	....	60,266	59,650	99.0	188	0.3	8	411
18 years	58,338	57,244	98.1	777	1.3	39	278	96,241	94,856	98.6	734	0.8	21	630
19 years	59,465	57,281	96.3	1,857	3.1	49	278	108,757	106,328	97.8	1,759	1.6	27	643
20 years	64,817	59,370	91.6	4,956	7.6	128	363	141,322	133,419	94.4	6,915	4.9	98	890
21 years	70,754	60,874	86.0	9,414	13.3	148	318	142,909	127,210	89.0	14,621	10.2	188	941
22 years	91,271	72,257	79.2	18,248	20.0	312	454	174,922	144,081	82.4	29,501	16.9	299	981
23 years	104,781	73,390	70.0	30,452	29.1	466	473	174,342	128,776	73.9	44,234	25.4	431	901
24 years	125,305	78,977	63.0	45,225	36.1	671	432	190,335	127,956	67.2	60,891	32.0	591	897
25 years	143,142	81,468	56.9	60,169	42.0	949	556	211,907	128,608	60.7	81,429	38.4	893	977
26 years	148,325	75,457	50.9	70,912	47.8	1,161	795	197,234	107,108	54.3	88,219	44.7	996	911
27 years	155,095	69,705	44.8	83,768	53.8	1,434	788	189,078	90,912	48.1	96,361	51.0	1,041	764
28 years	182,549	75,756	41.5	104,010	57.0	1,088	795	225,211	98,359	43.7	124,305	55.2	1,019	928
29 years	162,377	56,309	34.7	103,321	63.6	1,948	799	167,146	60,952	36.5	104,238	62.4	1,370	586
30 years	214,137	73,179	34.2	137,022	64.0	3,084	855	265,794	92,811	34.9	169,146	63.6	2,710	1,127
31 years	147,226	41,967	28.5	102,538	69.6	2,159	562	133,882	38,776	29.1	92,616	69.4	1,501	489
32 years	196,045	53,746	27.4	138,310	70.6	3,345	644	184,463	51,481	27.0	129,929	70.4	2,411	642
33 years	191,445	46,366	24.2	140,980	73.6	3,435	655	155,456	36,414	23.4	110,328	74.8	2,298	416
34 years	197,065	45,121	22.8	148,476	75.0	3,704	664	149,573	33,558	22.4	113,174	75.7	2,352	489

[1] Includes Indians, Chinese, Japanese, and "all other."   [2] Less than one-tenth of 1 per cent.

POPULATION.

TABLE 4.—MARITAL CONDITION OF THE POPULATION 15 TO 34 YEARS OF AGE, BY SEX AND SINGLE YEARS, FOR PRINCIPAL POPULATION CLASSES, FOR THE UNITED STATES: 1920 AND 1910—Continued.

CLASS OF POPULATION AND AGE.	Total.	SINGLE.		MARRIED.		Widowed or divorced.	Marital condition not reported.	Total.	SINGLE.		MARRIED.		Widowed or divorced.	Marital condition not reported.
		Number.	Per cent.	Number.	Per cent.				Number.	Per cent.	Number.	Per cent.		
				MALES: 1920							**MALES: 1910**			
Negro:														
15 years	103,063	102,805	99.7	246	0.2	12	....	101,921	101,133	99.2	119	0.1	11	658
16 years	106,028	105,415	99.4	584	0.6	29		106,679	105,427	98.8	219	0.2	29	1,004
17 years	100,059	98,441	98.4	1,568	1.6	50		100,185	98,436	98.3	806	0.8	57	886
18 years	107,218	100,882	94.1	5,560	5.2	255	521	108,316	104,136	96.1	3,068	2.8	151	961
19 years	97,048	84,100	86.7	12,085	12.5	409	454	90,844	83,021	91.4	6,852	7.5	272	699
20 years	87,789	66,456	75.7	20,164	23.0	736	433	92,494	75,738	81.9	15,265	16.5	739	752
21 years	100,001	61,911	61.9	36,459	36.5	1,249	382	100,178	68,576	68.5	29,684	29.6	1,213	705
22 years	105,414	56,167	53.3	47,008	44.6	1,847	392	101,974	59,215	58.1	40,155	39.4	1,958	646
23 years	96,854	44,293	45.7	50,145	51.8	2,077	339	92,960	44,994	48.4	45,186	48.6	2,280	401
24 years	97,111	38,768	39.9	55,577	57.2	2,472	294	94,551	39,471	41.7	51,820	54.8	2,770	490
25 years	99,348	35,011	35.2	60,946	61.3	3,057	334	101,523	37,236	36.7	60,052	59.2	3,718	517
26 years	85,079	26,695	31.4	55,392	65.1	2,720	272	83,100	26,809	32.3	52,793	63.5	3,113	385
27 years	82,241	23,105	28.1	56,154	68.3	2,722	260	77,595	22,170	28.6	51,961	67.0	3,142	322
28 years	90,327	23,126	25.6	63,752	70.6	3,159	290	93,921	24,389	26.0	65,246	69.5	3,941	345
29 years	67,357	15,476	23.0	49,151	73.0	2,506	224	65,666	14,835	22.6	47,770	72.7	2,829	232
30 years	97,320	22,822	23.5	69,737	71.7	4,457	304	114,699	26,225	22.9	81,822	71.3	6,178	474
31 years	48,377	10,063	20.8	36,136	74.7	2,058	120	45,572	8,948	19.6	34,137	74.9	2,311	176
32 years	63,499	12,782	20.1	47,571	74.9	2,953	193	63,470	11,859	18.7	48,064	75.7	3,341	206
33 years	57,278	10,052	17.5	44,349	77.4	2,710	167	52,894	8,457	16.0	41,318	78.2	2,939	150
34 years	65,105	10,469	16.1	51,448	70.0	3,022	166	55,528	8,268	14.9	43,950	79.2	3,157	147
				FEMALES: 1920							**FEMALES: 1910**			
All classes:[1]														
15 years	935,766	922,433	98.6	12,834	1.4	499	....	858,750	844,134	98.3	10,291	1.2	433	3,892
16 years	996,124	953,230	95.7	41,626	4.2	1,268		939,465	897,449	95.5	31,829	3.7	1,053	6,134
17 years	929,140	835,418	89.9	90,930	9.8	2,792		885,591	801,681	90.5	76,683	8.7	2,078	5,149
18 years	971,400	776,931	80.0	186,645	19.2	5,554	2,270	978,490	802,894	82.1	166,460	17.0	4,426	4,710
19 years	924,334	649,638	70.3	264,507	28.6	8,143	2,046	874,025	639,606	73.2	224,976	25.7	5,921	3,522
20 years	937,601	562,965	60.0	360,112	38.4	12,385	2,139	955,250	595,809	62.4	345,340	36.2	10,610	3,431
21 years	900,933	473,019	52.5	412,235	45.8	14,020	1,659	851,984	467,795	54.9	370,534	43.5	11,112	2,543
22 years	968,431	434,966	44.9	512,587	52.9	19,141	1,737	909,826	430,332	47.3	461,618	50.7	15,496	2,380
23 years	969,884	371,616	38.3	574,133	59.2	22,726	1,409	885,814	359,344	40.6	506,478	57.2	18,123	1,869
24 years	973,127	321,485	33.0	624,630	64.2	25,724	1,288	873,820	310,343	35.5	541,392	62.0	20,383	1,702
25 years	990,861	287,842	29.0	672,240	67.8	29,541	1,238	893,542	280,278	31.4	587,126	65.7	24,489	1,649
26 years	937,840	236,899	25.3	669,638	71.4	30,197	1,106	819,199	222,289	27.1	572,559	69.9	23,086	1,255
27 years	880,836	194,201	22.0	655,125	74.4	30,610	900	736,589	175,380	23.8	537,207	72.9	23,001	1,001
28 years	942,759	190,285	20.2	715,183	75.9	36,375	916	827,788	181,024	21.9	616,240	74.4	29,550	974
29 years	795,962	139,058	17.5	624,315	78.4	31,907	682	658,547	122,585	18.6	510,803	77.6	24,412	747
30 years	995,298	184,062	18.5	762,156	76.6	48,033	1,047	881,016	179,536	20.4	658,339	74.7	42,018	1,123
31 years	681,985	98,967	14.5	552,979	81.1	29,517	522	538,778	81,972	15.2	434,760	80.7	21,596	450
32 years	812,005	119,743	14.7	651,391	80.2	40,202	609	685,815	108,360	15.8	544,654	79.4	32,164	628
33 years	726,524	92,550	12.7	597,208	82.2	36,197	569	600,469	81,461	13.6	489,324	81.5	29,185	499
34 years	724,598	92,797	12.8	592,120	81.7	39,132	549	609,339	83,832	13.8	492,882	80.9	32,088	537
Native white—Native parentage:														
15 years	559,798	551,027	98.4	8,510	1.5	261	....	494,096	484,658	98.1	7,178	1.5	208	2,052
16 years	590,463	562,188	95.2	27,626	4.7	649		530,634	503,401	94.9	23,438	4.4	520	3,215
17 years	550,013	489,199	88.9	59,341	10.8	1,473		498,712	444,485	89.1	50,560	10.1	982	2,685
18 years	564,828	445,196	78.8	115,692	20.5	2,807	1,133	537,044	430,557	80.2	102,166	19.0	1,992	2,299
19 years	536,407	369,500	68.9	161,755	30.2	4,186	1,026	476,041	336,665	70.7	134,992	28.4	2,643	1,741
20 years	525,985	309,914	58.9	208,865	39.7	6,101	1,105	502,892	303,922	60.4	192,855	38.3	4,502	1,613
21 years	519,006	264,414	50.9	246,513	47.5	7,198	881	464,469	244,525	52.6	213,578	46.0	5,052	1,314
22 years	531,617	232,847	43.8	288,518	54.3	9,391	861	472,012	214,712	45.5	249,571	52.9	6,570	1,159
23 years	529,576	198,526	37.5	319,125	60.3	11,272	653	461,913	179,117	38.8	273,987	59.3	7,874	955
24 years	523,705	169,507	32.4	340,999	65.1	12,590	609	448,722	152,258	33.9	286,880	63.9	8,755	829
25 years	520,612	149,038	28.6	357,374	68.6	13,623	577	448,410	133,187	29.7	304,702	68.0	9,748	773
26 years	497,852	123,932	24.9	358,724	72.1	14,671	525	420,584	107,429	25.5	302,344	71.9	10,174	637
27 years	468,010	101,771	21.7	350,877	75.0	14,953	409	378,268	84,306	22.3	283,271	74.9	10,206	485
28 years	489,720	97,416	19.9	374,411	76.5	17,464	429	413,378	83,309	20.2	316,958	76.7	12,029	482
29 years	421,296	72,085	17.1	333,308	79.1	15,573	330	341,837	58,302	17.1	272,432	79.7	10,742	361
30 years	496,868	92,739	18.7	382,686	77.0	20,948	495	416,205	79,728	19.2	319,809	76.8	16,107	561
31 years	370,659	52,498	14.2	302,778	81.7	15,108	275	285,724	39,950	14.0	235,315	82.4	10,226	233
32 years	417,667	60,739	14.5	337,139	80.7	19,448	341	344,899	49,504	14.4	280,784	81.4	14,313	298
33 years	379,666	47,497	12.5	314,051	82.7	17,823	295	306,394	38,608	12.6	254,222	83.0	13,296	268
34 years	376,510	47,063	12.5	310,314	82.4	18,858	275	306,810	38,871	12.7	253,186	82.5	14,512	241
Native white—Foreign or mixed parentage:														
15 years	220,423	219,497	99.6	888	0.4	38	....	218,016	216,478	99.3	558	0.3	32	948
16 years	232,488	229,379	98.7	3,030	1.3	79		237,448	233,648	98.4	2,240	0.9	47	1,513
17 years	218,133	209,695	96.1	8,284	3.8	154		221,784	213,807	96.4	6,532	2.9	85	1,300
18 years	219,883	198,133	90.1	20,764	9.4	386	600	229,939	210,580	91.6	17,935	7.8	252	1,172
19 years	211,150	174,766	82.8	35,185	16.7	649	556	203,527	173,718	85.4	28,530	14.0	386	893
20 years	210,426	156,584	74.4	52,237	24.8	1,101	504	208,770	160,881	77.1	46,321	22.2	772	796
21 years	206,871	137,618	66.5	67,277	32.5	1,552	424	190,819	132,409	69.4	56,831	29.8	931	648
22 years	216,525	127,931	59.1	86,029	39.7	2,132	436	191,773	119,008	62.1	70,900	37.0	1,302	563
23 years	218,119	111,928	51.3	102,944	47.2	2,882	365	186,206	101,643	54.6	82,358	44.2	1,754	451
24 years	215,079	97,466	45.3	113,871	52.9	3,428	314	181,419	88,026	48.5	90,867	50.1	2,118	408
25 years	215,597	86,974	40.3	124,248	57.6	4,101	274	180,281	79,060	43.9	98,180	54.5	2,638	385
26 years	206,900	72,874	35.2	129,129	62.4	4,619	278	167,720	64,893	38.7	99,642	59.4	2,878	307
27 years	194,823	60,204	30.9	129,405	66.4	4,858	266	150,405	51,761	34.4	95,413	63.4	3,003	228
28 years	197,546	57,207	29.0	134,493	68.1	5,627	219	160,382	52,976	33.0	103,473	64.5	3,730	203
29 years	172,758	42,872	24.8	124,402	72.0	5,338	146	131,527	36,204	27.5	91,619	69.7	3,505	199
30 years	198,441	53,561	26.9	138,662	69.5	7,025	193	168,208	52,673	31.3	110,087	65.4	5,250	198
31 years	150,793	30,869	20.5	114,439	75.9	5,386	99	115,496	25,725	22.3	56,046	74.5	3,633	92
32 years	166,805	36,829	22.1	123,109	73.8	6,732	135	144,462	35,455	24.6	103,211	71.5	5,572	164
33 years	149,646	29,035	19.4	114,382	76.4	6,120	109	129,184	26,818	20.8	97,088	75.2	5,175	103
34 years	149,812	29,255	19.5	113,525	75.8	6,903	99	135,738	28,603	21.1	100,915	74.3	6,031	189

[1] Includes Indians, Chinese, Japanese, and "all other."

MARITAL CONDITION.

393

TABLE 4.—MARITAL CONDITION OF THE POPULATION 15 TO 34 YEARS OF AGE, BY SEX AND SINGLE YEARS, FOR PRINCIPAL POPULATION CLASSES, FOR THE UNITED STATES: 1920 AND 1910—Continued.

CLASS OF POPULATION AND AGE.	Total.	SINGLE. Number.	SINGLE. Per cent.	MARRIED. Number.	MARRIED. Per cent.	Widowed or divorced.	Marital condition not reported.	Total.	SINGLE. Number.	SINGLE. Per cent.	MARRIED. Number.	MARRIED. Per cent.	Widowed or divorced.	Marital condition not reported.
			FEMALES: 1920								FEMALES: 1910			
Foreign-born white:														
15 years	41,619	41,018	98.6	571	1.4	30	......	38,116	37,461	98.3	459	1.2	22	174
16 years	51,145	49,122	96.0	1,978	3.9	45	......	50,574	48,568	96.0	1,631	3.2	31	344
17 years	52,539	47,446	90.3	4,999	9.5	64	......	58,782	53,782	91.5	4,581	7.8	64	355
18 years	61,266	48,963	79.9	11,944	19.5	207	152	85,304	71,529	83.9	13,233	15.5	144	398
19 years	62,103	42,691	68.7	18,985	30.6	287	140	89,231	66,501	74.5	22,145	24.8	205	380
20 years	75,045	42,018	56.0	32,215	42.9	613	199	117,191	71,566	61.1	44,793	38.2	445	387
21 years	71,502	33,501	47.0	37,168	52.0	618	125	98,133	51,364	52.3	46,074	47.0	451	244
22 years	97,729	37,032	37.9	59,429	60.8	1,110	158	129,159	57,764	44.7	70,353	54.5	770	272
23 years	106,253	32,011	30.1	72,670	68.4	1,418	154	127,662	47,995	37.6	78,436	61.4	1,030	201
24 years	119,327	29,485	24.7	87,867	73.6	1,834	141	134,316	43,489	32.4	89,360	66.5	1,264	203
25 years	132,177	28,210	21.3	101,402	76.7	2,398	167	145,376	42,331	29.1	101,090	69.5	1,757	198
26 years	128,464	22,858	17.8	102,947	80.1	2,517	142	134,116	32,398	24.2	99,760	74.4	1,820	138
27 years	125,148	18,623	14.9	103,026	82.8	2,796	103	124,199	25,978	20.0	96,039	77.3	2,047	135
28 years	151,251	21,702	14.3	125,765	83.1	3,668	116	152,652	30,098	19.7	119,350	78.2	3,084	120
29 years	125,235	14,890	11.0	106,795	85.3	3,444	106	115,777	19,270	16.7	93,880	81.1	2,537	81
30 years	177,443	21,807	12.3	149,838	84.4	5,659	139	174,290	30,215	17.3	138,870	79.7	5,067	138
31 years	107,181	10,275	9.6	93,471	87.2	3,357	78	92,125	11,546	12.5	78,038	84.7	2,460	72
32 years	151,187	14,697	9.7	130,952	86.6	5,426	112	129,675	16,617	12.8	108,660	83.8	4,321	77
33 years	134,973	10,840	8.0	118,951	88.1	5,090	92	110,340	11,407	10.3	95,060	86.2	3,798	66
34 years	133,873	11,438	8.5	116,823	87.3	5,526	86	110,617	11,865	10.7	94,330	85.3	4,369	53
Negro:														
15 years	111,019	108,090	97.4	2,762	2.5	167	......	105,634	102,791	97.3	1,998	1.9	165	680
16 years	118,984	109,730	92.2	8,773	7.4	481	......	117,724	109,016	92.6	7,256	6.2	447	1,005
17 years	105,728	86,765	82.1	17,908	16.0	1,055	......	103,662	87,399	84.3	14,582	14.1	913	708
18 years	122,224	82,448	67.5	37,209	30.5	2,111	366	122,991	88,072	71.6	32,137	26.1	1,980	802
19 years	111,844	61,136	54.7	47,427	42.4	2,968	313	102,460	61,237	59.8	38,114	37.2	2,629	480
20 years	122,832	53,137	43.3	64,890	52.8	4,486	319	123,131	58,234	47.3	59,512	48.3	4,777	608
21 years	100,918	36,603	36.3	59,520	59.0	4,576	219	96,422	38,769	40.2	52,721	54.7	4,606	326
22 years	119,352	36,421	30.5	76,245	63.9	6,416	270	114,295	38,161	33.4	69,004	60.4	6,755	375
23 years	112,804	28,602	25.4	76,027	68.2	7,047	228	107,745	30,070	27.9	70,048	65.0	7,374	253
24 years	111,712	24,588	22.0	79,158	70.9	7,751	215	107,045	26,162	24.4	72,488	67.7	8,140	255
25 years	118,865	23,217	19.5	86,147	72.5	9,285	216	110,570	25,290	21.7	80,814	69.3	10,100	276
26 years	101,375	16,937	16.7	76,022	75.0	8,259	157	94,505	17,253	18.3	68,966	73.0	8,120	166
27 years	89,849	13,294	14.8	68,544	76.3	7,895	116	81,828	13,107	16.0	60,923	74.5	7,653	145
28 years	101,098	13,751	13.6	77,694	76.9	9,472	151	98,874	14,387	14.6	74,343	75.2	9,977	167
29 years	74,230	9,081	12.2	57,605	77.6	7,451	93	67,945	8,671	12.8	51,314	75.0	7,558	102
30 years	117,909	15,716	13.3	87,777	74.4	14,206	210	118,858	16,631	14.0	86,671	72.9	15,341	215
31 years	51,431	5,245	10.2	40,517	78.8	5,571	68	44,171	4,668	10.6	34,240	77.5	5,215	48
32 years	73,074	7,339	9.9	58,057	78.5	8,499	79	65,075	6,687	10.3	50,456	77.5	7,846	86
33 years	60,435	5,103	8.4	48,199	79.8	7,064	69	53,148	4,550	8.6	41,709	78.5	6,829	60
34 years	62,537	4,951	7.0	49,756	79.6	7,743	87	54,674	4,438	8.1	43,111	78.9	7,072	53

TABLE 5.—MARITAL CONDITION OF THE TOTAL POPULATION, BY SEX AND AGE PERIODS,

CLASS OF POPULATION AND AGE PERIOD.	MALES: 1920						MALES: 1910						MALES: 1900					
	Single.		Married.		Widowed or divorced.		Single.		Married.		Widowed or divorced.		Single.		Married.		Widowed or divorced.	
	Number.	Per cent.	Number.	Per cent.	Number.	Per cent.	Number.	Per cent.	Number.	Per cent.	Number.	Per cent.	Number.	Per cent.	Number.	Per cent.	Number.	Per cent.
All classes	**29,944,007**	**55.6**	**21,852,439**	**40.5**	**1,993,745**	**3.7**	**27,455,607**	**58.0**	**18,093,498**	**38.2**	**1,627,648**	**3.4**	**23,492,923**	**60.5**	**13,956,314**	**36.0**	**1,262,245**	**3.3**
Under 15 years of age	16,976,442	100.0	3,173	(1)	153	(1)	14,905,478	100.0	898	(1)	96	(1)	13,194,983	100.0	664	(1)	39	(1)
15 years and over	12,967,565	35.1	21,849,266	59.2	1,993,592	5.4	12,550,129	38.7	18,092,600	55.8	1,627,552	5.0	10,297,940	40.2	13,955,650	54.5	1,262,206	4.9
15 to 19 years	4,567,770	97.7	96,374	2.1	2,589	0.1	4,448,067	98.3	51,877	1.1	1,457	(1)	3,706,382	98.8	37,781	1.0	1,065	(1)
20 to 24 years	3,200,623	70.7	1,280,318	28.3	30,791	0.7	3,432,161	74.9	1,100,093	24.0	25,547	0.6	2,812,113	77.6	782,907	21.0	17,654	0.5
25 to 34 years	2,785,590	32.1	5,685,481	65.6	176,860	2.0	2,767,957	35.0	4,964,769	62.8	145,002	1.8	2,321,446	37.3	3,772,349	60.6	115,618	1.9
35 to 44 years	1,188,586	16.1	5,873,308	79.8	284,292	3.9	1,026,502	16.7	4,873,153	79.2	241,389	3.9	826,201	17.0	3,840,575	78.8	197,105	4.0
45 to 54 years	677,420	12.0	4,580,056	81.0	386,138	6.8	499,751	11.1	3,658,931	81.5	322,724	7.2	349,429	10.3	2,797,354	82.2	250,154	7.4
55 to 64 years	337,592	9.8	2,697,429	77.9	420,836	12.2	222,950	8.3	2,112,699	79.0	334,095	12.5	156,823	7.6	1,044,373	79.7	257,721	12.5
65 years and over	182,211	7.3	1,607,187	64.7	687,162	27.7	123,322	6.2	1,303,768	65.6	552,133	27.8	89,152	5.7	1,044,051	67.1	417,920	26.9
Age unknown	27,773	29.9	29,113	31.3	4,924	5.3	29,419	25.7	27,310	23.9	5,205	4.5	36,394	28.6	36,260	28.5	4,909	3.9
Native white—Native parentage	**17,319,288**	**58.4**	**11,246,113**	**37.9**	**1,009,690**	**3.4**	**15,180,989**	**60.2**	**9,144,513**	**36.2**	**816,383**	**3.2**	**12,956,535**	**62.1**	**7,194,236**	**34.5**	**635,907**	**3.0**
Under 15 years of age	10,542,770	100.0	1,824	(1)	80	(1)	8,995,665	100.0	414	(1)	44	(1)	7,761,272	100.0	314	(1)	20	(1)
15 years and over	6,776,518	35.5	11,244,289	58.9	1,009,610	5.3	6,185,324	38.1	9,144,099	56.3	816,339	5.0	5,195,263	39.7	7,193,922	55.0	635,887	4.9
15 to 19 years	2,727,715	97.5	64,392	2.3	1,460	0.1	2,504,473	98.1	33,818	1.3	706	(1)	2,094,924	98.7	24,687	1.2	570	(1)
20 to 24 years	1,747,256	68.6	774,580	30.4	17,011	0.7	1,691,385	72.5	618,300	26.5	12,633	0.5	1,445,161	75.9	444,361	23.3	8,945	0.5
25 to 34 years	1,272,312	28.8	3,046,796	68.9	94,329	2.1	1,181,751	31.2	2,524,551	66.6	72,167	1.9	1,023,796	34.0	1,918,933	63.8	57,951	1.9
35 to 44 years	491,663	13.9	2,909,069	82.0	140,745	4.0	415,192	14.5	2,319,342	81.3	114,435	4.0	337,156	14.7	1,852,064	80.9	95,827	4.2
45 to 54 years	280,785	10.6	2,184,378	82.4	180,708	6.8	209,014	9.8	1,757,732	82.8	152,575	7.2	157,321	9.0	1,405,221	83.8	123,923	7.1
55 to 64 years	149,315	8.8	1,347,772	79.1	204,812	12.0	106,387	7.5	1,144,917	80.4	170,767	12.0	72,914	6.7	887,317	81.5	127,269	11.7
65 years and over	91,915	6.7	902,207	66.1	367,953	26.9	61,042	5.6	733,401	67.3	290,510	26.7	43,703	5.1	585,534	68.9	219,240	25.8
Age unknown	15,557	26.5	15,095	25.7	2,592	4.4	16,080	23.4	12,038	17.5	2,546	3.7	20,288	26.4	15,805	20.6	2,162	2.8
Native white—Foreign or mixed parentage	**7,424,961**	**65.9**	**3,551,600**	**31.5**	**277,251**	**2.5**	**6,545,950**	**69.5**	**2,677,885**	**28.4**	**185,482**	**2.0**	**5,805,576**	**74.1**	**1,906,489**	**24.3**	**117,479**	**1.5**
Under 15 years of age	4,273,861	100.0	718	(1)	33	(1)	3,639,908	100.0	179	(1)	15	(1)	3,373,202	100.0	109	(1)	2	(1)
15 years and over	3,151,100	45.1	3,550,882	50.8	277,218	4.0	2,906,042	50.2	2,677,706	46.3	185,467	3.2	2,432,374	54.5	1,906,380	42.7	117,477	2.6
15 to 19 years	1,075,102	99.1	8,204	0.8	234	(1)	1,085,405	99.1	3,635	0.3	126	(1)	860,621	99.6	2,582	0.3	71	(1)
20 to 24 years	824,859	81.3	183,265	18.1	3,474	0.3	769,574	84.2	138,537	15.2	2,122	0.2	681,067	86.7	101,042	12.9	1,677	0.2
25 to 34 years	685,418	40.1	992,520	58.1	28,952	1.7	624,710	43.9	774,476	54.5	19,891	1.4	617,634	47.3	666,690	51.1	18,394	1.4
35 to 44 years	279,460	21.6	967,387	74.8	45,734	3.5	259,678	22.7	842,217	73.6	40,436	3.5	195,610	21.8	667,384	74.4	32,540	3.6
45 to 54 years	175,720	17.1	785,439	76.5	64,669	6.3	116,902	15.1	602,333	78.0	52,375	6.8	54,548	14.0	308,522	79.0	27,019	6.9
55 to 64 years	80,862	13.5	449,369	74.8	70,142	11.7	35,782	11.8	231,268	76.1	36,521	12.0	15,316	10.5	111,448	76.7	18,399	12.7
65 years and over	26,810	10.6	162,714	64.2	63,592	25.1	11,448	8.9	83,384	64.8	33,630	26.1	5,479	7.6	46,957	65.4	19,208	26.8
Age unknown	2,869	49.2	1,984	34.0	421	7.2	2,543	45.1	1,856	32.9	366	6.5	2,099	43.2	1,755	36.1	169	3.5
Native white—Foreign parentage [2]	**5,158,428**	**66.0**	**2,445,770**	**31.3**	**197,832**	**2.5**	**4,386,006**	**67.9**	**1,926,201**	**29.8**	**133,527**	**2.1**	...	...	...	...	...	...
Under 15 years of age	3,017,118	100.0	479	(1)	23	(1)	2,396,879	100.0	126	(1)	10	(1)	...	...	...	...	...	...
15 years and over	2,141,310	44.7	2,445,291	51.0	197,809	4.1	1,989,127	49.0	1,926,075	47.4	133,517	3.3	...	...	...	...	...	...
15 to 19 years	701,637	99.1	4,896	0.7	151	(1)	712,993	99.1	2,232	0.3	72	(1)	...	...	...	...	...	...
20 to 24 years	551,884	81.6	119,851	17.7	2,107	0.3	510,431	84.0	93,069	15.3	1,288	0.2	...	...	...	...	...	...
25 to 34 years	467,578	40.6	662,155	57.6	18,579	1.6	431,080	44.4	525,379	54.1	12,998	1.3	...	...	...	...	...	...
35 to 44 years	196,345	22.6	639,164	73.7	30,428	3.5	200,710	23.7	615,593	72.7	29,613	3.5	...	...	...	...	...	...
45 to 54 years	135,804	18.2	561,888	75.3	47,427	6.4	95,687	15.8	467,794	77.3	40,872	6.8	...	...	...	...	...	...
55 to 64 years	65,414	14.2	342,016	74.0	54,225	11.7	28,226	12.6	168,991	75.3	27,117	12.1	...	...	...	...	...	...
65 years and over	20,572	11.5	113,895	63.5	44,595	24.9	8,151	10.0	51,654	63.6	21,289	26.2	...	...	...	...	...	...
Age unknown	2,076	49.3	1,426	33.8	297	7.0	1,849	45.1	1,363	33.3	268	6.5	...	...	...	...	...	...
Native white—Mixed parentage [2]	**2,266,533**	**65.6**	**1,105,830**	**32.0**	**79,419**	**2.3**	**2,159,944**	**72.8**	**751,684**	**25.3**	**51,955**	**1.8**	...	...	...	...	...	...
Under 15 years of age	1,256,743	100.0	239	(1)	10	(1)	1,243,029	100.0	53	(1)	5	(1)	...	...	...	...	...	...
15 years and over	1,009,790	45.9	1,105,591	50.3	79,409	3.6	916,915	53.1	751,631	43.6	51,950	3.0	...	...	...	...	...	...
15 to 19 years	373,465	99.0	3,308	0.9	83	(1)	372,412	99.1	1,403	0.4	54	(1)	...	...	...	...	...	...
20 to 24 years	272,975	80.6	63,414	18.7	1,367	0.4	259,143	84.5	45,468	14.8	834	0.3	...	...	...	...	...	...
25 to 34 years	217,840	38.9	330,365	59.1	10,373	1.9	193,630	43.0	249,097	55.3	6,893	1.5	...	...	...	...	...	...
35 to 44 years	83,115	19.5	328,223	76.9	15,306	3.6	58,968	19.9	226,624	76.4	10,823	3.6	...	...	...	...	...	...
45 to 54 years	39,916	14.2	223,551	79.6	17,242	6.1	21,215	12.7	134,539	80.4	11,503	6.9	...	...	...	...	...	...
55 to 64 years	15,448	11.1	107,353	77.3	15,917	11.5	7,556	9.5	62,277	78.5	9,404	11.9	...	...	...	...	...	...
65 years and over	6,238	8.4	48,819	65.8	18,997	25.6	3,297	7.0	31,730	66.9	12,341	26.0	...	...	...	...	...	...
Age unknown	793	40.0	558	34.5	124	7.7	694	45.0	493	32.0	98	6.4	...	...	...	...	...	...
Foreign-born white	**2,130,562**	**28.3**	**4,903,186**	**65.1**	**470,023**	**6.2**	**2,652,619**	**35.3**	**4,432,298**	**58.9**	**407,814**	**5.4**	**1,803,634**	**32.7**	**3,355,624**	**60.8**	**339,786**	**6.2**
Under 15 years of age	275,515	99.9	244	0.1	24	(1)	383,703	99.9	163	(1)	29	(1)	257,841	100.0	68	(1)	2	(1)
15 years and over	1,855,047	25.6	4,902,942	67.6	469,999	6.5	2,268,916	31.8	4,432,135	62.1	407,785	5.7	1,545,793	29.4	3,355,556	63.8	339,784	6.5
15 to 19 years	255,327	98.5	3,258	1.3	129	(1)	346,672	98.6	2,851	0.8	78	(1)	269,028	99.1	1,815	0.7	65	(1)
20 to 24 years	344,868	75.5	108,295	23.7	1,725	0.4	661,481	80.3	156,222	19.0	1,607	0.2	375,442	82.3	78,117	17.1	918	0.2
25 to 34 years	619,161	35.6	1,089,515	62.7	23,207	1.3	738,979	39.3	1,115,745	59.4	17,191	0.9	485,308	38.8	747,770	59.8	13,729	1.1
35 to 44 years	317,080	17.5	1,436,395	79.3	53,228	2.9	269,854	17.3	1,246,128	79.7	43,482	2.8	219,013	17.8	971,973	79.0	36,786	3.0
45 to 54 years	170,915	12.2	1,137,747	81.5	84,084	6.0	137,594	11.6	970,464	82.1	72,309	6.1	103,458	11.4	741,917	81.7	61,536	6.8
55 to 64 years	89,194	10.0	700,795	78.2	104,611	11.7	64,807	9.1	557,016	78.2	89,100	12.5	54,942	8.7	493,193	78.2	81,693	12.9
65 years and over	52,979	7.8	422,265	62.2	202,153	29.8	43,229	7.1	379,197	62.5	183,161	30.2	32,898	6.7	315,040	63.8	144,097	29.2
Age unknown	5,523	40.2	4,672	34.0	862	6.3	6,300	32.0	4,512	22.9	857	4.3	5,704	35.3	5,725	35.5	960	5.9
Negro	**2,920,711**	**56.1**	**2,050,782**	**39.4**	**227,439**	**4.4**	**2,909,902**	**59.6**	**1,749,359**	**35.8**	**210,124**	**4.3**	**2,786,580**	**63.5**	**1,423,039**	**32.4**	**162,273**	**3.7**
Under 15 years of age	1,815,834	100.0	375	(1)	16	(1)	1,826,430	100.0	131	(1)	8	(1)	1,753,295	100.0	153	(1)	14	(1)
15 years and over	1,104,877	32.6	2,050,407	60.4	227,423	6.7	1,083,472	35.4	1,749,228	57.2	210,116	6.9	1,033,285	39.2	1,422,886	54.0	162,259	6.2
15 to 19 years	491,643	95.8	20,043	3.9	755	0.1	492,153	96.9	11,064	2.2	520	0.1	463,928	97.9	8,196	1.7	333	0.1
20 to 24 years	267,595	54.9	209,353	43.0	8,381	1.7	287,994	59.7	182,110	37.8	8,969	1.9	295,175	64.3	155,016	33.8	5,877	1.3
25 to 34 years	189,601	25.1	534,636	70.7	29,364	3.9	189,196	25.1	527,149	69.9	34,669	4.6	173,728	27.9	421,514	67.7	24,635	4.0
35 to 44 years	87,260	13.2	527,996	80.1	42,864	6.5	67,203	12.2	439,901	80.0	41,602	7.6	54,358	13.2	326,172	79.1	30,709	7.4
45 to 54 years	42,948	7.8	449,997	82.0	54,619	10.0	25,869	6.8	308,831	81.4	43,922	11.6	23,267	7.2	263,510	81.4	36,186	11.2
55 to 64 years	13,967	5.8	187,471	77.7	39,376	16.3	10,792	5.0	168,881	78.1	36,141	16.7	9,626	5.3	144,027	78.6	29,183	15.9
65 years and over	8,444	4.9	113,864	65.5	51,054	29.4	6,285	4.1	102,670	67.3	42,890	28.1	6,103	4.6	92,535	69.6	33,892	25.5
Age unknown	3,419	25.3	7,047	52.2	1,010	7.5	3,980	23.3	8,622	50.5	1,403	8.2	7,100	28.2	11,916	47.4	1,494	5.9
Indian, all ages	75,190	60.1	43,102	34.5	6,391	5.1	82,133	60.8	46,162	34.2	5,998	4.4	71,703	60.0	41,086	34.4	5,393	4.5
15 years and over	26,450	34.7	43,095	56.5	6,391	8.4	27,391	34.1	46,154	57.4	5,998	7.5	24,323	33.7	41,067	57.0	5,392	7.5
Chinese, all ages	27,167	50.4	24,784	46.0	1,421	2.6	36,790	55.0	26,451	39.6	1,184	1.8	50,704	59.4	31,794	37.3	1,329	1.6
15 years and over	23,096	46.4	24,782	49.7	1,421	2.9	34,330	53.3	26,449	41.1	1,184	1.8	48,997	58.6	31,794	38.0	1,329	1.6
Japanese, all ages	39,700	54.6	31,253	43.0	1,272	1.7	45,222	71.7	15,918	25.2	581	0.9	18,191	78.0	4,046	17.3	78	0.3
15 years and over	24,423	42.5	31,250	54.4	1,272	2.2	42,688	70.5	15,918	26.3	581	1.0	17,905	77.7	4,045	17.5	78	0.3
All other, all ages	6,428	74.1	1,619	18.7	258	3.0	2,002	64.7	912	29.5	82	2.7	...	...	...	...	...	...
15 years and over	6,054	72.9	1,619	19.5	258	3.1	1,966	64.4	911	29.8	82	2.7	...	...	...	...	...	...

[1] Less than one-tenth of 1 per cent.

FOR PRINCIPAL POPULATION CLASSES, FOR THE UNITED STATES: 1920, 1910, AND 1900.

CLASS OF POPULATION AND AGE PERIOD.	FEMALES: 1920						FEMALES: 1910						FEMALES: 1900					
	Single.		Married.		Widowed or divorced.		Single.		Married.		Widowed or divorced.		Single.		Married.		Widowed or divorced.	
	Number.	Per cent.	Number.	Per cent.	Number.	Per cent.	Number.	Per cent.	Number.	Per cent.	Number.	Per cent.	Number.	Per cent.	Number.	Per cent.	Number.	Per cent.
All classes	26,243,696	50.7	21,324,487	41.2	4,191,255	8.1	23,522,121	52.7	17,688,169	39.6	3,361,527	7.5	20,491,042	55.1	13,813,787	37.2	2,832,516	7.6
Under 15 years of age	16,626,794	100.0	5,554	(1)	326	(1)	14,588,951	100.0	3,482	(1)	231	(1)	12,924,512	100.0	3,730	(1)	154	(1)
15 years and over	9,616,902	27.3	21,318,933	60.6	4,190,929	11.9	8,933,170	29.7	17,684,687	58.9	3,361,296	11.2	7,566,530	31.2	13,810,057	57.0	2,832,362	11.7
15 to 19 years	4,137,650	87.0	596,542	12.5	18,256	0.4	3,985,704	87.9	513,239	11.3	13,011	0.3	3,374,814	88.7	415,682	10.9	11,754	0.3
20 to 24 years	2,104,051	45.0	2,483,607	52.3	93,906	2.0	2,163,683	48.3	2,225,302	49.7	75,724	1.7	1,913,552	51.0	1,726,296	46.5	65,009	1.8
25 to 34 years	1,636,404	19.3	6,492,355	76.5	351,711	4.1	1,510,726	20.9	5,443,804	75.1	281,589	3.9	1,324,284	22.6	4,281,055	73.0	249,636	4.3
35 to 44 years	767,882	11.4	5,426,434	80.3	560,520	8.3	628,516	11.4	4,410,310	80.1	461,165	8.4	481,608	11.1	3,451,375	79.5	402,630	9.3
45 to 54 years	404,838	9.0	3,587,704	74.0	787,620	16.3	331,573	8.5	2,904,043	74.8	642,320	16.6	234,413	7.8	2,212,223	73.9	545,507	18.2
55 to 64 years	257,029	8.4	1,878,478	61.2	929,813	30.3	167,901	7.1	1,470,454	62.2	720,652	30.7	128,954	6.6	1,172,904	60.5	635,837	32.6
65 years and over	173,442	7.1	830,160	33.9	1,440,230	58.8	124,223	6.3	687,335	35.0	1,147,461	58.4	90,858	6.0	521,220	34.2	900,259	59.8
Age unknown	15,606	28.0	23,473	42.0	8,783	15.7	14,604	26.9	21,050	38.5	9,474	17.3	17,987	24.6	29,302	40.1	12,010	16.4
Native white—Native parentage	15,520,296	53.9	11,190,314	38.9	2,037,916	7.1	13,377,257	55.1	9,221,615	38.0	1,623,705	6.7	11,428,302	56.9	7,258,852	36.1	1,304,988	6.9
Under 15 years of age	10,251,806	100.0	3,449	(1)	173	(1)	8,733,135	100.0	2,230	(1)	92	(1)	7,534,885	100.0	2,477	(1)	69	(1)
15 years and over	5,268,490	28.4	11,186,865	60.4	2,037,743	11.0	4,644,122	29.9	9,219,385	59.4	1,623,613	10.5	3,893,417	31.0	7,251,375	57.7	1,304,919	11.1
15 to 19 years	2,417,119	86.3	372,924	13.3	9,376	0.3	2,190,856	86.7	318,334	12.5	6,345	0.3	1,847,495	87.5	257,800	12.2	5,425	0.3
20 to 24 years	1,175,208	44.7	1,404,020	53.4	46,552	1.8	1,094,534	46.6	1,216,851	51.8	32,753	1.4	925,631	48.7	940,586	49.8	27,403	1.4
25 to 34 years	844,778	19.0	3,421,662	77.1	168,469	3.8	713,194	19.5	2,823,023	77.1	121,953	3.3	598,797	20.9	2,154,663	75.3	104,071	3.7
35 to 44 years	367,563	10.9	2,747,693	81.0	250,249	7.4	284,455	10.8	2,163,079	81.0	192,085	7.3	231,667	11.0	1,700,587	80.8	172,308	8.1
45 to 54 years	215,435	9.2	1,780,111	76.1	341,835	14.6	162,000	8.5	1,455,051	76.7	279,908	14.7	135,793	8.5	1,202,478	75.6	250,707	15.8
55 to 64 years	130,330	8.4	975,239	63.1	430,031	28.3	99,801	7.7	833,750	64.5	358,250	27.7	84,174	7.8	671,596	62.1	324,444	30.0
65 years and over	108,305	7.9	480,833	35.0	780,008	56.8	82,137	7.4	398,184	35.8	628,809	56.6	66,846	7.0	205,754	34.2	506,431	58.6
Age unknown	9,701	29.0	13,383	40.1	4,023	12.0	8,139	28.3	10,213	35.5	3,510	12.2	9,014	25.6	12,812	36.4	3,530	10.0
Native white—Foreign or mixed parentage	6,877,259	60.2	3,891,560	34.1	643,611	5.6	6,038,152	63.7	3,008,927	31.8	412,552	4.4	5,318,434	68.1	2,213,191	28.3	273,601	3.5
Under 15 years of age	4,208,816	100.0	690	(1)	38	(1)	3,585,135	100.0	304	(1)	28	(1)	3,333,145	100.0	245	(1)	14	(1)
15 years and over	2,668,443	37.0	3,890,870	54.0	643,573	8.9	2,453,017	41.7	3,008,623	51.1	412,524	7.0	1,985,289	44.4	2,212,946	49.4	273,587	6.1
15 to 19 years	1,031,470	93.6	68,151	6.2	1,306	0.1	1,048,201	94.4	55,795	5.0	802	0.1	837,120	94.9	43,832	5.0	712	0.1
20 to 24 years	631,527	59.2	422,358	39.6	11,002	1.0	601,067	62.8	347,277	36.2	6,877	0.7	534,754	64.9	282,517	34.3	6,270	0.8
25 to 34 years	499,800	27.7	1,245,794	69.1	56,709	3.1	454,177	30.6	985,683	66.5	41,415	2.8	416,387	31.5	864,820	65.3	41,548	3.1
35 to 44 years	242,258	18.0	1,005,802	74.7	97,196	7.2	207,030	17.8	867,878	74.7	85,361	7.4	139,149	16.0	655,016	75.4	73,724	8.5
45 to 54 years	156,500	15.3	710,571	69.6	153,718	15.0	99,148	13.2	531,859	70.9	119,027	15.9	39,244	10.7	261,969	71.5	64,732	17.7
55 to 64 years	77,012	12.9	346,364	57.5	177,365	29.4	29,302	10.1	174,054	59.9	87,022	29.9	11,744	8.5	81,219	58.9	44,900	32.5
65 years and over	26,582	10.1	89,813	34.2	145,530	55.5	10,899	8.0	44,426	35.0	71,428	56.3	5,502	7.9	22,379	32.3	41,377	59.7
Age unknown	2,394	44.4	2,017	37.4	657	12.2	2,143	44.0	1,651	33.9	592	12.2	1,389	42.3	1,194	36.4	315	9.6
Native white—Foreign parentage[2]	4,768,233	60.5	2,648,525	33.6	461,384	5.9	4,026,839	62.3	2,128,379	32.9	295,348	4.6	....	....	....	....	....	....
Under 15 years of age	2,976,962	100.0	471	(1)	28	(1)	2,366,719	100.0	214	(1)	13	(1)	....	....	....	....	....	....
15 years and over	1,791,271	36.5	2,648,054	54.0	461,356	9.4	1,660,120	40.6	2,128,165	52.0	295,335	7.2	....	....	....	....	....	....
15 to 19 years	674,765	93.5	45,336	6.3	747	0.1	689,242	94.2	37,924	5.2	458	0.1	....	....	....	....	....	....
20 to 24 years	417,140	58.9	283,156	40.0	6,809	1.0	392,180	62.0	234,717	37.1	4,135	0.7	....	....	....	....	....	....
25 to 34 years	327,577	27.0	823,381	69.3	36,170	3.0	307,391	31.0	656,285	66.2	26,092	2.7	....	....	....	....	....	....
35 to 44 years	166,760	18.8	656,869	73.9	64,442	7.3	159,071	18.7	630,802	74.0	62,334	7.3	....	....	....	....	....	....
45 to 54 years	120,476	16.2	509,685	68.5	112,858	15.2	80,946	13.8	412,518	70.3	93,318	15.9	....	....	....	....	....	....
55 to 64 years	63,214	13.5	264,796	56.8	138,020	29.6	22,630	10.0	127,107	59.3	64,393	30.0	....	....	....	....	....	....
65 years and over	19,654	10.6	63,422	34.2	101,787	55.0	7,087	9.0	27,550	35.2	43,622	55.7	....	....	....	....	....	....
Age unknown	1,685	44.5	1,409	37.2	463	12.2	1,573	45.1	1,172	33.6	413	11.8	....	....	....	....	....	....
Native white—Mixed parentage[2]	2,109,026	59.6	1,243,035	35.1	182,227	5.2	2,011,313	66.8	880,548	29.2	117,204	3.9	....	....	....	....	....	....
Under 15 years of age	1,231,854	100.0	219	(1)	10	(1)	1,218,416	100.0	90	(1)	15	(1)	....	....	....	....	....	....
15 years and over	877,172	38.1	1,242,816	53.9	182,217	7.9	792,897	44.2	880,458	49.1	117,189	6.5	....	....	....	....	....	....
15 to 19 years	356,705	93.8	22,815	6.0	559	0.1	350,049	94.7	17,871	4.7	344	0.1	....	....	....	....	....	....
20 to 24 years	214,387	59.8	139,202	38.8	4,223	1.2	209,787	64.3	112,560	34.5	2,742	0.8	....	....	....	....	....	....
25 to 34 years	172,223	28.0	422,413	68.6	20,530	3.3	146,786	29.9	329,398	67.0	14,753	3.0	....	....	....	....	....	....
35 to 44 years	75,498	16.5	348,933	76.3	32,754	7.2	47,959	15.6	237,079	76.9	23,027	7.5	....	....	....	....	....	....
45 to 54 years	36,024	13.0	200,886	72.3	40,860	14.7	18,202	11.1	119,341	73.1	25,709	15.7	....	....	....	....	....	....
55 to 64 years	14,698	10.8	81,568	60.1	39,345	29.0	6,732	8.8	46,857	61.4	22,629	29.7	....	....	....	....	....	....
65 years and over	6,928	9.0	26,391	34.2	43,743	56.7	3,812	7.9	16,876	34.8	27,806	57.3	....	....	....	....	....	....
Age unknown	709	44.0	608	37.7	194	12.0	570	41.4	479	34.8	179	13.0	....	....	....	....	....	....
Foreign-born white	1,105,893	17.9	4,123,806	66.7	946,961	15.3	1,369,303	23.5	3,624,215	62.3	820,700	14.1	1,121,558	23.9	2,855,654	60.8	715,114	15.2
Under 15 years of age	270,094	99.9	303	0.1	50	(1)	375,193	99.9	212	0.1	46	(1)	252,958	99.9	208	0.1	11	(1)
15 years and over	835,799	14.1	4,123,503	69.7	946,911	16.0	994,110	18.3	3,624,003	66.5	820,654	15.1	868,600	19.5	2,855,446	64.2	715,103	16.1
15 to 19 years	229,240	85.3	38,477	14.3	663	0.2	277,841	86.3	42,049	13.1	406	0.1	258,007	88.9	31,646	10.9	368	0.1
20 to 24 years	174,137	37.1	289,340	61.6	5,503	1.2	272,178	44.9	329,016	54.3	3,909	0.7	247,010	53.3	212,085	45.8	3,461	0.7
25 to 34 years	175,340	12.8	1,150,570	84.2	39,881	2.9	231,734	18.0	1,025,086	79.6	31,200	2.4	196,013	19.2	794,764	77.9	28,890	2.8
35 to 44 years	110,355	8.2	1,148,448	84.8	93,012	6.9	98,440	8.6	965,480	84.1	83,451	7.3	76,223	8.3	765,794	83.8	70,900	7.8
45 to 54 years	72,875	6.8	822,430	76.8	174,596	16.3	54,034	6.1	687,718	77.4	145,798	16.4	44,164	6.0	548,709	74.6	141,584	19.3
55 to 64 years	40,000	5.6	457,166	62.8	220,243	31.5	31,728	5.2	372,214	61.1	204,571	33.6	26,377	4.7	334,735	60.1	195,230	35.0
65 years and over	31,726	4.9	213,713	32.9	401,812	61.9	25,790	4.5	199,737	34.7	349,069	60.7	18,782	4.1	164,144	36.0	272,483	59.7
Age unknown	1,520	23.4	3,342	51.2	1,211	18.5	1,765	27.1	2,697	41.5	1,470	22.6	2,024	23.1	3,569	40.8	2,178	24.9
Negro	2,654,719	50.5	2,040,252	38.8	551,895	10.5	2,661,778	53.9	1,776,643	36.0	498,179	10.0	2,559,682	57.6	1,444,583	32.5	436,194	9.8
Under 15 years of age	1,829,461	99.9	1,071	0.1	63	(1)	1,837,782	100.0	694	(1)	62	(1)	1,755,999	100.0	716	(1)	54	(1)
15 years and over	825,258	24.1	2,039,181	59.6	551,832	16.1	823,996	26.6	1,775,949	57.2	498,117	15.9	803,683	29.9	1,443,817	53.7	436,140	16.2
15 to 19 years	448,169	78.7	114,169	20.0	6,782	1.2	448,515	81.2	94,087	17.0	6,134	1.1	423,040	83.2	79,400	15.6	5,054	1.0
20 to 24 years	179,411	31.6	356,740	62.8	30,276	5.3	191,396	34.9	323,773	59.0	31,652	5.8	202,802	39.8	278,436	54.6	27,891	5.5
25 to 34 years	114,634	13.5	650,348	76.4	85,445	10.0	115,682	14.5	592,547	74.5	85,801	10.8	111,523	17.4	453,660	71.0	73,101	11.4
35 to 44 years	46,996	7.0	508,417	75.4	117,707	17.5	38,105	7.1	401,609	74.4	98,887	18.4	34,144	8.0	310,650	72.3	84,001	19.6
45 to 54 years	19,683	4.9	266,087	66.2	115,747	28.8	15,537	4.7	220,800	66.4	95,853	28.8	14,933	5.1	191,912	65.3	86,359	29.4
55 to 64 years	7,973	4.2	95,605	50.7	84,682	44.9	6,946	3.9	95,023	52.8	77,547	43.1	6,499	4.1	81,799	51.9	68,900	43.7
65 years and over	6,516	4.1	43,271	27.2	108,343	68.2	5,243	3.7	42,404	29.9	93,421	66.0	5,557	4.3	37,076	28.9	85,100	66.3
Age unknown	1,876	18.8	4,484	44.9	2,790	27.9	2,572	18.4	6,246	44.7	3,822	27.4	5,005	21.5	10,785	45.6	5,734	24.2
Indian, all ages	65,136	54.6	43,961	36.8	10,045	8.4	69,850	53.5	49,134	37.6	11,033	8.5	60,427	51.3	43,990	37.4	12,334	10.5
15 years and over	16,238	23.1	43,923	62.4	10,043	14.3	16,324	21.2	49,095	63.8	11,030	14.3	14,350	20.1	43,906	61.4	12,328	17.2
Chinese, all ages	4,302	55.5	3,047	39.3	386	5.0	2,398	51.3	2,018	43.2	234	5.0	2,096	46.3	2,157	47.7	262	5.8
15 years and over	962	21.8	3,046	69.1	386	8.8	680	23.0	2,016	68.2	234	7.9	778	24.3	2,157	67.3	262	8.2
Japanese, all ages	15,663	40.9	22,195	57.9	411	1.1	3,346	36.8	5,582	61.4	113	1.2	543	55.1	410	41.6	23	2.3
15 years and over	1,604	6.6	22,193	91.5	411	1.7	908	13.7	5,581	84.0	113	1.7	413	48.3	410	48.0	23	2.7
All other, all ages	428	52.6	352	43.2	30	3.7	37	....	35	....	11	....	....	....	....	....	....	....
15 years and over	108	21.9	352	71.3	30	6.1	13	....	35	....	11	....	....	....	....	....	....	....

[2] The tabulation by marital condition was not made separately in 1900 for persons of foreign parentage and persons of mixed parentage.

396

POPULATION.

TABLE 6.—MARITAL CONDITION OF THE TOTAL POPULATION, BY SEX, BY DIVISIONS AND STATES: 1920.

DIVISION AND STATE.	Total population.	MALES.						FEMALES.					
		Total.	Single.	Married.	Widowed.	Divorced.	Marital condition not reported.	Total.	Single.	Married.	Widowed.	Divorced.	Marital condition not reported.
United States	105,710,620	53,900,431	29,944,007	21,852,439	1,758,426	235,319	110,240	51,810,189	26,243,696	21,324,487	3,917,894	273,361	50,751
GEOGRAPHIC DIVISIONS:													
New England	7,400,909	3,672,591	1,994,175	1,522,419	137,318	14,408	4,271	3,728,318	1,907,596	1,485,593	315,114	17,441	2,574
Middle Atlantic	22,261,144	11,206,445	6,131,062	4,659,423	368,608	23,741	23,611	11,054,699	5,607,137	4,519,088	888,799	29,377	10,298
East North Central	21,475,543	11,035,041	5,831,486	4,693,257	398,375	61,991	16,932	10,440,502	5,084,600	4,545,782	785,074	65,995	9,051
West North Central	12,544,249	6,459,067	3,610,512	2,597,238	206,480	31,543	13,294	6,085,182	3,075,632	2,556,312	411,497	34,730	7,011
South Atlantic	13,990,272	7,035,843	4,114,707	2,586,983	207,114	10,263	10,826	6,954,429	3,754,938	2,655,409	513,835	23,114	7,133
East South Central	8,893,307	4,471,690	2,566,250	1,742,287	142,313	15,263	5,577	4,421,617	2,331,908	1,726,261	334,731	24,931	3,786
West South Central	10,242,224	5,265,829	3,036,174	2,027,629	166,014	22,869	13,143	4,976,395	2,610,498	1,989,707	339,278	31,248	5,664
Mountain	3,336,101	1,789,299	1,027,684	683,270	56,181	13,432	8,732	1,546,802	780,426	654,620	98,283	11,514	1,959
Pacific	5,566,871	2,964,626	1,558,957	1,239,983	106,023	35,809	13,854	2,602,245	1,140,961	1,191,715	231,283	35,911	2,375
NEW ENGLAND:													
Maine	768,014	388,752	201,312	166,215	18,126	2,628	471	379,262	179,615	162,664	34,018	2,685	280
New Hampshire	443,083	222,112	114,855	94,804	10,325	1,762	366	220,971	106,040	92,362	20,437	1,845	287
Vermont	352,428	178,854	92,833	76,319	8,373	1,171	158	173,574	81,977	74,517	15,989	1,014	77
Massachusetts	3,852,356	1,890,014	1,038,825	775,781	67,586	5,825	1,997	1,962,342	1,026,961	758,994	167,264	8,000	1,123
Rhode Island	604,397	297,524	164,233	121,224	10,712	1,226	129	306,873	161,540	118,794	24,577	1,834	128
Connecticut	1,380,631	695,335	382,117	288,076	22,196	1,796	1,150	685,296	351,463	278,262	52,829	2,063	679
MIDDLE ATLANTIC:													
New York	10,385,227	5,187,350	2,804,260	2,183,574	173,125	10,166	15,925	5,197,877	2,594,446	2,134,985	448,698	13,569	6,179
New Jersey	3,155,900	1,590,075	862,078	672,837	50,580	2,593	1,987	1,565,825	784,399	653,672	123,086	3,298	1,370
Pennsylvania	8,720,017	4,429,020	2,464,724	1,802,712	144,903	10,082	5,699	4,290,997	2,228,292	1,730,431	317,015	12,510	2,749
EAST NORTH CENTRAL:													
Ohio	5,759,394	2,955,980	1,543,402	1,290,938	101,601	17,226	2,813	2,803,414	1,320,091	1,241,618	221,758	18,468	1,479
Indiana	2,930,390	1,489,074	756,681	663,650	55,552	10,339	2,852	1,441,316	663,965	650,275	114,250	10,724	2,102
Illinois	6,485,280	3,304,833	1,787,399	1,387,422	107,212	16,591	6,350	3,180,447	1,556,006	1,353,295	248,000	19,277	3,869
Michigan	3,668,412	1,928,436	1,031,283	820,170	62,420	12,359	2,204	1,739,976	827,131	782,746	118,419	10,768	912
Wisconsin	2,632,067	1,356,718	775,721	531,227	41,590	5,476	2,704	1,275,349	667,407	517,848	82,647	5,858	1,589
WEST NORTH CENTRAL:													
Minnesota	2,387,125	1,245,537	742,603	460,899	35,092	4,135	2,208	1,141,588	615,710	450,821	68,946	4,843	1,268
Iowa	2,404,021	1,229,392	667,534	512,134	40,764	6,946	2,014	1,174,629	579,280	505,396	81,124	7,510	1,319
Missouri	3,404,055	1,723,319	913,231	734,071	62,799	9,898	3,320	1,680,736	802,200	725,056	139,782	11,641	2,057
North Dakota	646,872	341,673	215,581	116,279	7,765	815	1,233	305,199	178,420	113,855	11,020	735	569
South Dakota	636,547	337,120	201,495	124,031	9,000	1,272	1,322	299,427	162,459	121,422	13,862	1,128	556
Nebraska	1,296,372	672,805	380,912	267,219	19,716	3,233	1,725	623,567	318,272	263,906	37,298	3,368	723
Kansas	1,769,257	909,221	489,156	382,605	30,744	5,244	1,472	860,036	419,291	375,856	58,865	5,505	519
SOUTH ATLANTIC:													
Delaware	223,003	113,755	59,942	48,867	4,264	307	375	109,248	52,092	47,481	9,095	358	222
Maryland	1,449,661	729,455	401,459	298,023	26,773	2,440	760	720,206	360,801	294,080	62,090	2,700	535
District of Columbia	437,571	203,543	105,505	88,699	7,616	884	839	234,028	115,878	88,615	27,762	1,381	392
Virginia	2,309,187	1,168,492	601,621	438,061	34,383	2,940	1,487	1,140,695	620,732	482,672	82,486	3,898	907
West Virginia	1,463,701	763,100	448,350	291,110	19,674	2,434	1,532	700,601	379,110	280,905	36,997	2,635	954
North Carolina	2,559,123	1,279,062	780,233	463,887	31,540	1,322	2,080	1,280,061	735,811	460,949	79,124	2,326	1,851
South Carolina	1,683,724	838,293	514,511	300,788	21,415	598	981	845,431	484,661	298,822	59,868	1,327	753
Georgia	2,895,832	1,444,823	843,278	554,434	42,318	3,242	1,551	1,451,009	776,332	551,926	115,840	5,927	984
Florida	968,470	495,320	269,808	203,004	19,131	2,096	1,221	473,150	229,521	199,959	40,573	2,562	535
EAST SOUTH CENTRAL:													
Kentucky	2,416,630	1,227,494	692,228	487,602	41,289	5,138	1,237	1,189,136	613,225	481,317	87,387	6,397	810
Tennessee	2,337,885	1,173,967	664,370	465,728	38,823	3,974	1,072	1,163,918	605,120	462,165	89,290	6,678	665
Alabama	2,348,174	1,173,105	680,192	444,243	34,421	3,486	1,763	1,175,069	636,270	440,478	90,380	6,654	1,287
Mississippi	1,790,618	897,124	520,460	344,714	27,780	2,665	1,505	893,494	477,293	342,301	67,674	5,202	1,024
WEST SOUTH CENTRAL:													
Arkansas	1,752,204	895,228	510,482	349,008	30,595	3,955	1,188	856,976	447,381	344,516	58,961	5,374	744
Louisiana	1,798,509	903,335	529,028	342,114	27,173	2,519	2,501	895,174	478,933	339,067	71,284	4,418	1,472
Oklahoma	2,028,283	1,058,044	605,125	412,295	32,254	5,424	2,940	970,239	508,198	403,036	51,991	5,886	1,128
Texas	4,663,228	2,409,222	1,391,539	924,152	75,992	10,971	6,568	2,254,006	1,175,986	903,088	157,042	15,570	2,320
MOUNTAIN:													
Montana	548,889	299,941	174,454	113,162	8,590	2,324	1,411	248,948	125,353	108,124	13,389	1,821	261
Idaho	431,866	233,919	137,527	87,989	6,409	1,667	327	197,947	102,769	84,569	9,391	1,146	72
Wyoming	194,402	110,359	64,154	41,418	3,180	966	641	84,043	40,990	38,176	4,089	660	128
Colorado	939,629	492,731	265,359	200,830	17,594	4,378	4,570	446,898	212,489	195,238	34,186	4,062	923
New Mexico	360,350	190,456	112,702	68,984	7,584	944	242	169,894	91,360	66,601	10,832	942	159
Arizona	334,162	183,602	107,789	67,757	6,185	1,166	705	150,560	75,019	63,721	10,812	852	156
Utah	449,396	232,051	139,074	86,406	5,078	1,246	247	217,345	118,820	83,722	13,169	1,531	103
Nevada	77,407	46,240	26,625	16,724	1,561	741	589	31,167	13,626	14,469	2,415	500	157
PACIFIC:													
Washington	1,356,621	734,701	400,660	298,987	23,918	8,605	2,531	621,920	283,863	287,913	41,890	7,816	438
Oregon	783,389	416,334	220,349	175,462	14,474	5,634	415	367,055	165,331	170,086	26,516	4,988	134
California	3,426,861	1,813,591	947,948	765,534	67,631	21,570	10,908	1,613,270	691,767	733,716	162,877	23,107	1,803

MARITAL CONDITION.

397

TABLE 7.—MARITAL CONDITION OF THE POPULATION 15 YEARS OF AGE AND OVER, BY SEX, BY DIVISIONS AND STATES: 1920.

DIVISION AND STATE.	MALES 15 YEARS OF AGE AND OVER.						FEMALES 15 YEARS OF AGE AND OVER.					
	Total.	Single.	Married.	Widowed.	Divorced.	Marital condition not reported.	Total.	Single.	Married.	Widowed.	Divorced.	Marital condition not reported.
United States	36,920,063	12,967,565	21,849,266	1,758,308	235,284	110,240	35,177,515	9,618,902	21,318,933	3,817,625	273,304	50,751
GEOGRAPHIC DIVISIONS:												
New England	2,614,119	935,919	1,522,214	137,307	14,408	4,271	2,681,138	890,653	1,485,377	315,093	17,441	2,574
Middle Atlantic	7,863,502	2,788,863	4,658,707	368,584	23,737	23,611	7,757,457	2,310,805	4,518,248	888,739	29,367	10,298
East North Central	7,844,734	2,764,777	4,692,684	368,357	61,984	16,932	7,321,833	1,916,579	4,545,175	785,038	65,090	9,951
West North Central	4,480,690	1,632,528	2,596,866	206,467	31,535	13,294	4,159,479	1,150,373	2,555,896	411,472	34,727	7,011
South Atlantic	4,459,049	1,538,338	2,686,520	207,103	16,262	10,826	4,420,837	1,222,561	2,654,236	513,797	23,110	7,133
East South Central	2,799,332	894,179	1,742,015	142,301	15,260	5,577	2,704,845	706,269	1,725,170	334,697	24,914	3,786
West South Central	3,375,273	1,145,995	2,027,272	166,000	22,863	13,143	3,131,029	766,117	1,658,774	339,238	31,236	5,664
Mountain	1,228,817	497,345	683,164	56,174	13,432	8,732	1,000,683	233,804	654,476	98,277	11,510	1,959
Pacific	2,255,117	859,621	1,239,824	106,015	35,803	13,854	1,910,811	449,681	1,101,572	231,274	35,009	2,375
NEW ENGLAND:												
Maine	279,478	92,085	166,171	18,123	2,028	471	271,764	72,159	162,623		35,000	
New Hampshire	161,931	54,688	94,791	10,324	1,762	366	161,208	46,292	92,353	20,431	1,845	287
Vermont	127,905	41,894	76,310	8,372	1,171	158	123,982	32,307	74,505	15,089	1,014	77
Massachusetts	1,347,788	406,697	775,687	67,582	5,825	1,997	1,425,443	490,170	758,807	167,253	8,000	1,123
Rhode Island	210,543	77,269	121,208	10,711	1,226	129	219,409	74,098	118,772	24,577	1,834	128
Connecticut	486,474	173,286	289,047	22,195	1,796	1,150	479,332	145,637	278,227	52,820	2,003	679
MIDDLE ATLANTIC:												
New York	3,732,828	1,350,088	2,183,536	173,113	10,166	15,925	3,767,540	1,164,525	2,134,004	448,670	13,562	6,179
New Jersey	1,110,387	382,481	672,749	50,577	2,593	1,987	1,092,623	311,293	653,587	123,076	3,207	1,370
Pennsylvania	3,020,287	1,056,294	1,802,422	144,894	10,978	5,699	2,807,294	834,987	1,730,657	316,993	12,508	2,749
EAST NORTH CENTRAL:												
Ohio	2,125,426	712,996	1,290,796	101,596	17,225	2,813	1,990,701	507,550	1,241,451	221,755	18,466	1,479
Indiana	1,059,890	327,582	663,577	55,540	10,339	2,852	1,021,915	244,659	650,187	114,244	10,723	2,102
Illinois	2,347,493	830,251	1,387,092	107,204	16,587	6,359	2,242,120	617,873	1,353,118	247,085	10,275	3,809
Michigan	1,371,116	474,065	820,071	62,418	12,358	2,204	1,108,037	285,297	782,648	118,412	10,768	3,899
Wisconsin	940,809	359,883	531,148	41,590	5,475	2,704	899,060	261,200	517,771	82,842	5,858	912
WEST NORTH CENTRAL:												
Minnesota	863,738	365,880	460,829	35,087	4,134	2,208	774,433	248,592	450,785	68,945	4,843	1,580
Iowa	865,407	303,626	512,060	40,703	6,044	2,014	819,947	224,700	505,294	81,118	7,510	1,268
Missouri	1,216,243	406,275	733,060	62,703	9,805	3,320	1,180,407	308,051	724,886	139,774	11,639	1,319
North Dakota	214,001	87,934	116,254	7,765	815	1,233	181,450	54,685	113,843	11,618	735	2,057
South Dakota	224,873	89,281	123,995	9,000	1,272	1,322	190,812	53,858	121,408	13,802	1,128	569
Nebraska	461,298	169,428	267,109	19,715	3,231	1,725	419,140	113,807	263,890	37,298	3,308	556
Kansas	630,130	210,101	382,599	30,744	5,244	1,472	587,284	146,614	375,790	58,857	5,504	723
SOUTH ATLANTIC:												
Delaware	81,611	27,815	48,850	4,204	307	375	77,105	19,962	47,469	9,094	858	519
Maryland	512,513	184,547	297,995	26,771	2,440	760	500,569	147,204	294,043	62,087	2,700	222
District of Columbia	159,013	60,976	88,698	7,616	884	839	188,406	70,330	88,002	27,701	1,381	535
Virginia	751,800	275,006	437,986	34,381	2,940	1,487	730,985	211,140	432,557	82,483	3,898	392
West Virginia	487,684	172,948	291,096	19,674	2,434	1,532	431,564	110,169	280,811	36,995	1,635	907
North Carolina	756,031	257,881	463,800	31,530	1,322	2,080	769,185	225,149	460,742	79,118	2,325	954
South Carolina	492,228	168,536	300,701	21,413	507	981	564,048	143,457	308,648	59,895	1,325	1,851
Georgia	884,801	283,338	554,356	42,314	3,242	1,551	900,117	225,856	551,522	115,829	5,926	763
Florida	332,078	107,291	203,020	19,131	2,096	1,221	312,798	69,294	199,842	40,565	2,502	984
EAST SOUTH CENTRAL:												
Kentucky	795,502	260,277	487,561	41,289	5,138	1,237	770,695	195,055	481,000	87,378	6,392	535
Tennessee	745,280	235,742	465,672	38,823	3,971	1,072	749,045	190,536	461,853	89,285	6,676	810
Alabama	710,229	226,392	444,168	34,420	3,486	1,763	720,780	182,268	440,207	90,369	6,649	665
Mississippi	548,321	171,768	344,614	27,769	2,665	1,505	554,325	138,410	342,020	67,665	5,197	1,287
WEST SOUTH CENTRAL:												
Arkansas	555,967	171,241	349,040	30,504	3,954	1,128	525,477	116,084	344,325	58,954	5,370	1,024
Louisiana	575,500	201,248	342,002	27,170	2,519	2,501	571,339	155,276	338,897	71,278	4,416	744
Oklahoma	671,835	219,012	412,202	32,252	5,423	2,946	594,679	132,818	402,863	51,984	5,886	1,472
Texas	1,571,981	554,494	923,968	75,984	10,967	6,568	1,439,534	361,939	902,689	157,022	15,564	1,128
MOUNTAIN:												
Montana	200,491	84,007	113,150	8,599	2,324	1,411	160,625	37,036	108,119	13,388	1,821	2,320
Idaho	156,167	59,795	87,969	6,409	1,667	327	123,287	28,124	84,554	9,391	1,146	201
Wyoming	79,366	33,171	41,408	3,180	966	641	54,169	11,120	38,172	4,089	660	72
Colorado	350,813	123,473	200,800	17,592	4,378	4,570	307,458	73,098	195,193	34,186	4,058	128
New Mexico	123,167	45,425	68,073	7,583	944	242	103,503	24,093	66,577	10,832	942	923
Arizona	127,117	51,329	67,735	6,182	1,186	705	95,671	20,170	63,685	10,808	852	159
Utah	146,202	53,294	86,897	5,078	1,246	247	133,642	35,127	82,713	13,108	1,531	156
Nevada	36,464	16,851	16,723	1,560	741	589	21,731	4,196	14,463	2,415	500	103
PACIFIC:												
Washington	546,019	212,021	298,950	28,915	8,602	2,531	438,357	100,343	287,871	41,889	7,816	157
Oregon	308,126	112,181	175,423	14,474	5,633	415	261,847	60,142	170,069	26,514	4,988	438
California	1,400,972	535,419	765,451	67,626	21,568	10,908	1,210,607	289,196	733,632	162,871	23,105	1,803

TABLE 8.—PER CENT DISTRIBUTION BY MARITAL CONDITION OF THE POPULATION 15 YEARS OF AGE AND OVER, BY SEX, BY DIVISIONS AND STATES: 1920, 1910, AND 1900.

[For numbers on which these percentages are based, see Table 11.]

DIVISION AND STATE.	MALES 15 YEARS OF AGE AND OVER.												FEMALES 15 YEARS OF AGE AND OVER.											
	Single.			Married.			Widowed.			Divorced.			Single.			Married.			Widowed.			Divorced.		
	1920	1910	1900	1920	1910	1900	1920	1910	1900	1920	1910	1900	1920	1910	1900	1920	1910	1900	1920	1910	1900	1920	1910	1900
United States	**35.1**	**38.7**	**40.2**	**59.2**	**55.8**	**54.5**	**4.8**	**4.5**	**4.6**	**0.6**	**0.5**	**0.3**	**27.3**	**29.7**	**31.2**	**60.6**	**58.9**	**57.0**	**11.1**	**10.6**	**11.2**	**0.8**	**0.6**	**0.5**
GEOGRAPHIC DIVISIONS:																								
New England	35.8	38.6	39.2	58.2	55.5	54.6	5.3	5.1	5.3	0.6	0.5	0.4	32.1	34.2	34.7	55.4	53.6	52.3	11.8	11.5	12.3	0.7	0.6	0.5
Middle Atlantic	35.5	39.0	39.7	59.2	56.1	55.3	4.7	4.3	4.6	0.3	0.2	0.2	29.8	32.6	33.3	58.2	56.1	54.7	11.5	10.8	11.6	0.4	0.3	0.2
East North Central	34.5	37.5	38.9	59.8	57.0	55.8	4.7	4.5	4.5	0.8	0.6	0.4	26.2	29.1	30.1	62.1	59.8	58.7	10.7	10.1	10.4	0.9	0.7	0.6
West North Central	36.4	40.5	41.8	58.0	54.1	53.3	4.0	4.3	4.2	0.7	0.5	0.4	27.7	29.7	30.3	61.4	60.4	60.0	9.9	9.0	9.0	0.8	0.7	0.5
South Atlantic	34.5	36.9	39.7	60.2	57.9	55.3	4.6	4.6	4.4	0.4	0.3	0.2	27.7	29.6	32.5	60.0	58.4	54.9	11.6	11.3	12.1	0.5	0.4	0.3
East South Central	31.9	34.9	38.6	62.2	59.2	56.0	5.1	5.1	4.8	0.5	0.5	0.3	25.3	26.8	29.9	61.7	60.3	56.7	12.0	11.8	12.7	0.9	0.8	0.6
West South Central	34.0	36.5	39.2	60.1	57.5	55.1	4.9	4.9	4.9	0.7	0.5	0.3	24.5	25.3	27.0	63.5	63.1	60.1	10.8	10.6	12.1	1.0	0.7	0.6
Mountain	38.0	45.1	47.3	55.6	49.5	47.0	4.6	3.8	4.1	1.1	0.8	0.6	23.4	25.2	25.2	65.4	64.5	64.0	9.8	9.0	9.8	1.2	1.0	0.8
Pacific	38.1	46.9	49.0	55.0	46.7	44.7	4.7	4.2	4.6	1.6	1.0	0.7	23.5	27.4	29.7	62.4	60.5	58.1	12.1	10.6	11.0	1.9	1.3	0.9
NEW ENGLAND:																								
Maine	32.9	34.6	36.0	59.5	57.8	56.5	6.5	6.4	6.3	0.9	1.0	0.7	26.6	27.4	28.8	59.8	59.2	57.5	12.5	12.3	12.8	1.0	0.9	0.7
New Hampshire	33.8	35.7	36.5	58.5	56.9	55.9	6.4	6.1	6.3	1.1	1.0	0.8	28.7	29.7	30.4	57.3	56.6	55.3	12.7	12.6	13.3	1.1	1.0	0.9
Vermont	32.8	34.3	35.1	59.7	58.5	57.4	6.5	6.2	6.3	0.9	0.9	0.6	26.1	26.4	26.9	60.1	60.6	59.6	12.9	12.2	12.6	0.8	0.8	0.7
Massachusetts	36.9	40.0	40.4	57.6	54.7	53.8	5.0	4.7	4.9	0.4	0.4	0.2	34.4	36.9	37.4	53.2	51.2	49.8	11.7	11.4	12.2	0.6	0.5	0.4
Rhode Island	36.7	40.1	40.5	57.6	54.0	53.5	5.1	5.0	5.1	0.6	0.6	0.5	33.8	35.8	36.9	54.1	52.2	50.6	11.2	10.9	11.7	0.8	0.8	0.7
Connecticut	35.6	39.3	40.4	59.2	55.3	54.1	4.6	4.8	5.0	0.4	0.3	0.3	30.4	33.6	34.1	58.0	54.6	53.0	11.0	11.2	12.3	0.4	0.4	0.4
MIDDLE ATLANTIC:																								
New York	36.2	39.8	39.7	58.5	55.2	55.1	4.6	4.4	4.8	0.3	0.2	0.2	30.9	33.7	33.7	56.7	54.5	53.6	11.9	11.3	12.4	0.4	0.3	0.2
New Jersey	34.4	37.9	38.2	60.6	57.3	56.7	4.6	4.4	4.7	0.2	0.2	0.1	28.5	31.6	32.3	59.8	57.3	55.7	11.3	10.7	11.6	0.3	0.2	0.2
Pennsylvania	35.0	38.4	40.0	59.7	56.8	55.1	4.8	4.3	4.3	0.4	0.3	0.2	28.8	31.4	33.2	59.7	57.9	55.9	10.9	10.2	10.5	0.4	0.3	0.3
EAST NORTH CENTRAL:																								
Ohio	33.5	36.1	38.3	60.7	58.2	56.4	4.8	4.8	4.7	0.8	0.6	0.4	25.5	28.9	31.1	62.4	59.5	57.2	11.1	10.7	11.0	0.9	0.7	0.5
Indiana	30.9	34.0	36.5	62.6	59.8	57.7	5.2	5.1	4.9	1.0	0.8	0.6	23.9	26.2	28.0	63.6	62.3	60.4	11.2	10.4	10.7	1.0	0.9	0.8
Illinois	35.4	39.3	40.7	59.1	55.2	54.2	4.6	4.2	4.3	0.7	0.5	0.4	27.6	30.4	31.0	60.3	58.6	57.7	11.1	10.1	10.6	0.9	0.7	0.5
Michigan	34.6	36.1	37.2	59.8	58.3	57.4	4.6	4.6	4.6	0.9	0.7	0.5	23.8	27.1	28.0	65.3	62.2	61.6	9.9	9.8	9.7	0.9	0.8	0.6
Wisconsin	38.3	41.4	41.1	56.5	53.6	53.9	4.4	4.2	4.3	0.6	0.5	0.4	30.1	32.6	31.6	59.6	57.7	58.5	9.5	9.0	9.3	0.7	0.6	0.5
WEST NORTH CENTRAL:																								
Minnesota	42.1	46.8	46.1	53.0	48.3	49.4	4.1	3.8	3.9	0.5	0.4	0.3	32.1	35.0	32.6	58.2	56.2	58.9	8.9	8.0	8.0	0.6	0.5	0.4
Iowa	35.1	38.6	40.1	59.2	55.9	54.9	4.7	4.4	4.3	0.8	0.6	0.4	27.4	29.8	30.7	61.6	60.0	59.9	9.9	9.1	8.6	0.9	0.7	0.6
Missouri	33.4	37.2	40.2	60.3	56.9	54.4	5.2	4.8	4.7	0.8	0.6	0.3	26.0	28.0	30.3	61.1	60.1	58.2	11.8	10.8	10.9	1.0	0.8	0.5
North Dakota	41.1	46.9	49.0	54.3	48.6	46.8	3.6	2.9	3.4	0.4	0.3	0.3	30.1	30.2	28.8	62.7	63.4	64.3	6.4	5.2	6.3	0.4	0.4	0.3
South Dakota	39.7	44.6	43.9	55.1	50.4	51.5	4.0	3.6	3.7	0.6	0.6	0.4	28.2	29.3	28.7	63.6	63.0	63.7	7.3	6.0	7.0	0.6	0.6	0.5
Nebraska	36.7	40.9	42.9	57.9	54.2	52.7	4.3	3.8	3.7	0.7	0.6	0.4	27.2	29.4	29.6	63.0	61.9	62.4	8.9	7.8	7.3	0.8	0.6	0.5
Kansas	33.3	37.4	39.5	60.7	56.8	55.3	4.9	4.5	4.3	0.8	0.6	0.4	25.0	26.6	28.4	64.0	63.7	62.1	10.0	8.7	8.6	0.9	0.7	0.6
SOUTH ATLANTIC:																								
Delaware	34.1	37.9	39.7	59.9	56.1	54.4	5.2	5.1	5.1	0.4	0.2	0.1	25.9	29.4	31.6	61.6	58.6	56.5	11.8	11.4	11.4	0.5	0.3	0.2
Maryland	36.0	38.7	40.9	58.1	55.8	53.6	5.2	5.0	4.8	0.5	0.3	0.2	29.1	33.1	35.0	58.0	54.8	52.4	12.3	11.5	12.1	0.5	0.4	0.3
District of Columbia	38.3	40.2	43.1	55.8	53.8	51.1	4.8	5.2	5.3	0.6	0.4	0.3	37.3	34.5	38.2	47.0	48.8	45.2	14.7	15.7	16.0	0.7	0.6	0.5
Virginia	36.6	38.5	41.6	58.3	56.1	53.1	4.6	4.9	4.8	0.4	0.3	0.2	28.9	31.6	35.0	59.2	56.5	52.6	11.3	11.3	12.0	0.5	0.4	0.3
West Virginia	35.5	38.9	41.0	59.7	56.7	54.5	4.0	3.7	3.7	0.5	0.3	0.2	25.5	28.0	31.6	65.1	63.3	59.4	8.6	7.9	8.5	0.6	0.5	0.4
North Carolina	34.1	36.3	39.0	61.3	59.1	56.5	4.2	4.1	4.1	0.2	0.2	0.1	29.3	31.2	34.1	59.9	58.0	54.4	10.3	10.3	11.1	0.3	0.3	0.3
South Carolina	34.2	35.5	38.2	61.1	59.7	57.3	4.4	4.4	4.2	0.1	0.1	0.1	28.5	29.0	31.4	59.2	58.4	55.8	11.9	12.1	12.5	0.3	0.2	0.2
Georgia	32.0	34.2	37.3	62.7	60.4	57.6	4.8	4.8	4.4	0.4	0.3	0.2	25.1	26.5	29.1	61.3	60.2	56.7	12.9	12.5	13.4	0.7	0.5	0.5
Florida	32.2	36.4	40.6	61.0	56.3	53.6	5.8	5.2	4.8	0.6	0.6	0.4	22.2	23.5	25.9	63.9	63.8	60.3	13.0	11.2	12.9	0.8	0.8	0.7
EAST SOUTH CENTRAL:																								
Kentucky	32.7	35.6	38.8	61.3	58.4	55.8	5.2	5.1	4.8	0.6	0.5	0.3	25.3	27.9	30.2	62.4	60.3	57.4	11.3	10.9	11.7	0.8	0.8	0.6
Tennessee	31.6	35.0	38.9	62.5	59.1	55.6	5.2	5.2	4.9	0.5	0.4	0.3	25.4	27.3	30.5	61.7	60.0	56.2	11.9	11.7	12.5	0.9	0.8	0.6
Alabama	31.9	34.5	38.2	62.5	60.0	56.7	4.8	4.9	4.6	0.5	0.4	0.3	25.3	26.3	29.7	61.1	60.3	56.2	12.5	12.4	13.5	0.9	0.9	0.6
Mississippi	31.3	34.3	38.3	62.8	59.5	56.2	5.1	5.2	5.0	0.5	0.5	0.3	25.0	25.6	29.0	61.7	60.7	56.6	12.2	12.5	13.6	0.9	0.9	0.6
WEST SOUTH CENTRAL:																								
Arkansas	30.8	34.3	37.6	62.8	58.9	56.1	5.5	5.9	5.6	0.7	0.5	0.3	22.1	23.7	26.0	65.5	64.0	60.8	11.2	11.3	12.5	1.0	0.8	0.6
Louisiana	35.0	37.9	39.8	59.4	56.1	54.6	4.7	5.0	5.1	0.4	0.3	0.3	27.2	28.3	29.6	59.3	57.6	55.0	12.5	13.2	14.7	0.8	0.6	0.6
Oklahoma	32.6	35.7	38.4	61.4	58.2	55.6	4.8	4.8	4.9	0.8	0.6	0.4	22.3	21.9	22.3	67.7	69.3	68.2	8.7	7.9	8.4	1.0	0.6	0.6
Texas	35.3	37.2	39.9	58.8	57.2	54.7	4.8	4.6	4.6	0.7	0.5	0.4	25.1	26.0	27.3	62.7	62.7	60.4	10.9	10.2	11.5	1.1	0.8	0.7
MOUNTAIN:																								
Montana	40.1	52.4	56.9	54.0	42.5	37.9	4.1	3.0	3.6	1.1	0.7	0.6	23.1	26.3	24.6	67.3	65.1	66.6	8.3	7.5	7.8	1.1	0.8	0.9
Idaho	38.3	45.9	49.2	56.3	49.2	45.7	4.1	3.4	4.0	1.1	0.7	0.7	22.8	24.7	23.7	68.0	67.8	68.1	7.6	6.4	7.4	0.9	0.7	0.8
Wyoming	41.8	56.3	58.2	52.2	39.7	37.1	4.0	2.8	3.5	1.2	0.7	0.5	20.5	23.5	24.7	70.5	69.1	68.2	7.5	6.2	6.4	1.2	1.0	0.6
Colorado	35.2	41.2	44.0	57.2	53.2	49.7	5.0	4.3	4.2	1.2	0.9	0.6	23.8	25.8	26.2	63.5	62.8	62.7	11.1	10.1	9.9	1.3	1.2	0.8
New Mexico	36.9	38.2	36.9	56.0	55.7	56.6	6.2	5.2	5.6	0.8	0.7	0.7	24.1	23.3	19.8	64.3	66.2	67.8	10.5	9.6	11.3	0.9	0.9	1.0
Arizona	40.4	45.8	49.5	53.3	47.7	43.6	4.9	4.4	5.1	0.9	0.8	0.7	21.1	22.2	21.0	66.6	65.7	64.8	11.3	10.5	12.6	0.9	1.0	1.0
Utah	36.4	41.0	41.0	59.1	54.2	54.8	3.5	2.9	3.3	0.9	0.6	0.4	26.3	27.9	29.5	62.6	61.3	59.3	9.9	9.2	10.2	1.1	0.8	0.9
Nevada	46.2	51.3	53.1	45.9	41.4	40.1	4.3	4.6	5.1	2.0	1.4	0.9	19.3	21.0	26.6	66.6	67.1	59.6	11.1	10.1	12.6	2.3	1.3	0.9
PACIFIC:																								
Washington	38.8	48.6	50.4	54.8	45.7	43.0	4.4	3.6	3.9	1.6	0.9	0.7	22.9	26.5	25.5	65.7	64.1	65.5	9.6	7.9	7.8	1.8	1.2	0.9
Oregon	36.4	47.5	47.8	56.9	46.6	46.1	4.7	4.3	4.8	1.8	1.2	0.8	23.0	27.1	28.9	64.9	63.0	61.4	10.1	8.6	8.6	1.9	1.1	0.9
California	38.2	45.8	48.8	54.6	47.3	44.9	4.8	4.4	4.7	1.5	1.0	0.7	23.9	27.9	31.1	60.6	58.4	55.2	13.5	12.2	12.5	1.9	1.3	0.9

MARITAL CONDITION.

399

TABLE 9.—PER CENT MARRIED, WIDOWED, OR DIVORCED IN THE POPULATION 15 YEARS OF AGE AND OVER, BY SEX, FOR PRINCIPAL POPULATION CLASSES, BY DIVISIONS AND STATES: 1920 AND 1910.

DIVISION AND STATE.	PER CENT OF MALES 15 YEARS AND OVER MARRIED, WIDOWED, OR DIVORCED.										PER CENT OF FEMALES 15 YEARS AND OVER MARRIED, WIDOWED, OR DIVORCED.									
	All classes.		Native white. Native parentage.		Native white. Foreign or mixed parentage.		Foreign-born white.		Negro.		All classes.		Native white. Native parentage.		Native white. Foreign or mixed parentage.		Foreign-born white.		Negro.	
	1920	1910	1920	1910	1920	1910	1920	1910	1920	1910	1920	1910	1920	1910	1920	1910	1920	1910	1920	1910
United States	64.6	60.8	64.2	61.4	54.8	49.5	74.1	67.8	67.1	64.0	72.5	70.0	71.4	69.8	62.9	58.1	85.7	81.6	75.7	73.1
GEOGRAPHIC DIVISIONS:																				
New England	64.0	61.2	65.7	65.0	46.2	42.0	70.1	68.2	60.8	58.2	67.8	65.7	68.0	68.2	50.8	48.0	81.9	74.9	72.7	67.7
Middle Atlantic	64.2	60.7	63.1	60.9	51.6	48.7	75.7	67.8	63.3	60.4	70.1	67.3	67.8	66.1	58.1	55.5	84.1	78.3	74.1	69.0
East North Central	65.3	62.1	64.0	61.9	58.6	52.5	75.8	72.2	64.6	60.5	73.7	70.7	71.5	69.8	66.7	60.5	89.0	86.3	81.6	75.3
West North Central	63.3	58.0	62.7	50.6	56.1	47.8	76.3	70.1	65.3	60.3	72.2	70.0	70.8	69.0	65.5	58.6	90.1	87.9	79.7	75.0
South Atlantic	65.3	62.7	64.8	62.3	58.2	56.0	69.3	68.4	66.6	63.8	72.2	70.1	71.3	69.3	65.5	61.9	85.5	82.9	73.6	71.5
East South Central	67.0	64.8	67.1	64.2	65.0	59.5	76.6	74.9	69.5	65.9	74.6	72.9	73.8	72.2	69.6	64.3	87.2	86.7	76.4	74.7
West South Central	65.7	62.0	64.9	62.2	60.3	55.7	69.0	70.5	68.0	64.9	75.4	74.4	74.7	74.2	70.1	66.4	82.5	85.6	77.1	74.9
Mountain	61.3	54.1	61.4	55.1	58.4	40.0	64.8	55.7	43.8	55.3	76.4	74.4	74.3	73.0	72.2	66.5	88.7	87.3	84.0	77.1
Pacific	61.3	51.9	63.2	54.9	55.3	45.6	63.4	54.4	62.7	52.6	76.3	72.4	75.4	72.1	69.3	62.2	86.4	84.2	82.0	76.0
NEW ENGLAND:																				
Maine	66.9	65.1	69.2	67.6	50.0	48.2	72.0	68.2	56.1	54.9	73.3	72.4	74.8	73.9	58.2	56.5	82.5	78.5	66.3	61.0
New Hampshire	66.0	64.1	69.5	69.2	47.5	44.2	73.7	65.2	55.0	58.1	71.1	70.1	73.7	73.7	53.0	51.0	81.4	74.7	71.0	58.8
Vermont	67.1	65.0	66.7	66.6	61.1	58.3	75.9	70.6	53.6	27.4	73.8	73.0	72.9	73.5	67.8	65.9	85.7	83.4	70.5	73.8
Massachusetts	63.0	59.8	64.3	63.6	44.0	41.5	76.1	68.1	60.3	57.8	65.5	63.0	64.3	64.5	48.7	45.7	80.4	73.1	71.8	67.1
Rhode Island	63.2	59.6	62.1	61.5	45.4	41.0	78.1	69.3	59.8	59.8	66.2	63.9	64.9	65.1	49.2	46.3	81.2	74.4	72.4	69.6
Connecticut	64.1	60.5	64.0	63.5	45.4	42.1	76.9	68.3	62.9	64.6	69.5	66.3	66.6	66.5	52.3	48.0	86.3	78.8	75.3	68.6
MIDDLE ATLANTIC:																				
New York	63.4	59.8	61.2	59.4	50.6	48.2	74.9	67.7	62.5	58.0	68.9	66.1	66.2	65.3	57.3	54.0	81.5	75.4	71.0	67.4
New Jersey	65.4	61.8	63.5	61.9	50.5	47.9	78.3	70.3	66.8	62.5	71.4	68.2	68.0	66.5	58.2	55.0	87.0	80.3	74.6	70.2
Pennsylvania	64.8	61.3	64.5	62.0	52.0	50.1	75.8	67.1	62.5	60.7	71.1	68.4	68.9	66.7	59.6	56.7	88.3	83.7	76.4	69.6
EAST NORTH CENTRAL:																				
Ohio	66.3	63.6	65.2	62.7	62.9	58.8	74.4	72.1	63.6	60.0	74.4	70.9	72.5	69.5	69.4	64.6	89.4	86.8	81.0	73.3
Indiana	68.8	65.6	68.1	65.3	69.0	63.7	76.2	71.8	66.7	61.7	75.0	73.6	75.0	73.3	73.5	68.3	90.3	89.5	81.0	75.8
Illinois	64.4	59.9	62.6	59.6	55.2	48.8	76.2	69.6	65.7	60.2	72.3	69.3	63.8	68.6	63.0	57.2	87.3	83.4	81.0	77.4
Michigan	65.3	63.6	64.6	64.7	57.1	50.6	74.4	74.3	62.3	62.4	76.1	73.7	74.0	73.0	67.8	60.1	89.6	87.6	84.7	75.2
Wisconsin	61.5	58.3	51.5	49.3	57.4	49.0	70.0	70.0	59.7	55.1	69.8	67.2	58.7	56.0	66.5	58.6	91.5	90.3	80.0	67.3
WEST NORTH CENTRAL:																				
Minnesota	57.6	52.5	53.0	48.6	48.2	39.0	73.0	66.8	62.3	50.4	67.7	64.0	60.2	58.8	59.4	50.5	89.9	86.6	82.8	72.0
Iowa	64.7	60.9	62.8	60.5	61.3	52.3	78.7	74.7	65.8	61.5	72.4	69.9	70.1	68.7	69.3	61.6	91.1	90.0	82.0	77.1
Missouri	66.3	62.3	65.1	61.8	65.0	58.1	78.0	72.7	65.2	60.5	73.9	71.7	72.8	71.3	71.2	65.4	87.6	86.8	78.9	74.9
North Dakota	58.3	51.8	55.4	50.3	40.1	37.0	74.5	63.7	48.7	38.4	60.5	60.0	65.0	68.4	58.4	53.2	80.5	84.7	77.9	69.7
South Dakota	59.7	54.5	57.3	52.8	52.7	43.5	75.5	63.6	56.7	54.4	71.5	70.2	68.1	68.7	65.7	59.1	90.8	88.5	77.4	69.8
Nebraska	62.9	58.6	61.3	58.6	56.5	46.4	78.4	73.4	61.8	56.3	72.7	70.4	70.9	70.0	66.1	58.1	91.3	89.8	84.4	76.4
Kansas	66.4	62.0	65.7	62.0	62.4	53.4	79.3	73.0	67.1	62.4	74.9	73.1	74.1	73.0	70.4	63.9	91.3	91.0	80.0	75.2
SOUTH ATLANTIC:																				
Delaware	65.5	61.4	66.0	63.0	55.0	50.1	71.9	66.8	61.3	58.5	73.8	70.3	73.7	70.6	64.2	59.2	87.8	82.8	72.5	68.8
Maryland	63.8	61.1	62.9	59.6	58.0	56.7	76.4	74.5	63.6	60.7	70.8	60.7	69.1	64.8	65.5	60.9	85.7	82.2	73.7	68.7
District of Columbia	61.1	59.4	59.5	58.0	56.7	55.2	66.4	65.3	65.3	52.0	62.5	65.1	58.0	63.4	57.4	62.0	76.9	75.9	71.2	66.5
Virginia	63.2	61.2	63.3	61.7	51.7	53.1	66.3	67.1	63.9	60.5	71.0	68.2	70.4	68.1	65.9	60.1	87.1	84.6	71.0	68.1
West Virginia	64.2	60.7	65.1	62.0	63.1	60.8	60.4	56.0	50.9	51.2	74.3	71.7	73.4	71.1	68.9	66.2	90.9	80.0	78.7	74.3
North Carolina	65.6	63.4	65.7	63.3	59.5	58.5	69.2	67.7	65.6	63.4	70.5	68.6	70.7	69.0	65.0	60.8	80.7	83.4	69.0	67.6
South Carolina	65.6	64.1	64.1	62.1	53.2	56.3	63.0	65.3	67.3	66.1	71.4	70.7	71.0	69.5	65.8	59.7	85.4	83.3	71.8	71.3
Georgia	67.8	65.4	66.6	64.3	58.5	54.0	68.1	65.0	69.8	67.2	74.8	73.2	73.4	71.8	67.4	63.0	83.5	84.2	76.7	75.0
Florida	67.4	62.0	67.2	62.4	61.8	53.2	73.0	64.7	67.6	61.0	77.7	75.8	76.7	74.5	71.9	66.3	85.3	83.4	79.0	77.5
EAST SOUTH CENTRAL:																				
Kentucky	67.1	64.1	67.0	64.3	67.0	60.2	76.2	79.3	66.5	61.4	74.6	71.9	74.4	72.2	69.3	63.5	87.0	86.6	77.2	72.3
Tennessee	68.2	64.7	68.0	64.7	65.6	58.6	77.5	72.4	69.0	64.5	74.5	72.5	73.8	72.1	70.0	65.6	86.7	85.6	76.9	73.8
Alabama	67.9	65.3	67.0	64.2	62.3	57.0	76.5	70.5	69.1	66.8	74.5	73.6	73.9	72.6	69.1	64.9	87.9	88.1	75.4	74.8
Mississippi	68.4	65.2	65.4	62.6	65.4	60.6	76.3	71.9	71.1	67.2	74.8	74.0	72.3	71.7	71.7	67.0	87.2	86.5	76.9	75.8
WEST SOUTH CENTRAL:																				
Arkansas	69.0	65.3	68.1	64.0	64.3	59.4	75.4	73.2	71.3	66.8	77.8	76.1	77.2	75.9	73.4	68.6	86.9	86.4	79.3	76.7
Louisiana	64.6	61.4	61.5	57.8	63.6	60.0	69.6	71.3	68.3	64.1	72.6	71.4	69.8	68.4	69.6	67.4	85.1	85.3	75.6	73.8
Oklahoma	67.0	63.6	66.8	63.5	65.2	59.7	71.8	70.1	68.4	64.0	77.5	77.8	77.3	77.7	75.0	72.7	91.2	91.5	77.7	77.8
Texas	64.3	62.3	63.7	61.0	57.5	52.4	68.3	70.2	67.9	64.7	74.7	73.7	74.0	73.5	68.6	63.9	81.1	84.7	77.2	74.5
MOUNTAIN:																				
Montana	59.2	46.2	60.8	47.6	52.4	39.7	62.7	47.6	57.0	40.3	76.8	73.4	75.1	72.3	69.8	62.8	90.0	85.2	84.4	74.0
Idaho	61.5	53.3	61.3	54.2	61.1	51.1	62.9	53.8	52.6	48.3	77.1	74.9	74.8	73.1	76.1	70.0	91.6	90.9	86.8	69.9
Wyoming	57.4	43.3	58.9	44.4	55.0	42.0	56.3	44.3	50.9	29.0	79.2	76.2	77.8	75.1	74.9	68.6	91.4	88.9	84.0	72.9
Colorado	63.5	58.3	63.9	54.7	57.8	50.2	70.4	66.1	65.4	63.4	75.0	74.0	75.1	73.4	68.8	64.9	88.9	88.9	81.8	78.4
New Mexico	62.9	61.6	64.5	62.3	58.7	53.0	67.4	60.4	26.2	60.2	75.7	76.7	75.0	76.1	70.6	68.4	85.4	87.0	80.2	79.2
Arizona	59.1	52.8	60.1	51.7	54.9	45.0	60.9	52.5	32.1	60.9	78.8	77.2	77.0	75.4	73.3	67.1	83.4	84.5	86.9	77.0
Utah	63.4	57.6	56.5	51.3	66.9	57.2	72.9	67.7	63.6	51.3	73.6	71.4	65.0	63.1	75.1	67.3	90.8	89.5	89.6	74.8
Nevada	52.2	47.4	54.3	49.3	53.1	45.6	46.5	44.0	57.1	55.5	80.0	78.5	76.4	76.4	78.1	73.2	92.6	89.4	79.0	76.1
PACIFIC:																				
Washington	60.7	50.2	63.3	53.2	53.4	43.4	62.7	51.6	58.2	44.1	77.0	73.1	76.2	73.2	68.5	61.7	88.4	84.5	85.1	74.6
Oregon	63.5	52.0	64.9	54.9	57.8	45.7	65.7	52.8	60.4	47.6	77.0	72.7	76.9	73.3	69.9	61.7	88.1	84.4	85.0	79.8
California	61.0	52.8	62.7	55.7	55.5	46.6	63.3	56.1	63.8	56.1	76.0	71.0	74.6	71.6						

400

POPULATION.

TABLE 10.—PER CENT MARRIED, WIDOWED, OR DIVORCED IN THE POPULATION 15 YEARS OF AGE AND OVER, BY SEX AND BROAD AGE GROUPS, BY DIVISIONS AND STATES: 1920 AND 1910.

DIVISION AND STATE.	PER CENT OF MALES MARRIED, WIDOWED, OR DIVORCED.										PER CENT OF FEMALES MARRIED, WIDOWED, OR DIVORCED.									
	15 to 19 years.		20 to 24 years.		25 to 34 years.		35 to 44 years.		45 years and over.		15 to 19 years.		20 to 24 years.		25 to 34 years.		35 to 44 years.		45 years and over.	
	1920	1910	1920	1910	1920	1910	1920	1910	1920	1910	1920	1910	1920	1910	1920	1910	1920	1910	1920	1910
United States	2.1	1.2	29.0	24.6	67.6	64.7	83.7	83.1	89.5	90.5	13.9	11.6	54.3	51.4	80.6	79.0	88.6	88.5	91.2	92.3
GEOGRAPHIC DIVISIONS:																				
New England	1.1	0.7	21.6	19.4	63.8	60.4	81.7	81.4	88.3	89.8	6.3	6.0	41.0	38.1	72.4	68.6	82.3	81.9	86.0	87.6
Middle Atlantic	1.3	0.7	24.0	20.9	65.6	63.3	82.9	82.7	88.8	90.1	8.1	7.0	46.8	43.6	76.8	74.4	85.6	85.4	88.6	89.8
East North Central	1.6	0.7	26.5	21.9	66.9	65.0	83.4	83.9	89.7	91.3	10.3	8.5	52.6	48.0	80.9	78.7	88.8	88.7	92.0	93.4
West North Central	1.4	0.7	24.6	19.8	65.5	61.1	82.4	81.7	89.1	90.9	9.9	9.4	50.1	48.3	80.2	79.6	89.4	90.6	93.6	95.3
South Atlantic	3.3	2.0	36.6	32.7	72.5	72.1	87.4	87.5	92.4	93.1	17.5	15.6	60.7	58.2	82.5	81.6	89.7	89.4	91.0	91.1
East South Central	4.0	2.6	41.4	37.5	76.3	75.9	89.6	89.3	93.7	94.2	20.4	19.3	64.8	63.3	85.2	84.7	91.6	91.5	93.1	93.5
West South Central	3.2	1.9	37.3	33.7	74.0	73.6	88.6	88.3	93.0	93.3	19.8	19.7	65.9	66.1	87.4	88.0	93.8	94.5	95.4	96.2
Mountain	1.5	0.9	25.6	18.7	63.8	53.6	79.6	75.0	84.6	82.9	14.2	13.5	61.3	59.2	86.5	85.2	93.4	93.4	95.4	96.1
Pacific	1.3	0.6	22.4	14.9	59.3	47.0	75.0	69.0	81.6	79.9	12.4	9.0	55.6	50.6	81.8	78.7	89.2	89.4	92.6	94.4
NEW ENGLAND:																				
Maine	1.8	1.1	27.1	22.4	67.5	64.4	82.6	82.8	88.8	90.3	10.2	9.6	50.1	47.8	78.9	77.1	87.9	87.5	89.9	90.9
New Hampshire	1.6	1.0	25.4	22.7	65.5	62.7	80.8	81.9	87.8	89.8	8.0	7.5	44.3	43.5	75.4	73.2	85.1	85.2	88.1	90.1
Vermont	1.5	0.8	26.2	22.4	67.4	64.6	83.3	83.5	89.1	91.1	9.8	10.0	49.4	50.0	79.6	78.1	88.0	87.8	90.2	91.6
Massachusetts	0.8	0.6	20.0	18.3	62.2	58.6	81.0	80.6	87.9	89.5	5.0	4.9	37.3	34.3	69.4	65.0	80.0	79.6	84.1	86.0
Rhode Island	0.9	0.7	21.3	19.3	64.8	61.3	82.5	82.0	89.2	90.3	5.7	5.6	39.8	37.0	71.0	67.8	80.9	81.1	85.3	87.1
Connecticut	0.9	0.5	21.0	18.7	64.8	60.8	82.7	81.8	88.7	89.6	6.3	5.8	44.6	40.1	76.3	71.3	84.8	83.5	87.3	88.4
MIDDLE ATLANTIC:																				
New York	1.0	0.5	20.8	18.9	63.6	61.1	81.9	81.5	88.1	89.5	6.5	5.8	42.7	40.3	74.5	72.3	84.3	84.5	88.0	89.5
New Jersey	1.1	0.7	23.8	21.7	67.5	64.9	84.6	84.0	90.3	90.8	7.6	6.9	48.3	44.9	78.9	75.8	87.2	86.8	89.6	90.4
Pennsylvania	1.7	0.8	28.0	23.0	67.6	65.4	83.5	83.7	89.3	90.8	10.0	8.5	51.7	47.7	79.0	76.5	86.6	86.1	88.9	89.9
EAST NORTH CENTRAL:																				
Ohio	1.7	0.8	28.8	23.8	68.3	67.1	83.7	84.3	89.6	91.3	11.5	9.0	55.8	49.0	81.4	78.2	88.2	87.3	90.7	91.6
Indiana	2.6	1.2	33.2	27.8	72.5	70.0	86.2	86.1	91.1	92.6	13.3	11.7	57.2	53.9	82.9	81.4	90.0	90.1	92.8	94.1
Illinois	1.3	0.6	24.8	20.7	66.0	62.7	82.5	82.6	88.9	90.4	9.3	8.2	49.3	47.3	79.3	77.6	87.8	88.4	91.8	93.4
Michigan	1.5	0.7	26.4	22.2	65.8	66.0	83.6	85.0	90.6	92.3	11.4	8.9	57.3	49.3	83.8	80.8	90.9	90.7	94.0	95.2
Wisconsin	0.7	0.3	18.6	14.6	62.4	59.6	81.5	82.3	88.7	90.7	5.7	4.7	43.1	39.7	77.7	76.9	88.3	89.0	92.2	94.0
WEST NORTH CENTRAL:																				
Minnesota	0.6	0.2	15.8	11.4	56.7	49.6	77.1	76.1	86.3	88.5	5.3	4.4	39.5	36.1	75.0	74.1	87.9	89.4	93.7	95.4
Iowa	1.4	0.6	25.5	20.3	67.7	63.1	83.2	82.8	89.6	91.6	9.4	7.9	50.0	46.0	80.1	78.0	88.4	89.1	92.7	94.5
Missouri	2.2	1.2	31.0	26.0	69.6	67.1	83.9	83.8	89.5	91.3	13.5	13.1	55.2	53.5	80.7	80.3	88.6	89.7	92.6	94.4
North Dakota	0.6	0.3	17.3	13.8	60.9	54.1	81.0	78.1	87.6	88.2	6.7	8.4	47.3	50.4	83.1	83.9	93.8	94.4	95.9	96.5
South Dakota	0.8	0.4	20.0	15.8	62.6	56.7	81.1	79.8	88.3	89.7	8.0	8.0	49.2	50.0	82.7	83.6	92.6	93.9	95.5	96.9
Nebraska	1.3	0.5	24.7	19.4	65.5	62.0	82.9	82.7	90.0	91.9	9.4	9.2	51.5	49.8	81.7	81.0	90.6	92.4	95.2	96.7
Kansas	1.8	0.8	28.6	23.1	70.8	66.5	85.9	84.7	91.1	92.5	12.1	11.2	55.7	54.1	83.5	83.2	91.2	92.4	95.1	96.6
SOUTH ATLANTIC:																				
Delaware	2.0	0.9	31.9	23.7	68.0	64.9	82.8	81.3	88.3	89.4	13.9	10.6	57.9	49.7	81.1	76.7	87.1	86.9	89.7	90.2
Maryland	1.6	0.7	29.5	24.0	68.3	65.1	82.8	83.1	88.7	89.7	12.3	8.2	54.4	45.7	78.1	73.9	85.1	84.7	87.3	88.0
District of Columbia	2.5	0.8	27.2	21.7	60.5	59.5	78.9	79.1	85.6	86.0	12.4	8.0	38.4	42.1	61.6	68.5	77.0	79.2	83.1	85.5
Virginia	2.2	1.1	30.8	26.9	69.4	68.8	86.2	86.7	91.7	92.3	13.7	11.8	57.0	52.2	81.6	79.2	89.2	88.4	90.2	90.2
West Virginia	2.6	1.3	32.8	26.3	70.1	68.5	85.5	86.0	91.7	93.3	18.4	15.8	63.8	59.4	85.8	83.5	91.3	90.7	92.6	92.9
North Carolina	3.1	1.9	38.7	34.8	75.8	76.1	90.5	90.4	94.3	94.8	16.1	14.5	59.2	56.9	82.5	81.5	90.1	89.7	91.0	90.2
South Carolina	3.2	3.2	42.4	42.4	76.5	78.7	90.7	91.2	94.8	95.1	17.0	17.9	63.3	63.5	84.3	84.6	91.6	91.8	92.8	93.0
Georgia	5.5	3.2	44.3	40.3	77.1	77.8	90.5	90.8	95.0	95.1	22.9	20.6	67.0	65.9	86.1	86.0	92.3	92.4	93.7	93.5
Florida	2.9	1.7	35.0	30.7	72.3	68.9	86.5	85.1	91.7	92.5	21.8	22.4	68.0	68.3	87.7	88.0	93.2	94.0	94.6	95.2
EAST SOUTH CENTRAL:																				
Kentucky	4.0	2.3	38.4	33.7	74.0	72.8	87.4	87.1	91.8	92.7	20.1	17.8	62.9	58.6	83.6	81.9	89.9	89.5	91.7	92.8
Tennessee	4.4	3.2	41.1	36.7	76.1	74.7	89.5	89.0	93.7	94.1	20.2	19.0	63.4	61.5	84.2	83.4	91.1	91.1	93.2	93.3
Alabama	3.6	2.3	42.1	39.5	77.8	78.0	90.8	90.7	94.9	95.3	20.4	20.0	66.2	60.2	86.5	86.5	92.8	92.6	93.6	93.7
Mississippi	4.1	2.4	44.8	40.6	78.2	78.8	91.5	91.3	94.9	95.2	21.1	20.7	67.0	67.4	86.9	87.4	93.2	93.4	94.5	94.9
WEST SOUTH CENTRAL:																				
Arkansas	4.0	2.1	43.5	37.7	78.6	77.9	91.1	90.4	94.6	95.1	23.2	22.0	71.2	69.7	90.1	90.2	95.2	95.9	96.4	96.9
Louisiana	2.9	1.6	37.6	33.3	73.0	71.7	87.0	86.2	91.7	91.5	18.2	17.0	62.9	61.8	84.2	83.9	90.8	90.6	92.0	93.3
Oklahoma	3.2	1.8	38.7	32.8	75.9	73.3	89.6	88.2	93.2	93.7	21.1	22.6	69.5	72.0	90.3	91.9	96.0	97.1	97.3	98.1
Texas	3.1	1.9	34.6	32.7	72.2	72.8	87.9	88.4	92.7	93.1	18.6	18.6	63.7	64.2	86.5	87.3	93.5	94.5	95.7	96.5
MOUNTAIN:																				
Montana	0.9	0.5	19.6	12.7	59.6	43.8	75.3	66.4	79.5	74.2	10.8	11.5	58.5	56.0	86.9	83.6	93.7	93.4	95.8	96.2
Idaho	1.4	0.7	26.0	17.5	65.5	53.5	80.2	74.4	83.6	82.1	13.1	11.8	63.0	61.9	89.2	88.3	95.4	95.0	96.8	97.5
Wyoming	1.2	0.6	23.3	12.3	58.3	40.6	74.2	64.9	80.3	77.0	15.3	14.7	67.1	63.4	88.9	87.7	95.2	95.0	96.7	96.5
Colorado	1.4	0.8	26.3	20.3	66.1	58.3	81.9	78.8	86.6	85.7	13.6	12.7	58.0	55.6	83.6	82.3	91.4	91.5	94.1	95.1
New Mexico	2.0	1.2	27.5	26.9	66.3	60.3	85.8	84.7	91.7	91.4	18.9	20.3	65.4	69.2	87.1	88.6	93.9	94.7	95.6	96.5
Arizona	2.1	2.2	27.0	21.1	62.4	53.7	78.8	71.3	82.3	76.7	22.2	21.1	69.8	67.4	88.6	87.0	94.3	94.3	95.9	96.2
Utah	1.5	0.8	29.4	22.4	70.4	62.9	85.1	84.4	91.2	91.2	10.1	8.5	56.9	53.6	86.5	85.7	93.8	94.1	96.3	97.3
Nevada	1.2	0.6	19.8	13.0	47.2	41.3	62.9	61.0	67.2	68.9	13.8	13.9	63.7	60.5	87.2	85.6	93.7	93.8	94.9	97.0
PACIFIC:																				
Washington	1.4	0.5	22.7	14.0	59.2	45.6	74.9	69.4	82.4	82.2	13.0	10.7	57.0	53.5	83.9	81.9	92.2	92.9	95.4	96.4
Oregon	1.3	0.5	23.9	15.6	63.1	47.1	77.7	68.9	84.2	81.4	12.7	10.7	57.0	51.9	83.7	80.3	91.2	92.4	95.2	96.4
California	1.2	0.6	21.9	15.1	58.5	47.7	74.4	69.9	80.7	78.6	12.0	9.3	54.6	48.8	80.5	76.9	87.7	87.3	91.2	93.2

469

CHAPTER V
STATE OF BIRTH OF THE NATIVE POPULATION

CHAPTER V.—STATE OF BIRTH OF THE NATIVE POPULATION.

INTRODUCTION.

The inquiry as to state of birth has been included at each census, beginning with that of 1850. At the censuses of 1850 and 1860, however, returns were made for the free population only. The statistics here presented relate to the resident population of continental United States. Statistics for Alaska, Hawaii, and Porto Rico are given in Volume III of the Fourteenth Census Reports.

The returns as to state of birth are valuable mainly for the light they throw on the migration of the native population within the United States. The term "native population" as ordinarily used by the Bureau of the Census comprises all persons born in continental United States or any of the outlying possessions, persons born at sea under the United States flag, and persons of native parentage born abroad and designated as "American citizens born abroad." Thus the term "native population," when used in the headings of tables presenting statistics by states, does not refer to the population native to (that is, born in) the particular states, but merely to the population born in the United States. The natives of individual states are designated in the table headings as persons born in those states.

Persons for whom the place of birth was not reported and for whom the returns gave no indication of foreign origin have been assumed to be natives of the United States and have been included with those for whom the place of birth was given as the United States without specification as to the particular state in which born. This practice has undoubtedly resulted in the inclusion of a few foreign-born persons, but it is certain that the great majority of those for whom the place of birth was not reported were born in the United States. In some of the tables the statistics for the population born in the United States relate only to persons for whom the state of birth was reported.

The fact that at each census since and including that of 1850 (excluding slaves in 1850 and 1860) more than one-fifth of the native Americans had migrated from the states of birth to other states indicates a rather high degree of mobility on the part of the population. (See Table 1.) It must be borne in mind that the census distinguishes as migrants only those persons who have migrated across state lines and are at the date of the census living in states other than those in which they were born. The statistics, therefore, afford no indication of the amount of migration within the same states from rural to urban communities or from one locality to another. There is no doubt that some of the intrastate migration involves greater changes of environment, and even longer journeys, than some of the interstate migration. Much of the movement from country to city takes place within the confines of single states; and, on the other hand, some of the interstate migration is merely from one border county or city to another just across the state line. Computations made in connection with the census of 1900 indicated that nearly one-half of the natives of the United States who were enumerated outside the states in which born were living in adjoining states.

Furthermore, the census figures do not show the migration from state to state outside the state of birth. A person who at one or at several times has removed from one state to another and has later returned to the state in which he was born is not reported as a migrant; and if he had not returned he would be classified simply as an interstate migrant but no account would be taken of the number of his migrations.

The proportion of migrants in the adult population at each census undoubtedly has exceeded the percentages given in Table 1 and other tables, since these percentages are based upon the total population born in and living in the United States, including children, among whom it is safe to assume that the proportion of migrants is smaller than among adults.

It is obvious that the statistics as to interstate migration do not represent the total number of persons who migrated from the states in which born to other states during any given period of time. Some of those who migrated have since died, others have returned to the states in which born, and still others have migrated to outlying possessions or to foreign countries. The statistics show only those living at the time of enumeration in the United States, outside the states in which born, who may be described as surviving migrants.

It must be remembered that the number of persons reported as born in any division or state by no means indicates what the native population of that division or state would have been had there been no migration on the part of the present generation. If all persons now living who were born in New England, for example, had remained there, the living children and grandchildren of such persons would have been added to the population of that division; but in fact the children and grandchildren of the migrants appear as natives of other divisions. The converse is true regarding descendants of persons born in other divisions and now living in New England. Thus while the census makes it possible to measure what may be termed the direct effects of the migration of persons still living, it affords no means of measuring the indirect effects.

(607)

608   POPULATION.

Nevertheless, the interstate-migration statistics, while supplying no definite information as to the total amount of migration from one locality to another within the United States or as to the total effect of such migration on the present population of the several divisions and states, do show in a general way the increase or decrease in the mobility of the native population from one decade to another and afford a good indication of the extent to which the population of certain states has been directly recruited from other states.

Migration east and west of the Mississippi River and between the North and the South.—In Tables 2 and 4, which give statistics as to migration between the sections of the country lying east and west of the line forming the eastern boundaries of Minnesota, Iowa, Missouri, Arkansas, and Louisiana, the terms "East of the Mississippi River," and "West of the Mississippi River" are employed for the sake of convenience, although portions of Minnesota and Louisiana lie east of the river.

In Tables 3 and 4, which present statistics as to migration between the North and South, the term "the North" is employed to designate the region comprising the New England, Middle Atlantic, East North Central, and West North Central divisions, while "the South" refers to the area embracing the South Atlantic, East South Central, and West South Central divisions. Except for the comparatively small part of Texas which lies south of New Mexico, the western boundaries of the two sections do not differ greatly in longitude. There has, of course, been a considerable amount of migration from both the North and the South to the West, and some of this migration—for example, from North Dakota to New Mexico or from Texas to Montana—has been more nearly northward or southward than eastward or westward. Nevertheless, the distinctly north-and-south migration can best be indicated by the presentation in Tables 3 and 4.

Gain or loss through interdivisional and interstate migration.—The net gain or loss through interdivisional migration (Table 7, column 8, and Table 9) and through interstate migration (Table 15) represents the difference, on the census date, between the total number of surviving native migrants out of the specified division or state and the total number of surviving native migrants into the specified division or state. Some of these migrants departed from or arrived in the division or state half a century or more before the census was taken.

The net gain or loss recorded for any division or state is, of course, no indication of the extent to which that division or state has participated in the total volume of migration, since on the one hand both the outward and inward migration may have been large but nearly evenly balanced, while on the other hand the opposing currents may have been relatively small but very different in volume. For example, Illinois

shows a net loss of only 358,780 in a total of 2,672,150 surviving inward and outward native migrants, while California shows a net gain of 1,222,727 in a total of 1,505,175.

The net gain or loss during a particular decade, as shown in column 9 of Table 7, represents the difference between the net gains or the net losses at the beginning and end of the decade, or is the sum of a net loss at the beginning and a net gain at the end of the decade, or vice versa. The net gain or loss of a division during a decade does not, however, represent exactly the difference between the number of native migrants out of and the number of native migrants into the division, being influenced also to some extent by differences between the two classes of migrants in regard to mortality, by emigration to foreign countries on the part of natives who had previously migrated from one division to another, and by the return to the United States of natives who had emigrated to foreign countries after migrating from one division to another.

Urban and rural communities.—Because of the differences between urban and rural communities in regard to the proportions of interstate migrants in their population, as well as in other respects, separate statistics for the two classes of communities are given in Tables 26 to 31. The extent of the migration to the two classes of communities within the same states can not, of course, be shown, as the census returns relate only to migration across state lines.

In drawing the distinction between urban and rural population, all incorporated places (and all towns in Massachusetts, Rhode Island, and New Hampshire) having 2,500 inhabitants or more are treated as urban and the remainder of the country as rural. In Massachusetts and Rhode Island it is not the practice, as in practically all the other states, to incorporate, as separate municipalities, the relatively densely populated portions of "towns" (which are the primary divisions of the counties), and no town as a whole is incorporated as a municipality until it attains a population greatly in excess of 2,500; and in New Hampshire a similar condition exists, although the state contains two incorporated villages, each of which has fewer than 2,500 inhabitants. For this reason those towns having 2,500 or more inhabitants in the three states named are treated as urban, although portions of their areas are rural in character. The urban areas in the three states in question, as classified by the census, thus contain relatively small numbers of inhabitants who in other sections of the country would be segregated as rural. Nevertheless, in most of the towns having 2,500 inhabitants or more in Massachusetts, Rhode Island, and New Hampshire by far the greater part of the population resides within the more densely settled areas, so that the proportion classed as urban, considering each state as a whole, is not greatly exaggerated by the practice adopted.

STATE OF BIRTH.

609

PER CENT WHICH POPULATION BORN IN EACH STATE AND LIVING IN OTHER STATES FORMED OF TOTAL BORN IN EACH STATE: 1920.

[District of Columbia, 29.2 per cent, not shown separately on the map.]

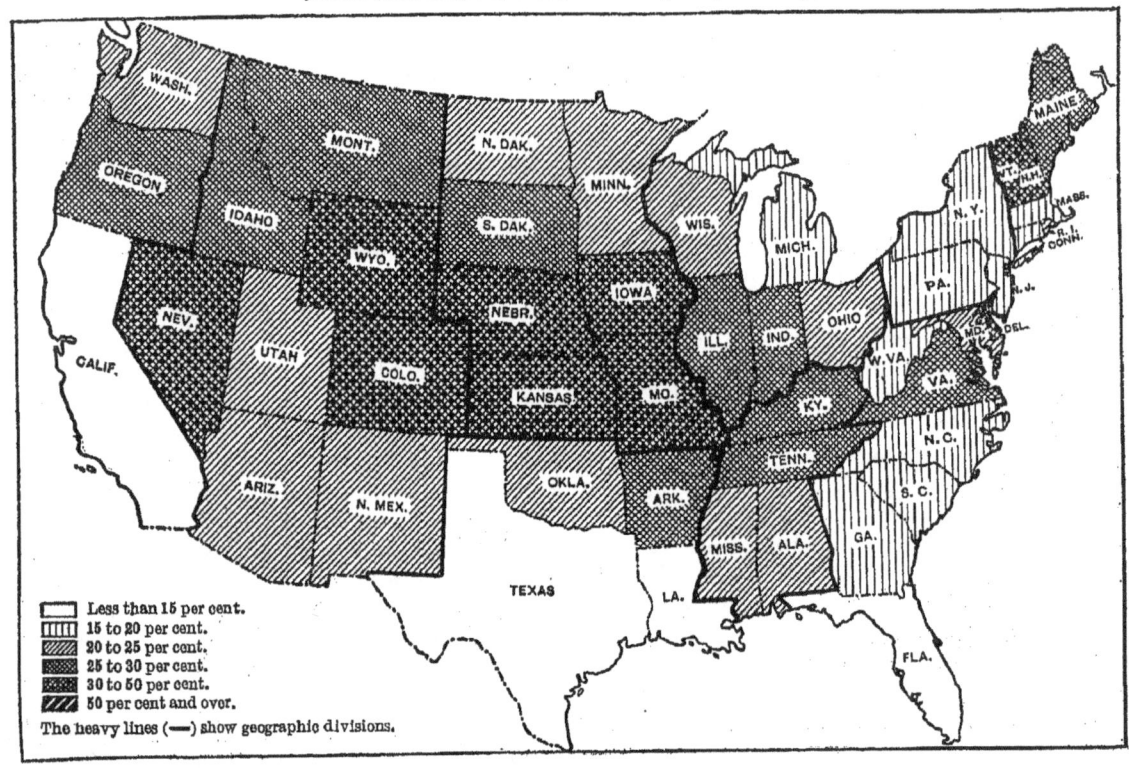

Less than 15 per cent.
15 to 20 per cent.
20 to 25 per cent.
25 to 30 per cent.
30 to 50 per cent.
50 per cent and over.
The heavy lines (—) show geographic divisions.

PER CENT WHICH POPULATION BORN IN OTHER STATES FORMED OF TOTAL NATIVE POPULATION LIVING IN EACH STATE: 1920.

[District of Columbia, 60.4 per cent, not shown separately on the map.]

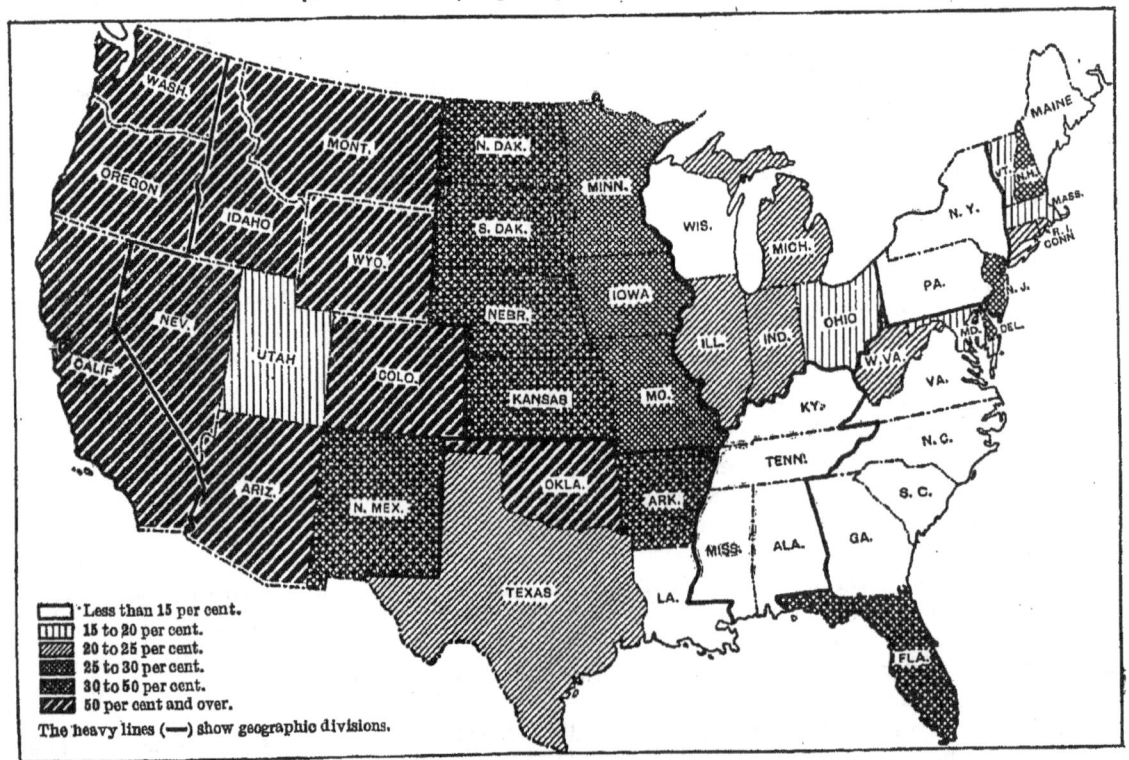

Less than 15 per cent.
15 to 20 per cent.
20 to 25 per cent.
25 to 30 per cent.
30 to 50 per cent.
50 per cent and over.
The heavy lines (—) show geographic divisions.

75647°—22——39

POPULATION.

STATES HAVING GAINED OR LOST THROUGH INTERSTATE MIGRATION: 1920.

[District of Columbia, with net gain, not shown separately on the map.]

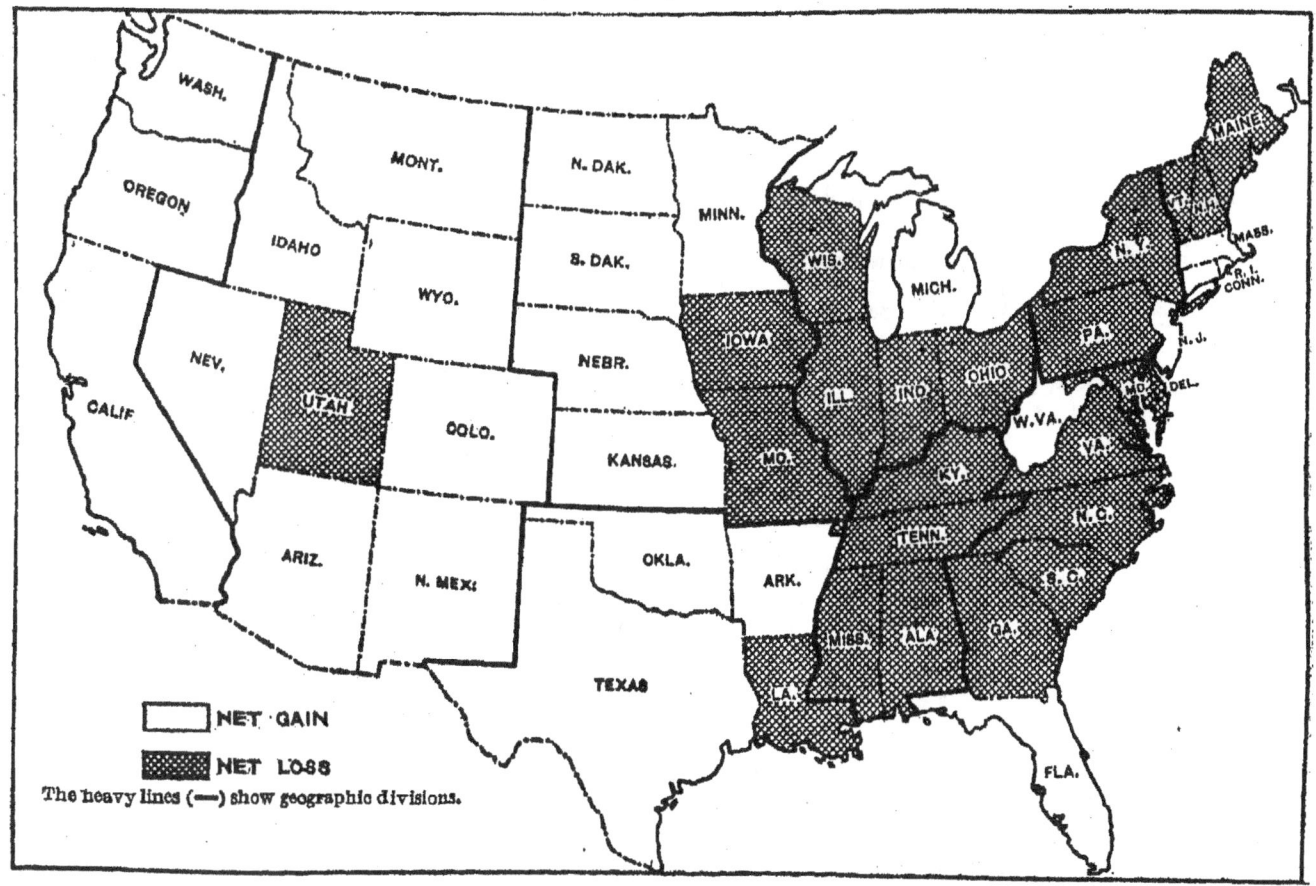

The heavy lines (—) show geographic divisions.

STATE OF BIRTH.

611

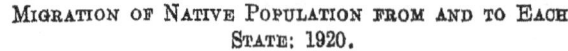

MIGRATION OF NATIVE POPULATION FROM AND TO EACH STATE: 1920.

NET GAIN OR NET LOSS THROUGH INTERSTATE MIGRATION: 1920.

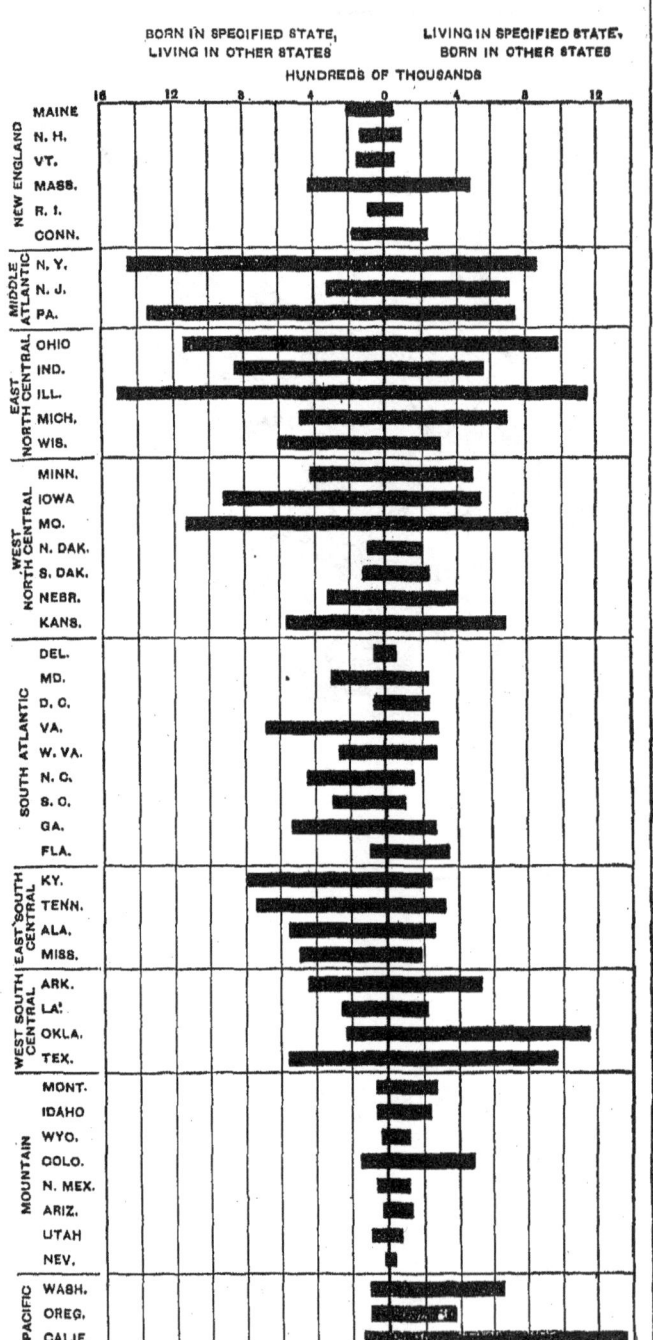

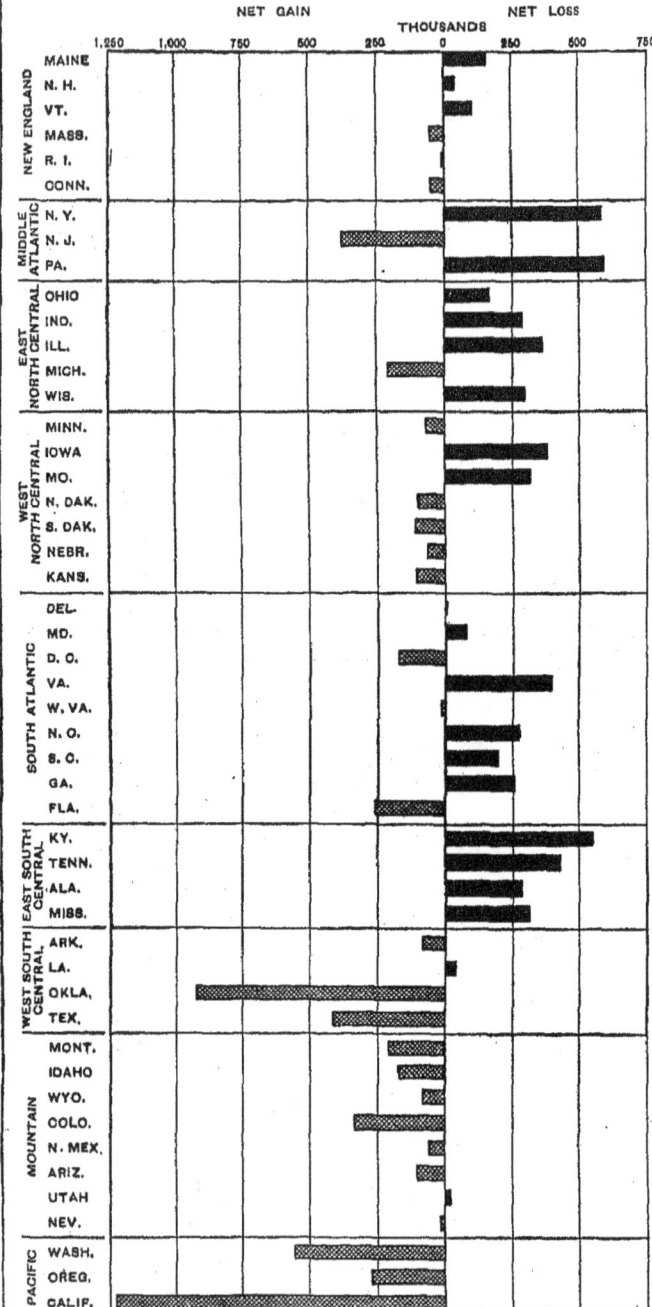

612

POPULATION.

DISTRIBUTION OF POPULATION BORN IN EACH STATE AS LIVING IN STATE OF BIRTH OR IN OTHER STATES: 1920.

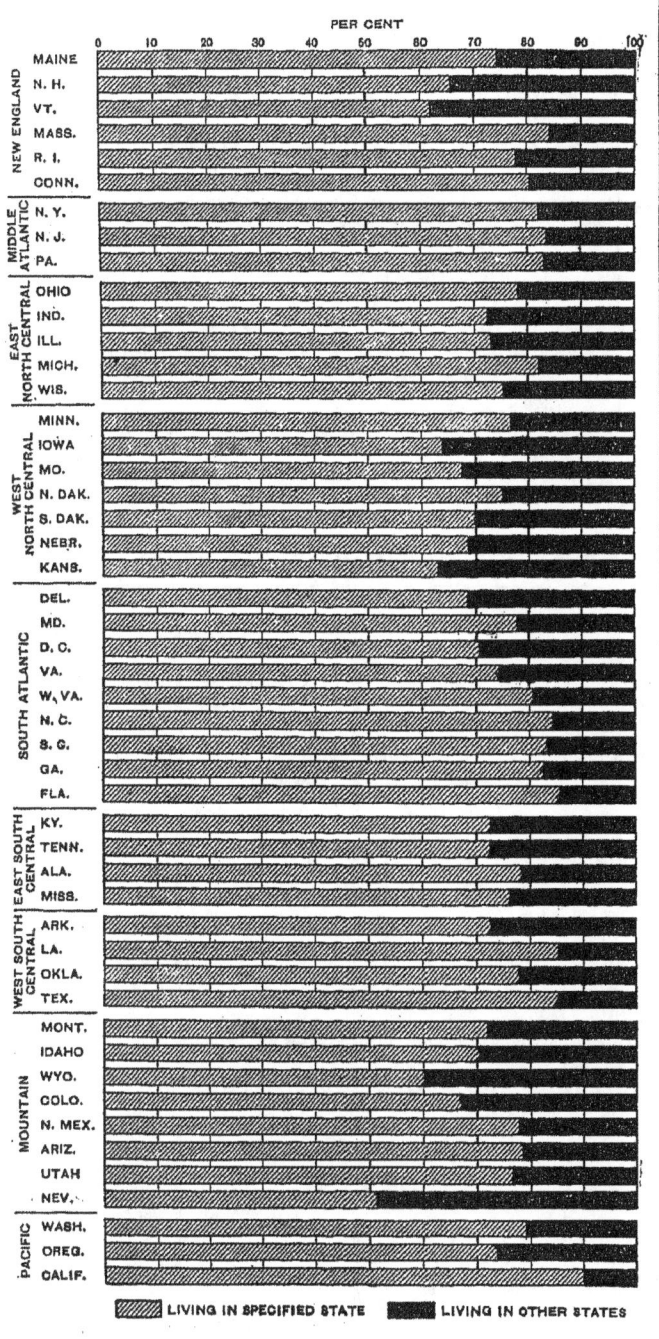

DISTRIBUTION OF TOTAL POPULATION OF EACH STATE AS BORN IN STATE OF RESIDENCE, IN OTHER STATES, OR IN FOREIGN COUNTRIES: 1920.

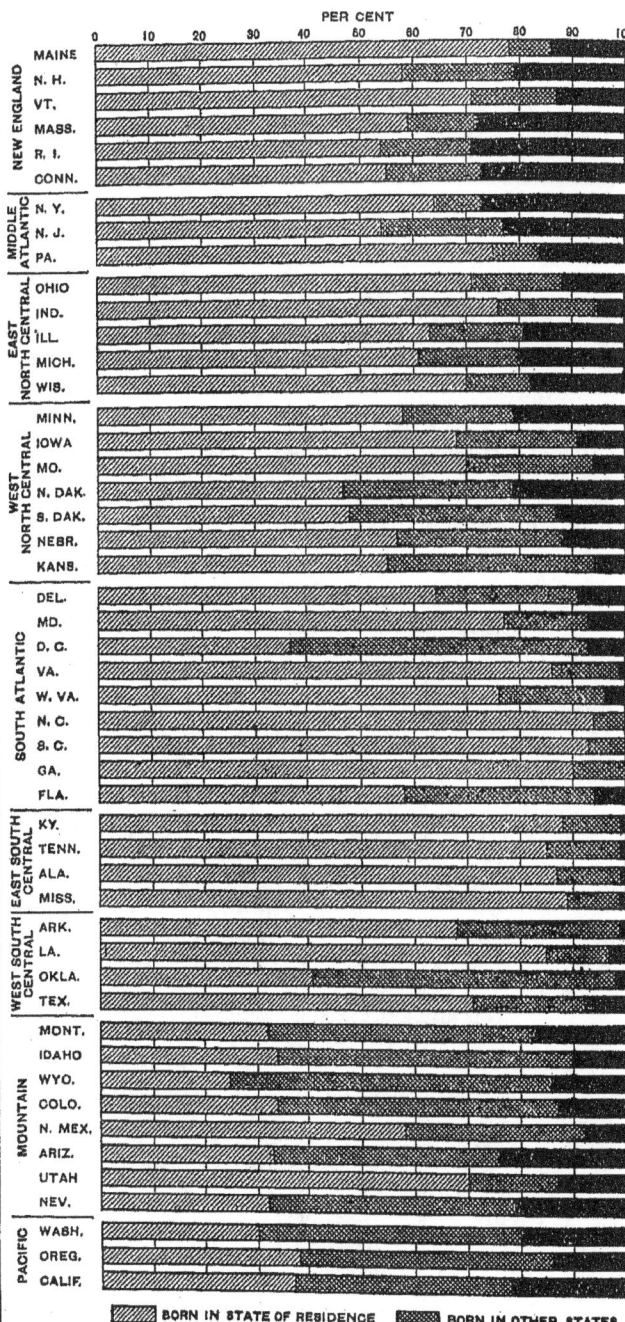

STATE OF BIRTH. 613

TABLE 1.—NUMBER AND PER CENT NATIVE AND FOREIGN BORN IN THE TOTAL POPULATION, WITH CLASSIFICATION OF NATIVE ACCORDING TO WHETHER BORN IN STATE OF RESIDENCE OR ELSEWHERE, FOR THE UNITED STATES: 1850–1920.

CENSUS YEAR.	Total population.	NATIVE POPULATION.											FOREIGN-BORN POPULATION.	
		Total.		With state of birth reported.						State of birth not reported.	Born in outlying possessions or at sea.	American citizens born abroad.		
				Born in state of residence.		Born in other states.						
		Number.	Per cent of total population.	Number.	Per cent of total population.	Number.	Per cent of total population.	Per cent of native population.					Number.	Per cent of total population.
1920	105,710,620	91,789,928	86.8	71,071,013	67.2	20,274,450	19.2	22.1	313,582	38,873	92,010	13,920,692	13.2
1910	91,972,266	78,456,380	85.3	61,185,305	66.5	16,910,114	18.4	21.6	285,685	8,925	66,351	13,515,886	14.7
1900	75,994,575	65,653,299	86.4	51,901,722	68.3	13,501,045	17.8	20.6	180,458	5,175	64,899	10,341,276	13.6
1890	¹ 62,622,250	53,372,703	85.2	41,871,611	66.9	11,094,108	17.7	20.8	396,652	1,785	8,547	9,249,547	14.8
1880	50,155,783	43,475,840	86.7	33,882,734	67.6	9,592,764	19.1	22.1		342		6,679,943	13.3
1870	38,558,371	32,991,142	85.6	25,321,340	65.7	7,657,320	19.9	23.2	12,262	220		5,567,229	14.4
1860	² 27,489,561	² 23,353,386	85.0	17,527,069	63.8	5,774,434	21.0	24.7	49,285	2,618		² 4,136,175	15.0
1850	² 19,987,563	² 17,742,961	88.8	13,457,049	67.3	4,251,250	21.3	24.0	34,662			² 2,244,602	11.2

¹ Exclusive of population of Indian Territory and Indian reservations, specially enumerated in 1890, with a native population of 325,451 and a foreign population of 13, not distributed by state of birth. These areas were not enumerated prior to 1890.
² White and free colored population only.

TABLE 2.—MIGRATION OF THE NATIVE POPULATION EAST AND WEST OF THE MISSISSIPPI RIVER: 1870–1920.

CENSUS YEAR.	NATIVE POPULATION WITH STATE OF BIRTH REPORTED.			MIGRANTS EAST AND WEST OF THE MISSISSIPPI RIVER.¹						Per cent of total trans-Mississippi migrants.		Per cent which column 6 forms of column 2.	Per cent which column 7 forms of column 3.
	Total.	Born east of the Mississippi.¹	Born west of the Mississippi.¹	Number.	Per cent of total.	Born east and living west of the Mississippi.	Born west and living east of the Mississippi.	Net gain of the west and loss of the east.		Moved west across the river.	Moved east across the river.		
	1	2	3	4	5	6	7	8		9	10	11	12
1920	91,345,403	67,487,718	23,857,745	6,266,755	6.9	5,227,850	1,038,905	4,188,945		83.4	16.6	7.7	4.4
1910	78,095,419	58,981,669	19,113,750	5,961,652	7.6	5,276,879	684,773	4,592,106		88.5	11.5	8.9	3.6
1900	65,402,767	51,163,588	14,239,179	5,030,640	7.7	4,512,097	518,543	3,993,554		89.7	10.3	8.8	3.6
1890	52,965,719	43,267,325	9,698,394	4,642,875	8.8	4,360,516	282,359	4,078,157		93.9	6.1	10.1	2.9
1880	43,475,498	37,196,027	6,279,471	3,721,096	8.6	3,510,737	210,359	3,300,378		94.3	5.7	9.4	3.3
1870	32,978,660	29,518,843	3,459,817	2,570,490	7.8	2,434,721	135,769	2,298,952		94.7	5.3	8.2	3.9

¹ In the preparation of this table the entire states of Minnesota and Louisiana have been treated as lying west of the Mississippi River.

TABLE 3.—MIGRATION OF THE NATIVE POPULATION BETWEEN THE NORTH AND THE SOUTH: 1870–1920.

CENSUS YEAR.	POPULATION BORN IN NORTH OR SOUTH,¹ WITH STATE OF BIRTH REPORTED.			MIGRANTS BETWEEN NORTH AND SOUTH.¹						Per cent of total North-and-South migrants.		Per cent which column 6 forms of column 2.	Per cent which column 7 forms of column 3.
	Total.	Born in the North.	Born in the South.	Number.	Per cent of total.	Born in North and living in South.	Born in South and living in North.	Net gain of North and loss of South.		From North to South.	From South to North.		
	1	2	3	4	5	6	7	8		9	10	11	12
1920	87,148,028	54,062,506	33,085,522	3,872,898	4.4	1,721,349	2,151,549	430,200		44.4	55.6	3.2	6.5
1910	75,189,257	46,179,002	29,010,255	2,976,336	4.0	1,449,229	1,527,107	77,878		48.7	51.3	3.1	5.3
1900	63,467,632	39,125,506	24,342,126	2,317,303	3.7	1,021,450	1,295,853	274,403		44.1	55.9	2.6	5.3
1890	51,771,684	31,933,974	19,837,710	1,771,214	3.4	635,594	1,135,620	500,026		35.9	64.1	2.0	5.7
1880	42,730,687	25,943,315	16,787,372	1,586,598	3.7	473,790	1,112,808	639,018		29.9	70.1	1.8	6.6
1870	32,589,747	19,899,822	12,689,925	1,349,151	4.1	298,298	1,050,853	752,555		22.1	77.9	1.5	8.3

¹ The North: New England, Middle Atlantic, East North Central, and West North Central divisions. The South: South Atlantic, East South Central, and West South Central divisions.

614   POPULATION.

TABLE 4.—MIGRATION OF THE NATIVE POPULATION EAST AND WEST OF THE MISSISSIPPI RIVER AND BETWEEN THE NORTH AND THE SOUTH, BY POPULATION CLASSES: 1920.

SECTION.[1]	Total.	WHITE.			Negro.	All other.
		Total.	Of native parentage.	Of foreign or mixed parentage.		
Born east and living west of the Mississippi River	5,227,850	4,882,520	3,745,681	1,136,839	342,931	2,399
Born west and living east of the Mississippi River	1,038,905	939,017	669,010	270,007	96,110	3,778
Net migration westward across the Mississippi River	4,188,945	3,943,503	3,076,671	866,832	246,821	
Net migration eastward across the Mississippi River						1,379
Born North and living South	1,721,349	1,675,085	1,363,190	311,895	44,536	1,728
Born South and living North	2,151,549	1,412,770	1,230,611	182,168	737,423	1,347
Net migration southward		262,306	132,579	129,727		381
Net migration northward	430,200				692,887	

[1] See footnotes to Tables 2 and 3.

TABLE 5.—PER CENT DISTRIBUTION, BY DIVISION OF BIRTH, OF THE NATIVE POPULATION LIVING IN EACH DIVISION: 1920 AND 1910.

DIVISION OF RESIDENCE.	PER CENT BORN IN—																			
	New England division.		Middle Atlantic division.		East North Central division.		West North Central division.		South Atlantic division.		East South Central division.		West South Central division.		Mountain division.		Pacific division.		United States, state not reported.		Outlying possessions.[1]	
	1920	1910	1920	1910	1920	1910	1920	1910	1920	1910	1920	1910	1920	1910	1920	1910	1920	1910	1920	1910	1920	1910
New England	91.4	91.8	5.6	5.3	0.9	0.8	0.3	0.3	0.9	0.9	0.1	0.1	0.1	0.1	0.1	0.1	0.1	0.1	0.2	0.2	0.3	0.3
Middle Atlantic	1.5	1.5	92.2	93.1	1.6	1.5	0.4	0.3	3.0	2.7	0.4	0.2	0.1	0.1	0.1	0.1	0.1	0.1	0.3	0.3	0.2	0.1
East North Central	0.6	0.6	4.1	4.3	86.6	88.3	2.6	2.2	1.8	1.3	3.1	2.2	0.4	0.2	0.2	0.1	0.2	0.1	0.3	0.4	0.1	0.1
West North Central	0.5	0.7	2.3	3.4	11.7	14.2	79.6	75.9	0.9	1.2	2.1	2.4	1.5	1.1	0.6	0.4	0.3	0.2	0.4	0.5	0.1	0.1
South Atlantic	0.4	0.3	2.0	1.7	1.3	1.0	0.4	0.2	93.1	94.9	2.1	1.5	0.3	0.1	0.1	(2)	0.1	(2)	0.2	0.2	(2)	(2)
East South Central	0.1	0.1	0.3	0.3	1.6	1.6	0.4	0.4	3.4	4.0	92.9	92.4	1.1	1.0	(2)	(2)	(2)	(2)	0.2	0.2	(2)	(2)
West South Central	0.1	0.1	0.8	0.7	3.2	3.7	5.6	5.9	2.3	3.3	8.6	10.2	78.3	75.3	0.4	0.2	0.2	0.1	0.5	0.4	0.1	(2)
Mountain	0.9	1.4	3.5	5.1	11.2	13.5	18.6	17.6	1.8	2.1	2.4	2.6	4.9	4.0	53.0	50.5	2.6	2.3	0.8	0.8	0.3	0.2
Pacific	2.4	3.1	6.1	7.2	15.3	16.9	15.4	15.6	1.9	2.1	2.3	2.4	2.9	2.1	4.1	2.9	48.2	46.4	0.6	1.0	0.8	0.4

[1] Includes, also, persons born at sea under United States flag and American citizens born abroad.   [2] Less than one-tenth of 1 per cent.

TABLE 6.—PER CENT DISTRIBUTION, BY DIVISION OF RESIDENCE, OF THE POPULATION BORN IN EACH DIVISION: 1920 AND 1910.

DIVISION OF BIRTH.	PER CENT LIVING IN—																	
	New England division.		Middle Atlantic division.		East North Central division.		West North Central division.		South Atlantic division.		East South Central division.		West South Central division.		Mountain division.		Pacific division.	
	1920	1910	1920	1910	1920	1910	1920	1910	1920	1910	1920	1910	1920	1910	1920	1910	1920	1910
New England	89.0	88.4	4.5	4.5	1.8	2.0	0.9	1.5	0.9	0.6	0.1	0.1	0.2	0.2	0.5	0.6	1.9	2.0
Middle Atlantic	1.7	1.6	88.5	87.7	4.2	4.3	1.4	2.2	1.5	1.3	0.2	0.2	0.4	0.4	0.6	0.7	1.5	1.5
East North Central	0.3	0.2	1.5	1.3	82.9	81.3	6.8	6.8	1.0	0.7	0.7	0.8	1.6	1.9	1.7	1.8	3.6	3.3
West North Central	0.2	0.1	0.7	0.5	4.3	3.6	78.6	80.5	0.5	0.3	0.3	0.3	4.8	5.3	4.7	4.1	6.0	5.3
South Atlantic	0.3	0.3	3.7	3.1	2.2	1.6	0.7	1.0	88.5	88.4	2.1	2.6	1.6	2.2	0.3	0.4	0.6	0.5
East South Central	0.1	0.1	0.6	0.3	5.5	3.6	2.3	2.5	2.8	1.9	79.0	81.1	8.1	9.1	0.7	0.6	1.0	0.8
West South Central	0.1	0.1	0.3	0.2	0.9	0.5	2.1	1.6	0.4	0.3	1.2	1.2	91.8	93.9	1.7	1.3	1.5	1.0
Mountain	0.3	0.3	0.8	0.9	1.8	1.4	3.5	3.0	0.4	0.3	0.2	0.2	1.9	1.3	81.3	85.4	9.8	7.2
Pacific	0.3	0.3	1.0	0.8	1.2	0.9	1.2	1.1	0.4	0.3	0.1	0.1	0.7	0.5	3.2	3.0	91.9	92.9

STATE OF BIRTH.   615

TABLE 7.—NATIVE POPULATION WITH STATE OF BIRTH REPORTED, BY DIVISION OF BIRTH AND DIVISION OF RESIDENCE, WITH NET GAIN OR LOSS THROUGH INTERDIVISIONAL MIGRATION: 1870–1920.

DIVISION AND CENSUS YEAR.	BORN IN THE SPECIFIED DIVISION.			Born in and living in the specified division.	LIVING IN THE SPECIFIED DIVISION.			Net gain (+) or loss (−) through interdivisional migration (col. 5−col. 1 or col. 6−col. 2).	Net gain (+) or loss (−) during preceding decade.
	Total (col. 4+col. 2).	Living in other divisions.			Total (col. 4+col. 6).	Born in other divisions.			
		Number.	Per cent.			Number.	Per cent.		
	1	2	8	4	5	6	7	8	9
NEW ENGLAND:									
1920	5,660,113	619,870	11.0	5,040,243	5,489,258	449,015	8.2	−170,855	+34,272
1910	4,907,215	568,763	11.6	4,338,452	4,702,088	363,636	7.7	−205,127	+13,638
1900	4,338,274	526,979	12.1	3,811,295	4,119,509	308,214	7.5	−218,765	+188,323
1890	3,898,003	564,572	14.5	3,333,431	3,540,915	207,484	5.9	−357,088	+60,446
1880	3,643,424	587,039	16.1	3,056,385	3,216,890	160,505	5.0	−426,534	+27,777
1870	3,293,103	568,707	17.3	2,724,396	2,838,792	114,396	4.0	−454,811	....
MIDDLE ATLANTIC:									
1920	18,019,528	2,069,953	11.5	15,949,575	17,214,224	1,264,649	7.3	−805,304	+127,163
1910	15,342,852	1,881,406	12.3	13,461,446	14,410,385	948,939	6.6	−932,467	+155,683
1900	13,178,117	1,808,060	13.7	11,370,057	12,089,967	719,910	6.0	−1,088,150	+248,899
1890	11,177,406	1,818,364	16.3	9,359,042	9,840,357	481,315	4.9	−1,337,049	+30,779
1880	9,843,732	1,785,831	18.1	8,057,901	8,475,904	418,003	4.9	−1,367,828	−116,551
1870	8,186,679	1,596,101	19.5	6,590,578	6,935,402	344,824	5.0	−1,251,277	....
EAST NORTH CENTRAL:									
1920	19,062,140	3,265,913	17.1	15,796,227	18,163,965	2,367,738	13.0	−898,175	+478,250
1910	16,479,755	3,077,070	18.7	13,402,685	15,103,330	1,700,645	11.3	−1,376,425	−520,976
1900	14,160,456	2,473,049	17.5	11,687,407	13,305,007	1,617,600	12.2	−855,449	−149,210
1890	11,596,441	2,194,018	18.9	9,401,523	10,890,202	1,488,679	13.7	−706,239	−817,075
1880	9,179,161	1,552,367	16.9	7,626,794	9,289,007	1,663,203	17.9	+110,836	−731,146
1870	6,618,328	930,119	14.1	5,688,209	7,460,310	1,772,101	23.8	+841,982	....
WEST NORTH CENTRAL:									
1920	11,320,725	2,426,788	21.4	8,893,937	11,109,954	2,216,017	19.9	−210,771	−723,058
1910	9,449,180	1,840,185	19.5	7,608,995	9,961,467	2,352,472	23.6	+512,287	−816,329
1900	7,448,659	1,101,856	14.8	6,346,803	8,777,275	2,430,472	27.7	+1,328,616	−687,769
1890	5,262,124	592,940	11.3	4,669,184	7,278,499	2,609,315	35.8	+2,016,375	+186,160
1880	3,276,998	333,539	10.2	2,943,459	5,157,213	2,213,754	42.9	+1,880,215	+498,626
1870	1,801,712	176,027	9.8	1,625,685	3,183,301	1,557,616	48.9	+1,381,589	....
SOUTH ATLANTIC:									
1920	14,377,095	1,658,241	11.5	12,718,854	13,627,901	909,047	6.7	−749,194	+151,972
1910	12,770,824	1,478,110	11.6	11,292,714	11,869,658	576,944	4.9	−901,166	+49,392
1900	11,161,575	1,372,186	12.3	9,789,389	10,211,017	421,628	4.1	−950,558	+40,633
1890	9,616,872	1,291,048	13.4	8,325,824	8,625,681	299,857	3.5	−991,191	+95,617
1880	8,509,714	1,335,735	15.7	7,173,979	7,422,906	248,927	3.4	−1,086,808	+55,849
1870	6,828,793	1,318,504	19.3	5,510,289	5,686,136	175,847	3.1	−1,142,657	....
EAST SOUTH CENTRAL:									
1920	10,368,842	2,178,394	21.0	8,190,448	8,803,425	612,977	7.0	−1,565,417	−388,496
1910	9,481,023	1,788,681	18.9	7,692,342	8,304,102	611,760	7.4	−1,176,921	−296,289
1900	8,325,166	1,482,208	17.8	6,842,958	7,444,534	601,576	8.1	−880,632	−194,042
1890	6,978,603	1,255,789	18.0	5,722,814	6,292,013	569,199	9.0	−686,590	−158,546
1880	6,019,996	1,146,840	19.1	4,873,156	5,480,952	616,796	11.2	−530,044	−237,855
1870	4,591,940	932,776	20.3	3,659,164	4,299,251	640,087	14.9	−292,689	....
WEST SOUTH CENTRAL:									
1920	8,339,585	680,706	8.2	7,658,879	9,725,508	2,066,629	21.2	+1,385,923	−248,650
1910	6,758,408	410,956	6.1	6,347,452	8,392,981	2,045,529	24.4	+1,634,573	+245,139
1900	4,855,385	231,088	4.8	4,624,297	6,244,819	1,620,522	25.9	+1,389,434	+351,731
1890	3,242,235	149,286	4.6	3,092,949	4,279,938	1,186,989	27.7	+1,037,703	+140,275
1880	2,257,662	108,456	4.8	2,149,206	3,155,090	1,005,884	31.9	+897,428	+266,693
1870	1,269,192	74,374	5.9	1,194,818	1,899,927	705,109	37.1	+630,735	....
MOUNTAIN:									
1920	1,870,479	349,873	18.7	1,520,606	2,836,393	1,315,787	46.4	+965,914	+96,594
1910	1,289,296	188,290	14.6	1,101,006	2,158,616	1,057,610	49.0	+869,320	+343,709
1900	835,858	84,466	10.1	751,392	1,361,469	610,077	44.8	+525,611	+112,210
1890	469,834	36,314	7.7	433,520	883,235	449,715	50.9	+413,401	+206,796
1880	285,621	17,969	6.3	267,652	492,226	224,574	45.6	+206,605	+134,039
1870	155,724	6,140	3.9	149,584	228,290	78,706	34.5	+72,566	....
PACIFIC:									
1920	2,326,956	189,210	8.1	2,137,746	4,374,835	2,237,089	51.1	+2,047,879	+471,953
1910	1,616,866	115,579	7.1	1,501,287	3,192,792	1,691,505	53.0	+1,575,926	+826,023
1900	1,099,277	74,379	6.8	1,024,898	1,849,170	824,272	44.6	+749,893	+139,215
1890	724,201	39,888	5.5	684,313	1,334,879	650,566	48.7	+610,678	+294,548
1880	459,190	25,332	5.5	433,858	775,320	341,462	44.0	+316,130	+102,068
1870	233,189	12,109	5.2	221,080	447,251	226,171	50.6	+214,062	....

616   POPULATION.

TABLE 8.—TOTAL POPULATION AND WHITE POPULATION DISTRIBUTED AS BORN IN DIVISION OF RESIDENCE, IN OTHER DIVISIONS, OR IN FOREIGN COUNTRIES, BY DIVISIONS, 1920, WITH PERCENTAGES FOR 1920, 1910, AND 1900.

DIVISION OF RESIDENCE.	Total.	BORN IN THE UNITED STATES AND WITH STATE OF BIRTH REPORTED. Born in division of residence.	Born in other divisions.	Foreign born.	BORN IN THE UNITED STATES AND WITH STATE OF BIRTH REPORTED. Born in the division of residence. 1920	1910	1900	Born in other divisions. 1920	1910	1900	FOREIGN BORN. 1920	1910	1900
		TOTAL POPULATION: 1920			PER CENT OF TOTAL POPULATION.								
United States........	[1] 105,710,620	77,906,515	13,438,948	13,920,692	73.7	72.6	74.0	12.7	12.3	12.0	13.2	14.7	13.6
New England.............	7,400,909	5,040,243	449,015	1,885,045	68.1	66.2	68.2	6.1	5.5	·5.5	25.5	27.9	25.8
Middle Atlantic.............	22,261,144	15,949,575	1,264,649	4,960,418	71.6	69.7	73.6	5.7	4.9	4.7	22.3	25.1	21.5
East North Central...........	21,475,543	15,790,227	2,367,738	3,232,141	73.6	73.4	73.1	11.0	9.3	10.1	15.1	16.8	16.4
West North Central...........	12,544,240	8,893,937	2,216,017	1,375,653	70.9	65.4	61.3	17.7	20.2	23.5	11.0	13.9	14.8
South Atlantic.............	13,990,272	12,718,854	909,047	330,537	90.9	92.6	93.7	6.5	4.7	4.0	2.4	2.5	2.1
East South Central...........	8,893,307	8,190,448	612,977	72,989	92.1	91.5	90.7	6.9	7.3	8.0	0.8	1.0	1.2
West South Central...........	10,242,224	7,658,879	2,066,629	464,828	74.8	72.3	70.8	20.2	23.3	24.8	4.5	4.0	4.1
Mountain.................	3,336,101	1,520,606	1,315,787	467,620	45.6	41.8	44.9	39.4	40.2	36.4	14.0	17.2	18.0
Pacific.................	5,566,871	2,137,746	2,237,089	1,130,561	38.4	35.8	42.4	40.2	40.3	34.1	20.3	22.8	22.5
		WHITE POPULATION: 1920			PER CENT OF WHITE POPULATION.								
United States........	[2] 94,820,915	68,601,740	12,119,885	13,712,754	72.3	70.6	72.0	12.8	12.7	12.4	14.5	16.3	15.3
New England.............	7,316,079	5,003,487	417,067	1,870,654	68.4	66.4	68.4	5.7	5.2	5.1	25.6	28.0	26.0
Middle Atlantic.............	21,641,840	15,714,467	930,794	4,912,575	72.6	70.3	74.1	4.3	3.9	3.7	22.7	25.6	21.9
East North Central...........	20,938,862	15,606,106	2,035,589	3,223,279	74.5	73.9	73.5	9.7	8.7	9.5	15.4	17.1	16.7
West North Central...........	12,225,387	8,699,489	2,099,261	1,371,961	71.2	65.3	61.0	17.2	20.0	23.4	11.2	14.2	15.2
South Atlantic.............	9,648,940	8,487,281	824,045	315,920	88.0	89.8	91.0	8.5	6.5	5.7	3.3	3.6	3.1
East South Central...........	6,367,547	5,791,383	495,062	71,939	91.0	90.3	89.5	7.8	8.0	8.6	1.1	1.5	1.8
West South Central...........	8,115,727	5,791,839	1,823,403	459,333	71.4	67.9	65.1	22.5	26.5	28.3	5.7	5.2	5.5
Mountain.................	3,212,899	1,442,878	1,287,952	453,225	44.9	40.7	43.4	40.1	41.2	37.7	14.1	17.3	18.3
Pacific.................	5,353,634	2,064,810	2,200,112	1,033,868	38.6	36.1	42.9	41.1	41.5	35.5	19.3	21.4	20.6

[1] Includes persons born in the United States, state of birth not reported; persons born in outlying possessions, or at sea under United States flag; and American citizens born abroad. The combined number of these classes in the United States in 1920 was 444,465, or four-tenths of 1 per cent of the total population.

[2] Includes white persons born in the United States, state of birth not reported; white persons born in outlying possessions, or at sea under United States flag; and white American citizens born abroad. The combined number of these classes in the United States in 1920 was 386,536, or four-tenths of 1 per cent of the total white population.

TABLE 9.—NATIVE POPULATION, NATIVE WHITE POPULATION, AND NATIVE NEGRO POPULATION, WITH STATE OF BIRTH REPORTED, BY DIVISION OF BIRTH AND DIVISION OF RESIDENCE, 1920, WITH GAIN OR LOSS THROUGH INTERDIVISIONAL MIGRATION, 1920 AND 1910.

DIVISION.	ALL NATIVE CLASSES: 1920 — Born in the specified division. Total.	Living in other divisions. Number.	Per cent.	Born in and living in the specified division.	Living in the specified division. Total.	Born in other divisions. Number.	Per cent.	NATIVE WHITE: 1920 — Born in the specified division. Total.	Living in other divisions. Number.	Per cent.	Born in and living in the specified division.	Living in the specified division. Total.	Born in other divisions. Number.	Per cent.
United States.	91,345,463	13,438,948	14.7	77,906,515	91,345,463	13,438,948	14.7	80,721,625	12,119,885	15.0	68,601,740	80,721,625	12,119,885	15.0
New England.........	5,660,113	619,870	11.0	5,040,243	5,489,258	449,015	8.2	5,613,387	609,900	10.9	5,003,487	5,420,554	417,067	7.7
Middle Atlantic......	18,019,528	2,069,953	11.5	15,949,575	17,214,224	1,264,649	7.3	17,754,221	2,039,754	11.5	15,714,467	16,651,261	936,794	5.6
East North Central...	19,062,140	3,265,913	17.1	15,796,227	18,163,965	2,367,738	13.0	18,836,603	3,230,497	17.2	15,606,106	17,641,695	2,035,589	11.5
West North Central...	11,320,725	2,426,788	21.4	8,893,937	11,109,954	2,216,017	19.9	11,077,968	2,378,479	21.5	8,699,489	10,798,750	2,099,261	19.4
South Atlantic......	14,377,095	1,658,241	11.5	12,718,854	13,627,901	909,047	6.7	9,605,593	1,118,312	11.6	8,487,281	9,311,926	824,045	8.8
East South Central..	10,368,842	2,178,394	21.0	8,190,448	8,803,425	612,977	6.9	7,445,580	1,654,197	22.2	5,791,383	6,286,445	495,062	7.9
West South Central..	8,339,585	680,706	8.2	7,658,879	9,725,508	2,066,629	21.2	6,358,200	566,361	8.9	5,791,839	7,615,242	1,823,403	23.9
Mountain............	1,870,479	349,873	18.7	1,520,606	2,836,393	1,315,787	46.4	1,785,103	342,225	19.2	1,442,878	2,730,830	1,287,952	47.2
Pacific.............	2,326,956	189,210	8.1	2,137,746	4,374,835	2,237,089	51.1	2,244,970	180,160	8.0	2,064,810	4,264,922	2,200,112	51.6

DIVISION.	NATIVE NEGRO: 1920 — Born in the specified division. Total.	Living in other divisions. Number.	Per cent.	Born in and living in the specified division.	Living in the specified division. Total.	Born in other divisions. Number.	Per cent.	GAIN (+) OR LOSS (−) THROUGH INTERDIVISIONAL MIGRATION. All native classes. 1920	1910	Native white. 1920	1910	Native Negro. 1920	1910
United States.	10,342,734	1,303,423	12.6	9,039,311	10,342,734	1,303,423	12.6	....	....	....	....	....	....
New England.........	44,786	9,842	22.0	34,944	66,111	31,167	47.1	−170,855	−205,127	−192,833	−226,219	+21,325	+20,310
Middle Atlantic......	258,303	29,748	11.5	228,555	554,967	326,412	58.8	−805,304	−932,407	−1,102,960	−1,120,678	+296,664	+186,384
East North Central...	209,080	34,308	16.4	174,772	505,191	330,419	65.4	−898,175	−1,376,425	−1,194,908	−1,496,074	+296,111	+119,649
West North Central...	205,853	45,552	22.1	160,301	274,075	113,774	41.5	−210,771	+512,287	−279,218	+472,566	+68,222	+40,497
South Atlantic......	4,757,142	539,327	11.3	4,217,815	4,301,732	83,917	2.0	−749,194	−901,166	−293,667	−507,454	−455,410	−392,827
East South Central..	2,920,718	523,270	17.9	2,397,448	2,515,207	117,759	4.7	−1,565,417	−1,176,921	−1,159,135	−974,185	−405,511	−200,876
West South Central..	1,923,083	112,716	5.9	1,810,367	2,050,433	240,066	11.7	+1,385,923	+1,634,573	+1,257,042	+1,434,780	+127,350	+194,658
Mountain............	9,671	4,814	49.8	4,857	29,756	24,899	83.7	+965,914	+869,320	+945,727	+856,683	+20,085	+13,229
Pacific.............	14,098	3,846	27.3	10,252	45,262	35,010	77.3	+2,047,879	+1,575,926	+2,019,952	+1,560,561	+31,164	+18,976

STATE OF BIRTH. 617

TABLE 10.—NATIVE WHITE POPULATION OF NATIVE PARENTAGE, OF FOREIGN PARENTAGE, AND OF MIXED PARENTAGE, WITH STATE OF BIRTH REPORTED, BY DIVISION OF BIRTH AND DIVISION OF RESIDENCE, 1920, WITH GAIN OR LOSS THROUGH INTERDIVISIONAL MIGRATION, 1920 AND 1910.

DIVISION.	NATIVE WHITE OF NATIVE PARENTAGE: 1920							NATIVE WHITE OF FOREIGN PARENTAGE: 1920						
	Born in the specified division.			Born in and living in the specified division.	Living in the specified division.			Born in the specified division.			Born in and living in the specified division.	Living in the specified division.		
	Total.	Living in other divisions.			Total.	Born in other divisions.		Total.	Living in other divisions.			Total.	Born in other divisions.	
		Number.	Per cent.			Number.	Per cent.		Number.	Per cent.			Number.	Per cent.
United States.	58,123,384	9,202,309	15.8	48,921,075	58,123,384	9,202,309	15.8	15,647,659	1,926,185	12.3	13,721,474	15,647,659	1,926,185	12.3
New England........	2,929,529	379,643	13.0	2,549,886	2,787,165	237,279	8.5	1,936,467	164,270	8.5	1,772,197	1,903,651	131,454	6.9
Middle Atlantic......	10,227,475	1,285,004	12.6	8,942,471	9,579,502	637,031	6.6	5,732,292	556,843	9.7	5,175,449	5,380,887	205,438	3.8
East North Central...	12,568,280	2,286,369	18.2	10,281,911	11,733,493	1,451,582	12.4	4,238,921	618,372	14.6	3,620,549	4,034,953	414,404	10.3
West North Central...	7,730,503	1,823,457	23.6	5,907,046	7,431,001	1,523,955	20.5	2,061,488	332,029	16.1	1,729,459	2,120,052	390,593	18.4
South Atlantic.......	9,081,279	1,000,006	11.0	8,081,273	8,760,192	678,919	7.8	333,939	74,703	22.4	259,236	352,850	93,614	26.5
East South Central...	7,214,624	1,564,982	21.7	5,649,642	6,084,164	434,522	7.1	125,575	49,151	39.1	76,424	115,224	38,800	33.7
West South Central...	5,751,584	494,099	8.6	5,257,485	6,921,543	1,664,058	24.0	368,038	43,335	11.8	324,703	414,549	89,846	21.7
Mountain............	1,222,832	239,477	19.6	983,355	1,977,527	994,172	50.3	329,703	58,951	17.9	270,752	449,742	178,990	39.8
Pacific.............	1,397,278	129,272	9.3	1,268,006	2,848,707	1,580,791	55.5	521,236	28,531	5.5	492,705	875,751	383,046	43.7

DIVISION.	NATIVE WHITE OF MIXED PARENTAGE: 1920							GAIN (+) OR LOSS (—) THROUGH INTERDIVISIONAL MIGRATION.					
	Born in the specified division.			Born in and living in the specified division.	Living in the specified division.			Native white of native parentage.		Native white of foreign or mixed parentage.			
	Total.	Living in other divisions.			Total.	Born in other divisions.		1920	1910	Total.		Foreign: 1920	Mixed: 1920
		Number.	Per cent.			Number.	Per cent.			1920	1910		
United States.	6,950,582	991,391	14.3	5,959,191	6,950,582	991,391	14.3						
New England........	747,391	65,987	8.8	681,404	720,738	48,334	6.6	—142,364	—180,137	—50,469	—46,082	—32,816	—17,653
Middle Atlantic......	1,794,454	197,907	11.0	1,596,547	1,890,872	94,325	5.6	—647,973	—741,207	—454,987	—379,471	—351,405	—103,582
East North Central...	2,029,402	325,756	16.1	1,703,646	1,873,249	184,713	14.8	—834,787	—1,067,279	—360,121	—428,795	—203,968	—156,153
West North Central...	1,285,977	222,993	17.3	1,062,984	1,247,097	184,713	14.8	—299,502	+281,575	+20,284	+190,991	+58,564	+8,509
South Atlantic.......	190,375	43,603	22.9	146,772	198,884	52,112	26.2	—321,087	—485,724	—28,675	—19,113	—10,351	—18,324
East South Central...	105,381	40,064	38.0	65,317	87,057	21,740	25.0	—1,130,460	—955,052	+87,083	+90,418	+46,511	+40,572
West South Central...	238,578	28,927	12.1	209,651	279,150	69,499	24.9	+1,169,959	+1,344,362	+191,082	+185,847	+120,039	+70,993
Mountain............	232,568	43,797	18.8	188,771	303,561	114,790	37.8	+754,695	+670,836	+568,433	+427,935	+354,515	+213,918
Pacific.............	326,456	22,357	6.8	304,099	540,374	236,275	43.7	+1,451,519	+1,132,626				

618

POPULATION.

TABLE 11.—PER CENT DISTRIBUTION, BY DIVISION OF BIRTH, OF THE NATIVE POPULATION LIVING IN EACH STATE: 1920 AND 1910.

[For geographic divisions, see Table 5.]

STATE OF RESIDENCE.	New England division.		Middle Atlantic division.		East North Central division.		West North Central division.		South Atlantic division.		East South Central division.		West South Central division.		Mountain division.		Pacific division.		United States, state not reported.		Outlying possessions.[2]	
	1920	1910	1920	1910	1920	1910	1920	1910	1920	1910	1920	1910	1920	1910	1920	1910	1920	1910	1920	1910	1920	1910
NEW ENGLAND:																						
Maine	97.1	97.3	1.1	1.1	0.4	0.4	0.3	0.2	0.3	0.2	0.1	0.1	(1)	(1)	0.1	0.1	0.1	0.1	0.2	0.2	0.4	0.3
New Hampshire	94.9	95.0	2.8	2.8	0.7	0.6	0.3	0.3	0.3	0.3	0.1	0.1	(1)	0.1	0.1	0.1	0.1	0.1	0.4	0.3	0.4	0.5
Vermont	90.1	89.9	7.3	7.2	0.8	0.7	0.4	0.4	0.2	0.3	0.1	0.2	0.1	0.1	0.1	0.1	0.1	0.1	0.2	0.4	0.7	0.7
Massachusetts	92.5	92.5	4.4	4.4	1.0	0.9	0.3	0.3	0.9	1.0	0.1	0.1	0.1	0.1	0.1	0.1	0.2	0.1	0.2	0.2	0.2	0.3
Rhode Island	92.5	91.4	4.6	5.1	0.7	0.8	0.3	0.3	1.1	1.5	0.1	0.1	0.1	0.1	0.1	0.1	0.1	0.1	0.2	0.3	0.2	0.2
Connecticut	83.3	84.8	12.9	11.9	1.0	0.9	0.3	0.3	1.5	1.3	0.2	0.1	0.1	0.1	0.1	0.1	0.1	0.1	0.3	0.3	0.1	0.1
MIDDLE ATLANTIC:																						
New York	2.3	2.4	92.2	92.9	1.7	1.5	0.5	0.4	1.8	1.7	0.3	0.2	0.2	0.1	0.1	0.1	0.2	0.1	0.5	0.3	0.3	0.2
New Jersey	2.0	1.9	91.4	92.2	1.3	1.1	0.4	0.3	3.8	3.6	0.4	0.2	0.2	0.1	0.1	0.1	0.1	0.1	0.3	0.3	0.1	0.1
Pennsylvania	0.5	0.5	92.5	93.5	1.7	1.6	0.3	0.3	4.1	3.5	0.4	0.2	0.1	0.1	0.1	0.1	0.1	0.1	0.2	0.2	0.1	0.1
EAST NORTH CENTRAL:																						
Ohio	0.5	0.4	6.1	5.0	84.4	88.4	0.9	0.7	3.6	2.6	3.8	2.3	0.3	0.1	0.1	0.1	0.1	0.1	0.2	0.3	0.1	0.1
Indiana	0.2	0.2	1.7	2.1	89.5	90.4	1.4	1.2	1.1	1.3	5.2	4.2	0.3	0.2	0.1	0.1	0.1	0.1	0.3	0.3	(1)	(1)
Illinois	0.6	0.8	3.2	4.1	85.1	85.4	4.7	4.3	1.2	1.2	3.4	2.8	0.8	0.4	0.3	0.2	0.2	0.1	0.4	0.6	0.1	0.1
Michigan	1.0	0.9	6.3	7.0	86.8	89.3	1.8	1.1	1.3	0.4	1.5	0.4	0.3	0.1	0.2	0.1	0.2	0.1	0.3	0.3	0.3	0.3
Wisconsin	0.6	0.9	2.2	3.3	91.4	91.2	4.4	3.5	0.2	0.2	0.3	0.2	0.1	0.1	0.2	0.1	0.2	0.1	0.3	0.3	0.1	0.1
WEST NORTH CENTRAL:																						
Minnesota	0.9	1.5	2.3	3.5	12.2	13.0	82.6	80.1	0.3	0.4	0.3	0.4	0.2	0.1	0.4	0.3	0.8	0.2	0.3	0.5	0.2	0.1
Iowa	0.5	0.7	2.6	4.1	12.4	14.7	81.5	77.8	0.7	0.9	0.8	0.7	0.5	0.2	0.4	0.2	0.2	0.1	0.4	0.4	0.1	0.1
Missouri	0.3	0.3	1.5	1.9	9.6	11.0	79.2	77.2	1.3	1.7	4.7	5.0	2.5	1.8	0.4	0.2	0.2	0.2	0.4	0.5	(1)	(1)
North Dakota	0.4	0.8	1.7	3.2	11.4	16.5	83.3	76.1	0.5	0.8	0.3	0.4	0.2	0.2	0.7	0.4	0.3	0.2	0.9	1.2	0.3	0.2
South Dakota	0.5	0.9	2.2	3.7	13.4	17.8	80.5	74.6	0.6	0.7	0.5	0.5	0.4	0.3	0.9	0.7	0.3	0.2	0.5	0.6	0.1	0.1
Nebraska	0.5	0.8	3.0	4.6	11.7	15.9	79.7	74.4	0.9	1.2	1.0	1.0	0.9	0.5	1.2	0.8	0.3	0.2	0.6	0.5	0.1	0.1
Kansas	0.4	0.6	3.0	4.3	13.7	18.1	73.2	68.3	1.4	1.8	2.7	3.2	3.9	2.3	0.9	0.6	0.3	0.2	0.5	0.5	0.1	0.1
SOUTH ATLANTIC:																						
Delaware	0.8	0.6	12.6	11.4	0.9	0.6	0.3	0.2	84.3	86.6	0.3	0.2	0.1	(1)	0.1	(1)	0.1	(1)	0.5	0.2	0.1	(1)
Maryland	0.6	0.4	5.3	4.5	1.1	0.8	0.4	0.2	91.5	93.5	0.4	0.2	0.2	0.1	0.1	(1)	0.1	0.1	0.2	0.1	0.1	(1)
District of Columbia	3.2	2.4	10.6	8.7	5.7	4.0	2.7	1.4	72.2	80.2	2.6	1.5	1.1	0.6	0.4	0.2	0.5	0.3	0.7	0.6	0.3	0.1
Virginia	0.3	0.2	1.6	1.3	0.9	0.6	0.3	0.2	94.8	96.3	1.5	1.2	0.2	0.1	0.1	(1)	0.1	(1)	0.2	0.1	(1)	(1)
West Virginia	0.1	0.1	3.3	3.7	4.3	4.5	0.3	0.2	88.6	89.1	2.9	1.9	0.1	0.1	0.1	(1)	0.1	0.1	0.3	0.2	(1)	(1)
North Carolina	0.1	0.1	0.3	0.3	0.2	0.2	0.1	0.1	98.3	98.7	0.7	0.5	0.1	0.1	(1)	(1)	(1)	(1)	0.1	0.1	(1)	(1)
South Carolina	0.1	0.1	0.3	0.2	0.2	0.1	0.1	(1)	98.4	99.1	0.6	0.4	0.1	0.1	(1)	(1)	(1)	(1)	0.1	0.1	(1)	(1)
Georgia	0.1	0.1	0.4	0.3	0.4	0.3	0.2	0.1	95.0	96.1	3.4	2.5	0.3	0.2	(1)	(1)	(1)	(1)	0.1	0.3	(1)	(1)
Florida	1.3	0.8	3.3	1.9	4.7	2.1	1.5	0.6	79.5	86.6	7.9	6.8	0.9	0.6	0.2	0.1	0.1	0.1	0.4	0.5	0.1	0.1
EAST SOUTH CENTRAL:																						
Kentucky	0.1	0.1	0.4	0.4	3.6	3.6	0.5	0.5	1.9	1.6	92.9	93.4	0.3	0.2	(1)	(1)	(1)	(1)	0.1	0.1	(1)	(1)
Tennessee	0.1	0.1	0.4	0.4	1.2	1.4	0.5	0.5	4.2	4.4	92.1	91.9	1.2	0.9	0.1	(1)	(1)	(1)	0.2	0.3	(1)	(1)
Alabama	0.1	0.1	0.3	0.3	0.7	0.7	0.2	0.2	5.6	7.0	92.2	91.0	0.7	0.5	(1)	(1)	(1)	(1)	0.2	0.2	(1)	(1)
Mississippi	(1)	(1)	0.1	0.1	0.6	0.5	0.3	0.2	1.5	2.7	94.6	93.5	2.5	2.6	(1)	(1)	(1)	(1)	0.2	0.3	(1)	(1)
WEST SOUTH CENTRAL:																						
Arkansas	0.1	0.1	0.4	0.5	3.7	4.2	4.8	4.4	2.8	4.2	13.3	13.6	74.3	72.4	0.1	0.1	0.1	0.1	0.4	0.5	(1)	(1)
Louisiana	0.1	0.1	0.4	0.4	0.9	0.8	0.7	0.6	1.2	1.7	5.9	5.6	90.1	90.2	0.1	(1)	0.1	(1)	0.3	0.4	0.1	(1)
Oklahoma	0.2	0.2	1.4	1.5	6.9	9.8	16.9	20.2	2.4	3.2	8.2	10.4	62.5	53.6	0.6	0.4	0.3	0.2	0.6	0.5	(1)	(1)
Texas	0.2	0.1	0.8	0.6	2.2	2.1	2.6	2.5	2.5	3.6	8.0	10.7	82.5	79.5	0.5	0.2	0.2	0.1	0.5	0.4	0.1	0.1
MOUNTAIN:																						
Montana	1.2	2.1	3.8	6.4	17.2	19.5	28.3	24.7	1.4	1.9	1.6	2.0	1.4	1.3	41.3	38.5	2.6	2.0	0.8	1.2	0.5	0.3
Idaho	0.7	1.2	2.6	4.0	11.1	14.5	19.2	20.6	1.8	2.2	1.8	1.9	2.4	1.9	52.8	46.0	6.8	6.7	0.3	0.8	0.4	0.2
Wyoming	0.9	1.8	4.2	6.9	13.6	16.2	32.5	28.7	1.8	2.6	1.8	2.4	2.8	2.3	39.8	37.3	1.3	1.0	1.0	0.6	0.2	0.2
Colorado	1.2	1.9	5.2	7.5	14.6	18.7	25.6	24.7	2.0	2.5	2.9	3.0	4.3	2.5	42.0	37.7	0.8	0.6	1.2	0.7	0.1	0.1
New Mexico	0.3	0.4	1.5	1.7	4.7	5.9	6.6	7.9	1.8	1.7	3.6	4.4	14.5	14.2	66.0	62.9	0.5	0.4	0.3	0.4	0.2	0.1
Arizona	1.0	1.3	3.4	4.1	8.7	9.0	9.0	7.9	2.8	2.4	4.6	3.5	12.8	8.6	50.3	57.5	5.0	4.6	1.7	0.9	0.8	0.4
Utah	0.4	0.6	1.6	2.3	3.4	4.4	4.1	4.4	0.8	1.0	0.9	1.0	0.7	0.5	86.4	83.7	1.1	0.9	0.2	1.0	0.4	0.2
Nevada	1.9	2.9	5.2	7.1	9.5	12.6	9.4	10.6	1.7	2.1	1.7	2.2	2.2	2.1	53.1	45.8	13.8	13.3	1.1	1.1	0.4	0.3
PACIFIC:																						
Washington	1.9	2.6	5.0	6.9	17.7	21.8	20.1	22.2	2.1	2.6	2.0	2.4	1.8	1.7	4.6	3.2	43.1	35.0	0.8	1.3	0.9	0.4
Oregon	1.3	1.8	4.0	5.5	14.7	17.3	18.2	18.9	1.5	1.9	1.9	2.2	2.1	1.8	4.2	3.2	51.2	46.6	0.4	0.7	0.4	0.2
California	3.0	3.8	7.1	7.9	14.4	14.3	12.8	11.3	1.9	2.0	2.5	2.4	3.5	2.3	3.9	2.6	49.5	51.9	0.6	0.9	0.8	0.5

[1] Less than one-tenth of 1 per cent.   [2] Includes, also, persons born at sea under United States flag and American citizens born abroad.

STATE OF BIRTH.   619

TABLE 12.—PER CENT DISTRIBUTION, BY DIVISION OF RESIDENCE, OF THE POPULATION BORN IN EACH STATE: 1920 AND 1910.

[For geographic divisions, see Table 6.]

STATE OF BIRTH.	PER CENT LIVING IN—																	
	New England division.		Middle Atlantic division.		East North Central division.		West North Central division.		South Atlantic division.		East South Central division.		West South Central division.		Mountain division.		Pacific division.	
	1920	1910	1920	1910	1920	1910	1920	1910	1920	1910	1920	1910	1920	1910	1920	1910	1920	1910
NEW ENGLAND:																		
Maine	89.6	88.5	2.4	2.2	1.5	1.7	1.4	2.1	0.9	0.6	0.1	0.1	0.3	0.3	0.7	1.0	3.1	3.5
New Hampshire	91.1	90.6	2.7	2.5	1.6	1.9	1.0	1.7	0.9	0.5	0.1	0.1	0.2	0.2	0.5	0.6	1.9	1.9
Vermont	81.5	79.1	7.0	7.0	3.5	4.6	2.6	4.0	1.1	0.6	0.1	0.1	0.4	0.4	0.9	1.2	2.9	2.9
Massachusetts	90.2	90.1	4.0	4.0	1.8	1.7	0.7	1.0	0.9	0.6	0.1	0.1	0.2	0.2	0.4	0.5	1.7	1.8
Rhode Island	90.7	91.7	4.2	4.0	1.4	1.1	0.6	0.7	1.0	0.6	0.2	0.1	0.3	0.2	0.3	0.3	1.3	1.2
Connecticut	86.8	85.8	7.6	8.0	1.9	2.1	0.7	1.2	1.0	0.7	0.1	0.1	0.2	0.2	0.4	0.5	1.3	1.4
MIDDLE ATLANTIC:																		
New York	2.9	2.8	87.8	86.4	3.9	4.7	1.4	2.3	1.0	0.7	0.1	0.2	0.4	0.4	0.6	0.8	1.8	1.8
New Jersey	1.6	1.4	93.3	93.5	1.7	1.7	0.6	0.9	1.3	1.0	0.1	0.1	0.2	0.2	0.3	0.4	1.0	0.9
Pennsylvania	0.5	0.5	88.0	87.8	5.1	4.5	1.6	2.4	2.1	2.0	0.2	0.2	0.5	0.5	0.6	0.8	1.4	1.3
EAST NORTH CENTRAL:																		
Ohio	0.2	0.2	2.5	2.4	85.7	83.9	3.7	5.6	1.8	1.5	1.1	1.2	1.2	1.3	1.1	1.3	2.6	2.5
Indiana	0.1	0.1	0.9	0.7	83.1	81.9	6.1	8.0	0.9	0.5	1.5	1.6	2.4	2.8	1.7	1.6	3.2	2.8
Illinois	0.2	0.2	1.1	0.9	78.2	76.2	10.8	13.0	0.6	0.3	0.5	0.5	2.5	3.1	2.2	2.2	3.9	3.5
Michigan	0.5	0.4	1.5	1.4	88.4	87.5	2.8	3.6	0.7	0.4	0.3	0.3	0.6	0.7	1.4	1.7	3.9	4.0
Wisconsin	0.2	0.2	0.8	0.6	81.0	80.0	9.9	11.5	0.4	0.2	0.2	0.2	0.6	0.6	2.2	2.1	4.8	4.5
WEST NORTH CENTRAL:																		
Minnesota	0.2	0.3	0.6	0.5	4.5	3.6	84.4	86.3	0.4	0.2	0.1	0.1	0.5	0.5	3.0	2.4	6.3	6.1
Iowa	0.2	0.1	0.7	0.5	5.1	4.3	79.9	81.4	0.5	0.2	0.2	0.2	2.3	2.7	4.6	4.6	6.5	5.9
Missouri	0.1	0.1	0.7	0.6	4.7	3.7	75.6	78.1	0.5	0.3	0.6	0.6	8.9	9.0	4.6	3.6	4.9	4.2
North Dakota	0.2	0.2	0.5	0.4	3.0	2.0	84.7	88.2	0.4	0.2	0.1	0.1	0.4	0.4	4.8	2.9	5.9	5.6
South Dakota	0.2	0.1	0.5	0.4	3.1	2.7	84.3	86.8	0.4	0.2	0.2	0.2	0.9	0.9	4.5	3.2	5.9	5.4
Nebraska	0.2	0.1	0.6	0.5	2.9	2.8	79.4	81.7	0.5	0.2	0.1	0.1	2.2	2.7	7.6	6.1	6.6	5.8
Kansas	0.1	0.1	0.7	0.5	3.3	3.0	72.5	74.6	0.6	0.3	0.3	0.3	8.9	9.8	6.6	5.4	7.1	6.0
SOUTH ATLANTIC:																		
Delaware	0.9	0.7	20.3	19.4	1.6	1.5	0.6	0.9	75.1	75.7	0.1	0.2	0.2	0.3	0.4	0.5	0.8	0.9
Maryland	0.6	0.5	8.7	8.2	2.4	2.1	0.8	1.1	85.9	86.3	0.2	0.3	0.3	0.4	0.3	0.4	0.7	0.7
District of Columbia	1.4	1.4	8.4	8.2	2.7	2.0	1.1	1.1	82.9	84.6	0.4	0.3	0.6	0.5	0.6	0.6	1.9	1.2
Virginia	0.6	0.6	5.9	5.4	2.8	2.6	1.5	2.1	84.9	84.2	1.9	2.3	1.1	1.6	0.5	0.5	0.8	0.8
West Virginia	0.1	0.1	2.9	2.7	7.8	5.9	1.3	1.9	84.3	86.0	0.9	0.8	1.0	0.9	0.6	0.7	1.0	1.0
North Carolina	0.2	0.3	1.7	1.4	1.0	0.8	0.5	0.7	92.9	91.9	1.6	2.2	1.3	1.9	0.3	0.3	0.5	0.5
South Carolina	0.2	0.2	1.9	0.9	0.8	0.3	0.2	0.2	94.0	94.1	1.1	1.8	1.4	2.1	0.1	0.1	0.2	0.2
Georgia	0.2	0.1	1.4	0.5	1.4	0.4	0.3	0.3	87.9	87.8	4.7	5.7	3.4	4.6	0.3	0.3	0.4	0.3
Florida	0.4	0.3	2.6	1.0	1.3	0.5	0.4	0.3	91.0	93.6	2.4	2.3	1.3	1.3	0.3	0.2	0.5	0.4
EAST SOUTH CENTRAL:																		
Kentucky	0.1	0.1	0.7	0.5	12.4	9.4	3.7	4.7	2.0	1.5	74.8	77.1	3.9	4.5	1.0	1.0	1.5	1.3
Tennessee	0.1	0.1	0.5	0.3	4.1	2.4	3.0	3.4	2.8	1.9	78.0	78.8	9.4	11.3	0.8	0.7	1.3	1.1
Alabama	0.1	0.1	0.8	0.3	2.2	0.5	0.6	0.5	5.3	3.7	83.0	85.0	7.4	9.4	0.3	0.3	0.4	0.3
Mississippi	(1)	(1)	0.3	0.1	1.8	0.5	1.5	0.7	0.8	0.5	81.3	85.4	13.4	12.2	0.4	0.3	0.5	0.3
WEST SOUTH CENTRAL:																		
Arkansas	(1)	(1)	0.2	0.1	1.2	0.7	3.6	2.9	0.4	0.3	1.6	1.6	90.1	92.2	1.3	1.0	1.6	1.3
Louisiana	0.1	0.2	0.5	0.4	1.2	0.5	0.6	0.5	0.5	0.3	2.4	2.5	93.6	94.8	0.3	0.2	0.8	0.5
Oklahoma	(1)	(1)	0.2	0.1	1.3	0.8	6.1	5.2	0.4	0.2	0.4	0.3	85.6	89.0	3.3	2.6	2.6	1.7
Texas	0.1	(1)	0.3	0.2	0.6	0.3	1.0	0.8	0.4	0.2	0.6	0.5	93.4	95.3	2.1	1.7	1.6	1.0
MOUNTAIN:																		
Montana	0.3	0.4	0.9	1.0	2.6	2.1	5.3	4.3	0.5	0.3	0.2	0.2	0.8	0.6	76.7	80.6	12.7	10.4
Idaho	0.1	0.3	0.4	1.0	1.7	1.9	2.7	2.1	0.3	0.5	0.1	0.4	0.8	1.0	78.4	80.7	15.4	12.2
Wyoming	0.3	0.4	1.8	1.8	2.6	2.4	7.8	8.3	0.7	0.6	0.2	0.2	1.4	1.1	76.5	78.3	8.7	7.0
Colorado	0.5	0.4	1.4	1.2	3.0	2.3	6.5	6.0	0.6	0.3	0.3	0.2	2.3	2.0	74.6	79.3	10.8	8.2
New Mexico	0.2	0.3	0.6	0.7	1.1	0.6	1.5	1.2	0.3	0.2	0.2	0.1	5.0	2.5	87.9	92.8	3.2	1.7
Arizona	0.2	0.2	0.6	1.6	1.0	1.2	1.0	1.0	0.5	0.3	0.3	0.2	2.6	1.7	82.5	86.1	11.3	7.7
Utah	0.1	0.1	0.4	0.3	0.6	0.4	0.7	0.7	0.3	0.1	0.1	(1)	0.5	0.3	91.9	94.4	5.4	3.7
Nevada	0.7	1.0	1.0	1.9	1.2	1.3	1.7	1.9	0.5	0.8	0.3	0.4	1.0	1.0	61.3	63.3	32.3	28.3
PACIFIC:																		
Washington	0.2	0.2	0.9	0.7	1.6	1.3	1.8	1.7	0.6	0.4	0.1	0.1	0.6	0.6	4.7	4.2	89.4	90.8
Oregon	0.2	0.1	0.6	0.4	1.1	0.7	1.5	1.3	0.3	0.3	0.1	0.1	0.6	0.5	4.4	4.0	91.3	92.6
California	0.4	0.4	1.1	1.0	1.1	0.9	0.9	0.8	0.4	0.2	0.1	0.1	0.7	0.5	2.8	2.4	92.9	93.6

1 Less than one-tenth of 1 per cent.

620

POPULATION.

TABLE 13.—TOTAL POPULATION DISTRIBUTED AS BORN IN STATE OF RESIDENCE, IN OTHER STATES, OR IN FOREIGN COUNTRIES, BY STATES, 1920, WITH PERCENTAGES FOR 1920, 1910, AND 1900.

[For geographic divisions, see Table 8.]

STATE OF RESIDENCE.	POPULATION: 1920				PER CENT OF TOTAL POPULATION.								
	Total.[1]	Born in the United States and with state of birth reported.		Foreign born.	Born in the United States and with state of birth reported.						Foreign born.		
		Born in state of residence.	Born in other states.		Born in state of residence.			Born in other states.					
					1920	1910	1900	1920	1910	1900	1920	1910	1900
United States.........	105,710,620	71,071,013	20,274,450	13,920,692	67.2	66.5	68.3	19.2	18.4	17.8	13.2	14.7	13.6
NEW ENGLAND:													
Maine.....................	768,014	598,345	58,475	107,814	77.9	78.0	80.7	7.6	6.7	5.3	14.0	14.9	13.4
New Hampshire..........	443,083	257,074	91,950	91,397	58.0	57.7	59.1	20.8	19.2	18.9	20.6	22.5	21.4
Vermont.................	352,428	250,538	54,748	44,558	71.1	70.4	72.2	15.5	14.7	13.9	12.6	14.0	13.0
Massachusetts.............	3,852,356	2,265,287	487,242	1,088,548	58.8	55.3	55.0	12.6	12.9	14.3	28.3	31.5	30.2
Rhode Island..............	604,397	324,792	102,790	175,189	53.7	49.2	49.9	17.0	17.5	18.4	29.0	33.0	31.4
Connecticut...............	1,380,631	756,212	241,805	378,439	54.8	54.5	57.0	17.5	15.7	16.6	27.4	29.6	26.2
MIDDLE ATLANTIC:													
New York...............	10,385,227	6,634,469	865,523	2,825,375	63.9	62.0	66.5	8.3	7.5	6.9	27.2	30.2	26.1
New Jersey...............	3,155,900	1,693,459	711,531	742,488	53.7	53.0	56.5	22.5	20.7	20.3	23.5	26.0	22.9
Pennsylvania..............	8,720,017	6,564,988	744,254	1,392,557	75.3	73.6	76.5	8.5	7.4	7.7	16.0	18.8	15.6
EAST NORTH CENTRAL:													
Ohio....................	5,759,394	4,079,758	983,017	680,452	70.8	74.4	76.7	17.1	12.7	12.0	11.8	12.6	11.0
Indiana..................	2,930,390	2,209,448	561,058	151,328	75.4	75.2	74.6	19.1	18.6	19.6	5.2	5.9	5.6
Illinois..................	6,485,280	4,090,918	1,156,685	1,210,584	63.1	60.4	60.0	17.8	17.7	19.6	18.7	21.4	20.1
Michigan.................	3,668,412	2,223,333	697,365	729,292	60.6	62.7	60.1	19.0	15.5	16.8	19.9	21.3	22.4
Wisconsin................	2,632,067	1,852,574	309,809	460,485	70.4	66.8	63.1	11.8	11.0	11.7	17.5	22.0	24.9
WEST NORTH CENTRAL:													
Minnesota...............	2,387,125	1,392,176	499,584	486,795	58.3	54.0	51.0	20.9	19.4	19.7	20.4	26.2	28.9
Iowa....................	2,404,021	1,624,606	543,565	225,994	67.6	63.7	59.1	22.6	23.6	26.9	9.4	12.3	13.7
Missouri.................	3,404,055	2,382,282	821,375	186,835	70.0	67.5	65.5	24.1	25.0	27.2	5.5	7.0	7.0
North Dakota............	646,872	304,679	204,092	131,863	47.1	34.3	34.1	31.6	37.6	30.0	20.4	27.1	35.4
South Dakota............	636,547	303,260	247,194	82,534	47.6	38.6	39.9	38.8	43.6	37.6	13.0	17.3	22.0
Nebraska.................	1,296,372	735,442	402,676	150,665	56.7	50.0	43.2	31.1	34.7	39.8	11.6	14.8	16.6
Kansas..................	1,769,257	967,838	681,185	110,967	54.7	48.7	42.9	38.5	42.8	48.2	6.3	8.0	8.6
SOUTH ATLANTIC:													
Delaware.................	223,003	142,963	50,045	19,901	64.1	67.8	70.1	26.5	23.4	22.2	8.9	8.6	7.5
Maryland................	1,449,661	1,107,290	236,134	103,179	76.4	79.2	80.5	16.3	12.5	11.4	7.1	8.1	7.9
District of Columbia.......	437,571	160,109	244,222	29,365	36.6	42.1	43.0	55.8	49.7	49.6	6.7	7.5	7.2
Virginia.................	2,309,187	1,978,940	293,493	31,705	85.7	89.4	91.7	12.7	9.2	7.1	1.4	1.3	1.0
West Virginia............	1,463,701	1,113,343	283,552	62,105	76.1	76.2	79.8	19.4	18.8	17.5	4.2	4.7	2.3
North Carolina...........	2,559,123	2,391,258	157,996	7,272	93.4	94.7	95.3	6.2	4.9	4.4	0.3	0.3	0.2
South Carolina...........	1,683,724	1,565,791	109,369	6,582	93.0	94.4	95.5	6.5	5.1	4.1	0.4	0.4	0.4
Georgia..................	2,895,832	2,595,423	279,246	16,564	89.6	90.6	90.7	9.6	8.5	8.6	0.6	0.6	0.6
Florida..................	968,470	560,103	349,624	53,864	57.8	61.5	64.9	36.1	32.5	30.2	5.6	5.4	4.5
EAST SOUTH CENTRAL:													
Kentucky................	2,416,630	2,134,989	247,732	30,906	88.3	88.7	87.8	10.3	9.4	9.7	1.3	1.8	2.3
Tennessee................	2,337,885	1,994,580	322,329	15,648	85.3	85.7	85.8	13.8	13.1	13.1	0.7	0.9	0.9
Alabama.................	2,348,174	2,055,273	269,981	18,027	87.5	86.9	86.3	11.5	12.0	12.8	0.8	0.9	0.8
Mississippi..............	1,790,618	1,595,136	183,405	8,408	89.1	87.0	85.5	10.2	12.2	13.9	0.5	0.5	0.5
WEST SOUTH CENTRAL:													
Arkansas.................	1,752,204	1,196,930	533,148	14,137	68.3	67.1	64.8	30.4	31.4	33.8	0.8	1.1	1.1
Louisiana................	1,798,509	1,522,615	223,013	46,427	84.7	84.9	84.6	12.4	11.5	11.4	2.6	3.2	3.8
Oklahoma................	2,028,283	819,229	1,155,880	40,432	40.4	31.1	26.5	57.0	65.9	70.4	2.0	2.4	2.6
Texas...................	4,663,228	3,306,311	968,382	363,832	70.9	70.1	66.6	20.8	23.3	27.2	7.8	6.2	5.9
MOUNTAIN:													
Montana.................	548,889	172,818	274,877	95,591	31.5	26.4	25.8	50.1	47.3	45.9	17.4	25.2	27.6
Idaho...................	431,866	148,028	240,313	40,747	34.3	27.7	29.9	55.6	58.4	54.5	9.4	13.1	15.2
Wyoming................	194,402	48,982	116,830	26,567	25.2	21.8	21.1	60.1	57.7	59.7	13.7	19.9	18.8
Colorado................	939,629	317,506	492,079	119,138	33.8	29.2	28.1	52.4	53.8	54.0	12.7	16.2	16.9
New Mexico..............	360,350	209,234	119,877	29,808	58.1	56.4	73.3	33.3	36.0	19.4	8.3	7.1	7.0
Arizona.................	334,162	109,776	137,573	80,566	32.9	38.6	42.9	41.2	36.6	36.7	24.1	23.9	19.7
Utah...................	449,396	314,006	73,999	59,200	69.9	65.1	65.7	16.5	16.2	14.5	13.2	17.6	19.4
Nevada..................	77,407	24,761	35,734	16,003	32.0	26.4	42.4	46.2	48.5	33.2	20.7	24.1	23.8
PACIFIC:													
Washington..............	1,356,621	410,175	662,451	265,292	30.2	23.0	25.7	48.8	53.3	51.3	19.6	22.4	21.5
Oregon..................	783,389	295,723	374,292	107,644	37.7	33.5	39.8	47.8	49.0	43.8	13.7	16.8	15.9
California................	3,426,861	1,268,243	1,363,951	757,625	37.0	38.0	44.5	39.8	36.3	29.9	22.1	24.7	24.7

[1] Includes persons born in the United States, state of birth not reported; persons born in outlying possessions, or at sea under United States flag; and American citizens born abroad. The combined number of these classes in the United States in 1920 was 444,465, or four-tenths of 1 per cent of the total population.

STATE OF BIRTH.

621

TABLE 14.—WHITE POPULATION DISTRIBUTED AS BORN IN STATE OF RESIDENCE, IN OTHER STATES, OR IN FOREIGN COUNTRIES, BY STATES, 1920, WITH PERCENTAGES FOR 1920, 1910, AND 1900.

[For geographic divisions, see Table 8.]

STATE OF RESIDENCE.	WHITE POPULATION: 1920				PER CENT OF WHITE POPULATION.								
	Total.[1]	Born in the United States and with state of birth reported.		Foreign born.	Born in the United States and with state of birth reported.						Foreign born.		
		Born in state of residence.	Born in other states.		Born in state of residence.			Born in other states.					
					1920	1910	1900	1920	1910	1900	1920	1910	1900
United States	94,820,915	62,524,789	18,196,836	13,712,754	65.9	64.6	66.3	19.2	18.7	18.1	14.5	16.3	15.3
NEW ENGLAND:													
Maine	765,695	596,893	58,109	107,349	78.0	78.0	80.8	7.6	6.7	5.3	14.0	14.9	13.4
New Hampshire	442,331	256,800	91,656	91,233	58.1	57.8	59.1	20.7	19.1	18.8	20.6	22.5	21.4
Vermont	351,817	250,196	54,519	44,526	71.1	70.6	72.3	15.5	14.4	13.8	12.7	14.1	13.0
Massachusetts	3,803,524	2,246,606	468,631	1,077,534	59.1	55.5	55.3	12.3	12.5	13.9	28.3	31.6	30.3
Rhode Island	593,980	320,269	98,665	173,499	53.9	49.4	50.1	16.6	16.9	17.7	29.2	33.4	31.9
Connecticut	1,358,732	748,187	230,023	376,513	55.1	54.6	57.1	16.9	15.2	16.1	27.7	29.9	26.6
MIDDLE ATLANTIC:													
New York	10,172,027	6,566,130	765,945	2,786,112	64.6	62.4	66.8	7.5	6.9	6.3	27.4	30.4	26.4
New Jersey	3,037,087	1,650,564	640,001	738,613	54.3	53.4	57.0	21.1	19.4	19.1	24.3	26.9	23.7
Pennsylvania	8,432,726	6,464,194	564,337	1,387,850	76.7	74.4	77.3	6.7	6.2	6.5	16.5	19.3	16.0
EAST NORTH CENTRAL:													
Ohio	5,571,893	4,012,837	865,637	678,697	72.0	74.9	77.2	15.5	12.0	11.3	12.2	12.8	11.8
Indiana	2,849,071	2,181,795	508,423	150,868	76.6	76.0	75.3	17.8	17.7	18.7	5.3	6.0	5.8
Illinois	6,299,333	4,046,455	1,020,859	1,206,951	64.2	61.0	60.5	16.2	16.8	18.8	19.2	21.8	20.4
Michigan	3,601,627	2,207,704	650,259	726,635	61.3	62.7	60.1	18.1	15.4	16.8	20.2	21.4	22.5
Wisconsin	2,616,938	1,842,264	305,462	460,128	70.4	66.7	63.0	11.7	11.0	11.7	17.6	22.1	25.1
WEST NORTH CENTRAL:													
Minnesota	2,368,936	1,382,057	492,350	486,164	58.3	54.0	50.9	20.8	19.3	19.6	20.5	26.4	29.1
Iowa	2,384,181	1,618,130	530,884	225,647	67.9	63.9	59.2	22.3	23.3	26.7	9.5	12.4	13.8
Missouri	3,225,044	2,280,498	746,767	186,026	70.7	67.4	65.0	23.2	24.8	27.3	5.8	7.3	7.3
North Dakota	639,954	298,954	203,361	131,503	46.7	33.8	33.1	31.8	37.9	30.3	20.5	27.4	36.1
South Dakota	619,147	288,924	244,501	82,391	46.7	37.2	38.3	39.5	44.5	38.2	13.3	17.8	23.2
Nebraska	1,279,219	731,066	391,329	149,652	57.1	50.1	43.3	30.6	34.5	39.7	11.7	14.9	16.8
Kansas	1,708,906	942,907	646,932	110,578	55.2	48.9	42.9	37.9	42.3	47.9	6.5	8.3	8.9
SOUTH ATLANTIC:													
Delaware	192,615	122,524	49,445	19,810	63.6	66.9	69.0	25.7	22.7	21.8	10.3	10.2	8.9
Maryland	1,204,737	910,534	189,777	102,177	75.6	77.6	78.5	15.8	12.4	11.5	8.5	9.8	9.8
District of Columbia	326,860	113,486	181,813	28,548	34.7	41.9	43.6	55.6	47.2	46.0	8.7	10.3	10.2
Virginia	1,617,909	1,360,807	223,106	30,785	84.1	87.7	90.1	13.8	10.2	8.2	1.9	1.9	1.6
West Virginia	1,377,235	1,079,987	231,288	61,906	78.4	78.1	81.3	16.8	16.7	16.0	4.5	4.9	2.4
North Carolina	1,783,779	1,665,379	109,612	7,099	93.4	94.5	95.1	6.1	5.0	4.5	0.4	0.4	0.3
South Carolina	818,538	718,524	92,445	6,401	87.8	89.8	91.8	11.3	9.3	7.2	0.8	0.9	1.0
Georgia	1,689,114	1,471,937	198,469	16,186	87.1	88.5	89.1	11.7	10.2	9.8	1.0	1.1	1.0
Florida	638,153	342,353	250,440	43,008	53.6	59.6	62.4	39.2	32.3	30.8	6.7	7.6	6.5
EAST SOUTH CENTRAL:													
Kentucky	2,180,560	1,933,612	213,855	30,780	88.7	88.6	87.3	9.8	9.3	9.9	1.4	2.0	2.7
Tennessee	1,885,993	1,628,768	238,751	15,478	86.4	86.5	86.3	12.7	12.2	12.4	0.8	1.1	1.1
Alabama	1,447,032	1,213,217	213,626	17,662	83.8	82.8	82.3	14.8	15.5	16.1	1.2	1.5	1.4
Mississippi	853,962	732,695	111,921	8,019	85.8	84.3	83.1	13.1	14.3	15.6	0.9	1.2	1.2
WEST SOUTH CENTRAL:													
Arkansas	1,279,757	885,648	375,105	13,975	69.2	67.2	64.5	29.3	30.9	33.7	1.1	1.5	1.5
Louisiana	1,096,611	887,092	160,368	44,871	80.9	81.0	80.7	14.6	13.0	12.0	4.1	5.5	7.1
Oklahoma	1,821,194	702,130	1,068,052	39,968	38.6	27.9	19.7	58.6	68.8	76.8	2.2	2.8	3.0
Texas	3,918,165	2,650,041	886,806	360,519	67.6	66.4	62.4	22.6	25.8	30.0	9.2	7.5	7.3
MOUNTAIN:													
Montana	534,260	162,852	272,356	93,629	30.5	24.9	23.6	51.0	48.5	48.1	17.5	25.4	27.6
Idaho	425,668	145,087	238,917	38,963	34.1	27.3	29.0	56.1	59.2	56.4	9.2	12.7	14.2
Wyoming	190,146	47,507	115,432	25,255	25.0	21.5	20.4	60.7	58.6	60.9	13.3	19.3	18.6
Colorado	924,103	313,547	482,961	116,054	33.9	29.4	28.2	52.3	53.7	53.7	12.7	16.2	17.1
New Mexico	334,673	189,989	114,398	29,077	56.8	53.9	72.2	34.2	38.2	20.1	8.7	7.4	7.4
Arizona	291,449	79,576	129,858	78,099	27.3	29.4	28.9	44.6	42.2	46.2	26.8	27.3	24.1
Utah	441,001	310,819	72,498	56,455	70.3	65.6	66.1	16.4	16.1	14.2	12.8	17.3	19.4
Nevada	70,699	19,962	35,071	14,802	28.2	22.6	36.6	49.6	52.2	38.6	20.9	24.2	24.2
PACIFIC:													
Washington	1,319,777	396,184	656,453	250,055	30.0	22.6	24.8	49.7	54.3	53.0	18.9	21.7	20.6
Oregon	769,146	290,378	371,416	102,151	37.8	33.6	40.4	48.3	50.0	45.4	13.3	15.7	13.7
California	3,264,711	1,216,634	1,333,857	681,662	37.3	38.6	45.4	40.9	37.5	31.2	20.9	22.9	22.6

[1] Includes white persons born in the United States, state of birth not reported; white persons born in outlying possessions, or at sea under United States flag; and white American citizens born abroad. The combined number of these classes in the United States in 1920 was 386,536, or four-tenths of 1 per cent of the total white population.

CHAPTER VI

COUNTRY OF BIRTH OF THE FOREIGN-BORN POPULATION

CHAPTER VI.—COUNTRY OF BIRTH OF THE FOREIGN-BORN POPULATION.

INTRODUCTION.

The inquiry as to country of birth of the foreign born has been made at each census, beginning with 1850. The statistics here presented relate to the population of continental United States, the states, and those cities having 25,000 inhabitants or more. Statistics for Alaska, Guam, Hawaii, Panama Canal Zone, and Porto Rico are given in Volume III of the Fourteenth Census Reports. No tabulation as to country of birth was made for American Samoa; and the Philippines and the Virgin Islands of the United States were not enumerated as a part of the Fourteenth Census.

The foreign-born population comprises all persons born outside of the United States or any of the outlying possessions, persons reported as born in any outlying possession being regarded as native, the same as persons born in continental United States.

The statistics here given except those in Table 1 relate to the foreign-born population of all races combined. Of the 13,920,692 persons of foreign birth who were enumerated in continental United States in 1920, 13,712,754 were white and 207,938 of nonwhite races, consisting mainly of Negroes, Chinese, and Japanese. (See Table 1.) As a general rule, to which natives of China, India, Japan, and the West Indies constitute the leading exceptions, the total number reported as born in a given country or region does not differ greatly from the number of white persons reported as born in that country or region.

CHANGES DUE TO WORLD WAR WHICH AFFECT COMPARABILITY OF STATISTICS.

The changes in the map of Europe and of Turkey in Asia which resulted from the World War of 1914–1918 have made difficult a comparison of the distribution of the foreign-born population in 1920 with that of preceding censuses. The following statement shows the various transfers of territory between 1910 and 1920 due to the World War which affect the comparability of the country-of-birth statistics:

NORTHWESTERN EUROPE.

Belgium.—Annexation of towns of Eupen and Malmedy from Germany.
Denmark.—Annexation of Northern Schleswig from Germany.
France.—Annexation of Alsace-Lorraine from Germany.

CENTRAL AND EASTERN EUROPE.

Austria.—Annexation of territory from Hungary. Detachments of territory to Czechoslovakia (q. v.), Poland (Galicia), Jugo-Slavia (q. v.), Rumania (Bukowina), and Italy (Trentino region,

Gorizia, Istrian peninsula, and Trieste); and detachment of Fiume (free state; see "Other Europe").

Bulgaria.—Detachments of territory to Greece (Bulgarian Thrace) and Jugo-Slavia (ceded territory includes towns of Strumitsa and Tsaribrod).

Czechoslovakia.—Created from territory formerly included in Austria-Hungary (Bohemia, Moravia, Ruthenia, and Slovakland).

Germany.—Detachments of territory to France (Alsace-Lorraine), Belgium (Eupen and Malmedy), Poland (West Prussia and Posen), and Denmark (Northern Schleswig); and of Saar Basin (now governed by a Commission of the League of Nations; see "Other Europe") and of Danzig (free city; see "Other Europe").

Hungary.—Detachments of territory to Austria, Czechoslovakia (Ruthenia and Slovakland), Rumania (ceded territory includes Transylvania and part of Banat), and Jugo-Slavia (q. v.).

Jugo-Slavia.—Created from territory formerly constituting Serbia and Montenegro and from territory formerly included in Austria-Hungary (Carniola, Dalmatia, Croatia, Slavonia, part of Banat, Bosnia, and Herzegovina) and Bulgaria (ceded territory includes towns of Strumitsa and Tsaribrod).

Lithuania.—Formerly included in Russia.

Poland.—Restored to its original status as an independent country by reuniting Austrian Poland (Galicia), German Poland (West Prussia and Posen), and Russian Poland.

Rumania.—Annexations of territory from Austria (Bukowina), Hungary (Transylvania, part of Banat, and other territory), and Russia (Bessarabia).

Russia.—Detachments of territory to Poland (Russian Poland) and Rumania (Bessarabia) and detachment of Lithuania.

Turkey in Europe.—Detachments of territory to Greece (Turkish Islands of the Aegean, Turkish Thrace, and Smyrna) and detachment of Albania.

SOUTHERN EUROPE.

Albania.—Formerly included in Turkey in Europe.

Greece.—Annexations of territory from Bulgaria (Bulgarian Thrace) and Turkey in Europe (Turkish Islands of the Aegean, Turkish Thrace, and Smyrna).

Italy.—Annexation of territory from Austria (Trentino region, Gorizia, Istrian peninsula, and Trieste).

OTHER EUROPE.

Danzig.—Free city; formerly included in Germany.
Fiume.—Free state; formerly included in Austria.
Saar Basin.—Under government of a Commission of the League of Nations; formerly included in Germany.

ASIA.

Armenia.—Formerly included in Turkey in Asia.
Palestine.—Formerly included in Turkey in Asia.
Syria.—Formerly included in Turkey in Asia.
Turkey in Asia.—Detachments of Armenia, Palestine, and Syria, and detachment of Hedjaz (now included in "Other Asia").
Other Asia.—Includes Hedjaz, formerly part of Turkey in Asia.

In Table 3 (p. 694) the foreign-born population is distributed by country of birth according to postwar boundaries for 1920 and according to prewar boundaries for 1910, and in using the statistics given therein cognizance must be taken of the changes in territory

688   POPULATION.

for certain countries, as has been indicated. It should also be remembered that the statistics given in other tables for preceding census years refer to the various foreign countries as constituted in the years to which the statistics relate,* except in the case of Poland, for which country the population figures have been adjusted.

Although Poland was not restored to its original status as an independent country until the close of the World War, many persons reported their birthplace as Poland and were so tabulated for several censuses. At the census of 1900 an attempt was made for the first time to distinguish Austrian, German, and Russian Poland, and separate statistics for each were presented. At the censuses of 1910 and 1920 the mother tongue, or native language, was reported for the foreign-born population, so that persons were enumerated at these censuses as of Polish mother tongue instead of as born in Poland.

* In taking the census of 1920 the enumerators were instructed to ask the name of the province or city, when a person reported himself or his parents as having been born in Germany, Austria, Russia, or any other country whose boundaries were affected by the war, so that it would be possible to present statistics on country of birth of person or parents according to the areas as constituted at the time of the census. This was found to be practicable in case of the person, but not of the parents; in many cases a person born in the United States does not know the name of the province or city in which his foreign parent or parents were born, so the statistics of birthplace of parents were compiled on the prewar basis and those of birthplace of person on the postwar basis. In the case of foreign-born persons, however, it is possible to present with some approximation to accuracy the increase on the basis of 1910 in the countries affected by the war, by arranging the detached areas, so far as separately reported, according to the countries of which they formed parts in 1910. This is done in the following statement:

COUNTRY OF BIRTH (basis of 1910).	1920	1910	Increase:[1] 1910-1920.	
			Number.	Per cent.
France	118,751	117,418	1,333	1.1
Germany	1,869,507	2,501,333	−631,826	−25.3
Germany	1,686,108			
Alsace-Lorraine	34,321			
Poland-German	146,766			
Danzig	2,049			
Saar Basin	263			
Italy	1,610,113	1,343,125	266,988	19.9
Austria-Hungary	2,021,926	1,670,582	351,344	21.0
Austria	575,627			
Bohemia-Moravia	214,841			
Bosnia-Herzegovina	5,911			
Jugo-Slavia	63,631			
Fiume	384			
Poland-Austrian	543,146			
Hungary	397,283			
Slovakland	144,507			
Croatia-Slavonia	73,506			
Ruthenia	3,090			
Russia-Finland	2,135,454	1,732,462	402,992	23.3
Russia	1,400,495			
Lithuania	135,068			
Poland-Russian	450,067			
Finland	149,824			
Balkan Peninsula	326,559	220,946	105,613	47.8
Rumania	102,823			
Bulgaria	10,477			
Serbia	20,754			
Montenegro	5,637			
Albania	5,608			
Greece	175,976			
Turkey, Europe	5,284			

[1] A minus sign (−) denotes decrease.

In all tables of this report showing comparative figures for 1910 it is assumed that the total number of Polish-speaking persons enumerated in 1910 as born in Austria, Germany, or Russia represents with substantial accuracy the total number of residents of the United States who were born in what is now Poland. Of course, some Polish-speaking persons were born in Austria, Germany, or Russia outside the limits of Poland; but, conversely, some non-Polish-speaking persons were born within those limits. In these comparative tables the 1910 figures for Austria, Germany, and Russia differ from those published in the Thirteenth Census Reports by the subtraction of the number of Polish-speaking persons in each of these countries; the figures for 1900 are used as published in the Twelfth Census Reports instead of as modified to meet the Thirteenth Census classification.

The composition of the foreign-born population of the United States has undergone a great change since 1850, and particularly since 1880, as will be seen by reference to Table 5. In studying the percentages in that table, it must be borne in mind that, since the foreign-born population enumerated at each census consists in large part of survivors of the foreign-born population enumerated at the preceding census, the changes in the proportions of the immigrants from certain countries have been much more pronounced from decade to decade than the changes in the proportions which the natives of these countries formed of the total foreign-born population enumerated at successive censuses.

To illustrate: Suppose that during the decade 1900–1910 the number of immigrants from a certain country was 880,000, or about one-tenth of the total immigration; that in 1910 the number of natives of that country who were enumerated in the United States was 1,350,000, or about one-tenth of the total foreign-born population; that during the decade 1910–1920 the number of immigrants from the country in question was only about 115,000, or about 2 per cent of the total immigration; and that, making due allowance for mortality, the number of natives of that country who were enumerated in the United States in 1920 was 1,200,000, or 8.6 per cent of the total foreign-born population in that year. In such a case a decline of four-fifths (from 10 per cent to 2 per cent) in the proportion of the total immigration from one decade to another would be accompanied by a decline of only about one-seventh (from 10 per cent to 8.6 per cent) in the proportion of the total foreign-born population from one census to another.

The increases in the numbers of persons born in those foreign countries whose areas have remained unchanged represent the excess of net immigration over mortality among immigrants already in the United States. Mortality depends largely on two

COUNTRY OF BIRTH.

factors, (1) the total number of persons in the United States who were born in the country in question and (2) their average age. In cases where large numbers of immigrants came to this country several decades ago—for instance, from Ireland—the number of deaths among such immigrants is considerably larger than in the case of countries—for example, Portugal—from which the immigration has been more recent, both because the total number of persons in the United States who were born in the countries from which the earlier immigration came is greater and because such persons belong, on the average, to an older age group and are consequently subject to a higher death rate; hence it would require a much larger net immigration to counterbalance the mortality among persons in the United States who were born in Ireland than to counterbalance the mortality among those born in Portugal.

URBAN AND RURAL COMMUNITIES.

Because of the great difference between the proportions of immigrants who go to urban and rural communities, separate statistics for the two classes of communities are given in Tables 18 and 19.

In drawing the distinction between urban and rural population, all incorporated places (and all towns in Massachusetts, Rhode Island, and New Hampshire) having 2,500 inhabitants or more are treated as urban and the remainder of the country as rural. In Massachusetts and Rhode Island it is not the practice, as in practically all the other states, to incorporate, as separate municipalities, the relatively densely populated portions of "towns" (which are the primary divisions of the counties), and no town as a whole is incorporated as a municipality until it attains a population greatly in excess of 2,500; and in New Hampshire a

75647°—22——44

similar condition exists, although the state contains two incorporated villages, each of which has fewer than 2,500 inhabitants. For this reason those towns having 2,500 or more inhabitants in the three states named are treated as urban, although portions of their areas are rural in character. The urban areas in the three states in question, as classified by the census, thus contain relatively small numbers of inhabitants who in other sections of the country would be segregated as rural. Nevertheless, in most of the towns having 2,500 inhabitants or more in Massachusetts, Rhode Island, and New Hampshire by far the greater part of the population resides within the more densely settled areas, so that the proportion classed as urban, considering each state as a whole, is not greatly exaggerated by the practice adopted.

In making comparisons between foreign countries in regard to the proportions of their natives who have settled in urban and in rural communities, respectively, consideration should be given to the fact that many of the immigrants from the Northwestern European countries and from Germany came to the United States at a time when land was to be had free or at low cost, while most of the immigrants from Central Europe, except Germany, and from Eastern and Southern Europe have arrived during a more recent period, when there has been comparatively little conveniently located and fertile land available for free settlement or obtainable at low prices. As a result, large numbers of the immigrants from Northwestern Europe and from Germany went to rural localities, while most of the immigrants from the remainder of Europe have settled in urban communities, despite the fact that many of them were farmers in their native countries.

POPULATION.

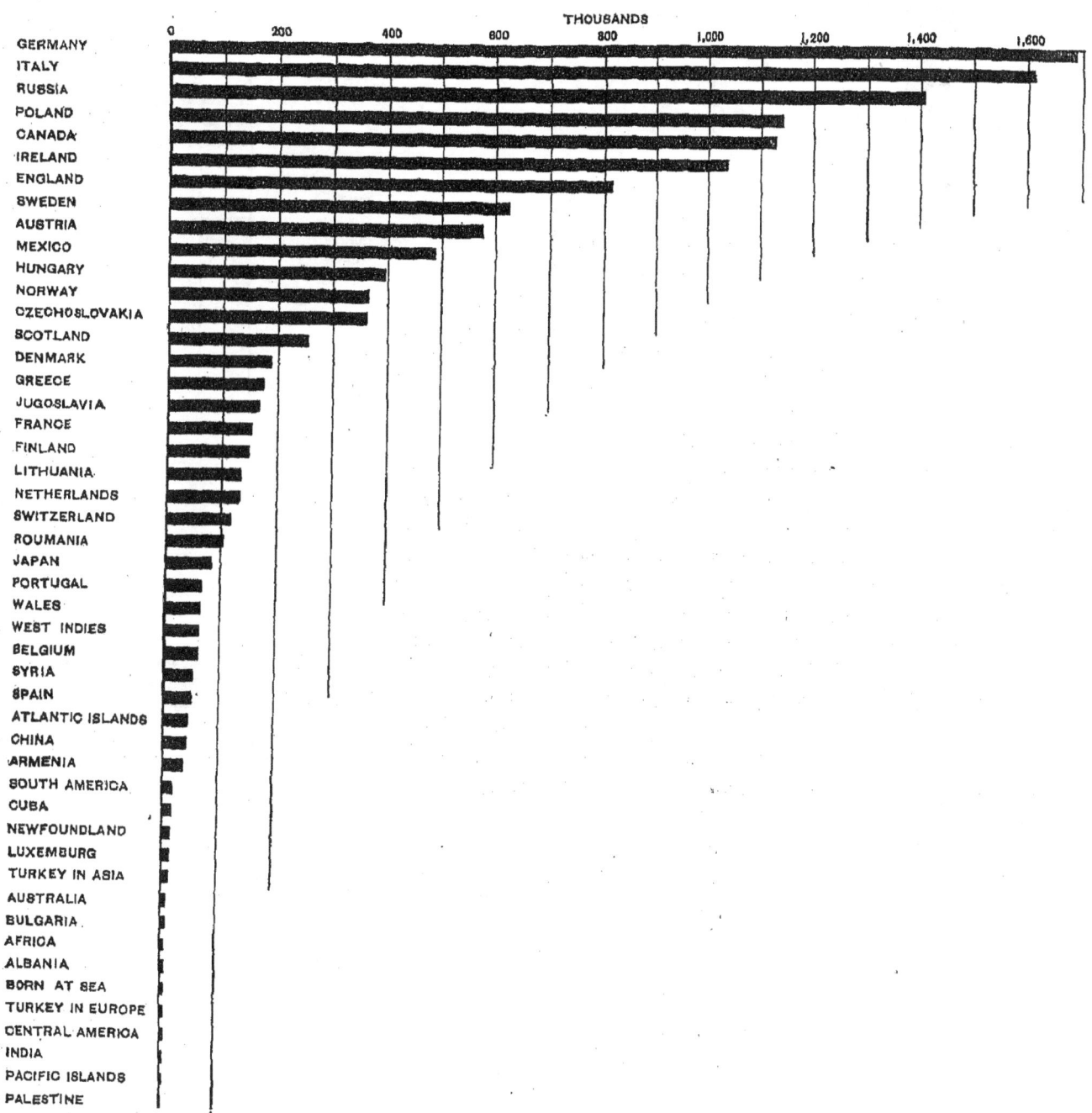

FOREIGN-BORN POPULATION OF THE UNITED STATES, BY COUNTRY OF BIRTH: 1920.

COUNTRY OF BIRTH.

DISTRIBUTION OF NATIVES OF PRINCIPAL FOREIGN COUNTRIES AND GROUPS OF COUNTRIES, BY STATES: 1920.

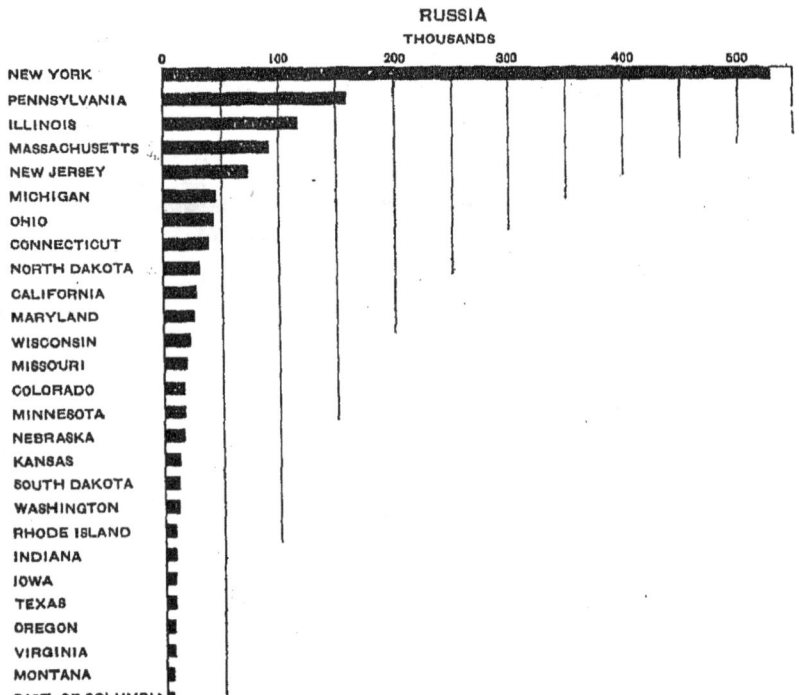

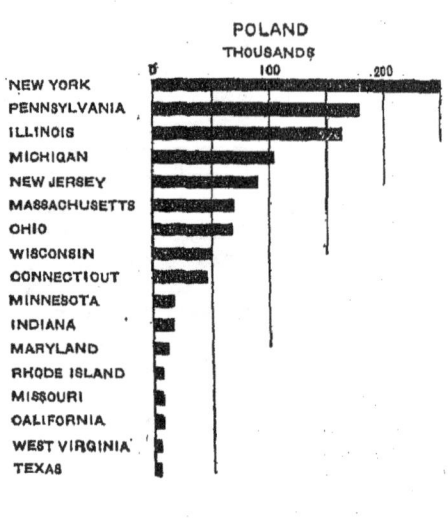

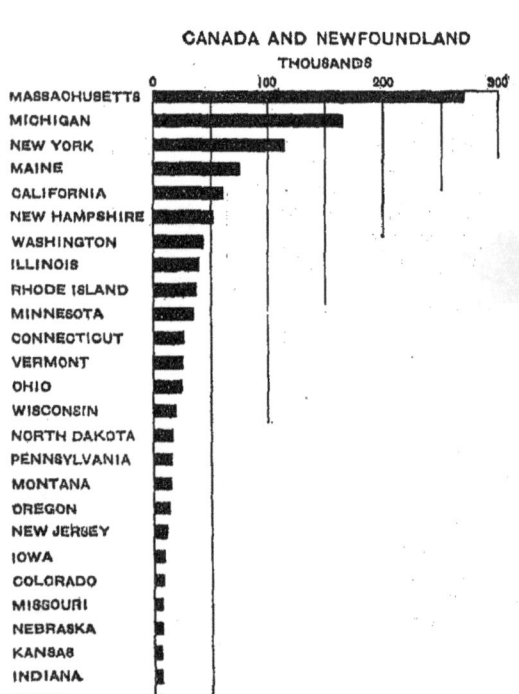

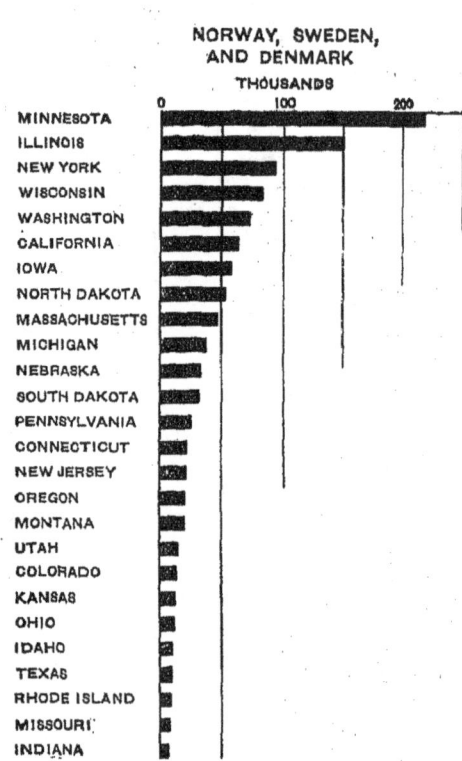

692

POPULATION.

DISTRIBUTION OF NATIVES OF PRINCIPAL FOREIGN COUNTRIES AND GROUPS OF COUNTRIES, BY STATES: 1920.

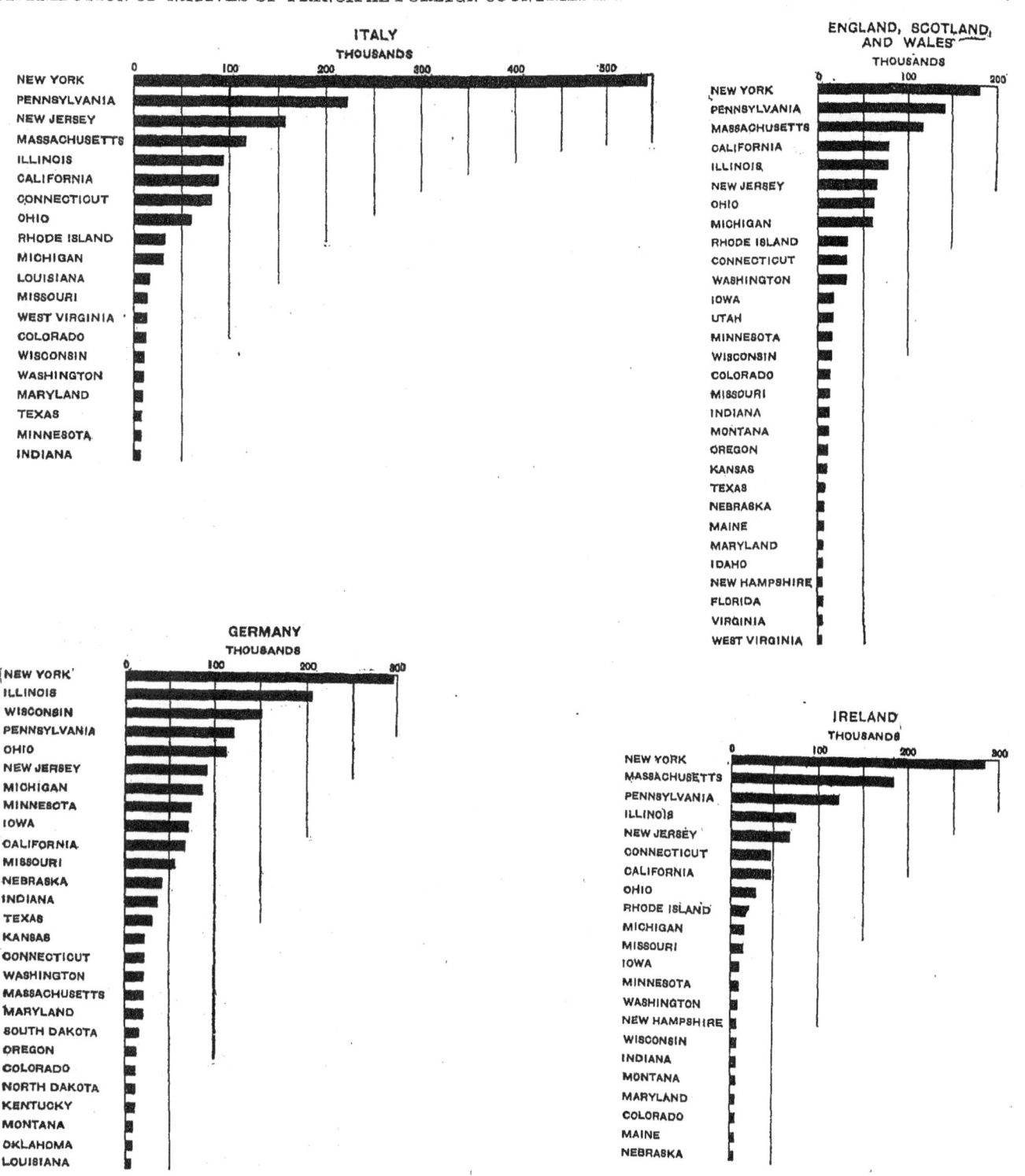

COUNTRY OF BIRTH.

693

TABLE 1.—PLACE OF BIRTH OF THE TOTAL, WHITE, AND NONWHITE POPULATION, FOR THE UNITED STATES: 1920.

COLOR OR RACE.	Total population: 1920	Native.	COUNTRY OF BIRTH OF FOREIGN BORN.																	
			Total foreign born.	Europe.	Asia.				America.					All other.					
					China.	Japan.	India.	Other Asia.	Canada and Newfoundland.	West Indies.[1]	Mexico.	Central America.	South America.	Africa.	Australia.	Atlantic Islands.	Pacific Islands.[1]	Not specified or born at sea.
All classes...	105,710,620	91,789,928	13,920,692	11,882,053	43,560	81,502	4,901	107,987	1,138,174	78,962	486,418	4,912	18,551	5,781	10,914	[2]44,340	3,712	6,925
White.........	94,820,915	81,108,161	13,712,754	11,877,991	716	278	2,532	106,924	1,131,120	26,369	478,383	4,074	16,855	5,222	10,801	38,984	3,643	8,862
Negro.........	10,463,131	10,389,328	73,803	3,996	6	....	....	21	5,657	52,422	3,123	816	1,660	556	107	5,349	40	44
Indian.........	244,437	238,138	6,299	....	....	....	....	....	1,329	58	4,871	14	20	....	....	2	....	5
Chinese.........	61,639	18,532	43,107	15	42,809	....	63	5	30	42	101	20	1	4	....	5	4	1	7
Japanese.........	111,010	29,672	81,338	39	28	81,160	4	42	23	9	21	1	2	....	1	1	3	4
All other [3]...	9,488	6,097	3,391	12	1	1	2,360	970	3	3	....	1	6	4	3	....	25	3

[1] Except possessions of the United States.
[2] Includes Azores (33,788 whites; 203 Negroes; 1 Chinese) and Cape Verde Islands (2,370 whites; 3,053 Negroes; 1 Japanese).
[3] Comprises Filipinos (5,593 native, 10 foreign born); Hindus (75 native, 2,432 foreign born); Koreans (309 native, 915 foreign born); Hawaiians (110 native); Malays (9 native, 10 foreign born); Siamese (17 foreign born); Samoans (1 native, 5 foreign born); and Maoris (2 foreign born).

TABLE 2.—COUNTRY OF BIRTH OF FOREIGN-BORN POPULATION, BY SEX, FOR THE UNITED STATES: 1920.

COUNTRY OF BIRTH.	NUMBER.			PER CENT.		Males to 100 females.	PER CENT DISTRIBUTION.		
	Total.	Male.	Female.	Male.	Female.		Total.	Male.	Female.
Total foreign born..............	13,920,692	7,675,435	6,245,257	55.1	44.9	122.9	100.0	100.0	100.0
Europe..................	11,882,053	6,570,781	5,311,272	55.3	44.7	123.7	85.4	85.6	85.0
Northwestern Europe..........	3,830,094	1,979,591	1,850,503	51.7	48.3	107.0	27.5	25.8	29.6
England........	813,853	425,664	388,189	52.3	47.7	109.7	5.8	5.5	6.2
Scotland........	254,570	133,956	120,614	52.6	47.4	111.1	1.8	1.7	1.9
Wales........	67,066	36,184	30,882	54.0	46.0	117.2	0.5	0.5	0.5
Ireland........	1,037,234	455,571	581,663	43.9	56.1	78.3	7.5	5.9	9.3
Norway........	363,863	202,758	161,105	55.7	44.3	125.9	2.6	2.6	2.6
Sweden........	625,585	344,938	280,647	55.1	44.9	122.9	4.5	4.5	4.5
Denmark........	189,154	114,063	75,091	60.3	39.7	151.9	1.4	1.5	1.2
Netherlands........	131,766	75,510	56,256	57.3	42.7	134.2	0.9	1.0	0.9
Belgium........	62,687	35,971	26,716	57.4	42.6	134.6	0.5	0.5	0.4
Luxemburg........	12,585	7,671	4,914	61.0	39.0	156.1	0.1	0.1	0.1
Switzerland........	118,659	67,830	50,829	57.2	42.8	133.4	0.9	0.9	0.8
France........	153,072	79,475	73,597	51.9	48.1	108.0	1.1	1.0	1.2
Alsace-Lorraine........	*34,321*	*19,197*	*15,124*	*55.9*	*44.1*	*126.9*	*0.2*	*0.3*	*0.2*
Central Europe..........	4,330,874	2,389,053	1,941,821	55.2	44.8	123.0	31.1	31.1	31.1
Germany........	1,686,108	891,293	794,815	52.9	47.1	112.1	12.1	11.6	12.7
Poland........	1,139,979	646,388	493,591	56.7	43.3	131.0	8.2	8.4	7.9
Czechoslovakia........	362,438	196,253	166,185	54.1	45.9	118.1	2.6	2.6	2.7
Austria........	575,627	323,453	252,174	56.2	43.8	128.3	4.1	4.2	4.0
Hungary........	397,283	216,914	180,369	54.6	45.4	120.3	2.9	2.8	2.9
Jugo-Slavia........	169,439	114,752	54,687	67.7	32.3	209.8	1.2	1.5	0.9
Eastern Europe..........	1,803,971	1,013,471	790,500	56.2	43.8	128.2	13.0	13.2	12.7
Russia........	1,400,495	774,017	626,478	55.3	44.7	123.6	10.1	10.1	10.0
Lithuania........	135,068	82,866	52,202	61.4	38.6	158.7	1.0	1.1	0.8
Finland........	149,824	85,287	64,537	56.9	43.1	132.2	1.1	1.1	1.0
Rumania........	102,823	58,135	44,688	56.5	43.5	130.1	0.7	0.8	0.7
Bulgaria........	10,477	9,508	969	90.8	9.2	981.2	0.1	0.1	(1)
Turkey in Europe........	5,284	3,658	1,626	69.2	30.8	225.0	(1)	(1)	(1)
Southern Europe..........	1,911,213	1,185,001	726,212	62.0	38.0	163.2	13.7	15.4	11.6
Greece........	175,976	143,606	32,370	81.6	18.4	443.6	1.3	1.9	0.5
Albania........	5,608	4,905	703	87.5	12.5	697.7	(1)	0.1	(1)
Italy........	1,610,113	958,277	651,836	59.5	40.5	147.0	11.6	12.5	10.4
Spain........	49,535	36,667	12,868	74.0	26.0	284.9	0.4	0.5	0.2
Portugal........	69,981	41,546	28,435	59.4	40.6	146.1	0.5	0.5	0.5
Other Europe [2]..........	5,901	3,665	2,236	62.1	37.9	163.9	(1)	(1)	(1)
Asia..................	237,950	172,460	65,490	72.5	27.5	263.3	1.7	2.2	1.0
Armenia........	36,628	25,352	11,276	69.2	30.8	224.8	0.3	0.3	0.2
Palestine........	3,203	2,062	1,141	64.4	35.6	180.7	(1)	(1)	(1)
Syria........	51,901	31,241	20,660	60.2	39.8	151.2	0.4	0.4	0.3
Turkey in Asia........	11,019	8,042	2,977	73.0	27.0	270.1	0.1	0.1	(1)
China........	43,560	40,754	2,806	93.6	6.4	1,452.4	0.3	0.5	(1)
Japan........	81,502	57,304	24,198	70.3	29.7	236.8	0.6	0.7	0.4
India........	4,901	3,774	1,127	77.0	23.0	334.9	(1)	(1)	(1)
Other Asia........	5,236	3,931	1,305	75.1	24.9	301.2	(1)	0.1	(1)
America..................	1,727,017	890,917	836,100	51.6	48.4	106.6	12.4	11.6	13.4
Canada and Newfoundland..........	1,138,174	556,837	581,337	48.9	51.1	95.8	8.2	7.3	9.3
Canada—French........	307,786	157,748	150,038	51.3	48.7	105.1	2.2	2.1	2.4
Canada—Other........	817,139	392,931	424,208	48.1	51.9	92.6	5.9	5.1	6.8
Newfoundland........	13,249	6,158	7,091	46.5	53.5	86.8	0.1	0.1	0.1
West Indies [3]........	78,962	43,263	35,699	54.8	45.2	121.2	0.6	0.6	0.6
Cuba........	14,872	8,341	6,531	56.1	43.9	127.7	0.1	0.1	0.1
Other West Indies [3]........	64,090	34,922	29,168	54.5	45.5	119.7	0.5	0.5	0.5
Mexico........	486,418	276,526	209,892	56.8	43.2	131.7	3.5	3.6	3.4
Central and South America........	23,463	14,291	9,172	60.9	39.1	155.8	0.2	0.2	0.1
Central America........	4,912	2,849	2,063	58.0	42.0	138.1	(1)	(1)	(1)
South America........	18,551	11,442	7,109	61.7	38.3	161.0	0.1	0.1	0.1
All other..................	73,672	41,277	32,395	56.0	44.0	127.4	0.5	0.5	0.5
Africa........	5,781	3,433	2,348	59.4	40.6	146.2	(1)	0.1	(1)
Australia........	10,914	6,019	4,895	55.1	44.9	123.0	0.1	0.1	0.1
Atlantic Islands........	44,340	24,523	19,817	55.3	44.7	123.7	0.3	0.3	0.3
Pacific Islands [3]........	3,712	2,050	1,662	55.2	44.8	123.3	(1)	(1)	(1)
Country not specified........	3,589	2,320	1,269	64.6	35.4	182.8	(1)	(1)	(1)
Born at sea........	5,336	2,932	2,404	54.9	45.1	122.0	(1)	(1)	(1)

[1] Less than one-tenth of 1 per cent.   [2] Comprises Danzig, Fiume, Saar Basin, and "Europe, not specified."   [3] Except possessions of the United States.

694

POPULATION.

TABLE 3.—COUNTRY OF BIRTH OF FOREIGN-BORN POPULATION, BY SEX, FOR THE UNITED STATES: 1920 AND 1910.

[For changes in area since 1910, see text, p. 687.]

COUNTRY OF BIRTH (postwar boundaries).	1920 Number.	Per cent of total foreign-born population.	Per cent of total population.	Male.	Female.	Males to 100 females.	COUNTRY OF BIRTH (prewar boundaries).	1910 Number.	Per cent of total foreign-born population.	Per cent of total population.	Male.	Female.	Males to 100 females.
Total foreign born	13,920,692	100.0	13.2	7,675,435	6,245,257	122.9	Total foreign born	13,515,886	100.0	14.7	7,667,748	5,848,138	131.1
Europe	11,882,053	85.4	11.2	6,570,781	5,311,272	123.7	Europe	11,791,841	87.2	12.8	6,702,997	5,088,844	131.7
Northwestern Europe	3,330,094	27.5	3.6	1,979,591	1,850,503	107.0	Northwestern Europe	4,239,037	31.4	4.6	2,226,363	2,012,674	110.6
England	813,853	5.8	0.8	425,664	388,189	109.7	England	877,719	6.5	1.0	477,320	400,399	119.2
Scotland	254,570	1.8	0.2	133,956	120,614	111.1	Scotland	261,076	1.9	0.3	144,659	116,417	124.3
Wales	67,066	0.5	0.1	36,184	30,882	117.2	Wales	82,488	0.6	0.1	45,397	37,091	122.4
Ireland	1,037,234	7.5	1.0	455,571	581,663	78.3	Ireland	1,352,251	10.0	1.5	611,556	740,695	82.6
Norway	363,863	2.6	0.3	202,758	161,105	125.9	Norway	403,877	3.0	0.4	230,156	173,721	132.5
Sweden	625,585	4.5	0.6	344,938	280,047	122.9	Sweden	665,207	4.9	0.7	369,953	295,254	125.3
Denmark	189,154	1.4	0.2	114,063	75,091	151.9	Denmark	181,649	1.3	0.2	109,120	72,529	150.5
Netherlands	131,766	0.9	0.1	75,510	56,256	134.2	Netherlands	120,063	0.9	0.1	68,363	51,700	132.2
Belgium	62,687	0.5	0.1	35,971	26,716	134.6	Belgium	49,400	0.4	0.1	29,895	19,505	153.3
Luxemburg	12,585	0.1	(1)	7,671	4,914	156.1	Luxemburg	3,071	(1)	(1)	1,963	1,108	177.2
Switzerland	118,659	0.9	0.1	67,830	50,829	133.4	Switzerland	124,848	0.9	0.1	72,726	52,122	139.5
France	153,072	1.1	0.1	79,475	73,597	108.0	France	117,418	0.9	0.1	65,285	52,133	125.2
Alsace-Lorraine	34,321	0.2	(1)	19,197	15,124	126.9							
Central Europe	4,330,874	31.1	4.1	2,389,053	1,941,821	123.0	Central Europe	4,600,298	34.0	5.0	2,636,069	1,964,229	134.2
Germany	1,686,108	12.1	1.6	891,293	794,815	112.1	Germany	[2]2,311,237	17.1	2.5	1,239,593	1,071,644	115.7
Poland	1,139,979	8.2	1.1	646,388	493,591	131.0	Poland	[2]937,884	6.9	1.0	588,030	399,854	153.6
Czechoslovakia	362,438	2.6	0.3	196,253	166,185	118.1							
Austria	575,627	4.1	0.5	323,453	252,174	128.3	Austria	[3]845,555	6.3	0.9	513,976	331,585	155.0
Hungary	397,283	2.9	0.4	216,914	180,369	120.3	Hungary	495,609	3.7	0.5	305,543	190,066	160.8
Jugo-Slavia	169,439	1.2	0.2	114,752	54,687	209.8							
							Serbia	4,639	(1)	(1)	3,837	802	478.4
							Montenegro	5,374	(1)	(1)	5,096	278	1,833.1
Eastern Europe	1,803,971	13.0	1.7	1,013,471	790,500	128.2	Eastern Europe	1,423,743	10.5	1.5	811,796	611,947	132.7
Russia	1,400,495	10.1	1.3	774,017	626,478	123.6	Russia	[2]1,184,412	8.8	1.3	656,856	527,556	124.5
Lithuania	135,068	1.0	0.1	82,866	52,202	158.7							
Finland	149,824	1.1	0.1	85,287	64,537	132.2	Finland	129,680	1.0	0.1	79,008	50,582	156.4
Rumania	102,823	0.7	0.1	58,135	44,688	130.1	Rumania	65,923	0.5	0.1	36,521	29,402	124.2
Bulgaria	10,477	0.1	(1)	9,508	969	981.2	Bulgaria	11,498	0.1	(1)	10,797	701	1,540.2
Turkey in Europe	5,284	(1)	(1)	3,658	1,626	225.0	Turkey in Europe [3]	32,230	0.2	(1)	28,524	3,706	769.7
Southern Europe	1,911,213	13.7	1.8	1,185,001	726,212	163.2	Southern Europe	1,525,875	11.3	1.7	1,026,951	498,924	205.8
Greece	175,976	1.3	0.2	143,606	32,370	443.6	Greece	101,282	0.7	0.1	93,447	7,835	1,192.7
Albania	5,608	(1)	(1)	4,905	703	697.7	(3)						
Italy	1,610,113	11.6	1.5	958,277	651,836	147.0	Italy	1,343,125	9.9	1.5	880,904	462,221	190.6
Spain	49,535	0.4	(1)	36,667	12,808	284.9	Spain	22,108	0.2	(1)	16,785	5,323	315.3
Portugal	69,981	0.5	0.1	41,546	28,435	146.1	Portugal	59,360	0.4	0.1	35,815	23,545	152.1
Other Europe	[4]5,901	(1)	(1)	3,665	2,236	163.9	Europe, not specified	2,853	(1)	(1)	1,788	1,070	167.1
Asia	237,950	1.7	0.2	172,460	65,490	263.3	Asia	191,484	1.4	0.2	162,050	29,434	550.6
Armenia	36,628	0.3	(1)	25,352	11,276	224.8							
Palestine	3,203	(1)	(1)	2,062	1,141	180.7							
Syria	51,901	0.4	(1)	31,241	20,660	151.2	Turkey in Asia	59,729	0.4	0.1	40,467	19,262	210.1
Turkey in Asia	11,019	0.1	(1)	8,042	2,977	270.1							
China	43,560	0.3	(1)	40,754	2,806	1,452.4	China	56,756	0.4	0.1	54,998	1,788	3,074.3
Japan	81,502	0.6	0.1	57,304	24,198	236.8	Japan	67,744	0.5	0.1	60,758	6,986	869.7
India	4,901	(1)	(1)	3,774	1,127	334.9	India	4,664	(1)	(1)	3,770	885	427.0
Other Asia	5,236	(1)	(1)	3,931	1,305	301.2	Other Asia	2,591	(1)	(1)	2,078	513	405.1
America	1,727,017	12.4	1.6	890,917	836,100	106.6	America	1,489,231	11.0	1.6	777,596	711,635	109.3
Canada and Newfoundland	1,138,174	8.2	1.1	556,837	581,337	95.8	Canada and Newfoundland	1,209,717	9.0	1.3	608,481	601,236	101.2
Canada—French	307,786	2.2	0.3	157,748	150,038	105.1	Canada—French	385,083	2.8	0.4	201,164	183,919	109.4
Canada—Other	817,139	5.9	0.8	392,931	424,208	92.6	Canada—Other	819,554	6.1	0.9	404,792	414,762	97.6
Newfoundland	13,249	0.1	(1)	6,158	7,091	86.8	Newfoundland	5,080	(1)	(1)	2,525	2,555	98.8
West Indies [5]	78,962	0.6	0.1	43,263	35,699	121.2	West Indies [5]	47,635	0.4	0.1	26,764	20,871	128.2
Mexico	486,418	3.5	0.5	276,526	209,892	131.7	Mexico	221,915	1.6	0.2	136,677	85,238	160.3
Central and South America	23,463	0.2	(1)	14,291	9,172	155.8	Central and South America	9,964	0.1	(1)	5,674	4,290	132.3
All other	73,672	0.5	0.1	41,277	32,395	127.4	All other	43,330	0.3	(1)	25,105	18,225	137.8
Africa	5,781	(1)	(1)	3,433	2,348	146.2	Africa	3,992	(1)	(1)	2,391	1,601	149.3
Australia	10,914	0.1	(1)	6,019	4,895	123.0	Australia	9,035	0.1	(1)	5,172	3,863	133.9
Atlantic Islands	44,340	0.3	(1)	24,523	19,817	123.7	Atlantic Islands	18,274	0.1	(1)	10,240	8,034	127.5
Pacific Islands [5]	3,712	(1)	(1)	2,050	1,662	123.3	Pacific Islands [5]	2,415	(1)	(1)	1,428	987	144.7
Country not specified	3,589	(1)	(1)	2,320	1,269	182.8	Country not specified	2,687	(1)	(1)	1,972	715	275.8
Born at sea	5,336	(1)	(1)	2,932	2,404	122.0	Born at sea	6,927	0.1	(1)	3,902	3,025	129.0

[1] Less than one-tenth of 1 per cent.

[2] Persons reported in 1910 as of Polish mother tongue born in Germany (98,182 males; 91,914 females), Austria (109,485 males; 129,933 females), and Russia (270,363 males; 148,007 females) have been deducted from the respective countries and combined as Poland for comparison with number reported in 1920 as born in Poland. (See text, p. 688.)

[3] Albania included with Turkey in Europe in 1910.

[4] Comprises Danzig (2,049), Fiume (384), Saar Basin (263), and "Europe, not specified" (3,205).

[5] Except possessions of the United States.

COUNTRY OF BIRTH.

695

TABLE 4.—COUNTRY OF BIRTH OF FOREIGN-BORN POPULATION, FOR THE UNITED STATES: 1850–1920.

[Figures are given for each country for all census years since 1850 for which data are available. For changes in area since 1910, see text, p. 687.]

COUNTRY OF BIRTH.	NUMBER.								PER CENT DISTRIBUTION.							
	1920	1910	1900	1890	1880	1870	1860	1850	1920	1910	1900	1890	1880	1870	1860	1850
Total foreign born	13,920,692	13,515,886	10,341,276	9,249,560	6,679,943	5,567,229	4,138,697	2,244,602	100.0	100.0	100.0	100.0	100.0	100.0	100.0	100.0
Europe	11,882,053	11,791,841	8,871,780	8,020,608	5,744,311	4,936,618	3,805,701	2,031,867	85.4	87.2	85.8	86.7	86.0	88.7	92.0	90.5
Northwestern Europe	3,830,094	4,239,067	4,202,683	4,380,752	3,494,484	3,124,638	2,472,211	1,437,475	27.5	31.4	40.6	47.4	52.3	56.1	59.7	64.0
England	813,853	877,719	840,513	909,092	664,160	555,046	433,494	278,675	5.8	6.5	8.1	9.8	9.9	10.0	10.5	12.4
Scotland	254,570	261,076	233,524	242,231	170,136	140,835	108,518	70,550	1.8	1.9	2.3	2.6	2.5	2.5	2.6	3.1
Wales	67,066	82,488	93,586	100,079	83,302	74,533	45,763	29,868	0.5	0.6	0.9	1.1	1.2	1.3	1.1	1.3
Ireland	1,037,234	1,352,251	1,615,459	1,871,509	1,854,571	1,855,827	1,611,304	961,719	7.5	10.0	15.6	20.2	27.8	33.3	38.9	42.8
Norway	363,863	403,877	336,388	322,065	181,729	114,246	43,995	12,678	2.6	3.0	3.3	3.5	2.7	2.1	1.1	0.6
Sweden	625,585	665,207	582,014	478,041	194,337	97,332	18,625	3,559	4.5	4.9	5.6	5.2	2.9	1.7	0.5	0.2
Denmark	189,154	181,649	153,690	132,543	64,196	30,107	9,962	1,838	1.4	1.3	1.5	1.4	1.0	0.5	0.2	0.1
Netherlands	131,766	120,063	94,931	81,828	58,090	46,802	28,281	9,848	0.9	0.9	0.9	0.9	0.9	0.8	0.7	0.4
Belgium	62,687	49,400	29,757	22,639	15,535	12,553	9,072	1,313	0.5	0.4	0.3	0.2	0.2	0.2	0.2	0.1
Luxemburg	12,585	3,071	3,031	2,882	12,836	5,802			0.1	(1)	(1)	(1)	0.2	0.1		
Switzerland	118,659	124,848	115,593	104,009	88,621	75,153	53,327	13,358	0.9	0.9	1.1	1.1	1.3	1.3	1.3	0.6
France	153,072	117,418	104,197	113,174	106,971	116,402	109,870	54,069	1.1	0.9	1.0	1.2	1.6	2.1	2.7	2.4
Central and Eastern Europe	6,134,845	6,024,041	4,136,646	3,420,629	2,187,776	1,784,449	1,311,722	586,240	44.1	44.6	40.0	37.0	32.8	32.1	31.7	26.1
Germany	1,686,108	2,311,237	2,663,418	2,784,894	1,966,742	1,690,533	1,276,075	583,774	12.1	17.1	25.8	30.1	29.4	30.4	30.8	26.0
Poland	1,139,979	937,884	383,407	147,440	48,557	14,436	7,298		8.2	6.9	3.7	1.6	0.7	0.3	0.2	
Czechoslovakia	362,438								2.6							
Austria	575,627	845,555	432,798	241,377	124,024	70,797	25,061	946	4.1	6.3	4.2	2.6	1.9	1.3	0.6	(1)
Hungary	397,283	495,609	145,714	62,435	11,526	3,737			2.9	3.7	1.4	0.7	0.2	0.1		
Jugo-Slavia	169,439								1.2							
Serbia		4,639								(1)						
Montenegro		5,374								(1)						
Russia	1,400,495	1,184,412	423,726	182,644	35,722	4,644	3,160	1,414	10.1	8.8	4.1	2.0	0.5	0.1	0.1	0.1
Lithuania	135,068								1.0							
Finland	149,824	120,680	62,641						1.1	1.0	0.6					
Rumania	102,823	65,923	15,032						0.7	0.5	0.1					
Bulgaria	10,477	11,498							0.1	0.1						
Turkey in Europe	5,284	32,230	9,910	1,839	1,205	302	128	106	(1)	0.2	0.1	(1)	(1)	(1)	(1)	(1)
Southern Europe	1,911,213	1,525,875	530,200	206,648	58,265	25,853	20,365	8,152	13.7	11.3	5.1	2.2	0.9	0.5	0.5	0.4
Greece	175,976	101,282	8,515	1,887	776	390	328	86	1.3	0.7	0.1	(1)	(1)	(1)	(1)	(1)
Albania	5,608								(1)							
Italy	1,610,113	1,343,125	484,027	182,580	44,230	17,157	11,677	3,679	11.6	9.9	4.7	2.0	0.7	0.3	0.3	0.2
Spain	49,535	22,108	7,050	6,185	5,121	3,764	4,244	3,113	0.4	0.2	0.1	0.1	0.1	0.1	0.1	0.1
Portugal	69,081	59,360	30,608	15,990	8,138	4,542	4,116	1,274	0.5	0.4	0.3	0.2	0.1	0.1	0.1	0.1
Other Europe [5]	5,901	2,858	2,251	12,570	3,786	1,678	1,403		(1)	(1)	(1)	0.1	0.1	(1)	(1)	.....
Asia	237,950	191,484	120,248	113,396	107,630	64,565	36,796	1,135	1.7	1.4	1.2	1.2	1.6	1.2	0.9	0.1
Armenia	36,628								0.3							
Palestine	3,203	59,729	(4)	(4)	(4)	(4)	(4)	(4)	(1)	0.4						
Syria	51,901								0.4							
Turkey in Asia	11,019								0.1							
China	43,560	56,756	81,534	106,701	104,468	63,042	35,565	758	0.3	0.4	0.8	1.2	1.6	1.1	0.9	(1)
Japan	81,502	67,744	24,788	2,292	401	73			0.6	0.5	0.2	(1)	(1)	(1)		
India	4,901	4,664	2,031	2,143	1,707	586			(1)	(1)	(1)	(1)	(1)	(1)		
Other Asia	5,236	2,591	11,895	2,200	1,054	864	1,231	377	(1)	(1)	0.1	(1)	(1)	(1)	(1)	(1)
America	1,727,017	1,489,231	1,317,380	1,088,245	807,230	551,335	288,285	168,484	12.4	11.0	12.7	11.8	12.1	9.9	7.0	7.5
Canada and Newfoundland [6]	1,138,174	1,209,717	1,179,922	980,938	717,157	493,464	249,970	147,711	8.2	9.0	11.4	10.6	10.7	8.9	6.0	6.6
Canada—French [6]	307,786	385,083	395,126	302,496					2.2	2.8	3.8	3.3				
Canada—Other [6]	817,139	819,554	784,796	678,442					5.9	6.1	7.6	7.3				
Newfoundland [6]	13,249	5,080							0.1	(1)						
West Indies:																
Cuba	14,872	15,133	11,081	23,256	6,917	5,319	7,353	5,772	0.1	0.1	0.1	0.3	0.1	0.1	0.2	0.3
Other West Indies	64,090	32,502	14,354		9,484	6,251			0.5	0.2	0.1		0.1	0.1		
Mexico	486,418	221,915	103,393	77,853	68,399	42,435	27,466	13,317	3.5	1.6	1.0	0.8	1.0	0.8	0.7	0.6
Central and South America:																
Central America	4,012	1,736	3,807	1,192	707	301	233	141	(1)	(1)	(1)	(1)	(1)	(1)	(1)	0.1
South America	18,551	8,228	4,733	5,006	4,566	3,565	3,263	1,543	0.1	0.1	(1)	0.1	0.1	0.1	0.1	0.1
All other	73,672	43,330	31,863	27,311	20,772	14,711	7,915	43,116	0.5	0.3	0.3	0.3	0.3	0.3	0.2	1.9
Africa	5,781	3,992	2,538	2,207	2,204	2,657	526	551	(1)	(1)	(1)	(1)	(1)	(1)	(1)	(1)
Australia	10,914	9,035	6,807	5,984	4,906	3,118	1,419		0.1	0.1	0.1	0.1	0.1	0.1	(1)	.....
Atlantic Islands	44,340	18,274	9,768	9,739	7,641	4,434	1,361		0.3	0.1	0.1	0.1	0.1	0.1	(1)	.....
Pacific Islands	3,712	2,415	2,013	3,309	1,953	910	721	588	(1)	(1)	(1)	(1)	(1)	(1)	(1)	1.9
Country not specified	3,589	2,687	2,546	479		954	1,366	41,977	(1)	(1)	(1)	(1)	.....	(1)	(1)	.....
Born at sea	5,336	6,927	8,196	5,533	4,068	2,638	2,522		(1)	0.1	0.1	0.1	0.1	(1)	0.1	.....

[1] Less than one-tenth of 1 per cent.
[2] Persons reported in 1910 as of Polish mother tongue born in Germany (190,096), Austria (329,418), and Russia (418,370), have been deducted from the respective countries and combined as Poland for comparison with number reported in 1920 as born in Poland. (See text, p. 688.)
[3] Albania included with Turkey in Europe in 1910.
[4] Turkey in Asia included with Turkey in Europe prior to 1910.
[5] Includes "Europe, not specified" at each census, and Danzig, Fiume, and Saar Basin in 1920.
[6] Newfoundland included with Canada prior to 1910.
[7] Except possessions of the United States.

696

POPULATION.

TABLE 5.—INCREASE IN FOREIGN-BORN POPULATION, BY COUNTRY OF BIRTH, FOR THE UNITED STATES: 1850–1920.

[For changes in area since 1910, see text, p. 687. Per cent not shown where base is less than 100. A minus sign (–) denotes decrease.]

COUNTRY OF BIRTH.	1910–1920		1900–1910		1890–1900		1880–1890		1870–1880		1860–1870		1850–1860	
	Number.	Per cent.	Number.	Per cent.	Number.	Per cent.	Number.	Per cent.	Number.	Per cent.	Number.	Per cent.	Number.	Per cent.
Total foreign born	404,806	3.0	3,174,610	30.7	1,091,716	11.8	2,569,617	38.5	1,112,714	20.0	1,428,532	34.5	1,854,095	84.4
Europe	90,212	0.8	2,920,061	32.9	851,172	10.8	2,278,297	39.6	807,693	16.4	1,130,917	29.7	1,773,534	87.3
Countries with unchanged boundaries since 1910:														
England	–63,866	–7.3	37,206	4.4	–68,579	–7.5	244,932	36.9	109,114	19.7	121,552	28.0	154,819	55.6
Scotland	–6,506	–2.5	27,552	11.8	–8,707	–3.6	72,095	42.4	29,301	20.8	32,317	29.8	37,968	53.8
Wales	–15,422	–18.7	–11,098	–11.9	–6,493	–6.5	16,777	20.1	8,769	11.8	28,770	62.9	15,895	53.2
Ireland	–315,017	–23.3	–263,208	–16.3	–266,050	–13.7	16,938	0.9	–1,256	–0.1	244,523	15.2	649,585	67.5
Norway	–40,014	–9.9	67,489	20.1	13,723	4.3	140,936	77.6	67,483	59.1	70,251	150.7	31,317	247.0
Sweden	–39,622	–6.0	83,193	14.8	103,973	21.7	283,704	146.0	97,005	99.7	78,707	422.6	15,060	423.3
Netherlands	11,703	9.7	25,132	26.5	13,103	16.0	23,738	40.9	11,288	24.1	18,521	65.5	18,433	187.2
Luxemburg	9,514	309.8	40	1.3	149	5.2	–9,954	–77.5	7,034	121.2	5,802			
Switzerland	–6,189	–5.0	9,255	8.0	11,524	11.1	15,448	17.4	13,468	17.9	21,826	40.9	39,909	299.2
Finland	20,144	15.5	67,039	107.0	(1)		(1)		(1)		(1)		(1)	
Spain	27,427	124.1	15,058	218.6	865	14.0	1,064	20.8	1,357	36.1	–480	–11.3	1,131	36.3
Portugal	10,621	17.9	28,752	93.9	14,612	91.3	7,858	96.6	3,596	79.2	426	10.3	2,842	223.1
Countries with changed boundaries since 1910:														
Denmark	7,505	4.1	27,959	18.2	21,147	16.0	68,347	106.5	34,089	113.2	20,145	202.2	8,124	442.0
Belgium	13,287	26.9	19,643	66.0	7,118	31.4	7,104	45.7	2,982	23.8	3,481	38.4	7,750	590.9
France	35,654	30.4	13,221	12.7	–8,977	–7.9	6,203	5.8	–9,431	–8.1	6,532	5.9	55,801	103.2
Germany	2–625,129	–27.0	2–352,181	–13.2	–121,476	–4.4	818,152	41.6	276,209	16.3	414,458	32.5	692,301	118.6
Austria	2–269,928	–31.9	2412,757	95.4	191,421	79.3	117,353	94.6	53,227	75.2	45,736	182.5	24,115	2,549.2
Hungary	–98,326	–19.8	349,895	240.1	83,270	133.4	50,900	441.7	7,789	208.4	3,737			
Russia and Lithuania	2 351,151	29.6	2760,686	179.5	1303,723	166.3	1 146,922	411.3	1 31,078	669.2	1 1,484	47.0	1 1,746	123.5
Rumania	36,900	56.0	50,891	388.6	15,032									
Bulgaria	–1,021	–8.9	11,498											
Turkey in Europe	–26,946	–83.6	3 22,320	225.2	3 8,071	438.9	3 634	52.6	3 903	290.0	3 174	135.0	3 22	20.8
Greece	74,694	73.7	92,767	1,089.5	6,628	351.2	1,111	143.2	386	99.0	62	18.9	242	
Italy	266,988	19.9	859,098	177.5	301,447	165.1	138,350	312.8	27,073	157.8	5,480	46.9	7,908	217.4
Countries organized since 1910:														
Poland	2 202,095	21.5	2 554,477	144.6	235,967	160.0	98,883	203.6	34,121	236.4	7,138	97.8	7,298	
Czechoslovakia	362,438													
Jugo-Slavia	159,426													
Albania	5,608		(2)											
Other Europe 4	3,043	106.5	10,620	471.8	–10,328	–82.1	8,793	232.3	2,108	125.6	275	19.6	1,403	
Asia	46,466	24.3	71,236	59.2	6,852	6.0	5,766	5.4	43,065	66.7	27,769	75.5	35,661	3,141.9
Armenia														
Palestine	43,022	72.0	3 59,729		(3)		(3)		(3)		(3)		(3)	
Syria														
Turkey in Asia														
China	–13,196	–23.3	–24,778	–30.4	–25,167	–23.6	2,233	2.1	41,426	65.7	27,477	77.3	34,807	4,592.0
Japan	13,758	20.3	42,956	173.3	22,496	981.5	1,801	471.6	328		73			
India	237	5.1	2,633	129.6	–112	–5.2	436	25.5	1,121	191.3	580			
Other Asia	2,645	102.1	–9,304	–78.2	9,635	426.3	1,206	114.4	190	22.0	–307	–20.8	854	220.5
America	237,786	16.0	171,851	13.0	229,135	21.1	281,015	34.8	255,895	46.4	263,050	91.2	119,801	71.1
Canada and Newfoundland 6	–71,543	–5.9	29,795	2.5	198,984	20.3	263,781	36.8	223,693	45.3	243,494	97.4	102,259	69.2
Canada—French 5	–77,297	–20.1	–10,043	–2.5	92,630	30.6								
Canada—Other 6	–2,415	–0.3	34,758	4.4	106,354	15.7								
Newfoundland 5	8,169	160.8	5,080											
West Indies 6	31,327	65.8	22,200	87.3	2,179	9.4	6,855	41.8	4,831	41.8	4,217	57.4	1,581	27.4
Mexico	264,503	119.2	118,522	114.6	25,540	32.8	9,454	13.8	25,064	61.2	14,909	54.5	14,140	106.2
Central and South America	13,499	135.5	1,334	15.5	2,432	39.2	925	17.5	1,407	36.4	370	10.6	1,812	107.6
All other	30,342	70.0	11,462	36.0	4,557	16.7	6,539	31.5	6,061	41.2	8,796	85.9	–35,201	–81.6

[1] Finland included with Russia prior to 1900.
[2] See note 2, Table 4.
[3] Albania included with Turkey in Europe in 1910. Turkey in Asia included with Turkey in Europe prior to 1910.
[4] Includes "Europe, not specified" at each census, and Danzig, Fiume, and Saar Basin in 1920.
[5] Newfoundland included with Canada prior to 1910.
[6] Except possessions of the United States.

495

COUNTRY OF BIRTH.

TABLE 6.—COUNTRY OF BIRTH OF FOREIGN-BORN POPULATION, BY DIVISIONS AND STATES: 1920.

DIVISION AND STATE.	Total foreign born: 1920	NORTHWESTERN EUROPE.											
		England.	Scotland.	Wales.	Ireland.	Norway.	Sweden.	Denmark.	Netherlands.	Belgium.	Luxemburg.	Switzerland.	France.
United States.......	13,920,692	813,853	254,570	67,066	1,037,234	363,863	625,585	189,154	131,766	62,687	12,585	118,659	153,072
GEOGRAPHIC DIVISIONS:													
New England........	1,885,945	147,320	47,501	2,999	267,429	8,564	67,286	8,458	2,912	4,411	114	3,763	13,252
Middle Atlantic.........	4,960,418	273,140	83,885	29,185	472,319	35,362	83,547	22,991	27,847	12,478	1,017	30,093	55,250
East North Central......	3,232,141	163,994	51,650	15,226	135,147	82,137	165,388	43,018	59,803	29,706	5,093	30,379	29,637
West North Central.....	1,375,653	53,551	17,196	5,693	49,558	166,280	187,629	61,748	24,399	7,159	4,846	15,838	11,443
South Atlantic.........	330,537	24,416	7,456	1,773	20,145	2,259	4,418	2,123	1,459	1,547	87	2,348	4,119
East South Central......	72,989	6,085	2,093	455	5,934	450	1,514	531	322	235	31	2,176	2,191
West South Central......	464,828	13,373	3,711	763	8,330	2,691	6,320	2,580	1,106	1,180	127	3,433	8,086
Mountain...............	467,620	44,588	12,986	4,907	19,634	17,400	32,232	17,023	5,252	1,608	372	6,695	4,968
Pacific.................	1,130,561	87,386	28,092	6,065	53,438	48,720	77,251	30,682	8,606	4,363	898	23,934	24,126
NEW ENGLAND:													
Maine.................	107,814	5,153	2,171	137	5,748	581	2,026	1,065	50	51	6	62	344
New Hampshire........	91,397	4,368	1,823	51	7,908	427	1,886	204	177	478	5	72	288
Vermont..............	44,558	2,197	1,854	540	2,884	106	1,123	155	32	15	2	187	197
Massachusetts.........	1,088,548	87,085	28,474	1,367	183,172	5,491	38,012	3,629	2,071	2,497	33	1,368	7,125
Rhode Island..........	175,189	25,791	5,092	245	22,253	545	6,542	365	138	968	14	211	1,971
Connecticut...........	378,439	22,726	7,487	650	45,464	1,414	17,697	3,040	444	402	54	1,863	3,327
MIDDLE ATLANTIC:													
New York.............	2,825,375	135,541	37,656	6,763	284,747	27,573	53,025	14,222	13,772	5,300	564	15,053	32,252
New Jersey...........	742,486	46,861	17,781	1,255	65,971	5,343	10,675	5,704	12,737	2,483	167	8,165	10,168
Pennsylvania.........	1,392,557	90,738	28,448	21,167	121,601	2,446	19,847	3,065	1,338	4,695	286	6,875	12,830
EAST NORTH CENTRAL:													
Ohio.................	680,452	43,172	12,148	7,772	29,262	1,487	7,266	2,353	2,529	1,902	273	9,656	8,067
Indiana..............	151,328	8,528	3,707	1,106	7,271	544	4,942	909	2,018	2,530	101	2,334	3,247
Illinois..............	1,210,584	54,272	19,598	3,444	74,274	27,785	105,577	17,098	14,344	11,329	3,211	7,837	12,006
Michigan.............	729,292	47,185	13,175	1,154	16,531	6,888	24,707	7,178	33,499	10,501	477	2,755	4,175
Wisconsin............	460,485	10,837	3,022	1,750	7,809	45,433	22,896	15,420	7,473	3,444	1,031	7,797	2,142
WEST NORTH CENTRAL:													
Minnesota............	486,795	10,964	3,928	854	10,289	90,188	112,117	16,904	5,380	2,056	1,782	2,720	1,806
Iowa.................	225,904	13,038	3,907	1,753	10,686	17,344	22,493	18,020	12,471	1,232	1,630	2,871	2,125
Missouri.............	186,835	10,407	2,969	903	15,022	610	4,741	1,688	906	1,113	140	4,934	3,831
North Dakota.........	131,863	2,289	1,220	120	1,660	38,190	10,543	4,552	903	456	229	506	350
South Dakota.........	82,534	2,944	832	346	1,954	16,813	8,573	5,983	3,218	251	480	761	337
Nebraska.............	150,665	6,006	1,695	547	5,422	2,165	18,825	12,338	846	551	301	1,808	858
Kansas...............	110,967	7,903	2,576	1,170	4,825	970	10,337	2,283	675	1,500	284	2,238	2,136
SOUTH ATLANTIC:													
Delaware.............	19,901	1,497	411	44	2,895	65	316	77	37	24	5	76	198
Maryland.............	103,179	5,113	1,692	499	6,580	536	630	382	314	135	22	509	818
District of Columbia.....	29,365	3,001	793	106	4,320	219	481	237	127	76	13	358	688
Virginia..............	31,705	3,776	1,327	163	1,732	491	664	459	335	122	7	239	455
West Virginia..........	62,105	3,435	998	704	1,459	51	326	121	66	938	6	545	633
North Carolina........	7,272	969	446	25	301	70	170	69	115	16	2	72	136
South Carolina........	6,582	493	190	10	442	85	133	76	30	61	1	31	78
Georgia..............	16,564	1,610	530	86	1,112	132	299	127	78	45	7	161	376
Florida...............	53,864	4,522	1,069	136	1,304	610	1,399	575	357	130	24	357	737
EAST SOUTH CENTRAL:													
Kentucky.............	30,900	1,865	520	149	3,422	75	214	89	150	90	12	1,315	984
Tennessee............	15,648	1,670	454	143	1,291	63	305	138	58	36	3	616	333
Alabama.............	18,027	1,951	975	145	809	215	748	191	83	73	8	174	616
Mississippi...........	8,408	599	144	18	412	97	247	113	31	36	8	71	258
WEST SOUTH CENTRAL:													
Arkansas.............	14,137	1,141	316	90	676	99	331	180	116	94	8	736	387
Louisiana............	46,427	1,841	447	76	2,000	555	522	331	260	350	9	378	4,193
Oklahoma............	40,432	2,687	1,120	319	1,321	297	931	561	176	289	52	629	962
Texas...............	363,832	7,704	1,828	278	4,333	1,740	4,536	1,508	554	447	58	1,690	2,544
MOUNTAIN:													
Montana.............	95,591	8,160	3,279	879	7,260	9,962	7,179	2,990	1,675	672	153	1,151	883
Idaho...............	40,747	4,451	1,228	575	1,410	2,482	5,112	2,240	439	123	60	1,347	482
Wyoming............	26,567	2,507	1,439	297	956	651	2,042	936	130	130	18	302	364
Colorado.............	119,138	9,588	3,357	1,482	6,191	1,525	10,112	2,823	853	430	91	1,510	1,420
New Mexico..........	29,808	889	440	78	434	128	310	115	70	76	6	148	377
Arizona..............	80,566	2,883	595	192	1,206	337	859	398	69	60	22	293	394
Utah................	59,200	14,839	2,310	1,304	1,207	2,109	6,073	6,970	1,980	90	18	1,566	434
Nevada..............	16,003	1,271	338	100	970	206	545	551	36	27	4	378	609
PACIFIC:													
Washington..........	265,292	20,821	7,886	2,040	8,927	30,305	34,793	8,359	3,097	1,439	315	3,671	2,452
Oregon..............	107,644	7,953	3,609	592	4,203	6,955	10,532	3,602	917	722	140	4,166	1,273
California............	757,625	58,612	16,597	3,433	45,308	11,460	31,926	18,721	4,592	2,202	443	16,097	20,401

698

POPULATION.

TABLE 6.—COUNTRY OF BIRTH OF FOREIGN-BORN POPULATION, BY DIVISIONS AND STATES: 1920—Continued.

DIVISION AND STATE.	CENTRAL EUROPE.						EASTERN EUROPE.						SOUTHERN EUROPE.					Other Europe.[1]
	Germany.	Po-land.	Czecho-slo-vakia.	Austria.	Hun-gary.	Jugo-Slavia.	Russia.	Lithu-ania.	Fin-land.	Ru-mania.	Bul-garia.	Tur-key in Eu-rope.	Greece.	Al-bania.	Italy.	Spain.	Por-tugal.	
United States........	1,686,108	1,139,979	362,438	575,627	397,283	169,439	1,400,495	135,068	149,824	102,823	10,477	5,284	175,976	5,608	1,610,113	49,535	69,981	5,601
GEOGRAPHIC DIVISIONS:																		
New England..........	51,129	131,378	9,653	23,081	15,137	2,405	147,371	35,361	19,543	3,128	214	631	32,185	2,819	238,798	2,864	40,302	290
Middle Atlantic........	508,227	515,708	123,863	310,844	190,224	48,087	763,894	58,594	17,431	55,910	1,336	2,634	44,531	1,156	925,222	16,921	3,090	1,412
East North Central.....	592,058	402,259	143,743	145,275	149,592	72,343	236,022	44,307	46,676	29,338	5,806	1,035	45,135	1,010	203,181	3,022	380	2,211
West North Central.....	293,035	38,262	50,906	37,504	17,640	18,159	110,707	2,098	31,035	6,950	1,095	124	11,236	262	34,488	776	59	465
South Atlantic.........	40,898	25,432	6,620	12,077	10,696	3,581	48,362	3,245	1,281	2,183	161	203	11,450	19	40,207	6,347	714	365
East South Central.....	16,652	2,590	617	2,023	1,829	766	7,408	76	219	441	51	50	2,014	23	8,584	215	29	89
West South Central....	47,217	7,206	15,438	9,195	1,664	1,267	14,652	219	455	663	241	101	3,484	12	27,724	2,522	199	336
Mountain...........	33,652	4,075	5,295	13,070	3,234	10,771	26,690	280	7,718	1,053	821	72	9,483	143	28,498	4,563	334	105
Pacific.............	103,240	12,469	6,303	22,558	7,217	12,030	45,329	888	24,960	3,177	752	534	16,457	155	103,641	12,105	24,834	718
NEW ENGLAND:																		
Maine.............	932	1,717	410	305	72	143	3,703	1,032	1,388	67	5	66	1,228	403	2,797	33	153	10
New Hampshire.......	1,714	3,997	75	389	68	120	3,407	1,017	1,558	25	8	....	5,280	118	2,074	29	142	2
Vermont...........	630	1,729	108	283	204	58	1,333	67	476	19	3	....	167	6	4,067	661	20	4
Massachusetts.......	22,113	69,157	2,238	8,698	1,387	850	92,034	20,789	14,570	1,445	120	451	20,441	1,947	117,007	821	29,191	199
Rhode Island........	3,126	8,158	264	1,307	176	146	8,055	794	320	370	45	45	1,219	142	32,241	80	8,999	11
Connecticut...........	22,614	46,623	6,558	12,699	13,222	990	38,719	11,662	1,226	1,202	33	66	3,851	203	80,322	1,237	1,788	82
MIDDLE ATLANTIC:																		
New York..........	295,051	247,519	38,247	151,172	78,374	8,547	529,243	12,121	12,504	40,116	614	2,050	26,117	415	545,173	12,722	1,484	842
New Jersey..........	92,382	90,419	16,747	36,917	40,470	3,313	73,527	9,246	2,109	4,564	66	195	4,521	54	157,285	2,002	687	170
Pennsylvania.........	120,194	177,770	68,869	122,755	71,380	36,227	161,124	30,227	2,818	11,230	656	289	13,893	687	222,764	2,197	919	400
EAST NORTH CENTRAL:																		
Ohio...........	111,863	67,570	42,121	48,073	73,281	30,377	48,690	4,095	6,406	13,058	2,535	569	13,540	432	60,658	1,281	149	351
Indiana.........	37,377	17,791	3,941	9,100	9,351	4,471	7,073	1,445	237	2,781	431	70	4,182	74	6,712	407	14	75
Illinois.........	205,401	162,405	66,709	46,457	34,437	19,285	117,809	30,358	3,080	6,238	940	181	20,405	151	94,497	754	110	524
Michigan.........	86,047	103,026	11,161	22,004	22,667	9,426	45,313	5,475	30,096	6,331	1,692	173	7,115	261	30,216	446	70	813
Wisconsin........	151,250	50,558	19,811	19,641	10,010	8,784	21,447	2,934	6,757	970	208	36	3,833	101	11,188	74	17	448
WEST NORTH CENTRAL:																		
Minnesota........	74,634	18,537	12,626	11,550	4,277	10,697	18,100	741	29,108	2,385	450	30	2,391	41	7,432	36	9	149
Iowa.............	70,842	2,028	9,150	4,334	747	1,603	7,319	687	107	297	209	18	2,834	7	4,956	41	15	78
Missouri.........	55,776	7,636	4,971	8,676	5,080	2,827	18,769	417	98	1,047	145	44	8,022	202	14,609	435	12	76
North Dakota......	11,960	2,236	2,086	2,659	2,519	199	29,617	32	1,108	1,811	31	17	420	....	176	0	2	25
South Dakota......	15,674	792	2,819	1,151	585	470	11,193	14	1,085	154	97	5	375	1	413	5	4	27
Nebraska.........	40,909	4,615	15,818	4,551	810	738	15,719	139	73	371	61	4	1,504	9	3,547	38	6	53
Kansas...........	23,380	2,418	3,466	5,183	822	2,155	12,050	68	55	285	36	6	640	2	3,355	215	11	57
SOUTH ATLANTIC:																		
Delaware.........	1,632	3,847	122	615	226	27	2,244	96	52	110	....	3	280	....	4,130	142	19	7
Maryland.........	22,032	12,061	3,553	2,690	1,947	359	24,781	2,206	175	537	18	10	984	1	9,543	226	63	79
District of Columbia....	3,382	716	122	525	219	43	5,181	38	104	86	5	72	1,207	8	3,764	111	14	17
Virginia.........	2,302	1,108	897	921	1,263	127	5,421	71	240	165	17	32	1,797	4	2,435	266	307	82
West Virginia......	3,798	5,799	1,549	5,115	6,260	2,802	3,911	717	232	625	98	23	3,186	2	14,147	1,543	17	71
North Carolina.....	703	210	20	149	68	29	932	29	15	31	1	17	551	....	453	18	14	7
South Carolina.....	1,079	351	45	206	68	22	1,187	9	53	26	1	10	878	....	344	19	7	10
Georgia.........	1,936	917	123	401	248	84	3,452	72	42	111	5	21	1,473	1	700	125	45	60
Florida.........	3,534	428	139	525	353	88	1,243	13	311	472	16	6	1,408	3	4,745	4,009	228	22
EAST SOUTH CENTRAL:																		
Kentucky........	11,137	1,037	240	906	1,084	354	2,736	66	50	192	28	22	401	1	1,932	98	8	30
Tennessee........	2,159	841	32	898	326	37	2,262	3	33	93	5	5	491	22	2,079	14	7	16
Alabama.........	2,427	394	232	583	372	155	1,582	12	74	120	18	22	915	....	2,732	71	7	33
Mississippi.......	929	318	63	136	47	220	828	5	62	36	....	1	207	....	1,841	62	7	10
WEST SOUTH CENTRAL:																		
Arkansas........	3,979	529	492	636	108	117	662	27	18	62	17	1	277	1	1,314	22	4	10
Louisiana........	5,147	377	302	725	305	312	1,928	23	147	93	49	14	910	2	16,264	1,293	112	74
Oklahoma........	7,029	1,253	1,825	1,393	311	218	5,005	132	101	65	105	11	020	1	2,122	126	13	49
Texas...........	31,062	5,047	12,819	6,441	940	620	7,057	37	189	443	70	75	1,977	8	8,024	1,081	70	203
MOUNTAIN:																		
Montana.........	7,873	1,219	1,895	3,298	935	3,782	5,203	80	3,577	344	204	28	1,465	38	3,842	63	31	13
Idaho.........	4,143	287	420	781	233	460	1,453	9	980	104	39	5	716	42	1,323	1,417	39	6
Wyoming........	2,292	544	518	1,183	349	1,189	1,482	33	856	71	72	2	1,236	5	1,948	139	20	4
Colorado........	11,991	1,867	2,953	5,722	1,157	2,109	15,669	115	678	394	349	12	1,802	11	12,580	297	33	43
New Mexico......	1,178	153	113	423	131	535	254	8	49	8	18	2	288	....	1,078	190	19	8
Arizona.........	1,516	261	148	483	210	1,167	816	16	407	51	28	10	329	6	1,261	1,013	30	8
Utah.........	3,589	240	163	987	179	836	684	12	779	69	30	12	3,029	41	3,225	250	4	19
Nevada.........	1,069	104	85	190	40	693	124	7	182	12	21	1	618	....	2,041	1,180	149	5
PACIFIC:																		
Washington.........	22,315	3,906	1,792	6,494	1,050	3,565	11,125	527	11,863	422	267	229	4,215	93	10,818	412	100	75
Oregon.........	13,740	1,480	1,132	2,798	909	1,186	6,979	101	6,050	352	214	41	1,928	13	4,324	553	125	34
California.........	67,185	7,083	3,379	13,266	5,252	7,279	27,225	260	7,053	2,403	271	264	10,314	49	88,504	11,140	24,609	609

[1] Comprises Danzig, Fiume, Saar Basin, and "Europe, not specified."

COUNTRY OF BIRTH.

TABLE 6.—COUNTRY OF BIRTH OF FOREIGN-BORN POPULATION, BY DIVISIONS AND STATES: 1920—Continued.

| DIVISION AND STATE. | ASIA. | | | | | | | | AMERICA. | | | | | | ALL OTHER. | | | | | |
	Armenia.	Palestine.	Syria.	Turkey in Asia.	China.	Japan.	India.	Other Asia.	Canada. French.	Canada. Other.	New-foundland.	West Indies.[1]	Mexico.	Central and South America.	Africa.	Australia.	Atlantic Islands.	Pacific Islands.(1)	Country not specified.	Born at sea.
United States	36,628	3,203	51,901	11,019	43,560	81,502	4,901	5,236	307,786	817,139	13,249	78,962	486,418	23,463	5,781	10,914	44,340	3,712	3,589	5,336
GEOG. DIVISIONS:																				
New England	11,964	271	11,181	2,267	2,594	315	332	550	240,385	235,871	8,201	5,400	224	1,805	400	537	32,715	176	305	384
Middle Atlantic	10,806	1,489	15,501	4,335	6,909	2,808	954	1,154	17,045	121,255	2,775	44,596	5,237	11,092	2,156	2,238	1,759	471	600	1,020
E. North Central	6,157	662	9,726	2,098	3,481	784	482	1,598	29,267	224,625	831	2,630	7,181	2,061	873	1,428	299	284	1,521	1,633
W. North Central	717	142	3,406	322	1,250	966	190	207	10,459	70,240	181	616	22,787	763	315	557	43	134	270	951
South Atlantic	402	143	4,064	456	1,313	304	163	80	813	12,228	230	21,256	641	1,025	315	283	231	104	85	171
E. South Central	61	77	1,501	93	366	20	46	32	179	3,022	32	686	570	265	98	82	15	21	29	92
W. South Central	148	156	3,436	206	1,056	406	130	105	590	8,178	100	1,799	261,478	1,550	346	624	150	356	212	218
Mountain	362	73	1,324	190	3,149	8,499	167	233	3,482	30,615	196	323	98,484	485	346	624	150	356	212	218
Pacific	6,011	190	1,762	1,052	23,442	67,331	2,437	1,268	5,566	111,099	703	1,656	89,816	4,417	940	4,848	9,051	2,085	282	611
NEW ENGLAND:																				
Maine	142	10	627	43	104	8	29	7	35,580	38,840	215	139	9	19	21	23	19	4	12	40
New Hampshire	276	7	523	60	63	8	5	2	38,277	14,035	182	52	10	31	12	21	45	4	14	11
Vermont	55	1	228	5	6	4	6	1	14,181	10,704	67	15	7	43	8	5	4	5	3	10
Massachusetts	8,640	180	7,128	1,672	1,807	170	202	107	108,691	154,787	7,168	4,176	146	1,156	317	340	28,294	103	62	216
Rhode Island	1,850	14	1,285	262	162	29	34	38	28,887	7,595	233	218	8	240	43	43	3,950	23	8	25
Connecticut	1,001	59	1,390	225	452	96	56	395	14,769	9,910	336	800	44	316	89	105	403	37	206	82
MIDDLE ATLANTIC:																				
New York	5,599	1,061	8,127	3,200	4,559	2,303	624	744	15,560	97,244	1,810	38,288	2,999	8,645	1,528	1,384	1,168	320	260	483
New Jersey	2,275	160	2,062	440	941	274	158	190	772	9,624	477	3,141	420	1,133	293	334	437	95	106	170
Pennsylvania	2,932	268	5,312	695	1,409	201	172	220	713	14,387	488	3,167	1,818	1,314	335	520	154	56	294	367
EAST NORTH CENTRAL:																				
Ohio	906	185	3,680	637	640	121	109	185	1,277	23,393	148	805	952	481	174	233	55	39	190	297
Indiana	134	26	717	158	205	58	21	128	406	4,741	44	145	686	89	44	78	7	26	43	133
Illinois	1,715	232	1,149	502	1,929	402	155	881	4,032	34,741	311	913	4,032	842	371	608	207	114	287	495
Michigan	2,498	176	3,648	663	524	161	152	349	18,635	147,267	245	592	1,333	475	225	400	23	81	128	314
Wisconsin	904	43	532	138	183	42	45	55	4,917	14,483	83	115	178	174	59	109	7	24	873	394
WEST NORTH CENTRAL:																				
Minnesota	174	25	818	100	364	61	51	45	6,796	27,066	56	102	248	125	92	107	16	29	67	266
Iowa	101	22	512	51	187	20	32	33	401	8,543	35	96	2,650	113	35	101	9	19	36	166
Missouri	181	63	848	83	310	109	38	31	299	6,263	38	247	3,411	222	94	140	8	23	41	180
North Dakota	75	5	289	21	97	67	5	18	1,533	14,210	20	9	29	39	10	35	......	9	23.	75
South Dakota	18	1	265	12	98	24	14	24	508	3,954	3	25	68	27	20	24	......	9	12	72
Nebraska	138	14	415	28	140	642	25	30	351	5,429	20	64	2,611	73	31	80	5	12	71	99
Kansas	30	12	259	27	54	43	25	26	571	4,781	9	73	13,770	164	33	70	5	20	20	93
SOUTH ATLANTIC:																				
Delaware	6	10	2	6	32	8	2	1	23	430	8	61	52	19	12	12	2	5	......	7
Maryland	43	15	72	39	283	23	24	15	117	1,777	61	737	87	215	57	62	32	36	11	49
Dist. of Columbia	63	10	211	62	345	97	23	11	147	1,570	18	365	73	186	54	25	17	7	13	17
Virginia	164	23	550	77	211	53	33	14	106	1,841	32	399	80	156	54	45	58	20	31	28
West Virginia	41	20	1,235	157	61	10	2	10	54	927	6	108	80	52	9	33	5	2	2	5
North Carolina	10	22	502	23	64	19	12	8	15	648	7	89	30	47	21	14	2	8	1	3
South Carolina	6	2	306	5	63	10	15	11	24	247	1	103	17	20	10	5	9	1	9	11
Georgia	28	16	473	49	147	11	14	8	50	915	22	223	55	69	40	28	11	8	17	27
Florida	41	16	533	38	107	73	38	11	277	3,864	75	19,171	167	261	58	59	95	17	8	27
EAST SOUTH CENTRAL:																				
Kentucky	20	16	309	22	42	6	12	12	50	853	13	80	138	38	10	38	2	11	13	54
Tennessee	18	30	127	20	39	13	18	5	47	941	9	85	176	62	28	15	3	4	9	16
Alabama	22	16	482	39	36	10	8	10	52	852	3	405	146	117	39	21	10	6	4	12
Mississippi	1	15	583	12	249	......	8	5	30	376	7	116	110	48	21	8	......		3	10
WEST SOUTH CENTRAL:																				
Arkansas	7	10	213	10	66	5	3	6	58	835	20	43	280	25	32	27	7	7	1	26
Louisiana	27	15	954	61	280	47	57	12	157	1,029	16	1,225	2,437	1,142	61	68	20	10	5	40
Oklahoma	15	20	691	21	169	56	10	42	126	2,363	11	59	6,884	72	30	54	2	13	20	51
Texas	99	105	1,578	114	561	298	60	45	249	3,951	53	472	251,827	311	125	173	39	51	199	139
MOUNTAIN:																				
Montana	140	8	192	62	641	896	14	39	2,211	12,489	63	43	236	72	50	81	5	39	66	41
Idaho	13	1	49	15	489	1,180	18	23	476	4,485	59	14	1,215	26	44	57	28	72	41	27
Wyoming	62	4	82	25	191	1,029	12	67	92	1,348	4	21	1,801	29	15	17	8	14	12	10
Colorado	46	41	289	30	208	1,762	44	33	418	7,224	39	114	11,037	185	56	112	9	40	22	63
New Mexico	2	2	198	5	124	198	3	8	42	696	3	38	20,272	26	26	14	5	4	2	5
Arizona	8	8	327	15	720	427	27	31	90	1,874	16	76	61,580	78	23	81	1	26	05	22
Utah	80	5	174	18	247	2,858	40	24	45	1,426	4	10	1,166	32	117	222	4	133	2	40
Nevada	11	4	13	20	529	649	9	8	108	1,073	8	7	1,177	37	15	40	104	23	2	10
PACIFIC:																				
Washington	259	18	318	288	1,727	12,971	206	201	2,581	40,598	318	258	450	322	133	612	46	246	126	180
Oregon	63	5	185	56	2,151	3,169	134	35	679	13,121	49	92	595	123	73	215	48	161	13	54
California	5,689	167	1,259	708	19,564	51,191	2,097	1,032	2,306	57,380	336	1,306	88,771	3,972	734	4,021	8,957	1,678	143	377

1 Except possessions of the United States.

700

POPULATION.

TABLE 7.—PER CENT DISTRIBUTION OF FOREIGN-BORN POPULATION

DIVISION AND STATE.	NORTHWESTERN EUROPE.												CENTRAL EUROPE.					
	England.	Scotland.	Wales.	Ireland.	Norway.	Sweden.	Denmark.	Netherlands.	Belgium.	Luxemburg.	Switzerland.	France.	Germany.	Poland.	Czechoslovakia.	Austria.	Hungary.	Jugo-Slavia.
United States	5.8	1.8	0.5	7.5	2.6	4.5	1.4	0.9	0.5	0.1	0.9	1.1	12.1	8.2	2.6	4.1	2.9	1.2
GEOGRAPHIC DIVISIONS:																		
New England	7.8	2.5	0.2	14.2	0.5	3.6	0.4	0.2	0.2	(1)	0.2	0.7	2.7	7.0	0.5	1.2	0.8	0.1
Middle Atlantic	5.5	1.7	0.6	9.5	0.7	1.7	0.5	0.6	0.3	(1)	0.6	1.1	10.2	10.4	2.5	6.3	3.8	1.0
East North Central	5.1	1.6	0.5	4.2	2.5	5.1	1.3	1.9	0.9	0.2	0.9	0.9	18.3	12.4	4.4	4.5	4.6	2.2
West North Central	3.9	1.3	0.4	3.6	12.1	13.6	4.5	1.8	0.5	0.4	1.2	0.8	21.3	2.8	3.7	2.7	1.3	1.3
South Atlantic	7.4	2.3	0.5	6.1	0.7	1.3	0.6	0.4	0.5	(1)	0.7	1.2	12.4	7.7	2.0	3.7	3.2	1.1
East South Central	8.3	2.9	0.6	8.1	0.6	2.1	0.7	0.4	0.3	(1)	3.0	3.0	22.8	3.5	0.8	2.8	2.5	1.0
West South Central	2.9	0.8	0.2	1.8	0.6	1.4	0.6	0.2	0.3	(1)	0.7	1.7	10.2	1.6	3.3	2.0	0.4	0.3
Mountain	9.5	2.8	1.0	4.2	3.7	6.9	3.6	1.1	0.3	0.1	1.4	1.1	7.2	1.0	1.1	2.8	0.7	2.3
Pacific	7.7	2.5	0.5	5.2	4.3	6.8	2.7	0.8	0.4	0.1	2.1	2.1	9.1	1.1	0.6	2.0	0.6	1.1
NEW ENGLAND:																		
Maine	4.8	2.0	0.1	5.3	0.5	1.9	1.0	(1)	(1)	(1)	0.1	0.3	0.9	1.6	0.4	0.3	0.1	0.1
New Hampshire	4.8	2.0	0.1	8.7	0.5	2.1	0.2	0.2	0.5	(1)	0.1	0.3	1.9	4.4	0.1	0.4	0.1	0.1
Vermont	4.9	4.2	1.2	6.5	0.2	2.5	0.3	0.1	(1)	(1)	0.4	0.4	1.4	3.9	0.2	0.0	0.0	0.1
Massachusetts	8.0	2.6	0.1	15.3	0.5	3.5	0.3	0.2	0.2	(1)	0.1	0.7	2.0	6.4	0.2	0.7	0.1	0.1
Rhode Island	14.7	3.2	0.1	12.7	0.3	3.7	0.2	0.1	0.6	(1)	0.1	1.1	1.8	4.7	0.2	0.7	0.1	0.1
Connecticut	6.0	2.0	0.2	12.0	0.4	4.7	0.8	0.1	0.1	(1)	0.5	0.9	6.0	12.3	1.7	3.4	3.5	0.3
MIDDLE ATLANTIC:																		
New York	4.8	1.3	0.2	10.1	1.0	1.9	0.5	0.5	0.2	(1)	0.5	1.1	10.5	8.8	1.4	5.4	2.8	0.3
New Jersey	6.3	2.4	0.2	8.9	0.7	1.4	0.8	1.7	0.3	(1)	1.1	1.4	12.4	12.2	2.3	5.0	5.5	0.4
Pennsylvania	6.5	2.0	1.5	8.7	0.2	1.4	0.2	0.1	0.3	(1)	0.5	0.9	8.6	12.8	4.9	8.8	5.1	2.0
EAST NORTH CENTRAL:																		
Ohio	6.3	1.8	1.1	4.3	0.2	1.1	0.3	0.4	0.3	(1)	1.4	1.2	16.4	9.9	6.2	7.1	10.8	4.5
Indiana	5.6	2.4	0.7	4.8	0.4	3.3	0.6	1.3	1.7	0.1	1.5	2.1	24.7	11.8	2.6	6.0	6.2	3.0
Illinois	4.5	1.6	0.3	6.1	2.3	8.7	1.4	1.2	0.9	0.3	0.6	1.0	17.0	13.4	5.5	3.8	2.8	1.6
Michigan	6.5	1.8	0.2	2.3	0.9	3.4	1.0	4.6	1.4	0.1	0.4	0.6	11.8	14.3	1.5	3.0	3.1	1.3
Wisconsin	2.4	0.7	0.4	1.7	9.9	5.0	3.3	1.6	0.7	0.2	1.7	0.5	32.8	11.0	4.3	4.3	2.2	1.9
WEST NORTH CENTRAL:																		
Minnesota	2.3	0.8	0.2	2.1	18.5	23.0	3.5	1.1	0.4	0.4	0.6	0.4	15.3	3.8	2.6	2.4	0.9	2.2
Iowa	5.8	1.8	0.8	4.7	7.7	10.0	8.0	5.5	0.5	0.7	1.8	0.9	31.3	0.9	4.0	1.9	0.3	0.7
Missouri	5.6	1.6	0.5	8.0	0.3	2.5	0.9	0.5	0.6	0.1	2.6	2.1	29.9	4.1	2.7	4.6	4.3	1.2
North Dakota	1.7	0.9	0.1	1.3	20.0	8.0	3.5	0.7	0.3	0.2	0.4	0.3	9.1	1.7	1.0	1.6	1.9	0.2
South Dakota	3.6	1.0	0.4	2.4	20.4	10.4	7.2	3.9	0.3	0.6	0.9	0.4	19.0	1.0	3.4	1.4	0.7	0.6
Nebraska	4.0	1.1	0.4	3.6	1.4	12.5	8.2	0.6	0.4	0.2	1.2	0.6	27.2	3.1	10.5	3.0	0.5	0.5
Kansas	7.1	2.3	1.1	4.3	0.9	9.3	2.0	0.6	1.4	0.3	2.0	1.9	21.1	2.2	3.1	4.7	0.6	1.0
SOUTH ATLANTIC:																		
Delaware	7.5	2.1	0.2	14.5	0.3	1.6	0.4	0.2	0.1	(1)	0.4	1.0	8.2	19.3	0.6	3.1	1.1	0.1
Maryland	5.0	1.6	0.5	6.6	0.4	0.6	0.4	0.3	0.1	(1)	0.5	0.8	21.4	11.7	3.4	3.5	1.0	0.3
District of Columbia	10.2	2.7	0.4	14.7	0.7	1.6	0.8	0.4	0.3	(1)	1.2	2.3	11.5	2.4	0.4	1.8	0.7	0.1
Virginia	11.9	4.2	0.5	5.5	1.5	2.1	1.4	1.1	0.4	(1)	0.8	1.4	8.8	3.5	2.8	2.9	4.1	0.4
West Virginia	5.5	1.6	1.1	2.3	0.1	0.5	0.2	0.1	1.5	(1)	0.0	1.0	6.1	9.3	2.5	8.2	10.1	4.5
North Carolina	13.3	6.1	0.3	4.1	1.0	2.3	0.9	1.6	0.2	(1)	1.0	1.9	9.7	2.9	0.3	2.0	0.0	0.4
South Carolina	7.5	2.9	0.2	6.7	1.3	2.0	1.2	0.5	0.9	(1)	0.5	1.2	16.4	5.3	0.7	3.1	0.9	0.3
Georgia	9.7	3.2	0.5	6.7	0.8	1.8	0.8	0.5	0.3	(1)	1.0	2.3	11.7	5.5	0.7	2.4	1.5	0.5
Florida	8.4	2.0	0.3	2.4	1.1	2.6	1.1	0.7	0.2	(1)	0.7	1.4	6.6	0.8	0.4	1.0	0.7	0.2
EAST SOUTH CENTRAL:																		
Kentucky	6.0	1.7	0.5	11.1	0.2	0.7	0.3	0.5	0.3	(1)	4.3	3.2	30.0	3.4	0.8	2.9	3.5	1.1
Tennessee	10.7	2.9	0.9	8.3	0.4	1.9	0.9	0.4	0.2	(1)	3.9	2.1	13.8	5.4	0.5	2.5	2.1	0.2
Alabama	10.8	5.4	0.8	4.5	1.2	4.1	1.1	0.5	0.4	(1)	1.0	3.4	13.5	2.2	1.3	3.2	2.1	0.9
Mississippi	7.1	1.7	0.2	4.9	1.2	2.9	1.3	0.4	0.4	0.1	0.8	3.1	11.0	3.8	0.7	1.6	0.6	2.6
WEST SOUTH CENTRAL:																		
Arkansas	8.1	2.2	0.6	4.8	0.7	2.3	1.3	0.8	0.7	0.1	5.2	2.7	28.1	3.7	3.5	4.5	0.8	0.8
Louisiana	4.0	1.0	0.2	4.3	1.2	1.1	0.7	0.6	0.8	(1)	0.8	9.0	11.1	0.8	0.7	1.6	0.7	0.7
Oklahoma	6.6	2.8	0.8	3.3	0.7	2.3	1.4	0.4	0.7	0.1	1.6	2.4	17.4	3.1	4.5	3.4	0.8	0.5
Texas	2.1	0.5	0.1	1.2	0.5	1.2	0.4	0.2	0.1	(1)	0.5	0.7	8.5	1.4	3.5	1.8	0.3	0.2
MOUNTAIN:																		
Montana	8.5	3.4	0.9	7.6	10.4	7.5	3.1	1.8	0.7	0.2	1.2	0.9	8.2	1.3	2.0	3.5	1.0	4.0
Idaho	10.9	8.0	1.4	3.5	6.1	12.5	5.5	1.1	0.3	0.1	3.8	1.2	10.2	0.7	1.0	1.9	0.6	1.1
Wyoming	9.4	5.4	1.1	3.6	2.5	7.7	3.5	0.5	0.5	0.1	1.1	1.4	8.6	2.0	1.9	4.5	1.3	4.5
Colorado	8.0	2.8	1.2	5.2	1.3	8.5	2.4	0.7	0.4	0.1	1.3	1.2	10.1	1.6	1.6	4.8	1.0	1.8
New Mexico	3.0	1.5	0.3	1.5	0.4	1.0	0.4	0.2	0.3	(1)	0.5	1.3	4.0	0.5	0.4	1.4	0.4	1.8
Arizona	3.6	0.7	0.2	1.5	0.4	1.1	0.5	0.1	0.1	(1)	0.4	1.2	1.9	0.3	0.2	0.6	0.3	1.4
Utah	25.1	3.9	2.2	2.0	3.6	10.3	11.8	3.3	0.2	(1)	2.6	0.7	6.1	0.4	0.3	1.7	0.3	1.4
Nevada	7.9	2.1	0.6	6.1	1.3	3.4	3.4	0.2	0.2	(1)	2.4	3.8	6.7	0.6	0.5	1.2	0.2	4.3
PACIFIC:																		
Washington	7.8	3.0	0.8	3.4	11.4	13.1	3.2	1.2	0.5	0.1	1.4	0.9	8.4	1.5	0.7	2.4	0.4	1.3
Oregon	7.4	3.4	0.5	3.9	6.5	9.8	3.3	0.9	0.7	0.1	3.9	1.2	12.8	1.4	0.7	2.4	0.8	1.3
California	7.7	2.2	0.5	6.0	1.5	4.2	2.5	0.6	0.3	0.1	2.1	2.7	8.0	0.9	1.1	2.6	0.8	1.3

1 Less than one-tenth of 1 per cent.

COUNTRY OF BIRTH.   701

BY COUNTRY OF BIRTH, BY DIVISIONS AND STATES: 1920.

DIVISION AND STATE.	EASTERN EUROPE.					SOUTHERN EUROPE.				ASIA.				AMERICA.					
	Russia.	Lithuania.	Finland.	Rumania.	Bulgaria and Turkey in Europe.	Greece.	Italy.	Spain.	Portugal.	Armenia.	Syria.	China.	Japan.	Canada. French.	Canada. Other.	Newfoundland.	West Indies.[2]	Mexico.	Central and South America.
United States	10.1	1.0	1.1	0.7	0.1	1.3	11.6	0.4	0.5	0.3	0.4	0.3	0.6	2.2	5.9	0.1	0.6	3.5	0.2
GEOGRAPHIC DIVISIONS:																			
New England	7.8	1.9	1.0	0.2	(1)	1.7	12.6	0.2	2.1	0.6	0.6	0.1	(1)	12.7	12.5	0.4	0.3	(1)	0.1
Middle Atlantic	15.4	1.0	0.4	1.1	0.1	0.9	18.7	0.3	0.1	0.2	0.3	0.1	0.1	0.3	2.4	0.1	0.9	0.1	0.2
East North Central	7.3	1.4	1.4	0.9	0.2	1.4	6.3	0.1	(1)	0.2	0.3	0.1	(1)	0.9	6.9	(1)	0.1	0.2	0.1
West North Central	8.1	0.2	2.3	0.5	0.1	0.8	2.5	0.1	(1)	0.1	0.2	0.1	0.1	0.8	5.1	(1)	(1)	1.7	0.1
South Atlantic	14.6	1.0	0.4	0.7	0.1	3.5	12.2	2.0	0.2	0.1	1.2	0.4	0.1	0.2	3.7	0.1	6.4	0.3	0.3
East South Central	10.1	0.1	0.3	0.6	0.1	2.8	11.8	0.3	(1)	0.1	2.1	0.5	(1)	0.2	4.1	(1)	0.9	0.8	0.4
West South Central	3.2	(1)	0.1	0.1	0.1	0.7	6.0	0.5	(1)	(1)	0.7	0.2	0.1	0.1	1.8	(1)	0.4	59.3	0.3
Mountain	5.7	0.1	1.7	0.2	0.2	2.0	6.1	1.0	0.1	0.1	0.3	0.7	1.8	0.7	6.5	(1)	0.1	21.1	0.1
Pacific	4.0	0.1	2.2	0.3	0.1	1.5	9.2	1.1	2.2	0.5	0.2	2.1	6.0	0.5	9.8	0.1	0.1	7.9	0.4
NEW ENGLAND:																			
Maine	3.5	1.0	1.3	0.1	0.1	1.1	2.6	(1)	0.1	0.1	0.6	0.1	(1)	33.0	36.0	0.2	0.1	(1)	(1)
New Hampshire	3.8	1.1	1.7	(1)	(1)	5.8	2.8	(1)	0.2	0.3	0.6	0.1	(1)	41.9	15.4	0.2	0.1	(1)	(1)
Vermont	3.0	0.2	1.1	(1)	(1)	0.4	9.1	1.5	0.1	0.1	0.5	(1)	(1)	31.8	24.0	0.2	(1)	(1)	0.1
Massachusetts	8.5	1.9	1.3	0.1	0.1	1.9	10.7	0.1	2.7	0.8	0.7	0.2	(1)	10.0	14.2	0.7	0.4	(1)	0.1
Rhode Island	4.6	0.5	0.2	0.2	0.1	0.7	18.4	0.1	5.1	1.1	0.7	0.1	(1)	16.5	4.3	0.1	0.1	(1)	0.1
Connecticut	10.2	3.1	0.3	0.3	(1)	1.0	21.2	0.3	0.5	0.3	0.4	0.1	(1)	3.9	2.6	0.1	0.2	(1)	0.1
MIDDLE ATLANTIC:																			
New York	18.7	0.4	0.4	1.4	0.1	0.9	19.3	0.5	0.1	0.2	0.3	0.2	0.1	0.6	3.4	0.1	1.4	0.1	0.3
New Jersey	9.9	0.8	0.3	0.6	(1)	0.6	21.2	0.3	0.1	0.3	0.3	0.1	(1)	0.1	1.3	0.1	0.4	0.1	0.2
Pennsylvania	11.6	2.2	0.2	0.8	0.1	1.0	16.0	0.2	0.1	0.2	0.4	0.1	(1)	0.1	1.0	(1)	0.2	0.1	0.1
EAST NORTH CENTRAL:																			
Ohio	6.4	0.6	0.9	1.9	0.5	2.0	8.9	0.2	(1)	0.1	0.5	0.1	(1)	0.2	3.4	(1)	0.1	0.1	0.1
Indiana	5.1	1.0	0.2	1.8	0.3	2.8	4.4	0.3	(1)	0.1	0.5	0.1	(1)	0.3	3.1	(1)	0.1	0.5	0.1
Illinois	9.7	2.5	0.3	0.5	0.1	1.4	7.8	0.1	(1)	0.1	0.1	0.2	(1)	0.3	2.9	(1)	0.1	0.3	0.1
Michigan	6.2	0.8	4.1	0.9	0.3	1.0	4.1	0.1	(1)	0.3	0.5	0.1	(1)	2.6	20.2	(1)	0.1	0.2	0.1
Wisconsin	4.7	0.6	1.5	0.2	0.1	0.8	2.4	(1)	(1)	0.2	0.1	(1)	(1)	1.1	3.1	(1)	(1)	(1)	(1)
WEST NORTH CENTRAL:																			
Minnesota	3.3	0.2	6.0	0.5	0.1	0.5	1.5	(1)	(1)	(1)	0.2	0.1	(1)	1.4	5.6	(1)	(1)	0.1	(1)
Iowa	3.2	0.3	(1)	0.1	0.1	1.3	2.2	(1)	(1)	(1)	0.2	0.1	(1)	0.2	3.8	(1)	(1)	1.2	0.1
Missouri	10.0	0.2	0.1	0.9	0.1	1.6	7.8	0.2	(1)	0.1	0.5	0.2	0.1	0.2	3.4	(1)	0.1	1.8	0.1
North Dakota	22.5	(1)	0.8	1.4	(1)	0.3	0.1	(1)	(1)	0.1	0.2	0.1	0.1	1.2	10.8	(1)	(1)	(1)	(1)
South Dakota	13.6	(1)	1.3	0.2	0.1	0.5	0.5	(1)	(1)	(1)	0.3	0.1	(1)	0.6	4.8	(1)	(1)	0.1	(1)
Nebraska	10.4	0.1	(1)	0.2	(1)	1.0	2.4	(1)	(1)	0.1	0.3	0.1	0.4	0.2	3.6	(1)	(1)	1.7	(1)
Kansas	10.9	0.1	0.1	0.3	(1)	0.6	3.0	0.2	(1)	(1)	0.2	(1)	(1)	0.5	4.3	(1)	(1)	12.4	0.1
SOUTH ATLANTIC:																			
Delaware	11.3	0.5	0.3	0.6	(1)	1.4	20.8	0.7	0.1	(1)	(1)	0.2	(1)	0.1	2.2	(1)	0.3	0.3	0.1
Maryland	24.0	2.1	0.2	0.5	(1)	0.9	9.2	0.2	0.1	(1)	0.1	0.3	(1)	0.1	1.7	0.1	0.7	0.1	0.2
District of Columbia	17.6	0.1	0.4	0.3	0.3	4.1	12.8	0.4	(1)	0.2	0.7	1.2	0.3	0.5	5.4	0.1	1.2	0.2	0.6
Virginia	17.1	0.2	0.8	0.5	0.2	5.7	7.7	0.8	1.0	0.5	1.7	0.7	0.2	0.3	5.8	0.1	1.3	0.3	0.5
West Virginia	6.3	1.2	0.5	1.0	0.2	5.1	22.8	2.5	(1)	0.1	2.0	0.1	(1)	0.1	1.5	(1)	0.2	0.1	0.1
North Carolina	12.8	0.4	0.2	0.4	0.2	7.6	6.2	0.2	0.2	0.1	8.1	0.9	0.2	0.2	8.9	0.1	1.2	0.4	0.6
South Carolina	18.0	0.1	0.8	0.4	0.2	8.8	5.2	0.3	0.1	0.1	6.0	1.0	0.2	0.4	3.8	(1)	1.6	0.3	0.3
Georgia	20.8	0.4	0.3	0.7	0.2	8.9	4.2	0.8	0.3	0.2	2.9	0.9	0.1	0.3	5.5	0.1	1.3	0.3	0.4
Florida	2.3	(1)	0.6	0.9	(1)	2.6	8.8	7.6	0.4	0.1	1.0	0.2	0.1	0.5	7.2	0.1	35.6	0.3	0.5
EAST SOUTH CENTRAL:																			
Kentucky	8.9	0.2	0.2	0.6	0.2	1.3	6.3	0.2	(1)	0.1	1.0	0.1	(1)	0.2	2.8	(1)	0.3	0.4	0.1
Tennessee	14.5	(1)	0.2	0.6	0.1	3.1	13.3	0.1	(1)	0.1	0.8	0.2	0.1	0.3	6.0	0.1	0.5	1.1	0.4
Alabama	8.8	0.1	0.4	0.7	0.2	5.1	15.2	0.4	(1)	0.1	2.7	0.2	0.1	0.3	4.7	(1)	2.2	0.8	0.6
Mississippi	9.8	0.1	0.7	0.4	(1)	2.5	21.9	0.7	0.1	(1)	6.9	3.0	....	0.4	4.5	0.1	1.4	1.3	0.6
WEST SOUTH CENTRAL:																			
Arkansas	4.7	0.2	0.1	0.4	0.1	2.0	9.8	0.2	(1)	(1)	1.5	0.5	(1)	0.4	5.9	0.1	0.3	2.0	0.2
Louisiana	4.2	(1)	0.3	0.2	0.1	1.3	35.0	2.8	0.2	0.1	2.1	0.6	0.1	0.3	2.2	(1)	2.6	5.4	2.5
Oklahoma	12.4	0.3	0.2	0.2	0.3	1.5	5.2	0.3	(1)	(1)	1.7	0.4	0.1	0.3	5.8	(1)	0.1	17.0	0.2
Texas	1.9	(1)	0.1	0.1	(1)	0.5	2.2	0.3	(1)	(1)	0.4	0.2	0.1	0.1	1.1	(1)	0.1	89.2	0.1
MOUNTAIN:																			
Montana	5.4	0.1	3.7	0.4	0.3	1.5	4.0	0.1	(1)	0.1	0.2	0.7	0.9	2.3	13.1	0.1	(1)	0.2	0.1
Idaho	3.6	(1)	2.4	0.3	0.1	1.8	3.2	3.5	0.1	(1)	0.1	1.2	2.9	1.2	11.0	0.1	(1)	3.0	0.1
Wyoming	5.6	0.1	3.2	0.8	0.3	4.7	7.3	0.5	0.1	0.2	0.3	0.7	3.9	0.3	5.1	(1)	0.1	6.8	0.1
Colorado	14.0	0.1	0.7	0.3	0.3	1.5	10.6	0.2	(1)	(1)	0.2	0.2	1.5	0.4	6.1	(1)	0.1	9.3	0.2
New Mexico	0.9	(1)	0.2	(1)	0.1	1.0	5.6	0.7	0.1	(1)	0.7	0.4	0.7	0.1	2.3	(1)	0.1	68.0	0.1
Arizona	1.0	(1)	0.5	0.1	(1)	0.4	1.6	1.3	(1)	(1)	0.4	0.9	0.5	0.1	2.8	(1)	0.1	76.4	0.1
Utah	1.2	(1)	1.3	0.1	0.1	5.1	5.4	0.4	(1)	0.1	0.8	0.4	4.0	0.1	2.4	(1)	(1)	2.0	0.1
Nevada	0.8	(1)	1.1	0.1	0.1	3.9	16.5	7.4	0.9	0.1	0.1	3.3	4.1	0.7	6.7	(1)	(1)	7.4	0.2
PACIFIC:																			
Washington	4.2	0.2	4.5	0.2	0.2	1.6	4.1	0.2	0.1	0.1	0.1	0.7	4.9	1.0	15.3	0.1	0.1	0.2	0.1
Oregon	3.5	0.1	3.6	0.3	0.2	1.3	4.0	0.5	0.1	0.1	0.2	2.0	2.9	0.6	12.2	(1)	0.1	0.6	0.1
California	3.6	(1)	0.9	0.3	0.1	1.4	11.7	1.5	3.2	0.8	0.2	2.6	6.8	0.3	7.6	(1)	0.2	11.7	0.5

[1] Less than one-tenth of 1 per cent.   [2] Except possessions of the United States.

702

POPULATION.

TABLE 8.—PER CENT DISTRIBUTION OF POPULATION BORN IN SPECIFIED

DIVISION AND STATE OF RESIDENCE.	Total foreign born; 1920	NORTHWESTERN EUROPE.												CENTRAL EUROPE.						EASTERN EUROPE.	
		England.	Scotland.	Wales.	Ireland.	Norway.	Sweden.	Denmark.	Netherlands.	Belgium.	Luxemburg.	Switzerland.	France.	Germany.	Poland.	Czechoslovakia.	Austria.	Hungary.	Jugo-Slavia.	Russia.	Lithuania.
United States	100.0	100.0	100.0	100.0	100.0	100.0	100.0	100.0	100.0	100.0	100.0	100.0	100.0	100.0	100.0	100.0	100.0	100.0	100.0	100.0	100.0
GEOGRAPHIC DIVISIONS:																					
New England	13.5	18.1	18.7	4.5	25.8	2.4	10.8	4.5	2.2	7.0	0.9	3.2	8.7	3.0	11.5	2.7	4.0	3.8	1.4	10.5	26.2
Middle Atlantic	35.6	33.6	33.0	43.5	45.5	9.7	13.4	12.2	21.1	19.9	8.1	25.4	36.1	30.1	45.2	34.2	54.0	47.9	28.4	54.5	36.0
East North Central	23.2	20.2	20.8	22.7	13.0	22.6	26.4	22.7	45.4	47.4	40.5	25.6	19.4	35.1	35.3	30.7	25.2	37.7	42.7	16.9	32.8
West North Central	9.9	6.6	6.8	8.5	4.8	45.7	30.0	32.6	18.5	11.4	38.5	13.3	7.5	17.4	3.4	14.0	6.5	4.4	10.7	7.9	1.6
South Atlantic	2.4	3.0	2.9	2.6	1.9	0.6	0.7	1.1	1.1	2.5	0.7	2.0	2.7	2.4	2.2	1.8	2.1	2.7	2.1	3.5	2.4
East South Central	0.5	0.7	0.8	0.7	0.6	0.1	0.2	0.3	0.2	0.4	0.2	1.8	1.4	1.0	0.2	0.2	0.4	0.5	0.5	0.5	0.1
West South Central	3.3	1.6	1.5	1.1	0.8	0.7	1.0	1.4	0.8	1.9	1.0	2.9	5.3	2.8	0.6	0.2	0.4	0.5	0.5	0.5	0.1
Mountain	3.4	5.5	5.1	7.3	1.9	4.8	5.2	9.0	4.0	2.6	3.0	5.6	3.2	2.0	0.4	4.3	1.6	0.4	0.7	1.0	0.2
Pacific	8.1	10.7	11.0	9.0	5.6	13.4	12.3	16.2	6.5	7.0	7.1	20.2	15.8	6.1	1.1	1.7	3.9	1.8	7.1	3.2	0.7
NEW ENGLAND:																					
Maine	0.8	0.6	0.9	0.2	0.6	0.2	0.3	0.6	(¹)	0.1	(¹)	0.1	0.2	0.1	0.2	0.1	0.1	(¹)	0.1	0.3	0.8
New Hampshire	0.7	0.5	0.7	0.1	0.8	0.1	0.3	0.1	0.1	0.8	(¹)	0.1	0.2	0.1	0.4	(¹)	0.1	(¹)	0.1	0.3	0.8
Vermont	0.3	0.3	0.7	0.8	0.3	(¹)	0.2	0.1	0.1	0.8	(¹)	0.1	0.2	0.1	0.4	(¹)	0.1	(¹)	0.1	0.2	0.8
Massachusetts	7.8	10.7	11.2	2.0	17.7	1.5	6.1	1.9	1.6	(¹)	(¹)	0.2	0.1	(¹)	0.2	(¹)	(¹)	0.1	(¹)	0.1	15.4
Rhode Island	1.3	3.2	2.2	0.4	2.1	0.1	1.0	0.2	0.1	4.0	0.3	1.2	4.7	1.3	6.1	0.6	1.4	0.3	0.6	6.6	0.6
Connecticut	2.7	2.8	2.9	1.0	4.4	0.4	2.8	1.6	0.3	1.5	0.1	0.2	1.3	0.2	0.7	0.1	0.2	(¹)	0.1	0.6	0.6
MIDDLE ATLANTIC:										0.6	0.4	1.6	2.2	1.3	4.1	1.8	2.2	3.3	0.6	2.8	8.6
New York	20.3	16.7	14.8	10.1	27.5	7.6	8.5	7.5	10.5	8.5	4.5	12.7	21.1	17.5	21.7	10.6	26.3	19.7	5.0	37.8	9.0
New Jersey	5.3	5.8	7.0	1.9	6.4	1.5	1.7	3.0	9.7	4.0	1.3	6.9	6.6	5.5	7.9	4.6	6.4	10.2	2.0	5.3	4.6
Pennsylvania	10.0	11.1	11.2	31.6	11.7	0.7	3.2	1.6	1.0	7.5	2.3	5.8	8.4	7.1	15.6	19.0	21.3	18.0	21.4	11.5	22.4
EAST NORTH CENTRAL:																					
Ohio	4.9	5.3	4.8	11.6	2.8	0.4	1.2	1.2	1.9	3.0	2.2	8.1	5.3	6.6	5.9	11.6	8.4	18.4	17.0	3.1	3.0
Indiana	1.1	1.0	1.5	1.6	0.7	0.1	0.8	0.5	1.5	4.0	0.8	2.0	2.1	2.2	1.6	1.1	1.6	2.4	2.6	0.5	1.1
Illinois	8.7	6.7	7.7	5.1	7.2	7.6	16.9	9.0	10.9	18.1	25.5	6.6	7.8	12.2	14.2	18.4	8.1	8.7	11.4	8.4	22.5
Michigan	5.2	5.8	5.2	1.7	1.6	1.9	3.9	3.8	25.4	16.8	3.8	2.3	2.7	5.1	9.1	3.1	3.8	5.7	5.6	3.2	4.1
Wisconsin	3.3	1.3	1.2	2.6	0.8	12.5	3.7	8.2	5.7	5.5	8.2	6.6	1.4	9.0	4.4	5.5	3.4	2.5	5.2	1.5	2.2
WEST NORTH CENTRAL:																					
Minnesota	3.5	1.3	1.5	1.3	1.0	24.8	17.9	8.9	4.1	3.3	14.2	2.3	1.2	4.4	1.6	3.5	2.0	1.1	6.3	1.1	0.5
Iowa	1.6	1.6	1.6	2.6	1.0	4.8	3.6	9.5	9.5	2.0	13.0	2.4	1.4	4.2	0.2	2.5	0.8	0.2	0.9	0.5	0.5
Missouri	1.3	1.3	1.2	1.3	1.4	0.2	0.8	0.9	0.7	1.8	1.1	4.2	2.5	3.3	0.7	1.4	1.5	2.0	1.4	1.3	0.3
North Dakota	0.9	0.3	0.5	0.2	0.2	10.5	1.7	2.4	0.7	0.7	1.8	0.4	2.5	3.3	0.7	1.4	1.5	2.0	1.4	2.1	(¹)
South Dakota	0.6	0.4	0.3	0.5	0.2	4.6	1.4	3.2	2.4	0.4	3.8	0.6	0.2	0.7	0.2	0.4	0.6	0.1	0.3	0.8	(¹)
Nebraska	1.1	0.7	0.7	0.8	0.5	0.6	3.0	6.5	0.6	0.9	2.4	0.6	0.2	0.9	0.1	0.8	0.2	0.1	0.3	0.8	(¹)
Kansas	0.8	1.0	1.0	1.7	0.5	0.3	1.7	1.2	0.5	2.4	2.3	1.5	0.6	2.4	0.4	4.4	0.8	0.2	0.4	1.1	0.1
SOUTH ATLANTIC:														1.9	1.4	1.4	0.2				
Delaware	0.1	0.2	0.2	0.1	0.3	(¹)	0.1	(¹)	(¹)	(¹)	(¹)	0.1	0.1	0.1	0.3	(¹)	0.1	0.1	(¹)	0.2	0.1
Maryland	0.7	0.6	0.7	0.7	0.6	0.1	0.1	0.2	0.2	0.2	0.2	0.4	0.5	1.3	1.1	1.0	0.6	0.5	0.2	1.8	1.0
District of Columbia	0.2	0.4	0.3	0.2	0.4	0.1	0.1	0.1	0.1	0.1	0.1	0.3	0.4	0.2	0.1	(¹)	0.1	0.1	(¹)	0.4	(¹)
Virginia	0.2	0.5	0.5	0.2	0.2	0.1	0.1	0.1	0.2	0.3	0.2	0.1	0.2	0.3	0.2	0.1	0.2	0.2	0.3	0.1	0.4
West Virginia	0.4	0.4	0.4	1.0	0.1	(¹)	0.1	0.1	0.1	1.5	(¹)	0.5	0.4	0.2	0.5	0.4	0.9	1.6	1.7	0.4	0.1
North Carolina	0.1	0.1	0.2	(¹)	(¹)	(¹)	0.1	0.1	0.1	(¹)	(¹)	0.1	0.1	(¹)	(¹)	(¹)	(¹)	(¹)	(¹)	0.3	0.5
South Carolina	(¹)	0.1	0.1	(¹)	(¹)	(¹)	(¹)	(¹)	0.1	0.1	(¹)	(¹)	0.1	0.1	(¹)	(¹)	(¹)	(¹)	(¹)	0.1	(¹)
Georgia	0.1	0.2	0.2	0.1	0.1	(¹)	(¹)	(¹)	(¹)	0.1	(¹)	0.2	0.1	0.1	(¹)	0.1	0.1	0.1	0.1	0.1	(¹)
Florida	0.4	0.6	0.4	0.2	0.1	0.2	0.2	0.3	0.3	0.2	0.2	0.3	0.5	0.2	(¹)	0.1	0.1	0.1	0.1	0.2	0.1
EAST SOUTH CENTRAL:																					
Kentucky	0.2	0.2	0.2	0.2	0.3	(¹)	(¹)	(¹)	0.1	0.1	0.1	1.1	0.6	0.7	0.1	0.1	0.1	0.1	0.1	0.1	(¹)
Tennessee	0.1	0.2	0.2	0.2	0.1	(¹)	(¹)	0.1	(¹)	0.1	0.1	0.5	0.2	0.1	0.1	(¹)	0.1	0.2	0.3	0.2	(¹)
Alabama	0.1	0.2	0.4	0.2	0.1	(¹)	(¹)	0.1	(¹)	0.1	(¹)	0.1	0.4	0.1	(¹)	0.1	0.1	0.1	0.1	0.2	(¹)
Mississippi	0.1	0.1	0.1	(¹)	(¹)	(¹)	(¹)	0.1	(¹)	0.1	0.1	0.1	0.2	0.1	(¹)	(¹)	0.1	0.1	0.1	0.1	(¹)
WEST SOUTH CENTRAL:														0.1							
Arkansas	0.1	0.1	0.1	0.1	0.1	(¹)	0.1	0.1	0.1	0.1	0.1	0.6	0.3	0.2	(¹)	0.1	0.1	(¹)	0.1	0.1	(¹)
Louisiana	0.3	0.2	0.2	0.1	0.2	0.2	0.1	0.2	0.2	0.6	0.1	2.7	0.8	(¹)	0.1	0.1	(¹)	0.1	(¹)	(¹)	(¹)
Oklahoma	0.3	0.8	0.4	0.5	0.1	0.1	0.1	0.3	0.1	0.5	0.4	0.5	0.6	0.4	0.1	0.5	0.2	0.1	0.1	0.4	0.1
Texas	2.6	0.9	0.7	0.4	0.4	0.5	0.7	0.8	0.4	0.7	0.5	1.4	1.7	1.8	0.4	3.5	1.1	0.2	0.4	0.5	(¹)
MOUNTAIN:																					
Montana	0.7	1.0	1.8	1.3	0.7	2.7	1.1	1.6	1.3	1.1	1.2	1.0	0.6	0.5	0.1	0.5	0.6	0.2	2.2	0.5	0.1
Idaho	0.3	0.5	0.5	0.9	0.1	0.7	0.8	1.2	0.3	0.2	0.5	1.1	0.8	0.2	(¹)	0.5	0.1	0.1	0.3	0.1	0.1
Wyoming	0.2	0.3	0.6	0.4	0.1	0.2	0.3	0.5	0.1	0.2	0.1	0.3	0.2	0.1	(¹)	0.1	0.2	0.1	0.7	0.1	(¹)
Colorado	0.9	1.2	1.3	2.2	0.6	0.4	1.6	1.5	0.6	0.7	0.7	1.3	0.9	0.7	0.2	0.5	1.0	0.8	1.2	0.1	0.1
New Mexico	0.2	0.1	0.2	0.1	(¹)	(¹)	(¹)	0.1	0.1	0.1	(¹)	0.2	0.3	0.2	(¹)	(¹)	0.1	0.1	0.5	(¹)	(¹)
Arizona	0.6	0.4	0.2	0.3	0.1	0.1	(¹)	0.1	0.1	0.1	(¹)	0.1	0.2	0.1	(¹)	(¹)	0.1	0.2	0.5	(¹)	(¹)
Utah	0.4	1.8	0.9	1.9	0.1	0.6	1.0	3.7	1.5	0.1	0.2	0.2	0.3	0.1	(¹)	(¹)	0.1	0.1	0.7	(¹)	(¹)
Nevada	0.1	0.2	0.1	0.1	0.1	0.1	0.1	0.3	(¹)	(¹)	(¹)	1.3	0.3	0.2	(¹)	(¹)	0.2	(¹)	0.5	(¹)	(¹)
PACIFIC:												0.3	0.4	0.1							
Washington	1.9	2.6	3.1	3.0	0.9	8.3	5.6	4.4	2.4	2.8	2.5	3.1	1.6	0.3	0.5	1.1	0.3	2.1	0.8	0.4	(¹)
Oregon	0.8	1.0	1.4	0.9	0.4	1.9	1.7	1.9	0.7	1.2	1.1	3.5	1.3	0.3	0.5	0.3	0.2	0.7	0.5	0.1	(¹)
California	5.4	7.2	6.5	5.1	4.4	3.1	5.1	9.9	3.5	3.5	3.5	13.6	13.3	4.0	0.6	0.9	2.3	1.3	4.3	1.9	0.2

¹ Less than one-tenth of 1 per cent.

COUNTRY OF BIRTH.

FOREIGN COUNTRIES, BY DIVISION OR STATE OF RESIDENCE: 1920.

DIVISION AND STATE OF RESIDENCE.	EASTERN EUROPE—continued.				SOUTHERN EUROPE.						ASIA.								AMERICA.						
	Finland	Rumania	Bulgaria	Turkey in Europe	Greece	Albania	Italy	Spain	Portugal	Other Europe[2]	Armenia	Palestine	Syria	Turkey in Asia	China	Japan	India	Other Asia	Canada French	Canada Other	Newfoundland	West Indies[3]	Mexico	Central and South America	All other
United States	100.0	100.0	100.0	100.0	100.0	100.0	100.0	100.0	100.0	100.0	100.0	100.0	100.0	100.0	100.0	100.0	100.0	100.0	100.0	100.0	100.0	100.0	100.0	100.0	100.0
GEOGRAPHIC DIVISIONS:																									
New England	13.0	3.0	2.0	11.9	18.3	50.3	14.8	5.8	57.6	3.5	32.7	8.5	21.5	20.6	6.0	0.4	6.8	10.5	78.1	28.9	61.9	6.8	[1]	7.7	47.0
Middle Atlantic	11.6	54.4	12.8	48.0	25.3	20.6	57.5	34.2	4.4	23.9	29.5	46.5	29.9	39.3	15.9	3.5	19.5	22.0	5.5	14.8	20.9	56.5	1.1	47.3	11.8
East North Central	31.1	28.5	55.4	19.6	25.6	18.2	12.6	6.1	0.5	37.5	16.8	20.7	18.7	19.0	8.0	1.0	9.8	30.5	9.5	27.5	6.3	3.3	1.5	8.8	8.2
West North Central	21.1	6.8	10.5	2.3	6.4	4.7	2.1	1.6	0.1	7.9	2.0	4.4	6.6	2.9	2.9	1.2	3.9	4.0	3.4	8.6	1.4	0.8	4.7	3.3	3.1
South Atlantic	0.9	2.1	1.5	3.8	6.5	0.3	2.5	13.2	1.0	6.0	1.1	4.5	7.8	4.1	3.0	0.4	3.3	1.7	0.8	1.5	1.7	26.9	0.1	4.4	1.6
East South Central	0.1	0.4	0.5	0.9	1.1	0.4	0.5	0.4	[1]	1.5	0.2	2.4	2.9	0.8	0.8	[1]	0.9	0.6	0.1	0.4	0.2	0.9	0.1	1.1	0.5
West South Central	0.3	0.6	2.3	1.9	2.0	0.2	1.7	5.1	0.3	5.7	0.4	4.9	6.6	1.9	2.4	0.5	2.7	2.0	0.2	1.0	0.8	2.3	53.8	6.0	1.6
Mountain	5.2	1.0	7.8	1.4	5.4	2.5	1.8	9.2	0.5	1.8	1.0	2.3	2.6	1.7	7.2	10.4	3.4	4.4	1.1	3.7	1.5	0.4	20.2	2.1	2.6
Pacific	16.7	3.1	7.2	10.1	9.4	2.8	6.4	24.4	35.6	12.2	16.4	5.9	3.4	9.5	53.8	82.0	49.7	24.2	1.8	13.6	5.3	2.1	18.5	18.8	24.2
NEW ENGLAND:																									
Maine	0.9	0.1	[1]	1.2	0.7	7.2	0.2	0.1	0.2	0.2	0.4	0.3	1.2	0.4	0.2	[1]	0.6	0.1	11.6	4.8	1.6	0.2	[1]	0.1	0.2
New Hampshire	1.0	[1]	0.1	....	3.0	2.1	0.1	[1]	0.2	[1]	0.8	0.2	1.0	0.5	0.1	[1]	0.1	[1]	12.4	1.7	1.4	0.1	[1]	0.1	0.1
Vermont	0.3	[1]	[1]	....	0.1	0.1	0.3	1.3	[1]	0.1	0.2	[1]	0.4	[1]	[1]	[1]	0.1	[1]	4.6	1.3	0.5	[1]	[1]	0.2	[1]
Massachusetts	9.7	1.4	1.1	8.5	11.6	34.7	7.3	1.7	41.7	1.7	23.6	5.6	13.7	15.2	4.1	0.2	4.1	2.0	35.3	18.9	54.1	5.3	[1]	4.9	39.8
Rhode Island	0.2	0.4	0.4	0.9	0.7	2.5	2.0	0.2	12.9	0.2	5.1	0.4	2.5	2.4	0.4	[1]	0.7	0.7	9.4	0.9	1.8	0.3	[1]	1.0	5.6
Connecticut	0.8	1.2	0.3	1.3	2.2	3.6	5.0	2.5	2.6	1.4	2.7	1.8	2.7	2.0	1.0	0.1	1.1	7.5	4.8	1.2	2.5	1.0	[1]	1.3	1.3
MIDDLE ATLANTIC:																									
New York	8.3	39.0	5.9	38.8	14.8	7.4	33.9	25.7	2.1	14.3	15.3	33.1	15.7	29.0	10.5	2.9	12.7	14.2	5.1	11.9	13.7	48.5	0.6	36.8	7.0
New Jersey	1.4	4.4	0.6	3.7	2.6	1.0	9.8	4.0	1.0	2.9	6.2	5.0	4.0	4.0	2.2	0.3	3.2	3.6	0.3	1.2	3.6	4.0	0.1	4.8	1.9
Pennsylvania	1.9	10.9	6.3	5.5	7.9	12.3	13.8	4.4	1.3	6.8	8.0	8.4	10.2	6.3	3.2	0.2	3.5	4.2	0.2	1.8	3.7	4.0	0.4	5.6	2.3
EAST NORTH CENTRAL:																									
Ohio	4.3	12.7	24.2	10.8	7.7	7.7	3.8	2.6	0.2	5.9	2.5	5.8	7.1	5.8	1.5	0.1	2.2	3.5	0.4	2.9	1.1	1.1	0.2	2.1	1.3
Indiana	0.2	2.7	4.1	1.3	2.4	1.3	0.4	0.9	[1]	1.3	0.4	0.8	1.4	1.4	0.5	0.1	0.4	2.4	0.1	0.6	0.3	0.2	0.1	0.4	0.4
Illinois	2.1	6.1	9.0	3.4	9.4	2.7	5.9	1.5	0.2	8.9	4.7	7.2	2.2	4.6	4.4	0.5	3.2	16.8	1.3	4.3	2.3	1.2	0.8	3.6	2.8
Michigan	20.1	6.2	16.1	3.4	4.0	4.7	1.9	0.9	0.1	13.8	6.8	5.5	7.0	6.0	1.2	0.2	3.1	6.7	6.1	18.0	1.8	0.7	0.3	2.0	1.6
Wisconsin	4.5	0.9	2.0	0.7	2.2	1.8	0.7	0.1	[1]	7.6	2.5	1.3	1.0	1.3	0.4	0.1	0.9	1.1	1.6	1.8	0.6	0.1	[1]	0.7	2.0
WEST NORTH CENTRAL:																									
Minnesota	19.4	2.3	4.4	0.6	1.4	0.7	0.5	0.1	[1]	2.5	0.5	0.8	1.6	0.9	0.8	0.1	1.0	0.9	2.2	3.3	0.4	0.1	0.1	0.5	0.8
Iowa	0.1	0.3	2.6	0.3	1.6	0.1	0.3	0.1	[1]	1.3	0.3	0.7	1.0	0.5	0.4	[1]	0.7	0.6	0.1	1.0	0.3	0.1	0.5	0.5	0.5
Missouri	0.1	1.6	1.4	0.8	1.7	3.6	0.9	0.9	[1]	1.3	0.5	2.0	1.6	0.8	0.7	0.1	0.8	0.6	0.1	0.8	0.3	0.3	0.7	0.9	0.7
North Dakota	0.7	1.8	0.3	0.3	0.2	....	[1]	[1]	[1]	0.4	0.2	0.2	0.6	0.2	0.2	0.1	0.1	0.3	0.5	1.7	0.2	[1]	[1]	0.2	0.2
South Dakota	0.7	0.1	0.9	0.1	0.2	[1]	[1]	[1]	[1]	0.5	0.1	0.2	0.3	0.5	0.1	0.2	0.3	0.5	0.2	0.5	[1]	[1]	0.1	0.1	0.2
Nebraska	[1]	0.4	0.6	0.1	0.0	0.2	0.2	0.1	[1]	0.9	0.4	0.4	0.3	0.8	0.5	0.6	0.1	0.7	0.2	0.1	0.5	0.3	0.4		
Kansas	[1]	0.3	0.3	0.1	0.4	[1]	0.2	0.4	[1]	1.0	0.1	0.4	0.5	0.2	0.1	0.1	0.5	0.5	0.2	0.6	0.1	0.1	2.8	0.7	0.3
SOUTH ATLANTIC:																									
Delaware	[1]	0.1	....	0.1	0.2	....	0.3	0.3	[1]	0.1	[1]	0.3	[1]	0.1	0.1	[1]	[1]	[1]	[1]	0.1	0.1	0.1	[1]	0.1	0.1
Maryland	0.1	0.5	0.2	0.4	0.5	[1]	0.6	0.5	0.1	1.3	0.1	0.5	0.1	0.4	0.6	[1]	0.5	0.3	[1]	0.2	0.5	0.9	[1]	0.9	0.3
District of Columbia	0.1	0.1	[1]	1.4	0.7	0.1	0.2	0.2	[1]	0.3	0.2	0.6	0.4	0.6	0.8	0.1	0.5	0.2	[1]	0.2	0.1	0.5	[1]	0.8	0.2
Virginia	0.2	0.2	0.2	0.6	1.0	0.1	0.2	0.5	0.4	1.4	0.4	0.7	1.1	0.7	0.5	0.1	0.7	0.8	[1]	0.2	0.2	0.5	[1]	0.7	0.3
West Virginia	0.2	0.6	0.9	0.4	1.8	[1]	0.9	3.1	[1]	1.2	0.1	0.6	2.4	1.4	0.1	[1]	[1]	0.2	[1]	0.1	[1]	0.1	[1]	0.2	0.1
North Carolina	[1]	[1]	[1]	0.3	0.3	....	[1]	[1]	[1]	0.1	[1]	0.7	1.1	0.2	0.1	[1]	0.2	0.2	[1]	0.1	0.1	0.1	[1]	0.2	0.1
South Carolina	[1]	[1]	[1]	0.2	0.3	....	[1]	[1]	[1]	0.2	[1]	0.1	0.8	[1]	0.1	[1]	0.3	0.2	[1]	[1]	[1]	0.1	[1]	0.1	[1]
Georgia	[1]	0.1	[1]	0.4	0.8	[1]	[1]	0.3	0.1	1.0	0.1	0.5	0.9	0.4	0.3	[1]	0.3	0.2	[1]	0.1	0.2	0.3	[1]	0.3	0.1
Florida	0.2	0.5	0.2	0.1	0.8	0.1	0.3	8.3	0.3	0.4	0.1	0.5	1.0	0.3	0.2	0.1	0.8	0.2	0.1	0.5	0.6	24.3	[1]	1.1	0.4
EAST SOUTH CENTRAL:																									
Kentucky	[1]	0.2	0.3	0.4	0.2	[1]	0.1	0.1	[1]	0.5	0.1	0.5	0.6	0.2	0.1	[1]	0.2	0.2	[1]	0.1	0.1	0.1	[1]	0.2	0.2
Tennessee	[1]	0.1	[1]	0.1	0.3	0.4	0.1	[1]	[1]	0.3	[1]	0.9	0.2	0.2	0.1	[1]	0.4	0.1	[1]	0.1	0.1	0.1	[1]	0.3	0.1
Alabama	[1]	0.1	0.2	0.4	0.5	....	0.2	0.1	[1]	0.6	0.1	0.5	0.9	0.4	0.1	[1]	0.2	0.2	[1]	0.1	[1]	0.5	[1]	0.5	0.1
Mississippi	[1]	[1]	....	[1]	0.1	....	0.1	0.1	[1]	0.2	[1]	0.5	1.1	0.1	0.6	....	0.2	0.1	[1]	[1]	0.1	0.1	[1]	0.2	0.1
WEST SOUTH CENTRAL:																									
Arkansas	[1]	0.1	0.2	[1]	0.2	[1]	0.1	[1]	0.1	0.2	[1]	0.5	0.4	0.1	0.2	[1]	0.1	0.1	[1]	0.1	0.2	0.1	0.1	0.1	0.1
Louisiana	0.1	0.1	0.5	0.3	0.3	[1]	1.0	2.6	0.2	1.3	0.1	0.5	1.8	0.6	0.6	0.1	1.2	0.2	0.1	0.1	0.1	1.6	0.5	4.9	0.3
Oklahoma	0.1	0.1	1.0	0.2	0.4	[1]	0.1	0.3	[1]	0.8	[1]	0.6	1.3	0.2	0.4	0.1	0.2	0.8	[1]	0.3	0.1	0.1	1.4	0.3	0.2
Texas	0.1	0.4	0.7	1.4	1.1	0.1	0.5	2.2	0.1	3.4	0.3	3.3	3.0	1.0	1.3	0.4	1.2	0.9	0.1	0.5	0.4	0.6	51.8	1.3	1.0
MOUNTAIN:																									
Montana	2.4	0.3	2.5	0.5	0.8	0.7	0.2	0.1	[1]	0.2	0.4	0.2	0.4	0.6	1.5	1.1	0.3	0.7	0.7	1.5	0.5	0.1	[1]	0.3	0.4
Idaho	0.7	0.1	0.4	0.1	0.4	0.7	0.1	2.9	0.1	0.1	[1]	[1]	0.1	0.1	1.1	1.4	0.4	0.4	0.2	0.5	0.4	[1]	0.2	0.1	0.4
Wyoming	0.6	0.1	0.7	[1]	0.7	0.1	0.1	0.3	[1]	0.1	0.2	0.1	0.2	0.2	0.4	1.3	0.2	1.3	[1]	0.2	[1]	[1]	0.4	0.1	0.1
Colorado	0.6	0.4	3.3	0.2	1.0	0.2	0.8	0.6	[1]	0.7	0.1	1.3	0.6	0.3	0.5	2.2	0.9	0.6	0.1	0.9	0.3	0.1	2.3	0.8	0.4
New Mexico	[1]	[1]	0.2	[1]	0.2	....	0.1	0.4	[1]	0.1	[1]	0.2	0.3	0.2	0.1	0.1	0.2	0.1	[1]	0.1	[1]	[1]	4.2	0.1	0.1
Arizona	0.3	[1]	0.3	0.2	0.2	0.1	0.1	2.0	[1]	0.1	[1]	0.2	0.6	0.1	1.7	0.5	0.6	0.6	[1]	0.2	0.1	0.1	12.7	0.3	0.3
Utah	0.5	0.1	0.3	0.2	1.7	0.7	0.2	0.5	[1]	0.3	0.2	0.2	0.3	0.2	0.6	2.9	0.8	0.5	[1]	0.2	[1]	[1]	0.2	0.1	0.7
Nevada	0.1	[1]	0.2	[1]	0.4	....	0.2	2.4	0.2	0.1	[1]	0.1	0.2	1.2	0.8	0.2	0.2	[1]	0.1	0.1	[1]	0.2	0.2	0.3	
PACIFIC:																									
Washington	7.9	0.4	2.5	4.3	2.4	1.7	0.7	0.8	0.2	1.3	0.7	0.6	0.6	2.6	4.0	15.9	4.2	3.8	0.8	5.0	2.4	0.8	0.1	1.4	1.8
Oregon	4.0	0.3	2.0	0.8	1.1	0.2	0.3	1.1	0.2	0.6	0.2	0.2	0.4	0.5	4.9	3.9	2.7	0.7	0.2	1.6	0.4	0.1	0.1	0.5	0.8
California	4.7	2.3	2.6	5.0	5.9	0.9	5.5	22.5	35.2	10.3	15.5	5.2	2.4	6.4	44.9	62.8	42.8	19.7	0.7	7.0	2.5	1.7	18.2	16.9	21.6

[1] Less than one-tenth of 1 per cent.   [2] Comprises Danzig, Fiume, Saar Basin, and "Europe, not specified."   [3] Except possessions of the United States.

704

POPULATION.

TABLE 9.—CONTINENT OF BIRTH OF FOREIGN-BORN POPULATION, BY DIVISIONS AND STATES: 1920, 1910, AND 1900.

DIVISION OR STATE AND CENSUS YEAR.	Total foreign born.	PERSONS BORN IN—							PER CENT OF TOTAL FOREIGN BORN.						
		Europe.				Asia.	America.	All other.	Europe.				Asia.	America.	All other.
		Total.[1]	North-western.	Central and Eastern.	Southern.				Total.[1]	North-western.	Central and Eastern.	Southern.			
UNITED STATES.															
1920	13,920,692	11,882,053	3,830,094	6,134,845	1,911,213	237,950	1,727,017	73,672	85.4	27.5	44.1	13.7	1.7	12.4	0.5
1910	13,515,886	11,781,841	4,239,067	6,024,041	1,525,875	191,484	1,489,231	43,330	87.2	31.4	44.6	11.3	1.4	11.0	0.3
1900	10,341,276	8,871,780	4,202,683	4,136,646	530,200	120,248	1,317,380	31,868	85.8	40.6	40.0	5.1	1.2	12.7	0.3
GEOGRAPHIC DIVISIONS.															
NEW ENGLAND:															
1920	1,885,945	1,329,978	574,009	439,081	316,679	29,474	491,886	34,607	70.5	30.4	23.3	16.8	1.6	26.1	1.8
1910	1,825,110	1,254,530	649,526	373,645	231,270	22,626	532,570	15,384	68.7	35.6	20.5	12.7	1.2	29.2	0.8
1900	1,445,237	915,823	656,647	179,572	80,553	7,534	513,962	6,918	63.4	45.4	12.4	5.6	0.5	35.6	0.5
MIDDLE ATLANTIC:															
1920	4,960,418	4,706,098	1,127,114	2,586,652	990,920	44,016	202,000	8,304	94.9	22.7	52.1	20.0	0.9	4.1	0.2
1910	4,851,173	4,642,436	1,298,479	2,537,934	805,307	25,987	176,260	6,490	95.7	26.8	52.3	16.6	0.5	3.6	0.1
1900	3,317,559	3,146,187	1,339,540	1,510,615	295,417	14,441	151,376	5,555	94.8	40.4	45.5	8.9	0.4	4.6	0.2
EAST NORTH CENTRAL:															
1920	3,232,141	2,934,520	811,238	1,868,354	252,717	24,988	266,595	6,038	90.8	25.1	57.8	7.8	0.8	8.2	0.2
1910	3,073,766	2,780,710	872,560	1,741,880	165,866	11,723	276,534	4,790	90.5	28.4	56.7	5.4	0.4	9.0	0.2
1900	2,625,226	2,316,021	924,565	1,343,656	47,353	4,567	299,958	4,680	88.2	35.2	51.2	1.8	0.2	11.4	0.2
WEST NORTH CENTRAL:															
1920	1,375,653	1,261,131	605,640	608,205	46,821	7,200	105,052	2,270	91.7	44.0	44.2	3.4	0.5	7.6	0.2
1910	1,616,695	1,492,707	711,084	728,400	52,996	6,223	115,005	2,760	92.3	44.0	45.1	3.3	0.4	7.1	0.2
1900	1,533,248	1,402,025	730,127	660,392	11,283	2,753	125,825	2,645	91.4	47.6	43.1	0.7	0.2	8.2	0.2
SOUTH ATLANTIC:															
1920	330,537	286,221	72,150	154,719	58,997	6,934	36,193	1,189	86.6	21.8	46.8	17.8	2.1	10.9	0.4
1910	299,994	266,885	71,790	146,623	48,103	4,407	27,756	946	89.0	23.0	48.9	16.0	1.5	9.3	0.3
1900	216,030	192,531	74,361	105,275	12,581	2,485	20,070	944	89.1	34.4	48.7	5.8	1.2	9.3	0.4
EAST SOUTH CENTRAL:															
1920	72,989	65,693	22,017	32,722	10,865	2,205	4,754	337	90.0	30.2	44.8	14.9	3.0	6.5	0.5
1910	87,825	81,227	28,943	42,368	9,797	1,827	4,380	391	92.5	33.0	48.2	11.2	2.1	5.0	0.4
1900	90,568	85,264	36,662	44,345	4,008	831	4,005	468	94.1	40.5	49.0	4.4	0.9	4.4	0.5
WEST SOUTH CENTRAL:															
1920	464,828	184,295	51,700	98,318	33,941	5,648	273,695	1,195	39.8	11.1	21.2	7.3	1.2	58.9	0.3
1910	352,192	207,939	57,300	114,907	35,253	4,229	139,212	812	59.0	16.3	32.6	10.0	1.2	39.5	0.2
1900	267,087	183,963	56,251	103,624	23,372	2,361	79,915	848	68.9	21.1	38.8	8.9	0.9	29.9	0.3
MOUNTAIN:															
1920	467,620	318,123	167,665	107,331	43,021	18,997	133,585	1,915	68.0	35.9	23.0	9.2	3.0	28.6	0.4
1910	453,322	351,907	186,341	114,048	51,379	16,542	83,133	1,740	77.6	41.1	25.2	11.3	3.6	18.3	0.4
1900	301,969	233,434	160,479	57,580	15,333	12,972	54,078	1,485	77.3	53.1	19.1	5.1	4.3	17.9	0.5
PACIFIC:															
1920	1,130,561	795,904	398,581	239,403	157,252	103,493	213,257	17,817	70.4	35.3	21.2	13.9	9.2	18.9	1.6
1910	955,809	713,500	363,094	224,236	125,904	97,920	134,381	10,008	74.6	38.0	23.5	13.2	10.2	14.1	1.0
1900	544,352	395,532	224,051	131,587	39,800	72,304	68,191	8,325	72.7	41.2	24.2	7.3	13.3	12.5	1.5
NEW ENGLAND.															
Maine:															
1920	107,814	31,923	17,394	9,905	4,614	970	74,802	119	29.6	16.1	9.2	4.3	0.9	69.4	0.1
1910	110,562	33,124	20,249	8,626	4,240	839	76,447	152	30.0	18.3	7.8	3.8	0.8	69.1	0.1
1900	93,330	25,604	20,878	3,293	1,423	413	67,178	135	27.4	22.4	3.5	1.5	0.4	72.0	0.1
New Hampshire:															
1920	91,397	37,759	17,687	12,436	7,634	944	52,587	107	41.3	19.4	13.6	8.4	1.0	57.5	0.1
1910	96,667	37,610	20,672	12,105	4,832	951	58,025	81	38.9	21.4	12.5	5.0	1.0	60.0	0.1
1900	88,107	28,791	23,489	4,275	1,025	184	59,003	129	32.7	26.7	4.9	1.2	0.2	67.0	0.1
Vermont:															
1920	44,558	19,200	9,301	4,965	4,930	306	25,017	35	43.1	20.9	11.1	11.1	0.7	56.1	0.1
1910	49,921	23,510	13,150	5,222	5,137	203	26,152	56	47.1	26.3	10.5	10.3	0.4	52.4	0.1
1900	44,747	18,860	14,496	2,095	2,263	161	25,680	46	42.1	32.4	4.7	5.1	0.4	57.4	0.1
Massachusetts:															
1920	1,088,548	763,186	360,324	233,352	169,410	19,906	276,124	29,332	70.1	33.1	21.4	15.6	1.8	25.4	2.7
1910	1,059,245	728,610	404,485	200,630	123,455	14,811	302,013	13,811	68.8	38.2	18.9	11.7	1.4	28.5	1.3
1900	846,324	540,977	402,962	93,680	44,320	5,050	294,808	5,489	63.9	47.6	11.1	5.2	0.6	34.8	0.6
Rhode Island:															
1920	175,189	130,242	64,735	22,806	42,690	3,674	37,181	4,092	74.3	37.0	13.0	24.4	2.1	21.2	2.3
1910	179,141	132,288	75,439	22,068	34,779	3,416	42,535	902	73.8	42.1	12.3	19.4	1.9	23.7	0.5
1900	134,519	93,456	72,023	9,805	11,624	812	39,530	721	69.5	53.5	7.3	8.6	0.6	20.4	0.5
Connecticut:															
1920	378,439	347,668	104,568	155,617	87,401	3,674	26,175	922	91.9	27.6	41.1	23.1	1.0	6.9	0.2
1910	329,574	299,388	115,551	124,994	58,827	2,406	27,398	382	90.8	35.1	37.9	17.8	0.7	8.3	0.1
1900	238,210	209,135	122,799	66,424	19,898	914	27,763	398	87.8	51.6	27.9	8.4	0.4	11.7	0.2
MIDDLE ATLANTIC.															
New York:															
1920	2,825,375	2,629,379	626,468	1,416,158	585,911	26,307	164,546	5,143	93.1	22.2	50.1	20.7	0.9	5.8	0.2
1910	2,748,011	2,582,946	708,954	1,386,954	486,724	15,904	145,421	3,740	94.0	25.8	50.5	17.7	0.6	5.3	0.1
1900	1,900,425	1,761,413	711,421	863,909	185,797	9,419	126,500	3,093	92.7	37.4	45.5	9.8	0.5	6.7	0.2
New Jersey:															
1920	742,486	718,984	187,310	366,955	164,549	6,500	15,567	1,435	96.8	25.2	49.4	22.2	0.9	2.1	0.2
1910	660,788	644,090	201,178	325,195	117,661	3,691	12,076	931	97.5	30.4	49.2	17.8	0.6	1.8	0.1
1900	431,884	420,922	192,813	185,885	42,187	1,753	8,422	787	97.5	44.6	43.0	9.8	0.4	2.0	0.2
Pennsylvania:															
1920	1,392,557	1,357,735	313,336	803,539	240,460	11,209	21,887	1,726	97.5	22.5	57.7	17.3	0.8	1.6	0.1
1910	1,442,374	1,415,400	388,347	825,785	200,922	6,392	18,763	1,819	98.1	26.9	57.3	13.9	0.4	1.3	0.1
1900	985,250	963,852	435,306	460,821	67,433	3,269	16,454	1,675	97.8	44.2	46.8	6.8	0.3	1.7	0.2

[1]Includes "Europe, not specified" at each census, and Danzig, Fiume, and Saar Basin in 1920.

503

COUNTRY OF BIRTH.

TABLE 9.—CONTINENT OF BIRTH OF FOREIGN-BORN POPULATION, BY DIVISIONS AND STATES: 1920, 1910, AND 1900—Continued.

DIVISION OR STATE AND CENSUS YEAR.	Total foreign born.	PERSONS BORN IN—							PER CENT OF TOTAL FOREIGN BORN.						
		Europe.				Asia.	America.	All other.	Europe.				Asia.	America.	All other.
		Total.[1]	North-western.	Central and Eastern.	Southern.				Total.[1]	North-western.	Central and Eastern.	Southern.			
EAST NORTH CENTRAL.															
Ohio:															
1920	680,452	645,885	125,887	443,587	76,060	6,463	27,116	988	94.9	18.5	65.2	11.2	0.9	4.0	0.1
1910	598,374	570,432	131,635	394,223	44,480	2,646	24,303	993	95.3	22.0	65.9	7.4	0.4	4.1	0.2
1900	458,734	433,836	146,624	275,432	11,695	900	23,142	856	94.6	32.0	60.0	2.5	0.2	5.0	0.2
Indiana:															
1920	151,828	143,439	37,297	94,618	11,449	1,447	6,111	331	94.8	24.6	62.5	7.6	1.0	4.0	0.2
1910	150,663	152,213	42,071	101,753	8,327	1,092	6,029	329	95.3	26.3	63.7	5.2	0.7	3.8	0.2
1900	142,121	135,204	48,636	85,069	1,488	427	6,043	387	95.2	34.2	59.9	1.0	0.3	4.3	0.3
Illinois:															
1920	1,210,584	1,156,666	350,775	693,480	111,887	6,965	44,871	2,082	95.5	29.0	57.3	9.2	0.6	3.7	0.2
1910	1,205,314	1,150,715	385,597	682,123	82,849	5,006	47,618	1,975	95.5	32.0	56.6	6.9	0.4	4.0	0.2
1900	966,747	911,177	391,701	493,798	25,520	2,274	51,423	1,873	94.3	40.5	51.1	2.6	0.2	5.3	0.2
Michigan:															
1920	729,292	551,403	168,225	344,257	38,108	8,171	168,547	1,171	75.6	23.1	47.2	5.2	1.1	23.1	0.2
1910	597,560	421,412	158,692	244,566	18,130	1,033	173,339	866	70.5	26.6	40.9	3.0	0.3	29.0	0.1
1900	541,653	355,514	163,507	185,504	6,383	561	184,748	830	65.6	30.2	34.3	1.2	0.1	34.1	0.2
Wisconsin:															
1920	460,485	437,127	129,054	292,412	15,213	1,942	19,950	1,466	94.9	28.0	63.5	3.3	0.4	4.3	0.3
1910	512,865	485,938	154,565	319,215	12,080	1,046	25,245	636	94.7	30.1	62.2	2.4	0.2	4.9	0.1
1900	515,971	480,230	174,097	303,793	2,267	405	34,602	734	93.1	33.7	58.9	0.4	0.1	6.7	0.1
WEST NORTH CENTRAL.															
Minnesota:															
1920	486,795	450,187	258,988	181,141	9,909	1,638	34,393	577	92.5	53.2	37.2	2.0	0.3	7.1	0.1
1910	543,595	500,186	287,272	201,466	11,398	1,084	41,422	903	92.0	52.8	37.1	2.1	0.2	7.6	0.2
1900	505,318	456,324	286,029	167,811	2,455	601	47,727	666	90.3	56.6	33.2	0.5	0.1	9.4	0.1
Iowa:															
1920	225,994	212,812	107,630	97,201	7,903	958	11,838	386	94.2	47.6	43.0	3.5	0.4	5.2	0.2
1910	273,765	260,182	127,029	123,852	9,250	774	12,408	401	95.0	46.4	45.2	3.4	0.3	4.5	0.1
1900	305,920	289,281	148,306	139,706	1,239	282	15,829	528	94.6	48.5	45.7	0.4	0.1	5.2	0.2
Missouri:															
1920	186,835	174,206	47,264	108,586	18,290	1,663	10,480	486	93.2	25.3	58.1	9.8	0.9	5.6	0.3
1910	220,779	217,560	60,912	140,475	16,084	1,094	9,950	575	94.7	26.5	61.1	7.0	0.4	4.3	0.3
1900	216,379	205,795	72,516	128,715	4,488	825	9,148	611	95.1	33.5	59.5	2.1	0.4	4.2	0.3
North Dakota:															
1920	131,883	115,301	61,027	53,645	604	577	15,840	145	87.4	46.3	40.7	0.5	0.4	12.0	0.1
1910	156,654	134,409	72,749	59,280	2,361	490	21,574	181	85.8	46.4	37.8	1.5	0.3	13.8	0.1
1900	113,091	84,544	51,239	32,590	707	240	28,182	125	74.8	45.3	28.8	0.6	0.2	24.9	0.1
South Dakota:															
1920	82,534	77,356	42,492	34,039	798	456	4,585	137	93.7	51.5	41.2	1.0	0.6	5.6	0.2
1910	100,790	94,154	49,875	42,874	1,396	426	6,070	140	93.4	49.5	42.5	1.4	0.4	6.0	0.1
1900	88,508	81,030	44,992	35,640	368	200	7,088	130	91.6	50.8	40.3	0.4	0.3	8.0	0.1
Nebraska:															
1920	150,665	140,387	51,362	83,868	5,104	1,432	8,548	298	93.2	34.1	55.7	3.4	1.0	5.7	0.2
1910	176,662	167,337	63,077	96,941	7,286	1,307	7,757	261	94.7	35.7	54.9	4.1	0.7	4.4	0.1
1900	177,347	167,506	69,219	97,291	963	429	9,137	275	94.5	39.0	54.9	0.5	0.2	5.2	0.2
Kansas:															
1920	110,967	90,882	36,877	49,725	4,223	476	19,368	241	81.9	33.2	44.8	3.8	0.4	17.5	0.2
1910	135,450	118,879	50,120	63,512	5,221	448	15,824	299	87.8	37.0	46.9	3.9	0.3	11.7	0.2
1900	126,685	117,545	57,826	58,639	1,063	116	8,714	310	92.8	45.6	46.3	0.8	0.1	6.9	0.2
SOUTH ATLANTIC.															
Delaware:															
1920	19,901	19,203	5,645	8,968	4,583	67	593	38	96.5	28.4	45.1	23.0	0.3	3.0	0.2
1910	17,492	16,857	6,619	7,299	2,933	45	552	38	96.4	37.8	41.7	16.8	0.3	3.2	0.2
1900	13,810	13,360	7,687	4,482	1,140	64	347	39	96.7	55.7	32.5	8.3	0.5	2.5	0.3
Maryland:															
1920	103,179	99,424	17,230	71,318	10,797	514	2,994	247	96.4	16.7	69.1	10.5	0.5	2.9	0.2
1910	104,944	102,272	19,752	74,879	7,553	428	2,017	227	97.5	18.8	71.4	7.2	0.4	1.9	0.2
1900	93,934	91,480	23,861	64,939	2,598	536	1,674	244	97.4	25.4	69.1	2.8	0.6	1.8	0.3
District of Columbia:															
1920	29,365	26,033	10,419	10,493	5,104	831	2,368	133	88.7	35.5	35.7	17.4	2.8	8.1	0.5
1910	24,902	22,826	10,360	9,209	3,150	474	1,507	95	91.7	41.6	37.3	12.7	1.9	6.1	0.4
1900	20,119	18,411	10,305	7,098	1,001	469	1,169	80	91.5	51.2	35.3	5.0	2.3	5.8	0.4
Virginia:															
1920	31,705	27,750	9,770	13,089	4,809	1,125	2,614	216	87.5	30.8	41.3	15.2	3.5	8.2	0.7
1910	27,057	24,587	9,222	11,948	3,324	877	1,656	137	90.9	34.1	44.2	12.3	2.5	6.1	0.5
1900	19,461	17,606	9,495	7,160	904	424	1,307	124	90.5	48.8	36.8	4.6	2.2	6.7	0.6
West Virginia:															
1920	62,105	59,234	9,282	30,986	18,895	1,536	1,227	108	95.4	14.9	49.9	30.4	2.5	2.0	0.2
1910	57,218	55,406	10,151	26,675	18,546	804	944	64	96.8	17.7	46.6	32.4	1.4	1.6	0.1
1900	22,451	21,444	8,607	9,780	3,034	198	763	46	95.5	38.3	43.6	13.5	0.9	3.4	0.2
North Carolina:															
1920	7,272	5,634	2,391	2,202	1,034	750	836	52	77.5	32.9	30.3	14.2	10.3	11.5	0.7
1910	6,092	4,955	2,119	2,095	723	471	611	55	81.3	34.8	34.4	11.9	7.7	10.0	0.9
1900	4,492	3,747	1,945	1,553	229	155	535	55	83.4	43.3	34.6	5.1	3.5	11.9	1.2
South Carolina:															
1920	6,582	5,633	1,630	3,045	948	508	412	29	85.6	24.8	46.3	14.4	7.7	6.3	0.4
1910	6,179	5,407	1,893	2,887	615	395	355	22	87.5	30.6	46.7	10.0	6.4	5.7	0.4
1900	5,528	5,054	2,157	2,623	263	151	276	47	91.4	39.0	47.4	4.8	2.7	5.0	0.9
Georgia:															
1920	16,564	14,377	4,563	7,410	2,344	746	1,334	107	86.8	27.5	44.7	14.2	4.5	8.1	0.6
1910	15,477	13,706	4,960	7,071	1,600	573	1,095	103	88.6	32.0	45.7	10.3	3.7	7.1	0.7
1900	12,403	11,022	5,228	5,267	486	290	983	108	88.9	42.2	42.5	3.9	2.3	7.9	0.9
Florida:															
1920	53,864	28,933	11,220	7,208	10,483	857	23,815	259	53.7	20.8	13.4	19.5	1.6	44.2	0.5
1910	40,633	20,869	6,714	4,470	9,653	540	19,019	205	51.4	16.5	11.0	23.8	1.3	46.8	0.5
1900	23,832	10,407	5,076	2,373	2,926	198	13,026	201	43.7	21.3	10.0	12.3	0.8	54.7	0.8

[1] Includes "Europe, not specified" at each census, and Danzig, Fiume, and Saar Basin in 1920.

POPULATION.

TABLE 9.—CONTINENT OF BIRTH OF FOREIGN-BORN POPULATION, BY DIVISIONS AND STATES: 1920, 1910, AND 1900—Continued.

DIVISION OR STATE AND CENSUS YEAR.	Total foreign born.	PERSONS BORN IN— Europe. Total.[1]	North-western.	Central and Eastern.	Southern.	Asia.	America.	All other.	PER CENT OF TOTAL FOREIGN BORN. Europe. Total.[1]	North-western.	Central and Eastern.	Southern.	Asia.	America.	All other.
EAST SOUTH CENTRAL.															
Kentucky:															
1920	30,906	29,167	8,885	17,842	2,410	439	1,172	128	94.4	28.7	57.7	7.8	1.4	3.8	0.4
1910	40,162	38,438	12,229	24,580	1,616	497	1,105	122	95.7	30.4	61.2	4.0	1.1	2.9	0.3
1900	50,249	48,546	17,722	30,017	725	219	1,318	166	96.6	35.3	59.7	1.4	0.4	2.6	0.3
Tennessee:															
1920	15,648	13,983	5,110	6,244	2,613	270	1,320	75	89.4	32.7	39.9	16.7	1.7	8.4	0.5
1910	18,607	16,976	6,980	7,539	2,436	232	1,310	89	91.2	37.5	40.5	13.1	1.2	7.0	0.5
1900	17,746	16,242	8,432	6,471	1,278	219	1,181	104	91.5	47.5	36.5	7.2	1.2	6.7	0.6
Alabama:															
1920	18,027	15,737	5,988	5,991	3,725	623	1,575	92	87.3	33.2	33.2	20.7	3.5	8.7	0.5
1910	19,286	17,534	7,078	7,003	3,407	444	1,204	104	90.9	36.7	36.3	17.7	2.3	6.2	0.5
1900	14,592	13,388	7,243	5,049	1,058	119	957	133	91.7	49.6	34.6	7.3	0.8	6.6	0.9
Mississippi:															
1920	8,408	6,806	2,034	2,645	2,117	873	687	42	80.9	24.2	31.5	25.2	10.4	8.2	0.5
1910	9,770	8,279	2,656	3,256	2,838	714	701	76	84.7	27.2	33.3	23.9	7.3	7.2	0.8
1900	7,981	7,093	3,265	2,808	947	274	549	65	88.9	40.9	35.2	11.9	3.4	6.9	0.8
WEST SOUTH CENTRAL.															
Arkansas:															
1920	14,137	12,450	4,174	6,648	1,618	326	1,261	100	88.1	29.5	47.0	11.4	2.3	8.9	0.7
1910	17,046	15,476	5,280	8,243	1,888	231	1,261	78	90.8	31.0	48.4	11.1	1.4	7.4	0.5
1900	14,289	12,901	4,893	7,398	589	92	1,212	84	90.3	34.2	51.8	4.1	0.6	8.5	0.6
Louisiana:															
1920	46,427	38,739	10,962	9,422	18,281	1,433	6,056	199	83.4	23.6	20.3	39.4	3.1	13.0	0.4
1910	52,766	47,985	13,430	13,175	21,262	1,390	3,184	207	90.9	25.5	25.0	40.3	2.6	6.0	0.4
1900	52,903	49,462	17,211	14,021	18,192	885	2,336	220	93.5	32.5	26.5	34.4	1.7	4.4	0.4
Oklahoma:[2]															
1920	40,432	29,723	9,344	17,448	2,882	1,024	9,515	170	73.5	23.1	43.2	7.1	2.5	23.5	0.4
1910	40,442	33,970	10,256	20,429	3,220	587	5,731	154	84.0	25.4	50.5	8.0	1.5	14.2	0.4
1900	20,538	18,322	6,407	11,262	638	181	1,970	65	89.2	31.2	54.8	3.1	0.9	9.6	0.3
Texas:															
1920	363,832	103,383	27,220	64,800	11,160	2,860	256,863	726	28.4	7.5	17.8	3.1	0.8	70.6	0.2
1910	241,938	110,508	28,334	73,060	8,883	2,021	129,036	373	45.7	11.7	30.2	3.7	0.8	53.3	0.2
1900	179,357	103,278	27,740	70,943	4,453	1,203	74,397	479	57.6	15.5	39.6	2.5	0.7	41.5	0.3
MOUNTAIN.															
Montana:															
1920	95,591	78,203	44,248	28,498	5,444	1,992	15,114	282	81.8	46.3	29.8	5.7	2.1	15.8	0.3
1910	94,713	77,529	41,178	27,756	8,577	2,913	14,039	232	81.9	43.5	29.3	9.1	3.1	14.8	0.2
1900	67,067	48,779	32,414	14,083	2,273	4,142	13,918	228	72.7	48.3	21.0	3.4	0.2	20.8	0.3
Idaho:															
1920	40,747	32,420	19,949	8,928	3,537	1,788	6,275	264	79.6	49.0	21.9	8.7	4.4	15.4	0.6
1910	42,578	34,564	20,590	8,931	5,006	2,208	5,582	224	81.2	48.4	21.0	11.8	5.2	13.1	0.5
1900	24,604	18,792	14,032	3,857	900	2,738	2,969	105	76.4	57.0	15.7	3.7	11.1	12.1	0.4
Wyoming:															
1920	26,567	21,724	9,772	8,591	3,357	1,472	3,295	76	81.8	36.8	32.3	12.6	5.5	12.4	0.3
1910	29,020	25,279	11,394	9,834	4,046	2,017	1,665	59	87.1	39.3	33.9	13.9	7.0	5.7	0.2
1900	17,415	15,208	9,252	4,928	1,028	831	1,317	59	87.3	53.1	28.3	5.9	4.8	7.6	0.3
Colorado:															
1920	119,138	97,366	39,382	43,218	14,723	2,453	19,017	302	81.7	33.1	36.3	12.4	2.1	16.0	0.3
1910	129,587	113,826	49,135	47,763	16,867	2,968	12,444	349	87.8	37.9	36.9	13.0	2.3	9.6	0.3
1900	91,155	79,712	46,775	26,004	6,924	782	10,351	310	87.4	51.3	28.5	7.6	0.9	11.4	0.3
New Mexico:															
1920	29,808	8,135	3,071	2,872	2,184	540	21,077	56	27.3	10.3	9.6	7.3	1.8	70.7	0.2
1910	23,146	9,488	3,608	3,632	2,238	587	12,983	88	41.0	15.6	15.7	0.7	2.5	56.1	0.4
1900	13,625	5,745	3,076	1,966	695	372	7,444	64	42.2	22.6	14.4	5.1	2.7	54.6	0.5
Arizona:															
1920	80,566	15,071	7,308	5,116	2,639	1,563	63,714	218	18.7	9.1	6.4	3.3	1.9	79.1	0.3
1910	48,765	15,214	7,971	4,746	2,494	1,518	31,898	135	31.2	16.3	9.7	5.1	3.1	65.4	0.3
1900	24,233	6,983	4,430	1,772	778	1,603	15,507	140	28.8	18.3	7.3	3.2	6.6	64.0	0.6
Utah:															
1920	59,200	53,048	38,900	7,580	6,549	2,946	2,683	523	89.6	65.7	12.8	11.1	5.0	4.5	0.9
1910	65,822	60,845	45,560	8,094	7,188	2,624	1,884	469	92.4	69.2	12.3	10.9	4.0	2.9	0.7
1900	53,777	50,879	46,207	3,583	1,081	994	1,404	500	94.6	85.9	6.7	2.0	1.8	2.6	0.9
Nevada:															
1920	16,003	12,156	5,035	2,528	4,588	1,243	2,410	194	76.0	31.5	15.8	28.7	7.8	15.1	1.2
1910	19,691	15,162	6,905	3,292	4,965	1,707	2,638	184	77.0	35.1	16.7	25.2	8.7	13.4	0.9
1900	10,093	7,336	4,293	1,387	1,654	1,510	1,168	79	72.7	42.5	13.7	16.4	15.0	11.6	0.8
PACIFIC.															
Washington:															
1920	265,292	203,434	124,105	63,561	15,693	15,988	44,527	1,343	70.7	46.8	24.0	5.9	6.0	16.8	0.5
1910	256,241	199,757	116,304	65,559	17,872	15,176	40,124	1,184	78.0	45.4	25.6	7.0	5.9	15.7	0.5
1900	111,364	80,865	53,030	25,431	2,380	9,332	20,570	597	72.6	47.6	22.8	2.1	8.4	18.5	0.5
Oregon:															
1920	107,644	86,623	44,664	34,982	6,943	5,798	14,659	564	80.5	41.5	32.5	6.4	5.4	13.6	0.5
1910	113,136	89,440	43,355	36,320	9,729	10,331	12,775	590	79.1	38.3	32.1	8.6	9.1	11.3	0.5
1900	65,748	45,802	25,662	18,822	1,307	11,948	7,634	364	69.7	39.0	28.6	2.0	18.2	11.6	0.6
California:															
1920	757,625	505,937	229,792	140,920	134,616	81,707	154,971	15,010	66.8	30.3	18.6	17.8	10.8	20.3	2.1
1910	586,432	424,303	203,435	122,357	98,303	72,413	81,482	8,234	72.4	34.7	20.9	16.8	12.3	13.9	1.4
1900	367,240	268,865	145,359	87,384	36,113	51,024	39,987	7,364	73.2	39.6	23.8	9.8	13.9	10.9	2.0

[1] Includes "Europe, not specified" at each census, and Danzig, Fiume, and Saar Basin in 1920.
[2] Includes population of Indian Territory for 1900.

CHAPTER VII
YEAR OF IMMIGRATION OF THE FOREIGN-BORN POPULATION

CHAPTER VII.—YEAR OF IMMIGRATION OF THE FOREIGN-BORN POPULATION.

INTRODUCTION.

The inquiry as to year of immigration supplies a basis for a comparison of the several geographic divisions and states in regard to the distribution of the foreign-born population by years of arrival in the United States. It also provides a means for determining what proportion of the immigrants who arrived during a given year or period of years, as shown by the immigration statistics, were still alive and residing in this country on the census date. This discussion does not cover the year of arrival of the foreign born who were enumerated in any of the outlying territories, but statistics for Alaska, Hawaii, and Porto Rico are given in the sections for those territories, in Volume III.

Data as to year of immigration have been collected at each of the last four decennial censuses. As the Fourteenth Census statistics show the numbers of surviving immigrants on January 1, 1920, who arrived in the United States during the periods 1906–1910 and 1901–1905, and in 1900 or earlier years, the statistics compiled from the returns of preceding censuses have little value for the purpose of comparison with those of the present census. Accordingly, the only comparative figures given are the Thirteenth Census statistics shown in Table 1. In that table the distribution of the immigrants for whom the year of arrival was not reported—about one-eleventh of the Fourteenth Census total and about one-tenth of the Thirteenth Census total—has been made on the assumption that the proportions arriving during each period of years were the same for the immigrants for whom the year was not reported as for those for whom data were secured. There is no way of determining whether the distribution thus made contains any considerable margin of error, but it is probably approximately correct.

In making use of the figures in Table 1, it must be remembered that the difference between the numbers of immigrants shown by the Thirteenth Census and by the Fourteenth Census as having arrived during a specified period, although due mainly to mortality, is affected to some extent by emigration of foreign-born persons.

It will be noted that the number shown by the Fourteenth Census as having arrived in 1900 or earlier was nearly one-fourth smaller than the corresponding number shown by the Thirteenth Census, whereas in the case of the group reported as having arrived during the period 1901–1905 the reduction between the two censuses was less than one-ninth. This condition is presumably due mainly to the fact that during the period between the two censuses the average age of the immigrants who arrived in 1900 or earlier was materially higher than that of the immigrants who reached this country during the period 1901–1905, so that the mortality between the two censuses would be greater for the former group than for the latter. It may be also that the proportion of emigrants among the foreign-born persons who arrived in 1900 or earlier was larger than among those who came during the years 1901 to 1905.

During the calendar years 1914 to 1919, inclusive, and especially the years 1915 to 1919, immigration to the United States was greatly reduced as a result of the World War, and therefore the number of foreign-born persons enumerated in 1920 as having arrived during the years from 1915 to 1918, inclusive, shows a marked decrease for each year of arrival as compared with the preceding one, but the foreign born enumerated as having arrived in 1919—the year following the termination of the war—outnumbered those who arrived in 1915 and who were still in the United States in 1920. The considerable numbers of these later arrivals enumerated in Texas, Arizona, and California were mainly Mexicans. (See Table 4.)

In making comparisons between the census statistics as to the numbers of immigrants arriving during specified years and the immigration and emigration statistics published by the Bureau of Immigration, it must be remembered that the census figures relate to calendar years, while the immigration and emigration figures are for fiscal years ended June 30.

Urban and rural communities.—Because of the great difference between the proportions of immigrants who go to urban and to rural communities, and because of the changes in these proportions from decade to decade, separate statistics for the two classes of communities are given in Tables 15 and 16.

In drawing the distinction between urban and rural population, all incorporated places (and all towns in Massachusetts, Rhode Island, and New Hampshire) having 2,500 inhabitants or more are treated as urban and the remainder of the country as rural. In Massachusetts and Rhode Island it is not the practice, as in practically all the other states, to incorporate, as separate municipalities, the relatively densely populated

(777)

778   POPULATION.

portions of "towns" (which are the primary divisions of the counties), and no town as a whole is incorporated as a municipality until it attains a population greatly in excess of 2,500; and in New Hampshire a similar condition exists, although the state contains two incorporated villages, each of which has fewer than 2,500 inhabitants. For this reason those towns having 2,500 or more inhabitants in the three states named are treated as urban, although portions of their areas are rural in character. The urban areas in the three states in question, as classified by the census, thus contain relatively small numbers of inhabitants who in other sections of the country would be segregated as rural. Nevertheless, in most of the towns having 2,500 inhabitants or more in Massachusetts, Rhode Island, and New Hampshire by far the greater part of the population resides within the more densely settled areas, so that the proportion classed as urban, considering each state as a whole, is not greatly exaggerated by the practice adopted.

It will be seen from Tables 15 and 16 that, considering the country as a whole, the foreign born in rural districts represent, on the average, a somewhat older immigration than those in urban communities, although in some sections of the country the reverse is true. Naturally, as the opportunities for acquiring land at low prices decreased, immigration to rural communities decreased. Moreover, the demand for labor in industrial communities has been greater in recent than in earlier decades. The fact that all transoceanic immigrants land in cities and that some remain there for more or less extended periods of time, even if their intention is ultimately to settle in rural districts, also may have some effect on the distribution as between urban and rural communities.

It may be noted, however, that of the comparatively few immigrants who arrived during the period from 1915 to 1919 and who were still living in the United States on the census date, the proportion who went to rural communities, 27.1 per cent (excluding those for whom the year of immigration was not reported), was materially larger than the corresponding proportion, 23.5 per cent, among the immigrants who arrived prior to 1915.

YEAR OF IMMIGRATION.

779

TABLE 1.—FOREIGN-BORN POPULATION, BY RACE AND YEAR OF IMMIGRATION, FOR THE UNITED STATES: 1920 AND 1910.

YEAR OF IMMIGRATION.	ALL CLASSES.		WHITE.		NEGRO.		INDIAN.		CHINESE.		JAPANESE.		ALL OTHER.	
	Number.	Per cent.	Number.	Per cent.	Number.	Per cent.	Number.	Per cent.	Number.	Per cent.	Number.	Per cent.	Number.	Per cent.
Total, 1920	13,920,692	100.0	13,712,754	100.0	73,803	100.0	6,299	100.0	43,107	100.0	81,338	100.0	3,391	100.0
Year of immigration:														
1919	214,123	1.5	201,280	1.5	5,938	8.0	644	10.2	1,141	2.6	5,027	6.2	93	2.7
1918	85,570	0.6	76,929	0.6	3,628	4.9	429	6.8	584	1.4	3,953	4.9	47	1.4
1917	116,222	0.8	106,059	0.8	4,537	6.1	435	6.9	952	2.2	4,120	5.1	119	3.5
1916	177,184	1.3	167,675	1.2	3,698	5.0	558	8.9	973	2.3	4,177	5.1	103	3.0
1915	203,098	1.5	193,684	1.4	3,213	4.4	374	5.9	1,299	3.0	4,396	5.4	132	3.9
1914	449,876	3.2	440,707	3.2	3,791	5.1	306	4.9	1,166	2.7	3,755	4.6	151	4.5
1911–1913	1,604,890	11.5	1,585,146	11.6	8,687	11.8	497	7.9	2,508	5.8	7,497	9.2	1,364	40.2
1906–1910	2,229,808	16.0	2,194,371	16.0	10,779	14.6	563	8.9	4,616	10.7	18,175	22.3	404	11.9
1901–1905	1,814,264	13.0	1,790,180	13.1	6,194	8.4	321	5.1	2,639	6.1	14,526	17.9	112	3.3
1900 or earlier	5,761,237	41.4	5,717,465	41.7	10,105	13.7	837	13.3	22,678	52.6	10,040	12.3	112	3.3
Not reported	1,264,360	9.1	1,239,258	9.0	13,233	17.9	1,335	21.2	4,551	10.6	5,672	7.0	311	9.2
Total, 1910	13,515,886	100.0	13,345,545	100.0	40,339	100.0	2,753	100.0	56,596	100.0	67,655	100.0	2,998	100.0
Year of immigration:														
1910, to Apr. 15	233,852	1.7	231,696	1.7	707	1.8	140	5.1	357	0.6	448	0.7	504	16.8
1909	579,419	4.3	573,585	4.3	2,331	5.8	101	3.7	1,409	2.5	1,624	2.4	369	12.3
1908	412,683	3.1	405,631	3.0	2,093	5.2	41	1.5	1,297	2.3	3,354	5.0	267	8.9
1907	705,771	5.2	694,362	5.2	2,596	6.4	34	1.2	951	1.7	8,200	12.1	628	20.9
1906	637,308	4.7	623,647	4.7	2,545	6.3	55	2.0	653	1.2	10,115	15.0	383	12.8
1905	530,808	3.9	520,161	3.9	2,153	5.3	40	1.5	545	1.0	7,704	11.4	205	6.8
1901–1904	1,505,214	11.1	1,479,844	11.1	5,557	13.8	170	6.2	1,884	3.3	17,523	25.9	236	7.9
1896–1900	1,053,099	7.9	1,046,500	7.8	4,044	10.0	147	5.3	3,723	6.6	9,244	13.7	41	1.4
1891–1895	1,157,513	8.6	1,148,645	8.6	2,708	6.7	131	4.8	4,253	7.5	1,763	2.6	13	0.4
1890 or earlier	5,347,710	39.6	5,302,515	39.7	7,675	19.0	895	25.2	34,863	61.6	1,868	2.8	94	3.1
Not reported	1,340,819	9.9	1,318,959	9.9	7,930	19.7	1,199	43.6	6,661	11.8	5,812	8.6	258	8.6
Period of immigration, including distribution of immigrants for whom year was not reported.[1]														
FOURTEENTH CENSUS.														
Total, 1920	13,920,692	100.0	13,712,754	100.0	73,803	100.0	6,299	100.0	43,107	100.0	81,338	100.0	3,391	100.0
1911–1919	3,136,743	22.5	3,045,410	22.2	40,812	55.3	4,115	65.3	9,608	22.4	35,411	43.5	1,327	39.1
1916–1919	654,610	4.7	607,215	4.4	21,692	29.4	2,622	41.6	4,096	9.5	18,582	22.8	403	11.9
1911–1915	2,482,133	17.8	2,438,195	17.8	19,120	25.9	1,493	23.7	5,572	12.9	16,829	20.7	924	27.2
1901–1910	4,443,964	31.9	4,376,966	31.9	20,680	28.0	1,122	17.8	8,116	18.8	35,140	43.2	1,940	57.2
1906–1910	2,450,805	17.6	2,410,766	17.6	13,134	17.8	714	11.3	5,165	12.0	19,532	24.0	1,494	44.1
1901–1905	1,993,159	14.3	1,966,200	14.3	7,546	10.2	408	6.5	2,951	6.8	15,608	19.2	446	13.2
1900 or earlier	6,339,985	45.5	6,290,378	45.9	12,311	16.7	1,062	16.9	25,323	58.7	10,787	13.3	124	3.7
THIRTEENTH CENSUS.														
Total, 1910	13,515,886	100.0	13,345,545	100.0	40,339	100.0	2,753	100.0	56,596	100.0	67,655	100.0	2,998	100.0
1901–1910, to Apr. 15	5,098,111	37.7	5,010,196	37.5	22,386	55.5	1,016	36.9	8,073	14.3	53,605	79.2	2,835	94.6
1906–1910, to Apr. 15	2,841,238	21.0	2,794,104	20.9	12,798	31.7	643	23.4	5,311	9.4	26,030	38.5	2,352	78.5
1901–1905	2,256,873	16.7	2,216,092	16.6	9,588	23.8	373	13.5	2,762	4.9	27,575	40.8	483	16.1
1900 or earlier	8,417,775	62.3	8,335,349	62.5	17,953	44.5	1,737	63.1	48,523	85.7	14,050	20.8	163	5.4

[1] See text, page 777.

POPULATION.

TABLE 2.—FOREIGN-BORN MALE POPULATION, BY RACE AND YEAR OF IMMIGRATION, FOR THE UNITED STATES: 1920 AND 1910.

YEAR OF IMMIGRATION.	ALL CLASSES.		WHITE.		NEGRO.		INDIAN.		CHINESE.		JAPANESE.		ALL OTHER.	
	Number.	Per cent.	Number.	Per cent.	Number.	Per cent.	Number.	Per cent.	Number.	Per cent.	Number.	Per cent.	Number.	Per cent.
Total, 1920...............	7,675,435	100.0	7,528,322	100.0	42,641	100.0	3,539	100.0	40,573	100.0	57,213	100.0	3,147	100.0
Year of immigration:														
1919.................	119,892	1.6	112,592	1.5	3,521	8.3	405	11.4	937	2.3	2,349	4.1	88	2.8
1918.................	47,320	0.6	42,723	0.6	1,953	4.6	237	6.7	460	1.1	1,908	3.3	39	1.2
1917.................	62,559	0.8	56,825	0.8	2,490	5.8	245	6.9	841	2.1	2,060	3.6	89	2.8
1916.................	96,056	1.3	90,676	1.2	2,004	4.7	305	8.6	859	2.1	2,123	3.7	89	2.8
1915.................	112,226	1.5	106,752	1.4	1,725	4.0	211	6.0	1,167	2.9	2,256	3.9	115	3.7
1914.................	256,216	3.3	250,808	3.3	2,136	5.0	181	5.1	1,052	2.6	1,904	3.3	135	4.3
1911-1913..........	933,333	12.2	921,758	12.2	4,796	11.2	295	8.3	2,222	5.5	3,733	6.5	529	16.8
1906-1910..........	1,288,152	16.8	1,261,115	16.8	6,326	14.8	331	9.4	4,269	10.5	14,783	25.8	1,328	42.2
1901-1905..........	1,057,498	13.8	1,037,662	13.8	3,883	9.1	178	5.0	2,492	6.1	12,014	22.0	369	11.7
1900 or earlier........	3,168,590	41.3	3,130,503	41.6	6,208	14.6	479	13.5	22,075	54.4	9,224	16.1	101	3.2
Not reported...........	533,593	7.0	516,908	6.9	7,599	17.8	672	19.0	4,199	10.3	3,050	0.9	265	8.4
Total, 1910...............	7,667,748	100.0	7,523,788	100.0	23,888	100.0	1,464	100.0	54,935	100.0	60,730	100.0	2,943	100.0
Year of immigration:														
1910, to Apr. 15........	172,170	2.2	170,459	2.3	487	2.0	126	8.6	340	0.6	254	0.4	504	17.1
1909.................	383,377	5.0	379,200	5.0	1,339	5.6	50	3.4	1,310	2.4	1,110	1.8	368	12.5
1908.................	256,638	3.3	251,148	3.3	1,214	5.1	21	1.4	1,235	2.2	2,754	4.5	266	9.0
1907.................	450,934	5.9	440,446	5.9	1,557	6.5	23	1.6	806	1.6	7,380	12.2	623	21.2
1906.................	394,289	5.1	382,537	5.1	1,532	6.4	30	2.0	612	1.1	9,202	15.2	376	12.8
1905.................	324,182	4.2	315,058	4.2	1,355	5.7	24	1.6	508	0.9	7,041	11.6	196	6.7
1901-1904..........	909,960	11.9	888,342	11.8	3,443	14.4	101	6.9	1,796	3.3	10,055	26.4	223	7.6
1896-1900..........	596,947	7.8	582,021	7.7	2,470	10.3	86	5.9	3,616	6.6	8,717	14.4	37	1.3
1891-1895..........	627,774	8.2	620,207	8.2	1,666	7.0	74	5.1	4,160	7.6	1,656	2.7	11	0.4
1890 or earlier........	2,999,822	39.1	2,958,741	39.3	4,723	19.8	398	27.2	34,155	62.2	1,717	2.8	88	3.0
Not reported...........	551,655	7.2	535,629	7.1	4,102	17.2	531	36.3	6,307	11.5	4,835	8.0	251	8.5
Period of immigration, including distribution of immigrants for whom year was not reported.[1]														
FOURTEENTH CENSUS.														
Total, 1920...............	7,675,435	100.0	7,528,322	100.0	42,641	100.0	3,539	100.0	40,573	100.0	57,213	100.0	3,147	100.0
1911-1919..........	1,750,905	22.8	1,698,775	22.6	22,664	53.2	2,320	65.6	8,408	20.7	17,554	30.7	1,184	37.6
1916-1919..........	351,606	4.6	325,141	4.3	12,130	28.4	1,472	41.6	3,454	8.5	9,076	15.9	333	10.6
1911-1915..........	1,399,299	18.2	1,373,634	18.2	10,534	24.7	848	24.0	4,054	12.2	8,478	14.8	851	27.0
1901-1910..........	2,520,449	32.8	2,408,252	32.8	12,423	29.1	628	17.7	7,542	18.6	29,751	52.0	1,853	58.9
1906-1910..........	1,384,286	18.0	1,354,089	18.0	7,698	18.1	408	11.5	4,762	11.7	15,879	27.8	1,450	46.1
1901-1905..........	1,136,163	14.8	1,114,163	14.8	4,725	11.1	220	6.2	2,780	6.9	13,872	24.2	403	12.8
1900 or earlier........	3,404,081	44.4	3,361,295	44.6	7,554	17.7	591	16.7	24,623	60.7	9,908	17.3	110	3.5
THIRTEENTH CENSUS.														
Total, 1910...............	7,667,748	100.0	7,523,788	100.0	23,888	100.0	1,464	100.0	54,935	100.0	60,730	100.0	2,943	100.0
1901-1910, to Apr. 15......	3,115,623	40.6	3,043,889	40.5	13,192	55.2	588	40.2	7,566	13.8	47,594	78.4	2,794	94.9
1906-1910, to Apr. 15......	1,785,841	23.3	1,748,251	23.2	7,399	31.0	392	26.8	4,963	9.0	22,500	37.0	2,336	70.4
1901-1905..........	1,329,782	17.3	1,295,638	17.2	5,793	24.3	196	13.4	2,603	4.7	25,094	41.3	458	15.6
1900 or earlier........	4,552,125	59.4	4,479,899	59.5	10,696	44.8	876	59.8	47,369	86.2	13,136	21.6	140	5.1

[1] See text, page 777.

YEAR OF IMMIGRATION.

781

TABLE 3.—FOREIGN-BORN FEMALE POPULATION, BY RACE AND YEAR OF IMMIGRATION, FOR THE UNITED STATES: 1920 AND 1910.

[Per cent not shown where base is less than 100.]

YEAR OF IMMIGRATION.	ALL CLASSES. Number.	Per cent.	WHITE. Number.	Per cent.	NEGRO. Number.	Per cent.	INDIAN. Number.	Per cent.	CHINESE. Number.	Per cent.	JAPANESE. Number.	Per cent.	ALL OTHER. Number.	Per cent.
Total, 1920	6,245,257	100.0	6,184,432	100.0	31,162	100.0	2,760	100.0	2,534	100.0	24,125	100.0	244	100.0
Year of immigration:														
1919	94,231	1.5	88,688	1.4	2,417	7.8	239	8.7	204	8.1	2,678	11.1	5	2.0
1918	38,250	0.6	34,206	0.6	1,675	5.4	192	7.0	124	4.9	2,045	8.5	8	3.3
1917	53,663	0.9	49,234	0.8	2,047	6.6	190	6.9	111	4.4	2,051	8.5	30	12.3
1916	81,128	1.3	76,909	1.2	1,694	5.4	253	9.2	114	4.5	2,054	8.5	14	5.7
1915	90,872	1.5	86,932	1.4	1,488	4.8	163	5.9	132	5.2	2,140	8.9	17	7.0
1914	193,660	3.1	189,899	3.1	1,655	5.3	125	4.5	114	4.5	1,851	7.7	16	6.6
1911–1913	671,557	10.8	663,388	10.7	3,891	12.5	202	7.3	286	11.3	3,764	15.6	26	10.7
1906–1910	941,716	15.1	933,250	15.1	4,453	14.3	232	8.4	347	13.7	3,392	14.1	36	14.8
1901–1905	756,760	12.1	752,518	12.2	2,311	7.4	143	5.2	147	5.8	1,612	6.7	35	14.3
1900 or earlier	2,592,647	41.5	2,586,962	41.8	3,897	12.5	358	13.0	603	23.8	816	3.4	11	4.5
Not reported	730,707	11.7	722,350	11.7	5,634	18.1	663	24.0	352	13.9	1,722	7.1	46	18.9
Total, 1910	5,848,138	100.0	5,821,757	100.0	16,451	100.0	1,289	100.0	1,661	100.0	6,925	100.0	55	....
Year of immigration:														
1910, to Apr. 15	61,682	1.1	61,237	1.1	220	1.3	14	1.1	17	1.0	194	2.8	....	....
1909	196,042	3.4	194,385	3.3	992	6.0	51	4.0	99	6.0	514	7.4	1	....
1908	156,045	2.7	154,483	2.7	879	5.3	20	1.6	62	3.7	600	8.7	5	....
1907	255,837	4.4	253,916	4.4	1,039	6.3	11	0.9	55	3.3	811	11.7	7	....
1906	243,109	4.2	241,110	4.1	1,013	6.2	25	1.9	41	2.5	913	13.2		
1905	205,626	3.5	205,103	3.5	798	4.9	16	1.2	37	2.2	663	9.6	9	....
1901–1904	595,254	10.2	591,502	10.2	2,114	12.9	69	5.4	88	5.3	1,468	21.2	13	....
1896–1900	466,752	8.0	464,479	8.0	1,574	9.6	61	4.7	107	6.4	527	7.6	4	....
1891–1895	520,739	9.1	528,438	9.1	1,042	6.3	57	4.4	93	5.6	107	1.5	2	....
1890 or earlier	2,347,888	40.1	2,343,774	40.3	2,952	17.9	297	23.0	708	42.6	151	2.2	6	....
Not reported	789,164	13.5	783,330	13.5	3,828	23.3	668	51.8	354	21.3	977	14.1	7	....
Period of immigration, including distribution of immigrants for whom year was not reported.[1]														
FOURTEENTH CENSUS.														
Total, 1920	6,245,257	100.0	6,184,432	100.0	31,162	100.0	2,760	100.0	2,534	100.0	24,125	100.0	244	100.0
1911–1919	1,385,838	22.2	1,346,635	21.8	18,148	58.2	1,795	65.0	1,260	49.7	17,857	74.0	143	58.6
1916–1919	303,004	4.9	282,074	4.6	9,502	30.7	1,150	41.7	642	25.3	9,506	39.4	70	28.7
1911–1915	1,082,834	17.3	1,064,561	17.2	8,586	27.6	645	23.4	618	24.4	8,351	34.6	73	29.9
1901–1910	1,923,515	30.8	1,908,714	30.9	8,257	26.5	494	17.9	574	22.7	5,389	22.3	87	35.7
1906–1910	1,066,519	17.1	1,056,677	17.1	5,436	17.4	306	11.1	403	15.9	3,653	15.1	44	18.0
1901–1905	856,996	13.7	852,037	13.8	2,821	9.1	188	6.8	171	6.7	1,736	7.2	43	17.6
1900 or earlier	2,935,904	47.0	2,929,083	47.4	4,757	15.3	471	17.1	700	27.6	879	3.6	14	5.7
THIRTEENTH CENSUS.														
Total, 1910	5,848,138	100.0	5,821,757	100.0	16,451	100.0	1,289	100.0	1,661	100.0	6,925	100.0	55	....
1901–1910, to Apr. 15	1,982,488	33.9	1,966,367	33.8	9,194	55.9	428	33.2	507	30.5	6,011	86.8	41	....
1906–1910, to Apr. 15	1,055,397	18.0	1,045,853	18.0	5,399	32.8	251	19.5	348	21.0	3,530	51.0	16	....
1901–1905	927,091	15.9	920,454	15.8	3,795	23.1	177	13.7	159	9.6	2,481	35.8	25	....
1900 or earlier	3,865,650	66.1	3,855,460	66.2	7,257	44.1	861	66.8	1,154	69.5	914	13.2	14	....

[1] See text, page 777.

782

POPULATION.

TABLE 4.—FOREIGN-BORN POPULATION BY YEAR OF IMMIGRATION, BY DIVISIONS AND STATES: 1920.

DIVISION AND STATE.	Total foreign born: 1920	YEAR OF IMMIGRATION.										
		1919	1918	1917	1916	1915	1914	1911-1913	1906-1910	1901-1905	1900 or earlier.	Year not reported.
United States..............	13,920,692	214,123	85,570	116,222	177,184	203,098	449,876	1,604,890	2,229,868	1,814,264	5,761,237	1,264,380
GEOGRAPHIC DIVISIONS:												
New England..................	1,885,945	29,877	9,160	16,766	29,248	31,142	59,020	214,966	304,735	250,235	832,443	108,353
Middle Atlantic.............	4,960,418	56,703	17,745	30,605	48,535	65,547	178,633	657,352	919,629	789,504	1,849,913	340,252
East North Central...........	3,232,141	27,055	8,818	13,569	25,994	34,008	106,821	412,127	511,268	379,564	1,389,247	323,670
West North Central..........	1,375,653	8,498	4,189	5,817	9,730	10,649	24,390	85,656	142,247	131,808	775,031	177,578
South Atlantic...............	330,537	5,916	2,586	3,040	5,209	5,218	12,452	38,856	53,817	42,176	118,650	42,637
East South Central..........	72,989	647	288	247	421	509	1,486	4,726	8,171	6,685	34,423	15,386
West South Central..........	464,828	33,994	16,082	16,358	20,225	18,850	20,112	45,929	50,287	31,854	131,588	79,549
Mountain...................	467,620	17,661	9,099	11,180	14,747	13,062	15,159	42,897	67,312	48,394	177,378	50,731
Pacific....................	1,130,561	33,772	17,623	18,640	23,075	24,113	31,803	102,381	172,402	133,984	452,504	120,204
NEW ENGLAND:												
Maine......................	107,814	3,842	1,147	1,385	2,019	1,950	2,887	8,289	13,359	11,687	48,103	13,146
New Hampshire.............	91,397	2,262	660	956	1,637	1,523	2,435	8,227	11,825	8,850	41,964	11,058
Vermont....................	44,558	2,065	586	752	1,077	996	1,260	3,909	5,723	4,665	19,122	4,403
Massachusetts..............	1,088,548	15,424	4,863	9,390	17,184	18,520	33,726	123,795	177,219	144,903	499,067	44,387
Rhode Island..............	175,189	2,670	742	1,700	2,720	2,580	4,829	17,743	27,577	23,463	79,195	11,970
Connecticut................	378,439	3,614	1,162	2,583	4,631	5,573	13,883	53,003	69,032	56,577	144,992	23,389
MIDDLE ATLANTIC:												
New York..................	2,825,375	42,568	12,748	21,380	31,089	39,678	101,615	352,344	519,916	448,411	1,058,145	197,481
New Jersey.................	742,486	5,827	2,048	3,673	6,528	8,891	26,316	99,215	139,734	115,086	286,803	48,365
Pennsylvania...............	1,392,557	8,308	2,949	5,552	10,918	16,978	50,702	205,793	259,979	226,007	504,965	100,406
EAST NORTH CENTRAL:												
Ohio.......................	680,452	4,999	1,591	3,154	6,304	8,252	30,191	110,308	124,243	91,414	248,824	51,112
Indiana....................	151,328	833	274	512	1,089	1,426	4,574	17,392	22,022	15,438	60,829	26,339
Illinois...................	1,210,584	6,157	2,707	4,140	7,311	11,249	36,540	143,818	203,726	156,792	517,963	120,181
Michigan..................	729,292	13,695	3,787	4,910	9,503	10,712	26,542	103,385	110,051	74,020	295,883	76,804
Wisconsin.................	460,485	1,371	459	853	1,787	2,369	8,974	37,164	50,626	41,900	265,748	49,234
WEST NORTH CENTRAL:												
Minnesota..................	486,795	2,481	765	1,435	3,157	3,755	9,125	31,853	52,035	52,276	287,015	42,898
Iowa.......................	225,994	1,421	512	845	1,399	1,701	4,042	13,758	18,633	14,794	130,092	32,797
Missouri..................	186,835	1,144	656	776	1,097	1,374	3,837	13,440	23,870	19,883	92,092	28,666
North Dakota..............	131,868	442	161	249	729	849	2,111	6,503	15,978	19,526	65,523	19,792
South Dakota..............	82,534	400	122	135	357	509	1,136	3,923	8,137	7,485	47,777	12,553
Nebraska..................	150,665	749	458	640	924	1,061	2,325	10,124	14,359	10,436	86,023	22,966
Kansas....................	110,967	1,861	1,515	1,737	2,067	1,400	1,814	6,055	9,235	7,468	59,909	17,906
SOUTH ATLANTIC:												
Delaware..................	19,901	174	66	106	204	279	816	3,130	3,447	2,022	6,607	2,450
Maryland..................	103,179	684	298	444	640	917	3,357	11,206	15,451	14,700	48,693	6,780
District of Columbia......	29,365	489	179	233	342	376	752	2,467	4,338	3,505	11,567	5,117
Virginia..................	31,705	655	366	411	559	539	995	3,013	4,892	3,873	10,487	5,915
West Virginia............	62,105	626	334	607	1,975	1,643	4,123	11,897	13,138	7,995	12,238	7,529
North Carolina...........	7,272	160	33	54	75	84	212	686	975	768	2,365	1,860
South Carolina...........	6,582	74	28	33	65	67	186	618	894	656	2,438	1,523
Georgia...................	16,564	228	87	90	171	184	436	1,469	2,594	2,006	6,456	2,843
Florida...................	53,864	2,826	1,175	1,062	1,178	1,129	1,575	4,370	8,088	6,042	17,799	8,620
EAST SOUTH CENTRAL:												
Kentucky..................	30,906	177	93	70	130	163	614	2,011	2,948	2,149	16,962	5,589
Tennessee.................	15,648	206	68	54	98	112	323	947	1,822	1,551	6,915	3,557
Alabama..................	18,027	190	100	96	124	154	379	1,225	2,306	1,915	7,022	4,516
Mississippi...............	8,408	74	32	27	69	80	170	543	1,095	1,070	3,524	1,724
WEST SOUTH CENTRAL:												
Arkansas..................	14,137	84	28	47	85	68	172	663	1,325	1,266	6,754	3,645
Louisiana.................	46,427	1,099	474	426	324	389	648	1,701	4,171	4,957	19,395	12,843
Oklahoma.................	40,432	1,516	748	648	687	552	665	2,178	3,843	3,043	17,476	9,066
Texas.....................	363,832	31,295	14,832	15,237	19,129	17,831	18,627	41,387	40,948	22,588	87,963	53,995
MOUNTAIN:												
Montana...................	95,591	842	342	576	1,454	1,276	2,780	8,692	15,091	11,376	38,870	14,292
Idaho.....................	40,747	715	571	480	562	598	935	2,943	5,421	4,122	20,253	4,147
Wyoming..................	28,567	578	333	378	536	498	924	3,255	4,764	3,128	8,550	3,623
Colorado..................	119,138	1,694	1,383	1,810	2,038	1,649	2,720	10,895	16,623	13,765	54,712	11,849
New Mexico...............	29,808	1,729	1,078	1,788	2,230	2,143	1,706	3,349	4,044	2,400	6,512	2,879
Arizona...................	80,566	10,879	4,566	5,299	6,720	5,559	3,928	7,333	9,903	5,677	12,777	7,925
Utah......................	59,200	798	589	635	858	985	1,655	4,972	8,799	6,039	30,007	3,808
Nevada....................	16,003	431	237	264	349	354	511	1,458	2,667	1,887	5,097	2,148
PACIFIC:												
Washington................	265,292	6,803	2,962	2,836	3,931	4,018	6,658	21,165	41,213	33,081	111,633	30,992
Oregon....................	107,644	2,224	690	860	991	1,246	2,590	8,895	16,736	12,605	52,641	8,166
California................	757,625	24,745	13,971	14,944	18,153	18,849	22,555	72,321	114,453	88,298	288,290	81,046

YEAR OF IMMIGRATION.

TABLE 4.—FOREIGN-BORN POPULATION BY YEAR OF IMMIGRATION, BY DIVISIONS AND STATES: 1920—Continued.

DIVISION AND STATE.	PER CENT OF TOTAL ARRIVING IN—										
	1919	1918	1917	1916	1915	1914	1911-1913	1906-1910	1901-1905	1900 or earlier.	Year not reported.
United States............	1.5	0.6	0.8	1.3	1.5	3.2	11.5	16.0	13.0	41.4	9.1
GEOGRAPHIC DIVISIONS:											
New England...........	1.6	0.5	0.9	1.6	1.7	3.1	11.4	16.2	13.3	44.1	5.7
Middle Atlantic.............	1.1	0.4	0.6	1.0	1.3	3.6	13.3	18.5	15.9	37.3	7.0
East North Central..........	0.6	0.3	0.4	0.8	1.1	3.3	12.8	15.8	11.7	43.0	10.0
West North Central.........	0.6	0.3	0.4	0.7	0.8	1.8	6.2	10.3	9.6	56.3	12.9
South Atlantic.............	1.8	0.8	0.9	1.6	1.6	3.8	11.8	16.3	12.8	35.9	12.9
East South Central..........	0.9	0.4	0.3	0.6	0.7	2.0	6.5	11.2	9.2	47.2	21.1
West South Central..........	7.3	3.5	3.5	4.4	4.1	4.3	9.9	10.8	6.9	28.3	17.1
Mountain.................	3.8	1.9	2.4	3.2	2.8	3.2	9.2	14.4	10.3	37.9	10.8
Pacific...................	3.0	1.6	1.6	2.0	2.1	2.8	9.1	15.2	11.9	40.0	10.6
NEW ENGLAND:											
Maine....................	3.6	1.1	1.3	1.9	1.8	2.7	7.7	12.4	10.8	44.6	12.2
New Hampshire.............	2.5	0.7	1.0	1.8	1.7	2.7	9.0	12.9	9.7	45.9	12.1
Vermont..................	4.6	1.3	1.7	2.4	2.2	2.8	8.8	12.8	10.5	42.9	9.9
Massachusetts..............	1.4	0.4	0.9	1.6	1.7	3.1	11.4	16.3	13.3	45.8	4.1
Rhode Island..............	1.5	0.4	1.0	1.6	1.5	2.8	10.1	15.7	13.4	45.2	6.8
Connecticut...............	1.0	0.3	0.7	1.2	1.5	3.7	14.0	18.2	15.0	38.3	6.2
MIDDLE ATLANTIC:											
New York................	1.5	0.5	0.8	1.1	1.4	3.6	12.5	18.4	15.9	37.5	7.0
New Jersey...............	0.8	0.3	0.5	0.9	1.2	3.5	13.4	18.8	15.5	38.6	6.5
Pennsylvania..............	0.6	0.2	0.4	0.8	1.2	3.6	14.8	18.7	16.2	36.3	7.2
EAST NORTH CENTRAL:											
Ohio.....................	0.7	0.2	0.5	0.9	1.2	4.4	16.2	18.3	13.4	36.6	7.5
Indiana..................	0.6	0.2	0.3	0.7	0.9	3.0	11.5	14.9	10.2	40.2	17.4
Illinois..................	0.5	0.2	0.3	0.6	0.9	3.0	11.9	16.8	13.0	42.8	9.9
Michigan.................	1.9	0.5	0.7	1.3	1.5	3.6	14.2	15.1	10.1	40.6	10.5
Wisconsin................	0.3	0.1	0.2	0.4	0.5	1.7	8.1	11.0	9.1	57.7	10.7
WEST NORTH CENTRAL:											
Minnesota................	0.5	0.2	0.3	0.6	0.8	1.9	6.5	10.7	10.7	59.0	8.8
Iowa....................	0.6	0.2	0.4	0.6	0.8	1.8	6.1	8.2	6.5	60.2	14.5
Missouri.................	0.6	0.4	0.4	0.6	0.7	2.1	7.2	12.8	10.6	49.3	15.3
North Dakota.............	0.3	0.1	0.2	0.6	0.6	1.6	4.9	12.1	14.8	49.7	15.0
South Dakota.............	0.5	0.1	0.2	0.4	0.6	1.4	4.8	9.9	9.1	57.9	15.2
Nebraska................	0.5	0.3	0.4	0.6	0.7	1.5	6.7	9.5	6.9	57.5	15.2
Kansas..................	1.7	1.4	1.6	1.9	1.3	1.6	5.5	8.3	6.7	54.0	16.1
SOUTH ATLANTIC:											
Delaware................	0.9	0.3	0.5	1.0	1.4	4.1	15.7	17.3	13.2	33.2	12.3
Maryland................	0.7	0.3	0.4	0.6	0.9	3.3	10.9	15.0	14.3	47.2	6.6
District of Columbia..........	1.7	0.6	0.8	1.2	1.3	2.6	8.4	14.8	11.9	39.4	17.4
Virginia.................	2.1	1.2	1.3	1.8	1.7	3.1	9.5	15.4	12.2	33.1	18.7
West Virginia.............	1.0	0.5	1.0	3.2	2.6	6.6	19.2	21.2	12.9	19.7	12.1
North Carolina.............	2.2	0.5	0.7	1.0	1.2	2.9	9.4	13.4	10.6	32.5	25.6
South Carolina.............	1.1	0.4	0.5	1.0	1.0	2.8	9.4	13.6	10.0	37.0	23.1
Georgia..................	1.4	0.5	0.5	1.0	1.1	2.6	8.9	15.7	12.1	39.0	17.2
Florida..................	5.2	2.2	2.0	2.2	2.1	2.9	8.1	15.0	11.2	33.0	16.0
EAST SOUTH CENTRAL:											
Kentucky................	0.6	0.3	0.2	0.4	0.5	2.0	6.5	9.5	7.0	54.9	18.1
Tennessee...............	1.3	0.4	0.3	0.6	0.7	2.1	6.1	11.6	9.9	44.2	22.7
Alabama.................	1.1	0.6	0.5	0.7	0.9	2.1	6.8	12.8	10.6	39.0	25.1
Mississippi...............	0.9	0.4	0.3	0.8	1.0	2.0	6.5	13.0	12.7	41.9	20.5
WEST SOUTH CENTRAL:											
Arkansas................	0.6	0.2	0.3	0.6	0.5	1.2	4.7	9.4	9.0	47.8	25.8
Louisiana................	2.4	1.0	0.9	0.7	0.8	1.4	3.7	9.0	10.7	41.8	27.7
Oklahoma................	3.7	1.9	1.6	1.7	1.4	1.6	5.4	9.5	7.5	43.2	22.4
Texas...................	8.6	4.1	4.2	5.3	4.9	5.1	11.4	11.3	6.2	24.2	14.8
MOUNTAIN:											
Montana.................	0.9	0.4	0.6	1.5	1.3	2.9	9.1	15.8	11.9	40.7	15.0
Idaho...................	1.8	1.4	1.2	1.4	1.5	2.3	7.2	13.3	10.1	49.7	10.2
Wyoming................	2.2	1.3	1.4	2.0	1.9	3.5	12.3	17.9	11.8	32.2	13.5
Colorado................	1.4	1.2	1.5	1.7	1.4	2.3	9.1	14.0	11.6	45.9	9.9
New Mexico..............	5.8	3.6	5.8	7.5	7.2	5.7	11.2	13.6	8.1	21.8	9.7
Arizona.................	13.5	5.7	6.6	8.3	6.9	4.9	9.1	12.3	7.0	15.9	9.8
Utah...................	1.3	1.0	1.1	1.4	1.7	2.8	8.4	14.9	10.2	50.7	6.5
Nevada.................	2.7	1.5	1.6	2.2	2.2	3.2	9.1	16.7	11.8	35.6	13.4
PACIFIC:											
Washington..............	2.6	1.1	1.1	1.5	1.5	2.5	8.0	15.5	12.5	42.1	11.7
Oregon.................	2.1	0.6	0.8	0.9	1.2	2.4	8.3	15.5	11.7	48.9	7.6
California................	3.3	1.8	2.0	2.4	2.5	3.0	9.5	15.1	11.7	38.1	10.7

POPULATION.

784

TABLE 5.—FOREIGN-BORN POPULATION AND FOREIGN-BORN WHITE POPULATION BY YEAR OF IMMIGRATION, BY DIVISIONS AND STATES: 1920.

DIVISION AND STATE.	YEAR OF IMMIGRATION OF—										PER CENT OF—							
	Foreign-born population.					Foreign-born white population.					Foreign-born population arriving in—				Foreign-born white population arriving in—			
	Total number: 1920	1911–1919	1901–1910	1900 or earlier.	Year not reported.	Total number: 1920	1911–1919	1901–1910	1900 or earlier.	Year not reported.	1911–1919	1901–1910	1900 or earlier.	Year not reported.	1911–1919	1901–1910	1900 or earlier.	Year not reported.
United States	13,920,692	2,850,963	4,044,132	5,761,237	1,264,360	13,712,754	2,771,480	3,984,551	5,717,465	1,239,258	20.5	29.1	41.4	9.1	20.2	29.1	41.7	9.0
GEOG. DIVISIONS:																		
New England	1,885,945	390,179	554,970	832,443	108,353	1,870,654	383,794	551,055	828,786	107,019	20.7	29.4	44.1	5.7	20.5	29.5	44.3	5.7
Middle Atlantic	4,960,418	1,055,120	1,709,133	1,849,913	346,252	4,912,575	1,032,848	1,697,568	1,843,171	338,988	21.3	34.5	37.3	7.0	21.0	34.6	37.5	7.0
E. North Central	3,232,141	628,392	890,832	1,389,247	323,670	3,223,279	626,316	888,997	1,386,473	321,493	19.4	27.6	43.0	10.0	19.4	27.6	43.0	10.0
W. North Central	1,375,653	148,929	274,115	775,031	177,578	1,371,961	148,024	273,302	774,080	176,555	10.8	19.9	56.3	12.9	10.8	19.9	56.4	12.9
South Atlantic	330,537	73,257	95,093	118,650	42,637	315,920	66,724	92,913	115,808	40,475	22.2	29.0	35.9	12.9	21.1	29.4	36.7	12.8
E. South Central	72,989	8,324	14,856	34,423	15,386	71,939	8,071	14,660	34,128	15,071	11.4	20.4	47.2	21.1	11.2	20.4	47.4	20.9
W. South Central	464,828	171,550	82,141	131,588	79,549	459,333	169,601	81,404	130,668	77,660	36.9	17.7	28.3	17.1	36.9	17.7	28.4	16.9
Mountain	467,620	123,805	115,706	177,378	50,731	453,225	119,327	111,035	173,998	48,865	26.5	24.7	37.9	10.8	26.3	24.5	38.4	10.8
Pacific	1,130,561	251,407	306,386	452,564	120,204	1,033,868	216,775	273,608	430,353	113,132	22.2	27.1	40.0	10.6	21.0	26.5	41.6	10.9
NEW ENGLAND:																		
Maine	107,814	21,519	25,046	48,103	13,146	107,349	21,390	24,943	47,946	13,070	20.0	23.2	44.6	12.2	19.9	23.2	44.7	12.2
New Hampshire	91,397	17,700	20,675	41,964	11,058	91,233	17,634	20,650	41,921	11,028	19.4	22.6	45.9	12.1	19.3	22.6	45.9	12.1
Vermont	44,558	10,645	10,388	19,122	4,403	44,526	10,639	10,377	19,111	4,399	23.9	23.3	42.9	9.9	23.9	23.3	42.9	9.9
Massachusetts	1,088,548	222,882	322,212	499,067	44,387	1,077,534	218,441	319,262	496,297	43,534	20.5	29.6	45.8	4.1	20.3	29.6	46.1	4.0
Rhode Island	175,189	32,984	51,040	79,195	11,970	173,499	32,179	50,626	78,874	11,820	18.8	29.1	45.2	6.8	18.5	29.2	45.5	6.8
Connecticut	378,439	84,449	125,609	144,992	23,389	376,513	83,511	125,107	144,637	23,168	22.3	33.2	38.3	6.2	22.2	33.3	38.4	6.2
MIDDLE ATLANTIC:																		
New York	2,825,375	601,422	968,327	1,058,145	197,481	2,786,112	581,741	958,779	1,053,613	191,979	21.3	34.3	37.5	7.0	20.9	34.4	37.8	6.9
New Jersey	742,486	152,498	254,820	286,803	48,365	738,613	151,232	253,864	285,874	47,643	20.5	34.3	38.6	6.5	20.5	34.4	38.7	6.5
Pennsylvania	1,392,557	301,200	485,986	504,965	100,406	1,387,850	299,875	484,925	503,684	99,366	21.6	34.9	36.3	7.2	21.6	34.9	36.3	7.2
E. NORTH CENTRAL:																		
Ohio	680,452	164,859	215,657	248,824	51,112	678,697	164,405	215,265	248,301	50,726	24.2	31.7	36.6	7.5	24.2	31.7	36.6	7.5
Indiana	151,328	26,100	38,060	60,829	26,339	150,868	26,032	37,953	60,686	26,197	17.2	25.2	40.2	17.4	17.3	25.2	40.2	17.4
Illinois	1,210,584	211,922	360,518	517,963	120,181	1,206,951	211,202	359,811	516,698	119,240	17.5	29.8	42.8	9.9	17.5	29.8	42.8	9.9
Michigan	729,292	172,534	184,071	295,883	76,804	726,635	171,785	183,508	295,190	76,152	23.7	25.2	40.6	10.5	23.6	25.3	40.6	10.5
Wisconsin	460,485	52,977	92,526	265,748	49,234	460,128	52,892	92,460	265,598	49,178	11.5	20.1	57.7	10.7	11.5	20.1	57.7	10.7
W. NORTH CENTRAL:																		
Minnesota	486,795	52,571	104,311	287,015	42,898	486,164	52,447	104,177	286,765	42,775	10.8	21.4	59.0	8.8	10.8	21.4	59.0	8.8
Iowa	225,994	23,678	33,427	136,092	32,797	225,647	23,566	33,363	136,011	32,707	10.5	14.8	60.2	14.5	10.4	14.8	60.3	14.5
Missouri	186,835	22,324	43,753	92,092	28,666	186,026	22,126	43,596	91,817	28,487	11.9	23.4	49.3	15.3	11.0	23.4	49.4	15.3
North Dakota	131,803	11,044	35,504	65,523	19,792	131,503	10,999	35,449	65,389	19,666	8.4	26.9	49.7	15.0	8.4	27.0	49.7	15.0
South Dakota	82,534	6,582	15,622	47,777	12,553	82,391	6,548	15,594	47,735	12,514	8.0	18.9	57.9	15.2	7.9	18.9	57.9	15.2
Nebraska	150,655	16,281	24,795	86,623	22,966	149,652	16,004	24,489	86,508	22,651	10.8	16.5	57.5	15.2	10.7	16.4	57.8	15.1
Kansas	110,967	16,449	16,703	59,909	17,906	110,578	16,334	16,634	59,855	17,755	14.8	15.1	54.0	16.1	14.8	15.0	54.1	16.1
SOUTH ATLANTIC:																		
Delaware	19,901	4,775	6,069	6,607	2,450	19,810	4,764	6,051	6,580	2,415	24.0	30.5	33.2	12.3	24.0	30.5	33.2	12.2
Maryland	103,179	17,546	30,160	48,693	6,780	102,177	17,281	29,941	48,362	6,593	17.0	29.2	47.2	6.6	16.9	29.3	47.3	6.5
Dist. of Columbia	29,365	4,838	7,843	11,567	5,117	28,548	4,589	7,697	11,342	4,920	16.5	26.7	39.4	17.4	16.1	27.0	39.7	17.2
Virginia	31,705	6,538	8,765	10,487	5,915	30,785	6,214	8,604	10,294	5,673	20.6	27.6	33.1	18.7	20.2	27.9	33.4	18.4
West Virginia	62,105	21,205	21,133	12,238	7,529	61,906	21,168	21,086	12,193	7,459	34.1	34.0	19.7	12.1	34.2	34.1	19.7	12.0
North Carolina	7,272	1,304	1,743	2,365	1,860	7,099	1,268	1,709	2,321	1,801	17.9	24.0	32.5	25.0	17.9	24.1	32.7	25.4
South Carolina	6,582	1,071	1,550	2,438	1,523	6,401	1,026	1,520	2,402	1,453	16.3	23.5	37.0	23.1	16.0	23.7	37.5	22.7
Georgia	16,504	2,665	4,600	6,456	2,843	16,186	2,599	4,533	6,328	2,729	16.1	27.8	39.0	17.2	16.0	28.0	39.1	16.9
Florida	53,864	13,315	14,130	17,799	8,620	43,008	7,818	11,772	15,986	7,432	24.7	26.2	33.0	16.0	18.2	27.4	37.2	17.3
E. SOUTH CENTRAL:																		
Kentucky	30,906	3,258	5,097	16,962	5,589	30,780	3,227	5,072	16,923	5,558	10.5	16.5	54.9	18.1	10.5	16.5	55.0	18.1
Tennessee	15,648	1,803	3,373	6,915	3,557	15,478	1,768	3,343	6,870	3,497	11.5	21.6	44.2	22.7	11.4	21.6	44.4	22.6
Alabama	18,027	2,268	4,221	7,022	4,516	17,662	2,165	4,163	6,946	4,388	12.6	23.4	39.0	25.1	12.3	23.6	39.3	24.8
Mississippi	8,408	995	2,165	3,524	1,724	8,019	911	2,091	3,389	1,628	11.8	25.7	41.9	20.5	11.4	26.1	42.3	20.3
W. SOUTH CENTRAL:																		
Arkansas	14,137	1,147	2,591	6,754	3,645	13,975	1,123	2,565	6,710	3,577	8.1	18.3	47.8	25.8	8.0	18.4	48.0	25.6
Louisiana	46,427	5,061	9,128	19,395	12,843	44,871	4,773	9,006	19,171	11,921	10.9	19.7	41.8	27.7	10.6	20.1	42.7	26.6
Oklahoma	40,432	7,004	6,886	17,476	9,066	39,968	6,901	6,828	17,333	8,906	17.3	17.0	43.2	22.4	17.3	17.1	43.4	22.3
Texas	363,832	158,338	63,536	87,963	53,995	360,519	156,804	63,005	87,454	53,256	43.5	17.5	24.2	14.8	43.5	17.5	24.3	14.8
MOUNTAIN:																		
Montana	95,591	15,962	26,467	38,870	14,292	93,620	15,583	26,008	38,199	13,830	16.7	27.7	40.7	15.0	16.6	27.8	40.8	14.8
Idaho	40,747	6,804	9,543	20,253	4,147	38,963	6,224	9,074	19,727	3,938	16.7	23.4	49.7	10.2	16.0	23.3	50.6	10.1
Wyoming	26,507	6,502	7,892	8,550	3,623	25,255	6,076	7,334	8,330	3,515	24.5	29.7	32.2	13.6	24.1	29.0	33.0	13.9
Colorado	119,138	22,189	30,388	54,712	11,849	116,954	21,453	29,525	54,383	11,593	18.6	25.5	45.9	9.9	18.3	25.2	46.5	9.9
New Mexico	29,808	13,973	6,444	6,512	2,879	29,077	13,627	6,266	6,390	2,794	46.9	21.6	21.8	9.7	46.9	21.5	22.0	9.6
Arizona	80,566	44,284	15,580	12,777	7,925	78,099	43,588	15,029	12,074	7,408	55.0	19.3	15.9	9.8	55.8	19.2	15.5	9.5
Utah	59,200	10,487	14,838	30,007	3,868	56,455	9,444	13,649	29,637	3,725	17.7	25.1	50.7	6.5	16.7	24.2	52.5	6.6
Nevada	16,003	3,604	4,554	5,697	2,148	14,802	3,332	4,150	5,258	2,062	22.5	28.5	35.6	13.4	22.5	28.0	35.5	13.9
PACIFIC:																		
Washington	265,292	48,373	74,294	111,633	30,992	250,055	42,204	68,930	109,366	29,555	18.2	28.0	42.1	11.7	16.9	27.6	43.7	11.8
Oregon	107,644	17,496	29,341	52,641	8,166	102,151	15,958	27,759	50,699	7,735	16.3	27.3	48.9	7.6	15.6	27.2	49.6	7.6
California	757,625	185,538	202,751	288,290	81,046	681,662	158,613	176,919	270,288	75,842	24.5	26.8	38.1	10.7	23.3	26.0	39.7	11.1

YEAR OF IMMIGRATION.   785

TABLE 6.—FOREIGN-BORN MALE POPULATION BY YEAR OF IMMIGRATION, BY DIVISIONS AND STATES: 1920.

DIVISION AND STATE.	Total foreign-born males: 1920	YEAR OF IMMIGRATION.							PER CENT OF TOTAL ARRIVING IN—						
		1918–1919	1916–1917	1911–1915	1906–1910	1901–1905	1900 or earlier	Year not reported.	1918–1919	1916–1917	1911–1915	1906–1910	1901–1905	1900 or earlier.	Year not reported.
United States	7,675,485	167,212	158,615	1,301,775	1,288,152	1,057,498	3,168,590	533,593	2.2	2.1	17.0	16.8	13.8	41.3	7.0
GEOGRAPHIC DIVISIONS:															
New England	956,111	19,192	22,224	164,243	161,596	133,173	415,262	40,421	2.0	2.3	17.2	16.9	13.9	43.4	4.2
Middle Atlantic	2,647,050	41,870	40,854	500,267	506,043	446,285	976,960	134,771	1.6	1.5	18.9	19.1	16.9	36.9	5.1
East North Central	1,816,081	19,944	22,768	335,702	309,365	228,596	769,016	130,690	1.1	1.3	18.5	17.0	12.6	42.3	7.2
West North Central	781,943	7,143	9,011	74,446	87,313	80,719	450,535	72,776	0.9	1.2	9.5	11.2	10.3	57.6	9.3
South Atlantic	194,364	4,883	5,526	36,522	32,911	25,810	67,610	21,102	2.5	2.8	18.8	16.9	13.3	34.8	10.9
East South Central	42,908	513	415	4,431	5,221	4,391	20,592	7,405	1.2	1.0	10.3	12.2	10.2	47.9	17.2
West South Central	264,915	30,945	19,593	45,690	28,777	18,613	79,548	41,749	11.7	7.4	17.2	10.9	7.0	30.0	15.8
Mountain	282,660	15,435	14,813	43,854	43,882	31,634	107,732	25,310	5.5	5.2	15.5	15.5	11.2	38.1	9.0
Pacific	689,343	27,287	23,411	96,620	113,044	88,277	281,335	59,369	4.0	3.4	14.0	16.4	12.8	40.8	8.6
NEW ENGLAND:															
Maine	56,098	2,632	1,708	7,458	7,289	6,386	25,744	4,881	4.7	3.0	13.3	13.0	11.4	45.9	8.7
New Hampshire	46,973	1,714	1,354	6,857	6,538	4,716	21,551	4,243	3.6	2.9	14.6	13.9	10.0	45.9	9.0
Vermont	23,733	1,359	957	3,418	3,175	2,670	10,349	1,805	5.7	4.0	14.4	13.4	11.3	43.6	7.6
Massachusetts	540,428	9,337	12,350	92,695	92,064	75,331	242,259	16,392	1.7	2.3	17.2	17.0	13.9	44.8	3.0
Rhode Island	87,450	1,649	2,100	13,205	14,353	12,322	39,637	4,184	1.9	2.4	15.1	16.4	14.1	45.3	4.8
Connecticut	201,429	2,501	3,755	40,610	38,177	31,748	75,722	8,916	1.2	1.9	20.2	19.0	15.8	37.6	4.4
MIDDLE ATLANTIC:															
New York	1,465,875	31,794	25,940	259,827	275,624	247,426	550,806	74,458	2.2	1.8	17.7	18.8	16.9	37.6	5.1
New Jersey	394,144	4,072	5,356	74,709	77,271	65,005	150,420	17,311	1.0	1.4	19.0	19.6	16.5	38.2	4.4
Pennsylvania	787,031	6,004	9,558	165,731	153,148	133,854	275,734	43,002	0.8	1.2	21.1	19.5	17.0	35.0	5.5
EAST NORTH CENTRAL:															
Ohio	392,668	3,695	5,990	93,679	76,556	55,283	135,588	21,877	0.9	1.5	23.9	19.5	14.1	34.5	5.6
Indiana	88,576	613	1,137	15,361	14,952	10,059	35,688	10,766	0.7	1.3	17.3	16.9	11.4	40.3	12.2
Illinois	660,269	4,391	6,062	108,511	118,063	92,694	282,175	48,373	0.7	0.9	16.4	17.9	14.0	42.7	7.3
Michigan	415,539	10,277	7,988	88,221	68,427	44,902	165,517	30,207	2.5	1.9	21.2	16.5	10.8	39.8	7.3
Wisconsin	259,029	968	1,591	29,930	31,367	25,658	150,048	19,467	0.4	0.6	11.6	12.1	9.9	57.9	7.5
WEST NORTH CENTRAL:															
Minnesota	279,099	1,652	2,542	28,119	32,514	32,058	165,642	16,572	0.6	0.9	10.1	11.6	11.5	59.3	5.9
Iowa	127,309	1,075	1,371	12,387	11,886	9,122	77,643	13,885	0.8	1.1	9.7	9.3	7.2	61.0	10.9
Missouri	104,079	969	1,059	10,754	14,164	12,249	52,958	11,926	0.9	1.0	10.3	13.6	11.8	50.9	11.5
North Dakota	75,641	301	495	5,740	9,348	11,678	40,657	7,422	0.4	0.7	7.6	12.4	15.4	53.7	9.8
South Dakota	47,728	288	305	3,585	5,124	4,636	28,543	5,247	0.6	0.6	7.5	10.7	9.7	59.8	11.0
Nebraska	85,072	735	1,015	8,352	8,782	6,438	50,356	9,394	0.9	1.2	9.8	10.3	7.6	59.2	11.0
Kansas	62,955	2,123	2,224	5,509	5,495	4,538	34,736	8,330	3.4	3.5	8.8	8.7	7.2	55.2	13.2
SOUTH ATLANTIC:															
Delaware	11,443	146	184	2,631	2,070	1,649	3,661	1,102	1.3	1.6	23.0	18.1	14.4	32.0	9.6
Maryland	55,486	544	653	9,207	8,510	8,327	25,384	2,861	1.0	1.2	16.6	15.3	15.0	45.7	5.2
District of Columbia	15,799	287	312	2,109	2,466	2,034	6,274	2,317	1.8	2.0	13.3	15.6	12.9	39.7	14.7
Virginia	19,870	725	727	3,158	3,125	2,496	6,729	2,910	3.6	3.7	15.9	15.7	12.6	33.9	14.6
West Virginia	42,084	585	2,064	12,688	9,039	5,568	7,774	4,366	1.4	4.9	30.1	21.5	13.2	18.5	10.4
North Carolina	4,483	92	84	654	629	512	1,555	957	2.1	1.9	14.6	14.0	11.4	34.7	21.3
South Carolina	4,243	54	62	656	630	454	1,565	822	1.3	1.5	15.5	14.8	10.7	36.9	19.4
Georgia	10,334	147	172	1,373	1,705	1,309	4,085	1,543	1.4	1.7	13.3	16.5	12.7	39.5	14.9
Florida	30,022	2,303	1,268	4,046	4,737	3,461	10,583	4,224	7.5	4.1	13.2	15.5	11.3	34.6	13.8
EAST SOUTH CENTRAL:															
Kentucky	17,578	147	181	2,004	2,019	1,445	9,448	2,384	0.8	0.7	11.4	11.5	8.2	53.7	13.6
Tennessee	9,159	143	93	826	1,096	980	4,245	1,776	1.6	1.0	9.0	12.0	10.7	46.3	19.4
Alabama	10,911	156	135	1,120	1,443	1,273	4,501	2,283	1.4	1.2	10.3	13.2	11.7	41.3	20.9
Mississippi	5,820	67	56	481	663	693	2,398	962	1.3	1.1	9.0	12.5	13.0	45.1	18.1
WEST SOUTH CENTRAL:															
Arkansas	8,728	67	83	601	869	813	4,411	1,884	0.8	1.0	6.9	10.0	9.3	50.5	21.6
Louisiana	28,120	992	483	1,724	2,451	2,974	11,937	7,559	3.5	1.7	6.1	8.7	10.6	42.5	26.9
Oklahoma	25,322	1,624	878	2,168	2,422	1,955	11,136	5,139	6.4	3.5	8.6	9.6	7.7	44.0	20.3
Texas	202,745	28,262	18,149	41,197	23,035	12,871	52,064	27,167	13.9	9.0	20.3	11.4	6.3	25.7	13.4
MOUNTAIN:															
Montana	59,818	638	1,176	8,264	10,197	7,665	25,012	6,866	1.1	2.0	13.8	17.0	12.8	41.8	11.5
Idaho	26,293	776	706	3,102	3,739	2,818	12,946	2,206	3.0	2.7	11.8	14.2	10.7	49.2	8.4
Wyoming	18,065	612	613	3,312	3,511	2,307	5,600	2,110	3.4	3.4	18.3	19.4	12.8	31.0	11.7
Colorado	69,798	1,776	2,246	9,294	10,307	8,603	32,078	5,494	2.5	3.2	13.3	14.8	12.3	46.0	7.9
New Mexico	17,375	1,651	2,159	4,086	2,512	1,484	4,174	1,309	9.5	12.4	23.5	14.5	8.5	24.0	7.5
Arizona	46,403	8,766	6,589	9,341	5,944	3,458	8,072	4,233	18.9	14.2	20.1	12.8	7.5	17.4	9.1
Utah	33,087	737	869	4,642	5,579	3,763	15,662	1,835	2.2	2.6	14.0	16.9	11.4	47.3	5.5
Nevada	11,821	479	455	1,813	2,093	1,536	4,188	1,257	4.1	3.8	15.3	17.7	13.0	35.4	10.6
PACIFIC:															
Washington	164,158	5,107	4,021	20,386	27,856	21,801	70,930	14,057	3.1	2.4	12.4	17.0	13.3	43.2	8.6
Oregon	66,798	1,568	1,084	7,958	11,117	8,264	32,809	3,998	2.3	1.6	11.9	16.6	12.4	49.1	6.0
California	458,387	20,612	18,306	68,276	74,071	58,212	177,596	41,314	4.5	4.0	14.9	16.2	12.7	38.7	9.0

75647°—22——50

786

POPULATION.

TABLE 7.—FOREIGN-BORN FEMALE POPULATION BY YEAR OF IMMIGRATION, BY DIVISIONS AND STATES: 1920.

DIVISION AND STATE.	Total foreign-born females: 1920	YEAR OF IMMIGRATION.							PER CENT OF TOTAL ARRIVING IN—						
		1918–1919	1916–1917	1911–1915	1906–1910	1901–1905	1900 or earlier.	Year not reported.	1918–1919	1916–1917	1911–1915	1906–1910	1901–1905	1900 or earlier.	Year not reported.
United States......	6,245,257	132,481	134,791	956,089	941,716	756,766	2,592,647	730,767	2.1	2.2	15.3	15.1	12.1	41.5	11.7
GEOGRAPHIC DIVISIONS:															
New England.........	929,834	19,845	23,790	140,885	143,139	117,062	417,181	67,932	2.1	2.6	15.2	15.4	12.6	44.9	7.3
Middle Atlantic......	2,313,368	32,578	38,286	401,265	413,586	343,219	872,953	211,481	1.4	1.7	17.3	17.9	14.8	37.7	9.1
East North Central....	1,416,060	15,929	16,795	217,254	201,903	150,968	620,231	192,980	1.1	1.2	15.3	14.3	10.7	43.8	13.6
West North Central....	593,710	5,544	6,536	46,249	54,934	51,149	324,496	104,802	0.9	1.1	7.8	9.3	8.6	54.7	17.7
South Atlantic........	136,173	3,599	2,723	20,004	20,906	16,366	51,040	21,535	2.6	2.0	14.7	15.4	12.0	37.5	15.8
East South Central....	30,021	422	253	2,290	2,950	2,294	13,831	7,981	1.4	0.8	7.6	9.8	7.6	46.1	26.6
West South Central....	199,913	19,131	16,990	39,201	21,510	13,241	52,040	37,800	9.6	8.5	19.6	10.8	6.6	20.0	18.9
Mountain............	184,960	11,325	11,114	27,264	23,430	16,760	69,646	25,421	6.1	6.0	14.7	12.7	9.1	37.7	13.7
Pacific..............	441,218	24,108	18,304	61,677	59,358	45,707	171,229	60,835	5.5	4.1	14.0	13.5	10.4	38.8	13.8
NEW ENGLAND:															
Maine..............	51,716	2,357	1,696	5,668	6,070	5,301	22,359	8,265	4.6	3.3	11.0	11.7	10.3	43.2	16.0
New Hampshire......	44,424	1,208	1,239	5,328	5,287	4,134	20,413	6,815	2.7	2.8	12.0	11.9	9.3	46.0	15.3
Vermont............	20,825	1,292	872	2,747	2,548	1,995	8,773	2,598	6.2	4.2	13.2	12.2	9.6	42.1	12.5
Massachusetts........	548,120	10,950	14,204	83,346	85,155	69,662	256,808	27,995	2.0	2.6	15.2	15.5	12.7	46.9	5.1
Rhode Island........	87,739	1,763	2,320	11,947	13,224	11,141	39,558	7,786	2.0	2.6	13.6	15.1	12.7	45.1	8.9
Connecticut..........	177,010	2,275	3,459	31,849	30,855	24,829	69,270	14,473	1.3	2.0	18.0	17.4	14.0	39.1	8.2
MIDDLE ATLANTIC:															
New York...........	1,359,500	23,522	26,529	233,810	244,292	200,985	507,339	123,023	1.7	2.0	17.2	18.0	14.8	37.3	9.0
New Jersey..........	348,342	3,803	4,845	59,713	62,463	50,081	136,383	31,054	1.1	1.4	17.1	17.9	14.4	39.2	8.9
Pennsylvania........	605,526	5,253	6,912	107,742	106,831	92,153	229,231	57,404	0.9	1.1	17.8	17.6	15.2	37.9	9.5
EAST NORTH CENTRAL:															
Ohio...............	287,784	2,895	3,468	55,132	47,687	36,131	113,236	29,235	1.0	1.2	19.2	16.6	12.6	39.3	10.2
Indiana.............	62,752	494	464	8,031	7,670	5,379	25,141	15,573	0.8	0.7	12.8	12.2	8.6	40.1	24.8
Illinois.............	550,315	4,473	5,389	83,096	85,663	64,098	235,788	71,808	0.8	1.0	15.1	15.6	11.6	42.8	13.0
Michigan............	313,753	7,205	6,425	52,418	41,624	29,118	130,366	46,597	2.3	2.0	16.7	13.3	9.3	41.6	14.9
Wisconsin...........	201,456	862	1,049	18,577	19,259	16,242	115,700	29,767	0.4	0.5	9.2	9.6	8.1	57.4	14.8
WEST NORTH CENTRAL:															
Minnesota...........	207,696	1,594	2,050	16,614	19,521	20,218	121,373	26,326	0.8	1.0	8.0	9.4	9.7	58.4	12.7
Iowa...............	98,625	858	873	7,114	6,747	5,672	58,449	18,912	0.9	0.9	7.2	6.8	5.8	59.3	19.2
Missouri............	82,756	831	814	7,897	9,706	7,634	39,134	16,740	1.0	1.0	9.5	11.7	9.2	47.3	20.2
North Dakota........	56,222	302	483	3,723	6,630	7,848	24,866	12,370	0.5	0.9	6.6	11.8	14.0	44.2	22.0
South Dakota........	34,806	234	187	1,983	3,013	2,849	19,234	7,306	0.7	0.5	5.7	8.7	8.2	55.3	21.0
Nebraska...........	65,593	472	549	5,158	5,577	3,998	36,267	13,572	0.7	0.8	7.9	8.5	6.1	55.3	20.7
Kansas.............	48,012	1,253	1,580	3,760	3,740	2,930	25,173	9,576	2.6	3.3	7.8	7.8	6.1	52.4	19.9
SOUTH ATLANTIC:															
Delaware...........	8,458	94	126	1,594	1,377	973	2,946	1,348	1.1	1.5	18.8	16.3	11.5	34.8	15.9
Maryland...........	47,693	438	431	6,273	6,941	6,382	23,309	3,919	0.9	0.9	13.2	14.6	13.4	48.9	8.2
District of Columbia....	13,566	381	263	1,486	1,872	1,471	5,293	2,800	2.8	1.9	11.0	13.8	10.8	39.0	20.6
Virginia............	11,835	296	243	1,389	1,767	1,377	3,758	3,005	2.5	2.1	11.7	14.9	11.6	31.8	25.4
West Virginia........	20,021	375	518	4,975	4,099	2,427	4,464	3,163	1.9	2.6	24.8	20.5	12.1	22.3	15.8
North Carolina.......	2,789	101	45	328	346	256	810	903	3.6	1.6	11.8	12.4	9.2	29.0	32.4
South Carolina.......	2,339	48	36	215	264	202	873	701	2.1	1.5	9.2	11.3	8.6	37.3	30.0
Georgia.............	6,230	168	89	716	889	697	2,371	1,300	2.7	1.4	11.5	14.3	11.2	38.1	20.9
Florida.............	23,242	1,698	972	3,028	3,351	2,581	7,216	4,396	7.3	4.2	13.0	14.4	11.1	31.0	18.9
EAST SOUTH CENTRAL:															
Kentucky...........	13,328	123	69	784	929	704	7,514	3,205	0.9	0.5	5.9	7.0	5.3	56.4	24.0
Tennessee...........	6,489	126	59	556	726	571	2,670	1,781	1.9	0.9	8.6	11.2	8.8	41.1	27.4
Alabama............	7,116	134	85	638	863	642	2,521	2,233	1.9	1.2	9.0	12.1	9.0	35.4	31.4
Mississippi..........	3,088	39	40	312	432	377	1,126	762	1.3	1.3	10.1	14.0	12.2	36.5	24.7
WEST SOUTH CENTRAL:															
Arkansas...........	5,409	45	49	302	456	453	2,343	1,761	0.8	0.9	5.6	8.4	8.4	43.3	32.6
Louisiana...........	18,307	581	267	1,014	1,720	1,983	7,458	5,284	3.2	1.5	5.5	9.4	10.8	40.7	28.9
Oklahoma...........	15,110	640	457	1,237	1,421	1,088	6,340	3,927	4.2	3.0	8.2	9.4	7.2	42.0	26.0
Texas..............	161,087	17,865	16,217	36,648	17,913	9,717	35,899	26,828	11.1	10.1	22.8	11.1	6.0	22.3	16.7
MOUNTAIN:															
Montana............	35,773	546	854	4,484	4,894	3,711	13,858	7,426	1.5	2.4	12.5	13.7	10.4	38.7	20.8
Idaho..............	14,454	510	336	1,874	1,682	1,304	7,307	1,941	3.5	2.3	9.5	11.6	9.0	50.6	13.4
Wyoming...........	8,502	299	301	1,365	1,253	821	2,950	1,513	3.5	3.5	16.1	14.7	9.7	34.7	17.8
Colorado...........	49,340	1,301	1,602	5,970	6,316	5,162	22,634	6,355	2.6	3.2	12.1	12.8	10.5	45.9	12.9
New Mexico.........	12,433	1,156	1,809	3,112	1,532	916	2,338	1,570	9.3	14.5	25.0	12.3	7.4	18.8	12.6
Arizona............	34,163	6,679	5,430	7,479	3,959	2,219	4,705	3,692	19.6	15.9	21.9	11.6	6.5	13.8	10.8
Utah...............	26,113	645	624	2,970	3,220	2,276	14,345	2,033	2.5	2.4	11.4	12.3	8.7	54.9	7.8
Nevada............	4,182	189	158	510	574	351	1,509	891	4.5	3.8	12.2	13.7	8.4	36.1	21.3
PACIFIC:															
Washington..........	101,134	4,658	2,746	11,455	13,357	11,280	40,703	16,935	4.6	2.7	11.3	13.2	11.2	40.2	16.7
Oregon.............	40,846	1,346	767	4,773	5,619	4,341	19,832	4,168	3.3	1.9	11.7	13.8	10.6	48.6	10.2
California...........	299,238	18,104	14,791	45,449	40,382	30,086	110,694	39,732	6.1	4.9	15.2	13.5	10.1	37.0	13.3

YEAR OF IMMIGRATION.

787

TABLE 8.—FOREIGN-BORN NEGROES, INDIANS, CHINESE, AND JAPANESE, BY YEAR OF IMMIGRATION, FOR SELECTED STATES: 1920.

[The states for which figures are presented in this table are those having 500 or more foreign-born inhabitants of the specified race.]

CLASS OF POPULATION AND STATE.	Total foreign born of specified race: 1920	YEAR OF IMMIGRATION.										
		1919	1918	1917	1916	1915	1914	1911–1913	1906–1910	1901–1905	1900 or earlier.	Year not reported.
NEGRO.												
United States	73,803	5,938	3,628	4,537	3,698	3,213	3,791	8,687	10,779	6,194	10,105	13,233
California	1,123	48	33	36	29	33	28	92	150	103	282	289
Connecticut	1,363	34	52	115	82	117	124	229	198	106	147	159
Florida	10,665	1,559	740	567	507	405	484	1,210	1,578	731	1,752	1,152
Illinois	1,245	27	38	31	23	16	27	84	102	73	296	528
Louisiana	1,217	64	63	27	14	22	15	34	38	35	107	798
Maryland	696	34	8	22	10	25	33	75	101	66	195	127
Massachusetts	9,037	352	249	476	514	419	583	1,333	1,508	1,012	1,830	761
Michigan	1,769	60	50	55	51	40	56	118	190	158	483	502
New Jersey	2,634	75	90	129	110	96	117	308	440	231	428	610
New York	31,971	3,193	1,883	2,594	1,902	1,614	1,829	4,173	5,057	2,665	2,263	4,798
Ohio	951	23	6	15	24	22	25	84	103	90	276	283
Pennsylvania	3,020	103	96	122	106	97	120	267	415	292	541	861
Rhode Island	1,496	38	55	110	92	117	124	237	213	163	221	126
Texas	1,532	129	77	71	62	52	66	112	134	94	207	528
Virginia	656	24	30	33	44	35	33	59	67	43	92	196
All other states	4,428	175	158	134	128	103	147	272	479	332	985	1,515
INDIAN.												
United States	6,299	644	429	435	558	374	306	497	563	321	837	1,335
Arizona	1,112	48	28	55	56	53	53	51	107	97	187	377
California	1,993	212	174	241	238	178	148	198	222	101	105	176
Texas	929	168	90	44	136	47	34	143	79	34	58	96
All other states	2,265	216	137	95	128	96	71	105	155	89	487	686
CHINESE.												
United States	43,107	1,141	584	952	973	1,299	1,166	2,508	4,616	2,639	22,678	4,551
Arizona	726	17	11	24	9	20	16	39	76	17	415	82
California	19,458	457	238	331	454	649	533	1,188	2,154	959	10,740	1,753
Illinois	1,906	49	25	27	47	58	37	96	220	157	908	282
Massachusetts	1,788	54	37	43	61	60	60	111	242	146	896	78
Michigan	512	16	7	14	19	26	26	45	75	31	173	80
Montana	650	4	1	4	9	6	6	18	33	16	344	209
Nevada	531	2	....	13	7	14	9	13	44	29	367	33
New Jersey	920	26	18	28	15	30	24	51	115	76	455	82
New York	4,486	258	90	107	98	113	157	310	506	566	1,965	316
Ohio	621	13	13	17	22	33	28	60	107	31	219	78
Oregon	2,146	10	14	9	15	16	26	76	118	71	1,553	238
Pennsylvania	1,385	22	21	39	34	50	48	79	185	109	676	122
Texas	545	3	4	122	24	14	7	14	33	17	223	84
Washington	1,692	79	29	24	26	44	25	85	152	71	970	187
All other states	5,743	131	76	150	133	166	164	323	556	343	2,774	927
JAPANESE.												
United States	81,338	5,027	3,953	4,120	4,177	4,396	3,755	7,497	18,175	14,526	10,040	5,672
California	51,138	2,837	2,373	2,488	2,710	2,966	2,477	4,830	10,998	9,824	6,819	2,816
Colorado	1,762	72	76	94	88	88	79	186	395	386	166	187
Idaho	1,176	56	51	45	61	59	46	114	227	181	200	136
Montana	883	56	47	27	35	29	31	55	205	156	148	94
Nebraska	640	12	9	16	16	21	18	40	143	91	29	245
Nevada	649	25	27	33	26	31	28	42	186	140	69	42
New York	2,374	354	169	145	112	104	91	187	408	288	258	260
Oregon	3,157	176	164	164	179	181	144	310	819	491	362	167
Utah	2,359	124	112	145	125	125	103	182	632	491	224	96
Washington	12,966	1,061	762	762	664	607	596	1,268	3,212	1,742	1,194	1,098
Wyoming	1,029	52	47	48	42	51	38	90	279	196	101	85
All other states	3,205	202	116	153	124	134	104	243	671	542	470	446

POPULATION.

788

TABLE 9.—FOREIGN-BORN POPULATION BY YEAR OF IMMIGRATION, FOR CITIES HAVING 100,000 INHABITANTS OR MORE: 1920.

CITY.	Total foreign born: 1920	1919	1918	1917	1916	1915	1914	1911-1913	1906-1910	1901-1905	1900 or earlier.	Year not reported.
Akron, Ohio	38,021	569	209	380	840	835	3,240	10,612	8,410	4,160	6,967	1,799
Albany, N. Y.	17,695	95	51	70	110	217	509	1,951	2,814	2,175	9,165	528
Atlanta, Ga.	4,789	102	10	27	42	44	118	375	746	677	1,800	758
Baltimore, Md.	84,809	528	235	333	523	769	2,900	9,692	13,278	12,970	40,870	2,702
Birmingham, Ala.	6,140	51	17	31	42	73	146	406	857	647	2,200	1,580
Boston, Mass.	242,619	2,977	966	1,708	2,774	3,884	7,894	27,733	39,614	33,202	106,342	15,575
Bridgeport, Conn.	46,782	434	220	361	637	713	2,222	7,155	8,918	6,807	14,070	5,155
Buffalo, N. Y.	121,824	1,050	549	701	1,051	1,383	3,886	15,582	16,736	13,512	50,253	17,121
Cambridge, Mass.	33,296	626	218	383	650	646	1,157	4,025	5,340	4,420	15,500	331
Camden, N. J.	20,354	191	50	97	176	318	841	3,420	3,696	2,744	6,721	2,100
Chicago, Ill.	808,558	3,988	1,737	2,775	4,876	8,238	27,928	106,717	148,603	111,372	327,286	65,038
Cincinnati, Ohio	42,921	178	55	107	175	275	973	3,029	5,512	4,281	24,939	3,397
Cleveland, Ohio	240,173	1,604	490	963	1,786	3,143	11,188	42,884	49,162	37,010	78,171	12,872
Columbus, Ohio	16,187	100	29	49	137	182	497	1,601	2,110	1,680	6,670	3,033
Dallas, Tex	8,801	454	259	184	200	166	281	680	903	719	2,900	2,055
Dayton, Ohio	13,165	94	29	59	88	113	469	1,920	2,344	1,609	5,621	819
Denver, Colo.	38,230	400	300	293	429	364	714	2,559	4,894	4,427	21,984	1,806
Des Moines, Iowa	11,269	93	30	46	91	111	242	904	1,390	1,229	5,303	1,680
Detroit, Mich.	290,884	8,884	2,461	3,136	5,021	6,660	15,703	58,568	56,096	33,068	77,754	22,033
Fall River, Mass.	42,421	308	175	358	739	818	822	3,872	6,009	5,769	21,917	1,634
Fort Worth, Tex.	7,502	1,079	558	407	349	270	209	526	552	315	1,292	1,945
Grand Rapids, Mich.	28,427	114	42	98	167	216	633	2,823	3,807	2,028	13,941	3,663
Hartford, Conn.	40,912	394	105	374	592	680	1,678	6,479	8,051	5,952	15,634	973
Houston, Tex.	12,088	774	444	384	380	288	328	1,035	1,212	980	4,020	2,243
Indianapolis, Ind.	17,096	87	15	44	130	146	465	1,486	2,058	1,480	7,896	3,283
Jersey City, N. J.	76,294	450	154	208	631	860	2,518	9,003	13,755	11,199	34,091	2,756
Kansas City, Kans.	11,721	297	303	424	420	273	437	1,615	1,849	1,217	4,006	880
Kansas City, Mo.	27,583	411	267	318	384	431	634	2,135	3,524	2,972	11,331	5,176
Los Angeles, Calif.	122,131	5,909	2,965	3,000	3,166	3,213	8,714	11,630	19,327	14,748	44,092	10,367
Louisville, Ky.	11,667	44	10	8	21	33	122	379	833	713	7,081	2,423
Lowell, Mass.	38,116	484	197	490	807	840	1,118	3,814	5,527	4,381	10,913	545
Memphis, Tenn.	5,844	47	24	12	31	63	120	435	755	722	2,280	1,355
Milwaukee, Wis.	110,160	308	119	303	556	750	3,659	14,208	17,317	12,071	52,884	7,985
Minneapolis, Minn.	88,248	756	236	401	1,010	1,236	2,518	7,759	12,727	12,068	43,855	5,682
Nashville, Tenn.	2,412	28	1	11	24	9	76	130	295	202	1,159	477
New Bedford, Mass.	51,078	1,513	515	1,501	2,092	1,743	1,927	6,012	8,987	6,622	18,835	731
New Haven, Conn.	46,124	292	95	256	482	704	1,383	5,087	8,416	7,581	18,058	3,170
New Orleans, La.	27,365	716	840	345	230	232	398	924	2,116	2,192	10,811	9,055
New York, N. Y.	2,028,160	34,005	9,631	16,900	24,012	30,584	77,416	250,196	393,860	348,602	726,634	110,320
Bronx borough	267,742	1,282	466	1,048	1,738	2,813	7,795	27,313	52,765	51,314	103,855	17,343
Brooklyn borough	666,188	8,946	2,531	4,631	6,231	8,414	22,274	75,051	126,475	110,701	254,710	37,224
Manhattan borough	950,264	21,126	6,314	10,630	14,989	17,982	44,025	141,429	193,909	158,334	297,007	44,519
Queens borough	112,171	794	178	355	707	949	2,457	9,117	16,111	15,039	58,165	8,299
Richmond borough	31,795	1,857	142	236	347	426	865	3,286	4,000	4,214	12,887	2,935
Newark, N. J.	117,549	1,006	383	649	1,059	1,422	4,089	15,819	22,532	19,042	43,884	7,664
Norfolk, Va.	6,998	297	179	232	249	168	283	787	1,219	846	1,963	775
Oakland, Calif.	49,895	820	413	546	695	889	1,220	4,189	7,812	6,108	23,558	3,645
Omaha, Nebr.	35,645	211	123	183	342	449	1,100	4,031	5,765	3,912	15,180	4,349
Paterson, N. J.	45,342	324	98	281	554	535	1,378	5,108	7,094	6,707	19,750	2,728
Philadelphia, Pa.	400,744	2,665	1,036	1,727	3,152	4,577	14,684	52,040	73,974	63,995	158,448	24,446
Pittsburgh, Pa.	120,792	603	180	404	788	1,229	3,781	15,468	20,078	19,713	52,305	6,243
Portland, Oreg.	49,778	1,205	412	452	445	619	1,337	4,678	9,148	6,428	22,840	2,205
Providence, R. I.	69,895	606	224	491	760	904	1,948	7,176	11,343	10,237	31,522	4,084
Reading, Pa.	9,573	55	20	49	202	145	310	1,445	1,819	1,558	3,800	670
Richmond, Va.	4,713	50	7	29	53	70	122	434	691	638	1,737	882
Rochester, N. Y.	71,411	948	301	419	828	981	2,726	10,399	13,405	8,805	25,188	7,411
St. Louis, Mo.	103,526	452	195	309	523	729	2,585	9,070	16,389	13,534	49,603	10,237
St. Paul, Minn.	51,722	342	89	218	337	539	1,410	4,048	6,405	5,610	28,219	4,505
Salt Lake City, Utah	19,897	263	184	204	238	335	487	1,549	3,115	2,222	10,536	764
San Antonio, Tex.	36,824	4,763	1,462	1,673	2,054	2,021	1,988	3,981	3,825	2,004	6,698	6,355
San Francisco, Calif.	149,195	3,553	1,733	1,850	2,216	3,147	4,116	13,901	23,251	18,548	60,705	16,025
Scranton, Pa.	28,587	90	49	70	93	189	646	2,536	4,200	3,796	13,315	3,544
Seattle, Wash.	80,976	3,061	1,531	1,843	1,675	1,717	2,388	6,986	13,016	10,040	28,204	11,015
Spokane, Wash.	17,096	454	136	141	260	185	338	994	2,400	2,003	9,009	1,007
Springfield, Mass.	31,461	420	139	218	486	460	1,074	4,159	5,721	4,405	13,253	1,066
Syracuse, N. Y.	32,383	295	126	179	332	432	1,048	4,155	5,584	4,100	13,969	2,163
Toledo, Ohio	38,296	341	86	149	287	373	1,609	5,480	5,545	4,462	17,859	2,155
Trenton, N. J.	30,168	213	84	130	248	303	1,391	5,114	6,093	4,961	9,844	1,097
Washington, D. C.	29,365	489	179	238	342	376	752	2,467	4,383	3,505	11,567	5,117
Wilmington, Del.	16,387	120	55	85	187	241	705	2,743	2,911	2,259	5,424	1,607
Worcester, Mass.	53,527	434	211	344	951	774	1,651	7,176	9,177	7,240	23,355	2,214
Yonkers, N. Y.	25,796	205	82	111	206	244	745	2,825	4,747	3,902	11,926	803
Youngstown, Ohio	33,945	198	64	216	466	494	2,040	7,289	7,117	4,849	9,082	2,130

YEAR OF IMMIGRATION.

789

TABLE **9.**—FOREIGN-BORN POPULATION BY YEAR OF IMMIGRATION, FOR CITIES HAVING 100,000 INHABITANTS OR MORE: 1920—Continued.

CITY.	PER CENT OF TOTAL ARRIVING IN—										
	1919	1918	1917	1916	1915	1914	1911-1913	1906-1910	1901-1905	1900 or earlier.	Year not reported.
Akron, Ohio	1.5	0.5	1.0	2.2	2.2	8.5	27.9	22.1	10.9	18.3	4.7
Albany, N. Y	0.5	0.3	0.4	0.6	1.2	2.0	11.1	15.9	12.3	51.8	3.0
Atlanta, Ga	2.1	0.2	0.6	0.9	0.9	2.5	7.8	15.6	14.1	39.5	15.8
Baltimore, Md	0.6	0.3	0.4	0.6	0.9	3.4	11.4	15.7	15.3	48.2	3.2
Birmingham, Ala	0.8	0.3	0.5	0.7	1.2	2.4	8.1	14.0	10.5	35.8	25.7
Boston, Mass	1.2	0.4	0.7	1.1	1.6	3.8	11.4	16.3	13.7	43.8	6.4
Bridgeport, Conn	0.9	0.5	0.8	1.4	1.5	4.7	15.3	19.1	14.7	30.1	11.0
Buffalo, N. Y	0.9	0.5	0.6	0.9	1.1	3.2	12.8	13.7	11.1	41.3	14.1
Cambridge, Mass	1.9	0.7	1.2	2.0	1.9	3.5	12.1	16.0	13.3	46.6	1.0
Camden, N. J	0.9	0.2	0.5	0.9	1.6	4.1	16.8	18.2	13.5	33.0	10.3
Chicago, Ill	0.5	0.2	0.3	0.6	1.0	3.5	13.2	18.4	13.8	40.5	8.0
Cincinnati, Ohio	0.4	0.1	0.2	0.4	0.6	2.3	7.1	12.8	10.0	58.1	7.9
Cleveland, Ohio	0.7	0.2	0.4	0.7	1.3	4.7	17.9	20.5	15.8	32.5	5.4
Columbus, Ohio	0.6	0.2	0.3	0.8	1.1	3.1	10.4	13.0	10.4	41.3	18.7
Dallas, Tex	5.2	2.0	2.1	2.3	1.9	3.2	7.7	10.3	8.2	33.0	23.3
Dayton, Ohio	0.7	0.2	0.4	0.7	0.9	3.6	14.6	17.8	12.2	42.7	6.2
Denver, Colo	1.0	0.8	0.8	1.1	1.0	1.9	6.7	12.8	11.6	57.5	4.9
Des Moines, Iowa	0.8	0.3	0.4	0.8	1.0	2.1	8.6	12.3	10.9	47.9	14.9
Detroit, Mich	3.1	0.8	1.1	2.0	2.3	5.4	20.1	19.3	11.4	26.7	7.8
Fall River, Mass	0.7	0.4	0.8	1.7	1.9	1.9	9.1	14.2	13.6	51.7	3.9
Fort Worth, Tex	14.4	7.4	5.4	4.7	3.6	2.8	7.0	7.4	4.2	17.2	25.9
Grand Rapids, Mich	0.4	0.1	0.3	0.6	0.8	2.2	9.9	13.4	10.3	49.0	12.9
Hartford, Conn	1.0	0.3	0.9	1.4	1.7	4.1	15.8	19.7	14.5	38.2	2.4
Houston, Tex	6.4	3.7	3.2	3.1	2.4	2.7	8.6	10.0	8.1	33.3	18.6
Indianapolis, Ind	0.5	0.1	0.3	0.8	0.9	2.7	8.7	12.0	8.7	46.2	10.2
Jersey City, N. J	0.6	0.2	0.4	0.8	1.1	3.3	12.0	18.0	14.7	44.7	3.6
Kansas City, Kans	2.5	2.6	3.6	3.6	2.3	3.7	13.8	15.8	10.4	34.2	7.5
Kansas City, Mo	1.5	1.0	1.2	1.4	1.6	2.3	7.7	12.8	10.8	41.1	18.8
Los Angeles, Calif	4.8	2.4	2.5	2.6	2.6	3.0	9.5	15.8	12.1	36.1	8.5
Louisville, Ky	0.4	0.1	0.1	0.2	0.3	1.0	3.2	7.1	6.1	60.7	20.8
Lowell, Mass	1.3	0.5	1.3	2.1	2.2	2.9	10.0	14.5	11.5	52.2	1.4
Memphis, Tenn	0.8	0.4	0.2	0.5	1.1	2.1	7.4	12.9	12.4	39.0	23.2
Milwaukee, Wis	0.3	0.1	0.3	0.5	0.7	3.3	12.9	15.7	11.0	48.0	7.2
Minneapolis, Minn	0.9	0.3	0.5	1.1	1.4	2.9	8.8	14.4	13.7	49.7	6.4
Nashville, Tenn	1.2	(1)	0.5	1.0	0.4	3.2	5.4	12.2	8.4	48.1	19.8
New Bedford, Mass	3.0	1.0	2.9	4.1	3.8	3.8	12.9	17.6	13.0	36.9	1.4
New Haven, Conn	0.6	0.2	0.6	1.0	1.5	3.0	12.3	18.2	16.4	39.2	6.9
New Orleans, La	2.0	1.2	1.3	0.9	0.8	1.5	3.4	7.7	8.0	39.5	33.1
New York, N. Y	1.7	0.5	0.8	1.2	1.5	3.8	12.6	19.4	17.2	35.8	5.4
Bronx borough	0.5	0.2	0.4	0.6	1.1	2.9	10.2	19.7	19.2	38.8	6.5
Brooklyn borough	1.3	0.4	0.7	0.9	1.3	3.3	11.3	19.0	18.0	38.2	5.6
Manhattan borough	2.2	0.7	1.1	1.6	1.9	4.6	14.9	20.4	16.7	31.3	4.7
Queens borough	0.7	0.2	0.3	0.6	0.8	2.2	8.1	14.4	13.4	51.9	7.4
Richmond borough	5.8	0.4	0.7	1.1	1.3	2.7	10.3	14.5	13.3	40.5	9.2
Newark, N. J	0.9	0.3	0.6	0.9	1.2	3.5	13.5	19.2	16.2	37.3	6.5
Norfolk, Va	4.2	2.6	3.3	3.6	2.4	4.0	11.2	17.4	12.1	28.1	11.1
Oakland, Calif	1.6	0.8	1.1	1.4	1.8	2.4	8.4	15.7	12.2	47.2	7.3
Omaha, Nebr	0.6	0.3	0.5	1.0	1.3	3.1	11.3	16.2	11.0	42.6	12.2
Paterson, N. J	0.7	0.2	0.6	1.2	1.2	3.0	11.3	17.0	15.0	43.7	6.0
Philadelphia, Pa	0.7	0.3	0.4	0.8	1.1	3.7	13.0	18.5	16.0	39.5	6.1
Pittsburgh, Pa	0.5	0.1	0.3	0.7	1.0	3.1	12.8	16.6	16.3	43.3	5.2
Portland, Oreg	2.4	0.8	0.9	0.9	1.2	2.7	9.4	18.4	12.9	45.9	4.4
Providence, R. I	0.9	0.3	0.7	1.1	1.3	2.8	10.3	16.2	14.6	45.1	6.7
Reading, Pa	0.6	0.2	0.5	2.1	1.5	3.2	15.1	19.0	16.3	34.5	7.0
Richmond, Va	1.1	0.1	0.6	1.1	1.5	2.6	9.2	14.7	13.5	36.9	18.7
Rochester, N. Y	1.3	0.4	0.6	1.2	1.4	3.8	14.6	18.8	12.3	35.3	10.4
St. Louis, Mo	0.4	0.2	0.3	0.5	0.7	2.5	8.8	15.8	13.1	47.9	9.9
St. Paul, Minn	0.7	0.2	0.4	0.7	1.0	2.7	7.8	12.4	10.8	54.6	8.7
Salt Lake City, Utah	1.3	0.9	1.0	1.2	1.7	2.4	7.8	15.7	11.2	53.0	3.8
San Antonio, Tex	12.9	4.0	4.5	5.6	5.5	5.4	10.8	10.4	5.4	18.2	17.3
San Francisco, Calif	2.4	1.2	1.2	1.5	2.1	2.8	9.4	15.6	12.4	40.7	10.7
Scranton, Pa	0.3	0.2	0.2	0.3	0.7	2.3	8.9	14.9	13.3	46.6	12.4
Seattle, Wash	3.8	1.9	1.7	2.1	2.1	2.9	8.6	16.1	12.4	34.8	13.6
Spokane, Wash	2.7	0.8	0.8	1.5	1.0	2.0	5.8	14.6	11.7	53.2	5.9
Springfield, Mass	1.3	0.4	0.7	1.5	1.5	3.4	13.2	18.2	14.2	42.1	3.4
Syracuse, N. Y	0.9	0.4	0.6	1.0	1.3	3.2	12.8	17.2	12.7	43.1	6.7
Toledo, Ohio	0.9	0.2	0.4	0.7	1.0	4.2	14.2	14.5	11.7	46.6	5.6
Trenton, N. J	0.7	0.3	0.4	0.8	1.3	4.6	17.0	22.2	16.4	32.6	3.6
Washington, D. C	1.7	0.6	0.8	1.2	1.3	2.6	8.4	14.8	11.9	39.4	17.4
Wilmington, Del	0.7	0.3	0.5	1.1	1.5	4.3	16.8	17.8	13.8	33.2	9.8
Worcester, Mass	0.8	0.4	0.6	1.1	1.8	3.1	13.4	17.1	13.5	43.6	4.1
Yonkers, N. Y	0.8	0.3	0.4	0.8	0.9	2.9	11.0	18.4	15.1	46.2	3.1
Youngstown, Ohio	0.6	0.2	0.6	1.4	1.5	6.0	21.5	21.0	14.3	26.8	6.3

[1] Less than one-tenth of 1 per cent.

TABLE 10.—FOREIGN-BORN POPULATION AND FOREIGN-BORN WHITE POPULATION BY YEAR OF IMMIGRATION, FOR CITIES HAVING 100,000 INHABITANTS OR MORE: 1920.

CITY.	YEAR OF IMMIGRATION OF—										PER CENT OF—							
	Foreign-born population.					Foreign-born white population.					Foreign-born population arriving in—				Foreign-born white population arriving in—			
	Total number: 1920	1911–1919	1901–1910	1900 or earlier.	Year not reported.	Total number: 1920	1911–1919	1901–1910	1900 or earlier.	Year not reported.	1911–1919	1901–1910	1900 or earlier.	Year not reported.	1911–1919	1901–1910	1900 or earlier.	Year not reported.
Akron, Ohio	38,021	16,685	12,570	6,967	1,799	37,889	16,642	12,544	6,933	1,770	43.9	33.1	18.3	4.7	43.9	33.1	18.3	4.7
Albany, N. Y.	17,695	3,013	4,989	9,165	528	17,636	3,002	4,974	9,140	520	17.0	28.2	51.8	3.0	17.0	28.2	51.8	2.9
Atlanta, Ga.	4,789	718	1,423	1,890	758	4,738	710	1,415	1,871	742	15.0	20.7	39.5	15.8	15.0	29.9	39.5	15.7
Baltimore, Md.	84,809	14,980	26,257	40,870	2,702	83,911	14,733	26,057	40,572	2,549	17.7	31.0	48.2	3.2	17.6	31.1	48.4	3.0
Birmingham, Ala.	6,140	856	1,504	2,200	1,580	6,084	836	1,497	2,187	1,564	13.9	24.5	35.8	25.7	13.7	24.6	35.9	25.7
Boston, Mass.	242,619	47,886	72,816	106,342	15,575	238,919	46,537	71,930	105,507	14,945	19.7	30.0	43.8	6.4	19.5	30.1	44.2	6.3
Bridgeport, Conn.	46,782	11,742	15,815	14,070	5,155	46,414	11,526	15,760	14,011	5,117	25.1	33.8	30.1	11.0	24.8	34.0	30.2	11.0
Buffalo, N. Y.	121,824	24,202	30,248	50,253	17,121	121,530	24,127	30,197	50,168	17,038	19.9	24.8	41.3	14.1	19.9	24.8	41.3	14.0
Cambridge, Mass.	33,296	7,705	9,760	15,500	331	32,104	7,126	9,403	15,264	311	23.1	29.3	46.6	1.0	22.2	29.3	47.5	1.0
Camden, N. J.	20,354	5,093	6,440	6,721	2,100	20,262	5,079	6,426	6,677	2,080	25.0	31.6	33.0	10.3	25.1	31.7	33.0	10.3
Chicago, Ill.	808,558	156,259	259,975	327,286	65,038	805,482	155,659	259,385	326,178	64,260	19.3	32.2	40.5	8.0	19.3	32.2	40.5	8.0
Cincinnati, Ohio	42,921	4,792	9,793	24,939	3,397	42,827	4,774	9,772	24,901	3,380	11.2	22.8	58.1	7.9	11.1	22.8	58.1	7.9
Cleveland, Ohio	240,173	62,058	87,072	78,171	12,872	239,538	61,903	86,902	77,989	12,744	25.8	36.3	32.5	5.4	25.8	36.3	32.6	5.3
Columbus, Ohio	16,187	2,685	3,790	6,679	3,033	16,055	2,658	3,772	6,651	2,979	16.6	23.4	41.3	18.7	16.5	23.5	41.4	18.6
Dallas, Tex.	8,801	2,224	1,622	2,900	2,055	8,730	2,195	1,612	2,889	2,034	25.3	18.4	33.0	23.3	25.1	18.5	33.1	23.3
Dayton, Ohio	13,165	2,772	3,953	5,621	819	13,111	2,759	3,945	5,600	807	21.1	30.0	42.7	6.2	21.0	30.1	42.7	6.2
Denver, Colo.	38,230	5,059	9,321	21,984	1,866	37,620	4,911	9,103	21,825	1,781	13.2	24.4	57.5	4.9	13.1	24.2	58.0	4.7
Des Moines, Iowa	11,269	1,577	2,619	5,393	1,680	11,224	1,568	2,610	5,371	1,675	14.0	23.2	47.9	14.9	14.0	23.3	47.9	14.9
Detroit, Mich.	290,884	101,333	89,164	77,754	22,633	289,297	100,842	88,788	77,397	22,270	34.8	30.7	26.7	7.8	34.9	30.7	26.8	7.7
Fall River, Mass.	42,421	7,092	11,778	21,917	1,634	42,331	7,064	11,755	21,882	1,630	16.7	27.8	51.7	3.9	16.7	27.8	51.7	3.9
Fort Worth, Tex.	7,502	3,398	867	1,292	1,945	7,359	3,334	859	1,249	1,917	45.3	11.6	17.2	25.9	45.3	11.7	17.0	26.0
Grand Rapids, Mich.	28,427	4,088	6,735	13,941	3,663	28,355	4,074	6,725	13,920	3,636	14.4	23.7	49.0	12.9	14.4	23.7	49.1	12.8
Hartford, Conn.	40,912	10,302	14,003	15,634	973	40,667	10,180	13,957	15,580	950	25.2	34.2	38.2	2.4	25.0	34.3	38.3	2.3
Houston, Tex.	12,088	3,633	2,192	4,020	2,243	12,012	3,618	2,172	4,008	2,214	30.1	18.1	33.3	18.6	30.1	18.1	33.4	18.4
Indianapolis, Ind.	17,096	2,373	3,544	7,896	3,283	16,958	2,350	3,520	7,850	3,238	13.9	20.7	46.2	19.2	13.9	20.8	46.3	19.1
Jersey City, N. J.	76,294	14,493	24,954	34,091	2,756	75,981	14,424	24,856	33,996	2,705	19.0	32.7	44.7	3.6	19.0	32.7	44.7	3.6
Kansas City, Kans.	11,721	3,769	3,066	4,006	880	11,656	3,756	3,031	3,996	873	32.2	26.2	34.2	7.5	32.2	26.0	34.3	7.5
Kansas City, Mo.	27,583	4,580	6,496	11,331	5,176	27,320	4,481	6,457	11,290	5,092	16.6	23.6	41.1	18.8	16.4	23.6	41.3	18.6
Los Angeles, Calif.	122,131	33,597	34,075	44,092	10,367	112,057	29,627	30,280	42,452	9,698	27.5	27.9	36.1	8.5	26.4	27.0	37.9	8.7
Louisville, Ky.	11,667	617	1,546	7,081	2,423	11,621	607	1,534	7,066	2,414	5.3	13.3	60.7	20.8	5.2	13.2	60.8	20.8
Lowell, Mass.	38,116	7,750	9,908	19,913	545	38,040	7,737	9,888	19,870	545	20.3	26.0	52.2	1.4	20.3	26.0	52.2	1.4
Memphis, Tenn.	5,844	732	1,477	2,280	1,355	5,775	723	1,461	2,256	1,335	12.5	25.3	39.0	23.2	12.5	25.3	39.1	23.1
Milwaukee, Wis.	110,160	19,903	29,388	52,884	7,985	110,068	19,873	29,366	52,856	7,973	18.1	26.7	48.0	7.2	18.1	26.7	48.0	7.2
Minneapolis, Minn.	88,248	13,916	24,795	43,855	5,682	88,032	13,867	24,738	43,778	5,649	15.8	28.1	49.7	6.4	15.8	28.1	49.7	6.4
Nashville, Tenn.	2,412	279	497	1,159	477	2,387	266	497	1,158	466	11.6	20.6	48.1	19.8	11.1	20.8	48.5	19.5
New Bedford, Mass.	51,078	15,903	15,609	18,835	731	48,689	14,624	14,962	18,395	708	31.1	30.6	36.9	1.4	30.0	30.7	37.8	1.5
New Haven, Conn.	40,124	8,899	15,997	18,058	3,170	45,686	8,678	15,914	17,985	3,109	19.3	34.7	39.2	6.9	19.0	34.8	39.4	6.8
New Orleans, La.	27,365	3,191	4,308	10,811	9,055	25,992	2,930	4,209	10,658	8,195	11.7	15.7	39.5	33.1	11.3	16.2	41.0	31.5
New York, N. Y.	2,028,160	448,744	742,462	726,634	110,320	1,991,547	429,916	733,473	722,746	105,412	22.1	36.6	35.8	5.4	21.6	36.8	36.3	5.3
Bronx borough	267,742	42,455	104,079	103,865	17,343	266,971	42,193	103,876	103,729	17,173	15.9	38.9	38.8	6.5	15.8	38.9	38.9	6.4
Brooklyn borough	666,188	128,078	246,176	254,710	37,224	659,287	124,733	244,662	253,876	36,016	19.2	37.0	38.2	5.6	18.9	37.1	38.5	5.5
Manhattan borough	950,264	256,495	352,243	297,007	44,519	922,080	241,553	345,152	294,233	41,142	27.0	37.1	31.3	4.7	26.2	37.4	31.9	4.5
Queens borough	112,171	14,557	31,150	58,165	8,299	111,676	14,422	31,001	58,057	8,196	13.0	27.8	51.9	7.4	12.9	27.8	52.0	7.3
Richmond borough	31,795	7,159	8,814	12,887	2,935	31,533	7,015	8,782	12,851	2,885	22.5	27.7	40.5	9.2	22.2	27.9	40.8	9.1
Newark, N. J.	117,549	24,427	41,574	43,884	7,664	117,003	24,284	41,451	43,703	7,565	20.8	35.4	37.3	6.5	20.8	35.4	37.4	6.5
Norfolk, Va.	6,998	2,195	2,065	1,963	775	6,587	2,007	1,981	1,892	707	31.4	29.5	28.1	11.1	30.5	30.1	28.7	10.7
Oakland, Calif.	49,895	8,772	13,920	23,558	3,645	45,162	7,589	12,672	21,429	3,472	17.6	27.9	47.2	7.3	16.8	28.1	47.4	7.7
Omaha, Nebr.	35,645	6,439	9,677	15,180	4,349	35,381	6,376	9,584	15,115	4,306	18.1	27.1	42.6	12.2	18.0	27.1	42.7	12.2
Paterson, N. J.	45,242	8,273	14,491	19,750	2,728	45,145	8,242	14,474	19,722	2,707	18.3	32.0	43.7	6.0	18.3	32.1	43.7	6.0
Philadelphia, Pa.	400,744	79,881	137,969	158,448	24,446	397,927	79,110	137,303	157,670	23,844	19.9	34.4	39.5	6.1	19.9	34.5	39.6	6.0
Pittsburgh, Pa.	120,792	22,453	39,791	52,305	6,243	120,266	22,287	39,661	52,171	6,147	18.6	32.9	43.3	5.2	18.5	33.0	43.4	5.1
Portland, Oreg.	49,778	9,148	15,576	22,849	2,205	47,114	8,442	14,844	21,701	2,127	18.4	31.3	45.9	4.4	17.9	31.5	46.1	4.5
Providence, R. I.	69,895	12,109	21,580	31,522	4,684	68,951	11,627	21,381	31,353	4,590	17.3	30.9	45.1	6.7	16.9	31.0	45.5	6.7
Reading, Pa.	9,573	2,226	3,377	3,300	670	9,553	2,222	3,370	3,295	666	23.3	35.3	34.5	7.0	23.3	35.3	34.5	7.0
Richmond, Va.	4,713	765	1,329	1,737	882	4,637	748	1,311	1,721	857	16.2	28.2	36.9	18.7	16.1	28.3	37.1	18.5
Rochester, N. Y.	71,411	16,602	22,210	25,188	7,411	71,321	16,574	22,188	25,166	7,393	23.2	31.1	35.3	10.4	23.2	31.1	35.3	10.4
St. Louis, Mo.	103,626	13,863	29,923	49,603	10,237	103,239	13,804	29,838	49,420	10,177	13.4	28.9	47.9	9.9	13.4	28.9	47.9	9.9
St. Paul, Minn.	51,722	6,983	12,015	28,219	4,505	51,595	6,965	11,984	28,168	4,478	13.5	23.2	54.6	8.7	13.5	23.2	54.6	8.7
Salt Lake City, Utah	19,897	3,260	5,337	10,536	764	19,434	3,117	5,183	10,416	718	16.4	26.8	53.0	3.8	16.0	26.7	53.6	3.7
San Antonio, Tex.	36,824	17,942	5,829	6,698	6,355	36,646	17,908	5,794	6,649	6,295	48.7	15.8	18.2	17.3	48.9	15.8	18.1	17.2
San Francisco, Calif.	149,195	30,606	41,799	60,765	16,025	140,200	27,235	39,187	58,437	15,341	20.5	28.0	40.7	10.7	19.4	28.0	41.7	10.9
Scranton, Pa.	28,587	3,673	8,055	13,315	3,544	28,568	3,669	8,053	13,308	3,538	12.8	28.2	46.6	12.4	12.8	28.2	46.6	12.4
Seattle, Wash.	80,976	18,701	23,056	28,204	11,015	73,875	15,598	20,574	27,225	10,478	23.1	28.5	34.8	13.6	21.1	27.8	36.9	14.2
Spokane, Wash.	17,096	2,488	4,502	9,099	1,007	16,826	2,437	4,417	8,982	990	14.6	26.3	53.2	5.9	14.5	26.3	53.4	5.9
Springfield, Mass.	31,461	6,956	10,186	13,253	1,066	31,250	6,879	10,134	13,184	1,053	22.1	32.4	42.1	3.4	22.0	32.4	42.2	3.4
Syracuse, N. Y.	32,383	6,567	9,684	13,969	2,163	32,321	6,547	9,668	13,956	2,150	20.3	29.9	43.1	6.7	20.3	29.9	43.2	6.7
Toledo, Ohio	38,296	8,275	10,007	17,859	2,155	38,145	8,247	9,979	17,793	2,126	21.6	26.1	46.6	5.6	21.6	26.2	46.6	5.6
Trenton, N. J.	30,168	7,573	11,654	9,844	1,097	30,073	7,539	11,631	9,812	1,091	25.1	38.6	32.6	3.6	25.1	38.7	32.6	3.6
Washington, D. C.	29,365	4,838	7,843	11,567	5,117	28,548	4,589	7,697	11,342	4,920	16.5	26.7	39.4	17.4	16.1	27.0	39.7	17.2
Wilmington, Del.	16,337	4,136	5,170	5,424	1,607	16,279	4,126	5,161	5,408	1,584	25.3	31.6	33.2	9.8	25.3	31.7	33.2	9.7
Worcester, Mass.	53,527	11,541	16,417	23,355	2,214	53,418	11,511	16,391	23,313	2,203	21.6	30.7	43.6	4.1	21.5	30.7	43.6	4.1
Yonkers, N. Y.	25,796	4,418	8,649	11,926	803	25,700	4,383	8,629	11,899	789	17.1	33.5	46.2	3.1	17.1	33.6	46.3	3.1
Youngstown, Ohio	33,945	10,767	11,966	9,082	2,130	33,834	10,727	11,941	9,064	2,102	31.7	35.3	26.8	6.3	31.7	35.3	26.8	6.2

YEAR OF IMMIGRATION.

791

TABLE 11.—FOREIGN-BORN MALE POPULATION BY YEAR OF IMMIGRATION, FOR CITIES HAVING 100,000 INHABITANTS OR MORE: 1920.

CITY.	Total foreign-born males: 1920	YEAR OF IMMIGRATION.							PER CENT OF TOTAL ARRIVING IN—						
		1918-1919	1916-1917	1911-1915	1906-1910	1901-1905	1900 or earlier	Year not reported.	1918-1919	1916-1917	1911-1915	1906-1910	1901-1905	1900 or earlier.	Year not reported.
Akron, Ohio	24,731	491	896	10,105	5,672	2,669	4,016	882	2.0	3.6	40.9	22.9	10.8	16.2	3.6
Albany, N. Y	9,022	56	79	1,471	1,570	1,298	4,374	174	0.6	0.9	16.3	17.4	14.4	48.5	1.9
Atlanta, Ga	2,741	47	37	308	447	420	1,128	354	1.7	1.3	11.2	16.3	15.3	41.2	12.9
Baltimore, Md	44,805	409	499	7,779	7,148	7,235	20,708	1,027	0.9	1.1	17.4	16.0	16.1	46.2	2.3
Birmingham, Ala	3,545	36	46	424	498	431	1,309	801	1.0	1.3	12.0	14.0	12.2	36.9	22.6
Boston, Mass	120,122	1,767	2,018	20,956	20,719	17,521	51,481	5,660	1.5	1.7	17.4	17.2	14.6	42.9	4.7
Bridgeport, Conn	25,598	373	595	5,899	5,138	3,998	7,703	1,892	1.5	2.3	23.0	20.1	15.6	30.1	7.4
Buffalo, N. Y	64,938	817	921	12,529	10,105	8,090	27,077	5,399	1.3	1.4	19.3	15.6	12.5	41.7	8.3
Cambridge, Mass	15,837	382	439	2,890	2,733	2,170	7,096	127	2.4	2.8	18.2	17.3	13.7	44.8	0.8
Camden, N. J	11,162	115	155	2,687	2,237	1,619	3,607	742	1.0	1.4	24.1	20.0	14.5	32.3	6.6
Chicago, Ill	434,307	2,871	3,960	79,494	84,251	64,804	173,801	25,126	0.7	0.9	18.3	19.4	14.9	40.0	5.8
Cincinnati, Ohio	21,855	119	189	2,365	3,081	2,472	12,570	1,129	0.5	0.8	10.8	13.9	11.3	57.5	5.2
Cleveland, Ohio	133,508	1,061	1,445	33,983	28,741	22,161	41,284	4,833	0.8	1.1	25.4	21.5	16.6	30.9	3.7
Columbus, Ohio	9,221	76	121	1,533	1,340	1,090	3,627	1,434	0.8	1.3	16.6	14.5	11.8	39.3	15.6
Dallas, Tex	5,153	519	238	708	587	461	1,739	901	10.1	4.6	13.7	11.4	8.9	33.7	17.5
Dayton, Ohio	7,438	68	95	1,502	1,453	1,001	2,989	330	0.9	1.3	20.2	19.5	13.5	40.2	4.4
Denver, Colo	21,420	398	438	2,244	2,934	2,613	11,965	828	1.9	2.0	10.5	13.7	12.2	55.9	3.9
Des Moines, Iowa	6,252	73	86	762	820	727	3,056	728	1.2	1.4	12.2	13.1	11.6	48.9	11.6
Detroit, Mich	170,150	6,825	5,034	51,415	35,386	20,348	42,037	9,105	4.0	3.0	30.2	20.8	12.0	24.7	5.4
Fall River, Mass	20,408	239	484	2,704	2,949	2,902	10,581	549	1.2	2.4	13.2	14.5	14.2	51.8	2.7
Fort Worth, Tex	4,851	1,210	484	685	377	204	856	1,035	24.9	10.0	14.1	7.8	4.2	17.6	21.3
Grand Rapids, Mich	15,047	73	123	2,127	2,191	1,737	7,464	1,332	0.5	0.8	14.1	14.6	11.5	49.6	8.9
Hartford, Conn	21,683	241	449	4,922	4,441	3,299	7,973	358	1.1	2.1	22.7	20.5	15.2	36.8	1.7
Houston, Tex	6,861	708	439	973	737	601	2,432	971	10.3	6.4	14.2	10.7	8.8	35.4	14.2
Indianapolis, Ind	9,470	50	107	1,362	1,331	940	4,429	1,251	0.5	1.1	14.4	14.1	9.9	46.8	13.2
Jersey City, N. J	40,423	295	489	7,452	7,732	6,320	17,328	807	0.7	1.2	18.4	19.1	15.6	42.9	2.0
Kansas City, Kans	6,911	378	485	1,442	1,109	788	2,291	358	5.5	7.0	20.9	16.9	11.4	33.2	5.2
Kansas City, Mo	15,584	390	414	1,904	2,165	1,849	6,615	2,247	2.5	2.7	12.2	13.9	11.9	42.4	14.4
Los Angeles, Calif	67,312	4,379	3,200	10,283	11,037	8,979	24,746	4,688	6.5	4.8	15.3	16.4	13.3	36.8	7.0
Louisville, Ky	5,921	23	13	327	474	443	3,764	877	0.4	0.2	5.5	8.0	7.5	63.6	14.8
Lowell, Mass	18,532	319	622	3,041	2,811	2,187	9,337	215	1.7	3.4	16.4	15.2	11.8	50.4	1.2
Memphis, Tenn	3,324	34	27	363	460	438	1,348	654	1.0	0.8	10.9	13.8	13.2	40.6	19.7
Milwaukee, Wis	60,776	214	504	11,136	10,587	7,453	27,692	3,190	0.4	0.8	18.3	17.4	12.3	45.6	5.2
Minneapolis, Minn	48,596	501	744	6,765	7,615	7,087	23,943	1,941	1.0	1.5	13.9	15.7	14.6	49.3	4.0
Nashville, Tenn	1,305	10	19	127	170	122	646	202	0.8	1.5	9.7	13.7	9.3	49.5	15.5
New Bedford, Mass	25,474	1,104	1,744	5,251	4,552	3,849	9,225	249	4.3	6.8	20.6	17.9	13.1	36.2	1.0
New Haven, Conn	23,828	186	347	4,108	4,446	4,216	9,369	1,156	0.8	1.5	17.2	18.7	17.7	39.3	4.9
New Orleans, La	16,671	655	362	986	1,296	1,399	6,424	5,549	3.9	2.2	5.9	7.8	8.4	38.5	33.3
New York, N. Y	1,041,723	26,006	20,169	186,303	203,566	189,407	374,914	41,358	2.5	1.9	17.9	19.5	18.2	36.0	4.0
Bronx borough	135,865	749	1,272	18,974	26,942	27,769	54,553	5,606	0.6	0.9	14.0	19.8	20.4	40.2	4.1
Brooklyn borough	345,597	7,417	5,448	54,313	65,565	66,180	132,495	14,179	2.1	1.6	15.7	19.0	19.1	38.3	4.1
Manhattan borough	485,229	16,341	12,651	103,843	99,841	84,655	150,421	17,477	3.4	2.6	21.4	20.6	17.4	31.0	3.6
Queens borough	57,412	432	463	6,460	8,620	8,360	30,171	2,906	0.8	0.8	11.3	15.0	14.6	52.6	5.1
Richmond borough	17,620	1,067	335	2,713	2,598	2,443	7,274	1,190	6.1	1.9	15.4	14.7	13.9	41.3	6.8
Newark, N. J	62,319	858	947	11,769	12,267	10,763	23,097	2,618	1.4	1.5	18.9	19.7	17.3	37.1	4.2
Norfolk, Va	4,822	403	404	919	829	563	1,306	398	8.4	8.4	19.1	17.2	11.7	27.1	8.3
Oakland, Calif	29,252	640	751	3,801	4,872	3,850	13,796	1,542	2.2	2.6	13.0	16.7	13.2	47.2	5.3
Omaha, Nebr	20,122	195	328	3,457	3,514	2,420	8,388	1,820	1.0	1.6	17.2	17.5	12.0	41.7	9.0
Paterson, N. J	23,268	183	390	3,750	4,114	3,748	10,305	778	0.8	1.7	16.1	17.7	16.1	44.3	3.3
Philadelphia, Pa	207,699	1,892	2,650	39,096	39,735	35,163	80,085	9,078	0.9	1.3	18.8	19.1	16.9	38.6	4.4
Pittsburgh, Pa	65,783	374	591	11,976	11,586	11,296	27,505	2,455	0.6	0.9	18.2	17.6	17.2	41.8	3.7
Portland, Oreg	29,520	783	496	3,882	5,782	4,026	13,634	926	2.7	1.7	13.1	19.6	13.6	46.2	3.1
Providence, R. I	34,829	390	560	5,331	5,952	5,412	15,491	1,693	1.1	1.6	15.3	17.1	15.5	44.5	4.9
Reading, Pa	5,475	45	129	1,132	1,079	972	1,841	277	0.8	2.4	20.7	19.7	17.8	33.6	5.1
Richmond, Va	2,596	26	40	392	389	377	1,004	368	1.0	1.5	15.1	15.0	14.5	38.7	14.2
Rochester, N. Y	37,051	575	527	7,409	7,580	5,175	13,180	2,605	1.6	1.4	20.0	20.5	14.0	35.6	7.0
St. Louis, Mo	56,600	322	454	6,999	9,575	8,214	27,397	3,645	0.6	0.8	12.4	16.9	14.5	48.4	6.4
St. Paul, Minn	28,093	201	295	3,685	3,881	3,395	15,126	1,510	0.7	1.1	13.1	13.8	12.1	53.8	5.4
Salt Lake City, Utah	10,112	218	209	1,253	1,682	1,229	5,124	397	2.2	2.1	12.4	16.6	12.2	50.7	3.9
San Antonio, Tex	19,639	4,224	1,852	4,031	2,020	1,062	3,729	2,721	21.5	9.4	20.5	10.3	5.4	19.0	13.9
San Francisco, Calif	89,905	2,930	2,372	12,893	14,927	11,910	36,006	8,867	3.3	2.6	14.3	16.6	13.2	40.0	9.9
Scranton, Pa	15,153	66	81	1,944	2,441	2,202	7,043	1,376	0.4	0.5	12.8	16.1	14.5	46.5	9.1
Seattle, Wash	48,725	2,360	1,699	6,809	8,774	6,738	17,594	4,751	4.8	3.5	14.0	18.0	13.8	36.1	9.8
Spokane, Wash	9,683	265	211	867	1,515	1,150	5,289	386	2.7	2.2	9.0	15.6	11.9	54.6	4.0
Springfield, Mass	16,049	265	357	3,161	3,084	2,418	6,384	380	1.7	2.2	19.7	19.2	15.1	39.8	2.4
Syracuse, N. Y	17,473	208	259	3,338	3,295	2,401	7,065	907	1.2	1.5	19.1	18.9	13.7	40.4	5.2
Toledo, Ohio	21,857	286	269	4,923	3,473	2,690	9,321	895	1.3	1.2	22.5	15.9	12.3	42.6	4.1
Trenton, N. J	16,556	131	174	3,855	3,846	2,940	5,158	452	0.8	1.1	23.3	23.2	17.8	31.2	2.7
Washington, D. C	15,799	287	312	2,109	2,466	2,034	6,274	2,317	1.8	2.0	13.3	15.6	12.9	39.7	14.7
Wilmington, Del	9,396	102	165	2,296	1,768	1,407	2,941	722	1.1	1.8	24.4	18.8	15.0	31.3	7.7
Worcester, Mass	27,961	326	741	5,400	5,080	3,903	11,700	811	1.2	2.7	19.3	18.2	14.0	41.8	2.9
Yonkers, N. Y	13,048	120	152	1,951	2,469	2,124	5,946	286	0.9	1.2	15.0	18.9	16.3	45.6	2.2
Youngstown, Ohio	20,793	139	437	6,493	4,619	2,998	5,211	896	0.7	2.1	31.2	22.2	14.4	25.1	4.3

POPULATION.

TABLE 12.—FOREIGN-BORN FEMALE POPULATION BY YEAR OF IMMIGRATION, FOR CITIES HAVING 100,000 INHABITANTS OR MORE: 1920.

CITY.	Total foreign-born females: 1920	YEAR OF IMMIGRATION.							PER CENT OF TOTAL ARRIVING IN—						
		1918–1919	1916–1917	1911–1915	1906–1910	1901–1905	1900 or earlier.	Year not reported.	1918–1919	1916–1917	1911–1915	1906–1910	1901–1905	1900 or earlier.	Year not reported.
Akron, Ohio	13,290	287	324	4,582	2,738	1,491	2,951	917	2.2	2.4	34.5	20.6	11.2	22.2	6.9
Albany, N. Y.	8,673	90	101	1,216	1,244	877	4,791	354	1.0	1.2	14.0	14.3	10.1	55.2	4.1
Atlanta, Ga.	2,048	65	32	229	299	257	762	404	3.2	1.6	11.2	14.6	12.5	37.2	19.7
Baltimore, Md.	40,004	354	357	5,582	6,130	5,744	20,162	1,675	0.9	0.9	14.0	15.3	14.4	50.4	4.2
Birmingham, Ala.	2,595	32	27	291	359	216	891	779	1.2	1.0	11.2	13.8	8.3	34.3	30.0
Boston, Mass.	122,497	2,176	2,464	18,505	18,895	15,681	54,861	9,915	1.8	2.0	15.1	15.4	12.8	44.8	8.1
Bridgeport, Conn.	21,184	281	403	4,191	3,780	2,899	6,367	3,263	1.3	1.9	19.8	17.8	13.7	30.1	15.4
Buffalo, N. Y.	58,886	782	831	8,322	6,631	5,422	23,176	11,722	1.4	1.5	14.6	11.7	9.5	40.7	20.6
Cambridge, Mass.	17,459	462	594	2,938	2,607	2,250	8,404	204	2.6	3.4	16.8	14.9	12.9	48.1	1.2
Camden, N. J.	9,192	126	118	1,892	1,459	1,125	3,114	1,358	1.4	1.3	20.6	15.9	12.2	33.9	14.8
Chicago, Ill.	374,251	2,854	3,691	63,389	64,352	46,568	153,485	39,912	0.8	1.0	16.9	17.2	12.4	41.0	10.7
Cincinnati, Ohio	21,066	114	113	1,912	2,481	1,809	12,369	2,268	0.5	0.5	9.1	11.8	8.6	58.7	10.8
Cleveland, Ohio	106,665	1,033	1,304	23,282	20,421	15,749	36,887	7,989	1.0	1.2	21.8	19.1	14.8	34.6	7.5
Columbus, Ohio	6,966	53	65	837	770	590	3,052	1,599	0.8	0.9	12.0	11.1	8.5	43.8	23.0
Dallas, Tex.	3,648	194	146	419	316	258	1,161	1,154	5.3	4.0	11.5	8.7	7.1	31.8	31.6
Dayton, Ohio	5,727	55	52	1,000	891	608	2,632	489	1.0	0.9	17.5	15.6	10.6	46.0	8.5
Denver, Colo.	16,810	302	284	1,393	1,960	1,814	10,019	1,038	1.8	1.7	8.3	11.7	10.8	59.6	6.2
Des Moines, Iowa	5,017	50	51	555	570	502	2,337	952	1.0	1.0	11.1	11.4	10.0	46.6	19.0
Detroit, Mich.	120,734	4,520	4,023	29,516	20,710	12,720	35,717	13,528	3.7	3.3	24.4	17.2	10.5	29.6	11.2
Fall River, Mass.	22,013	244	613	2,808	3,060	2,867	11,336	1,085	1.1	2.8	12.8	13.9	13.0	51.5	4.9
Fort Worth, Tex.	2,651	427	272	320	175	111	436	910	16.1	10.3	12.1	6.6	4.2	16.4	34.3
Grand Rapids, Mich.	13,380	83	137	1,545	1,616	1,191	6,477	2,331	0.6	1.0	11.5	12.1	8.9	48.4	17.4
Hartford, Conn.	19,229	258	517	3,915	3,610	2,653	7,661	615	1.3	2.7	20.4	18.8	13.8	39.8	3.2
Houston, Tex.	5,227	510	325	678	475	379	1,588	1,272	9.8	6.2	13.0	9.1	7.3	30.4	24.3
Indianapolis, Ind.	7,626	52	67	735	727	546	3,467	2,032	0.7	0.9	9.6	9.5	7.2	45.5	26.6
Jersey City, N. J.	35,871	309	410	5,538	6,023	4,879	16,763	1,949	0.9	1.1	15.4	16.8	13.6	46.7	5.4
Kansas City, Kans.	4,810	222	359	883	680	429	1,715	522	4.6	7.5	18.4	14.1	8.9	35.7	10.9
Kansas City, Mo.	11,999	288	288	1,296	1,359	1,123	4,716	2,920	2.4	2.4	10.8	11.3	9.4	39.3	24.4
Los Angeles, Calif.	54,819	4,495	2,966	8,274	8,290	5,769	19,346	5,679	8.2	5.4	15.1	15.1	10.5	35.3	10.4
Louisville, Ky.	5,746	31	16	207	359	270	3,317	1,546	0.5	0.3	3.6	6.2	4.7	57.7	26.9
Lowell, Mass.	19,584	362	675	2,731	2,716	2,194	10,576	330	1.8	3.4	13.9	13.0	11.2	54.0	1.7
Memphis, Tenn.	2,520	37	16	255	295	284	932	701	1.5	0.6	10.1	11.7	11.3	37.0	27.8
Milwaukee, Wis.	49,384	213	355	7,481	6,730	4,618	25,192	4,795	0.4	0.7	15.1	13.6	9.4	51.0	9.7
Minneapolis, Minn.	39,652	491	667	4,748	5,112	4,981	19,912	3,741	1.2	1.7	12.0	12.0	12.6	50.2	9.4
Nashville, Tenn.	1,107	19	16	88	116	80	513	275	1.7	1.4	7.9	10.5	7.2	46.3	24.8
New Bedford, Mass.	25,604	924	1,849	5,031	4,435	3,273	9,610	482	3.6	7.2	19.6	17.3	12.8	37.5	1.9
New Haven, Conn.	22,296	201	391	3,666	3,970	3,365	8,689	2,014	0.9	1.8	16.4	17.8	15.1	39.0	9.0
New Orleans, La.	10,694	401	219	568	820	793	4,387	3,506	3.7	2.0	5.3	7.7	7.4	41.0	32.8
New York, N. Y.	986,437	17,630	20,743	177,893	190,294	159,195	351,720	68,962	1.8	2.1	18.0	19.3	16.1	35.7	7.0
Bronx borough	131,877	999	1,514	18,947	25,823	23,545	49,312	11,737	0.8	1.1	14.4	19.6	17.9	37.4	8.9
Brooklyn borough	320,591	4,060	5,414	51,426	60,910	53,521	122,215	23,045	1.3	1.7	16.0	19.0	16.7	38.1	7.2
Manhattan borough	465,035	11,099	12,968	99,593	94,068	73,679	146,586	27,042	2.4	2.8	21.4	20.2	15.8	31.5	5.8
Queens borough	54,759	540	599	6,063	7,491	6,679	27,904	5,393	1.0	1.1	11.1	13.7	12.2	51.1	9.8
Richmond borough	14,175	932	248	1,864	2,002	1,771	5,613	1,745	6.6	1.7	13.1	14.1	12.5	39.6	12.3
Newark, N. J.	55,230	531	761	9,561	10,265	8,279	20,787	5,046	1.0	1.4	17.3	18.6	15.0	37.6	9.1
Norfolk, Va.	2,176	73	77	319	390	283	657	377	3.4	3.5	14.7	17.9	13.0	30.2	17.3
Oakland, Calif.	20,643	503	490	2,497	2,940	2,258	9,762	2,103	2.9	2.4	12.1	14.2	10.9	47.3	10.2
Omaha, Nebr.	15,523	139	197	2,123	2,251	1,492	6,792	2,529	0.9	1.3	13.7	14.5	9.6	43.8	16.3
Paterson, N. J.	21,974	234	445	3,271	3,580	3,049	9,445	1,950	1.1	2.0	14.9	16.3	13.9	43.0	8.9
Philadelphia, Pa.	193,045	1,809	2,229	32,205	34,239	28,832	78,363	15,368	0.9	1.2	16.7	17.7	14.9	40.6	8.0
Pittsburgh, Pa.	55,009	409	601	8,502	8,492	8,417	24,800	3,788	0.7	1.1	15.5	15.4	15.3	45.1	6.9
Portland, Oreg.	20,249	834	401	2,752	3,366	2,402	9,215	1,279	4.1	2.0	13.6	16.6	11.9	45.5	6.3
Providence, R. I.	35,066	440	691	4,697	5,391	4,825	16,031	2,991	1.3	2.0	13.4	15.4	13.8	45.7	8.5
Reading, Pa.	4,098	30	122	768	740	586	1,459	393	0.7	3.0	18.7	18.1	14.3	35.6	9.6
Richmond, Va.	2,117	31	42	234	302	261	733	514	1.5	2.0	11.1	14.3	12.3	34.6	24.3
Rochester, N. Y.	34,360	674	720	6,697	5,825	3,630	12,008	4,806	2.0	2.1	19.5	17.0	10.6	34.9	14.0
St. Louis, Mo.	47,020	325	378	5,385	6,814	5,320	22,206	6,592	0.7	0.8	11.5	14.5	11.3	47.2	14.0
St. Paul, Minn.	23,629	230	260	2,312	2,524	2,215	13,093	2,995	1.0	1.1	9.8	10.7	9.4	55.4	12.7
Salt Lake City, Utah	9,785	229	233	1,118	1,433	993	5,412	367	2.3	2.4	11.4	14.6	10.1	55.3	3.8
San Antonio, Tex.	17,185	2,001	1,875	3,959	1,805	942	2,969	3,634	11.6	10.9	23.0	10.5	5.5	17.3	21.1
San Francisco, Calif.	59,290	2,356	1,694	8,361	8,324	6,638	24,759	7,158	4.0	2.9	14.1	14.0	11.2	41.8	12.1
Scranton, Pa.	13,434	73	82	1,427	1,819	1,593	6,272	2,168	0.5	0.6	10.6	13.5	11.9	46.7	16.1
Seattle, Wash.	32,251	2,232	1,319	4,282	4,242	3,302	10,610	6,264	6.9	4.1	13.3	13.2	10.2	32.9	19.4
Spokane, Wash.	7,413	325	190	630	984	853	3,810	621	4.4	2.6	8.5	13.3	11.5	51.4	8.4
Springfield, Mass.	15,412	294	347	2,532	2,637	2,047	6,869	686	1.9	2.3	16.4	17.1	13.3	44.6	4.5
Syracuse, N. Y.	14,910	213	252	2,297	2,289	1,699	6,904	1,256	1.4	1.7	15.4	15.4	11.4	46.3	8.4
Toledo, Ohio	16,439	141	167	2,489	2,072	1,772	8,538	1,260	0.9	1.0	15.1	12.6	10.8	51.9	7.7
Trenton, N. J.	13,012	166	204	3,043	2,847	2,021	4,686	645	1.2	1.5	22.4	20.9	14.8	34.4	4.7
Washington, D. C.	13,566	381	263	1,486	1,872	1,471	5,293	2,800	2.8	1.9	11.0	13.8	10.8	39.0	20.6
Wilmington, Del.	6,941	73	107	1,393	1,148	852	2,483	885	1.1	1.5	20.1	16.5	12.3	35.8	12.8
Worcester, Mass.	25,566	319	554	4,201	4,097	3,337	11,655	1,403	1.2	2.2	16.4	16.0	13.1	45.6	5.5
Yonkers, N. Y.	12,748	167	165	1,863	2,278	1,778	5,980	517	1.3	1.3	14.6	17.9	13.0	46.9	4.1
Youngstown, Ohio	13,152	123	245	3,330	2,498	1,851	3,871	1,234	0.9	1.9	25.3	19.0	14.1	29.4	9.4

YEAR OF IMMIGRATION.   793

TABLE 13.—FOREIGN-BORN POPULATION BY YEAR OF IMMIGRATION, FOR CITIES HAVING FROM 25,000 TO 100,000 INHABITANTS: 1920.

CITY.	Total foreign born: 1920	YEAR OF IMMIGRATION. 1916–1919	1911–1915	1906–1910	1901–1905	1900 or earlier.	Year not reported.
Alabama.							
Mobile	2,157	134	141	225	197	724	736
Montgomery	771	26	93	106	83	334	129
Arizona.							
Phoenix	4,146	909	615	524	333	1,323	442
Arkansas.							
Fort Smith	855	7	50	72	84	461	181
Little Rock	1,815	19	94	161	76	749	716
California.							
Alameda	6,353	317	724	879	743	3,166	524
Berkeley	10,506	850	1,235	1,393	1,295	5,105	628
Fresno	9,715	851	1,550	1,696	1,266	2,931	1,421
Long Beach	7,100	1,049	607	700	506	3,415	823
Pasadena	7,169	614	804	806	611	3,283	1,051
Sacramento	12,988	981	1,780	2,023	1,628	5,134	1,492
San Diego	14,088	1,429	1,834	1,537	1,223	6,278	1,787
San Jose	8,274	252	888	967	991	3,631	1,545
Stockton	8,341	525	1,001	1,136	934	3,534	1,211
Colorado.							
Colorado Springs	2,639	92	136	169	215	1,539	488
Pueblo	7,489	1,097	952	854	871	2,222	1,493
Connecticut.							
Meriden	7,916	203	1,099	1,198	908	3,846	662
New Britain	21,340	659	5,610	4,843	3,345	6,603	280
New London	5,935	246	1,016	988	941	2,606	138
Norwalk	6,008	123	861	1,080	904	2,471	569
Stamford	10,764	438	2,056	2,272	1,749	3,425	824
Waterbury	29,974	1,420	7,415	5,340	4,231	9,980	1,588
Florida.							
Jacksonville	4,144	226	468	632	550	1,427	841
Miami	7,398	2,301	1,599	1,170	575	1,157	536
Pensacola	1,499	55	105	148	125	550	516
Tampa	11,352	974	1,633	2,492	2,052	3,292	909
Georgia.							
Augusta	999	23	115	109	95	360	297
Columbus	333	11	47	60	42	155	18
Macon	703	17	97	116	120	248	105
Savannah	3,336	165	413	520	355	1,600	283
Illinois.							
Aurora	6,482	71	1,035	1,057	667	3,110	542
Bloomington	2,841	26	215	229	162	1,670	539
Cicero town	15,471	157	2,666	3,346	2,694	5,836	772
Danville	1,926	22	118	180	152	1,191	263
Decatur	2,595	28	301	303	264	1,400	299
East St. Louis	6,798	115	1,370	1,330	1,018	1,971	994
Elgin	5,061	35	245	361	233	2,505	1,682
Evanston	6,811	148	1,219	1,009	778	2,938	721
Joliet	8,522	170	1,419	1,372	1,143	3,737	681
Moline	7,398	280	1,206	1,225	820	3,538	329
Oak Park village	5,648	99	360	496	437	3,417	839
Peoria	7,821	118	696	808	652	4,112	1,435
Quincy	2,417	9	53	80	81	1,747	447
Rock Island	5,365	125	655	745	516	2,764	560
Rockford	17,373	618	2,898	2,776	1,998	7,159	1,924
Springfield	6,268	71	522	889	846	2,886	1,104
Indiana.							
Anderson	946	18	126	124	70	405	203
East Chicago	14,701	368	4,738	3,619	2,003	2,183	1,790
Evansville	3,164	32	107	127	125	2,241	532
Fort Wayne	6,657	105	880	664	523	3,865	560
Gary	16,510	772	4,583	3,961	2,226	2,317	2,651
Hammond	8,136	73	1,831	1,746	1,240	2,612	634
Kokomo	1,170	24	212	181	112	532	109
Muncie	828	24	63	66	51	366	258
Richmond	1,135	25	155	131	93	558	173
South Bend	13,415	174	2,116	2,675	1,785	4,591	2,074
Terre Haute	3,683	35	339	497	411	1,767	634
Iowa.							
Cedar Rapids	5,873	125	934	744	507	2,820	743
Council Bluffs	4,002	131	399	411	247	1,772	1,042
Davenport	7,663	169	455	474	455	4,380	1,730
Dubuque	4,224	61	283	195	185	2,971	529
Sioux City	11,250	348	2,097	1,913	1,211	5,063	618
Waterloo	2,938	75	486	303	189	1,139	746
Kansas.							
Topeka	4,035	432	591	404	189	1,878	541
Wichita	3,044	435	333	277	169	1,151	679

CITY.	Total foreign born: 1920	YEAR OF IMMIGRATION. 1916–1919	1911–1915	1906–1910	1901–1905	1900 or earlier.	Year not reported.
Kentucky.							
Covington	2,894	18	85	118	134	2,182	357
Lexington	817	27	92	98	74	343	183
Newport	2,094	18	131	170	175	1,422	178
Louisiana.							
Shreveport	1,316	56	139	170	154	428	369
Maine.							
Bangor	3,839	177	333	388	435	1,668	838
Lewiston	10,277	1,006	1,511	1,472	1,039	4,583	666
Portland	13,346	644	1,878	1,949	1,602	6,122	1,061
Maryland.							
Cumberland	1,168	13	108	110	106	336	495
Hagerstown	435	11	55	60	48	202	59
Massachusetts.							
Brockton	17,191	651	2,701	2,987	2,477	7,896	479
Brookline town	9,502	631	1,531	1,309	1,027	4,756	188
Chelsea	17,286	394	3,939	3,813	3,121	5,055	964
Chicopee	12,190	460	2,215	2,551	1,754	4,907	313
Everett	11,227	374	1,265	1,758	1,469	6,212	149
Fitchburg	13,180	805	2,078	2,012	1,616	5,377	1,292
Haverhill	13,335	580	2,243	2,212	1,719	6,152	429
Holyoke	20,280	912	2,957	3,215	2,501	10,223	472
Lawrence	39,201	1,709	8,297	8,147	5,318	14,859	871
Lynn	28,138	1,307	4,597	4,920	4,172	12,824	318
Malden	14,158	441	1,794	2,422	2,200	7,242	59
Medford	8,598	279	938	1,142	1,123	5,043	73
Newton	10,296	496	1,559	1,453	1,245	5,381	162
Pittsfield	8,247	239	1,645	1,436	994	3,224	709
Quincy	13,776	578	2,322	2,297	2,016	6,207	356
Revere	8,857	168	930	1,501	1,506	4,012	740
Salem	11,258	372	1,559	1,606	1,601	5,819	211
Somerville	24,254	1,117	3,072	3,268	3,115	13,497	185
Taunton	10,185	638	1,666	1,465	1,274	4,708	434
Waltham	8,126	455	1,204	1,282	962	4,135	138
Michigan.							
Battle Creek	3,427	144	614	455	252	1,289	673
Bay City	8,956	107	486	619	588	6,291	865
Flint	15,213	1,227	3,788	2,623	1,341	4,535	1,699
Hamtramck village	23,099	451	11,326	6,291	2,706	2,051	274
Highland Park	12,721	1,264	3,662	2,275	1,232	2,917	1,371
Jackson	5,379	149	995	707	520	2,141	777
Kalamazoo	7,232	129	1,099	998	742	2,505	1,759
Lansing	6,042	205	1,220	784	429	2,061	1,343
Muskegon	6,791	132	754	657	543	3,805	900
Pontiac	5,228	396	900	528	234	1,185	1,985
Port Huron	6,368	458	805	530	486	3,748	341
Saginaw	11,055	263	1,201	1,195	849	5,828	2,319
Minnesota.							
Duluth	30,196	809	3,864	4,755	4,573	13,601	2,594
Missouri.							
Joplin	734	4	43	61	60	461	105
St. Joseph	6,438	227	787	864	505	2,780	1,275
Springfield	977	10	51	36	38	535	307
Montana.							
Butte	11,634	394	1,448	1,715	1,332	4,584	2,161
Nebraska.							
Lincoln	7,235	169	1,224	1,274	796	2,914	858
New Hampshire.							
Manchester	27,537	1,692	4,387	4,507	2,850	12,253	1,808
Nashua	8,821	607	1,687	1,248	769	3,361	1,149
New Jersey.							
Atlantic City	7,509	247	1,090	1,190	1,148	3,247	587
Bayonne	25,514	682	6,162	5,824	4,489	7,963	394
Clifton	9,634	235	1,950	2,200	1,600	3,418	231
East Orange	6,890	173	694	839	786	3,359	1,039
Elizabeth	28,276	660	6,514	6,073	4,511	9,100	1,418
Hoboken	23,543	962	4,182	4,184	3,696	9,878	641
Irvington town	5,520	40	503	731	688	2,693	885
Kearny town	7,925	222	1,363	1,639	1,047	3,439	215
Montclair town	5,575	347	880	869	664	2,192	623
New Brunswick	8,969	323	2,127	2,009	1,586	2,098	826
Orange	7,039	173	923	918	1,164	3,413	448
Passaic	26,396	340	6,856	6,594	4,589	6,949	1,068
Perth Amboy	15,046	285	3,181	3,285	2,566	4,529	1,200
Plainfield	5,559	216	971	1,050	840	2,084	398
West Hoboken town	14,097	368	2,114	2,535	2,322	6,555	203
West New York town	8,933	173	1,429	1,619	1,416	3,570	726

794

POPULATION.

TABLE **13.**—FOREIGN-BORN POPULATION BY YEAR OF IMMIGRATION, FOR CITIES HAVING FROM 25,000 TO 100,000 INHABITANTS: 1920—Continued.

CITY.	Total foreign born: 1920	YEAR OF IMMIGRATION.					
		1916–1919	1911–1915	1906–1910	1901–1905	1900 or earlier.	Year not reported.
New York.							
Amsterdam	9,808	140	1,913	2,229	1,558	3,226	742
Auburn	7,607	285	1,775	1,595	998	2,741	213
Binghamton	10,401	107	2,440	2,152	1,373	2,674	1,655
Elmira	4,735	81	527	510	415	2,152	1,050
Jamestown	11,427	330	1,596	1,601	1,586	5,395	919
Kingston	2,769	33	180	261	330	1,393	572
Mount Vernon	10,171	284	1,333	1,595	1,818	4,877	264
New Rochelle	8,666	309	1,092	1,469	1,393	3,947	396
Newburgh	4,957	93	585	731	613	2,260	675
Niagara Falls	17,948	1,344	4,725	3,006	2,280	4,318	2,275
Poughkeepsie	5,556	148	833	889	738	2,113	835
Rome	5,240	262	1,409	1,147	691	1,530	201
Schenectady	20,504	543	3,679	3,882	3,659	7,625	1,176
Troy	11,525	124	938	1,221	1,036	6,132	2,074
Utica	23,201	529	4,655	4,955	3,799	9,015	338
Watertown	5,844	269	654	824	773	2,661	663
North Carolina.							
Asheville	561	18	29	56	67	237	154
Charlotte	522	29	63	55	70	155	150
Wilmington	647	31	95	83	45	199	194
Winston-Salem	317	19	48	63	44	94	49
Ohio.							
Canton	14,729	1,185	4,939	2,509	1,676	3,476	944
East Cleveland	3,847	120	414	488	416	2,283	126
Hamilton	2,667	30	331	306	234	1,487	279
Lakewood	7,263	113	1,549	1,874	944	2,859	424
Lima	1,983	46	318	211	169	776	413
Lorain	11,941	346	3,393	2,867	2,152	2,867	316
Mansfield	3,209	77	690	751	429	951	311
Marion	955	24	132	110	64	483	142
Newark	1,508	26	341	270	102	569	140
Portsmouth	698	17	63	53	35	379	151
Springfield	2,772	61	367	207	165	1,528	384
Steubenville	5,593	227	1,571	1,315	866	1,232	382
Warren	4,687	260	1,725	1,059	468	1,036	139
Zanesville	1,273	6	209	162	150	612	134
Oklahoma.							
Muskogee	556	37	29	38	66	249	137
Oklahoma City	3,565	534	380	389	292	1,422	548
Tulsa	2,066	118	228	264	198	645	613
Pennsylvania.							
Allentown	8,622	97	2,273	2,028	1,517	2,288	419
Altoona	5,326	162	1,007	976	911	2,077	193
Bethlehem	10,975	614	3,345	2,592	1,683	2,051	690
Chester	11,389	565	3,801	2,366	1,326	2,789	542
Easton	4,040	127	971	781	615	1,258	288
Erie	17,396	387	3,163	2,859	1,954	6,662	2,371
Harrisburg	4,190	100	674	730	550	1,263	873
Hazleton	6,026	75	580	731	981	3,352	307
Johnstown	12,172	175	2,970	2,687	2,310	3,746	284
Lancaster	2,718	56	275	296	231	1,497	363
McKeesport	11,887	203	2,389	2,121	1,915	4,367	892
New Castle	8,703	230	2,090	1,755	1,383	2,697	548
Norristown borough	4,337	90	558	680	759	1,727	543
Wilkes-Barre	14,580	80	2,187	2,287	2,065	6,969	992
Williamsport	2,272	47	308	256	216	971	474
York	1,200	22	117	87	131	629	214

CITY.	Total foreign born: 1920	YEAR OF IMMIGRATION.					
		1916–1919	1911–1915	1906–1910	1901–1905	1900 or earlier.	Year not reported.
Rhode Island.							
Cranston	7,551	175	1,018	1,091	1,112	3,462	693
Newport	5,916	159	635	677	695	3,180	570
Pawtucket	21,138	1,075	3,165	3,288	2,476	9,656	1,478
Woonsocket	10,082	1,350	2,215	2,514	1,663	6,020	1,720
South Carolina.							
Charleston	2,234	77	250	244	190	965	502
Columbia	547	19	65	88	75	199	101
South Dakota.							
Sioux Falls	2,977	62	212	290	212	1,333	868
Tennessee.							
Chattanooga	1,253	18	129	171	151	615	169
Knoxville	821	14	61	98	74	409	165
Texas.							
Austin	2,562	203	175	147	118	1,015	904
Beaumont	1,949	210	187	274	270	819	183
El Paso	33,655	9,781	12,777	4,197	2,337	3,701	862
Galveston	7,030	1,024	963	836	663	2,391	1,213
Waco	1,788	101	185	180	138	654	524
Wichita Falls	1,726	516	154	135	122	315	484
Utah.							
Ogden	4,925	253	507	666	592	2,359	548
Virginia.							
Lynchburg	354	8	39	43	37	157	70
Newport News	2,218	153	209	357	281	647	481
Petersburg	520	16	86	113	72	162	71
Portsmouth	1,582	65	255	307	212	682	61
Roanoke	878	26	105	95	89	413	150
Washington.							
Bellingham	5,378	264	596	714	615	2,342	847
Everett	5,822	342	597	826	671	2,772	614
Tacoma	21,705	1,103	2,408	3,370	2,641	9,306	2,777
West Virginia.							
Charleston	1,382	40	124	159	176	449	434
Clarksburg	1,043	71	340	324	287	587	325
Huntington	735	23	94	101	61	269	187
Wheeling	5,808	149	900	730	529	2,605	889
Wisconsin.							
Green Bay	3,568	17	112	203	200	2,432	604
Kenosha	12,725	272	3,353	2,890	1,796	3,346	1,068
La Crosse	4,449	23	143	170	205	3,577	331
Madison	4,888	127	639	651	518	2,486	467
Oshkosh	5,796	16	247	371	404	3,822	936
Racine	16,215	476	3,472	2,870	1,895	6,524	978
Sheboygan	8,275	51	1,640	1,274	837	3,687	786
Superior	10,788	212	1,133	1,499	1,570	4,904	1,464

YEAR OF IMMIGRATION. 795

TABLE 14.—FOREIGN-BORN NEGROES, CHINESE, AND JAPANESE, BY YEAR OF IMMIGRATION, FOR SELECTED CITIES: 1920.

[The cities for which figures are presented in this table are those having 500 or more foreign-born inhabitants of the specified race.]

CLASS OF POPULATION AND CITY.	Total foreign born of specified race: 1920	YEAR OF IMMIGRATION.										
		1919	1918	1917	1916	1915	1914	1911-1913	1906-1910	1901-1905	1900 or earlier.	Year not reported.
NEGRO.												
Florida:												
Miami	4,815	860	464	403	318	259	267	728	865	300	275	76
Tampa	660	25	17	7	25	12	16	36	93	69	249	120
Illinois:												
Chicago	1,020	20	18	20	18	8	20	75	81	62	245	453
Louisiana:												
New Orleans	1,146	58	60	27	13	19	14	34	36	23	93	769
Maryland:												
Baltimore	625	30	7	21	9	23	32	73	96	57	177	100
Massachusetts:												
Boston	2,879	105	72	135	140	100	171	424	466	240	453	573
Cambridge	1,116	37	44	60	74	62	88	175	218	121	217	20
New Bedford	2,342	141	68	161	194	137	178	387	345	292	416	23
Michigan:												
Detroit	1,141	40	33	50	42	28	39	79	143	104	268	315
New York:												
New York	30,436	3,100	1,836	2,516	1,855	1,554	1,779	4,051	4,871	2,533	1,960	4,381
Pennsylvania:												
Philadelphia	1,976	68	72	79	72	76	88	166	281	212	348	514
Rhode Island:												
Providence	835	21	36	76	56	76	67	132	98	78	114	81
CHINESE.												
California:												
Los Angeles	1,260	29	21	21	32	29	24	68	134	64	705	133
Oakland	2,596	43	17	43	51	112	64	124	227	121	1,717	77
Sacramento	580	28	19	13	22	25	25	63	95	37	226	27
San Francisco	4,450	200	89	122	162	230	187	448	713	250	1,755	294
Stockton	784	3	5	7	19	31	14	49	102	34	475	45
Illinois:												
Chicago	1,645	45	24	20	42	50	34	85	194	133	810	208
Massachusetts:												
Boston	742	15	20	19	25	19	21	41	106	57	369	50
New York:												
New York	3,958	247	80	100	83	102	141	287	435	517	1,708	258
Oregon:												
Portland	1,237	8	7	5	11	10	14	54	87	38	964	39
Pennsylvania:												
Philadelphia	702	10	12	12	10	13	12	26	83	57	401	66
Washington:												
Seattle	806	76	22	18	22	20	15	51	99	45	460	68
JAPANESE.												
California:												
Berkeley	666	37	38	35	40	38	33	74	171	115	61	24
Fresno	780	45	36	43	31	45	28	78	146	127	143	60
Los Angeles	8,519	566	466	434	459	493	420	769	1,990	1,528	877	467
Oakland	1,924	56	79	73	71	92	89	195	461	387	370	51
Sacramento	1,366	78	68	80	73	78	74	131	304	266	168	46
San Diego	601	26	39	26	34	33	25	45	123	80	99	71
San Francisco	4,175	328	248	228	214	253	180	364	907	647	496	310
Stockton	557	25	22	24	30	40	32	47	105	119	73	40
New York:												
New York	2,061	329	148	123	89	90	78	156	354	245	211	238
Oregon:												
Portland	1,340	78	86	70	71	73	57	147	368	198	164	28
Washington:												
Seattle	6,011	642	409	391	301	268	276	550	1,486	783	487	418
Tacoma	1,061	103	67	57	68	50	51	124	265	126	98	52

POPULATION.

TABLE 15.—FOREIGN-BORN POPULATION AND FOREIGN-BORN WHITE POPULATION OF URBAN AND RURAL COMMUNITIES, BY SEX AND YEAR OF IMMIGRATION, FOR THE UNITED STATES: 1920.

CLASS OF POPULATION AND YEAR OF IMMIGRATION.	BOTH SEXES.				MALE.				FEMALE.			
	Urban.		Rural.		Urban.		Rural.		Urban.		Rural.	
	Number.	Per cent.	Number.	Per cent.	Number.	Per cent.	Number.	Per cent.	Number.	Per cent.	Number.	Per cent.
Foreign-born population	10,500,942	100.0	3,419,750	100.0	5,660,719	100.0	2,014,716	100.0	4,840,223	100.0	1,405,034	100.0
Year of immigration:												
1919	152,493	1.5	61,630	1.8	83,498	1.5	36,394	1.8	68,995	1.4	25,236	1.8
1918	57,363	0.5	28,207	0.8	31,060	0.5	16,260	0.8	26,303	0.5	11,947	0.9
1917	84,364	0.8	31,858	0.9	44,313	0.8	18,246	0.9	40,051	0.8	13,612	1.0
1916	131,386	1.3	45,798	1.3	69,663	1.2	26,393	1.3	61,723	1.3	19,405	1.4
1915	154,813	1.5	48,285	1.4	83,432	1.5	28,794	1.4	71,381	1.5	19,491	1.4
1914	364,541	3.5	85,335	2.5	203,799	3.6	52,417	2.6	160,742	3.3	32,918	2.3
1911–1913	1,303,789	12.4	301,101	8.8	746,998	13.2	186,335	9.2	556,791	11.5	114,766	8.2
1906–1910	1,787,112	17.0	442,756	12.9	1,012,374	17.9	275,778	13.7	774,738	16.0	166,978	11.9
1901–1905	1,443,128	13.7	371,136	10.9	825,715	14.6	231,783	11.5	617,413	12.8	139,353	9.9
1900 or earlier	4,175,275	39.8	1,585,962	46.4	2,217,610	39.2	950,980	47.2	1,957,665	40.4	634,982	45.2
Not reported	846,678	8.1	417,682	12.2	342,257	6.0	191,336	9.5	504,421	10.4	226,346	16.1
Foreign-born white population	10,356,983	100.0	3,355,771	100.0	5,560,396	100.0	1,967,926	100.0	4,796,587	100.0	1,387,845	100.0
Year of immigration:												
1919	143,212	1.4	58,068	1.7	78,054	1.4	34,538	1.8	65,158	1.4	23,530	1.7
1918	51,329	0.5	25,600	0.8	27,760	0.5	14,963	0.8	23,569	0.5	10,637	0.8
1917	77,132	0.7	28,927	0.9	40,164	0.7	16,661	0.8	36,968	0.8	12,266	0.9
1916	124,881	1.2	42,794	1.3	65,915	1.2	24,761	1.3	58,966	1.2	18,033	1.3
1915	148,457	1.4	45,227	1.3	79,639	1.4	27,113	1.4	68,818	1.4	18,114	1.3
1914	358,160	3.5	82,547	2.5	199,986	3.6	50,822	2.6	158,174	3.3	31,725	2.3
1911–1913	1,289,714	12.5	295,432	8.8	738,584	13.3	183,174	9.3	551,130	11.5	112,258	8.1
1906–1910	1,763,726	17.0	430,645	12.8	995,348	17.9	265,767	13.5	768,378	16.0	164,878	11.9
1901–1905	1,428,308	13.8	361,872	10.8	814,106	14.6	223,556	11.4	614,202	12.8	138,316	10.0
1900 or earlier	4,144,032	40.0	1,573,433	46.9	2,190,978	39.4	939,525	47.7	1,953,054	40.7	633,908	45.7
Not reported	828,032	8.0	411,226	12.3	329,862	5.9	187,046	9.5	498,170	10.4	224,180	16.2

YEAR OF IMMIGRATION.   797

TABLE 16.—FOREIGN-BORN POPULATION OF URBAN AND RURAL COMMUNITIES BY YEAR OF IMMIGRATION, BY DIVISIONS AND STATES: 1920.

DIVISION AND STATE.	URBAN COMMUNITIES.										RURAL COMMUNITIES.									
	Total foreign born: 1920	Year of immigration.					Per cent of total arriving in—				Total foreign born: 1920	Year of immigration.					Per cent of total arriving in—			
		1916–1919	1911–1915	1901–1910	1900 or earlier.	Year not reported.	1911–1919	1901–1910	1900 or earlier	Year not reported.		1916–1919	1911–1915	1901–1910	1900 or earlier.	Year not reported.	1911–1919	1901–1910	1900 or earlier	Year not reported.
United States.	10,500,942	425,608	1,823,143	3,230,240	4,175,275	846,678	21.4	30.8	39.8	8.1	3,419,750	167,493	434,721	813,892	1,585,952	417,682	17.6	23.8	46.4	12.2
GEOG. DIVISIONS:																				
New England...	1,656,120	72,623	274,037	493,620	728,764	87,076	20.9	29.8	44.0	5.3	229,825	12,428	31,091	61,350	103,679	21,277	18.9	26.7	45.1	9.3
Middle Atlantic..	4,286,036	189,376	781,885	1,488,126	1,599,005	277,644	21.5	34.7	37.3	6.5	674,382	14,212	119,647	221,007	250,908	68,608	19.8	32.8	37.2	10.2
E. North Central.	2,519,957	66,229	486,560	744,964	992,962	229,222	21.9	29.6	39.4	9.1	712,204	9,207	66,896	145,803	396,285	94,448	10.6	20.5	55.6	13.3
W. North Central.	609,942	17,417	71,980	143,654	300,903	75,988	14.7	23.6	49.3	12.5	765,711	10,817	48,715	130,461	474,128	101,590	7.8	17.0	61.9	13.3
South Atlantic...	233,879	10,874	35,435	68,227	93,116	26,227	19.8	29.2	39.9	11.2	96,658	5,857	21,091	27,786	25,534	16,410	27.9	28.7	26.4	17.0
E. South Central.	49,015	987	3,886	9,543	24,356	10,243	9.9	19.5	49.7	20.9	23,974	616	2,835	5,313	10,067	5,143	14.4	22.2	42.0	21.5
W. South Central.	223,424	42,304	44,500	39,067	56,798	40,749	38.9	17.5	25.4	18.2	241,404	44,355	40,385	43,074	74,790	38,800	35.1	17.8	31.0	16.1
Mountain........	186,147	15,201	24,318	44,313	81,564	20,751	21.2	23.8	43.8	11.1	281,478	37,486	46,800	71,393	95,814	29,980	29.9	25.4	34.0	10.7
Pacific...........	736,442	60,595	100,536	198,726	297,807	78,778	21.9	27.0	40.4	10.7	394,119	32,515	57,761	107,660	154,757	41,426	22.9	27.3	39.3	10.5
NEW ENGLAND:																				
Maine............	59,465	4,419	7,642	13,898	27,135	6,401	20.3	23.3	45.6	10.8	48,349	3,974	5,484	11,178	20,968	6,745	19.6	23.1	43.4	14.0
New Hampshire.	71,574	4,253	10,184	16,977	32,176	7,984	20.2	23.7	45.0	11.2	19,823	1,262	2,001	3,698	9,788	3,074	16.5	18.7	49.4	15.5
Vermont.........	18,167	873	2,478	4,974	8,200	1,642	18.4	27.4	45.1	9.0	26,391	3,607	3,687	5,414	10,922	2,761	27.6	20.5	41.4	10.5
Massachusetts...	1,055,640	45,803	171,973	318,764	481,651	42,359	20.6	29.7	45.6	4.0	32,008	948	4,068	8,448	17,416	2,028	15.2	25.7	52.9	6.2
Rhode Island....	173,305	7,778	24,924	50,575	78,352	11,736	18.9	29.2	45.2	6.8	1,824	54	228	465	843	234	15.5	25.5	46.2	12.8
Connecticut.....	277,909	9,407	56,836	93,462	101,250	16,954	23.8	33.6	36.4	6.1	100,530	2,583	15,623	32,147	43,742	6,435	18.1	32.0	43.5	6.4
MIDDLE ATLANTIC:																				
New York.......	2,623,903	102,036	468,153	917,761	966,917	169,036	21.7	35.0	36.9	6.4	201,472	5,749	25,484	50,566	91,228	28,445	15.5	25.1	45.3	14.1
New Jersey......	631,873	15,692	117,065	218,250	242,751	38,109	21.0	34.5	38.4	6.1	110,613	2,384	17,357	36,564	44,052	10,256	17.8	33.1	39.8	9.3
Pennsylvania....	1,030,260	21,648	196,667	352,109	389,337	70,499	21.2	34.2	37.8	6.8	362,297	6,079	76,806	133,877	115,628	29,907	22.9	37.0	31.9	8.3
E. NORTH CENTRAL:																				
Ohio............	572,098	14,361	131,608	184,365	203,519	38,245	25.5	32.2	35.6	6.7	108,354	1,687	17,203	31,292	45,305	12,867	17.4	28.9	41.8	11.9
Indiana.........	119,251	2,387	21,268	32,988	43,576	19,032	19.8	27.7	36.5	16.0	32,077	321	2,124	5,072	17,253	7,307	7.6	15.8	53.8	22.8
Illinois.........	1,050,200	18,034	175,935	325,579	435,448	95,204	18.5	31.0	41.5	9.1	160,384	2,281	15,672	34,939	82,515	24,977	11.2	21.8	51.4	15.8
Michigan.......	523,978	28,287	122,361	143,088	177,439	52,803	28.8	27.3	33.9	10.1	205,314	3,608	18,278	40,983	118,444	24,001	10.7	20.0	57.7	11.7
Wisconsin.......	254,410	3,160	35,388	58,944	132,980	23,938	15.2	23.2	52.3	9.4	206,075	1,310	13,119	33,582	132,768	25,296	7.0	16.3	64.4	12.3
W. NORTH CENTRAL:																				
Minnesota......	242,008	5,393	29,777	62,054	122,633	21,551	14.5	25.9	50.7	8.9	244,787	2,445	14,956	41,657	164,382	21,347	7.1	17.0	67.2	8.7
Iowa...........	90,285	2,404	9,608	15,059	49,304	13,910	13.3	16.7	54.6	15.4	135,709	1,773	9,893	18,368	86,788	18,887	8.6	13.5	64.0	13.9
Missouri........	149,551	3,247	16,032	39,238	70,215	19,919	13.5	26.2	47.0	13.3	37,284	426	1,719	4,515	21,877	8,747	5.8	12.1	58.7	23.5
North Dakota...	16,308	253	1,300	3,474	7,593	3,688	9.5	21.3	46.6	22.6	115,555	1,328	8,168	32,080	57,930	16,104	8.2	27.7	50.1	13.9
South Dakota...	12,236	192	903	2,322	5,984	2,835	8.9	19.0	48.9	23.2	70,298	822	4,685	13,300	41,793	9,718	7.8	18.9	59.5	13.8
Nebraska.......	59,905	1,056	8,592	14,224	27,522	7,911	17.1	23.7	45.9	13.2	90,760	1,115	4,918	10,571	59,101	15,055	6.6	11.6	65.1	16.6
Kansas..........	39,049	4,272	4,868	6,683	17,652	6,174	23.1	16.9	44.5	15.6	71,318	2,908	4,401	10,020	42,257	11,732	10.2	14.0	59.3	16.5
SOUTH ATLANTIC:																				
Delaware........	16,878	454	3,851	5,331	5,566	1,676	25.5	31.0	33.0	9.9	3,023	96	374	738	1,041	774	15.5	24.4	34.4	25.6
Maryland........	88,678	1,680	13,762	27,054	42,290	3,892	17.4	30.5	47.7	4.4	14,501	386	1,712	3,106	6,403	2,888	14.5	21.4	44.2	19.9
Dist. Columbia[1].	29,385	1,243	3,595	7,843	11,567	5,117	16.5	26.7	39.4	17.4										
Virginia.........	20,018	1,524	2,975	5,694	6,689	3,136	22.5	28.4	33.4	15.7	11,687	467	1,572	3,071	3,798	2,779	17.4	26.3	32.5	23.8
West Virginia...	19,804	683	3,592	5,655	6,803	3,131	21.5	28.5	34.2	15.8	42,241	2,359	14,071	15,478	5,435	4,898	40.1	36.6	12.9	10.4
North Carolina..	4,373	171	567	1,119	1,351	1,165	16.9	25.6	30.9	26.6	2,899	151	415	624	1,014	695	19.5	21.5	35.0	24.0
South Carolina..	4,356	134	555	1,027	1,666	974	15.8	23.6	38.2	22.4	2,226	66	316	523	772	549	17.2	23.5	34.7	24.7
Georgia.........	12,733	469	1,522	3,548	5,170	2,024	15.6	27.9	40.6	15.9	3,831	107	567	1,052	1,286	819	17.6	27.5	33.6	21.4
Florida.........	37,614	4,516	5,016	10,956	12,014	5,112	25.3	29.1	31.9	13.6	16,250	1,725	2,058	3,174	5,785	3,508	23.3	19.5	35.6	21.6
E. SOUTH CENTRAL:																				
Kentucky.......	21,667	206	1,230	3,062	13,210	3,959	6.6	14.1	61.0	18.3	9,239	264	1,558	2,085	3,752	1,630	19.7	22.0	40.6	17.6
Tennessee.......	11,621	340	1,113	2,697	5,003	2,468	12.5	23.2	43.1	21.2	4,027	81	269	676	1,912	1,089	8.7	16.8	47.5	27.0
Alabama........	11,431	351	1,167	2,677	4,257	2,979	13.3	23.4	37.2	26.1	6,590	159	591	1,544	2,765	1,537	11.4	23.4	41.9	23.3
Mississippi......	4,296	90	376	1,107	1,880	837	10.8	25.8	43.8	19.5	4,112	112	417	1,058	1,688	837	12.9	25.7	39.8	21.6
W. SOUTH CENTRAL:																				
Arkansas........	5,647	52	293	891	2,644	1,767	6.1	15.8	46.8	31.3	8,490	192	610	1,700	4,110	1,878	9.4	20.0	48.4	22.1
Louisiana.......	34,093	1,829	2,065	5,880	13,682	10,637	11.4	17.2	40.1	31.2	12,334	494	673	3,248	5,713	2,206	9.5	26.3	46.3	17.9
Oklahoma......	14,449	1,675	1,420	2,576	5,405	3,373	21.4	17.8	37.4	23.3	25,983	1,924	1,985	4,310	12,071	5,693	15.0	16.6	46.5	21.9
Texas..........	169,235	38,748	40,728	29,720	35,067	24,972	47.0	17.6	20.7	14.8	194,597	41,745	37,117	33,816	52,896	29,023	40.5	17.4	27.2	14.9
MOUNTAIN:																				
Montana........	33,482	1,091	3,802	8,462	13,998	6,129	14.6	25.3	41.8	18.3	62,109	2,123	8,946	18,005	24,872	8,163	17.8	29.0	40.0	13.1
Idaho..........	11,801	647	1,249	2,513	6,010	1,382	16.1	21.3	50.9	11.7	28,946	1,681	3,227	7,030	14,243	2,765	17.0	24.3	49.2	9.5
Wyoming.......	8,966	717	1,339	2,458	3,181	1,271	22.9	27.4	35.5	14.2	17,601	1,108	3,388	5,434	5,369	2,352	25.3	30.9	30.5	13.4
Colorado.......	60,483	3,062	6,144	14,082	31,643	5,552	15.2	23.3	52.3	9.2	58,655	3,863	9,120	16,308	23,069	6,207	17.8	27.8	39.3	10.7
New Mexico.....	5,754	775	937	1,135	2,037	870	29.8	19.7	35.4	15.1	24,054	6,000	6,261	5,309	4,475	2,009	51.0	22.1	18.6	8.4
Arizona........	29,704	7,438	6,657	6,643	6,015	2,951	47.5	22.4	20.2	9.9	50,862	20,026	10,163	8,937	6,762	4,974	59.4	17.6	13.3	9.8
Utah...........	33,152	1,332	3,909	8,324	17,694	1,893	15.8	25.1	53.4	5.7	28,048	1,543	3,703	6,514	12,313	1,975	20.1	25.0	47.3	7.6
Nevada........	2,805	139	281	696	986	703	15.0	24.8	35.2	25.1	13,198	1,142	2,042	3,858	4,711	1,445	24.1	29.2	35.7	10.9
PACIFIC:																				
Washington....	159,291	11,543	19,761	44,406	63,637	19,944	19.7	27.9	40.0	12.5	106,001	4,989	12,080	29,888	47,996	11,048	16.1	28.2	45.3	10.4
Oregon.........	65,073	3,103	8,214	19,331	30,314	4,111	17.4	29.7	46.6	6.3	42,571	1,662	4,517	10,010	22,327	4,055	14.5	23.5	52.4	9.5
California......	512,078	45,949	72,561	134,989	203,850	54,723	23.1	26.4	39.8	10.7	245,547	25,864	41,164	67,762	84,434	26,323	27.3	27.6	34.4	10.7

[1] No rural population, as Washington city is coextensive with the District of Columbia.

Chapter VIII
CITIZENSHIP OF THE FOREIGN-BORN POPULATION

CHAPTER VIII.—CITIZENSHIP OF THE FOREIGN-BORN POPULATION.

INTRODUCTION.

The inquiry as to citizenship of the foreign born has been made at each census, beginning with 1890. In that year, however, no tabulation was made by color or race; and in 1890, 1900, and 1910 the returns related only to foreign-born men 21 years of age and over. The census of 1920 is thus the first at which complete data as to citizenship have been secured for foreign-born persons of both sexes and all ages. The statistics here presented relate to the population of continental United States, the states, and those cities having 25,000 inhabitants or more. Statistics for Alaska, Hawaii, and Porto Rico are given in Volume III of the Fourteenth Census Reports.

The classification in regard to citizenship embraces four groups, namely, naturalized, having first papers, alien, and citizenship not reported. The first papers constitute the declaration of intention to become a citizen of the United States, which declaration may be made by any eligible alien 18 years of age or more at any time after arrival in the United States. The process of naturalization can not be completed, however, until at least two years and not more than seven years have elapsed after the declaration of intention, and the applicant has resided at least five years continuously in the United States and at least one year continuously in the state of which he seeks to become a citizen. In some cases, however, the requirement of five years' continuous residence in the United States is waived on account of military or naval service.

Under the provisions of the naturalization laws at the time the Fourteenth Census was taken, the citizenship status of a married woman was the same as that of her husband (but if the husband had taken out his first naturalization papers only, his wife was classified in the census returns as an alien); for an unmarried woman the process of naturalization was the same as for a man; a foreign-born widow or foreign-born divorced wife of a citizen of the United States retained the citizenship status of her former husband so long as she continued to reside in this country; a foreign-born widow or foreign-born divorced wife of an alien might become naturalized in the same manner as a man; and, in general, foreign-born minors have the same citizenship status as their parents.

Since the foreign-born population of the United States consists mainly of white persons, the statistics in most of the tables relate to foreign-born whites only; but in Tables 1, 2, 5, and 11 figures are given for the total foreign-born population, of all races, and in Table 1 a separate presentation is made for each of the several color or race classes. It will be noted that a few foreign-born Chinese and Japanese are reported as naturalized, although the members of these races are not legally eligible to citizenship unless born in the United States. A small number of Chinese may have been naturalized prior to 1882, in which year their legal ineligibility was made more explicit, and a few more Chinese and some Japanese may have been illegally admitted to citizenship prior to 1906, when the Federal Government undertook a closer supervision of the matter. It is possible, however, that the number reported as naturalized was somewhat exaggerated by false returns, especially in the case of the Chinese. (See Table 1.)

In comparing the percentages naturalized, having first papers, and alien for 1920 with those for earlier census years, the varying proportion of foreign-born persons for whom returns as to citizenship were not made should be taken into consideration. This proportion in 1920 for men 21 years of age and over (5.2 per cent) was less than one-half as large as the corresponding proportion in 1910 (11.8 per cent) and only a little more than one-third as large as that for 1900 (14.9 per cent). The proportion naturalized for 1920 (47 per cent of the total) thus represented slightly less than one-half of the proportion for whom explicit returns as to citizenship were made (94.8 per cent of the total), and the proportion naturalized for 1910 (44.8 per cent of the total) represented slightly more than one-half of the proportion for whom explicit returns were made (88.2 per cent of the total), while for 1900 and 1890 the proportions naturalized were approximately two-thirds of the total for whom returns as to citizenship were made.

In making use of these statistics account should also be taken of the proportion of the foreign-born population which had been in the United States less than five years, the length of time necessary for the acquirement of eligibility for citizenship (except in cases of certain aliens who had rendered military or naval service). In 1900 slightly less than one-tenth

75647°—22——51

(801)

POPULATION.

of the foreign-born population had been in the United States less than five years; in 1910, more than one-fifth; and in 1920, about one-sixteenth. It might be expected, therefore, that, other things being equal, the proportion naturalized in 1920 would be materially larger than in 1910 and slightly larger than in 1900; but, in fact, the proportion naturalized for men 21 years of age and over, as shown by the 1920 returns, did not differ greatly from that for 1910 and was considerably below that for 1900. This condition is presumably to be explained by the difference between the character of the earlier immigration and that which has arrived during the past two decades. Moreover, the procedure and requirements for naturalization are now more rigid than they were prior to 1900.

If, however, the proportions naturalized and having first papers are combined, the proportion of the foreign-born men who had become citizens, or at least had declared their intention to do so, is shown to be larger for 1920 than for 1910, although not so large for 1920 as for 1900 or 1890.

The first three diagrams on the next page show the percentages naturalized and not naturalized for white persons born in those countries or groups of countries each of which had contributed 200,000 or more to the entire foreign-born white population of the United States, enumerated as of January 1, 1920, the countries being arranged in descending order according to numbers. The fourth diagram shows the percentages naturalized for white persons born in those countries each of which had contributed at least 50,000 to the foreign-born white population of the United States in 1920, the order of arrangement being determined by the percentages.

Urban and rural communities.—Because of the pronounced difference between urban and rural communities in regard to the proportions of native and foreign-born persons in their population, separate statistics for the two classes of communities are given in Tables 18 to 20.

In drawing the distinction between urban and rural population, all incorporated places (and all towns in Massachusetts, Rhode Island, and New Hampshire) having 2,500 inhabitants or more are treated as urban and the remainder of the country as rural. In Massachusetts and Rhode Island it is not the practice, as in practically all the other states, to incorporate as separate municipalities the relatively densely populated portions of "towns" (which are the primary divisions of the counties), and no town as a whole is incorporated as a municipality until it attains a population greatly in excess of 2,500; and in New Hampshire a similar condition exists, although the state contains two incorporated villages, each of which has fewer than 2,500 inhabitants. For this reason, those towns having 2,500 or more inhabitants in the three states named are treated as urban, although portions of their areas are rural in character. The urban areas in the three states in question, as classified by the census, thus contain relatively small numbers of inhabitants who in other sections of the country would be segregated as rural. Nevertheless, in most of the towns having 2,500 inhabitants or more in Massachusetts, Rhode Island, and New Hampshire by far the greater part of the population resides within the more densely settled areas, so that the proportion classed as urban, considering each state as a whole, is not greatly exaggerated by the practice adopted.

CITIZENSHIP.

CITIZENSHIP OF FOREIGN WHITE PERSONS BORN IN SPECIFIED COUNTRIES OR GROUPS OF COUNTRIES: 1920.

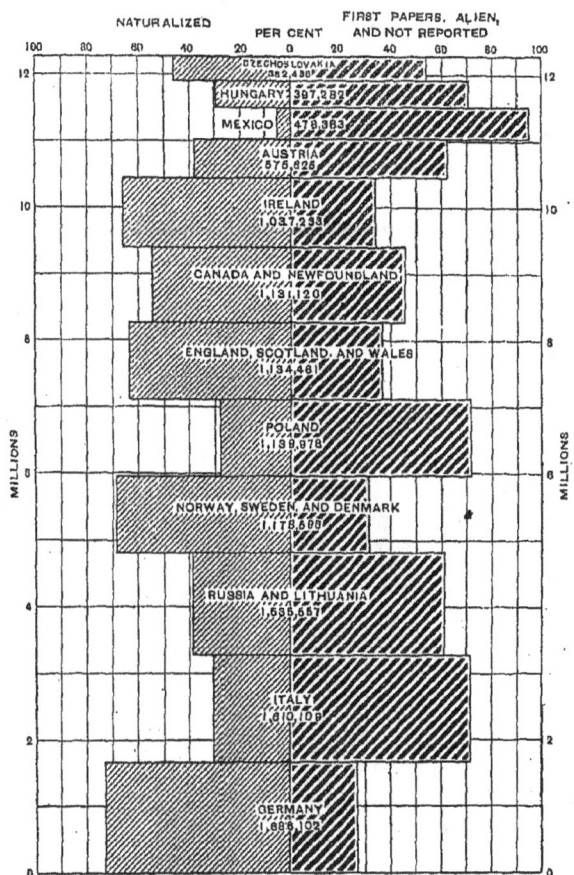

CITIZENSHIP OF FOREIGN WHITE MEN 21 YEARS OF AGE AND OVER BORN IN SPECIFIED COUNTRIES OR GROUPS OF COUNTRIES: 1920.

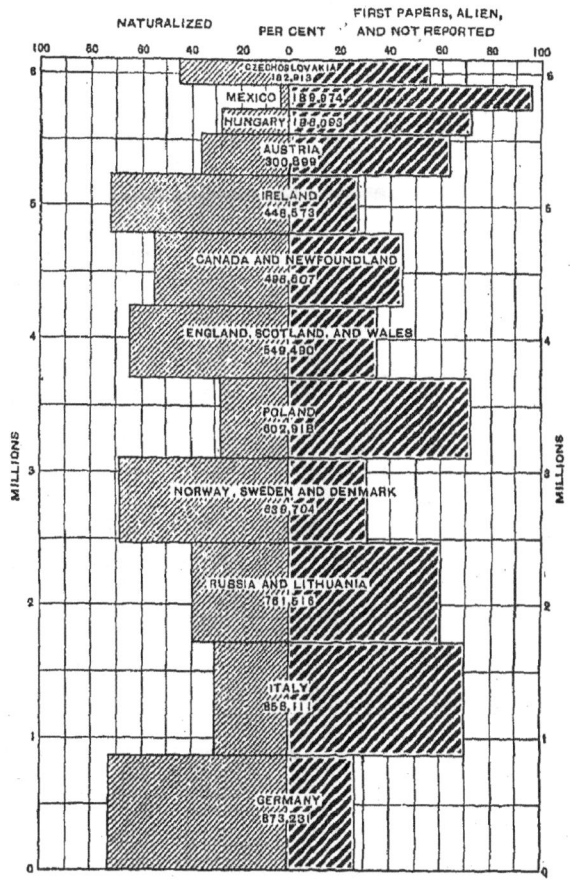

CITIZENSHIP OF FOREIGN WHITE WOMEN 21 YEARS OF AGE AND OVER BORN IN SPECIFIED COUNTRIES OR GROUPS OF COUNTRIES: 1920.

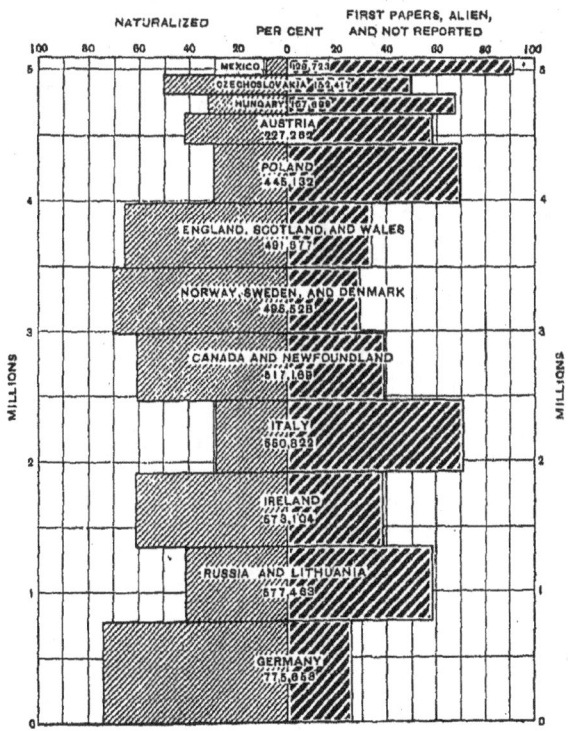

PER CENT NATURALIZED IN FOREIGN-BORN WHITE POPULATION, BY COUNTRY OF BIRTH: 1920.

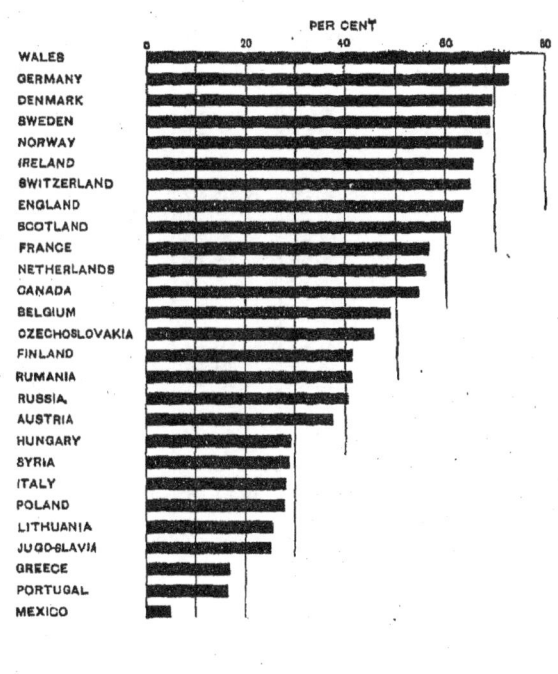

804

POPULATION.

TABLE 1.—CITIZENSHIP OF THE POPULATION BY COLOR OR RACE AND NATIVITY, FOR ALL AGES AND FOR PERSONS 21 YEARS OF AGE AND OVER, BY SEX, FOR THE UNITED STATES: 1890–1920.

[Figures are given for age and sex under each class for all census years for which data are available.]

CENSUS YEAR, SEX, AGE, AND COLOR OR RACE.	Total.	Native.	FOREIGN-BORN. Number. Total.	Naturalized.	Having first papers.	Alien.	Citizenship not reported.	FOREIGN-BORN. Per cent. Naturalized.	Having first papers.	Alien.	Citizenship not reported.	CITIZENS, NATIVE OR NATURALIZED. Number.	Per cent of total of specified class.
1920													
Both sexes, all ages	105,710,620	91,789,928	13,920,692	6,493,088	1,223,490	5,398,605	805,509	46.6	8.8	38.8	5.8	98,283,016	93.0
White	94,820,915	81,108,161	13,712,754	6,479,150	1,219,057	5,223,715	790,823	47.2	8.9	38.1	5.8	87,587,320	92.4
Negro	10,463,131	10,389,328	73,803	10,724	3,496	48,930	10,653	14.5	4.7	66.3	14.4	10,400,052	99.4
Indian	244,437	238,138	6,299	665	59	4,946	629	10.6	0.9	78.5	10.0	238,803	97.7
Chinese	61,639	18,532	43,107	1,834	430	39,436	1,407	4.3	1.0	91.5	3.3	20,306	33.0
Japanese	111,010	29,672	81,338	572	270	78,740	1,756	0.7	0.3	96.8	2.2	30,244	27.2
All other	9,488	6,097	3,391	134	178	2,888	241	4.0	5.2	83.7	7.1	6,231	65.7
Males, all ages	53,900,421	46,224,996	7,675,435	3,451,609	1,137,911	2,688,929	396,986	45.0	14.8	35.0	5.2	49,676,805	92.2
White	48,430,655	40,902,333	7,528,392	3,443,968	1,133,727	2,562,917	387,710	45.7	15.1	34.0	5.2	44,346,301	91.6
Negro	5,209,436	5,166,795	42,641	5,579	3,294	27,653	6,115	13.1	7.7	64.9	14.3	5,172,374	99.3
Indian	125,068	121,529	3,539	213	51	2,900	375	6.0	1.4	81.9	10.6	121,742	97.3
Chinese	53,891	13,318	40,573	1,342	423	37,514	1,294	3.3	1.0	92.5	3.2	14,660	27.2
Japanese	72,707	15,494	57,213	399	239	55,296	1,279	0.7	0.4	96.6	2.2	15,893	21.9
All other	8,674	5,527	3,147	108	177	2,649	213	3.4	5.6	84.2	6.8	5,635	65.0
Females, all ages	51,810,189	45,564,932	6,245,257	3,041,479	85,579	2,709,676	408,523	48.7	1.4	43.4	6.5	48,606,411	93.8
White	46,390,260	40,205,828	6,184,432	3,035,191	85,330	2,660,798	403,113	49.1	1.4	43.0	6.5	43,241,019	93.2
Negro	5,253,695	5,222,533	31,162	5,145	202	21,277	4,538	16.5	0.6	68.3	14.6	5,227,678	99.5
Indian	119,369	116,609	2,760	452	8	2,046	254	16.4	0.3	74.1	9.2	117,061	98.1
Chinese	7,748	5,214	2,534	492	7	1,922	113	19.4	0.3	75.8	4.5	5,706	73.6
Japanese	38,303	14,178	24,125	173	31	23,444	477	0.7	0.1	97.2	2.0	14,351	37.5
All other	814	570	244	26	1	189	28	10.7	0.4	77.5	11.5	596	73.2
Both sexes, 21 years and over	60,886,520	48,200,127	12,686,393	6,221,705	1,198,588	4,522,359	743,741	49.0	9.4	35.6	5.9	54,421,832	89.4
White	55,113,461	42,614,741	12,498,720	6,208,697	1,194,276	4,364,909	730,838	49.7	9.6	34.9	5.8	48,823,438	88.6
Negro	5,522,475	5,458,063	64,412	10,104	3,422	41,586	9,300	15.7	5.3	64.6	14.4	5,468,167	99.0
Indian	116,486	112,044	4,442	603	56	3,297	486	13.6	1.3	74.2	10.9	112,647	96.7
Chinese	50,625	10,131	40,494	1,637	407	37,149	1,301	4.0	1.0	91.7	3.2	11,768	23.2
Japanese	75,727	658	75,069	541	254	72,679	1,595	0.7	0.3	96.8	2.1	1,199	1.6
All other	7,746	4,490	3,256	123	173	2,739	221	3.8	5.3	84.1	6.8	4,613	59.6
Males, 21 years and over	31,403,370	24,339,776	7,063,594	3,322,104	1,120,833	2,253,691	366,966	47.0	15.9	31.9	5.2	27,661,880	88.1
White	28,442,400	21,513,948	6,928,452	3,314,910	1,116,744	2,138,237	358,561	47.8	16.1	30.9	5.2	24,828,858	87.3
Negro	2,792,006	2,753,772	38,234	5,316	3,238	24,165	5,515	13.9	8.5	63.2	14.4	2,750,088	98.8
Indian	61,229	58,670	2,559	187	49	2,026	297	7.3	1.9	79.2	11.6	58,857	96.1
Chinese	46,979	8,694	38,285	1,199	402	35,470	1,214	3.1	1.1	92.6	3.2	9,893	21.1
Japanese	53,411	412	52,999	390	228	51,207	1,174	0.7	0.4	96.6	2.2	802	1.5
All other	7,845	4,280	3,565	102	172	2,586	205	3.3	5.6	84.4	6.7	4,382	59.7
Females, 21 years and over	29,483,150	23,860,351	5,622,799	2,899,601	77,755	2,268,668	376,775	51.6	1.4	40.3	6.7	26,759,952	90.8
White	26,671,061	21,100,793	5,570,268	2,893,787	77,532	2,226,672	372,277	52.0	1.4	40.0	6.7	23,994,580	90.0
Negro	2,730,469	2,704,291	26,178	4,788	184	17,421	3,785	18.3	0.7	66.5	14.5	2,709,079	99.2
Indian	55,257	53,374	1,883	416	7	1,271	189	22.1	0.4	67.5	10.0	53,790	97.3
Chinese	3,646	1,437	2,209	438	5	1,679	87	19.8	0.2	76.0	3.9	1,875	51.4
Japanese	22,316	246	22,070	151	26	21,472	421	0.7	0.1	97.3	1.9	397	1.8
All other	401	210	191	21	1	153	16	11.0	0.5	80.1	8.4	231	57.6
1910													
Males, 21 years and over	28,999,151	20,218,937	6,780,214	3,040,302	572,421	2,370,398	797,093	44.8	8.4	35.0	11.8	23,259,239	86.1
White	24,357,514	17,710,697	6,646,817	3,034,117	570,772	2,266,535	775,393	45.6	8.6	34.1	11.7	20,744,814	85.2
Negro	2,458,873	2,437,725	21,148	4,186	749	11,642	4,571	19.8	3.5	55.1	21.6	2,441,911	99.3
Indian	62,967	61,742	1,225	191	10	406	618	15.6	0.8	33.1	50.4	61,933	98.4
Chinese	60,421	8,463	51,958	1,368	483	42,710	7,397	2.6	0.9	82.2	14.2	9,831	16.3
Japanese	56,638	209	56,429	420	387	46,860	8,762	0.7	0.7	83.0	15.5	629	1.1
All other	2,738	101	2,637	20	20	2,245	352	0.8	0.8	85.1	13.3	121	4.4
1900													
Males, 21 years and over	21,134,299	16,124,013	5,010,286	2,849,981	412,790	1,001,595	745,920	56.9	8.2	20.0	14.9	18,973,994	89.8
White	18,918,697	14,014,427	4,904,270	2,845,473	411,898	914,917	731,982	58.0	8.4	18.7	14.9	16,859,900	89.1
Negro	2,060,302	2,049,958	10,344	3,834	373	3,630	3,007	32.2	3.6	35.1	29.1	2,053,292	99.7
Indian	57,077	56,071	1,006	138	33	378	457	13.7	3.3	37.6	45.4	56,209	98.5
Chinese	81,018	3,520	77,498	805	373	68,627	7,303	1.2	0.5	88.9	9.4	4,415	5.4
Japanese	17,205	37	17,168	141	113	13,743	3,171	0.8	0.7	80.1	18.5	178	1.0
1890 [1]													
Males, 21 years and over	16,940,311	12,591,852	4,348,459	2,545,753	236,061	1,189,452	377,193	58.5	5.4	27.4	8.7	15,137,605	89.4

[1] Exclusive of population of Indian Territory and Indian reservations, specially enumerated in 1890 but not distributed by age.

CITIZENSHIP.

TABLE 2.—CITIZENSHIP OF FOREIGN-BORN AND FOREIGN-BORN WHITE MALES 21 YEARS OF AGE AND OVER, 1920, 1910, AND 1900, AND OF FEMALES, 1920 ONLY, FOR THE UNITED STATES.

[No inquiry as to the citizenship of females prior to 1920. A minus sign (−) denotes decrease.]

CITIZENSHIP.	MALES 21 YEARS OF AGE AND OVER.							Females 21 years of age and over: 1920	Males to 100 females in population 21 years and over: 1920
	1920	1910	1900	Increase: 1910–1920		Increase: 1900–1910			
				Number.	Per cent.	Number.	Per cent.		
Foreign born	7,063,594	6,780,214	5,010,286	283,380	4.2	1,769,928	35.3	5,622,799	125.6
Naturalized	3,322,104	3,040,302	2,849,981	281,802	9.3	190,321	6.7	2,899,601	114.6
Having first papers	1,120,833	572,421	412,790	548,412	95.8	159,631	38.7	77,755	1,441.5
Alien	2,253,691	2,370,398	1,001,595	−116,707	−4.9	1,368,803	136.7	2,268,668	99.3
Not reported	366,966	797,093	745,920	−430,127	−54.0	51,173	6.9	376,775	97.4
Foreign-born white	6,926,452	6,646,817	4,904,270	281,635	4.2	1,742,547	35.5	5,570,266	124.4
Naturalized	3,314,910	3,034,117	2,845,473	280,793	9.3	188,644	6.6	2,893,787	114.6
Having first papers	1,116,744	570,772	411,898	545,972	95.7	158,874	38.6	77,532	1,440.4
Alien	2,138,237	2,266,535	914,917	−128,298	−5.7	1,351,618	147.7	2,226,672	96.0
Not reported	358,561	775,393	731,982	−416,832	−53.8	43,411	5.9	372,277	96.3

TABLE 3.—CITIZENSHIP OF FOREIGN-BORN WHITE POPULATION, BY SEX AND COUNTRY OF BIRTH, FOR THE UNITED STATES: 1920.

COUNTRY OF BIRTH.	FOREIGN-BORN WHITE POPULATION.						FOREIGN-BORN WHITE MALES.						FOREIGN-BORN WHITE FEMALES.					
	Total.	Naturalized.		Having first papers.	Alien.	Citizenship not reported.	Total.	Naturalized.		Having first papers.	Alien.	Citizenship not reported.	Total.	Naturalized.		Having first papers.	Alien.	Citizenship not reported.
		Number.	Per cent.					Number.	Per cent.					Number.	Per cent.			
All countries	13,712,754	6,479,159	47.2	1,219,057	5,223,715	790,823	7,528,322	3,443,968	45.7	1,123,727	2,562,917	387,710	6,184,432	3,035,191	49.1	95,330	2,660,798	403,113
EUROPE.																		
Northwestern Europe:																		
England	812,828	512,670	63.1	56,331	175,447	68,380	425,038	265,820	62.5	51,297	73,377	34,544	387,790	246,850	63.7	5,034	102,070	33,836
Scotland	254,567	154,931	60.9	20,268	58,824	20,544	133,955	82,425	61.5	18,464	22,827	10,239	120,612	72,506	60.1	1,804	35,997	10,305
Wales	67,066	48,897	72.9	3,264	8,271	6,634	36,184	26,152	72.3	3,009	3,574	3,449	30,882	22,745	73.7	255	4,697	3,185
Ireland	1,037,288	681,362	65.7	52,707	206,959	96,205	455,571	327,146	71.8	44,297	50,286	33,852	581,662	354,216	60.9	8,420	156,673	62,353
Norway	363,862	244,743	67.3	32,386	63,035	23,698	202,757	134,659	66.4	29,551	27,167	11,390	161,105	110,084	68.3	2,835	35,868	12,318
Sweden	625,580	431,556	69.0	53,007	105,445	35,572	344,933	236,614	68.6	48,173	42,369	17,777	280,647	194,942	69.5	4,834	63,076	17,795
Denmark	189,154	130,826	69.2	16,862	28,987	12,479	114,063	78,030	68.4	15,671	18,175	7,187	75,091	52,796	70.3	1,191	15,812	5,292
Netherlands	131,766	73,773	56.0	13,465	36,550	7,978	75,510	41,383	54.8	12,567	17,216	4,344	56,256	32,390	57.6	898	19,334	3,634
Belgium	62,686	30,740	49.0	8,255	19,635	4,056	35,970	17,604	48.9	7,759	8,344	2,263	26,716	13,136	49.2	496	11,291	1,793
Luxemburg	12,585	9,124	72.5	669	1,507	985	7,671	5,543	72.3	895	695	538	4,914	3,581	72.9	74	812	447
Switzerland	118,659	76,957	64.9	8,756	22,635	10,311	67,830	43,332	63.9	7,983	11,194	5,321	50,829	33,625	66.2	773	11,441	4,990
France	152,890	86,740	56.7	11,205	41,229	13,716	79,351	45,875	57.8	10,010	16,945	6,521	73,539	40,865	55.6	1,195	24,284	7,195
Central Europe:																		
Germany	1,686,102	1,227,713	72.8	116,479	210,922	130,988	891,289	646,579	72.5	102,322	83,570	58,812	794,813	581,134	73.1	14,157	127,346	72,176
Poland	1,139,978	319,383	28.0	148,420	338,468	333,468	646,387	176,197	27.3	141,320	311,785	17,085	493,591	143,186	29.0	7,100	326,922	16,383
Czechoslovakia	362,436	165,997	45.8	49,244	132,176	15,019	196,251	85,444	43.5	46,110	57,565	7,132	166,185	80,553	48.5	3,134	74,611	7,887
Austria	575,625	216,968	37.7	67,913	265,054	25,115	323,451	115,481	35.7	54,227	129,355	14,888	252,174	101,487	40.2	3,686	133,335	13,666
Hungary	397,282	115,736	29.1	54,002	212,429	15,115	216,914	59,695	27.5	50,950	99,018	7,251	180,368	56,041	31.1	3,052	113,411	7,864
Jugo-Slavia	169,437	42,686	25.2	28,892	92,971	4,888	114,750	25,064	21.8	27,952	58,470	3,264	54,687	17,622	32.2	940	34,501	1,624
Eastern Europe:																		
Russia	1,400,489	562,930	40.2	139,149	644,966	53,444	774,013	310,284	40.1	130,870	305,541	27,018	626,476	252,646	40.3	8,279	339,125	26,426
Lithuania	135,068	34,627	25.6	16,890	80,428	3,123	82,856	20,891	25.2	16,304	43,869	1,802	52,202	13,736	26.3	586	36,559	1,321
Finland	149,824	61,902	41.3	18,797	63,000	6,125	85,287	33,065	38.8	17,661	31,449	3,112	64,537	28,837	44.7	1,136	31,551	3,013
Rumania	102,823	42,225	41.1	12,694	43,952	3,952	58,135	23,169	39.9	11,948	21,045	1,973	44,688	19,056	42.6	746	22,907	1,979
Bulgaria	10,477	1,268	12.1	1,716	7,023	470	9,508	994	10.5	1,696	6,395	423	969	274	28.3	20	628	47
Turkey in Europe	5,284	1,070	20.2	665	3,349	200	3,658	711	19.4	640	2,173	134	1,626	359	22.1	25	1,176	66
Southern Europe:																		
Greece	175,972	29,479	16.8	21,451	117,295	7,747	143,602	23,786	16.6	21,080	92,381	6,355	32,370	5,693	17.6	371	24,914	1,392
Albania	5,608	413	7.4	517	4,551	127	4,905	335	6.8	513	3,950	107	703	78	11.1	4	601	20
Italy	1,610,109	452,753	28.1	163,499	941,602	52,255	958,274	275,609	28.8	157,159	495,385	29,621	651,835	177,144	27.2	6,340	445,717	22,634
Spain	49,247	4,881	9.9	2,428	39,623	2,315	36,434	3,021	8.3	2,355	29,428	1,630	12,813	1,860	14.5	73	10,195	685
Portugal	67,453	11,049	16.4	2,481	51,590	2,333	39,372	6,319	16.0	2,337	29,322	1,384	28,081	4,730	16.8	144	22,258	949
Other Europe[1]	5,901	2,835	48.0	675	1,821	570	3,665	1,560	42.6	631	1,172	302	2,236	1,275	57.0	44	649	268
ASIA.																		
Armenia	36,626	10,574	28.9	4,630	20,125	1,297	25,351	6,948	27.4	4,472	13,055	876	11,275	3,626	32.2	158	7,070	421
Palestine	3,202	1,201	37.5	358	1,433	210	2,061	729	35.4	341	863	128	1,141	472	41.4	17	570	82
Syria	51,900	15,001	28.9	6,023	28,119	2,757	31,240	9,312	29.8	5,733	14,648	1,547	20,660	5,689	27.5	290	13,471	1,210
Turkey in Asia	11,014	2,768	25.1	1,148	6,511	587	8,039	1,868	23.2	1,108	4,089	374	2,975	900	30.3	40	1,822	213
Other Asia	7,708	2,815	36.5	838	3,379	676	5,082	1,642	32.3	803	2,193	444	2,626	1,173	44.7	35	1,186	232
AMERICA.																		
Canada—French	307,786	138,019	44.8	23,777	129,975	16,015	157,748	68,802	43.6	22,447	58,909	7,590	150,038	69,217	46.1	1,330	71,066	8,425
Canada—Other	810,092	469,284	57.9	48,937	215,582	76,289	389,609	212,579	54.6	43,972	94,586	38,472	420,483	256,705	61.1	4,965	120,996	37,817
Newfoundland	13,242	6,271	47.4	1,234	4,624	1,113	6,154	2,868	46.6	1,143	1,659	484	7,088	3,403	48.0	91	2,965	629
Mexico	478,383	22,732	4.8	2,989	433,028	19,634	271,564	8,527	3.1	2,658	248,519	11,860	206,819	14,205	6.9	331	184,509	7,774
West Indies[2]	26,309	7,419	28.1	1,232	14,351	3,367	14,133	3,822	27.0	1,119	7,431	1,761	12,236	3,597	29.4	113	6,920	1,606
Central and South America	20,929	5,046	24.1	1,232	12,413	2,238	12,624	2,592	20.5	1,131	7,575	1,326	8,305	2,454	29.5	101	4,838	912
OTHER COUNTRIES.																		
Africa	5,222	2,276	43.6	405	2,087	454	2,981	1,228	41.2	373	1,114	266	2,241	1,048	46.8	32	973	188
Australia	10,801	5,345	49.5	916	3,415	1,125	5,985	2,613	44.0	837	1,814	671	4,866	2,732	56.1	79	1,601	454
Atlantic Islands	38,984	8,138	20.9	1,312	28,353	1,181	21,005	4,597	21.9	1,246	14,508	654	17,979	3,541	19.7	66	13,845	527
Pacific Islands[2]	3,643	1,824	50.1	287	1,123	409	1,993	911	45.7	272	570	240	1,650	913	55.3	15	553	169
All other	8,862	4,212	47.5	352	1,578	2,720	5,209	2,143	41.1	331	926	1,809	3,653	2,069	56.6	21	652	911

[1] Comprises Danzig, Fiume, Saar Basin, and "Europe, not specified."   [2] Except possessions of the United States.

806

POPULATION.

TABLE 4.—CITIZENSHIP OF FOREIGN-BORN WHITE MALES 21 YEARS OF AGE AND OVER, BY COUNTRY OF BIRTH, FOR THE UNITED STATES: 1920 AND 1910.

1920

COUNTRY OF BIRTH (postwar boundaries).	Foreign-born white males 21 years of age and over.	Naturalized. Number.	Naturalized. Per cent.	Having first papers.	Alien.	Citizenship not reported.
All countries	6,928,452	3,314,910	47.8	1,116,744	2,138,237	358,561
EUROPE.						
Northwestern Europe:						
England	392,116	253,937	64.8	50,338	55,148	32,693
Scotland	122,568	77,903	63.6	18,125	16,942	9,598
Wales	34,806	25,591	73.5	2,967	2,885	3,363
Ireland	448,573	324,100	72.3	43,995	47,181	33,297
Norway	195,101	131,322	67.3	29,223	23,640	10,916
Sweden	334,849	232,761	69.5	47,632	37,257	17,199
Denmark	109,754	76,412	69.6	15,447	10,978	6,917
Netherlands	67,901	39,462	58.1	12,304	12,135	4,000
Belgium and Luxemburg	39,295	21,722	55.3	8,504	6,515	2,554
Switzerland	65,656	42,623	64.9	7,915	9,934	5,184
France	73,937	44,421	60.1	9,811	13,567	6,138
Central Europe:						
Germany	873,231	639,843	73.3	101,473	74,277	57,638
Poland	602,918	168,354	27.9	139,759	279,386	15,419
Czechoslovakia	182,913	81,705	44.7	45,520	49,119	6,569
Austria	300,899	109,615	36.4	63,446	114,712	13,126
Hungary	196,093	55,188	28.1	50,215	84,406	6,284
Jugo-Slavia	107,974	23,140	21.4	27,687	54,134	3,013
Eastern Europe:						
Russia	682,208	284,320	41.7	127,879	246,604	23,405
Lithuania	79,308	20,254	25.5	16,186	41,194	1,674
Finland	80,407	31,550	39.2	17,466	28,511	2,880
Rumania	52,979	21,602	40.8	11,718	17,949	1,710
Bulgaria and Turkey in Europe	12,530	1,605	12.8	2,310	8,083	532
Southern Europe:						
Greece	135,207	23,093	17.1	20,736	85,459	5,919
Italy	858,111	259,547	30.2	154,330	418,583	25,651
Spain	31,540	2,814	8.9	2,285	25,061	1,380
Portugal	33,837	5,854	17.3	2,274	24,527	1,182
Other Europe [2]	7,916	1,814	22.9	1,112	4,610	380
ASIA.						
Armenia	23,746	6,664	28.1	4,419	11,851	812
Palestine	1,703	610	35.8	327	655	111
Syria	28,478	8,821	31.0	5,610	12,683	1,364
Turkey in Asia	7,383	1,719	23.3	1,090	4,250	324
Other Asia	4,453	1,488	33.4	779	1,810	376
AMERICA.						
Canada—French	141,514	66,579	47.0	21,997	46,094	6,844
Canada—Other and Newfoundland	355,093	205,794	58.0	44,257	69,690	35,352
Mexico	189,974	6,363	3.3	2,506	172,127	8,978
West Indies [3]	11,690	3,461	29.0	1,088	5,673	1,468
Central and South America	9,215	2,147	23.3	1,038	5,052	978
All other	32,576	10,712	32.9	2,976	15,555	3,333

1910

COUNTRY OF BIRTH (prewar boundaries).	Foreign-born white males 21 years of age and over.	Naturalized. Number.	Naturalized. Per cent.	Having first papers.	Alien.	Citizenship not reported.
All countries	6,646,817	3,034,117	45.6	570,772	2,266,535	775,393
EUROPE.						
Northwestern Europe:						
England	437,152	259,571	59.4	29,959	82,358	65,264
Scotland	133,116	75,101	56.5	10,340	28,600	19,015
Wales	43,054	29,772	69.2	1,986	4,438	6,858
Ireland	597,860	405,590	67.8	34,383	82,230	75,057
Norway	213,042	121,651	57.1	32,324	34,478	24,589
Sweden	349,022	219,057	62.8	40,248	52,041	37,676
Denmark	102,308	63,068	61.6	12,938	14,107	12,285
Netherlands	59,752	33,922	56.8	6,410	11,706	7,714
Belgium and Luxemburg	27,619	11,869	43.0	3,976	8,691	3,083
Switzerland	69,241	42,760	61.8	6,604	10,338	9,539
France	59,601	29,613	49.6	4,852	16,605	8,591
Central Europe:						
Germany [1]	1,278,667	889,007	69.5	92,030	127,103	170,527
Austria [1]	609,347	149,914	24.6	58,636	349,341	51,456
Hungary	255,844	36,610	14.3	25,750	174,518	18,960
Serbia	3,332	298	8.9	218	2,584	232
Montenegro	4,520	120	2.7	200	3,862	278
Eastern Europe:						
Russia [1]	737,120	192,264	26.1	95,562	385,970	63,324
Finland	70,716	21,669	30.6	11,279	32,458	5,310
Rumania	27,835	8,014	28.8	4,920	12,500	2,323
Bulgaria and Turkey in Europe	32,460	1,877	5.8	1,895	26,187	2,501
Southern Europe:						
Greece	74,975	4,946	6.6	4,550	58,208	7,271
Italy	712,812	126,523	17.7	55,522	468,442	62,325
Spain	14,170	2,318	16.4	824	9,213	1,815
Portugal	28,603	7,141	24.9	1,113	18,444	1,905
Europe, not specified	1,586	564	35.6	102	521	399
ASIA.						
Turkey in Asia	32,691	6,940	21.2	3,363	10,413	2,975
Other Asia	2,558	855	33.4	290	965	448
AMERICA.						
Canada—French	170,987	76,367	44.7	6,745	68,807	19,068
Canada—Other and Newfoundland	362,372	195,395	53.9	19,405	81,911	65,661
Mexico	102,009	10,932	10.7	2,358	67,930	20,789
West Indies [3]	9,671	2,961	30.6	611	4,271	1,828
Central and South America	3,315	1,152	34.8	272	1,240	651
All other	19,220	6,210	32.3	1,032	6,986	4,986

[1] Poland included with Germany, Austria, and Russia in 1910.
[2] Comprises Albania, Danzig, Fiume, Saar Basin, and "Europe, not specified."
[3] Except possessions of the United States.

CITIZENSHIP.

807

TABLE 5.—CITIZENSHIP OF FOREIGN-BORN AND FOREIGN-BORN WHITE POPULATION, BY DIVISIONS AND STATES: 1920.

DIVISION AND STATE.	FOREIGN-BORN POPULATION.									FOREIGN-BORN WHITE POPULATION.								
	Total.	Naturalized.		Having first papers.		Alien.		Citizenship not reported.		Total.	Naturalized.		Having first papers.		Alien.		Citizenship not reported.	
		Number.	Per cent.	Number.	Per cent.	Number.	Per cent.	Number.	Per cent.		Number.	Per cent.	Number.	Per cent.	Number.	Per cent.	Number.	Per cent.
United States.....	13,920,692	6,493,088	46.6	1,223,490	8.8	5,398,605	38.8	805,509	5.8	13,712,754	6,479,159	47.2	1,219,057	8.9	5,223,715	38.1	790,823	5.8
GEOGRAPHIC DIVISIONS:																		
New England......	1,885,945	788,403	41.8	141,726	7.5	884,984	46.9	70,832	3.8	1,870,654	786,429	42.0	140,811	7.5	873,456	46.7	69,958	3.7
Middle Atlantic....	4,960,418	2,134,347	43.0	413,125	8.3	2,162,891	43.6	250,055	5.0	4,912,575	2,129,416	43.3	411,046	8.4	2,128,166	43.3	243,947	5.0
East North Central.	3,232,141	1,643,240	50.8	392,887	12.2	995,148	30.8	200,866	6.2	3,223,279	1,641,238	50.9	392,466	12.2	990,000	30.7	199,575	6.2
West North Central.	1,375,653	901,448	65.5	109,998	8.0	252,010	18.3	112,197	8.2	1,371,981	900,871	65.7	109,904	8.0	249,478	18.2	111,708	8.1
South Atlantic.....	330,537	139,923	42.3	23,202	7.0	139,500	42.2	27,906	8.4	315,920	138,249	43.8	22,934	7.3	128,507	40.7	26,230	8.3
East South Central.	72,989	39,992	54.8	4,124	5.7	17,533	24.0	11,340	15.5	71,939	39,788	55.3	4,082	5.7	16,968	23.6	11,101	15.4
West South Central.	464,828	121,441	26.1	15,338	3.3	291,133	62.6	36,916	7.9	459,333	120,903	26.3	15,235	3.3	287,115	62.5	36,080	7.9
Mountain..........	467,020	221,914	47.5	32,998	7.1	186,904	40.0	25,804	5.5	453,225	221,327	48.8	32,894	7.3	173,832	38.4	25,172	5.6
Pacific............	1,130,561	502,380	44.4	90,092	8.0	468,496	41.4	69,593	6.2	1,033,808	500,938	48.5	89,685	8.7	376,193	36.4	67,052	6.5
NEW ENGLAND:																		
Maine............	107,814	42,768	39.7	6,947	6.4	50,579	46.9	7,520	7.0	107,349	42,662	39.7	6,925	6.5	50,291	46.8	7,471	7.0
New Hampshire....	91,397	38,147	41.7	5,156	5.6	41,661	45.6	6,433	7.0	91,233	38,131	41.8	5,151	5.6	41,527	45.5	6,424	7.0
Vermont..........	44,558	21,086	47.3	2,295	5.2	19,065	42.8	2,112	4.7	44,526	21,077	47.3	2,292	5.1	19,047	42.8	2,110	4.7
Massachusetts....	1,088,548	459,321	42.2	82,119	7.5	518,365	47.6	28,743	2.6	1,077,534	457,889	42.5	81,414	7.6	510,025	47.3	28,206	2.6
Rhode Island.....	175,189	82,276	47.0	15,325	8.7	69,903	39.9	7,685	4.4	173,499	82,070	47.3	15,212	8.8	68,043	39.6	7,574	4.4
Connecticut......	378,439	144,805	38.3	29,884	7.9	185,411	49.0	18,339	4.8	376,513	144,600	38.4	29,817	7.9	183,923	48.8	18,173	4.8
MIDDLE ATLANTIC:																		
New York.........	2,825,375	1,216,185	43.0	241,335	8.5	1,220,801	43.2	147,054	5.2	2,786,112	1,212,638	43.5	239,591	8.6	1,191,604	42.8	142,279	5.1
New Jersey.......	742,486	320,935	43.2	65,384	8.8	321,897	43.4	34,270	4.6	738,613	320,374	43.4	65,246	8.8	319,308	43.2	33,685	4.6
Pennsylvania.....	1,392,557	597,227	42.9	106,406	7.6	620,193	44.5	68,731	4.9	1,387,850	596,404	43.0	106,209	7.7	617,254	44.5	67,983	4.9
EAST NORTH CENTRAL:																		
Ohio.............	680,452	307,527	45.2	81,007	12.0	257,738	37.9	33,580	4.9	678,697	307,078	45.2	81,527	12.0	256,769	37.8	33,323	4.9
Indiana..........	151,328	66,351	43.8	25,263	16.7	42,423	28.0	17,291	11.4	150,868	66,273	43.9	42,183	27.9	17,206	11.4		
Illinois..........	1,210,584	667,056	55.1	136,450	11.3	329,506	27.2	77,572	6.4	1,206,951	666,460	55.2	136,346	11.3	327,119	27.1	77,026	6.4
Michigan.........	729,292	345,709	47.4	93,011	12.8	250,350	34.3	40,222	5.5	726,635	344,909	47.5	92,830	12.8	249,044	34.3	39,852	5.5
Wisconsin........	460,485	256,597	55.7	56,556	12.3	115,131	25.0	32,201	7.0	460,128	256,518	55.7	56,537	12.3	114,905	25.0	32,168	7.0
WEST NORTH CENTRAL:																		
Minnesota........	486,795	328,421	67.5	44,710	9.2	85,585	17.6	28,079	5.8	486,164	328,278	67.5	44,688	9.2	85,181	17.5	28,017	5.8
Iowa.............	225,994	156,593	69.3	12,228	5.4	36,128	16.0	21,045	9.3	225,647	156,551	69.4	12,224	5.4	35,875	15.9	20,997	9.3
Missouri.........	186,835	108,063	57.8	15,027	8.0	45,522	24.4	18,223	9.8	186,020	107,942	58.0	15,000	8.1	44,960	24.2	18,118	9.7
North Dakota.....	131,863	96,680	73.3	7,144	5.4	17,990	13.6	10,049	7.6	131,503	96,568	73.4	7,135	5.4	17,823	13.6	9,977	7.6
South Dakota.....	82,534	56,990	69.1	6,906	8.4	9,598	11.6	9,040	11.0	82,391	56,955	69.1	6,901	8.4	9,508	11.5	9,027	11.0
Nebraska.........	150,665	92,243	61.2	15,273	10.1	28,365	18.8	14,784	9.8	149,652	92,170	61.6	15,261	10.2	27,558	18.4	14,663	9.8
Kansas...........	110,967	62,458	56.3	8,710	7.8	28,822	26.0	10,977	9.9	110,578	62,407	56.4	8,689	7.9	28,573	25.8	10,909	9.9
SOUTH ATLANTIC:																		
Delaware.........	19,901	8,405	42.2	1,635	8.2	8,264	41.5	1,597	8.0	19,810	8,388	42.3	1,632	8.2	8,222	41.5	1,568	7.9
Maryland.........	103,179	52,016	50.4	9,700	9.4	37,249	36.1	4,214	4.1	102,177	51,837	50.7	9,649	9.4	36,577	35.8	4,114	4.0
District of Columbia	29,365	15,626	53.2	2,204	7.5	7,952	27.1	3,583	12.2	28,548	15,507	54.3	2,186	7.7	7,427	26.0	3,428	12.0
Virginia..........	31,705	15,181	47.9	2,555	8.1	10,198	32.2	3,771	11.9	30,785	15,038	48.8	2,499	8.1	9,658	31.4	3,590	11.7
West Virginia.....	62,105	15,122	24.3	3,275	5.3	38,490	62.0	5,218	8.4	61,906	15,080	24.4	3,272	5.3	38,389	62.0	5,165	8.3
North Carolina....	7,272	3,453	47.5	301	4.1	2,201	30.3	1,317	18.1	7,099	3,420	48.2	298	4.2	2,104	29.6	1,277	18.0
South Carolina.....	6,582	3,243	49.3	451	6.9	1,847	28.1	1,041	15.8	6,401	3,223	50.4	448	7.0	1,735	27.1	995	15.5
Georgia...........	16,564	8,912	53.8	1,097	6.6	4,734	28.6	1,821	11.0	16,186	8,846	54.7	1,083	6.7	4,506	27.8	1,751	10.8
Florida...........	53,864	17,965	33.4	1,984	3.7	28,571	53.0	5,344	9.9	43,008	16,910	39.3	1,867	4.3	19,889	46.2	4,342	10.1
EAST SOUTH CENTRAL:																		
Kentucky.........	30,906	18,972	61.4	1,694	5.5	6,024	19.5	4,216	13.6	30,780	18,942	61.5	1,689	5.5	5,957	19.4	4,192	13.6
Tennessee........	15,648	8,101	51.8	822	5.3	4,118	26.3	2,607	16.7	15,478	8,054	52.0	817	5.3	4,042	26.1	2,565	16.6
Alabama..........	18,027	9,059	50.3	1,224	6.8	4,637	25.7	3,107	17.2	17,662	8,990	50.9	1,203	6.8	4,471	25.3	2,998	17.0
Mississippi........	8,408	3,860	45.9	384	4.6	2,754	32.8	1,410	16.8	8,019	3,802	47.4	373	4.7	2,498	31.2	1,346	16.8
WEST SOUTH CENTRAL:																		
Arkansas.........	14,137	7,841	55.5	826	5.8	2,916	20.6	2,554	18.1	13,975	7,809	55.9	824	5.9	2,845	20.4	2,497	17.9
Louisiana........	46,427	15,920	34.3	2,307	5.0	21,982	47.3	6,218	13.4	44,871	15,783	35.2	2,274	5.1	20,855	46.5	5,959	13.3
Oklahoma........	40,432	20,145	49.8	1,971	4.9	12,565	31.1	5,751	14.2	39,968	20,064	50.2	1,967	4.9	12,259	30.7	5,688	14.2
Texas...........	363,832	77,535	21.3	10,234	2.8	253,670	69.7	22,393	6.2	360,519	77,247	21.4	10,180	2.8	251,156	69.7	21,936	6.1
MOUNTAIN:																		
Montana.........	95,591	60,181	63.0	9,340	9.8	19,066	19.9	7,004	7.3	93,620	60,015	64.1	9,318	10.0	17,491	18.7	6,796	7.3
Idaho...........	40,747	24,982	61.3	3,347	8.2	9,953	24.4	2,465	6.0	38,963	24,959	64.1	3,340	8.6	8,218	21.1	2,446	6.3
Wyoming.........	26,567	12,654	47.6	2,537	9.5	9,391	35.3	1,986	7.5	25,255	12,630	50.0	2,530	10.0	8,135	32.2	1,960	7.8
Colorado.........	119,138	64,738	54.3	9,481	8.0	38,961	32.7	5,958	5.0	116,954	64,686	55.3	9,457	8.1	36,991	31.6	5,840	5.0
New Mexico.......	29,808	6,352	21.3	831	2.8	21,092	70.8	1,533	5.1	29,077	6,294	21.6	821	2.8	20,476	70.4	1,486	5.1
Arizona..........	80,586	11,900	14.8	1,964	2.4	63,437	78.7	3,205	4.0	78,099	11,757	15.1	1,953	2.5	61,339	78.5	3,050	3.9
Utah............	59,200	34,601	58.4	4,069	6.9	18,178	30.7	2,352	4.0	56,455	34,576	61.2	4,048	7.2	15,517	27.5	2,314	4.1
Nevada..........	16,003	6,446	40.3	1,429	8.9	6,826	42.7	1,302	8.1	14,802	6,430	43.4	1,427	9.6	5,665	38.3	1,280	8.6
PACIFIC:																		
Washington.......	265,292	140,426	52.9	30,296	11.4	78,516	29.6	16,054	6.1	250,055	140,166	56.1	30,191	12.1	63,981	25.6	15,717	6.3
Oregon..........	107,644	57,726	53.6	12,219	11.4	33,092	30.7	4,607	4.3	102,151	57,627	56.4	12,159	11.9	27,823	27.2	4,542	4.4
California........	757,625	304,228	40.2	47,577	6.3	356,888	47.1	48,932	6.5	681,662	303,145	44.5	47,335	6.9	284,389	41.7	46,793	6.9

808

POPULATION.

TABLE **6.**—CITIZENSHIP OF FOREIGN-BORN WHITE MALES AND FEMALES, BY DIVISIONS AND STATES: 1920.

DIVISION AND STATE.	FOREIGN-BORN WHITE MALES.									FOREIGN-BORN WHITE FEMALES.								
	Total.	Naturalized.		Having first papers.		Alien.		Citizenship not reported		Total.	Naturalized.		Having first papers.		Alien.		Citizenship not reported	
		Number.	Per cent.	Number.	Per cent.	Number.	Per cent.	Number.	Per cent.		Number.	Per cent.	Number.	Per cent.	Number.	Per cent.	Number.	Per cent.
United States.....	7,528,322	3,443,968	45.7	1,133,727	15.1	2,562,917	34.0	387,710	5.2	6,134,432	3,035,191	49.1	85,330	1.4	2,660,798	43.0	403,113	6.5
GEOGRAPHIC DIVISIONS:																		
New England.......	945,786	381,815	40.4	131,196	13.9	403,482	42.7	29,243	3.1	924,918	404,614	43.7	9,615	1.0	469,974	50.8	40,715	4.4
Middle Atlantic.....	2,617,566	1,115,431	42.6	380,474	14.5	1,016,419	38.8	105,242	4.0	2,295,009	1,013,985	44.2	30,572	1.3	1,111,747	48.4	138,705	6.0
East North Central.	1,809,384	874,857	48.4	367,160	20.3	468,362	25.9	98,955	5.5	1,413,945	766,381	54.2	25,306	1.8	521,638	36.9	100,620	7.1
West North Central.	779,022	496,624	63.7	101,622	13.0	121,676	15.6	59,100	7.6	592,939	404,247	68.2	8,282	1.4	127,802	21.6	52,608	8.9
South Atlantic.....	185,143	76,007	41.1	21,311	11.5	72,980	39.4	14,845	8.0	130,777	62,242	47.6	1,623	1.2	55,527	42.5	11,385	8.7
East South Central..	42,093	22,744	54.0	3,764	8.9	9,419	22.4	6,166	14.6	20,846	17,044	57.1	318	1.1	7,549	25.3	4,935	16.5
West South Central..	260,777	67,539	25.9	13,879	5.3	158,577	60.8	20,782	8.0	198,556	53,364	26.9	1,350	0.7	128,538	64.7	15,298	7.7
Mountain..........	271,373	125,014	46.1	30,899	11.4	100,107	36.9	15,353	5.7	181,852	96,313	53.0	1,995	1.1	73,725	40.5	9,819	5.4
Pacific............	617,278	283,937	46.0	83,422	13.5	211,895	34.3	38,024	6.2	416,590	217,001	52.1	6,263	1.5	164,298	39.4	29,028	7.0
NEW ENGLAND:																		
Maine.............	55,807	19,013	34.1	6,688	12.0	26,645	47.7	3,461	6.2	51,542	23,649	45.9	237	0.5	23,646	45.9	4,010	7.8
New Hampshire.....	46,844	18,080	38.6	4,930	10.5	21,060	45.0	2,774	5.9	44,389	20,051	45.2	221	0.5	20,467	46.1	3,650	8.2
Vermont...........	23,711	10,189	43.0	2,155	9.1	10,341	43.6	1,026	4.3	20,815	10,888	52.3	137	0.7	8,700	41.8	1,084	5.2
Massachusetts.......	533,319	221,087	41.5	75,186	14.1	225,897	42.4	11,149	2.1	544,215	236,802	43.5	6,228	1.1	284,128	52.2	17,057	3.1
Rhode Island.......	86,164	40,045	46.5	13,818	16.0	29,180	33.9	3,121	3.6	87,335	42,025	48.1	1,394	1.6	39,463	45.2	4,453	5.1
Connecticut.........	199,891	73,401	36.7	28,419	14.2	90,359	45.2	7,712	3.9	176,622	71,199	40.3	1,398	0.8	93,564	53.0	10,461	5.9
MIDDLE ATLANTIC:																		
New York..........	1,442,575	632,112	43.8	218,599	15.2	533,084	37.0	58,780	4.1	1,343,537	580,526	43.2	20,992	1.6	658,520	49.0	83,499	6.2
New Jersey.........	391,655	165,859	42.3	61,641	15.7	150,530	38.4	13,625	3.5	346,958	154,515	44.5	3,605	1.0	168,778	48.6	20,000	5.8
Pennsylvania........	783,336	317,460	40.5	100,234	12.8	332,805	42.5	32,837	4.2	604,514	278,944	46.1	5,975	1.0	284,449	47.1	35,146	5.8
EAST NORTH CENTRAL:																		
Ohio..............	391,344	163,227	41.7	77,674	19.8	133,363	34.1	17,080	4.4	287,353	143,851	50.1	3,853	1.3	123,406	42.9	16,243	5.7
Indiana............	88,180	36,131	41.0	23,767	27.0	19,266	21.8	9,016	10.2	62,688	30,142	48.1	1,459	2.3	22,897	36.5	8,190	13.1
Illinois............	657,264	354,892	54.0	127,218	19.4	137,944	21.0	37,210	5.7	549,087	311,568	56.7	9,128	1.7	189,175	34.4	39,816	7.2
Michigan..........	413,806	182,236	44.0	87,779	21.2	123,684	29.9	20,107	4.9	312,829	162,673	52.0	5,051	1.6	125,360	40.1	19,745	6.3
Wisconsin..........	258,740	138,371	53.5	50,722	19.6	54,105	20.9	15,542	6.0	201,388	118,147	58.7	5,815	2.9	60,800	30.2	16,620	8.3
WEST NORTH CENTRAL:																		
Minnesota..........	278,588	181,733	65.2	41,197	14.8	41,503	14.9	14,155	5.1	207,576	146,545	70.6	3,491	1.7	43,678	21.0	13,862	6.7
Iowa..............	127,065	85,777	67.5	11,339	8.9	18,851	14.8	11,098	8.7	98,582	70,774	71.8	885	0.9	17,024	17.3	9,899	10.0
Missouri...........	103,418	59,177	57.2	13,930	13.5	21,100	20.4	9,211	8.9	82,608	48,765	59.0	1,076	1.3	23,860	28.9	8,907	10.8
North Dakota......	75,386	54,090	71.8	6,668	8.8	9,114	12.1	5,514	7.3	56,117	42,478	75.7	467	0.8	8,709	15.5	4,463	8.0
South Dakota......	47,610	31,915	67.0	6,422	13.5	4,165	8.7	5,108	10.7	34,781	25,040	72.0	479	1.4	5,343	15.4	3,919	11.3
Nebraska..........	84,277	50,171	59.5	14,052	16.7	12,245	14.5	7,809	9.3	65,375	41,999	64.2	1,200	1.8	15,313	23.4	6,854	10.5
Kansas............	62,678	33,761	53.9	8,014	12.8	14,698	23.5	6,205	9.9	47,900	28,646	59.8	675	1.4	13,875	29.0	4,704	9.8
SOUTH ATLANTIC:																		
Delaware...........	11,369	4,498	39.6	1,559	13.7	4,547	40.0	765	6.7	8,441	3,890	46.1	73	0.9	3,675	43.5	803	9.5
Maryland..........	54,628	27,088	49.6	8,926	16.3	16,619	30.4	1,995	3.7	47,549	24,749	52.0	723	1.5	19,958	42.0	2,119	4.5
District of Columbia.	15,142	8,179	54.0	1,838	12.1	3,376	22.3	1,749	11.6	13,406	7,328	54.7	348	2.6	4,051	30.2	1,679	12.5
Virginia...........	19,051	8,862	46.5	2,376	12.5	5,653	29.7	2,160	11.3	11,734	6,170	52.6	123	1.1	4,005	34.1	1,430	12.2
West Virginia......	41,910	8,760	20.9	3,157	7.5	26,731	63.8	3,262	7.8	19,996	6,320	31.6	115	0.6	11,658	58.3	1,903	9.5
North Carolina.....	4,341	1,981	45.6	288	6.6	1,294	29.8	778	17.9	2,758	1,439	52.2	10	0.4	810	29.4	499	18.1
South Carolina.....	4,095	2,017	49.3	425	10.4	1,039	25.4	614	15.0	2,306	1,206	52.3	23	1.0	696	30.2	381	16.5
Georgia............	10,004	5,275	52.7	997	10.0	2,677	26.8	1,055	10.5	6,182	3,571	57.8	86	1.4	1,829	29.6	696	11.3
Florida............	24,603	9,347	38.0	1,745	7.1	11,044	44.9	2,467	10.0	18,405	7,563	41.1	122	0.7	8,845	48.1	1,875	10.2
EAST SOUTH CENTRAL:																		
Kentucky..........	17,479	10,490	60.0	1,522	8.7	3,395	19.4	2,072	11.9	13,301	8,452	63.5	167	1.3	2,562	19.3	2,120	15.9
Tennessee..........	9,021	4,592	50.9	751	8.3	2,182	24.2	1,496	16.6	6,457	3,462	53.6	66	1.0	1,860	28.8	1,069	16.6
Alabama...........	10,625	5,274	49.6	1,139	10.7	2,455	23.1	1,757	16.5	7,037	3,716	52.8	64	0.9	2,016	28.6	1,241	17.6
Mississippi.........	4,968	2,388	48.1	352	7.1	1,387	27.9	841	16.9	3,051	1,414	46.3	21	0.7	1,111	36.4	505	16.6
WEST SOUTH CENTRAL:																		
Arkansas...........	8,591	4,707	54.8	759	8.8	1,565	18.2	1,560	18.2	5,384	3,102	57.6	65	1.2	1,280	23.8	937	17.4
Louisiana..........	26,808	9,607	35.8	2,185	8.2	12,145	45.3	2,871	10.7	18,063	6,176	34.2	89	0.5	8,710	48.2	3,088	17.1
Oklahoma..........	24,931	11,559	46.4	1,809	7.3	7,817	31.4	3,746	15.0	15,037	8,505	56.6	148	1.0	4,442	29.5	1,942	12.9
Texas.............	200,447	41,666	20.8	9,126	4.6	137,050	68.4	12,605	6.3	160,072	35,581	22.2	1,054	0.7	114,106	71.3	9,331	5.8
MOUNTAIN:																		
Montana...........	58,229	35,631	61.2	8,815	15.1	9,613	16.5	4,170	7.2	35,391	24,384	68.9	503	1.4	7,878	22.3	2,626	7.4
Idaho.............	24,877	14,715	59.2	3,184	12.8	5,357	21.5	1,621	6.5	14,086	10,244	72.7	156	1.1	2,861	20.3	825	5.9
Wyoming..........:	16,934	7,582	44.8	2,450	14.5	5,532	32.7	1,370	8.1	8,321	5,048	60.7	80	1.0	2,603	31.3	590	7.1
Colorado...........	68,219	35,804	52.5	8,791	12.9	20,225	29.6	3,399	5.0	48,735	28,862	59.2	666	1.4	16,766	34.4	2,441	5.0
New Mexico........	16,845	3,557	21.1	765	4.5	11,663	69.2	860	5.1	12,232	2,737	22.4	56	0.5	8,813	72.0	626	5.1
Arizona............	44,557	6,462	14.5	1,854	4.2	34,463	77.2	1,878	4.2	33,442	5,295	15.8	99	0.3	26,876	80.4	1,172	3.5
Utah..............	30,875	17,038	55.2	3,639	11.8	8,935	28.9	1,263	4.1	25,580	17,538	68.6	409	1.6	6,582	25.7	1,051	4.1
Nevada............	10,737	4,225	39.3	1,401	13.0	4,319	40.2	792	7.4	4,065	2,205	54.2	26	0.6	1,346	33.1	488	12.0
PACIFIC:																		
Washington........	153,118	80,164	52.4	28,626	18.7	35,376	23.1	8,952	5.8	96,937	60,002	61.9	1,565	1.6	28,605	29.5	6,765	7.0
Oregon............	62,310	32,902	52.8	11,367	18.2	15,247	24.5	2,794	4.5	39,841	24,725	62.1	792	2.0	12,576	31.6	1,748	4.4
California..........	401,850	170,871	42.5	43,429	10.8	161,272	40.1	26,278	6.5	279,812	132,274	47.3	3,906	1.4	123,117	44.0	20,515	7.3

CITIZENSHIP.

TABLE 7.—CITIZENSHIP OF FOREIGN-BORN WHITE MALES 21 YEARS OF AGE AND OVER, 1920, 1910, AND 1900, AND OF FEMALES, 1920 ONLY, BY DIVISIONS AND STATES.

[No inquiry as to the citizenship of females prior to 1920.]

DIVISION AND STATE.	FOREIGN-BORN WHITE MALES 21 YEARS OF AGE AND OVER—NUMBER.														
	Total.			Naturalized.			Having first papers.			Alien.			Citizenship not reported.		
	1920	1910	1900	1920	1910	1900	1920	1910	1900	1920	1910	1900	1920	1910	1900
United States..	6,928,452	6,646,817	4,904,270	3,314,910	3,034,117	2,845,473	1,116,744	570,772	411,598	2,138,237	2,266,535	914,917	358,561	775,393	731,952
GEOGRAPHIC DIVS.:															
New England.....	866,042	796,847	597,823	367,478	323,994	268,304	128,790	48,508	24,167	343,403	366,161	215,304	26,371	58,184	90,048
Middle Atlantic...	2,406,975	2,272,271	1,510,875	1,065,420	879,348	825,262	374,400	202,012	100,091	871,495	965,101	381,823	95,660	225,810	203,699
E. North Central..	1,687,728	1,573,343	1,284,617	843,952	812,489	802,666	302,436	148,254	141,461	388,827	426,278	136,308	92,513	186,322	204,182
W. North Central.	738,673	869,408	790,009	483,504	510,918	516,440	100,226	76,934	86,650	98,487	144,177	61,899	56,456	137,379	125,020
South Atlantic....	170,407	150,665	104,183	72,664	61,134	64,513	20,810	8,997	4,252	63,077	57,127	17,263	13,850	23,407	18,155
E. South Central..	39,697	46,308	47,445	22,056	25,955	32,037	3,683	2,220	1,719	8,079	8,647	4,662	5,879	9,486	9,027
W. South Central.	208,431	171,940	130,931	64,503	70,765	61,511	13,516	10,071	18,466	111,736	52,853	25,953	18,676	38,251	25,001
Mountain.........	241,321	257,537	164,862	119,979	113,670	99,129	30,452	23,219	16,485	76,754	85,619	27,158	14,136	35,029	22,090
Pacific..........	569,178	508,498	273,525	275,354	235,844	175,611	82,425	50,557	18,607	176,379	160,572	44,547	35,020	61,525	34,760
NEW ENGLAND:															
Maine............	49,355	48,464	38,515	18,028	14,994	13,242	6,553	1,490	784	21,676	23,672	17,148	3,098	8,308	7,346
New Hampshire..	42,432	41,956	34,769	17,395	16,415	14,022	4,839	1,421	958	17,724	19,377	12,850	2,474	4,743	6,939
Vermont.........	20,462	23,759	20,846	9,540	10,811	9,560	2,106	1,164	689	7,886	9,652	6,949	930	2,132	3,698
Massachusetts.....	491,107	453,801	343,522	213,477	189,126	150,919	73,725	30,016	14,752	193,844	212,033	127,172	10,061	22,426	50,679
Rhode Island.....	78,118	75,899	53,768	38,212	32,040	27,840	13,521	5,314	2,071	23,562	31,996	17,027	2,823	6,549	6,830
Connecticut.......	184,568	153,168	106,403	70,826	60,608	52,721	28,046	9,103	4,963	78,711	69,431	34,163	6,985	14,026	14,556
MIDDLE ATLANTIC:															
New York.......	1,318,883	1,221,013	829,474	604,256	502,083	481,362	214,958	131,085	59,748	446,859	475,259	189,715	52,810	112,586	98,649
New Jersey.......	360,902	309,648	196,598	158,727	128,438	109,460	60,708	24,511	12,765	129,137	122,076	45,591	12,330	34,623	28,782
Pennsylvania.....	727,190	741,610	484,803	302,437	248,827	234,440	98,734	46,416	27,578	295,499	367,766	146,517	30,520	78,601	76,268
E. NORTH CENTRAL:															
Ohio............	363,504	308,478	225,688	156,820	142,465	157,323	76,524	17,509	7,069	114,287	113,856	26,335	15,873	34,648	34,961
Indiana..........	82,908	88,927	73,087	34,871	42,533	44,364	23,563	13,320	9,830	15,980	18,354	3,155	8,494	14,720	15,738
Illinois..........	613,797	604,524	467,123	341,910	317,389	326,538	125,752	43,482	16,188	111,349	174,581	51,576	34,786	69,122	72,821
Michigan.........	381,808	302,177	261,415	175,631	167,304	153,377	86,400	26,285	31,122	101,206	76,550	37,449	18,511	32,088	39,467
Wisconsin........	245,711	269,237	257,304	134,720	142,848	121,064	50,137	47,708	77,252	46,005	42,937	17,793	14,849	35,744	41,195
W. NORTH CENTRAL:															
Minnesota........	266,856	298,282	260,753	177,355	179,187	160,373	40,727	20,222	35,684	35,245	58,132	24,801	13,529	34,741	33,895
Iowa............	121,392	146,880	157,906	84,160	90,573	117,507	11,109	6,654	5,627	15,384	20,275	11,372	10,739	29,378	23,400
Missouri..........	97,345	121,404	112,483	57,561	65,612	78,829	13,765	10,117	5,215	17,240	25,835	10,427	8,779	19,840	18,012
North Dakota.....	70,043	79,721	55,558	51,350	46,636	31,534	6,558	9,824	10,515	7,017	10,965	5,488	5,118	12,296	8,021
South Dakota.....	45,340	54,528	45,446	31,030	32,495	26,684	6,318	8,020	7,918	3,103	4,376	2,411	4,889	9,637	8,433
Nebraska.........	79,821	94,345	90,925	49,012	57,270	54,241	13,868	9,924	14,368	9,490	12,347	4,846	7,451	14,804	17,470
Kansas...........	57,876	74,248	66,938	33,036	39,145	41,272	7,881	6,173	7,823	11,008	12,247	2,554	5,951	16,683	15,789
SOUTH ATLANTIC:															
Delaware.........	10,614	8,776	6,747	4,329	3,707	4,109	1,539	658	275	4,033	3,189	1,287	713	1,222	1,076
Maryland.........	50,363	47,973	42,011	26,077	24,256	28,528	8,720	3,278	1,276	13,720	13,573	5,706	1,846	6,866	6,506
Dist. of Columbia.	14,042	11,738	9,600	7,786	6,474	6,733	1,775	1,058	657	2,842	2,304	1,294	1,639	1,902	916
Virginia..........	17,431	14,882	11,085	8,356	6,411	6,801	2,294	859	484	4,792	4,693	1,492	1,989	2,919	2,308
West Virginia....	38,471	34,687	12,878	8,315	7,263	6,429	3,105	1,358	507	23,996	22,545	3,714	3,055	3,521	2,228
North Carolina....	4,035	3,296	2,451	1,886	1,439	1,444	285	194	67	1,124	827	313	740	836	627
South Carolina....	3,850	3,355	2,979	1,924	1,602	1,801	417	184	79	921	739	494	588	830	605
Georgia..........	9,319	8,513	6,707	5,023	4,023	3,952	958	625	363	2,340	1,846	949	998	2,019	1,443
Florida..........	22,282	17,445	9,725	8,968	5,959	4,721	1,723	788	544	9,309	7,411	2,014	2,282	3,292	2,446
E. SOUTH CENTRAL:															
Kentucky.........	16,827	20,440	25,139	10,278	13,225	18,731	1,472	815	682	3,060	2,754	1,692	2,022	3,646	4,034
Tennessee........	8,428	10,112	9,509	4,430	5,444	5,746	739	464	280	1,821	1,867	1,193	1,438	2,337	2,290
Alabama.........	9,814	10,521	8,082	5,031	4,841	4,895	1,125	684	618	2,030	2,793	995	1,628	2,203	1,574
Mississippi........	4,628	5,235	4,715	2,322	2,445	2,665	347	257	139	1,168	1,233	782	791	1,300	1,129
W. SOUTH CENTRAL:															
Arkansas.........	8,166	9,718	8,278	4,593	5,284	4,730	753	595	527	1,319	1,388	795	1,501	2,451	2,226
Louisiana.........	24,848	26,519	25,340	9,350	10,024	12,848	2,121	1,166	962	10,708	9,151	7,302	2,669	6,178	4,228
Oklahoma [1]......	22,817	23,551	11,540	11,239	12,074	6,609	1,777	1,477	1,447	6,233	4,449	693	3,568	5,551	2,791
Texas............	152,600	112,152	85,773	39,321	43,383	37,324	8,865	6,833	15,530	93,476	37,865	17,163	10,938	24,071	15,756
MOUNTAIN:															
Montana.........	54,250	59,313	39,983	34,009	27,635	26,268	8,714	6,749	4,018	7,636	16,937	5,397	3,891	7,992	4,300
Idaho...........	23,366	25,844	13,491	14,186	12,817	9,127	3,156	2,478	1,400	4,489	6,215	1,228	1,535	4,334	1,736
Wyoming........	15,796	18,263	10,611	7,289	6,837	6,224	2,427	1,937	1,071	4,791	8,125	2,226	1,289	1,364	1,090
Colorado........	62,089	70,514	51,162	34,630	35,245	29,678	8,648	6,536	7,317	15,696	19,615	6,539	3,115	9,118	7,628
New Mexico......	13,244	12,502	7,251	3,381	4,267	3,568	750	709	432	8,390	6,048	1,973	723	1,478	1,278
Arizona.........	33,582	25,682	12,161	5,986	5,912	4,684	1,801	1,113	657	24,147	14,574	5,507	1,648	4,083	1,313
Utah............	28,791	32,652	24,406	16,377	15,351	15,826	3,563	2,415	1,334	7,664	9,626	3,181	1,187	5,260	4,085
Nevada..........	10,203	12,767	5,797	4,121	5,606	3,754	1,393	1,282	256	3,941	4,479	1,107	748	1,400	680
PACIFIC:															
Washington.......	143,258	147,224	61,745	77,156	68,895	39,466	28,308	15,258	5,511	29,572	43,202	8,012	8,222	19,869	8,756
Oregon..........	58,580	63,909	31,486	31,899	29,675	21,814	11,255	7,591	3,584	12,800	17,430	2,842	2,626	9,213	3,246
California........	367,340	297,365	180,294	166,299	137,274	114,331	42,862	27,708	9,512	134,007	99,940	33,693	24,172	32,443	22,758

[1] Includes population of Indian Territory for 1900.

810

POPULATION.

TABLE 7.—CITIZENSHIP OF FOREIGN-BORN WHITE MALES 21 YEARS OF AGE AND OVER, 1920, 1910, AND 1900, AND OF FEMALES, 1920 ONLY, BY DIVISIONS AND STATES—Continued.

[No inquiry as to the citizenship of females prior to 1920.]

DIVISION AND STATE.	FOREIGN-BORN WHITE MALES 21 YEARS OF AGE AND OVER—PER CENT.												FOREIGN-BORN WHITE FEMALES 21 YEARS OF AGE AND OVER: 1920								
	Naturalized.			Having first papers			Alien.			Citizenship not reported			Total.	Naturalized.		Having first papers		Alien.		Citizenship not reported	
	1920	1910	1900	1920	1910	1900	1920	1910	1900	1920	1910	1900		Number.	Per cent.	Number.	Per cent.	Number.	Per cent.	Number.	Per cent.
United States....	47.8	45.6	58.0	16.1	8.6	8.4	30.9	34.1	18.7	5.2	11.7	14.9	5,570,268	2,893,787	52.0	77,532	1.4	2,226,672	40.0	372,277	6.7
GEOGRAPHIC DIVISIONS:																					
New England.......	42.4	40.7	44.9	14.9	6.1	4.0	39.7	46.0	36.0	3.0	7.3	15.1	839,249	388,049	46.2	8,521	1.0	405,170	48.3	37,509	4.5
Middle Atlantic.....	44.3	38.7	54.6	15.6	8.9	6.6	36.2	42.5	25.3	4.0	9.9	13.5	2,070,777	959,199	46.3	27,691	1.3	956,162	46.2	127,725	6.2
East North Central.	50.0	51.6	62.5	21.5	9.4	11.0	23.0	27.1	10.6	5.5	11.8	15.9	1,290,847	732,715	56.8	23,179	1.8	441,004	34.2	93,949	7.3
West North Central.	65.5	58.8	65.4	13.6	8.8	11.0	13.3	16.6	7.8	7.6	15.8	15.8	553,121	390,628	70.6	7,572	1.4	105,135	19.0	49,786	9.0
South Atlantic.....	42.6	40.6	61.9	12.2	6.0	4.1	37.0	37.9	16.6	8.1	15.5	17.4	116,808	58,759	50.3	1,461	1.3	46,150	39.5	10,438	8.9
East South Central.	55.6	56.0	67.5	9.3	4.8	3.6	20.4	18.7	9.8	14.8	20.5	19.0	27,545	16,279	59.1	297	1.1	6,283	22.8	4,686	17.0
West South Central.	30.9	41.2	47.0	6.5	5.9	14.1	53.6	30.7	19.8	9.0	22.2	19.1	148,789	49,755	33.4	1,219	0.8	84,503	56.8	13,312	8.9
Mountain...........	49.7	44.1	60.1	12.6	9.0	10.0	31.8	33.2	16.5	5.9	13.6	13.4	152,087	90,885	59.5	1,790	1.2	51,321	33.6	8,691	5.7
Pacific...........	48.4	46.4	64.2	14.5	9.9	6.8	31.0	31.6	16.3	6.2	12.1	12.7	370,445	207,518	56.0	5,802	1.6	130,944	35.3	26,181	7.1
NEW ENGLAND:																					
Maine.............	36.5	30.9	34.4	13.3	3.1	2.0	43.9	48.8	44.5	6.3	17.1	19.1	44,974	22,451	49.9	189	0.4	18,751	41.7	3,583	8.0
New Hampshire.....	41.0	39.1	40.3	11.4	3.4	2.8	41.8	46.2	37.0	5.8	11.3	20.0	39,617	19,226	48.5	201	0.5	16,874	42.6	3,316	8.4
Vermont...........	46.6	45.5	45.9	10.3	4.9	3.1	38.5	40.6	33.3	4.5	9.0	17.7	17,770	10,285	57.9	117	0.7	6,377	35.9	991	5.6
Massachusetts.......	43.5	41.7	43.9	15.0	6.6	4.3	39.5	46.7	37.0	2.0	4.9	14.8	497,806	227,939	45.8	5,555	1.1	248,507	49.9	15,805	3.2
Rhode Island.......	48.9	42.2	51.8	17.3	7.0	3.9	30.2	42.2	31.7	3.6	8.6	12.7	78,748	39,963	50.7	1,232	1.6	33,445	42.5	4,108	5.2
Connecticut........	38.4	39.6	49.5	15.2	5.9	4.7	42.6	45.3	32.1	3.8	9.2	13.7	160,334	68,185	42.5	1,227	0.8	81,210	50.7	9,700	6.1
MIDDLE ATLANTIC:																					
New York..........	45.8	41.1	58.0	16.3	10.7	7.2	33.9	38.9	22.9	4.0	9.2	11.9	1,209,614	549,557	45.4	19,140	1.6	564,261	46.6	76,656	6.3
New Jersey.........	44.0	41.5	55.7	16.8	7.9	6.5	35.8	39.4	23.2	3.4	11.2	14.6	314,320	146,789	46.7	3,185	1.0	145,890	46.4	18,456	5.9
Pennsylvania.......	41.6	33.6	48.4	13.6	6.3	5.7	40.6	49.6	30.2	4.2	10.6	15.7	546,843	262,853	48.1	5,366	1.0	246,011	45.0	32,613	6.0
EAST NORTH CENTRAL:																					
Ohio..............	43.1	46.2	69.7	21.1	5.7	3.1	31.4	36.9	11.7	4.4	11.2	15.5	259,019	136,715	52.8	3,350	1.3	104,001	40.2	14,953	5.8
Indiana...........	42.1	47.8	60.7	28.4	15.0	13.4	19.3	20.6	4.3	10.2	16.6	21.5	57,465	28,696	49.9	1,353	2.4	19,682	34.3	7,734	13.5
Illinois...........	55.7	52.5	69.9	20.5	7.2	3.5	18.1	28.9	11.0	5.7	11.4	15.6	504,131	297,536	59.0	8,380	1.7	161,042	31.9	37,167	7.4
Michigan..........	46.0	55.4	58.7	22.6	8.7	11.9	26.5	25.3	14.3	4.8	10.6	15.1	281,352	155,327	55.2	4,553	1.6	103,843	36.7	18,129	6.4
Wisconsin..........	54.8	53.1	47.1	20.4	17.7	30.0	18.7	15.9	6.9	6.0	13.3	16.0	188,880	114,441	60.6	5,537	2.9	52,936	28.0	15,966	8.5
WEST NORTH CENTRAL:																					
Minnesota.........	66.5	60.1	63.8	15.3	8.8	13.7	13.2	19.5	9.5	5.1	11.6	13.0	195,726	142,035	72.6	3,211	1.6	37,404	19.1	13,076	6.7
Iowa..............	69.3	61.7	74.4	9.2	4.5	3.6	12.7	13.8	7.2	8.8	20.0	14.8	93,087	69,111	74.2	781	0.8	13,686	14.7	9,509	10.2
Missouri...........	59.1	54.0	70.1	14.1	8.3	4.6	17.7	21.3	9.3	9.0	16.3	16.0	76,206	46,887	61.5	993	1.3	19,853	26.1	8,473	11.1
North Dakota......	73.3	58.5	56.8	9.4	12.3	18.9	10.0	13.8	9.9	7.3	15.4	14.4	51,004	39,837	78.1	407	0.8	6,702	13.1	4,058	8.0
South Dakota.......	68.4	59.6	58.7	13.9	14.7	17.4	6.8	8.0	5.3	10.8	17.7	18.6	32,687	24,134	73.8	433	1.3	4,397	13.5	3,723	11.4
Nebraska..........	61.4	60.7	59.7	17.4	10.5	15.8	11.9	13.1	5.3	9.3	15.7	19.2	61,078	40,771	66.8	1,119	1.8	12,705	20.8	6,483	10.6
Kansas............	57.1	52.7	61.7	13.6	8.3	10.9	19.0	16.5	3.8	10.3	22.5	23.6	43,333	27,853	64.3	628	1.4	10,388	24.0	4,464	10.3
SOUTH ATLANTIC:																					
Delaware..........	40.8	42.2	60.9	14.5	7.5	4.1	38.0	36.3	19.1	6.7	13.9	15.9	7,631	3,698	48.5	67	0.9	3,131	41.0	735	9.6
Maryland..........	51.8	50.6	67.9	17.3	6.8	8.0	27.2	28.3	13.6	3.7	14.3	15.5	43,261	23,687	54.8	647	1.5	16,914	39.1	2,013	4.7
District of Columbia.	55.4	55.2	70.1	12.6	9.0	6.8	20.2	19.6	13.5	11.7	16.2	9.5	12,334	6,926	56.2	324	2.6	3,491	28.3	1,593	12.9
Virginia...........	47.9	43.1	61.4	13.2	5.8	4.4	27.5	31.5	13.5	11.4	19.6	20.8	10,420	5,701	54.7	108	1.0	3,327	31.9	1,284	12.3
West Virginia......	21.6	20.9	49.9	8.1	3.9	3.9	62.4	65.0	28.8	7.9	10.2	17.3	16,994	5,826	34.3	100	0.6	9,386	55.2	1,082	9.0
North Carolina.....	46.7	43.7	58.9	7.1	5.6	2.7	27.9	25.1	12.8	18.3	25.4	25.6	2,453	1,349	55.0	10	0.4	648	26.4	446	18.2
South Carolina.....	50.0	47.7	60.5	10.8	5.5	2.7	23.9	22.0	16.6	15.3	24.7	20.3	2,091	1,138	54.4	21	1.0	583	27.9	349	16.7
Georgia...........	53.9	47.3	58.0	10.3	7.3	5.4	25.1	21.7	14.1	10.7	23.7	21.5	5,536	3,293	59.5	73	1.3	1,533	27.7	637	11.5
Florida...........	40.2	34.2	48.5	7.7	4.5	5.6	41.8	42.5	20.7	10.2	18.9	25.2	16,088	7,141	44.4	111	0.7	7,137	44.4	1,699	10.6
EAST SOUTH CENTRAL:																					
Kentucky..........	61.1	64.7	74.5	8.7	4.0	2.7	18.2	13.5	6.7	12.0	17.8	16.0	12,661	8,220	64.9	159	1.3	2,212	17.5	2,070	16.3
Tennessee..........	52.6	53.8	60.4	8.8	4.6	2.9	21.6	18.5	12.5	17.1	23.1	24.1	5,891	3,278	55.6	62	1.1	1,535	26.1	1,016	17.2
Alabama..........	51.3	46.0	60.6	11.5	6.5	7.6	20.7	26.5	12.3	16.6	20.9	19.5	6,291	3,472	55.2	59	0.9	1,639	26.1	1,121	17.8
Mississippi........	50.2	46.7	56.5	7.5	4.9	2.9	25.2	23.6	16.6	17.1	24.8	23.9	2,702	1,309	48.4	17	0.6	897	33.2	479	17.7
WEST SOUTH CENTRAL:																					
Arkansas..........	56.2	54.4	57.1	9.2	6.1	6.4	16.2	14.3	9.6	18.4	25.2	26.9	5,000	2,976	59.5	64	1.3	1,066	21.3	894	17.9
Louisiana..........	37.6	37.8	50.7	8.5	4.4	3.8	43.1	34.5	28.8	10.7	23.3	16.7	16,380	5,846	35.7	82	0.5	7,586	46.3	2,866	17.5
Oklahoma [1]......	49.3	51.3	57.3	7.8	6.3	12.5	27.3	18.9	6.0	15.6	23.6	24.2	13,291	8,133	61.2	124	0.9	3,266	24.6	1,768	13.3
Texas.............	25.8	38.7	43.5	5.8	6.1	18.1	61.3	33.8	20.0	7.2	21.5	18.4	114,118	32,800	28.7	949	0.8	72,585	63.6	7,784	6.8
MOUNTAIN:																					
Montana..........	62.7	46.6	65.7	16.1	11.4	10.0	14.1	28.6	13.5	7.2	13.5	10.8	31,459	22,618	71.9	479	1.5	5,990	19.0	2,372	7.5
Idaho.............	60.7	49.6	67.7	13.5	9.6	10.4	19.2	24.0	9.1	6.6	16.8	12.9	12,804	9,708	75.8	189	1.1	2,217	17.3	740	5.8
Wyoming..........	46.1	37.4	58.7	15.4	10.6	10.1	30.3	44.5	21.0	8.2	7.5	10.3	7,261	4,719	65.0	72	1.0	1,965	27.1	505	7.0
Colorado..........	55.8	50.0	58.0	13.9	9.3	14.3	25.3	27.8	12.8	5.0	12.9	14.9	42,928	27,688	64.5	603	1.4	12,446	29.0	2,191	5.1
New Mexico.......	25.5	34.1	49.2	5.7	5.7	6.0	63.3	48.4	27.2	5.5	11.8	17.6	8,689	2,500	28.8	45	0.5	5,642	64.9	502	5.8
Arizona...........	17.8	23.0	38.5	5.4	4.3	5.4	71.9	56.7	45.3	4.9	15.9	10.8	22,391	4,722	21.1	79	0.4	16,638	74.3	952	4.3
Utah..............	56.9	47.0	64.8	12.4	7.4	5.5	26.6	29.5	13.0	4.1	16.1	16.7	23,463	16,815	71.7	348	1.5	5,320	22.7	980	4.2
Nevada...........	40.4	43.9	64.8	13.7	10.0	4.4	38.6	35.1	19.1	7.3	11.0	11.7	3,692	2,115	57.3	25	0.7	1,103	29.9	449	12.2
PACIFIC:																					
Washington........	53.9	46.8	63.9	19.8	10.4	8.9	20.6	29.3	13.0	5.7	13.5	14.2	87,177	56,761	65.1	1,443	1.7	22,954	26.3	6,019	6.9
Oregon...........	54.5	46.4	69.3	19.2	11.9	11.4	21.9	27.3	9.0	4.5	14.4	10.3	36,227	23,581	65.1	726	2.0	10,326	28.5	1,594	4.4
California.........	45.3	46.2	63.4	11.7	9.3	5.3	36.5	33.6	18.7	6.6	10.9	12.6	247,041	127,176	51.5	3,633	1.5	97,664	39.5	18,568	7.5

[1] Includes population of Indian Territory for 1900.

CITIZENSHIP.

811

TABLE 8.—NUMBER AND PER CENT NATURALIZED AMONG FOREIGN-BORN WHITE MALES AND FEMALES 21 YEARS OF AGE AND OVER, FOR SELECTED COUNTRIES OF BIRTH, BY DIVISIONS AND STATES: 1920.

[The countries for which figures are given in this table are those which contributed 2 per cent or more of the total number of foreign-born white persons 21 years of age and over, of both sexes combined, enumerated in the specified division or state.]

FOREIGN-BORN WHITE POPULATION 21 YEARS OF AGE AND OVER: 1920

DIVISION OR STATE OF RESIDENCE AND COUNTRY OF BIRTH.	Male. Total number.	Male. Naturalized. Number.	Male. Naturalized. Per cent.	Female. Total number.	Female. Naturalized. Number.	Female. Naturalized. Per cent.
UNITED STATES.						
All countries	6,928,452	3,314,910	47.8	5,570,268	2,893,787	52.0
Germany	873,281	639,843	73.3	775,653	573,608	74.0
Italy	858,111	259,547	30.2	550,822	160,166	29.1
Russia	682,208	284,320	41.7	529,129	225,241	42.6
Poland	602,918	168,354	27.9	445,132	134,281	30.2
Canada and Newfoundland	496,607	272,373	54.8	517,169	315,185	60.9
Canada—French	141,514	66,579	47.0	132,662	66,402	50.1
Ireland	448,573	324,100	72.3	573,104	350,821	61.2
England	392,116	253,937	64.8	353,282	233,702	66.2
Sweden	334,849	232,761	69.5	270,700	190,931	70.5
Austria	300,899	109,015	36.4	227,262	95,045	41.8
Hungary	190,098	55,188	28.1	157,690	50,995	32.3
Norway	195,101	131,322	67.3	159,784	106,710	69.4
Czechoslovakia	182,913	81,705	44.7	152,417	76,630	50.3
Mexico	180,974	6,363	3.3	129,723	11,261	8.7
Scotland	122,508	77,903	63.6	108,966	67,769	62.2
Denmark	109,754	76,412	69.6	71,044	51,127	72.0
Greece	135,207	23,093	17.1	26,308	5,036	19.1
Jugo-Slavia	107,974	23,140	21.4	47,982	15,676	32.7
France	73,937	44,421	60.1	66,959	38,309	57.2
Finland	80,407	31,550	39.2	59,608	27,323	45.8
Lithuania	79,308	20,254	25.5	48,334	12,979	26.9
Netherlands	67,901	39,462	58.1	49,276	30,459	61.8
Switzerland	65,056	42,023	64.9	48,736	32,885	67.5
Rumania	52,979	21,602	40.8	39,138	17,278	44.1
Belgium and Luxemburg	39,295	21,722	55.3	27,228	15,213	55.0
Wales	34,800	25,591	73.5	29,429	22,169	75.3
Portugal	33,837	5,854	17.3	22,739	4,211	18.5
Syria	28,478	8,821	31.0	18,097	5,236	28.9
Spain	31,540	2,814	8.9	9,896	1,636	16.5
Armenia	23,746	6,664	28.1	9,780	3,340	34.2
West Indies[1]	11,690	3,461	29.6	9,969	3,220	32.3
Bulgaria and Turkey in Europe	12,530	1,005	12.8	2,035	530	26.0
Central and South America	9,215	2,147	23.3	5,331	1,903	35.7
All other	54,031	16,343	30.2	33,537	12,903	38.5
GEOG. DIVISIONS.						
NEW ENGLAND.						
All countries	866,042	367,478	42.4	839,249	388,049	46.2
Canada and Newfoundland	202,389	91,199	45.1	231,300	120,220	52.0
Canada—French	106,203	44,505	41.9	104,712	47,592	45.5
Ireland	108,713	77,007	70.8	155,295	92,160	59.3
Italy	122,027	29,386	24.1	84,408	19,361	22.9
England	65,222	43,090	66.1	60,085	44,188	64.0
Russia	72,882	20,340	36.1	56,605	21,615	38.1
Poland	67,397	10,638	15.8	54,594	8,770	16.1
Sweden	32,028	21,141	66.0	32,655	20,776	63.6
Germany	25,591	18,824	73.6	24,130	17,733	73.5
Scotland	20,419	13,078	64.0	22,521	13,477	59.8
MIDDLE ATLANTIC.						
All countries	2,406,975	1,065,420	44.3	2,070,777	959,199	46.3
Italy	477,135	151,841	31.8	329,929	97,218	29.5
Russia	363,742	148,783	40.9	299,497	119,306	39.8
Germany	254,970	181,812	71.3	242,070	171,630	71.0
Poland	268,079	70,338	26.2	204,131	57,598	28.2
Ireland	193,130	139,601	72.3	271,887	161,366	59.4
Austria	155,940	55,101	35.4	129,780	50,159	38.6
England	124,774	81,802	65.6	122,640	80,336	65.5
Hungary	90,873	26,640	29.3	81,263	26,370	32.5
Canada and Newfoundland	55,936	31,445	56.2	68,308	42,795	62.7
Canada—French	7,751	4,256	54.9	7,668	4,715	61.5
Czechoslovakia	63,601	19,168	30.1	51,260	18,328	35.8
EAST NORTH CENTRAL.						
All countries	1,687,728	843,952	50.0	1,290,847	732,715	56.8
Germany	299,283	219,878	73.5	279,136	207,007	74.2
Poland	216,288	64,836	30.0	153,234	51,676	33.7
Canada and Newfoundland	116,204	73,419	63.2	113,942	79,777	70.0
Canada—French	15,761	10,183	64.2	12,296	8,484	69.2
Russia	121,730	45,551	37.4	81,134	33,962	41.9
Italy	114,271	36,409	31.9	62,775	21,132	33.7
Sweden	86,696	62,860	72.5	73,888	53,330	72.2
England	81,852	53,250	65.1	67,455	45,655	67.7
Ireland	63,301	47,680	75.3	69,144	47,171	68.2
Czechoslovakia	70,682	38,829	47.9	60,822	32,480	53.4
Austria	78,248	25,206	32.2	52,914	21,452	40.5
Hungary	75,631	18,167	24.0	54,517	15,799	29.0
Norway	41,938	27,839	66.4	37,193	24,832	66.8
Jugo-Slavia	44,755	9,469	21.2	21,551	6,787	31.5
WEST NORTH CENTRAL.						
All countries	738,673	483,504	65.5	553,121	390,628	70.6
Germany	157,753	121,934	77.3	129,568	102,108	78.8
Sweden	104,470	77,281	74.0	77,195	59,360	76.9
Norway	89,966	66,071	73.4	70,776	53,046	75.8
Russia	52,091	30,006	56.9	41,309	25,174	60.9
Canada and Newfoundland	40,087	27,006	67.4	33,989	25,547	75.2
Canada—French	5,854	4,096	70.0	4,227	3,199	75.7
Denmark	36,039	25,770	71.5	22,951	17,133	74.7
England	28,531	19,410	68.0	22,114	15,904	71.9
Ireland	25,202	18,776	74.3	24,041	16,276	67.7
Czechoslovakia	25,904	17,010	65.7	22,402	15,744	70.3
Poland	20,995	10,394	49.5	14,653	8,128	55.5
Austria	20,198	10,443	51.7	14,600	9,033	61.9
Italy	19,848	6,287	31.7	10,445	3,346	32.0
Finland	18,218	8,167	44.8	11,331	6,677	58.9
SOUTH ATLANTIC.						
All countries	170,407	72,664	42.6	116,808	58,759	50.3
Russia	24,650	11,539	46.8	17,933	8,986	50.1
Germany	21,448	15,858	73.9	18,500	13,809	74.8
Italy	22,648	5,800	24.8	11,584	2,797	24.1
Poland	13,900	3,804	27.4	9,162	2,802	30.6
England	12,058	6,794	56.3	10,048	6,087	60.6
Ireland	8,874	6,168	69.5	10,965	6,661	60.7
Greece	8,987	1,600	17.8	1,505	361	24.0
Canada and Newfoundland	5,552	2,647	47.7	5,639	3,347	59.4
Canada—French	390	172	44.1	308	169	51.6
Austria	6,951	2,235	32.2	4,073	1,742	42.8
Hungary	6,169	1,106	17.9	3,303	849	25.7
West Indies[1]	3,890	982	25.2	3,747	1,113	29.7
Scotland	3,814	2,149	56.3	3,027	1,797	59.4
Czechoslovakia	3,372	1,545	45.8	2,720	1,446	53.0
EAST SOUTH CENTRAL.						
All countries	39,697	22,056	55.6	27,545	16,279	59.1
Germany	8,867	6,716	75.7	7,572	5,405	71.4
Italy	4,801	1,472	30.7	2,742	813	29.6
Russia	3,919	2,311	59.0	2,630	1,502	60.5
Ireland	2,852	1,830	64.2	3,042	1,667	54.8
England	3,266	1,850	56.6	2,436	1,521	62.4
Greece	1,641	440	26.8	251	88	35.1
Canada and Newfoundland	1,604	715	44.6	1,250	783	62.6
Canada—French	98	49	(2)	69	34	(2)
Poland	1,484	800	53.9	853	479	56.2
Switzerland	1,223	880	72.0	921	650	70.6
France	1,097	719	65.5	947	576	60.8
Scotland	1,154	683	59.2	790	495	62.7
Austria	1,209	622	51.4	673	401	59.6
Hungary	1,057	359	34.0	569	233	40.9
Sweden	959	632	65.9	526	382	72.6
Syria	825	326	39.5	530	192	36.2
WEST SOUTH CENTRAL.						
All countries	208,431	64,503	30.9	148,789	49,755	33.4
Mexico	96,305	3,241	3.4	72,967	6,197	8.5
Germany	26,176	17,838	68.1	20,085	13,066	65.5
Italy	15,063	4,773	31.7	10,295	2,836	27.5
Czechoslovakia	7,487	4,766	63.7	6,572	4,288	65.2
Russia	7,783	4,538	58.3	5,094	3,034	59.6
England	7,791	4,348	55.8	4,901	3,147	64.2
Austria	4,970	2,974	59.8	3,470	2,216	63.9
Ireland	4,424	2,766	62.5	3,801	1,795	47.2
Canada and Newfoundland	4,804	2,257	47.0	3,246	2,069	63.7
Canada—French	331	157	47.4	197	105	53.3
France	4,283	2,297	53.6	3,480	1,639	47.1
MOUNTAIN.						
All countries	241,821	119,979	49.7	152,687	90,885	59.5
Mexico	38,264	1,412	3.7	26,005	2,442	9.4
England	22,600	16,054	71.0	19,108	14,698	76.9
Germany	19,505	14,504	74.1	12,788	10,173	79.5
Sweden	18,281	13,021	71.2	12,964	10,060	77.6
Canada and Newfoundland	17,416	11,975	68.8	12,162	9,326	76.7
Canada—French	2,055	1,448	70.5	1,173	908	74.0
Italy	18,000	6,934	38.5	8,062	3,877	48.1
Russia	11,821	5,066	42.9	8,850	3,015	44.2
Ireland	11,073	8,218	74.2	8,277	6,288	75.9
Norway	10,038	7,161	71.3	6,596	5,044	76.5
Denmark	9,333	7,059	75.6	6,816	5,464	80.2
Austria	8,138	3,568	43.8	4,125	2,503	60.7
Scotland	7,207	5,141	71.3	4,890	3,759	76.9
Jugo-Slavia	7,608	2,346	30.8	2,632	1,271	48.3
Greece	8,526	1,157	13.6	601	125	20.8

[1] Except possessions of the United States.

[2] Per cent not shown, base being less than 100.

812

POPULATION.

TABLE 8.—NUMBER AND PER CENT NATURALIZED AMONG FOREIGN-BORN WHITE MALES AND FEMALES 21 YEARS OF AGE AND OVER, FOR SELECTED COUNTRIES OF BIRTH, BY DIVISIONS AND STATES: 1920—Continued.

[The countries for which figures are given in this table are those which contributed 2 per cent or more of the total number of foreign-born white persons 21 years of age and over, of both sexes combined, enumerated in the specified division or state.]

DIVISION OR STATE OF RESIDENCE AND COUNTRY OF BIRTH.	Male. Total number.	Male. Naturalized. Number.	Male. Naturalized. Per cent.	Female. Total number.	Female. Naturalized. Number.	Female. Naturalized. Per cent.
GEOG. DIVISIONS—Con.						
PACIFIC.						
All countries..........	589,178	275,354	48.4	370,445	207,518	56.0
Germany	59,578	42,479	71.3	41,708	31,487	75.5
Canada and Newfoundland	52,615	31,710	60.3	47,333	31,321	66.2
Canada—French	*2,981*	*1,773*	*59.5*	*2,092*	*1,226*	*60.5*
Italy	63,318	16,579	26.2	30,582	8,786	28.7
England	46,022	27,249	59.2	35,495	22,171	62.5
Sweden	45,135	27,892	61.8	29,080	20,554	69.3
Mexico	37,694	1,058	2.8	23,704	2,000	8.7
Ireland	30,944	22,054	71.3	26,652	17,442	65.4
Norway	28,147	17,164	61.0	18,547	12,603	68.0
Russia	22,990	10,186	44.3	16,017	7,657	47.8
Denmark	18,917	13,164	69.6	10,841	7,841	72.3
Scotland	15,479	9,291	60.0	10,786	6,447	59.8
Finland	14,538	5,404	37.2	9,345	4,541	48.6
Switzerland	14,651	8,230	56.2	8,321	5,372	64.6
France	12,793	6,924	54.1	10,012	5,670	56.6
Portugal	13,911	3,360	24.2	8,032	2,380	29.0
Austria	14,128	5,814	41.2	7,284	4,059	55.7
NEW ENGLAND.						
Maine.						
All countries..........	49,255	18,028	36.5	44,974	22,451	49.9
Canada and Newfoundland	32,051	10,844	33.8	31,952	15,904	49.8
Canada—French	*15,164*	*5,587*	*35.5*	*14,279*	*6,000*	*42.0*
Ireland	2,400	1,498	62.4	3,267	1,818	55.6
England	2,379	1,362	57.3	2,327	1,438	61.8
Russia	2,147	763	35.5	1,240	593	47.8
Italy	1,593	384	24.1	787	188	23.9
Sweden	1,133	666	58.8	817	575	70.4
Scotland	942	518	55.0	988	576	58.3
New Hampshire.						
All countries..........	42,432	17,395	41.0	39,617	19,226	48.5
Canada and Newfoundland	22,981	9,989	43.5	23,236	11,850	51.0
Canada—French	*16,934*	*7,009*	*41.7*	*16,185*	*7,260*	*44.9*
Ireland	3,257	2,378	73.0	4,573	2,780	60.8
Greece	3,087	250	8.1	1,409	73	5.2
England	1,994	1,240	62.2	2,051	1,320	64.4
Poland	2,030	182	9.0	1,706	168	9.8
Russia	2,041	449	22.0	1,129	361	32.0
Sweden	905	606	67.0	913	616	67.5
Italy	1,149	324	28.2	627	200	31.9
Scotland	755	480	63.6	940	544	57.9
Germany	866	623	71.9	761	587	77.1
Vermont.						
All countries..........	20,462	9,540	46.6	17,770	10,285	57.9
Canada and Newfoundland	10,289	4,629	45.0	10,040	5,842	58.2
Canada—French	*5,884*	*2,548*	*43.3*	*5,102*	*2,664*	*52.2*
Italy	2,222	1,062	47.8	1,358	727	53.5
Ireland	1,214	920	75.8	1,638	1,139	69.5
England	1,091	551	50.5	917	589	64.2
Poland	970	122	12.6	621	82	13.2
Scotland	862	615	71.3	747	550	73.6
Russia	798	221	27.9	412	179	43.4
Sweden	582	444	76.3	504	390	77.4
Massachusetts.						
All countries..........	491,107	213,477	43.5	497,806	227,939	45.8
Canada and Newfoundland	110,272	52,517	47.6	137,635	71,086	51.6
Canada—French	*48,898*	*20,132*	*41.3*	*49,749*	*21,670*	*43.6*
Ireland	74,417	52,587	70.7	106,381	62,079	58.4
Italy	60,071	13,089	21.8	41,041	8,204	20.0
Russia	44,208	16,882	38.2	36,088	13,812	38.3
England	38,420	25,736	67.0	41,096	25,998	63.3
Poland	35,233	5,469	15.5	29,061	4,460	15.3
Sweden	17,797	11,538	64.8	18,639	11,438	61.4
Scotland	12,167	7,771	63.9	13,567	7,884	58.1
Portugal	12,488	1,286	10.3	10,450	1,130	10.8
Germany	11,127	8,130	73.1	10,386	7,514	72.3
Lithuania	11,604	1,659	14.3	8,120	1,081	13.3

DIVISION OR STATE OF RESIDENCE AND COUNTRY OF BIRTH.	Male. Total number.	Male. Naturalized. Number.	Male. Naturalized. Per cent.	Female. Total number.	Female. Naturalized. Number.	Female. Naturalized. Per cent.
NEW ENGLAND—Con.						
Rhode Island.						
All countries..........	78,118	38,212	48.9	78,748	39,963	50.7
Canada and Newfoundland	15,702	8,341	53.1	17,007	9,480	55.8
Canada—French	*12,630*	*6,595*	*52.2*	*12,849*	*6,804*	*53.7*
Italy	16,035	5,033	31.4	12,280	3,605	29.4
England	11,150	7,719	69.2	12,391	8,226	66.4
Ireland	8,492	6,416	75.6	13,497	8,502	63.0
Poland	3,093	711	17.8	3,549	630	17.8
Russia	3,846	1,751	45.5	3,212	1,530	47.6
Portugal	3,761	484	12.9	3,046	406	13.3
Sweden	3,025	2,119	70.0	3,273	2,177	66.5
Scotland	2,382	1,679	70.5	2,817	1,837	65.2
Connecticut.						
All countries..........	184,568	70,826	38.4	160,334	68,185	42.5
Italy	40,957	9,494	23.2	28,315	6,437	22.7
Ireland	18,933	13,208	69.8	25,939	15,842	61.1
Poland	24,152	3,950	16.4	19,108	3,293	17.2
Russia	19,852	6,274	31.6	14,584	5,140	35.2
Canada and Newfoundland	11,094	4,879	44.0	11,430	6,049	52.9
Canada—French	*6,783*	*2,724*	*40.2*	*6,548*	*3,104*	*47.4*
Germany	11,244	8,314	73.9	10,806	7,976	73.8
England	10,179	6,482	63.7	10,303	6,617	64.2
Sweden	8,586	5,768	67.2	8,509	5,580	65.6
Hungary	6,229	1,385	22.2	5,729	1,453	25.4
Austria	6,063	1,829	30.4	5,839	1,924	33.0
Lithuania	6,723	1,064	15.8	4,355	731	16.8
Scotland	3,311	2,015	60.9	3,462	2,086	60.3
MIDDLE ATLANTIC.						
New York.						
All countries..........	1,318,883	604,256	45.8	1,209,614	549,557	45.4
Italy	272,399	84,035	30.8	202,595	55,205	27.3
Russia	247,112	101,341	41.0	211,127	80,798	38.3
Germany	148,971	104,665	70.3	141,316	98,042	69.8
Ireland	114,982	82,712	71.9	105,526	60,486	57.4
Poland	123,623	36,393	29.4	101,170	30,578	30.2
Austria	70,380	30,818	43.8	67,899	28,311	41.7
England	60,953	37,608	61.7	59,346	36,501	61.5
Canada and Newfoundland	45,102	25,394	56.3	56,348	35,080	62.3
Canada—French	*7,088*	*3,865*	*55.0*	*7,050*	*4,312*	*61.2*
Hungary	34,222	14,169	41.4	37,191	14,532	39.1
Sweden	24,990	14,825	59.3	26,124	14,233	54.5
New Jersey.						
All countries..........	360,902	158,727	44.0	314,320	146,789	46.7
Italy	80,019	26,571	33.2	57,026	17,788	30.9
Germany	46,227	32,292	69.9	43,469	30,875	71.0
Poland	46,679	9,130	19.6	36,664	7,532	20.5
Russia	36,719	14,566	39.7	28,083	11,988	42.7
Ireland	26,872	19,894	74.0	37,860	24,677	65.2
England	21,158	14,057	66.4	21,658	14,252	65.8
Hungary	19,442	4,659	24.0	16,966	4,646	27.4
Austria	17,892	6,398	35.8	16,144	6,292	39.0
Sweden	7,842	4,954	63.2	8,036	4,803	60.5
Czechoslovakia	8,105	2,581	31.8	6,976	2,509	36.0
Pennsylvania.						
All countries..........	727,190	302,437	41.6	546,843	262,853	48.1
Italy	124,717	41,235	33.1	69,708	24,135	34.6
Poland	98,377	24,815	25.2	66,201	19,488	29.4
Russia	79,911	32,876	41.1	60,287	26,520	44.0
Ireland	51,276	36,995	72.1	68,492	41,723	60.9
Germany	59,772	44,855	75.0	57,291	42,313	73.9
Austria	67,668	17,945	26.5	45,737	15,556	34.0
England	42,663	30,227	70.9	41,636	29,583	71.1
Hungary	37,209	7,812	21.0	27,100	7,192	26.5
Czechoslovakia	37,958	9,569	25.2	25,682	8,320	32.4
Jugo-Slavia	23,533	3,376	14.3	9,537	2,452	25.7
Lithuania	17,681	6,700	37.9	11,033	4,594	41.6
Scotland	12,950	8,807	68.0	12,782	8,695	68.0

CITIZENSHIP.

TABLE 8.—NUMBER AND PER CENT NATURALIZED AMONG FOREIGN-BORN WHITE MALES AND FEMALES 21 YEARS OF AGE AND OVER, FOR SELECTED COUNTRIES OF BIRTH, BY DIVISIONS AND STATES: 1920—Continued.

[The countries for which figures are given in this table are those which contributed 2 per cent or more of the total number of foreign-born white persons 21 years of age and over, of both sexes combined, enumerated in the specified division or state.]

DIVISION OR STATE OF RESIDENCE AND COUNTRY OF BIRTH.	FOREIGN-BORN WHITE POPULATION 21 YEARS OF AGE AND OVER: 1920					
	Male.			Female.		
	Total number.	Naturalized. Number.	Per cent.	Total number.	Naturalized. Number.	Per cent.
EAST NORTH CENTRAL.						
Ohio.						
All countries	363,504	156,820	43.1	259,019	136,715	52.8
Germany	56,028	45,089	80.5	53,371	42,456	79.5
Hungary	37,772	8,558	22.7	26,537	7,443	28.0
Poland	37,194	9,840	26.5	24,435	7,546	30.9
Italy	35,116	9,360	26.7	17,629	5,186	29.4
Austria	26,715	6,848	25.6	16,757	5,809	34.7
England	21,216	14,369	67.7	18,255	12,881	70.6
Czechoslovakia	20,865	8,547	41.0	17,388	8,368	48.1
Russia	22,652	8,507	37.6	15,000	6,470	43.1
Ireland	13,412	10,126	75.5	15,437	10,682	69.2
Jugo-Slavia	18,769	3,327	17.7	9,236	2,501	27.1
Canada and Newfoundland	10,528	6,466	61.4	11,144	7,880	70.7
Canada—French	*648*	*411*	*64.0*	*555*	*393*	*71.7*
Greece	11,681	1,409	12.1	1,105	248	22.4
Indiana.						
All countries	82,908	34,871	42.1	57,465	28,696	49.9
Germany	19,240	12,212	63.5	17,357	11,184	64.4
Poland	9,648	2,395	24.8	6,586	1,798	27.3
Austria	5,188	1,237	23.8	3,138	929	29.6
Hungary	4,955	1,247	25.2	3,243	944	29.1
England	4,302	2,546	59.2	3,532	2,275	64.4
Ireland	3,470	2,238	64.5	3,717	2,076	55.9
Russia	4,319	1,481	34.3	2,466	974	39.5
Italy	4,014	1,224	30.5	1,887	592	31.4
Sweden	2,732	1,746	63.9	2,094	1,411	67.4
Canada and Newfoundland	2,486	1,244	50.0	2,179	1,452	66.6
Canada—French	*237*	*136*	*57.4*	*159*	*103*	*64.8*
Jugo-Slavia	3,082	532	17.3	1,072	279	26.0
Greece	3,534	547	15.5	379	97	25.6
Czechoslovakia	2,196	627	28.6	1,441	469	32.5
Scotland	1,742	955	54.8	1,370	812	59.3
France	1,649	931	56.5	1,286	727	56.5
Illinois.						
All countries	613,797	341,910	55.7	504,131	297,536	59.0
Germany	103,054	82,522	80.1	97,395	76,974	79.0
Poland	83,854	28,768	34.3	66,129	24,085	36.4
Sweden	52,761	39,302	74.5	49,767	35,628	71.6
Russia	58,641	25,238	43.0	43,081	19,448	45.1
Italy	50,950	18,141	35.6	31,412	11,343	36.1
Ireland	34,150	27,060	79.2	38,371	26,762	69.7
Czechoslovakia	31,913	17,627	55.2	29,576	17,305	58.5
England	26,606	18,756	70.5	22,532	16,087	71.4
Austria	23,773	9,811	41.3	18,261	8,590	47.0
Canada and Newfoundland	17,527	12,264	70.0	18,515	13,224	71.4
Canada—French	*1,980*	*1,472*	*76.0*	*1,963*	*1,451*	*74.3*
Hungary	16,224	5,428	33.5	13,652	5,048	37.0
Lithuania	18,207	5,298	29.1	10,470	3,318	31.7
Norway	12,912	9,427	73.0	13,638	9,308	68.3
Michigan.						
All countries	381,808	175,631	46.0	281,352	155,327	55.2
Canada and Newfoundland	75,388	47,066	62.4	74,145	51,658	69.7
Canada—French	*10,017*	*6,445*	*64.3*	*7,665*	*5,340*	*69.6*
Poland	58,672	13,238	22.6	36,296	9,481	26.1
Germany	43,486	29,895	68.7	40,405	28,933	71.6
England	24,118	14,046	58.2	18,618	11,401	61.2
Russia	25,003	6,547	26.2	13,780	4,392	31.9
Netherlands	16,673	10,161	60.9	13,738	8,752	63.7
Finland	16,299	7,967	48.9	11,596	6,688	57.7
Italy	17,756	5,484	30.9	8,510	2,850	33.6
Sweden	13,841	9,950	71.9	10,196	7,790	76.4
Austria	12,072	2,886	23.9	7,441	2,300	30.9
Hungary	11,653	1,688	14.5	7,599	1,350	17.8
Ireland	8,414	5,565	66.1	7,737	5,044	65.2
Wisconsin.						
All countries	245,711	134,720	54.8	188,880	114,441	60.6
Germany	77,475	50,160	64.7	70,608	47,460	67.2
Poland	26,920	10,595	39.4	19,788	8,766	44.3
Norway	24,222	15,194	62.7	19,839	12,837	64.7
Sweden	13,263	9,242	69.7	8,968	6,602	73.6
Czechoslovakia	10,013	5,260	52.5	8,300	4,783	57.6
Russia	11,115	3,778	34.0	6,807	2,678	39.3
Austria	10,500	4,424	42.1	7,317	3,824	52.3

DIVISION OR STATE OF RESIDENCE AND COUNTRY OF BIRTH.	FOREIGN-BORN WHITE POPULATION 21 YEARS OF AGE AND OVER: 1920					
	Male.			Female.		
	Total number.	Naturalized. Number.	Per cent.	Total number.	Naturalized. Number.	Per cent.
EAST NORTH CENTRAL—Con.						
Wisconsin—Con.						
Canada and Newfoundland	10,275	6,379	62.1	7,959	5,563	69.9
Canada—French	*2,929*	*1,659*	*56.6*	*1,906*	*1,186*	*61.2*
Denmark	8,853	6,293	71.1	5,997	4,272	71.2
England	5,610	3,533	63.0	4,518	3,011	66.6
Italy	3,435	2,200	34.2	3,337	1,155	34.6
Hungary	5,027	1,206	24.0	3,486	1,014	29.1
WEST NORTH CENTRAL.						
Minnesota.						
All countries	266,856	177,355	66.5	195,726	142,035	72.6
Sweden	62,622	45,968	73.4	45,535	34,950	76.8
Norway	48,439	35,484	73.3	38,881	29,108	74.9
Germany	39,727	31,377	79.0	33,465	27,236	81.4
Canada and Newfoundland	17,142	11,951	69.7	13,653	10,335	75.7
Canada—French	*3,916*	*2,795*	*71.4*	*3,672*	*2,080*	*75.8*
Finland	16,854	7,313	43.4	10,301	5,916	57.4
Poland	10,182	5,556	54.6	7,314	4,600	62.9
Denmark	9,957	7,241	72.7	6,243	4,786	76.7
Russia	8,072	3,866	47.9	5,542	3,029	54.7
Czechoslovakia	6,630	4,324	65.2	5,445	3,852	70.7
Austria	6,362	3,163	49.7	4,487	2,855	63.6
England	5,838	3,953	67.7	4,393	3,064	69.7
Ireland	5,358	4,047	75.5	4,816	3,486	72.4
Jugo-Slavia	7,261	1,668	23.0	2,865	1,145	40.0
Iowa.						
All countries	121,392	84,160	69.3	93,087	69,111	74.2
Germany	37,781	30,728	81.3	31,411	26,003	82.8
Sweden	12,228	9,499	77.7	9,738	7,646	78.5
Denmark	10,389	7,463	71.8	6,731	4,909	73.8
Norway	9,194	6,835	74.3	7,738	5,915	76.4
England	6,913	4,836	70.0	5,413	3,931	72.6
Netherlands	6,149	3,515	57.2	4,566	2,845	62.3
Ireland	5,357	4,018	75.0	5,181	3,545	68.4
Czechoslovakia	4,491	3,223	71.8	4,146	3,156	76.1
Canada and Newfoundland	4,356	2,859	65.6	4,153	3,105	74.8
Canada—French	*204*	*144*	*70.6*	*190*	*145*	*76.3*
Russia	3,609	1,666	46.2	2,487	1,237	49.7
Italy	2,951	807	27.3	1,376	432	31.4
Missouri.						
All countries	97,345	57,561	59.1	76,206	46,887	61.5
Germany	29,686	23,012	77.5	25,334	19,080	75.3
Russia	8,685	4,289	49.4	7,027	3,382	48.1
Ireland	7,109	5,413	76.1	7,780	5,017	64.5
Italy	8,105	2,508	30.9	4,690	1,387	29.6
England	5,323	3,491	65.6	4,427	3,077	69.5
Austria	4,498	2,260	50.2	3,356	1,850	55.1
Poland	4,035	1,639	40.6	2,976	1,246	41.9
Hungary	3,782	1,353	35.8	3,198	1,186	37.1
Canada and Newfoundland	3,230	1,801	55.8	2,941	1,978	67.3
Canada—French	*160*	*80*	*50.0*	*124*	*80*	*64.6*
Switzerland	2,817	2,032	72.1	2,017	1,482	73.5
Sweden	2,589	1,839	71.0	2,061	1,493	72.4
Czechoslovakia	2,427	1,379	56.8	2,222	1,310	59.0
France	2,021	1,411	69.8	1,638	1,143	69.8
North Dakota.						
All countries	70,043	51,350	73.3	51,004	39,837	78.1
Norway	21,210	15,863	74.8	15,361	12,082	78.7
Russia	13,733	10,114	73.0	11,352	8,827	77.8
Canada and Newfoundland	7,683	5,645	74.4	6,406	5,023	78.4
Canada—French	*785*	*585*	*74.5*	*687*	*508*	*77.0*
Germany	6,751	5,298	78.5	4,840	3,951	81.6
Sweden	6,423	4,741	73.8	3,684	2,938	79.8
Denmark	2,684	2,029	75.6	1,686	1,304	77.3
South Dakota.						
All countries	45,340	31,030	68.4	32,687	24,134	73.8
Norway	9,137	6,563	71.8	7,153	5,397	75.5
Germany	8,801	6,407	72.8	6,466	4,997	77.3
Russia	5,446	3,848	70.7	4,555	3,418	75.0
Sweden	5,048	3,533	70.0	3,198	2,402	75.1

POPULATION.

TABLE 8.—NUMBER AND PER CENT NATURALIZED AMONG FOREIGN-BORN WHITE MALES AND FEMALES 21 YEARS OF AGE AND OVER, FOR SELECTED COUNTRIES OF BIRTH, BY DIVISIONS AND STATES: 1920—Continued.

[The countries for which figures are given in this table are those which contributed 2 per cent or more of the total number of foreign-born white persons 21 years of age and over, of both sexes combined, enumerated in the specified division or state.]

DIVISION OR STATE OF RESIDENCE AND COUNTRY OF BIRTH.	Male. Total number.	Naturalized. Number.	Per cent.	Female. Total number.	Naturalized. Number.	Per cent.
W. NORTH CENTRAL—Con.						
South Dakota—Con.						
Denmark	3,509	2,378	67.8	2,104	1,509	71.7
Canada and Newfoundland	2,327	1,495	64.2	1,831	1,394	76.1
Canada—French	299	208	69.6	197	153	77.7
Netherlands	1,684	859	51.0	1,124	645	57.4
England	1,620	1,156	71.4	1,157	879	76.0
Czechoslovakia	1,493	1,017	68.1	1,171	849	72.5
Ireland	1,064	752	70.7	854	563	65.9
Nebraska.						
All countries	79,821	49,012	61.4	61,078	40,771	66.8
Germany	22,285	15,879	71.3	17,890	13,156	73.5
Sweden	10,046	7,338	73.0	8,314	6,191	74.5
Czechoslovakia	8,007	5,166	64.5	7,014	4,817	68.7
Russia	7,070	2,697	38.1	5,611	2,305	41.1
Denmark	7,089	4,892	69.0	4,701	3,488	73.3
England	3,179	2,154	67.8	2,565	1,846	72.0
Ireland	2,873	2,072	72.1	2,497	1,714	68.6
Canada and Newfoundland	2,822	1,702	60.3	2,538	1,883	74.2
Canada—French	185	105	56.8	140	103	73.6
Poland	2,549	1,164	45.7	1,752	822	46.9
Austria	2,398	1,271	53.0	1,878	1,192	63.5
Italy	1,911	523	27.4	1,115	256	23.0
Kansas.						
All countries	57,876	33,036	57.1	43,333	27,853	64.3
Germany	12,722	9,233	72.6	10,162	7,085	75.6
Russia	6,076	3,526	58.0	4,735	2,976	62.9
Sweden	5,514	4,363	79.1	4,665	3,740	80.2
Mexico	5,868	95	1.6	3,050	56	1.8
England	4,342	2,914	67.1	3,313	2,481	74.9
Canada and Newfoundland	2,627	1,553	59.1	2,467	1,829	74.1
Canada—French	305	179	58.7	247	186	75.3
Ireland	2,548	1,746	68.5	2,246	1,500	66.8
Austria	2,722	1,311	48.2	2,061	1,181	57.3
Czechoslovakia	1,758	1,121	63.8	1,540	1,089	70.4
Italy	1,927	564	29.3	1,036	272	26.3
Scotland	1,381	960	69.5	1,089	810	74.4
Switzerland	1,252	887	70.8	955	686	71.8
Denmark	1,345	1,002	74.5	859	669	77.9
Poland	1,325	536	40.5	876	393	44.9
SOUTH ATLANTIC.						
Delaware.						
All countries	10,614	4,329	40.8	7,631	3,698	48.5
Italy	2,518	631	25.1	1,112	323	29.0
Poland	2,136	395	18.5	1,374	310	22.6
Ireland	1,283	939	73.2	1,567	978	62.4
Russia	1,220	467	38.3	822	380	46.2
Germany	818	610	74.6	768	557	72.5
England	730	480	65.8	636	419	65.9
Austria	322	114	35.4	260	102	39.2
Scotland	197	120	60.9	189	122	64.6
Canada and Newfoundland	178	94	52.8	199	133	66.8
Canada—French	11	6	(1)	11	7	(1)
Maryland.						
All countries	50,363	26,077	51.8	43,261	23,687	54.8
Germany	10,869	8,309	76.4	10,735	8,192	76.3
Russia	11,723	5,370	45.8	9,791	4,580	46.8
Poland	6,111	1,871	30.6	4,934	1,629	33.0
Italy	5,310	1,475	27.8	3,031	754	24.9
Ireland	2,638	2,025	76.8	3,861	2,474	64.1
England	2,380	1,486	62.4	2,142	1,396	65.2
Czechoslovakia	1,673	1,034	61.8	1,664	1,058	63.6
Austria	1,772	880	49.7	1,545	822	53.2
Lithuania	1,196	394	32.9	906	313	34.5
District of Columbia.						
All countries	14,042	7,786	55.4	12,334	6,926	56.2
Russia	2,529	1,410	55.8	1,950	1,070	54.9
Ireland	1,724	1,217	70.6	2,539	1,529	60.2
Italy	2,195	744	33.9	1,168	371	31.8
Germany	1,736	1,359	78.3	1,607	1,232	76.7
England	1,314	828	63.0	1,436	823	57.3

DIVISION OR STATE OF RESIDENCE AND COUNTRY OF BIRTH.	Male. Total number.	Naturalized. Number.	Per cent.	Female. Total number.	Naturalized. Number.	Per cent.
SOUTH ATLANTIC—Con.						
District of Columbia—Con.						
Canada and Newfoundland	616	401	65.1	958	546	57.0
Canada—French	56	32	(1)	80	30	(1)
Greece	844	154	18.2	227	45	19.8
Scotland	345	220	66.4	389	225	57.8
France	291	105	56.7	353	180	51.0
Poland	382	238	62.3	244	142	58.2
Virginia.						
All countries	17,431	8,356	47.9	10,420	5,701	54.7
Russia	2,816	1,527	54.2	2,010	1,140	56.7
England	1,970	980	49.7	1,441	806	55.9
Germany	1,667	1,188	71.3	1,074	779	72.5
Italy	1,513	690	45.6	657	305	46.4
Ireland	964	612	63.5	719	447	62.2
Greece	1,420	283	19.9	225	60	26.7
Canada and Newfoundland	862	369	42.8	751	448	59.7
Canada—French	63	28	(1)	31	16	(1)
Scotland	688	374	54.4	500	292	58.4
Hungary	705	174	24.7	456	122	26.8
Poland	596	284	47.7	373	102	43.4
Austria	485	248	51.1	346	166	48.0
Czechoslovakia	439	209	47.6	364	172	47.3
Sweden	453	237	52.3	189	121	64.0
West Virginia.						
All countries	38,471	8,315	21.6	16,994	5,826	34.3
Italy	8,853	1,434	16.2	3,407	608	17.8
Hungary	3,932	281	7.1	1,615	181	11.2
Poland	3,578	346	9.7	1,611	195	12.1
Austria	3,283	387	11.8	1,320	281	21.3
Germany	2,061	1,436	69.7	1,617	1,160	71.7
Russia	2,677	536	20.0	963	341	35.4
England	1,727	958	55.5	1,367	882	64.5
Greece	2,625	157	6.0	283	27	9.5
Jugo-Slavia	2,134	135	6.3	488	73	15.0
Ireland	735	449	61.1	706	397	56.2
Czechoslovakia	933	118	12.6	456	93	20.4
Syria	763	317	41.5	366	171	46.7
North Carolina.						
All countries	4,035	1,886	46.7	2,453	1,349	55.0
England	510	247	48.4	393	226	57.5
Russia	540	333	61.7	311	207	66.6
Germany	415	306	73.7	270	201	72.0
Canada and Newfoundland	301	100	33.2	292	169	57.9
Canada—French	10	4	(1)	4	3	(1)
Syria	340	103	30.3	184	64	34.8
Greece	442	97	21.9	68	19	(1)
Italy	277	119	43.0	125	50	40.0
Scotland	233	98	42.1	156	84	53.8
Ireland	147	81	55.1	149	61	40.9
Poland	126	58	46.0	68	39	(1)
Sweden	118	59	50.0	50	31	(1)
Austria	88	52	(1)	52	23	(1)
South Carolina.						
All countries	3,850	1,924	50.0	2,091	1,138	54.4
Germany	586	380	66.4	473	312	66.0
Russia	679	359	52.9	371	201	54.2
Greece	454	114	25.1	90	25	(1)
England	259	98	37.8	188	107	56.9
Ireland	231	144	62.3	206	103	50.0
Syria	222	63	28.4	141	34	24.1
Italy	257	139	54.1	67	33	(1)
Poland	225	134	59.6	98	42	(1)
Canada and Newfoundland	140	60	42.9	107	70	65.4
Canada—French	15	6	(1)	7	5	(1)
Austria	139	84	60.4	59	42	(1)
Scotland	109	57	52.3	70	44	(1)
Sweden	99	59	(1)	31	20	(1)
Georgia.						
All countries	9,319	5,023	53.9	5,536	3,293	59.5
Russia	1,805	1,155	64.0	1,251	791	63.2
Germany	1,215	816	67.2	687	488	71.0

1 Per cent not shown, base being less than 100.

CITIZENSHIP. 815

TABLE 8.—NUMBER AND PER CENT NATURALIZED AMONG FOREIGN-BORN WHITE MALES AND FEMALES 21 YEARS OF AGE AND OVER, FOR SELECTED COUNTRIES OF BIRTH, BY DIVISIONS AND STATES: 1920—Continued.

[The countries for which figures are given in this table are those which contributed 2 per cent or more of the total number of foreign-born white persons 21 years of age and over, of both sexes combined, enumerated in the specified division or state.]

DIVISION OR STATE OF RESIDENCE AND COUNTRY OF BIRTH.	Male. Total number.	Male. Naturalized. Number.	Male. Naturalized. Per cent.	Female. Total number.	Female. Naturalized. Number.	Female. Naturalized. Per cent.
SOUTH ATLANTIC—Con.						
Georgia—Con.						
England	837	424	50.7	631	376	59.6
Greece	1,121	307	27.4	226	73	32.3
Ireland	548	353	64.4	540	299	55.4
Canada and Newfoundland	448	200	44.6	412	256	62.1
Canada—French	_28_	_8_	(1)	_19_	_14_	(1)
Poland	520	348	66.9	301	210	69.8
Italy	476	201	42.2	164	79	48.2
Scotland	317	164	51.7	183	98	53.6
Syria	256	105	41.0	168	60	35.7
Austria	262	124	47.3	111	66	59.5
France	174	105	60.3	167	101	60.5
Florida.						
All countries	22,282	8,968	40.2	16,088	7,141	44.4
West Indies [2]	3,619	894	24.7	3,538	1,022	28.9
England	2,331	1,293	55.5	1,814	1,052	58.0
Italy	2,249	433	19.3	1,853	274	14.8
Spain	2,697	273	10.1	973	106	10.9
Canada and Newfoundland	1,742	818	47.0	1,769	1,025	57.9
Canada—French	_118_	_51_	_43.2_	_96_	_47_	(1)
Germany	2,081	1,445	69.4	1,350	978	72.4
Sweden	775	488	63.0	592	399	67.4
Greece	1,151	280	24.3	178	64	36.0
Ireland	604	348	57.6	678	373	55.0
Russia	661	382	57.8	404	276	59.5
Scotland	594	314	52.9	415	224	54.0
EAST SOUTH CENTRAL.						
Kentucky.						
All countries	16,827	10,273	61.1	12,661	8,220	64.9
Germany	5,666	4,552	80.3	5,390	3,989	74.0
Ireland	1,504	1,023	68.0	1,899	1,070	56.3
Russia	1,477	867	58.7	961	628	65.3
Italy	1,313	419	31.9	456	183	40.1
England	979	630	64.4	770	495	64.3
Switzerland	733	549	74.9	570	408	71.6
Poland	661	318	48.1	303	169	55.8
Hungary	653	123	18.8	288	75	26.0
Austria	578	269	46.5	270	168	62.2
France	495	362	73.1	457	300	65.6
Canada and Newfoundland	460	224	48.7	374	230	61.5
Canada—French	_26_	_13_	(1)	_20_	_13_	(1)
Tennessee.						
All countries	8,428	4,430	52.6	5,891	3,278	55.6
Germany	1,256	874	69.6	871	593	68.1
Russia	1,083	567	52.4	865	432	49.9
Italy	1,138	342	30.1	730	207	28.4
England	914	475	52.0	659	387	58.7
Ireland	678	420	61.9	603	354	58.7
Canada and Newfoundland	474	206	43.5	411	250	60.8
Canada—French	_23_	_14_	(1)	_16_	_7_	(1)
Poland	435	261	60.0	290	174	60.0
Switzerland	343	239	69.7	202	186	71.0
Greece	338	94	24.2	67	16	(1)
Scotland	276	157	56.9	147	89	60.5
Austria	203	116	57.1	162	91	56.2
France	153	101	66.0	152	100	65.8
Hungary	185	131	70.8	118	80	67.8
Sweden	183	119	65.0	119	93	78.2
Alabama.						
All countries	9,814	5,031	51.3	6,291	3,472	55.2
Italy	1,460	445	30.5	899	250	27.8
Germany	1,380	901	65.3	961	631	65.7
England	1,029	569	55.3	793	510	64.3
Russia	862	503	58.3	546	364	66.7
Scotland	512	312	60.9	384	245	63.8
Greece	715	185	25.9	140	53	37.9
Ireland	422	243	57.6	379	163	43.0
Canada and Newfoundland	444	206	46.4	323	213	65.9
Canada—French	_31_	_15_	(1)	_17_	_10_	(1)

DIVISION OR STATE OF RESIDENCE AND COUNTRY OF BIRTH.	Male. Total number.	Male. Naturalized. Number.	Male. Naturalized. Per cent.	Female. Total number.	Female. Naturalized. Number.	Female. Naturalized. Per cent.
EAST SOUTH CENTRAL—Con.						
Alabama—Con.						
Sweden	461	309	67.0	271	191	70.5
France	299	170	56.9	242	121	50.0
Austria	340	185	54.4	199	119	59.8
Syria	245	91	37.1	182	67	36.8
Poland	210	125	59.5	143	76	53.1
Hungary	193	92	47.7	144	69	47.9
Mississippi.						
All countries	4,628	2,322	50.2	2,702	1,309	48.4
Italy	890	266	29.9	657	173	26.3
Germany	565	389	68.8	350	192	54.9
Russia	497	314	63.2	258	168	65.1
England	344	176	51.2	214	129	60.3
Syria	313	112	35.8	219	78	35.6
Ireland	248	144	58.1	161	80	49.7
Canada and Newfoundland	226	79	35.0	142	90	63.4
Canada—French	_18_	_7_	(1)	_6_	_4_	(1)
Poland	178	96	53.9	117	60	51.3
France	150	86	51.3	96	55	(1)
Sweden	169	109	64.5	74	54	(1)
Jugo-Slavia	132	76	57.6	73	40	(1)
Greece	174	65	37.4	21	10	(1)
WEST SOUTH CENTRAL.						
Arkansas.						
All countries	8,166	4,593	56.2	5,000	2,976	59.5
Germany	2,270	1,491	65.7	1,589	1,092	68.7
Italy	727	233	32.0	405	96	23.7
England	677	409	60.4	420	284	67.6
Canada and Newfoundland	517	220	42.6	331	217	65.6
Canada—French	_34_	_14_	(1)	_22_	_16_	(1)
Switzerland	348	233	67.0	360	168	46.7
Ireland	420	253	60.2	250	135	54.0
Russia	421	263	62.5	193	127	65.8
Austria	349	189	54.2	242	149	61.6
Poland	349	221	63.3	164	96	58.5
Czechoslovakia	247	130	52.6	204	121	59.3
France	221	132	59.7	153	89	58.2
Sweden	221	151	68.3	103	76	73.8
Scotland	190	115	60.5	110	80	72.7
Greece	223	77	34.5	35	14	(1)
Louisiana.						
All countries	24,848	9,350	37.6	16,380	5,846	35.7
Italy	8,650	2,332	27.0	6,553	1,520	23.2
Germany	2,835	1,816	64.1	2,236	1,277	57.1
France	2,194	1,055	48.1	1,883	699	37.1
Ireland	871	512	58.8	1,112	429	38.6
England	1,050	469	44.7	641	316	49.3
Russia	1,029	502	48.8	623	320	51.4
Mexico	990	48	4.8	585	95	16.2
Spain	905	138	14.3	181	44	24.3
Canada and Newfoundland	715	257	35.9	363	176	48.5
Canada—French	_90_	_33_	(1)	_41_	_15_	(1)
Syria	520	209	40.2	353	123	34.8
Oklahoma.						
All countries	22,817	11,239	49.3	13,291	8,133	61.2
Germany	4,189	3,081	73.5	2,682	2,084	77.7
Mexico	3,710	83	2.2	1,111	51	4.6
Russia	2,619	1,654	63.2	1,928	1,285	66.6
England	1,573	919	58.4	1,000	702	70.2
Canada and Newfoundland	1,341	676	50.4	988	691	69.9
Canada—French	_75_	_40_	(1)	_48_	_31_	(1)
Italy	1,206	350	29.0	655	192	29.3
Czechoslovakia	925	632	68.3	762	559	73.4
Ireland	810	535	66.0	504	338	67.1
Austria	730	380	52.1	537	321	59.8
Poland	711	292	41.1	415	170	41.0
Scotland	616	347	56.3	425	292	68.7
Sweden	581	414	71.3	329	237	72.0
France	525	300	57.1	364	229	62.9

[1] Per cent not shown, base being less than 100.   [2] Except possessions of the United States.

816

POPULATION.

TABLE 8.—NUMBER AND PER CENT NATURALIZED AMONG FOREIGN-BORN WHITE MALES AND FEMALES 21 YEARS OF AGE AND OVER, FOR SELECTED COUNTRIES OF BIRTH, BY DIVISIONS AND STATES: 1920—Continued.

[The countries for which figures are given in this table are those which contributed 2 per cent or more of the total number of foreign-born white persons 21 years of age and over, of both sexes combined, enumerated in the specified division or state.]

DIVISION OR STATE OF RESIDENCE AND COUNTRY OF BIRTH.	FOREIGN-BORN WHITE POPULATION 21 YEARS OF AGE AND OVER: 1920					
	Male.			Female.		
	Total number.	Naturalized.		Total number.	Naturalized.	
		Number.	Per cent.		Number.	Per cent.
WEST SOUTH CENTRAL—Con.						
Texas.						
All countries..........	152,600	39,321	25.8	114,118	32,800	28.7
Mexico..................	91,483	3,104	3.4	71,223	6,045	8.5
Germany................	16,882	11,450	67.8	13,578	9,513	70.1
Czechoslovakia.........	6,162	3,920	63.6	5,486	3,539	64.5
England................	4,491	2,551	56.8	2,840	1,845	65.0
Italy..................	4,480	1,858	41.5	2,682	1,028	38.3
Russia.................	3,714	2,119	57.1	2,350	1,302	55.4
Austria................	3,405	2,154	63.3	2,483	1,647	66.3
MOUNTAIN.						
Montana.						
All countries..........	54,250	34,009	62.7	31,459	22,618	71.9
Canada and Newfoundland.	7,124	5,083	71.4	4,712	3,643	77.3
Canada—French........	*1,276*	*912*	*71.5*	*747*	*538*	*72.0*
Norway.................	5,981	4,407	73.7	3,536	2,741	77.5
Germany................	4,788	3,543	74.0	2,802	2,280	81.4
England................	4,407	3,034	68.8	3,132	2,353	75.1
Ireland................	4,135	3,005	72.7	3,013	2,270	75.3
Sweden.................	4,419	3,166	71.6	2,538	1,995	78.6
Russia.................	2,338	1,089	46.6	1,686	841	49.9
Jugo-Slavia............	2,556	1,054	41.2	1,021	574	56.2
Italy..................	2,580	1,057	41.0	918	502	54.7
Finland................	2,028	911	44.9	1,355	790	58.3
Austria................	1,971	975	49.5	1,092	684	62.6
Scotland...............	1,858	1,313	70.7	1,100	823	74.8
Denmark................	1,896	1,413	74.5	927	740	79.8
Czechoslovakia.........	1,084	635	58.6	681	449	65.9
Idaho.						
All countries..........	23,366	14,186	60.7	12,804	9,708	75.8
Sweden.................	3,198	2,185	68.3	1,724	1,387	80.5
Canada and Newfoundland.	2,810	1,914	68.1	1,645	1,326	80.6
Canada—French........	*303*	*211*	*69.6*	*148*	*111*	*75.0*
England................	2,316	1,704	73.6	1,876	1,529	81.5
Germany................	2,494	1,951	78.2	1,506	1,241	82.4
Norway.................	1,545	1,058	68.5	859	679	79.0
Denmark................	1,282	999	77.9	822	697	84.8
Ireland................	916	640	69.9	464	342	73.7
Switzerland............	727	550	75.7	570	454	79.6
Spain..................	1,006	75	7.5	260	51	19.6
Italy..................	909	379	41.7	312	180	57.7
Scotland...............	755	527	69.8	417	327	78.4
Russia.................	689	419	60.8	481	338	70.3
Finland................	635	264	41.6	311	184	59.2
Mexico.................	562	12	2.1	186	16	8.6
Austria................	545	222	40.7	192	135	70.3
Wyoming.						
All countries..........	15,796	7,289	46.1	7,261	4,719	65.0
England................	1,331	930	69.9	969	762	78.6
Germany................	1,456	865	59.4	728	552	75.8
Sweden.................	1,299	858	66.1	676	543	80.3
Italy..................	1,308	424	32.4	485	218	44.9
Mexico.................	1,141	24	2.1	265	12	4.5
Scotland...............	849	580	68.3	494	378	76.5
Canada and Newfoundland.	780	489	64.3	522	413	79.1
Canada—French........	*50*	*53*	*(1)*	*30*	*25*	*(1)*
Greece.................	1,101	146	13.3	79	13	(1)
Jugo-Slavia............	893	199	22.3	225	87	38.7
Russia.................	658	249	37.8	444	172	38.7
Austria................	761	249	32.7	309	155	50.2
Ireland................	601	400	66.6	332	264	79.5
Denmark................	599	441	73.6	314	254	80.9
Finland................	535	220	41.1	262	150	57.3
Norway.................	402	271	67.4	222	172	77.5
Poland.................	359	132	36.8	152	62	40.8
Czechoslovakia.........	300	128	42.7	163	94	57.7

DIVISION OR STATE OF RESIDENCE AND COUNTRY OF BIRTH.	FOREIGN-BORN WHITE POPULATION 21 YEARS OF AGE AND OVER: 1920					
	Male.			Female.		
	Total number.	Naturalized.		Total number.	Naturalized.	
		Number.	Per cent.		Number.	Per cent.
MOUNTAIN—Continued.						
Colorado.						
All countries..........	62,089	34,630	55.8	42,928	27,688	64.5
Russia.................	7,095	2,781	39.2	5,660	2,276	40.2
Germany................	6,696	5,326	79.5	4,966	4,119	82.9
Italy..................	7,348	3,154	42.9	4,148	2,101	50.7
Sweden.................	5,474	4,119	75.2	4,436	3,454	77.9
England................	5,075	3,797	74.8	4,135	3,315	80.2
Mexico.................	4,912	140	2.9	2,470	92	3.7
Canada and Newfoundland.	3,730	2,673	71.7	3,396	2,614	77.0
Canada—French........	*230*	*166*	*72.2*	*168*	*134*	*79.8*
Ireland................	3,122	2,549	81.6	3,016	2,401	79.6
Austria................	3,486	1,645	47.2	1,943	1,221	62.8
Scotland...............	1,816	1,368	75.3	1,330	1,035	77.8
Denmark................	1,658	1,215	73.3	1,033	776	75.1
New Mexico.						
All countries..........	13,244	3,381	25.5	8,689	2,500	28.8
Mexico.................	7,705	508	6.6	5,730	757	13.2
Italy..................	1,029	382	37.1	460	188	40.9
Germany................	697	524	75.2	437	315	72.1
England................	497	336	67.6	322	218	67.7
Canada and Newfoundland.	383	227	59.3	286	186	65.0
Canada—French........	*26*	*18*	*(1)*	*13*	*10*	*(1)*
Jugo-Slavia............	368	66	17.9	135	34	25.2
Ireland................	244	184	75.4	184	114	62.0
Arizona.						
All countries..........	33,582	5,986	17.8	22,391	4,722	21.1
Mexico.................	22,400	672	3.0	10,984	1,514	8.9
England................	1,550	804	57.7	1,053	680	64.6
Canada and Newfoundland.	1,131	631	55.8	689	470	68.2
Canada—French........	*68*	*40*	*(1)*	*21*	*16*	*(1)*
Germany................	1,001	651	65.0	485	347	71.5
Ireland................	751	498	66.3	442	300	67.9
Italy..................	872	357	40.9	302	144	47.7
Jugo-Slavia............	893	212	23.7	217	84	38.7
Utah.						
All countries..........	28,791	16,377	56.9	23,463	16,815	71.7
England................	6,681	4,890	73.2	7,154	5,524	77.2
Denmark................	3,209	2,524	78.7	3,392	2,754	81.2
Sweden.................	2,759	1,989	72.1	3,036	2,280	75.1
Germany................	1,722	1,144	66.4	1,523	1,059	69.5
Italy..................	2,092	582	27.8	856	316	36.9
Greece.................	2,665	258	9.7	235	45	19.1
Scotland...............	1,120	848	75.7	1,082	883	81.6
Norway.................	910	614	67.5	1,007	772	72.4
Netherlands............	726	321	44.2	820	392	47.8
Switzerland............	688	527	76.6	779	588	75.5
Canada and Newfoundland.	730	474	64.9	540	410	75.9
Canada—French........	*29*	*19*	*(1)*	*14*	*10*	*(1)*
Wales..................	653	510	78.1	610	514	84.3
Ireland................	697	509	73.0	474	350	73.8
Nevada.						
All countries..........	10,203	4,121	40.4	3,692	2,115	57.3
Italy..................	1,802	599	32.2	581	228	39.2
England................	743	469	63.1	407	312	66.8
Canada and Newfoundland.	748	484	64.7	372	264	71.0
Canada—French........	*73*	*49*	*(1)*	*32*	*24*	*(1)*
Spain..................	942	68	7.2	150	36	23.9
Germany................	711	500	70.3	341	260	76.2
Ireland................	607	433	71.3	352	242	68.8
Mexico.................	773	14	1.8	150	16	10.7
Jugo-Slavia............	514	106	20.6	150	37	24.7
Greece.................	580	54	9.3	27	4	(1)
France.................	422	133	31.5	161	86	53.4
Sweden.................	390	250	64.1	148	116	78.4
Denmark................	352	242	68.8	168	121	72.0
Switzerland............	271	155	57.2	99	59	(1)
Scotland...............	213	137	64.3	105	79	75.2

¹ Per cent not shown, base being less than 100.

CITIZENSHIP.

817

Table 8.—NUMBER AND PER CENT NATURALIZED AMONG FOREIGN-BORN WHITE MALES AND FEMALES 21 YEARS OF AGE AND OVER, FOR SELECTED COUNTRIES OF BIRTH, BY DIVISIONS AND STATES: 1920—Continued.

[The countries for which figures are given in this table are those which contributed 2 per cent or more of the total number of foreign-born white persons 21 years of age and over, of both sexes combined, enumerated in the specified division or state.]

DIVISION OR STATE OF RESIDENCE AND COUNTRY OF BIRTH.	FOREIGN-BORN WHITE POPULATION 21 YEARS OF AGE AND OVER: 1920					
	Male.			Female.		
	Total number.	Naturalized.		Total number.	Naturalized.	
		Number.	Per cent.		Number.	Per cent.
PACIFIC.						
Washington.						
All countries	143,258	77,156	53.9	87,177	56,761	65.1
Canada and Newfoundland	19,557	11,668	59.7	15,848	11,025	69.6
Canada—French	*1,404*	*840*	*59.8*	*946*	*578*	*61.2*
Sweden	21,003	12,315	58.6	12,359	8,535	69.1
Norway	17,450	10,496	60.1	11,453	7,765	67.8
Germany	13,162	9,577	72.8	8,615	6,807	79.0
England	11,167	6,317	56.6	8,076	5,094	63.1
Finland	7,101	2,474	34.5	4,147	1,980	47.7
Italy	7,164	2,082	29.1	2,692	962	35.7
Russia	5,953	2,714	45.6	3,711	2,071	55.8
Ireland	5,412	3,565	65.9	3,336	2,240	67.1
Denmark	5,197	3,572	68.7	2,870	2,098	73.1
Scotland	4,405	2,462	55.9	2,903	1,711	58.9
Austria	4,160	1,663	40.0	1,986	1,166	58.7
Oregon.						
All countries	58,580	31,899	54.5	36,227	23,581	65.1
Germany	7,925	5,769	72.8	5,483	4,289	78.2
Canada and Newfoundland	6,430	3,945	61.4	5,259	3,831	72.8
Canada—French	*347*	*206*	*59.4*	*270*	*146*	*54.1*
Sweden	6,445	3,730	57.9	3,748	2,603	69.5
England	4,370	2,692	61.6	3,084	2,066	67.0
Norway	4,079	2,423	59.4	2,600	1,765	67.9
Russia	3,329	1,403	42.1	2,519	1,174	46.6
Finland	3,456	1,325	38.3	2,302	1,092	47.4

DIVISION OR STATE OF RESIDENCE AND COUNTRY OF BIRTH.	FOREIGN-BORN WHITE POPULATION 21 YEARS OF AGE AND OVER: 1920					
	Male.			Female.		
	Total number.	Naturalized.		Total number.	Naturalized.	
		Number.	Per cent.		Number.	Per cent.
PACIFIC—Con.						
Oregon—Con.						
Ireland	2,566	1,742	67.9	1,500	1,081	69.3
Switzerland	2,428	1,430	58.9	1,510	1,000	66.2
Italy	2,716	764	28.1	1,149	372	32.4
Denmark	2,219	1,561	70.3	1,269	954	75.2
Scotland	2,032	1,253	61.7	1,315	823	62.6
Austria	1,750	606	34.6	866	498	57.5
Greece	1,755	284	16.2	114	30	26.3
California.						
All countries	367,340	166,299	45.3	247,041	127,176	51.5
Italy	53,438	13,733	25.7	26,741	7,452	27.9
Germany	38,491	27,133	70.5	27,610	20,301	73.8
Mexico	36,962	1,005	2.7	23,584	2,003	8.5
England	30,455	18,240	59.8	24,335	15,011	61.7
Canada and Newfoundland	26,628	16,097	60.5	26,226	16,465	62.8
Canada—French	*1,230*	*727*	*59.1*	*877*	*542*	*61.8*
Ireland	22,966	16,747	72.9	21,756	14,121	64.9
Sweden	17,687	11,847	67.0	13,578	9,416	69.3
Russia	13,708	6,069	44.3	9,787	4,412	45.1
Portugal	13,728	3,249	23.7	7,947	2,270	28.6
France	10,761	5,722	53.2	8,593	4,755	55.3
Denmark	11,501	8,031	69.8	6,702	4,789	71.5
Scotland	9,042	5,576	61.7	6,568	3,913	59.6
Switzerland	9,925	5,449	54.9	5,591	3,508	62.7
Austria	8,218	3,545	43.1	4,432	2,395	54.0

75647°—22——52

CHAPTER IX

COUNTRY OF ORIGIN OF THE FOREIGN WHITE STOCK

CHAPTER IX.—COUNTRY OF ORIGIN OF THE FOREIGN WHITE STOCK.

INTRODUCTION.

The inquiry as to birthplace of foreign parents was first made at the census of 1880, but only a part of the data secured was tabulated. The earliest complete statistics pertaining to this inquiry are those for 1890. As the number of nonwhites in the United States who were born abroad or whose parents were born abroad is proportionally very small, statistics as to country of origin are presented for white persons only.

FOREIGN WHITE STOCK.

For brevity, the term "foreign white stock" is used to indicate the combined total of three classes, namely, the foreign-born whites, the native whites of foreign parentage (both parents born abroad), and the native whites of mixed parentage (one parent native and the other foreign born).

COUNTRY OF ORIGIN.

Because of the many changes in the map of Europe which have resulted from the World War, the classification of the white population of foreign birth or foreign parentage according to country of origin was made peculiarly difficult. Many natives of foreign or mixed parentage knew the countries, according to the prewar map, but not the provinces or cities, in which their parents were born. For this reason it was impossible to make a proper classification of the foreign parents of natives with reference to European countries as now constituted, and therefore the statistics for this class have been compiled on the prewar basis. As the country of birth of foreign-born white persons was tabulated according to postwar areas, it was necessary to make a new tabulation of this class according to prewar areas in order to secure comparability with natives of foreign or mixed parentage. This was done by tabulating the foreign-born whites by birthplace of father,[1] classified on the prewar basis.

The term "country of origin," therefore, as used in the reports of the Fourteenth Census, signifies the country of birth of the father of a foreign-born person or of the foreign parent or parents of a native. At previous censuses the distribution of the foreign born themselves was made according to their own countries

[1] For 29,025 foreign-born white persons reported as having native fathers, the birthplace of the foreign-born mother was used.

of birth. The distribution of the foreign born according to country of birth is given in Chapter VI and of the foreign-born white in Chapter VIII.

FOREIGN WHITE STOCK FROM SPECIFIC COUNTRIES.

The foreign white stock from any specific country of origin represents the total of three classes, namely, native whites having both parents born in that country, or one parent so born the other being native, and foreign-born whites having fathers born in that country. Native white persons having one parent born in a specified country and the other in some other foreign country are designated as "of mixed foreign parentage," and while included in the foreign white stock as a whole, are not included in that for any specific country (see Table 1). The term "mixed foreign parentage" must not be confused with "mixed parentage," the latter representing persons having one parent foreign born and the other native. For the distribution of persons of mixed foreign parentage by birthplace of father with reference to birthplace of mother, for the United States, see Table 4 (page 900).

No totals are given for continents or groups of countries, for the reason that in the case of the native whites of foreign parentage the true total is not the same as the sum of the figures for the separate countries, there being some persons having one parent born in one country and the other in another country of the same continent or group. For instance, a person of mixed foreign parentage may have a father born in England, and mother born in France, but both parents born in Northwestern Europe. It is very evident that the number of persons of mixed foreign parentage would be considerably diminished if considered with reference to continents or groups of countries.

The proportions of the foreign white stock originating in certain countries are shown graphically by the diagrams, and, as in the tables, the distribution relates to countries as constituted prior to the World War. In the series of bar diagrams for states, the countries and groups of countries are those represented by more than 1,000,000 persons of foreign white stock as enumerated in the United States in 1920; and only those states are shown in which there were enumerated more than 10,000 persons belonging to the stock originating in the specified country or group of countries.

892   POPULATION.

The following statement shows the numerical distribution of the white population of the United States in 1920 according to nativity and parentage, together with the per cent distribution for 1920, 1910, 1900, and 1890:

CLASS OF POPULATION.	Number: 1920	PER CENT OF TOTAL POPULATION.				PER CENT OF TOTAL WHITE POPULATION.			
		1920	1910	1900	1890	1920	1910	1900	1890
Total population....	105,710,620	100.0	100.0	100.0	100.0	.....	.....	.....	.....
Total white population...	94,820,915	89.7	88.9	87.9	87.5	100.0	100.0	100.0	100.0
Native, native parentage	58,421,957	55.3	53.8	53.9	54.8	61.6	60.5	61.3	62.6
Foreign white stock.....	36,398,958	34.4	35.1	34.0	32.8	38.4	39.5	38.7	37.4
Foreign born..........	13,712,754	13.0	14.5	13.4	14.5	14.5	16.3	15.3	16.6
Native, foreign parentage..............	15,694,539	14.8	14.0	14.0	12.8	16.6	15.8	15.9	14.7
Native, mixed parentage..............	6,991,665	6.6	6.5	6.6	5.4	7.4	7.3	7.5	6.2
Nonwhite classes..........	10,889,705	10.3	11.1	12.1	12.5	.....	.....	.....	.....

URBAN AND RURAL COMMUNITIES.

Since marked differences exist between urban and rural communities in regard to the distribution of the foreign white stock by country of origin, separate statistics are given for the two classes of communities in Tables 13 and 14.

In drawing the distinction between urban and rural population, all incorporated places (and all towns in Massachusetts, Rhode Island, and New Hampshire) having 2,500 inhabitants or more are treated as urban and the remainder of the country as rural.

In Massachusetts and Rhode Island it is not the practice, as in practically all the other states, to incorporate, as separate municipalities, the relatively densely populated portions of "towns" (which are the primary divisions of the counties), and no town as a whole is incorporated as a municipality until it attains a population greatly in excess of 2,500; and in New Hampshire a similar condition exists, although the state contains two incorporated villages, each of which has fewer than 2,500 inhabitants. For this reason those towns having 2,500 or more inhabitants in the three states named are treated as urban, although portions of their areas are rural in character. The urban areas in the three states in question, as classified by the census, thus contain relatively small numbers of inhabitants who in other sections of the country would be segregated as rural. Nevertheless, in most of the towns having 2,500 inhabitants or more in Massachusetts, Rhode Island, and New Hampshire by far the greater part of the population resides within the more densely settled areas, so that the proportion classed as urban, considering each state as a whole, is not greatly exaggerated by the practice adopted.

COUNTRY OF ORIGIN.

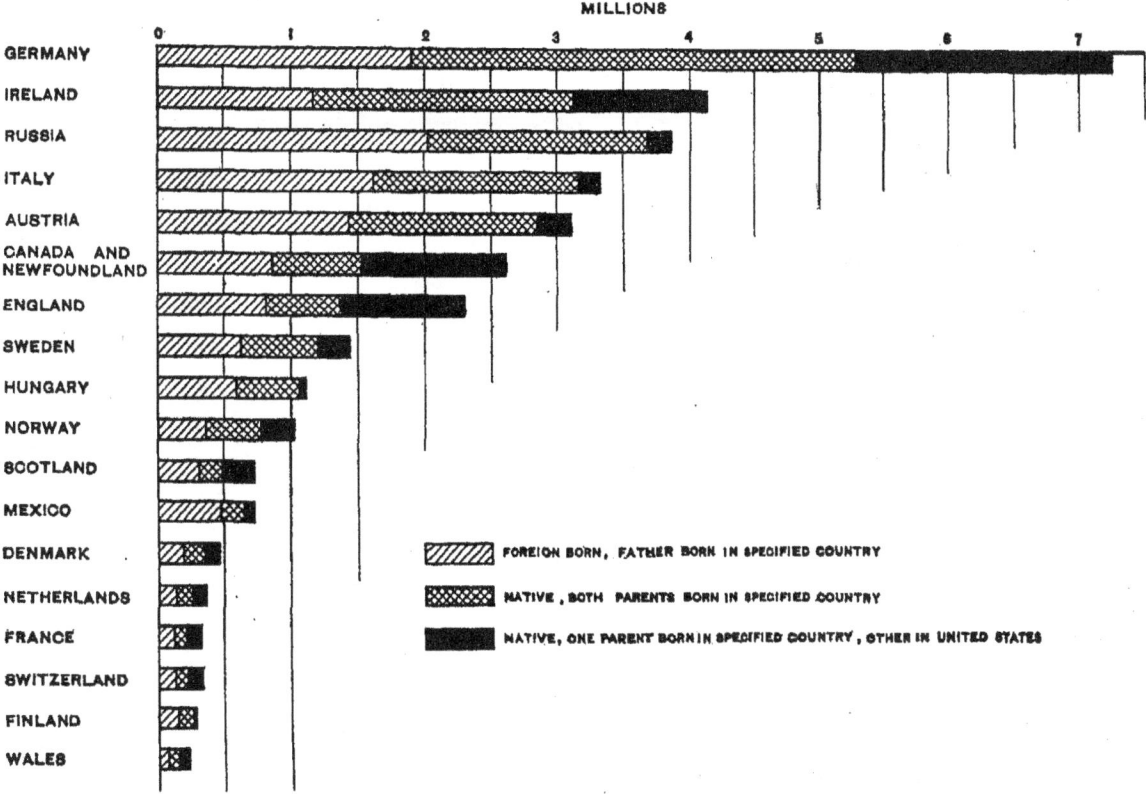

FOREIGN WHITE STOCK BY PRINCIPAL COUNTRIES OF ORIGIN: 1920.

MILLIONS

GERMANY
IRELAND
RUSSIA
ITALY
AUSTRIA
CANADA AND NEWFOUNDLAND
ENGLAND
SWEDEN
HUNGARY
NORWAY
SCOTLAND
MEXICO
DENMARK
NETHERLANDS
FRANCE
SWITZERLAND
FINLAND
WALES

FOREIGN BORN, FATHER BORN IN SPECIFIED COUNTRY

NATIVE, BOTH PARENTS BORN IN SPECIFIED COUNTRY

NATIVE, ONE PARENT BORN IN SPECIFIED COUNTRY, OTHER IN UNITED STATES

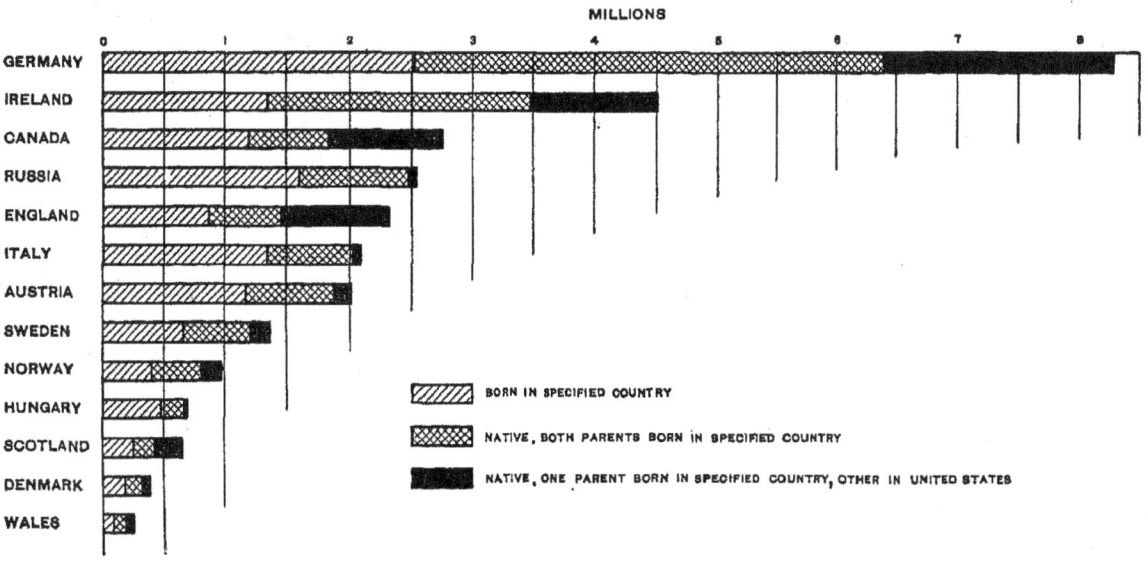

FOREIGN WHITE STOCK BY PRINCIPAL COUNTRIES OF ORIGIN: 1910.

MILLIONS

GERMANY
IRELAND
CANADA
RUSSIA
ENGLAND
ITALY
AUSTRIA
SWEDEN
NORWAY
HUNGARY
SCOTLAND
DENMARK
WALES

BORN IN SPECIFIED COUNTRY

NATIVE, BOTH PARENTS BORN IN SPECIFIED COUNTRY

NATIVE, ONE PARENT BORN IN SPECIFIED COUNTRY, OTHER IN UNITED STATES

894

POPULATION.

PER CENT DISTRIBUTION OF THE FOREIGN WHITE STOCK BY PRINCIPAL COUNTRIES OF ORIGIN.

1920

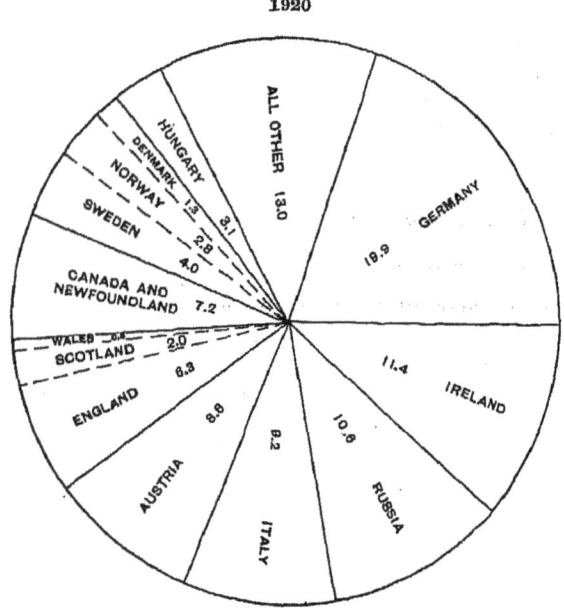

1910

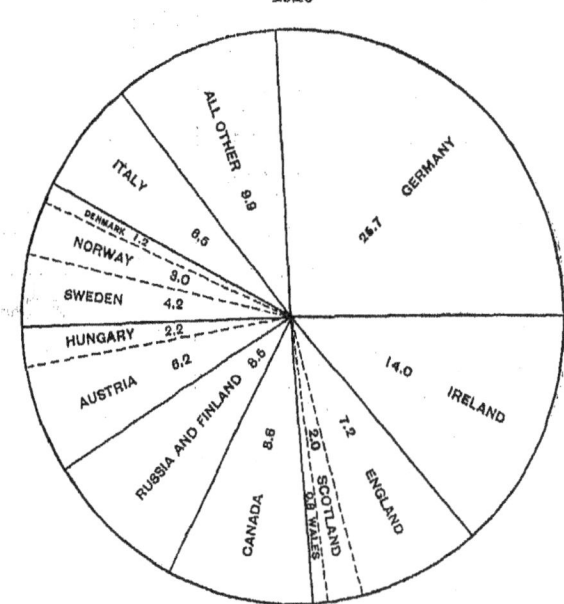

COUNTRY OF ORIGIN.

DISTRIBUTION OF THE FOREIGN WHITE STOCK ORIGINATING IN SELECTED COUNTRIES AND GROUPS OF COUNTRIES, BY STATES: 1920 AND 1910.

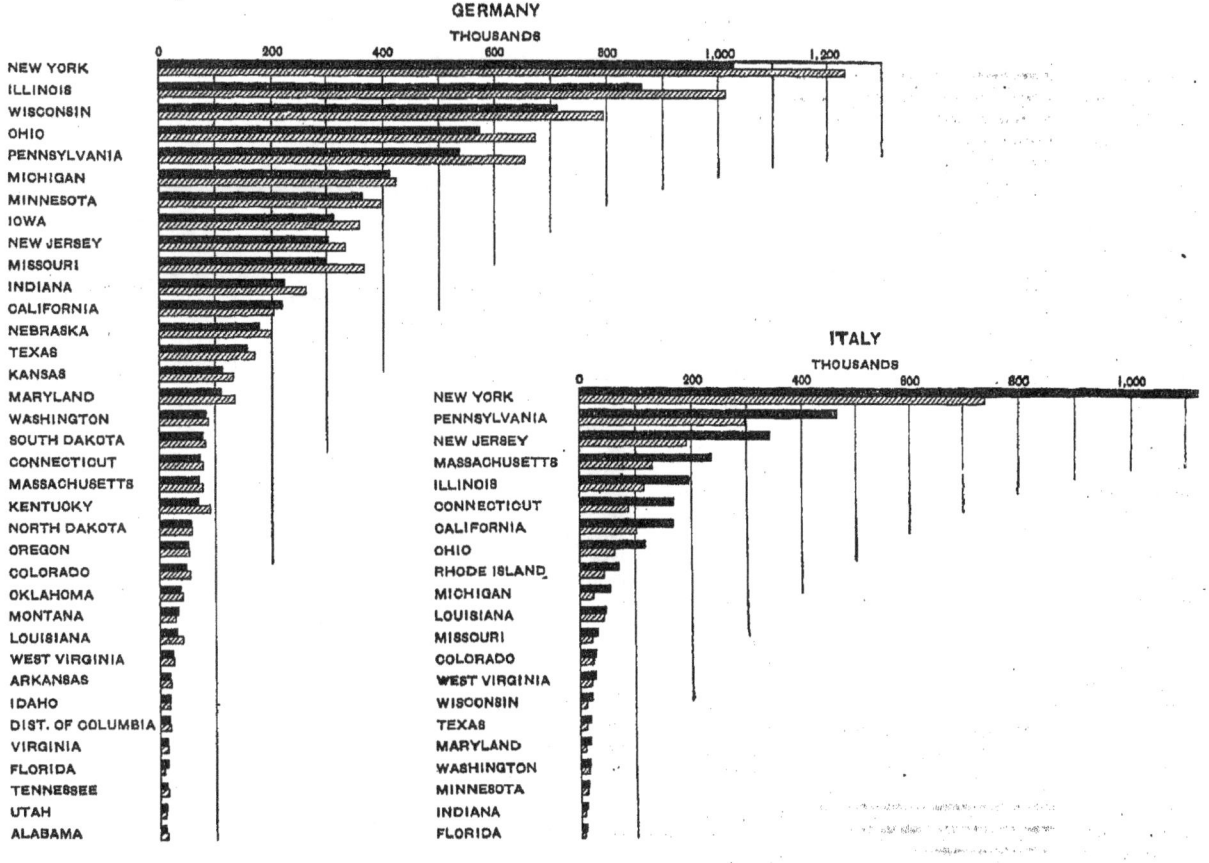

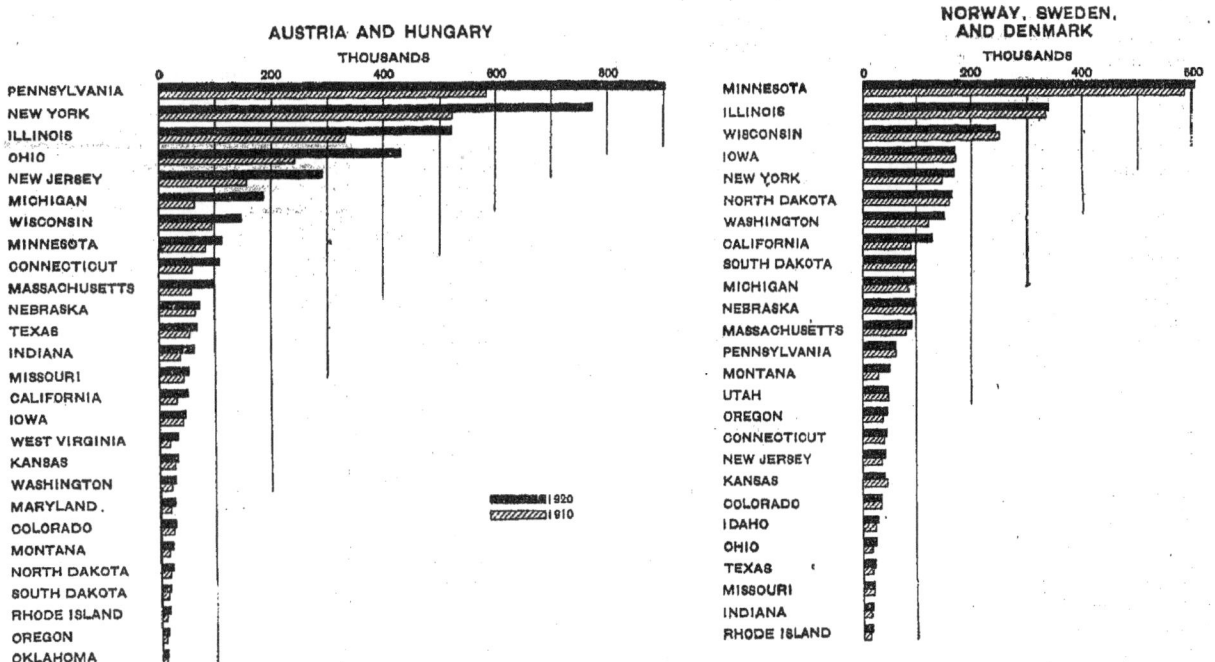

896

POPULATION.

DISTRIBUTION OF THE FOREIGN WHITE STOCK ORIGINATING IN SELECTED COUNTRIES AND GROUPS OF COUNTRIES, BY STATES: 1920 AND 1910.

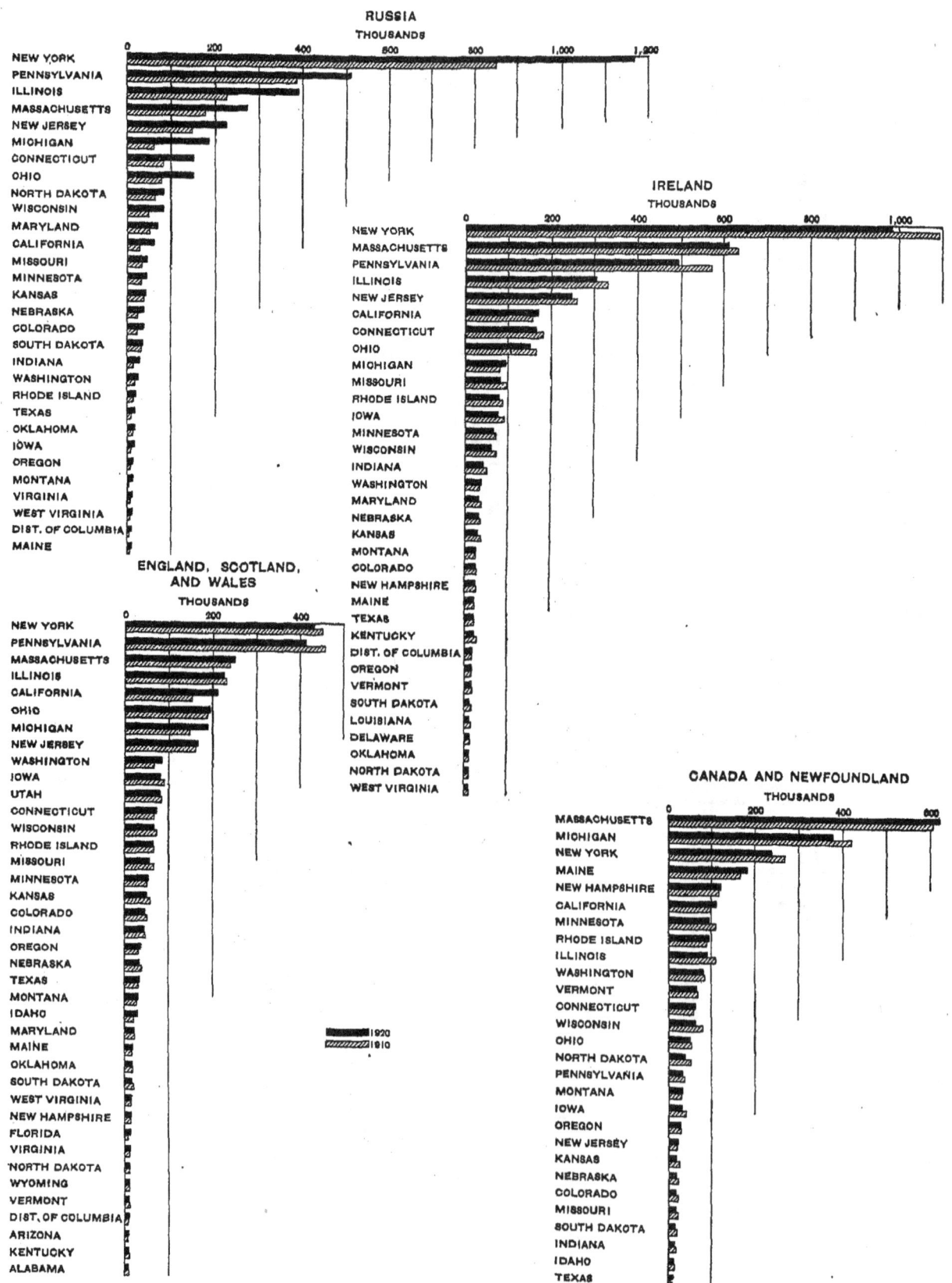

COUNTRY OF ORIGIN.   897

TABLE 1.—COUNTRY OF ORIGIN OF THE FOREIGN WHITE STOCK, BY NATIVITY AND PARENTAGE, FOR THE UNITED STATES: 1890–1920.

[Figures for 1920 relate to countries as constituted prior to the World War (see text, p. 891).]

COUNTRY OF ORIGIN.	Total foreign white stock.	Foreign-born white.[1]	NATIVE WHITE OF FOREIGN OR MIXED PARENTAGE.				Total foreign white stock.	Foreign-born white.[1]	NATIVE WHITE OF FOREIGN OR MIXED PARENTAGE.			
			Total.	Both parents foreign.	Father foreign.	Mother foreign.			Total.	Both parents foreign.	Father foreign.	Mother foreign.
	1920						**1910**					
Total	36,398,958	13,712,754	22,686,204	15,694,539	4,539,776	2,451,889	32,243,382	13,345,545	18,897,837	12,916,311	3,923,845	2,057,681
Northwestern Europe:												
England	2,307,112	824,088	1,483,024	574,499	571,560	336,965	2,322,442	876,455	1,445,987	592,285	546,215	307,487
Scotland	731,239	310,092	421,147	178,638	153,917	88,592	659,663	261,034	398,629	175,391	145,227	78,011
Wales	230,380	66,962	163,418	78,114	54,889	30,415	248,947	82,479	166,468	84,934	52,555	28,979
Ireland	4,136,395	1,164,707	2,971,688	1,966,968	573,021	431,699	4,504,360	1,352,155	3,152,205	2,141,577	603,013	407,615
Norway	1,023,225	362,051	661,174	437,623	143,314	80,237	979,099	403,858	575,241	410,051	106,805	57,485
Sweden	1,457,382	632,656	824,726	599,744	144,382	80,600	1,364,215	665,183	699,032	546,788	97,504	54,740
Denmark	467,525	191,496	276,029	170,702	73,915	31,412	400,064	181,621	218,443	147,648	40,721	21,074
Netherlands	362,318	134,229	228,089	142,547	57,301	28,241	293,574	120,053	173,521	116,831	38,199	18,991
Belgium	122,686	63,234	59,452	37,525	15,420	6,507	89,264	49,397	39,867	26,448	9,802	3,617
Luxemburg	43,109	12,837	30,272	16,263	10,847	3,162	6,945	3,068	3,877	2,381	1,244	252
Switzerland	327,797	117,270	210,527	103,452	75,315	31,760	301,650	124,834	176,816	90,669	61,244	24,903
France	333,678	124,727	208,951	90,073	86,549	32,329	292,389	117,236	175,153	78,937	73,085	23,131
Central and Eastern Europe:												
Germany	7,250,992	1,915,864	5,344,128	3,397,370	1,367,805	578,953	8,282,618	2,501,181	5,781,437	3,911,847	1,337,651	531,939
Austria	3,129,798	1,445,141	1,684,657	1,435,524	171,678	77,455	2,001,559	826,635	1,174,924	709,070	80,595	36,970
Hungary	1,110,905	598,170	512,735	472,521	29,510	10,704	700,227	495,600	204,627	191,059	10,106	3,462
Russia	3,871,109	2,020,646	1,850,463	1,671,949	135,098	43,416	2,541,649	1,602,752	938,897	873,055	51,856	13,986
Finland	296,276	150,770	145,506	130,083	9,765	5,658	211,026	129,669	81,357	76,261	3,319	1,777
Rumania	134,318	85,255	49,063	43,683	3,820	1,560	87,721	65,920	21,801	20,707	821	273
Bulgaria, Serbia, and Montenegro	43,703	32,681	11,022	9,696	1,191	135	22,685	21,451	1,234	948	239	47
Turkey in Europe	23,268	18,907	4,361	3,948	372	41	35,314	32,221	3,093	2,560	423	110
Southern Europe:												
Greece	212,342	166,786	45,556	36,990	8,287	279	109,665	101,264	8,401	5,524	2,400	477
Italy	3,336,941	1,615,180	1,721,761	1,550,065	146,304	19,392	2,098,360	1,343,070	755,290	695,187	52,047	7,156
Spain	77,947	52,686	25,261	14,973	7,972	2,316	33,134	21,977	11,157	4,387	5,364	1,406
Portugal	134,794	67,048	66,846	52,794	11,673	2,379	111,122	57,623	53,499	41,680	10,359	1,460
Europe, not specified	10,998	8,342	7,656	5,019	1,900	737	7,576	2,853	4,723	2,926	1,281	516
Asia:												
Turkey in Asia	164,480	100,843	63,637	57,915	4,827	895	78,631	59,702	18,929	17,480	1,255	194
All other countries	10,735	5,139	5,596	1,791	2,343	1,462	7,264	4,612	2,652	517	1,329	806
America:												
Canada—French	848,309	302,675	545,634	326,435	129,203	89,996	932,238	385,083	547,155	330,976	133,990	82,180
Canada—Other	1,755,519	558,775	1,196,744	343,546	467,206	385,943	1,822,377	810,987	1,011,390	307,291	387,617	316,482
Newfoundland	25,448	12,320	13,128	7,163	2,780	3,185	8,635	5,076	3,559	1,836	853	870
West Indies[2]	45,496	21,909	23,587	9,987	9,005	4,595	41,842	23,169	18,673	8,681	6,743	3,249
Mexico	725,332	473,287	252,045	178,309	45,720	28,016	382,002	219,802	162,200	107,866	34,995	19,339
Central and South America	19,487	11,782	7,705	1,424	3,595	2,686	13,510	9,069	4,441	807	2,050	1,584
All other	116,458	48,299	68,159	38,700	19,292	10,167	74,523	40,167	34,356	14,214	13,029	7,113
Of mixed foreign parentage	1,502,457	....	1,502,457	1,502,457	....	....	1,177,092	....	1,177,092	1,177,092	....	....
	1900						**1890**					
All foreign countries	25,859,834	10,213,817	15,646,017	10,632,280	3,346,652	1,667,085	20,625,542	9,121,867	11,503,675	8,085,019	2,378,729	1,039,927
Northwestern Europe:												
England	2,173,741	839,830	1,333,911	565,461	494,929	273,521	1,977,595	909,092	1,068,503	488,661	386,711	193,131
Scotland	594,297	233,473	360,824	163,991	129,735	67,098	519,252	242,231	277,021	134,243	97,661	45,117
Wales	253,045	93,560	159,485	86,899	47,498	25,088	225,582	100,079	125,503	75,375	34,863	15,265
Ireland	4,826,904	1,615,232	3,211,672	2,244,241	605,987	361,444	4,795,681	1,871,509	2,924,172	2,164,397	502,155	257,620
Norway	788,758	336,379	452,379	349,220	67,649	35,510	606,316	322,665	283,651	238,679	29,883	15,089
Sweden	1,082,388	581,986	500,402	414,772	55,479	30,151	730,569	478,041	252,528	217,217	23,810	11,501
Denmark	310,127	153,644	156,483	115,173	29,514	11,796	216,995	132,543	84,452	66,196	13,677	4,579
Switzerland	257,426	115,581	141,845	74,951	48,806	18,088	(4)	(4)	(4)	....	....	....
France	268,292	104,031	164,261	71,263	72,110	20,888	258,919	113,174	145,745	68,572	61,187	15,986
Central, Eastern, and Southern Europe:												
Germany	8,111,453	2,813,413	5,298,040	3,709,706	1,180,880	407,454	6,857,229	2,784,894	4,072,335	3,006,342	827,828	238,170
Austria	895,500	491,259	404,241	344,070	42,295	17,876	341,549	241,377	100,172	90,195	6,744	3,233
Hungary	218,447	145,709	72,738	66,713	4,895	1,130	77,121	62,435	14,686	13,048	1,390	248
Russia	955,918	578,072	377,846	356,249	17,719	3,878	258,583	182,044	75,939	69,802	4,962	1,175
Italy	727,844	483,963	243,881	218,750	22,442	2,689	249,544	182,580	66,964	54,742	11,096	1,126
All other:												
Canada—French	830,335	394,461	435,874	265,947	106,833	63,094	526,984	302,496	224,438	157,104	42,356	24,978
Canada—Other	1,637,603	778,399	859,204	260,471	317,988	280,745	1,255,629	[5] 673,000	582,629	183,602	227,144	171,883
All other countries	871,604	454,825	416,779	268,251	101,893	46,635	1,013,774	523,107	490,667	342,574	107,267	40,826
Of mixed foreign parentage	1,056,152	....	1,056,152	1,056,152	....	....	714,270	....	714,270	714,270	....	....

[1] For 1920, according to birthplace of father; for 1910, 1900, and 1890, according to birthplace of person. (See p. 891.)
[2] Except possessions of the United States.
[3] The report for 1890 classified the foreign born by country of birth without distinction as to color or race. For the purposes of this table it is assumed that, with the exception of "Canada—Other" (see note 5), the number reported for each specified country represented white persons only. The number for "All other countries" has been obtained by deducting the sum of the items for the specified countries from the United States total, which represents foreign-born white only.
[4] Switzerland included in "All other countries" in tabulation by birthplace of parents. Number of persons born in Switzerland, 104,069, also included in "All other countries" in this table.
[5] Partly estimated; total reported for "Canada—Other" was 678,442, of whom eight-tenths of 1 per cent were estimated to be nonwhites, this proportion being based upon returns of later censuses.

75647°—22——57

898   POPULATION.

TABLE 2.—COUNTRY OF ORIGIN OF THE FOREIGN WHITE STOCK, BY NATIVITY AND PARENTAGE, WITH PER CENT OF INCREASE, FOR THE UNITED STATES: 1920 AND 1910.

[Figures for 1920 relate to countries as constituted prior to the World War (see text, p. 891). A minus sign (−) denotes decrease.]

| COUNTRY OF ORIGIN. | TOTAL FOREIGN WHITE STOCK. | | | FOREIGN-BORN WHITE.[1] | | | NATIVE WHITE OF FOREIGN OR MIXED PARENTAGE. | | | | | | | | |
| | | | | | | | Total. | | | Foreign parentage. | | | Mixed parentage. | | |
	1920	1910	Per cent of increase.	1920	1910	Per cent of increase.	1920	1910	Per cent of increase.	1920	1910	Per cent of increase.	1920	1910	Per cent of increase
Total	36,398,958	32,243,382	12.9	13,712,754	13,345,545	2.8	22,686,204	18,897,837	20.0	15,694,539	12,916,311	21.5	6,991,665	5,981,526	16.9
Northwestern Europe:															
England	2,307,112	2,322,442	−0.7	824,088	876,455	−6.0	1,483,024	1,445,987	2.6	574,499	592,285	−3.0	908,525	853,702	6.4
Scotland	731,239	659,603	10.9	310,092	261,034	18.8	421,147	398,629	5.6	178,638	175,391	1.9	242,509	223,238	8.6
Wales	230,380	248,947	−7.5	66,962	82,479	−18.8	163,418	166,468	−1.8	78,114	84,934	−8.0	85,304	81,534	4.6
Ireland	4,136,395	4,504,360	−8.2	1,164,707	1,352,155	−13.9	2,971,688	3,152,205	−5.7	1,966,968	2,141,577	−8.2	1,004,720	1,010,628	−0.6
Norway	1,023,225	979,099	4.5	362,051	403,858	−10.4	661,174	575,241	14.9	437,623	410,951	6.5	223,551	164,290	36.1
Sweden	1,457,382	1,364,215	6.8	632,656	665,183	−4.9	824,726	699,032	18.0	599,744	546,788	9.7	224,982	152,244	47.8
Denmark	467,525	400,064	16.9	191,496	181,621	5.4	276,029	218,443	26.4	170,702	147,648	15.0	105,327	70,795	48.8
Netherlands	362,318	293,574	23.4	134,229	120,053	11.8	228,089	173,521	31.4	142,547	116,331	22.5	85,542	57,190	49.6
Belgium	122,686	89,264	37.4	63,234	49,397	28.0	59,452	39,867	49.1	37,525	26,448	41.9	21,927	13,419	63.4
Luxemburg	43,109	6,945	520.7	12,837	3,068	318.4	30,272	3,877	680.8	16,263	2,381	583.0	14,009	1,496	836.4
Switzerland	327,797	301,650	8.7	117,270	124,834	−6.1	210,527	176,816	19.1	103,452	90,669	14.1	107,075	86,147	24.3
France	333,678	292,389	14.1	124,727	117,236	6.4	208,951	175,153	19.3	90,073	78,937	14.1	118,878	96,216	23.6
Central and Eastern Europe:															
Germany	7,259,992	8,282,618	−12.3	1,915,864	2,501,181	−23.4	5,344,128	5,781,437	−7.6	3,397,370	3,911,847	−13.2	1,946,758	1,869,590	4.1
Austria	3,129,798	2,001,559	56.4	1,445,141	1,174,924	23.0	1,684,657	826,635	103.8	1,435,524	709,070	102.5	249,133	117,565	111.9
Hungary	1,110,905	700,227	58.6	598,170	495,600	20.7	512,735	204,627	150.6	472,521	191,059	147.3	40,214	13,568	196.4
Russia	3,871,109	2,541,049	52.3	2,020,646	1,602,752	26.1	1,850,463	938,897	97.1	1,671,949	873,055	91.5	178,514	65,842	171.1
Finland	296,291	211,026	40.4	150,770	129,669	16.3	145,506	81,357	78.8	130,083	76,201	70.6	15,423	5,096	202.6
Rumania	134,318	87,721	53.1	85,255	65,920	29.3	49,063	21,801	125.0	43,683	20,707	111.0	5,380	1,094	391.8
Bulgaria, Serbia, and Montenegro	43,703	22,685	92.7	32,081	21,451	52.4	11,022	1,234	793.2	9,696	948	922.8	1,326	286	363.6
Turkey in Europe	23,268	35,314	−34.1	18,907	32,221	−41.3	4,361	3,093	41.0	3,948	2,560	54.2	413	533	−22.5
Southern Europe:															
Greece	212,342	109,665	93.6	166,786	101,264	64.7	45,556	8,401	442.3	36,990	5,524	569.6	8,566	2,877	197.7
Italy	3,336,941	2,098,360	59.0	1,615,180	1,343,070	20.3	1,721,761	755,290	128.0	1,556,065	695,187	123.8	165,696	60,103	175.7
Spain	77,947	33,134	135.2	52,686	21,977	139.7	25,261	11,157	126.4	14,973	4,387	241.3	10,288	6,770	52.0
Portugal	134,794	111,122	21.3	67,948	57,623	17.9	66,846	53,499	24.9	52,704	41,680	26.7	14,052	11,819	18.9
Europe, not specified	10,998	7,576	45.2	3,342	2,853	17.1	7,656	4,723	62.1	5,019	2,926	71.5	2,637	1,797	46.7
Asia:															
Turkey in Asia	164,480	78,631	109.2	100,843	59,702	68.9	63,637	18,929	236.2	57,915	17,480	231.3	5,722	1,449	294.9
All other countries	10,735	7,264	47.8	5,139	4,612	11.4	5,596	2,652	111.0	1,791	517	246.4	3,805	2,135	78.2
America:															
Canada—French	848,309	932,238	−9.0	302,675	385,083	−21.4	545,634	547,155	−0.3	326,435	330,970	−1.4	219,199	216,170	1.4
Canada—Other	1,755,519	1,822,377	−3.7	558,775	810,987	−31.1	1,196,744	1,011,390	18.3	343,595	307,291	11.8	853,149	704,099	21.2
Newfoundland	25,448	8,635	194.7	12,320	5,076	142.7	13,128	3,559	268.9	7,103	1,836	290.1	5,965	1,723	246.2
West Indies[2]	45,496	41,842	8.7	21,909	23,169	−5.4	23,587	18,673	26.3	9,987	8,681	15.0	13,600	9,992	36.1
Mexico	725,382	382,002	89.9	473,287	219,802	115.3	252,045	162,200	55.4	178,309	107,866	65.3	73,736	54,334	35.7
Central and South America	19,487	13,510	44.2	11,782	9,069	29.9	7,705	4,441	73.5	1,424	807	76.5	6,281	3,634	72.8
All other	116,458	74,523	56.3	48,299	40,167	20.2	68,159	34,356	98.4	38,700	14,214	172.3	29,459	20,142	46.3
Of mixed foreign parentage	1,502,457	1,177,092	27.6	....	....	....	1,502,457	1,177,092	27.6	1,502,457	1,177,092	27.6	....	....	....

[1] For 1920, according to birthplace of father; for 1910, according to birthplace of person. (See p. 891.)　　　[2] Except possessions of the United States.

COUNTRY OF ORIGIN.   899

TABLE 3.—PER CENT DISTRIBUTION OF THE FOREIGN WHITE STOCK BY COUNTRY OF ORIGIN FOR NATIVITY AND PARENTAGE CLASSES, AND BY NATIVITY AND PARENTAGE CLASSES FOR COUNTRIES OF ORIGIN, FOR THE UNITED STATES: 1920 AND 1910.

[Figures for 1920 relate to countries as constituted prior to the World War (see text, p. 891).]

COUNTRY OF ORIGIN	PER CENT DISTRIBUTION BY COUNTRY OF ORIGIN												PER CENT DISTRIBUTION BY NATIVITY AND PARENTAGE CLASSES									
	Total foreign white stock		Foreign-born white[1]		Native white of foreign or mixed parentage								Foreign-born white[1]		Native white of foreign or mixed parentage							
					Total		Both parents foreign		Father foreign		Mother foreign				Total		Both parents foreign		Father foreign		Mother foreign	
	1920	1910	1920	1910	1920	1910	1920	1910	1920	1910	1920	1910	1920	1910	1920	1910	1920	1910	1920	1910	1920	1910
Total	100.0	100.0	100.0	100.0	100.0	100.0	100.0	100.0	100.0	100.0	100.0	100.0	37.7	41.4	62.3	58.6	43.1	40.1	12.5	12.2	6.7	6.4
Northwestern Europe:																						
England	6.3	7.2	6.0	6.6	6.5	7.7	3.7	4.6	12.6	13.9	13.7	14.9	35.7	37.7	64.3	62.3	24.9	25.5	24.8	23.5	14.6	13.2
Scotland	2.0	2.0	2.3	2.0	1.9	2.1	1.1	1.4	3.4	3.7	3.6	3.8	42.4	39.6	57.6	60.4	24.4	26.6	21.0	22.0	12.1	11.8
Wales	0.6	0.8	0.5	0.6	0.7	0.9	0.5	0.7	1.2	1.3	1.2	1.4	29.1	33.1	70.9	66.9	33.9	34.1	23.8	21.1	13.2	11.6
Ireland	11.4	14.0	8.5	10.1	13.1	16.7	12.5	16.6	12.6	15.4	17.6	19.8	28.2	30.0	71.8	70.0	47.6	47.5	13.9	13.4	10.4	9.0
Norway	2.8	3.0	2.6	3.0	2.9	3.0	2.8	3.2	3.2	2.7	3.3	2.8	35.4	41.2	64.6	58.8	42.8	42.0	14.0	10.9	7.8	5.9
Sweden	4.0	4.2	4.6	5.0	3.6	3.7	3.8	4.2	3.2	2.5	3.3	2.7	43.4	48.8	56.6	51.2	41.2	40.1	9.9	7.1	5.5	4.0
Denmark	1.3	1.2	1.4	1.4	1.2	1.2	1.1	1.1	1.6	1.3	1.3	1.0	41.0	45.4	59.0	54.6	36.5	36.9	15.8	12.4	6.7	5.3
Netherlands	1.0	0.9	1.0	0.9	1.0	0.9	0.9	0.9	1.3	1.0	1.2	0.9	37.0	40.9	63.0	59.1	39.3	39.6	15.8	13.0	7.8	6.5
Belgium	0.8	0.3	0.5	0.4	0.3	0.2	0.2	0.2	0.3	0.2	0.3	0.2	51.5	55.3	48.5	44.7	30.6	29.6	12.0	11.0	5.3	4.1
Luxemburg	0.1	(2)	0.1	(2)	0.1	(2)	0.1	(2)	0.2	(2)	0.1	(2)	29.8	44.2	70.2	55.8	37.7	34.3	25.2	17.9	7.3	3.6
Switzerland	0.9	0.9	0.9	0.9	0.9	0.9	0.7	0.7	1.7	1.6	1.3	1.2	35.8	41.4	64.2	58.6	31.6	30.1	23.0	20.3	9.7	8.3
France	0.9	0.9	0.9	0.9	0.9	0.9	0.6	0.6	1.9	1.9	1.3	1.1	37.4	40.1	62.6	59.9	27.0	27.0	25.9	25.0	9.7	7.9
Central and Eastern Europe:																						
Germany	19.9	25.7	14.0	18.7	23.6	30.6	21.6	30.3	30.1	34.1	23.6	25.9	26.4	30.2	73.6	69.8	46.8	47.2	18.8	16.2	8.0	6.4
Austria	8.6	6.2	10.5	8.8	7.4	4.4	9.1	5.5	3.8	2.1	3.2	1.8	46.2	58.7	53.8	41.3	45.9	35.4	5.5	4.0	2.5	1.8
Hungary	3.1	2.2	4.4	3.7	2.3	1.1	3.0	1.5	0.7	0.3	0.4	0.2	53.8	70.8	46.2	29.2	42.5	27.3	2.7	1.4	1.0	0.5
Russia	10.6	7.9	14.7	12.0	8.2	5.0	10.7	6.8	3.0	1.3	1.8	0.7	52.2	63.1	47.8	36.9	43.2	34.3	3.5	2.0	1.1	0.6
Finland	0.8	0.7	1.1	1.0	0.6	0.4	0.8	0.6	0.2	0.1	0.2	0.1	50.9	61.4	49.1	38.6	43.9	36.1	3.3	1.6	1.9	0.8
Rumania	0.4	0.3	0.6	0.5	0.2	0.1	0.3	0.2	0.1	(2)	0.1	(2)	63.5	75.1	36.5	24.9	32.5	23.6	2.8	0.9	1.2	0.3
Bulgaria, Serbia, and Montenegro	0.1	0.1	0.2	0.2	(2)	(2)	0.1	(2)	(2)	(2)	(2)	(2)	74.8	94.6	25.2	5.4	22.2	4.2	2.7	1.1	0.3	0.2
Turkey in Europe	0.1	0.1	0.1	0.2	(2)	(2)	(2)	(2)	(2)	(2)	(2)	(2)	81.3	91.2	18.7	8.8	17.0	7.2	1.6	1.2	0.2	0.3
Southern Europe:																						
Greece	0.6	0.3	1.2	0.8	0.2	(2)	0.2	(2)	0.2	0.1	(2)	(2)	78.5	92.3	21.5	7.7	17.4	5.0	3.9	2.2	0.1	0.4
Italy	9.2	6.5	11.8	10.1	7.6	4.0	9.9	5.4	3.2	1.3	0.8	0.3	48.4	64.0	51.6	36.0	40.6	33.1	4.4	2.5	0.6	0.3
Spain	0.2	0.1	0.4	0.2	0.1	0.1	0.1	(2)	0.2	0.1	0.1	0.1	67.6	66.3	32.4	33.7	19.2	13.2	10.2	16.2	3.0	4.2
Portugal	0.4	0.3	0.5	0.4	0.3	0.3	0.3	0.3	0.3	0.3	0.1	0.1	50.4	51.9	49.6	48.1	39.2	37.5	8.7	9.3	1.8	1.3
Europe, not specified	(2)	(2)	(2)	(2)	(2)	(2)	(2)	(2)	(2)	(2)	(2)	(2)	30.4	37.7	69.6	62.3	45.6	38.6	17.3	16.9	6.7	6.8
Asia:																						
Turkey in Asia	0.5	0.2	0.7	0.4	0.3	0.1	0.4	0.1	0.1	(2)	(2)	(2)	61.3	75.9	38.7	24.1	35.2	22.2	2.9	1.6	0.5	0.2
All other countries	(2)	(2)	(2)	(2)	(2)	(2)	(2)	(2)	0.1	(2)	0.1	(2)	47.9	63.5	52.1	36.5	16.7	7.1	21.8	18.3	13.6	11.1
America:																						
Canada—French	2.3	2.9	2.2	2.9	2.4	2.9	2.1	2.6	2.8	3.4	3.7	4.0	35.7	41.3	64.3	58.7	38.5	35.5	15.2	14.4	10.6	8.8
Canada—Other	4.8	5.7	4.1	6.1	5.3	5.4	2.2	2.4	10.3	9.9	15.7	15.4	31.8	44.5	68.2	55.5	19.6	16.9	26.6	21.3	22.0	17.4
Newfoundland	0.1	0.1	0.1	(2)	0.1	(2)	(2)	(2)	0.1	(2)	0.1	(2)	48.4	58.8	51.6	41.2	28.1	21.3	10.9	9.9	12.5	10.1
West Indies[3]	0.1	0.1	0.2	0.2	0.1	0.1	0.1	0.1	0.2	0.2	0.2	0.2	48.2	55.4	51.8	44.6	22.0	20.7	19.8	16.1	10.1	7.8
Mexico	2.0	1.2	3.5	1.6	1.1	0.9	1.1	0.8	1.0	0.9	1.1	0.9	65.3	57.5	34.7	42.5	24.6	28.2	6.3	9.2	3.9	5.1
Central and South America	0.1	(2)	0.1	0.1	(2)	(2)	(2)	(2)	0.1	0.1	0.1	0.1	60.5	67.1	39.5	32.9	7.3	6.0	18.4	15.2	13.8	11.7
All other	0.3	0.2	0.4	0.3	0.3	0.2	0.2	0.1	0.4	0.3	0.4	0.3	41.5	53.9	58.5	46.1	33.2	19.1	16.6	17.5	8.7	9.5
Of mixed foreign parentage	4.1	3.7	....	....	6.6	6.2	9.6	9.1	....	....	....	....	....	....	100.0	100.0	100.0	100.0	....	....	....	....

[1] For 1920, according to birthplace of father; for 1910, according to birthplace of person. (See p. 891.)
[2] Less than one-tenth of 1 per cent.
[3] Except possessions of the United States.

900

POPULATION.

TABLE 4.—NATIVE WHITE POPULATION OF MIXED FOREIGN PARENTAGE, BY COUNTRY OF BIRTH

[Figures relate to countries as constituted prior to the World War (see text, p. 891).]

| COUNTRY OF BIRTH OF FATHER. | Total native white of mixed foreign parentage: 1920 | COUNTRY OF BIRTH OF MOTHER. | | | | | | | | | | | | | | | | |
| | | Northwestern Europe. | | | | | | | | | | | | Central and Eastern Europe. | | | | |
		England.	Scotland.	Wales.	Ireland.	Norway.	Sweden.	Denmark.	Netherlands.	Belgium.	Luxemburg.	Switzerland.	France.	Germany.	Austria.	Hungary.	Russia.	Finland.
1 Total	1,502,457	165,689	79,350	21,028	213,202	55,539	61,467	26,046	18,501	8,314	5,321	46,300	66,165	269,987	140,709	39,093	78,362	10,931
Northwestern Europe:																		
2 England	199,019		27,175	12,311	72,015	2,464	4,788	3,218	1,480	371	62	1,632	4,474	20,161	2,147	393	3,594	463
3 Scotland	93,280	27,509		2,252	34,325	813	1,616	634	368	104	28	383	1,167	4,783	427	90	456	102
4 Wales	18,884	10,252	1,725		3,178	94	262	203	58	12	2	170	194	1,067	81	82	31	17
5 Ireland	150,325	51,382	20,667	3,088		1,062	1,888	614	648	172	49	765	3,318	12,348	1,018	1,017	288	106
6 Norway	39,922	1,506	505	71	1,940		22,046	4,338	742	81	11	226	204	3,417	498	72	145	1,813
7 Sweden	63,771	2,920	1,279	228	3,951	29,077		6,120	322	78	26	807	496	7,579	607	109	642	6,127
8 Denmark	44,381	2,991	660	198	2,757	10,002	11,118		229	62	48	541	362	11,557	645	88	216	287
9 Netherlands	21,250	1,762	360	53	1,913	1,084	535	266		1,457	92	448	717	10,221	618	145	284	46
10 Belgium	9,509	489	104	26	786	87	129	56	1,306		378	277	2,082	2,361	336	64	102	27
11 Luxemburg	6,491	50	9	3	167	36	51	21	133	357		193	415	4,249	446	93	89	4
12 Switzerland	46,814	1,548	432	132	2,276	358	816	299	411	150	152		3,430	31,288	2,107	351	413	61
13 France	79,399	4,464	1,121	191	7,616	259	701	279	642	1,976	505	3,681		46,137	1,487	218	691	83
Central and Eastern Europe:																		
14 Germany	272,895	21,973	5,197	1,143	36,699	4,766	8,018	7,228	8,610	1,813	3,496	31,941	37,945		47,344	8,767	24,206	507
15 Austria	108,213	2,739	343	63	2,032	418	563	200	267	209	235	1,580	1,233	41,999		17,251	30,454	118
16 Hungary	25,783	422	45	49	1,227	61	86	28	42	32	42	208	171	7,049	12,133		3,101	38
17 Russia	132,700	7,370	810	60	956	206	893	108	217	90	30	379	1,016	42,633	57,920	7,231		732
18 Finland	6,655	502	29	6	221	1,469	3,570	99	17	17	4	10	78	207	50	5	205	
19 Rumania	15,718	280	14	1	21	11	31	4	17	5	2	25	74	552	4,106	928	9,274	8
20 Bulgaria	595	17	11	1	9	3	4		5	3	1	3	16	61	182	115	68	
21 Serbia	1,162	15			13	3	4		7	1	8	8	15	89	486	298	88	2
22 Montenegro	197	1			1	1						4	1	1	87	87	6	3
23 Turkey in Europe	1,114	30	8		35	4	11	9	1	5		10	23	74	170	74	287	5
Southern Europe:																		
24 Greece	6,527	224	71	9	555	82	176	56	21	25	10	78	221	2,111	917	224	419	22
25 Italy	29,330	2,104	490	83	3,327	159	561	145	87	488	16	1,753	4,138	4,372	3,807	1,025	1,304	125
26 Spain	5,809	392	84	17	801	10	29	10	14	24	1	71	703	453	119	11	67	6
27 Portugal	2,605	191	45	8	685	8	35	24	83	3	3	19	62	156	35	2	29	4
28 Europe, not specified	636	48	14	2	52	3	27	6	7	9		21	43	241	67	9	33	
Asia:																		
29 Turkey in Asia	2,824	133	49		165	32	53	10	7	24	1	13	82	214	251	96	621	6
30 China	109	21	1		9	4	16		3				1	11	11		4	
31 Japan	139	23	9		17	8	8	1	2			5	8	14	11	1	6	
32 India	734	262	57	4	151	8	7	4	25	4		6	16	45	1	4	3	1
33 Asia, not specified	392	13	6		26	1	6	1	3		5	7	13	75	46	11	108	
America:																		
34 Canada	99,227	22,047	8,466	920	37,336	2,730	3,120	1,947	561	717	113	851	3,015	12,023	1,842	182	630	221
35 Newfoundland	2,117	207	94	12	908	13	27	7	7		1	6	12	44	8	1	4	4
36 Cuba	1,021	121	13	1	164	1	9	10	6	10	1	7	73	95	31	11	4	2
37 Other West Indies[1]	1,355	245	77	4	433	24	28	13	15	2		15	83	114	24	9	18	2
38 Mexico	1,131	88	26	4	94	9	15	6	28	4		10	79	156	50	17	24	1
39 Central America	129	11			4							5	11	10	9		1	1
40 South America	2,217	171	37	7	142	5	14	6	20	4		29	70	290	79	13	112	
All other:																		
41 Africa	851	129	24	1	71	15	38	14	14			12	30	127	40	16	79	4
42 Australia	1,718	467	93	30	346	16	44	7	7		1	19	21	250	51	19	92	3
43 Atlantic Islands	1,458	130	37	13	264	6	20	10	1			2	3	71	12	6		
44 Pacific Islands[1]	634	170	45	8	110	8	24	9	28	1		6	6	72	12	6	7	3
45 Country not specified	1,434	87	24	9	161	19	27	8	16	6	5	21	41	507	123	26	92	18
46 Born at sea	1,979	183	94	20	243	100	44	21	28	4	5	47	40	703	88	6	64	9

[1] Except possessions of the United States.

COUNTRY OF ORIGIN.

OF FATHER ACCORDING TO COUNTRY OF BIRTH OF MOTHER, FOR THE UNITED STATES: 1920.

[Figures relate to countries as constituted prior to the World War (see text, p. 891).]

COUNTRY OF BIRTH OF MOTHER—continued.

Central and Eastern Europe—Continued.					Southern Europe.				Europe, not specified.	Asia.					America.							All other.						
Rumania.	Bulgaria.	Serbia.	Montenegro.	Turkey in Europe.	Greece.	Italy.	Spain.	Portugal.		Turkey in Asia.	China.	Japan.	India.	All other.	Canada.	Newfoundland.	Cuba.	Other West Indies.[1]	Mexico.	Central America.	South America.	Africa.	Australia.	Atlantic Islands.	Pacific Islands.[1]	Country not specified.	Born at sea.	
14,743	206	368	61	710	1,850	8,872	3,018	2,016	647	1,234	79	51	611	495	133,838	2,755	1,765	1,350	4,466	191	3,169	1,059	2,552	1,046	817	2,263	3,171	1
186	6	7	...	11	90	421	402	132	50	28	19	13	245	5	37,054	552	74	387	509	31	207	193	774	125	284	165	301	2
6	...	...	1	1	25	73	125	18	10	8	5	...	60	5	16,987	168	25	105	86	6	46	75	180	29	62	56	94	3
1	...	1	...	...	6	29	25	6	1	...	1	...	12	...	1,187	36	...	18	3	1	11	13	57	2	4	20	22	4
2	1	2	...	4	62	333	286	97	40	10	6	4	132	2	39,551	654	23	131	189	6	107	48	420	48	109	289	339	5
...	1	...	...	...	12	38	16	9	2	3	...	1	5	...	1,842	20	...	12	18	1	19	13	62	7	25	22	179	6
8	...	3	...	...	135	65	28	45	2	6	6	8	3	2	2,577	65	23	24	41	1	38	6	46	19	30	43	88	7
7	...	...	...	...	20	21	9	18	6	3	6	2	2	7	2,219	35	5	48	24	4	24	10	52	12	15	30	41	8
8	...	...	...	2	16	26	18	59	19	5	3	...	9	2	810	12	5	29	35	6	28	22	22	...	29	42	42	9
10	4	5	...	1	2	76	19	1	7	6	...	...	...	1	705	...	...	8	8	1	14	8	8	...	...	4	16	10
...	...	...	...	...	1	14	...	...	1	...	...	...	...	4	125	...	...	...	2	...	...	1	1	...	...	16	10	11
4	2	2	1	1	44	952	45	12	35	9	1	...	2	7	1,117	5	14	11	76	3	61	15	29	3	8	60	62	12
67	5	5	1	16	118	1,756	675	83	31	33	1	2	11	8	5,420	34	55	50	487	16	161	47	42	26	12	95	82	13
449	14	37	...	28	647	760	330	88	229	62	12	9	47	53	16,268	117	63	161	566	31	893	133	316	20	70	880	1,444	14
3,874	35	148	30	52	71	1,700	49	30	58	74	2	...	3	20	1,728	27	7	8	131	1	92	32	71	10	19	127	10	15
459	19	70	1	9	34	149	10	1	3	29	...	...	...	2	155	1	6	5	12	...	22	11	11	...	7	23	10	16
9,195	31	6	2	144	93	121	22	31	41	428	...	1	12	204	1,108	17	12	6	34	3	164	62	98	1	5	105	103	17
8	...	...	...	...	2	...	4	4	3	...	...	...	...	2	121	8	1	5	...	...	...	...	2	...	...	5	3	18
...	55	12	...	64	14	20	...	15	2	61	...	...	...	3	55	...	12	...	1	...	8	19	7	...	...	10	2	19
30	...	1	...	18	8	3	1	1	...	14	...	...	...	2	20	...	...	...	...	...	...	2	...	...	...	...	1	20
33	...	...	19	...	4	26	...	...	...	2	...	...	...	...	10	1	...	...	10	...	7	6	1	5	...	1	...	21
...	...	36	...	4	5	8	...	...	...	...	...	...	...	1	...	...	...	...	1	...	...	...	...	...	...	...	...	22
86	4	1	...	...	146	18	...	3	2	41	...	...	...	7	37	3	4	4	...	...	6	5	...	...	...	1	...	23
76	5	13	...	141	102	302	43	30	5	167	...	2	1	17	339	3	...	11	83	...	9	47	4	...	1	6	3	24
60	...	11	...	41	2	626	335	351	16	117	...	2	...	1	1,706	15	14	22	637	7	1,285	153	60	51	28	40	23	25
6	...	...	6	1	2	626	131	...	7	3	...	...	...	1	127	5	1,274	49	637	7	57	18	4	28	521	2	2	26
17	...	...	...	1	...	44	95	...	2	2	...	...	...	1	247	2	6	22	89	...	135	4	2	521	9	2	12	27
1	...	...	...	2	4	17	5	...	...	6	...	...	...	1	11	...	...	...	...	...	...	...	3	...	8	1	...	28
74	18	4	...	167	124	110	7	12	13	...	...	...	1	122	201	6	2	11	52	...	36	93	8	...	2	4	...	29
...	...	...	...	1	...	...	...	...	...	...	...	...	...	...	11	...	...	...	14	...	1	...	...	...	...	...	...	30
...	...	...	...	...	1	...	2	...	...	1	...	...	...	...	10	...	...	...	12	...	...	...	...	...	...	...	...	31
1	...	...	...	1	2	13	3	...	1	...	3	...	1	...	109	...	1	4	5	...	5	...	2	...	5	2	...	32
3	...	...	...	...	...	...	...	...	...	22	3	...	1	...	10	...	1	8	...	3	1	3	...	...	2	...	...	33
27	6	3	...	1	36	171	78	70	14	25	9	5	51	5	...	949	30	117	154	11	61	17	202	50	82	163	163	34
...	...	...	...	...	...	3	1	5	...	6	...	...	...	3	742	1	4	2	1	...	22	1	...	5	2	...	...	35
1	...	...	...	...	...	153	130	...	...	6	...	...	...	...	44	2	51	44	2	22	...	1	...	5	17	1	...	36
2	...	...	...	1	127	162	4	15	...	1	1	3	...	2	204	...	7	9	7	12	...	2	7	2	6	20	6	37
...	...	...	...	2	3	6	1	...	...	1	...	...	...	...	41	1	53	5	6	48	2	...	2	...	...	...	6	38
...	...	...	...	...	1	523	45	212	...	11	...	...	...	1	3	2	1	6	48	...	...	2	...	...	...	...	...	39
8	...	3	...	1	...	...	...	...	...	...	...	...	...	...	106	2	19	11	202	10	...	1	45	1	1	6	...	40
16	...	...	...	3	18	80	6	1	...	49	...	...	...	1	51	...	2	1	...	...	4	...	2	1	1	...	...	41
13	...	...	...	...	1	14	1	...	...	1	...	...	...	...	165	2	3	22	22	...	6	...	2	19	2	...	...	42
...	...	...	...	...	...	8	11	522	...	...	...	...	1	1	197	6	27	22	5	1	71	1	26	...	2	1	...	43
...	...	...	...	...	...	1	2	...	...	...	...	1	...	7	64	1	...	2	8	...	2	1	...	1	...	1	2	44
3	...	...	...	...	...	39	9	...	1	42	...	...	...	...	117	...	...	1	26	...	1	2	...	2	...	...	1	45
...	...	...	...	...	1	19	...	...	8	3	...	1	...	...	228	5	...	2	...	...	...	6	...	...	...	7	...	46

[1] Except possessions of the United States.

POPULATION.

TABLE 5.—COUNTRY OF ORIGIN OF THE FOREIGN WHITE

[Figures for 1920 relate to countries as constituted prior to the World War (see text, p. 891).]

	DIVISION AND STATE.	TOTAL FOREIGN WHITE STOCK.		NORTHWESTERN EUROPE.											
				England.		Scotland.		Wales.		Ireland.		Norway.		Sweden.	
		1920	1910	1920	1910	1920	1910	1920	1910	1920	1910	1920	1910	1920	1910
1	United States	36,398,958	32,243,382	2,307,112	2,322,442	731,239	659,663	280,380	248,947	4,136,395	4,504,360	1,023,225	979,099	1,457,382	1,364,215
	GEOGRAPHIC DIVISIONS:														
2	New England	4,512,930	3,867,095	324,095	320,834	111,369	97,740	7,264	8,225	925,051	978,352	15,551	13,367	138,102	126,471
3	Middle Atlantic	12,010,828	10,417,491	700,177	752,940	214,891	211,237	95,586	109,310	1,724,888	1,922,099	61,118	49,719	170,730	160,208
4	East North Central	9,148,492	8,175,654	514,407	503,085	157,105	132,743	55,323	58,348	657,662	706,740	235,795	246,136	382,816	365,310
5	West North Central	4,749,839	4,827,934	218,740	245,227	72,941	73,652	23,966	28,129	314,177	369,020	542,330	543,681	497,264	491,949
6	South Atlantic	869,524	730,398	72,408	64,317	24,898	21,692	6,251	5,791	102,689	111,597	5,198	3,101	10,139	6,062
7	East South Central	274,765	301,834	22,328	26,230	8,170	8,736	1,976	2,433	41,229	51,346	1,214	1,161	3,768	3,580
8	West South Central	1,155,942	954,042	52,985	53,203	15,531	14,933	3,166	3,097	55,250	59,331	7,519	6,493	19,020	16,498
9	Mountain	1,210,391	1,053,831	166,553	171,028	44,778	42,087	18,313	19,810	86,710	93,697	48,005	32,136	79,887	73,329
10	Pacific	2,466,247	1,915,103	235,419	184,678	81,556	50,843	18,535	13,804	228,789	212,178	106,486	83,305	155,650	120,748
	NEW ENGLAND:														
11	Maine	269,915	245,088	13,544	12,572	6,041	5,101	448	551	24,216	24,949	1,221	1,086	4,668	4,308
12	New Hampshire	216,819	109,675	11,230	11,340	4,951	4,308	122	125	27,891	30,589	887	852	3,826	3,550
13	Vermont	123,492	124,916	6,880	6,422	5,097	5,373	1,464	2,202	16,428	19,625	228	175	2,377	2,421
14	Massachusetts	2,572,751	2,221,497	185,546	184,347	65,536	55,482	3,122	3,228	610,696	633,022	9,663	8,370	75,927	68,468
15	Rhode Island	420,427	372,671	52,942	53,727	12,444	12,423	549	655	79,640	88,205	973	916	13,571	13,214
16	Connecticut	909,526	703,248	53,953	52,426	17,300	15,053	1,559	1,464	166,180	181,962	2,579	1,908	37,733	34,504
	MIDDLE ATLANTIC:														
17	New York	6,503,751	5,736,520	317,179	341,429	94,021	90,678	19,703	19,726	983,036	1,091,140	46,220	37,404	99,069	90,235
18	New Jersey	1,824,412	1,435,985	120,811	122,041	42,071	38,091	3,946	3,283	248,652	260,492	10,104	8,352	21,690	18,348
19	Pennsylvania	3,682,655	3,244,986	262,187	289,470	78,799	82,468	71,937	86,301	493,200	570,467	4,794	3,963	49,977	51,685
	EAST NORTH CENTRAL:														
20	Ohio	1,902,771	1,621,638	131,502	128,112	35,034	30,133	29,574	31,505	151,698	166,848	3,181	2,031	16,505	11,055
21	Indiana	519,527	509,873	32,121	34,666	11,412	10,517	3,631	4,090	44,962	53,208	1,541	1,193	12,685	11,801
22	Illinois	3,232,770	2,926,407	159,304	168,396	55,872	53,609	10,851	11,637	304,924	330,434	66,088	68,438	235,329	230,131
23	Michigan	1,931,180	1,560,406	144,733	120,323	42,084	25,477	3,739	2,359	94,201	81,415	17,325	16,774	61,377	56,937
24	Wisconsin	1,502,244	1,557,330	46,747	52,488	12,703	13,007	7,518	8,757	61,887	74,835	147,660	157,700	56,920	55,386
	WEST NORTH CENTRAL:														
25	Minnesota	1,541,309	1,484,146	36,873	36,506	14,860	12,655	3,730	3,932	65,869	72,775	280,982	279,606	280,077	268,018
26	Iowa	855,628	905,665	56,786	63,423	17,725	18,864	7,170	8,576	75,924	92,015	62,568	66,902	63,788	60,195
27	Missouri	688,108	747,097	41,598	48,413	11,983	12,437	3,769	4,477	82,213	98,636	1,925	1,740	13,339	13,527
28	North Dakota	431,988	407,394	8,913	9,323	5,352	4,118	606	781	11,336	11,701	127,561	123,284	28,606	26,800
29	South Dakota	310,549	318,119	12,601	14,875	3,885	4,182	1,653	2,063	14,619	17,399	58,866	60,746	24,128	23,292
30	Nebraska	522,155	538,218	26,438	30,591	7,864	8,529	2,507	3,082	32,151	37,662	7,092	7,707	55,057	58,486
31	Kansas	400,102	427,295	35,531	42,096	11,272	12,867	4,531	5,218	32,065	38,832	3,345	3,696	32,289	35,631
	SOUTH ATLANTIC:														
32	Delaware	52,739	43,293	4,541	4,580	1,117	897	205	150	12,211	14,038	110	65	702	625
33	Maryland	311,649	296,012	15,645	15,841	6,483	6,844	1,904	2,022	33,533	39,699	1,076	671	1,491	891
34	District of Columbia	87,372	69,417	9,085	7,695	2,759	2,017	511	334	19,727	19,306	725	318	1,346	661
35	Virginia	83,415	64,571	10,588	9,431	3,751	3,179	555	542	9,385	9,487	1,008	697	1,405	721
36	West Virginia	144,378	114,710	10,887	10,309	3,460	3,324	2,239	2,209	11,107	13,118	134	79	822	598
37	North Carolina	18,576	14,793	2,329	2,045	1,305	1,197	89	101	1,545	1,399	156	80	376	218
38	South Carolina	19,120	17,191	1,677	1,536	725	793	42	29	2,675	3,321	179	141	276	183
39	Georgia	46,417	40,744	5,043	4,866	1,947	1,744	269	232	6,607	7,544	331	286	774	638
40	Florida	105,858	69,667	12,113	7,414	3,351	1,697	437	172	5,899	3,665	1,479	764	2,947	1,527
	EAST SOUTH CENTRAL:														
41	Kentucky	141,426	164,757	7,864	9,846	2,241	2,448	679	838	23,595	29,686	191	132	578	442
42	Tennessee	53,236	56,826	5,758	6,496	1,827	1,913	693	841	8,846	11,144	194	242	806	881
43	Alabama	52,903	51,373	6,301	6,967	3,363	3,521	536	686	5,283	6,059	561	548	1,634	1,507
44	Mississippi	27,200	28,878	2,405	2,921	739	854	68	58	3,505	4,457	208	239	750	750
	WEST SOUTH CENTRAL:														
45	Arkansas	53,065	53,517	5,256	5,712	1,585	1,607	387	553	5,053	5,508	300	202	1,016	935
46	Louisiana	154,887	164,499	6,818	7,737	1,783	1,820	259	273	14,104	18,858	964	638	1,297	936
47	Oklahoma	142,087	134,128	13,032	13,494	4,676	4,581	1,419	1,305	11,878	11,901	1,095	1,208	3,329	3,029
48	Texas	805,903	601,898	27,879	26,260	7,487	6,835	1,101	966	24,215	22,914	5,160	4,445	13,378	11,598
	MOUNTAIN:														
49	Montana	258,457	198,453	22,809	20,736	9,175	6,911	2,515	2,320	28,448	28,431	27,824	13,942	16,841	11,802
50	Idaho	131,416	115,622	22,883	21,056	5,418	4,455	3,083	3,156	7,327	7,319	7,061	6,076	13,002	10,985
51	Wyoming	67,262	59,622	9,061	8,886	4,134	3,866	1,106	1,229	4,942	5,236	1,664	1,249	4,884	4,550
52	Colorado	321,062	308,279	32,150	36,648	11,257	11,688	4,672	5,417	28,370	33,097	4,111	4,034	24,384	25,413
53	New Mexico	61,356	48,985	3,034	3,394	1,386	1,419	257	270	2,406	2,722	380	331	839	749
54	Arizona	140,304	89,000	8,094	7,274	2,113	1,522	601	561	5,450	4,901	809	542	2,035	1,574
55	Utah	196,120	194,920	64,209	68,016	10,123	10,476	5,716	6,367	5,034	5,989	5,738	5,509	16,762	17,083
56	Nevada	34,414	38,950	4,313	5,038	1,172	1,387	363	481	4,073	6,002	418	453	1,080	1,193
	PACIFIC:														
57	Washington	608,071	523,725	56,178	46,478	22,572	16,230	6,111	5,227	39,607	35,556	65,613	52,724	68,075	56,079
58	Oregon	271,420	238,239	25,525	22,712	10,965	8,455	2,024	1,642	18,355	18,943	16,120	13,485	22,004	18,108
59	California	1,586,756	1,153,139	153,716	115,488	48,019	32,158	10,400	6,935	170,777	159,679	24,753	17,146	65,571	46,471

COUNTRY OF ORIGIN.

STOCK, BY DIVISIONS AND STATES: 1920 AND 1910.

[Figures for 1920 relate to countries as constituted prior to the World War (see text, p. 891).]

NORTHWESTERN EUROPE—continued.												CENTRAL AND EASTERN EUROPE.						
Denmark.		Netherlands.		Belgium.		Luxemburg.		Switzerland.		France.		Germany.		Austria.		Hungary.		
1920	1910	1920	1910	1920	1910	1920	1910	1920	1910	1920	1910	1920	1910	1920	1910	1920	1910	
467,525	400,064	362,318	293,574	122,686	89,264	43,109	6,945	327,797	301,650	333,678	292,389	7,259,992	8,282,618	3,129,798	2,001,559	1,110,905	700,227	1
17,097	14,199	5,993	3,910	6,389	4,159	203	17	7,629	6,620	21,887	18,985	162,381	176,945	194,105	107,127	41,962	26,016	2
44,468	36,326	67,725	58,081	21,504	16,426	2,185	200	65,418	61,143	95,216	82,524	1,871,619	2,222,900	1,411,112	873,407	553,644	389,738	3
102,847	92,602	175,721	153,406	61,295	46,223	16,863	2,109	100,011	93,897	73,202	63,430	2,789,953	3,172,097	958,258	556,527	388,690	214,885	4
167,079	150,465	72,080	54,961	16,477	11,832	19,764	4,054	56,819	56,971	34,437	32,563	1,407,203	1,601,182	292,995	256,972	58,228	35,111	5
4,606	2,522	3,428	1,528	2,672	1,699	208	30	6,435	5,178	10,320	7,487	195,706	228,285	56,970	33,820	24,672	14,154	6
1,424	1,305	1,389	1,031	542	364	84	6	7,509	7,872	6,912	6,888	96,191	125,572	7,440	5,461	4,334	2,570	7
7,183	5,922	3,458	2,435	2,818	1,808	411	102	11,364	10,386	29,362	29,549	246,190	275,451	80,831	67,376	5,234	3,454	8
55,078	48,377	12,010	7,223	3,128	1,634	1,155	121	19,091	16,187	12,247	9,981	135,662	134,967	53,502	49,228	17,439	6,402	9
67,743	48,346	19,914	10,909	7,861	5,119	2,258	306	53,521	43,396	50,095	40,382	355,087	347,219	74,585	52,081	16,702	7,897	10
2,411	1,984	128	72	90	50	8	....	154	118	757	609	2,889	3,285	1,348	1,220	1,145	227	11
404	255	300	83	648	209	5	....	171	163	546	368	4,464	4,533	7,718	3,428	201	109	12
345	314	103	60	54	47	2	....	266	312	539	489	2,146	2,146	2,699	1,523	684	632	13
7,021	6,072	4,176	2,881	3,441	2,162	72	3	2,814	2,408	11,391	9,909	71,568	77,728	94,521	53,711	4,332	3,129	14
659	589	272	242	1,415	1,172	25	2	415	368	2,531	2,375	9,622	11,021	15,035	9,080	584	452	15
6,257	4,985	1,014	572	741	519	91	12	3,809	3,251	6,123	5,235	71,692	78,232	72,784	38,165	35,066	21,467	16
25,516	20,709	32,841	27,901	7,830	5,017	1,200	127	30,743	29,553	52,822	45,945	1,029,448	1,234,580	614,102	382,158	158,895	141,327	17
12,277	9,667	30,892	27,503	4,144	2,868	325	30	16,333	13,759	16,471	13,036	303,194	333,636	193,591	88,207	98,086	68,699	18
6,675	5,950	3,992	2,677	9,530	8,541	640	43	18,342	17,831	25,923	23,843	538,977	654,684	603,419	403,102	298,663	179,712	19
5,390	3,795	8,055	5,870	3,883	2,696	1,146	126	35,235	33,947	20,274	18,862	572,756	673,795	246,890	125,600	183,466	116,135	20
2,688	2,174	6,458	5,371	4,997	4,205	388	26	10,438	10,225	10,052	9,087	225,661	264,198	36,948	17,835	24,622	18,622	21
37,004	33,519	37,759	32,404	19,696	14,858	9,111	1,434	22,524	21,658	25,377	21,757	865,311	1,014,408	424,054	280,844	98,191	52,764	22
17,668	14,799	98,705	88,031	18,581	10,505	1,350	284	8,913	7,191	12,002	8,667	413,284	424,753	132,336	50,522	53,845	14,198	23
40,138	38,815	24,744	21,820	14,138	13,959	4,868	289	22,901	20,876	5,407	5,057	712,941	794,943	118,030	81,726	28,566	13,166	24
44,487	37,524	15,007	8,934	4,882	3,161	7,100	1,285	9,368	8,581	4,920	4,482	385,933	396,859	87,214	75,178	24,116	8,560	25
47,252	41,741	35,587	28,748	2,987	1,786	6,919	1,972	10,798	11,134	6,464	6,118	314,491	360,005	42,100	39,885	3,951	2,027	26
4,733	4,256	3,550	2,932	2,582	1,911	411	36	16,944	17,207	11,607	10,994	298,177	367,511	36,941	29,786	16,000	14,574	27
12,728	12,203	2,790	1,911	839	489	800	93	1,841	1,717	1,134	894	57,477	59,767	15,634	11,200	6,096	4,668	28
16,975	14,963	9,074	6,678	711	584	2,040	327	2,592	2,450	1,128	1,102	76,263	82,793	14,054	13,255	1,782	1,062	29
33,956	32,562	3,355	3,091	1,147	855	1,319	202	6,236	6,367	2,786	2,387	180,572	201,713	68,804	62,810	2,196	2,142	30
6,948	7,216	2,717	2,667	3,329	3,046	1,175	139	9,040	9,515	6,398	6,886	114,290	132,534	28,248	24,857	4,087	2,078	31
187	88	90	42	38	8	6	1	156	142	496	431	6,393	7,565	4,919	1,399	539	376	32
851	483	843	498	230	103	60	11	1,172	945	2,009	1,689	110,119	135,325	23,228	16,256	4,071	2,789	33
610	323	366	178	127	74	33	2	835	605	1,447	1,068	16,178	18,298	1,570	810	435	250	34
855	474	628	267	208	86	25	9	682	550	1,275	810	12,957	13,785	4,417	2,293	3,561	2,482	35
268	166	237	131	1,577	1,148	9	1	1,981	1,903	1,506	1,320	20,929	24,911	18,797	10,855	14,469	7,591	36
135	77	182	62	36	10	2	1	218	183	357	292	2,902	3,347	307	224	132	57	37
190	128	78	34	98	108	3	....	63	87	338	280	4,861	5,699	785	416	103	71	38
308	217	235	141	120	67	12	....	437	425	1,083	804	8,547	9,867	1,254	658	536	414	39
1,252	566	769	180	238	95	58	5	891	338	1,809	784	12,820	7,488	1,603	409	776	124	40
282	214	749	464	237	188	40	2	4,473	4,577	2,858	2,799	70,217	92,258	3,010	1,717	2,219	858	41
363	369	278	226	82	52	14	1	2,112	2,397	1,218	1,091	11,063	14,582	1,295	1,141	767	735	42
468	430	262	234	152	76	13	3	628	589	1,686	1,738	10,099	12,127	1,924	1,661	1,216	885	43
311	292	100	107	71	48	17	....	296	309	1,150	1,260	4,812	6,655	1,211	942	182	92	44
510	448	423	380	207	183	20	6	2,049	1,955	1,556	1,390	18,751	20,603	3,264	2,557	505	555	45
839	756	586	308	967	731	16	1	1,225	1,325	16,524	19,911	30,699	41,287	3,221	2,883	849	701	46
1,790	1,645	849	757	624	352	202	50	2,597	2,490	3,170	2,443	37,521	41,785	10,268	8,830	1,036	700	47
4,044	3,073	1,000	990	1,020	542	173	36	5,493	4,616	8,112	5,805	159,219	171,776	64,078	53,100	2,844	1,498	48
7,456	3,041	3,937	2,016	1,214	394	492	45	2,924	2,024	2,130	1,385	33,845	26,668	15,505	12,820	6,439	2,142	49
9,132	7,466	1,194	639	259	159	210	17	4,326	3,358	1,325	959	17,855	17,223	3,033	2,274	744	269	50
2,730	2,340	390	171	240	136	61	10	953	654	822	666	8,944	8,133	5,923	5,490	1,303	607	51
6,850	5,710	2,553	1,734	901	654	278	36	3,999	3,984	3,918	3,053	49,323	55,882	21,252	21,334	5,755	2,630	52
332	282	250	207	154	70	24	1	447	438	877	813	5,086	6,143	1,815	1,707	709	281	53
1,227	702	273	112	105	85	50	6	788	632	1,083	698	6,399	5,656	2,069	1,934	1,038	178	54
25,966	26,611	3,913	2,253	151	93	32	3	4,749	4,239	1,037	783	10,567	9,928	2,975	2,628	1,000	241	55
1,385	1,316	100	91	44	43	8	3	905	858	1,055	1,024	3,643	5,334	930	1,041	385	54	56
18,913	15,078	7,517	4,805	2,590	1,804	840	127	8,898	7,205	6,073	5,044	82,790	87,478	28,564	18,930	4,142	1,707	57
8,703	6,773	2,558	1,687	1,531	1,081	395	67	9,921	8,173	3,216	2,725	51,224	53,359	9,904	7,573	2,260	1,538	58
40,127	26,495	9,829	4,417	3,740	2,234	1,021	112	34,702	28,018	40,806	32,613	221,073	206,382	41,117	25,578	10,300	4,652	59

904

POPULATION.

TABLE 5.—COUNTRY OF ORIGIN OF THE FOREIGN WHITE STOCK,

[Figures for 1920 relate to countries as constituted prior to the World War (see text, p. 891).]

| | DIVISION AND STATE. | CENTRAL AND EASTERN EUROPE—continued. | | | | | | | | | | SOUTHERN EUROPE. | | | | | | | |
| | | Russia. | | Finland. | | Rumania. | | Bulgaria, Serbia, and Montenegro. | | Turkey in Europe. | | Greece. | | Italy. | | Spain. | | Portugal. | |
		1920	1910	1920	1910	1920	1910	1920	1910	1920	1910	1920	1910	1920	1910	1920	1910	1920	1910
1	United States......	3,871,109	2,541,649	296,276	211,026	134,318	87,721	43,703	22,685	23,268	35,314	212,342	109,685	3,336,941	2,098,360	77,947	33,134	134,794	111,122
	GEOGRAPHIC DIVISIONS:																		
2	New England......	470,118	291,618	35,253	21,378	4,307	2,821	649	386	4,460	8,250	43,404	18,131	494,708	277,361	4,124	1,767	67,304	53,721
3	Middle Atlantic.......	1,908,800	1,382,493	26,796	17,451	77,876	60,491	8,342	2,852	9,979	9,136	50,878	18,009	1,939,300	1,299,462	22,515	6,892	4,228	1,827
4	East North Central...	838,762	424,124	103,097	76,042	33,570	11,894	19,179	5,253	5,070	7,936	53,309	19,943	406,075	226,150	4,656	1,100	1,024	1,431
5	West North Central...	301,845	232,940	68,761	50,711	8,466	7,012	4,501	4,697	783	3,252	13,206	14,631	70,558	55,123	1,481	1,060	173	203
6	South Atlantic........	131,635	82,208	1,995	620	3,144	1,479	1,369	196	427	1,845	14,630	5,294	81,326	55,206	11,388	6,764	765	814
7	East South Central...	18,276	14,118	403	320	656	456	191	247	94	394	2,779	1,642	19,849	14,838	806	745	62	39
8	West South Central...	40,568	29,799	724	466	991	574	705	468	185	818	4,595	2,192	74,446	63,645	6,049	3,582	469	454
9	Mountain.............	60,950	30,389	14,843	14,078	1,144	902	4,150	4,848	555	1,379	10,807	13,438	56,525	50,562	6,893	3,680	639	784
10	Pacific..............	100,155	53,965	44,404	29,960	4,164	2,092	4,617	3,738	1,765	2,304	18,734	16,385	194,064	126,013	20,035	7,544	60,130	52,369
	NEW ENGLAND:																		
11	Maine...............	10,983	7,167	2,435	1,214	76	26	23	51	525	773	1,624	632	5,589	4,588	114	177	292	195
12	New Hampshire......	9,143	5,891	3,038	1,834	28	34	23	21	311	2,003	6,647	2,722	3,922	2,942	48	35	184	153
13	Vermont.............	4,554	3,621	884	467	18	18	3	4	6	77	236	131	7,704	6,617	1,032	428	68	119
14	Massachusetts.......	274,600	176,490	26,173	16,170	1,893	1,110	409	179	2,958	3,943	28,230	12,416	238,178	130,577	1,341	875	49,215	41,431
15	Rhode Island........	20,429	14,888	581	462	541	587	74	52	283	706	1,622	1,053	70,665	42,804	164	72	15,387	10,393
16	Connecticut.........	150,409	83,552	2,142	1,231	1,751	1,046	117	79	377	748	5,045	1,177	168,740	89,773	1,425	180	2,158	1,430
	MIDDLE ATLANTIC:																		
17	New York...........	1,168,518	848,324	18,158	11,505	58,886	47,103	1,727	1,113	7,662	5,554	28,830	11,277	1,124,433	739,059	16,872	5,548	2,208	1,150
18	New Jersey..........	227,963	146,683	3,524	2,258	5,302	3,237	386	167	396	466	5,848	1,882	344,468	191,849	2,719	717	863	198
19	Pennsylvania........	512,319	387,486	5,114	3,688	13,688	10,151	6,229	1,572	1,921	3,116	16,200	4,850	470,399	298,554	2,924	627	1,097	479
	EAST NORTH CENTRAL:																		
20	Ohio...............	150,074	76,149	12,764	7,301	12,928	4,508	7,749	1,862	2,125	2,164	14,624	2,954	119,501	62,332	1,607	225	374	369
21	Indiana.............	29,526	14,585	402	315	3,562	785	1,856	597	841	2,306	4,235	1,478	12,703	9,140	793	101	46	27
22	Illinois.............	391,415	227,900	4,885	3,182	8,901	5,382	3,885	1,965	991	2,572	21,589	11,178	195,804	116,685	1,448	603	459	937
23	Michigan...........	185,816	60,023	70,365	55,548	7,270	669	4,501	396	784	423	8,178	1,343	55,877	24,753	663	101	114	49
24	Wisconsin...........	81,931	45,407	14,681	9,696	909	550	1,188	433	329	471	4,683	2,990	22,190	13,240	145	70	31	49
	WEST NORTH CENTRAL:																		
25	Minnesota..........	42,526	30,277	61,640	44,463	3,523	2,681	2,255	2,471	164	569	2,794	1,840	14,806	13,007	108	102	21	34
26	Iowa...............	16,465	9,822	164	191	412	461	791	652	72	514	3,341	3,510	9,689	7,560	19	88	34	20
27	Missouri............	44,945	34,262	198	184	2,136	1,919	664	467	375	1,038	3,681	2,951	31,141	21,118	786	416	44	62
28	North Dakota.......	84,132	62,186	3,306	2,610	1,650	1,453	86	270	32	286	440	1,103	338	1,365	17	22	8	10
29	South Dakota.......	35,500	33,013	3,235	3,075	169	72	212	507	40	256	383	242	827	1,603	22	9	9	8
30	Nebraska...........	37,525	24,885	112	125	478	352	330	189	38	281	1,748	3,514	6,725	4,840	68	64	21	32
31	Kansas.............	40,752	38,495	106	63	98	74	163	141	12	308	819	1,471	7,032	5,630	361	359	36	37
	SOUTH ATLANTIC:																		
32	Delaware...........	8,919	5,427	60	9	181	51	2	1	1	11	377	49	8,319	4,529	169	26	21	4
33	Maryland...........	69,306	46,965	252	55	699	294	197	32	29	64	1,288	624	19,720	11,160	332	172	54	68
34	District of Columbia..	11,481	5,733	151	27	140	55	24	14	98	48	1,724	415	7,500	4,553	224	110	38	9
35	Virginia............	12,662	7,605	347	78	258	127	58	15	45	190	2,277	792	5,505	4,069	391	112	102	96
36	West Virginia.......	12,256	7,294	455	164	722	280	958	104	135	489	3,541	517	26,808	21,183	2,129	555	18	6
37	North Carolina......	2,520	1,339	29	38	56	24	29	2	20	120	734	203	998	770	53	23	29	18
38	South Carolina......	2,881	1,447	78	47	31	14	8	1	19	57	770	331	776	548	66	46	14	9
39	Georgia.............	8,676	5,478	68	65	202	128	33	7	54	113	2,026	1,086	1,301	972	202	192	62	33
40	Florida.............	2,934	915	555	137	855	508	60	20	26	753	1,893	977	10,300	7,413	7,762	5,528	337	71
	EAST SOUTH CENTRAL:																		
41	Kentucky...........	6,536	5,617	77	32	253	142	75	93	23	73	544	303	4,180	2,545	120	65	15	10
42	Tennessee..........	5,986	4,241	64	85	149	98	21	23	29	30	704	440	4,867	3,758	79	68	15	10
43	Alabama...........	3,645	2,633	123	75	197	166	65	129	40	159	1,255	759	6,457	4,676	264	242	17	11
44	Mississippi.........	2,109	1,627	139	178	57	50	30	2	2	132	276	140	4,345	3,859	343	370	15	8
	WEST SOUTH CENTRAL:																		
45	Arkansas...........	1,965	1,414	25	30	85	52	33	36	3	58	405	215	2,977	2,652	72	35	14	2
46	Louisiana..........	4,297	3,185	220	186	128	134	147	35	36	262	813	379	46,403	42,911	3,127	2,405	225	238
47	Oklahoma.........	16,501	14,585	127	32	86	35	160	149	21	188	812	634	4,755	4,069	203	80	30	30
48	Texas.............	17,805	10,615	352	218	692	353	365	248	125	310	2,565	964	20,311	14,013	2,557	1,062	200	184
	MOUNTAIN:																		
49	Montana...........	13,013	3,443	7,155	6,623	320	291	1,193	2,170	263	494	1,413	1,934	6,535	8,001	123	70	47	41
50	Idaho..............	3,642	1,512	1,954	954	73	20	167	579	56	130	826	1,869	2,493	2,627	2,046	1,179	69	79
51	Wyoming...........	3,237	1,097	1,669	2,154	86	69	596	336	82	274	1,388	1,937	2,657	2,489	201	133	62	58
52	Colorado...........	36,675	22,425	1,675	1,857	482	454	653	649	51	242	2,078	2,318	28,527	24,190	629	302	71	88
53	New Mexico........	672	386	69	26	13	6	129	170	14	26	328	170	3,471	2,826	399	151	57	16
54	Arizona............	1,856	460	636	696	74	25	642	389	20	49	413	88	2,334	2,189	1,578	916	62	38
55	Utah...............	1,528	880	1,417	1,535	88	27	361	371	64	147	3,667	4,062	6,024	4,228	377	49	25	24
56	Nevada............	327	186	268	233	8	10	409	184	5	17	694	1,060	4,484	4,012	1,540	880	246	420
	PACIFIC:																		
57	Washington........	26,430	17,986	21,053	13,257	473	274	1,074	1,663	1,087	769	4,092	4,316	18,754	16,576	723	521	469	423
58	Oregon............	14,745	8,793	11,398	7,711	372	310	480	1,120	244	574	2,011	3,671	7,550	6,819	888	580	335	327
59	California..........	58,980	27,186	11,953	8,992	3,319	1,508	3,063	955	434	961	12,631	8,398	167,760	102,618	18,424	6,443	59,326	51,619

[1] Except possessions of the United States.

COUNTRY OF ORIGIN.

905

BY DIVISIONS AND STATES: 1920 AND 1910—Continued.

[Figures for 1920 relate to countries as constituted prior to the World War (see text, p. 891).]

| Europe, not specified. | | ASIA. | | | | AMERICA. | | | | | | | | | | | | All other countries. | | Of mixed foreign parentage. | | |
| | | Turkey in Asia. | | All other. | | Canada—French. | | Canada—Other. | | Newfoundland. | | West Indies.[1] | | Mexico. | | Central and South America. | | | | | | |
1920	1910	1920	1910	1920	1910	1920	1910	1920	1910	1920	1910	1920	1910	1920	1910	1920	1910	1920	1910	1920	1910	
10,998	7,576	164,480	78,631	10,735	7,264	848,309	932,238	1,755,519	1,822,377	25,448	8,635	45,496	41,842	725,332	382,002	19,487	13,510	116,458	74,523	1,502,457	1,177,002	1
258	192	41,112	24,377	1,206	833	620,157	609,241	510,069	495,143	16,017	3,887	2,358	2,212	281	197	1,080	1,039	53,357	23,601	158,590	127,973	2
2,073	1,674	48,127	20,982	2,713	2,022	53,726	76,146	234,110	247,729	5,170	2,720	16,600	13,009	5,437	1,153	8,219	4,080	7,787	10,107	477,885	361,972	3
2,963	1,217	28,127	10,170	2,631	1,318	102,655	145,255	490,220	533,884	1,625	746	1,656	1,191	7,966	1,212	1,529	1,255	8,354	9,620	366,070	287,385	4
1,510	894	8,572	5,425	745	671	42,027	61,047	192,348	235,172	419	345	680	787	26,485	11,296	734	719	3,611	5,784	208,475	180,096	5
741	884	9,220	3,987	391	475	2,047	1,963	24,356	17,165	351	150	20,538	21,475	797	338	898	446	1,594	1,657	35,306	23,168	6
494	409	3,490	2,030	129	143	508	1,028	7,271	7,709	69	27	482	324	756	340	254	171	570	678	13,116	11,621	7
1,715	1,451	7,634	3,787	442	321	2,141	3,542	22,803	22,277	176	94	1,544	1,360	410,009	237,893	1,331	650	1,725	1,635	37,068	28,996	8
228	280	3,328	1,729	429	282	10,014	13,509	69,132	73,239	386	222	371	286	146,353	78,029	371	412	3,323	3,496	65,792	56,091	9
1,016	506	14,564	6,144	2,049	1,199	15,034	20,507	205,210	190,059	1,235	438	1,267	1,198	127,248	51,544	5,121	4,132	31,137	17,945	140,149	99,790	10
17	16	1,555	1,037	40	55	86,110	75,507	93,947	90,789	406	189	124	104	12	31	31	25	222	279	6,716	6,101	11
10	2	1,417	1,140	17	15	90,246	81,354	32,642	36,947	336	115	51	52	9	8	40	21	152	140	5,191	4,328	12
6	2	554	272	19	12	39,419	40,519	25,949	27,434	124	63	21	22	10	7	22	21	81	106	3,520	3,235	13
112	109	27,954	15,805	478	414	287,897	295,282	318,502	308,487	14,007	3,007	1,408	1,336	178	106	679	668	50,198	21,202	98,517	80,901	14
20	8	5,352	3,892	95	66	75,058	73,214	10,846	15,345	517	255	236	362	12	13	91	135	6,608	1,175	14,569	12,088	15
93	55	4,280	2,231	551	271	40,827	43,365	22,183	16,141	627	258	520	336	60	32	187	109	1,096	639	30,077	20,720	16
1,015	587	25,233	11,839	1,604	1,244	49,730	69,695	185,474	198,806	3,211	1,066	12,834	9,780	3,134	761	6,437	3,252	4,322	5,561	272,788	204,767	17
287	140	7,652	3,152	534	332	2,004	2,775	19,246	16,661	989	650	1,894	1,527	462	163	862	746	1,357	1,388	75,069	52,982	18
771	947	15,242	5,991	575	446	1,992	3,676	29,390	32,262	970	404	1,872	1,702	1,841	229	920	688	2,108	3,158	130,028	104,223	19
532	281	8,748	2,631	369	260	4,030	7,361	46,450	46,890	329	80	566	278	1,019	159	374	280	1,570	1,905	72,434	53,139	20
256	225	1,837	1,102	257	91	1,763	3,003	12,511	13,547	97	36	89	96	740	88	86	62	568	778	18,815	14,203	21
1,127	406	5,210	3,282	1,250	641	14,322	23,577	74,437	86,092	615	378	570	538	4,592	782	629	556	2,768	3,741	126,458	90,659	22
790	99	10,127	2,081	621	237	62,206	82,909	314,844	337,059	438	134	303	190	1,387	124	285	213	1,453	1,873	84,925	69,997	23
258	206	2,205	1,074	124	89	20,334	28,405	41,972	50,296	146	118	128	89	228	59	155	144	1,995	1,323	63,444	50,297	24
329	152	1,926	959	173	151	26,430	35,207	67,004	75,126	148	73	93	108	383	89	100	139	829	1,814	70,623	56,828	25
317	154	1,180	744	137	124	2,032	4,136	29,109	36,312	54	30	151	140	3,093	553	118	91	691	996	33,089	30,169	26
396	325	2,110	1,507	130	147	1,272	2,954	16,738	20,451	81	67	296	347	3,815	1,578	177	206	883	1,183	32,468	27,483	27
78	44	835	641	44	26	5,774	7,136	33,013	44,468	34	47	6	12	35	11	16	15	219	311	20,212	16,429	28
71	49	646	342	72	62	2,126	3,898	12,948	16,198	17	14	17	47	92	25	37	35	179	316	13,576	12,577	29
147	71	1,231	864	95	78	1,401	2,791	17,153	21,732	63	88	60	59	2,800	318	87	68	370	504	20,133	19,177	30
172	99	644	368	94	83	2,992	4,925	16,263	20,885	22	26	57	68	16,227	8,727	193	165	440	660	18,374	17,433	31
13	16	43	20	6	7	42	124	860	803	9	......	43	39	61	4	6	15	38	85	1,909	1,666	32
145	256	272	109	52	61	339	277	3,639	2,813	98	80	390	315	100	28	209	126	408	443	11,402	7,994	33
68	29	624	223	55	34	467	293	3,747	2,402	44	17	191	179	71	37	170	94	197	180	4,604	3,081	34
166	181	1,608	784	86	97	296	304	3,749	2,676	59	30	140	105	108	23	141	39	236	173	3,791	2,262	35
104	73	2,553	1,015	13	20	137	276	1,949	1,953	5	7	25	13	81	11	31	19	127	102	3,909	2,646	36
22	41	1,097	529	42	26	43	95	1,276	1,106	6	2	71	36	33	14	45	11	85	87	727	416	37
30	41	788	379	14	125	63	71	584	547	9	4	67	42	11	6	32	10	32	39	754	592	38
138	159	1,085	549	43	42	185	194	1,912	1,665	25	3	156	221	88	37	52	42	109	159	2,317	1,698	39
55	88	1,156	379	80	63	495	329	6,640	8,200	96	13	19,449	20,525	244	178	215	90	362	339	5,898	2,803	40
210	67	791	499	41	44	150	307	2,180	2,469	27	10	51	49	172	46	47	24	235	296	6,486	5,597	41
77	116	350	234	22	34	149	315	2,153	2,505	18	14	70	43	245	70	86	31	136	144	2,700	2,546	42
140	130	1,111	574	29	10	138	261	1,967	1,762	12	3	279	181	185	126	90	85	125	121	2,638	2,289	43
67	96	1,238	723	37	55	71	145	991	973	12	......	82	101	154	98	31	31	74	117	1,292	1,189	44
32	140	478	219	23	27	213	427	2,360	2,599	21	16	40	29	366	198	38	25	166	185	2,867	2,414	45
369	428	2,175	1,416	100	69	424	705	2,571	2,462	33	20	1,018	952	3,139	1,641	896	362	277	398	8,338	8,146	46
171	125	1,661	564	83	68	700	1,336	7,685	8,644	33	10	94	84	8,330	3,134	56	75	289	318	6,714	5,293	47
1,143	758	8,620	1,588	236	157	804	1,074	10,187	8,572	89	48	392	295	398,174	232,920	341	188	993	734	19,149	13,143	48
34	51	633	285	61	44	6,041	6,604	25,194	23,057	134	58	40	43	264	95	50	60	401	375	13,989	9,137	49
17	41	148	104	54	35	1,376	2,017	11,036	11,456	110	69	21	15	1,271	170	20	33	602	488	8,523	6,834	50
10	10	244	162	25	13	297	459	3,593	3,386	7	4	28	20	2,025	334	34	13	126	150	3,738	2,949	51
114	118	713	503	135	108	1,404	2,531	17,043	21,541	75	61	163	132	14,533	3,330	93	164	461	669	15,714	14,683	52
15	33	454	215	38	10	163	404	1,664	2,228	8	3	30	19	34,083	21,048	15	17	75	144	1,603	1,361	53
17	6	634	183	54	20	279	410	4,056	3,509	29	6	53	37	91,514	51,102	81	53	268	241	3,510	2,206	54
13	26	447	250	48	31	211	463	4,138	4,599	12	8	19	8	1,311	184	34	19	1,065	1,185	16,633	16,675	55
8	4	55	27	14	21	243	621	2,408	3,463	11	13	17	12	1,352	866	44	53	325	294	2,082	2,256	56
114	47	1,213	533	371	212	7,175	9,378	73,205	74,555	539	131	145	150	507	216	296	287	1,488	1,736	35,380	26,223	57
53	61	505	240	141	133	1,977	3,063	27,359	26,585	112	44	109	84	655	291	109	106	813	1,043	18,849	12,323	58
849	458	12,846	5,371	1,537	854	5,882	8,066	104,646	88,919	584	263	1,013	964	126,080	51,037	4,716	3,739	28,836	15,168	87,920	61,244	59

906

POPULATION.

TABLE 6.—PER CENT DISTRIBUTION OF THE FOREIGN WHITE STOCK,

[Figures relate to countries as constituted prior to the World War (see text, p. 891).]

PER CENT WHICH SPECIFIED COUNTRY OF ORIGIN CONTRIBUTED TO TOTAL FOREIGN WHITE STOCK IN SPECIFIED DIVISION OR STATE.

	DIVISION AND STATE.	Northwestern Europe.												Central and Eastern Europe.		
		England.	Scotland.	Wales.	Ireland.	Norway.	Sweden.	Denmark.	Netherlands.	Belgium.	Luxemburg.	Switzerland.	France.	Germany.	Austria.	Hungary.
1	United States	6.3	2.0	0.6	11.4	2.8	4.0	1.3	1.0	0.3	0.1	0.9	0.9	19.9	8.6	3.1
	GEOGRAPHIC DIVISIONS:															
2	New England	7.2	2.5	0.2	20.5	0.3	3.1	0.4	0.1	0.1	(1)	0.2	0.5	3.6	4.3	0.9
3	Middle Atlantic	5.8	1.8	0.8	14.4	0.5	1.4	0.4	0.6	0.2	(1)	0.5	0.8	15.6	11.7	4.6
4	East North Central	5.6	1.7	0.6	7.2	2.6	4.2	1.1	1.9	0.7	0.2	1.1	0.8	30.5	10.5	4.2
5	West North Central	4.6	1.5	0.5	6.6	11.4	10.5	3.5	1.5	0.3	0.4	1.2	0.7	29.6	6.2	1.2
6	South Atlantic	8.3	2.9	0.7	11.8	0.6	1.2	0.5	0.4	0.3	(1)	0.7	1.2	22.5	6.6	2.8
7	East South Central	8.1	3.0	0.7	15.0	0.4	1.4	0.5	0.5	0.2	(1)	2.7	2.5	35.0	2.7	1.6
8	West South Central	4.6	1.3	0.3	4.8	0.7	1.6	0.6	0.3	0.2	(1)	1.0	2.5	21.3	7.0	0.5
9	Mountain	13.8	3.7	1.5	7.2	4.0	6.6	4.6	1.0	0.3	0.1	1.6	1.0	11.2	4.4	1.4
10	Pacific	9.5	3.3	0.8	9.3	4.3	6.3	2.7	0.8	0.3	0.1	2.2	2.0	14.4	3.0	0.7
	NEW ENGLAND:															
11	Maine	5.0	2.2	0.2	9.0	0.5	1.7	0.9	(1)	(1)	(1)	0.1	0.3	1.1	0.5	0.4
12	New Hampshire	5.2	2.3	0.1	12.9	0.4	1.8	0.2	0.1	0.3	(1)	0.1	0.3	2.1	3.6	0.1
13	Vermont	5.6	4.1	1.2	13.3	0.2	1.9	0.3	0.1	(1)	(1)	0.2	0.4	1.7	2.2	0.5
14	Massachusetts	7.2	2.5	0.1	23.7	0.4	3.0	0.3	0.2	0.1	(1)	0.1	0.4	2.8	3.7	0.2
15	Rhode Island	12.6	3.0	0.1	18.9	0.2	3.2	0.2	0.1	0.3	(1)	0.1	0.6	2.3	3.6	0.1
16	Connecticut	5.9	1.9	0.2	18.3	0.3	4.1	0.7	0.1	0.1	(1)	0.4	0.7	7.9	8.0	3.9
	MIDDLE ATLANTIC:															
17	New York	4.9	1.4	0.3	15.1	0.7	1.5	0.4	0.5	0.1	(1)	0.5	0.8	15.8	9.4	2.4
18	New Jersey	6.6	2.3	0.2	13.6	0.6	1.2	0.7	1.7	0.2	(1)	0.9	0.9	10.6	10.6	5.4
19	Pennsylvania	7.1	2.1	2.0	13.4	0.1	1.4	0.2	0.1	0.3	(1)	0.5	0.7	14.6	16.4	8.1
	EAST NORTH CENTRAL:															
20	Ohio	6.9	1.8	1.6	8.0	0.2	0.9	0.3	0.4	0.2	0.1	1.9	1.1	30.1	13.0	9.6
21	Indiana	6.2	2.2	0.7	8.7	0.3	2.4	0.5	1.2	1.0	0.1	2.0	1.9	43.4	7.1	4.7
22	Illinois	4.9	1.7	0.3	9.4	2.0	7.3	1.1	1.2	0.6	0.3	0.7	0.8	26.8	13.1	3.0
23	Michigan	7.5	2.2	0.2	4.9	0.9	3.2	0.9	5.1	1.0	0.1	0.5	0.6	21.4	6.9	2.8
24	Wisconsin	3.0	0.8	0.5	4.0	9.5	3.6	2.6	1.6	0.9	0.3	1.5	0.3	45.6	7.6	1.8
	WEST NORTH CENTRAL:															
25	Minnesota	2.4	1.0	0.2	4.3	18.2	18.2	2.9	1.0	0.3	0.5	0.6	0.3	23.7	5.7	1.6
26	Iowa	6.6	2.1	0.8	8.9	7.3	7.5	5.5	4.2	0.3	0.8	1.3	0.8	36.8	4.9	0.5
27	Missouri	6.0	1.7	0.5	11.9	0.3	1.9	0.7	0.5	0.4	0.1	2.5	1.7	43.3	5.4	2.3
28	North Dakota	2.1	1.2	0.1	2.6	29.5	6.6	2.9	0.6	0.2	0.2	0.4	0.3	13.3	3.6	1.4
29	South Dakota	4.1	1.3	0.5	4.7	19.0	7.8	5.5	2.9	0.2	0.7	0.8	0.4	24.6	4.5	0.6
30	Nebraska	5.1	1.5	0.5	6.2	1.4	10.5	6.5	0.6	0.2	0.3	1.2	0.5	34.6	13.2	0.4
31	Kansas	8.9	2.8	1.1	8.0	0.8	8.1	1.7	0.7	0.8	0.3	2.3	1.6	28.6	7.1	1.0
	SOUTH ATLANTIC:															
32	Delaware	8.6	2.1	0.4	23.2	0.2	1.3	0.3	0.2	0.1	(1)	0.3	0.9	12.1	9.3	1.0
33	Maryland	5.0	2.1	0.6	10.8	0.3	0.5	0.3	0.3	0.1	(1)	0.4	0.6	35.3	7.5	1.3
34	District of Columbia	10.4	3.2	0.6	22.6	0.8	1.5	0.7	0.4	0.1	(1)	1.0	1.7	18.5	1.8	0.5
35	Virginia	12.7	4.5	0.7	11.3	1.2	1.7	1.0	0.8	0.2	(1)	0.8	1.5	15.5	5.3	0.5
36	West Virginia	7.5	2.4	1.6	7.7	0.1	0.6	0.2	0.2	1.1	(1)	1.4	1.0	14.5	13.0	10.0
37	North Carolina	15.2	7.0	0.5	8.3	0.8	2.0	0.7	1.0	0.2	(1)	1.2	1.9	15.6	2.1	0.7
38	South Carolina	8.8	3.8	0.2	14.0	0.9	1.4	1.0	0.4	0.5	(1)	0.3	1.8	25.4	4.1	0.5
39	Georgia	10.9	4.2	0.6	14.2	0.7	1.7	0.7	0.5	0.3	(1)	0.9	2.3	18.4	2.7	1.3
40	Florida	11.4	3.2	0.4	5.6	1.4	2.8	1.2	0.7	0.2	0.1	0.8	1.7	12.1	1.5	0.7
	EAST SOUTH CENTRAL:															
41	Kentucky	5.6	1.6	0.5	16.7	0.1	0.4	0.2	0.5	0.2	(1)	3.2	2.0	49.6	2.1	1.6
42	Tennessee	10.8	3.4	1.3	16.6	0.4	1.5	0.7	0.5	0.2	(1)	4.0	2.3	20.8	2.4	1.4
43	Alabama	11.9	6.4	1.0	10.0	1.1	3.1	0.9	0.5	0.3	(1)	1.2	3.2	19.1	3.6	2.3
44	Mississippi	8.8	2.7	0.3	12.9	1.0	2.8	1.1	0.4	0.3	0.1	1.1	4.2	17.7	4.5	0.5
	WEST SOUTH CENTRAL:															
45	Arkansas	9.9	3.0	0.7	9.5	0.6	1.9	1.0	0.8	0.4	(1)	3.9	2.9	35.3	6.2	1.0
46	Louisiana	4.4	1.2	0.2	9.1	0.6	0.8	0.5	0.4	0.6	(1)	2.6	10.7	19.8	2.1	0.5
47	Oklahoma	9.2	3.3	1.0	8.4	0.8	2.3	1.3	0.6	0.4	0.1	1.8	2.2	26.4	7.2	0.7
48	Texas	3.5	0.9	0.1	3.0	0.6	1.7	0.5	0.2	0.1	(1)	0.7	1.0	19.8	8.0	0.4
	MOUNTAIN:															
49	Montana	8.8	3.5	1.0	11.0	10.8	6.5	2.9	1.5	0.5	0.2	1.1	0.8	13.1	6.0	2.5
50	Idaho	17.4	4.1	2.3	5.6	5.4	9.9	6.9	0.9	0.2	0.2	3.3	1.0	13.6	2.3	0.6
51	Wyoming	13.5	6.1	1.6	7.3	2.5	7.3	4.1	0.6	0.4	0.1	1.4	1.2	13.3	8.8	1.9
52	Colorado	10.0	3.5	1.5	8.8	1.3	7.6	2.1	0.8	0.3	0.1	1.2	1.2	15.4	6.6	1.8
53	New Mexico	4.9	2.3	0.4	4.0	0.6	1.4	0.5	0.4	0.3	(1)	0.7	1.4	8.3	3.0	1.2
54	Arizona	5.8	1.5	0.4	3.9	0.6	1.5	0.9	0.2	0.1	0.1	0.6	0.8	4.6	1.5	0.7
55	Utah	32.7	5.2	2.9	2.9	2.9	8.5	13.2	2.0	0.1	(1)	2.4	0.5	5.4	1.5	0.5
56	Nevada	12.5	3.4	1.1	11.8	1.2	3.1	4.0	0.3	0.1	(1)	2.6	3.1	10.6	2.7	1.1
	PACIFIC:															
57	Washington	9.2	3.7	1.0	6.5	10.8	11.2	3.1	1.2	0.4	0.1	1.5	1.0	13.6	3.9	0.7
58	Oregon	9.4	4.0	0.7	6.8	5.9	8.1	3.2	0.9	0.6	0.1	3.7	1.2	18.9	3.6	0.8
59	California	9.7	3.0	0.7	10.8	1.6	4.1	2.5	0.6	0.2	0.1	2.2	2.6	13.9	2.6	0.6

[1] Less than one-tenth of 1 per cent.

COUNTRY OF ORIGIN.

907

BY COUNTRY OF ORIGIN, BY DIVISIONS AND STATES: 1920.

[Figures relate to countries as constituted prior to the World War (see text, p. 891).]

PER CENT WHICH SPECIFIED COUNTRY OF ORIGIN CONTRIBUTED TO TOTAL FOREIGN WHITE STOCK IN SPECIFIED DIVISION OR STATE.

Central and Eastern Europe—Continued.					Southern Europe.				Europe, not specified.	Asia.		America.						All other countries.	Of mixed foreign parentage.	
Russia.	Finland.	Rumania.	Bulgaria, Serbia, Montenegro.	Turkey in Europe.	Greece.	Italy.	Spain.	Portugal.		Turkey in Asia.	All other.	Canada French.	Canada Other.	New found-land.	West Indies.	Mexico.	Central and South America.			
10.6	0.8	0.4	0.1	0.1	0.6	9.2	0.2	0.4	[1]	0.5	[1]	2.3	4.8	0.1	0.1	2.0	0.1	0.3	4.1	1
10.4	0.8	0.1	[1]	0.1	1.0	11.0	0.1	1.5	[1]	0.9	[1]	13.7	11.3	0.4	0.1	[1]	[1]	1.3	3.5	2
15.9	0.2	0.6	0.1	0.1	0.4	16.1	0.2	[1]	[1]	0.4	[1]	0.4	1.9	[1]	0.1	[1]	0.1	0.1	4.0	3
9.2	1.1	0.4	0.2	0.1	0.6	4.4	0.1	[1]	[1]	0.3	[1]	1.1	5.4	[1]	[1]	0.1	[1]	0.1	4.0	4
6.4	1.4	0.2	0.1	[1]	0.3	1.5	[1]	[1]	[1]	0.2	[1]	0.9	4.0	[1]	[1]	0.6	[1]	0.1	4.4	5
15.1	0.2	0.4	0.2	[1]	1.7	9.4	1.3	0.1	0.1	1.1	[1]	0.2	2.8	[1]	2.4	0.1	0.1	0.2	4.1	6
6.7	0.1	0.2	0.1	[1]	1.0	7.2	0.3	[1]	0.2	1.3	[1]	0.2	2.6	[1]	0.2	0.3	0.1	0.2	4.8	7
3.5	0.1	0.1	0.1	[1]	0.4	6.4	0.5	[1]	0.1	0.7	[1]	0.2	2.0	[1]	0.1	35.5	0.1	0.1	3.2	8
5.0	1.2	0.1	0.3	[1]	0.9	4.7	0.6	0.1	[1]	0.3	[1]	0.8	5.7	[1]	[1]	12.1	[1]	0.3	5.4	9
4.1	1.8	0.2	0.2	0.1	0.8	7.9	0.8	2.4	[1]	0.6	0.1	0.6	8.3	0.1	0.1	5.2	0.2	1.3	5.7	10
4.1	0.9	[1]	[1]	0.2	0.6	2.1	[1]	0.1	[1]	0.6	[1]	31.9	34.8	0.2	[1]	[1]	[1]	0.1	2.5	11
4.2	1.4	[1]	[1]	0.1	3.1	1.8	[1]	0.1	[1]	0.7	[1]	41.6	15.1	0.2	[1]	[1]	[1]	0.1	2.4	12
3.7	0.7	[1]	[1]	[1]	0.2	6.2	0.8	0.1	[1]	0.4	[1]	31.9	21.0	0.1	[1]	[1]	[1]	0.1	2.9	13
10.7	1.0	0.1	[1]	0.1	1.1	9.3	0.1	1.9	[1]	1.1	[1]	11.2	12.4	0.5	0.1	[1]	[1]	2.0	3.8	14
4.9	0.1	0.1	[1]	0.1	0.4	16.8	[1]	3.7	[1]	1.3	[1]	18.0	4.0	0.1	0.1	[1]	[1]	1.6	3.5	15
16.5	0.2	0.2	[1]	[1]	0.6	18.6	0.2	0.2	[1]	0.5	0.1	4.5	2.4	0.1	0.1	[1]	[1]	0.1	3.3	16
18.0	0.3	0.9	[1]	0.1	0.4	17.3	0.3	[1]	[1]	0.4	[1]	0.8	2.9	[1]	0.2	[1]	0.1	0.1	4.2	17
12.5	0.2	0.3	[1]	[1]	0.3	18.9	0.1	[1]	[1]	0.4	[1]	0.1	1.1	0.1	0.1	[1]	[1]	0.1	4.1	18
13.9	0.1	0.4	0.2	0.1	0.4	12.8	0.1	[1]	[1]	0.4	[1]	0.1	0.8	[1]	0.1	[1]	[1]	0.1	3.5	19
7.9	0.7	0.7	0.4	0.1	0.8	6.3	0.1	[1]	[1]	0.5	[1]	0.2	2.4	[1]	[1]	0.1	[1]	0.1	3.8	20
5.7	0.1	0.7	0.4	0.2	0.8	2.4	0.2	[1]	[1]	0.4	[1]	0.3	2.4	[1]	[1]	0.1	[1]	0.1	3.6	21
12.1	0.2	0.3	0.1	[1]	0.7	6.1	[1]	[1]	[1]	0.2	[1]	0.4	2.3	[1]	[1]	0.1	[1]	0.1	3.9	22
9.6	3.6	0.4	0.2	[1]	0.4	2.9	[1]	[1]	[1]	0.5	[1]	3.2	16.3	[1]	[1]	0.1	[1]	0.1	4.4	23
5.2	0.9	0.1	0.1	[1]	0.3	1.4	[1]	[1]	[1]	0.1	[1]	1.3	2.7	[1]	[1]	[1]	[1]	0.1	4.1	24
2.8	4.0	0.2	0.1	[1]	0.2	1.0	[1]	[1]	[1]	0.1	[1]	1.7	4.4	[1]	[1]	[1]	[1]	0.1	4.6	25
1.9	[1]	[1]	0.1	[1]	0.4	1.1	[1]	[1]	[1]	0.1	[1]	0.2	3.4	[1]	[1]	0.4	[1]	0.1	3.9	26
8.5	[1]	0.3	0.1	0.1	0.5	4.5	0.1	[1]	0.1	0.3	[1]	0.2	2.4	[1]	[1]	0.6	[1]	0.1	4.7	27
19.5	0.8	0.4	[1]	[1]	0.1	0.1	[1]	[1]	[1]	0.2	[1]	1.8	7.6	[1]	[1]	[1]	[1]	0.1	4.7	28
11.4	1.0	0.1	0.1	[1]	0.1	0.3	[1]	[1]	[1]	0.2	[1]	0.7	4.2	[1]	[1]	[1]	[1]	0.1	4.4	29
7.2	[1]	0.1	0.1	[1]	0.3	1.3	[1]	[1]	[1]	0.2	[1]	0.3	3.3	[1]	[1]	0.6	[1]	0.1	3.9	30
10.2	[1]	[1]	[1]	[1]	0.2	1.8	0.1	[1]	[1]	0.2	[1]	0.7	4.1	[1]	[1]	4.1	[1]	0.1	4.6	31
16.9	0.1	0.3	[1]	[1]	0.7	15.8	0.3	[1]	[1]	0.1	[1]	0.1	1.6	[1]	0.1	0.1	[1]	0.1	3.6	32
22.2	0.1	0.2	0.1	[1]	0.4	6.3	0.1	[1]	[1]	0.1	[1]	0.1	1.2	[1]	0.1	[1]	0.1	0.1	3.7	33
13.1	0.2	0.2	[1]	0.1	2.0	8.6	0.3	[1]	0.1	0.7	0.1	0.5	4.3	0.1	0.2	0.1	0.2	0.2	5.3	34
15.2	0.4	0.3	0.1	0.1	2.7	6.6	0.5	0.2	0.2	1.9	0.1	0.4	4.5	0.1	0.2	0.1	0.2	0.3	4.5	35
8.5	0.3	0.5	0.7	0.1	2.5	18.6	1.5	[1]	0.1	1.8	[1]	0.1	1.3	[1]	[1]	0.1	[1]	0.1	2.7	36
13.6	0.2	0.3	0.2	0.1	4.0	5.4	0.3	0.2	0.1	5.9	0.2	0.2	6.9	[1]	0.4	0.2	0.2	0.5	3.9	37
15.1	0.4	0.2	[1]	0.1	4.0	4.1	0.3	0.1	0.2	4.1	0.1	0.3	3.1	[1]	0.4	0.1	0.2	0.2	3.9	38
18.7	0.1	0.4	0.1	0.1	4.4	3.0	0.6	0.1	0.3	2.3	0.1	0.4	4.1	0.1	0.3	0.2	0.1	0.2	5.0	39
2.8	0.5	0.8	0.1	[1]	1.8	9.7	7.3	0.3	0.1	1.1	0.1	0.5	6.3	0.1	18.4	0.2	0.2	0.3	5.6	40
4.6	0.1	0.2	0.1	[1]	0.4	3.0	0.1	[1]	0.1	0.6	[1]	0.1	1.5	[1]	[1]	0.1	[1]	0.2	4.6	41
11.2	0.1	0.3	[1]	0.1	1.3	9.1	0.1	[1]	0.1	0.6	[1]	0.3	4.0	[1]	0.1	0.5	0.2	0.3	5.1	42
6.9	0.2	0.4	0.1	0.1	2.4	12.2	0.5	[1]	0.3	2.1	0.1	0.3	3.7	[1]	0.5	0.3	0.2	0.2	5.0	43
7.8	0.5	0.2	0.1	[1]	1.0	16.0	1.3	0.1	0.2	4.6	0.1	0.3	3.6	[1]	0.3	0.6	0.1	0.3	4.8	44
3.7	[1]	0.2	0.1	[1]	0.8	5.6	0.1	[1]	0.1	0.9	[1]	0.4	4.4	[1]	0.1	0.7	0.1	0.3	5.4	45
2.8	0.1	0.1	0.1	[1]	0.5	30.0	2.0	0.1	0.2	1.4	0.1	0.3	1.7	[1]	0.7	2.0	0.6	0.3	5.4	46
11.6	0.1	0.1	0.1	[1]	0.6	3.3	0.2	[1]	0.1	1.2	0.1	0.5	5.4	[1]	0.1	5.9	[1]	0.2	4.7	47
2.2	[1]	0.1	[1]	[1]	0.3	2.5	0.3	[1]	0.1	0.4	[1]	0.1	1.8	[1]	[1]	49.4	[1]	0.1	2.4	48
5.0	2.8	0.1	0.5	0.1	0.5	2.5	[1]	[1]	[1]	0.2	[1]	2.3	9.7	0.1	[1]	0.1	[1]	0.2	5.4	49
2.8	1.5	0.1	0.1	[1]	0.6	1.9	1.6	0.1	[1]	0.1	[1]	1.0	8.4	0.1	[1]	1.0	[1]	0.5	6.5	50
4.8	2.5	0.1	0.9	0.1	2.1	4.0	0.3	0.1	[1]	0.4	[1]	0.4	5.3	[1]	[1]	3.0	0.1	0.2	5.6	51
11.4	0.5	0.2	0.2	[1]	0.6	8.9	0.2	[1]	[1]	0.2	[1]	0.4	5.3	[1]	0.1	4.5	[1]	0.1	4.9	52
1.1	0.1	[1]	0.2	[1]	0.5	5.7	0.7	0.1	[1]	0.7	0.1	0.3	2.7	[1]	[1]	55.5	[1]	0.1	2.6	53
1.3	0.5	0.1	0.5	[1]	0.3	1.7	1.1	[1]	[1]	0.5	[1]	0.2	2.9	[1]	[1]	65.2	0.1	0.2	2.5	54
0.8	0.7	[1]	0.2	[1]	1.9	3.1	0.2	[1]	[1]	0.2	[1]	0.1	2.1	[1]	[1]	0.7	[1]	0.5	8.5	55
1.0	0.8	[1]	1.2	[1]	2.0	13.0	4.5	0.7	[1]	0.2	[1]	0.7	7.0	[1]	[1]	3.9	0.3	0.9	6.0	56
4.3	3.5	0.1	0.2	0.2	0.7	3.1	0.1	0.1	[1]	0.2	0.1	1.2	12.0	0.1	[1]	0.1	[1]	0.2	5.8	57
5.4	4.2	0.1	0.2	0.1	0.7	2.8	0.3	0.1	[1]	0.2	0.1	0.7	10.1	[1]	[1]	0.2	[1]	0.3	6.2	58
3.7	0.8	0.2	0.2	[1]	0.8	10.6	1.2	3.7	0.1	0.8	0.1	0.4	6.6	[1]	0.1	7.9	0.3	1.8	5.5	59

908

POPULATION.

TABLE 7.—PER CENT DISTRIBUTION OF THE FOREIGN WHITE STOCK

[Figures relate to countries as constituted prior to the World War (see text, p. 891).]

	DIVISION AND STATE.	Total foreign white stock: 1920	NORTHWESTERN EUROPE.												CENTRAL AND EASTERN EUROPE.		
			England.	Scotland.	Wales.	Ireland.	Norway.	Sweden.	Denmark.	Netherlands.	Belgium.	Luxemburg.	Switzerland.	France.	Germany.	Austria.	Hungary.
1	United States.......	100.0	100.0	100.0	100.0	100.0	100.0	100.0	100.0	100.0	100.0	100.0	100.0	100.0	100.0	100.0	100.0
	GEOGRAPHIC DIVISIONS:																
2	New England...........	12.4	14.0	15.2	3.2	22.4	1.5	9.5	3.7	1.7	5.2	0.5	2.3	6.6	2.2	6.2	3.8
3	Middle Atlantic.........	33.0	30.3	29.4	41.5	41.7	6.0	11.7	9.5	18.7	17.5	5.0	20.0	28.5	25.8	45.1	49.8
4	East North Central......	25.1	22.3	21.5	24.0	15.9	23.0	26.3	22.0	48.5	50.0	39.1	30.5	21.9	38.4	30.0	35.0
5	West North Central.....	13.0	9.5	10.0	10.4	7.6	53.0	34.1	35.7	19.9	13.4	45.8	17.3	10.3	19.4	9.4	5.2
6	South Atlantic.........	2.4	3.1	3.4	2.7	2.5	0.5	0.7	1.0	0.9	2.2	0.5	2.0	3.1	2.7	1.8	2.2
7	East South Central.....	0.8	1.0	1.1	0.9	1.0	0.1	0.3	0.3	0.4	0.4	0.2	2.3	2.1	1.3	0.2	0.4
8	West South Central.....	3.2	2.3	2.1	1.4	1.3	0.7	1.3	1.5	1.0	2.3	1.0	3.5	8.8	3.4	2.6	0.5
9	Mountain.............	3.3	7.2	6.1	7.9	2.1	4.7	5.5	11.8	3.5	2.5	2.7	5.8	3.7	1.9	1.7	1.6
10	Pacific...............	6.8	10.2	11.2	8.0	5.5	10.4	10.7	14.5	5.5	6.4	5.2	16.3	15.0	4.9	2.4	1.5
	NEW ENGLAND:																
11	Maine...............	0.7	0.6	0.8	0.2	0.6	0.1	0.3	0.5	(1)	0.1	(1)	(1)	0.2	(1)	(1)	0.1
12	New Hampshire........	0.6	0.5	0.7	0.1	0.7	0.1	0.3	0.1	0.1	0.5	(1)	0.1	0.2	0.1	0.2	(1)
13	Vermont.............	0.3	0.3	0.7	0.6	0.4	(1)	0.2	0.1	(1)	(1)	(1)	0.1	0.2	(1)	0.1	0.1
14	Massachusetts..........	7.1	8.0	9.0	1.4	14.8	0.9	5.2	1.5	1.2	2.8	0.2	0.9	3.4	1.0	3.0	0.4
15	Rhode Island..........	1.2	2.3	1.7	0.2	1.9	0.1	0.9	0.1	0.1	1.2	0.1	0.1	0.8	0.1	0.5	0.1
16	Connecticut...........	2.5	2.3	2.4	0.7	4.0	0.3	2.6	1.3	0.3	0.6	0.2	1.2	1.8	1.0	2.3	3.2
	MIDDLE ATLANTIC:																
17	New York.............	17.9	13.7	12.9	8.6	23.8	4.5	6.8	5.5	9.1	6.4	2.8	9.4	15.8	14.2	19.6	14.1
18	New Jersey...........	5.0	5.2	5.8	1.7	6.0	1.0	1.5	2.6	8.5	3.4	0.8	5.0	4.9	4.2	6.2	8.8
19	Pennsylvania..........	10.1	11.4	10.8	31.2	11.9	0.5	3.4	1.4	1.1	7.8	1.5	5.6	7.8	7.4	19.3	26.9
	EAST NORTH CENTRAL:																
20	Ohio................	5.2	5.7	4.8	12.8	3.7	0.3	1.1	1.2	2.2	3.2	2.7	10.7	6.1	7.9	7.9	16.5
21	Indiana..............	1.4	1.4	1.6	1.6	1.1	0.2	0.9	0.6	1.8	4.1	0.9	3.2	3.0	3.1	1.2	2.2
22	Illinois..............	8.9	6.9	7.6	4.7	7.4	6.5	16.1	7.9	10.4	16.1	21.1	6.9	7.6	11.9	13.5	8.8
23	Michigan.............	5.3	6.3	5.8	1.6	2.3	1.7	4.2	3.8	27.2	15.1	3.1	2.7	3.6	5.7	4.2	4.8
24	Wisconsin............	4.3	2.0	1.7	3.3	1.5	14.4	3.9	8.6	6.8	11.5	11.3	7.0	1.6	9.8	3.8	2.6
	WEST NORTH CENTRAL:																
25	Minnesota............	4.2	1.6	2.0	1.6	1.6	27.5	19.2	9.5	4.1	4.0	16.5	2.9	1.5	5.0	2.8	2.2
26	Iowa................	2.4	2.5	2.4	3.1	1.8	6.1	4.4	10.1	9.8	2.4	16.1	3.3	1.9	4.3	1.3	0.4
27	Missouri.............	1.9	1.8	1.6	1.6	2.0	0.2	0.9	1.0	1.0	2.1	1.0	5.2	3.5	4.1	1.2	1.4
28	North Dakota.........	1.2	0.4	0.7	0.3	0.3	12.5	2.0	2.7	0.8	0.7	1.9	0.6	0.3	0.8	0.5	0.5
29	South Dakota.........	0.9	0.5	0.5	0.7	0.4	5.8	1.7	3.6	2.5	0.6	4.7	0.8	0.3	1.1	0.4	0.2
30	Nebraska............	1.4	1.1	1.1	1.1	0.8	0.7	3.8	7.3	0.9	0.9	3.1	1.9	0.8	2.5	2.2	0.2
31	Kansas..............	1.1	1.5	1.5	2.0	0.8	0.3	2.2	1.5	0.7	2.7	2.7	2.8	1.9	1.6	0.9	0.4
	SOUTH ATLANTIC:																
32	Delaware............	0.1	0.2	0.2	0.1	0.3	(1)	(1)	(1)	(1)	(1)	(1)	(1)	0.1	0.1	0.2	(1)
33	Maryland............	0.9	0.7	0.9	0.8	0.8	0.1	0.1	0.2	0.2	0.2	0.1	0.4	0.6	1.5	0.7	0.4
34	District of Columbia.....	0.2	0.4	0.4	0.2	0.5	0.1	0.1	0.1	0.1	0.1	0.1	0.3	0.4	0.2	0.1	(1)
35	Virginia..............	0.2	0.5	0.5	0.2	0.2	0.1	0.1	0.2	0.2	0.2	0.1	0.2	0.4	0.2	0.1	0.3
36	West Virginia.........	0.4	0.5	0.5	1.0	0.3	(1)	0.1	0.1	0.1	1.3	(1)	0.6	0.5	0.3	0.6	1.3
37	North Carolina........	0.1	0.1	0.2	(1)	(1)	(1)	(1)	(1)	0.1	(1)	(1)	0.1	0.1	(1)	(1)	(1)
38	South Carolina........	0.1	0.1	0.1	(1)	0.1	(1)	(1)	(1)	(1)	0.1	(1)	(1)	0.1	0.1	(1)	(1)
39	Georgia..............	0.1	0.2	0.3	0.1	0.2	(1)	0.1	0.1	0.1	0.1	(1)	0.1	0.3	0.1	(1)	0.1
40	Florida..............	0.3	0.5	0.5	0.2	0.1	0.1	0.2	0.3	0.2	0.2	0.1	0.3	0.5	0.2	0.1	0.1
	EAST SOUTH CENTRAL:																
41	Kentucky.............	0.4	0.3	0.3	0.3	0.6	(1)	(1)	0.1	0.2	0.2	0.1	1.4	0.9	1.0	0.1	0.2
42	Tennessee............	0.1	0.2	0.2	0.3	0.2	(1)	0.1	0.1	0.1	0.1	(1)	0.6	0.4	0.2	(1)	0.1
43	Alabama.............	0.1	0.3	0.5	0.2	0.1	0.1	0.1	0.1	0.1	0.1	(1)	0.2	0.5	0.1	0.1	0.1
44	Mississippi...........	0.1	0.1	0.1	(1)	0.1	(1)	0.1	0.1	(1)	0.1	(1)	0.1	0.3	0.1	(1)	(1)
	WEST SOUTH CENTRAL:																
45	Arkansas.............	0.1	0.2	0.2	0.2	0.1	(1)	0.1	0.1	0.1	0.2	(1)	0.6	0.5	0.3	0.1	(1)
46	Louisiana............	0.4	0.3	0.2	0.1	0.3	0.1	0.1	0.2	0.2	0.8	(1)	0.4	5.0	0.4	0.1	0.1
47	Oklahoma............	0.4	0.6	0.6	0.6	0.3	0.1	0.2	0.4	0.2	0.5	0.5	0.8	1.0	0.5	0.3	0.1
48	Texas...............	2.2	1.2	1.0	0.5	0.6	0.5	0.9	0.9	0.4	0.8	0.4	1.7	2.4	2.2	2.0	0.3
	MOUNTAIN:																
49	Montana.............	0.7	1.0	1.3	1.1	0.7	2.7	1.2	1.6	1.1	1.0	1.1	0.9	0.9	0.5	0.5	0.6
50	Idaho...............	0.4	1.0	0.7	1.3	0.2	0.7	0.9	2.0	0.3	0.2	0.5	1.3	0.4	0.2	0.1	0.1
51	Wyoming............	0.2	0.4	0.6	0.5	0.1	0.2	0.3	0.6	0.1	0.2	0.1	0.3	0.2	0.1	0.2	0.1
52	Colorado.............	0.9	1.4	1.5	2.0	0.7	0.4	1.7	1.5	0.7	0.7	0.1	1.2	1.2	0.7	0.7	0.5
53	New Mexico..........	0.2	0.1	0.2	0.1	0.1	(1)	0.1	0.1	0.1	0.1	0.1	0.1	0.1	0.1	0.1	0.1
54	Arizona..............	0.4	0.4	0.3	0.3	0.1	0.1	0.1	0.3	0.1	0.1	0.1	0.2	0.3	0.1	0.1	0.1
55	Utah................	0.5	2.8	1.4	2.5	0.1	0.6	1.2	5.6	1.1	0.1	0.1	1.4	0.3	0.1	0.1	0.1
56	Nevada..............	0.1	0.2	0.2	0.2	0.1	(1)	0.1	0.3	(1)	(1)	(1)	0.3	0.3	0.1	(1)	(1)
	PACIFIC:																
57	Washington...........	1.7	2.4	3.1	2.7	1.0	6.4	4.7	4.0	2.1	2.1	1.9	2.7	1.8	1.1	0.8	0.4
58	Oregon..............	0.7	1.1	1.5	0.9	0.4	1.6	1.5	1.9	0.7	1.2	0.9	3.0	1.0	0.7	0.3	0.2
59	California............	4.4	6.7	6.6	4.5	4.1	2.4	4.5	8.6	2.7	3.0	2.4	10.6	12.2	3.0	1.3	0.9

[1] Less than one-tenth of 1 per cent.

COUNTRY OF ORIGIN.

909

HAVING SPECIFIED COUNTRIES OF ORIGIN, BY DIVISIONS AND STATES: 1920.

[Figures relate to countries as constituted prior to the World War (see text, p. 891).]

| | | CENTRAL AND EASTERN EUROPE—con. | | | | SOUTHERN EUROPE. | | | | Europe, not specified. | ASIA. | | AMERICA. | | | | | | All other countries. | Of mixed foreign parentage. | |
Russia.	Finland.	Rumania.	Bulgaria, Serbia, and Montenegro.	Turkey in Europe.	Greece.	Italy.	Spain.	Portugal.		Turkey in Asia.	All other.	Canada. French.	Canada. Other.	Newfoundland.	West Indies.	Mexico.	Central and South America.			
100.0	100.0	100.0	100.0	100.0	100.0	100.0	100.0	100.0	100.0	100.0	100.0	100.0	100.0	100.0	100.0	100.0	100.0	100.0	100.0	1
12.1	11.9	3.2	1.5	19.1	20.4	14.8	5.3	49.9	2.3	25.0	11.2	73.1	29.1	62.9	5.2	(1)	5.3	50.1	10.6	2
49.3	9.0	58.0	19.1	42.9	24.0	58.1	28.9	3.1	18.8	29.3	25.3	6.3	13.3	20.3	36.5	0.7	42.2	6.7	31.8	3
21.7	34.8	25.0	43.9	21.8	25.1	12.2	6.0	0.8	26.9	17.1	24.5	12.1	27.9	6.4	3.6	1.1	7.8	7.2	24.4	4
7.8	23.2	6.3	10.3	3.1	6.2	2.1	1.0	0.1	13.7	5.2	6.9	5.0	11.0	1.6	1.5	3.7	3.8	3.1	13.9	5
3.4	0.7	2.3	3.1	1.8	6.9	2.4	14.6	0.6	6.7	5.6	3.6	0.2	1.4	1.4	45.1	0.1	4.6	1.4	2.3	6
0.5	0.1	0.5	0.4	0.5	1.3	0.6	1.0	(1)	4.5	2.1	1.2	0.1	0.4	0.3	1.1	0.1	1.3	0.5	0.9	7
1.0	0.2	0.7	1.6	0.8	2.2	2.2	7.8	0.3	15.6	4.8	4.1	0.3	1.3	0.7	3.4	56.5	6.8	1.5	2.5	8
1.6	5.0	0.9	9.5	2.4	5.1	1.7	8.8	0.5	2.1	2.0	4.0	1.2	3.9	1.5	0.8	20.2	1.9	2.9	4.4	9
2.6	15.0	3.1	10.6	7.6	8.8	5.8	25.7	44.6	9.2	8.8	19.1	1.8	11.7	4.9	2.8	17.5	26.3	26.7	9.3	10
0.3	0.8	0.1	0.1	2.3	0.8	0.2	0.1	0.2	0.2	0.9	0.4	10.2	5.4	1.6	0.3	(1)	0.2	0.2	0.4	11
0.2	1.0	(1)	0.1	1.3	3.1	0.1	0.1	0.1	0.1	0.9	0.2	10.6	1.9	1.3	0.1	(1)	0.2	0.1	0.3	12
0.1	0.3	(1)	(1)	(1)	0.1	0.2	1.3	0.1	0.1	0.3	0.2	4.6	1.5	0.5	(1)	(1)	0.1	0.1	0.2	13
7.1	8.8	1.4	0.9	12.7	13.3	7.1	1.7	36.5	1.0	17.0	4.5	33.9	18.1	55.0	3.1	(1)	3.5	43.1	6.6	14
0.5	0.2	0.4	0.2	1.2	0.8	2.1	0.2	11.4	0.2	3.8	0.9	8.9	1.0	2.0	0.5	(1)	0.5	5.7	1.0	15
3.9	0.7	1.3	0.3	1.6	2.4	5.1	1.8	1.6	0.8	2.6	5.1	4.8	1.3	2.5	1.1	(1)	0.9	0.9	2.0	16
30.2	6.1	43.8	4.0	32.9	13.6	33.7	21.6	1.7	9.2	15.3	14.9	5.9	10.6	12.6	28.2	0.4	33.0	3.7	18.2	17
5.9	1.2	3.9	0.9	1.7	2.8	10.3	3.5	0.6	2.6	4.6	5.0	0.2	1.1	3.9	4.2	0.1	4.4	1.2	5.0	18
13.2	1.7	10.2	14.2	8.3	7.6	14.1	3.8	0.8	7.0	9.3	5.4	0.2	1.7	3.8	4.1	0.8	4.7	1.8	8.7	19
3.9	4.3	9.6	17.7	9.1	6.9	3.6	2.1	0.3	4.8	5.3	3.4	0.5	2.6	1.3	1.2	0.1	1.9	1.3	4.8	20
0.8	0.1	2.7	4.2	3.6	2.0	0.4	1.0	(1)	2.3	1.1	2.4	0.2	0.7	0.4	0.2	0.1	0.4	0.5	1.3	21
10.1	1.6	6.6	8.9	4.3	10.2	5.9	1.9	0.3	10.2	3.2	11.7	1.7	4.2	2.4	1.3	0.6	3.2	2.4	8.4	22
4.8	23.7	5.4	10.3	3.4	3.9	1.7	0.9	0.1	7.2	6.2	5.8	7.3	17.9	1.7	0.7	0.2	1.5	1.2	5.7	23
2.1	5.0	0.7	2.7	1.4	2.2	0.7	0.2	(1)	2.3	1.3	1.1	2.4	2.4	0.6	0.3	(1)	0.8	1.7	4.2	24
1.1	20.8	2.6	5.2	0.7	1.3	0.4	0.1	(1)	3.0	1.2	1.6	3.1	3.8	0.6	0.2	(1)	0.5	0.7	4.7	25
0.4	0.1	0.3	1.8	0.3	1.6	0.3	0.1	(1)	2.9	0.7	1.3	0.2	1.7	0.2	0.3	0.4	0.6	0.6	2.2	26
1.2	0.1	1.6	1.5	1.6	1.7	0.9	1.0	(1)	3.6	1.3	1.2	0.1	1.0	0.3	0.7	0.5	0.9	0.8	2.2	27
2.2	1.1	1.2	0.2	0.1	0.2	(1)	(1)	(1)	0.7	0.5	0.4	0.7	1.9	0.1	(1)	(1)	0.1	0.2	1.3	28
0.9	1.1	0.1	0.5	0.2	0.2	(1)	(1)	(1)	0.6	0.4	0.7	0.3	0.7	0.1	(1)	(1)	0.2	0.2	0.9	29
1.0	(1)	0.4	0.8	0.2	0.8	0.2	0.1	(1)	1.3	0.7	0.9	0.2	1.0	0.2	0.1	0.4	0.4	0.3	1.3	30
1.1	(1)	0.1	0.4	(1)	0.4	0.2	0.5	(1)	1.6	0.4	0.9	0.4	0.9	0.1	0.1	2.2	1.0	0.4	1.2	31
0.2	(1)	0.1	(1)	(1)	0.2	0.2	0.2	(1)	0.1	(1)	0.1	(1)	(1)	(1)	0.1	(1)	(1)	(1)	0.1	32
1.8	0.1	0.5	0.5	0.1	0.6	0.6	0.4	(1)	1.3	0.2	0.5	(1)	0.2	0.4	0.9	(1)	1.1	0.4	0.8	33
0.3	0.1	0.1	0.1	0.4	0.8	0.2	0.3	(1)	0.6	0.4	0.5	0.1	0.2	0.2	0.4	(1)	0.9	0.3	0.3	34
0.3	0.1	0.2	0.1	0.2	1.1	0.2	0.5	0.1	1.5	1.0	0.8	(1)	0.2	0.2	0.3	(1)	0.7	0.2	0.3	35
0.3	0.2	0.5	2.2	0.6	1.7	0.8	2.7	(1)	0.9	1.6	0.1	(1)	0.1	(1)	0.1	(1)	0.2	0.1	0.3	36
0.1	(1)	(1)	(1)	0.1	0.3	(1)	0.1	(1)	0.2	0.7	0.4	(1)	0.1	(1)	0.1	(1)	0.2	0.1	(1)	37
0.1	(1)	(1)	(1)	0.1	0.4	(1)	0.1	(1)	0.3	0.5	0.1	(1)	(1)	(1)	0.1	(1)	0.2	(1)	0.1	38
0.2	(1)	0.2	0.1	0.2	1.0	(1)	0.3	(1)	1.3	0.7	0.4	(1)	0.1	0.1	0.3	(1)	0.3	0.1	0.2	39
0.1	0.2	0.6	0.1	0.1	0.9	0.3	10.0	0.3	0.5	0.7	0.7	0.1	0.4	0.4	42.8	(1)	1.1	0.3	0.4	40
0.2	(1)	0.2	0.2	0.1	0.3	0.1	0.2	(1)	1.9	0.5	0.4	(1)	0.1	0.1	0.1	(1)	0.2	0.2	0.4	41
0.2	(1)	0.1	(1)	0.2	0.8	0.1	0.1	(1)	0.7	0.2	0.2	(1)	0.1	0.1	0.2	(1)	0.4	0.1	0.2	42
0.1	(1)	0.1	0.1	0.2	0.6	0.2	0.3	(1)	1.3	0.7	0.3	(1)	0.1	(1)	0.6	(1)	0.5	0.1	0.2	43
0.1	(1)	(1)	0.1	(1)	0.1	0.1	0.4	(1)	0.6	0.8	0.3	(1)	0.1	(1)	0.2	(1)	0.2	0.1	0.1	44
0.1	(1)	0.1	0.1	(1)	0.2	0.1	0.1	(1)	0.3	0.3	0.2	(1)	0.1	0.1	0.1	0.1	0.2	0.1	0.2	45
0.1	0.1	0.1	0.3	0.2	0.4	1.4	4.0	0.2	3.4	1.3	0.9	(1)	0.1	0.1	2.2	0.4	4.6	0.2	0.6	46
0.4	(1)	0.1	0.4	0.1	0.4	0.1	0.4	(1)	1.6	1.0	0.8	0.1	0.4	0.1	0.2	1.1	0.3	0.2	0.4	47
0.5	0.1	0.5	0.8	0.5	1.2	0.6	3.3	0.1	10.4	2.2	2.2	0.1	0.6	0.3	0.9	54.9	1.7	0.9	1.3	48
0.3	2.4	0.2	2.7	1.1	0.7	0.2	0.2	(1)	0.3	0.4	0.6	0.7	1.4	0.5	0.1	(1)	0.3	0.8	0.9	49
0.1	0.7	0.1	0.4	0.2	0.4	0.1	2.6	0.1	0.2	0.1	0.5	0.2	0.6	0.4	(1)	0.2	0.1	0.5	0.6	50
0.1	0.6	0.1	1.4	0.4	0.7	0.1	0.3	(1)	0.1	0.1	0.2	(1)	0.2	(1)	0.1	0.3	0.2	0.1	0.2	51
0.9	0.6	0.4	1.5	0.2	1.0	0.9	0.8	0.1	1.0	0.4	1.3	0.2	1.0	0.3	0.4	2.0	0.5	0.4	1.0	52
(1)	(1)	(1)	0.3	0.1	0.2	0.1	0.5	(1)	0.1	0.3	0.4	(1)	0.1	(1)	0.1	4.7	0.1	0.1	0.1	53
(1)	0.2	(1)	1.5	0.1	0.2	0.1	2.0	(1)	0.2	0.4	0.5	(1)	0.2	0.1	0.1	12.6	0.4	0.2	0.2	54
(1)	0.5	0.1	0.8	0.3	1.7	0.2	0.5	(1)	0.1	0.3	0.4	(1)	0.2	(1)	(1)	0.2	0.2	0.9	1.1	55
(1)	0.1	(1)	0.9	(1)	0.3	0.1	2.0	0.2	0.1	(1)	0.1	(1)	0.1	(1)	(1)	0.2	0.2	0.8	0.1	56
0.7	7.1	0.4	2.5	4.7	1.9	0.6	0.9	0.3	1.0	0.7	3.5	0.8	4.2	2.1	0.3	0.1	1.5	1.3	2.4	57
0.4	3.8	0.3	1.1	1.0	0.9	0.2	1.1	0.2	0.5	0.3	1.3	0.2	1.6	0.4	0.2	0.1	0.6	0.7	1.1	58
1.5	4.0	2.5	7.0	1.9	5.9	5.0	23.6	44.0	7.7	7.8	14.3	0.7	6.0	2.3	2.2	17.4	24.2	24.8	5.9	59

CHAPTER X

MOTHER TONGUE OF THE FOREIGN WHITE STOCK

CHAPTER X.—MOTHER TONGUE OF THE FOREIGN WHITE STOCK.

INTRODUCTION.

The inquiry as to mother tongue of the foreign white stock was first made at the census of 1910. The statistics here presented relate to the population of continental United States, the states, and those cities having 25,000 inhabitants or more.

Although information as to "mother tongue"— that is, the language of customary speech in the homes of the immigrants prior to immigration—was secured for all persons of foreign birth or parentage, it has been tabulated only for white persons, partly because statistics as to mother tongue for nonwhites are of little significance and partly in order to secure exact comparability with the statistics as to country of origin of the foreign white stock (Chapter IX). The foreign white stock comprises the aggregate white population which is foreign either by birth or by parentage. It embraces three classes, namely, foreign-born whites, native whites both of whose parents were foreign born, and native whites having one foreign and one native parent. The foreign white stock as defined by the census thus includes only immigrants and the native children of immigrants, so that the statistics do not bring out completely the relative importance of the several ethnic stocks in the total population of the United States. The entire English and Celtic foreign white stock, for instance, would include all living descendants of English, Irish, Scotch, and Welsh immigrants—their grandchildren, great-grandchildren, and still more remote generations—as well as the first and second generations.

While this report and that on country of origin treat of the same aggregate population—namely, 36,398,958 white persons reported in 1920 as being either foreign born or of foreign or mixed parentage— they treat of essentially different characteristics. In the report on country of origin the classification is with reference to geographic origin, while the present report deals with native language or mother tongue. Since, however, the mother tongue is to a considerable degree determined by geographic origin, the two classifications are closely related.

Mother tongue in relation to ethnic stock.—In most cases the returns for mother tongue may be taken as indicative of ethnic stock. The principal exception to this rule appears in the case of persons reported under the head English and Celtic, which group includes four ethnically distinct peoples, namely, the English, the Irish, the Scotch, and the Welsh. In the case of these peoples country-of-origin statistics throw much more light on ethnic composition than do mother-tongue statistics. As a matter of fact, some persons were returned by the enumerators as Irish, Scotch, or Welsh in mother tongue, but it was evident that in very many such cases the returns indicated nationality rather than mother tongue and would therefore, if published, greatly exaggerate the number of persons using these languages in customary speech, while at the same time they would come far short of indicating the total number of persons of Irish, Scotch, or Welsh extraction.

While English and Celtic as a mother tongue thus covers more than one group of peoples, the opposite is true of Yiddish, which is the mother tongue reported for only a part of the Hebrews, the others being returned as speaking Polish, Russian, German, etc. In particular, it is probable that a large proportion of the persons reported in 1920 as Russian in mother tongue were in reality Hebrews; and it is possible also that the very great increase between 1910 and 1920 in the number of persons thus reported is due in some measure to the return of certain persons in 1910 as Yiddish and in 1920 as Russian in mother tongue. (See Table 1.)

Statistics as to mother tongue are of greatest significance with reference to the foreign white stock originating in seven countries, Austria, Hungary, Russia, Czechoslovakia, Jugo-Slavia, Rumania, and Canada, as at present constituted, or in six countries, Germany, Austria, Hungary, Russia, Rumania, and Canada, as constituted in 1910. Immigrants from Canada include both English-speaking and French-speaking persons, while those from the other countries named, especially Austria and Hungary as constituted in 1910, include widely different ethnic groups. There is also more or less mixture in the cases of Poland, Finland, Switzerland, and Belgium; but in the case of each of these countries one language is spoken by a large majority of the immigrants.

Mother tongue in relation to country of origin.—In Table 4 the various mother tongues are shown by countries of origin for 1920 and 1910. Because of the numerous changes in the map of Europe which resulted from the World War, it was impossible to make an accurate classification of the foreign parents of natives with reference to European countries as now constituted, and it was therefore necessary to classify them on the prewar basis. (See Country of Origin of the Foreign White Stock, p. 891.) In Table 4, therefore, the distribution of the foreign-born white has been made according to birthplace of father, in order that

(967)

968   POPULATION.

the statistics for this class may be comparable with those for the natives of foreign or mixed parentage. Tables 5 and 6, however, show, for 1920, the distribution of the foreign-born white population alone by mother tongue and country of birth on the postwar basis, the distribution in Table 5 being primarily by mother tongue and secondarily by country of birth, while in Table 6 the distribution is primarily by country of birth and secondarily by mother tongue.

Classification of mother tongues.—The mother tongues for which statistics are here presented are classified according to linguistic groups as follows:

English and Celtic (includes Irish, Scotch, and Welsh).
Germanic:
    German.
    Dutch and Frisian.
    Flemish.
Scandinavian:
    Swedish.
    Norwegian.
    Danish (includes Icelandic).
Latin and Greek:
    Italian (includes Romansh and Friulian).
    French (includes Breton).
    Spanish (includes Basque).
    Portuguese.
    Rumanian.
    Greek.
Slavic and Lettic:
    Polish.
    Czech.
    Slovak.
    Russian.
    Ruthenian.
    Slovenian.
    Serbo-Croatian—
       Croatian.
       Dalmatian.
       Serbian.
       Montenegrin.
    Bulgarian.
    Slavic, not specified (includes Wendish).
    Lithuanian and Lettish.
Unclassified:
    Yiddish and Hebrew.
    Magyar.
    Finnish (includes Lappish and Esthonian).
    Armenian.
    Syrian and Arabic.
    Turkish.
    Albanian.
    All other (includes Persian, Gypsy, Georgian, Kurdish, and Egyptian).
Unknown.

The same classification was used at the Thirteenth Census, except that Czech was then shown as Bohemian and Moravian.

The classification is based largely on linguistic relationship. The first three groups named—the English and Celtic, Germanic, and Scandinavian—embrace all "Teutonic" mother tongues, in the broad sense of this word, together with those Celtic languages which in the census figures could not be accurately separated from the English. The remaining Celtic tongue, the Breton, could not be accurately separated from and is therefore counted with the French.

Other combinations which have been made because the returns often showed that one mother tongue had been wrongly reported for the other are the following: Dutch and Frisian, Lithuanian and Lettish, Yiddish and Hebrew, and Syrian and Arabic. The Hebrew and the Syrian, which are practically dead languages, have been reported by many who really speak Yiddish and Arabic, respectively, and therefore have been counted with the latter two mother tongues. Many more were reported as Syrian than as Arabic in mother tongue, and yet Arabic was undoubtedly the language of customary speech, before immigration, of virtually the entire number of persons in this country reporting Syrian.

With the Latin has been included the numerically less important and somewhat related mother tongue, the Greek; and with the Slavic have been grouped the related Lithuanian and Lettish.

The subgroup "Slavic, not specified" requires explanation. At the census of 1920 this subgroup consisted principally of Wendish. At the preceding census it also included the small number of Wendish shown by the returns, but was then composed mainly of persons who were reported, contrary to the instructions given the enumerators, as "Slavs," "Slavic," "Slavish," or "Slavonian." Some of these persons should doubtless have been reported as Slovak or Slovenian. (These two languages are also sometimes confused with each other and must be considered as having a larger margin of error than perhaps any other languages in the regular classification.) The figures for "Slavic, not specified" for 1910 are not, therefore, comparable with those for 1920.

The subdivisions of the Serbo-Croatian subgroup are not, properly speaking, separate languages, but correspond in reality to certain divisions of the Serbo-Croatian population which arise from political and religious differences. The Serbo-Croatian total is consequently much more trustworthy than the numbers given for the respective subdivisions (Table 1), which are often confused one with another. The Dalmatian may properly be considered for the most part as Croatian, and the Montenegrin as Serbian.

Mixed mother tongue.—At the census of 1910 all native white persons of foreign parentage were classified according to the mother tongue of the father. This resulted in the inclusion, under each mother tongue, of certain numbers of persons whose mothers were reported as belonging to different linguistic classifications. At the census of 1920, however, all native whites whose foreign-born parents were of different mother tongues have been separately classified as "of mixed mother tongue"; and, in order to secure proper comparisons, the figures for 1910 in Tables 1, 4, and 7 have been revised by deducting

MOTHER TONGUE OF THE FOREIGN WHITE STOCK.   969

from the total for each mother tongue, as shown in the Thirteenth Census Reports, the number of native whites of mixed mother tongue who were included in that total.

Leading mother tongues of foreign countries.—The following statement shows the leading languages spoken by the white immigrants from those countries each of which had contributed at least 5,000 to the foreign-born white population of the United States as enumerated in 1920. Where two or more languages are shown for a given country they are named in the order of their importance as determined by the extent to which they are spoken by the immigrants from that country. All languages spoken by as many as 2 per cent of the immigrants from the specified country are listed. (See Table 6.)

Northwestern Europe:

England—English and Celtic.
Scotland—English and Celtic.
Wales—English and Celtic.
Ireland—English and Celtic.
Norway—Norwegian.
Sweden—Swedish.
Denmark (as constituted both in 1920 and in 1910)—Danish.
Netherlands—Dutch and Frisian.
Belgium (as constituted both in 1920 and in 1910)—Flemish, French, Dutch and Frisian, German.
Luxemburg—German, French.
Switzerland—German, French, Italian.
France (as constituted both in 1920 and in 1910)—French, German.

Central Europe:

Germany (as constituted in 1920)—German.
Germany (as constituted in 1910)—German, Polish.
Poland—Polish, Yiddish and Hebrew, Ruthenian, German.
Czechoslovakia—Czech, Slovak, German.
Austria (as constituted in 1920)—German, Yiddish and Hebrew, Slovak, Slovenian, Polish, Czech, Croatian, Russian.
Austria (as constituted in 1910)—Polish, Czech (Bohemian and Moravian), German, Yiddish and Hebrew, Slovenian, Croatian, Slovak.
Hungary (as constituted in 1920)—Magyar, German, Slovak, Yiddish and Hebrew.
Hungary (as constituted in 1910)—Magyar, Slovak, German, Yiddish and Hebrew, Rumanian.
Jugo-Slavia—Croatian, Slovenian, Serbian, Slovak, German, Montenegrin.

Eastern Europe:

Russia (as constituted in 1920)—Yiddish and Hebrew, Russian, German, Polish, Lithuanian and Lettish.
Russia (as constituted in 1910, not including Finland)—Yiddish and Hebrew, Polish, Lithuanian and Lettish, German, Russian.
Lithuania—Lithuanian and Lettish, Yiddish and Hebrew.
Finland—Finnish, Swedish.
Rumania (as constituted in 1920)—Rumanian, Yiddish and Hebrew, German, Magyar.
Rumania (as constituted in 1910)—Yiddish and Hebrew, Rumanian, German.
Bulgaria (as constituted both in 1920 and in 1910)—Bulgarian.
Turkey in Europe (as constituted in 1920)—Greek, Spanish, Turkish, Armenian, Yiddish and Hebrew, Bulgarian, German.
Turkey in Europe (as constituted in 1910)—Greek, Bulgarian, Syrian and Arabic, Turkish, Albanian, Serbian, Yiddish and Hebrew.

Southern Europe:

Greece (as constituted both in 1920 and in 1910)—Greek.
Albania—Albanian, Greek.
Italy (as constituted both in 1920 and in 1910)—Italian.
Spain—Spanish.
Portugal—Portuguese.

Asia:

Armenia—Armenian.
Syria—Syrian and Arabic.
Turkey in Asia (as constituted in 1920)—Turkish, Syrian and Arabic, Greek, Yiddish and Hebrew, Armenian.
Turkey in Asia (as constituted in 1910)—Syrian and Arabic, Armenian, Greek, Turkish.

America:

Canada—English and Celtic, French.
Newfoundland—English and Celtic.
West Indies (except possessions of United States)—Spanish, English and Celtic.
Mexico—Spanish.
Central and South America—Spanish, Italian, English and Celtic, Portuguese, German.

Other countries:

Atlantic Islands—Portuguese, English and Celtic.
Australia—English and Celtic, German.

More detailed information in regard to the mother tongue of white immigrants, as enumerated in 1920, from each of the principal countries contributing to the foreign-born white population of the United States is given in Table 5.

970 POPULATION.

FOREIGN WHITE STOCK, BY PRINCIPAL MOTHER TONGUES: 1920 AND 1910.

TOTAL.

ELEMENTS.

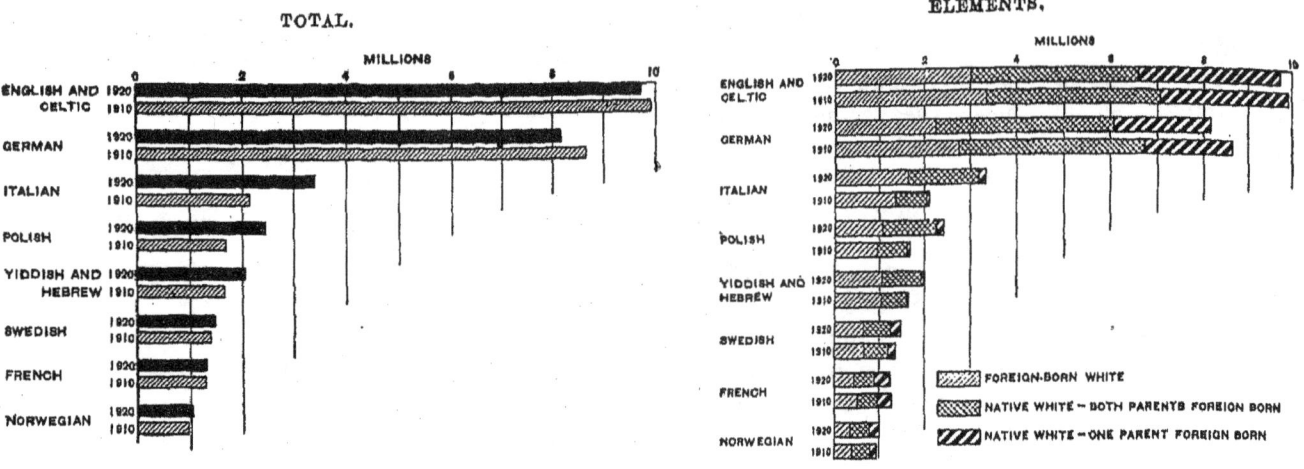

ELEMENTS OF FOREIGN WHITE STOCK, BY LINGUISTIC GROUPS.

TOTAL FOREIGN WHITE STOCK.

1920

FOREIGN-BORN WHITE.

1920

NATIVE WHITE OF FOREIGN STOCK.

1920

1910

1910

1910

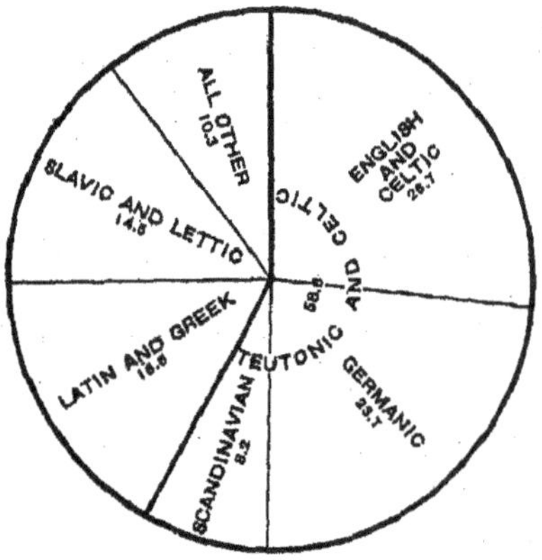

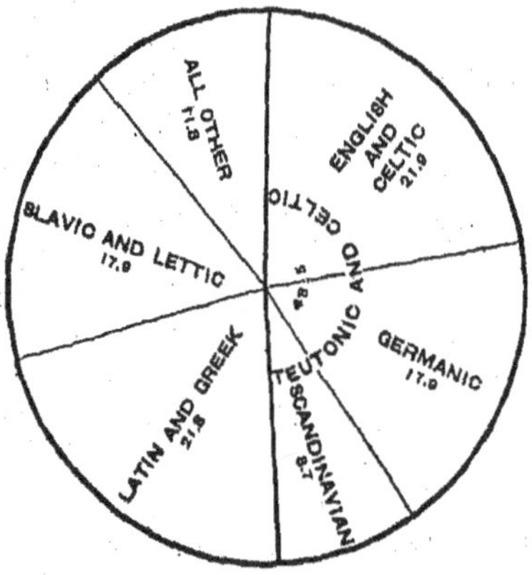

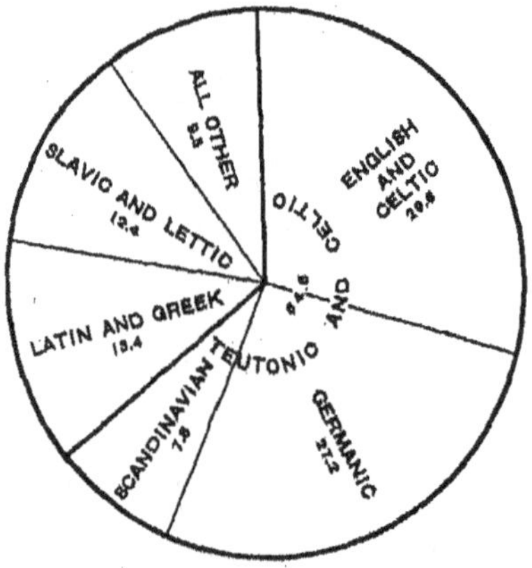

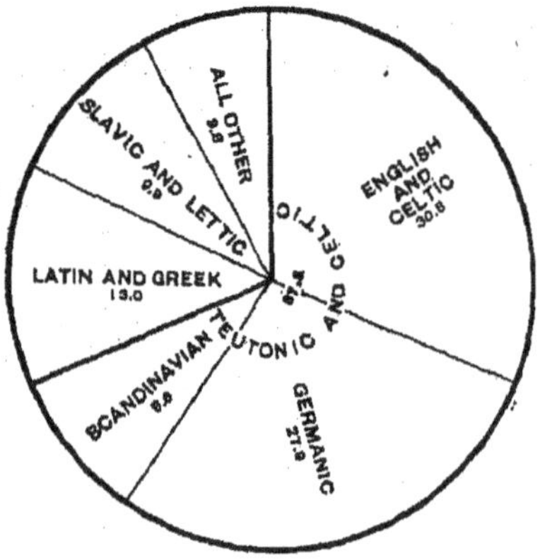

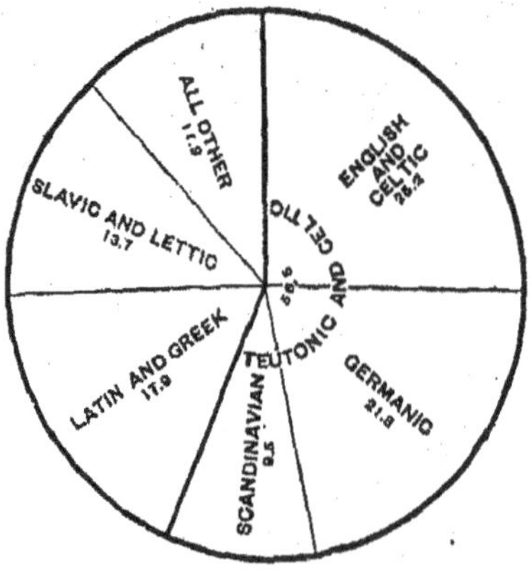

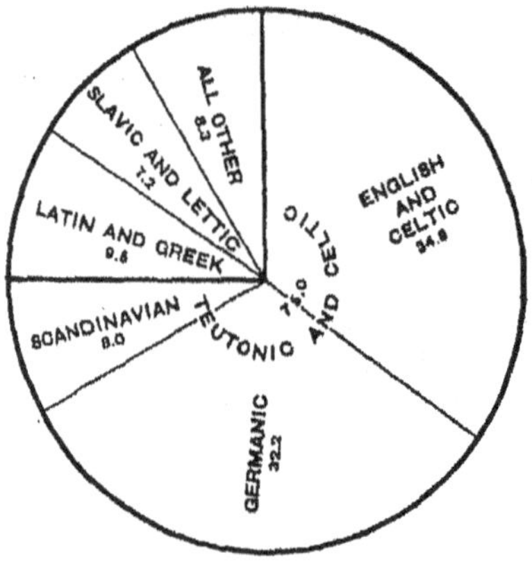

MOTHER TONGUE OF THE FOREIGN WHITE STOCK.   971

DISTRIBUTION OF FOREIGN WHITE STOCK HAVING SPECIFIED MOTHER TONGUES, FOR SELECTED STATES: 1920 AND 1910.

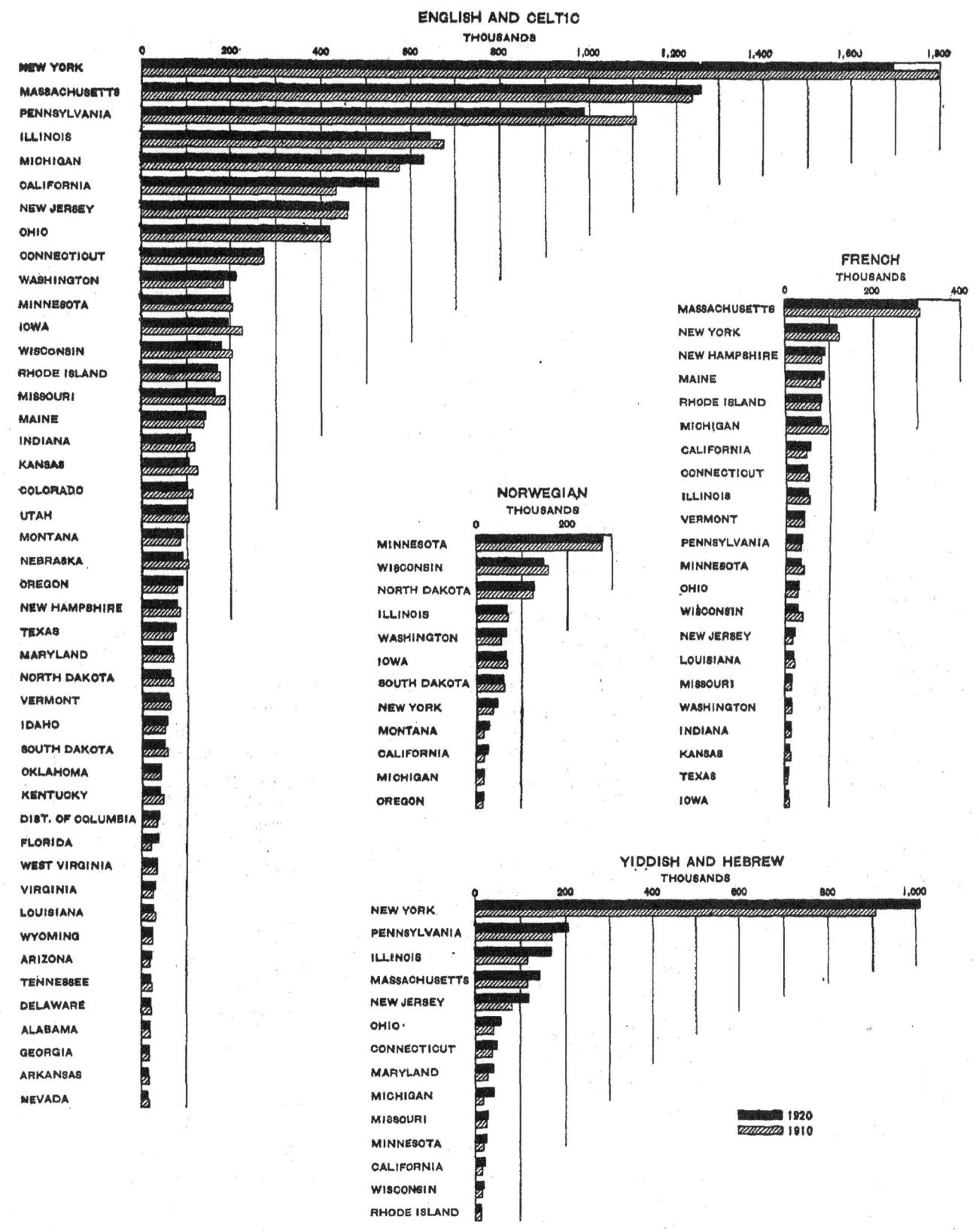

972

POPULATION.

DISTRIBUTION OF FOREIGN WHITE STOCK HAVING SPECIFIED MOTHER TONGUES, FOR SELECTED STATES:
1920 AND 1910.

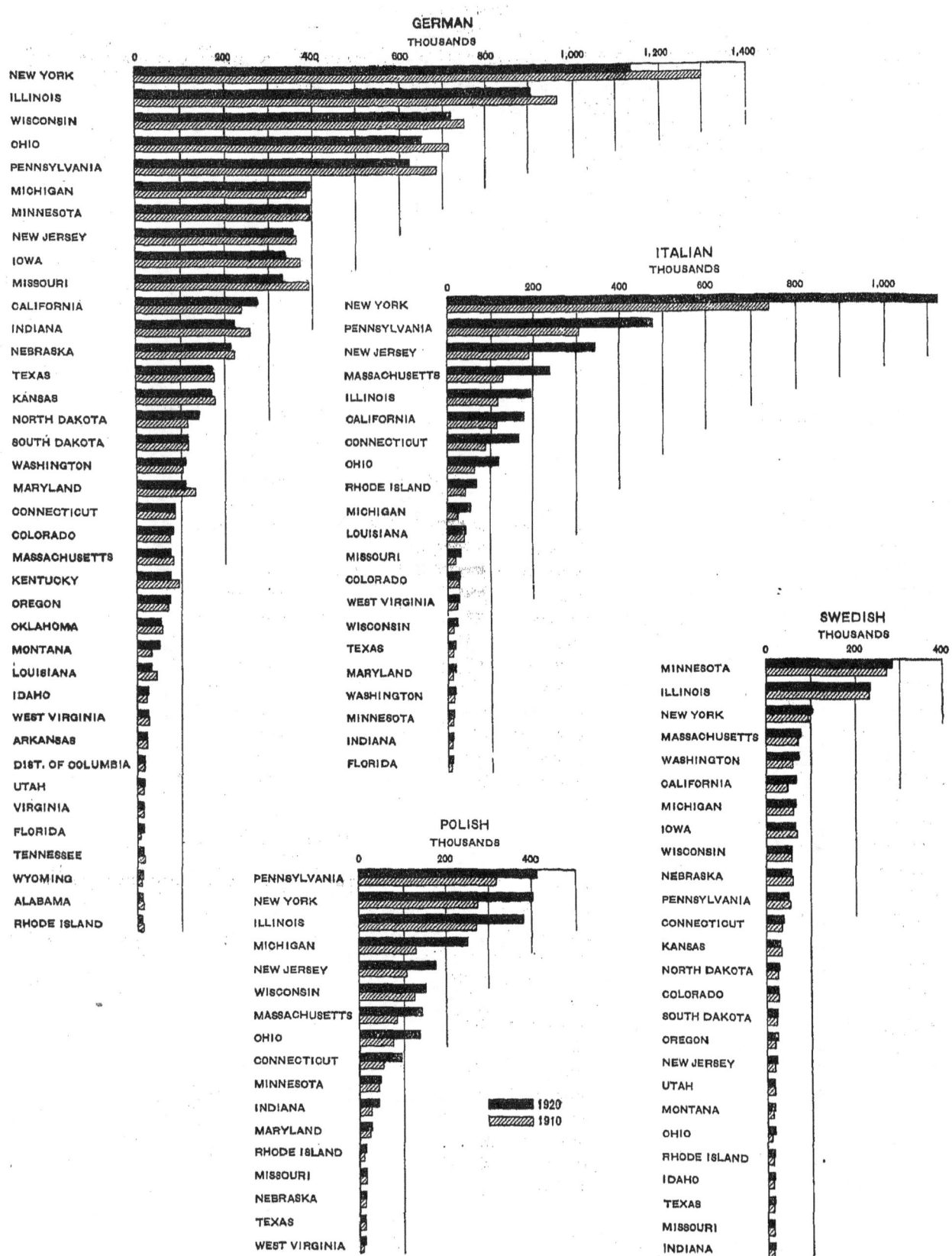

MOTHER TONGUE OF THE FOREIGN WHITE STOCK.

TABLE 1.—MOTHER TONGUE OF THE FOREIGN WHITE STOCK BY NATIVITY AND PARENTAGE, FOR THE UNITED STATES: 1920 AND 1910.

[Figures for 1910 revised (see text, p. 968).]

| MOTHER TONGUE. | TOTAL FOREIGN WHITE STOCK. | | FOREIGN-BORN WHITE. | | NATIVE WHITE OF FOREIGN OR MIXED PARENTAGE. | | | | | | | |
| | | | | | Total. | | Both parents foreign. | | Father foreign. | | Mother foreign. | |
	1920	1910	1920	1910	1920	1910	1920	1910	1920	1910	1920	1910
All mother tongues	36,398,958	32,243,382	13,712,754	13,345,545	22,686,204	18,897,837	15,694,539	12,916,311	4,539,776	3,923,845	2,451,889	2,057,681
English and Celtic [1]	9,729,365	9,930,861	3,007,932	3,363,792	6,721,433	6,567,069	3,585,586	3,706,885	1,845,808	1,727,987	1,290,039	1,132,197
Germanic	8,622,500	9,000,139	2,449,364	2,910,857	6,173,136	6,089,282	3,976,338	4,113,643	1,535,215	1,412,238	661,583	563,401
Scandinavian	2,972,796	2,781,402	1,194,933	1,272,150	1,777,863	1,509,252	1,224,919	1,120,801	360,891	254,807	192,053	133,644
Latin and Greek	6,036,001	4,185,932	2,990,954	2,385,388	3,045,047	1,800,544	2,383,187	1,329,954	473,995	330,049	187,865	140,541
Slavic and Lettic	5,270,581	3,194,647	2,460,332	1,831,666	2,810,249	1,362,981	2,474,746	1,207,837	245,232	111,357	90,271	43,797
Unclassified	2,956,321	2,261,563	1,602,073	1,465,420	1,354,248	796,143	1,252,219	754,828	73,980	31,337	28,049	9,978
Unknown or mixed mother tongue	811,394	888,838	7,166	116,272	804,228	772,566	797,544	682,373	4,655	56,070	2,029	34,123
English and Celtic [1]	9,729,365	9,930,861	3,007,932	3,363,792	6,721,433	6,567,069	3,585,586	3,706,885	1,845,808	1,727,987	1,290,039	1,132,197
Germanic:												
German	8,164,111	8,646,402	2,267,128	2,759,032	5,896,983	5,887,370	3,801,349	3,976,902	1,466,770	1,368,278	628,864	542,190
Dutch and Frisian	370,499	311,015	136,540	126,045	233,959	184,970	146,371	124,382	58,825	40,523	28,763	20,065
Flemish	87,890	42,722	45,696	25,780	42,194	16,942	28,618	12,359	9,620	3,437	3,956	1,146
Scandinavian:												
Swedish	1,485,062	1,394,410	643,203	683,218	841,859	711,192	616,225	558,230	144,699	97,906	80,935	55,056
Norwegian	1,020,788	976,827	362,199	402,587	658,589	574,240	436,365	410,364	142,448	106,531	79,776	57,345
Danish [2]	466,946	410,165	189,531	186,345	277,415	223,820	172,329	152,207	73,744	50,370	31,342	21,243
Latin and Greek:												
Italian [3]	3,365,864	2,135,393	1,624,998	1,365,110	1,740,866	770,283	1,571,605	707,710	149,444	55,153	19,817	7,420
French	1,290,110	1,288,897	466,956	528,842	823,154	760,055	455,918	435,671	236,788	215,510	130,448	108,874
Spanish [4]	850,848	444,132	556,111	258,131	294,737	186,001	203,175	119,991	58,958	44,215	32,604	21,795
Portuguese	215,728	139,221	105,895	72,649	109,833	66,572	87,788	52,562	18,137	12,180	3,908	1,830
Rumanian	91,683	49,588	62,336	42,277	29,347	7,311	26,236	6,727	2,300	443	811	141
Greek	221,768	128,701	174,658	118,379	47,110	10,322	38,465	7,293	8,368	2,548	277	481
Slavic and Lettic:												
Polish	2,436,895	1,684,108	1,077,392	943,781	1,359,503	740,327	1,208,425	666,535	115,952	56,455	35,126	17,337
Czech	622,796	531,193	234,564	228,738	388,232	302,455	291,005	237,283	60,757	41,724	36,470	23,448
Slovak	619,866	281,707	274,948	166,474	344,918	115,233	319,040	110,749	20,346	3,482	5,532	1,002
Russian [5]	731,949	91,341	392,049	57,926	339,900	33,415	303,090	30,467	27,644	2,366	9,166	582
Ruthenian	95,458	34,837	55,672	25,131	39,786	9,706	37,850	9,468	1,589	200	347	38
Slovenian	208,552	181,594	102,744	123,631	105,808	57,963	96,509	54,810	7,488	2,659	1,811	494
Serbo-Croatian—												
Croatian	140,559	92,260	83,063	74,036	57,496	18,224	54,330	17,557	2,780	583	386	84
Dalmatian	3,119	5,372	2,112	4,344	1,007	1,028	902	877	103	145	2	6
Serbian	52,208	26,483	36,471	23,403	15,737	3,080	14,742	2,771	888	259	107	50
Montenegrin	4,535	3,949	4,198	3,886	337	63	288	58	41	5	8	....
Bulgarian	14,420	19,183	12,853	18,341	1,567	842	1,104	644	441	154	22	44
Slavic, not specified [6]	3,624	34,799	2,039	21,012	1,585	13,787	1,539	13,117	27	499	19	171
Lithuanian and Lettish	336,600	207,821	182,227	140,963	154,373	66,858	145,922	63,491	7,176	2,826	1,275	541
Unclassified:												
Yiddish and Hebrew	2,043,618	1,664,142	1,091,820	1,051,767	951,798	612,375	884,591	584,301	49,707	21,748	17,495	6,326
Magyar	473,538	315,283	268,112	229,094	205,426	86,189	189,969	79,630	10,708	4,927	4,749	1,632
Finnish [7]	265,472	197,515	133,567	120,086	131,905	77,429	118,191	72,189	8,681	3,404	5,033	1,836
Armenian	52,840	29,690	37,647	23,938	15,193	5,752	14,047	5,312	1,063	410	83	30
Syrian and Arabic	104,139	46,495	57,557	32,868	46,582	13,627	42,724	12,799	3,270	704	588	124
Turkish	8,505	5,310	6,627	4,709	1,878	601	1,538	477	305	100	35	24
Albanian	6,426	2,358	5,515	2,312	911	46	761	37	137	9	13	....
All other [8]	1,788	770	1,228	646	560	124	398	83	109	35	53	6
Unknown	20,336	297,918	7,166	116,272	13,170	181,646	6,486	91,453	4,655	56,070	2,029	34,123
Of mixed mother tongue	791,058	590,920	....	....	791,058	590,920	791,058	590,920	....	....	....	....

[1] Includes persons reporting Irish, Scotch, or Welsh.
[2] Includes Icelandic (5,634 in 1920; 5,105 in 1910).
[3] Includes Romansh and Friulian (2,206 in 1920; 3,183 in 1910).
[4] Includes Basque (527 in 1920; 656 in 1910).
[5] Probably includes a considerable proportion of Hebrews erroneously reported as of Russian mother tongue.
[6] Practically all Wendish in 1920; 395 reported as Wendish in 1910.
[7] Includes Lappish and Esthonian (1,390 in 1920; 2,533 in 1910).
[8] Comprises Persian (1,159 in 1920; 592 in 1910), Gypsy (173 in 1920; 156 in 1910), Georgian (65 in 1920; 14 in 1910), Kurdish (122 in 1920; 8 in 1910), and Egyptian (269 in 1920).

POPULATION.

TABLE 2.—INCREASE IN THE FOREIGN WHITE STOCK BY MOTHER TONGUE, FOR NATIVITY AND PARENTAGE CLASSES, FOR THE UNITED STATES: 1910-1920.

[Per cent not shown where base is less than 100. A minus sign (−) denotes decrease.]

MOTHER TONGUE.	INCREASE: 1910-1920											
	Total foreign white stock.		Foreign-born white.		Native white of foreign or mixed parentage.							
					Total.		Both parents foreign.		Father foreign.		Mother foreign.	
	Number.	Per cent.	Number.	Per cent.	Number.	Per cent.	Number.	Per cent.	Number.	Per cent.	Number.	Per cent.
All mother tongues	4,155,576	12.9	367,209	2.8	3,788,367	20.0	2,778,228	21.5	615,931	15.7	394,208	19.2
English and Celtic	−201,496	−2.0	−355,860	−10.6	154,364	2.4	−121,290	−3.3	117,821	6.8	157,842	13.9
Germanic	−377,639	−4.2	−461,493	−15.9	83,854	1.4	−137,305	−3.3	122,977	8.7	98,182	17.4
Scandinavian	191,394	6.9	−77,217	−6.1	268,611	17.8	104,118	9.3	116,084	41.6	58,409	43.7
Latin and Greek	1,850,069	44.2	605,566	25.4	1,244,503	69.1	1,053,233	79.2	143,946	43.6	47,324	33.7
Slavic and Lettic	2,075,934	65.0	628,666	34.3	1,447,268	106.2	1,266,919	104.9	133,875	120.2	46,474	106.1
Unclassified	694,758	30.7	136,653	9.3	558,105	70.1	497,301	65.9	42,643	136.1	18,071	181.1
Unknown or mixed mother tongue	−77,444	−8.7	−109,106	−93.8	31,662	4.1	115,171	16.9	−51,415	−91.7	−32,094	−94.1
English and Celtic	−201,496	−2.0	−355,860	−10.6	154,364	2.4	−121,290	−3.3	117,821	6.8	157,842	13.9
Germanic:												
German	−482,291	−5.6	−491,904	−17.8	9,613	0.2	−175,553	−4.4	98,492	7.2	86,674	16.0
Dutch and Frisian	59,484	19.1	10,495	8.3	48,989	26.5	21,989	17.7	18,302	45.2	8,698	43.3
Flemish	45,168	105.7	19,916	77.3	25,252	149.0	16,259	131.6	6,183	170.9	2,810	245.2
Scandinavian:												
Swedish	90,652	6.5	−40,015	−5.9	130,667	18.4	57,995	10.4	46,793	47.8	25,879	47.0
Norwegian	43,961	4.5	−40,388	−10.0	84,349	14.7	26,001	6.3	35,917	33.7	22,431	39.1
Danish	56,781	13.8	3,186	1.7	53,595	23.9	20,122	13.2	23,374	46.4	10,099	47.5
Latin and Greek:												
Italian	1,230,471	57.6	259,888	19.0	970,583	126.0	863,895	122.1	94,291	171.0	12,397	167.1
French	1,213	0.1	−61,886	−11.7	63,099	8.3	20,247	4.6	21,278	9.9	21,574	19.8
Spanish	406,716	91.6	297,980	115.4	108,736	58.5	83,184	69.3	14,743	33.3	10,809	49.6
Portuguese	76,507	55.0	33,246	45.8	43,261	65.0	35,226	67.0	5,957	48.9	2,078	113.6
Rumanian	42,095	84.9	20,059	47.4	22,036	301.4	19,509	290.0	1,857	410.2	670	475.2
Greek	93,067	72.3	56,279	47.5	36,788	356.4	31,172	427.4	5,820	228.4	−204	−42.4
Slavic and Lettic:												
Polish	752,787	44.7	133,611	14.2	619,176	83.6	541,890	81.3	59,497	105.4	17,789	102.6
Czech	91,603	17.2	5,826	2.5	85,777	28.4	53,722	22.6	19,033	45.6	13,022	55.5
Slovak	338,159	120.0	108,474	65.2	229,685	199.3	208,201	188.1	16,804	484.3	4,530	452.1
Russian[1]	640,608	701.3	334,123	576.8	306,485	917.2	272,623	894.8	25,278	1,068.4	8,584	1,474.9
Ruthenian	60,621	174.0	30,541	121.5	30,080	309.9	28,382	299.8	1,389	604.5	309	....
Slovenian	26,958	14.8	−20,887	−16.9	47,845	82.5	41,699	76.1	4,829	181.6	1,317	266.6
Serbo-Croatian—												
Croatian	48,299	52.4	9,027	12.2	39,272	215.5	36,773	209.4	2,197	376.8	302	....
Dalmatian	−2,253	−41.9	−2,232	−51.4	−21	−2.0	25	2.9	−42	−29.0	−4	....
Serbian	25,725	97.1	13,068	55.8	12,657	410.9	11,971	432.0	629	242.9	57	....
Montenegrin	586	14.8	312	8.0	274	....	230	....	36	....	8	....
Bulgarian	−4,763	−24.8	−5,488	−29.9	725	86.1	460	71.4	287	180.4	−22	....
Slavic, not specified	−31,175	−89.6	−18,973	−90.3	−12,202	−88.5	−11,578	−88.3	−472	−94.6	−152	−88.9
Lithuanian and Lettish	128,779	62.0	41,264	29.3	87,515	130.9	82,431	129.8	4,350	153.9	734	135.7
Unclassified:												
Yiddish and Hebrew	379,471	22.8	40,053	3.8	339,418	55.4	300,290	51.4	27,959	128.6	11,169	176.6
Magyar	158,255	50.2	39,018	17.0	119,237	138.3	110,339	138.6	5,781	117.3	3,117	191.0
Finnish	67,957	34.4	13,481	11.2	54,476	70.4	46,002	63.7	5,277	155.0	3,197	174.1
Armenian	23,150	78.0	13,709	57.3	9,441	164.1	8,735	164.4	653	159.3	53	....
Syrian and Arabic	57,644	124.0	24,689	75.1	32,955	241.8	29,025	233.8	2,566	364.5	404	374.2
Turkish	3,195	60.2	1,918	40.7	1,277	212.5	1,061	222.4	205	205.0	11	....
Albanian	4,068	172.5	3,203	138.5	865	....	724	....	128	....	13	....
All other	1,018	132.2	582	90.1	436	351.6	315	....	74	....	47	....
Unknown	−277,582	−93.2	−109,106	−93.8	−168,476	−92.7	−84,967	−92.9	−51,415	−91.7	−32,094	−94.1
Of mixed mother tongue	200,138	33.9	....	....	200,138	33.9	200,138	33.9	....	....	....	....

[1] It is probable that a considerable proportion of the persons returned as Russian in mother tongue were in reality Hebrews. The increase between 1910 and 1920 is, therefore, probably exaggerated.

MOTHER TONGUE OF THE FOREIGN WHITE STOCK.   975

TABLE 3.—PER CENT DISTRIBUTION OF THE FOREIGN WHITE STOCK BY MOTHER TONGUE FOR NATIVITY AND PARENTAGE CLASSES, AND BY NATIVITY AND PARENTAGE CLASSES FOR MOTHER TONGUES, FOR THE UNITED STATES: 1920 AND 1910.

MOTHER TONGUE.	PER CENT DISTRIBUTION BY MOTHER TONGUE.												PER CENT DISTRIBUTION BY NATIVITY AND PARENTAGE CLASSES.										
	Total foreign white stock.		Foreign-born white.		Native white of foreign or mixed parentage.								Foreign-born white.		Native white of foreign or mixed parentage.									
					Total.		Both parents foreign.		Father foreign.		Mother foreign.				Total.		Both parents foreign.		Father foreign.		Mother foreign.			
	1920	1910	1920	1910	1920	1910	1920	1910	1920	1910	1920	1910	1920	1910	1920	1910	1920	1910	1920	1910	1920	1910		
All mother tongues	100.0	100.0	100.0	100.0	100.0	100.0	100.0	100.0	100.0	100.0	100.0	100.0	37.7	41.4	62.3	58.6	43.1	40.1	12.5	12.2	6.7	6.4		
English and Celtic	26.7	30.8	21.9	25.2	29.6	34.8	22.8	28.7	40.7	44.0	52.6	55.0	30.9	33.9	69.1	66.1	36.9	37.3	19.0	17.4	13.3	11.4		
Germanic	23.7	27.9	17.9	21.8	27.2	32.2	25.3	31.8	33.8	36.0	27.0	27.4	28.4	32.3	71.6	67.7	46.1	45.7	17.8	15.7	7.7	6.3		
Scandinavian	8.2	8.6	8.7	9.5	7.8	8.0	7.8	8.7	7.9	6.5	7.8	6.5	40.2	45.7	59.8	54.3	41.2	40.3	12.1	9.2	6.5	4.8		
Latin and Greek	16.6	13.0	21.8	17.9	13.4	9.5	15.2	10.3	10.4	8.4	7.7	6.8	49.6	57.0	50.4	43.0	39.5	31.8	7.9	7.0	3.1	3.4		
Slavic and Lettic	14.5	9.9	17.9	13.7	12.4	7.2	15.8	9.4	5.4	2.8	3.7	2.1	46.7	57.3	53.3	42.7	47.0	37.8	4.7	3.5	1.7	1.4		
Unclassified	8.1	7.0	11.7	11.0	6.0	4.2	8.0	5.8	1.6	0.8	1.1	0.5	54.2	64.8	45.8	35.2	42.4	33.4	2.5	1.4	0.9	0.4		
Unknown or mixed mother tongue	2.2	2.8	0.1	0.9	3.5	4.1	5.1	5.3	0.1	1.4	0.1	1.7	0.9	13.1	99.1	86.9	98.3	76.8	0.6	6.3	0.3	3.8		
English and Celtic	26.7	30.8	21.9	25.2	29.6	34.8	22.8	28.7	40.7	44.0	52.6	55.0	30.9	33.9	69.1	66.1	36.9	37.3	19.0	17.4	13.3	11.4		
Germanic:																								
German	22.4	26.8	16.5	20.7	26.0	31.2	24.2	30.8	32.3	34.9	25.6	26.3	27.8	31.9	72.2	68.1	46.6	46.0	18.0	15.8	7.7	6.3		
Dutch and Frisian	1.0	1.0	1.0	0.9	1.0	1.0	1.0	1.0	1.3	1.0	1.2	1.0	36.9	40.5	63.1	59.5	39.5	40.0	15.9	13.0	7.8	6.5		
Flemish	0.2	0.1	0.3	0.2	0.2	0.1	0.2	0.1	0.2	0.1	0.2	0.1	52.0	60.3	48.0	39.7	32.6	28.9	10.9	8.0	4.5	2.7		
Scandinavian:																								
Swedish	4.1	4.3	4.7	5.1	3.7	3.8	3.9	4.3	3.2	2.5	3.3	2.7	43.3	49.0	56.7	51.0	41.5	40.0	9.7	7.0	5.4	3.9		
Norwegian	2.8	3.0	2.6	3.0	2.9	3.0	2.8	3.2	3.1	2.7	3.3	2.8	35.5	41.2	64.5	58.8	42.7	42.0	14.0	10.9	7.8	5.9		
Danish	1.3	1.3	1.4	1.4	1.2	1.2	1.1	1.2	1.6	1.3	1.3	1.0	40.6	45.4	59.4	54.6	36.9	37.1	15.8	12.3	6.7	5.2		
Latin and Greek:																								
Italian	9.2	6.6	11.9	10.2	7.7	4.1	10.0	5.5	3.3	1.4	0.8	0.4	48.3	63.9	51.7	36.1	46.7	33.1	4.4	2.6	0.6	0.3		
French	3.5	4.0	3.4	4.0	3.6	4.0	2.9	3.4	5.2	5.5	5.3	5.3	36.2	41.0	63.8	59.0	35.3	33.8	18.4	16.7	10.1	8.4		
Spanish	2.3	1.4	4.1	1.9	1.3	1.0	1.3	0.9	1.3	1.1	1.3	1.1	65.4	58.1	34.6	41.9	23.9	27.0	6.9	10.0	3.8	4.9		
Portuguese	0.6	0.4	0.8	0.5	0.5	0.4	0.6	0.4	0.4	0.3	0.2	0.1	49.1	52.2	50.9	47.8	40.7	37.8	8.4	8.7	1.8	1.3		
Rumanian	0.3	0.2	0.5	0.3	0.1	(1)	0.2	0.1	0.1	(1)	(1)	(1)	68.0	85.3	32.0	14.7	28.6	13.6	2.5	0.9	0.9	0.3		
Greek	0.6	0.4	1.3	0.9	0.2	0.1	0.2	0.1	0.2	0.2	0.1	(1)	78.8	92.0	21.2	8.0	17.3	5.7	3.8	2.0	0.1	0.4		
Slavic and Lettic:																								
Polish	6.7	5.2	7.9	7.1	6.0	3.9	7.7	5.2	2.6	1.4	1.4	0.8	44.2	56.0	55.8	44.0	49.6	39.6	4.8	3.4	1.4	1.0		
Czech	1.7	1.6	1.7	1.7	1.7	1.6	1.9	1.8	1.3	1.1	1.5	1.1	37.7	43.1	62.3	56.9	46.7	44.9	9.8	7.9	5.9	4.4		
Slovak²	1.7	0.9	2.0	1.2	1.5	0.6	2.0	0.9	0.4	0.1	0.2	0.1	44.4	59.1	55.6	40.9	51.5	39.3	3.3	1.2	0.9	0.4		
Russian²	2.0	0.3	2.9	0.4	1.5	0.2	1.9	0.2	0.6	0.1	0.4	(1)	53.6	63.4	46.4	36.6	33.4	28.6	3.8	2.6	1.3	0.6		
Ruthenian	0.3	0.1	0.4	0.2	0.2	0.1	0.2	0.1	(1)	(1)	(1)	(1)	58.3	72.1	41.7	27.9	39.7	27.2	1.7	0.6	0.4	0.1		
Slovenian	0.6	0.6	0.7	0.9	0.5	0.3	0.6	0.4	0.2	0.1	0.1	(1)	49.3	68.1	50.7	31.9	46.3	30.2	3.6	1.5	0.9	0.3		
Serbo-Croatian—																								
Croatian	0.4	0.3	0.6	0.6	0.3	0.1	0.3	0.1	0.1	(1)	(1)	(1)	59.1	80.2	40.9	19.8	38.7	19.0	2.0	0.6	0.3	0.1		
Dalmatian	(1)	(1)	(1)	(1)	(1)	(1)	(1)	(1)	(1)	(1)	(1)	(1)	67.7	80.9	32.3	19.1	28.9	16.3	3.3	2.7	0.1	0.1		
Serbian	0.1	0.1	0.3	0.2	0.1	0.1	0.1	0.1	(1)	(2)	(1)	(2)	69.9	88.4	30.1	11.6	28.2	10.5	1.7	1.0	0.2	0.2		
Montenegrin	(1)	(1)	(1)	(1)	(1)	(1)	(1)	(1)	(1)	(1)	(1)	.....	92.6	98.4	7.4	1.6	6.4	1.5	1.0	0.9	0.1	0.2		
Bulgarian	(1)	0.1	0.1	0.1	(1)	(1)	(1)	(1)	(1)	(1)	(1)	(1)	89.1	95.6	10.9	4.4	7.7	3.4	3.1	0.8	0.8	0.2		
Slavic, not specified	(1)	0.1	(1)	0.2	(1)	0.1	(1)	0.1	(1)	(1)	(1)	(1)	56.3	60.4	43.7	39.6	42.5	37.7	0.7	1.4	0.5	0.5		
Lithuanian and Lettish	0.9	0.6	1.3	1.1	0.7	0.4	0.9	0.5	0.2	0.1	0.1	(1)	54.1	67.8	45.9	32.2	43.4	30.6	2.1	1.4	0.4	0.3		
Unclassified:																								
Yiddish and Hebrew	5.6	5.2	8.0	7.9	4.2	3.2	5.6	4.5	1.1	0.6	0.7	0.3	53.4	63.2	46.6	36.8	43.3	35.1	2.4	1.3	0.9	0.4		
Magyar	1.3	1.0	2.0	1.7	0.9	0.5	1.2	0.6	0.2	0.1	0.2	0.1	56.6	72.7	43.4	27.3	40.1	25.3	2.8	1.6	1.0	0.5		
Finnish	0.7	0.6	1.0	0.9	0.6	0.4	0.8	0.6	0.2	0.1	0.2	0.1	50.3	60.8	49.7	39.2	44.5	36.5	3.3	1.7	1.9	0.9		
Armenian	0.1	0.1	0.3	0.2	0.1	(1)	0.1	(1)	(1)	(1)	(1)	(1)	71.2	80.6	28.8	19.4	26.0	17.9	2.0	1.4	0.2	0.1		
Syrian and Arabic	0.3	0.1	0.4	0.2	0.2	0.1	0.3	0.1	0.1	(1)	(1)	(1)	55.3	70.7	44.7	29.3	41.0	27.5	3.1	1.5	0.6	0.3		
Turkish	(1)	(1)	(1)	(1)	(1)	(1)	(1)	(1)	(1)	(1)	(1)	(1)	77.9	88.7	22.1	11.3	18.1	9.0	3.6	1.9	0.4	0.5		
Albanian	(1)	(1)	(1)	(1)	(1)	(1)	(1)	(1)	(1)	(1)	(1)	.....	85.8	98.0	14.2	2.0	11.8	1.6	2.1	0.4	0.4	0.2		
All other	(1)	(1)	(1)	(1)	(1)	(1)	(1)	(1)	(1)	(1)	(1)	(1)	68.7	83.9	31.3	16.1	22.3	10.8	6.1	4.5	3.0	0.8		
Unknown	0.1	0.9	0.1	0.9	0.1	1.0	(1)	0.7	0.1	1.4	0.1	1.7	35.2	39.0	64.8	61.0	31.9	30.7	22.9	18.8	10.0	11.5		
Of mixed mother tongue	2.2	1.8	.....	.....	3.5	3.1	5.0	4.6	.....	.....	.....	.....	.....	.....	100.0	100.0	100.0	100.0	100.0	100.0	.....	.....		

¹ Less than one-tenth of 1 per cent.   ² See footnote to Table 2, p. 974.

976

POPULATION.

TABLE 4.—MOTHER TONGUE OF THE FOREIGN WHITE STOCK BY COUNTRY OF ORIGIN, FOR THE UNITED STATES: 1920 AND 1910.

[Countries shown in this table represent their prewar areas. Figures for 1910 revised (see text, p. 968). Per cent not shown where base is less than 100.]

MOTHER TONGUE AND COUNTRY OF ORIGIN.	Number 1920	Number 1910	Per cent distribution 1920	Per cent distribution 1910	Increase[1] 1910–1920 Number.	Increase[1] 1910–1920 Per cent.
All mother tongues	36,393,958	32,243,382	100.0	100.0	4,155,576	12.9
English and Celtic	9,729,365	9,930,861	26.7	30.8	−201,496	−2.0
Germanic	8,622,500	9,000,139	23.7	27.9	−377,639	−4.2
Scandinavian	2,972,796	2,781,402	8.2	8.6	191,394	6.9
Latin and Greek	6,036,001	4,185,932	16.6	13.0	1,850,069	44.2
Slavic and Lettic	5,270,581	3,194,647	14.5	9.9	2,075,934	65.0
Unclassified	2,956,321	2,261,563	8.1	7.0	694,758	30.7
Unknown or mixed mother tongue	811,394	888,838	2.2	2.8	−77,444	−8.7
English and Celtic	9,729,365	9,930,861	100.0	100.0	−201,496	−2.0
Ireland	4,131,751	4,627,636	42.5	46.6	−495,885	−10.7
England	2,300,130	2,408,690	23.6	24.3	−108,560	−4.5
Canada	1,727,125	1,778,934	17.8	17.9	−51,809	−2.9
Scotland	729,754	733,350	7.5	7.4	−3,596	−0.5
Wales	230,097	264,678	2.4	2.7	−34,581	−13.1
Germany	36,669	675	0.4	(2)	35,994	5,332.4
Newfoundland	25,207	8,253	0.3	0.1	16,954	205.4
West Indies[3]	19,628	14,306	0.2	0.1	5,322	37.2
Russia	18,478	162	0.2	(2)	18,316	11,306.2
Australia	12,018	14,943	0.1	0.2	−2,925	−19.6
France	7,262	580	0.1	(2)	6,682	1,152.1
Austria	6,579	356	0.1	(2)	6,223	1,748.0
Sweden	5,377	82	0.1	(2)	5,295	......
Other countries	41,855	20,439	0.4	0.2	21,416	104.8
Mixed foreign	437,435	57,777	4.5	0.6	379,658	657.1
Germanic:						
German	8,164,111	8,646,402	100.0	100.0	−482,291	−5.6
Germany	6,701,603	7,577,749	82.1	87.6	−876,147	−11.6
Austria	456,751	267,735	5.6	3.1	189,016	70.6
Russia	303,532	243,361	3.7	2.8	60,171	24.7
Switzerland	275,920	255,518	3.4	3.0	20,402	8.0
Hungary	143,766	98,490	1.8	1.1	45,276	46.0
Luxemburg	38,537	6,428	0.5	0.1	32,109	499.5
Canada	14,407	36,995	0.2	0.4	−22,588	−61.1
France	10,776	9,957	0.1	0.1	819	8.2
Netherlands	6,118	12,129	0.1	0.1	−6,011	−49.6
Rumania	4,565	2,390	0.1	(2)	2,175	91.0
Belgium	4,416	2,705	0.1	(2)	1,711	63.3
Other countries	19,266	16,862	0.2	0.2	2,404	14.3
Mixed foreign	184,455	116,083	2.3	1.3	68,372	58.9
Dutch and Frisian	370,499	311,015	100.0	100.0	59,484	19.1
Netherlands	351,624	280,084	94.9	90.1	71,540	25.5
Germany	6,155	20,365	1.7	6.5	−14,210	−69.8
Belgium	4,787	5,432	1.3	1.7	−645	−11.9
Switzerland	1,283	209	0.3	0.1	1,074	513.9
Canada	1,182	1,265	0.3	0.4	−83	−6.6
Russia	1,072	255	0.3	0.1	817	320.4
Austria	500	204	0.1	0.1	296	145.1
Luxemburg	419	106	0.1	(2)	313	295.3
Denmark	390	66	0.1	(2)	324	......
Hungary	307	140	0.1	(2)	227	162.1
West Indies[3]	309	91	0.1	(2)	218	......
Africa	231	211	0.1	0.1	20	9.5
Other countries	1,016	1,400	0.3	0.5	−384	−27.4
Mixed foreign	1,164	1,187	0.3	0.4	−23	−1.9
Flemish	87,890	42,722	100.0	100.0	45,168	105.7
Belgium	86,297	41,620	98.2	97.4	44,677	107.3
Netherlands	463	283	0.5	0.7	180	63.6
France	253	390	0.3	0.9	−137	−35.1
Luxemburg	191	20	0.2	(1)	171	......
Germany	64	80	0.1	0.2	−16	......
Finland	51	....	0.1	......	51	......
Other countries	193	178	0.2	0.4	15	8.4
Mixed foreign	378	151	0.4	0.4	227	150.3
Scandinavian:						
Swedish	1,485,062	1,394,410	100.0	100.0	90,652	6.5
Sweden	1,443,237	1,358,736	97.2	97.4	84,501	6.2
Finland	32,101	26,363	2.2	1.9	5,738	21.8
Norway	1,910	2,286	0.1	0.2	−376	−16.4
Denmark	947	846	0.1	0.1	101	11.9
Other countries	1,337	2,555	0.1	0.2	−1,218	−47.7
Mixed foreign	5,530	3,624	0.4	0.3	1,906	52.6
Norwegian	1,020,788	976,827	100.0	100.0	43,961	4.5
Norway	1,016,436	974,285	99.6	99.7	42,151	4.3
Sweden	2,339	524	0.2	0.1	1,815	346.4
Other countries	1,259	1,435	0.1	0.1	−176	−12.3
Mixed foreign	754	583	0.1	0.1	171	29.3
Danish	466,946	410,165	100.0	100.0	56,781	13.8
Denmark	458,189	396,697	98.1	96.6	62,092	15.7
Germany	4,478	9,032	1.0	2.2	−4,554	−50.4
Sweden	832	211	0.2	0.1	621	294.3
Norway	546	344	0.1	0.1	202	58.7
Other countries	860	1,451	0.2	0.4	−591	−40.7
Mixed foreign	2,041	3,030	0.4	0.7	−989	−32.6

MOTHER TONGUE AND COUNTRY OF ORIGIN.	Number 1920	Number 1910	Per cent distribution 1920	Per cent distribution 1910	Increase[1] 1910–1920 Number.	Increase[1] 1910–1920 Per cent.
Latin and Greek:						
Italian	3,365,864	2,135,393	100.0	100.0	1,230,471	57.6
Italy	3,324,701	2,096,029	98.8	98.2	1,228,762	58.6
Austria	16,102	16,621	0.5	0.8	−519	−3.1
Switzerland	15,622	14,354	0.5	0.7	1,268	8.8
Other countries	3,424	5,501	0.1	0.3	−2,077	−37.8
Mixed foreign	5,925	2,888	0.2	0.1	3,037	105.2
French	1,290,110	1,288,897	100.0	100.0	1,213	0.1
Canada	847,879	932,238	65.7	72.3	−84,359	−9.0
France	312,207	277,814	24.2	21.6	34,393	12.4
Germany	45,311	6,863	3.5	0.5	38,448	560.2
Switzerland	28,404	23,398	2.2	1.8	5,000	21.4
Belgium	25,155	31,843	1.9	2.5	−6,688	−21.0
Luxemburg	3,084	221	0.2	(2)	2,863	1,295.5
Italy	2,296	868	0.2	0.1	1,428	164.5
England	1,538	858	0.1	0.1	680	79.3
Austria	1,231	257	0.1	(2)	974	379.0
Russia	1,125	208	0.1	(2)	917	440.9
Ireland	822	115	0.1	(2)	707	614.8
Other countries	5,030	2,992	0.4	0.2	2,038	68.1
Mixed foreign	16,028	11,222	1.2	0.9	4,800	42.8
Spanish	850,848	444,132	100.0	100.0	406,716	91.0
Mexico	723,500	379,844	85.0	85.5	343,656	90.5
Spain	76,814	32,547	9.0	7.3	44,267	136.0
West Indies[3]	23,892	22,856	2.8	5.1	1,036	4.5
South America	9,995	3,997	1.2	0.9	5,998	150.1
Turkey in Europe	5,820	590	0.7	0.1	5,230	886.4
Central America	3,501	1,189	0.4	0.3	2,312	194.4
Italy	951	51	0.1	(2)	900	......
France	903	166	0.1	(2)	737	444.0
Greece	537	4	0.1	(2)	533	......
Turkey in Asia	524	229	0.1	0.1	295	128.8
Atlantic Islands[4]	527	241	0.1	0.1	286	118.7
Germany	495	51	0.1	(2)	444	......
Other countries	2,563	1,155	0.3	0.3	1,408	121.9
Mixed foreign	826	1,212	0.1	0.3	−386	−31.8
Portuguese	215,728	139,221	100.0	100.0	76,507	55.0
Portugal	133,720	110,643	62.0	79.5	23,077	20.9
Atlantic Islands[4]	78,052	26,923	36.2	19.3	51,129	189.9
South America	1,080	557	0.5	0.4	523	93.9
West Indies[3]	252	473	0.1	0.3	−221	−46.7
Austria	214	14	0.1	(2)	200	......
Italy	116	5	0.1	(2)	111	......
Other countries	630	395	0.3	0.3	235	59.5
Mixed foreign	1,664	211	0.8	0.2	1,453	688.6
Rumanian	91,683	49,588	100.0	100.0	42,095	84.9
Rumania	71,805	27,943	78.3	56.4	43,862	157.0
Hungary	10,819	16,523	11.8	33.3	−5,704	−34.5
Austria	7,241	3,688	7.9	7.4	3,553	96.3
Russia	484	359	0.5	0.7	125	34.8
Turkey in Europe	416	559	0.5	1.1	−143	−25.6
Greece	209	9	0.2	(2)	200	......
Turkey in Asia	97	43	0.1	0.1	54	......
Bulgaria	68	39	0.1	0.1	29	......
Serbia	65	67	0.1	0.1	−2	......
Other countries	125	297	0.1	0.6	−172	−57.9
Mixed foreign	354	61	0.4	0.1	293	......
Greek	221,768	128,701	100.0	100.0	93,067	72.3
Greece	208,939	109,006	94.2	84.7	99,933	91.7
Turkey in Europe	6,842	12,655	3.1	9.8	−5,813	−45.9
Russia	1,301	1,885	0.6	1.5	−584	−20.2
Austria	1,251	1,445	0.6	1.1	−194	−13.4
Turkey in Asia	1,717	2,441	0.8	1.9	−724	−29.7
Europe, not specified	263	259	0.1	0.2	4	1.5
Italy	190	244	0.1	0.2	−54	−22.1
Hungary	166	234	0.1	0.2	−68	−29.1
Bulgaria	134	54	0.1	(2)	80	......
Africa	114	79	0.1	0.1	35	......
Serbia	114	13	0.1	(2)	101	......
Rumania	113	46	0.1	(2)	67	......
Other countries	240	239	0.1	0.2	1	0.4
Mixed foreign	294	101	0.1	0.1	193	191.1
Slavic and Lettic:						
Polish	2,436,895	1,684,108	100.0	100.0	752,787	44.7
Austria	1,036,131	490,178	42.5	29.1	545,953	111.4
Russia	911,634	644,212	37.4	38.3	267,422	41.5
Germany	426,744	506,177	17.5	30.1	−79,433	−15.7
Hungary	5,293	3,941	0.2	0.2	1,352	34.3
Other countries	3,078	4,234	0.1	0.3	−1,156	−27.3
Mixed foreign	54,015	35,306	2.2	2.1	18,649	52.7
Czech	622,796	531,103	100.0	100.0	91,693	17.2
Austria	611,738	507,921	98.2	95.6	103,817	20.4
Hungary	4,953	2,783	0.8	0.5	2,170	78.0
Russia	1,476	1,651	0.2	0.3	−175	−10.6
Germany	1,279	16,626	0.2	3.1	−15,347	−92.3
Europe, not specified	1,101	401	0.2	0.1	700	174.6
Other countries	774	862	0.1	0.2	−88	−10.2
Mixed foreign	1,475	949	0.2	0.2	526	55.4

[1] A minus sign (—) denotes decrease.
[2] Less than one-tenth of 1 per cent.
[3] Except possessions of the United States.
[4] Includes Azores and Cape Verde Islands.

MOTHER TONGUE OF THE FOREIGN WHITE STOCK. 977

TABLE 4.—MOTHER TONGUE OF THE FOREIGN WHITE STOCK BY COUNTRY OF ORIGIN, FOR THE UNITED STATES: 1920 AND 1910—Continued.

[Countries shown in this table represent their prewar areas. Figures for 1910 revised (see text, p. 968). Per cent not shown where base is less than 100.]

MOTHER TONGUE AND COUNTRY OF ORIGIN.	Number. 1920	Number. 1910	Per cent distribution. 1920	Per cent distribution. 1910	Increase:[1] 1910-1920 Number.	Increase:[1] 1910-1920 Per cent.
Slavic and Lettic—Con.						
Slovak	619,866	281,707	100.0	100.0	338,159	120.0
Austria	320,849	109,870	51.8	39.0	210,979	192.0
Hungary	287,508	166,931	46.4	59.3	120,577	72.2
Russia	4,221	2,875	0.7	1.0	1,346	46.8
Germany	1,013	732	0.2	0.3	281	38.4
Serbia	576	54	0.1	(²)	522	.....
Europe, not specified	335	291	0.1	0.1	44	15.1
Other countries	1,449	525	0.2	0.2	924	176.0
Mixed foreign	3,915	429	0.6	0.2	3,486	812.6
Russian	731,949	91,341	100.0	100.0	640,608	701.3
Russia[3]	681,311	62,463	93.1	68.4	618,848	990.7
Austria	39,967	23,268	5.5	25.5	16,699	71.8
Hungary	5,000	2,210	0.7	2.4	2,796	126.5
Germany	626	911	0.1	1.0	−285	−31.3
Rumania	476	188	0.1	0.2	288	153.2
Asia, not specified	408	53	0.1	0.1	355	.....
Other countries	1,198	1,936	0.2	2.1	−738	−38.1
Mixed foreign	2,957	312	0.4	0.3	2,645	847.8
Ruthenian	95,458	34,837	100.0	100.0	60,621	174.0
Austria	86,942	23,512	91.1	67.5	63,430	269.8
Hungary	6,299	6,531	6.6	18.7	−232	−3.6
Russia	1,549	4,643	1.6	13.3	−3,094	−66.6
Rumania	151	12	0.2	(²)	139	.....
Other countries	177	101	0.2	0.3	76	75.2
Mixed foreign	340	38	0.4	0.1	302	.....
Slovenian	208,552	181,594	100.0	100.0	26,958	14.8
Austria	161,340	173,224	77.4	95.4	−11,884	−6.9
Hungary	43,449	7,804	20.8	4.3	35,645	456.8
Russia	992		0.5		992	.....
Serbia	553	26	0.3	(²)	527	.....
Germany	360		0.2		360	.....
Montenegro	194		0.1		194	.....
Italy	187	158	0.1	0.1	29	18.4
Other countries	657	240	0.3	0.1	417	173.8
Mixed foreign	820	142	0.4	0.1	678	477.5
Serbo-Croatian	200,421	128,064	100.0	100.0	72,357	56.5
Hungary	87,171	16,581	43.5	12.9	70,590	425.7
Austria	80,525	99,070	40.2	77.4	−18,545	−18.7
Serbia	26,929	5,115	13.4	4.0	21,814	426.5
Montenegro	2,694	5,159	1.3	4.0	−2,465	−47.8
Russia	369	437	0.2	0.3	−68	−15.6
Germany	297	182	0.1	0.1	115	63.2
Turkey in Europe	295	979	0.1	0.8	−684	−69.9
Greece	208	13	0.1	(²)	195	.....
Italy	146	27	0.1	(²)	119	.....
Turkey in Asia	134	116	0.1	0.1	18	15.5
Other countries	611	330	0.3	0.3	281	85.2
Mixed foreign	1,042	55	0.5	(²)	987	.....
Bulgarian	14,420	19,183	100.0	100.0	−4,763	−24.8
Bulgaria	10,400	11,152	72.1	58.1	−752	−6.7
Turkey in Europe	2,235	5,845	15.5	30.5	−3,610	−61.8
Greece	945	16	6.6	0.1	929	.....
Hungary	251	1,851	1.7	9.6	−1,600	−86.4
Austria	147	156	1.0	0.8	−9	−5.8
Russia	126	12	0.9	0.1	114	.....
Serbia	120	1	0.8	(²)	119	.....
Turkey in Asia	60	50	0.4	0.3	10	.....
Rumania	47	53	0.3	0.3	−6	.....
Germany	37	13	0.3	0.1	24	.....
Other countries	33	27	0.2	0.1	6	.....
Mixed foreign	19	7	0.1	(²)	12	.....
Slavic, not specified	3,624	34,799	100.0	100.0	−31,175	−89.6
Hungary	2,807	9,293	77.5	26.7	−6,486	−69.8
Austria	660	21,541	18.2	61.9	−20,881	−96.9
Germany	122	1,043	3.4	3.0	−921	−88.3
Other countries	25	2,886	0.7	8.3	−2,861	−99.1
Mixed foreign	10	36	0.3	0.1	−26	.....
Lithuanian and Lettish	336,600	207,821	100.0	100.0	128,779	62.0
Russia	330,710	200,937	98.3	96.7	129,773	64.6
Austria	2,346	1,883	0.7	0.9	463	24.6
Germany	1,655	3,645	0.5	1.8	−1,990	−54.6
Hungary	523	179	0.2	0.1	344	192.2
Rumania	175		0.1		175	.....
Other countries	525	1,012	0.2	0.5	−487	−48.1
Mixed foreign	666	165	0.2	0.1	501	303.6
Unclassified and unknown:						
Yiddish and Hebrew	2,043,613	1,664,142	100.0	100.0	379,471	22.8
Russia	1,591,115	1,306,650	77.9	78.5	284,466	21.8
Austria	276,609	196,181	13.5	11.8	80,428	41.0
Rumania	54,372	56,202	2.7	3.4	−1,830	−3.3
Hungary	32,734	32,358	1.6	1.9	376	1.2
Germany	13,470	15,190	0.7	0.9	−1,720	−11.3
Turkey in Asia	2,542	1,029	0.1	0.1	1,513	147.0
England	2,445	14,950	0.1	0.9	−12,505	−83.6
Other countries	6,635	6,214	0.3	0.4	421	6.8
Mixed foreign	63,690	35,368	3.1	2.1	28,322	80.1
Unclassified and unknown—Continued.						
Magyar	473,568	315,283	100.0	100.0	158,255	50.2
Hungary	469,449	313,311	99.1	99.4	156,138	49.8
Germany	699	816	0.1	0.3	−117	−14.3
Rumania	640	237	0.1	0.1	403	170.0
Russia	455	325	0.1	0.1	130	40.0
Other countries	546	499	0.1	0.2	47	9.4
Mixed foreign	1,749	95	0.4	(²)	1,654	.....
Finnish	265,472	197,515	100.0	100.0	67,957	34.4
Finland	260,143	183,136	98.0	92.7	77,007	42.0
Russia	1,941	8,662	0.7	4.4	−6,721	−77.6
Sweden	1,060	2,729	0.4	1.4	−1,669	−61.2
Norway	397	1,236	0.1	0.6	−839	−67.9
Other countries	218	386	0.1	0.2	−168	−43.5
Mixed foreign	1,713	1,366	0.6	0.7	347	25.4
Armenian	52,840	29,690	100.0	100.0	23,150	78.0
Turkey in Asia	50,416	27,111	95.4	91.3	23,305	86.0
Russia	829	1,206	1.6	4.1	−377	−31.3
Asia, not specified	522	189	1.0	0.6	333	176.2
Turkey in Europe	395	731	0.7	2.5	−336	−46.0
Austria	112		0.2		112	.....
Greece	50	11	0.1	(²)	45	.....
Africa	33	43	0.1	0.1	−10	.....
Bulgaria	33	45	0.1	0.2	−12	.....
Hungary	30	16	0.1	0.1	14	.....
Other countries	134	304	0.3	1.0	−170	−55.9
Mixed foreign	280	34	0.5	0.1	246	.....
Syrian and Arabic	104,139	46,495	100.0	100.0	57,644	124.0
Turkey in Asia	99,181	39,663	95.2	85.3	59,518	150.1
Asia, not specified	2,139	760	2.1	1.6	1,379	181.4
Europe, not specified	1,009	167	1.0	0.4	842	504.2
Africa	600	395	0.6	0.8	205	51.9
Serbia	181	26	0.2	0.1	155	.....
Turkey in Europe	147	5,038	0.1	10.8	−4,891	−97.1
Austria	130		0.1		130	.....
Russia	126	49	0.1	0.1	77	.....
Other countries	405	367	0.4	0.8	38	10.4
Mixed foreign	221	30	0.2	0.1	191	.....
Turkish	8,505	5,310	100.0	100.0	3,195	60.2
Turkey in Asia	7,341	2,471	86.3	46.5	4,870	197.1
Turkey in Europe	593	2,449	7.0	46.1	−1,856	−75.8
Greece	215	255	2.5	4.8	−40	−15.7
Russia	77	13	0.9	0.2	64	.....
Austria	51	3	0.6	0.1	48	.....
Asia, not specified	42	32	0.5	0.6	10	.....
Bulgaria	34	21	0.4	0.4	13	.....
Other countries	115	65	1.4	1.2	50	.....
Mixed foreign	37	1	0.4	(²)	36	.....
Albanian	6,426	2,358	100.0	100.0	4,068	172.5
Turkey in Europe	5,885	1,951	91.6	82.7	3,934	201.6
Italy	247	85	3.8	3.6	162	.....
Greece	86	51	1.3	2.2	35	.....
Turkey in Asia	52	246	0.8	10.4	−194	−78.9
Austria	41	3	0.6	0.1	38	.....
Other countries	110	22	1.7	0.9	88	.....
Mixed foreign	5		0.1		5	.....
All other	1,788	770	100.0	100.0	1,018	132.2
Asia, not specified	1,060	554	59.3	71.9	506	91.8
Africa	233	37	13.0	4.8	196	.....
Russia	108	59	6.0	7.7	49	.....
Serbia	87	1	4.9	0.1	86	.....
Turkey in Asia	61	9	3.4	1.2	52	.....
Austria	64	4	3.6	0.5	60	.....
Hungary	58	51	3.2	6.6	7	.....
Germany	26	11	1.5	1.4	15	.....
Other countries	81	43	4.5	5.6	38	.....
Mixed foreign	10	1	0.6	0.1	9	.....
Unknown	20,336	297,918	100.0	100.0	−277,582	−93.2
Germany	4,391	103,957	21.6	34.9	−99,566	−95.8
Austria	4,177	56,642	20.5	19.0	−52,465	−92.6
Europe, not specified	3,128	3,898	15.4	1.3	−770	−19.8
Russia	1,995	51,176	9.8	17.2	−49,181	−96.1
Switzerland	1,100	6,652	5.4	2.2	−5,552	−83.5
Hungary	738	18,138	3.6	6.1	−17,400	−95.9
West Indies[4]	594	3,323	2.9	1.1	−2,729	−82.1
South America	501	1,862	2.5	0.6	−1,361	−73.1
Luxemburg	445	145	2.2	(²)	300	206.9
Turkey in Asia	428	4,610	2.1	1.5	−4,182	−90.7
Finland	317		1.6		317	.....
Atlantic Islands[5]	312	1,082	1.5	0.4	−770	−71.2
Belgium	256	6,802	1.3	2.3	−6,546	−96.2
Africa	209	750	1.0	0.3	−541	−72.1
At sea	160	7,611	0.8	2.6	−7,451	−97.9
Pacific Islands[4]	133	666	0.7	0.2	−533	−80.0
India	127	397	0.6	0.1	−270	−68.0
Asia, not specified	112	566	0.6	0.2	−454	−80.2
Central America	74	327	0.4	0.1	−253	−77.4
Turkey in Europe	38	2,645	0.2	0.9	−2,607	−98.6
Other countries	852	23,374	4.2	7.8	−22,522	−96.4
Mixed foreign	249	3,295	1.2	1.1	−3,046	−92.4

[1] A minus sign (−) denotes decrease.
[2] Less than one-tenth of 1 per cent.
[3] See footnote to Table 2, p. 974.
[4] Except possessions of the United States.
[5] Includes Azores and Cape Verde Islands.

75647°—22——62

978

POPULATION.

TABLE 5.—MOTHER TONGUE OF THE FOREIGN-BORN WHITE POPULATION BY PRINCIPAL COUNTRIES OF BIRTH, FOR THE UNITED STATES: 1920.

[Countries shown in this table represent their postwar areas.]

MOTHER TONGUE AND COUNTRY OF BIRTH.	FOREIGN-BORN WHITE: 1920	
	Number.	Per cent distri-bution.
All mother tongues	13,712,754	100.0
English and Celtic	3,007,932	21.9
Germanic	2,449,364	17.9
Scandinavian	1,194,933	8.7
Latin and Greek	2,990,954	21.8
Slavic and Lettic	2,460,332	17.9
Unclassified	1,602,073	11.7
Unknown	7,166	0.1
English and Celtic	3,007,932	100.0
Ireland	1,035,944	34.4
England	797,358	26.5
Canada	789,347	26.2
Scotland	252,994	8.4
Wales	66,914	2.2
Newfoundland	13,075	0.4
West Indies¹	11,364	0.4
Australia	9,838	0.3
Germany	3,917	0.1
Pacific Islands¹	3,057	0.1
India	2,287	0.1
Africa	2,094	0.1
Russia	1,934	0.1
At sea	1,842	0.1
South America	1,734	0.1
Other countries	14,233	0.5
Germanic:		
German	2,267,128	100.0
Germany	1,641,482	72.4
Austria	201,603	8.9
Russia	116,535	5.1
Switzerland	97,087	4.3
Hungary	76,845	3.4
Poland	38,179	1.7
France	21,997	1.0
Czechoslovakia	16,446	0.7
Canada	11,136	0.5
Luxemburg	10,844	0.5
Rumania	8,187	0.4
Jugo-Slavia	7,787	0.3
Belgium	1,910	0.1
At sea	1,825	0.1
Danzig	1,685	0.1
Netherlands	1,677	0.1
Italy	1,497	0.1
England	1,488	0.1
Denmark	1,487	0.1
Other countries	7,451	0.3
Dutch and Frisian	136,540	100.0
Netherlands	128,905	94.4
Belgium	2,383	1.7
Germany	1,614	1.2
Canada	687	0.5
Switzerland	348	0.3
West Indies¹	294	0.2
Russia	290	0.2
Africa	285	0.2
Hungary	207	0.2
Austria	206	0.2
Pacific Islands¹	191	0.1
Denmark	183	0.1
England	178	0.1
Luxemburg	144	0.1
South America	144	0.1
Other countries	486	0.4
Flemish	45,696	100.0
Belgium	44,776	98.0
Netherlands	252	0.6
France	249	0.5
Luxemburg	87	0.2
Canada	104	0.2
Other countries	228	0.5
Scandinavian:		
Swedish	643,203	100.0
Sweden	621,545	96.6
Finland	17,721	2.8
Norway	1,546	0.2
Canada	658	0.1
Denmark	619	0.1
Other countries	1,114	0.2
Norwegian	362,199	100.0
Norway	360,754	99.6
Canada	462	0.1
Sweden	308	0.1
At sea	184	0.1
Other countries	491	0.1
Scandinavian—Continued.		
Danish	189,531	100.0
Denmark	185,564	97.9
Germany	2,589	1.4
Canada	361	0.2
Norway	269	0.1
Sweden	197	0.1
Other countries	551	0.3
Latin and Greek:		
Italian	1,624,998	100.0
Italy	1,604,492	98.7
Switzerland	7,527	0.5
Austria	4,256	0.3
South America	2,580	0.2
France	1,918	0.1
Canada	847	0.1
Other countries	3,378	0.2
French	466,956	100.0
Canada	307,790	65.9
France	125,589	26.9
Belgium	12,793	2.7
Switzerland	12,605	2.7
Germany	1,540	0.3
Luxemburg	1,283	0.3
Italy	406	0.1
Austria	417	0.1
England	415	0.1
Africa	370	0.1
South America	364	0.1
West Indies¹	371	0.1
Denmark	269	0.1
Other countries	2,684	0.6
Spanish	556,111	100.0
Mexico	476,618	85.7
Spain	48,535	8.7
West Indies¹	13,125	2.4
South America	8,263	1.5
Central America	3,228	0.6
Greece	3,188	0.6
Turkey in Europe	1,313	0.2
Other countries	1,841	0.3
Portuguese	105,895	100.0
Portugal	66,726	63.0
Atlantic Islands²	37,314	35.2
South America	1,419	1.3
West Indies¹	110	0.1
Other countries	326	0.3
Rumanian	62,336	100.0
Rumania	51,682	82.9
Hungary	4,646	7.5
Austria	4,399	7.1
Greece	383	0.6
Jugo-Slavia	220	0.4
Canada	188	0.3
Russia	164	0.3
Turkey in Asia	100	0.2
Albania	98	0.2
Poland	77	0.1
England	64	0.1
Bulgaria	64	0.1
Other countries	251	0.4
Greek	174,658	100.0
Greece	168,276	96.3
Turkey in Europe	2,034	1.2
Turkey in Asia	1,451	0.8
Austria	634	0.4
Poland	245	0.1
Europe, not specified	215	0.1
Russia	202	0.1
Africa	197	0.1
Jugo-Slavia	194	0.1
Albania	187	0.1
Italy	135	0.1
Bulgaria	134	0.1
Rumania	129	0.1
Armenia	110	0.1
Syria	105	0.1
Other countries	410	0.2
Slavic and Lettic:		
Polish	1,077,392	100.0
Poland	922,812	85.7
Russia	72,065	6.7
Austria	43,618	4.0
Germany	27,853	2.6
Hungary	2,138	0.2
Lithuania	1,840	0.2
Czechoslovakia	1,537	0.1
Canada	978	0.1
England	852	0.1
Jugo-Slavia	809	0.1
Other countries	2,890	0.3
Czech	234,564	100.0
Czechoslovakia	190,868	81.4
Austria	38,820	16.5
Hungary	1,287	0.5
Russia	908	0.4
Germany	700	0.3
Jugo-Slavia	637	0.3
Poland	404	0.2
Europe, not specified	245	0.1
Canada	136	0.1
Other countries	550	0.2
Slovak	274,948	100.0
Czechoslovakia	133,179	48.4
Austria	90,370	32.9
Hungary	28,771	10.5
Jugo-Slavia	13,815	5.0
Poland	4,730	1.7
Russia	1,730	0.6
Germany	374	0.1
Rumania	343	0.1
Italy	245	0.1
Canada	187	0.1
Europe, not specified	141	0.1
Other countries	1,063	0.4
Russian	392,049	100.0
Russia³	361,843	92.3
Austria	12,117	3.1
Poland	8,781	2.2
England	1,327	0.3
Hungary	1,255	0.3
Lithuania	1,157	0.3
Canada	984	0.3
Rumania	936	0.2
Czechoslovakia	928	0.2
Jugo-Slavia	427	0.1
Asia, not specified	412	0.1
Germany	397	0.1
Other countries	1,485	0.4
Ruthenian	55,672	100.0
Poland	43,534	78.2
Austria	7,482	13.4
Czechoslovakia	3,228	5.8
Russia	545	1.0
Hungary	339	0.6
Rumania	203	0.4
Jugo-Slavia	111	0.2
Canada	90	0.2
Other countries	170	0.3
Slovenian	102,744	100.0
Jugo-Slavia	46,388	45.1
Austria	44,611	43.4
Czechoslovakia	5,678	5.5
Hungary	3,290	3.2
Poland	605	0.6
Russia	547	0.5
Italy	490	0.5
Germany	305	0.3
Rumania	128	0.1
Other countries	702	0.7
Serbo-Croatian	125,844	100.0
Jugo-Slavia	94,114	74.8
Austria	24,028	19.1
Hungary	4,466	3.5
Czechoslovakia	908	0.7
Italy	528	0.4
Poland	268	0.2
Greece	205	0.2
Russia	155	0.1
Fiume	143	0.1
Rumania	140	0.1
Germany	136	0.1
Canada	114	0.1
Other countries	609	0.5

¹ Except possessions of the United States.   ² Includes Azores and Cape Verde Islands.   ³ See footnote 5 to Table 1, p. 973.

MOTHER TONGUE OF THE FOREIGN WHITE STOCK. 979

TABLE 5.—MOTHER TONGUE OF THE FOREIGN-BORN WHITE POPULATION BY PRINCIPAL COUNTRIES OF BIRTH, FOR THE UNITED STATES: 1920—Continued.

[Countries shown in this table represent their postwar areas.]

MOTHER TONGUE AND COUNTRY OF BIRTH.	FOREIGN-BORN WHITE: 1920 Number.	Per cent distri- bution.	MOTHER TONGUE AND COUNTRY OF BIRTH.	FOREIGN-BORN WHITE: 1920 Number.	Per cent distri- bution.	MOTHER TONGUE AND COUNTRY OF BIRTH.	FOREIGN-BORN WHITE: 1920 Number.	Per cent distri- bution.
Slavic and Lettic—Continued.			**Unclassified and unknown—Con.**			**Unclassified and unknown—Con.**		
Bulgarian	12,853	100.0	Magyar	268,112	100.0	Turkish	6,627	100.0
Bulgaria	9,462	73.6	Hungary	253,780	94.7	Turkey in Asia	5,326	80.4
Greece	2,651	20.6	Czechoslovakia	6,682	2.5	Turkey in Europe	416	6.8
Turkey in Europe	177	1.4	Jugo-Slavia	2,678	1.0	Armenia	263	4.0
Jugo-Slavia	129	1.0	Rumania	2,606	1.0	Greece	223	3.4
Russia	93	0.7	Poland	817	0.3	Syria	107	1.6
Germany	78	0.6	Germany	375	0.1	Palestine	48	0.7
Austria	76	0.6	Canada	281	0.1	Albania	41	0.6
Hungary	64	0.5	Russia	244	0.1	Bulgaria	32	0.5
Other countries	123	1.0	Other countries	649	0.2	Asia, not specified	35	0.5
						Other countries	136	2.1
Slavic, not specified	2,039	100.0						
Hungary	1,615	79.2	Finnish	133,567	100.0	Albanian	5,515	100.0
Austria	343	16.8	Finland	130,808	97.9	Albania	5,086	92.2
Germany	33	1.6	Russia	1,294	1.0	Greece	119	2.2
Other countries	48	2.4	Sweden	580	0.4	Italy	118	2.1
			Canada	388	0.3	Turkey in Europe	39	0.7
Lithuanian and Lettish	182,227	100.0	Norway	313	0.2	France	32	0.6
Lithuania	126,441	69.4	Other countries	184	0.1	Other countries	121	2.2
Russia	49,140	27.0						
Poland	3,446	1.9				All other	1,228	100.0
Austria	682	0.4	Armenian	37,647	100.0	Asia, not specified	802	65.3
Germany	634	0.3	Armenia	35,321	93.8	Africa	173	14.1
Scotland	415	0.2	Turkey in Asia	524	1.4	Russia	51	4.2
England	404	0.2	Russia	471	1.3	Jugo-Slavia	42	3.4
Czechoslovakia	179	0.1	Turkey in Europe	391	1.0	Austria	23	1.9
Jugo-Slavia	146	0.1	Asia, not specified	313	0.8	Other countries	137	11.2
Canada	139	0.1	Syria	131	0.3			
Other countries	601	0.3	Africa	78	0.2	Unknown	7,166	100.0
			Greece	55	0.1	Austria	1,327	18.5
Unclassified and unknown:			Austria	54	0.1	Unknown	1,196	16.7
Yiddish and Hebrew	1,091,820	100.0	Bulgaria	51	0.1	Poland	662	9.2
Russia	791,181	72.5	Other countries	258	0.7	Russia	507	7.1
Poland	114,362	10.5				West Indies[1]	471	6.6
Austria	99,279	9.1				Hungary	369	5.1
Rumania	37,287	3.4	Syrian and Arabic	57,557	100.0	South America	348	4.9
Hungary	16,964	1.6	Syria	50,727	88.1	Europe, not specified	343	4.8
England	9,845	0.9	Turkey in Asia	1,656	2.9	Germany	300	4.2
Lithuania	4,971	0.5	Asia, not specified	1,640	2.8	Jugo-Slavia	203	2.8
Germany	3,100	0.3	Palestine	1,183	2.1	At sea	199	2.8
Canada	2,687	0.2	Europe, not specified	807	1.4	Atlantic Islands[2]	137	1.9
Czechoslovakia	2,024	0.2	Africa	495	0.9	Luxemburg	132	1.8
Palestine	1,568	0.1	Jugo-Slavia	160	0.3	Africa	115	1.6
France	897	0.1	Canada	139	0.2	Turkey in Asia	103	1.4
Turkey in Asia	796	0.1	South America	96	0.2	Central America	102	1.4
Italy	712	0.1	Armenia	93	0.2	Switzerland	90	1.3
Scotland	694	0.1	Mexico	77	0.1	Asia, not specified	78	1.1
Ireland	694	0.1	Turkey in Europe	62	0.1	Belgium	72	1.0
Jugo-Slavia	645	0.1	Greece	58	0.1	Finland	69	1.0
Other countries	4,114	0.4	Austria	52	0.1	France	51	0.7
			Other countries	312	0.5	Other countries	292	4.1

[1] Except possessions of the United States.　　　　[2] Includes Azores and Cape Verde Islands.

980 POPULATION.

TABLE 6.—COUNTRY OF BIRTH OF THE FOREIGN-BORN WHITE POPULATION BY PRINCIPAL MOTHER TONGUES, FOR THE UNITED STATES: 1920.

[Countries shown in this table represent their postwar areas.]

COUNTRY OF BIRTH AND MOTHER TONGUE	Number	Per cent distribution
All foreign countries........	13,712,754	100.0
Europe....	11,877,991	86.6
Northwestern Europe....	3,828,876	27.9
Central Europe....	4,330,860	31.6
Eastern Europe....	1,803,965	13.2
Southern Europe....	1,908,389	13.9
Other Europe....	5,901	(1)
America....	1,656,801	12.1
All other....	177,962	1.3
Northwestern Europe.		
England....	812,828	100.0
English and Celtic....	797,358	98.1
Yiddish and Hebrew....	9,845	1.2
German....	1,488	0.2
Russian....	1,327	0.2
All other....	2,810	0.3
Scotland....	254,567	100.0
English and Celtic....	252,994	99.4
All other....	1,573	0.6
Wales....	67,066	100.0
English and Celtic....	66,914	99.8
All other....	152	0.2
Ireland....	1,037,233	100.0
English and Celtic....	1,035,944	99.9
All other....	1,289	0.1
Norway....	363,862	100.0
Norwegian....	360,754	99.1
Swedish....	1,546	0.4
All other....	1,562	0.4
Sweden....	625,580	100.0
Swedish....	621,545	99.4
English and Celtic....	1,221	0.2
German....	1,043	0.2
All other....	1,771	0.3
Denmark....	189,154	100.0
Danish....	185,564	98.1
German....	1,487	0.8
All other....	2,103	1.1
Netherlands....	131,766	100.0
Dutch and Frisian....	128,905	97.8
German....	1,677	1.3
All other....	1,184	0.9
Belgium....	62,686	100.0
Flemish....	44,776	71.4
French....	12,793	20.4
Dutch and Frisian....	2,383	3.8
German....	1,910	3.0
All other....	824	1.3
Luxemburg....	12,585	100.0
German....	10,844	86.2
French....	1,283	10.2
Dutch and Frisian....	144	1.1
All other....	314	2.5
Switzerland....	118,659	100.0
German....	97,087	81.8
French....	12,605	10.6
Italian....	7,527	6.3
All other....	1,440	1.2
France....	152,890	100.0
French....	125,589	82.1
German....	21,997	14.4
Italian....	1,918	1.3
English and Celtic....	1,072	0.7
All other....	2,314	1.5

COUNTRY OF BIRTH AND MOTHER TONGUE	Number	Per cent distribution
Central Europe.		
Germany....	1,686,102	100.0
German....	1,641,482	97.4
Polish....	27,853	1.7
English and Celtic....	3,917	0.2
Yiddish and Hebrew....	3,100	0.2
Danish....	2,589	0.2
Dutch and Frisian....	1,614	0.1
French....	1,540	0.1
All other....	4,007	0.2
Poland....	1,139,978	100.0
Polish....	922,812	80.9
Yiddish and Hebrew....	114,962	10.0
Ruthenian....	43,534	3.8
German....	38,179	3.3
Russian....	8,781	0.8
Slovak....	4,730	0.4
Lithuanian and Lettish....	3,446	0.3
All other....	4,134	0.4
Czechoslovakia....	362,438	100.0
Czech....	190,868	52.7
Slovak....	133,179	36.7
German....	16,446	4.5
Magyar....	6,682	1.8
Slovenian....	5,678	1.6
Ruthenian....	3,228	0.9
Yiddish and Hebrew....	2,024	0.6
Polish....	1,537	0.4
All other....	2,794	0.8
Austria....	575,625	100.0
German....	201,603	35.0
Yiddish and Hebrew....	99,279	17.2
Slovak....	90,370	15.7
Slovenian....	44,611	7.8
Polish....	43,618	7.6
Czech....	38,820	6.7
Croatian....	17,886	3.1
Russian....	12,117	2.1
Ruthenian....	7,452	1.3
Serbian....	5,825	1.0
Rumanian....	4,399	0.8
Italian....	4,258	0.7
English and Celtic....	1,039	0.2
All other....	4,348	0.8
Hungary....	397,282	100.0
Magyar....	253,780	63.9
German....	76,845	19.3
Slovak....	28,791	7.2
Yiddish and Hebrew....	16,964	4.3
Rumanian....	4,646	1.2
Slovenian....	3,290	0.8
Croatian....	2,785	0.7
Polish....	2,138	0.5
Serbian....	1,675	0.4
Wendish....	1,615	0.4
Czech....	1,287	0.3
Russian....	1,255	0.3
All other....	2,231	0.6
Jugo-Slavia....	169,437	100.0
Croatian....	60,204	35.5
Slovenian....	46,388	27.4
Serbian....	27,954	16.5
Slovak....	13,815	8.2
German....	7,787	4.6
Montenegrin....	4,191	2.5
Magyar....	2,678	1.6
Dalmatian....	1,765	1.0
All other....	4,655	2.7

COUNTRY OF BIRTH AND MOTHER TONGUE	Number	Per cent distribution
Eastern Europe.		
Russia....	1,400,489	100.0
Yiddish and Hebrew....	791,181	56.5
Russian[2]....	361,843	25.8
German....	116,535	8.3
Polish....	72,065	5.1
Lithuanian and Lettish....	49,140	3.5
All other....	9,725	0.7
Lithuania....	135,068	100.0
Lithuanian and Lettish....	126,441	93.6
Yiddish and Hebrew....	4,971	3.7
Polish....	1,840	1.4
Russian....	1,157	0.9
All other....	659	0.5
Finland....	149,824	100.0
Finnish....	130,808	87.3
Swedish....	17,721	11.8
All other....	1,295	0.9
Rumania....	102,823	100.0
Rumanian....	51,682	50.3
Yiddish and Hebrew....	37,287	36.8
German....	8,167	7.9
Magyar....	2,606	2.5
All other....	3,081	3.0
Bulgaria....	10,477	100.0
Bulgarian....	9,462	90.3
All other....	1,015	9.7
Turkey in Europe....	5,284	100.0
Greek....	2,034	38.5
Spanish....	1,313	24.8
Turkish....	416	7.9
Armenian....	391	7.4
Yiddish and Hebrew....	265	5.0
Bulgarian....	177	3.3
German....	151	2.9
All other....	537	10.2
Southern Europe.		
Greece....	175,072	100.0
Greek....	168,276	95.6
Spanish....	3,188	1.8
Bulgarian....	2,551	1.5
All other....	1,857	1.1
Albania....	5,608	100.0
Albanian....	5,086	90.7
Greek....	187	3.3
All other....	335	6.0
Italy....	1,610,109	100.0
Italian....	1,604,492	99.7
German....	1,497	0.1
All other....	4,120	0.3
Spain....	49,247	100.0
Spanish....	48,535	98.6
English and Celtic....	351	0.7
All other....	361	0.7
Portugal....	67,453	100.0
Portuguese....	66,726	98.9
All other....	727	1.1
Other Europe.		
Other Europe....	5,901	100.0
German....	2,334	39.6
Syrian and Arabic....	809	13.7
Polish....	443	7.5
English and Celtic....	425	7.2
Czech....	248	4.2
Greek....	215	3.6
Slovak....	200	3.4
Yiddish and Hebrew....	152	2.6
Croatian....	144	2.4
Italian....	117	2.0
Spanish....	108	1.8
All other....	706	12.0

1 Less than one-tenth of 1 per cent.

2 See footnote 5 to Table 1, p. 973.

MOTHER TONGUE OF THE FOREIGN WHITE STOCK. 981

TABLE 6.—COUNTRY OF BIRTH OF THE FOREIGN-BORN WHITE POPULATION BY PRINCIPAL MOTHER TONGUES, FOR THE UNITED STATES: 1920—Continued.

[Countries shown in this table represent their postwar areas.]

COUNTRY OF BIRTH AND MOTHER TONGUE.	FOREIGN-BORN WHITE: 1920 Number.	Per cent distri-bution.	COUNTRY OF BIRTH AND MOTHER TONGUE.	FOREIGN-BORN WHITE: 1920 Number.	Per cent distri-bution.	COUNTRY OF BIRTH AND MOTHER TONGUE.	FOREIGN-BORN WHITE: 1920 Number.	Per cent distri-bution.
Asia.			**Asia—Continued.**			**America—Continued.**		
Armenia	36,626	100.0	Other Asia	7,708	100.0	Central and South America	20,929	100.0
Armenian	35,321	96.4	English and Celtic	3,223	41.8	Spanish	11,491	54.9
Yiddish and Hebrew	312	0.9	Syrian and Arabic	1,653	21.4	Italian	2,603	12.4
All other	993	2.7	Persian	801	10.4	English and Celtic	2,284	10.9
			Russian	454	5.9	Portuguese	1,430	6.8
Palestine	3,202	100.0	German	365	4.7	German	965	4.6
Yiddish and Hebrew	1,568	49.0	Armenian	320	4.2	French	406	1.9
Syrian and Arabic	1,183	36.9	Yiddish and Hebrew	235	3.7	Yiddish and Hebrew	328	1.6
All other	451	14.1	All other	607	7.9	All other	1,422	6.8
Syria	51,900	100.0	**America.**			**Other countries.**		
Syrian and Arabic	50,727	97.7	Canada	1,117,878	100.0	Atlantic Islands[2]	38,984	100.0
All other	1,173	2.3	English and Celtic	789,347	70.6	Portuguese	37,314	95.7
			French	307,790	27.5	English and Celtic	1,245	3.2
Turkey in Asia	11,014	100.0	German	11,136	1.0	All other	425	1.1
Turkish	5,326	48.4	Yiddish and Hebrew	2,687	0.2			
Syrian and Arabic	1,656	15.0	All other	6,918	0.6	Australia	10,801	100.0
Greek	1,451	13.2				English and Celtic	9,838	91.1
Yiddish and Hebrew	796	7.2	Newfoundland	13,242	100.0	German	405	3.7
Armenian	524	4.8	English and Celtic	13,075	98.7	All other	558	5.2
Spanish	212	1.9	All other	167	1.3			
English and Celtic	173	1.6				All other	17,727	100.0
German	160	1.5	West Indies[1]	26,369	100.0	English and Celtic	7,179	40.5
French	151	1.4	Spanish	13,125	49.8	German	3,294	18.6
Rumanian	100	0.9	English and Celtic	11,364	43.1	Unknown	1,558	8.8
All other	465	4.2	French	371	1.4	French	720	4.1
			All other	1,509	5.7	Yiddish and Hebrew	636	3.6
						Dutch and Frisian	559	3.2
			Mexico	478,383	100.0	Syrian and Arabic	514	2.9
			Spanish	476,618	99.6	Italian	492	2.8
			All other	1,765	0.4	Polish	413	2.3
						All other	2,362	13.3

[1] Except possessions of the United States.   [2] Includes Azores and Cape Verde Islands.

982

POPULATION.

TABLE 7.—MOTHER TONGUE OF THE FOREIGN WHITE

	All mother tongues		English and Celtic		Germanic						Scandinavian			
DIVISION AND STATE.					German		Dutch and Frisian		Flemish		Swedish		Norwegian	
	1920	1910	1920	1910	1920	1910	1920	1910	1920	1910	1920	1910	1920	1910
1 United States.......	36,398,958	32,243,382	9,729,365	9,930,861	8,164,111	8,646,402	370,499	311,015	87,890	42,722	1,485,062	1,394,410	1,020,788	976,827
GEOGRAPHIC DIVISIONS:														
2 New England.......	4,512,930	3,867,095	1,981,954	1,974,417	185,564	193,670	6,045	4,327	3,971	2,069	142,307	130,631	15,274	13,157
3 Middle Atlantic......	12,010,828	10,417,491	3,145,076	3,368,176	2,111,589	2,351,155	69,729	60,392	11,913	5,335	174,190	164,357	60,309	48,952
4 East North Central...	9,148,492	8,175,654	1,984,717	1,996,683	2,896,993	3,073,613	178,484	162,612	49,570	26,311	389,506	373,514	245,434	245,485
5 West North Central..	4,749,839	4,827,034	871,419	980,695	1,716,113	1,795,401	73,240	58,966	12,041	5,435	500,194	495,773	542,150	543,602
6 South Atlantic......	869,524	730,398	251,295	232,471	205,640	222,795	3,839	1,774	1,497	267	10,202	6,609	5,699	3,084
7 East South Central..	274,765	301,834	86,454	99,779	106,659	133,860	1,732	1,087	247	96	3,732	3,603	1,196	1,145
8 West South Central..	1,155,942	954,042	162,499	159,432	277,264	291,869	4,318	2,599	1,652	512	18,836	16,637	7,311	6,413
9 Mountain..........	1,210,391	1,053,831	413,455	421,592	205,994	170,753	12,817	7,705	2,130	495	81,791	75,843	47,896	31,998
10 Pacific............	2,466,247	1,915,103	832,496	697,616	458,295	413,286	20,295	11,553	4,860	2,202	164,295	127,983	106,038	83,011
NEW ENGLAND:														
11 Maine.............	269,915	245,088	142,531	137,200	3,005	3,378	130	114	37	8	4,720	4,388	1,150	1,071
12 New Hampshire......	216,819	199,675	79,832	85,063	4,996	4,774	293	122	605	79	3,828	3,564	883	856
13 Vermont...........	128,492	124,916	57,655	62,391	2,526	2,538	153	99	22	21	2,395	2,505	218	177
14 Massachusetts.......	2,572,751	2,221,497	1,257,891	1,235,850	76,341	82,593	4,109	3,205	2,260	1,478	78,037	71,429	9,475	8,238
15 Rhode Island........	420,427	372,671	171,485	178,632	10,663	12,191	276	245	566	208	13,823	13,398	975	906
16 Connecticut.........	909,526	703,248	272,758	275,281	88,033	88,196	1,024	542	472	275	38,604	35,347	2,567	1,909
MIDDLE ATLANTIC:														
17 New York..........	6,503,761	5,736,520	1,696,877	1,799,142	1,134,050	1,300,109	33,188	29,729	4,160	1,924	101,365	93,235	45,787	36,924
18 New Jersey.........	1,824,412	1,435,985	460,197	459,824	355,235	362,919	31,785	27,399	2,440	1,412	22,394	18,904	9,904	8,237
19 Pennsylvania........	3,682,655	3,244,986	988,502	1,109,210	622,304	688,127	4,756	3,264	5,313	1,999	50,440	52,218	4,618	3,791
EAST NORTH CENTRAL:														
20 Ohio..............	1,902,771	1,621,638	419,481	420,297	652,728	713,433	8,320	7,325	1,771	463	16,422	11,100	3,065	2,013
21 Indiana...........	519,527	509,873	110,818	119,295	223,894	257,546	6,749	5,690	3,889	2,248	12,565	11,845	1,513	1,163
22 Illinois............	3,232,770	2,926,407	643,522	676,588	904,730	965,732	38,341	33,173	15,925	10,180	235,075	231,237	66,077	68,222
23 Michigan..........	1,931,180	1,560,406	629,660	574,397	396,602	386,896	100,295	91,363	16,856	7,927	66,807	61,680	17,055	16,269
24 Wisconsin.........	1,562,244	1,557,330	181,236	206,106	719,039	750,006	24,770	25,061	11,129	5,493	58,637	57,052	147,724	157,818
WEST NORTH CENTRAL:														
25 Minnesota.........	1,541,309	1,484,146	200,677	206,940	395,682	395,916	15,160	10,621	3,754	1,884	283,815	271,343	281,046	279,617
26 Iowa.............	855,628	905,665	197,624	227,292	341,301	371,951	35,787	29,511	2,280	873	63,461	66,198	62,513	66,851
27 Missouri...........	688,108	747,097	166,426	190,678	335,471	392,609	3,769	3,028	1,735	956	13,206	13,593	1,826	1,717
28 North Dakota.......	431,988	407,894	62,559	70,834	142,826	115,090	2,936	2,016	668	92	28,371	26,901	127,532	123,352
29 South Dakota.......	310,549	318,119	48,489	56,846	115,672	116,510	9,039	7,305	582	308	24,115	23,366	58,946	60,787
30 Nebraska..........	522,155	538,218	90,636	104,206	216,148	224,957	3,382	3,606	920	439	55,010	58,666	7,014	7,645
31 Kansas............	400,102	427,295	105,008	123,899	169,013	178,368	3,167	2,870	2,102	883	32,215	35,700	3,273	3,823
SOUTH ATLANTIC:														
32 Delaware..........	52,739	43,293	19,783	21,164	6,120	6,603	96	45	15	4	703	631	113	65
33 Maryland..........	311,649	296,012	65,176	69,597	110,684	131,759	955	500	107	26	1,501	888	1,054	651
34 District of Columbia..	87,372	69,417	38,473	33,121	17,495	17,789	403	181	51	18	1,311	661	719	315
35 Virginia...........	83,415	64,571	30,039	26,270	14,416	14,092	647	279	85	32	1,406	722	987	692
36 West Virginia.......	144,378	114,710	31,180	31,996	24,885	27,034	326	298	928	99	829	603	128	78
37 North Carolina......	18,576	14,793	7,598	6,596	3,145	3,228	198	72	26	3	369	223	148	70
38 South Carolina......	19,120	17,191	6,126	6,416	5,068	5,474	109	55	66	58	270	182	178	140
39 Georgia...........	46,417	40,744	16,864	15,589	9,435	9,864	292	144	64	12	763	628	314	283
40 Florida...........	105,858	69,667	36,056	20,722	14,392	6,952	813	200	155	15	3,050	1,531	1,449	761
EAST SOUTH CENTRAL:														
41 Kentucky..........	141,426	164,757	38,956	46,814	76,036	96,779	902	483	124	57	548	441	187	136
42 Tennessee.........	53,236	56,826	20,318	23,552	13,686	17,009	350	228	22	7	802	886	192	240
43 Alabama..........	52,903	51,873	18,792	19,801	11,715	13,421	337	264	60	11	1,645	1,528	553	538
44 Mississippi.........	27,200	28,878	8,388	9,602	5,222	6,651	143	112	41	21	737	748	264	231
WEST SOUTH CENTRAL:														
45 Arkansas..........	53,065	53,517	15,920	16,671	21,328	21,779	878	383	126	20	975	950	288	193
46 Louisiana..........	154,887	164,499	28,406	33,071	32,203	41,687	750	316	544	140	1,266	954	953	631
47 Oklahoma.........	142,087	134,128	41,590	41,388	52,536	53,627	1,029	826	350	86	3,273	3,037	1,067	1,205
48 Texas............	805,903	601,898	76,593	68,302	171,197	174,776	1,961	1,074	632	266	13,322	11,606	5,003	4,384
MOUNTAIN:														
49 Montana..........	258,457	198,453	93,539	84,412	50,142	31,080	3,999	2,084	945	128	17,158	12,256	27,793	13,949
50 Idaho............	131,416	115,622	53,316	49,802	26,259	21,361	1,224	851	196	82	13,432	11,212	7,023	6,056
51 Wyoming.........	67,262	59,622	24,568	24,279	12,519	9,360	389	195	121	8	4,885	4,576	1,038	1,245
52 Colorado..........	321,062	308,279	100,189	113,847	82,195	74,953	2,587	1,830	576	182	24,808	26,119	4,061	3,946
53 New Mexico........	61,356	48,985	9,519	10,600	5,984	6,947	284	219	97	18	853	767	363	830
54 Arizona...........	140,304	89,000	21,960	18,702	7,697	6,420	283	112	93	32	2,163	1,682	787	528
55 Utah.............	196,120	194,920	96,969	102,478	16,772	14,690	3,955	2,320	72	14	17,218	17,054	5,819	5,490
56 Nevada...........	34,414	38,950	13,395	17,472	4,426	5,942	96	94	30	31	1,179	1,277	412	454
PACIFIC:														
57 Washington........	608,071	523,725	213,638	185,233	110,690	104,198	7,499	5,091	1,773	908	72,864	59,099	65,405	52,654
58 Oregon...........	271,420	238,239	90,501	79,928	74,531	69,248	2,711	1,801	1,161	535	23,609	19,580	16,119	13,322
59 California..........	1,586,756	1,153,139	528,357	432,455	273,074	239,840	10,085	4,661	1,935	759	67,822	49,304	24,514	17,035

[1] Figures for 1910 revised (see text, p. 968).

MOTHER TONGUE OF THE FOREIGN WHITE STOCK. 988

STOCK, BY DIVISIONS AND STATES: 1920 AND 1910.

Scandinavian—Continued.		Latin and Greek.												Slavic and Lettic.				
Danish.		Italian.		French.		Spanish.		Portuguese.		Rumanian.		Greek.		Polish.		Czech.		
1920	1910	1920	1910	1920	1910	1920	1910	1920	1910	1920	1910	1920	1910	1920	1910	1920	1910	
466,946	410,165	3,365,864	2,135,393	1,290,110	1,288,897	850,848	444,132	215,728	139,221	91,683	49,588	221,768	128,701	2,436,895	1,684,108	622,796	531,193	1
16,703	14,581	494,924	279,069	651,788	633,533	5,417	2,573	124,252	74,458	2,285	1,111	44,710	22,837	275,342	161,494	8,306	5,895	2
43,673	37,123	1,943,798	1,238,438	181,048	173,675	47,081	15,145	4,722	2,088	41,248	19,534	55,497	25,009	992,522	703,204	82,289	66,164	3
102,565	94,064	411,536	231,515	204,149	231,103	14,775	2,907	1,897	1,929	35,443	18,802	54,895	22,006	969,902	636,380	266,313	228,609	4
168,181	154,507	72,035	56,496	89,274	101,789	28,584	12,503	299	230	5,445	5,391	13,428	15,979	94,078	93,343	167,477	156,993	5
4,513	2,577	81,408	55,275	15,504	11,181	27,396	23,998	878	298	2,328	1,513	15,217	6,680	56,045	42,868	13,611	11,192	6
1,379	1,313	19,929	15,049	9,443	8,711	1,813	1,253	98	43	515	515	2,893	1,916	3,444	3,747	934	683	7
7,087	5,962	74,660	64,270	36,511	35,550	418,064	241,934	505	433	623	413	4,824	2,536	17,470	19,230	57,959	47,219	8
55,149	48,673	60,474	55,570	26,282	25,853	153,704	81,778	905	817	908	622	10,967	14,162	9,035	8,848	10,911	6,382	9
67,746	50,765	207,100	139,711	76,111	67,502	154,014	61,956	82,172	58,925	2,908	1,627	19,337	17,576	19,057	14,994	14,996	8,056	10
2,427	2,143	5,574	4,594	87,356	76,296	171	239	309	201	27	23	1,704	876	2,706	2,028	66	41	11
373	239	3,902	2,957	91,246	81,911	87	65	237	181	41	48	6,850	4,461	9,205	5,244	97	29	12
338	301	8,085	7,134	40,304	41,226	1,046	447	68	124	12	9	241	140	3,722	2,668	155	39	13
6,670	6,043	237,858	131,330	303,821	307,316	2,169	1,360	99,096	61,061	834	356	29,044	14,340	145,822	86,241	3,648	2,805	14
616	600	70,699	43,020	79,801	76,860	228	153	22,022	11,378	389	288	1,623	1,200	16,578	10,613	258	338	15
6,279	5,255	168,806	90,034	49,260	49,924	1,716	309	2,520	1,513	962	387	5,248	1,820	97,309	54,700	4,082	2,583	16
24,912	21,040	1,124,162	741,932	119,622	122,069	36,373	12,039	2,559	1,340	28,552	11,037	31,230	14,333	403,969	278,351	52,730	46,378	17
12,277	10,073	344,765	192,707	24,103	17,634	4,524	1,468	953	215	3,480	1,430	6,203	2,354	176,342	106,219	9,720	6,364	18
6,484	6,010	474,871	303,799	37,323	33,972	6,184	1,638	1,210	533	9,216	7,067	18,064	8,322	412,211	318,634	19,839	13,427	19
5,227	3,933	121,511	63,427	32,578	29,389	3,277	484	457	398	16,576	10,640	15,376	3,676	138,106	77,045	59,206	49,562	20
2,559	2,189	12,862	9,188	14,806	14,348	1,744	245	49	31	4,071	3,924	4,388	2,120	46,251	28,793	3,666	2,077	21
36,995	34,505	196,925	118,137	49,124	50,660	6,860	1,708	1,220	1,406	4,998	2,955	22,006	11,648	382,101	272,122	140,011	122,993	22
17,591	15,091	57,475	26,876	77,572	94,517	2,400	297	121	47	9,229	929	8,360	1,481	251,381	130,967	17,005	9,839	23
40,193	38,946	22,763	13,887	30,069	42,180	494	173	50	47	569	414	4,765	3,081	152,063	127,453	46,425	44,138	24
44,600	38,078	15,306	13,390	33,630	41,060	516	220	27	36	2,253	1,853	2,812	2,037	49,490	48,240	35,394	32,644	25
47,970	43,504	9,812	7,680	10,653	11,159	3,263	658	77	48	324	524	3,408	3,795	3,082	4,083	32,859	31,803	26
4,605	4,256	31,500	21,569	17,350	16,205	4,825	2,127	91	60	1,814	1,968	3,751	3,304	15,603	15,809	13,746	13,701	27
12,750	12,501	341	1,377	7,267	8,213	60	38	5	11	365	395	508	1,173	4,751	4,680	8,401	7,167	28
17,015	15,332	1,007	1,764	3,660	5,262	135	41	9	9	120	79	408	291	1,861	2,301	10,982	9,831	29
34,260	33,507	6,730	4,911	5,114	5,812	3,011	406	34	28	514	483	1,747	3,642	14,720	13,421	54,024	50,376	30
6,931	7,329	7,339	5,805	11,600	14,078	16,774	9,103	56	38	55	89	794	1,737	4,571	4,809	11,981	11,471	31
147	87	8,325	4,538	626	583	256	45	22	5	117	19	387	56	9,194	6,134	217	115	32
827	485	19,692	11,179	2,788	2,119	729	357	87	38	420	283	1,855	672	29,129	24,460	9,752	9,102	33
574	324	7,561	4,548	2,342	1,551	562	286	43	14	88	51	1,814	425	946	1,052	343	124	34
838	498	5,506	4,077	1,919	1,212	649	175	226	99	152	93	2,366	909	1,752	2,543	1,548	1,035	35
263	175	27,033	21,242	2,544	2,551	2,298	572	18	6	823	600	3,699	1,132	12,663	6,917	918	526	36
141	78	830	699	664	490	129	53	31	15	27	20	765	256	298	261	52	16	37
195	128	769	546	446	388	127	70	21	9	20	9	802	358	585	470	116	70	38
306	225	1,410	989	1,458	1,088	520	364	77	34	149	81	2,080	1,153	782	791	241	116	39
1,222	577	10,282	7,457	2,717	1,199	22,126	22,076	353	78	532	377	1,949	1,719	696	240	424	88	40
270	230	4,194	2,563	4,107	3,477	337	128	21	10	278	248	583	384	1,307	1,283	266	283	41
372	371	4,873	3,817	1,846	1,682	375	150	44	10	88	78	719	485	966	1,044	248	174	42
445	423	6,507	4,761	2,094	2,052	558	458	18	16	116	122	1,308	865	611	934	255	174	43
292	289	4,355	3,908	1,396	1,500	543	517	15	7	38	67	283	182	560	486	165	52	44
499	445	3,019	2,731	2,299	2,272	460	231	17	1	67	48	415	242	1,292	1,382	1,006	769	45
808	758	46,394	43,017	18,950	21,508	7,603	4,605	224	219	92	92	849	504	605	1,543	689	155	46
1,773	1,636	4,863	4,234	4,592	4,125	8,658	3,221	30	26	45	26	823	734	2,530	2,900	6,335	5,581	47
4,007	3,123	20,384	14,288	10,670	7,645	401,843	233,877	234	187	419	247	2,737	1,056	13,043	13,405	49,929	40,714	48
7,441	4,052	6,927	8,497	8,968	8,349	432	213	43	42	374	384	1,472	2,168	2,923	2,089	4,389	1,634	49
9,142	7,473	2,653	2,694	3,301	3,256	3,303	1,362	120	73	61	9	835	1,924	390	596	1,305	640	50
2,709	2,375	3,632	3,279	1,321	1,319	2,257	473	69	62	62	70	1,407	2,022	1,663	1,445	1,007	656	51
6,878	5,819	30,145	27,196	6,658	7,104	15,313	3,654	79	90	258	109	2,109	2,524	3,024	3,830	2,957	2,846	52
327	276	3,637	2,941	1,272	1,338	34,497	22,118	59	12	8	0	334	174	246	244	297	172	53
1,161	721	2,385	2,311	1,622	1,207	93,278	51,965	67	38	55	9	431	94	441	228	391	96	54
26,066	26,554	6,167	4,287	1,769	1,565	1,658	213	30	24	34	21	3,682	4,177	256	279	393	255	55
1,425	1,403	4,928	4,365	1,371	1,715	2,966	1,775	438	476	6	11	697	1,079	92	137	172	83	56
18,782	15,397	19,205	17,152	15,330	15,921	2,216	889	524	438	324	327	4,375	4,674	7,805	6,307	4,329	2,873	57
8,665	6,885	7,689	7,028	6,481	6,541	1,715	901	416	349	253	268	2,069	3,889	2,190	2,537	2,897	1,685	58
40,299	28,483	180,206	115,531	54,800	45,040	150,083	60,166	81,232	58,138	2,331	1,032	12,893	9,013	9,062	6,150	7,770	3,498	59

POPULATION.

984

TABLE 7.—MOTHER TONGUE OF THE FOREIGN WHITE

FOREIGN WHITE STOCK [1]—continued.

Slavic and Lettic—Continued.

	Slovak.		Russian.[2]		Ruthenian.		Slovenian.		Serbo-Croatian.		Bulgarian.		Slavic, not specified.		Lithuanian and Lettish.	
DIVISION AND STATE.	1920	1910	1920	1910	1920	1910	1920	1910	1920	1910	1920	1910	1920	1910	1920	1910
1 United States....	619,866	281,707	731,949	91,341	95,458	34,837	208,552	181,594	200,421	128,064	14,420	19,183	3,624	34,799	336,600	207,821
GEOGRAPHIC DIVISIONS:																
2 New England.....	25,834	12,393	67,745	6,280	5,728	1,454	4,014	4,424	1,646	842	189	627	604	545	75,185	40,629
3 Middle Atlantic.....	391,285	186,694	411,516	60,708	72,461	27,804	72,176	83,120	66,346	42,866	8,290	6,260	169	6,388	108,678	58,774
4 East North Central.	159,310	64,126	107,788	10,111	13,146	3,164	81,029	51,370	79,956	42,016	1,594	3,491	0	545	5,107	6,101
5 West North Central.	13,006	6,660	49,687	5,848	2,228	1,668	19,184	14,526	22,150	17,097	228	303	23	332	8,060	5,808
6 South Atlantic......	9,600	4,359	29,591	3,266	1,067	355	4,323	2,860	4,416	2,112	629	358	83	142	94	216	187
7 East South Central..	1,252	641	6,053	654	48	45	942	521	629	358	289	310	117	485	1,192	1,291
8 West South Central.	2,404	1,095	11,380	906	211	53	1,804	1,664	1,072	1,085	1,080	3,028	7	1,064	873	703
9 Mountain..........	9,064	3,724	13,104	1,007	209	104	12,452	11,645	12,421	11,064	908	2,108	2	429	2,870	1,784
10 Pacific............	7,511	2,015	35,087	2,561	360	190	12,628	11,464	11,785	9,721	908	2,108	2	429	2,870	1,784
NEW ENGLAND:																
11 Maine.............	1,232	607	2,241	163	27	2	30	147	61	43	3	24	......	1	2,185	1,245
12 New Hampshire....	59	14	2,886	251	203	44	18	12	72	10	11	38	1	5	2,304	1,594
13 Vermont...........	323	139	1,245	115	107	157	73	79	82	13	4	35	......	15	104	141
14 Massachusetts......	2,732	1,367	32,617	2,607	1,296	427	614	704	796	205	95	227	......	90	44,064	24,493
15 Rhode Island......	284	199	4,122	211	1,306	221	22	54	142	6	43	66	......	8	1,333	824
16 Connecticut........	21,204	10,067	24,634	2,933	2,789	603	3,257	3,338	493	565	33	237	603	417	25,045	12,332
MIDDLE ATLANTIC:																
17 New York.........	46,209	22,515	255,265	32,728	17,055	4,540	15,025	9,017	8,143	5,308	655	971	7	3,595	27,006	17,457
18 New Jersey........	48,857	23,285	48,613	3,873	8,092	4,441	6,894	6,926	1,720	850	90	179	18	3,705	15,884	8,503
19 Pennsylvania.......	296,219	140,894	107,638	24,107	47,314	18,823	50,257	67,177	56,483	36,708	1,005	1,764	2,668	17,617	91,430	60,584
EAST NORTH CENTRAL:																
20 Ohio...............	78,982	32,780	31,318	3,642	6,213	1,276	39,012	21,349	25,595	11,897	3,418	1,546	18	1,634	10,532	4,784
21 Indiana............	11,750	3,202	5,977	470	223	262	3,039	2,588	7,846	4,201	1,008	1,306	......	622	3,741	1,908
22 Illinois............	44,010	20,585	38,750	3,889	2,891	1,258	21,595	16,482	24,844	15,966	1,352	2,613	110	3,718	74,805	44,910
23 Michigan..........	12,776	2,841	23,630	1,226	3,337	203	6,808	5,556	14,818	6,466	2,007	446	3	197	12,022	2,899
24 Wisconsin..........	11,792	4,718	8,111	884	482	165	9,575	5,395	6,853	3,486	355	349	38	217	7,578	4,269
WEST NORTH CENTRAL:																
25 Minnesota..........	6,478	2,672	8,562	1,477	715	79	13,803	10,567	9,003	7,866	621	1,205	4	212	1,031	614
26 Iowa..............	1,880	1,209	5,145	503	53	52	649	788	3,526	2,331	323	427	3	19	1,613	959
27 Missouri...........	2,531	1,786	10,530	1,073	711	381	1,021	1,010	3,814	3,487	262	697	1	128	800	677
28 North Dakota.......	333	113	11,365	1,878	682	1,001	101	108	177	123	154	346	......	13	132	2,486
29 South Dakota......	221	161	3,416	233	18	42	341	291	404	698	120	479	......	41	74	147
30 Nebraska.........	281	139	4,973	453	20	12	334	269	1,608	825	60	144	......	38	1,093	593
31 Kansas............	1,282	580	5,696	231	29	101	2,935	1,493	3,558	2,667	45	133	1	94	274	625
SOUTH ATLANTIC:																
32 Delaware..........	165	69	1,909	170	307	121	106	32	21	11	......	10	......	3	267	101
33 Maryland..........	1,398	604	10,074	1,806	356	36	536	309	375	240	34	40	23	39	5,074	3,697
34 District of Columbia.	72	19	3,422	179	11	9	50	8	44	20	5	13	......	......	76	104
35 Virginia..........	1,670	480	3,546	280	27	36	376	206	94	42	20	41	......	29	150	234
36 West Virginia......	5,901	3,121	3,937	365	332	130	3,043	2,271	3,661	1,778	126	172	......	269	2,282	1,492
37 North Carolina.....	94	19	821	30	2	2	42	6	37	5	5	1	......	......	38	64
38 South Carolina.....	19	5	1,144	82	7	......	19	......	14	1	......	1	......	1	19	19
39 Georgia............	83	35	3,524	291	14	7	77	24	100	9	7	4	......	1	63	82
40 Florida...........	198	7	1,214	63	11	14	74	4	70	6	30	12	......	......	91	15
EAST SOUTH CENTRAL:																
41 Kentucky..........	373	181	2,328	129	42	4	207	29	354	163	38	11	......	17	137	63
42 Tennessee.........	90	56	1,662	283	4	21	71	33	34	44	13	25	......	2	28	58
43 Alabama..........	648	342	1,289	103	2	......	206	185	174	135	36	105	......	52	32	28
44 Mississippi.........	141	62	794	139	......	20	458	274	67	16	1	1	......	23	19	38
WEST SOUTH CENTRAL:																
45 Arkansas..........	769	501	677	45	3	11	125	475	95	47	28	35	......	18	77	103
46 Louisiana..........	337	111	2,242	185	1	8	694	480	188	255	53	32	......	20	45	42
47 Oklahoma.........	465	178	3,371	382	157	9	326	236	171	179	124	111	1	27	848	926
48 Texas............	833	305	5,090	294	50	25	659	473	618	607	84	132	116	420	230	220
MOUNTAIN:																
49 Montana..........	2,264	1,095	3,521	262	83	45	3,622	2,592	4,839	4,518	407	1,018	......	31	258	157
50 Idaho............	150	71	734	47	12	......	281	114	507	576	53	413	7	33	49	50
51 Wyoming.........	1,075	499	554	86	36	12	1,297	1,378	946	750	136	335	......	77	77	73
52 Colorado..........	5,322	1,608	6,052	524	64	36	5,246	5,923	1,831	2,151	366	501	......	866	322	331
53 New Mexico.......	244	183	277	17	2	......	453	170	767	832	34	29	......	7	21	44
54 Arizona...........	154	220	1,201	22	5	11	381	359	1,788	802	35	28	......	28	65	26
55 Utah.............	364	36	621	38	6	......	846	869	1,013	981	34	94	......	5	70	8
56 Nevada...........	91	12	144	11	1	......	326	240	730	454	15	10	......	17	11	15
PACIFIC:																
57 Washington........	4,220	1,268	6,976	623	222	82	3,445	3,715	4,174	4,417	314	873	......	155	1,408	965
58 Oregon...........	598	120	3,676	273	71	19	975	1,077	1,223	1,463	302	805	......	35	497	239
59 California..........	2,693	627	24,435	1,665	67	89	8,208	6,672	6,388	3,841	292	340	2	239	974	580

[1] Figures for 1910 revised (see text, p. 968).

MOTHER TONGUE OF THE FOREIGN WHITE STOCK.   985

STOCK, BY DIVISIONS AND STATES: 1920 AND 1910—Continued.

FOREIGN WHITE STOCK [1]—continued.

Unclassified.

Yiddish and Hebrew.		Magyar.		Finnish.		Armenian.		Syrian and Arabic.		Turkish.		Albanian.		All other.		Unknown.		Of mixed mother tongue.		
1920	1910	1920	1910	1920	1910	1920	1910	1920	1910	1920	1910	1920	1910	1920	1910	1920	1910	1920	1910	
2,043,613	1,664,142	473,538	315,283	265,472	197,515	52,840	29,690	104,139	46,495	8,505	5,310	6,426	2,358	1,788	770	20,336	297,918	791,058	590,920	1
211,232	168,819	23,418	15,754	31,051	19,096	18,603	13,211	20,846	10,991	1,841	1,744	3,261	1,302	217	103	735	10,230	61,959	44,229	2
1,339,275	1,160,910	232,426	173,219	22,565	14,926	14,121	7,350	29,785	13,050	3,663	1,204	1,414	477	524	255	4,639	85,011	244,987	160,775	3
289,880	188,242	177,461	100,448	95,842	73,198	7,558	2,947	20,117	7,450	1,467	862	1,070	219	591	349	5,547	59,203	194,416	154,334	4
69,678	55,798	10,538	8,853	65,683	49,977	821	689	7,409	4,081	209	545	298	233	139	10	3,127	62,622	125,064	111,097	5
71,109	44,964	14,798	8,226	1,792	664	548	239	8,221	3,163	254	112	29	6	45	9	1,302	19,944	18,655	11,654	6
10,656	8,664	2,446	1,107	335	317	85	126	3,292	1,730	89	92	26	......	15	1	865	7,950	7,265	6,405	7
13,338	7,863	2,265	1,462	589	423	213	235	7,589	2,958	103	174	12	2	45	7	1,655	20,938	22,081	18,079	8
11,350	9,459	3,280	2,440	12,575	12,747	405	322	2,706	1,289	190	187	158	29	48	2	765	13,990	36,686	29,941	9
27,095	19,423	6,906	3,774	35,040	25,567	10,486	4,571	4,174	1,783	689	390	158	90	164	34	1,701	18,030	78,945	54,406	10
4,954	4,029	64	29	2,365	1,201	230	265	1,308	781	24	58	451	394	1	......	46	1,135	2,774	2,364	11
2,036	1,145	64	50	3,010	1,847	428	454	912	495	57	97	131	95	......	......	28	2,127	2,264	1,804	12
1,308	1,434	388	453	822	425	63	20	486	334	......	1	6	......	......	1	9	370	1,441	1,365	13
141,228	113,757	1,606	1,335	23,120	15,272	13,204	8,307	13,270	7,253	1,334	1,146	2,354	764	38	11	354	4,667	35,985	25,061	14
12,257	12,014	203	162	325	360	2,950	2,902	2,203	958	265	364	127	49	......	11	44	557	4,798	3,675	15
49,449	36,440	21,093	13,725	1,409	591	1,728	1,263	2,667	1,170	161	78	192	......	178	80	254	1,374	14,697	9,960	16
1,013,289	907,922	93,606	76,100	15,362	9,405	7,054	4,006	14,752	7,312	2,891	958	496	371	309	161	2,117	28,868	145,894	95,769	17
119,018	83,059	59,190	34,340	2,690	1,990	3,519	1,942	3,871	1,092	326	84	168	7	72	32	777	18,547	40,192	25,971	18
206,968	169,929	79,630	62,779	4,518	3,531	3,548	1,402	11,162	4,646	440	162	750	99	143	62	1,745	37,596	59,401	39,095	19
57,039	39,989	97,962	59,040	12,491	7,415	1,028	344	7,159	2,442	506	137	456	36	103	66	1,505	15,552	35,324	24,574	20
6,672	5,360	15,357	10,290	377	307	163	169	1,512	986	98	161	85	45	80	18	689	9,781	10,096	7,497	21
167,806	115,949	29,041	19,270	4,233	3,238	2,210	1,556	3,064	1,568	308	422	124	75	288	253	1,548	19,551	71,886	53,832	22
40,687	14,270	27,763	7,653	65,936	54,255	3,175	521	7,195	1,642	465	71	274	24	99	6	904	8,095	40,812	35,459	23
17,676	12,724	7,338	4,195	12,805	7,983	982	357	1,187	812	90	71	131	39	26	6	901	6,224	36,298	32,972	24
24,572	17,563	2,823	2,286	58,705	43,283	213	261	1,649	694	50	120	27	63	13	2	602	10,000	48,276	41,243	25
7,399	5,771	743	381	138	313	118	50	1,026	626	46	60	7	2	89	2	549	9,185	17,907	17,047	26
27,984	24,465	4,414	3,756	134	190	233	176	1,782	1,055	61	178	216	157	17	3	948	12,017	16,841	14,281	27
1,668	1,744	705	583	3,398	2,728	42	30	731	497	15	34	......	11	2	......	204	11,243	12,849	10,616	28
728	615	501	478	3,184	3,240	30	40	624	309	8	52	5	......	4	3	194	3,298	8,567	7,951	29
6,210	4,400	853	908	64	124	154	110	1,025	651	14	79	40	......	6	......	288	6,062	11,888	11,306	30
1,117	1,240	499	461	60	99	31	13	572	249	15	22	3	......	8	......	342	10,817	8,756	8,653	31
2,521	1,264	361	247	57	4	8	1	17	26	2	1	......	......	5	......	44	512	828	627	32
41,057	28,281	1,686	975	243	69	55	25	164	99	18	20	2	......	4	2	237	3,436	6,057	4,229	33
7,385	3,959	283	138	127	28	75	7	502	138	21	1	2	......	8	5	244	2,798	2,320	1,531	34
8,670	4,268	2,156	1,632	352	87	232	119	1,277	601	54	5	3	3	3	2	165	2,623	2,084	1,155	35
1,871	1,808	9,420	4,866	423	166	62	18	2,372	1,001	108	38	5	3	4	......	173	2,194	2,123	1,199	36
1,468	593	92	23	18	36	12	9	1,072	438	3	15	......	......	17	......	67	1,268	365	195	37
1,572	541	69	27	64	50	6	18	793	371	2	1	......	......	......	......	40	1,336	454	365	38
4,867	3,956	334	286	61	96	29	31	1,016	375	35	16	5	......	6	......	93	2,191	1,354	979	39
1,698	294	397	82	447	128	69	11	1,008	114	11	15	12	......	4	......	239	3,586	4,069	1,874	40
3,668	4,643	1,542	286	59	25	31	21	704	417	25	9	2	......	5	......	304	2,393	3,496	3,050	41
3,790	2,526	505	435	32	44	20	29	279	138	4	56	24	......	4	1	207	1,989	1,573	1,343	42
2,251	1,082	340	338	108	66	32	49	1,056	463	51	15	......	......	1	......	253	1,772	1,430	1,270	43
947	413	59	48	136	182	2	27	1,253	712	9	12	......	......	5	......	101	1,796	766	742	44
749	440	119	61	15	22	6	8	461	184	......	10	......	......	3	......	167	2,260	1,482	1,180	45
1,840	1,530	638	412	187	152	39	57	2,096	852	60	125	2	......	6	......	421	5,141	5,702	5,897	46
1,424	1,056	422	367	109	50	30	50	1,628	527	7	8	2	......	20	6	242	4,800	3,264	2,564	47
9,325	4,837	1,086	622	278	199	138	120	3,404	1,395	36	31	8	2	16	1	825	8,737	11,633	8,438	48
607	441	704	515	6,736	6,339	144	80	430	209	62	47	34	......	23	......	144	4,217	8,034	4,950	49
146	120	178	98	1,590	1,178	12	23	123	76	4	16	45	......	2	1	87	1,527	4,876	3,888	50
516	164	495	359	1,689	2,170	58	101	147	67	34	43	10	......	3	......	33	791	1,909	1,354	51
8,702	8,025	1,344	1,067	1,061	1,360	43	52	612	435	27	20	13	10	13	1	309	4,422	7,808	6,898	52
130	65	164	176	65	19	2	23	461	166	1	8	......	......	6	......	24	379	934	702	53
378	198	158	55	502	612	19	3	622	177	7	4	6	......	6	......	58	980	2,102	1,330	54
777	358	187	140	802	908	117	40	284	143	38	41	50	19	......	......	82	1,225	9,919	9,694	55
94	88	52	30	130	161	10	......	27	16	17	8	......	......	1	......	28	449	1,104	1,125	56
3,584	3,696	759	593	15,925	11,655	279	90	602	404	149	149	88	24	23	2	388	8,652	20,756	15,210	57
2,700	2,312	588	555	9,738	6,741	95	40	375	237	32	56	15	......	9	2	222	3,187	9,297	6,482	58
20,811	13,415	5,559	2,626	9,377	7,171	10,112	4,441	3,197	1,142	508	185	55	66	132	30	1,091	6,191	48,892	32,714	59

[1] See footnote to Table 2, p. 974.

POPULATION.

TABLE 8.—PER CENT DISTRIBUTION OF THE FOREIGN WHITE

PER CENT OF TOTAL FOREIGN WHITE STOCK IN SPECIFIED DIVISION OR STATE.

	DIVISION AND STATE.	English and Celtic.	Germanic.			Scandinavian.			Latin and Greek.						Slavic and Lettic.	
			German.	Dutch and Frisian.	Flemish.	Swedish.	Norwegian.	Danish.	Italian.	French.	Spanish.	Portuguese.	Rumanian.	Greek.	Polish.	Czech.
1	United States	26.7	22.4	1.0	0.2	4.1	2.8	1.3	9.2	3.5	2.3	0.6	0.3	0.6	6.7	1.7
	GEOGRAPHIC DIVISIONS:															
2	New England	43.9	4.1	0.1	0.1	3.2	0.3	0.4	11.0	14.4	0.1	2.8	0.1	1.0	6.1	0.2
3	Middle Atlantic	26.2	17.6	0.6	0.1	1.5	0.5	0.4	16.2	1.5	0.4	(1)	0.3	0.5	8.3	0.7
4	East North Central	21.7	31.7	2.0	0.5	4.3	2.6	1.1	4.5	2.2	0.2	(1)	0.4	0.6	10.6	2.9
5	West North Central	18.3	36.1	1.5	0.3	10.5	11.4	3.5	1.5	1.9	0.6	(1)	0.1	0.3	2.0	3.5
6	South Atlantic	28.9	23.6	0.4	0.2	1.2	0.6	0.5	9.4	1.8	3.2	0.1	0.3	1.8	6.4	1.6
7	East South Central	31.5	38.8	0.6	0.1	1.4	0.4	0.5	7.3	3.4	0.7	(1)	0.2	1.1	1.3	0.3
8	West South Central	14.1	24.0	0.4	0.1	1.6	0.6	0.6	6.5	3.2	36.2	(1)	0.1	0.4	1.5	5.0
9	Mountain	34.2	17.0	1.1	0.2	6.8	4.0	4.6	5.0	2.2	12.7	0.1	0.1	0.9	0.7	0.9
10	Pacific	33.8	18.6	0.8	0.2	6.7	4.3	2.7	8.4	3.1	6.2	3.3	0.1	0.8	0.8	0.6
	NEW ENGLAND:															
11	Maine	52.8	1.1	(1)	(1)	1.7	0.4	0.9	2.1	32.4	0.1	0.1	(1)	0.6	1.0	(1)
12	New Hampshire	36.7	2.3	0.1	0.3	1.8	0.4	0.2	1.8	42.1	(1)	0.1	(1)	3.2	4.2	(1)
13	Vermont	46.7	2.0	0.1	(1)	1.9	0.2	0.3	6.5	32.6	0.8	0.1	(1)	0.2	3.0	0.1
14	Massachusetts	48.9	3.0	0.2	0.1	3.1	0.4	0.3	9.2	11.8	0.1	3.0	(1)	1.1	5.7	0.1
15	Rhode Island	40.8	2.5	0.1	0.1	3.3	0.2	0.1	16.8	19.0	0.1	5.2	0.1	0.4	3.9	0.1
16	Connecticut	30.0	9.7	0.1	0.1	4.2	0.3	0.7	18.6	5.4	0.2	0.3	0.1	0.6	10.7	0.4
	MIDDLE ATLANTIC:															
17	New York	26.1	17.4	0.5	0.1	1.6	0.7	0.4	17.3	1.8	0.6	(1)	0.4	0.5	6.2	0.8
18	New Jersey	25.2	19.5	1.7	0.1	1.2	0.5	0.7	18.9	1.3	0.2	0.1	0.2	0.3	9.7	0.5
19	Pennsylvania	26.8	16.9	0.1	0.1	1.4	0.1	0.2	12.9	1.0	0.2	(1)	0.3	0.5	11.2	0.5
	EAST NORTH CENTRAL:															
20	Ohio	22.0	34.3	0.4	0.1	0.9	0.2	0.3	6.4	1.7	0.2	(1)	0.9	0.8	7.8	3.1
21	Indiana	21.3	43.1	1.3	0.7	2.4	0.8	0.5	2.5	2.8	0.3	(1)	0.8	0.8	8.9	0.7
22	Illinois	19.9	28.0	1.2	0.6	7.3	2.0	1.1	6.1	1.5	0.2	(1)	0.2	0.7	11.8	4.3
23	Michigan	32.6	20.5	5.2	0.9	3.5	0.9	0.9	3.0	4.0	0.1	(1)	0.5	0.4	13.0	0.9
24	Wisconsin	11.6	46.0	1.6	0.7	3.8	9.5	2.6	1.5	1.9	(1)	(1)	(1)	0.3	9.7	3.0
	WEST NORTH CENTRAL:															
25	Minnesota	13.0	25.7	1.0	0.2	18.4	18.2	2.9	1.0	2.2	(1)	(1)	0.1	0.2	3.2	2.3
26	Iowa	23.1	39.9	4.2	0.3	7.4	7.3	5.6	1.1	1.2	0.4	(1)	(1)	0.4	0.4	3.8
27	Missouri	24.2	48.8	0.5	0.3	1.9	0.3	0.7	4.6	2.5	0.7	(1)	0.3	0.5	2.3	2.0
28	North Dakota	14.5	33.1	0.7	0.2	6.6	29.5	3.0	0.1	1.7	(1)	(1)	0.1	0.1	1.1	2.0
29	South Dakota	15.6	37.2	2.9	0.2	7.8	19.0	5.5	0.3	1.2	(1)	(1)	(1)	0.1	0.6	3.5
30	Nebraska	17.4	41.4	0.6	0.2	10.5	1.3	6.6	1.3	1.0	0.6	(1)	0.1	0.3	2.8	10.3
31	Kansas	26.2	42.2	0.8	0.5	8.1	0.8	1.7	1.8	2.9	4.2	(1)	(1)	0.2	1.1	3.0
	SOUTH ATLANTIC:															
32	Delaware	37.5	11.6	0.2	(1)	1.3	0.2	0.3	15.8	1.2	0.5	(1)	0.2	0.7	17.4	0.4
33	Maryland	20.9	35.5	0.3	(1)	0.5	0.3	0.3	6.3	0.9	0.2	(1)	0.1	0.4	9.3	3.1
34	District of Columbia	44.0	20.0	0.5	0.1	1.5	0.8	0.7	8.7	2.7	0.6	(1)	0.1	2.1	1.1	0.4
35	Virginia	36.0	17.3	0.8	0.1	1.7	1.2	1.0	6.6	2.8	0.8	0.3	0.2	2.8	2.1	1.9
36	West Virginia	21.6	17.2	0.2	0.6	0.6	0.1	0.2	18.7	1.8	1.6	(1)	0.6	2.6	8.8	0.6
37	North Carolina	40.9	16.9	1.1	0.1	2.0	0.8	0.8	4.5	3.6	0.7	0.2	0.1	4.1	1.6	0.3
38	South Carolina	32.0	26.5	0.6	0.3	1.4	0.9	1.0	4.0	2.3	0.7	0.1	0.1	4.2	3.1	0.6
39	Georgia	36.3	20.3	0.6	0.1	1.6	0.7	0.7	3.0	3.1	1.1	0.2	0.3	4.5	1.7	0.5
40	Florida	34.1	13.6	0.8	0.1	2.9	1.4	1.2	9.7	2.6	20.9	0.3	0.5	1.8	0.7	0.4
	EAST SOUTH CENTRAL:															
41	Kentucky	27.5	53.8	0.6	0.1	0.4	0.1	0.4	3.0	2.9	0.2	(1)	0.2	0.4	0.0	0.2
42	Tennessee	38.2	25.7	0.7	(1)	1.5	0.4	0.7	9.2	3.5	0.7	0.1	0.2	1.4	1.8	0.5
43	Alabama	35.5	22.1	0.6	0.1	3.1	1.0	0.8	12.3	4.0	1.1	(1)	0.2	2.5	1.2	0.5
44	Mississippi	30.8	19.2	0.5	0.2	2.7	1.0	1.1	16.0	5.1	2.0	0.1	0.1	1.0	2.1	0.6
	WEST SOUTH CENTRAL:															
45	Arkansas	30.0	40.2	1.1	0.2	1.8	0.5	0.9	5.7	4.3	0.9	(1)	0.1	0.8	2.4	1.9
46	Louisiana	18.3	20.8	0.5	0.4	0.8	0.6	0.5	30.0	12.2	4.9	0.1	0.1	0.5	0.4	0.4
47	Oklahoma	29.3	37.0	0.7	0.2	2.3	0.8	1.2	3.4	3.2	6.1	(1)	(1)	0.6	1.8	4.5
48	Texas	9.5	21.2	0.2	0.1	1.7	0.6	0.5	2.5	1.3	49.8	(1)	0.1	0.3	1.0	6.2
	MOUNTAIN:															
49	Montana	36.2	19.4	1.5	0.4	6.6	10.8	2.9	2.7	3.5	0.2	(1)	0.1	0.6	1.1	1.7
50	Idaho	40.6	20.0	0.9	0.1	10.2	5.3	7.0	2.0	2.5	2.5	0.1	(1)	0.6	0.3	1.0
51	Wyoming	36.5	18.6	0.6	0.2	7.3	2.4	4.0	5.4	2.0	3.4	0.1	0.1	2.1	2.5	1.5
52	Colorado	31.2	25.6	0.8	0.2	7.8	1.3	2.1	9.4	2.1	4.8	(1)	0.1	0.7	0.9	0.9
53	New Mexico	15.5	9.8	0.5	0.2	1.4	0.6	0.5	5.9	2.1	58.2	0.1	(1)	0.5	0.4	0.5
54	Arizona	15.7	5.5	0.2	0.1	1.5	0.6	0.8	1.7	1.2	66.5	(1)	(1)	0.5	0.3	0.3
55	Utah	49.4	8.6	2.0	(1)	8.8	3.0	13.3	3.1	0.9	0.8	(1)	(1)	1.9	0.1	0.2
56	Nevada	38.9	12.9	0.3	0.1	3.4	1.2	4.1	14.3	4.0	8.6	1.3	(1)	2.0	0.3	0.5
	PACIFIC:															
57	Washington	35.1	18.2	1.2	0.3	12.0	10.8	3.1	3.2	2.5	0.4	0.1	0.1	0.7	1.3	0.7
58	Oregon	33.3	27.5	1.0	0.4	8.7	5.9	3.2	2.8	2.4	0.6	0.2	0.1	0.8	0.8	1.1
59	California	33.3	17.2	0.6	0.1	4.3	1.5	2.5	11.4	3.4	9.5	5.1	0.1	0.8	0.6	0.5

1 Less than one-tenth of 1 per cent.

MOTHER TONGUE OF THE FOREIGN WHITE STOCK.   987

STOCK BY MOTHER TONGUE, BY DIVISIONS AND STATES: 1920.

PER CENT OF TOTAL FOREIGN WHITE STOCK IN SPECIFIED DIVISION OR STATE—continued.																		
Slavic and Lettic—Continued.								Unclassified.								Un-known.	Of mixed mother tongue.	
Slovak.	Russian.²	Ruthe-nian.	Slove-nian.	Serbo-Croa-tian.	Bul-garian.	Slavic, not speci-fied.	Lithu-anian and Lettish.	Yiddish and Hebrew.	Magyar.	Finnish.	Armen-ian.	Syrian and Arabic.	Turkish.	Alba-nian.	All other.			
1.7	2.0	0.3	0.6	0.6	(¹)	(¹)	0.9	5.6	1.3	0.7	0.1	0.3	(¹)	(¹)	(¹)	0.1	2.2	1
0.6	1.5	0.1	0.1	(¹)	(¹)	(¹)	1.7	4.7	0.5	0.7	0.4	0.5	(¹)	0.1	(¹)	(¹)	1.4	2
3.3	3.4	0.6	0.6	0.6	(¹)	(¹)	1.1	11.2	1.9	0.2	0.1	0.2	(¹)	(¹)	(¹)	(¹)	2.0	3
1.7	1.2	0.1	0.9	0.9	0.1	(¹)	1.2	3.2	1.9	1.0	0.1	0.2	(¹)	(¹)	(¹)	0.1	2.6	4
0.3	1.0	(¹)	0.4	0.5	(¹)	(¹)	0.1	1.5	0.2	1.4	(¹)	0.2	(¹)	(¹)	(¹)	0.1	2.6	5
1.1	3.4	0.1	0.5	0.5	(¹)	(¹)	0.9	8.2	1.7	0.2	0.1	0.9	(¹)	(¹)	(¹)	0.1	2.3	6
0.5	2.2	(¹)	0.3	0.2	(¹)	....	0.1	3.9	0.9	0.1	(¹)	1.2	(¹)	(¹)	(¹)	0.3	2.6	7
0.2	1.0	(¹)	0.2	0.1	(¹)	(¹)	0.1	1.2	0.2	0.1	(¹)	0.7	(¹)	(¹)	(¹)	0.1	1.9	8
0.8	1.1	(¹)	1.0	1.0	0.1	(¹)	0.1	0.9	0.3	1.0	(¹)	0.2	(¹)	(¹)	(¹)	0.1	3.0	9
0.3	1.4	(¹)	0.5	0.5	(¹)	(¹)	0.1	1.1	0.3	1.4	0.4	0.2	(¹)	(¹)	(¹)	0.1	3.2	10
0.5	0.8	(¹)	(¹)	(¹)	(¹)	....	0.8	1.8	(¹)	0.9	0.1	0.5	(¹)	0.2	(¹)	(¹)	1.0	11
(¹)	1.3	0.1	(¹)	(¹)	(¹)	(¹)	1.1	0.9	(¹)	1.4	0.2	0.4	(¹)	0.1	....	(¹)	1.0	12
0.3	1.0	0.1	0.1	0.1	(¹)	....	0.2	1.1	0.3	0.7	0.1	0.4	....	(²)	....	(¹)	1.2	13
0.1	1.3	0.1	(¹)	(¹)	(¹)	....	1.7	5.5	0.1	0.9	0.5	0.5	0.1	0.1	....	(¹)	1.4	14
0.1	1.0	0.3	(¹)	(¹)	(¹)	....	0.3	2.9	(¹)	0.1	0.7	0.5	0.1	(¹)	....	(¹)	1.1	15
2.3	2.7	0.3	0.4	0.1	(¹)	0.1	2.8	5.4	2.3	0.2	0.2	0.3	(¹)	(¹)	(¹)	(¹)	1.6	16
0.7	3.9	0.3	0.2	0.1	(¹)	(¹)	0.4	15.6	1.4	0.2	0.1	0.2	(¹)	(¹)	(¹)	(¹)	2.2	17
2.7	2.7	0.4	0.4	0.1	(¹)	(¹)	0.9	6.5	3.2	0.1	0.2	0.2	(¹)	(¹)	(¹)	(¹)	2.2	18
8.0	2.9	1.3	1.4	1.5	(¹)	0.1	2.5	5.6	2.2	0.1	0.1	0.3	(¹)	(¹)	(¹)	(¹)	1.6	19
4.2	1.6	0.3	2.1	1.3	0.2	(¹)	0.6	3.0	5.1	0.7	0.1	0.4	(¹)	(¹)	(¹)	0.1	1.9	20
2.3	1.2	(¹)	0.8	1.5	0.2	....	0.7	1.3	3.0	0.1	(¹)	0.3	(¹)	(¹)	(¹)	0.1	1.9	21
1.4	1.2	0.1	0.7	0.8	(¹)	(¹)	2.3	5.2	0.6	0.1	0.1	0.1	(¹)	(¹)	(¹)	(¹)	2.2	22
0.7	1.2	0.2	0.4	0.8	0.1	(¹)	0.6	2.1	1.4	3.4	0.2	0.4	(¹)	(¹)	(¹)	(¹)	2.1	23
0.8	0.5	(¹)	0.6	0.4	(¹)	(¹)	0.5	1.1	0.5	0.8	0.1	0.1	(¹)	(¹)	(¹)	0.1	2.3	24
0.4	0.6	(¹)	0.9	0.6	(¹)	(¹)	0.1	1.6	0.2	3.8	(¹)	0.1	(¹)	(¹)	(¹)	(¹)	3.1	25
0.2	0.6	(¹)	0.1	0.4	(¹)	(¹)	0.2	0.9	0.1	(¹)	(¹)	0.1	(¹)	(¹)	(¹)	0.1	2.1	26
0.4	1.5	0.1	0.1	0.6	(¹)	(¹)	0.1	4.1	0.6	(¹)	(¹)	0.3	(¹)	(¹)	(¹)	0.1	2.4	27
0.1	2.6	0.2	(¹)	(¹)	(¹)	....	(¹)	0.4	0.2	0.8	(²)	0.2	(¹)	....	(¹)	(¹)	3.0	28
0.1	1.1	(¹)	0.1	0.1	(¹)	....	(¹)	0.2	0.2	1.0	(¹)	0.2	(¹)	(¹)	(¹)	0.1	2.8	29
0.1	1.0	(¹)	0.1	0.3	(¹)	....	0.2	1.2	0.2	(¹)	(¹)	0.2	(¹)	(¹)	(¹)	0.1	2.3	30
0.3	1.4	(¹)	0.7	0.9	(¹)	(¹)	0.1	0.3	0.1	(¹)	(¹)	0.1	(¹)	(¹)	(¹)	0.1	2.2	31
0.3	3.6	0.6	0.2	(¹)	....	....	0.5	4.8	0.7	0.1	(¹)	(¹)	(¹)	....	(¹)	0.1	1.6	32
0.4	3.2	0.1	0.2	0.1	(¹)	(¹)	1.6	13.2	0.5	0.1	(¹)	0.1	(¹)	(¹)	(¹)	0.1	1.9	33
0.1	3.9	(¹)	0.1	0.1	(¹)	....	0.1	8.5	0.3	0.1	0.1	0.6	(¹)	(¹)	(¹)	0.3	2.7	34
2.0	4.3	(¹)	0.5	0.1	(¹)	....	0.2	10.4	2.6	0.4	0.3	1.5	0.1	(¹)	(¹)	0.2	2.5	35
4.1	2.7	0.2	2.1	2.5	0.1	(¹)	1.0	1.3	6.5	0.3	(¹)	1.6	0.1	(¹)	(³)	0.1	1.5	36
0.5	4.4	(¹)	0.2	0.2	(¹)	(¹)	0.2	7.9	0.5	0.1	0.1	5.8	(¹)	....	0.1	0.4	2.0	37
0.1	6.0	(¹)	0.1	0.1	....	....	0.1	8.2	0.4	0.3	(¹)	4.1	(¹)	....	....	0.2	2.4	38
0.2	7.6	(¹)	0.2	0.2	(¹)	....	0.1	10.5	0.7	0.1	0.1	2.2	0.1	(¹)	....	0.2	2.9	39
0.2	1.1	(¹)	0.1	0.1	(¹)	(¹)	0.1	1.6	0.4	0.4	0.1	1.0	(¹)	(¹)	(¹)	0.2	3.8	40
0.3	1.6	(¹)	0.1	0.3	(¹)	....	0.1	2.6	1.1	(¹)	(¹)	0.5	(¹)	(¹)	(¹)	0.2	2.5	41
0.2	3.1	(¹)	0.1	0.1	(¹)	....	0.1	7.1	0.9	0.1	(¹)	0.5	(¹)	(¹)	(¹)	0.4	3.0	42
1.2	2.4	(¹)	0.4	0.3	0.1	(¹)	0.1	4.3	0.6	0.2	0.1	2.0	0.1	(¹)	(¹)	0.5	2.7	43
0.5	2.9	....	1.7	0.2	(¹)	(¹)	0.1	3.5	0.2	0.5	(¹)	4.6	(¹)	(¹)	(¹)	0.4	2.8	44
1.4	1.3	(¹)	0.2	0.2	0.1	(¹)	0.1	1.4	0.2	(¹)	(¹)	0.9	....	....	(¹)	0.3	2.8	45
0.2	1.4	(¹)	0.4	0.1	(¹)	....	(¹)	1.2	0.4	0.1	(¹)	1.4	(¹)	(¹)	(¹)	0.3	3.7	46
0.3	2.4	0.1	0.2	0.1	0.1	(¹)	0.6	1.0	0.3	0.1	(¹)	1.1	(¹)	(¹)	(¹)	0.2	2.3	47
0.1	0.6	(¹)	0.1	0.1	(¹)	(¹)	(¹)	1.2	0.1	(¹)	(¹)	0.4	(¹)	(¹)	(¹)	0.1	1.4	48
0.9	1.4	(¹)	1.4	1.9	0.2	....	0.1	0.2	0.3	2.6	0.1	0.2	(¹)	(¹)	(¹)	0.1	3.1	49
0.1	0.6	(¹)	0.2	0.4	(¹)	(¹)	(¹)	0.1	0.1	1.2	(¹)	0.1	(¹)	(¹)	(¹)	0.1	3.7	50
1.6	0.8	0.1	1.9	1.4	0.2	....	0.1	0.8	0.7	2.5	0.1	0.2	0.1	(¹)	(¹)	(¹)	2.8	51
1.7	1.9	(¹)	1.6	0.6	0.1	(¹)	0.1	2.7	0.4	0.8	(¹)	0.2	(¹)	(¹)	(¹)	0.1	2.4	52
0.4	0.5	(¹)	0.7	1.3	0.1	(¹)	(¹)	0.2	0.3	0.1	(¹)	0.8	(¹)	....	....	(¹)	1.5	53
0.1	0.9	(¹)	0.3	1.3	(¹)	....	(¹)	0.3	0.1	0.4	(¹)	0.4	(¹)	(¹)	(¹)	(¹)	1.5	54
0.2	0.3	(¹)	0.4	2.5	(¹)	(¹)	(¹)	0.4	0.1	0.4	0.1	0.1	(¹)	(¹)	....	(¹)	5.1	55
0.3	0.4	(¹)	0.9	2.1	(¹)	(¹)	(¹)	0.3	0.2	0.4	(¹)	0.1	(¹)	(¹)	(¹)	0.1	3.2	56
0.7	1.1	(¹)	0.6	0.7	0.1	....	0.2	0.6	0.1	2.6	(¹)	0.1	(¹)	(¹)	(¹)	0.1	3.4	57
0.2	1.4	(¹)	0.4	0.5	0.1	(¹)	0.2	1.0	0.2	3.6	(¹)	0.1	(¹)	(¹)	(¹)	0.1	3.4	58
0.2	1.5	(¹)	0.5	0.4	(¹)	(¹)	0.1	1.3	0.4	0.6	0.6	0.2	(¹)	(¹)	(¹)	0.1	3.1	59

² See footnote 5 to Table 1, p. 973.

988

POPULATION.

TABLE 9.—PER CENT DISTRIBUTION OF THE FOREIGN WHITE STOCK

			GERMANIC.			SCANDINAVIAN.			LATIN AND GREEK.						SLAVIC AND LETTIC.	
DIVISION AND STATE.	All mother tongues: 1920	English and Celtic.	German.	Dutch and Frisian.	Flemish.	Swedish.	Norwegian.	Danish.	Italian.	French.	Spanish.	Portuguese.	Rumanian.	Greek.	Polish.	Czech.
1 United States........	100.0	100.0	100.0	100.0	100.0	100.0	100.0	100.0	100.0	100.0	100.0	100.0	100.0	100.0	100.0	100.0
GEOGRAPHIC DIVISIONS:																
2 New England..........	12.4	20.4	2.3	1.6	4.5	9.6	1.5	3.6	14.7	50.5	0.6	57.6	2.5	20.2	11.3	1.3
3 Middle Atlantic........	33.0	32.3	25.9	18.8	13.6	11.7	5.9	9.4	57.8	14.0	5.5	2.2	45.0	25.0	40.7	13.2
4 East North Central......	25.1	20.4	35.5	48.2	56.4	26.2	23.1	22.0	12.2	15.8	1.7	0.0	38.7	24.8	39.8	42.8
5 West North Central.....	13.0	9.0	21.0	19.8	13.7	33.7	53.1	36.0	2.1	6.9	3.4	0.1	5.9	6.1	3.9	26.9
6 South Atlantic..........	2.4	2.6	2.5	1.0	1.7	0.7	0.5	1.0	2.4	1.2	3.2	0.4	2.5	6.0	2.3	2.2
7 East South Central......	0.8	0.9	1.3	0.5	0.3	0.3	0.1	0.3	0.6	0.7	0.2	(¹)	0.6	1.3	0.1	0.1
8 West South Central......	3.2	1.7	3.4	1.2	1.9	1.3	0.7	1.5	2.2	2.8	49.1	0.2	0.7	2.2	0.7	9.3
9 Mountain...............	3.3	4.2	2.5	3.5	2.4	5.5	4.7	11.8	1.8	2.0	18.1	0.4	1.0	4.0	0.4	1.8
10 Pacific.................	6.8	8.6	5.6	5.5	5.5	11.1	10.4	14.5	6.2	5.9	18.1	38.1	3.2	8.7	0.8	2.4
NEW ENGLAND:																
11 Maine.................	0.7	1.5	(¹)	(¹)	(¹)	0.3	0.1	0.5	0.2	6.8	(¹)	0.1	(¹)	0.8	0.1	(¹)
12 New Hampshire.........	0.6	0.8	0.1	0.1	0.7	0.3	0.1	0.1	0.1	7.1	(¹)	0.1	(¹)	3.1	0.4	(¹)
13 Vermont..............	0.3	0.6	(¹)	(¹)	(¹)	0.2	(¹)	0.1	0.2	3.1	0.1	(¹)	(¹)	0.1	0.2	(¹)
14 Massachusetts..........	7.1	12.9	0.9	1.1	2.6	5.3	0.9	1.4	7.1	23.6	0.3	45.9	0.9	13.1	6.0	0.6
15 Rhode Island..........	1.2	1.8	0.1	0.1	0.6	0.9	0.1	0.1	2.1	6.2	(¹)	10.2	0.4	0.7	0.7	(¹)
16 Connecticut..........	2.5	2.8	1.1	0.3	0.5	2.6	0.3	1.3	5.0	3.8	0.2	1.2	1.0	2.4	4.0	0.7
MIDDLE ATLANTIC:																
17 New York.............	17.9	17.4	13.9	9.0	4.7	6.8	4.5	5.3	33.4	9.3	4.3	1.2	31.1	14.1	16.6	8.5
18 New Jersey...........	5.0	4.7	4.4	8.6	2.8	1.5	1.0	2.6	10.2	1.9	0.5	0.4	3.8	2.8	7.2	1.0
19 Pennsylvania.........	10.1	10.2	7.6	1.3	6.0	3.4	0.5	1.4	14.1	2.9	0.7	0.6	10.1	8.1	16.9	3.2
EAST NORTH CENTRAL:																
20 Ohio.................	5.2	4.3	8.0	2.2	2.0	1.1	0.3	1.1	3.6	2.5	0.4	0.2	18.1	6.9	5.7	9.5
21 Indiana..............	1.4	1.1	2.7	1.8	4.4	0.8	0.1	0.6	0.4	1.1	0.2	(¹)	4.4	2.0	1.9	0.6
22 Illinois..............	8.9	6.6	11.1	10.3	18.1	15.8	6.5	7.9	5.9	3.8	0.8	0.6	5.5	9.9	15.7	22.5
23 Michigan.............	5.3	6.5	4.9	27.1	19.2	4.5	1.7	3.8	1.7	6.0	0.3	0.1	10.1	3.8	10.3	2.7
24 Wisconsin............	4.3	1.9	8.8	6.7	12.7	3.9	14.5	8.6	0.7	2.3	0.1	(¹)	0.6	2.1	6.2	7.5
WEST NORTH CENTRAL:																
25 Minnesota............	4.2	2.1	4.8	4.1	4.3	19.1	27.5	9.6	0.5	2.6	0.1	(¹)	2.5	1.3	2.0	5.7
26 Iowa.................	2.4	2.0	4.2	9.7	2.6	4.3	6.1	10.3	0.3	0.8	0.4	(¹)	0.4	1.5	0.1	5.3
27 Missouri.............	1.9	1.7	4.1	1.0	2.0	0.9	0.2	1.0	0.9	1.3	0.6	(¹)	2.0	1.7	0.6	2.2
28 North Dakota.........	1.2	0.6	1.7	0.8	0.8	1.9	12.5	2.7	(¹)	0.6	(¹)	(¹)	0.4	0.2	0.2	1.4
29 South Dakota.........	0.9	0.5	1.4	2.4	0.7	1.6	5.8	3.6	(¹)	0.3	(¹)	(¹)	0.1	0.2	0.1	1.8
30 Nebraska.............	1.4	0.9	2.6	0.9	1.0	3.7	0.7	7.3	0.2	0.4	0.4	(¹)	0.6	0.8	0.6	8.7
31 Kansas...............	1.1	1.1	2.1	0.9	2.4	2.2	0.3	1.5	0.2	0.9	2.0	(¹)	0.1	0.4	0.2	1.9
SOUTH ATLANTIC:																
32 Delaware.............	0.1	0.2	0.1	(¹)	(¹)	(¹)	(¹)	0.2	0.2	(¹)	(¹)	(¹)	0.1	0.2	0.4	(¹)
33 Maryland.............	0.9	0.7	1.4	0.8	0.1	0.1	0.1	0.2	0.6	0.2	0.1	(¹)	0.5	0.6	1.2	1.6
34 District of Columbia.....	0.2	0.4	0.2	0.1	0.1	0.1	0.1	0.1	0.2	0.2	0.1	(¹)	0.1	0.8	(¹)	0.1
35 Virginia.............	0.2	0.3	0.2	0.2	0.1	0.1	0.1	0.2	0.2	0.1	0.1	0.1	0.2	1.1	0.1	0.2
36 West Virginia..........	0.4	0.3	0.3	0.1	1.1	0.1	(¹)	0.1	0.8	0.2	0.3	(¹)	0.9	1.7	0.5	0.1
37 North Carolina........	0.1	0.1	(¹)	0.1	(¹)	(¹)	(¹)	0.1	(¹)	0.1	(¹)	(¹)	0.1	0.3	(¹)	(¹)
38 South Carolina........	0.1	0.1	0.1	(¹)	0.1	(¹)	(¹)	(¹)	(¹)	(¹)	(¹)	(¹)	(¹)	0.4	(¹)	(¹)
39 Georgia..............	0.1	0.2	0.1	0.1	0.1	0.1	(¹)	0.1	(¹)	0.1	0.1	(¹)	0.2	0.9	(¹)	(¹)
40 Florida..............	0.3	0.4	0.2	0.2	0.2	0.2	0.1	0.3	0.3	0.2	2.6	0.2	0.6	0.9	(¹)	0.1
EAST SOUTH CENTRAL:																
41 Kentucky.............	0.4	0.4	0.9	0.2	0.1	(¹)	(¹)	0.1	0.1	0.3	(¹)	(¹)	0.3	0.3	0.1	(¹)
42 Tennessee............	0.1	0.2	0.2	0.1	(¹)	0.1	(²)	0.1	0.1	0.1	(¹)	(¹)	0.1	0.3	(¹)	(¹)
43 Alabama.............	0.1	0.2	0.1	0.1	0.1	0.1	0.1	0.1	0.2	0.2	0.1	(¹)	0.1	0.6	(¹)	(¹)
44 Mississippi...........	0.1	0.1	0.1	(¹)	(¹)	(¹)	(²)	0.1	0.1	0.1	0.1	(¹)	(¹)	0.1	(¹)	(¹)
WEST SOUTH CENTRAL:																
45 Arkansas.............	0.1	0.2	0.3	0.2	0.1	0.1	(¹)	0.1	0.1	0.2	0.1	(¹)	0.1	0.2	0.1	0.2
46 Louisiana............	0.4	0.3	0.4	0.2	0.6	0.1	0.1	0.2	1.4	1.5	0.9	0.1	0.1	0.4	(¹)	0.1
47 Oklahoma............	0.4	0.4	0.6	0.3	0.4	0.2	0.1	0.4	0.1	0.4	1.0	(¹)	(¹)	0.4	0.1	1.0
48 Texas................	2.2	0.8	2.1	0.5	0.7	0.9	0.5	0.9	0.6	0.8	47.2	0.1	0.5	1.2	0.5	8.0
MOUNTAIN:																
49 Montana..............	0.7	1.0	0.6	1.1	1.1	1.2	2.7	1.6	0.2	0.7	0.1	(¹)	0.4	0.7	0.1	0.7
50 Idaho................	0.4	0.5	0.3	0.3	0.2	0.9	0.7	2.0	0.1	0.3	0.4	0.1	0.1	0.4	(¹)	0.2
51 Wyoming.............	0.2	0.3	0.2	0.1	0.1	0.3	0.2	0.6	0.1	0.1	0.3	(¹)	0.1	0.6	0.1	0.2
52 Colorado.............	0.9	1.0	1.0	0.7	0.7	1.7	0.4	1.5	0.9	0.5	1.8	(¹)	0.3	1.0	0.1	0.5
53 New Mexico...........	0.2	0.1	0.1	0.1	0.1	0.1	(¹)	0.1	0.1	0.1	4.1	(¹)	(¹)	0.2	(¹)	(¹)
54 Arizona..............	0.4	0.2	0.1	0.1	0.1	0.1	0.1	0.2	0.1	0.1	11.0	(¹)	(¹)	0.2	(¹)	(¹)
55 Utah.................	0.5	1.0	0.2	1.1	0.1	1.2	0.6	5.6	0.2	0.1	0.2	(¹)	0.1	1.7	(¹)	0.1
56 Nevada..............	0.1	0.1	0.1	(¹)	(¹)	0.1	(¹)	0.3	0.1	0.1	0.3	0.2	(¹)	0.3	(¹)	(¹)
PACIFIC:																
57 Washington...........	1.7	2.2	1.4	2.0	2.0	4.9	6.4	4.0	0.6	1.2	0.3	0.2	0.4	2.0	0.3	0.7
58 Oregon...............	0.7	0.9	0.9	0.7	1.3	1.6	1.6	1.9	0.2	0.5	0.2	0.2	0.3	0.9	0.1	0.5
59 California............	4.4	5.4	3.3	2.7	2.2	4.6	2.4	8.6	5.4	4.2	17.6	37.7	2.5	5.8	0.4	1.2

¹ Less than one-tenth of 1 per cent.

MOTHER TONGUE OF THE FOREIGN WHITE STOCK.   989

HAVING SPECIFIED MOTHER TONGUES, BY DIVISIONS AND STATES: 1920.

SLAVIC AND LETTIC—continued.								UNCLASSIFIED.										
Slovak.	Russian.[2]	Ruthenian.	Slovenian.	Serbo-Croatian.	Bulgarian.	Slavic, not specified.	Lithuanian and Lettish.	Yiddish and Hebrew.	Magyar.	Finnish.	Armenian.	Syrian and Arabic.	Turkish.	Albanian.	All other.	Unknown.	Of mixed mother tongue.	
100.0	100.0	100.0	100.0	100.0	100.0	100.0	100.0	100.0	100.0	100.0	100.0	100.0	100.0	100.0	100.0	100.0	100.0	1
4.2	9.3	6.0	1.9	0.8	1.3	16.7	22.3	10.3	4.9	11.7	35.2	20.0	21.6	50.7	12.1	3.6	7.8	2
63.1	56.2	75.9	34.6	33.1	12.2	74.3	39.9	65.5	49.1	8.5	26.7	28.6	43.1	22.0	29.3	22.8	31.0	3
25.7	14.7	13.8	38.0	39.9	57.5	4.7	32.3	14.2	37.5	36.1	14.3	19.3	17.2	16.7	33.1	27.3	24.6	4
2.1	0.8	2.3	9.2	11.1	11.1	0.2	1.5	3.4	2.2	24.7	1.6	7.1	2.5	4.6	7.8	15.4	15.8	5
1.5	4.0	1.1	2.1	2.2	1.6	0.6	2.4	3.5	3.1	0.7	1.0	7.9	3.0	0.5	2.5	6.4	2.5	6
0.2	0.8	0.1	0.5	0.3	0.6	....	0.1	0.5	0.5	0.1	0.2	3.2	1.0	0.4	0.8	4.3	0.9	7
0.4	1.6	0.2	0.9	0.5	2.0	3.2	0.4	0.7	0.5	0.2	0.4	7.3	1.2	0.2	2.5	8.1	2.8	8
1.6	1.8	0.2	6.0	6.2	7.5	0.2	0.3	0.6	0.7	4.7	0.8	2.6	2.2	2.5	2.7	3.8	4.6	9
1.2	4.8	0.4	6.1	5.9	6.3	0.1	0.9	1.3	1.5	13.2	19.8	4.0	8.1	2.5	9.2	8.4	10.0	10
0.2	0.3	(¹)	(¹)	(¹)	(¹)	....	0.8	0.2	(¹)	0.9	0.4	1.3	0.3	7.0	0.1	0.2	0.4	11
(¹)	0.4	0.2	(¹)	(¹)	0.1	(¹)	0.7	0.1	(¹)	1.1	0.8	0.9	0.7	2.0	....	0.1	0.3	12
0.1	0.2	0.1	(¹)	(¹)	(¹)	....	0.1	0.1	0.1	0.3	0.1	0.5	....	0.1	....	(¹)	0.2	13
0.4	4.5	1.4	0.3	0.4	0.7	....	13.1	6.9	0.3	8.7	25.0	12.7	15.7	35.6	2.1	1.7	4.5	14
(¹)	0.6	1.4	(¹)	0.1	0.3	....	0.4	0.6	(¹)	0.1	5.6	2.1	3.1	2.0	....	0.2	0.6	15
3.4	3.4	2.9	1.6	0.2	0.2	16.6	7.4	2.4	4.5	0.5	3.3	2.6	1.9	3.0	10.0	1.2	1.9	16
7.5	34.9	17.9	7.2	4.1	4.5	0.2	8.0	49.6	19.8	5.8	13.3	14.2	34.0	7.7	17.3	10.4	18.4	17
7.9	6.6	8.5	3.3	0.9	0.7	0.5	4.7	5.8	12.5	1.0	6.7	3.7	3.8	2.6	4.0	3.8	5.1	18
47.8	14.7	49.6	24.1	28.2	7.0	73.6	27.2	10.1	16.8	1.7	6.7	10.7	5.2	11.7	8.0	8.6	7.5	19
12.7	4.3	6.5	18.7	12.8	23.7	0.5	3.1	2.8	20.7	4.7	1.9	6.9	5.9	7.1	5.8	7.4	4.5	20
1.9	0.8	0.2	3.9	7.6	7.6		1.1	0.3	3.2	0.1	0.3	1.5	1.2	1.3	4.5	3.4	1.3	21
7.1	5.3	3.0	10.4	12.4	9.4	3.0	22.2	8.2	6.1	1.6	4.2	2.9	3.6	1.9	15.8	7.6	9.1	22
2.1	3.2	3.5	3.3	7.4	14.3	0.1	3.6	2.0	5.9	24.8	6.0	6.9	5.5	4.3	5.5	4.4	5.2	23
1.9	1.1	0.5	4.6	3.4	2.5	1.0	2.3	0.9	1.5	4.8	1.9	1.1	1.1	2.0	1.5	4.4	4.6	24
1.0	1.2	0.7	6.6	4.5	4.3	0.1	0.3	1.2	0.6	22.1	0.4	1.6	0.6	0.4	0.7	3.0	0.1	25
0.3	0.7	0.1	0.3	1.8	2.2	0.1	0.5	0.4	0.2	0.1	0.2	1.0	0.5	0.1	5.0	2.7	2.3	26
0.4	1.4	0.7	0.5	1.9	1.8	(¹)	0.3	1.4	0.9	0.1	0.4	1.7	0.7	3.4	1.0	4.7	2.1	27
0.1	1.6	0.7	(¹)	0.1	1.1	....	(¹)	0.1	0.1	1.3	0.1	0.7	0.2	....	0.1	1.0	1.6	28
(¹)	0.5	(¹)	0.2	0.3	0.9	....	(¹)	(¹)	0.1	1.2	0.1	0.6	0.1	0.1	0.2	1.0	1.1	29
(¹)	0.7	(¹)	0.2	0.8	0.4	(¹)	0.3	0.3	0.2	(¹)	0.3	1.0	0.2	0.6	0.3	1.4	1.5	30
0.2	0.8	(¹)	1.4	1.8	0.3	(¹)	0.1	0.1	0.1	(¹)	0.1	0.5	0.2	(¹)	0.4	1.7	1.1	31
(¹)	0.3	0.3	0.1	(¹)	....		0.1	0.1	0.1	(¹)	(¹)	(¹)	(¹)	....	0.3	0.2	0.1	32
0.2	1.4	0.4	0.3	0.2	0.2	0.6	1.5	2.0	0.4	0.1	0.1	0.2	0.2	(¹)	0.2	1.2	0.8	33
(¹)	0.5	(¹)	(¹)	(¹)	(¹)	....	(¹)	0.4	0.1	(¹)	0.1	0.5	0.2	(¹)	0.4	1.2	0.3	34
0.3	0.5	(¹)	0.2	(¹)	0.1	....	(¹)	0.4	0.5	0.1	0.4	1.2	0.6	(¹)	0.2	0.8	0.3	35
1.0	0.5	0.3	1.5	1.8	0.9	....	0.7	0.1	2.0	0.2	0.1	2.3	1.3	0.1	0.2	0.9	0.3	36
(¹)	0.1	(¹)	(¹)	(¹)	(¹)	....	(¹)	0.1	(¹)	(¹)	(¹)	1.0	(¹)	....	1.0	0.3	(¹)	37
(¹)	0.2	(¹)	(¹)	(¹)	....	....	(¹)	0.1	(¹)	(¹)	(¹)	0.8	(¹)	....		0.2	0.1	38
(¹)	0.5	(¹)	(¹)	(¹)	(¹)	....	(¹)	0.2	0.1	(¹)	0.1	1.0	0.4	0.1	....	0.5	0.2	39
(¹)	0.2	(¹)	(¹)	(¹)	0.2	....	(¹)	0.1	0.1	0.2	0.1	1.0	0.1	0.2	0.2	1.2	0.5	40
0.1	0.3	(¹)	0.1	0.2	0.2	....	(¹)	0.2	0.3	(¹)	0.1	0.7	0.3	(¹)	0.3	1.5	0.4	41
(¹)	0.2	(¹)	(¹)	(¹)	0.1	....	(¹)	0.2	0.1	(¹)	(¹)	0.3	(¹)	0.4	0.2	1.0	0.2	42
0.1	0.2	(¹)	0.1	0.1	0.2	....	(¹)	0.1	0.1	(¹)	0.1	1.0	0.6	....	0.1	1.2	0.2	43
(¹)	0.1	....	0.2	(¹)	(¹)	....	(¹)	(¹)	(¹)	0.1	(¹)	1.2	0.1	....	0.3	0.5	0.1	44
0.1	0.1	(¹)	0.1	(¹)	0.2	....	(¹)	(¹)	(¹)	(¹)	(¹)	0.4	....	....	0.2	0.8	0.2	45
0.1	0.3	(¹)	0.3	0.1	0.4	....	(¹)	0.1	0.1	0.1	0.1	2.0	0.7	(¹)	0.3	2.1	0.7	46
0.1	0.5	0.2	0.2	0.1	0.9	(¹)	0.2	0.1	0.1	(¹)	0.1	1.6	0.1	(¹)	1.1	1.2	0.4	47
0.1	0.7	0.1	0-3	0.3	0.6	3.2	0.1	0.5	0.2	(¹)	0.3	3.3	0.4	0.1	0.9	4.1	1.5	48
0.4	0.5	0.1	1.7	2.4	2.8	....	0.1	(¹)	0.1	2.5	0.3	0.4	0.7	0.5	1.8	0.7	1.0	49
(¹)	0.1	(¹)	0.1	0.3	0.4	0.2	(¹)	(¹)	(¹)	0.6	(¹)	0.1	(¹)	0.7	0.1	0.4	0.6	50
0.2	0.1	(¹)	0.6	0.5	0.9	....	(¹)	(¹)	0.1	0.6	0.1	0.1	0.4	0.2	0.2	0.2	0.2	51
0.9	0.8	0.1	2.5	0.9	2.5	....	0.1	0.4	0.8	0.4	0.1	0.6	0.3	0.2	0.7	1.5	1.0	52
(¹)	(¹)	(¹)	0.2	0.4	0.2	....	(¹)	(¹)	(¹)	(¹)	(¹)	0.4	(¹)	....	....	0.1	0.1	53
(¹)	0.2	(¹)	0.2	0.9	0.2	....	(¹)	(¹)	(¹)	(¹)	(¹)	0.6	0.1	0.1	0.3	0.3	0.3	54
0.1	0.1	(¹)	0.4	0.5	0.2	....	(¹)	(¹)	(¹)	0.3	0.2	0.3	0.4	0.8	....	0.4	1.3	55
(¹)	(¹)	(¹)	0.2	0.4	0.1	....	(¹)	(¹)	(¹)	(¹)	(¹)	(¹)	0.2	....	0.1	0.1	0.1	56
0.7	1.0	0.2	1.7	2.1	2.2	....	0.4	0.2	0.2	6.0	0.5	0.6	1.8	1.4	1.8	1.9	2.6	57
0.1	0.5	0.1	0.5	0.6	2.1	....	0.1	0.1	0.1	8.7	0.2	0.4	0.4	0.2	0.5	1.1	1.2	58
0.4	3.3	0.1	3.9	3.2	2.0	0.1	0.3	1.0	1.2	3.5	19.1	3.1	6.0	0.9	7.4	5.4	6.2	59

² See footnote 5 to Table 1, p. 973.

CHAPTER XI

SCHOOL ATTENDANCE

CHAPTER XI.—SCHOOL ATTENDANCE.

INTRODUCTION.

The statistics of school attendance compiled from the returns of the census of 1920 are based upon the answers to a question on the population schedule as to whether the person enumerated had attended school between September 1, 1919, and the census date, January 1, 1920. If the person had attended any kind of school, college, or other educational institution for any length of time within the period in question an affirmative answer was to be made. The total number of persons returned as attending school is, therefore, larger than the number who were simultaneously in attendance at any one time between September 1, 1919, and January 1, 1920. Although this period represents considerably less than half the entire school year 1919–20, the number of persons who attended school in that year subsequently but not prior to January 1 would form an insignificant proportion of the total enrollment. The figures are, therefore, fairly comparable with those for preceding censuses, at which the enumerations were made later in the year.

The statistics on school attendance here presented are limited to continental United States and cover the United States as a whole, the states, and cities having 25,000 inhabitants or more. Less detailed statistics for states, for counties, and for incorporated places having 2,500 inhabitants or more, and complete statistics for the outlying possessions enumerated at the Fourteenth Census, are presented in Volume III of the Fourteenth Census Reports.

For the sake of simplicity, the school years 1919–20, 1909–10, etc., are designated in the tables by "1920," "1910," etc.

Ages of school attendance.—Ages of compulsory school attendance vary in the different states, beginning at 7 years in 21 states and at 8 years in 27 states and the District of Columbia. Table 3 (p. 1045) presents, for the United States, the number and per cent of persons attending school by single years of age from 5 to 20, inclusive, so that from this table it is possible to compile the number of children attending school for any desired age group. Tables 13 and 18 give similar statistics for states and for large cities, respectively. In the remaining tables school-attendance figures are presented for persons 7 to 20 years of age, sometimes grouped into the age periods 7 to 13, 14 and 15, 16 and 17, and 18 to 20, and several of the tables also show the number attending school under 7 and 21 years of age and over.

Population classes.—The differences among the proportions attending school for the several classes of the population are due in part to differences in distribution as between urban and rural communities. The native whites of foreign or mixed parentage and the foreign-born whites are found mainly in urban communities, in which school attendance begins and, in general, ends at somewhat earlier ages than in rural communities. (See Table 20.) It is probable, however, that the decidedly higher proportions for the native stock, 14 years of age and over, are due in part to the better economic and social position of this class of population. Attendance at school, college, or any other educational institution at the older school ages is more clearly indicative of a higher economic level than school attendance at the younger ages, when local school facilities and legal requirements are dominant factors. (See Table 2.)

The smaller proportions attending school at the ages of 14 and over among the foreign-born whites than among the natives are not due wholly to the fact that those in school leave before reaching this age, but result in part from the influx of immigrants at and above the age of 14, most of whom never attend school in the United States. The difference between the proportions attending school for the two sexes in the foreign-born white population at and above the age of 14 is probably due to the feeling, common in many foreign countries, that education is much more important for men than for women.

UNITED STATES AS A WHOLE.

Comparison with preceding censuses.—Because of a difference in the form of the census inquiry regarding school attendance, the statistics for 1890 and 1900 are probably not exactly comparable with those for the other census years covered by Table 1. At the censuses prior to 1890 and subsequent to 1900 the inquiry was merely as to whether the person enumerated had attended school at any time during the period between the beginning of the school year and the census date; but in 1890 and 1900 the enumerators were required to ascertain also the number of months of school attendance. It is undoubtedly true that in some cases, when the person interviewed by the enumerator was not the one to whom the information applied, the fact of school attendance was known, while the number of months of attendance was unknown. In such cases enumerators might sometimes have been disposed to make no reply whatever to the inquiry, rather than to give only a partial one. The returns for 1910 and 1920 are, therefore, doubtless more nearly complete than those for 1890 and 1900.

75647°—22——66

(1041)

POPULATION.

DIVISIONS AND STATES.

In making comparisons among the geographic divisions and states, it must be borne in mind that the census inquiry as to school attendance ascertains only the fact that a certain number of persons in a given state or division attended school during the census year, throwing no light on the duration of attendance. In other words, the census figures indicate merely the fact that education was being obtained but not the relative amount of education obtained. There are very considerable differences among the geographic divisions and states in regard to the average length of time schools are in session during the year, and consequently in regard to the average annual duration of school attendance.

URBAN AND RURAL COMMUNITIES.

Because of the marked differences between urban and rural communities in regard to school facilities, and also in regard to the composition and characteristics of their population, separate statistics for school attendance are given for the two classes of communities in Tables 19 to 21. In drawing the distinction between urban and rural population, all incorporated places (and all towns in Massachusetts, Rhode Island, and New Hampshire) having 2,500 inhabitants or more are treated as urban and the remainder of the country as rural.

In Massachusetts and Rhode Island it is not the practice, as in practically all the other states, to incorporate, as separate muncipalities, the relatively densely populated portions of "towns" (which are the primary divisions of the counties), and no town as a whole is incorporated as a muncipality until it attains a population greatly in excess of 2,500; and in New Hampshire a similar condition exists, although the state contains two incorporated villages, each of which has fewer than 2,500 inhabitants. For this reason those towns having 2,500 or more inhabitants in the three states named are treated as urban, although portions of their areas are rural in character. The urban areas in the three states in question, as classified by the census, thus contain relatively small numbers of inhabitants who in other sections of the country would be segregated as rural. Nevertheless, in most of the towns having 2,500 inhabitants or more in Massachusetts, Rhode Island, and New Hampshire by far the greater part of the population resides within the more densely settled areas, so that the proportion classed as urban, considering each state as a whole, is not greatly exaggerated by the practice adopted.

The proportions attending school at the earlier ages are somewhat smaller, and at the later school ages somewhat larger, in rural than in urban communities.

The explanation is probably to be found in the facts that in rural districts, where schools are less accessible, children begin their schooling at somewhat older ages than in cities and towns, and that larger proportions of rural youth at and above the age of 14 remain in school because employment on the farm does not preclude school attendance, at least during a part of the school year, while employment in the city frequently does.

The slightly larger proportion of persons attending school in rural than in urban communities in 1920, considering the combined 7 to 20 age group as a whole, does not indicate, of course, that the rural population of the United States was receiving more schooling than the urban. This condition is due merely to the fact that in many parts of the country the schools in rural districts are in session for shorter periods during each year than those in urban communities, and consequently the amount of schooling received by rural inhabitants, while not larger in the aggregate, is often prolonged through a greater number of years. (See Table 19.)

PER CENT ATTENDING SCHOOL IN THE TOTAL POPULATION AND IN CERTAIN CLASSES AT EACH YEAR OF AGE FROM 7 TO 20, INCLUSIVE: 1920.

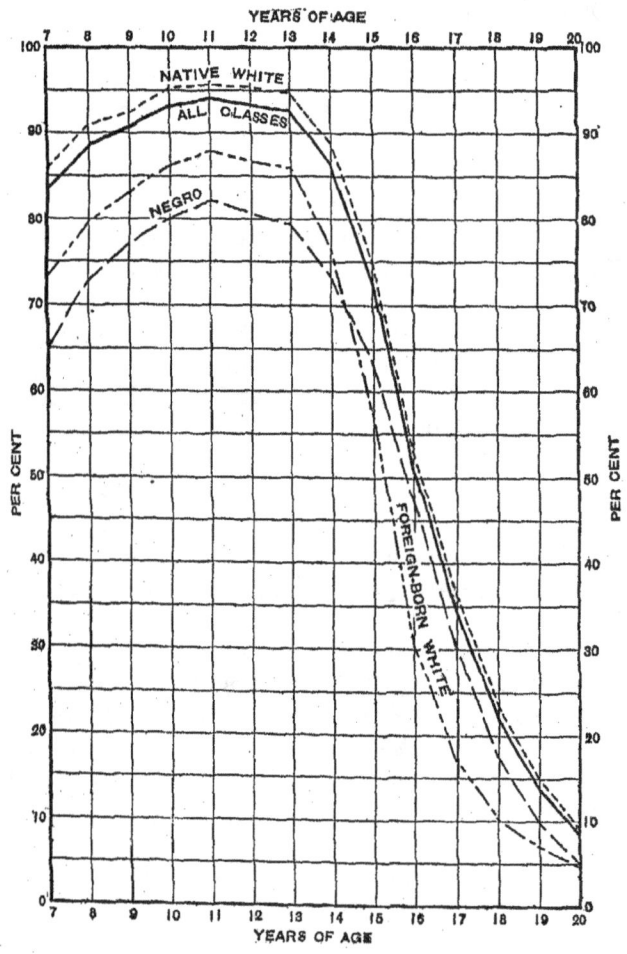

SCHOOL ATTENDANCE.

1043

TABLE 1.—SCHOOL ATTENDANCE, BY SEX, FOR PRINCIPAL POPULATION CLASSES, FOR THE UNITED STATES: 1850-1920.

[Because of variations from census to census in the manner of presenting statistics of school attendance, it is impossible to give comparative figures for any specified age group. The school-attendance percentages are, however, based on the population 5 to 20 years of age, inclusive, for the reason that the numbers of persons attending school at ages above and below these limits are insignificant. For all classes and for the white and Negro population in 1860 and 1850 the number 5 to 20 years of age has been calculated by adding estimates for age 20 to the numbers returned as in the 5 to 19 group; and for the Negro population in 1890 and 1880 the number in the 5 to 20 group was estimated on the assumption that the proportion which this group formed of the total at all ages was the same for the Negro population as for the total colored population (Negroes, Indians, Chinese, Japanese, and other nonwhites).]

CLASS OF POPULATION AND CENSUS YEAR.	POPULATION 5 TO 20 YEARS OF AGE, INCLUSIVE.			TOTAL PERSONS ATTENDING SCHOOL.					
				Both sexes.		Male.		Female.	
	Both sexes.	Male.	Female.	Number.	Per cent.	Number.	Per cent.	Number.	Per cent.
All classes:									
1920	33,250,870	16,639,600	16,611,270	21,763,275	65.5	10,886,703	65.4	10,876,572	65.5
1910	29,785,997	14,952,530	14,833,467	18,009,891	60.5	9,037,655	60.4	8,972,236	60.5
1900	26,041,940	13,048,537	12,993,403	13,387,147	51.3	6,668,823	51.1	6,698,324	51.6
1890	22,447,392	11,242,700	11,204,692	11,674,878	52.0	5,954,142	53.0	5,720,736	51.1
1880	18,319,830	9,180,762	9,139,068	9,951,608	54.3	5,123,507	55.8	4,828,101	52.8
1870	14,507,658	7,253,307	7,254,351	6,596,466	45.5	3,416,153	47.1	3,180,313	43.8
1860	11,980,728	6,029,870	5,950,858	5,692,954	47.5	2,978,292	49.4	2,714,662	45.6
1850	9,204,908	4,629,874	4,575,034	4,089,507	44.4	2,160,296	46.7	1,929,211	42.2
White:									
1920	29,333,533	14,727,541	14,605,992	19,644,508	67.0	9,870,374	67.0	9,774,134	66.9
1910	25,902,293	13,092,081	12,900,212	16,279,292	62.6	8,220,847	62.8	8,058,445	62.5
1900	22,441,947	11,271,583	11,170,364	12,231,004	54.5	6,137,874	54.5	6,093,130	54.5
1890	19,250,565	9,655,372	9,595,193	10,667,171	55.4	5,464,413	56.6	5,202,758	54.2
1880	15,618,617	7,838,446	7,780,171	9,095,485	58.2	4,690,093	59.8	4,405,392	56.6
1870	12,528,178	6,274,555	6,253,623	6,414,740	51.2	3,326,797	53.0	3,087,943	49.4
1860	10,099,266	5,086,975	5,012,291	5,660,325	56.0	2,961,698	58.2	2,698,627	53.8
1850	7,681,163	3,868,917	3,812,246	4,063,046	52.9	2,146,432	55.5	1,916,614	50.3
Negro:									
1920	3,796,957	1,848,797	1,948,160	2,049,791	54.0	979,246	53.0	1,070,545	55.0
1910	3,677,860	1,797,688	1,880,172	1,670,650	45.4	783,869	43.6	886,781	47.2
1900	3,499,187	1,721,758	1,777,429	1,096,734	31.3	509,984	29.6	586,750	33.0
1890	3,126,497	1,560,122	1,566,375	999,324	32.0	484,969	31.1	514,355	32.8
1880	2,633,683	1,301,039	1,332,644	856,014	32.5	433,375	33.3	422,639	31.7
1870	1,958,237	963,965	994,272	180,372	9.2	88,594	9.2	91,778	9.2
1860	1,859,370	929,994	929,376	32,629	1.8	16,594	1.8	16,035	1.7
1850	1,524,829	761,229	763,600	26,461	1.7	13,864	1.8	12,597	1.6
Native white—Native parentage:									
1920	20,048,170	10,090,524	9,957,646	13,655,361	68.1	6,846,934	67.9	6,808,427	68.4
1910	17,246,081	8,691,250	8,554,831	11,110,583	64.4	5,611,901	64.6	5,498,682	64.3
1900	14,876,715	7,506,903	7,369,812	8,244,687	55.4	4,141,997	55.2	4,102,690	55.7
1890	12,604,550	6,341,747	6,262,803	7,204,755	57.2	3,695,420	58.3	3,509,335	56.0
Native white—Foreign or mixed parentage:									
1920	8,116,313	4,060,004	4,056,309	5,434,720	67.0	2,733,322	67.3	2,701,398	66.6
1910	7,157,099	3,575,800	3,581,299	4,517,203	63.1	2,270,706	63.5	2,246,497	62.7
1900	6,372,199	3,180,232	3,191,967	3,605,128	56.6	1,801,303	56.6	1,803,825	56.5
1890	5,313,470	2,648,167	2,665,303	2,948,534	55.5	1,500,893	56.7	1,447,641	54.3
Foreign-born white:									
1920	1,169,050	577,013	592,037	554,427	47.4	290,118	50.3	264,309	44.6
1910	1,589,113	825,031	764,082	651,506	41.0	338,240	41.0	313,266	41.0
1900	1,193,033	584,448	608,585	381,189	32.0	194,574	33.3	186,615	30.7
1890	1,332,545	665,458	667,087	513,882	38.6	268,100	40.3	245,782	36.8

1044

POPULATION.

TABLE 2.—SCHOOL ATTENDANCE, BY SEX AND AGE PERIODS, FOR POPULATION CLASSES, FOR THE UNITED STATES: 1920 AND 1910.

[Per cent not shown where base is less than 100.]

CENSUS YEAR, CLASS OF POPULATION, AND SEX	Total number of persons attending school	PERSONS 7 TO 13 YEARS OF AGE			PERSONS 14 AND 15 YEARS OF AGE			PERSONS 16 AND 17 YEARS OF AGE			PERSONS 18 TO 20 YEARS OF AGE			OTHERS ATTENDING SCHOOL	
		Total number.	Attending school Number.	Per cent.	Total number.	Attending school Number.	Per cent.	Total number.	Attending school Number.	Per cent.	Total number.	Attending school Number.	Per cent.	Under 7 years of age	21 years of age and over
1920															
All classes	21,763,275	15,306,793	13,869,010	90.6	3,907,710	3,124,129	79.9	3,828,131	1,644,081	42.9	5,522,082	814,651	14.8	1,966,635	344,789
Male	10,886,703	7,723,238	6,984,902	90.4	1,953,976	1,556,519	79.5	1,902,867	767,533	40.3	2,688,747	397,847	14.8	978,621	201,281
Female	10,876,572	7,583,555	6,884,108	90.8	1,943,734	1,567,610	80.4	1,925,264	876,528	45.5	2,833,335	416,804	14.7	988,014	143,508
White	19,644,608	13,515,118	12,490,436	92.5	3,432,889	2,797,409	81.5	3,384,559	1,468,476	43.4	4,851,302	739,268	15.2	1,815,677	324,242
Male	9,870,374	6,827,330	6,309,623	92.4	1,726,962	1,405,367	81.4	1,680,778	693,491	41.0	2,384,143	366,165	15.4	900,290	189,438
Female	9,774,134	6,687,788	6,180,813	92.6	1,705,927	1,392,042	81.6	1,694,781	774,985	45.7	2,467,159	373,103	15.1	900,387	134,804
Negro	2,049,791	1,738,822	1,331,043	76.5	461,778	317,355	68.7	430,799	168,760	39.2	648,955	70,124	10.8	145,571	10,938
Male	979,246	869,045	655,699	75.5	225,122	146,225	65.0	206,087	70,365	34.1	292,055	28,349	9.7	69,672	8,936
Female	1,070,545	869,777	675,344	77.6	236,656	171,130	72.3	224,712	98,395	43.8	356,900	41,775	11.7	75,899	8,002
Indian	51,865	44,256	31,054	70.2	11,216	7,851	70.0	10,167	5,320	52.3	14,769	3,346	22.7	8,464	830
Male	25,902	22,203	15,543	70.0	5,658	3,920	69.3	5,041	2,536	50.3	7,358	1,755	23.9	1,647	501
Female	25,963	22,053	15,511	70.3	5,558	3,931	70.7	5,126	2,784	54.3	7,411	1,591	21.5	1,817	329
Chinese	6,081	2,944	2,609	88.6	842	703	83.5	959	555	57.9	2,235	708	31.7	555	951
Male	4,045	1,712	1,502	87.7	587	479	81.6	726	398	54.8	1,812	562	31.0	301	803
Female	2,036	1,232	1,107	89.9	255	224	87.8	233	157	67.4	423	146	34.5	254	148
Japanese	9,942	5,429	4,672	86.1	924	765	82.8	1,538	890	57.0	3,906	997	25.5	1,334	1,284
Male	6,221	2,834	2,438	86.0	617	505	81.8	1,152	696	60.4	2,518	819	32.5	693	1,070
Female	3,721	2,595	2,234	86.1	307	260	84.7	386	194	50.3	1,388	178	12.8	641	214
All other	1,088	224	196	87.5	61	46		109	60	55.0	915	208	22.7	34	544
Male	915	114	97	85.1	30	23		83	47		861	197	22.9	18	533
Female	173	110	99		31	23		26	13		54	11		16	11
Native white	19,090,081	13,136,967	12,181,396	92.7	3,272,950	2,690,787	82.2	3,179,688	1,420,296	44.7	4,470,268	712,478	15.9	1,797,722	287,402
Male	9,580,256	6,636,501	6,148,896	92.7	1,647,491	1,351,089	82.0	1,588,501	668,716	42.1	2,201,523	350,519	15.9	897,151	163,885
Female	9,509,825	6,500,466	6,032,500	92.8	1,625,459	1,339,698	82.4	1,591,097	751,580	47.2	2,268,745	361,959	16.0	900,571	123,517
Native parentage	13,655,361	9,315,013	8,584,679	92.2	2,303,091	1,982,664	83.9	2,283,004	1,111,509	48.7	3,209,876	562,322	17.5	1,201,706	212,421
Male	6,846,934	4,713,879	4,338,518	92.0	1,193,040	994,541	83.4	1,143,128	522,656	45.7	1,582,596	274,761	17.3	599,140	118,318
Female	6,808,427	4,601,134	4,246,161	92.3	1,170,651	988,123	84.4	1,140,476	588,913	51.6	1,627,280	288,561	17.7	602,566	94,103
Foreign parentage	3,697,784	2,664,732	2,505,236	94.0	598,719	453,603	75.8	585,970	179,726	30.7	824,353	84,290	10.2	428,784	46,145
Male	1,863,285	1,338,859	1,259,560	94.1	299,293	229,744	76.8	290,421	80,436	29.8	403,530	44,462	11.0	214,490	28,593
Female	1,834,499	1,325,873	1,245,676	94.0	299,426	223,859	74.8	295,549	98,290	31.6	420,823	39,828	9.5	214,294	17,552
Mixed parentage	1,736,936	1,157,222	1,091,481	94.3	310,540	254,520	82.0	310,114	129,001	41.6	436,039	65,806	15.1	167,232	28,836
Male	870,087	583,763	550,818	94.4	155,518	126,804	81.7	155,042	59,624	38.5	215,397	32,296	15.0	83,521	16,974
Female	866,809	573,459	540,663	94.3	155,382	127,716	82.2	155,072	69,377	44.7	220,642	33,570	15.2	83,711	11,862
Foreign-born white	554,427	378,151	318,040	84.1	159,939	106,622	66.7	204,871	48,180	23.5	381,034	26,790	7.0	17,955	36,840
Male	290,118	190,829	160,727	84.2	79,471	54,278	68.3	101,187	24,775	24.5	182,620	15,646	8.6	9,139	25,553
Female	264,309	187,322	157,313	84.0	80,468	52,344	65.0	103,684	23,405	22.6	198,414	11,144	5.6	8,816	11,287
1910															
All classes	18,009,891	12,950,418	11,146,173	86.1	3,569,347	2,676,465	75.0	3,650,951	1,573,377	43.1	5,546,049	844,836	15.2	1,455,784	313,256
Male	9,037,655	6,539,326	5,608,062	85.8	1,798,449	1,337,710	74.4	1,825,895	762,029	41.7	2,738,284	424,801	15.5	725,816	179,237
Female	8,972,236	6,411,092	5,538,111	86.4	1,770,898	1,338,755	75.6	1,825,056	811,348	44.5	2,807,765	420,035	15.0	729,968	134,019
White	16,279,292	11,252,886	10,057,883	89.4	3,113,894	2,409,311	77.4	3,209,712	1,414,376	44.1	4,881,708	704,479	15.7	1,345,467	287,776
Male	8,220,847	5,690,176	5,079,331	89.3	1,572,638	1,216,478	77.4	1,611,778	694,806	43.1	2,431,769	300,483	10.1	673,546	166,113
Female	8,058,445	5,562,710	4,978,552	89.5	1,541,256	1,192,833	77.4	1,597,934	719,480	45.0	2,449,939	373,996	15.3	671,921	121,663
Negro	1,670,650	1,648,753	1,058,791	64.1	442,103	257,894	58.3	428,250	152,145	35.5	640,236	74,745	11.7	106,684	22,391
Male	783,869	824,097	512,609	62.2	218,560	116,209	53.2	206,864	63,327	30.6	291,054	30,617	10.5	50,503	10,604
Female	886,781	824,656	544,182	66.0	223,543	141,685	63.4	221,386	88,818	40.1	348,582	44,128	12.7	56,181	11,787
Indian	53,458	46,034	29,415	63.9	12,246	8,596	70.2	11,292	6,188	54.8	17,143	4,500	26.2	3,306	1,453
Male	27,843	23,469	14,885	63.4	6,347	4,488	70.7	5,765	3,235	56.1	8,661	2,683	31.0	1,590	962
Female	25,615	22,565	14,530	64.4	5,899	4,108	69.6	5,527	2,953	53.4	8,482	1,817	21.4	1,716	491
Chinese	3,887	1,840	1,418	77.1	918	556	60.6	1,258	540	42.9	2,701	628	23.3	185	560
Male	2,977	1,109	874	78.8	777	461	59.3	1,109	461	41.6	2,492	563	23.3	94	524
Female	910	731	544	74.4	141	95	67.4	149	79	53.0	209	65	24.2	91	36
Japanese	2,512	882	647	73.4	170	102	60.0	395	120	30.4	3,993	461	11.5	142	1,040
Male	2,036	462	351	76.0	111	68	61.3	336	103	30.7	3,504	432	12.3	83	999
Female	476	420	296	70.5	59	34		59	17		489	29	5.9	59	41
All other	92	23	19		16	6		44	8		268	23	8.6		36
Male	83	13	12		16	6		43	7		264	23	8.7		35
Female	9	10	7					1	1		4				1
Native white	15,627,786	10,773,631	9,640,513	89.5	2,963,982	2,321,048	78.3	2,990,669	1,376,133	46.0	4,243,662	734,855	17.3	1,303,075	252,162
Male	7,882,607	5,448,095	4,867,727	89.3	1,497,505	1,170,305	78.1	1,502,091	674,701	44.9	2,085,449	373,719	17.9	652,012	144,143
Female	7,745,179	5,325,536	4,772,786	89.6	1,466,177	1,150,743	78.5	1,488,578	701,432	47.1	2,158,213	361,130	16.7	651,063	108,019
Native parentage	11,110,583	7,647,477	6,744,539	88.2	2,071,568	1,664,279	80.3	2,073,051	1,060,244	51.1	2,988,189	586,302	19.6	862,610	192,203
Male	5,611,901	3,875,729	3,409,430	88.0	1,051,381	838,613	79.8	1,044,805	520,842	49.9	1,472,212	301,538	20.5	431,091	110,389
Female	5,498,682	3,771,748	3,335,109	88.4	1,020,187	825,666	80.9	1,029,346	539,402	52.4	1,515,977	285,172	18.8	431,519	81,814
Foreign parentage	2,867,327	2,015,386	1,864,944	92.5	584,765	414,773	70.9	604,600	210,475	72.0	825,400	81,648	9.9	285,767	36,232
Male	1,444,938	1,012,837	938,745	92.7	292,290	210,475	72.0	301,181	90,939	30.2	402,392	40,762	10.1	143,503	20,514
Female	1,422,389	1,002,549	926,199	92.4	292,475	204,298	69.9	303,425	90,024	30.7	423,014	40,886	9.7	142,264	15,718
Mixed parentage	1,649,876	1,110,768	1,031,030	92.8	307,649	241,996	78.7	312,112	131,926	42.3	430,007	66,499	15.5	154,698	23,727
Male	825,768	559,529	519,552	92.9	154,134	121,217	78.6	156,305	62,920	40.3	210,845	35,078	16.0	77,418	13,240
Female	824,108	551,239	511,478	92.8	153,515	120,779	78.7	155,807	69,006	44.3	219,222	35,078	16.0	77,280	10,487
Foreign-born white	651,506	479,255	417,370	87.1	149,912	88,263	58.9	219,043	38,243	17.5	638,046	29,624	4.6	42,392	35,614
Male	338,240	242,081	211,604	87.4	74,833	46,173	61.7	109,087	20,195	18.4	346,820	16,764	4.8	21,534	21,970
Female	313,266	237,174	205,766	86.8	75,079	42,090	56.1	109,356	18,048	16.5	291,726	12,860	4.4	20,858	13,644

SCHOOL ATTENDANCE.

TABLE 3.—SCHOOL ATTENDANCE OF POPULATION 5 TO 20 YEARS OF AGE, BY SINGLE YEARS, FOR POPULATION CLASSES, BY SEX, FOR THE UNITED STATES: 1920 AND 1910.

AGE AND CENSUS YEAR.	NUMBER AND PER CENT OF TOTAL AT SPECIFIED AGE ATTENDING SCHOOL.																	
	All classes.						White.				Negro.				Indian, Chinese, Japanese, and all other.			
	Both sexes.		Male.		Female.		Male.		Female.		Male.		Female.		Male.		Female.	
	Number.	Per cent.	Number.	Per cent.	Number.	Per cent.	Number.	Per cent.	Number.	Per cent.	Number.	Per cent.	Number.	Per cent.	Number.	Per cent.	Number.	Per cent.
5 years:																		
1920	441,411	18.8	217,446	18.3	223,965	19.3	202,686	19.2	207,736	20.2	14,122	11.2	15,638	12.3	638	12.7	591	11.9
1910	346,673	17.0	171,687	16.7	174,986	17.4	159,467	17.8	161,229	18.4	11,774	9.3	13,286	10.3	446	10.6	471	11.6
6 years:																		
1920	1,480,714	63.3	739,300	62.8	741,414	63.9	683,070	65.5	680,447	66.5	54,306	41.7	58,921	44.1	1,924	38.9	2,046	41.4
1910	1,059,353	52.1	529,244	51.7	530,109	52.4	490,944	55.2	487,723	55.8	37,051	28.5	41,073	30.9	1,249	30.1	1,313	31.3
7 years:																		
1920	1,905,404	83.3	959,128	83.1	946,276	83.5	874,634	85.6	859,058	85.9	81,807	64.0	84,650	65.9	2,687	61.0	2,568	60.1
1910	1,464,730	75.0	737,137	74.7	727,593	75.2	677,023	79.0	663,813	79.2	58,270	46.3	61,834	49.2	1,844	46.7	1,946	50.2
8 years:																		
1920	2,010,894	88.5	1,011,506	88.3	999,388	88.6	915,061	90.5	901,117	90.7	93,447	72.1	95,296	73.3	2,998	67.9	2,975	68.3
1910	1,586,572	82.7	797,445	82.5	789,127	82.8	724,680	86.5	711,404	86.6	70,609	56.5	75,577	59.3	2,156	56.0	2,146	56.7
9 years:																		
1920	1,944,314	90.4	982,227	90.3	962,087	90.5	889,955	92.1	869,151	92.1	89,558	76.4	90,287	77.7	2,714	73.8	2,649	73.4
1910	1,567,665	86.2	792,754	86.1	774,911	86.3	719,310	89.4	699,450	89.4	71,232	63.7	73,308	65.4	2,212	64.3	2,153	63.6
10 years:																		
1920	2,077,965	93.0	1,048,389	92.9	1,029,576	93.2	940,070	94.8	921,080	94.9	105,328	79.1	105,560	80.9	2,991	74.8	2,936	75.4
1910	1,681,342	90.0	848,141	89.6	833,201	90.4	761,994	92.9	745,176	93.3	83,575	68.0	85,580	71.5	2,572	68.5	2,445	68.2
11 years:																		
1920	1,970,255	93.9	989,744	93.8	980,511	94.1	898,983	95.3	887,392	95.4	88,166	81.0	90,688	83.2	2,595	80.7	2,451	80.7
1910	1,555,301	91.2	779,675	90.9	775,626	91.5	708,698	93.6	700,644	93.8	68,730	70.8	72,993	74.5	2,247	74.6	1,989	72.6
12 years:																		
1920	2,082,749	93.2	1,052,583	93.0	1,030,166	93.4	940,739	95.0	914,973	95.1	108,801	79.0	112,307	82.1	3,043	77.5	2,826	77.2
1910	1,716,810	89.8	864,799	89.2	851,511	90.3	773,524	92.7	754,321	93.2	88,619	67.5	94,648	72.8	2,656	70.8	2,542	73.3
13 years:																		
1920	1,877,429	92.5	941,325	92.4	936,104	92.7	850,181	94.3	837,042	94.3	88,592	77.3	96,516	81.3	2,552	79.2	2,546	80.5
1910	1,574,253	88.8	788,111	88.3	786,142	89.3	714,102	91.7	703,744	91.8	71,574	64.9	80,242	71.9	2,435	73.9	2,156	74.7
14 years:																		
1920	1,766,784	86.3	890,571	86.2	876,213	86.5	802,209	88.4	777,753	88.0	85,701	70.2	96,060	76.5	2,661	75.1	2,400	74.0
1910	1,501,456	81.2	755,379	80.7	746,077	81.8	685,670	84.1	664,734	84.0	66,988	57.4	79,046	67.0	2,721	72.3	2,297	71.5
15 years:																		
1920	1,357,345	72.9	665,948	71.9	691,397	73.9	603,158	73.6	614,289	74.7	60,524	58.7	75,070	67.6	2,266	67.6	2,038	70.1
1910	1,175,009	68.3	582,331	67.5	592,678	69.0	530,808	70.1	528,099	70.4	49,221	48.3	62,639	59.3	2,302	66.0	1,940	67.2
16 years:																		
1920	1,001,701	50.8	470,433	48.2	531,268	53.3	424,156	48.9	467,659	53.5	44,260	41.7	61,785	51.9	2,017	57.3	1,824	59.9
1910	943,511	50.6	456,081	49.3	487,430	51.9	415,308	51.0	431,179	52.7	38,600	36.2	54,455	46.3	2,173	57.2	1,796	58.2
17 years:																		
1920	642,360	34.6	297,100	32.1	345,260	37.2	269,335	32.7	307,326	37.4	26,105	26.1	36,610	34.6	1,660	47.6	1,324	48.6
1910	629,866	35.3	305,948	34.0	323,918	36.6	279,588	35.1	288,301	37.0	24,727	24.7	34,363	33.1	1,633	47.3	1,254	47.3
18 years:																		
1920	413,619	21.7	192,481	20.5	221,138	22.8	175,296	21.2	196,272	23.2	15,842	14.8	23,906	19.6	1,343	33.4	960	30.0
1910	434,864	22.6	209,687	22.1	225,177	23.0	191,480	22.9	199,331	23.4	16,613	15.3	24,894	20.2	1,594	34.3	952	29.6
19 years:																		
1920	252,680	13.8	127,011	14.0	125,669	13.6	117,229	14.6	113,112	14.0	8,631	8.9	11,984	10.7	1,154	27.7	573	20.7
1910	254,421	14.4	131,514	14.8	122,907	14.1	121,347	15.3	110,169	14.3	8,964	9.9	12,146	11.9	1,203	25.0	592	21.4
20 years:																		
1920	148,352	8.3	78,355	9.3	69,997	7.5	73,643	9.8	63,719	7.9	3,876	4.4	5,885	4.8	836	19.2	393	11.9
1910	155,551	8.4	83,600	9.3	71,951	7.5	77,656	9.7	64,496	7.8	5,040	5.4	7,088	5.8	904	16.7	367	11.2

1046

POPULATION.

TABLE 3.—SCHOOL ATTENDANCE OF POPULATION 5 TO 20 YEARS OF AGE, BY SINGLE YEARS, FOR POPULATION CLASSES, BY SEX, FOR THE UNITED STATES: 1920 AND 1910—Continued.

AGE AND CENSUS YEAR.	NUMBER AND PER CENT OF TOTAL AT SPECIFIED AGE ATTENDING SCHOOL.																			
	Native white.																Foreign-born white.			
	Total.				Native parentage.				Foreign parentage.				Mixed parentage.							
	Male.		Female.		Male.		Female.		Male.		Female.		Male.		Female.		Male.		Female.	
	Number.	Per cent.	Number.	Per cent.	Number.	Per cent.	Number.	Per cent.	Number.	Per cent.	Number.	Per cent.	Number.	Per cent.	Number.	Per cent.	Number.	Per cent.	Number.	Per cent.
5 years:																				
1920......	200,917	19.2	206,016	20.2	125,461	17.1	129,580	18.2	54,653	23.9	55,081	24.5	20,803	24.5	21,355	26.0	1,709	18.6	1,720	18.9
1910......	154,339	17.7	150,208	18.4	94,883	15.1	96,679	15.8	39,230	24.6	38,951	24.7	20,226	23.7	20,576	24.7	5,128	21.5	5,023	21.6
6 years:																				
1920......	675,933	65.7	673,543	66.7	461,847	63.9	460,692	65.3	153,442	69.4	152,805	69.3	60,644	71.7	60,046	72.4	7,137	53.3	6,904	52.8
1910......	475,192	55.2	472,528	55.8	323,323	52.2	322,098	53.0	97,672	62.6	96,836	62.5	54,197	63.3	53,594	63.8	15,752	55.7	15,195	55.3
7 years:																				
1920......	861,388	85.8	845,933	86.1	599,742	84.7	588,693	85.2	186,519	88.4	183,784	88.2	75,127	88.8	73,456	88.8	13,246	73.0	13,125	72.8
1910......	652,902	79.1	640,190	79.3	455,622	76.9	447,054	77.4	126,168	84.4	123,833	83.6	71,112	85.0	69,303	84.8	24,121	77.2	23,623	76.6
8 years:																				
1920......	898,147	90.7	884,426	90.9	631,393	90.0	619,292	90.3	188,727	92.5	188,255	92.4	78,027	92.5	76,879	92.4	16,914	79.8	16,691	79.8
1910......	696,345	86.6	683,455	86.7	491,955	85.0	480,502	85.3	130,763	90.4	130,170	90.3	73,627	90.7	72,783	90.8	28,335	84.5	27,049	83.8
9 years:																				
1920......	870,449	92.3	849,984	92.3	611,500	91.7	595,336	91.8	181,680	93.6	179,406	93.6	77,269	93.7	75,242	93.7	19,506	82.9	19,167	83.3
1910......	689,752	89.4	670,667	89.5	486,151	88.2	471,252	88.4	130,169	92.5	127,058	92.3	73,432	92.5	71,757	92.5	29,558	87.5	28,783	87.4
10 years:																				
1920......	914,502	95.0	896,152	95.2	648,691	94.5	632,778	94.8	185,568	96.3	184,126	96.2	80,243	96.2	79,248	96.2	25,568	80.3	24,028	80.3
1910......	727,847	93.1	711,745	93.4	511,385	92.0	497,843	92.5	139,034	95.6	137,822	95.8	76,828	95.7	76,080	95.8	34,147	90.3	33,431	90.3
11 years:																				
1920......	873,369	95.5	862,019	95.7	620,380	95.1	610,489	95.3	173,513	96.6	173,136	96.6	79,476	96.7	78,394	96.6	25,614	88.0	25,373	87.5
1910......	678,112	93.6	670,898	93.9	475,668	92.6	470,411	93.1	129,281	96.1	128,427	96.0	73,163	96.1	72,060	96.0	30,586	91.7	29,746	91.1
12 years:																				
1920......	910,842	95.3	880,132	95.4	644,264	94.7	624,208	95.0	183,346	96.5	180,941	96.5	83,232	96.6	80,923	96.5	29,897	86.6	28,841	86.6
1910......	739,070	92.9	720,917	93.3	516,120	91.7	501,638	92.4	145,253	95.6	142,787	95.5	77,697	95.7	76,492	95.7	34,454	90.5	33,404	89.9
13 years:																				
1920......	820,199	94.7	807,854	94.7	582,548	94.1	575,305	94.3	160,207	95.8	156,028	95.3	77,444	96.1	76,521	95.8	29,982	86.3	29,188	85.4
1910......	683,699	91.8	674,914	92.1	472,529	90.6	466,409	91.3	137,477	94.6	135,502	93.6	73,693	94.9	73,003	94.4	30,403	88.7	28,830	86.8
14 years:																				
1920......	771,677	88.9	748,585	88.6	563,367	89.2	546,793	89.5	136,394	87.0	131,111	84.5	71,916	89.8	70,681	89.3	30,532	77.9	29,108	75.1
1910......	657,669	84.6	639,244	84.8	463,852	84.8	451,616	85.8	124,565	82.4	120,114	80.3	69,252	86.8	67,514	80.2	28,001	74.1	25,490	69.0
15 years:																				
1920......	579,412	74.4	591,113	75.8	431,174	76.8	441,330	78.8	93,350	65.5	92,748	64.3	54,888	73.1	57,035	74.9	23,746	59.0	23,176	55.7
1910......	512,636	71.2	511,499	71.8	374,761	74.3	374,050	75.7	85,910	60.9	84,184	58.9	51,965	69.9	53,265	70.9	18,172	49.0	16,600	43.6
16 years:																				
1920......	408,751	50.0	452,596	55.0	317,034	53.9	351,939	59.6	54,902	36.6	58,895	38.5	36,815	46.4	41,702	52.6	15,405	31.0	15,063	29.5
1910......	402,819	52.6	420,003	54.7	306,104	57.7	319,365	60.2	57,980	37.4	58,851	37.5	38,675	48.0	41,787	52.0	12,480	25.3	11,176	22.1
17 years:																				
1920......	259,965	33.7	298,984	38.9	205,622	37.1	230,974	43.1	31,534	22.5	34,395	24.1	22,809	30.1	27,615	36.5	9,370	18.2	8,342	15.9
1910......	271,882	36.9	281,429	39.1	214,678	41.8	220,037	44.1	32,959	22.5	34,173	23.4	24,245	31.6	27,219	36.1	7,706	12.8	6,872	11.7
18 years:																				
1920......	168,506	21.9	190,927	24.3	133,360	24.0	153,043	27.1	20,277	14.6	20,609	14.3	14,869	20.0	17,275	22.8	6,790	11.6	5,345	8.7
1910......	184,811	25.0	193,594	25.2	149,276	28.6	153,198	28.5	20,145	14.0	21,814	14.4	15,390	20.5	18,582	23.7	6,669	6.9	5,737	6.7
19 years:																				
1920......	112,103	15.0	109,734	14.7	87,189	16.2	87,316	16.3	14,487	10.7	12,112	8.8	10,477	14.4	10,306	14.0	5,123	8.6	3,878	5.4
1910......	115,865	16.9	106,149	15.6	93,432	19.4	83,633	17.6	12,655	9.5	12,058	9.0	9,778	14.0	10,458	15.0	5,482	5.0	4,020	4.5
20 years:																				
1920......	69,910	10.2	61,298	8.3	53,262	10.9	48,202	9.2	9,698	7.5	7,107	5.1	6,950	10.2	5,989	8.4	3,733	5.8	2,421	3.2
1910......	73,043	11.1	61,303	8.6	58,828	12.5	48,341	9.6	7,962	6.3	7,014	5.1	6,253	9.5	6,038	8.5	4,613	3.3	3,103	2.6

SCHOOL ATTENDANCE. 1047

TABLE 4.—SCHOOL ATTENDANCE, BY BROAD AGE GROUPS, BY DIVISIONS AND STATES: 1920 AND 1910.

| DIVISION AND STATE. | TOTAL NUMBER OF PERSONS ATTENDING SCHOOL. | | PERSONS 7 TO 20 YEARS OF AGE. | | | | | | PERSONS UNDER 7 YEARS OF AGE ATTENDING SCHOOL. | | PERSONS 21 YEARS OF AGE AND OVER ATTENDING SCHOOL. | |
| | | | 1920 | | | 1910 | | | | | | |
	1920	1910	Total number.	Attending school Number.	Per cent.	Total Number.	Attending school Number.	Per cent.	1920	1910	1920	1910
United States	21,763,275	18,009,891	28,564,716	19,451,851	68.1	25,716,765	16,240,851	63.2	1,966,635	1,455,784	344,789	313,256
GEOGRAPHIC DIVISIONS:												
New England	1,424,088	1,222,228	1,768,290	1,223,623	69.2	1,610,552	1,051,485	65.3	174,175	149,077	26,290	21,666
Middle Atlantic	4,260,677	3,531,373	5,527,757	3,746,560	67.8	4,979,935	3,131,190	62.9	447,445	339,656	66,672	60,527
East North Central	4,236,641	3,576,003	5,350,637	3,728,706	69.7	4,870,168	3,197,292	65.7	427,749	315,207	80,186	63,504
West North Central	2,741,410	2,530,591	3,393,143	2,420,929	71.3	3,318,977	2,271,448	68.4	270,428	209,562	50,053	49,581
South Atlantic	3,080,686	2,418,444	4,323,620	2,818,406	65.2	3,815,749	2,226,901	58.4	225,573	154,223	36,707	37,320
East South Central	2,018,295	1,730,191	2,818,595	1,858,659	65.9	2,665,236	1,589,551	59.6	141,808	114,264	17,828	26,376
West South Central	2,247,456	1,795,100	3,259,000	2,097,596	64.4	2,815,947	1,673,480	59.4	125,955	94,808	23,905	26,812
Mountain	732,593	505,191	896,406	656,638	73.3	684,190	460,193	67.3	63,174	35,122	12,781	9,876
Pacific	1,021,429	700,770	1,227,268	900,734	73.4	956,011	639,311	66.9	90,328	43,865	30,367	17,594
NEW ENGLAND:												
Maine	154,163	140,831	188,822	134,299	71.1	181,632	122,218	67.3	17,622	16,257	2,242	2,356
New Hampshire	81,850	77,550	104,581	73,063	69.9	104,082	68,048	65.4	7,298	8,374	1,489	1,128
Vermont	68,745	70,531	87,302	62,544	71.6	88,177	62,064	70.4	5,254	7,549	947	918
Massachusetts	741,029	630,119	907,212	633,124	69.8	820,931	539,615	65.7	91,931	78,259	15,974	12,245
Rhode Island	110,838	96,242	149,774	95,499	63.8	138,015	83,312	60.4	13,822	10,877	1,517	2,053
Connecticut	267,463	206,955	330,599	225,094	68.1	277,715	176,228	63.5	38,248	27,761	4,121	2,966
MIDDLE ATLANTIC:												
New York	1,900,039	1,650,863	2,461,306	1,656,905	67.3	2,289,201	1,452,179	63.4	206,238	166,968	36,896	31,716
New Jersey	613,575	469,272	786,040	525,979	66.9	658,328	405,496	61.6	80,202	56,840	7,394	6,938
Pennsylvania	1,747,063	1,411,238	2,280,411	1,563,676	68.6	2,032,406	1,273,515	62.7	161,005	115,848	22,382	21,875
EAST NORTH CENTRAL:												
Ohio	1,125,097	898,088	1,386,799	989,417	71.3	1,223,240	810,136	66.2	107,461	72,575	28,219	15,377
Indiana	572,310	529,742	745,281	515,237	69.1	723,663	482,597	66.7	48,998	36,416	8,075	10,729
Illinois	1,251,189	1,064,346	1,619,847	1,108,216	68.4	1,502,604	955,869	63.6	120,945	88,269	22,028	20,208
Michigan	723,639	568,926	893,744	626,165	70.1	739,692	500,305	67.6	85,894	59,416	11,580	9,205
Wisconsin	564,406	514,901	704,966	489,671	69.5	680,969	448,385	65.8	64,451	58,531	10,284	7,985
WEST NORTH CENTRAL:												
Minnesota	510,238	462,867	643,287	451,096	70.1	603,310	417,496	69.2	47,778	35,728	11,364	9,643
Iowa	526,864	490,272	627,248	454,078	72.4	628,492	434,117	69.1	62,457	54,961	10,329	10,194
Missouri	609,809	665,972	901,694	624,395	69.2	922,695	608,226	65.9	65,014	46,280	10,400	11,466
North Dakota	161,221	121,649	198,020	146,289	73.9	168,166	110,459	65.7	12,162	8,793	2,770	2,397
South Dakota	146,956	126,903	181,271	131,943	72.8	170,033	115,592	68.0	12,691	8,840	2,322	2,471
Nebraska	298,619	275,829	358,143	256,961	71.7	347,607	242,625	69.8	36,565	27,671	5,098	5,533
Kansas	397,703	378,099	483,480	356,167	73.7	478,674	342,933	71.6	33,761	27,289	7,775	7,877
SOUTH ATLANTIC:												
Delaware	41,713	36,330	54,739	37,759	69.0	53,994	33,362	61.8	3,391	2,409	563	559
Maryland	270,968	234,628	381,106	246,056	64.6	360,868	213,622	59.2	20,730	16,967	4,182	4,039
District of Columbia	70,886	54,688	89,931	58,005	64.5	73,955	47,662	64.4	6,704	4,726	6,177	2,300
Virginia	495,674	401,696	709,980	460,037	64.8	646,000	381,532	59.1	29,746	14,868	5,891	5,296
West Virginia	324,747	267,411	437,703	297,044	67.9	365,700	244,996	67.0	24,439	18,519	8,264	3,896
North Carolina	626,981	495,196	839,574	576,239	68.6	721,114	455,109	63.1	44,817	32,032	5,925	8,055
South Carolina	427,962	300,359	576,564	393,077	68.2	518,817	277,210	53.4	31,070	18,663	3,815	4,486
Georgia	624,776	494,781	953,304	570,386	59.8	851,147	452,234	53.1	49,264	36,007	5,126	6,540
Florida	196,979	133,355	280,719	179,803	64.1	224,154	121,174	54.1	15,412	10,032	1,764	2,149
EAST SOUTH CENTRAL:												
Kentucky	524,342	473,481	717,667	480,526	67.0	698,446	437,863	62.7	39,203	28,520	4,613	7,098
Tennessee	528,993	451,190	724,688	488,543	67.4	681,513	417,862	61.3	35,533	26,094	4,917	7,234
Alabama	527,595	396,845	774,048	499,888	64.6	691,822	371,850	53.7	23,270	18,641	4,437	6,354
Mississippi	437,365	408,675	602,192	389,702	64.7	593,455	361,976	61.0	43,802	41,009	3,861	5,690
WEST SOUTH CENTRAL:												
Arkansas	410,853	333,795	569,870	375,115	65.8	506,549	304,909	60.2	31,911	23,450	3,827	5,436
Louisiana	356,690	257,027	574,202	327,546	57.0	529,497	235,264	44.4	25,584	18,124	3,280	3,639
Oklahoma	487,013	394,201	647,939	444,247	68.6	519,327	361,376	69.6	37,546	27,689	5,220	5,136
Texas	992,900	810,077	1,466,989	950,688	64.8	1,260,574	771,931	61.2	30,614	25,545	11,598	12,601
MOUNTAIN:												
Montana	115,367	62,755	135,886	102,021	75.5	86,625	56,976	65.8	10,975	4,638	1,771	1,141
Idaho	104,456	68,603	122,278	95,027	77.7	89,215	63,613	71.3	7,976	3,798	1,453	1,192
Wyoming	38,827	23,745	47,474	34,387	72.4	33,042	21,475	65.0	3,793	1,842	647	428
Colorado	198,060	153,412	239,926	175,745	73.2	200,022	138,467	69.2	18,176	11,642	4,139	3,303
New Mexico	83,370	66,717	109,738	75,119	68.5	96,859	60,704	62.7	7,171	5,201	1,080	812
Arizona	60,688	31,346	89,464	54,387	60.8	52,248	28,753	55.0	5,271	2,092	1,030	501
Utah	118,934	88,056	136,039	107,908	79.3	111,284	80,725	72.5	8,615	5,052	2,411	2,279
Nevada	12,891	10,557	15,601	11,444	73.4	14,895	9,480	63.6	1,197	857	250	220
PACIFIC:												
Washington	265,051	201,695	321,410	238,012	74.1	272,793	185,795	68.1	19,568	11,329	7,471	4,571
Oregon	157,552	121,409	187,704	141,613	75.4	163,739	111,597	68.2	10,778	6,599	5,161	3,222
California	598,826	377,666	718,154	521,109	72.6	519,479	341,919	65.8	59,982	25,946	17,735	9,801

597

1048

POPULATION.

TABLE 5.—SCHOOL ATTENDANCE OF POPULATION 7 TO 20 YEARS OF AGE, BY SEX, BY DIVISIONS AND STATES: 1920 AND 1910.

DIVISION AND STATE.	MALES 7 TO 20 YEARS OF AGE.						FEMALES 7 TO 20 YEARS OF AGE.					
	1920			1910			1920			1910		
	Total number.	Attending school. Number.	Per cent.	Total number.	Attending school. Number.	Per cent.	Total number.	Attending school. Number.	Per cent.	Total number.	Attending school. Number.	Per cent.
United States	14,273,823	9,706,801	68.0	12,901,954	8,132,602	63.0	14,290,888	9,745,050	68.2	12,814,811	8,108,249	63.3
GEOGRAPHIC DIVISIONS:												
New England	878,176	608,434	69.3	803,599	523,899	65.2	890,114	615,189	69.1	806,953	527,586	65.4
Middle Atlantic	2,748,199	1,879,234	68.4	2,476,904	1,566,531	63.2	2,779,558	1,867,326	67.2	2,503,031	1,504,059	62.5
East North Central	2,687,570	1,869,629	69.6	2,450,080	1,610,601	65.7	2,663,067	1,859,077	69.8	2,420,088	1,586,691	65.6
West North Central	1,702,169	1,208,596	71.0	1,677,888	1,144,488	68.2	1,690,974	1,212,333	71.7	1,641,089	1,126,900	68.7
South Atlantic	2,151,766	1,395,324	64.8	1,902,650	1,101,477	57.9	2,171,854	1,423,082	65.5	1,913,099	1,125,424	58.8
East South Central	1,403,750	925,257	65.9	1,333,442	793,545	59.5	1,414,845	933,402	66.0	1,331,794	790,006	59.8
West South Central	1,628,633	1,040,793	63.9	1,412,878	839,147	59.4	1,630,367	1,056,803	64.8	1,403,069	834,333	59.5
Mountain	453,004	328,957	72.6	351,406	232,644	66.2	443,402	327,681	73.9	332,784	227,549	68.4
Pacific	620,561	450,577	72.6	493,107	320,270	64.9	606,707	450,157	74.2	462,904	319,041	68.9
NEW ENGLAND:												
Maine	94,350	66,239	70.2	91,353	60,941	66.7	94,472	68,060	72.0	90,279	61,277	67.9
New Hampshire	51,982	36,128	69.5	52,492	33,805	64.4	52,599	36,935	70.2	51,590	34,243	66.4
Vermont	44,150	31,266	70.8	45,014	31,030	68.9	43,152	31,278	72.5	43,103	31,034	71.9
Massachusetts	448,959	314,927	70.1	406,779	267,791	65.8	458,253	318,197	69.4	414,152	271,824	65.6
Rhode Island	74,634	47,336	63.4	69,610	42,589	61.2	75,140	48,163	64.1	68,405	40,723	59.5
Connecticut	164,101	112,538	68.6	138,351	87,743	63.4	166,498	112,556	67.0	139,364	88,485	63.5
MIDDLE ATLANTIC:												
New York	1,219,837	832,157	68.2	1,127,719	723,463	64.2	1,241,469	824,748	66.4	1,161,482	728,716	62.7
New Jersey	390,937	263,928	67.5	326,391	203,327	62.3	395,103	262,051	66.3	331,937	202,169	60.9
Pennsylvania	1,137,425	783,149	68.9	1,022,794	639,741	62.5	1,142,986	780,527	68.3	1,009,612	633,774	62.8
EAST NORTH CENTRAL:												
Ohio	696,509	494,519	71.0	615,169	409,085	66.5	690,290	404,898	71.7	608,071	401,051	66.0
Indiana	374,852	259,245	69.2	365,674	243,500	66.6	370,429	255,992	69.1	357,989	239,097	66.8
Illinois	809,763	557,008	68.8	751,167	480,526	64.0	810,084	551,208	68.0	751,437	475,343	63.3
Michigan	452,535	314,630	69.5	374,281	251,550	67.2	441,209	311,535	70.6	365,411	248,755	68.1
Wisconsin	353,911	244,227	69.0	343,789	225,940	65.7	351,055	245,444	69.9	337,180	222,445	66.0
WEST NORTH CENTRAL:												
Minnesota	323,064	225,043	69.7	305,057	210,343	69.0	320,223	226,053	70.6	298,258	207,153	69.5
Iowa	314,822	226,107	71.8	317,775	218,044	68.6	312,426	227,911	72.9	310,717	216,073	69.5
Missouri	449,804	312,866	69.6	460,960	305,552	66.3	451,890	311,520	68.9	461,735	302,674	65.6
North Dakota	99,346	73,083	73.6	80,761	55,380	65.0	98,074	73,206	74.2	81,405	54,079	66.4
South Dakota	92,081	66,151	71.8	87,654	59,038	67.4	89,190	65,792	73.8	82,379	56,554	68.7
Nebraska	180,616	128,304	71.0	176,285	122,544	69.5	177,527	128,657	72.5	171,322	120,081	70.1
Kansas	242,436	176,982	73.0	243,396	172,587	70.9	241,044	179,185	74.3	235,278	170,346	72.4
SOUTH ATLANTIC:												
Delaware	27,300	18,957	69.4	27,549	17,144	62.2	27,439	18,802	68.5	26,445	16,218	61.3
Maryland	191,855	124,602	64.9	179,155	107,311	59.9	189,251	121,454	64.2	181,713	106,311	58.5
District of Columbia	42,647	28,720	67.3	35,607	23,135	65.0	47,284	29,285	61.9	38,348	24,527	64.0
Virginia	357,586	226,508	63.3	323,465	188,141	58.2	352,394	233,529	66.3	322,535	193,391	60.0
West Virginia	220,917	148,588	67.3	188,168	124,686	66.3	216,786	148,456	68.5	177,532	120,310	67.8
North Carolina	417,912	286,398	68.5	360,461	227,744	63.2	421,662	289,841	68.7	360,653	227,365	63.0
South Carolina	284,150	193,276	68.0	256,852	134,767	52.5	292,414	199,801	68.3	261,965	142,443	54.4
Georgia	470,774	279,458	59.4	419,930	219,420	52.3	482,530	290,928	60.3	431,217	232,814	54.0
Florida	138,625	88,817	64.1	111,463	59,129	53.0	142,094	90,986	64.0	112,691	62,045	55.1
EAST SOUTH CENTRAL:												
Kentucky	361,539	239,915	66.4	351,504	220,640	62.8	356,128	240,611	67.6	346,942	217,223	62.6
Tennessee	362,072	244,777	67.6	343,050	209,798	61.2	362,616	243,766	67.2	338,463	208,004	61.5
Alabama	382,161	248,315	65.0	343,893	184,397	53.6	391,887	251,573	64.2	348,019	187,453	53.9
Mississippi	297,978	192,250	64.5	295,085	178,710	60.6	304,214	197,452	64.9	298,370	183,266	61.4
WEST SOUTH CENTRAL:												
Arkansas	283,750	187,438	66.1	253,025	152,402	60.2	286,120	187,677	65.6	253,524	152,507	60.2
Louisiana	282,282	159,544	56.5	261,479	114,896	43.9	291,920	168,002	57.6	268,018	120,368	44.9
Oklahoma	326,159	222,124	68.1	264,489	185,149	70.0	321,780	222,123	69.0	254,838	176,227	69.2
Texas	736,442	471,687	64.0	633,885	386,700	61.0	730,547	479,001	65.6	626,689	385,231	61.5
MOUNTAIN:												
Montana	68,710	51,244	74.6	45,249	28,409	62.8	67,176	51,377	76.5	41,376	28,567	69.0
Idaho	62,478	47,975	76.8	46,530	32,616	70.1	59,800	47,052	78.7	42,685	30,997	72.6
Wyoming	24,629	17,274	70.1	17,817	10,813	60.7	22,845	17,113	74.9	15,225	10,602	70.0
Colorado	120,608	87,277	72.4	101,327	69,139	68.2	119,318	88,468	74.1	98,695	69,328	70.2
New Mexico	54,960	37,662	68.5	49,203	31,391	63.8	54,778	37,457	68.4	47,656	29,313	61.5
Arizona	45,363	27,363	60.3	27,053	14,633	54.1	44,101	27,024	61.3	25,195	14,120	56.0
Utah	68,184	54,429	79.8	56,231	40,858	72.7	67,855	53,479	78.8	55,053	39,867	72.4
Nevada	8,072	5,733	71.0	7,996	4,785	59.8	7,529	5,711	75.9	6,899	4,695	68.1
PACIFIC:												
Washington	161,954	118,386	73.1	140,962	93,199	66.1	159,456	119,626	75.0	131,831	92,596	70.2
Oregon	94,215	70,622	75.0	84,716	56,570	66.8	93,489	70,991	75.9	79,023	55,027	69.6
California	364,392	261,569	71.8	267,429	170,501	63.8	353,762	259,540	73.4	252,050	171,418	68.0

SCHOOL ATTENDANCE.

TABLE 6.—SCHOOL ATTENDANCE OF POPULATION 7 TO 20 YEARS OF AGE, BY AGE PERIODS, BY DIVISIONS AND STATES: 1920 AND 1910.

DIVISION AND STATE.	PERSONS 7 TO 13 YEARS OF AGE ATTENDING SCHOOL.				PERSONS 14 AND 15 YEARS OF AGE ATTENDING SCHOOL.				PERSONS 16 AND 17 YEARS OF AGE ATTENDING SCHOOL.				PERSONS 18 TO 20 YEARS OF AGE ATTENDING SCHOOL.			
	1920		1910		1920		1910		1920		1910		1920		1910	
	Number.	Per cent.	Number.	Per cent.	Number.	Per cent.	Number.	Per cent.	Number.	Per cent.	Number.	Per cent.	Number.	Per cent.	Number.	Per cent.
United States...	13,869,010	90.6	11,146,173	86.1	3,124,129	79.9	2,676,465	75.0	1,644,061	42.9	1,573,377	43.1	814,651	14.8	844,836	15.2
GEOGRAPHIC DIVISIONS:																
New England......	898,605	95.3	751,547	95.2	179,963	75.3	163,585	73.6	92,749	39.0	85,293	36.8	52,306	15.0	51,060	13.9
Middle Atlantic....	2,805,986	94.3	2,269,431	93.0	582,517	79.3	496,046	73.5	240,079	32.3	240,434	33.4	117,978	11.0	125,279	10.9
East North Central.	2,603,634	95.1	2,239,718	93.5	598,227	82.5	528,507	77.9	293,581	40.4	284,439	40.0	143,264	13.4	144,628	13.3
West North Central.	1,679,682	93.9	1,512,644	91.5	401,680	85.3	386,893	83.6	224,014	48.1	243,032	51.1	115,553	17.3	128,879	17.7
South Atlantic.....	1,997,008	85.6	1,508,993	75.6	452,330	75.4	360,081	67.1	249,134	43.7	229,240	43.8	119,934	14.6	128,587	16.9
East South Central.	1,283,921	83.6	1,043,420	75.0	307,840	77.5	265,274	70.4	181,363	48.8	178,509	47.8	85,535	16.8	102,348	19.6
West South Central.	1,447,653	82.5	1,106,205	74.7	351,732	76.9	286,521	72.8	208,180	48.1	187,674	48.9	90,031	14.7	93,080	16.7
Mountain..........	452,896	91.8	302,970	86.4	104,983	86.7	76,661	83.4	65,231	57.0	51,831	55.7	33,528	20.0	28,731	19.3
Pacific.............	609,625	94.1	411,245	91.2	144,857	89.2	112,897	85.3	89,730	55.4	72,925	52.3	56,522	22.1	42,244	18.1
NEW ENGLAND:																
Maine.............	93,615	94.2	83,590	92.3	21,967	83.7	20,350	78.6	12,082	46.5	11,807	45.4	6,635	17.8	6,471	16.5
New Hampshire....	51,544	93.4	48,314	94.9	12,312	86.6	10,991	75.5	5,979	41.7	5,646	37.1	3,228	15.5	3,097	13.2
Vermont...........	43,336	93.9	42,700	95.7	10,577	86.2	10,613	85.1	5,611	46.0	5,813	46.3	3,020	18.1	2,938	15.9
Massachusetts.....	464,752	96.1	385,813	96.0	90,290	73.9	82,672	73.5	49,260	40.6	43,519	37.3	28,822	16.0	27,611	14.5
Rhode Island.......	74,872	95.6	61,436	93.9	11,327	59.0	11,968	62.5	5,527	26.3	5,889	28.4	3,273	10.8	4,019	12.3
Connecticut.......	170,486	94.7	129,694	95.6	32,990	74.9	26,991	71.6	14,290	33.0	12,619	31.3	7,328	11.6	6,924	10.8
MIDDLE ATLANTIC:																
New York.........	1,226,918	93.9	1,032,247	93.7	265,353	81.5	240,687	78.7	107,688	32.6	116,077	34.7	56,946	11.4	63,168	11.5
New Jersey........	404,928	94.9	300,367	92.6	74,841	71.8	62,658	69.9	31,016	29.9	28,917	30.7	15,194	10.0	13,554	9.0
Pennsylvania.......	1,174,140	94.5	936,817	92.3	242,323	79.6	192,701	69.0	101,375	32.8	95,440	32.9	45,838	10.8	48,557	10.8
EAST NORTH CENTRAL:																
Ohio.............	703,560	96.0	560,731	94.1	162,380	87.8	133,706	79.0	82,659	44.4	76,376	42.4	40,818	14.4	39,323	14.1
Indiana...........	369,713	94.9	335,541	93.3	82,964	80.2	78,746	77.2	41,405	39.9	43,997	42.1	21,155	14.2	24,313	15.4
Illinois...........	815,080	94.7	678,407	92.5	171,810	79.0	156,528	75.4	81,699	37.1	80,928	36.8	39,627	12.3	40,006	11.7
Michigan.........	453,652	94.9	345,005	94.1	103,747	86.6	85,713	84.5	47,055	39.4	47,279	43.7	21,711	12.3	22,308	13.6
Wisconsin.........	351,629	94.5	320,034	93.7	77,326	77.8	73,814	75.4	40,763	42.2	35,859	36.2	19,953	14.6	18,678	13.1
WEST NORTH CENTRAL:																
Minnesota.........	314,905	93.9	279,592	93.0	76,759	86.2	74,209	88.4	38,055	42.5	42,443	48.8	21,377	16.6	21,252	16.1
Iowa.............	309,744	95.0	291,643	93.2	74,732	85.5	72,278	81.8	45,078	51.4	45,618	50.5	24,524	19.4	24,578	17.9
Missouri..........	440,394	93.4	408,655	90.1	103,959	82.1	102,823	78.4	54,963	43.9	63,730	47.5	25,079	14.1	33,018	16.2
North Dakota.....	102,876	92.1	75,340	86.1	23,489	87.3	17,760	79.9	13,417	53.4	11,089	49.4	6,507	19.0	6,270	17.4
South Dakota.....	91,322	93.5	76,479	87.7	21,411	86.7	19,286	84.1	12,757	52.6	12,979	55.1	6,453	18.6	6,848	18.8
Nebraska..........	178,910	93.9	160,389	92.9	42,315	86.0	41,546	86.5	23,830	49.7	26,461	52.9	11,906	16.9	14,229	18.5
Kansas............	241,531	94.5	220,546	92.3	59,015	87.9	58,991	88.8	35,914	54.4	40,712	59.5	19,707	20.8	22,684	21.6
SOUTH ATLANTIC:																
Delaware..........	27,336	95.2	22,977	87.6	5,997	80.7	5,841	73.9	2,968	39.1	3,090	39.8	1,458	13.2	1,454	12.2
Maryland..........	182,147	92.6	157,223	86.4	38,525	73.6	32,278	63.6	16,812	31.7	16,690	32.1	8,572	10.9	7,431	9.8
District of Columbia	38,962	93.5	31,101	90.4	9,530	83.2	8,271	84.1	5,566	44.8	5,277	47.6	3,947	16.2	3,013	16.2
Virginia...........	324,292	84.8	254,237	74.5	73,671	75.5	64,373	70.1	41,769	44.3	41,057	46.5	20,305	15.0	21,805	17.5
West Virginia.....	213,053	89.1	166,925	87.8	48,331	82.3	39,863	79.7	24,599	42.3	24,316	48.4	11,061	13.6	13,892	18.4
North Carolina.....	400,846	87.0	291,608	76.5	91,619	77.4	73,078	71.8	54,942	50.1	53,737	54.1	28,832	19.1	36,686	26.4
South Carolina.....	274,429	87.1	184,535	67.6	64,264	78.0	45,005	61.9	36,318	49.2	30,380	42.8	18,066	17.2	17,290	16.9
Georgia...........	409,754	79.1	318,189	70.5	90,718	78.7	71,843	59.3	49,133	39.7	42,271	37.3	20,781	11.7	19,931	12.1
Florida...........	126,189	83.2	82,198	70.5	29,675	78.6	19,529	64.2	17,027	45.5	12,422	40.9	6,912	12.8	7,025	15.0
EAST SOUTH CENTRAL:																
Kentucky..........	342,974	88.5	293,068	81.3	78,178	77.6	73,107	73.6	40,983	42.5	46,482	46.9	18,391	13.8	25,206	18.1
Tennessee.........	333,118	85.3	289,064	77.2	80,780	79.4	70,524	73.2	49,669	50.7	49,976	50.2	24,976	18.6	29,198	21.0
Alabama.........	344,699	80.4	243,275	66.3	83,417	77.5	61,866	63.5	49,559	48.8	41,866	44.0	22,213	16.3	24,843	18.8
Mississippi........	263,130	80.1	238,013	75.4	65,465	75.2	59,777	71.1	41,152	51.7	41,085	50.5	19,955	18.6	23,101	20.5
WEST SOUTH CENTRAL:																
Arkansas..........	256,263	82.0	195,383	74.2	62,632	77.0	50,816	71.7	38,423	50.8	36,652	51.8	17,797	17.7	22,058	21.7
Louisiana.........	234,249	75.9	165,194	58.8	53,736	65.6	38,362	51.7	28,053	36.8	21,343	30.0	11,508	10.7	10,365	10.0
Oklahoma.........	304,665	85.8	235,528	86.1	73,720	82.0	61,953	86.3	46,088	54.2	42,400	60.1	19,774	16.8	21,495	20.8
Texas.............	652,476	83.7	510,100	76.8	161,644	79.1	135,390	76.7	95,616	48.8	87,279	51.0	40,952	14.2	39,162	15.7
MOUNTAIN:																
Montana..........	71,513	92.8	37,910	87.1	16,058	89.1	9,669	83.9	10,036	58.3	6,106	53.0	5,014	21.2	3,282	16.4
Idaho.............	65,102	95.5	40,606	87.4	15,342	91.6	10,901	89.3	9,741	62.3	8,010	66.7	4,842	22.3	4,096	22.1
Wyoming..........	24,554	92.8	14,406	88.8	5,294	86.2	3,389	84.3	3,047	52.6	2,372	54.9	1,492	16.4	1,308	15.5
Colorado..........	121,353	93.9	90,911	90.9	28,076	86.2	23,136	85.0	16,997	53.2	15,526	54.7	9,319	20.2	8,894	20.0
New Mexico.......	52,829	87.4	39,696	77.2	12,002	80.4	9,763	74.6	6,885	50.6	6,995	53.7	3,403	16.4	4,250	22.0
Arizona...........	38,179	78.8	19,483	71.8	8,663	73.8	4,832	70.0	4,874	45.3	2,900	43.8	2,671	14.4	1,538	13.3
Utah.............	71,611	95.5	53,644	91.6	17,719	93.7	13,408	88.8	12,456	71.4	8,894	58.4	6,122	24.7	4,779	21.3
Nevada...........	7,755	90.5	6,305	87.9	1,829	88.8	1,563	82.6	1,195	61.4	1,028	53.0	665	22.0	584	15.0
PACIFIC:																
Washington.......	162,750	94.7	120,345	91.1	38,442	88.6	32,555	87.0	23,105	54.5	21,034	53.7	13,715	21.5	11,861	18.5
Oregon...........	94,312	94.7	70,141	90.3	23,224	90.6	19,924	87.7	14,931	59.7	13,693	57.1	9,146	24.4	7,839	19.9
California..........	352,563	93.7	220,759	91.6	83,191	89.1	60,418	83.6	51,694	54.7	38,198	50.1	33,661	21.9	22,544	17.3

1050   POPULATION.

TABLE 7.—SCHOOL ATTENDANCE OF POPULATION 7 TO 20 YEARS OF AGE, FOR PRINCIPAL POPULATION CLASSES, BY DIVISIONS AND STATES: 1920.

[Per cent not shown where base is less than 100.]

DIVISION AND STATE.	ALL CLASSES.			NATIVE WHITE.						FOREIGN-BORN WHITE.			NEGRO.		
				Native parentage.			Foreign or mixed parentage.								
	Total number.	Attending school.		Total number.	Attending school.		Total number.	Attending school.		Total number.	Attending school.		Total number.	Attending school.	
		Number.	Per cent.		Number.	Per cent.		Number.	Per cent.		Number.	Per cent.		Number.	Per cent.
United States.....	28,564,716	19,451,851	68.1	17,172,184	12,241,234	71.3	6,887,689	4,763,723	69.2	1,123,995	498,632	44.5	3,280,354	1,887,282	57.5
GEOGRAPHIC DIVISIONS:															
New England.........	1,768,290	1,223,623	69.2	668,252	489,081	73.2	928,867	653,535	70.4	153,693	69,351	45.1	16,710	11,167	66.8
Middle Atlantic.......	5,527,757	3,746,560	67.8	2,603,372	1,818,582	69.9	2,382,080	1,669,684	70.1	414,050	179,409	43.3	125,222	77,076	61.6
East North Central...	5,350,637	3,728,706	69.7	3,377,218	2,434,054	72.1	1,631,454	1,112,886	68.2	230,668	111,095	48.2	106,177	67,374	63.5
West North Central...	3,393,143	2,420,929	71.3	2,293,464	1,696,658	74.0	950,927	642,546	67.6	74,430	34,657	46.6	62,513	39,737	63.6
South Atlantic.......	4,323,020	2,818,406	65.2	2,694,259	1,855,629	68.9	149,498	102,119	68.3	26,881	12,101	45.0	1,448,023	845,820	58.4
East South Central...	2,818,595	1,858,659	65.9	1,943,812	1,369,090	70.4	36,526	25,740	66.8	4,403	2,105	47.8	831,205	461,566	55.5
West South Central...	3,259,000	2,097,596	64.4	2,265,347	1,565,028	69.1	207,759	117,437	56.5	86,894	24,771	28.5	676,744	375,356	55.5
Mountain............	896,406	656,608	73.3	598,723	460,004	76.8	216,070	157,950	73.1	50,451	23,342	46.3	4,772	2,867	60.1
Pacific.............	1,227,268	900,734	73.4	727,737	553,108	76.0	382,518	281,920	73.7	82,525	42,801	51.9	8,988	6,319	70.3
NEW ENGLAND:															
Maine..............	188,822	134,299	71.1	117,909	86,367	73.3	58,850	42,320	71.9	11,552	5,255	45.5	278	176	63.3
New Hampshire......	104,581	73,063	69.9	49,973	36,391	72.8	46,098	32,396	70.3	8,356	4,176	50.0	134	93	69.4
Vermont............	87,302	62,544	71.6	59,678	43,449	72.8	22,154	16,002	72.2	5,315	2,989	56.2	148	101	68.2
Massachusetts........	907,212	633,124	69.8	290,030	217,865	75.1	524,636	371,485	70.8	82,849	37,111	44.8	9,312	6,420	68.9
Rhode Island........	149,774	95,499	63.8	43,537	29,858	68.6	88,421	58,227	65.9	15,651	6,038	38.6	2,114	1,338	63.3
Connecticut........	330,599	225,094	68.1	107,125	75,131	70.1	188,608	133,096	70.5	29,970	13,782	46.0	4,724	3,039	64.3
MIDDLE ATLANTIC:															
New York...........	2,461,306	1,656,905	67.3	954,820	665,970	69.7	1,222,725	861,480	70.5	245,090	106,552	43.5	36,112	21,267	58.9
New Jersey...........	786,040	525,979	66.9	322,926	224,392	69.5	375,464	258,658	68.9	60,394	25,389	42.0	27,120	17,471	64.4
Pennsylvania........	2,280,411	1,563,676	68.6	1,325,626	928,220	70.0	783,891	549,496	70.1	108,566	47,468	43.7	61,990	38,338	61.8
EAST NORTH CENTRAL:															
Ohio..............	1,386,799	989,417	71.3	991,441	717,654	72.4	302,490	219,026	72.4	53,353	27,064	50.7	39,401	25,618	65.0
Indiana............	745,281	515,237	69.1	642,549	449,571	70.0	74,347	49,507	66.6	9,971	4,536	45.5	18,375	11,604	63.2
Illinois............	1,619,847	1,108,216	68.4	901,858	650,122	72.1	596,067	396,067	66.5	85,261	38,170	44.8	36,306	23,008	63.4
Michigan............	893,744	626,165	70.1	467,475	341,313	73.0	355,874	248,259	69.8	57,690	29,130	50.5	11,028	6,445	58.4
Wisconsin..........	704,966	489,671	69.5	373,895	275,394	73.7	302,676	199,377	65.9	24,393	12,195	50.0	1,067	699	65.5
WEST NORTH CENTRAL:															
Minnesota..........	643,287	451,096	70.1	280,012	211,607	75.6	337,204	226,365	67.1	21,958	10,656	48.5	1,421	969	68.2
Iowa..............	627,248	454,078	72.4	464,074	347,895	75.0	148,277	98,050	66.1	10,426	5,111	49.0	4,291	2,897	67.5
Missouri...........	901,694	624,895	69.2	754,513	534,214	70.8	95,498	60,911	63.8	11,877	5,106	43.0	36,709	24,118	60.7
North Dakota........	198,020	146,289	73.9	70,273	55,305	78.7	115,856	85,302	73.6	9,781	4,637	47.4	89	67	.....
South Dakota........	181,271	131,943	72.8	100,200	77,199	77.0	72,073	49,634	68.9	4,131	1,899	46.0	206	131	63.6
Nebraska..........	358,143	256,961	71.7	236,491	177,652	75.1	109,814	73,016	66.5	8,273	4,062	49.1	2,578	1,630	63.4
Kansas............	483,480	356,167	73.7	387,901	292,786	75.5	72,205	49,268	68.2	7,984	3,186	39.9	14,224	9,925	69.8
SOUTH ATLANTIC:															
Delaware...........	54,739	37,759	69.0	35,215	24,748	70.3	9,802	6,855	69.9	1,457	656	45.0	8,263	5,498	66.5
Maryland..........	381,106	246,056	64.6	248,137	166,109	66.9	56,663	36,711	64.8	8,225	3,429	41.7	68,046	39,789	58.5
District of Columbia..	89,931	58,005	64.5	50,638	33,491	66.1	11,684	8,030	68.7	2,064	1,062	51.5	25,462	15,375	60.4
Virginia...........	709,980	460,037	64.8	469,449	317,087	67.5	15,352	10,310	67.2	2,738	1,235	45.2	222,125	131,284	59.1
West Virginia........	437,703	297,044	67.9	386,185	263,542	68.2	22,810	16,844	73.8	6,010	2,731	45.4	22,680	13,922	61.4
North Carolina........	839,574	576,239	68.6	504,782	399,852	70.8	3,169	2,302	72.6	557	256	46.0	266,953	171,379	64.2
South Carolina........	576,534	393,077	68.2	256,367	187,341	73.3	3,042	1,981	65.1	431	190	44.1	316,022	203,028	64.1
Georgia...........	953,304	570,386	59.8	526,435	352,408	66.9	7,463	5,333	71.5	1,259	591	46.9	418,086	212,041	50.7
Florida...........	280,719	179,803	64.1	157,061	110,551	70.4	19,513	13,753	70.5	4,145	1,951	47.1	99,786	53,504	53.6
EAST SOUTH CENTRAL:															
Kentucky...........	717,667	480,526	67.0	638,043	431,095	67.6	15,912	9,704	61.0	1,230	583	47.4	62,458	39,133	62.7
Tennessee..........	724,688	488,543	67.4	575,837	406,847	70.7	7,997	5,787	72.4	1,085	575	53.0	139,751	75,324	53.9
Alabama..........	774,048	499,888	64.6	456,507	325,110	71.2	10,090	7,083	70.2	1,442	708	49.1	305,861	166,943	54.6
Mississippi.........	602,192	389,702	64.7	273,425	206,032	75.4	4,527	3,166	69.9	646	239	37.0	323,135	180,166	55.8
WEST SOUTH CENTRAL:															
Arkansas..........	569,870	375,115	65.8	404,152	283,477	70.1	9,897	6,574	66.4	789	308	41.7	155,034	84,729	54.7
Louisiana..........	574,202	327,546	57.0	314,604	205,661	65.4	27,580	16,906	61.3	3,320	1,247	37.6	228,238	103,598	45.4
Oklahoma..........	647,939	444,247	68.6	547,268	379,331	69.3	27,037	18,895	69.9	3,325	1,139	34.3	49,369	30,387	61.6
Texas............	1,466,989	950,688	64.8	999,323	696,559	69.7	143,245	75,062	52.4	79,510	22,077	27.8	244,103	156,642	64.2
MOUNTAIN:															
Montana............	135,886	102,621	75.5	75,854	59,404	78.3	49,354	37,003	75.0	7,107	4,024	56.6	243	171	70.4
Idaho.............	122,278	95,027	77.7	93,627	74,526	79.6	24,966	18,607	74.5	2,498	1,217	48.8	149	97	65.1
Wyoming..........	47,474	34,387	72.4	33,338	24,776	74.3	11,487	8,237	71.7	1,986	962	48.4	219	114	52.1
Colorado...........	239,926	175,745	73.2	165,284	124,402	75.3	60,590	44,156	72.5	10,828	5,309	49.0	2,240	1,524	68.0
New Mexico........	109,738	75,119	68.5	86,427	61,868	71.6	9,577	6,330	66.1	5,953	2,690	45.2	671	298	44.4
Arizona............	89,454	54,387	60.8	41,740	30,947	74.1	18,156	12,322	67.9	17,410	6,709	38.5	990	490	49.5
Utah..............	136,039	107,908	79.3	93,448	77,103	82.5	37,381	28,070	75.1	3,884	2,101	54.1	214	145	67.8
Nevada............	15,601	11,444	73.4	9,010	6,978	77.4	4,259	3,225	75.7	790	330	41.8	46	28	.....
PACIFIC:															
Washington........	321,410	238,012	74.1	190,271	144,865	76.1	108,028	79,843	73.9	16,826	9,285	55.2	1,111	785	70.7
Oregon...........	187,704	141,613	75.4	132,897	102,108	76.8	45,274	33,669	74.4	6,627	3,686	55.6	352	254	72.2
California..........	718,154	521,109	72.6	404,569	306,135	75.7	229,216	168,414	73.5	59,072	29,830	50.5	7,525	5,280	70.2

SCHOOL ATTENDANCE.

1051

TABLE 8.—SCHOOL ATTENDANCE OF POPULATION 7 TO 20 YEARS OF AGE, FOR PRINCIPAL POPULATION CLASSES, BY DIVISIONS AND STATES: 1920 AND 1910.

[Per cent not shown where base is less than 100.]

DIVISION AND STATE.	ALL CLASSES. 1920 Number.	Per cent.	1910 Number.	Per cent.	NATIVE WHITE. Native parentage. 1920 Number.	Per cent.	1910 Number.	Per cent.	Foreign or mixed parentage. 1920 Number.	Per cent.	1910 Number.	Per cent.	FOREIGN-BORN WHITE. 1920 Number.	Per cent.	1910 Number.	Per cent.	NEGRO. 1920 Number.	Per cent.	1910 Number.	Per cent.
United States.	19,451,851	68.1	16,240,851	63.2	12,241,234	71.3	10,055,770	68.0	4,763,723	69.2	4,016,779	64.9	409,632	44.5	573,500	38.6	1,887,282	57.5	1,541,575	43.8
GEOG. DIVISIONS:																				
New England..	1,223,623	69.2	1,051,485	65.3	489,081	73.2	445,343	71.8	653,535	70.4	507,030	68.6	69,351	45.1	89,145	37.9	11,167	66.8	9,461	65.3
Middle Atlantic	3,746,560	67.8	3,131,190	62.9	1,818,582	69.9	1,625,956	67.8	1,669,634	70.1	1,193,976	65.2	179,409	43.3	257,783	39.0	77,076	61.6	51,124	57.6
E. N. Central..	3,728,706	69.7	3,197,292	65.7	2,434,054	72.1	2,027,808	70.0	1,112,836	68.2	1,016,626	62.5	111,095	48.2	107,194	39.3	67,374	63.5	41,742	61.3
W. N. Central..	2,420,929	71.3	2,271,448	68.4	1,696,658	74.0	1,441,569	71.5	642,546	67.6	738,217	66.5	34,657	46.6	47,872	40.5	39,737	63.6	35,152	58.7
South Atlantic	2,818,406	65.2	2,226,901	58.4	1,855,629	68.9	1,468,802	64.6	102,119	68.3	71,973	60.3	12,101	45.0	11,797	34.5	845,820	58.4	672,549	48.6
E. S. Central...	1,858,659	65.9	1,589,551	59.6	1,369,090	70.4	1,131,194	65.2	25,740	66.8	29,800	60.0	2,105	47.8	2,607	39.1	461,566	55.5	425,687	48.7
W. S. Central...	2,097,596	64.4	1,673,480	59.4	1,565,028	69.1	1,235,891	65.6	117,437	56.5	106,784	54.1	24,771	28.5	12,881	26.4	375,356	55.5	300,143	45.5
Mountain......	656,638	73.3	460,193	67.3	400,004	76.8	298,535	71.2	157,950	73.1	135,219	69.1	23,342	46.3	15,521	38.2	2,867	60.1	2,373	61.3
Pacific..........	900,734	73.4	639,311	66.9	553,108	76.0	380,672	70.6	281,926	73.7	217,154	67.5	42,801	51.9	28,700	41.2	6,319	70.3	3,344	61.0
NEW ENGLAND:																				
Maine..........	134,299	71.1	122,218	67.3	86,387	73.3	81,554	70.7	42,329	71.9	33,912	68.4	5,255	45.5	6,378	39.6	176	63.3	213	62.5
New Hampshire	73,063	69.9	68,048	65.4	36,391	72.8	35,297	71.9	32,396	70.3	27,606	68.9	4,176	50.0	5,061	34.3	93	69.4	74	55.6
Vermont.......	62,544	71.6	62,064	70.4	43,449	72.8	43,261	72.9	16,002	72.2	15,646	70.5	2,989	56.2	3,033	47.1	101	68.2	120	51.1
Massachusetts.	633,124	69.6	539,615	65.7	217,865	75.1	189,613	73.1	371,485	70.8	294,097	69.4	37,111	44.8	50,254	38.9	6,420	68.9	5,410	66.1
Rhode Island..	95,499	63.8	83,312	60.4	29,858	68.6	27,054	69.3	58,227	65.9	45,731	64.6	6,038	38.6	9,150	35.2	1,338	63.3	1,320	62.6
Connecticut....	225,094	68.1	176,228	63.5	75,131	70.1	68,564	69.9	133,090	70.5	90,038	67.6	13,782	46.0	15,269	35.7	3,039	64.3	2,324	66.9
MIDDLE ATLANTIC:																				
New York.....	1,656,905	67.3	1,452,179	63.4	665,970	69.7	619,070	69.1	861,480	70.5	652,280	67.1	106,552	43.5	155,321	42.0	21,267	58.9	14,159	55.6
New Jersey....	525,979	66.9	405,496	61.6	224,392	69.5	188,413	67.1	258,058	68.9	174,856	64.5	25,389	42.0	30,235	35.2	17,471	64.4	11,938	58.7
Pennsylvania...	1,563,676	68.6	1,273,515	62.7	928,220	70.0	818,473	67.0	549,496	70.1	366,840	62.5	47,468	43.7	62,227	34.5	38,338	61.8	25,027	58.4
E. N. CENTRAL:																				
Ohio..........	989,417	71.3	810,136	66.2	717,654	72.4	607,631	69.8	219,026	72.4	162,724	61.3	27,064	50.7	23,481	38.9	25,618	65.0	16,242	62.2
Indiana........	515,237	69.1	482,597	66.7	449,571	70.0	421,401	68.3	49,507	66.6	47,541	59.5	4,536	45.5	4,350	36.9	11,604	63.2	9,136	62.5
Illinois........	1,108,216	68.4	955,869	63.6	650,122	72.1	545,474	69.5	396,667	66.5	353,182	61.2	38,170	44.8	43,466	37.2	23,008	63.4	13,617	58.9
Michigan.......	626,165	70.1	500,305	67.6	341,313	73.0	248,051	72.4	248,259	69.8	226,244	66.4	29,130	50.5	22,217	44.2	6,445	58.4	2,375	63.9
Wisconsin......	489,671	69.5	448,385	65.8	275,394	73.7	205,161	73.1	199,377	65.9	226,935	62.5	12,195	50.0	13,680	41.0	699	65.5	372	62.8
W. N. CENTRAL:																				
Minnesota......	451,096	70.1	417,496	69.2	211,607	75.6	144,057	75.4	226,365	67.1	255,505	68.6	10,656	48.5	15,010	41.9	989	68.2	741	65.7
Iowa..........	454,078	72.4	434,117	69.1	347,895	75.0	296,204	72.5	98,050	66.1	130,013	64.8	5,111	49.0	5,569	35.7	2,897	67.5	2,209	63.4
Missouri.......	624,395	69.2	608,226	65.9	534,214	70.8	505,627	68.5	60,911	63.8	74,230	58.0	5,106	43.0	6,767	39.1	24,118	60.7	21,531	55.3
North Dakota..	146,289	73.9	110,459	65.7	55,305	78.7	34,166	71.1	85,302	73.6	66,157	68.0	4,637	47.4	8,677	42.4	67	.....	50	.....
South Dakota..	131,943	72.8	115,592	68.0	77,199	77.0	53,997	71.9	49,634	63.9	55,002	67.7	1,899	46.0	3,213	40.2	131	63.6	117	67.2
Nebraska......	256,961	71.7	242,625	69.8	177,652	75.1	143,755	73.2	73,016	66.5	92,636	67.4	4,002	49.1	4,595	41.4	1,630	63.4	874	61.1
Kansas........	356,167	73.7	342,933	71.6	292,786	75.5	263,763	73.4	49,268	68.2	64,674	68.9	3,186	39.9	4,041	41.1	9,925	68.9	9,564	65.6
SOUTH ATLANTIC:																				
Delaware......	37,759	69.0	33,362	61.8	24,748	70.3	22,462	64.4	6,855	69.9	4,784	61.0	656	45.0	587	30.2	5,498	66.5	5,544	59.0
Maryland......	246,056	64.6	213,622	59.2	166,109	66.9	143,102	62.8	36,711	64.8	29,698	55.4	3,429	41.7	4,288	37.6	39,789	58.5	36,503	53.8
Dist. Columbia.	58,005	64.5	47,662	64.4	33,491	66.1	26,914	67.1	8,030	68.7	6,606	67.8	1,062	51.5	900	49.1	15,375	60.4	13,147	59.5
Virginia........	460,037	64.8	381,532	59.1	317,087	67.5	261,753	64.3	10,310	67.2	7,183	65.7	1,235	45.2	1,204	42.1	131,284	59.1	111,337	49.5
West Virginia..	297,044	67.9	244,996	67.0	263,542	68.2	225,257	68.9	16,844	73.8	8,501	64.6	2,731	45.4	2,054	24.8	13,922	61.4	9,169	53.5
North Carolina.	576,239	65.6	455,109	55.1	399,852	70.8	316,067	66.8	2,302	72.6	1,926	72.3	256	46.0	274	40.1	171,379	54.2	135,297	56.0
South Carolina.	393,077	68.2	277,210	53.4	187,841	73.3	130,390	61.9	1,981	65.1	1,755	63.5	190	44.1	195	36.4	203,028	64.1	144,803	47.5
Georgia........	570,386	59.8	452,234	53.1	352,408	66.9	272,317	62.1	5,333	71.5	4,392	65.3	591	46.9	639	41.9	212,041	50.7	174,871	43.3
Florida........	179,803	64.1	121,174	54.1	110,551	70.4	70,540	61.8	13,753	70.5	7,128	60.2	1,951	47.1	1,616	31.7	53,504	53.6	41,878	45.0
E. S. CENTRAL:																				
Kentucky......	480,526	67.0	437,863	62.7	431,095	67.6	380,683	64.1	9,704	61.0	14,377	55.7	583	47.4	701	37.5	39,133	62.7	42,081	55.0
Tennessee.....	488,543	67.4	417,862	61.3	406,847	70.7	336,860	64.9	5,787	72.4	6,224	65.5	575	53.0	787	45.9	75,324	53.9	73,980	48.8
Alabama.......	499,888	64.6	371,850	53.7	325,116	71.2	235,970	62.5	7,083	70.2	6,104	63.0	708	49.1	815	41.1	166,943	54.6	128,850	42.6
Mississippi.....	389,702	64.7	361,976	61.0	206,032	75.4	177,681	72.8	3,166	69.9	3,095	65.8	239	37.0	324	28.5	180,166	55.8	180,776	52.7
W. S. CENTRAL:																				
Arkansas.......	375,115	65.8	304,909	60.2	283,477	70.1	224,305	64.6	6,574	66.4	6,734	62.6	308	41.7	481	34.9	84,729	54.7	73,287	49.9
Louisiana......	327,546	57.0	235,204	44.4	205,001	65.4	150,002	56.9	16,906	61.3	13,671	52.6	1,247	37.6	1,522	27.9	103,598	45.4	69,992	29.9
Oklahoma......	444,247	68.6	361,376	69.6	379,331	69.3	292,864	70.4	18,895	69.9	20,398	70.5	1,139	34.3	1,391	43.1	30,387	61.6	29,208	65.1
Texas.........	950,688	64.8	771,931	61.2	696,559	69.7	568,720	66.5	75,062	52.4	65,981	50.2	22,077	27.8	9,487	24.4	156,642	64.2	127,656	54.4
MOUNTAIN:																				
Montana.......	102,621	75.5	56,976	65.8	59,404	78.3	28,191	69.0	37,003	75.0	24,693	70.3	4,024	56.6	2,400	33.9	171	70.4	176	62.2
Idaho..........	95,027	77.7	63,613	71.3	74,526	79.6	44,826	73.0	18,607	74.5	17,334	72.5	1,217	48.8	1,004	34.8	97	65.1	47	.....
Wyoming......	34,387	72.4	21,475	65.0	24,776	74.3	13,974	68.1	8,237	71.7	6,332	67.4	962	48.4	745	31.4	114	52.1	132	49.6
Colorado......	175,745	73.2	138,467	69.2	124,402	75.9	91,252	71.3	44,156	72.5	40,073	60.7	5,309	49.0	5,248	45.6	1,524	58.0	1,462	63.3
New Mexico....	75,119	68.5	60,704	62.7	61,868	71.6	52,456	66.9	6,830	66.1	5,243	64.2	2,690	45.2	1,070	33.0	298	44.4	200	60.2
Arizona.......	54,387	60.8	28,753	55.0	30,947	74.1	14,582	68.8	12,322	67.9	7,985	59.6	6,709	38.5	2,580	35.7	490	49.5	234	61.1
Utah..........	107,908	79.3	80,725	72.5	77,103	82.5	47,856	77.8	28,070	75.1	30,416	69.9	2,101	54.1	2,228	44.0	145	67.8	105	57.7
Nevada........	11,444	73.4	9,480	63.6	6,978	77.4	5,398	72.2	3,225	75.7	3,143	69.2	330	41.8	240	19.2	28	.....	27	.....
PACIFIC:																				
Washington....	238,012	74.1	185,795	68.1	144,865	76.1	108,709	71.1	79,843	73.9	65,874	69.3	9,285	55.2	8,700	44.0	785	70.7	498	57.7
Oregon........	141,613	75.4	111,597	68.2	102,108	76.8	77,769	70.7	33,669	74.4	29,163	67.6	3,686	55.6	3,018	37.2	254	72.2	95	52.8
California......	521,109	72.6	341,919	65.8	306,135	75.7	194,194	70.3	168,414	73.5	122,117	66.5	29,830	50.5	16,982	40.6	5,280	70.2	2,751	62.0

POPULATION.

TABLE 9.—SCHOOL ATTENDANCE OF POPULATION 7 TO 13 YEARS OF AGE, FOR PRINCIPAL POPULATION CLASSES, BY DIVISIONS AND STATES: 1920 AND 1910.

[Per cent not shown where base is less than 100.]

DIVISION AND STATE.	ALL CLASSES. 1920 Number.	Per cent.	1910 Number.	Per cent.	NATIVE WHITE Native parentage 1920 Number.	Per cent.	1910 Number.	Per cent.	Foreign or mixed parentage 1920 Number.	Per cent.	1910 Number.	Per cent.	FOREIGN-BORN WHITE. 1920 Number.	Per cent.	1910 Number.	Per cent.	NEGRO. 1920 Number.	Per cent.	1910 Number.	Per cent.
United States..	13,869,010	90.6	11,146,173	86.1	8,564,679	92.2	6,744,539	88.2	3,596,717	94.1	2,895,974	92.6	318,040	84.1	417,370	87.1	1,331,043	76.5	1,056,781	64.1
GEOG. DIVISIONS:																				
New England..	898,605	95.3	751,547	95.2	341,324	95.2	297,192	95.2	504,143	95.8	384,594	95.8	44,727	90.1	62,704	92.2	8,079	95.1	6,672	94.7
Middle Atlantic	2,805,986	94.3	2,269,431	93.0	1,313,475	94.7	1,135,936	93.3	1,323,749	94.4	907,992	93.4	110,784	88.8	187,273	90.0	56,685	93.4	37,217	89.7
E. N. Central..	2,693,634	95.1	2,239,718	93.5	1,729,506	95.4	1,391,070	93.6	840,339	95.0	734,462	93.8	72,659	90.5	82,694	89.4	48,791	94.7	28,832	90.6
W. N. Central..	1,679,682	93.9	1,512,644	91.5	1,184,836	94.3	958,914	91.7	441,521	94.0	492,073	92.3	21,007	85.7	33,584	84.1	27,669	89.7	23,179	83.7
South Atlantic.	1,997,008	85.6	1,508,993	75.0	1,304,485	89.2	977,037	82.1	77,736	93.6	52,788	87.8	7,316	87.9	8,948	78.7	605,539	77.8	469,114	64.0
E. S. Central..	1,283,921	83.6	1,043,420	75.0	944,921	88.5	736,782	80.9	17,997	92.0	20,295	90.0	1,187	82.1	1,803	74.2	319,750	71.6	284,395	62.5
W. S. Central..	1,447,653	82.5	1,100,205	74.7	1,077,986	87.0	808,729	81.1	84,135	76.1	73,565	72.1	17,256	47.5	9,078	45.9	258,306	72.5	203,599	58.5
Mountain......	452,896	91.8	302,970	86.4	317,320	93.6	190,158	88.1	110,020	93.3	89,085	90.0	15,814	74.0	11,107	78.0	1,927	91.5	1,576	87.8
Pacific.........	609,625	94.1	411,245	91.2	370,826	94.8	242,741	91.5	197,077	94.5	141,120	92.4	27,250	86.2	20,089	87.4	4,297	93.9	2,207	91.0
NEW ENGLAND:																				
Maine.......	93,615	94.2	83,590	92.3	59,314	94.3	53,725	92.7	30,639	94.7	24,998	92.3	3,414	89.9	4,630	87.7	122	93.1	133	92.4
New Hampshire	51,544	93.4	48,314	94.9	25,305	93.5	23,428	94.8	23,702	94.0	21,074	95.5	2,458	88.1	3,756	92.6	74	.....	51	.....
Vermont......	43,336	93.9	42,700	95.7	29,686	94.0	29,250	95.9	11,548	94.4	11,194	96.0	2,026	88.4	2,101	92.2	74	.....	91	.....
Massachusetts..	464,752	96.1	385,813	96.0	151,889	96.5	125,693	96.2	284,578	96.4	222,095	96.4	23,549	90.1	34,072	92.3	4,508	95.9	3,832	95.8
Rhode Island..	74,872	95.6	61,436	93.9	22,110	96.1	18,148	94.7	47,477	96.0	35,385	94.2	4,272	90.6	6,932	90.6	981	92.2	931	92.5
Connecticut....	170,486	94.7	129,694	95.6	53,020	94.1	46,948	95.3	106,199	95.3	69,848	96.2	9,008	91.2	11,243	93.3	2,230	95.0	1,634	93.8
MIDDLE ATLANTIC:																				
New York.....	1,226,918	93.9	1,032,247	93.7	473,682	93.9	420,711	93.5	673,873	94.4	485,444	94.5	62,690	88.8	115,079	92.0	15,534	93.1	10,131	91.3
New Jersey.....	404,928	94.9	300,367	92.6	164,326	95.4	133,409	93.0	210,496	95.1	135,073	93.0	17,104	89.2	23,224	89.1	12,952	94.1	8,634	89.6
Pennsylvania...	1,174,140	94.5	936,817	92.3	675,467	95.0	581,816	93.2	439,380	94.2	287,475	91.8	30,990	88.4	48,970	85.9	28,199	93.2	18,452	88.8
E. N. CENTRAL:																				
Ohio..........	703,560	90.0	560,731	94.1	501,839	90.1	413,055	94.3	106,213	96.2	118,070	94.4	16,950	92.3	18,373	80.8	18,538	95.8	11,208	91.8
Indiana.......	309,713	94.9	335,541	93.3	320,233	95.1	291,719	93.5	37,777	94.0	33,950	92.9	3,099	89.3	3,401	87.7	8,595	94.2	6,413	92.7
Illinois.......	815,080	94.7	678,407	92.5	463,333	95.1	373,507	92.6	310,016	94.5	261,272	93.2	25,105	90.3	34,133	88.9	16,443	93.7	9,351	87.3
Michigan.......	453,652	94.9	345,005	94.1	244,696	95.3	168,498	94.4	183,595	95.0	157,772	94.3	19,886	90.3	16,141	90.7	4,717	95.2	1,620	93.7
Wisconsin......	351,629	94.5	320,034	93.7	199,405	94.5	144,201	93.9	142,738	94.9	163,398	93.9	7,559	88.9	10,646	88.9	498	95.0	240	91.3
W. N. CENTRAL:																				
Minnesota......	314,905	93.9	279,592	93.0	150,740	94.1	97,156	93.0	155,990	94.1	170,345	93.3	6,439	88.6	10,287	89.6	660	95.5	456	92.7
Iowa..........	309,744	95.0	291,643	93.2	238,772	95.2	198,977	93.2	65,582	94.7	86,997	93.7	3,267	88.0	4,024	86.0	2,046	95.0	1,612	92.4
Missouri.......	440,394	93.4	408,655	90.1	376,201	93.6	337,924	90.3	44,245	94.3	51,107	92.4	3,060	88.7	5,215	86.4	16,857	86.8	14,363	80.4
North Dakota..	102,876	92.1	75,340	86.1	39,780	93.0	23,387	88.0	59,903	92.4	45,308	87.3	2,521	86.8	5,760	74.0	47	.....	33	.....
South Dakota..	91,322	93.5	76,479	87.7	54,802	94.1	35,978	88.3	33,233	93.8	36,431	88.9	1,105	85.9	2,097	77.6	95	85.6	74	.....
Nebraska......	178,910	93.9	160,389	92.9	125,030	93.9	94,895	92.9	49,819	94.3	61,213	93.4	2,508	86.5	3,280	88.3	1,143	94.0	604	90.8
Kansas........	241,531	94.5	220,546	92.3	199,508	94.9	170,597	92.4	32,749	94.5	40,672	93.1	2,197	71.3	2,921	82.7	6,821	94.5	6,037	88.8
SOUTH ATLANTIC:																				
Delaware......	27,336	95.2	22,977	87.0	17,512	95.5	15,133	88.2	5,476	95.4	3,554	89.3	425	92.2	457	83.7	3,922	94.2	3,830	81.1
Maryland......	182,147	92.6	157,223	86.4	121,786	94.2	103,721	89.2	28,737	95.6	23,360	87.8	2,016	91.9	3,897	83.0	29,600	84.0	26,733	76.4
Dist. Columbia.	38,962	93.5	31,101	90.4	22,062	93.6	17,436	91.5	5,451	94.1	4,260	91.8	503	94.0	642	89.2	10,924	93.0	8,743	87.7
Virginia.......	324,292	84.8	254,237	74.5	222,093	87.7	171,795	79.9	7,520	92.7	4,922	87.3	695	87.3	874	78.3	93,907	78.1	76,608	64.2
West Virginia..	213,053	89.1	166,925	87.8	187,581	89.1	152,685	88.2	13,444	90.2	6,179	89.4	1,942	83.2	1,598	72.5	10,103	88.6	6,456	81.2
North Carolina.	400,846	87.0	291,608	76.5	278,799	89.5	200,597	80.6	1,548	89.1	1,244	86.1	133	78.2	182	70.5	118,612	81.8	88,618	68.6
South Carolina.	274,429	87.1	184,535	67.6	130,660	93.0	84,968	77.9	1,412	95.0	1,176	86.7	103	83.1	135	77.6	142,232	82.3	98,216	60.4
Georgia.......	409,754	79.1	318,189	70.5	247,712	85.9	184,636	79.7	3,769	94.8	2,950	90.1	286	89.7	436	81.8	157,977	70.2	130,157	60.3
Florida........	126,189	83.2	82,198	70.5	76,300	88.2	46,066	77.1	10,379	92.1	5,143	81.2	1,213	87.4	1,227	70.8	38,262	73.1	29,753	61.0
E. S. CENTRAL:																				
Kentucky......	342,974	88.5	293,068	81.3	308,311	88.7	254,869	81.6	6,831	93.9	10,103	93.2	311	81.0	486	87.7	27,514	85.9	27,599	74.9
Tennessee.....	333,118	85.3	269,034	77.2	277,342	88.4	216,179	80.5	3,910	94.0	3,935	89.1	289	90.3	509	82.2	51,569	71.1	48,423	64.7
Alabama.......	344,699	80.4	243,275	66.3	223,138	87.5	152,372	76.2	5,027	89.7	4,231	85.3	411	85.4	591	75.8	116,093	69.2	86,004	53.4
Mississippi....	263,130	80.1	238,013	75.4	136,180	90.0	113,342	87.3	2,229	88.0	2,026	86.8	126	63.0	217	45.5	124,574	71.5	122,369	67.0
W. S. CENTRAL:																				
Arkansas......	256,263	82.0	195,383	74.2	194,873	86.2	143,553	79.1	4,480	90.9	4,490	86.5	167	78.4	326	60.1	56,726	69.9	46,946	61.8
Louisiana......	234,249	75.9	165,194	58.8	146,771	85.7	103,524	73.3	12,860	85.6	9,945	75.0	702	76.1	1,094	53.8	73,821	61.0	50,577	40.7
Oklahoma.....	304,665	85.8	235,528	86.1	261,744	86.5	191,343	87.0	12,275	91.9	13,204	89.9	688	63.9	928	79.7	20,336	77.8	18,992	80.2
Texas.........	652,476	83.7	510,100	76.8	474,598	88.0	370,309	81.4	54,520	70.6	45,926	66.6	15,699	46.0	6,730	42.0	107,423	84.0	87,084	70.2
MOUNTAIN:																				
Montana......	71,513	92.8	37,919	87.1	41,463	93.5	18,650	88.2	25,966	94.0	16,640	90.1	2,634	84.9	1,639	80.5	112	90.3	102	84.3
Idaho.........	65,102	95.5	40,608	87.4	51,536	95.9	29,073	87.6	12,409	95.4	10,606	88.7	696	81.4	664	81.7	66	.....	25	.....
Wyoming......	24,554	92.9	14,406	88.8	17,722	93.1	9,320	89.2	5,935	93.4	4,268	89.5	647	82.2	551	82.0	70	.....	91	90.1
Colorado......	121,353	93.9	90,911	90.9	85,123	94.1	59,009	90.7	31,419	95.2	28,884	92.5	3,592	83.7	3,833	86.1	999	93.2	974	89.6
New Mexico....	52,829	87.4	39,666	77.2	43,259	90.0	34,151	81.3	4,749	85.7	3,507	80.6	2,035	75.5	773	61.3	213	85.9	126	79.2
Arizona.......	38,179	78.8	19,483	71.8	21,434	92.8	9,772	85.5	9,295	88.7	5,683	78.1	4,820	61.3	1,926	66.4	355	90.6	166	86.9
Utah.........	71,611	95.5	53,644	91.6	52,021	96.0	32,546	91.9	17,989	95.8	19,404	93.1	1,196	89.0	1,563	88.8	95	94.1	70	.....
Nevada.......	7,755	90.5	6,305	87.9	4,757	93.3	3,637	91.4	2,258	93.1	2,093	93.1	194	72.7	158	83.6	17	.....	22	.....
PACIFIC:																				
Washington....	162,750	94.7	120,345	91.1	99,306	95.1	69,757	91.3	55,048	95.2	42,902	92.3	5,790	89.2	6,142	88.7	552	94.5	328	85.0
Oregon........	94,312	94.7	70,141	90.3	68,455	94.8	48,863	90.0	22,606	95.6	18,311	91.8	2,148	89.9	2,094	87.7	175	93.6	66	.....
California......	352,563	93.7	220,759	91.6	203,065	94.7	124,121	92.2	119,423	94.1	79,907	92.6	19,312	85.0	11,853	86.7	3,570	93.8	1,813	92.4

SCHOOL ATTENDANCE.

TABLE 10.—SCHOOL ATTENDANCE OF INDIAN POPULATION, BY SEX AND AGE PERIODS, BY DIVISIONS AND STATES: 1920.

DIVISION AND STATE.	MALE.							FEMALE.						
	Total number attending school: 1920	7 to 13 years of age.		14 to 20 years of age.		Others attending school.		Total number attending school: 1920	7 to 13 years of age.		14 to 20 years of age.		Others attending school.	
		Total number.	Attending school.	Total number.	Attending school.	Under 7 years of age.	21 years of age and over.		Total number.	Attending school.	Total number.	Attending school.	Under 7 years of age.	21 years of age and over.
United States.....	25,302	22,203	15,543	18,057	8,211	1,647	501	25,963	22,053	15,511	18,095	8,306	1,817	329
GEOGRAPHIC DIVISIONS:														
New England........	152	108	104	89	27	17	4	170	121	113	108	36	21	....
Middle Atlantic......	600	450	408	402	133	50	9	652	496	444	397	152	50	6
East North Central...	1,616	1,254	1,081	990	390	126	19	1,674	1,298	1,084	982	419	151	20
West North Central..	3,737	3,169	2,235	2,603	1,272	159	71	3,961	3,061	2,254	2,689	1,430	212	65
South Atlantic.......	1,404	1,302	905	1,011	391	86	22	1,403	1,384	955	992	338	96	14
East South Central...	84	175	54	139	23	6	1	70	153	48	127	15	6	1
West South Central..	8,083	6,318	4,921	4,686	2,526	539	97	8,099	6,286	4,954	4,743	2,472	601	72
Mountain.............	6,728	6,965	3,827	5,738	2,239	473	189	6,338	6,784	3,662	5,689	2,120	457	99
Pacific...............	3,498	2,462	2,008	2,399	1,210	191	89	3,596	2,470	1,997	2,368	1,324	223	52
NEW ENGLAND:														
Maine.............	83	63	61	40	11	11	....	84	64	59	51	13	12	....
New Hampshire......	4	4	4	....	....	....	....	1	1	1	3	....	....	....
Vermont...........	3	4	2	1	1	....	....	....	....	....	1	....	....	....
Massachusetts........	38	25	25	29	8	2	3	57	30	29	47	20	8	....
Rhode Island........	11	7	7	9	2	2	....	11	10	10	2	1	....	....
Connecticut.........	13	5	5	10	5	2	1	17	16	14	4	2	1	....
MIDDLE ATLANTIC:														
New York...........	563	426	386	371	122	48	7	614	461	413	383	147	49	5
New Jersey.........	6	3	2	8	2	....	2	5	4	4	2	1	....	....
Pennsylvania........	31	21	20	23	9	2	....	33	31	27	12	4	1	1
EAST NORTH CENTRAL:														
Ohio.............	4	2	2	5	1	....	1	6	4	4	4	2	....	....
Indiana...........	8	4	4	6	3	1	....	5	2	2	5	3	....	....
Illinois...........	6	5	5	5	1	....	....	10	2	2	10	7	....	1
Michigan...........	526	427	361	357	115	45	5	532	447	365	331	111	52	4
Wisconsin.........	1,072	816	709	617	270	80	13	1,121	843	711	632	296	99	15
WEST NORTH CENTRAL:														
Minnesota..........	718	770	494	541	182	38	4	822	767	558	541	219	43	2
Iowa.............	51	40	37	31	14	....	....	57	35	34	30	17	6	....
Missouri...........	16	10	8	13	3	3	2	15	8	8	15	6	1	....
North Dakota........	471	579	308	412	149	18	1	544	563	317	445	203	19	5
South Dakota........	1,630	1,355	1,071	995	475	73	11	1,653	1,277	1,011	1,015	515	103	24
Nebraska...........	327	270	201	192	83	21	22	337	255	190	210	96	30	21
Kansas............	524	145	116	419	366	11	31	533	156	136	433	374	10	13
SOUTH ATLANTIC:														
Delaware........	....	....	....	....	....	....	....	....	....	....	....	....	....	....
Maryland...........	3	2	2	3	1	....	....	3	2	2	3	1	....	....
District of Columbia..	3	2	2	1	....	....	1	1	1	1	3	....	....	....
Virginia...........	55	82	42	53	7	5	1	46	72	28	58	12	5	1
West Virginia......	....	....	....	....	....	....	....	....	....	....	1	....	....	....
North Carolina......	1,315	1,145	840	884	375	80	20	1,331	1,218	912	850	317	89	13
South Carolina.......	16	23	9	20	7	....	....	15	31	8	23	6	1	....
Georgia.............	1	8	1	12	....	....	....	3	11	1	11	1	1	....
Florida.............	11	40	9	38	1	1	....	4	49	3	43	1	....	....
EAST SOUTH CENTRAL:														
Kentucky...........	2	4	1	4	1	....	....	3	4	2	3	....	1	....
Tennessee..........	8	5	5	6	2	1	....	3	3	3	1	....	....	....
Alabama...........	22	51	14	25	5	2	1	20	45	16	24	3	1	....
Mississippi.........	52	115	34	104	15	3	....	44	101	27	99	12	4	1
WEST SOUTH CENTRAL:														
Arkansas...........	15	8	5	9	6	2	2	10	7	6	11	3	1	....
Louisiana...........	57	113	29	74	15	12	1	60	107	35	96	18	6	1
Oklahoma..........	7,869	6,013	4,796	4,416	2,459	521	93	7,882	5,986	4,819	4,499	2,408	589	66
Texas.............	142	184	91	187	46	4	1	147	186	94	137	43	5	5
MOUNTAIN:														
Montana...........	1,061	911	666	703	325	60	10	1,026	881	628	679	335	57	8
Idaho.............	273	249	171	199	81	13	8	259	234	173	195	71	13	2
Wyoming..........	156	99	91	92	58	6	1	135	87	77	84	46	11	1
Colorado...........	102	136	69	85	25	6	2	126	133	78	83	36	12	....
New Mexico........	2,243	1,955	1,306	1,612	685	195	57	2,116	1,894	1,256	1,616	667	170	23
Arizona............	2,223	3,002	1,143	2,548	852	129	99	2,013	2,955	1,071	2,497	752	133	57
Utah.............	200	250	123	179	46	29	2	203	230	128	169	36	38	1
Nevada..........	470	363	258	320	167	35	10	460	370	253	361	177	23	7
PACIFIC:														
Washington........	873	689	553	614	256	53	11	948	750	595	585	271	72	10
Oregon............	759	371	324	518	386	21	28	707	367	304	491	374	17	12
California...........	1,866	1,402	1,131	1,267	568	117	50	1,941	1,353	1,098	1,292	679	134	30

1054

POPULATION.

TABLE 11.—SCHOOL ATTENDANCE OF CHINESE AND JAPANESE POPULATION, BY SEX AND AGE PERIODS, FOR DIVISIONS AND SELECTED STATES: 1920.

DIVISION AND STATE.	MALE.							FEMALE.						
	Total number attending school: 1920	7 to 13 years of age.		14 to 20 years of age.		Others attending school.		Total number attending school: 1920	7 to 13 years of age.		14 to 20 years of age.		Others attending school.	
		Total number.	Attending school.	Total number.	Attending school.	Under 7 years of age.	21 years of age and over.		Total number.	Attending school.	Total number.	Attending school.	Under 7 years of age.	21 years of age and over.
CHINESE.														
United States	4,045	1,712	1,502	3,125	1,439	301	803	2,036	1,232	1,107	911	527	254	148
GEOGRAPHIC DIVISIONS:														
New England	194	67	61	161	59	15	59	80	46	42	34	23	11	4
Middle Atlantic	547	188	171	336	145	43	188	309	146	144	102	74	30	61
East North Central	403	87	76	266	130	14	183	104	58	54	40	20	16	14
West North Central	78	20	14	114	36	5	23	37	28	25	15	4	4	4
South Atlantic	83	35	30	98	32	4	17	41	32	28	19	8	4	1
East South Central	17	16	10	27	3	1	3	6	6	4	3	......	1	1
West South Central	46	31	27	54	15	2	2	34	28	24	13	7	3	......
Mountain	160	88	71	171	66	7	16	76	63	51	45	16	8	1
Pacific	2,517	1,180	1,042	1,898	953	210	312	1,349	825	735	640	375	177	62
SELECTED STATES:														
Arizona	62	41	33	48	26	3	......	26	21	17	21	7	2	......
California	2,087	1,001	885	1,596	764	190	248	1,172	700	624	556	326	166	56
District of Columbia	24	7	7	30	10	......	7	12	10	9	5	2	1	......
Illinois	233	61	56	127	70	8	99	72	40	38	24	16	12	6
Massachusetts	149	48	44	111	51	11	43	68	37	33	30	20	11	4
Michigan	66	12	10	55	25	1	30	16	9	9	8	2	1	4
Minnesota	26	7	3	32	16	2	5	12	11	10	6	2	......	......
Montana	25	17	13	28	7	......	5	15	13	10	8	4	1	......
New Jersey	30	11	10	42	10	1	9	9	7	7	6	......	2	......
New York	447	146	136	219	118	38	155	288	124	123	82	64	21	60
Ohio	75	10	7	56	24	3	41	10	5	3	6	1	2	4
Oregon	206	105	94	125	76	11	25	116	79	72	64	34	6	4
Pennsylvania	70	31	25	75	17	4	24	32	15	14	14	10	7	1
Washington	224	74	63	177	113	9	39	61	46	39	20	15	5	2
JAPANESE.														
United States	6,221	2,834	2,438	4,287	2,020	693	1,070	3,721	2,595	2,234	2,081	632	641	214
GEOGRAPHIC DIVISIONS:														
New England	32	3	3	5	1	1	27	13	6	6	6	4	......	3
Middle Atlantic	204	64	61	75	24	16	103	104	55	52	55	25	17	10
East North Central	105	11	10	30	17	7	71	39	22	20	15	4	6	9
West North Central	46	18	14	38	12	5	15	17	12	9	6	1	5	2
South Atlantic	16	2	1	5	1	1	13	19	9	9	6	6	3	1
East South Central	1	......	......	1	......	......	1	......						
West South Central	26	20	16	14	8	......	2	25	27	19	6	4	1	1
Mountain	413	125	94	445	190	35	94	156	115	96	123	23	30	7
Pacific	5,378	2,591	2,239	3,674	1,767	628	744	3,348	2,349	2,023	1,864	565	579	181
SELECTED STATES:														
California	4,190	2,035	1,754	2,751	1,369	528	539	2,627	1,887	1,595	1,447	436	478	118
Colorado	112	32	26	95	56	12	18	53	39	34	38	9	10	......
Idaho	47	21	16	53	22	5	4	35	23	22	25	5	7	1
Illinois	62	9	8	18	11	3	40	21	12	11	7	1	3	6
Montana	28	12	10	48	11	2	5	8	5	5	15	2	1	......
New Jersey	22	17	17	11	2	1	2	18	11	10	6	4	4	......
New York	149	38	35	58	17	14	83	74	36	35	43	18	11	10
Oregon	178	73	61	186	69	16	32	108	83	64	57	15	22	7
Pennsylvania	33	9	9	8	5	1	18	12	8	7	6	3	2	......
Texas	20	18	14	10	6	......	......	24	24	18	5	4	1	1
Utah	182	38	30	158	83	7	62	40	32	22	25	4	8	6
Washington	1,010	483	424	737	329	84	173	613	429	364	360	114	79	56

CHAPTER XII

ILLITERACY

CHAPTER XII.—ILLITERACY.

INTRODUCTION.

Illiteracy, as defined by the Census Bureau, signifies inability to write in any language, not necessarily English, regardless of ability to read. The statistics of illiteracy here presented relate to the population 10 years of age and over and cover continental United States as a whole, the states, and cities having 25,000 inhabitants or more. Less detailed statistics for states, for counties, and for incorporated places having 2,500 inhabitants or more, and complete statistics for the outlying possessions enumerated at the Fourteenth Census, are presented in Volume III of the Fourteenth Census Reports.

It should be noted that ability to read or write can not be defined so precisely as to cover all cases with certainty. A person may know the alphabet and a small number of printed words, but may not be able to read in any true sense; or he may be able to write his name but may be wholly unable to express his thoughts in writing in an intelligible manner. In general, the illiterate population as shown by the census figures should be understood as comprising only those persons who have had no education whatever. Thus the statistics do not show directly or definitely the proportion of the population which may be termed illiterate when the word is used to imply lack of ability to read and write with a reasonable degree of facility; but they do afford a fairly reliable measure of the effect of the improvement in educational opportunities from decade to decade.

There is undoubtedly a margin of error in the statistics of illiteracy, resulting from a variety of causes. In some cases there may be unwillingness to admit illiteracy on the part of persons enumerated. Furthermore, in parts of the country where practically all native white persons are literate the enumerators are likely to acquire the habit of returning them as such without the formality of an inquiry, and in this way a few isolated cases of illiteracy may be overlooked. On the other hand, in the case of Negroes the opposite assumption may sometimes be made by white enumerators, while, in the case of the foreign born, inability to write in English may sometimes be taken as constituting illiteracy, although the instructions make it clear that a person able to write in any language is to be returned as literate. For the United States as a whole and for the states and large cities the figures are probably nearly enough accurate to supply a sound basis for judgment as to the relative illiteracy of different classes of the population, of persons in different age groups, and of males as compared with females. Beyond question comparisons between different censuses show the general tendencies with substantial accuracy. The returns for small areas, however, may be open to question in some cases.

The population schedule for the census of 1920, like those for several previous censuses, contained two inquiries relating to illiteracy, namely, as to whether the person enumerated was able to read, and as to whether he was able to write. In most of the tables here presented the figures relate only to the total number of illiterates, but in Tables 4, 13, 20, and 23 statistics are given showing the number of illiterates classified according to the degree of illiteracy, that is, as unable to read or write and as able to read but not to write.

Population classes.—The variations in the proportion of illiterates in the several population classes reflect the educational opportunities, past and present, which have been open to them in the different sections of the United States and, in the case of the foreign born, in the countries from which they have come. (See Table 3.)

The decidedly higher percentage of illiteracy for the native whites of native parentage than for the native whites of foreign or mixed parentage is due mainly to the fact that a much larger proportion of the former than of the latter class is found in rural communities, in some of which, because of the inaccessibility of the schools or for other reasons, school attendance has been less general, especially during the childhood and youth of the older generations, than in urban communities. Moreover, most of the rural native whites of foreign or mixed parentage live in sections of the country where educational facilities are good. In order to make a fair comparison between these two elements of the population in regard to illiteracy, the statistics for individual cities and for urban and rural communities in individual states should be examined. (See Tables 18, 19, and 22.)

Age periods.—The extension of educational opportunities from decade to decade is brought out by the statistics for age groups. The illiteracy of each age group measures the lack of educational advantages during the childhood and youth of that group. If the development of school facilities were to be arrested completely at the present time, there would nevertheless be a gradual diminution in illiteracy for some decades to come, as the older and more illiterate age classes would dwindle and the general level of illiteracy gradually approach that found at present in the

(1145)

younger age classes. The improvement in educational facilities since 1890 can also be studied by making a comparison of the percentages of illiteracy for the age groups 10–14 and 15–19 as shown by the census figures for 1900, 1910, and 1920. It will be noted, for example, that for the native whites of native parentage in the 10–14 group the percentage of illiteracy was only half as large in 1910 as in 1900, and only half as large in 1920 as in 1910. (See Table 3.)

Urban and rural communities.—Because of the marked differences between urban and rural communities in regard to school facilities, and also in regard to the composition and characteristics of their population, separate statistics for illiteracy are given for the two classes of communities in Tables 21 to 23. In drawing the distinction between urban and rural population, all incorporated places (and all towns in Massachusetts, Rhode Island, and New Hampshire) having 2,500 inhabitants or more are treated as urban and the remainder of the country as rural.

In Massachusetts and Rhode Island it is not the practice, as in practically all the other states, to incorporate, as separate municipalities, the relatively densely populated portions of "towns" (which are the primary divisions of the counties), and no town as a whole is incorporated as a municipality until it attains a population greatly in excess of 2,500; and in New Hampshire a similar condition exists, although the state contains two incorporated villages, each of which has fewer than 2,500 inhabitants. For this reason those towns having 2,500 or more inhabitants in the three states named are treated as urban, although portions of their areas are rural in character. The urban areas in the three states in question, as classified by the census, thus contain relatively small numbers of inhabitants who in other sections of the country would be segregated as rural. Nevertheless, in most of the towns having 2,500 inhabitants or more in Massachusetts, Rhode Island, and New Hampshire by far the greater part of the population resides within the more densely settled areas, so that the proportion classed as urban, considering the New England division as a whole, is not greatly exaggerated by the practice adopted.

Each class of the native population shows a decidedly lower percentage of illiteracy in urban than in rural communities, and even in the case of the foreign-born whites there is, on the average, a slight difference in favor of the urban communities. This condition is attributable in part to the fact that the urban population is found mainly in those states in which illiteracy generally is low, while a large part of the rural population resides in states in which illiteracy generally is high. This does not constitute the entire explanation, however, since in almost every state a lower percentage of illiteracy is shown for each native class of the population in urban than in rural communities. The relatively large proportion of rural illiteracy is due principally to the inadequacy of the country school facilities in certain regions, a condition which was more conspicuous a few decades ago than at present. (See Table 22.)

ILLITERACY.

PER CENT ILLITERATE IN POPULATION 10 YEARS OF AGE AND OVER: 1920.

ALL CLASSES.

[District of Columbia, 2.8 per cent, not shown separately on the map.]

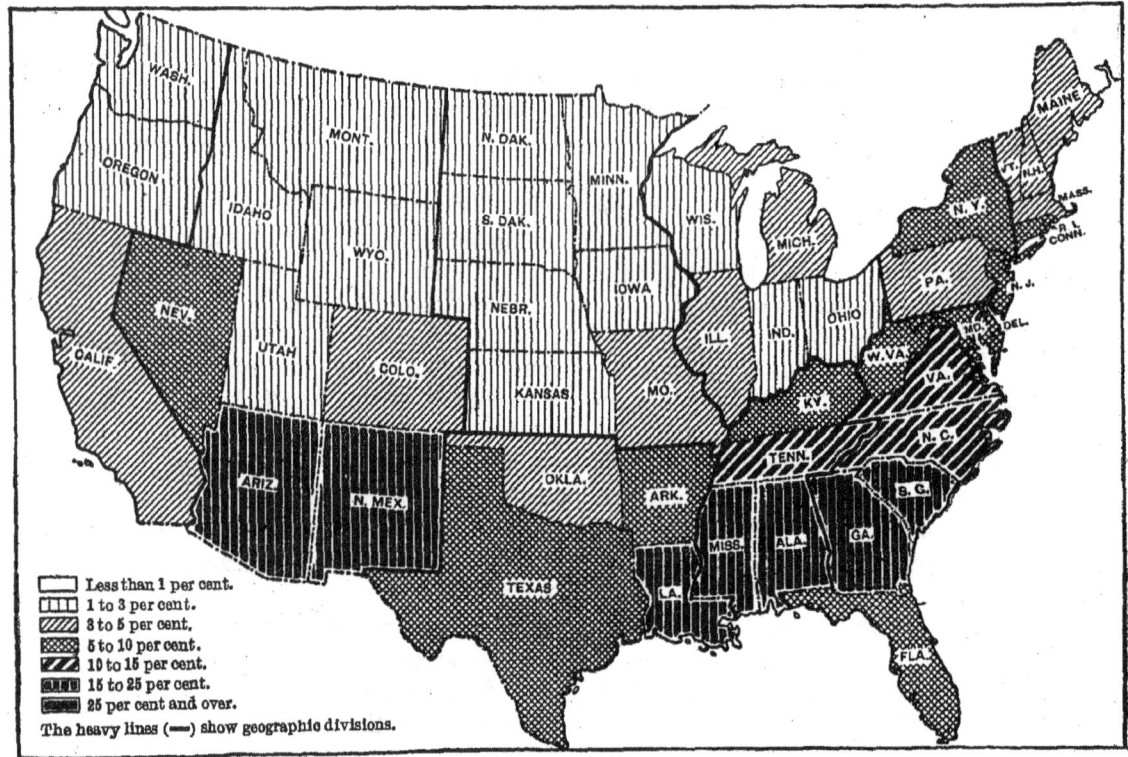

NATIVE WHITE OF NATIVE PARENTS.

[District of Columbia, 0.3 per cent, not shown separately on the map.]

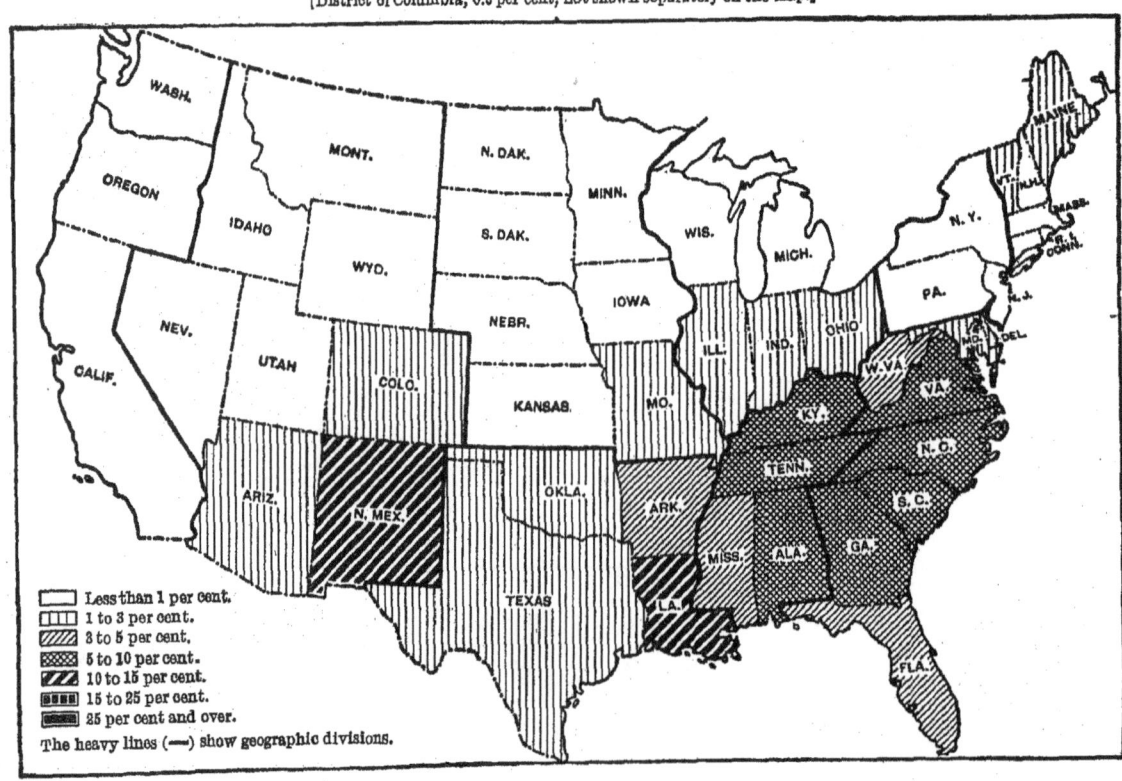

48   POPULATION.

PER CENT ILLITERATE IN POPULATION 10 YEARS OF AGE AND OVER: 1920.

FOREIGN-BORN WHITE.

[District of Columbia, 6.1 per cent, not shown separately on the map.]

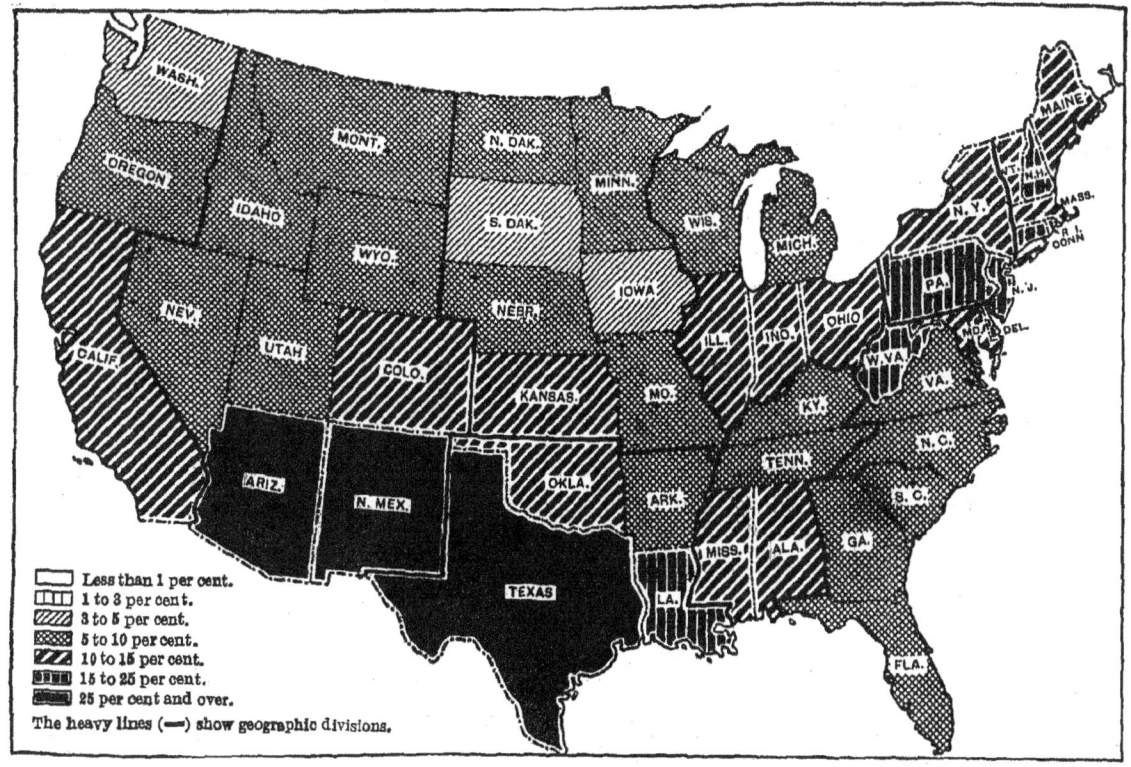

Less than 1 per cent.
1 to 3 per cent.
3 to 5 per cent.
5 to 10 per cent.
10 to 15 per cent.
15 to 25 per cent.
25 per cent and over.

The heavy lines (—) show geographic divisions.

NEGRO.

[District of Columbia, 8.6 per cent, not shown separately on the map.]

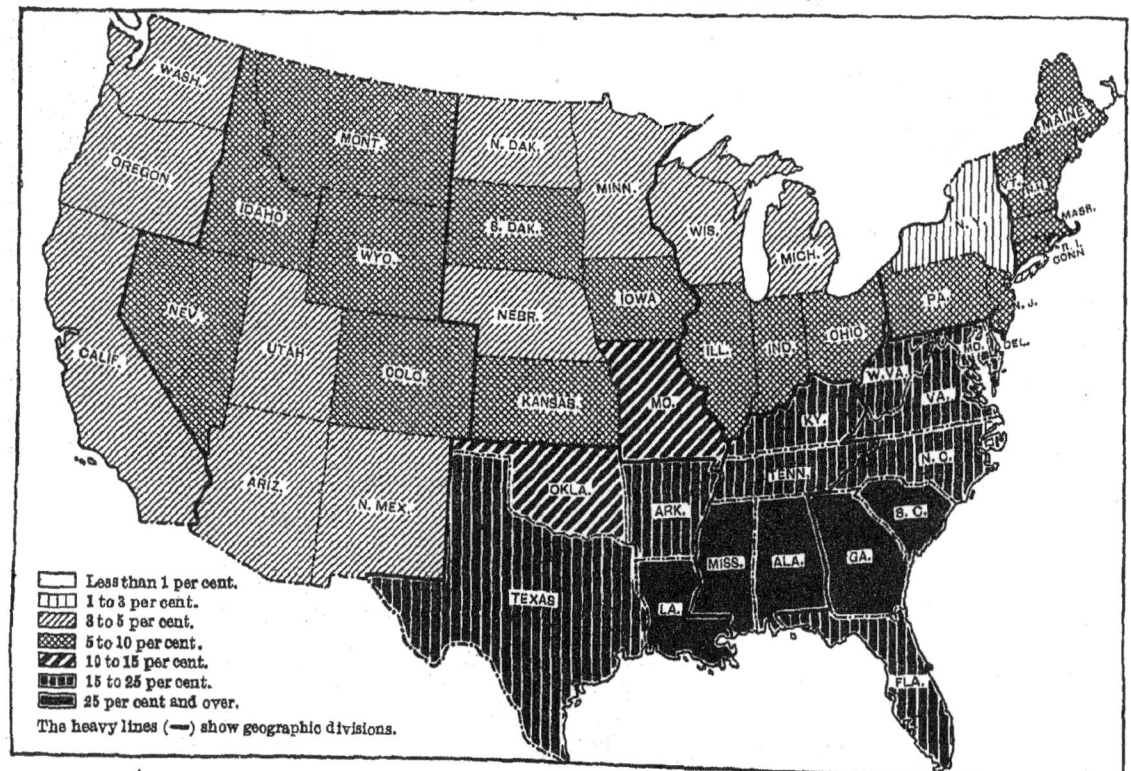

Less than 1 per cent.
1 to 3 per cent.
3 to 5 per cent.
5 to 10 per cent.
10 to 15 per cent.
15 to 25 per cent.
25 per cent and over.

The heavy lines (—) show geographic divisions.

ILLITERACY.

PER CENT ILLITERATE IN POPULATION 10 YEARS OF AGE AND OVER, BY STATES: 1920 AND 1910.

ALL CLASSES.

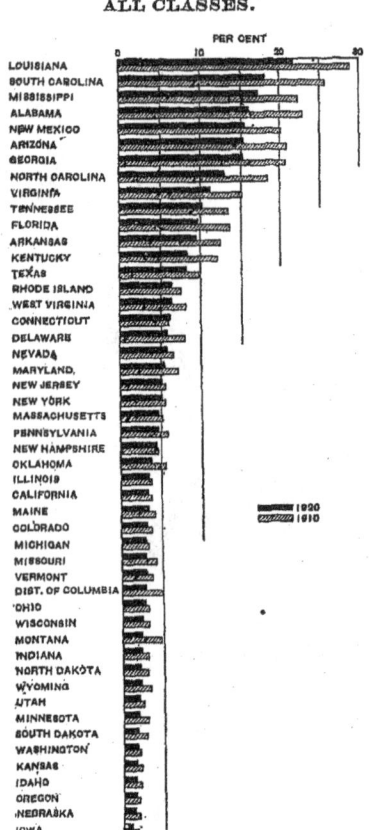

NATIVE WHITE—NATIVE PARENTAGE.

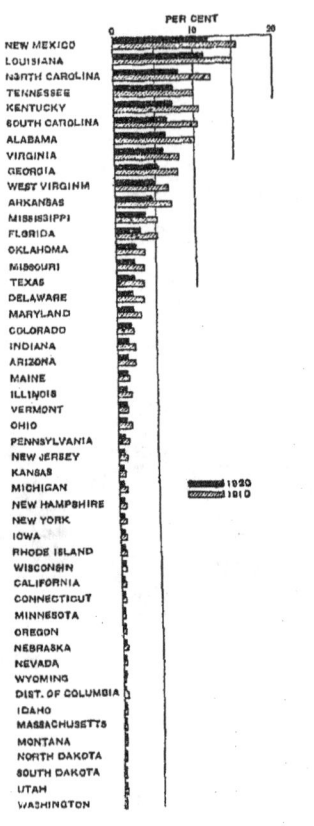

FOREIGN-BORN WHITE.

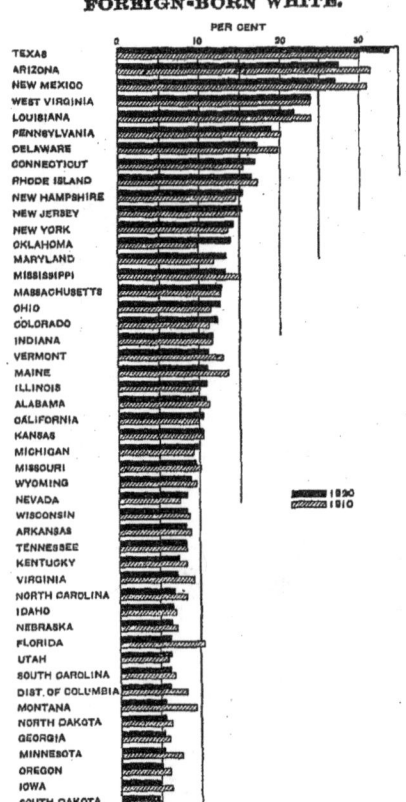

NEGRO.

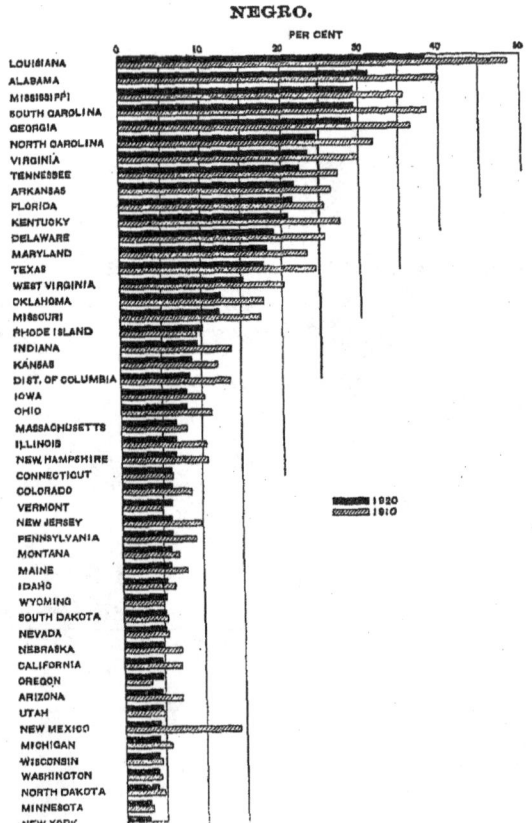

1150

POPULATION.

TABLE 1.—NUMBER AND PER CENT ILLITERATE IN POPULATION 10 YEARS OF AGE AND OVER, BY SEX, FOR POPULATION CLASSES, FOR THE UNITED STATES: 1870–1920.

[Figures are given under each class for all census years for which data are available.]

CENSUS YEAR AND CLASS OF POPULATION.	POPULATION 10 YEARS OF AGE AND OVER.								
	Both sexes.			Male.			Female.		
	Total number.	Illiterate.		Total number.	Illiterate.		Total number.	Illiterate.	
		Number.	Per cent.		Number.	Per cent.		Number.	Per cent.
1920									
All classes	82,739,315	4,931,905	6.0	42,289,969	2,540,209	6.0	40,449,346	2,391,696	5.9
White	74,359,749	3,006,312	4.0	38,070,736	1,551,529	4.1	36,289,013	1,454,783	4.0
Colored [1]	8,379,566	1,925,593	23.0	4,219,233	988,680	23.4	4,160,333	936,913	22.5
Negro	8,053,225	1,842,161	22.9	4,009,462	942,368	23.5	4,043,763	899,793	22.3
Native white	60,861,863	1,242,572	2.0	30,651,045	684,707	2.2	30,210,818	557,865	1.8
Native parentage	44,077,564	1,109,875	2.5	22,361,495	614,612	2.7	21,716,069	495,263	2.3
Foreign or mixed parentage	16,784,299	132,697	0.8	8,289,550	70,095	0.8	8,494,749	62,602	0.7
Foreign parentage	11,462,926	98,076	0.9	5,679,128	50,442	0.9	5,783,798	47,634	0.8
Mixed parentage	5,321,373	34,621	0.7	2,610,422	19,653	0.8	2,710,951	14,968	0.6
Foreign-born white	13,497,886	1,763,740	13.1	7,419,691	866,822	11.7	6,078,195	896,918	14.8
1910									
All classes	71,580,270	5,516,163	7.7	37,027,558	2,814,950	7.6	34,552,712	2,701,213	7.8
White	63,933,870	3,184,633	5.0	33,164,229	1,662,505	5.0	30,769,041	1,522,128	4.9
Colored [1]	7,646,400	2,331,530	30.5	3,863,329	1,152,445	29.8	3,783,071	1,179,085	31.2
Negro	7,317,922	2,227,731	30.4	3,637,386	1,096,000	30.1	3,680,536	1,131,731	30.7
Native white	50,989,341	1,534,272	3.0	25,843,033	796,055	3.1	25,146,308	738,217	2.9
Native parentage	37,081,278	1,378,884	3.7	18,933,751	715,926	3.8	18,147,527	662,958	3.7
Foreign or mixed parentage	13,908,063	155,388	1.1	6,909,282	80,129	1.2	6,998,781	75,259	1.1
Foreign parentage	9,602,968	117,336	1.2	4,788,825	59,240	1.2	4,814,143	58,090	1.2
Mixed parentage	4,305,095	38,052	0.9	2,120,457	20,883	1.0	2,184,638	17,169	0.8
Foreign-born white	12,944,529	1,650,361	12.7	7,321,196	866,450	11.8	5,623,333	783,911	13.9
1900									
All classes	57,949,824	6,180,069	10.7	29,703,440	3,011,224	10.1	28,246,384	3,168,845	11.2
White	51,250,918	3,200,746	6.2	26,327,931	1,567,153	6.0	24,922,987	1,633,593	6.6
Colored [1]	6,698,906	2,979,323	44.5	3,375,509	1,444,071	42.8	3,323,397	1,535,252	46.2
Negro	6,415,581	2,853,194	44.5	3,181,650	1,371,432	43.1	3,233,931	1,481,762	45.8
Native white	41,236,652	1,913,611	4.6	20,912,940	955,517	4.6	20,323,722	958,094	4.7
Native parentage	30,310,261	1,734,764	5.7	15,452,855	862,175	5.6	14,857,406	872,589	5.9
Foreign or mixed parentage	10,926,401	178,847	1.6	5,460,085	93,342	1.7	5,466,316	85,505	1.6
Foreign-born white	10,014,256	1,287,135	12.9	5,414,991	611,636	11.3	4,599,265	675,499	14.7
1890									
All classes	[2] 47,413,559	[2] 6,324,702	13.3	24,352,659	3,008,222	12.4	23,060,900	3,316,480	14.4
White	41,931,074	3,212,574	7.7	21,578,245	1,517,722	7.0	20,352,829	1,694,852	8.3
Colored [1]	5,482,485	3,112,128	56.8	2,774,414	1,490,500	53.7	2,708,071	1,621,628	59.9
Negro	5,328,972	3,042,668	57.1	2,646,171	1,438,923	54.4	2,682,801	1,603,745	59.8
Native white	33,144,187	2,065,003	6.2	16,796,497	978,408	5.8	16,347,690	1,086,595	6.6
Native parentage	25,375,766	1,890,723	7.5	12,901,102	888,415	6.9	12,474,664	1,002,308	8.0
Foreign or mixed parentage	7,768,421	174,280	2.2	3,895,395	89,993	2.3	3,873,026	84,287	2.2
Foreign-born white	8,786,887	1,147,571	13.1	4,781,748	539,314	11.3	4,005,139	608,257	15.2
1880									
All classes	36,761,607	6,239,958	17.0	18,735,980	2,966,421	15.8	18,025,627	3,273,537	18.2
White	32,160,400	3,019,080	9.4	16,425,250	1,410,805	8.6	15,735,150	1,608,275	10.2
Colored [1]	4,601,207	3,220,878	70.0	2,310,730	1,555,616	67.3	2,290,477	1,665,262	72.7
Native white	25,785,789	2,255,460	8.7	......	......	......	......	......	......
Foreign-born white	6,374,611	763,620	12.0	......	......	......	......	......	......
1870									
All classes	28,228,945	5,658,144	20.0	14,258,866	2,603,888	18.3	13,970,079	3,054,256	21.9
White	24,717,870	2,851,911	11.5	12,526,487	1,250,970	10.0	12,191,383	1,600,941	18.1
Colored [1]	3,511,075	2,806,233	79.9	1,732,379	1,352,918	78.1	1,778,696	1,453,315	81.7
Negro	3,428,757	2,789,689	81.4	1,664,656	1,342,347	80.6	1,764,101	1,447,342	82.0

[1] Persons of Negro descent, Indians, Chinese, Japanese, and "all other."
[2] Exclusive of persons in Indian Territory and on Indian reservations, areas specially enumerated in 1890, but for which illiteracy statistics are not available.

ILLITERACY.

TABLE 2.—NUMBER AND PER CENT ILLITERATE IN POPULATION 10 YEARS OF AGE AND OVER, BY AGE PERIODS, FOR POPULATION CLASSES, BY SEX, FOR THE UNITED STATES: 1920.

[Per cent not shown where base is less than 100.]

CLASS OF POPULATION AND SEX.	POPULATION 10 YEARS OF AGE AND OVER: 1920 [1] Total number.	Illiterate. Number.	Per cent.	10 TO 14 YEARS. Total number.	Illiterate. Number.	Per cent.	15 TO 19 YEARS. Total number.	Illiterate. Number.	Per cent.	20 TO 24 YEARS. Total number.	Illiterate. Number.	Per cent.
All classes	82,739,315	4,931,905	6.0	10,641,137	246,360	2.3	9,430,556	283,316	3.0	9,277,021	392,353	4.2
Male	42,289,969	2,540,209	6.0	5,369,306	141,576	2.6	4,673,792	171,489	3.7	4,527,045	203,773	4.5
Female	40,449,346	2,391,696	5.9	5,271,831	104,784	2.0	4,756,784	111,827	2.4	4,749,976	189,080	4.0
White	74,359,749	3,006,312	4.0	9,369,322	100,643	1.1	8,314,155	125,495	1.5	8,185,341	207,649	2.5
Male	38,070,736	1,551,529	4.1	4,735,150	57,150	1.2	4,141,831	74,455	1.8	4,018,576	103,958	2.6
Female	36,289,013	1,454,783	4.0	4,634,172	43,493	0.9	4,172,324	51,040	1.2	4,166,765	103,691	2.5
Negro	8,053,225	1,842,161	22.9	1,236,914	140,892	11.4	1,083,215	152,998	14.1	1,054,847	179,124	17.0
Male	4,009,462	942,368	23.5	616,251	81,944	13.3	513,416	94,455	18.4	487,169	96,895	19.9
Female	4,043,763	899,793	22.3	620,663	58,948	9.5	569,799	58,543	10.3	567,678	82,229	14.5
Indian	176,925	61,730	34.9	30,173	4,751	15.7	25,417	4,373	17.2	20,009	4,211	21.0
Male	91,546	30,010	32.8	15,225	2,427	15.9	12,710	2,247	17.7	10,413	2,054	19.7
Female	85,379	31,720	37.2	14,948	2,324	15.5	12,707	2,126	16.7	9,596	2,157	22.5
Chinese	56,230	11,262	20.0	2,005	40	2.0	2,760	145	5.3	4,845	545	11.2
Male	51,041	10,064	19.7	1,223	28	2.3	2,161	132	6.1	4,122	427	10.4
Female	5,189	1,198	23.1	782	12	1.5	599	13	2.2	723	118	16.3
Japanese	84,238	9,276	11.0	2,569	29	1.1	4,342	292	6.7	9,636	1,226	12.7
Male	58,806	5,145	8.7	1,379	22	1.6	3,081	189	6.1	4,535	360	7.9
Female	25,432	4,131	16.2	1,190	7	0.6	1,261	103	8.2	5,101	866	17.0
All other	8,948	1,164	13.0	154	5	3.2	667	13	1.9	2,343	98	4.2
Male	8,378	1,093	13.0	78	5	......	593	11	1.9	2,230	79	3.5
Female	570	71	12.5	76	......	......	74	2	......	113	19	16.8
Native white	60,861,863	1,242,572	2.0	9,037,960	85,856	0.9	7,788,213	97,013	1.2	7,258,497	98,938	1.4
Male	30,651,045	684,707	2.2	4,567,998	49,650	1.1	3,882,561	60,731	1.6	3,561,588	57,040	1.6
Female	30,210,818	557,865	1.8	4,469,962	36,206	0.8	3,903,652	36,282	0.9	3,696,909	41,898	1.1
Native parentage	44,077,564	1,109,875	2.5	6,455,709	71,845	1.1	5,599,046	83,303	1.5	5,176,707	86,669	1.7
Male	22,361,495	614,612	2.7	3,269,388	42,349	1.3	2,797,477	53,406	1.9	2,546,818	50,891	2.0
Female	21,716,069	495,263	2.3	3,186,321	29,496	0.9	2,801,569	29,897	1.1	2,629,889	35,778	1.4
Foreign parentage	11,462,926	98,076	0.9	1,763,468	10,032	0.6	1,429,368	9,934	0.7	1,384,755	9,207	0.7
Male	5,679,128	50,442	0.9	886,217	5,181	0.6	707,722	5,132	0.7	676,135	4,396	0.7
Female	5,783,798	47,634	0.8	877,251	4,851	0.6	721,646	4,802	0.7	708,620	4,811	0.7
Mixed parentage	5,321,373	34,621	0.7	818,783	3,979	0.5	757,799	3,776	0.5	697,035	3,062	0.4
Male	2,610,422	19,653	0.8	412,393	2,120	0.5	377,362	2,193	0.6	338,635	1,753	0.5
Female	2,710,951	14,968	0.6	406,390	1,859	0.5	380,437	1,583	0.4	358,400	1,309	0.4
Foreign-born white	13,497,886	1,763,740	13.1	331,362	14,787	4.5	527,942	28,482	5.4	926,844	108,711	11.7
Male	7,419,691	866,822	11.7	167,152	7,500	4.5	259,270	13,724	5.3	456,988	46,918	10.3
Female	6,078,195	896,918	14.8	164,210	7,287	4.4	268,672	14,758	5.5	469,856	61,793	13.2

CLASS OF POPULATION AND SEX.	25 TO 34 YEARS. Total number.	Illiterate. Number.	Per cent.	35 TO 44 YEARS. Total number.	Illiterate. Number.	Per cent.	45 TO 54 YEARS. Total number.	Illiterate. Number.	Per cent.	55 TO 64 YEARS. Total number.	Illiterate. Number.	Per cent.	65 YEARS AND OVER. Total number.	Illiterate. Number.	Per cent.
All classes	17,157,664	961,200	5.6	14,120,838	988,961	7.0	10,498,493	857,776	8.2	6,531,672	594,573	9.1	4,933,215	591,385	12.0
Male	8,669,016	486,217	5.6	7,359,904	509,107	6.9	5,653,095	453,950	8.0	3,461,865	292,511	8.4	2,483,071	273,000	11.0
Female	8,488,668	474,983	5.6	6,760,934	479,854	7.1	4,845,398	403,826	8.3	3,069,807	302,062	9.8	2,450,144	318,385	13.0
White	15,480,480	660,706	4.3	12,721,352	662,629	5.2	9,505,306	518,918	5.5	6,077,104	370,421	6.1	4,583,026	352,525	7.7
Male	7,870,567	336,106	4.3	6,652,753	355,103	5.3	5,072,779	279,937	5.5	3,202,280	181,988	5.7	2,298,475	158,298	6.9
Female	7,609,913	324,600	4.3	6,068,599	307,526	5.1	4,432,527	238,981	5.4	2,874,824	188,433	6.6	2,284,551	194,227	8.5
Negro	1,607,604	287,063	17.9	1,333,632	310,538	23.3	950,699	323,924	34.1	430,098	212,682	49.4	332,718	227,310	68.3
Male	755,931	143,515	19.0	659,513	144,961	22.0	548,501	164,954	30.1	241,290	103,407	42.9	173,881	108,473	62.4
Female	851,673	143,548	16.9	674,119	165,577	24.6	402,198	158,970	39.5	188,808	109,275	57.9	158,832	118,837	74.8
Indian	30,011	8,769	29.2	25,325	10,212	40.3	19,534	10,644	54.5	12,526	8,328	66.5	13,139	10,043	76.4
Male	15,521	4,078	26.3	13,284	4,803	36.2	10,751	5,297	49.3	6,730	4,131	61.4	6,512	4,792	73.6
Female	14,490	4,691	32.4	12,041	5,409	44.9	8,783	5,347	60.9	5,796	4,197	72.4	6,627	5,251	79.2
Chinese	9,961	1,543	15.5	10,664	2,106	19.7	11,572	2,595	22.4	10,098	2,789	27.6	4,065	1,432	35.2
Male	8,636	1,174	13.6	9,702	1,781	18.4	11,092	2,400	21.6	9,892	2,680	27.1	3,971	1,380	34.8
Female	1,325	369	27.8	962	325	33.8	480	195	40.6	206	109	52.9	94	52	......
Japanese	26,523	2,779	10.5	28,156	3,082	10.9	10,696	1,487	13.9	1,703	299	17.6	201	38	18.9
Male	15,419	1,029	6.7	23,039	2,078	9.0	9,313	1,156	12.4	1,537	254	16.5	173	27	15.6
Female	11,104	1,750	15.8	5,117	1,004	19.6	1,383	331	23.9	166	45	27.1	28	11	......
All other	3,105	340	11.0	1,709	394	23.1	686	208	30.3	143	54	37.8	71	37	......
Male	2,942	315	10.7	1,613	381	23.6	659	206	31.8	136	51	37.5	59	30	......
Female	163	25	15.3	96	13	......	27	2	......	7	3	......	12	7	......
Native white	12,374,642	190,913	1.5	9,555,448	201,739	2.1	7,038,254	202,196	2.9	4,452,651	177,515	4.0	3,254,799	185,133	5.7
Male	6,131,661	108,587	1.8	4,840,881	112,982	2.3	3,676,810	113,275	3.1	2,305,862	92,008	4.0	1,619,091	88,662	5.5
Female	6,242,981	82,326	1.3	4,714,567	88,757	1.9	3,361,444	88,921	2.6	2,146,789	85,507	4.0	1,635,708	96,471	5.9
Native parentage	8,860,843	168,484	1.9	6,915,182	182,209	2.6	4,989,713	183,398	3.7	3,249,319	160,362	4.9	2,738,876	170,603	6.2
Male	4,421,983	97,189	2.2	3,546,880	102,180	2.9	2,649,866	102,506	3.9	1,704,797	82,986	4.9	1,365,527	81,498	6.0
Female	4,438,860	71,295	1.6	3,368,302	80,089	2.4	2,339,847	80,892	3.5	1,544,522	77,376	5.0	1,373,349	89,105	6.5
Foreign parentage	2,338,688	17,124	0.7	1,755,761	14,317	0.8	745,976	7,754	0.9	462,180	6,680	1.4	364,554	10,472	2.9
Male	1,150,323	8,407	0.7	866,975	7,778	0.9	743,634	6,009	0.8	406,532	6,285	1.3	179,375	4,980	2.8
Female	1,188,365	8,717	0.7	888,786	6,539	0.7	558,931	5,035	0.9	274,610	4,188	1.5	185,179	5,492	3.0
Mixed parentage	1,175,111	5,305	0.5	884,505	5,153	0.6	558,931	4,014	0.7	274,610	4,188	1.5	151,369	4,058	2.9
Male	559,355	2,991	0.5	427,026	3,024	0.5	280,968	2,020	0.7	135,735	1,846	1.4	74,189	2,184	2.9
Female	615,756	2,314	0.4	457,479	2,129	0.5	277,963	1,994	0.7	138,875	2,342	1.7	77,180	1,874	2.4
Foreign-born white	3,105,838	469,793	15.1	3,165,904	450,890	14.6	2,467,052	316,722	12.8	1,624,453	192,906	11.9	1,328,227	167,392	12.6
Male	1,738,906	227,519	13.1	1,811,872	242,121	13.4	1,395,969	166,662	11.9	896,418	89,980	10.0	679,384	69,636	10.2
Female	1,366,932	242,274	17.7	1,354,032	218,769	16.2	1,071,083	150,060	14.0	728,035	102,926	14.1	648,843	97,756	15.1

[1] Totals include persons of unknown age.

TABLE 3.—NUMBER AND PER CENT ILLITERATE IN POPULATION 10 YEARS OF AGE AND OVER, BY AGE PERIODS, FOR POPULATION CLASSES, BY SEX, FOR THE UNITED STATES: 1920, 1910, AND 1900.

CLASS OF POPULATION AND AGE PERIOD.	ILLITERATES IN THE POPULATION 10 YEARS OF AGE AND OVER.																	
	1920						1910						1900					
	Both sexes.		Male.		Female.		Both sexes.		Male.		Female.		Both sexes.		Male.		Female.	
	Number.	Per cent.	Number.	Per cent.	Number.	Per cent.	Number.	Per cent.	Number.	Per cent.	Number.	Per cent.	Number.	Per cent.	Number.	Per cent.	Number.	Per cent.
All classes	4,931,905	6.0	2,540,209	6.0	2,391,696	5.9	5,516,163	7.7	2,814,950	7.6	2,701,213	7.8	6,180,069	10.7	3,011,224	10.1	3,168,845	11.2
10 to 14 years	246,360	2.8	141,576	2.6	104,784	2.0	370,136	4.1	211,703	4.6	158,373	3.5	577,640	7.1	325,984	8.0	251,665	6.3
15 to 19 years	283,316	3.0	171,489	3.7	111,827	2.4	448,414	4.9	262,770	5.8	185,644	4.1	576,978	7.6	326,370	8.7	250,608	6.6
20 to 24 years	392,853	4.2	203,773	4.5	189,080	4.0	622,073	6.9	343,450	7.5	278,623	6.2	644,273	8.8	329,093	9.1	315,180	8.5
25 to 34 years	961,200	5.6	486,217	5.6	474,983	5.6	1,102,384	7.3	597,657	7.6	504,727	7.0	1,103,478	9.1	545,508	8.8	557,970	9.5
35 to 44 years	988,961	7.0	509,107	6.9	479,854	7.1	940,510	8.1	466,287	7.6	474,223	8.6	1,033,591	11.2	473,419	9.7	560,142	12.9
45 to 54 years	857,776	8.2	453,950	8.0	403,826	8.3	829,153	9.9	389,608	8.7	439,545	11.3	943,607	14.7	439,572	12.9	504,035	16.8
55 to 64 years	594,573	9.1	292,511	8.4	302,062	9.8	607,754	12.0	283,076	10.6	324,678	13.6	642,257	16.0	290,417	14.1	351,840	18.1
65 years and over	591,385	12.0	273,000	11.0	318,385	13.0	573,709	14.5	248,875	12.5	324,924	16.5	611,440	19.8	259,180	16.7	352,260	23.1
Age unknown	15,481	10.4	8,586	9.2	6,895	12.4	21,940	13.0	11,464	10.0	10,476	19.2	46,790	23.3	21,651	17.0	25,139	34.4
White	3,006,312	4.0	1,551,529	4.1	1,454,783	4.0	3,184,633	5.0	1,662,505	5.0	1,522,128	4.9	3,200,746	6.2	1,567,153	6.0	1,633,593	6.4
10 to 14 years	100,643	1.1	57,150	1.2	43,493	0.9	144,675	1.8	82,569	2.1	62,106	1.6	240,580	3.5	138,241	3.9	102,339	3.0
15 to 19 years	125,495	1.5	74,455	1.8	51,040	1.2	226,432	2.8	132,616	3.3	93,816	2.4	255,707	3.9	147,557	4.5	108,150	3.3
20 to 24 years	207,649	2.5	103,958	2.6	103,691	2.5	367,669	4.6	211,861	5.2	155,808	4.0	292,468	4.6	157,930	5.0	134,538	4.2
25 to 34 years	660,706	4.3	336,106	4.3	324,600	4.3	702,962	5.2	403,285	5.7	299,677	4.7	583,293	5.4	309,311	5.6	273,982	5.3
35 to 44 years	662,629	5.2	355,103	5.3	307,526	5.1	569,403	5.4	303,719	5.5	265,684	5.4	569,810	6.0	279,773	6.3	290,046	7.4
45 to 54 years	518,918	5.5	279,937	5.5	238,981	5.4	477,080	6.3	232,105	5.7	244,975	6.9	501,571	8.7	234,121	7.7	267,450	9.9
55 to 64 years	370,421	6.1	181,988	5.7	188,433	6.6	344,877	7.4	155,476	6.4	189,401	8.6	362,297	9.9	148,574	8.0	213,723	12.0
65 years and over	352,525	7.7	158,298	6.9	194,227	8.5	342,420	9.4	135,102	7.4	207,318	11.4	378,071	13.5	143,152	10.1	234,919	16.9
Age unknown	7,326	5.9	4,534	5.8	2,792	6.2	9,115	6.8	5,712	6.1	3,403	8.5	16,940	11.7	8,494	8.7	8,446	17.9
Negro	1,842,161	22.9	942,368	23.5	899,793	22.3	2,227,731	30.4	1,096,000	30.1	1,131,731	30.7	2,853,194	44.5	1,371,432	43.1	1,481,762	45.8
10 to 14 years	140,892	11.4	81,944	13.3	58,948	9.5	218,555	18.9	125,616	21.7	92,939	16.1	328,992	30.1	183,540	33.5	145,452	26.8
15 to 19 years	152,998	14.1	94,455	18.4	58,543	10.3	214,860	20.3	126,459	24.9	88,401	16.0	312,094	31.8	173,891	36.7	138,203	27.2
20 to 24 years	179,124	17.0	96,895	19.9	82,229	14.5	245,860	23.9	126,970	26.3	118,890	21.7	340,516	35.1	165,085	36.0	175,431	34.4
25 to 34 years	287,063	17.9	143,515	19.0	143,548	16.9	380,742	24.6	183,993	24.4	196,749	24.7	496,180	39.3	222,516	35.7	273,664	42.8
35 to 44 years	310,538	23.3	144,961	22.0	165,577	24.6	351,858	32.3	152,132	27.7	199,726	37.1	437,503	52.0	177,199	43.0	260,304	60.6
45 to 54 years	323,924	34.1	164,954	30.1	158,970	39.5	334,930	47.0	147,542	38.9	187,388	56.3	420,438	68.1	191,883	59.3	228,555	77.3
55 to 64 years	212,682	49.4	103,407	42.9	109,275	57.9	249,584	63.0	120,046	55.5	129,538	72.0	267,312	78.4	134,535	73.4	132,777	84.3
65 years and over	227,310	68.3	108,473	62.4	118,837	74.8	219,255	74.5	107,877	70.7	111,378	78.6	223,124	85.4	111,158	83.6	111,966	87.2
Age unknown	7,630	32.5	3,764	27.9	3,866	33.7	12,087	38.9	5,365	31.4	6,722	48.1	27,035	55.4	11,625	46.2	15,410	65.1
Ind., Chi., Jap., and all other	83,432	25.6	46,312	22.1	37,120	31.8	103,799	31.6	56,445	25.0	47,354	46.2	126,129	44.5	72,639	37.5	53,490	59.8
10 to 14 years	4,825	13.8	2,482	13.9	2,343	13.8	6,906	20.6	3,578	20.4	3,328	20.9	8,077	27.8	4,203	27.8	3,874	27.9
15 to 19 years	4,823	14.5	2,579	13.9	2,244	15.8	7,122	20.5	3,695	18.3	3,427	23.5	9,177	20.7	4,922	20.4	4,255	34.7
20 to 24 years	6,080	16.5	2,920	13.7	3,160	20.3	8,544	21.5	4,619	17.0	3,925	31.2	11,289	36.7	6,078	30.1	5,211	49.1
25 to 34 years	13,431	19.3	6,596	15.5	6,835	25.2	18,080	23.8	10,379	18.0	8,301	40.1	24,005	42.9	13,681	34.4	10,324	63.9
35 to 44 years	15,794	24.0	9,043	19.0	6,751	37.1	19,249	33.9	10,436	24.8	8,813	60.0	26,269	45.8	16,477	36.8	9,792	78.1
45 to 54 years	14,934	35.1	9,059	28.5	5,875	55.0	17,143	41.2	9,901	31.0	7,242	74.4	21,598	53.4	13,568	44.1	8,030	83.3
55 to 64 years	11,470	46.9	7,116	38.9	4,354	70.5	13,293	54.4	7,554	42.0	5,739	83.7	12,648	63.9	7,308	53.4	5,340	87.5
65 years and over	11,550	66.1	6,229	58.1	5,321	78.7	12,124	78.7	5,896	69.6	6,228	90.0	10,251	82.6	4,870	75.3	5,381	90.5
Age unknown	525	34.2	288	27.7	237	48.1	738	19.5	387	11.9	351	65.5	2,815	41.0	1,532	34.5	1,283	56.2
Native white	1,242,572	2.0	684,707	2.2	557,865	1.8	1,534,272	3.0	796,055	3.1	738,217	2.9	1,913,611	4.6	955,517	4.6	958,094	4.7
10 to 14 years	85,856	0.9	49,650	1.1	36,206	0.8	131,991	1.7	76,359	2.0	55,632	1.5	223,208	3.4	129,027	3.8	94,181	2.9
15 to 19 years	97,013	1.2	60,731	1.6	36,282	0.9	140,323	1.9	85,510	2.3	54,813	1.5	196,393	3.3	117,661	3.9	78,732	2.6
20 to 24 years	98,938	1.4	57,040	1.6	41,898	1.1	148,541	2.3	84,586	2.6	63,955	1.9	185,966	3.4	102,564	3.8	83,402	3.1
25 to 34 years	190,913	1.5	108,587	1.8	82,326	1.3	247,774	2.4	136,583	2.6	111,101	2.2	307,890	3.6	159,643	3.7	148,256	3.5
35 to 44 years	201,739	2.1	112,982	2.3	88,757	1.9	235,489	3.0	120,488	3.0	115,001	3.0	314,950	5.1	140,203	4.7	165,756	5.6
45 to 54 years	202,196	2.9	113,275	3.1	88,921	2.6	248,900	4.5	122,110	4.2	126,790	4.8	292,643	7.1	140,410	6.0	152,233	7.8
55 to 64 years	177,515	4.0	92,008	4.0	85,507	4.0	197,955	6.0	95,273	5.5	102,682	6.5	187,727	7.7	79,495	6.4	108,232	8.9
65 years and over	185,133	5.7	88,662	5.5	96,471	5.9	179,219	7.3	73,035	6.0	106,184	8.6	194,713	10.5	72,692	7.9	122,021	13.1
Age unknown	3,269	3.2	1,772	2.7	1,497	3.9	4,080	3.8	2,111	2.8	1,969	5.0	10,103	8.4	4,822	5.9	5,281	13.7
Native parentage	1,109,875	2.5	614,612	2.7	495,263	2.3	1,378,884	3.7	715,928	3.8	662,958	3.7	1,734,764	5.7	868,175	5.6	872,589	5.8
10 to 14 years	71,845	1.1	42,349	1.3	29,496	0.9	117,973	2.2	69,087	2.6	48,886	1.9	205,735	4.4	110,221	5.0	86,514	3.8
15 to 19 years	83,303	1.5	53,406	1.9	29,897	1.1	121,878	2.4	75,304	3.0	46,484	1.8	175,505	4.1	105,248	5.0	70,257	3.3
20 to 24 years	86,609	1.7	50,891	2.0	35,778	1.4	130,991	2.8	75,103	3.2	55,798	2.4	166,884	4.4	91,737	4.8	75,147	4.0
25 to 34 years	168,484	1.9	97,189	2.2	71,295	1.6	220,707	3.0	121,983	3.2	98,814	2.7	272,557	4.0	140,465	4.7	132,092	4.3
35 to 44 years	182,269	2.6	102,180	2.9	80,089	2.4	210,694	3.8	107,355	3.8	103,339	3.9	280,240	6.4	131,664	5.8	148,582	7.0
45 to 54 years	183,398	3.7	102,506	3.9	80,892	3.5	224,421	5.0	109,758	5.2	114,663	6.0	266,889	8.0	128,073	7.3	138,816	8.7
55 to 64 years	160,362	4.9	82,986	4.9	77,376	5.0	181,363	6.7	87,500	6.1	93,863	7.3	174,080	8.0	73,320	6.7	100,763	9.3
65 years and over	170,603	6.2	81,498	6.0	89,105	6.5	167,099	7.0	67,752	6.2	99,347	8.9	183,428	10.7	67,955	8.0	115,473	13.4
Age unknown	2,942	3.2	1,607	2.7	1,335	4.0	3,668	3.8	1,904	2.8	1,764	6.1	9,431	8.4	4,486	5.8	4,945	14.0
Foreign or mixed parentage	132,697	0.8	70,095	0.8	62,602	0.7	155,388	1.1	80,129	1.2	75,259	1.1	178,847	1.6	93,342	1.7	85,505	1.6
10 to 14 years	14,011	0.5	7,301	0.6	6,710	0.5	14,018	0.6	7,272	0.6	6,746	0.6	17,473	0.9	9,806	1.0	7,667	0.8
15 to 19 years	13,710	0.6	7,325	0.7	6,385	0.6	18,445	0.8	10,116	0.9	8,329	0.7	20,888	1.2	12,413	1.4	8,475	1.0
20 to 24 years	12,269	0.6	6,149	0.6	6,120	0.6	17,550	0.9	9,393	1.0	8,157	0.9	19,082	1.2	10,827	1.4	8,255	1.0
25 to 34 years	22,429	0.6	11,398	0.7	11,031	0.6	26,977	0.9	14,600	1.0	12,377	0.8	35,342	1.3	19,178	1.5	16,164	1.2
35 to 44 years	19,470	0.7	10,802	0.8	8,668	0.6	24,795	1.1	13,133	1.1	11,662	1.0	34,713	2.0	17,539	2.0	17,174	2.0
45 to 54 years	18,798	0.9	10,769	1.0	8,029	0.8	24,479	1.6	12,352	1.6	12,127	1.6	25,754	3.4	12,337	3.2	13,417	3.7
55 to 64 years	17,153	1.4	9,022	1.5	8,131	1.4	16,592	2.8	7,773	2.6	8,810	3.0	13,638	4.8	6,169	4.2	7,469	5.4
65 years and over	14,530	2.8	7,164	2.8	7,366	2.8	12,120	4.7	5,283	4.1	6,837	5.4	11,285	8.0	4,737	6.6	6,548	9.4
Age unknown	327	2.9	165	2.8	162	3.0	412	3.9	207	3.7	205	4.2	672	8.3	336	6.9	336	10.2
Foreign-born white	1,763,740	13.1	866,822	11.7	896,918	14.8	1,650,361	12.7	866,450	11.8	783,911	13.9	1,287,135	12.9	611,636	11.3	675,499	14.7
10 to 14 years	14,787	4.5	7,500	4.5	7,287	4.4	12,684	3.5	6,210	3.4	6,474	3.7	17,372	5.0	9,214	5.8	8,158	5.3
15 to 19 years	28,482	5.4	13,724	5.3	14,758	5.5	86,109	12.8	47,106	13.4	39,003	12.1	59,314	10.6	29,896	11.0	29,418	10.1
20 to 24 years	108,711	11.7	46,918	10.3	61,793	13.2	219,128	15.3	127,275	15.4	91,853	15.1	106,502	11.6	55,366	12.1	51,136	11.0
25 to 34 years	469,793	15.1	227,519	13.1	242,274	17.7	455,188	14.4	266,702	14.2	188,486	14.6	275,394	12.1	149,668	12.0	125,726	12.3
35 to 44 years	460,890	14.6	242,121	13.4	218,769	16.2	333,914	12.3	183,231	11.7	150,683	13.1	254,860	11.9	130,570	10.6	124,290	13.6
45 to 54 years	316,722	12.8	166,662	11.9	150,060	14.0	228,180	11.0	110,055	9.3	118,125	13.3	208,928	12.7	93,711	10.3	115,217	15.7
55 to 64 years	192,906	11.9	89,980	10.0	102,926	14.1	146,922	11.1	60,203	8.5	86,719	14.2	174,570	14.7	69,079	10.9	105,491	18.9
65 years and over	167,392	12.6	69,636	10.2	97,756	15.1	163,201	13.8	62,067	10.2	101,134	17.5	183,358	19.3	70,460	14.3	112,898	24.7
Age unknown	4,057	20.0	2,762	20.1	1,295	19.8	5,035	19.2	3,601	18.3	1,434	22.0	6,837	27.5	3,672	22.8	3,165	30.2

ILLITERACY.

TABLE 4.—ILLITERATE POPULATION 10 AND 21 YEARS OF AGE AND OVER, RESPECTIVELY, CLASSIFIED BY SEX AND DEGREE OF ILLITERACY, FOR POPULATION CLASSES, FOR THE UNITED STATES: 1920 AND 1910.

[Per cent not shown where base is less than 100.]

CENSUS YEAR, AGE, AND CLASS OF POPULATION.	ILLITERATE POPULATION.									CAN READ BUT NOT WRITE—PER CENT OF TOTAL ILLITERATE.		
	Both sexes.			Male.			Female.					
	Total.	Can neither read nor write.	Can read but not write.	Total.	Can neither read nor write.	Can read but not write.	Total.	Can neither read nor write.	Can read but not write.	Both sexes.	Male.	Female.
1920												
All classes, 10 years and over	4,931,905	4,483,565	448,340	2,540,209	2,324,149	216,060	2,391,696	2,159,416	232,280	9.1	8.5	9.7
Native white:												
Native parentage	1,109,875	962,292	147,583	614,612	542,894	71,718	495,263	419,398	75,865	13.3	11.7	15.3
Foreign parentage	98,076	84,157	13,919	50,442	43,758	6,684	47,634	40,399	7,235	14.2	13.3	15.2
Mixed parentage	34,621	29,320	5,301	19,653	16,958	2,695	14,968	12,362	2,606	15.3	13.7	17.4
Foreign-born white	1,763,740	1,611,529	152,211	866,822	796,187	70,635	896,918	815,342	81,576	8.6	8.1	9.1
Negro	1,842,161	1,715,132	127,029	942,368	879,576	62,792	899,793	835,556	64,237	6.9	6.7	7.1
Indian	61,730	60,531	1,199	30,010	29,396	614	31,720	31,135	585	1.9	2.0	1.8
Chinese	11,262	10,611	651	10,064	9,457	607	1,198	1,154	44	5.8	6.0	3.7
Japanese	9,276	8,873	403	5,145	4,870	275	4,131	4,003	128	4.3	5.3	3.1
All other	1,164	1,120	44	1,093	1,053	40	71	67	4	3.8	3.7	......
All classes, 21 years and over	4,333,111	3,933,793	399,318	2,192,368	2,005,697	186,671	2,140,743	1,928,096	212,647	9.2	8.5	9.9
Native white:												
Native parentage	938,311	809,159	129,152	509,343	449,228	60,115	428,968	359,931	69,037	13.8	11.8	16.1
Foreign parentage	76,136	64,088	12,048	39,234	33,534	5,700	36,902	30,554	6,348	15.8	14.5	17.2
Mixed parentage	26,222	21,678	4,544	14,969	12,696	2,273	11,253	8,982	2,271	17.3	15.2	20.2
Foreign-born white	1,707,145	1,557,478	149,667	840,063	770,592	69,471	867,082	786,886	80,196	8.8	8.3	9.2
Negro	1,512,987	1,411,122	101,865	748,229	700,517	47,712	764,758	710,605	54,153	6.7	6.4	7.1
Indian	51,439	50,457	982	24,788	24,282	506	26,651	26,175	476	1.9	2.0	1.8
Chinese	10,964	10,329	635	9,812	9,220	592	1,152	1,109	43	5.8	6.0	3.7
Japanese	8,776	8,393	383	4,865	4,601	264	3,911	3,792	119	4.4	5.4	3.0
All other	1,131	1,089	42	1,065	1,027	38	66	62	4	3.7	3.6	......
1910												
All classes, 10 years and over	5,516,163	4,803,770	712,393	2,814,950	2,489,451	325,499	2,701,213	2,314,319	386,894	12.9	11.6	14.3
Native white:												
Native parentage	1,378,884	1,115,316	263,568	715,926	597,693	118,233	662,958	517,623	145,335	19.1	16.5	21.9
Foreign parentage	117,336	98,505	18,831	59,246	51,101	8,145	58,090	47,404	10,686	16.0	13.7	18.4
Mixed parentage	38,052	31,493	6,559	20,883	17,811	3,072	17,169	13,682	3,487	17.2	14.7	20.3
Foreign-born white	1,650,361	1,463,465	186,896	866,450	787,780	78,670	783,911	675,685	108,226	11.3	9.1	13.8
Negro	2,227,731	1,993,752	233,979	1,096,000	980,284	115,716	1,131,731	1,013,468	118,263	10.5	10.6	10.4
Indian	85,445	83,747	1,698	40,104	39,233	871	45,341	44,514	827	2.0	2.2	1.8
Chinese	10,891	10,382	509	9,849	9,364	485	1,042	1,018	24	4.7	4.9	2.3
Japanese	6,213	5,885	328	5,247	4,965	282	966	920	46	5.3	5.4	4.8
All other	1,250	1,225	25	1,245	1,220	25	5	5	....	2.0	2.0	......
All classes, 21 years and over	4,570,017	3,958,639	611,378	2,273,603	2,007,531	266,072	2,296,414	1,951,108	345,306	13.4	11.7	15.0
Native white:												
Native parentage	1,113,427	887,460	225,967	557,042	462,585	94,457	556,385	424,875	131,510	20.3	17.0	23.6
Foreign parentage	90,269	73,605	16,664	45,233	38,262	6,971	45,036	35,343	9,693	18.5	15.4	21.5
Mixed parentage	28,649	22,828	5,821	15,458	12,845	2,613	13,191	9,983	3,208	20.3	16.9	24.3
Foreign-born white	1,507,493	1,329,749	177,744	788,631	714,212	74,419	718,862	615,537	103,325	11.8	9.4	14.4
Negro	1,742,648	1,559,716	182,932	819,135	733,019	86,116	923,513	826,697	96,816	10.5	10.5	10.5
Indian	70,215	68,784	1,431	32,603	31,865	738	37,612	36,919	693	2.0	2.3	1.8
Chinese	10,383	9,891	492	9,452	8,982	470	931	909	22	4.7	5.0	2.4
Japanese	5,808	5,503	305	4,928	4,662	266	880	841	39	5.3	5.4	4.4
All other	1,125	1,103	22	1,121	1,099	23	4	4	....	2.0	2.0	......

75647°—22——73

1154   POPULATION.

TABLE 5.—NUMBER AND PER CENT ILLITERATE IN POPULATION 10 YEARS OF AGE AND OVER, FOR PRINCIPAL POPULATION CLASSES, BY DIVISIONS AND STATES: 1920.

	All classes: 1920			Native white. Native parentage.			Native white. Foreign or mixed parentage.			Foreign-born white.			Negro.		
DIVISION AND STATE.	Total number.	Illiterate. Number.	Per cent.	Total number.	Illiterate. Number.	Per cent.	Total number.	Illiterate. Number.	Per cent.	Total number.	Illiterate. Number.	Per cent.	Total number.	Illiterate. Number.	Per cent.
United States	82,739,315	4,931,905	6.0	44,077,564	1,109,875	2.5	16,784,299	132,697	0.8	13,497,886	1,763,740	13.1	8,053,225	1,842,161	22.9
GEOGRAPHIC DIVISIONS:															
New England	5,945,989	289,700	4.9	2,226,085	13,185	0.6	1,805,558	13,759	0.8	1,813,026	257,207	14.0	63,271	4,607	7.0
Middle Atlantic	17,666,354	805,382	4.9	7,471,675	52,924	0.7	4,816,496	24,048	0.5	4,834,236	760,010	15.7	508,031	25,537	5.0
East North Central	17,130,786	495,470	2.9	8,931,324	88,793	1.0	4,557,935	28,390	0.6	3,183,790	342,832	10.8	440,129	32,052	7.3
West North Central	9,889,740	193,221	2.0	5,491,297	50,954	1.1	2,772,958	14,678	0.5	1,358,323	86,760	6.4	237,277	24,887	10.5
South Atlantic	10,513,447	1,212,942	11.5	6,547,732	352,907	5.4	421,140	3,878	0.9	311,385	39,745	12.8	3,221,691	812,343	25.2
East South Central	6,677,229	845,450	12.7	4,502,712	299,025	6.6	176,884	2,626	1.5	71,211	6,457	9.1	1,924,714	536,583	27.9
West South Central	7,739,536	773,637	10.0	5,146,751	199,408	3.9	531,661	35,021	6.6	430,053	128,723	29.9	1,587,020	402,233	25.3
Mountain	2,564,463	132,659	5.2	1,456,002	35,163	2.4	575,344	5,697	1.0	436,304	55,422	12.7	27,741	1,487	5.4
Pacific	4,611,771	123,435	2.7	2,303,106	8,516	0.4	1,126,314	4,600	0.4	1,010,536	80,570	8.0	41,348	1,912	4.6
NEW ENGLAND:															
Maine	621,233	20,240	3.3	400,506	5,106	1.3	114,256	3,290	2.9	101,585	11,601	11.1	1,091	64	5.2
New Hampshire	361,930	15,788	4.4	184,676	1,023	0.6	87,168	950	1.1	89,472	13,746	15.4	490	33	6.7
Vermont	284,472	8,488	3.0	181,212	1,904	1.1	60,074	1,709	2.8	42,791	4,837	11.3	451	28	6.2
Massachusetts	3,106,709	146,607	4.7	970,471	2,926	0.3	1,032,063	4,854	0.5	1,063,572	133,730	12.8	37,003	2,565	6.9
Rhode Island	483,788	31,312	6.5	134,973	694	0.5	169,252	1,561	0.9	171,032	28,169	16.5	8,192	839	10.2
Connecticut	1,087,797	67,265	6.2	355,147	1,532	0.4	342,745	1,395	0.4	371,066	63,131	17.0	17,441	1,078	6.2
MIDDLE ATLANTIC:															
New York	8,402,786	425,022	5.1	2,876,032	16,150	0.6	2,589,703	12,256	0.5	2,752,055	389,601	14.2	171,303	5,032	2.9
New Jersey	2,494,246	127,661	5.1	942,438	6,797	0.7	723,716	2,899	0.4	726,790	111,595	15.3	96,701	5,910	6.1
Pennsylvania	6,769,322	312,699	4.6	3,652,305	29,977	0.8	1,503,077	8,893	0.6	1,371,402	258,812	18.9	240,027	14,545	6.1
EAST NORTH CENTRAL:															
Ohio	4,624,456	131,006	2.8	2,864,260	28,535	1.0	931,113	5,191	0.6	669,924	84,387	12.6	157,912	12,715	8.1
Indiana	2,356,214	52,034	2.2	1,832,594	24,981	1.4	305,549	2,948	1.0	149,239	17,355	11.8	68,361	6,476	9.5
Illinois	5,184,943	173,987	3.4	2,304,980	24,437	1.1	1,524,345	6,470	0.4	1,194,970	131,996	11.0	157,205	10,476	6.7
Michigan	2,895,606	88,046	3.0	1,235,017	7,580	0.6	889,958	6,592	0.7	713,528	70,535	9.9	52,193	2,203	4.2
Wisconsin	2,069,567	50,397	2.4	604,473	3,260	0.5	906,970	7,189	0.8	456,420	38,359	8.4	4,458	182	4.1
WEST NORTH CENTRAL:															
Minnesota	1,877,132	34,487	1.8	537,758	1,088	0.4	842,657	3,967	0.5	482,230	26,242	5.4	7,776	241	3.1
Iowa	1,913,155	20,680	1.1	1,180,271	5,921	0.5	542,534	2,354	0.4	223,752	11,001	4.9	15,902	1,283	8.1
Missouri	2,737,771	83,403	3.0	1,950,927	43,031	2.2	442,882	4,035	0.9	184,394	17,569	9.6	182,861	18,898	12.1
North Dakota	470,210	9,937	2.1	126,602	335	0.3	208,432	972	0.5	129,901	7,238	5.6	405	16	4.0
South Dakota	482,195	8,109	1.7	205,083	660	0.3	182,519	830	0.5	81,781	3,848	4.7	678	35	5.2
Nebraska	1,012,552	13,784	1.4	542,380	2,184	0.4	307,534	1,176	0.4	148,200	9,468	6.4	11,480	536	4.7
Kansas	1,396,725	22,821	1.6	992,166	5,835	0.6	246,400	1,344	0.5	108,006	11,291	10.5	48,156	4,223	8.8
SOUTH ATLANTIC:															
Delaware	178,930	10,508	5.9	111,963	2,295	2.0	22,778	132	0.6	19,541	3,373	17.3	24,598	4,700	19.1
Maryland	1,158,953	64,434	5.6	695,984	13,884	2.0	166,509	1,484	0.9	101,155	13,575	13.4	194,825	35,404	18.2
District of Columbia	377,295	10,509	2.8	204,354	504	0.2	50,168	76	0.2	28,292	1,728	6.1	93,782	8,361	8.9
Virginia	1,748,868	195,159	11.2	1,150,561	70,081	6.1	40,359	394	1.0	30,325	2,150	7.1	520,657	122,322	23.5
West Virginia	1,083,395	69,413	6.4	902,071	43,573	4.8	51,151	751	1.5	60,679	14,548	24.0	68,786	10,513	15.3
North Carolina	1,844,673	241,603	13.1	1,275,432	104,073	8.2	8,776	171	1.9	6,981	474	6.8	545,542	133,074	24.5
South Carolina	1,219,816	220,667	18.1	583,300	38,039	6.5	10,409	103	1.0	6,327	391	6.2	618,928	181,422	29.3
Georgia	2,150,230	328,838	15.3	1,213,122	66,537	5.5	24,654	259	1.1	16,029	861	5.4	896,127	261,115	29.1
Florida	751,787	71,811	9.0	404,345	12,661	3.1	46,285	508	1.1	42,057	2,657	6.3	258,449	55,639	21.5
EAST SOUTH CENTRAL:															
Kentucky	1,837,434	155,014	8.4	1,512,456	110,902	7.3	101,608	1,304	1.3	30,603	2,244	7.3	192,657	40,548	21.0
Tennessee	1,770,762	182,629	10.3	1,308,626	101,317	7.4	32,291	492	1.5	15,297	1,263	8.3	354,426	79,532	22.4
Alabama	1,730,421	278,082	16.1	1,011,213	64,925	6.4	27,479	469	1.7	17,363	1,893	10.9	674,004	210,690	31.3
Mississippi	1,338,612	229,734	17.2	610,417	21,881	3.6	15,506	361	2.3	7,918	1,057	13.3	703,627	205,813	29.3
WEST SOUTH CENTRAL:															
Arkansas	1,302,905	121,837	9.4	892,310	40,753	4.6	33,164	658	2.0	13,834	1,145	8.3	363,403	79,245	21.8
Louisiana	1,360,066	299,092	21.9	693,683	78,818	11.4	90,515	3,139	3.5	44,214	9,707	21.9	530,362	206,730	38.5
Oklahoma	1,513,951	56,864	3.8	1,235,330	29,413	2.4	85,068	1,005	1.2	39,020	5,456	14.0	114,536	14,205	12.4
Texas	3,556,614	295,844	8.3	2,325,419	50,424	2.2	322,914	30,219	9.4	332,955	112,417	33.8	572,719	102,053	17.8
MOUNTAIN:															
Montana	421,443	9,544	2.3	196,637	609	0.3	121,895	398	0.3	91,729	5,178	5.6	1,450	87	6.0
Idaho	326,051	4,924	1.5	207,601	654	0.3	75,066	260	0.3	38,379	2,501	6.5	814	44	5.4
Wyoming	150,993	3,149	2.1	90,771	320	0.4	31,867	101	0.3	24,762	2,233	9.0	1,251	66	5.3
Colorado	747,485	24,208	3.2	463,431	7,655	1.7	150,732	969	0.6	114,285	14,224	12.4	9,909	619	6.2
New Mexico	267,595	41,687	15.6	199,359	23,757	11.9	21,534	1,762	8.2	20,786	7,250	27.1	5,382	228	4.2
Arizona	255,461	39,131	15.3	114,238	1,454	1.3	38,637	1,779	4.6	70,053	19,291	27.5	7,369	333	4.6
Utah	331,530	6,264	1.9	155,751	535	0.3	113,990	390	0.3	55,724	3,504	6.3	1,273	59	4.6
Nevada	63,905	3,802	5.9	28,214	119	0.4	15,623	38	0.2	14,586	1,241	8.5	313	16	5.1
PACIFIC:															
Washington	1,101,929	18,526	1.7	549,796	1,628	0.3	277,938	751	0.3	244,881	11,630	4.7	6,061	245	4.0
Oregon	638,987	9,317	1.5	389,438	1,529	0.4	137,081	461	0.3	100,672	5,172	5.1	1,893	89	4.7
California	2,870,855	95,592	3.3	1,363,872	5,359	0.4	711,295	3,388	0.5	664,983	69,768	10.5	33,391	1,579	4.7

ILLITERACY.

TABLE 6.—NUMBER AND PER CENT ILLITERATE IN POPULATION 21 YEARS OF AGE AND OVER, FOR PRINCIPAL POPULATION CLASSES, BY DIVISIONS AND STATES: 1920.

	All classes: 1920			Native white — Native parentage			Native white — Foreign or mixed parentage			Foreign-born white			Negro		
DIVISION AND STATE.	Total number.	Illiterate Number.	Per cent.	Total number.	Illiterate Number.	Per cent.	Total number.	Illiterate Number.	Per cent.	Total number.	Illiterate Number.	Per cent.	Total number.	Illiterate Number.	Per cent.
United States	60,886,520	4,333,111	7.1	31,007,257	938,311	3.0	11,607,484	102,358	0.9	12,498,720	1,707,145	13.7	5,522,475	1,512,937	27.4
GEOGRAPHIC DIVISIONS:															
New England	4,591,477	280,826	6.1	1,715,664	11,058	0.6	1,113,673	11,805	1.1	1,705,291	252,584	14.8	52,315	4,466	8.5
Middle Atlantic	13,451,656	843,582	6.3	5,472,931	47,443	0.9	3,077,035	19,664	0.6	4,477,752	749,227	16.7	409,441	24,531	6.0
East North Central	13,025,595	480,238	3.7	6,356,539	81,372	1.3	3,320,377	25,360	0.8	2,978,575	339,165	11.4	358,341	31,084	8.7
West North Central	7,278,548	180,616	2.5	3,759,084	53,246	1.4	2,018,791	12,722	0.6	1,291,794	84,598	6.5	187,865	23,550	12.5
South Atlantic	7,212,523	1,006,764	14.0	4,496,540	297,595	6.6	309,020	3,273	1.1	287,215	38,785	13.5	2,111,952	664,235	31.5
East South Central	4,523,944	700,098	15.5	3,024,782	252,934	8.4	146,635	2,391	1.6	67,242	6,249	9.3	1,284,069	438,003	34.1
West South Central	5,243,770	611,363	11.7	3,423,881	157,177	4.6	372,942	19,330	5.2	357,220	104,076	29.1	1,062,244	323,869	30.5
Mountain	1,888,921	113,384	6.0	1,010,072	30,136	3.0	411,787	4,077	1.0	394,008	49,959	12.7	23,881	1,386	5.8
Pacific	3,670,077	110,240	3.2	1,747,764	7,350	0.4	837,224	3,730	0.4	939,623	82,502	8.8	34,367	1,863	5.4
NEW ENGLAND:															
Maine	475,191	18,572	3.9	309,621	4,156	1.3	69,735	2,886	4.1	94,329	11,302	12.0	876	60	6.8
New Hampshire	281,026	15,257	5.4	146,345	897	0.6	52,136	858	1.6	82,049	13,437	16.4	388	30	7.7
Vermont	217,042	8,152	3.8	135,135	1,715	1.3	43,307	1,627	3.8	38,232	4,772	12.5	342	28	8.2
Massachusetts	2,411,507	142,750	5.9	749,761	2,469	0.3	639,680	8,930	0.6	988,913	133,330	13.5	30,412	2,491	8.2
Rhode Island	368,687	30,319	8.2	101,761	633	0.6	103,155	1,339	1.3	156,866	27,480	17.5	6,554	820	12.5
Connecticut	838,074	65,776	7.8	273,041	1,188	0.4	205,660	1,165	0.6	344,902	62,263	18.1	13,743	1,037	7.5
MIDDLE ATLANTIC:															
New York	6,514,681	415,359	6.4	2,141,646	14,497	0.7	1,691,206	10,270	0.6	2,528,497	383,862	15.2	142,544	4,815	3.4
New Jersey	1,897,884	124,858	6.6	695,049	6,073	0.9	450,457	2,285	0.5	675,222	109,893	16.3	75,671	5,668	7.5
Pennsylvania	5,039,091	303,805	6.0	2,636,236	26,873	1.0	935,372	7,109	0.8	1,274,033	255,472	20.1	191,226	14,048	7.3
EAST NORTH CENTRAL:															
Ohio	3,558,481	126,645	3.6	2,100,309	26,100	1.2	707,565	4,644	0.7	622,523	83,415	13.4	126,940	12,316	9.7
Indiana	1,779,820	50,147	2.8	1,335,975	23,545	1.8	249,101	2,803	1.1	140,373	17,393	12.4	53,935	6,336	11.7
Illinois	3,944,197	169,127	4.3	1,619,477	22,362	1.4	1,075,200	5,547	0.5	1,117,928	130,474	11.7	128,450	10,146	7.9
Michigan	2,215,436	85,613	3.9	883,685	6,798	0.8	621,222	5,875	0.9	663,160	69,759	10.5	43,407	2,111	4.9
Wisconsin	1,527,661	48,706	3.2	417,093	2,567	0.6	667,289	6,491	1.0	434,591	38,124	8.8	3,609	175	4.8
WEST NORTH CENTRAL:															
Minnesota	1,380,834	32,869	2.4	332,198	1,406	0.4	574,612	3,305	0.6	462,582	26,047	5.6	6,666	234	3.5
Iowa	1,428,682	19,444	1.4	778,247	5,267	0.7	422,833	2,065	0.5	214,479	10,749	5.0	12,568	1,249	9.9
Missouri	2,038,814	77,348	3.8	1,376,435	38,780	2.8	366,878	3,834	1.0	173,551	17,269	10.0	121,328	17,333	14.3
North Dakota	322,918	9,373	2.9	77,101	258	0.3	121,244	717	0.6	121,047	7,126	5.9	336	16	4.8
South Dakota	344,846	7,640	2.2	132,212	520	0.4	125,383	671	0.5	78,027	3,795	4.9	520	35	6.7
Nebraska	738,310	12,972	1.8	366,189	1,832	0.5	219,564	965	0.4	140,899	9,253	6.6	9,437	538	5.7
Kansas	1,024,144	20,970	2.0	690,702	5,183	0.7	188,277	1,165	0.6	101,209	10,359	10.2	37,010	4,145	11.2
SOUTH ATLANTIC:															
Delaware	136,521	10,088	7.4	84,468	2,190	2.6	15,646	110	0.7	18,245	3,327	18.2	18,113	4,453	24.6
Maryland	862,391	58,877	6.8	503,732	12,533	2.5	122,656	1,318	1.1	93,624	13,398	14.3	141,991	31,544	22.2
District of Columbia	305,255	10,190	3.3	163,781	521	0.3	41,023	64	0.2	26,376	1,699	6.4	73,448	7,823	10.7
Virginia	1,207,074	162,376	13.5	798,586	56,917	7.1	28,686	318	1.1	27,551	2,086	7.5	351,231	102,884	29.3
West Virginia	752,344	61,468	8.2	609,811	37,099	6.1	35,830	619	1.7	55,465	14,062	25.4	51,145	9,662	18.9
North Carolina	1,210,727	204,492	16.9	850,173	90,642	10.7	6,394	155	2.4	6,488	453	7.0	342,758	111,109	32.4
South Carolina	779,991	179,482	23.0	388,821	32,894	8.5	8,034	94	1.2	5,941	385	6.5	376,930	146,027	38.7
Georgia	1,421,606	261,294	18.4	812,254	54,339	6.7	18,919	241	1.3	14,855	839	5.6	575,330	205,819	35.8
Florida	536,614	58,497	10.9	284,914	10,460	3.7	31,832	354	1.1	38,370	2,536	6.6	181,008	44,914	24.8
EAST SOUTH CENTRAL:															
Kentucky	1,289,496	136,235	10.6	1,027,352	94,829	9.2	88,685	1,263	1.4	29,488	2,202	7.5	143,881	37,926	26.4
Tennessee	1,214,947	153,163	12.6	929,098	85,527	9.2	26,027	459	1.8	14,319	1,240	8.7	245,395	65,913	26.9
Alabama	1,143,395	228,565	20.0	666,083	55,004	8.3	19,843	379	1.9	16,105	1,825	11.3	441,130	171,283	38.8
Mississippi	876,106	182,135	20.8	402,249	17,574	4.4	12,080	290	2.4	7,380	982	13.4	453,663	162,881	35.9
WEST SOUTH CENTRAL:															
Arkansas	867,292	99,413	11.5	586,481	33,403	5.7	25,256	584	2.3	13,166	1,088	8.3	242,234	64,309	26.5
Louisiana	924,184	229,980	24.9	453,319	61,049	13.5	69,470	1,819	2.6	41,228	9,328	22.6	359,251	157,294	43.8
Oklahoma	1,021,588	48,076	4.7	821,069	24,096	2.9	63,676	834	1.3	36,108	4,854	13.4	76,331	12,491	16.4
Texas	2,430,715	233,894	9.6	1,563,012	38,629	2.5	214,540	16,093	7.5	266,718	88,806	33.3	384,428	89,775	23.4
MOUNTAIN:															
Montana	320,562	9,071	2.8	141,429	550	0.4	84,926	303	0.4	85,709	5,104	6.0	1,262	84	6.7
Idaho	234,076	4,510	1.9	138,149	545	0.4	55,669	220	0.4	36,170	2,377	6.6	699	41	5.9
Wyoming	115,739	2,940	2.5	66,343	269	0.4	23,282	77	0.3	23,057	2,120	9.2	1,065	65	6.1
Colorado	564,529	22,080	3.9	338,339	6,671	2.0	110,442	769	0.7	105,017	13,427	12.8	8,106	599	7.4
New Mexico	185,186	34,952	18.9	134,623	20,396	15.2	14,601	1,211	8.3	21,933	6,275	28.6	4,809	213	4.4
Arizona	187,929	30,636	16.3	82,841	1,197	1.4	25,815	1,159	4.5	55,973	16,057	28.7	6,559	316	4.8
Utah	228,682	5,679	2.5	86,833	410	0.5	84,542	309	0.4	52,254	3,413	6.5	1,104	55	5.0
Nevada	52,218	3,516	6.7	21,515	98	0.5	12,510	29	0.2	13,895	1,186	8.5	277	13	4.7
PACIFIC:															
Washington	857,079	17,777	2.1	406,544	1,394	0.3	195,544	575	0.3	230,435	11,494	5.0	5,208	241	4.6
Oregon	494,968	8,905	1.8	288,455	1,303	0.5	102,268	400	0.4	94,807	5,097	5.4	1,620	89	5.5
California	2,318,030	83,558	3.9	1,052,765	4,653	0.4	539,412	2,761	0.5	614,381	65,911	10.7	27,539	1,533	5.6

1156 POPULATION.

TABLE 7.—PER CENT ILLITERATE IN POPULATION 10 YEARS OF AGE AND OVER, BY SEX AND PRINCIPAL POPULATION CLASSES, BY DIVISIONS AND STATES: 1920, 1910, AND 1900.

PER CENT ILLITERATE IN POPULATION 10 YEARS OF AGE AND OVER.

Division and State	All classes — Both sexes 1920	1910	1900	Male 1920	1910	1900	Female 1920	1910	1900	Native white, native parentage 1920	1910	1900	Native white, foreign or mixed parentage 1920	1910	1900	Foreign-born white 1920	1910	1900	Negro 1920	1910	1900
United States	6.0	7.7	10.7	6.0	7.6	10.1	5.9	7.8	11.2	2.5	3.7	5.7	0.8	1.1	1.6	13.1	12.7	12.9	22.9	30.4	44.5
GEOGRAPHIC DIVISIONS:																					
New England	4.9	5.3	6.0	4.8	5.3	5.9	5.0	5.2	6.1	0.6	0.7	0.9	0.8	1.3	2.1	14.0	13.8	16.2	7.1	7.8	11.6
Middle Atlantic	4.9	5.7	5.8	4.7	5.6	5.6	5.1	5.7	6.0	0.7	1.2	2.0	0.5	0.8	1.2	15.7	15.8	15.8	5.0	7.9	14.2
East North Central	2.9	3.4	4.3	3.0	3.5	4.1	2.8	3.3	4.5	1.0	1.7	2.8	0.6	0.9	1.4	10.8	10.1	10.2	7.3	11.0	18.5
West North Central	2.0	2.9	4.1	2.0	2.9	3.7	1.9	2.9	4.4	1.1	1.7	2.9	0.5	0.7	1.1	7.6	7.6	8.0	10.5	14.9	25.4
South Atlantic	11.5	16.0	23.9	12.1	16.0	23.1	11.0	16.1	24.7	5.4	8.0	12.0	0.9	1.2	2.1	12.8	13.5	12.9	25.2	32.5	47.1
East South Central	12.7	17.4	24.9	13.8	17.4	24.1	12.0	17.3	25.8	6.6	9.6	13.6	1.5	1.7	2.6	9.1	9.7	10.4	27.9	34.8	49.2
West South Central	10.0	13.2	20.5	10.0	12.7	19.3	10.0	13.8	21.8	3.9	5.6	9.2	6.6	7.7	9.1	29.9	25.6	27.2	25.8	33.1	48.0
Mountain	5.2	6.9	9.6	4.7	6.3	8.2	5.7	7.5	11.6	2.4	3.6	7.1	1.0	1.2	1.9	12.7	12.5	10.6	5.3	8.0	13.5
Pacific	2.7	3.0	4.2	2.8	3.3	4.5	2.5	2.5	3.7	0.4	0.4	0.8	0.4	0.5	0.9	8.0	8.0	7.3	4.6	6.3	12.7
NEW ENGLAND:																					
Maine	3.3	4.1	5.1	3.9	4.9	5.9	2.5	3.2	4.3	1.3	1.4	1.7	2.9	4.5	6.7	11.1	13.7	19.4	5.9	8.0	14.2
New Hampshire	4.4	4.6	6.2	4.5	5.2	7.1	4.2	4.1	5.3	0.6	0.8	1.0	1.1	2.1	3.7	16.4	14.5	20.5	6.7	10.6	11.9
Vermont	3.0	3.7	5.8	3.6	4.4	6.7	2.4	3.1	4.9	1.1	1.2	1.8	2.8	4.0	6.8	11.3	13.1	21.4	6.2	4.8	14.6
Massachusetts	4.7	5.2	5.9	4.5	5.0	5.4	4.9	5.3	6.4	0.3	0.4	0.5	0.5	0.7	1.2	12.8	12.7	14.6	6.8	8.1	10.7
Rhode Island	6.5	7.7	8.4	6.0	7.4	8.1	7.0	8.0	8.8	0.5	0.7	1.0	0.9	1.8	2.8	16.5	17.8	18.7	10.2	9.5	14.1
Connecticut	6.2	6.0	5.9	5.8	5.7	5.7	6.6	6.3	6.0	0.4	0.5	0.6	0.4	0.8	0.9	17.0	15.4	16.3	6.2	6.3	11.5
MIDDLE ATLANTIC:																					
New York	5.1	5.5	5.5	4.5	5.0	5.0	5.6	5.9	6.0	0.6	0.8	1.3	0.5	0.7	1.1	14.2	13.7	14.0	2.9	5.0	10.8
New Jersey	5.1	5.6	5.9	4.9	5.5	5.8	5.3	5.7	5.9	0.7	1.1	2.1	0.4	0.7	1.0	15.3	14.7	14.1	6.1	9.9	17.2
Pennsylvania	4.6	5.9	6.1	4.7	6.4	6.3	4.5	5.4	5.9	0.8	1.4	2.5	0.6	1.1	1.6	18.9	20.1	19.9	6.1	9.1	15.1
EAST NORTH CENTRAL:																					
Ohio	2.8	3.2	4.0	3.0	3.5	3.8	2.6	3.0	4.2	1.0	1.7	2.8	0.6	0.9	1.4	12.6	11.5	11.1	8.1	11.1	17.8
Indiana	2.2	3.1	4.6	2.4	3.2	4.3	2.0	2.9	4.9	1.4	2.2	3.9	1.0	1.4	2.2	11.8	11.7	11.4	9.5	13.7	22.6
Illinois	3.4	3.7	4.2	3.3	3.7	3.9	3.4	3.8	4.6	1.1	1.7	2.9	0.4	0.6	0.9	11.0	10.1	9.1	6.7	10.5	18.1
Michigan	3.0	3.3	4.2	3.1	3.0	4.4	2.9	3.1	4.1	0.6	1.0	1.5	0.7	1.2	1.8	9.9	9.3	10.3	4.2	5.7	10.9
Wisconsin	2.4	3.2	4.7	2.5	3.1	4.2	2.4	3.2	5.3	0.5	0.6	1.0	0.8	1.0	1.5	8.4	8.7	11.1	4.1	4.5	11.4
WEST NORTH CENTRAL:																					
Minnesota	1.8	3.0	4.1	1.8	2.9	3.3	1.9	3.1	5.0	0.4	0.4	0.5	0.5	0.6	0.9	5.4	7.6	8.4	3.1	3.4	7.9
Iowa	1.1	1.7	2.3	1.2	1.7	2.1	1.0	1.7	2.6	0.5	0.9	1.4	0.4	0.6	0.8	4.9	6.8	7.1	8.1	10.8	18.5
Missouri	3.0	4.3	6.4	3.3	4.4	6.2	2.8	4.2	6.8	2.2	3.4	5.6	0.9	1.2	1.7	9.6	10.1	9.3	12.1	17.4	28.1
North Dakota	2.1	3.1	5.6	1.9	2.8	4.7	2.4	3.5	6.7	0.3	0.3	0.6	0.3	0.3	0.6	5.6	6.3	7.3	4.0	4.8	12.8
South Dakota	1.7	2.9	5.0	1.5	2.5	3.8	1.9	3.3	6.5	0.3	0.3	0.5	0.5	0.4	0.8	4.7	5.0	6.7	5.2	5.5	13.3
Nebraska	1.4	1.9	2.6	1.3	1.9	1.9	1.4	2.0	2.7	0.4	0.6	0.8	0.4	0.5	0.7	6.4	7.1	6.8	4.8	7.2	11.8
Kansas	1.6	2.2	2.9	1.7	2.3	2.6	1.6	2.1	3.2	0.6	0.8	1.3	0.5	0.8	1.0	10.5	10.5	8.5	8.8	12.0	22.3
SOUTH ATLANTIC:																					
Delaware	5.9	8.1	12.0	6.2	8.4	11.9	5.5	7.8	12.2	2.0	3.3	6.3	0.6	0.9	1.4	17.3	19.8	18.3	19.1	25.6	38.1
Maryland	5.6	7.2	11.1	5.7	7.2	10.8	5.4	7.1	11.4	2.0	3.0	4.7	0.9	1.0	1.9	13.4	11.9	13.4	18.2	23.4	35.1
District of Columbia	2.8	4.9	8.6	2.5	4.1	7.2	3.0	5.7	9.9	0.6	0.6	0.9	0.2	0.4	0.5	6.1	8.2	7.0	8.6	13.5	24.3
Virginia	11.2	15.2	22.9	12.1	15.7	23.2	10.2	14.6	22.5	6.1	8.2	11.4	1.0	1.2	2.1	7.1	9.2	10.9	23.5	30.0	44.6
West Virginia	6.4	8.3	11.4	7.2	8.8	11.3	5.6	7.7	11.6	4.8	6.7	10.4	1.5	2.0	3.2	14.0	9.8	10.8	15.3	20.3	32.8
North Carolina	13.1	18.5	28.7	13.7	18.2	27.4	12.5	18.7	29.9	8.2	12.3	19.6	3.0	5.1	6.8	24.0	23.9	21.5	24.5	31.9	47.0
South Carolina	18.1	25.7	35.9	18.8	25.0	34.3	17.9	26.3	37.5	6.6	10.5	13.9	1.9	3.0	5.1	6.8	8.3	6.1	29.3	38.7	52.8
Georgia	15.3	20.7	30.5	16.2	20.9	29.6	14.4	20.5	31.3	5.5	8.0	12.2	1.1	1.6	2.5	6.2	6.8	6.5	29.3	38.7	52.8
Florida	9.6	13.8	21.9	9.6	13.2	20.4	9.5	14.4	23.5	3.1	5.2	9.0	1.1	2.2	3.6	6.3	10.5	11.6	21.5	25.5	38.4
EAST SOUTH CENTRAL:																					
Kentucky	8.4	12.1	16.5	9.3	12.6	16.3	7.6	11.6	16.7	7.3	10.7	13.9	1.3	1.5	2.1	7.3	8.3	10.9	21.0	27.6	40.1
Tennessee	10.3	13.6	20.7	11.2	13.8	20.1	9.5	13.4	21.4	7.4	9.9	14.5	1.5	1.8	3.2	8.3	8.3	9.7	22.4	27.3	41.6
Alabama	16.1	22.9	34.0	16.4	22.5	32.6	15.8	23.3	35.4	6.4	10.1	15.2	1.7	2.3	3.5	10.9	11.3	9.3	31.3	40.1	57.4
Mississippi	17.2	22.4	32.0	18.1	22.4	30.9	16.3	22.5	33.1	3.6	5.3	8.1	2.3	2.2	3.8	13.3	15.1	10.7	29.8	35.6	49.1
WEST SOUTH CENTRAL:																					
Arkansas	9.4	12.6	20.4	9.6	12.1	18.9	9.1	13.1	22.1	4.6	7.1	11.8	2.0	2.8	4.9	8.3	8.9	8.0	21.8	26.4	43.0
Louisiana	21.9	29.0	38.5	21.6	28.0	36.9	22.2	30.1	40.1	11.4	15.0	20.4	3.5	3.6	3.8	21.9	24.0	28.6	38.5	48.4	61.1
Oklahoma [1]	3.8	5.6	12.1	4.1	5.5	11.6	3.4	5.8	12.7	2.4	3.5	8.1	1.2	1.3	3.1	14.0	9.8	10.8	12.4	17.7	37.0
Texas	8.3	9.9	14.5	8.5	9.8	13.9	8.2	10.1	15.2	2.2	3.3	5.1	9.4	11.6	13.2	33.8	30.0	30.3	17.8	24.6	38.2
MOUNTAIN:																					
Montana	2.3	4.8	6.1	2.3	5.2	5.6	2.3	4.0	7.1	0.3	0.3	0.6	0.8	0.4	0.8	5.6	9.4	7.0	6.0	7.0	11.4
Idaho	1.5	2.2	4.6	1.7	2.6	4.5	1.3	1.6	4.7	0.3	0.4	0.8	0.3	0.4	0.8	6.5	6.9	6.0	5.4	6.4	14.5
Wyoming	2.1	3.3	4.0	2.5	3.7	3.9	1.5	2.5	4.2	0.4	0.3	0.7	0.8	0.4	0.5	9.0	9.7	8.2	5.3	5.0	17.2
Colorado	3.2	3.7	4.2	2.9	3.6	3.7	3.6	3.8	4.8	1.7	2.0	3.3	0.6	0.9	0.9	12.4	11.3	8.1	6.2	8.6	13.0
New Mexico	15.6	20.2	33.2	12.7	15.9	25.7	18.9	25.4	42.2	11.9	15.5	30.8	8.2	8.9	16.8	27.1	31.0	34.8	4.3	14.2	19.1
Arizona	15.3	20.9	29.0	13.9	19.2	25.3	17.1	23.5	34.8	1.9	2.3	3.8	4.6	8.4	10.9	27.5	31.5	35.3	4.6	7.2	12.7
Utah	1.9	2.5	3.1	2.1	2.7	2.8	1.6	2.2	3.5	0.3	0.4	1.1	0.3	0.4	0.6	6.3	5.9	6.1	4.0	4.8	6.3
Nevada	5.9	6.7	13.3	5.8	6.1	12.1	6.2	8.0	15.2	0.4	0.4	0.7	0.2	0.5	0.6	8.5	7.6	7.5	5.1	5.5	23.0
PACIFIC:																					
Washington	1.7	2.0	3.1	1.7	2.1	3.0	1.6	1.8	3.4	0.3	0.3	0.5	0.3	0.3	0.5	4.7	4.8	4.5	4.0	4.3	11.6
Oregon	1.5	1.9	3.3	1.6	2.2	3.3	1.3	1.4	2.3	0.4	0.4	0.9	0.4	0.4	0.7	5.1	6.1	4.1	4.7	3.4	8.8
California	3.3	3.7	4.8	3.5	4.2	5.3	3.1	3.1	4.2	0.4	0.5	1.0	0.5	0.6	1.0	10.5	10.0	8.7	4.7	7.1	13.4

[1] Includes Indian Territory for 1900.

ILLITERACY.

TABLE 8.—PER CENT ILLITERATE IN POPULATION 21 YEARS OF AGE AND OVER, BY SEX AND PRINCIPAL POPULATION CLASSES, BY DIVISIONS AND STATES: 1920, 1910, AND 1900.

DIVISION AND STATE	Both sexes			Male			Female			Native parentage			Foreign or mixed parentage			Foreign-born white			Negro		
	1920	1910	1900	1920	1910	1900	1920	1910	1900	1920	1910	1900	1920	1910	1900	1920	1910	1900	1920	1910	1900
United States	7.1	8.9	12.0	7.0	8.4	10.8	7.3	9.4	13.2	3.0	4.3	6.4	0.9	1.3	2.0	13.7	12.9	13.3	27.4	35.7	51.7
GEOGRAPHIC DIVISIONS:																					
New England	6.1	6.3	7.1	6.0	6.3	6.9	6.2	6.3	7.2	0.6	0.8	1.0	1.1	1.8	2.7	14.8	14.3	17.0	8.5	9.4	13.9
Middle Atlantic	6.3	6.9	7.1	5.9	6.8	6.8	6.6	7.0	7.4	0.9	1.5	2.6	0.6	1.1	1.6	16.7	16.4	16.3	6.0	9.4	17.1
East North Central	3.7	4.3	5.6	3.7	4.3	5.1	3.6	4.2	6.0	1.3	2.2	3.7	0.8	1.2	1.9	11.4	10.3	10.8	8.7	13.6	23.5
West North Central	2.5	3.7	5.3	2.5	3.5	4.5	2.5	3.9	6.2	1.4	2.2	3.5	0.6	0.9	1.4	6.5	7.5	8.4	12.5	18.3	32.6
South Atlantic	14.0	18.6	26.9	14.0	17.6	24.5	13.9	19.6	29.3	6.6	9.3	13.4	1.1	1.4	2.5	13.5	13.6	13.1	31.5	39.1	55.4
East South Central	15.5	20.4	28.5	15.7	19.4	26.0	15.2	21.4	31.1	8.4	11.3	15.5	1.6	1.9	3.1	9.3	9.4	10.6	34.1	41.4	57.9
West South Central	11.7	15.0	23.0	11.3	13.7	20.3	12.1	16.5	26.1	4.6	6.4	9.7	5.2	6.4	7.6	29.1	24.4	26.3	30.5	38.5	55.2
Mountain	6.0	7.7	10.8	5.4	6.9	8.9	6.8	8.9	13.8	3.0	4.3	8.1	1.0	1.3	2.1	12.7	12.2	10.6	5.8	9.1	15.8
Pacific	3.2	3.4	5.1	3.3	3.7	5.3	3.0	3.1	4.7	0.4	0.5	1.0	0.4	0.6	1.1	8.8	7.9	7.4	5.4	7.3	15.4
NEW ENGLAND:																					
Maine	3.9	4.7	5.7	4.7	5.5	6.4	3.1	3.8	4.9	1.3	1.5	1.7	4.1	6.3	8.1	12.0	14.5	20.5	6.8	10.3	17.1
New Hampshire	5.4	5.5	6.9	5.6	6.2	7.9	5.2	4.8	6.0	0.6	0.9	1.1	1.6	3.1	4.8	16.4	15.4	21.8	7.7	13.3	12.8
Vermont	3.8	4.6	7.0	4.5	5.3	7.9	3.0	3.8	6.1	1.3	1.5	2.0	3.8	5.3	8.8	12.5	14.1	23.0	8.2	5.0	18.8
Massachusetts	5.9	6.2	7.0	5.7	6.1	6.4	6.1	6.3	7.6	0.3	0.4	0.5	0.6	1.0	1.6	13.5	13.1	15.5	6.2	7.2	12.7
Rhode Island	8.2	9.2	9.8	7.6	8.8	9.2	8.8	9.6	10.5	0.6	0.9	1.2	1.3	2.4	3.5	17.5	18.1	19.7	12.5	11.4	17.3
Connecticut	7.8	7.2	7.0	7.4	6.8	6.8	8.4	7.5	7.2	0.4	0.6	0.3	0.6	1.1	1.2	18.1	16.0	17.0	7.5	7.8	14.1
MIDDLE ATLANTIC:																					
New York	6.4	6.6	6.6	5.7	6.0	5.9	7.1	7.2	7.2	0.7	1.1	1.6	0.6	0.9	1.4	15.2	14.3	14.5	3.4	5.8	12.9
New Jersey	6.6	6.7	7.1	6.3	6.6	6.9	6.9	6.8	7.2	0.9	1.4	2.6	0.5	0.8	1.2	16.3	14.8	14.5	7.5	11.9	20.5
Pennsylvania	6.0	7.3	7.7	6.2	7.8	7.7	5.9	6.8	7.6	1.0	1.8	3.3	0.8	1.4	2.0	20.1	20.8	20.5	7.3	11.0	18.4
EAST NORTH CENTRAL:																					
Ohio	3.6	4.0	5.2	3.8	4.2	4.8	3.3	3.8	5.5	1.2	2.2	3.7	0.7	1.1	1.9	13.4	11.8	11.6	9.7	13.9	23.1
Indiana	2.8	3.9	6.1	3.0	4.1	5.6	2.6	3.8	6.6	1.8	3.0	5.2	1.1	1.7	2.8	12.4	11.8	11.9	11.7	17.5	29.7
Illinois	4.3	4.7	5.4	4.1	4.6	4.8	4.4	4.8	6.1	1.4	2.2	3.7	0.5	0.8	1.3	11.7	10.3	9.6	7.9	12.4	22.1
Michigan	3.9	4.2	5.4	3.9	4.4	5.5	3.8	4.0	5.4	0.8	1.3	1.9	0.9	1.6	2.4	10.5	9.6	11.0	4.9	6.9	13.9
Wisconsin	3.2	4.2	6.3	3.2	4.0	5.5	3.2	4.4	7.3	0.6	0.9	1.3	1.0	1.3	2.0	8.8	8.9	11.8	4.8	5.3	14.0
WEST NORTH CENTRAL:																					
Minnesota	2.4	4.0	5.4	2.2	3.7	4.1	2.6	4.4	7.0	0.4	0.5	0.7	0.6	0.9	1.3	5.6	7.7	9.0	3.5	3.9	9.2
Iowa	1.4	2.2	3.1	1.4	2.1	2.7	1.3	2.2	3.6	0.7	1.2	1.8	0.5	0.8	1.1	5.0	6.3	7.5	9.9	12.8	23.8
Missouri	3.8	5.4	7.9	4.0	5.3	7.0	3.6	5.5	8.7	2.8	4.3	6.7	1.0	1.4	2.2	10.0	10.2	9.6	14.3	21.1	35.5
North Dakota	2.9	3.7	6.8	2.5	3.1	5.4	3.5	4.5	8.9	0.3	0.4	0.7	0.6	0.6	1.0	5.9	6.2	8.0	4.8	5.3	17.5
South Dakota	2.2	3.7	6.9	1.9	3.1	5.0	2.6	4.6	9.3	0.4	0.4	0.6	0.5	0.5	1.0	4.9	5.0	7.0	6.7	8.5	17.3
Nebraska	1.8	2.5	3.1	1.7	2.4	2.5	1.9	2.7	3.8	0.5	0.8	1.1	0.4	0.7	0.9	6.6	7.1	7.2	5.7	8.5	15.0
Kansas	2.0	2.8	3.9	2.1	2.9	3.4	2.0	2.8	4.5	0.7	1.1	1.8	0.6	1.0	1.4	10.2	10.3	8.8	11.2	15.9	31.2
SOUTH ATLANTIC:																					
Delaware	7.4	10.0	14.5	7.7	10.1	14.0	7.0	9.8	15.1	2.6	4.2	7.9	0.7	1.0	1.8	18.2	19.7	18.7	24.6	32.9	46.8
Maryland	6.8	8.7	13.3	6.9	8.5	12.5	6.7	8.9	14.1	2.5	3.7	5.8	1.1	1.1	2.3	14.3	12.3	13.8	22.2	28.6	43.1
District of Columbia	3.3	6.0	10.4	3.0	4.9	8.4	3.6	7.0	12.2	0.3	0.7	1.1	0.2	0.5	0.6	6.4	8.3	7.1	10.7	16.8	30.3
Virginia	13.5	17.9	26.4	14.1	17.7	25.3	12.7	18.0	27.4	7.1	9.4	12.5	1.1	1.5	2.1	7.5	9.3	11.0	29.3	37.1	54.6
West Virginia	8.2	10.2	13.9	8.9	10.4	12.9	7.3	10.0	14.9	6.1	8.4	12.7	1.7	2.3	3.8	25.4	23.9	21.4	32.4	40.4	57.5
North Carolina	16.9	22.6	32.8	17.0	21.3	29.4	16.8	24.0	36.2	10.7	15.0	21.7	2.4	4.0	5.6	7.0	8.1	6.1	38.7	46.9	60.7
South Carolina	23.0	29.6	39.3	22.3	27.1	35.1	23.8	32.0	43.4	8.5	11.4	14.0	1.2	1.4	1.8	6.5	6.5	6.3	35.8	43.8	61.1
Georgia	18.4	24.1	34.6	18.4	22.8	31.6	18.4	25.5	37.5	6.7	9.2	13.5	1.3	1.8	2.9	5.9	5.9	7.3	36.5	45.1	61.1
Florida	10.9	15.5	25.3	10.6	14.0	22.1	11.3	17.3	29.2	3.7	5.7	10.3	1.1	1.9	3.8	6.6	10.5	11.3	24.8	28.8	45.2
EAST SOUTH CENTRAL:																					
Kentucky	10.6	14.5	20.0	11.3	14.5	18.8	9.8	14.6	21.2	9.2	12.8	16.6	1.4	1.7	2.6	7.5	8.2	11.2	26.4	34.7	50.9
Tennessee	12.6	16.3	24.0	13.2	15.7	21.7	12.0	17.0	26.3	9.2	11.9	16.4	1.8	2.1	3.7	8.7	8.2	9.6	26.9	33.3	50.5
Alabama	20.0	26.2	37.4	19.5	24.3	33.7	20.5	28.2	41.1	8.3	11.5	16.1	1.9	2.7	4.0	11.3	11.1	9.2	38.8	46.4	64.7
Mississippi	20.8	26.8	37.2	20.9	25.3	33.8	20.7	28.4	40.6	4.4	6.2	8.9	2.4	2.3	4.0	13.4	13.6	10.6	35.9	43.2	58.2
WEST SOUTH CENTRAL:																					
Arkansas	11.5	15.1	23.5	11.1	13.5	20.0	11.8	16.9	27.5	5.7	8.5	13.1	2.3	3.2	5.3	8.3	8.2	8.1	26.5	32.0	51.1
Louisiana	24.9	31.1	40.9	23.6	28.6	37.6	26.2	33.7	44.3	13.5	16.8	21.8	2.6	2.7	3.6	22.6	23.2	26.8	43.8	52.2	66.5
Oklahoma [1]	4.7	6.9	12.2	4.9	6.4	10.6	4.5	7.6	14.3	2.9	4.2	7.1	1.3	1.6	3.1	13.4	9.7	11.0	16.4	22.7	42.6
Texas	9.6	11.6	17.3	9.6	10.9	15.4	9.7	12.4	19.4	2.5	3.7	5.7	7.5	10.0	11.4	33.3	28.8	29.6	23.4	31.4	49.3
MOUNTAIN:																					
Montana	2.8	5.5	7.0	2.7	5.7	6.1	2.9	5.1	8.8	0.4	0.4	0.7	0.4	0.5	0.9	6.0	9.2	7.1	6.7	8.0	12.6
Idaho	1.9	2.7	5.8	2.1	3.1	5.4	1.6	2.2	6.5	0.4	0.4	1.3	0.4	0.4	0.9	6.6	6.6	6.2	5.9	6.8	17.6
Wyoming	2.5	3.8	4.7	2.9	4.1	4.3	1.9	3.2	5.5	0.4	0.4	0.9	0.3	0.3	0.6	9.2	9.5	8.3	6.1	5.3	20.6
Colorado	3.9	4.4	4.8	3.5	4.2	4.1	4.4	4.7	5.7	2.0	2.4	3.7	0.7	0.6	1.1	12.8	11.3	8.2	7.4	10.0	15.9
New Mexico	18.9	23.4	38.1	14.7	17.6	28.3	24.1	30.8	50.5	15.2	18.8	36.2	8.3	9.0	18.3	28.6	31.2	35.1	4.4	15.9	21.5
Arizona	16.3	21.9	30.4	14.5	19.5	25.4	18.8	25.8	39.1	1.4	2.4	4.0	4.5	7.9	9.4	28.7	31.4	35.3	4.8	8.4	13.4
Utah	2.5	3.1	4.3	2.8	3.3	3.7	2.2	2.9	5.0	0.5	0.7	1.7	0.4	0.4	0.8	6.5	5.9	6.4	5.0	5.3	7.6
Nevada	6.7	6.8	14.4	6.4	6.0	12.8	7.3	8.7	17.3	0.5	0.3	0.8	0.2	0.5	0.7	8.5	7.0	7.3	4.7	6.0	25.0
PACIFIC:																					
Washington	2.1	2.3	3.8	2.1	2.4	3.4	2.1	2.2	4.5	0.3	0.3	0.6	0.3	0.3	0.6	5.0	4.7	4.7	4.6	4.8	13.6
Oregon	1.8	2.2	4.2	2.0	2.5	4.8	1.6	1.8	3.2	0.5	0.5	1.2	0.4	0.5	1.0	5.4	5.9	4.4	5.5	3.7	9.7
California	3.9	4.3	5.7	4.0	4.6	6.2	3.0	3.7	5.2	0.4	0.6	1.2	0.5	0.7	1.2	10.7	9.8	8.8	5.6	8.4	16.6

[1] Includes Indian Territory for 1900.

POPULATION.

1158

TABLE 9.—NUMBER AND PER CENT ILLITERATE IN POPULATION 10 TO 15 YEARS OF AGE, INCLUSIVE, FOR PRINCIPAL POPULATION CLASSES, 1920, WITH COMPARATIVE PERCENTAGES FOR 1910, BY DIVISIONS AND STATES.

[Per cent not shown where base is less than 100.]

	POPULATION 10 TO 15 YEARS OF AGE, INCLUSIVE.																				
DIVISION AND STATE.	All classes.				Native white.								Foreign-born white.				Negro.			
					Native parentage.				Foreign or mixed parentage.											
	Total number: 1920	Illiterate.			Total number: 1920	Illiterate.			Total number: 1920	Illiterate.			Total number: 1920	Illiterate.			Total number: 1920	Illiterate.		
		Number: 1920	Per cent. 1920	1910		Number: 1920	Per cent. 1920	1910		Number: 1920	Per cent. 1920	1910		Number: 1920	Per cent. 1920	1910		Number: 1920	Per cent. 1920	1910
United States	12,502,582	292,467	2.3	4.1	7,576,827	85,485	1.1	2.2	3,020,339	16,632	0.6	0.8	413,261	18,183	4.4	4.2	1,450,996	166,416	11.5	18.9
GEOGRAPHIC DIVISIONS:																				
New England	768,131	2,472	0.3	0.5	292,555	1,012	0.3	0.3	412,544	914	0.2	0.3	55,801	515	0.9	2.4	6,953	30	0.4	0.3
Middle Atlantic	2,397,736	6,448	0.3	0.5	1,138,793	2,566	0.2	0.2	1,062,587	2,140	0.2	0.3	145,600	1,466	1.0	2.8	49,600	252	0.5	1.1
East North Central	2,312,711	5,587	0.2	0.3	1,473,221	3,398	0.2	0.3	707,208	1,404	0.2	0.3	87,700	538	0.6	1.6	42,444	196	0.5	1.2
West North Central	1,477,863	5,682	0.4	0.6	1,010,792	3,207	0.3	0.5	407,567	944	0.2	0.3	27,516	663	2.2	3.0	26,579	654	2.5	3.6
South Atlantic	1,911,574	97,032	5.1	10.0	1,192,583	26,147	2.2	5.0	64,639	289	0.4	0.8	9,308	147	1.6	5.9	642,881	70,112	10.9	19.0
East South Central	1,267,275	77,670	6.1	10.6	878,541	23,508	2.7	5.7	16,401	130	0.8	0.9	1,637	51	3.1	11.3	375,323	53,830	14.3	20.6
West South Central	1,449,764	86,336	6.0	9.3	1,018,056	23,037	2.3	4.0	89,955	9,527	10.6	11.0	34,367	11,724	34.1	34.8	301,663	41,288	13.7	22.2
Mountain	393,503	8,932	2.3	3.5	265,942	2,032	0.8	1.7	94,354	856	0.9	1.1	20,110	2,145	10.7	8.8	1,790	24	1.3	1.3
Pacific	524,465	2,328	0.4	0.5	315,744	583	0.2	0.1	165,094	422	0.3	0.3	31,132	994	3.2	3.0	3,763	21	0.6	0.7
NEW ENGLAND:																				
Maine	82,829	628	0.8	1.0	52,396	432	0.8	0.7	26,101	147	0.6	1.0	4,041	47	1.2	3.8	111	1	0.9	0.7
New Hampshire	45,691	131	0.3	0.5	22,218	66	0.3	0.2	20,390	39	0.2	0.4	3,014	25	0.8	2.4	67	1		
Vermont	38,579	109	0.3	0.3	26,415	67	0.3	0.3	9,876	39	0.3	0.4	2,218	12	0.5	1.9	60			
Massachusetts	394,026	977	0.2	0.3	127,038	221	0.2	0.1	232,962	482	0.2	0.2	30,029	255	0.8	1.9	3,867	19	0.5	0.4
Rhode Island	63,739	204	0.3	0.9	18,343	31	0.2	0.2	39,006	93	0.2	0.5	5,480	76	1.4	4.1	886	4	0.5	0.3
Connecticut	143,267	423	0.3	0.4	46,145	195	0.4	0.1	84,119	123	0.1	0.2	11,019	100	0.9	2.2	1,956	5	0.3	0.1
MIDDLE ATLANTIC:																				
New York	1,059,635	2,530	0.2	0.4	415,040	778	0.2	0.2	545,727	972	0.2	0.2	84,201	718	0.9	2.1	13,640	50	0.4	0.5
New Jersey	341,185	911	0.3	0.6	140,560	283	0.2	0.3	166,920	300	0.2	0.4	22,427	260	1.2	3.5	11,242	58	0.5	1.4
Pennsylvania	996,916	3,007	0.3	0.6	583,193	1,505	0.3	0.3	349,940	868	0.2	0.4	38,972	488	1.3	4.0	24,718	144	0.6	1.2
EAST NORTH CENTRAL:																				
Ohio	596,741	1,621	0.3	0.3	429,175	1,155	0.3	0.3	131,991	269	0.2	0.2	19,718	122	0.6	1.7	15,820	75	0.5	1.0
Indiana	323,979	748	0.2	0.3	280,625	620	0.2	0.3	31,902	69	0.2	0.2	3,842	19	0.5	2.0	7,509	35	0.5	0.8
Illinois	699,310	1,657	0.2	0.4	393,723	923	0.2	0.4	258,445	425	0.2	0.2	32,265	232	0.7	1.7	14,775	77	0.5	1.8
Michigan	384,213	811	0.2	0.3	203,592	340	0.2	0.2	153,016	325	0.2	0.3	22,117	110	0.5	1.2	3,802	8	0.2	0.5
Wisconsin	308,468	755	0.2	0.3	166,106	355	0.2	0.2	130,864	316	0.2	0.3	9,758	55	0.6	1.7	439	1	0.2	0.9
WEST NORTH CENTRAL:																				
Minnesota	277,528	814	0.3	0.3	123,089	315	0.3	0.1	144,678	358	0.2	0.2	8,034	42	0.5	1.3	569	1	0.2	0.2
Iowa	270,217	518	0.2	0.3	202,391	330	0.2	0.2	61,903	137	0.2	0.2	4,081	42	1.0	2.0	1,784	9	0.5	1.4
Missouri	395,682	2,738	0.7	1.2	334,177	1,949	0.6	1.1	40,381	84	0.2	0.3	4,221	96	2.3	2.7	16,899	609	3.6	5.2
North Dakota	87,883	246	0.3	1.2	31,205	42	0.1	0.1	52,260	120	0.2	0.7	3,444	19	0.6	6.1	46			
South Dakota	78,427	250	0.3	0.6	44,003	75	0.2	0.2	30,824	81	0.3	0.2	1,534	15	1.0	2.5	95			
Nebraska	155,920	319	0.2	0.3	104,672	165	0.2	0.2	40,594	84	0.2	0.2	3,240	58	1.8	2.1	1,025	3	0.3	0.4
Kansas	211,706	777	0.4	0.3	171,255	331	0.2	0.2	30,918	80	0.3	0.2	2,072	331	11.1	4.3	6,191	32	0.5	0.6
SOUTH ATLANTIC:																				
Delaware	23,809	125	0.5	1.6	15,434	41	0.3	0.4	4,278	10	0.2	0.4	513	6	1.2	3.7	3,584	68	1.9	6.4
Maryland	184,846	2,444	1.5	2.6	107,595	558	0.5	1.0	24,739	60	0.2	0.5	2,703	21	0.9	2.7	29,499	1,802	6.1	9.6
District of Columbia	35,230	78	0.2	0.4	19,920	16	0.1	0.1	4,700	6	0.1	0.2	657	4	0.6	1.1	9,927	52	0.5	1.0
Virginia	311,915	16,976	5.4	9.2	206,223	7,010	3.4	5.6	6,281	50	0.8	0.6	949	18	1.9	4.8	98,338	9,897	10.0	16.0
West Virginia	191,299	3,505	1.8	2.7	169,967	3,161	1.9	2.5	10,051	78	0.8	0.7	2,281	61	2.7	10.6	8,996	206	2.3	6.7
North Carolina	373,484	15,711	4.2	10.1	251,333	5,645	2.2	6.8	1,302	10	0.7	0.5	191	4	2.1	2.2	118,749	9,830	8.3	16.6
South Carolina	260,204	15,909	6.1	17.2	114,910	1,999	1.7	8.4	1,167	2	0.2	1.8	150	2	1.3	7.3	143,919	13,884	9.6	23.4
Georgia	427,235	35,263	8.3	13.6	236,959	6,531	2.8	5.6	3,225	8	0.2	0.9	424	6	1.4	5.0	186,602	28,713	15.4	22.3
Florida	123,852	7,020	5.7	10.0	70,242	1,186	1.7	4.7	8,727	65	0.7	3.2	1,530	22	1.4	11.7	43,267	5,690	13.2	17.5
EAST SOUTH CENTRAL:																				
Kentucky	318,408	8,767	2.8	6.0	284,337	7,617	2.7	5.9	6,465	21	0.3	0.4	466	13	2.8	3.0	27,129	1,116	4.1	8.6
Tennessee	323,548	16,482	5.1	7.4	258,066	8,356	3.2	5.6	3,985	13	0.4	1.0	309	4	1.0	5.2	61,593	8,109	13.2	15.0
Alabama	349,537	26,649	7.6	16.2	206,198	4,981	2.4	7.5	4,494	47	1.0	1.5	537	15	2.8	10.0	138,384	21,590	15.6	27.4
Mississippi	275,782	25,772	9.3	12.9	125,080	2,554	2.0	3.4	2,047	49	2.4	1.0	325	19	8.1	30.7	148,217	23,024	15.5	19.5
WEST SOUTH CENTRAL:																				
Arkansas	259,503	13,463	5.2	7.9	184,919	4,459	2.4	4.5	4,374	38	0.9	1.8	248	10	4.0	23.3	70,036	8,954	12.8	16.3
Louisiana	258,052	36,266	14.1	24.5	141,649	8,925	6.3	11.5	12,336	763	6.2	8.2	1,618	104	9.9	32.7	102,821	26,355	25.6	40.8
Oklahoma	289,533	5,232	1.8	2.4	245,332	3,309	1.3	1.6	11,520	109	0.9	0.7	1,066	184	17.3	5.7	22,005	1,063	4.8	6.1
Texas	642,586	31,375	4.9	6.2	441,756	6,344	1.4	2.6	61,725	8,617	14.0	14.5	32,005	11,426	35.7	37.4	106,801	4,916	4.6	10.8
MOUNTAIN:																				
Montana	60,045	228	0.4	1.3	33,635	69	0.2	0.1	21,790	57	0.3	0.2	3,066	23	0.8	3.0	100	2	1.9	
Idaho	54,641	197	0.4	0.4	42,286	63	0.1	0.2	10,913	21	0.2	0.1	948	7	0.7	3.1	57	1		
Wyoming	20,387	58	0.3	0.5	14,418	22	0.2	0.3	4,939	9	0.2	0.4	796	20	2.5	2.5	73			
Colorado	104,790	854	0.8	0.9	72,707	381	0.5	0.8	26,604	97	0.4	0.3	4,270	289	6.8	4.5	948	10	1.1	0.9
New Mexico	48,032	2,820	5.9	11.3	38,165	1,328	3.5	7.1	4,170	272	6.5	8.5	2,308	308	13.5	24.1	194	5	2.0	6.3
Arizona	38,278	4,394	11.5	15.3	18,298	96	0.5	0.5	7,920	348	4.4	7.3	6,844	1,305	19.0	21.5	312	2	0.6	1.3
Utah	60,675	272	0.4	0.7	42,445	61	0.1	0.1	16,105	45	0.3	0.2	1,545	22	1.4	1.5	86	2		
Nevada	6,715	109	1.6	4.4	3,988	12	0.3	0.5	1,817	7	0.4	0.2	273	16	5.9	2.5	14	2		
PACIFIC:																				
Washington	138,645	293	0.2	0.4	82,939	122	0.1	0.1	46,974	80	0.2	0.2	6,507	24	0.4	0.9	459	1	0.2	0.3
Oregon	81,500	189	0.2	0.2	58,485	121	0.2	0.1	19,242	36	0.2	0.1	2,607	14	0.5	1.3	150			
California	304,320	1,846	0.6	0.7	174,320	340	0.2	0.2	98,878	306	0.3	0.3	22,018	956	4.3	4.3	3,154	20	0.6	0.8

ILLITERACY.

1159

TABLE 10.—NUMBER AND PER CENT ILLITERATE IN POPULATION 16 TO 20 YEARS OF AGE, INCLUSIVE, FOR PRINCIPAL POPULATION CLASSES, 1920, WITH COMPARATIVE PERCENTAGES FOR 1910, BY DIVISIONS AND STATES.

[Per cent not shown where base is less than 100.]

DIVISION AND STATE.	POPULATION 16 TO 20 YEARS OF AGE, INCLUSIVE.																				
	All classes.			Native white.									Foreign-born white.				Negro.				
				Native parentage.				Foreign or mixed parentage.													
	Total number: 1920	Illiterate.		Total number: 1920	Illiterate.			Total number: 1920	Illiterate.			Total number: 1920	Illiterate.			Total number: 1920	Illiterate.			
		Number: 1920	Per cent.		Number: 1920	Per cent.			Number: 1920	Per cent.			Number: 1920	Per cent.			Number: 1920	Per cent.		
			1920	1910			1920	1910			1920	1910			1920	1910			1920	1910	
United States..........	9,350,213	306,327	3.3	5.5	5,493,480	86,079	1.6	2.5	2,156,476	13,707	0.6	0.9	585,905	38,412	6.6	14.6	1,079,754	162,758	15.1	21.3
GEOGRAPHIC DIVISIONS:																				
New England.........	586,381	6,402	1.1	3.7	218,766	1,115	0.5	0.6	279,341	1,040	0.4	0.8	81,936	4,108	5.0	13.3	6,003	111	1.8	3.4
Middle Atlantic........	1,816,962	15,352	0.8	3.8	859,951	2,915	0.3	0.5	676,874	2,238	0.3	0.7	229,904	9,317	4.1	16.0	48,990	804	1.6	2.8
East North Central.....	1,792,480	9,645	0.5	1.5	1,101,564	4,028	0.4	0.6	530,350	1,626	0.3	0.5	117,515	3,129	2.7	10.7	41,344	772	1.9	2.4
West North Central.....	1,133,829	6,943	0.6	1.2	721,401	3,501	0.5	0.7	346,600	1,012	0.3	0.4	39,013	1,559	4.0	9.6	22,833	683	3.0	4.5
South Atlantic.........	1,389,350	109,146	7.9	11.5	858,609	29,165	3.4	5.4	47,590	316	0.7	1.0	14,772	825	5.6	16.9	466,861	78,495	16.8	22.5
East South Central.....	886,010	67,691	7.6	12.1	604,389	22,583	3.7	6.6	13,758	105	0.8	0.9	2,332	157	6.7	15.8	265,322	44,741	16.9	23.7
West South Central.....	1,045,993	75,938	7.3	10.0	709,214	19,194	2.7	4.3	68,764	6,164	9.0	9.7	38,466	12,925	33.6	33.5	228,113	37,076	16.6	23.6
Mountain.............	281,979	10,343	3.7	5.5	179,988	2,995	1.7	2.5	69,203	764	1.1	1.4	22,186	3,318	15.0	19.7	2,070	47	2.3	3.6
Pacific..............	417,229	4,867	1.2	2.1	239,598	583	0.2	0.3	123,996	442	0.4	0.5	39,781	3,074	7.7	13.1	3,218	29	0.9	2.5
NEW ENGLAND:																				
Maine...............	63,213	1,040	1.6	3.3	38,489	518	1.3	1.6	18,330	257	1.4	3.6	6,215	255	4.1	10.9	104	3	2.9	1.4
New Hampshire.......	35,213	400	1.1	3.4	16,113	60	0.4	0.4	14,642	53	0.4	1.4	4,409	284	6.4	11.8	35	2		
Vermont.............	28,851	227	0.8	1.7	19,662	122	0.6	0.7	6,891	52	0.8	1.7	2,251	53	2.4	7.4	46			0.9
Massachusetts........	301,236	2,880	1.0	3.6	93,672	236	0.3	0.3	159,421	442	0.3	0.4	44,630	2,135	4.8	12.7	3,324	55	1.7	4.3
Rhode Island.........	51,412	789	1.5	5.4	14,869	30	0.2	0.3	27,091	129	0.5	1.4	8,686	613	7.1	16.7	752	15	2.0	4.2
Connecticut..........	106,456	1,066	1.0	4.2	35,961	149	0.4	0.3	52,966	107	0.2	0.5	15,745	768	4.9	15.4	1,742	36	2.1	1.4
MIDDLE ATLANTIC:																				
New York............	828,470	7,133	0.9	3.9	320,246	875	0.3	0.4	352,770	1,014	0.3	0.5	139,357	5,023	3.6	13.6	15,119	167	1.1	1.8
New Jersey...........	255,177	2,392	0.9	4.4	106,829	441	0.4	0.5	106,339	308	0.3	0.7	32,150	1,442	4.5	18.3	9,788	184	1.9	4.1
Pennsylvania.........	733,315	5,827	0.8	3.5	432,876	1,599	0.4	0.5	217,765	916	0.4	1.0	58,397	2,852	4.9	20.2	24,083	453	1.9	2.9
EAST NORTH CENTRAL:																				
Ohio................	469,234	2,740	0.6	1.5	334,776	1,280	0.4	0.6	91,557	278	0.3	0.3	27,683	850	3.1	12.6	15,143	324	2.1	2.3
Indiana.............	252,415	1,144	0.5	1.0	215,994	816	0.4	0.6	24,456	76	0.3	0.4	5,024	143	2.8	13.6	6,917	105	1.5	1.7
Illinois.............	541,436	3,203	0.6	1.9	291,780	1,152	0.4	0.7	190,700	498	0.3	0.3	44,786	1,290	2.9	11.2	13,980	253	1.8	3.2
Michigan............	295,957	1,022	0.5	1.4	147,740	442	0.3	0.5	114,820	302	0.3	0.7	27,951	666	2.4	8.0	4,894	84	1.7	1.0
Wisconsin...........	233,438	936	0.4	1.2	111,274	338	0.3	0.4	108,817	382	0.4	0.6	12,071	180	1.5	7.9	410	6	1.5	1.2
WEST NORTH CENTRAL:																				
Minnesota...........	218,770	804	0.4	1.2	82,471	267	0.3	0.2	123,367	304	0.2	0.4	11,614	153	1.3	8.5	541	6	1.1	0.6
Iowa................	214,256	718	0.3	0.7	149,633	324	0.2	0.4	57,798	152	0.3	0.4	5,192	213	4.1	7.0	1,550	25	1.6	2.2
Missouri............	303,275	3,317	1.1	1.9	246,315	2,302	0.9	1.5	35,623	117	0.3	0.4	6,622	304	4.6	13.4	14,664	586	4.0	6.1
North Dakota........	59,409	318	0.5	2.1	18,386	35	0.2	0.2	34,919	135	0.4	0.3	8,460	93	1.7	8.2	23			
South Dakota........	58,922	219	0.4	1.0	28,868	65	0.2	0.2	26,312	78	0.3	0.3	2,220	38	1.7	6.1	63			
Nebraska............	118,322	493	0.4	0.9	71,519	187	0.3	0.3	41,376	127	0.3	0.4	4,080	157	3.8	10.3	1,027	15	1.5	1.2
Kansas..............	160,875	1,074	0.7	0.9	124,209	321	0.3	0.3	27,205	99	0.4	0.4	3,825	601	15.7	16.6	4,965	51	1.0	1.5
SOUTH ATLANTIC:																				
Delaware............	18,600	295	1.6	4.4	12,061	64	0.5	1.1	2,854	12	0.4	0.6	783	40	5.1	28.1	2,901	179	6.2	11.6
Maryland............	132,016	3,113	2.4	4.0	84,587	793	0.9	1.6	19,174	106	0.6	0.9	4,828	153	3.2	11.4	23,335	2,058	8.8	12.6
District of Columbia.....	36,810	241	0.7	1.7	20,653	27	0.1	0.3	4,436	6	0.1	0.3	1,259	25	2.0	9.8	10,407	178	1.7	3.6
Virginia.............	229,879	15,807	6.9	9.9	151,752	6,154	4.1	5.8	5,392	26	0.5	0.6	1,525	46	3.0	11.8	71,088	9,571	13.5	17.7
West Virginia........	139,752	4,439	3.2	5.7	122,893	3,313	2.7	4.3	5,270	54	1.0	1.4	2,933	425	14.5	28.2	8,645	645	7.5	12.3
North Carolina.......	260,462	21,400	8.2	11.5	173,926	8,386	4.8	7.6	1,020	6	0.6	0.7	302	17	5.6	15.2	84,037	12,735	15.2	19.2
South Carolina.......	179,121	25,276	14.1	21.4	79,569	3,746	4.7	9.1	1,208	7	0.6	1.6	236	4	1.7	10.5	98,070	21,511	21.9	30.5
Georgia.............	301,389	32,281	10.7	14.8	163,909	5,667	3.5	5.1	2,510	10	0.4	1.1	749	16	2.1	8.1	134,195	26,583	19.8	25.9
Florida.............	91,821	6,294	6.9	9.8	49,189	1,015	2.1	3.4	5,726	89	1.6	2.2	2,157	99	4.6	10.6	34,174	5,035	14.7	18.2
EAST SOUTH CENTRAL:																				
Kentucky............	229,530	10,012	4.4	7.5	200,767	8,456	4.2	7.3	6,458	20	0.3	0.5	649	29	4.5	14.7	21,647	1,506	7.0	12.0
Tennessee...........	232,267	12,984	5.6	8.8	181,462	7,434	4.1	6.9	2,779	20	0.7	1.0	579	19	3.3	11.7	47,438	5,510	11.6	15.2
Alabama............	237,480	22,868	9.6	16.0	130,072	4,940	3.6	6.9	3,142	43	1.4	1.5	751	53	7.1	16.1	94,400	17,817	18.9	29.4
Mississippi..........	186,724	21,827	11.7	16.4	83,088	1,753	2.1	3.5	1,379	22	1.6	2.4	353	56	15.9	24.7	101,747	19,908	19.6	25.7
WEST SOUTH CENTRAL:																				
Arkansas............	176,020	8,961	5.1	7.5	120,910	2,891	2.4	4.3	3,534	36	1.0	1.5	420	47	11.2	14.3	51,133	5,982	11.7	15.3
Louisiana...........	183,830	32,846	17.9	25.3	98,715	8,844	9.0	12.8	8,709	557	6.4	5.2	1,968	275	14.0	30.9	74,290	23,081	31.1	41.2
Oklahoma...........	202,830	3,556	1.8	3.8	168,938	2,008	1.2	2.7	9,872	62	0.6	0.9	1,846	418	22.6	13.8	16,200	651	4.0	9.8
Texas...............	483,313	30,575	6.3	7.3	320,651	5,451	1.7	2.5	46,640	5,509	11.8	13.4	34,232	12,185	35.6	36.7	81,490	7,362	9.0	14.3
MOUNTAIN:																				
Montana............	40,836	245	0.6	3.3	21,573	50	0.2	0.2	15,173	38	0.3	0.4	2,954	51	1.7	16.2	82	1		1.7
Idaho...............	37,334	217	0.6	1.3	27,166	46	0.2	0.2	8,484	19	0.2	0.1	1,261	82	6.5	14.5	58	2		
Wyoming............	14,867	151	1.0	2.2	10,010	29	0.3	0.2	3,646	15	0.4	0.4	909	93	10.2	14.5	113	1	0.9	3.6
Colorado............	78,166	1,274	1.6	2.4	52,355	603	1.2	1.4	19,986	103	0.5	0.5	4,998	508	10.2	15.9	855	10	1.2	3.6
New Mexico..........	34,377	3,865	11.2	15.2	26,571	2,033	7.7	9.9	2,763	279	10.1	8.7	2,485	607	24.4	33.0	359	10	2.8	7.6
Arizona.............	29,254	4,101	14.0	21.2	13,009	161	1.2	2.6	4,902	272	5.5	11.9	7,236	1,869	25.8	39.2	498	20	4.0	1.5
Utah...............	42,173	313	0.7	1.4	26,473	64	0.2	0.2	13,253	36	0.3	0.2	1,925	69	3.6	7.9	83	2		
Nevada.............	4,972	177	3.6	7.9	2,711	9	0.3	0.5	1,296	2	0.2	0.3	418	39	9.3	18.0	22	1		
PACIFIC:																				
Washington..........	106,205	456	0.4	1.2	60,313	112	0.2	0.2	35,420	96	0.3	0.2	7,939	112	1.4	7.5	397	3	0.8	1.3
Oregon.............	62,519	223	0.4	1.2	42,498	105	0.2	0.2	15,571	25	0.2	0.3	3,258	61	1.9	11.0	123			
California...........	248,505	4,188	1.7	2.7	136,787	366	0.3	0.3	73,005	321	0.4	0.7	28,584	2,901	10.1	16.1	2,698	26	1.0	2.8

POPULATION.

1160

TABLE 11.—NUMBER AND PER CENT ILLITERATE IN THE INDIAN, CHINESE, JAPANESE, AND "ALL OTHER" POPULATION 10 YEARS OF AGE AND OVER, 1920, WITH COMPARATIVE PERCENTAGES FOR 1910, BY DIVISIONS AND STATES.

[Per cent not shown where base is less than 100.]

DIVISION AND STATE.	INDIAN POPULATION 10 YEARS OF AGE AND OVER.				CHINESE POPULATION 10 YEARS OF AGE AND OVER.				JAPANESE POPULATION 10 YEARS OF AGE AND OVER.				ALL OTHER POPULATION 10 YEARS OF AGE AND OVER.			
	Total number: 1920	Illiterate.			Total number: 1920	Illiterate.			Total number: 1920	Illiterate.			Total number: 1920	Illiterate.		
		Number: 1920	Per cent.			Number: 1920	Per cent.			Number: 1920	Per cent.			Number: 1920	Per cent.	
			1920	1910			1920	1910			1920	1910			1920	1910
United States	176,925	61,730	34.9	45.3	56,230	11,262	20.0	15.8	84,238	9,276	11.0	9.2	8,948	1,164	13.0	39.8
GEOGRAPHIC DIVISIONS:																
New England	1,368	177	12.9	16.7	3,357	747	22.3	14.7	320	16	5.0	4.3	102	2	2.0	
Middle Atlantic	4,589	710	15.5	21.3	8,321	1,915	23.0	14.3	2,930	123	4.2	3.5	1,056	65	6.2	
East North Central	11,582	2,403	33.2	33.2	4,764	952	20.0	17.7	826	28	3.4	2.6	436	20	4.6	
West North Central	27,175	6,525	24.0	41.7	1,560	300	19.2	21.4	996	111	11.1	8.0	174	6	3.4	
South Atlantic	9,139	3,223	35.3	44.5	1,687	317	18.8	22.7	317	8	2.5	11.9	344	10	2.9	
East South Central	1,176	679	57.7	60.3	478	86	18.0	21.6	26				28	3		
West South Central	42,050	7,813	18.6	25.8	1,415	367	25.9	24.9	426	28	6.6	10.7	100	42	26.3	35.5
Mountain	56,103	32,576	58.1	71.4	4,046	853	21.1	23.1	8,589	1,448	16.9	14.7	334	43	12.0	11.9
Pacific	23,743	7,624	32.1	46.0	30,602	5,725	18.7	14.4	69,808	7,514	10.8	8.4	6,314	973	15.4	43.1
NEW ENGLAND:																
Maine	631	151	23.9	31.8	155	25	16.1	13.9	7				2			
New Hampshire	25	2			91	34			8							
Vermont	16	7			11	3			4							
Massachusetts	460	5	1.1	3.8	2,359	530	22.5	14.2	172	5	2.9	2.1	69	2		
Rhode Island	100	5	5.0	4.4	201	43	21.4	21.8	31	1			7			
Connecticut	136	7	5.1	10.7	540	112	20.7	15.0	98	10			24			
MIDDLE ATLANTIC:																
New York	4,226	695	16.4	27.9	5,438	1,149	21.1	11.8	2,430	94	3.9	2.6	699	43	6.2	
New Jersey	90	9		18.8	1,159	422	36.4	23.0	278	15	5.4	4.2	65	14		
Pennsylvania	273	6	2.2	0.6	1,724	344	20.0	15.9	222	14	6.3	8.5	292	8	2.7	
EAST NORTH CENTRAL:																
Ohio	137	9	6.6	10.2	898	154	17.1	18.9	125	7	5.6		87	8		
Indiana	113	7	6.2	13.5	281	67	23.8	25.5	61				16			
Illinois	182	17	9.3	8.5	2,602	580	22.3	15.9	425	11	2.6	1.9	225			
Michigan	4,187	1,011	24.1	34.4	752	110	14.6	20.7	160	4	2.4		102	11	10.8	
Wisconsin	6,963	1,359	19.5	33.7	231	41	17.7	18.0	46	6			6	1		
WEST NORTH CENTRAL:																
Minnesota	6,155	1,968	32.0	40.2	466	79	17.0	13.1	67	2			23			
Iowa	407	80	19.7	46.6	223	34	15.2		25	1			41	3		
Missouri	152	18	11.8	15.1	393	95	24.2	25.8	114	27	23.7		48			
North Dakota	4,541	1,344	29.6	46.0	121	26	21.5		67	5			1	1		
South Dakota	11,979	2,705	22.6	45.5	123	29	23.6	34.2	28	2			4			
Nebraska	2,095	298	14.2	35.5	169	28	16.6	20.7	649	73	11.2	6.8	27	1		
Kansas	1,846	112	6.1	18.7	65	9			46	1		7.7	30	1		
SOUTH ATLANTIC:																
Delaware	2				40	7			8	1						
Maryland	30	5			352	81	23.0	26.9	26	1			12			
District of Columbia	31	2			434	85	19.6	23.4	97				137	1	0.7	
Virginia	551	173	31.4	24.2	258	34	13.2	27.4	54	2			103	3	2.9	
West Virginia	7	1			88	26			10				3	1		
North Carolina	7,840	2,598	33.1	47.2	80	10			21	3			55			
South Carolina	204	93	45.6	41.0	82	19			11				8	2		
Georgia	90	22			192	42	21.9	16.4	9				8	2		
Florida	384	329	85.7		161	13	8.1	10.6	81	1			25	3		
EAST SOUTH CENTRAL:																
Kentucky	42	10		52.3	56	0			8				4			
Tennessee	46	12		37.7	56	13			7				13			
Alabama	258	92	35.7	40.8	55	10			11				8	3		
Mississippi	830	565	68.1	79.0	311	57	18.3	21.5					3			
WEST SOUTH CENTRAL:																
Arkansas	81	19		13.4	105	15	14.3		5	1			3	1		
Louisiana	789	551	71.7	73.9	337	103	30.6	30.9	40	8			107	36	33.6	
Oklahoma	39,669	6,723	16.9	25.2	248	58	23.4	9.8	57	3			14	1		
Texas	1,531	520	34.0	43.4	725	191	26.3	22.2	315	16	5.1	11.4	36	4		
MOUNTAIN:																
Montana	7,963	2,849	35.8	55.8	815	218	26.7	28.8	892	138	15.5	23.0	62	7		
Idaho	2,415	1,106	45.8	59.4	562	145	25.8	20.9	1,194	211	17.7	13.7	20	3		
Wyoming	979	184	18.8	51.2	248	23	9.3	23.8	1,031	219	21.2	10.1	84	3		
Colorado	1,001	527	52.6	48.6	261	28	10.7	22.5	1,800	179	9.9	13.0	60	7		
New Mexico	14,180	8,553	60.3	81.7	160	40	30.6	13.2	207	38	18.4	14.6	7			
Arizona	23,692	16,068	67.8	72.9	1,009	175	17.3	25.1	435	22	5.1	10.6	28	4		
Utah	2,026	1,249	61.6	83.0	333	67	20.1	38.2	2,378	444	18.7	12.5	55	16		
Nevada	3,847	2,040	53.0	71.7	658	148	22.5	11.1	652	197	30.2	4.3	12	3		
PACIFIC:																
Washington	6,714	2,127	31.7	45.8	2,138	472	22.1	19.0	13,283	1,605	12.1	6.8	1,115	68	6.1	38.9
Oregon	3,664	847	23.1	36.6	2,768	782	28.3	7.6	3,222	409	12.7	11.1	249	28	11.2	51.6
California	13,365	4,650	34.8	49.0	25,696	4,471	17.4	15.5	53,303	5,500	10.3	8.0	4,950	877	17.7	42.3

CHAPTER XIII

INABILITY TO SPEAK ENGLISH

CHAPTER XIII.—INABILITY TO SPEAK ENGLISH.

INTRODUCTION.

The inquiry as to ability to speak English has been made at each of the last four censuses. The statistics here presented relate to persons 10 years of age and over and cover continental United States as a whole, the states, and cities having 25,000 inhabitants or more. Statistics for the outlying possessions enumerated are given in Volume III of the Fourteenth Census Reports.

Population classes.—With two exceptions (Tables 1 and 7), all the tables on inability to speak English relate to the foreign-born white class of population, this being the only class for which the statistics are of special value. Table 1 presents a United States summary for the several classes of population covered at each of the four censuses which included an inquiry on this subject, and Table 7 shows, by states, for 1920 and 1910, the numbers of males and females in each of the nonwhite classes reported as unable to speak English. At the census of 1890 statistics were compiled for the native white classes, and at the census of 1900 for the native white of foreign or mixed parentage. Examination of the statistics for the various states for those years shows that the native white persons reported as unable to speak English were enumerated mainly in a few of the border states, such as Arizona, New Mexico, and Texas, where there is a more or less constant immigration of Mexicans whose descendants continue to speak Spanish, and in Louisiana, whose population includes a relatively large number of French-speaking natives, both white and Negro. Of the non-English-speaking Negroes in 1920, 46 per cent were enumerated in Louisiana.

At the census of 1890 the figures for Negroes unable to speak English were not presented separately but were included with those for the total colored population, and at the census of 1900 these statistics were not published for the Negro population. Returns were made for the Negroes in 1900, but were valueless. The error was due to the grouping on the census schedule, under the general head "Education," of the four inquiries relating, respectively, to school attendance, ability to read, ability to write, and ability to speak English. Thus in the great majority of cases for the whites, and in a large number of cases for the Negroes, correct returns necessitated writing "Yes," "Yes," "Yes," in answer, respectively, to the three inquiries "Can read," "Can write," and "Can speak English." It would be natural, therefore, for a careless enumerator occasionally to write "Yes," "Yes,"

"Yes," in the case of a foreign-born person able to read and write in his own language but unable to speak English, or "No," "No," "No," in the case of an illiterate person able to speak English. The latter error appears to have been made in the returns for a few Negroes, whose number has been roughly estimated at about 1 per cent of the illiterate Negro population 10 years of age and over, or about one-third of 1 per cent of the total Negro population 10 years of age and over; and, because the number of Negroes actually unable to speak English was very small, the error resulted in a proportionally large overstatement of this number.

It is likely that similar errors were made in the returns for the foreign-born white population in 1900, but the effect of such errors on the proportion of foreign-born whites reported as unable to speak English would be very much less than in the case of the Negro population. In other words, if it be assumed that 1 per cent of the illiterate foreign-born whites were erroneously returned as unable to speak English, and that, on the other hand, 1 per cent of the literate foreign-born whites (that is, those who were able to read and write in any language, not necessarily English) were erroneously returned as able to speak English, the net result of these errors would be an understatement of about 74,000 in the number of foreign-born whites unable to speak English. This would represent a little more than 6 per cent of the total number of foreign-born whites returned as unable to speak English, and the correction of such an error would increase the percentage of foreign-born whites 10 years of age and over unable to speak English from 12.2 to 12.9.

In 1910 and 1920 the inquiry as to inability to speak English was so placed on the schedule as to eliminate any possibility that a careless enumerator would make an incorrect return of the kind described above. The 1910 and 1920 statistics for both the foreign-born whites and the Negroes are, therefore, considered to be reasonably reliable; and the 1900 statistics for the foreign-born whites are believed to have some value, although less nearly accurate than those for 1910 and 1920; but the 1900 statistics for the Negroes are valueless and, therefore, have not been published.

Urban and rural communities.—Because of the marked difference between urban and rural communities in regard to the composition and characteristics of their population, separate statistics are given for the two classes of communities in Table 11. In

1250

POPULATION.

drawing the distinction between urban and rural population, all incorporated places (and all towns in Massachusetts, Rhode Island, and New Hampshire) having 2,500 inhabitants or more are treated as urban and the remainder of the country as rural.

In Massachusetts and Rhode Island it is not the practice, as in practically all the other states, to incorporate, as separate municipalities, the relatively densely populated portions of "towns" (which are the primary divisions of the counties), and no town as a whole is incorporated as a municipality until it attains a population greatly in excess of 2,500; and in New Hampshire a similar condition exists, although the state contains two incorporated villages, each of which has fewer than 2,500 inhabitants.

For this reason those towns having 2,500 or more inhabitants in the three states named are treated as urban, although portions of their areas are rural in character. The urban areas in the three states in question, as classified by the census, thus contain relatively small numbers of inhabitants who in other sections of the country would be segregated as rural. Nevertheless, in most of the towns having 2,500 inhabitants or more in Massachusetts, Rhode Island, and New Hampshire by far the greater part of the population resides within the more densely settled areas, so that the proportion classed as urban, considering each state as a whole, is not greatly exaggerated by the practice adopted.

TABLE 1.—NUMBER AND PER CENT UNABLE TO SPEAK ENGLISH, FOR POPULATION CLASSES, BY SEX, IN POPULATION 10 YEARS OF AGE AND OVER, 1890-1920, AND IN POPULATION 21 YEARS OF AGE AND OVER, 1920 AND 1910, FOR THE UNITED STATES.

[Figures are given under each class for all census years for which data are available.]

CENSUS YEAR AND CLASS OF POPULATION.	BOTH SEXES.			MALE.			FEMALE.		
	Total number.	Unable to speak English.		Total number.	Unable to speak English.		Total number.	Unable to speak English.	
		Number.	Per cent.		Number.	Per cent.		Number.	Per cent.
POPULATION 10 YEARS OF AGE AND OVER.									
1920									
Foreign-born white	13,497,886	1,488,948	11.0	7,419,691	680,033	9.2	6,078,195	808,915	13.3
Negro	8,053,225	14,644	0.2	4,009,462	7,207	0.2	4,043,763	7,437	0.2
Indian	176,925	36,752	20.8	91,546	17,469	19.1	85,379	19,283	22.6
Chinese	56,230	10,020	17.8	51,041	8,903	17.4	5,189	1,117	21.5
Japanese	84,238	19,068	22.6	58,806	8,709	14.8	25,432	10,359	40.7
All other [1]	8,948	982	11.0	8,378	916	10.9	570	66	11.6
1910									
Foreign-born white	12,944,529	2,953,011	22.8	7,321,196	1,683,949	23.0	5,623,333	1,269,062	22.6
Negro	7,317,922	22,110	0.3	3,637,386	10,870	0.3	3,680,536	11,240	0.3
Indian	188,758	59,055	31.3	96,582	26,705	27.7	92,176	32,350	35.1
Chinese	68,924	28,370	41.2	65,479	26,632	40.7	3,445	1,738	50.4
Japanese	67,061	26,564	39.3	60,809	22,848	37.6	6,852	3,716	54.2
All other [2]	3,135	2,097	66.9	3,073	2,077	67.6	62	20	([3])
1900									
Native white—foreign or mixed parentage	10,926,401	65,008	0.6	5,460,085	28,164	0.5	5,466,316	36,844	0.7
Foreign-born white	10,014,256	1,217,280	12.2	5,414,991	563,982	10.4	4,599,265	653,298	14.2
Indian	171,552	72,583	42.3	86,504	32,309	37.3	85,048	40,274	47.4
Chinese	87,682	33,498	38.2	84,141	31,191	37.1	3,541	2,307	65.2
Japanese	24,091	14,843	61.6	23,214	14,448	62.2	877	395	45.0
1890									
Native white—native parentage	25,375,766	168,149	0.7	12,901,102	75,874	0.6	12,474,664	92,275	0.7
Native white—foreign or mixed parentage	7,768,421	69,876	0.9	3,895,395	30,659	0.8	3,873,026	39,217	1.0
Foreign-born white	8,786,887	1,371,044	15.6	4,781,748	666,496	13.9	4,005,139	704,548	17.6
Colored	5,482,485	109,427	2.0	2,774,414	85,860	3.1	2,708,071	23,567	0.9
POPULATION 21 YEARS OF AGE AND OVER.									
1920									
Foreign-born white	12,498,720	1,399,759	11.2	6,928,452	637,830	9.2	5,570,268	761,929	13.7
Negro	5,522,475	10,223	0.2	2,792,006	4,989	0.2	2,730,469	5,234	0.2
Indian	116,486	29,023	24.9	61,229	13,662	22.3	55,257	15,361	27.8
Chinese	50,625	9,629	19.0	46,979	8,565	18.2	3,646	1,064	29.2
Japanese	75,727	17,624	23.3	53,411	7,942	14.9	22,316	9,682	43.4
All other [1]	7,746	938	12.1	7,345	875	11.9	401	63	15.7
Foreign born—									
Negro	64,412	2,509	3.9	38,234	1,459	3.8	26,178	1,050	4.0
Indian	4,442	2,769	62.3	2,559	1,495	58.4	1,883	1,274	67.7
Chinese	40,494	8,873	21.9	38,285	7,981	20.8	2,209	892	40.4
Japanese	75,069	17,600	23.4	52,999	7,940	15.0	22,070	9,660	43.8
1910									
Foreign-born white	11,653,925	2,565,612	22.0	6,646,817	1,462,134	22.0	5,007,108	1,103,478	22.0
Negro	4,886,615	13,870	0.3	2,458,873	6,768	0.3	2,427,742	7,102	0.3
Indian	123,136	47,411	38.5	62,967	21,118	33.5	60,169	26,293	43.7
Chinese	62,902	26,338	41.9	60,421	24,816	41.1	2,481	1,522	61.3
Japanese	62,710	24,882	39.7	56,638	21,484	37.9	6,072	3,398	56.0
All other [2]	2,792	1,877	67.2	2,738	1,858	67.9	54	19	([3])

[1] Comprises Filipinos, Hindus, Koreans, Hawaiians, Malays, Siamese, Samoans, and Maoris.
[2] Comprises Filipinos, Hindus, Koreans, and Maoris.
[3] Per cent not shown, base being less than 100.

INABILITY TO SPEAK ENGLISH.

TABLE 2.—NUMBER AND PER CENT UNABLE TO SPEAK ENGLISH, BY SEX AND AGE PERIODS, IN FOREIGN-BORN WHITE POPULATION 10 YEARS OF AGE AND OVER, FOR THE UNITED STATES: 1920 AND 1910.

CENSUS YEAR AND AGE PERIOD.	FOREIGN-BORN WHITE POPULATION 10 YEARS OF AGE AND OVER.								
	Both sexes.			Male.			Female.		
	Total number.	Unable to speak English.		Total number.	Unable to speak English.		Total number.	Unable to speak English.	
		Number.	Per cent.		Number.	Per cent.		Number.	Per cent.
1920									
Total, 10 years and over	13,497,886	1,488,948	11.0	7,419,691	680,033	9.2	6,078,195	808,915	13.3
10 to 14 years	331,362	28,149	8.5	167,152	14,163	8.5	164,210	13,986	8.5
15 to 19 years	527,942	43,711	8.3	259,270	20,651	8.0	268,672	23,060	8.6
20 to 24 years	926,844	119,092	12.8	456,988	48,971	10.7	469,856	70,121	14.9
25 to 29 years	1,454,363	203,676	14.0	792,088	85,814	10.8	662,275	117,862	17.8
30 to 34 years	1,651,475	210,593	12.8	946,818	97,449	10.3	704,657	113,144	16.1
35 to 39 years	1,737,805	207,035	11.9	1,008,677	101,796	10.1	729,128	105,239	14.4
40 to 44 years	1,428,099	154,877	10.8	803,195	75,745	9.4	624,904	79,132	12.7
45 to 49 years	1,299,675	132,442	10.2	744,428	67,487	9.1	555,252	64,955	11.7
50 to 54 years	1,167,377	107,053	9.2	651,546	50,538	7.8	515,831	56,515	11.0
55 to 59 years	908,722	78,121	8.6	503,789	33,907	6.7	404,933	44,214	10.9
60 to 64 years	715,731	69,639	9.7	392,629	29,257	7.5	323,102	40,382	12.5
65 years and over	1,328,227	129,445	9.7	679,384	50,847	7.5	648,843	78,598	12.1
Age unknown	20,264	5,115	25.2	13,732	3,408	24.8	6,532	1,707	26.1
1910									
Total, 10 years and over	12,944,529	2,953,011	22.8	7,321,196	1,683,949	23.0	5,623,333	1,269,062	22.6
10 to 14 years	358,330	56,405	15.7	181,303	28,307	15.6	177,027	28,098	15.9
15 to 19 years	673,761	227,649	33.8	351,754	130,930	37.2	322,007	96,719	30.0
20 to 24 years	1,430,381	497,511	34.8	823,920	310,276	37.7	606,461	187,235	30.9
25 to 29 years	1,662,696	511,695	30.8	990,576	324,067	32.7	672,120	187,628	27.9
30 to 34 years	1,505,715	391,254	26.0	888,668	244,551	27.5	617,047	146,703	23.8
35 to 39 years	1,408,093	301,273	21.4	812,007	180,579	22.2	596,086	120,694	20.2
40 to 44 years	1,303,475	237,525	18.2	751,519	136,638	18.2	551,956	100,887	18.3
45 to 49 years	1,146,360	179,383	15.6	656,455	92,570	14.1	489,905	86,813	17.7
50 to 54 years	925,055	145,482	15.7	526,256	68,781	13.1	398,799	76,701	19.2
55 to 59 years	693,520	100,696	14.5	380,110	42,303	11.1	313,410	58,393	18.6
60 to 64 years	627,583	91,792	14.6	331,914	37,069	11.2	295,669	54,723	18.5
65 years and over	1,183,349	201,709	17.0	607,008	78,903	13.0	576,341	122,806	21.3
Age unknown	26,211	10,637	40.6	19,706	8,975	45.5	6,505	1,662	25.5

1252

POPULATION.

TABLE 3.—NUMBER AND PER CENT UNABLE TO SPEAK ENGLISH IN FOREIGN-BORN WHITE POPULATION 10 YEARS OF AGE AND OVER, BY DIVISIONS AND STATES: 1920, 1910, AND 1900.

DIVISION AND STATE.	FOREIGN-BORN WHITE POPULATION 10 YEARS OF AGE AND OVER.									INCREASE (+) OR DECREASE (−) IN NUMBER UNABLE TO SPEAK ENGLISH.	
	1920			1910			1900				
	Total number.	Unable to speak English.		Total number.	Unable to speak English.		Total number.	Unable to speak English.		1910–1920	1900–1910
		Number.	Per cent.		Number.	Per cent.		Number.	Per cent.		
United States	13,497,886	1,488,943	11.0	12,944,529	2,953,011	22.8	10,014,256	1,217,280	12.2	−1,464,063	+1,735,731
GEOGRAPHIC DIVISIONS:											
New England	1,843,028	180,851	9.8	1,757,244	326,890	18.6	1,392,969	155,429	11.2	−146,039	+171,461
Middle Atlantic	4,853,256	525,849	10.8	4,661,990	1,217,698	26.1	3,227,687	430,188	13.3	−691,849	+757,510
East North Central	3,183,790	328,981	10.3	2,985,823	693,981	23.2	2,583,504	302,531	11.7	−364,980	+391,430
West North Central	1,358,323	85,259	6.3	1,579,694	274,620	17.4	1,511,527	168,887	11.2	−189,361	+105,733
South Atlantic	311,385	32,042	10.3	280,387	71,389	25.5	205,209	19,518	9.5	−39,347	+51,871
East South Central	71,211	2,363	3.3	84,893	9,983	11.8	88,774	3,618	4.1	−7,620	+6,365
West South Central	430,053	181,799	42.3	330,431	148,028	44.8	254,168	82,043	32.3	+33,771	+65,985
Mountain	436,304	71,096	16.3	423,068	96,637	22.8	283,167	30,359	10.7	−25,541	+66,278
Pacific	1,010,536	80,708	8.0	840,999	113,805	13.5	467,161	24,707	5.3	−33,097	+89,098
NEW ENGLAND:											
Maine	104,585	10,333	9.9	105,336	19,589	18.6	88,796	13,919	15.7	−9,256	+5,670
New Hampshire	89,472	11,339	12.7	92,976	26,783	28.8	83,542	17,107	20.5	−15,444	+9,676
Vermont	42,701	3,065	7.2	47,654	8,342	17.5	43,105	3,921	9.1	−5,277	+4,421
Massachusetts	1,063,572	96,426	9.1	1,020,594	171,014	16.8	816,808	76,637	9.4	−74,588	+94,377
Rhode Island	171,032	21,620	12.6	171,904	36,961	21.5	128,901	17,029	13.2	−15,341	+19,932
Connecticut	371,666	38,068	10.2	318,780	64,201	20.1	231,817	26,816	11.6	−26,133	+37,385
MIDDLE ATLANTIC:											
New York	2,752,055	290,200	10.5	2,634,578	597,012	22.7	1,844,333	220,306	11.9	−306,812	+376,706
New Jersey	729,799	73,409	10.1	636,848	153,861	24.2	420,765	48,709	11.6	−80,452	+105,152
Pennsylvania	1,371,402	162,240	11.8	1,390,564	466,825	33.6	962,589	161,173	16.7	−304,585	+305,652
EAST NORTH CENTRAL:											
Ohio	669,924	81,161	12.1	579,274	163,722	28.3	452,120	51,752	11.4	−82,561	+111,970
Indiana	149,239	13,269	8.9	155,596	40,731	26.2	140,402	11,339	8.1	−27,462	+29,392
Illinois	1,194,979	121,965	10.2	1,168,559	266,557	22.8	951,701	103,301	10.9	−144,592	+163,256
Michigan	713,228	68,105	9.5	579,803	102,286	17.6	529,731	49,342	9.3	−34,181	+52,944
Wisconsin	456,420	44,481	9.7	502,591	120,665	24.0	509,640	86,797	17.0	−76,184	+33,868
WEST NORTH CENTRAL:											
Minnesota	482,230	28,311	5.9	533,915	89,850	16.8	498,866	68,894	13.8	−61,539	+20,956
Iowa	223,752	9,559	4.3	269,246	37,169	13.8	303,226	25,544	8.4	−27,610	+11,625
Missouri	184,394	11,126	6.0	223,578	37,747	16.9	214,091	14,511	6.8	−26,621	+23,236
North Dakota	129,951	10,189	7.8	150,451	33,491	22.3	103,167	18,082	16.7	−23,302	+15,409
South Dakota	81,781	4,861	5.9	98,334	18,486	18.8	86,770	13,104	15.1	−13,625	+5,382
Nebraska	148,209	9,186	6.2	172,497	29,519	17.1	175,262	17,908	10.2	−20,333	+11,611
Kansas	108,006	12,027	11.1	131,673	28,358	21.5	125,145	10,844	8.7	−16,331	+17,514
SOUTH ATLANTIC:											
Delaware	19,541	2,733	14.0	16,940	4,824	28.5	13,524	1,529	11.3	−2,091	+3,295
Maryland	101,155	7,765	7.7	100,951	17,544	17.4	91,609	7,520	8.2	−9,779	+10,024
District of Columbia	28,292	779	2.8	23,755	1,349	5.7	19,309	254	1.3	−570	+1,095
Virginia	30,325	1,135	3.7	25,639	3,983	15.5	18,742	827	4.4	−2,848	+3,156
West Virginia	60,679	11,121	18.3	54,646	27,461	50.3	22,025	3,612	16.4	−16,340	+23,849
North Carolina	6,981	190	2.7	5,734	779	13.6	4,314	123	2.9	−589	+656
South Carolina	6,327	116	1.8	5,911	447	7.6	5,320	52	1.0	−331	+395
Georgia	16,028	285	1.8	14,656	953	6.5	11,829	177	1.5	−668	+776
Florida	42,057	7,918	18.8	32,155	14,049	43.7	18,537	5,424	29.3	−6,131	+8,625
EAST SOUTH CENTRAL:											
Kentucky	30,603	688	2.2	39,571	3,816	9.6	49,860	1,850	3.7	−3,128	+1,966
Tennessee	15,297	506	3.3	17,985	1,648	9.2	17,339	675	3.9	−1,142	+973
Alabama	17,393	724	4.2	18,291	3,028	16.6	14,060	759	5.4	−2,304	+2,269
Mississippi	7,918	445	5.6	9,046	1,491	16.5	7,515	334	4.4	−1,046	+1,157
WEST SOUTH CENTRAL:											
Arkansas	13,834	697	5.0	16,454	2,741	16.7	13,971	877	6.3	−2,044	+1,864
Louisiana	44,244	3,683	8.3	50,333	11,547	22.9	50,132	7,817	15.6	−7,864	+3,730
Oklahoma[1]	39,020	5,362	13.7	39,064	7,975	20.4	20,029	1,718	8.6	−2,613	+6,257
Texas	332,955	172,057	51.7	224,580	125,765	56.0	170,036	71,631	42.1	+46,292	+54,134
MOUNTAIN:											
Montana	91,729	3,098	3.4	89,456	13,718	15.3	61,306	3,109	5.1	−10,620	+10,609
Idaho	38,379	1,956	5.1	39,619	5,805	14.7	21,638	921	4.3	−3,849	+4,884
Wyoming	24,762	2,003	8.1	26,381	5,970	22.6	16,374	1,962	12.0	−3,967	+4,008
Colorado	114,285	10,650	9.3	123,026	22,610	18.4	89,158	6,429	7.2	−11,960	+16,181
New Mexico	26,786	13,225	49.4	21,235	11,776	55.5	12,620	5,478	43.4	+1,449	+6,298
Arizona	70,053	36,352	51.9	43,724	25,072	57.3	21,379	9,775	45.7	+11,280	+15,297
Utah	55,724	2,303	4.1	61,840	8,129	13.1	52,148	2,208	4.2	−5,826	+5,921
Nevada	14,586	1,509	10.3	17,787	3,557	20.0	8,544	477	5.6	−2,048	+3,080
PACIFIC:											
Washington	244,881	7,796	3.2	234,928	25,568	10.9	100,482	3,815	3.8	−17,772	+21,753
Oregon	100,672	3,342	3.3	100,759	13,531	13.4	53,309	2,087	3.9	−10,189	+11,444
California	664,983	69,570	10.5	505,312	74,706	14.8	313,370	18,805	6.0	−5,136	+55,901

[1] Includes population of Indian Territory for 1900.

INABILITY TO SPEAK ENGLISH.

1253

TABLE 4.—NUMBER AND PER CENT UNABLE TO SPEAK ENGLISH IN FOREIGN-BORN WHITE POPULATION 10 YEARS OF AGE AND OVER, BY SEX, BY DIVISIONS AND STATES: 1920 AND 1910.

DIVISION AND STATE.	FOREIGN-BORN WHITE MALES 10 YEARS OF AGE AND OVER. 1920 Total number.	Unable to speak English. Number.	Per cent.	1910 Total number.	Unable to speak English. Number.	Per cent.	FOREIGN-BORN WHITE FEMALES 10 YEARS OF AGE AND OVER. 1920 Total number.	Unable to speak English. Number.	Per cent.	1910 Total number.	Unable to speak English. Number.	Per cent.	INCREASE (+) OR DECREASE (−) IN NUMBER UNABLE TO SPEAK ENGLISH: 1910-1920 Males.	Females.
United States	7,419,691	680,033	9.2	7,321,196	1,683,949	23.0	6,078,195	808,915	13.3	5,623,333	1,269,062	22.6	−1,003,916	−460,147
GEOGRAPHIC DIVISIONS:														
New England	931,845	70,213	7.5	899,625	164,929	18.3	911,183	110,638	12.1	857,619	161,961	18.9	−94,716	−51,323
Middle Atlantic	2,587,798	231,273	8.9	2,558,973	695,299	27.2	2,265,458	294,576	13.0	2,103,017	522,399	24.8	−464,026	−227,823
East North Central	1,789,466	152,312	8.5	1,699,847	397,275	23.4	1,394,324	176,669	12.7	1,285,976	296,686	23.1	−244,963	−120,017
West North Central	772,147	35,467	4.6	927,721	147,656	15.9	588,176	49,792	8.5	651,973	126,964	19.5	−112,189	−77,172
South Atlantic	182,846	17,777	9.7	167,727	47,878	28.5	128,539	14,265	11.1	112,660	23,511	20.9	−30,101	−9,246
East South Central	41,729	1,110	2.7	49,514	5,928	12.0	29,482	1,253	4.3	35,379	4,055	11.5	−4,818	−2,802
West South Central	245,597	93,160	37.9	193,328	79,092	40.9	184,456	88,639	48.1	137,103	68,936	50.3	+14,068	+19,703
Mountain	262,733	37,261	14.2	279,095	67,800	24.3	173,571	33,835	19.5	143,973	28,837	20.0	−30,539	+4,998
Pacific	605,530	41,460	6.8	545,366	78,092	14.3	405,006	39,248	9.7	295,633	35,713	12.1	−36,632	+3,535
NEW ENGLAND:														
Maine	54,308	3,486	6.4	55,564	8,940	16.1	50,187	6,847	13.6	49,772	10,649	21.4	−5,454	−3,802
New Hampshire	45,952	4,350	9.5	48,912	13,412	27.4	43,520	6,989	16.1	44,064	13,371	30.3	−9,062	−6,382
Vermont	22,800	1,348	5.9	26,826	4,821	18.0	19,895	1,717	8.6	20,828	3,521	16.9	−3,473	−1,804
Massachusetts	526,272	37,556	7.1	508,878	85,783	16.9	537,300	58,870	11.0	511,716	85,231	16.7	−48,227	−26,361
Rhode Island	84,933	7,993	9.4	87,501	17,341	19.8	86,099	13,627	15.8	84,403	19,620	23.2	−9,348	−5,993
Connecticut	197,484	15,480	7.8	171,944	34,632	20.1	174,182	22,588	13.0	146,836	29,569	20.1	−19,152	−6,981
MIDDLE ATLANTIC:														
New York	1,425,461	123,304	8.7	1,384,830	305,414	22.1	1,326,594	166,896	12.6	1,249,748	291,598	23.3	−182,110	−124,702
New Jersey	387,251	31,661	8.2	345,789	86,366	25.0	342,548	41,748	12.2	291,059	67,495	23.2	−54,705	−25,747
Pennsylvania	775,086	76,308	9.8	828,354	303,519	36.6	596,316	85,932	14.4	562,210	163,306	29.0	−227,211	−77,374
EAST NORTH CENTRAL:														
Ohio	386,901	41,785	10.8	337,157	103,193	30.6	283,023	39,376	13.9	242,117	60,529	25.0	−61,408	−21,153
Indiana	87,396	6,517	7.5	95,297	28,234	29.6	61,843	6,752	10.9	60,299	12,497	20.7	−21,717	−5,745
Illinois	651,256	53,389	8.2	656,301	148,692	22.7	543,723	68,576	12.6	512,258	117,865	23.0	−95,303	−49,289
Michigan	407,057	32,432	8.0	325,735	57,957	17.8	306,171	35,673	11.7	254,088	44,329	17.4	−25,525	−8,656
Wisconsin	256,856	18,189	7.1	285,357	59,199	20.7	199,564	26,292	13.2	217,234	61,466	28.3	−41,010	−35,174
WEST NORTH CENTRAL:														
Minnesota	276,630	10,900	3.9	315,895	45,995	14.6	205,600	17,411	8.5	218,020	43,855	20.1	−35,095	−26,444
Iowa	126,109	4,239	3.4	155,230	20,721	13.3	97,643	5,320	5.4	114,016	16,448	14.4	−16,482	−11,128
Missouri	102,587	5,065	4.9	129,201	22,370	17.3	81,807	6,061	7.4	94,377	15,377	16.3	−17,305	−9,316
North Dakota	74,633	3,532	4.7	89,680	15,962	17.8	55,318	6,657	12.0	60,771	17,529	28.8	−12,430	−10,872
South Dakota	47,289	1,768	3.7	58,512	8,911	15.2	34,492	3,093	9.0	39,822	9,575	24.0	−7,143	−6,482
Nebraska	83,542	3,873	4.6	99,839	16,002	16.0	64,667	5,313	8.2	72,658	13,517	18.6	−12,129	−8,204
Kansas	61,357	6,090	9.9	79,364	17,695	22.3	46,649	5,937	12.7	52,309	10,663	20.4	−11,605	−4,726
SOUTH ATLANTIC:														
Delaware	11,280	1,429	12.7	9,687	3,180	32.8	8,311	1,304	15.7	7,253	1,644	22.7	−1,751	−340
Maryland	54,102	3,396	6.3	52,082	9,206	17.5	47,053	4,369	9.3	48,269	8,338	17.3	−5,810	−3,969
District of Columbia	15,022	329	2.2	12,606	710	5.6	13,270	450	3.4	11,149	639	5.7	−381	−189
Virginia	18,812	588	3.1	16,288	2,826	17.4	11,513	547	4.8	9,351	1,157	12.4	−2,238	−610
West Virginia	41,295	7,655	18.5	40,036	22,091	55.2	19,384	3,466	17.9	14,610	5,370	36.8	−14,436	−1,904
North Carolina	4,287	87	2.0	3,639	509	14.0	2,694	103	3.8	2,095	270	12.9	−422	−167
South Carolina	4,063	67	1.6	3,657	287	7.8	2,264	49	2.2	2,254	160	7.1	−220	−111
Georgia	9,923	141	1.4	9,201	585	6.3	6,105	144	2.4	5,365	368	6.9	−444	−224
Florida	24,112	4,085	16.9	19,841	8,484	42.8	17,945	3,833	21.4	12,314	5,565	45.2	−4,399	−1,732
EAST SOUTH CENTRAL:														
Kentucky	17,401	347	2.0	21,354	2,277	10.7	13,202	341	2.6	18,217	1,539	8.4	−1,930	−1,198
Tennessee	8,928	230	2.6	10,896	942	8.6	6,369	276	4.3	7,089	706	10.0	−712	−430
Alabama	10,484	319	3.0	11,479	1,847	16.1	6,909	405	5.9	6,812	1,181	17.3	−1,528	−776
Mississippi	4,916	214	4.4	5,785	862	14.9	3,002	231	7.7	3,261	629	19.3	−648	−398
WEST SOUTH CENTRAL:														
Arkansas	8,528	303	3.6	10,368	1,533	14.8	5,306	394	7.4	6,086	1,208	19.8	−1,230	−814
Louisiana	26,477	1,656	6.3	28,935	6,049	20.9	17,767	2,027	11.4	21,398	5,498	25.7	−4,393	−3,471
Oklahoma	24,412	3,348	13.7	25,148	5,098	20.3	14,608	2,014	13.8	13,916	2,877	20.7	−1,750	−863
Texas	186,180	87,853	47.2	128,877	66,412	51.5	146,775	84,204	57.4	95,703	59,353	62.0	+21,441	+24,851
MOUNTAIN:														
Montana	57,287	1,384	2.4	63,504	11,068	17.4	34,442	1,714	5.0	25,952	2,650	10.2	−9,684	−936
Idaho	24,565	1,191	4.8	27,676	4,748	17.2	18,814	765	5.5	11,943	1,057	8.9	−3,557	−292
Wyoming	16,700	1,301	7.8	19,743	4,921	24.9	8,062	702	8.7	6,638	1,049	15.8	−3,620	−347
Colorado	66,869	4,982	7.5	76,165	14,640	19.2	47,416	5,668	12.0	46,861	7,970	17.0	−9,658	−2,302
New Mexico	15,685	7,024	44.8	14,117	7,686	54.4	11,101	6,201	55.9	7,118	4,090	57.5	−662	+2,111
Arizona	40,476	19,009	47.0	29,035	15,702	54.1	29,577	17,343	58.6	14,689	9,370	63.8	+3,307	+7,973
Utah	30,516	1,342	4.4	35,149	5,988	17.0	25,208	961	3.8	26,691	2,141	8.0	−4,646	−1,180
Nevada	10,635	1,028	9.7	13,706	3,047	22.2	3,951	481	12.2	4,081	510	12.5	−2,019	−29
PACIFIC:														
Washington	150,510	3,772	2.5	157,493	18,455	11.7	94,371	4,024	4.3	77,435	7,113	9.2	−14,683	−3,089
Oregon	61,575	1,769	2.9	68,619	10,518	15.3	39,097	1,573	4.0	32,140	3,013	9.4	−8,749	−1,440
California	393,445	35,919	9.1	319,254	49,119	15.4	271,538	33,651	12.4	186,058	25,587	13.8	−13,200	+8,064

POPULATION.

1254

TABLE 5.—NUMBER UNABLE TO SPEAK ENGLISH IN FOREIGN-BORN WHITE POPULATION

DIVISION AND STATE.	TOTAL, 10 YEARS OF AGE AND OVER.			10 TO 14 YEARS.			15 TO 19 YEARS.			20 TO 24 YEARS.			25 TO 34 YEARS.		
	Both sexes.	Male.	Female.	Both sexes.	Male.	Female.	Both sexes.	Male.	Female.	Both sexes.	Male.	Female.	Both sexes.	Male.	Female.
United States	1,488,948	680,033	808,915	28,149	14,163	13,986	43,711	20,651	23,060	119,092	48,971	70,121	414,269	183,263	231,006
GEOGRAPHIC DIVISIONS:															
New England	180,851	70,213	110,638	1,437	686	751	4,042	1,650	2,302	15,827	4,602	11,225	55,693	20,743	34,950
Middle Atlantic	525,849	231,273	294,576	2,377	1,169	1,208	6,326	2,790	3,536	34,421	11,079	23,342	151,775	63,532	88,243
East North Central	328,981	152,312	176,669	1,254	653	601	2,557	1,166	1,391	19,436	6,660	12,776	99,861	44,434	55,427
West North Central	85,259	35,467	49,792	848	432	416	1,509	729	780	4,284	2,154	2,130	15,177	6,815	8,362
South Atlantic	32,042	17,777	14,265	294	155	139	814	467	347	2,756	1,539	1,217	10,280	5,870	4,410
East South Central	2,363	1,110	1,253	54	29	25	64	26	38	153	86	72	515	243	272
West South Central	181,799	93,160	88,639	16,224	8,221	8,003	19,382	9,400	9,982	24,376	13,079	11,297	39,203	19,791	19,412
Mountain	71,096	37,261	33,835	3,890	1,943	1,947	5,480	2,618	2,862	9,560	5,215	4,345	19,428	10,231	9,197
Pacific	80,708	41,460	39,248	1,771	875	896	3,537	1,805	1,732	8,274	4,557	3,717	22,337	11,604	10,733
NEW ENGLAND:															
Maine	10,333	3,486	6,847	339	148	191	606	251	355	1,010	361	649	2,192	715	1,477
New Hampshire	11,339	4,350	6,989	126	58	68	317	145	172	1,080	336	744	3,268	1,247	2,021
Vermont	3,065	1,348	1,717	113	62	51	144	80	64	271	132	139	816	336	480
Massachusetts	96,426	37,556	58,870	506	237	269	1,832	657	1,175	8,520	2,376	6,144	30,920	11,608	19,312
Rhode Island	21,620	7,993	13,627	178	85	93	597	245	352	1,842	542	1,300	5,881	2,098	3,783
Connecticut	38,068	15,480	22,588	175	96	79	546	272	274	3,104	855	2,249	12,616	4,739	7,877
MIDDLE ATLANTIC:															
New York	290,200	123,304	166,896	1,451	693	758	3,895	1,600	2,295	18,051	5,804	12,247	76,870	31,743	45,127
New Jersey	73,409	31,661	41,748	334	166	168	901	392	509	6,006	1,680	4,326	23,324	9,668	13,656
Pennsylvania	162,240	76,308	85,932	592	310	282	1,530	798	732	10,364	3,595	6,769	51,581	22,121	29,460
EAST NORTH CENTRAL:															
Ohio	81,161	41,785	39,376	254	134	120	647	318	329	5,522	2,320	3,202	26,669	13,262	13,407
Indiana	13,269	6,517	6,752	47	27	20	101	57	44	686	241	445	3,861	1,668	2,193
Illinois	121,965	53,389	68,576	538	277	261	1,089	478	611	7,395	2,203	5,192	38,526	15,765	22,761
Michigan	68,105	32,432	35,673	316	158	158	568	247	321	4,624	1,454	3,170	22,815	10,470	12,345
Wisconsin	44,481	18,189	26,292	99	57	42	152	66	86	1,209	442	767	7,990	3,269	4,721
WEST NORTH CENTRAL:															
Minnesota	28,311	10,900	17,411	73	44	29	153	82	71	616	269	347	4,430	1,794	2,636
Iowa	9,559	4,239	5,320	90	46	44	194	98	96	480	265	215	1,683	880	803
Missouri	11,126	5,065	6,061	124	62	62	240	108	132	720	297	423	2,588	1,121	1,467
North Dakota	10,189	3,532	6,657	36	19	17	90	33	57	356	101	255	1,467	433	1,034
South Dakota	4,861	1,768	3,093	18	7	11	55	28	27	115	59	56	465	197	268
Nebraska	9,186	3,873	5,313	62	36	26	127	65	62	439	233	206	1,501	723	778
Kansas	12,027	6,090	5,937	445	218	227	650	315	335	1,558	930	628	3,043	1,667	1,376
SOUTH ATLANTIC:															
Delaware	2,733	1,429	1,304	9	3	6	36	18	18	263	106	157	972	470	502
Maryland	7,765	3,396	4,369	27	17	10	82	38	44	415	173	242	1,946	838	1,108
District of Columbia	779	329	450	15	9	6	15	8	7	44	13	31	193	73	120
Virginia	1,135	588	547	17	10	7	22	14	8	94	58	36	307	152	155
West Virginia	11,121	7,655	3,466	87	47	40	301	225	76	1,181	846	335	4,462	3,065	1,397
North Carolina	190	87	103	5	3	2	12	3	9	15	8	7	39	19	20
South Carolina	116	67	49				3	2	1	10	5	5	22	13	9
Georgia	285	141	144	3		3	9	4	5	29	9	20	62	34	28
Florida	7,918	4,085	3,833	131	66	65	334	155	179	705	321	384	2,277	1,206	1,071
EAST SOUTH CENTRAL:															
Kentucky	688	347	341	16	8	8	19	9	10	41	22	19	140	81	59
Tennessee	506	230	276	14	8	6	8	1	7	41	28	13	110	49	61
Alabama	724	319	405	8	5	3	16	7	9	30	12	18	177	76	101
Mississippi	445	214	231	16	8	8	21	9	12	46	24	22	88	37	51
WEST SOUTH CENTRAL:															
Arkansas	697	303	394	12	8	4	24	14	10	41	22	19	109	40	69
Louisiana	3,683	1,656	2,027	74	35	39	144	66	78	281	133	148	573	259	314
Oklahoma	5,362	3,348	2,014	200	91	109	357	228	129	931	707	224	1,400	903	497
Texas	172,057	87,853	84,204	15,938	8,087	7,851	18,857	9,092	9,765	23,123	12,217	10,906	37,121	18,589	18,532
MOUNTAIN:															
Montana	3,098	1,384	1,714	26	13	13	35	17	18	132	57	75	834	392	442
Idaho	1,956	1,191	765	51	30	21	94	68	26	255	167	88	616	391	225
Wyoming	2,003	1,301	702	27	17	10	67	38	29	299	217	82	600	377	223
Colorado	10,650	4,982	5,668	369	186	183	532	248	284	999	533	466	2,729	1,281	1,448
New Mexico	13,225	7,024	6,201	921	466	455	1,269	626	643	1,786	929	857	3,279	1,673	1,606
Arizona	36,352	19,009	17,343	2,443	1,209	1,234	3,350	1,538	1,812	5,585	2,955	2,630	10,207	5,385	4,822
Utah	2,303	1,342	961	29	13	16	66	34	32	242	158	84	606	362	244
Nevada	1,509	1,028	481	24	9	15	67	49	18	262	199	63	557	370	187
PACIFIC:															
Washington	7,796	3,772	4,024	47	29	18	99	51	48	346	174	172	1,776	889	887
Oregon	3,342	1,769	1,573	24	12	12	67	36	31	223	162	61	749	407	342
California	69,570	35,919	33,651	1,700	834	866	3,371	1,718	1,653	7,705	4,221	3,484	19,812	10,308	9,504

INABILITY TO SPEAK ENGLISH.

1255

10 YEARS OF AGE AND OVER, BY SEX AND AGE PERIODS, BY DIVISIONS AND STATES: 1920.

DIVISION AND STATE.	35 TO 44 YEARS.			45 TO 54 YEARS.			55 TO 64 YEARS.			65 YEARS AND OVER.			AGE UNKNOWN.		
	Both sexes.	Male.	Female.	Both sexes.	Male.	Female.	Both sexes.	Male.	Female.	Both sexes.	Male.	Female.	Both sexes.	Male.	Female.
United States	361,912	177,541	184,371	239,495	118,025	121,470	147,760	63,164	84,596	129,445	50,847	78,598	5,115	3,408	1,707
GEOGRAPHIC DIVISIONS:															
New England	43,996	18,720	25,276	29,343	12,603	16,740	17,446	6,517	10,929	12,896	4,617	8,279	171	75	96
Middle Atlantic	141,725	67,585	74,140	94,702	45,415	49,287	56,460	23,922	32,538	35,964	14,507	21,457	2,099	1,274	825
East North Central	85,788	45,223	40,565	52,241	27,407	24,834	32,491	13,707	18,784	34,593	12,479	22,114	760	583	177
West North Central	15,491	7,054	8,437	12,873	5,505	7,388	12,545	4,565	7,980	22,336	8,102	14,234	196	111	85
South Atlantic	8,222	4,727	3,495	5,007	2,848	2,159	2,647	1,285	1,362	1,914	792	1,122	108	94	14
East South Central	544	259	285	421	205	216	205	129	136	338	130	208	4	3	1
West South Central	31,853	15,881	15,972	23,809	12,650	11,159	14,394	7,514	6,880	11,644	5,934	5,710	914	690	224
Mountain	15,067	8,011	7,056	9,090	4,994	4,096	4,656	2,342	2,314	3,603	1,687	1,916	322	220	102
Pacific	19,226	10,081	9,145	12,009	6,398	5,611	6,856	3,183	3,673	6,157	2,599	3,558	541	358	183
NEW ENGLAND:															
Maine	2,004	709	1,295	1,786	561	1,225	1,265	350	915	1,126	387	739	5	4	1
New Hampshire	2,518	1,074	1,444	1,898	745	1,153	1,223	439	784	884	293	591	25	13	12
Vermont	711	324	387	491	235	256	261	101	160	249	72	177	9	6	3
Massachusetts	24,003	10,314	13,689	15,335	6,768	8,567	8,802	3,300	5,502	6,442	2,271	4,171	66	25	41
Rhode Island	4,983	1,930	3,053	3,770	1,472	2,298	2,512	933	1,579	1,836	684	1,152	21	4	17
Connecticut	9,777	4,369	5,408	6,063	2,822	3,241	3,383	1,394	1,989	2,359	910	1,449	45	23	22
MIDDLE ATLANTIC:															
New York	74,503	33,969	40,534	53,542	24,115	29,427	36,497	14,935	21,562	23,935	9,703	14,232	1,456	742	714
New Jersey	19,467	9,248	10,219	12,119	5,888	6,231	6,709	2,849	3,860	4,480	1,730	2,750	69	40	29
Pennsylvania	47,755	24,368	23,387	29,041	15,412	13,629	13,254	6,138	7,116	7,549	3,074	4,475	574	492	82
EAST NORTH CENTRAL:															
Ohio	23,386	13,159	10,227	13,253	7,678	5,575	6,561	3,117	3,444	4,792	1,734	3,058	77	63	14
Indiana	3,606	1,935	1,671	2,276	1,299	977	1,193	584	609	1,276	496	780	223	210	13
Illinois	32,358	16,076	16,282	19,805	9,880	9,925	11,507	4,759	6,748	10,488	3,779	6,709	259	172	87
Michigan	17,499	9,718	7,781	9,766	5,249	4,517	6,222	2,681	3,541	6,167	2,367	3,800	128	88	40
Wisconsin	8,939	4,335	4,604	7,141	3,301	3,840	7,008	2,566	4,442	11,870	4,103	7,767	73	50	23
WEST NORTH CENTRAL:															
Minnesota	4,956	2,201	2,755	4,130	1,683	2,447	4,439	1,478	2,961	9,473	3,329	6,144	41	20	21
Iowa	1,518	790	728	1,255	626	629	1,291	506	785	3,018	1,006	2,012	30	22	8
Missouri	2,675	1,364	1,311	1,846	942	904	1,220	539	681	1,696	625	1,071	17	7	10
North Dakota	1,975	587	1,388	2,023	680	1,343	1,992	760	1,232	2,239	915	1,324	11	4	7
South Dakota	711	261	450	853	275	578	1,019	353	666	1,610	578	1,032	15	10	5
Nebraska	1,439	635	804	1,372	593	779	1,509	516	993	2,708	1,052	1,656	29	20	9
Kansas	2,217	1,216	1,001	1,394	706	688	1,075	413	662	1,592	597	995	53	28	25
SOUTH ATLANTIC:															
Delaware	688	405	283	420	248	172	216	104	112	99	46	53	30	29	1
Maryland	1,872	887	985	1,446	672	774	1,025	397	628	949	372	577	3	2	1
District of Columbia	192	87	105	138	67	71	83	34	49	97	37	60	2	1	1
Virginia	292	156	136	182	95	87	115	66	49	104	36	68	2	1	1
West Virginia	3,083	2,118	965	1,337	945	392	433	288	145	199	88	111	38	33	5
North Carolina	30	13	17	37	19	18	27	10	17	25	12	13	......	......	......
South Carolina	36	21	15	20	13	7	13	7	6	12	6	6	......	......	......
Georgia	68	41	27	54	29	25	35	14	21	25	10	15	33	28	5
Florida	1,961	999	962	1,373	760	613	700	365	335	404	185	219			
EAST SOUTH CENTRAL:															
Kentucky	145	85	60	121	67	54	57	31	26	148	43	105	1	1	......
Tennessee	116	46	70	89	44	45	56	25	31	71	28	43	1	1	......
Alabama	187	79	108	136	60	76	94	45	49	70	35	41	2	1	1
Mississippi	96	49	47	75	34	41	58	28	30	43	24	19	2	1	1
WEST SOUTH CENTRAL:															
Arkansas	134	58	76	131	61	70	109	45	64	137	55	82	......	......	......
Louisiana	687	296	391	713	298	415	575	259	316	630	306	324	6	4	2
Oklahoma	948	606	342	619	347	272	421	208	213	411	185	226	75	73	2
Texas	30,084	14,921	15,163	22,346	11,944	10,402	13,289	7,002	6,287	10,466	5,388	5,078	833	613	220
MOUNTAIN:															
Montana	815	349	466	599	271	328	343	153	190	299	120	179	15	12	3
Idaho	409	252	157	236	142	94	140	77	63	152	63	89	3	1	2
Wyoming	481	310	171	248	175	73	98	56	42	59	26	33	124	85	39
Colorado	2,578	1,189	1,389	1,670	793	877	958	406	552	779	323	456	36	23	13
New Mexico	2,511	1,344	1,167	1,732	1,009	723	995	556	439	705	403	302	27	18	9
Arizona	7,399	3,994	3,405	4,118	2,279	1,839	1,851	952	899	1,290	621	669	109	76	33
Utah	544	346	198	336	220	116	205	101	104	269	105	164	6	3	3
Nevada	330	227	103	151	105	46	66	25	41	50	26	24	2	2	......
PACIFIC:															
Washington	1,927	995	932	1,429	732	697	1,006	452	554	1,139	429	710	27	21	6
Oregon	834	476	358	529	272	257	435	204	231	477	198	279	4	2	2
California	16,465	8,610	7,855	10,051	5,394	4,657	5,415	2,527	2,888	4,541	1,972	2,569	510	335	175

1256

POPULATION.

TABLE 6.—NUMBER AND PER CENT UNABLE TO SPEAK ENGLISH IN FOREIGN-BORN WHITE POPULATION 21 YEARS OF AGE AND OVER, BY SEX, 1920, WITH COMPARATIVE PERCENTAGES FOR 1910, BY DIVISIONS AND STATES.

	FOREIGN-BORN WHITE POPULATION 21 YEARS OF AGE AND OVER.											
	Both sexes.				Male.				Female.			
	Total number: 1920	Unable to speak English.			Total number: 1920	Unable to speak English.			Total number: 1920	Unable to speak English.		
DIVISION AND STATE.		Number: 1920	Per cent.			Number: 1920	Per cent.			Number: 1920	Per cent.	
			1920	1910			1920	1910			1920	1910
United States	12,498,720	1,399,759	11.2	22.0	6,928,452	637,830	9.2	22.0	5,570,268	761,929	13.7	22.0
GEOGRAPHIC DIVISIONS:												
New England	1,705,291	173,515	10.2	17.3	866,042	67,350	7.8	17.0	839,249	106,165	12.7	17.6
Middle Atlantic	4,477,752	513,768	11.5	25.7	2,406,975	226,306	9.4	26.7	2,070,777	287,462	13.9	24.6
East North Central	2,978,575	323,675	10.9	22.7	1,687,728	149,946	8.9	22.5	1,290,847	173,729	13.5	22.9
West North Central	1,291,794	82,212	6.4	16.8	738,673	33,964	4.6	14.9	553,121	48,248	8.7	19.4
South Atlantic	287,215	30,504	10.6	24.2	170,407	16,881	9.9	27.0	116,808	13,623	11.7	20.0
East South Central	67,242	2,216	3.3	11.1	39,697	1,043	2.6	11.1	27,545	1,173	4.3	11.0
West South Central	357,220	140,308	39.3	41.9	208,431	72,655	34.9	37.9	148,789	67,653	45.5	47.7
Mountain	394,008	59,736	15.2	21.4	241,321	31,717	13.1	22.7	152,687	28,019	18.4	19.0
Pacific	939,623	73,825	7.9	12.7	569,178	37,968	6.7	13.2	370,445	35,857	9.7	11.9
NEW ENGLAND:												
Maine	94,329	9,190	9.7	16.9	49,355	3,013	6.1	14.3	44,974	6,177	13.7	20.0
New Hampshire	82,049	10,723	13.1	26.1	42,432	4,097	9.7	24.3	39,617	6,626	16.7	28.1
Vermont	38,232	2,761	7.2	16.3	20,462	1,181	5.8	16.5	17,770	1,580	8.9	16.0
Massachusetts	988,913	93,150	9.4	15.6	491,107	36,448	7.4	15.7	497,806	56,702	11.4	15.5
Rhode Island	156,866	20,648	13.2	20.2	78,118	7,601	9.7	18.4	78,748	13,047	16.6	22.1
Connecticut	344,902	37,043	10.7	19.1	184,568	15,010	8.1	19.1	160,334	22,033	13.7	19.1
MIDDLE ATLANTIC:												
New York	2,528,497	282,902	11.2	22.4	1,318,883	120,426	9.1	21.7	1,209,614	162,476	13.4	23.3
New Jersey	675,222	71,587	10.6	23.0	360,902	30,962	8.6	24.0	314,320	40,625	12.9	21.7
Pennsylvania	1,274,033	159,279	12.5	33.1	727,190	74,918	10.3	35.9	546,843	84,361	15.4	28.8
EAST NORTH CENTRAL:												
Ohio	622,523	79,813	12.8	27.7	363,504	41,136	11.3	29.7	259,019	38,677	14.9	24.8
Indiana	140,373	13,064	9.3	25.3	82,908	6,405	7.7	28.5	57,465	6,659	11.6	20.4
Illinois	1,117,928	119,788	10.7	22.1	613,797	52,462	8.5	21.8	504,131	67,326	13.4	22.5
Michigan	663,160	66,873	10.1	17.2	381,808	31,915	8.4	17.1	281,352	34,958	12.4	17.4
Wisconsin	434,591	44,137	10.2	23.9	245,711	18,028	7.3	20.2	188,880	26,109	13.8	28.8
WEST NORTH CENTRAL:												
Minnesota	462,582	28,024	6.1	16.6	266,856	10,749	4.0	13.9	195,726	17,275	8.8	20.5
Iowa	214,479	9,210	4.3	13.2	121,392	4,066	3.3	12.4	93,087	5,144	5.5	14.4
Missouri	173,551	10,668	6.1	16.4	97,345	4,857	5.0	16.6	76,206	5,811	7.6	16.1
North Dakota	121,047	10,021	8.3	20.8	70,043	3,467	4.9	15.8	51,004	6,554	12.8	28.3
South Dakota	78,027	4,771	6.1	18.1	45,340	1,722	3.8	14.0	32,687	3,049	9.3	24.1
Nebraska	140,899	8,941	6.3	16.7	79,821	3,749	4.7	15.2	61,078	5,192	8.5	18.6
Kansas	101,209	10,577	10.5	20.5	57,876	5,354	9.3	20.8	43,333	5,223	12.1	20.0
SOUTH ATLANTIC:												
Delaware	18,245	2,665	14.6	26.6	10,614	1,398	13.2	31.1	7,631	1,267	16.6	20.6
Maryland	93,624	7,623	8.1	17.2	50,363	3,328	6.6	17.1	43,261	4,295	9.9	17.3
District of Columbia	26,376	740	2.8	5.5	14,042	311	2.2	5.4	12,334	429	3.5	5.7
Virginia	27,851	1,081	3.9	15.2	17,431	556	3.2	16.7	10,420	525	5.0	12.4
West Virginia	55,465	10,506	18.9	48.6	38,471	7,195	18.7	53.3	16,994	3,311	19.5	36.0
North Carolina	6,488	170	2.6	12.4	4,035	80	2.0	12.9	2,453	90	3.7	11.6
South Carolina	5,941	113	1.9	7.1	3,850	65	1.7	7.3	2,091	48	2.3	6.8
Georgia	14,855	269	1.8	6.1	9,319	136	1.5	5.8	5,536	133	2.4	6.6
Florida	38,870	7,337	19.1	40.9	22,282	3,812	17.1	40.1	16,088	3,525	21.9	42.1
EAST SOUTH CENTRAL:												
Kentucky	29,488	643	2.2	9.2	16,827	327	1.9	10.1	12,661	316	2.5	8.3
Tennessee	14,319	479	3.3	8.5	8,428	218	2.6	7.8	5,891	261	4.4	9.7
Alabama	16,105	694	4.3	16.2	9,814	306	3.1	15.7	6,291	388	6.2	17.1
Mississippi	7,330	400	5.5	14.2	4,628	192	4.1	12.5	2,702	208	7.7	17.2
WEST SOUTH CENTRAL:												
Arkansas	13,166	650	4.9	15.2	8,166	273	3.3	13.1	5,000	377	7.5	18.7
Louisiana	41,228	3,414	8.3	22.2	24,848	1,534	6.2	20.2	16,380	1,880	11.5	25.1
Oklahoma	36,108	4,616	12.8	19.6	22,817	2,896	12.7	19.2	13,291	1,720	12.9	20.2
Texas	266,718	131,628	49.4	52.9	152,600	67,952	44.5	48.2	114,118	63,676	55.8	59.6
MOUNTAIN:												
Montana	85,709	3,020	3.5	14.5	54,250	1,342	2.5	16.3	31,459	1,678	5.3	10.1
Idaho	36,170	1,761	4.9	13.4	23,366	1,055	4.5	15.5	12,804	706	5.5	8.7
Wyoming	23,057	1,870	8.1	21.6	15,796	1,218	7.7	23.6	7,261	652	9.0	15.6
Colorado	105,017	9,555	9.1	17.7	62,089	4,445	7.2	18.3	42,928	5,110	11.9	16.7
New Mexico	21,933	10,630	48.5	53.3	13,244	5,736	43.3	52.2	8,689	4,894	56.3	55.6
Arizona	55,973	29,357	52.4	55.2	33,582	15,704	46.8	51.9	22,391	13,653	61.0	62.4
Utah	52,254	2,170	4.2	12.6	28,791	1,277	4.4	16.1	23,463	893	3.8	8.0
Nevada	13,895	1,373	9.9	17.7	10,203	940	9.2	19.6	3,692	433	11.7	11.7
PACIFIC:												
Washington	230,435	7,602	3.3	10.3	143,258	3,669	2.6	10.9	87,177	3,933	4.5	9.3
Oregon	94,807	3,209	3.4	12.5	58,580	1,689	2.9	14.0	36,227	1,520	4.2	9.4
California	614,381	63,014	10.3	13.9	367,340	32,610	8.9	14.2	247,041	30,404	12.3	13.4

INABILITY TO SPEAK ENGLISH.   1257

TABLE 7.—NUMBER UNABLE TO SPEAK ENGLISH IN COLORED POPULATION 10 YEARS OF AGE AND OVER, BY RACE AND SEX, BY DIVISIONS AND STATES: 1920 AND 1910.

DIVISION AND STATE.	1920 Negro Male	Negro Female	Indian Male	Indian Female	Chinese Male	Chinese Female	Japanese Male	Japanese Female	All other, both sexes	1910 Negro Male	Negro Female	Indian Male	Indian Female	Chinese Male	Chinese Female	Japanese Male	Japanese Female	All other, both sexes
United States	7,207	7,437	17,469	19,283	8,903	1,117	8,709	10,359	¹982	10,870	11,240	26,705	32,350	26,632	1,738	22,848	3,716	²2,097
GEOGRAPHIC DIVISIONS:																		
New England	640	502	4	10	384	45	9	3		870	487	5	12	848	18	13	3	1
Middle Atlantic	525	475	46	123	1,066	41	105	49	69	259	186	191	292	3,776	70	111	30	13
East North Central	204	175	210	402	708	35	17	12	40	102	45	890	1,434	1,105	8	23	7	1
West North Central	233	181	1,647	2,288	276	15	127	75	2	169	33	4,508	5,944	435	9	391	11	7
South Atlantic	1,060	971	233	244	152	9	4	3	6	726	518	222	219	396	7	22	8	2
East South Central	495	448	16	22	18	3		1		85	65	119	146	84	3	1		
West South Central	3,837	4,544	1,352	1,618	270	11	21	20	10	8,288	9,786	3,603	4,691	432	5	106	23	39
Mountain	115	76	12,502	12,652	598	55	1,321	928	14	146	71	15,575	17,002	1,753	57	5,233	178	98
Pacific	98	65	1,459	1,924	5,431	903	7,105	9,270	841	225	49	1,592	2,610	17,803	1,561	16,948	3,456	1,936
NEW ENGLAND:																		
Maine	2	2	2	8	15	2	2			4		4	12	21				
New Hampshire	13	5		1	5						1			10				
Vermont			1		2						8	1		3				
Massachusetts	372	377		1	307	40	2	1		678	398			658	15	8	2	1
Rhode Island	130	86	1		12	1	1			167	79			58		1	1	
Connecticut	123	32			43	2	4	2		20	1			98	3	4		
MIDDLE ATLANTIC:																		
New York	312	330	45	122	667	24	94	42	56	112	120	174	285	2,896	59	77	21	13
New Jersey	35	39	1	1	200	8	9	7		24	11	12	6	314	6	23	5	
Pennsylvania	178	106			199	9	2		13	123	55	5	1	566	5	11	4	
EAST NORTH CENTRAL:																		
Ohio	80	51	3		139	5	2	3	10	16	8			197	3	5		
Indiana	21	24	5		54				6	4	12	2	2	71		4		
Illinois	69	65	1	1	410	24	7	5	3	67	15		1	720	3	5	5	1
Michigan	29	30	45	124	67	5	5	2	21	8	3	445	675	62		9	1	
Wisconsin	5	5	156	277	38	1	3	2		7	7	443	755	55	2	1		
WEST NORTH CENTRAL:																		
Minnesota	4	3	356	615	43	7				35	6	729	1,014	58	3	8		
Iowa	41	24	3	10	28	1	1			12	1	115	30	19		5	2	
Missouri	130	103	2	1	118	2	25	4	2	77	11	3	2	267		8		
North Dakota	1		380	471	26	1	1	3		3	3	941	1,110	11		23		
South Dakota	1	2	848	1,108	14	2	1	1		2		2,422	3,327	38	4	16		
Nebraska	7	14	36	53	37	2	100	67		22	1	201	386	41	2	201	8	7
Kansas	49	35	22	30	10					18	11	97	75	1		40	1	
SOUTH ATLANTIC:																		
Delaware	10	8			2									7		1		
Maryland	34	33			40	1	2			3	5			123	1	1	1	
District of Columbia	11	13			51	4			1	8	4	1		114	2	2	2	2
Virginia	213	142		1	11			2		28	4			30	1	4		
West Virginia	39	31			14				2	21	9			23		2		
North Carolina	167	147	73	98	5	3			1	9	3	220	219	16	1	1	1	
South Carolina	228	242			7	1								9	1			
Georgia	162	166			13		1	1	1	14	1			35	1	1	1	
Florida	196	189	160	145	9		1			639	492	1		39		11	3	
EAST SOUTH CENTRAL:																		
Kentucky	47	34			6					3	5	1		9				
Tennessee	79	85			2	1				9				11		1		
Alabama	74	81			3		1			7	3			10				
Mississippi	295	248	16	22	7	2				66	57	118	146	54	3			
WEST SOUTH CENTRAL:																		
Arkansas	56	93			2	1				3	2	1		9	1			
Louisiana	2,991	3,745	67	77	41	4	11		9	7,789	9,465	77	95	126	3	6		39
Oklahoma	63	45	911	1,256	37	1		2		23	319	3,457	4,523	65		24	23	
Texas	727	661	374	285	190	5	10	18	1	473		68	73	232	1	76		
MOUNTAIN:																		
Montana	3	2	647	780	100	2	106	63		21		1,588	1,908	527	7	842	9	4
Idaho	13	1	230	253	167	4	131	143	3	6	1	473	607	316	9	671	27	5
Wyoming	3		110	134	35		173	78	3	8	1	197	253	87	2	950	20	65
Colorado	30	21	237	235	21	3	141	270	1	30	22	232	252	120	6	1,093	52	
New Mexico	5	7	4,348	4,130	23		16	12		47	36	5,414	5,562	47	2	122	6	
Arizona	46	38	6,323	6,495	126	34	35	49	1	17	10	6,594	7,132	325	13	73	10	14
Utah	15	7	504	450	39	4	471	266	3	16	1	747	789	138	6	1,102	39	10
Nevada			103	175	87	8	248	45	3	1		330	519	193	12	380	15	
PACIFIC:																		
Washington	12	5	300	531	383	53	1,555	1,587	42	34	8	608	1,086	927	87	4,037	661	88
Oregon	1		156	305	929	57	356	303	18	8		213	466	1,203	51	1,093	142	237
California	85	60	1,003	1,088	4,119	793	5,194	7,380	781	183	41	711	1,058	15,673	1,423	11,818	2,653	1,611

¹ Includes 66 females, credited to states as follows: New York, 2; Idaho, 1; Wyoming, 1; Arizona, 1; Washington, 6; Oregon, 1; California, 54.
² Includes 20 females, credited to states as follows: New York, 3; District of Columbia, 1; Utah, 3; California, 13.

1258

POPULATION.

TABLE 8.—NUMBER UNABLE TO SPEAK ENGLISH IN FOREIGN-BORN WHITE POPULATION 10 YEARS OF AGE AND OVER AND 21 YEARS OF AGE AND OVER, BY SEX, WITH PERCENTAGES FOR BOTH SEXES COMBINED, FOR CITIES HAVING, IN 1920, 100,000 INHABITANTS OR MORE: 1920 AND 1910.

CITY.	Total number: 1920	Both sexes Number: 1920	Per cent 1920	Per cent 1910	Male 1920	Male 1910	Female 1920	Female 1910	Total number: 1920	Both sexes Number: 1920	Per cent 1920	Per cent 1910	Male 1920	Male 1910	Female 1920	Female 1910
Akron, Ohio	37,213	4,354	11.7	32.6	2,607	2,739	1,747	1,382	33,912	4,229	12.5	32.1	2,536	2,524	1,693	1,176
Albany, N.Y.	17,471	1,669	9.5	12.4	777	1,318	892	880	16,348	1,617	9.9	11.4	755	1,129	862	751
Atlanta, Ga.	4,676	90	1.9	5.9	36	125	54	127	4,272	85	2.0	5.8	34	103	51	117
Baltimore, Md.	83,083	6,768	8.1	17.5	2,834	6,134	3,934	6,901	76,647	6,654	8.7	17.7	2,787	5,538	3,867	6,230
Birmingham, Ala.	5,997	320	5.3	20.0	133	634	187	460	5,470	307	5.6	19.8	129	565	178	407
Boston, Mass.	236,320	14,069	6.0	10.8	5,662	12,151	8,407	13,161	221,036	13,758	6.2	10.5	5,553	10,509	8,205	11,553
Bridgeport, Conn.	45,795	5,980	13.1	21.3	2,746	4,250	3,234	3,221	42,308	5,853	13.8	21.0	2,682	3,564	3,171	2,630
Buffalo, N.Y.	119,685	17,157	14.3	26.8	8,250	16,354	8,907	14,472	111,716	16,879	15.1	26.6	8,162	14,912	8,717	13,102
Cambridge, Mass.	31,624	1,482	4.7	8.1	524	1,364	958	1,357	29,490	1,435	4.9	7.6	511	1,154	924	1,186
Camden, N.J.	19,955	2,832	14.2	17.2	1,310	1,520	1,522	1,105	18,380	2,754	15.0	16.3	1,284	1,310	1,470	913
Chicago, Ill.	797,618	89,092	11.2	24.4	38,612	98,443	50,480	86,441	743,803	87,699	11.8	23.7	38,020	86,915	49,679	75,115
Cincinnati, Ohio	42,564	1,768	4.2	17.3	773	5,315	995	4,246	40,849	1,739	4.3	16.5	766	4,715	983	3,829
Cleveland, Ohio	236,244	35,390	15.0	31.3	16,319	32,359	19,071	26,768	217,793	35,001	16.1	31.4	16,189	28,788	18,812	23,885
Columbus, Ohio	15,891	1,087	6.8	19.5	579	1,985	508	1,108	14,726	1,058	7.2	18.9	563	1,756	495	1,040
Dallas, Tex.	8,394	1,660	19.8	7.0	991	187	669	187	7,495	1,329	17.7	6.5	811	145	518	163
Dayton, Ohio	12,960	1,363	10.5	34.3	722	3,227	641	1,375	12,060	1,338	11.1	32.7	710	2,843	628	1,171
Denver, Colo.	37,203	1,808	4.9	7.3	740	1,300	1,068	1,494	35,282	1,699	4.8	7.1	692	1,163	1,007	1,376
Des Moines, Iowa	11,110	619	5.6	9.7	306	559	313	420	10,441	584	5.6	9.2	298	493	286	376
Detroit, Mich.	282,257	33,007	11.7	25.2	17,101	23,380	15,906	14,658	257,510	32,318	12.6	24.8	16,827	20,697	15,491	12,967
Fall River, Mass.	41,736	8,441	20.2	28.0	2,978	5,485	5,463	8,250	38,145	8,114	21.3	27.2	5,211	4,605	2,903	6,761
Fort Worth, Tex.	6,860	2,443	35.6	23.9	1,562	811	881	167	5,868	1,989	33.9	23.2	1,306	724	683	139
Grand Rapids, Mich.	28,065	2,084	7.4	18.8	845	2,639	1,239	2,515	26,181	2,062	7.9	18.4	836	2,362	1,226	2,273
Hartford, Conn.	40,176	3,192	7.9	13.1	1,370	1,869	1,822	2,088	37,021	3,122	8.4	12.6	1,350	1,592	1,772	1,792
Houston, Tex.	11,459	1,827	15.9	11.2	880	379	947	312	10,123	1,466	14.5	10.4	715	332	751	259
Indianapolis, Ind.	16,818	617	3.7	17.7	313	2,512	304	929	16,000	610	3.8	16.5	308	2,145	302	858
Jersey City, N.J.	75,232	6,249	8.3	18.6	2,876	8,372	3,373	5,698	70,677	6,114	8.7	17.5	2,820	7,200	3,294	4,731
Kansas City, Kans.	11,253	1,387	12.3	24.4	709	1,718	678	738	10,334	1,224	11.8	22.5	645	1,447	579	615
Kansas City, Mo.	26,810	2,216	8.3	10.9	1,040	1,539	1,176	1,138	24,728	2,008	8.1	10.3	945	1,313	1,063	1,030
Los Angeles, Calif.	108,684	10,619	9.8	12.8	4,722	4,006	5,897	3,485	98,710	9,492	9.6	11.9	4,238	3,352	5,254	3,021
Louisville, Ky.	11,569	180	1.6	8.3	59	767	121	655	11,182	166	1.5	7.8	56	690	110	593
Lowell, Mass.	37,549	6,141	16.4	27.6	2,426	6,228	3,715	5,421	35,023	5,806	16.6	24.5	2,332	4,865	3,474	4,155
Memphis, Tenn.	5,704	174	3.1	8.8	62	294	112	261	5,294	168	3.2	7.7	59	226	109	215
Milwaukee, Wis.	108,934	17,074	15.7	35.4	7,162	20,437	9,912	17,865	101,684	16,969	16.7	35.7	7,118	18,670	9,851	16,886
Minneapolis, Minn.	87,083	1,952	2.2	9.8	636	4,658	1,316	3,604	82,735	1,915	2.3	9.4	617	4,123	1,298	3,198
Nashville, Tenn.	2,365	29	1.2	3.7	11	47	18	61	2,197	26	1.2	3.2	9	31	17	54
New Bedford, Mass.	47,636	9,983	21.0	26.7	4,020	4,774	5,963	6,071	42,486	9,277	21.8	25.9	3,776	3,864	5,501	4,924
New Haven, Conn.	45,101	5,234	11.6	17.0	1,988	3,282	3,296	3,761	41,634	5,119	12.3	17.1	1,887	2,849	3,232	3,368
New Orleans, La.	25,632	1,510	5.9	12.3	626	1,541	884	1,779	23,814	1,401	5.9	12.1	584	1,428	817	1,625
New York, N.Y.	1,968,535	208,125	10.6	22.7	86,536	196,969	121,589	224,982	1,797,882	202,651	11.3	23.0	84,342	172,112	118,309	192,235
Bronx borough	264,475	17,633	6.7	14.1	6,678	9,714	10,955	10,746	243,093	17,203	7.1	13.7	6,517	8,417	10,686	9,333
Brooklyn borough	651,941	71,835	10.9	21.0	29,463	52,340	41,872	62,852	593,266	69,507	11.7	21.1	28,054	46,382	40,853	54,541
Manhattan borough	910,438	109,288	12.0	25.3	46,121	125,302	63,167	143,308	827,420	106,258	12.8	26.0	44,978	108,923	61,280	121,208
Queens borough	110,736	6,815	6.2	17.8	2,863	7,251	3,952	6,526	105,012	6,687	6.4	17.1	2,809	6,323	3,878	5,820
Richmond borough	30,945	3,054	9.9	16.0	1,411	2,362	1,643	1,550	29,091	2,996	10.3	15.8	1,384	2,037	1,612	1,333
Newark, N.J.	115,609	11,222	9.7	23.8	5,111	12,453	6,111	12,832	105,959	10,880	10.3	23.8	4,950	10,932	5,930	11,136
Norfolk, Va.	6,511	199	3.1	7.3	112	148	87	99	5,946	186	3.1	7.3	103	133	83	89
Oakland, Calif.	44,575	1,383	3.1	9.6	567	1,908	816	1,559	41,953	1,334	3.2	9.3	539	1,723	795	1,434
Omaha, Nebr.[1]	35,017	2,132	6.1	18.7	938	4,045	1,194	2,283	32,585	2,049	6.3	18.1	894	3,662	1,155	2,007
Paterson, N.J.	44,564	4,230	9.5	18.6	1,729	4,103	2,501	4,055	40,746	4,090	10.0	18.1	1,683	3,502	2,407	3,532
Philadelphia, Pa.	393,747	31,742	8.1	18.5	13,324	34,280	18,418	34,005	361,648	31,138	8.6	18.2	13,092	30,055	18,046	29,104
Pittsburgh, Pa.	119,182	10,324	8.7	27.8	4,938	23,795	5,386	14,262	111,907	10,180	9.1	27.6	4,879	21,200	5,301	12,565
Portland, Oreg.	46,338	1,220	2.6	9.9	539	2,875	681	1,325	43,133	1,188	2.8	9.3	524	2,468	664	1,184
Providence, R.I.	68,278	7,416	10.9	19.8	2,713	7,398	4,703	7,246	63,441	7,259	11.4	19.1	2,663	6,180	4,596	6,141
Reading, Pa.	9,449	1,407	14.9	44.1	601	2,350	806	1,390	8,693	1,361	15.7	43.6	581	2,009	780	1,213
Richmond, Va.	4,576	97	2.1	7.9	31	181	66	131	4,252	95	2.2	7.7	30	155	65	121
Rochester, N.Y.	70,085	6,362	9.1	19.4	2,447	6,292	3,915	4,734	63,668	6,165	9.7	18.5	2,366	5,342	3,799	4,080
St. Louis, Mo.	102,490	5,658	5.5	18.6	2,391	12,944	3,267	9,816	95,716	5,549	5.8	18.1	2,351	11,493	3,198	8,791
St. Paul, Minn.	51,086	1,693	3.3	11.1	589	3,235	1,104	2,887	48,314	1,674	3.5	10.8	583	2,890	1,091	2,681
Salt Lake City, Utah	19,182	595	3.1	8.4	306	950	289	596	17,814	553	3.1	8.0	285	814	268	549
San Antonio, Tex.	33,977	16,466	48.5	46.1	8,274	3,376	8,192	4,114	27,109	13,580	50.1	44.6	7,001	2,775	6,579	3,449
San Francisco, Calif.	138,475	7,110	5.1	7.4	3,245	5,255	3,871	4,282	130,867	6,790	5.2	7.0	3,080	4,635	3,710	3,859
Scranton, Pa.	28,321	2,462	8.7	22.8	1,045	4,692	1,417	3,078	26,687	2,428	9.1	22.1	1,034	4,120	1,394	2,701
Seattle, Wash.	71,988	1,985	2.8	6.5	1,017	2,937	968	942	67,540	1,918	2.8	6.2	989	2,570	929	845
Spokane, Wash.	16,488	317	1.9	7.0	124	1,080	193	371	15,483	315	2.0	6.7	123	953	192	334
Springfield, Mass.	30,857	2,185	7.1	16.4	820	1,744	1,365	1,906	28,724	2,121	7.4	15.5	799	1,480	1,322	1,580
Syracuse, N.Y.	31,936	2,832	8.9	21.3	1,310	4,117	1,522	2,256	29,793	2,781	9.3	19.8	1,294	3,462	1,487	1,857
Toledo, Ohio	37,667	5,300	14.1	21.0	2,702	3,605	2,598	2,963	35,311	5,215	14.8	20.8	2,652	3,261	2,563	2,733
Trenton, N.J.	29,676	3,697	12.5	29.5	1,672	4,595	2,025	2,901	27,091	3,601	13.3	28.3	1,638	3,975	1,963	2,323
Washington, D.C.	28,292	779	2.8	5.7	329	710	450	639	26,376	740	2.8	5.5	311	632	429	593
Wilmington, Del.	16,075	2,459	15.3	32.0	1,255	2,770	1,204	1,495	15,073	2,404	15.9	30.0	1,236	2,377	1,168	1,212
Worcester, Mass.	52,821	3,318	6.3	15.4	1,230	4,236	2,088	3,023	49,389	3,249	6.6	14.6	1,196	3,572	2,053	2,627
Yonkers, N.Y.	25,439	2,581	10.1	20.8	1,111	3,089	1,470	2,301	23,962	2,529	10.6	18.8	1,099	2,544	1,430	1,711
Youngstown, Ohio	33,343	5,073	15.2	33.6	3,108	5,984	1,965	2,078	30,943	4,987	16.1	33.1	3,063	5,285	1,924	1,796

[1] Includes population of South Omaha for 1910.

INABILITY TO SPEAK ENGLISH.   1259

TABLE 9.—NUMBER UNABLE TO SPEAK ENGLISH IN FOREIGN-BORN WHITE POPULATION 10 YEARS OF AGE AND OVER, BY SEX, WITH PERCENTAGES FOR BOTH SEXES COMBINED, FOR CITIES HAVING, IN 1920, FROM 25,000 TO 100,000 INHABITANTS: 1920 AND 1910.

[Figures for 1910 not available for cities having a population of less than 25,000 at that census.]

CITY.	Total number: 1920	Both sexes. Number: 1920	Per cent. 1920	Per cent. 1910	Male 1920	Male 1910	Female 1920	Female 1910
Alabama.								
Mobile	1,973	27	1.4	3.1	10	40	17	26
Montgomery	744	20	2.7	6.4	7	23	13	21
Arizona.								
Phoenix	3,838	1,355	35.3	......	673		682	
Arkansas.								
Fort Smith	848	29	3.4	......	11		18	
Little Rock	1,788	23	1.3	6.1	12	60	11	58
California.								
Alameda	5,781	115	2.0	......	51		64	
Berkeley	9,434	194	2.1	5.4	96	224	98	183
Fresno	8,319	918	11.0	......	353		565	
Long Beach	6,581	306	4.6	......	153		153	
Pasadena	6,622	197	3.0	4.8	72	107	125	94
Sacramento	10,705	705	6.6	8.4	314	468	391	267
San Diego	12,918	1,110	8.6	12.0	441	473	669	382
San Jose	7,728	771	10.0	10.2	299	253	472	330
Stockton	6,874	521	7.6	......	240		281	
Colorado.								
Colorado Springs	2,586	61	2.4	5.1	28	131	33	20
Pueblo	7,073	1,137	16.1	38.4	566	2,181	571	944
Connecticut.								
Meriden	7,846	656	8.4	10.8	291	368	365	474
New Britain	20,982	3,721	17.7	34.3	1,444	3,392	2,277	2,602
New London	5,770	427	7.4	......	117		310	
Norwalk	5,891	550	9.3	......	207		343	
Stamford	10,554	802	7.6	13.8	257	550	545	514
Waterbury	29,432	2,606	8.9	16.8	1,131	2,357	1,475	1,777
Florida.								
Jacksonville	3,825	87	2.3	4.1	50	54	37	46
Miami	2,492	8	0.3	......	1		7	
Pensacola	1,428	15	1.1	......	9		6	
Tampa	10,413	5,293	50.8	66.5	2,650	3,379	2,643	2,746
Georgia.								
Augusta	920	21	2.3	10.0	9	59	12	28
Columbus	323	1	0.3	......		1	1	
Macon	686	7	1.0	9.1	4	43	3	17
Savannah	3,215	35	1.1	3.4	9	70	26	41
Illinois.								
Aurora	6,427	245	3.8	22.1	84	1,019	161	428
Bloomington	2,818	137	4.9	7.3	56	83	81	161
Cicero town	15,360	3,226	21.0	......	1,267		1,959	
Danville	1,904	46	2.4	5.1	19	39	27	63
Decatur	2,555	80	3.1	17.1	36	146	44	253
East St. Louis	6,711	678	10.1	45.4	365	3,162	313	953
Elgin	5,021	160	3.2	12.5	71	381	89	315
Evanston	6,704	219	3.3	......	79		140	
Joliet	8,408	1,222	14.5	39.1	624	2,854	598	1,120
Moline	7,305	263	3.6	......	128		135	
Oak Park village	5,604	70	1.2	......	30		40	
Peoria	7,734	357	4.6	18.2	236	1,121	121	461
Quincy	2,407	79	3.3	11.4	38	151	41	260
Rock Island	5,296	170	3.2	......	73		97	
Rockford	17,160	1,514	8.8	19.1	709	1,581	805	991
Springfield	6,188	223	3.6	13.2	98	481	125	397
Indiana.								
Anderson	929	82	8.8	......	44		38	
East Chicago	14,440	2,906	20.1	......	1,487		1,419	
Evansville	3,106	29	0.9	12.5	9	244	20	312
Fort Wayne	6,573	282	4.3	16.8	147	755	135	433
Gary	16,198	1,377	8.5	......	729		648	
Hammond	8,032	1,085	13.5	......	556		529	
Kokomo	1,149	52	4.5	......	38		14	
Muncie	813	36	4.4	......	24		12	
Richmond	1,122	25	2.2	......	10		15	
South Bend	13,222	2,237	16.9	48.4	992	3,682	1,245	2,509
Terre Haute	3,636	177	4.9	13.4	110	349	67	151

CITY.	Total number: 1920	Both sexes. Number: 1920	Per cent. 1920	Per cent. 1910	Male 1920	Male 1910	Female 1920	Female 1910
Iowa.								
Cedar Rapids	5,784	594	10.3	20.9	265	526	329	550
Council Bluffs	3,944	206	5.2	12.5	131	417	75	109
Davenport	7,574	243	3.2	10.4	146	438	97	396
Dubuque	4,193	170	4.1	13.4	77	490	93	319
Sioux City	11,119	638	5.7	16.3	359	1,350	279	305
Waterloo	2,836	140	4.9	16.0	71	349	69	73
Kansas.								
Topeka	3,846	518	13.5	14.4	263	347	255	232
Wichita	2,891	539	18.6	16.5	324	373	215	87
Kentucky.								
Covington	2,878	25	0.9	6.5	15	109	10	147
Lexington	791	8	1.0	4.1	3	19	5	19
Newport	2,082	37	1.8	8.3	15	160	22	117
Louisiana.								
Shreveport	1,275	48	3.8	3.7	19	21	29	15
Maine.								
Bangor	3,688	88	2.4	......	48		40	......
Lewiston	9,974	2,614	26.2	40.0	688	1,257	1,926	2,311
Portland	12,995	262	2.0	7.4	94	547	168	327
Maryland.								
Cumberland	1,153	139	12.1	......	91		48	......
Hagerstown	428	9	2.1	......	5		4	......
Massachusetts.								
Brockton	16,917	688	4.1	12.1	257	922	431	894
Brookline town	9,307	8	0.1	0.7	3	15	5	39
Chelsea	16,980	2,423	14.3	18.5	1,093	1,195	1,330	1,217
Chicopee	12,025	2,557	21.3	40.7	946	1,780	1,611	2,178
Everett	10,952	509	4.6	3.8	212	183	297	172
Fitchburg	12,900	1,459	11.3	24.8	502	1,355	957	1,913
Haverhill	13,165	785	6.0	15.2	264	999	521	660
Holyoke	19,973	2,083	10.4	21.6	765	1,979	1,318	2,864
Lawrence	38,463	6,723	17.5	29.8	2,676	5,772	4,047	6,029
Lynn	27,544	1,309	4.8	11.6	588	1,869	721	1,205
Malden	13,968	327	2.3	4.4	97	272	230	309
Medford	8,456	157	1.9	......	50		107	
Newton	10,073	272	2.7	8.2	68	564	204	338
Pittsfield	8,094	790	9.8	16.4	346	642	444	424
Quincy	13,532	914	6.8	9.4	378	518	536	466
Revere	8,761	567	6.5	......	154		413	
Salem	11,062	1,412	12.8	23.9	502	1,466	910	1,665
Somerville	23,835	582	2.4	5.6	230	678	352	466
Taunton	9,832	1,734	17.6	25.8	752	1,189	982	1,259
Waltham	8,024	262	3.3	6.0	94	239	168	213
Michigan.								
Battle Creek	3,331	144	4.3	9.4	92	197	52	44
Bay City	8,895	409	4.6	9.8	159	327	250	727
Flint	14,709	949	6.5	14.6	518	759	431	167
Hamtramck village	22,471	6,843	30.5	......	3,260		3,583	
Highland Park	12,266	357	2.9	......	126		231	
Jackson	5,256	315	6.0	16.3	148	462	167	226
Kalamazoo	7,118	619	8.7	15.9	307	593	312	453
Lansing	5,870	467	8.0	17.1	289	466	178	198
Muskegon	6,742	314	4.7	......	150		164	
Pontiac	5,052	441	8.7	......	363		78	
Port Huron	6,166	123	2.0	......	65		58	
Saginaw	11,435	530	4.6	9.9	172	494	358	632
Minnesota.								
Duluth	29,807	1,366	4.6	14.5	711	2,929	655	1,410
Missouri.								
Joplin	722	6	0.8	3.1	......	20	6	8
St. Joseph	6,333	888	14.0	13.3	506	701	382	353
Springfield	967	49	5.1	2.8	25	20	24	12
Montana.								
Butte	11,301	232	2.1	5.0	98	386	134	243

1260

POPULATION.

TABLE 9.—NUMBER UNABLE TO SPEAK ENGLISH IN FOREIGN-BORN WHITE POPULATION 10 YEARS OF AGE AND OVER, BY SEX, WITH PERCENTAGES FOR BOTH SEXES COMBINED, FOR CITIES HAVING, IN 1920, FROM 25,000 TO 100,000 INHABITANTS: 1920 AND 1910—Continued.

[Figures for 1910 not available for cities having a population of less than 25,000 at that census.]

CITY.	Total number: 1920	Unable to speak English.							
		Both sexes.			Male.		Female.		
		Number: 1920	Per cent.						
			1920	1910	1920	1910	1920	1910	
Nebraska.									
Lincoln	7,015	617	8.8	19.1	206	537	411	746	
New Hampshire.									
Manchester	27,060	4,509	16.7	37.7	1,431	5,287	3,078	5,407	
Nashua	8,598	1,890	22.0	45.4	792	2,023	1,098	1,901	
New Jersey.									
Atlantic City	6,928	330	4.8	14.1	164	593	166	281	
Bayonne	25,199	3,152	12.5	25.1	1,432	2,984	1,720	1,981	
Clifton	9,502	1,744	18.4		589		1,155		
East Orange	6,714	214	3.2	7.5	92	170	122	249	
Elizabeth	27,873	2,914	10.5	27.9	1,391	3,933	1,523	2,476	
Hoboken	23,215	1,287	5.5	16.8	488	2,379	799	2,120	
Irvington town	5,465	129	2.4		52		77		
Kearny town	7,800	166	2.1		62		104		
Montclair town	5,078	684	13.5		345		339		
New Brunswick	8,794	762	8.7		230		532		
Orange	6,894	504	7.3	21.5	148	896	356	803	
Passaic	26,089	5,479	21.0	55.2	2,136	6,215	3,343	8,892	
Perth Amboy	14,759	1,690	11.5	36.6	710	2,965	980	2,078	
Plainfield	5,438	454	8.3		165		289		
West Hoboken town	13,936	1,386	9.9	18.3	543	1,052	843	1,374	
West New York town	8,805	631	7.2		203		428		
New York.									
Amsterdam	9,732	1,653	17.0	42.5	590	2,206	1,063	2,191	
Auburn	7,485	1,002	13.4	27.0	402	1,203	600	808	
Binghamton	10,271	2,100	20.4	30.0	962	978	1,138	1,181	
Elmira	4,657	253	5.4	8.3	109	228	144	197	
Jamestown	11,299	827	7.3	17.2	286	991	541	785	
Kingston	2,748	92	3.3	16.3	26	287	66	255	
Mount Vernon	9,957	980	9.8	21.3	344	858	636	791	
New Rochelle	8,347	283	3.4	23.2	105	1,124	178	826	
Newburgh	4,898	394	8.0	14.4	183	381	211	297	
Niagara Falls	17,370	2,751	15.8	20.7	1,502	1,673	1,249	728	
Poughkeepsie	5,466	617	11.3	22.2	278	602	339	381	
Rome	5,152	993	19.3		522		471		
Schenectady	20,250	2,655	13.1	23.5	962	2,628	1,693	1,608	
Troy	11,404	308	2.7	10.7	117	898	191	719	
Utica	23,000	4,090	17.8	29.7	1,590	3,053	2,500	3,052	
Watertown	5,725	208	3.6	12.1	113	534	95	196	
North Carolina.									
Asheville	549	15	2.7		6		9		
Charlotte	503	3	0.6	11.7	1	28	2	24	
Wilmington	608	7	1.2	3.4	5	10	2	5	
Winston-Salem	293	4	1.4		3		1		
Ohio.									
Canton	14,437	2,506	17.4	36.1	1,899	2,348	607	689	
East Cleveland	3,804	18	0.5		4		14		
Hamilton	2,639	157	5.9	18.2	82	379	75	210	
Lakewood	7,196	1,000	13.9		426		574		
Lima	1,889	80	4.2	8.2	40	77	40	52	
Lorain	11,770	1,100	9.3	50.2	606	3,669	494	1,554	
Mansfield	3,154	198	6.3		95		103		
Marion	948	75	7.9		44		31		
Newark	1,485	162	10.9	41.2	97	709	65	115	
Portsmouth	662	23	3.3		14		9		
Springfield	2,731	157	5.7	10.1	86	239	71	77	
Steubenville	5,488	1,077	19.6		663		414		
Warren	4,593	1,068	23.3		771		297		
Zanesville	1,266	161	12.7	25.3	105	300	56	97	
Oklahoma.									
Muskogee	533	32	6.0	8.4	18	33	14	12	
Oklahoma City	3,354	511	15.2	17.3	301	460	210	88	
Tulsa	1,988	47	2.4		25		22		
Pennsylvania.									
Allentown	8,505	1,263	14.9	48.8	490	1,311	773	1,045	
Altoona	5,228	636	12.2	26.7	269	865	367	470	
Bethlehem	10,795	2,686	24.9		1,482		1,204		

CITY.	Total number: 1920	Unable to speak English.							
		Both sexes.			Male.		Female.		
		Number: 1920	Per cent.						
			1920	1910	1920	1910	1920	1910	
Pennsylvania—Contd.									
Chester	11,133	1,784	16.0	31.1	1,096	1,487	688	521	
Easton	3,944	487	12.3	29.1	216	502	271	372	
Erie	17,103	2,716	15.9	33.3	1,440	2,846	1,276	1,975	
Harrisburg	4,093	430	10.5	27.5	184	624	246	464	
Hazleton	5,971	474	7.9	22.9	137	579	337	756	
Johnstown	12,013	1,416	11.8	59.7	682	6,752	734	2,052	
Lancaster	2,692	127	4.7	19.6	53	325	74	291	
McKeesport	11,769	1,848	15.7	35.0	1,072	2,802	776	1,499	
New Castle	8,551	1,437	16.8	41.1	652	2,504	785	928	
Norristown borough	4,250	840	19.8	27.0	389	610	451	462	
Wilkes-Barre	14,460	2,037	14.1	26.2	902	2,448	1,135	1,633	
Williamsport	2,244	337	15.0	15.0	176	200	161	140	
York	1,182	58	4.9	16.0	29	175	29	73	
Rhode Island.									
Cranston	7,437	667	9.0		198		469		
Newport	5,708	59	1.0	5.0	22	199	37	111	
Pawtucket	20,723	1,892	9.1	10.2	871	841	1,021	933	
Woonsocket	15,619	3,287	21.0	37.3	1,111	2,460	2,176	3,353	
South Carolina.									
Charleston	2,125	22	1.0	4.2	14	59	8	40	
Columbia	538	16	3.0	10.7	12	33	4	13	
South Dakota.									
Sioux Falls	2,928	171	5.8		80		91		
Tennessee.									
Chattanooga	1,230	17	1.4	5.1	6	24	11	41	
Knoxville	803	11	1.4	3.0	3	10	8	13	
Texas.									
Austin	2,470	334	13.5	15.8	138	157	196	222	
Beaumont	1,875	310	16.5		189		121		
El Paso	29,736	18,292	61.5	70.7	7,137	3,764	11,155	5,214	
Galveston	6,711	1,141	17.0	7.6	723	268	418	187	
Waco	1,716	268	15.6	9.2	138	48	130	69	
Wichita Falls	1,661	458	27.6		376		82		
Utah.									
Ogden	4,517	130	2.9	9.2	70	274	60	123	
Virginia.									
Lynchburg	344	3	0.9	3.4	2	6	1	9	
Newport News	2,018	25	1.2		10		15		
Petersburg	508	10	2.0		4		6		
Portsmouth	1,520	37	2.4	2.7	12	9	25	20	
Roanoke	861	9	1.0	2.3	4	11	5	6	
Washington.									
Bellingham	5,173	110	2.1		42		68		
Everett	5,618	51	0.9		18		33		
Tacoma	20,234	791	3.9	10.0	424	1,876	367	717	
West Virginia.									
Charleston	1,336	47	3.5		18		29		
Clarksburg	1,901	280	14.7		148		132		
Huntington	724	15	2.1	3.0	6	5	9	10	
Wheeling	5,736	552	9.6	21.0	306	711	246	407	
Wisconsin.									
Green Bay	3,554	182	5.1	10.0	55	151	127	251	
Kenosha	12,523	869	6.9		387		482		
La Crosse	4,434	172	3.9	12.4	59	289	113	454	
Madison	4,814	444	9.2	13.1	224	322	220	214	
Oshkosh	5,764	273	4.7	17.3	98	577	175	677	
Racine	15,982	1,057	6.6	26.7	552	2,129	505	1,111	
Sheboygan	8,105	1,652	20.4	50.3	773	2,392	879	1,799	
Superior	10,650	441	4.1	13.7	219	1,268	222	558	

INABILITY TO SPEAK ENGLISH.

TABLE **10.**—NUMBER UNABLE TO SPEAK ENGLISH IN FOREIGN-BORN WHITE POPULATION 10 YEARS OF AGE AND OVER, BY SEX AND AGE PERIODS, FOR SELECTED CITIES: 1920.

[Cities of 25,000 inhabitants or more having 5,000 or more foreign-born whites 10 years of age and over unable to speak English.]

CITY.	TOTAL, 10 YEARS OF AGE AND OVER.			10 TO 14 YEARS.			15 TO 19 YEARS.			20 TO 24 YEARS.			25 TO 34 YEARS.		
	Both sexes.	Male.	Female.	Both sexes.	Male.	Female.	Both sexes.	Male.	Female.	Both sexes.	Male.	Female.	Both sexes.	Male.	Female.
Baltimore, Md.	6,768	2,834	3,934	21	12	9	69	28	41	345	124	221	1,681	695	986
Boston, Mass.	14,069	5,662	8,407	67	34	33	159	58	101	785	250	535	4,141	1,553	2,588
Bridgeport, Conn.	5,980	2,746	3,234	20	12	8	72	36	36	474	140	334	2,075	902	1,173
Buffalo, N. Y.	17,157	8,250	8,907	82	34	48	127	41	86	1,086	357	729	5,385	2,671	2,714
Chicago, Ill.	89,092	38,612	50,480	355	188	167	672	300	372	5,658	1,493	4,165	29,412	12,041	17,371
Cleveland, Ohio	35,390	16,319	19,071	77	38	39	164	58	106	2,464	740	1,724	11,913	5,251	6,662
Detroit, Mich.	33,007	17,101	15,906	169	83	86	313	132	181	2,733	852	1,881	12,679	6,191	6,488
El Paso, Tex.	18,292	7,137	11,155	1,335	576	759	1,955	709	1,246	2,332	833	1,499	4,333	1,547	2,786
Fall River, Mass.	8,441	2,978	5,463	24	10	14	199	56	143	817	208	609	2,232	788	1,444
Hamtramck village, Mich.	6,843	3,260	3,583	18	14	4	30	11	19	819	190	629	3,479	1,522	1,957
Jersey City, N. J.	6,249	2,876	3,373	36	20	16	60	22	38	472	140	332	2,161	954	1,207
Lawrence, Mass.	6,723	2,676	4,047	27	11	16	82	23	59	577	117	460	2,359	859	1,500
Los Angeles, Calif.	10,619	4,722	5,897	295	135	160	570	249	321	1,190	515	675	2,905	1,309	1,596
Lowell, Mass.	6,141	2,426	3,715	68	35	33	174	45	129	695	188	507	1,942	777	1,165
Milwaukee, Wis.	17,074	7,162	9,912	24	13	11	47	20	27	601	188	413	3,925	1,628	2,297
New Bedford, Mass.	9,983	4,020	5,963	87	31	56	433	161	272	1,348	422	926	3,329	1,470	1,859
New Haven, Conn.	5,234	1,938	3,296	37	21	16	51	21	30	319	86	233	1,412	443	969
New York, N. Y.	208,125	86,536	121,589	1,063	507	556	2,961	1,225	1,736	12,235	3,948	8,287	50,215	20,322	29,893
Bronx borough	17,633	6,678	10,955	90	34	56	237	98	139	889	207	622	4,005	1,475	2,530
Brooklyn borough	71,335	29,463	41,872	322	157	165	1,011	458	553	4,224	1,487	2,737	17,837	7,298	10,539
Manhattan borough	109,288	46,121	63,167	611	297	314	1,605	625	980	6,654	2,050	4,604	26,137	10,626	15,511
Queens borough	6,815	2,863	3,952	29	14	15	77	32	45	340	87	253	1,713	701	1,012
Richmond borough	3,054	1,411	1,643	11	5	6	31	12	19	128	57	71	523	222	301
Newark, N. J.	11,222	5,111	6,111	61	31	30	185	93	92	827	302	525	3,372	1,575	1,797
Passaic, N. J.	5,479	2,136	3,343	8	5	3	46	10	36	899	159	740	2,356	961	1,395
Philadelphia, Pa.	31,742	13,324	18,418	114	51	63	311	136	175	2,076	637	1,439	8,958	3,563	5,395
Pittsburgh, Pa.	10,324	4,938	5,386	26	13	13	76	38	38	558	189	369	3,106	1,409	1,697
Providence, R. I.	7,416	2,713	4,703	25	9	16	84	23	61	455	129	326	2,080	711	1,369
Rochester, N. Y.	6,362	2,447	3,915	37	24	13	120	48	72	441	100	341	1,800	610	1,190
St. Louis, Mo.	5,658	2,391	3,267	18	8	10	61	26	35	309	96	213	1,333	502	831
San Antonio, Tex.	16,466	8,274	8,192	1,048	514	534	1,366	555	811	2,727	1,652	1,075	3,998	2,071	1,927
San Francisco, Calif.	7,116	3,245	3,871	87	40	47	166	82	84	529	252	277	1,867	822	1,045
Tampa, Fla.	5,293	2,650	2,643	87	44	43	243	110	133	517	233	284	1,589	824	765
Toledo, Ohio	5,300	2,702	2,598	13	8	5	40	26	14	356	152	204	1,595	854	741
Youngstown, Ohio	5,073	3,108	1,965	15	10	5	41	20	21	382	179	203	2,000	1,168	832

CITY.	35 TO 44 YEARS.			45 TO 54 YEARS.			55 TO 64 YEARS.			65 YEARS AND OVER.			AGE UNKNOWN.		
	Both sexes.	Male.	Female.	Both sexes.	Male.	Female.	Both sexes.	Male.	Female.	Both sexes.	Male.	Female.	Both sexes.	Male.	Female.
Baltimore, Md.	1,606	730	876	1,268	567	701	922	346	576	855	331	524	1	1	—
Boston, Mass.	3,838	1,666	2,172	2,445	1,078	1,367	1,577	613	964	1,045	404	641	6	4	2
Bridgeport, Conn.	1,683	859	824	1,008	518	490	427	201	226	215	74	141	13	8	5
Buffalo, N. Y.	4,445	2,468	1,977	2,859	1,367	1,492	1,960	810	1,150	1,200	494	706	123	75	48
Chicago, Ill.	23,558	11,774	11,784	14,263	6,984	7,279	8,461	3,389	5,072	6,590	2,368	4,222	16	9	7
Cleveland, Ohio	10,023	5,215	4,808	5,759	3,060	2,699	3,016	1,293	1,723	1,958	655	1,303	63	52	11
Detroit, Mich.	8,678	5,424	3,254	4,525	2,704	1,821	2,335	1,076	1,259	1,512	587	925	13	8	5
El Paso, Tex.	3,573	1,418	2,155	2,617	1,141	1,476	1,356	585	771	789	345	444	2	1	1
Fall River, Mass.	1,985	727	1,258	1,554	585	969	944	349	595	684	254	430	2	1	1
Hamtramck village, Mich.	1,677	1,035	642	535	360	175	197	92	105	86	51	35	2	1	1
Jersey City, N. J.	1,741	881	860	961	494	467	505	242	263	309	122	187	4	1	3
Lawrence, Mass.	1,776	828	948	1,015	461	554	592	252	340	294	125	169	49	36	13
Los Angeles, Calif.	2,415	1,123	1,292	1,580	707	873	919	361	558	696	287	409	2	1	1
Lowell, Mass.	1,399	626	773	967	437	530	512	180	332	382	137	245	12	7	5
Milwaukee, Wis.	3,980	2,013	1,967	2,976	1,397	1,579	2,582	925	1,657	2,927	971	1,956	12	5	7
New Bedford, Mass.	2,174	913	1,261	1,373	606	767	736	259	477	498	156	342	5	2	3
New Haven, Conn.	1,331	523	808	962	395	567	647	249	398	471	198	273	4	2	2
New York, N. Y.	52,759	23,123	29,636	40,443	17,605	22,838	28,687	11,613	17,074	18,418	7,525	10,893	1,344	668	676
Bronx borough	4,040	1,621	2,419	3,474	1,367	2,107	2,844	1,037	1,807	2,037	769	1,268	17	10	7
Brooklyn borough	18,195	7,881	10,314	13,395	5,720	7,675	9,646	3,858	5,788	6,653	2,577	4,076	52	27	25
Manhattan borough	28,254	12,554	15,700	21,965	9,760	12,205	15,159	6,306	8,853	8,819	3,856	4,963	84	47	37
Queens borough	1,800	833	967	1,257	587	670	853	342	511	728	247	481	18	9	9
Richmond borough	470	234	236	352	171	181	185	70	115	181	65	116	1,173	575	598
Newark, N. J.	2,958	1,443	1,515	1,852	897	955	1,163	466	697	800	302	498	4	1	3
Passaic, N. J.	1,225	574	651	564	271	293	251	106	145	129	49	80	1	1	—
Philadelphia, Pa.	8,292	3,788	4,504	5,942	2,677	3,265	3,729	1,520	2,209	2,298	939	1,359	22	13	9
Pittsburgh, Pa.	3,049	1,608	1,441	1,905	1,035	870	951	394	557	651	250	401	7	2	5
Providence, R. I.	1,870	685	1,185	1,391	562	829	903	336	567	601	256	345	14	11	3
Rochester, N. Y.	1,598	673	925	1,040	491	549	747	271	476	585	239	346	14	11	3
St. Louis, Mo.	1,442	696	746	1,013	481	532	698	296	402	774	282	492	10	4	6
San Antonio, Tex.	3,076	1,450	1,626	2,142	1,019	1,123	1,205	568	637	844	425	419	60	26	34
San Francisco, Calif.	1,840	870	970	1,202	590	612	723	493	230	677	453	224	27	25	2
Tampa, Fla.	1,297	635	662	827	446	381	461	201	260	262	118	144	10	5	5
Toledo, Ohio	1,350	757	593	919	467	452	555	245	310	459	180	279	13	13	—
Youngstown, Ohio	1,552	1,057	495	734	513	221	230	112	118	116	46	70	3	3	—

POPULATION.

1262

TABLE 11.—NUMBER AND PER CENT UNABLE TO SPEAK ENGLISH IN THE URBAN AND RURAL FOREIGN-BORN WHITE POPULATION 10 YEARS OF AGE AND OVER, BY SEX, 1920, WITH COMPARATIVE PERCENTAGES FOR 1910, BY DIVISIONS AND STATES.

DIVISION AND STATE.	FOREIGN-BORN WHITE MALES 10 YEARS OF AGE AND OVER.								FOREIGN-BORN WHITE FEMALES 10 YEARS OF AGE AND OVER.							
	In urban communities.				In rural communities.				In urban communities.				In rural communities.			
	Total number: 1920	Unable to speak English. Number: 1920	Per cent 1920	Per cent 1910	Total number: 1920	Unable to speak English. Number: 1920	Per cent 1920	Per cent 1910	Total number: 1920	Unable to speak English. Number: 1920	Per cent 1920	Per cent 1910	Total number: 1920	Unable to speak English. Number: 1920	Per cent 1920	Per cent 1910
United States	5,485,144	482,570	8.8	22.0	1,934,547	197,463	10.2	25.2	4,722,319	607,224	12.9	21.7	1,355,876	201,691	14.9	25.3
GEOGRAPHIC DIVISIONS:																
New England	812,741	63,574	7.8	18.5	119,104	6,639	5.6	17.0	806,150	101,209	12.6	19.1	105,033	9,429	9.0	15.3
Middle Atlantic	2,208,232	198,032	9.0	24.7	379,566	33,241	8.8	38.3	1,981,537	257,484	13.0	24.4	283,921	37,092	13.1	27.7
East North Central	1,385,974	129,521	9.3	25.7	403,492	22,791	5.6	17.8	1,093,036	145,741	13.3	23.7	301,288	30,928	10.3	21.5
West North Central	333,223	15,117	4.5	15.5	438,924	20,350	4.6	16.2	266,895	18,254	6.8	13.8	319,281	31,538	9.9	23.3
South Atlantic	122,316	9,997	8.2	20.8	60,530	7,780	12.9	40.5	97,463	10,834	11.1	19.5	31,076	3,431	11.0	24.7
East South Central	26,737	537	2.0	8.5	14,992	573	3.8	18.0	21,222	739	3.5	8.9	8,260	514	6.2	18.0
West South Central	114,268	35,779	31.3	26.7	131,329	57,381	43.7	49.5	92,671	39,096	42.2	36.3	91,785	49,543	54.0	60.4
Mountain	98,765	9,262	9.4	15.8	163,968	27,999	17.1	29.0	77,778	10,585	13.6	14.5	95,793	23,250	24.3	25.2
Pacific	382,888	20,751	5.4	10.0	222,642	20,709	9.3	20.3	285,567	23,282	8.2	9.7	119,430	15,966	13.4	17.0
NEW ENGLAND:																
Maine	28,505	2,168	7.6	17.6	25,893	1,318	5.1	12.7	29,227	5,154	17.6	24.7	20,960	1,693	8.1	11.5
New Hampshire	34,956	3,271	9.4	30.6	10,996	1,079	9.8	17.3	35,017	6,089	17.4	33.3	8,503	900	10.6	19.2
Vermont	9,217	738	8.0	21.0	13,589	610	4.5	12.6	8,564	888	10.4	20.1	11,331	829	7.3	10.5
Massachusetts	510,069	36,889	7.2	16.8	16,203	667	4.1	17.7	521,482	57,627	11.1	16.7	15,818	1,243	7.9	15.0
Rhode Island	84,015	7,931	9.4	19.9	918	62	6.8	15.6	85,227	13,518	15.9	23.3	872	109	12.5	17.6
Connecticut	145,979	12,577	8.6	19.8	51,505	2,903	5.6	24.3	126,633	17,933	14.2	20.1	47,549	4,655	9.8	20.7
MIDDLE ATLANTIC:																
New York	1,318,801	117,337	8.9	21.8	106,660	5,967	5.6	24.4	1,235,277	159,401	12.9	24.1	91,317	7,495	8.2	14.3
New Jersey	328,662	26,786	8.2	23.8	58,589	4,875	8.3	30.2	292,321	36,229	12.4	23.7	50,227	5,519	11.0	20.5
Pennsylvania	560,769	53,909	9.6	31.4	214,317	22,399	10.5	47.5	453,939	61,854	13.6	25.6	142,377	24,078	16.9	39.8
EAST NORTH CENTRAL:																
Ohio	323,311	36,255	11.2	31.0	63,590	5,530	8.7	29.2	239,706	34,329	14.3	25.5	43,317	5,047	11.7	22.8
Indiana	69,348	5,674	8.2	33.2	18,048	843	4.7	21.6	48,092	5,753	12.0	22.9	13,751	999	7.3	15.7
Illinois	559,414	48,950	8.8	24.1	91,842	4,439	4.8	16.1	476,875	62,958	13.2	23.9	66,848	5,618	8.4	18.5
Michigan	293,601	26,658	9.1	20.7	113,456	5,774	5.1	14.0	216,975	26,707	12.3	17.9	89,196	9,066	10.1	16.7
Wisconsin	140,300	11,984	8.5	25.3	116,556	6,205	5.3	16.3	111,388	15,994	14.4	28.0	88,176	10,298	11.7	28.6
WEST NORTH CENTRAL:																
Minnesota	134,240	4,019	3.0	13.7	142,390	6,881	4.8	15.2	104,848	6,078	5.8	13.6	100,752	11,333	11.2	25.5
Iowa	49,100	2,032	4.1	14.3	77,009	2,207	2.9	12.9	39,995	1,962	4.9	10.1	57,048	3,358	5.8	16.7
Missouri	81,069	4,123	5.1	16.5	21,518	942	4.4	19.7	66,314	4,994	7.5	15.9	15,493	1,067	6.9	17.6
North Dakota	8,528	188	2.2	13.6	66,105	3,344	5.1	18.2	7,390	300	4.1	10.3	47,928	6,357	13.3	31.0
South Dakota	6,516	293	4.5	11.4	40,773	1,475	3.6	15.8	5,528	313	5.7	9.4	28,964	2,780	9.6	26.2
Nebraska	32,624	1,656	5.1	18.9	50,918	2,217	4.4	14.7	25,924	2,141	8.3	15.9	38,743	3,172	8.2	19.9
Kansas	21,146	2,806	13.3	22.0	40,211	3,284	8.2	22.4	16,896	2,466	14.6	14.1	29,753	3,471	11.7	22.9
SOUTH ATLANTIC:																
Delaware	9,559	1,302	13.6	36.5	1,671	127	7.6	18.9	7,046	1,258	17.8	25.1	1,265	51	4.0	11.2
Maryland	45,788	3,045	6.7	16.6	8,314	351	4.2	20.1	41,089	4,041	9.8	18.3	5,964	328	5.5	13.3
District of Columbia	15,022	329	2.2	5.6	(1)	(1)	......	......	13,270	450	3.4	5.7	(1)	(1)	......	......
Virginia	11,725	325	2.8	6.7	7,087	263	3.7	27.3	7,252	301	4.2	6.6	4,261	246	5.8	20.1
West Virginia	11,758	1,193	10.1	34.1	29,537	6,462	21.9	61.8	7,719	943	12.2	20.1	11,665	2,528	21.6	47.1
North Carolina	2,504	39	1.6	6.3	1,783	48	2.7	21.4	1,685	43	2.7	7.1	1,009	60	5.9	20.6
South Carolina	2,507	49	2.0	6.4	1,556	18	1.2	10.5	1,672	28	1.7	5.1	592	21	3.5	11.6
Georgia	7,241	81	1.1	6.0	2,682	60	2.2	7.2	5,052	120	2.4	6.2	1,053	24	2.3	10.2
Florida	16,212	3,634	22.4	49.0	7,900	451	5.7	29.6	12,678	3,655	28.8	54.1	5,267	178	3.4	13.8
EAST SOUTH CENTRAL:																
Kentucky	11,244	114	1.0	7.7	6,157	233	3.8	18.0	10,218	194	1.9	7.3	2,984	147	4.9	12.9
Tennessee	6,429	154	2.4	5.8	2,499	76	3.0	13.9	4,915	182	3.7	7.9	1,454	94	6.5	15.6
Alabama	6,516	183	2.8	13.3	3,968	136	3.4	19.4	4,494	257	5.7	14.8	2,415	148	6.1	20.8
Mississippi	2,548	86	3.4	8.4	2,368	128	5.4	20.8	1,595	106	6.6	11.5	1,407	125	8.9	28.2
WEST SOUTH CENTRAL:																
Arkansas	3,230	46	1.4	4.4	5,298	257	4.9	20.3	2,322	87	3.7	6.4	2,984	307	10.3	28.4
Louisiana	19,051	809	4.2	11.0	7,428	847	11.4	36.1	13,129	1,113	8.5	14.9	4,638	914	19.7	50.9
Oklahoma	8,723	1,212	13.9	20.6	15,689	2,136	13.6	20.1	5,113	636	12.4	14.4	9,495	1,378	14.5	22.9
Texas	83,264	33,712	40.5	35.7	102,916	54,141	52.6	59.8	72,107	37,260	51.7	49.2	74,668	46,944	62.9	70.0
MOUNTAIN:																
Montana	19,098	352	1.8	12.9	38,189	1,032	2.7	19.8	13,157	442	3.4	7.4	21,285	1,272	6.0	12.6
Idaho	6,423	375	5.8	17.1	18,142	816	4.5	17.2	4,529	244	5.4	7.3	9,285	521	5.6	9.3
Wyoming	5,249	399	7.6	14.0	11,451	902	7.9	29.2	3,028	221	7.3	7.2	5,034	481	9.6	21.1
Colorado	32,434	1,824	5.6	13.0	34,435	3,158	9.2	24.4	26,157	2,271	8.7	11.4	21,259	3,397	16.0	24.9
New Mexico	3,004	590	19.6	23.2	12,681	6,434	50.7	60.1	2,398	638	26.6	34.8	8,703	5,563	63.9	65.1
Arizona	14,594	5,124	35.1	41.2	25,882	13,885	53.6	60.2	12,000	6,206	51.7	58.1	17,577	11,137	63.4	68.5
Utah	16,339	489	3.0	10.8	14,177	853	6.0	22.9	15,562	466	3.0	7.0	9,646	495	5.1	9.5
Nevada	1,624	109	6.7	10.3	9,011	919	10.2	23.9	947	97	10.2	10.7	3,004	384	12.8	13.0
PACIFIC:																
Washington	86,911	2,105	2.4	9.4	63,599	1,667	2.6	14.7	59,395	2,085	3.5	6.6	34,976	1,939	5.5	13.3
Oregon	35,565	847	2.4	10.7	26,010	922	3.5	20.4	24,968	890	3.6	8.6	14,129	683	4.8	10.7
California	260,412	17,799	6.8	10.2	133,033	18,120	13.6	23.2	201,204	20,307	10.1	11.0	70,334	13,344	19.0	20.5

[1] No rural population, as Washington city is coextensive with the District of Columbia.

637

CHAPTER XIV

DWELLINGS AND FAMILIES

CHAPTER XIV.—DWELLINGS AND FAMILIES.

INTRODUCTION.

The statistics on dwellings and families here presented represent, for states and for cities having 25,000 inhabitants or more, a summarization of the data on this subject which were collected at the Fourteenth Decennial Census. The state reports on the composition and characteristics of the population give the number of dwellings and the number of families in 1920 for each county or equivalent division and for each incorporated place (and each town in Massachusetts, Rhode Island, and New Hampshire) having 2,500 inhabitants or more.

Dwellings.—A dwelling, for census purposes, is a place in which one or more persons regularly sleep. It need not be a house in the usual sense of the word, but may be a hotel, boarding house, institution, or the like. A boat, a tent, a freight car, or a room in a factory, store, or office building, although occupied by only one person, is also counted as a dwelling, while, on the other hand, an entire apartment house, although containing many families, constitutes but one dwelling.

Variations among the divisions and states in regard to the number of persons per dwelling are due in great part to differences in the proportion of the population living in large cities, where there are many apartment or tenement buildings housing more than one family and often large numbers of families.

For the United States as a whole, a decrease in the average number of persons per dwelling has been shown at each census from 1850 to 1920 for which comparative figures are available. During the same period, however, as a result of the increased construction of apartment houses and tenements, the number of families per dwelling has increased from 1.07 to 1.18. (See Table 1.) In all geographic divisions and in 38 states the number of persons to a dwelling either decreased or remained stationary between 1910 and 1920, but increases are shown for the District of Columbia and 10 states—New York, Michigan, North Dakota, South Dakota, North Carolina, South Carolina, Alabama, Colorado, New Mexico, and Nevada. (See Table 2.)

Of the 68 cities having 100,000 inhabitants or more, 25 show increases and 33 decreases in the number of persons to a dwelling between 1910 and 1920, while in the remaining 10 there was no change in this respect. In most, but not all, of the cities in which the population increased with especial rapidity during the decade, the number of persons to a dwelling was larger in 1920 than in 1910. For example, in Akron, whose population increased by 201.8 per cent, the number of persons to a dwelling was 30 per cent larger in 1920 than in 1910; and in Detroit, with a population increase of 113.3 per cent, the number of persons to a dwelling increased by 16 per cent. On the other hand, in Los Angeles, in which the rate of increase (80.7 per cent) in population was also very large, the number of persons to a dwelling remained unchanged. (See Table 3.)

Families.—The term "family," as used in the census, signifies a group of persons, whether related by blood or not, who live together as one household, usually sharing the same table. One person living alone is counted as a family, and, on the other hand, all the occupants and employees of a hotel, boarding house, or lodging house, if that is their usual place of abode, and all the inmates of an institution, however numerous, are treated as constituting a single family. Thus the census family may be either a private family or an "economic family." The economic family, of course, is likely to be much larger than the private family. Moreover, the private family is not necessarily identical with the natural family, since many private families include servants, boarders, or other members not related by blood, or members of more or less distant blood relationship. The natural family commonly comprises husband, wife, and children. The members of a natural family, however, in many cases do not live together in the same private family. In particular, the older sons and daughters are likely to be members of other households, perhaps in other parts of the country.

In the case of entire states or of large cities there is probably no great difference between the average size of private families and the average size of all census families, but this is not true of small communities in which large institutions are situated. It is believed, however, that the changes in the average size of census families from decade to decade, as well as the variations in this respect among the geographic divisions and states, are due mainly to differences in the size of private families and particularly in the number of children. In the cases of certain cities, however, and particularly western cities, changes from census to census in the average size of families are due in considerable measure to reductions in the proportion of the population living in economic families. In a new city or town the floating population—that is, the population living in lodging houses, construction camps, and the like—constitutes a considerably larger proportion of the total than in older communities.

The number of persons to a family, like the number to a dwelling, has decreased from census to census since 1850, having been nearly one-third larger in that year than in 1920. (See Table 1.) During the decade 1910–1920 this average decreased in every geographic division as a whole and in 40 states and the District of Columbia. Of the remaining 8 states, only one, New Mexico, shows an increase, no change having taken place in the other 7—Michigan, North Dakota, South Dakota, North Carolina, South Carolina, Colorado, and Nevada. (See Table 2.)

Nearly all the cities having 100,000 inhabitants or more show decreases in the average number of persons to a family between 1910 and 1920, the only exceptions being Akron, in which an increase took place, and Toledo, Hartford, and Camden, in which the average remained unchanged. The increase in Akron was undoubtedly due to the very large rate of increase (201.8 per cent) in population, with the resultant growth in the size of hotel, boarding-house, and lodging-house families. (See Table 3.)

Urban and rural communities.—Since marked differences exist between urban and rural communities in regard to the family grouping and housing of the population, statistics for the two classes of communities are shown separately. In drawing the distinction between urban and rural population, all incorporated places (and all towns in Massachusetts, Rhode Island, and New Hampshire) having 2,500 inhabitants or more are treated as urban and the remainder of the country as rural.

In Massachusetts and Rhode Island it is not the practice, as in practically all the other states, to incorporate, as separate municipalities, the relatively densely populated portions of "towns" (which are the primary divisions of the counties), and no town as a whole is incorporated as a municipality until it attains a population greatly in excess of 2,500; in New Hampshire a similar condition exists, although the state contains two incorporated villages, each of which has fewer than 2,500 inhabitants. For this reason it is necessary in the case of the three states named to treat as urban those towns having 2,500 inhabitants or more, although their areas contain relatively small numbers of inhabitants who in other sections of the country would be segregated as rural.

In some cases a decrease in the average number of persons to a dwelling in urban communities or in rural communities, or in both urban and rural communities, has taken place without causing any change in the average for both classes of communities combined.

For example, in the Middle Atlantic division the average number of persons to a dwelling decreased from 7.3 to 7.1 in urban communities and from 4.6 to 4.5 in rural communities, although the average for both classes of communities combined remained unchanged at 6.2. In this and similar cases the effect of the decrease in one or both classes of communities was offset by the increase in the proportion which the population of urban communities (whose averages are larger than those for rural communities) formed of the total population of the division or state. (See Table 6.)

Excess of Families over dwellings.—The excess of families over dwellings in the United States in 1920 was equal to 15 per cent of the total number of families. This, of course, does not mean that only 15 per cent of the total number of families were living on January 1, 1920, in plural-family dwellings. To illustrate: Suppose that 120 families were housed in 100 dwellings and that no more than two families occupied one dwelling. In this case 80 families would occupy 80 dwellings and 40 families would occupy 20 dwellings, and the number of families living in dwellings housing more than one family each would be 40, or exactly twice the excess of families over dwellings. If, however, 98 families occupied 98 dwellings and each of the remaining 2 dwellings was occupied by 11 families, the number of families living in plural-family dwellings (22) would be only slightly greater than the excess of families over dwellings (20).

The number of families living in plural-family dwellings is, therefore, somewhat more than the excess of families over dwellings, but the precise number can not be ascertained from the tabulations made. It is possible, however, to obtain a rough approximation of the trend toward plural-family dwellings by comparing the percentage which the excess of families over dwellings represented of the total number of families for a given area in 1920 with the corresponding percentages for earlier censuses. (See Tables 5 and 7.)

TABLE 1.—DWELLINGS AND FAMILIES, FOR THE UNITED STATES: 1850–1920.

CENSUS YEAR.	Population.	Number of dwellings.	Number of families.	Persons to a dwelling.	Persons to a family.	Families to a dwelling.
1920	105,710,620	20,697,204	24,351,676	5.1	4.3	1.18
1910	91,972,266	17,805,845	20,255,555	5.2	4.5	1.14
1900	75,994,575	14,430,145	16,187,715	5.3	4.7	1.12
1890	[1] 62,622,250	11,483,318	12,690,152	5.5	4.9	1.11
1880	50,155,783	8,955,812	9,945,916	5.6	5.0	1.11
1870	38,558,371	[2]	7,579,363	[2]	5.1	[2]
1860	[3] 27,489,561	[2]	[3] 5,210,934	[2]	5.3	[2]
1850	[3] 19,987,563	[3] 3,362,337	[3] 3,598,240	[3] 5.9	[3] 5.6	[3] 1.07

[1] Exclusive of population (325,464) specially enumerated in Indian Territory and on Indian reservations, for which statistics of dwellings and families are not available.
[2] Dwellings reported in 1860 and 1870 include both occupied and unoccupied dwellings.
[3] Statistics for 1850 and 1860 relate to free population only.

DWELLINGS AND FAMILIES.

1267

TABLE 2.—DWELLINGS AND FAMILIES, BY DIVISIONS AND STATES: 1920, 1910, AND 1900.

DIVISION AND STATE.	1920			1910			1900			PERSONS TO A DWELLING.			PERSONS TO A FAMILY.		
	Population.	Dwellings.	Families.	Population.	Dwellings.	Families.	Population.	Dwellings.	Families.	1920	1910	1900	1920	1910	1900
United States	105,710,620	20,697,204	24,351,676	91,972,266	17,805,845	20,255,555	75,994,575	14,430,145	16,187,715	5.1	5.2	5.3	4.3	4.5	4.7
GEOGRAPHIC DIVISIONS:															
New England	7,400,909	1,255,964	1,703,812	6,552,681	1,099,336	1,464,942	5,592,017	989,018	1,253,970	5.9	6.0	5.7	4.3	4.5	4.5
Middle Atlantic	22,261,144	3,566,549	5,085,080	19,315,892	3,093,464	4,235,675	15,454,678	2,592,450	3,369,770	6.2	6.2	6.0	4.4	4.6	4.6
East North Central	21,475,543	4,385,541	5,143,913	18,250,621	3,743,779	4,214,820	15,985,581	3,175,632	3,526,261	4.9	4.9	5.0	4.2	4.3	4.5
West North Central	12,544,249	2,716,968	2,957,849	11,637,921	2,448,083	2,592,069	10,347,423	2,052,776	2,168,989	4.6	4.8	5.0	4.2	4.3	4.8
South Atlantic	13,990,272	2,781,684	2,991,628	12,194,895	2,424,935	2,539,270	10,443,480	2,006,696	2,101,757	5.0	5.0	5.2	4.7	4.8	5.0
East South Central	8,893,307	1,867,167	1,977,381	8,409,901	1,732,152	1,796,832	7,547,757	1,472,820	1,533,303	4.8	4.9	5.1	4.5	4.7	4.9
West South Central	10,242,224	2,110,879	2,242,810	8,784,534	1,780,510	1,827,105	6,532,290	1,264,981	1,303,013	4.9	4.9	5.2	4.6	4.8	5.0
Mountain	3,336,101	743,775	803,853	2,633,517	586,451	614,656	1,674,657	368,410	384,571	4.5	4.5	4.5	4.2	4.3	4.4
Pacific	5,566,871	1,268,677	1,445,350	4,192,304	897,135	970,186	2,416,692	507,362	546,081	4.4	4.7	4.8	3.9	4.3	4.4
NEW ENGLAND:															
Maine	768,014	162,304	186,106	742,371	159,437	177,960	694,466	148,507	163,344	4.7	4.7	4.7	4.1	4.2	4.3
New Hampshire	443,083	92,184	108,334	430,572	88,871	103,156	411,588	86,635	97,902	4.8	4.8	4.8	4.1	4.2	4.2
Vermont	352,428	77,158	85,804	355,956	77,466	85,178	343,641	75,021	81,462	4.6	4.6	4.6	4.1	4.2	4.2
Massachusetts	3,852,356	597,052	874,798	3,366,416	511,926	734,013	2,805,346	451,362	613,659	6.5	6.6	6.2	4.4	4.6	4.6
Rhode Island	604,397	98,861	137,160	542,610	79,725	117,976	428,556	67,816	94,179	6.1	6.8	6.3	4.4	4.6	4.6
Connecticut	1,380,631	228,405	311,610	1,114,756	181,911	246,659	908,420	159,677	203,424	6.0	6.1	5.7	4.4	4.5	4.5
MIDDLE ATLANTIC:															
New York	10,385,227	1,325,114	2,441,125	9,113,614	1,178,686	2,046,845	7,268,894	1,035,180	1,634,523	7.8	7.7	7.0	4.3	4.5	4.4
New Jersey	3,155,900	515,211	721,841	2,537,167	407,295	558,202	1,883,669	321,032	415,222	6.1	6.2	5.9	4.4	4.5	4.5
Pennsylvania	8,720,017	1,726,224	1,922,114	7,665,111	1,507,483	1,630,628	6,302,115	1,236,238	1,320,025	5.1	5.1	5.1	4.5	4.7	4.8
EAST NORTH CENTRAL:															
Ohio	5,759,394	1,216,542	1,414,068	4,767,121	1,024,800	1,138,165	4,157,545	857,636	944,433	4.7	4.7	4.8	4.1	4.2	4.4
Indiana	2,930,390	696,466	737,707	2,700,876	631,554	654,891	2,516,462	552,495	571,513	4.2	4.3	4.6	4.0	4.1	4.4
Illinois	6,485,280	1,190,414	1,534,077	5,638,591	1,006,848	1,264,717	4,821,550	845,836	1,036,158	5.4	5.6	5.7	4.2	4.5	4.7
Michigan	3,668,412	755,931	862,745	2,810,173	618,222	657,418	2,420,982	521,648	548,094	4.9	4.5	4.6	4.3	4.3	4.4
Wisconsin	2,632,067	526,188	595,316	2,333,860	462,355	499,629	2,069,042	398,017	426,063	5.0	5.0	5.2	4.4	4.7	4.9
WEST NORTH CENTRAL:															
Minnesota	2,387,125	469,652	526,026	2,075,708	380,809	416,452	1,751,394	317,037	342,658	5.1	5.5	5.5	4.5	5.0	5.1
Iowa	2,404,021	559,188	586,070	2,224,771	498,943	512,515	2,231,853	468,682	480,878	4.3	4.5	4.8	4.1	4.3	4.6
Missouri	3,404,055	717,256	829,043	3,293,335	677,196	749,812	3,106,665	593,528	654,383	4.7	4.9	5.2	4.1	4.4	4.7
North Dakota	646,872	129,905	134,881	577,056	118,757	120,910	319,146	63,319	64,690	5.0	4.9	5.0	4.7	4.8	4.9
South Dakota	636,547	138,512	142,793	583,888	127,739	131,060	401,570	81,863	83,536	4.7	4.6	4.9	4.5	4.5	4.8
Nebraska	1,296,372	288,390	303,436	1,192,214	258,967	265,549	1,066,300	213,972	220,947	4.5	4.6	5.0	4.3	4.5	4.8
Kansas	1,769,257	416,065	435,600	1,690,949	385,672	395,771	1,470,495	314,375	321,947	4.3	4.4	4.7	4.1	4.3	4.6
SOUTH ATLANTIC:															
Delaware	223,003	47,868	52,030	202,322	43,183	44,951	184,735	38,191	39,446	4.7	4.7	4.8	4.3	4.5	4.7
Maryland	1,449,661	288,261	324,742	1,295,346	253,805	274,824	1,188,044	221,706	242,331	5.0	5.1	5.4	4.5	4.7	4.9
District of Columbia	437,571	72,175	96,194	331,069	58,513	71,339	278,718	49,385	56,678	6.1	5.7	5.6	4.5	4.6	4.9
Virginia	2,309,187	450,229	483,363	2,061,612	400,445	419,452	1,854,184	347,159	364,517	5.1	5.1	5.3	4.8	4.9	5.1
West Virginia	1,463,701	293,002	310,098	1,221,119	239,128	248,480	958,800	180,715	186,291	5.0	5.1	5.3	4.7	4.9	5.1
North Carolina	2,559,123	495,299	513,377	2,206,287	430,570	440,334	1,893,810	360,491	370,072	5.2	5.1	5.3	5.0	5.0	5.1
South Carolina	1,683,724	330,500	349,126	1,515,400	302,842	315,204	1,340,316	259,302	269,864	5.1	5.0	5.2	4.8	4.8	5.0
Georgia	2,895,832	586,509	628,525	2,609,121	530,631	553,264	2,216,331	436,153	455,587	4.9	4.9	5.1	4.6	4.7	4.9
Florida	968,470	217,871	234,133	752,619	165,818	171,422	528,542	113,594	117,001	4.4	4.5	4.7	4.1	4.4	4.5
EAST SOUTH CENTRAL:															
Kentucky	2,416,630	510,981	546,306	2,289,905	469,669	494,788	2,147,174	413,974	437,054	4.7	4.9	5.2	4.4	4.6	4.9
Tennessee	2,337,885	488,892	519,108	2,184,789	444,814	462,553	2,020,616	385,588	402,536	4.8	4.9	5.2	4.5	4.7	5.0
Alabama	2,348,174	480,892	508,769	2,138,093	441,249	454,767	1,828,697	362,295	374,765	4.9	4.8	5.0	4.6	4.7	4.9
Mississippi	1,790,618	387,402	403,198	1,797,114	376,420	384,724	1,551,270	310,963	318,948	4.6	4.8	5.0	4.4	4.7	4.9
WEST SOUTH CENTRAL:															
Arkansas	1,752,204	375,316	390,960	1,574,449	327,625	333,368	1,311,564	259,004	265,238	4.7	4.8	5.1	4.5	4.7	4.9
Louisiana	1,798,509	370,377	389,913	1,656,388	331,220	344,144	1,381,625	269,395	284,875	4.9	5.0	5.1	4.6	4.8	4.8
Oklahoma	2,028,283	418,557	444,524	1,657,155	342,488	351,167	[1]790,391	[1]160,848	[1]153,609	4.8	4.8	4.9	4.6	4.7	4.8
Texas	4,663,228	946,629	1,017,413	3,896,542	779,177	798,426	3,048,710	575,734	589,291	4.9	5.0	5.3	4.6	4.9	5.2
MOUNTAIN:															
Montana	548,889	130,670	139,912	376,053	82,811	86,602	243,329	53,779	55,889	4.2	4.5	4.5	3.9	4.3	4.4
Idaho	431,866	95,299	100,500	325,594	71,830	73,669	161,772	36,487	37,491	4.5	4.5	4.4	4.3	4.4	4.3
Wyoming	194,402	44,710	48,476	145,965	30,969	32,092	92,531	19,664	20,116	4.3	4.7	4.7	4.0	4.5	4.6
Colorado	939,629	211,103	230,843	799,024	183,874	194,467	539,700	120,384	127,459	4.5	4.3	4.5	4.1	4.1	4.2
New Mexico	360,350	78,024	83,706	327,301	75,888	78,883	195,310	44,903	46,355	4.6	4.3	4.3	4.3	4.1	4.2
Arizona	334,162	73,673	80,208	204,354	45,386	47,927	122,931	28,763	29,875	4.5	4.5	4.3	4.2	4.3	4.1
Utah	449,396	89,587	98,346	373,351	72,649	77,339	276,749	53,490	56,196	5.0	5.1	5.2	4.6	4.8	4.9
Nevada	77,407	20,709	21,862	81,875	23,044	23,677	42,335	10,960	11,190	3.7	3.6	3.9	3.5	3.5	3.8
PACIFIC:															
Washington	1,356,621	304,735	342,228	1,141,990	238,822	254,692	518,103	106,622	113,086	4.5	4.8	4.9	4.0	4.5	4.5
Oregon	783,389	185,081	202,890	672,765	144,832	151,858	413,536	87,523	91,214	4.2	4.6	4.7	3.9	4.4	4.5
California	3,426,861	778,861	900,232	2,377,549	513,481	563,636	1,485,053	313,217	341,781	4.4	4.6	4.7	3.8	4.2	4.3

¹ Includes Indian Territory.

1268

POPULATION.

TABLE 3.—DWELLINGS AND FAMILIES, FOR CITIES HAVING, IN 1920, 100,000 INHABITANTS OR MORE: 1920, 1910, AND 1900.

CITY.	1920			1910			1900			PERSONS TO A DWELLING.			PERSONS TO A FAMILY.		
	Popula-tion.	Dwell-ings.	Families.	Popula-tion.	Dwell-ings.	Families.	Popula-tion.	Dwell-ings.	Families.	1920	1910	1900	1920	1910	1900
Akron, Ohio	208,435	32,030	44,195	69,067	13,701	15,851	42,728	8,649	9,746	6.5	5.0	4.9	4.7	4.4	4.4
Albany, N. Y	113,344	18,402	28,097	100,253	15,437	24,069	94,151	13,567	21,027	6.2	6.5	6.9	4.0	4.2	4.4
Atlanta, Ga	200,616	38,098	49,523	154,839	30,308	35,813	89,872	16,555	20,593	5.3	5.1	5.4	4.1	4.3	4.4
Baltimore, Md	733,826	136,324	166,857	558,485	101,905	118,851	508,957	89,442	105,584	5.4	5.5	5.7	4.4	4.7	4.8
Birmingham, Ala	178,806	35,100	43,040	132,685	26,989	31,050	38,415	6,618	8,453	5.1	4.9	5.8	4.2	4.3	4.5
Boston, Mass	748,060	79,597	164,785	670,585	73,919	139,700	560,892	66,482	117,244	9.4	9.1	8.4	4.5	4.8	4.8
Bridgeport, Conn	143,555	22,328	31,994	102,054	14,934	21,689	70,996	11,329	15,553	6.4	6.8	6.3	4.5	4.7	4.6
Buffalo, N. Y	506,775	73,880	116,201	423,715	62,335	91,328	352,387	49,914	73,631	6.9	6.8	7.1	4.4	4.6	4.8
Cambridge, Mass	109,694	15,113	25,293	104,839	14,577	22,765	91,886	13,414	19,434	7.3	7.2	6.9	4.3	4.6	4.7
Camden, N. J	116,309	24,921	26,645	94,538	20,260	21,482	75,935	16,856	17,390	4.7	4.7	4.5	4.4	4.4	4.4
Chicago, Ill	2,701,705	335,777	623,912	2,185,283	246,744	473,141	1,698,575	193,895	359,960	8.0	8.9	8.8	4.3	4.6	4.7
Cincinnati, Ohio	401,247	62,885	106,239	363,591	49,525	87,541	325,902	40,634	74,536	6.4	7.3	8.0	3.8	4.2	4.4
Cleveland, Ohio	796,841	116,545	182,692	560,663	90,465	124,822	381,768	63,205	81,519	6.8	6.2	6.0	4.4	4.5	4.7
Columbus, Ohio	237,031	51,663	58,913	181,511	39,580	42,645	125,560	24,219	27,582	4.6	4.6	5.2	4.0	4.3	4.6
Dallas, Tex	158,976	30,860	36,754	92,104	18,536	20,516	42,638	8,254	9,168	5.2	5.0	5.2	4.3	4.5	4.7
Dayton, Ohio	152,559	33,918	38,138	116,577	26,692	28,370	85,333	17,987	19,617	4.5	4.4	4.7	4.0	4.1	4.3
Denver, Colo	256,491	50,636	61,916	213,381	44,736	51,339	133,859	27,100	30,936	5.1	4.8	4.9	4.1	4.2	4.3
Des Moines, Iowa	126,468	27,127	31,644	86,368	18,694	20,599	62,139	12,708	14,110	4.7	4.6	4.9	4.0	4.2	4.4
Detroit, Mich	993,678	153,208	218,973	465,766	83,124	100,356	285,704	52,040	60,505	6.5	5.6	5.5	4.5	4.6	4.7
Fall River, Mass	120,485	13,807	26,399	119,295	10,962	24,378	104,863	9,509	21,027	8.7	10.9	11.0	4.6	4.9	5.0
Fort Worth, Tex	106,482	19,679	25,052	73,312	14,585	16,295	26,688	5,418	5,933	5.4	5.0	4.9	4.3	4.5	4.5
Grand Rapids, Mich	137,634	29,157	33,703	112,571	23,432	26,925	87,565	18,049	20,550	4.7	4.8	4.9	4.1	4.2	4.3
Hartford, Conn	138,036	16,495	30,813	98,915	11,535	21,925	79,850	9,609	17,231	8.4	8.6	8.2	4.5	4.5	4.6
Houston, Tex	138,276	28,452	33,932	78,800	15,903	17,040	44,633	8,541	9,554	4.9	5.0	5.2	4.1	4.6	4.7
Indianapolis, Ind	314,194	71,648	81,256	233,650	53,359	58,045	169,164	36,160	39,710	4.4	4.4	4.7	3.9	4.0	4.3
Jersey City, N. J	298,103	31,145	67,288	267,779	27,805	56,790	206,433	23,627	44,700	9.6	9.6	8.7	4.4	4.7	4.6
Kansas City, Kans	101,177	22,641	25,000	82,331	18,279	19,677	51,418	10,454	11,802	4.5	4.5	4.9	4.0	4.2	4.4
Kansas City, Mo	324,410	61,321	82,056	248,381	47,978	59,296	163,752	28,027	36,490	5.3	5.2	5.8	4.0	4.2	4.5
Los Angeles, Calif	576,673	125,004	159,476	319,198	69,061	78,678	102,479	22,531	25,207	4.6	4.6	4.5	3.6	4.1	4.1
Louisville, Ky	234,891	47,449	60,490	223,928	41,686	52,155	204,731	34,655	44,012	5.0	5.4	5.9	3.9	4.3	4.6
Lowell, Mass	112,759	17,488	25,034	106,294	15,056	21,932	94,969	13,671	19,279	6.4	7.1	6.9	4.5	4.8	4.9
Memphis, Tenn	162,351	35,295	42,309	131,105	26,710	31,154	102,320	17,443	21,600	4.6	4.9	5.9	3.8	4.2	4.7
Milwaukee, Wis	457,147	66,915	106,101	373,857	60,724	80,566	285,315	45,809	59,806	6.8	6.2	6.2	4.3	4.6	4.8
Minneapolis, Minn	380,582	65,568	91,843	301,408	46,903	63,241	202,718	31,836	42,536	5.8	6.4	6.4	4.1	4.8	4.8
Nashville, Tenn	118,342	24,992	30,220	110,364	22,118	26,077	80,865	15,239	18,422	4.7	5.0	5.3	3.9	4.2	4.4
New Bedford, Mass	121,217	14,961	26,858	96,652	11,504	20,820	62,442	8,744	13,924	8.1	8.4	7.1	4.5	4.6	4.5
New Haven, Conn	162,537	22,536	36,257	133,605	17,466	29,271	108,027	15,240	23,001	7.2	7.6	7.1	4.5	4.6	4.6
New Orleans, La	387,219	76,969	85,188	339,075	67,192	73,377	287,104	52,988	61,775	5.0	5.0	5.4	4.5	4.6	4.6
New York, N. Y	5,620,048	365,963	1,278,341	4,766,883	305,698	1,020,827	3,437,202	249,991	735,621	15.4	15.6	13.7	4.4	4.7	4.7
Bronx borough	732,016	33,985	166,260	430,980	28,733	93,897	200,507	19,044	42,266	21.5	15.0	10.1	4.4	4.6	4.7
Brooklyn borough	2,018,356	173,847	453,587	1,634,351	147,666	353,606	1,166,582	113,972	255,821	11.6	11.1	10.2	4.4	4.6	4.6
Manhattan borough	2,284,103	75,534	525,154	2,331,542	75,410	493,545	1,850,093	80,603	391,087	30.2	30.9	23.0	4.3	4.7	4.7
Queens borough	469,042	64,323	109,559	284,041	39,764	62,001	152,909	24,221	32,121	7.3	7.1	6.3	4.3	4.6	4.8
Richmond borough	116,531	18,274	23,781	85,969	14,125	17,718	67,021	11,251	13,726	6.4	6.1	6.0	4.9	4.9	4.9
Newark, N. J	414,524	41,535	93,274	347,469	38,603	77,039	246,070	30,307	54,654	10.0	9.0	8.1	4.4	4.5	4.5
Norfolk, Va	115,777	19,934	26,782	67,452	11,958	15,498	46,624	7,664	10,050	5.8	5.6	6.1	4.3	4.4	4.6
Oakland, Calif	216,261	47,297	55,793	150,174	31,740	35,723	66,960	13,974	15,270	4.6	4.7	4.8	3.9	4.4	4.4
Omaha, Nebr	191,601	37,997	44,499	[1]150,855	[1]28,619	[1]31,604	[1]128,556	[1]22,290	[1]25,608	5.0	5.3	5.8	4.3	4.8	5.0
Paterson, N. J	135,875	18,769	32,186	125,600	15,812	27,978	105,171	13,501	23,472	7.2	7.9	7.7	4.2	4.5	4.5
Philadelphia, Pa	1,823,779	352,944	402,946	1,549,008	295,220	327,263	1,293,697	241,589	265,880	5.2	5.2	5.4	4.5	4.7	4.9
Pittsburgh, Pa	588,343	93,890	130,274	533,905	86,942	110,457	[2]451,512	[2]71,345	[2]90,517	6.3	6.1	6.3	4.5	4.8	5.0
Portland, Oreg	258,288	54,664	67,045	207,214	37,436	42,029	90,426	14,025	16,724	4.7	5.5	6.2	3.9	4.9	5.4
Providence, R. I	237,595	35,634	54,720	224,326	28,705	49,129	175,597	25,204	39,236	6.7	7.8	7.0	4.3	4.6	4.5
Reading, Pa	107,784	22,759	25,202	96,071	20,798	21,809	78,961	16,185	17,002	4.7	4.6	4.9	4.3	4.4	4.6
Richmond, Va	171,667	30,753	39,191	127,628	22,205	26,914	85,050	14,201	17,845	5.6	5.7	6.0	4.4	4.7	4.8
Rochester, N. Y	295,750	56,502	68,247	218,149	38,850	46,787	162,608	29,531	34,402	5.2	5.6	5.5	4.3	4.7	4.7
St. Louis, Mo	772,897	118,102	190,640	687,029	105,650	155,555	575,238	82,260	123,719	6.5	6.5	7.0	4.1	4.4	4.6
St. Paul, Minn	234,698	42,462	54,409	214,744	32,616	41,548	163,065	24,681	30,919	5.5	6.6	6.6	4.3	5.2	5.3
Salt Lake City, Utah	118,110	23,685	28,216	92,777	17,856	20,283	53,531	10,233	11,707	5.0	5.2	5.2	4.2	4.6	4.5
San Antonio, Tex	161,379	30,264	36,405	96,614	19,574	21,096	53,321	10,415	11,326	5.3	4.9	5.1	4.4	4.6	4.7
San Francisco, Calif	506,676	90,132	123,349	416,912	65,025	86,414	342,782	53,323	71,697	5.6	6.4	6.4	4.1	4.8	4.8
Scranton, Pa	137,783	23,952	29,768	129,867	22,143	26,312	102,026	17,438	20,636	5.8	5.9	5.8	4.6	4.9	4.9
Seattle, Wash	315,312	60,516	80,048	237,194	43,559	51,042	80,671	11,852	14,254	5.2	5.4	6.8	3.9	4.6	5.7
Spokane, Wash	104,437	22,389	27,178	104,402	20,282	22,676	36,848	6,500	8,159	4.7	5.1	5.6	3.8	4.6	4.5
Springfield, Mass	129,614	18,945	30,361	88,926	13,352	19,968	62,059	10,165	14,057	6.8	6.7	6.1	4.3	4.5	4.4
Syracuse, N. Y	171,717	28,725	41,558	137,249	23,200	31,551	108,374	19,081	25,347	6.0	5.9	5.7	4.1	4.4	4.3
Toledo, Ohio	243,164	49,501	57,951	168,497	35,888	39,677	131,822	26,632	28,923	4.9	4.7	4.9	4.2	4.3	4.6
Trenton, N. J	119,289	22,373	25,319	96,815	17,932	19,678	73,307	14,441	15,095	5.3	5.4	5.1	4.7	4.9	4.9
Washington, D. C	437,571	72,175	96,194	331,069	58,513	71,330	278,718	49,385	58,678	6.1	5.7	5.6	4.5	4.6	4.8
Wilmington, Del	110,168	20,876	24,488	87,411	17,223	18,637	76,508	14,737	15,667	5.3	5.1	5.2	4.5	4.7	4.9
Worcester, Mass	179,754	19,337	39,230	145,986	15,109	30,743	118,421	13,130	24,841	9.3	9.7	9.0	4.6	4.7	4.8
Yonkers, N. Y	100,176	10,302	22,126	79,803	7,857	16,219	47,931	5,349	9,629	9.7	10.2	9.0	4.5	4.9	5.0
Youngstown, Ohio	132,358	24,007	28,699	79,066	14,280	16,228	44,885	8,343	9,090	5.5	5.5	5.4	4.6	4.9	4.9

[1] Includes South Omaha, annexed to Omaha since 1910.   [2] Includes Allegheny, annexed to Pittsburgh between 1900 and 1910.

DWELLINGS AND FAMILIES.

1269

TABLE 4.—DWELLINGS AND FAMILIES, 1920, AND NUMBER OF PERSONS TO A DWELLING AND TO A FAMILY, 1920, 1910, AND 1900, FOR CITIES HAVING, IN 1920, FROM 25,000 TO 100,000 INHABITANTS.

CITY.	1920 Population.	Dwellings.	Families.	PERSONS TO A DWELLING. 1920	1910	1900	PERSONS TO A FAMILY. 1920	1910	1900
Alabama.									
Mobile	60,777	12,350	15,148	4.9	4.6	5.0	4.0	4.2	4.2
Montgomery	43,464	9,437	11,568	4.6	4.7	4.8	3.8	4.0	4.1
Arizona.									
Phoenix	29,053	5,867	7,354	5.0	4.3	4.1	4.0	4.0	3.9
Arkansas.									
Fort Smith	28,870	5,916	6,872	4.9	4.9	5.0	4.2	4.6	4.6
Little Rock	65,142	13,156	15,059	5.0	4.8	5.2	4.3	4.5	4.6
California.									
Alameda	28,806	7,191	7,886	4.0	4.3	4.5	3.7	4.0	4.2
Berkeley	56,036	12,936	15,159	4.3	4.6	4.6	3.7	4.1	4.4
Fresno	45,086	9,493	11,234	4.7	4.8	4.8	4.0	4.3	4.3
Long Beach	55,593	12,758	17,169	4.4	3.7	(1)	3.2	3.4	(1)
Pasadena	45,354	11,712	12,657	3.9	3.9	4.0	3.6	3.7	3.9
Sacramento	65,908	13,779	17,263	4.8	5.1	4.9	3.8	4.4	4.3
San Diego	74,683	18,532	22,723	4.0	4.0	4.0	3.3	3.7	3.7
San Jose	39,642	9,391	10,669	4.2	4.4	4.7	3.7	4.0	4.3
Stockton	40,296	8,470	9,981	4.8	5.1	5.2	4.0	4.6	4.9
Colorado.									
Colorado Springs	30,105	7,680	8,332	3.9	4.1	4.9	3.6	3.9	4.4
Pueblo	43,050	8,956	10,484	4.8	5.1	4.9	4.1	4.8	4.5
Connecticut.									
Meriden	29,867	4,412	6,955	6.8	7.0	6.3	4.3	4.4	4.5
New Britain	59,316	6,109	12,072	9.7	9.3	7.8	4.9	5.1	4.8
New London	25,688	4,730	5,937	5.4	5.7	6.0	4.3	4.2	4.3
Norwalk	27,743	5,139	6,791	5.4	²6.0	⁴4.9	4.1	²4.3	²4.1
Stamford	35,096	4,656	7,839	7.5	6.8	5.5	4.5	4.6	4.5
Waterbury	91,715	11,583	19,124	7.9	9.5	8.3	4.8	5.0	4.9
Florida.									
Jacksonville	91,558	19,571	23,265	4.7	4.7	4.5	3.9	4.4	3.9
Miami	29,571	6,698	7,497	4.4	4.0	(1)	3.9	3.5	(1)
Pensacola	31,035	6,353	7,448	4.9	4.3	4.7	4.2	4.1	4.4
Tampa	51,608	10,492	12,137	4.9	5.0	5.0	4.3	4.6	4.5
Georgia.									
Augusta	52,548	11,988	13,966	4.4	4.4	4.9	3.8	3.8	4.0
Columbus	31,125	6,224	7,245	5.0	4.7	5.0	4.3	4.2	4.2
Macon	52,995	11,299	13,730	4.7	4.7	5.0	3.9	4.0	3.9
Savannah	83,252	16,999	21,207	4.9	4.8	5.3	3.9	4.0	4.1
Illinois.									
Aurora	36,397	7,920	8,973	4.6	4.8	4.7	4.1	4.3	4.3
Bloomington	28,725	6,829	7,451	4.2	4.2	4.6	3.9	4.0	4.3
Cicero town	44,995	6,463	9,770	7.0	7.3	(1)	4.6	5.2	(1)
Danville	33,776	7,947	8,907	4.3	4.1	4.7	3.8	3.9	4.2
Decatur	43,818	9,768	10,874	4.5	4.4	4.4	4.0	4.1	4.2
East St. Louis	66,767	14,081	15,768	4.7	5.0	5.2	4.2	4.5	4.6
Elgin	27,454	5,776	6,490	4.8	4.8	5.1	4.2	4.3	4.6
Evanston	37,234	6,411	8,472	5.8	5.8	5.8	4.4	4.7	4.9
Joliet	38,442	6,865	8,654	5.6	5.8	5.7	4.4	4.8	4.9
Moline	30,734	6,535	7,564	4.7	5.0	5.5	4.1	4.4	4.6
Oak Park village	39,858	8,112	9,737	4.9	5.1	....	4.1	4.5	....
Peoria	76,121	16,743	19,397	4.5	4.7	5.2	3.9	4.4	4.7
Quincy	35,978	8,445	9,378	4.3	4.3	4.9	3.8	4.2	4.4
Rock Island	35,177	7,910	8,824	4.4	4.5	5.0	4.0	4.2	4.6
Rockford	65,651	12,668	16,027	5.2	5.2	5.2	4.1	4.4	4.3
Springfield	59,183	13,006	14,255	4.6	4.6	4.9	4.2	4.3	4.5
Indiana.									
Anderson	29,767	6,827	7,523	4.4	4.2	4.4	4.0	3.9	4.3
East Chicago	35,967	5,100	7,080	7.1	8.7	6.5	5.1	5.8	4.9
Evansville	85,264	19,072	20,648	4.5	4.6	5.1	4.1	4.3	4.8
Fort Wayne	86,549	18,879	20,406	4.6	4.6	4.7	4.2	4.4	4.5
Gary	55,378	8,264	12,022	6.7	7.5	....	4.6	5.8	....
Hammond	36,004	6,910	7,983	5.2	5.4	5.4	4.5	4.8	4.9
Kokomo	30,067	6,968	7,505	4.3	4.1	4.1	4.0	3.9	3.9
Muncie	36,524	8,645	9,529	4.2	4.1	4.5	3.8	3.9	4.2
Richmond	26,765	6,506	7,055	4.1	4.0	4.1	3.8	3.8	3.9
South Bend	70,983	14,626	16,113	4.9	4.8	5.1	4.4	4.5	4.3
Terre Haute	66,083	15,476	16,745	4.3	4.3	4.7	3.9	4.1	4.3
Iowa.									
Cedar Rapids	45,566	10,645	11,612	4.3	4.3	4.6	3.9	4.1	4.3
Council Bluffs	36,162	8,278	8,789	4.4	4.6	4.9	4.1	4.4	4.7
Davenport	56,727	12,042	14,388	4.7	4.8	5.0	3.9	4.2	4.4
Dubuque	39,141	8,173	9,314	4.8	5.2	5.5	4.2	4.6	4.4
Sioux City	71,227	14,014	16,234	5.1	5.1	5.2	4.4	4.7	4.6
Waterloo	36,230	8,348	9,071	4.3	4.7	4.5	4.0	4.4	4.1
Kansas.									
Topeka	50,022	12,021	13,039	4.2	4.2	4.3	3.8	3.9	4.1
Wichita	72,217	15,846	18,596	4.6	4.6	4.7	3.9	4.1	4.3

CITY.	1920 Population.	Dwellings.	Families.	PERSONS TO A DWELLING. 1920	1910	1900	PERSONS TO A FAMILY. 1920	1910	1900
Kentucky.									
Covington	57,121	11,100	14,809	5.1	5.4	5.9	3.9	4.2	4.5
Lexington	41,534	9,500	10,720	4.4	4.5	4.8	3.9	4.1	4.4
Newport	29,317	5,621	7,792	5.2	5.5	5.8	3.8	4.1	4.5
Louisiana.									
Shreveport	43,874	9,175	10,618	4.8	4.6	4.5	4.1	4.2	3.9
Maine.									
Bangor	25,978	5,234	6,145	5.0	4.9	5.0	4.2	4.3	4.4
Lewiston	31,791	3,676	6,750	8.6	8.3	8.0	4.7	4.9	4.9
Portland	69,272	11,036	16,801	6.3	6.2	6.1	4.1	4.3	4.4
Maryland.									
Cumberland	29,837	5,894	6,438	5.1	4.9	5.1	4.6	4.7	4.9
Hagerstown	28,064	5,991	6,609	4.7	4.6	4.6	4.2	4.2	4.4
Massachusetts.									
Brockton	66,254	10,388	16,084	6.4	6.9	6.0	4.1	4.3	4.3
Brookline town	37,748	5,036	8,603	7.5	7.4	7.1	4.4	4.7	5.0
Chelsea	43,184	4,403	8,533	9.8	9.1	9.1	4.9	4.9	4.5
Chicopee	36,214	4,625	7,004	7.8	7.7	7.0	5.2	5.7	5.5
Everett	40,120	6,870	9,187	5.8	6.0	5.4	4.4	4.4	4.4
Fitchburg	41,029	6,180	9,273	6.6	7.8	6.8	4.4	4.8	4.7
Haverhill	53,884	9,165	12,814	5.9	6.0	5.8	4.2	4.4	4.2
Holyoke	60,203	5,706	12,948	10.6	11.9	10.9	4.6	5.1	5.1
Lawrence	94,270	12,700	19,715	7.4	8.2	7.7	4.8	5.0	4.9
Lynn	99,148	14,841	23,308	6.7	6.8	6.2	4.3	4.5	4.4
Malden	49,103	8,495	11,238	5.8	6.0	5.3	4.4	4.5	4.4
Medford	39,038	7,632	9,351	5.1	5.0	5.0	4.2	4.3	4.5
Newton	46,054	8,944	10,189	5.1	5.4	5.4	4.5	4.8	4.9
Pittsfield	41,763	7,693	9,499	5.4	5.5	5.2	4.4	4.8	4.7
Quincy	47,876	9,483	11,146	5.0	5.3	5.3	4.3	4.6	4.7
Revere	28,823	3,942	6,375	7.3	6.4	5.0	4.5	4.6	4.6
Salem	42,529	5,902	9,353	7.2	7.4	6.8	4.5	4.7	4.5
Somerville	93,091	15,112	22,653	6.2	6.4	5.7	4.1	4.2	4.3
Taunton	37,137	5,989	8,062	6.2	6.3	6.2	4.6	4.7	4.7
Waltham	30,915	5,681	6,566	5.4	5.9	5.4	4.7	4.8	4.9
Michigan.									
Battle Creek	36,164	8,240	9,347	4.4	4.1	4.4	3.9	3.8	3.9
Bay City	47,554	10,466	11,002	4.5	4.7	5.0	4.3	4.5	4.7
Flint	91,599	16,228	19,570	5.6	5.2	4.4	4.7	4.5	4.1
Hamtramck village	48,615	5,702	9,117	8.5	5.4	....	5.3	5.0	....
Highland Park	46,499	8,051	10,401	5.8	4.3	(1)	4.5	4.2	(1)
Jackson	48,374	10,565	11,551	4.6	4.2	4.4	4.1	4.0	4.1
Kalamazoo	48,487	10,467	11,854	4.6	4.7	4.7	4.1	4.3	4.3
Lansing	57,327	12,089	13,811	4.7	4.6	4.3	4.2	4.2	4.2
Muskegon	36,570	7,397	8,696	4.9	4.7	4.8	4.2	4.3	4.5
Pontiac	34,273	6,295	7,090	5.4	5.0	5.0	4.8	4.7	4.7
Port Huron	25,944	5,918	6,407	4.4	4.0	4.5	4.0	3.9	4.4
Saginaw	61,903	14,035	14,908	4.4	4.4	4.5	4.2	4.2	4.4
Minnesota.									
Duluth	98,917	17,320	21,294	5.7	6.6	6.5	4.6	5.3	5.3
Missouri.									
Joplin	29,902	7,414	8,012	4.0	4.2	4.8	3.7	4.0	4.5
St. Joseph	77,939	17,359	19,189	4.5	4.8	6.7	4.1	4.5	5.0
Springfield	39,631	9,578	10,412	4.1	4.5	4.8	3.8	4.2	4.4
Montana.									
Butte	41,611	8,287	10,098	5.0	5.2	5.4	4.1	4.6	4.7
Nebraska.									
Lincoln	54,948	12,241	13,812	4.5	4.6	5.8	4.0	4.2	5.1
New Hampshire.									
Manchester	78,384	10,657	17,415	7.4	8.1	7.7	4.5	4.9	4.9
Nashua	28,379	5,111	6,305	5.6	5.5	5.5	4.5	4.6	4.6
New Jersey.									
Atlantic City	50,707	9,807	12,468	5.2	5.8	5.6	4.1	4.7	5.1
Bayonne	76,754	8,299	15,513	9.2	9.0	7.4	4.9	5.1	5.0
Clifton	26,470	4,036	5,800	6.6	....	....	4.6	....	....
East Orange	50,710	8,277	12,416	6.1	5.6	5.5	4.1	4.5	4.9
Elizabeth	95,783	13,408	20,641	7.1	7.3	6.7	4.6	4.8	4.8
Hoboken	68,166	4,617	15,877	14.8	15.9	14.2	4.3	4.5	4.4
Irvington town	25,480	3,889	6,098	6.6	6.0	5.2	4.2	4.4	4.5
Kearny town	26,724	3,811	5,706	7.0	7.0	6.3	4.7	4.9	5.0
Montclair town	28,810	4,989	6,294	5.8	6.2	6.0	4.6	5.0	5.2
New Brunswick	32,779	5,128	7,404	6.4	6.0	5.6	4.4	4.5	4.4
Orange	33,268	4,842	7,289	6.9	6.7	6.3	4.6	4.7	4.9
Passaic	63,841	6,380	13,393	10.0	10.7	9.0	4.8	5.3	5.1
Perth Amboy	41,707	5,475	8,605	7.6	7.6	7.2	4.8	5.0	5.1
Plainfield	27,700	5,282	6,375	5.2	5.2	5.2	4.3	4.6	4.7
West Hoboken town	40,074	4,234	10,131	9.5	9.5	8.0	4.0	4.2	4.3
West New York town	29,926	3,063	7,410	9.8	8.3	6.5	4.0	4.6	4.7

¹ Figures not available.

² Based on figures for Norwalk and South Norwalk cities, consolidated and made coextensive with Norwalk town since 1910.

1270   POPULATION.

TABLE 4.—DWELLINGS AND FAMILIES, 1920, AND NUMBER OF PERSONS TO A DWELLING AND TO A FAMILY, 1920, 1910, AND 1900, FOR CITIES HAVING, IN 1920, FROM 25,000 TO 100,000 INHABITANTS—Continued.

CITY.	1920 Population.	1920 Dwellings.	1920 Families.	Persons to a dwelling 1920	1910	1900	Persons to a family 1920	1910	1900
New York.									
Amsterdam	33,524	5,013	7,726	6.7	7.6	6.5	4.3	4.7	4.5
Auburn	36,192	7,263	8,719	5.0	5.1	5.3	4.2	4.4	4.5
Binghamton	66,800	10,421	16,000	6.4	5.7	5.6	4.2	4.2	4.2
Elmira	45,393	9,209	11,357	4.9	4.7	4.9	4.0	4.1	4.3
Jamestown	38,917	7,926	10,206	4.9	5.5	5.2	3.8	4.0	4.1
Kingston	26,688	5,233	6,701	5.1	5.4	5.7	4.0	4.3	4.5
Mount Vernon	42,726	5,856	9,715	7.3	6.7	6.0	4.4	4.5	4.8
New Rochelle	36,213	5,491	7,725	6.6	6.7	6.1	4.7	5.0	4.9
Newburgh	30,366	4,944	7,647	6.1	6.6	6.1	4.0	4.2	4.2
Niagara Falls	50,760	8,307	10,857	6.1	5.4	5.3	4.7	4.6	4.2
Poughkeepsie	35,000	5,583	8,732	6.3	6.1	6.0	4.0	4.1	4.2
Rome	26,341	4,486	5,416	5.9	5.6	5.0	4.9	4.7	4.4
Schenectady	88,723	13,782	20,657	6.4	6.8	7.0	4.3	4.6	4.7
Troy	72,013	11,554	17,895	6.2	7.1	7.8	4.0	4.2	4.5
Utica	94,156	13,969	21,657	6.7	7.2	6.2	4.3	4.6	4.6
Watertown	31,285	6,610	7,835	4.7	4.6	4.8	4.0	4.1	4.2
North Carolina.									
Asheville	28,504	5,575	6,477	5.1	5.4	6.1	4.4	4.6	4.3
Charlotte	46,338	9,641	10,720	4.8	4.8	5.2	4.3	4.4	4.6
Wilmington	33,372	7,012	7,847	4.8	4.7	4.7	4.8	4.4	4.1
Winston-Salem	48,395	8,542	9,895	5.7	[1]5.2	[1]5.2	4.9	[1]4.7	[1]4.6
Ohio.									
Canton	87,091	17,506	20,496	5.0	4.7	4.6	4.2	4.2	4.3
East Cleveland	27,292	5,611	7,122	4.9	4.4	4.4	3.8	4.0	4.3
Hamilton	39,675	8,570	9,706	4.6	4.6	5.0	4.1	4.3	4.5
Lakewood	41,732	8,534	10,537	4.9	4.8	4.7	4.0	4.2	4.6
Lima	41,326	9,638	10,659	4.3	4.4	4.6	3.9	4.1	4.3
Lorain	37,295	6,562	8,004	5.7	5.7	6.0	4.7	4.8	5.1
Mansfield	27,824	6,230	7,215	4.5	4.4	4.7	3.9	3.9	4.1
Marion	27,891	6,798	7,231	4.1	4.0	4.4	3.9	3.9	4.2
Newark	26,718	6,928	7,322	3.9	4.1	4.6	3.6	3.9	4.3
Portsmouth	33,011	6,961	7,967	4.7	4.7	4.9	4.1	4.4	4.4
Springfield	60,840	14,242	15,484	4.3	4.2	4.8	3.9	4.0	4.4
Steubenville	28,508	5,736	6,516	5.0	5.1	4.9	4.4	4.7	4.6
Warren	27,050	5,670	6,561	4.8	4.2	4.5	4.1	4.0	4.2
Zanesville	29,569	7,356	7,958	4.0	4.1	4.4	3.7	3.9	4.2
Oklahoma.									
Muskogee	30,277	6,506	7,414	4.7	4.9	4.7	4.1	4.4	4.5
Oklahoma City	91,295	17,285	21,346	5.3	5.6	5.4	4.3	4.7	4.7
Tulsa	72,075	13,559	16,910	5.3	5.1	(2)	4.3	4.5	(2)
Pennsylvania.									
Allentown	73,502	15,316	17,298	4.8	4.6	4.7	4.2	4.4	4.5
Altoona	60,331	12,482	13,740	4.8	4.7	4.9	4.4	4.5	4.8
Bethlehem	50,358	10,190	11,265	4.9	[3]5.3	[4]4.9	4.5	[3]4.6	[4]4.6
Chester	58,030	10,894	12,259	5.3	5.0	5.1	4.7	4.8	4.9
Easton	33,813	7,652	8,257	4.4	4.3	4.5	4.1	4.1	4.3
Erie	93,372	17,387	21,425	5.4	5.3	5.4	4.4	4.5	4.7
Harrisburg	75,917	16,935	19,158	4.5	4.4	4.6	4.0	4.3	4.5
Hazleton	32,277	6,320	6,584	5.1	5.4	5.0	4.9	5.1	4.9
Johnstown	67,327	12,444	13,858	5.4	5.7	5.4	4.9	5.2	5.1
Lancaster	53,150	12,002	12,344	4.4	4.5	4.7	4.1	4.4	4.6
McKeesport	46,781	7,781	9,916	6.0	5.7	5.6	4.7	4.9	4.9
New Castle	44,938	9,181	10,897	4.9	4.8	4.9	4.3	4.5	4.6
Norristown borough	32,319	5,931	6,624	5.4	5.4	5.3	4.9	5.2	5.2
Wilkes-Barre	73,833	13,464	15,378	5.5	5.5	5.3	4.8	5.1	5.0
Williamsport	36,198	8,079	8,927	4.5	4.4	4.6	4.1	4.2	4.4
York	47,512	10,886	11,692	4.4	4.4	4.7	4.1	4.3	4.5

CITY.	1920 Population.	1920 Dwellings.	1920 Families.	Persons to a dwelling 1920	1910	1900	Persons to a family 1920	1910	1900
Rhode Island.									
Cranston	29,407	5,311	6,360	5.5	5.9	5.8	4.6	4.9	5.0
Newport	30,255	4,895	6,440	6.2	6.1	5.8	4.7	4.9	4.5
Pawtucket	64,248	10,609	14,675	6.1	7.7	6.7	4.4	4.6	4.6
Woonsocket	43,496	5,341	9,080	8.1	9.1	9.1	4.8	5.1	5.1
South Carolina.									
Charleston	67,957	11,714	17,824	5.8	6.1	6.4	3.8	3.9	4.0
Columbia	37,524	6,704	8,151	5.6	5.3	5.7	4.6	4.6	4.8
South Dakota.									
Sioux Falls	25,202	5,176	6,208	4.9	4.9	5.3	4.1	4.3	4.8
Tennessee.									
Chattanooga	57,895	11,458	14,021	5.1	4.9	5.2	4.0	4.2	4.3
Knoxville	77,818	15,494	17,474	5.0	5.3	5.6	4.5	4.6	4.8
Texas.									
Austin	34,876	7,392	7,925	4.7	5.1	5.3	4.4	4.8	5.0
Beaumont	40,422	7,867	9,495	5.1	4.9	5.4	4.3	4.6	5.2
El Paso	77,560	11,158	18,159	7.0	4.9	5.0	4.3	4.5	4.6
Galveston	44,255	9,273	10,588	4.8	5.0	5.2	4.2	4.5	4.7
Waco	38,500	8,011	9,374	4.8	5.0	5.3	4.1	4.7	4.9
Wichita Falls	40,079	6,595	7,878	6.1	5.6	(2)	5.1	4.9	(2)
Utah.									
Ogden	32,804	6,483	7,803	5.1	5.2	5.1	4.2	4.7	4.9
Virginia.									
Lynchburg	30,070	5,878	6,558	5.1	5.4	5.7	4.6	4.7	4.7
Newport News	35,596	6,012	7,835	5.9	5.5	5.6	4.5	4.5	5.0
Petersburg	31,012	6,832	7,540	4.5	4.7	4.8	4.1	4.2	4.2
Portsmouth	54,387	11,210	12,568	4.9	5.0	5.4	4.3	4.7	4.9
Roanoke	50,842	9,090	11,200	5.6	5.6	5.6	4.5	4.9	4.9
Washington.									
Bellingham	25,585	6,009	6,640	4.3	4.6	[5]4.8	3.9	4.3	[5]4.6
Everett	27,644	6,149	7,109	4.5	5.0	5.1	3.9	4.7	4.7
Tacoma	96,965	21,512	24,662	4.5	5.2	5.4	3.9	4.6	4.8
West Virginia.									
Charleston	39,608	7,725	9,069	5.1	5.1	4.9	4.4	4.7	4.6
Clarksburg	27,869	5,604	6,453	5.0	5.2	5.3	4.3	4.5	5.0
Huntington	50,177	9,804	11,350	5.1	5.2	5.1	4.4	4.8	4.8
Wheeling	56,208	11,226	13,019	5.0	5.4	5.5	4.0	4.2	4.5
Wisconsin.									
Green Bay	31,017	6,020	6,914	5.2	5.0	5.2	4.5	4.6	4.8
Kenosha	40,472	6,350	8,098	6.4	5.9	5.5	5.0	4.9	4.8
La Crosse	30,421	6,866	7,526	4.4	4.9	5.1	4.0	4.5	4.7
Madison	38,378	7,515	9,413	5.1	4.9	5.4	4.1	4.3	4.8
Oshkosh	33,162	7,523	8,027	4.4	4.0	4.9	4.1	4.4	4.6
Racine	58,593	10,439	12,799	5.6	5.4	5.3	4.6	4.6	4.7
Sheboygan	30,955	5,823	7,215	5.3	5.0	5.6	4.3	4.5	4.7
Superior	39,671	7,347	8,602	5.4	6.0	6.3	4.0	5.7	5.5

[1] Based on figures for Winston city and Salem town, consolidated as a city under name of Winston-Salem since 1910.
[2] Figures not available.
[3] Based on figures for Bethlehem and South Bethlehem boroughs, consolidated and incorporated as Bethlehem city since 1910.
[4] Based on figures for Bethlehem, South Bethlehem, and West Bethlehem boroughs; West Bethlehem annexed to Bethlehem between 1900 and 1910.
[5] Based on figures for Fairhaven and New Whatcom, consolidated as Bellingham between 1900 and 1910.

DWELLINGS AND FAMILIES.

TABLE 5.—DWELLINGS, FAMILIES, AND EXCESS OF FAMILIES OVER DWELLINGS, FOR CITIES HAVING, IN 1920, 100,000 INHABITANTS OR MORE: 1920, 1910, AND 1900.

CITY AND CENSUS YEAR.	Dwellings.	Families.	Excess of families over dwellings. Number.	Excess of families over dwellings. Per cent of total families.
Akron, Ohio:				
1920	32,030	44,195	12,165	27.5
1910	13,701	15,851	2,150	13.6
1900	8,649	9,746	1,097	11.3
Albany, N.Y.:				
1920	18,402	28,097	9,695	34.5
1910	15,437	24,069	8,632	35.9
1900	13,567	21,627	8,060	37.8
Atlanta, Ga.:				
1920	38,098	49,523	11,425	23.1
1910	30,308	35,813	5,505	15.4
1900	16,555	20,563	4,008	19.5
Baltimore, Md.:				
1920	136,324	166,857	30,533	18.3
1910	101,905	118,851	16,946	14.3
1900	89,442	105,584	16,142	15.3
Birmingham, Ala.:				
1920	35,100	43,040	7,940	18.4
1910	26,989	31,050	4,061	13.1
1900	6,618	8,453	1,835	21.7
Boston, Mass.:				
1920	79,597	164,785	85,188	51.7
1910	73,919	139,700	65,781	47.1
1900	66,482	117,244	50,762	43.3
Bridgeport, Conn.:				
1920	22,328	31,994	9,666	30.2
1910	14,934	21,689	6,755	31.1
1900	11,329	15,553	4,224	27.2
Buffalo, N.Y.:				
1920	73,880	116,201	42,321	36.4
1910	62,335	91,328	28,993	31.7
1900	49,914	73,631	23,717	32.2
Cambridge, Mass.:				
1920	15,113	25,293	10,180	40.2
1910	14,577	22,765	8,188	36.0
1900	13,414	19,434	6,020	31.0
Camden, N.J.:				
1920	24,921	26,645	1,724	6.5
1910	20,260	21,482	1,222	5.7
1900	16,850	17,390	534	3.1
Chicago, Ill.:				
1920	335,777	623,912	288,135	46.2
1910	246,724	473,141	226,397	47.8
1900	193,895	359,960	166,065	46.1
Cincinnati, Ohio:				
1920	62,885	106,239	43,354	40.8
1910	49,525	87,541	38,016	43.4
1900	40,634	74,536	33,902	45.5
Cleveland, Ohio:				
1920	116,545	182,692	66,147	36.2
1910	90,465	124,822	34,357	27.5
1900	63,205	81,519	18,314	22.5
Columbus, Ohio:				
1920	51,663	58,913	7,250	12.3
1910	39,580	42,645	3,065	7.2
1900	24,219	27,582	3,363	12.2
Dallas, Tex.:				
1920	30,860	36,754	5,894	16.0
1910	18,536	20,516	1,980	9.7
1900	8,254	9,168	914	10.0
Dayton, Ohio:				
1920	33,918	38,138	4,220	11.1
1910	26,692	28,370	1,678	5.9
1900	17,987	19,617	1,630	8.3
Denver, Colo.:				
1920	50,636	61,916	11,280	18.2
1910	44,736	51,339	6,603	12.9
1900	27,100	30,936	3,836	12.4
Des Moines, Iowa:				
1920	27,127	31,644	4,517	14.3
1910	18,694	20,599	1,905	9.2
1900	12,708	14,119	1,411	10.0
Detroit, Mich.:				
1920	153,206	218,973	65,767	30.0
1910	83,124	100,356	17,232	17.2
1900	52,046	60,505	8,459	14.0
Fall River, Mass.:				
1920	13,807	26,399	12,592	47.7
1910	10,962	24,378	13,416	55.0
1900	9,509	21,027	11,518	54.8
Fort Worth, Tex.:				
1920	19,679	25,052	5,373	21.4
1910	14,585	16,295	1,710	10.5
1900	5,418	5,933	515	8.7
Grand Rapids, Mich.:				
1920	29,157	33,703	4,546	13.5
1910	23,432	26,925	3,493	13.0
1900	18,049	20,550	2,501	12.2

CITY AND CENSUS YEAR.	Dwellings.	Families.	Excess of families over dwellings. Number.	Excess of families over dwellings. Per cent of total families.
Hartford, Conn.:				
1920	16,495	30,813	14,318	46.5
1910	11,535	21,925	10,390	47.4
1900	9,699	17,231	7,532	43.7
Houston, Tex.:				
1920	28,452	33,932	5,480	16.1
1910	15,903	17,040	1,137	6.7
1900	8,541	9,554	1,013	10.6
Indianapolis, Ind.:				
1920	71,648	81,256	9,608	11.8
1910	53,359	58,645	5,286	9.0
1900	36,160	39,710	3,550	8.9
Jersey City, N.J.:				
1920	31,145	67,288	36,143	53.7
1910	27,805	56,790	28,985	51.0
1900	23,627	44,760	21,133	47.2
Kansas City, Kans.:				
1920	22,641	25,009	2,368	9.5
1910	18,279	19,677	1,398	7.1
1900	10,454	11,802	1,348	11.4
Kansas City, Mo.:				
1920	61,321	82,056	20,735	25.3
1910	47,978	59,296	11,318	19.1
1900	28,027	36,496	8,469	23.2
Los Angeles, Calif.:				
1920	125,004	159,476	34,472	21.6
1910	69,061	78,678	9,617	12.2
1900	22,531	25,207	2,676	10.6
Louisville, Ky.:				
1920	47,449	60,490	13,041	21.6
1910	41,686	52,155	10,469	20.1
1900	34,655	44,912	10,257	22.8
Lowell, Mass.:				
1920	17,488	25,034	7,546	30.1
1910	15,056	21,932	6,876	31.4
1900	13,671	19,279	5,608	29.1
Memphis, Tenn.:				
1920	35,295	42,369	7,074	16.7
1910	26,710	31,154	4,444	14.3
1900	17,443	21,666	4,223	19.5
Milwaukee, Wis.:				
1920	66,915	106,101	39,186	36.9
1910	60,724	80,566	19,842	24.6
1900	45,809	59,806	13,997	23.4
Minneapolis, Minn.:				
1920	65,568	91,843	26,275	28.6
1910	46,903	63,241	16,338	25.8
1900	31,836	42,536	10,700	25.2
Nashville, Tenn.:				
1920	24,992	30,220	5,228	17.3
1910	22,118	26,077	3,959	15.2
1900	15,239	18,422	3,183	17.3
New Bedford, Mass.:				
1920	14,961	26,858	11,897	44.3
1910	11,504	20,820	9,316	44.7
1900	8,744	13,924	5,180	37.2
New Haven, Conn.:				
1920	22,536	36,257	13,721	37.8
1910	17,466	29,271	11,805	40.3
1900	15,240	23,601	8,361	35.4
New Orleans, La.:				
1920	76,969	85,188	8,219	9.6
1910	67,192	73,377	6,185	8.4
1900	52,988	61,775	8,787	14.2
New York, N.Y.:				
1920	365,963	1,278,341	912,378	71.4
1910	305,698	1,020,827	715,129	70.1
1900	249,991	735,621	485,630	66.0
Bronx boro.—				
1920	33,985	166,260	132,275	79.6
1910	28,733	93,897	65,164	69.4
1900	19,944	42,266	22,322	52.8
Brooklyn boro.—				
1920	173,847	453,587	279,740	61.7
1910	147,666	353,666	206,000	58.2
1900	113,972	255,821	141,849	55.4
Manhattan boro.—				
1920	75,534	525,154	449,620	85.6
1910	75,410	493,545	418,135	84.7
1900	80,603	391,687	311,084	79.4
Queens boro.—				
1920	64,323	109,559	45,236	41.3
1910	39,764	62,001	22,237	35.9
1900	24,221	32,121	7,900	24.6
Richmond boro.—				
1920	18,274	23,781	5,507	23.2
1910	14,125	17,718	3,593	20.3
1900	11,251	13,726	2,475	18.0

CITY AND CENSUS YEAR.	Dwellings.	Families.	Excess of families over dwellings. Number.	Excess of families over dwellings. Per cent of total families.
Newark, N.J.:				
1920	41,535	93,274	51,739	55.5
1910	38,693	77,039	38,346	49.8
1900	30,397	54,654	24,257	44.4
Norfolk, Va.:				
1920	19,934	26,732	6,798	25.4
1910	11,953	15,498	3,545	22.9
1900	7,664	10,050	2,386	23.7
Oakland, Calif.:				
1920	47,297	55,793	8,496	15.2
1910	31,740	36,723	4,983	13.6
1900	13,974	15,276	1,302	8.5
Omaha, Nebr.:				
1920	37,997	44,499	6,502	14.6
1910	[1] 28,619	[1] 31,604	2,985	9.4
1900	[1] 22,296	[1] 25,608	3,312	12.9
Paterson, N.J.:				
1920	18,769	32,186	13,417	41.7
1910	15,812	27,978	12,186	43.5
1900	13,591	23,472	9,881	42.1
Philadelphia, Pa.:				
1920	352,944	402,946	50,002	12.4
1910	295,220	327,263	32,043	9.8
1900	241,589	265,880	24,291	9.1
Pittsburgh, Pa.:				
1920	93,890	130,274	36,384	27.9
1910	86,942	110,457	23,515	21.3
1900	[2] 71,345	[2] 90,517	19,172	21.2
Portland, Oreg.:				
1920	54,664	67,045	12,381	18.5
1910	37,436	42,029	4,593	10.9
1900	14,625	16,724	2,099	12.6
Providence, R.I.:				
1920	35,634	54,726	19,092	34.9
1910	28,705	49,129	20,424	41.6
1900	25,204	39,236	14,032	35.8
Reading, Pa.:				
1920	22,759	25,202	2,443	9.7
1910	20,798	21,809	1,011	4.6
1900	16,185	17,002	817	4.8
Richmond, Va.:				
1920	30,753	39,191	8,438	21.5
1910	22,205	26,914	4,709	17.5
1900	14,201	17,845	3,644	20.4
Rochester, N.Y.:				
1920	56,502	68,247	11,745	17.2
1910	38,860	46,787	7,927	16.9
1900	29,531	34,402	4,871	14.2
St. Louis, Mo.:				
1920	118,102	190,640	72,538	38.0
1910	105,650	155,555	49,905	32.1
1900	82,260	123,719	41,459	33.5
St. Paul, Minn.:				
1920	42,462	54,409	11,947	22.0
1910	32,616	41,548	8,932	21.5
1900	24,681	30,919	6,238	20.2
Salt Lake City, Utah:				
1920	23,685	28,216	4,531	16.1
1910	17,856	20,283	2,427	12.0
1900	10,233	11,797	1,564	13.3
San Antonio, Tex.:				
1920	30,264	36,405	6,141	16.9
1910	19,574	21,096	1,522	7.2
1900	10,415	11,326	911	8.0
San Francisco, Calif.:				
1920	90,132	123,349	33,217	26.9
1910	65,025	86,414	21,389	24.8
1900	53,323	71,697	18,374	25.6
Scranton, Pa.:				
1920	23,952	29,768	5,816	19.5
1910	22,143	26,312	4,169	15.8
1900	17,433	20,636	3,203	15.5
Seattle, Wash.:				
1920	60,516	80,048	19,532	24.4
1910	43,559	51,042	7,483	14.7
1900	11,852	14,254	2,402	16.9
Spokane, Wash.:				
1920	22,389	27,178	4,789	17.6
1910	20,282	22,676	2,394	10.6
1900	6,560	8,159	1,599	19.6
Springfield, Mass.:				
1920	18,945	30,361	11,416	37.6
1910	13,352	19,968	6,616	33.1
1900	10,165	14,057	3,892	27.7
Syracuse, N.Y.:				
1920	28,725	41,558	12,833	30.9
1910	23,200	31,551	8,351	26.5
1900	19,081	25,347	6,266	24.7

[1] Includes South Omaha, annexed to Omaha since 1910.   [2] Includes Allegheny, annexed to Pittsburgh between 1900 and 1910.

1272   POPULATION.

TABLE 5.—DWELLINGS, FAMILIES, AND EXCESS OF FAMILIES OVER DWELLINGS, FOR CITIES HAVING, IN 1920, 100,000 INHABITANTS OR MORE: 1920, 1910, AND 1900—Continued.

| CITY AND CENSUS YEAR. | Dwell-ings. | Fami-lies. | EXCESS OF FAMILIES OVER DWELLINGS. | | CITY AND CENSUS YEAR. | Dwell-ings. | Fami-lies. | EXCESS OF FAMILIES OVER DWELLINGS. | | CITY AND CENSUS YEAR. | Dwell-ings. | Fami-lies. | EXCESS OF FAMILIES OVER DWELLINGS. | |
			Num-ber.	Per cent of total fami-lies.				Num-ber.	Per cent of total fami-lies.				Num-ber.	Per cent of total fami-lies.
Toledo, Ohio:					Wilmington, Del.:					Yonkers, N. Y.:				
1920	49,501	57,951	8,450	14.6	1920	20,876	24,488	3,612	14.8	1920	10,302	22,126	11,824	53.4
1910	35,888	39,677	3,789	9.5	1910	17,223	18,637	1,414	7.6	1910	7,857	16,219	8,362	51.6
1900	26,632	28,923	2,291	7.9	1900	14,737	15,667	930	5.9	1900	5,349	9,629	4,280	44.4
Trenton, N. J.:					Worcester, Mass.:					Youngstown, Ohio:				
1920	22,373	25,319	2,946	11.6	1920	19,337	39,230	19,893	50.7	1920	24,007	28,699	4,692	16.3
1910	17,932	19,678	1,746	8.9	1910	15,109	30,743	15,634	50.9	1910	14,280	16,228	1,948	12.0
1900	14,441	15,095	654	4.3	1900	13,130	24,841	11,711	47.1	1900	8,343	9,090	747	8.2
Washington, D. C.:														
1920	72,175	96,194	24,019	25.0										
1910	58,513	71,339	12,826	18.0										
1900	49,385	56,678	7,293	12.9										

DWELLINGS AND FAMILIES.

1273

TABLE 6.—DWELLINGS AND FAMILIES, FOR URBAN AND RURAL COMMUNITIES, BY DIVISIONS AND STATES: 1920 AND 1910.

DIVISION, STATE, AND CLASS OF COMMUNITY.	1920			1910			PERSONS TO A DWELLING.		PERSONS TO A FAMILY.	
	Population.	Dwellings.	Families.	Population.	Dwellings.	Families.	1920	1910	1920	1910
United States	105,710,620	20,697,204	24,351,676	91,972,266	17,805,845	20,255,555	5.1	5.2	4.3	4.5
Urban	54,304,603	9,484,550	12,803,047	42,166,120	7,160,349	9,395,436	5.7	5.9	4.2	4.5
Rural	51,406,017	11,212,654	11,548,629	49,806,146	10,645,496	10,860,119	4.6	4.7	4.5	4.6
GEOGRAPHIC DIVISIONS.										
NEW ENGLAND	7,400,909	1,255,964	1,703,812	6,552,681	1,099,336	1,464,942	5.9	6.0	4.3	4.5
Urban	5,865,073	903,949	1,325,076	4,998,082	744,219	1,084,898	6.5	6.7	4.4	4.6
Rural	1,535,836	352,015	378,736	1,554,599	355,117	380,044	4.4	4.4	4.1	4.1
MIDDLE ATLANTIC	22,261,144	3,566,549	5,085,080	19,315,892	3,093,464	4,235,675	6.2	6.2	4.4	4.6
Urban	16,672,595	2,332,383	3,788,850	13,723,373	1,879,460	2,966,286	7.1	7.3	4.4	4.6
Rural	5,588,549	1,234,166	1,296,230	5,592,519	1,214,004	1,269,389	4.5	4.6	4.3	4.4
EAST NORTH CENTRAL	21,475,543	4,385,541	5,143,913	18,250,621	3,743,779	4,214,820	4.9	4.9	4.2	4.3
Urban	13,049,272	2,406,316	3,119,157	9,617,271	1,775,153	2,213,296	5.4	5.4	4.2	4.3
Rural	8,426,271	1,979,225	2,024,756	8,633,350	1,968,626	2,001,524	4.3	4.4	4.2	4.3
WEST NORTH CENTRAL	12,544,249	2,716,968	2,957,849	11,637,921	2,448,083	2,592,069	4.6	4.8	4.2	4.5
Urban	4,727,372	959,775	1,164,089	3,873,716	755,821	879,829	4.9	5.1	4.1	4.4
Rural	7,816,877	1,757,193	1,793,760	7,764,205	1,692,262	1,712,240	4.4	4.6	4.4	4.5
SOUTH ATLANTIC	13,990,272	2,781,684	2,991,628	12,194,895	2,424,935	2,539,270	5.0	5.0	4.7	4.8
Urban	4,338,792	846,647	1,006,440	3,092,153	602,959	688,260	5.1	5.1	4.3	4.5
Rural	9,651,480	1,935,037	1,985,188	9,102,742	1,821,976	1,851,010	5.0	5.0	4.9	4.9
EAST SOUTH CENTRAL	8,893,307	1,867,167	1,977,381	8,409,901	1,732,152	1,796,832	4.8	4.9	4.5	4.7
Urban	1,994,207	422,751	496,765	1,574,229	325,380	371,179	4.7	4.8	4.0	4.2
Rural	6,899,100	1,444,416	1,480,616	6,835,672	1,406,772	1,425,653	4.8	4.9	4.7	4.8
WEST SOUTH CENTRAL	10,242,224	2,110,879	2,242,810	8,784,534	1,780,510	1,827,105	4.9	4.9	4.6	4.8
Urban	2,970,829	606,625	695,135	1,957,456	403,347	432,089	4.9	4.9	4.3	4.5
Rural	7,271,395	1,504,254	1,547,675	6,827,078	1,377,163	1,395,016	4.8	5.0	4.7	4.9
MOUNTAIN	3,336,101	743,775	803,853	2,633,517	586,451	614,656	4.5	4.5	4.2	4.3
Urban	1,214,980	254,491	295,327	947,511	197,088	215,987	4.8	4.8	4.1	4.4
Rural	2,121,121	489,284	508,526	1,686,006	389,363	398,669	4.3	4.3	4.2	4.2
PACIFIC	5,566,871	1,268,677	1,445,350	4,192,304	897,135	970,186	4.4	4.7	3.9	4.3
Urban	3,471,483	751,613	912,208	2,382,329	476,922	543,612	4.6	5.0	3.8	4.4
Rural	2,095,388	517,064	533,142	1,809,975	420,213	426,574	4.1	4.3	3.9	4.2
NEW ENGLAND.										
MAINE	768,014	162,304	186,106	742,371	159,437	177,960	4.7	4.7	4.1	4.2
Urban	299,569	53,647	70,672	282,248	47,769	60,164	5.6	5.5	4.2	4.4
Rural	468,445	108,657	115,434	480,123	111,668	117,796	4.3	4.3	4.1	4.1
NEW HAMPSHIRE	443,083	92,184	108,334	430,572	88,871	103,156	4.8	4.8	4.1	4.2
Urban	279,761	51,456	65,051	255,099	45,885	57,245	5.4	5.6	4.3	4.5
Rural	163,322	40,728	43,283	175,473	42,986	45,911	4.0	4.1	3.8	3.8
VERMONT	352,428	77,158	85,804	355,956	77,466	85,178	4.6	4.6	4.1	4.2
Urban	109,976	20,722	25,994	98,917	18,136	22,415	5.3	5.5	4.2	4.4
Rural	242,452	56,436	59,810	257,039	59,330	62,763	4.3	4.3	4.1	4.1
MASSACHUSETTS	3,852,356	597,052	874,798	3,366,416	511,926	734,013	6.5	6.6	4.4	4.6
Urban	3,650,248	547,896	822,425	3,125,367	455,381	673,167	6.7	6.9	4.4	4.6
Rural	202,108	49,156	52,373	241,049	56,545	60,846	4.1	4.3	3.9	4.0
RHODE ISLAND	604,397	98,861	137,160	542,610	79,725	117,978	6.1	6.8	4.4	4.6
Urban	589,180	95,027	133,118	524,654	75,461	113,368	6.2	7.0	4.4	4.6
Rural	15,217	3,834	4,042	17,956	4,264	4,610	4.0	4.2	3.8	3.9
CONNECTICUT	1,380,631	228,405	311,610	1,114,756	181,911	246,659	6.0	6.1	4.4	4.5
Urban	936,339	135,201	207,816	731,797	101,587	158,541	6.9	7.2	4.5	4.6
Rural	444,292	93,204	103,794	382,959	80,324	88,118	4.8	4.8	4.3	4.3
MIDDLE ATLANTIC.										
NEW YORK	10,385,227	1,325,114	2,441,125	9,113,614	1,178,686	2,046,845	7.8	7.7	4.3	4.5
Urban	8,589,844	889,174	1,983,762	7,185,494	723,425	1,570,617	9.7	9.9	4.3	4.6
Rural	1,795,383	435,940	457,363	1,928,120	455,261	476,228	4.1	4.2	3.9	4.0
NEW JERSEY	3,155,900	515,211	721,841	2,537,167	407,295	558,202	6.1	6.2	4.4	4.5
Urban	2,474,936	366,650	562,334	1,907,210	272,788	413,710	6.8	7.0	4.4	4.6
Rural	680,964	148,561	159,507	629,957	134,507	144,492	4.6	4.7	4.3	4.4
PENNSYLVANIA	8,720,017	1,726,224	1,922,114	7,665,111	1,507,483	1,630,628	5.1	5.1	4.5	4.7
Urban	5,607,815	1,076,559	1,242,754	4,630,669	883,247	981,959	5.2	5.2	4.5	4.7
Rural	3,112,202	649,665	679,360	3,034,442	624,236	648,669	4.8	4.9	4.6	4.7
EAST NORTH CENTRAL.										
OHIO	5,759,394	1,216,542	1,414,068	4,767,121	1,024,800	1,138,165	4.7	4.7	4.1	4.2
Urban	3,677,136	714,734	898,839	2,665,143	529,435	633,664	5.1	5.0	4.1	4.2
Rural	2,082,258	501,808	515,229	2,101,978	495,365	504,501	4.1	4.2	4.0	4.2
INDIANA	2,930,390	696,466	737,707	2,700,876	631,554	654,891	4.2	4.3	4.0	4.1
Urban	1,482,855	338,981	373,802	1,143,835	262,137	280,781	4.4	4.4	4.0	4.1
Rural	1,447,535	357,485	363,905	1,557,041	369,417	374,110	4.0	4.2	4.0	4.2
ILLINOIS	6,485,280	1,190,414	1,534,077	5,638,591	1,006,848	1,264,710	5.4	5.6	4.2	4.5
Urban	4,403,153	706,812	1,040,938	3,476,929	524,355	774,962	6.2	6.6	4.2	4.5
Rural	2,082,127	483,602	493,139	2,161,662	482,493	489,755	4.3	4.5	4.2	4.4
MICHIGAN	3,668,412	755,931	862,745	2,810,173	618,222	657,418	4.9	4.5	4.3	4.3
Urban	2,241,560	416,154	515,020	1,327,044	269,806	302,881	5.4	4.9	4.4	4.4
Rural	1,426,852	339,777	347,725	1,483,129	348,416	354,537	4.2	4.3	4.1	4.2
WISCONSIN	2,632,067	526,188	595,316	2,333,860	462,355	499,629	5.0	5.0	4.4	4.7
Urban	1,244,568	229,635	290,558	1,004,320	189,420	221,008	5.4	5.3	4.3	4.5
Rural	1,387,499	296,553	304,758	1,329,540	272,935	278,621	4.7	4.9	4.6	4.8

1274   POPULATION.

TABLE 6.—DWELLINGS AND FAMILIES FOR URBAN AND RURAL COMMUNITIES, BY DIVISIONS AND STATES: 1920 AND 1910—Continued.

DIVISION, STATE, AND CLASS OF COMMUNITY.	1920 Population.	1920 Dwellings.	1920 Families.	1910 Population.	1910 Dwellings.	1910 Families.	PERSONS TO A DWELLING. 1920	PERSONS TO A DWELLING. 1910	PERSONS TO A FAMILY. 1920	PERSONS TO A FAMILY. 1910
WEST NORTH CENTRAL.										
MINNESOTA	2,387,125	469,652	526,026	2,075,708	380,809	416,452	5.1	5.5	4.5	5.0
Urban	1,051,593	191,734	241,261	850,294	188,499	170,308	5.5	6.1	4.4	5.0
Rural	1,335,532	277,918	284,765	1,225,414	242,310	246,144	4.8	5.1	4.7	5.0
IOWA	2,404,021	559,188	586,070	2,224,771	498,943	512,515	4.3	4.5	4.1	4.3
Urban	875,495	202,124	222,669	680,054	153,001	163,193	4.3	4.4	3.9	4.2
Rural	1,528,526	357,064	363,401	1,544,717	345,942	349,322	4.3	4.5	4.2	4.4
MISSOURI	3,404,055	717,256	829,043	3,293,335	677,196	749,812	4.7	4.9	4.1	4.4
Urban	1,586,903	295,055	398,030	1,398,817	257,777	325,256	5.4	5.4	4.0	4.3
Rural	1,817,152	422,201	431,013	1,894,518	419,419	424,556	4.3	4.5	4.2	4.5
NORTH DAKOTA	646,872	129,905	134,881	577,056	118,757	120,910	5.0	4.9	4.8	4.8
Urban	88,239	16,575	19,413	63,236	11,266	12,207	5.3	5.6	4.5	5.1
Rural	558,633	113,330	115,468	513,820	107,491	108,613	4.9	4.8	4.8	4.7
SOUTH DAKOTA	636,547	136,512	142,793	583,888	127,739	131,060	4.7	4.6	4.5	4.5
Urban	101,872	21,200	24,348	76,673	15,189	16,886	4.8	5.0	4.2	4.5
Rural	534,675	115,312	118,445	507,215	112,550	114,174	4.6	4.5	4.5	4.4
NEBRASKA	1,296,372	288,390	303,436	1,192,214	258,967	265,549	4.5	4.6	4.3	4.5
Urban	405,306	86,761	97,810	310,852	64,585	69,144	4.7	4.8	4.1	4.5
Rural	891,066	201,629	205,626	881,362	194,382	196,105	4.4	4.5	4.3	4.5
KANSAS	1,769,257	416,065	435,600	1,690,949	385,672	395,771	4.3	4.4	4.1	4.3
Urban	617,964	146,326	160,558	493,790	115,504	122,445	4.2	4.3	3.8	4.0
Rural	1,151,293	269,739	275,042	1,197,159	270,168	273,326	4.3	4.4	4.2	4.4
SOUTH ATLANTIC.										
DELAWARE	223,003	47,868	52,070	202,322	43,183	44,951	4.7	4.7	4.3	4.5
Urban	120,767	23,655	27,314	97,085	19,588	21,053	5.1	5.0	4.4	4.6
Rural	102,236	24,213	24,756	105,237	23,595	23,898	4.2	4.5	4.1	4.4
MARYLAND	1,449,661	288,261	324,742	1,295,346	253,805	274,824	5.0	5.1	4.5	4.7
Urban	869,422	165,383	198,198	658,192	123,572	141,607	5.3	5.3	4.4	4.6
Rural	580,239	122,878	126,544	637,154	130,233	133,217	4.7	4.9	4.6	4.8
DISTRICT OF COLUMBIA	437,571	72,175	96,194	331,069	58,513	71,339	6.1	5.7	4.5	4.6
Urban	437,571	72,175	96,194	331,069	58,513	71,330	6.1	5.7	4.5	4.6
Rural [1]										
VIRGINIA	2,309,187	450,229	483,363	2,061,612	400,445	419,452	5.1	5.1	4.8	4.9
Urban	673,984	127,674	152,826	476,529	89,156	103,049	5.3	5.3	4.4	4.6
Rural	1,635,203	322,555	330,537	1,585,083	311,289	316,403	5.1	5.1	4.9	5.0
WEST VIRGINIA	1,463,701	293,002	310,098	1,221,119	239,128	248,480	5.0	5.1	4.7	4.9
Urban	369,007	74,472	85,483	228,242	44,755	50,149	5.0	5.1	4.3	4.6
Rural	1,094,694	218,530	224,615	992,877	194,373	198,331	5.0	5.1	4.9	5.0
NORTH CAROLINA	2,559,123	495,269	513,377	2,206,287	430,570	440,334	5.2	5.1	5.0	5.0
Urban	490,370	98,136	107,915	318,474	64,642	69,436	5.0	4.9	4.5	4.6
Rural	2,068,753	397,133	405,462	1,887,813	365,928	370,898	5.2	5.2	5.1	5.1
SOUTH CAROLINA	1,683,724	330,500	349,126	1,515,400	302,842	315,204	5.1	5.0	4.8	4.8
Urban	293,987	57,309	69,825	224,832	43,178	52,178	5.1	5.2	4.2	4.3
Rural	1,389,737	273,191	279,301	1,290,568	259,664	263,026	5.1	5.0	5.0	4.9
GEORGIA	2,895,832	586,509	628,525	2,609,121	530,631	553,264	4.9	4.9	4.6	4.7
Urban	727,859	150,141	179,410	538,650	112,250	128,494	4.8	4.8	4.1	4.2
Rural	2,167,973	436,368	449,115	2,070,471	418,381	424,770	5.0	4.9	4.8	4.9
FLORIDA	968,470	217,871	234,133	752,619	165,818	171,422	4.4	4.5	4.1	4.4
Urban	355,825	77,702	89,275	219,080	47,305	50,955	4.6	4.6	4.0	4.3
Rural	612,645	140,169	144,858	533,539	118,513	120,467	4.4	4.5	4.2	4.4
EAST SOUTH CENTRAL.										
KENTUCKY	2,416,630	510,981	546,306	2,289,905	469,669	494,788	4.7	4.9	4.4	4.6
Urban	633,543	134,688	161,733	555,442	111,823	131,247	4.7	5.0	3.9	4.2
Rural	1,783,087	376,293	384,573	1,734,463	358,346	363,541	4.7	4.8	4.6	4.8
TENNESSEE	2,337,885	488,392	519,108	2,184,789	444,814	462,553	4.8	4.9	4.5	4.7
Urban	611,226	129,488	151,637	441,045	90,286	103,183	4.7	4.9	4.0	4.3
Rural	1,726,659	358,904	367,471	1,743,744	354,528	359,370	4.8	4.9	4.7	4.9
ALABAMA	2,348,174	480,392	508,769	2,138,093	441,240	454,767	4.9	4.8	4.6	4.7
Urban	509,317	104,695	123,392	370,431	78,675	87,375	4.9	4.7	4.1	4.2
Rural	1,838,857	375,697	385,377	1,767,662	362,574	367,392	4.9	4.9	4.8	4.8
MISSISSIPPI	1,790,618	387,402	403,198	1,797,114	376,420	384,724	4.6	4.8	4.4	4.7
Urban	240,121	53,880	60,003	207,311	45,096	49,374	4.5	4.6	4.0	4.2
Rural	1,550,497	333,522	343,195	1,589,803	331,324	335,350	4.6	4.8	4.5	4.7
WEST SOUTH CENTRAL.										
ARKANSAS	1,752,204	375,316	390,960	1,574,449	327,625	333,368	4.7	4.8	4.5	4.7
Urban	290,497	63,603	71,001	202,681	43,736	46,152	4.6	4.6	4.1	4.4
Rural	1,461,707	311,713	319,959	1,371,768	283,889	287,216	4.7	4.8	4.6	4.8
LOUISIANA	1,798,509	370,377	389,913	1,656,388	331,220	344,144	4.9	5.0	4.6	4.8
Urban	628,163	128,684	141,294	496,516	100,662	108,705	4.9	4.9	4.4	4.6
Rural	1,170,346	241,693	248,619	1,159,872	230,558	235,439	4.8	5.0	4.7	4.9
OKLAHOMA	2,028,283	418,557	444,524	1,657,155	342,488	351,167	4.8	4.8	4.6	4.7
Urban	539,480	111,317	128,357	320,155	65,858	71,173	4.8	4.9	4.2	4.5
Rural	1,488,803	307,240	316,167	1,337,000	276,630	279,994	4.8	4.8	4.7	4.8
TEXAS	4,663,228	946,629	1,017,413	3,896,542	779,177	798,426	4.9	5.0	4.6	4.9
Urban	1,512,689	303,021	354,483	938,104	193,091	206,059	5.0	4.9	4.3	4.6
Rural	3,150,539	643,608	662,930	2,958,438	586,086	592,367	4.9	5.0	4.8	5.0

[1] No rural population, as Washington city is coextensive with the District of Columbia.

DWELLINGS AND FAMILIES.

1275

TABLE 6.—DWELLINGS AND FAMILIES, FOR URBAN AND RURAL COMMUNITIES, BY DIVISIONS AND STATES: 1920 AND 1910—Continued.

DIVISION, STATE, AND CLASS OF COMMUNITY.	1920			1910			PERSONS TO A DWELLING.		PERSONS TO A FAMILY.	
	Population.	Dwellings.	Families.	Population.	Dwellings.	Families.	1920	1910	1920	1910
MOUNTAIN.										
MONTANA	548,889	130,670	139,912	376,053	82,811	86,602	4.2	4.5	3.9	4.3
Urban	172,011	36,135	42,525	133,420	26,247	28,812	4.8	5.1	4.0	4.6
Rural	376,878	94,535	97,387	242,633	56,564	57,790	4.0	4.3	3.9	4.2
IDAHO	431,866	95,299	100,500	325,594	71,830	73,669	4.5	4.5	4.3	4.4
Urban	119,037	25,386	28,416	69,898	14,045	15,009	4.7	5.0	4.2	4.7
Rural	312,829	69,913	72,084	255,696	57,785	58,660	4.5	4.4	4.3	4.4
WYOMING	194,402	44,710	48,476	145,965	30,969	32,092	4.3	4.7	4.0	4.5
Urban	57,348	11,588	13,652	43,221	7,999	8,637	4.9	5.4	4.2	5.0
Rural	137,054	33,122	34,824	102,744	22,970	23,455	4.1	4.5	3.9	4.4
COLORADO	939,629	211,103	230,843	799,024	183,874	194,467	4.5	4.3	4.1	4.1
Urban	453,259	95,904	112,380	404,840	88,420	97,456	4.7	4.6	4.0	4.2
Rural	486,370	115,199	118,463	394,184	95,454	97,011	4.2	4.1	4.1	4.1
NEW MEXICO	360,350	78,024	83,706	327,301	75,888	78,883	4.6	4.3	4.3	4.1
Urban	64,960	13,911	15,858	46,571	10,262	11,080	4.7	4.5	4.1	4.2
Rural	295,390	64,113	67,848	280,730	65,626	67,803	4.6	4.3	4.4	4.1
ARIZONA	334,162	73,673	80,208	204,354	45,386	47,927	4.5	4.5	4.2	4.3
Urban	117,527	24,964	28,814	63,260	13,660	14,782	4.7	4.6	4.1	4.3
Rural	216,635	48,709	51,394	141,094	31,726	33,145	4.4	4.4	4.2	4.3
UTAH	449,396	89,587	98,346	373,351	72,649	77,339	5.0	5.1	4.6	4.8
Urban	215,584	43,262	49,931	172,934	33,592	37,126	5.0	5.1	4.3	4.7
Rural	233,812	46,325	48,415	200,417	39,057	40,213	5.0	5.1	4.8	5.0
NEVADA	77,407	20,709	21,862	81,875	23,044	23,677	3.7	3.6	3.5	3.5
Urban	15,254	3,341	3,751	13,367	2,863	3,085	4.6	4.7	4.1	4.3
Rural	62,153	17,368	18,111	68,508	20,181	20,592	3.6	3.4	3.4	3.3
PACIFIC.										
WASHINGTON	1,356,621	304,735	342,228	1,141,990	238,822	254,692	4.5	4.8	4.0	4.5
Urban	748,735	156,661	190,272	605,530	116,767	130,783	4.8	5.2	3.9	4.6
Rural	607,886	148,074	151,956	536,460	122,055	123,909	4.1	4.4	4.0	4.3
OREGON	783,389	185,081	202,890	672,765	144,832	151,858	4.2	4.6	3.9	4.4
Urban	391,019	86,224	101,728	307,060	58,764	64,817	4.5	5.2	3.8	4.7
Rural	392,370	98,857	101,162	365,705	86,068	87,041	4.0	4.2	3.9	4.2
CALIFORNIA	3,426,861	778,861	900,232	2,377,549	513,481	563,636	4.4	4.6	3.8	4.2
Urban	2,331,729	508,728	620,208	1,469,739	301,391	348,012	4.6	4.9	3.8	4.2
Rural	1,095,132	270,133	280,024	907,810	212,090	215,624	4.1	4.3	3.9	4.2

1276   POPULATION.

TABLE 7.—EXCESS OF FAMILIES OVER DWELLINGS, FOR TOTAL POPULATION AND POPULATION LIVING IN CITIES HAVING, IN 1920, 100,000 INHABITANTS OR MORE, 1920, 1910, AND 1900, AND FOR RURAL AND URBAN POPULATION, 1920 AND 1910, BY DIVISIONS AND STATES.

[Rural population is that living in unincorporated places or in cities, towns, or villages having fewer than 2,500 inhabitants.]

DIVISION AND STATE.	TOTAL. Excess of families over dwellings. Number: 1920	Per cent of total families. 1920	1910	1900	RURAL. Excess of families over dwellings. Number: 1920	Per cent of total families. 1920	1910	URBAN. Excess of families over dwellings. Number: 1920	Per cent of total families. 1920	1910	CITIES OF 100,000 OR MORE. Excess of families over dwellings. Number: 1920	Per cent of total families. 1920	1910	1900
United States	3,654,472	15.0	12.1	10.9	335,975	2.9	2.0	3,318,497	25.9	23.8	2,393,234	37.5	35.3	34.5
GEOGRAPHIC DIVISIONS:														
New England	447,848	26.3	25.0	21.1	26,721	7.1	6.6	421,127	31.8	31.4	215,509	43.8	43.5	39.6
Middle Atlantic	1,518,531	29.9	27.0	23.1	62,064	4.8	4.4	1,456,467	38.4	36.6	1,201,410	50.3	48.0	43.9
East North Central	758,372	14.7	11.2	9.9	45,531	2.2	1.6	712,841	22.9	19.8	553,520	35.0	32.6	32.3
West North Central	240,881	8.1	5.6	5.4	36,567	2.0	1.2	204,314	17.6	14.1	144,882	27.9	23.7	25.6
South Atlantic	209,944	7.0	4.5	4.5	50,151	2.5	1.6	159,793	15.9	12.4	84,825	21.0	15.7	15.2
East South Central	110,214	5.6	3.6	3.9	36,200	2.4	1.3	74,014	14.9	12.3	33,283	18.9	16.3	20.9
West South Central	131,931	5.9	2.6	2.9	43,421	2.8	1.3	88,510	12.7	6.7	31,107	14.3	8.5	12.4
Mountain	60,078	7.5	4.6	4.2	19,242	3.8	2.3	40,836	13.8	8.8	15,811	17.5	12.6	12.6
Pacific	176,673	12.2	7.5	7.1	16,078	3.0	1.5	160,595	17.6	12.3	112,887	22.0	15.9	18.8
NEW ENGLAND:														
Maine	23,802	12.8	10.4	9.1	6,777	5.9	5.2	17,025	24.1	20.6				
New Hampshire	16,150	14.9	13.8	11.5	2,555	5.9	6.4	13,595	20.9	19.8				
Vermont	8,646	10.1	9.1	7.9	3,374	5.6	5.5	5,272	20.3	19.1				
Massachusetts	277,746	31.7	30.3	26.4	3,217	6.1	7.1	274,529	33.4	32.4	158,712	47.0	44.9	41.2
Rhode Island	38,299	27.9	32.4	28.0	208	5.1	7.5	38,091	28.6	33.4	19,002	34.0	41.6	35.8
Connecticut	83,205	26.7	26.3	21.5	10,590	10.2	8.8	72,615	34.9	35.9	37,705	38.1	39.7	35.7
MIDDLE ATLANTIC:														
New York	1,116,011	45.7	42.4	36.7	21,423	4.7	4.4	1,094,588	55.2	53.9	1,000,796	64.4	63.2	59.2
New Jersey	206,630	28.6	27.0	22.7	10,946	6.9	6.9	195,084	34.8	34.1	105,960	43.3	40.6	36.3
Pennsylvania	195,890	10.2	7.6	6.3	29,695	4.4	3.8	166,195	13.4	10.1	94,045	10.1	12.5	12.1
EAST NORTH CENTRAL:														
Ohio	197,526	14.0	10.0	9.2	13,421	2.6	1.8	184,105	20.5	16.4	140,278	28.3	23.9	24.4
Indiana	41,241	5.6	3.6	3.3	6,420	1.8	1.3	34,821	9.3	6.6	9,608	11.8	9.0	8.9
Illinois	343,663	22.4	20.4	18.4	9,537	1.9	1.5	334,126	32.1	32.3	288,135	40.2	47.8	46.1
Michigan	106,814	12.4	6.0	4.8	7,948	2.3	1.7	98,866	19.2	10.9	70,813	27.8	16.3	13.5
Wisconsin	69,128	11.6	7.5	6.6	8,205	2.7	2.0	60,923	21.0	14.3	39,186	36.9	24.6	23.4
WEST NORTH CENTRAL:														
Minnesota	56,374	10.7	8.6	7.5	6,847	2.4	1.6	49,527	20.5	18.7	38,222	26.1	24.1	23.1
Iowa	26,882	4.6	2.6	2.5	6,337	1.7	1.0	20,545	9.2	6.2	4,517	14.3	9.2	10.0
Missouri	111,787	13.5	9.7	9.3	8,812	2.0	1.2	102,975	25.9	20.7	93,273	34.2	28.5	31.2
North Dakota	4,976	3.7	1.8	2.1	2,138	1.9	1.0	2,838	14.6	8.4				
South Dakota	6,281	4.4	2.5	2.0	3,133	2.6	1.4	3,148	12.9	10.0				
Nebraska	15,046	5.0	2.5	3.2	3,997	1.9	0.9	11,049	11.3	7.0	6,502	14.6	9.4	12.9
Kansas	19,535	4.5	2.6	2.4	5,303	1.9	1.2	14,232	8.9	5.7	2,368	9.5	7.1	11.4
SOUTH ATLANTIC:														
Delaware	4,202	8.1	3.9	3.2	543	2.2	1.3	3,659	13.4	7.0	3,612	14.8	7.6	5.9
Maryland	36,481	11.2	7.6	8.5	3,666	2.9	2.2	32,815	16.6	12.7	30,533	18.3	14.3	15.3
District of Columbia	24,019	25.0	18.0	12.9	(1)	(1)	(1)	24,019	25.0	18.0	24,019	25.0	18.0	12.9
Virginia	33,134	6.9	4.5	4.8	7,982	2.4	1.6	25,152	16.5	13.5	15,236	23.1	19.5	21.6
West Virginia	17,096	5.5	3.8	3.0	6,085	2.7	2.0	11,011	12.9	10.8				
North Carolina	18,108	3.5	2.2	2.6	8,329	2.1	1.3	9,779	9.1	6.9				
South Carolina	18,626	5.3	3.9	3.9	6,110	2.2	1.3	12,516	17.9	17.2				
Georgia	42,016	6.7	4.1	4.3	12,747	2.8	1.5	29,269	16.3	12.6	11,425	23.1	15.4	19.5
Florida	10,262	6.9	3.3	2.9	4,689	3.2	1.6	11,573	13.0	7.2				
EAST SOUTH CENTRAL:														
Kentucky	35,325	6.5	5.1	5.3	8,280	2.2	1.4	27,045	16.7	15.2	13,041	21.6	20.1	22.8
Tennessee	30,716	5.9	3.8	4.2	8,587	2.3	1.3	22,149	14.6	12.5	12,302	16.9	14.7	18.5
Alabama	28,377	5.6	3.0	3.3	9,680	2.5	1.3	18,697	15.2	10.0	7,940	18.4	13.1	21.7
Mississippi	15,796	3.9	2.2	2.5	9,673	2.8	1.2	6,123	10.2	8.7				
WEST SOUTH CENTRAL:														
Arkansas	15,644	4.0	1.7	2.4	8,246	2.6	1.2	7,398	10.4	5.2				
Louisiana	19,536	5.0	3.8	5.4	6,926	2.8	2.1	12,610	8.9	7.4	8,219	9.6	8.4	14.2
Oklahoma	25,967	5.8	2.5	1.7	8,927	2.8	1.2	17,040	13.3	7.5				
Texas	70,784	7.0	2.4	2.3	19,322	2.9	1.1	51,462	14.5	6.3	22,888	17.3	8.5	9.8
MOUNTAIN:														
Montana	9,242	6.6	4.4	3.8	2,852	2.9	2.1	6,390	15.0	8.9				
Idaho	5,201	5.2	2.5	2.7	2,171	3.0	1.5	3,030	10.7	6.4				
Wyoming	3,766	7.8	3.5	2.2	1,702	4.9	2.1	2,064	15.1	7.4				
Colorado	19,740	8.6	5.4	5.6	3,264	2.8	1.6	16,476	14.7	9.3	11,280	18.2	12.9	12.4
New Mexico	5,682	6.8	3.8	3.1	3,735	5.5	3.2	1,947	12.3	7.4				
Arizona	6,535	8.1	5.3	3.7	2,685	5.2	4.3	3,850	13.4	7.6				
Utah	8,759	8.9	6.1	4.8	2,090	4.3	2.9	6,669	13.4	9.5	4,531	16.1	12.0	13.3
Nevada	1,153	5.3	2.7	2.1	743	4.1	2.0	410	10.9	7.2				
PACIFIC:														
Washington	37,493	11.0	6.2	5.7	3,882	2.6	1.5	33,611	17.7	10.7	24,321	22.7	13.4	17.9
Oregon	17,809	8.8	4.6	4.0	2,305	2.3	1.1	15,504	15.2	9.3	12,381	18.5	10.9	12.6
California	121,371	13.5	8.9	8.4	9,891	3.5	1.6	111,480	18.0	13.4	76,185	22.5	17.8	19.9

[1] No rural population, as Washington city is coextensive with the District of Columbia.

CHAPTER XV

OWNERSHIP OF HOMES

CHAPTER XV.—OWNERSHIP OF HOMES.

INTRODUCTION.

The inquiry as to ownership of homes has been made at each of the last four censuses. The statistics here presented relate to continental United States as a whole, states, counties, and those incorporated places having 10,000 inhabitants or more. Statistics for Alaska, Hawaii, and Porto Rico are given in Vol. III of the Fourteenth Census Reports.

At the census of 1920, as in 1890, but not in 1900 or 1910, the inquiry as to encumbrance covered value of mortgaged homes, amount of mortgage indebtedness, and rate of interest paid. Statistics on these branches of the subject, however, are to be published separately in a special report, and the tables in this chapter relate solely to the facts of proprietorship and encumbrance. The term "proprietorship," as here used, is not restricted to ownership but has its full legal meaning and covers both ownership and tenancy.

At the censuses of 1920, 1910, and 1890 the returns on home ownership were tabulated with reference to "census families," which include certain groups that may be termed "economic families," such as occupants or inmates of hotels, boarding houses, or institutions. Thus the census family is not in all cases identical with the private family. At the census of 1900 the statistics for the total population of the United States and of each state were tabulated with reference to both census families and private families, but the statistics for cities and those as to color or race were tabulated only with reference to private families. Accordingly the figures for 1900 given in Tables 3, 5, 6, and 7 are not exactly comparable with those for 1910 and 1920.

For census purposes a home is treated as owned if it is owned wholly or in part by the head of the family living in it, or by his wife, or by a son or a daughter, or by any other relative living in the same house with the head of the family. (But if the home is owned by a lodger or boarder who is not related to the head of the family occupying it, it is treated as a rented home.) Every home not owned, either wholly or in part, by the family living in it is classed as rented, whether rent is actually paid or not.

In the case of an apartment house or other plural-family dwelling, the portion occupied by each family is treated as a separate home and is returned as rented, owned free, or owned encumbered, as the case may be.

Apportionment of "unknown."—For a small proportion of the homes (2.2 per cent in 1920) no returns were made as to proprietorship; and for a small proportion of those returned as owned (2.6 per cent in 1920) information as to encumbrance was lacking. In tabulating the census of 1890 these unknown items were distributed in the same proportions as the known items; and in Table 1, in which figures for 1890 are shown, the statistics for the other census years have been distributed in the same manner, in order to make them comparable with those for 1890. In computing the percentages in Tables 4, 5, and 7 the unknown items have also been distributed. The method employed was as follows:

The "Tenure Unknown" for each state were distributed between "Rented" and "Owned" in the proportions of the known figures for rented and owned homes. The number thus allotted as owned was then added to the number returned as owned but unknown as to encumbrance, and the sum of these two unknown items was distributed between the "Free" and "Encumbered" groups on the basis of the proportions which these two groups formed of the total number of owned homes for which returns as to encumbrance were made.

TABLE 1.—DISTRIBUTION OF HOMES ACCORDING TO PROPRIETORSHIP AND ENCUMBRANCE, FOR THE UNITED STATES: 1890–1920.

[In compiling this table, the unknown items as to proprietorship and encumbrance have been distributed as explained in the Introduction.]

| CENSUS YEAR. | HOMES. | | | | | PER CENT OF TOTAL HOMES. | | | | PER CENT OF OWNED HOMES. | |
| | Total. | Rented. | Owned. | | | Rented. | Owned. | | | | |
			Total.	Free.	Encumbered.		Total.	Free.	Encumbered.	Free.	Encumbered.
1920	24,351,676	13,236,709	11,114,967	6,862,520	4,252,447	54.4	45.6	28.2	17.5	61.7	38.3
1910	20,255,555	10,982,380	9,273,175	6,236,074	3,037,101	54.2	45.8	30.8	15.0	67.2	32.8
1900	16,187,715	8,719,060	7,468,655	5,127,935	2,340,720	53.9	46.1	31.7	14.5	68.7	31.3
1890	12,690,152	6,623,735	6,066,417	4,369,527	1,696,890	52.2	47.8	34.4	13.4	72.0	28.0

(1279)

1280

POPULATION.

TABLE 2.—NUMBER OF HOMES, DISTRIBUTED ACCORDING TO PROPRIETORSHIP

		1920						
	DIVISION AND STATE.	Total homes.	Rented.	Owned.				Tenure unknown.
				Total.	Free.	Encumbered.	Unknown.	
1	United States..............	24,351,676	12,943,596	10,866,960	6,522,119	4,059,593	285,248	541,118
	GEOGRAPHIC DIVISIONS:							
2	New England.............	1,703,812	1,010,586	668,324	335,753	322,064	10,507	24,902
3	Middle Atlantic...........	5,085,080	3,144,533	1,864,123	934,703	892,787	36,633	76,424
4	East North Central........	5,143,913	2,407,639	2,644,052	1,510,174	1,069,927	63,951	92,222
5	West North Central.......	2,957,849	1,257,816	1,626,771	952,049	631,238	43,484	73,262
6	South Atlantic............	2,991,628	1,684,936	1,221,214	896,122	281,864	43,228	85,478
7	East South Central........	1,977,381	1,101,352	823,131	617,367	181,669	24,095	52,898
8	West South Central.......	2,242,810	1,252,703	913,378	613,789	262,404	37,185	76,729
9	Mountain................	803,853	349,755	431,039	269,907	149,458	11,674	23,059
10	Pacific..................	1,445,350	734,278	674,928	392,255	268,182	14,491	36,144
	NEW ENGLAND:							
11	Maine...................	188,106	73,860	108,829	80,540	25,979	2,310	3,417
12	New Hampshire..........	108,334	53,159	52,778	36,195	15,193	1,390	2,397
13	Vermont.................	85,804	35,706	48,370	29,029	18,571	770	1,728
14	Massachusetts............	874,798	564,097	301,245	126,312	171,741	3,192	9,456
15	Rhode Island.............	137,160	92,800	41,921	19,889	21,352	680	2,439
16	Connecticut.............	311,610	190,964	115,181	43,788	69,228	2,165	5,465
	MIDDLE ATLANTIC:							
17	New York...............	2,441,125	1,670,088	738,738	342,452	381,776	14,510	32,299
18	New Jersey..............	721,841	438,911	271,914	101,598	165,844	4,472	11,016
19	Pennsylvania............	1,922,114	1,035,534	853,471	490,653	345,167	17,651	33,109
	EAST NORTH CENTRAL:							
20	Ohio....................	1,414,068	673,858	719,097	432,804	271,872	14,421	21,113
21	Indiana.................	737,707	326,192	395,402	243,851	139,796	11,755	16,113
22	Illinois.................	1,534,077	846,071	658,260	370,221	268,446	19,593	29,746
23	Michigan................	862,745	349,054	499,471	268,287	220,467	10,717	14,220
24	Wisconsin...............	595,316	212,464	371,822	195,011	169,346	7,465	11,030
	WEST NORTH CENTRAL:							
25	Minnesota...............	526,026	202,222	312,367	181,253	123,786	7,328	11,437
26	Iowa....................	586,070	239,880	332,567	205,115	119,289	8,163	13,623
27	Missouri.................	829,043	409,068	401,667	229,129	163,824	8,714	18,308
28	North Dakota............	134,881	45,050	84,904	37,268	43,375	4,261	4,927
29	South Dakota............	142,793	53,099	84,712	40,438	34,621	3,653	4,982
30	Nebraska................	303,436	125,713	169,098	99,715	63,973	5,410	8,625
31	Kansas..................	435,600	182,784	241,456	153,131	82,370	5,955	11,360
	SOUTH ATLANTIC:							
32	Delaware................	52,070	28,287	22,829	12,858	9,072	799	954
33	Maryland...............	324,742	160,219	159,202	94,095	60,857	3,710	5,261
34	District of Columbia......	96,194	65,654	28,503	12,354	15,375	774	2,037
35	Virginia.................	483,363	231,563	242,062	187,547	48,614	5,901	9,738
36	West Virginia...........	310,098	160,528	141,362	109,732	26,477	5,153	8,208
37	North Carolina..........	513,877	261,303	235,842	186,460	38,498	10,884	16,232
38	South Carolina..........	349,126	227,657	108,179	80,911	21,977	5,291	13,290
39	Georgia.................	628,525	421,047	188,185	141,809	39,546	6,740	19,293
40	Florida.................	234,133	128,678	94,990	70,166	20,848	3,976	10,465
	EAST SOUTH CENTRAL:							
41	Kentucky...............	546,306	258,643	275,993	209,239	59,846	6,908	11,670
42	Tennessee...............	519,108	264,982	241,875	186,199	50,056	5,620	12,251
43	Alabama................	508,769	319,756	172,363	124,456	41,445	6,462	16,650
44	Mississippi.............	403,198	257,971	132,900	97,473	30,322	5,105	12,327
	WEST SOUTH CENTRAL:							
45	Arkansas...............	390,960	208,491	171,253	119,279	46,727	5,247	11,216
46	Louisiana...............	389,913	248,802	126,410	94,420	24,515	7,475	14,701
47	Oklahoma [1]............	444,524	231,813	193,840	109,001	74,586	10,253	18,871
48	Texas...................	1,017,413	563,597	421,875	291,089	116,576	14,210	31,941
	MOUNTAIN:							
49	Montana................	139,912	53,362	81,840	43,776	35,559	2,505	4,710
50	Idaho...................	100,500	38,013	59,208	30,974	26,957	1,277	3,279
51	Wyoming................	48,476	22,271	24,060	14,167	8,579	1,314	2,145
52	Colorado................	230,843	109,501	116,781	71,155	43,244	2,382	4,561
53	New Mexico.............	83,706	32,907	48,152	38,593	8,208	1,351	2,647
54	Arizona.................	80,208	44,163	33,075	24,605	7,797	673	2,970
55	Utah...................	98,346	38,598	57,985	38,842	17,582	1,561	1,763
56	Nevada.................	21,862	10,940	9,938	7,795	1,532	611	984
	PACIFIC:							
57	Washington.............	342,228	151,513	183,322	106,729	72,655	3,938	7,393
58	Oregon.................	202,890	89,588	108,772	66,491	40,054	2,227	4,530
59	California...............	900,232	493,177	382,834	219,035	155,473	8,326	24,221

[1] Includes Indian Territory.

OWNERSHIP OF HOMES.   1281

AND ENCUMBRANCE, BY DIVISIONS AND STATES: 1920, 1910, AND 1900.

1910 Total homes.	Rented.	Owned. Total.	Free.	Encumbered.	Unknown.	Tenure unknown.	1900 Total homes.	Rented.	Owned. Total.	Free.	Encumbered.	Unknown.	Tenure unknown.	
20,255,555	10,697,895	9,083,711	5,984,284	2,931,695	167,732	473,949	16,187,715	8,365,739	7,259,382	4,761,211	2,196,375	301,776	562,614	1
1,464,942	870,210	574,590	332,124	236,025	6,441	20,142	1,253,970	703,491	513,478	300,908	200,295	12,275	37,001	2
4,235,675	2,672,232	1,475,393	825,620	627,696	22,077	88,050	3,369,770	2,078,480	1,194,109	672,022	481,913	40,174	97,175	3
4,214,820	1,950,268	2,187,573	1,380,040	777,892	29,641	76,979	3,526,261	1,579,215	1,860,540	1,150,262	652,063	58,215	86,506	4
2,592,069	1,053,539	1,474,343	928,712	523,329	22,302	64,187	2,168,989	874,385	1,230,351	746,179	445,004	39,168	64,253	5
2,539,270	1,451,523	1,017,823	793,024	197,122	27,677	69,924	2,101,757	1,183,682	813,010	618,853	140,397	53,750	105,065	6
1,798,832	1,008,776	746,057	574,722	154,070	17,265	41,999	1,533,303	844,691	624,783	488,388	100,466	35,929	63,829	7
1,827,105	1,010,563	762,702	554,998	184,095	23,609	53,840	1,303,013	691,329	553,466	427,502	86,344	39,620	58,218	8
614,656	242,311	346,796	272,080	65,806	8,910	25,549	384,571	151,699	210,054	171,222	27,616	11,216	22,818	9
970,186	438,473	498,434	322,964	165,660	9,810	33,279	546,081	258,761	259,571	185,865	62,277	11,429	27,749	10
177,960	65,523	109,298	82,262	25,481	1,555	3,139	163,344	55,994	103,142	75,651	24,471	3,020	4,208	11
103,156	49,549	52,052	38,344	13,017	691	1,555	97,902	43,622	51,017	36,078	13,154	1,785	3,263	12
85,178	35,112	49,489	29,332	19,807	350	577	81,462	31,487	48,094	26,892	19,813	1,389	1,881	13
734,013	484,982	240,445	121,681	116,492	2,272	8,636	613,659	385,959	207,579	109,494	94,176	3,909	20,121	14
117,976	83,134	32,849	17,790	14,503	556	1,993	94,179	65,422	26,256	14,617	10,905	734	2,501	15
246,659	151,960	90,457	42,715	46,725	1,017	4,242	203,424	121,007	77,390	38,176	37,776	1,438	5,027	16
2,046,845	1,387,900	622,125	327,186	287,294	7,645	36,820	1,634,523	1,061,267	528,152	280,673	234,363	13,116	45,104	17
558,202	355,076	191,177	82,790	104,966	3,421	11,949	415,222	263,851	137,743	62,360	70,805	4,578	13,628	18
1,630,628	929,256	662,091	415,644	235,436	11,011	39,281	1,320,025	753,368	528,214	328,989	176,745	22,480	38,443	19
1,138,165	545,519	574,085	383,346	183,683	7,056	18,561	944,433	437,618	484,142	318,553	150,254	15,335	22,673	20
654,891	290,727	352,295	280,099	116,515	5,681	11,869	571,513	245,366	313,516	200,822	104,042	8,652	12,631	21
1,264,717	698,683	545,999	340,677	195,713	9,609	25,635	1,036,158	555,438	454,139	275,137	162,469	16,533	26,581	22
657,418	247,152	398,616	241,966	152,441	4,209	11,650	548,094	201,041	332,334	193,190	129,550	9,594	14,719	23
499,629	173,787	316,578	183,952	129,540	3,086	9,204	426,063	139,752	276,409	162,560	105,748	8,101	9,902	24
416,452	154,340	251,092	160,913	86,913	3,266	11,020	342,658	120,694	209,797	127,265	75,084	7,448	12,167	25
512,515	208,344	292,951	186,763	101,962	4,226	11,220	480,878	185,270	284,230	164,519	113,414	6,297	11,378	26
749,812	358,514	374,461	219,577	149,878	5,006	16,837	654,333	312,807	323,725	194,190	119,173	10,362	17,801	27
120,910	28,123	87,641	51,364	34,437	1,840	5,146	64,690	12,425	49,696	33,754	13,853	2,089	2,569	28
131,060	40,302	86,539	58,789	25,633	2,117	4,219	83,536	23,145	57,288	37,483	17,249	2,556	3,103	29
265,549	106,099	153,155	103,165	47,780	2,210	6,295	220,947	92,479	121,465	71,617	44,465	5,383	7,003	30
395,771	157,817	228,504	148,141	76,726	3,637	9,450	321,947	127,565	184,150	117,351	61,766	5,033	10,232	31
44,951	25,951	17,794	10,501	6,646	647	1,206	39,446	24,101	13,747	7,809	5,165	773	1,598	32
274,824	149,201	117,297	77,814	37,202	2,281	8,326	242,331	136,995	91,180	58,881	27,246	5,053	14,156	33
71,339	51,607	17,375	9,918	7,178	279	2,357	56,678	41,721	13,161	8,557	4,304	300	1,796	34
419,452	198,860	211,322	171,476	35,636	4,210	9,270	364,517	179,670	171,258	134,287	26,692	10,279	4,831	35
248,480	123,068	120,583	100,076	17,784	2,723	4,829	186,291	82,473	98,987	78,324	14,935	5,728	14,552	36
440,334	227,239	203,552	162,914	35,074	5,564	9,543	370,072	189,794	165,726	131,029	24,800	9,897	16,788	37
315,204	210,904	93,757	70,912	19,419	3,426	10,543	269,864	175,780	77,346	57,341	14,048	5,957	30,522	38
553,264	373,887	164,116	130,896	27,588	5,632	15,261	455,557	294,530	130,205	101,494	17,674	11,037	7,283	39
171,422	90,806	72,027	58,517	10,595	2,915	8,589	117,001	58,318	51,400	41,141	5,533	4,726	7,283	40
494,788	235,433	251,059	198,329	47,659	5,071	8,296	437,054	205,793	218,842	172,522	35,182	11,138	12,419	41
482,553	240,515	213,125	172,779	35,238	5,108	8,913	402,536	208,473	179,836	147,219	21,098	11,519	14,227	42
454,767	285,722	154,716	114,719	36,125	3,872	14,329	374,765	234,064	122,904	95,048	20,605	7,251	17,797	43
384,724	247,106	127,157	88,895	35,048	3,214	10,461	318,948	196,361	103,201	73,599	23,581	6,021	19,386	44
333,368	173,251	151,002	116,947	30,085	3,970	9,115	265,238	132,055	120,481	95,977	16,571	7,933	12,702	45
344,144	225,433	106,953	85,230	17,322	4,401	11,758	284,875	183,943	84,108	65,265	12,260	6,583	16,824	46
351,167	186,109	154,571	99,390	49,764	5,417	10,487	163,609	71,756	84,888	68,471	7,076	9,321	6,985	47
798,426	425,770	350,176	253,431	86,924	9,821	22,480	589,291	303,575	264,009	197,789	50,437	15,783	21,707	48
86,602	32,511	48,757	38,680	8,118	1,959	5,334	55,859	22,714	29,611	24,526	3,499	1,586	3,564	49
73,669	22,035	47,045	33,577	12,155	1,313	4,589	37,491	9,936	25,056	20,727	3,274	1,055	2,499	50
32,092	14,159	16,961	13,556	3,081	324	972	20,116	8,138	10,015	8,059	1,114	842	1,963	51
194,467	90,929	96,728	68,528	25,653	2,547	6,810	127,459	64,529	56,249	39,933	13,141	3,175	6,681	52
78,883	22,704	54,537	50,632	2,996	909	1,642	46,355	13,568	29,478	26,846	658	1,974	3,309	53
47,927	23,408	22,712	18,846	3,217	649	1,807	29,875	11,742	15,871	13,701	1,048	1,122	2,202	54
77,339	26,144	48,131	37,732	9,639	760	3,064	56,196	17,601	36,990	31,567	4,316	1,107	1,605	55
23,677	10,421	11,925	10,529	947	449	1,331	11,190	3,471	6,784	5,863	566	355	935	56
254,692	104,471	140,367	94,215	43,163	2,989	9,854	113,086	48,776	58,403	45,560	10,565	2,278	5,907	57
151,858	58,279	87,688	60,500	25,270	1,918	5,891	91,214	35,954	51,074	37,951	10,897	2,226	4,186	58
583,636	275,723	270,379	168,249	97,227	4,903	17,534	341,781	174,031	150,094	102,354	40,815	6,925	17,656	59

1282

POPULATION.

TABLE 3.—NUMBER OF HOMES OF WHITE AND COLORED [1] FAMILIES, DISTRIBUTED ACCORDING

DIVISION OR STATE AND COLOR.	1920						
	Total homes.	Rented.	Owned.				Tenure unknown.
			Total.	Free.	Encumbered.	Unknown.	
SOUTHERN STATES.							
1 White	5,147,960	2,526,308	2,485,497	1,783,659	617,239	84,599	136,155
2 Colored	2,063,859	1,512,683	472,226	343,619	108,698	19,909	78,950
SOUTH ATLANTIC:							
3 White	2,032,225	990,093	992,711	727,829	231,884	32,908	49,421
4 Colored	959,403	694,843	228,503	168,293	49,980	10,230	36,057
EAST SOUTH CENTRAL:							
5 White	1,370,388	635,380	703,838	530,893	153,197	19,748	31,170
6 Colored	606,993	465,972	119,293	86,474	28,472	4,347	21,728
WEST SOUTH CENTRAL:							
7 White	1,745,347	900,835	788,948	524,937	232,158	31,853	55,564
8 Colored	497,463	351,868	124,430	88,852	30,246	5,332	21,165
SOUTH ATLANTIC.							
DELAWARE:							
9 White	45,157	23,171	21,230	11,396	9,077	757	756
10 Colored	6,913	5,116	1,599	962	595	42	198
MARYLAND:							
11 White	269,751	120,039	145,833	86,064	56,556	3,213	3,879
12 Colored	54,991	40,180	13,429	8,631	4,301	497	1,382
DISTRICT OF COLUMBIA:							
13 White	71,044	44,668	25,059	10,611	13,809	639	1,317
14 Colored	25,150	20,986	3,444	1,743	1,566	135	720
VIRGINIA:							
15 White	334,708	147,492	180,755	140,548	36,114	4,093	6,461
16 Colored	148,655	84,071	61,307	46,999	12,500	1,808	3,277
WEST VIRGINIA:							
17 White	289,284	143,950	137,802	107,230	25,541	5,031	7,532
18 Colored	20,814	16,578	3,560	2,502	936	122	676
NORTH CAROLINA:							
19 White	356,297	156,106	189,933	153,148	28,526	8,259	10,258
20 Colored	157,080	105,197	45,909	33,312	9,972	2,625	5,974
SOUTH CAROLINA:							
21 White	164,326	87,422	71,660	53,603	14,919	3,138	5,244
22 Colored	184,800	140,235	36,519	27,308	7,058	2,153	8,046
GEORGIA:							
23 White	351,952	195,797	147,982	112,414	30,594	4,974	8,173
24 Colored	276,573	225,250	40,203	29,485	8,952	1,766	11,120
FLORIDA:							
25 White	149,706	71,448	72,457	52,815	16,748	2,894	5,801
26 Colored	84,427	57,230	22,533	17,351	4,100	1,082	4,664
EAST SOUTH CENTRAL.							
KENTUCKY:							
27 White	483,583	217,141	256,621	194,258	56,067	6,296	9,821
28 Colored	62,723	41,502	19,372	14,981	3,779	612	1,849
TENNESSEE:							
29 White	407,653	185,075	213,805	165,421	43,616	4,768	8,773
30 Colored	111,455	79,907	28,070	20,778	6,440	852	3,478
ALABAMA:							
31 White	300,051	155,147	136,961	99,441	32,414	5,106	7,943
32 Colored	208,718	164,609	35,402	25,015	9,031	1,356	8,707
MISSISSIPPI:							
33 White	179,101	78,017	96,451	71,773	21,100	3,578	4,633
34 Colored	224,097	179,954	36,449	25,700	9,222	1,527	7,694
WEST SOUTH CENTRAL.							
ARKANSAS:							
35 White	276,427	125,337	144,095	101,554	38,036	4,505	6,995
36 Colored	114,533	83,154	27,158	17,725	8,691	742	4,221
LOUISIANA:							
37 White	224,131	119,614	97,504	72,430	19,217	5,857	7,013
38 Colored	165,782	129,188	28,906	21,990	5,298	1,618	7,688
OKLAHOMA: [2]							
39 White	400,401	209,236	175,024	96,444	69,888	8,692	16,141
40 Colored	44,123	22,577	18,816	12,557	4,698	1,561	2,730
TEXAS:							
41 White	844,388	446,648	372,325	254,509	105,017	12,799	25,415
42 Colored	173,025	116,949	49,550	36,580	11,559	1,411	6,528

[1] The term "colored" refers to persons of Negro descent, Indians, Chinese, Japanese, and all other nonwhites.

OWNERSHIP OF HOMES. 1283

TO PROPRIETORSHIP AND ENCUMBRANCE, FOR SOUTHERN STATES: 1920, 1910, AND 1900.

	1910							1900 [b]							
	Total homes.	Rented.	Owned.				Tenure unknown.	Total homes.	Rented.	Owned.				Tenure unknown.	
			Total.	Free.	Encumbered.	Unknown.				Total.	Free.	Encumbered.	Unknown.		
1	4,227,905	2,049,676	2,084,664	1,598,958	435,082	50,624	93,565	3,235,904	1,488,209	1,643,506	1,290,376	253,820	99,310	103,289	
2	1,935,302	1,421,186	441,918	323,786	100,205	17,927	72,198	1,651,809	1,197,661	337,790	237,168	71,749	28,873	116,358	
3	1,653,891	808,454	808,660	634,521	154,915	19,224	36,777	1,315,663	621,550	648,981	501,229	107,936	39,816	45,132	
4	885,379	643,069	209,163	158,503	42,207	8,453	33,147	762,940	546,214	160,276	115,068	31,710	13,498	56,450	
5	1,192,765	545,020	626,578	492,994	120,541	13,043	21,167	991,712	433,976	530,934	425,561	76,889	28,484	26,802	
6	604,067	463,756	119,479	81,728	33,529	4,222	20,832	528,627	401,927	91,477	61,095	23,206	7,176	35,223	
7	1,381,249	696,202	649,426	471,443	159,626	18,357	35,621	927,629	432,688	463,591	363,586	68,995	31,010	31,355	
8	445,856	314,361	113,276	83,555	24,469	5,252	18,219	360,242	249,520	86,037	61,005	16,833	8,199	24,685	
9	38,453	21,261	16,293	9,617	6,103	573	899	32,957	19,535	12,342	7,087	4,625	630	1,080	
10	6,498	4,690	1,501	884	543	74	307	6,050	4,300	1,299	672	490	137	451	
11	227,420	116,226	105,220	69,727	33,708	1,785	5,974	194,255	104,276	80,298	51,790	24,345	4,163	9,681	
12	47,404	32,975	12,077	8,087	3,494	496	2,352	45,582	31,077	10,404	6,787	2,763	854	4,101	
13	51,906	35,002	15,297	8,618	6,431	248	1,607	38,015	25,858	11,083	7,171	3,621	241	1,124	
14	19,433	16,605	2,078	1,300	747	31	750	17,450	14,895	1,965	1,270	640	55	590	
15	281,489	121,690	154,325	126,148	25,374	2,803	5,474	232,060	101,080	124,273	99,571	17,475	7,227	6,707	
16	137,963	77,170	56,997	45,328	10,262	1,407	3,796	128,689	76,007	46,301	34,265	9,055	2,981	6,381	
17	234,241	112,088	117,838	98,058	17,150	2,630	4,315	175,507	74,848	96,485	76,588	14,398	5,499	4,174	
18	14,239	10,980	2,745	2,018	634	93	514	8,278	5,911	1,984	1,384	433	167	378	
19	298,956	131,272	162,637	132,958	26,063	3,616	5,047	244,524	102,315	135,584	109,948	18,606	7,030	6,625	
20	141,378	95,967	40,915	29,956	9,011	1,948	4,496	123,041	85,847	29,638	20,702	6,129	2,807	7,556	
21	135,608	71,588	60,574	45,656	12,973	1,945	3,446	107,280	53,228	50,170	37,428	9,068	3,674	3,882	
22	179,596	139,316	33,183	25,256	6,446	1,481	7,097	160,579	121,220	26,884	19,710	4,926	2,248	12,475	
23	289,920	158,275	125,380	101,773	19,771	3,836	6,265	229,329	117,078	103,028	81,989	12,614	8,425	9,223	
24	263,344	215,612	38,736	29,123	7,817	1,796	8,996	221,383	174,369	26,639	19,125	4,989	2,525	20,375	
25	95,898	41,052	51,096	41,966	7,342	1,788	3,750	61,736	23,332	35,768	29,657	3,184	2,927	2,636	
26	75,524	49,754	20,931	16,551	3,253	1,127	4,839	51,893	32,588	15,162	11,153	2,285	1,724	4,143	
27	432,500	195,020	231,265	182,959	44,102	4,204	6,215	373,880	164,833	200,225	158,785	31,660	9,780	8,822	
28	62,288	40,413	19,794	15,370	3,557	867	2,081	60,348	39,176	17,917	13,257	3,374	1,286	3,255	
29	355,934	163,629	186,107	152,589	29,426	4,092	6,198	302,539	136,127	158,145	131,615	17,316	9,214	8,267	
30	106,619	76,886	27,018	20,190	5,812	1,016	2,715	96,478	69,950	21,030	15,148	3,679	2,203	5,498	
31	247,666	121,558	120,715	91,946	26,006	2,763	5,393	192,564	88,330	98,897	79,197	14,349	5,351	5,337	
32	207,101	164,164	34,001	22,773	10,119	1,109	8,936	178,416	142,850	23,552	15,495	6,200	1,857	12,014	
33	156,665	64,813	88,491	65,500	21,007	1,984	3,361	122,729	44,686	73,667	55,964	13,564	4,139	4,376	
34	228,059	182,293	38,666	23,395	14,041	1,230	7,100	193,385	149,951	28,978	17,195	9,953	1,830	14,456	
35	235,469	103,969	126,959	101,029	23,200	2,730	4,541	185,583	76,060	102,987	84,552	12,032	6,403	6,536	
36	97,899	69,282	24,043	15,918	6,885	1,240	4,574	76,838	54,351	16,840	10,958	4,437	1,445	5,647	
37	184,379	99,203	79,636	64,362	12,123	3,151	5,540	140,765	72,568	63,042	49,759	8,263	5,020	5,155	
38	159,765	126,230	27,317	20,868	5,199	1,250	6,218	140,684	109,009	20,533	15,102	3,941	1,490	11,142	
39	309,231	166,301	134,358	84,373	46,001	3,984	8,572	138,942	64,817	69,007	56,385	6,468	6,154	5,118	
40	41,036	19,808	20,213	15,017	3,763	1,433	1,915	23,004	6,086	15,286	11,670	527	3,089	1,632	
41	652,170	326,729	308,473	221,679	78,302	8,492	16,968	462,339	219,238	228,555	172,890	42,232	13,433	14,546	
42	146,256	99,041	41,703	31,752	8,622	1,329	5,512	119,716	80,074	33,378	23,275	7,928	2,175	6,264	

[a] In 1900 the tabulation as to color or race was made for private families only. (See p. 1279.)

[b] Includes Indian Territory for 1900.

1284

POPULATION.

TABLE 4.—PER CENT DISTRIBUTION OF HOMES ACCORDING TO PROPRIETORSHIP AND ENCUMBRANCE, BY DIVISIONS AND STATES: 1920, 1910, AND 1900.

[In computing the percentages in this table, the numbers representing the unknown items as to proprietorship and encumbrance have been distributed as explained in the Introduction. (See p. 1279.)]

DIVISION AND STATE.	1920						1910						1900					
	Per cent of all homes.				Per cent of owned homes.		Per cent of all homes.				Per cent of owned homes.		Per cent of all homes.				Per cent of owned homes.	
	Rented.	Owned.	Owned free.	Owned encumbered.	Free.	Encumbered.	Rented.	Owned.	Owned free.	Owned encumbered.	Free.	Encumbered.	Rented.	Owned.	Owned free.	Owned encumbered.	Free.	Encumbered.
United States	54.4	45.6	28.2	17.5	61.7	38.3	54.2	45.8	30.8	15.0	67.2	32.8	53.9	46.1	31.7	14.5	68.7	31.3
GEOGRAPHIC DIVISIONS:																		
New England	60.2	39.8	20.4	19.5	51.1	48.9	60.3	39.7	23.2	16.5	58.5	41.5	58.0	42.0	25.2	16.8	60.1	39.9
Middle Atlantic	62.8	37.2	19.0	18.2	51.2	48.8	64.5	35.5	20.2	15.3	56.8	43.2	63.7	36.3	21.2	15.2	58.3	41.7
East North Central	47.7	52.3	30.6	21.7	58.5	41.5	47.2	52.8	33.8	19.0	64.0	36.0	46.1	53.9	34.4	19.5	63.9	36.1
West North Central	43.6	56.4	33.9	22.5	60.1	39.9	41.8	58.2	37.3	20.8	64.2	35.8	41.8	58.2	36.6	21.6	62.9	37.1
South Atlantic	58.0	42.0	32.0	10.0	76.2	23.8	59.1	40.9	32.8	8.2	80.0	20.0	59.9	40.1	32.4	7.7	80.8	19.2
East South Central	57.3	42.7	33.0	9.7	77.2	22.8	57.7	42.3	33.4	8.9	78.9	21.1	58.0	42.0	34.9	7.2	83.0	17.0
West South Central	57.8	42.2	29.5	12.6	70.0	30.0	57.1	42.9	32.3	10.6	75.3	24.7	55.9	44.1	36.8	7.3	83.5	16.5
Mountain	44.8	55.2	35.5	19.7	64.4	35.6	41.5	58.5	47.1	11.4	80.5	19.5	42.4	57.6	49.6	7.9	86.2	13.8
Pacific	52.1	47.9	28.4	19.4	59.4	40.6	47.0	53.0	35.1	18.0	66.1	33.9	50.3	49.7	37.3	12.4	75.0	25.0
NEW ENGLAND:																		
Maine	40.4	59.6	45.0	14.5	75.6	24.4	37.7	62.3	47.6	14.7	76.4	23.6	35.5	64.5	48.8	15.7	75.6	24.4
New Hampshire	50.2	49.8	35.1	14.7	70.4	29.6	49.0	51.0	38.1	12.9	74.7	25.3	46.5	53.5	39.2	14.3	73.3	26.7
Vermont	42.5	57.5	35.1	22.4	61.0	39.0	41.6	58.4	34.9	23.5	59.8	40.2	39.9	60.1	34.7	25.4	57.7	42.3
Massachusetts	65.2	34.8	14.8	20.1	42.4	57.6	66.9	33.1	16.9	16.2	51.1	48.9	65.1	34.9	18.7	16.1	53.7	46.3
Rhode Island	68.9	31.1	15.0	16.1	48.2	51.8	71.7	28.3	15.6	12.7	55.0	45.0	71.4	28.6	16.4	12.2	57.4	42.6
Connecticut	62.4	37.6	14.6	23.0	38.7	61.3	62.8	37.2	17.8	19.5	47.7	52.3	61.1	38.9	19.5	19.4	50.2	49.8
MIDDLE ATLANTIC:																		
New York	69.3	30.7	14.5	16.2	47.3	52.7	69.1	30.9	16.4	14.4	53.2	46.8	66.9	33.1	18.0	15.0	54.5	45.5
New Jersey	61.7	38.3	14.5	23.7	38.0	62.0	65.0	35.0	15.4	19.5	44.1	55.9	65.8	34.2	16.0	18.2	46.8	53.2
Pennsylvania	54.8	45.2	26.5	18.7	58.7	41.3	58.5	41.5	26.5	15.0	63.8	36.2	58.9	41.1	26.7	14.4	65.0	35.0
EAST NORTH CENTRAL:																		
Ohio	48.4	51.6	31.7	19.9	61.4	38.6	48.8	51.2	34.6	16.6	67.6	32.4	47.6	52.4	35.6	16.8	67.9	32.1
Indiana	45.2	54.8	34.8	20.0	63.6	36.4	45.3	54.7	36.3	18.3	66.4	33.6	44.1	55.9	36.9	19.1	65.9	34.1
Illinois	56.2	43.8	25.4	18.4	58.0	42.0	56.0	44.0	28.0	16.1	63.5	36.5	55.1	44.9	28.2	16.7	62.9	37.1
Michigan	41.1	58.9	32.3	26.6	54.9	45.1	38.4	61.6	37.8	23.7	61.5	38.5	38.0	62.0	37.3	24.7	60.1	39.9
Wisconsin	36.4	63.6	34.1	29.6	53.5	46.5	35.6	64.4	37.9	26.5	58.8	41.2	33.8	66.2	40.2	26.0	60.8	39.2
WEST NORTH CENTRAL:																		
Minnesota	39.3	60.7	36.1	24.6	59.4	40.6	38.3	61.7	40.2	21.5	65.2	34.8	37.0	63.0	39.8	23.2	63.2	36.8
Iowa	41.9	58.1	36.7	21.4	63.2	36.8	41.6	58.4	38.0	20.4	65.0	35.0	39.5	60.5	35.9	24.5	59.4	40.6
Missouri	50.5	49.5	28.9	20.7	58.3	41.7	49.1	50.9	30.3	20.6	59.6	40.4	49.5	50.5	31.4	19.1	62.1	37.9
North Dakota	34.7	65.3	30.2	35.1	46.2	53.8	24.9	75.1	45.4	29.7	60.4	39.6	20.8	79.2	56.4	22.7	71.2	28.8
South Dakota	38.5	61.5	35.2	26.3	57.3	42.7	32.1	67.9	47.5	20.4	69.9	30.1	29.1	70.9	48.8	22.1	68.8	31.2
Nebraska	42.6	57.4	34.9	22.4	60.9	39.1	41.0	59.0	40.4	18.6	68.5	31.5	43.4	56.6	35.1	21.5	62.0	38.0
Kansas	43.1	56.9	37.0	19.9	65.0	35.0	40.9	59.1	39.1	20.0	66.1	33.9	41.1	58.9	38.7	20.2	65.8	34.2
SOUTH ATLANTIC:																		
Delaware	55.3	44.7	25.1	19.6	56.1	43.9	59.4	40.6	24.8	15.7	61.2	38.8	63.8	36.2	21.8	14.4	60.1	39.9
Maryland	50.1	49.9	30.3	19.5	60.9	39.1	56.1	43.9	29.7	14.2	67.7	32.3	60.3	39.7	27.1	12.5	68.5	31.5
District of Columbia	69.7	30.3	13.5	16.8	44.6	55.4	74.8	25.2	14.6	10.6	58.0	42.0	76.0	24.0	16.0	8.0	66.5	33.5
Virginia	48.9	51.1	40.6	10.5	79.4	20.6	48.5	51.2	42.3	8.9	82.7	17.3	51.8	48.2	38.7	9.5	80.2	19.8
West Virginia	53.2	46.8	37.7	9.1	80.6	19.4	50.8	49.2	41.6	7.5	84.7	15.3	45.9	54.1	45.3	8.8	83.8	16.2
North Carolina	52.6	47.4	39.3	8.1	82.9	17.1	53.0	47.0	38.6	8.3	82.2	17.8	54.0	46.0	38.6	7.3	84.1	15.9
South Carolina	67.8	32.2	25.8	6.4	78.6	21.4	69.4	30.6	24.0	6.6	78.6	21.4	70.1	29.9	24.0	5.8	80.4	19.6
Georgia	69.1	30.9	24.2	6.7	78.2	21.8	69.6	30.4	25.1	5.3	82.6	17.4	70.0	30.0	25.6	4.5	85.2	14.8
Florida	57.5	42.5	32.7	9.7	77.1	22.9	56.3	43.7	36.9	6.7	84.6	15.4	53.9	46.1	40.6	5.5	88.0	12.0
EAST SOUTH CENTRAL:																		
Kentucky	48.4	51.6	40.1	11.5	77.8	22.2	48.6	51.4	41.4	10.0	80.6	19.4	48.8	51.2	42.4	8.7	82.9	17.1
Tennessee	52.3	47.7	37.6	10.1	78.8	21.2	53.3	46.7	38.8	7.9	83.0	17.0	54.2	45.8	40.0	5.8	87.3	12.7
Alabama	65.0	35.0	26.3	8.7	75.0	25.0	65.1	34.9	26.6	8.3	76.2	23.8	66.1	33.9	27.9	6.0	82.4	17.6
Mississippi	66.0	34.0	25.9	8.1	76.3	23.7	66.0	34.0	24.5	9.5	72.1	27.9	65.8	34.2	26.1	8.1	76.3	23.7
WEST SOUTH CENTRAL:																		
Arkansas	54.9	45.1	32.4	12.7	71.9	28.1	53.6	46.4	36.9	9.5	79.5	20.5	52.8	47.2	40.2	7.0	85.2	14.8
Louisiana	66.3	33.7	26.7	6.9	79.4	20.6	68.0	32.0	26.6	5.3	83.2	16.8	69.0	31.0	26.1	4.9	84.3	15.7
Oklahoma[1]	54.5	45.5	27.0	18.5	59.4	40.6	54.6	45.4	30.4	15.0	67.0	33.0	46.0	54.0	49.2	4.8	91.0	9.0
Texas	57.2	42.8	30.6	12.2	71.4	28.6	54.9	45.1	33.7	11.4	74.8	25.2	53.7	46.3	37.0	9.3	79.9	20.1
MOUNTAIN:																		
Montana	39.5	60.5	33.4	27.1	55.2	44.8	40.7	59.3	49.1	10.2	82.7	17.3	44.0	56.0	49.1	7.0	87.6	12.4
Idaho	39.1	60.9	32.6	28.3	53.5	46.5	32.7	67.3	49.6	17.7	73.7	26.3	29.3	70.7	61.2	9.5	86.6	13.4
Wyoming	48.1	51.9	32.4	19.6	62.3	37.7	45.9	54.1	44.1	10.0	81.5	18.5	46.1	53.9	47.4	6.5	87.9	12.1
Colorado	48.4	51.6	32.1	19.5	62.2	37.8	48.7	51.3	37.3	14.0	72.7	27.3	53.7	46.3	34.9	11.4	75.3	24.7
New Mexico	40.6	59.4	49.0	10.4	82.5	17.5	29.7	70.3	66.3	4.0	94.4	5.6	32.0	68.0	66.4	1.6	97.6	2.4
Arizona	57.2	42.8	32.5	10.8	75.9	24.1	51.1	48.9	41.8	7.2	85.4	14.6	43.2	56.8	52.7	4.1	92.8	7.2
Utah	40.0	60.0	41.3	18.7	68.8	31.2	35.4	64.6	51.4	13.1	79.6	20.4	32.5	67.5	59.3	8.1	88.0	12.0
Nevada	52.4	47.6	39.8	7.8	83.6	16.4	46.7	53.3	48.9	4.3	91.9	8.1	34.2	65.8	60.2	5.5	91.6	8.4
PACIFIC:																		
Washington	45.3	54.7	32.6	22.2	59.5	40.5	42.9	57.1	39.1	17.9	68.6	31.4	46.1	53.9	43.8	10.1	81.3	18.7
Oregon	45.2	54.8	34.2	20.6	62.4	37.6	40.3	59.7	42.2	17.5	70.6	29.4	41.9	58.1	45.2	12.9	77.9	22.1
California	56.3	43.7	25.6	18.1	58.5	41.5	50.6	49.4	31.3	18.1	63.4	36.6	54.0	46.0	32.9	13.1	71.6	28.4

[1] Includes Indian Territory for 1900.

OWNERSHIP OF HOMES.

1285

TABLE 5.—PER CENT DISTRIBUTION OF HOMES OF WHITE AND COLORED [1] FAMILIES ACCORDING TO PROPRIETORSHIP AND ENCUMBRANCE, FOR SOUTHERN STATES: 1920, 1910, AND 1900.

[In computing the percentages in this table, the numbers representing the unknown items as to proprietorship and encumbrance have been distributed as explained in the Introduction. (See p. 1279.)]

DIVISION OR STATE AND COLOR.	1920						1910						1900 [2]					
	Per cent of all homes.				Per cent of owned homes.		Per cent of all homes.				Per cent of owned homes.		Per cent of all homes.				Per cent of owned homes.	
	Rented.	Owned.	Owned free.	Owned encumbered.	Free.	Encumbered.	Rented.	Owned.	Owned free.	Owned encumbered.	Free.	Encumbered.	Rented.	Owned.	Owned free.	Owned encumbered.	Free.	Encumbered.
SOUTHERN STATES.																		
White	50.4	49.6	36.8	12.8	74.3	25.7	49.8	50.2	39.5	10.7	78.6	21.4	47.9	52.1	43.5	8.6	83.6	16.4
Colored	76.2	23.8	18.1	5.7	76.0	24.0	76.3	23.7	18.1	5.6	76.5	23.5	78.3	21.7	16.8	5.0	77.2	22.8
SOUTH ATLANTIC:																		
White	49.9	50.1	38.0	12.1	75.9	24.1	50.3	49.7	39.9	9.8	80.3	19.7	49.4	50.6	41.6	9.0	82.2	17.8
Colored	75.3	24.7	19.1	5.7	77.1	22.9	75.6	24.4	19.3	5.1	79.0	21.0	77.7	22.8	17.5	4.8	78.5	21.5
EAST SOUTH CENTRAL:																		
White	47.4	52.6	40.8	11.8	77.6	22.4	46.8	53.2	42.8	10.5	80.4	19.6	45.4	54.6	46.3	8.4	84.7	15.3
Colored	79.6	20.4	15.3	5.0	75.2	24.8	79.5	20.5	14.6	5.9	71.2	28.8	81.5	18.5	13.5	5.0	73.1	26.9
WEST SOUTH CENTRAL:																		
White	53.3	46.7	32.3	14.3	69.3	30.7	51.9	48.1	36.1	12.1	74.9	25.1	48.5	51.5	43.3	8.1	84.2	15.8
Colored	73.9	26.1	19.5	6.6	74.6	25.4	73.5	26.5	20.5	6.0	77.5	22.5	74.6	25.4	20.2	5.3	79.2	20.8
SOUTH ATLANTIC.																		
DELAWARE:																		
White	52.2	47.8	26.6	21.2	55.7	44.3	56.7	43.3	26.4	16.8	61.1	38.9	61.4	38.6	23.4	15.3	60.5	39.5
Colored	76.2	23.8	14.7	9.1	61.8	38.2	75.9	24.1	14.9	9.2	62.0	38.0	77.0	23.0	13.3	9.7	57.8	42.2
MARYLAND:																		
White	45.1	54.9	33.1	21.8	60.3	39.7	52.6	47.4	32.0	15.4	67.5	32.5	56.8	43.2	29.5	13.8	68.1	31.9
Colored	75.0	25.0	16.7	8.3	66.7	33.3	73.5	26.5	18.6	8.0	70.0	30.0	75.3	24.7	17.6	7.1	71.1	28.9
DISTRICT OF COLUMBIA:																		
White	64.1	35.9	15.6	20.3	43.5	56.5	69.6	30.4	17.4	13.0	57.3	42.7	70.1	29.9	19.9	10.0	66.4	33.6
Colored	85.9	14.1	7.4	6.7	52.7	47.3	88.9	11.1	7.1	4.1	63.5	36.5	88.3	11.7	7.7	3.9	66.5	33.5
VIRGINIA:																		
White	44.9	55.1	43.8	11.3	79.6	20.4	44.4	55.6	46.2	9.4	83.1	16.9	45.3	54.7	46.4	8.2	84.9	15.1
Colored	57.8	42.2	33.3	8.9	79.0	21.0	57.9	42.1	34.3	7.8	81.4	18.6	62.7	37.3	29.4	7.8	79.0	21.0
WEST VIRGINIA:																		
White	51.1	48.9	39.5	9.4	80.8	19.2	49.1	50.9	43.3	7.7	84.9	15.1	44.1	55.9	47.0	8.9	84.0	16.0
Colored	82.3	17.7	12.9	4.8	72.8	27.2	80.1	19.9	15.1	4.8	75.9	24.1	75.1	24.9	18.9	6.0	75.8	24.2
NORTH CAROLINA:																		
White	45.1	54.9	46.3	8.6	84.3	15.7	44.9	55.1	46.0	9.1	83.6	16.4	43.5	56.5	48.3	8.2	85.5	14.5
Colored	69.6	30.4	23.4	7.0	77.0	23.0	70.2	29.8	23.0	6.9	77.0	23.0	74.6	25.4	19.6	5.7	77.4	22.6
SOUTH CAROLINA:																		
White	55.0	45.0	35.2	9.8	78.2	21.8	54.5	45.5	35.5	10.0	77.9	22.1	52.1	47.9	38.6	9.3	80.6	19.4
Colored	79.3	20.7	16.4	4.2	79.5	20.5	80.9	19.1	15.3	3.9	79.7	20.3	82.2	17.8	14.2	3.5	80.2	19.8
GEORGIA:																		
White	57.0	43.0	33.8	9.2	78.6	21.4	56.0	44.0	36.9	7.2	83.7	16.3	53.7	46.3	40.1	6.2	86.7	13.3
Colored	84.9	15.1	11.6	3.5	76.7	23.3	84.7	15.3	12.1	3.2	79.0	21.0	86.8	13.2	10.5	2.7	79.7	20.3
FLORIDA:																		
White	49.6	50.4	38.2	12.1	75.9	24.1	45.1	54.9	46.7	8.3	85.0	15.0	40.1	59.9	54.0	5.9	90.2	9.8
Colored	71.7	28.3	22.9	5.4	80.9	19.1	70.7	29.3	24.5	4.8	83.6	16.4	68.7	31.3	26.0	5.3	83.0	17.0
EAST SOUTH CENTRAL.																		
KENTUCKY:																		
White	45.8	54.2	42.0	12.1	77.6	22.4	46.0	54.0	43.5	10.5	80.5	19.5	45.5	54.5	45.4	9.1	83.3	16.7
Colored	68.2	31.8	25.4	6.4	79.9	20.1	67.3	32.7	26.6	6.1	81.3	18.7	68.8	31.2	24.9	6.3	79.7	20.3
TENNESSEE:																		
White	46.4	53.6	42.4	11.2	79.1	20.9	47.0	53.0	44.4	8.6	83.8	16.2	46.7	53.3	47.1	6.2	88.3	11.7
Colored	74.0	26.0	19.8	6.2	76.3	23.7	74.0	26.0	20.2	5.8	77.7	22.3	77.0	23.0	18.5	4.5	80.5	19.5
ALABAMA:																		
White	53.1	46.9	35.4	11.5	75.4	24.6	50.4	49.6	38.7	10.9	78.0	22.0	47.6	52.4	44.4	8.0	84.7	15.3
Colored	82.3	17.7	13.0	4.7	73.5	26.5	82.8	17.2	12.0	5.2	69.6	30.4	85.9	14.1	10.2	3.9	72.1	27.9
MISSISSIPPI:																		
White	44.7	55.3	42.7	12.6	77.3	22.7	42.5	57.5	43.7	13.8	75.9	24.1	38.2	61.8	49.9	11.9	80.7	19.3
Colored	83.2	16.8	12.4	4.4	73.6	26.4	82.4	17.6	11.1	6.5	63.1	36.9	83.7	16.3	10.5	5.7	64.7	35.3
WEST SOUTH CENTRAL.																		
ARKANSAS:																		
White	46.5	53.5	38.9	14.6	72.8	27.2	45.2	54.8	44.5	10.2	81.3	18.7	43.0	57.0	49.9	7.2	87.4	12.6
Colored	75.4	24.6	16.5	8.1	67.1	32.9	74.1	25.9	18.2	7.7	70.2	29.8	76.5	23.5	16.8	6.7	71.7	28.3
LOUISIANA:																		
White	55.1	44.9	35.5	9.4	79.0	21.0	55.8	44.2	37.2	7.0	84.2	15.8	53.9	46.1	39.5	6.5	85.8	14.2
Colored	81.7	18.3	14.7	3.5	80.6	19.4	82.3	17.7	14.2	3.5	80.2	19.8	84.2	15.8	12.6	3.2	79.8	20.2
OKLAHOMA: [3]																		
White	54.5	45.5	26.4	19.1	58.0	42.0	55.3	44.7	29.1	15.6	65.1	34.9	48.5	51.5	46.2	5.3	89.7	10.3
Colored	54.5	45.5	33.1	12.4	72.8	27.2	49.7	50.3	40.3	10.0	80.1	19.9	29.0	71.0	67.9	3.1	95.0	4.4
TEXAS:																		
White	54.5	45.5	32.2	13.3	70.8	29.2	51.5	48.5	36.0	12.5	74.2	25.8	49.1	50.9	41.0	9.9	80.6	19.4
Colored	70.2	29.8	22.6	7.1	76.0	24.0	70.4	29.6	23.3	6.3	78.7	21.3	70.7	29.3	22.0	7.3	75.0	25.0

[1] The term "colored" refers to persons of Negro descent, Indians, Chinese, Japanese, and all other nonwhites.
[2] In 1900 the tabulation as to color or race was made for private families only. (See p. 1279.)
[3] Includes Indian Territory for 1900.

POPULATION.

TABLE 6.—NUMBER OF HOMES, DISTRIBUTED ACCORDING TO PROPRIETORSHIP AND ENCUM-

	CITY.	1920		Owned.				
		Total homes.	Rented.	Total.	Free.	Encumbered.	Unknown.	Tenure unknown.
1	Akron, Ohio	44,195	24,081	19,504	6,703	12,376	425	610
2	Albany, N. Y.	28,097	19,673	7,911	4,359	3,324	228	513
3	Atlanta, Ga.	49,523	36,787	12,076	6,159	5,676	241	660
4	Baltimore, Md.	166,857	88,595	76,298	40,730	34,900	668	1,964
5	Birmingham, Ala.	43,040	29,700	11,632	6,481	4,821	330	1,708
6	Boston, Mass.	164,785	132,658	30,132	9,998	19,609	525	1,995
7	Bridgeport, Conn.	31,994	23,311	7,612	1,639	5,792	181	1,071
8	Buffalo, N. Y.	116,201	70,572	44,297	17,168	26,744	385	1,332
9	Cambridge, Mass.	25,293	20,790	4,454	1,774	2,668	12	49
10	Camden, N. J.	26,645	15,591	10,628	3,492	7,038	98	426
11	Chicago, Ill.	623,912	447,407	165,866	58,382	102,719	4,765	10,639
12	Cincinnati, Ohio.	106,239	75,092	30,266	17,040	12,935	291	881
13	Cleveland, Ohio.	182,692	117,374	63,502	25,777	37,075	650	1,816
14	Columbus, Ohio.	58,913	36,895	21,258	9,936	11,177	145	760
15	Dallas, Tex.	36,754	22,696	13,280	7,058	6,026	196	778
16	Dayton, Ohio.	38,138	21,997	15,889	6,526	9,196	167	252
17	Denver, Colo.	61,916	37,768	23,436	13,325	9,930	181	712
18	Des Moines, Iowa.	31,644	15,123	15,810	7,674	7,823	313	711
19	Detroit, Mich.	218,973	133,253	82,679	31,506	49,509	1,664	3,041
20	Fall River, Mass.	26,399	21,099	5,165	1,927	3,202	36	135
21	Fort Worth, Tex.	25,052	14,566	8,974	4,644	3,923	407	1,512
22	Grand Rapids, Mich.	33,703	16,522	16,661	7,655	8,239	767	520
23	Hartford, Conn.	30,813	24,277	6,372	1,155	5,137	80	164
24	Houston, Tex.	33,932	22,136	11,518	7,460	3,962	96	278
25	Indianapolis, Ind.	81,256	51,874	27,356	11,479	15,220	657	2,026
26	Jersey City, N. J.	67,288	53,045	13,040	4,585	8,066	389	1,203
27	Kansas City, Kans.	25,009	12,001	11,706	6,300	5,281	125	402
28	Kansas City, Mo.	82,056	52,407	27,879	10,009	17,317	493	1,770
29	Los Angeles, Calif.	159,476	102,077	54,278	28,360	25,361	557	3,121
30	Louisville, Ky.	60,490	41,797	17,714	11,356	5,899	459	979
31	Lowell, Mass.	25,034	18,468	6,513	3,032	3,462	19	53
32	Memphis, Tenn.	42,369	29,281	11,925	6,833	4,389	703	1,163
33	Milwaukee, Wis.	106,101	67,853	37,382	14,994	22,031	357	866
34	Minneapolis, Minn.	91,843	53,527	37,090	16,606	19,924	560	1,226
35	Nashville, Tenn.	30,220	20,225	9,470	6,757	2,618	95	525
36	New Bedford, Mass.	26,858	19,105	7,651	2,936	4,678	87	102
37	New Haven, Conn.	36,257	25,859	9,563	2,550	6,814	199	835
38	New Orleans, La.	85,188	63,373	19,003	12,446	5,352	1,205	2,812
39	New York, N. Y.	1,278,341	1,105,900	160,707	33,358	123,865	3,484	11,734
40	Bronx borough.	166,260	151,789	13,591	2,839	10,391	361	880
41	Brooklyn borough.	453,587	362,292	86,818	16,191	69,104	1,523	4,477
42	Manhattan borough.	525,154	510,183	10,768	3,813	6,075	880	4,203
43	Queens borough.	109,559	68,322	39,589	6,980	32,094	515	1,648
44	Richmond borough.	23,781	13,314	9,941	3,535	6,201	205	526
45	Newark, N. J.	93,274	73,517	18,600	4,931	13,286	383	1,157
46	Norfolk, Va.	26,732	20,451	6,171	3,338	2,740	93	110
47	Oakland, Calif.	55,793	31,776	22,966	12,087	10,538	341	1,051
48	Omaha, Nebr.[1]	44,499	22,453	21,028	9,077	10,874	477	1,018
49	Paterson, N. J.	32,186	23,075	8,729	3,333	5,280	116	382
50	Philadelphia, Pa.	402,946	239,698	156,354	45,802	107,974	2,578	6,894
51	Pittsburgh, Pa.[1]	130,274	91,934	36,363	19,151	16,500	712	1,977
52	Portland, Oreg.	67,045	36,911	29,752	15,998	13,552	202	382
53	Providence, R. I.	54,726	41,119	12,641	5,203	7,315	123	966
54	Reading, Pa.	25,202	13,291	11,603	5,379	5,963	261	308
55	Richmond, Va.	39,191	28,492	9,958	6,444	3,345	169	741
56	Rochester, N. Y.	68,247	38,532	28,535	8,678	19,501	356	1,180
57	St. Louis, Mo.	190,640	143,106	44,700	24,202	19,666	832	2,834
58	St. Paul, Minn.	54,409	28,843	24,623	13,723	10,606	294	943
59	Salt Lake City, Utah.	28,216	15,445	12,308	6,138	5,808	362	463
60	San Antonio, Tex.	36,405	22,076	13,388	9,070	3,985	333	941
61	San Francisco, Calif.	123,349	87,754	33,159	19,252	13,100	807	2,436
62	Scranton, Pa.	29,768	18,871	10,371	7,021	3,286	64	526
63	Seattle, Wash.	80,048	42,219	36,420	17,543	18,010	867	1,409
64	Spokane, Wash.	27,178	14,980	12,083	6,862	5,154	67	115
65	Springfield, Mass.	30,361	21,713	8,411	1,907	6,442	62	237
66	Syracuse, N. Y.	41,558	25,446	15,563	5,233	10,053	277	549
67	Toledo, Ohio.	57,951	29,009	28,295	13,844	14,182	269	647
68	Trenton, N. J.	25,319	15,566	9,583	2,550	6,960	73	170
69	Washington, D. C.	96,194	65,054	28,503	12,354	15,375	774	2,037
70	Wilmington, Del.	24,488	14,839	9,192	3,380	5,683	149	457
71	Worcester, Mass.	39,230	28,061	10,749	1,966	8,674	109	420
72	Yonkers, N. Y.	22,126	16,788	5,161	1,244	3,890	27	177
73	Youngstown, Ohio.	28,699	14,821	13,561	6,096	7,319	146	317

[1] Figures for 1900 relate to private families only. (See p. 1279.)

OWNERSHIP OF HOMES.

1287

BRANCE, FOR CITIES HAVING, IN 1920, 100,000 INHABITANTS OR MORE: 1920, 1910, AND 1900.

Total homes.	Rented.	Owned. Total.	Owned. Free.	Owned. Encumbered.	Owned. Unknown.	Tenure unknown.	Total homes.	Rented.	Owned. Total.	Owned. Free.	Owned. Encumbered.	Owned. Unknown.	Tenure unknown.	
15,851	7,687	7,824	4,158	3,577	89	340	9,605	4,288	4,977	2,912	2,001	64	340	1
24,009	17,189	6,338	4,347	1,885	106	542	21,243	15,141	5,407	3,598	1,626	183	695	2
35,813	26,213	8,580	5,553	2,947	80	1,020	20,185	15,841	3,625	2,582	977	66	719	3
118,851	75,381	38,400	26,795	11,006	599	5,070	104,146	69,761	26,989	19,286	6,960	743	7,396	4
31,050	21,115	8,910	5,475	3,303	132	1,025	8,091	6,691	1,067	794	234	39	333	5
139,700	114,312	23,496	10,540	12,731	225	1,892	114,705	89,083	20,696	9,944	10,395	357	4,926	6
21,089	10,504	4,671	1,531	3,055	85	514	15,275	11,491	3,443	1,271	2,113	59	341	7
91,328	58,745	30,592	14,277	16,033	282	1,991	72,436	47,298	23,168	10,965	11,844	359	1,970	8
22,765	18,378	4,282	2,187	2,064	31	105	19,163	14,690	3,950	2,055	1,844	51	523	9
21,482	14,750	6,087	2,583	3,356	148	645	17,176	12,303	4,245	1,912	2,164	169	628	10
473,141	342,472	121,447	55,025	64,981	1,441	9,222	354,036	258,582	86,435	39,246	43,735	3,454	9,019	11
87,541	66,153	19,965	12,983	6,801	181	1,423	73,519	56,384	14,891	9,725	4,915	251	2,244	12
124,822	80,005	43,473	21,701	21,526	246	1,344	80,014	48,844	29,139	16,240	12,246	653	2,031	13
42,645	26,787	14,862	7,468	7,184	210	996	27,013	17,822	8,093	4,445	3,204	444	1,098	14
20,516	12,641	7,123	4,733	2,307	83	752	8,705	5,685	2,828	2,233	539	56	192	15
28,370	17,244	10,596	5,425	5,071	100	530	19,384	11,943	7,335	3,738	3,414	183	106	16
51,339	31,342	17,774	10,732	6,779	263	2,223	29,979	21,215	8,269	5,000	3,114	155	495	17
20,599	10,894	9,123	5,138	3,762	223	582	13,912	8,228	5,141	2,912	2,164	65	543	18
100,356	57,831	40,471	20,752	19,501	218	2,054	59,836	35,178	22,540	12,378	9,172	990	2,118	19
24,378	19,926	4,317	1,881	2,411	25	135	20,874	16,711	3,659	1,473	2,098	88	504	20
16,295	10,202	5,412	3,240	1,967	205	681	5,659	3,290	2,014	1,424	500	90	355	21
26,925	13,690	12,599	6,184	6,230	185	636	20,360	11,534	8,152	3,742	4,184	226	674	22
21,925	16,879	4,632	1,380	3,200	52	414	16,730	12,604	3,513	1,109	2,296	108	613	23
17,040	11,235	5,132	3,783	1,227	122	673	9,224	5,800	2,691	1,907	435	349	733	24
58,045	38,702	19,036	9,829	8,985	222	907	38,978	25,004	12,729	6,741	5,832	156	1,245	25
56,790	44,394	11,209	4,899	6,104	206	1,187	44,367	34,060	8,536	4,569	3,729	238	1,771	26
19,677	10,381	8,872	4,580	4,131	161	424	11,660	7,450	3,794	2,451	1,227	116	416	27
59,296	36,537	20,711	8,595	11,870	246	2,048	35,341	26,466	8,443	4,501	3,774	168	432	28
78,678	42,202	34,159	17,249	16,671	239	2,317	24,180	12,745	10,049	5,969	3,743	347	1,386	29
52,155	37,621	13,603	10,232	3,251	120	931	44,098	31,640	11,363	8,361	2,692	310	1,095	30
21,932	16,761	4,848	2,689	2,182	27	323	18,763	13,910	4,130	2,330	1,730	70	723	31
31,154	22,363	7,541	4,906	2,441	194	1,250	20,956	15,851	3,665	2,678	607	382	1,440	32
80,566	50,352	28,824	12,875	15,720	229	1,390	58,889	37,466	20,955	9,541	11,278	136	468	33
63,241	36,195	24,539	13,571	10,515	453	2,507	41,704	28,522	11,473	6,287	4,903	283	1,709	34
26,077	17,868	7,879	5,797	1,972	110	330	18,060	12,564	4,419	3,320	628	471	1,077	35
20,820	15,190	5,144	2,543	2,547	54	486	13,786	9,596	3,720	2,144	1,480	96	470	36
29,271	21,394	7,326	2,792	4,467	67	551	23,275	16,722	6,062	2,413	3,598	51	491	37
73,377	54,113	16,273	12,615	3,058	600	2,991	60,796	45,129	12,886	10,034	1,698	554	2,781	38
1,020,827	884,616	117,740	34,951	81,007	1,782	18,471	722,670	617,474	85,169	35,050	48,002	2,117	20,027	39
93,897	80,114	12,071	2,654	9,267	150	1,712	41,735	32,233	7,846	2,643	4,882	321	1,656	40
353,666	284,739	63,842	17,335	45,954	553	5,085	252,519	205,154	44,960	18,611	25,763	586	2,405	41
493,545	468,927	14,103	5,358	7,909	838	10,515	383,726	352,116	16,316	6,305	9,056	955	15,294	42
62,001	40,020	21,176	6,410	14,601	165	805	31,340	19,681	11,241	4,828	6,197	216	418	43
17,718	10,816	6,548	3,196	3,276	76	354	13,350	8,290	4,806	2,663	2,104	39	254	44
77,039	60,473	15,119	4,979	9,999	141	1,447	53,965	41,270	11,041	4,415	6,517	109	1,654	45
15,498	12,024	3,056	2,232	762	62	418	9,742	7,922	1,624	1,284	326	14	196	46
36,723	19,263	16,870	9,683	7,084	103	590	14,906	8,362	6,035	3,846	2,124	65	509	47
31,604	17,778	12,590	7,231	5,142	217	1,236	24,583	16,384	6,971	4,089	2,755	127	1,228	48
27,978	20,714	6,538	2,695	3,770	73	726	23,153	17,285	5,230	2,016	3,088	126	638	49
327,263	229,354	83,262	35,950	46,312	1,000	14,647	263,093	196,124	55,528	29,033	24,013	2,482	11,441	50
110,457	77,288	29,983	16,052	13,445	486	3,186	89,090	63,347	23,072	13,062	9,502	508	2,671	51
42,029	21,495	18,509	11,089	7,131	289	2,025	15,513	10,004	4,586	3,041	1,334	211	923	52
49,129	38,276	10,071	4,795	5,107	169	782	38,516	29,696	7,895	4,087	3,708	100	925	53
21,809	12,865	8,418	4,408	3,974	36	526	16,769	10,191	6,018	3,189	2,825	54	580	54
26,914	19,801	6,255	4,609	1,318	328	858	17,549	12,408	3,565	2,259	748	558	1,576	55
46,787	26,525	19,321	7,876	11,306	139	941	33,964	20,481	12,469	6,001	6,289	179	1,014	56
155,555	113,515	37,761	22,178	15,197	386	4,279	121,123	90,983	26,804	16,097	9,699	1,008	3,336	57
41,548	23,826	16,665	10,910	5,621	134	1,057	30,221	20,266	8,652	5,556	2,851	245	1,303	58
20,283	10,500	8,623	4,806	3,694	123	1,160	11,554	6,700	4,472	3,189	1,202	81	382	59
21,096	12,080	8,315	6,031	1,990	294	701	10,999	6,411	3,937	3,252	470	215	651	60
86,414	55,946	27,500	16,329	10,996	175	2,968	67,592	49,656	15,774	10,186	5,139	449	2,162	61
26,312	16,116	9,711	5,524	3,935	252	485	20,299	12,209	7,436	4,600	2,583	253	654	62
51,042	27,245	22,167	13,464	8,508	195	1,630	13,139	8,711	3,779	2,780	903	96	1,189	63
22,076	10,610	11,165	5,869	5,112	184	901	7,608	4,642	2,747	1,789	811	147	219	64
19,968	14,009	5,821	2,064	3,711	46	138	13,868	9,009	4,494	1,842	2,607	45	365	65
31,551	18,547	12,202	4,873	7,225	104	802	24,928	15,439	9,238	4,082	5,115	41	251	66
39,677	21,609	17,170	9,622	7,438	110	898	28,319	15,851	11,962	6,793	4,990	179	506	67
19,678	13,274	6,019	2,083	3,839	97	385	14,884	10,593	3,768	1,411	2,316	41	523	68
71,339	51,607	17,875	9,918	7,178	279	2,357	55,465	40,753	12,998	8,441	4,261	296	1,714	69
18,637	12,567	5,500	2,348	2,948	204	570	15,410	10,630	3,950	1,661	2,209	80	830	70
30,743	23,057	7,431	2,196	5,162	73	255	24,044	17,875	5,913	2,055	3,807	51	756	71
16,219	12,239	3,764	1,132	2,583	49	216	9,480	6,692	2,042	729	1,193	120	746	72
16,228	9,272	6,372	3,665	2,430	277	584	8,949	4,750	3,910	2,524	1,280	104	289	73

2 Includes South Omaha for 1910 and 1900.   1 Includes Allegheny for 1900.

1288   POPULATION.

TABLE 7.—PER CENT DISTRIBUTION OF HOMES ACCORDING TO PROPRIETORSHIP AND ENCUMBRANCE, FOR CITIES HAVING, IN 1920, 100,000 INHABITANTS OR MORE: 1920, 1910, AND 1900.

[In computing the percentages in this table, the numbers representing the unknown items as to proprietorship and encumbrance have been distributed as explained in the Introduction. (See p. 1279.)]

CITY.	1920 Per cent of all homes. Rented.	Owned.	Owned free.	Owned encumbered.	1920 Per cent of owned homes. Free.	Encumbered.	1910 Per cent of all homes. Rented.	Owned.	Owned free.	Owned encumbered.	1910 Per cent of owned homes. Free.	Encumbered.	1900¹ Per cent of all homes. Rented.	Owned.	Owned free.	Owned encumbered.	1900¹ Per cent of owned homes. Free.	Encumbered.
Akron, Ohio	55.3	44.7	15.7	29.0	35.1	64.9	49.6	50.4	27.1	23.3	53.8	46.2	46.3	53.7	31.8	21.9	59.3	40.7
Albany, N.Y	71.3	28.7	16.3	12.4	56.7	43.3	73.1	26.9	18.8	8.1	69.8	30.2	73.7	26.3	18.1	8.2	68.9	31.1
Atlanta, Ga	75.3	24.7	12.9	11.9	52.0	48.0	75.3	24.7	16.1	8.6	65.3	34.7	81.4	18.6	13.5	5.1	72.5	27.5
Baltimore, Md	53.7	46.3	24.9	21.4	53.9	46.1	66.3	33.7	23.9	9.8	70.9	29.1	72.1	27.9	20.5	7.4	73.5	26.5
Birmingham, Ala	71.9	28.1	16.1	12.0	57.3	42.7	70.3	29.7	18.5	11.2	62.4	37.6	86.2	13.8	10.6	8.1	77.3	22.7
Boston, Mass	81.5	18.5	6.3	12.3	33.8	66.2	82.9	17.1	7.7	9.3	45.3	54.7	81.1	18.9	9.2	9.6	48.9	51.1
Bridgeport, Conn	75.4	24.6	5.4	19.2	22.1	77.9	77.9	22.1	7.4	14.7	33.4	66.6	76.9	23.1	8.7	14.4	37.6	62.4
Buffalo, N.Y	61.4	38.6	15.1	23.5	39.1	60.9	65.8	34.2	16.1	18.1	47.1	52.9	67.1	32.9	15.8	17.1	48.1	51.9
Cambridge, Mass	82.4	17.6	7.0	10.6	39.9	60.1	81.1	18.9	9.7	9.2	51.4	48.6	78.8	21.2	11.2	10.0	52.7	47.3
Camden, N.J	59.5	40.5	13.4	27.1	33.2	66.8	70.8	29.2	12.7	16.5	43.5	56.5	74.3	25.7	12.0	13.6	46.9	53.1
Chicago, Ill	73.0	27.0	9.8	17.2	36.2	63.8	73.8	26.2	12.0	14.2	45.9	54.1	74.9	25.1	11.8	13.2	47.3	52.7
Cincinnati, Ohio	71.3	28.7	16.3	12.4	56.8	43.2	76.8	23.2	15.2	8.0	65.6	34.4	79.1	20.9	13.9	7.0	66.4	33.6
Cleveland, Ohio	64.9	35.1	14.4	20.7	41.0	59.0	64.8	35.2	17.7	17.5	50.2	49.8	62.6	37.4	21.3	16.1	57.0	43.0
Columbus, Ohio	63.4	36.6	17.2	19.4	47.1	52.9	64.3	35.7	18.2	17.5	51.0	49.0	68.8	31.2	18.1	13.1	58.1	41.9
Dallas, Tex	63.1	36.9	19.9	17.0	53.9	46.1	64.0	36.0	24.2	11.8	67.2	32.8	66.8	33.2	26.8	6.5	80.6	19.4
Dayton, Ohio	58.1	41.9	17.4	24.5	41.5	58.5	61.9	38.1	19.7	18.4	51.7	48.3	62.0	38.0	19.9	18.2	52.3	47.7
Denver, Colo	61.7	38.3	21.9	16.4	57.3	42.7	63.8	36.2	22.2	14.0	61.3	38.7	72.0	28.0	17.3	10.8	61.6	38.4
Des Moines, Iowa	48.9	51.1	25.3	25.8	49.5	50.5	54.4	45.6	26.3	19.3	57.7	42.3	61.5	38.5	22.1	16.4	57.4	42.6
Detroit, Mich	61.7	38.3	14.9	23.4	38.9	61.1	58.8	41.2	21.2	19.9	51.6	48.4	60.9	39.1	22.4	16.6	57.4	42.6
Fall River, Mass	80.3	19.7	7.4	12.3	37.6	62.4	82.2	17.8	7.8	10.0	43.8	56.2	82.0	18.0	7.4	10.6	41.3	58.7
Fort Worth, Tex	61.9	38.1	20.7	17.5	54.2	45.8	65.3	34.7	21.6	13.1	62.2	37.8	62.0	38.0	28.1	9.9	74.0	26.0
Grand Rapids, Mich	49.8	50.2	24.2	26.0	48.2	51.8	52.1	47.9	23.9	24.1	49.8	50.2	58.6	41.4	19.5	21.9	47.2	52.8
Hartford, Conn	79.2	20.8	3.8	17.0	18.4	81.6	78.5	21.5	6.5	15.0	30.1	69.9	78.2	21.8	7.1	14.7	32.6	67.4
Houston, Tex	65.8	34.2	22.4	11.9	65.3	34.7	68.6	31.4	23.7	7.7	75.5	24.5	68.3	31.7	25.8	5.9	81.4	18.6
Indianapolis, Ind	65.5	34.5	14.8	19.7	43.0	57.0	67.0	33.0	17.2	15.7	52.2	47.8	66.3	33.7	18.1	15.6	53.6	46.4
Jersey City, N.J	80.3	19.7	7.2	12.6	36.2	63.8	79.8	20.2	9.0	11.2	44.5	55.5	80.0	20.0	11.0	9.0	55.1	44.9
Kansas City, Kans	52.4	47.6	25.9	21.7	54.4	45.6	53.9	46.1	24.2	21.9	52.6	47.4	66.3	33.7	22.5	11.3	66.6	33.4
Kansas City, Mo	65.3	34.7	12.8	22.0	36.8	63.2	63.8	36.2	15.2	21.0	42.0	58.0	75.8	24.2	13.2	11.0	54.4	45.6
Los Angeles, Calif	65.3	34.7	18.3	16.4	52.8	47.2	55.3	44.7	22.7	22.0	50.9	49.1	61.4	38.6	21.7	17.0	61.4	38.6
Louisville, Ky	70.2	29.8	19.6	10.2	65.8	34.2	73.4	26.6	20.2	6.4	75.9	24.1	73.6	26.4	20.0	6.4	75.6	24.4
Lowell, Mass	73.9	26.1	12.2	13.9	46.7	53.3	77.6	22.4	12.5	9.9	55.8	44.2	77.1	22.9	13.1	9.8	57.4	42.6
Memphis, Tenn	71.1	28.9	17.6	11.3	60.9	39.1	74.8	25.2	16.3	8.9	64.6	35.4	81.2	18.8	15.3	3.5	81.5	18.5
Milwaukee, Wis	64.5	35.5	14.4	21.1	40.5	59.5	63.6	36.4	16.4	20.0	45.0	55.0	64.1	35.9	16.4	19.4	45.8	54.2
Minneapolis, Minn	59.1	40.9	18.6	22.3	45.5	54.5	59.6	40.4	22.8	17.6	56.3	43.7	71.3	28.7	16.1	12.6	56.2	43.8
Nashville, Tenn	68.1	31.9	23.0	8.9	72.1	27.9	69.4	30.6	22.8	7.8	74.6	25.4	74.0	26.0	21.9	4.1	84.1	15.9
New Bedford, Mass	71.4	28.6	11.0	17.6	38.6	61.4	74.7	25.3	12.6	12.7	50.0	50.0	72.1	27.9	16.5	11.4	59.2	40.8
New Haven, Conn	73.0	27.0	7.4	19.6	27.2	72.8	74.5	25.5	9.8	15.7	38.5	61.5	73.4	26.6	10.7	15.9	40.1	59.9
New Orleans, La	76.9	23.1	16.1	6.9	69.9	30.1	76.9	23.1	18.6	4.5	80.5	19.5	77.8	22.2	19.2	3.1	86.2	13.8
New York, N.Y.	87.3	12.7	2.7	10.0	21.3	78.7	88.3	11.7	3.5	8.2	30.2	69.8	87.9	12.1	5.1	7.0	42.2	57.8
Bronx borough	91.8	8.2	1.8	6.5	21.5	78.5	86.9	13.1	2.9	10.2	22.3	77.7	80.4	19.6	6.9	12.7	35.1	64.9
Brooklyn borough	80.7	19.3	3.7	15.7	19.0	81.0	81.7	18.3	5.0	13.3	27.4	72.6	82.0	18.0	7.5	10.4	41.9	58.1
Manhattan borough	97.9	2.1	0.8	1.3	38.6	61.4	97.1	2.9	1.2	1.7	40.4	59.6	95.6	4.4	1.8	2.6	41.0	59.0
Queens borough	63.3	36.7	6.6	30.1	17.9	82.1	65.4	34.6	10.6	24.0	30.5	69.5	63.8	36.2	15.9	20.4	43.8	56.2
Richmond borough	57.3	42.7	15.5	27.2	36.3	63.7	62.3	37.7	18.6	19.1	49.4	50.6	63.3	36.7	20.5	16.2	55.9	44.1
Newark, N.J	79.8	20.2	5.5	14.7	27.1	72.9	80.0	20.0	6.6	13.4	33.2	66.8	78.9	21.1	8.5	12.6	40.4	59.6
Norfolk, Va	76.8	23.2	12.7	10.4	54.9	45.1	79.7	20.3	15.1	5.2	74.6	25.4	83.0	17.0	13.6	3.4	79.7	20.3
Oakland, Calif	58.0	42.0	22.4	19.5	53.4	46.6	53.3	46.7	27.0	19.7	57.7	42.3	58.1	41.9	27.0	14.9	64.4	35.6
Omaha, Nebr.²	51.6	48.4	22.8	25.6	47.1	52.9	58.4	41.6	24.2	17.2	58.4	41.6	70.2	29.8	17.8	12.0	59.7	40.3
Paterson, N.J	72.6	27.4	10.6	16.8	38.7	61.3	76.0	24.0	10.0	14.0	41.7	58.3	76.8	23.2	9.2	14.1	39.5	60.5
Philadelphia, Pa.	60.5	39.5	11.8	27.7	29.8	70.2	73.4	26.6	11.6	15.0	43.7	56.3	77.9	22.1	12.1	10.0	54.7	45.3
Pittsburgh, Pa.³	71.7	28.3	15.2	13.1	53.7	46.3	72.0	28.0	15.2	12.7	54.4	45.6	73.3	26.7	15.5	11.2	57.9	42.1
Portland, Oreg	55.4	44.6	24.2	20.5	54.1	45.9	53.7	46.3	28.2	18.1	60.9	39.1	68.6	31.4	21.8	9.6	69.5	30.5
Providence, R.I	76.5	23.5	9.8	13.7	41.6	58.4	79.2	20.8	10.1	10.7	48.4	51.6	79.0	21.0	11.0	10.0	52.4	47.6
Reading, Pa	53.4	46.6	22.1	24.5	47.4	52.6	60.4	39.6	20.8	18.8	52.6	47.4	62.9	37.1	19.5	17.6	52.6	47.4
Richmond, Va	74.1	25.9	17.0	8.8	65.8	34.2	76.0	24.0	18.7	5.3	77.8	22.2	77.7	22.3	16.8	5.6	75.1	24.9
Rochester, N.Y	57.5	42.5	13.1	29.4	30.8	69.2	57.9	42.1	17.3	24.8	41.1	58.9	62.2	37.8	18.5	19.4	48.8	51.2
St. Louis, Mo	76.2	23.8	13.1	10.7	55.2	44.8	75.0	25.0	14.8	10.1	59.3	40.7	77.2	22.8	14.2	8.6	62.4	37.6
St. Paul, Minn	53.9	46.1	26.0	20.1	56.4	43.6	58.8	41.2	27.2	14.0	66.0	34.0	70.1	29.9	19.8	10.1	66.1	33.9
Salt Lake City, Utah	55.7	44.3	22.8	21.6	51.4	48.6	54.9	45.1	25.5	19.6	56.5	43.5	60.0	40.0	29.1	11.0	72.6	27.4
San Antonio, Tex	62.3	37.8	26.2	11.5	69.5	30.5	59.2	40.8	30.7	10.1	75.2	24.8	62.0	38.0	33.2	4.8	87.4	12.6
San Francisco, Calif	72.6	27.4	16.3	11.1	59.5	40.5	67.0	33.0	19.7	13.3	59.8	40.2	75.9	24.1	16.0	8.1	66.5	33.5
Scranton, Pa	64.5	35.5	24.2	11.3	68.1	31.9	62.8	37.2	22.0	15.6	58.4	41.6	62.1	37.9	24.2	13.6	64.0	36.0
Seattle, Wash	53.7	46.3	22.9	23.5	49.3	50.7	55.1	44.9	27.5	17.4	61.3	38.7	68.4	31.6	23.9	7.8	75.5	24.5
Spokane, Wash	55.4	44.6	25.5	19.2	57.1	42.9	48.7	51.3	27.4	23.9	53.4	46.6	62.8	37.2	25.6	11.6	68.8	31.2
Springfield, Mass	72.1	27.9	6.4	21.5	22.8	77.2	70.6	29.4	10.5	18.9	35.7	64.3	66.7	33.3	13.8	19.5	41.4	58.6
Syracuse, N.Y	62.1	37.9	13.0	25.0	34.2	65.8	60.3	39.7	16.0	23.7	40.3	59.7	62.6	37.4	16.6	20.8	44.4	55.6
Toledo, Ohio	50.6	49.4	24.4	25.0	49.4	50.6	55.7	44.3	25.0	19.3	56.4	43.6	57.0	43.0	24.8	18.2	57.7	42.3
Trenton, N.J	61.9	38.1	10.2	27.9	26.9	73.2	69.0	31.0	11.0	20.2	35.2	64.8	73.8	26.2	9.9	16.3	37.8	62.2
Washington, D.C	69.7	30.3	13.5	16.8	44.6	55.4	74.8	25.2	14.6	10.6	58.0	42.0	75.8	24.2	16.1	8.1	66.5	33.5
Wilmington, Del	61.7	38.3	14.2	24.0	37.2	62.8	69.6	30.4	13.5	16.9	44.3	55.7	72.9	27.1	11.6	15.5	42.9	57.1
Worcester, Mass	72.3	27.7	5.1	22.6	18.5	81.5	75.6	24.4	7.3	17.1	29.8	70.2	75.1	24.9	8.7	16.1	35.1	64.9
Yonkers, N.Y	76.5	23.5	5.7	17.8	24.2	75.8	76.5	23.5	7.2	16.4	30.5	69.5	75.1	24.9	8.9	14.5	38.0	62.0
Youngstown, Ohio	52.2	47.8	21.7	26.1	45.4	54.6	59.3	40.7	24.5	16.2	60.1	39.9	54.9	45.1	30.0	15.2	66.4	33.6

¹ Percentages for 1900 relate to private families only. (See p. 1279.)   ² Includes South Omaha for 1910 and 1900.   ³ Includes Allegheny for 1900.

BIBLIOGRAPHY

General

Blanke, David. *The 1910s.* Westport, CT: Greenwood Press, 2002.

Bradley, Patricia. *Making American Culture: A Social History, 1900-1920.* New York: Palgrave Macmillan, 2009.

Furnas, J. C. *Great Times; An Informal Social History of the United States, 1914-1929.* New York: Putnam, 1974.

Hawley, Ellis W. *The Great War and the Search for a Modern Order; A History of the American People and Their Institutions, 1917-1933,* 2d ed. New York: St. Martin's Press, 1992.

Lears, T. Jackson. *No Place of Grace: Antimodernism and the Transformation of American Culture, 1880-1920.* Chicago: University of Chicago Press, 1994.

Leuchtenberg, William E. *The Perils of Prosperity, 1914-1932,* 2d ed. Chicago: University of Chicago Press, 1993.

Mencken, H. L. *The American Language,* 2d ed., rev. and enl. New York: Knopf, 1921.

Moskowitz, Marina. *Standard of Living: The Measure of the Middle Class in Modern America.* Baltimore: Johns Hopkins University Press, 2004.

Nash, Roderick. *The Nervous Generation; American Thought, 1917-1930.* 1970; reprint, Chicago: Elephant Paperbacks, 1990.

Proctor, Tammy M. *Civilians in a World at War, 1914-1918.* New York: New York University Press, 2010.

Saunders, Nicholas. *Killing Time: Archaeology and the First World War.* Stroud, Gloucestershire, UK: Sutton, 2007.

Shevin-Coetzee, Marilyn, and Frans Coetzee, eds. *Empires, Soldiers and Citizens: A World War I Sourcebook,* 2d ed. Malden, MA: Wiley, 2012.

Shi, David E. *Facing Facts: Realism in American Thought and Culture, 1850-1920.* New York: Oxford University Press, 1995.

Sklar, Martin J. *The United States as a Developing Country: Studies in U.S. History in the Progressive Era and the 1920s.* New York: Cambridge University Press, 1992.

Sklar, Robert, ed. *The Plastic Age (1917-1930).* New York: G. Braziller, 1970.

Stevenson, D. *Armaments and the Coming of War: Europe, 1904-1914.* Oxford, UK: Clarendon Press/New York: Oxford University Press, 1996.

Sullivan, Mark. *Our Times; America at the Birth of the Twentieth Century,* ed. with new material by Dan Rather. Abridged ed. New York: Scribner, 1996.

Whalan, Mark. *American Culture in the 1910s.* Edinburgh: Edinburgh University Press, 2010.

Wohl, Robert. *The Generation of 1914.* Cambridge, MA: Harvard University Press, 1979.

Woodiwiss, Michael. *Crime, Crusades, and Corruption: Prohibitions in the United States, 1900-1987.* Totowa, NJ: Barnes & Noble, 1988.

Zieger, Robert H. *America's Great War: World War I and the American Experience.* Lanham, MD: Rowman & Littlefield, 2000.

African Americans

Anderson, Jervis. *This Was Harlem: A Cultural Portrait, 1900-1950.* New York: Farrar, Straus & Giroux, 1982.

Aycock, Colleen, and Mark Scott, eds. *The First Black Boxing Champions: Essays on Fighters from the 1800s to the 1920s.* Jefferson, NC: McFarland, 2010.

Binder, Frederick M. and David M. Reimers. *All the Nations under Heaven: An Ethnic and Racial History of New York City.* New York: Columbia University Press 1995.

Bracey, John H., Jr., August Meier, and Elliott Rudwick, eds. *Black Workers and Organized Labor.* Belmont, CA: Wadsworth Publishing, 1971.

Brundage, W. Fitzhugh, ed. *Beyond Blackface: African American and the Creation of American Popular Culture, 1890-1930.* Chapel Hill: University of North Carolina Press, 2011.

Candaele, Kerry. *Bound for Glory: From the Great Migration to the Harlem Renaissance, 1910-1930.* New York: Chelsea House, 1996.

Chicago Commission on Race Relations. *The Negro in Chicago: A Study of Race Relations and a Race Riot.* Chicago: University of Chicago Press, 1922.

Doetsch, Ethan. "Veteran Status, Race, and Labor Mobility in the United States." PhD diss., University of Utah, 2012.

Du Bois, W. E. B. *Selections from The Crisis,* ed. by Herbert Aptheker. Millwood, NY: Kraus-Thompson, 1983.

Gates, Henry Louis, Jr., and Gene Andrew Jarrett, eds. *The New Negro: Readings on Race, Representation, and African American Culture, 1892-1938.* Princeton, NJ: Princeton University Press, 2007.

Grossman, James R. *Land of Hope: Chicago, Black Southerners, and the Great Migration.* Chicago: University of Chicago Press, 1989.

Hagedorn, Ann. *Savage Peace; Hope and Fear in America, 1919.* New York: Simon & Schuster, 2007.

McWhirter, Cameron. *Red Summer: The Summer of 1919 and the Awakening of Black America.* New York: H. Holt, 2011.

Meier, August, and Elliott M. Rudwick. *Black Detroit and the Rise of the UAW.* 1979; reprint, Ann Arbor: University of Michigan Press, 2007.

Moreno, Paul D. *Black Workers and Organized Labor: A New History.* Baton Rouge: Louisiana State University Press, 2006.

Sandburg, Carl. *The Chicago Race Riots, July, 1919.* Introductory note by Walter Lippmann; preface by Paul Buhle. Mineola, NY: Dover Publications, 2013.

Trotter, Joe William Jr., ed. *The Great Migration in Historical Perspective: New Dimensions of Race, Class, and Gender.* Bloomington: Indiana University Press, 1991.

Tuttle, William H. *Race Riot: Chicago in the Red Summer of 1919.* 1970; reprint, Urbana: University of Illinois Press, 1996.

Wilkerson, Isabel, *The Warmth of Other Suns: The Epic Story of America's Great Migration.* New York: Random House, 2010.

Williams, Chad L. *Torchbearers of Democracy: African American Soldiers in the World War I Era.* Chapel Hill: University of North Carolina Press, 2011.

Woodward, C. Vann. *The Strange Career of Jim Crow,* commemorative edition with a new afterword by William F. McFeely. New York: Oxford University Press, 2002. [First edition, 1955.]

Art and Design

Blaszczyk, Regina Lee. *Imagining Consumers: Design and Innovation from Wedgwood to Corning.* Baltimore: Johns Hopkins University Press, 2000.

Chipp, Herschel B., with contributions by Peter Zelz and Joshua C. Taylor. *Theories of Modern Art; A Sourcebook by Artists and Critics.* 1968; reprint, Berkeley: University of California Press, 1984.

Cork, Richard. *A Bitter Truth: Avant-Garde Art and the Great War.* New Haven: Yale University Press/Barbican Art Gallery, 1994.

Cornebise, Alfred E. *Art from the Trenches: America's Uniformed Artists in World War I.* College Station: Texas A & M University Press, 1991.

Crunden, Robert M. *American Salons: Encounters with European Modernism, 1885-1917.* New York: Oxford University Press, 1993.

Davidson, Abraham A. *Early American Modernist Painting, 1910-1935.* 1981; reprint, New York: Da Capo Press, 1994.

Eberle, Matthias. *World War I and the Weimar Artists: Dix, Grosz, Beckmann, Schlemmer,* tr. by John Gabriel. New Haven: Yale University Press, 1985.

Foglesong, Richard F. *Planning the Capitalist City: The Colonial Era to the 1920s.* Princeton, NJ: Princeton University Press, 1986.

Franck, Dan. *Bohemian Paris: Picasso, Modigliani, Matisse, and the Birth of Modern Art,* tr. by Cynthia Hope Liebow. New York: Grove Press, 2001. [A translation of Franck's *Bohèmes.*]

Fuglie, Gordon L., curator. *Images of the Great War: 1914-1918,* ed. by Lucinda H. Gedeon. Los Angeles: Grunwald Center for the Graphic Arts, University of California at Los Angeles, 1983.

Gosling, Lucinda. *Brushes and Bayonets; Cartoons, Sketches, and Paintings of World War I.* Oxford, UK: Osprey, 2008.

Gough, Paul. *A Terrible Beauty: British Artists in the First World War.* Bristol: Sansom & Co., 2010.

Green, Christopher. *Cubism and Its Enemies: Modern Movements and Reaction in French Art, 1916-1928.* New Haven: Yale University Press, 1987.

Green, Hardy. *The Company Town: The Industrial Edens and Satanic Mills That Shaped the American Economy.* New York: Basic Books, 2010.

Harries, Meirion. *The War Artists: British Official War Art of the Twentieth Century.* London: M. Joseph/Imperial War Museum/Tate Gallery, 1983.

Howell, Edgar, curator and ed. *Battle Art: American Expeditionary Forces, 1918; An Exhibition in the Museum of History and Technology.* Washington, DC: Smithsonian Institution/USGPO, 1967.

Hughes, Gordon, and Philipp Blom, eds. *Nothing but the Clouds Unchanged; Artists in World War I.* Los Angeles: Getty Research Institute, 2014.

James, Pearl. *Picture This: World War I Posters and Visual Culture.* Lincoln: University of Nebraska Press, 2010.

Jones, Barbara, and Bill Howell. *Popular Arts of the First World War.* New York: McGraw-Hill, 1972.

Kimball, Jane A. *Trench Art: An Illustrated History.* Davis, CA: Silverpenny Press, 2004.

Krass, Peter. *Portrait of War: The U.S. Army's First Combat Artists and the Doughboys' Experience of WWI.* Hoboken, NJ: Wiley, 2007.

Kroes, Rob, and Alessandro Portelli, eds. *Social Change and New Modes of Expression; The United States, 1910-1930.* Amsterdam: Free University Press, 1986.

Kunst- und Ausstellungshalle der Bundesrepublik. *1914: The Avant-Garde Goes to War,* ed. by Uwe M. Schneede. Köln: Snoek, 2013.

Lemke, Sieglinde. *Primitivist Modernism: Black Culture and the Origins of Transatlantic Modernism.* New York: Oxford University Press, 1998.

Ludington, Townsend, with Thomas Fahy and Sarah P. Reuning, eds. *A Modern Mosaic: Art and Modernism in the United States.* Chapel Hill: University of North Carolina Press, 2000.

Malvern, Sue. *Modern Art, Britain, and the Great War: Witnessing, Testimony, and Remembrance.* New Haven; London: Published for the Paul Mellon Centre for Studies in British Art by Yale University Press, 2004.

Roshwald, Aviel, and Richard Stites, eds. *European Culture in the Great War: The Arts, Entertainment, and Propaganda, 1914-1918.* New York: Cambridge University Press, 1999. [Studies in the Social and Cultural History of Modern Warfare 6.]

Saunders, Nicholas J. *Trench Art: A Brief History and Guide, 1914-1939.* London: Leo Cooper, 2001.

Sillars, Stuart. *Art and Survival in First World War Britain.* New York: St. Martin's Press, 1987.

Smith, Terry. *Making the Modern: Industry, Art, and Design in America.* Chicago: University of Chicago Press, 1993.

Spencer, Herbert. *Pioneers of Modern Typography,* rev. ed. Cambridge, MA: MIT Press, 2004.

Swinth, Kirsten. *Painting Professionals: Women Artists and the Development of Modern American Art, 1870-1930.* Chapel Hill: University of North Carolina Press, 2001.

Tartsinis, Ann Marguerite. *An American Style: Global Sources for New York Textile and Fashion Design, 1915-1928.* New York: Bard Graduate Center, 2013.

Tippett, Maria. *Art at the Service of War: Canada, Art, and the Great War.* Buffalo, NY: University of Toronto Press, 1984.

Troy, Virginia Gardner. *The Modernist Textile: Europe and America, 1890-1940.* Aldershot, Hampshire, UK: Lund Humphries, 2006.

Viney, Nigel. *Images of Wartime: British Art and Artists of World War I.* Newton Abbey, Devon: David & Charles, 1991. [Pictures from the collection of the Imperial War Museum.]

Wardle, Marian, ed. *American Women Modernists; The Legacy of Robert Henri, 1910-1945.* Provo, UT: Brigham Young University Museum of Art/New Brunswick, NJ: Rutgers University Press, 2005.

White, Michael. *Generation Dada: The Berlin Avant-Garde and the First World War.* New Haven: Yale University Press, 2013.

Business and Economy

Benson, Susan Porter. *Counter Cultures: Saleswomen, Managers, and Customers in American Department Stores, 1890-1940*. Urbana: University of Illinois Press, 1986.

Blatz, Perry K. *Democratic Miners: Work and Labor Relations in the Anthracite Coal Industry, 1875-1925*. Albany: State University of New York Press, 1994.

Broadberry, S. N, and Mark Harrison, eds. *The Economics of World War I*. New York: Cambridge University Press, 2005.

Burk, Kathleen. *Britain, America and the Sinews of War, 1914-1918*. Boston: G. Allen & Unwin, 1985.

Carlson, Linda. *Company Towns of the Pacific Northwest*. Seattle: University of Washington Press, 2003.

Chandler, Alfred D., Jr. *The Visible Hand: The Managerial Revolution in American Business*. Cambridge, MA: Belknap Press of Harvard University Press, 1993.

Cook, Daniel Thomas. *The Commodification of Childhood: The Children's Clothing Industry and the Rise of the Child Consumer*. Durham, NC: Duke University Press, 2004.

Crawford, Margaret. *Building the Workingman's Paradise: The Design of American Company Towns*. London: Verso, 1995.

Garbade, Kenneth D. *Birth of a Market: The U.S. Treasury Securities Market from the Great War to the Great Depression*. Cambridge, MA: MIT Press, 2012.

Gidlow, Liette. *The Big Vote: Gender, Consumer Culture, and the Politics of Exclusion, 1890s-1920s*. Baltimore: Johns Hopkins University Press, 2004.

Gilbert, Charles. *American Financing of World War I*. Westport, CT: Greenwood Press, 1970.

Green, Hardy. *The Company Town: The Industrial Edens and Satanic Mills That Shaped the American Economy*. New York: Basic Books, 2010.

Hardach, Gerd. *The First World War, 1914-1918*. Berkeley: University of California Press, 1977. [History of the World Economy in the Twentieth Century 2.]

Horowitz, Daniel. *The Morality of Spending: Attitudes toward the Consumer Society in America, 1875-1940*. 1985; reprint, Chicago: Ivan Dee, 1992.

Hounshell, David A. *From the American System to Mass Production, 1800-1932: The Development of Manufacturing Technology in the United States*. Baltimore: Johns Hopkins University Press, 1984.

Jablonsky, Thomas J. *Pride in the Jungle: Community and Everyday Life in Back of the Yards Chicago*. Baltimore: Johns Hopkins University Press, 1993.

Jacobson, Lisa. *Raising Consumers: Children and the American Mass Market in the Early Twentieth Century*. New York: Columbia University Press, 2004.

Lambert, Nicholas A. *Planning Armageddon: British Economic Warfare and the First World War*. Cambridge, MA: Harvard University Press, 2012.

Leach, William. *Land of Desire: Merchants, Power, and the Rise of a New American Culture*. New York: Pantheon Books, 1993.

Mandell, Nikki. *The Corporation as Family: The Gendering of Corporate Welfare, 1890-1930*. Chapel Hill: University of North Carolina Press, 2002.

Offer, Avner. *The First World War: An Agrarian Interpretation*, new ed. New York: Oxford University Press, 1991.

Pak, Susie J. *Gentlemen Bankers: The World of J. P. Morgan*. Berlin: De Gruyter, 2013.

Schwartz, Michael. *Broadway and Corporate Capitalism; The Rise of the Professional-Managerial Class, 1900-1920*. New York: Palgrave Macmillan, 2009.

Steen, Kathryn. *American Synthetic Organic Chemicals Industry: War and Politics, 1910-1930*. Chapel Hill: University of North Carolina Press, 2014.

Strachan, Hew. *Financing the First World War*. New York: Oxford University Press, 2004. [Originally appeared in Strachan's *To Arms*, vol. 1 of his *The First World War* (2001).]

Tunc, Tanfer Emin. "Less Sugar, More Warships: Food as American Propaganda in the First World War." *War in History* 19, no. 2 (April 1, 2012): 193-216.

Wrigley, Chris, ed. *The First World War and the International Economy*. Cheltenham, UK: E. Elgar, 2000.

Education

Axtell, James. *The Educational Legacy of Woodrow Wilson: From College to Nation*. Charlottesville: University of Virginia Press, 2012.

Barzansky, Barbara, and Norman Gevitz, eds. *Beyond Flexner: Medical Education in the Twentieth Century*. New York: Greenwood Press, 1992.

Berliner, Howard S. *A System of Scientific Medicine; Philanthropic Foundations of the Flexner Era*. New York: Tavistock, 1985.

Cohen, Ronald D., and Raymond A, Mohl. *The Paradox of Progressive Education: The Gary Plan and Urban Schooling*. Port Washington, NY: Kennikat Press, 1979.

Flexner, Abraham. *Medical Education in the United States and Canada; A Report to the Carnegie Foundation for the Advancement of Teaching*. 1910; reprint, Buffalo: Heritage Press, 1973.

Van Slyck, Abigail. *Free to All: Carnegie Libraries and American Culture, 1890-1920*. Chicago: University of Chicago Press, 1995.

Wallace, James M. *Liberal Journalism and American Education, 1914-1941*. New Brunswick, NJ: Rutgers University Press, 1991.

Weiner, Melissa F. "Resources, Riots, and Race: The Gary Plan and the Harlem 9," in her *Power, Protest, and the Public Schools; Jewish and African American Struggles in New York City*. New Brunswick, NJ: Rutgers University Press, 2010.

Weiss, Bernard J., ed. *American Education and the European Immigrant, 1840-1940*. Urbana: University of Illinois Press, 1982.

Wheatley, Steven C. *The Politics of Philanthropy: Abraham Flexner and Medical Education*. Madison: University of Wisconsin Press, 1988.

Wirt, William. *Newer Ideals in Education; The Complete Use of the School Plant*. Philadelphia: Public Education Association of Philadelphia, 1912.

Film, Music, and Popular Culture

Basinger, Jeanine. *Silent Stars*. New York: Knopf, 1999.

Bilton, Alan. *Silent Film Comedy and American Culture*. New York: Palgrave Macmillan, 2013.

Blake, Angela M. *How New York Became American, 1890-1924*. Baltimore: Johns Hopkins University Press, 2006.

Blaszczyk, Regina Lee. *Imagining Consumers: Design and Innovation from Wedgwood to Corning*. Baltimore: Johns Hopkins University Press, 2000.

Boyer, Paul S. *Purity in Print: Book Censorship in America from the Gilded Age to the Computer Age*, 2d ed. Madison: University of Wisconsin Press, 2002.

Bradley, Patricia. *Making American Culture: A Social History, 1900-1920*. New York: Palgrave Macmillan, 2009.

Bristow, Nancy K. *Making Men Moral: Social Engineering during the Great War.* New York: New York University Press, 1996.

Brown, Elspeth H. *The Corporate Eye: Photography and the Rationalization of American Commercial Culture, 1884-1929.* Baltimore: Johns Hopkins University Press, 2005.

Brundage, W. Fitzhugh, ed. *Beyond Blackface: African Americans and the Creation of American Popular Culture, 1890-1930.* Chapel Hill: University of North Carolina Press, 2011.

Budreau, Lisa M. *Bodies of War: World War I and the Politics of Commemoration in America, 1919-1933.* New York: New York University Press, 2010.

Capozzola, Christopher J. N. *Uncle Sam Wants You: World War I and the Making of the Modern American Citizen.* New York: Oxford University Press, 2008.

Collins, L. J. *Theatre at War, 1914-18.* New York: St. Martin's Press, 1998.

Conolly-Smith, Peter. *Translating America: An Immigrant Press Visualizes American Popular Culture, 1895-1918.* 2004; reprint, Washington, DC: Smithsonian Books, 2010.

Cook, Daniel Thomas. *The Commodification of Childhood: The Children's Clothing Industry and the Rise of the Child Consumer.* Durham, NC: Duke University Press, 2004.

Cooper, Patricia A. *Once a Cigar Maker: Men Women, and Work Culture in American Cigar Factories, 1900-1919.* Urbana: University of Illinois Press, 1987.

Crafton, Donald. *Before Mickey: The Animated Film, 1898-1928.* Chicago: University of Chicago Press, 1993.

Doyle, Peter. *The First World War in 100 Objects.* Stroud, Gloucestershire, UK: History Press, 2014.

Doyle, Peter, and Julian Walker. *Trench Talk: Words of the First World War.* Stroud, Gloucestershire, UK: History Press, 2012.

Dulles, Foster Rhea. *A History of Recreation; America Learns to Play,* 2d ed. New York: Appleton Century Crofts, 1965.

Feuerlicht, Roberta Strauss. *America's Reign of Terror: World War I, the Red Scare and the Palmer Raids.* New York: Random House, 1971.

Finnegan, Margaret Mary. *Selling Suffrage: Consumer Culture and Votes for Women.* New York: Columbia University Press, 1999.

Flink, James J. *The Automobile Age.* Cambridge, MA: MIT Press, 1988.

Fraser, Alastair H., Andrew Robertshaw, and Steve Roberts. *Ghosts on the Somme: Filming the Battle, June-July 1916.* Barnsley, South Yorkshire, UK: Pen & Sword Military, 2009.

Fussell, Paul. *The Great War and Modern Memory.* 1975; reprint, New York: Oxford University Press, 2000.

Gidlow, Liette. *The Big Vote: Gender, Consumer Culture, and the Politics of Exclusion, 1890s-1920s.* Baltimore: Johns Hopkins University Press, 2004.

Gjerde, Jon. *The Minds of the West: Ethnocultural Evolution in the Rural Middle West, 1830-1917.* Chapel Hill: University of North Carolina Press, 1997.

Golden, Eve. *Golden Images: Forty-One Essays on Silent Film Stars.* Jefferson, NC: McFarland, 2001.

Gordon, Ian. *Comic Strips and Consumer Culture, 1890-1945.* Washington, DC: Smithsonian Institution Press, 1998.

Green, Hardy. *The Company Town: The Industrial Edens and Satanic Mills That Shaped the American Economy.* New York: Basic Books, 2010.

Gusfield, Joseph R. *Symbolic Crusade: Status Politics and the American Temperance Movement.* 1963; reprint, Urbana, IL: Illini Books, 1986.

Hagedorn, Ann. *Savage Peace; Hope and Fear in America, 1919.* New York: Simon & Schuster, 2007.

Hammond, Michael, ed. *British Silent Cinema and the Great War.* New York: Palgrave Macmillan, 2011.

Hansen, Miriam. *Babel and Babylon: Spectatorship in American Silent Film.* 1991; reprint, Cambridge, MA: Harvard University Press, 1994.

Heller, Adele, ed. *1915, the Cultural Moment; The New Politics, the New Woman, the New Psychology, the New Art and the New Theatre in America.* New Brunswick, NJ: Rutgers University Press, 1991.

Horowitz, Daniel. *The Morality of Spending: Attitudes toward the Consumer Society in America, 1875-1940.* 1985; reprint, Chicago: Ivan Dee, 1992.

Jacobs, Lewis. *The Rise of the American Film: A Critical History.* 1939; reprint, New York: Teachers College Press, 1968.

Jacobson, Lisa. *Raising Consumers: Children and the American Mass Market in the Early Twentieth Century.* New York: Columbia University Press, 2004.

James, Pearl. *Picture This: World War I Posters and Visual Culture.* Lincoln: University of Nebraska Press, 2010.

Keil, Hartmut, ed. *German Workers' Culture in the United States, 1850 to 1920.* Washington, DC: Smithsonian Institution Press, 1988.

Kelly, Andrew. *Cinema and the Great War.* New York: Routledge, 1997.

Kennedy, Kate, and Trudi Tate, eds. *Literature and Music of the First World War,* a special issue of *First World War Studies* 2, no. 4 (June 2011).

Lasswell, Harold D. *Propaganda Technique in World War I.* Cambridge, MA: MIT Press, 1971.

Lawson, Kenneth Gregory. "War at the Grassroots: The Great War and the Nationalization of Civic Life." PhD diss., University of Washington, 2000.

Lears, T. Jackson. *No Place of Grace: Antimodernism and the Transformation of American Culture, 1880-1920.* Chicago: University of Chicago Press, 1994.

Lewinnek, Elaine. *The Working Man's Reward: Chicago's Early Suburbs and the Roots of American Sprawl.* New York: Oxford University Press, 2014.

Mandell, Nikki. *The Corporation as Family: The Gendering of Corporate Welfare, 1890-1930.* Chapel Hill: University of North Carolina Press, 2002.

May, Lary. *Screening Out the Past: The Birth of Mass Culture and the Motion Picture Industry.* Oxford: Oxford University Press, 1980.

Mayo, Katherine. *"That Damn Y": A Record of Overseas Service.* Boston: Houghton Mifflin, 1920.

Nasaw, David. *Going Out: The Rise and Fall of Public Amusements.* Cambridge, MA: Harvard University Press, 1999.

Nolan, Michael E. *The Inverted Mirror: Mythologizing the Enemy in France and Germany, 1898-1914.* New York: Berghahn Books, 2005.

Orvell, Miles. *The Real Thing: Imitation and Authenticity in American Culture, 1880-1940.* Chapel Hill: University of North Carolina Press, 1989.

Paddock, Troy R. E. *A Call to Arms: Propaganda, Public Opinion, and Newspapers in the Great War.* Westport, CT: Greenwood Publishing Group, 2004.

Paris, Michael, ed. *The First World War and Popular Cinema: 1914 to the Present.* New Brunswick, N.J.: Rutgers University Press, 2000.

Ritter, Lawrence S. *The Glory of Their Times: The Story of the Early Days of Baseball Told by the Men Who Played It,* new enl. ed. New York: Morrow, 1984.

Roshwald, Aviel, and Richard Stites, eds. *European Culture in the Great War.* New York: Cambridge University Press, 1999. [Studies in the Social and Cultural History of Modern Warfare 6.]

Ross, Steven J. *Working Class Hollywood: Silent Film and the Shaping of Class in America.* Princeton, NJ: Princeton University Press, 1998.

Sadler, John, and Rosie Serdiville. *Tommy Rot: WW1 Poetry They Didn't Let You Read.* Stroud, Gloucestershire, UK: History Press, 2013.

Saunders, Nicholas J, ed. *Matters of Conflict: Material Culture, Memory and the First World War.* New York: Routledge, 2004.

Sears, Roebuck Company. Sears, *Roebuck Home Builders Catalog: The Complete Illustrated 1910 Edition.* New York: Dover, 1990.

Seymour, Harold. *Baseball: The Golden Age,* vol. 2 of *Baseball,* 3 vols. 1960-1971; reprint, New York: Oxford University Press, 1989-1990.

Shi, David E. *Facing Facts: Realism in American Thought and Culture, 1850-1920.* New York: Oxford University Press, 1995.

Strasser, Susan. *Never Done; A History of American Housework.* 1982; reprint, New York: H. Holt, 2013.

Van Slyck, Abigail. *Free to All: Carnegie Libraries and American Culture, 1890-1920.* Chicago: University of Chicago Press, 1995.

Whalan, Mark. *American Culture in the 1910s.* Edinburgh: Edinburgh University Press, 2010.

Wright, Gwendolyn. *Building the Dream: A Social History of Housing in America.* 1981; reprint, Cambridge, MA: MIT Press, 1983.

Zieger, Robert H. *America's Great War: World War I and the American Experience.* Lanham, MD: Rowman & Littlefield, 2000.

Immigration and Nativism

Binder, Frederick M., and David M. Reimers. *All the Nations under Heaven: An Ethnic and Racial History of New York City.* New York: Columbia University Press, 1995.

Bodnar, John. *The Transplanted: A History of Immigrants in Urban America* Bloomington: Indiana University Press, 1985.

Briggs, John W. *An Italian Passage: Immigrants to Three American Cities, 1890-1930.* New Haven: Yale University Press, 1978.

Chermayeff, Ivan, Fred Wasserman, and Mary J. Shapiro. *Ellis Island: An Illustrated History of the Immigrant Experience.* New York: Macmillan, 1991.

Conolly-Smith, Peter. *Translating America: An Immigrant Press Visualizes American Popular Culture, 1895-1918.* 2004; reprint, Washington, DC: Smithsonian Books, 2010.

Dinnerstein, Leonard, and David M. Reimers. *Ethnic Americans: A History of Immigration and Assimilation,* 2d ed. New York: Harper & Row, 1982.

Ewen, Elizabeth. *Immigrant Women in the Land of Dollars: Life and Culture on the Lower East Side, 1890-1925.* New York: Monthly Review Press, 1985.

Gabaccia, Donna: *From the Other Side: Women, Gender, and Immigrant Life in the U.S.* Bloomington: Indiana University Press, 1994.

Gjerde, Jon. *The Minds of the West: Ethnocultural Evolution in the Rural Middle West, 1830-1917.* Chapel Hill: University of North Carolina Press, 1997.

Higham, John. *Strangers in the Land: Patterns of American Nativism, 1865-1925.* 1955; reprint, New Brunswick, NJ: Rutgers University Press, 2002.

Hoerder, Dirk. *American Labor and Immigration History, 1877-1920s; Recent European Research.* Urbana: University of Illinois Press, 1983.

Irving, Katrina. *Immigrant Mothers: Narratives of Race and Maternity, 1890-1925.* Urbana: University of Illinois Press, 2000.

Keil, Hartmut, ed. *German Workers' Culture in the United States, 1850 to 1920.* Washington, DC: Smithsonian Institution Press, 1988.

Knobel, Dale T. *America for the Americans: The Nativist Movement in the United States.* New York: Twayne Publishers/London: Prentice Hall International, 1996.

Kraut, Alan. *Silent Travelers: Germs, Genes, and the "Immigrant Menace."* New York: Basic Books, 1994.

Lee, Erika. *At America's Gates; Chinese Immigration during the Exclusion Era, 1882-1943.* Chapel Hill: University of North Carolina Press, 2003.

Luebke, Frederick. *Bonds of Loyalty: German America and World War I.* DeKalb: Northern Illinois University Press, 1974.

Moreno, Barry. *Encyclopedia of Ellis Island.* Westport, CT: Greenwood Press, 2004.

Mormino, Gary R., and George E. Pozzetta. *The Immigrant World of Ybor City: Italians and Neighbors in Tampa, 1885-1985.* Urbana: University of Illinois Press, 1987.

Ostergren, Robert C. *A Community Transplanted: The Trans-Atlantic Experience of a Swedish Immigrant Settlement in the Upper Middle West, 1835-1915.* Madison: University of Wisconsin Press, 1988.

Preston, William, Jr. *Aliens and Dissenters: Federal Suppression of Radicals, 1903-1933.* 1963; reprint, Urbana: University of Illinois Press, 1994.

Ramirez, Bruno, with Yves Otis. *Crossing the 49th Parallel; Migration from Canada to the United States, 1900-1930.* Ithaca, NY: Cornell University Press, 2001.

Rappaport, Joseph. *Hands across the Sea: Jewish Immigrants and World War I.* Lanham, MD: Hamilton Books, 2005.

Sterba, Christopher M. *Good Americans: Italian and Jewish Immigrants during the First World War.* New York: Oxford University Press, 2003.

Van Nuys, Frank. *Americanizing the West: Race, Immigrants, and Citizenship, 1890-1930.* Lawrence: University Press of Kansas, 2002.

Wan, Amy J. *Producing Good Citizens; Literacy Training in Anxious Times.* Pittsburgh, PA: University of Pittsburgh Press, 2014.

Watson, Bruce. *Bread and Roses: Mills, Migrants, and the Struggle for the American Dream.* New York, Viking, 2005.

Weiss, Bernard J., ed. *American Education and the European Immigrant, 1840-1940.* Urbana: University of Illinois Press, 1982.

Wilson, Sarah. *Melting-Pot Modernism.* Ithaca, NY: Cornell University Press, 2010.

Labor

Arnesen, Eric. *Brotherhoods of Color: Black Railroad Workers and the Struggle for Equality.* Cambridge, MA: Harvard University Press, 1992.

Bracey, John H., Jr., August Meier, and Elliott Rudwick, eds. *Black Workers and Organized Labor.* Belmont, CA: Wadsworth Publishing, 1971.

Brody, David. *Labor in Crisis: The Steel Strike of 1919.* 1965; reprint, Urbana: University of Illinois Press, 1987.

Cahn, William. *Lawrence, 1912: The Bread and Roses Strike.* New York: Pilgrim Press, 1980.

Cooper, Patricia A. *Once a Cigar Maker: Men Women, and Work Culture in American Cigar Factories, 1900-1919.* Urbana: University of Illinois Press, 1987.

Cronin, James E., and Carmen Sirianni, eds. *Work, Community, and Power: The Experience of Labor in Europe and America, 1900-1925.* Philadelphia: Temple University Press, 1983.

Davin, Eric Leif. *Crucible of Freedom: Workers' Democracy in the Industrial Heartland, 1914-1960.* Lanham, MD: Lexington Books, 2010.

Doetsch, Ethan. "Veteran Status, Race, and Labor Mobility in the United States." PhD diss., University of Utah, 2012.

Dubofsky, Melvyn. *Industrialism and the American Worker, 1865-1920,* 3d ed. Wheeling, IL: H. Davidson, 1996.

Dubofsky, Melvyn. *We Shall Be All; A History of the Industrial Workers of the World*, 2d ed. Urbana: University of Illinois Press, 1988.

Forrant, Robert, and Jurg Siegenthaler, eds. *The Great Lawrence Textile Strike of 1912; New Scholarship on the Bread and Roses Strike.* Amityville, NY: Baywood Publishing, 2014.

Gregory, Adrian. *The Last Great War: British Society and the First World War.* New York: Cambridge University Press, 2008.

Gulick, Charles Adams. *Labor Policy of the United States Steel Corporation.* 1924; reprint, New York: AMS Press, 1968.

Hoerder, Dirk. *American Labor and Immigration History, 1877-1920s; Recent European Research.* Urbana: University of Illinois Press, 1983.

Jacoby, Sanford M. *Employing Bureaucracy: Managers, Unions, and the Transformation of Work in the Twentieth Century.* Mahwah, NJ: Lawrence Erlbaum, 2004.

Keil, Hartmut, ed. *German Workers' Culture in the United States, 1850 to 1920.* Washington, DC: Smithsonian Institution Press, 1988.

McCartin, Joseph A. *Labor's Great War: The Struggle for Industrial Democracy and the Origins of Modern American Labor Relations, 1912-1921.* Chapel Hill: University of North Carolina Press, 1997.

Meier, August, and Elliott M. Rudwick. *Black Detroit and the Rise of the UAW.* 1979; reprint, Ann Arbor: University of Michigan Press, 2007.

Peterson, Joyce Shaw, "Black Automobile Workers in Detroit, 1910-30," *Journal of Negro History* 64 (1979).

Renshaw, Patrick: *The Wobblies; The Story of the IWW and Syndicalism in the United States,* new ed. Chicago: Ivan R. Dee, 1999.

Schmidt, James D. *Industrial Violence and the Legal Origins of Child Labor.* New York: Cambridge University Press, 2010.

Watson, Bruce. *Bread and Roses: Mills, Migrants, and the Struggle for the American Dream.* New York: Viking, 2005.

Literature and Drama

Boyer, Paul S. *Purity in Print: Book Censorship in America from the Gilded Age to the Computer Age,* 2d ed. Madison: University of Wisconsin Press, 2002.

Buitenhuis, Peter. *The Great War of Words: British, American, and Canadian Propaganda and Fiction, 1914-1933.* Vancouver: University of British Columbia Press, 1987.

Childs, Peter. *Modernist Literature: A Guide for the Perplexed.* New York: Continuum, 2011.

Cork, Richard. *A Bitter Truth: Avant-Garde Art and the Great War.* New Haven: Yale University Press/Barbican Art Gallery, 1994.

Cross, Tim. *The Lost Voices of World War I: An International Anthology of Writers, Poets & Playwrights.* London: Bloomsbury, 1998.

Das, Santanu. *Race, Empire and First World War Writing.* New York: Cambridge University Press, 2011.

Fielding, Raymond. *The American Newsreel: A Complete History, 1911-1967,* 2d ed. Jefferson, NC: McFarland & Co, 2006.

Fussell, Paul. *The Great War and Modern Memory.* 1975; reprint, New York: Oxford University Press, 2000.

Gilbert, Sandra M. "Soldier's Heart: Literary Men, Literary Women, and the Great War," in *Behind the Lines: Gender and the Two World Wars,* ed. Margaret R. Higonnet. New Haven: Yale University Press, 1987.

Goldman, Dorothy, with Jane Gledhill and Judith Hattaway. *Women Writers and the Great War.* New York: Twayne, 1995.

Halliwell, Martin. *Transatlantic Modernism: Moral Dilemma in Modernist Fiction.* 2001; reprint, Edinburgh: Edinburgh University Press, 2006. [First edition entitled *Modernism and Morality.*]

Haytock. Jennifer. *At Home, At War; Domesticity and World War I in American Literature.* Columbus: Ohio State University Press, 2003.

Higonnet, Margaret R. "Authenticity and Art in Trauma Narratives of World War I." *Modernism/Modernity* 9 (2002): 91-107.

Higonnet, Margaret R. *Lines of Fire: Women Writers of World War I.* New York: Plume, 1999.

Higonnet, Margaret R., ed. *Nurses at the Front: Writing the Wounds of the Great War.* Boston: Northeastern University Press, 2001.

Marcus, Leonard S. *Minders of Make-Believe: Idealists, Entrepreneurs, and the Shaping of American Children's Literature.* Boston: Houghton Mifflin, 2008.

Matsen, William E. *The Great War and the American Novel: Versions of Reality and the Writer's Craft in Selected Fiction of the First World War.* New York: Peter Lang, 1993.

Sherry, Vincent. *The Great War and the Language of Modernism.* New York: Oxford University Press, 2003.

Stromberg, Roland N. *Redemption by War: The Intellectuals and 1914.* Lawrence: Regents Press of Kansas, 1982.

Van Wienen, Mark W. *Partisans and Poets: The Political Work of American Poetry in the Great War.* New York: Cambridge University Press, 1997.

Walter, George, ed. *Penguin Book of First World War Poetry,* rev. ed. New York: Penguin, 2007.

Wilson, Sarah. *Melting-Pot Modernism.* Ithaca, NY: Cornell University Press, 2010.

Politics and the Presidency

Afflerbach, Holger, and David Stevenson, eds. *An Improbable War?: The Outbreak of World War I and European Political Culture before 1914.* New York: Berghahn Books, 2007.

Benbow, Mark. *Leading Them to the Promised Land; Woodrow Wilson, Covenant Theology, and the Mexican Revolution, 1913-1915.* Kent, OH: Kent State University Press, 2010.

Berg, A. Scott. *Wilson.* New York: G. P. Putnam, 2013.

Budreau, Lisa M. *Bodies of War: World War I and the Politics of Commemoration in America, 1919-1933.* New York: New York University Press, 2010.

Capozzola, Christopher J. N. *Uncle Sam Wants You: World War I and the Making of the Modern American Citizen.* New York: Oxford University Press, 2008.

Cook, Brian J. *Democracy and Administration: Woodrow Wilson's Ideas and the Challenges of Public Management.* Baltimore: Johns Hopkins University Press, 2007.

Cooper, John Milton, Jr. *Breaking the Heart of the World; Woodrow Wilson and the Fight for the League of Nations.* New York: Cambridge University Press, 2001.

Cooper, John Milton, Jr. *Woodrow Wilson.* New York: Knopf, 2009.

Davis, Donald E., and Eugene P. Trani. *The First Cold War: The Legacy of Woodrow Wilson in U.S.-Soviet Relations.* Columbia: University of Missouri Press, 2002.

Ernst, Daniel R., *Tocqueville's Nightmare: The Administrative State Emerges in America, 1900-1940.* New York: Oxford University Press, 2014.

Feuerlicht, Roberta Strauss. *America's Reign of Terror: World War I, the Red Scare and the Palmer Raids.* New York: Random House, 1971.

Fic, Victor M. *The Collapse of American Policy in Russian and Siberia, 1918: Wilson's Decision Not to Intervene (March-October, 1918).* Boulder, CO: East European Monographs, 1995.

Flanagan, Maureen A. *America Reformed: Progressives and Progressivisms, 1890s-1920s.* New York: Oxford University Press, 2007.

Ford, Nancy Gentile. *The Great War and America: Civil-Military Relations during World War I.* Westport, CT: Praeger, 2008.

Gardner, Lloyd C. *Wilson and Revolution, 1913-1921.* 1976; reprint, Washington, DC: University Press of America, 1982.

Hagedorn, Ann. *Savage Peace; Hope and Fear in America, 1919.* New York: Simon & Schuster, 2007.

Jaffe, Julian F. *Crusade against Radicalism; New York during the Red Scare, 1914-1924.* Port Washington, NY: Kennikat Press, 1972.

Kennedy, Ross A., ed. *Companion to Woodrow Wilson.* New York: Wiley, 2013.

Kirby, D. G. *War, Peace, and Revolution: International Socialism at the Crossroads, 1914-1918.* New York: St. Martin's Press, 1986.

Langhorne, Richard. *The Collapse of the Concert of Europe: International Politics, 1890-1914.* New York: St. Martin's Press, 1981.

Lasswell, Harold D. *Propaganda Technique in World War I.* Cambridge, MA: MIT Press, 1971.

Lawson, Kenneth Gregory. "War at the Grassroots: The Great War and the Nationalization of Civic Life." PhD diss., University of Washington, 2000.

Levin, Phyllis Lee. *Edith and Woodrow: The Wilson White House.* New York: Scribner, 2001.

Levy, Jack S, and John A Vasquez, eds. *The Outbreak of the First World War: Structure, Politics, and Decision-Making.* New York: Cambridge University Press, 2014.

MacMillan, Margaret. *Paris 1919: Six Months That Changed the World.* New York: Random House, 2001.

Morrisey, Will. *The Dilemma of Progressivism: How Roosevelt, Taft, and Wilson Reshaped the American Regime of Self-Government.* Lanham, MD: Rowman & Littlefield, 2009.

Mulligan, William. *The Great War for Peace.* New Haven: Yale University Press, 2014.

Murphy, Paul L. *World War I and the Origin of Civil Liberties in the United States.* New York: W. W. Norton, 1979.

Noble, David W. *The Progressive Mind, 1890-1917,* rev. ed. Minneapolis: Burgess, 1981.

Rabin, Jack, and James S. Bowman. *Politics and Administration; Woodrow Wilson and American Public Administration.* New York: M. Dekker, 1984.

Romero, Francine Sanders, comp. *Presidents from Theodore Roosevelt through Coolidge, 1901-1929; Debating the Issues in Pro and Con Documents.* Westport, CT: Greenwood Press, 2002.

Stevenson, D. *Cataclysm: The First World War as Political Tragedy.* New York: Basic Books, 2004.

Stivers, Camilla. *Bureau Men, Settlement Women: Constructing Public Administration in the Progressive Era.* Lawrence: University Press of Kansas, 2000.

Thorsen, Niels Aage. *The Political Thought of Woodrow Wilson, 1875-1910.* Princeton, NJ: Princeton University Press, 1988.

Tilchin, William N., and Charles E. Neu, eds. *Artists of Power: Theodore Roosevelt, Woodrow Wilson, and Their Enduring Impact on U.S. Foreign Policy.* Westport, CT: Praeger, 2006.

Van Riper, Paul P. *The Wilson Influence on Public Administration; From Theory to Practice.* Washington, DC: American Society for Public Administration, 1990.

Wan, Amy J. *Producing Good Citizens; Literacy Training in Anxious Times.* Pittsburgh, PA: University of Pittsburgh Press, 2014.

Religion

Anderson, Robert Mapes. *Vision of the Disinherited; The Making of American Pentecostalism.* New York: Oxford University Press, 1979.

Baker, Kelly G. *Gospel according to the Klan: The KKK's Appeal to Protestant America, 1915-1930.* Lawrence: University Press of Kansas, 2011.

Boniface, Xavier. *Histoire religieuse de la Grande Guerre.* Paris: Fayard, 2014.

Bristow, Nancy K. *Making Men Moral: Social Engineering during the Great War.* New York: New York University Press, 1996.

Curtis, Susan. *Consuming Faith: The Social Gospel and Modern American Culture.* Baltimore: Johns Hopkins University Press, 1991.

Drapac, Vesna. "The Devotion of French Prisoners of War and Requisitioned Workers to Thérèse of Lisieux: Transcending the 'Diocese behind Barbed Wire.'" *Journal of War & Culture Studies* 7, no. 3 (July 17, 2014): 283-96.

Ebel, Jonathan H. *Faith in the Fight: Religion and the American Soldier in the Great War.* Princeton, NJ: Princeton University Press, 2010.

Gamble, Richard M. *The War for Righteousness: Progressive Christianity, the Great War, and the Rise of the Messianic Nation.* Wilmington, DE: ISI Books, 2003.

Granick, Jaclyn. "Waging Relief: The Politics and Logistics of American Jewish War Relief in Europe and the Near East (1914-1918)." *First World War Studies* 5, no. 1 (2014): 55-68.

Gregory, Adrian. "Redemption through War: Religion and Languages of Sacrifice," in his *The Last Great War: British Society and the First World War.* New York: Cambridge University Press, 2008.

Hutchinson, William R. *The Modernist Impulse in American Protestantism.* 1976; reprint, Durham, NC: Duke University Press, 1992.

Jenkins, Philip. *The Great and Holy War: How World War I Changed Religion Forever.* San Francisco: HarperCollins, 2014.

McKeown, Elizabeth. *War and Welfare; American Catholics and World War I.* New York: Garland, 1988.

Putney, Clifford. *Muscular Christianity; Manhood and Sports in Protestant America, 1880-1920.* 2001; reprint, Cambridge, MA: Harvard University Press, 2003.

Raphael, Marc Lee, ed. *Columbia History of Jews and Judaism in America.* New York: Columbia University Press, 2008.

Schweitzer, Richard. *The Cross and the Trenches: Religious Faith and Doubt among British and American Great War Soldiers.* Westport, CT: Praeger, 2003.

Smith, Christian, ed. *The Secular Revolution: Power, Interests, and Conflict in the Secularization of American Public Life.* Berkeley: University of California Press, 2003.

Smith, Gary Scott. *The Seeds of Secularization: Calvinism, Culture, and Pluralism in America, 1870-1915.* Grand Rapids, MI: Christian University Press, 1985.

Sorin, Gerald. *A Time for Building: The Third Migration, 1880-1920,* vol. 3 of *The Jewish People in America,* ed. by Henry L. Feingold. Baltimore: Johns Hopkins University Press, 1992.

Synan, Vinson. *The Holiness-Pentecostal Tradition; Charismatic Movements in the Twentieth Century,* 2d ed. Grand Rapids, MI: W. B. Eerdmans, 1997.

Wacker, Grant. *Heaven Below: Early Pentecostals and American Culture.* Cambridge, MA: Harvard University Press, 2001.

Weissbach, Lee Shai. *Jewish Life in Small-Town America: A History* (New Haven: Yale University Press, 2005.

Sports

Asinoff, Eliot. *Eight Men Out; the Black Sox and the 1919 World Series.* 1963; reprint, New York: H. Holt, 1987.

Aycock, Colleen, and Mark Scott, eds. *The First Black Boxing Champions: Essays on Fighters from the 1800s to the 1920s.* Jefferson, NC: McFarland, 2010.

Boddy, Kasia. *Boxing: A Cultural History.* London: Reaktion Books, 2008.

Burgess, Charles D. *Golf Links, Chay Burgess, Francis Ouimet, and the Bringing of Golf to America.* Cambridge, MA: Rounder Books, 2005.

Burk, Robert F. *Never Just a Game: Players, Owners, and American Baseball to 1920.* Chapel Hill: University of North Carolina Press, 2001.

Carney, Gene. *Burying the Black Sox: How Baseball's Cover-Up of the 1919 World Series Fix Almost Succeeded.* Washington, DC: Potomac Books, 2006.

Dulles, Foster Rhea. *A History of Recreation; America Learns to Play,* 2d ed. New York: Appleton Century Crofts, 1965.

Frost, Mark. *The Greatest Game Ever Played: Harry Vardon, Francis Ouimet, and the Birth of Modern Golf.* New York: Hyperion, 2002.

Jerris, Rand, et al. *Golf's Golden Age: Robert T. Jones, Jr. and the Legendary Players of the '10s, '20s, and '30s.* Photographs by George S. Pietzcker. Far Hills, NJ: U.S. Golf Association/Washington, DC: National Geographic, 2005.

Ouimet, Francis. *A Game of Golf.* Boston: Northeastern University Press, 2004. [Foreword by Ben Crenshaw; introduction by Richard A. Johnson; afterword by Robert Donovan.]

Putney, Clifford. *Muscular Christianity; Manhood and Sports in Protestant America, 1880-1920.* 2001; reprint, Cambridge, MA: Harvard University Press, 2003.

Ribowsky, Mark. *Complete History of the Negro Leagues; 1884 to 1955.* Secaucus, NJ: Citadel Press, 1995.

Riess, Steven A. *City Games: The Evolution of American Urban Society and the Rise of Sports.* 1989; reprint, Urbana, IL: Illini Books, 1991.

Riess, Steven A. *Sport in Industrial America, 1850-1920,* 2d ed. New York: Wiley, 2013.

Riess, Steven A. *Touching Base: Professional Baseball and American Culture in the Progressive Era,* rev. ed. Urbana: University of Illinois Press, 1999.

Ritter, Lawrence S. *The Glory of Their Times: The Story of the Early Days of Baseball Told by the Men Who Played It,* new enl. ed. New York: Morrow, 1984.

Seymour, Harold. *Baseball: The Golden Age,* vol. 2 of *Baseball,* 3 vols. 1960-1990; reprint, New York: Oxford University Press, 1989-1991.

Streible, Dan. *Fight Pictures: A History of Boxing in Early Cinema.* Berkeley: University of California Press, 2008.

Tygiel, Jules. *Past Time: Baseball as History.* New York: Oxford University Press, 2000.

Wiggins, David K., ed. *Sport in America: From Colonial Leisure to Celebrity Figures and Globalization.* Champaign, IL: Human Kinetics, 2010.

Wiggins, David K., ed. *Sport in America: From Wicked Amusement to National Obsession.* Champaign, IL: Human Kinetics, 1995.

Wilson, Elizabeth. *Love Game; A History of Tennis, from Victorian Pastime to Global Phenomenon.* London: Serpent's Tail, 2014.

Women's History

Ewen, Elizabeth. *Immigrant Women in the Land of Dollars: Life and Culture on the Lower East Side, 1890-1925.* New York: Monthly Review Press, 1985.

Fell, Alison S., and Christine E. Hallett, eds. *First World War Nursing: New Perspectives.* New York: Routledge, 2013.

Finnegan, Margaret Mary. *Selling Suffrage: Consumer Culture and Votes for Women.* New York: Columbia University Press, 1999.

Foster, Catherine. *Women for All Seasons: The Story of the Women's International League for Peace and Freedom.* Athens: University of Georgia Press, 1989.

Gabaccia, Donna. *From the Other Side: Women, Gender, and Immigrant Life in the U.S.* Bloomington: Indiana University Press, 1994.

Gavan, Lettie. *American Women in World War I: They Also Served.* Boulder Springs: University Press of Colorado, 1999.

Gidlow, Liette. *The Big Vote: Gender, Consumer Culture, and the Politics of Exclusion, 1890s-1920s.* Baltimore: Johns Hopkins University Press, 2004.

Hallett, Christine E. *Containing Trauma: Nursing Work in the First World War.* Manchester, UK: Manchester University Press, 2012.

Hallett, Christine E. *Veiled Warriors; Allied Nurses of the First World War.* New York: Oxford University Press, 2014.

Higonnet, Margaret R., et al. *Behind the Lines: Gender and the Two World Wars.* New Haven: Yale University Press, 1987.

Higonnet, Margaret R., ed. *Lines of Fire: Women Writers of World War I.* New York: Plume, 1999.

Jensen, Kimberly. *Mobilizing Minerva: American Women in the First World War.* Urbana: University of Illinois Press, 2008.

Kraditor, Aileen S. *The Ideas of the Woman Suffrage Movement: 1890-1920,* new ed. New York: W. W. Norton, 1981.

Mandell, Nikki. *The Corporation as Family: The Gendering of Corporate Welfare, 1890-1930.* Chapel Hill: University of North Carolina Press, 2002.

Marshall, Susan E. *Splintered Sisterhood: Gender and Class in the Campaign against Woman Suffrage.* Madison: University of Wisconsin Press, 1997.

Mayhew, Emily. *Wounded: A New History of the Western Front in World War I.* New York: Oxford, 2014.

Parker, Alison M. *Purifying America: Women, Cultural Reform, and Pro-Censorship Activism, 1873-1933.* Urbana: University of Illinois Press, 1997.

Patterson, Martha H., ed. *The American New Woman Revisited: A Reader, 1894-1930.* New Brunswick, NJ: Rutgers University Press, 2008.

Satter, Beryl. *Each Mind a Kingdom; American Women, Sexual Purity, and the New Thought Movement, 1875-1920.* Berkeley: University of California Press, 1999.

Stivers, Camilla. *Bureau Men, Settlement Women: Constructing Public Administration in the Progressive Era.* Lawrence: University Press of Kansas, 2000.

Swinth, Kirsten. *Painting Professionals: Women Artists and the Development of Modern American Art, 1870-1930.* Chapel Hill: University of North Carolina Press, 2001.

Woollacott, Angela. *On Her Their Lives Depend: Munitions Workers in the Great War.* Berkeley: University of California Press, 1994.

Zeiger, Susan. *In Uncle Sam's Service: Women Workers with the American Expeditionary Force, 1917-1919.* Ithaca, NY: Cornell University Press, 1999.

World War I

Adams, R. J. Q. *The Great War, 1914-18: Essays on the Military, Political and Social History of the First World War.* London: Macmillan, 1990.

Afflerbach, Holger, and David Stevenson, eds. *An Improbable War?: The Outbreak of World War I and European Political Culture before 1914.* New York: Berghahn Books, 2007.

Albrecht-Carrié, René. *The Meaning of the First World War.* Englewood Cliffs, NJ: Prentice-Hall, 1965.

Ashworth, Tony. *Trench Warfare, 1914-1918; The Live and Let Live System.* London: Macmillan, 1980.

Beckett, Ian F. W. *The Making of the First World War.* New Haven: Yale University Press, 2013.

Black, Jeremy. *The Great War and the Making of the Modern World.* New York: Continuum, 2011.

Buitenhuis, Peter. *The Great War of Words: British, American, and Canadian Propaganda and Fiction, 1914-1933.* Vancouver: University of British Columbia Press, 1987.

Chasseaud, Peter. *Mapping the First World War: The Great War through Maps from 1914-1918.* London: Collins, 2013.

Chickering, Roger, and Stig Förster, eds. *Great War, Total War: Combat and Mobilization on the Western Front, 1914-1918.* Washington, DC: German Historical Institute/New York: Cambridge University Press, 2000.

Controvich, James T. *The United States in World War I: A Bibliographic Guide.* Lanham, MD: Scarecrow Press, 2012.

Crownover, Roger. *The United States Intervention in North Russia, 1918, 1919; The Polar Bear Odyssey.* Lewiston, NY: Edwin Mellen, 2001.

Doyle, Peter, and Julian Walker. *Trench Talk: Words of the First World War.* Stroud, Gloucestershire, UK: History Press, 2012.

Faulkner, Richard S. *The School of Hard Knocks; Combat Leadership in the American Expeditionary Forces.* College Station: Texas A & M University Press, 2012.

Fic, Victor M. *The Collapse of American Policy in Russia and Siberia, 1918; Wilson's Decision Not to Intervene (March-October, 1918).* Boulder, CO: East European Monographs, 1995.

First World War Studies, the Journal of the International Society for First World War Studies. Abingdon, UK: Routledge/Taylor & Francis, March 2010-.

Ford, Nancy Gentile. *The Great War and America: Civil-Military Relations during World War I.* Westport, CT: Praeger, 2008.

Gavan, Lettie. *American Women in World War I: They Also Served.* Boulder Springs: University Press of Colorado, 1999.

Gilbert, Martin. *The First World War: A Complete History.* New York: H. Holt, 1994.

Gilbert, Martin. *Routledge Atlas of the First World War.* London: Routledge, 2008.

Gregory, Adrian. *A War of Peoples 1914-1919.* New York: Oxford University Press, 2014.

Grotelueschen, Mark Ethan. *The AEF Way of War: The American Army and Combat in World War I.* New York: Cambridge University Press, 2007.

Haber, L. F. *The Poisonous Cloud: Chemical Warfare in the First World War.* Oxford, UK: Clarendon Press/New York: Oxford University Press, 1986.

Halliday, E. M. *The Ignorant Armies.* New York: Harper, 1960.

Hart, Peter. *The Great War: A Combat History of the First World War.* New York: Oxford University Press, 2013.

Hastings, Max. *Catastrophe 1914; Europe Goes to War.* New York: Knopf, 2013.

Herman, Gerald. *The Pivotal Conflict: A Comprehensive Chronology of the First World War, 1914-1919.* New York: Greenwood Press, 1992.

Herrmann, David G. *The Arming of Europe and the Making of the First World War.* Princeton, NJ: Princeton University Press, 1996.

Herwig, Holger H., and Neil M. Heyman. *Biographical Dictionary of World War I.* Westport, CT: Greenwood Press, 1982.

Higham, Robert, and Dennis Showalter. *Researching World War I: A Handbook.* Westport, CT: Greenwood Press, 2003.

Horne, John, ed. *A Companion to World War I.* Malden, MA: Wiley, 2010.

Horne, John, ed. *State, Society, and Mobilization in Europe during the First World War.* New York: Cambridge University Press, 1997.

Hughes, Matthew, and William James Philpott. *The Palgrave Concise Historical Atlas of the First World War.* New York: Palgrave Macmillan, 2005.

Hull, Isabel V. *A Scrap of Paper: Breaking and Making International Law during the Great War.* Ithaca, NY: Cornell University Press, 2014.

Jackson, Robert. *At War with the Bolsheviks; The Allied Intervention.* London: Tom Stacy Ltd., 1972.

Jahns, Lewis E., Joel R. Moore, and Harry H. Mead. *History of the American Expedition Fighting the Bolsheviki; Campaigning in North Russia 1918-1919.* 1920; reprint, St. Petersburg, FL: Red and Black, 2007.

Keegan, John. *The First World War.* New York: A. Knopf, 1999.

Keene, Jennifer D. *World War I: The American Soldier Experience.* Lincoln: University of Nebraska Press, 2011.

Kennedy, Kate, and Trudi Tate, eds. "Literature and Music of the First World War." Special issue, *First World War Studies* 2, no. 4 (June 2011).

Kinvig, Clifford. *Churchill's Crusade: The British Invasion of Russia 1918-1920.* New York: Hambledon-Continuum, 2006.

Lawson, Kenneth Gregory. "War at the Grassroots: The Great War and the Nationalization of Civic Life." PhD diss., University of Washington, 2000.

Leed, Eric J. *No Man's Land: Combat & Identity in World War I.* New York: Cambridge University Press, 1979.

Lengel, Edward. *World War I Memories: An Annotated Bibliography of Personal Accounts Published in English since 1919.* Lanham, MD: Scarecrow Press, 2004.

Levy, Jack S., and John A. Vasquez, eds. *The Outbreak of the First World War: Structure, Politics, and Decision-Making.* New York: Cambridge University Press, 2014.

Little, Branden, ed. "Humanitarianism in the Era of the First World War." Special issue, *First World War Studies* 5, no. 1 (2014).

Luebke, Frederick. *Bonds of Loyalty: German America and World War I.* DeKalb: Northern Illinois University Press, 1974.

MacMillan, Margaret. *Paris 1919: Six Months That Changed the World.* New York: Random House, 2001.

Massie, Robert K. *Castles of Steel: Britain, Germany, and the Winning of the Great War at Sea.* New York: Random House, 2003.

Massie, Robert K. *Dreadnought: Britain, Germany, and the Coming of the Great War.* New York: Random House, 1991.

Mayhew, Emily. *Wounded: A New History of the Western Front in World War I.* New York: Oxford, 2014.

Morrow, John. *The Great War: An Imperial History.* New York: Routledge, 2004.

Mulligan, William. *The Great War for Peace.* New Haven: Yale University Press, 2014.

Murray, Nicholas. *The Rocky Road to the Great War: The Evolution of Trench Warfare to 1914.* Washington, DC: Potomac Books, 2013.

National War Council, Young Men's Christian Associations. *Summary of World War Work of the American Y.M.C.A; with Soldiers and Sailors of American at Home, on the Sea, and Overseas; with the Men of the Allied Armies and with the Prisoners of War in All Parts of the World.* New York: 1920.

Neiberg, Michael S. *Dance of the Furies: Europe and the Outbreak of World War I.* Cambridge, MA: Belknap Press of Harvard University Press, 2011.

Neiberg, Michael S. *Fighting the Great War: A Global History.* Cambridge, MA: Harvard University Press, 2005.

Nelson, Clifford L. *German-American Political Behavior in Nebraska and Wisconsin, 1916-1920.* Lincoln: University of Nebraska, 1972. [University of Nebraska-Lincoln publication no. 217.]

Nicolson, Colin. *Longman Companion to the First World War: Europe 1914-1918.* New York: Routledge, 2014.

Nolan, Michael E. *The Inverted Mirror: Mythologizing the Enemy in France and Germany, 1898-1914*. New York: Berghahn Books, 2005.

Pearson, Chris. *Mobilizing Nature: The Environmental History of War and Militarization in Modern France*. Manchester, UK: Manchester University Press, 2012.

Proctor, Tammy M. *Civilians in a World at War, 1914-1918*. New York: New York University Press, 2010.

Read, Christopher. *War and Revolution in Russia, 1914-22*. New York: Palgrave Macmillan, 2013.

Richard, Carl. *When the United States Invaded Russia; Woodrow Wilson's Siberian Disaster*. Lanham, MD: Rowman & Littlefield, 2012.

Shevin-Coetzee, Marilyn, and Frans Coetzee, eds. *Empires, Soldiers and Citizens: A World War I Sourcebook*, 2d ed. Malden, MA: Wiley, 2012.

Snell, Mark A., ed. *Unknown Soldiers: The American Expeditionary Forces in Memory and Remembrance*. Kent, OH: Kent State University Press, 2008.

Sondhaus, Lawrence. *World War I: The Global Revolution*. New York: Cambridge University Press, 2011.

Steuer, Kenneth. *Pursuit of an "Unparalleled Opportunity": The American WMCA and Prisoner of War Diplomacy among the Central Power Nations during World War I, 1914-1923*. New York: Columbia University Press, 2009.

Stevenson, D. *Armaments and the Coming of War: Europe, 1904-1914*. Oxford, UK: Clarendon Press/New York: Oxford University Press, 1996.

Stevenson, D. *Cataclysm: The First World War as Political Tragedy*. New York: Basic Books, 2004.

Stone, Norman. *The Eastern Front, 1914-1917*. London: Hodder and Stoughton, 1975.

Strachan, Hew. *The First World War: A New Illustrated History*. New York: Simon & Schuster, 2003.

Strachan, Hew. *To Arms*, vol. 1 of *The First World War*. New York: Oxford University Press, 2001.

Strohn, Matthias, ed. *World War I Companion*. Oxford, UK: Osprey Publishing, 2013.

Travers, Timothy. *The Killing Ground: The British Army, the Western Front, and the Emergence of Modern Warfare, 1900-1918*. London: Allen & Unwin, 1987.

Williams, Chad L. *Torchbearers of Democracy: African American Soldiers in the World War I Era*. Chapel Hill: University of North Carolina Press, 2011.

Winter, Denis. *Death's Men: Soldiers of the Great War*. London: Allen Lane, 1978.

Winter, J. M. *The Experience of World War I*. New York: Oxford University Press, 1989.

Winter, J. M. *The Great War in History: Debates and Controversies, 1914 to the Present*. New York: Cambridge University Press, 2005.

Winter, J. M., ed. *The Cambridge History of the First World War*. 3 vols. New York: Cambridge University Press, 2014.

Woollacott, Angela. *On Her Their Lives Depend: Munitions Workers in the Great War*. Berkeley: University of California Press, 1994.

Zeiger, Susan. *In Uncle Sam's Service: Women Workers with the American Expeditionary Force, 1917-1919*. Ithaca, NY: Cornell University Press, 1999.

	Same House			No	Yes							40		Foreman
	Same House			No	No	No	No	No	H					
	Same House			No	No	No	No	No	S					
	Same House			No	Yes									Laborer

INDEX

2014 Title List

Visit **www.HwWilsonInPrint.com** for Product Information, Table of Contents and Sample Pages

Current Biography

Current Biography Cumulative Index 1946-2013
Current Biography Magazine
Current Biography Yearbook-2004
Current Biography Yearbook-2005
Current Biography Yearbook-2006
Current Biography Yearbook-2007
Current Biography Yearbook-2008
Current Biography Yearbook-2009
Current Biography Yearbook-2010
Current Biography Yearbook-2011
Current Biography Yearbook-2012
Current Biography Yearbook-2013
Current Biography Yearbook-2014

Core Collections

Senior High Core Collection
Middle & Junior High School Core
Children's Core Collection
Fiction Core Collection
Public Library Core Collection: Nonfiction

Sears List

Sears List of Subject Headings
Sears: Lista de Encabezamientos de Materia

The Reference Shelf

Aging in America
Revisiting Gender
The U.S. National Debate Topic, 2014/2015
Embracing New Paradigms in education
Marijuana Reform
Representative American Speeches 2013-2014
Reality Television
The Business of Food
The Future of U.S. Economic Relations: Mexico, Cuba, and Venezuela
Sports in America
Global Climate Change
Representative American Speeches, 2012-2013
Conspiracy Theories
The Arab Spring
U.S. National Debate Topic: Transportation Infrastructure
Families: Traditional and New Structures
Faith & Science
Representative American Speeches 2011-2012
Social Networking
Dinosaurs
Space Exploration & Development
U.S. Infrastructure
Politics of the Ocean
Representative American Speeches 2010-2011
Robotics
The News and its Future
American Military Presence Overseas
Russia
Graphic Novels and Comic Books
Representative American Speeches 2009-2010

Readers' Guide

Readers Guide to Periodicals Literature
Abridged Readers' Guide to Periodical Literature
Short Story Index

Indexes

Short Story Index
Index to Legal Periodicals & Books

Facts About Series

Facts About the Presidents, Eighth Edition
Facts About China
Facts About the 20th Century
Facts About American Immigration
Facts About World's Languages

Nobel Prize Winners

Nobel Prize Winners, 2002-2013

World Authors

World Authors 2000-2005
World Authors 2006-2013

Famous First Facts

Famous First Facts, Seventh Edition
Famous First Facts About American Politics
Famous First Facts About Sports
Famous First Facts About the Environment
Famous First Facts, International Edition

American Book of Days

The American Book of Days, Fifth Edition
The International Book of Days

Junior Authors & Illustrators

Tenth Book of Junior Authors & Illustrations

Monographs

The Barnhart Dictionary of Etymology
Celebrate the World
Indexing from A to Z
Radical Change: Books for Youth in a Digital Age
The Poetry Break
Guide to the Ancient World

Wilson Chronology

Wilson Chronology of Asia and the Pacific
Wilson Chronology of Human Rights
Wilson Chronology of Ideas
Wilson Chronology of the Arts
Wilson Chronology of the World's Religions
Wilson Chronology of Women's Achievements

Book Review Digest

Book Review Digest, 2014

Grey House Publishing | Salem Press | H.W. Wilson
4919 Route, 22 PO Box 56, Amenia NY 12501-0056

2014 Title List

Visit **www.SalemPress.com** for Product Information, Table of Contents and Sample Pages

History and Social Science

A 2000s in America
50 States
African American History
Agriculture in History (check)
American First Ladies
American Heroes
American Indian Tribes
American Presidents
American Villains
Ancient Greece
Bill of Rights, The
Cold War, The
Defining Documents: American Revolution 1754-1805
Defining Documents: Civil War 1860-1865
Defining Documents: Emergence of Modern America, 1868-1918
Defining Documents: Exploration & Colonial America 1492-1755
Defining Documents: Manifest Destiny 1803-1860
Defining Documents: Reconstruction, 1865-1880
Defining Documents: The 1920s
Defining Documents: The 1930s
Defining Documents: World War I
Eighties in America
Encyclopedia of American Immigration
Fifties in America
Forties in America
Great Athletes
Great Events from History: 17th Century
Great Events from History: 18th Century
Great Events from History: 19th Century
Great Events from History: 20th Century, 1901-1940
Great Events from History: 20th Century, 1941-1970
Great Events from History: 20th Century, 1971-200
Great Events from History: Ancient World
Great Events from History: Middle Ages
Great Events from History: Modern Scandals
Great Events from History: Renaissance & Early Modern Era
Great Lives from History: 17th Century
Great Lives from History: 18th Century
Great Lives from History: 19th Century
Great Lives from History: 20th Century
Great Lives from History: African Americans
Great Lives from History: Ancient World
Great Lives from History: Asian & Pacific Islander Americans
Great Lives from History: Incredibly Wealthy
Great Lives from History: Inventors & Inventions
Great Lives from History: Jewish Americans
Great Lives from History: Latinos
Great Lives from History: Middle Ages
Great Lives from History: Notorious Lives
Great Lives from History: Renaissance & Early Modern Era
Great Lives from History: Scientists & Science
Historical Encyclopedia of American Business
Immigration in U.S. History
Magill's Guide to Military History
Milestone Documents in African American History
Milestone Documents in American History
Milestone Documents in World History
Milestone Documents of American Leaders
Milestone Documents of World Religions
Musicians & Composers 20th Century
Nineties in America
Seventies in America

Sixties in America
Survey of American Industry and Careers
Thirties in America
Twenties in America
U.S. Court Cases
U.S. Laws, Acts, and Treaties
U.S. Legal System
U.S. Supreme Court
United States at War
USA in Space
Weapons and Warfare
World Conflicts: Asia and the Middle East

Grey House Publishing | Salem Press | H.W. Wilson
4919 Route, 22 PO Box 56, Amenia NY 12501-0056

2014 Title List

Visit **www.SalemPress.com** for Product Information, Table of Contents and Sample Pages

SALEM PRESS

Literature

American Ethnic Writers
Critical Insights: Authors
Critical Insights: New Literary Collection Bundles
Critical Insights: Themes
Critical Insights: Works
Critical Survey of Drama
Critical Survey of Graphic Novels: Heroes & Super Heroes
Critical Survey of Graphic Novels: History, Theme & Technique
Critical Survey of Graphic Novels: Independents & Underground Classics
Critical Survey of Graphic Novels: Manga
Critical Survey of Long Fiction
Critical Survey of Mystery & Detective Fiction
Critical Survey of Mythology and Folklore: Heroes and Heroines
Critical Survey of Mythology and Folklore: Love, Sexuality & Desire
Critical Survey of Mythology and Folklore: World Mythology
Critical Survey of Poetry
Critical Survey of Poetry: American Poetry
Critical Survey of Poetry: British, Irish & Commonwealth Poets
Critical Survey of Poetry: European Poets
Critical Survey of Poetry: European Poets
Critical Survey of Poetry: Topical Essays
Critical Survey of Poetry: World Poets
Critical Survey of Science Fiction & Fantasy Literature
Critical Survey of Shakespeare's Sonnets
Critical Survey of Short Fiction
Critical Survey of Short Fiction: American Writers
Critical Survey of Short Fiction: British, Irish & Commonwealth Poets
Critical Survey of Short Fiction: European Writers
Critical Survey of Short Fiction: Topical Essays
Critical Survey of Short Fiction: World Writers
Cyclopedia of Literary Characters
Introduction to Literary Context: American Post-Modernist Novels
Introduction to Literary Context: American Short Fiction
Introduction to Literary Context: English Literature
Introduction to Literary Context: World Literature
Magill's Literary Annual 2014
Magill's Survey of American Literature
Magill's Survey of World Literature
Masterplots
Masterplots II: African American Literature
Masterplots II: Christian Literature
Masterplots II: Drama Series
Masterplots II: Short Story Series
Notable African American Writers
Notable American Novelists
Notable Playwrights
Short Story Writers

Science, Careers & Mathematics

Applied Science
Applied Science: Engineering & Mathematics
Applied Science: Science & Medicine
Applied Science: Technology
Biomes and Ecosystems
Careers in Chemistry
Careers in Communications & Media
Careers in Healthcare
Careers in Hospitality & Tourism
Careers in Law & Criminology
Careers in Physics
Computer Technology Inventors
Contemporary Biographies in Chemistry
Contemporary Biographies in Communications & Media
Contemporary Biographies in Healthcare
Contemporary Biographies in Hospitality & Tourism
Contemporary Biographies in Law & Criminology
Contemporary Biographies in Physics
Earth Science
Earth Science: Earth Materials & Resources
Earth Science: Earth's Surface and History
Earth Science: Physics & Chemistry of the Earth
Earth Science: Weather, Water & Atmosphere
Encyclopedia of Energy
Encyclopedia of Environmental Issues
Encyclopedia of Global Resources
Encyclopedia of Global Warming
Encyclopedia of Mathematics and Society
Encyclopedia of the Ancient World
Forensic Science
Internet Innovators
Introduction to Chemistry
Magill's Encyclopedia of Science: Animal Life
Magill's Encyclopedia of Science: Plant life
Magill's Medical Guide
Notable Natural Disasters
Solar System

Health

Addictions & Substance Abuse
Cancer
Complementary & Alternative Medicine
Genetics & Inherited Conditions
Infectious Diseases & Conditions
Magill's Medical Guide
Psychology & Mental Health
Psychology Basics

Grey House Publishing | Salem Press | H.W. Wilson
4919 Route, 22 PO Box 56, Amenia NY 12501-0056

2014 Title List

Visit **www.GreyHouse.com** for Product Information, Table of Contents and Sample Pages

General Reference

America's College Museums
American Environmental Leaders: From Colonial Times to the Present
An African Biographical Dictionary
An Encyclopedia of Human Rights in the United States
Constitutional Amendments
Encyclopedia of African-American Writing
Encyclopedia of the Continental Congress
Encyclopedia of Gun Control & Gun Rights
Encyclopedia of Invasions & Conquests
Encyclopedia of Prisoners of War & Internment
Encyclopedia of Religion & Law in America
Encyclopedia of Rural America
Encyclopedia of the United States Cabinet, 1789-2010
Encyclopedia of War Journalism
Encyclopedia of Warrior Peoples & Fighting Groups
From Suffrage to the Senate: America's Political Women
Nations of the World
Political Corruption in America
Speakers of the House of Representatives, 1789-2009
The Environmental Debate: A Documentary History
The Evolution Wars: A Guide to the Debates
The Religious Right: A Reference Handbook
The Value of a Dollar: 1860-2009
The Value of a Dollar: Colonial Era
This is Who We Were: A Companion to the 1940 Census
This is Who We Were: The 1920s
This is Who We Were: The 1950s
This is Who We Were: The 1960s
US Land & Natural Resource Policy
Working Americans 1770-1869 Vol. IX: Revolutionary War to the Civil War
Working Americans 1880-1999 Vol. I: The Working Class
Working Americans 1880-1999 Vol. II: The Middle Class
Working Americans 1880-1999 Vol. III: The Upper Class
Working Americans 1880-1999 Vol. IV: Their Children
Working Americans 1880-2003 Vol. V: At War
Working Americans 1880-2005 Vol. VI: Women at Work
Working Americans 1880-2006 Vol. VII: Social Movements
Working Americans 1880-2007 Vol. VIII: Immigrants
Working Americans 1880-2009 Vol. X: Sports & Recreation
Working Americans 1880-2010 Vol. XI: Inventors & Entrepreneurs
Working Americans 1880-2011 Vol. XII: Our History through Music
Working Americans 1880-2012 Vol. XIII: Education & Educators
World Cultural Leaders of the 20th & 21st Centuries

Business Information

Complete Television, Radio & Cable Industry Directory
Directory of Business Information Resources
Directory of Mail Order Catalogs
Directory of Venture Capital & Private Equity Firms
Environmental Resource Handbook
Food & Beverage Market Place
Grey House Homeland Security Directory
Grey House Performing Arts Directory
Hudson's Washington News Media Contacts Directory
New York State Directory
Sports Market Place Directory

Education Information

Charter School Movement
Comparative Guide to American Elementary & Secondary Schools
Complete Learning Disabilities Directory
Educators Resource Directory
Special Education

Health Information

Comparative Guide to American Hospitals
Complete Directory for Pediatric Disorders
Complete Directory for People with Chronic Illness
Complete Directory for People with Disabilities
Complete Mental Health Directory
Diabetes in America: A Geographic & Demographic Analysis
Directory of Health Care Group Purchasing Organizations
Directory of Hospital Personnel
HMO/PPO Directory
Medical Device Register
Older Americans Information Directory

Statistics & Demographics

America's Top-Rated Cities
America's Top-Rated Small Towns & Cities
America's Top-Rated Smaller Cities
American Tally
Ancestry & Ethnicity in America
Comparative Guide to American Hospitals
Comparative Guide to American Suburbs
Profiles of America
Profiles of... Series – State Handbooks
The Hispanic Databook
Weather America

Financial Ratings Series

TheStreet.com Ratings Guide to Bond & Money Market Mutual Funds
TheStreet.com Ratings Guide to Common Stocks
TheStreet.com Ratings Guide to Exchange-Traded Funds
TheStreet.com Ratings Guide to Stock Mutual Funds
TheStreet.com Ratings Ultimate Guided Tour of Stock Investing
Weiss Ratings Consumer Guides
Weiss Ratings Guide to Banks & Thrifts
Weiss Ratings Guide to Credit Unions
Weiss Ratings Guide to Health Insurers
Weiss Ratings Guide to Life & Annuity Insurers
Weiss Ratings Guide to Property & Casualty Insurers

Bowker's Books In Print®Titles

Books In Print®
Books In Print® Supplement
American Book Publishing Record® Annual
American Book Publishing Record® Monthly
Books Out Loud™
Bowker's Complete Video Directory™
Children's Books In Print®
El-Hi Textbooks & Serials In Print®
Forthcoming Books®
Law Books & Serials In Print™
Medical & Health Care Books In Print™
Publishers, Distributors & Wholesalers of the US™
Subject Guide to Books In Print®
Subject Guide to Children's Books In Print®

Canadian General Reference

Associations Canada
Canadian Almanac & Directory
Canadian Environmental Resource Guide
Canadian Parliamentary Guide
Financial Services Canada
Governments Canada
Health Services Canada
Libraries Canada
Major Canadian Cities
The History of Canada

Grey House Publishing | Salem Press | H.W. Wilson
4919 Route, 22 PO Box 56, Amenia NY 12501-0056